D0004399

Artist's rendition of Canada as seen from far above Central America. Projection courtesy M. Feuchtwanger and S.L. Pattison, Department of Geography, Simon Fraser University. Artwork by Michael J. Lee.

THE CANADIAN ENCYCLOPEDIA

SECOND EDITION

VOLUME II
Edu – Min

Hurtig Publishers
Edmonton

Hurtig Publishers Ltd.
10560 – 105 Street
Edmonton, Alberta
Canada T5H 2W7

Every attempt has been made to identify and credit sources for photographs. The publisher would appreciate receiving information as to any inaccuracies in the credits for subsequent editions.

Canadian Cataloguing in Publication Data

Main entry under title:
The Canadian Encyclopedia

Editor in Chief: James H. Marsh.

ISBN 0-88830-326-2 (set) –ISBN 0-88830-327-0 (v. 1). –ISBN 0-88830-328-9 (v. 2). –ISBN 0-88830-329-7 (v. 3). –ISBN 0-88830-330-0 (v.4)

1. Canada–Dictionaries and encyclopedias.
I. Marsh, James H.
FCwe.C36 1985 971'.003'21 C84-091250-1
F1006.C36 1985

Designed, typeset and manufactured in Canada

Education, Alternate The philosophical roots of "alternate education" derive from 2 related but conflicting educational traditions. One is the modern progressive tradition represented by American philosopher John Dewey and his followers in the US, by the post-WWI New Schools Movement in Great Britain, by the Steiner (Waldorf) schools on the European continent and, more recently, by the Hall-Dennis (Committee on Aims and Objectives of Education) and Worth (Commission on Educational Planning) reports for Ontario and Alberta, respectively. This tradition stresses both the need to accommodate curriculum and teaching to the stages of child development and the gradual integration of the child into adult society through planned experiential learning. Education is also viewed as a major vehicle for social reform and for the broad dissemination of democratic principles and practices. The second tradition is strongly libertarian, stressing the rights of parents and children to make their own educational and life choices. Writers in this tradition, eg, A.S. Neill in Great Britain and John Holt in the US, uphold the individual freedom and innate goodness of the child against institutional and social conformity and the corrupting influences of modern society. Some writers, eg, Ivan Illich in *Deschooling Society*, have attacked conventional schooling and compulsory education as ethnocentric, paternalistic, bureaucratic, etc. Independent "free" schools which flowered in Canada and the US in the middle and late 1960s (and soon disappeared) were rooted in this libertarian tradition.

While both traditions share certain attitudes, eg, accommodation of individual needs and interests and a critical stance toward modern corporate society, the progressive tradition leans toward intervention and the careful planning of the child's educational experiences and activities while the libertarian tradition stresses noninterference with "natural" growth and learning processes and the importance of personal choice and freedom in educational matters. Both traditions intermingled in Canada in the open-education movement in public elementary education in the late 1960s and in the alternative schools that emerged in the 1970s. The term "alternative school" first came into general usage in Canada with the establishment in the early 1970s of several small elementary and secondary schools, mainly initiated under the jurisdiction of public boards of education. The term "alternative" was adopted partly to distinguish these schools from the independent, parent-student-teacher-run "free" schools that preceded them (and from which some of them actually evolved) and to emphasize the board's commitment to options within the public system.

With the increasing stress on educational pluralism and choice in the 1970s the alternative-school label was adopted by many newer independent private schools that wished to identify themselves as alternatives to "mainstream" public education. Simultaneously, political pressures within public systems to provide for the "special" learning needs of students who were doing poorly in or dropping out of regular schools persuaded more SCHOOL BOARDS to establish re-entry and work-study programs for high-school dropouts, community-oriented outreach programs, and independent study programs for bright, self-motivated secondary students. In the early 1980s attention shifted to special schools and programs for the academically gifted and artistically talented as well as to programs linking schooling with the workplace ("co-operative education"). In the public sector most alternative schools offer independent study programs, basic-skills programs, mini-high schools with a mixture of conventional and nonconventional courses, and schools with an arts focus. A growing number of parent-teacher co-operative elementary alternative schools have also emerged, mainly organized along the lines of the family-grouped, activity-based British Infant Schools. This development is most prominent in Toronto. It is very difficult to estimate the number of alternate schools currently operating under public school boards in urban centres across Canada. It is likely, however, that the total exceeds 100. For some adolescents and young adults they provide an escape from the large, seemingly impersonal, modern comprehensive high school. They offer smaller classes, closer and more informal relations with teachers, and greater flexibility in course selection and timetabling. Finally, alternative schools resemble the liberal arts college more than the high school in style and format, easing the transition from the highly programmed high school to the more loosely structured pace of university student life.

For parents, co-operatively governed elementary-school alternative programs provide not only a choice of program philosophies but also opportunities to be involved more closely with the schooling of their children. Parents may sit on various internal governance committees, assist in the classroom, serve as resource people in the program and have direct access to the teachers. Co-operative/alternative elementary schools have also pioneered the extension of early-childhood education through all-day kindergarten programs and the provision of after-school day-care programs for children of working parents (especially single mothers). As well, the Canadian Alliance of Home Schooling estimates that 1000 families in Canada have chosen to educate their children at home; the parents usually work out the curriculums with the local school board.

The expanding network of co-operatively run new elementary alternatives may be viewed as a renaissance of the spirit of the small community school in the face of a general trend toward increased centralization and bureaucratization in school systems. In addition, for those parents and teachers who remain committed to the ideals and principles of progressive, open education in the face of the "back to basics" movement, these alternative schools represent islands of progressivism in a sea of educational conservatism. Judged by curriculum, pedagogy and, in the case of elementary alternatives, even size, the differences are not great between alternative and traditional schools. Teachers in public alternative schools are drawn by and large from the same universities and teacher-training programs as teachers in traditional schools, and most teach in traditional schools before moving to an alternative school. Basic curriculum and materials are similar in both types of alternative schools. Practices probably vary more from teacher to teacher than from school to school. With declining enrolments even some mainstream elementary schools have shrunk to the size of alternative schools. At the secondary level in particular, stiffer university admission requirements and a general trend toward curriculum standardization threatens to reduce even further any curriculum differences between mainstream and alternative schools.

What seems to differentiate many alternative schools from the others is the sense of ownership, autonomy and control that teachers, parents and students enjoy in relation to the system. At the same time there is a clear move to assert and maintain stronger administrative control over alternative schools. If present trends continue, alternate education may well be incorporated under an expanding "special education" network within school systems. In a more optimistic scenario, alternative schools might serve as forerunners of a more decentralized, pluralistic, community-based education system. MALCOLM LEVIN

Education, Early-Childhood, embraces a variety of group care and education programs for young children (primarily 2-8 years old) and some services for parents. The traditional focus on DAY-CARE, NURSERY-SCHOOL and KINDERGARTEN programs has expanded recently to include attention to the needs of infants and school-aged children in primary grades, but programs designed for children in the 2-to-8 age range still outnumber those for older and younger children. Various types of day-care and nursery programs are designed for the care and education needs of preschool children. Although different kinds of day care exist, there is increasing demand for the kind of group program associated with a centre. In schools, kindergarten and the early primary grades are considered within the purview of early-childhood education. For some Canadian children, entry to kindergarten or first grade represents the first organized early-education experience.

Although, depending on the age and experience of the children involved, programs may emphasize either the care or the education of the child at a particular time, all early-childhood education is guided by concern for the individual child and by an awareness of the need to nurture all aspects of his or her development. Early-education practice reflects the thinking of Johann Pestalozzi (1746-1829), the renowned Swiss educator whose concern for and work with young orphan children is generally acknowledged as being responsible for the birth of early-childhood education. The influence of European educators, such as Friedrich Froebel, Maria Montessori and Margaret McMillarn is obvious in N American and European early-childhood education. The Montessori schools in Canada are a concrete example, but the more widespread and enduring impact of these educators is reflected in classroom practices based on their beliefs about child development and their respect for a child's individuality. In the latter part of the 20th century, early-childhood education has been strongly influenced by Swiss psychologist Jean Piaget's theories. Piaget's studies of children's thinking, in particular, have stimulated a wave of research exploring children's intellectual development, resulting in many innovations in early-childhood programs.

There is controversy over what constitutes the best educational experience for the young child, although generally the goals and purposes of this experience are in less dispute than the means by which they are to be achieved. For example, the extent to which the teacher, or any adult, should intervene in a child's learning is debatable, particularly when intervention takes the form of direct instruction in teacher-directed lessons. A second, related question, concerns the desirability of a prespecified learning objective. Sometimes this controversy is described as the "play" versus "instruction" approach to learning. At issue are conflicting beliefs about when children can and should direct their own learning. Much of the debate concerns school programs for children in the 5-to-8 age range, but it has spilled over into preschool programs as well.

Compensatory education for preschool children, developed principally in the US with extensive government funding, was intended to meet the needs of socially and economically disadvantaged children. Some programs designed by groups of educational researchers and developers challenged the long-standing early-childhood education emphasis on social and emotional development and emphasized intellectual development. The conflict between the more traditional and the experimental programs and the effect of these programs on the children became part of the general discussion about the means and ends of the preschool experience. This discussion, in Canada, has centered around "at risk" children, ie, those who because of one or more factors in their background may face some difficulties in school achievement or social adjustment, or both.

In Canada, some of the questions related to special needs are associated with the needs of second-language learners and of children identified as having particular learning or developmental needs. Children of parents who have recently immigrated to Canada frequently enter kindergarten or first grade with little or no facility in English or French. Opinions differ regarding the best approach to developing the child's competence with the language of the school. The identification of other special needs and capabilities at the time the child enters school is the objective of the early-identification procedures adopted by many school boards. Again, there are different views regarding the best means of identifying existing and potential problems and of meeting the needs that are identified. The early-identification movement is concerned with identifying physical, social, emotional and learning problems in preschool and early-primary children. Screening procedures have been designed for this purpose, and some follow-up in response to the identified needs of individual children is encouraged.

Perhaps the greatest influence on early-childhood education in Canada today has been the philosophy and practice of the British infant and primary schools. Frequently referred to as "informal" or "open" education, this approach is viewed by many as the embodiment of the "child-centered" philosophy. Attempts to implement "informal" education in Canada and the US have been directed, in particular, to kindergarten and primary-grade programs. In Ontario alone, almost 400 open-area schools were constructed between 1967 and 1972. Even where the open areas were not provided, water tables, "junk" boxes and other materials used in British classrooms appeared in Canadian classrooms. Multi-age grouping practised in Britain was also tried in Canada.

Other developments within the field of education and society have also influenced the scope and direction of early-childhood education. For many years the study of child development and early-education practice were dominated by the child developmentalists, who resisted direct intervention by teachers in children's learning. However, since the 1960s scholars and researchers in other disciplines and professions have turned their attention to the study of children and the early-education setting. In Canada today a number of university departments of education and psychology are engaged in research exploring the dimensions of child development and learning, and the dimensions and outcomes of early-childhood practice. The research of linguists, eg, has provided new understanding of the development of and relationship between language and thought. These findings have generated new discussions about the teacher's role in language development.

Changing ways of life and other social change have also affected early education because of changing needs and demands for child care and education. The increasing number of working women, many of whom are mothers of young children, has resulted in a demand for increased day-care facilities. In Canada this demand and the related issue of day-care funding have attracted the attention of many interest groups and policymakers, and the role of the school in providing day-care needs has become a subject of debate.

Perhaps the greatest challenge to early-childhood practitioners and researchers today is finding a way to determine whether early-childhood education achieves its objectives. Developing valid and reliable measures to assess program effectiveness, or even to define the criteria of effectiveness, has been difficult because some early-childhood educators are reluctant to support formal evaluation of program effects on children. This reluctance seems to stem from concern that any formal assessment of children promotes a kind of child evaluation that is antithetical to the notion of respecting individual differences. However, advances in research design and methodology and an awareness of the need to support claims with evidence have combined to support a growing body of research in the field. This research increasingly demonstrates concern with long-term, as well as immediate effects of early-childhood programs, and with determining relationships between different types of programs and different learning development outcomes.

ELLEN M. REGAN

Reading: A. Biemiller, "Early Childhood Education," *Canadian Research in Education* (1982); S.J. Braun and E.P. Edwards, *History and Theory of Early Childhood Education* (1972); E.D. Evans, *Contemporary Influences in Early Childhood Education* (1975); L.M. Logan and V.G. Logan, *Educating Young Children* (1974).

Education, Higher, usually refers to education and training in universities, colleges and institutes of technology or art. What would now be called higher education was first organized by the churches, in the 17th century (*see* EDUCATION, HISTORY OF), but it was not until 1789 that the first "church-sponsored" UNIVERSITY, University of King's College (NS), was chartered in Canada. MCGILL UNIVERSITY (founded in 1821) was the first private nondenominational university to receive a charter. The establishment of provincial universities began with UNIVERSITY OF TORONTO in 1850. There are 3 federal government foundations, all military colleges, of which the first, the ROYAL MILITARY COLLEGE OF CANADA, was founded in 1874 and opened in 1876. There are more than 70 universities and other institutions with the power to grant degrees. Of these, 8 use French as the principal language of instruction, 5 use both French and English. The rest teach mainly in English, although a few have French-language constituent or affiliated colleges and some teach individual courses in French. The universities' chief functions are teaching, research and community service. Programs of study leading to the degrees of bachelor, master and doctor are offered in the arts and sciences and in the professions. The universities undertake most of the country's basic research and some of its applied research. Community service includes the provision of opportunities for study in nondegree programs of both general and professional interest.

Until the mid-1960s, post-secondary vocational education was provided by a variety of specialized institutions. At that time, systems of colleges were introduced, mostly by provincial governments. In some cases the colleges absorbed former institutions of post-secondary education (PSE). There are now nearly 200 such nonuniversity institutions, most teaching in English, some in French and a few in both, and they are called by a variety of names – college, COMMUNITY COLLEGE, regional college, college of applied arts and technology, COLLÈGE D'ENSEIGNEMENT GÉNÉRAL ET PROFESSIONNEL (CEGEP), institute of technology, etc. These colleges offer programs leading to diplomas rather than degrees. Some provide academic education for transfer to university, almost all provide vocational training, covering a vast array of occupations, while others offer both academic and vocational programs. The colleges are not expected to undertake research, but do provide a wealth of community services.

Enrolment in PSE has risen steadily since WWII and the participation rate (total of full-time students in PSE as a percentage of the population 18-24 years old) was 24.5% in 1985-86. Full-time students in universities and community colleges in 1986-87 were estimated at 792 000, of these, 471 000 attended university. An additional 286 000 students attended university part-time. According to Statistics Canada, in 1986, 10.4% of the population over 15 years of age had a degree and 12% had another post-secondary qualification. PSE is funded primarily by governments (approximately 83% in 1985-86), the balance coming from tuition fees and other sources. Both the provincial and federal governments contribute, but in the context of overall federal-provincial fiscal arrangements the federal share is being constantly renegotiated (*see also* EDUCATIONAL OPPORTUNITY).

Recurrent issues in higher education include who should be served; what mix of general and specialized courses should be offered by universities and colleges; how good teaching can be assured; what the desirable balance is between teaching and research; how costs should be shared by the student and society; what the respective roles and responsibilities of institutions and governments should be; how co-operation with business and industry can be encouraged; and whether aims and outcomes are commensurate.

EDWARD SHEFFIELD

Reading: Robin S. Harris, *A History of Higher Education in Canada, 1663-1960* (1976); Edward Sheffield et al, *Systems of Higher Education: Canada* (1982); J.D. Dennison and P. Gallagher, *Canada's Community Colleges* (1986).

Education, History of The history of education is a central theme in Canada's social, economic and political development. Among the NATIVE PEOPLES and in NEW FRANCE, education was usually an informal process in which skills and values were passed from one generation to the next by parents, relatives and older siblings. Three hundred years later, informal learning has become an adjunct to extensive systems of formal schooling. The growth of schooling in Canada reflects a transformation in the nature of social organization, which has become increasingly based on institutional structures.

During the French regime in Canada, the process of learning was integrated into everyday life. While the French government supported the responsibility of the Catholic Church for schooling, the FAMILY was the basic unit of social organization and the main context within which almost all learning took place. In the labour-intensive economy of the 17th and 18th centuries, families relied on the economic contributions of their children, who were actively engaged in productive activity. Children learned skills such as gardening, spinning and land clearing from other family members. Young males were trained for various trades through an APPRENTICESHIP system. Similarly, because the population was small and dispersed, it was the family that undertook religious instruction and, in some cases, instruction in reading and writing. In certain areas, parish priests established *petites écoles* in which they taught catechism and other subjects. However, the majority of the population in New France, particularly in the rural areas, could not read and write.

In the towns of New France, formal education was more important for a variety of purposes. The Jesuits, Récollects, Ursulines, the Congregation of Notre Dame and other religious orders provided elementary instruction in catechism, reading, writing and arithmetic. More advanced instruction was available for young men who might become priests or enter the professions. By the mid-17th century, a course in classical studies, grammar and theology was available at the COLLEGE DES JÉSUITES, founded in 1635. In the 1660s Bishop LAVAL founded the SÉMINAIRE DE QUÉBEC, which later became UNIVERSITÉ LAVAL. Formal instruction for females was quite limited and usually did not extend beyond religious instruction and skills such as needlework. However, girls who lived in the countryside may have been better educated than boys as a result of the efforts of the sisters of the Congregation of Notre Dame, who established schools in rural areas as well as in towns, and travelled as itinerant teachers.

While only a minority of colonists in New France received instruction in an institutional setting, Catholic missionaries played an important role in formal education. The Recollects hoped to undermine the traditional culture and belief systems of the native people by educating the young boys and girls in the Catholic religion and in French customs. The Jesuits, who also embarked on an ambitious program to "francisize" the native people, compiled translations of the native tongues and established various schools. Other groups, such as the Ursulines, focused their educational efforts on native girls. However, the Catholic Church's missionary efforts met with minimal success and the educational programs had little impact on the society of native people, in which learning continued to be viewed as an ongoing part of everyday activity (*see* NATIVE PEOPLE, EDUCATION).

During the 18th and early 19th centuries, the family remained the unrivalled setting for education; few children in what was then British N America received formal instruction either from tutors or in schools. The pattern began to change during this period, however, as the British government looked to education as a way of promoting cultural identification with Protestantism, the English language and British customs.

In the years after the Conquest of 1759-60, the British authorities were exceedingly concerned about the strong French Canadian presence in the colony, and they tried repeatedly to assist in the establishment of schools that were outside the control of religious authorities. These efforts were undermined by the Catholic Church and, more importantly, by the disinterest of local communities, in which education was associated more with households than classrooms. However, the concept of schooling as an agent of cultural change became more widespread among social leaders during the 19th century, especially as American influence and IRISH immigration added to concern about the cultural complexion of British N America. In these years, politicians, churchmen and educators debated questions of educational financing, control and participation, and as early as the 1840s the structure of the modern SCHOOL SYSTEMS can clearly be discerned in an emerging official consensus.

The consensus involved a fundamental redefinition of the content and structure of education, eg, formal education became a public responsibility under secular rather than religious control. Schools were promoted as components of educational systems rather than as products of single communities. In most regions, the financing of schools became compulsory and attendance by all children (and not just the more affluent) was encouraged. One of the major promoters of these developments was Egerton RYERSON, who as a Methodist minister in UPPER CANADA began a long career of educational leadership when he took up the cause of nondenominational schooling in the late 1820s. The position of superintendent to which he was appointed in 1844 had been created by the School Act of 1841, which was intended to provide for a uniform school system for the United Province of Canada. However, the Act did not effectively resolve the complicated issue of control, administration and finance, and Ryerson sought possible solutions in the US and Europe. During 1844 and 1845 he visited more than 20 countries and was particularly impressed by teaching methods in Prussia, by textbook use in Ireland, and by educational administration in New York and Massachusetts. The recommendations for legislative change included in his 1846 report were based partly on his impressions of education in these countries. These recommendations were incorporated into the Common School Acts of 1846 and 1850 and refined in the 1871 Act to Improve the Common and Grammar Schools. This legislation was not only the foundation for the contemporary Ontario school system, but served as the model for school Acts in most other regions of Canada.

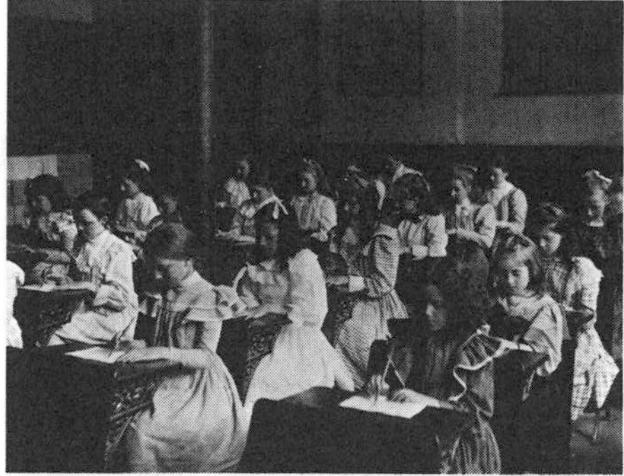

Model school, Ottawa June 1899 (*courtesy National Archives of Canada/PA-28094/photo by W.J. Topley*).

Ryerson and other school promoters such as Alexander FORRESTER in NS and John Jessop in BC sought to establish a system of universal tax-supported elementary education based on Christian morality. Ideally the administration of this system would blend centralized control and local responsibility. In most cases, property taxes would finance the new institutions to guarantee free access to all children. Teachers would be trained and certified and pupils would be provided with standardized textbooks. Fulfilment of these ambitions depended upon a complex array of circumstances. To begin with, school promoters had to convince property owners that they should pay taxes to support the schooling not only of their own children but also, and most importantly, of poorer children. To do so, educators argued that schooling had become necessary as a result of widespread political, social and economic changes. The association of formal education with social purpose was potent in the mid-19th century; school promoters believed that common schooling not only provided an opportunity for general social improvement but that it would serve as an antidote to social instability. Canadian leaders interpreted the REBELLIONS OF 1837 as a sign that the future political stability of their society depended upon achieving a new consensus on the importance of social order and the moral value of self-regulation.

At the same time, economic changes were transforming the family, especially the position of women and children. Until around 1920, Canada was a predominantly rural society, but throughout the 19th century rapid commercial and manufacturing development spurred the growth of major cities in which productive activity moved out of the home and into centralized workplaces (*see* WORK). This transition redefined production as employment. Women and children were most affected, because the emerging wage-labour economy generally offered job opportunities only to men. Older children and unmarried women were employed in sectors such as the textile industry, but by the mid-1800s the number of these potential workers greatly exceeded the number of jobs available for them.

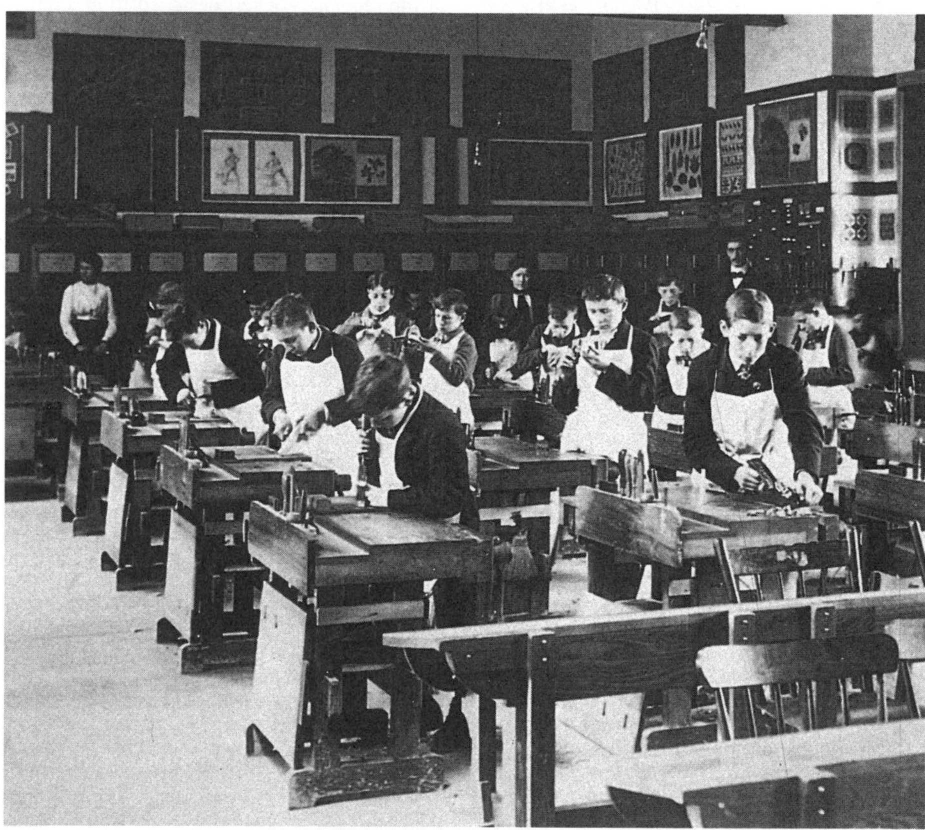

Manual Training Room, OAAC, Ottawa 1901 (*courtesy National Archives of Canada/PA-28236*).

Kindergarten was meant to promote spontaneous learning through song and play but came to be seen as a bridge between home and school (*courtesy Archives of Ontario*).

Social leaders viewed the dislocation of children from productive activity with concern, fearing that cities such as Toronto and Hamilton might be threatened by the appearance on the streets of numerous idle children from working-class families. These children were generally considered by educators to be ignorant, criminally inclined and in need of social training. In the mid-19th century, therefore, school promoters argued that public systems could respond to the emerging political, social and economic dimensions of a new Canadian society, and that free schools would create social harmony by providing a common experience for children of disparate socioeconomic groups. Of course, common schooling was not intended to alter the actual social structure but to preserve it by shaping the behaviour and attitudes of what were perceived as certain potentially disruptive groups, eg, immigrants and the poor. The role of education was to engender a "proper" appreciation (and acceptance) of one's place in society and to promote shared values and customs, thereby ensuring social stability. School promoters considered taxation a small price to pay for these benefits, and although some ratepayers in communities as disparate as Toronto and Victoria did oppose the taxation, the promise of education was sufficiently attractive to encourage support at the local level. The rapid construction of school systems during the mid-19th century resulted not only from official promotion of public schooling but also from the willingness of parents to send their children to school. Even before compulsory attendance legislation was enacted in the late 19th century, most children between the ages of 7 and 12 attended school at least several months each year. Children from affluent families attended regularly and stayed in school until they were older, while children from poorer families only attended irregularly because other demands were more pressing. Official motivation for promoting school construction and local motivation for sending children to school have been distinct from each other; therefore the history of education since the 19th century has been one of conflict and controversy.

Educational development since Ryerson's day has been characterized by an increase in the years of formal attendance at school. SECONDARY SCHOOLS became commonplace in cities. By 1921 many Canadian children registered at school until age 16, while a smaller percentage continued to higher levels. However, social position continued to influence attendance patterns. Children from working-class families received far less schooling than those from more affluent backgrounds. In addition, children in rural areas had less EDUCATIONAL OPPORTUNITY than their counterparts in cities, where population density encouraged the construction of high schools and UNIVERSITIES. The development of public school systems in the 19th century was marked by the standardization of textbooks, teacher training, classroom organization and curriculum. Children were viewed as clay to be molded in desired forms, but over time a view of children as inherently distinct with varying levels of potential (ie, seedlings that had to be cultivated according to their individual natures) came to prevail. The changing view of children contributed to the growth of new educational programs (especially at the secondary level) designed to accommodate the differing abilities and potential of different students. Most importantly, technical and vocational courses were developed for students who were deemed unsuitable for further academic study. Not surprisingly, the criteria used for assigning children to various courses reflected cultural and social prejudices more than intellectual assessments. Measures such as IQ tests, developed by the 1920s, revealed unintentionally more about the school administrators than the students, but they were nevertheless used to place different students in different courses of study after the elementary years. This approach has been constantly revised during the 20th century, especially after WWII, when the expansion of post-secondary institutions provided a new way of sorting different students into different programs. In these years, educational debate focused on the content of the appropriate CURRICULUM for various age groups. Questions of administration, financing, teacher training and other structural features of school systems have tended to follow the general pattern established during the 19th century.

A great deal of educational conflict and controversy has involved religion and language. The establishment of schools brought local practice under official scrutiny and forced communities to conform to prescribed standards of formal instruction which did not accord with the reality of a diverse society. For example, religious groups did not always agree on the desirability of nondenominational Christian curricula, and their protests led to the growth of parallel Catholic and Protestant school systems in Québec, the provision for SEPARATE SCHOOLS in provinces such as Ontario, and a completely denominationally based school system in Newfoundland. These developments were legally guaranteed by the Constitution Act, 1867, which not only assigned education to the provinces but also enshrined the continued legitimacy of denominational schools that were in place in the provinces at the time that they joined Confederation.

Canada's educational history has been marked by constant conflict over minority-language education. Most controversies have involved Francophones outside Québec, but recently the language question has affected Québec Anglophones and has also concerned heritage language instruction to children of immigrant groups (*see* SECOND-LANGUAGE INSTRUCTION). These conflicts reflect the fact that within the general expansion of standardized public schooling, there have been competing educational visions both among policymakers and parents.

Similarly, within the concept of a standard education, there was a sharp distinction between males and females. The ideal public schoolhouse of the mid-19th century included separate entrances, classrooms and recess areas for boys and for girls. In addition, the redefinition of the family as less of an economic unit of production than an association based on emotional attachment was accompanied by the idea that girls should be educated for household responsibility while boys should be trained as breadwinners. By the late 19th century, girls attended HOME ECONOMICS programs to learn cooking and cleaning skills while boys, especially from working-class families, learned manual skills related to factory production. The idealization of women as wives and mothers, as well as the relative paucity of other employment opportunities for females, contributed to the feminization of the elementary-school teaching force. While the proper sphere for women was considered the home, young single women came to be viewed as ideal teachers for younger children who could benefit from their supposedly inherent nurturing qualities. Women teachers were poorly paid and were supervised by male officials who saw themselves as the real educators. Even in the later 20th century, many of the earlier patterns remain unchanged. The history of education has therefore been quite different for males and females.

Formal education also had different implications for Canadians of non-European ancestry. The ambitions of educators to encourage the assimilation of native peoples continued unchanged after the time of New France. In the 19th and 20th centuries, boarding schools were a major strategy for separating native children from their own people, but this approach only served to confuse the children culturally and damage them psychologically. Recently, there have been attempts by official educators to collaborate with native peoples in developing educational programs that respect cultural identity, but thus far the political, social and economic context of NATIVE-WHITE RELATIONS has worked against effective educational collaboration.

Similarly, the history of Canadian education includes the establishment in the 19th century of separate schools for blacks in Ontario and Nova Scotia and special regulations for Asians in BC. Such discrimination is no longer official policy in Canada, but more subtle and informal racism is still apparent in some educational programs and textbooks.

Conclusion The history of education in Canada, as in other Western countries, has involved the growth of formal instruction funded by taxes and supervised by the state. This growth resulted from concern about cultural, moral and political behaviour, from the emergence of a wage-labour economy, from changing concepts of childhood and the family, and from the general reorganization of society into institutions. By the late 20th century, schooling has become part of an institutional network which includes hospitals, businesses, prisons and welfare agencies. Various groups have experienced this development in different ways, sometimes by official design and sometimes by their own choice. As a result, there are many histories of Canadian education and important distinctions within the general trends.

CHAD GAFFIELD

Education, Special, is remedial education designed to help children and young adults who are exceptional in some way as a result of low intelligence, visual or auditory impairment, or emotional or specific learning difficulties or problems. Any individual may present more than one disability. At the other end of the scale are very gifted children who are exceptional because of high intelligence and/or creativity. Remedial or enrichment techniques may include the use of special schools or classes, individual instruction, and specifically designed programs in reading, language or other areas. Up to 40% of youngsters may at some time require special educational help, but as a field, special education is particularly concerned with the 10-15% of the population who suffer major or chronic handicaps (*see* DISABILITIES).

The behaviour of exceptional children varies, but one of the more common characteristics associated with a handicap is instability of behaviour, eg, the motivation to learn may increase or decrease markedly from day to day or even during the course of a day. Teachers, psychologists, social workers and medical practitioners frequently collaborate as an interdisciplinary team, assessing the problems of exceptional children and designing programs suited to the children's individual needs.

Categories of Exceptional Persons The largest group of exceptional persons consists of those who have below average intelligence and below average social and educational attainment. The majority suffer mild handicaps, but they may be afflicted with physical handicaps as well, although multiple handicaps are most common among persons with a severe intelligence handicap. Children who are mildly or moderately handicapped frequently attend special classes, but others study at regular schools. Some severely handicapped children also attend special schools.

There is a large group of persons who have seemingly normal cognitive ability and physique but have difficulty learning to read, spell, etc. These children and adults are often referred to as learning disabled, but the causes of disability are not agreed upon although brain injury and genetic issues have been commonly cited. Others believe environmental factors are also important. Specific techniques and specialized learning centres have been designed to help alleviate these problems. Learning centres may be run by a school board or private agency. Sometimes they are attached to universities such as the learning centre at McGill U, which was started by Dr S. Rabinovitch. Generally, they provide assessment of learning problems and intensive individualized or small-group (3-5 persons) instruction. Children usually attend 2 or 3 times per week. The centre staff sometimes support and advise the child's regular teacher. New centres, such as the Response Centres in Alberta, are being developed to deal with exceptional children. Educationalists are beginning to recognize that the label or category of disability is not as important as the process of assessment and remediation, for general principles of intervention are common to most, if not all, disabilities.

Emotional disabilities and behavioural problems are also common but vary in their duration. Prevalence figures vary from 2 to 20%, but authorities do not agree on the definition of emotional disturbance. Personal as well as environmental factors are important in their development and frequently they result in educational and allied learning difficulties. In many cases it is difficult to know whether the learning difficulty causes the emotional disturbance or vice versa. However, one disability, autism, is regarded as distinct and is recognized as typically beginning during the first 3 years of life and as a disturbance of brain development. Specialized treatment facilities, some of them involving residential schools, are available across Canada. Other children with delinquent and violent behaviour may also be placed in residential facilities.

Visual and hearing impairments are less common handicaps. The majority of those so impaired enjoy partial sight or hearing and often attend special classes using technological aids such as opticon and loop induction. An opticon, used by persons with very restricted vision, magnifies the size of print; with the loop system, designed to aid those with auditory difficulties, a wire around the classroom passes amplified signals to hearing aids. Physical handicaps include problems of the motor system and diseases such as diabetes. Many people with physical or sensory handicaps exhibit average or above average intelligence and many attend regular schools.

Gifted children, who form about 5% of the population, may be permitted to attend grades higher than normally warranted by their chronological age (acceleration). Special enrichment programs are developed for them and a few go to university at an early age. Such children are sometimes unmotivated by regular school programs, and need greater educational challenge. Issues relating to emotional development and experience often arise which necessitate counselling or other professional advice.

Educational Services In many cases the severity of a child's handicap decreases over time through the use of remedial techniques and because of changes in personal or social circumstances. For example, with adulthood different demands are made upon exceptional individuals and there may as well be a change in the perception of what constitutes "normality." Skills learned in school (eg, reading, mathematics) are not necessarily of major importance in certain occupations of the work force. Frequently, intelligence increases substantially during late adolescence and early adult years.

Provincial governments have developed curricula for exceptional children. Special education now involves not just remediation of basic school subjects, but emphasizes social education, eg, the development of basic language and self-help skills, and may include vocational preparation and training. Day-to-day skills used in a home (eg, meal preparation, cleaning) and skills used in leisure activities, which include not only skills learned through participation in sports but those involved in choosing and planning leisure activities at home, are also taught as part of special education and are considered very important to adult adjustment. Development of this approach has already begun to change the concept of the sheltered workshop. Although special schools and special classes are provided for exceptional children, these children are integrated, wherever possible, into regular classes, and remedial education is provided though there are different requirements in different provinces. Exceptional learners may be integrated with their age group for some subjects but not for others. Preschool education within integrated settings is now encouraged for very young children with disabilities. The most normal life-style possible is now accepted as relevant to all forms of disability and the integration of disabled persons into regular educational and social environments is encouraged.

Assessment of Exceptional Children Assessment procedures involving diagnostic and attainment tests are used to ascertain if a child is suffering serious difficulties with hearing or visual impairment, with levels of motor attainment, education (reading or math) or cognitive ability. Intelligence tests have been used frequently for administrative purposes and have resulted in the unjustified segregation of children. Tests of social adaptation, to assess levels of social, vocational and home-living skills, have been developed recently. Staff, parents and sometimes the child discuss goals and procedures and progress. Ideally an individual program plan (sometimes called Individual Education Plan) is developed to achieve very specific goals, eg, what the child needs to learn, in what sequence he or she will do so, which techniques of special education will be used to assist the child, who the teacher will be, and where the child will be taught. Assessment techniques are now being used in Canada which concentrate on how children learn and the methods children use to solve problems. The development of learning strategies is believed to be very important in designing appropriate remedial programs.

The process of "normalization," which is designed to assist a handicapped person to develop as normal and valued a way of life as possible, took root in Canada in the early 1970s. The Canadian Assn for the Mentally Retarded (now the Canadian Assn for Community Living) played an important part in this development, although the evidence relating to its successful application is still, to some degree, wanting. The application of such ideas to education is leading to changes in the environment, for example, barrier-free environments for physically disabled persons, and to a recognition of the social connotations of handicapping conditions.

A requirement for compulsory education in other countries during the mid-1970s led to the development of the individual program plan which is now a required procedure within many Canadian educational institutions. During the early 19th century, some medical facilities were provided for handicapped children, but educational institutions gradually assumed greater responsibility for their welfare. Until the 1970s, handicapped children were isolated in special schools, often run by private agencies; others were sent to institutions or remained at home. With the development of the Individual Education Plan, the labelling has waned, and there has been some recognition that standardized performance tests are of limited help in assessing and developing educational procedures for such children. Denis Stott from University of Guelph has played an important role in the development of curriculum material in special education and in the change of concepts in this area. At the provincial level, pioneers in this field include Dr Christine Meikle from Alberta, who began a school and training centre for mentally handicapped children and initiated the internationally recognized Vocational and Rehabilitation Research Institute in Calgary. John Dolan promoted developments in Saskatchewan, notably the Alvin Buckwold Centre.

Professional Education Many universities provide courses in special education; BEd degrees often include majors in special education, and such studies can be pursued at the graduate level. In a number of Canadian universities, student teachers are now required to take a course in special education because all teachers will become involved with handicapped persons as the process of integration accelerates. Specialized qualifications in counselling and school psychology also exist in many Canadian universities and provide education for specialists who work with exceptional children. Beyond the school system, Canada developed, through the National Institute on Mental Retardation under Allan Roeher, the internationally recognized National Manpower model, which provides for the training of rehabilitation practitioners through diploma programs in community colleges and calls for education beyond this level – at undergraduate and graduate levels in universities. The community-college diploma courses have been in place since the early 1970s in many provinces.

Future of Special Education Regular class teachers generally know too little about learning difficulties and the common behavioural signs of handicapped children. Exceptional children require considerable structure in learning processes. Reading kits using specialized techniques, and social and allied programs have been developed. Computer-assisted instruction increasingly helps physically handicapped people who can use modified terminals. Microcomputers can be used to teach a range of verbal and nonverbal skills in a structured manner. Reading, math and social-skill training are among the programs available on computers, and these lend themselves to education of all exceptional children, including gifted individuals. Major developments in the future will be associated with an examination of the quality of life-style for disabled persons: the accent will be on the development of positive self-image and planned changes to the environment to enable disabled persons to function as effectively as possible in society. Gradually it is being recognized that exceptionality has for many persons lifelong implications. Tertiary institutes of learning are adapting their facilities for physically handicapped persons, but they are also recognizing that many able students have specific learning difficulties that require specialized assistance.

Agencies that provide services to exceptional persons include the Council for Exceptional Children, Canadian National Institute for the Blind, Canadian Rehabilitation Council for the Disabled, National Institute on Mental Retardation (now the Allan G. Roeder Institute), and Institut national canadien-français pour la déficience mentale. There are many parent associations. Some of them are large, such as the Canadian Association for Children and Adults with Learning Disabilities, while others are relatively small and are only just beginning to make themselves felt in Canada (eg, Association for Parents of Children with Prader Willi Syndrome). ROY I. BROWN

Reading: N.J. Marlett, R. Gall and A. Wight-Felske, eds, *Dialogue on Disability: A Canadian Perspective*, Vol I, *The Service System* (1984); M. Csapo, *Children with Behaviour and Social Disorders: A Canadian Focus* (1981); *Canadian Journal of Special Education*.

Education, Technical, combines education and training in preparing persons for gainful employment in occupations that require an understanding of applied scientific principles. Education fosters the development of the whole person without regard to practical applications, while training focuses on transmitting certain practical skills. The terms "vocational education" and "technical education" are often used interchangeably, but vocational education may refer to preparation for nontechnical work or it may describe a series of learning activities that concentrate on narrow training and have little value beyond the immediate application. Technical education, on the other hand, incorporates both training and educational components, although the emphasis on each will vary according to subject matter. Students who enrol in technical-education courses handle materials and tools, gain a degree of technological literacy (in a society that depends almost totally upon technology for material needs), and develop skills for utilitarian or recreational purposes. The standard of living in Canada is tied to the ability of its population to compete with other industrial nations in the international market. There is a growing awareness in Canada that technical and engineering education of a high quality must be available to produce graduates for industry and for governmental agencies.

History The beginnings of formal technical education in Canada can be traced to trade schools established by church authorities in Québec City and St-Joachim, *c* 1668. At these schools, not only were sculpture and painting taught both as trades and as arts, but basic instruction was given in cabinetmaking, carpentry, masonry, roofing, shoemaking and tailoring. By 1700, Jesuit colleges in Québec City and Montréal were training pilots, ships' captains, explorers and surveyors by instruction in mathematics, surveying and hydrography. Significant developments in technical education did not occur, however, until the latter half of the 19th century, and even then growth was slow and unsteady, partly because immigration provided much of the skilled labour (a pattern that has persisted until very recently) and because of APPRENTICESHIP programs. Some of the early developments across Canada included the establishment of MECHANICS' INSTITUTES in Saint John in 1838 and another in Victoria in 1864; and the founding of the Halifax Marine School in 1872 (now Nova Scotia Nautical Institute), the Ontario Society of Artists' School (later the Ontario College of Art) in 1876, 13 trade schools in Québec in 1880, industrial schools for Indians in Saskatchewan and Alberta in 1884, and a manual training centre in Manitoba in 1900.

Role of Governments Involvement by provincial governments in technical education increased in the early part of this century when legislation covering matters such as authorization, financial grants and supervision was passed. Various other schools were founded, eg, a technical school in Montréal (1907), and the Nova Scotia Technical College (1907) and Agricultural College (1905). The Ontario Industrial Education Act (1911) led to the construction of several technical and commercial high schools within the decade. Several other events also reflected the role of provincial governments. A royal commission to enquire into the state of vocational education was created in Manitoba (1910); an amendment to the Secondary Education Act (1911), which initiated manual training, was passed in Saskatchewan; in Alberta in 1913 the Agricultural Schools Act created the Board of Agricultural Education, which in turn established schools of agriculture in Olds, Vermilion and Claresholm; and BC's Department of Education extended manual training to high schools (1909).

The federal government became active in this area in 1910 when it set up the Royal Commission on Industrial Training and Technical Education. Since then, 18 major federal government Acts and agreements have been passed; each has provided funds for use by provincial authorities in the development of a wide range of technical or vocational training.

During the first half of this century, 2 of these Acts were particularly important. The first was the Technical Education Act (1919) under which the Dominion agreed to share up to 50% of provincial expenditures for technical education, resulting in federal grants of $10 million over a 10-year period. The second was the Youth Training Act (1939), out of which the War Emergency Training Program (1940-46) was developed as a special schedule. This provided technical training to both skilled and semiskilled levels for individuals in war industries and in the armed services. Nearly $24 million was expended under this program, and more than 300 000 persons received training.

By far the most influential of government actions was the Technical and Vocational Training Assistance Act of 1960. Under this legislation, the federal government helped the provinces undertake the construction of new vocational high schools, institutes of technology, and adult-training centres. Under the stimulus of this Act, projects valued at over $2 billion were approved within a decade, providing nearly 600 000 new student places.

Although the term "technical education" does not extend to degree programs offered by universities, it does encompass the COMMUNITY COLLEGES and institutes of technology. These post-secondary institutions emerged in considerable numbers during the 1960s, although a few, such as the prestigious Ryerson Institute of Technology (*see* RYERSON POLYTECHNICAL INSTITUTE) in Toronto, had been established soon after WWII.

Courses Offered The range of technical subjects covered in Canadian secondary schools, post-secondary institutes and industry, is extensive. From the first years of secondary school to technological courses at community colleges, the emphasis shifts from manual operations to intellectual comprehension as the content becomes more complex and theoretical. Courses in basic electricity are expanded into computer electronics or industrial power circuits; simple woodworking evolves into building construction, drafting into machine design or architectural planning, and machining operations into automated, programmed sequences.

Until recently, technical courses were taken almost exclusively by males, but an increasing number of females now enrol in high-school technical courses and in technology programs at the post-secondary level. Another trend is toward "co-operative education," whereby students are employed part-time in work situations under the supervision of employers and school staff.

D.E. LONEY

Education Organization The wide diversity in organizational structures in Canadian schools and post-secondary institutions largely reflects the fact that Canada has never had a co-ordinated EDUCATION POLICY and is not likely to have one in the future. Co-ordinated action in education has been frustrated by the economic, cultural and demographic differences between regions in Canada. While each province has attempted to develop its own educational organization, the federal government has also introduced many policies that influence provincial structures (*see* SCHOOL SYSTEMS). There are 6 main legal bases for education in Canada: the Constitution Act, 1867; the stipulations related to the admittance of other provinces to Confederation after 1867; provincial legislation; provincial department of education regulations; rules set by post-secondary institutions and local SCHOOL BOARDS; and court precedents and quasi-judicial decisions.

Types of Organization Elementary and secondary schools in Canada are under public, federal or private control. Publicly controlled schools in all provinces are run by local SCHOOL BOARDS that operate under provincial jurisdiction and are supported either by local taxation or provincial grants, or by both. This includes publicly supported Protestant and Roman Catholic SEPARATE SCHOOLS in some provinces. Education in local school districts is a provincial-local arrangement that allows some local adaptation to provincially set curriculum. Nearly 95% of the 4.94 million pupils enrolled in all schools (1986-87) were enrolled in public schools.

Federal schools are operated by the federal government. The Department of Indian Affairs and Northern Development is responsible for Indian education in all provinces except Newfoundland (*see* NATIVE PEOPLE, EDUCATION). Federal schools generally follow the curriculum of the province in which they are located. The Department of National Defence operates a handful of schools in Canada and overseas. The overseas schools generally follow the curriculum of Ontario, whereas those in Canada follow the curriculum guidelines for public schools of the province in which they are located.

The term PRIVATE SCHOOLS generally describes schools that are not under the direct control of either the federal or provincial governments, although some provinces do provide some financial support. Religious organizations or other groups are directly responsible for the administration of these schools, which nevertheless usually operate within the guidelines determined by provincial departments of education. In 1985-86 private schools represented 5% of total enrolment, an increase of 3% in 15 years.

At the local level, the provinces are divided into public school districts that are typically governed by elected boards of trustees and administered by superintendents and their staffs. These local districts implement provincial educational policy; evaluate and promote students; employ, transfer and dismiss teachers and administrators; develop some local curricula; select texts; and raise supplementary funds through local property taxation (which is usually incorporated without review into municipal tax levies). They also assume responsibility for functions, such as CURRICULUM DEVELOPMENT, which may be decentralized by provincial governments. Several western provinces allow locally developed courses to be counted towards high-school graduation credits.

There are degree-granting post-secondary institutions (eg, universities, and liberal-arts colleges with degree-granting authority) and nondegree-granting institutions (eg, COMMUNITY COLLEGES, the one remaining teachers' college in Nova Scotia, and hospital NURSING schools). An extensive number of nondegree-granting organizations (eg, labour unions, libraries, churches, private companies, museums) are involved in providing ADULT EDUCATION.

Post-secondary institutions are organized differently in the various provinces. In some provinces, eg, public school boards are actively involved in delivering courses, while in others they are represented on the boards of colleges.

By 1986-87 full-time enrolment in undergraduate programs in colleges and universities had reached 733 090. The enrolment rate, ie, full-time enrolment, in post-secondary institutions as a proportion of the 18-24 age group, rose from 10% in 1960 to 24.5% by 1986-87. The size and variety of the post-secondary system has also increased since the 1960s. New professional schools have been created within the universities and graduate programs have increased.

Provincial Systems of Education Because the Constitution Act, 1867, made the provinces responsible for education, 12 autonomous education systems have developed in the 10 provinces and 2 territories. Each province has at least one minister of education, who is an elected member of the legislature (or, in Québec, the National Assembly). Each minister has one or more deputy ministers, appointed civil servants who administer their departments and advise the minister on policy. The minister and the department of education establish curricula, certify staff, approve textbooks, authorize capital developments and allocate the majority of operating funds to local school districts.

The typical provincial financing scheme is the foundation program, whereby a province guarantees a basic level of support for each public-school child and provides the difference between the funds raised by local school districts and the foundation level of support. A variety of special grant mechanisms to meet the special needs of particular school districts and pupils supplement this scheme.

The proportional contribution of local municipalities varies. For example, in 1986-87, no municipal dollars were raised in PEI or New Brunswick, but Ontario municipalities contributed 30.9% of elementary-secondary school expenditures. Provincial and territorial governments supplied between 47.7% and 96.9% of direct funding; federal government contributions ranged between 0.2% and 10.6%.

Pluralism in school organization is most marked in the treatment of religious schools. Each province has developed its own solution to the issue of state-supported sectarian (usually Roman Catholic) schools. The pre-Confederation arrangement in Ontario led to the recognition of elementary separate schools organized as part of the public school system. Saskatchewan and Alberta adopted the same arrangement in 1905 when they became provinces (Alberta also has separate high schools). Québec's dual system (Catholic and Protestant) has been administered by a department of education since 1964. Unofficial local arrangements for public support to Catholic schools evolved in New Brunswick, Nova Scotia and PEI, although no legal provisions for sectarian schools existed when these provinces joined Confederation. Manitoba rejected legal and political attempts to re-establish state support for Roman Catholic schools in the 1890s (*see* MANITOBA SCHOOLS QUESTION), but by the 1960s modest state assistance was extended to them as well as to private schools. BC has a single public-school system but has provided tax support to private schools since 1977. The Terms of Union under which Newfoundland entered Confederation in 1949 guaranteed an exceptional denominational system, which has 3 types of school boards divided among several groups.

The difference among the 12 education systems in Canada is also reflected in the establishment of different levels of schooling. New Brunswick does not support kindergartens in the elementary schools. The elementary level spans only the first 6 grades in 6 of the provinces and in the NWT. Other provinces include seventh or eighth grade in their elementary divisions. Secondary education (high school), covers 3 to 5 grades and is subdivided into junior high schools, senior high schools, or junior-senior high schools. Grade 12 is the highest grade in most provinces, but in Newfoundland and Québec it is grade 11, and in Ontario it is grade 13.

The institutional bases of post-secondary education have been brought increasingly under provincial authority. The development of college systems under close provincial control has been the most significant change in post-secondary education since the mid-1960s. Most universities, with few exceptions, operate under provincial charters. Until 1960 the majority of universities were considered private institutions and were not fully integrated with the provincial systems of education. Then provincially supported universities were established in Manitoba, PEI, Ontario, Québec, New Brunswick, Alberta and BC. Government review of university expenditures became more stringent, although in many cases it was conducted by an intermediate buffer authority such as a grants council. The Maritime Provinces Higher Education Commission plans and co-ordinates higher education systems and advises the 3 provincial governments. All provinces are increasingly exerting their authority in the overall planning, development and programming of universities.

The Federal Role Canada has no national ministry of education. By 1966 the Education Support Branch of the Dept of Secretary of State was established to co-ordinate national efforts in this sector. The federal government intervenes in education through a variety of programs operated by a multitude of departments and agencies. Although the most visible programs are sponsored by the Canada Employment and Immigration Commission and the Department of the Secretary of State, the federal presence in education is also manifest through the educational work of agencies such as the NATIONAL FILM BOARD and the CANADIAN BROADCASTING CORPORATION.

Education is no longer what it was in 1867: the simplest of government services, easily administered and financed locally. The federal government has had to act to meet many national educational demands, financial and otherwise. The incursion of the federal government into a constitutional area where it had no legal jurisdictional powers commenced with very modest federal agricultural grants in 1912 to provinces and agricultural institutions and continued through the Technical Education Act of 1919, which provided grants to the provinces for upgrading vocational, technical, and industrial education. Powerful forces – the state of the economic system, regional financial disparities, national unity – compelled a re-examination of the federal stance by the 1960s. Two programs in particular, one respecting vocational training (the Technical and Vocational Training Act, 1960) and the other official language instruction (OFFICIAL LANGUAGES ACT, 1969), effectively restructured these aspects of education in provincial schools and led to the growth of vocational education (some provinces built comprehensive high schools incorporating academic and vocational courses) and the growth of SECOND-LANGUAGE INSTRUCTION.

The federal role in post-secondary education expanded after WWII. By 1981 federal educational expenditures had reached $5.7 billion, of which more than $5 billion went towards post-secondary education. By 1986-87, direct federal education expenditures reached $6.2 billion, of which $3.7 million went towards post-secondary education. Under the 1960 Technical and Vocational Training Act, the 1967 Adult Occupational Training Act and the 1982 National Training Act, Parliament authorized the payment of allowances to individuals selected by the federal government to take occupational training. The Canada Student Loans Act (1964) authorized the federal government to subsidize bank loans to full-time students (Québec operates its own program) and the Fiscal Arrangements Act (1967, revised 1977) authorized federal unconditional grants to the provinces to defray 50% of the operating costs of post-secondary education.

The COUNCIL OF MINISTERS OF EDUCATION, CANADA (CMEC), which has operated at the national level since 1967 (on an interprovincial rather than a federal basis), sees itself as the official channel for decisions affecting Canada-wide educational policy. A small staff co-ordinates and supports committees on research related to reviewing federal legislation and financing and interprovincial coordination on concerns such as educational media and statistics.

An Assessment One of the most illuminating evaluations of Canadian education was made in the 1976 Report on Education in Canada by the Organization for Economic Cooperation and Development (OECD). Its declaration that "Canadian education policy may be one of the least 'politicized' in the world" explains the absence of a broad public dialogue about ends and means in education. The OECD Report concludes that "reforms in education are almost totally pragmatic, or so generally conceived and relying so heavily on United States, British, and French models, more or less adapted to Canadian conditions, that the opportunity for conflict is, for all practical purposes, excluded."

This absence of open political controversy helps maintain the status quo. The report also noted the dominance of unplanned development in education which can be traced largely to the inadequate funding of educational research. As a result, shifts in education often occur in response to public and political pressures rather than to well-researched systematic policy. In the 1960s, school organizations responded to the winds of change with "continuous progress" plans, vocational education, community colleges and more course options, "alternative" schools, decentralization and faculty power. The 1970s and 1980s saw a shift back to a more subject-oriented regime, centralization of power and "back to the basics" programs. It is doubtful that these shifts did much to relieve the problems of Canadian educators identified by the OECD examiners concerning the poor treatment of the arts and the educational handicaps of underprivileged groups. In addition, it may well be that the greater centralization of decision making in government bureaucracies, the priorities of government and demographic trends are all likely to generate increased uncertainty with respect to the organization (and implicitly of the goals) of education in Canada. LIONEL ORLIKOW

Education Policy in each province is meant to develop the personal capacities of individuals, but also to impart skills useful to society, to induce conformity to community values and generally to encourage socialization. The tension between these aims has resulted in controversies over various aspects of the structure of EDUCATION systems, including curriculum (especially concerning sensitive subjects, eg, religious instruction or sex education); rights of ethnic, linguistic and religious minorities; the extent and forms of public financial support at the local, provincial and federal levels; and the related question of government control relative to the rights of pupils or students, parents and teachers.

Historically, education was essentially a local and private matter (*see* EDUCATION, HISTORY OF), undertaken largely at the initiative of parents and clergy. Colonial and later provincial governments legislated a general framework within which municipalities and religious or charitable institutions might establish and operate schools, especially where local taxes provided a public subsidy. The law ensured general public access to tax-supported schools even where these were confessional or sectarian. Provincial governments also licensed teachers and approved textbooks mainly to ensure that public funds would not be expended on schooling that catered only to a particular religious denomination. In some places special provision was made for religious and, implicitly, for linguistic minorities by establishing sectarian or "dissentient" schools. An attempt was made to offer constitutional protection for minority education rights in the CONSTITUTION ACT, 1867 and in the Acts creating Manitoba (1870), Saskatchewan (1905) and Alberta (1905). Canadian education history is marked by controversies over separate schools in one province after another: NB, 1871; Manitoba, 1891-96; Alberta and Saskatchewan, 1905; Ontario, 1912; Québec, 1969 and afterwards. In every case constitutionally enshrined education rights were ineffective in protecting minorities increasingly concerned with questions of language and religion. In recent years, however, minority language instruction in several provinces has become far more widespread, and under the Constitution Act, 1982, language rights (in English or French) in education are guaranteed where numbers warranted. Although the courts can enforce these rights, it remains to be seen how extensive they will become in practice; in most provinces the language rights set out in the Constitution are still more of a goal than an achievement.

The protection of minority rights is the most visible feature of education policy, historically and currently; but of equal and perhaps even more fundamental importance has been the extension of the government's role in supporting and controlling educational institutions. The provincial governments, and in some respects also the federal government, feel responsible for ensuring universal access to high-quality instruction. From the age of 5 to about 16, school attendance is compulsory. Increasing attendance rates and the average number of years spent in school are major policy goals. Correspondingly, the control by provincial departments of education over local school boards has increased. The trend towards larger, eg, county, SCHOOL BOARDS and the extension of government control over some private but state-supported educational institutions (most universities in Ontario and eastwards, and several schools in Québec) also reflect centralization. The extension of the state's role has been the most far-reaching of the changes in Canadian education policies over the past century and has transformed the machinery for implementing education policy.

Policy Formation and Implementation In each province locally elected school boards are legally responsible for providing free and public schooling up to but not including the college or university level. The school system is typically divided into a primary level and a secondary level. Some programs of instruction terminate at grades 9 or 10, but most continue for 1 to 3 years after that. The BNA Act assigned education "in and for each province" exclusively to the provincial legislatures, except for the never-used federal power of remedial legislation if the rights of religious minorities were being disregarded. Provincial jurisdiction is jealously guarded, and there is considerable variation among the provinces in the structure of education systems. Overall policy is normally set by provincial departments of education. Departmental regulations or ministerial directives prescribe the basic components of the curriculum (*see* CURRICULUM DEVELOPMENT) as well as the range of courses that may be offered at the option of local boards or individual schools. The provincial government also approves instructional materials, establishes qualifications for teachers, specifies the rights of parents and students (eg, in the case of handicapped or gifted children), and sets expenditure ceilings on a per-student basis. Within the fairly narrow limits set by provincial regulations and financial constraints, the trustees elected to county or district boards exercise discretion over curriculum, the hiring, placement and remuneration of teachers, the location of schools and the range of programs offered by each. The degree of centralization in the system varies by province.

The extension of provincial government control has not always been achieved without controversy. The most wrenching conflict occurred in Québec, where prior to the reforms of the 1960s most students going on to university attended private – mainly church-sponsored and -administered – "classical colleges" (*see* COLLÈGE CLASSIQUES). Traditionally, it was felt the state's role in education should consist mainly of providing financial support for a system of schooling (both public and private institutions) controlled in all important respects by the Roman Catholic Church. In policymaking structures the supervision of the school system was the responsibility of 2 advisory committees, one Catholic (effectively the council of bishops) and the other Protestant. The latter was actually nonsectarian and served the entire English-language population of the province except for the Anglo-Catholics. By the late 1950s the Catholic system's deficiencies had become obvious, partly from the very low percentage of youth who obtained secondary schooling and partly from the curriculum's weakness in scientific and technical subjects. The plans of Paul GÉRIN-LAJOIE, minister of youth in the newly elected government of Jean LESAGE, to create a Ministry of Education (1964) and to modernize the system were strongly opposed by many traditional leaders of Québec society, who rightly perceived that the transformation of the education system would transform the entire society; it was also opposed by much of the rural and lower-income population who would have to finance a system which they believed benefited primarily the aspiring urban middle class. Many rural dwellers also resented having to send their children to distant regional comprehensive schools ("polyvalentes"). Successive governments nevertheless succeeded in remaking the system from kindergarten to university, revamping the curriculum and creating a network of comprehensive secondary schools and post-secondary institutions, or COLLÈGES D'ENSEIGNEMENT GÉNÉRAL ET PROFESSIONEL (CEGEPs).

The controversial changes in Québec, which still generate bitter public disputes over curriculum and administrative structures, are in some way similar to those experienced elsewhere in Canada at an earlier period and over a longer time. Nonetheless the Québec situation was and is unique; because of the minority position of the Francophones within Canada and because of the former economic dominance of the Anglophones (a linguistic and religious minority within the province), Québec has a special interest in preserving full control over the educational system at all levels.

Provincial autonomy in education has recently been challenged by the federal government. At the primary and secondary levels its interest has been limited to the extension of minority-language education through bilingualism grants. However, since WWII it has initiated manpower-training programs and has also attempted to broaden access to and rates of participation in post-secondary education. Over the past 30 years Ottawa has actively pursued all these policy aims through a variety of direct-expenditure programs (student aid, purchase of retraining services from vocational colleges, and from 1951 to 1967 direct grants to universities) and fiscal transfers to provincial governments. In 1986-87 the federal government transferred some $2.3 billion in cash to the provinces annually, nominally for post-secondary education but in fact without conditions. There has also been since 1977 a transfer of a portion of the income tax, enabling provinces to swell revenues by an amount almost as large as the cash transfer (*see* INTERGOVERNMENTAL FINANCE). These sums, the cash transfer and the value of the tax points, grow each year at a rate faster than provincial spending. The provinces now finance a decreasing proportion of post-secondary education costs from their own revenue, which the federal government has stated flatly it does not like. It has hinted that it will intervene more directly in post-secondary education in the future if the provinces do not support colleges and universities more generously and otherwise act to further national objectives in post-secondary education.

Critique of Education Policies Policies in any area must be evaluated according to their objectives. With education policy, individual and community preferences vary considerably. In matters of curriculum it is argued that pupils or students should be allowed to study what they choose at their own pace, while others demand a return to basics and a less liberal classroom atmosphere. Some critics urge respect for linguistic and religious particularities, while others insist that the building and preservation of community requires a common educational experience for the young, according to norms established by the majority. A single issue – whether education is primarily for the development of the individual's personal capacities or for molding character and imparting skills so that people become useful and well-adjusted social beings – underlies these disagreements; it is also at the root of controversies over the extent of public support for education (particularly at the post-secondary level), the importance of private institutions and the degree of government control over the system. There is, however, widespread agreement that the largest possible number of young people should complete a high-school program and that access to post-secondary education ought not to be restricted by the finances of individuals or their families. Internationally, Canada is second only to the US in rates of educational attainment (number of years of formal schooling commonly achieved). Within Canada, Québec now has the highest rates of attendance at educational institutions; otherwise, they tend to rise from E to W, probably because of varying community values and expectations and of differences in educational philosophy and practice.

Access to post-secondary education is commonly discussed as if it were primarily a question of financial means (*see* EDUCATIONAL OPPORTUNITY). This factor is undeniably important; its recognition in government policy explains the continuing decline in the proportion of university operating costs borne by fees (26% in 1955; now about half that). Grants and loans are now far more generous and available than in the past; each province (except Québec) administers the federally funded Canada Student Loans Plan and supplements it with its own grants and loans. In most cases the restrictions on access to post-secondary education are now probably traceable to other than financial factors, eg, the program a student takes at the secondary level and whether he or she completes it. Here family background and the encouragement given or withheld by teachers at the primary and secondary levels are probably crucial.

PETER M. LESLIE

Educational Broadcasting refers to TELEVISION PROGRAMMING and RADIO PROGRAMMING providing or related to courses of study. The term "educational" is also applied at times to other programs that are particularly enlightening, informative or stimulating. Educational broadcasting can be received in the home or in an educational institution. Learning by yourself, in the home, is often called "distance education" and broadcasting is only one of several media that can be used to provide the course contents. Films, videotape recording and playback facilities, computer communications, and videodisc recordings are used to supplement written materials and the teacher's work.

Educational programming on radio has had an interesting history in Canada going back to the late 1920s. The University of Alberta was probably the first educational institution to get a radio-broadcasting licence in Canada (CKUA in 1927). Since then, many universities and colleges have become broadcasting licensees. Some stations are owned by the institutions themselves and others are owned and operated by student societies or associations. The most active in producing and broadcasting educational radio programs has been the CANADIAN BROADCASTING CORPORATION (CBC). From its start (1936), the CBC has used radio in original and innovative ways. Aside from the programs for preschool and school-age children, the CBC has received international recognition for its FARM RADIO FORUM programming (1941-65).

These programs discussed major issues and topics of interest to a farming community and were designed to be heard by adults in voluntarily organized listening groups, which would hold their own discussions after each program. The group's response to the program as well as suggestions for future action were collected into provincial reports and broadcast nationally through the CBC to inform all the Forum listeners. The Canadian Association for Adult Education was instrumental in organizing the listener groups on a nationwide basis and in providing the listener responses to the CBC. Because of the Forum's great success, a similar program, called "Citizens' Forum" (1943-52), was established for a broader audience. However, "Citizens' Forum" was considered less successful because there were fewer listening groups and interests were too diffuse to be easily focused. The "Farm Forum" idea has been copied widely in developing countries since the 1950s as an excellent method for distributing information to rural people isolated from modern sources of agricultural knowledge and for encouraging people to exchange information and ideas among themselves.

The CBC's traditions in educational programming on radio are still carried on today although to a lesser extent. When TV services were introduced, the demands on CBC resources increased. It was impossible to engage in the more costly TV production on the same scale as had been possible for radio. The CBC's position as national broadcaster of educational programs has always been complicated because the CBC is a federal CROWN CORPORATION and education is a provincial responsibility. So all CBC instructional programs for schools have been produced and aired under arrangements whereby the provincial educational departments would be responsible for the content of a program though CBC produced the program and transmitted it to the audience. At present, the COUNCIL OF MINISTERS OF EDUCATION works with the CBC to develop programming plans and to work out cost-sharing arrangements. In addition to the broadcasts for each province alone, some programs are shared by several provinces. Programs produced by the CBC for countrywide distribution are called Canadian Schools Broadcasts and Canadian Schools Telecasts.

Some provinces indicated in the 1960s that they wanted educational TV facilities of their own. In metropolitan areas such as Toronto, local school boards began producing TV programming

Scene from the popular children's program "The Polka Dot Door" (*courtesy TVOntario*).

and using CABLE TV channels to reach viewers at home and in schools. Furthermore, several provinces, particularly Ontario, indicated that they wanted to control their own educational TV programs. A satisfactory agreement was reached in 1969 when it was decided that a province could establish a specially incorporated provincial educational authority that would hold any broadcasting licences issued. Each such authority depends entirely on funds voted by the provincial legislature to pay for its broadcasting service. Radio-Québec was first established in 1968 as the "Office de la radio du Québec" but it undertook no production of broadcast materials until it was reorganized in late 1969 as the "Office de radio-télédiffusion du Québec." The Ontario Educational Communications Authority (OECA) was set up in 1970 to provide educational programs for all ages; this authority is called TVOntario, or TVO. The Ontario and Québec authorities each hold licences for several TV stations. Both provinces will be able to reach more people when new transmitters or satellite distribution systems can be set up. In Alberta, the Alberta Educational Communications Corp (ACCESS) was set up (1973) to carry out the educational broadcasting goals of the Alberta Educational Communications Authority. ACCESS now operates the radio station CKUA, which has become the basis for a province-wide radio service. ACCESS also engages in TV production to provide programs through cable TV systems, satellite distribution and some private TV stations. In BC, another approach was taken when the Knowledge Network of the West Communications Authority (KNOW) was established (1980). KNOW does not engage in program production but provides a communications distribution system for all universities and colleges in the province who wish to use it. KNOW uses a satellite linkage from the Vancouver area to one of the Anik satellites, which then beams the signal throughout the province to cable TV systems for distribution. Much of the programming schedule distributed by KNOW is produced outside the province, principally by OECA, the Open University in Britain, and some American sources. There have been discussions about the development of a nationwide educational TV network using the existing authorities' resources, with contributions from the others of programs or funding. The Agency for Tele-Education in Canada (ATEC), made up of representatives from Radio Québec, OECA, ACCESS and KNOW, has put forward proposals for such a network that would be received by most Canadians.

JEAN MCNULTY

Educational Foundations and Endowments The *Canadian Directory of Foundations and Granting Agencies* lists 595 agencies that exist primarily to disburse funds. Within the directory's subcategory of "Education," only 14 FOUNDATIONS and endowments (terms used interchangeably) are listed. Of these 14 the oldest,

McLean, was established in 1945, and most of the others were established between 1960 and 1975. On the basis of 1981 data, this group was responsible for grants of approximately $20 million annually, ranging from $60 000 (A.E. Lepage Charitable Foundation) to over $6 million (Hospital for Sick Children). A number of the endowments are in fact limited to projects either in medicine or in areas related to medicine. None of the 14 foundations is either exclusively or even primarily concerned with education itself.

On the other hand, a number of Canadian foundations and endowments not listed under "Education" do support work in this field. Most of these funds were established after WWII. Some of the better known include Atkinson, Donner Canadian, Bronfman Family, Laidlaw, McConnell and Max Bell. These funds represent median annual disbursements of over $2 million whereas the corresponding figure for the first group is less than $1 million. In addition, there are agencies, such as the Canadian Education Association and the Canada Studies Foundation, that provide some funding for research and program development. In relation to the annual Canadian public investment in education of $10 billion, the effective contribution of Canadian endowments and foundations is marginal at best.

Several of the Canadian educational foundations and endowments (eg, Macdonald Stewart, Jackman, McConnell) are general purpose in scope; much more common (at least with regard to education) are endowments for specialization. For example, Max Bell is likely to be focused on health care and medicine; Bronfman on learning disabilities; Harry E. Foster on mental retardation; and Donner on law reform and Canadian foreign policy. Moreover, even when published guidelines are general in nature, funds are frequently disbursed for particular purposes. There is at least one fund that specifies the eligibility of broad areas of education research but which in fact supports university-based research only in medicine. Individuals and institutions who are in search of funding support need to develop a very detailed knowledge of the particular preferences of each fund. BERNARD J. SHAPIRO

Educational Opportunity Education has been seen in modern industrial societies, as the way to provide equality of opportunity. Education, it is argued, can provide this opportunity because it prepares young people for jobs in a continually changing world and allows the most able to develop their talents and to rise to the top. Inequalities in a society can be justified if everyone has a chance to acquire the rewards that the society has to offer. One of the goals of education since the early 1960s, in Canada as well as in the rest of the Western world, has been to eliminate barriers that are based on race, ethnicity, sex and social class.

Although equality of opportunity has always been seen as a reason for the expansion of education, economic and social reasons have been equally important. In Upper Canada, Egerton RYERSON, the first superintendent of education, lauded education as "the most effectual preventative of pauperism and its natural companions, misery and crime." In the 19th century, the goal of educational reformers was not access to higher education but the provision of free, universal, compulsory, elementary education (*see* EDUCATION, HISTORY OF). This goal was strenuously opposed by those who were not prepared to have their taxes used for the benefit of other people's children and by those who resisted the intervention of the state in the lives of families.

By the 1960s, the new goal, accessibility to UNIVERSITY for all who wished it and were able to benefit from it, was endorsed by the 1948 Universal Declaration of Human Rights adopted by the UN General Assembly with the qualification: "Higher education shall be made equally accessible to all on the basis of merit." In the 1960s the expansion of education was promoted as being essential in order to provide a post-industrial society with the skills it would require.

In Canada, until the 1960s, there were few educational opportunities for high-school students (only 4% went on to university). During the 1960s, however, post-secondary education expanded enormously. COMMUNITY COLLEGES were established, existing universities were expanded and new ones created. Full-time enrolments to all post-secondary institutions increased by 214% in a decade. Simultaneously, expenditures increased. These expenditures and the economic crisis of the 1980s led to a questioning of the educational system and the policy of accessibility on which it was based.

In the 1960s, however, post-secondary education was seen as a panacea for personal, social and economic ills. To widen accessibility, student assistance plans were implemented in all provinces (*see* STUDENTS, FINANCIAL AID TO). The federal government's involvement began with aid to veterans after both world wars. The Dominion-Provincial Student Aid Program (1939) was supplanted by the Canada Student Loans Plan (CSLP) in 1964. Under the CSLP the federal government assumed responsibility for providing guaranteed loans to all students who demonstrated need. The provinces were to administer the program under jointly agreed criteria. All provinces and territories, except Québec, which provides its own program, participated. Provincial governments supplemented the Canada Student Loans with loans, grants and bursaries.

Both the idea that education could ensure equality of opportunity and the belief that the post-industrial world would require an upgrading of the labour force were later challenged. In *The Rise of the Meritocracy* (1970), author Michael Young predicted that in a society based on meritocracy, ruthless competition and rigorous selection would create an upper class of masters and an under class of drones. Others have questioned the idea that a just society can emerge based on equality of opportunity. In *Labour and Monopoly Capital*, Harry Braverman argued that in a technologically advanced society there would be a degrading of the labour force; a relatively few highly trained workers would be necessary, and the mass of workers would require fewer skills.

Others have argued that the society that develops as a result of the expansion of higher education is one in which credentials, rather than job requirements or a person's inherent skills and ability, determine accessibility to occupations. This argument is based on evidence that the increasing educational requirements for jobs are not a result of the increasing complexity of jobs; rather, they are caused by employers using educational credentials as screening devices.

Finally, there are critics who believe that the educational system does not provide opportunities for equality but perpetuates the inequalities that already exist, and that one way that it does so is by "streaming" students from different socioeconomic backgrounds into different programs (*see also* SOCIAL CLASS). Moreover, these critics claim that attitude and personality are more important than intelligence and ability in determining who is "successful" in school.

Canadian society has not found easy answers to these questions, but general support still exists for the belief that it is profoundly unfair to limit opportunities for higher education to those who through their socialization in privileged families can best meet rigid selection procedures.

MARION PORTER

Reading: H. Braverman, *Labor and Monopoly Capital* (1974); John Porter, "Education, Equality and the Just Society," in John Porter, *The Measure of Canadian Society* (1979); Porter, Marion Porter and B.R. Blishen, *Stations and Callings* (1982).

Edwards, Henrietta Louise, née Muir, women's rights activist, reformer (b at Montréal 18 Dec 1849; d at Ft Macleod, Alta 10 Nov 1931). Of a wealthy family, Edwards early evinced feminist sympathies; in 1875 she founded the Working Girls' Assn to provide vocational training and edited a journal, *Women's Work in Canada*. She helped Lady ABERDEEN found the National Council of Women (1893) and also helped found the VICTORIAN ORDER OF NURSES. One of Alberta's "Famous Five" in the PERSONS CASE and a supporter of divorce on equal grounds, prison reform and mother's allowances, she aimed to expand women's rights in the political and especially the legal sphere. She wrote *The Legal Status of Women in Alberta* (1921) and pressed for the 1917 DOWER ACT. ELIANE LESLAU SILVERMAN

Henrietta Louise Edwards, an early women's rights activist (*courtesy Glenbow Archives, Calgary*).

Edwards, Robert Chambers, "Bob," newspaper publisher (b at Edinburgh, Scot 12 Sept 1864; d at Calgary 14 Nov 1922). Related to the Chambers publishing family, he immigrated to western Canada in 1894; in 1897 he launched the *Wetaskiwin Free Lance*, forerunner of the Calgary *Eye Opener*, an itinerant newspaper first published in High River in 1902 that gained a reputation for originality and wit. Lampooning society and political personalities, the *Eye Opener* was the target of legal actions that included one on behalf of Prem A.L. SIFTON. The *Eye Opener* called the 3 biggest liars in Alberta "Robert Edwards, Gentleman; Hon A.L. Sifton (premier); and Bob Edwards, Editor of the Eye Opener." The suit was dropped when Edwards filed a similar action on behalf of Robert Edwards, Gentleman, and Bob Edwards, Editor. An alcoholic, usually in debt, Edwards moved to Toronto in 1909, then to Montréal, Port Arthur, Ont, and Winnipeg, returning to Calgary in 1911. Unconventional to the end, he supported PROHIBITION in the referendum of 1916, then won election as an Indepen-

Bob Edwards, *c*1910. His wit and his lampooning of society and political personalities landed him with several legal suits but gained him an unmatched reputation as a maverick journalist (*courtesy Provincial Archives of Alberta/H. Pollard Coll*).

dent in the 1921 provincial elections. He was able to attend only one sitting before his death. His reputation was such that police in dress uniform were his pallbearers, and today his status as a maverick publisher has become a western legend. JOHN PATRICK GILLESE

Edwards, William Cameron, industrialist, politician (b in Clarence Twp, Russell County, Canada W 7 May 1844; d at Ottawa 17 Sept 1921). Edwards entered the lumbering business in Thurso but moved to Rockland in 1868 and founded W.C. Edwards and Co, building large sawmills at Rockland and New Edinburgh. A noted stockbreeder and agriculturalist, he represented Russell in Parliament 1887-1903, when he was appointed to the Senate. He accompanied PM Wilfrid LAURIER to Queen Victoria's Diamond Jubilee in 1897 and King Edward's coronation in 1902. Edwards was president of Canada Cement and the Russell Agricultural Soc, and director of many companies, including the Canadian Bank of Commerce, Canada Central Railway, Canadian Forestry Association and the Central Canada Exhibition. In 1920 he helped organize a $60-million merger involving Riordon Pulp and Paper Company. RICHARD REID

Eel, snakelike fish of class Osteichthyes, order Anguilliformes (or Apodes). There are about 20 families, 130 genera and 600 species, including moray, conger, snake and snipe eels. Except for the freshwater family Anguillidae, they are marine, abounding in shallow waters of tropical and subtropical seas. Some inhabit deep seas. There are 11 species in 11 genera in Canadian Atlantic waters, including deep- and shallow-water forms; 4 species in 4 genera of deep-water forms occur in Canadian Pacific waters. The American eel (*Anguilla rostrata*) occurs widely in eastern Canadian fresh waters. Eels, typically, are elongated, round in cross section at the front and laterally compressed toward the back. They lack pelvic fins; the dorsal and anal fins are usually continuous with the tail fin. Most species lack scales. Eels are predaceous and tend to be nocturnal. The American and European eels are catadromous, ie, spend their lives in fresh water, returning to the ocean (the Atlantic, near the West Indies) to spawn and die. Larvae take one year to reach the N American coast and probably 3 years to reach the European coast. Spawning behaviour and exact place and time of spawning are subjects of continuing research. These eels are highly regarded as food, especially when smoked. W.B. SCOTT

Eenoolooapik, "Bobbie," Inuk traveller, guide (b at Qimisuk, Cumberland Sound, NWT 1820?; d at Cumberland Sound 1847), brother of TOOKOOLITO. He travelled to Britain in 1839 with whaling captain William Penny, who had hoped to establish a wintering base for whalers in Cumberland Sd. Penny's plan was rejected, but Eenoolooapik's friendliness and sense of humour endeared him to the British, who followed newspaper reports of his activities. In 1840, after helping Penny enter Cumberland Sd, he returned to his birthplace where he married and lived as a hunter and trader. Not long after his death, wintering in Cumberland Sd became common practice among whalers, and thus the knowledge Eenoolooapik provided to his European friends served to accelerate the colonization of his homeland. JOHN BENNETT

Eggleston, Wilfrid, journalist (b at Lincoln, Eng 25 Mar 1901; d at Ottawa 13 June 1986). Raised on an Alberta homestead, he took a BA at Queen's (1926) before becoming a journalist, briefly in Lethbridge and then in Toronto. He was Ottawa correspondent for the Toronto *Star* and Reuters, 1929-36, a member of the secretariat of the Royal Commission on FEDERAL-PROVINCIAL RELATIONS, 1937-39, chief press censor during WWII and founding director of Carleton U's School of Journalism, 1947-66. He was considered the father of journalism education in Canada, emphasizing its roots in the liberal arts and social sciences. His literary works include 2 novels, literary criticism, histories of Ottawa, nuclear energy in Canada and the National Research Council and 2 memoirs, *While I Still Remember* (1968) and *Literary Friends* (1980). D.M.L. FARR

Eggplant (*Solanum melongena* var. *esculentum*), or aubergine, perennial herbaceous plant of the NIGHTSHADE family. The genus contains about 1500 tropical and temperate climate species; one wild and 5 cultivated species occur in Canada. Native to SW Asia, eggplant was derived from a wild species with egg-shaped fruits. Plants are either bushy or upright, 45-100 cm tall; flowers (2-4 cm across) are purple and usually occur singly. Fruits (20-25 cm long) are a glossy purplish black with a green calyx. A long-season crop, eggplants require a greenhouse or hotbed start of 9-10 weeks and reach maturity 55-80 days after transplanting. INSECT PESTS are fleas and Colorado potato beetles; plant diseases, *Verticillium* and bacterial wilts. Eggplants are comparable to TOMATOES in nutrition but have better shelf life. Eggplants are a low-hectarage commercial crop in Canada but are grown in gardens across the country. V.W. NUTTALL

Ehattesaht, a NOOTKA Indian tribe on the W coast of Vancouver I. They formerly consisted of 3 tribes who, decimated by disease and warfare, amalgamated in the historic period. Their traditional territories include the N shore of Esperanza Inlet and the outer coast, Zeballos Inlet and part of Espinosa Inlet. The main Ehattesaht villages were Oke and Tatchu, but today the tribal village is Chenahkint at Queen's Cove. The Ehattesaht traditionally were major suppliers of dentalia shells, highly valued as trade objects by native peoples of the Northwest Coast. *See also* NATIVE PEOPLE: NORTHWEST COAST. JOHN DEWHIRST

Elbow, Sask, Village, pop 323 (1986c), 313 (1981c), inc 1909, is situated midway between SASKATOON and MOOSE JAW. It received its name because of a configuration of the S Saskatchewan R, on which it sits. While the village of Elbow dates only from the early years of this century, the general location had been so designated for more than 100 years. The first known use of the term "elbow" is found in the journal of John Macdonald of Garth, a fur trader of the NWC, who wrote, "There is an elbow in the river parallel to that of the north branch, a most beautiful place." The first settlers appear to have been ranchers. By 1903 settlers were taking up homesteads near Elbow, and by the end of the decade lands in the elbow were extensively occupied. The CANADIAN PACIFIC RY, which arrived in 1908, has accounted for the continued existence of the village. The level of activity in the community increased with the long-anticipated South Saskatchewan River Dam Project in 1958. The completion of GARDINER DAM and Qu'Appelle Dam a decade later created DIEFENBAKER LAKE which provides irrigation and recreation in the area. DON HERPERGER

Elder, shrub of genus *Sambucus*, family Caprifoliaceae (honeysuckle). Elders grow up to 3 m high and spread to form thickets. About 20 species are known worldwide; 3 are native to Canada. The leaves are large, opposite and pinnate with 5-11 leaflets. They are usually hairy underneath. Several stems arise from one root. The pithy-cored stems are sometimes hollowed out and used for peashooters and whistles; however, the roots, stems and leaves are poisonous. Their emetic and purgative properties were used in European and N American folk medicine. The small, cream-coloured flowers are borne in dense clusters. They are edible and are used to flavour beverages. The juicy, berrylike fruits are blue, black or red, depending on species. The fruits of blue- and black-fruited species are seedy, and not very palatable when raw, but make excellent wine, jelly and pie, alone or combined with other fruits. *See also* PLANTS, NATIVE USES. NANCY J. TURNER

Elder, James, equestrian (b at Toronto, Ont 27 July 1934). An illustrious international equestrian for over a quarter-century, Elder was a member of the bronze-medal Canadian team in the 3-day event at the 1956 Olympics and of the winning 1959 Pan-American Games team. With the Canadian show-jumping team since 1952 – for several years as captain – he formed a trio with James DAY and Thomas GAYFORD that brought Canadian equestrians to the fore in the late 1960s. Their victories included the Grand Prix at the 1968 Mexico City Olympics, the World Championships (1970) and the Pan-American Games (1971). Elder represented Canada in the 1972, 1976 and 1984 Olympics, and was on the winning teams at the Olympic Games alternate Nation's Cup in Rotterdam (1980) and at the CSIO Nation's Cup in Sydney, Australia (1982). He was individual international champion at the Royal Horse Show 3 times. In 1983 he was appointed an Officer of the Order of Canada and in 1985 he was honoured for his longtime and outstanding contribution to EQUESTRIAN SPORT. BARBARA SCHRODT

Elder, Richard Bruce, filmmaker, critic (b at Hawkesbury, Ont 12 June 1947). Internationally recognized for his avant-garde films and his writing on film and computer technology, Elder studied cinema at Ryerson and the University Film Study Centre after graduating from U of T with an MA 1970. His *Barbara is a Vision of Loveliness* won the 1976 Canadian Film Award for best experimental film and his autobiographical *The Art of Worldly Wisdom* (1979) was named Best Independent Experimental Film by the Los Angeles Critics Circle. Elder's *1857: Fool's Gold* (1980) and *Illuminated Texts* (1982) are characterized by their incorporation of written texts and their use of computer-generated optical printing and sound.

Elder's 8-hour experimental film, *Lamentations* (1985), was shown as part of an Art Gallery of Ontario retrospective that year. Also in 1985, he published "The Cinema We Need," an article that has been called "the first Canadian film manifesto since Grierson," and elicited considerable controversy. *Consolations*, a 14-hour work, was released in 1987. SETH FELDMAN

Eldorado Gold Mines Limited, later Eldorado Mining & Refining Ltd and later still Eldorado Nuclear Ltd, a uranium mining company with properties in Saskatchewan and Ontario. It is a subsidiary of Eldorado Nuclear Ltd and has been owned since 1944 by the Government of Canada. Eldorado began as a gold mine in Manitoba; when that failed, its owners, the LABINE brothers, took what remained of the treasury and invested it in exploration in the Subarctic around Great Bear Lake. Gilbert LaBine discovered a silver and pitchblende deposit at Port Radium (Echo Bay) in 1930; a mine was established and the product was refined into radium at Port Hope, Ont. Eldorado did not prosper in the radium market, but it was rescued from near-bankruptcy by the sudden rise in importance of its waste product, uranium, in 1942 with the Allied drive to make an atomic bomb. Because of Eldorado's strategic importance it was bought secretly that year by the Canadian government and nationalized in 1944. Because of the LaBines' incompetent management, they were replaced by C.D. HOWE's choice as president, W.J. BENNETT, in 1947. Bennett turned the company into a wildly prosperous supplier of the US Atomic Energy Commission, and expanded its operations into Beaverlodge (URANIUM CITY), Sask, in 1948. Production there began in 1953.

Eldorado also served as compulsory marketing agent for all private Canadian uranium companies during the 1950s. With the collapse of the world uranium market in 1959, however, Eldorado knew tough times, especially since, as a crown company, it was not allowed to be fully competitive with its private rivals. It recovered with the uranium boom of the mid- to late 1970s, but when the price of the product descended once more, in the 1980s, it was obliged to close its Beaverlodge mine and concentrate on more abundant mining deposits farther south in Saskatchewan. Although the company accounts for almost 20% of Canadian production of uranium, it suffered a net loss of $64 million at its 1986 year-end. ROBERT BOTHWELL

Election Expenses Act, which came into effect on 1 Aug 1974, made important changes to federal ELECTION and income tax laws. The laws provide that a certain proportion of an individual's contribution to a federal registered political party or a federal election candidate could be deducted from payable federal income tax. Some provinces have now made similar provisions for their own elections. The legislation also limits the amount of money that could be spent in an election campaign (*see* ELECTORAL SYSTEMS). This provision was designed to reduce any unfair advantages to the wealthiest parties and candidates and to encourage a broader participation. The amount that a registered party may spend is limited to a total based on the number of electors in each district where it is running candidates. Individual candidates' campaign expenses are also limited by the number of names on the list of electors in their district. After an election, candidates and parties must file audited reports detailing expenses incurred and contributions received. Candidates who receive at least 15% of the votes cast in their district are entitled to a partial reimbursement of their expenses.

Problems have arisen in the interpretation and application of the new legislation, partly as a consequence of imprecise or ambiguous wording. There may be disputes about what actually constitutes an election expense limited by the Act. There are also some obvious weaknesses in the enforcement procedures.

Following the 1984 election, the RCMP began an investigation of a number of members, including one Cabinet minister, Marcel MASSE, for alleged violations of the Election Expenses Act. Masse, who resigned his portfolio when the investigation began, was exonerated and returned to Cabinet amid complaints of slow progress with the investigation, damaging publicity and heavy-handed use of the RCMP. Problems have also risen over the promotion of, or opposition to, parties, candidates or issues by agencies not directly involved in the election (what is referred to as "third-party advertising"). TERENCE H. QUALTER

Elections Canadian elections are held under a process that reflects well-understood principles and is an integral part of the country's political culture. Despite the varying regional differences that often appear in election results, the process itself is national; the same basic rules are in force from coast to coast. The first few federal elections were held under disparate provincial laws, but in the 1870s the first national election provisions were enacted, laying the foundations for the present system. Seats are shared first among the provinces, and then constituency boundaries are drawn by commissions established under federal law. Between elections, by-elections can be held to fill vacancies in the HOUSE OF COMMONS; one of the duties of the Chief Electoral Officer is to keep the whole system under continual review, with improvements constantly in mind. The apparent stability of the process can be misleading. A political party can poll more votes than a rival but still lose an election, as the CONSERVATIVE PARTY did in 1896. A party can win almost identical shares of the popular vote in consecutive elections but lose the first disastrously and score a triumph in the second, as the LIBERAL PARTY did in 1930 and 1935. A party can be weak nationally but, if its support is concentrated in one area, may elect several members, as the SOCIAL CREDIT PARTY did in Alberta through several elections beginning in 1940. A party can have a stable national support but, if votes for it are scattered across the country, its share of victories in any election may lag far behind its share of the vote, as both the CO-OPERATIVE COMMONWEALTH FEDERATION (CCF) and its successor, the NEW DEMOCRATIC PARTY (NDP), have experienced.

The unbalanced nature of many election results can be attributed chiefly to the single-member constituency system (*see* ELECTORAL SYSTEM), in which a candidate need poll only one vote more than the runner-up to win the seat, no matter how many votes the other candidates amass, and to the federal distribution of the seats in the House of Commons (*see* REDISTRIBUTION). The distribution not only makes it easier for a party concentrating in one area to win seats there, but the disproportionate size of Ontario and Québec (which between them have always had more than half the seats in the Commons) permits a party to do reasonably well in either of them without necessarily winning many seats. The classic case is that of the federal Conservative party in Québec prior to the 1984 election, but since the 1950s the Liberals have had similar difficulties in the West. A relatively new factor, the extent of whose influence on election results is as yet unknown, is the combined use of television and advertising agencies in campaign strategies.

Prime Minister Louis St. Laurent with children, during election campaign of 1949 (*courtesy National Archives of Canada/PA-123988*).

National elections can occur for several reasons. A House of Commons ceases to exist 5 years after the writs for the last election are returned, and an election may be necessary because the existing Commons has constitutionally expired, as happened in 1896 and (almost) in 1935, and might have happened in 1916 if the CONSTITUTION had not been temporarily amended to prolong the life of the Parliament chosen in 1911. A PRIME MINISTER has the power to advise the dissolution of Parliament when he considers it wise or expedient, and elections have been held as close together as 1872 and 1874, 1925 and 1926, 1957 and 1958, and 1962 and 1963. A change of prime minister may bring on an election; eg, when Pierre TRUDEAU became prime minister in 1968, one of his first official acts was to advise the dissolution of Parliament. The defeat of a government in the House of Commons may precipitate an election (1926, 1963 and 1979): if the government loses the ensuing election, it is replaced; if it wins, it simply continues in office. While elections and changes in either the prime minister or the government as a whole may be related to each other, there is no necessary connection between elections and changes in the executive. The Conservatives won in 1872, but their leader, Sir John A. MACDONALD, resigned in 1873 because he was convinced he had lost the support of too many of his own party members in the Commons to carry on; the next election, called by his Liberal successor, Alexander MACKENZIE, was in 1874. Macdonald, who died after the election of 1891, was followed by 4 consecutive Conservative prime ministers, one of whom also died in office, but there was no election until 1896. In 1925 the Conservatives won more seats than the Liberals, but remained in Opposition. In 1926 the Conservative leader, Arthur MEIGHEN, did become prime minister without an election, but when he called an election in that year and lost it, he also lost the prime ministership. Sometimes there is a connection between an election and executive changes, and sometimes there is not.

All the prime ministers mentioned above were party leaders, and the election system relies wholly on parties (*see* PARTY SYSTEM); Parliament provides through elaborate laws for the holding of elections, but the laws do not require anybody to come forth to hold one. Each party assumes that function in its own interests, providing can-

Canadian General Elections 1867-1984
Party Standing in House of Commons
(*Source:* Elections Canada)

Date of Election	*Con*	*Lib*	*Prog*	*UFA*	*CCF*	*NDP*	*SC*	*Ral Créd*	*Others*	*Ind*	*No Aff*	*Total Seats*
7 Aug-20 Sept 1867	101	80	-	-	-	-	-	-	-	-	-	181
20 July-3 Sept 1872	103	97	-	-	-	-	-	-	-	-	-	200
22 Jan 1874	73	133	-	-	-	-	-	-	-	-	-	206
17 Sept 1878	137	69	-	-	-	-	-	-	-	-	-	206
20 June 1882	139	71	-	-	-	-	-	-	-	-	-	210
22 Feb 1887	123	92	-	-	-	-	-	-	-	-	-	215
5 Mar 1891	123	92	-	-	-	-	-	-	-	-	-	215
23 June 1896	88	118	-	-	-	-	-	-	7	-	-	213
7 Nov 1900	81	132	-	-	-	-	-	-	-	-	-	213
3 Nov 1904	75	139	-	-	-	-	-	-	-	-	-	214
26 Oct 1908	85	133	-	-	-	-	-	-	1	2	-	221
21 Sept 1911	133	86	-	-	-	-	-	-	1	1	-	221
17 Dec 1917	153[1]	82	-	-	-	-	-	-	-	-	-	235
6 Dec 1921	50	116	65	-	-	-	-	-	2	2	-	235
29 Oct 1925	116	99	24	-	-	-	-	-	4	2	-	245
14 Sept 1926	91	116	13	11	-	-	-	-	12	2	-	245
28 July 1930	137	91	2	10	-	-	-	-	4	1	-	245
14 Oct 1935	39	171	-	-	7	-	17	-	10	1	-	245
26 Mar 1940	39	178	-	-	8	-	10	-	6	4	-	245
11 June 1945	67	125	-	-	28	-	13	-	7	5	-	245
27 June 1949	41	190	-	-	13	-	10	-	3	5	-	262
10 Aug 1953	51	171	-	-	23	-	15	-	2	3	-	265
10 June 1957	112	105	-	-	25	-	19	-	2	2	-	265
31 Mar 1958	208	49	-	-	8	-	-	-	-	-	-	265
18 June 1962	116	99	-	-	-	19	30	-	1	-	-	265
8 Apr 1963	95	129	-	-	-	17	24	-	-	-	-	265
8 Nov 1965	97	131	-	-	-	21	5	9	1	1	-	265
25 June 1968	72	155	-	-	-	22	-	14	-	1	-	264
30 Nov 1972	107	109	-	-	-	31	15	-	-	1	1	264
8 July 1974	95	141	-	-	-	16	11	-	-	1	-	264
22 May 1979	136	114	-	-	-	26	6	-	-	-	-	282
18 Feb 1980	103	147	-	-	-	32	-	-	-	-	-	282
4 Sept 1984	211	40	-	-	-	30	-	-	-	1	-	282

Notes
[1] Unionists
Con - Conservative
Lib - Liberal
Prog - Progressives
UFA - United Farmers of Alberta
Ind - Independents
CCF - Co-operative Commonwealth Federation
NDP - New Democratic Party
Ral Créd - Ralliement des Créditistes
SC - Social Credit
No Aff - No Affiliation

didates, planning and financing the campaigns, selecting the issues over which each election is fought, and providing the leader who, each party hopes, will become prime minister or at least leader of the Opposition (*see* LEADERSHIP CONVENTION). While it is not impossible for independents to get elected to Parliament, it is unusual; the parties, in effect, provide candidates for each election. They use an elaborate and closely regulated administrative machine provided by the state, but in so doing they privately raise and spend large amounts of money. The amounts, and the purposes on which the money can be spent, are now also regulated (*see* ELECTION EXPENSES ACT) but the limits on both parties and candidates are generous.

The law of elections also provides for reimbursement of candidates for certain legitimate expenses (provided they win a prescribed share of the vote), so that serious aspirants to Parliament need not be deterred from running solely for financial reasons.

Each general election is unique, for while the basic principles on which elections are conducted have varied remarkably little since the beginning, the personnel involved and the issues fought over are never entirely the same. Some elections are fought mainly on one clear-cut issue: eg, in 1911, the governing Liberals favoured a comprehensive reciprocal trade agreement with the US; the Conservatives opposed it and won.

In 1917 the Conservatives favoured CONSCRIPTION for overseas service, and the issue so deeply divided the Liberals in Opposition that they could not mount a united campaign either for or against it; the leader, LAURIER, opposed conscription, and while the issue in 1917 reduced Liberal strength in Parliament to its lowest ebb since CONFEDERATION, the Conservatives thereafter found Québec all but closed to them for several consecutive decades. If a government has been long in power, as the Conservatives were under Macdonald to 1891 and the Liberals were under KING and ST. LAURENT to 1957, its record is invariably an issue in each election.

Rising prosperity is generally good for a governing party, as the Liberals showed after 1896 and 1945, and its opposite, depression, can haunt a party for decades, as the Conservatives found after 1935. Modern electronics has created new kinds of issues, since the parties' credibility on television, and in particular the leaders' image, have become factors in attracting and repelling voters. In a manner that successful former electioneers such as Macdonald, Laurier, BORDEN and King might find difficult to approve, a modern election produces a series of selling campaigns in which each leader and party is packaged for marketing as enticingly as possible. In a modern election an individual party leader may become an issue.

Few Canadian elections have been fought on issues as fundamental as free trade versus protectionism, monarchy versus republicanism, or democracy versus authoritarianism, although there have been elections in which basic issues have been important. The 1911 election, for example, created heated arguments over Canada's relations with the US, and that of 1926 was exploited by King to challenge Canada's relationship with the UK in a way that soon altered the relationship. But the raising of fundamental principles as election issues in Canada is not often attractive to political parties because of 2 considerations that are also fundamental.

Quite apart from the difficulties of making abstract principles comprehensible as useful material in election campaigns, the Canadian electorate is so varied that a basic issue can provoke vastly different and even opposing responses in different parts of the country. The clearest single historical example is the question of whether Canadians should be conscripted to fight in wars abroad: in 1917 the Government gave one answer, and the party chiefly responsible for it suffered electorally for decades; in WWII the Government believed that a yes or no answer at the national level was not possible and produced a slogan that is a Canadian model of its kind, "Conscription if necessary, but not necessarily conscription."

The diversity of the country produces the other basic consideration; any party hoping to find electoral success in Canada has to have a broad appeal, and the result is that the parties rarely differ deeply on fundamental issues. All parties successful in elections contain individuals of enormously varied opinions, but during elections the parties generally present a united front which does not encourage the expression of the extremes of opinion within the party. All the parties agree on the retention of the monarch, of Parliament, of the party system and of free elections. All are committed to a broad range of health and welfare policies and to a mixture of public and private enterprise. All recognize that foreign investment in Canada can have undesirable effects but that it is necessary. No "extreme" party in Canada has ever, in fact, successfully used elections to produce a regular contingent of members of Parliament. *See also* ELECTORAL BEHAVIOUR.

NORMAN WARD

Electoral Behaviour About 76% of those Canadians eligible to vote went to the polls in Sept 1984 to elect a new Progressive Conservative government headed by Brian MULRONEY. At a time when participation in elections has been declining in many countries, voting turnout in most elections in Canada has remained high. The 1984 turnout, for example, compares favourably with the 54% turnout in the US presidential election of the same year.

The 1984 federal election produced the third change of government in 3 consecutive elections, but it was a dramatic change indeed as Mulroney's Conservatives overwhelmed the short-lived Liberal government of John TURNER, who had succeeded Pierre TRUDEAU as prime minister only a few months earlier.

Winning a record 211 seats, the Conservatives won support in all parts of the country, including Québec where the party had enjoyed little electoral success in recent times. The Liberals were reduced to a record low of 40 seats in the House of Commons, while the New Democratic Party under Edward BROADBENT managed to hold 30 seats, only a slight decline from its previous standing.

While the sharp swing to the Conservatives in 1984 seemed to represent a dramatic change, volatile political trends have become fairly commonplace in Canada. John DIEFENBAKER swept to power with a record majority in 1958 but was ousted by the Liberals under Lester PEARSON only 5 years later. The sudden rise and fall of provincial political movements such as the SOCIAL CREDIT PARTY or the PARTI QUÉBÉCOIS provides further evidence of the Canadian electorate's capacity for sudden and sometimes dramatic political change.

The results of federal elections are not always clear and decisive. Canadians have elected MINORITY GOVERNMENTS in 6 of the last 11 federal elections, partly because no single political party consistently enjoys the support of a majority of all voters.

Even in the massive sweep of 1984, only a bare 50% of those voting supported the Conservatives, while nearly as many voted for one of the other parties. The electoral system, with its emphasis on the distribution of seats in Parliament, sometimes gives a distorted picture of the actual behaviour of the electorate. Within 2 years of his massive victory, public opinion polls were suggesting that Mulroney may have considerable difficulty in repeating his 1984 success. A recent poll found the Conservatives enjoying the support of only 24% of the sampled electorate, placing them behind both the Liberals and New Democrats at the time of the poll. The next federal election will very likely contain as much drama and uncertainty as the last one.

While most Canadians identify themselves at least nominally with one of the 3 main political parties, these ties are not as durable as they tend to be in some European countries where the political parties reflect strong SOCIAL CLASS, religious feelings, or deep ideological divisions. Feelings about class, religion or ethnic ties are capable of explaining behaviour of Canadians in no more than about 10% of the elections, although some general patterns have tended to persist. In this century the Liberal Party has tended to enjoy greater support among Roman Catholics and among people of French ancestry. Regional patterns have also been fairly persistent. Until 1984, the Liberals had generally done well in Québec in most elections, and ever since 1958 the Conservatives have exhibited considerable strength in the 4 western provinces. The New Democratic Party has sought to consolidate its support among members of organized labour. But none of these patterns are highly reliable. In most elections, the NDP does only slightly better among members of unions than among other voters. And, as 1984 demonstrated, traditional Liberal strength in Québec is not invulnerable to other forces.

Shorter-term factors such as particular political issues or feelings about individual political leaders have generally had more to do with voting behaviour, and these factors are much more subject to change from one election to another or vary considerably among the different regions of the country. Economic issues, particularly the persistent high rate of unemployment and the general performance of the economy, were among the principal election issues in 1984. Because both Turner and Mulroney were leading their respective parties in an election campaign for the first time in the 1984 federal election, voters' impressions of them were somewhat unformed and highly subject to change, even during the course of the campaign period. Turner's relationship to the government of former PM Trudeau was also a factor, in part because the image of his party was closely intertwined with that of Trudeau in the minds of many voters.

Because of the nature of the federal system in Canada, it is not always possible to completely separate federal and provincial politics, even though the elections take place at different times. Some Canadians feel more strongly about the politics of their own province or region, and several provinces have party systems which are quite distinct from that found at the federal level. The Social Credit Party, which has held power provincially in BC and Alta, has never been a significant political force in Ontario or in the Atlantic provinces. The NDP has been a "third" party in much of the East, but has held power in BC, Sask and Man. The Liberals have been very weak in the provincial politics of the western provinces, but have recently won provincial elections in Ontario, Québec, NB (a clean sweep of the seats), and PEI.

The pattern of volatility which has been evident in recent Canadian politics both at the federal and provincial level, is characteristic of both Canada's decentralized political system and of the weak ties of individual voters to existing political alignments. It is not likely to change soon, as younger generations of voters now entering the electorate exhibit many of the same traits. While it is possible that some of the political trends of recent years may eventually solidify, it is more likely that the capacity for abrupt change will continue to provide both challenge and opportunity to the political leaders of the future. LAWRENCE LEDUC

Electoral Systems, methods of choosing political representatives. The Canadian federal ELECTION system is governed by the Canada Elections Act, as amended from time to time. The provincial election systems, governed by provincial election Acts, are similar to the federal system, but all differ slightly from each other in important details. Federal election practices are not therefore an accurate guide to provincial elections. The Canadian election process is extremely complicated; the rules apply to most people, most of the time, but in every case there are exceptions and special circumstances.

Voting Until 1917, in Canada, only men were allowed to vote, and even then only those who met a property qualification (*see* HUMAN RIGHTS and FRANCHISE). Now, subject to only a very few special constraints, any Canadian citizen at least 18 years old and living in Canada may vote. Generally the voter's name must appear on an official list of voters. In urban areas, enumerators go from door to door some weeks before an election, compiling a list of people entitled to vote. In rural areas the rules are less strict. Enumerators, for example, may compile lists from personal knowledge of people in the area, information from neighbours, etc. Also, in rural areas those not on the list may vote if vouched for by another qualified voter. The enumeration procedure is one reason for the length of Canadian federal election campaigns (normally about 60 days). It takes a great deal of time to appoint and instruct enumerators, to visit every urban resident in Canada, and to collect, check and print a list of names. The alternative – a permanent voters' list – has many advantages but is extremely expensive to maintain. With a maximum interval of 5 years, a federal election may be called at any time, largely at the discretion of the PRIME MINISTER.

Candidates With some exceptions, and after complying with certain legal requirements, any voter may also be a candidate. Because most candidates are judged by their party affiliation rather than their personal qualifications, the only candidates with any real chance of being elected are those with a party label. Since 1972 the candidate's party has appeared following his or her name on the ballot paper. This may have made it even more difficult for an independent candidate to win more than a few hundred votes except in the most unusual circumstances. However, the procedures by which the parties nominate their candidates are determined by the parties themselves, and are not subject to election laws (*see* ELECTION EXPENSES ACT).

Example 1		Example 2	
Candidate	*No. of Votes*	*Candidate*	*No. of Votes*
A	37400(91%)	A	7999(26%)
B	1965	B	7940
C	1583	C	7662
D	182	D	7121

Constituencies Canada is divided into single-member constituencies – increased from 282 in 1976 to 295 in 1987 (*see* REDISTRIBUTION). Voters may vote only in the constituency in which they have been enumerated and for one of the candidates running in that constituency. The constituencies are divided into a number of polling divisions, each with about 250 electors. Voters must cast their ballots in the polling division where their names are registered.

Voting System Some parts of the world have very complicated voting systems, but Canada's, known as the plurality system, is very simple. In any constituency the voter casts a single vote and the candidate with the greatest number of votes is elected. This can produce some strange results; while the winning candidate in a constituency contested by only two candidates must have a majority of the votes cast, a candidate among three or more in another constituency may be elected with far less than a complete majority. More often than not a Canadian government will be elected with a majority of seats and considerably less than a majority of votes. A further consequence of this political arithmetic is a regional concentration of political party representation. A party may appear strong in one region and weak in another, because the disparity in the number of seats may be far greater than the actual distribution of the popular vote. Over recent decades about 75% of eligible voters have chosen to exercise their franchise. There are many alternative voting systems, but none is perfect. Any of the defects of the present Canadian system could be corrected, but not without creating new and perhaps even more serious problems.

Election Administration The actual operation of a federal election is under the overall authority of a Chief Electoral Officer. Authority in each constituency is vested in a permanent Returning Officer, appointed by the Governor-in-Council. Returning officers may be removed only on attaining the age of 65, or for cause, as defined in the Act, although they may resign at any time. New Returning Officers must be appointed following any redistribution or significant readjustment of existing boundaries. Voting in a federal election is on the same day across the country, with the hours of voting extensive enough to give all who want to vote a reasonable opportunity to do so. Employers are required to ensure that their employees have adequate time to vote. Those who have reason to suppose they will not be able to vote on the day of the general election may vote in special advance polls a few days before. To prevent voters being influenced on the main polling day, the ballots from the advance polls are not counted until the polls have closed on election day. Candidates or their representatives may be present in the polling stations to witness the votes being cast and to ensure the honesty of the count. The results of an election determine not only who the representatives will be, but which party will form the government. If a party wins a majority of the seats in the House of Commons, either alone or in alliance with another party, it is said to have "won the election." The leader of the winning party will then be appointed prime minister, and will in turn appoint some fellow party members to the CABINET, which is the effective Government of Canada.

Electoral Fraud Electoral fraud, from ballot box stuffing, impersonation of voters, bribery and intimidation to gerrymandering, was once an acknowledged and largely tolerated aspect of Canadian elections. It has now been virtually eliminated and is nowhere a significant factor. Improved anti-fraud procedures, the greatly increased populations of electoral districts, and a changed climate of public opinion, have all made former practices obsolete. TERENCE H. QUALTER

Electric Power Electricity is a property of the atomic structure of matter, and is manifested as attraction between 2 oppositely charged bodies or repulsion between 2 similarly charged bodies. Subatomic particles may have a positive charge (proton), a neutral charge (neutron) or a negative charge (electron). Electrons are mobile and can be activated to create electric currents if a low resistance path (conductor) is provided. These currents provide a clean, controllable, versatile ENERGY commodity, which has been largely responsible for profound changes in the quality of life of all Canadians, reducing, for example, drudgery in homes, farms and factories. Some uncontrolled forms (eg, LIGHTNING) occur in nature. The widespread availability of cheap electric energy (notably HYDROELECTRICITY), made possible by large, integrated power systems, has given rise to major industrial developments across Canada. Many Canadian industries such as aluminum, pulp and paper, iron and steel and chemicals consume large amounts of electricity.

Gravitational energy, SOLAR ENERGY and its derivatives (eg, COAL, PETROLEUM, BIOMASS, WIND), TIDAL ENERGY, NUCLEAR ENERGY, etc, are primary energy sources. In contrast, electricity is usually regarded as a secondary energy source, since it must be generated by the conversion of gravitational (falling water), chemical (fossil fuels) or nuclear energy. Conversion typically requires 3 units of input energy (eg, burning coal or falling water) to produce one unit of electricity; the other 2 units are wasted as low-quality heat.

History The generic inventions that gave birth to ELECTRIC-POWER GENERATION were the water wheel (used in Roman times to grind corn), the steam engine and the dynamo or electric generator. The harnessing of water power in the 19th century, notably to drive textile mills, corn mills and woodworking and metal-shaping machinery, was largely responsible for Canada's emergence as an industrial nation (*see* TECHNOLOGY). With the development during the 1870s of reliable electric generators of adequate capacity, it was logical to generate electricity based on hydro power as well as on wood- and coal-fueled steam engines. The product was used originally for electric lighting and later for the host of applications that characterize contemporary society. In 1881 a 1.86 kW steam-driven electric generator was installed in downtown Toronto and the first skating rink was lit by arc lamps. Electric arc lights were installed at the CANADIAN NATIONAL EXHIBITION in 1882 and in 1883 street lighting was installed in Toronto and Montréal.

In 1884 the Ottawa Parliament Buildings and University of Ottawa were lighted electrically with generators powered by steam engines. All the streets of Ottawa were electrically lighted in 1885; it was the first city in the world to achieve this distinction. Several other Canadian cities such as Montréal, Québec City and Sherbrooke were supplied with electric power in varying degrees before 1900, but the transmission of electric power from NIAGARA FALLS to local communities in 1906 heralded the real dawn of the age of electric power in Canada.

Subsequently, in 1910, the Hydro-Electric Power Commission of Ontario, one of the world's first integrated public ELECTRIC UTILITIES, completed the first 110 000-volt bulk electric-power transmission lines to supply several municipalities in SW Ontario. This major achievement placed Canada in the forefront of electric-power pioneering nations.

The first Canadian thermal-electric (coal-burning) power station with an installed capacity of 1 million kW was put in service in 1951 in Toronto. Canada's first NUCLEAR-POWER PLANT, at

Energy Conversion Processes

Source	*Processes*	*Conversions*	*Characteristics*
Gravity	falling water rotates water turbine coupled to electric generator	gravitational to mechanical to electrical	renewable; can maintain 24 hour/day operation, also valuable for providing peak power; very efficient
Fossil fuels	heat of combustion powers steam turbine, diesel engine, gas turbine or internal combustion engine coupled to electric generator	chemical to high-quality thermal to mechanical to electrical	nonrenewable; high-cost fuel; comparatively low efficiency; potential for POLLUTION
Nuclear-fission fuels	fission of uranium-235 atoms creates heat to power steam turbine coupled to electric generator	nuclear to high-quality thermal to mechanical to electrical	nonrenewable, but virtually extendable indefinitely; low cost fuel; 24 hour/day operation; comparatively low efficiency; safety and environmental concerns

Rolphton, Ont, first delivered power to the grid in 1962. It was based on the Canadian Deuterium Uranium reactor (CANDU) subsequently used in Ontario's Pickering and Bruce generating stations, which have proved the world's most reliable commercial nuclear plants.

Capacity and Consumption From 1900 to 1986 the installed generating capacity in Canada increased from 130 MW to 98 508 MW. During 1986, the total consumption of electric energy in Canada was approximately 422 000 GWh. The average power demand approximated 48 200 MW; the peak demand, about 73 470 MW. The overall load factor (average/peak x 100) was 65.6%. The reserve margin (installed generating capacity minus peak-power demand) was 25 038 MW, an amount essential for the maintenance of acceptable system-reliability levels during scheduled maintenance or forced outages of generating units. Industrial users consumed 42% of the generated electric energy; the commercial sector, 22%; domestic and farm customers, 28%. Losses, mostly in transmission lines and transformers, account for the remaining 8%.

Government Regulations Under Canada's CONSTITUTION, electricity production falls within provincial jurisdiction. Because of the importance of electricity to Canadian life, it is understandable that most provinces have created publicly owned electric-power utilities to provide electricity at the lowest possible cost, a high level of reliability and minimal environmental impact. To ensure the regulation and orderly growth of the electric-power utilities, each province has passed legislation which sets out mandates and standards and establishes regulatory boards concerned with setting rates, emission standards and safety standards in connection with the generation, transmission and distribution of electricity.

Some aspects of electric-power regulation are undertaken by the federal government. Of primary importance is the licensing of CANDU-based steam-generating units – the responsibility of the ATOMIC ENERGY CONTROL BOARD (AECB). Before issuing a licence, the board assesses reactor safety, health and environmental factors relating to radioactive discharges, and the handling of spent nuclear fuel. The AECB also develops codes and standards for the mining and milling of uranium ores. The export of uranium and nuclear materials in general is controlled by the federal government. Several of Canada's provincial power networks are interconnected across provincial and international boundaries to ensure optimal reliability and to reduce costs. Export of energy is regulated by the NATIONAL ENERGY BOARD (NEB), a federal agency.

Type of Generation	*Generating Capacity (MW)*
hydroelectric	56 848
fossil-fueled thermal	30 676
nuclear-fueled thermal	10 984
Total	98 508

Research and Development The Canadian electric-power industry has pioneered many significant developments in nuclear power, the design of electric-power stations and the production of generators, transformers, transmission lines and energy-conservation systems. Major research programs are conducted by HYDRO-QUÉBEC, ONTARIO HYDRO and the national laboratories of Atomic Energy of Canada Ltd and the NATIONAL RESEARCH COUNCIL.

Some research areas deserving special mention include the safety, reliability and efficiency of nuclear-power stations; the management and storage of spent nuclear fuel; the environmental impacts of burning coal (eg, ACID RAIN) and methods of minimizing them (eg, SO_2 "scrubbers"); the design of ultra-high-voltage transmission lines; the development of renewable sources of energy for electric-power generation and small-scale hydroelectric plants. The total national research and development budget for electric-power related projects exceeds $100 million annually. ARTHUR PORTER

Reading: Canadian Enerdata, *Canadian Energy Trends* (May 1983).

Electric-Power Development The early history of the use of electrical energy in Canada is quite complex and lacks complete documentation. As is common in the introduction of any new technology, various aspects of the scientific phenomena are used to develop practical applications that have economic or social benefits to industry and the general public.

As these new inventions are being tested in the field, new discoveries constantly appear to alter the situation. Also, if the new technology becomes a rival for a firmly entrenched existing business, then an additional factor of competition affects the rate of acceptance and development of new equipment. In addition, another complication is that the new technology usually has a new terminology that is slowly introduced, gradually modified and may even become obsolete.

The first experiments with current electricity (as opposed to static electricity) were carried out with various kinds of batteries producing electricity chemically. The power was called continuous current (now called direct current – DC). DC has some very specific technical characteristics and in many ways is the simplest form of electrical energy.

When the first dynamos (generators) were built, creating electricity using mechanical energy, the current that was generated alternated forward and backward (now known as alternating current – AC). The early experimenters did not know how to use this AC current and had to adapt their dynamos to produce DC by adding a commutator.

With the new dynamos and batteries, scientists and engineers now had a reliable source of power with which to experiment. The obvious practical applications were communication (the telegraph) and lighting (the arc lamp), both of which required very simple apparatus. The arc lamps created light by causing a spark to jump

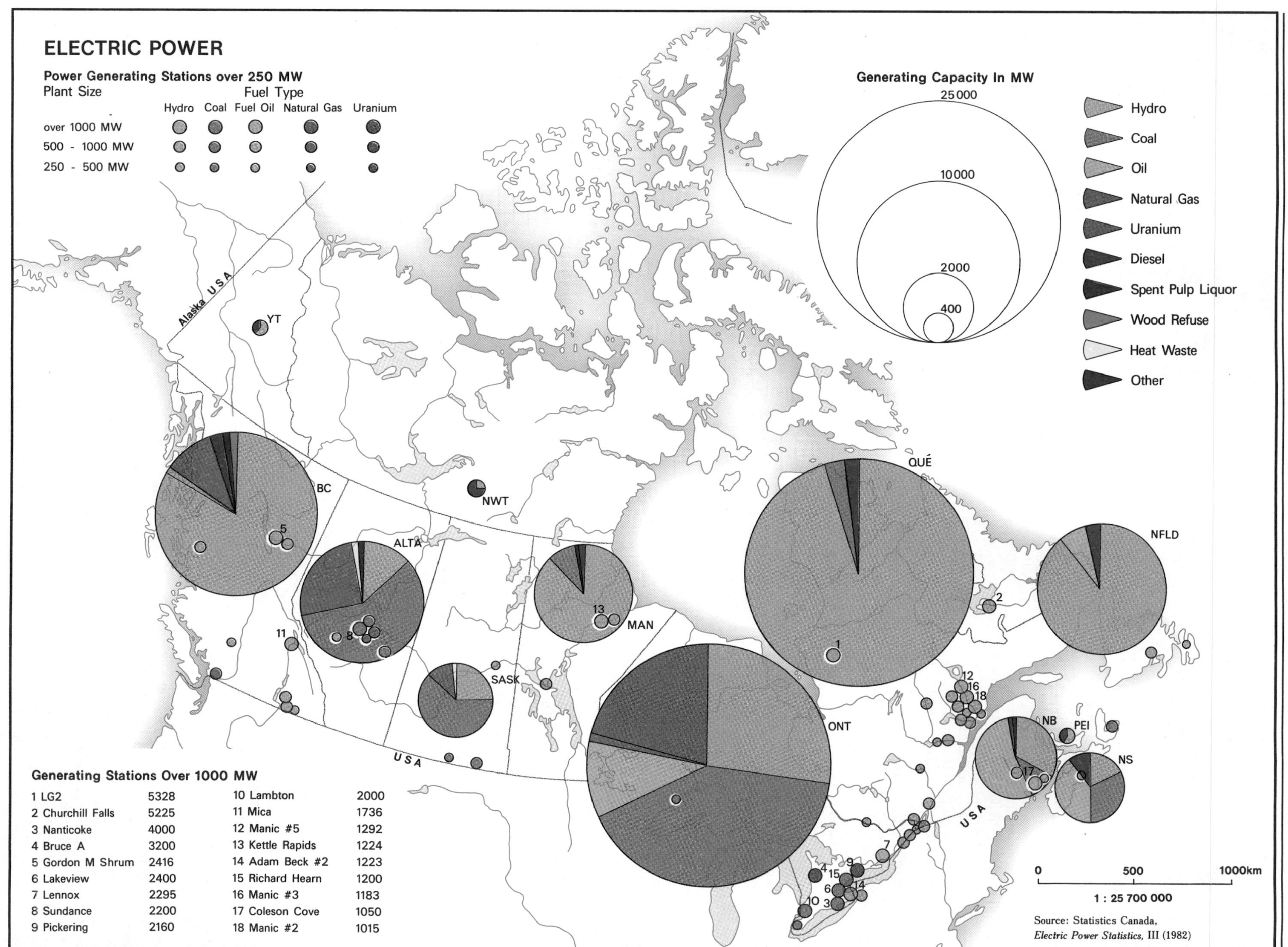
ELECTRIC POWER
Power Generating Stations over 250 MW
Plant Size
Fuel Type
Hydro Coal Fuel Oil Natural Gas Uranium
over 1000 MW
500 - 1000 MW
250 - 500 MW
Generating Capacity In MW
25 000
10000
2000
400
Hydro
Coal
Oil
Natural Gas
Uranium
Diesel
Spent Pulp Liquor
Wood Refuse
Heat Waste
Other
Alaska U S A
YT
NWT
BC
ALTA
SASK
MAN
ONT
QUÉ
NFLD
NB
PEI
NS
U S A
U S A
0 500 1000km
1 : 25 700 000
Source: Statistics Canada, *Electric Power Statistics*, III (1982)
Generating Stations Over 1000 MW
1 LG2 5328
2 Churchill Falls 5225
3 Nanticoke 4000
4 Bruce A 3200
5 Gordon M Shrum 2416
6 Lakeview 2400
7 Lennox 2295
8 Sundance 2200
9 Pickering 2160
10 Lambton 2000
11 Mica 1736
12 Manic #5 1292
13 Kettle Rapids 1224
14 Adam Beck #2 1223
15 Richard Hearn 1200
16 Manic #3 1183
17 Coleson Cove 1050
18 Manic #2 1015

from one electrode to another. Although the light was far brighter than any previous source of man-made illumination, arc lighting did have some disadvantages such as having to use fairly high voltages to create the spark. The lights connected in series had to have a continuous level of current, which meant that it was difficult to turn individual lights on and off. Finally, the early lights had to be short-circuited to start, which means that the electrodes had to be touching and then drawn apart after the spark was created. The operation of the lights caused one electrode to erode and thus the lights would have to be adjusted manually nearly every day. These disadvantages meant that arc lamps were not very suitable for use indoors but were good for outdoor, street or area lighting.

Demonstration installations of arc lighting were set up in Europe and N America and small trial installations were made in Montréal and Toronto in 1878 and 1879. One of the earliest permanent arc lighting systems was designed and installed by J.J. Wright in Toronto in 1881: several stores including Timothy Eaton's were illuminated but the lights were far more effective on the adjacent streets. Demonstrations of arc lights using steam-driven generators were set up by several companies and eventually the Toronto Electric Light Co, an amalgamation of them, was granted the exclusive franchise to provide electric light in Toronto. In Ottawa arc lighting was installed in several mills and the Ottawa Electric Co later provided arc lighting using equipment consisting of 3 dynamos driven by a waterwheel.

By 1883 permanent arc lighting systems were in operation in the streets of Toronto, Montréal and Winnipeg and by 1890 many other centres, including Ottawa, Hamilton, Pembroke, London, Victoria, Vancouver, Halifax, Saint John, St John's, Moncton and Sherbrooke, were also arc lit. During this experimental period, new types of arc lamps were developed, such as the Jablochkov Candle, the Brush, the Hochhausen-Vandepoele and the Thomson-Houston systems which gave a more regular light.

In the meantime, several inventors were trying to develop a better kind of lamp that produced light for human eyes that was not so harsh indoors. Gaslight had been popular for years: various mantles that gave a bright incandescent flame had been produced, and a stick of lime could be inserted in the flame to increase its brilliance ("limelight"). Thomas Edison in the US and J.W. Swan in the UK were experimenting with electric incandescent lamps enclosed in glass globes. Demonstration installations of the Edison lighting systems were made in Montréal as early as 1879 and later in 1882, and in Toronto in 1883. They did not work very well and were removed. The first successful installation was completed at the Canada Cotton Co Mill at Cornwall, Ont, in the fall of 1882, and the Montréal Cotton Co Mills at Valleyfield, Qué, installed an Edison system in Sept 1883 (electric light was a godsend to the dusty textile and lumber mills as it was much less of a fire hazard). In 1886 a small plant producing incandescent light was installed in the Parliament Buildings in Ottawa and in Jan 1887 a station was completed in Victoria, BC, which was reputed to be the first public incandescent lighting station in Canada. Edison soon became the main promoter of DC incandescent electric light in the US and Canada. The light bulbs used generally had carbon filaments which had a short life and low efficiency. They would be improved in time with tungsten filaments, better wiring and control systems. Incandescent lamps were tried for street lighting in various areas, but the early bulbs were not bright enough to compete with gas or arc lamps. DC generators also had the advantage of being able to charge storage batteries.

Electrical-Generating Capacity, Production, Consumption

(Source: E. W. Humphrys based on material from the Dept of Energy, Mines and Resources, 1986)

	Installed Capacity				*Production*				*Consumption*[5]		
	Total		*Hydro*		*Total*		*Hydro*		*Total*		*Source*
	MW	*%*	*MW*	*%*	*GWH*	*%*	*GWH*	*%*	*GWH*	*Hyd %*	*Other %*
Nfld	7 174[1]	7.3	6 417	89	40 407	8.9	39 129	97	9 712	97	3-oil[2]
PEI	122	.1	0	0	12	.01	0	0	622	0	2-oil 98-imp (NB)[3]
NS	2 355	2.4	366	1.5	7 411	1.6	1 001	13.5	7 960	12.5	81-coal/oil 7-imp (NB)
NB	3 434	3.5	903	26	12 192	2.7	3 146	26	11 653	26	43-nuclear 21-oil/coal
Qué	27 561	28	25 812	93.6	148 260	32.5	144 328	97	151 837	98	2-nuclear 17-imp (Nflnd)
Ont	30 404	30.9	7 172	23.6	125 225	27.5	41 050	33	126 966	32	21-coal 47 nuclear
Man	4 141	4.2	3 641	88	24 052	5.3	23 840	99	16 210	99	1-coal/oil
Sask	2 963	3.0	829	27.9	11 913	2.6	3 764	32	11 961	31	68-coal 1-oil and gas
Alta	7 598	7.7	734	9.7	34 716	7.6	1 800	5	34 655	5	92-coal 3-gas
BC	12 443	12.6	10 844	87	50 772	11.1	48 923	96	49 407	96	1-oil 3-gas
YT	123	.12	82	.12	337	.07	315	93	337	94	6-oil
NWT	190	.19	49	.19	480	.11	347	72	480	65	35-oil
Canada	98 508	100	56 849	57.7	455 832	100	307 643	67.5	421 855	64.6	18 conv th 15 nuclear

[1] Includes the 5225 MW Churchill Falls hydro station; most of its output is exported to Qué

[2] Imp(NB) = imported from NB, etc; 3-oil = 3% produced by oil-fired generation; conv th = conventional thermal generation

[3] In 1986 there were net interprovincial transfers from Nfld to Qué 30 695 GWH; NB to PEI 610, to NS 549; Qué to NB 7204, to Ont 7275; Man to Ont 730, to Sask 135; Alta to BC 64.

[4] Production exceeds consumption by exports to the US totalling 33 977 GWH, ex NB (6584), Qué (12 639), Ont (6264), Man (6977), Sask (87) and BC (1429)

[5] Includes transmission losses — approx 8.5%

All of these installations were designed to provide power for the immediate area only and could serve an area up to one-quarter-mile radius. Edison devised a 3-wire system of 220/110 volts that increased the distance to one-half mile, but beyond that the voltage losses as a result of the resistance in the wire were too great.

During this period, experimentation continued with AC current. Engineers discovered that the disadvantage of the power alternately increasing and decreasing with single-phase AC could be mitigated by altering the wiring in the generator which could produce 2- or 3-phase current that would deliver smoother power. They also adapted AC to arc and incandescent lighting and some AC motors were being developed that would rival the existing DC motors. One of the most important early inventions was the converter (now called transformer) which consisted of two coils of different sizes. Voltage in the first coil induced a higher or lower voltage (depending on the number of windings) in the second coil with a corresponding lower or higher amperage – the current remained constant. It was discovered that the higher the voltage, the lower the power losses. Thus if you could transform (or step up) the voltage from the generator from 2200 volts to 11 000 or 50 000 or more (now 750 000), the power losses were greatly reduced, which made possible the efficient long-distance transmission of power for the first time.

A vigorous competition ensued between proponents of DC (Edison) and AC (Westinghouse). DC advocates referred to AC as "killer" voltage among other things. In 1888 the first recorded permanent installation of a Westinghouse AC system in Canada was installed in Cornwall, Ont. By 1890 similar installations were constructed in other locations across Canada. It appears from the statistics that several companies added AC capability to their DC plants primarily to supply customers who wanted indoor lighting.

Another major user of electrical power appeared in the 1880s. Street cars using DC motors were quickly established with considerable success in urban areas. Street-car companies usually generated and distributed their own power. The first use of the power of Niagara Falls in Canada for electricity was in 1893 when a railway company (later the International Railway Co) installed two 1000 hp generators to operate its electric tramway as well as to supply power for distribution. This transmission was at generator voltage and not long distance.

The competition between advocates of AC and DC came to a climax during the massive development of Niagara Falls power in the US. The plan called for the generation and transmission of power for industry, including the new electrochemical and electro-metallurgical industries, in the Buffalo, NY, area. Proponents of DC proposed to generate electrical power, convert it to mechanical power and transmit it by cables and pulleys, or compressed air, or hydraulically. AC advocates suggested using the new transformer (which would not work on DC) to step up the power from 2200 to 11 000 volts and then transmit the power by wire to Buffalo. The AC system of George Westinghouse was selected and in 1895 one of the world's most influential power developments was opened.

The concept of transmitting electrical power over long distances was enormously important to Canada, where numerous hydroelectric power sites in remote areas could be harnessed for industry. One of the earliest long-distance transmissions in Canada was from a power station on the Batiscan R 16 miles to Trois-Rivières in 1897. This line carried 11 000 volts. The power of nearby Shawinigan Falls was first harnessed for the pulp and paper industry and the new aluminum industry in 1901. By 1903 a power line from here carrying 50 000 volts reached Montréal and within a decade it carried 100 000 volts.

The whole electrical equipment industry developed almost as rapidly. The new power source required generators, alternators, motors, lights, meters, switches and, above all, good cheap copper wire, and all of it needed to be standardized to make the equipment universally interchangeable. Building codes had to be altered to ensure the safe installation and use of electrical equipment. Most of this technology was imported to Canada as the Westinghouse Co established a branch plant in Hamilton and General Electric (previously Edison Electric) in Peterborough. However, many Canadian companies manufactured some of their own equipment. The demand for copper wire stimulated Canadian mining. The mines and pulp and paper companies were also major consumers and developers of electrical power; the development of hydroelectric power and Canadian resources went hand in hand.

W.G. RICHARDSON

Electric-Power Generation In Canada the 2 basic methods of producing ELECTRIC POWER are hydroelectric generation, based on the energy contained in flowing water, and thermal generation, based on the production of steam. Thermal generation may be conventional, using COAL and PETROLEUM products, or nuclear, using URANIUM in thermonuclear fission (*see* NUCLEAR ENERGY). Canada is abundantly supplied with most of the resources from which electric power can be generated, and Canadians are among the world's highest per capita producers and consumers of electricity. Canada's installed electrical generating capacity in 1987 was 97.9 gigawatts (GW = 10^9 watts): 57.5% derived from HYDROELECTRICITY, 17.5% from coal, 8% from oil, 11.5% from nuclear power, 5% from natural gas, and 0.5% from other sources. Installed capacity is the amount of power that could be generated at a given instant if all power plants were working simultaneously at full capacity. Actual production depends on the amount of time particular generators are running and on load (appliances, motors, etc) placed on the system. ELECTRIC UTILITIES build 10-25% extra capacity into their systems, above the expected maximum load, to serve as backup during emergencies and maintenance shutdowns. In 1985, total actual production in Canada was 446 413 GWh. Of this, nearly 67.5% was hydroelectric, 17.5% coal, 13% nuclear, 1.5% oil and .5% gas. The difference between the various sources' shares of capacity and production (ie, a higher proportional production from hydro and nuclear, lower from fossil fuels) reflects the economics of electric-power generation, and the pressures placed by CONSERVATION concerns on petroleum-based thermal development.

Hydroelectric Generation converts the energy of Canada's RIVERS into electrical energy for industrial, commercial and residential use. Building a dam to retain water requires a large capital investment, but the method has several major advantages, being nonpolluting, being based on a renewable resource and requiring no expensive fuels. Canada's principal hydroelectric generating stations and their installed capacity are LG-2, on the La Grande R, Qué, 5328 MW; Churchill Falls, on the Churchill R, Lab, 5225 MW; and Gordon M. Shrum, on the Peace R, BC, 2416 MW. LG-4, also on the La Grande R, was installed but testing in 1986; its proposed capacity is 2650.50 MW. Others are listed on the map.

Thermal Generation uses the heat energy of fossil fuels or uranium to produce steam to drive a steam turbine which is coupled to a generator. In addition to its fuel requirements, a thermal plant must have a supply of water to cool and condense the exhaust steam from the turbine so that it can be reused in the steam cycle. Conventional thermal plants have relatively low capital costs but high operating costs. Their disadvantages include pollution from exhaust gases (*see* ACID RAIN, AIR POLLUTION) and low efficiency. Efficiency is limited by the Carnot cycle of a heat engine, which effectively means that less than 40% of the heat

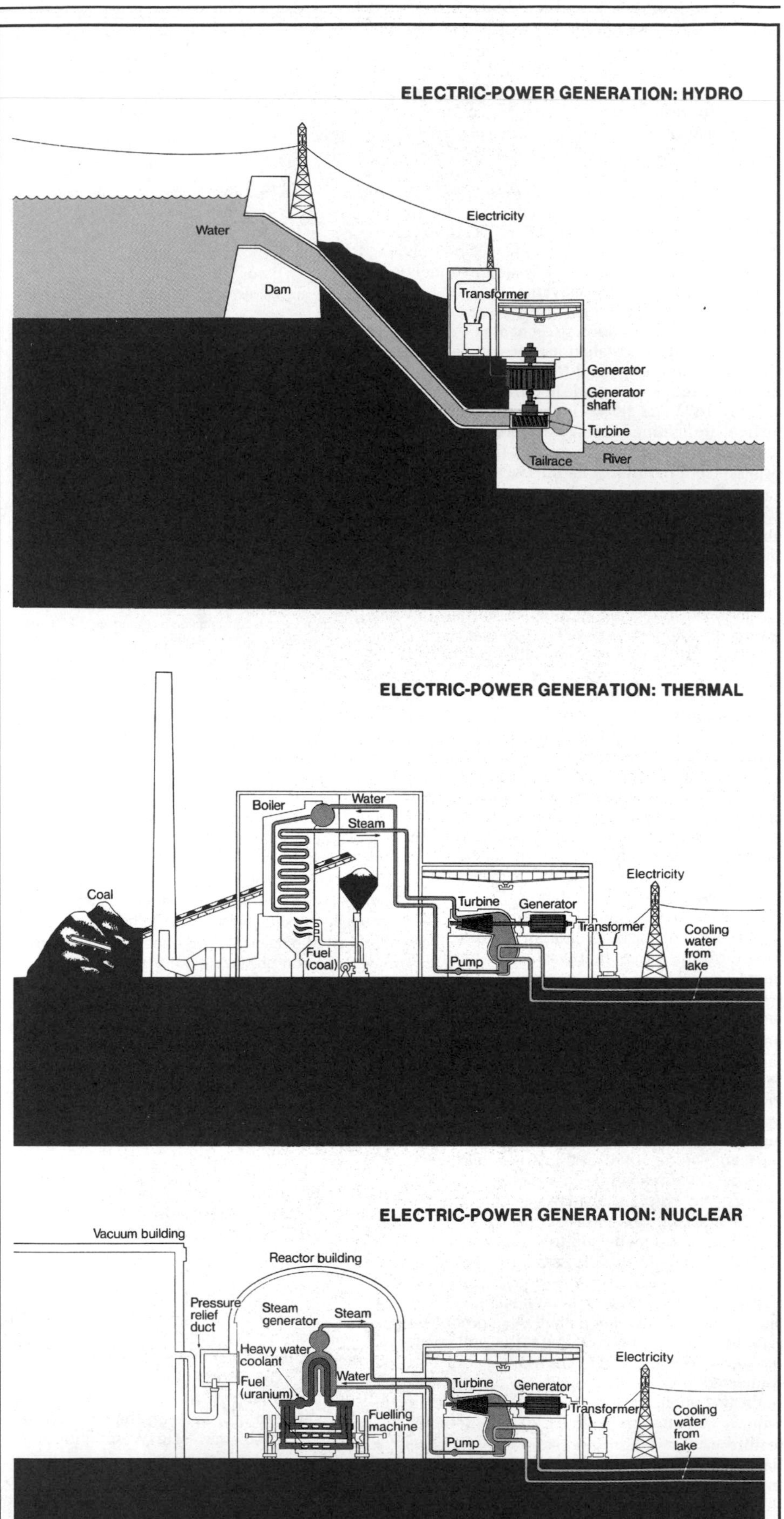

(courtesy Ontario Hydro)

energy of the fuel is converted into electricity, the remainder being lost as waste heat. Several research projects are exploring ways to use this waste heat for agriculture, AQUACULTURE or industrial purposes. Canada's principal coal-fired generating stations are Nanticoke, Ont, 4000 MW; Lakeview, Ont, 2400 MW; Lambton, Ont, 2000 MW; and Sundance, Alta, 2200 MW. The partly natural gas-fired and partly coal-fired Richard L. Hearn facility in Ontario has been mothballed. Oil-fired facilities at Lennox, Ont (2295 MW), have also been mothballed.

A NUCLEAR POWER PLANT is a thermal plant in that steam is produced by a nuclear reaction and used to drive a conventional steam turbine. However, the economics are quite different since the capital cost of the plant is high and the construction time longer than for a conventional thermal plant. The complexity of the plant also adds to the operating cost. Such expenses are offset by the low cost of fuel and the absence of atmospheric pollution, factors that make nuclear generation using the Canadian CANDU system economically attractive in parts of Canada, notably Ontario and the Maritimes. Concern remains about the long-term storage of the spent radioactive fuel (*see* NUCLEAR SAFETY). Canada's principal nuclear generating stations are Bruce "A" and "B" (6400 MW) and Pickering "A" and "B" (4300 MW). A 4-unit nuclear-fueled generating station being constructed at Darlington, Ont, will have an installed capacity of 3600 MW when completed in 1992.

Unlike most other forms of energy, electricity cannot be stored economically in large quantities. Instead, the energy is stored in fuel stockpiles or in water held above hydroelectric dams, and power is produced on demand. The demand on a typical power system varies significantly with time of day, season and general economic activity; hence, the number of generators and the load on each must be varied. To meet this varying demand, 2 types of generating plant are required, for base-load generation and for peaking generation. The base load is the continuous minimum demand; the peak load is the maximum demand. Thermal plants are more suited to base-load operations because they take a long time to warm up and bring on line, and they operate most efficiently at a constant load. Nuclear plants have an added base-load advantage in that their capital cost is high and their fuel cost low; hence, they are most economical when run at a high, constant load. Hydro plants can be designed as either peaking plants or base-load plants, depending on the ratio of electrical capacity to water flow and water-storage capacity. If a hydro plant is operated in parallel with a thermal plant, the hydro plant is typically used for peak loads, as it can be brought on line quickly. Gas turbines are also well suited to peaking generation since they start up quickly and have low capital cost and high fuel costs.

The location of electric-generating plants is always a compromise between the location of the population to be served and the location of the energy resource to be tapped: the longer the transmission line to the service area, the higher the effective cost of the plant. Hydroelectric sites require a stable base for a dam and geographic features that minimize the necessary size of the dam and control structures; the effects of flooding above the dam must also be considered. For thermal plants, the availability of cooling water is a crucial consideration. Proximity to a fuel source or cheap transportation is a major factor in choosing a location for coal-fired plants; electricity is cheaper to transport than coal. The safety concerns of neighbouring populations can influence the siting of nuclear plants.

The mix of electric-generating sources varies considerably across Canada. In 1980, hydroelectricity provided most electricity in Newfoundland, Québec, Manitoba, BC and the YT; coal, in NS, Saskatchewan and Alberta; and oil, in NB, PEI and the NWT. Nuclear power provided about 28% of Ontario's electricity production, ranking a close third after hydro and coal. Nuclear generation began in NB in 1983. Many alternative means of electric-power generation are under active study. These include TIDAL ENERGY, WIND ENERGY, photovoltaic SOLAR ENERGY, ocean thermal energy, OCEAN WAVE ENERGY, GEOTHERMAL ENERGY, magnetohydrodynamic generators, NUCLEAR FUSION energy, low-head and small-scale hydroelectric dams, and thermal plants burning BIOMASS and PEAT. Cogeneration, the production of both heat and electricity, can substantially improve the economics of thermal stations. Two of the alternatives, vertical-axis windmills and tidal power, are being used in small-scale trials at present, but it will be some years before they offer a significant alternative to the resources now in use. Canada is also participating in nuclear fusion research to a limited extent, because it will be at least several decades before fusion is available to generate electricity commercially.

M.M.C. COLLINS

Electric-Power Transmission lines carry power from generating plants (*see* ELECTRIC-POWER GENERATION) to the distribution systems that feed electricity to domestic, commercial and industrial users. Transmission lines vary from a few kilometres long in an urban environment to over 1000 km for lines carrying power from remote hydroelectric plants. They may differ greatly in the amount of power carried. Because requirements vary, many technical, economic and environmental factors must be considered when new lines are planned.

The basic modes of transmission are direct current (DC) and alternating current (AC). In direct current, the current flows in one direction only; in alternating current it reverses its direction many times per second. It is difficult to transform direct current from one voltage to another; hence, initially, DC had to be transmitted at the low voltage at which it was generated and used. This fact limited its applicability: if transmission of large amounts of electricity or transmission over long distances was required, the cost of the conductor (copper wire) was prohibitive. Alternating current may be generated at a low voltage, boosted to a higher voltage by a transformer, transmitted and converted back to a lower voltage before use. Consequently, following the development of the transformer in the 1890s, most electricity was transmitted as AC. However, DC transmission has a number of advantages and is being more widely used. For example, a DC line, requiring only 2 conductors instead of the 3 needed for an AC line, costs about two-thirds as much. Further, in DC transmission the effective voltage is equal to the peak voltage, while in AC transmission the peak voltage is 40% higher. Since radio interference increases with the peak voltage and decreases as the conductor size is increased, the DC system can carry a higher effective voltage than an AC line of equivalent size and still maintain an acceptable radio interference level. Thus, in some long lines carrying bulk power from remote generating sites, power is generated as AC, boosted to a high voltage, converted to DC for transmission, then reconverted to AC and transformed to a lower voltage for use. The cost of the converter stations at either end is offset by the lower cost of the line. An example of DC transmission is Manitoba's Nelson R line which carries power from generating plants on the Nelson R to Winnipeg, almost 1000 km south. DC transmission is also advantageous for transmitting power through submarine cables, such as the line from the BC mainland to Vancouver I.

Electric transmission lines in Québec. Technological developments in power transmission have been largely responsible for profound changes in the quality of life and for major industrial developments across Canada (*photo by J.A. Kraulis*).

AC and DC can be transmitted in overhead lines or underground cables. The cost of underground cables is much greater than that of overhead lines, but this increase may be acceptable in urban areas where space for overhead lines is lacking or where aesthetics are a major concern. Transmission across bodies of water also requires the use of cables if the distance is too great to span with overhead lines.

Overhead power lines have 3 major components: support structure, insulation and conductors. Support structures can be wooden poles, free-standing steel towers or guyed towers of steel or aluminum. Glass or porcelain suspension insulators have traditionally separated the live conductors from the grounded towers. Each insulator consists of a metal cap on top and a metal pin underneath separated by the glass or porcelain insulation. These units are used to form insulator strings which vary in length depending on the voltage level and application. Several strings may be used in parallel to carry the weight of the conductors. For 735 kV about 30 insulators are used. New types of insulators have been developed using polymers; field testing and full-scale use have become more prevalent during the 1980s. In the early days of electrical transmission, copper was used extensively as a conductor, but now virtually all conductors are aluminum. Each conductor is made of many strands (1-5 mm in diameter) combined to give an overall diameter of 4-50 mm. In most conductors, steel or a high-strength aluminum alloy is used for the core strands to give the conductor added strength. In a transmission line, up to 4 conductors may be used in parallel to form a conductor bundle.

Transmission voltages can vary considerably. Early in this century Canada's fledgling power industry transmitted a few tens of kilowatts (kW) of power over transmission lines operating at a few tens of kilovolts (kV). Today one of HYDRO-QUÉBEC's James Bay transmission lines may carry over 2000 megawatts (MW) of power more than 1000 km at 735 kV. As the amount of power carried and the distances increased, it was necessary to increase the voltage to reduce losses and permit more power to be carried on a single line. Losses are proportional to distance and to the square of the current. Thus, for the same amount of power, if the voltage is doubled, the current is halved and the distance can be quadrupled for the same losses. Unfortunately, as voltages increase, so do costs: virtually everything must be larger and insulation problems become more complex. Electric power is generated at relatively low voltages, 25 kV or less. It must be transformed to a higher voltage for transmission, then transformed down to the distribution voltage, typically less than 25 kV. As the cost of the transformers also increases with voltage, the optimum voltage must be chosen carefully. For complex technical reasons the use of higher transmission voltages is beneficial to the stability of the power system.

Because of the long transmission distances in this country, Canadian ELECTRICAL UTILITIES have often been pioneers in the field of transmission technology. As of 1982 Manitoba Hydro's Nelson R system, which began service in 1972, was the largest high-voltage DC transmission system in the world. In 1965 Hydro-Québec inaugurated its 735 kV Manicouagan line, thus becoming the first utility to go above 500 kV AC for transmission. Since even higher voltages will probably be needed in the future, the utilities are supporting research into transmission at voltages in excess of 1000 kV. M.M.C. COLLINS

Electric Utilities are private or government organizations involved in the production, transmission, distribution, marketing and sale to consumers of ELECTRIC POWER. Canadian electric UTILITIES account for approximately 90% of the total production of electrical energy in Canada; the remaining 10% is produced by industrial establishments for their own use, chiefly in the MINING, metal-processing and PULP AND PAPER industries. In 1985 about 90% of the utilities' production was consumed in Canada, the remainder being exported to the US.

The electrical-utility industry started in the 1880s as a multitude of privately owned enterprises which supplied electrical ENERGY in specific communities or regions. Many also provided other services such as gas distribution and street railways. As the use of electricity increased, many of the original companies were absorbed by larger, investor-owned corporations. In most instances, nonelectrical energy activities were split off, eg, STREET RAILWAYS were taken over by municipalities. Early in this century, PUBLIC OWNERSHIP of the electrical-utility business emerged, beginning with municipal ownership of electrical generation or distribution. A significant development was the creation of a provincially owned utility, now ONTARIO HYDRO, in 1906.

Increasing demand for adequate supply of electrical energy at roughly uniform rates created a trend towards provincial ownership of the industry. Provincial government takeover of municipally and investor-owned electric utilities accelerated after WWII. Provincial ownership was intended to provide electricity at lower cost to consumers as a result of such factors as provincial guarantee of capital debt, co-ordinated planning and absence of profit-taking and income-tax burden. By the 1980s, Canada's electrical-utility industry was characterized by a mix of investor, municipal and provincial ownership. Except in Alberta and PEI, provincial bodies play the dominant role in generating capacity, transmission network and assets. These bodies are BC Hydro and Power Authority (BC HYDRO); Saskatchewan Power Corporation (SPC); Manitoba Hydro-Electric Board (Manitoba Hydro); Hydro-Electric Power Commission of Ontario (Ontario Hydro); HYDRO-QUÉBEC; New Brunswick Electric Power Commission (NB Power); Nova Scotia Power Corp (NS Power); and Newfoundland and Labrador Hydro.

In the northern territories, the Northern Canada Power Commission (NCPC), a federal crown corporation, has been the principal electrical utility, dating from 1948 in the NWT and 1952 in the YT. An investor-owned utility operates several diesel-generating stations supplying isolated communities, and purchases power from the NCPC for distribution in Whitehorse and several smaller communities. In 1987 the NCPC assets in the YT were transferred from federal to YT control and ownership; concurrently, the government of YT established the Yukon Energy Corp to hold and manage the new territorial enterprise. In the NWT the NCPC is the principal supply authority pending negotiations leading to devolution of the federal interest in the NCPC to the government of the NWT. In addition, an investor-owned utility supplies 3 communities that are not connected to the the NCPC system, and a second investor owned utility distributes electrical power in the city of Yellowknife.

Investor-owned utilities dominate in Alberta and PEI, and play a minor but significant role in BC, Ontario and Newfoundland. Municipal ownership is a minor element in BC, Québec and PEI but is very significant in Alberta, Manitoba and Ontario. In Ontario, distribution and some generation in urban municipalities is provided by 316 municipal hydroelectric commissions, most of which purchase supply from Ontario Hydro in a quasi co-operative arrangement.

Two investor-owned utilities are responsible for generation and transmission of about 80% of the power consumed in Alberta. Distribution in major urban centres is by municipal utilities, and 2 of these produce the remaining 20% of the provincial consumption. Planning and operations are co-ordinated by an Electric Utility Planning Council which includes representatives of the municipally and investor-owned utilities and the provincial government. The agency does not set final rates to consumers.

While the electrical-utility industry is structured on a provincial basis, electric-power transmission interconnections for interchange of supply have been established between all adjacent provinces, except that construction of a Saskatchewan/Alberta interconnection is scheduled for completion in 1989. Interconnections with US utilities have been developed by NB Power, Hydro-Québec, Ontario Hydro, Manitoba Hydro, SPC and BC Hydro. These cross-border connections are primarily for export of electricity from Canada, but they also permit some imports when needed. Electrical-energy exports and export facilities are licensed by the NATIONAL ENERGY BOARD (NEB).

An important component of the electrical-utility industry is the Canadian Electrical Association (CEA, est 1891). All major investor-owned and provincially owned utilities, and some municipal utilities, are corporate members of the association, and many manufacturers of electrical equipment have nonvoting membership status. The CEA co-ordinates the exchange of general and technical information, and provides a liaison with the provincial and federal governments. It also sponsors and co-ordinates research which supplements activities of the 4 utilities that have research divisions: Hydro-Québec, Ontario Hydro, SPC and BC Hydro.

Because investor-owned utilities are profit oriented and operate in a monopolistic environment, their rate structures are generally subject to review and regulation by public authorities. Formerly, publicly owned utilities were generally autonomous in setting rates within guidelines requiring them to provide service at cost, in some instances, subject to approval by the parent government. A trend has developed toward having public boards examine the rate structures of the publicly owned utilities, but final jurisdiction remains with the government concerned. A development in this area was the 1981 decision by the government of Québec to depart from the service-at-cost principle in favour of a rate-setting philosophy tied to government policy; hence rates now reflect energy CONSERVATION objectives, the cost of other forms of energy and any profits above a specified minimum level, and accrue to the government as dividends. E.W. HUMPHRYS

Electrical Appliances Industry The dominant activity of the electrical appliance industry in Canada is the design, manufacture and sale of major household appliances. The core products (ie, those with very high saturation levels, approaching the category of necessities) are refrigerators, ranges, automatic washers and dryers. Other major appliances include dishwashers, freezers, microwave ovens and room air conditioners. Manufacturing takes place entirely in Ontario and Québec.

History in Canada To many Canadians in the 1920s, 1930s and 1940s, the purchase of a major appliance, such as a washing machine, was a major expenditure. There were some Canadian appliance manufacturers, eg, Beatty headquartered in Fergus, Ont, and having a reputation built on the reliability and service facilities relative to washing machines. The modern major appliance industry, however, has its roots in the American consumer-products boom of the 1950s. By that time most major appliance products originated in the US and initially reached Canada as imports. Brands such as Kelvinator, Frigidaire, Philco, General Electric (GE) and Westinghouse became household words in Canada. Because of high Canadian import tariffs, most US manufacturers found it more economical to produce major appliances in Canada once the Canadian sales volume had climbed to permit reasonable economies of scale. The result was an industry dominated by high levels of foreign ownership, although the tariffs permitted a number of Canadian entrepreneurs to operate profitably as small regional manufacturers.

Among the most successful Canadian entrepreneurs were W.C. Wood and Ralph Barford, both of whom developed major appliance companies that have survived the ups and downs of the industry and the recession of the early 1980s. Wood survived by specializing in a single product (freezers) and exporting to the US. By 1984 Wood was the largest and most modern freezer manufacturer in Canada. Mainly by acquiring existing small businesses (eg, McClary, Easy, Moffat), Barford put together the only Canadian-owned, full-line appliance company (GSW Inc). The Moffat acquisition, probably Barford's largest, brought GSW into the big 6 full-line appliance makers. The other 5, all foreign controlled, were Admiral, GE, Inglis, White and Westinghouse.

As early as the mid-1970s, the federal government had begun to urge the industry to consolidate to achieve greater economies of scale and become more competitive. An opportunity for consolidation arose in 1975 when White agreed to purchase the major appliance division of Westinghouse in the US. The Canadian assets were contingently part of the agreement; however, Canada's FOREIGN INVESTMENT REVIEW AGENCY (FIRA) intervened to block the sale in Canada. If it had gone through, White-Westinghouse would have had the scale potential to put pressure on the other 4 full-line competitors, particularly GSW. Barford, in an attempt to protect GSW's position, negotiated a merger with Canadian General Electric (CGE), each firm contributing its major appliance activities to a joint venture called Camco. Camco then proceeded to purchase the Canadian major appliance division of Westinghouse, and because GSW held 50% of the voting shares of Camco, the purchase was exempted from FIRA procedures. By 1976 there were only 4 full-line competitors: Admiral, Camco, Inglis and White. The number was reduced to 3 in 1982 when Inglis, with some government assistance, bought out ailing Admiral.

Economic Performance Although industry exports had increased and imports declined (largely because of weakness in the Canada dollar), a trade deficit in major appliances still prevailed in 1982, which was the worst year the industry had faced in over a decade as sales declined by 20%. A recovery began in 1983 and continued at a somewhat slower pace in 1984. Microwave ovens represent the only bright spot in the industry. Sales of microwaves had climbed steadily since 1976, when 65 000 units were sold, to 1986, when sales reached 1 075 000 units. Unit sales of appliances as a whole, however, had been in decline since 1978. The decline was caused by high saturation levels of core products and low replacement buying. For example, the same proportion of Canadian households (over 99%) owned a refrigerator in 1986 as in 1976. Saturation levels for electric ranges (93%) and automatic washers (76%) had not grown either. Clothes dryers had grown modestly from 55% in 1976 to 69% in 1986.

Beyond the core products, saturation levels varied. Freezers reached 58% in 1986, but room air conditioners had reached only 18%. With the newer products, Canadian saturation levels were still catching up with those in the US. Dishwashers reached 26% in Canada in 1979, compared to 43% in the US. By 1986 the Canadian figure was 38%. A similar pattern arose with microwaves: in 1982 US saturation was around 27%; Japanese, 31%; and Canadian, 10%. By 1986 the Canadian figure had reached 44% and US ownership of microwaves was about 60%.

The Modern Industry in Canada

Since import tariffs were scheduled to drop in the early 1980s to 12.5% by 1987, industry participants realized that more INDUSTRIAL RESEARCH AND DEVELOPMENT would be needed for the industry to prosper under international competition. By 1984 the US could not ship core products to Canada below Canadian costs, and it is expected that under the FREE TRADE agreement US core products will still have difficulty penetrating the Canadian market with its 75¢ dollar. However, it is more likely that some agreed specialization in Canadian and US markets will capture greater scale economies in Canada. In 1986 exports of refrigerators and freezers reached 143 847 units, valued at almost $40 million, following an upward trend since 1984. International trade in newer products was governed less by cost than by innovation. Products such as dishwashers and microwaves were imported because the design and development were done abroad. They were manufactured in Canada only when the sales volume was high enough to make it economical. Industry sources estimated in 1986 that Canadian production costs were 15-20% higher than US costs in core products and 30-40% higher in new products, assuming parity between the Canadian and US dollars.

All of the surviving full-line manufacturers expect to expand employment in both Ontario and Québec. Camco, now 51% owned by CGE, will compete largely through the Hotpoint, GE and Moffat brand names, and will manufacture part of the Beaumark line for the Bay and Simpsons. Inglis, 43% owned by Whirlpool, will compete with the Admiral, Inglis and Whirlpool names and will manufacture the Kenmore line for Sears. White, almost wholly owned by Electrolux of Sweden, will compete with the White-Westinghouse, Kelvinator and Frigidaire names and will manufacture much of the Viking line for Eaton's and certain models in the Beaumark line.

Associations The Canadian work force in the industry is represented by several unions, including the United Electrical Workers (UEW). Employment in the industry has declined from 11 888 in 1976 to 6902 in 1981, partly because of reduced output but largely as a result of improved efficiency. Canadian wage rates in the major-appliance industry, on average, were higher than those in the US in the mid-1970s, but the relative decline in the Canadian dollar had reversed this situation by the early 1980s. By 1984 both countries were facing strong competition from manufacturers in the Far East and Latin America in low-cost component parts. The industry was represented by the Canadian Appliance Manufacturers Assn which, in turn, was a section of the Electrical and Electronic Manufacturers Assn of Canada, with head offices in Toronto. HAROLD CROOKELL

Electrical Engineering, discipline in the ENGINEERING profession which deals with the application of electricity to serve the needs of society. Electrical engineers are involved in a wide range of activities, from designing and manufacturing computer and COMMUNICATION systems, to planning and overseeing the operation of large ELECTRIC-POWER stations. The field is expanding rapidly and, over the past decade, many universities have modified their programs to provide a degree of specialization. Upon graduation, many electrical engineers form their own companies to manufacture electrically based products or to provide consulting services. Others are employed in salaried positions and become involved in research, design, manufacture, sales or maintenance of electrical equipment. Electrical engineering has many applications which affect our daily lives.

Communications Systems Electrical engineers are involved in the design, manufacture and operation of devices and systems for voice, video and data transmission. Communication systems are made up of transmitters, in which voice or other information is used to modulate a "carrier" signal. The carrier is transmitted through space or conductors, and the information is extracted at the receiving end. The transmission of radio waves through space has been the key to worldwide and interplanetary communication systems. Electrical engineers are involved in many of these applications, including SATELLITE COMMUNICATION facilities. Canada's first satellite, the Alouette I, was launched in 1962 and the first communication satellite, the Anik A-1, was put into orbit in 1972 by Telesat Canada (*see* SPACE TECHNOLOGY). Communication satellites are used to relay signals from ground-based sending stations to ground-based receiving stations. Canadian satellites now relay television, radio, telephone and computer data to ground-based receiving stations, but future satellites may be used for defence purposes, plotting mineral deposits, monitoring crops, etc.

Computers Electrical engineers are involved in the design and manufacture of computer components and peripheral devices (eg, printers, video terminals), and also in many areas where a more fundamental knowledge of computer hardware is required, eg, at the design stage of business and personal computers. Electrical engineers use computers to solve technical problems or to monitor and control complicated processes. In other situations, eg, ROBOTICS and feedback control systems, they use microcomputers and related hardware as part of a total system (*see* ARTIFICIAL INTELLIGENCE).

Electrical Power Before building new generating plants, electrical engineers use simulation studies to determine generator size, control hardware characteristics and provide other pertinent information. During commissioning of large power generators and, subsequently, during operation, electrical engineers are involved in analysing operational problems and applying their skills to maintaining and improving the quality of service to homes and industry. Electric generators and their energy sources, steam turbines and hydraulic turbines, are controlled by electronic modules made up of transistors, microprocessors and electromagnetic devices. An understanding of feedback control theory is a necessary part of an electrical engineer's training, along with COMPUTER SCIENCE and fundamentals of power systems.

Recent advances in superconductivity, eg, where the resistance of a conductor is lowered by refrigeration, are being applied to electric generator design. Magnetohydrodynamics (MHD), where a liquid conductor carries electric current by interaction with a magnetic field, provides an alternate means of generating electricity. Electrical engineers are involved with these new innovations and in developing alternate energy sources such as wind, solar and tidal energy.

Transportation Electrical engineers were initially involved with electric motor drives in the transportation field but this involvement has expanded to other areas. The use of computers for scheduling and controlling traffic provides a greater degree of safety for the public, as does use of electronics in communication systems at airport control towers and in aircraft. Transporting payloads into space, using disposable rockets and recoverable vehicles (eg, the Space Shuttle) is expected to continue as a dynamic area.

Biomedical The use of electronics and microcomputers in MEDICAL RESEARCH, hospital patient care and operating rooms is another area of application. Electrical engineers are involved in the design and manufacture of devices that monitor and analyse electrocardiograms and electroencephalograms, and control life-support systems. Applications of LASERS to medicine and the use of X rays and ultrasonic scanners for 3-dimensional viewing of body organs have involved electrical engineering skills.

Military and Defence The use of microprocessor-controlled guidance systems for rockets and sophisticated electronics for detection and interception of incoming missiles has meant a greater dependence on electrical engineering support for the military. World War II hastened the development of RADAR for aiming guns at incoming aircraft. Since that time, the military establishments of many countries have accelerated the development of many devices that incorporate microprocessors and other electronic components.

Training One of the earliest programs in electrical engineering was established at McGill U in 1891. In 1907 U of New Brunswick had 3 professors offering courses in electrical engineering. Since that time enrolments have increased in universities across Canada to a level of 6675 in 1982 and 11 943 in 1985-86. The curriculum is regulated by the Canadian Council of Professional Engineers, with periodic reviews made at each university by the Canada Accreditation Board. Technical societies such as the Institute of Electrical and Electronics Engineers sponsor conferences and meetings, in Canada and the US, for the exchange of technical information. Other organizations, eg, the Canadian Electrical Assn, which is funded by many Canadian ELECTRIC UTILITIES, organize technical conferences and provide funds for research projects related to the electric power industry.

K.E. BOLLINGER

Electroacoustic Music is composed, performed or reproduced with the aid of electronic technology, excluding instrumental and vocal music heard via loudspeakers. The term includes tape, electronic and computer music, each with its own techniques. Tape music includes any composition created with magnetic tape using prerecorded or electronic sounds that have been modified and assembled through techniques of mixing, splicing, speed changes, tape reversal, tape loops, tape echo and feedback, as well as electronic modifications. Electronic music refers to compositions produced with sounds generated electronically by oscillators and modified with filters, modulators or other equipment. Early work in electronic music occurred after WWII in Europe and N America, although many electric musical instruments (the Theremin, Ondes Martenot and Hammond organ) were invented earlier in the century. Since the 1960s electronic music has become associated with commercially produced sound synthesizers, which are groupings of sound-generating and -modifying units using the principle of voltage control to determine the sound parameters. Live electronics refers to musical performance with any combination of synthesizers and associated equipment, whereas studio composition involves mixing all materials onto tape for later playback.

Computer music is the application of digital technology to musical activity, such as computer-assisted composition, digital sound synthesis and, most recently, live performance with digital synthesizers using the MIDI (Musical Instrument Digital Interface) communications scheme. Computer music differs from other forms by using programs or software to control the process, and by representing sound as a series of numbers called samples. Digital technology is being integrated into all aspects of music and audio engineering, including signal processing and digital recording, most notably in the CD (Compact Disk) and DAT (Digital Audio Tape) formats. Some early computer-music systems in Canada were developed by Ken Pulfer of the National Research Council in 1969, Gustav Ciamaga and William Buxton at the University of Toronto, and Barry Truax at Simon Fraser University.

Electroacoustic techniques are used for both commercial and artistic types of music, the former usually associated with multi-track recording studios, and the latter with university and private studios as well as national radio networks in Europe. The first Canadian studios were established at U of T (1959) by Myron Schaeffer and at McGill (1964) by Istvan Anhalt, and now are found in almost every university music faculty. Hugh LE CAINE of the NRC was the most significant pioneer of electronic music in Canada through his design and construction of many specialized devices for composers and performers, including the first synthesizer, the Sackbut, in 1945. Today, electroacoustic music, despite the public's lack of familiarity with its artistic forms, is an important aspect of musical life. BARRY D. TRUAX

Electronics Industry The Canadian electronics industry consists of more than 1000 firms that manufacture products such as advanced telephones, COMPUTER SYSTEMS and software, word processors and other electronic office systems, televisions and radios, communications SATELLITES and other TELECOMMUNICATIONS systems, and electronic control and monitoring devices used in many industrial and scientific applications. In 1986 industry shipments were valued at over $7.1 billion, divided among 4 subsectors: COMMUNICATIONS and components, 59% ($4.2 billion); office machines and computers, 21% ($1.5 billion); instrumentation, 13% ($900 million); consumer electronics, 7% ($500 million). The apparent domestic market (shipments plus imports minus exports) was $12.9 billion in 1986.

Despite some strengths, notably in telecommunications, Canada has traditionally been a net importer of electronic goods, mostly from the US and Japan. The sector's trade deficit grew steadily between 1973 ($850 million) and 1986 ($5.79 billion), with office machines and computers accounting for more than half ($1.68 billion). In fact, between 1973 and 1986, all 4 major subsectors were in deficit. The only bright light was provided by telephone-apparatus commodities, which produced a 1982 surplus of over $336 million. Exports of these commodities had increased by a third ($116 million) over the previous year. However, the continuing serious deficits in this industry, coupled with the growing importance of electronics to a nation's economic health and international competitiveness, have caused grave concern about Canada's ability to maintain its status as a technologically advanced industrialized nation.

It is difficult for Canada to compete with the US and Japan in major areas of electronics research and development (R & D); in the early 1980s, for example, the US and Japan started a cutthroat multi-billion-dollar competition to develop the most advanced computer technologies; that race is simply out of Canada's league.

The preferred Canadian strategy has been to find "niches" (specialized subsections of the market) and to move into them before anyone else, in the hope of establishing momentum and a lasting reputation. In part, this strategy is dictated by the fact that, by world standards, Canadian electronics firms are comparatively small (most have sales of under $10 million). Northern Telecom Ltd, which makes advanced telecommunications devices, is the largest, with worldwide revenues of over $4.38 billion in 1986.

In 1986 the electronics industry employed about 86 500 people, up from the 1985 total of 81 800. The industry is "knowledge intensive"; ie, it is the largest employer of technically and scientifically trained people in Canada and accounts for more than a third of all industrial R & D in Canada, more than any other industry. The electronics industry spends a greater percentage of sales on R & D than most other sectors of industry.

There is a high degree of FOREIGN INVESTMENT in Canada's electronics industry. Although about 80% of Canadian electronics firms are Canadian owned, they account for less than half the industry's sales (less than 20%, if Northern's sales are excluded). Nearly three-quarters of the 100 largest firms are foreign owned, a degree of foreign ownership virtually unparalleled in other industrialized countries.

Most of Canada's electronics output comes from firms located in Ontario and Québec, mostly in large cities, such as Montréal, Ottawa and Toronto, which provide the necessary technological support structure and skilled workers. The main centre in the West is Vancouver. There are now several hundred technology centres across the country. Some of these, as well as a sampling of the companies that produce the range of technologies included in this industry sector are described below.

Northern Telecom Ltd, Mississauga, Ont, a public company 52% owned by BELL CANADA ENTERPRISES INC, is Canada's largest telecommunications/electronics firm, specializing mainly in sophisticated telephone and telephone-switching technology. In 1986 its sales exceeded $6 billion and it had nearly $5.5 billion in assets. Employees numbered 46 202, making it one of the country's largest employers. Northern produces a very wide range of telecommunications products, including business communications systems (data-switching networks, electronic telephone systems, electronic private-branch-exchange telephone systems); electronic office equipment (a wide variety of voice and data terminals, including the Displayphone, a combination telephone and desk-top computer terminal); several types of telephones (rotary dial, push-tone, coin-operated, electronic, etc) and related equipment (headsets, hands-free speaker units); a wide range of telecommunications wire and cable products; several telephone-switching systems; telecommunications test equipment; power equipment; and voice- and data-transmission systems. The last category includes fibre-optics technology, which involves transmitting information (eg, a telephone conversation) as light signals through ultra-thin fibres made of extremely pure glass. Northern has as its research arm, Bell-Northern Research Ltd of Ottawa.

In 1986 Northern spent 11% of its sales on R & D. The company does a great deal of research on semiconductors (microelectronic chips). It is among the world's top 10 users of semiconductors and is one of very few Canadian companies able to design and fabricate custom MICROCHIPS. Northern's products are used in about 90 countries by telephone companies, businesses, governments and educational and military institutions. It has a large number of offices or plants in Canada, the US, England, Switzerland, Singapore, Ireland, France, Malaysia and Brazil.

Spar Aerospace Ltd, Toronto, is a company engaged in the design, development, manufacturing and servicing of systems and products for the space, aviation, communications, defence, and remote manipulator markets. It was founded in 1968 and employs over 2000 people. It has one of the largest staffs of highly qualified scientific and technical workers in private industry in Canada. Spar's sales in 1985 totalled over $223 million, about half from exports.

Spar is famous as the developer of the CANADARM, the remote manipulator system used on the US Space Shuttle. The Canadian government paid $110 million for development of the first arm, which was given to the United States National Aeronautics and Space Administration (NASA) and flown on a shuttle flight for the first time in 1981. Spar subsequently received a $74-million contract from NASA to build 3 more arms, which were delivered between 1982 and 1985. The company is studying the potential uses of remote-manipulator technology in such industrial applications on Earth as mining and nuclear-reactor work. Spar is also a major supplier, both in Canada and internationally, of satellite communications systems (including satellites and subsystems); it produces components and systems for satellite-Earth receiving stations. It has also developed remote heat-sensing technology for detecting ships, missiles and aircraft for defence and navigation purposes.

AES Data Ltd is a Montréal firm that designs, manufactures and distributes OFFICE AUTOMATION equipment, ranging from stand-alone desk-top word-processing machines to sophisticated shared-logic, multiple work-station systems. The company, which was established in 1974, had sales of about $133 billion and its products are sold in more than 55 countries; employees number 1300. In 1987 the firm was sold by the Canada Development Corp to Kinburn Technology Corp of Ottawa.

Canadian Astronautics Ltd, Ottawa, does R&D in aerospace, electronics and computers. Its products include satellite-ground receiving stations and other equipment for receiving satellite signals; space-hardware subsystems (eg, high-reliability batteries, deployable antennas); space-related computer software; airborne RADAR; electronic warfare systems; scientific and engineering minicomputers and microcomputers and various instruments.

Gandalf Data Ltd, Nepean, Ont, specializes in data-transmission technologies, including private automatic computer exchanges, mobile computer terminals and various communications modems for linking computers together using telephone or cable lines. The company has sold over 400 000 devices to telephone companies, educational institutions, government departments and industries around the world. Perhaps its most well-known product is a computerized receiving device for taxi drivers. A major product is PACXnet, a sophisticated, intelligent "switching" system that connects many different computers, computer terminals and switching networks, allowing users access to electronic mail, information data banks and other electronic services. In its fiscal year ending July 1986, it had sales of almost $108 billion and assets of $80.8 billion. Twelve percent of its sales went to R & D. It employed 1361 people and it was 27% foreign owned.

Lumonics Inc is a Kanata firm that designs, develops and manufactures a variety of LASERS and laser systems for marking, materials processing, and scientific and medical applications. Founded in 1970, it is now the third-largest company in the world manufacturing commercial laser-based products. It has subsidiaries in the US, UK, Germany, France and Japan; 95% of its sales are outside Canada. By the end of 1985, annual sales were running about $70 million. Its 1986 R & D budget was about $9 million. It employs about 600 people worldwide (175 in Canada). The company's products include Lasermark®, a high-speed, noncontact laser-marking system used to put product codes, part numbers, serial numbers, etc, on packaged foods, beverages, drugs, electronic components, etc; WaferMark®, used to put data on semiconductor wafers; TagMarkers; and pulsed solid-state and carbon-dioxide lasers for materials processing applications in industry for cutting, welding, drilling and heat treating. Other systems are used for scientific purposes in such things as spectroscopy and photochemistry and in holography for industrial purposes.

Mitel Corp, Kanata, is an international manufacturer of telecommunications products and semiconductor devices. The company had sales of $413 billion in 1986 and employed 4655 people; 9% of its sales went to R & D. It was 51% foreign owned, with British Telecom being the major shareholder. Major products include microchip-controlled telephone switching systems for office use, Earth-terminal switching devices for satellite systems, special telephone handsets and a successful IBM-compatible personal computer called Hyperion. Mitel is also one of the few Canadian companies designing and manufacturing advanced microelectronic circuits, including the latest generation of VLSI (very large-scale integration) chips.

CAE Electronics Ltd, Montréal, a wholly owned subsidiary of CAE Industries Ltd, Toronto, is a major designer and manufacturer of commercial digital flight simulators for civilian and military aircraft and helicopters (devices used primarily for pilot training). The company makes simulators for major aircraft manufactured by Boeing, Airbus, Lockheed and McDonnell Douglas; customers include major international airlines such as British Airways, KLM, Swissair, United Airlines and Air Canada. CAE also makes control-room simulators for training nuclear-power plant operators, as well as supervisory control and data acquisition systems for nuclear and fossil-fuel power stations, electric substations and oil and gas pipelines. The company also makes a computerized data processing and display system for use in AIR TRAFFIC CONTROL and it was one of the companies that contributed to development of the CANADARM. CAE Electronics GmbH is a West German division of the company that provides maintenance and service for military flight simulators and various commercial and military communications and electronic systems throughout Europe. This division also designs and manufactures communications equipment for worldwide telecommunications services. About 300 Europeans are employed.

NORPAK Corp, Kanata, founded in 1975, develops and markets a wide range of colour-graphics computer-display terminals and associated computer hardware. The company was the major developer of Canada's TELIDON videotex system. Videotex is a computerized, interactive (2-way) system for the electronic delivery of text and graphics information to special Telidon-receiving terminals or personal computers for use in homes or offices. NORPAK's products include the Telidon Information Provider System (the terminals used to create and edit Telidon text and graphics information); the MK IV Videotex Decoder (the receiving terminal that displays the information and a number key pad and keyboard that allow the user to request the information desired); and an Electronic Projection System (a decoder with added memory so that it can call up already stored information, either from its own memory storage or from a remote computer data base). The company also makes similar teletex equipment. Unlike 2-way videotex, teletex involves a one-way broadcast of information to a receiving set, eg, by regular or cable TV. NORPAK also makes products for use in education and computer-aided design and in electronic warfare, command and control and training applications. It is developing a videotex military information handling system. The company has several facilities in Canada and the US.

Electrohome Ltd, Kitchener, Ont, is one of the oldest firms in Canada belonging to the electronics sector. It was incorporated in 1933, but predecessor companies date back to 1907. The company had sales of $160.6 billion in 1986 and a work force of 2185 people. In the early 1970s its main product was TV sets; later it concentrated its electronics capabilities in industrial markets, specializing in video display units. Products include monitors for computer terminals and personal computers, electronic games and medical and industrial control equipment; Telidon terminals; and systems and electronic circuit boards for satellite receiving stations.

SED Systems Inc, Saskatoon, Sask, makes a variety of products for the aerospace, communications and instrumentation and control markets in Canada, the US, Europe and Australia. Aerospace products include satellite ground-station control facilities; satellite-systems test equipment; defence electronics and support; payloads (scientific instrument packages) for the Space Shuttle and rockets. It also operates an Earth station, receiving data from the Landsat REMOTE-SENSING satellite. Communications products include equipment for transmitting and receiving a wide range of signals via satellite; transportable satellite-Earth receiving stations; mobile test facilities; and automatic telephone dialers. Instrumentation and control systems include farm monitoring systems for tractors, seeders, sprayers, grain loss and combines that provide farmers with instant information on all farming operations; sprayer-control systems; storage tank and bin monitors; and control systems used in industry.

The Ontario Centre for Microelectronics, based in Ottawa, is an Ontario government CROWN CORPORATION set up in 1982 to provide technical expertise and assistance, advice and information for industry in the field of microelectronics. The centre offers consulting services, feasibility studies, training programs and information services. It also contracts to design integrated electronic circuits. The purpose of the centre is to help small and medium-sized companies exploit the latest advances in microelectronic technology. The Ontario government has also set up 2 other centres that focus on electronics technologies: one, in Cambridge, Ont, specializes in CAD/CAM (computer-aided design and computer-aided MANUFACTURING); the other, in Peterborough, specializes in ROBOTICS.

In 1982 the federal government also helped to establish a number of microelectronic centres across Canada, in collaboration with provincial governments. An example is the Alberta Microelectronic Centre, based at University of Alberta, Edmonton. This nonprofit centre was designed to help Alberta businesses learn about and apply new electronic technologies – to increase productivity and international competitiveness. It offers laboratory facilities, machine shops, computers, CAD/CAM systems and other equipment to industry in return for fees and will conduct research on microelectronic applications in collaboration with industry and university researchers.

Industrial trade associations and technical societies whose members belong to the electronics sector include the Canadian Advanced Technology Association, Electrical and Electronic Manufacturers Association of Canada, Aerospace Industries Association of Canada, Canadian Society for Electrical Engineering, Information Technology Assn of Canada, Canadian Information Processing Society and Institute of Electrical and Electronics Engineers. *See also* COMPUTER INDUSTRY; ELECTRICAL ENGINEERING; SATELLITE COMMUNICATIONS; SPACE TECHNOLOGY. LYDIA DOTTO

Elgin, James Bruce, 8th Earl of, governor general of Canada 1847-54 (b at London, Eng 20 July 1811; d at Dharmsala, India 20 Nov 1863). As a student at Eton and Oxford, Elgin displayed the brilliance that sparked his later reputation as an inspired orator, cultured humanist and judicious administrator. Appointed as governor of Jamaica in 1842, Elgin was named governor general of Canada in 1846 and arrived in Montréal on 30 Jan 1847. The Colonial Office had previously resisted the concession of RESPONSIBLE GOVERNMENT as demanded by Canadian Reformers, but Elgin and the new Colonial Secretary, Earl Grey, believed it offered the best way to settle Canadian political strife. When the Draper-Viger administration lost the election of 1848 to a Reform majority, Elgin commissioned Louis-Hippolyte LAFONTAINE to form the first truly responsible gov-

James Bruce, 8th Earl of Elgin, was governor general of Canada 1847-54. In 1848 he commissioned L.-H. LaFontaine to form the first responsible government in Canada (*courtesy National Archives of Canada/C-10720*).

ernment. The new administration passed the REBELLION LOSSES BILL in 1849, evoking vehement Tory opposition. When Elgin gave the bill his assent he was attacked by angry mobs and the Parliament buildings in Montréal were burned. Elgin weathered this crisis without compromise, ensuring that responsible government would prevail. Elgin is also noted for the diplomatic finesse with which he secured ratification by the US Senate of the RECIPROCITY Treaty in 1854, a measure much desired by Canadians at the time as an antidote to economic stagnation.

After leaving Canada in 1854, Elgin was special commissioner to China 1857-59 and 1860-61. In between these appointments he served as postmaster general in the Palmerston Cabinet. In 1862 he was appointed viceroy to India.

JACQUES MONET, S.J.

Reading: J.M.S. Careless, *The Union of the Canadas* (1972); Jacques Monet, s.j., *The Last Cannon Shot* (1969).

Elites, used in an everyday sense, refers to those who are best at any given activity, eg, top athletes, artists, or soldiers. More precisely, elites are those who hold the uppermost decision-making positions in any powerful activity organized in a definite hierarchy; those who occupy these positions are powerful by virtue of the positions they hold, not necessarily because they are "the best." To examine elites it is necessary first to locate the most powerful activities within society; second, to identify the uppermost or decision-making positions within these activities; and finally to specify the characteristics of the people holding these positions.

Power may be defined as the ability to mobilize resources, including people, money, military strength, opinions and goods or services. At a given time, the military, politicians, religious leaders or economic leaders may be the most powerful group in a society. To determine which activity or activities are most powerful the organization of a society must be understood. According to the materialist perspective, no matter what institution is the most powerful, a society reproduces itself through the production of a means of living (food, clothing, shelter) and therefore the economy is always a fundamental activity, whether organized by religious, political, military or business leaders. Those who control the economy are a powerful elite within any modern society. To determine which are the uppermost positions within the most powerful activities, it is necessary to examine how these activities are organized, eg, the church, labour unions, the military, corporations or the state. In government, for example, PRIME MINISTERS or PREMIERS and their CABINETS occupy the most powerful positions; in corporations it is the executive (chairman of the board and president) and board of directors; in the military, generals; in labour, the executive positions within unions and labour centrals; in the church, archbishops.

"Uppermost positions" refers to 2 phenomena, both related to the idea of hierarchy. In the corporate world, corporations such as the Royal Bank of Canada (22 times the size of General Motors, Canada) are very large while others, eg, the BANK OF BRITISH COLUMBIA, are relatively small. The most powerful banks can be identified by their assets or profits. The uppermost banks ("dominant corporations") clearly stand above the others. In Canada's case these include the ROYAL BANK OF CANADA, the CANADIAN IMPERIAL BANK OF COMMERCE, the BANK OF MONTREAL, the BANK OF NOVA SCOTIA and the TORONTO DOMINION BANK. Among themselves these 5 banks control over 90% of the assets, income and profits of all banks in Canada. The Toronto Dominion Bank (which alone is almost 2.5 times the size of Canada's top 4 oil companies combined) is the smallest of the 5 dominants but has twice the assets of its closest rival, the NATIONAL BANK OF CANADA. These dominant corporations are the power bases for the economic elite.

The next hierarchy is reflected in the internal structure of the corporation. Those in the uppermost positions, eg, executive and directors, determine the corporation's direction. In the case of the banks, the executive and board of directors establish policy, review the performance of management and approve or disapprove large loans or investments. The elite of Canadian BANKING are the executive and directors of the 5 dominant banks. Frequently one person holds more than one position. In the case of the banks, however, a director of one bank cannot sit on the board of another bank in Canada, although he or she may sit on the boards of other corporations. Directors of the 5 banks hold 41% of the highest positions of power in the dominant life-insurance companies in Canada, and 28% of the top positions in the dominant banks are held by people who occupy the same positions in one of the dominant life-insurance companies.

Among the 113 dominant corporations (each controlling many other corporations or subsidiaries) that command the economy in Canada are 1848 interlocked positions, called interlocking directorships, 56% of which are interlocked with important positions on American corporations.

Economic Elite The more elites tend to resemble one another as particular social types and are distinguishable from the society in general, the more it can be concluded that access to an elite is exclusive and biased in favour of certain social types. Of all the elites in Canada, the economic elite is the most exclusive. It is overwhelmingly male; only 8 of its 798 members (or 1%) are women. People of British origins comprise about 87% of the economic elite but only 45% of the entire population; in contrast French Canadians comprise only 8% of this elite but 29% of the population. Of the "non-charter" (neither French nor British) ethnic groups, only Jewish Canadians surpass their proportion of the population (4% of the elite and 1% of the population), while all other ethnic groups are seriously underrepresented (1% of the elite but 25% of the population). Region of birth is also a factor; those born in Ontario and those currently resident in Ontario have a disproportionate chance of entering the economic elite, reflecting Ontario's traditional position as the centre of the Canadian economy and the location for most head offices of major financial, transportation and manufacturing companies. At least 41% of the members of the economic elite characteristically attend private schools, eg, Upper Canada College. The parents of the economic elite could afford such luxuries because they were themselves from privileged positions in society (*see* SOCIAL MOBILITY). Only about 1% of the society can be classified as upper class, but in 1972, 61% of the elite had these class origins; 33% came from the middle class, compared to about 15% of the population; and 6% from the working class, which accounts for about 85% of the population. Over the past 20 years the social-class origins of the elite have become more exclusive. John PORTER's classic study, *The Vertical Mosaic,* revealed that 50% of the economic elite in 1951 had upper-class origins, 32% had middle-class origins and 18% were of working-class origins. (*See also* BUSINESS ELITES.)

Media Elite The elite of the mass media, which controls the major private media complexes in Canada, is similar to the economic elite. Nearly 50% of its members are also members of the economic elite, the 2 overlapping to such an extent that together they can be categorized as the "corporate elite." The media elite tend to be even more upper class in origin than the economic elite, have a slightly higher proportion of women (4%) and slightly higher proportion of French Canadians (13%).

State Elite Members of the state elite share some common features with the corporate elite, but there are important differences. In *The State Elite,* an update of Porter's work, Dennis Olsen divides the state elite into political, bureaucratic and judicial elites. The first comprises prime ministers, premiers, federal Cabinet members, and provincial Cabinet members holding the top posts in the largest provinces (Québec, Ontario, Alberta and BC). Women, again, are seriously underrepresented, accounting for only 2% of these office holders between 1961 and 1973. French Canadian representation in the political elite is greater than it is in the corporate elite; between 1961 and 1973 it rose to 25% from 22% between 1940 and 1960. Only 8% of noncharter ethnic groups are represented. Individuals with British origins comprise 68% of the political elite, which, like all the state elites, is overwhelmingly middle class in its origins (69%). Nevertheless, the upper class is still overrepresented (22%), and the working class underrepresented (9%). The bureaucratic elite, eg, deputy ministers and assistant deputy ministers or their equivalents in government departments, crown corporations, regulatory boards and commissions at the federal level and in the 4 largest provinces, are overwhelmingly middle class in their origins (75%) with fewer from the upper class (10%). Only 2% are women. Ethnically the bureaucratic elite resembles the political elite, and the number of French Canadians in the federal bureaucracy increased from 13% in 1953 to 24% in 1973. The judicial elite, eg, justices of the Supreme Court and chief justices of the federal and provincial courts, are drawn overwhelmingly from the 2 charter groups and are almost all male and somewhat more upper middle class in origin than the other state elites.

Labour and Religious Elites Although Porter attempted to identify labour, intellectual and religious elites in Canada, none of these have been studied as intensively as state or corporate elites and it is difficult to argue that they wield the same degree of power. Labour is not organized in the same hierarchical way as the corporate and state worlds. The Canadian Labour Congress, the main labour central in Canada, cannot direct its constituent members in binding ways and the member unions and locals enjoy considerable autonomy. Moreover, only about 33% of Canada's labour force is organized into unions. Porter's survey of labour leaders in the early 1950s revealed that they were more representative of a variety of ethnic groups and more representative of the working class. Porter attempted to identify intellectual leaders in Canada by examining members of the Royal Society of Canada, but this is an honorific organization with no decision-making power of its own. While religion has had an important place historically in Canada's power structure, its influence is clearly waning. The power structure of the dominant churches, particularly Roman Catholic and Anglican, and the uppermost positions, eg, archbishops and bishops, can be identified, but the extent of their power relative to other societal elites is doubtful.

The most powerful elites, those that command the greatest resources in Canada today, are the corporate and state elites. Studies have demonstrated that entrance to these elites is strongly affected by social-class origins, region of birth and residence, ethnic origins and gender; the most powerful decision-making positions in Canada

Elk Island National Park, Alta, est 1913, a 194 km² sanctuary for moose, elk, mule deer, bison and over 200 species of birds (*courtesy Environment Canada, Parks/R.D. Muir*).

are therefore held by people who do not represent a cross-section of Canadians. WALLACE CLEMENT

Reading: Wallace Clement, *The Canadian Corporate Elite: An Analysis of Economic Power* (1975); Dennis Olsen, *The State Elite* (1980).

Elk, *see* WAPITI.

Elk Island National Park (est 1913) is a 194 km² sanctuary of rolling woodlands and meadows dotted with lakes, bogs and ponds, 48 km E of Edmonton. Preserved within the park's fenced boundary is a remnant of Alberta's Beaver Hills. Frequent fires have created a mosaic of aspen and mixed-wood forests, meadows and wetlands, which provide ideal habitat for wildlife, including moose, elk, mule deer, some 450 Plains bison and 225 wood bison, various smaller mammals and over 200 species of birds. In presettlement days, Cree inhabited the park area, trading beaver pelts and harvesting plains bison. Europeans settled in the late 1800s in anticipation of railway construction. Advertisements for homesteading properties brought large ethnic populations westward, and the Ukrainian influence remains strong in the area. Semiserviced camping facilities are available in the park, as are canoeing, swimming, golf, cross-country skiing and hiking. LILLIAN STEWART

Elkford, BC, District Municipality, pop 3187 (1986c) situated on the W side of the Elk R, a tributary to the Kootenay R, in the East Kootenay district of southeastern BC. Located among the Rocky Mts near the old coal-mining communities of the CROWSNEST PASS, Elkford, at 1400 m elevation, is the highest community in Canada. The population was 605 in 1971 when Fording Coal opened its coal mine nearby. The development of various coal mines in the region since then has created an economic and population boom for Elkford. Besides mining, the community is the gateway to a large wilderness area, particularly Elk Lakes Provincial Park 70 km north. In spite of its elevation Elkford has a relatively sheltered climate and is subject to numerous warming CHINOOK winds in the winter. JOHN STEWART

Ellef Ringnes Island, 11 295 km², is part of the SVERDRUP group that borders the Arctic Ocean. Most of the island consists of great thicknesses of sedimentary rock, except for an occurrence of the arctic coastal plain in the NW corner. The island's topography reflects these structural and lithological controls, and is characterized by broad lowlands and dissected uplands. Domal structures, like the 250 m high Isachsen Dome, are the most striking feature of the landscape. Despite generally arid conditions the surface becomes saturated in summer, owing to an active layer derived from water-retentive shale, underlain by impermeable PERMAFROST. DOUG FINLAYSON

Ellesmere Island, 196 236 km², third-largest island in Canada and most northerly island in the ARCTIC ARCHIPELAGO. It is separated from Greenland by Kane Basin and Kennedy Channel, which is a mere 30 km wide in places, and from Devon I to the S by Jones Sound. Cape Columbia (88°07′ N lat) is Canada's most northerly point of land. The entire island is deeply incised by fjords, and the N coast is extended by ice shelves – aprons of sea ice which are fused to the shore. The N is dominated by the Grant Land Mts, a jagged chain of sedimentary rocks, some 100 000 years old, and shrouded in ice nearly 2000 m thick – remnants of the last ICE AGE. Rock spires project through the ice; Barbeau Peak (2616 m) is the highest mountain in eastern N America. The land descends southward to Hazen Plateau, dominated by Lk Hazen – the largest lake in the polar region. In central Ellesmere, mountains of the Central Ellesmere Fold Belt rise to 2000 m.

Ellesmere is distinguished by a spectacular landscape and an exceptional and fragile environment. Small herds of MUSKOXEN are dispersed across Hazen Plateau, along with the remnants of a CARIBOU herd decimated by Robert E. Peary in 1900 during his attempt to reach the NORTH POLE. There are numerous species of birds and several other land mammals, but coastal SEA ICE discourages sea mammals. Thirteen species of SPIDERS occur on Ellesmere I. Though the climate is extreme, a peculiar "thermal oasis" at Lk Hazen produces surprisingly warm summers. The frost-free period at Tanquary Fjord averages 50-60 days. Ellesmere is a true polar desert, with only 2.5 cm of precipitation annually in some places. Consequently vegetation is sparse.

One of the most remote places on Earth, Ellesmere I has experienced little human activity (*see* ARCTIC EXPLORATION). However, archaeological evidence shows that the fjords of Hazen Plateau were occupied some 4200 years ago. Excavations of THULE-culture winter houses in Bache Pen, dating from 1250-1350 AD, have uncovered numerous Norse artifacts. The island was sighted by William BAFFIN in 1616, but was not explored until the 19th century. John ROSS discovered parts of the coastline in 1818 and the island was named for the earl of Ellesmere during the Inglefield expedition of 1852. Sir George Nares carried out extensive observations in 1875. As part of the First INTERNATIONAL POLAR YEAR activities, an American group led by A.W. Greely explored widely in N Ellesmere in 1881 from a base on Discovery Harbour. The expedition ended tragically when sup-

Ellesmere Island, NWT, 3rd-largest island in Canada and one of the most remote places on Earth. The Northern Mts are shown (*photo by John Foster/Masterfile*).

ply ships failed to arrive, and only 7 of 26 men survived. Much of the exploration was incidental to the search for the North Pole. Otto SVERDRUP between 1898 and 1902 mapped several islands in the area of Ellesmere I. In 1903-04 the Canadian government was moved to send A.P. LOW to the area to demonstrate Canadian sovereignty; he placed a cairn at the farthest "northing" and installed a flag. A research camp was established at Lk Hazen during the International Geophysical Year (1957-58), and today there are stations at Craig Harbour and Alexandra Fjord. Grise Fjord is an important native community. HIGH ARCTIC WEATHER STATIONS are maintained at Eureka and Alert – the northernmost station in the Canadian Arctic (82°31′ N lat). In 1986 Ellesmere I National Park Reserve was created on the N part of the island, scheduled to become a national park when claims in the area are settled. JAMES MARSH

Ellesmere Island Archaeological Sites were occupied about 4200 years ago by hunting bands believed to have originated from NE Asia and Alaska. Remains of seasonal hunting camps have been found in northern interior valleys and on raised marine terraces along the south and northeast coast of Ellesmere I. Artifacts include small, finely made stone tools of the Arctic Small Tool tradition and artistic carvings from the late DORSET period. Around 1000 AD the THULE-culture Inuit, direct ancestors of all the present-day INUIT, arrived from the Bering Sea and replaced the Dorset population. The remains of their settlements are found along the coastlines of fjords and islands advantageous to hunting sea-mammals, including large bowhead whales. Contact with Norsemen seems to have occurred *c*1250 AD in the Smith Sd region. Ellesmere I was abandoned by the Inuit sometime during the Little Ice Age, between 1650 and 1850 AD. PETER SCHLEDERMANN

Ellice, Edward, fur trader, merchant, politician (b at London, Eng 23 or 27 Sept 1783; d near Glengarry, Scot 17 Sept 1863). He was the son of a prominent London merchant and was educated at Marischall College, Aberdeen, before being sent to Canada where he assisted in 1804 in the merger of the XY COMPANY and NORTH WEST COMPANY. As a NWC partner, Ellice (always known as "Bear") was active in the pamphlet warfare with Lord SELKIRK, and he was a major party in the negotiations for unification of the NWC and HBC, completed in 1821. For years thereafter he was involved in litigation over the claims against the NWC. From 1818 on Ellice almost continuously, until his death, represented Coventry in the House of Commons, and after the Whigs took office in 1830 he held several Cabinet posts 1830-34. With large landholdings in Canada, including the seigneury of Beauharnois, Ellice followed developments there closely and behind the scenes greatly influenced British policy. J.M. BUMSTED

Elliot Lake, Ont, Town, pop 17 984 (1986c), 16 723 (1981c), is located 140 km W of SUDBURY. Elliot Lake formally came into existence in 1955, only 2 years after the famous "backdoor staking bee" of J.H. HIRSHHORN had alerted the mining world to the area's URANIUM potential. Stimulated by the American military demand for uranium, Elliot Lake boomed 1956-63. By 1959 a dozen mining companies were in operation and nearly 25 000 people resided in the carefully laid out, government-planned community. The American government's decision that year not to renew its contracts was a devastating blow. By 1965 Elliot Lake's population had dwindled to 6600, and by 1970 only Denison Mines and Rio Algom were in operation. In the later 1960s and 1970s the uranium industry was revived by the advent of nuclear-generated electrical power. In the early 1980s, long-range sales to ONTARIO HYDRO brought a second surge in growth, but by mid-decade falling prices once more brought a decline in population. MATT BRAY

Elliott, Andrew Charles, lawyer, judge, politician, premier of BC (b in Ire *c*1828; d at San Francisco, Calif 9 Apr 1889). A barrister of Lincoln's Inn, London, Elliott held several judicial and administrative posts in colonial British Columbia, was a member of the Legislative Council (1865-66) and in 1875 was elected to the provincial legislature, replacing William SMITHE as leader of the Opposition. On the defeat of G.E. WALKEM'S government (1876) he became premier, but he was no match for Walkem, who attacked his attempts at conciliation in the Pacific railway dispute with Ottawa. Heavy tax increases and the end of Victoria's hopes of being the transcontinental terminus caused Elliott to lose his seat in the electoral defeat of his government (1878). H. KEITH RALSTON

Elliott, George Alexander, economist, professor, civil servant (b at Napier, Ont 22 July 1901). A man whose imagination, exactitude and humanity inspired his students, Elliott made important contributions to economic theory in articles in learned journals while professor at U of Alberta 1929-46 and U of Toronto 1946-57. References to his work still appear in scientific literature. Turning his attention to Canadian trade policy, he published *Tariff Procedures and Trade Practices* in 1954 and was appointed to the Tariff Board of Canada from 1957 to 1971. He was elected to the Royal Society of Canada in 1947 and was elected president of the Canadian Political Science Assn in 1957; he was awarded an LLD by Queen's in 1965. H.C. EASTMAN

Elliott, Kenneth Allan Caldwell, biochemist-neurochemist (b at Kimberley, S Africa 24 Aug 1903; d at Montréal 28 Apr 1986). A founder of the study of the brain's chemistry, Allan Elliott was the first person officially titled neurochemist at the Montreal Neurological Institute (1944). He was the first director of the Donner Lab of Experimental Neurochemistry (MNI) and then chairman of the dept of biochemistry at McGill and Gilman Cheney Professor of Biochemistry. Elliott did original research on brain swelling following trauma, inhibitory and excitatory neurotransmitters, and the biochemistry of epilepsy as well as analysis for the chemical composition of the fluid that bathes the brain. His chemical analysis of the cerebrospinal fluid led to "Elliott's solution," which is in standard use by neurosurgeons. Elliott wrote over 140 publications and was senior editor of 2 editions of *Neurochemistry*. After retirement from McGill he joined CUSO and taught biochemistry to medical students in Enugu, Nigeria. He was the first Norman Bethune Exchange Professor from McGill to the Chinese Medical College, Beijing. LEONHARD S. WOLFE

Elm (*Ulmus*), genus of trees of elm family (Ulmaceae), found only in temperate regions of the Northern Hemisphere. Twenty-five species occur worldwide; 3 are native to Canada. White elm occurs as far W as central Saskatchewan; rock and slippery elms are restricted to parts of extreme SW Ontario and SE Québec. Elms, especially white or American elm, may reach imposing heights and are characterized by an umbrella-shaped crown. Leaves are simple, short stalked, oval (slightly asymmetrical at base) and veined, and have teeth of 2 sizes along the margin. They alternate along the twig. The flat, winged fruit develops in very early spring. Elms can grow in various habitats but are usually found in wet, fertile ones (eg, alluvial flats). The very hard wood is used for specialized items, eg, hockey sticks, and for piano bodies, caskets and furniture. Elms are often planted as ORNAMENTALS but many have died from Dutch elm disease. ESTELLE LACOURSIÈRE

White elm (*Ulmus americana*), with fruit (*artwork by Claire Tremblay*).

Elmira, Ontario, UP, pop 6972 (1986c), 7063 (1981c), is located about 17 km NW of KITCHENER. Founded on the banks of the Canagagigue R, it was part of the original Six Nations Reserve and a stopping point on the CANADA COMPANY'S Guelph-Goderich Road. Its first settlers were English and Irish, then predominantly German from the 1850s. It has been a supply centre for Kitchener's agricultural hinterland. Now part of the Township of Woolwich, Elmira achieved town status in 1923 but disappeared as a legal corporation with the inauguration of Waterloo Regional Government. KEN MCLAUGHLIN

Elora, Ontario, pop 2799 (1986c), 2666 (1981c), inc 1858, is a picturesque village at the junction of the Grand and Irvine rivers; the sheer beauty of the junction rivals NIAGARA FALLS. Elora was founded 1832 by Capt William Gilkison of Irvine, Scotland, and named after *Ellora*, his brother's East Indian merchantman. Gilkison, a cousin of

Kosso Eloul, *Innercity Gate* (1978) stelcoloy, TD Centre, Toronto (*courtesy Kosso Eloul*).

John GALT, the CANADA COMPANY promoter, was impressed by the magnificence of the limestone gorge. Development ceased in the 1870s but there remains a magnificent unspoiled array of 19th-century Ontario architecture in brick and stone to complement the natural landscape.

KEN MCLAUGHLIN

Eloul, Kosso, sculptor (b at Mourom, USSR 22 Jan 1920). Eloul's art training started in Tel Aviv in 1938 and continued in 1939 at the Art Institute of Chicago, where he studied with Frank Lloyd Wright, and at the Chicago School of Design with Laszlo Moholy-Nagy. After service in WWII and the War of Independence in Palestine, he returned to his art in 1948. In 1959 he represented Israel at the 29th Venice Biennale. After the First Sculpture Symposium in Yugoslavia in 1961 he set up a similar event in the Negev Desert in 1962; his lifelong involvement with international SCULPTURE conferences began then. He settled permanently in Toronto in 1969 and was the moving force behind the 10th Sculpture Conference held there in 1978. Eloul's characteristic monumental sculptures grace the public spaces of many Canadian cities. His gleaming rectangles of highly polished aluminum or stainless steel are balanced precariously at unusual angles, testing and probing the laws of gravity. Although usually described as minimalist, their inherent energy and restless potential for movement transcend the contemplative minimalist sensibility.

CLARA HARGITTAY

Elsa, YT, UP, pop 294 (1986c), located 108 km NE of the Klondike Highway, 452 km by road N from Whitehorse. In 1924, Charles Brefalt staked the Elsa silver claim on the northern slope of Galena Hill in the Mayo district. Within 5 years, miners working in the silver-lead deposits had established a village on the hill. At first, low silver prices hindered development but in 1936 the Treadwell Yukon Co constructed a 150-ton ore mill and a camp at the site. Falling metal prices drove the company into dissolution in 1942 but independent miners kept Elsa alive. It received a post office in 1949 and in the 1950s was the starting point for the first oil exploration winter road to drilling sites 500 km to the north. Elsa remains a service centre for the few miners in the district.

H. GUEST

Emblems of Canada At Confederation in 1867 no armorial bearings were assigned to the new Dominion of Canada. In 1868 the original provinces, Nova Scotia, New Brunswick, Québec and Ontario, received arms by a royal warrant that also provided for a great seal of Canada, a shield bearing the quartered arms of the 4 provinces. Although not intended as arms of federal authority, the shield came to be considered the arms of the Dominion. As additional provinces entered Confederation, armorial bearings assigned to them were added to the federal shield, creating an unsatisfactory aggregation. A Canadian committee appointed in 1919 had decided within a year on the basic elements of a new design, which was forwarded to the College of Arms in London, Eng, for its consideration. On 21 Nov 1921 King George V, by royal proclamation, assigned armorial bearings for Canada.

The blazon (heraldic description) of Canada's arms is as follows: Tierced in fesse: the first and second divisions containing the quarterly coat following, namely, 1st, gules, three lions passant guardant in pale or; 2nd, or, a lion rampant within a double tressure fleury-counter-fleury gules; 3rd, azure, a harp or stringed argent; 4th, azure, three fleurs-de-lis or; and the third division argent three maple leaves conjoined on one stem proper. Upon the royal helm mantled argent doubled gules a wreath of the colours surmounted by a lion passant guardant or imperially crowned proper and holding in the dexter paw a maple leaf gules nerved or; the whole ensigned with St Edward's Crown. *Supporters:* on the dexter a lion rampant or holding a lance argent, point or, flying therefrom to the dexter the Union flag; and on the sinister an unicorn argent armed, crined and unguled or, gorged with a coronet composed of crosses patée and fleurs-de-lis a chain affixed thereto reflexed of the last, and holding a like lance flying therefrom to the sinister a banner azure charged with three fleurs-de-lis or. (For a guide to the specialized vocabulary used here, *see* EMBLEMS, PROVINCIAL AND TERRITORIAL; HERALDRY.)

The design is traditional, with the shield displaying the arms of England, Scotland, Ireland and France to symbolize the nation's founding races. Underneath the 4 quarters, on a white field, is a sprig of 3 maple leaves to indicate the new nation of many peoples. Originally green, in 1957 the leaves officially became red, a common autumnal colour, and thus were in accord with Canada's national colours, red and white. The crest and the shield's supporters are strikingly similar to the royal arms of Great Britain. The motto A MARI USQUE AD MARE ("From sea to sea") is from Psalm 72:8, "He shall have dominion also from sea to sea, and from the river unto the ends of the earth" (King James version).

Flag

The red and white flag featuring a stylized maple leaf was proclaimed Canada's national flag by Queen Elizabeth II on 15 Feb 1965. Its

Canada's flag (*courtesy National Archives of Canada/Karen E. Bailey*).

Arms of Alberta (*NAC/Karen E. Bailey*).

Arms of British Columbia (*Province of British Columbia*).

Arms of Manitoba (*NAC/Karen E. Bailey*).

Arms of New Brunswick (*courtesy New Brunswick Information Service*).

Arms of Newfoundland (*NAC/Karen E. Bailey*).

Arms of Northwest Territories (*NAC/Karen E. Bailey*).

Arms of Nova Scotia (*NAC/Karen E. Bailey*).

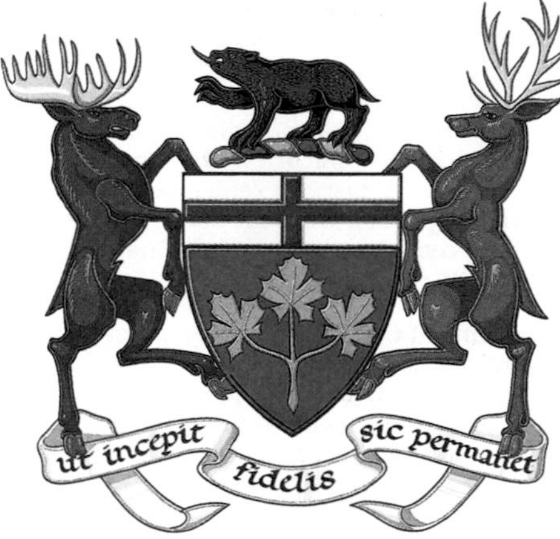

Arms of Ontario (*NAC/Karen E. Bailey*).

Arms of Prince Edward Island (*NAC/Karen E. Bailey*).

Arms of Québec (*NAC/Karen E. Bailey*).

Arms of Saskatchewan (*Province of Saskatchewan*).

Arms of Yukon Territory (*NAC/Karen E. Bailey*).

adoption was the culmination of many years of discussion, hundreds of designs and the heated FLAG DEBATE in Parliament. Its blazon is "Gules on a Canadian pale argent a maple leaf of the first." The proportions of the flag are 2 by length and one by width, with a white square in the centre the width of the flag.

Before 1965 Canada did not have an official flag. During the French regime the flag flown was the royal banner of France, "Azure, three fleurs-de-lis or, arranged two and one." The golden lilies symbolized the Holy Trinity. After the Conquest in 1760 the flags most commonly flown were Great Britain's Union Flag (Union Jack) and the Canadian Red Ensign. The latter was the flag of the British merchant marine, red, with the Union Jack in the canton (ie, near the staff). In 1892 the British Admiralty authorized its use, with the addition of a shield for Canada in the fly, on vessels registered in Canada. In 1924 a Canadian order-in-council decreed that the flag could be flown over Canadian government buildings abroad. The Red Ensign was later carried by Canadian athletes at the Olympics and by Canadian troops in WWII. In 1945 another order-in-council approved the flying of the flag over federal buildings within Canada. To many Canadians the Red Ensign was the national flag, and this led to intense feeling when Parliament proposed to replace it with a new design.

Emblems

Beaver The BEAVER, most significant of the fur-bearing animals sought in the FUR TRADE, was identified early as an emblem suitable to represent portions of the vast territories that in the 19th century became Canada. In 1621 King James I granted Nova Scotia to Sir William ALEXANDER. In 1633 when Alexander became earl of Stirling and Viscount Canada, his new arms featured a beaver to symbolize his fiefdom in the New World.

From 1678 the HUDSON'S BAY COMPANY (chartered 1670) possessed an armorial seal charged with 4 beavers and separated into compartments formed by a St George's cross. About the same time Gov Frontenac of NEW FRANCE suggested the beaver as a suitable emblem for the colony, but arms were never authorized. In 1690, to commemorate Frontenac's successful defence of the QUÉBEC CITADEL against the naval attack by Sir William Phips, the Kebeca Liberata MEDAL was struck. It bore a representation of France as a seated woman, and of Canada as a beaver at her feet. The use of the beaver as a Canadian emblem declined in the second half of the 19th century, perhaps because Montréal ceased to be a major fur entrepôt. The animal's emblematic importance was revived by Sir Sandford FLEMING when he designed Canada's first postage stamp, the 1851 3-penny beaver. Today the beaver, noted for its industry and perseverance, qualities considered suitable for a nation to emulate, decorates the reverse of the Canadian 5-cent coin.

Maple Leaf Along the St Lawrence the leaf of the indigenous common MAPLE, with its distinctive shape and beautiful autumnal colouring, seems to have been considered as an emblem by 1700. When the first ST-JEAN-BAPTISTE SOCIETY was founded in 1834, the maple leaf was made its emblem. In Toronto the 1848 issue of Rev John McCaul's literary annual, *Maple Leaf*, referred to the leaf as the chosen emblem of Canada. In 1860 the leaf was incorporated into the badge of the 100th Regiment (Royal Canadians), and that year the leaves were used extensively in decorations for the Prince of Wales's visit. In 1867 Alexander Muir composed "The Maple Leaf," a song which for decades was regarded as a national hymn. By royal warrant on 26 May 1868 the designs of arms granted to Québec and Ontario each incorporated a sprig of 3 maple leaves. The maple leaf was the badge of the Canadian Expeditionary Force in WWI. When national armorial bearings were assigned in 1921, a sprig of leaves was an important feature, and in 1965 it became the dominant element in the new national flag. BRUCE PEEL

Reading: Conrad Swan, *Canada: Symbols of Sovereignty* (1977); Canada, Secretary of State, *The Arms, Flags and Emblems of Canada* (1981).

Emblems, Provincial and Territorial Each Canadian province and territory has, at some point, chosen or been granted formal emblems to symbolize such things as its history, its flora and fauna, its geographical setting, and its existence as a sovereign entity. These emblems are coats of arms, flags and PROVINCIAL FLORAL EMBLEMS, and sometimes a tartan or an animal or mineral. Coats of arms are properly described in the formal language of HERALDRY, which, among English speakers, is a vocabulary derived from Norman French with borrowings from Latin and other languages. Since their descriptions are in words, the emblems may vary in their visual execution from artist to artist, but the basic elements must always appear in correct relation to one another. The following glossary is intended as an aid to interpretation of the heraldic description both here and in EMBLEMS OF CANADA.

Glossary addorsed: back to back; *argent:* silver; *azure:* blue; *bar:* narrow horizontal stripe; *barrulet:* narrow bar; *barry:* divided by horizontal lines; *base:* horizontal band occupying bottom third of shield (also called "champagne"); *bezant:* gold roundel; *billety:* strewn with billets (upright, oblong figures); *charged:* bearing a heraldic figure; *chief:* horizontal band occupying top third of shield; *compartment:* the base on which a shield rests, particularly with supporters; *crined:* referring to colour of mane, hair or beard; *cross patée:* cross with expanding arms; *dexter:* right side as seen from behind shield, hence viewer's left; *escutcheon:* shield; *fesse:* horizontal band occupying centre third of shield; *field:* background; *fimbriated:* bordered with a different tincture; *fleury-counter-fleury:* with fleurs-de-lis placed alternately in opposite directions; *fructed:* bearing fruit, *garb:* sheaf of grain; *gorged:* wearing a collar; *guardant:* with head turned to face viewer; *gules:* red; *haurient* (of fish or sea animal): vertical, with head upwards; *helm:* helmet; *langued:* referring to tincture of tongue; *mantle:* cloth hanging from helmet; *mullet:* a star; *of the first, last,* etc: of the first, last, etc, tincture mentioned in the description; *or:* gold; *pale:* vertical band occupying centre third of shield; *pallet:* 2 or more narrow vertical stripes; *passant:* walking; *pile:* wedge-shaped figure with point downward; *proper:* in normal colours; *rampant:* with one hind paw on ground, the other three raised, tail erect; *reflexed:* looped; *roundel:* circular shape; *sable:* black; *sinister:* left side as seen from behind shield, hence viewer's right; *slipped:* torn from stock or branch; *statant:* standing; *tierced:* in 3 parts of different colours; *tinctures:* colours and metals, the metals are argent and or; *tressure:* narrow band bordering shield, often double; *unguled:* referring to colour of hoofs, nails, claws; *vair:* bell-like shapes, white and blue; *vert:* green; *wavy:* formed like waves; *wreath:* garland on which the crest is borne.

Alberta

Coat of Arms was granted by King Edward VII, 30 May 1907. The crest and supporters were granted 13 July 1980. *Arms:* Azure, in front of a range of snow mountains proper, a range of hills vert, in base a wheatfield surmounted by a prairie both also proper, on a chief argent, a St George's Cross. *Crest:* Upon a helm with wreath argent and gules, a beaver couchant upholding on its back the royal crown, both proper. *Supporters:* On the dexter side, a lion or armed and langued gules, and, on the sinister side, a pronghorn antelope proper; the compartment comprising a grassy mount with the floral emblem of the province of Alberta growing therefrom proper. *Motto:* "Fortis et liber" (Strong and Free).

Flag consists of a royal ultramarine blue field bearing in the centre the provincial arms. It was approved by Queen Elizabeth II on 1 May 1968 and proclaimed on June 1. The proportions are 2 by length and one by width. The arms are in length seven-elevenths of the flag's width.

British Columbia

Coat of Arms and motto were granted by King Edward VII, 31 Mar 1906; crest, supporters and compartment by Elizabeth II, 15 Oct 1987. *Arms:* Argent, 3 bars wavy azure, issuant from the base a demi-sun in splendour proper, on a chief, the Union Device charged in the centre point with an antique crown or. *Crest:* Upon a helm with a wreath argent and gules the royal crest of general purpose of our royal predecessor Queen Victoria differenced for us and our successors in right of British Columbia with the lion thereof garlanded about the neck with the provincial flower that is to say the pacific dogwood (*Cornus nuttallii*) with leaves all proper mantled gules doubled argent. *Supporters:* On the dexter side, a wapiti stag (*Cervus canadensis*) proper and on the sinister side a bighorn sheep ram (*Ovis canadensis*) argent armed and unguled or. *Compartment:* Beneath the shield a scroll entwined with pacific dogwood flowers slipped and leaved proper inscribed with the motto assigned by the said warrant of our royal predecessor King Edward VII that is to say "Splendor sine occasu" ("Splendor without diminishment").

Flag The royal warrant of 1906 authorized the use of the arms for the provincial flag. This was put into effect by a provincial order-in-council, 20 June 1960. The proportions are 5 by length and 3 by width.

Manitoba

Coat of Arms was granted by King Edward VII, 10 May 1905. *Arms:* Vert, on a rock, a buffalo statant proper, on a chief argent, the Cross of St George.

Flag The Red Ensign, bearing in the fly the provincial arms, received royal approval 11 May 1965 and was proclaimed 12 May 1966. The proportions are 2 by length and one by width.

New Brunswick

Coat of Arms was granted by Queen Victoria, 26 May 1868. The crest, supporters, compartment and motto were granted by Elizabeth II 24 Sept 1984. *Arms:* Or, on waves, a lymphad, or ancient galley, with oars in action proper, on a chief gules, a lion passant guardant or. *Crest:* Upon a helm with wreath or and gules within a coronet comprising 4 maple leaves (3 manifest) set upon a rim or water barry wavy azure and argent leaping thereform an atlantic salmon (*Salmo salar*) upholding on its back our royal crown both proper mantled gules doubled or. *Supporters:* On either side a white tailed deer (*Odocoileus virginianus*) each gorged with a collar of Maliseet wampum proper and pendant therefrom an escutcheon that to the dexter bearing our union badge and that to the sinister the arms azure 3 fleur-des-lys or otherwise France modern. *Compartment:* Comprising a grassy mount with the floral emblem of the said province of New Brunswick the purple violet (*Viola cucullata*) and young ostrich fern (*Matteuccia struthiopteris*) commonly called fiddlehead growing therefrom all proper. *Motto:* "Spem reduxit" (Hope was restored).

Flag The royal warrant of 1868 authorized the use of the arms for the provincial flag. This was put into effect by provincial proclamation, 24 Feb 1963. The proportions are 4 by length and 2.5 by width. The red portion with the lion occupies one-third of the surface.

Newfoundland

Coat of Arms was granted by King Charles I, 1 Jan 1637. *Arms:* Gules, a cross argent, in the first and fourth quarters, a lion passant guardant crowned or; in the second and third quarters, an unicorn passant of the second, armed, maned and unguled of the third, and gorged with a crown, thereto a chain affixed passing between the forelegs and reflected over his back, of the last. *Mantling:* Gules doubled argent. *Crest:* On a wreath or and gules an elk passant proper. *Supporters:* Two "savages of the clime" armed and apparelled according to their guise when they go to war. *Motto:* "Quaerite prime regnum dei" (Seek ye first the Kingdom of God).

Flag Adopted by the provincial legislature, 28 May 1980. The flag is white. In the portion near the staff 4 right-angle triangles, all separated by the field, are arranged in pairs to form rectangular patterns horizontally. In the fly, a gold arrow bordered red between 2 red right-angle triangles, completely voided in their centre, point away from the staff.

Northwest Territories

Coat of Arms was authorized and approved by Queen Elizabeth II, 24 Feb 1956. *Arms:* Per bendwavy gules and vert billety or, in sinister chief, the mask of an arctic fox argent, on a chief indented also argent, a barrulet wavy azure. *Crest:* On a wreath argent and gules, a compass rose proper between 2 narwhals haurient and addorsed or.

Flag The flag adopted by the territorial council, 1 Jan 1969, is divided vertically in the proportions: one blue (near staff), 2 white (middle), one blue (fly). The white square displays in its centre the arms of the Northwest Territories.

Nova Scotia

Coat of Arms was first granted by King Charles I in 1626. It was reinstated by King George V, 19 Jan 1929, to supersede the coat of arms granted 26 May 1868. *Arms:* Argent, a Cross of St Andrew azure charged with an escutcheon of the Royal Arms of Scotland. *Crest:* On a wreath of the colours, a branch of laurel and a thistle issuing from two hands conjoined, the one being armed and the other naked, all proper. *Supporters:* On the dexter side, an unicorn argent armed, crined and unguled or, and crowned with the imperial crown proper, and gorged with a coronet composed of crosses patée and fleurs-de-lis a chain affixed thereto passing through the forelegs and reflexed over the back, or. And on the sinister side, a savage holding in the exterior hand an arrow, proper. *Motto:* "Munit haec et altera vincit" (One defends and the other conquers).

Flag The royal warrant of 1929 authorized the use of the arms for the provincial flag.

Ontario

Coat of Arms The arms were granted by Queen Victoria, 26 May 1868; the crest, supporters and motto were granted by King Edward VII, 27 Feb 1909. *Arms:* Vert, a sprig of 3 leaves of maple slipped or, on a chief argent, the Cross of St George. *Crest:* On a wreath of the colours, a bear passant sable. *Supporters:* On the dexter side, a moose, and on the sinister side a Canadian deer both proper. *Motto:* "Ut incepit fidelis sic permanet" (Loyal it began, loyal it remains).

Flag The Red Ensign, bearing in the fly the provincial arms, received royal approval as the provincial flag, 14 Apr 1965, and was proclaimed on May 21. The proportions are 2 by length and one by width.

Prince Edward Island

Coat of Arms was granted by King Edward VII, 30 May 1905. *Arms:* Argent, on an island vert, to the sinister an oak tree fructed, to the dexter thereof 3 oak saplings sprouting all proper, on a chief gules, a lion passant guardant or. *Motto:* "Parva sub ingenti" (The small under the protection of the great).

Flag The 1905 warrant authorized the use of the provincial arms for the flag. On 24 Mar 1964 the province adopted a design bearing the arms within a red and white border. The proportions are 6′ (183 cm) by length and 4′ (122 cm) by width including the border, which is 3″ (7.6 cm) wide. The alternating strips of the border are each 10″ (25 cm) long.

Québec

Coat of Arms was authorized by a provincial order-in-council on 9 Dec 1939. These arms resemble those granted by Queen Victoria in 1868 except that the upper portion bears 3 gold fleurs-de-lis on a blue field instead of 2 blue fleurs-de-lis on a gold field. The same order-in-council approved the use of the royal crown above the shield. The motto, adopted 1883, was suggested by Eugène Taché, architect of the "palais législatif." *Arms:* Tierced in fesse: 1, azure, 3 fleurs-de-lis or; 2, gules, a lion passant guardant or; 3, or, a sprig of three leaves of sugar maple vert veined of the field. *Motto:* "Je me souviens" (I remember), in letters azure within a scroll argent edged azure.

Flag Adopted 21 Jan 1948 by an order-in-council and by an Act assented to 9 Mar 1950, the fleurdelisé flag is described as "Azure a cross between four fleurs-de-lis argent." The proportions are 6 units by length, 4 by width, and the arms of the cross are one unit wide.

Saskatchewan

Coat of Arms was granted by King Edward VII, 25 Aug 1906; the crest, supporters and motto by Elizabeth II, 16 Sept 1986. *Arms:* Vert, 3 garbs in fesse or, on a chief of the last, a lion passant guardant gules. *Crest:* Upon a helm with a wreath argent and gules a beaver upholding with its back the royal crown and holding in the dexter fore-claws a western red lily (*Lilium philadelphicum andinum*) slipped all proper, mantled gules doubled argent. *Supporters:* Or the dexter side a lion or gorged with a collar of prairie indian beadwork proper and dependent thereupon a 6-pointed mullet faceted argent fimbriated and garnished or charged with a maple leaf gules and on the sinister side a white tailed deer (*Odocoileus virginianus*) proper gorged with a like collar and dependent therefrom a like mullet charged with a western red lily slipped and leaved proper. *Motto:* Beneath the shield a scroll entwined with western red lilies slipped and leaved proper inscribed with the motto "*Multis e gentibus vires*" (out of many peoples, strength).

Flag Saskatchewan's flag was officially dedicated 22 Sept 1969. It is divided horizontally, green above and yellow below. On the green portion near the staff are the provincial arms. In the fly over both tinctures is the provincial floral emblem.

Yukon

Coat of Arms was authorized by Queen Elizabeth II on 24 Feb 1956. *Arms:* Azure, on a pallet wavy argent a like pallet of the field, issuant from base 2 piles reversed gules edged also argent each charged with 2 bezants in pale, on a chief argent, a cross gules surmounted of a roundel vair. *Crest:* On a wreath or and gules, a husky dog standing on a mount of snow proper.

Flag The flag, adopted by the territorial council in 1967, is divided vertically in equal parts: green (near the staff), white (middle), blue (fly). On the white field above a wreath of fireweed are the arms of the Yukon with the crest.

AUGUSTE VACHON

Reading: A.B. Beddoe, *Beddoe's Canadian Heraldry* (1981); Canada, Secretary of State, *The Arms, Flags and Emblems of Canada* (1981); C. Swan, *Canada: Symbols of Sovereignty* (1977).

Emerson, John Norman, professor, archaeologist (b at Toronto 13 Mar 1917; d there 18 Nov 1978). As a Huron-Iroquois specialist, he was the first in Canada to establish a continuing training program for Canadian archaeologists. Educated at U of T and Chicago, and supervisor of archaeological studies at U of T for 30 years, Emerson was a humanitarian teacher and a socially minded scientist. He firmly believed in the "learn by doing" philosophy of teaching. His prodigious excavations at nearly 50 sites helped expose numerous students and the general public to Ontario archaeology. He founded the modern Ontario Archaeological Soc. and helped establish the Canadian Archaeological Assn in 1968. W.C. NOBLE

Emery, John, bobsledder (b at Montréal 4 Jan 1932). Infected by brother Vic EMERY's enthusiasm for BOBSLEDDING, John teamed with Vic, Doug Anakin and Peter Kirby to provide Canada with a 1964 Innsbruck Olympics gold medal in a sport few Canadians dared attempt because of cost and inadequate training facilities.

BOB FERGUSON

Emery, Victor, Vic, bobsledder (b at Montréal, 28 June 1933). Sailing and skiing were his first loves, but Emery became captivated with BOBSLEDDING and luge while watching the 1956 Cortina Olympic Games. He assembled a crew, including his brother John EMERY, that won startling gold-medal victories at the 1964 Innsbruck Olympics and 1965 world championships.

BOB FERGUSON

Emigration, the act of leaving a place of residence or country to live elsewhere. Of the 4 major components of Canadian POPULATION change (births, deaths, IMMIGRATION and emigration), emigration is the most statistically uncertain. Canada does not maintain an exit-visa register. Intercensal estimates of emigration measured by collecting data from the US and UK and combining them with a figure of 48 000 (the annual estimate for emigration to all other countries in the world) are published annually by Statistics Canada. Emigration from Canada between 1851 and 1971 was as volatile as immigration, especially since, during the period of early settlement, Canada was a way station for immigrants travelling to the US. Early estimates of emigration, which vary from 170 000 (1851-61) to 1 089 000 (1911-21), were based on the population census conducted every 10 years from 1851 to 1951 (the 1851 and 1861 data are aggregates of separate censuses for Canada E, Canada W, NS and NB). Since 1951 a national census has been taken every 5 years.

Demographers use 3 methods in making emigration assumptions when projecting Canadian population growth. The first method is to use emigration as an absolute number over a period of time as mentioned above. The second method is estimate emigration as a percentage of gross immigration since a significant part of emigrants are either returning to their original country or re-migrating to another country. In 1975 a Special Joint Committee of Parliament on immigration policy indicated that future emigration from Canada could be estimated as one-third of gross immigration. However, the use of immigration statistics creates problems, eg, the difficulty of distinguishing between nationality, country of birth and country of last residence. Immigration data usually record only the last residence. Thirdly, emigration could be estimated as a proportion of the total population. Since there is no foolproof technique, there is no way to prove that one approach is superior to another. To complicate matters further, often a number of Canadian emigrants in previous years came back as "returning residents" and as such are not registered as "immigrants."

Evidence indicates that 3 out of 5 emigrants from Canada had been immigrants at some time. About 25% of them had immigrated in the previous 5-year period. As an average for the period 1851 to 1951, it is estimated that the extent of emigration relative to immigration has been as high as 80 per 100 immigrants. During the postwar period this ratio seems to have declined to 50 emigrants per 100 immigrants. The figures for 1971-81 are estimated to be in the range of 35 to 46 emigrants per 100 immigrants.

Since a large number of Canadian emigrants have gone to the United States, it is necessary to focus attention on this exchange. The number of Canadians born in the United States was at its peak in 1930 at 1.3 million, representing 12.6% of the population of Canada in 1931. In 1980, however, the Canadians born in the US amounted to 843 000 or 3.5% of the 1981 Canadian population (*see* AMERICANS).

Over the period 1945-64 the emigration to the US increased, but has slowed down since 1965, partly owing to more restrictive US immigration laws. After 1969, Canada has barely filled half of its annual US quota of 20 000 immigrants. Available information shows that over a million Canadians were counted in the censuses of 59 countries sometime between 1970 and 1985. It is notable that the only countries with figures of 10 000 or more Canadians were France at 12 000, Australia at 18 000, Italy 18 000, the UK at 56 000 and the US at 843 000. With changing patterns of immigration to Canada several other countries would be added to the above list in the next few years.

Three aspects of Canadian emigration to the US needs mention. First, many emigrants from Canada are former immigrants to this country. In 1979-85 period the proportion of foreign-born among emigrants to the US from Canada was close to one-third. Second, in recent years more Canadian emigrants settled in the Pacific, southeastern and southwestern regions of the US where high-tech industries were located, unlike in earlier years when they settled in Illinois, New York and Pennsylvania. Third, occupationally, more than half of those destined to the labour force in 1985 belonged to professional, technical or managerial occupations as in previous years.

Various theories have been advanced to explain the relationship between economic development and the movement of people. For example, Britain was once the world's largest exporter of capital, technical skills and unskilled labour to the developing countries overseas. Whether international flow of human capital is an economic blessing or a curse depends on the stage of development, the supply of skilled labour in the sending country, the demand for the same in the receiving country and the behaviour of the migrants in terms of remittances and of transfer of technology and capital to the sending country. Canada has attracted large numbers of skilled workers to its shores while the number of departures of such workers has declined.

CHRIS TAYLOR AND J. SAMUEL

Emmerson, Henry Robert, lawyer, businessman, premier of NB (b at Maugerville, NB 25 Sept 1853; d at Dorchester, NB 9 July 1914). A successful businessman and lawyer, Emmerson was an MLA 1888-90, a legislative councillor 1891-92 and MLA 1892-1900 (during which he was commissioner of public works). In the years 1897 to 1900 he was premier of NB and held the post of attorney general. Emmerson was elected MP in 1900 and became minister of railways and canals in Sir Wilfrid LAURIER's Cabinet 1904-07. In that capacity he played an important role in the development of railway terminals, docks and canals. Forced to resign over a scandal in his private life, he continued to sit in the House of Commons until his death.

ARTHUR T. DOYLE

Empire Day, observed annually on the school day preceding the May 24 holiday for Queen Victoria's birthday, was the most important patriotic rite for children in English-speaking Canada during the half century following its first observance 23 May 1899. The idea originated with Clementina Fessenden of Hamilton, and was publicized across the country by George Ross, Ontario education minister. Empire Day celebrations were associated with IMPERIALISM, militarism and immigrant assimilation. After an initial decline in the 1930s, the celebrations were rejuvenated by WWII. In later years various provinces renamed the day Commonwealth or Citizenship Day. *See also* VICTORIA DAY.

ROBERT M. STAMP

Employment and Income, White Paper on, described the government's immediate postwar fiscal and economic policies. Presented to Parliament in 1945 by the Hon C.D. HOWE, minister of reconstruction, it outlined the government's intention to adopt Keynesian economic policies to maintain a high level of employment and income. Deficits would be incurred and national debt increased when unemployment threatened, but would be balanced by surpluses in periods of prosperity. The White Paper led to policy changes and preceded the period of greatest prosperity in Canadian history; as well, it helped set the style of federal-provincial relations for 15 years.

C.E.S. FRANKS

Employment Law in Canada generally refers to the law governing the relationship of an individual employee to an employer, as distinguished from LABOUR LAW, the law of unionized COLLECTIVE-BARGAINING relationships. Employment law includes both the common, or judge-made, law of "master and servant," which is concerned mainly with wrongful dismissal, and a complex mass of statute law dealing with minimum labour standards, human rights, occupational health and safety, workers' compensation, etc.

With some important exceptions, unionized employees are also protected by the statutory part of employment law, although they are seldom concerned with minimum standards because their collective agreements almost always establish higher levels of wages and benefits. Other statutes, such as those regarding human rights, wage-payment protection, occupational health and safety, workers' compensation, pension and unemployment-insurance laws, do concern them.

In all provinces except Québec the law of wrongful dismissal is largely inherited from England, but Canadian courts now rarely refer to English case law. The equivalent Québec law is based on the French Civil Code. Generally an employee cannot be dismissed without cause unless he or she has been given due notice or pay in lieu thereof, but outside of these conditions the law of wrongful dismissal provides no protection against firing.

What constitutes cause and how much notice is "due" notice have been the subjects of countless court cases. The essence of cause for dismissal is usually an employee's failure to fulfil an obligation, within the scope of the job, to obey the employer's lawful directions. The period of notice to which the employee is entitled depends, first, on any agreement or understanding with the employer arising from the practice of the industry or the particular workplace. For example, in some industries or types of job, layoffs are a matter of course. In others, in the absence of employee misconduct, employment is assumed to be long term, and in that case an employer's economic difficulties will not justify dismissal without due notice.

Where there is no agreement or understanding, the length of the notice to which the employee is entitled depends on the character or status of the employment, the employee's length of service and age, and the availability of similar employment. Some minimum periods of notice are tied directly to the way wages are paid; eg, if payment is made every week, a week's notice may be all that is required. In the majority of jurisdictions, the minimum protection is only available to employees who have been employed for a specified period of time, usually 3 months.

A wrongfully dismissed employee can sue in the ordinary courts and will be awarded money damages equal to the pay he or she would have received if proper notice had been given, but the employee is under a duty to mitigate the damages; ie, any money earned at a new job or which could have been earned if a reasonable effort had been made to find a new job will be deducted. Because of court costs, wrongful dismissal cases usually involve executive-level employees. Unionized employees working under collective agreements cannot sue for wrongful dismissal. They must go through their grievance procedures and finally to ARBITRATION. This may be preferable because arbitrators, unlike the courts, order employers to put employees who are found to have been dismissed without just cause back on the job. Moreover, grievance arbitration normally costs the employee nothing.

Master and servant law may be thought of as the "old" employment law and the statute law as the "new" employment law, although there has been statutory regulation of the terms and conditions of employment since the Middle Ages. The earliest regulation of employment was largely for the benefit of employers, but since the 1900s, Factory Acts legislation, however inadequate it actually was, has existed for the protection of employees.

Whether or not a person is subject to any employment law depends on whether he or she is in fact the employee of an employer. There are a surprising number of cases where legally it is unclear whether people are employees or independent contractors. For example, taxi drivers or truckers may do work for only one company but not be considered employees by the law. The courts, or the administrators of labour legislation, will ask whether the driver, or any other person who claims to be an employee, owns the equipment or tools of the trade, stands to make a profit or take a loss and, most important, whether he or she is subject to control not only regarding what will be done on the job but how it will be done.

In each province and in the federal jurisdiction the Labour Standards Code or its equivalent regulates minimum wages, hours of work, overtime, the mode and interval of wage payments, wage statements, daily rest, weekly rest, statutory holidays, vacations and vacation pay, time off to vote, maternity leave and equal pay for men and women. In some jurisdictions the equal-pay law is found in the human rights code, which prohibits discrimination based on sex, race, religion, ethnic or national origin and a variety of other grounds that differ somewhat from province to province. In every province and as part of the federal government's Canada Labour Code there are statutory provisions that buttress the law of wrongful dismissal by setting minimum periods of notice to be given employees prior to their dismissal. The Canada Labour Code, applicable to employees in industries under federal constitutional jurisdiction, eg, banks, also provides that employees who have been employed for more than one year are entitled to reinstatement if they are found by special adjudicators to have been dismissed without just cause. Many other statutes, eg, corporations legislation and debt-collection legislation, can be considered part of employment law, as can legislation governing various aspects of public employment, eg, the civil service and public-school teaching.

Through the 1970s the individual-employer relationship in Canada became increasingly regulated, as is exemplified by the changes in the Canada Labour Code which gave wrongfully dismissed employees the right to claim reinstatement through a special low-cost administrative procedure. Judges became increasingly generous in the damages they awarded to wrongfully dismissed executives, to the point where a year's pay became quite common – a measure of damages far in excess of that normally given by American courts. With the adverse economic climate of the early 1980s, however, the momentum for greater employee protection appears to have been lost, and the question is whether economic pressure will result in the recall of protections already gained. INNIS CHRISTIE

Empress of Ireland, Canadian Pacific ocean-going passenger ship that sank in the St Lawrence R near Rimouski, Qué 29 May 1914. She was rammed in dense fog by the Norwegian collier *Storstad* and sank in only 14 minutes; 1014 passengers and crew died, while 465 managed to abandon ship. Bodies recovered from the *Empress* were gathered in the village of Ste-Luce and buried near Métis-sur-Mer, where a monument stands to their memory. Capt Anderson of the *Storstad* was later held responsible for the DISASTER. JAMES MARSH

Emslie, Robert Daniel, baseball player (b at Guelph, Canada W 27 Jan 1859; d at St Thomas, Ont 26 Apr 1943). Emslie played baseball in Ontario and Kansas before a brief major-league pitching career in which he won 32 games for Baltimore in 1884. He started umpiring in 1887 as the only official on the field. During his National League tenure (1891-1924), he helped improve the working conditions, wages and image of the umpire, and on retirement served the league in an advisory capacity. In 1946 the Baseball Hall of Fame in Cooperstown, NY, named him to its honour roll. WILLIAM HUMBER

Encyclopedia, a written work containing numerous entries, usually in alphabetical arrangement, attempting to cover all branches of knowledge or all aspects of one subject. The late Latin word is a misconstruction based on the Greek expression for "complete education." Various efforts were made in ancient times to encompass all knowledge in a single work. The first modern encyclopedia, with broad coverage and elaborate cross-referencing, was the *Cyclopaedia* (London, 1728) edited by Ephraim Chambers. With Denis Diderot's *Encyclopédie* (Paris, vol 1, 1751) the encyclopedia reached its apogee of literary excellence and social influence. The greatest English-language encyclopedia, *Encyclopaedia Britannica,* was first issued in 1768 in 3 volumes, and by the scholarly 11th edition of 1910-11 it had grown to 29 volumes.

The first attempt to produce an encyclopedic work entirely on Canada was *Canada: An Encyclopaedia of the Country* (6 vols, Toronto, 1898-1900), edited by J. Castell HOPKINS. More comprehensive was *The Encyclopedia of Canada* (6 vols, Toronto, 1935-37), edited by W.S. WALLACE, which was arranged alphabetically and included numerous biographies and descriptions of places. A supplementary volume on Newfoundland, compiled by Robert Blackburn, was published in 1949. The encyclopedia was sold to the Grolier Society, an American publisher, and provided the core of *Encyclopedia Canadiana* (10 vols, Toronto, 1957), edited by John ROBBINS. *The Canadian Encyclopedia* (3 vols, Edmonton, 1985; rev ed 1988) was an entirely new work.

Attempts have been made to compile encyclopedic works on aspects of Canada. Sir Arthur DOUGHTY and L.J. BURPEE compiled the *Index and Dictionary of Canadian History* (1911) as a companion to the Makers of Canada series, and Doughty and Adam SHORTT edited the 23-volume *Canada and Its Provinces* (1913-17). *The Oxford Companion to Canadian History and Literature,* by Norah Story, was published in 1967, and a supplement edited by William Toye appeared in 1970. A new *Oxford Companion to Canadian Literature,* edited by Toye, was published in 1983. The comprehensive ENCYCLOPEDIA OF MUSIC IN CANADA was published in 1981. A recent attempt to produce a modern encyclopedia of a province is the *Encyclopedia of Newfoundland and Labrador,* edited by Joseph SMALLWOOD (vol 1, 1981; vol 2, 1984). JAMES MARSH

Encyclopedia of Music in Canada, edited by Helmut KALLMANN, Gilles Potvin and Kenneth Winters and comprising over 3100 articles and 500 illustrations, was the first music encyclopedia published in Canada. Entries include biographies and histories of organizations involved with any facet of music in Canada. National topics such as Inuit music, piano building, and awards, and regional topics such as education, instrument collections and folk music are treated, as are music activities in Canadian cities and Canada's relations in music with other countries. Bibliographies, discographies, lists of compositions, filmographies and cross-references to other articles are included, and 15 000 index entries locate subjects which are mentioned in the articles.

Prompted initially in 1971 by Floyd S. CHALMERS, preparation began in 1973. With the editors, a peak staff of 23, aided by consultants, processed original articles from 400 writers. Equal attention was paid to all areas of music. Information was gathered from records of individuals and organizations, from personal interviews and from research of related documents. *EMC* was published in English by U of T Press (1981) and in French by Éditions Fides (1983). Procedures for continual editorial revision have been established. MABEL H. LAINE

Endangered Animals Animal species already extinct (extc) or extirpated (extp) from Canada include swift fox (extp), sea mink (extc, 1500s), great auk (extc, 1844), Labrador duck (extc, 1878), passenger pigeon (extc, 1914), timber rattlesnake (extp, 1941), paddlefish (extp, 1800s), Banff longnose dace (extc, 1950s), blue walleye (extc, 1960s), longjaw cisco (extc, 1970s) and gravel chub (extp, 1958). A number of other animal species are on the brink of extinction. The endangered species listed as of Apr 1987 by the Committee on the Status of Endangered Wildlife in Canada (COSEWIC) is provided on the accompanying table (next page).

The major factors involved in the disappearance or endangering of Canadian species have been exploitation (hunting, fishing, gathering of eggs or young), destruction of habitat and pollution. Factors affecting the quality of the ENVIRONMENT and leading to a steady loss of habitat include decrease in FOREST cover (cutting exceeds reforestation in most provinces); lack of natural VEGETATION to control EROSION on stream banks and woodlots on many farms; AIR POLLUTION by acid and other toxic substances; and WATER POLLUTION by industry, individuals and municipalities. A study of case histories is instructive. For example, the sea otter was exploited on the W Coast by hunters who sold as many as 1200 pelts per year during the late 1700s and 1800s. By 1900, sea otters were on the verge of extinction; the last documented sighting in BC was in 1929. An international treaty (1911) gave protection, and by the late 1960s the Alaskan population had grown to about 30 000. Transplants to BC (1969-72) were successful and 70 individuals were sighted in 1977.

The introduction of mammalian predators onto Langara I reduced the population of ancient murrelets and of the peregrine falcon which fed on them. Many populations of peregrines were

The peregrine falcon was one of Canada's endangered species; it is still rare (*courtesy Alberta Fish and Wildlife Division*).

Endangered Species List, 1987

	Mammals	*Birds*	*Reptiles, Amphibians & Fish*
Extinct	Dawson Caribou Sea Mink	Great Auk Labrador Duck Passenger Pigeon	*Banff Longnose Dace Blue Walleye Longjaw Cisco
Extirpated	*Atlantic Gray Whale *Atlantic Walrus St Lawrence population Black-footed Ferret Swift Fox		*Gravel Chub *Paddlefish
Endangered	Bowhead Whale Eastern Cougar Right Whale St Lawrence River Beluga Whale Sea Otter Vancouver Island Marmot Wood Bison	Eskimo Curlew Greater Prairie Chicken Kirtland's Warbler Peregrine Falcon subspecies anatum Piping Plover Spotted Owl Whooping Crane	Acadian Whitefish *Aurora Trout Leatherback Turtle Salish Sucker
Threatened	Maritime Woodland Caribou Newfoundland Pine Marten North Pacific Humpback Whale Peary Caribou Prairie Long-tailed Weasel	Burrowing Owl Ferruginous Hawk Henslow's Sparrow Loggerhead Shrike Peregrine Falcon subspecies undrius Roseate Tern	*Copper Redhorse *Great Lakes Deepwater Sculpin *Lake Simcoe Whitefish Shorthead Sculpin *Shortjaw Cisco *Shortnose Cisco
Rare	Black-tailed Prairie Dog Blue Whale Eastern Mole *Fin Whale Grey Fox Northwest Atlantic Humpback Whale Plains Pocket Gopher Queen Charlotte Islands Ermine Western Woodland Caribou Wolverine	Common Barn Owl Caspian Tern Cooper's Hawk Eastern Bluebird Great Gray Owl Ipswich Sparrow Ivory Gull King Rail Peregrine Falcon subspecies pealei Prairie Warbler Prothonotary Warbler Red-shouldered Hawk Ross's Gull Trumpeter Swan	Bigmouth Shiner Blackstripe Top minnow Brindled Madtom Central Stoneroller Charlotte Unarmoured Stickleback Fowler's Toad Giant Stickleback *Green Sturgeon Lake Lamprey *Pacific Sardine Pugnose Minnow Pugnose Shiner *Redside Dace River Redhorse Shortnose Sturgeon Silver Chub Silver Shiner Speckled Dace Spotted Gar Spotted Sucker *Squanga Whitefish

* Status designated 1987
(Source: Committee on the Status of Endangered Wildlife in Canada, 1987)

decimated by DDT, which when metabolized to DDE reduces calcium in eggshells, causing them to break.

The greater prairie chicken originally occurred in Alberta, Saskatchewan, Manitoba and Ontario. The species occupied large blocks of ungrazed or lightly grazed grasslands where preferred habitat included native bluestem and Indian grass, wild rye, switch grass and sand dropseed. The birds flourished amid the small-scale farming activities of the early 1900s, but when vast amounts of native prairie grassland were converted to cultivated crops and cattle grazing, the habitat was destroyed. The greater prairie chicken has been extirpated from all provinces except Saskatchewan, where there were 15 reports, some of which might not have been valid, between 1965 and 1977. GRASSLANDS NATIONAL PARK RESERVE, Sask, established in 1981, is sufficiently large and protected, and might permit re-establishment of this species.

The leatherback turtle is a large (up to 680 kg), unique, mainly tropical, open-sea species. Sparse sightings have occurred in the Atlantic Ocean north to Nain, Lab, and along the West Coast to Cordova, Alaska. Estimates place world population at 30 000-40 000, but up to 20-30% of some populations are killed annually. Although adults are occasionally tangled in fishing gear or harpooned as curiosities in Canadian waters, most mortality takes place in tropical waters, where eggs are collected for human consumption. The world population is believed to be declining and endangered. Only adult leatherback turtles are seen in Canadian waters. They may be migrants or strays, but they feed in this country and appear to be vigorous. Thus, in some cases, protection of species occurring in Canada may require international co-operation.

The Acadian whitefish was discovered as a distinct species only in 1967. Scarcely anything is known of the whitefish's life history. When discovered, it was already being threatened by a dam blocking its upstream spawning migration from the sea. The dam was provided with an inadequate fish ladder. Recently, ACID RAIN, originating in the US and Ontario, has decimated Atlantic salmon in southern NS and has probably had the same effect on Acadian whitefish.

The brindled madtom is a tiny, spotted catfish reaching 87 mm at most in Canadian waters. It inhabits rivers, streams and lakes, where it is most active at night. It once occurred in tributaries of Lk Erie, and in the Niagara and Sydenham rivers of southern Ontario. The parents share nest-building activities and guarding of young. Madtoms guard themselves with a sharp, pectoral-fin spine which could sting a would-be predator. The species was last reported in Canada in 1976, although suitable habitats and localities known to support the species have been searched since then. Because of the madtom's size and habitats, it is difficult to be certain whether population levels are exceedingly low or whether the species has already been extirpated in Canadian waters.

The shorthead sculpin was discovered in Canadian waters in 1957, in the lower 24 km of the tiny Flathead R drainage of BC, between elevations of 1000-1400 m. Sculpins are most abundant on gravel or stony bottoms that are not heavily sedimented and have summer temperatures up to 13-17°C. They reach 100 mm in length, may lay up to 690 eggs, probably on undersides of rocks, and feed on insects and small fish. A proposal to develop surface coal mines in the Flathead Basin for export of coal to Japan, and to redirect the flow of Howell Creek, a Flathead tributary, may threaten the species. Sedimentation, acidification or modification of flow and temperature regimes could be harmful.

While it is obvious that protection from overhunting is needed to save a species from extinction, it is less apparent that many subtle features of the habitat may also have to be protected. Habitat requirements for a fish might include stream spawning grounds, nursery area for feeding of fry in a lake, unobstructed river for migration to sea, estuarine and offshore feeding grounds for young and adults and, again, an unobstructed river for return to spawning ground.

The spawning ground itself may require clear, oxygenated water, free of pollutants, running at the correct velocity, and gravel of a certain size, free of both organic and inorganic sediments. The gravel bed may have to be within a certain temperature range, neither too warm nor freezing, and never exposed by dropping water levels. Stream-bank trees, often removed by common logging and farming practices, are important to stream life. Summer temperatures, runoff from snowmelt and rain, and bank soil erosion are moderated by trees, bushes and herbaceous plants. Leaf fall into streams is an important food-energy component of the ecological network. Leaves are fed on by bacteria and single-celled animals, which in turn are eaten by insects and other invertebrates that serve as food for birds and fishes. A species habitat is complex and small changes may make it unsuitable. If a single habitat requirement is unavailable, a species may not survive. Terrestrial habitats are equally vulnerable; salt licks, summer and winter ranges, and undisturbed calving grounds may be necessary for certain ungulates inhabiting them. Slow degeneration of the environment may be more dangerous to survival of a species, as it is less apt to be noticed and corrected than dramatic spills of pollutants. The gradual buildup of pollutants may have catastrophic effects. It took several years before DDT began significantly to thin eggshells of falcons. The advance of acid rain, clear-cutting of forests and drainage of wetlands clearly portend serious ecological (and economic) consequences if they are not reversed.

Several organizations are engaged in the study and management of rare and endangered species. The NATIONAL MUSEUM OF NATURAL SCIENCES, Ottawa, has for many years evaluated the status of Canada's fauna and flora, although it has never been given special resources for this task. The CANADIAN WILDLIFE SERVICE has had a role in managing and studying Canada's migratory birds; the Dept of Fisheries and Oceans in managing and studying fishes and sea mammals. Canada is a signatory to the Convention on International Trade in Endangered Species (CITES), which

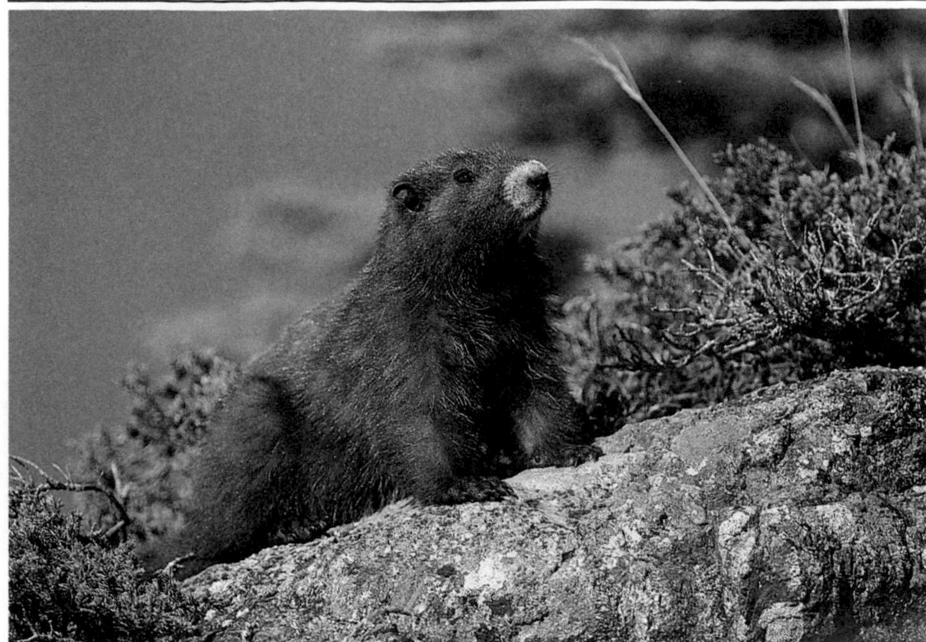

The habitat of the Vancouver Island marmot is threatened by logging (*photo by Tim Fitzharris*).

regulates trade in these species or their by-products. Provinces and territories have mandates in WILDLIFE CONSERVATION AND MANAGEMENT. The Committee on the Status of Endangered Wildlife in Canada is an organization of specialists from federal, provincial and territorial governments and national, private conservation organizations. It decides which plant or animal species (the future of which is in doubt in Canada) is in what category (rare, threatened, endangered, extirpated or extinct). COSEWIC provides status reports, but it is up to the appropriate management agency to correct adverse factors. A number of other organizations are active in protection of Canadian species and the environment, including the World Wildlife Fund (Canada), Toronto; CANADIAN WILDLIFE FEDERATION, Ottawa; CANADIAN NATURE FEDERATION, Ottawa; and POLLUTION PROBE, Toronto.

To protect now-endangered species may require natural-history preserves, public education, protective legislation, enforcement and other measures such as artificial breeding. Individuals and industries are coming to realize that many wastes do not disappear when dumped into air, earth or water, but spread through the biosphere; that we shall have to consider the environmental effects of each of society's requirements (eg, energy, transportation, sewage disposal, wetlands and leisure time); and that the habitat of choice of mankind includes nature.

D.E. McALLISTER

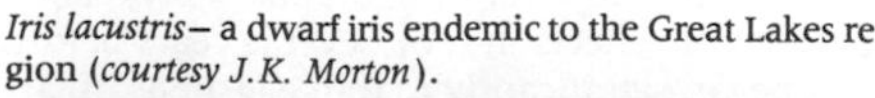

Iris lacustris– a dwarf iris endemic to the Great Lakes region (*courtesy J.K. Morton*).

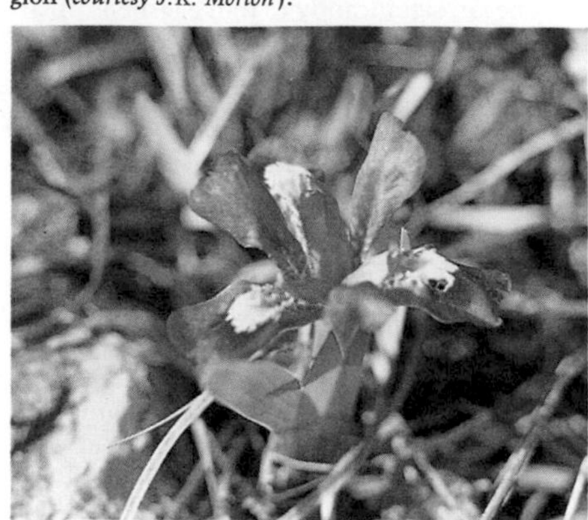

Endangered Plants are those in imminent danger of extinction. The International Union for Conservation of Nature and Natural Resources (IUCN) recognizes 4 stages in endangerment: rare, vulnerable, endangered and extinct. A plant may be endangered locally, nationally or throughout its range. The yellow LADY'S SLIPPER (*Cypripedium calceolus*), familiar in many parts of Canada, is probably Britain's rarest plant, with only 3 or 4 individuals surviving in the wild. The lost Franklinia (*Franklinia alatamaha*), named for Benjamin Franklin, is extinct in the wild but survives in cultivation.

Extinction, a natural process that has occurred throughout world history, takes place when an organism is unable to adapt to a changing environment or to compete with better-adapted species. In recent times humans have become the major threat to the survival of many plants. Technological developments in industrial nations and increasing pressure for agricultural land in developing countries can cause rapid environmental changes that threaten the survival of thousands of plants. Because destruction of habitat is now the principal cause of endangerment, habitat protection is the only effective way to save plants from extinction. Growing a plant in a BOTANICAL GARDEN is no substitute for maintaining it in its wild habitat. Botanical gardens can, however, be useful in providing a reservoir of material to restock wild populations of endangered plants.

Legislation protecting rare plants in Canada is fragmentary and of limited effect. As a natural resource, plants are a provincial rather than a federal responsibility; hence, each province must enact its own endangered-species legislation. However, the federal government, as a signatory of the Convention on International Trade in Endangered Species, 1973 (CITES), can provide protection for some plants (eg, all cacti, orchids and other plants traded across international boundaries). GINSENG (*Panax quinquefolius*), of the deciduous forests of eastern and central Canada, is one such plant. The roots are harvested and sold for their reputed medicinal properties. Most of Canada's flora falls outside these regulations. Several provinces have endangered-species legislation; however, as yet, very few plants are protected by it, although protection could be extended to other species with sufficient pressure from botanists and the public. More effective protection comes from national and provincial parks, and through some local conservation authorities and natural-history societies. National parks provide the most stringent, effective and lasting protection for Canadian flora. Many are situated in areas where rare plants occur, and part of the mandate of Parks Canada is to ensure the protection for all time of rare plants and their habitats. The effectiveness of provincial parks and conservation authorities in protecting endangered species varies considerably. Many place greater emphasis on exploiting the natural environment for human enjoyment than on protecting habitats or rare plants; furthermore, any protection provided can be overridden without reference to Parliament. Rare plants can also be protected if environmental assessments and impact studies are required

Isopyrum savilei – a small anemonelike herb found in the Queen Charlotte Islands (*courtesy J.K. Morton*).

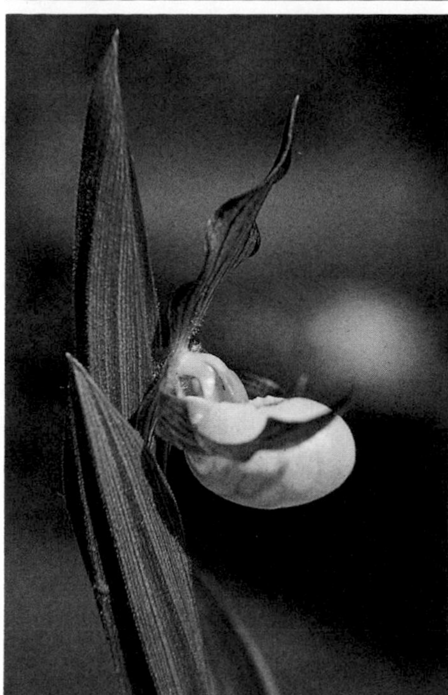

Cypripedium candidum– the white lady's slipper orchid which is now rare throughout its range of distribution (*courtesy J.K. Morton*).

before major development work can begin. In Canada, however, the impact of this type of legislation has been minimal. The presence of a few rare plants usually is not sufficient to persuade those in power that development should be stopped or moved elsewhere. Canada has a long way to go to provide effective legislation protecting rare plants.

Canada's flora includes about 3300 native species of vascular plants, of which an estimated 500 are endangered. Lists of rare plants for each province have been published by the National Museums of Canada and a national list is in preparation. Ontario's list contains over 600 species; Alberta's, over 300; and the national list will contain 1000 species, about one-third of our flora. These lists do not apply to Canada as a whole, since many species rare in one province are common in another. Rare or potentially endangered plants can be divided into 3 groups: endemic species that occur only in Canada or in restricted areas straddling the borders; plants of widespread occurrence that have become so rare throughout their range that they are in danger of extinction; and plants of widespread occurrence that are only endangered in the Canadian part of their range.

Canadian endemic plants tend to be concentrated in several centres. Important centres from W to E are the region straddling the Alaska-YT border – endemics include an anemone (*Anemone multiceps*), 2 fleabanes (*Erigeron mexiae* and *E. muiri*) and a rare chickweed (*Stellaria alaskana*); the Queen Charlotte Is – a ragwort (*Senecio newcombei*), an avens (*Geum schofieldii*) and an isopyrum (*Isopyrum savilei*); sand dunes on the S shore of Lk Athabasca – a chickweed (*Stellaria arenicola*), several dwarf willows and sea thrift (*Armeria maritima* ssp. *interior*); the shores of the Great Lakes, 2 thistles (*Cirsium pitcheri* and *C. pumilum*), an iris (*Iris lacustris*), Houghton's goldenrod (*Solidago houghtonii*) and an alpine sunflower (*Hymenoxys acaulis* var. *glabra*); the Gulf of St Lawrence (eg, the mountains of the Gaspé Pen, Mingan I and Île d'Anticosti and the limestone and serpentine tablelands of Newfoundland) – a sandwort (*Minuartia marcescens*), a gentian (*Gentianella crinita* ssp. *victorinii*), 2 roses and several willows.

In Canada, several species occur that are now so rare and restricted that their continued survival is endangered. Their rarity is usually caused by destruction of natural habitats. For example, the small white lady's slipper orchid (*Cypripedium candidum*), which was the first plant to be protected under Ontario law, now occurs only in 3 small colonies in SW Ontario and in several isolated stations in the US.

The main threats to Canada's flora are to those plants that reach the northern limit of their range in southern Canada. Unfortunately, population density is high and agriculture and industry are concentrated in this region. Little now remains of the deciduous forests that once covered southern Ontario and Québec, but these forests support a large and very special assemblage of plants found nowhere else in Canada. Most are now rare; some are on the verge of extinction; a few are extinct. Many trees are included in the list: magnolia (*Magnolia acuminata*), pignut hickory (*Carya glabra*), pitch pine (*Pinus rigida*), black walnut (*Juglans nigra*) and no less than 6 oaks. Associated with them are many herbaceous plants, shrubs and climbers, including the beautiful trumpet flower (*Campsis radicans*), the redbud (*Cercis canadensis*, extinct in Canada) and the medicinally important goldenseal (*Hydrastis canadensis*).

Most survive in small woodlots or conservation areas, fragments of the continuous forest that covered this region before European settlement. Similar problems exist in other provinces. In NS and NB, many plants characteristic of the Atlantic seaboard and the eastern forests are threatened by cottage developments, agriculture, forestry and dam construction. These include the Canada lily (*Lilium canadense*), an iris (*Iris prismatica*) and the redroot (*Lachnanthes tinctoria*). On the prairies, almost all the natural grassland has succumbed to the plough or is heavily grazed. Many prairie plants now survive precariously along roadsides and railway tracks, where they escape the pressures of agriculture but are threatened by herbicides. Examples include legumes such as *Astragalus purshii*, and *Bahia oppositifolia*, prairie parsley (*Lomatium orientale*) and ironweed (*Vernonia fasciculata*). The western mountains have their own unique assemblage of alpine flowers. Many species, although common in the US, reach their northern limit here and are rare. Examples include the western white trillium (*Trillium ovatum*), a lowly sandwort (*Minuartia nuttallii*) and the very beautiful Townsendia daisy (*Townsendia condensata*).

Why protect plants from extinction? Why not let nature take its course and allow the plants to die out? There are many reasons, including aesthetic ones. Plants afford pleasure and relaxation to many people, and provide a source of inspiration in most art forms: painting, photography, poetry and prose. All life, as well as the quality of life, depends on plants, yet only about 30 kinds have been exploited to form the world's major food crops (eg, rice, wheat, corn, potatoes). The potential for producing new crops and for improving existing ones is unlimited, but this depends on using the genetic diversity found in wild plants.

Plants vary depending on where they grow; eg, northern populations often differ genetically from southern ones. Each has become adapted to the habitat and climate in which it grows. For the continued survival of a species, it is essential that the diversity of its gene pool be maintained so that it can adapt to the continual small changes in environment, shifts in climate, changing pressures from predators, disease, competition, etc. For this reason, we must protect those plants that reach the limits of their range in Canada, even though they may be abundant in the US. In addition, agriculturalists must be concerned to protect wild ancestors of cultivated plants and to ensure the survival of others that may be potential new crops, new horticultural varieties or new sources of useful products.

Plants have been a major source of medicines since prehistoric times. Modern research is discovering an apparently unlimited source of new chemicals in wild plants, many of which can form the basis for new drugs or other products important to human well-being and development. Cortisones were originally developed from wild yams (*Dioscorea*), and recently an obscure bush in the semidesert of Arizona, the jojoba bean (*Simmondsia chinensis*), has been found to be a potential commercial source of an oil for car transmissions, similar to that obtained from the endangered sperm whale. Recent work in Canada and Britain indicates that an effective treatment for eczema may have been found in evening primroses (*Oenothera*). The potential for economic and material benefit is unlimited, for we have barely begun to exploit the wealth of useful products contained in wild plants. At this early stage, we cannot afford to let plants become extinct for, once lost, a species can never be recreated.

JOHN MORTON

Enderby, BC, City, pop 1714 (1986c), 1879 (1981c), area 265 ha, inc 1905, is located on the Shuswap R 13 km N of Armstrong and 19 km S of Salmon Arm. Notable for its plethora of names, it was variously known after its first settlement in 1876 as Spallumcheen, Steamboat Landing, Lambly's Landing or Belvidere, before the present name was settled upon in 1887. During an afternoon tea party, the sight of the spring flood of the Shuswap R inspired the recitation of a poem by Jean Ingelow, "High Tide on the Coast of Lincolnshire," and the place-name Enderby mentioned in the poem so enchanted the ladies that they adopted it for their community. Grain was the main crop of the district until 1923 when Enderby's flour mill closed, resulting in a shift to dairying. Three sawmills are fed by the local logging industry. The weekly *Enderby Commoner* has appeared under various names since 1904.

DUANE THOMSON

Endicott, James, missionary, clergyman (b in Devonshire, Eng 8 May 1865; d at Toronto 9 Mar 1954). Coming to Canada at age 17, he served Methodist home missions until he returned to school at Wesley Coll, Winnipeg, and was ordained in 1893. That same year, he went to Sichuan, China, and was active in church publishing and education at Chengdu. He returned to Canada in 1910 and from 1913 to 1937 headed the Foreign Missions Board of the Methodist Church and, after 1925, of The United Church of Canada. He was the second Moderator of the UNITED CHURCH 1926-28 and explained the new church to missionaries in the field. A respected preacher and pamphleteer, Endicott worked hard for world peace and especially for aid to the Third World. He led the way in explaining the needs of the Orient to Canadians.

NEIL SEMPLE

Endive, or escarole (*Cichorium endivia*), herbaceous biennial vegetable belonging to the Compositae family. In continental Europe the term is used to refer to the closely related species *C. intybus*, CHICORY (Belgian or French endive). Endive is cultivated much like LETTUCE, although it is sometimes blanched (ie, bleached by excluding sunlight) before harvest to reduce its bitter taste.

ADRIANA A. DAVIES

Energy The term "energy" is often used interchangeably with the term "power," but incorrectly so. Energy is defined as the capacity to do work and is measured in joules (J) or watt hours (1 Wh = 3600 J). Power is the work done per unit time and is measured in watts (W), ie, joules per second.

Energy is subdivided into 2 categories, primary and secondary. Primary energy is recovered from

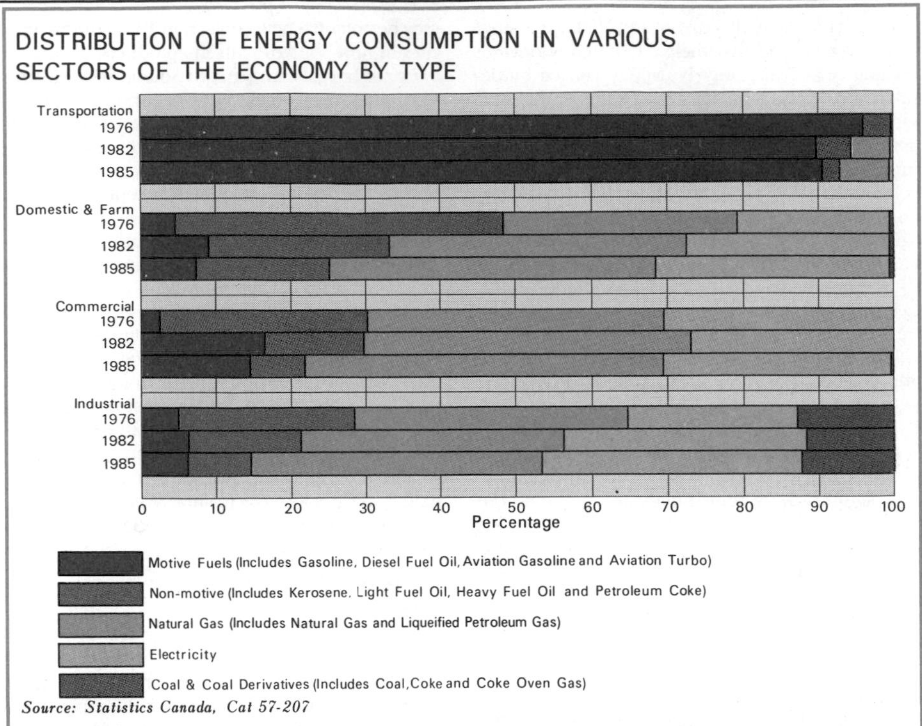

Source: Statistics Canada, Cat 57-207

natural resources such as solar radiation, falling water, wind, coal, petroleum products and uranium. It is consumed by primary energy industries such as ELECTRIC-POWER generating stations and oil refineries. A significant portion is lost in storage, processing and transportation before primary energy is delivered to consumers as secondary energy. Further energy is lost through the inefficiencies of conversion devices (cars, appliances, heaters, etc) that transform the secondary energy into useful work.

Primary energy resources are frequently described as renewable or nonrenewable. Renewable energy resources include geothermal heat, falling water, tidal forces, wind action, solar input, vegetable and animal matter, and ocean thermal gradients. Nonrenewable resources include hydrocarbon materials such as natural gas, crude oil, bitumen and coal, as well as isotopes from which energy may be extracted through nuclear fission or NUCLEAR FUSION. The extraction of primary energy resources and their use, either direct or after conversion to secondary forms, have resulted in the evolution of sophisticated technologies and systems during the 20th century. There have been rapid developments in resource exploitation, mining, refining, machine design and operation, pipeline transportation, electric-power transmission and energy marketing. Since 1900 world annual energy consumption has increased more than tenfold. The expected large growth in future world population would mean that continued increase in per capita energy demand would double the world's energy requirement again between 1980 and 2000. Human ingenuity would be taxed to meet such a supply challenge.

Nonrenewable resources now provide the bulk of purchased secondary energy. In 1985 some 89% of the consumption of commercially provided energy, totalling 330 exajoules (EJ = 10^{18} J), came from crude oil, coal and natural gas. The balance was produced in hydroelectric and NUCLEAR POWER PLANTS. An estimated 30 EJ of additional energy was derived from noncommercial renewable sources such as wood wastes and animal refuse (BIOMASS ENERGY), SOLAR ENERGY, wind action and geothermal steam (*see* WIND ENERGY, GEOTHERMAL ENERGY). Renewable energy forms are particularly important to those developing areas of the world where crude oil and natural gas are neither indigenous nor affordable, and where sophisticated systems of power generation, transmission and distribution have not yet been introduced. In many such areas, population pressure is leading to an increased demand for energy and other resources and consequently to a rapid denudation of the world's forested tropical and subtropical zones. Concern is growing therefore about serious future climatic and ecological changes that may be precipitated on a worldwide scale as a result of the existing, often rapacious, exploitation of the forests.

In the past 40 years, world dependence on crude oil as an energy source has grown remarkably, so that now nearly 40% of all primary energy is provided by oil. A peak in production may already have been reached in 1979, with an output of 10.5 million m^3/day. By 1985 production had dropped to 9.1 million m^3/day. The decrease was partly caused by a glut of oil which developed following a twofold price increase imposed in 1979-80 by the Organization of Petroleum Exporting Countries (OPEC). Another factor affecting the decrease was the increased cost of developing replacement reserves for those being consumed so rapidly; at the end of 1985, proved reserves were only some 33 times the 1985 consumption rate. Many analysts have concluded that serious worldwide depletion of both crude oil and natural gas will have occurred by about the middle of the next century. By then the world population may have more than doubled.

Hence, even assuming that judicious use and conservation of energy supplies will be pursued in the coming decades, it appears that increased reliance must be placed on coal, nuclear power and renewable energy sources. Unfortunately the development of each of these is likely to be impeded. The mining, transportation and combustion of coal impose severe environmental hazards which could restrict the industry's growth rate. Not the least of the concerns is that burning vast quantities of coal would cause a significant increase in the carbon-dioxide content of the Earth's atmosphere, and this might have a serious effect on the world's climate.

The direct environmental damage resulting from the installation and operation of nuclear power plants is much less severe. In fact, many technical experts consider nuclear power to be the most benign of all energy sources available for future long-term use. Antinuclear activists, however, have campaigned against this energy option on the basis of perceived hazards of low-level radiation effects, nuclear accidents, management of spent nuclear fuel, and the proliferation of nuclear weapons.

The development of renewable energy resources has been curtailed by economic constraints. Meaningful sources of geothermal steam, for example, are few in number, and many of them are located far from large consumer centres. Similar limitations apply to the relatively small number of large hydroelectric sites remaining to be developed. Perhaps the most promising future prospect for renewable resource development is in the utilization of solar energy for direct use in heating, and for conversion to hydrocarbons or for generation of electricity. Many technical and economic challenges remain to be overcome, however, before solar energy can successfully compete with the traditional nonrenewable energy sources. Most industrialized countries are not expected to become self-sufficient in long-term energy supplies because of the paucity of indigenous sources. Canada is an exception. It has a large landmass, a relatively small population and a profusion of proven and potential resources that include crude oil, natural gas, oil sands, coal, undeveloped hydroelectric sites, large uranium deposits and a highly sophisticated nuclear technology. The federal-provincial sharing of responsibility for resource control, ownership and taxation imposes barriers to efficient development, but the plethora of resource wealth may be large enough to overcome such man-made obstacles. O.J.C. RUNNALLS

Reading: Energy, Mines and Resources, *Current Energy Statistics* (1987); W. Häfele, *Energy in a Finite World* (1986); National Energy Board of Canada, *Canadian Energy Supply and Demand, 1985-2005* (1986); W. Sassin, "Energy," *Scientific American* (Sept 1980).

Energy, Mines and Resources, Department of, established in 1966 by the federal Government Organization Act. Some of the department's components have long histories. The Department of Mines, created in 1907, was reorganized as the Department of Mines and Resources in 1936. The Department of Mines and Technical Surveys was formed in 1949. In 1966 the department took on a new and important role of energy development. The main objective of EMR is to enhance the discovery, development and use of Canada's mineral and energy resources through national policies based on research, data collection and social and economic analyses. The Energy Sector is responsible for the development and implementation of a national ENERGY POLICY. The Mineral Policy Sector performs a similar role for nonrenewable resources, supporting appropriate exploration, development and movement of minerals. A Science and Technology Section was replaced in July 1981 by 2 science sectors: the Earth Sciences Sector, comprising Geological Survey, Surveys and Mapping Branch and Polar Continental Shelf Project; and the Research and Technology Sector, comprising CANMET (Canada Centre for Mineral and Energy Technology), Canada Centre for Remote Sensing and Explosive Branch. ATOMIC ENERGY OF CANADA LTD, Eldorado Nuclear Ltd, the NATIONAL ENERGY BOARD, Uranium Canada Ltd and PETRO-CANADA report to Parliament through the minister. Published estimates indicate a 1986-87 departmental budget of \$1.6 billion. The greater than 50% drop from \$4 billion in 1984-85 reflects the termination of major energy-related incentive programs (PIP, CHIP, etc).

Energy, Royal Commission on (Borden Commission), established (1957) by the government of John DIEFENBAKER, under chairman Henry BORDEN, the president of Brazilian Traction, Light and Power Co, Ltd to investigate "a number of questions relating to sources of energy." The most important issue before the commission was the demand by the Alberta independent oil producers to find a market for their crude oil by building a pipeline from Edmonton to Montréal. Their opponents, the large, international oil companies, found it more profitable to use imported oil in their Montréal refineries. Probably the most influential individual at the hearings was Walter J. Levy, a New York oil consultant, who proposed that the pipeline not be built and that Alberta oil be exported to the US while Montréal continued to be supplied from abroad. In its reports (1958 and 1959), the commission accepted this recommendation, called the National Oil Policy (NOP), thereby securing the market west of the Ottawa Valley for the western oil producers. The NATIONAL ENERGY BOARD, proposed by the commission to administer the policy, was established by Parliament in 1959. The NOP, established in 1961, remained in effect until the events of the 1970s precipitated dramatic changes in ENERGY POLICY.

ED SHAFFER

Energy in Society Energy plays a unique and critical role in the world; no activity of any kind (no "work") can take place without the movement or conversion of energy. Energy use in society is a flow that begins with a source (eg, COAL, URANIUM, PETROLEUM, the SUN) and passes through several intermediate processes for refinement or conversion to a different form (eg, electricity, diesel oil, methane), finally reaching a home, vehicle or industrial plant where it is introduced into a consuming device (eg, furnace, motor). In between are imports, exports and losses of various kinds, including the energy needed to operate the energy system itself. The final consumer does not want energy as such but only the services it can provide, services that are not measured in litres or joules but in warmth, motion, sound, etc.

Two thermodynamic laws govern all aspects of energy use. The first states that a given system will always contain the same amount of energy. The second states that every time an amount of energy is used its quality declines, not the quantity of the energy itself. Hence, we keep track of both the quantity and quality of the energy we use. Quantity is measured in familiar units, such as litres (L) of oil, kilowatt-hours (kWh) of electricity, and tonnes (t) of coal, all of which can be converted to one standard unit of energy content, the joule (J). Quality is more difficult to measure: scientific measures do exist, but for many purposes it is sufficient to define higher-quality energy as being hotter or denser (ie, containing much energy in a small volume, eg, gasoline) or more versatile (eg, electricity). The market value of high-quality energy is generally higher. Energy conservation involves not only saving quantities of energy but also ensuring that high-quality forms are used only when necessary. Thus, dense fuels are most useful for transportation; electricity is most appropriate for lighting, electronics and motors; and heating buildings requires only low-quality energy because the temperatures of buildings are raised by relatively small amounts.

There are 3 ways to measure the efficiency with which energy is used. First-law efficiency indicates how much energy is being used compared with the service provided (eg, L of gasoline per 100 km of car travel). Calculations using this measure suggest that the Canadian economy may be 40% efficient. A second measure, second-law efficiency, relates the energy used to obtain a service to the theoretical minimum needed under ideal conditions. Estimates using this measure suggest that the Canadian economy is less than 10% efficient (or as low as 1-2% if materials use and RECYCLING are considered). The third measure of efficiency is cost effectiveness, which relates the dollar value of inputs to the energy services obtained. This type of measure is needed for decisions in which energy must be balanced against other economic activities (eg, adding more insulation versus buying more fuel to warm a building). Calculations indicate that most sectors of the economy spend twice as much on energy (ie, they are only half as cost effective as they could be).

Four sets of factors determine how much energy is used in a society. First are demographic and geographic factors: the greater the population, the bigger the area and the colder the climate, the more energy will be used. Thus Canada's relatively small, dispersed population requires that a lot of energy be used for transportation. Canada is colder than most countries, although new building techniques are conserving energy.

The second set of factors determining energy use is economic. There is no direct relationship between national income and energy use, and countries with similar levels of per capita income can use different amounts of energy. However, higher-income countries with more industry do tend to use more energy than poorer, less-industrialized ones. In Canada industry is concentrated in the primary sectors (pulp and paper, smelting and refining, agriculture) which tend to use more energy per dollar value of production than manufacturing or service industries do. Energy use also reflects the availability and cost of energy resources. Historically, for example, Canada and the US have had an abundance of relatively low-cost energy (eg, large, easily accessible waterfalls) and, hence, have used it extensively. Consumers use less energy as its price goes up. This effect, called price elasticity, has been estimated to lie between -0.5 and -1.2, which means that for each 10% increase in the price of energy, use will drop 5 to 12%.

The third set of factors is technological. Until the 1970s, when all energy prices began to rise, little attention was paid to the technology of energy use. Examples of this neglect occurred in housing and the American automobile, and others occurred throughout industry. With the rise in prices, many old techniques involving more efficient energy use were reintroduced and research into new ones began (*see* SCIENTIFIC RESEARCH AND DEVELOPMENT). For example, Canadians have become world leaders in constructing energy-efficient buildings. Typical single-family homes built around 1973 require about 175 gigajoules (GJ = 10^9 J, roughly the energy content of 4500 L of heating oil) for heating each year. Homes being built today to the federal government's R-2000 design use 40-50 GJ annually; the most efficient ones (modelled on the Saskatchewan Conservation House) need only 15 GJ. In 1973 typical high-rise office buildings required 600 kWh per m^2 each year for operation; many being built since then have cut this to 200 kWh. The Gulf Canada Square tower in Calgary requires only 125 kWh, and a federal office building in Scarborough, using underground storage and solar panels, has cut the figure to 20 kWh.

The fourth set of factors involves life-styles. For example, some people choose to live in smaller houses or in apartments, to buy more efficient cars or use public transit, and to buy goods in returnable or recyclable containers, thereby using less energy. Other people choose a life-style reflecting more "conspicuous consumption."

Measurement of Energy Use

Energy use can be measured at various points and in various ways. The most useful results are obtained from measurement at the point of purchase by the final consumer. This measurement is called secondary energy consumption to distinguish it from primary and tertiary energy consumption. Primary consumption is measured at the point of production and includes the energy required for production. Tertiary consumption indicates the amount of energy available for, say, heating a room or turning the wheels of a vehicle after deducting efficiency losses in the furnace or motor. Tertiary energy consumption is very important but difficult to measure.

Statistics on secondary energy use typically are divided according to the form of energy used (eg, gasoline, electricity) and according to the sector in which it is used (eg, residential, commercial, industrial, transportation). Completely separate from this secondary energy is use in the energy supply sector, to cover the energy consumed or lost in energy production, conversion, transportation and transmission. In recent years the amount of this energy supply sector has been 20% as great as the amount of secondary energy use.

Modern approaches to energy analysis and the most effective method for energy forecasts depend on a breakdown according to the use made of the energy. Heating and cooling include all space and water heating plus low-temperature process heat. Higher temperature heat is used only in industry. Electricity-specific uses such as electronics, lighting or appliances depend on the properties of electricity. Liquid fuels are for portable uses such as transportation. This breakdown takes account of quality and shows, for example, that in 1984 most Canadian energy requirements are for heat at various temperatures (55% of total use, 75% of industrial use) and that electricity-specific uses represent little more than 13% of the total. However, 2 adjustments must be made to the energy data: it must allow for nonenergy products such as plastics, fertilizers and coking coal made from energy raw materials, and it must allow for energy that does not pass through the organized market, such as wood sold at a rural lot. The latter adjustment means, for example, that wood as a residential fuel never fell as low as indicated by Canadian statistics.

A statistical problem particularly important to Canada involves ELECTRIC POWER, a form of energy that can be manufactured from diverse sources such as falling water, burning coal or controlled nuclear reactions, each with its own rate of conversion (the difference between the energy content of the source input and that of the electricity output). The best approach for preparation of energy-use statistics is to ignore the source of the electricity and convert directly from electrical output to joules (3.6 MJ per kWh). However, in most international and some Canadian statistics, electricity is converted to energy units expressed as the amount of coal or oil that would be needed to produce it, which, for thermodynamic reasons, is about 3 times as large. This practice leads to the calculation that 35% of Canada's energy is used in the form of electricity, when the correct figure is about 17%. If electricity in Canada were used only for those specific applications where it is truly efficient, the figure would be further reduced to the 13% described above.

Secondary Energy Use in 1984

Total secondary energy use in Canada in 1984 was approximately 6.6 exajoules (EJ = 10^{18}J). Ontario and Québec account for about three-fifths of this use. The levels of energy use per capita in these 2 provinces are about equal, but Ontario is well below Québec and most other provinces in energy use per dollar of provincial product (because Ontario has relatively more light manufacturing compared with primary industries). Other provincial variations follow mainly from geographic and economic differences. BC uses more energy in the forest industry and less for heating than elsewhere. The Atlantic provinces are the lowest per capita users of energy; the Prairie provinces are the highest.

Residential Uses account for 19% of total secondary use in Canada. Nearly 91% of this energy is used for space and water heating, while the remaining 9% represents electricity-specific uses. Coal and wood, which used to provide much residential heating, have declined in favour of more convenient fuels. Use of coal remains negligible but wood now has an 11% share. Other fuels for residential heating are oil, 23% (1980, 46%), natural gas, 43% (1980, 38%) and electricity, 24% (1980, 14%). Clearly, use of oil products has declined substantially in the face of higher prices and government subsidy programs supporting other sources. Residential and agricultural uses are often combined, although agriculture is more of an industry. These statistics show that energy use on farms accounts for 4% of secondary energy use in Canada, 9-12% on the prairies.

Commercial Uses account for 14% (1980, 12%) of Canadian energy use, of which two-thirds (1980, three-quarters) is used for heating and cooling buildings and for water heating and one-third for electricity-specific uses. Energy for this sector is increasingly supplied by natural gas and electricity or by electricity alone.

Industrial Uses, including primary industries, manufacturing and construction, account for more energy than any other sector – 35% (1980, 37%) of the total – and most projections show this share growing to one-half.

In contrast to other sectors, industry uses energy of all qualities and forms. Nearly three-quarters (1980, two-thirds) of industrial energy is used as heat, some 40% (1980, 25%) for temperatures above 260°C. Energy forms are divided among oil products, 16% (1980, 36%), natural gas, 9% (1980, 28%), and electricity, 7% (1980, 21%). Apart from electric utilities the industrial sector is the only significant user of coal and wood for energy – 10% and 17% respectively (1980, 8% each) – and the latter is mainly generated from forest industry waste.

In 1984 only 7 industries – pulp and paper, chemicals, primary metals, food and beverage, mining, industrial minerals and construction – account for nearly 75% of all industrial energy use. The first 3 alone account for about half of industrial energy use (and for two-thirds of all high-temperature heat and perhaps three-quarters of all water used by industry). The subsectors vary widely in the forms of energy used: for example, the chemicals and petrochemicals industries use large volumes of oil and gas as fuel and also as inputs to produce plastics and other nonenergy products, and the aluminum industry is a particularly heavy user of electricity.

Transportation Uses account for more energy use in Canada than in most other countries: 28% of total use and, more significantly, 60% (1980, half) of oil use. Automobiles and light trucks account for 53% of transportation use (14% of Canada's total energy use); larger trucks take 27% and buses 5%; therefore, road modes use a total of 85%. The remaining sectors – air, marine and rail – follow in declining order (although in some provinces the positions vary; eg, in Newfoundland marine rises to second place).

About half of transportation energy is used within urban areas, the remainder between cities. The transportation sector is unique in depending almost exclusively on one form of energy, liquid fuel (primarily gasoline, diesel oil and aviation turbo fuel), derived from one source, oil; a fraction is electricity, used for urban public transit. A small number of vehicles run on propane, compressed natural gas or methanol (a form of alcohol derived from natural gas).

International Energy Use

World energy use in 1984 was about 313 EJ, or an average of about 66 GJ per capita. Variations around the average are large. Industrial countries typically use 150-200 GJ per capita; Canada uses 260 GJ per capita; Third World countries, 20-25 GJ per capita; and the poorest countries in Africa, 2.5 GJ per capita. Canada, with about 0.5% of the world's population, accounts for 2% of world energy use. It is often said that Canadians consume more energy per capita or per dollar of Gross Domestic Product than any other country, but international statistics tend to make Canada appear more energy-intensive than it actually is. For example, the manner in which the use of electricity is calculated overstates Canada's energy production and use. In addition, Canada exports a great deal of energy in the form of raw or semifinished goods. This "embodied" energy should in principle be counted against the country where the steel, paper or aluminum is used. Despite these qualifications, Canada remains one of the world's most energy-intensive nations.

Changes in Energy Use

With growth in population, economy and income, Canadians have used more and more energy. Before WWII secondary energy use in Canada climbed at about 3% per year, but during the era of cheap energy after the war this rate climbed to 5% and higher. Such growth ended quickly with the energy crisis of 1973. Since then the rate has fallen, partly because of slower economic growth, but largely because of gains in efficiency. Between 1974 and 1980 energy use grew by an average of 2.3% annually; between 1980 and 1984 this rate was 1% per year. Oil use has dropped by about 15%: fears of shortage and a return to higher prices work against its use except for transportation or in regions where other heating fuels are unavailable or more expensive.

Projections of future energy use abound, but one thing is striking: the projections are falling. A 1973 report of the federal Dept of Energy, Mines and Resources expected 4.5% annual growth; a 1976 report envisioned 3.7%; the 1980 National Energy Program projected 1.9%; and a 1986 report from the staff of the National Energy Board expected 1.5-1.9%. The decline reflects mainly the growing potential for energy efficiency. Since 1973 the energy required to produce a dollar of GDP in Canada has fallen by 12% (34% for oil) and the decline is continuing. Federal policy dictated that average fuel consumption of new cars had to be halved between 1975 and 1985 (to 8.5 L per 100 km); this target was achieved about a year ahead of schedule. Industry has planned to cut its energy use by 30% per unit of output by 1990; thereafter continued annual gains of about 1% are likely.

Even the lowest official projections may be too high. Some recent analyses begin with end-use demand for energy services and try to match the quality of energy supplied to end-use requirements. These studies are called "soft energy" studies because they emphasize smaller scale, decentralized and environmentally less destructive means of providing energy. Soft energy studies show that it is possible to satisfy our needs for energy without threatening either global climate or local land use. They also show that it is possible to increase the availability of energy for lower income regions and countries. Soft energy studies have been prepared for many nations, including Canada. They allow for population and economic growth and for reasonable time for investment in energy-efficient structures, equipment and vehicles to permit a smooth transition to greater economic efficiency.

Canada's rate of energy use will be determined in part by physical laws and technology, but to a large extent by individual choices and government policies. The limits to energy production and use are set by physics and geology, but those limits are wide; within them the rates actually achieved are mainly determined by politics and economics. As values change, conservation plays a greater and greater role in ENERGY POLICY. DAVID B. BROOKS

Reading: Robert Bott et al, *Life After Oil: A Renewable Energy Strategy for Canada* (1983); David B. Brooks, *Zero Energy Growth for Canada* (1981); International Energy Agency, *Energy Conservation in IEA Countries* (1987), World Commission on Energy and Development, *Our Common Future,* Chapter 7 (1987).

Energy Policy comprises government measures concerned with the production, transportation and use of energy commodities. Governments may adopt energy policies to meet goals such as economic growth, the distribution of income, industrial diversification and the protection of the ENVIRONMENT. Since the large jump in energy prices in the early 1970s, governments around the world have played an increasingly active role in energy policy. Although Canada appears to be generously endowed with major forms of ENERGY, eg, COAL, OIL AND NATURAL GAS, URANIUM and HYDROELECTRICITY, and although its production of certain fuels has occasionally exceeded domestic requirements, it has never been entirely self-sufficient in energy. Historically, Canada has been dependent on energy imports largely because of the great distances separating indigenous sources of supply from markets. It is therefore primarily as a result of geography, rather than geology, that questions concerning the importation, export and particularly the transportation of energy have preoccupied energy policymakers.

The attempt to reconcile diverse economic interests in overcoming the transportation challenge has been a central theme of Canadian energy policy. These interests have traditionally pitted energy producers – whether of Nova Scotia coal before WWI, of Nova Scotia and Alberta coal between the 2 wars, or Alberta oil and gas since WWII – against energy consumers, the majority of whom live in Ontario and Québec.

A second major determinant of Canadian energy policy derives from Canada's system of government. As a result of the constitutional DISTRIBUTION OF POWERS, strong powers over resource management (*see* RESOURCE RIGHTS) are vested in both levels of government. Section 109 of the CONSTITUTION ACT, 1867, grants the provinces control over all the natural resources within their territory. A province also has the right to levy direct taxes (royalties) on these resources. The federal government, however, enjoys broad taxation powers and has jurisdiction over all aspects of interprovincial and international trade. The federal government also has the constitutional power to void provincial legislation and to assume control over provincial works "for the general advantage of Canada," although neither power has been invoked in recent years.

Because this division of power gives the 2 levels of government overlapping responsibilities, Canadian energy policy has often been the product of federal-provincial bargaining. The bargaining can become acrimonious when the federal government and the producing provinces diverge in their views, as they did for most of the 1970s and early 1980s (Canada is perhaps unique in encompassing in a single country the interests that globally divide energy producers and consumers).

The influence exerted by the US constitutes a third major element that has shaped Canadian energy policy. Over the years, the US has both supplied and bought energy from Canada; Canadian-American energy trade exceeded $10.7 billion in 1985. The US has also represented an important source of investment capital and has consequently played a large role in the development of Canada's oil and gas resources.

Canadian Energy Policy to 1973 After Confederation, 1867, Canadian energy policy was designed to promote the greater use of domestic coal reserves by the imposition of a tariff on American imports. This tariff was part of the 1879 NATIONAL POLICY. Nevertheless, Canadian coal rarely comprised more than 50% of the domestic market. Ontario, the largest consumer, was (and still is) supplied by Pennsylvania mines, while Nova Scotia and Alberta producers supplied the eastern and western provinces, respectively. Following WWI, as a result of the increased penetration of American imports and growing concerns about energy security, new policies (including the subsidy of transportation costs) were introduced to protect the Canadian coal industry. These policies had limited success in relieving the industry's chronic productive overcapacity, a problem that was aggravated by the discovery of oil in 1947 at Leduc, Alta. After WWII, government policy was aimed at sustaining coal communities. The importance of coal as a dominant source of energy declined (which deeply affected New Brunswick and Nova Scotia) until Canadian domestic consumption rose between the mid-1960s and late 1970s by some 150%. The US has increased its coal consumption as well, and the expanded use of coal in both countries has contributed to environmental problems, particularly that of acid rain. As a result, some Alberta coal producers have demanded that they supply central Canada, partly because Alberta coal contains 8 times less sulphur (the main ingredient of acid rain) than American coal. However, as in the 1920s, the counterargument is that Alberta coal is too expensive.

Oil and Gas Although oil was being produced in southern Ontario as early as 1857, reserves and domestic consumption were small. The modern oil era was triggered by the 1947 strike in Leduc and by several subsequent oil and gas finds in the 3 western provinces. Coincidentally, demand for oil in Canada and internationally had increased rapidly as a result of the war and the subsequent economic boom.

The overriding objective of Canadian energy policy for the next 20 years was to stimulate the growth of the domestic PETROLEUM INDUSTRIES. As a result, major oil and gas PIPELINES were built from the producing provinces to markets in both Canada and the US, encouraging investment and promoting exports.

From the beginning, the US played a large role in the development of Canada's oil and gas reserves, not only because the industry was largely American owned but because of the distribution of Canada's petroleum resources. Economic efficiency dictated that Alberta supply the markets closest to itself, ie, the American Pacific Northwest and Midwest, while eastern Canada continued to rely on American imports. When pipelines were finally built from the western provinces to domestic markets, the western provinces exported part of the throughput to amortize the costs of transporting oil over these considerable distances. As a result of Canada's reliance on the export of oil and gas, first to serve its own energy needs and then to spur the growth of the oil industry, an increasing share of domestic oil and gas production was dedicated to the American market. This share peaked in 1971 when Canada exported to the US 57% of its oil production and 47% of its gas production.

The oil industry's rapid growth in the 1950s, the controversy surrounding the construction of Canada's first 2 major gas pipelines (the 1956 Trans-Canada PIPELINE DEBATE contributed to the electoral defeat of the Liberal government the following year), and an acknowledgement that the government's information concerning energy matters was inadequate, led in 1957 to the creation of the Borden Commission (*see* ENERGY, ROYAL COMMISSION ON) to study Canadian energy policy. The commission's recommendations resulted in the creation of the NATIONAL ENERGY BOARD (1959) to regulate the interprovincial pipelines and the interprovincial marketing of energy resources, and to advise the federal government on energy matters. The commission also championed the establishment of a national oil policy (NOP) to shelter the Canadian oil industry against imports of cheaper foreign oil. This policy, introduced in 1961, established a protected market for domestic oil W of the Ottawa Valley, which freed the industry from foreign competition, while the 5 eastern provinces continued to rely on imports. The NOP remained the cornerstone of Canadian energy policy for the next decade.

The 1960s were a period of consolidation; no new major policy initiatives were launched until the early 1970s. Canadian oil and gas consumption grew steadily, prices were stable, and the country's hydrocarbon potential appeared virtually unlimited. This uneventful decade made the adjustment to the energy crisis of the early 1970s traumatic.

Hydroelectrical and Nuclear Policy The public sector has played an important role in the development of Canada's electricity resources since the early 1900s, when the Hydro-Electric Power Commission of Ontario was created. Today, every province except Alberta and PEI manages its own power utility. The federal government's involvement in hydroelectricity, however, has historically been limited, partly because electricity-generating sources are more evenly distributed across the country and the interprovincial trade in electricity has therefore been on a smaller scale. Nevertheless, in 1907 Parliament passed the Electricity and Fluid Exportation Act to regulate the export of electricity and natural gas, a function that was transferred to the National Energy Board in 1959. In 1963 the federal government announced a National Power Policy (the basic tenets of which still endure) to encourage development of power resources, the greater interconnection of provincial transmission systems and the export of surplus power to the US.

Hydropower in the 1980s provided fully 70% of Canada's electricity needs. Expansion of hydroelectrical power presents significant difficulties, as most remaining potential hydro sites are far from centres of population and long-distance transmission lines are costly to build. The building of dams can also cause severe environmental damage. The federal government was deeply involved in the development of NUCLEAR ENERGY, largely as a result of its expropriation in 1944 (for military reasons) of Canada's only (at the time) uranium mine. The government strengthened its control over uranium resources in 1946 with the passage of the Atomic Energy Control Act, which transferred jurisdiction over uranium from provincial to federal authorities and regulated the production and uses of uranium in Canada. Two important federal crown corporations have been involved in atomic energy: ATOMIC ENERGY OF CANADA LTD (AECL) and ELDORADO Nuclear Ltd. The former is responsible for nuclear research; the latter for the mining and refining of uranium.

Canada's nuclear energy program was born in 1953 when feasibility studies on the CANDU reactor design were initiated. Although the first commercial CANDU reactor began operations only in 1971 in Pickering, Ont, by 1980 nuclear energy accounted for 38% of Ontario's electricity consumption. In 1985 there were NUCLEAR POWER PLANTS in Ontario, Québec and New Brunswick.

Canadian Energy Policy after OPEC Canada, like most industrialized countries, was unprepared for the consequences of the fourfold increase in international oil prices and the partial oil embargo imposed by the Arab members of the Organization of Petroleum Exporting Countries (OPEC) in the wake of the 1973 Middle East war. Canadian energy policy entered a decade of unprecedented turmoil as a result of the fight between the western provinces and the federal government for control over growing energy revenues and over the issue of whether domestic oil and gas prices should track world levels.

Some of the federal government's initiatives between 1973 and 1974 provoked forceful provincial reaction. In March 1973 Ottawa moved to control the export of oil when a rapid jump in shipments to the United States threatened to disrupt domestic supplies. Then, in September, Ottawa froze the domestic price of oil for 6 months and imposed an export tax on oil to ensure fair returns from US sales and to help subsidize eastern Canadians dependent on oil imports. Interpreting these actions as federal intrusions into their traditional areas of responsibility, the western provinces retaliated through new legislation that purported to control the production, regulation, marketing and pricing of their resources. Included were new royalty schemes designed to capture a larger share of revenues.

Alberta also created the Alberta Petroleum Marketing Commission, with broad powers over the production, pricing and provincial marketing of oil. The federal government responded by amending the Income Tax Act to disallow the deductibility of provincial royalties from corporate income tax, and by enacting the Petroleum Administration Act, under which Ottawa assumed broader powers to control oil and gas pricing in Canada.

In Dec 1973, as part of its response to the "energy crisis," the federal government announced the creation of PETRO-CANADA – to boost oil and gas exploration in the North and offshore, to assist in the development of the tar sands (*see* BITUMEN) and to secure reliable oil imports. By the 1980s Petro-Canada had become one of Canada's largest petroleum companies. As the federal government's "window on industry," it has both acted as a source of information to the government about oil and gas and served as a policy instrument, eg, in frontier drilling.

Between 1973 and 1978, the price of oil and natural gas in Canada rose quickly through agreements reached between the federal government and the producing provinces, but did not reach world levels. By mid-1978 the gap between domestic and international prices had closed to less than $3 per barrel. In the wake of the 1979 Iranian Revolution, however, world prices increased by 150% and the federal government renounced its intention of ensuring eventual parity between domestic and world prices. This left Canadian prices far below international ones and created difficult strains between Alberta and the federal government.

The 1980 National Energy Program The 1979 increase in world oil prices aggravated some of the problems Canada already faced. First, it represented a large transfer of wealth from consumers to producers. In Canada this wealth transfer had 2 significant dimensions: a large interregional transfer of wealth from Ontario and Québec (which together accounted for 58% of domestic oil consumption in 1980) to Alberta (which produced 86% of Canada's oil), and an international transfer of wealth from Canada to the US as a re-

Sources of Canadian Energy Consumption
(Source: NEB, *Report on Canadian Energy Supply and Demand, 1986*)

							Forecast (percentages)		
	1920	*1930*	*1940*	*1950*	*1960*	*1970*	*1980*	*1990*	*2000*
Petroleum	7	15	20	33	54	55	51	36	31
Natural Gas	–	2	3	3	13	18	21	29	30
Coal and Coke	75	63	58	49	17	12	12	12	16
Hydroelectricity*	1	4	7	7	11	9	10	12	13
Nuclear Electricity*	–	–	–	–	–	–	2	4	4
Others	17	16	12	8	5	6	4	7	6
Total	100	100	100	100	100	100	100	100	100
Consumption (petajoules)	1 204	1 492	1 681	2 546	3 350	5 997	8 019	8 538	9 829

* Converted at 3.6 MJ/kWh

sult of the high level of American ownership of the oil and gas industry (*see* FOREIGN INVESTMENT).

Second, the rapid increase in international prices made it difficult for the federal government to manage the national economy. It aggravated inflation and strained the EQUALIZATION PAYMENTS system. It contributed to the federal deficit as well, because the federal government continued to subsidize oil imports to maintain a uniform domestic price across the country. The increase in the world oil price, however, also represented an opportunity to achieve a higher level of oil self-sufficiency through the development of high-cost oil in the frontier and increased synthetic production from the tar sands.

In 1980 the federal government introduced the National Energy Program (NEP). Its objectives were to increase Canadian ownership of the oil industry, to achieve oil self-sufficiency and gain a greater share of energy revenues. Although all 3 objectives were controversial to some degree, the third aroused the most debate because it raised the concerns of the producing provinces and the oil industry that "their" revenues would be reduced if the federal government increased its share. The means chosen to advance the NEP's objectives also proved contentious because they represented an unprecedented degree of federal intervention and were imposed without prior consultation with industry or with the producing provinces. For example, to "Canadianize" the industry, the federal government introduced a tax to fund acquisitions by Petro-Canada and favoured Canadian-owned companies when distributing exploration grants. In addition, the federal government continued to hold domestic oil prices below international ones. Finally, to achieve oil self-sufficiency, the government sponsored expensive frontier exploration and instituted a system of grants to encourage consumers to conserve energy and switch to alternative fuels.

Previously, energy policy had reflected the assumption that demand can only rise and that new supplies must therefore be developed continually. But the the NEP's recognition that the solution to a "shortfall" in energy lay in controlling demand and supply was an innovation. Although most conservation and "off-oil" programs have been eliminated since the NEP came into being, the government still encourages conservation.

Coming after 2 years of unsuccessful negotiations with Alberta, however, the NEP precipitated an intense confrontation between the province and the federal government. Alberta cut back its oil production and withheld approval of 2 large tar-sand and heavy-oil projects, and challenged in court the legality of the proposed federal tax on gas exports. As energy producers, Saskatchewan and BC also denounced the NEP without, however, retaliating directly against the federal government. An understanding between Alberta and Ottawa was only reached when the federal government substantially altered the NEP's pricing and taxation provisions to bring domestic prices closer to world levels. Although this agreement put an end to the political conflict, it failed to bring stability in energy policy.

Adjustments to the NEP and provincial fiscal regimes were required almost immediately in response to the 1983 drop in world oil prices, the fall in gas exports and the recession. The 1984 election of a market-oriented Conservative government led to more dramatic changes as most of the NEP's interventionist policies – price controls, consumer subsidies, exploration incentives, production taxes and the 25% crown share on federal lands, or "back-in" – were gradually eliminated.

Although both the oil industry and the western provinces welcomed these changes, they soon had to confront an even greater threat than the NEP: the 50% drop in world oil prices in 1986. The collapse in international prices forced the cancellation of energy investments across the country and battered the economy of the western provinces. It also led to renewed calls for government intervention to stabilize prices and revenues.

As 1987 drew to a close, the oil industry's prospects improved: oil prices had rebounded from the previous year's low and revenues were up. More important still was the FREE TRADE agreement negotiated between Canada and the US. By committing both countries to let market forces dictate the pattern of energy development, the free trade agreement represented a far-reaching commitment to energy deregulation and the integration of continental markets.

Conclusion Oil and gas will continue to fill a large share of Canadian energy requirements into the next century, although oil's importance is already declining. The depletion of western conventional reserves will force Canada to become dependent on imports as well as on oil from the tar sands, on heavy oils, and on arctic and offshore oils. New domestic sources of oil will be more expensive to find, will in some instances pose new environmental risks, and will often require the development of new technology.

The rising cost of energy – oil, gas, electricity – has already led to a greater emphasis on conservation and to a search for alternative sources of energy, particularly liquid fuels and renewable forms of energy, such as SOLAR ENERGY, WIND ENERGY and BIOMASS ENERGY. These and other forms may eventually replace much contemporary oil and gas uses, although hydrocarbons are likely to remain important in transportation fuels and as components of petrochemical products. FRANÇOIS BREGHA

Reading: Canada, Department of Energy, Mines and Resources, *The National Energy Program* (1980); B. Doern and G. Toner, *The NEP and the Politics of Energy* (1984); J. McDougall, *Fuels and the National Policy* (1982).

Energy Resources Conservation Board Established by the Government of Alberta in 1938 and known first as the Petroleum and Natural Gas Conservation Board, the agency's purpose was to ensure proper procedures were followed in oil and gas development and production throughout the province and to stop the wasteful flaring of natural gas at TURNER VALLEY. This independent quasi-judicial body developed and applied policies for the effective conservation of Alberta's oil and gas resources. Since the period of excess productive capacity following the major Leduc discovery in 1947, it has regulated rates of production to permit equitable access to markets by all producers. It also ensures that only natural gas which is surplus to Alberta's long-term needs is sold outside the province. In 1971, the board's mandate was expanded to include pipelines, coal and electricity, and its name was changed to the Energy Resources Conservation Board. Composed of up to 6 Cabinet-appointed members, the board's responsibilities are set forth in Acts of the Legislature. The board, supported by a substantial technical and professional staff, must regulate the operation of existing energy facilities, and evaluate and decide on applications for new or expanded energy projects. Its decisions are final in many areas, but comprise recommendations to the government when they relate to matters which have far-reaching implications. Public hearings are typically part of the process whenever the issues are complex or controversial. The ERCB also provides comprehensive statistics and information to the public, government, and industry on all aspects of Alberta's energy resource sector. DAVID H. BREEN

Enfranchisement was the most common of the legal processes by which Indians lost their INDIAN status under the INDIAN ACT. The term was used both for those who give up their status by choice, and for the much larger number of Indian women who lost status automatically upon marriage to non-Indian men (*see* Jeannette LAVELL). Only the former were entitled to take with them a share of band reserve lands and funds, but both groups lost their treaty and statutory rights as Indians, and their right to live in the reserve community. The right to vote, often confused with "enfranchisement" in the technical sense discussed here, was only one of the supposed advantages of loss of status before Indians acquired the federal vote in 1960. From its first enactment in 1857 up to at least the 1960s, voluntary enfranchisement was the cornerstone of Canadian Indian policy (*see* NATIVE PEOPLE, GOVERNMENT POLICY). By enfranchising, a person was supposed to be consenting to abandon Indian identity and communal society (with its artificial legal disabilities) in order to merge with the "free," individualistic and non-Indian majority. There were in fact relatively few such enfranchisements over the years; a law to force enfranchisement of Indians whom the government thought should be removed from band lists (in force 1920-22, 1933-51) was unpopular and a failure. A 1985 amendment to the Indian Act eliminated the idea of enfranchisement as used here: as well as eliminating the Act's discriminatory section the government gave individual bands the right to decide their own conditions for membership. BENNETT MCCARDLE

Reading: DIAND, *The Historical Development of the Indian Act* (1978), *Indian Acts and Amendments 1868-1950* and *Contemporary Indian Legislation, 1951-1978* (1981).

Engel, Howard, novelist, cartoonist (under the pen-name "Foo"), story writer, poet (b at Toronto 2 Apr 1931). He was raised in St Catharines, Ont, and educated at McMaster U and the Ontario College of Education. During his career as a producer of literary and cultural programs at the CBC, Engel published a few stories and poems, but he did not begin to write seriously until he became interested in detective fiction. A founding member of Crime Writers of Canada, Engel recognized that while Canada has produced some detective writers, ordinary Canadian locales have never achieved literary prominence. Determined to rectify this oversight, Engel has vividly brought to life southern Ontario, setting his work – *The Suicide Murders* (1980), *The Ransom Game* (1981), *Murder on Loca-*

tion (1982), *Murder Sees the Light* (1984) and *A City Called July* (1986) – in fictional Grantham (based on his hometown). Engel's gumshoe, Benny Cooperman, a Jewish bachelor, is an atypical sleuth, but his self-deprecating humour and timorous personality make him a quintessential Canadian private eye. *Murder on Location* has been serialized for radio, and *The Suicide Murders* and *Murder Sees the Light* filmed for television by the CBC. DONNA COATES

Engel, Marian, née Passmore, writer (b at Toronto 24 May 1933; d there 16 Feb 1985). Engel grew up in Galt, Sarnia and Hamilton, Ont. Educated at McMaster, McGill and Aix-en-Provence, France, she taught in the US, Canada and Cyprus. She married and subsequently divorced Howard ENGEL. She was widely known and respected, particularly because of her Gov Gen's Award-winning novel, *Bear* (1976). She was also influential in the movement to enable Canadian writers to deal collectively with publishers and other institutions. She was the first chairman of the WRITERS' UNION OF CANADA (1973-74). In her novels and stories, Engel wrote with wit and grace about the everyday lives of contemporary people, especially women. Among her 6 novels are *No Clouds of Glory* (1968), *Monodromos* (1974) and *Lunatic Villas* (1981). She also wrote 2 juvenile books and 2 collections of short stories called *Inside the Easter Egg* (1975) and *The Tattooed Woman* (1985). A special issue of *Room of One's Own* (9:2, 1984) is devoted to Engel and features an interview, articles on her work, original writing by her and a bibliography.

JEAN WILSON

Engineering, in its broadest sense, is any activity that applies scientific and mathematical knowledge to the solution of material problems. The modern profession of engineering is involved with designing, building and manufacturing most of the devices, systems and structures that characterize technical civilization. Engineering touches virtually every human activity in industrial society, from computers, space vehicles, lasers and satellite communications to buildings, roads, harbours, sewage systems, food packaging and paper manufacturing. To some extent, the history of engineering is the history of humanity's progress in using tools and observations on the nature of matter to overcome physical limitations and to modify, harness and control the natural environment. Highly organized, complex engineering works were a prominent feature of many of the civilizations of antiquity, where abundant technical skill developed in the design and construction of fortifications, monuments, roads, aqueducts, irrigation networks and other installations, some of which are still in use (*see* ENGINEERING, HISTORY OF).

The Modern Profession

The engineering profession is the result of 2 important developments which took place in Europe during the 18th and 19th centuries: the Industrial Revolution and the increasing reliability of science. As the industrial production of factories surpassed the output of craftsmen and artisans, both the scope of engineering and the demand for engineering skills greatly increased. Science became the principal means of technical advance, allowing engineers to predict the behaviour of materials and natural forces with increasing accuracy. Engineering schools were founded around the world during this time; specialized engineering disciplines began to develop and the stage was set for an explosion of technical knowledge in the 20th century.

Estimates suggest that the volume of scientific and technical knowledge now doubles every 20 years or less. Since no one person can possibly be familiar with all knowledge relevant to a given field, today's engineer most commonly works as part of an engineering team, with scientists, technologists, technicians and other specialists. Thus, in addition to training in mathematics, physics, systems analysis, chemistry and other sciences required by a particular engineering discipline, engineers require good communications skills to be effective in a team context. As most engineering requires compromise between the competing demands of economy, performance, compatibility with existing systems, environmental concerns and other factors, engineers also require good judgement, creativity and diplomacy to achieve the best use of limited materials, energy and human resources.

While the rapid pace of technical development continues to produce new areas of engineering specialization, most of these new fields are related to one or more of the principal branches, which include AGRICULTURAL ENGINEERING, CHEMICAL ENGINEERING, CIVIL ENGINEERING, ELECTRICAL ENGINEERING, MECHANICAL ENGINEERING, MINERAL AND MINING ENGINEERING, and SURVEYING, as well as the fields discussed briefly below.

Bioengineering involves the use and control of biological systems, through the application of engineering methods in fields such as human engineering, biochemical engineering, medical engineering and environmental engineering. Human engineering concerns the optimal integration of tools, procedures and environments to human dimensions and performance criteria. Medical engineering produces technology for use in medicine, including diagnostic devices, monitoring and life-support systems such as pacemakers and artificial organs, and tools such as surgical instruments. Biochemical engineering uses the processes and physical properties of living organisms in applications such as the production of chemicals and drugs. Bioengineers usually complete advanced study in a related life-science discipline.

Naval Architecture concerns the design of oceangoing vessels and includes both an understanding of the physical influence of the sea and the ability to conceive designs integrating the piping, electrical circuits, structural members and other subcomponents into a compact and functional whole (*see* SUBMERSIBLES).

Marine Engineering concentrates on the technical aspects of SHIPBUILDING, eg, establishing design specifications and installing and testing shipboard machinery.

Industrial Engineering is the field dealing with the effective management of manpower, machinery and materials in the industrial production environment. Using systems analysis, queuing theory (ie, the study of waiting-line processes), statistics and other mathematics-based disciplines, the industrial engineer assumes direction of such industrial functions as plant design, materials handling, automation and industrial quality control, and implements the use of computers and data-processing procedures in the production cycle (*see* ROBOTICS).

Aeronautical Engineering deals with the design, construction, testing and maintenance of aircraft and their components and may include many specialized areas related to AERODYNAMICS, materials, propulsion and the myriad problems related to flight.

Metallurgical and Materials Engineering is concerned with the extraction, alloying, shaping and fabrication of metals and related materials. The practitioner is well versed in chemistry and physics, with a strong emphasis on thermodynamics, high-temperature and solution chemistry and electrochemistry, the principles of solidification, phase transformations in the solid state, corrosion and deformation, and is familiar with an extensive range of chemical, optical and microanalytical techniques and physical testing methods. Thus, there is very little professional distinction between the metallurgical engineer and the metallurgist.

Nuclear Engineering is broadly concerned with discovering practical applications for nuclear physics in the areas of medicine, nondestructive testing, NUCLEAR-POWER generation and weaponry.

Petroleum Engineering Natural or artificial forces may cause fluids to be stored or to move within structures or traps in the porous rocks of the Earth's crust. Petroleum engineering is concerned with locating and delineating such traps (reservoirs), determining the nature and quantity of the fluids they contain and the orderly and economic exploitation of such fluids. Another concern is the injection of fluids into reservoirs to store or dispose of them, or to use them to remove the reservoir's original contents. Discovery, production, transportation, processing and marketing of petroleum and petroleum products requires the interaction of many specialists during road building and the preparation of well sites and production, pumping and treatment facilities, pipelines, etc.

Engineers may also be classified according to the work they do. Thus, for example, the design engineer creates the plans and specifications for a particular job, drawing plans and details of each part, indicating how the parts fit together and preparing specifications of the materials to be used and performance standards to be maintained. Design may be in satellites, heart-lung machines, offshore drilling rigs, etc. The construction engineer supervises building, working from detailed plans. In industrial processes the research engineer performs applied science and engineering research on processes and products. The development engineer develops products based on scientific and engineering research. The operating engineer manages industrial operations and production facilities. The production engineer works to find the most economical way of transforming raw materials into finished products. The service engineer supervises the installation or repair of equipment delivered to a client.

Relationship with Other Sciences

Engineering calls upon knowledge from all the disciplines of science in combinations which reflect the engineer's specialization and the nature of a given project. Mathematics, physics and their applications in the materials sciences are fundamental to the study and practice of engineering. While computers and computerized design aids have reduced the burden of performing extensive calculations, skill in advanced mathematical procedures remains essential for engineering work. Depending on the area of specialization, an engineer may require advanced study of one or more related disciplines, eg, physics, chemistry, geology, oceanography, biology and medicine. Engineering training in Canada also involves study of the humanities and social sciences; economics and sociology help the engineer evaluate the impact of new technologies and assess the socioeconomic dimensions of technological problems. Business management studies can be invaluable assets to the financial and management aspects of engineering.

Engineering generalists are concerned with integrating the work of specialists from the engineering and scientific communities, a role that demands wide general knowledge of engineering and the sciences. Many problems require an engineer to use knowledge outside the scope of formal engineering training. This factor, combined with rapidly changing technology, leads most engineers to continue to study throughout their careers.

Training

In the first half of the 19th century, Canadian engineers were trained as apprentices in the offices of established professionals, such as Samuel KEEFER or Sir Casimir GZOWSKI. In 1854 the first engineering school in Canada was established at King's College (now University of New Brunswick). Other applied science courses were established by the 1870s at McGill and l'École polytechnique de Montréal and at the School of Practical Sciences (now part of U of Toronto). Engineering education has continued to grow in Canada throughout the 20th century. One of the most significant areas of development, in which Canada is a world leader, has been in petroleum engineering. The U of Alberta established the first petroleum engineering degree program in Canada in 1948 and continues to offer BSc, MSc and PhD degrees. In 1986, 39 Canadian institutions offered 181 accredited engineering programs, monitored by the engineering profession through the Canadian Accreditation Board, a committee of the Canadian Council of Professional Engineers, and certified to meet minimum quality standards for entry into the profession. University graduates normally undergo a 2-year apprenticeship, before being registered with the provincial engineering association as a Professional Engineer (PEng). Prospective engineers who lack the necessary educational requirements may become registered by passing exams offered by the associations.

Engineering Organizations

Canada's engineering organizations fulfil several different roles: some regulate and administer the profession; others facilitate an interchange of technical ideas between engineers working in the same field or arrange exchanges between engineers and other groups within society or with engineers in other countries; still others are concerned with advancing the purposes of an engineering occupation or industrial sector. The engineering profession is regulated by provincial legislation, administered through the 10 provincial and 2 territorial engineering associations. The CANADIAN COUNCIL OF PROFESSIONAL ENGINEERS was organized in 1936 to co-ordinate the activities of the provincial associations. Its membership of nearly 130 000 represents about 95% of Canadian engineers. Civil, electrical and mechanical engineers each make up about 25% of its membership; chemical engineers, 10%; others, including mining and petroleum engineers, 15%. Its activities include monitoring (accrediting) university engineering undergraduate education and providing statistics on engineering manpower. The first association of practising engineers in Canada was the Canadian Society of Civil Engineers, formed in 1887, which became the Engineering Institute of Canada in 1918. It now represents approximately 12 000 Canadian professional engineers. Other engineering organizations are the Canadian Society for Chemical Engineering, the Canadian Institute of Mining and Metallurgy, the Association of Consulting Engineers of Canada and the Institute of Electrical and Electronics Engineers.

Engineering Law

The professional engineer's conduct is governed by a code of ethics which determines professional duties to the public, the employer, the client, other engineers and to the profession. In addition, the extensive financial and public safety responsibilities of engineering require professional engineers to be aware of the law relevant to practice.

Contracts, primarily covered by common law (civil law in Québec), are usually written documents stating terms and conditions of a purchase or agreement, but may be considered to exist without writing. Engineers routinely contract for goods and services where a failure to live up to the terms of the contract (eg, late delivery) may involve extensive financial loss and result in lawsuits for damages.

Specifications determine the required characteristics of contracted goods and are important in determining the warranty obligations of the manufacturer or seller and in settling lawsuits resulting from damages or injury in the event of product failure.

Corporate Law The corporation is normally recognized as a legal entity separate from its holders, whose personal liability for its indebtedness is limited. Corporate liability is an important consideration for the engineer embarking on a career in private practice (*see* CORPORATE LAW).

Industrial (or Intellectual) Property Industrial property rights are covered by PATENTS, COPYRIGHTS and TRADE MARKS. Patents and copyrights are means of protecting original creative ideas; trademarks offer rights to an original trade name. Patents are granted to a new invention meeting certain conditions, giving the patent holder a monopoly of rights to the invention for a specified period. Copyrights cover every original literary, dramatic, musical and artistic work and generally refer to the sole right to reproduce the work or any part of it. Of special interest to engineers are provisions of the copyright act dealing with engineering drawings, which preclude a client from reproducing or repeating the design without permission from the engineer who produced the drawing.

Safety The professional engineer is responsible for the health and safety of people who may be affected by his or her work, and may be held liable for injuries resulting from failure to perform to a reasonable level of competence.

CLAUDE LAJEUNESSE

Engineering, History of Although engineering is a major Canadian industry, profession and export, its history has attracted little attention from Canada's scholars or cultural institutions. Notwithstanding the fact that 2 of the world's 10 largest engineering firms are of Canadian origin and ownership, there are more Canadian university courses and positions in the history of mediaeval technology than in the history of Canadian engineering and technology. It remains to be seen whether or not engineering will experience a level of newly awakened cultural awareness and scholarly study comparable to that in other areas such as Canadian literature and fine arts. Critical factors will include funding for research outside the traditional academic environment and the degree to which universities see the field as a legitimate area of scholarly research.

With the beginning of sustained European settlement in what is now Canada a new set of goals, values, demands and expectations were placed upon the land. The indigenous population had created a material culture and social organization well adapted to the land and, although much of this was of considerable use to the settlers, the new expectations were based on another technological tradition and demanded that it be an important platform on which the new society be erected.

Thus, for example, although both societies depended on water transportation and the newcomers made good use of indigenous craft, the large sailing ship was the basis of transoceanic trade and Great Lakes trade. Consequently the newcomers needed protected harbours, wharves and deeper water along with a different type of knowledge of watercourses. Water more than deep enough for the most heavily laden of the largest of canoes might be treacherously shallow for larger European-style sailing craft. Hence, there developed a need not necessarily for better but for different hydrographic knowledge and work in the St Lawrence R by early French hydrographers, trained first in France and then in Québec.

Construction on the Lachine Canal, beyond Wellington Bridge, Montréal, from the *Canadian Illustrated News*, vol XIV, no 15 (*courtesy National Archives of Canada/C-64628*).

Early hydrographic surveys clearly demonstrated one of the fundamental lessons of Canadian engineering history, namely that differing expectations bring with them the need for different types of engineering and technological knowledge and expertise. This is clearly illustrated by the massive masonry FORTIFICATION erected for protection against attackers with gunpowder. Early fortifications such as those at LOUISBOURG and Québec City reflect a high level of military engineering skills.

For centuries "engineer" meant military engineer, one who built defensive works, engines of war and other military requirements. During the 19th century more and more engineering became civil, that is to say nonmilitary. This was the beginning of a continuing trend towards greater specialization in engineering. Although the lifestyle and expectations of the newcomers demanded the erection of large sawmills and flour mills, some of which were built by military engineers, these civilian structures were largely built by millwrights and only in the late 19th or early 20th century would industrial structures become increasingly designed by engineers. However, it was the demand for vastly improved transportation systems in the form of canals and railways which brought the civilian engineers to the forefront.

The need for improved inland water communications led to a period of intense CANAL building activity during the 19th century which left Canada with such engineering monuments as the Rideau and Welland canals, as well as a host of smaller ones such as the Lachine and Beauharnois. Completed in 1832 under the supervision of Lt-Col John BY as part of a defensive military network, the RIDEAU CANAL is one of the continent's major 19th-century engineering achievements. To build a 200 km long canalized river and lake network through wilderness was in itself a major feat greatly enhanced by the high level of quality and permanence that characterized its construction. But in the long term, perhaps the greatest contribution of the Rideau Canal is that it marked a major benchmark in learning to be a Canadian engineer rather than being an engineer in Canada. Although there are canal sites such as Jones Falls (the largest true masonry arch dam in N America at the time), which represented European technique transported to N America virtually unaltered, much of

Grand Trunk single-arch, double-track steel bridge over the Niagara R, 1898 (*courtesy National Archives of Canada/C-28859*).

the canal represented new adaptive thinking to correspond with Canadian conditions.

At the sudden narrowing and precipitous drop in the Rideau R known as the Hog's Back, the violent spring and summer floods could raise water levels as much as 5 m above normal. A dam at this spot would have to withstand these sudden onslaughts both during and after construction. Conventional European construction methods were too slow and the dam was washed out 3 times before it could be brought to a point where it was strong enough to withstand the violence of the floods. On the fourth try traditional European based approaches were abandoned and the dam was built with stone-filled timber cribs which, although very unattractive to some eyes, could be built quickly using readily available materials. The Hog's Back embodied an important lesson: engineering is often best when it relies heavily on local materials and labour along with the adaptation of known technology to fit local circumstances. These characteristics were to become hallmarks of Canadian engineering and serve Canadian engineers well in jobs throughout the world, particularly on those requiring flexibility and imagination in the face of unusual circumstances.

As Canada strove to increase Great Lakes commerce and to compete with the Erie Canal which drew trade through the US instead of Canada, Niagara Falls stood as the most spectacular impediment to trade and prosperity. The WELLAND CANAL bypassed the falls but, as a privately funded exercise in frontier capitalism, it was plagued by financial troubles which resulted in the form of engineering and construction which tried to economize too heavily. Eventually the canal was taken over as a government project and successive rebuildings attained much higher standards. However, the canal yielded another of the engineering lessons that has served Canada well.

"Sourcing" is the modern jargon to describe the exercise of drawing engineering expertise from various areas for a particular job. Royal Engineers, trained military engineers in the employ of the British government, provided most of the Rideau Canal engineering. Of necessity the first Welland Canal, which was a private venture, depended on civilian engineers who were hired as needed. When the Welland Canal became a government-owned canal, more options opened up for sourcing engineering talent. When Royal Engineers finished a job such as the Rideau Canal, they almost invariably moved on, leaving the area as poor in engineering talent as it was when they arrived. Massive engineering projects therefore did little or nothing to build up a pool of trained engineering talent committed to the area or country which could be used on other jobs. There were rare exceptions as with the Royal Engineers who stayed on in BC after the completion of the CARIBOO ROAD. It was therefore decided, after greater controversy in Upper Canada, that the re-engineering of the Welland Canal would rely on civil servant engineers in key positions who would hire or contract with civilian engineers as needed. As a result, a number of Canadians had the opportunity to work on a major project and to lay the foundations of successful engineering careers.

The same general growth and economic development in the country which gave rise to engineering opportunities on canals also created other needs. In cities such as Toronto, Hamilton, Montréal and Halifax, higher population densities created serious fire hazards as well as medical problems caused by inadequate water supply systems and by improper sewage treatment and disposal. As a result, around mid-century various Canadian cities embarked on major water supply engineering projects. Cities such as Hamilton, where Thomas Coltrin KEEFER built one of his numerous water pumping stations, engineered a better quality of life and also provided engineers with continuing opportunities for further professional development.

Although road and highway transportation was certainly uncomfortable during all or most of the 19th century, by the end of the third quarter of the 19th century the combination of canals, roads and bridges plus the water and sanitary needs of cities – projects known collectively as public works – had given engineers such as T.C. Keefer, his brother Samuel, Pierre Gauvreau, Charles BAILLAIRGÉ and Casimir GZOWSKI a chance to develop and shine as major engineers. As one would expect in a multicultural country such as Canada, engineers represented a wide range of cultural, national and linguistic groups.

Railways were the most important single 19th-century training and proving ground for Canadian engineers. The INTERCOLONIAL RAILWAYS and the CANADIAN PACIFIC in particular illustrate a number of major themes in Canadian engineering history. From an engineering point of view some of the most important characteristics of 19th-century Canadian railways include vast distances; difficult and varied terrain; wide temperature ranges sometimes coupled with hazardous snow loads and conditions; and chronic underfunding, particularly in the initial and early construction phases. Consequently, Canadian engineers very early became world-renowned for their ability to build railways quickly and relatively inexpensively and then, as finances allowed, to improve the quality and permanence of the railway after it was operational and generating revenue. One of the ways this reputation was achieved was to rely very heavily on local building materials. In much of Canada this meant using timber and, where this was combined with breathtaking terrain such as in the mountains of BC, it produced spectacular feats of timber construction. The massive timber trestles of Canadian railways which Canadians took for granted, or even found embarrassing because they were not of iron and steel, were much admired in Europe as engineering feats on a par with the still standing aqueducts of the ancient Romans. Then because wooden structures had to be replaced they gave both Canadian engineers and manufacturers such as Dominion Bridge the opportunity to work in, learn and demonstrate their capability in more modern materials.

While the increasing knowledge and self-confidence of Canadian engineers led to much better value for funds expended, it could also lead to conflict between client and engineer, particularly when the client might not be solely interested in best value as defined by an engineer. Perhaps the most spectacular and openly public case of 19th century engineer-client conflict came from Sandford FLEMING's fights over whether bridges on the Intercolonial should be timber or iron. Fleming saw that with changing technology and the closeness of much of the Intercolonial route to economical water transportation, it made sense to depart from common Canadian convention and build with iron; his colleagues and masters overruled him. Undeterred, he appealed first to PM Macdonald and, when that did not have the desired effect, to the Privy Council in Britain which upheld him.

Fleming's dispute emphasized that the rate of change in technology and the circumstances surrounding engineering were beginning to outstrip society's ability to absorb new information and decide on its best utilization. Other errors of judgement were less nobly intentioned. Too many engineering projects, particularly railways, were undertaken primarily to make money for unscrupulous promoters and not to serve the best interests of the governments and individual investors who were talked into backing them. And in this process it was all too often the engineer who played a major role in creating a favourable climate of opinion for dubious ventures.

Engineers were clearly the key to much that an emerging industrial society and country both needed, yet they were often treated with little or no respect and had few avenues to offer independent views. Engineers who were too scrupulous, or believed to be on the side of what sud-

Massive timber trestles were built over spectacular terrain, such as the CPR bridge at Lethbridge, Alta (*photo by Harry Savage*).

denly became the wrong political party, might suddenly find themselves not merely out of a job but virtually unemployable. In response to problems such as these a group of engineers in 1887 formed the Canadian Society of Civil Engineers. Although it lacked the power to enforce standards or impose licensing requirements, the new society represented the first and most important step in a long series of events that today has made engineering a highly specialized profession with strict licensing requirements and high standards.

By the late 19th century numerous changes were occurring which accelerated engineering towards ever-greater specialization and diversity. The causes behind this trend were the emergence of entirely new areas of activity as well as the redefining of other traditional areas of activity. In the former one finds developments such as the emergence of electricity as both an industrial force and part of daily domestic life and with it the growth of engineering specialists in the field of ELECTRICAL ENGINEERING. Many later developments were as entirely new, computer engineering. In other areas it was not the field that was new but the way in which things were done. Here mining is an excellent example: although mining is almost as old as human technological history, it was radically transformed by new knowledge in areas as diverse as chemistry, metallurgy and electricity. A never-before-equalled need for sophisticated technical understanding in a number of areas was then embodied in the new profession of the mining engineer.

During the last 2 decades of the 19th century electricity became less of a curiosity and more of a domestic servant and an industrial driving force (*see* ELECTRIC-POWER DEVELOPMENT). Because of the difficulties associated with ELECTRIC POWER TRANSMISSION over distances, early power users had to be close to the source; numerous generating sites, many driven by steam, grew up with each serving a very limited number of customers or uses. Thus was started a long-standing Canadian tradition of building hydroelectric generation stations in undeveloped areas and then using them as a stimulus for local development or as a source of power transmitted over long distances to existing centres of population and industry. One of the best early examples of this latter trend comes from Shawinigan Falls on the St Maurice R in Québec. Here innovative entrepreneurs recognized the potential and invested even before being assured of customers. However, customers were attracted by the prospects of cheap, abundant, reliable power and soon Shawinigan Water and Power Company signed contracts to supply power to manufacturers of calcium carbide, aluminum and pulp and paper. In addition it built a transmission line over what then seemed the excessively long distance of 137 km to Montréal.

Most of the excellent hydroelectric power sites are far from the major centres of population that grew up along the more placid water routes of little use for hydroelectric generation but of great use for transportation. This feature is a quirk of Canadian geography that has meant that one of the continuing challenges and limiting factors in numerous Canadian hydroelectric developments has been the need to transmit power over long distances, and this means at high voltages. Various utilities in Canada have contributed to the growing capability in this area but the achievements are most dramatically illustrated by Hydro-Québec where power is now transmitted from James Bay at 735 000 volts, the highest transmission voltage in the world; it is a feat recognized by the Engineering Council Awards Jury as one of the 10 great engineering achievements of the past century.

The grain elevator, which made possible a storage network for western farmers, became one of the great symbols of Canada (*photo by Richard Harrington*).

The role of engineers in completely transforming the nature of Canadian roads, streets and highways is a good example of how engineering feats are taken for granted. Throughout much of its history Canada was noted internationally for its abysmal roads. Burgeoning cities and changing patterns of agriculture made better roads if not an absolute necessity then certainly a business asset. Similar pressures came from the growth of manufacturing aimed at serving more than a simple local market. Before the outbreak of WWI, and even more strongly after, engineers became increasingly involved in building long-distance networks of durable, year-round arteries for rapid mechanized travel. The same conditions held in the cities which, considering the total length of roads within a city was on an even larger scale. To withstand the wear and tear of mechanized vehicles engineers turned increasingly to concrete and asphalt and in so doing greatly stimulated the demand for these materials and the growth of industries associated with them. This relationship was just one part of the intricate network of change coupled to engineering and automobiles. Because automobiles made it possible to live farther from work than before, large suburban areas surrounded Canadian cities. These in turn stimulated the demand for further engineering services such as sewers and water supply and supplying electric power. At another level there was engineering for the host of mining, lumbering and other industries supplying construction needs. As cities became increasingly congested engineers in many areas were assigned the task of building suburban industrial parks and factory locations in order to reduce both the costs of construction and, more important, the shipping time delays often associated with an urban location. Thus in Canada, paradoxical as it may seem, the automobile provided far more work for engineers outside of its direct manufacture than within.

The rapid growth of western Canada was another of the major early 20th-century changes transforming Canadian life and economy. Some settled areas required elaborately engineered water storage and irrigation networks. Grain that could not get to market had little or no value and feeder roads leading to rail lines were not enough. Nationwide transfer and storage networks had to be built and this made the modern GRAIN ELEVATOR one of the great symbols of Canada. Although some of these early installations were of wood, concrete became the universal building material and so both material and scale dictated careful engineering. Concrete is a symbol of both the 20th century and of the greater importance of the engineer, for here was a man-made material for which there was great potential but no traditional rules of thumb for its use; success came from careful calculation and supervised use by professional engineers who alone understood how to take it to ever-increasing levels of utility.

In western Canada urban growth also demanded public utilities. It also required dealing with special problems such as the development of alkali-resistant concrete which would withstand western soils without premature decay and failure. Much of this was achieved under C.J. MACKENZIE, later head of the NATIONAL RESEARCH COUNCIL OF CANADA in Ottawa, while dean of engineering at U Sask in Saskatoon. It was in western Canada where petroleum engineering became a mature professional field both with conventional deposits and with heavy crude deposits which were long known to exist but difficult to process. Successful processing resulted only after decades of research dating back to early work by the GEOLOGICAL SURVEY OF CANADA and more importantly the ALBERTA RESEARCH COUNCIL.

Although relatively sparsely populated, northern Canada has seen some of the most dramatic 20th-century growth and change. Hydroelectric development, mining, pulp and paper, along with the northward extension of the transportation systems, have been responsible for the greater engineering input. There are numerous aspects to this involvement, but one area in which Canada has made an exceptional impact on world engineering is the development and manufacture of special-purpose vehicles.

The airplane has played a crucial role in transforming the North (*see* BUSH FLYING). The response to northern requirements has given birth to Canadian leadership in short-take-off-and-landing aircraft (STOL). STOL capability and other requirements were admirably met by the DE HAVILLAND BEAVER, another of the 10 engineering achievements celebrated by the Engineering Centennial Board. The Beaver was a brilliantly designed and engineered Canadian plane built to meet the identified needs of northern bush pilots. Extensive forested areas of northern Canada have led to world renown in the engineering and production of water bombers.

As an eminently suitable engineering response to Canadian needs, the de Havilland Beaver is the spiritual brother of the BOMBARDIER snow vehicles which range in size from single to multi-passenger. Both of these vehicles embody very innovative original engineering and have spread worldwide after proving themselves in Canada. Perhaps even more specialized are the off-road and specialized exploration and service vehicles manufactured in Calgary by Canadian Foremost Ltd. With the post-WWII increase in exploration, particularly for oil reserves, new vehicle types were needed to carry crews and equipment in the often swampy muskeg-filled areas of northern Canada. Satisfying this need, first on a small-scale, led to the growth of a company which now exports specialty vehicles worldwide for construction and exploration and for firefighting in the USSR.

Foremost Husky 8 in use in the oil fields of Indonesia. Special-purpose vehicles, initially designed for use in the rugged terrain of the North, are now used worldwide (*courtesy Canadian Foremost Ltd*).

Massive underground powerhouse at the James Bay Project (*photo by Mike Dobel/Masterfile*).

During the Depression of the 1930s engineering assignments often took on a new complexion. While there was still some new construction and expansion along traditional lines, for many companies simple survival became the major goal. Make-work projects had to be designed to find work for the staggering numbers of unemployed. The still used and very beautiful Broadway Bridge in Saskatoon, Sask, is an excellent example of such a project. A less labour-intensive structural steel design was rejected in favour of one put forward by C.J. Mackenzie, whose graceful multiple arch concrete bridge was designed so that most of the work could be carried out by inexperienced labourers with minimal reliance on machinery. Other engineers made their contributions to combatting the problems of the Depression through their work with the PRAIRIE FARM REHABILITATION ACT on projects such as small dams, water catch basins and erosion control projects.

Canada's industrial contribution to the war effort in WWII ranged from socks and boots to explosives, tanks, ships and airplanes. In many instances Canadian engineers converted existing factories into units capable of producing war materials unlike anything they had ever built before. For example, Dominion Bridge as well as producing ships and other heavy steel products also produced precision-made automatic weapons. In other areas pre-existing industries were force-fed into growth. The Canadian aircraft industry, with 4000 people, 8 plants and 46 500 m^2 of floor space and annual production of 40 airplanes, stood by the end of the war at 116 000 employees, 1.4 million m^2 of floor space and annual production of 4000 airplanes. Part of that impressive growth and production record represented a then scarce and relatively new component in Canadian engineering history: women professional engineers. Elsie MACGILL was the chief aeronautical engineer at Canadian Car & Foundry Co in Fort William, Ont. She had designed the Maple Leaf Trainer and, with a work force of up to 4500 managed the production of approximately 2000 Hawker Hurricane fighters. A rarity when she graduated from U of Toronto in 1927, Elsie MacGill was one of the pioneers of an important trend which would not begin to make significant inroads until several decades after the end of the war.

Other engineering needs of WWII demanded the creation of entirely new production facilities. Special aluminum alloys and forms were required for aircraft and in Kingston the Aluminium Co of Canada (ALCAN) built an entirely new plant in only 13 months to supply aluminum alloy sheets, tubes, forgings and extrusions for aircraft builders in Canada, Britain and the US. In Québec, where the world's largest hydroelectric power installation had been completed at Îsle Maligne in 1925, the giant Shipshaw generating station was designed by the consulting engineers of H.G. Acres and Co and then built in only 18 months by The Foundation Co of Canada. It was a remarkable feat of construction but Canadians were well known for speed. In Sarnia, Ont, an equally remarkable feat of high-speed design engineering and construction was the creation of the strategically crucial synthetic rubber plant for the Polymer Corp Ltd, now Polysar. This was another achievement recognized by the Engineering Centennial Awards Jury.

By the end of WWII in 1945 Canada had endured over a decade and a half of deprivation and much of the country's roads, sewers, communications systems and housing stock were inadequate. The massive postwar immigration to Canada would add to the pressure on these inadequate facilities and help to fuel a major construction boom. Many factories which had limped along with outdated equipment during the Depression and war years soon found that, without modernization, they would face the prospect of going out of business. In addition, new materials and processes developed or advanced during the war now offered considerable potential to those willing and able to seize them. In all of these areas engineers were called upon to conceptualize, plan and supervise a radical transformation of Canada.

Between 1949 and 1970 Canada spent nearly $1.5 billion to create the TRANS-CANADA HIGHWAY. At a length of 7821 km (4784 miles) it was the longest paved highway in the world. At one level it represented a massive engineering achievement, the road traffic equivalent of the building of the transcontinental railways with all of the attendant engineering and construction difficulties which had plagued these projects. It also marks a major political achievement, the first time all provinces had agreed on a joint project involving uniform construction standards nationwide.

Paralleling road needs was the need for improved electronic communications. Business, government and private individuals were demanding a rapidly escalating volume of telephone, AM and FM radio and television signals which were far beyond what existing technology and systems could handle. During the war microwaves have proven themselves for communications but never on a scale demanded for a trans-Canada network. Nonetheless it was decided to place Canada at the forefront of COMMUNICATIONS TECHNOLOGY and in a project marked by significant electrical engineering as well as extremely difficult feats of construction the Trans-Canada Microwave system was officially completed on 1 July 1958. It was the largest microwave transmission network in the world. The microwave system served the major population corridor of Canada very well but was not well adapted to isolated and sparsely populated far northern areas. Here the solution lay with SATELLITE technology and in 1962 with the launching of Alouette I Canada became the third nation in space behind the USSR and US.

Outer space is a very hostile environment and as befits a nation whose engineers have an enviable record of achievement in engineering for our own hostile natural environment, the Alouette satellites set records for reliability and longevity. The careful engineering and high performance of the antennae, known more formally as STEM ("storable tubular extendible module"), set new world standards and led directly to the development of the CANADARM. In the interval between the achievements the basic technology has been adapted for use in other hostile environments such as the interiors of nuclear reactor fuel cells.

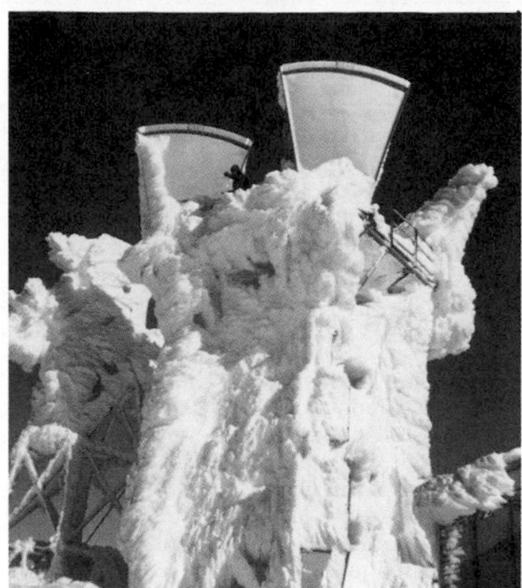

Snow-covered BC Tel transmission tower on Dog Mt. The construction of the TransCanada Microwave system was an extremely difficult feat of engineering (*courtesy BC Telephone Co/photo by Graeme Stuart*).

The Microwave System and the Alouette satellites were recognized by the Engineering Centennial Board as among the 10 outstanding Canadian engineering achievements of the last century, as was the CANDU Nuclear Reactor System. The latter was another outgrowth of wartime technology, although after the war Canada made a commitment to use nuclear power for peaceful purposes. In so doing Canada was set on the path towards not just a sound nuclear electric generating system but also becoming a major player in the medical and industrial applications of nuclear knowledge.

Another important facet of Canadian engineering is the growing amount of foreign work done by Canadian consulting engineers. Expertise, experience and reputation gained in major Canadian projects has led to opportunities for work abroad. After the completion of the Trans-Canada Microwave System Canadian engineers went on to build the PANAFTEL network linking the 5 African countries of Benin, Niger, Upper Volta, Mali and Senegal. Even more dramatically, the experience gained by Canadian engineering firms on the world's largest hydroelectric projects in Northern Québec has been a major factor in the rapid growth of a number of Canadian engineering firms and their ability to gain contracts abroad.

The importance of leading-edge work as the springboard to other work underlies a central but often little understood facet of engineering, namely its fragility. Although engineering demands years of formal education and preparation, engineers rely heavily on continuing experience to keep their skills and knowledge up to date; without the opportunity for significant experience it is all too easy to become outmoded, no longer competitive, no longer capable of giving best value for money expended by clients and no longer desirable. Thus, in the long run, a nation whose overall economy is not healthy and balanced is unlikely to be able to continue to create and support a healthy engineering profession as Canada has done in the past. It is for this reason that it is essential to develop an understanding of the role of Canada's engineers, not a recitation of major jobs and achievements but an understanding of how they are central to and one of the very foundations of Canadian history and culture.

NORMAN R. BALL

Reading: Norman R. Ball, *Mind, Heart, and Vision: Professional Engineering in Canada 1877 to 1987* (1987).

Englehart, Jacob Lewis, industrialist (b at Cleveland, Ohio 2 Nov 1847; d at Toronto 6 Apr 1921). In 1869, at age 19, he established Englehart and Co, one of the most successful producers in the Petrolia, Ont, fields, where the world's first commercial oil production had begun in 1857. Englehart started by acquiring the remains of a refinery, used to distill kerosene from crude oil, which had been destroyed by fire. He was one of 16 operators at Petrolia who merged their interests in 1880 to form IMPERIAL OIL, which in turn was soon exporting kerosene around the world. Englehart was a major shareholder and VP of Imperial. Unable to raise capital for expansion elsewhere, Imperial in 1898 turned to John Rockefeller's Standard Oil Co, which purchased controlling interest. In 1905 Englehart was appointed chairman of the board of the Temiskaming and Northern Ontario Ry (ONTARIO NORTHLAND), which he administered with outstanding success for 15 years.

EARLE GRAY

Reading: Earle Gray, *The Great Canadian Oil Patch* (1970).

English The English were among the first Europeans to reach Canadian shores and waters after the Norse seafarers of the 10th and 11th centuries. English mariners probably fished in Canadian waters even before John CABOT's voyage of 1497; Dr John Dee, Queen Elizabeth I's astrologer who was interested in the discovery of the NORTHWEST PASSAGE, found evidence to suggest that 2 Bristol merchants – Thorne and Eliot – may have reached Newfoundland *c*1494. British merchants financed several voyages at the beginning of the 16th century, and as early as 1527 the harbour of ST JOHN'S became a rendezvous site for fishing vessels. When Sir Humphrey GILBERT arrived to claim the land for Queen Elizabeth I in 1583 he found a makeshift town to serve the Devon fishermen already there. In 1610 John Guy, also of Bristol, founded the well-known English settlement at Cupers Cove, later known as CUPIDS, and from this point onwards settlement continued, people from the English West Country outnumbering the Irish immigrants 2 to 1. To this day Newfoundland remains, by descent, the most English province of Canada.

Another early direction of English penetration was through the Northwest Passage to Hudson Bay. Some of the famous Elizabethan captains went in search of the passage, including Martin FROBISHER, who received an Inuit arrow in his rump at Frobisher Bay in 1577. In 1610 Henry HUDSON entered the inland sea now called Hudson Bay. In 1670 the foundation of the HUDSON'S BAY COMPANY brought an influx of English traders and employees, largely recruited from the urban unemployed. Englishmen based in the company's forts on the bay conducted pioneer explorations of the West and the North, including Henry KELSEY's 1690 travels in the Canadian prairies, Anthony HENDAY's sighting of the Rockies in 1754 and Samuel HEARNE's epic journey down the Coppermine R to the Arctic Sea in 1771-72.

Origins People of English descent came to Canada either directly from England or indirectly through the American colonies. In the first case their motives were largely economic. In the early 19th century, many working people were unemployed, and among the upper and middle classes, younger sons and discharged officers emigrated because they were unable to keep up appearances at home. In the later period of the settlement of the PRAIRIE WEST, many English immigrants were attracted to Canada by the offer of free land. The motives of those of English descent who emigrated from the US were largely political, for most of them were LOYALISTS, although it is true that many English-Americans immigrated to Upper Canada and later to the Prairies because of the farming opportunities. Apart from the special connection between Newfoundland and the western counties of Devon and Dorset, no part of England can be singled out as having contributed particularly to the Canadian population; immigrants have come from all parts of the country, and from urban as well as rural areas.

Migration Because England was the imperial centre and by definition the "old country" of English Canada, many of the English, at least until 1867, came in official capacities as public servants and soldiers who, on release from service, remained in the country. For example, almost all the officials in BC, when it entered Confederation in 1871, were English or Anglo-Irish. Migration in the broader sense began on the mainland with the foundation of HALIFAX in 1749. Two-thirds of its early population of 3000 were Englishmen based there as a counterbalance to the French force at LOUISBOURG. With the capture of Louisbourg in 1758 and of Québec in 1759 and with the Treaty of PARIS, (1763) New France became another British colony. Shortly afterwards, in the 1760s, New England farmers of English descent began to settle around the Bay of Fundy on former Acadian lands, and in the early 1770s a group of Yorkshiremen put down roots in northern Nova Scotia. Then, at the end of the American War of Independence, the Loyalists came northward and carved out in 1784 the province of New Brunswick, whose population – apart from the returning Acadians – has remained largely English in descent.

Some of the Loyalists travelled to the region which in 1791 became Upper Canada. Here they were joined after the Napoleonic Wars by a considerable influx of English from England suffering the effects of high unemployment and depressed wages. By 1819 one-half of the British subjects who sailed for British N America were English from the British Isles. Many of these emigrated in various ways with official encouragement or assistance. The imperial authorities hoped to reproduce, at least partially, the English graded social system in Canada, and for this reason they encouraged ex-officers and other members of the gentry with generous grants of land, hoping to establish a kind of aristocracy. Speculative companies such as the CANADA COMPANY acquired large tracts of land on condition that they bring in suitable settlers from England. At the bottom of the scale were the schemes by which English parishes unloaded into Canada the paupers who were victims of crop failures and economic recession and who reached Canada with no means and none of the skills they needed in a pioneer environment. By 1851 this wave of immigration had settled down, and after a considerable inflow into the US some 93 000 people actually born in England remained in Canada West [Ont], constituting about one-tenth of the population. They were almost matched in number by the Scottish born (90 000) and greatly outnumbered by the 227 000 Irish born.

There were at least 3 other great waves of English immigration. After Confederation, children from private homes, industrial schools and poor-law schools were given free passage to Canada, where they became wards of various societies. Between 1867 and the 1920s thousands of British children, the majority of them English, were settled across Canada (*see* IMMIGRANT CHILDREN). Between 1890 and 1914, in response to the opening of the Prairie provinces, there was another large influx of English settlers. In 1901 they numbered less than 10 000, but in 1906, 3 years after an immigration office was established in central London, 65 000 immigrants arrived in Canada and in 1913 the number peaked at 113 004. Although the British government, under the Empire Settlement Act (1922), helped 130 000 British immigrants settle in Canada after WWI, the number of English immigrants did not rise significantly until after WWII. In 1947 over 7000 English, many of them trained industrial workers, artisans and technicians, immigrated to Canada; in 1957 the number rose to 75 546 and in 1967 it was 43 000.

Over the years, despite immigration, the proportion of Canadians of English descent has remained fairly steady. In 1871 those of English descent numbered 706 369 out of a total population of 3 689 257; in 1931, 2 741 419 out of 10 376 786. Although Statistics Canada no longer distinguished "English" from "British" immigrants in its census, in 1984, 3516 immigrants arrived from England (out of a total of 4657 from Britain).

Settlement Patterns Proportionately the most heavy English settlement has been in Newfoundland, BC, the Maritime provinces, and later in Ontario. In Québec the English are found mainly in enclaves in Montréal and the Eastern Townships. But wherever they have settled, except in Québec, they have tended to become assimilated quickly into the local community, largely because they have not had to learn a new language and have encountered little prejudice. Outbursts of anglophobia have been rare enough for such manifestations as the "Englishmen Need Not Apply" job notices of the early 1900s to have passed into Prairie legend as historic curiosities. Popular resentment against the English (as indeed against immigrants generally) was most acute during periods of economic crisis. During the depression of the early 1900s the government dealt as harshly with the English as with other immigrants; of nearly 1800 persons deported in 1908, 1100 were returned to the British Isles. The few cases of all-English agrarian settlements have usually existed because their members shared the same class attitudes or the same opinions rather than because they shared "Englishness." An example of the former was the colony of English gentlemen founded at CANNINGTON MANOR in Saskatchewan in 1882; one of the latter was the Barr Colony (*see* BARR COLONISTS) on the Alta-Sask border.

Economic Life The English entered into every level of Canadian life. They have been prominent in government and have shared the control of Canadian business with the SCOTS not only in the English-speaking parts of Canada but also in Montréal (*see* ELITES; BUSINESS ELITES). The Canadian armed forces were created and have largely been staffed by officers of English descent.

The first waves of English immigration contributed greatly to the farming population in the rural areas and to the skilled artisan population in the towns, but after WWII many English immigrants were professionals, technicians or individuals concerned in various ways with the arts. English immigrants have made important contributions to many Canadian institutions, including the NFB, the CBC, the Canada Council, the National Ballet and the Stratford Festival.

Social and Cultural Life The English, perhaps because they are so widely and evenly spread across Canada and because they consider them-

Mrs Corbett and family from Surrey, England, coming to meet her husband at Québec *c* 1911 (*courtesy National Archives of Canada/PA-10150*).

selves a founding race, have tended to be less self-defensively clannish than other groups. The family unit facilitated and promoted their ethnic identity. The ratio of male to female English prior to WWI was 5:3 while for other groups it was 5:1. The largest and most important English cultural society was the Sons of England, which in 1913 had 40 000 Canadian members. Lodges formed across Canada were usually led by affluent Englishmen, professionals, clergymen and former military officers who had joined local elites. The most important vehicle for maintaining traditions was the social evening "At home," which was modelled on the English music hall. On these occasions the Sons were expected to thrill to jingoistic songs, weep at evocations of England, savour warm, dark ale and revert to regional dialects. As a mutual benefit society, the Sons organized receptions for newcomers, provided medical services and paid unemployment and disability benefits.

The English were often perceived by other ethnic groups as xenophobic and industrious. English ethnicity could be asserted productively in Canada, because it provided not only status but a competitive advantage in securing employment. Companies such as The T. EATON CO were so partial to English workers that they imported them from London to work in their stores and factories, and the CPR used the union which had organized metal-trade workers in Britain as a supplier of labour.

Unlike the Scottish and Irish groups, the English pay scant attention to national days; only in Newfoundland is St George's Day celebrated seriously. They maintain few organizations to nurture group ties, and as the generations passed and the class accents of England dissolved into Canadian speech, the divisions of the homeland's sharply stratified society have blurred. If the descendants of the English in Canada are now vertically divided, it is more by wealth than by birth. The snobbish English enclaves of Westmount and Victoria are almost as obsolete as that uniquely English institution, the once numerous corps of REMITTANCE MEN – feckless sons of wealthy families paid to stay in Canada. Many of the remittance men died during WWI; the rest finally vanished when currency restrictions ended their English subsidies during WWII.

A number of Canadian institutions – some of them very important – have been profoundly influenced by English models and are still largely supported by Canadians of English stock. Representative institutions and the traditions of the British and English COMMON LAW are among the most important inheritances Canada has received from Great Britain. The parliamentary system, under which the Cabinet, which rules the country, is responsible to Parliament, is an extension of the British Cabinet system to colonial government, embodied in the British North America Act of 1867. In the realm of LAW, the civil law in 9 of Canada's provinces (the exception is Québec where French CIVIL LAW is maintained) is based largely on English common law; the system of courts follows the English model closely.

Another institution is the exclusive club frequented by businessmen and professionals which exists in all Canadian cities and is modelled directly on the clubs of London's West End; many of them still, like their English counterparts, exclude women and some have only recently abandoned policies of racial exclusion. These are inherited from a transformed English class system now based less on descent than on fortune. The PRIVATE SCHOOL, of which UPPER CANADA COLLEGE is the best example, is based on the English public school. The English maintain private schools in Canada not to preserve their culture but to maintain, in a changed form, their traditional class system.

English Camp at San Juan, Vancouver I, BC, 1860. Though many of the English came to Canada as officials, those who came for economic motives made up a significant proportion of the Canadian population, particularly in BC and the Maritimes (*courtesy Provincial Archives of British Columbia/HP 12720*).

The Anglican Church, formerly the Church of England in Canada, is perhaps the largest of the distinctively English institutions, transplanted almost unchanged from the homeland (*see* ANGLICANISM). About 50% of Canadians of English descent adhere to it; the rest belong to the United Church and some smaller Protestant sects, with a relatively small minority being Roman Catholics.

The RCMP, founded as the North-West Mounted Police, was originally modelled closely on British light cavalry units. Institutions such as the RED CROSS, the Boy SCOUTS and the GIRL GUIDES were also brought from England.

Finally, English workingmen brought to Canada their own traditions of trade unions and social democracy. Canadian labour unions as they exist today are a hybrid of American and English forms, but their militancy is Anglo-Scottish in character. Politically, Canada is distinct in N America because, unlike the US, it has a viable party (the NEW DEMOCRATIC PARTY, previously the CO-OPERATIVE COMMONWEALTH FEDERATION) dedicated to democratic socialism, which was founded and built mainly by English, Welsh and Scots reared in the traditions of the British Independent Labour Party and later of the Labour Party. To this day the NDP operates more like an Anglo-Scottish party than an American one, and its structure – of constituency branches combined with labour unions – reflects that of the Labour Party in Britain.

English cultural activities have permeated Canada, largely through the dominance of the English language outside Québec and NW New Brunswick. This is true especially in literature. The influence of English traditions and English models has inevitably been profound, and it is only within the present generation that a distinctive English Canadian literature has really emerged. Yet there has never been a distinctive literature of Englishmen writing to preserve or portray English culture in Canada, as there has been one of, for example, Icelanders writing to preserve an Icelandic culture. Again, the English person's sense of being part of the dominant culture precludes particularism; immigrant writers from England have quickly found their places in the Canadian setting and in helping to form a Canadian literature an English tradition has been freely modified to its N American milieu.

GEORGE WOODCOCK

English Language Although English was used in Canada before the 19th century, there were neither enough speakers nor enough significant features in the language for it to be regarded as anything other than British English. However, between 1825 and 1846 more than half a million immigrants came to Canada directly from Britain, and by 1871 over 2 million people in Canada listed the British Isles as their land of origin. These new Canadians brought with them the kind of English that they had learned from their parents, and it bore little similarity to what is now often called Standard British English, or simply Standard English. Since the 14th century the regional dialect used in London, the centre of British government, and in nearby Oxford and Cambridge universities, had become associated with British educated and upper-class speakers. However, very few people spoke it. It was not until 1880 that education became compulsory in England; and it is unlikely that most British immigrants to Canada in the early 19th century had received much schooling or had had any opportunity to acquire a form of British English associated with educated or upper-class people. Those who were educated often objected to the English they heard in Canada, as did Susanna MOODIE in *Roughing It in the Bush* (1852) and Rev A.C. Geikie in the *Canadian Journal* (1857). The kind of English introduced to Canada in the early 19th century was by no means standard. It was spoken English, often typical of the region from which the speakers came, such as Ireland, Yorkshire or Devon.

When people move to a new land isolated from their homeland, two things happen to their language: first, it escapes the direct influences of changes in grammar or pronunciation that take place in the parent language; and second, it undergoes great changes in vocabulary in order to allow its users to accommodate their speech to their new circumstances. In Canada one rarely hears, for example, "clerk" pronounced to rhyme with "dark." Acceptable late-18th-century British pronunciation rhymed "clerk" with "lurk," "caught" with "cot," and "aunt" with "ant," and those pronunciations are the ones immigrants brought with them. In some instances, more than one pronunciation of a word came to Canada. This is true of the common ways of saying "schedule": one with an initial *sk* sound and one with *sh*, both acceptable in British English until the mid-19th century. The former pronunciation has been reinforced in Canada by American influence; but it did not, in fact, reach Canada from the US: the source for both countries was pre-19th-century British English. Similarly, although the pronunciation of "new" to rhyme with "do" rather than with "few," as in British English, is often regarded as due to American influence in Canada, this is not the case. Until the late 19th century both pronunciations were current in British English, and immigrants brought both with them.

Grammatical differences between British and Canadian English are very few, since the major changes that were to affect the grammatical structure of English had taken place in Britain well before the periods of heavy immigration to Canada. The grammatical differences that exist are minor ones, concerning choices in the use of prepositions and verbs, which late 18th-century British English had not yet decided. Both "dived" and "dove" are heard as the past tense of "dive" in Canada, but the latter no longer has currency in British English. Two verbs heard occasionally in every Canadian province date from the Old English period (approximately 6th-12th centuries AD): "snuck" and "clumb" for "sneaked" and "climbed." Since the 19th century both verbs have become parts of British regional dialects, but they are not dialect usage in Canada, although "snuck" is often regarded as a rather amusing past tense of "sneak." Of the three prepositions used after "sick" in "sick to," "sick at" and "sick in" the stomach, British English has largely dropped "to," which survives in Canada as majority usage. Standard British English no longer uses the phrasal prepositions "back of" and "in back of," but Canadian English preserves both. In 18th-century British English the omission of the infinitive ("to go" or "to come") in "wants out" and "wants in" was frequent, but it is now rarely heard except in Scotland; Canadian English preserves this feature.

It is in vocabulary that the English language in Canada has undergone the greatest change, largely because of the settlers' need for new words to describe new things. Vocabulary may be increased in predictable ways: words are borrowed from other languages; existing words are given new meanings; new compounds are created; people and places give their names to things with which they are associated. Canadian English has used all these ways. Borrowings from the Canadian Indians include *moose, muskeg, caribou* and *chipmunk;* and from the Inuit, *parka, mukluk, kayak, umiak* and *igloo.* From Inuit also comes *tupek,* the skin tent that is the Inuit equivalent of the Indians' *wigwam* or *tepee* (TIPI).

It was from French Canadians that the English and Scots fur traders learned to navigate the rivers of the new land. From the French Canadian VOYAGEUR the English learned about the problem of *rapids* (the turbulent sections of a river), and how to avoid them by lifting the canoe from the water and making a PORTAGE. Canadian Indians showed the travellers how to prepare PEMMICAN (meat prepared with fat), and how to make *watap* (the roots of trees used as thread in repairing damaged canoes). From the Canadian French, the British learned about the *travois,* an A-shaped frame devised by the Indians that allowed a dog or a horse to carry a heavy load by trailing the legs of the frame on the ground, with the load fastened low on the frame.

In addition to borrowing words, English the world over has always followed the practice of giving new meanings to existing words. Thus, in North America, "section" gained a new meaning during the settlement of the West: one square mile (640 acres, or 259 ha). With the Canadian movement towards representative government, the British word "riding," borrowed centuries ago from Scandinavian (meaning "a third"), and used to refer to administrative areas in English counties, came into general Canadian usage to refer to an electoral district. In the gold camps of the Cariboo, "hurdy gurdy," an old name for a barrel organ, was used to refer to dance hostesses because their music was provided by that instrument.

The English language in Canada has also followed the practice of the parent language of creating new compounds from existing words. Thus, "sour" and "dough" become "sourdough," a name for both a fermenting dough used as a starter in baking bread and the gold seekers who used such dough on their travels. From the French *la crosse* ("hooked stick") comes "lacrosse," the name used for the game that Algonquian Indians called *baggataway* ("playing ball"). To combat the lampreys in the Great Lakes, Canadian biologists developed a hybrid fish by crossing the speckled trout with the lake trout and named the hybrid "splake" by compounding elements of "speckled" and "lake."

Since the Renaissance, English has drawn freely on Latin and Greek to create new words, especially in medicine. That tradition was followed in Canada when the drug developed to control diabetes was named *insulin* (Lat *insula,* "island"). "Kerosene" was coined from Gk *keros* ("wax") by Dr Abraham GESNER, a 19th-century scientist in the Maritimes who developed a process for extracting "coal oil."

The British named *sherry* after its place of origin (Xeres, or Jerez, Sp) and called policemen *bobbies* after Robert (Bobby) Peel. A similar naming practice has occasionally been used in Canada. The *malpeque oyster* carries the name of the bay in Prince Edward Island where it originates. The *malemute,* a dog made popular by Robert SERVICE, is named after the Inuit people of that name who first bred it. A BOMBARDIER in Canada is not a soldier but a tracked snow vehicle, developed by Armand Bombardier of Valcourt, Qué. From Digby, NS, comes the *Digby chicken,* a variety of smoked herring; and from Labrador comes the *Labrador* dog.

Until the end of the 14th century, Standard English was no more standard than any other regional dialect of British English, but from that time until the mid-20th century it was held as the ideal to which speakers of regional dialects should aspire. Canadian English, on the other hand, has never elevated any one form of regional speech to a position of prestige. The federal government is in Ottawa; but Ottawa English is not held up as a model of the best speech. However, a form of Canadian English, the language stripped of its regional features, is used by English-speaking Canadians across the country. Although Canadian English does not have the regional dialects of British English, French or German that have developed over the centuries, it does have marked differences in speech among the various regions. Newfoundland is the most obvious example, with its undertones of Irish and the regional speech of southwestern England. What is often called the Ottawa Valley twang reminds one that thousands of Irish immigrants settled there in the 1840s. In general, local dialect boundaries in English-speaking Canada may be considered to be Newfoundland, the Maritimes, eastern Ontario, western Ontario, the Prairies and British Columbia (the most "British" region in Canada).

M.H. SCARGILL

Reading: J.K. Chambers, ed, *Canadian English* (1975); R.E. McConnell, *Our Own Voice* (1979); M.M. Orkin, *Speaking Canadian English* (1970); M.H. Scargill, *A Short History of Canadian English* (1977).

Ense, Donald Orion Henry, artist, illustrator, poet (b at Mindemoya, Manitoulin I, Ont 17 May 1953). An early member of the Manitoulin group of native painters, he found his theme in the teachings of the Anishabec (Ojibwa) and genre paintings of reserve life. His style reflects the 2-dimensionality of the pictographic native style plus some post-impressionistic influences; he paints in a simplified realistic manner with black form line and areas filled in flat colour. He has great narrative ability and is an excellent illustrator.

MARY E. SOUTHCOTT

Reading: Mary E. Southcott, *The Sound of the Drum: The Sacred Art of the Anishabec* (1984).

Entomology is the branch of zoology dealing with INSECTS, although which organisms are included is open to interpretation. Probably, those animals covered by the Gk word *entomon* ("cut up, segmented") are appropriately considered insects, ie, the arthropods, but CRUSTACEANS (except for a few terrestrial species) and a few small, marine arthropod groups, such as sea spiders and horseshoe crabs, are generally excluded. Entomologists study the following groups: Insecta; Myriapoda (eg, MILLIPEDES, CENTIPEDES); and Arachnida (eg, SCORPIONS, SPIDERS, MITES). Hence, entomology embraces the study of the majority of known species of organisms.

Entomology has made contributions to almost all life sciences, from ecology and taxonomy to genetics, nuclear biology and medicine. The science comprises many subdisciplines including, among its more theoretical aspects, insect morphology, taxonomy, ecology, ethology, physiology and biochemistry. Agricultural, forest, medical and veterinary entomology (aimed at pest and disease control) and related branches (eg, environmental and POLLINATION biology and quarantine services) are among its applied aspects. Ethnoentomology studies the role of insects in human culture.

In Canada, entomology began as an applied discipline. In 1856, the Bureau of Agriculture and Statistics for the Province of Canada offered prizes for essays on various pests of wheat. The winners were amateurs; in fact, many early contributions were made by amateurs, eg, H.H. CROFT, first president of the Entomological Society of Canada (est 1863), was professor of chemistry at King's College (University of Toronto). In 1884, James FLETCHER became the first honorary Dominion Entomologist. He was officially appointed Dominion Entomologist and Botanist in 1886 and was transferred, in 1887, to the newly created Dominion Experimental Farm, Ottawa. In 1914, the Division of Entomology, Experimental Farms

Branch, became a branch of the Dept of Agriculture – the Entomological Service, now part of the Biosystematics Research Centre.

Largely because of increased public awareness of the numbers of insects, the destruction that a small percentage of them do to crops and other products, and the distress caused by their transmission of diseases to humans and livestock, the demand for professional entomologists has increased enormously in the last 100 years. This demand, particularly in government, necessitated the establishment of university-level schools of entomology. In Canada independent university departments of entomology are found at U of Manitoba, at U of Alberta and at Macdonald College, McGill, which until the end of the 1950s was responsible for training half of Canada's professional entomologists. The department of environmental biology, U of Guelph, successor to what was virtually a fourth independent department, also remains predominantly entomologically oriented. Several other Canadian universities have departments of zoology or biology, with strong entomological leanings (and often traditions), offering excellent education and research facilities. These include the following universities: British Columbia, Simon Fraser, Saskatchewan, Toronto, McMaster, Carleton, Montréal, Laval, New Brunswick and Memorial. Some entomological research is carried on at most other Canadian universities. Most professional entomologists are employed by the federal government in the departments of Agriculture and Environment (especially the Forestry Service of Environment Canada). Both have research laboratories and advisory services across the country. Provincial governments employ entomologists in similar capacities, and the larger municipalities engage a few. Various industries have staff entomologists and, of course, universities and museums hire some. Entomologists may also become schoolteachers or may work with private firms undertaking environmental studies. Many are associated with government and international organizations and with exchange programs that deal with entomological or other problems.

The principal entomological collections in Canada are those at Agriculture Canada, Ottawa (Canadian National Insect Collection); McGill (Macdonald Campus, Lyman Entomological Museum and Research Laboratory); U of T (Royal Ontario Museum); and those associated with departments of entomology at the universities of Alta and Man, and the department of zoology, UBC. The first 3 are of international importance. Insect collections are also held in provincial museums, notably at Halifax and Victoria. Canadian entomological societies are the Entomological Soc of Canada (the oldest national Canadian scientific society) which since 1868 has published its journal, *The Canadian Entomologist*; the Acadian Entomological Soc (serving the Atlantic Provinces and northern New England); La Société entomologique du Québec; entomological societies of Ont, Man, Sask, Alta and BC; and a few amateur, local societies. La Société de protection des plantes du Québec is largely oriented to entomology, and Canadian Soc of Zoologists has a very large entomological contingent. D.K. McEwan Kevan

Environment, the physical, social and psychological milieu in which we exist, which affects us and is in turn affected by us. Throughout its 4-billion-year history, profound changes have occurred in the geological and ecological systems of planet Earth. As long as human populations remained small and communities were part of local ecosystems, most changes took place slowly and seemingly without major disturbances in the global system. Mass extinctions and major disturbances did take place as results of climate changes or catastrophic events such as earthquakes, volcanic eruptions, floods, etc. However, the geometric increase in the human population and the extensive industrialization of the last 200 years have placed stresses on the complex processes that maintain the stability of the biosphere (the relatively thin but highly complex layer on and above the surface of the planet, consisting of the atmosphere, water, minerals and organisms). Disturbances in one part of the biosphere do not necessarily remain localized but can affect its composition and stability elsewhere (*see* BIOGEOGRAPHY). Thus the burning of fossil fuels in the Northern Hemisphere has increased the carbon-dioxide content of the air over the South Pole. Sulphur compounds produced by industrial activity in the UK and continental Europe have caused a marked decline in the biological productivity of lakes in Sweden; while deleterious changes in lakes in Ontario are attributable to pollutants from the US and from Ontario itself (*see* ACID RAIN).

The growth of ENVIRONMENTAL AND CONSERVATION MOVEMENTS originated in the 19th century in the initiatives of private individuals and groups largely concerned with the despoliation of their immediate surroundings. Increasing knowledge and sophistication in analysis has broadened this largely middle-class preoccupation with the more visible aspects of POLLUTION to include concerns about sustained economic development resource shortages, impacts on human mental and physical health (eg, contamination of food, indoor AIR POLLUTION), aesthetics and appropriate land-use policies. In the 1950s, an early worker in the area of creating systems for assessing the degree of environmental degradation was the Canadian environmentalist Pierre DANSEREAU. He created a model of the ecosystem, the "Ball of Arrows," which attempted to show the intricate web of relationships among its living and nonliving components.

A rational conservation strategy requires adequate knowledge of processes governing interactions within and among highly complex ecosystems; a knowledge of the sources of damage (types and nature of pollutants), changes in habitats and of the technology available for counteracting their effects; promotion of economic policies which accept that development and conservation programs should be linked and that "diseconomies" which reduce the quality of the environment should be minimized; and development of legal and administrative structures which designate standards and ensure their maintenance. Canadian zoologist and systems analyst C.S. Holling and his co-workers have used computer models to deal with these complex issues.

Global Perspectives

Environmental problems require international co-operation because many of them cross international boundaries; the benefits of work done must be maximized by sharing experiences to avoid duplication of effort (particularly in developing countries); and the establishment of "pollution havens" must be prevented.

Over the last 2 decades, considerable progress has been made towards achieving a global strategy for the maintenance of the health of the biosphere. Concern for the environment received international recognition through the 1972 United Nations Conference on the Human Environment, held in Stockholm. The conference, under the chairmanship of Maurice STRONG, provided an international forum for discussion of global environmental problems by government and nongovernment personnel. A major result of the conference was establishment of the UN Environment Programme (UNEP), which now funds and co-ordinates many studies concerned with conservation. Governments are also linked through other specialist bodies of the UN (eg, Food and Agriculture Organization, World Health Organization and, especially, United Nations Educational, Scientific and Cultural Organization). Many of these programs are carried out co-operatively, facilitated by UNEP. UNESCO is responsible for environmental matters and promotes education programs about the processes operating in the biosphere. These programs involve governmental organizations and nongovernmental bodies, eg, the International Council of Scientific Unions (ICSU) and the International Union for the Conservation of Nature and Natural Resources (IUCN). UNESCO receives financial help from the World Bank and the UN Interim Fund for Science and Technology for Development. The following UNESCO programs are concerned with the environment.

Man and the Biosphere Programme (MAB) Planned in 1973-75, largely as a successor to the International Biological Programme (IBP, 1967-72), this program in 1983 involved 95 countries. Priority is now given to studies in the humid tropics, arid zones and urban systems. A network of biosphere reserves is being developed to promote conservation of important natural systems and to ensure preservation of genetic material. Over 260 reserves in 70 countries have already been named. More than 3000 sites have been surveyed in Canada. In 1987 there were 4 biosphere reserves designated in Canada: Waterton Lakes National Park (Alta), Riding Mountain National Park (Man), Long Point National Wildlife Area (Ont), and Mont-Saint-Hilaire (Qué). An additional site was under consideration.

International Geological Correlation Programme (IGCP) was concerned with developing knowledge of the processes governing the evolution of the Earth's crust, with special emphasis on the rational use of MINERAL and ENERGY resources.

International Hydrological Programme (IHP) The first 6-year phase has been completed and a second phase is underway. The major aim is to advance understanding of hydrologic processes and their interactions with human activities (*see* HYDROLOGY). The World Meteorological Organization is closely associated with many parts of this program (*see* METEOROLOGY).

The World Commission on Environment and Development Called the Brundtland Commission after its chairman, Dr Gro Harlem Brundtland, PM of Norway, it was formed in 1984 by the UN General Assembly to take a fresh look at environment and development and to propose concrete and practical actions that promote needed economic development without compromising environmental quality. Among 22 environmental, political and economic experts from 21 countries were 2 Canadians, Maurice Strong and James MacNeill. The commission's work was based on the increasingly recognized fact that short-term economic gains that cause environmental damage generally impose serious economic problems in the longer term. The commission held hearings in Canada in 1986. Its report, issued in Apr 1987, stressed the serious threat to the environment posed by humanity and reasserted the fact that environmental protection is not at odds with economic development.

The publication in March 1980 of the World Conservation Strategy was a major step towards the development of a unified approach to conservation of the biosphere. The document, prepared by IUCN, commissioned by UNEP and financially supported by the World Wildlife Fund, represents a compromise statement of conservation priori-

Pond ecosystem. A national conservation strategy requires knowledge of the processes governing interaction within and between highly complex ecosystems (*artwork by Claire Tremblay*).

ties among organizations with very different viewpoints. It aims to stimulate a global approach to the management of living resources and provide guidelines to the policymakers and their advisers, and to conservationists and development agencies. Government acceptance and implementation of the strategy would ensure maintenance of essential ecological processes and life-support systems; of genetic diversity in important animals, plants and micro-organisms; and of renewable resources (species and ecosystems) at levels which will permit their use and guarantee their continued existence. In 1986 Canada was host to an international conference of 110 nations. Environment Canada reported on national efforts to meet 3 of the WCS objectives: the maintenance of essential ecological objectives and life-support systems; the preservation of genetic diversity; and the sustainable utilization of species and ecosystems. The federal government, at least 6 provinces and the 2 territories have started development of conservation strategies.

Canadian Scene

The increasing power of the TECHNOLOGY available for manipulation of the environment and its resources has produced in Canada a complete turnaround in attitudes towards the natural environment. In Canada's early development the wilderness was considered something to be fought, although it provided apparently unlimited resources. Exploited at a small-to-modest scale, those resources provided wealth without severe repercussions other than the extermination of several wildlife species (eg, passenger pigeon, Plains grizzly). Increasingly powerful and large-scale technologies started to overwhelm parts of the environment to the point where the resource base and human well-being were sometimes threatened. Under these circumstances, wilderness is now perceived as a valuable and dwindling resource to be respected and protected.

In this respect, the Federal Environmental Assessment Review Office (FEARO) was formed in 1973 to report to the minister of environment. Since then reviews have been carried out on the biophysical and social impacts at 34 major projects. The review process included public hearings to provide opportunities for the public to express its concerns. In addition, in keeping with the ongoing concern about environmental quality in Canada, fines for infractions of environmental regulations have been sharply increased and jail sentences have been imposed. Environment Canada has produced the first state of the environment report.

The actors in the environment drama can be divided into 4 overlapping groups: the general public and special-interest groups, industry, governments and academia. Public interest in and concerns about environmental issues have been increasing since the late 1960s, but have not yet been translated into action. The special-interest groups have been largely responsible for raising and maintaining public interest. Most environmental organizations have become increasingly knowledgeable and skilled, and now depend less on vociferous protest and more on quiet discussion and hard work. A small minority has come to advocate violence in pursuit of its aims, eg, bombing power facilities in BC or threatening to ram sealing vessels on the East Coast. Industrial representatives who still maintain that environmental protection infringes on free enterprise and is too expensive have become a small minority. Legal requirements, the importance of public image and the discovery that environmentally acceptable planning and operations can be cost-effective have caused industry, with exceptions, to become increasingly inclined to incorporate sound environmental planning into its developments.

In the early 1970s the federal and all provincial governments passed legislation regarding environmental issues (*see* ENVIRONMENTAL AGENCIES). In most jurisdictions, experience and increasing knowledge have led to amendments in the legislation and changes in its application (*see* ENVIRONMENTAL LAW). In education, courses, programs, textbooks and other resource materials have greatly improved. New environment units within universities have established credibility with their academic colleagues, and with industry and government. Consequently, graduates with greatly improved skills and knowledge can move quickly to resolve problems rather than having to learn on the job, as was often the case in the past. The most important remaining transition is in development of the will and ability to anticipate and avoid environmental problems rather than simply reacting to them as they arise. This development will be accomplished through monitoring and evaluating new and existing policies, projects and products. It will also be essential to move social and environmental concerns to the beginning of research and development, design and planning processes rather than having them tacked on at the end. DIXON THOMPSON

Reading: Pierre Dansereau, *Harmony and Disorder in the Canadian Environment* (1975).

Environmental Agencies In Canada environmental problems may require action by governments at 4 levels: international, national, provincial and municipal. At the international level, activities include protection of whales, control of ACID RAIN, and the work of the INTERNATION-

AL JOINT COMMISSION on water-quality questions. At the other 3 levels of government, powers and responsibilities are divided, but the divisions are frequently ambiguous and uncertain. A great deal of co-operation and co-ordination is required. With 3 levels of government, and with different departments at each level and sometimes numerous legislative requirements for each department or agency, industries seeking approval for projects face a maze of legislation which is costly and time consuming. At the federal and provincial levels, some governments are attempting to reduce costs without reducing standards by moving to a "single window" approval process in which one government agency would be responsible for co-ordinating all requirements for proposed projects.

In addition, legislation or responsibility for various environmental issues often rests in such other government departments as agriculture, culture, health, fish and wildlife, transportation, housing and municipal affairs and recreation, as well as other agencies and tribunals. Jurisdiction is frequently transferred from one agency to another, or may involve interdepartmental or intergovernmental agencies. *See also* ENVIRONMENTAL LAW. DIXON THOMPSON

Environmental and Conservation Movements Probably Canada's first conservationists were its native peoples, who had for centuries lived off the land with little apparent destruction. Such practices as clearing areas or driving game by lighting fires would have affected forests, but there is little evidence that such activities caused any long-term damage. Furthermore, Indian bands and Inuit family groups often moved their settlements to new areas for better HUNTING, allowing the regions left to grow back and repopulate with wildlife. Hence there was no need for concern about CONSERVATION problems before the first permanent European settlement in the 17th century. In Canada since that time, attitudes towards the conservation of nature and natural RESOURCES have developed in 5 overlapping but distinct periods.

The first period, from about the 1670s to 1860, has been called the "Tree Reserves Period." In this period the French and English tried to ensure a steady supply of ship timber. During the second, the "Land Reserves Period" (1860-1885), land was reserved by church and state for schools, universities and railways. Sales of land and land taxes were the only sources of wealth for governments. The first Canadian naturalist club was established in Ontario in this period (1863). A wide variety of parks, forest reserves, BIRD SANCTUARIES and wildlife preserves were created during the third period, the "Resource Reserve Period" (1880-present). Emphasis was placed on using wildlife wisely, rather than merely preserving or protecting it. During the fourth period, called the "Recreation Reserves Period" (1885-present), recreation facilities such as parks, historic sites and fish and game reserves were established, especially near urban areas. The "Nature and Wilderness Reserves Period" dates from about 1960, when Canadians began to see value in setting aside areas of wild country. Emphasis is less on resource use or recreation than on retaining areas where only the forces of nature are allowed to shape the environment.

The first Canadians to study the natural environment were probably the amateurs (doctors, diviners, etc) who began to catalogue the natural history of the country (eg, flora, fauna, rocks, fossils) and laid the bases of the sciences of biology, botany, geology, paleontology, entomology and zoology in Canada. The view they took of nature and the environment was shaped initially by European art and scientific traditions. European experiences of forestry and game preserves also had an effect. Writers such as Jean Jacques Rousseau, William Wordsworth and Lord Byron influenced Canadians, as did the writings of Grey Owl (A.S. BELANEY), an Englishman who settled in Canada. American thinkers had an even greater effect. These included the eminent ornithologist John James Audubon, who visited Canada in the 1830s, and the writers James Fenimore Cooper, Ralph Waldo Emerson and Henry David Thoreau. The American conservationists John Muir, the founder of the Sierra Club (1892), and Gifford Pinchot, who with President Theodore Roosevelt launched the American conservation movement in the early 1900s, were also significant.

Americans were generally ahead of Canadians in concern for the conservation of resources. This concern probably resulted from the more extensive settlement in the US, which demonstrated the harm that civilization could do. In Canada a pioneer mentality of "unlimited" forests, lakes and wildlife persisted longer. The development of national parks clearly illustrates the difference between early American and Canadian conservation action. The first N American national park was Yellowstone created in the US in 1872. From the beginning, such parks were intended to protect scenic attractions. In Canada the first national parks were established in the Rocky Mts (BANFF in 1885, YOHO and GLACIER in 1886), but their purpose was economic: to produce revenue from forest reserves and tourist travel. Parks were not conceived as wilderness preserves at this stage. In 1916 the US passed the National Park Service Act, which stated that parks were to be "unimpaired for the enjoyment of future generations." This wording was not used in the Canadian National Parks Act until 1930. In this respect, 1930 is a kind of turning point in Canadian conservation thought.

In the area of wildlife conservation, however, Canada did react to some emergency situations quite early. The first bird sanctuary was created in Saskatchewan in 1887. By 1889 the plains BISON had been reduced from about 60 million to less than 2000 animals. In 1907 and 1909 the government purchased about 700 bison and placed them in national parks. Between 1910 and 1920, 3 areas were set aside as reserves for ANTELOPE in Alberta and Saskatchewan; these were later abolished as unnecessary. In 1911 Canada formally established a parks branch; James HARKIN was appointed Dominion parks commissioner. Harkin, probably the first leading Canadian to argue for protection of wilderness for its own sake, was deeply influenced by the American conservation movement. Canada's first significant international conservation effort was a treaty with the US (1916) for the protection of migratory birds.

Until 1945 conservation in Canada focused on establishing national and provincial parks in remote areas. After WWII emphasis was on park expansion for recreational purposes. National and provincial park systems grew slowly during this period. The 1960s marked a different era for conservation and the environmental movement in Canada. Conservationist attitudes were no longer restricted primarily to naturalist groups. A growing number of Canadians became concerned not only about using resources wisely but also about the effects of human activity on the environment. During the 1960s, concern about POLLUTION became a major public issue. Specialized groups such as the Society for the Promotion of Environmental Conservation (in the West), Pollution Probe (in the East) and the Ecology Action Centre (in the Maritimes) were born. Such groups were led by scientists such as Donald CHANT, who was deeply concerned about issues such as AIR POLLUTION and WATER POLLUTION, HAZARDOUS WASTES and the careless use of PESTICIDES (documented by American conservationist Rachel Carson in her 1962 book *Silent Spring)*. Preservation of the natural environment had come to be seen as more than a question of recreation or preserving scenic beauty, but as being important to human survival.

The nature conservation movement received a boost from the environmental interest of the 1960s. The National and Provincial Parks Association of Canada was established in 1963, the Sierra Club in Canada in 1970 and, in 1971, the Canadian Audubon Society and several of its affiliates established the Canadian Nature Federation, a national assembly of naturalist groups from across the country. Scientific biological associations and groups traditionally less active in conservation issues, such as game and fish associations, also increased their emphasis on environmental issues.

During this period, the concern for nature conservation centered on preserving wilderness and protecting unique areas or ecosystems as ecological reserves. Each province experienced a burst in the growth of local groups focusing on local conservation and environmental issues, and provincial naturalist and conservation federations became increasingly active and vocal. In a single decade, federal and provincial governments established ministries or departments of the environment, environmental protection Acts and environmental assessment legislation. Acts to protect endangered species, such as that passed in Ontario in 1971, were unique in the world because they sought to protect rare or endangered species of all plants and animals (including insects). In 1978 the intergovernmental Committee on the Status of Endangered Wildlife in Canada began to define a national list of species at risk.

In 1972 the United Nations convened in Stockholm an international Conference on the Human Environment. Canada was well represented and, as a result, Canadian conservation concern became increasingly international through participation in agencies such as the Convention on International Trade in Endangered Species and the International Union for the Conservation of Nature and Natural Resources. Environmental concerns are now seen in a global context as awareness grows that all people depend on clean air and water and healthy ecosystems. MONTE HUMMEL

Reading: J. Foster, *Working for Wildlife: The Beginning of Preservation in Canada* (1978); J.I. Nicol, *The National Parks Movement in Canada* (1969).

Environmental Law is a relatively new field of law comprising laws designed to protect the natural environment.

Constitutional Jurisdiction In Canada the power to pass laws relating to the environment is divided between federal and provincial governments. The Constitution gives the federal government power to pass laws relating to fisheries, shipping, interprovincial trade and commerce, and criminal law. The federal residuary power to pass general legislation for the "Peace, Order, and Good Government of Canada" might also justify environmental legislation. Federal legislation enacted under these powers includes the Oil Pollution Prevention Regulations (under the Canada Shipping Act), the Arctic Waters Pollution Prevention Act, the Canada Water Act, the Clean Air Act, the Environmental Contaminants Act, the Fisheries Act and the Transportation of Dangerous Goods Act. In late 1987 Parliament was considering new legislation, Bill C-74 (the Canadian Environmental Protection Act), which would replace the Clean Air Act and the Environment Contaminants Act.

Provincial powers cover all matters of a local nature, and property and civil rights within the province. These powers give the provinces ample authority to pass most kinds of environmental laws. Provincial governments also "own" most natural resources. Provincial provisions for exploitation of these resources may include measures intended to protect the environment. Most provinces have now passed legislation concerning WATER POLLUTION and AIR POLLUTION. Provincial legislation also includes most WILDLIFE CONSERVATION AND MANAGEMENT regulations, the creation of ecological reserves and wilderness areas, and environmental controls in forestry and mining. Migratory bird regulations, however, are administered federally, in co-operation with the US and Mexico. Other wildlife regulations increasingly involve interprovincial arrangements.

The Common Law Historically, the law left private individuals to solve what are now considered pollution problems by negotiation or, if that failed, by suing one another in the COMMON LAW courts. Judges developed 2 key principles for dealing with these problems. The first TORT of significance to environmental law is the nuisance action, which dates back to the early common law, long before Confederation. Any landowner has the right to sue another who injures him by creating a "nuisance," defined as a use of land that causes physical injury to neighbouring land or substantially and unreasonably interferes with the use and enjoyment of neighbouring lands. The second kind of tort, a specialized form of the first, arises from the principle established in the leading case *Rylands* v *Fletcher,* decided by the British House of Lords in 1866. It holds that people who bring dangerous substances onto their land and allow them to escape are strictly liable for resulting damages. These 2 kinds of actions are still the key legal means by which private persons may bring POLLUTION problems before the courts.

However, these torts do not provide an effective means of pollution control. Air pollution in your neighbourhood might be caused by several factories. In order to sue one of them, you would be required to identify injuries that it caused and to prove that the specific factory caused them. Such proof would be very difficult to establish in most cases and the legal costs very high.

Since the late 1960s and early 1970s, Parliament and the provincial legislatures have passed numerous laws intended to protect the natural environment. One legal reference book, for example, contains 6 volumes devoted exclusively to federal and provincial legislation relating to the environment. It catalogues hundreds of separate statutes and regulations dealing with the environment (*see* ENVIRONMENTAL AGENCIES). Obviously, regulating environmental quality is complex.

Water-Pollution Control A key law in Canada pertaining to water pollution is the federal Fisheries Act, which prohibits discharge or deposition of substances harmful to fish if that discharge or deposition can contaminate waters where fish might be found. The term "fish" is used broadly to include all aquatic animals and including their immature stages. Steep penalties are provided ($50 000 for the first offence and $100 000 for any subsequent offence); each day on which the violation continues is considered a separate offence. Court decisions hold firms convicted in violation of this Act as strictly liable, ie, guilty regardless of intention. However, a firm will not be found guilty if it establishes "due diligence"; ie, that it took reasonable steps to avoid causing the pollution. These provisions play a leading role in Canadian environmental law because of vigorous enforcement by the Environmental Protection Service of the federal Dep of the Environment. The Fisheries Act also gives certain regulatory powers to the federal Cabinet, which may pass regulations establishing standards for certain industries. They have been established for the following industries: chlorine manufacturers, petroleum refineries, pulp and paper mills, metal-mining and -finishing plants, meat- and poultry-products plants and potato-processing plants.

Other federal laws also concern water pollution. The Canada Water Act was intended to establish a basic framework for federal and provincial co-operation on water quality management. Instead the federal government has relied on the Fisheries Act and the provinces have relied on their own laws. Informal co-operation between officials of both levels of government seems to work well; consequently the Canada Water Act has been little needed. The federal International Boundary Waters Treaty Act implements a treaty between the US and Canada (entered into by Great Britain on behalf of Canada). The treaty established the INTERNATIONAL JOINT COMMISSION, which is empowered to report on water quality issues referred to it by the 2 nations. The IJC has been instrumental in establishing water quality standards and cleanup programs in the Great Lakes Basin. Water quality in the Territories is regulated under the federal Northern Inland Waters Act. The Canada Shipping Act prohibits discharge of certain pollutants, notably oil, by ships operating in Canadian waters and includes elaborate safety standards (*see* HAZARDOUS WASTES). The Arctic Waters Pollution Prevention Act accomplishes the same objective for the Arctic. The Ocean Dumping Control Act regulates disposal of waste at sea.

All provinces have passed legislation regulating water pollution. Some follow an approach similar to the federal Fisheries Act. For example, Ontario prohibits discharge of contaminants that would impair water quality in the province. The minister responsible for the environment may order firms to clean up environmental pollution that they have caused. Some provinces, such as BC, use a licensing or permit approach to pollution control; ie, firms may not discharge any contaminants until they have received a permit from the appropriate agency. The firm must outline the system of pollution control that it intends to use. The permit sets limits to what the company may discharge, and usually specifies the kind of pollution-control equipment the company must use.

Air Pollution Control The federal government has elected to play a leading role in development of standards for air pollution. The key legislation is the Clean Air Act. One of its most important provisions allow the federal government to establish "ambient air quality objectives" or goals with respect to air pollution. The objectives specify "desirable" levels of concentration for most significant air contaminants. In themselves, these objectives have no legal effect, ie, it is not illegal to create pollution in excess of that allowed by the objectives. However, the federal objectives have been incorporated into most provincial schemes. When a company applies to provincial agencies for a permit to discharge contaminants to the air, most agencies check to ensure that federal objectives will not be exceeded.

Another important provision of the Clean Air Act allows the federal Cabinet to establish National Emission Standards specifying the maximum allowable quantities and concentrations of air contaminants from particular classes of stationary sources. This power is limited to situations where the emissions would constitute a significant danger to health or would violate the terms of an international treaty. Pursuant to this provision the government has issued National Emission Standards for the following industries: secondary lead smelters, asbestos mining and milling, chlor-alkali mercury processing plants, and vinyl-chloride and polyvinyl-chloride manufacturing. The proposed Canadian Environmental Protection Act would repeal the Clean Air Act, replacing these provisions with similar, but stronger provisions of its own. The standards issued under the Clean Air Act would probably be continued under the new Act.

Provincial air pollution control measures are similar to water pollution control schemes. A company planning to build a plant that will emit contaminants into the air must get a permit before beginning construction. Additional permits are required before the plant can begin operation. Air pollution standards or guidelines are set by provincial authorities, usually based on the federal objectives. Most provincial authorities also have the power to issue control orders to prevent significant air pollution.

Ecotoxicity and Impact Assessment Long-term ecotoxicity also presents governments with difficult problems. Over 100 000 chemicals are now in commercial use, with hundreds of new chemicals each year. Most have never been tested, and we know little about them, but inevitably they end up in the environment. Many are both toxic and persistent (ie, do not break down quickly) and build up in food chains. The challenge for government is to detect and regulate dangerous chemicals before they become a problem.

PESTICIDES and herbicides are regulated federally under the Pest Control Products Act. Basically, the Act imposes control over the manufacturing, importing, labelling and distribution of these products. Other toxic substances are regulated under the federal Environmental Contaminants Act, which allows the government to designate substances that are likely to pose a significant danger to the environment. The government may prohibit anyone from releasing these chemicals into the environment. In addition, the Act establishes a kind of early-warning system with respect to new chemical compounds. It requires anyone who manufactures or imports more than 500 kg of a chemical compound to report this to the minister of the environment. The report is made only once, when the chemical is first manufactured or imported, but it informs government of the new chemical and thus allows government to consider whether it should be regulated.

The proposed Canadian Environmental Protection Act would repeal the Environmental Contaminants Act, replacing the provisions with similar, but stronger provisions of its own. It would, for example, allow the ministers of the environment and national health and welfare temporarily to permit, or to prohibit, the manufacture or import of new substances. It would also require the ministers to assess the information on new substances within a reasonable time.

Environmental impact assessment is another tool that government uses to prevent or reduce environmental problems. An environmental impact assessment is usually required when a company plans to build a new mine, dam or other facility that is likely to have significant impact on the environment. The legal source of this requirement varies. Some provinces have statutes providing for environmental impact assessments. The federal Parliament has not passed a law requiring such assessments, but a Cabinet order requires assessments before approval can be given to projects under federal regulatory control.

Environmental law has made great strides, but many challenges remain. ACID RAIN, ecotoxicity and the transportation and disposal of hazardous wastes are among the unsolved problems. The development of offshore resources and the North will require new legal approaches. A number of aspects of private ownership versus public access to major developments need to be clarified. Few areas of the law are completely static; however, environmental law will probably continue to change with unusual rapidity as governments try new solutions to environmental problems created by development and new technologies. It will continue to offer a challenge for judges, lawmakers and lawyers. ROBERT T. FRANSON

Reading: L.F. Duncan, ed, *Environmental Enforcement* (1985); Robert T. Franson and A.R. Lucas, eds, *Canadian Environmental Law* (1976); Law Reform Commission of Canada, *Crimes Against the Environment* (1985); A.R. Thompson, *Environmental Regulation in Canada* (1980).

Epidemic The application of the principles of hygiene in recent decades has virtually eliminated epidemic outbreaks of the most deadly of the contagious diseases. Canada, at least until the last century, had no overcrowded cities and all the benefits of alternating hot and cold seasons, but it did not manage to escape the devastation of epidemic outbreaks. Two main reasons explain this fact. The overcrowded, unhealthy ships which linked America to Europe favoured the development of contagious diseases such as SMALLPOX, TYPHUS, CHOLERA and INFLUENZA among their passengers. Ignorance of the causes of these diseases and how they were transmitted helped spread them into port cities. The outbreak of an epidemic almost always coincided with the arrival of a vessel full of sick passengers. The second factor had to do with the native population. Since they had had no contact with the germs of these diseases, they had no natural defences against them and so formed an ideal reservoir for the multiplication of the responsible bacteria or virus.

By the end of the 18th century inoculation against smallpox (the introduction beneath the skin of smallpox pus) had become a popular preventive method in Europe. Soon after, vaccination – more effective and less dangerous – appeared in N America. Epidemics of smallpox continued to affect the population, however, and Montréal was particularly hard hit. The epidemic of 1885 was especially dramatic; its scale persuaded municipal authorities to make vaccination obligatory but medical opinion divided into pro- and anti-vaccination camps, with the latter accusing the former of spreading the disease. The population, terrified, refused to be vaccinated. On 18 Sept 1885 a riot broke out in the city. People tore down the pro-vaccination posters and ransacked the home of the official medical vaccinater, the city hall, pharmacies and the homes of municipal magistrates. The extent of the catastrophe (it took 3164 lives, 2117 of them children) finally sobered Montréalers into more reasonable behaviour and they obeyed the sanitary authorities and the clergy.

Typhus first reached Canada in 1659, but the episode of 1746 was notable for its severity. France had sent a large flotilla of warships to Canada to retake Port-Royal in Acadia. Of the 3150 soldiers aboard, 1270 died at sea and another 1130 in Bedford Basin where they were supposed to rendezvous with an army coming from Québec. The disease hit the Micmacs of the region and more than one-third died. 1847 was "the year of the typhus," when 9293 British immigrants died during the Atlantic crossing. Another 10 037 died at GROSSE-ÎLE, the quarantine station in the St Lawrence R below Québec, or in the hospitals of Québec, Montréal, Kingston and Toronto. Monuments at CAP DES ROSIERS on the Gaspé coast commemorate those who died at sea.

The Canadian government feared the introduction of cholera by European immigrants, especially in 1831 when Asian cholera devastated Europe. New regulations forbade the local population to visits ships in port. A sanitation committee was set up early in 1832, quarantine laws were strengthened and Grosse Île was placed under military command. One ship was permitted to leave the quarantine station, however, and was responsible for the cholera epidemic in 1832 which was responsible for the deaths of some 6000 people. Barely 2 years later the disease struck again and sporadic outbreaks occurred throughout the century.

Influenza mortality was usually low, but some epidemics of it occurred during outbreaks of typhus or other diseases. Since the post-WWI outbreak of Spanish Influenza, scientific discoveries have rendered infectious diseases less deadly. Recent influenza epidemics, for example, have caused much sickness but few deaths.

Epidemics of other diseases included yellow fever, leprosy and tuberculosis. In 1710, the germs of a disease as yet unknown in Canada, at the time called "the Siamese disease" and today known as yellow fever, arrived in the port of Québec from the West Indies. The vector insect is *Stegomya fasciata*. This mosquito found the heat and humidity on board ship ideal for its reproduction and infected the vulnerable passengers with the dangerous virus. The sick sailors were taken to HÔTEL-DIEU in Québec where they died – as did 6 nurses and 12 priests. The epidemic must have claimed many victims, but the exact number is unknown. Once winter came, the insect and its disease both disappeared. There do not seem to have been any other such epidemics in Canada, even if a few sporadic cases occurred in the country's port cities. The Canadian government has on occasion declared quarantine against American ports where the disease is raging.

In 1773 a mysterious disease appeared in the Baie Saint-Paul area which spread through neighbouring parishes and finally reached the Montréal region. It was marked by buccal ulcers, pain in the limbs and finally the destruction of the bones of the nose, the palate, the gums and the appearance of swellings on the head, the clavicles and the bones of the limbs. Men, women and children were all afflicted. After some hesitation and discussion, medical opinion decided that this malady, known as the Baie Saint-Paul Disease, was of syphilitic origins.

There were a few cases of leprosy in Canada in the 19th century, even if the cases cannot be called an epidemic. In 1815 the disease was brought to the Tracadie region of NB by 2 Norwegian sailors. Cases multiplied and the authorities built a leprosarium which was run by the sisters of Hôtel-Dieu in Montréal and, from 1815-1924, received 319 lepers. Some cases of leprosy were also observed in Cape Breton, Manitoba and PEI. In 1882, in New Westminster, BC, the compatriots of a Chinese leper hanged him in the hope of choking off the infection. After other lepers were discovered in the province, a leprosarium was opened at D'Arcy Island in 1907. There has been an increase in leprosy in Canada in recent years, almost all of its victims being recent immigrants, usually from the Orient or the West Indies.

Because of the insidious beginnings of a tubercular attack and the chronic nature of its evolution, tuberculosis cannot be defined as an epidemic. However tuberculosis, that universal social scourge, existed in endemic state in the Canadian population during the 19th century and early 20th century. Poor hygiene, urban overcrowding and malnutrition all encouraged the outbreak and spread of the illness. Thanks to better living conditions and the discovery of antibiotics, TB has been contained and is now quite rare. Unfortunately it persists in endemic form among certain disadvantaged populations such as Canada's native peoples.

Epidemics have had a great impact on society, preoccupying whole communities and making severe demands on the abilities of individuals and their societies to cope with the crisis. Epidemics also spur the development of control and prophylactic measures. MARCEL CADOTTE

Epp, Arthur Jacob, "Jake," politician (b at St Boniface, Man 1 Sept 1939). The son of a Mennonite preacher, Epp graduated from U of Man in 1961 and then taught high school for 11 years in Steinbach, Man, where he was a town councillor 1970-71. Elected to the House of Commons for Provencher in 1972, he was minister of Indian affairs and northern development in the CLARK government 1979-80. Epp was Clark's most trusted parliamentary ally in the leadership battles that followed the election defeat of 1980, and he was prominent in opposing the TRUDEAU government's plan to patriate the constitution unilaterally. PM Brian MULRONEY named Epp minister of health and welfare and chairman of the Cabinet committee on social development in 1984. In the Mulroney government from 1984, Epp was an effective and respected minister involved in issues such as child care and the government's campaign against smoking. NORMAN HILLMER

Equal Rights Association for the Province of Ontario (ERA) est June 1889 in Toronto, was formed in response to Québec's JESUITS' ESTATES ACT. The ERA criticized Catholic interference in politics and what it saw as the subservience of politicians to the Roman Catholic Church. At first it agitated for disallowance of the Estates Act, and later, at the behest of Tory MP D'Alton MCCARTHY, extended its attack to include Catholic separate schools and French-language schooling in the North-West Territories and Manitoba as well as Ontario. This extension, coming on the eve of the 1890 Ontario election, alienated many Liberals, including ERA president Rev William Caven. The ERA won only one seat in Ontario, but the movement forced both political parties to adopt parts of its program. Weakened by the election, the ERA was spent by the 1891 federal contest, although McCarthy's rhetoric contributed to the acrimony of the developing MANITOBA SCHOOLS QUESTION. Some members later supported the PROTESTANT PROTECTIVE ASSOCIATION. J.R. MILLER

Equalization Payments are payments that the federal government makes to the poorer provinces. The monies come from Ottawa's general revenues and are unconditional transfers that can be spent as the recipient provinces please (*see also* TRANSFER PAYMENT). Their purpose is to reduce the horizontal imbalance among the provinces.

In general, 2 kinds of fiscal imbalance can arise in a federation – vertical and horizontal. The former is an imbalance between the 2 levels of government, federal and provincial, eg, when the responsibilities of the provinces are disproportionately large compared with their share of revenues. Such an imbalance can be remedied by a transfer of responsibilities to the federal government (eg, family allowances and UNEMPLOYMENT INSURANCE) or by a transfer of revenues from Ottawa to the provinces. By contrast, horizontal imbalance is a fiscal imbalance among the provinces themselves – the fact that some provinces have more sources of revenue and are therefore richer than other provinces. Equalization payments can help adjust these horizontal imbalances. The Constitution Act, 1982, states "Parliament and the Government of Canada are committed to the principle of making equalization payments to ensure that provincial governments have sufficient revenues to provide reasonably comparable levels of public services and reasonably comparable levels of taxation."

The concept of equalization can be traced to the statutory subsidies in the CONSTITUTION ACT, 1867, and more recently to the National Adjustment Grants recommended by the Royal Commission on DOMINION-PROVINCIAL RELATIONS as part of an overall reorganization of federal-provincial financial arrangements (*see also* INTERGOVERNMENTAL FINANCE; FEDERAL-PROVINCIAL RELATIONS). The first formal equalization program was introduced in 1957. The transfers were designed to ensure that per-capita revenues of all provinces from shared taxes (*see* TAXATION) – personal income taxes, corporate income taxes and succession duties – matched those of the wealthiest provinces, at that time BC and Ontario.

In the first of the required 5-year revisions, the level up to which these transfers were equalized became the all-province average, rather than matching the wealthiest 2 provinces. As compensation, the recipient provinces were also guaranteed revenues equal to 50% of the all-province per-capita average of resource revenues. Throughout this time equalization payments rose, largely because the federal government transferred increasing proportions of the personal income tax to the provinces; from 10% in 1957 to 24% by 1967.

The comprehensive nature of the current equalization program dates from 1967. In effect, most of the categories of revenues collected by the provinces were equalized to the national average level. With one major exception (energy) and with some modifications, eg, increasing the number of revenue sources included, the system remained unchanged until 1982. Canada's equalization program became the most comprehensive and most generous in the world.

However, problems began to develop in 1973 with the increase in world energy prices. Maintaining full equalization of energy revenues and increasing domestic energy prices would have meant a tripling of total equalization flows and the inclusion of Ontario as a recipient province. Temporary steps were adopted in 1973-74 to reduce the impact of energy on the system and in the 1977 revision only 50% of resource revenues was eligible for equalization. In spite of this modification, Ontario still qualified for equalization payments over the 1977-82 period and was retroactively excluded from receiving payments by what has come to be known as the "personal income override," ie, essentially, no province whose per capita income exceeds the national-average level is eligible for equalization.

In the 1982 version of the program, provinces are eligible to receive sufficient equalization to raise their revenues from all provincial and local revenue sources to a level that is calculated by applying national average tax rates to the average per capita tax bases of 5 designated provinces (Ontario, Québec, Saskatchewan, Manitoba and BC). As a result, Ontario will no longer qualify for payments and energy revenues will have less impact on equalization flows, chiefly because Alberta is not one of the 5 provinces.

The scheduled 1987 revision of the equalization formula has effectively been postponed for a year or two. Part of this relates to the proposed tax reform measures. Since taxation will shift from income toward consumption, this may require significant alterations in the formula. Moreover, the proposed federal day-care program contains shared-cost measures that cover 90% of costs for Newfoundland and only 50% of Ontario. This represents a major departure in that we are now embarked on expenditure-side equalization, which in turn may influence the negotiations on the revenue-equalization formula.

Finally, the 1985 Atlantic Accord on energy (with Newfoundland and Labrador) and the 1986 Canada-Nova Scotia Offshore Petroleum Resource Accord gives these 2 provinces a sort of special status with respect to equalization. Carried to the extreme, this would move equalization away from a formula-based system and toward a bilateral approach. Thus, the forthcoming negotiations might constitute a watershed in the evolution of equalization payments. T.J. COURCHENE

Equestrian Sports Today's major equestrian sports have developed principally from the 17th- and 18th-century activities of academic horsemanship, the fox hunt and the steeplechase, although the use of horses in competitions dates back at least to the ancient Olympic Games.

The first modern Olympic equestrian events, held in Paris in 1900, consisted of show jumping, the long jump and the high jump. Dressage and the 3-day event were included with show jumping in Stockholm in 1912. The 3-day event tests the all-round ability of horse and rider, and consists of dressage, endurance tests and show jumping, each on a separate day. These 3 disciplines have been an integral part of the summer Olympics since that time. Dressage (from the French term for the training of horses) consists of a series of movements of varying difficulty that test the harmonious development of the physique and ability of a horse. (Individual and team competitions at the Olympics feature the Grand Prix test, the most accomplished form of dressage.) In show jumping, horse and rider jump a set course of obstacles. Nation's Cups, which include the Olympics, are premier invitational international competitions for jumpers.

Women have long been active in equestrian competition, but were not admitted to the Olympics until 1952 in dressage, until 1956 in jumping and until 1964 in the 3-day event; equestrian sports is one of the few Olympic activities where women and men compete in the same events. They are also included in the Pan-American Games. The international governing body, Fédération equestre internationale (FEI), was founded in 1921.

Equestrian activities have been part of Canada's sporting scene since the early 1800s. The Montreal Fox Hunt was established in the late 1820s, and the first steeplechase race in British N America was held in Montréal in 1840. By 1873 women were active participants in hunts. A hunters' and jumpers' stake was part of a Toronto hunt meeting in 1875, and by the late 1880s competitions in hunting and jumping classes were included in the programs of agricultural fairs across Canada. The first Dominion equestrian championships took place in Toronto in 1895, with several events for both men and women. The Royal Agricultural Winter Fair, held in Toronto every Nov since 1922, signalled the emergence of the Royal Horse Show, Canada's premier international equestrian event.

Equestrian sport in Canada is controlled by the Canadian Equestrian Federation (CEF), formed in 1977 from the National Equestrian Federation of Canada (sport) and the Canadian Horse Council (industry). CEF membership includes all 10 provincial associations and many affiliated ones. Horse shows in Canada are licensed by the CEF; there are now more than 500 recognized shows. The Canadian Equestrian Team is a semiautonomous committee of the CEF, responsible for the selection and authorization to compete of Canada's international teams in dressage, show jumping and the 3-day event.

Canadian equestrians began making international appearances as early as 1909, when a team of jumpers entered the Military Tournament in the International Horse Show at Olympia, London. Canadian Army teams continued to compete abroad after WWI; Maj R.S. Timmis became the first Canadian to win an international contest, at the Toronto Coliseum (1923).

In 1926, the first official Canadian jumping team entered the Royal Winter Fair and competed in Boston and London. The military monopoly of Canadian teams continued until the early 1950s, when reduced cavalry units and a broadened equestrian base resulted in an increase in civilian participants.

Canada's first Olympic equestrian team (3-day event, Helsinki, 1952) had a majority of civilian members. At the 1956 Olympic equestrian events, held in Stockholm, the Canadian 3-day team captured the bronze medal. Canadian 3-day eventers have also performed well at the Pan-American Games, winning the team gold and individual bronze medals (Norman Elder) in 1959; the individual silver (Elder) in 1967; the team gold and individual silver (Clint Banbury) in 1971; and the team silver in 1975. The 1978 world championship 3-day event was won by Canada in Lexington, Ky.

International competition in dressage has attracted Canadians since the early 1950s. Christilot Hanson (now Boylen) earned the distinction of membership on 4 consecutive Olympic teams. In 1972, she became the first Canadian to place in the top 12 international individual dressage riders, when she was 9th in the Olympics; in 1976, she was 7th. In Pan-American Games competition, she won gold medals in 1971 and 1975. In team dressage, Hanson, Cynthia Neale and Zoltan Sztehlo won the gold medal at the 1971 Pan-American Games; in 1975, Hanson-Boylen teamed with Barbara Stracey and Lorraine Stubbs to place 2nd at the Games; and the Canadian

Equalization and Provincial Revenues

	Nfld	*PEI*	*NS*	*NB*	*Qué*	*Ont*	*Man*	*Sask*	*Alta*	*BC*	*Total*
1981-82[a]											
Equalization ($ million)	427	103	509	414	2 320	*	387	–	–	–	4 162
Equalization ($ per capita)	750	840	600	596	361	*	376	–	–	–	176
Own source revenues (% of all-province revenue raising) [b] (Index)	59	55	66	66	78	94	79	112	217	111	100
Own source revenues plus equalization [b] (Index)	83	83	84	84	86	88	88	105	203	104	100
Own source revenues plus all transfers [b] (Index)	90	96	89	92	90	87	90	106	186	102	100
1987-88[c]											
Equalization ($ million)	754	156	681	699	2983	–	506	153	–	–	5931

Notes: Ontario is excluded by the personal income override. According to the formula, it would qualify as a recipient province for this year.

[a] Ontario Budget, 1982; [b] per capita; [c] Department of Finance Estimates.

team was 5th at the 1976 Montréal Olympics. In 1984, Hansen-Boylen finished 10th individually and the team placed 7th. At the 1986 world championships (held at Cedar Valley, Ont, the first time outside of Europe), Cynthia Ishoy [Neale] finished 7th individually and the team placed 5th.

Canadian equestrians have garnered their highest honours in show jumping. In 1953, Dorinda Fuller [Hall-Holland] won the first FEI international jumping class event held at the Royal Horse Show. In 1967, James DAY became the first Canadian to win an individual equestrian gold in the Pan-American Games and the jumping team placed 3rd. On the final day of the 1968 Mexico City Olympics, James Day, James ELDER and Thomas GAYFORD thrilled Canada by winning the team gold medal. This same team won the N American Grand Prix and Royal Horse Show events in 1969, and the World Championship at La Baule, France, in 1970. 1971 saw Canadian jumpers win the gold at the Pan-American Games (Terrance Millar, individual bronze), NY National Horse Show and Royal Horse Show. The 1972 Olympic team placed 6th; James Day was 4th in the individual event, losing the bronze by one-quarter of a time fault. Barbara Simpson Kerr placed 3rd in the Ladies World Show Jumping Championships in 1974, and the Canadian team won the Pan-American bronze medal in 1975. A highlight of the 1976 Olympics was Michel Vaillancourt's silver medal performance in individual jumping. With the equestrian boycott of the 1980 Moscow Olympics, the designated alternative competition was the Nation's Cup in Rotterdam, where the Canadians won the team gold medal. Canadians were also successful in the 1980 Washington International Horse Show pair relay test; the NY National Horse Show Cavcotte Challenge (1980) and speed class (1981); and the Nation's Cup in Sydney, Australia (1982). Mario Deslauriers won the jumping World Cup in Sweden in 1984. At Aachen, W Germany, in 1986, Gail GREENOUGH won the world show-jumping championship with a no-fault performance. At the Pan-Am Games in Aug 1987 show-jumper Ian Miller became the second Canadian to win an individual gold; Canada's 3-day team took the silver behind the US. An important development in Canadian show jumping was the construction, in 1975, of the show-jumping complex at Spruce Meadows, S of Calgary. The finest outdoor competition site in N America, it is ranked among the best in the world, and has brought a much-needed practice and competition facility to western Canada. Spruce Meadows' Masters, offering prize money of more than $600 000, is now the richest show-jumping event in the world. BARBARA SCHRODT

Erasmus, Georges, politician (b at Fort Rae, NWT 8 Aug 1948). Erasmus has been a central figure in NWT Indian territorial politics of the 1970s and 1980s (*see* NATIVE PEOPLE; LAND CLAIMS). After a period with the Company of Young Canadians he moved into native politics, becoming president of the DENE NATION (1976-83) and continuing thereafter as an active member of NWT and national native organizations such as the ASSEMBLY OF FIRST NATIONS. He became national chief of AFN in 1985 and was made a Member of the Order of Canada in 1987. BENNETT MCCARDLE

Erasmus, Peter, interpreter (b at Red River Colony [Man] 27 June 1833; d at Whitefish Lk, Alta 28 May 1931). Of Danish-Cree parentage, he studied to become an Anglican clergyman, but was drawn to the free life farther west. In 1855 he agreed to serve as interpreter for a Methodist missionary in the Ft Edmonton region and in 1858-59 he was interpreter and guide for the PALLISER EXPEDITION, working mainly with James HECTOR. Returning to the Methodists, he helped build a mission at Smoky Lk and then worked for 3 years with G.M. and J.C. MCDOUGALL. In 1865 he became a free trader, trapper and hunter around Whitefish Lk. Having acted as an interpreter for Treaty No 6 at Forts Carlton and Pitt in 1876, he was employed by the Indian Dept, off and on, for the rest of his life. A man of great influence, he encouraged the Saddle Lk Indians to remain loyal during the NORTH-WEST REBELLION of 1885. HUGH A. DEMPSEY

Eric the Red, Eirikr Thorvaldsson, explorer (*fl* 985). According to the *Saga of Eric the Red,* he spent 3 years of outlawry exploring the coast of Greenland and in 985 AD established 2 settlements there. Eric's son LEIF ERICSSON was likely the first European to set foot in N America. JAMES MARSH

Erickson, Arthur Charles, architect (b at Vancouver 14 June 1924). Erickson studied at UBC and McGill and completed his architectural training in 1950. Army service took him to Asia, and after graduation he travelled in Europe and the Middle East. In partnership with Geoffrey Massey he began private practice in Vancouver in 1953; their success in the design competition for SFU in 1963 brought them international attention. A series of major commissions followed, including theme buildings at EXPO 67 in Montréal; the MacMillan Bloedel office tower in Vancouver in 1969; the Canadian Pavilion, Expo 70, Osaka, Japan; U of Lethbridge, 1971; the Museum of Anthropology at UBC 1971-77; the provincial government offices and courthouse (and Vancouver Art Gallery) complex, begun in 1973; the Bank of Canada, Ottawa, 1980, in association with Marani, Rounthwaite & Dick; and Roy Thomson Hall, Toronto, 1982. Erickson has also received numerous commissions from Middle Eastern countries, S America and the US, where he was architect for the Canadian embassy in Washington (scheduled completion and opening, May 1988). Among many awards and honours, Erickson received the Royal Bank Award (1971) and the Chicago Architectural Award (1984, with Philip Johnson and Joan Burgee); as well, he received gold medals from the Royal Architectural Institute of Canada (1984) and the American Institute of Architects (1986).

Perhaps the first Canadian architect to be widely known by the international public, he has gained high popular regard by his ability to create places of great drama with apparently simple means. A consistent theme through many of his buildings is the simple frame to create a welcoming and sheltering portal, a motif found in West Coast Indian building. Such restricted means, and muted colours, are used in his best buildings to create a sense of occasion, and places that are striking in themselves as objects in the landscape. Erickson's success in recent years reflects his ability to attract and effectively supervise the work of talented associates in widely separated offices (Vancouver, Toronto, Los Angeles, Abu Dhabi). The work continues and extends the mainstream 20th-century architecture. MICHAEL MCMORDIE

Architect Arthur Erickson has gained wide popular regard for his ability to create places of great drama (*courtesy Arthur Erickson Architects/photo by V. Tony Hauser*).

Law Court, Vancouver, designed by Arthur Erickson (*courtesy* The Capilano Review *Issue #40/photo by Robert G. Sherrin*).

Erie, Lake, 25 700 km^2 (including islands), of which 12 800 km^2 lie in Canada, elev 173.3 m; 388 km long, 92 km wide and 64 m deep. The shallowest of the 5 major GREAT LAKES (excluding Lk St Clair), it receives most of its waters from Lk HURON via the DETROIT R. Other major inflowing streams are the Maumee and Cuyahoga rivers in Ohio, and the Grand R in Ontario. The lake outflows through the NIAGARA R at FORT ERIE, falling almost 100 m to Lk Ontario; more than 50 m of this drop occurs at NIAGARA FALLS. It is also joined to Lk Ontario by the WELLAND CANAL. The lake drainage basin measures 58 800 km^2 in area, and is home to over 15 million people in Canada and the US, making it the most densely populated of all the Great Lakes basins. Buffalo, NY; Erie, Pa; Toledo and Cleveland, Ohio, are large, heavily industrialized cities on the US side. NANTICOKE is the only sizable community on the Canadian shore.

Lk Erie is the southernmost of the Great Lks (lat similar to northern California), and this, combined with its relatively shallow depth and large nutrient inflows from the urban areas and intensively cultivated farmlands making up its watershed, contributes to a high level of biological productivity. Excessive productivity caused the proliferation of unsightly algae, which later sank and decomposed during the summer. This decomposition caused the thin, cold, lower layer of water (hypolmnion) to be devoid of oxygen. Phosphorus loading controls agreed upon by Canada and the US in 1972 and 1978 have gradually resulted in lower nutrient levels. By 1987 the offshore waters were now quite clear in the summer, with visibility of up to 8 m. The response of oxygen conditions is being closely monitored. Despite pollution and LAMPREY infestations, the lake supports the largest commercial fishery in the Great Lks, yielding more than 20 000 t annually, consisting mainly of yellow perch. Warm summers, excellent beaches and well-preserved coastal marshes make Erie a favourite rendezvous for summer recreationists and wildlife enthusiasts (*see* POINT PELÉE NATIONAL PARK). Bird-watchers

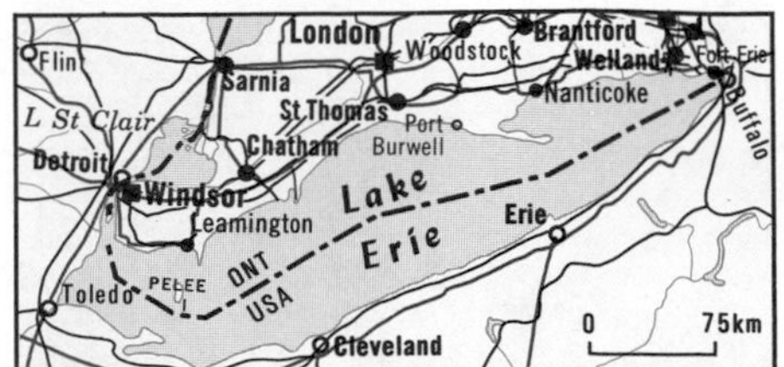

flock to these areas to take advantage of the lake's position on the major migration routes. Although Erie freezes over most winters, it remains an important part of the ST LAWRENCE SEAWAY system.

Like most of the other Great Lks, Erie occupies a glacier-deepened river drainage system, in which the less resistant shales and limestones of the Paleozoic rock column were differentially eroded to create the huge elongated depressions in which the lakes formed. These Pleistocene glaciers, hundreds of metres thick, periodically occupied much of the basin and left behind extensive deposits of clay and silt, which now comprise much of the rapidly eroding shoreline. More resistant dolomites form the shoreline only in the extreme eastern and western portions of the lake.

The N shore was frequented intermittently by NEUTRAL Indians, who lived around the Niagara Peninsula and along the Niagara Escarpment. Étienne BRÛLÉ (*c*1592-1633) was likely the first European to sight the lake. The decisive naval battle at PUT-IN-BAY was fought on the lake during the War of 1812. Called Lac du Chat by the French explorers, the lake came to be called after the Erie, an Iroquoian tribe inhabiting the S shore.

J.P. COAKLEY AND M.N. CHARLTON

Ermine, *see* WEASEL.

Erosion is the collective result of all processes that pick up and transport material at or very close to the Earth's surface. The main erosional agents are water, wind, ice and gravity, each of which acts in several ways.

Water Erosion, the most complex form, encompasses rain splash, unconcentrated surface erosion by sheetwash or rill wash, channel erosion in rivers or in gullies flowing only during storms, erosion by water flowing through surface materials, and erosion in the shallow zone of lakes and oceans by tides, currents and wave action. Rain splash is rather specialized and is effective only on agricultural fields and exposed loose materials; otherwise, water erosion can be classified as chemical or physical. Chemical erosion occurs primarily when material is dissolved and transported by water. It depends on such factors as water chemistry, surface materials and temperature. Most commonly its effects are hidden, but up to 70% of the load carried by many rivers is in solution. Where the surface is formed of soluble rocks such as limestone, KARST LANDFORMS develop. In Canada excellent examples occur in the Nahanni region, YT, and in many parts of the Rocky Mts.

Physical water erosion occurs when moving water achieves sufficient velocity to pick up or move loose particles or to pry fragments loose from SOIL or bedrock. In some rivers this is continual, but in many perennial streams and in gully erosion, sheetwash and rilling, such velocities occur only during rainstorms or snowmelt; therefore, erosion is closely controlled by patterns of storm activity. This is also true in lakes and oceans, but the key factor in these cases is wind force, which generates severe wave action. Water erosion rates differ greatly with location, depending on the mixture of processes and on the nature of surface materials. Available data on sediment loads in Canadian rivers show a range from below 2 to over 400 tonnes/km^2/year. If equally distributed, the upper rate (found in north-central BC) would correspond to a surface lowering of approximately 0.1 mm/year. The actual rate of surface lowering in most parts of Canada is much lower, but in some highly erodible areas, such as the Alberta BADLANDS, measurements have shown surface lowering rates as high as 4 mm per year.

Wind Erosion acts in essentially the same manner as physical water erosion but, because air is less dense than water, higher wind velocities are required to effect erosion. Theoretically, almost any material is vulnerable but, in practice, wind speed is rarely high enough to move material larger than sand grains, and these only if dry and unbound by vegetation. Significant wind erosion is, therefore, confined almost entirely to coastal areas and to glacial outwash plains and agricultural fields, where vegetation is minimal. The most severe wind erosion recorded in Canada occurred in the southern Prairies during the prolonged DROUGHT of the 1930s. Vulnerable soils were disturbed by tillage and blown in immense clouds, creating the "Dust Bowl." Erosion was sporadic and varied but surface lowering of 0.5 m in one storm was not uncommon.

Ice Erosion As ice moves over the surface or is constricted through valleys it can pluck protruding or loose material away from adjacent surfaces and transport it on or in the GLACIER. This matter joins with material falling onto the glacier and into crevasses to form an englacial MORAINE, which makes the ice an extremely effective abrasive agent capable of planing off surfaces and scouring out valleys. Valley or alpine glaciers tend to increase local relief by scouring valleys while adjacent peaks protrude above the ice. Continental glaciers spreading over the complete surface tend to reduce relief. Most of Canada was covered by ice during the Pleistocene epoch (2.5 million-10 000 years ago) and excellent examples of both effects are found in many areas. Although glacial erosion now occurs only in the Cordillera and the Arctic, residual features formed during the Pleistocene still dominate most landscapes.

Gravity is an important erosional agent because it acts continually on all sloping surfaces. Gravitational stress at any location does not vary, but the resistance of surface materials does alter, particularly in response to moisture changes. Many of the most dramatic movements tend, therefore, to follow prolonged periods of wet weather. By definition, material can only be moved relatively short distances to the base of the original slope, but very large amounts of material can be moved in a few minutes. Among the classic examples of major gravitational erosion in Canada are the FRANK SLIDE, Alta (1903), and the Hope

These cross sections show the formation of the Eardley Escarpment, near Ottawa. The first (left) shows the Canadian Shield buried beneath a thick layer of shale and limestone. Several million years later (centre) faults have formed along weaknesses in the bedrock; tensions in the Earth's crust cause immense blocks to move. The depression became the Ottawa Valley. The third drawing (right) shows the layer of shale and limestone eroded over millions of years, exposing the Shield (*courtesy National Capital Commission, artwork by Kiyomi Shoyama*).

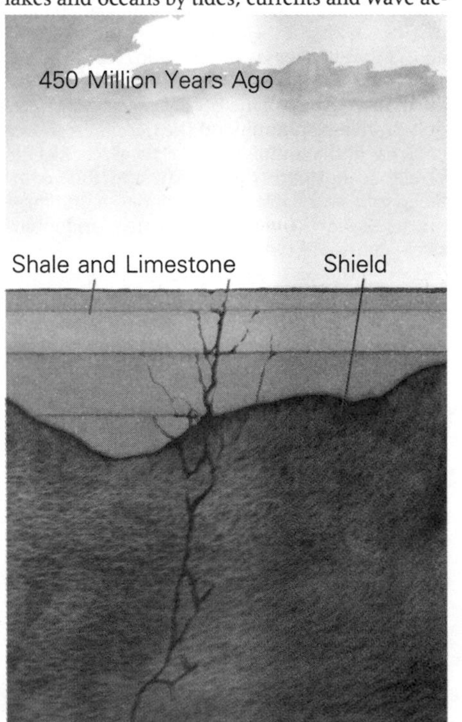

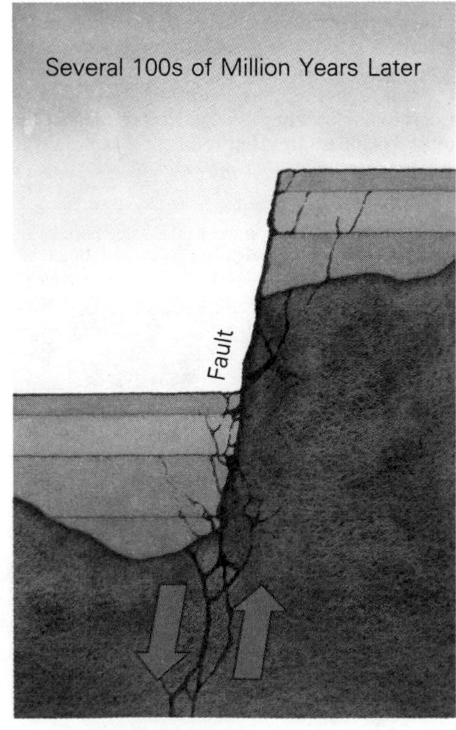

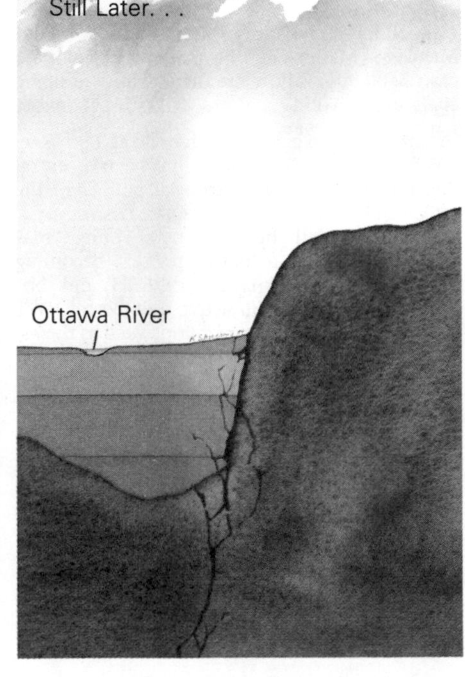

Slide, BC (1965), and numerous quick clay slides in the old marine deposits of the CHAMPLAIN SEA in the St Lawrence Valley (*see* LANDSLIDE).

R.B. BRYAN

Escarpment, steep or vertical cliff which usually extends over a considerable distance. The most common type of escarpment occurs where more resistant strata form a cap rock over easily eroded rocks. As EROSION takes place, the lower rock erodes more rapidly so that the cliff remains very steep. The NIAGARA ESCARPMENT continues from Tobermory, Ont, into New York state. Its resistant cap rock, formed by the Lockport Dolomite, overlies several weaker shale and sandstone beds. Some escarpments are formed by tectonic activity (ie, deformational movements of the Earth's crust or volcanism), particularly uplift along fault lines, and are distinguished as fault scarps. An excellent example is in the Aspy Valley of northern Cape Breton I, NS. The angle of the fault scarp is controlled by the inclination of the fault plane and is often more gentle than that of the classic escarpment formed by strata of differing resistance. The latter can vary, however, from the flat, vertically sided feature, eg, the Niagara Escarpment, to a cuesta (with a steep scarp face and gentle dip face), or to a hogback ridge in which both faces are equally inclined. *See also* PLATE TECTONICS.

R.B. BRYAN

Esker, narrow, sinuous ridge of gravel and sand emplaced during glacial retreat by the deposition of sediments from meltwater streams flowing on the ice or in tunnels on, through or, most frequently, under glacial ice. Eskers were deposited in segments, each ending in a delta formed in a proglacial lake (ie, a lake formed beside the margin of a GLACIER). As the wall of ice melted, esker sediments collapsed to the angle of repose (ie, the steepest slope at which loose material will stand, about 30°). The sides are generally covered by finer, proglacial lake sediments. Eskers may run for tens of kilometres and are generally 1-2 km wide. The sediments may reach 50 m deep in depressions. Sediment grain size varies from sand to coarse gravel, suggesting that meltwater in the ice tunnel was under high pressure. One of the world's best areas to observe eskers is the mining region of NW Québec, where many eskers, generally aligned N-S, were emplaced during the last deglaciation. Eskers do not generally survive from one GLACIATION to another. They are features of a deglaciation phase and are usually destroyed when ice readvances over them. Their orientation is affected by various factors, but generally they are roughly parallel to the ice flow and the general slope of the subglacial topography. However, as they have been reported to cross divides between valleys, meltwater pressure may also play a role in their orientation. Eskers form good, confined aquifers (water-bearing strata) when covered by fine, impermeable sediments. Esker sediments help locate ore deposits upstream from the ore-indicator-bearing esker bed (*see* PROSPECTING).

PIERRE LASALLE

Eskimo, a group of N American aborigines, forming part of the Eskimoan linguistic stock. They inhabit the coasts and islands of arctic N America, from eastern Greenland and Labrador to western Alaska and Siberia. The name "Eskimo" comes from one of the Algonquian languages, most likely Montagnais or Naskapi. The Eskimo of arctic Canada call themselves INUIT, meaning "people." They constitute a distinct physical type, whose language, Inuktitut, and customs are relatively homogeneous throughout the arctic and subarctic zones. Ethnological groups differentiated on the basis of territory are, however, recognized by the Inuit. *See also* NATIVE PEOPLE: ARCTIC.

RENÉ R. GADACZ

Eskimo Lakes, 880 km^2, lie along the southern edge of the Tuktoyaktuk Pen, NWT, and drain into Liverpool Bay on the Beaufort Sea. They are tidal lakes, with tide heights averaging 2 m, and occupy a fault zone separating geological blocks. The lakes are almost partitioned into several separate water bodies by bow-shaped, nearly parallel, ridgelike peninsulas that project across them from N and S shores. These relic ice-pushed ridges narrow the lakes to less than 50 m in places and are highest at the inland end of the lakes, reaching heights of 30 m. Inland the lakes are shallow (10 m) and flat bottomed, deepening towards the outlet to 66 m with uneven lake beds.

DOUGLAS FINLAYSON

Eskimo Point, NWT, Hamlet, pop 1189 (1986c), 1022 (1981c), is located on the W coast of HUDSON BAY, 1086 air km E of YELLOWKNIFE. The site was a summer camp for the inland Pallirmiut INUIT of S Keewatin until the 1900s. It acquired permanent settlement status when an HBC trading post and a Roman Catholic mission were built in the early 1920s. Today the community is one of the major settlements of the eastern Arctic. It is known for its Inuit Cultural Institute, which was established to preserve and encourage Inuit culture. The community has the largest number of independent entrepreneurs in the Keewatin.

ANNELIES POOL

Espanola, Ont, Town, pop 5491 (1986c), inc 1958, 70 km W of Sudbury on the Spanish R, started in 1899 by the Spanish River Pulp and Paper Co. Evidence indicates that the name relates to Indian contacts with Spaniards when they claimed the central US. (Espanola, when used as a noun, means Spanish woman.) In 1928 Abitibi Power & Paper Co Ltd purchased the mill but shut it down in 1929 because of depression conditions. Espanola was practically a "ghost town" for a decade. In 1940 the mill was converted into a prisoner-of-war camp, a function it served into 1943. That year the mill and townsite were purchased by the Kalamazoo Vegetable Parchment Co, which switched from spruce to jackpine for its main wood supply. The company town and its fringe development united and became incorporated in 1958. Currently, the mill is operated by E.B. Eddy Forest Products, a Canadian company. Although basically a one-industry town, Espanola is the centre for an active tourist area and has many regional mining developments.

GEORGE R. MORRISON

Esposito, Philip Anthony, hockey player (b at Sault Ste Marie, Ont 20 Feb 1942). He began his NHL career as a centre in 1963 with the Chicago Black Hawks and was traded to the Boston Bruins in 1967. He and Bobby ORR led the Bruins to STANLEY CUP victories in 1970 and 1972, but his best season was 1970-71 when he scored 76 goals, a record that stood until Wayne GRETZKY's 92-goal performance of 1981-82. Although not a fast or graceful skater, Esposito's large and immovable presence in front of the opposition net and his ability to score from all angles won him the ART ROSS TROPHY 5 times (1969, 1971-74), and the HART TROPHY in 1969 and 1974. He was the inspirational leader of Team Canada during the dramatic CANADA-SOVIET HOCKEY SERIES of 1972. He was traded to the New York Rangers in 1975 and retired in 1982, second then only to Gordie HOWE in both goals (717) and points (1590) on the all-time NHL scoring list. He became general manager of the New York Rangers in 1986, rapidly transforming the team with a flurry of trades.

DEREK DRAGER

Esquimalt, BC, District Municipality, pop 15 972 (1986c), 15 870 (1981c), area 1000 ha, inc 1912, is located on the SE coast of VANCOUVER I adjacent to VICTORIA. It is the most established residential area of Metropolitan Victoria and its excellent harbour has made it an important Pacific coast naval establishment. It is governed by a mayor and 6 aldermen, and shares some responsibilities with the Capital Regional Dist. SALISH Indians first occupied the site ("a place gradually shoaling"). James DOUGLAS surveyed the harbour in 1843, and later purchased land in the area from the Indians for the HBC. Esquimalt's quiet development was shattered by the GOLD RUSH of the late 1850s. By the 1880s rapid growth was occurring through the building of Royal Navy dry docks, the construction of the Esquimalt to Nanaimo railway, and the founding of a military base at Work Point.

Of the region's original economic supports, agriculture and the military, only the latter has remained important. A large Canadian Forces Base in Esquimalt and shipyards, dry docks and attendant enterprises are prominent in the economy. Several structures inside or adjacent to the naval dockyard have been listed as heritage buildings. St Paul's Anglican Church (1866) contains relics and plaques covering over a century of naval history. Some of Esquimalt's pleasant residential neighbourhoods make effective use of the community's extensive waterfront with its bays and beaches.

ALAN F.J. ARTIBISE

Reading: F.V. Longstaff, *Esquimalt Naval Base: A History of its Work and Defences* (1941); A.C. Wurtele, *Esquimalt, 1912-1962* (1962).

Essay in English An essay is a brief, discursive piece of prose which develops a single theme from a personal point of view, following the prototype established by French essayist Michel de Montaigne (1533-92). The earliest Canadian resemblance to this form emerged during the 19th century in the Maritimes, where the primary intention of writers such as Joseph HOWE and George Stewart was usually descriptive or hortatory. JOURNALISM has always provided the greatest stimulus to the essay in Canada. In *The Week* (Toronto, 1883-96) appeared articles discussing current political or religious questions. Those by Goldwin SMITH or his private secretary Theodore A. Haultain have less in common with the traditional form than the unpretentious and intimate "Saunterings" of Sara Jeannette DUNCAN. Yet the only contributor who really deserves the title "essayist" is Archibald MacMechan. His collections, *The Porter of Bagdad, and Other Fantasies* (1901) and *The Life of a Little College, and Other Papers* (1914), contain whimsical reveries that recreate an innocent era of nature and art reminiscent of essays by Victorian writers John Ruskin and Matthew Arnold, whom he admired.

Physician Sir William OSLER, concerned that his medical students might miss "those gentler influences which make life worth living," enunciated in *Aequanimitas* (1903) the need to harmonize the humanities and sciences. Bliss CARMAN's *The Kinship of Nature* (1904) treats his recurring didactic theme of self-betterment and personal harmony. Sir Andrew MACPHAIL, a medical professor at McGill University and editor of *The* UNIVERSITY MAGAZINE, published *Essays in Puritanism* (1905), *Essays in Politics* (1909) and *Essays in Fallacy* (1910), which are distinguished by their pungency and winsome vigour. Of less literary interest are the moralizing articles of journalist Thomas O'Hagan, which originally appeared in the *Catholic Register* and were published as *Chats by the Fireside* (1911).

In Pastures Green (1915), *The Red Cow and her Friends* (1919) and *Around Home* (1925) are collections of another journalist, Peter McArthur, from his farm column in the Toronto *Globe*. His humorous and often rambling depiction of Ontario pastoral life reflects the freshness and earthiness of the countryside. The simple natural settings were also celebrated by Toronto lawyer William Hume Blake, who describes angling in the Laurentians in *Brown Waters, and Other Sketches* (1915) and *A Fisherman's Creed* (1923).

Essays and Literary Studies (1916) by Stephen LEACOCK, although primarily humorous, sometimes presents serious themes. His satiric pieces reflect the advance made by the essay form in Canada since its early didactic and descriptive precursors. The *Canadian Forum* (fd 1920) encouraged the journalistic essay. Perhaps its most eloquent contributor was scholar Douglas Bush, who displayed a gift for phrasing and allusion, along with a genial irreverence for some of his colleagues' preoccupation with a national literature and identity. W.D. Woodhead and John D. Robins wrote with more overt humour. The essays of other contributors such as Barker FAIRLEY, Margaret Fairley, John Macnaughton, Frederick Philip GROVE, E.K. Broadus, B.K. SANDWELL, Frank UNDERHILL and A.J.M. SMITH treated art, the humanities, criticism, contemporary poetry, education and socialist politics with an academic rather than a familiar tone.

That the critical spirit continued to dominate the form is indicated in the title of Malcolm ROSS's anthology covering much of this period, *Our Sense of Identity* (1954). William Arthur DEACON, for example, moved from the whimsy and humour of *Pens and Pirates* (1923) to the critical *My Vision of Canada* (1933). Lucid and scholarly essays on people, books and ideas were also being published by Maurice Hutton, John Charles Robertson and Gilbert Norwood, professors at U of T. Less detached and contemplative are the collections of newspaper feature writers, yet many of these in their use of description, anecdote, reminiscence and humour approach the timeless quality of the essay. Noteworthy among them are *One Thing After Another* (1948) by C.B. Pyper and *From Our Town* (1959) by Jack Scott. The most widely read columnists were the humorists. The sketches of Peter Donovan from *Saturday Night* were collected in *Imperfectly Proper* (1920). Newton MacTavish of *Canadian Magazine* published *Thrown In* (1923), recollections of a rural childhood which are amplified in *Newton MacTavish's Canada* (posth 1965). In 1959 *The Best of Gregory Clark* was culled from his anecdotes in *Weekend Magazine*. Eric NICOL has recorded refreshingly satirical anecdotes, some of which were collected from columns in the Vancouver *Province*, in illustrated books including *The Roving I* (1950) and *Canada Cancelled Because of Lack of Interest* (1977). Common sense, tolerance and gentle amusement at human foibles permeate the style of these journalists.

A significant journalistic theme of the period was the return to nature. Cecil Francis Lloyd describes its attraction in *Sunlight and Shadow* (1928). His *Malvern Essays* (1930), modelled after Montaigne's, express a wistful if weary acceptance of "The Burden of Existence." More in the tradition of American writer Henry David Thoreau were Harry Lutz Symons in *Friendship* (1943) and *Canadian Forum* contributors and academics E.K. Broadus (*Saturday and Sunday*, 1935) and John D. Robins (*The Incomplete Anglers*, 1943). Roderick HAIG-BROWN, a fisherman in the Waltonian tradition, describes outdoor delights and their value for the individual in *A River Never Sleeps* (1946) and *Measure of the Year* (1950). His *Fisherman's Spring* (1951), *Fisherman's Winter* (1954) and *Fisherman's Summer* (1959) as well as his posthumous *Writings and Reflections* (1982) provide a pattern of civilized life. Kenneth McNeil Wells collected into 4 books a series of articles from the Toronto *Telegram* chronicling life at *The Owl Pen* (1947) farm, which was *Up Medonte Way* (1951), and was successful in transcribing Ontario rustic idiom.

Various writers used the essay to increase the awareness or appreciation of the "average reader." B.K. SANDWELL, editor of *Saturday Night*, employs Swiftian irony in *The Privacity Agent and Other Modest Proposals* (1928) to contrast the 20th century with happier past eras. F.P. Grove in *Over Prairie Trails* (1922) describes natural scenery with cosmic implications, tracing changing moods and emotions during 7 journeys over one Manitoba road. His *The Turn of the Year* (1923) is more forbidding and less personal. Morley CALLAGHAN, in monthly commentaries for *New World* magazine (1940-48) and pieces in *Saturday Night*, *Maclean's* and other journals, dealt with topical themes from an imaginative point of view. In *Cross-Country* (1949) Hugh MACLENNAN treats the Canadian character in a cultivated style marked by personal memories and biases. His *Thirty and Three* (1954), *Scotchman's Return* (1960) and *The Other Side of Hugh MacLennan* (1978]) attempt to define and reconcile transition with the world around him.

Novelist, dramatist and editor Robertson DAVIES ignores the "average reader" as being incapable of understanding "good talk." In *Diary* (1947) and *Table Talk* (1949) are portrayed the tastes and opinions of the fictional Samuel Marchbanks, who like Dr Samuel Johnson "loved tea, conversation and pretty women, and had not much patience with fools." *A Voice from the Attic* (1960) pursues the theme that reading as a private, individual art is the mark of the cultivated mind and the central activity of the good life; and *Samuel Marchbanks' Almanack* (1967) continues Davies's examination of Canadian society. Somewhat different are the essays of arctic explorer Vilhjalmur STEFANSSON. The logical and even philosophical structure of his pieces in *Adventures in Error* (1936) conceals an ironical exploration of man's mental processes which affirms that "errors" of the human imagination are true and that human desires, even when self-deceptive, are important.

Northrop FRYE has maintained the tradition of the scholarly essayists in volumes such as *The Educated Imagination* (1963), *The Modern Century* (1967), *The Bush Garden* (1971) and *Spiritus mundi* (1976). He provocatively explores literature, education and other aspects of contemporary society. George WOODCOCK, a less academic but wider ranging "man of letters," displays an easy competence in the essay form in such books as *The World of Canadian Writing* (1980). Eli MANDEL's *A Passion for Identity: An Introduction to Canadian Studies* (1987) expands on his earlier *Contexts of Criticism* (1971). In a similar vein is David Staine's *The Canadian Imagination: Dimensions of A Canadian Culture* (1977). Established writers of fiction have always found the genre challenging. In *Hunting Tigers Under Glass* (1968), *Shovelling Trouble* (1972) and *The Great Comic Book Heroes* (1978), Mordecai RICHLER expatiates on such themes as the Jewish experience, "Why I write" and the changing national scene. Hugh HOOD, in *The Governor's Bridge Is Closed* (1973), expresses his cheerful belief in Canadian life and culture. Margaret LAWRENCE's *Heart of a Stranger* (1976) and Margaret ATWOOD's *Second Words* (1982) are collections of personal pieces which, like Gabrielle ROY's *The Fragile Lights of Earth* (1982), provide perceptive insights into the writer's world and social history.

Running to Paradise (1962) by Kildare Dobbs (although largely autobiographical reminiscence), *Reading the Time* (1968) and *Pride and Fall* (1981) are marked by a versatile style befitting the wide range of topics treated. Norman WARD in *Mice in the Beer* (1960) and *The Fully Processed Cheese* (1964) displays an attitude of tolerance and amusement toward topical themes and toward his academic colleagues. The posthumous collection of contributions by Ralph ALLEN to the *Toronto Star* and *Maclean's* are entitled *The Man from Oxbow* (1967). *Crisis at the Victory Burlesk* (1968) is a collecton of Robert FULFORD's early journalism, which is less reflective than his regular essays in *Saturday Night*. The waspish miscellanies of Richard Needham, originally published in the *Globe and Mail*, have appeared in several collections, including *Needham's Inferno* (1966) and *The Wit & Wisdom of Richard Needham* (1977). Columnist Allan FOTHERINGHAM has collected a number of his acerbic, irreverent political essays in *Malice in Blunderland* (1982). Another exemplar of *persona* journalism is Harry Bruce, whose collection of *Toronto Star* columns, *The Short Happy Walks of Max MacPherson* (1968), combines history and description.

Neurosurgeon Wilder PENFIELD, emulating his mentor Osler, in *The Second Career* (1964) and *Second Thoughts* (1970) reflects on the need for "eternal vigilance and resolute action" in a changing world. Economist John Kenneth GALBRAITH gives an ironic and acerbic account of his boyhood in *The Scotch* (1964), and presents the viewpoint of a perceptive and versatile diplomat in *A Contemporary Guide to Economics, Peace, and Laughter* (1971). Others who write in a discursive fashion about their special interests include George GRANT (philosophy), John BECKWITH (music) and Greg CURNOE (art).

Folksy and nostalgic memories of rural simplicity form H. Gordon Green's central theme in a number of books, including *A Time to Pass Over* (1962) and *With My Sock Feet on the Oven Door* (1975). Harry J. BOYLE exploits the same vein, beginning with *Mostly in Clover* (1961) and continuing through *Memories of a Catholic Boyhood* (1973). Another variation of the pastoral mode is *The Battle of Mole Run and Other Offenses* (1967) by Howard T. Mitchell. A more enduring presentation of farm life is *Western Windows* (1967) by Bruce HUTCHISON. In *The Far Side of the Street* (1976) his informal essays cover 50 years of change in Canadian life.

In *The Medium is the Message* (1967), Marshall MCLUHAN developed a type of *essai concret*, involving a mosaic of verbal and visual, spatial and durational material, in what he called a "collideoscope of interface situations" without linear sequence. His unique technique has been assimilated rather than imitated by other writers.

During the second half of the 20th century the Canadian essay continues to be influenced chiefly by journalism, although television's slickness has made it difficult for the columnist to maintain freshness. The increased tempo and pragmatic urgency of technological life have militated against undogmatic attention to theme and easy discursiveness, which survive mainly in reminiscences of more relaxed eras. *See also* SHORT FICTION. A.B. CONRON

Essay in French The hallmark of the French Canadian essay is that it is both personal (or subjective) and creative. The essay stands apart from any writing that claims to offer an objective explanation of reality or explores a preordained, objective truth that is assumed to be valid for any time and place. The essayist is not at the service of the truth, a cause or a class: he proclaims and defends his own irreducible sincerity and recognizes that, while his experience and the account he gives of it are subjective, they may still serve as a model to others. The essay may range from popular to scholarly treatment of a subject. The writer may just as easily deal with a scientific subject as with a theological, literary or political one, and his tone may be polemical or discursive. The literary quality of an essay, as of any other genre, rests in the quality of the writing, in the capacity of the author to interpret the world about him, to reconstruct it and awaken in the reader as much admiration and wonder for the interpretation as for the reality being interpreted. ANDRÉ GIROUARD

Pamphlets and Polemics

Philosophical and political essays, pamphlets, manifestos and polemic exchanges are all arguably forms of the essay. When placed in their original contexts, they afford excellent opportunities to observe sociopolitical and cultural phenomena of their eras. Polemical texts and pamphlets are not always self-evidently critical in nature, and they are made all the more effective when the author's indignation is camouflaged. A complete polemic structure is to be found as an undercurrent in accounts of early voyages, in private and administrative correspondence and in the writings of religious orders in New France. Generally addressed to authorities in the mother country, these texts crystallize metropolitan antagonisms around Canadian situations. They contain a double contradiction, expressing the New World in the linguistic and cultural codes of the mother country, which is itself replete with antagonisms such as those between Recollets and Jesuits or, at another level, proponents of evangelization and champions of exploitation.

The texts of Cartier, Champlain, Lescarbot, Biard and Sagard, and the JESUIT RELATIONS (*see* EXPLORATION AND TRAVEL LITERATURE IN FRENCH), should be read in the context of the actual conditions in which they were written (literary strategies, thinly veiled battles to obtain local credit, privilege and power). So, too, should one read the protests of Canadian naval personnel against French officers during the Seven Years' War. Essays of protest continued to be written after the Conquest, and pamphlets regarding the GUIBORD AFFAIR (1869-74) and the battle between Mgr BOURGET and the INSTITUT CANADIEN carried the genre into the late 19th century. Parliamentary battles in the Canadas gave scope to the pamphleteer and essayist as well: oratorical jousts were taken up and exaggerated in the polemics between francophone and anglophone newspapers (eg, in the *Anti-Gallic Letters).*

Striking examples of the use of polemical essays in political settings include exchanges during the MANITOBA SCHOOLS QUESTION (1890-96), the anticommunist campaigns of the 1930s (*Pamphlets de Valdombre,* 1936-43) and the CONSCRIPTION debates during the 2 world wars. In 1960 Jean-Paul DESBIENS, in *Les* INSOLENCES DU FRÈRE UNTEL, and Gilles Leclerc, in *Journal d'un inquisiteur,* took up the language debate and other matters with vehemence. The authors offer pragmatic commentary on current events, using this as a device to discredit the targets of their scorn, hoping thus to alter the attitudes of the reading public. Since the QUIET REVOLUTION there has been an explosion of polemical writings about independence, unionism and native people by leftist individuals, groups and magazines. More recently feminism held the limelight, with its radical challenge to all the institutions that have traditionally excluded women. BERNARD ANDRÈS

Political Essay

Political essays may be distinguished from other works in the fields of history, sociology and political science as the products of a more personal and untrammelled quest. Memoirs, reminiscences, notebooks, diaries and autobiographical fragments all overlap partially and unevenly with the political essay. Among the best political memoirs in French are the 3 volumes by Georges-Émile LAPALME, the leader of the Québec Liberal Party who was caught between Prem Maurice DUPLESSIS and PM Louis ST. LAURENT. He makes some lucid comments on the subject of the limits of political action.

The major political or ideological essays of the 19th century were not the work of orators or public figures (Papineau, Mercier, Laurier) but the discussions and chronicles of some leading journalists (Étienne PARENT, Arthur BUIES). *L'Avenir du peuple canadien-français* (1896), by sociologist Edmond de Nevers, was a cultural and deeply political essay, a mixture of idealism, pessimism and prophecy. In the 20th century as well, the best political essays have been the work of a few well-educated journalists (Olivar Asselin, Jules Fournier, André LAURENDEAU) and nationalist historians (Lionel GROULX, Michel Brunet). They raised (or revived) the question of Québec's relations with London and Paris and with English Canadians; they were as concerned about war and conscription as about elections.

The birth of political magazines free from party affiliation – CITÉ LIBRE (1950-66) and PARTI PRIS (1963-68) – led to a proliferation of the political essay. The collection of articles, studies and testimonials about the ASBESTOS STRIKE, *La Grève de l'amiante* (1956), which appeared with a comprehensive introduction by Pierre Elliott TRUDEAU, was the prototype for numerous other collections. Many were the products of conferences, such as that held in Cerisy-la-Salle, France (*Le Canada au seuil du siècle de l'abondance,* 1969), which had brought together Francophones of every persuasion. Independentists produced manifestos, declarations and testimonies, but also a few essays of a more structured nature, such as *Le Colonialisme au Québec* (1966) by André d'Allemagne. A Marxist-tinged theory of decolonization, inspired by the experiences and rhetoric of the Third World, marked a number of the essays published at the beginning of the Quiet Revolution, in particular NÈGRES BLANCS D'AMÉRIQUE (1968) by Pierre Vallières. Neo-federalists (most of them in the group around Trudeau and Gérard PELLETIER) began countering the arguments of the fervent neo-nationalists. They seemed to be calmer and more staid than their antagonists, but they were just as lively in their use of history and statistics. Essays in their true form were rare: the writers slid easily from a constitutional treatise or thesis to a circumstantial or journalistic approach.

Some of the meatiest and most thought-provoking essays written since the late 1960s are *Le Canada français après deux siècles de patience* (1967) by political scientist Gérard Bergeron; La DERNIÈRE HEURE ET LA PREMIÈRE (1973) by Pierre VADEBONCOEUR, trade unionist turned writer; *La Question du Québec* (1971) by sociologist Marcel Rioux; and *Le Développement des idéologies au Québec* (1977) by political scientist Denis Monière. The most trenchant political essays are perhaps to be found in certain novels (eg, those of Hubert AQUIN and Jacques FERRON).

Québec political essayists have been obsessed since the mid-1960s by the state and the constitution. Subjects now discussed move beyond partisanship and dogma to a new definition of the central issue: the division of powers is not solely a Québec-Ottawa dispute; it is also an issue for Montréal and its suburbs, the regions of Québec, women and ethnic and marginal groups. The post-referendum period was marked by important essays on language and culture as well as economics and the role of the state. Among the less systematic but more intense and vivid of the collections were those of columnists Lysiane Gagnon (*Chroniques politiques*, 1985) and of Lise Bissonnette (*La Passion du présent*, 1987), whose "Les Yvettes" served as a stimulus for the NON faction; as well, René Lévesque contributed his memoirs (*Attendez que je me rappelle...*, 1986). Then there was a study of international as well as national politics, more precisely, the Québec-Ottawa-Paris triangle, by former minister of intergovernmental affairs Claude Morin.

LAURENT MAILHOT

Literary Essay

Unlike literary criticism, which necessarily passes judgement on the work under study, the literary essay freely considers the written work, offering nondefinitive, personal comments on its aesthetic value. The literary essay first appeared in newspapers and magazines of the mid-19th century as well as in papers presented in literary circles, at the Institut canadien and in similar reading groups. These first stirrings prepared the way for true literary essayists, Étienne Parent and Napoléon Aubin, Abbé Henri-Raymond CASGRAIN, Octave CRÉMAZIE, Arthur Buies and a few others who were prompted by religious and moral concerns to deal with aesthetic questions.

The literary essay developed along nationalist and regionalist lines in Québec in the early 20th century, thanks to Laval professor Camille ROY, who explored the "nationalization" of French Canadian literature in some 30 essays. He was followed by Olivier Maurault and Émile Chartier of U de Montréal, and other major voices of nationalism such as Lionel Groulx, who concentrated on the land, the parish, the family, religion, customs and ancestral traditions; and by the next wave, regionalist writers associated with the journals *Le Pays laurentien, La Revue nationale* and L'ACTION FRANÇAISE (later *L'Action canadienne-française* and then *L'Action nationale).* The "Parisianists" ("exotics"), who followed modern French thought in their subjects and writings and often sharply disagreed with the first group, included Paul Morin, Marcel Dugas, Jean Charbonneau, Robert de Roquebrune, Olivar Asselin, Victor Barbeau and his *Cahiers de Turc* (1921-22; 1926-27), and the people associated with *Le* NIGOG, *Cahiers des Jeunes-Canada* and *La* RELÈVE. In the long run, the often vigorous disagreements led to an affirmation of a French Canadian literature that was autonomous yet always strongly influenced by France.

With this ideological battle behind them, writers could finally pay serious attention to the different genres of expression. From 1940 to 1960 the literary essay was particularly important. The many publications included writings about Canadian as well as French authors; general studies of French Canadian literature by critics such as Roger Duhamel, Benoît Lacroix and Séraphin Marion; specialized studies of THEATRE by Léopold Houlé and Jean Béraud, of poetry by Jeanne Crouzet and of the novel by Dostaler O'Leary; and histories of literature by Samuel Baillargeon, Berthelot Brunet and Auguste Viatte.

The proliferation of literary essays has been boosted, since the Quiet Revolution, by the development of the teaching of Québec literature (*see* LITERATURE IN FRENCH, SCHOLARSHIP AND TEACHING). Analyses of literature and of literary movements (the historical novel, the novel of the soil, literary nationalism, *Parti pris,* the AUTOMATISTES, surrealism) were accompanied by many essays dealing with literary genres: the novel (Gérard Bessette, Yves Dostaler, Jacques Blais, Maurice Lemire, Gilles Marcotte, Mireille Servais-Maquoi, Henri Tuchmaïer); theatre (Michel Belair, Beaudoin Burger, Jacques Cotnam, Martial Dassylva, Jan Doat, Jean-Cléo Godin and Laurent Mailhot, Chantal Hébert, G.E. Rinfret); poetry (Paul Gay,

Philippe Haeck, Jeanne d'Arc Lortie, Axel Maugey); and the literary essay (Jean Terrasse). There were treatments of specific subject-matter (themes of the family, of winter, etc), a host of monographs on French Canadian writers, general studies of Québec literature (Guy Laflèche, Gilles Marcotte, Jean Ménard, Guy Robert) and histories of literature (Pierre de Grandpré, Laurent Mailhot, Gérard Tougas). There are also collective literary essays, such as the *Archives des lettres canadiennes*, and anthologies, including *L'Anthologie de la littérature québécoise* (directed by Gilles Marcotte) and the *Dictionnaire des oeuvres littéraires du Québec* (directed by Maurice Lemire) – highly useful works, although their contents tend to be literary criticism rather than essays. Only rarely do Québec essayists study broad issues the way Europeans do. Finally, most Québec literary essays are aimed at students and professors in both foreign and Québec colleges and universities, though they are occasionally intended to reach a larger public. GILLES DORION

Esson, James, photographer (b at Preston [Cambridge, Ont] 10 Aug 1853; d at Toronto 1933). He learned PHOTOGRAPHY from his father and in 1875 established his own business. At age 30, he built a large, 3-storey brick "atelier" – purportedly the most elegant, complete and costly establishment in the country. A familiar name in art circles throughout Ontario, Esson attracted patrons of social and political prominence, including the marquess of LORNE and Princess Louise.
JOAN M. SCHWARTZ

Estate, all property owned by an individual. From 1958 to 1972 Parliament levied an estate tax on all property left when people died (*see* TAXATION). More technically, an estate refers to ownership of an interest in land. As a result of the feudal system imposed on England by William the Conqueror in 1066, all land in Canada's common law provinces is still owned by the CROWN.

Strictly speaking, an individual does not own land but an estate "in land." The largest and most common estate is a "fee simple absolute" (grant of an estate on land to a person or his heirs absolutely). Another freehold estate (an interest in land of indefinite duration) in land is a "life estate." Owner of the fee simple can divide part of the full estate by creating a life estate in A, who now has a freehold estate determinable by A's own death; if the owner dies before A, the freehold estate reverts to his estate only after A's death. If A conveyed his life estate in the land to B, B would acquire a life estate not measured by B's own life but measured by A's. The owner of a fee simple may also lease the land. The leasehold is an estate in land entitling the tenant to exclusive possession for the term of the lease. Other land interests, eg, easements, licences and restrictive covenants, are not classified as estates (*see* PROPERTY LAW).

Québec civil law does not have a doctrine of estates. In the modern civil law, ownership of property is absolute and contains all rights of disposition, management and enjoyment.
GORDON BALE

Esterhazy, Sask, Town, pop 3083 (1986c), 3065 (1981c), inc as a village in 1903 and as a town in 1957, is located in E-central Saskatchewan, 65 km SE of Yorkton. It is named after Count Paul Esterhazy, who founded a colony of Hungarian families S of the future townsite in 1886. The Kirkella branch of the CPR reached the area in 1902 and the community served the mixed farming area surrounding it. Potash was discovered in the 1950s and the "world's largest potash mine" went into production in 1962. DON HERPERGER

Estevan, Sask, City, pop 10 161 (1986c), 9174 (1981c), inc 1957, is located on the SOURIS R, 210 km SE of Regina and 16 km N of the US border. The townsite was surveyed in 1892 where the Soo Line of the CPR crossed the river, and grew steadily from that date, largely because of its dual role as a trading and energy centre. The large lignite coal deposits in the area were quickly recognized as a valuable source of fuel for the treeless plains, and coal mining developed rapidly. It has remained significant and the construction of the coal-fueled Boundary Dam generating station of the Saskatchewan Power Corp during the late 1950s confirmed the city's position as the "energy capital" of Saskatchewan. Oil was discovered in the 1950s and the oil industry plays an important role in the local economy. DON HERPERGER

Estevan Coal Miners' Strike, 1931 Coal miners at Bienfait, Sask, had joined the militant Mine Workers' Union of Canada in 1931. In Sept of that year they went on strike to win recognition of their union as a prelude to pressing demands for a restoration of wages cut by the local coal operators. When the mine operators proved intransigent, the miners and their families decided to demonstrate in nearby Estevan to gain community support for the strike. Estevan's mayor banned the demonstration and called upon the RCMP to aid local police in crushing the march which occurred Sept 29. Three miners were murdered in the ensuing melee and many others were injured. The suppression of the miners' strike contributed to working-class anger with the governments of that period and aided the cause of the MWUC and the WORKERS UNITY LEAGUE of which it was a part.
ALVIN FINKEL

Estey Commission (Inquiry into the collapse of the CCB and Northland Bank) The Honourable Willard Z. Estey of the Supreme Court of Canada was commissioned by the federal government 29 Sept 1985 to investigate the failures of the CANADIAN COMMERCIAL BANK and the Northland Bank, the causes of these failures and the regulatory approach to these banks and to make recommendations to improve the regulation of the banking system. The report issued by the commission in Aug 1986 claimed that management, directors, auditors and regulators were all seriously lacking in the performance of their duties. It criticized the bank's management for improvident lending policies and bizarre banking procedures, overstated income and loan values and misleading financial statements. The external auditors, the report stated, accepted financial statements that did not follow accepted banking practices nor reflect the true financial position of the banks. The commission claimed that the directors had relied heavily on management and had not performed their customary function of setting policy and directing management and that the regulators had made no independent assessment of the loan portfolio, and did not support the auditors when they challenged management. Furthermore, it claimed that the Inspector General had full knowledge of the situation but refused to act and therefore must bear much of the blame.

All depositors were fully compensated for their losses because, according to the report, public officials continued to express confidence in both banks during the failed rescue attempt. Investors have been less fortunate because there was no equity remaining. The report concluded by recommending that the office of Inspector General of Banks be combined with a strengthened Canada Deposit Insurance Corp to improve the banking supervision system. ALIX GRANGER

Estonians belong to the Finno-Ugrian (and not the Indo-European) language group. From 1900 to 1944, fewer than 3000 Estonians immigrated to Canada. Of the 72 000 Estonian political refugees who had fled their home country in 1944 for Sweden and Germany, nearly 14 000 immigrated to Canada between 1946 and 1955. Between 1947 and 1949, almost 1600 of them crossed the Atlantic in 9-20 m "Viking" boats that they had bought in Sweden. Since 1960 practically no Estonians have immigrated and the 1986 census estimated that there were 13 200 Canadians of Estonian origin.

Migration and Settlement A few small Estonian farming communities emerged in southern Alberta during the first half of the century, but most prewar Estonian immigrants settled in urban areas. The postwar immigrants settled in industrial cities, especially in Toronto, where, since 1960, more than 50% of all Estonians in Canada have lived. Other sizable Estonian communities are found in Montréal, Vancouver and Hamilton.

Social and Cultural Life Because of their professional and occupational skills, Estonian immigrants did not encounter serious adjustment problems, although few were able to maintain their former professions. At present, Canadians of Estonian origin are among the ethnic groups with the highest average educational levels and incomes. The Estonians have contributed particularly to the development of amateur sports and, particularly in Toronto and Vancouver, to architecture and the construction industry.

Group Maintenance Since the 1950s the Estonians have maintained an elaborate structure of ethnic organizations, especially in Toronto. They continue to co-operate closely with similar communities of the Estonian diaspora in the US, Sweden, Australia, England and West Germany. Every fourth year these communities organize a well-attended, week-long Estonian World Festival that rotates among Canada (Toronto), the US, Sweden and Australia. The Estonian communities abroad continue to maintain strong choir singing, theatre, folk dancing, amateur sports and scouting traditions. However, because Estonians have been well assimilated into Canadian society, only in Toronto do a significant number of second- and third-generation Estonians use Estonian as their home language.
K. AUN

Reading: K. Aun, *The Political Refugees: A History of Estonians in Canada* (1985).

Estrogen, female sex hormone produced primarily in the ovaries. Many of the female body's vital metabolic and physiologic processes are controlled by estrogen. Estrogen has specific effects on the female sex organs and sex characteristics. It also acts as a building block and metabolic regulator on other tissues and systems such as the skin, skeletal musculature and probably the cardiovascular system. Pharmaceutical estrogen products are divided into those used for conception control and those used for their metabolic and physiologic effects alone.

In 1885 the French physiologist Claude Bernard discovered that, in addition to external excretions, many of the body's glands produce internal secretions which may affect all or specific body organs. In 1906 investigators discovered that the ovaries secrete a hormone that produces the phenomenon of estrus (hence, estrogen). Other researchers made further explorations into the action of estrogen. At McGill, J.B. COLLIP, D.L. Thomson and J.S.L. Browne studied placental and ovarian hormones and, in 1930, published 3 papers in the *Canadian Medical Assn Journal*, describing isolation of the estrogen complex in pure form from a human placenta. They named this natural compound Emmenin. In collaboration with the McGill investigators and with the approval of McGill's biochemistry department, Ayerst, McKenna and Harrison in Montréal manufactured Emmenin, the first orally active, female sex hormone available for clinical use.

In 1938 another group of researchers published data describing the isolation of estrogens from pregnant mares' urine. Drs Stanley Cook and Gordon Grant, of Ayerst, decided to investigate this estrogenic complex as a possible source of an orally active product. On 17 Jan 1939 the first gallon of pregnant mares' urine was processed at Ayerst. During the following years, Ayerst researchers determined the biologic and metabolic effects of the various estrogenic components of the new compound, which they named Premarin. When Premarin became available for general clinical use (1941), physicians recognized its powerful metabolic and therapeutic effects. Ayerst still processes Premarin at its estrogen-extraction plant in Manitoba, depending on prairie farmers to deliver urine from thousands of pregnant mares. The finished product is exported all over the world. *See* also BIOLOGICAL PRODUCTS.

ELVIRA STAHL

Etcheverry, Sam, football player (b at Carlsbad, NM 20 May 1930). Etcheverry turned professional with the MONTREAL ALOUETTES in 1952, and later earned his nickname of "The Rifle" as a quarterback. His CANADIAN FOOTBALL LEAGUE statistics show 1630 completions from 2829 passes for 25 582 yards, including 163 interceptions and 174 touchdowns. In 1956 he obtained the CFL single-season passing mark of 4723 yards, with a completion total of 276 in 446 attempts. In the same year, he also obtained the record for the longest completed pass, 109 yards to Hal PATTERSON against Hamilton at Montréal. Etcheverry played in 3 Grey Cup finals, and coached the Alouettes to their 1970 Grey Cup win. He won several awards, including Schenley Player of the Year in 1954 and induction to the Canadian Football Hall of Fame in 1969. GERALD REDMOND

Éthier-Blais, Jean, professor, writer, literary critic (b at Sturgeon Falls, Ont 15 Nov 1925). Professor of French literature at McGill since 1962, Éthier-Blais regularly contributed literary criticism to *Le Devoir* from 1961. Some of these articles were published in *Signets* (3 vols, 1967, 1973). His original works include poems, stories, essays and novels (*Mater Europa*, 1968, and *Les Pays étrangers*, 1982). Éthier-Blais handles the universal themes of love and death, but always through the perspective of his own experience and the cultural situation of French Canadians. He became a member of the French Canadian Academy in 1971; in 1983 the St-Jean-Baptiste Society of Montréal awarded him its prestigious Prix Duvernay. NICOLE BOURBONNAIS

Ethnic and Race Relations Canadian society can be described, at one level, as a complex network of relations among ethnic groups which occupy unequal economic, political and social positions in Canadian society. Within this complexity 3 main axes of ethnic differentiation are identifiable: the relationship between natives and nonnatives, between English and French and between the colonizing (or "charter") groups and other immigrants and their descendants. These distinctions are relevant not only to the private experiences of individuals but also to public issues, eg, aboriginal rights and land claims; linguistic rights; IMMIGRATION POLICY; PREJUDICE AND DISCRIMINATION; and MULTICULTURALISM. Although interrelated, these issues pertain to different matters largely because they concern different groups. For example, the controversy over language between English and French differs from that between other ethnolinguistic groups (eg, Ukrainians, Italians, Greeks) and the English-speaking or French-speaking communities because the *official* languages of Canada are English and French.

The relations among ethnic groups must be understood in terms of the access to and control of the society's resources and of the functioning of rules and practices that may benefit or disadvantage particular groups. Inequality among groups can result from several factors, including the circumstances of their arrival in Canada (eg, establishment of a colony by a European power; individual or family immigration); their size; their visibility; their internal economic, political and social organization; the direct or indirect support received from other groups or countries; and the power and status of the country of origin in the international order.

Groups who have achieved control over certain resources (eg, jobs, capital, institutional authority) will protect their gains and attempt to extend them. They are likely to try to deny access to power and control to other groups, and the institutional and bureaucratic barriers are designed to preclude or defuse attempts by such groups to bring about change. The relatively disadvantaged may indeed pressure for change in the economic or political situation, but their chances of success depend on the very factors which brought about inequality. As a result, improvements in the situation of disadvantaged minorities are frequently very slow (*see* ELITES).

Natives and Canadian Society The relationship between native peoples and the rest of Canadian society is characterized first by "marginality" and dependence. The historical settlement and expansion of English and French societies led to the displacement of the native population. Land was the main concern of the successive Indian Acts and of the treaties. Total control of Indian lands was given first (1850) to the Commission of Indian Lands and then, through the BRITISH NORTH AMERICA ACT, to the federal government. Through INDIAN TREATIES, from 1850 to 1921, large tracts of land in central and western Canada were surrendered in exchange for reserve lands, money and promises of social assistance.

An objective of the INDIAN ACT of 1876 and of its subsequent versions was the control and management of the native population. For this purpose, it defined "status Indians" as those registered in 1874, their closest dependants in the male line, and their wives and children (they numbered 348 809 in 1984). It also established a bureaucracy for the administration of Indian affairs, which was staffed almost entirely by non-Indians. Recently, this situation has begun to change: Indians have been recruited in the government bureaucracy; the administration of Indian affairs has been decentralized; and moves in the direction of self-government have been undertaken, although progress in that direction is encountering considerable resistance, including from provincial governments.

The population of native ancestry also includes non-status Indians, Métis and Inuit. They do not have the special relationship that the status Indians have with the federal government. All, however, are affected by the dominant society's ideology of superiority and inferiority and tend to be located at the lower levels of the stratification system. The formation of native organizations, including Pan-Indian national associations whose primary objective is the defence of Indian interests in land, may restore both objective and subjective equality to native peoples. However, in their efforts at social, economic and political organization, native people will have to overcome the legacy of marginality and dependence. They will also have to transcend the numerous cleavages within the native population arising from different cultural and linguistic backgrounds, from the division of status Indians into some 592 bands, and the division of status from non-status Indians.

Francophone-Anglophone Relations After the Conquest, the British progressively constructed a society parallel to the one that the French had already established. The institutions of the 2 subsocieties are critical for their respective members because they provide them with economic and political opportunities and because they embody their language, cultural values and traditions. As a result, the 2 groups have struggled, unequally, for the control of cultural, economic and political institutions.

The competition between the English and French societies has always been manifested in the struggle over the control of government institutions. The Quebec Act of 1774, the 1791 Constitutional Act, the Act of Union of 1841, the BNA Act and its modifications, the 1982 patriation of the Constitution and the MEECH LAKE ACCORD of 1987 have all been concerned with the DISTRIBUTION OF POWERS and the symbolic recognition of the language and culture of both groups. The issues of job distribution, of control of economic institutions, of culture and of the size of their respective populations have been reflected in conflicts over policies dealing with matters such as immigration, international relations, industry and trade, education, family allowances, language of education and work, and mass communication. Of course, issues change with time and circumstances, but the fundamental questions of political power, population size, access to capital for development, and of the cultural character of the society and its institutions will always be there as long as the 2 groups are in the same society. The competition is unequal, however, largely because of differences in population and wealth, and because of the Conquest and its implications, the British influence in the shaping of Canadian society and government institutions, and the anglophone character of N American society.

Immigrants and Canadian Society The decrease in British representation led to a concomitant decrease in their control of the economy or of the political system or to a change in the status of Canada as a "white" society. Other European immigrants do not share equality with the charter groups. John PORTER in *The Vertical Mosaic* argued that the crucial fact of Canadian life was the "exclusion of minority groups from the main loci of decision making within the corporate sector of the economy" (*see* BUSINESS ELITES).

In politics the composition of federal Cabinets since 1867 has reflected only the struggle to balance English and French interests. The decision by certain groups, eg, Finns and Ukrainians and other central and eastern European immigrants, to become engaged in radical political activities has reflected their decision to challenge what has been called "the notion of Canadian society on the one hand and the existence of ethnic groups as something independent of the society on the other."

Conflicts between immigrant and charter groups are a result of unequal access to employment and education, and unequal security and social respect. Several groups have been the victims of systematic exploitation, discrimination and social exclusion, but their situation has largely improved as a result of their own individual and collective efforts, and because of legislation and economic prosperity.

For the first generation of immigrants the structure of social networks and organizations is formed largely for adaptive purposes, ie, to advance or defend shared interests and to provide social support. The structure tends to weaken in succeeding generations if the group has achieved some measure of economic advancement and assimilation. At the individual level, this manifests itself in the loss of language and culture and in a decreased participation in the group's associations and social networks. This does not mean a complete loss of identity and culture. However, what the second and subsequent generations retain as their lives evolve in Canada is a selection and transformation of what was brought from the country of origin.

Visible Minorities The visibility of certain groups adds a dimension to the question of their full incorporation in Canadian society. Racism in Canada has been well documented in historical studies of immigration. Canadians manifest an ostrichlike approach to the problem, although studies reveal that PREJUDICE AND DISCRIMINATION are a reality in Canada (*see also* ANTI-SEMITISM BLACKS; JAPANESE; CHINESE; JEWS). To the extent that negative attitudes and behaviour exist, it is more difficult for visible than for other minorities to avoid being subjected to them.

The Relationship of Ethnic Groups to Anglophone and Francophone Cultures raises the question of how certain manifestations of individual and collective ethnicity (if they are to exist) are to be recognized and incorporated into Canadian society and how social institutions are to be modified to accommodate and recognize various cultural traditions. The multiculturalism policies and programs of the various levels of government have been a step in that direction. But their aim has not been to restructure institutions to reflect the composition of the population. What such a restructuring would entail has by and large yet to be defined. And whether or not it should be attempted remains a highly controversial question.

RAYMOND BRETON

Ethnic Identity Ethnic identification describes the relation of an individual to a group with whom the individual believes he has common ancestry based on shared individual characteristics, shared sociocultural experiences, or both. An individual may identify with an important person, eg, a parent or a friend, with a group from which he draws values, eg, family or co-workers, or with a broad category of persons, eg, ethnic or occupational groups. Ethnic identification can exist at all 3 levels.

An ethnic group is often a distinct category of the population in a larger society with a (generally) different culture. Distinct ethnic and cultural groups were recorded by Herodotus 2500 years ago. Scholars note that ethnic groups may be the result of migrations of whole societies (or parts of them), military conquest or altered political boundaries. Many factors characterize ethnic groups. First, they usually control a territory, tightly knit community or network, within which their offspring may perpetuate their heritage. Different ethnic groups may occupy the same area but use different resources. The French in Québec retain control of the provincial territory; the Hutterites are a rural segregated ethnic community; Indian reserves are communities segregated by the state within which various ethnic groups may exist. Second, ethnic institutions often generate forces of attraction. A minority can develop its own social system, with control over its own institutions, so that interaction of the group will take place largely within the system. The French and Jews frequently maintain a comprehensive set of religious, educational and welfare institutions. Residential segregation and ethnic institutional independence therefore tend to reinforce each other. Third, individuals need to identify clearly with the heritage and culture of the group, perhaps through language, endogamy, choice of friends, religion, parochial schools, voluntary organizations, etc. Territorial, institutional and cultural identity factors reinforce each other, so that ethnic individuals can remain distinct and less prone to assimilation. Historical symbols are also important. Without ethnic pride and knowledge, the desire to perpetuate tradition rapidly diminishes. The Jews have ritualized their history and their youth are exposed to the symbols, eg, special days, fasting, food habits, etc. Fourth, a political or religious ideology that promotes values considered more important than cultural and institutional ones may give ethnic youth purpose and impetus. There is often a very strong correlation between religion and ethnicity, eg, most French and Polish Canadians are Roman Catholic. Sixth, individuals with a sense of mission often use sociopsychological means to adapt an ideology to a current situation, linking it symbolically with the past. Charismatic leaders of minority movements have included Louis RIEL and René LÉVESQUE. Minorities may identify with other dimensions of ethnicity, but identity, territory, institutions, culture, heritage, ideology and leaders are crucial.

Various theories have been developed to explain the fate of ethnic groups in an industrial society. The assimilation theory assumes that ethnic groups are constantly becoming more like the dominant culture, which in N America is represented by white, Anglo-Saxon protestants. The "melting pot" or amalgamation theory has been criticized as deterministic because it assumes that minority groups will not be able to withstand the power of the dominant group and will be synthesized into a new group. Canada's relatively open IMMIGRATION POLICY has provided the potential opportunity for many peoples to contribute to a melting pot, but the synthesis of the many into a recognizable national character has been a long time coming, perhaps partly because it was not until 1971 that Canadians ceased to be described as British subjects. Cultural pluralism theorists maintain that different ethnic groups maintain their unique identities over time. It has been argued that people do not choose their ancestry, that each of the minority groups has something of value to contribute to a country and that the Canadian Constitution assumes that all people are created equal, even though there may be many distinct differences. Cultural pluralism holds that the trend toward permissive differentiation has been established in Canada by acceptance of pluralist religious expressions and a diversity of political parties and ideologies, and that multiculturalism is therefore a logical policy for all. Some social scientists argue that ethnic change is not a single social process but a number of subprocesses and that the opposing processes of assimilation and pluralism may therefore occur simultaneously, depending on change of cultural patterns to those of the larger society, significant entrance into institutions of the larger society, intermarriage, development of a sense of "peoplehood" based on a modification of ingroup and outgroup networks.

Other social scientists study the processes of ethnic conflict. Marx believed conflict resulted from class struggle, but most ethnic groups in Canada do not aspire to such an extensive power struggle. While conflict may occasionally be manifested by revolution and secession, eg, the FLQ movement in Québec, it also exists in less intense forms. When many subgroups and a multitude of cultures coexist they will maintain distinct identities, providing a potential for conflict of values, territorial interests and power relationships. Québec's QUIET REVOLUTION, the quest of the native peoples for equal rights and the relations between adjacent ethnic communities all demonstrate a constant potential for dissension.

LEO DRIEDGER

Reading: Leo Driedger, *Ethnic Canada: Identities and Inequalities* (1987); A.B. Anderson and J.S. Frideres, *Ethnicity in Canada: Theoretical Perspectives* (1981).

Ethnic Languages There have been several distinct periods of IMMIGRATION into Canada by groups of non-British or non-French origin. By 1901, only slightly less than 10% of the total population consisted of members of ethnic minority groups (primarily European, but also a significant number of Chinese who came to Canada to work on the railway). The early 20th century saw a spectacular increase in European immigration, particularly from Ukraine and Germany. This period was also marked by the appearance of substantial numbers of Serbo-Croatian and Greek immigrants, as well as smaller groups from countries as diverse as Lebanon, Romania and Turkey. During WWI immigration was insignificant, but the period between the wars brought a new wave – again mostly from Europe. Immigration virtually stopped once more during WWII, but the postwar period brought a steady stream of newcomers, over half a million of them from Italy. In this later period significant numbers of non-European immigrants arrived, particularly Asians. Since 1979 Canada has accepted thousands of Indo-Chinese REFUGEES through both government and private sponsorship. Today Canadians of non-British, non-French origins represent more than 35 different ethnic groups and constitute more than 30% of the country's total population.

Although immigrants are free to settle where they choose, a disproportionate number live in Ontario. The Royal Commission on BILINGUALISM AND BICULTURALISM reported that in 1961 almost 42% of Toronto residents were born outside the country. Fully 58% of the population of the Prairie provinces, 21% of the population of BC and 18% of Ontario's population is composed of immigrants of other than British or French origin (1986c).

These statistics do not reflect the number of Canadians who have declared a nonofficial language as a mother tongue. According to the 1981 census, just over 3 million of the 8 million ethnic population learned a language other than English or French in childhood, and of these over 1.5 million now use an OFFICIAL LANGUAGE in the home. They understand the first language but use it infrequently. These individuals have integrated into Canadian society.

The Royal Commission on Bilingualism and Biculturalism states that *integration* "does not imply the loss of an individual's identity and original characteristics or of his original language and culture." *Assimilation*, on the other hand, is "almost total absorption into another linguistic and cultural group. An assimilated individual gives up his cultural identity and may even ... change his name." It was the impression of the commission that immigrants of non-British, non-French origin clearly preferred integration to assimilation. Obviously, the maintenance of a mother tongue together with mastery of an official language is indicative of integration; however, loss of the mother tongue by an ethnic community does not necessarily imply total assimilation. A variety of factors such as religion, folk traditions, race, marriage outside the community, geographic concentration, size of the group, its economic strength and the ratio of foreign-born to native-born individuals within it all interact in determining the degree of assimilation undergone in a given group.

Certain ethnic groups have maintained strong linguistic and cultural ties with their places of origin, as well as developing new ethnic-Canadian, integrated cultures here. The Ukrainians in western Canada are a case in point. It has been suggested that a principal factor in their retention of the Ukrainian language was their settlement in rural areas. The combination of isolation and a fierce pride in the culture of the homeland resulted in the development of very strong Ukrainian communities which survived and flourished when Canada underwent mass urbanization. The unique set of circumstances faced by the first Ukrainian immigrants upon their arrival had a major impact on their successful integration. Other groups, under different circumstances, have been assimilated to a greater extent (eg, Scandinavians).

A powerful force that leads to both integration and assimilation is the desire for identification with the prestige (majority) group: the anglophone community in English Canada and the francophone community in Québec. This is particularly evident in the children of various ethnic groups. The desire for identification pervades all aspects of their behaviour: play, mode of dress, recreation, food, values and language. Linguistic identification means speaking the official language grammatically, without accent. It ensures that the individual will be recognized and accepted as one of the prestige group. The desire to identify with the majority is so strong that it entails the rejection of everything that could delay this identification, including one's mother tongue. The process often takes place against the will of parents who wish their children to maintain the language and culture of origin. Identification with peers is usually stronger than the influence of the family; however, if other cultural factors (eg, a strong religious influence, as is present in most Canadian Jewish communities) contribute to ethnic identity, the child can integrate successfully without assimilating completely. The educational systems across Canada have recently provided for increased opportunity for ethnic groups to maintain their mother tongues. The number of immersion programs in other than official languages (*see* SECOND-LANGUAGE INSTRUCTION) is on the rise; in the 1980s the Edmonton Public School Board, for example, offered immersion schooling in Arabic, Mandarin, Hebrew, Ukrainian and German.

It is inevitable that many ethnic groups settling in Canada should undergo linguistic assimilation; what is remarkable is the revival of interest in the languages of origin and the ongoing integration into Canadian society of cultural traditions that originated elsewhere. *See also* ETHNIC LITERATURE; LANGUAGES IN USE.

BERNARD SAINT-JACQUES

Reading: W.H. Coons et al, eds, *The Individual, Language and Society in Canada* (1977); H. Giles, ed, *Language, Ethnicity and Intergroup Relations* (1977); Giles and Bernard Saint-Jacques, eds, *Language and Ethnic Relations* (1979); Stanley Lieberson, *Language and Ethnic Relations in Canada* (1970); Bernard Saint-Jacques, "The Languages of Immigrants" in J.K. Chambers, ed, *The Languages of Canada* (1979).

Ethnic Literature In Canadian English, the term "ethnic" has been used to designate those immigrants who do not belong to Canada's founding European cultures: the Catholic French and the Protestant Anglo-Celtic. It also embraces the aboriginal inhabitants of Canada, the native Indian and Inuit who have stood distant and often alienated from Canadian society. Literature by ethnic writers or about ethnic experience has generally been regarded as outside the literary mainstream and has often been overlooked by scholars. The expression "Canadian ethnic literature" is itself complex, dependent on combinations of such variables as the writer's ethnic identity, the language of writing or translation and the literary expression of ethnic themes. To be fair, a definition of Canadian ethnic literature must be comprehensive and include émigré writing, both in the nonofficial languages and in translation; literature by writers who perceive themselves as belonging to an ethnic minority and write from this perspective (usually in English or French); and works that deal with immigrant or ethnic experience but are not necessarily written by a member of the group portrayed.

The relationship between ethnic literature and mainstream writing is very much in flux. The latter is increasingly defined in the light of Canada's ethnic diversity. This can be seen in re-evaluations of the separate Irish, Scots and Welsh traditions in mainstream writing; the recognition in English Canadian letters of Jewish writers; the increasing thematic significance of ethnicity in the works of contemporary writers; and the growing number of authors of ethnic descent who are making their mark on Canadian literature. The work of second and later generations of ethnic writers such as George RYGA, W.D. Valgardson, Rudy WIEBE, Andrew SUKNASKI and Pier Giorgio DI CICCO is permeating the mainstream sensibility; the work of émigré writers such as George Faludy, Josef ŠKVORECKÝ, Waclaw Iwaniuk and Robert Zend is becoming increasingly available in translation; and the work of new immigrants such as Kristjana Gunnars, Pablo Urbanyi and Cyril Dabydeen is becoming accessible as it receives critical acclaim.

Canadian literature was born of the colonial mentality of early immigrants from the British Isles and France. The earliest form of ethnic bias may be seen marginally in the period 1841-55, which is described by Carl F. Klinck in *Literary History of Canada* (2nd ed 1976) as that of "genteel colonialism." The period's prominent English-language writers desired to be English and aristocratic in every sense, not only in life-style but in language. Thus some objected to "uncivilized" Irish and Scottish pronunciations invading Canadian speech patterns. Susanna MOODIE expressed a more blatant prejudice against the Irish in ROUGHING IT IN THE BUSH (1852), calling the Irish "savages" without "common decency." Although British Canadian writers like Moodie may sometimes have perpetuated Old World prejudices against the "ethnic" Irish and Scots, the Anglo-Celtic community remained fundamentally united as a social and literary force.

A more deeply significant ethnic subject of early English Canadian literature was one who, ironically, most deserves not to be considered foreign: the native Indian. Yet no other group has been as persistently portrayed as "the other" in the white man's literary world, nor has any other "ethnic" group registered as strongly on the consciousness of writers. Whether the fictional Indian was depicted as the barbaric antagonist or the noble savage – in such early works as John RICHARDSON'S gothic novel, WACOUSTA (1832), and the romantic poetry of Charles MAIR, Charles SANGSTER and Duncan Campbell SCOTT – he became a projection of the imaginative needs of colonial culture. Even in late 20th-century works where the Indian is sympathetically drawn, he remains the "other" and thus a touchstone for white culture. In works such as George Ryga's *The Ecstasy of Rita Joe* (1970) and W.O. MITCHELL'S *The Vanishing Point* (1973), the Indian is a fitting vehicle through which to express dissent from white society. Nonetheless, contemporary writers such as Mitchell and Margaret LAURENCE portray with some realism, and a great deal of sympathy, the condition and status of the modern Indian and the Métis. Several writers, particularly in the West, have created fiction and poetry in which aboriginal mythology and perspectives shape literary forms or contribute to the definition of the artist, his contemporary characters and his region. These writers include John NEWLOVE, Dale Zieroth, Andy Suknaski, George BOWERING, Sheila WATSON, Robert KROETSCH, Susan Musgrave, Leonard COHEN, Margaret ATWOOD and Marian ENGEL. Rudy Wiebe has made honest attempts to realize the Indian's point of view in his historical novels *The Temptations of Big Bear* (1973) and *The Scorched-Wood People* (1977).

If the legacy of British colonialism meant the literary interpretation of the Indian through the view of whites, it also meant that other ethnic groups were dimly seen. English Canadian literature, if it treated the ethnic as a subject at all, demonstrated less interest in ethnic character than in assimilation. This is true of the work of Presbyterian minister Charles W. GORDON (pseudonym Ralph Connor) in the novel *The Foreigner* (1909), in which the protagonist, Kalmar Kalman, a "Slav," lives in the "foreign colony" of North Winnipeg of 1884. Ascribing to Kalman the stereotyped "Slavic" traits of exotic features and primitive passions, Connor "Canadianizes" and "civilizes" his hero by having him adopt the religion and moral values of the Anglo-Saxon Protestant.

The pressure to assimilate necessarily affected the ethnic person's view of himself and his people. A crisis of identity is particularly evident in those second-generation, English-speaking ethnic writers who write of themselves in relation to their immigrant parents, eg, Ukrainian Canadian Vera Lysenko, in *Yellow Boots* (1954), and Hungarian Canadian John Marlyn, in *Under the Ribs of Death* (1957). In more recent literature, the second-generation ethnic writer may express similar dislocation but does so with less shame and with a new authority and pride in ethnic roots, at the same time often protesting against racial discrimination or unfair treatment of ethnic minorities. Joy KOGAWA, for example, vindicates her Japanese Canadian people in OBASAN (1981). Immigrant writers, too, can write with self-confidence about injustice. Bharati MUKHERJEE, an accomplished writer born in Calcutta, writes bitterly but with self-esteem of her unsatisfactory life in Canada, as both an Indian woman and an ethnic writer; Guyana-born Cyril Dabydeen records the hard ironies of being a black immigrant in Canada, without relinquishing his self-respect. Assimilation continues to be problematic also for the characters in ethnic literature, but their authors are making increasingly bold pleas for equal rights and opportunities.

Inuit Literature The Inuit did not develop a written language; Christian missionaries introduced written Inuktitut early in the 18th century. Consequently the first Inuktitut literature consisted of translations of the Bible and other religious materials, to which secular classics were soon added. The first major scholarly sources of traditional Inuit poetry are *Expedition – the Danish Ethnographical Expedition to Arctic North America, 1921-24* (1928-45, 1976), by Knud Rasmussen, and *Songs of the Copper Eskimos* (1925), collected by Helen Roberts and Diamond JENNESS. Among southern Canadians there has been a growing interest in Inuit literature. Drawing on the pioneering work of Rasmussen, Roberts and Jenness, others such as John Robert COLOMBO (*Poems of the Inuit,* 1981) have collected traditional Inuit literature.

Contemporary Inuit literature, published in both Inuktitut and English, includes important diaries and autobiographies, such as *Sketches of Labrador Life* (1980), by Lydia Campbell. *People from Our Side* (1975), by Dorothy Eber and Peter PITSEOLAK, depicts, often humorously, recent Inuit culture, shaped by contact with the N American mainstream. Modern Inuit culture is depicted in darker tones by Anthony Apakark Thrasher in *Thrasher: Skid Row Eskimo* (1976). Recently a number of Inuktitut-English journals, such as *Inuit Today*, have published the work of contemporary Inuit writers. Both traditional and contemporary Inuit literature are included in Robin Gedalof's *An Annotated Bibliography of Canadian Inuit Literature* (1979).

Indian Literature Indian literature in Canada is rooted in the oral tradition of storytelling and includes all types of traditional narratives, such as myths, legends, fairy tales, animal stories and fables (*see* ORAL LITERATURE). Such narratives have proven to be fascinating to white culture, beginning in the 17th century when Jesuit missionaries first recorded Huron and Algonquian tales in the JESUIT RELATIONS, and continuing into the 19th and 20th centuries when scores of anthropologists, folklorists and sociologists studied various tribes and recorded their FOLKLORE. Thus, there is a wealth of transcribed Indian legends and myths. However, written translation has unavoidably lessened both the nuances and the oral impact of the narratives; the imposition of Christian value systems has altered aboriginal meanings; the tendency of folklorists to place Indian folklore in a European context of storytelling has often led to distorted interpretations; and the many Indian tales that deal, often humorously, with the body processes have been left out of anthologies because they have been unacceptable to white morality. As a result of the early influence of white contact, a purely aboriginal tradition of Indian narrative is difficult to trace. Moreover, because the Indians are not a homogenous cultural or linguistic group, the mythology as expressed in their narratives is vast and complex. Indian storytelling also allowed the storyteller to invent and alter narratives as he pleased; thus there can be many variants of a story, although certain motifs and narrative patterns appear to be common (eg, the trickster figure as the source of creation).

Contemporary native authors are finding their own voice. Their writing includes rhetorical and political works, such as Harold CARDINAL's *The Rebirth of Canada's Indians* (1977) and Duke Redbird's *We Are Metis* (1980); retrospectives of the Indian way of life, such as *Potlatch* (1969) by George CLUTESI of the Northwest Coast Indians, *These Mountains Are Our Sacred Places* (1977) by Chief John SNOW of the Stoney and *The Ways of My Grandmothers* (1980) by Beverly Hungry Wolf of the Blood Tribe; autobiographies, biographies and memoirs such as Anahareo's *Devil in Deerskins* (1972); and creative literature including poetry, legend and drama, such as Norval MORRISSEAU's Ojibwa *Legends of My People* (1965) and Chief Dan GEORGE's poetic volume *My Heart Soars* (1974). A milestone in the recognition of Indian literature was the publication of the anthology *I Am an Indian* (1969), edited by non-Indian Kent Gooderham.

Acadian Literature ACADIA first referred to the French Atlantic-seaboard colonies in the New World. In 1755, during the SEVEN YEARS' WAR, British authorities stripped the Acadians of their lands and rights and deported most of them. Some returned when French-English hostilities abated. The Acadian story first found sympathetic literary expression in T.C. HALIBURTON's *An Historical and Statistical Account of Nova Scotia* (1829), which influenced American poet Henry Wadsworth Longfellow to write EVANGELINE (1847), a narrative poem of the expulsion. This romantic tale received international attention and inspired mainstream writers, such as Charles G.D. ROBERTS, to write fictional romances of Acadian history and induced Acadian writers themselves to express an Acadian consciousness.

The theme of cultural survival is synonymous with Acadian literature, which often celebrates a lost past, extols Acadian traditions and language, and protests past and present treatment. Since the publication of Napoléon Landry's *Poèmes de mon pays* (1949), Acadian literature has flourished; its impetus has come, in part, from the example of cultural nationalism in Québec, from the election in 1960 of the first Acadian premier of New Brunswick, L.J. ROBICHAUD, from the establishment in 1972 of the first publishing house in Acadia, les Éditions d'Acadie, and from the national and international recognition of Acadian writer Antonine MAILLET for such works as *Pointe-aux-Coques* (1958) and *La Sagouine* (1971; tr 1979). Notable modern Acadian writers include poets Ronald Després (*Silences à nourrir de sang*, 1958) and Raymond LeBlanc (*Cri de terre*, 1973).

Irish, Scottish and Welsh Literature Some Scottish Irish from largely Protestant Ulster immigrated in the mid-18th century, as did SCOTS from Scotland. By the end of the century Scots were immigrating in droves, followed by many IRISH in the first decades of the 19th century and scores more with the potato famine of 1846-47. The greatest WELSH immigration coincided with economic depressions in Wales in the 19th and early 20th centuries. These groups were integrated into the culture around them and their literature has been considered mainstream. Thomas D'Arcy MCGEE, for example, attempted to foster a national spirit in Canada through such works as his *Canadian Ballads* (1858), which were based on Irish ballad forms. Scotsman Alexander MCLACHLAN was a popular poet who wrote such "Canadian" works as *The Emigrant, and Other Poems* (1861) in the tradition of Robert Burns. Much scholarship remains to be done in assessing the nature of Irish and Scottish immigrant literature and in tracing the Irish and Scottish literary heritage from the colonial period until the present day, when such contemporary writers as Brian MOORE, Morley CALLAGHAN, Alice MUNRO and Margaret Laurence have continued to demonstrate an Irish or Scottish sensibility.

Many early Scottish settlers were Scottish Gaels (Highlanders) who brought with them to settlements in the Maritimes, Manitoba and parts of Ontario the Gaelic language and the ancient, oral, bardic tradition of songs, folktales and epic narratives. Gaelic poets, such as pioneer bards John McLean (who came to Nova Scotia in 1819) and Rev Duncan Black Blair, have had little effect on mainstream literature, but their poetry has remained intact and is of interest to those who know the language, as Margaret MacDonell's translated edition, *The Emigrant Experience* (1982), bears witness.

Later Arrivals Other immigrants who came later and settled primarily in the West brought literary traditions, both oral and written. One early group was the ICELANDERS, who came to Canada in the mid-1870s fleeing volcanic eruptions in their homeland. Despite their small numbers, they produced a notable body of literature in Canada. In Manitoba the new settlers quickly established newspapers, which became vehicles for lively debate as well as for creative writing. A number of writers, exemplified by Thorsteinn Thorsteinsson and Sigurbjorn Johannson, wrote poetry and stories in their native language but about the Canadian immigrant experience. The literary achievement of one pioneer, Stephan STEPHANSSON, was particularly remarkable. Though he was largely unknown to Canadians until recently, Stephansson received the title of poet laureate of Iceland on the strength of poems he composed in Canada. He profoundly revitalized the Icelandic language and tradition in which he wrote, while addressing the Canadian experience with insight and a freshness of imagery that are not altogether lost even in translations of his lyric poetry. The pioneers were followed by a generation of writers who, though continuing to write in Icelandic and out of an essentially Icelandic tradition, addressed Canadian experience. Notable among them are Guttormur Guttormsson and Einar Pall Jonsson. Jonsson's well-known poem "The Laundress" captures the sense of loss engendered by assimilation. Like the work of numerous early ethnic writers, that of Stephansson, Guttormsson and Jonsson first became available to English-speaking Canadians through the efforts of Watson Kirkconnell, an English professor who translated and compiled collections of poetry in languages other than English and French, most notably his 1935 *Canadian Overtones*. Kirkconnell also wrote the "Publications in Other Languages" section of UNIVERSITY OF TORONTO QUARTERLY from 1935 to 1966.

Caught between the remnants of the immigrant culture and the evolving mainstream, the ethnic writer of the second or third generation typically becomes a "mediator" between cultures. Icelandic Canadian writer Laura Goodman SALVERSON, in her romantic novel *The Viking Heart* (1923), tells the story of her people through fictional characters who gradually commit themselves to Canada and find acceptance here. In her more realistic autobiography, *Confessions of an Immigrant's Daughter* (1939), she explores with some frankness the problems the immigrant family faces. Some contemporary writers of Icelandic background, eg, W.D. Valgardson and recent immigrant Kristjana Gunnars, still explore Icelandic characters and themes. Valgardson's collections of short stories, *Bloodflowers* (1973), *God is Not a Fish Inspector* (1975) and *Red Dust* (1978), his book of poetry, *In the Gutting Shed* (1976), and his novel, *Gentle Sinners* (1980), present with stark clarity a dark vision of the interface between ethnicity and the post-modern world. In her poetry, particularly *The Settlement Poems* (1980), and in her book of short stories, *The Axe's Edge* (1983), Gunnars attempts to merge historical research and a poetic, almost mystical, vision to provide a narrative vehicle for the Icelandic Canadian experience.

Other Scandinavians have been present in Canadian literature as well, either as writers or as characters. Norwegian-born Martha Ostenso contributed to the emergence of realism in Canada through her prairie novel, *Wild Geese* (1925), which portrays an authoritarian farmer's impact on his wife and children. German immigrant Frederick Philip GROVE brought naturalism to his treatment of Scandinavian immigrant characters in *Settlers of the Marsh* (1925), and Anglo-Canadian writer Nellie MCCLUNG presented a Finnish immigrant as her main character in *Painted Fires* (1925). Danish-Norwegian writer Aksel Sandemose spent several years in the Maritimes and the western provinces, and wrote several novels dealing with the Canadian immigrant experience; perhaps the most notable is *Ross Dane* (1928), which is well known in Scandinavia.

Many Ukrainians came to Canada from eastern Europe after 1896, and they have produced a significant body of literature in Canada. Its evolution has been distinctive and complex, because of the Ukrainians' large numbers, their pioneer status in western Canada, their continuing immigration in significant numbers after WWII and the unique political history of their homeland. Combined, these factors have fostered a vital émigré tradition that finds its ultimate raison d'être in the belief of many Ukrainian writers and intellectuals that Ukrainian is a legitimate Canadian language (albeit not an official one) and that the Ukrainian literary tradition can continue to develop in Canada (*see* UKRAINIAN WRITING).

A natural offshoot of this tradition has been writing in English by authors of Ukrainian background. The writer best exemplifying the second-generation apologist's stance is Vera Lysenko, whose novel *Yellow Boots* tells the story of second-generation character Lili Landash, who assimilates into Anglo-Canadian culture through education and intermarriage. Other writers have been less willing to glorify the shedding of ethnic culture. George Ryga, for example, who does not directly fictionalize his own experience as the son of Ukrainian immigrants, nevertheless portrays ethnic characters from the inside while looking at Canadian society from the outsider's perspective, as in his play *The Ecstasy of Rita Joe* (1970) or his novels *Hungry Hills* (1963) and *Ballad of a Stonepicker* (1966). Andrew Suknaski, in *Wood Mountain Poems* (1976) and *The Land They Gave Away* (1982) attempts to create and give earthy expression to a personal mythology that embraces ethnicity and fuses it with Canadian experience.

GERMANS, Canada's third-largest ethnic group, settled in Canada as early as the 1750s and continue to do so. German Canadians have produced a significant body of literature, though it is difficult to generalize about it since the group is remarkably diverse. It includes, for example, Catholics and various ANABAPTIST sects (eg, MENNONITES) and secular immigrants from postwar Germany. In addition, Germans have settled throughout the country, though there are concentrations in Nova Scotia and Ontario and in the Prairie provinces. Their linguistic heritage is complex, including both High and Low German and a variety of dialects (*see* GERMAN WRITING).

Jewish writing is perhaps the most impressive of Canada's ethnic literatures, despite the relatively small number of JEWS in Canada. Shaped by successive waves of immigration that began in the early 1890s, Jewish writing reflects a variety of cultural and linguistic influences. Most of the early immigrants spoke Yiddish; consequently, though some writers chose to write in Hebrew, Jewish Canadian literature before WWII was written primarily in Yiddish. Jewish writers, principally those born in Canada, have also written in English. A.M. KLEIN, Irving LAYTON, Miriam WADDINGTON, Eli MANDEL and Mordecai RICHLER, as well as Fredelle Maynard, Morley Turgov and others, have so skilfully articulated Jewish experience in Canada that it has penetrated the mainstream sensibility, earning Jewish writing a major place in modern Canadian literature. Regardless of the language in which it is written, Jewish literature in Canada characteristically reflects an international vision, a minority sensibility and the profound influence of the WWII Holocaust (*see* JEWISH WRITING).

A number of the other small European groups in Canada, most notably HUNGARIANS, CZECHS and ITALIANS, have also produced substantial bodies of literature; as well, significant works have appeared in Estonian, Latvian, Lithuanian, Slovak, Croatian, Romanian, Russian and Spanish. Although the presence in Canada of a number of these groups dates back to the turn of the century, their literary activity has been most notable since WWII. Postwar European immigrants, often fleeing political upheaval in their own countries, were generally educated, urban people, and included writers and intellectuals who revitalized the cultural life of the group in Canada. Toronto, which attracted a majority of postwar European immigrants, has become the major centre of émigré writing.

Hungarians came to Canada during the early waves of immigration primarily as farmers and miners. They produced some literature, such as the epic poem written in the early 1900s by John Szatmari in which he describes his immigrant experiences, and the 1919 collection of poetry by Hungarian Canadians, *Mezel Virägok* (*Prairie Flowers*). But the Hungarian Canadians' most substantial literary achievement has been since WWII, as a result of the coming of age of second and subsequent generation writers such as John Marlyn, and in the work of postwar émigré writers, particularly those who fled Hungary after the uprising of 1956. Many Hungarian émigré writers, particularly the older ones such as poets Ferenc Fay, Tamas Tuz, Robert Zend and George Faludy, continue to write in Hungarian, whereas younger writers such as George Jonas write in English (although some, such as Gyorgy Vitez and Kemenes Gefin, also write in Hungarian). As Hungarian Canadian scholar John Miska points out, the Hungarian writer often wishes to be a "champion of freedom," and this "self-imposed crusading function" is reflected in the nationalistic, "heroic-emotional" tone of Hungarian Canadian poetry. A number of these writers also deal with Canadian subjects, exploring the tensions of émigré marginality. In 1969, Hungarian Canadian writers formed an association which has published several anthologies in Hungarian and one in English translation, *The Sound of Time* (1974).

POLES have also had a literary presence in Canada. In his epic novel *Three Generations* (1973), Melchior Wánkowicz, who immigrated to Canada in 1950, depicts the life of early Polish immigrants. The most notable second-generation writer of Polish descent is poet and literary scholar Louis DUDEK, whose achievements are very much a part of the mainstream. The postwar period brought to Canada writers such as poet Waclaw Iwaniuk. In his *Ciemny Czas* (1968; tr *Dark Times*, 1979) and most recently in his *Evenings on Lake Ontario* (1981) Iwaniuk explores, in tightly controlled verse and from both European and N American perspectives, the condition of contemporary man, but idealizes neither the Old World nor the New.

Postwar émigré writers from other European countries explore similar themes. Czech Canadian Josef Škvorecký was already a known literary figure before he immigrated to Canada following the Soviet invasion of Czechoslovakia in 1968. He has published a number of books in Canada that have been translated into English, such as his novella, *The Bass Saxophone* (1977) and *The Engineer of Human Souls* (1977; tr 1984). Although Škvorecký's work has political overtones, it is preoccupied with the universal themes of the individual's fate in history and the importance of art. Also noteworthy as a postwar émigré who writes about WWII and its political aftermath is Estonian Arved Viirlaid, who came to Canada in 1954.

Postwar immigration also revitalized ITALIAN WRITING in Canada, and literary activity among Italians has burgeoned, particularly since 1970. As with other groups, this growth follows as the result of an infusion of immigrants and increasing educational levels and affluence in Canada, but, unlike Hungarians, Czechs and others displaced by the war and subsequent political events, the Italians are not political expatriates. Most have come to find a better material life, and the old country remains at least partially accessible to them. Consequently, Italian Canadian writers, who most often write in English or French, are not preoccupied with European politics or a sense of exile. Rather, in the works of contemporary authors Frank PACI, Giorgio DI CICCO, Mary DI MICHELE and Alexandre Amprimoz, there is an attempt to balance material and spiritual values as the authors explore the price their parents, often labourers, paid for success in Canada. Their writing, which expresses a cosmopolitan sensibility, explores the contrasts and connections between Italy and Canada, often fusing the authors' Italian and Canadian identities. Italians in Canada can also claim the "protean literary force," John Robert COLOMBO, whose translations and anthologies have been crucial to bringing the work of ethnic writers into the mainstream of Canadian literature.

Asian Canadian literature also came of age during the 1970s. Although CHINESE and JAPANESE Canadians have lived in Canada for over a century, the earlier waves of immigrants produced little significant literature. This is true for a variety of reasons, not the least being the discrimination and hard labour they faced. However, some literature from early immigrants does exist, such as the poetry of Japanese-born Takeo Nakano, who came to Canada in 1920. He published a number of poems, many in the traditional Japanese 31-syllable *tanka*, such as "My Hands" (which appears in English translation in Colombo's *The Poets of Canada*, 1978). *Maple*, an anthology of *tanka* poems by Nakano and other first-generation Japanese Canadians, was published in 1975. Nakano also wrote of his WWII INTERNMENT experience in *Within the Barbed Wire Fence* (1980). The Chinese Canadian immigrant experience has been addressed by Charlie Jang, though his work has not yet been translated into English. In the 1970s, influenced by FRENCH CANADIAN NATIONALISM and by the Asian cultural revival that occurred in the US in the mid- and late 1960s in the wake of the black power movement, a number of young writers began to write about the Asian Canadian experience. These new writers, such as Roy KIYOOKA, Paul Yee and Kevin Irie, are preoccupied with the question of their identity as they articulate the experience of growing up as N Americans, albeit often with a second-class status, while being regarded by the predominantly white society as culturally "other." Asian Canadian writers, perhaps most notably Joy Kogawa, are examining their roots, thus bringing the missing perspective to the standard interpretations of events. In addition, these writers often reject assimilation. Their work has appeared in the journals *Asianadian* and *Rikka* as well as in an issue of *West Coast Review* (1981).

Recent Arrivals Since the 1970s ethnic literature has proliferated remarkably, largely because of the increased diversity of recent immigrants. Responding to the liberalization of Canada's immigration law in 1967, immigrants, most of them well educated and many of them members of visible minorities, have come from all parts of the globe. Just as they have changed and enriched Canadian society generally, they have also brought new dimensions to Canadian literature. Now, in addition to *belles lettres* in the traditional European nonofficial languages, ethnic literature includes such work in languages previously considered exotic to Canadian culture. Moreover, in bringing a Third World perspective to their writing, the new immigrant writers have extended the landscape of Canadian literature, enriched its forms and broadened its concerns.

For example, working in several languages, including Punjabi, Urdu and English, contemporary SOUTH ASIAN writers in Canada, such as Urdu poets Shaheen, Irfana Azia and Abdul Qavi Zia; Pakistani short-story writer M. Athar Tahir; Indian short-story writer Rohintin Mistry and novelist Reshard Gool; and Sri Lankan poet Rienzi Crusz depict in various ways the sharp contrasts between South Asian and Canadian life. Many of these writers publish in the *Toronto South Asian Review*.

West Indian writers in Canada also explore the tensions between "have" and "have-not" nations, and the racial and cultural hostilities that are the residue of British colonialism, as well as the problems faced by the visible immigrants in Canada. Perhaps the most distinguished is Austin Clarke, whose impressive body of fiction is set in both Barbados and Toronto, and includes a trilogy that in portraying West Indian immigrants reveals a deep undercurrent of racism in Canadian society. Younger West Indian writer, Cyril Dabydeen, explores similar themes in both poetry and prose.

Recent Canadian ethnic literature also includes the work of S American writers, the most substantial being that of the Chileans. With the exception of Ludwig Zeller, perhaps the best known of the Chilean writers through his iconoclastic poetry collected in *In the Country of the Antipodes* (1979), most are political REFUGEES, either having been forced to flee or having chosen to leave Chile following the 1973 coup d'état. Most, in the early 1980s, were relatively young, and went to Ontario, where they continued to write in Spanish. Among them are Jorge Etchevérry, Erik Martínez and Naín Nómez, members of an avant-garde poetry movement known in Chile as the "Santiago School." Their sophisticated poetry, which draws on both European and Chilean traditions of surrealism, is both political and personal. Though they are preoccupied with Chile, the émigrés also address Canadian experience, as do Gonzalo Millan, Manuel Aránguiz, Claudio Durán, Ramón Sepúlveda and José Leandro Urbina. An anthology, *Chilean Literature in Canada*, was published in 1982. The S American voice also includes the work of Argentinian writer Pablo Urbanyi, who came to Canada in 1977 and has since published a novel, *The Nowhere Idea* (1982), which comments on Canadian life.

Before 1970, for English-speaking Canadians, access to and information about ethnic writing in nonofficial languages were very limited. Kirkconnell's pioneering translations, collections and bibliographic work stood practically alone. In the 1970s and 1980s, partially as a result of the federal government's 1971 announcement of a policy of MULTICULTURALISM, several significant translations and anthologies of ethnic literature have been published, including *Volvox* (1971) and 2 translation issues of *Canadian Fiction Magazine* (1976, 1980), as well as a number of anthologies representative of particular groups. Scholarship in the field has also proliferated. The most ambitious bibliographic effort to date is John Miska's *Ethnic and Native Canadian Literature 1850-1979* (1980).

Conclusion The profile of Canadian ethnic literature is currently being strengthened both within and outside the country. Canadian ethnic writers today are receiving international acclaim: in the early 1980s, Jewish Canadian Irving Layton was nominated for the Nobel Prize; Japanese Canadian Joy Kogawa won 3 international awards, including the American Book Award for *Obasan;* and Czech Canadian Josef Škvorecký was awarded the Neustadt Prize for *The Bass Saxophone*, an honour which is generally considered a prerequisite for the Nobel Prize. These authors are celebrated for their art, but theirs is also a contribution to the history of the Canadian mosaic.

TAMARA J. PALMER AND BEVERLY J. RASPORICH

Ethnic Studies are concerned with the study of groups who share a sense of peoplehood, based on a belief in a common origin, culture or physical traits. It embraces a wide range of disciplines, eg, history, the social sciences, education and the humanities. The development of ethnic studies has reflected developments in Canadian society, in government policy and in the various academic disciplines.

While Canadian society has always been ethnically heterogeneous, the interest in ethnic studies began in the 1920s. The concept of the cultural "mosaic," developed in the 1920s, was later criticized by John PORTER as being a stratified or VERTICAL MOSAIC. The emergence of the concept of cultural pluralism, or MULTICULTURALISM, in the 1960s and 1970s was sparked by the "ethnic revival" in the US, the expansion of Canadian universities, the advent of non-British and non-French scholars, and the Royal Commission on BILINGUALISM AND BICULTURALISM. In the 1970s the federal government proclaimed a policy of multiculturalism within a bilingual framework and a new Citizenship Act and a new immigration Act. Several provinces also proclaimed policies of multiculturalism. Since 1972, a number of federal programs have initiated or encouraged ethnic studies. Provincial departments of education have increased opportunities to study not only mother tongues and cultural origins, but also ethnic diversity as a dimension of Canadian society.

Ethnic studies' research and publication have burgeoned, especially since the 1960s, with the journal *Canadian Ethnic Studies* and the Canadian Ethnic Studies Assn.

Ethnic studies have tended to develop unevenly. In particular, studies have often concentrated on changes in ethnic groups that have apparently resulted from "assimilation," or adjustment. These studies have ignored other changes. They have also tended to deal with single groups, to be descriptive rather than analytical and interpretive, and to deal with European groups rather than the "visible minorities," except for studies of attitudes, which have focused on the latter. *See also* ETHNIC AND RACE RELATIONS. JEAN BURNET

Reading: H. Palmer, ed, *Immigration and the Rise of Multiculturalism* (1975).

Etrog, Sorel, sculptor, writer, philosopher (b at Iaşi, Romania 29 Aug 1933). After a turbulent and traumatic childhood, Etrog began his formal art training in Tel Aviv after his family immigrated to Israel. A chance meeting with Toronto collector Samuel J. Zacks resulted in a solo show in Toronto in 1959, and Etrog moved to that city in 1963. His reputation as an intense, dynamic sculptor was quickly established and in 1966 he was chosen as one of the 3 artists representing Canada at the Venice Biennale. Etrog has important private and public commissions to his credit, some of which, such as *Ritual Head* (Calgary, 1976), are monumental in scale. Crafted predominantly in bronze and more recently in rolled sheet metal, Etrog's sculptures are reminiscent of the structures of the human body or of the massive bolts and hinges of heavy machinery, always suggesting a latent potential for movement.

CLARA HARGITTAY

Ritual Head (1976), bronze by Sorel Etrog, is typical of this sculptor's monumental public commissions (*courtesy Sorel Etrog/Gallery Moos*).

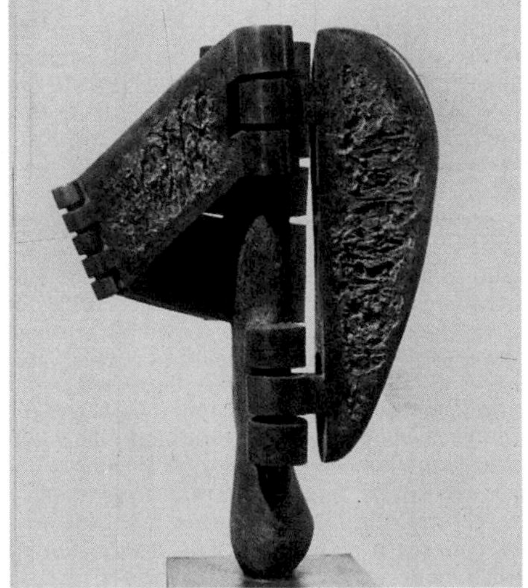

Evaluarjuk, Henry, sculptor (b at Igloolik region, north Melville Pen 1923), directly related to the Evaluarjuk who was so important as an informant to the Danish anthropologist Knud Rassmussen. Evaluarjuk moved from Igloolik to Frobisher Bay [Iqaluit], southeast Baffin Island, during the DEW Line construction era in the mid-1950s. He had done some earlier ivory and stone carving but began his development as a sculptor in Frobisher. Following this period, he went to Yellowknife, NWT, and remained there for several years. During that period, he greatly perfected his carving skills, drawing on his great hunter's memory for human and animal forms, most especially sleek, lively bear sculptures for which he has become justly famous. In addition, Evaluarjuk also possesses an outstanding talent for drawing. JAMES HOUSTON

Evangelical and Fundamentalist Movements include Protestant Christian denominations and subgroups, and nondenominational and paradenominational organizations whose designation indicates their differentiation from "liberal" or "modernist" religious, social and cultural currents, and which define themselves with reference to the Christian scriptures exclusively. Evangelical, the broader category, has the longer and richer history. A derivative of the Gk *euangelion* ("good news," or "gospel"), "evangelical" is a virtual equivalent of "Christian." Throughout Christian history, however, it has been used by certain groups to differentiate themselves from those considered less true to the Christian gospel. Accordingly, LUTHERANS claimed to be evangelical in contrast to Roman CATHOLICS, METHODISTS to ANGLICANS, low church Anglicans to their high church brethren, and the more revivalist BAPTISTS and Methodists on the American frontier to the more liturgical Anglicans and Lutherans. Hence, the term lacks precision historically and even today some Christians resist the co-opting of the term by a particular Protestant movement.

Evangelicalism, in current usage, is shaped by the fundamentalist-modernist controversy. Believing that liberals were abandoning the Christian essence in accommodating to the modern era's evolving ideology, conservatives in most Protestant denominations fought back in the late 19th and early 20th centuries. The Baptists bore the brunt of the conflict in Canada. MCMASTER UNIVERSITY, still Baptist in the 1920s, became the centre of the controversy when Thomas Todhunter SHIELDS, pastor of Toronto's Jarvis Street Baptist Church, accused the board of harbouring a modernist professor of divinity. Shields's refusal to compromise led to his congregation's censure by the Baptist Convention of Ontario and Quebec in 1926. In turn, he organized the Union of Regular Baptist Churches with 70 churches and its own college; URBC members were expelled from the BCOQ in 1928. Other dissenters formed the Fellowship of Independent Baptist Churches, which in 1953 united with URBC to form the Fellowship of Evangelical Baptist Churches. Lesser conflicts, eg, one surrounding Brandon College (now BRANDON UNIVERSITY), similarly caused schisms that, in turn, added to this new alliance of fundamentalist Baptists.

Outside Baptist circles the controversy (which reached its zenith in 1925 with the Scopes "monkey" trial in the US), seemed upstaged in

Canada by the union that year of more liberal denominations in the UNITED CHURCH OF CANADA. Some more traditionalist PRESBYTERIANS refused to join, considering United Church theology too compromised. The resistance of others to the "liberalization" of major Protestant churches contributed to a redrawing of the denominational map in Canada, if only gradually. The various HOLINESS and PENTECOSTAL groups, for example, shared in the fundamentalist cause in earlier decades and are partners in the larger evangelical movement today.

By the 1940s numerous Evangelicals sought to distance themselves from the strident militancy, rigorous separatism, anti-intellectualism and premillennial primacy identified with fundamentalism, and instead claimed the label evangelical. In the US, the National Association of Evangelicals, fd 1942, embraced the likes of evangelist Billy Graham, theologian Carl F.H. Henry, the journal *Christianity Today* and Fuller Theological Seminary. The Evangelical Fellowship of Canada followed in 1964. Adherents affirm the full authority of Scripture in matters of faith and conduct; the necessity of personal faith in Jesus as saviour; and the urgency of converting the sinful. Fundamentalists saw this movement as a betrayal and in Canada formed the Canadian Council of Evangelical Protestant Churches in 1953, parallel to the American Council of Christian Churches, to emphasize premillennialism and strict separation from all liberalism. On the other hand, the 1960s and 1970s produced young evangelicals more open to biblical HIGHER CRITICISM and critical of the identification with conservative and even reactionary politics common in the US.

Already in the 1930s Canadian fundamentalism had proved much less reactionary politically than the American parallel. The dispensationalist founder of the Calgary Prophetic Bible Institute and preacher on the *Back to the Bible Hour,* William ABERHART, and his lieutenant, Ernest MANNING, combined belief in the imminent end of the world with SOCIAL CREDIT, a populist mixture of social reform and small-time capitalism. This was the first and only time before the use of the so-called "moral majority" in the US that fundamentalism in N America sought and won political power. Although strongly opposed to socialism, as well as to the SOCIAL GOSPEL as preached by the more liberal Christians, Aberhart and Manning, together with most Canadian fundamentalists, rarely identified Christianity with raw anticommunism as did some of their US counterparts. Even the Renaissance Canada movement – directed against secular humanism in family, school and government – and the TV show *100 Huntley Street* are restrained versions of their US parallels and exemplify Canadian moderation.

The continuum from the closed fundamentalist to the more open evangelicals is evident in several representative denominations. Plymouth Brethren (Christian Brethren) separated from the Church of England in the 1820s to regain certain emphases of primitive Christianity. Their renowned leader John Nelson Darby travelled extensively in Ontario in mid-century, drawing Baptists and Presbyterians among others to his unique "dispensationalist" reading of the Bible. His premillennialism, a conviction that Christ's second coming would precede the millennium (*see* MILLENARIANISM), undergirded a long series of late-19th-century international "prophetic" Bible conferences, several of them in Niagara-on-the-Lake, Ont. The fundamentalist movement drew ideology, leadership and organization from these conferences, but most of Darby's disciples did not follow him into the Brethren churches. Nonetheless, Brethren assemblies, of some 8 varieties according to degrees of exclusivism, were established in Canada and are growing today. Regent College, a major evangelical graduate theological school in Vancouver, owes much to the Christian Brethren.

The Christian and Missionary Alliance, centered in Nyack, NY, where the denomination established one of the first BIBLE SCHOOLS, was founded in the 1880s by former Canadian Presbyterian minister A.B. Simpson. Emphasizing conversion, holy living and missionary endeavours, the CMA became a classical evangelical denomination. This church operates the Canadian Bible College and Seminary in Regina. With a theology much like the CMA's, the Missionary Church arose from the 1969 union of the United Missionary Church and the Missionary Church Association, which originated in several late-19th-century MENNONITE divisions. The new body, emphasizing mission work, has Bible colleges in Kitchener, Ont, and Didsbury, Alta. The Associated Gospel Churches of Canada were organized in 1925 in Ontario to serve fundamentalists leaving other denominations. Their belief in premillennialism, an inerrant Scripture, holy living, and sect-like separation from the world were typically fundamentalist in contrast to the more evangelical stance of The Missionary Church. This group has 105 churches in Canada today.

Fundamentalist separatism and internecine conflicts between various types of fundamentalism and evangelicalism obscure their role in Canada. Yet these movements must not be underestimated. Nondenominational fundamentalist and evangelical Bible schools, colleges and seminaries teach theology alongside the liberal arts to increasingly more students each year than all mainline Protestant and Catholic schools combined. Evangelically oriented renewal movements are growing even in such denominations as the United Church. *Faith Today*, a new Canadian evangelical magazine, symbolizes the vitality of this sector of Canadian Protestantism in the late 1980s. Fundamentalism and evangelicalism are very much a part of modern Canada.

RODNEY J. SAWATSKY

Reading: J. Barr, *Fundamentalism* (1977); G. Marsden, *Fundamentalism and American Culture* (1980); D.F. Wells and J.D. Woodbridge, *The Evangelicals* (1975).

Evangelical Fellowship of Canada, a national church agency, organized in 1964 to foster cooperation among evangelical (conservative) Christian denominations and individuals. With headquarters in Markham, Ont, the group includes 24 denominations and many interchurch service agencies. The largest member denomination is Pentecostal Assemblies of Canada, with about 11 000 congregations. Others are smaller evangelical denominations, such as the SALVATION ARMY, Mennonite Brethren Church, The Christian Reformed Church, and Christian and Missionary Alliance churches. The member denominations have a constituency of over 1 million, and the individual members are evangelicals who are members of mainline denominations or of other denominations not aligned with EFC. Members of all Protestant denominations are on the general council, and 3 of its presidents have been ministers of mainline Protestant denominations.

Previous attempts to organize Canada's estimated 1-2 million evangelicals have been frustrated by their preference for independent initiative. EFC seeks to promote renewal among the churches and to serve as a forum for interaction and stimulation. It also represents an evangelical voice to the media, government and the general public. A full-time executive director, 1 commission (social action) and 2 task forces (family and evangelism) implement its program. A bimonthly, *Faith Today* (formerly *Faith Alive*), is the official EFC publication. *See* also EVANGELICAL AND FUNDAMENTALIST MOVEMENTS.

LESLIE K. TARR

Evangeline: A Tale of Acadie (Boston, 1847), a poem by American poet Henry Wadsworth Longfellow. In 1841 he had heard the story of young lovers parted by the deportation of the ACADIANS, to be reunited only at the end of their lives. His imagination was the main source for his poem, but he used the work of Abbé Raynal (a contributor to Diderot's *Encyclopédie*) and of T.C. HALIBURTON to provide background material. The poem quickly gained worldwide popularity. Its first translation into French in N America was by Pamphile Le May in 1865, but 1851 had already seen its translation into German and Polish, and in 1853 a French translation was published in London. For Longfellow the story was "the best illustration of the faithfulness and constancy of women that I have ever heard of or read." But for many Acadians, especially those of the elite at the turn of the 19th century, it was the true story of their ancestors, "those simple Acadian farmers" who "Dwelt in the love of God and of man. Alike were they free from/Fear, that reigns with the tyrant, and envy, the vice of republics." To them it was the poetic distillation of their history, the true legend of their past.

N.E.S. GRIFFITHS

Reading: N.E.S. Griffiths, "Longfellow's *Evangeline...*," *Acadiensis* II (1982).

Evangelism [Gk *euangelion,* "good news," or "gospel"] is the attempt to win new converts, or to revive existing commitments, to Christ, usually through fervent preaching. The term has been used since the Reformation to identify the proselytizing activities of Protestants who believed in divine grace through faith and the supreme authority of the "gospel." It is currently applied to those who lay special stress on personal conversion, as in the "born-again" movement.

The history of evangelism in Canada can be traced to Henry ALLINE, who in 1776 launched the GREAT AWAKENING movement among the scattered settlers of Nova Scotia. During the 1830s and 1840s, Mgr de Forbin-Janson, bishop of Nancy, France, and other charismatic preachers mounted a Roman Catholic revival to combat the active Protestant evangelists. By the 1860s Anglicans, Roman Catholics and Methodists were all vying for converts in Upper and Lower Canada.

Most Methodist preachers were self-educated natives of Upper Canada who conducted informal services at camp meetings. Ralph HORNER, a Methodist minister, introduced the use of the large tent in 1886. He laid claim to "cyclones of power," which were capable of converting the most stubborn sinner in an instant. Expelled from the Methodist Church, he founded the Holiness Movement Church in 1897 and the Standard Church of America in 1916.

The SALVATION ARMY tried tents but soon abandoned them in favour of street services, which municipal authorities tried to suppress. Angry mobs attacked the street-corner evangelists, and both Montréal and Québec were scenes of mass arrests. Nonetheless, the Army's popularity spread rapidly through Canadian urban centres. Numerous Methodist ministers switched to the more evangelically minded Salvation Army. In an attempt to counteract this movement the Methodists supported the efforts of Hugh T. Crossley and John E. Hunter, who toured Ontario and the West in 1887-89. These evangelists formed the Gospel Band movement, out of which evolved the Epworth League. Anglicans, for their part, organized the Church Army.

Since about 1880 American evangelists have had a profound effect on Canadian religious life.

Usually unconnected with any church, often unordained, they made their appeals to regular church followers. One, Dwight L. Moody, held gigantic rallies in Toronto, where in 1884 his Christian convention attracted half the adult population of the city. Two years later, Georgia evangelists Sam Jones and Sam Small held an even more successful 3-week campaign in Toronto.

Although most evangelicals maintained that transformation of society could come about only through the conversion of individuals, there was a growing trend to become more involved in Canadian social and political issues (*see* SOCIAL GOSPEL). As the evangelical movements became more established and urbanized, their early political radicalism changed to conservatism. This was true in 19th-century Upper Canada, where Methodist leader Egerton RYERSON led his following away from the REFORM MOVEMENT and thus contributed to Tory victories. In 20th-century Alberta, William ABERHART's Prophetic Bible Institute provided the basis for the formation of the SOCIAL CREDIT party. His successor, Ernest MANNING, was once referred to as the "unofficial pope to Canada's evangelicals." The movements tended to serve those largely ignored by the larger and wealthier church bodies.

A Pentecostal revival in England in 1907 led several Canadian Anglican clergymen to identify with the movement. One who became prominent in the PENTECOSTAL MOVEMENT in western Canada was J.E. Purdie, who later became principal of Western Bible College, Winnipeg (this is now Central Pentecostal College, Saskatoon).

American evangelists found in Canada fertile ground for successful revivalist campaigns and evangelical rallies. The best known and most widely accepted was Billy Graham, whose appearance in Canada in the mid-1950s was welcomed not only by crowds of eager worshippers but by most local churches, which saw him as a means of renewing their members' Christian commitment. Canadian churches launched their own campaigns in the 1950s, principally that of Charles TEMPLETON, a Toronto-born evangelist who conducted several cross-country missions for the UNITED CHURCH. Graham's Canadian brother-in-law, Leighton Ford, headed revival crusades in the 1960s.

Ken Campbell, a Canadian Baptist from near Milton, Ont, who in the 1970s conducted numerous annual crusades across the country, is head of Renaissance International. This is a political pressure group organized in 1974 to lobby on issues of morality, particularly against permissive education and homosexuality.

Electronic Evangelism The advent of radio gave the evangelists a powerful tool to spread their gospel. Aberhart, one of the most popular radio evangelists, began a series of "prophetic lectures" from a Calgary theatre in 1925. In his broadcasts he mingled prophecies on political and economic events with premillennial theology (*see* MILLENARIANISM). During the Depression years these economic ideas became popular, and he soon built a large political as well as religious following. He became premier of Alberta in 1935.

In 1925, the newly formed United Church started its own radio station (VOWR: "Voice of Wesley Radio") in Newfoundland. By 1928 various churches operated stations. In Vancouver the United and Presbyterian churches and the International Bible Students Assn (an organization of the JEHOVAH'S WITNESSES) all had stations. The latter also had stations in Edmonton and Saskatoon. Another Edmonton station belonged to the Christian and Missionary Alliance. In Toronto, CJYC was operated by Universal Radio of Canada, which was later revealed to be the International Bible Students Assn. In 1928, because of complaints concerning the "unpatriotic and abusive" nature of CJYC, the Canadian government closed it down. The ensuing controversy contributed to the movement toward greater government control of BROADCASTING.

One of the most popular evangelists in N America was Canadian Aimee Semple MCPHERSON. For 20 years, until her death in 1944, she attracted large audiences at her $1.25 million Angelus Temple in California and through her own radio stations. She also started a BIBLE SCHOOL and a magazine, wrote several books and spread her gospel through some 200 missions. She founded the International Church of the Foursquare Gospel (fundamentalist, perfectionist, adventist and charismatic).

With the coming of network television the "electronic evangelists" from the US were able to reach all of Canada with appeals for converts and money. In 1987 about 60 syndicated American religious television programs were available in Canada. Purchase of religious air time in Canada and the US totalled over $600 million annually. American TV evangelists in 1987 took in close to $2 billion. Canada's dozen TV evangelists raise some $25 million per year; the most prominent is David Mainse of Toronto, whose program *100 Huntley Street* is broadcast daily over the Global Television network and numerous independent Canadian and American stations. About 18 faith groups in Canada participate in Vision TV, an organization that applied to the CRTC on 30 July 1987 for permission to operate a satellite to cable an all-religious, nonprofit network. The regulatory board approved the application in Dec 1987. Many denominations, faced with declining membership, now see television as a means to spread the Gospel and achieve conversion as did the tent meetings and revival missions of the past. *See also* EVANGELICAL AND FUNDAMENTALIST MOVEMENTS. ROY BONISTEEL

Reading: S.D. Clark, *Church and Sect in Canada* (1948).

Evans, Arthur "Slim" (b at Toronto 1890; d at Vancouver 1944). Slim Evans was a colourful socialist and trade union organizer who played the leading role in organizing the ONTO OTTAWA TREK of 1935. He apprenticed as a carpenter and moved west in 1911 where he soon got caught up in the radical movements of the period. Active in the INDUSTRIAL WORKERS OF THE WORLD, he spent several months of 1912 in a Kansas jail for making radical speeches without a municipal permit for an assembly. Back in Canada, he found work in the Drumheller coal mines and became active in the ONE BIG UNION. Later, as secretary of the Drumheller district of the United Mine Workers of America, he authorized funds for a wildcat strike in 1923 and spent 3 years in penitentiary after UMWA's American leaders prosecuted him for "embezzlement." He joined the Communist Party in 1926 and became their leading British Columbia organizer of the unemployed during the Depression. He was arrested and charged with membership in an illegal organization (National Unemployed Workers Association) for his role in the ON TO OTTAWA TREK; the charges were later dropped. In his last years, he organized metal miners in Trail, BC, and wartime shipyard workers in BC. ALVIN FINKEL

Reading: B. Swankey and J.E. Shiels, *"Work and Wages!" A Semi-Documentary Account of the Life and Times of Arthur H. (Slim) Evans* (1977); V. Howard, *We Were the Salt of the Earth...* (1985).

Evans, Hubert Reginald, writer (b at Vankleek Hill, Ont 9 May 1892; d at Sechelt, BC 17 June 1986). He became a reporter in 1910 and, after service overseas in WWI, was a fisheries officer in northern BC. In 1925 he decided to write full-time and in 1927 began supporting his family by writing articles, short stories, serials, radio plays and books for juveniles. His first novel, *The New Front Line* (1927), was about a returned veteran. *Mist on the River* (1954), described cultural conflicts in an Indian village. While in his 80s he wrote 3 books of poetry and published a new novel, *O Time in Your Flight* (1979), about a boy in Ontario in 1899. Evans's writing career spanned 7 decades; Margaret LAURENCE called him the "elder of the tribe." In 1984 he received an honorary degree from Simon Fraser U, and BC Book Prizes gives an annual Hubert Evans Award. BERT (A.E.) NELSON

Evans, James, Methodist minister, linguist, creator of Cree syllabic writing (b at Kingston-upon-Hull, Eng 18 Jan 1801; d at Kelby, Eng 23 Nov 1846). Ordained in 1833, Evans served in various missions in Upper Canada, learning Ojibwa and translating and printing various texts. In 1840 he was appointed superintendent of the British Wesleyan mission to the Hudson's Bay Co Territories and stationed at NORWAY HOUSE. He established a thriving mission at Rossville, and his experience enabled him to create the CREE SYLLABIC form of writing. He again translated and printed materials and travelled extensively. His life and work were shortened by ill health, by increasing conflict with the HBC and by his accidental shooting of a man in 1844. In 1845 HBC Governor George SIMPSON requested Evans's removal. The Wesleyan Society invited Evans to London to discuss this request, as well as charges of immorality against him, but he died before the investigation was completed. GERALD M. HUTCHINSON

Evans, Thomas Dixon Byron, soldier (b at Hamilton, Ont 22 Mar 1860; d at Battle Creek, Mich 23 Aug 1908). The outstanding Canadian soldier of his generation, he joined the 43rd (Ottawa and Carleton) Rifles in 1880, and was promoted captain and adjutant in 1884. After serving with the Midland Battalion in the NORTH-WEST REBELLION (1885) he joined the Permanent Force in 1888, serving with the infantry, mounted rifles and cavalry, and commanding the Canadian cavalry contingent sent to England for Queen Victoria's Diamond Jubilee (1897). He was promoted lieutenant-colonel to command the YUKON FIELD FORCE in 1898, and commanded the 2nd Battalion, 1st Canadian Mounted Rifles, in S Africa (1900) and the 2nd Canadian Mounted Rifles (1901-02). In 1907 he was appointed District Officer Commanding at Winnipeg but the following summer he fell suddenly ill and died.
BRERETON GREENHOUS

Evans, William, journalist, agronomist (b at Carana, Ire 22 Nov 1786; d at Côte St-Paul, Canada E 1 Feb 1857). Evans immigrated to Lower Canada in 1819 and settled on a farm in Côte St-Paul near Montréal. His first work, *A Treatise on the Theory and Practice of Agriculture in Canada,* was published in 1835 and translated into French a year later. An early agronomist, Evans published other books and agricultural journals, including the first agricultural journal to be published in French (1844), trying by writing and example to change and reform traditional farming techniques. JEAN-CLAUDE ROBERT

Evanshen, Terrance Anthony, football player (b at Montréal 13 June 1944). During a 14-year career in the CANADIAN FOOTBALL LEAGUE he developed into one of the most skilled pass receivers in CFL history. Known for his intense concentration, Evanshen caught 600 passes for 4 different CFL teams, totalling 9697 yards and 80 touchdowns, while fumbling only 3 times. In 1987 he ranked 4th on the all-time CFL list in receptions and yardage and third in touchdowns receiving.

He began his career in 1965 with the Montreal Alouettes, leading the Eastern Conference in pass receptions and was named the EFC rookie of the year. He twice won the SCHENLEY AWARD as the Outstanding Canadian Player, in 1967 with Calgary and 1971 with Montreal. He still holds the CFL record for most games catching a pass (181) and most consecutive games catching a touchdown pass (10), and he shares the record for the longest pass reception in CFL history with Hal PATTERSON (109 yds). With Calgary in 1967 he established a single season record of 96 receptions and tied the record for most touchdown receptions; both records have since been broken. He retired after the 1978 season and was elected to the Canadian Football Hall of Fame in 1985.
PETER WONS

Everson, Ronald Gilmour, poet (b at Oshawa, Ont 18 Nov 1903). Educated at U of T and Osgoode Hall, Everson practised law before moving into public relations. His poetic career began in the 1920s, though his poems have appeared in book form only since the late 1950s. He cofounded the publishing company Delta Books in Montréal, where he has spent most of his life. Most of his poems are concise and direct responses to his environment and personal situation, his later work turning darker and more plaintive. A gathering of his poetry is found in *Selected Poems 1920-1970* (1970). PETER STEVENS

Evolution Modern understanding of evolution began in 1859 with publication of Charles Darwin's *On The Origin of Species by Means of Natural Selection.* In this revolutionary work, Darwin presented an extensive catalogue of evidence to show that all living creatures have descended from ancestors unlike themselves. He also proposed a dynamic, natural mechanism, which he called "natural selection," to explain "descent with modification." The theory of natural selection was developed independently by A.R. Wallace at the same time, and the 2 explanations were presented jointly to the Linnaean Society of London (1858). Throughout the next decades, biologists such as T.H. Huxley improved the theory, defended it from attack by antievolutionists, publicized it and contributed further evidence to it. Three outstanding sources of evidence are discussed below.

Fossil Record Creatures have not always been of the same kinds as they are today. Fossil evidence shows that there has been a unique succession of life forms, progressing from simple to complex, and involving groups replacing other groups which, once extinct, never originate again. Fossils in older rocks are less like living organisms than fossils in younger rocks; and groups recognized as being distantly related can be seen to be more and more alike the farther back their fossil ancestors are traced. At local exposures of undisturbed sedimentary rock strata, geologically older fossils occur at lower horizons (layers) and younger fossils at higher (eg, at the BURGESS SHALE, BC, and the dinosaur BADLANDS, Alta). Some successions allow direct observation of evolutionary change through time, ie, of species giving rise to new and different species directly, through intermediate generations.

Comparative Anatomy and Embryology Organisms of different species show resemblances in anatomy and embryonic development that are inexplicable unless the species are descended from a single ancestral species, different from any descendant. For example, the forelimbs of bats, moles, horses and humans are superficially very different, and function in different ways in accordance with their varying designs. Yet the underlying anatomy and development of forelimb bones, muscles, nerves and blood vessels are the same in all. The differences are only in proportions: forelimb anatomy in each group has been modified, from an original pattern in ancestral mammals, to meet diverse adaptive needs in the descendants.

Biogeography Organisms are distributed geographically according to their relationships, not according to their ecological role; hence similar environments, if widely separated, do not necessarily support similar species. For example, most native Australian mammals are MARSUPIALS (they do not develop placentae and young incubate in external pouches), but marsupials do not occur in Africa or SE Asia, which have climates similar to that of Australia. Nothing in the climate or geography of Australia suggests that pouches would be especially advantageous there. The diversity of Australian marsupials results from their descent with modification from a primitive, opossumlike ancestor that entered Australia from S America at least 50 million years ago. When land connections between continents were severed, Australian marsupials evolved in isolation, filling niches occupied elsewhere by placental mammals. Marsupials were prevented from dispersing to Africa and Asia by ocean barriers surrounding the island continent.

How does evolution happen? Darwin realized, and contemporary evolutionary BIOLOGY confirms, that natural selection is the major mechanism governing evolutionary change. Because organisms vary, no 2 members of a species (the basic evolutionary unit) are identical. Many variations can be passed, by genetic inheritance, from parent to offspring. Population size of any organism is limited by the resources of the environment and, in each generation, more offspring are produced than can survive and reproduce. Some individuals in each generation will survive longer and will produce more offspring than others. If enhanced survival and reproduction are caused by heritable variations, offspring that have inherited the favourable variations will also survive longer and reproduce more. Consequently, unless the environment changes to make a favourable variation neutral or disadvantageous, individuals carrying the variation will make up an increasingly high proportion of the species, ie, evolutionary change will occur. It will tend inevitably towards the accumulation of favourable changes. Selection of the variants will be brought about by environmental factors (physical and biological) acting directly on individual organisms (ie, selection is not random). If variations do not occur to meet changing environmental demands, fewer individuals survive and reproduce, and ultimately the species will become extinct. Selection was once thought to be either "natural," leading to the longer reproductive life of the organism, or "sexual," leading to the easier attraction of mates. Physical characteristics, eg, antler size or feather coloration, and some genetically patterned behaviours, were thought to have resulted from sexual selection. Sexual selection is now considered simply as natural selection.

In recent years, particularly in North America, both the fact and the mechanism of evolution have come under attack by some Christian groups espousing "Creationism," the belief that earth and its creatures were miraculously created, as is, only 6000 years ago. Creationist beliefs make no contribution to the scientific explanation of adaptation in plants and animals or of the history and diversity of life; therefore, they lack credibility in the scientific community. *See also* SOCIAL DARWINISM. RICHARD C. FOX

Reading: S.J. Gould, *Ever Since Darwin* (1977).

Ewart, John Skirving, lawyer, publicist (b at Toronto, 11 Aug 1849; d at Ottawa 21 Feb 1933). Educated at Upper Canada College and Osgoode Hall, Toronto, Ewart moved to Winnipeg to practise law in 1882. He was counsel for the French-speaking minority in the MANITOBA SCHOOLS dispute, 1890-96. He settled in Ottawa in 1904 to facilitate his many appearances before the Supreme Court of Canada and the Judicial Committee of the Privy Council, London. He wrote a series of essays urging Canadian constitutional independence, as well as other works on law, Canadian constitutional development and the diplomatic origins of WWI. D.M.L. FARR

Ewen, William Paterson, painter (b at Montréal 7 Apr 1925). Studying at McGill and the Art Assn of Montreal's School of Art and Design in the late 1940s, Ewen was attracted to abstract art through the AUTOMATISTE and PLASTICIEN movements. In 1968 he moved to London, Ont, where painting on gouged plywood sheets led to his return to figuration and a new subject, meteorological phenomena. Included in numerous Canadian group shows, he has had 2 retrospective exhibitions and in 1982 represented Canada at the Venice Biennale. Through his intentionally awkward drawing, emotionally charged images and exceptional handling of materials, he has revitalized Canadian landscape painting. In 1987 he received the Banff Centre's National Award.
SANDRA PAIKOWSKY

Ewert, Arthur (b Germany 1890; d Germany 1959), early communist agent in Canada. Ewert immigrated to Canada with his wife Elise in 1914, was arrested in Toronto 23 Mar 1919 under the pseudonym Arthur Brown and expelled as a subversive alien. In Germany he became a member of the communist Politburo and was elected to the Reichstag. He went to the US in 1927 to enforce Stalin's doctrines on American communists and later served as an agent in China, where he is supposed to have met members of the British "Fifth Man" group in 1935, was arrested and expelled. From 1947 he was hospitalized in Germany as a result of torture in Brazil. Hardly anything is publicly known of Ewert's life in Canada (or anywhere else) except for British MI5 information published by the British author Chapman Pincher. DONALD J.C. PHILLIPSON

Ewing, Walter Hamilton, trapshooter (b at Montréal 11 Feb 1878; *fl* 1908). The records of the Amateur Athletic Union of Canada claim incorrectly that Ewing won a gold medal at the 1900 Paris Olympics. There is scant evidence of Ewing's career, though indications are that he was one of Canada's best marksmen at the turn of the century. Even as a member of the 1908 Olympic team, he competed in relative obscurity as media attention was focused on the Canadian runner, Tom LONGBOAT. Despite having to adjust to a more difficult style of shooting – British rules for the sport were used – Ewing proved himself the most consistent competitor. He had a score of 72 points out of 80 for the 3-day event, 12 more than his nearest competitor, and won the gold medal. J. THOMAS WEST

Examination for Discovery is a legal proceeding, also known as examination on discovery, which enables a party to a civil action to examine another person orally and before trial. This proceeding assists the examining party in preparing for trial by compelling the disclosure of relevant facts and by bringing to a focus the issues in dispute. Examination for discovery also serves as a means of obtaining admissions from an adverse party and of evaluating the evidence in his hands; finally, it may, as a side effect, open avenues for out-of-court settlements. The transcript of the examination does not generally form part of the evidence on which the court will decide the case, but at trial the examining party may introduce

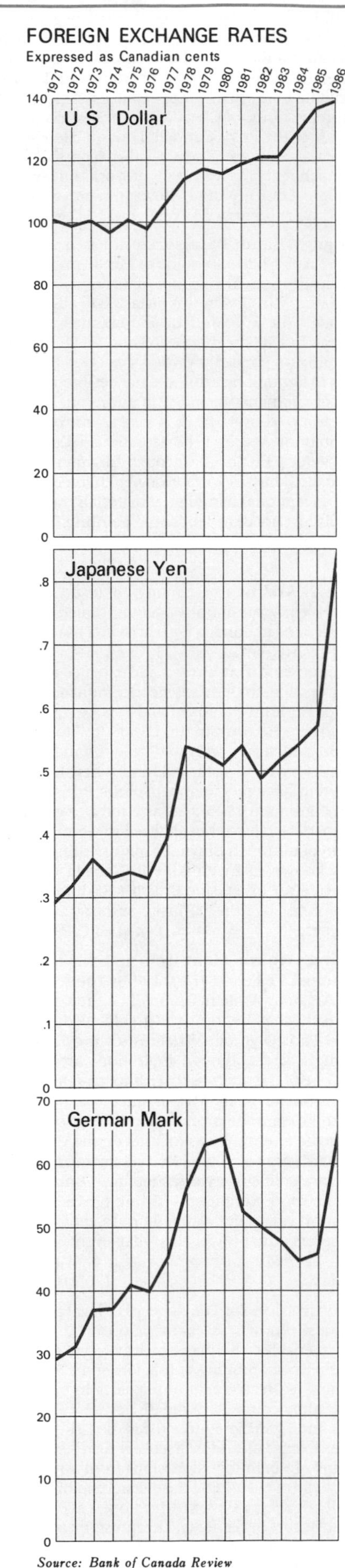

any part of the transcript into the record or may use the transcript to point to contradictions or variations between a witness's testimony in court and prior statements made by the same witness on discovery. *See also* LAW OF EVIDENCE.

YVES-MARIE MORISSETTE

Exchange Rates are rates at which nations' currencies are exchanged, or the price of one currency as opposed to another. Almost all countries now use the American dollar (US$) as the standard against which to measure the value of their own currency. As the majority of Canada's international trade and financial transactions are with the US, the value of the Canadian dollar (Cdn$) in relation to the US$ is of prime importance to Canada.

The dollar became the official monetary unit of the Province of Canada on 1 Jan 1858 and the official currency of Canada after Confederation. Its "spot" or current market value has approximated the US$ until the former's recent decline, the significant exception being during the US Civil War when the Cdn$ rose to US$1.45. From 1879 to 1914 Canadian and US currencies were defined by fixed and equal units of gold. Following WWI, except for the brief period between 1926 and 1929, the Cdn$ has been either pegged at a particular value in relation to the US$ (1962-70) or allowed to fluctuate according to international demand and supply. From 1952 and 1962 and since 1970, the Cdn$ has fluctuated or "floated." During these periods the BANK OF CANADA has bought and sold foreign exchange to smooth out daily fluctuations in the rate. It has also raised or lowered Canadian interest rates, relative to those in the US, to encourage or discourage funds flowing into Canada that increase or decrease the value of the Cdn$.

The exchange rate of the Cdn$ is influenced by several factors besides direct government policy. Good grain harvests, new resource developments, improved labour productivity and prosperous business conditions abroad all help to stimulate exports and put upward pressure on the dollar's foreign worth. An increase in either foreign investment in Canada or foreign tourists visiting Canada has a similar effect. Conversely the opposite of these forces places downward pressure on the dollar's external value. Concurrently the dollar's worth abroad affects the international competitiveness of Canadian products, especially manufactured goods. If increased capital inflows cause the value of the Canadian dollar to rise, Canada's manufacturing industry could be adversely affected because foreign products would be cheaper.

BRUCE W. WILKINSON

Experimental Farm, *see* RESEARCH STATIONS.

Exploits River, 246 km long, the longest river on the island of Newfoundland. Its tributaries, the Lloyds and Victoria rivers, rise in the SW corner of the Island and flow NW into Red Indian Lk (250 km^2). The Exploits begins at the NE outlet of the lake, where a dam regulates its flow. The river valley is flat and the river wide and shallow. At GRAND FALLS, the river turns NE and empties into the Bay of Exploits on NOTRE DAME BAY. It is dammed at numerous points and harnessed for hydroelectric power, notably at Grand Falls and Bishop's Falls. The origin of the name, which appeared as early as James COOK's charts of 1774, is unknown. In 1810-11 an expedition led by David Buchan travelled up the river on snowshoes, encountering a camp of BEOTHUK at Red Indian Lk.

JAMES MARSH

Exploration Until well into the 16th century, Europe's knowledge of the nearest part of America, its eastern extremity at Newfoundland, was misty and uncertain. Stimulated by the thought

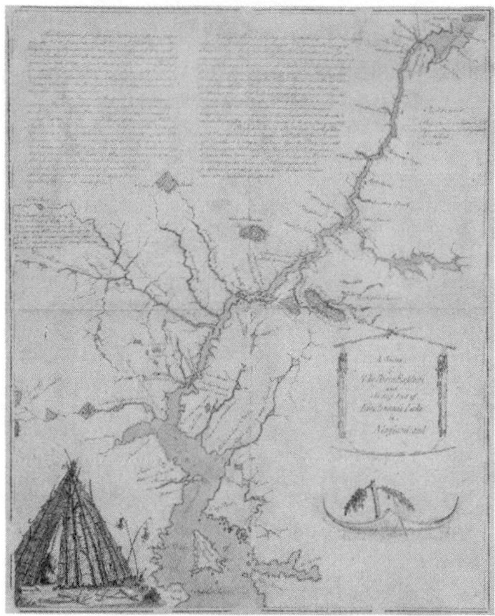

Exploits R, from an early sketch, also showing a native canoe and wigwam. The description notes the river's frequent shoals (*courtesy National Archives of Canada*).

that, even with primitive vessels and navigation, the northern crossing to that region could be made in the summer by island hopping via the Faroes, Iceland and Greenland, scholars have debated "prior discovery." Claims have been made for the sighting of some part of Canada's Atlantic coastline by the Irish monk St Brendan in the 6th century, and more credibly for the landing of NORSE adventurers and settlers in the late 10th and early 11th centuries. Archaeological excavations at L'ANSE AUX MEADOWS near the northern tip of Newfoundland have lent substance to the ambiguous evidence in the sagas. These show that the earliest sighting was probably made by BJARNI HERJOLFSSON in 985 or 986, and that in about 1000 LEIF ERICSSON landed in the first of a series of expeditions culminating in the establishment of a short-lived Norse settlement. But the sagas are far from clear as to precise locations, and the crucial question of the identity of the Norse seafarers' "Vinland" has never been definitely resolved. Further, if we judge exploration to involve not only discovery but also recording and placing for posterity lands hitherto unknown, then it should be noted that the Norse saga evidence was lost to sight until the end of the 16th century. When Europeans again approached NE America in the late 15th century, they were likely unaware of the routes and discoveries of their predecessors.

A leap forward of 500 years might be expected to produce firmer evidence of voyages attempted and discoveries made. On the contrary, such documents as exist for the half century before the 1520s are fragmentary and obscure. There has been speculation that seamen from Bristol reached Newfoundland, or thereabouts, as early as the 1480s, thus predating Columbus's voyage of 1492. But the only hard evidence points to John CABOT's English expedition of 1497 as the first known voyage to mainland N America in the new era of overseas discovery. Cabot probably coasted the shores of Maine, NS, Newfoundland and Labrador; certainly he saw enough to organize a more ambitious but totally disastrous venture the next year. Equally difficult to pinpoint is the activity in that area of the Portuguese CORTE-REAL family 1500-03; and a rumoured expedition in about 1508-09 by John Cabot's son, Sebastian, may simply have been a hoax. Maps of the period show the rudimentary and hesitant outline of a coast stretching from the Spanish discoveries

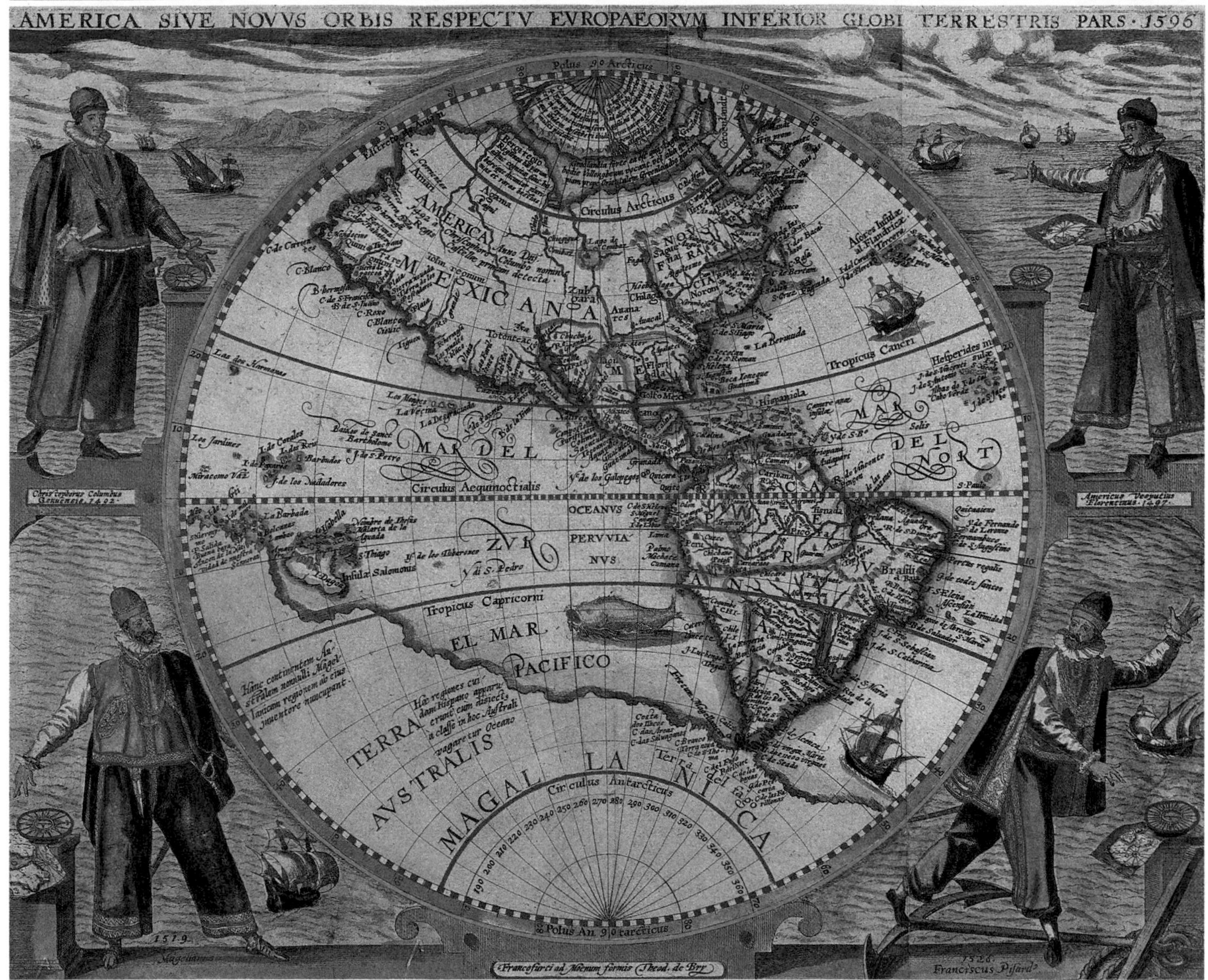

T. de Bry's 1596 map of N and S America gives an impression of the state of geographical knowledge shortly after the voyages of Columbus (*courtesy National Archives of Canada/NMC-8589*).

around the Carolinas NE to the cod fisheries; but there was as yet no realization that Newfoundland was an island, nor any clear idea as to the nature of the coastline between the area of Spanish knowledge and the fishing banks 3000 km N where the English, Portuguese and Bretons were active. Although Giovanni da VERRAZZANO sailed from N Carolina to Newfoundland in 1524 in French service, he stayed too far from shore to sight the strait separating Cape Breton from Newfoundland, and so remained ignorant of the Gulf of St Lawrence.

This major discovery fell to the Breton, Jacques CARTIER, who in 3 voyages in 1534, 1535-36 and 1541-42 (this last for colonization, rather than discovery) began to give recognizable shape to eastern Canada. On his first voyage he entered and explored the Gulf of St Lawrence by way of the Str of Belle Isle. On his second he followed the St Lawrence to the Indian townships of Stadacona [Québec] and Hochelaga [Montréal]. At the latter spot, 1600 km into the continent, Cartier's native informants insisted that the river, now broken by rapids, stretched 3 months' travel to the W. For the first time, Europeans were given some idea of the vastness of the continent in northern latitudes. On his return voyage Cartier discovered Cabot Str between Cape Breton and Newfoundland: he had now navigated both northern and southern entrances into the gulf, and had shown Newfoundland to be insular. The achievement was remarkable. Cartier had discovered the great river which, with its tributaries, was to enable the French to explore and dominate much of the NE of the continent in the 17th century. He also discovered the Canadian winter, for in 1535-36, frozen in at Stadacona, he lost almost a quarter of his men through cold and scurvy. The very extent of Cartier's explorations showed a close, if increasingly uneasy, relationship with the native inhabitants of the St Lawrence Valley. The IROQUOIS, so important in Canada's history, now enter the journals and the consciousness of the French. Cartier had not found the "great quantity of gold, and other precious things" mentioned in his instructions; but to the gulf's teeming fisheries he added the mainland's furs to tempt Europe's commercial acquisitiveness; and if he had not reached the Pacific and so, like Cabot and Verrazzano, failed in that obsessive quest, he had at least found a route pointing straight west.

For the remainder of the century there was no significant advance. The French and other Europeans continued to exploit the FISHERIES and the FUR TRADE, but after Cartier the limits of French enterprise stopped at TADOUSSAC. New explorations, which began in the 1570s, were far to the N (*see* ARCTIC EXPLORATION) where the English, in particular, made repeated attempts along the ice-bound shores of the eastern Arctic to find a water route to the Pacific. Martin FROBISHER, John DAVIS, William BAFFIN and Henry HUDSON were among the long list of explorers who sought a NORTHWEST PASSAGE in vain. One effect of the search was that it opened up to European view, and eventual English domination, the great inland sea of Hudson Bay, which was explored by a series of expeditions culminating in those of Luke FOX (1631) and Thomas JAMES (1631-32).

An alternative entry into the continent was essential if the English were to challenge the French, for in the early 17th century the activities of Samuel de CHAMPLAIN confirmed and extended Cartier's claims. The century began with a new departure: in 1600 the first European trading post in Canada was established at Tadoussac. In 1603 Champlain followed Cartier's old route to Hochelaga, and also explored more of the Saguenay and Richelieu rivers. The next year he landed in ACADIA, where he explored the Bay of Fundy, and in 1605 he established PORT-ROYAL Habitation [Annapolis Royal]. By 1607 the French had mapped the Atlantic coastline from Cape Breton to Cape Cod (Cap Blanc). Champlain's writings and his last great map of 1632 show the extent of his achievement: the opening up of the difficult country N of the St Lawrence by way of the

Saguenay and St Maurice rivers, the crucial discovery of the route from the St Lawrence to the Hudson R by way of Lk Champlain, the exploration of much of the Acadian coastline, and above all the indications of the Great Lakes, based on European exploration and native accounts.

For the explorations of the 40 years following Champlain's death in 1635, the JESUIT RELATIONS provide a unique source. The missionaries' first concern was to record the life and, they hoped, the conversion of the Indians, but their travels brought them a close knowledge of the land itself; and in the *Relations* there is telling detail of its rivers and forests, swamps and portages, its harsh winters and brief, insect-ridden summers. For the first time, perhaps, the Canadian environment took shape and form for European readers. From their mission stations in HURONIA, the JESUITS in the 1640s reached as far west as Sault Ste Marie, while back on the St Lawrence they helped found a post at VILLE-MARIE [Montréal] where the Ottawa R offered a new route to the W. Dominating the Jesuit reports now were Indian and then missionary descriptions of Lk Superior, thought by some to be the gateway to the Pacific. Other French groups prospected new portage routes that linked Lk Superior, Georgian Bay and Lk Ontario, reached the Niagara R from Lk Ontario and wintered (in 1669-70) on Lk Erie. The information from these scattered sources was brought together and given graphic form in the impressive 1672 Jesuit map of the Great Lakes. In the *Relations* we catch glimpses of the COUREURS DE BOIS, the rough outriders of French expansion and discovery, pushing westward in search of furs. The importance of the Indians as guides and helpers emerges clearly in the French accounts. Although the Indians lacked European surveying techniques (*see* CARTOGRAPHY), it was Indian knowledge of the terrain ahead, its peoples and animal life, and the ability to act as interpreters and mediators, that opened the way to the French advance. At least as valuable as direct native assistance to the European was observing and imitating Indian methods of travel, such as the birchbark canoe in summer and the snowshoe in winter.

One of the most authentic and vivid accounts of life among the HURON and Mohawk in the mid-17th century comes from the narrative of Pierre-Esprit RADISSON, whose explorations with Médard Chouart DES GROSEILLIERS, if often obscure in location and direction, were to have profound commercial significance. In their wanderings, which took them as far as Lk Superior, they learned that many prime furs brought down to the French came from the CREE, who lived near "the Bay of the North Sea" (Hudson Bay). Groseilliers and Radisson were convinced that the most direct route for these furs was not the long canoe journey to the St Lawrence and Montréal, but the shorter way N to Hudson Bay, and then to Europe by ship. By 1670 this idea resulted, not in French exploitation of the scheme, but in the establishment of the HUDSON'S BAY COMPANY. It marked the beginning of a 150-year rivalry between the St Lawrence and the Hudson Bay approaches to the fur country, which in the end would take the competing traders, and with them the course of exploration, to the Pacific coast. Although the French in the 1670s finally managed to cross the height of land from the St Lawrence to James Bay by way of the Saguenay R and Lk MISTASSINI, that tortuous route could never compete with Hudson Str. By the 1690s the new company not only had posts on the shores of James Bay, but had established YORK FACTORY at the mouths of the Nelson and Hayes rivers – waterways which led deep into the western interior.

As yet the HBC showed little interest in inland exploration, but from 1690 to 1692 one of its servants, Henry KELSEY, made a remarkable journey. Travelling with the Cree, he reached the Saskatchewan R, a busy waterway of the Indian trade, and from there the great plains, thick with herds of buffalo, and with an Indian population that included Siouan-speaking Assiniboine and Algonquian-speaking BLACKFOOT. To the N the prairie broke into wooded areas where moose, deer and beaver were plentiful – a lush region compared to the immediate hinterland of York Factory. The key to Kelsey's achievement was his ability to speak Cree, and to live and travel with the Indians. He was the first European to reach the Saskatchewan R and the Canadian prairies, the first to leave a description of the grizzly bear and bison. His journey disappeared into an obscurity from which it was not rescued until the 20th century, and long afterwards the only English interior explorations of any note from Hudson Bay were the ventures of William Stuart (1715-16) and Richard Norton (1717-18) northwestward among the CHIPEWYAN. On the canoe routes west from Superior the French took the lead. In 1688 Jacques de Noyon reached Rainy Lk, and the next year possibly Lake of the Woods; on these journeys he heard garbled reports of the Winnipeg R and Lk Winnipeg. Here the westward movement halted until the Treaty of UTRECHT (1713) ended the prolonged Anglo-French wars in N America.

This map shows the forts established by La Vérendrye and his men: Ft Maurépas, at the mouth of the Winnipeg R; Ft La Reine (Portage la Prairie); Ft Bourbon, to the NW of Lk Winnipeg; Ft Paskoya, on the Saskatchewan R and others (*courtesy Service historique de la Marine, Vincennes, France: Service hydrographique, recueil 67, 0°10*).

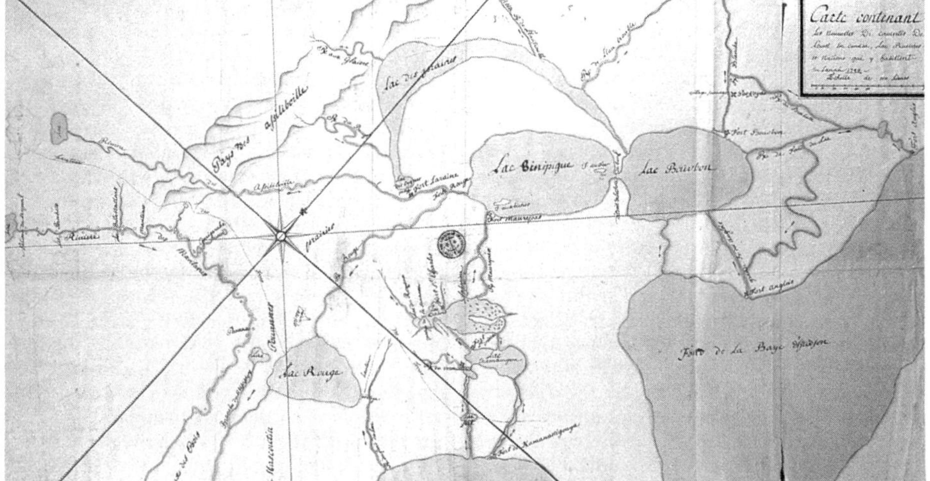

Roald Amundsen's ship *Maud* at Cambridge Bay *c*1934. The *Maud*, built for arctic exploration, made several voyages 1918-25 under the command of Capt Amundsen, including the "North-East Passage" (north of Siberia) (*photo by H.R. Rokeby-Thomas*).

Dominating French concepts of the "upper country" was the conviction that not far to the west lay the MER DE L'OUEST, envisaged as a N American Mediterranean, connected to the Pacific by a strait (perhaps that alleged to have been discovered on the Pacific coast by Juan de FUCA in 1592), and linked on its other shore with the rivers and lakes along which the French were advancing. The belief distorted all views of western Canada's geography because it could not coexist with a range of mountains running N-S; no indication of the Rockies appears on maps until late in the 18th century. To search for this western sea, and to find new fur areas, was the task of the last great French explorers, the LA VÉRENDRYE family. Much of their exploration took place in what is now the US, but toward the end of the father's life he turned back to the N. In 1739 one son, Louis-Joseph, reached the Saskatchewan R, and in the absence of contemporary knowledge of Kelsey's route must be accounted the effective European discoverer of the river. Indians told him of "very lofty mountains" to the W, but geographers obsessed by inland seas, westward-flowing rivers and a nearby Pacific could not assimilate them. More important was that French posts were being built in a steady westward progression – on or near Rainy Lk, Lk Winnipeg, Cedar Lk, and finally, in 1753, Ft St-Louis near the Forks.

Even though the French seemed poised to capture the northwestern fur trade, the HBC was slow to react. Attempts by the ADMIRALTY, by private groups and, rather unenthusiastically, by the company, to find a strait on the west coast of Hudson Bay to the South Sea – the traditional English concept of the NW Passage – had petered out by the late 1740s, but in the following decade the company began to move in different directions. Efforts were made to survey the bleak shores of the Labrador-Québec peninsula with coastal expeditions along the "East Main" of Hudson Bay, and of more far-reaching significance were probes deep inland from York Factory, of which Anthony HENDAY's in 1754-55 was the most spectacular. His method of travelling and his objectives were much the same as Kelsey's. Living with an Indian woman, Henday followed the Cree along their canoe route from York Factory to the lower Saskatchewan R, across the South Branch and the North Branch, to the great buffalo herds of the plains and the horsed Blackfoot Indians. At his farthest W, somewhere near modern Innisfail, Alta, Henday should have been within sight of the Rocky Mts. It is a puzzle that his journals nowhere specifically mention the great mountain range; as with the La Vérendryes' slightly earlier ventures, conclusive evidence of the first European sighting of the Canadian Rockies is missing.

The SEVEN YEARS' WAR and the CONQUEST affected expansion and exploration. The campaign against Québec in 1759 produced the next year a superb published chart of the St Lawrence by James COOK and other naval surveyors. This work, combined with Cook's subsequent hydrographic surveys around Newfoundland, set a new standard, and brought a new precision to Europe's knowledge of the region. Far to the W the Conquest led to the abandonment by the French of the interior posts; but the pause was brief. Within 10 years the posts had been reoccupied by "pedlars" from Montréal, thrustful, energetic traders supported by British and American capital, and using many of the French canoemen and interpreters. Once more the HBC reacted, if slowly, by sending its servants to and beyond the Saskatchewan R, notably Matthew Cocking in 1772-73, and in 1774 the company established its first inland post at CUMBERLAND HOUSE, 100 km beyond The Pas (Man). In command was Samuel HEARNE, newly returned from an impressive overland journey from Ft Churchill down the Coppermine R with a Chipewyan band to the shores of the Arctic Ocean, becoming on 17 July 1771 the first European to sight the continent's northern coastline. Although Hearne's single observation of latitude (71°54′ N) was almost 4° too far north, it established approximately the continent's northern extent, and pushed future searches for a salt-water passage into the icy maze of the ARCTIC ARCHIPELAGO.

Hearne apart, the most extensive explorations were being carried out by NORTH WEST COMPANY traders. The commercial struggle had begun which was to take the rival companies westward into Athabasca, across the Rockies and finally to the Pacific. As the traders battled westward, naval expeditions from Europe were also heading for the unknown NORTHWEST COAST. Vitus Bering's Russian expedition of 1741 had made several landfalls along the Alaskan coast, but there was no southern approach until the 1770s. In 1774 and 1775 Spanish expeditions from Mexico coasted northwards towards Alaska (*see* SPANISH EXPLORATION), and in 1778 Cook made his more comprehensive, but still incomplete, survey northward from NOOTKA SOUND to Bering Str. The approximate outline and location of the coast were at last established, in the same decade as Hearne had reached the polar shore, but neither the British nor their predecessors had determined whether the stretches of coastline glimpsed through mist and rain were islands or mainland. And on the major problem of how far N the Rockies extended, these seaborne expeditions provided no help.

Also in 1778, the NWC, in the person of Peter POND, moved decisively westward. Using Grand Portage at the western end of Lk Superior rather than Montréal as a supply base, Pond tracked NW across the height of land at the Methye Portage and into the Athabasca region. He had crossed the watershed separating the Hudson Bay and Arctic Ocean drainage basins, opened a magnificent new fur-producing region, and taken European enterprises nearer the mountains and the Pacific. By placing Lk Athabasca 1100 km too far W, Pond greatly underestimated its distance from the Pacific, and he made the same error when he discovered Great Slave Lk, from where he suggested a river ran into Cook's R [Cook Inlet, Alaska] on the NW Coast. Lacking formal surveying skills, Pond was one of the last of the old explorers, men tough in body and mind, but often unable to represent accurately in map form where they had been or what they had seen. In 1789 Alexander MACKENZIE followed Pond's river out of Great Slave Lk, only to discover that it led to the Arctic Ocean, not the Pacific. He reinforced the foreboding lesson of Hearne's arctic journey, pointing out that permanent ice virtually ended all hopes of a navigable NW passage. In 1793 Mackenzie again sought a route to the Pacific. From Lk Athabasca he followed the Peace R into the Rockies, crossed the Continental Divide, followed the turbulent Fraser R down the western slopes, and finally reached the coast by way of the Bella Coola R.

With this magnificent journey Mackenzie became the first European to cross the Canadian Rockies, but the difficulty of his route meant that the discovery had little commercial importance. Coastal and overland exploration were now working together to define the features of the Northwest, for the spot where Mackenzie reached the Pacific coast in July 1793 had been mapped 7 weeks earlier by George VANCOUVER'S British naval expedition, in its middle season of a 3-year survey of the coast. Spanish survey expeditions were also on the coast, as were a number of trading vessels; but it was Vancouver's meticulous survey, published in 1798, which formed the definitive record of that intricate shoreline. For the first time the outline of modern Canada was emerging on the maps – most notably on those of Aaron Arrowsmith, who had access to the surveys of the British Admiralty, the HBC and the NWC, and whose maps of N America from 1795 onwards traced the accelerating pace of exploration across the continent.

The overland expeditions had spun thin lines of knowledge across the plains, through the mountains and down to the Pacific and Arctic oceans. After Mackenzie, Duncan MCGILLIVRAY organized an expedition which crossed the Rockies by White Man's Pass in 1801, although it stopped well short of the sea; in 1808 Simon FRASER followed the river which was to bear his name down to tidal waters; and in 1811 David THOMPSON made the crucial commercial discovery when he traced the Columbia R down to its Pacific outlet (by then, he found, in American hands). But away from these trails, all was uncertainty, ignorance and rumour; and on both sides of the mountains serious if sporadic exploration continued. While NWC men made the more dramatic journeys, the HBC had since the late 1770s trained and used explorers of considerable technical ability – Philip TURNOR, Thompson, Peter FIDLER – who with the aid of Indian guides mapped the fur-country waterways with a care and accuracy previously unknown. Thompson, in particular, was a prodigious traveller; switching to the NWC, he had by the turn of the century carried out extensive surveys along both the N and S Saskatchewan rivers, in Athabasca, along the Churchill R and around Lesser Slave Lk. It was estimated that he travelled 80 000 km on his surveys, on foot, on horseback and by canoe.

After the union of the rival companies in 1821 the enlarged HBC continued filling in the blank spaces on the maps. With settlement confined to the Atlantic colonies, the St Lawrence Valley, Upper Canada and RED RIVER, the fur trade still provided the main motivation and resources for exploration, opening up new fur regions, or finding better routes in existing areas of exploitation. In the frontier areas of the fur trade such as the Mackenzie Valley and, across the mountains, NEW CALEDONIA, exploration of the waterways continued. Across terrain rugged even by the rigorous standards of the fur trade, Samuel BLACK, John McLeod and Robert Campbell followed rivers on both flanks of the northern Rockies – the upper reaches of the Peace, the Liard flowing into the Mackenzie, the Pelly and Lewes rivers leading into the Yukon, and the Stikine which reached the sea in Alaska. In the E, similar commercial motives led James Clouston, William Hendry and John MCLEAN to make the first crossings of the inhospitable Labrador-Québec peninsula, until then inviolate.

Far to the N the British government and the HBC joined forces in tracing the polar shoreline. The Admiralty sent seaborne expeditions into the Arctic after the Napoleonic Wars in search of the Northwest Passage, while fur traders helped John FRANKLIN'S land journeys across the barrens to Hearne's Coppermine R, from which he explored E and W along the coast in 1819-22 and 1825-27. In 1837-39 the HBC's Peter Warren DEASE and Thomas Simpson made long sweeps along the polar shoreline from Point Barrow in the west to Rae Str in the E. From 1846 onwards John RAE, one of the most self-sufficient explorers of the North, whose techniques for travel and survival owed much to the INUIT, crisscrossed the huge area bounded by Great Bear Lk, the Boothia Peninsula and the NW coast of Hudson Bay in a series of arduous journeys that soon became directed towards the search for the missing Franklin Expedition.

These explorations were for the most part taking place on or even beyond the margins of profitable fur-trading areas, but slowly the trade was losing its predominance. In the S, interest in settlement overtook the claims of the fur trade, and for this different sorts of surveys were needed. The prospects for agriculture, settlement, telegraph lines and railways became major concerns. It is in this context that the mid-century surveys of S.J. DAWSON, H.Y. HIND and, above all, Capt John PALLISER must be seen. They were less explorations of wholly unknown territory than efforts to determine the productive resources of a land previously viewed through the narrow vision of the fur traders. Exploration in the conventional sense remained to be done, particularly in the Arctic; but by the mid-19th century most of the main geographical features of Canada were known and mapped. GLYNDWR WILLIAMS

Reading: J.B. Brebner, *The Exploration of North America 1492-1806* (1964); W.P. Cumming et al, *The Discovery of North America* (1971) and *The Exploration of North America 1630-1776* (1974); S. Milligan and W. Kupsch, *Living Explorers of the Canadian Arctic* (1987); S.E. Morison, *The European Discovery of America* (1971); D.B. Quinn, *England and the Discovery of America* (1973).

Exploration and Travel Literature in English Although innocent of literary ambition, the accounts of primary geographical EXPLORATION in Canada are not without literary interest, for they constitute the foundation upon which much of our imaginative literature is built. These documents record the first European images of the Canadian landscape and articulate the experience of entering into it. The significance of this writing extends beyond a Canadian context as well, for the narrators deal with the same universal themes of quest, journey and initiation as are found in the works of Homer and Melville. The importance of exploration writing to modern poetry and prose has gained recognition since the 1960s. The narratives of Alexander MACKENZIE and David THOMPSON have been edited by scholars with literary backgrounds, and Canadian anthologies have begun to include excerpts from the writings of Jacques CARTIER, Alexander HENRY, Samuel HEARNE and others. The notion that the origins of Canadian literature lie almost wholly in the creative efforts of a handful of 19th-century immigrants is beginning to make way for other views.

The initial survey of the land occurred on 3 fronts: overland from Montréal and Hudson Bay, largely motivated by the FUR TRADE'S search for profits; through the arctic islands, spurred by the

*Falls of the Chaudière, c*1812, watercolour by George Heriot, whose *Travels Through the Canadas* appeared in 1807 (*courtesy of the Royal Ontario Museum*).

quest for a NORTHWEST PASSAGE; and up the Pacific coast, where British, Spanish, American and Russian mariners rapidly reduced the sea otter population. The fur industry produced many accounts of interest only to the geographer or historian; yet curiously this profit-oriented enterprise also spawned writing of considerably greater literary significance than did the somewhat less materialistic search for the Northwest Passage. One reason for this may be that the fur trade tolerated personal idiosyncrasies so long as they did not hinder profits. Several fur-trade narratives – particularly Hearne's *Journey from Prince of Wales's Fort in Hudson's Bay to the Northern Ocean* (1795) and Thompson's unfinished *Travels* – rise to the level of literature through their success in conveying the author's personality and palpable narrative presence. Hearne's horror at his own powerlessness as he watches his Indian companions slaughter a camp of Inuit, for example, becomes our horror, not by virtue of the event itself, but through the emotional intensity of observing with the explorer's own eyes. Numerous other fur-trade documents, such as Mackenzie's *Voyages from Montreal* (1801), Alexander Henry the Elder's *Travels and Adventures* (1809) and Alexander ROSS's satiric *The Fur Hunters of the Far West* (1855), achieve literary significance to the extent that they create a convincing narrative point of view, presenting models for later writers to draw upon.

The same is true of the writing about the Northwest Passage. *The Strange and Dangerous Voyage of Captain Thomas James* (1633) has intrinsic merit in its vivid description of a winter in the Arctic. James's expedition was privately financed; like the fur traders, he had the freedom to create a firm narrator's perspective. However, even though the imaginative and dramatic potential of the search is immense, that potential remains dormant in all but a few accounts, a situation arising because the narratives fail to create individual human voices through which experience can be communicated. Most of this failure in 19th-century accounts can be attributed to the influence of the British ADMIRALTY, the agency which dominated ARCTIC EXPLORATION between 1818 and 1859. The Admiralty expected of and nurtured in its officers an objective and impersonal sensibility, one that served naval interests well, but limited the subjective dimension of literature. John Ross's *A Voyage of Discovery* (1819), W. E. PARRY's *Journal of a Voyage for the Discovery of a Northwest Passage* (1821) and Robert MCCLURE's *The Discovery of the North-West Passage* (1856) all suffer from this restriction. Johann Miertsching, a Moravian missionary travelling aboard McClure's ship as interpreter, kept an evocative and powerful journal that McClure apparently tried, but failed, to suppress. The author's compassion and sensitivity to the human suffering on the nearly disastrous journey of 1850 to 1854 are freely expressed, a freedom from naval restrictions granted by Miertsching's civilian status.

There are other literary dimensions to these records: some accounts became catalysts for imaginative works, and Northwest Passage accounts, when read together, have the flavour of epic. The intrinsic value of an isolated piece, however, depends very much on the image we receive of the man behind the journal or narrative.
RICHARD C. DAVIS

Travel Literature

Hundreds of travel books on Canada have been published in the last 2 centuries, packed with cultures and climate, people and places. Long subtitles specify their scope, eg, George Head's *Forest Scenes and Incidents in the Wilds of North America; being a Diary of a winter's route from Halifax to the Canadas, and during four months' residence in the woods on the borders of Lakes Huron and Simcoe* (1829). Most titles are shortened here.

Earliest English reports, in Richard Hakluyt's *Divers Voyages* (1582) and *The Principall Navigations* (1589; 1598-1600), and Samuel Purchas's *Hakluytus Posthumus* (1625), mostly described rocky shorelines; but late 17th- and early 18th-century French travellers Louis HENNEPIN, L. A. de LAHONTAN and P.F.X. de CHARLEVOIX, and the Swede Pehr KALM moved inland to describe Québec life. French Canadian culture retained dominant interest for British writers from Isaac Weld, *Travels Through the States of North America and the Provinces of Upper and Lower Canada* (1799), George HERIOT, *Travels through the Canadas* (1807) and John Lambert, *Travels* (1810 – beautifully illustrated in aquatint), to William Teeling, *England's French Dominion* (1932). American writers who also relished the quaint Old World flavour of convent and citadel included John Ogden (*A Tour*, 1799), H.D. Thoreau (*A Yankee in Canada*, 1866), Walt Whitman (*Diary in Canada*, 1904), Anson Gard (*The Last West*, 1906) and Dorothy Duncan (*Here's to Canada*, 1941). Some American travellers also felt the charm of the Maritimes, eg, John Cozzens in *Acadia* (1859); and later the attractions of the northern frontier, eg, Warburton Pike (*Through the Subarctic Forest*, 1896).

To British tourists the American presence in Canada was puzzling. Those Britons who tucked a Canadian tour into a visit to America in order to test the difference between colonial and republican life included Basil Hall (*Travels*, 1829), Frederick Marryat (*A Diary in America*, 1839), Charles Dickens (*American Notes*, 1842), Anthony Trollope (*North America*, 1862) and Basil Newman (*American Journey*, 1943). Military men reported on GARRISON life as a distinctive imperial feature. Gentlemanly sports, flirtations, road building and marches added verve to Col Richard Levinge's *Echoes from the Backwoods* (1846), George Warburton's *Hochelaga* (1846), Col J.E. Alexander's *L'Acadie* (1849) and Sir Richard Bonnycastle's *The Canadas in 1841* (1842) and *Canada and the Canadians* (1846). Lt Francis Duncan described *Our Garrisons in the West* (1864). Anywhere in Canada, "a face yet burned by the suns of India, encircled in a fur cap," might appear to "a friend from China or Aldershot." Officers and other British gentlemen wrote often about sporting pleasures, eg, Capt F. Tolfrey's *The Sportsman in Canada* (1845), Campbell Hardy's *Sporting Adventures in the New World* (1855) and P.E. Doolittle's *Wheel Outings in Canada* (1895).

Other observers described the alternate culture – or lack of it – outside the garrisons, in backwoods settlements. Sour reports on narrow, isolated lives appear in John Howison's *Sketches of Upper Canada* (1821) and Isaac Fidler's *Observations on Professions, Literature, Manners, and Emigration* (1833). The unglamorous life of pioneers is described by E.A. Talbot in *Five Years' Residence* (1824), which parodies the colonizer's glowing accounts of the trip upriver to Ontario; disillusionment is tinged with bitterness in comparable later reports, such as W.H.P. Jarvis's *The Letters of a Remittance Man* (1908), N.P.R. Noel's *Blanket-Stiff* (1912) and E.F.G. Fripp's *The Outcasts of Canada* (1932). But some settlers' stories strike a happier note of acceptance of this strange, ungenteel life: Samuel Strickland's *Twenty-Seven Years in Canada West* presents advice for prospective British immigrants, and A.J. Church edited the letters of his 2 young sons in the cheery *Making a Start in Canada* (1889).

Canadian women appear in all these reports, as pretty French Canadian "muffins" or as indomitable ladies in the lonely bush. Some women, temporarily based in Canada, contributed excellent books on their travels: Anna Jameson, *Winter Studies and Summer Rambles in Canada* (1838), Lady Monck, *My Canadian Leaves* (1873), Lady Dufferin, *My Canadian Journal, 1872-78* (1891), Lady Aberdeen, *Through Canada With a Kodak* (1893), Marion Cran, *A Woman in Canada* (1910), Georgina Binnie-Clark, *A Summer on the Canadian Prairie* (1910) and Eva Hasell, *Across the Prairie* (1922). Other ladies, birds of passage, also published their impressions, among them Isabella Bishop (1856) and the duchess of Somerset (1890). They were particularly aware of the environment – winter cold, mosquitoes, autumn colours and wild flowers – although they also comment on social conditions. John Mactaggart in *Three Years in Canada* (1829) and John Bigsby in *The Shoe and Canoe* (1850) give an equally vivid sense of harsh conditions and varied terrain.

Travel books add to our sense of life in the Canadian art world: Horton Rhys in *A Theatrical Tour for a Wager!* (1861) and Peggy Webling in *Peggy* (1924) give inside glimpses of touring life on provincial stages; T.R. Richman in *Short Notes* (1886) recounts discussions with fellow architects; and Marion Cran spends a chapter on Canadian art and artists.

In *Wanderings of an Artist* (1859) Paul KANE combines glimpses of the artist's life with notes on his dominant subject, the Canadian Indian. Other travellers emphasized the Indian peoples as well. George SIMPSON in *An Overland Journey Around the World* (1847) begins with an account of the great treaty gatherings; L. Oliphant in *Minnesota and the Far West* (1855) and J.G. Colmer in *Across Canadian Prairies* (1894) extend the story to the Plains Indians; S.P. Day in *English America* (1864) updates the Manitoulin gatherings; and *B.C. 1887* (1888) by J.A. Lees and W.J. Clutterbuck adds an effective mix of comic and sympathetic vignettes of West Coast Indians to its many other excellences. Travellers generalize from very selective experience, but the travel books are the best, and for many decades the only, reports on contact between native peoples and other Canadians. In this as in many other ways, W.F. BUTLER'S *The Great Lone Land* (1872) is a most important document.

In the later 19th century the journey across the prairies to, and sometimes through, the Rocky Mts became increasingly popular. British visitors included the earl of Southesk, who published a record of his travels of 1859-60 in *Saskatchewan and the Rocky Mountains* (1875), and Viscount Milton and W.B. Cheadle, whose *Northwest Passage by Land* (1865) gives a good picture of the prairies. Fraser Rae reported on his travels from *Newfoundland to Manitoba* (1876), and in 1884 Gov Gen the marquess of Lorne published *Canadian Pictures.* Canadians too began to write travel books in increasing numbers; G.M. GRANT (*Ocean to Ocean,* 1873) and Charles HORETZKY (*Canada on the Pacific,* 1874) both recorded their experiences on the difficult overland journey. Sandford FLEMING, surveyor and chief engineer for the Canadian Pacific Railway, wrote about his travels in *England and Canada* (1884). The opening of the CPR in 1885 made transcontinental travel very much faster and easier, and travel books proliferated. The new style of travel was reflected in Edward Roper's *By Track and Trail* (1891) and Douglas Sladen's *On the Cars and Off* (1895). Twentieth-century accounts of the transcontinental tour include Bruce Hutchison's *The Unknown Country* (1942) and Eugene Cloutier's *Le Canada sans passeport* (2 vols, 1967; tr *No Passport,* 1968), a Québecois account that is tinged with tension over biculturalism.

Even the great West, however, could not supplant Niagara Falls as the showpiece of Canadian travel books. Most tourists would agree with George Warburton: "The sight was precisely what I expected – the sensations it caused, totally different." Of all Niagara pieces, the most exciting is perhaps Charles Lyell's in *Travels in North America* (1845): this geologist expanded his theory of fossil life as he explored the escarpment, then topped his fine description of the falls with the report of a ride northwards, presenting a vision of great land terraces circling upward from the Great Lakes to the Ontario northlands.

Air travel has ended the slow experience of distance, the passage through changing regions, the encounters by the way that were once the staple of Canadian travel books. Few travellers keep travel diaries, and fewer publish them. One modern development is the appearance of travel poems, such as Earle Birney's in *Ice Cod Bell and Stone* (1962), Al Purdy's in *North of Summer* (1965) and John Newlove's in *Black Night Window* (1968). These poems continue the function of travel books: by creating and clarifying our image, at home and abroad, they help create Canada.

ELIZABETH WATERSTON

Reading: E. Kröller, *Canadian Travellers in Europe 1851-1900* (1987); G. Warkentin, "Exploration Literature," and Elizabeth Waterston, "Travel Literature," in W. Toye, ed, *The Oxford Companion to Canadian Literature* (1983).

Exploration and Travel Literature in French Travel accounts, in their dual capacity as documentation and literature, were the founding texts of Québec culture. The early narratives offer eyewitness accounts of how a small group of Europeans established settlements in N America. For the years 1534-1634 in particular, they are our richest sources for the reconstruction of both the period's mentality and its events. As literature, they established subjects that later writers picked up: nomadic life in the open spaces, the St Lawrence R, the seasons and the process of settling a country. The accounts of travel in NEW FRANCE fall into 3 somewhat overlapping categories: the investigations and explorations reported by Jacques CARTIER and Samuel de CHAMPLAIN; the more encyclopedic accounts written by Gabriel Sagard, Nicholas DENYS and the Jesuits; and the critical analyses of Louis HENNEPIN and Baron de LAHONTAN.

Cartier studied the St Lawrence R, offered the first overall view of the Montréal region and attempted to develop a comprehensive profile of the Indian. Champlain left the waterways behind, penetrated the land and its villages, formed alliances and waged war. Sagard, whose descriptive narrative is predominantly ethnological in approach, takes a narrow but perceptive look at the Huron, pores over the details of their daily life, and attempts to draw conclusions about their sexual, religious. dietary and political practices.

The JESUITS, on the other hand, in their comprehensive 60-year inquiry recorded in the JESUIT RELATIONS, produced a more fragmented but also more systematic study. Their knowledge was informed by a mixture of mysticism and militant evangelism and a vision of the world as a vast theatre where God and Satan fight a bitter, unending battle, in this case through the "savages." Finally, Lahontan, in his *Nouveaux Voyages, Mémoires* and *Dialogues*, sought not so much to record new knowledge about the new land as to challenge the nature of what was already known. Whereas P.F.X. de CHARLEVOIX had presented N American history as a coherent, comprehensible whole, Lahontan argued that because it was forever changing, it could have no lasting meaning.

The travel account, a complex genre, is both a description of individual experiences and a means through which existing general knowledge can be disputed or expanded. Yet how can the author convey the uniqueness of his own adventures when, in many cases, others have travelled his route before him? It is not enough to stress exotic and curious events and places; they must be dramatized, ordered and put into an appropriate context for the understanding of the reader. This explains the numerous dissertations on the climate and on the Indians' origins and religion; the many charts and drawings of N American Indians, and of *septentrional* (northern) and *méridional* (southern) plants and animals; the long descriptions of certain pet phenomena – for Lahontan, the beaver; for Hennepin, Niagara Falls; for the Jesuits and MARIE DE L'INCARNATION, the earthquake of 1663, war, hunting, and the elaborate Huron marriage rituals and festival of the dead.

From 1760 on, travel accounts fall into 3 main categories. Reports written by the VOYAGEURS, traders and explorers comprise the first of these groups. Although relatively few first-hand narratives are extant, 20th-century Canadian and American scholars have brought to light interesting accounts written between 1779 and 1810 by Joseph-François Perrault, Jean-Baptiste Perrault, Charles Le Raye, Jean-Baptiste Trudeau, Pierre-Antoine Tabeau, François-Antoine Larocque and Gabriel Franchère.

A second category, which flourished in the first half of the 19th century, consists of missionary reports replete with observations on Indian and Métis life. *Les Missions* by Frs Modeste Demers and François-Norbert Blanchet and descriptions of the Pacific coast region by Frs Jean-Baptiste Brouillet and Jean-Baptiste Bolduc are typical of such accounts. By the 1880s French Canadian missionary orders were sending their members out to labour in the far corners of the British Empire, Latin America, French Africa, Japan and China, and reports of their travels were published in a plethora of mission-oriented periodicals (*see* MISSIONS AND MISSIONARIES).

The third and by far the largest category of travel literature produced since the end of the French regime belongs to the golden age of transatlantic luxury tourism, from the mid-19th century to the early 1960s. More than 70 accounts of travel to the "Old World" were published between 1815 and 1914. France is described in 46 of these, Italy (especially Rome) in 38 and England in 20. Tourists and pilgrims also visited the Holy Land, Algeria, Egypt, Spain and Greece. All these narratives provide valuable insights into the mentality of the clerical and intellectual elite of Québec at the time.

Accounts still recognized for their literary merit include Mgr J.O. PLESSIS'S *Journal d'un voyage en Europe... 1819-1820*; François-Xavier GARNEAU'S *Voyage en Angleterre et un France [1831-33]* (1854-55); and a variety of accounts by Adolphe-Basile Routhier, Honoré Beaugrand, Narcisse-Henri-Edouard Faucher de Saint-Maurice, Jules-Paul TARDIVEL, Fr Léon PROVANCHER, Fr Jean-Baptiste Proulx and Fr Henri Cimon. Quality declined after 1914, but there were exceptions to the general banality, eg, the writings of Henri BOURASSA, Jean Bruchési; Charles-Joseph Magnan, Dr Jules Dorion, Germaine Bernier (*Impressions*, 1954) and Alain GRANDBOIS (*Visages du monde*). Eugène Cloutier also wrote a series of fine personal travel reports (*En Suède*, 1970; *À Cuba*, 1971; *Au Chili*, 1972).

Travel writers also wrote about trips through Québec, Canada, the US and even Africa. Arthur BUIES was clearly the best of those writing on Québec. Others wrote of specific historical events such as the War of 1812; the Rebellions of 1837-38 (seen through the eyes of political exiles, who described their adventures as deportees in Bermuda and Australia); the California gold rush; the expedition to Mexico (Faucher de Saint-Maurice); the experiences of the pontifical ZOUAVES; the North-West campaign of 1885; the KLONDIKE GOLD RUSH; and the 2 world wars.

In sum, travel accounts in French were at their richest – from every point of view – during the French regime. Thereafter, the adventurous missionary and colonial expeditions, with all their suspense, sense of purpose and excitement of discovery, were followed by relatively uneventful tourist excursions. In the 19th century autobiography and the novel supplanted travel literature as expressions of personal adventure. By the 1960s, as a result of mass tourism and the competition of mass media, this genre had virtually disappeared from French Canadian literature.

P. SAVARD AND R. OUELLET

Reading: J. Hare, *Les Canadiens français aux quatre coins du monde* (1964); E. Kröller, *Canadian Travellers in Europe 1851-1900* (1987); Maurice Lemire, ed, *Dictionnaire des oeuvres littéraires du Québec,* vols I-III (1980-82); G. Rousseau, *L'Image des États Unis...* (1981).

Expo 67, the "Universal and International Exhibition," was the highlight of Canada's CENTENNIAL celebrations in 1967. Senator Mark Drouin of Québec first developed the idea of a world exhibition in Montréal to serve as a focal point for Canada's celebrations of its 100th birthday. Senator Drouin and Senator Sarto Fournier, former mayor of Montréal, first presented the idea to the Bureau International des Expositions (BIE) in Paris, but that body initially decided that the 1967 world exhibition should be held in Moscow. In late 1962, however, the USSR cancelled its plans and Montréal's mayor Jean DRAPEAU made a fresh presentation to the BIE and the exhibition was awarded to Canada. That Expo 67 was sanctioned by the BIE virtually assured participation by a majority of the countries of the world. What is more, the BIE designated it as an exhibition of the "first category," the first to be held in N America. The most important aspect of this "first category" classification is that the exposition must cover the full range of activities of contemporary man.

Implementing legislation passed by the House of Commons in late 1962 established a crown company, the Canadian Corporation for the 1967 World Exhibition, to build and run the exposition. The exhibition was to be a 3-way partnership, with 50% participation by the federal government, 37.5% by the Québec government and 12.5% by the city of Montréal. With time pressing, the 3 governments called a conference of educators, literary figures, and intellectuals at Montebello, Qué, to choose a central theme and evolve a philosophy for the exhibition. "Man and His World," the theme chosen at the Montebello conference, derived from the title of a book by the French author, poet and aviator, Antoine de Saint-Exupery, *Terre des Hommes*. On schedule, in late 1963, the master plan was completed and submitted to Parliament. By late 1966 the corporation listed approximately $320 million as capital-incurred costs of Expo 67, and $138 million as anticipated revenue, yielding an expected deficit of $82 million.

The choice of a site for the exhibition presented many difficulties, not the least of which was the shortage of time. Many proposals were studied, but it was finally decided Île Ste-Hélène, a park in the centre of the St Lawrence linked to Montréal by the Jacques Cartier Bridge, would be expanded by land reclamation techniques using silt and rock dredged from the bottom of the river. In addition, a new island, Île Notre- Dame, would be created adjoining Île Ste-Hélène and alongside the St Lawrence Seaway. River bottom sources of landfill proved insufficient and for months parades of dump trucks bringing landfill moved to the site on a 24-hour-a-day basis, and the cost of building the site rose from the original estimate of $10 million to $40 million. Despite all the problems, the site was formally turned over to the exhibition corporation on 1 July 1964. As finally developed, it was divided into 4 main areas. The entrance at Cité du Havre was formerly known as Mackay Pier, a part of the port of Montréal. From the Cité du Havre, the new Concordia Bridge across the St Lawrence led to the first exhibition area on the western section of Île Ste-Hélène. The third area was the Île Notre-Dame. The fourth, La Ronde, at the eastern end of Île Ste-Hélène, contained most of the amusement activities.

The theme program was divided into 5 main groups: Man the Creator, Man the Explorer, Man the Producer, Man the Provider, and Man and the Community. These, in turn, were divided into subgroups. To implement the theme, the exhibition corporation invested almost $40 million in theme buildings, strategically located around the site to serve as "points of polarization" for the theme groups. Illustrating Man the Creator was an exhibit of approximately 160 paintings borrowed from museums and individuals worldwide. Also part of this subtheme were exhibitions of sculpture, photography and industrial design. The social sciences and humanities were grouped under Man and the Community.

Expo 67 was held on an island landfill site in the St Lawrence R. More than 50 million visitors attended the fair (*photo by Gordon F. Callaghan, Montréal*).

The nations that agreed to participate in Expo 67 either built their own pavilions or combined with other nations in regional pavilions. Among them, the Soviet Union spent approximately $15 million; Czechoslovakia, $10 million; and the United States, more than $9 million. The approaches taken by some of the world's greatest architects in designing the pavilions were varied and frequently breathtaking. Arthur ERICKSON's pyramidal Man in His Community was built from hexagonal frames of Douglas fir; the German pavilion, a 15-storey, multi-peaked tent of plastic, indicated how concept and materials might radically alter the design of buildings such as auditoriums; and Buckminster Fuller's geodesic dome for the US became the prototype for a new trend in construction. The interiors of the pavilions also varied greatly. Some presented prosaic displays of consumer goods and machinery while others imaginatively depicted their history and cultural traditions. Montréal architect Moshe SAFDIE's revolutionary Habitat '67 was a graphic demonstration that by industrializing the building process, there are better and cheaper ways to house people. Expo also witnessed the development of new approaches to viewing film. The multi-screen technique was omnipresent, transforming everyday sights and sounds into more vital images.

Expo 67 also encouraged participation by private industry and by special groups. In the latter category, 7 Christian churches combined to present a Christian pavilion; others included the United Nations Association, the European Economic Community, the House of Judaism, sponsored by the Canadian Jewish community, and the Youth Pavilion.

Under BIE rules, each country taking part in the exhibition may send performing artists as a part of its participation. The World Arts Festival was thus able to include on its schedule such internationally known groups as La Scala Opera Company from Milan, Sir Laurence Olivier's National Theatre from Great Britain, the New York Philharmonic, the Amsterdam Concertgebouw, and classical theatre from Greece. Expo 67 and the Montréal International Film Festival combined to present a festival of more than 30 feature films during August. Sports events included an international soccer tournament, a lacrosse tournament and a European-American track meet. Spectacles such as a western rodeo and the first N American appearance of the Gendarmerie française rounded out the festivities at this, the crowning event of Canada's birthday celebration.

There were some 120 governments present at Expo in 60 pavilions, and thousands of private exhibitors and sponsors participated in 53 private pavilions and through various facilities on the site. The exhibition site was planned to accommodate 26 million individual visits over a 183-day period. In fact, there were over 50 million paid admissions recorded from Apr 28 to Oct 27, not counting over 5 million admissions by performers, the press, official visitors and employees. Expo 67 cost Canada, Québec and Montréal $283 million to put together and to run. Independent economic studies indicated that the return to federal, provincial and municipal taxpayers was almost double that amount. For example, the increase in tourist revenues in 1967 directly related to Expo was calculated at $480 million.

Expo 86, Vancouver, BC, was opened 2 May 1986 by the Prince and Princess of Wales and closed 13 Oct 1986 after 20 111 578 visits. Two sites covered 70 ha: the main site of 67 ha ran 4.5 km along the N and E shores of False Creek, and the Canada Pavilion, located off the main site, covered 3 ha.

In 1978, Sam Bawlf, provincial minister for recreation and conservation, had proposed an international exposition to celebrate Vancouver's centenary based on a concept study by architect Randle Iredale. A formal application for a fair called Transpo 86 was submitted June 1979 to the Bureau International des Expositions (BIE), Paris. Various sites and plans were proposed. The BIE approved the fair in Nov 1980. Patrick Reid, Ambassador and Commissioner General, changed the name to Expo 86 in Oct 1981, eliminating any connotations of a trade fair. Unlike EXPO 67 this was a special category exposition, the largest ever held, with a single theme of transportation and communications. The theme statement of "World in Motion – World in Touch" was symbolized by a logo of 3 concentric circles using the figures 8 and 6 intersecting to represent transportation by land, sea and air. After difficulties with funding through 1980-81, plans were finalized. The project was sponsored by the federal and provincial governments. Expo 86 Corp was established as a nonprofit agency to plan and operate the fair and was headed by Jim PATTISON, chairman of the board and later president. Creative director was Ron Woodall, chief architect was Bruno Freschi and Bob Smith was in charge of production and design.

Construction of the first pavilion began in Oct 1983. Labour disputes for 5 months in 1984 disrupted work but the pavilions were completed on schedule and $8 million under budget. Expo Centre opened 2 May 1985 as a preview of the fair. The site was divided into 6 coloured zones, each containing pavilions, theatres, rides and restaurants. The centre of the site was dominated by the 4.5 ha BC Place which remains after Expo. It included a covered stadium, Expo Theatre and the Plaza of Nations where national and special day ceremonies were held. There were 65 pavilions: 41 were international; 7 provinces, 2 territories, 3 states and 9 corporations had pavilions; 2 were theme pavilions and one was special (Ramses II containing treasures from the life of the pharaoh). Pavilions were built and leased to international participants according to BIE rules. The international pavilions were constructed of steel modular units, each unit 250 m^2, with some pavilions comprising up to 10 units (eg, USSR). All other participants were responsible for planning, design and construction of their pavilions. Two theme pavilions remain after the fair: the Roundhouse exhibiting "The Golden Age of Ingenuity" in transportation is a renovated 100-year-old railway roundhouse, and the Expo Centre

Expo Centre, Vancouver, opened in May 1985 as a preview of the fair. BC Place is to the left (*photo by K. Nagai/Miller Comstock*).

"Futures Pavilion" is a 17-storey geodesic dome with a 500-seat Omnimax theatre, a Futures Theatre with push-button voting and Design 2000, an exhibit of futuristic vehicles. The Expo Centre will reopen as Science World by 1990. One of the most popular pavilions was the Northwest Territories designed by architect Bing Thom. It was constructed of pale blue plaster with reflective blue glass to resemble icebergs and glaciers. The NWT exhibits, combining film, photos with text, displays and models, were visually stunning and thought provoking, giving the visitor insights into the dramatic effects of transportation and communications on the life and culture of northern Canadians.

The most frequent features of many pavilions were films. Among the more popular were *Carrying Things*, a 3-D IMAX film; Canadian Pacific's *Rainbow War*; Telecom Canada's *Portraits of Canada – Images du Canada* in circlevision; *A Freedom to Move; Zargon*, a 70mm Showscan film; and *Northwest Passage*, a 69-slide projector show in which viewers were transported along a moving walkway. Perhaps the most popular film was General Motor's *Spirit Lodge*, produced by Bob Rogers, a live presentation combined with holographic effects presented in a darkened Big House, prepared with the assistance of the Nimpkish Band of the Kwagulth (KWAKIUTL) people of Alert Bay, BC.

There were 9 plazas on the site, 3 related to transportation. The Land Plaza was filled with land vehicles from all nations centered around the sculpture "Transcending the Traffic," a 26 m tall "traffic jam" by sculptor Bill Lishman. The Air Plaza's "Flight Dream" was a celebration of forms of air and space travel. Examples of water craft in the Marine Plaza were located near the 33 m high brightly painted, steel sculpture "Dream Ship," which resembled the superstructure of a large sailing vessel. This plaza hosted a gathering of hundreds of water craft from around the world, including Japan's tall ship, the *Nippon Maru*.

Six theatres operated by Expo provided free entertainment daily. The Royal Bank/Expo 86 World Festival was held at venues throughout Vancouver including Expo Theatre. Among performers were world-renowned ballet and opera companies, dancers, singers, comedians, musicians and rock groups.

All on-site transportation was free. A 5.4 km monorail gave a 20-minute ride through the site to 10.5 million passengers. Two gondola skyrides carried 9.75 million people. Free, direct transportation to the Canada Pavilion was by Skytrain, Vancouver's newly opened light-rail transit system. Access to Skytrain from the main site was through the Canada Portal marked by the world's tallest freestanding 86 m flagpole, a Canadian flag 12 m x 24 m and a hockey stick 61 m high.

The Canada Pavilion, with 10 800 m^2 of exhibit and performance space, extended 3.5 city blocks into Burrard Inlet and cost $145 million. This dramatic white building with mountains, water and city as backdrop was constructed to resemble a ship with 5 large "sails" of suspended fabric. The pavilion now serves as a convention centre and cruise ship terminal. An old Haida war canoe from the Canadian Museum of Civilization in Ottawa was the centrepiece of the exhibit hall and was juxtaposed with Hystar, a "flying saucer" being developed as a carrier for heavy cargo in remote areas, which was flown around the hall once every hour.

Among the most entertaining spectacles were the sculptures: Ron Baird's "Spirit Catcher," a huge iron bird; "Rowingbridge" by Geoffrey Smedley; Miho Saawada's "Locomotive People #4"; and John Gilbert's bright, colourful, popular "UFO H2O," a children's water playground that resembled a Martian spaceship. The largest sculpture was "Highway 86" designed by S.I.T.E. Projects (NY), a 217 m undulating steel and concrete 4-lane freeway for pedestrians. Many forms of air, land and water vehicles, painted grey, were cemented to the freeway.

Expenditures for the fair were $802 million and revenues were $491 million. The federal government contributed $75 million to build Canada Pavilion, $60 million to build Skytrain and $25 million toward the deficit. More than 36 corporate sponsors committed $173 million. Participants spent $698 million for total expenditures at Expo of $1.5 billion. The final deficit was $311 million. However, the Canadian economy received an extra $3.7 billion as a result of Expo 86. The fair proved so popular that restaurants and clubs on-site remained open after pavilions closed each evening. Expo 86 will be remembered for the warm, friendly spirit that existed among the exhibitors, staff, 8000 volunteers and visitors.

KIM PATRICK O'LEARY

Exports are goods or services which a nation sells to other nations. During 1986 Canadian sales abroad amounted to $145 billion, consisting of $121 billion (or 83%) merchandise, $17 billion (or 12%) services and $7 billion (or 5%) investment income.

Merchandise Over the decades, the US has been an increasingly important destination for Canadian merchandise exports. Its share has risen from 36% in 1928 to 78% in 1986. Japan has become the second most significant market, although taking only 5% of Canadian shipments it lags far behind the US. All the countries of the European Economic Community, including the United Kingdom, account for only 6.7% of EXPORTS. The remaining 11% of exports are to all the other countries of the world. These include wheat shipments to our two largest markets for grain, the Soviet Union and the People's Republic of China; coal to S Korea; and asbestos, sulphur, newsprint, woodpulp, fertilizers and a range of machinery and equipment to a wide variety of countries such as India, Brazil and Morocco.

Canadian exports are dominated by one commodity group, automobiles and parts. These, of which 98% are destined for the US, amounted to $34 billion or 29% of all merchandise exports in 1986. Apart from these, the great majority of Canada's other important exports are based on the nation's abundant natural resources. These include, in order of their importance in 1986, forest products such as newsprint, lumber and woodpulp (14.5%); metals and minerals (12.8%); energy products such as oil, gas, coal and electricity (9.4%); food products such as grains, red meats and fish (7.0%); and fertilizers and chemicals (4.1%). A few highly manufactured goods of growing importance in recent years are aircraft engines and parts (2.6%) and telecommunications equipment (2.2%).

Over the last 15 years, the value of merchandise exports has expanded at an average annual compound rate of nearly 13.5%. Of this, about 7.5% reflects merely the increase in prices, while 6.0% is the growth in the actual volume or quantity of shipments. The most rapidly expanding categories in volume terms during the 1980s have been crude petroleum, office machinery, automobiles, precious metals and miscellaneous chemical products.

Services Receipts to Canada from sales of services to nonresidents consist of 3 main categories: travel receipts from foreigners coming to Canada for business or pleasure trips; freight and shipping receipts from the use of Canadian-operated transportation systems for exports or the shipment of foreign-owned goods in Canada or abroad; and business services such as engineering or consulting services sold abroad as well as commissions, insurance, communications and other such receipts. These 3 groups each account for about 30% of service receipts. There are also some receipts from foreign governments covering costs of their diplomatic offices in Canada and a variety of miscellaneous items. The proportion of total receipts coming from the US is less than for merchandise – only 60%.

Investment Income includes interest and dividend receipts plus miscellaneous income from lending and investing abroad. The latter category is the largest, accounting for about 55% of total investment income receipts. Dividends in turn amounted to about 37% in 1986, although if the earnings retained in Canadian-owned firms abroad were included with dividends, this category would be expanded somewhat. Receipts from the US account for only about 40% of total investment income from abroad. *See also* BALANCE OF PAYMENTS; FREE TRADE; INTERNATIONAL TRADE.

BRUCE W. WILKINSON

External Affairs, Department of After CONFEDERATION in 1867, British diplomats continued to handle Canada's boundary disputes and treaty negotiations with other countries. In 1909 PM Sir Wilfrid Laurier created the Dept of External Affairs. Under a distinguished civil servant, Sir Joseph POPE, and a handful of clerks, the department functioned as an archive, issued passports to Canadians travelling abroad, provided the focus for liaison with the British COLONIAL OFFICE and foreign consuls in Canada, and handled routine relations with the US. Diplomacy, however, remained largely in the hands of the British. Transformation to a proper foreign office began in the mid-1920s under PM Mackenzie King and his undersecretary of state for external affairs, O.D. SKELTON. As Canada acquired more autonomy within the COMMONWEALTH, it needed its own diplomatic representatives abroad. A foreign service was established and, between 1925 and 1929, a Dominion of Canada Advisory Office was opened in Geneva and diplomatic missions (legations) were established at Washington, Paris and Tokyo (the latter 3 became embassies). During and after WWII, additional posts were opened and Canada emerged as a MIDDLE POWER. With the department as their headquarters, Canadian diplomats played important roles in creating the UNITED NATIONS, NATO and various PEACEKEEPING forces.

The department's headquarters in the Lester B. Pearson Building on Ottawa's Sussex Drive coordinates activities of 113 posts in 86 countries. The department provides policy guidance to other government departments and agencies; plans and interprets the international impact of domestic decisions; ensures international representation of Canadian interests through its ambassadors, high commissioners and consuls; negotiates international agreements; fosters an awareness and understanding of Canada abroad; and provides assistance and guidance to Canadians travelling and working abroad. Since 1982 a restructuring and integration of government departments has brought international trade, export promotion, immigration policy and development assistance under the department's control. Its policies are designed to present a coherent and unified foreign policy, to protect our sovereignty and independence, to promote social justice and democracy, to preserve peace and security, to promote economic prosperity and to protect the natural environment. D.M. PAGE

External Relations To a great extent, the history of Canada's external relations is the history of the development of a British colony into an independent nation within the COMMONWEALTH. Colonial foreign relations were normally controlled by the mother country. In the case of BRITISH NORTH AMERICA, foreign relations largely meant relations with the neighbouring US. The implicit understanding was that the imperial government controlled relations with foreign states, and that as a corollary it had the obligation to defend the colony. This assumption did not lose all its force until well into the 20th century.

Concession of RESPONSIBLE GOVERNMENT to the N American colonies in the late 1840s did not alter this situation. The colonies that united in CONFEDERATION were essentially self-governing in internal affairs. Nevertheless, the BRITISH NORTH AMERICA ACT which effected the union said nothing about external relations. It was assumed that those relations were virtually the exclusive concern of the UK. The authorities conducting Canada's business with the US were the GOVERNOR GENERAL, the British minister in Washington and the foreign secretary in London. The governor general consulted his Canadian ministers and transmitted their views to London; but final authority rested with the British government.

The Canadian government acquired influence over the relationship only gradually. An important landmark was the Treaty of WASHINGTON in 1871, which liquidated dangerous issues between Britain and the US left over from the AMERICAN CIVIL WAR. The British government nominated as one of its 5 negotiators PM Sir John A. MACDONALD. This recognized both Canada's growing status and its concern with the issues; but Macdonald was present as a British plenipotentiary, not as a representative of his country. To a large extent the negotiation was triangular: Macdonald had serious disagreements with his British associates, particularly over the Atlantic fisheries. Although unhappy over this aspect of the treaty, he signed it; and the treaty was in fact advantageous to Canada, simply because it restored friendly relations between the British Empire and the US.

In 1874 the Liberal government of Alexander MACKENZIE prevailed on Britain to accredit George BROWN (along with the British minister in Washington) to seek a RECIPROCITY treaty similar to that of 1854, which the US had terminated in 1866. Macdonald and his colleagues had tried for this in 1871, without success. Brown failed likewise. Macdonald, on returning to power in Sept 1878, enacted the NATIONAL POLICY. Tariff reciprocity with the US continued to be a Canadian goal, but successive American administrations gave no encouragement. Trade policy remained Canada's most persistent problem with the US, with fishery troubles a close second. In 1880, with Britain's reluctant consent, Sir Alexander Galt was appointed Canadian high commissioner in London. In 1882 a *commissaire général* was appointed in Paris; he doubled as a representative of Québec until 1912. He had no diplomatic status. No further development of Canadian representation abroad took place until after WWI.

In the latter part of Queen Victoria's reign, British anti-imperialism (reflected in the withdrawal of British garrisons from central Canada in 1870-71) had given place to its opposite. In Canada, IMPERIALISM gave an outlet to growing NATIONALISM and the desire to play an expanding part in the world. When British Gen C.G. Gordon was cut off in Khartoum in 1884, there was considerable demand in Canada for a contingent to go to the Sudan. Macdonald deliberately damped this down. But when Britain sought to raise at its own expense a body of Canadian voyageurs to help a rescue expedition surmount the cataracts of the Nile (*see* NILE EXPEDITION), no objection was made.

The beginning of the SOUTH AFRICAN WAR in 1899 raised more serious questions. Sir Wilfrid LAURIER's Liberals were now in power in Canada. Québec, the citadel of Laurier's political authority, was largely unmoved by the imperial enthusiasm of other provinces. On the question of contributing a contingent, Cabinet was deeply divided. Ultimately, Laurier was forced by the majority to send a battalion of volunteers. Further contingents followed, and in spite of Laurier's disclaimers when attacked by his Québec compatriots (notably Henri BOURASSA), it was clear that a precedent had been set.

Relations with the US continued to turn largely on commercial policy. In 1888 the Liberals had adopted "Unrestricted Reciprocity"; on it they fought and lost the election of 1891, Macdonald's last. Thereafter the Liberals abandoned unrestricted reciprocity and, death having removed Macdonald from the scene in 1891, were elected, headed by Laurier, in 1896. Laurier's government would come to grief, in due course, over reciprocity, but meanwhile he had to confront the ALASKA BOUNDARY DISPUTE, the last great boundary dispute between Canada and the US. This old controversy acquired new importance during the KLONDIKE GOLD RUSH. The handling of the question by US Pres Theodore Roosevelt aroused bitter resentment in Canada, as did the behaviour of British representative Lord Alverstone, who, when the tribunal on the matter met, voted with the Americans. Nevertheless, as with the Treaty of Washington, this settlement served Canada's paramount interest by removing an obstacle to friendly relations between the empire and the US.

Canada's relationship with the empire found a focus in the series of COLONIAL AND IMPERIAL CONFERENCES, the first of which was held in London in 1887. During Lord Salisbury's Conservative government (1895-1902), the colonial secretary was the energetic Joseph Chamberlain, who envisaged an empire more organized and centralized than the informal affair that had grown up. In Laurier he met a determined defender of the status quo. Sir Wilfrid regularly declared that Canada was well satisfied with things as they were and had no demands to make; it had its autonomy and, he more than hinted, intended to keep it. After the turn of the century, the menace presented by the growing German navy led to demands both in Canada and in Britain for some Canadian naval assistance. Sir Wilfrid's ultimate response was not a contribution to the Royal Navy but an autonomous Canadian navy, provided for by the NAVAL SERVICE ACT of 1910.

The general election of 1911 turned to an unprecedented extent on questions of external policy. Any naval policy was unpopular in Québec. Robert Laird BORDEN, the Conservative leader, argued that no permanent policy should be adopted until approved by the people; meanwhile there should be a contribution to the RN. His campaign played down the naval issue; but the Naval Service Act did Laurier much harm in Québec. Elsewhere the paramount issue was reciprocity with the US. The agricultural West had been pressing for freer trade, and there was similar agitation in the US. The result had been the 1911 reciprocity agreement which provided for free trade in a wide range of agricultural products and a limited number of manufactured goods. Violent nationalistic opposition developed against this measure; manufacturers assailed it as a menace to Canadian industry, and it was claimed that it would open the door to political union. Laurier lost the election, and Borden became prime minister.

The predominantly British province of Ontario now succeeded Québec as the main seat of the government's political power, and external policy reflected this fact. Borden was as much of a nationalist as Laurier, though his nationalism found different expression. Where Laurier had sought to stand aside from imperial entanglements, and had asserted no claim to influence in the imperial system, Borden was prepared to participate but attempted to exact a price. In England in 1912 he told British statesmen that Canadians would now expect "a voice" in the formation of imperial policy. When later that year he proposed that Canada should contribute 3 battleships to the RN, he clearly expected a quid pro quo in the form of such influence. Britain's Liberal government was loath to commit itself; and the Canadian Senate rejected Borden's naval bill.

Everything changed with the outbreak of WORLD WAR I. Canada was united behind the decision of Borden's government to give full support to Britain and to dispatch a CANADIAN EXPEDITIONARY FORCE. There was now a stronger argument than ever before for a Canadian "voice" in the making of policy; but British PM Lord Asquith still had nothing to offer.

In Dec 1916 Asquith fell and David Lloyd George became prime minister. Lloyd George realized that the Dominions could not be expected to continue making sacrifices without being called to Britain's councils. He therefore summoned an Imperial War Cabinet and an Imperial War Conference, which first met in Mar 1917, and between them discussed both the conduct of the war and imperial matters generally. In Apr 1917 the conference passed Resolution IX, largely Borden's work, which placed on record the opinion that any postwar readjustment of constitutional relations "should be based upon a full recognition of the Dominions as autonomous nations of an Imperial Commonwealth," and should give the Dominions and India "an adequate voice in foreign policy."

There was a second series of sessions of the Imperial War Cabinet and War Conference in 1918, in which Borden was active; and in 1919 the Imperial War Cabinet in effect became the British Empire Delegation to the Paris Peace Conference. Largely as a result of Borden's insistence, the Dominions were accorded what amounted to dual representation at the conference: as nations in their own right, along with other small Allied nations, and as units of the British Empire. In both capacities Canada signed the Treaty of VERSAILLES and became a member of the LEAGUE OF NATIONS, whose covenant was part of the treaty. Thus the country acquired a new international status, won by its soldiers on the battlefield and confirmed by its statesmen's pertinacity at the conference table.

A small Department of EXTERNAL AFFAIRS had been instituted by statute in 1909, principally to ensure the businesslike conduct of the country's external concerns. In 1912 an amendment made the prime minister also secretary of state for external affairs – an arrangement that lasted until 1946. For many years the department's most important official was Loring C. CHRISTIE, appointed by Borden in 1913 with the title of legal adviser. He was Borden's confidential assistant at the Imperial War Cabinet and the Peace Conference, and a major contributor to the national achievements of the period. When in July 1920 Borden retired and Arthur MEIGHEN became prime minister, Christie remained as Meighen's trusted adviser.

Meighen represented Canada at the Imperial Conference of 1921. This conference proceeded on the general assumption that it was desirable that the empire should pursue a common foreign policy arrived at by consultation. Difficulties arose, however, over the renewal of the Anglo-Japanese alliance. Meighen, influenced by Christie, argued that the alliance constituted a serious obstacle to amicable relations with the US, so vital to the empire and particularly to Canada; whereas Australia regarded the alliance as important to its security. A disastrous break was avoided by Lloyd George's diplomatic tactics; at the subsequent Washington Conference of 1922 (attended by Borden and Christie), the alliance was abandoned, to be replaced by a 4-power treaty signed by Britain, the US, Japan and France, who agreed to respect one another's rights and possessions in the Pacific. This conference was the last important occasion when a British Empire delegation functioned as a unit at an international negotiation.

In the Dec 1921 general election Meighen was defeated by Mackenzie KING's Liberals. Although external policy was not an ostensible issue, in fact 1921 marks a reversal even more striking than that of 1911. The Liberals took every one of Québec's 65 seats in the Commons, and it was inevitable that King's policies should be tailored accordingly. In 1921 Québec was strongly isolationist; the war and CONSCRIPTION had left deep marks. The result was the abandonment of unified diplomacy in partnership with the other countries of what was now increasingly being called the Commonwealth, and the substitution of separate national policy. At Paris, Canada had been recognized both as a member country of the British Empire and as a separate nation; King's policies consistently emphasized the latter aspect at the expense of the former. Symbolically, Christie was frozen out of the Dept of External Affairs in 1923. His successor as the prime minister's confidential adviser was O.D. SKELTON, who became undersecretary in 1925 and held that appointment until his death in 1941.

Skelton was not the deviser of King's policies, which were well developed before Skelton joined him, nor were their opinions exactly the same. Skelton has been called anti-British, not without reason, whereas King would have wholly repudiated that label. King was an admirer of British institutions and practices, and always considered that in another world war Canada would have to stand by Britain. But King and Skelton entirely agreed in rejecting a common foreign policy for the Commonwealth and maintaining that in normal conditions Canada and the UK should pursue their own national policies. At the Imperial Conference of 1923 King made it clear to Britain that he had no intention of maintaining Borden's policies. In his memoranda for King, Skelton gave no recognition to the nationalistic aspect of the Canadian Conservative proceedings of 1911 to 1921, and even avoided mention of Resolution IX of the Imperial War Conference; he represented those events as, in effect, a centralizing British plot. The CHANAK AFFAIR of 1922, with its bungled British request for a Canadian expeditionary force, had provided only too convincing a background for King's attitude. And he had given a striking example of his view of policy when in Mar 1923 he insisted that the HALIBUT TREATY with the US be signed by Canada alone, without the traditional participation of the British ambassador. He was delighted when the Imperial Conference accepted this procedure as normal. He was unaware that the British Foreign Office was as hostile as he to the idea of an imperial policy formed in consultation with the Dominions; to the Foreign Office such consultation was merely a trammel on British freedom of action.

Under King, Canada achieved separate diplomatic representation in Washington. An arrangement for this had in fact been made in Borden's time, but no action had been taken. In 1926 Vincent MASSEY became the first Canadian minister to the US. Legations were opened in France in 1928 and in Japan in 1929. Early in 1939 missions were established in Belgium and the Netherlands (served by the same minister); this was the extent of Canadian representation abroad before WWII.

Canada's relations with the League of Nations began at Paris in 1919 with an effort to weaken Article 10 of the Covenant, which bound members to defend the territorial integrity and independence of all other members. Successive Canadian governments continued to fight against this article (especially unpopular in Québec) until 1923, when a resolution leaving to each member the decision as to how far it was bound to use force in fulfilment of Article 10 failed of the necessary unanimous support in the Assembly by one vote. In 1927 Canada was elected to a nonpermanent seat on the League Council, with the reluctant assent of King, who feared unnecessary commitments and complications.

The Imperial Conference of 1926 resulted in a formal widening of Dominion autonomy. South Africa insisted on a definition of Britain's relation with the Dominions. The result was the BALFOUR REPORT, which led to the 1931 STATUTE OF WESTMINSTER giving the Dominions complete legislative independence so far as they desired it. In Canada's case this stopped short only of the right to amend its own constitution, the core of which was found in the 1867 British North America Act. This reservation was the result of pressure from Ontario and Québec. It ceased to be operative only as a result of the CONSTITUTION ACT, 1982. The word "independence" is not found in the Statute of Westminster, largely because King would not hear of it in the discussions of 1926; but Canada's independence may be said to date from that statute (11 Dec 1931).

By this time the GREAT DEPRESSION had brought the Conservatives, led by R.B. BENNETT, to power in the 28 July 1930 election. Bennett, motivated by the desperate state of the economy, raised the tariff, primarily as retaliation against the US's new Hawley-Smoot tariff, though British preferential rates were also raised. At the Imperial Conference of 1930 he made a dramatic gesture, inviting the delegates to a special economic conference at Ottawa and proposing, not a general reduction of imperial rates, but a 10% increase in rates levied against countries outside the Commonwealth. British politicians saw how little the offer was worth; nevertheless, the Imperial Economic Conference finally met at Ottawa in 1932 (*see* OTTAWA AGREEMENTS) amid hopes that something might be done to alleviate the depression. Bennett, theoretically an imperialist, was in fact an economic nationalist of the first order. The Anglo-Canadian trade agreement made at the conference contained some concessions on both sides. But the achievement was much less than optimists had hoped, and there was ill will between British and Canadian negotiators. Relations between the 2 countries were at a low ebb.

PM Lester B. Pearson and US President John F. Kennedy at Hyannis Port, Mass, spring 1963. Canadian-American relations were less acerbic under Pearson than under his predecessor, John Diefenbaker (*courtesy National Archives of Canada/C-90482*).

As the general election of 1935 approached, the world situation was threatening. Hitler had come to power in Germany in 1933, Japan was engaged in aggression against China, and Italy was preparing to attack Ethiopia. The League of Nations' effort to restrain Italy led to apprehension of an Anglo-Italian war. The Bennett government showed itself prepared to support sanctions against Italy, but after the election of 14 Oct 1935 returned the Liberals to power, PM King adopted a policy of economic conciliation, putting an end to a trade war with Japan and (more important) reaching a trade agreement with the US – an object Bennett had lately pursued without success. King's cautious policy as the danger of war in Europe grew (*see* MUNICH CRISIS), much criticized as pusillanimous, was to be justified by the fact that Canada entered WWII a united country.

After WORLD WAR II King still pursued a cautious and generally isolationist policy, apprehensive of the growing American influence in Canadian affairs, hostile as ever to imperial centralization, and tending to resist the increasing involvement of Canada in world affairs. Nevertheless the movement seemed irresistible. By 1947 Canada had 36 missions abroad, and in 1946 the office of secretary of state for external affairs was finally separated from that of prime minister, the first secretary of state under the new regime being Louis ST. LAURENT. King's own retirement from politics in Nov 1948 was the end of an era.

O.D. Skelton's best legacy to the Dept of External Affairs had been the group of able civil servants he recruited beginning in 1927, notably L.B. PEARSON, Norman ROBERTSON and Hume WRONG. The professional standard established by these men and their colleagues was a great asset to a country beginning to make its way in diplomacy. Robertson became undersecretary in 1941, succeeding Skelton, and Pearson succeeded Robertson in 1946. When St. Laurent was about to become prime minister, Pearson entered Cabinet as secretary of state for external affairs.

After King's retirement, Canadian external policy took a rather bolder tone. Tendencies to assume commitments had already appeared, notably in Canada's actions at the founding conference of the UNITED NATIONS in 1945. When faith in the UN's effectiveness was undermined by the COLD WAR between the Soviet Union and the West, Canada not only accepted but even advocated the idea of a western regional union for collective defence, and signed the North Atlantic Treaty in 1949. As a result, Canadian military units were sent to Europe in 1951 to serve under the North Atlantic Treaty Organization (NATO). During the same period the Canadian government (somewhat reluctantly) dispatched a brigade group to fight under UN command in the KOREAN WAR.

These commitments led to large increases in Canada's ARMED FORCES.

Joining NATO marked a turning point in Canadian policy. Traditionally, Canada had been loath to accept commitments either to Britain or the US individually; it was easier to accept commitments to an organization of which both were members, the more so as they too were abandoning isolationist positions. These new attitudes reflected the experience of WWII and the traumatic effect of the advent of atomic weapons. At the same time it was becoming clear that the war had greatly weakened Britain's world position; that confrontation between the superpowers, the capitalist US and the communist USSR, was now the dominant fact of the international situation (*see* MIDDLE POWER); and that relations with the American neighbour eclipsed all other Canadian external problems.

As Britain gave up its imperial obligations, the Commonwealth became increasingly multiracial, a development that the Canadian government encouraged. The new polity was severely strained in 1956 by the SUEZ CRISIS, when Britain and France made a military attack on Egypt following Egyptian nationalization of the Suez Canal Co. The UN, including the US, condemned the aggression, which was also strongly reprobated by the nonwhite Commonwealth countries. It was a classic example of the difficulty in which a serious Anglo-American dispute places Canada. Canada abstained from voting on a resolution demanding a cease-fire and Anglo-French withdrawal, but proposed an international PEACEKEEPING force to supervise the cessation of hostilities. The Commonwealth stayed together, and L.B. Pearson received the Nobel Peace Prize for his peace initiatives. Canada was at the height of its diplomatic influence.

An electoral upset on 10 June 1957 brought the Progressive Conservatives under John DIEFENBAKER to power. During his period in power, until 1963, foreign relations turned largely on the military connection with the US. At the very beginning, accepting a proposal that had been before their predecessors, the new government associated Canada with the US in the North American Air Defence Command (NORAD). Diefenbaker's personal relations with Pres John F. Kennedy (1961-63) were poor (*see* CUBAN MISSILE CRISIS), and there was trouble over whether or not Canada should accept nuclear weapons (*see* BOMARC MISSILE CRISIS). Early in 1963 Pearson, now Opposition leader, reversing his earlier stand, advocated accepting them in order to carry out obligations to the US. Diefenbaker's vacillations led to resignations from his Cabinet, and finally to the government's defeat.

Under Pearson, leader of the new minority government, CANADIAN-AMERICAN RELATIONS were less acerbic than under Diefenbaker, but US participation in the Vietnam War contributed to poisoning them. A positive development of 1965 was the so-called Autopact providing for free trade between the 2 countries in motor cars and parts, one result of which was that large numbers of cars were produced in Canada for sale in the US. The large lines of Canadian policy changed little under Pearson, who had done so much to lay them down. The lesson the generation that had fought WWII had drawn from its experience – that security could be best ensured by the Western nations being united and strong – was still accepted.

With Pearson's retirement in 1968 and his replacement by Pierre TRUDEAU, there was a change of atmosphere. Trudeau was not, like Pearson, a member of the Ottawa establishment, and he had played no part in the war. The PRIME MINISTER'S OFFICE became more important and the Dept of External Affairs less influential. In 1969 there was a drastic reduction in the armed forces and a considerable reduction in the foreign service. The cut in military strength certainly contributed to a decline in Canadian diplomatic influence, though this had already been in progress as the result of the postwar recovery of France and West Germany. In 1970 a series of government pamphlets entitled *Foreign Policy for Canadians* defined Canada's goals: to "foster economic growth, safeguard sovereignty and independence, work for peace and security, promote social justice, enhance the quality of life, [and] ensure a harmonious natural environment." These high-sounding phrases seemed to traditional diplomatists hardly a practicable basis for foreign policy, and some feared that, taken with the measures of 1969, they were harbingers of a new isolationism.

Economic relations with the US provided the worst problems of the Trudeau era. There was considerable popular anti-Americanism, sparked by resentment of growing US investment and therefore control in Canada (though this FOREIGN INVESTMENT had been welcomed in earlier times) and by continuing dislike of the Vietnam adventure, which terminated only in 1973. Energy problems following a crisis caused by the Organization of Petroleum Exporting Countries (OPEC) in 1973-74 were a violent irritant, particularly in view of the domination of the Canadian oil market by American companies. In the autumn of 1980 the Trudeau government announced the National Energy Program, one objective of which was at least 50% Canadian ownership of oil and gas production by 1990. This almost coincided with the election of US Pres Ronald Reagan, and to his conservative Republican administration the NEP, much hated by the US oil companies, was an object of hostility. So was another Trudeau institution, the FOREIGN INVESTMENT REVIEW AGENCY, which began to monitor foreign investment in Canada in 1974.

During the last generation the pattern of Canadian external trade has been transformed. Before WWII Canada had 2 great trading partners, Britain and the US. Exports to Britain exceeded imports; with the US the situation was the reverse. After the war, Canada's British market never wholly revived. In recent years Japan has been Canada's second-largest trading partner, and in imports Venezuela, from which Canada takes large quantities of oil, stood ahead of Britain in 1983. Canada has recently sold great quantities of wheat to China and the USSR. The US dominates the Canadian trading scene as never before: over 75% of all Canada's trade is with that country. Canadian commercial policy has been influenced in the direction of freer trade by adherence to the General Agreement on Tariffs and Trade, first drawn up in 1947 and modified since.

The overwhelming victory of the Conservatives, now led by Brian MULRONEY, in the federal general election of Sept 1984 produced changes of policy. Mulroney cultivated Pres Reagan, and the 2 leaders' supposed closeness was emphasized during Reagan's visit to Québec City (the so-called "Shamrock Summit") in Mar 1985. The new attitude appeared in the abandonment of the National Energy Program and the weakening of the Foreign Investment Review Agency, now to be called Investment Canada. The leading element in Mulroney's policy, however, was the proposal, concurred in by Reagan, for a comprehensive FREE TRADE agreement with the US. Teams from the 2 countries began negotiations, but 16 months of discussion failed to produce the desired result. At the last moment, just before a deadline set by the US Congress, the intervention of Cabinet-level negotiators from both countries brought about an "agreement in principle" (3 Oct 1987), within minutes of a deadline set by the US Congress. Even then negotiations continued, and the document was modified in certain particulars before it was finally published on 11 Dec 1987. The complicated arrangement, which included a declaration that all bilateral tariffs between Canada and the US would be eliminated in the course of 10 years, had a mixed reception in Canada. Business interests in general favoured it, organized labour opposed it; the West was broadly though not unanimously – owing to Manitoba's resistance – favourable. The Québec government supported it and Atlantic Canada seemed uncertain about it, but Ontario was officially hostile. The great Conservative majority in the Canadian Parliament ensured its acceptance there, in spite of Liberal and NDP attacks; but protectionist feeling was strong in Washington, and the agreement's fate in Congress seemed uncertain. It seems likely that the issue will be a dominant issue in the next Canadian federal election.

C.P. STACEY

Reading: Canadian Annual Review of Politics and Public Affairs (1960, continuing); *Documents on Canadian External Relations* (1967, continuing); James Eayrs, *In Defence of Canada*, 5 vols (1964-83); G.P. de T. Glazebrook, *A History of Canadian External Relations*, 2 vols (rev ed, 1966); C.P. Stacey, *Canada and the Age of Conflict*, 2 vols (1977-81).

Eyre, Ivan Kenneth, painter (b at Tulleymet, Sask 15 Apr 1935). Raised on the Saskatchewan prairie and in the suburbs of Saskatoon, Eyre developed a perception that enabled him to see the aesthetic content of natural scenes. After studying sporadically under Ernest LINDNER and Eli BORNSTEIN, he began art training in 1953 at the University of Manitoba School of Art. In 1959 he joined the faculty and has taught there ever since. His studies of the old European and Japanese masters gave him a broad perspective, and when he began to develop his individual style in 1961, through concentrated drawing followed by painting, he stayed aloof from the changing novelties of the art scene. His first show was in 1962, and since then he has exhibited in Canada, Germany and the US. A major retrospective was held at the Robert McLaughlin Gallery, Oshawa, in 1980. Eyre is also a fine draftsman, sculptor and printmaker. In all his work, he seeks to interpret the human condition, man's relationship to reality. For him, form, like words, must have a meaning beyond itself.

GEORGE WOODCOCK

Ivan Eyre, *Sky Terrace* (1971-72), acrylic and oil on canvas (*courtesy Robert McLaughlin Gallery, Oshawa*).

Faba Bean, or broad bean (*Vicia faba* or *Faba vulgaris*), legume family member, which is not a true bean but a VETCH. It originated in Eurasia, and archaeological evidence indicates that it was known to various ancient Western civilizations. The faba bean has a high protein content (25%) and has played a key role in human nutrition, being used in the green, immature state (as a shelled green vegetable) or dried and stored for future use. A cool-season plant, the faba bean does not thrive where summers are hot and dry. Black APHIDS constitute its principal pest. Plant height varies among the half dozen or so cultivars (commercial varieties), from 59-118 cm. Leaves are pinnately compound (ie, featherlike) and turn blackish with age. Flowers are white with wings marked by a large black spot.

The main cultivar is Broad Windsor, of English origin. Selections have been made resulting in varying plant size and heat resistance. Seeded in spring (mid-May), the bean matures in 65-85 days, depending on location and cultivar. Broad beans for home consumption may be produced in most garden areas across Canada. Commercial production in Canada began in 1972; by 1980, 23 000 ha were cultivated, but hectarage decreased substantially in 1987 to 10 900 as a result of limitations in the export market. Faba beans are grown as a silage crop and as a vegetable; there is increasing interest in smaller-seeded types for use as a source of vegetable oil. CROP RESEARCH is concentrated at Morden, Man, and Lethbridge, Alta. *See also* OILSEED CROPS.

I.L. NONNECKE

Fabre, Édouard-Raymond, bookseller, Patriote, politician (b at Montréal 15 Sept 1799; d there 16 July 1854). As Lower Canada's first prominent bookseller, Fabre was a focal point of provincial intellectual life during the 1820s and 1830s, serving a clientele ranging from members of the Catholic hierarchy to numbers of L.-J. PAPINEAU's radical followers. An active participant in PATRIOTE causes – providing financial assistance to and holding office in various Patriote organizations – he exerted an important influence on the movement during the decade preceding the REBELLIONS OF 1837. An ardent admirer and close associate of Papineau, he was arrested and briefly imprisoned in 1838; thereafter he worked tirelessly to help Patriotes in exile and to hasten their return to Canada. During the last years of his life, he was active in Montréal municipal politics, serving 2 terms as mayor 1849-51.

STANLEY GORDON

Fackenheim, Emil Ludwig, philosopher, theologian (b at Halle, Germany 22 June 1916). Educated at U of Halle, and ordained a rabbi in 1939, he fled Germany after a short imprisonment in a concentration camp. He studied at U of Aberdeen and then at U of T (PhD, 1945) where he taught 1948-84. Profoundly affected by the anti-Semitism and genocide of the Nazi era, he developed, from interests in 19th- and 20th-century European thought, particularly on questions of religion and history, a Jewish response to the Holocaust and to Western culture in general. He discusses God's presence in history and maintains that, since Auschwitz, there is a divine command to the Jews to survive and to struggle for justice. Fackenheim's writings include *Metaphysics and Historicity* (1961), *Quest for Past and Future* (1968), *The Religious Dimension in Hegel's Thought* (1968), *God's Presence in History* (1970), *The Jewish Return into History* (1978) and *To Mend the World* (1982). Since 1986 he has been a fellow of the Institute of Contemporary Jewry, Hebrew U, in Jerusalem.

THOMAS MATHIEN

Fafard, Joseph, sculptor (b at Ste-Marthe-Rocanville, Sask 2 Sept 1942). He began his career making kinetic sculpture, but soon after his appointment at U of Sask in 1968 he turned to satirical plaster portraits of his colleagues and people in the art world. He started working in ceramic around 1972, broadening his range of subjects to respond to the life and people of his community. Through his ceramic portraits of people and animals in the FOLK ART tradition, he has gained considerable recognition across the country. In 1985 his work *The Pasture*, comprising 7 bronze cows with varying patinas, was completed for an area outside the IBM tower of the Toronto Dominion Centre, Toronto. In 1987 he moved his studio to Regina.

MARILYN BURNETT

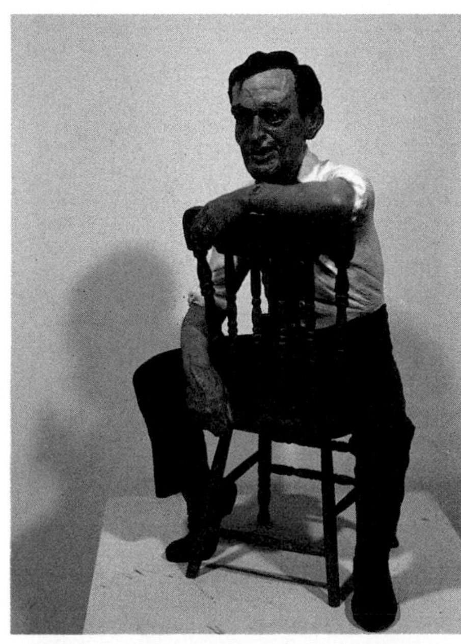

Joe Fafard, *The Candidate*, 1987, bronze patina and painted (*courtesy Woltjen/Udell Gallery*).

Fagundes, João Alvares, explorer (*fl* 1521). In 1520 he explored the coast S and W of Cape Race, Nfld, and perhaps entered the St Lawrence R. He may have sighted Saint-Pierre and Miquelon, Cape Breton I and Sable I. Fagundes may have established a Portuguese colony but no trace has been found.

JAMES MARSH

Fairclough, Ellen Louks, politician (b at Hamilton, Ont 28 Jan 1905). A chartered accountant by profession, she became secretary of state and Canada's first woman federal Cabinet minister in the 1957 DIEFENBAKER government. Owner of a Hamilton accounting firm, she was a member of city council 1946-49. She won a federal seat in a May 1950 by-election. The quietly persuasive Tory labour critic soon introduced a bill requiring equal pay for equal work and advocated equal opportunity and the creation of a Dept of Labour Women's Bureau. She moved to the Dept of Citizenship and Immigration in 1958 and became postmaster general in 1962. She was defeated in the 1963 election. After leaving politics, she served first as a senior executive in a trust company, then as chairman of Hamilton Hydro and finally as treasurer of the Zonta International women's group. In 1985 she was invested Dame of Grace, Order of St John of Jerusalem, Knights Hospitaler.

PATRICIA WILLIAMS

Fairley, Barker, scholar, literary and art critic, painter (b at Barnsley, Eng 21 May 1887; d at Toronto 11 Oct 1986). One of the foremost German scholars of the century and author of 2 epoch-making books on Goethe (*Goethe as Revealed in His Poetry*, 1932; *A Study of Goethe*, 1947), Fairley was co-founder of the CANADIAN FORUM, and friend and promoter of the GROUP OF SEVEN. His wide-ranging opinions on art and literature were always expressed in a provocative and felicitous prose style that appealed to the general reader. After graduating from U of Leeds, he began his academic career at U of Jena (1907-10) and was then invited to join the newly founded U of A in Edmonton (1910-15). From 1915 until his retirement in 1957 (except 1932-36) he taught at University Coll, U of T. In retirement he devoted considerable time to his painting (see his 1981 book, *Portraits*) and enjoyed increasing recognition as a painter of portraits, landscapes and still lifes. Although first and foremost a scholar of German literature, he wrote articles and books on many writers and was instrumental, chiefly through his columns in *Canadian Forum*, in focusing public attention on Canadian art in general and on the Group of Seven in particular.

RODNEY SYMINGTON

Fairn, Leslie Raymond, architect (b at Waterville, NS 26 June 1875; d at Halifax 13 Aug 1971). Fairn attended Acadia U, studied architecture in Boston, Mass, and apprenticed with Edward Elliot, architect of the Halifax City Hall. In 1904 he began a career that lasted 65 years. His commissions include county courthouses at Kentville, NS (1903); Digby, NS (1908-10); and Newcastle, NB (1912-13); Killam Library, Dalhousie; and Memorial Library and Grace Maternity Hospital in Halifax. A fellow of the Royal Soc of Arts and the Royal Architectural Inst of Canada, he was also one of the founders of the NS Assn of Architects.

GRANT WANZEL AND KAREN KALLWEIT

Fairvale, NB, Village, pop 4660 (1986c), inc 1966, located on the Kennebecasis R, 20 km north of Saint John. Settled in 1819, it remained a farming area until early in the 20th century. The only variation from agricultural pursuits was a period of shipbuilding in the latter half of the 19th century. Called Fair Leigh in the 1880s, it later became Fair Vale and was eventually named Fairvale in 1926. The early 20th century saw it develop as a summer community for Saint John residents, and recently it has also become a dormitory community for that city.

BURTON GLENDENNING

Fairweather, Eugene Rathbone, theologian, ecumenist (b at Ottawa 2 Nov 1920). An ordained priest of the Anglican Church of Canada, Fairweather was a member of the theological faculty of Trinity Coll, U of T, from 1944 until his retirement in 1986. He was dean of divinity 1983-85. He is known as a Thomist, and is intensely interested in ecumenical conversations, particularly with the Roman Catholic Church. He served on the Anglican-Roman Catholic International Commission, for which he received the Cross of the Order of St Augustine's of Canterbury in 1981. He has been a member of the Canadian and World Council of Churches' Commissions on Faith and Order and was a delegated observer at Vatican II. He is a member of the Board of Patrons of the Ecumenical Institute for Advanced Theological Research, Tantur, Jerusalem. Fairweather assisted in the founding of the *Canadian Journal of Theology* and was its editor (1960-70). He has worked to promote ecumenical co-operation in theological education in the university.

WILLIAM O. FENNELL

Fairweather, Mount, elev 4663 m, located at the S end of the St Elias Range, on the BC-Alaska border, where a segment of the BC border juts SW, nearly cutting off the Alaska Panhandle. Named in 1778 by Captain James COOK and considered to be one of the highest coastal mountains in the world, glaciers spawned on its flanks flow to the Gulf of Alaska, 35 km to the W. Despite its name, the mountain and its environs are noted for foul weather conditions. First climbed on 7 June 1931 by Americans Allen Carpé and Terris Moore, a second ascent was made in June 1958 by a Canadian party of 8, commemorating British Columbia's centennial.

GLEN BOLES

Faith, Percy, conductor, arranger, composer (b at Toronto 7 Apr 1908; d at Los Angeles 9 Feb 1976). After an injury to his hands interrupted an early career as a concert pianist, he turned to composition and arranging. Faith joined CRBC Toronto in 1933 as conductor-arranger for a series of programs. One of these, "Music by Faith" (1938-40), also gained him popularity in the US. As a result, Faith joined NBC radio as music director of the "Carnation Contented Hour" 1940-47. He became one of the best known arrangers in the US, working for Columbia Records until his death. Faith's many recordings include his own film scores and popular songs and choruses.

ANN SCHAU

Falcon (family Falconidae), small- to medium-sized predatory bird noted for swiftness in flight. Falcons range in size from sparrow sized (falconet of SE Asia) to raven sized (powerful, arctic-dwelling gyrfalcon). Falcons tend to have more distinctive plumages than most other BIRDS OF PREY, frequently having striking facial patterns or contrasting markings. They are characterized by large, dark brown eyes, a hooked beak with a toothlike projection on the mandible and a small tubercle in the centre of each nostril. Most have very distinctive, long, pointed wings and a long tail.

Female falcons are noticeably larger than males. Because of their speed, many species have long been prized by falconers, who train them to hunt. Gyrfalcons and PEREGRINE FALCONS have become status symbols for falconers worldwide. Five falcon species breed in Canada. The brightly coloured, robin-sized American kestrel (*Falco sparverius*) is relatively common and, except in winter, may be seen perched or hovering along roadsides from coast to coast. The more elusive merlin (*F. columbarius*) also occurs across the country. Recently, merlins have become more common in urban areas in western Canada. The crow-sized, sandy-coloured prairie falcon (*F. mexicanus*) is restricted to grasslands and, although fairly abundant, is seen only in very specific habitats in the Prairie provinces or in some interior valleys of BC. The peregrine falcon (*F. peregrinus*), similar in size to the prairie falcon, formerly bred wherever suitable nesting habitat and prey were found. The gyrfalcon (*F. rusticolus*) of the Canadian Arctic feeds mainly on ptarmigan and arctic hare. Although its population fluctuates in relation to prey, it has not been affected to any great extent by pesticides or other pollutants.

R.W. FYFE

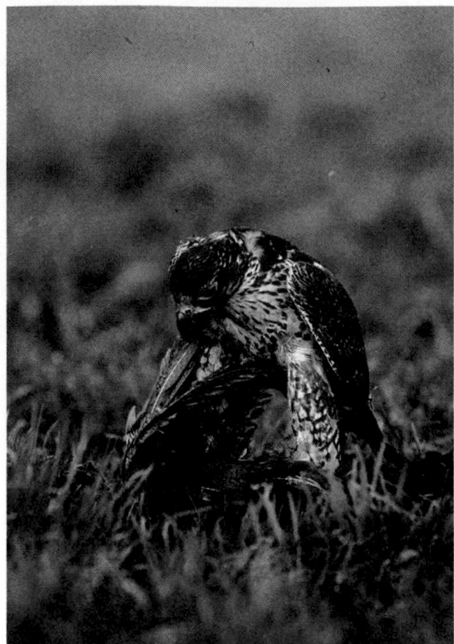

The gyrfalcon (*F. rusticolus*) of the Canadian Arctic feeds mostly on ptarmigan and hare (*photo by Tim Fitzharris*).

Falcon, Pierre, poet, troubadour, magistrate (b at Elbow Ft [near Swan R, Man] 4 June 1793; d at Grantown, now St-François-Xavier, Man 26 Oct 1876). Of Cree and French parentage, he was the son of a North West Co employee. Sent to Montréal for education, he returned to the North-West and became a clerk with the NWC and worked for the Hudson's Bay Co 1821-25. He then moved to Grantown, on the White Horse Plain, where he farmed and later became a magistrate. Throughout his life, he spontaneously composed poems or songs about any stirring event, and they were sung by voyageurs across the country. The ballad "La Chanson de la Grenouillère," for example, was occasioned by the SEVEN OAKS INCIDENT. His songs that survived are found in M.A. MacLeod's *Songs of Old Manitoba* (1960). Falcon Lk on the Manitoba-Ontario border was named in his memory.

MARGARET CHARTRAND

Falconer, Sir Robert Alexander, clergyman, scholar, educator (b at Charlottetown 10 Feb 1867; d at Toronto 4 Nov 1943). Falconer spent much of his youth in Trinidad, where his Presbyterian clergyman father had been posted. He was educated at London and Edinburgh universities, concentrating on classics and philosophy, and pursued postgraduate work at Leipzig, Berlin and Marburg, Germany. In 1892 he was ordained a minister in the Presbyterian Church in Canada and took up a lectureship in New Testament Greek at Pine Hill Divinity Hall, Halifax. Becoming a professor there in 1895, he was appointed principal in 1904.

Falconer is most important, however, for his 25-year tenure as president of UNIVERSITY OF TORONTO (1907-32). A royal commission appointed to investigate all aspects of the university had found administrative chaos and low morale. It recommended a complete constitutional reorganization and implicitly a new president in 1906. To the surprise of many, the 40-year-old Falconer was asked to replace James LOUDON. Much of Falconer's time and energy for the next 2 decades was given to executing the recommendations of the 1906 commission. He inherited a collection of colleges; he left behind him an integrated university that led the country in industrial and scientific, as well as humanistic, research.

An unemotional and cerebral scholar, Falconer was much in demand as a public speaker, particularly on the importance of maintaining the British imperial connection, the nurturing of "idealism in national character" (the title of his 1920 collection of wartime addresses), and the integrity and place of the humanities in an increasingly scientific and practical university environment. Active in the Presbyterian Church in Canada, Falconer was one of those who sought to bring his denomination into union with Canada's Methodists and Congregationalists in the 1920s. Such was his reputation within the British Empire that in 1929 Edinburgh University broke with tradition to offer him its principalship, a position that he declined.

A.B. MCKILLOP

Falher, Alta, Town, pop 1178 (1986c), 1102 (1981c), inc 1955, is located 60 km S of Peace River. It was named (1929) for Rev Constant Falher, OMI, who brought the first French Canadian settlers to the area Aug 1912. In 1916 the Edmonton, Dunvegan and BC Ry arrived, and Falher grew as a distribution centre for a prosperous cereal grain and CANOLA growing area. Two alfalfa pelletizing plants produce 50 000 t annually and more than 25 000 beehives in the region produce more than 2 million kg of honey, earning the town the nickname "Honey Capital of Canada."

ERIC J. HOLMGREN

Falk, Gathie, artist (b at Alexander, Man 31 Jan 1928). A multimedia artist with a strong national reputation, Falk began a successful artistic career in 1965 when she left teaching to study art. In 1967 she abandoned formal studies at UBC to become a self-supporting artist and in 1968 her Home Environment show at the Douglas Gallery, Vancouver, established her reputation. From 1968 to 1977 her many exhibitions were counterpointed by her work as a performance artist. After 1974 she turned to drawing, watercolour and oil-painted images in an impressionist vein. Her works are owned by major public galleries and the Vancouver Art Gallery staged solo exhibitions of her work in 1981, 1982, 1983, 1985 and 1987.

ANN ROSENBERG

Fallon, Michael Francis, Roman Catholic bishop (b at Kingston, Canada W 17 May 1867; d at London, Ont 22 Feb 1931). After graduating from U of O in 1889, he entered the Congregation of the Oblates of Mary Immaculate, and after studies in Holland and Rome was ordained a priest in 1894. He was professor of English, then vice-rector of U of O before becoming pastor of parishes in Ottawa 1888-1901 and Buffalo, NY, 1901-09, where he became an American citizen. Made provincial superior of his order, he was appointed bishop of London, Ont, in Dec 1909. He became the leader of Ontario's Irish Catholics who were endeavouring to keep Franco-Ontarians "in their place," ie, trying to prevent the acceptance of bilingual schooling. During his more than 20 years as bishop, Fallon stood at the centre of the ethnolinguistic fighting during the ONTARIO SCHOOLS QUESTION 1912-27. He died a hero to many Irish Catholics but a demon to Franco-Ontarians.

ROBERT CHOQUETTE

Reading: Robert Choquette, *Language and Religion* (1975).

Falls, Robert Hilborn, naval officer (b at Welland, Ont 29 Apr 1924). Falls joined the RCAF in late 1942 and trained as a pilot. He transferred to the navy after WWII, moving through a series of naval flying and command responsibilities (including HMCS BONAVENTURE) to senior management positions at headquarters and a period as commander of the Canadian Flotilla Atlantic. Vice-chief of the defence staff 1974-77, he became the first naval officer to serve as chief of the defence staff 1977-80. He was the first Canadian to be chairman of the NATO Military Committee, the alliance's senior military authority, 1980-83. He caused controversy with farewell remarks in 1983 suggesting that NATO might have more nuclear weapons in Europe than necessary. He involved himself thereafter in disarmament causes, becoming, in 1985, president of the Canadian Centre for Arms Control and Disarmament.

NORMAN HILLMER

False Face Society, the best known of several curing societies among the IROQUOIS of the lower Great Lakes. Curing, the restoration of well-being for the community and health for the individual, was a vital part of native religious practice. The False Faces had special powers over the winds, ill luck and illness affecting the joints and shoulders, as well as toothaches, earaches, swelling and nosebleeds. Public and private ceremonies were held at certain times of the year to drive out disease; amid dancing and chanting the sick were cured by having ashes rubbed onto their heads or having hands laid on them. In return, the False Faces demanded tobacco and hot corn mush. False Face MASKS represented portraits of mythological beings whose help was requested; the performers themselves were initiated into the society, originally secret, upon seeing Faces in dreams or being cured by them. Members were men, but the leader or keeper of the False Faces was always a woman. Masks, which were given curative powers by offerings of tobacco, were carved from specially selected living trees, then painted and adorned with fibres of hair. The distorted or exaggerated features, although human, were often terrifying or even comic. The society was witnessed by Europeans in the late 17th century, and has continued into the 20th century. Masks are still carved in traditional styles, for sale rather than for ritual use. *See also* NATIVE PEOPLE, RELIGION.

RENÉ R. GADACZ

Family There is no such thing as the "Canadian" family. Membership in a family, the activities of those members in and out of the household, and the relationship among members varies with economic conditions and also with regions, historical periods, SOCIAL CLASS and ethnicity. Yet most people eat, sleep, work, procreate, recuperate, learn, love, laugh, cry and die within what most would agree is a family. While the variations are in many ways endless, there is usually a dominant pattern, one that is more common than others in each region and time.

Before the arrival of the Europeans, family patterns among Canada's native peoples were enormously varied, as were the subsequent interpretations of those patterns by scholars. While some of the many societies and language groups functioned as nomadic hunting bands, others had complex organizations for agriculture, fishing and hunting. Family structures reflected the varying economic conditions. Agricultural societies frequently engaged in the co-operative production and preparation of food, and provided collective child care and other "family activities." Women did much of the farming and men often lived with their wives' relatives ("matrilocal residence") after marriage. Among fishing communities on the Pacific coast, on the other hand, separation of property was often practised, there were greater social differences within the group, women moved in with their husbands' relatives ("patrilocal residence") and the men fished. There was a division of labour by age and sex, but the specific tasks assigned to each group were different from society to society. In many of these families, women exercised a not inconsiderable amount of power as well as contributing directly to the survival of the group. What are often considered modern trends – premarital sex, adoption of children, divorce and trial marriages – were not uncommon among the native people, particularly in seminomadic societies.

With the arrival of the Europeans, economic conditions and family structures altered, but the variety remained. The organization of rival fur-trading companies led to the formation of different family relationships between whites and Indians. The temporary stations of the NORTH WEST COMPANY often permitted only short-term liaisons, the Indian women being left to tend their MÉTIS offspring. The HUDSON'S BAY COMPANY, however, had permanent posts and allowed or encouraged relatively stable relationships to develop, at least with regard to officers of the company. What today would be called common-law marriages were frequently established, and some of the children – but rarely the wives – were taken back to England when the officers returned home. These practices, and the introduction of private property, disrupted family patterns within Indian societies, discouraged co-operative production, and created single-parent households.

Meanwhile, in the central and eastern regions of the country, Europeans were establishing more settled agricultural communities and, along with them, different kinds of families. Patterns from the Old World were adapted to the new economic, social and physical conditions. While from the beginning of New France some people survived by working for the government, for the fur-trading companies, for the church, or as independent artisans, an increasingly dominant group produced most of what they needed for survival by working the land. Women, men and children laboured together to grow or to make the necessities of life. Men held most of the legal power in these families, but the mutual economic dependency that existed in most households contributed to the women's strength.

The scarcity of women, combined with the fact that their work was essential to household survival and that – except for a career as a nun or work as a domestic – marriage offered practically the sole means of support, meant that almost all women married. As a result of the high casualties of war, disease, accidents and death in childbirth, few marriages lasted long. Unlike the custom in France, widows and widowers did not wait long to remarry; consequently, many households contained children from 2 or more marriages. Women born in Canada married early, especially if their families were poor, but those who immigrated were often prevented from marrying at a younger age by long contracts for domestic service. These early marriages, the need for labourers in agricultural communities, the high proportion of children dying at birth or in their early years, the lack of contraception (*see* BIRTH CONTROL) and the religious proscription against it, all contributed to the high birthrates, especially among those families working the land (*see* MARRIAGE AND DIVORCE).

Although remarriage was strongly encouraged, religious beliefs and the desire for legitimate children to inherit the property in these settled communities accounted for the strong sanctions against premarital and extramarital sex, especially for women. Marriages were frequently arranged, for the wealthier to ensure the protection of their property, and for the poorer to ensure their own survival.

The British, and many of the other European settlers who came later, brought with them a firm belief in private property and self-reliance, but those who worked the land formed families that were similar in many ways to those of New France. The household was the place where the majority of goods and services were produced. Therefore, for most people – even those earning wages – home and workplace were one. Households were large, including as they often did an average of 4 or 5 children, hired help, single relatives and paying boarders. Few contained grandparents because most people did not live to be elderly and because many children left at an early age. In these early agricultural communities, the differences in family assets and resources tended to be small because almost everyone worked the land for a living.

Labour was divided by sex and age. Women centered their activities around the house, performing highly skilled and visible tasks such as baking bread, preserving food, and making soap, candles and clothes. In addition to bearing primary responsibility for teaching children to read and write and for the family's health care, women also frequently tended the vegetable gardens and the small animals, looked after the milking, and worked in the fields at sowing and harvest times. Men tended the larger animals, constructed furniture and buildings, slaughtered animals, felled and chopped trees, and planted and harvested the fields. Children worked alongside their parents, carrying out the more menial tasks and learning the skills necessary for survival. While this meant that men were actively involved in child rearing, infants were primarily cared for by women, older children and the hired help. And while women sometimes did "men's work," men rarely did any "women's work" other than looking after older children. In English common law, men were the decision makers, although women and children had some basis for power, because they contributed in obvious and visible ways to the maintenance of the household.

The physical distances between many of these households meant that entertainment was mainly a family affair. Even in more populated areas, social gatherings tended to involve the entire family, allowing the parents to supervise many of their children's contacts with others. In these households, the selection of marriage partners was less likely to be arranged formally. The idea of romantic love was gaining popularity, but economic and family considerations were still the most important factors in most decisions to marry, and marriages, particularly among wealthier families, usually required parental approval.

Although most Canadians lived in rural areas until after the turn of this century, some people worked for wages from the earliest years of settlement. Both women and men frequently began life in Canada by working for someone else, often as servants or on farms, in shops, in hotels and, somewhat later, in factories, but only men held jobs in the army and in the government. At first, readily accessible land meant that there was a way out of this work and a large proportion of men married and left the paid labour force to establish their own farms. When good land was no longer available and when new technology reduced the need for workers in the fields and forest, it was primarily men who were cut off from the means of directly producing for their needs and who thus had to work for others.

A large number of single women, and women whose husbands were dead or disabled, did work for pay, but for the overwhelming majority of women, marriage meant the end of such labour. Until well into this century, most women could still contribute directly to the family's survival by growing, preserving and preparing food, making clothes and baking bread. Many also generated cash income by selling their produce, by sewing clothes, and by taking in laundry and boarders. As job possibilities expanded in the labour force, many single women rejected domestic labour in favour of the somewhat greater freedom and pay associated with other work. The decline in domestic servants coincided with changing household technology, a technology that made it increasingly possible for one married woman to do the work alone.

Some children worked in factories and shops, or as hired help on farms or in other households, although from the 17th century on, the government restricted CHILD LABOUR. The application of these laws, combined with the declining need for labour and the increasing need for a literate labour force (which contributed to the introduction of compulsory schooling), meant that from the latter part of the 19th century, the number of employed young children dwindled. The need for children's labour in the household also decreased as fewer goods and services were produced in the household. Children became economic liabilities rather than economic assets. This, along with better health care, which meant that more children survived, contributed to declining birthrates.

These changes, which started in central Canada, gradually spread to the western and eastern parts of the country. Increasingly, families were distinguished from each other by social and class differences. Wealthier farmers and industrialists were able to send their children away to PRIVATE SCHOOLS long before compulsory schooling was introduced, and some households could afford to pay servants long after DOMESTIC SERVICE disappeared from the majority of homes.

It was not until the early part of the 20th century that what came to be called the "traditional" family – mother at home, father in the labour force, children at school and no other hired help or related individuals – appeared as the dominant family form in Canada. Although it has lasted only some 50 years, this kind of family structure has come to be popularly regarded as ideal.

Today the majority of married women (just over 3 million) are working or are actively looking for work in the labour force. Even mothers with very young children are returning to their paid jobs after the birth of their babies, although the overwhelming majority of small children are still looked after mainly by their parents and other relatives. Fewer and fewer women can contribute directly to family maintenance by earning money or making goods at home. This, combined with the fact that the expenses of a family can often be met only through 2 incomes, means that most married women have sought some form of paid employment.

The legalization and increasing accessibility of contraceptive devices have helped to lower birthrates, as have rising prices. Most families now have only one or 2 children and are having them closer together. These children are staying in school and often in the home longer, especially with current unemployment rates. These declining birthrates and increasing education levels have in turn contributed to the rising number of women in the labour force. That most women now keep their paid jobs after marriage and childbirth may also help explain why bridegrooms are younger now; fewer men have to anticipate being the sole income earners in the household.

As more and more women have entered the labour force, they have demanded fairer marital and PROPERTY LAWS. While earning wages has probably increased women's power in some areas, low wages, part-time jobs and segregation into poorly paid occupations reinforces and is reinforced by their continued responsibility for household chores and child care. Rising unemployment rates may also, in some households, severely threaten male authority.

Unidentified family studio portrait *c* 1910, Dong Yee Studio (*courtesy City of Vancouver Archives*).

Such changes contribute to tension in families, which not infrequently erupts in violence directed against women and children. Domestic violence is not new and it is difficult to tell how much it may have increased over time. It is clear, however, that because of the nuclear family structure, there are few individuals to witness or stop the violent acts, or to support the victims.

Divorce is certainly more common in Canada now than in the past, particularly since the advent of the 1968 Divorce Act. Divorces are easier and are less humiliating to obtain. People are living longer, making "happily ever after" much longer than it ever was before. One out of 4 couples can anticipate being divorced at least once. Rising divorce rates and the increase in legal separations and in the number of unmarried women having babies mean that the number of single-parent households is growing. This does not necessarily mean, however, that there is now a higher proportion of households in which children are living without both their biological parents, because high death rates in early Canada ensured that this situation was common in the past.

The growing participation of women in the labour force has helped many families to maintain their standard of living, but it has not prevented some families from living in POVERTY. Although estimates vary (depending on how poverty is defined), in 1985 approximately 15% of all Canadian families were living at or below the poverty line (*see* INCOME DISTRIBUTION). The majority of these households contain 2 parents and 50% of poor families have a "head" who is in the labour force. However, low wages for women and women's child care responsibilities help explain why female-headed households have a very high poverty rate. Women's greater life expectancy, their low wages, lack of private pensions and disrupted employment patterns also explain why the majority of the elderly poor are widows. At the other end of the scale, families in the top 20% of income brackets collect almost twice their share of total family income. It is these households that are most likely to contain a married couple (at least one of whom generally has a university degree) who live in a major city, own a home and a car. Women in these families (which are the most likely to conform to the popular but distorted image of the family) generally do not work in the labour force.

Conclusion Most Canadians today marry and stay married to the same person throughout life. The majority of men marry in their mid-twenties. The brides – a couple of years younger – usually share with their husbands a similar education and a similar ethnic and religious background. Most of these couples have children. Moreover, most children are born and raised in 2-parent households. The children are usually born to women who are in their mid- to late twenties. Since most women complete their child bearing within a short period of time, the children are separated from each other by only a few years. While there is little information available on the sexual practices and attitudes of these families, the numbers and spacing of children clearly indicate that most couples are practising some form of birth control. Most do not beat their children and most wives escape physical assault.

Although most women now hold paid jobs for much of their lives and although there have been some important moves towards greater equality in the household, women still do most of the HOUSEWORK. These are dominant patterns, but the important variations on these patterns must be kept in mind. The number of unmarried couples living together has certainly increased, although this is not an entirely new phenomenon. Perhaps the only really new family form is the older couple whose children have grown and left home.

PAT ARMSTRONG

Reading: Pat and Hugh Armstrong, *The Double Ghetto: Canadian Women and Their Segregated Work* (1978); J. Brown, *Strangers in Blood* (1980); M. Eichler, *Families in Canada* (1983); F. Elkin, *The Family in Canada* (1964); M. Kronby, *Canadian Family Law* (1983); M. Luxton, *More Than a Labour of Love* (1980); J. Parr, ed, *Childhood and Family in Canadian History* (1982); A. Prentice and S. Houston, eds, *Family, School and Society in Nineteenth Century Canada* (1975); D. Ross, *The Canadian Fact Book on Poverty* (1983); S.M. Trofimenkoff and A. Prentice, *The Neglected Majority* (1977).

Family Allowance, a monthly allowance paid to families with children to help cover the costs of child maintenance. Canada's first universal welfare program, it was introduced by the federal government in 1945. Under it, all families were paid a monthly sum on behalf of children under 16 years of age who were attending school. Critics called it a waste of taxpayers' money, claiming the "baby bonus" would encourage poor families to procreate. Some suggested that the money should be distributed by way of services to needy families instead. Supporters of family allowances argued that the service approach was paternalistic and that money distributed to mothers on behalf of their children would enhance the autonomy of families.

Furthermore, because studies counted family size a significant cause of poverty, family allowances would ensure a basic income for families with children. Their universality was defended on the grounds that the administrative costs involved in determining who was poor would be substantial. In fact, family allowances did not result in an increase in the birthrate, which has steadily declined since the mid-1950s.

In 1973 a new Family Allowances Act increased allowances from an average of between $6 and $7 to $20, which was paid to all dependent children – under age 18 – of Canadian citizens or landed immigrants. The allowances, indexed to the cost of living, were made taxable.

Beginning in 1978, a major restructuring of social security benefits for families occurred with the merging of social security and income tax provisions in support of families with children. A refundable child tax credit, aimed at low and moderate income families, was introduced. It was to be financed by cutting back family allowances and reducing or eliminating some tax exemptions for dependent children. This new measure attempted to provide more precise targeting of benefits without the stigma that typically adheres to such efforts. Critics contended that the measure was an attack on universality. In response to mounting government deficits, in 1985 the federal government announced a 4-year plan to restructure family benefits. Beginning in 1986, family allowances were only partly indexed to the cost of living, rising in line with increases in excess of 3%. Child tax credits were to be increased for 3 successive years, from 1987 to 1989, to a total of $524 per child, and beginning in 1989 were to be partly indexed in the same manner as family allowances. The income threshold, above which the child tax credit is phased out as income rises, was reduced to $23 500 from $26 300 and also partly indexed to the cost of living. Over the same time period, the child tax exemption will be substantially reduced. Critics have charged that these changes will represent a spending cut in child benefits of $550 million by 1991 and that the poorest families will receive only a token increase in their net family benefits over the years 1985 to 1989. A further measure to assist low-income families was announced in 1986 when a federal sales tax credit of $50 for persons 18 and over and $25 for children under 18 was announced for families and individuals with less than $15 000 of income. The universal family allowance paid to all children regardless of family income has been a unique feature of the Canadian social security system since its inception 1 July 1945. In 1986 over 3.6 million families received family allowances on behalf of 6.6 million children in the amount of $31.58 per child per month in most provinces and territories. Repeated calls for reduction in government spending threaten the program's existence, a situation made more probable as Canada gains experience in the use of the tax system to deliver selective benefits in a nonstigmatizing manner. DENNIS GUEST

Reading: Dennis Guest, *The Emergence of Social Security in Canada* (2nd ed, rev 1985).

Family Compact, disparaging epithet applied by contemporaries to the small group of officials who dominated the executive and legislative councils, senior bureacratic positions and the judiciary of UPPER CANADA until the 1830s. The group emerged after John Graves SIMCOE, UC's first lieutenant-governor, attempted to create a local aristocracy by appointing his Loyalist friends to government posts and granting them land. The next generation, including John Beverley ROBINSON, was supplemented by Britons, including John STRACHAN, who arrived before 1812 and were drawn into the governing TORY elite. The compact, centered at York [Toronto], was linked by family, patronage and shared political and social beliefs to the professional and mercantile upper middle class. It was sustained by conservative groups throughout the province. The compact gave vitality to the political ideology that shaped UC: drawing upon Loyalist beliefs, the Tories envisaged the development of a society strengthened by the imperial connection and hostile to the US. It idealized British institutions such as a balanced constitution, a hierarchical society and an established church. By the 1830s the compact was losing influence. Its exclusiveness provoked opponents to seek to reform the political system, and helped provoke the discontent that led to the REBELLIONS OF 1837. The rebellion was easily crushed, but the victorious Family Compact Tories in the government were soon squeezed out of politics by a new group of moderates who accepted the legitimacy of political opposition and the development of a PARTY SYSTEM. DAVID MILLS

Family Court, the common name of courts established by provincial statutes to administer FAMILY LAW. Judges are appointed by the provincial government. Although the 3 main consequences of the breakup of a marriage or common-law relationship – custody of and access to children; support obligations among spouses, parents and children; and division of property – fall under family law, provincially appointed judges cannot adjudicate on property division or divorce and its consequences – matters which must be heard by a superior court. Family courts also deal with adoption. Most provinces have a family division of their provincial court; Québec's is the Social Welfare Court, PEI's is the Family Division of the Supreme Court of PEI. Judges of unified family courts in Saskatchewan and parts of Newfoundland and Ontario are appointed by both the federal and provincial governments and can thus deal with all aspects of family law. PETER K. DOODY

Family Law governs relations between spouses and between parents and children, as well as covering some other areas. In family law some matters, such as MARRIAGE AND DIVORCE (including custody and maintenance arising on divorce), are under federal jurisdiction; but most matters (including adoption, matrimonial property disputes, and custody and maintenance unrelated to divorce) are governed by provincial laws that vary widely from province to province. However, even within areas of provincial jurisdiction, certain matters, eg, occupation of the family home, can only be dealt with by judges appointed under s96 of the Constitution Act (*see* JUDICIARY). There is a growing trend in Canada towards the creation of unified family courts in which all family law matters, whether federal or provincial, could be dealt with before one judge.

Family Law in Common-Law Provinces

Marriage The licensing and formalities of a valid marriage ceremony are governed by provincial law, but Parliament has jurisdiction over marriage, eg, the age at which individuals may marry, the laws forbidding marriage between certain persons, and divorce.

Annulment makes a marriage legally void, retroactively, on the grounds that it was never fully legal owing to some disqualification. A marriage may be annulled if the parties are within the prohibited degrees (of consanguinity or through marriage), if one is or was under age (unless the consent of both parents had been granted), or as a result of bigamy, a defective marriage ceremony, duress, mental incapacity, or the failure to consummate the marriage because of the physical or mental inability of one of the parties.

Separation is a legally recognized parting by spouses or the agreed cessation of cohabitation. It can be cited as grounds for divorce.

Divorce is the legal termination of a valid marriage. Until the federal Divorce Act of 1968, divorce was governed by pre-Confederation provincial statutes. In Newfoundland and Québec, where no divorce legislation existed, divorces could only be obtained through a private Act of Parliament. The 1968 Divorce Act provides that if the petitioner is domiciled in Canada and either party has been ordinarily resident for one year in the province in which the divorce is sought, the provincial supreme court can hear the case. Grounds for divorce include fault grounds, eg, adultery, mental or physical cruelty, homosexual conduct, imprisonment of the respondent for a certain period of time, or gross addiction to alcohol or narcotics (as defined under the Narcotic Control Act) for at least 3 years; and breakdown grounds, eg, separation for 3 years or, if the deserting spouse wishes to petition for divorce, desertion for 5 years. Over 90% of divorces are undefended and are usually granted after a short hearing. A divorce is granted in 2 parts, but only the decree absolute entitles the parties to remarry. In 1969, 26 093 divorces were granted; in 1982, 70 436; and in 1985, 61 980. In 1984 the federal government introduced a bill intending to make a one-year separation the only ground for divorce. The bill died on the order paper. However, in June 1986 the Divorce Act, 1985, became effective. Under the new Act, there is one ground for divorce – breakdown of marriage – which can be established by proof of either adultery or mental or physical cruelty, or separation of the parties for one year.

Maintenance can fall under federal law in connection with divorce, and under provincial law otherwise. Spouses, parents, children (who may have to support dependent parents) and guardians of children all have a legal obligation to support dependants. Increasingly, spouses are expected to become self-supporting where this is possible. The means and resources of the parties are important factors in establishing the amount of maintenance, as is their tax status, because the payer of periodical maintenance (but not lump sum maintenance) can deduct it from taxable income. Wives may have to support their husbands and children, and in some provinces common-law relationships may result in support obligations. Maintenance orders made under the Divorce Act are effective throughout Canada upon registration, but the enforcement of orders made under provincial laws, when spouses live in different provinces, depends upon the more cumbersome Reciprocal Enforcement of Maintenance legislation. New federal legislation, the Family Orders and Agreements Enforcement Assistance Act, 1986, which is not expected to be fully operational until the spring of 1988, contains 2 important parts: the first will govern access to federal data banks in order to locate missing children or spouses who are in default of their support obligations, and the second will enable monies due from the federal government to a spouse who is in default of support obligations to be intercepted and transferred to the person who is entitled to a support order. This legislation requires the co-operation of the provincial authorities, and provincial legislation has had to be passed which is compatible with the federal Act.

Matrimonial Property Under old COMMON LAW, a husband acquired the right to own or manage his wife's property. The one recompense allowed the wife was a "dower," ie, a life interest in the freehold property the husband owned when he died (*see* PROPERTY LAW). Married women had limited contractual capacity except as agents for their husbands. In the 1890s, married women's property Acts introduced into all Canadian provinces the concept of separation of property. This gave wives contractual and tortious rights and responsibilities, though in several provinces actions between husband and wife in TORT are still forbidden. Giving women power to acquire property, however, did not alter the fact that employment opportunities for women were restricted and that most property was paid for by husbands and bought in the husband's name. A wife obtained no property ownership for her work of looking after the home and rearing the children, although she did obtain a measure of protection in her occupation of the matrimonial home under Dominion Lands Acts in the West and, to a lesser extent, DOWER Acts in the East. The traditional rules required that for a wife to own property it must be bought in her name or she must have made some direct contribution to its purchase, so cases arose such as the MURDOCH CASE, in which the wife obtained no rights of ownership in what she thought were family assets. The harshness of this rule led all of the provinces to amend their legislation to give married women a fairer share in the division of the family's assets (*see* HUMAN RIGHTS), though the court has a discretion to vary the proportions according to certain criteria, eg, the date and manner of acquisition of assets, whether there is an agreement between the spouses about the property, etc. Frequently the Acts distinguish between family and other assets. In *Leatherdale* v *Leatherdale*, however, the Supreme Court of Canada (1982) upheld an Ontario court judgement (1980) that a wife has no right to an equal sharing of the shares that the husband has acquired under a scheme available to employees. Spouses who contribute to the business assets of their partner are entitled to compensation.

Recent case law developments suggest that common-law spouses who contribute money, or money's worth, to property purchased in their partner's name may acquire an interest in the property (eg, *Pettkus* v *Becker*, 1980; *Re Sorochan*, 1986). This is important, because common-law spouses are not usually covered by the matrimonial property laws. These systems have been revised but they generally operate to give a wife ownership rights in property acquired after marriage, which has meant that spouses have not had the almost complete freedom of testation once available under common law (*see* SUCCESSION).

Custody refers to the legal rights of parents regarding possession of children. Once a marriage has broken down these rights are not usually shared (joint custody) without both parents' consent, since the courts, particularly after a 1979 Ontario Court of Appeal decision, are generally reluctant to look favourably on joint custody. Custody and rights of visitation are increasingly seen as a parental privilege rather than a right. There is no law requiring that the custody of young children be granted to mothers. Where both parents are working full-time, fathers are increasingly winning custody (in 1985, 5762 husbands were granted custody of their children, representing 32% of total petitions by husbands). The courts do operate, however, on certain premises of common sense, eg, their unwillingness to disturb a satisfactory status quo and their reluctance to separate siblings, accordingly, 32 124 wives were granted custody of their children in 1985. In some provinces separate representation of children is permitted. Third parties, such as aunts or uncles, can also seek custody of a child. The Divorce Act, 1985, provides for increased contact between the child and both its parents, without expressly mandating joint custody. The Act also provides for third parties, eg, grandparents, to apply for visitation rights, or even custody, with the court's permission.

Illegitimacy Historically an illegitimate child was "filius nullius" or the "son of no man." References to children in wills were usually taken as referring only to legitimate children, but the harshness of this rule has been gradually eroded. Illegitimate children in several provinces have rights of intestate succession against their mothers, or the right to ask for proper provision from their parents' estate under dependents' relief legislation. The obligation to support illegitimate children has been imposed on both parents under provincial maintenance legislation and the distinction between legitimate and illegitimate children in Ontario, for example, was abolished under the Children's Law Reform Act (1977). Similar legislation has been passed in Manitoba. The procedure for establishing paternity is called filiation; blood tests may be used to prove or contest such allegations.

Where spouses cannot have children of their own they may seek medical help. Artificial insemination of the mother by the husband generally produces no legal problems for a child born in consequence, but a child born as a result of insemination by semen from a donor might well be illegitimate or have a right to maintenance against the donor, though in many cases the presumption of legitimacy, unless rebutted by blood tests, would presume the husband of the mother to be the father. Only in Québec is a husband who consents to the insemination of his wife the legal father of the child; any attempt to establish a link between donor and child is barred.

In the case of in vitro fertilization and embryo transfers, an ovum is retrieved from the mother-to-be by laparoscopy and fertilized in a culture medium with sperm from the father before reintroduction into the womb of the gestational mother. If the mother who provides the ovum and the gestational mother are different persons, questions can arise about who is legally the mother. Problems can also arise about additional ova which are fertilized but not reintroduced into the gestational mother. If such ova are allowed to develop and are subjected to research before disposal, their status, and whether their disposal is an offence, is unclear.

If a woman agrees to have a child by artificial insemination by the husband of an infertile wife, the current view is that the agreement is probably not legally enforceable and that payments to secure the surrender of the mother's rights of custody may constitute an offence under provincial adoption Acts. The father of such a child could, however, rely on his own rights as biological father to retain his child if the mother was prepared to surrender it to him, but his wife would have no legal ties to the child in the absence of adoption. With regard to sterilization, the Supreme Court of Canada has expressed, in the decision *Re Eve* (1986), its reluctance to allow the sterilization of a mentally retarded adult unless a clear therapeutic advantage can be demonstrated. ALASTAIR BISSETT-JOHNSON

Family Law, Québec

Québec family law is largely of French origin, but because marriage and divorce are within federal jurisdiction, there is a strong common-law influence. Moreover, because Québec law has been revised drastically by legislation in the last 20 years, differences in family law between Québec and the rest of Canada are not as strong as they once were. Traditionally the Québec Civil Code consecrated a notion of "paternal authority," which made the husband the head of the family and gave him considerable powers over his wife and children. This notion was recently applied by the court of appeal in *Cheyne* v *Cheyne* (1977), but the decision has since been repealed and the revised Civil Code (1980) insists on absolute equality of spouses.

Other aspects of Québec family law have also changed drastically. Traditional Québec family law was heavily influenced by the church. Divorce was utterly prohibited; separation and annulment of marriage were difficult to obtain. Women could be deprived of their part of community property as punishment for adultery. Illegitimate children were subject to various discriminatory rules and even adopted children were denied full equality. All of this has now changed and has been replaced by modern, liberal provisions. One aspect of the new Québec law has been questioned, however, and that is the marked tendency to delegate discretion to courts instead of to individuals. For example, a minor who wishes to marry will, in the future, ask the court and not his parents for permission.

Marriage Marriage law in Québec reflects principles similar to those underlying marriage law in other provinces, ie, it is strictly monogamous, requires capacity and consent of both parties and must include a ceremony, either civil or religious.

Separation and Divorce Separation can now be obtained in Québec with a minimum of formality. It does not break the marriage tie. Divorce is obtained under federal law. Québec adopted fairly liberal divorce provisions in the 1982 Code but these articles have not been proclaimed because they are not constitutional.

Children The 1982 Code abolished the concept of illegitimacy. Adoption is included in the Civil Code and creates the same relationship as birth. It is illegal to trade in children or to accept payment for a private adoption and presumably any contract to have a child and give it up to someone would be void, unenforceable and unlawful. Parents and children owe each other support even when the child has reached majority, although both parties must strive to be as independent as possible.

Matrimonial Property Québec law has kept the civilian concept of matrimonial regime, ie, the system of sharing or separating property between spouses. Couples are free under the Marriage Act to choose one of 3 regimes and to change it. The most common regimes are separation of property and partnership of acquests.

If no regime is chosen by marriage contract, the couple is presumed to have selected partnership of acquests. Under this system, each partner keeps the property he or she had at the time of marriage and each administers his own property after marriage. However, when the marriage or the regime end, the property acquired after marriage is generally divided equally between the parties.

Marriage contracts must be drafted by a notary. In addition to the choice of regimes, contracts often contain gifts from one spouse to the other, either while both spouses are alive or in contemplation of death. Such gifts are enforceable notwithstanding a subsequent will. In case of divorce or separation, the court may reduce or eliminate the gifts, and it appears that those contracted in contemplation of death lapse automatically since the 1982 change of law.

Since 1982 the Civil Code has protected the spouse's interest in the matrimonial home and the furniture. In the case of a home owned by one spouse, the other spouse's rights are not protected unless a "declaration of matrimonial domicile" is registered at the appropriate registry office. One spouse is not entitled to dispose of furniture garnishing the matrimonial domicile without the other spouse's consent; however, purchases for value in good faith are protected. There is at present insufficient jurisprudence to judge what constitutes "good faith."

Procedure The Québec Civil Code and Code of Civil Procedure have been amended to provide remedies suitable for family law. The most controversial features include provision for separate representation of children and for adoption and return of children. In December 1983 a new set of rules for the recognition of foreign adoptions came into effect and as a result it is very difficult for Quebeckers to adopt foreign children.

The most debated issue has been the new law under which all family law trials take place behind closed doors. Lawyers have protested but the validity of the law has yet to be contested. It has also provided that, in reporting cases, names not be published. JULIUS GREY

Family Studies Because marriage and the family are so important to the lives of many people, the study of the family attracts individuals from different disciplines. Basic to most approaches is a knowledge about how families exist – their composition, duration, economic behaviour, etc. This descriptive task, mainly the responsibility of Statistics Canada, is complex. Definitions change (eg, that of a head of a household) over time, and the information Statistics Canada can gather is limited. Nevertheless, through its periodic censuses, correlated with vital statistics (births, deaths, marriages, divorces) registered by the provinces, Statistics Canada maintains an extensive body of information about Canadian family life. In addition, many limited or special studies, eg, those on consumer spending or sickness and health care, contribute to our knowledge of the family. However, no comprehensive guide to all the information gathered by governments exists.

Following the 1968 changes of laws regarding divorce, the number and rate of marriage breakups increased dramatically from 26 093 in 1969 to 61 980 in 1985 (34% of marriages). Marriage and remarriage rates are also very high, creating concern about divorce and its impact on children, and concern as well about the new, "blended" families. In family studies, an increasingly popular approach is to study marriage and the family as relationships regulated by law and social policy. In recent years the federal government and most provinces have set up law reform commissions to examine how laws affect family relationships and how they might be changed to reflect and shape current realities. No general analyses or interpretations have yet been published, though M. Eichler's *Families in Canada Today* is a long step in this direction. Sociologists and anthropologists have studied how people live within families and how the family is linked to other social institutions. Many particular aspects of marriage and family life in various communities or groups have been documented, eg, in *The Canadian Family* and *The Canadian Family in Comparative Perspective*. Families are intimately involved in and affected by local, regional and national economies, and by changing ideologies about the status of women, the rights of children, the dissolution of marriage, etc. The Vanier Institute of the Family in Ottawa has been active in documenting and publicizing some of these aspects and changes.

Many psychologists and other social scientists have studied the family as the matrix within which adults exist and children are socialized; their work has been mainly academic, though their conclusions have been applied in school programs, parent effectiveness training programs, etc. Family-life education is taught in many school curriculums; although it is frequently a euphemism for sex education, the current trend is to expand the subject to include homemaking, child rearing and interpersonal skills. Family studies are offered as a course or specialization in colleges and universities; they have developed from what was earlier known as home economics or household science and have broadened to include many courses on household skills, consumer behaviour, interpersonal skills, etc, although critics of these courses argue that the image of the family in school and college courses is biased, is inherently conservative and idealized, and does not reflect the experience of most people.

The recognition that it is within families that much individual and interpersonal pathology develops has spurred a new "science" of family diagnosis and family treatment, which is applied in SOCIAL WORK, psychology, psychiatry and family medicine, although there is as yet no national organization in Canada specifically devoted to this type of study and practice. *See also* MARRIAGE AND DIVORCE. NORMAN BELL

Reading: M. Baker, ed, *The Family: Changing Trends in Canada* (1984); M. Eichler, *Families in Canada Today* (1973); K. Ishwaran, *The Canadian Family* (rev 1976); L. Larson, *The Canadian Family in Comparative Perspective* (1976); R. Pike and E. Zureik, eds, *Socialization and Values in Canadian Society*, 2 vols (1975).

Fantasy Fiction, *see* POPULAR LITERATURE IN ENGLISH; POPULAR LITERATURE IN FRENCH.

Farm Credit Corporation, a federal crown agency set up in 1959 under the Farm Credit Act to develop efficient farm businesses through the use of long-term mortgage credit. The FCC succeeded the Canadian Farm Loan Board, which had been in operation since 1929. Corporation headquarters are in Ottawa with regional offices in each province except NS, PEI and Nfld, which are served by the NB office. The corporation's board is composed of 7 members appointed by the federal minister of agriculture. Regional appeal boards hear appeals from farmers not satisfied with FCC decisions on loan applications. A national advisory committee, with members appointed by the minister of agriculture, advises the minister or corporation on lending policies and practices. The FCC may borrow from the Consolidated Revenue Fund or may raise funds in private money markets. The corporation provides standard loans and phase-in loans. Standard loans may be made of up to 100% of the appraised farm value to a maximum dollar ceiling set by the corporation. Phase-in loans aid beginning farmers under 35 years of age, permitting them to phase into farming over a 5-year period. Either type may be used to acquire farmland, modernize or erect buildings, and purchase equipment and livestock. The corporation also administers the Farm Syndicates Credit Act, under which 3 or more farmers may apply co-operatively for a loan to purchase equipment or erect buildings. This type of loan reduces production costs by encouraging joint ownership and use of machinery and equipment. J.C. GILSON

Farm Drainage Drainage problems are caused by an excess of water at the SOIL surface or in the root zone. Drainage work is carried out to improve the root-zone environment for crop growth, to improve conditions for cultivation, planting and harvesting, to allow earlier spring planting for better use of the short Canadian growing season, and to convey salts out of the soil in areas where salinity is a problem. The problem of excess water and inadequate drainage is obvious wherever pondings remain after rainfall or snowmelt. A less obvious problem exists when the root zone is saturated but no water is present on the surface. Most crops prefer moist, unsaturated soil, with over 6% of the volume filled with air. Air space allows roots to respire, grow and obtain nutrients from greater depth.

Land drainage work began in Canada more than 200 years ago. As the population increased in the 19th century, the limitations of Canada's CLIMATE and soils became obvious. Eastern Canada and the coastal valleys of BC had a cool, moist climate; frequently, there was more rain than needed. Much of the higher land, which had adequate natural drainage, lacked fertility, or was stony or had a shallow soil which suffered from DROUGHT; flatter lands and river valleys usually had greater food-production potential after drainage work was carried out. Before 1900 some rivers and streams were deepened to provide better outlets. Ditches were dug by human and animal power to improve field drainage. Dikes were constructed to protect lands from high TIDES around the Bay of FUNDY and along the S shore of the ST LAWRENCE R estuary. The construction of additional drainage ditches and the cleaning of former ditches has continued through the 20th century to allow increased food production and to improve marginal land to replace farmland lost to expanding cities. Steam shovels, employed on the larger drainage jobs from 1870 to 1930, have been replaced by diesel shovels and draglines. Since 1970 most channel excavation has been done by high-capacity hydraulic backhoes. Approximately 1000 km of main ditches are dug annually in Canada.

Subsurface drainage by means of tiles, stones and wooden drains was introduced in the mid-19th century. The work was done by hand. The prospect for increased subsurface drainage came with the introduction of wheel-type ditching machines in 1907. The power and speed of new trenching machines have increased steadily since 1945. Drain-laying plows, pulled by bulldozers, were introduced in 1968. Since 1971, LASER grade-control systems have improved the accuracy and speed of trenchers and drain-laying plows. The installation of subsurface drains to intercept seepage from IRRIGATION canals and to help reduce soil salinity in Alberta and Saskatchewan proceeded after field experiments conducted before 1970. Construction of drainage systems to reduce waterlogging and salinity is accelerating now, as the need is great.

Canadian drainage engineers, contractors and drainage material manufacturers have made rapid advances in drainage technology in the past 20 years, as subsurface drainage installations have increased from 22 000 km to more than 100 000 km per year. This technology has made it possible for a construction crew of 5 persons to install 7000 m of pipe per day, compared with 800 m per day in 1968. Less than one-third of the farmland that needs subsurface drains to achieve its crop production potential has had drains installed. R.S. BROUGHTON

Farm Law In Canada more than 99% of farm businesses are family operations; these operations involve about one million people. The total capital value of Canadian farms in 1986 was about $110 billion; the average capital value per farm was $375 000; and, on average, farm real estate was worth more than $375/ha. Because of the economic and social importance of the family farm and the dramatic increase in farm bankruptcies in the 1980s, farm groups have emphasized the importance of establishing the farm business on a sound legal footing, both to protect individual farmers and to maintain the family farm as a viable unit. Because of its special social and economic problems, the rigid marketing structures that surround it and the high risks attached to it, farming requires a more sophisticated approach to legal matters than many other businesses do. Regulations relating to marketing vary according to the product, the part of the country in which it is produced, the intended market (eg, domestic or export), etc. A general outline can be drawn, however, of business arrangements and taxation rulings affecting farm businesses.

The 2 broad areas of business relationship are the connection between the owner and his business and that between the owner, his estate and his family. These kinds of relationship have special implications in farming because the farm family is the major source of farm labour and management. Business arrangements between fathers and children are the most frequently encountered in farming, and each party has problems that must be resolved. The father has accumulated substantial, usually nonliquid, assets (ie, land, buildings, machinery, inventories of grain and livestock), and wishes to make an adequate arrangement to assure the continuance of the child or children in the farm business, while maintaining some control of business management and income. Finally, he desires to assure succession of the business to the child, but wishes to be paid for the capital he transfers to the child and to provide income and capital for his wife and for beneficiaries not involved in the business. The child desires an adequate income, means of acquiring a controlling capital interest in the farm, and eventual, guaranteed succession.

Both parties must consider certain areas of mutual interest, eg, evaluation and ownership of assets, amount of time each shall contribute to the enterprise, apportionment of income now and in future, regular transfer of capital from father to child (by gift, purchase or both), agreements regulating purchase and sale of shares in the farm, and the means by which other children may acquire interest in the business.

The farmer considering his farm as an estate is faced with the problem of how to divide control of his business. Related questions include continuity of management, the effect of his death on the availability of business credit and funds for the purchase of his business by his children, and the need to make funds available for executors to pay debts and taxes and provide an income for dependants. A properly thought-out estate plan will do much to establish credit, create acceptable collateral, provide retirement funds, prevent the sale of assets at distress prices, establish the value of the business and achieve continuity in business activity. In most instances, funding for the purchase by the son from the father is secured by mortgage financing from a bank, the FARM CREDIT CORPORATION or a provincial government credit association. Any outstanding balance owed to the father is secured by additional financing which ranks second to the aforementioned mortgage obligation. Accordingly, the father's equity, on which he relies to support himself and his wife during retirement, is at risk and, in difficult times, is often obliterated. It is therefore essential that other methods be sought to secure protection for the father.

The farm business involving 2 or more people can be carried on by 2 major methods, the partnership (general or limited) and the limited corporation, each with its own advantages and disadvantages. In certain instances a combination may be warranted.

The Farm Partnership

A partnership is the relation between persons carrying on a business in common with a view to profit. It is not a legal entity; all rights and obligations accrue to the individuals in the partnership. Each partner is regarded as the agent of the other and is capable of making the other liable. The relationship between the partners is separately liable for all debts and obligations incurred by the partnership. A general partnership consists of 2 or more general partners who are jointly and severally liable for the firm's debts, not only to the extent of their investment in the partnership but, if this investment is insufficient to satisfy the creditors, to the extent that their private property is required for this purpose. Each partner has a right of indemnity against the other. A limited partnership consists of one or more general partners and one or more limited partners. A limited partner is liable for the firm's debts only to the extent of his investment, but his liabilities increase to those of a general partner if he allows his name to appear in the firm's name and if he publicly helps conduct the business. To be considered a limited partner, one must be so designated in a declaration filed with the government. A limited partnership must be registered and all partners are considered general partners until so registered.

Capital contributions from the different partners may vary, as is often the case in family farm partnerships. In some such cases the partner with the higher capital investment may be paid interest on such excess by the partnership. Such interest is charged as an expense to the partnership; therefore the partner is, in effect, paying part of his own interest. In other instances the partner contributing least capital may contribute most labour. These positions are sometimes equated so that profits are divided equally. Alternatively, excess labour may be compensated by payment of a wage, leaving the rate of return of profit related to the amount of capital contribution. The cost of labour is charged to the partnership and the partner being paid for his labour contributes personally to his own wage.

The division of income from a farm partnership is often difficult. The father needs cash to support and educate other members of the family; the child may also have a growing family and require a maximum amount of income. In such a case, capital acquisition must either be limited or have payment amortized over a long period to make the maximum amount of cash available. At the same time the goal may have to be towards the immediate expansion of the farm unit. Thus, there may be a most difficult conflict between the capital needs for expansion and the immediate need for cash. To resolve such a conflict the first necessity is to determine whether the existing farm unit can support the partners and, if not, what can be done to alter it to allow it to do so. The various factors that must be taken into account in the division of income are the amount required by each party for family spending, contributions to labour, management or capital made by each party, and a formula that relates the minimum wage to be earned by each partner, plus a division of surplus, to the growth of the business. The arrangement chosen must be flexible and must recognize the changing needs of each partner.

The Farm Corporation

A corporation is a legal person with the capacity (subject to the Corporations Act), rights, powers and privileges of a natural person. It is an advantageous form of business association because it gives potential income tax advantages, accommodates the many variations of business relationships, can be a vehicle for estate planning, and its liability is usually limited to the assets it owns. Finally, a corporation has an identity distinct from that of its shareholders and potentially can exist forever. Thus it offers opportunities for investment and management decisions that are largely independent of an individual owner or partner. An individual invests in a corporation by purchasing shares. Shares are allotted for amounts fixed by the directors, and such values, determined at the time of issue, become the paid-up or "stated" capital of those shares. There may be more than one class of shares, each carrying different rights and restrictions. The directors should determine the nature and attributes of the shares to be issued by considering the nature of the business the corporation will carry on, the relationship between the persons who will be shareholders and the method of securing the repayment of any monies owed by the corporation.

A farmer considering incorporation must consider various aspects of CORPORATION LAW as they will affect his business. For example, the appointment of directors and the rules governing voting (including the definition of a quorum) will influence who has managing control over farm-business decisions. Similarly, regulations established within the corporation to govern purchase and sale of shares will affect how shares in the farm may be traded within the family or to persons outside the family corporation. The means of repayment to a retiring shareholder or to the estate of a deceased shareholder can influence the continued economic health of the farm corporation. In this connection the importance of insurance on the lives of the principals should be emphasized.

The corporation offers certain advantages to the farm business. For example, a farmer may incorporate his farm business by selling assets to a corporation owned by himself or by members of his family without incurring tax liability. Such a sale must comply with s85 of the Income Tax Act. Further, a corporation lends itself particularly well to the estate plan. Provided it is adequately established, it can freeze the value of the farmer's estate so that all future growth will go to those persons he wishes it to benefit. It allows the farmer to give nonvoting participating shares during his lifetime, without affecting his control of the corporation, its assets or its income. It permits the farmer to give his heirs specific interests in such proportions as he desires, immediately and in the future. It allows for the maintenance of control by the farmer's executors beyond his death to maintain the farm's value, carry on business and protect the farmer's wife and dependants. Finally, it allows a farmer to complete arrangements with those of his children who wish to operate the farm, so that they share in the income and continued growth of the assets, obtain eventual control and thus stay with the business.

Taxation

The Income Tax Act generally requires that business income must be computed on an accrual basis; however, if the taxpayer chooses, income from a farming or fishing business can be computed on a cash basis. Thus a farmer may include only amounts actually received in that year and deduct amounts actually paid in that year.

Livestock herds are now treated as ordinary inventory. Livestock acquisition costs, deducted from income on a cash basis, may result in the farmer realizing a loss for the year. Losses may only be carried forward and applied against income for 5 years. To allow a farmer to use these losses without having to reduce his herd to generate income against which the losses could be charged, the Act permits a farmer in each year to include as income any amount up to the fair market value of his livestock at the end of that year (the amount claimed in the previous year being deducted the following year). Thus livestock acquisition costs can be carried forward indefinitely for deduction against actual future income.

Restricted Farm Loss TAXATION law distinguishes 3 categories of farmers. Farmers who are in the "business" of farming can deduct fully all losses incurred in farming. Those persons who farm as a sideline with a reasonable expectation of profit can deduct losses to a maximum of $5000 per year, the balance (ie, restricted farm losses) being carried forward. Persons who farm for enjoyment (ie, as a hobby) are not entitled to any deductions.

Transfer of Farm Property To preserve the family farm, the Income Tax Act contains certain provisions that allow a farmer to transfer farm property to his spouse or children on a tax-deferred (rollover) basis. Included in the type of property that may be transferred are farm property, shares in a family farm corporation and an interest in a family farm partnership. In each case the property must be used by the taxpayer, his spouse or his child in the business of farming. *See also* AGRICULTURAL ECONOMICS; FAMILY LAW; PROPERTY LAW.

Y.M. HENTELEFF AND M.S. PALAY

Farm Radio Forum, 1941-65, was a national rural listening-discussion group project sponsored by the Canadian Assn for Adult Education, the Canadian Federation of Agriculture and CBC. Up to 27 000 persons met in neighbourhood groups Monday nights, Nov through Mar, using half-hour radio broadcasts, printed background material and pretested questions as aids to discussion of social and economic problems. Farm Forum provided an antidote to the hard times of the 1930s economic depression, and meeting and discussing new ideas in neighbours' homes helped restore rural confidence, often leading to positive group action in the community. Farm Forum innovations included a regional report-back system, whereby group conclusions were collected centrally and broadcast regularly across Canada, occasionally being sent to appropriate governments. In addition, discussion – leading to self-help – resulted in diverse community "action projects" such as co-operatives, new forums and folk schools. Farm and community leaders claimed that the give-and-take of these discussions provided useful training for later public life. In 1952, UNESCO commissioned research into Farm Forum techniques. The report was published in 1954, and consequently India, Ghana and France utilized Canadian Farm Forum models in their programs. O.J.W. SHUGG

Reading: J. Dumazedier, *Television and Rural Adult Education* (1956); R. Faris, *The Passionate Educators* (1975); R.A. Sim, ed, *Canada's Farm Radio Forum* (1954).

Farm Silo, storage structure for silages and high-moisture grains used for livestock feeds. Silos are a common fixture in livestock and mixed-farming operations across Canada. Silage is formed by microbial fermentation of plant material under anaerobic (oxygen-free) or near-anaerobic conditions. Whole-plant corn silage (30-35% dry matter) is made by chopping the entire plant finely (1-2 cm); haylage is silage composed of wilted grass or alfalfa dried to 35-50% dry matter. High-moisture grains (eg, whole shelled, ground shelled and ground ear corns and barley) go through the same fermentation process as silage. Under normal conditions, silage-producing microbial fermentation produces lactic and acetic acids until acidity is such that growth of all microorganisms stops (after 2-3 weeks). With well-ensiled material in anaerobic storage, the quality and palatability of the feed is maintained until the material is exposed to oxygen, which causes silage to deteriorate quickly. Silos are of bunker or tower type. The bottom-unloading tower silo allows a greater degree of automation but is somewhat more expensive to build. Bunker silos are the cheapest but allow little automation and have the greatest feed loss by oxidation.

Bunker Silos are paved areas surrounded on 3 sides by concrete or 3-5 m-high timber walls. Forage is dumped within the walled area, compacted, covered with polyethylene sheets and weighed down with old tires. Unloading is by front-end loader or by allowing cattle to feed directly from the exposed face of the silage.

Tower Silos are 15-30 m-high, cylindrical, concrete or steel structures, usually closed with a domed roof. Forage is blown into the top via a pipe mounted on the silo's side. Special unloading equipment is mounted inside. Top-unloading silos have a rotating scraper that sweeps silage through openings in the wall into a chute mounted on the side. Silage falls into a feeding cart, or onto a conveyor belt for distribution to livestock. Bottom-unloading silos have a screw-type unloader, which moves silage into a central hopper from which it is conveyed further by belt or screw conveyor. J.C. JOFRIET

Typical farm in Huron County, Ont. Silos, such as the one shown here, are common in mixed farming operations across Canada (*photo © Hartill Art Associates, London, Ont*).

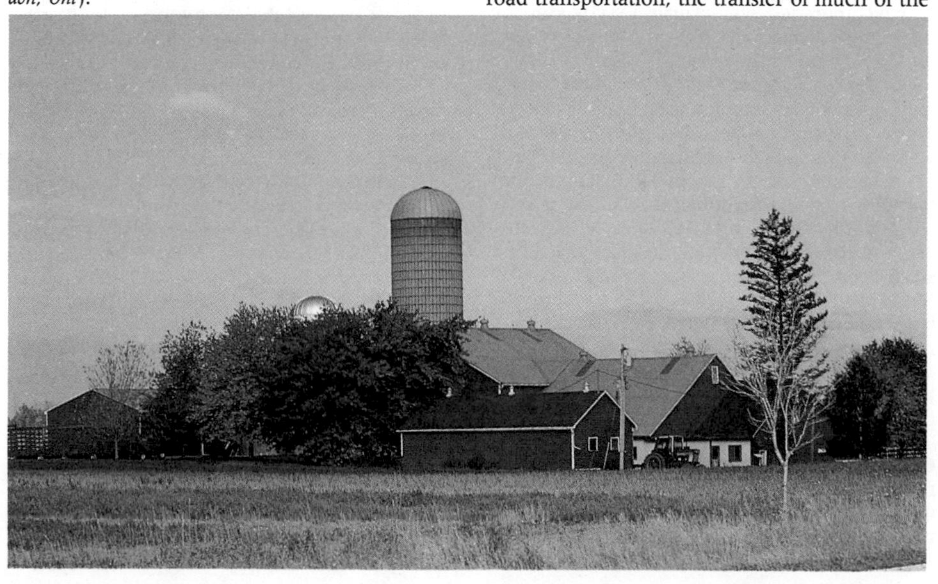

Farnham, Qué, Town, pop 6102 (1986c), 6476 (1981c), inc 1876, is located about 65 km SE of Montréal on the N branch of the Yamaska R, at the boundary between the plain of Montréal and the Eastern Townships. The township of West Farnham (created 20 Oct 1798) was settled in the early 19th century by colonists from northern New England, mainly Vermont. Later, Francophones migrated from regions around the Richelieu and Yamaska rivers (Rouville and St-Hyacinthe counties). The village of West Farnham was incorporated in 1862. Francophones have long been in the majority and now represent over 90% of the population. During the first 40 years (1817-57), the chief source of revenue was the manufacture of potash. The construction of the Stanstead-Shefford & Chambly Ry in 1857 began Farnham's remarkable progress as a railway centre, thanks to its geographic position and competition among railway promoters. The South Eastern Ry was constructed from West Farnham to Richford and reached Newport, Vt, in 1873. It established its headquarters, roundhouse and repair shop in Farnham. Later, no fewer than 5 CPR lines converged here. In the early 20th century, the CPR employed some 500 men from Farnham (pop 3114, 1901c); however, these activities diminished in the following decades. The growth of road transportation, the transfer of much of the repair work to Montréal, and the removal of several regional railway lines after 1925 tended to limit Farnham's development. Through the years, Farnham's industries have also included sugar-beet refining, woodworking, and organ, safe and vault, clothing and rubber manufacturing. Today the main industries are textiles, carpets and iron cable. JOHANNE LEDOUX

Farnon, Robert Joseph, composer, arranger, conductor (b at Toronto 24 July 1917). A successful purveyor of good, light music, he is considered one of the most influential film composers of his generation in Europe and N America. Farnon became trumpeter in several 1930s Toronto dance bands and in the Canadian Radio Broadcasting Commission's orchestras of Percy FAITH and Geoffrey WADDINGTON. He was a member of CBC Radio's "Happy Gang" 1937-43. After serving overseas during WWII as musical director of the Army Show, Farnon settled permanently in Great Britain and built a solid reputation as orchestral conductor, arranger and composer through a series of BBC radio programs and recordings for Chappell and Co Mood Music. His arrangements have been recorded by such well-known performers as Vera Lynn, Lena Horne and Frank Sinatra. As well as numerous film scores, Farnon's own compositions include the popular suite *Canadian Impressions* and *Rhapsody* for violin and orchestra (recorded by Steven STARYK). ANN SCHAU

Faro, YT, Town, pop 400 (1986c), 1652 (1981c) is located 6 km N of the Campbell Hwy, 200 km by air NE of Whitehorse. The Cyprus Anvil Mines Co built the town in 1969 to house employees of its open-pit lead and zinc mine. Ravaged by a forest fire in its first year, it was quickly rebuilt and became the territory's second-largest community. The mine was Canada's largest producer of LEAD, and its exports became a mainstay of the Yukon economy in the 1970s. As a result of depressed lead and zinc prices, the mine shut down in 1982. By 1986 the population had suffered a -75.8% change since 1981. The mine was sold to Curragh Resources and in Oct 1986 was reopened. Faro's name is derived from a game of chance, popular in Klondike saloons, in which the cards bore a stylized portrait of an Egyptian pharaoh. H. GUEST

Farquharson, Donald, politician, premier of PEI (b at Mermaid, PEI 27 July 1834; d at Charlottetown 26 June 1903). A teacher by training, Farquharson subsequently entered the wholesale and shipping business and in 1876 won election to the PEI Assembly as a Liberal. He was a member of the government in 1878-79 and from 1891 to 27 Dec 1901, serving as premier after 1 Aug 1898. He resigned to contest Queens W successfully in a federal by-election for the House of Commons 15 Jan 1902 and died while sitting as a member. PETER E. RIDER

Farquharson, Ray Fletcher, physician, medical educator (b at Claude, Ont 4 Aug 1897; d at Ottawa 1 June 1965). Farquharson was Sir John and Lady Eaton Professor of Medicine, U of T (1947-60), and first chairman of the Medical Research Council (Canada) in 1960, and held the position until his sudden death during a council meeting. Farquharson did significant research in pernicious anemia, Simmond's disease, anorexia nervosa and hyperparathyroidism. He was an excellent teacher and an outstanding consultant, much revered by his patients for his warm and sympathetic personality. He was consultant to the RCAF during WWII and president of the Royal Coll of Physicians and Surgeons of Canada (1945-47). ROBERT B. KERR

Farrally, Betty, née Hey, dancer, teacher, ballet director (b at Bradford, Eng 5 May 1915). As co-founder of the ROYAL WINNIPEG BALLET and later through her teaching, Farrally, renowned for her vivacity and energy, has become one of the most respected figures in Canadian BALLET. Following completion of dance studies in England, she immigrated to Canada with her former teacher Gweneth LLOYD in 1938. She was instrumental in helping Lloyd establish the Winnipeg Ballet (Royal Winnipeg Ballet) and, following her colleague's move to Toronto in 1950, remained artistic director until 1957 when she founded a new school in Kelowna, BC. Farrally was also longtime co-head and continues as an artistic adviser to the Banff Centre's summer dance program. She was made an Officer of the Order of Canada in 1981 and received the Dance in Canada Award in 1984. MICHAEL CRABB

Farrer, Edward, journalist (b near Castlebar?, Ire; d at Ottawa 27 Apr 1916). An outstanding craftsman and promoter of Canada-US union, he was said to have studied for the priesthood in Rome before coming to Canada about 1870. He worked for various papers, including the Winnipeg *Times*, 1882-84 and *Sun*, 1884. As editor of the Toronto *Daily Mail*, 1885-90, he made it perhaps the leading paper of the day, and helped to provoke its break from the control of PM Sir John A. MACDONALD. The paper brilliantly promoted an outbreak of anti-French, anti-Catholic feeling in the wake of the NORTH-WEST REBELLION, with Farrer evidently using the campaign to alienate English Canada from Confederation. In 1890 he transferred to the Liberal *Globe* as premier editor and again subtly promoted annexation. In the 1891 election, Macdonald disclosed a pamphlet – allegedly written by Farrer – as evidence of Liberal sympathy for annexation. Farrer left the *Globe* in 1892, worked for the annexationist movement, and later served PM Sir Wilfrid LAURIER, as a propagandist and agent, consistently promoting anti-imperial policies. CARMAN CUMMING

Fascism is a term often loosely used to describe military dictatorships and extreme right-wing governments and organizations (or individuals) known to be either violently anticommunist or violently anti-Semitic, or both. These are often important elements within fascism (as are the institutionalization of sexual repression and strong antifemale, antihomosexual and profamily biases), but the term should be more precisely confined to those mass movements and political parties that originated in the capitalist economies of Europe in the late 19th and early 20th centuries, culminating in Mussolini's Italy and Hitler's Germany. (Fascism existed but was not very influential in Britain, the US and Canada [mainly Québec] during the 1930s.) It is characterized by a hatred for liberalism, socialism, democracy and the parliamentary system; by extreme and aggressive nationalism, and hostility to other nations and races; by a glorification of power, violence and war; by dreams of conquest and expansion; by a hankering after a supposedly glorious past; by paramilitary associations; by the myth of the "leader" to whom superhuman qualities are attributed; and by the creation of a convenient scapegoat – usually JEWS – for all social, national and economic ills.

Fascist movements became prominent after WWI among the losing nations that had suffered humiliating defeats, lost large territories and faced harsh terms of peace. Reconquest of old colonies and territories and restoration of prewar positions in the world was a major theme of all fascist movements. Fascism attracted not only the military but also those who had lost their traditional place in society and were frightened of the future, particularly the lower-middle classes. Essential to the rise of fascism was the devastating economic crisis that threw millions out of work and threatened the economic security of many more millions, but other conditions were important as well: a capitalist class fearful of powerful working-class organization and of strong communist and socialist parties who seemed on the verge of taking power, and the existence of weak and ever-changing minority governments in countries where parliamentary institutions and liberal democratic social values were poorly developed and where leadership was widely discredited by indecision, paralysis and corruption.

Once in power, fascist parties banned all opposition parties, independent trade unions and strikes, eliminated the independent press, established one-party states and reorganized industry along corporatist lines. In practice, CORPORATISM severely curtailed the rights of workers while emphasizing and protecting the rights of employers. Fascism ceased to be a powerful force with the defeat of the Axis powers of WWII and the long wave of postwar prosperity, but elements of fascism flourish in some underdeveloped Third World countries and survive in some fully developed capitalist countries. In Canada fascist elements are evident in organizations such as the KU KLUX KLAN. CY GONICK

A page from *Simpson's Catalogue* shows the fashion range of the 1920s (*courtesy National Archives of Canada/ C-49409*).

Fashion Design is the creation of styles for wearing apparel that will satisfy more than the physical needs of men, women and children for protection against the elements and for modesty. It is characterized by seasonal changes that often reflect social, political, historical and economic influences. Canada's contribution to international fashion dates back to the 16th century when French explorers returned to Europe with luxurious beaver pelts. For centuries, Canada struggled to become self-reliant in satisfying its clothing needs. Pioneer settlers not only produced fabrics and clothing, but fashioned the necessary tools by hand, importing the first machines from England and Scotland after 1846. Increased immigration brought skilled tailors from Europe, who became the basis for the apparel industry.

In the past, most designers and manufacturers depended on Europe and the US for inspiration; however, Elen Henderson was known internationally by 1949 and John Warden by 1963. The international Association of Clothing Designers (men's fine clothing) has had Toronto and Montréal chapters since before 1929. The 1967 Centennial celebration inspired the fashion industry to enhance its own identity. Fashion/Canada, a crown corporation, was set up by the government to promote Canadian fashion and designers during the formative years, 1968-71, and it became a major force in design. Fashion designers turned their attention to furs and made impressive inroads into export markets. Designers established, with Fashion/Canada's help, the Fashion Designers Association of Canada in 1974. Among the founders were internationally acclaimed designers Leo Chevalier, John Warden, Michel Robichaud and Hugh Garber of Montréal and Alfred SUNG, Elen Henderson, Claire Haddad and Pat McDonaugh of Toronto. Chevalier has received both the Designer of the Year Award and the Merit Award of Québec as well as the Order of Canada. Haddad, until recently a manufacturer of ladies' lounge and sleep-wear, was the first Canadian to receive the coveted Coty Award, the top fashion award in the US, and holds the Order of Canada and 6 Eedee Awards (Ontario government awards for fashion). Robichaud apprenticed with foremost French designers before returning to Montréal to open his own boutique and to design ready-to-wear clothing. Henderson is internationally known as a designer of children's clothes. She received the Eedee Award for 6 consecutive years and designed the uniform of the Canadian Girl Guides and Brownies. Alfred Sung, Emily Zarb, Mariola Mayer, Bernard McGee and Shelly Wickabrod are among the many young, up-and- coming designers who are now becoming internationally recognized. Gabriel Levy and Albert Shu are famous Canadian fashion designers working in Vancouver.

There are annual incentives for young and aspiring designers offered by government and industry. Ten universities, 23 community colleges and 30 private and technical schools offer fashion design courses and programs across Canada; these vary from one to 4 years in duration. Some of their graduates, such as Linda Lundstrom and Wayne Clarke, are internationally known designers today. Ryerson Polytechnical Institute is now offering Canada's first 4-year degree programs in fashion design.

S. SCHIPPER, C. GONZALES AND E. SHANNON

Fathers of Confederation No one has adequately defined a Father of CONFEDERATION. Some definitions include the delegates from the RED RIVER COLONY who created Manitoba in 1870, and those who came to Ottawa to bring in Newfoundland in 1949. The conventional meaning includes all who represented colonies of BRITISH NORTH AMERICA at the CHARLOTTETOWN CONFERENCE and the QUÉBEC CONFERENCE (1864), or the LONDON CONFERENCE (1866-67).

Charlottetown Conference Province of Canada: George Brown, Alexander Campbell, George-Étienne Cartier, Alexander Galt, Hector Langevin, John A. Macdonald, William McDougall, Thomas D'Arcy McGee; NB: E.B. Chandler, J.H. Gray, J.M. Johnson, W.H. Steeves, Samuel L. Tilley; NS: Adams G. Archibald, R.B. Dickey, W.A. Henry, Jonathan McCully, Charles Tupper; PEI: George Coles, J.H. Gray, A.A. Macdonald, Edward Palmer, W.H. Pope.

Québec Conference Those named above were joined by, for Canada, J.Ç. Chapais, James Cockburn, Oliver Mowat, Sir Étienne P. Taché; for NB, Charles Fisher, Peter Mitchell; for PEI, T.H. Haviland, Edward Whelan; and for Nfld, F.B.T. Carter, Ambrose Shea.

London Conference Some of the above did not

attend, and there were 3 new delegates: for Canada, W.P. Howland; for NS, J.W. Ritchie; and for NB, R.D. Wilmot. P.B. WAITE

Reading: G.P. Browne, ed, *Documents on the Confederation of British North America* (1969); P.B. Waite, *The Life and Times of Confederation, 1864-1867* (1962).

Fauquier, John Emilius, air force officer (b at Ottawa 19 Mar 1909; d at Toronto 3 Apr 1981). Educated at Ashbury College, Fauquier, a commercial pilot, joined the RCAF in 1939, eventually commanding 405 (Pathfinder) Squadron, RCAF, and from Dec 1944, 617 (Dambuster) Squadron, RAF. He was awarded the DFC for gallantry and the DSO for his "skillful and courageous example" over Peenemünde and Berlin, Aug 1943. He received a bar to his DSO in Jan 1944 and at war's end became the only Canadian airman to be awarded a second bar, for his "brilliant leadership, undoubted skill and iron determination." He also received the Croix de Guerre avec palme and was made Chevalier de la légion d'honneur. He returned to private business and in 1973 was named to the Aviation Hall of Fame. JEAN PARISEAU

Fauteux, André, sculptor (b at Dunnville, Ont 15 Mar 1946). He received his basic art education at Central Technical School in Toronto and worked with Anthony Caro (York U, 1974-75). Fauteux is known for the elegant, controlled line of drawing that characterizes his abstract sculptures. Profoundly influenced by the minimalist paintings of Kenneth Noland, Fauteux has successfully dealt with and transformed Noland's painterly concerns to his sculptures. The carefully articulated thin outlines enclose the volume of each work, but the flatness of the steel, the convergence of verticals and horizontals at sharp, dramatic angles, and the surrounding negative space defy the mass and weight of the sculptures. Fauteux's approach uses the interaction of geometric shapes as a point of departure in the building of a sculptural form. In 1987 his work was displayed at the Jack Gallery (Manhattan) and at the Miro Godard Gallery (Toronto). CLARA HARGITTAY

Favreau, Guy, lawyer, politician (b at Montréal 20 May 1917; d there 11 July 1967). Favreau was a prominent Montréal lawyer who was elected to the House of Commons in the 1963 election. A member of the "new guard" of Québec Liberals, Favreau quickly rose to prominence under PM Lester PEARSON's patronage. His first appointment on 22 Apr 1963 was as minister of citizenship and immigration. On 3 Feb 1964 Pearson appointed Favreau minister of justice and attorney general as well as Liberal house leader. In this period, Favreau carried on the work done by the former Conservative justice minister, E.D. FULTON, in seeking an amending formula for Canada's constitution. The so-called Fulton-Favreau formula was much debated but never approved. In Apr 1964 Favreau also became Québec Liberal Party leader. The tasks were too much for him, and press criticism of Favreau intensified as a result of the Lucien RIVARD scandal. The Dorion Commission criticized Favreau's handling of the scandal, and on 29 June 1965 he resigned as justice minister. On 7 July 1965 Pearson, in a controversial move, appointed Favreau president of the Privy Council. His political reputation was tarnished beyond repair. He faded quickly from public view, his health failed, and in 1967 this tragic figure died. JOHN ENGLISH

Reading: Peter C. Newman, *The Distemper of Our Times* (1968).

Favreau, Marc, actor, author, monologist (b at Montréal 9 Nov 1929). Originally a commercial designer, he enrolled in the school of the THÉÂTRE DU NOUVEAU MONDE (1950) and studied in Paris (1955-57). Thereafter, he had roles in top Canadian TV series (*Jeunesse dorée, Le Survenant, Les Enquêtes Jobidon* and *Les Forges du Saint-Maurice*) and also TV series for children (*Le Courrier du roy, Le Boîte à surprise* and, above all, *Sol et Gobelet*). He created the Sol clown role for the program *Bim et Sol* (which later became *Sol et Bouton* and then *Sol et Gobelet*) in 1958, and in 1972 began a theatrical career as the naive clown. While presenting an image of society shaped by his own eternal poverty, the ignorant Sol announces great truths about the world and the way it leads him about in his verbally acrobatic and imaginative monologues. Having delighted Canadian critics and audiences, Favreau has also known lasting success overseas. *L'Univers est dans la pomme* was well received in France (1986) and Québec. CARMEN LANGLOIS

Favro, Murray, artist (b at Huntsville, Ont 24 Dec 1940). Favro began his career painting brightly coloured works on masonite. Around 1965 he abandoned painting for other-than-art interests – guitars, machines, airplanes, experiments with film images and inventions. A Canada Council Arts Bursary in 1970 allowed him to devote himself to his art. That year he developed his first successful "projected reconstruction," in which images on a slide are projected onto their wooden, white, life-sized counterparts, giving them colour, detail and identity. He later produced modified inventions (*Windmill Electric Generator*, 1975-76; *Perpetual Motion Machine*, 1976-77), evolved inventions (*Propeller Engine*, 1978), and material, 3-dimensional renderings of airplanes (*Flying Flea*, 1976-77, and *Sabre Jet, 55% Size*, 1979-83). Favro's work deals with the nature of perception, reality and art itself, as well as with the insistent presence of the machine environment. His art has its own language of form – a vocabulary of constituent properties, a grammar of particular functions. It has a touch presence, a poetic logic and an integrity of being.

Reading: M.L. Fleming, *Murray Favro: A Retrospective* (1983); P. Smith and P. Theberge, *Boucherville, Montreal, Toronto, London* (1975).

Fear, Alfred Henry, "Cap," football player (b at Old Sailbury, Eng 11 June 1901; d at St Catharines, Ont 12 Feb 1978). He played with the TORONTO ARGONAUTS (1919-26, 1 Grey Cup) and Hamilton Tigers (1927-32, 3 Grey Cups) as an outside wing in an era when, with no forward pass, this position was noted for defensive tackling. He was also an accomplished hockey player in the Toronto Mercantile League, was runner up for the N American welterweight boxing title and, as a member of the Toronto Argonaut Rowing Club, won victories at the Royal Canadian Henley Regatta. But it was on the football field where the square-jawed, stocky Fear became famous for his "bonecrunching" tackling. FRANK COSENTINO

Feast of the Dead, held by the HURON whenever a large village shifted location, every 10-15 years. The bodies of all those who had not died violent deaths were removed from their temporary tombs and buried in a common ossuary – a deep pit lined with beaver robes. The ceremony expressed the great affection the Huron held for their dead relatives and exercised a powerful reinforcement of the alliances among the tribes and villages. The final burial was believed to release the souls of the dead and to allow them to travel westward to the land where Iouskeha and Aataentsic lived. JAMES MARSH

Federal Court of Canada, established 1971 to replace the Exchequer Court, enjoys jurisdiction chiefly over matters involving the federal government, eg, lawsuits against it and supervision of actions by federal government bodies and officials. The Federal Court is also the only court in Canada with jurisdiction over certain specialized areas, eg, maritime law, patent and copyright law, although in some specialized areas it shares concurrent jurisdiction with provincial superior courts. The court is divided into the Federal Court of Appeal and the Federal Court, Trial Division. The Trial Division hears lawsuits and initial applications to review some types of governmental actions; the Court of Appeal hears appeals from the Trial Division and supervises the formal decisions of government tribunals. Decisions of the Court of Appeal can be appealed, with leave, to the SUPREME COURT OF CANADA. The Federal Court's main office is in Ottawa, but it sits throughout the country. The number of judges was expanded in 1983 from 14 to 21 and had reached 25 by 1987. *See also* JUDICIARY; COURTS OF LAW. PETER K. DOODY

Federal Cultural Policy Review Committee was established 28 Aug 1980 to review CULTURAL POLICIES for Canada. Its chairman was Louis APPLEBAUM and its co-chairman was Jacques HÉBERT. Other members included Thomas SYMONS, Mary PRATT and Rudy WIEBE. The report was published Nov 1982, after hearings in 18 centres and 1369 briefs. The committee recommended that the operations of key cultural agencies, such as the CANADA COUNCIL and CBC, be immune from political direction. It also recommended the establishment of several new agencies, including a Canadian Heritage Council, and that more funds be given to art galleries. It called for support for book publishing through subsidies and for the film industry through increased funding for Telefilm Canada. Its suggestion for payment to authors for library use of their books was acted upon in 1986. It also recommended changes in the CBC, particularly that it relinquish TV production and acquire programs from independent producers.

In minority reports, Albert Breton protested the committee's policy of recommending that grants be given only to Canadian-owned film companies, and Guy Robert felt that the committee placed too much stress on the role of institutions. *See also* ARTS FUNDING. JAMES MARSH

Federal Government popularly refers to the national or dominion level of GOVERNMENT, and in its most general sense includes the executive, legislative and judicial branches, along with the numerous departments and agencies comprising the administrative branch. The 3 principles regulating the powers of the various components of government and the relationships between them are inherited from Britain: parliamentary supremacy, meaning that the SENATE and HOUSE OF COMMONS acting in conjunction with the CROWN possess constitutional plenary powers to legislate; the fusion of executive and legislative instruments, eg, as opposed to the US principle of separation of powers; and the RULE OF LAW, applied and maintained by an independent JUDICIARY. The relationship between the legislature and the CABINET is held in equilibrium by the doctrine of individual and collective ministerial responsibility to the legislature. If the executive can maintain the confidence of the legislature, it can continue to govern. If not, a Cabinet must resign or seek dissolution of the legislature and call an ELECTION.

A more precise definition of federal government focuses on the term "federal." A federal government is distinct from a unitary government, eg, that of Britain. In the latter, there is only one seat of ultimate authority. In a federal government, there are 2 independent seats of authority. Parliament and the provinces are each assigned certain powers and jurisdictional terrain. In practice, this subdivision modifies the principle of parliamentary supremacy; each separate level

of government is supreme as long as it does not trespass on the preserve of the other. The umpire for resolving jurisdictional disputes is the SUPREME COURT OF CANADA. *See also* FEDERALISM; DISTRIBUTION OF POWERS. J.E. HODGETTS

Federal-Provincial Relations, are the complex and multifaceted networks of influence which have developed in the relationships between Canada's federal and provincial governments. These relationships have become a central element of Canadian government and policy-making, and a fundamental characteristic of Canadian federalism. These relationships are a result of the pervasive interdependence which exists between the 2 levels of government. Central and provincial government activities are intertwined in a pattern of shared and overlapping responsibilities, shared authority and shared funding in many if not most areas of public policy. Many of the concerns of modern government cut across the loose jurisdictional boundaries found in the constitution. National purposes can often only be achieved with provincial co-operation; provincial goals often require federal assistance. As government roles in social, economic and other policy areas grew, then the need for co-operation and co-ordination – and the costs of failing to achieve it – also expanded. Through federal-provincial relations – and the related tools of INTERGOVERNMENTAL FINANCE, shared cost programs and the like – the federal government is deeply involved in fields largely within provincial jurisdiction; and provinces have increasingly sought to influence federal policies in areas such as foreign trade and transportation. Thus federal-provincial relations have grown primarily in response to the changing roles of government within Canadian federalism.

They have also been sustained by more political factors. The weakness of mechanisms for regional representation in the federal government, and the regional concentration of support for the major national parties throughout much of recent history, have stengthened the ability of provinces to act as the primary articulators of regional interests. The difficulty of achieving changes in the constitutional allocations of power has played a premium on informal mechanisms of accommodation.

Federal-provincial relations takes place in many arenas. They range from the multitude of informal day-to-day contacts between bureaucrats, to more formal, set-piece meetings between ministers and first ministers. Most attention is focused on the multilateral meetings of representatives of all 11 governments, but there are also many exchanges which are bilateral or involve only a few governments. While the relationships among governments are often influenced by developments in the wider political setting, and while governments also frequently undertake unilateral actions without extensive consultation with others, the term federal-provincial relations is most often used to refer to exchanges among bureaucrats and ministers, summarized in the descriptive term "executive federalism."

The Nov 1978 First Ministers Conference, at the National Conference Centre in Ottawa. PM Pierre Trudeau presides (*courtesy SSC Photocentre*).

No complete inventory of federal-provincial interactions exists, and the intensity and subject matter has varied over time. One estimate for 1977 records a total of 335 meetings of 158 different intergovernmental bodies for that year. The frequency appears to have diminished somewhat during the Liberal government of 1980-84, with an average of 132 meetings recorded per year. In the first year of the Progressive Conservative government elected in 1984, the number of federal-provincial meetings rose to 438, including 123 at the first ministers level, and 353 at the ministerial level. In recent years, constitutional issues and economic development matters, including international trade, have become the predominant subjects of intergovernmental discussion; in the postwar generation, the process played a central role in the development of the Canadian welfare state. In terms of programs, a 1982-83 inventory listed 316 shared activities, ranging from major national programs, such as EQUALIZATION and MEDICARE to a host of minor agreements. Joint arrangements are crucial parts of INTERGOVERNMENTAL FINANCE and TAXATION. Regional development activities are expressed through intergovernmental Economic and Regional Development Agreements (ERDAs).

The tone and style of federal-provincial relations varies considerably over time. In the postwar period, the term "co-operative federalism" referred to a pattern of federal financial and policy leadership. In the 1960s and 1970s, as the strength and assertiveness of provinces grew, relationships became more equal, and federal-provincial relations were widely seen as a vehicle for the expression of successful provincial claims for a greater share of fiscal resources, greater freedom for provincial policy initiatives, and greater provincial influence over federal policies in its areas of jurisdiction. The rise of a more assertive Québec nationalism, and later of interregional tensions of energy matters in the 1960s and 1970s, along with deep divisions over the constitution led many to see intergovernmental forms less as an arena for harmony and co-operation, and more as one for exacerbating disagreement.

The Liberal government of 1980-84, concerned with what it saw as a drift towards greater provincial power, sought to minimize the role of federal-provincial relations in shared decision making, acting unilaterally in many areas, and seeking to establish direct relations with citizens and groups in the provinces, without going through the intermediary of the provinces. By contrast, the Conservative government made "national reconciliation" a central goal, and sought to restore more harmonious relations, with consultation on a variety of matters.

The most important federal-provincial mechanism is the FIRST MINISTERS CONFERENCE. It is chaired by the prime minister. These conferences have become major public events, attracting national media attention and often gavel-to-gavel television coverage. Nevertheless, much of the hard bargaining takes place in closed sessions and in back-room meetings of ministers and officials. Below the first ministers conferences, and often reporting to them, are many ministerial conferences, some meeting regularly, and others, such as a ministerial committee on the US free trade negotiations, convened on an ad hoc basis. It has become common for such meetings to be held outside Ottawa and to be chaired by provincial ministers. Numerous parallel committees of officials exist, the most important of which is the Continuing Committee on Economic and Fiscal Matters, est 1955. The success of such meetings in achieving policy harmonization and a co-ordinated approach to new problems varies widely. Many federal-provincial meetings are provided with organizational and secretarial services through an intergovernmental body, the Canadian Intergovernmental Conference Secretariat. As federal-provincial relations have become more important, all governments have established offices, attached to the first minister, to oversee the province's intergovernmental affairs.

In addition to the federal-provincial mechanisms, interprovincial relationships are also important. Annual meetings of premiers have been held since 1960, not only to attempt to harmonize provincial policies but also to develop common provincial policies on matters of federal-provincial concern. On many issues such co-operation is limited by divergent political orientations and regional, interests. There are also 2 regional groupings of provinces, the Prairie Provinces Economic Council and the Council of Maritime Premiers, which hold regular meetings to resolve interprovincial issues and develop common positions. The Maritimes Council has a secretariat and operates a number of joint programs for the region. Provinces have also established several interprovincial minsterial bodies.

Despite their importance, federal-provincial relations have arisen in an informal and ad hoc way; they are nowhere mentioned in the constitution. The MEECH LAKE ACCORD of 1987, however, does give a constitutional status to them, by providing a constitutional requirement for annual meetings of first ministers on the constitution and the economy. It will also give greater prominence to intergovernmental relations in the shaping of major national institutions by providing for joint selection of judges and senators, and by ensuring joint federal-provincial discussion of proposed new federal spending programs in areas of provincial jurisdiction.

Assessments of the importance and value of federal-provincial relations vary widely. Virtually all observers agree that a high degree of co-ordination between the 2 orders of government is essential to effective policymaking, and that many vital programs could not have been achieved without it. But there have been many criticisms. First, it has been argued that federal-provincial conferences have too often become forums in which governments exacerbate conflict as they compete for resources and popular support. Second, it is suggested that too great an emphasis on intergovernmental consensus leads to excessive delay and a subordination of policy to the lowest common denominator. Supporters of a stronger federal government have argued that highly visible federal-provincial conferences give undue prominence to provincial governments as national policymakers, thus undermining federal authority. Others argue that the secrecy and closed-door nature of much federal-provincial activity undermines citizen participation and reduces the ability effectively to consult with interest groups representing "non-territorial" interests. To the extent that intergovernmental agreements are made in the federal-provincial arena and then presented as faits accomplis to the 11 legislatures, it is felt that the process undermines responsible government and legislative sovereignty. The high degree of interaction in financial and policy matters, it is argued, also undermines governmental accountability.

Such critics have tended to argue for placing less emphasis on extensive intergovernmental co-operation, and more on encouraging each government to act independently within its area of jurisdiction. This model of "competitive federalism" suggests that government responsiveness and policy effectiveness is to be found more in vigorous competition than in a search for intergovernmental agreement for its own sake. Advocates of a more collaborative, or partnership, model, by contrast, emphasize the costs of competition, and the sense that in few areas can governments effectively achieve their goals alone. With 2 powerful and equal orders of government, co-operation is seen as essential. Neither side in the debate denies the importance of federal-provincial relations: the issue is whether they should constitute something like a third order of government, with real decision-making power, or whether, instead, they should be seen primarily as opportunities for consultation and debate. Each side also tends to argue for somewhat different reforms in the process; those advocating a more competitive model call for "disentanglement" and a clarification of the powers of each level and argue for reforms in the central government which will make it more regionally responsive, and therefore more able to bypass provinces. Advocates of collaborative federalism call for a more formalized network of intergovernmental machinery designed to make co-operation more effective. RICHARD SIMEON

Reading: Richard Simeon, *Intergovernmental Relations*, vol 63, Research Studies of the Royal Commission on the Economic Union and Canada's Development Prospects (1985) and, ed, *Division of Powers and Public Policy*, vol 61, Research Studies of the Royal Commission on the Economic Union and Canada's Development Prospects (1985); G. Stevenson, *Unfulfilled Union: Canadian Federalism and National Unity* (1982).

Federalism is a type of political system in which legislative power is divided between a central or federal legislature and a number of state or provincial legislatures. The FEDERAL GOVERNMENT has jurisdiction over the entire national territory and population; a PROVINCIAL GOVERNMENT has jurisdiction only over particular portions of territory and population. Both levels of government derive their authority from a written CONSTITUTION. In a centralized federation the powers of provincial governments are relatively narrow; in a decentralized federation the provincial sphere of authority is wider. Federalism is distinguished from unitary government, in which subnational institutions derive their authority from the central government and are therefore subordinate to it; it is also different from various forms of association, such as economic communities or military alliances, whose members retain sovereign powers and can withdraw from the arrangement at will. A true federation, in the modern sense, means a STATE in which the component units are not sovereign and cannot legally secede (*see* CONSTITUTIONAL LAW).

Although imaginative efforts have been made to trace the history of federalism back into antiquity, the US Constitution (1787) is the earliest example of a modern federal constitution. The possibility of establishing a federal union among the remaining British colonies of N America was considered sporadically early in the 19th century, and more seriously from 1857 onwards. Negotiations among political leaders from the PROVINCE OF CANADA, NB and NS resulted later in the Imperial Parliament's adoption of the BRITISH NORTH AMERICA ACT, which united those 3 colonies into a federal state in 1867. CONFEDERATION marks the beginning of Canadian federalism. Unification was desired, particularly by commercial interests, as a means of facilitating economic growth, territorial expansion and military defence. Retention of existing governments and boundaries, however, was desired by many influential people for a variety of reasons. French Canadians, a majority only in Québec, were unwilling to place all powers in the hands of a central government where they would be a minority. There was also a strong sense of provincial identity in NS and NB. Federalism was therefore a necessary compromise. PM John A. MACDONALD was not enthusiastic about federalism and would have preferred a unitary state. Moreover, the American Civil War had contributed to a belief that powerful provincial governments would be a source of instability. For these reasons the Canadian Constitution includes features incompatible with a strict theory of federalism. The lieutenant-governor of each province, who is appointed by the central government, can prevent provincial legislation from taking effect until the central government has approved it. The central government can also disallow any provincial statute within a year of its adoption (*see* DISALLOWANCE). Parliament can adopt legislation concerning education within a province to protect the rights of certain religious minorities and can also declare that "works and undertakings" within a province fall under its jurisdiction, regardless of the normal DISTRIBUTION OF POWERS. The BNA Act, because of these unitary features, has been described as quasi-federal rather than strictly federal, but the quasi-federal powers have fallen into disuse.

Although Canadian politicians have a reputation for being uninterested in political theory, they have actually articulated a variety of different concepts of Canadian federalism. Differences of opinion over federalism have been sharper in Canada over a longer period than in most federations, and no consensus has ever been achieved regarding the appropriate relationship between the 2 levels of government, either in theory or in practice. National and provincial politicians tend to espouse different views, and these have become associated with partisan conflict when one party has held office at the national level for a long period while enjoying less success at the provincial level. Macdonald's quasi-federal concept was associated with the CONSERVATIVE PARTY until about 1900, when the generation of politicians that had been involved in drafting the BNA Act ceased to be influential in that party. It has had little support during this century, although a centralist view of federalism, emphasizing the importance of a strong and active central government, continues to enjoy considerable support. Modern centralists do not normally emphasize using the quasi-federal powers of disallowance and reservation. Instead, they argue for a broad interpretation of Parliament's legislative powers and believe that the central government should be permitted to make policy in its areas of jurisdiction without consulting the provincial governments. They also believe that the central government should have access to a predominant share of revenue from taxation and that it should be entitled to make conditional grants to provincial governments even in relation to matters not strictly within its jurisdiction.

A centralist view of federalism, with certain qualifications, was expressed in the 1940 report of the Royal Commission on DOMINION-PROVINCIAL RELATIONS (the Rowell-Sirois Commission). Since then, centralist ideas about federalism have been influential in the LIBERAL PARTY. The NEW DEMOCRATIC PARTY also tends towards a centralist position. Politicians and political thinkers who have articulated a centralist concept of federalism include Louis ST. LAURENT, F.R. SCOTT, Eugene FORSEY, David LEWIS, Bora LASKIN and, in his last years as prime minister, Pierre Elliott TRUDEAU. Macdonald's view that the provincial governments should be subordinated to the central government was controversial from the outset, and in the early 1880s a Québec judge, T.J.J. LORANGER, wrote that the central government had been created by the provincial governments and that no increase in the central government's powers, and indeed no substantial change in the Constitution, was permissible without the unanimous consent of the provincial governments. This view became known as the Compact Theory of Confederation and was expressed at the interprovincial conference of 1887, organized by Québec PM Honoré MERCIER. A similar view was expressed by certain premiers during the constitutional discussions of 1980-81. The emphasis on the importance of provincial autonomy has been influential since 1939 in the Progressive Conservative Party, in the SOCIAL CREDIT Party and in all parties at the provincial level in Québec. Supporters of the anticentralist view believe that the functions of the central government should be limited to those that the provincial governments cannot perform for themselves, and that its control over revenue should be restricted accordingly. They have also argued, particularly in recent years, that the central government should consult the provincial governments before initiating major policies. An eloquent statement of the anticentralist view was the 1956 report of the Québec Royal Commission on CONSTITUTIONAL PROBLEMS and a more recent expression of the concept may be found in the 1979 report of the task force on CANADIAN UNITY.

Canadian federalism, in practice, has fluctuated between the extremes of centralization and DECENTRALIZATION in response to a variety of political, economic and social circumstances. Macdonald's preference for a highly centralized regime seems to have triumphed for a few years after Confederation, but by the time he died, in 1891, the provincial governments were becoming as powerful as their US counterparts, if not more so. Provincial control over natural resources facilitated the development of largely self-contained provincial economies, and the concentration of secondary manufacturing in Ontario made its government particularly important and influential. Deteriorating relations between francophone and anglophone Canadians undermined Macdonald's Conservative Party and increased anticentralist sentiment in Québec. Centralization revived temporarily during WWI and immediately after, when the central government levied an income tax for the first time in 1917, imposed military conscription and exercised an unprecedented control over the economy. These tendencies were largely reversed after 1921, and the Great Depression demonstrated that the central government lacked the power to deal effectively with a severe economic crisis. Efforts were made to ensure that centralization during WWII would have more lasting effects than it had had during WWI. The central government monopolized personal income tax from 1941 until 1954, and constitutional amendments gave Parliament the power to establish UNEMPLOYMENT INSURANCE and universal PENSIONS paid from a special fund in 1940 and 1951 respectively. Interpretation of the BNA Act by the JUDICIAL COMMITTEE OF THE PRIVY COUNCIL, which was considered to be favourable to provincial autonomy, was terminated in 1949. During the postwar period, extensive conditional grants were introduced to encourage provincial spending on health and welfare, and federal grants were given direct to universities.

A shift of power towards the provincial governments, however, became evident after 1960, when a dynamic and interventionist Québec government, headed by Jean LESAGE, emerged as an effective opponent of centralization. Other contributing factors included the growing importance of provincial natural resources, the decline of the old commercial and financial elite based in Montréal, economic integration between Canada and the US, and the development of a more competitive party system at the national level after the defeat of St. Laurent's Liberal government in 1957. Between 1960 and 1980 these circumstances led to a substantial increase in the provincial share of TAXATION and PUBLIC EXPENDITURE. Grants to universities were replaced by subsidies to the provinces. By OPTING OUT of certain conditional grant programs, Québec received unconditional grants in return and established its own contributory pension plan, although the central government established one for residents of other provinces. Conferences between the PM and provincial premiers became more frequent, a phenomenon described as "executive federalism." Provincial governments began to intervene more aggressively in provincial economies and also challenged the right of the central government to make economic policy without their collaboration or consent. Provincial relations with foreign governments also became significant, particularly in the case of Québec, whose nationalist movement was encouraged by President Charles de Gaulle of France. The dramatic increase in Alberta's petroleum revenues after 1972 imposed further strains on the federal system and made that province's government increasingly contemptuous of the federal authorities. In Québec the emergence of a major political party dedicated to seeking independence for that province, the PARTI QUÉBÉCOIS, suggested that the survival of Canadian federalism could not be taken for granted. A separatist movement in western Canada also attracted considerable attention 1980-82.

Formal changes in a country's constitution usually follow, rather than precede, informal shifts in economic and political power. The trend away from centralization in Canadian federalism was under way by 1960, and demands for a formal transfer of constitutional authority towards the provincial level of government became widespread in Québec shortly afterwards. Other provinces, with the partial exception of Ontario, had little interest in constitutional change at that time; this encouraged the idea of "special status," whereby only Québec would receive additional powers. After 1972, increasing natural-resource revenues caused a number of other provincial governments to demand additional powers in a revised constitution, Alberta being the most militant. In response to these pressures, the central government convened a number of intergovernmental conferences on constitutional change between 1968 and 1981, although it insisted that a charter of individual rights and the restructuring of national institutions be discussed in addition to the distribution of legislative powers. A related problem was the absence of an amending formula in the BNA Act. The constitutional negotiations included efforts to devise such a formula as a necessary prelude to "patriating" the Constitution, a matter that had been sporadically and inconclusively discussed as far back as 1927. In 1980 the Trudeau government attempted to patriate the Constitution with an amending formula that would require the support of Ontario, Québec, 2 western provinces and 2 Atlantic provinces for any subsequent change, and simultaneously to entrench a CANADIAN CHARTER OF RIGHTS AND FREEDOMS in the Constitution. This initiative, which followed the breakdown of negotiations over the distribution of powers, was opposed by 8 provincial governments, and was ruled unconstitutional in the conventional sense, although not illegal, by the Supreme Court of Canada. Further negotiations led to qualifications in the charter of rights and replacement of the original amending formula by one that required the approval of 7 provinces comprising at least half of Canada's population, but permitted dissenting provinces to exempt themselves from the application of amendments that would reduce their powers. All provincial governments except Québec accepted this compromise, which took effect when the constitution was formally "patriated" on 17 Apr 1982. Québec regarded the federal concessions as inadequate, and particularly objected to the entrenchment of language rights for its anglophone minority. Although the Supreme Court subsequently ruled that Québec's consent had not been required to amend and patriate the constitution, efforts to secure a constitutional settlement acceptable to Québec resumed in 1986. These efforts culminated in an agreement among the 11 first ministers in the MEECH LAKE ACCORD of Apr 1987, which recognized Québec as a distinct society; provided for provincial participation in the selection of senators and justices of the Supreme Court; restricted the federal power to spend in areas of provincial jurisdiction; recognized provincial powers over immigration; and made slight changes on the amending formula. Constitutional amendments based on this agreement were approved by 3 provincial legislatures and the House of Commons by the end of 1987 and were awaiting approval from the remaining legislatures and the Senate.

The future evolution of Canadian federalism is difficult to predict because it will depend on economic and political developments throughout Canada and the world. The 1982 amending formula is conducive to further decentralization since it makes it easier to increase the formal powers of provincial governments and allows dissident provinces to exempt themselves from amendments that would increase the powers of the central government. On the other hand, the charter may create a new focus of national identity and gradual erosion of interprovincial differences in public policy, as the Bill of Rights has apparently done in the US. The independence movement in Québec appears to have lost substantial support since the referendum, and the western provincial governments have become less truculent as the price of oil has declined. The federal government has taken some steps to reassert its authority, notably the Canada Health Act of 1984, which imposed more rigid conditions on provincial health-insurance programs and was supported by all 3 parties in Parliament.

Whatever the future may hold in store, patriation of the Constitution has brought Canada no closer to achieving consensus on the direction in which federalism should evolve. Supporters of greater provincial autonomy emphasize the diversity of provincial interests and argue that a more stable and legitimate political order would result if the distribution of power between the 2 levels of government was adjusted to accord with what they view as the socioeconomic realities. On the other hand, those who support the retention or enlargement of the central government's powers argue that decentralization is more the cause than the consequence of interprovincial diversities and that it ignores the significant common interests of Canadians, which can only be expressed through a strong central government. They also argue that excessive decentralization weakens Canada's economy and Canada's influence in the world. It is unlikely that these differences of opinion will be resolved soon. GARTH STEVENSON

Reading: D.V. Smiley, *Canada in Question: Federalism in the Eighties* (1980); Garth Stevenson, *Unfulfilled Union: Canadian Federalism and National Unity* (1982).

Federated Women's Institutes of Canada is the national organization that co-ordinates the activities of the provincial Women's Institutes. The first institute was founded in 1897 in Stoney Creek, Ont, by Adelaide HOODLESS, and by 1913 institutes were established in all the provinces. In 1919 provincial representatives met in Winnipeg to form the FWIC and a national office was established in Ottawa in 1958. The motto "For Home and Country" reflects FWIC aims: to promote an appreciation of rural living, to develop informed citizens through the study of national and international issues (particularly those affecting women and children), and to initiate national programs to achieve common goals. Each provincial organization is represented on the board of directors, which meets annually; new executives are elected at triennial conventions. Reflecting the urbanization of Canadian society, FWIC membership has slowly declined; in 1987 there were 43 000 members. JEAN E. DRYDEN

Federation of Medical Women of Canada was founded in Ottawa in 1924 and held its first annual meeting in Victoria in 1926. Membership numbers 650 (1987), composed of practising physicians and medical students from across the country. The federation is an independent member of the Medical Women's International Assn and has been affiliated with the CANADIAN MEDICAL ASSN since 1964. The objects of the federation are the promotion of interests of medical women, the aid of women medical students at all levels, and the establishment and administration of scholarship and loan funds. The major scholarship fund is named for Dr Maude ABBOTT, a founding member. JANICE DICKIN MCGINNIS

Feild, Edward, bishop (b at Worcester, Eng 7 June 1801; d at Hamilton, Bermuda 8 June 1876). Ordained in the Church of England in 1827, Feild displayed organizational ability and his arrangements became known as the "Feild System." Offered the see of Newfoundland in 1844, he faced unusual difficulty and was embroiled in strife for the greater part of his episcopacy. By temperament an uncompromising rigorist and extremist, he battled local politicians, Roman Catholics, Methodists, and Evangelicals of his own church to build a strong, independent Anglican Church with a distinctly high-church tone. Newfoundlanders in time gave this man of iron will not only respect but also appreciation and affection. Feild served Newfoundland with devotion, personal humility and kindliness, visiting his people, scattered along a rugged shore of some 5000 km, in the church ship *Hawk*. J. ROGERS

Feinberg, Abraham, né Nisselevicz, rabbi, singer, peace activist (b at Bellaire, Ohio 14 Sept 1899; d at Reno, Nev 5 Oct 1986). Raised and educated in the US, he held rabbinical pulpits there in the 1920s. He left the rabbinate in 1930, and after changing his name to Anthony Frome embarked on a new career as a singer. With his own radio show in New York, 1932-35, he became known as the "Poet Prince of the Air Waves." Alarmed by the rise of Hitler and Nazi Germany, Feinberg became a rabbi again. In 1943 he came to Toronto as rabbi of Holy Blossom Temple, Canada's largest Reform Jewish congregation. During his tenure at Holy Blossom, 1943-61, he earned a worldwide reputation for his championship of the downtrodden, his embrace of radical causes, and his efforts to remove the barriers between Jews and non-Jews. Dedicated to world peace and social justice, he protested against the VIETNAM WAR, and perhaps his greatest moment as a peace activist was his 1967 visit to Vietnam when he met with Ho Chi Minh. In the 1970s, Feinberg moved back to the US where he became rabbi-in-residence at the Glide Memorial Church in San Francisco. He was the author of 3 books, *Storm the Gates of Jericho* (1964), *Hanoi Diary* (1968) and *Sex and the Pulpit* (1981), and wrote for *Saturday Night*, *Maclean's*, the *Globe and Mail* and the Toronto *Star*. SHARON DRACHE

Feldbrill, Victor, conductor (b at Toronto 4 Apr 1924). A versatile conductor with an international reputation, Feldbrill is widely known for his enthusiastic promotion of Canadian music and for his support of young musicians. Following his TORONTO SYMPHONY conducting debut at age 18, he was active as a violinist and guest conductor and was conductor of the Winnipeg Symphony Orchestra 1958-68. Since 1968 he has been associated with U of T as a lecturer and conductor. With the Toronto Symphony he was director of youth programming (1968-78), resident conductor (1973-77) and music director and conductor of its youth orchestra (1974-78). All Feldbrill's concerts include at least one Canadian work. He became an Officer of the Order of Canada and was named the first recipient of the Roy Thomson Hall Award (1985). BARCLAY MCMILLAN

Fencing, or duelling with a sword according to established rules, was practised in ancient times as a pastime as well as in war. Skilful swordplay with light weapons developed in the 14th century when gunpowder made heavy armour obsolete. As DUELS were gradually outlawed, fencers refined their skills into the elegant art of fencing. The organized sport of fencing emerged at the end of the 19th century as a contest in which the number of hits are counted to determine the winner of a bout. Fencing was included in the first modern Olympic Games in 1896. Fencers today compete in categories determined by the type of sword used. The foil is light and flexible; the épée is as long as the foil but heavier and less flexible; and the sabre is a cut-and-thrust weapon. The target area of the body varies with the type of sword (generally, the foil target is the trunk of the fencer, the sabre target the trunk and arms, and the épée target the entire body). Women usually compete in the foil and épée events. Electrical scoring machines, first developed in the 1930s, are used to record hits in foil and épée bouts; foil fencers wear an electrically conductive jacket over the target area. With protective masks, gloves and jackets, there is little danger in the sport, which demands subtle tactics, poise, speed and balance.

In Canada, fencing schools were well attended in the late 18th and early 19th centuries, and the sport began to flourish again in the late 19th century. The Toronto Fencing Club and a women's fencing club at Toronto's University College were formed in 1895. During the next decade, fencing clubs were established in eastern universities, and in 1902 the first Canadian championships were held. The 1930s saw further development, and after WWII immigration from Europe brought distinguished fencers and masters. Fencing is organized by the Canadian Fencing Assn. Canadian fencers, both men and women, have competed in the Olympic Games since 1932, but have been most successful in the Commonwealth and Pan-Am Games. Several silver and bronze medals have been won at the Commonwealth Games, and in 1954 the men's sabre team won the gold medal. At the Pan-Am Games, Canadians have won a number of bronze medals; silver medals were won by the women's foil teams in 1975 and 1979. In the 1986 Commonwealth Games, Canadian fencers swept the sabre and épée individual gold, silver and bronze medals, and also the team gold. The 1987 Pan-Am Games saw Jean-Paul Banos of Montréal win a gold medal in men's sabre. Canada also won 2 silver and 4 bronze medals. BARBARA SCHRODT

Fenerty, Charles, inventor (b at Upper Sackville, NS Jan 1821; d at Lower Sackville 10 June 1892). Concerned about the difficulty a local paper mill was having in obtaining an adequate supply of rags to make quality paper, Fenerty succeeded in producing paper from wood pulp as early as 1841. Fenerty's inspiration has been attributed to either a study of spruce fibres, influenced by the reports of Titus SMITH concerning its possible usefulness, or to his observation of how wasps made a form of paper from vegetable fibres; but most likely it came from perceiving that the fibrous matter formed by the constant friction of wood upon wood in the moving parts of sawmills could be used to make paper. Fenerty neglected to publicize his discovery until 1844, by which time others had patented papermaking processes based on wood fibre. TERRENCE M. PUNCH

Fenians, members of a movement initiated in 1857 by Irish-Americans to secure Irish independence from Britain. Its titular chief, James Stephens, organized an underground movement in Ireland with the aid of funds collected by his American deputy, John O'Mahony. The American wing emerged as a powerful force, and by the end of 1865 the Fenians had nearly $500 000 and about 10 000 AMERICAN CIVIL WAR veterans organized in military clubs. At this time they split into 2 factions, one led by O'Mahony, favouring an uprising in Ireland, and another led by William Roberts, intent on invading Canada. A small group of Canadian Fenians was headed initially by Michael Murphy of Toronto, who supported the O'Mahony wing. When it became obvious that there was to be no immediate uprising in Ireland, O'Mahony launched a raid against the New Brunswick frontier in Apr 1866. Murphy was summoned to join O'Mahony's forces by cipher telegram, but the telegram was intercepted and deciphered, bringing about his arrest in Cornwall. The raid collapsed and its only lasting consequence was to turn opinion in the Maritimes in favour of CONFEDERATION. The Roberts wing crossed the Niagara frontier on June 1, defeated Canadian militiamen at RIDGEWAY, and withdrew. A second group crossed the Québec frontier at Missisquoi Bay on June 7, and remained 48 hours. After the failure of an Irish uprising in 1867, the movement fragmented. Yet a Fenian apparently assassinated Thomas D'Arcy MCGEE in 1868, and in 1870 the faction led by "General" John O'Neill launched 2 small raids over the Québec frontier. O'Neill attempted one more raid in the fall of 1871, this time against Manitoba, hoping to receive support from Louis Riel and the Métis. This was checked by American authorities before it reached the Canadian border. Instead of supporting O'Neill, Riel raised loyalist volunteers to defend the frontier. After 1871, some sections of the fragmented Fenian movement carried on and were still in being at the time of the Easter 1916 uprising in Dublin, Ireland. Fenianism added a page to Irish folklore and helped to unite Canadians by providing an external threat during the period of Confederation. HEREWARD SENIOR

Fennario, David, né Wiper, playwright, novelist (b at Montréal 26 Apr 1947). Fennario grew up in Pointe-Ste-Charles, an English working-class ghetto in Montréal, where he still lives. A 1960s dropout, Fennario drifted through a series of dead-end jobs until he enrolled in Montréal's Dawson College, where his creative writing teacher arranged a private publication of his journal entries on life in "The Pointe" – *Without a Parachute* (1972). Fortuitously, the book caught the attention of Maurice Podbrey, artistic director of the CENTAUR THEATRE, who encouraged Fennario to write plays and subsequently appointed him the theatre's first playwright-in-residence. Podbrey also premiered *On the Job* (1975), *Nothing to Lose* (1976), *Toronto* (1978), *Balconville* (1979) and *Moving* (1983). *Balconville*, which won the Chalmers Award in 1979, contains one-third French dialogue, and has been billed as Canada's first bilingual play. It was produced in London's Old Vic theatre and broadcast on CBC TV in 1985. Fennario sets his naturalistic dramas in grimy factories, smoky taverns or decaying tenements, where he realistically depicts ordinary labourers who struggle against the economic imbalance that exists between management and workers. His unpublished plays include *Changes* (1980), an autobiographical one-man show adapted from *Without a Parachute*, and *Joe Beef* (1984), a history play about "The Pointe." *Blue Mondays* (1984), a prose journal, picks up where *Without a Parachute* leaves off. DONNA COATES

Ferguson, George Howard, lawyer, Conservative politician, premier of Ontario 1923-30 (b at Kemptville, Ont 18 June 1870; d at Toronto 21 Feb 1946). He personified Ontario in the 1920s: a mix of 19th-century values and 20th-century

Hon G. Howard Ferguson, premier of Ontario (*courtesy Archives of Ontario*).

ambitions. As premier at the climax of industrialization's first great wave, he set a style of government that prevails still. Confident that industry, protected by the tariff, and the development of natural resources would provide work and wealth for all, his government tried to create the climate and facilities conducive to private investment in Ontario's forests, mines and factories. Yet his administration did not permit untrammelled exploitation; measures to conserve and regulate were instituted. Action to meet the social problems of industrialization was slow and parsimonious, yet at times innovative, designed to extend educational and medical services to all regions and groups. He lifted some of the restrictions placed on Ontario's bilingual schools by the infamous Regulation 17 (1912), his earlier answer to mounting FRENCH CANADIAN NATIONALISM and a factor in national disunity during WWI. A master of brokerage politics, he maintained harmony among the classes and regions of Ontario. BARBARA A. MCKENNA

Reading: P. Oliver, *G. Howard Ferguson* (1977).

Ferguson, George Victor, newspaper editor (b at Cupar, Scot 20 Apr 1897; d at Montréal 26 Jan 1977). One of John W. DAFOE'S newspaper "pupils" and a distinguished journalist in his own right, Ferguson was educated at U of A and Oxford, where he was a Rhodes scholar. He served in WWI as a private soldier and joined the *Manitoba Free Press* in 1925, rising to managing editor under Dafoe in 1933. Like Dafoe, he took a strong nationalist view and sought to understand the roots of Canadian unity. In 1944, when Dafoe died, Ferguson became executive editor of the *Free Press*, but soon after left for Montréal where he served as editor in chief of the *Montreal Star* and where his editorials on French-English relations were important reading. Ordinarily Liberal in politics, Ferguson, much like Dafoe, had the capacity to take issue with his party and was positively exultant when the Conservatives won power under DIEFENBAKER in 1957. J.L. GRANATSTEIN

Ferguson, Ivan Graeme, film director, executive (b at Toronto 7 Oct 1929). He was a summer student at the National Film Board, 1950, and then made a number of films in the US before returning to Canada in 1970. He formed his own company (now IMAX SYSTEMS CORP) which developed the multiscreen system that was used at Ontario Place and other locations. His multiscreen films include *North of Superior* (1971) and *Snow Job* (1974). In 1984 an IMAX/OMNIMAX camera was flown aboard US space shuttle flights, taking footage released as "The Dream is Alive." He won a Special Achievement Award, Academy of Canadian Cinema and Television 1986 Genies. GAYLE BONISH

Ferguson, John Bright, "Fergie," chemist, professor (b at Londesborough, Ont 2 Nov 1889; d at Toronto 7 Jan 1963). Associate professor of physical chemistry at U of T 1920-48, he also spent 7 years with the Geophysical Laboratory in the Carnegie Institute, Washington, DC, where he solved problems in the manufacturing of optical glass for the War Industry Board, and he spent a short time with Western Electric Co, New York C. During WWII, he and his students undertook studies for the Canadian Army, including the development of a method for testing activated charcoals for use in respirators. He was the author of over 100 scientific papers. HARRY SHEFFER

Ferguson, Maynard, jazz trumpeter (b at Verdun, Qué 4 May 1928). Renowned in jazz for his exhibitionistic, high-note trumpet style, Ferguson worked in Montréal until 1948 with Stan Wood and Johnny Holmes, and with his own band. Thereafter based in the US, he was featured in the bands of Boyd Raeburn, Jimmy Dorsey, Charlie Barnet and, from 1950 to 1953, Stan Kenton. In 1956 he formed the first of a succession of big bands which, by the 1970s, had taken up a brash, rock-oriented music, showcasing Ferguson's remarkable range. He recorded some 50 albums under his own name, 1954-87, and had a hit recording with "Gonna Fly Now," the theme from the US film *Rocky*. In 1987 he returned to a small-group format with the fusion-jazz septet High Voltage. MARK MILLER

Ferguson, Robert George, physician (b at Joliette, ND 12 Sept 1883; d at Regina 1 Mar 1964). Ferguson studied arts, theology and medicine at U of Man and in 1917 became medical superintendent of the Saskatchewan Anti-tuberculosis League at Fort Qu'Appelle. His 31-year tenure achieved many "firsts": a school survey for TUBERCULOSIS (1921); province-wide free diagnosis and treatment of tuberculosis (1929) ; BCG vaccination of native infants (1930) and of student nurses (1938); and a province-wide radiographic survey for tuberculosis (1941-47). His book, *Studies in Tuberculosis* (1955), reported the striking drop in mortality from the disease. His honours included the King's Medallion (1934), OBE (1935), and an honorary LLD from U of Sask (1946). An island in Montreal Lake and a professorship at U of Sask bear his name. C. STUART HOUSTON

Ferguson, Robert, businessman (b at Logierait, Scot 17 Apr 1768; d at Campbellton, NB 10 Aug 1851). He came to the RESTIGOUCHE R in 1796 and was soon the most prominent merchant and largest landowner in the region. He farmed, built ships and exported timber and fish to Europe, his large house and store becoming the business centre of the Restigouche. In 1826 he began selling lots in what became the town of CAMPBELLTON. Along with Hugh Munro, he controlled the trade of northern NB until his authority was challenged with the arrival of Irish immigrants in the late 1820s. He was in part responsible for the creation of Restigouche County in 1837. One of the commissioners for laying out the first highway between NB and Lower Canada, he was active in the agricultural society, in the militia and as a magistrate. He was referred to as "the founder and father of Restigouche." WILLIAM A. SPRAY

Ferland, Jean-Pierre, author, composer, singer (b at Montréal 24 June 1934). In 1959 he won fame as one of the singing group the Bozos, of which he was co-founder, and also as a singer and host on Radio-Canada television. He wrote the words for the song "*Feuilles de gui*," which won a Radio-Canada competition and the grand prize at the Gala international de la chanson in Brussels (1962), and has twice been awarded the grand prize of the Festival du disque de Montréal (1965, 1968). Ferland also received first prize for recordings from the Académie Charles-Cros in Paris (1968) and has sung in France, Poland and Japan. In Canada, Ferland has toured in Québec, Ontario and the Maritimes, and in 1971 he appeared at the Place des Arts, accompanied by the Montreal Symphony. Whatever the subject of his songs, he almost always produces a spine-tingling emotional impact. Among his greatest successes are *Les Fleurs de macadam; Le Petit Roi; Saint-Adèle, Qué; Un Peu plus haut, un peu plus loin; Je reviens chez nous* and *Quand on aime on a toujours vingt ans*. In 1985 he was host of Radio-Québec's summer show "Stratim soleil." HÉLÈNE PLOUFFE

Fern, common name for a diverse group (division Polypodiophyta) of usually perennial, spore-producing plants with divided, evergreen or deciduous leaves (fronds) arising from slender, horizontal rhizomes (underground stems) or stout, ascending rootstalks. Tropical and subtropical tree ferns may grow several metres high. Related tree-like species, dating to the Devonian period (408-360 million years ago) and reaching highest development in the Carboniferous period (360-286 million years ago), comprised some of the vegetation forming coal beds (*see* FOSSILS). Recent advances in knowledge have necessitated taxonomic realignments: 21 families encompassing 308 genera (each containing 1-200 or more species) are now recognized; 11 families, 31 genera and 97 species have been recorded for Canada.

Licorice ferns with frost (*photo by Tim Fitzharris*).

Ferns show alternation of generations, ie, a sexual stage (gametophyte) alternates with an asexual, spore-producing stage (sporophyte). Each stage is an independent plant. Spores are produced in spore cases, which may be naked on a leafless branch, as in primitive *Ophioglossum* and *Botrychium;* arranged in clusters (sori) on the backs or margins of sometimes drastically modified leaflets (pinnae), as in several families, eg, Polypodiaceae, Schizaeaceae; or in fruiting bodies (sporocarps), as in *Azolla* and *Marsilea*. Spores germinate to form tiny, often heart-shaped plants (prothallia) that bear antheridia (structures producing sperm) and archegonia (structures producing eggs). The prothallia are the gametophyte generation. Fertilization of the egg, and subsequent development, produces the familiar fern plant, the sporophyte generation, and completes the life cycle. Many ferns also reproduce vegetatively (eg, by buds on roots or fronds).

Most ferns are tropical or subtropical; *Woodsia ilvensis, W. alpina, W. glabella, Cystopteris fragilis* and *Dryopteris fragrans* grow in Canada's arctic islands. Ferns are usually terrestrial; some, such as *Polypodium glycyrrhiza* of coastal BC, are partly or wholly epiphytic (growing on other plants); others, such as *Marsilea* and *Azolla*, are aquatic, the latter free floating. Habitats are usually moist. Most Canadian ferns grow in wooded regions, but bracken (*Pteridium aquilinum*) and hay-scented fern (*Dennstaedtia punctilobula*) thrive in open areas. Species of *Pellaea*, with leatherlike blades, grow in dry crevices of cliffs.

Most Canadian ferns have relatively wide distributions. Some are restricted in range: curly grass, *Schizaea pusilla*, grows in *Sphagnum* moss or wet depressions in NS and Newfoundland; netted chain fern, *Woodwardia areolata*, in southern NS; hart's tongue fern, *Phyllitis scolopendrium*, is associated with the limestone of the Niagara Escarpment; polypody, *Polypodium scouleri*, grows along the BC coast, often in reach of salt spray; filmy fern, *Mecodium wrightii*, forms mats on shaded cliff faces and tree bases from the Alaska Panhandle to Vancouver I.

Ferns have little economic value, but many are beautiful. Edible FIDDLEHEADS or ostrich fern, *Matteuccia struthiopteris*, are gathered commercially in NB; this species is also used in foundation plantings. Boston fern, *Nephrolepis exaltata* var. *bostoniensis*, is a common houseplant. Some woodland ferns are excellent for cool, moist, shaded gardens. Bracken, sometimes eaten as a green, has been shown to be carcinogenic in rats

Sporedots on the underside of a fern leaf (*courtesy National Museums of Canada/National Museum of Natural Sciences/G.L. Christie*).

and responsible for livestock diseases. It is not recommended for human consumption. W.J. CODY

Reading: W.J. Cody and D.M. Britton, *Ferns and Fern Allies of Canada* (1984).

Fernandes, João, explorer (*fl* 1486-1505). A Portuguese of the Azores, he had traded with Bristol from 1486. He likely sailed with John CABOT in 1498 as a pilot. Cabot's ship went down, but Fernandes returned with charts of discoveries around Greenland and Newfoundland. It is thought that the name Labrador derives from Fernandes's discoveries; he was likely the *labrador* ("landowner") of the Azores referred to in contemporary documents. He may later have taken part in the voyages of the CORTE-REAL brothers. JAMES MARSH

Fernie, BC, City, pop 5188 (1986c), 5444 (1981c), inc 1904, lies in the broad valley of the Elk R, between prominent mountain ranges, about 35 km N of its junction with the Kootenay R. It is 970 km E of Vancouver. Originally called Coal Creek, the city was later named for William FERNIE. It was founded in 1898 with the construction of the Crow's Nest Pass Ry. Wiped out by fire in 1908, it was rebuilt in impressive fashion. Referred to in its early years as the "Pittsburgh of the West," it became the centre for the region's coal mines, particularly Coal Creek Mines. At the end of WWI, 4500 people resided there. A recession followed that was prolonged by the switch from coal to oil on American railroads and intensified by the Great Depression. The first coal was shipped to Japanese steelmakers in 1970 and Fernie's economy today is dependent on coal-mining developments in the Elk Valley. The Snow Valley ski area is a popular attraction for local people and tourists from Alberta. WILLIAM A. SLOAN

Fernie, William, prospector, miner, entrepreneur (b at Kimbolton, Eng 2 Apr 1837; d at Victoria 15 May 1921). After travelling through Australasia and S America, he came to Vancouver I in 1860. He soon moved to the Kootenay district, where he worked as a miner, cattle rancher and in various provincial government posts, including that of gold commissioner 1873-82. In the summer of 1887, with his brother Peter, Fernie discovered coal while laying a trail through the CROWSNEST PASS. He became an original director of the Crow's Nest Pass Coal Co, promoter of the BC Southern Ry and founder of the BC city that bears his name. A bachelor, he retired to Victoria in 1906, where he was noted for his beautiful Oak Bay home and his philanthropy. PATRICIA E. ROY

Ferrer Maldonado, Lorenzo, apocryphal navigator, adventurer (b in Spain; d 1625). In 1601 he submitted to King Philip III of Spain a document about his purported 1588 voyage through the NORTHWEST PASSAGE from E to W. His descriptions bear little semblance to reality, though his account received some support from geographers. In 1791 the Spanish government diverted Alejandro Malaspina's expedition to search the NORTHWEST COAST for the passage's entrance. *See also* MALASPINA EXPEDITION. CHRISTON I. ARCHER

Ferret, Black-footed (*Mustela nigripes*), large WEASEL, probably extinct in Canada and almost so in the US. It is mink sized, long, slender and short legged. Males reach about 53 cm in length, females 10% less. They are sandy buff in colour, with face, neck, legs and tail tip dark-brown or black, and with white on the face, throat and underparts. The black-footed ferret was a prairie animal usually associated with PRAIRIE DOG towns, but ranged beyond them in southern Alberta and Saskatchewan. Food was prairie dogs, ground squirrels and other small mammals. In the US, it was virtually extirpated as a result of the prairie dog eradication program. Nothing is known of its reproductive biology. The last specimen taken in Canada was captured in 1937. The European ferret (*M. putorius*) has been introduced. *See also* ENDANGERED ANIMALS. IAN MCTAGGART-COWAN

Ferries are vessels that carry passengers and vehicles across a body of water, such as a lake, river or harbour, on a regular schedule. Simple ferries have operated across rivers and lakes for centuries. The earliest ferries were skiffs or rafts, rowed by oars, or towed by men or horses using ropes. The modern car ferry employs the roll-on, roll-off (RO-RO) method of loading and unloading vehicles through bow and stern doors. Although the Scandinavians claim to have pioneered the RO-RO concept, the first purpose-built RO-RO ferry was the *Motor Princess*, launched at Esquimalt, BC, in 1923 for Canadian Pacific. It ended its long career with British Columbia Ferry Corporation in the 1970s as the *Pender Queen*. The distinction between ferries and other vessels has become less clear during the past decade. The RO-RO method is used in many oceangoing cargo vessels, while ferries are being built larger and used on longer routes, necessitating the provision of staterooms and other passenger facilities similar to those provided on cruise ships and passenger liners.

In addition to car, truck and train ferries, there are also passenger-only ferries that generally operate over very short distances, such as across harbours (eg, Vancouver and Halifax). New marine technologies have increased the speed and efficiency of ferries. The *Abegweit*, a CN Marine ferry, has icebreaking capacity and is fitted with an air-bubbler system that eases the vessel through the ice by lubricating the sides with air. Hydrofoils, hovercraft and catamarans are all surface-effect ships that attempt to maximize speed by reducing the friction between water and hull. Hovercraft can attain speeds of 60 knots; hydrofoils and catamarans can attain 45 knots; whereas large, conventional car ferries generally operate at less than 22 knots.

The tremendous increase in the size of modern ferries has led to some safety concerns. The operational efficiency of ferries is largely the result of the vast, easily accessible car decks, but their very nature makes these car decks a potential danger. Should the deck become only slightly flooded, the vessel could become unstable very quickly owing to the tremendous weight of the water and its propensity to shift quickly on the wide-open deck. Although a flooded car deck is a rare event, this phenomenon has resulted in some quick capsizings in recent years, the most notable of which was the *Herald of Free Enterprise* disaster in 1987. Having failed to close its watertight doors, the vessel capsized in less than 2 minutes after taking water on its car deck just off Zeebrugge, Belgium. The loss of 188 lives has prompted regulatory authorities worldwide to re-evaluate safety measures for modern ferries.

Old ferry, Niagara, 1830, watercolour by J.P. Cockburn (*courtesy National Archives of Canada/C-40053*).

Operators of large ferries around the world include Sealink (operating between Britain, Ireland and Europe), Danish State Rail, Hong Kong and Yaumati Ferry Co, Washington State Ferries and the British Columbia Ferry Corporation. The largest ferries carry more than 2000 passengers and up to 700 vehicles on 3 car decks. To berth these large, new ferries most major ferry terminals are now equipped with ramps that enable vehicles to be loaded and unloaded from 2 decks simultaneously. The BC Ferry Corporation operates some of the busiest terminals in the world. It also has the 4 largest double-ended ferries in the world. The *Queen of Cowichan, Queen of Coquitlam, Queen of Surrey* and *Queen of Oak Bay* carry 1500 passengers, plus 360 cars on 3 decks, and travel at up to 22 knots. The term double-ended refers to the propellers at each end, which alleviate the necessity of turning the ferry around and backing into a dock. Because of the variety of services provided in Atlantic Canada, the CN Marine fleet includes vessels ranging from 30 m high-speed craft to a 148 m ship capable of carrying 39 railway freight cars; from vessels that take a dozen passengers with a load of cargo to others capable of carrying 1100 people and their automobiles, trucks and tractor trailers. Some vessels operate between 15 main terminals and others between 100 Newfoundland and Labrador outports, many of which have no other transportation link with the outside world.

In Canada there are also dozens of small ferries operating across rivers and lakes, eg, those plying Toronto Harbour to Centre I, or the service on Georgian Bay from Tobermory to Manitoulin I. Over the past 20 or 30 years, many of these small ferries have been replaced by bridges. The major ferry systems in the country, however, are saltwater operations. CN Marine, owned by the federal government, operates 18 ships on routes between Newfoundland, PEI, NS, NB and Maine. The Société des traversiers du Québec, owned by the province of Québec, operates 9 vessels on 6 routes across the St Lawrence R. The BC Ferry Corporation, owned by the province of BC, operates 38 vessels on 25 routes along the BC coast. The BC

CN ferry approaches the docks at Wood Island, PEI (*photo by Jim Merrithew*).

Ferry Corporation is a provincial crown corporation that receives a small federal subsidy (because one of its routes is an extension of the Trans-Canada Highway to Vancouver I), but the bulk of its subsidization comes from the provincial government. In Québec, the government ferries are a separate organization subsidized by the provincial government. CN Marine receives its entire subsidy from the federal government because it provides a transport link between provinces.

LEONARD ROUECHE

Ferron, Jacques, doctor, writer (b at Louiseville, Qué 20 Jan 1921; d at St-Lambert, Qué 22 Apr 1985). His father was a Liberal Party organizer, and Ferron (brother of Marcelle FERRON) was early attracted to political opposition. His earliest works, published in the late 1940s in Montréal newspapers and directed against the DUPLESSIS regime, carried the profoundly humanist and socialist stamp that helped earn him a reputation as the Voltaire of Québec letters. His commitment to socialist principles, partly owing to his first wife's affiliation with the Communist Party, was expressed in his involvement with left-wing magazines (*Situations, La Revue socialiste, Parti pris*) and in his political campaign as a candidate for the Co-operative Commonwealth Federation (CCF) in the 1958 federal election. He was later approached by the Rassemblement pour l'indépendance nationale and was a RIN candidate in the 1966 provincial election. Meanwhile, in 1963, he and friends founded the RHINOCEROS PARTY, which turned its main weapon – irony – on the increasingly dominant power of the federal government.

A remarkable and prolific stylist, Ferron tackled the full range of literary genres. He wrote some 20 plays, none frequently performed. Some are traditional intimist works (*L'Ogre, La Sortie*); others are theoretical reflections on drama as a genre (*Le Coeur d'une mère*); some are strongly nationalistic (*Les Grands Soleils, La Tête du roi*). Ferron used his experience as a physician in poor neighbourhoods as subject matter for most of his stories and novels. His narrative works all denounce the social and cultural alienation of the Québécois. These works mix memories with allusions to current events, thereby creating a new fiction that is peopled by both historical characters and imaginary beings (*Le Ciel de Québec, Papa Boss, Le Saint-Elias*), or puts the common people at the centre of the fictional universe (*Cotnoir, Les Roses sauvages, La Chaise du maréchal-Ferrant*), or is autobiographical (*Les Confitures de coings, L'Amélanchier*).

An observant and lucid chronicler, Ferron demonstrated his historical knowledge in a genre he rescued from oblivion: the satirical chronicle (*Historiettes, Du fond de mon arrière-cuisine, Escarmouches*). He wrote more than 1000 of these pieces, in almost sloganeering style, skilfully bringing irony and sarcasm to bear on Québec's political, social and literary life. In addition to these chronicles, Ferron wrote about 200 "letters to the editor," most of them directed to the Montréal dailies (*Le Canada, Le Devoir, La Presse*), in which he showed himself to be a critical and lucid observer of the last 40 years of Québec history. Ferron won several literary awards: the Gov Gen's Award in 1962 for *Contes du pays incertain;* the Prix France-Québec in 1972 for *Les Roses sauvages;* the Prix Duvernay also in 1972; and the Prix David in 1977.

PIERRE CANTIN

Ferron, Marcelle, artist (b at Louiseville, Qué 20 Jan 1924). Sister of Jacques FERRON, she was an active participant in Les AUTOMATISTES, led by Paul-Émile BORDUAS, and has pursued an innovative artistic career, where her work in stained glass is noteworthy. After studying at the École du Meuble in Montréal and the École des beaux-arts in Québec City, Ferron became part of Les Automatistes, signing that association's polemical manifesto REFUS GLOBAL. Her nonfigurative paintings were hung in all the major Automatiste exhibitions. She lived in Paris 1953-66 and continued to show in avant-garde exhibitions, including the 1961 São Paulo Biennial where she won the silver medal. The paintings of this dynamic artist became progressively more forceful. Vibrant colours and larger, fluid forms dominated the canvas. After 1964 her interest in light was effectively translated into a new medium – stained glass – examples of which can be seen in the Champ-de-Mars and Vendôme metro stations in Montréal. Ferron is represented in Canadian and foreign collections, including the Musée des beaux-arts de Montréal.

ANN DAVIS

Ferry Command was established early in WWII to improve aircraft deliveries to Britain from US factories, since surface shipping was too slow and the ships themselves were needed for other cargoes. Against the British Air Ministry's advice, Lord Beaverbrook (Maxwell AITKEN), the Canadian-born minister of aircraft production, asked Sir Edward BEATTY of the CPR to assemble an organization to fly new multiengined aircraft across the Atlantic. A handful of experienced transatlantic flyers from British Overseas Airways Corporation worked with servicemen and civilians of virtually every Allied nation from headquarters in Montréal. At the time, transatlantic flight was in its infancy, yet knowledgeable observers, believing such a scheme to be impossible, were proved wrong. The CP Air Services Department, established in July 1940, and its successors, Royal Air Force Ferry Command and No 45 Group of RAF Transport Command, eventually delivered more than 900 warplanes – losing only about 100 – and paved the way for mass postwar transatlantic air travel.

CARL A. CHRISTIE

Ferryland, Nfld, Community, pop 762 (1986c), 795 (1981c), inc 1971, is located 60 km S of St John's on the shores of a picturesque harbour, dominated by a large lighthouse. The name Ferryland is probably derived from the French (*forillon*) or Portuguese (*farelhao*) for "steep rock" or "reef," and was first noted on maps as early as 1529. A seasonal fishing station for migratory European fishing ships in the 1600s, Ferryland was founded in 1621 as the capital of the English colony of Avalon by George CALVERT, first Lord Baltimore. In 1638 it was forcibly possessed by David KIRKE and it remained in the immediate Kirke family until 1708, despite claims by Calvert's heirs. The fishing settlement was fortified from Baltimore's time, and was further fortified 1743, 1746, 1776 and 1812 during periods of Anglo-French and Anglo-American conflict. The predominantly English colony received a great influx of Irish fishing servants in the 1700s. In the 1800s it was a major supply and fishing centre, controlled by local and St John's merchants. Modern Ferryland is a fishing community that continues to be a regional services and administrative centre.

JANET E.M. PITT AND ROBERT D. PITT

Fertility, *see* POPULATION.

Fertilizer, any material, natural or manufactured, which may be added to the soil to supply plant nutrients. Fertilizers are most commonly used to provide 3 of the 17 elements essential for plant growth: nitrogen (N), phosphorus (P_2O_5) and potassium (K_2O). Other less commonly required elements are sulphur, calcium, magnesium, iron, copper, manganese, boron and zinc. Manufactured or commercial fertilizers are sold on the basis of the N, P_2O_5 and K_2O content (expressed as percentages) and usually contain a high proportion of one or more of these elements. For example, urea, a commonly used fertilizer, has the analysis 46-0-0, indicating that it contains 46% N but no P_2O_5 or K_2O. The 11-55-0 analysis of a commonly used ammonium-phosphate fertilizer indicates that it contains 11% N and 55% P_2O_5 but no K_2O.

Natural organic fertilizers (eg, barnyard MANURE, sewage sludge) are much lower in nutrient content and higher in bulk than are manufactured fertilizers. Manure, although variable in composition, commonly contains about 0.5% N, 0.25% P_2O_5, 0.5% K_2O and small amounts of other essential elements. It is an important fertilizer on livestock farms and may also be used on land close to large livestock-feeding enterprises. Because of their low nutrient content and high bulk, it is impractical to transport natural organic fertilizers long distances.

The use of manufactured commercial fertilizers is unavoidable in the agricultural systems of urbanized societies. Not surprisingly, where fertilizers are available at prices that farmers can afford, crop yields are much higher than in countries where very little fertilizer is used. In Canada the highest rates of fertilizer application are in eastern Canada; the lowest in the prairies.

R.A. HEDLIN

Fertilizer Industry

The fertilizer industry is one of the CHEMICAL INDUSTRIES. The major fertilizer types are potassium, nitrate and phosphate fertilizers; various sulphate compounds are also important. As each depends upon different chemical processes, each has a somewhat different history in Canada.

Nitrogen Fertilizers originally had to be derived from natural sources (eg, Chile's nitrate deposits). Large-scale synthetic nitrate production became possible after the 1908 discovery, by German chemists Fritz Haber and Carl Bosch, of a process for producing ammonia from atmospheric nitrogen and hydrogen. The process was applied to fertilizer production after WWI. The ammonia, known as anhydrous (ie, water-free) ammonia, may itself be used as a fertilizer or may be used to produce other fertilizers. For example, ammonium nitrate is produced by combining anhydrous ammonia and nitric acid; urea is produced by combining anhydrous ammonia and carbon dioxide from the atmosphere; ammonium phosphate is produced by combining anhydrous ammonia with phosphoric acid. In 1930, Cominco Ltd constructed an anhydrous ammonia plant at Trail, BC. Cominco Ltd became the world's first producer of granular fertilizers in 1932, of granular ammonium nitrate in 1963, and of granular urea in 1965.

Phosphate Fertilizers are made from phosphate rock (about 25% phosphorus), treated with sulphuric acid to produce phosphoric acid which, in turn, is used to manufacture fertilizers such as ammonium phosphate. Canada lacks suitable phosphate rock deposits and imports the rock, mainly from the US.

Potassium Fertilizer production in Canada began before the 19th century, with the manufacture of POTASH from wood ashes. The industry expanded until the late 19th century, when Germany became the world's major potash supplier. Potash deposits were found in Saskatchewan in 1943 but development did not begin until 1954, when the Potash Corporation of America sank the first shaft at Patience Lk, Sask. Of the major fertilizer companies, only Cominco Ltd is engaged in developing the potash resource; however, by the mid-1980s, potash mines had been developed in Sussex, NB, and Salt Springs, NB, by the Potash Corporation of America and Dennison Mines, respectively.

Sulphate Compounds Sulphuric acid was first produced from metallic sulphides in 1866 and, in the 1920s, sulphuric acid production from base metal smelter gases began at Sudbury, Ont, and Trail. The first sour-gas recovery plant in Canada was built in 1951, and there are now 45 such plants in Alta, 3 in BC and one in Sask. Cominco Ltd, Sherritt Gordon and Esso Chemical produce sulphur dioxide gas as a by-product of their mining and gas operations. This gas was first emitted into the atmosphere, but because of its dangerously high concentration government controls were instituted to limit emissions. In addition to being used to produce phosphate fertilizers, sulphur dioxide gas is combined with water to produce sulphuric acid, which is mixed with anhydrous ammonia to produce ammonium sulphate.

S.R. MacMillan

Fessenden, Reginald Aubrey, radio inventor (b at Milton-Est, Canada E 6 Oct 1866; d at Hamilton, Bermuda 22 July 1932). After attending Bishop's U, Fessenden joined Thomas Edison's laboratory in 1886 and later worked for Westinghouse, the US Weather Service and 2 American universities, making several fundamental discoveries in radio, including the superheterodyne principle, the basis of all modern broadcasting. In 1902 Fessenden formed his own company. In 1906 he achieved 2-way voice transmission by radio between Machrihanish, Scot, and Brant Rock, Mass (Marconi had sent radio signals from England to Newfoundland in 1901, but only one way and in Morse code). On Christmas Eve 1906 Fessenden made the first public broadcast of music and voice. In 1910 he lost control of his company and thereafter lived in relative seclusion, although continuing his research. Many of his patents were widely adopted (without his consent) during WWI, and in 1928, in recognition of his contributions to radio technology, the US Radio Trust paid him $2.5 million.

Donald J.C. Phillipson

Reading: O. Raby, *Radio's First Voice* (1970).

Festival Lennoxville opened in 1972 at bishop's university in the Eastern Townships of Québec. Drama department chairman David Rittenhouse and director William Davis founded it to present new productions of outstanding Canadian plays staged earlier by other theatres across the country. Their first season included Ann Henry's *Lulu Street,* George ryga's *Captives of the Faceless Drummer,* and Mavor moore's *The Ottawa Man.* Robertson davies's *A Jig for the Gypsy* and *Hunting Stuart,* Lister sinclair's *The Blood is Strong* and Ted Allan's *The Secret of the World* were 4 older plays revived. Plays by Michael cook, Sharon pollock, Betty Lambert, David Freeman, Herschel Hardin and Michel tremblay were presented. Richard Ouzounian, artistic director from 1978 to 1980, had to adopt a more commercial version of the original policy, selecting more musicals and comedies to attract larger audiences and increase revenue. Festival Lennoxville cancelled its 1981 season to reduce its deficit and to give new artistic director Scott Swan time to plan. However, in spite of Swan's efforts to design a repertoire that would appeal to both anglophone and francophone audiences, Festival Lennoxville closed permanently after a truncated 1982 season.

Ross Stuart

Festival Singers of Canada Founded in 1954 by Elmer iseler as the Festival Singers of Toronto, the chorus reached professional status in 1968 when it became the core of the toronto mendelssohn choir. Early concerts brought the 25 singers recognition and, expanded to 36 voices, the choir performed regularly on the CBC and soon won international acclaim. A 1967 performance in the White House, Washington, DC, was the beginning of tours which, in 1971, 1972 and 1977, took the choir to Britain, France, Germany, Austria, Yugoslavia and the USSR. Further concerts were performed in the US in 1972, 1976 and 1977, in western Canada in 1974 and 1977, and in eastern Canada in 1975. The repertoire included music of all periods and styles, with emphasis on Canadian choral music. The Festival Singers commissioned and premiered compositions by Canadian composers, bringing an artistry to the performance that earned the selections a place in universal choral literature. Recordings made by the choir reflected this varied repertoire. In 1978 Giles Bryant succeeded Iseler as director, one year before the chorus suspended activities.

Isabelle Margaret Mills

Festivals began in antiquity as religious and ritual observance of the seasons, often including sacred community meals or feasts. Today, festivals are held to commemorate, celebrate or reenact events and seasons. Close to 200 major and numerous minor festivals are held in Canada each year. These celebrations have both indigenous and borrowed sources. Long before European contact, the native people marked seasonal changes with religious festivals. Among the ojibwa there were 2 thanksgiving celebrations, one in spring at the rising of the sap to give thanks for deliverance from winter, and one in fall at harvest time. On the NW Coast there were potlatches (ceremonial feasts marked by lavish gift giving), and among the Plains Indians, powwows are still held as social events to maintain and promote their culture. Religious observances marked festivals imported from Europe in the 17th century. From the earliest days of colonization, French-speaking settlers celebrated, on June 24, the Fête St Jean-Baptiste, a Christian overlay to earlier pagan celebrations of the summer solstice.

Since the climate strongly shapes the Canadian way of life, it is not surprising to find these ancient threads of seasonal celebration in festivals held today. The awakening of nature after the winter provides the focus for several spring festivals. In NS, there is the annual Annapolis Valley Apple Blossom Festival; in Ontario's fruit belt the Niagara Falls Blossom Festival, featuring horticultural exhibits and the Blossom Festival Parade; and in BC the Creston Blossom Festival. Other spring events are the maple syrup festivals held in April in Ontario, NS and Québec. There are 32 held in southern Ontario alone, and in Plessisville, Qué, the Maple Syrup Festival is held in the heart of Québec's maple sugar belt. Here numerous sugaring-off parties celebrate the process of converting maple syrup into sugar. Tied to history as much as the season is the week-long Festival of Spring (Tulip Festival) held in Ottawa each year. To express her thanks to Canadians for their hospitality during her war exile, Queen Juliana of the Netherlands gave 10 000 tulip bulbs to the city. The royal family of Holland and the tulip producers continue to send 25 000 bulbs each year, which bloom as an annual reminder.

The warm weather lingers briefly in Canada and more festivals are held in summer than in any other season. Food is the focus of many: potatoes, strawberries, salmon and shrimp, blueberries, oysters and trout are all feted where they are grown or harvested. In mid-July, the NS Pictou Lobster Carnival marks the end of the lobster-fishing season, with fishermen's boat races a reminder of the traditional way of letting off steam after gruelling weeks at sea. Outdoor seafood suppers add to the festivities. In late July in Altona, Manitoba, there is the annual Sunflower Festival highlighting agriculture, with displays of sunflower seeds and also Mennonite cooking. In August, at L'Anse Amour in Labrador, the annual Bakeapple Festival celebrates the tasty bakeapple berry, with food, dancing and storytelling. Pine Days in Pine Point, NWT, in mid-June, has a more unusual focus. During a 2-day celebration, residents and visitors celebrate the longest day of the year in the land of the midnight sun, with horseshoe tournaments and canoe jousting.

By fall, there are fewer seasonal festivals. These are held in recognition of the coming hard winter months, and in thanksgiving for the harvests. In the European tradition, Oktoberfests are held in many communities, particularly in areas where German immigrants have settled. One notable event is the Kitchener-Waterloo Oktoberfest in Ontario, attracting many students to a last fling before hard studying begins. And in Rimouski, Qué, the Fall Festival focuses on the relationship between man and the land. Survival skills are emphasized with a pheasant hunt and a clay pigeon shooting contest.

As a relief from winter, several festivals, usually beginning in late January and lasting through April in northernmost latitudes, ease the notorious "cabin fever." Most famous is the Québec Winter Carnival, a pre-Lenten celebration which first ran from 1894 to 1900 and was revived during the 1950s. The symbol of the carnival is a talking snowman, "Bonhomme Carnaval," who holds court in an ice palace and comes out to celebrate with the crowds. Ottawa holds the 10-day Winterlude festival along the rideau canal, one of the world's most famous skating rinks.

In Whitehorse, YT, a Sourdough Rendezvous features dogsled and snowshoe races (and more modern competition between snowmobiles), contests for flour-packing, and 1898 costumes and beards. The namesake food, first eaten in the north by prospectors, is featured at sourdough hotcake breakfasts. Most festivals in the Far North test survival skills, such as tea-making and animal-skinning under frigid conditions; these are featured activities at gatherings such as the Hay River, NWT, Ookpik Carnival and Yellowknife's Caribou Carnival.

As nature was tamed and European civilization took root, Canadians began to look back and started celebrating the events that formed the country. St John's Day celebrations in Newfoundland commemorate the day (24 June 1497) when John Cabot first sailed into the quiet water off the coast of Newfoundland. Loyalist Days in Saint John, NB, commemorates the arrival (1783) of 4200 United Empire Loyalists, fleeing the aftermath of the American Revolution. On Prince Edward Island, Charlottetown Natal Day, in June, honours both the birth of the city (1855) and the fact that Charlottetown is the birthplace of Canada, as the setting for meetings of the fathers of confederation.

In Ontario in August, Simcoe Day honours the first governor of what was then Upper Canada, as well as the beginnings of the province in the 1790s. The opening of the Canadian West is celebrated with events such as Winnipeg's Red River Exhibition in June, Saskatoon's Pioneer Days in July, and Edmonton's Klondike Days, looking back to the late 1890s when prospectors surged north from the city in search of gold. In the Yukon, Discovery Day, held in August, commemorates the 1896 founding of dawson City on the last frontier.

Another mark of Canadian development is multiculturalism, which has fostered the growth of many ethnic and multicultural festivals celebrating heritage and ancestry. Appropriately,

Canada's original peoples celebrate with various Indian Days festivities held across Canada. In Ontario, the Brantford Six Nations Indian Pageant in August features crafts and theatre based on native history. The Opasquia Indian Days in The Pas, Man, is organized by residents of the Opasquia reserve to spotlight native woodland games, traditional foods, crafts and canoe races. In the NWT the unique ARCTIC WINTER GAMES are celebrated each year, roving from town to town, with Inuit and Dene sports, dances, drumming, competitions and displays. The Fête acadienne in PEI celebrates French settlement on Île St-Jean (as PEI was first called). The distinctive nature of Acadian culture is illustrated in festivities that include Acadian drama, song, fiddling and step-dancing contests, and in NB's Foire Brayonne (celebrated late July) founded in 1979 to showcase folksinging and culture. In Manitoba in June there is the Fête Franco-Manitobaine, celebrating the French presence in Manitoba, dating from the mid-1700s. Folk concerts in the traditional boîte-à-chanson style, French Canadian dancing and food are part of the entertainment. In Québec, there are events such as Sherbrooke's Festival des cantons and Québec City's annual Festival d'été.

Other groups who helped build Canada also pay tribute to their ancestral heritage. In NS, descendants of Scottish settlers celebrate throughout the summer. In Pugwash, the Gathering of the Clans with caber tossing and drum and pipe-band contests is the first event of the season, followed by the Antigonish HIGHLAND GAMES in July and the Festival of Tartans in New Glasgow in Aug. The influence of Ukrainian settlers was felt most on the Prairies, and in Dauphin, Man, Canada's fifth-largest ethnic group hosts Canada's National Ukrainian Festival. At Gimli, Man, where a self-governing New Iceland flourished 1875-81, the Icelandic Festival or Islendingadagurinn is held each year with parades, songs and poetry.

The newest entrants on the festival calendar are the multicultural festivals: Toronto's Caravan, Winnipeg's Folklorama, Regina's Mosaic and Edmonton's Heritage Days. All gather together and share the food, culture and spirit of the various ethnic groups. The Canadian Heritage Festival is an annual amateur folkloric performing arts event co-sponsored by the federal government and the host province, while the Festival de Drummondville in Québec, which has added the word "folklothèque" to the French language, annually celebrates folklore and popular culture, including that of the local Abenaki people. Heritage festivals are often held in conjunction with other major events (Olympic Games, Montréal, 1976; Saskatchewan's 75th Anniversary, 1980; Newfoundland's 400th Anniversary in 1983).

Other aspects of culture (art, music, theatre and film) have come to be celebrated in Canada as well. Festivals such as the Guelph Spring Festival in Ontario focus on music; the Banff Festival of the Arts in Alberta encompasses music, theatre and art. Individual styles of music are also celebrated: Toronto's Mariposa Folk Festival, the Winnipeg Folk Festival and the Festival International de Jazz in Montréal or Jazz City in Edmonton are 4 examples. Other festivals focus on styles and eras of music: baroque, classical and religious music are the themes of several smaller gatherings held in Ontario each summer, while a newer celebration, the Montréal New Music Festival, features roots rock, ska, and electronic pop. Canadian theatre festivals have also grown up over the years in cottage country, finding ready audiences among vacationers from the cities. Others are long-established traditions drawing international audiences: the STRATFORD FESTIVAL in Ontario, founded in 1953, and the SHAW FESTIVAL, at Niagara-on-the-Lake, established in 1962, both balance Canadian and international works. A newer festival is Edmonton's Fringe Festival, featuring short works and street theatre. All summer long, the CHARLOTTETOWN SUMMER FESTIVAL celebrates theatre (*see* MUSICAL THEATRE), and in St John's, the Summer Festival is a well-known mecca for theatre lovers. And in Québec, festivals commemorate related art forms, such as mime, at the Festival international de mime — Montréal, and humour, Festival Juste pour rire. Film has also attracted followers and is now fêted: the World Film Festival in Montréal each Aug and Toronto's Festival of Festivals in Sept feature new international and Canadian films and retrospectives of genres, performers and directors.

Other festival celebrations range from the CANADIAN NATIONAL EXHIBITION in Toronto, the world's oldest and largest permanent exhibition, to the CALGARY STAMPEDE (July), calling itself the Greatest Outdoor Show on Earth with 10 days of World Cup Rodeo and chuckwagon races; and from Vancouver Island's All Sooke Day in July, celebrating pioneering woodsmen with log rolling, tree chopping, high rigging and axe throwing, to Yellowknife's Annual Midnight Golf Tournament, another commemoration of the longest day of the year. Whatever the season, the day, the occasion or the people, Canadians show with their festivals that they have much to celebrate. *See also* FOLK FESTIVALS. DEBORAH C. SAWYER

Feux Follets, Les, begun as an amateur folk ensemble in the 1950s, it turned professional in 1964. Its repertoire, at the insistence of founding director Michel Cartier, was inspired by indigenous native lore and historical events. In 1972 the troupe became associated with the CHARLOTTETOWN SUMMER FESTIVAL under artistic director Alan LUND. Feux follets, meaning "dancing fire" or "fireflies," was recognized for its lavish costumes, stage sets and special effects. It has not presented public performances since 1975. CAROL BISHOP

Fiddlehead, The, LITERARY MAGAZINE fd 1945 at Fredericton, NB, by A.G. BAILEY as a mimeographed in-house organ of the Bliss Carman Poetry Society. Prominent in the magazine's early years were Bailey, Elizabeth BREWSTER, Fred COGSWELL, Frances Firth, Donald Gammon (the first editor), Robert Gibbs, Desmond PACEY, Robert Richards and A. Robert Rogers. During its early years, the magazine reflected strongly both the poetic techniques of T.S. Eliot and W.B. Yeats and those masters' desire to fuse the present with the traditional past through the use of myth and symbol. In 1952, to fill a publishing vacuum among Canadian magazines, *The Fiddlehead* was converted to an international magazine of poetry and issued in a printed format. Between 1952 and 1966, under Cogswell, it became a quarterly, added a book review section, undertook to publish prose fiction, and established a reputation for eclecticism. In 1967 the magazine became officially the property of UNB; editorial and managerial duties were subdivided among individuals connected with the university and, after a brief flirtation with monthly publication, the magazine continued as a quarterly with an expanded and improved format. FRED COGSWELL

Fiddlehead Greens (*Matteuccia struthiopteris*), edible plant of the FERN family (Polypodiaceae) considered a delicacy in parts of Canada. The new leaves are tightly coiled and look like violin-tuning heads (hence the name). The shoot and main axis uncoil upwards; the lateral parts, outwards. This perennial fern, also called ostrich fern, sends up a ring of leaves from a circular, brownish rootstock. It should not be confused with the bracken fern, which is carcinogenic and sends up a single leaf from below ground. Fiddleheads are most popular in the Maritimes. The MALISEET in NB, with a long tradition of harvesting this delicacy, considered it medicine as well as food. In BC it remains part of the diet of coastal Indians. Ostrich fern grows in moist, rich soil (bottomlands, swamps) and in alluvial areas alongside streams across Canada. The fern propagates through spores released from under the leaves, or through the rootstock, which spreads numerous underground runners. The growing season is restricted to a few weeks around the beginning of May. Fiddleheads are best harvested when young shoots are 10-20 cm high, leaving 2 or 3 leaves so that the clump will not be weakened. Commercial demand far exceeds supply because the fern has not yet been successfully cultivated on a large scale. It is sold frozen out of season. Fiddleheads are eaten raw or cooked. Raw fiddleheads contain the enzyme thiaminase which attacks vitamin B when ingested in sufficient quantities; therefore, caution is recommended. NICOLE BERNSHAW

Fiddlehead greens (*Matteuccia struthiopteris*) grow in alluvial lands alongside streams across Canada. They are harvested commercially for a few weeks around the beginning of May (*photo by Bill Ivy*).

Fidler, Peter, fur trader, mapmaker, explorer (b at Bolsover, Eng 16 Aug 1769; d at Fort Dauphin [Man] 17 Dec 1822). Long obscured by his contemporary, David THOMPSON, Fidler has come to be recognized for his contribution to the mapping of western Canada. Fidler joined the HUDSON'S BAY CO as a labourer in 1788 and was appointed chief surveyor and mapmaker in 1796. His surveys took him to Lk Athabasca and Great Slave Lk (1790-92), the foothills of the Rockies (1792-93), N Manitoba (1793-95) and the Assiniboine R (1795-96). After 3 years as a trader at YORK FACTORY and on the Saskatchewan R, he was sent to spearhead competition against the NORTH WEST CO on the Beaver R (1799-1800), S Saskatchewan R (1800-02) and Lk Athabasca (1802-06). Two years completing surveys around Lk Winnipeg and REINDEER LK were followed by 3 difficult ones competing against the NWC on the Churchill R. After leave in England, he served the company in the Red River area until his death; his last job as a surveyor was to lay out river lots for the RED RIVER COLONY. JOHN S. NICKS

Field Hockey is a stick-and-ball goal game of 11 players per team, with many of its rules patterned after soccer. A noncontact game, its distinctive features are a stick, of which only one side can be used to play the ball, and an obstruction rule that prohibits a player from turning between the ball and a nearby opponent. The game's origins are lost in antiquity. As an organized team sport, it developed in England, the first club being formed sometime before 1861. Women in the British Isles started playing the game late in the 19th century, and it spread throughout the world, played as much by women as by men.

In Canada, field hockey is generally restricted to spring, summer and early autumn seasons, except in southwestern BC, where it can be played year-round. It is principally a girls' sport in schools, but is played by both men and women in adult leagues across the country. In 1980, there were approximately 2500 adult players in Canada. The modern form of field hockey was first played in BC; in 1896, the first recorded match in Canada was played by Vancouver girls, and the Vancouver Ladies Club was formed. Men were also playing at the turn of the century in Vancouver and Victoria, and a Vancouver league was in existence in 1902. The first women's organization in Canada was formed in Vancouver in 1927. During the first half of the 20th century, field hockey was played on Vancouver I and in the Vancouver area, and contests were recorded with teams from California and Australia in the 1930s.

After WWII, the immigration of players to Canada from all parts of the British Commonwealth influenced the establishment of field hockey across the country, and by 1959 the game was being played in the Maritimes, Ontario and Alberta. The Canadian (men's) Field Hockey Assn was founded in 1961; the Canadian Women's FHA a year later. International contests have increased markedly since the 1950s. The Canadian women's team participated in the women's international tournament for the first time in 1956, and in 1979 Canada hosted 18 countries in Vancouver for that world event; Canada placed 8th. The 1978 Canadian team was the first to enter the Women's World Cup, placing 5th; since then the team has finished 2nd in 1983 (Malaysia) and 3rd in 1986 (Amsterdam). The women's team placed 5th in the 1984 Olympic Games at Los Angeles and took the bronze medal at the 1987 Pan-Am Games. The men's team first qualified for the Olympic Games in 1964, and placed 10th in 1984. The team qualified for the World Cup in 1977, and placed 10th in 1986 (London, Eng). They have also participated in the Pan-Am Games, placing 4th in 1967, 3rd in 1971, 2nd in 1975 and 1979, and 1st in 1983. In the 1987 games after a promising preliminary-round performance, the team was unable to win any playoff medals. BARBARA SCHRODT

Fielding, William Stevens, journalist, politician, premier of NS (b at Halifax 24 Nov 1848; d at Ottawa 23 June 1929). He rose from clerk to managing editor of Halifax's *Morning Chronicle* by 1874 and retained that post until he became premier in 1884. Concerned with the province's precarious economic condition and the refusal of federal assistance, he led his Liberal Party – pledged to withdrawal from Confederation – to victory in 1886. When he failed in his pledge, he attempted to rescue the province's economy by developing its coal resources. In 1896 he resigned as premier to become the minister of finance and receiver general in LAURIER's government. Apart from lowering the tariff against British goods (called the Fielding, or imperial preferential, tariff), Fielding retained the high tariff policy of his Conservative predecessors. In 1910 he negotiated a reciprocity agreement with the US, but when it was opposed in Parliament an election was called for Sept 1911. Fielding and his party were defeated, and he accepted the editorship of Montréal's *Daily Telegraph*. Seen as Laurier's successor, Fielding's support of CONSCRIPTION cost him the leadership of his party in 1919, when Mackenzie KING won by 38 votes on the third ballot. After King became PM in 1921, Fielding resumed his position as minister of finance for 4 years.
CARMAN MILLER

Fields, John Charles, mathematician (b at Hamilton 14 May 1863; d at Toronto 9 Aug 1932). Educated at U of T (BA, 1884) and Johns Hopkins U (PhD, 1887), Fields taught mathematics for 4 years in Pennsylvania, then continued his studies at Paris, Göttingen and Berlin. On his return to Toronto (1902), he was appointed a lecturer in the mathematics department at U of T, becoming Research Professor of Mathematics in 1923. Fields was an ardent campaigner for both business and state support for scientific research, taking his message to the Canadian Manufacturers' Assn and boards of trade. He was active in the creation of the School of Graduate Studies at U of T, and the ONTARIO RESEARCH FOUNDATION. Fields was instrumental in arranging the first postwar meeting of the International Congress of Mathematicians (1924), at which he presided. With funds left from organizing the meeting, he attempted to establish a mathematics prize to be awarded at congress meetings, held every 4 years. These efforts resulted in the Fields Medal, named in his honour and first awarded in 1932. Fields was elected a fellow of the Royal Soc of Canada (1909), of London (1913), and to honorary membership in nearly all the world's mathematical societies, including the Academy of Sciences, USSR. He was president of the Royal Canadian Institute, 1919-25. MARGARET E. MCCALLUM

Fife, David, farmer, wheat breeder (b at Kincardine, Scot 1805; d near Peterborough, Ont 9 Jan 1877). Fife immigrated to Otonabee, UC, with his parents in 1820. In 1842 he planted seeds of wheat obtained by a friend in Scotland from Danzig [Gdansk, Poland]. All but one plant perished over the winter and most of the survivor was eaten by a cow, but the remaining seeds, later identified as Galician, produced plants of better rust resistance, threshing quality, yield and flour than previously available. At first distributed locally, the strain was used widely after 1848, becoming the leader in Ontario by 1851 and virtually replacing all others there by 1860. The strain, eventually known as Red Fife, was also popular in the US and was introduced into Manitoba about 1870, ranking as the leading variety there from 1882 to 1909. Red Fife served as the male parent of the Marquis strain which proved more frost tolerant and even less susceptible to rusts, allowing wheat farming in Manitoba to spread farther W and N. MARTIN K. MCNICHOLL

Fifth Business, novel by Robertson DAVIES (New York and Toronto, 1970; London, 1971). The first of 3 novels called the Deptford Trilogy opens with Percy Staunton throwing a snowball at Dunstable Ramsay but hitting the pregnant Mary Dempster, causing the premature birth of Paul. These characters' fates intertwine for the rest of their lives. When Dunstable is gravely injured in WWI, he associates an apparition of a saintly figure with Mary Dempster. Ramsay returns to Canada, becomes a historian and hagiographer (a writer of the lives of saints) and tells the story of his self-discovery, which occurred through encounters with an unusual cast of characters. As he discovers he is "fifth business" (ie, an actor in a secondary role, but who is nevertheless essential to the development of a drama), Ramsay gains deep insight into the mysterious relations between myth and history, spirit and flesh, fiction, fact and faith. *Fifth Business* has been translated into French, as *Cinquième emploi* (Montréal, 1975), and Polish.
NEIL BESNER

Figure Skating is a sport for solo and pair skaters, in which style and technical skill are tested. Competition is conducted in single skating for men and women, pairs skating and ice dancing. Single skaters are judged in school figures, a short program with prescribed elements of free skating, and an original program of free skating. Pairs perform in compulsory and free-skating sections. Ice dancers demonstrate skill in compulsory dances, original set pattern dance and free dance, with no jumps, spins or lifts above the waist, and partners separate only to change positions. International competition in figure skating is organized by the International Skating Union, founded in 1892. The most important championships are the Olympic Games, and the world and European championships. The N American championships (last held in 1971) were also a top-ranked event. Among the important international invitational competions is Skate Canada, first staged in 1973. In world championships and Olympic Games, the number of entries are determined by previous results, with a maximum of 3 entries allowed per nation for each event.

Figure skating, in which prescribed patterns or figures are etched on the ice with precision, began to evolve after 1742, when the Edinburgh Skating Club was established. In the 1880s the centre of the activity became St Moritz, Switzerland, where skaters from Great Britain developed more figures and established a graduated system of figure tests. Meanwhile, free skating was being promoted by the "Viennese" school, a more theatrical approach that incorporated elements of dance with jumps and spins. Jackson Haines, an American ballet master, introduced music to the ice in the 1860s, producing the style that became free skating. Organized ice dancing dates from the 1880s in Vienna, and the waltz was danced on ice in Halifax as early as 1885. The first official world championship in figure skating for men was held in St Petersburg, Russia, in 1896. Separate women's championships began in 1906, with pairs starting 2 years later. World ice-dancing championships date from 1952.

In Canada, what was then called "fancy" skating began to develop a strong following in the 1860s, in part inspired by Haines, who toured eastern and central Canada in 1864. Exhibitions were staged at the opening of new rinks, and gala balls and carnivals were frequently held at the Victoria Rink in Montréal. F. Perkins, of Toronto, was the leading skater of this period and won the Gold Medal of Canada in 1867. That same year, the Montreal Skating Club offered a championship cup for amateurs, "open to the world." The most important Canadian figure skater in the late 1800s was Louis RUBENSTEIN, who won the unofficial world championship in St Petersburg, Russia, in 1890. He also won the United States amateur title in 1885 and 1889. George Meagher of Montréal won an open competition in 1891 that was claimed as the world championship. Figure skating grew in popularity during the next decades, and in 1903 the Minto prizes were presented by Governor General Lord MINTO to encourage the development of skilful performance in figures.

In 1914, figure skating was recognized as a separate sport, distinct from speed skating, with the formation of the Figure Skating Department of Canada as a section of the Amateur Skating Assn of Canada. Louis Rubenstein was the first president, and the membership consisted of the Minto Skating Club of Ottawa and the Earl Grey Skating Club of Montréal. In 1939, the department be-

World gold medalist pair, Barbara Underhill and Paul Martini, Ottawa, 1984 (*photo by Jim Merrithew*).

came the Canadian Figure Skating Assn, which became autonomous in 1951 with direct affiliation to the International Skating Union. Although figure skating had been included in the Olympic Games since 1908, Canadians did not participate until 1924, when the first Winter Olympic Games were held in Chamonix, France. Cecil Smith and Melville Rogers were Canada's first participants. Smith was also the first woman to represent Canada in any Olympic event, and when she placed 2nd in the 1930 women's world championship, she became the first Canadian woman to earn a top position in international figure-skating competition. In 1932, the world championships were held in Canada for the first time (in Montréal), and the Canadian skaters, Montgomery WILSON and Constance Wilson-Samuel, placed 2nd and 3rd, respectively, in their singles events. That same year, Wilson won the bronze medal in the Olympic Games at Lake Placid; as Canadian men's champion, he has been unequalled, winning that title 8 times between 1929 and 1939.

After WWII, Barbara Ann SCOTT of Ottawa established Canada as an important figure-skating nation. She won her first Canadian title in 1944 at age 15, and was such an excellent skater that in 1947 she became world champion in her first attempt at overseas competition. In 1948 she won the Canadian, US, N American, European and world championships as well as the Olympic gold medal. In 1948, the Olympic bronze medal win by Suzanne Morrow and Wallace Diestelmeyer began an era of outstanding pairs combinations from Canada. Frances Dafoe and Norris Bowden won the world championship in 1954 and 1955, and placed 2nd in the 1956 Olympics. Barbara WAGNER and Robert PAUL won their first of 4 consecutive pairs world titles in 1957; in 1960 they became the first non-European pair to win the Olympic title. Maria and Otto Jelinek followed with a 1962 world championship win, and Debbie Wilkes and Guy Revell placed 2nd in the 1964 Olympics. In the late 1970s, Canadian junior pairs made excellent showings in the world junior championships. Outstanding Canadian singles men skaters include Donald JACKSON who placed 3rd in the 1960 Olympics and won the 1962 world championships, and Donald MCPHERSON who won the 1963 world title. The 1970s were dominated by the innovative skater Toller CRANSTON, Canadian champion from 1971 to 1976. He won the free-skating segment of the world championship 4 times and was awarded the bronze medal in the 1976 Olympics. A number of women skaters have also gained international recognition. Wendy Griner placed 2nd in the 1962 world championships, the same year that a young Petra BURKA demonstrated her potential by executing a triple salchow – the first by a woman in competition. Burka placed 3rd in the 1964 Olympics, and next year won the world championship. In the early 1970s, after overcoming stress fractures in both legs, Karen MAGNUSSEN placed 2nd in the 1972 Olympics and won the 1973 world title.

In the 1980s, Canadian skaters were again among the world's best. In 1984, Barbara UNDERHILL of Oshawa, Ont, and Paul MARTINI of Woodbridge, Ont, culminated a long career by winning the world pairs championship in Ottawa. Brian ORSER of Belleville, Ont, holder of the Canadian senior title from 1981, placed third in the world championship in 1983, followed by 3 years in second place and a silver medal at the 1984 Olympic Games. Then, in 1987, he won the world title, the first competitor to complete 3 triple axels successfully in one program.

The CFSA, the association responsible for amateur figure skating in Canada, is the largest of its kind in the world. From 2 clubs in 1914, it grew to a membership of 360 in 1967, and 1410 in 1986. There were 156 143 skaters registered with affiliated clubs in 1986. The CFSA National Skating Test program operates 8 tests, from preliminary to gold. In 1977, a system was introduced to separate test and competitive skaters, and the program is used to determine the eligibility of skaters for novice events, the first stage of competition. Only skaters registered with a CFSA affiliated club may try official tests. The CFSA also operates courses for amateur and professional coaches.

BARBARA SCHRODT

Reading: N. Brown, *Ice Skating: A History* (1959).

Filibuster, the use of delaying tactics, used most often by the Opposition, in a parliamentary body. Opposition filibusterers speak as often and as long as possible, raising many points of privilege and order to prevent votes they expect to lose. Their aim is to kill the government's bill or motion, to create the impression that chaos reigns, or to cause an election – possibly all 3. Filibustering is also resorted to by the government, and is used effectively to resist the Opposition's proposals, eg, in "talking out" a bill. The length of a filibuster, or even whether one has occurred, is a matter of opinion. Generally accepted examples of filibusters in Parliament include the CPR bill, 1881; the Manitoba remedial bill, 1896; the reciprocity bill, 1911; the naval bill, 1913; the PIPELINE DEBATE, 1956; and the FLAG DEBATE, 1964. The CLOSURE rule was introduced to end the naval bill filibuster. *See also* ALLOTMENT OF TIME.

JOHN B. STEWART

Filion, Gérard, publisher (b on Île Verte, Qué 18 Aug 1909). Educated at Laval and Montréal's École des hautes études commerciales, he became editor of *Terre de chez nous* in 1935, and then secretary general of the Union des cultivateurs catholiques, the journal's proprietor. As publisher of *Le Devoir* (1947-63), French Canada's most renowned independent daily, Filion was able, with his editorial staff headed by a close friend, André LAURENDEAU, to make the paper the most vocal critic of Québec's Union Nationale government during the 1950s. Championing the modernization of Québec society at all levels, he helped redefine traditional FRENCH CANADIAN NATIONALISM by demanding the creation of an activist, interventionist Québec state to help the nascent French Canadian bourgeoisie gain control over Québec's economy through a range of state corporations. In the 1960s Filion promoted the modernization and secularization of education as a member of Québec's Royal Commission on Education, was VP and director general of the Société générale de financement du Québec, and headed several of Québec's provincial government corporations.

M. D. BEHIELS

Filion, Hervé, harness-racing trainer and driver (b at Angers, Qué 1 Feb 1940). Filion was the sixth child of a harness-racing family and drove his first race at age 12. Adept, aggressive and horse-wise, he became a leading driver at Aylmer's Connaught Park Raceway when only 17. He soon was a popular idol on Québec, Ontario and northern NY tracks. Ten times – from 1968 to 1978 – Filion was the leading N American driver. With more than 1 1/2 times the wins of his nearest competitor, he leads all drivers in life purse earnings. He is a member of the US Hall of Fame of the Trotter and the Canadian Horse Racing and Sports Halls of Fame, was named French-speaking athlete of the world, and won the LOU MARSH TROPHY as outstanding Canadian sportsman.

MARGARET NEAL

Filipinos The Philippines are an archipelago of 7083 islands off the Asian mainland with a population of about 56 million, some 80% of whom are Roman Catholics, 14% Protestants and 10% Muslims. Filipinos belong to the Indo-Malay group that spread out from the southern tip of Asia to settle as far as Polynesia in the South Pacific. The Philippines were a colony of Spain from 1564 to 1898, when they were ceded to the US following the SPANISH-AMERICAN WAR. Americans governed the country until 1941, when it was lost to Japan in WWII. It was subsequently retaken by the Americans and granted independence on 4 July 1946.

Filipinos were first reported as a separate listing in Canadian immigration statistics in 1965, when 1467 entered Canada, nearly twice the number admitted in the previous 2 decades. This new emphasis in the federal IMMIGRATION POLICY on

Canada's own labour needs enabled the skilled and well-trained Filipinos – the result of compulsory mass public education – to enter Canada in large numbers. Overpopulation and economic and political difficulties have inspired emigration, and by the late 1980s more than 90 000 Filipino citizens, generally young (20 to 34 years), predominantly female, well-educated, Roman Catholic and proficient in English, had entered Canada. A 1972 survey of Canadian Filipinos revealed that some 85% of immigrants held at least a BA degree. Their intended occupations were in health, manufacturing, and in the mechanical, sales, service and clerical categories. However, as parents and dependent minors joined the original migrants, the percentage of college graduates among the new arrivals decreased significantly. Filipinos usually settle in metropolitan areas, but not in ethnic enclaves. Because of their relatively high education and good incomes they have tended to become integrated into suburban communities. Over the past 20 years, more than 50% of all Filipino immigrants have settled in Ontario; about 60 000 have chosen Metro Toronto. Others settled in Manitoba, BC and Alberta.

Social and Cultural Life The Roman Catholic Church serves as the centre of much Filipino social interaction outside the home. The religious holidays are celebrated with traditional rites, featuring native songs and special foods and decorations. Most Filipino clubs and associations, which include the Filipino-Canada Assn and regional associations affiliated with the United Council of Filipino Assns, participate in festivals and civic celebrations. ELEANOR R. LAQUIAN

Filles du Roi, women of marriageable age who were shipped (the term is appropriate) to New France under royal auspices, 1663-73. As private interests preferred to send male indentured servants, the French state and religious communities had to rectify the imbalance of the sexes in the colonies. In Canada's case, although women began crossing in the 1630s, only the approximately 800 who disembarked during the first 11 years of royal government are commonly referred to as the *filles du roi*. Equipped with a trousseau and in some cases a small dowry, almost all found husbands quickly. Some were Parisian beggars and orphans; others were recruited from the La Rochelle and Rouen areas. Administrators' reports suggest that many were ill prepared for the arduous life of the Canadian peasant. TOM WIEN

Film A nation is rich in proportion to the pride it takes in its image of itself, an image that can be created most persuasively in our cinemas and on our TV screens. If an iconographical study were made of Canadian films of the 1960s and 1970s, whether French or English, certain images would recur. There would be many shots of landscapes depicting the vastness and beauty of the land. There would be the recurring presence of winter and streets clogged with snow, and there would be Canadian beer. Does this ubiquitous presence of beer in films suggest that Canada is a nation of drinkers? Does it suggest that the national cinema depicts the people living on the fringes of society, people from the regions, people out of work, more than it does the secure middle class? Or does it express a kind of pride that in this country, where so many industries are controlled by foreign interests, Canadians, at least in the 1960s and 1970s always used to drink Canadian beer? Any of these images can help us to see our cinema as our own, but because Canada is considered part of the American domestic market, Canadian films have no guaranteed access to our theatres and only intermittent access to our TV screens. When Canadian films appear, they are generally compared with the more familiar American

Nell Shipman, writer and star of the movie *Back to God's Country* (1919). The romantic adventure of an embattled heroine was released worldwide (*courtesy National Archives of Canada/MISA/4833*).

product. Like our dollar, films often are considered inferior rather than different. Most Canadians do not see Canadian films. Children are brought up with American TV and graduate to American movies shown on Canadian screens. Except for the occasional short film from the NATIONAL FILM BOARD, there is scant exposure to Canadian films in schools. Even in the post-secondary institutions that have ambitious film departments – UBC, York, Ryerson, Concordia and UQAM – there is no effort to base production training on a thorough knowledge of Canadian achievement. From *Back to God's Country* (1919) to *Les Fleurs sauvages* (1982), Canadian films have been shot mostly on location, using the local terrain less as decorative backdrop than as one of the protagonists. Films have been structured at such a pace that we are allowed to look at, feel and even at times to think about what we are experiencing. In classic Canadian films, we are seldom driven along by an identification with larger-than-life characters or held firmly in the grip of suspenseful narrative. There are fewer "jolts-per-minute" than in most American films, and since Canadian films are often about families and groups of people (*Mon oncle Antoine* or *Who Has Seen the Wind*), there are no outstanding heroes and no international stars.

Canadian cinema is not a fantasy cinema, or a cinema of escape. Repeatedly, it is an observational cinema. Characters are placed within their milieu and the films seem to ask why the characters behave as they do. Frequently the protagonists seem trapped, yet judgements are seldom made. The characters in *Between Friends, Paperback Hero, Entre la mer et l'eau douce, The Rowdyman,* or even in *Les Bons Débarras*, rarely understand their own dilemmas. Since the films do not move inexorably towards a resolution, a sense of understanding is withheld from the audience as well. Canadian scripts are often inconclusive, reflecting the uncertainties of the world. There is the sense of an inner, private journey as in some of our finest novels (Margaret ATWOOD's *Surfacing* or Marion ENGEL's *Bear*). Films such as *Goin' Down the Road, Isabel, The Hard Part Begins, Les Maudits sauvages* and *Family Viewing* all depict a feeling of isolation, a movement through a hostile or unknown world. Canadian films seldom provide the easy comfort that is possible when personalities are depicted whose characteristics are familiar enough to lend themselves to satire. This is why most Canadian films are so serious, especially films made at the NFB or the CBC. Perhaps we do not know ourselves well enough to satirize.

Since 1977, advantageous tax incentives have created a flurry of filmmaking activity, much of it a limp imitation of American films. In a bid to gain access to US screens, Canadian locations have been disguised and the Canadian identity denied. Toronto has been passed off as Houston, and Montréal has had to stand in for New York. Though an industry might be created through these deceptions, such an industry would be culturally as important to Canadians as General Motors or Imperial Oil. For Canadian cinema to survive and be important, the cultural integrity of the films of the 1960s and early 1970s must be combined with the production skills that have been developed in the late 1970s and early 1980s. If large-scale productions can be made successfully, so much the better, but small-scale productions are also needed to give a stronger sense of Canadian identity. Indeed, in recent years, although Telefilm Canada funds continue to focus on big-budget, Hollywood-style productions, it is still the extremely local, low-budget films – *The Grey Fox, My American Cousin, The* DECLINE OF THE AMERICAN EMPIRE, *I've Heard the Mermaids Singing* and *Family Viewing* – that earn both the critical and financial success. Perhaps, in this way, Canadian films are now becoming of interest both to Canada and the rest of the world. PETER HARCOURT

Film History

The first Canadian films were produced in the fall of 1897, a year after the first public exhibition of motion pictures on 27 June 1896 in Montréal. They were made by James Freer, a Manitoba farmer, and depicted life on the Prairies. In 1898-99, the Canadian Pacific Railway showed them throughout the UK to promote immigration. They were so successful that the federal government sponsored a second tour by Freer in 1902 and the CPR began directly financing production of immigration films. The CPR hired a British company to bring together a group of filmmakers, known as the Bioscope Co of Canada, to produce *Living Canada,* a series of 35 films depicting Canadian life, plus one 15-min drama (the first one in Canada): *"Hiawatha," the Messiah of the Ojibway* (1903). In 1910, the CPR hired the Edison Co to produce 13 story films, to dramatize the special virtues of settling in the West. These promotional films are characteristic of most Canadian production through 1912: financed by Canadians but made by non-Canadians to sell Canada or Canadian products abroad. The few Canadians (such as Ernest OUIMET in Montréal, Henry Winter in Newfoundland and James Scott in Toronto) who initiated their own production made only newsreels or travelogues. Meanwhile, American film companies were beginning to use Canada as the setting for story films that featured villainous French Canadian lumberjacks, Métis, gold prospectors and noble Mounties.

After 1912, film companies in several Canadian cities began producing fiction as well as factual films. In Halifax, Canadian Bioscope Co made the first Canadian feature, *Evangeline* (1913), based on the Longfellow poem about the expulsion of the Acadians. It was a critical and financial success. The company made several other less successful films before folding in 1915. The British American Film Co of Montréal, one of several short-lived companies in that city, produced *The Battle of the Long Sault* (1913). In Toronto, the Conness Till Film Co made several comedy and adventure films (1914-15), and in Windsor, the All Red Feature Co produced *The War Pigeon* (1914), a drama of the War of 1812.

The growth of Canadian nationalism around WWI promoted Canadian production and other aspects of the industry. The first widely released Canadian newsreels appeared, feature film production expanded, as did the Canadian-owned Allen Theatres chain and associated distribution companies, and motion picture bureaus were established by the Ontario government (1917) and the federal government (1923). This optimistic period of expansion was led by such producers as George Brownridge, principal promoter of studios at Trenton, Ont, and producer of 3 features including *The Great Shadow* (1919); Ernest Ouimet, producer, exhibitor and distributor, who had also opened the world's first luxury movie theatre in Montréal in 1907; Blaine Irish, head of Filmcraft Industries, producer of the feature *Satan's Paradise* (1922) and of 2 successful theatrical short film series; Ben Norrish, first head of the Canadian Government Motion Picture Bureau and later head of Associated Screen News; Charles and Len Roos, producers, directors and cameramen of many films, including the feature *Self Defence* (1916); and A.D. "Cowboy" Kean, cameraman and producer since 1912. The most successful producer was Ernest SHIPMAN, who had already established his reputation as a promoter in the US when he returned to Canada in 1919 with his author/actress wife, Nell Shipman, to produce *Back to God's Country* in Calgary. This romantic adventure story of an embattled heroine triumphing over villainy was released worldwide and returned a 300% profit to its Calgary backers. During the next 3 years Shipman established companies in several Canadian cities and made 6 more features based on Canadian novels and filmed not in studios, as was then common, but on location. Though these films – eg, *God's Crucible* (1920), *Cameron of the Royal Mounted* (1921), *The Man from Glengarry* (1922) and *The Rapids* (1922) – were not as profitable as his first, they were not failures. Only his last film, *Blue Water* (1923), made in NB, was a disaster. Shipman left Canada and died in 1931 in relative obscurity.

Shipman's departure also marked the end of a minor boom in Canadian production that had begun during WWI. Only 2 features were in production in 1923 (there had been 9 in 1922) and even the production of short films showed a sharp decline. But the number of Hollywood films with Canadian plots increased markedly. At this same time Canadian box-office receipts began to be included under domestic receipts for the US, and distribution companies and theatres came under direct Hollywood control. The takeover of the Allen Theatres chain (1923) by Famous Players Canadian Corp gave Famous Players control of the Canadian exhibition market. European film industries also faced the threat of Hollywood domination in the 1920s, but most governments moved quickly to protect their domestic industries by controlling ownership of exhibition and distribution companies, or by stimulating national production. Canada took no comparable action. Throughout the 1920s, production in Canada was mainly restricted to inserts for American newsreels, sponsored short films, and documentaries produced by government motion picture bureaus and a handful of private companies.

There was one brief resurgence in 1927 when private investors contributed $500 000 to produce *Carry on Sergeant!*, a drama about Canadians in WWI written and directed by British author and cartoonist Bruce Bairnsfather. Though well received by critics, it died within weeks of its release. Apart from the work of Associated Screen News and government production (which also suffered funding cutbacks during the Depression), the Canadian film industry in the 1930s became virtually a branch plant of Hollywood. Feature production was restricted to the making of "quota quickies" for the British market under a British law requiring that a certain number of British or Commonwealth films be shown in British theatres. "Quota" companies, legally Canadian but financed by Hollywood, were established in Calgary, Montréal and Toronto, but the most active was Central Films of Victoria, which produced 12 films from 1935 to 1937. Several of these low-budget adventure films were not even set in Canada and none can be considered Canadian in a cultural sense. Even this level of production ended in 1938 when the British excluded Commonwealth production from protection, mainly because of the way the Canadian government had allowed Hollywood to circumvent the intent of the original law. The only memorable feature of this period is *The Viking*, a dramatic depiction of the hazardous life of Newfoundland's seal hunters, produced in Newfoundland in 1930-31 by the American Varick Frissell (and, technically, not a Canadian production). It is a key example of what was to become a characteristic Canadian genre: documentary dramas and films blending fiction and nonfiction, often rich in a sense of place and connotation, which explore the relationship between people and their environment. This approach emerged early in Canadian film and distinguished many later Canadian features.

But in the 1930s this approach was scarcely evident. The commercial industry had died, the Ontario Motion Picture Bureau had been closed down, and even the federal Motion Picture Bureau had lapsed into sterility. Only in the work of a few individuals (especially Bill Oliver in Alberta and Albert Tessier in Québec) and at Associated Screen News (founded 1920, active until 1958) was there any continuing sense of creative vitality. Though this Montréal company's mainstay was newsreels and sponsored films, it did produce 2 widely released short-film series: *Kinograms* in the 1920s and the *Canadian Cameo* series from 1932 to 1953. Supervised and usually directed by Gordon SPARLING, these films showed flair and imagination, and were almost the only film representation of Canada either at home or abroad. This arid scene began to change in the late 1930s. New film companies were established, Odeon Theatres emerged to compete with Famous Players, and John GRIERSON wrote a report (1938) that led to the creation of the NFB.

PETER MORRIS

Film in English Canada

The history of English Canadian cinema has been one of sporadic achievement accomplished in isolation against great odds. It has existed within a hostile environment where access to capital for production, to the marketplace for distribution, and to theatres for exhibition has been extremely difficult. It has largely been a concurrent history of a struggle against an entertainment monopoly (Hollywood), which has a vested interest in delaying its development, and a search for an audience that is still largely unaware of an indigenous industry. The lack of production can only be understood against this economic backdrop, where the major distribution and exhibition outlets have been owned and controlled by foreigners. Without access to the marketplace, any industry will have to remain underdeveloped.

Before the outbreak of war in 1939, Canadian film production was almost nonexistent. The war changed all this, owing entirely to the establishment of the NFB, which naturally began to train and develop Canadian filmmakers. The NFB acted as a kind of film school and it was only natural that with time these people would restlessly turn their energies to the more complex form offered by the fiction-feature film, which commanded the greatest popular attention. There is evidence that in the immediate postwar period this was beginning to happen. However, these visions remained unrealized for 2 decades as Hollywood moved ruthlessly and efficiently to protect its interests. The problem was complex and involved the Hollywood hegemony in Canada. After the war, Canada, like many other countries, experienced a balance of payments problem with the US. The government restricted imports on a large number of goods in 1947. Money made on films was also discussed, and there were rumours that some kind of quota system would be conceived to force Hollywood to invest part of its box-office profits in Canada. This never happened. Instead, an arrangement was made and formalized into the Canadian Co-operation Project. In return for the uninterrupted flow of dollars out of Canada, the American film lobby attempted to boost tourism to Canada by (among other things) placing Canadian references in American films. The nationalistic lobbying on behalf of Canadians was successfully defeated, and the chance to create a pool of capital by taxing US dollars was lost. The NFB, which had lobbied for fiscal restrictions on Hollywood money, was also thwarted. This episode is important because it helps us to understand the 20 years after the war, in which there was virtually no production in Canada.

Only one English Canadian feature film was made outside Québec in the 1940s – *Bush Pilot* (1946), an imitation of Hollywood's *Captains of the Clouds* (1942). A half-dozen or so English feature films were made in the 1950s. Tyrone GUTHRIE, who was instrumental in establishing the theatre at Stratford, Ont, directed a production of Sophocles' *Oedipus Rex* (1956), the only film to this date that has used the resources of Stratford. A young Canadian, Sidney FURIE, directed 2 films of considerable promise, dealing with young people in rebellion against society. Both *A Dangerous Age* (1957) and *A Cool Sound from Hell* (1959) attracted international critical attention, especially in Britain; but the neglect the films suffered in Canada persuaded Furie to immigrate to Britain in 1960, and he has never returned to Canada to direct. Furie is typical of the emigration of talent from Canada at this time.

The 1960s started in much the same way as the previous decade had ended, with insipid and pedestrian films occasionally appearing, one of which employed the fashionable 3-D process–*The Mask* (1961). However, times were about to change and a new optimism was apparent. Ottawa filmmaker and producer F.R. "Budge" CRAWLEY turned his limitless energies towards features and produced *Amanita Pestilens* (1963) and the gritty story of an immigrant, *The Luck of Ginger Coffey* (1964). The NFB, although primarily focusing on documentary films, produced 2 features in the early 1960s that were a harbinger of things to come. *Drylanders* (1963) turned to history for its subject matter, and *Nobody Waved Good-bye* (1964), directed by Don OWEN, followed the problems of 2 teenagers in contemporary Toronto. Production also began to flourish in other ways. The aesthetic advances made by the French "New Wave" of filmmakers led to a more "personalist" cinema, and the development of the cheap mobile 16 mm camera allowed more access to a medium that had hitherto been the preserve of few. A wave of low-budget feature production swept Canada, much of it from university campuses. The first film, made by Larry Kent while studying at UBC, created the most controversy. The sex scenes in his *The Bitter Ash* (1963) turned it into an overnight sensation. Kent went on to direct 2 more features on the

West Coast before moving east. Many other student features were made, some by one-time directors, others by people who continued to work in the industry. Films such as *Winter Kept Us Warm* (1965), *Slow Run* (1968), *The Columbus of Sex* (1969), *The Plastic Mile* (1968) and *Great Coups of History* (1968) were all low-budget films of some interest. An important figure was David CRONENBERG, who made 2 experimental, futuristic films as a student before turning his talents to commercial production. The emerging filmmakers of the 1960s, both English and French, looked to government to protect their fledgling interests. In 1967 the federal government took a significant step by creating the CANADIAN FILM DEVELOPMENT CORPORATION, funded with $10 million to develop a feature film industry that would last. The CFDC was only to concern itself with production, and not with commercial distribution or exhibition.

At first the CFDC gave money to some of the student filmmakers. Many of the subsequent films were artistic and commercial failures. A few attempts to imitate American models of filmmaking were supported, but with a similar lack of success. However, 2 films indicated future directions. Paul ALMOND, without CFDC money, directed *Isabel* (1968), a story set in the Gaspé starring Geneviève BUJOLD. In 1970, Toronto filmmaker Don SHEBIB appeared with the landmark *Goin' Down the Road* (1970), an artistic and commercial success that received national distribution and attracted large audiences. Both films were unmistakably Canadian, using regional landscapes and characters with sensitivity. They spawned a number of films such as *Paperback Hero* (1973), *The Hard Part Begins* (1973), *Wedding in White* (1972), *The Only Thing You Know* (1971), *Montreal Main* (1973) and *The Rowdyman* (1972). The first fiction feature made by a woman, *Madeleine Is ...* (1971), was made on the West Coast during this vibrant period. Most of these films were made on modest budgets; none of them were major commercial successes. The CFDC was pressured to raise the visibility of the material it was funding, either by legislating the marketplace so the distribution and exhibition of Canadian films would be guaranteed, or by employing foreign talent in conjunction with Canadians. In 1973 a voluntary quota on Canadian films was negotiated with the 2 theatre chains. The quota was not successful, but it was the furthest the federal government would go. Instead, foreign stars and directors were used with increasing regularity, a number of them employed on co-productions. The government did act decisively to provide financial incentives for investment in the domestic film industry through tax benefits and the Capital Cost Allowance program, which resulted in a massive increase in the amount invested in Canadian production. This policy shift marked a new aggressiveness within the industry, and within government agencies responsible for film. Priorities shifted from the low-budget, cultural film to high-budget, commercial projects. At the CFDC a shift in management was made (1978) to reflect the new orientation. The emphasis was placed on film as an industry, not as an art form. Producers, not directors, were given priority.

Initially the use of foreign talent was fortuitous, producing 2 films of high quality that went on to become commercial hits: *The Apprenticeship of Duddy Kravitz* (1974) and *Lies My Father Told Me* (1975). Unfortunately, these films were the exception and not the rule. The string of international co-productions and films using international stars in trite commercial vehicles, littering the second half of the 1970s, was an almost complete disaster.

Anne Wheeler and Denys Arcand, 2 Canadian film directors who came to prominence in the 1970s and 1980s (*photo by Ron Levine*).

Though the majority of Canadian films in the late 1970s suffered from identity crises, a few worthy films emerged from this commercial period. *Why Shoot the Teacher* (1976) and *Who Has Seen the Wind* (1977), both adapted from Canadian novels, retained their integrity and did well at the box office. David CRONENBERG'S horror films, *Rabid* (1977), *The Brood* (1979) and *Scanners* (1980), established his reputation at home and abroad. As attrition depleted the number of opportunists attracted solely by the financial benefits of the film industry, those producers who had something to contribute began to prosper. In 1983 the CFDC changed its name to Telefilm Canada, reflecting its new orientation. Projects were geared more for potential television release, as opposed to theatrical distribution, but it proved impossible to suppress those brave individuals who kept insisting on making feature films for regular exhibition. Regional co-operatives sprinkled across the country began to train young filmmakers who remained committed to the concept of a cultural cinema, and a generation of talented producers began to emerge.

Phillip BORSOS'S *The Grey Fox* (1982) restored pride to an industry and again gave Canadians the sense that they could produce indigenous material of high quality. A newfound confidence led to a resurgence, much of it low-budget independent production from every region of the country. Sandy Wilson directed *My American Cousin* (1985) in BC, Anne WHEELER made *Loyalties* (1986) in Alberta, John Paizs appeared with the zany *Crime Wave* (1985) from Manitoba, while Bill MacGillivray drew on his NS roots in *Stations* (1983) and *Life Classes* (1987). Atom Egoyan, a Toronto filmmaker, followed *Next of Kin* (1984) with *Family Viewing* (1987), while Leon Marr and Patricia Rozema had their films, *Dancing in the Dark* (1986) and *I've Heard the Mermaids Singing* (1987), premiere at Cannes to favourable reviews.

These successes all augur well for the future. Nevertheless, the English Canadian cinema remains a fragile and precarious adventure. The past 20 years are dotted with occasional successes and a fair share of mistakes. Access to the marketplace is still not guaranteed and capital is difficult to raise. The tension between film as industry or art is still being debated by those who define future directions. The industry is still at the mercy of governments who seem to lack consistent policies and change the rules regularly. What seems incontrovertible is the capacity of our filmmakers to survive. PIERS HANDLING

Film in Québec

In 1939, when the Canadian government founded the NFB, Québec films consisted of the work of a few enthusiastic amateurs, most of them priests, such as Maurice PROULX and Albert Tessier. These works today, in addition to their undeniable cinematic qualities, contribute valuable ethnographic documentation. The early filmmakers found a natural outlet in the Service de ciné-photographie, founded in 1942 by the Québec government. Its mandate was to meet certain propaganda and educational needs, but it was ill equipped to do so with a minimum of staff, and working only in 16 mm. The NFB did not have these constraints, but in the early years it was primarily an anglophone organization.

Dubbed versions of English-language films were made for Québec, and little thought was given to French-language production. Under the circumstances, Vincent Paquette, Jean Palardy and a few others did heroic work. After the war they were joined by Roger Blais, Raymond Garçeau and Bernard Devlin. A francophone team took shape and encouraged the emergence of Québec filmmaking within the NFB. In its infancy it was not always differentiated from anglophone production, and sometimes it even produced in English. It achieved its best results when reacting to some specific event: *Les Reportages* was a noteworthy series that began offering biweekly newsreels in French in Sept 1941.

After WWII there was a period of active feature film production in Québec. The war caused a scarcity of French-language films, and sent some French filmmakers into exile in Québec. As a result, feature filmmaking awakened in 1944 with *Le Père Chopin*. This film helped create a new, vertically integrated (from production to exhibition) industry, with international contacts and religious support (financial and ideological). Other Québecois were eager to produce films, hoping to recoup their expenses on the local market and find distribution abroad. In 1947 Québec-Productions brought out *Whispering City/La Forteresse*, in English and French versions. This psychological thriller did not achieve the commercial success for which the producers had hoped. The US film industry at the time was in poor shape, and QP had to modify its aspirations and be content with local markets. The company therefore drew on the highly popular subject matter of RADIO DRAMAS for its next 3 films (1949-50). Another company, Renaissance, wanted to make Catholic films and finally brought one out in 1949. Both companies tried to break out of the strictly domestic market by arranging co-productions with French companies but these efforts failed, and they reverted to Québec themes. Their relative success did inspire several other smaller outfits to produce a total of 7 feature films, 2 of them in English and most of them adapted from theatrical dramas. Paradoxically, 2 of these became the most famous of the era: *La Petite Aurore l'enfant martyre* (1951) by J.Y. Bigras, the story of a child tortured to death by a stepmother destined to be hanged, and *Tit-Coq* (1953) by G. GÉLINAS, the drama of an illegitimate orphan whose fiancée was persuaded to marry another man while Tit-Coq was overseas during the war. In 1954, after 19 films, the feature-film industry collapsed. Television dealt a fatal blow to an industry made vulnerable by its mediocrity. Today, the quality of these films is not important, but they have great value as social documents. In the 1940s and 1950s, Québec transformed from a traditional, agricultural society to an urban one. The films seem to defend the traditional social order, especially the role of the clergy, but a closer look reveals the contrary. The characters and themes of these films, despite the negative impressions of Québec society that they evoke, depict a society in transition, a society in which the traditional Catholic values were being questioned, and thus contradict the surface message of the plot.

Throughout the next decade, feature films and private production were virtually nonexistent, although a few semiprofessionals produced work for the Québec government. Thus, the only place where Québec film survived was within the NFB. A number of brilliant filmmakers joined the NFB during the 1950s: L. Portugais, M. BRAULT, G. GROULX, C. JUTRA and others. They, and the NFB "old-timers," finally had opportunities worthy of their talents. This explosion was the result of 3 developments. First, the NFB moved from Ottawa to Montréal (1956), which meant that Québec filmmakers could live and work in Québec. Second, in 1957 public attention focused on francophone filmmakers who were not being given the same opportunities as their anglophone colleagues; the result was that French and English productions were separated administratively and financially, leading ultimately to the creation of a distinct francophone service. Third, TV demanded large amounts of material; this meant that both popular entertainment and artistic innovation received as much support as films for government departments and educational institutions (eg, 39 films in the *Passe-Partout* series, 1955-57; 26 dramatic episodes of *Panoramique*, 1957-59, a landmark for Québec fictional cinema; *Temps présent*, late 1950s and early 1960s). Filmmakers were also pushing the technological limitations, trying to improve their equipment and its capacity to capture natural sound and images while mobile on location. In 1958 Brault and Groulx produced *Les Raquetteurs*, which was important technologically as a key step in the development of direct cinema, and socially as a statement of the nation's awakening.

The period was one of profound social change. Duplessis died in 1959; the Liberals came to power in 1960 and the QUIET REVOLUTION began. French Canadians became Québecois, and film met the need to give expression to the change. *Les Raquetteurs* went beyond picturesque scenes to stress membership in a national community. The early 1960s accelerated the development of Québec cinema, both within and outside the NFB. People such as Brault, Pierre PERRAULT, Jutra, P. Patry and F. Dansereau were eager to try new directions. In 1963, a new era began with 2 categories (documentary and fiction) and 2 films: *Pour la suite du monde*, by Perrault and Brault; *A tout prendre*, by Jutra. The first, through its technique and the importance it gave to the spoken word, marked another major step in the development of direct cinema. The second was an example of films being produced by nationalistic filmmakers throughout the world and was a personal statement by Jutra. Groulx's *Le Chat dans le sac* (1964) was one of the best films to that time about petit-bourgeois youth. J.P. LEFEBVRE, a prolific filmmaker, brought out *Le Révolutionnaire* (1965), a fable/commentary on society. Gilles CARLE, who had been with the NFB since 1961, was working on his first feature, a comedy, *La Vie heureuse de Léopold Z* (1965). Coopératio, a private company, tried to get the film industry moving again. Its director, P. Patry, made *Trouble-fête* in 1964 and then, in the space of just over a year, 3 more films. Others also tried feature films, working privately or for the NFB or the Québec government (A. LAMOTHE, D. ARCAND, R. Lavoie, A.C. POIRIER, J. GODBOUT, B. Gosselin, G. Dufaux, C. Perron, J.C. Labrecque and others). Ferment and change were occurring in all aspects of the arts, and film forms evolved to meet the needs of the filmmakers. Direct cinema in all its variations, auteur films (documentary or docudrama) and every genre of commercial film were attempted.

View of Jean Duceppe and Jacques Gagnon in a scene from Claude Jutra's *Mon oncle Antoine* (1971), one of the finest Canadian films *(courtesy National Archives of Canada/MISA/3283)*.

Perrault dominated direct filmmaking of these years with his saga of the people of Île-aux-Coudres. With his cameramen Brault and Gosselin, he wanted not only to observe and record the awakening of the Québec nation but to play a part in that awakening as well. Yet direct cinema was not limited to nationalistic subjects. Some producers wanted to use the techniques for social action films. A number of these efforts took place within the framework of the NFB program Société nouvelle (francophone equivalent of Challenge for Change), which made its début in 1968 with *St-Jérôme* by F. Dansereau and lasted more than a decade. Others at the NFB concentrated on workers, eg, Denys Arcand, whose extraordinary *On est au coton* (1970) was the victim of political censorship for 6 years. Others (including Dansereau and, most notably, A. Lamothe) left the NFB in order to work more freely. Lamothe's *Le Mépris n'aura qu'un temps* (1970) gave us an economic, social and political analysis that film had not previously offered. Between Perrault's approach and that of the activist films arose many other forms of direct cinema, united only by their technique and their methods. This kind of film moved steadily to the forefront. Another significant figure in the late 1960s and early 1970s was Labrecque, particularly with his *La Visite du général de Gaulle au Québec* (1967) and *La Nuit de la poésie* (1970).

But the movement began to falter at the beginning of the 1970s, partly because some of its practitioners (Labrecque, Gosselin and, especially, Brault and Groulx) were attracted by the possibilities of fiction film. Brault made his first solo feature film in 1967, *Entre la mer et l'eau douce*, which showed the marks of his long apprenticeship as a cameraman/producer.

In 1974, with *Les Ordres*, Brault once again put documentary skills at the service of fiction and, with his reconstruction of Québec under the WAR MEASURES ACT in 1970, made the perfect synthesis of the flexibility, improvisation and attention to detail of direct cinema with the dramatic progression and structured narrative of fiction. Groulx went exactly the opposite way, in both style and content. He offered a clear personal statement for discussion and criticism. Three features illustrate his methodology, *Où êtes-vous donc?* (1969), *Entre tu et vous* (1969) and *24 heures ou plus* (1972). His films integrated documentary and fiction at the editing stage, a technique in which he still leads.

Fiction moved away from direct cinema and won new adherents for a second reason. In 1967, the CFDC was born, and with it avenues of financing. The next year D. HÉROUX brought out *Valérie*, Quebec's first erotic film and commercial success. These 2 factors opened the way for commercial filmmaking and explain the 1970s production boom. Québec had its various waves – erotic films (including C. Fournier's box-office hit *Deux femmes en or*, 1970), subtle comedies and thrillers. But this boom in commercial films soon ran into trouble, made even worse by foreign control of the key sectors of distribution. Some commercial films surmounted the problems of quality versus commercial viability. Gilles Carle, essentially a storyteller, knew how to lace his films with humour and sex, ideology and social colour, showmanship and stars, making them much more interesting than most of the others in his field. With his fifth feature, *La Vraie Nature de Bernadette* (1972), Carle won lasting international acclaim.

Others also knew how to combine quality with commercial success. The best known is probably Denys Arcand, whose *Réjeanne Padovani* (1973) and *Gina* (1974) blended social observation and colour with perfect artistic harmony; or Claude Jutra, who won acclaim for his NFB film *Mon oncle Antoine* (1971), one of the finest Québec films ever made. Unfortunately, he did not have the same commercial success with *Kamouraska* (1973), a period film based on the celebrated novel, and an expensive co-production. A number of other NFB producers (M. Carrière, C. Perron, J. Godbout, etc) made films that could scarcely be distinguished from private ones. The trailblazer of this kind was J. BEAUDIN's tender and simple period film, *J.A. Martin, photographe* (1976).

J.P. Lefebvre dominated the field of the more personal statement for 15 years, with 18 very important features to his credit. His work evolved from 2 fundamental approaches to filmmaking: the first, social, concrete, reflective and critical; the second, abstract, symbolic and intimate. Jacques LEDUC, who concentrated on nondramatic moments of daily life and the state of the soul, belonged to that same generation. Leduc's work, marginal yet high profile, belonged both to the school of direct cinema (*On est loin du soleil*, 1970) and to fiction (*Chronique de la vie quotidienne*, 1973-78).

A group of women filmmakers within the NFB produced *En tant que femmes* (1973-74), a series of films, some direct and some fictional, about issues that concerned women. Women had very recently found their voice in Québec film with the appearance of the first feature made by a woman in Québec (*De mère en fille*, by A.C. POIRIER, 1968), followed in 1972 by the first feature privately made by a woman, *La Vie rêvée*, by M. DANSEREAU. The NFB series encouraged film production by women. Dansereau now has several films to her credit, as does Poirier (including the famous *Mourir à tue-tête*, 1979, about the psychological, social and political implications of rape). Filmmakers such as L. Carré, P. Baillargeon, M. Lanctôt and L. Pool explored new and unexpected paths in fiction. Direct films moved onto uncharted ground (eg, sexism, domestic work, the couple, violence, racism) with the work of L. Guilbeault, H. Girard, D. Létourneau, T. Rached and others. The work done was much more important than its numerical output would indicate, and was a sign of awakening, renewal and dynamism.

Another kind of dynamism in the 1970s originated with young producers who concentrated more on individual, even marginal, problems than on social ones. Some excelled in film for children (A. Melançon); others went happily from fiction to direct (J. Chabot and R. Frappier). Some were more traditional, more narrative, one of the best being F. MANKIEWICZ (*Les Bons Débarras*, 1980). Three names dominated the ironical fringe: M.A. FORCIER (4 features, including *Bar salon*, 1973), J.G. Noel (3 features, including *Ti-cul Tougas*, 1976) and P. Harel. These filmmakers had in common that several of their films were produced or co-produced by the Association coopérative de productions audio-visuelles, which receives funding from the INSTITUT QUÉBECOIS DU CINEMA (IQC) for shorts and first films. This production by young people assures Québec film a vitality and creativity that otherwise would be lacking – especially in fiction, since this field has been dominated for some years by large established companies. An exception to this is the astonishing *Les Plouffe* (1981) by G. Carle, in which historical authenticity is matched by emotional accuracy.

In the late 1970s and early 1980s, direct films have once again become the best part of Québec cinema. This is primarily because of the work of the veterans: Perrault, with his 2 major film cycles on Abitibi and the MONTAGNAIS-NASKAPI (including the *Pays de la terre sans arbre ou le Mouchouânipi*, 1980); Gosselin, Brault, André Gladu and a few others with films that mix ethnology, pop culture and nationalism; M. Moreau's pedagogic and ideological films; A. Lamothe's 2 social and political series about Indian life and culture (*Carcajou et le péril blanc*, 1973-76; *Innu asi*, 1979-80; *Mémoire battante*, 1983); and G. Dufaux, a director/cameraman of sensitivity and humanity whose subjects have included everything from old age to education to China.

Nick Mancuso and Carole Laure in the film *Maria Chapdelaine*, directed by Gilles Carle, 1983 (*courtesy National Archives of Canada/MISA/12439*).

As the 1980s began, Québec film was again in crisis. The number of private productions was declining dangerously; even the NFB faced cutbacks. Filmmakers with high hopes for the 1975 Loi sur le cinéma were disillusioned. The IQC's 5-year plan also closed down some possibilities. The CFDC and the Société générale du cinéma were interested in a profitable, commercial film industry based on international markets, and this is not always compatible with filmmakers' definitions of a national film industry. Direct and documentary filmmaking decreased, even at the NFB. Fewer productions, money problems, higher costs, unemployment for competent producers, technicians and artists, and huge international-content productions were elements of Québec filmmaking in the early 1980s. Feature co-productions are being made by the NFB, private industry, the IQC, the CFDC and TV. Since the crisis in Québec film is not primarily one of creativity or quality but of production, this multiple participation may provide the means for continuing growth. This seems to be indicated in the recent success of such films as Melançon's *Bach et Bottine*, 1986, and *La Guerre des tuques*, 1987; Pool's *Anne Trister*, 1986; Y. Simoneau's *Pouvoir in time*, 1986; J.C. Lauzon's *Un Zoo, la nuit*, 1987; and especially Arcand's Le Déclin de l'empire américain, 1986 (*see* DECLINE OF THE AMERICAN EMPIRE, THE). PIERRE VÉRONNEAU

Reading: M. Knelman, *Home Movies* (1987); Peter Morris, *Embattled Shadows, A History of Canadian Cinema 1895-1939* (1978); Pierre Véronneau and Piers Handling, eds, *Self Portrait: Essays on the Canadian and Québec Cinemas* (1980).

Film, Documentary The genre is virtually synonymous with the NATIONAL FILM BOARD, but earlier work preceded this development. In the first decade of the century, companies such as Canadian Pacific and Massey-Harris used film for promotional purposes. The federal government established its own agency, mainly as a result of its involvement with film in WWI. From this evolved the Canadian Government Motion Picture Bureau in 1923, which for a brief time in the 1920s led the world in using film to spread information. The bureau's most notable film was *Lest We Forget* (1935), a documentary history of the Canadian effort in WWI, compiled from newsreels, graphics and re-enacted scenes. Another successful documentary was *The Royal Visit* (1939), a record of the Royal Tour of that year. In the 1930s Associated Screen News, a private film company in Montréal, produced many films and series, such as *Canadian Cameo*, for theatrical release. Gordon SPARLING spent most of his career at ASN, and *Rhapsody in Two Languages* (1934) remains a classic prewar documentary. In Québec, a number of priests, notably Maurice PROULX and Albert Tessier, shot films extolling the land and Catholic virtues, documents depicting a life-style now disappeared.

With the arrival of John GRIERSON, who was responsible for creating the NFB in 1939, the documentary began to flourish. The coming of war meant that Canada needed propaganda films, and series such as *Canada Carries On* and *The World in Action* reached audiences of millions. Grierson also promoted films that dealt with ethnic groups, Indians, social problems and Canadian art. The arrival of peace in 1945 signalled a new direction for the NFB. By the early 1950s a group of young NFB filmmakers, part of Unit B, began to produce a unique body of work based on the Canadian experience. *Corral* (1954), *City of Gold* (1957) and *Lonely Boy* (1961) dealt with issues of the past and the present in a quiet, delicate fashion. The *Candid Eye* series, made for TV, examined socially relevant issues in *The Days Before Christmas* (1958) and *The Back-Breaking Leaf* (1959). Unit B produced much of its work for TV in the period 1952-58 before the CBC developed its own capability.

In 1956 the NFB moved from Ottawa to Montréal and this provided a great incentive to French Canadian production. The French Unit made socially active films of commitment and contestation. In direct cinema, which relies on portable, lightweight 16 mm cameras and magnetic sound-recording equipment, the director does not preplan but allows events to dictate the direction of the finished film. This direct cinema movement produced classics in Québec such as *Les Raquetteurs* (1958) and *La Lutte* (1961). The feature documentary *Pour la suite du monde* (1963) captured the vanishing life-style of islanders in the St Lawrence. Its directors, Pierre PERRAULT and Michel BRAULT, went on to make outstanding contributions to the Québec documentary film. By the late 1960s the material emerging from French production at the NFB took on a more political bias and some films were banned. Meanwhile, in the rest of the NFB the objective documentary still flourished. Donald BRITTAIN rose to the fore with *Memorandum* (1965) and followed this with numerous finely crafted films, many of which employed archival footage. Other filmmakers produced excellent work of a diverse nature at this time: Don OWEN, Robin Spry and Tony Ianzelo, to mention a few. More personal statements were made by people such as Derek May and Michael Rubbo, whose film on Vietnam, *Sad Song of Yellow Skin* (1971), won the prestigious Robert Flaherty Award.

In the private sector, Allan KING gained international repute with his *cinéma-vérité* films, *Warrendale* (1967) and *A Married Couple* (1969). King formed his own company to produce documentaries before moving on to direct fiction features. F.R. "Budge" CRAWLEY, an Ottawa filmmaker who formed his own company (1938), won an Oscar for *The Man Who Skied Down Everest* (1975), the pinnacle of a long, distinguished career that also included *The Loon's Necklace* (1948). Harry Rasky achieved prominence with his portraits of famous people: Marc Chagall, Will and Ariel Durant, Leonard COHEN, Arthur Miller and Anne Frank.

The NFB began to revitalize itself in the 1970s through a new program entitled "Challenge for Change," which had an overt social and political function. This program produced some of Canada's finest documentaries. Another fortuitous development resulted from the "Challenge for Change" program: the establishment (1974) of a women's studio at the NFB. Studio D has produced a number of fine works on a variety of problems, from a woman's perspective. Its most controversial effort has been its film on pornography, *Not a Love Story* (1981). Québec women filmmakers have had an illustrious history at the NFB. Anne-Claire POIRIER has made feature documentaries, her film on rape, *Mourir à tue-tête*, garnering many accolades. Women have contributed a number of highly interesting films in the private sector: *Les Servantes du bon Dieu* (1979), *D'abord menagères* (1978) and *P4W – Prison for Women* (1981).

Regional filmmakers began to make their own distinctive contributions: on the West Coast Phil BORSOS with his film *Nails* (1979); on the Prairies, Tom Radford, *China Mission* (1980) and Anne WHEELER, *War Story* (1982); Michael Scott, *For Gentlemen Only* (1976) and Bob Lower, *Something Hidden* (1981) from Winnipeg; Kent Martin, *Empty Harbours, Empty Dreams* (1979) from Halifax; Québec began to reassert its documentary prowess in the late 1970s and made films about its music (*Le Son des français d'Amérique* series, 1973-77), Indians (*Carcajou et le péril blanc* series, 1973-76), its heritage (*La Belle Ouvrage* series, 1977-80), deprived people (*Les Exclus* series, 1978) and daily life (*Chronique de la vie quotidienne* series 1973-78). Despite the fact that television has begun to affect the manner in which documentary films are made, some notable efforts are still being made in this area. Ron Mann made 2 feature documentaries of considerable power, *Imagine the Sound* (1981) and *Poetry in Motion* (1982). Sturla Gunnarsson works consistently within the cinéma-vérité style in films such as *After the Axe* (1981) and *Final Offer* (1985). Paul Cowan stirred controversy with his film on Billy Bishop, *The Kid Who Couldn't Miss* (1982), and experimented with the docudrama style in *Democracy on Trial: The Morgenthaler Affair* (1984). Donald Brittain continues to produce excellent work, most notably his study of the Trudeau and Lévesque years, *The Champions* (1978) and *The Final Battle* (1986), and *Canada's Sweetheart: The Saga of Hal C. Banks* (1985). Brigitte Berman's *Artie Shaw: Time Is All You've Got* (1985), a film on the famous American clarinetist, won the Academy Award for Best Documentary Film.

The documentary idea has unique significance in Canadian art, and most especially for Canadian cinema. Indeed, the realist tradition dominates even our fictional cinema. Perhaps its roots can be traced to a number of sources. This distrust of the "imaginary" and the irrational could arise out of a utilitarian philosophy that provides the cornerstone for our educational and social system. Others feel that the documentary form has been rooted in a need to comprehend the alien and hostile landscape that surrounds us. Grierson's philosophy, which had a great influence on documentary film in Canada, was essentially educative and informative. He wanted to bridge the gap between people by showing them how others lived. This pragmatic approach found its natural form in the factual or documentary film. PIERS HANDLING

Film, Experimental Even though the avant-garde has produced some of Canada's most accomplished films, it has been involved in the medium a comparatively short time. Film artists in Germany, France, the US and the Soviet Union began making experimental films in the 1920s. Although political censorship brought the movement to an end in the Soviet Union permanently, and in Germany for a time, artists in France and the US continued to produce experimental films throughout the 1930s and 1940s. During the 1950s and 1960s, especially in the US, production accelerated as artists attempted to reformulate the cinema according to modernist ideals. In Canada, except for Norman MCLAREN, an animator, there was almost no experimental filmmaking until the mid-1960s. There are 2 major reasons for this delayed development. Traditionally Canada has lacked the political and intellectual interest in the arts that accompanies the growth of an avant-garde, and Canadian artists have retained a long-standing dedication to representation and documentation – not only through documentary films but also through depictions of landscape and of social life in painting, poetry and fiction. The artistic doctrine that dominated experimental film until the mid-1960s – and was known as modernism – was largely committed to abstraction. There were a few filmmakers who made experimental films, eg, Burton Rubenstein (*The Hyacinth Child Bedtime Story*, 1966), Peter Rowe (*Buffalo Airport Visions*, 1967) and John Hofsess (*The Palace of Pleasure*, 1966, and *The Columbus of Sex*, 1969).

Still from Norman McLaren's film *Neighbours* (1952), a political fable in which he used a technique of stop-motion cinematography called pixilation (*courtesy National Film Board of Canada*).

Not until the development in the late 1960s of postmodernism, with its greater concern with representation and its interest in photography, did avant-garde filmmaking became widespread in Canada. Given Canada's commitment to representational art, it is not surprising that a Canadian, Michael SNOW, became one of the key innovators within postmodernist forms of cinema, and that several other Canadians (Joyce WIELAND, Jack CHAMBERS, David RIMMER and Bruce ELDER) have also made significant contributions. Many of Snow's films attempt to reconcile the demands of photographic representation with the material and formal interests of the modernist tradition. His film ↔, or *Back and Forth* (1968-69), suggests how abstraction, depiction and construction, haptic space and optical space, illusionistic devices and devices revealing the work's material construction can be brought into a balanced, integrated form. Jack Chambers, like Snow, worked in painting before making films. In his films *Mosaic* (1966), *Hart of London* (1970) and *CCCI* (1971), Chambers developed structures to convey his ideas about light, mind and nature.

In the work of Canadian avant-garde filmmakers, there are several forms that have found special importance; all are based on characteristics of the photographic image. One is the landscape film exemplified in such films as Snow's *La Région centrale* (1971); Wieland's *Reason over Passion* (1969); Rimmer's *Real Italian Pizza* (1971) and *Canadian Pacific I* (1974) and *II* (1975); and Chambers's *Circle* (1968). None of these works is a simple or straightforward representation of a landscape; all explore the capacity of the photographic and cinematographic image to represent nature, metanature or the relation of self to nature. The second form is the diary film which chronicles the daily life of the filmmaker. Here the subject explored is usually the affinity of the photographic and filmic image for the ordinary matter of everyday life and the manner in which a photograph converts natural matter into art. Examples are Judy Steed's *Hearts in Harmony* (1973), Rich Hancox's *Home for Christmas* (1978) and Elder's *The Art of Worldly Wisdom* (1980). The final form depends on the use of theme and variations in a structure. The different variations are generated by optical printing, a process that enables the filmmaker to rephotograph an already existent film image. In such works, the cinematic image becomes the subject of the film. Filmmakers who have done work in this form include Rimmer (*Surfacing on the Thames*, 1970, *Watching for the Queen*, 1973), Al RAZUTIS (*98.3KHZ Bridge at Electrical Storm*, 1973, *Lumière's Train*, 1980) and Elder (*1857: Fool's Gold*, 1981). Canadian experimental films, like Canadian documentaries and animation films, enjoy an international reputation.

As the 1980s progressed, economic factors became increasingly important, not without detriment to the art form. As the cost of making films soared, they became more conventional. The large public investment required to sustain the experimental film movement lent some appearance of validity to comments that experimental film becomes socially useful by becoming politicized. A hybrid form known as the "New Narrative" emerged that incorporated some of the politically useful strategies of experimental film, largely strategies for defeating the appeals of cinematic illusionism. In Canada, as elsewhere, this form has been associated with the feminist movement. The best known example is Patricia Gruben's *Low Visibility* (1984). This cinematic form became controversial and caused a rift in experimental film between its supporters and detractors.

Film Animation Canada commands worldwide respect for work in film animation. This reputation has been built over the last 40 years and is largely, though not entirely, based on the work of Norman MCLAREN and the films produced by the NATIONAL FILM BOARD. Some Canadian pioneers in animation were Walter Swaffield, Harold Peberdy and Bert Cob; however, the first animated films, all predating 1920, have disappeared. In the 1920s a Toronto painter and illustrator, Bryant Fryer, began work on the first of a series of animated films entitled *Shadow Laughs;* only 2 films in the series of 12 were completed, both in 1927. Six years later he embarked on a new series, *Shadowettes*, producing 3 films using the silhouette technique made famous in Germany by Lotte Reiniger. Shortly afterwards, Fryer was forced to suspend his activities, and he moved into commercial production. These early attempts were all necessarily sporadic and unconnected. With the founding of the NFB (1939), conditions were established that would guarantee continuity of production, free from commercial pressures. Shortly after John GRIERSON was appointed to head the NFB, he asked his friend and former colleague, the gentle Scotsman, Norman McLaren, to join him in Canada. McLaren was put in charge of the fledgling animation department to produce short propaganda messages for the war effort. McLaren's effervescent imagination was applied to this task immediately. He also began to recruit young artists from across Canada to assist him, thereby laying the foundation for future success. With a minimum of means, animators such as George Dunning, Grant Munro and René Jodoin produced films of charm and vitality.

After WWII McLaren turned his attention towards more personal projects, leaving a legacy that is legendary. His technical innovations in animation, for instance, drawing directly on film and eliminating the need for a camera, were revolutionary. His pixilation techniques of animating live actors were also extraordinarily imaginative. Both *Neighbours* (1952) and *A Chairy Tale* (1957) were made this way, the former winning him an Academy Award. McLaren dazzled audiences around the world with his colourful, innovative films, reaching millions of people. In the 1960s he became fascinated with dance and broke new ground with the beautiful *Pas de deux* (1967), a black-and-white visual poem which uses multiple exposures.

While McLaren was quietly absorbed in his own work, a generation of animators began to develop their own techniques in the 1950s. Colin Low's *The Romance of Transportation in Canada* (1952) was only one of many interesting efforts, but it signalled the arrival of Canadian animation. By this time Robert Verrall, Wolf Koenig and Sidney Goldsmith had joined the animation section at the NFB to make their own singular contributions. The move of the NFB to Montréal in 1956 stimulated French animators Bernard Longpré, Yvon Mallette, Pierre Moretti and Pierre HÉBERT. The styles were as numerous as the animators. Some became interested in using computers, others used charcoal, watercolours, photographs and the pin screen. By the late 1960s animation production had split along linguistic lines, but with no deterioration in quality; diversity was rampant. Don Arioli used his acerbic wit to amuse; Co HOEDEMAN created fantastic creatures out of sand in *The Sand Castle* (1977); Caroline Leaf used watercolour and ink on glass in *The Street* (1976); Ishu Patel employed thousands of beads in *Bead Game* (1977); Laurent Coderre utilized painstaking cutout animation in *Zikkaron* (1971); and Bernard Longpré and André Leduc returned to pixilation with *Monsieur Pointu* (1975). The NFB's stress on regional production in the 1970s resulted in many entertaining efforts from Vancouver, Winnipeg and Halifax. The board has won prizes worldwide for its animated films and 3 of its films have won the coveted Oscar: *Neighbours, The Sand Castle* and *Special Delivery* (1977). Filmmakers in the private sector were making equally intriguing films. Crawley Films had established an animation studio very early in its history and the award-winning *The Loon's Necklace* (1948), which recounts an old Indian legend, is still in active distribution. In the 1960s Crawley began to produce animation for American TV, notably *The Tales of the Wizard of Oz* (1962) and *Return to Oz* (1963).

In the 1950s, Jim McKay and George Dunning left the NFB to found Graphic Associates, and after Dunning's departure in 1955, under its new name Film Design Ltd, it has continued production to the present. Al Guest formed his own company in the same year and at one time it was the third largest of its type in the world. Guest now runs Rainbow Animation. On the West Coast, the self-educated Al Sens opened his own studio and continues to make films. *The See Hear Talk Think Dream and Act Film* (1965) combines live action and animation into one of his best pieces. Gerald Potterton, another ex-NFB animator, formed his own company in Montréal (1968); it produced many films of note, among them the feature-length *Tiki Tiki* (1970-71), before its demise in the mid-1970s. Potterton recently returned to the spotlight by directing Canada's most expensive animated feature film, *Heavy Metal* (1981), which became a box-office success. Many animators and production companies shared in this effort. Interestingly, there had been an animated feature made in Canada as early as 1955, *Le Village enchanté*, directed by Marcel and Réal Racicot, which drew on Québec folk legends. Another independent animator is John Straiton, an advertising executive who works in animation in his spare time. *Portrait of Lydia* (1964) uses a succession of sexual images and symbols, and *Eurynome* (1970) is a technical wonder employing plasticine. Straiton's films have won numerous awards. Canada's unique and innovative animated films continue to elicit the respect of critics and the public everywhere. PIERS HANDLING

Film Censorship has existed in Canada for almost as long as films have been shown. CENSORSHIP takes a variety of forms: customs officials may forbid entry to pornographic films, cities may ban films within their municipal limits and provincial attorneys general may lay criminal charges. Production houses, especially governmental agencies, practise self-censorship. The NATIONAL FILM BOARD has demonstrated this a number of times, most notably in 1972 when on political grounds the presiding government film commissioner banned several Québec films made by the French unit.

Censorship is a provincial responsibility. With the exception of PEI and Newfoundland, each province has its own censorship, supervisory or classification board. Between 1911 and 1913, 5 provinces passed censorship laws and then established boards to apply them. In Québec, where censorship was seen as an extension of family rights and responsibilities, the emphasis was placed on protecting children from corruption. Western provinces took the same approach and added an element of anti-Americanism. For about 50 years, censorship boards have had almost unchallenged control over the fate of films. Reasons for banning a film or demanding certain cuts are extremely diverse and vary from province to province. In the post-WWII years, censorship was justified on the grounds of protecting the public interest against outrages to morality. In Québec everything that ran counter to church teaching and morality was forbidden; but this censorship began to be criticized and, paradoxically, Québec became the most liberal province. In 1963, following a commission of inquiry, Québec established a classification policy, and in 1967 the censorship board became the supervisory board. The following year, Manitoba substituted classification for censorship. In 1976, the Superior Court of NS ruled that censorship was not under provincial jurisdiction. Five provinces appealed this ruling and won its reversal in the Supreme Court of Canada. Their powers reaffirmed, the provinces continue to impose 10 different sets of cinematic standards. A modest form of liberalization has triumphed lately – except in Ontario which, since 1975, has become the stronghold of conservatism and the object of protests and anticensorship movements. Canadian censorship, subject to institutional, political, police and religious interference, remains a matter of provincial control and continuing controversy. In the late 1980s, the provinces are occupied in dealing with the classification of videotapes. PIERRE VÉRONNEAU

Reading: M. Dean, *Censored! Only in Canada* (1981).

Film Distribution is the marketing branch of the industry and a necessary, though often resented, link between production and exhibition. It is also the most predictably profitable of the 3 branches, at least for the large multinational conglomerates that dominate the industry internationally. Since the early 1920s, the Canadian distribution sector has been overwhelmed by these multinationals: though there are approximately 80 Canadian distribution companies, the largest 8 (all subsidiaries of Hollywood multinationals and members of the Motion Picture Export Association of America) receive about 80% of total rental revenues. Although Canada is the largest foreign market for US films, most of this revenue is exported, and this has had a profound impact not only on the viability of the Canadian distribution sector (few independent Canadian companies are profitable) but also on Canadian production. The reason for this lies in the close links established between distribution and production in the early years of the industry.

Although distribution was the last of the 3 branches of the industry to develop, it increasingly came to dominate the industry's economic structure. By the early 1920s the largest, Wall Street-financed US distributors had acquired both production companies and theatre chains, thus creating vertically integrated combines that enabled 8 "major" companies to dominate first the US and then the international film industry. Although the original vertical combines of the majors were broken up after WWII under US anti-trust legislation, the basic operating principle continued; most Hollywood production is controlled, and usually financed, by the majors. Consequently, US distributors have only minimal interest in marketing films in which they do not have a direct stake in producing. These 2 consecutive patterns (first vertical integration, then distributor-controlled production) have seriously affected the viability of the Canadian film industry since the early 1920s. At that time, Hollywood majors acquired direct or indirect control, and through tied contracts, first with Famous Players theatres and also, since the 1940s, with Odeon (now CINEPLEX ODEON CORP) theatres, ensured a constant flow of Hollywood films to Canadian theatres. Independent Canadian distributors, lacking significant access to the 2 chains as well as to major Hollywood films, have traditionally emphasized the marketing of independently produced films, low budget exploitation films and art films; they have also been the principle distributors of Canadian films. Since the late 1970s, the majors have extended activities to include independently produced films (though rarely Canadian ones) and consequently have seriously affected the economic viability of Canadian distributors and have continued to deny Canadian films more than minimal market access. As a result, few Canadian distribution companies survive more than a few years. The exceptions, such as Astral Bellevue-Pathé and Cineplex Odeon, have followed vertically integrated models, and a recent loosening of anti-trust regulations in the US may lead the industry as a whole in this direction (a notion not discouraged by heavy US purchases of Cineplex Odeon shares).

Proposals made in 1987 by the federal government to diminish domination of Canadian distribution would allow the majors to distribute in Canada any films they had participated in the production of or for which they owned world rights, whereas independently produced films would have to be sold separately in Canada and would have to allow Canadian companies access to their distribution. These proposals have met stiff opposition from Hollywood and have generated intense lobbying of the government. As of Jan 1988, the federal government had not yet tabled legislation. PETER MORRIS

Film Festivals, Prizes The first major film festival in Canada was started in Montréal (1960), and it included a competitive section for Canadian films. In the mid-1960s Vancouver started its own festival, and both Ottawa and Stratford hosted a number of events in the early and mid-1970s. Of these, only Vancouver still hosts a film festival. In 1976 the first Festival of Festivals was held in Toronto and it has continued to be a success. A year later the World Film Festival, a competitive festival that awards the Grand Prix of the Americas, started in Montréal. In 1979 the Banff Television Festival was inaugurated as a competitive event.

The oldest film festival, and one which still runs biennially, was begun in 1950 as a documentary film festival in Yorkton, Saskatchewan. The Yorkton Short Film and Video Festival has now expanded to include all short films; its major prize is the Golden Sheaf. Other competitive festivals include the Canadian International Animation Festival, the Banff Festival of Mountain Films, and the Canadian Student Film Festival. Important noncompetitive events are Montréal's Festival international du nouveau cinéma et de la video de Montréal, the Grierson Documentary Seminar and Festival, the Rendez-vous du cinéma québecois, the Atlantic Film Festival, the Festival du cinéma international en Abitibi-Témiscamingue, and the Festival de films et video "Femmes en Focus."

In 1948 the first Canadian Film Awards were organized; they became an annual occurrence. By 1979 the Academy of Canadian Cinema was established to continue this work, and it gives Genie awards as symbols of film excellence in a range of categories. It also awards Gemini awards for TV production. The Canadian Motion Picture Distributors Assn awards the Golden Reel Award to the top-earning film of each year. Another prize of importance, given by the Québec critics' organization, is the Prix de la critique québecoise. The Alberta Motion Picture Industries Assn presents a number of prizes at its annual Alberta Film and Television Awards. Toronto's Festival of Festivals awards the Toronto City Award for Excellence in Canadian Production each year, accompanied by a cash prize. PIERS HANDLING

Fils de la Liberté, an association of 700-800 young PATRIOTES fd 5 Sept 1837 in Montréal. Inspired by the ideals of the American Revolution, the Fils de la Liberté published a manifesto on Oct 4 which proclaimed their belief in the right of a people to choose its own government and of a colony to become independent. André Ouimet led the civil and political arm of the movement, while Thomas Storrow Brown looked after its military wing. On 6 Nov 1837 the Fils de la Liberté clashed violently with the anglophone DORIC CLUB in Montréal. The association died with the outbreak of the Rebellions of 1837. FERNANDE ROY

Finance, Department of, was formally created by statute in 1869, inheriting its title, structure and personnel from the tiny finance department of the pre-Confederation Province of Canada. Originally, its primary function was bookkeeping: administering the collecting and spending of public monies, and servicing the national debt. During WWI the federal government borrowed from and taxed individual Canadians directly for the first time (through Victory Loans and income taxes), which complicated but did not fundamentally alter the department's task. The Great Depression and WWII transformed the department into a hive of national economic managers. For the first time, university-trained economists, such as Clifford Clark, W.A. MACKINTOSH, R.B. BRYCE, and Ken Eaton, occupied senior offices. Massive expansion of the economy during the war (Gross National Product doubled and total annual federal spending increased to 10 times that of the 1939 figure) led to an expansion of the influence of the department and, more generally, of the federal government as a whole. Financial structure was changed permanently in WWII with the introduction of UNEMPLOYMENT INSURANCE (1941) and FAMILY ALLOWANCES (1944). More significantly, in 1939 departmental officials developed a new approach to the federal budget. Instead of simply attempting to balance expenditures with revenues – the prewar practice – they began to use taxing powers and spending policies to influence economic development in general. Management of the economy, especially through its FISCAL POLICIES, remains the most important function of today's department. The BANK OF CANADA and the AUDITOR GENERAL report to Parliament through the minister of finance. DAVID FRANSEN

Finance Act, Aug 1914, emergency measure ending Canada's GOLD STANDARD and giving the Department of Finance new powers. The same name applied to a 1923 measure continuing these new powers while providing for the return to the gold standard on 1 July 1926, and for its suspension in certain emergencies. Before 1914 each bank had issued its own paper currency while the federal government issued Dominion notes in exchange for gold, or vice versa. Thus when gold flowed in, the Dominion would issue more paper money; chartered bank notes were convertible into gold or Dominion notes.

After 1914 the government could issue new Dominion notes without gold backing to finance the war effort and to lend to the chartered banks at their request. This arrangement continued until 1935 when the BANK OF CANADA was formed; it meant that the chartered banks could never be short of cash, because they could always borrow newly printed Dominion notes, whose quantity was no longer related to the amount of gold in Ottawa's vaults. Thus the note issue was unlikely to be proportionate to the gold, although from 1 July 1926 Dominion notes were convertible into gold, at a fixed price, as they were before 1914. In late 1928 gold did run short, and the emergency provisions of the 1923 Act were invoked. *See also* EXCHANGE RATES. IAN DRUMMOND

About 14 species of finch are known in Canada, including the common redpoll (*Acanthis hornemanni*), which nests in northern Canada and winters in southern Canada (*photo by Bill Ivy*).

Financial Post, a newspaper founded by John Bayne MACLEAN, who also founded MACLEAN'S magazine. Intended to provide reliable investment information, especially to the Toronto business community, the *Financial Post* published its first issue on 12 Jan 1912. In 1987 it was published weekly at 777 Bay Street, Toronto, by MACLEAN HUNTER LIMITED. In Oct 1987 it was announced that the paper had been bought by the Toronto Sun Publishing Corp and that a new daily *Financial Post*, published in conjunction with the existing national weekly, would be launched in 1988. Its circulation was 198 000 at the time. The publisher is Neville J. Nankivell and the editor is John F. Godfrey. The *Financial Post* reflects orthodox Canadian business opinion but has no political affiliation. D. MCGILLIVRAY

Financial Times The *Financial Times* of Canada is a weekly, tabloid-sized, business newspaper, first published as the *Montreal Financial Times* on 21 June 1912. It was purchased in 1961 by Southam-Maclean Publications Limited, a subsidiary of the Southam Company Limited, now SOUTHAM INC. The headquarters of Financial Times were in Montréal until 1 July 1975 when it was moved to Toronto. Noted editors of the past include Bernard Keble SANDWELL, later editor of *Saturday Night*, and Michael Barkway. David Tafler is now publisher and Terence Corcoran is editor (1987). Average total paid circulation as of Dec 1986 was 102 361. The viewpoint of *Financial Times* is orthodox business, leaning towards free-market economics. D. MCGILLIVRAY

Finch, common name for one of the largest bird families, Fringillidae, which occurs worldwide (excluding Australia). It includes some GROSBEAKS, crossbills, Hawaiian honey creepers, redpolls, siskins and birds specifically named finches. In Canada, about 14 species are known, ranging in length from the redpolls (*Acanthis hornemanni, A. flammea*), pine siskin (*Spinus pinus*) and American goldfinch (*S. tristis*), as small as 11 cm, to the pine grosbeak (*Pinicola enucleator*), up to 25 cm. Although a diverse group, all members of the family have a stout, conical bill with a cutting edge angling sharply near its base. This makes it ideal for crushing seeds, principal food of most finches; insects are also eaten. Bill dimensions vary considerably: grosbeaks and cardinals have large, deep bills; goldfinches and siskins have relatively slender bills; the mandibles of crossbills overlap. Both plumage and song show tremendous variability. Males have bright and often strikingly patterned plumages, and most species have elaborate, tuneful songs.

In northern Canada, most species raise one brood annually. As the summer is longer in southern Canada, most species attempt to raise 2 broods. In southern Canada, a few species are resident, eg, house finches (*Carpodacus mexicanus*) in southern BC. Some species perform altitudinal MIGRATIONS: gray-crowned rosy finch (*Leucosticte tephrocotis*) nests at the summit of mountains in Alta, BC and YT, but winters in lowlands and foothills of western Canada.

Southern Canada is a wintering area for species nesting in northern Canada, for example, redpolls, crossbills (*Loxia curvirostra* and *L. leucoptera*) and pine grosbeaks, but numbers vary considerably from year to year, depending on food availability farther north. Only a very few hardy species can survive winters in northern Canada; eg, at Churchill, Man, only hoary redpolls attempt to overwinter and even they are not found in some winters.

RICHARD W. KNAPTON

Finch, Robert Duer Claydon, poet, scholar (b at Freeport, Long Island, NY 14 May 1900). He was educated at University College, U of T, and the Sorbonne, Paris, and was a professor of French at the U of T 1928-68. His scholarship is chiefly evident in *The Sixth Sense: Individualism in French Poetry 1686-1760* (1966), as well as in several volumes of poetry, the first of which, *Poems* (1946), received the Gov Gen's Award. The same award was also bestowed upon *Acis in Oxford* (1961). He is also the recipient of the Lorne Pierce medal for literature, an LLD from U of T and a FRSC. Finch is one of Canada's modernists, initially anthologized in *New Provinces*. His work, deeply imbued with the classical tradition, is characterized by an intense care for form and graced by a rare subtlety and elegance. Among his recent works are *Twelve for Christmas* (1982), *The Grand Duke of Moscow's Favourite Solo* (1983), *Double Tuning* (1984) and *For the Back of a Likeness* (1986). E.D. BLODGETT

Findley, Timothy, writer, actor (b at Toronto 30 Oct 1930). For years a successful actor (charter member, Stratford Shakespearean Festival, 1953; original Edinburgh Festival cast of Thornton Wilder's *The Matchmaker*, 1954), Findley published his first novel, *The Last of the Crazy People*, in 1967 and the second, *The Butterfly Plague*, in 1969. *The Wars* (1977) won a Gov Gen's Award and an international reputation for the author, which *Famous Last Words* (1981) enhanced. *Not Wanted on the Voyage* appeared in 1984, and *The Telling of Lies* in 1986. A play, *Can You See Me Yet?*, was performed at the National Arts Centre, Ottawa, in 1976 (published 1977). He has also written TV scripts, including *The National Dream* (1974) and *The Whiteoaks of Jalna* (1971-72). *The Wars* depicts the experiences of a young Ontario man during WWI, and *Famous Last Words* deals with the life of a fictional international man of letters during and before WWII. *Not Wanted on the Voyage* handles the tale of Noah with considerable wit and invention, while *The Telling of Lies* is a mystery story. Despite their differences, all his novels display considerable imagination, as does his short-story collection, *Dinner Along the Amazon* (1984). A broad range of subject matter and narrative device enables Findley's *oeuvre* to resist easy categorization. Recent awards include the Canadian Authors Assn Award (1985). In 1986-87, he was president of the Canadian division of PEN International. DENNIS DUFFY

Finn, Henry James William, expatriate actor, playwright (b at Sydney, NS 17 June 1787; d 13 Jan 1840). Taken to New York as a child, he travelled to London, eventually acting small parts at Haymarket Theatre 1811-12. He returned to America in 1815 and appeared in New York, Philadelphia and Boston, playing Hamlet, Richard III and Othello. With his triumphant Aguecheek in *Twelfth Night* (1824), he eschewed tragedy for farce, becoming a comic favourite. He managed Boston's Federal St and Tremont theatres 1825-30 and wrote about 9 plays, *Montgomery; or, the Falls of Montmorency* (1825) and *Removing the Deposits* (1835) being best known. He died aboard a burning steamship on the way to his summer home on Rhode I. DAVID GARDNER

Finns The first Finnish immigrants to arrive in N America were part of a group of settlers who established the colony of New Sweden along the banks of the Delaware R between 1641 and 1655. The total number of settlers was small and was soon assimilated into the American mainstream. Between 1835 and 1865, several hundred Finns settled in Alaska (which at that time was a part of Russia) and many moved down the coast to BC (*see* SOINTULA). Some early Finnish immigrants to Ontario worked on the construction of the first WELLAND CANAL, which was completed in 1829. The 1986 census estimated that there were 40 565 residents of Finnish origin in Canada.

Origins Finland was part of Sweden until 1808 when it was ceded to the Russian Empire. In Dec 1917 the Finnish Parliament declared its independence from Russia; there followed a bitter civil war in 1918, in which the conservative White Guard defeated the Red Guard workers. Finns had been immigrating to N America in large numbers prior to WWI and continued to do so in the first decade of Finnish independence, primarily for economic reasons. A large population explosion in rural areas coincided with a lack of available farmland, forcing many rural inhabitants to look elsewhere. The overseas migration was mainly from the provinces of Vaasa, Oulu and Turku-Pori in southeastern Finland, and later from Helsinki. Other factors encouraging immigration included religious freedom and a desire to escape compulsory military service in the Russian army.

Migration and Settlement Until 1914, most Finnish emigrants went to the US, although a small minority came directly to Canada and others came to Canada via the US during periods when the Canadian economy was attractive. Canada became the main destination of emigrants from Finland in the 1920s when the US established entry quotas. Landless groups, with no economic prospects in their homeland, made up the largest proportion of overseas emigrants.

Finns again immigrated to Canada in large numbers (20 000) between 1950 and 1960, seeking better economic opportunities than were available in postwar Finland. These Finns were generally from urban areas, were better skilled and educated, and were more willing to settle in the urban areas of Canada than pre-1930 Finnish immigrants. Since 1960, with the expansion of the Finnish economy, few Finns have immigrated to Canada.

Ontario and BC have traditionally attracted the largest numbers of Finnish immigrants. Finns settled as pioneers in Thunder Bay, Sault Ste Marie, Sudbury, Kirkland Lake and Timmins, Ont. Before WWI some Finns settled in Toronto and their population there increased after WWII. Small Finnish communities were also established in Windsor, Hamilton and St Catharines, Ont, in the 1950s. There has been an active Finnish community in Montréal since the 1920s, but few settled elsewhere in Québec. Some small rural Finnish communities were established in Alberta and Saskatchewan.

Economic Life Many of the first Finnish settlers worked on the construction of the CPR. Later, jobs were found in mining and lumbering. Many of these early Finnish immigrants worked in industry and then settled on small farms outside these urban centres. This was particularly the pattern in northern Ontario. Many single women arrived to work in DOMESTIC SERVICE. It was not until after WWII that children of Finnish farmers left the farms for jobs in industry. Finnish immigrants arriving in Canada in the 1950s settled immediately in the urban centres, where some established businesses and moved into the professions.

Social Life and Community Finns established temperance societies, sports clubs, churches, and clubs for dances, drama, choirs, bands, and folk dancing, to meet their community and cultural needs. Many of the Finns of the pre-1930 period were of working age and spoke only Finnish; consequently, there was a very real need for these social activities and a close bond linked the members. The Finnish Organization of Canada (FOC), est 1911 (originally the Finnish Socialist Organization of Canada), is the oldest Canadian nationwide cultural organization for Finns. The prolabour activism of some of its leaders in the 1920s and 1930s occasionally brought it into confrontation with the Canadian authorities and caused some dissension within the Finnish community itself. Today the few remaining FOC locals provide activities for their members, who are mainly senior citizens.

In 1940, a number of Lutheran churches and non-FOC clubs organized the first of the Finnish Grand Festivals that was held to raise funds for Finland during WWII. These festivals, featuring track and field, gymnastics, folk dancing, choirs, drama, and a wide range of social activities, have continued as an annual summer event. The Finnish Canadian Cultural Federation (with some 40 member groups) was founded in 1971 to undertake the activities of the Grand Festival and to serve as a nationwide organization to promote Finnish culture in Canada.

Religion and Cultural Life Most of the Finns in Canada are Lutherans, although only a minority participate actively in the Lutheran churches. Finnish Lutheran congregations have been established in Montréal, Toronto, Timmins, Sudbury, Sault Ste Marie, Thunder Bay and Vancouver. Some Finns support the United Church, others the Finnish Pentecostal Church, which has a number of active Finnish-language congregations, primarily in Ontario. Several significant Finnish-language newspapers were founded in Canada, eg, the independent *Vapaa Sana* (1931), published in Toronto, the leftist *Vapaus*, published in Sudbury from 1917 to 1975; and the independent *Canadan Uutiset*, published in Thunder Bay since 1915. However, since few Finnish immigrants have arrived in Canada since 1960, the readership of the Finnish-language press in Canada will probably decline.

Education The children of Finnish immigrants adapted readily to the Canadian educational system, but the Great Depression prevented many from moving up the social scale. The children of many of the earlier Finnish immigrants who settled in the rural areas of northern Ontario retained the Finnish language and customs. In the 1970s, as a result of a growing cultural consciousness and support from various government agencies, a number of Finnish-language schools were established.

Politics Many Finns played a leading role in the Canadian labour movement and in the establishment of co-operatives; during the 1930s some FOC leaders were prosecuted by the authorities for supporting communism. A large number of Finns within the FOC at that time opposed this activism and broke away.

Electoral data indicates that, for many years, a large number of Finns in northern Ontario supported the CO-OPERATIVE COMMONWEALTH FEDERATION in elections. Today the political support of the Finnish Canadian voter tends to be based on social status rather than on any ethnic factors. Each of the 3 main political parties has nominated Finnish Canadians in recent federal and provincial elections. LENNARD SILLANPAA

Fir, Scandinavian for "pine," designates the "true" firs, ie, evergreen CONIFERS (genus *Abies*) of the pine family (Pinaceae). About 50 species occur worldwide, all in the Northern Hemisphere; 4 are native to Canada. Balsam fir (*A. balsamea*) occurs from Alberta to the Atlantic provinces. Alpine fir (*A. lasiocarpa*) grows at high elevations in the West, from Alaska to Mexico. Pacific silver fir (*A. amabilis*) and grand fir (*A. grandis*) grow along the BC, Washington and Oregon coasts. Three introduced species (white, shasta and Spanish firs) are planted as ORNAMENTALS. Firs are stately trees with single, straight trunks and nar-

Balsam fir (*Abies balsamea*), with male cones (left) and female cones (right) (*artwork by Claire Tremblay*).

Alpine fir (*Abies lasiocarpa*). Firs are stately trees with straight trunks and pyramidal crowns (*photo by Tim Fitzharris*).

row, pyramidal crowns. Branches are regularly whorled; leaves are flat and needlelike. Cones are erect and usually restricted to upper branches. POLLINATION occurs in spring; seeds are mature in fall. The bracts (modified leaves) and scales (ovule-bearing structures) are shed from the cone axis with the winged seeds. The relatively light, soft, weak wood is used extensively for pulp, paper and lumber. JOHN N. OWENS

Firearm It is not known exactly when or where firearms were invented, but cannons that could fire a ball of stone or iron were sufficiently well developed to be used in the siege of Trent (1278). Firearms are mentioned frequently in literature, but the earliest datable illustration found comes from 1326. Most early guns were muzzle loading; ie, the powder was put into the breech from the muzzle and a ball was put on top of it. A red-hot wire was used to ignite a small "train" of powder leading, through a vent at the breech, to the main charge. The burning powder produced a tremendous amount of gas, which propelled the ball out of the barrel and towards the target.

The early development of firearms was very slow. "Hand cannons" light enough to be carried by one man were produced, but the method of firing did not change for about 100 years. About 1400 a mechanical device was invented, consisting of a lighted wick of twisted hemp that could be drawn by means of a lever into a pan at the breech. The result was the first self-contained small arm, the matchlock musket. When Sir Humphrey GILBERT landed in Newfoundland in 1583, his ship was armed with cannon and some of his men carried matchlock muskets.

In the late 15th century a wheel-lock mechanism, which used a stone (iron pyrite) rubbed against a revolving steel wheel to produce a spark, was invented in Italy. The spark ignited the priming powder to discharge the gun. News of this improvement moved slowly through Europe. The device was fragile and expensive and, although it was made in large quantities for hunting by the nobility, it did not become a "general issue" military arm. When Pierre du Gua de MONTS and Samuel de CHAMPLAIN were outfitting their expeditions to inhabit Canada, they brought with them cannons and matchlock muskets. By 1619 there were also at least 2 of the expensive wheel locks in the habitation at Québec, along with 3 small cannons and 6 breech-loading swivel guns.

About the time Champlain was establishing Québec (1608), a French gunsmith of the Le Bourgeoys family was perfecting an inexpensive and efficient lock mechanism that represented a real advance in metallurgical knowledge. The flintlock, as it was known, positioned a piece of flint in the jaws of a vise or "cock" powered by a strong "V" spring. When the trigger was pulled, the cock fell forward, the flint struck a steel plate (battery), the sparks produced fell into a small pan of priming powder, and this ignited the main charge. The flintlock rapidly became the most common and best form of firearm available. It was rapidly adopted by the settlers of America and quickly found its way into the hands of the Indians. Gunsmiths and gunmakers in Canada copied designs originating in France or England and supplied a small portion of the local requirement, although most guns were imported by the trading companies or merchants.

The flintlock remained fundamentally unchanged until replaced in the first half of the 19th century. In 1807 Alexander Forsyth, a Scottish clergyman, patented a lock that used a small amount of fulminate to ignite the main charge. This development quickly led to the invention of the percussion cap (about 1818), the separate primed paper or metallic cartridge (about 1821) and the self-contained cartridge (about 1826). Canadian gunmakers quickly adopted these innovations and developed improvements of their own. The first guns found that are known to have been made in Canada date from the 1830s. William Gurd of York [Toronto] made guns that had locks converted from flintlocks. The pistols and rifles made by J. Woods of Brantford are marked with an Upper Canada address, indicating that Woods was the proprietor of a "Rifle Factory" prior to 1840.

The greatest difficulty in perfecting a breech-loading gun was preventing the escape of gas through the breech. This problem was resolved by the invention of a thin-walled metallic cartridge, which expanded to produce a seal and then contracted, after the gas had left the barrel, to allow removal of the cartridge case. Development of the cartridge took place mainly in the US, Britain and France. Dudley Booth of Ottawa invented an unsuccessful breech loader and its cartridge in 1867, and several other Canadians obtained patents for breech-loading guns in the period 1850-80. A few of these obtained some local acceptance, but none achieved national recognition.

"Brown Bess" flintlock musket, English, *c*1770-80; steel, walnut stock, brass mounts (*courtesy Royal Canadian Military Institute Museum*).

Officer's light flintlock musket, English, *c*1775-80; steel with walnut (*courtesy Royal Ontario Museum*).

Flintlock musket, India pattern, English, marked by the Tower Armouries, *c*1805-15. A piece of flint positioned in the jaws of a "cock" was sprung forward by the trigger, striking a steel plate and igniting the powder (*courtesy Royal Ontario Museum*).

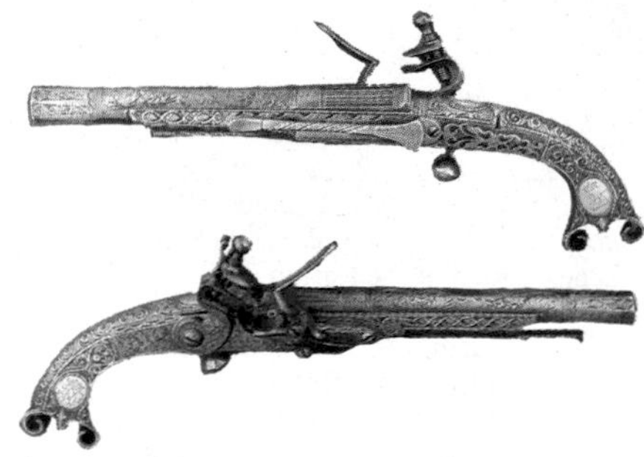

Flintlock pistols, Scottish, Thomas Murdoch (1730-85), Leith, *c*1785; steel and silver (*courtesy Royal Ontario Museum*).

Flintlock musket, French pattern of 1717, French marks of Mauberge Arsenal, *c*1717-24; steel, walnut stock. The flintlock was a French invention of *c*1610 and remained in use until the 19th century (*courtesy National Museums of Canada/Canadian Museum of Civilization/83-978*).

Most of the firearms used in Canada were imported from England or the US: fine shotguns from Britain, rifles from the US, pistols and revolvers from both countries. Arms with serial numbers under 100, by all major US makers, have been found in Canada. In 1866 Smith and Wesson, the large revolver manufacturers of Springfield, Mass, first advertised in the Oshawa, Ont, *Vindicator*.

Military weapons were supplied in large quantities from England. Canada was usually used as a proving ground for cold-weather trials of most new weapons, and many were not produced because of the experience gained. The first shipment of Snider-Enfield breech-loading rifles was sent to Canada in 1866, when threats of a FENIAN invasion from the US were prevalent. Smaller quantities of American-made weapons were purchased for Canadian militia use. In 1855-56, 800 Colt Navy Model 1851 revolvers were purchased for the militia cavalry of the Province of Canada. These are easily recognized by the company markings and numbers on the grips. In the 1860s a quantity of Spencer repeating rifles and carbines was purchased along with those of other manufacturers. In 1885 the NORTH-WEST MOUNTED POLICE placed the first of many orders for Winchester Model 1876 carbines. In the same year the Colt Repeating Arms Co lent Canada 2 Gatling guns, under the command of A. L. Howard of the Connecticut National Guard, for use in the suppression of the NORTH-WEST REBELLION. Howard remained in Canada to establish the Dominion Cartridge Co at Brownsburg, Qué.

At the same time, Canadian gunmakers were supplying fine-quality target rifles to the militia and sporting rifles to farmers, hunters and sportsmen. The skills of some gunmakers were as good as any in the world, and the accuracy of their rifles was equal to that of the finest English makers. James Paris Lee came to Canada as a youngster from Scotland and was educated in Galt [Cambridge, Ont]. He was trained as a jeweller and set up business in Chatham (Canada W) in 1850. Lee later moved to Janesville, Wis, where he developed a number of firearm designs, one of which was the bolt-action rifle, which later became the basis of the Lee-Enfield rifle, manufactured for Commonwealth troops until 1950. The Lee-Enfield rifle was used by Canadian troops through 2 world wars.

About 1900, Sir Charles Ross, the designer of a bolt-action rifle which was being made for him in the US, moved to Canada and interested the Canadian government in his design. A factory was established at Québec City, and the first shipment of the Canadian-made ROSS RIFLE was turned over to the government in 1905. The Ross went through many variations until it was replaced by the Lee-Enfield rifle during WWI.

Beginning in the mid-1860s, the demand for custom-made guns was slowly replaced by that for machine-made repeating rifles, most of which could be produced more economically in the US. Nevertheless a few excellent gunmakers have continued to work in Canada. Although very few of them have made much money, they have continued a tradition by making fine rifles to meet the requirements of Canadian sportsmen. *See also* ARMAMENTS. S. JAMES GOODING

Fireweed, common name for *Epilobium angustifolium,* a member of a genus of herbaceous or shrubby plants of the evening primrose family (Onagraceae). Roughly 160 species of *Epilobium* (willow herbs) are found throughout temperate regions; 12 are native to Canada. Willow herbs have alternate or opposed leaves, and regular or slightly irregular flowers. The calyx forms a 4-part tube; the flower has 4 petals. Eight stamens surround the compound ovary; the fruit is a long, narrow capsule. Seeds are numerous and tufted at the top. The Yukon Territory adopted fireweed as its floral emblem in 1957. The flowers are arranged in an elongated cluster, situated terminally on a stem 50-200 cm long with alternate, spear-shaped leaves. The large purple, magenta or occasionally white flowers blossom from the bottom up. This species propagates quickly after forest fires (hence the name). Because it tends to overrun the area where it grows, fireweed should be grown in dry, poorish soil. It may be grown from seeds, shoots or root cuttings. *See also* PROVINCIAL FLORAL EMBLEMS. CÉLINE ARSENEAULT

First Canadian Army was an army of some 170 000 men organized in 2 corps (5 divisions and 2 armoured brigades) formed overseas in 1942 under Lt-Gen A.G.L. MCNAUGHTON. McNaughton's aim was to keep the Canadian Army together to lead the cross-channel assault on NW Europe; instead, the Canadian government dispatched I Canadian Corps from McNaughton's command to serve in the Italian campaign in 1943 so that Canadian troops could see action. Because the existence of an identifiably Canadian army was important at home, Allied formations were added to First Canadian Army to keep it up to strength. Accordingly, when First Canadian Army (now commanded by Lt-Gen H.D.G. CRERAR) went into battle on the left flank in France, Belgium and Holland, clearing the Channel coast after the NORMANDY INVASION, it had more Allied than Canadian troops. The balance was redressed in Mar 1945 following the RHINELAND campaign, when the Canadians in Italy rejoined First Canadian Army for the LIBERATION OF HOLLAND. *See also* ORTONA, BATTLE OF; WORLD WAR II. STEPHEN HARRIS

First Ministers Conferences, gatherings of Canada's provincial premiers with the federal prime minister, a term that has overtaken the older "dominion-provincial" and "federal-provincial" usages. The term appears to have originated in the constitutional conference that led to the abortive Victoria Charter of 1971, which specifically established a "Constitutional Conference of First Ministers." The charter also provided for annual meetings to take place among the prime minister of Canada and the "first ministers" of the provinces – unless of course a majority of those comprising the conference decided otherwise. Since that time the terminology of "first ministers" has been followed, even though the Victoria Charter was never adopted, and despite the omission of any reference at all to the meetings in the CONSTITUTION ACT, 1982 (*see also* CONSTITUTION, PATRIATION OF).

The term has the advantage of distinguishing top-level, federal-provincial meetings from more specialized gatherings of ministers and civil servants, and it avoids the issue of whether the first ministers of the provinces are to be called premiers or prime ministers, an issue of importance to some provincial leaders.

To some observers, the first ministers' meetings fill a gap in the Canadian constitution by providing a forum for consultation and regulation of federal-provincial relations; to others they furnish an opportunity for gratuitous grandstanding by politicians. *See also* FEDERAL-PROVINCIAL RELATIONS; MEECH LAKE ACCORD.

ROBERT BOTHWELL

Fireweed (*Epilobium angustifolium*) off the Alaska Highway, near the Liard R. Fireweed propagates quickly after forest fires. Fireweed is the floral emblem of the Yukon (*photo by J.A. Kraulis*).

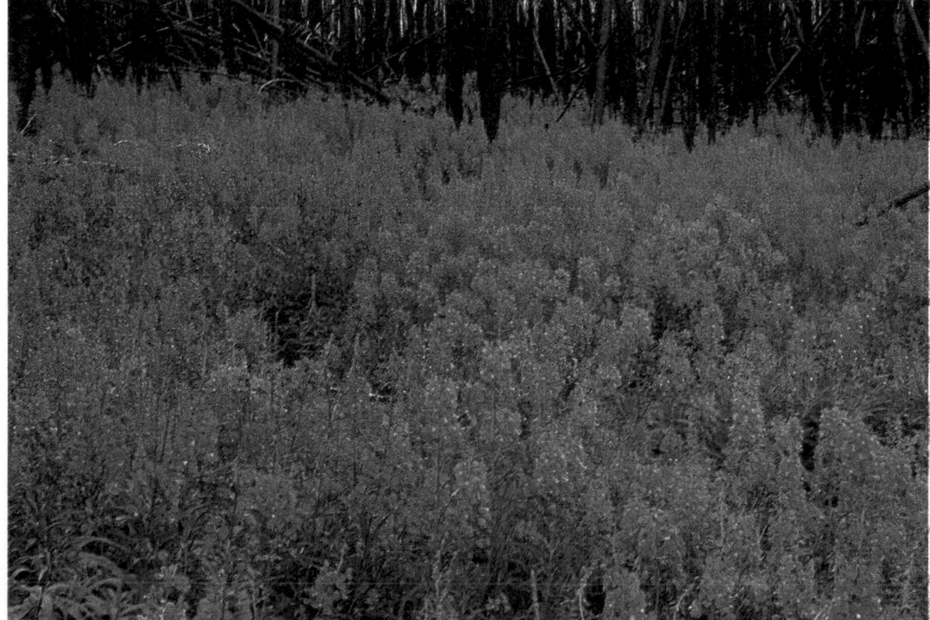

Fiscal Policy, the use of government taxing and spending powers to affect the behaviour of the economy. The economy's total output, income and employment levels are directly related to total private and public spending or *aggregate demand.* Private spending consists of purchases of goods and services by consumers, by businesses for investment, and net exports (exports minus imports). For their part, governments raise revenues from a variety of taxes and other sources to spend on such things as health care, education, defence and social assistance.

Fiscal policy refers to government action to change the total or composition of these revenues and expenditures for demand management purposes – to keep a growing labour force and the country's stock of industrial plants and machinery employed at high levels but without inflation or excessive borrowing to pay for goods from other countries. Revenue increases, of themselves, reduce aggregate demand; additional expenditures increase it. Thus, if private expenditures fall (eg, if consumers buy fewer cars), governments might prevent aggregate demand and, in turn, total output, income and employment from declining by increasing their expenditures or reducing taxes.

Although some tax and expenditure changes affect the ECONOMY more than others, the balance of government revenues and expenditures provides a rough estimate of the impact. An excess of revenues over expenditures (*a surplus*), of itself, reduces aggregate demand. Depending upon what is happening in other sectors, the economy has a tendency to contract. If expenditures exceed revenues (*a deficit*), there will be a tendency for incomes, output and employment to expand and eventually for prices to rise. However, a deficit has to be financed by borrowing.

Under some circumstances, government may end up by competing with private borrowers for funds, driving interest rates up and making private investment, for example, more costly. That could offset some of the original expansionary impact. Moreover, if deficits continue for prolonged periods, the accumulation of public debt and rising interest payments on that debt may jeopardize government's ability to undertake further revenue and expenditure changes for stabilization purposes. Thus, the effects of fiscal policy cannot be viewed in isolation from those of MONETARY POLICY – and of changes in government debt.

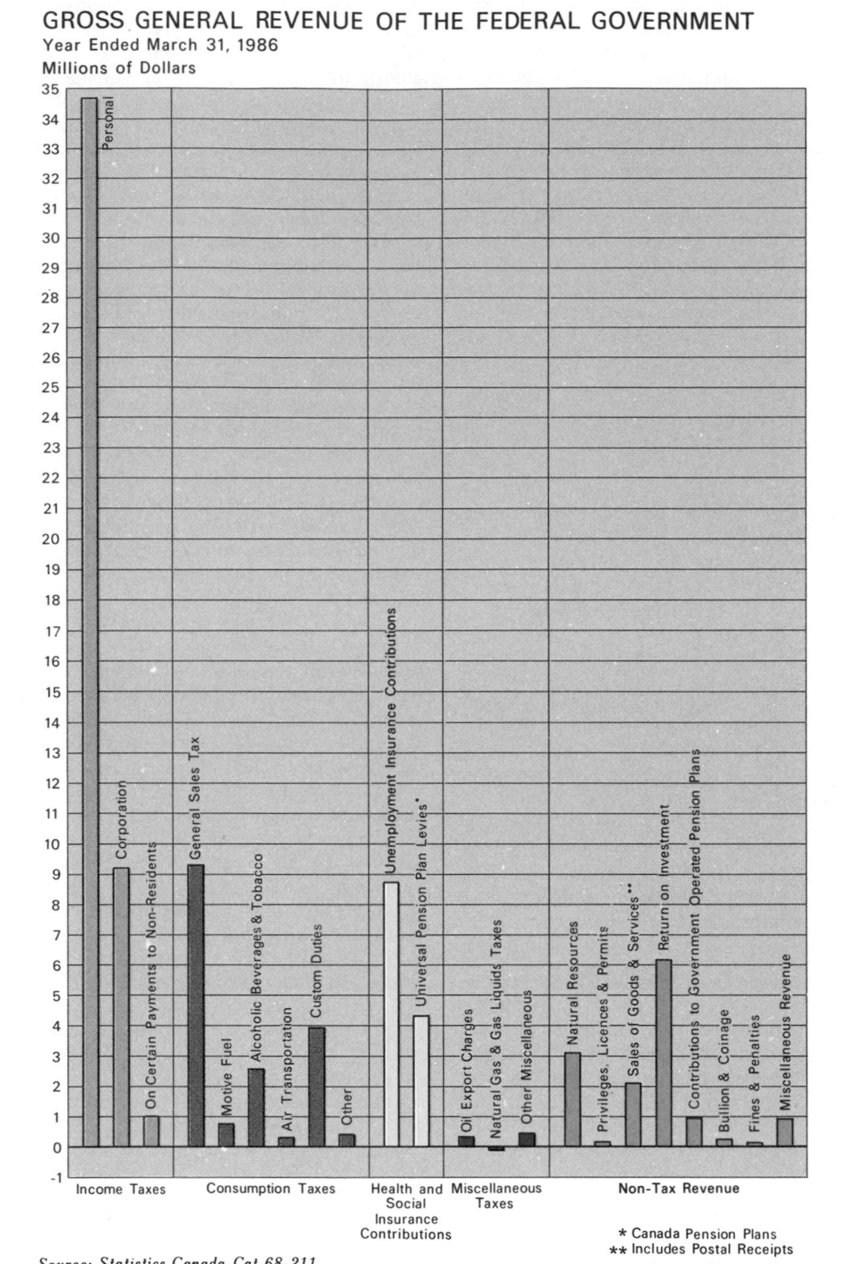

Source: Statistics Canada, Cat 68-211

Fiscal policy is primarily the responsibility of the federal government, although the provinces are certainly not without a role. In his budget papers, the federal minister of finance summarizes the coming expenditures of the government, the revenues anticipated and, if a deficit is expected, how much borrowing will be required (total financial requirements, including "nonbudgetary" transactions such as loans and investments). For fiscal policy purposes, he also presents the budget (*see* BUDGETARY PROCESS) on a *national accounts basis*, in which various revenues and expenditures are grouped under headings related to their impact on the economy (eg, purchases of goods and services), rather than – as in the *administrative budget*– by department or broad purpose (eg, social affairs).

Even the government's actual surplus or deficit on the national accounts basis can be misleading. For example, particularly from 1979 on, the federal government took action to make fiscal policy more restrictive by reducing some expenditures and increasing taxes. Yet its actual deficit became very large by 1982 and continued to rise relative to the economy's total ouput until mid-decade. In part, this was because some tax collections and some expenditure items responded automatically to changes in the level of economic activity and prices. Such "built-in stabilizers" as personal and corporate income taxes fall and unemployment insurance payments rise as economic activity declines, thus increasing aggregate demand and income even without policy action. Also, interest payments on the public debt tend to rise with inflation. To separate these effects from deliberate policy actions, the minister may also present "cyclically adjusted" and "inflation-adjusted surplus/deficit" figures to show respectively what the fiscal position would be with higher average levels of employment and without the effects of inflation on debt charges.

History of Canadian Fiscal Policy Prior to the 1930s, many economists felt that swings in the level of economic activity were by and large self-correcting, though perhaps with some assistance from monetary policy to prevent excessive movement in prices. Governments, like prudent households, were simply expected to balance their budgets annually. Unfortunately, this sometimes led to raising taxes or reducing expenditures when economic activity was already low, thus making the business cycle even worse.

The severe and prolonged unemployment of the GREAT DEPRESSION ended the optimism about self-correction and brought increasing demands for positive action by governments. Economists differed widely in their prescription for what could be done. The blueprint for action was provided by John Maynard Keynes's book, *General Theory of Employment, Interest and Money* (1936), which provided a comprehensive explanation of how total output and unemployment were determined (*see* KEYNESIAN ECONOMICS). Indeed, the Depression and Keynes's book, along with the illustration of what governments could do provided by their greatly expanded wartime role, brought a revolution in thinking, including a strong emphasis on fiscal policy and, for a while, a downgrading of monetary policy for the achievement of economic stability. In 1945, Canada's federal government committed itself to use fiscal policy "to maintain a high and stable level of employment and income" by setting the budgetary position as the business cycle required.

During the 1950s, especially after the Korean War, the government was reasonably successful in keeping unemployment low and prices stable, partly through fiscal policy, although monetary policy too became more active after mid-decade. Indeed, those economists (such as Milton Freedman at U of Chicago) who stressed the importance of the supply of money and the neglect of monetary policy by Keynesians, applied increasing pressure to what had become the mainstream of economic thought.

By the early 1960s, it was recognized that simply trying to smooth the ups and downs of the business cycle sometimes choked off recovery before the economy reached full growth. Attention shifted to using a combination of fiscal and monetary policies to "fine-tune" the economy, steering it along a path of continually growing output and employment, even if that called for balancing the budget only over periods much longer than the usual business cycle. The strong growth that developed in the mid-1960s served to create great optimism about the use of "aggregate demand" policies: any desired level of unemployment could be achieved, once people were prepared to accept the rate of inflation that went with it.

This optimism disappeared in the 1970s, and was replaced by increasing controversy which continued in the 1980s. Events proved that the choices among growth, unemployment and inflation were not so simple.

Stagflation – weak output growth, high unemployment and accelerating inflation – was particularly acute after 1975, partly as a result of external shocks – especially major increases in the price of oil. That experience culminated in 1981-82 with the deepest recession Canada has undergone since the 1930s. Inflation peaked only in late 1981 and unemployment reached extremely high levels in 1982. Despite a reasonably strong economic recovery, output did not surpass its prerecession level until late 1984, and it remained below capacity into the second half of the decade. Unemployment fell back to the 9-10% range, and stabilized at that level only in 1986.

The continuation first of increasing inflation in the face of little or no economic growth and, more recently, high unemployment despite renewed growth, underscored the problems of demand management. The federal government has had a deficit every year since 1976, with particularly large increases 1982-85, so that its debt has risen substantially relative to the economy's total output. Policymakers tried at first to keep output and

The Fiscal Plan
Government of Canada
Summary Statement of Transactions
Source: Government of Canada, Dept of Finance, *The Fiscal Plan* (Feb 1986)

	1979-80	1980-81	1981-82	1982-83	1983-84 (millions $)	1984-85	1985-86	1986-87 (projected)	1987-88 (projected)
Budgetary transactions									
Revenues	41 912	48 763	59 859	60 682	64 059	70 869	78 000	87 275	94 025
Expenditures	53 422	62 292	74 611	88 371	96 482	109 115	116 740		119 965
Surplus or deficit (-)	-11 510	-13 529	-14 752	-27 689	-32 423	-38 246	-34 250	-29 465	-25 940
Nonbudgetary transactions	1 380	3 492	5 516	3 896	7 224	8 445	5 932	6 909	8 258
Financial requirements (excluding foreign exchange transactions)	-10 130	-10 037	-9 236	-23 793	-25 199	-29 801	-28 818	-22 556	-17 682
Surplus or deficit (-) National Accounts Basis	-9 176	-9 472	-8 993	-21 985	-25 283	-32 208	-26 370	-23 220	-19 550
(As percent of Gross Domestic Product)	(3.5)	(3.2)	(2.6)	(6.1)	(6.4)	(7.7)	(5.8)	(4.8)	(3.4)

employment up by a series of tax reductions, while checking inflation through wage and price controls (1975-78), slowing down new expenditures programs and, most important, adopting an increasingly restrictive monetary policy. From 1979 to 1982 the emphasis on inflation control and monetary policy increased. Although there were some tax hikes and further attempts to reduce expenditure growth, fiscal policy remained basically expansionary. The latter tendency continued into the recovery as rising debt charges and the costs of statutory programs proved difficult to cut back. However, increasing concern with the accumulation of government debt led to both tax and expenditure measures to reduce the deficit to a more manageable level in the budgets of May 1985 and Feb 1986.

These events brought to the surface a long-simmering controversy between the Keynesian-based view that fiscal policy was the most effective way of controlling the economy – with monetary policy playing only a supporting role – and the "monetarists" who took the opposite stance. At the extremes, the schools differ sharply on the causes of fluctuations in the economy, the importance of interest rate changes (monetarists stress monetary causes and sensitivity to interest rates), and the degree of government intervention required (monetarists, especially those who stress the influence of inflationary expectations on people's views of the economy, favour less; Keynesians more). More traditional Keynesian views have also been weakened somewhat by the increasing concern in the 1980s with the longer-term, cumulative effects of deficits on the growth in public debt and its implications for stabilizing the economy, as well as by greater realization of the limits of fiscal policy in an economy as open to international shocks as Canada's is.

Policy Formulation and Implementation Although the actual fiscal policy followed may reflect a tug-of-war among many conflicting interests, responsibility for its implementation in Canada rests largely, though not entirely, with the federal Department of Finance. The federal budget is based on the *Fiscal Plan*, a set of recommendations on the level of total federal expenditures and their distribution among various policy "envelopes" (eg, economic development), as well as projections of revenue from existing taxes. The *Plan* is a co-operative effort among the Treasury Board, the Department of Finance and other government departments and agencies. Final decisions on spending and its distribution among the various "envelopes" are made by the Priorities and Planning Committee of Cabinet. Proposals for tax changes, the other input to the budget, are much more the product of a small group centered on the minister of finance. There is some discussion of possible tax changes outside this group, but because of a tradition of budget secrecy the Department of Finance has felt constrained in its ability to have open consultations with the provinces or private groups on such proposals in advance of the budget.

In practice, it is not easy to use fiscal policy to control the economy closely. It takes time to produce the figures for employment, output and prices required to see where the economy is moving, or to set required policy changes, particularly expenditure changes, in motion. Even when tax and expenditure changes are implemented, they may take 2 or more years to have a major impact on the economy, and since Canada's economy is relatively small compared to those of other major industrial countries, the effects of policy action here may be swamped by events elsewhere. Moreover, as the monetarist controversy of the early 1980s has shown, we still do not know enough about the detailed working of the economy to be certain that fiscal (or monetary) policy will always have the desired results. These difficulties are compounded by the presence of 2 major levels of government in Canada. For example, total government expenditures, including both direct purchases of goods and services and transfer payments to individuals, rose from the equivalent of about 30% of Gross Domestic Product (GDP) in 1960 to 46% in 1980. But federal expenditures rose from 14% to only 16% of GDP, while the proportion of provincial-local expenditures shot up from 16% to more than 30%, raising questions about the scope of federal government action for stabilization. Fortunately, provincial-local expenditures grow in a reasonably stable fashion, since many are related to long-term factors such as population growth. Moreover, some provinces have come to stress the role they too can play in stabilization.

Nor are the disagreements confined to economists and governments. Even if the authorities could be absolutely sure of what should be done, fiscal policy, like politics, is at best "an art of the possible." Large changes in taxes or expenditures, or again in monetary policy, may simply not be acceptable to all groups in the country, especially to organized groups such as business and labour, partly because they disagree on objectives and partly because they question the methods.

Critique of Policy Judged by actual results in recent years, neither fiscal policy nor the combination of fiscal and monetary policies have been very successful in stabilizing the Canadian economy. On the plus side, inflation has declined to much lower levels than its peak in 1981 and the country's international payments position has improved. On the other hand, economic growth was very poor from the mid-1970s to the early 1980s, and even in the mid-1980s output remained below the country's capabilities. Unemployment, although down from its 1982 peak, has remained high by historical standards, and the deficits of the federal and some provincial governments have remained very large into the second half of the 1980s. There has been a loss of confidence in government's ability to manage the economy, and controversy about the proper course of policy has been greater in the 1980s than at any time since the 1930s. The federal budgetary process was improved through a new expenditure management system (1979) and attempts have been made to widen consultation on it – the use of a committee of outside experts to examine proposed tax changes (1982) and government papers to stimulate public discussion of the process (1982, 1985).

Co-ordination of fiscal policy changes between the federal and provincial governments continues to be somewhat weak, although there have been a number of examples of co-operation as well as regular meetings of federal and provincial finance ministers. The tools of fiscal policy, including statistical material and econometric models of the economy, continue to improve.

The ability of government to change aggregate demand is well established, but much more needs to be known about how such changes will affect income, output and employment, on the one hand, and prices on the other. Some economists feel that fiscal and monetary policies for the control of inflation will have to be supplemented by wage and price controls.

There is a need too for better public education on fiscal policy. At times, even when the direction that policy should take has seemed clear to many economists, governments have been restricted in their actions or in the ways they explain their budgets because of public opinion. Controversy about policy goes far beyond disputes over how fiscal (or monetary) changes work, and disagreement over objectives has sharpened in recent years because broader social considerations have grown in importance. Should control of inflation take priority over reduction of unemployment? Should employment be increased by tax reductions, which reduce the role of government in the economy, or by expenditure increases, which expand it? How does one choose among proposed tax changes that will affect certain income groups or regions more than others? Such questions are more political than technical, and can be resolved only by public debate. PETER M. CORNELL

Reading: R.M. Bird, ed, *Fiscal Dimensions of Canadian Federalism* (1980); D.J. Daly, "Fiscal Policy – An Assessment" in *Canadian Perspectives in Economics* (1972); D.C. Smith, ed, *Economic Policy Advising in Canada* (1981).

Fish, member of a large, heterogeneous group of VERTEBRATES, living in a wide variety of aquatic habitats. There are slightly more species of fish than of all other vertebrates combined. They include jawless species (Agnatha), such as hagfishes and lampreys, and species with jaws (Pisces). Living members of the latter are fishes with cartilaginous skeletons (Chondrichthyes), eg, sharks and rays, or with bony skeletons (Osteichthyes), eg, salmon, perch and flatfishes. The term "fish" is used by some ichthyologists (zoologists studying them) in a more restricted sense than that used here. Some would include only forms with jaws. A few would include only the Osteichthyes, the largest and most diverse class of vertebrates. As the term is used here, fishes may be defined as cold-blooded vertebrates with gills throughout life, and limbs, if any, in the shape of fins. Most have scales and paired fins; however, many unrelated groups lack scales (eg, lampreys, bullhead catfishes), or one or both of the paired fins (eg, lampreys, eels, sand lances).

Body Covering Sharks and rays have placoid scales resembling tiny teeth. Most species of bony fishes with scales have either cycloid scales (smooth bordered) or ctenoid scales (rough bordered). Teleosts, the largest and most recently evolved (termed advanced or derived versus primitive or ancestral) group of bony fishes, display both forms of true scale: cycloid scales characterize relatively primitive teleosts (eg, salmon, minnows); ctenoid scales characterize advanced teleosts (eg, perch, sunfishes). Generally, fishes with cycloid scales have pelvic fins in the mid-portion of their bodies and lack spines in the fins; those with ctenoid scales have pelvic fins beneath the pectoral fin and have spines in some of their fins. Although frequently used to tell a fish's age, scales are not always reliable; certain bones in the head may be more accurate.

Buoyancy and Respiration Most bony fishes possess a swim or air bladder which helps them attain neutral buoyancy in water. Many bottom fishes lack the bladder, enabling them to stay on the bottom, even in relatively fast streams, with minimum energy expenditure. Some species (eg, longnose dace) can change bladder volume over relatively short periods of time, increasing it when in a lake, decreasing it in a river. Although a few fishes have lungs or other organs for breathing air, all fishes possess gills. In Canada, fishes are virtually always confined to water for respiration, but elsewhere there are species that can breathe in the atmosphere and even make journeys onto land.

Form and Colour Fishes exhibit a wide variety of shapes, sizes and colours. They range from highly elongate, almost stringlike, to globular in form. They can look like a lumpy rock, a leaf or a snake. Most have a tapering, variably compressed body with smooth contours, a torpedolike shape exemplified by trout. Fishes range in size from a whale shark, exceeding 15 m, to a tiny, 8 mm goby. In Canadian waters, the smallest fishes (eg, some minnows, darters, sculpins) may not exceed 10 cm; those over 3 m include Atlantic sturgeon and bluefin tuna; several may even exceed 5 m (eg, white sturgeon and thresher, white and basking sharks). Fishes are highly variable in colour. In the tropics, many brilliantly coloured freshwater and marine fishes occur, but those in Canadian waters, as in other northern areas, are generally drab. There are some exceptions, however, and males of several species can develop bright colours at spawning time (eg, arctic char, sockeye salmon, northern redbelly dace, longnose sucker, some darters). There tends to be more variation in colour among populations of the same species of northern freshwater fishes than among tropical fishes. The marked colour variations of rainbow trout or northern pike have convinced some anglers that there are different species of these fishes in different localities.

Nutrition Fish consume a wide variety of foods. Northern fishes have more generalized feeding habits than tropical fishes, tending to eat what is available. Most species are carnivorous; some are herbivorous, usually consuming ALGAE. The latter tend to have longer intestines. Many species are primarily bottom feeders (eg, sturgeons, suckers); others feed on PLANKTON in open water (eg, herring, cisco). Piscivorous fishes (eg, northern pike) feed primarily on other fishes. Insects and crustaceans are generally the most important diet items for nonpiscivorous, freshwater species in Canadian waters. The lamprey is the only parasitic northern fish; adults of many species feed on the blood of other fishes.

Reproduction Reproductive habits vary greatly. Chondrichthyes have internal fertilization; most Osteichthyes have external fertilization. In Canadian waters, most Osteichthyes have distinct spawning seasons. Eggs laid in fresh water by fall-spawning fish generally hatch in spring; those laid in summer hatch in a few days or weeks. Some (eg, sticklebacks, sunfish) build nests in which eggs are deposited and sometimes guarded. Herring and cod abandon their eggs after spawning. Individuals of most species can spawn for several years but lampreys and Pacific salmon spawn once and die. Many species migrate great distances to reach spawning grounds. One of the longest migrations is made by chinook salmon, which swim, without feeding, for about 2800 km up the Yukon R.

Habitat In marine and fresh water, various species can be characterized as bottom dwelling (benthic, these are the "groundfishes" of commercial FISHERIES) or open water dwelling (ie, pelagic in oceans, limnetic in lakes). Littoral zone fishes are inshore and, in oceans, may occur in tide pools. In the Arctic Ocean and arctic lakes, fish may spend most of their lives under ice. There waters can be superchilled, colder than -1°C.

Freshwater habitats of fishes are diverse, including hot springs, cold torrential mountain streams, deep lakes and saline waters. In the Cave and Basin Hot Springs drainage system near Banff, Alta, a form of longnose dace, normally found in cold lakes and streams, lives in temperatures up to 26°C and in close proximity to introduced, tropical aquarium fishes (eg, sailfin molly and mosquitofish, which live in temperatures of up to 30°C and give birth to live young). In Wood Buffalo National Park, fishes live in sinkhole lakes, formed by the surface collapsing through dissolved-out bedrock. In some cases, they got to the small ponds by underground channels.

Evolution Fishes probably evolved from descendants of ECHINODERMS and in turn gave rise to AMPHIBIANS. Their origin dates back to about 500 million years ago. In Canada, there is an extensive FOSSIL record of fishes, including Agnatha, Chondrichthyes and Osteichthyes. Placoderms and acanthodians are 2 other large groups known only from the fossil record.

Canada has a diverse fauna of living species, including representatives of all classes. This fauna is rich in numbers of individuals, but not in numbers of species, especially when the vast amount of freshwater lakes and rivers and the extensive coastline are considered. There are about 22 000 recognized species of living fishes worldwide, in about 450 families; almost 40% of the species live in fresh water. D.E. McAllister, National Museum of Natural Science, Ottawa, has calculated numbers of native species in Canadian waters at about 950, in 190 families. Of this number, about 760 are confined to marine waters (Pacific, Arctic and Atlantic oceans). Several species are diadromous, ie, spend part of their life in the ocean and part in fresh water. Of these, some (Pacific salmon, many lampreys) are anadromous, spawning in fresh water, while the American eel of the Atlantic coast is catadromous, spawning in the ocean. The native species confined to fresh water (about 190) occur in drainages of the Pacific, Arctic and Atlantic oceans, Hudson Bay and the Gulf of Mexico. The Great Lakes and southern Ontario have the greatest number of species; YT, NWT, Alberta and Saskatchewan have relatively few, considering their area and extent of water.

The ice ages had a profound effect on Canada's fish fauna. Differences in species numbers across Canada can be explained by glacial events. Until about 15 000 years ago, most of Canada was covered by ice. A reinvasion of fishes occurred from ice-free areas (refugia), with most of our modern freshwater fish coming from the Mississippi-Missouri refugium. Most of British Columbia's species came from the Columbian R refugium; in other areas of Canada, the Yukon R and Atlantic coast refugia were important. As the ice sheet melted, species could cross from one drainage basin to another, eg, from the Columbia R to the Fraser R. Only fishes with some salt tolerance could reach offshore areas (Newfoundland, Vancouver I, Queen Charlotte Is).

More new species of fishes are described each year around the world than species of any other vertebrate group. It is unlikely that many species new to science will be found in Canadian waters (although range extensions may continue to be found). Few species appear to be confined to Canadian waters. A species of whitefish (*Coregonus huntsmani*, formerly called *Coregonus canadensis*), confined to part of NS, has been described, but its existence may be threatened by ACID RAIN. Although biologists in provincial and federal government agencies, universities and consulting companies are involved in fish studies, many gaps remain in our knowledge. Collecting trips often reveal a species not previously recorded in a particular province or even in Canada, particularly off the Pacific coast. The observant fisherman, interested in identifying his catch, can provide valuable distributional records. Important gaps also exist in our knowledge of the life history of many commercially important species (eg, very little is known about habitats of larval herring and lake whitefish). *See also* ATLANTIC SALMON; BASS; CATFISH; CHAR; CHIMAERA; COD; EEL; FLATFISH; GAR; GRAYLING; HAGFISH; HERRING; LAMPREY; MACKEREL; MINNOW; MUSKELLUNGE; PACIFIC SALMON; PERCH; PICKEREL; PIKE; RAY; SALMON; SCORPIONFISH; SCULPIN; SHARK; SMELT; SPORTFISHING; STICKLEBACK; STURGEON; SUCKER; TROUT; TUNA; WHITEFISH. JOSEPH S. NELSON

Reading: J.L. Hart, *Pacific Fishes of Canada* (1973); A.H. Leim and W.B. Scott, *Fishes of the Atlantic Coast of Canada* (1966); Scott and E.J. Crossman, *Freshwater Fishes of Canada* (1973).

Fish Classification There is no single, accepted classification system for fishes, and there are more disagreements among ichthyologists about the interrelationships of fishes than exist among other vertebrate systematists about their groups. This results, in part, from our relatively poor knowledge of the 22 000 or so living species and numerous fossil groups, and also from differing approaches to classification. It is not necessarily the result of differing views on evolutionary relationships. Many ichthyologists have adopted a relatively new method, cladistics, which classifies strictly according to the recency of common descent. Others use the more conventional approach, evolutionary or synthetic systematics, where the inferred amount of divergence among groups is considered, as is the history of their evolutionary relationships (phylogeny — the determination of these relationships is another matter). These perspectives can result in markedly different classifications. For example, in a cladistic system, HAGFISHES probably would be placed in a category separate from LAMPREYS and other vertebrates because, relative to hagfishes, lampreys are thought to share a common genealogical branching point with all other vertebrates. Systematists using the evolutionary approach could express the relationship in several ways but would tend to place hagfishes and lampreys in the single category of jawless fishes, separate from all jawed vertebrates, although recognizing that they are very distantly related. Cladists may use terms in ways that differ significantly from classical usage, eg, cladists would include all evolutionary derivatives of Osteichthyes within that category and would therefore consider the tetrapods (including mammals) as Osteichthyes. Differences may also exist among classification systems, depending on whether the worker is a "lumper" or a "splitter." A lumper constructs a classification with categories containing more groups than that of a splitter. There are no rules for the amount of difference necessary to designate various categories. A lumper recognizes one family for salmon, whitefish and grayling; a splitter, 2 or 3 families. JOSEPH S. NELSON

Reading: Joseph S. Nelson, *Fishes of the World* (1984).

Fisher (*Martes pennanti*), cat-sized MARTEN with relatively short legs, long tapering tail, and feet clawed for climbing. Its heavy pelage includes a dense grey underfur overlain by brown, silver-banded guard hairs. Females have finer, more lustrous fur than males. Males may reach 100 cm in length and 7 kg in weight; females seldom exceed 90 cm and 2.7 kg. Fishers are a forest species, formerly distributed from coast to coast, N to lat 65°. They were exterminated S of the St Lawrence R but have been reintroduced to NS and NB. Food is mainly hares, squirrels and mice, but porcupines, and other species, as available, are regularly killed. Fishers are generally solitary except for the female and her young. Mating is polygamous, during Mar-Apr. The gestation period is about 350 days because of delayed implantation. The young (1-4) are born in Mar. Sexual maturity is reached in 2 years. Fishers are among the most valuable furbearing animals but are not abundant and only 6000-9000 furs are marketed annually. *See also* FUR TRAPPING. IAN MCTAGGART-COWAN

Fisher, Charles, lawyer, politician, judge, premier of NB (b at Fredericton 15 Aug or 16 Sept 1808; d there 8 Dec 1880). He led the first RESPONSIBLE GOVERNMENT in NB (1854-61) and was the leading constitutional lawyer of his day. He was educated at King's College (UNB) and was elected to the Assembly in 1837. A somewhat tardy convert to responsible government because he considered Newbrunswickers "too loyal and too ignorant" to reject the ruling clique, he served on the compact Council 1848-50 before leading the Opposition to power as attorney general in 1854. His Cabinet, perhaps the province's most talented, then implemented its administrative, electoral and educational reforms. Ousted by S.L. TILLEY as premier in 1861 over a crown lands scandal, Fisher later joined with Tilley as a Father of Confederation at the QUÉBEC CONFERENCE and LONDON CONFERENCE. Elected to the House of Commons in 1867, Fisher resigned when he was appointed a judge of the NB Supreme Court (3 Oct 1868). CARL M. WALLACE

Fisher, Douglas Mason, politician, journalist (b at Sioux Lookout, Ont 19 Sept 1919). Educated at U of T, Queen's and U of London, he served overseas during WWII. Known as "The Giant Killer" after his first political campaign and smashing victory over C.D. HOWE in 1957, Fisher represented Port Arthur [Thunder Bay] for the CCF-NDP until his resignation in 1965. He became a syndicated columnist for the Toronto *Telegram*, 1963-71, and then the Toronto *Sun*, and since 1963 has had his own weekly TV political interview program on CJOH Ottawa. His interest in sports led to his appointment as a director of Hockey Canada (1971-78). Fisher co-authored *Canada's Sporting Heroes* (1975) and, with Dalton CAMP, 5 reports of the Ontario Commission on the Legislature (1971-74). As a newspaper columnist and TV host, he is seen as unbiased politically, one who emphasizes parliament, the federal party system, and the individuality of Canada's political figures. JEAN MARGARET CROWE

Fisher, Gordon Neil, publisher (b at Montréal 9 Dec 1928; d at Toronto 8 Aug 1985). Fisher was president of SOUTHAM INC, one of the largest newspaper chains in Canada. He attended Lower Canada Coll, Trinity Coll School and McGill, where he studied engineering. At Southam, as president and director, he played an important role in keeping the firm's interests diversified into radio, TV, print and other areas. J.L. GRANATSTEIN

Fisher, Hugh, canoeist (b in New Zealand 1 Oct 1955). He finished first in the K-2 500 m and K-4 500 m events at the 1976 national championships and was 1979 and 1980 outrigger world champion. He missed the 1981 season because of injury but managed a second-place finish (K-2 1000 m, time 3:37.45) at the 1982 world championships, a third-place finish at the 1983 world championships (K-2 500 m, 1:49.58) and a second (K-2 500 m) and third (K-2 1000 m) at the Brandenburg Regatta in 1984. With Alwyn MORRIS he won a gold medal in the K-2 1000 m (3:24.22) and bronze in the K-2 500 m (1:35.41) at the 1984 Los Angeles Olympics. At recent national championships, he finished first in the K-4 1000 m (3:12.136) in 1985, but had a second-place finish in the K-1 500 m and K-2 500 m events in 1986. Along with numerous other awards, he was named a Member of the Order of Canada in 1985, and in 1987 was a medical student at UBC. JAMES MARSH

Hugh Fisher and Alwyn Morris in action at the 1984 Los Angeles Olympics, at which they won a gold medal (*courtesy Athlete Information Bureau/Service Information Athlètes*).

Fisher, John, broadcaster, publicist (b at Sackville, NB 29 Nov 1912; d at Boynton Beach, Fla 15 Feb 1981). A law graduate from Dalhousie U, he was a reporter and broadcaster in Halifax before joining the CBC as a "roving reporter." From 1943 to 1955, he travelled throughout the country, broadcasting its wonders on "John Fisher Reports," a popular, live, quarter-hour program heard 3 times a week over the national radio network. He called his scripts "pride builders" and was unofficially dubbed "Mr Canada." Thereafter, he served as executive director of the Canadian Tourist Association; special assistant to PM John DIEFENBAKER; chief centennial commissioner; and finally head of John Fisher Enterprises Ltd, a public-relations firm. JOHN ROBERT COLOMBO

Fisheries In 1985 Canada's commercial fisheries contributed slightly over $1 billion (GDP value added) to the national economy (less than 1% of that of all goods-producing industries). In the Atlantic provinces, however, the industry contributed about $750 million in 1985, or 10% of the value of all goods-producing industries in the region. Along the Atlantic coast, about 1000 communities are mostly or wholly dependent upon the fisheries. Lesser numbers of such communities are found on the Pacific coast and around the lakes of the interior. Most are hamlets with less than 500 people, but the industry also supports larger urban centres in all 3 regions. The fisheries of BC, NS and Newfoundland are of greatest significance. BC's is usually the leader in value of production. In the Atlantic provinces, Newfoundland leads in volume and NS in value of production; together they account for 75-80% of Atlantic output. The fisheries also have a strong regional impact through links with suppliers of goods and services, especially the SHIPBUILDING industry but also ship-chandlers, and other intermediaries. These links, plus the interaction between fishermen's households and the local community, mean that the effect of economic change in the fishing industry is transmitted and multiplied throughout the general economy; eg, in NS a 1% change in fishery production causes a 1.4% change in total provincial income.

The industry has many part-time fishermen; half of the fishermen registered in the Atlantic region, two-thirds of those in the Pacific region and three-quarters of those in the central region receive the larger part of their income from sources other than fishing. Some of these people depend on fishing to augment other income; others participate because of cultural or family tradition and are often strongly attached to their identity as fishermen.

Those who claim fishing as their principal source of income derive, on the average, about 65% of total income from it. In the Pacific and central regions, the balance comes mainly from nonfishing activities; in the Atlantic region the major income supplement is unemployment insurance benefits to which self-employed fishermen (owner/operators) and crewmen are entitled. In all regions, the typical net annual income from all sources is $5000-12 500 (fishermen in the Pacific region are near the top of the range; those in the central region near the bottom; those in the Atlantic region in the middle). The evidence suggests that most fishing enterprises at present are incapable not only of generating surplus revenue for capital accumulation and investment but even of providing adequate personal incomes.

Resource Base Fishery resources may be classified as finfish (including major marine species and all commonly used freshwater species) and shellfish (CRUSTACEANS and MOLLUSCS). Aquatic mammals and SEAWEEDS also are considered fishery resources. Marine species are classified as littoral or inshore (found within the 50-60 fathom contour adjacent to the coastline); demersal (dwelling near the seafloor, chiefly on offshore banks); and pelagic (occupying the surface of the open sea). Littoral stocks include crustaceans (LOBSTER and CRAB species) and molluscs (most CLAM species and OYSTERS). Demersal stocks include some crustaceans (crabs), a mollusc (SCAL-

LOP) and a great variety of finfish (eg, COD, and related species, FLATFISHES, rockfishes). The important pelagic species are all finfish (eg, HERRING, TUNA), except for one mollusc (the common SQUID).

Certain species – eg, redfish (ocean perch), which combine demersal and pelagic features – elude this classification. Others, particularly the anadromous species that swim upstream to spawn (eg, SALMON), must be classified separately. Because of their dependence on watershed and estuarine habitats, anadromous species are, along with the sedentary littoral species, most vulnerable to environmental damage. Demersal species and the larger or predator pelagic species are relatively long-lived and subject to low natural mortality. Stocks tend to be quite stable, eg, the year-to-year variation in the Atlantic cod catch averages about 10%, compared with about a 30% variation in the PACIFIC SALMON catch. The smaller or forage pelagic species feed on PLANKTON and, being located at a low trophic level, generally occur in relative abundance. Because of high mortality in the younger stages, these stocks fluctuate widely, some (eg, common squid) in the short term and others (eg, some herring stocks) over the long term. A fish community as a whole has far greater stability than the many individual species it contains.

Stocks of most pelagic species have a regular seasonal north-south migration pattern, sometimes over long distances. Some of these species, as well as anadromous and certain demersal species, also exhibit a seasonal inshore-offshore migration. The presence inshore of these stocks and of sedentary littoral stocks provides the basis for various small-boat fisheries. Operations on the offshore fishing grounds are based on schools (ie, feeding and spawning concentrations) of demersal and pelagic stocks and involve larger craft.

Canada has abundant fishery resources on the Atlantic and Pacific coasts and in inland waters but, while renewable, they are limited and exhaustible. Stock restoration and enhancement projections indicate that, even with full use of all available species stocks, the total yield or nominal catch is unlikely to exceed 2.5 million t annually, ie, somewhat less than twice the 1985 level of 1.4 million (valued at just over $1 billion). This amount would be only about 3% of the annual world catch, which appears to have reached a limit at 70-75 million t.

Resource Harvesting A peculiarity of fishery resources is that typically they are common property, ie, under the "rule of capture," fish in a wild stock become the private property of a fishing enterprise only when caught and removed from the water. Each such enterprise therefore tries to maximize its share of a harvest limited by nature or regulation. The results are large fleets, high production costs, increased wastage and spoilage, and idle periods for vessels and handling/processing facilities. Because of mounting pressure to circumvent and subvert existing CONSERVATION measures, fish stocks are jeopardized.

Most Canadian enterprises are individually owned and operated; partnerships are common in some fisheries and there are influential producers' co-operatives on both coasts and in the inland fisheries. Native bands run communal enterprises in certain areas. Vertical integration (ie, fleet ownership by corporations involved in fish processing) is predominant in the Atlantic trawling and scallop-dragging fisheries and, although declining in importance, still occurs in the Pacific purse-seining fishery and elsewhere. Remuneration is generally made on the basis of shares in the proceeds of the catch. Typically the owner receives a fixed percentage as the "boat's" share and deductions are made to cover certain expenses and, in larger operations, officers' bonuses; the balance is then divided equally among the crew. Sharing ("lay") formulae vary with the scale of the operation; the owner's share in the Pacific purse-seining fleet is about 35%; in the Atlantic trawler fleet, 60%. With the unionization of crews, such arrangements are subject to bargaining and modification (for example, providing a basic rate of pay, regardless of the success of the trip).

Herring fishing on Deer Island, NB, using weirs and seines (*courtesy Tourism New Brunswick*).

A distinction is often made between small-scale and large-scale (ie, industrial) fishing enterprises, usually called "inshore" and "offshore," respectively. Inshore craft, defined for administrative purposes as those under 25 gross t, account for 95% of all vessels in the Canadian fleets but only 35% of the tonnage. The distinction, however, is an oversimplification: vessels of all sizes, except perhaps the smallest, sometimes fish the same grounds. More significant is the distinction between vessels with year-round versus seasonal operating capability and between those capable of versatile operation versus specialization.

Fish Processing At least 95% of the Canadian fish harvest is converted to food products: 70-75% is fresh chilled or frozen; 10-15%, cured; 10%, canned. About 98% of the total is handled by the fish-processing industry, which (at $2.4 billion in 1985) more than doubles the value of the fish caught. Advanced processing (eg, canning, curing, filleting/freezing, etc) predominates. This is because of the need for storage (in view of the seasonal peaking of raw-material supplies) and because products must be transported over long distances; it is also a response to the increasing use of "convenience" foods.

Processing companies range from small, usually specialized firms to large, integrated ones supplying a wide range of products. In the Pacific region, consolidation of operations around the major coastal centres has been accompanied by a massive concentration of ownership through mergers and acquisitions. In the early 1980s the 4 largest firms produced 60-65% of the regional output of frozen salmon and about 80% of canned salmon and herring roe. The central region is dominated in the West by the Freshwater Fish Marketing Corp (FFMC), which handles about half the region's production, and in the Great Lakes area by a private firm. Concentration has also occurred in the Atlantic region where about 60% of the regional output of groundfish products comes from the 4 largest firms (40% from the catch of their own fleets). With the Canadian Saltfish Corp, a crown trading company, these firms account for possibly 80-90% of the export trade in groundfish products. Concentration in the Atlantic region has not been associated with consolidation of processing activity. On the contrary, as the traditional cottage industry declined, plant processing dispersed to replace it. At present some 450 coastal communities have processing facilities, most of them being independently owned, but many also belonging to (horizontally) integrated companies and co-operatives. More critical, perhaps, is the fact that redundance in processing capacity causes an obsession with plant throughput and leads to counterproductive competition for raw material.

Marketing Although a significant part of total fish production is handled in the marketplace by specialized dealers, brokers and export/import houses, most is marketed by processing companies and co-operatives. Substantial quantities of some products (eg, canned salmon, frozen groundfish) are prepared for export under labels of foreign buyers. The Canadian market absorbs about one-third of the annual production, the proportion varying among products from virtually zero to 100%. Canned salmon probably is the major product for which the domestic market is the more important outlet; conversely, only 20% of Atlantic groundfish is consumed in Canada. When domestic sources are deficient, some products (eg, canned and frozen shrimp and canned tuna) are supplemented with imports (valued at almost $500 million in 1985), of which two-thirds are from the US.

The Canadian fish trade has always been strongly export oriented and is likely to remain so. By the end of the 1970s, Canada had become the world's foremost fish-exporting nation. But, in 1985 Canada commands only an 8% share of international fish trade, about $1.4 billion (US) in a $17-billion (US) international market. Canadian exports go to many countries but are highly concentrated in the US, which takes 60% of the total, including most of the freshwater fish, chilled and frozen Atlantic groundfish, lobster and scallop; Japan takes close to 20%; western Europe (especially the European Economic Community) takes somewhere around 15%.

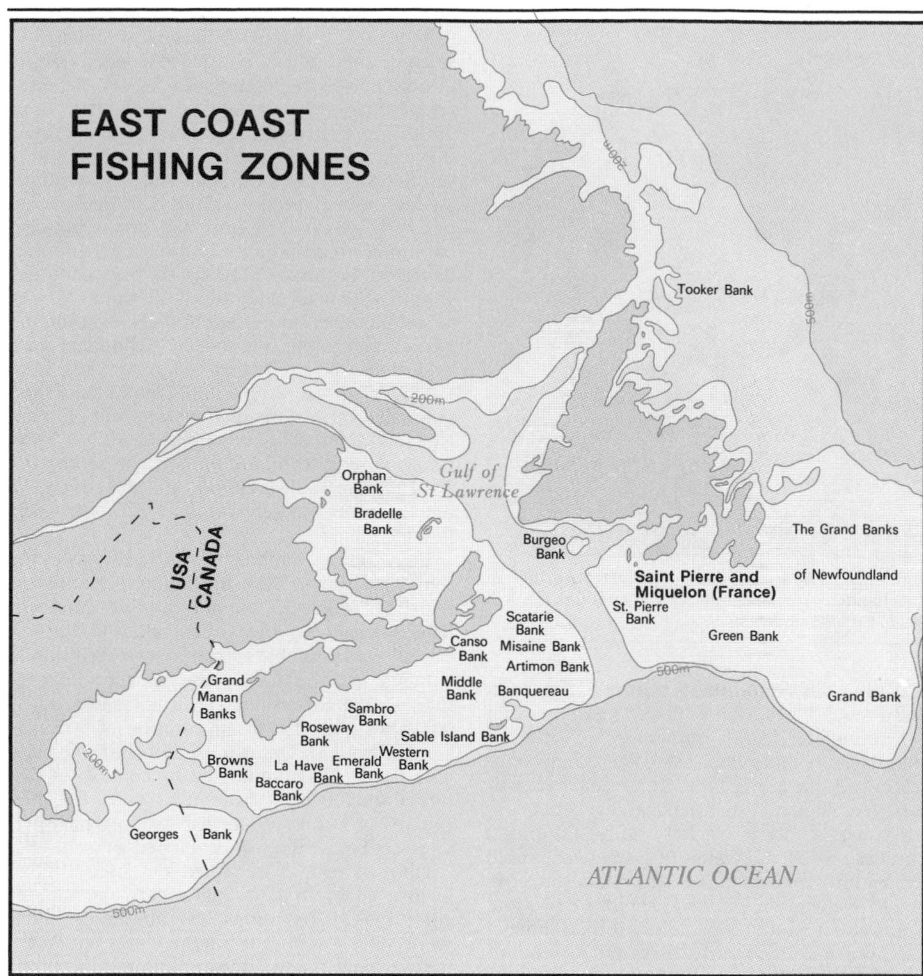

The EEC is the most important market for canned salmon and frozen herring; Japan is the major market for frozen salmon and almost an exclusive market for herring roe. Cured fish, chiefly salted and dried codfish, is exported mainly to Mediterranean and Caribbean countries; canned herring products are exported worldwide.

Institutional Aspects The 2 large fishermen's unions at present, in BC and Newfoundland, comprise fish-plant workers and some vessel owners as well as crewmen – groups with partially conflicting economic interests. Otherwise, fishermen on the Pacific coast, in inland waters and on the Atlantic coast outside Newfoundland are generally organized into associations based on a particular fishery, gear type or other special interest. In the Maritimes, many of these associations are linked by an umbrella federation. Unlike unions, which negotiate with buyers, mainly over fish prices, associations tend to represent members to government on matters of fishery regulation. In addition, fishermen's co-operatives, which embrace processing and marketing as well as fish-harvesting operations, operate in BC, Saskatchewan, Québec and the Maritimes. Co-operatives and private firms in the processing and marketing divisions of commercial fisheries support associations representing the interests of those divisions. These associations, organized provincially, are federated in the Fisheries Council of Canada in Ottawa, the principal channel of communication between the fishing industry and the federal government.

The federal government has exclusive jurisdiction over fishing operations and over interprovincial and export trade in fishery products. The port market and fish handling and processing come under provincial jurisdiction. Subject to federal approval of regulations, management authority has been delegated to Ontario and to the Prairie provinces for commercial freshwater fisheries and to Québec for littoral marine fisheries.

All provincial governments and various federal agencies are active in fishery development activities; co-ordination of policy is sought, with mixed success, through a number of formal and ad hoc arrangements. The federal powers are exercised through the Department of Fisheries and Oceans and through certain special agencies which report directly to the minister of fisheries. The national headquarters are in Ottawa; regional administrative headquarters are located in Vancouver, Winnipeg, Halifax, St John's and Moncton, NB. There are major research stations and laboratories at Nanaimo, BC; Winnipeg; Burlington, Ont; St Andrews, NB; Dartmouth, NS; and St John's (*see also* FISHERIES RESEARCH BOARD; FRESHWATER INSTITUTE).

The basic statute administered by the Department of Fisheries and Oceans is the Fisheries Act, under which regulations are made for fishery management, including the patrol of coastal waters, the protection of fish life in streams, etc. The Coastal Fisheries Protection Act empowers the government to control the conduct of foreign fishing vessels in Canadian ports and territorial waters, and the Fish Inspection Act provides for control of the quality of fishery products. Assistance programs and intervention in industrial and trade development fall under a group of statutes, eg, the Fisheries Development Act, the Fisheries Prices Support Act, the Freshwater Fish Marketing Act and the Canadian Saltfish Act. *See also* SEALING; WHALING.

W.C. MACKENZIE AND JOSEPH GOUGH

Fisheries History Canada's Atlantic fishery was the attraction that drew the first Europeans to the northern half of N America. Economist Harold INNIS and others have argued that the fishery encouraged the growth of the British, French and Dutch empires, partly because of its value as a "nursery for seamen," but more because fishing, shipbuilding, shipping and trading economically reinforced one another. The fishery also encouraged the development of the N American colonies, and it still sustains large coastal and inland regions. The fishing industry has been complex, contradictory and varied, with a "boom and bust" economic nature. Its independent participants, who have traditionally faced hazards and hardships in the pursuit of the trade, in the 20th century have formed many organizations of varying strength to protect themselves against loss and to lobby governments for improved conditions in the industry.

Beginnings: 1500-1750 Europeans, including the English, French, Spanish, Portuguese and Basques, began fishing off Newfoundland in the 16th century. The plentiful, easy-to-catch COD was the most valuable commodity: dried or salted, it could be transported long distances and would keep for several months. Fleets of fishing boats were numerous, for they required little capital investment. Fishermen arrived in the spring and stayed until about September. They fished directly from the boats using hooks and lines.

By the late 16th century the English and French were the chief rivals. The English fishery, operated primarily by West Countrymen, was concentrated in semipermanent fishing stations in protected harbours on Newfoundland's SE coast. The captain of the first ship to arrive at a harbour became the FISHING ADMIRAL and governed the station. Fish were caught close to shore from small boats brought from England. The day's catch was unloaded directly onto a "stage" (wharf), where the fish were cleaned, split and lightly salted. They were then dried on "flakes" (open tables that allowed maximum circulation of air). This shore-based DRY FISHERY resulted in a "hard-cure" cod suitable for trade to distant markets, and it became the basis for England's territorial claims to Newfoundland.

By contrast, French fishermen from widely scattered ports more commonly fished off the GRAND BANKS and other banks (productive, relatively shallow areas off the coast). They had access to more salt than the English, and most French fishermen processed the catch aboard their ships. This GREEN FISHERY yielded a shorter-lived product more suited to home use than distant travel, but it allowed French fishermen to get the fish to markets faster than the English, and they could return to the banks more than

Drawing of a 16th-century Newfoundland fishing ship. The cod were so plentiful that they could be hauled in with baskets (*courtesy National Archives of Canada/C-92348*).

once in a season. PLACENTIA, Nfld, served as French headquarters until the Treaty of UTRECHT in 1713, when French territorial claims to Newfoundland and mainland Nova Scotia were lost. The French fishery then became dispersed, with fishermen using Cape Breton and temporary fishing stations on Newfoundland's N and W coast. Cape Breton was lost through the Treaty of PARIS, 1763, but French fishermen were allowed continued use of Newfoundland's W and part of the NE coasts (*see* FRENCH SHORE).

Meanwhile, a British fishery had developed in the Maritimes. Although SALMON received increasing attention, cod still dominated. In all Atlantic areas, settlers fished in small, open boats from shore using single lines with hooks, like the Europeans. Some European fishing vessels gradually began to bring passengers who fished from small boats (*see* BYE-BOAT) and might return or settle; some took aboard fish cured by settlers (called PLANTERS in Newfoundland). Some ships only brought trade goods and took away salt fish. By the mid-18th century, the WHALE fishery around Newfoundland and the WALRUS fishery at the Îles de la Madeleine had practically disappeared.

1750-1867 From the second half of the 18th century, a great schooner fleet developed in the Atlantic fishery. Schooners (fore-and-aft rigged vessels such as the BLUENOSE), in search of cod, halibut and haddock on banks, carried dories; fishermen would set out in these rowboats and bring fish back for splitting and salting on board the schooners. In Newfoundland a large schooner fleet fished the banks and the Labrador coast. LIVEYERS were permanent residents, "floaters" moved along the coast, and "stationers" set up fishing stations where they could cure fish ashore. Conception Bay schooners also developed a large SEAL fishery which became important in Newfoundland's growth.

The AMERICAN REVOLUTION and the NAPOLEONIC WARS increased British dependence on northwestern Atlantic fish and lumber. The mutually reinforcing fisheries, lumbering and trade, all related to wooden vessels, brought vigour to the Atlantic economy, so that even today the period is considered a golden age. But most fishermen appear to have been poor: most operated small shore boats rather than schooners, and many, especially in the southern areas, alternated between fishing and the shipping trade. Southwestern Nova Scotia and New Brunswick's Bay of Fundy shore began to lead the Atlantic fishery. The region had a good lumber and trading base, a long ice-free fishing season, an abundance of fish, a good mix of species, a short coastline allowing some concentration of enterprise, nearby markets, and nearby alternative employment in the US. Although small enterprises dominated the southern areas, elsewhere large fish-curing and schooner-owning firms, such as St John's firms and the Robin interests in the Gulf of St Lawrence, controlled much of the fishery. In Newfoundland, smaller-scale local merchants and schooner owners made some gains.

New methods emerged in the 19th century. For example, fishermen had used the beach seine, which required points of land to help in the encirclement of fish with nets. The new purse seine, developed by American fishermen, operated in open water by surrounding surface-schooling fish with a net hanging down from a line of corks. The fishermen then tightened a purse line at the bottom of the net to enclose the fish in what looked like a floating bowl. As well, French fishermen introduced bultows (now "longlines"), which were long "groundlines" anchored near or on the bottom with many short sections of hook and line. Instead of a single hook on the line, as before, hundreds could be used.

Fishermen hauling trawl into dory. The rubber rings on their hands are nippers to protect the hands (*courtesy Wilfred L. Eisnor/Knickle's Studio*).

During this period the presence of American and French fleets fishing off the Maritimes and Newfoundland led to numerous incidents, as colonial authorities laboured to keep foreign vessels outside the 3-mile limit. By the CONVENTION OF 1818 New England fishermen could generally use BNA waters only for shelter and repair, and to purchase wood and water. But Americans could fish within 3 miles at the Îles de la Madeleine, SW and W Newfoundland, and Labrador E of about Natashquan; and they could dry fish on shore at Labrador and in unsettled bays off Newfoundland's SW coast. Between 1854 and 1866 a RECIPROCITY treaty with the US allowed fishermen from each jurisdiction to fish within the other's territorial waters and provided some measure of free trade. The end of reciprocity coincided with some economic distress among Nova Scotia and Newfoundland fishermen.

Confederation to WWI After Confederation in 1867, Canadian politicians attempted to turn from a commercial-marine economy and to develop a continental economy. Maritime leaders tried to take advantage of new opportunities in railways and manufacturing, and made little effort to promote the self-reinforcing lumbering-fishing-exporting marine economy. By WWI only fishing remained a major employer. But the dispersion of its facilities along the coastline – attributable to a harvesting technology requiring proximity to the resources and a curing technique (drying on flakes) needing enormous spaces – persisted, and since WWI the fishery has never been able to support its scattered communities properly.

The growing urban and industrial economy of the late 19th century brought changes to the fishery. Steel vessels with greater reliability, safety and size began to displace wooden trading vessels. In Newfoundland's seal fishery, steamers replaced sail in the 1860s. From about 1870 to 1900, improved canning technology encouraged the creation of the lobster and Bay of Fundy sardine industries. Although salted groundfish (white-fleshed species such as cod, halibut and haddock which feed near the ocean bottom) continued to dominate the industry, American fishermen began to sell fresh fish. Fast schooners enabled them to get groundfish from GEORGES BANK and other banks near Nova Scotia onto the market before the fish spoiled. Schooners from LUNENBURG, NS, followed the Americans from Labrador to the Grand and other banks, and gradually other Canadian vessels did so also. Newfoundland schooners, despite some Grand Banks fishing, continued to depend largely on the Labrador saltfish fishery, and the codtrap (a net enclosure) largely replaced the hook-and-line technique.

Elsewhere in Canada, Ontario fisheries in the 19th century had fresh-fish markets nearby and depended less on salting and canning. Persistent fishing trends in the Great Lakes led to the depletion of desirable species, which allowed less valuable ones to take over. As well, environmental changes resulting from increased population caused the disappearance of ATLANTIC SALMON from Lk Ontario. In the West, the early lake fishery was dominated by companies that rented small boats to fishermen, who were often Indians. A strong winter fishery, in which nets were set below the ice, developed as well.

On the Pacific coast, salted and dried fish had been used by Indians, fur traders and miners. After the 1870s numerous salmon canneries were built. Canning technology and settlement patterns gave the BC industry a more concentrated character than that of the Atlantic, because even in isolated places the industry depended on bringing together many plant workers and many boats to take advantage of the seasonal migrations of PACIFIC SALMON. Railways provided transport to larger markets for the growing salmon industry, and later for the halibut fishery. Increased bait requirements encouraged the herring fishery.

Conflicts primarily with the United States over fisheries continued to test and strengthen Canadian sovereignty. Between 1871 and 1885 the Treaty of WASHINGTON settled some fisheries disputes and slightly boosted the fishing industry. Conflicts in the 1880s between Americans and Canadians sealing on the Bering Sea were settled by international tribunal in 1893 (*see* BERING SEA DISPUTE). Colonial authorities established bounties (subsidies) or regulations to encourage fishing; some (eg, Newfoundland's BAIT ACTS) were in response to heavy subsidies provided by the French fishery on the northwestern Atlantic. Newfoundland won more respect from the United States and Canada, and more independence from Great Britain, through its stubborn and partly successful efforts to govern foreign fishing (*see* BOND-BLAINE TREATY).

At Confederation the federal government was given authority over the fisheries. In the Province of Canada early legislation had included a system of licensing largely designed to protect private ownership of salmon-fishing stands. The emphasis after Confederation was on conservation, and the 1868 Fisheries Act provided for licensing on a much broader scale. Various royal commissions provided the rationale for regulatory action, and the resulting restrictions usually applied to fishing times and seasons, fish size, equipment (eg, the purse seine was banned for many years from the Atlantic fishery) and, in BC,

Dories from the schooner *Albert J. Lutz*, 1913, being towed astern prior to being dropped off. In dory fishing, fishermen set out in rowboats and brought back fish to the schooner for splitting and salting (*courtesy Maritime Museum of the Atlantic*).

the number of boats and plants. The original Fisheries Act also contained provisions to outlaw the introduction to the water of substances deleterious to fish. These provisions, and the Act's clauses on licensing, remain the pillars of Canadian fishery management. Despite frequent difficulties in the industry, Canadian fishery management is among the best in the world.

The Canadian Fisheries Service was established after Confederation, and over the next half-century the Dept of Marine and Fisheries developed an extensive hatchery program (*see* AQUACULTURE). Although fishery authorities claimed excellent results, by the mid-1930s the program's success was minimal and most hatcheries were closed. Scientific research commenced in 1898 when the federal government established the first of several fisheries biological and technical stations. The Biological Board of Canada (later the FISHERIES RESEARCH BOARD) was independent until the early 1970s, when the federal fisheries department took control of research.

WWI interrupted fish supplies to Europe and made manpower scarce. A brief postwar period of prosperity, plus the need of veterans for employment, ended "limited entry" (licence limitation), which had been applied in the BC salmon fishery since 1889. The federal government also abandoned the system, established before the war, of transport subsidies for fish. Finally, decisions by Britain's JUDICIAL COMMITTEE OF THE PRIVY COUNCIL in this period and the 1920s weakened the federal government's authority over the fisheries relative to that of the provinces.

Boom and Depression: 1919-39 The GREAT DEPRESSION started early in the Atlantic fisheries. After WWI, while Newfoundland and Gulf of St Lawrence fisheries were served largely by superannuated fishing craft from Nova Scotia, European fleets used trawlers (large vessels that drag conical nets along the bottom), which were more reliable than either the hook-and-line fishery or the seasonal codtrap fishery. In the 1920s, after losing some of its market to European suppliers, Newfoundland competed more strongly in the West Indies markets traditionally supplied by the Maritimes, causing prices to decline. Some Maritime companies acquired trawlers, and small-boat fishermen believed that some of this price drop was a consequence. As overseas competition damaged salt-fish markets for Newfoundland and Canadian producers, New England fishermen and processors developed the filleting and quick-freezing processes and were able to sell packaged fresh or frozen fillets, instead of whole fish, to a wider market.

Increasing economic difficulties brought about a 1927 royal commission, whose findings had 2 main effects. First, the trawler fleet was reduced to only 3 or 4 vessels during the 1930s. This restriction, combined with decreased markets and investment capital, extended an existing technological lag and retarded development for many years; and, although the Lunenburg fleet in particular began winter-fishing for the fresh-fish market, the restriction also blocked the growth of a fresh and fresh-frozen fishery and of a year-round fishery. Second, the commission prompted the federal government to help set up fishermen's co-operatives (*see* CO-OPERATIVE MOVEMENT), leading to the creation of the United Maritimes Fishermen's Co-operative and the Québec United Fishermen. In Newfoundland a remarkable fishermen's movement had begun before WWI when William COAKER built the Fishermen's Protective Union (FPU) into a powerful industrial and political force. Coaker's attempts to reform fishery marketing failed, and the FPU faded away during the 1930s.

In the Prairie province fisheries, overfishing and overcrowding, lack of organization and weak marketing created an unstable, low-income fishery. Governments tried various schemes of amelioration, including lake and boat quotas and fleet limitations, but without thorough and effective application.

BC fishermen weathered the Depression better than their Atlantic counterparts. The salmon industry, with roughly 100 plants at the beginning of the century, began to consolidate in the late 1920s (as it did again in the 1950s and the late 1970s). In 1923 the HALIBUT TREATY with the US regulated the Pacific halibut fishery. The pilchard (California sardine) fishery, developed in the late 1920s and the 1930s, suited the purse seine and the "reduction" fishery, which reduced fish flesh and bones into fertilizer or fish meal. The pilchard fishery boomed in the 1930s but failed in the 1940s when the resource declined. BC fishermen continued to organize more than did Atlantic fishermen, and their organizations have been influential for decades. One, the Prince Rupert Fishermen's Co-operative Assn, took hold in the 1930s and became one of the world's most successful fishermen's co-operatives; in the early 1980s it dominated the northern BC fishery.

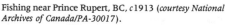

Fishing near Prince Rupert, BC, *c*1913 (*courtesy National Archives of Canada/PA-30017*).

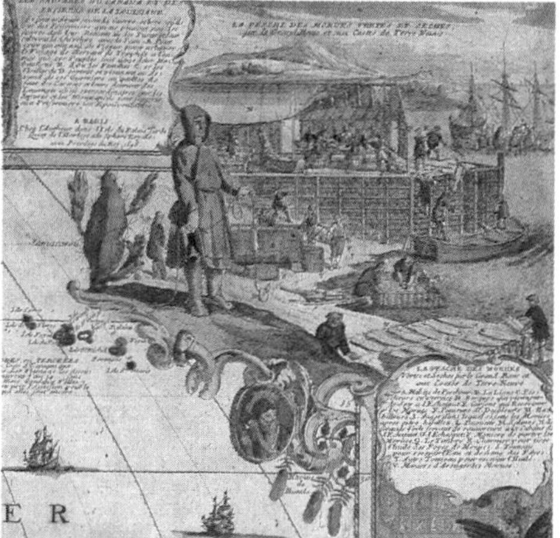

Detail from the upper right portion of Nicolas de Fer's wall map of the Americas, 1698, showing activities in the cod fishery (*courtesy National Archives of Canada/NMC-26825*).

Though continuing extensive regulation for conservation, federal fisheries management showed little vigour or innovation in this period. In 1922 the federal government allowed Québec to manage its own fixed-gear fisheries, and in 1930 it turned over fishery management to the Prairie provinces and separated the Dept of Fisheries from the Dept of Marine. It also set up a Salt Fish Board to regulate and subsidize exporters. Newfoundland exporters remained weak; exports were finally regulated 2 decades after Coaker's attempt.

The Age of "Productivity": 1940-67 The onset of WWII brought increased prosperity and productivity through a high demand for fish and a new technology (radios, radar, sonar) which fishing fleets rapidly adopted. The fishing industry began to emphasize development. A special example of this occurred when Saskatchewan's CCF government enacted a series of interventionist measures, eventually producing a system of producer co-operatives. The federal government extended generous subsidies to help build vessels and plants, chiefly for groundfish. It set up the Fisheries Prices Support Board (1947), extended UNEMPLOYMENT INSURANCE to self-employed fishermen and extended loan and vessel-insurance program to fishermen. On the Atlantic coast provincial loan boards offered advantageous interest rates to fishermen, allowing them to modernize their fleets.

Development in the Atlantic region came as refrigeration in transportation and storage facilities, stores and homes led to increased demand for frozen fish. The federal government had withdrawn the ban on purse seining in the 1930s, and now ended the ban on groundfish trawlers. In the groundfish industry, which rapidly switched to frozen-fish production, a few vertically integrated companies (fishing, processing and marketing) began to dominate; they have since extended partial dominance into lobster, SCALLOP and HERRING fisheries.

Government explorations and demonstrations of techniques helped open a number of

The modern fish dragger *Cape Brier* operates out of Lunenburg, NS (*courtesy Wildred L. Eisnor/Knickle's Studio*).

fisheries, all of them – except the Great Lakes smelt fishery – on the Atlantic: redfish, flounder and other flatfish, sea scallop, crab and shrimp. In the 1940s and 1950s Bay of Fundy fishermen built up a purse-seine herring fishery. In the 1960s the federal government encouraged purse-seining on the Atlantic, despite the overfishing of herring stocks on the Pacific coast, where purse-seining of herring was banned 1967-72. Atlantic provincial governments helped get more boats and plants into the herring fishery. The result has been a series of unresolved crises stemming from overfishing and overcapacity.

Before the war, a main problem had been too little capacity to catch offshore fish; after the war, the problem was too great a capacity. The Canadian fleet of vessels 50 t and over multiplied its capacity fivefold from 1959 to 1974, and the groundfish catch actually fell as both domestic and foreign fleets added pressure. Overexpansion of fleets depleted stocks and drove down average incomes. The International Commission for the Northwest Atlantic Fisheries, est 1949, gathered comprehensive data on fish abundance and location and established mild restrictions, but it lacked the power of enforcement and the political will to take effective measures. In Atlantic Canada scientists seemed carried away by the stress on development, and few voices in government warned of the consequences of overfishing.

By contrast, federal fisheries officials in BC developed a superb corps of salmon managers who kept stocks fairly stable despite increasing pressure from the fishing fleet and from the encroachment of urban-industrial society on fish habitats. The department led public opinion in a struggle that held back potential damage to salmon stocks from hydroelectric dams. BC fishermen's organizations such as the United Fishermen and Allied Workers Union and processor organizations more actively influenced fishery management. Although a few major Atlantic processing companies developed a powerful fleet of 150 or more large trawlers, in BC vessel ownership by processors decreased. The BC fleet became more independent and the salmon-canning industry increasingly consolidated.

Conservation and Economics: 1968-80s The expansionist trend brought on a number of crises and semicollapses in the Canadian fishery. When the BC herring fishery reopened in 1972, a new and rich Japanese market for herring roe helped to fuel investment. By that time, the federal government had limited entry by fishermen into the herring and salmon fleet, on the principle that a fishery open to all comers tends toward overfishing and overinvestment, while limiting participation can benefit both conservation and average incomes. But Pacific fleet limitation, while increasing incomes, helped make more money available for investment. By the early 1980s, overinvestment had partly thwarted the intent of licence limitation: increased fishing power endangered the stocks and the fishermen's profit margins. The Commission on Pacific Fisheries Policy in 1982 recommended further fleet reduction and a system of licence fees and landing taxes that would remove windfall profits and dampen the boom-and-bust pattern. No such action had emerged by 1987, but good catches and markets had, at least temporarily, reduced the urgency. And the huge Salmonid Enhancement Program, begun by the federal and provincial governments in 1977, promised to increase abundance.

In 1974-75 the Atlantic groundfish industry faced depleted stocks and high fuel and other costs; poor markets threatened major companies with bankruptcy. The federal government authorized some $200 million in special aid and undertook other measures. It extended Canadian fishing limits to 200 nautical miles (370 km) on 1 Jan 1977 (*see* LAW OF THE SEA). Licence limitation had been established in 1967 for the Atlantic lobster fishery, and gradually from 1973 for all other major fisheries on the Atlantic and Pacific coasts. The federal Dept of Fisheries and Oceans (as it became in 1979) tried to take a more comprehensive approach to management and imposed tight quotas and other conservation measures on Atlantic groundfish stocks. As well, between 1974 and 1982, fisheries minister Roméo LeBlanc encouraged organization of fishermen. Incomes generally increased, and Canada became the world's leading fish exporter.

Excessive optimism after 1977 brought overinvestment (especially in plants, despite federal advice to the contrary) and a near-collapse of major Atlantic groundfish companies. The fisheries are common property, and each fisherman tries to carve out the biggest possible share of the catch. This naturally leads to a race for the biggest and best vessels. To remedy this, in 1982 the federal Task Force on Atlantic Fisheries recommended "enterprise allocations," a system that would entitle each licensed fisherman to a portion of the total catch and would reduce the perceived need to upgrade equipment uneconomically; and the task force recommended reforms in quality and marketing. Although progress has been less than envisaged, some improvements took place, and the report cleared the air by dispelling some old arguments. In 1984 a financial restructuring of major companies took place, the federal government alone contributing some $200 million in temporary equity investment. Two companies, Fishery Products International and National Sea Products, now dominate the offshore groundfish industry.

During the 1970s and early 1980s, tensions were frequent between Atlantic processing companies, traditionally the main influence on government, and newly powerful fishermen's organizations such as the Newfoundland Fisherman, Food and Allied Workers' Union and the Maritime Fishermen's Union. In 1983, fishermen's organizations suggested that government should force the major, vertically integrated groundfish producers to relinquish their trawler fleets, which supply 30-40% of Atlantic groundfish, so that independent fishermen would control the supply. Processing companies have been sensitive to suggestions of further government intervention, especially after federal and provincial governments created 2 crown corporations: in 1969 the Freshwater Fish Marketing Corp, which has a monopoly on selling fish in interprovincial and export trade in the Prairie provinces, the Northwest Territories and parts of northwestern Ontario, and in 1970 the Canadian Saltfish Corp, which has a monopoly on marketing salt fish from Newfoundland and parts of Québec.

The fishery has fared best in places such as BC and the SW Nova Scotia-Bay of Fundy area, where more favourable conditions allow fishermen and processors alike to display a great deal of independence. Elsewhere – especially in Newfoundland – more difficult conditions have created an industry that has alternated between expressions of independence and requests for government help. Fishermen often resent regulations affecting their own vessels, yet ask the government to regulate vessels using different methods or coming from different areas. The built-in conflicts of a private-enterprise yet common-property industry (with fishing under federal jurisdiction and processing under provincial jurisdiction) continue to foster tensions. Yet, fishing and coastal life have their built-in pleasures, and the fishing industry has made some progress over the years. Management and understanding of the fishery, and consultation between fishermen, processors and governments, improved during the 1970s and 1980s—and since the mid-1980s, a new consciousness of both the dietary and health benefits of seafood has improved markets.

Notwithstanding its difficulties, the fishing industry now has increasingly good chances for stability and prosperity because of the 200-mile limit, the greater understanding by all parties and the new approach that tries to tailor production capacity to the size of the resource and to get the maximum value per fish. Despite the turmoil and crises that have beset the fisheries, the fish keep coming in, the boats keep fishing and communities generally stay alive. JOSEPH GOUGH

Reading: Canada, *Navigating Troubled Waters* (1983); J.E. Forester and A.D. Forester, *Fishing: BC's Commercial Fishing History* (1975); C. G. Head, *Eighteenth Century Newfoundland* (1976); H.A. Innis, *The Cod Fisheries* (ed, 1978).

Fisheries Policy The management and development of fishing is a significant area of public policy. Federal jurisdiction over Canada's coastal and inland fisheries dates to the CONSTITUTION ACT, 1867, and a federal fisheries administration has existed, either as a separate department or as a branch of another department or ministry, since that time. In 1979 the federal government established the Department of Fisheries and Oceans (DFO). However, the provinces are responsible for certain areas of fisheries jurisdiction, including fish processing and the training of fishermen.

The challenge of fisheries policy is to preserve fish stocks while maximizing economic benefit to the people involved in the industry, to the communities that depend on it, and to the nation as a whole. The fishing industry is complex and difficult to administer, made up as it is of many different and often conflicting interest groups.

Some of the difficulties stem from the "common property" nature of the resource. There is no arrangement for proprietary tenure over fish, which tends to result in a "free-for-all" race for limited fish stocks. The first priority of fishery policy is to maintain and if possible expand the resource by annually setting an overall quota or Total Allowable Catch (TAC) for discretely identifiable species stock. This procedure is applied particularly in the management of demersal (groundfish) and pelagic (open-sea) fisheries. In other fisheries, different approaches are used, eg, an optimal necessary "escapement" (salmon) and a minimum legal size (lobster), etc. The federal government has also pursued a policy of limited entry into the fishing industry and of restricted licences to fish certain species. Recently, there has been a trend in federal policy toward the introduction of quasi-property rights or enterprise allocations, whereby each fishing enterprise is given its own individual quota. Proponents of this approach believe it will help solve the problem of overinvestment and self-defeating competition associated with the common-property resource.

Fish stocks were severely depleted during the 1960s and early 1970s as a result of overfishing off Canadian coasts by foreign factory freezer-trawler fleets. Following a series of multinational negotiations, a new fisheries management regime came into effect in 1977 when Canada's jurisdiction was extended to 200 nautical miles (370 km). The federal government then moved to reverse the decline in fish stocks by gradually reducing foreign fishing within the 200-mile limit while increasing Canada's own effort. The subsequent growth of northern cod stock off Labrador has been one of the success stories in fisheries management, although by 1983-84 this appeared to have slowed.

Some fish stocks that are important to Canada's fishing industry remain outside the 200-mile management zone. Organizations set up to protect stocks in international waters include the Northwest Atlantic Fisheries Organization (NAFO) and the International North Pacific Fisheries Commission (INPFC). Problems can still arise between individual countries. In the early 1980s, for instance, Canada charged Spain (which had not then signed the NAFO treaty) with overfishing just outside the 200-mile limit in the area known as the Tail of the Grand Banks. This led to some curtailment of trade between the 2 nations. The jurisdictional boundary around the French-owned islands of SAINT-PIERRE AND MIQUELON off the S coast of Newfoundland is still disputed between Canada and France; however, disputes with the US have for the most part been resolved. In 1984, the International Court of Justice ruled that a zonal boundary be fixed in the Gulf of Maine and allowed a joint management of some fisheries in the area. The 1985 Pacific Salmon Treaty with the US provides for innovations in fishery management and includes conditions for restoration of fish stocks and harvest sharing.

In the 1980s the Atlantic and to a lesser extent the Pacific fishing industries found themselves in deep economic trouble. On both coasts, it was charged that there were "too many boats chasing too few fish." With the introduction of the 200-mile limit, fishermen and processors had been encouraged to overexpand their operations in anticipation of a boom that never materialized. Many went heavily into debt, only to be hit with extremely high interest rates that coincided with a periodic slump in the world market. In response, the federal government created 2 royal commissions (under Peter Pearse and Michael Kirby, respectively) to study the Pacific and Atlantic fisheries. The policy issues on each coast are different. On the West Coast, the most important issues are conservation, rationalization of effort, reduction of fleet size, and market stabilization. On the East Coast, the main issues involve the upgrading of the quality and therefore the market value of fish products (particularly cod and herring); the development of markets for abundant, underutilized species, eg, hake, mackerel, herring, alewife; some reduction in numbers of fishermen; improved and stabilized income for fishermen; and the creation of a proper and stable balance between inshore, nearshore and offshore fleets and effort.

The recommendations produced by the 2 commissions were and remain controversial. On the West Coast, the DFO met resistance from fishermen in its efforts to implement the Pearse Commission's plan to reduce the fishing fleet drastically through a system of royalties and buy backs. The Pearse Commission Report suggested that a government-appointed board should offer compensation to holders of fishing licences for voluntarily giving up their licences, thus reducing the total number of fishermen involved in the salmon and roe herring fisheries. The report proposed that the cost of such a program should be shared between government and the remaining holders of fishing licences, who would supposedly benefit from the fleet reduction by increasing their individual catches. Revenue would be derived from fishermen in the form of royalties, which would be a fixed percentage of the value of fish landings.

On the East Coast, a "restructuring" process was set in motion, involving the infusion of public money to refinance 5 major offshore fishing companies that were virtually bankrupt. Out of this restructuring emerged 2 new "super-companies," one based in Newfoundland and the other in Nova Scotia. The Newfoundland-based company is owned by the federal and provincial governments, while the Nova Scotia-based company remains in private hands. The restructuring deals were sharply criticized, particularly because nothing was done to assist independent fishermen who were caught in a financial squeeze as a result of steep increases in operating costs.

Just what role government should play in the fishing industry is a question that underlies much of the debate on restructuring and indeed on fishery policy in general. Fish-plant owners subscribe to a private enterprise philosophy, but critics charge that private enterprise has been responsible for the crises in the fishery industry, crises that have necessitated government intervention.

Under the Fisheries Prices Support Act, in force since the 1940s, government programs have helped shield primary producers from periodic fluctuations in international commodity markets, and many argue that such programs should be expanded. The Norwegians, who are among Canada's leading competitors in the fish trade, have similar programs for their fishermen. In 1969 the Canadian government established the Freshwater Fish Marketing Corp (FFMC), a crown trading corporation modelled on the Canadian Wheat Board, to control the export of freshwater fish and fish products from the Prairie provinces, the NWT and northern Ontario. The traditional salt-fish trade to Mediterranean and Caribbean countries has declined in Canada because of undisciplined marketing by a multitude of small exporters and because of effective competition from Norway and Iceland. In 1970, in response to an initiative from the Newfoundland government, the federal government established the Canadian Saltfish Corporation (CSC), modelled on the FFMC but with a slightly different mandate. It handles the export of (and interprovincial trade in) dried salt codfish and similar products originating in Newfoundland, Labrador and the lower North Shore of Québec. Both the FFMC and the CSC are joint federal-provincial companies.

Role of Unions While more government involvement in fish marketing is generally opposed by processors it is supported by most unions representing Canadian fishermen and fish-plant workers. Increasing numbers of fishermen and plant workers have banded together into unions and other organizations to protect their interests in dealing with fish companies and governments. Unions bargain directly with fish companies to establish fish prices and plant wages, and lobby governments for fishing policies they favour.

An early example of unionization in Newfoundland was the founding of the Fishermen's Protective Union by William COAKER in 1908. This was a social and political movement aimed at breaking the old credit or "truck" system which kept fishermen in a condition of semiserfdom. A fisherman never saw any cash throughout the year; instead the merchant supplied him on credit with staple goods such as flour and molasses. At the end of the season the merchant took the fisherman's cured fish, calculating its worth at a price set not by fishermen but by traders. In this way fishermen were kept permanently in debt and completely dependent on the merchant. Coaker attempted to assure the fishermen of some financial independence by creating a shareholding company that operated cash stores which supplied staple goods at noninflated prices. Coaker's movement declined after 1919 when as minister of fisheries in a coalition government he tried unsuccessfully to introduce certain reforms in fisheries policy, including co-ordination of salt-fish exporting.

On the West Coast, the chief union in the fishing industry is the United Fishermen and Allied Workers Union, which was founded in 1945 and remains an effective bargaining agent for fishermen and shoreworkers. In BC, however, there is no provincial legislation giving independent fishermen the formal right to collective bargaining. The first province to pass collective bargaining legislation for fishermen was Newfoundland, which did so in 1971 as a result of political pressure from the newly formed Newfoundland Fishermen, Food and Allied Workers Union (NFFAWU). New Brunswick fishermen obtained collective bargaining rights in 1982, but Nova Scotia and PEI still have no collective bargaining legislation for self-employed fishermen. The NFFAWU, representing some 28 000 inshore fishermen, offshore trawlermen and plant workers in Newfoundland and Nova Scotia, is now Canada's largest fishing-industry union. It is affiliated to the United Food and Commercial Workers International Union, which also has several fishing industry locals across Canada. The NFFAWU has played a major role in increasing fish prices and wages, influencing public policy and introducing social benefits, such as workers' compensation, for fishermen. Unions influence government policy through representation on various committees that advise the federal government on establishing quotas for different species, eg, the NFFAWU has representatives on the Atlantic Groundfish Advisory Commmittee (AGAC).

When fishermen and processors' organizations mount conflicting lobbies to influence policy, fishermen sometimes prevail. For example, government policy allows "over-the-side sales" (which are opposed by processors) whereby self-employed fishermen who are unable to sell their catch to a fish plant may sell directly to foreign factory ships. When fishing-industry unions perceive that government policy favours the interests of the fish companies, their last resort may be an attempt to mobilize their membership at the ballot box, eg, in 1984 they mounted the "Unity '84" campaign against Ottawa's restructuring policy, which involved 7 different fishing-industry unions in the Atlantic provinces.

RICHARD CASHIN

Reading: H.A. Innis, *The Cod Fisheries* (rev ed, 1978).

Fisheries Research Board Until the transfer of its staff to the Department of the Environment in 1973 and its demise in 1979, the FRB was the principal federal research organization working on aquatic science and fisheries. Many of Canada's eminent marine scientists were associated with the FRB, which descended from a board of management (1898), established to run a floating biological station on the Atlantic coast, to become the Biological Board of Canada in 1912. In 1908, permanent biological stations were opened at St Andrews, NB, and Nanaimo, BC, staffed by summer volunteers from universities. In the 1920s, the board hired full-time employees and opened laboratories concerned with the fishing industry and food processing. By 1937, when the Biological Board of Canada became the FRB, it had a distinguished record of marine biological and physical oceanographic research. After WWII the FRB opened new laboratories and expanded its work on physical oceanography, Pacific salmon, Atlantic fish stocks and eastern Arctic marine biology. With the opening of the BEDFORD INSTITUTE OF OCEANOGRAPHY, the expansion of the Department of Mines and Technical Surveys into oceanography, and the recommendations of the Glassco Commission (*see* GOVERNMENT ORGANIZATION, ROYAL COMMISSION ON) in the 1960s, the FRB, which was not affiliated with a department, became an administrative anomaly. Several federal government departments now conduct research originally done by the FRB. *See also* FRESHWATER INSTITUTE.

ERIC L. MILLS

Reading: K. Johnstone, *The Aquatic Explorers: A History of the Fisheries Research Board of Canada* (1977).

Fisherman Lake, archaeological site located in the foothills of the Mackenzie Mts, in the extreme SW corner of the NWT. Archaeological work since 1952 has exposed a long and problematic history of human occupation extending from the early Holocene until historic times. Of the 154 sites found and evaluated, 10 have been excavated. The earliest occupations are poorly represented and difficult to interpret, but by at least 6000 or 5000 BC the area may have been inhabited by a Northern Cordilleran/Plano culture moving north in the wake of optimal climatic conditions. These people may have been bison hunters, although no bone remains have been preserved. About 4000 BC, new people entered the area from Alaska and the Yukon, characterized by a distinctive stone technology based on tiny stone blades ("microblades"). Eventually, many of the more distinctive aspects of this technology disappeared, but these people may be the ancestors of the SLAVEY who inhabit Fisherman Lake to the present day. *See also* ARCHAEOLOGY; PREHISTORY.

DAVID A. MORRISON

Fishing, Ice Ice provides a seasonal platform for fishing by netting, spearing and angling. Net, spear and hook were in use in northern Europe and N America, winter and summer, long before the dawn of history.

Ice fishing near Tuktoyaktuk, NWT (*photo by Karl-Heinz Raach*).

Netting Nets are used by people fishing commercially, or requiring regular supplies of fish for feeding families or dog teams, or supplying fox or mink ranches. They are easiest to set before ice is thick. A line must be stretched 50 m or more under the ice. A series of holes is cut in the ice and a line is passed from one to the next, often by means of a long, straight pole. The line is then used to pull through a rope which, in turn, is used to extend the net, floats and weights beneath the ice. Another method uses a prairie ice jigger, a sled-like, wooden device that slides along the underside of the ice. The jigger is launched under the ice, towing a rope. When the rope is pulled, a lever is raised; when the rope is released, the lever springs back in such a way that it pushes against the ice and jerks the jigger forward. It can be traced by watching through clear ice, or by listening through snow-covered ice. When the appropriate length of rope has been drawn out, the jigger is retrieved through another hole cut over it. The net is retrieved from the opposite direction when the catch is removed. Nets must be deployed well below the bottom surface of ice or floats may become frozen-in. A rope or net header embedded in the new ice that forms in the hole is almost certain to be cut when the hole is reopened; therefore, headers are best held down by poles extending well into the water.

Spearing Fish spearing may date from the Paleolithic. N American natives often were accomplished fish spearers, eg, Inuit speared lake trout and arctic char through ice. The fish spear (*kakivak*) of the eastern Arctic had a central prong to transfix fish and lateral, reverse prongs to hold them. Bone, antler or ivory decoys were dangled to attract cruising fish into range. In Canada, the fish spear is prohibited, except for taking eels wintering in estuaries in the Atlantic provinces, and for game fishing in Québec.

Angling Hooks were derived from earlier devices, eg, gorges, which date from Paleolithic times and were designed to be swallowed by animals. Bright metal and enamelled lures have largely replaced baited tackle designed to be swallowed by fish. Ice angling is a widespread Canadian pastime: from Labrador to the Okanagan Valley, from Lancaster Sound to Lk St Clair. Catches range from perch and pike to Greenland shark on the fast ice off Pond Inlet, inconnu on a quiet channel of the Mackenzie Delta, pickerel in the Bay of Quinte, smelt in Lk Erie, poulamons at Ste-Anne-de-la-Pérade, and brook trout in Halifax County ponds. Most Canadians have access to waters inhabited by more than one of the following: lake whitefish, yellow perch, pickerel (walleye), ling (burbot), northern pike and rainbow trout.

A.H. MACPHERSON

Fishing Admiral, a position of authority claimed by the first fishing ship's captain to enter each Newfoundland harbour every year, although in some harbours in the 1500s each ship's captain may have taken a turn during the fishing season. The practice was in effect by the late 1500s and continued to some extent until the late 1700s. Their authority confirmed by a British charter in 1633, the fishing admirals, in addition to having the choice location in their harbour, were responsible for enforcing British regulations and law. Together with the second and third captains to enter the harbour – the vice-admiral and rear-admiral – the fishing admiral administered the earliest form of "government" in Newfoundland. Since they were simply ships' captains, the justice they dispensed was often wanting, and many accounts of abuses appeared in the historical records. *See also* FISHERIES HISTORY.

ROBERT D. PITT

Fishing Islands, an archipelago of about 15 islets in Lk HURON (scattered in an area of 10 km²), lie off the W coast of the BRUCE PENINSULA in western Ontario between Chiefs Pt and Pike Bay. The archipelago is named for the teeming shoals of fish that were once caught there.

DAVID EVANS

Fitness Broadly defined, fitness is a state of physical, mental and social well-being. Concern for becoming and staying fit is increasingly important to Canadians. Interest is reflected in all age groups, but involvement in physical activity by people 60 years of age and over has increased 3 times faster than that of younger people over the past few years. One consequence of the interest in fitness has been a renewed effort to implement daily PHYSICAL EDUCATION in Canadian schools.

In the Canada Fitness Survey (1981), which involved nearly 12 000 households in 80 urban and rural communities across Canada, 16 000 people, aged 7 to 69 years, participated in a fitness test, and 22 000 people completed a questionnaire about their physical activity and life-style. The results of the survey provided a comprehensive picture of fitness in Canada.

Physical Activity Patterns According to the survey, 11.5 million Canadians (56% of those aged 10 and over) are physically active in their leisure time; walking is a favourite activity, followed by bicycling, swimming, jogging and gardening. Active Canadians are more likely to be young and to be westerners, managers and professionals, single and better educated. The survey also found that active Canadians score higher on all measures of health and emotional well-being; that strength and muscular endurance decline rapidly after age 25; that females are more supple than males but that suppleness in both sexes declines precipitously after age 25. Based on the survey results, an estimated 46% of Canadians would achieve a recommended level of cardiovascular (aerobic) fitness, 33% would reach the minimal level of fitness and the remaining 20% of Canadians would be assessed as unfit. Males are fitter than females and the young are generally fitter than the old. The findings are somewhat biased as an ever-increasing number of Canadians over the age of 40 were screened out of the testing for medical reasons. Seventy-eight percent of persons in the survey placed "regular physical activity" in the top 5 components of a healthy life, behind such basic components as adequate sleep and nutrition. In a 1985 survey of health attitudes, exercise was the most cited activity that Canadians did to improve their health.

International Comparisons In 1972 PARTICIPaction introduced the famous comparison between the 60-year-old Swede and the 30-year-old Canadian in a 15-second television commercial. The idea that a 60-year-old Swede was fitter than a 30-year-old Canadian captured the nation's imagination. In fact, only when Sweden and other countries undertake a survey as comprehensive as the Canada Fitness Survey of 1981 can true comparisons be made.

Canadian researchers are well recognized in the international fitness community. In 1988 Canada will host the first international conference on exercise, fitness and health. Researchers from around the world will meet in Toronto to review the latest scientific evidence and make recommendations for new programs and policies.

Federal and Provincial Fitness Programs The fitness movement of the 1970s and 1980s was generated partly through the efforts of the federal and provincial governments. Fitness Canada, the federal government agency with a mandate to "encourage, promote and develop increased participation of physical activity leading towards fitness for all Canadians," has created a number of national programs and resources and has undertaken co-operative work with national agencies in the physical activity and health field. Fitness Canada was formed in 1979 from the Fitness and Recreation branches of the Fitness and Amateur Sports Directorate. PARTICIPaction, an independent nonprofit communications company funded by Fitness Canada, is a unique and successful model for encouraging Canadians to become involved in regular physical activity. Fitness Canada sponsors Canada's "Fitweek" in May of each year. Millions of Canadians get involved in physical activity during this week.

Every provincial government in Canada, through departments of recreation, youth, culture, tourism or health, promotes fitness through physical activity. The organization of each program varies, ranging from the large Kino Québec network with over 100 community offices to the typical agency in a smaller province in which a small core of professionals work with voluntary agencies across the province.

Voluntary Fitness Agencies and Organizations in Canada work in the fields of fitness, SPORT and recreation. More than a million Canadians are actively involved in these organizations as coaches, board members, officials and helpers, and many millions more are involved as participants. Some of the voluntary organizations, such as running clubs, serve one community; others, such as those created for organized sport, sponsor community clubs across the country and are organized into provincial chapters and a national organization to govern the sport nationally and internationally. In the field of fitness development, the YMCA and the YWCA have been very influential.

Commercial Fitness Centres have developed rapidly in the late 1980s, and facilities now exist in racquet clubs, shopping centres and office buildings. Standard qualifications for leaders conducting fitness testing have been developed by the Fitness Accreditation and Certification program (FACA) of the Canadian Assn for Sports Sciences. While national guidelines for fitness leadership exist no certification program exists in Canada. Good program leaders should have completed a recognized training program from the provincial agency, the YMCA or YWCA, or a university or national association. Fitness centres can apply for accreditation if they meet the standards set by the FACA program.

P. EDWARDS AND J. HAUSER

Fitzgerald, Francis Joseph, RNWMP inspector (b at Halifax 12 Apr 1869; d Yukon Territory Feb 1911). He enlisted in the NORTH-WEST MOUNTED POLICE in 1888 and was released for a year's service in the SOUTH AFRICAN WAR with the Canadian Mounted Rifles, but most of his career was spent with the police in the North. He served in the Yukon during the gold rush, and in 1903 was put in command of the new police detachment at Herschel Island in the western Arctic. Here he demonstrated Canadian sovereignty over the region with firmness and tact. In 1910 he was chosen to attend the coronation of George V in London, and on his way south was put in command of the annual winter mail patrol to Dawson. Though highly experienced in northern patrols, he travelled light, hoping for a speed record, and refused to hire a native guide. The patrol became lost, and in late Feb 1911 Fitzgerald and his companions eventually died, 3 from starvation and one by suicide.

W.R. MORRISON

Reading: D. North, *The Lost Patrol* (1978).

FitzGerald, Lionel LeMoine, painter (b at Winnipeg 17 Mar 1890; d there 7 Aug 1956). FitzGerald spent almost his whole life in Winnipeg painting, drawing and sketching quiet contemplative scenes. He trained in Winnipeg, Pittsburgh and NY. He was principal of the Winnipeg School of Art, 1929-47, and exhibited with the GROUP OF SEVEN in 1930 – joining the Group formally in 1932 – but remained a loner. From a decorative and impressionistic style FitzGerald moved to a pointillist technique. *Williamson's Garage* (1927), *Doc Snider's House* (1931) and *Farm Yard* (1931) illustrated the fine texture he built up, using dry paint, tiny brushstrokes, bleached tones and subtle colour. *The Pool* (1934) explores geometric relationships. In *Jar* (1938) he uses glistening daubs of paint to illuminate the jar from within.

In the 1940s FitzGerald turned to coloured chalks, pen and ink, and sometimes oil on a palette knife. After his death a set of self-portraits and drawings of the nude were found, unusual for the shy painter. He painted the apple in all media and was stimulated by visits to the West Coast. Retired in 1949, he painted *From an Upstairs Window* in 1951, one of his best works. On a trip to BC he met Lawren HARRIS and afterwards did pen and ink studies with thousands of tiny dots and dashes shaping the forms. *Still Life with Hat* (1955) creates his characteristically mysterious world, made with weightless cross-hatching. By *Autumn Sonata* (1954) and *Abstract in Blue and Gold* (1955), FitzGerald became totally abstract. The surface rhythms give way to a smooth brushstroke. His entire body of work is distinguished by a painstaking, original way of handling brush, pen, pencil, crayon or paintbrush to get his own look and texture.

ANNE MCDOUGALL

Doc Snider's House (1931), oil on canvas, is one of Lionel LeMoine FitzGerald's masterpieces (*courtesy National Gallery of Canada/Gift of Dr P.D. Ross, 1932*).

The great Pangnirtung Fjord, on the SE coast of Baffin I, NWT (*courtesy Environment Canada, Parks/Prairie & Northern Region*).

Fitzpatrick, Sir Charles, minister of justice, chief justice of Canada (b at Québec City, Canada E 19 Dec 1853; d there 17 June 1942). After studying law at Laval, he was called to the bar 1876. Fitzpatrick quickly made a name as a criminal lawyer and acted as chief counsel for Louis RIEL in 1885, and for Honoré MERCIER after his dismissal from office in 1891. Fitzpatrick sat as a Liberal in the Legislative Assembly of Québec 1890-96 and the House of Commons 1896-1906, and served as solicitor general 1896 and minister of justice 1902 during the LAURIER administration. He resigned in 1906 to become chief justice of Canada. Upon retirement, he was lt-gov of Québec 1918-23. DAVID EVANS

Fjord, long, narrow bay formed by glacial erosion of river valleys during the ICE AGES and consisting of one or more basins separated by sills. Fjords occur on the coasts of BC and eastern Canada, Alaska, Chile, New Zealand, Greenland and Norway. In cross section they are U-shaped, often with a flat bottom. The fjords of the Pacific coast are 3-400 km long, 0.6-15 km wide, and 20-500 m in average depth. Sill depths range from a few metres to 500 m below the water surface. The water in fjords comes from 2 sources: the ocean supplies salt water, which being dense fills most of the fjord basin; rivers provide lighter fresh water, which forms a layer on top of the salt water. The rivers flowing into fjords are fed by rainfall draining from their watersheds and, in summer, by meltwater from mountain snowfields and glaciers. Glacial meltwater usually carries finely ground rock (rock flour), which gives it a milky appearance. Most of this material is deposited to form the flat bottom which is so typical of many fjords.

In oceanographic terminology, fjords are estuaries, ie, semienclosed bodies of water in which seawater is measurably diluted by fresh water from land drainage. As there is a continual supply of river water, usually at the landward end of the fjord, the upper layer (a few metres thick) flows toward the sea, picking up some salt water from below en route and carrying it out to sea. An inflow of salt water from the ocean balances this export. The combination of surface-layer outflow of low-salinity water and deeper inflow of more saline ocean water is known as an estuarine circulation. It serves to exchange or ventilate the basin water. If the outer sill is very shallow, projecting up into the outflowing upper layer, this ventilation is hindered. In this case the basin water stagnates and most or all of its dissolved oxygen is used up by bacterial processes; therefore, fish may be unable to live in it. In some shallow-silled fjords stagnation may persist for years; in others there is an annual cycle in which inflow of deeper salt water occurs seasonally when dense water upwells outside the mouth of the fjord. The degree of ventilation of a fjord basin is important when experts are considering whether or not it may be permissible to discharge industrial effluent or mine tailings into it. Of the many fjords that have been investigated, only a small minority exhibit marked stagnation.

Most of the fjords on the West Coast have been studied. In particular the seasonal variations of water properties in Bute Inlet have been observed for more than 30 years, and intensive studies in Knight Inlet since 1977 have revealed many features of subsurface motions and internal waves. On the East Coast, fewer fjords have been investigated, but the physics, chemistry and geology of Saguenay Fjord, 100 km long and 275 m deep, off the north shore of the St Lawrence estuary, have been investigated in some detail. *See also* SAGUENAY RIVER. G.L. PICKARD

Flag of Canada A national flag is a simple, effective way of identifying both individual citizens and the nation as a whole – expressing its collective will and SOVEREIGNTY. Before 1763, rather than a flag, the royal arms represented the king of France in Canada. The British, on the other hand, were accustomed to flying either the Red Ensign or the Union Flag from their forts. This confusion worsened after Confederation when the quartered coats of arms of the provinces were placed in the fly of the Red Ensign, giving it a form of popular sanction as Canada's flag. PM Mackenzie KING'S attempts to adopt a national flag in 1925 and again in 1946 failed, and eventually, in 1964, PM Lester B. PEARSON assigned the task of evolving a suitable design to an all-party, 15-member special committee.

After considerable debate, the final design adopted by Parliament, and approved by royal proclamation, became Canada's flag 15 Feb 1965. Red and white had been sanctioned as national colours by the royal proclamation granting a coat of arms to Canada in 1921, and the maple

Members of Parliament with flag at the time of closure during the flag debate, Ottawa, Dec 1964 (*courtesy National Archives of Canada/PA-142624/Duncan Cameron*).

leaf had enjoyed a long tradition as a symbol of Canada. *See also* EMBLEMS OF CANADA.

AUGUSTE VACHON

Reading: J.R. Matheson, *Canada's Flag* (1986).

Flag Debate, the debate over the proposed new Canadian FLAG, which opened in the House of Commons 15 June 1964 and ended by CLOSURE 15 Dec 1964. Canada's official flag from 1867 had been Britain's Union Flag, although the Red Ensign with the Canadian badge was regularly flown for qualified purposes. In 1925 PM Mackenzie KING appointed an armed services committee to investigate possible designs, but it did not report. In 1946 a committee of both Senate and Commons presented a design with the Red Ensign charged with a golden maple leaf but it was not adopted. The issue was raised again by Lester PEARSON, as leader of the Opposition in 1960 and as PM in 1963. John Matheson MP sought strict adherence to the colours, red and white, and the maple leaf emblem authorized by George V on 21 Nov 1921 as advocated by A. Fortescue Duguid. Alan B. Beddoe added 2 blue bars to what became known as the "Pearson pennant." This proposal for design, 3 maple leaves on a white centre square with blue bars on each side, was introduced to Parliament in June 1964.

The ensuing controversy raged not over whether there should be a new flag, but on its design. The French Canadian members followed with keen interest a debate wherein feelings ran high among many English-speaking Canadians. John DIEFENBAKER demanded that the flag honour the "founding races," with the Union Jack in the canton of honour. Pearson insisted on a design denoting allegiance to Canada devoid of colonial association. After prolonged, rancorous debate the issue was referred to a 15-member all-party committee which recommended a design inspired by the Royal Military College flag theme, red-white-red, but with one red maple leaf in a white squared centre. Debate in the House continued until Léon Balcer, a prominent Conservative MP from Québec, invited the Liberals to invoke closure, which would limit speeches to 20 minutes and force a vote. After some 250 speeches, a vote was taken 15 Dec 1964 at 2 AM and the committee's recommendation was accepted 163 to 78. Senate approval followed on Dec 17. The royal proclamation was signed by Her Majesty 28 Jan 1965 and the national flag was officially unfurled 15 Feb 1965. *See also* HERALDRY; EMBLEMS OF CANADA.

JOHN ROSS MATHESON

Reading: John Ross Matheson, *Canada's Flag* (1986); G.F.G. Stanley, *The Story of Canada's Flag* (1965).

Flatfish, common name for bottom-living, primarily marine fishes, of class Osteichthyes, order Pleuronectiformes (Heterosomata). Among the flatfishes are some of the most valuable food fishes, eg, halibut, plaice, flounder, turbot and sole. About 520 species in 6 families inhabit Continental Shelf waters of world oceans, but a few occur in deep seas and some ascend rivers. Most occur in temperate and tropical seas but some penetrate the Arctic. In Canada, 34 species in 25 genera and 3 families occur in coastal waters: 21 species in the Pacific and 13 in the Atlantic. The family Pleuronectidae, the right-eyed flounders, with 26 species (including halibut, genus *Hippoglossus*, and plaice, genus *Hippoglossoides*), is best represented in Canadian waters. The other families are the Bothidae (left-eyed flounders, eg, sand dabs, genus *Citharichthys*) and the Cynoglossidae (tonguefishes).

The loss of bilateral symmetry sets the flatfishes apart from all others. Newly hatched flatfishes swim upright and are symmetrical, but a few days after hatching, one eye begins to migrate across the skull and eventually both eyes are on one side. The dorsal fin grows forward onto the head. Changes in jaw structure, pelvic fins and anatomy also occur. Finally, young flatfish drop to the bottom to lie eyed side uppermost, blind side on the bottom. The left eye migrates in some species; the right in others. Flatfish with both eyes on the right side are said to be right-eyed (dextral); those with both eyes on the left side are left-eyed (sinistral). The eyed side is pigmented; the blind side is usually white. Some flatfishes have a highly developed ability to vary body colouring to match the ocean bottom. Most flatfishes are small (30-38 cm long) but the halibuts may attain lengths of 267 cm and weights up to 316 kg. The mouth is usually small (except in halibut). The lower jaw is prominent in most species but in true soles (found in European waters) the rounded snout projects beyond the mouth. Dorsal and anal fins are usually soft rayed and long. Flatfishes are carnivorous, eating various fishes, crustaceans and bottom-dwelling invertebrates. They are caught mainly by otter trawl, Danish seines or longlines; some are angled. In Canada, Atlantic and Pacific halibut (*H. hippoglossus* and *H. stenolepsis*, respectively) are the most highly esteemed flatfishes and command the highest price on both domestic and foreign markets. The smaller flatfishes, known locally as flounder, sole, yellowtail, dab, witch or plaice, are marketed as fresh or frozen fillets under the name sole.

W.B. SCOTT

Flatworm (Platyhelminthes), phylum of soft, bilaterally symmetrical INVERTEBRATES. Flatworms vary in shape from leaflike to ribbonlike; size ranges from microscopic to over 15 m long (some parasitic forms). Flatworms have an identifiable "head," sometimes highly modified as an attachment organ in parasitic forms. A body cavity is lacking; internal organs are suspended in a spongy matrix (parenchyma). Flatworms lack circulatory and respiratory systems, but have well-developed reproductive and excretory ones. A simple alimentary tract (gut) occurs in most forms, but is absent in tapeworms and one group of free-living flatworms (Acoela). With few exceptions among the flukes, the gut has only a ventral-surface opening, often close to the front end, serving both as mouth and anus. Most flatworms are hermaphroditic; however, cross-fertilization between 2 individuals is the rule. Flatworms occur worldwide. Most of the roughly 15 000 known species are parasitic. Probably thousands of species occur in Canada, but only a fraction of them have been discovered. Platyhelminthes are subdivided into 5 classes: Turbellaria, Temnocephalida, Monogenea, Trematoda and Cestoidea. Some zoologists include Temnocephalida in Turbellaria.

Turbellaria are mainly free-living in fresh and coastal waters; some live in tropical, terrestrial habitats, and others are commensals or parasites of aquatic invertebrates or, rarely, fish. They have hairlike cilia on the body, used for gliding over surfaces. Some are brightly coloured; most are whitish, brown, grey, black or colourless, and rather difficult to see.

Temnocephalida have tentacles and a posterior adhesive organ, and lack cilia on the body surface. Almost all live attached to freshwater invertebrates, especially CRUSTACEANS, in the tropics and subtropics.

Monogenea are primarily parasitic on body surface and gills of freshwater and marine fishes. The posterior end forms an attachment organ, bearing hooks, suckers or clamps.

Trematoda (flukes) are internal parasites of freshwater, marine and terrestrial vertebrates, some causing disease in humans and animals. Most possess one anterior and one ventral-surface muscular sucker for attachment; body cilia are absent but spines may be present. The most distinctive feature of Trematodes is a complex life cycle, requiring alternate development in 2 or more hosts, one of which is almost always a mollusc.

Cestoidea (tapeworms) are intestinal parasites of vertebrates, also with developmental stages in alternate hosts. They are usually ribbonlike, segmented animals with anterior end modified into an attachment organ frequently bearing suckers or hooks. Each segment contains one or more sets of female and male reproductive organs. Lacking a gut, tapeworms absorb nutrients through the body surface. Like the flukes, some tapeworms cause disease in humans and animals.

Nemertea (proboscis or ribbon worms) resemble flatworms, but have a tubular, muscular organ (proboscis) that can be turned inside out, for capturing food. They differ also in having a circulatory system, an anus and separate sexes. They are mainly free-living, littoral, marine organisms; some live in fresh water or moist terrestrial areas; a few are commensals of invertebrates. Length ranges from under 1 mm to several metres. Often they are brightly coloured. About 500 species are known.

L. MARGOLIS

Flavelle, Sir Joseph Wesley, meat packer, financier, philanthropist (b at Peterborough, Canada W 15 Feb 1858; d at Palm Beach, Fla 7 Mar 1939). Inspired by Methodism's demand for personal holiness, self-denial and careful stewardship, Flavelle rose from humble origins to become one of Canada's most able, respected and influential businessmen, as president of the British Empire's largest pork packer, William Davies Co of Toronto, and as chairman of the Bank of Commerce, the National Trust Co and Simpsons Ltd. Successful in business, he devoted much of his wealth and energy after 1900 to charities, needy individuals and public service. He played a major role in the affairs of U of T, the Methodist Church, the Toronto General Hospital and the CNR. Chairman of the Imperial Munitions Board in WWI, Flavelle converted a scandal-ridden and inefficient industry into a vast, well-organized operation and received a baronetcy in 1917 – the last resident citizen of Canada to receive a hereditary title. Shortly thereafter, he and the William Davies Co were accused of profiteering from the wartime bacon business and, though an inquiry exonerated him, the episode sullied Flavelle's reputation.

J. LINDSEY

Reading: M. Bliss, *A Canadian Millionaire* (1978).

Flax (*Linum usitatissimum*), annual plant belonging to the family of the same name (Linaceae). Flax is sown and harvested much like a spring CEREAL CROP and matures at the same time as wheat. The flowers have 5 petals (usually blue but sometimes white) and produce a boll (fruit capsule) with up to 10 small, flattened, ovate seeds, 2-6 mm in diameter. Mature seeds contain approximately 40% oil, 25% protein. The seed coat is usually brown but some varieties are yellow. Although the place of origin of flax is unknown, it was cultivated in ancient Egypt, where its stem fibres were used to produce linen cloth. Oil crushed from the seed (linseed oil) was initially a by-product of linen-fibre production, but with the Industrial Revolution it came into demand as an industrial drying oil (eg, in paints, steelworks and oilcloths). By the 20th century, flax was grown primarily for oil. In Europe, one type is produced for linen fibre, used in producing linen cloth, and for industrial purposes where toughness under water and in corrosive conditions is required.

In Canada, flax is produced only as an industri-

Common Flax (*Linum usitatissimum*) is grown as an oilseed crop on more than 60 000 ha in western Canada (*artwork by Claire Tremblay*).

al OILSEED CROP and is grown annually on more than 750 000 ha in western Canada (55% of which is in Manitoba). The average yield in 1985 was more than 1320 kg/ha. Some seed is crushed in Canada for the domestic paint industry, but most is exported to the US, Europe and Japan. The meal, which remains after crushing, is used as a protein supplement in animal feeds. Flax straw can be processed to produce fine paper, used primarily as cigarette paper since it is clean burning and tasteless. The fibres are also used in paper money, giving it toughness. G.G. ROWLAND

Flea, very small, wingless, laterally flattened insect of order Siphonaptera. Of the 180 species and subspecies indigenous to Canada, 23 are PARASITES of birds, the remainder being mammal parasites. Six species, introduced from Europe or Asia, are common parasites of humans and domestic animals. Worldwide, the flea fauna is much larger, but incompletely documented. Adult fleas are highly specialized: their tough, bristly integument (outer covering) helps adapt them to existence as external parasites of warm-blooded hosts. Ancestors originated in Asia and evolved, primarily, as temporary parasites of small mammals. The life cycle begins with an egg, laid in fur or feathers, which drops to the host's nest or the ground. The larva is nonparasitic, feeding on organic debris. It develops into a pupa, enclosed in a cocoon. Both stages are sedentary. Adult fleas can leap 200 times their own length. Fleas are most numerous in dry climates, being as much as 4 times as numerous in BC and Alberta as in Québec and the Maritimes. Their habits of feeding on blood and occupying filthy places make fleas potential transmitters of disease, particularly bubonic or sylvatic plague. W.O. HAUFE

Fleming, Archibald Lang, Church of England bishop of the Arctic 1933-49 (b at Greenock, Scot 8 Sept 1883; d at Toronto 17 May 1953). In 1906 he went to Canada to train at Wycliffe Coll, Toronto, and in 1909 he established a mission at Lake Harbour, Baffin I, where he stayed until 1916. For his crossing of Fox Pen on his return, he was made a member of the Royal Geographic Soc. Until his first appointment as archdeacon of the Arctic in 1927, he served first as financial secretary and chaplain to Wycliffe Coll and then as rector of Old Stone Church, Saint John, NB. His incredible travels as bishop of the Arctic earned him the title "The Flying Bishop." He was author of *The History of St. John's Church, Saint John, New Brunswick* (1925) and *Archibald the Arctic* (1956). FRITS PANNEKOEK

Fleming, Donald Methuen, lawyer, politician (b at Exeter, Ont 23 May 1905; d at Toronto 31 Dec 1986). Minister of finance in the DIEFENBAKER government (1957-62), Fleming is best remembered for his dispute with Bank of Canada Governor James COYNE. Elected to the House in 1945, he contested the Tory leadership in 1948, 1956 and 1967. In May 1956, during the PIPELINE DEBATE, Fleming was ruled out of order in asking a question – incorrectly as history has shown – and expelled from the House by the Speaker. A highly publicized debate with Coyne over monetary and fiscal policy overshadowed his hard work when finance minister. In 1962 Fleming became minister of justice and attorney general and, apart from a brief flirtation with the leadership in 1967, resigned from public life in 1963. PATRICIA WILLIAMS

Fleming, May Agnes, née Early, novelist (b at Saint John 15 Nov 1840; d at Brooklyn, NY 24 Mar 1880). She began publishing while still a schoolgirl, her early stories appearing in New York and Boston, Mass, as well as in local papers. By the time she moved to Brooklyn, around 1875, she was an established writer. Her novels were serialized in New York and London before being published in book form. Prolific and highly paid, she combined in her fiction elements of romance and gothic mystery and introduced into her later work a private detective. Her best novels are enlivened by fast-moving plots, brisk dialogue and flashes of humour. LORRAINE MCMULLEN

Fleming, Michael Anthony, Roman Catholic bishop of Newfoundland (b at Carrick-on-Suir, Ire 1792?; d at St John's 14 July 1850). A Franciscan priest, Fleming came to St John's in 1823. Initially assistant to Bishop Thomas SCALLAN, Fleming became coadjutor bishop in 1829, and succeeded Scallan in 1830. He completely restructured Newfoundland Catholicism, vastly increasing the number of priests and parishes, introducing sisters for the education of females, and building schools, convents and churches. His advocacy of the rights of Roman Catholics who had no vote until 1832 and no major government office until 1840, his support of "radical" politicians, and the treatment of Catholics who rejected his political views led to accusations of undue clerical influence, especially during the 1830s. Fleming's major achievement was the construction of the Roman Catholic cathedral (Basilica) in St John's. Begun in 1841, it was N America's largest church when completed in 1855. RAYMOND J. LAHEY

Fleming, Robert James Berkeley, composer, educator (b at Prince Albert, Sask 12 Nov 1921; d at Ottawa 28 Nov 1976). One of the most prolific Canadian composers of his generation, Fleming won an international reputation through his work at the National Film Board as a staff composer 1946-58 and as music director 1958-70. Some 250 film scores are complemented by his large output of music for other performance media – ballet, orchestra, chamber ensemble, band, organ, piano and voice. His ballet *Shadow on the Prairie* (1952) and the song cycle *The Confession Stone*, composed for Maureen FORRESTER in 1966, both recorded, are representative of the appealing blend of traditional and 20th-century techniques typical of Fleming's style. A devout churchman, Fleming served several parishes as organist-choirmaster. A number of his hymns, carols and settings of the Anglican Eucharist have been published. From 1970 until his death, Fleming taught at Carleton U. BARCLAY MCMILLAN

Sir Sandford Fleming was Canada's foremost railway surveyor and construction engineer. He was also instrumental in the adoption of standard time (*courtesy National Archives of Canada/C-14128*).

Fleming, Sir Sandford, civil engineer (b at Kirkcaldy, Scot 7 Jan 1827; d at Halifax 22 July 1915). He was Canada's foremost railway surveyor and construction engineer of the 19th century and a distinguished inventor and scientist. He came to Canada in 1845 and, after studying science and engineering in both Scotland and Canada, joined the engineering staff of the Ontario, Simcoe and Huron Ry, becoming engineer in chief of the successor Northern Ry in 1857. In 1863 the Canadian government appointed him chief surveyor of the first portion of a proposed railway from Québec City to Halifax and Saint John. Subsequently built as the INTERCOLONIAL RY, Fleming was its chief engineer. In 1871 he was appointed engineer of the proposed new Canadian railway from Montréal to the Pacific coast. He was in charge of the major surveys across the prairies and through the Rocky Mts. He proposed constructing the railway along a northerly route through Edmonton and the YELLOWHEAD PASS and then turning S to Burrard Inlet on the Pacific. Although his specific recommendations regarding the route were not followed, his extensive survey work of various routes, including the KICKING HORSE PASS through which the Canadian Pacific main line was built, greatly facilitated Canadian railway construction. In the early years of the 20th century, the CANADIAN NORTHERN RY was built along the survey route advocated by Fleming.

Fleming retired from the CPR when the Canadian government turned the project over to a private syndicate in 1880, but he continued to do consultative railway work. He also turned his attention to other projects. He was a strong advocate of a telecommunications cable from Canada to Australia, which he believed would become a vital communications link of the British Empire. The Pacific Cable was successfully laid in 1902. He was also interested in the development of a satisfactory world system of keeping time.

The railway had made obsolete the old system where every major centre set its clocks according to local astronomical conditions. Fleming advocated the adoption of a standard or mean time and hourly variations from that according to established time zones. He was instrumental in convening an International Prime Meridian Conference in Washington in 1884 at which the system of international standard time – still in use today – was adopted. Fleming also designed the first Canadian postage stamp, the threepenny beaver, issued in 1851. He was created a CMG in 1877 and a KCMG in 1897.

T.D. REGEHR

Flemming, Hugh John, lumberman, politician, premier of NB (b at Peel, NB 5 Jan 1899; d at Fredericton 16 Oct 1982). Elected in 1921 as a municipal councillor for Carleton, Flemming became Conservative MLA for Carleton in 1944. In 1951 he was selected Conservative leader; he led the party to victory in 1952, ending 17 years of Liberal government. He served as premier 1952-60 and also as minister of public works and minister of municipal affairs, modernizing NB's hydroelectric system through construction of the Beechwood complex. His government was defeated over hospital taxes. Named federal minister of forestry in 1960 by PM John Diefenbaker, he sat for Royal. In 1962 he was elected MP for Victoria-Carleton and appointed minister of national revenue. He continued as MP until 1972 and served on the Atlantic Development Board.

DELLA M.M. STANLEY

Flemming, James Kidd, businessman, premier of NB 1911-14 (b at Woodstock, NB 27 Apr 1868; d there 10 Feb 1927). Flemming served as provincial secretary and receiver general before becoming premier in 1911. Three years later he was forced to resign after a royal commission found him guilty of fund-raising irregularities. In 1925 and again the following year he ran for the House of Commons and won resounding victories. He is remembered more for his oratorical ability and colourful personality than for his legislative accomplishments.

ARTHUR T. DOYLE

Fletcher, James, entomologist, botanist (b at Ashe, Eng 28 Mar 1852; d at Montréal 8 Nov 1908). Fletcher had been a bank clerk (1874-76) and library assistant (1876-86), without formal training in biology, before his appointment as Canada's first official Dominion entomologist and botanist in 1886, after 2 years as an honorary entomologist in Ottawa. He became a recognized specialist on moth, butterfly and weed identification. Through correspondence, he determined the types and number of insect pests in Canada and the damage they caused. The San José Scale Act of 1898, permitting import restrictions and fumigation of insect-infested material and the first federal legislation pertaining to insects, was enacted under his direction. He pressed for government entomological research, instructed the public in practical insect and weed control, established an insect-identification service and founded the Canadian National Collection of insects. The annual reports (1886-1908) and numerous bulletins of the federal Dept of Agriculture and many scientific papers illustrate his achievements. *See also* ENTOMOLOGY.

P.W. RIEGERT

Reading: P.W. Riegert, *From Arsenic to DDT: A History of Entomology in Western Canada* (1980).

Flett, John A., carpenter, trade-union organizer (b at Hamilton 1860; d there 19 Mar 1941). Flett began a long, distinguished labour career in his local carpenters' union. By the end of the 1890s, he had filled several important posts in the Hamilton labour movement and was emerging as a leader within the fledgling TRADES AND LABOR CONGRESS OF CANADA (TLC), where he was an early and outspoken advocate of independent political action for labour. In 1900 the American Federation of Labor (AFL) chose him as its Canadian organizer, and Flett travelled across the country adding new recruits. At its 1902 convention, the TLC decided to consolidate international unionism in Canada by expelling any "dual unions" competing in the same field with AFL affiliates. That meeting also confirmed its commitment to the continental connection by choosing Flett as its president. He remained AFL organizer for Canada until 1925.

CRAIG HERON

Flin Flon, Man, City, pop 7243 in Man, 348 in Sask (1986c); 7894 in Man, 367 in Sask (1981c), inc 1970, is situated along the Manitoba-Saskatchewan border, 870 km NW of Winnipeg. The Saskatchewan part of Flin Flon is jointly administered by the 2 provinces. Despite the discovery of extensive mineral deposits at the site in 1915, it was more than a decade before production began. Construction of a railway link with THE PAS (1928), development of a power source at Island Falls on the Churchill R (1929) and successful extraction processes facilitated development, as did the involvement of H.P. Whitney of New York, who by 1927 had formed Hudson Bay Mining and Smelting Co Ltd.

By 1930 production began at what became Canada's largest zinc refinery and third-largest copper smelter. Many families left the Prairies for Flin Flon during the 1930s, determined to make new lives for themselves. Flin Flon is still dependent on mining. In recent years HBMS has established satellite mines within the region, including a new concentrator at SNOW LAKE, a community to the E. The city has a trade population of about 15 000 and is also a tourism/recreation centre.

Flin Flon is likely named after the fictional character Professor Josiah *Flin*tabbatey *Flon*atin (created by J.E.P. Murddock , and the adventurer-explorer hero of *The Sunless City*, 1905), and was developed initially in an unplanned manner near the mine and plant. Costs of materials and the rocky terrain led to construction of small houses and businesses with minimal amenities. Redevelopment and newer residential areas have improved the townscape. The city hosts an annual Trout Festival in July and is known for its production of fine hockey talent.

D.M. LYON

Reading: V. Hedman et al, *Flin Flon* (1974).

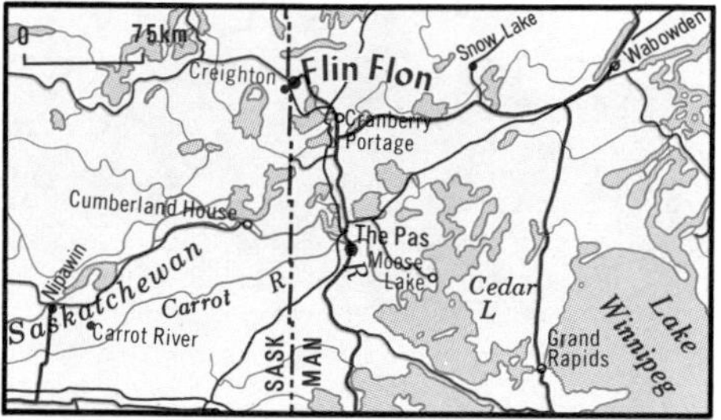

Floods and Flood Control Floods are the result of naturally occurring variations in the height of rivers, lakes and oceans. Flood damage occurs when people knowingly or unknowingly locate their activities, buildings and other property within range of the variations that occur above "normal" levels. There are 2 definitions of a flood: the hydrological definition, ie, when water levels exceed their "normal" range (flood stage); and the economic definition, when damage begins (flood damage stage).

The main cause of riverine flooding is excessive runoff following heavy RAINS. Runoff is augmented by snowmelt in early spring; for much of Canada spring is the peak flood season. Floods can also be caused by ice jams, when upstream water is blocked by accumulations of ice downstream, and by heavy convectional storms in summer. Similar high-water problems occur on lakes. Damage to shoreline facilities is not uncommon on the Great Lakes and occurs occasionally on most other lakes (eg, Lk Winnipeg). Coastal flooding may be caused when seasonally high tides are augmented by storm activity, or when a TSUNAMI, generated by EARTHQUAKES, is driven ashore. This phenomenon occurs occasionally on the West Coast. Coastal flooding related to hurricanes sometimes occurs in Atlantic Canada.

One of Canada's most difficult flood problems is on the RED R in Manitoba. Snowmelt waters from the US flow N through a wide, flat plain, and severe flooding sometimes creates havoc in many small communities as well as in Winnipeg. Major floods occurred in Winnipeg in 1950 and 1966. To alleviate the danger to the city a major flood diversion channel has been constructed. Major floods also occur in the lower FRASER R valley, S of Vancouver. In 1948, 16 000 people were evacuated from their homes, and damage was estimated at over $20 million (1948 dollars).

In 1954 heavy rains associated with the passage of HURRICANE HAZEL caused flooding on the Don and Humber rivers in Toronto and resulted in 81 deaths and severe damages. In July 1986, 900 Edmonton residents fled their homes as the rain-swollen waters of the N Saskatchewan R rose 7.6 m above their normal level, causing the worst flooding since 1915. Damaging floods have also occurred at Red Deer, Alta (Red Deer R); Swift Current and Moose Jaw, Sask; Fredericton (Saint John R); along the Châteauguay, Richelieu, Yamaska, St François and Chaudière rivers, Qué; and at many other localities in Canada.

Many residents trapped by rising waters in the Winnipeg flood of May 1950 were picked up by military personnel and transported to special trains which carried them to safety (*courtesy U of Manitoba/Dept of Archives and Special Coll/Winnipeg Tribune Coll*).

Flood Control A traditional approach to flooding has been to attempt to control high flows by construction of dams, dikes and diversion channels. While there are no accurate statistics on national flood damage, some evidence suggests that such engineering works have not prevented a rise in nationwide damages. In many regions, urban and suburban developments for housing, industry and commercial activities have been located on floodplains. When floods occur they cause more damage than in the past because more property lies in the path of floodwaters.

In an attempt to reverse this trend the federal government invited the provinces to join in a coordinated program to tackle the increasing toll of flood damage in a more comprehensive way. A flood-damage reduction program was announced in 1975, its main element being the preparation of flood-risk maps to identify hazard areas. Provincial and municipal policies, regulations, bylaws and public information activities are based on such maps. The program is intended to alert communities to the need for a comprehensive approach to reducing flood damage, including flood forecasting and warning systems, emergency measures, structural measures for flood control and land-use planning. The concept of adjusting the location, pattern and type of human settlement to flood hazard has replaced the concept of simply trying to control floods. The new program has been well received by most provinces and is being carried out under federal-provincial agreements. *See also* DISASTERS.

IAN BURTON

Floras and Botanical Journals Before 1900 a published "flora" may be defined loosely as a comprehensive, itemized description of the plants of a specific geographical region. Usually more than a mere list, it should involve an analytical description, discussing habitats and distribution and citing previous authorities. This definition would not apply to travelogues, natural histories, botanical art books or popular manuals, of which there were several in Canada by the late 19th century. Before that time, floras dealing with the area now comprising Canada were published elsewhere and written by botanical explorers and by sedentary scholars who identified specimens received from colonial residents, travellers and professional collectors.

Until the 19th century the only published floras containing predominantly Canadian plants were those of Jacques Phillipe Cornut in 1635 (*Canadensium Plantarum Historia*) and Pierre-François-Xavier de CHARLEVOIX in 1744 (*Histoire et description générale de la Nouvelle-France*). The manuscripts of Canadian flora known to have been started in the 18th century by Michel SARRAZIN, Jean-François GAULTIER and Pehr KALM were not published. Early in the 19th century, André MICHAUX and Frederick PURSH included more than 400 Canadian locales in their northern American floras, and Auguste Jean Marie Bachelot de la Pylaie wrote a modest flora of Newfoundland but never completed the expected sequel. In 1815 Pursh began collecting for a Canadian flora but died in Montréal in 1820, shortly after his collection was destroyed by fire.

The era of the itinerant botanical visitor or absentee scholar reached its climax in Canada with William Jackson Hooker, who amassed the collections of explorers, collectors and residents from coast to coast for his monumental *Flora Boreali Americana* (1833-40). Among his contributors in Québec was a small group of botanizers, including Harriet and William Sheppard, who were encouraged by Pursh, and who also sent specimens to John Torrey and Asa Gray for their *Flora of North America* (1838-43). Sheppard, a lumber merchant, did not confine his communications to foreign professionals. In 1829 Canada's first scholarly journal, the *Transactions of the Literary and Historical Society of Quebec*, contained Sheppard's identifications and popular descriptions of Charlevoix's plants, and in 1831 and 1837 his articles titled "Notes on some of the plants of Lower Canada." Although intended for local amateurs, this pioneer work gave Linnaean classification and synonyms, translated Pursh's Latin descriptive specifications, and elaborated on habitats, uses and points of interest.

Botanical articles including plant lists were carried in the *Canadian Journal* (est 1852) in Toronto, the *Canadian Naturalist and Geologist* (est 1856) in Montréal, the short-lived *Annals of the Botanical Society of Canada* (est 1861) in Kingston and the *Proceedings and Transactions of the Nova Scotian Institute of Science* (est 1863) in Halifax. Their pages frequently announced intentions to compile regional or national floras, but none were published. Credit for the first extensive flora by a Canadian belongs to another Québec amateur, Abbé Léon PROVANCHER, whose 2-volume *Flore Canadienne* appeared in 1862. Because he openly borrowed numerous illustrations from 2 books by the influential Asa Gray, this flora was seldom cited by contemporary botanists; subsequently, Provancher successfully shifted his scientific efforts to entomology, much of it published in his *Naturaliste canadien* (est 1868).

Later regional periodicals, such as the *Transactions of the Ottawa Field-Naturalists' Club* (est 1880) and the *Bulletin of the Natural History Society of New Brunswick* (est 1882) carried detailed local floras as well as botanical notes. The more professional Canadian botanists, such as George LAWSON in Halifax, continued to publish articles of high quality abroad or in the *Transactions of the Royal Society of Canada* (est 1882). Throughout this period, abbreviated floras were appended to many botanical textbooks and manuals published in Canada, and lists of plants from remote regions were included in the reports of the GEOLOGICAL SURVEY by such indefatigable field men as Robert BELL and John MACOUN.

The ultimate in historic Canadian floras, the first that could compare favourably with the best from abroad, was the *Catalogue of Canadian Plants*, compiled by Macoun and published in 7 parts (1883-1902). Despite its thousands of species, some with descriptions, synonyms, habitats, locales and authorities, Macoun modestly considered it only preliminary to a "Flora of Canada," which would have to await the 20th century. Nonetheless, the development of Canadian botanical description could be considered to have come of age after a painful adolescence marked by catastrophic losses, disappointed hopes and deplorable neglect. This slow maturation deserves recognition as pioneering scholarship under adverse conditions. *See also* BOTANY HISTORY.

J.M. NEELIN

Reading: M.A. Downie and M. Hamilton, *'and some brought flowers': Plants in a New World* (1980).

Florenceville, NB, Village, pop 725 (1986c), 709 (1981c), inc 1966, is situated 146 km up the SAINT JOHN R from Fredericton. Originally known as Buttermilk Cr, it was renamed in honour of Crimean War heroine Florence Nightingale. The initial wave of Loyalist settlers was augmented by 19th-century immigrants to form the basis of Florenceville's population. The community's initial growth flourished on the W bank of the Saint John R, but the completion of a bridge in 1884 and a spectacular fire in 1911 shifted the centre of commerce activity to the E bank. In the 20th century, Florenceville's development has been synonymous with the development of a small dealer in potatoes and other agricultural products into an international frozen-food industry.

FRED FARRELL

Flounder, *see* FLATFISH.

Flour Milling is the process of grinding grain into flour or meal. Canada's flour milling industry comprises mills which produce flour and other products for use in baked goods, pasta and other food products. By-products of the milling process, such as bran, shorts (fine bran) and wheat germ, are used mainly in the production of animal feeds, but small quantities of bran and wheat germ are also required for human consumption. Flour milling predates agricultural production; its evolution from a tedious manual chore to a highly automated, efficient and exact industrial process reflects many social changes and significant technological developments.

In N America, in precontact times, native people hand-ground corn and other substances (eg, acorns) into flour used in porridge, flat cakes, etc. By the middle of the 16th century, the first European settlers had arrived in NEW FRANCE, bringing with them their flour milling technology. The first water-powered mill commenced operation in 1607 at PORT-ROYAL. Many of the early wind- and water-driven mills have been preserved and may be seen in Ontario, Québec and the Maritimes. Pairs of circular millstones were used for grinding the grain. The best millstones, made of burr, a hard silicate found in France's Seine River valley, were constructed in segments, cemented together and bound with heavy iron bands. Both milling faces of the stones were grooved. The miller's skill lay in maintaining the grinding faces of the stones, since the precision of the millstone dressing determined the fineness of the grist. Stones were dressed with a chisel-faced hammer, called a "mill-bill." A flour miller also required a "true-steel" (ie, a straightedge used to test the evenness of the millstones), a bar scale for weighing, and a slate for tallying the incoming grain and the outgoing grist.

For most of history, flour milling has been a very manpower-intensive operation with grain, ground stocks in process and finished products requiring handling at every stage. The 18th century saw a growth of scientific ideas which brought significant changes to the process. Vertical and horizontal conveying of grain and ground materials by mechanical means (achieved by 1785) halved the manpower requirements in a mill and transformed flour milling into a completely mechanized continuous-process industry. Flour milling was one of the earliest applications of the steam engine. James Watt used one to drive a mill which he built in London, UK, in 1786. The mill used 6 pairs of millstones and, before its destruction by fire in 1791, was enlarged to 20 pairs, driven by 2 steam engines. In the latter part of the 19th century, Canadian millers were quick to replace millstones with steel rolls and to adopt the "gradual reduction system," a milling method developed in Hungary, which proved to be much more efficient with the use of steel rolls. The method involves milling in stages, the ground stock at each stage being sifted to remove the product and classify the remaining stocks for further gradual reduction. Many more-or-less successful variations have appeared throughout the past century.

The construction of a railway linking the prairie grain-producing region with the Great Lakes markedly influenced Canada's milling industry, permitting western Canadian wheat to be shipped to the eastern seaboard ports for export and to the mills in eastern Canada for processing. The railway was extended to the western seaboard by 1885. Canadian wheat was already known for its excellent milling and breadmaking qualities and, as domestic and export demands increased, wheat production in the Prairies expanded to meet it. By 1900, annual flour exports exceeded 80 000 t. The first decades of the 20th century were a period of competition and rationalization in the industry. The number of mills decreased from 2550 in 1891 to 801 in 1922. The industry was affected by the Great Depression of the 1930s but expanded during WWII. Since that time, the industry has been further rationalized and modernized as flour exports have fallen and most trading partners have developed domestic milling industries.

Modern flour mills are very highly automated and some parts of the process are easily adapted to computer control. Automation, improvements in transportation and declining trade have led to a further reduction of the number of mills in operation. As of Sept 1987, Canada had 36 flour mills: Ont had 17; Qué, 5; Alta, Man and Sask, 4 each; BC and NS, one each. Total milling capacity, over 11 000 t of wheat ground per day, produces slightly over 8200 t of flour. The industry employs 3000 people and has an annual payroll of over $81 million.

White flour for the Canadian market is enriched in accordance with regulations outlined in the Food and Drugs Act (*see* FOOD LEGISLATION). Other optional additives are used to meet customer specifications; however, the kinds and quantities of each FOOD ADDITIVE are also controlled through the Food and Drugs Act and a system of inspection ensures a strict adherence to all regulations.

The Canadian National Millers Association is a national trade association representing virtually 100% of Canada's millers. The CNMA was founded 29 Oct 1920 and its permanent office is in Ottawa. Most of the information distributed from the CNMA national office is of a technical nature (eg, relating to contracts, traffic considerations, statistical details, metrication). In the recent past, the CNMA has made representations on numerous government policies and has acted on the industry's behalf in a successful appeal to the Supreme Court of Canada. The CNMA maintains ongoing contact with officials from various departments and agencies, including the CANADIAN WHEAT BOARD and the Dept of Regional Economic Expansion. Each year CNMA executives negotiate Canada's yearly sale of flour to the Soviet Union for export to Cuba. The most recent contract was for 260 000 t, a significant percentage of the industry's overall production. PAUL W. BRENNAN

Flowers, Cultivated Flowers are cultivated by both commercial growers and hobbyists. In Canada, most commercial production is carried out under glass or plastic, with rare exceptions (eg, gladiolus, baby's breath, Shasta daisy). Commercial greenhouse production is a year-round enterprise with crops such as carnation, ROSE and chrysanthemum, but is seasonally oriented with crops such as poinsettia (Christmas) and Bermuda lily (Easter). Houseplants (eg, cyclamen, cineraria, pelargonium, African violet) are produced in many commercial greenhouses but the volume is not large, relative to the previously mentioned crops. In 1986 the commercial flower and vegetable industry in Canada had 9.8 million m^2 under glass or plastic; the sales of flowers in the same year amounted to approximately $299 million.

For those who grow flowers for sheer enjoyment, the culture of perennial flowers appears to offer the greatest satisfaction. Regional, national and international societies exist to promote interest in and improvement of special kinds of flowers, eg, lily, dahlia, peony and gladiolus. A brochure titled *Canadian Specialist Plant Societies,* compiled by T.J. Cole of the Ottawa Research Station, Agriculture Canada, lists 47 societies catering to the interests of the growers of 17 plant specialties. Public interest is also fostered by participation in flower shows which are sponsored by local societies.

Flowers in great variety may be seen in all parts of Canada, from the time the last snow disappears until the first killing frost of autumn. The earliest flowers, the small flowering bulbs (eg, crocus, puschkinia, chionodoxa, scilla), are followed by the larger narcissus and tulip. In many parts of Canada the primrose (*Primula*) and its relative the cortusa have become very popular spring flowers. Low cushion plants (eg, phlox, aubretia, arabis) also provide colour at this time of year.

In summer, gardeners will generally opt for the use of annual flowers only, or for a combination of long-blooming perennials with annuals. The first option limits the gardener to a constant, unchanging array of colour from the time the plants reach full bloom in late June (in most parts of Canada) until they are killed by autumn frost. The second option provides the grower with greater variety by employing the more ephemeral perennials in key positions, with annual flowers being supplementary. The perennials most commonly used are Shasta daisy, peony, oriental poppy, lythrum, hollyhock, anthemis, day lily, monkshood and delphinium. The most common annuals used are snapdragon, petunia, aster, verbena, bush balsam and marigold.

The sources of information for the amateur flower grower are abundant. The popular literature is immense, and the information is generally of universal acceptibility. Commercial growers are also generally well supported by specialists employed by Agriculture Canada (eg, at RESEARCH STATIONS across the country), provincial departments of agriculture, and HORTICULTURE departments in some colleges and universities. *See also* BOTANICAL GARDENS. R.H. KNOWLES

Reading: Reader's Digest, *Illustrated Guide to Gardening in Canada* (1979).

Fluke, *see* FLATWORM.

Fly, term commonly applied to many actively flying insects; restricted by scientists to 2-winged flies of order Diptera. This order includes BLACK FLIES, blow flies, bot flies, crane flies, deer flies, face flies, flesh flies, gnats, horn flies, horse flies, house flies, MIDGES, MOSQUITOES, no-see-ums, stable flies and warble flies. Four-winged "flies," eg, ALDERFLIES, BUTTERFLIES, CADDISFLIES, DAMSELFLIES, DRAGONFLIES, LACEWINGS, MAYFLIES, SAWFLIES, scorpionflies, snakeflies, STONEFLIES and whiteflies, are not true flies. About 100 000 species of Diptera have been described worldwide; the actual number may be double that. Over 7000 species have been reported in Canada, a figure also estimated to represent only half the species present. Flies range in size from 1 mm to 5.5 cm. Their relative abundance in the insect fauna increases northwards; in the most severe arctic localities, they outnumber all other winged insects, both as species and as individuals. The most obvious characteristic distinguishing true flies from other insects is the modification of the hind wings into knob-shaped, gyroscopic organs (halteres), essential for maintaining balance in flight. They allow flies to perform outstanding feats of aerobatics (eg, landing upside-down on ceilings).

Adult flies have sucking or piercing mouthparts and lack mandibles with which other insects bite food. The term "biting flies" is incorrect, since all such flies (eg, horse flies, mosquitoes, etc) pierce skin with a stabbing action. It is thought that adult flies were, primitively, predators of other insects, using their mouthparts to pierce prey's integument (body covering) and that the habit of sucking vertebrate blood evolved from this. Many modern flies, including voracious predators such as robber flies and dance flies, still attack only other insects. Most predatory flies feed on carbohydrates, eg, honeydew and nectar, as well as on animal prey. Some flies have abandoned predation and use pollen (hover flies) or decaying material (house flies) as their protein source. Adult warble and bot flies do not feed, relying on fat reserves accumulated in the larval stage.

Dipteran larvae are legless. Most are maggots living concealed within a moist substrate, but some hoverflies have free-living larvae, which prey on APHIDS. Specialized swimming larvae have evolved in mosquitoes and related groups of nonbiting midges. Most fly larvae feed on microorganisms or decaying matter. A few are predatory or parasitic: larvae of marsh flies (sciomyzids) kill snails; those of horse flies (tabanids), robber flies (asilids) and dance flies (empidids) prey on other insect larvae; those of tachinids (parasitic flies) are specialized internal parasites, important in biological control of INSECT PESTS. Although few groups of flies have evolved exclusively plant-eating larvae (notably fruit flies, gall midges and leaf-mining flies), those that have are unusually diverse and actively evolving. Among aquatic larvae, those of nonbiting midges form a major part of the invertebrate biomass in Canadian waters.

Flies are holometabolous insects, ie, they pass through a nonfeeding pupal stage before becoming adult. In higher flies, the pupa is enclosed in an outer shell (puparium) which gives added protection against drying, drowning, etc. The earliest described fossil Diptera date from Upper Triassic (225-208 million years ago). More advanced Diptera probably did not appear until late Cretaceous, but dating is uncertain. Western Canadian amber from the Cretaceous (144-66.4 million years ago) is a promising source of fossil Diptera. The enlarged salivary glands of many Diptera contain giant chromosomes convenient for genetic studies. This trait, and their willingness to breed in bottles, make *Drosophila* a popular experimental animal. G.C.D. GRIFFITHS

Reading: G.C.D. Griffiths, ed, *Flies of the Nearctic Region* (1980).

Flycatcher, Tyrant (Tyrannidae), large, diverse New World family of birds. The name flycatcher also refers to some members of Old World family Muscicapidae and to some other birds. Of the 367 known species of Tyrannidae, 16 regularly breed in Canada (10 called flycatchers, 2 kingbirds, 2 pewees, 2 phoebes); 7 others stray here. Tyrannidae range from robin to warbler size. Many are dull olive green; some are strikingly coloured. All feed by capturing a flying insect and returning to a perch to eat it. They are the only representatives in Canada of the suboscine perching birds (ie, those without true songs), and their loud, abrupt calls are the easiest means of distinguishing many species in the field. Canadian Tyrannidae are present May-Sept, when insects are available. Great crested flycatcher (*Myiarchus crinitus*) of eastern broad-leaved woodlands and olive-sided flycatcher (*Contopus borealis*) of coniferous forests across Canada are large compared with species of genus *Empidonax*. Yellow-bellied flycatcher (*E. flaviventris*) of northern spruce forests, least flycatcher (*E. minimus*) of broad-leaved stands and alder flycatcher (*E. alnorum*) of alder and willow thickets are widespread from Newfoundland to northern BC. Three others (*E. oberholseri, E. hammondii* and *E. difficilis*) occur only in the West, and 2 southern species (*E. virescens, E. traillii*) breed only a short distance N of the US border. The kingbirds are large, pugnacious flycatchers. Eastern kingbirds (*Tyrannus tyrannus*) breed from the NWT to NS; western kingbirds (*T. verticalis*) are found in the southern prairies and southern BC. Pewees are little larger than *Empidonax* flycatchers. Eastern wood pewees (*Contopus virens*) breed in southern Canada from Man to NS. Western wood pewees (*C. sordidulus*) are found from SW Man to southern YT, including coastal BC. Phoebes are bluebird sized. Eastern phoebes (*Sayornis phoebe*) are found from southeastern YT across southern Ontario and SW Québec to NB. Say's phoebe (*S. saya*) breeds in the NWT, YT, BC, Alberta and southern Saskatchewan.

A.J. ERSKINE

Alder flycatcher (*E. alnorum*) found in alder and willow thickets from Newfoundland to British Columbia (*artwork by Claire Tremblay*).

Flynn, Edmund James, premier of Québec 1896-97 (b at Percé, Canada E 16 Nov 1847; d at Québec C 7 June 1927). A meticulous politician, he proved a highly competent minister of natural resources, but when asked to succeed Premier TAILLON, he was unable to breathe life into the moribund Conservative Party. He served as premier from May 1896 to May 1897. His party was defeated in the elections of 1897, 1900 and 1904, thereby ushering in a Liberal regime that was to last until the 1936 election of Maurice DUPLESSIS.

DANIEL LATOUCHE

Fog, concentration of atmospheric particles (usually minute water droplets or ICE crystals) of sufficient density to reduce visibility. For practical purposes, in Canada, a reduction of visibility to 1000-9600 m is arbitrarily called mist; reduction to under 1000 m is called fog. In contrast, haze is a condition where such dry atmospheric particles as dust, ocean salt, natural oils from forest vegetation or forest-fire smoke are present in sufficient quantity to obscure vision. Near or downwind from industrial centres, combustion products such as smoke, soot, sulphuric and nitric oxides can combine with and acidify fog (*see* ACID RAIN). The major centres in Canada that experience most fog are St. John's, Nfld, with fog reported on an average of 126 days per year; Halifax, NS, with 74; Vancouver, BC, with 62. Penticton, BC, receives least fog, an average of 4 days per year.

Radiation fog forms most commonly as moist air is cooled below its dew point, ie, the critical temperature at which air can no longer hold all its water vapour. A dense fog develops if the liquid water droplets or ice crystals formed by condensation are trapped and concentrated in a shallow layer near the ground by a temperature inversion (in which temperature increases with height rather than decreasing with height as is usual). Such special meteorological conditions arise quite frequently. For example, in Canada's coastal regions the cool waters of the Pacific and Atlantic oceans chill warm, moist air masses moving over them, especially in spring and early summer, causing huge banks of persistent fog (called advection fog). Inland fog is commonly caused by the cooling of the lower atmosphere through the radiation of heat into space on cloudless nights. In early morning (particularly in autumn), dense fog banks form and persist until dissipated by the heat of the sun. Weather satellite pictures show that this drying out process proceeds inwards from the outer edges of the fog bank. Warm fronts of weather systems also cause fog when the cool air below the frontal surface becomes saturated by rain falling into it from the warmer air above. This type usually persists until swept away by drier air.

Occasionally, freezing fogs form (mainly of the radiation and frontal types) when liquid water droplets exist at temperatures a little below freezing. Such droplets are said to be supercooled and freeze into beautiful fringes of hoar frost on wires, trees and other objects. In the depths of Canada's arctic winters, the air is so bitterly cold that it can hold very little water vapour. When cooled further, what little vapour there is condenses into a fog of tiny, sparkling ice crystals rather than liquid droplets. Any extra moisture placed into the atmosphere (eg, by vehicle exhaust) also expands into an immediate ice-crystal fog. Arctic sea smoke, another type of winter fog, is formed when air, made warm and moist by contact with open water, rises through convection and condensation takes place immediately.

MICHAEL J. NEWARK

Fogo Island, 260 km^2, 15 km off Newfoundland's NE coast, was named *fuego,* "fire," by the Portuguese. The irregularly shaped island, heavily forested in the S, lies on shallow Fogo Shelf, which attracts salmon, cod and other species. Until the late 1700s Fogo was a summer home of the BEOTHUK. European fishermen visited its waters from the early 1500s and settlement began at Fogo Harbour (now Fogo), an outpost of Devon and Dorset businesses, in the early 1700s. The island, connected by ferry with Carmanville across Hamilton Sound, now supports 10 settlements though it once had 26. In the 1960s attempts to resettle Fogo I were countered by a movement towards rural development, aided by the National Film Board, whose short documentaries helped to unite residents, crossing traditional social, cultural and religious lines. The "Fogo Process," the interactive use of film and videotape to foster community awareness and identity, is now used for the same purpose in underdeveloped countries. In Fogo, resettlement was abandoned, a fishermen's co-operative was founded, educational facilities were integrated, and a near-shore, long-liner fishery was developed. JANET E.M. PITT

Folk Art embraces a wide range of artistic works, a mixture of naivety and sophistication, cultural tradition and individual innovation. Although varied definitions abound, folk art in general falls into 2 categories: cultural and individual. Cultural art has an ethnic basis (French, English, German, Polish, Ukrainian), tends to be conservative, and reflects the common ethos in a community; individual art is innovative, the expression of a unique if sometimes eccentric personality. Whether they are paintings, sculptures, carvings or objects embellished with pictorial and decorative motifs, all folk-art products have popular appeal. The people who fashioned them intended them to interest the ordinary citizens who were their neighbours, friends and acquaintances. Traditionally, folk art sprang from a desire to make human and meaningful the daily round of work and home life, and thus reflected the cultural and regional diversity in Canada. Contemporary folk art, often shut off from traditional sources and responding to the demand by museums and collectors for "goods," is an art of individual and aesthetic expression, employing new techniques and responding to influences in modern society. While traditional folk art is usually anonymous, recent artists are known and specialize in particular media and styles.

Folk art mirrors the basic ideas and customs that regulate life-styles, and may be based in religion, patriotic affection for king and country, satisfaction with daily living or appreciation for na-

Much folk art relating to the sea was produced by craftsmen carving figures to illustrate a ship's name. The carving of explorer Marco Polo graced the stern of the famous NB clipper of the same name (*courtesy New Brunswick Museum*).

ture. Folk art is sometimes described as "primitive," for the artists are untrained, work by instinct and deal in a simple way with the basic truths as known to ordinary people.

Folk art based on religious belief has flourished in Canada from the days of early European settlement and embraces a sense of continuity and tradition. Visitors to 18th- and 19th-century Catholic Québec described the pious decorative mottoes, the religious paintings depicting old themes, and the cocks on church steeples, which reminded parishioners of St Peter's in Rome. They had been painted or fashioned by simple, devout people who lacked artistic training but had in common a great desire to express their inner artistic sensibilities. A significant form of early religious folk art, copied from France, was the VOTIVE PAINTING that illustrated miraculous happenings such as escape from impending shipwreck through the intervention of Ste-Anne (collection of Ste-Anne-de-Beaupré, Québec). The sculptured figures of the Holy Family and favourite saints that adorned many churches inspired the carving of more primitive copies for private religious devotion. Wayside crosses throughout Québec were erected at many crossroads and the crucified Christ who hung on some of them was often carved by a local worker. Such carvings sometimes rose to the level of the finest folk art. An example originating in the Gaspé Pen and now in the Musée des beaux-arts de Montréal is a massive, simple, austere, Christ figure, with dignified simple planes; it does not strive for the realism of high art. Local people carved nativity figures for the Christmas crib, painted pictures of the lamb on banners that were carried in religious processions, or carved sugar molds with biblical motifs. All these artifacts were reminders of religious teachings and emphasized the importance of religious life in an agreeable way. In Charlevoix County during the 1930s and 1940s a group of local artists pictured well-known themes, some of them religious, such as the wise men visiting a local home and mingling informally with the family at Christmas.

The religious art of Protestant provinces in Canada seems less obvious because they did not allow representations of God. Yet wall memorials to departed relatives or samplers embroidered in Nova Scotia during the early 1800s demonstrate deep religious piety. Protestant ORANGE ORDER lodges carried painted banners with religious symbols in their street processions, and many Protestant homes had little paintings of King Billy on his white horse. Religious banners hung in Sharon Temple, built by a Protestant group N of Toronto. A century ago Anna WEBER, a Mennonite, painted motifs in Waterloo County, Ont, that symbolized nature as described in the "Songs of Solomon." Early TOMBSTONES in local cemeteries almost everywhere in Canada are often overlooked as folk art. One such stone in Ontario recalls graphically how a pioneer was killed by a falling tree when clearing the primeval forest. An 18th-century Halifax tombstone shows Ezekiel blowing his trumpet on Judgement Day, and nearby another stone pictures Adam and Eve flanking the serpent encircling an apple tree. Another example of religious folk art is the "corn dolly" artistically woven from the last sheaf of the harvest and sometimes thrown into the fire to propitiate the gods, which harks back to superstitions in England during the Druid age.

Loyalty to country, racial origin and religion have been common themes of the folk artist in Canada, whether British, French, German, Italian, Mennonite, Ukrainian, Doukhobor or Polish. Battle memorials in the form of descriptive paintings or soldiers carved in full uniform are numerous, and patriotic mothers hooked pictures of tanks and flags on mats during both world wars. Loyalist immigrants to Canada left no doubt of their continuing British sympathies; they erected a signboard on which was painted the head of George III in front of the King's Head Inn at Burlington, Ont. A local carver fashioned a statue of General WOLFE that stood in a niche at a Québec street corner for many years. Lutheran immigrants from the Palatine region of Germany who settled along the upper St Lawrence in 1784 fashioned a weather vane in the form of a swan because the Swan of St Lothair had been a traditional symbol in their homeland. It declared their ancestry. Inn and trade signs in English and French towns were like a popular picture gallery which fascinated the people, and in imitation similar signs were painted in Canada. Traditional designs for clothes and decorations used in Europe were continued in the New World. Ukrainian Easter eggs are an ancient and sophisticated folk art with religious and symbolic significance. The tradition of hand-lettered and decorated documents, books and miscellaneous items was brought by Mennonite immigrants to Ontario between the 1780s and 1830s (*see* GERMANIC FRAKTUR AND CALLIGRAPHY). Gradually, Canadian loyalties and heroes developed. John A. MACDONALD was featured on a sampler in the 1880s, and designs incorporated maple leaves, beavers and Mounties on any number of objects. Other occupational figures, particularly the cowboy and the pioneer settler, were favourite motifs in folk art.

When sailing ships were links with distant places, up to the early 20th century, much distinctive folk art relating to the sea was produced, particularly in the schooner and lighthouse motifs on the eastern seaboard (*see* SCULPTURE). Crews had an affection for their ships and named vessels in honour of celebrated naval heroes such as Admiral Nelson, or after more personal associations, such as the "Mary W." Craftsmen in the shipyards of Québec City, Saint John, Digby or Summerside carved figureheads of buxom women or a tall admiral to illustrate the name. A notable carving graced the clipper MARCO POLO, which had been built near Saint John and made record-breaking voyages to the Orient. Sailors on distant voyages passed long hours in a myriad of activities; some made models or paintings of their ship to be displayed at home, often with intricate riggings; others carved trinket boxes or whalebone ivory, engraving the polished surfaces with pictures of unicorns, polar bears, or tokens of endearment for absent loved ones.

Similarly, much Canadian folk art relates to farming, which played a major role in national life. Agriculture in Ontario and Québec reached a peak of visible prosperity in the later 19th century when vast BARNS were constructed, many of them crowned by decorative metal and wooden weather vanes fashioned as horses, cows or sheep. Progressive farmers of the day exhibited their finest livestock at country fairs or at provincial exhibitions in Toronto, Québec City and Fredericton, and artist/craftsmen such as J.W. Swift of Toronto were commissioned to paint the best stock in watercolour or oil. Some farmers still hang hand-painted signs depicting their particular herd type at the entrance to their property. Dutch immigrant Jan Wyers has produced some of the country's finest popular paintings of the last half century, especially of farm life, and William Panko, a western artist of the 1940s who knew nothing about perspective, painted scenes that reveal a direct joy in the fresh outdoors. On the self-sufficient farm, where a variety of tasks were performed in the fields and in the home, many useful objects were fashioned in an attractive shape and with fine, meaningful ornamentation. Hand tools, trivets, molds, and combs used in spinning were often examples of high craftsmanship (*see* LEATHERWORKING). Wooden butter stamps served as a trademark and as proof of the farmer's aesthetic sensibility. Rural women recycled textile fibres into decorative hooked RUGS and QUILTS whose blocks of colour and design rival fine contemporary nonobjective painting. They embroidered pillowcases, table linen and handkerchiefs with pictorial tokens of love. Whittlers in the family created models of family pets and dancing dolls, and carved wall shelves and cabinets, rocking horses and TOYS for the children (*see* FURNITURE, COUNTRY). More sophisticated sculptors turned out elaborate decoys for the hunting season, painted to depict every detail of the species.

These Good Old Thrashing Days by Jan Wyers, oil on fabric (*courtesy Norman Mackenzie Art Gallery, Regina*).

Wooden chests served as travelling trunks and as storage boxes in the home.

With increasing industrialization, many craftsmen turned their skills to creating miniatures of a passing rural life, recording the skills, amusements and tales of the past in tangible form for the next generation. Other carvers depicted the new technology, in steam engines that worked and in intricate models of farm machinery.

Folk art does not have to be useful, or based on culture or tradition. It may be purely whimsical, rooted in the particular imagination of the artist. Garden ornaments, birdhouses, shadowboxes and figurines may be exotic, erotic, humorous or fanciful, though always direct and spontaneous in their "folksiness." The sculptor J.B. Côté of Québec once carved a wooden figure, a gaunt, gangling youth who sang in the choir and had about him the air of a young "man-about-town" but who was trussed or strangled by his starched Sunday collar. His attractive human qualities gave him immediate popular appeal and, like all successful folk art, enlivened the life of ordinary people around him. *See also* FOLK DANCE; FOLKLORE.

J. RUSSELL HARPER

Reading: M. Bird, *Canadian Folk Art* (1983) and *Ontario Fraktur* (1977); P. Crépeau et al, *From the Heart: Folk Art in Canada* (1983); J. Russell Harper, *A People's Art* (1974).

Folk Dance exists on a variety of levels and folk dancers think of it in many ways. A definition includes several key elements. Folk dance is vernacular in that it is characteristic of a particular time and place and relates to a popular rather than an elite aspect of a culture. Folk dance belongs to the "little" tradition within the "great" tradition of a society since it is primarily an oral or customary tradition, unwritten and unofficial. "Survival" folk dances are those that serve an integral function within a community; "revival" folk dances lack this stature and are performed by a select group of people who dance for various personal reasons.

One result of an oral, as opposed to a written, tradition is that people see, hear and perform differently; therefore they transmit the material in a variety of ways. With folk dance, no particular version of a dance is the definitive one. If variants do not exist, then a dance was undoubtedly passed on in a nontraditional way, perhaps by written official sources or by a group that zealously guarded the "purity" of the dance. Although documents that record the historical development of folk dance are scarce, some researchers believe that many dance forms grew from religious rituals. Each culture area has experienced its own evolution, although some areas have had more contact with external influences than have others.

Social dance, although not usually considered so, is an important form of folk dance and exists at several levels. Dance studios teach the "right" way, but in practice people invent, simplify and change the order, thereby creating variants in dances such as the waltz, cha-cha, disco or jitterbug. Social dance is part of the "little" tradition in a culture, and is vernacular. At its most sophisticated, social dancing can be executed as a performance. In the western European tradition, social dance is performed in couples and its usual function is courtship, a valuable ritual. Most social dances enjoy a short but intense popularity, which then declines. Some, however, possess an unusual longevity: the waltz, polka, square dance and longways forms and the minuet of the 18th and 19th centuries are good examples. Not as popular as it was in past periods, social dancing is still considered a convenient and acceptable way to meet people. Companies, clubs, university groups, high schools and community centres host social dance events regularly.

In Canada, with the exception of social dancing, there is little activity on the level of survival folk dancing. As there are few studies in folk dance, it is difficult to determine precisely the amount of survival dancing. However, it is found among relatively isolated (geographically or psychologically) communities, such as the native peoples, and the francophone and Hassidic cultures. Urban-based minority groups, such as Indian, Chinese, Italian, Portuguese, Ukrainian, Macedonian, Greek, Polish, German, Armenian, Irish, Latin-American and West Indian, might have retained some of the dances unique to their regional origins. But as the first- and second-generation immigrants die off, the third and subsequent generations tend to assimilate into mainstream society, and with them go the dances which were once an important part of their social, occupational or religious spheres.

Revival dances are more frequent and more visible. They are especially noticeable among groups who have strong feelings for their ethnic roots. One way to preserve, express and perpetuate this sentiment is to perform "national" or "ethnic" dances. Dances may be acquired either when older group members recall dances from the past, or when an outside expert is summoned to teach the dance. The dances are then "set" for the group, who enjoy dancing them on suitable occasions.

Another area of activity is "international" folk dancing, performed by people who seek not cultural identity but the enjoyment of dances from many countries. A large proportion of the dances are from the Balkans, for line dances with intricate footwork seem to hold the greatest attraction. Again the dances are "set" by an expert, and as such are indicative of only one of the possible variants which may be found in the native milieu.

A third type of revival dancing involves the groups whose goal is to execute the dances "perfectly," eg, square-dance clubs. Here participants casually perform for each other, although some groups have costumes for more formal, presentational occasions. Another type of group whose emphasis is on perfection is the theatrical folk-dance troupe. Choreography, costumes and lighting designs combine to create a particular effect. Dances are presented in a highly theatrical manner and sometimes several dances are combined into one. The labelling of this material as "folk dance" is misleading, since it is "set" and variants are not encouraged. A better designation might be "folk-inspired" or "folk-derived" dance, labels that might help audiences to discriminate between theatrical presentations and survival folk dancing. In spite of these limitations, perfection-oriented groups express a vernacular form of dance within the "little" traditions of society, and this can be classified as folk dance.

The French Canadian dance tradition is a good example of a culture with both survival and revival forms. In Québec, folk dances are those based on square and longways formations, on sung-circle dances, and on the percussive, rhythmic pattering of the feet called step dancing or *gigue*. Many of these dances have an elite and noble history, such as the complex quadrille of Île d'Orléans. Simpler square dances and others such as the longways *la contredanse* and *le brandy* were probably the result of British or American influence. All of these styles have emerged as folk dances, complete with variants and a paucity of documentation.

The *gigue* is traditionally passed down from parent (usually father) to child. Though its origins are not certain, it seems likely that it derives from the Irish jig. Because the *gigue* has always been an oral dance form, contemporary manifestations clearly demonstrate the process of a folk tradition – a vibrant dance form where structural and stylistic variants abound. Sung-circle dances, which were once popular with adults, have now mostly passed into the children's repertoire. A couple of adult *rondes* have been documented in isolated communities and from time to time they are resurrected at workshops. Some of these dances represent part of the rich store of culture brought from France in the 17th century.

Survival dance in Québec usually revolves around the home *veillée*, where dancing is one of many activities such as gossiping, eating, card playing and music. Dancing serves as a catalyst to socialization, an important aspect of individual and community development. Today, as a result of television, smaller families and a rejection of "old-fashioned" ways, many "dancing families" no longer dance. There is, however, an active revival movement. The workshops sponsored by the Fédération des loisirs-danse du Québec emphasize learning the dances and having fun. In Québec City, Les Danseries offers weekly lessons in pedagogy, calling for dances, and fiddle and accordion playing. The performance troupe has been a popular entertainment spectacle in Québec for many years. In the 1950s les Folkloristes du Québec were the first to theatricalize, in that they wore period costumes. Later, troupes such as les FEUX FOLLETS, les Danseurs du St-Laurent, les Gens de mon pays and the present les Sortilèges performed to enthusiastic audiences.

In English Canadian folk dance, the square dance is the most widely disseminated dance, popular from Newfoundland to BC. However, recent growth of the step-dance contest, especially in Ontario, has catapulted this form into the limelight. Step dancing is an interesting mixture: it is both a vehicle for performance and a dance in a constant state of evolution. Younger contestants usually take lessons from experts, or learn from within the family. Only the "old timers" purport to dance in a traditional or old-fashioned style, while the others appear to have some of the exhibitionistic tap-dance influence. Nontraditional taps are worn on the shoes in order to accentuate the sound. The music remains within the folk genre – a certain amount each of hornpipe, jig and reel. Only the tempo has increased.

Native peoples' dance is often connected with important rituals, and thus cannot properly be considered folk. Dances of lesser consequence, however, can be shared with other tribes or with non-Indians. The most visible occasion for folk dancing is the pan-Indian POWWOW, where prizes are won by dance competitors and there is dancing for noncontestants. The BLOOD of Alberta, for example, present 2 types of dances at powwows: collective solo dances such as the Sioux Dance, Grass Dance and War Dance, and Couples Ring Dances, such as the Owl Dance. Another opportunity to do powwow dancing is at the annual SUN DANCE, where many of the younger participants are unfamiliar with ritual dancing. Pan-Indian powwow dancing limits the attention given to specific tribal dances, but promotes identification with general Indian culture.

Non-native folk dances are also popular among some tribes. Square dances are probably the most pervasive; they have been reported among the Blood as Spi-ye-Buska/Mexican Dance and among the HARE at Fort Good Hope. The Hare also enjoyed the 2-step, waltz, jive and Scots reel.

Across Canada then, there are many types of folk-dance activities. Dancing is usually associated with an ethnic community and often parents encourage children to participate in folk dance as a means of learning about and identifying with their cultural heritage. However, elementary school children in general are obliged to learn squares or other types of folk dance, depending on their teachers' expertise. Carefully graded record and book sets are available to interested educators. The children usually perform these dances in a cultural void, considering them tedious and unimportant.

Organizations, clubs and societies cater to the revival in folk dancing. A recent publication, *People's Folk Dance Directory*, has compiled an extensive list of folk-dance places, teachers and societies for both the US and Canada. Though useful as a general guide, the directory is far from comprehensive since many of the groups are not even mentioned.

Along with regularly scheduled folk-dance classes, special events such as folk festivals and ethnic celebrations are open to folk-dance enthusiasts. Some of the more easily identified festivals include the Irish *feis*, Scottish highland-dancing contests, May Day festivities (often involving English Morris-dance teams), Québec winter carnival, Caribana and Israeli Independence Day. Other events, such as Caravan in Toronto, Man and his World in Montréal, and Folk Fest in BC, are multicultural in scope and provide an opportunity to watch and participate in the activities of a variety of cultures.

The university campus is often a major force in the folk-dance community, sponsoring clubs that are usually open to all. Academically, faculty and students at U Laval (Québec) and Memorial U (Newfoundland) have researched dance in their regions, and dance departments at York and Waterloo have also contributed to folk-dance studies.

Several umbrella-type organizations both prepare folk-dance events and act as a storehouse and information centre on activities in the area. The Canadian Folk Arts Council has branches throughout Canada, with head offices in Toronto and Montréal that have documentation centres. The Ontario Folkdance Assn publishes *Ontario Folkdancer*, a magazine/newsletter that includes notices of events across Canada and in parts of the US. In Montréal the Fédération des loisirs-danse du Québec organizes soirées and weekend workshops, houses archival material and publishes the folk journal *La Jarnigoine*. *See also* FOLK MUSIC. ELLEN SHIFRIN

Reading: C. Carpenter, *Many Voices: A Study of Folklore Activities in Canada* (1979); G. Emmerson, *A Social History of Scottish Dance* (1972); B. Everett, *Canadian Square Dances* (nd) and *Traditional Canadian Dances* (1967); L. Melamed, *All Join Hands: Connecting People Through Folk Dance* (1977); R.L. Séguin, *Les Divertissements en Nouvelle-France* (1968); R. Witmer, *The Musical Life of the Blood Indians* (1982); film: *The Longhouse People*; *Le Reel du pendu*; *Circle of the Sun*; *Canadians Can Dance*; *L'Art de la gigue*.

Folk Festivals The Canadian Folk Festival Directory lists 132 major and minor summer festivals in every province. Almost half of them were in Ontario, and another one-third in the Maritimes. Hundreds of old-time fiddling contests also take place throughout Canada in summer and fall. These festivals resulted from the widespread popularity of traditional music in the 1950s and 1960s. Early festivals such as Miramichi (est 1958) in NB were devoted to preserving the authentic FOLK MUSIC of local performers who rarely appeared outside of their rural communities. As interest in folk music continued and festivals grew, urban "revival" performers who learned their music from books and records became popular. At the peak of the folk-music revival in the mid-1960s, urban folksingers were composing their own songs and music on folk models. Singer-songwriters such as Stan ROGERS were featured at all major festivals. By the late 1980s, some larger festivals, responding to financial problems, had moved beyond folk music in order to attract larger and more varied audiences.

A handful of Canadian festivals have attained international recognition and draw performers and listeners from all parts of Canada as well as the US and Europe. Best known of these is the Mariposa Folk Festival, founded in 1961. It began modestly in Orillia, Ont, but by 1968, when it moved to TORONTO ISLAND, it was the largest festival in N America, capable of attracting international performers such as Joni MITCHELL, Joan Baez, IAN AND SYLVIA Tyson and Gordon LIGHTFOOT. Mariposa's use of multiple workshop and concert stages and its development of separate craft, children's and other specialty areas became the model for other major festivals.

The Winnipeg Folk Festival, now the largest, began in July 1974. It offers a wide variety of music, song, dance and stories from all over the continent. Urban singer-songwriters are popular but traditional music is still featured. Folk festivals are scheduled in August in Vancouver (est 1979) and Edmonton (est 1980). These festivals draw 10 000 – 20 000 people of all ages and backgrounds. Dozens of workshops are offered during the day and concerts take place at night.

Many of the small Maritime festivals still feature traditional performers rather than the more popular urban artists. Other festivals throughout Canada offer a mixture of traditional and contemporary material. Ontario, for example, offers dozens of medium-sized festivals such as the Owen Sound Summer Folk Festival in August and the Toronto Festival of Storytelling in Feb. KAY F. STONE

Folk Music, Anglo-Canadian Folk music is the music of ordinary people: songs and tunes that are passed on from one to another by ear rather than by print and thus acquire variations. They are sung or played for pleasure rather than for profit, and usually the composer is unknown. The largest number of Anglo-Canadian folk songs came to this country with the early settlers from Britain and Ireland and were passed from generation to generation over the last 300 years. They include 77 of the *English and Scottish Popular Ballads* catalogued by Francis James Child and several hundred of the later broadside ballads, as well as lullabies, love songs, sea shanties and music-hall songs.

Newfoundland is particularly rich in the ancient supernatural ballads that are rare elsewhere in N America. The most popular ballad in Canada, as throughout the English-speaking world, is "the little Scotch song of Barbry Allen" which delighted Samuel Pepys in 1666: over 60 different versions of it have turned up across the country. Other popular titles include "Lady Isabel and the Elf Knight," "Little Musgrave and Lady Barnard," "Lord Randall," "The Cruel Mother," "The Gypsy Laddie," "The Sweet Trinity" and "The Farmer's Curst Wife."

Even more numerous than the Child ballads are the later broadside ballads (printed on single sheets known as "broadsides"). Some 240 of the 290 that G. Malcolm Laws, Jr, catalogued in *American Balladry from British Broadsides* were sung in Canada, and many more have turned up since his guide appeared. Most of these are romantic tales of family opposition to lovers, of lovers' disguises and tricks, or of faithful and unfaithful lovers. The most popular of all the plots was that of the broken ring or returned lover which has been told and retold in dozens of different ballads.

Fewer songs were composed in Canada than were imported from the British Isles, and nearly all the native Canadian songs borrowed their tunes from Old World sources. Most of our native Anglo-Canadian songs were inspired by the occupations of the early settlers, the 2 largest groups springing from men who earned their living on the sea or in the woods. Nova Scotia and Newfoundland are noted for sea shanties, songs of whaling, sealing and fishing, and ballads about disasters at sea. In New Brunswick and Ontario most of the native songs came from the lumber camps, some telling of the winter's work, others describing tragic accidents in the woods or on the rivers, and still others relating the shantyboys' experiences when they left the camps in spring. Smaller numbers of songs came from sailors on the Great Lakes, miners in Cape Breton and BC, and homesteaders and cowboys on the Prairies. Western Canada produced few Anglo-Canadian songs, but some American songs found their way across the border. Canadians adopted or adapted some pioneer American ditties such as "The Little

Old Sod Shanty" and "Bury Me Not on the Lone Prairie." The most widespread Prairie song, known variously as "Prairie Land," "Alberta Land" or "Saskatchewan," was a localized form of American verses based on "Beulah Land."

Other native songs reflect outstanding events in our history. The Battle of the Plains of Abraham inspired the earliest known Anglo-Canadian ballad, "Brave Wolfe" or "Bold Wolfe." The War of 1812 produced such lively songs as "Come All You Bold Canadians" and "The *Chesapeake* and the *Shannon.*" Other ballads recall the Rebellions of 1837-38 and the Fenian raids of 1866, and Confederation inspired some anti-Confederation songs in Newfoundland.

Besides the occupational and historical songs, there are various accounts of local happenings: murders, disasters, celebrations or other newsworthy incidents. Ballads tell of the murderer J.R. BIRCHALL, the Miramichi fire, the Halifax Explosion and the Springhill mine disasters, and ditties such as "The Kelligrews Soiree" and "The Feller from Fortune" immortalize the lively Newfoundland parties.

The most notable characteristic of the native Anglo-Canadian songs is their predominantly Irish quality, which is evident not only in Newfoundland but also in the Maritimes and Ontario. Both sea ballads and lumbering songs fall into the typical "come-all-ye" pattern and nearly all are set to Irish tunes.

Traditional folksingers always sang unaccompanied until very recently, and "mouth music" or lilting was sometimes used to accompany dancing. The fiddle was by far the most popular folk instrument, followed by the accordion and tin whistle. The most common fiddle tunes were Scottish and Irish, and some were composed by local fiddlers.

Anglo-Canadian collectors have concentrated on folk songs to a far greater extent than on any other type of FOLKLORE. There are over 20 major books of folk songs and few devoted to any other single genre. The pioneer collectors were W. Roy Mackenzie in NS and Elisabeth Greenleaf in Newfoundland, followed by Helen CREIGHTON and Kenneth Peacock. Edith FOWKE has collected in Ontario and P.J. Thomas in BC. An American, Edward D. Ives, has produced 3 books dealing with Maritime singer-composers. EDITH FOWKE

Reading: Canadian Folk Music Journal (1973-); H. Creighton, *Songs and Ballads from Nova Scotia* (1932); Edith Fowke, *The Penguin Book of Canadian Folk Songs* (1973); Fowke and Alan Mills, *Singing our History: Canada's Story in Song* (1984); Fowke and R. Johnston, *Folk Songs of Canada, I and II* (1954; 1967); G. Lehr, *Come and I Will Sing to You: A Newfoundland Song Book* (1985); K. Peacock, *Songs of the Newfoundland Outports* (3 vols, 1965); P.J. Thomas, *Songs of the Pacific Northwest* (1979).

Folk Music, Franco-Canadian French colonists brought their customs, way of life and music with them to the shores of the St Lawrence. From the Conquest, 1759-60, until well into the 20th century these French communities, mostly rural, persisted in a linguistic and cultural isolation that helped maintain the vitality and strength of their traditional culture.

French Canadian instrumental music is derived from several sources. Unfettered by the linguistic constraints affecting song, it has benefited from its contact with CELTIC MUSIC and the music of France and the British Isles. While retaining some characteristics of the country of origin, French Canadian folk music has become freer and more lyrical, and has adapted to the rigours of the country and the Latin temperament of its inhabitants. It is essentially functional music, and meant to accompany dances such as quadrilles, the cotillion, the jig (a solo demonstration of skill) and various *rondes* and *jeux dansés.*

The violin (fiddle), the most common instrument in French Canadian folk music, dates back to New France. Joseph Allard, Jean CARIGNAN and Jos Bouchard established reputations as masters of the fiddle. The harmonica came from Germany, via the US, in 1866 and quickly became popular. In 1892 the diatonic accordion also arrived from Germany and became a favourite instrument among French Canadians. Two of its best-known interpreters in Québec were Alfred Montmarquette and Philippe Bruneau. The jew's harp and simple percussion instruments such as spoons, bones and feet are also characteristic of the traditional music of French Canada.

Folk Songs seem to have come from the people, the peasant classes, and were passed down from generation to generation through oral tradition, renewing and transforming along the way. The songs have basic, straightforward verses, rudimentary metre and simple vocabulary. Some French Canadian folk songs derive from a medieval French tradition brought over by the early colonists; they exist today as an old form of folkloric repertory, richer than anything now found in France. Other songs are of more recent composition with rough and imitative lyrics. Expressed as lament or satire, these songs reflect the social conditions of the French Canadian community: the life of the voyageurs, the lumber camps, disasters and misfortunes, and political and communal life. Acadia has long been a rich source of this form of music.

Research on folk songs, which began in France in 1853, had an impact in Canada. In 1863 Hubert LaRue published an article entitled "Les chansons populaires et historique du Canada" in *Le Foyer canadien.* He persuaded Ernest GAGNON to collect and transcribe tunes for some of the lyrics he had collected. Two years later Gagnon published a work entitled *Chansons populaires du Canada,* with melodies and abundant commentary. In 1916 Marius BARBEAU, an anthropologist with the National Museum of Canada, began collecting folk songs. His collection of more than 10 000 songs is preserved in the Canadian Centre for Folk Culture Studies in Ottawa. His major books on traditional songs are *Romancero du Canada* (1937), *Jongleur Songs of Old Quebec* (1962), *Le Rossignol y chante* (1962), and *En roulant ma boule* (1982). In 1944 Luc Lacourcière founded the Archives de folklore at Laval. Conrad Laforte began classifying folk songs in 1954 and between 1977 and 1983 published 5 of his 6 volumes of *Catalogue de la chanson folklorique française.* From 1942 to 1983 Anselme Chiasson published *Chansons d'Acadie* in 6 volumes; he is also one of the founders of the Centre d'études acadiennes at U Moncton. Another collector of note is Germain Lemieux at the Centre franco-ontarien de folklore at Laurentian U (Sudbury). *See also* FOLKLORE; FOLK DANCE.

DONALD DESCHÊNES

Reading: M. Béland, *Chansons de voyageurs, coureurs de bois et forestiers* (1982); M. and R. Harcourt, *Chansons folkloriques françaises au Canada* (1956); C. Laforte, *Poétique de la chanson traditionelle française* (1976); J.P. Joyal, "Le processus de composition dans la musique instrumentale du Québec," *Canadian Folk Music Journal* 8 (1980); L. Ornstein, "Instrumental Folk Music of Quebec," *Canadian Folk Music Journal* 10 (1982).

Folklore was first introduced as a term in England in 1846 and today refers to information, wisdom and human expression that is passed on, usually anonymously, from generation to generation or transmitted and circulated as traditional cultural behaviour. Folkloric materials can be found anywhere and in any form, although past scholarship has favoured verbal folklore or oral literature – folk songs, folktales, epic, myth, legend, folk drama, riddles, proverbs, sayings and a variety of verses. Nonverbal folklore includes material culture such as folk architecture, folk art and crafts, dance, music, custom, ritual and belief, traditional folkways and amusements.

To become folklore, a song, story, custom or belief must go through a process of "folklorization" and meet the criteria and approval of the receiving community. During this filtering process, the item may undergo one or more revisions before it definitely enters into the community's cultural heritage. Along with general recognition and appreciation, anonymity and variation are also features that characterize the folkloric process; thus, jokes come in many versions, folk songs in many variations and Easter eggs with different designs. Folk life is another general term that is sometimes used interchangeably with folklore, popular culture and folk tradition, although each has its own history and bias.

The main purposes of folklore are to instruct, support, entertain and express communal and individual artistic taste and creativity. Modern scholarship has shown that folklore is an important aspect of all cultures because it helps people to comprehend and cope with their social and natural environment. The myths of Canada's Indian and Inuit peoples exemplify how large bodies of folklore in many parts of the world depend on nature (eg, the seasons and the cycle of life itself) to provide a meaningful framework for their folkloric traditions.

Folklore continues to be important in industrialized societies, where the growth of literacy has spawned various forms of "paper folklore" ranging from chain letters to photocopied office jokes. These and other forms of the new urban folklore provide safety valves by helping to dissipate hostilities (eg, ethnic-joke cycles) and by offering the individual and the group a sense of identity.

The urge to see and experience something out of the ordinary partly accounts for the periodic revival of interest in ethnic folklore and folk traditions, as illustrated by the popularity of Toronto's "Caravan," Winnipeg's "Folklorama," Edmonton's "Heritage Festival" and similar events. New interest in folklore focuses on sensory, nonlingual phenomena: the taste and smell of unusual foods, the moving colour and visual excitement of the ethnic FOLK DANCE, the detail of FOLK ART and handiwork, and the unique acoustic appeal of folk song and FOLK MUSIC. These manifestations of folklore thrive in modern settings, as shown by the popular annual Winnipeg Folk Festival. Sophisticated marketing techniques produce a highly compressed showcase of talent, ranging from contemporary folksingers to demonstrations of traditional weaving.

The trained folklorist sees a continuity from the winged deities of classical mythology to N America's "Superman." Folklore is able to bridge old and new by selecting and reinterpreting elements from the past in order to meet present needs.

Canadian Folklore Geography and a diverse linguistic and ethnocultural composition prohibit a concise description of Canadian folklore. Most books structure folklore in chronological fashion, with 4 main bodies of lore reflecting the traditions of Canada's main population groups: aboriginal (native Indian and Inuit), French Canadian, Anglo-Canadian (English, Irish, Scottish, Welsh) and other ethnic groups. Various factors favoured the preservation and development of folklore throughout the country: the prevalence of a rural population (at least until after WWII), a high percentage of illiteracy among certain groups in earlier times, and the use of folklore to foster local and national self-consciousness. French Canada, for instance, enjoyed a "golden age" of oral literature lasting into the 20th century. This was largely a result of French colonial policy, which did not allow the establishment of a press in New France, and later of the policies of English authorities, who consistently used English to introduce that language and Protestantism. The lack of publication in French and the scarcity of French schools helped to maintain a culture rooted in folklore. Early French Canadian writers incorporated many traditional customs and legends into their works and fostered the recognition and admiration of the folk heritage. French Canada's rich contact with the native population and Anglo-Canada's predilection for life by and on the sea helped to differentiate further the bodies of lore from one another. Since the 19th century the intermittent waves of immigrants and refugees from all parts of the world have greatly expanded the bounds of Canadian folklore by introducing new elements.

Canadian folklore has always been influenced by the US as well as other countries, and vice versa (eg, the impact of the Canadian wilderness and the Mountie hero on the imagination of Americans). Elsewhere abroad, the exodus of native sons and daughters to Canada, and their early experiences as immigrants in this country, have stimulated the production of entire cycles of songs and stories about immigrating to Canada, cycles which in turn enter into the folklore of the original countries.

Travel notes and reports of 17th-century explorers, traders and missionaries are the earliest records of Canadian folklore. The first conscious efforts at recording and publishing folklore appear in the 19th century in French Canada. The search for a national identity and the corresponding reaction against foreign influences in Canadian life and letters provoked, after WWII, a renewed interest in the national past and popular tradition. Folklore recordings and publications in folklore, partly in its genuine form, partly reshaped, began to appear in increasing numbers. The initiation of 2 especially important serial publications, Les Archives de folklore (published by Laval U since 1946) and the Mercury Series (published by the Canadian Centre for Folk Culture Studies at the Canadian Museum of Civilization in Ottawa since 1972), enriched scholarly research. Centennial celebrations in 1967 stimulated further interest in folklore and emphasized the attractiveness of the nation's folklore heritage. As the country became more urbanized, transitional forms emerged. Television and other mass-communication media have played an important role in this process, although their impact on Canadian folklore has not yet been fully researched or fully evaluated.

All categories and types of folklore appear in Canada, but their distribution varies from culture to culture. Efforts to identify this lore properly and to assess and characterize the nature of distribution are frustrated by the lack of suitable, comparative data. The particularly rich and multiform development of folklore among Canada's native peoples is largely explained by the delayed impact of European influence. This situation has long attracted the attention of scholars and enthusiasts whose collections and studies of native lore tended to focus on spoken narrative and ritual activities. The SUN DANCE and ceremonies associated with the medicine man (SHAMAN) and native healing practices (eg, the SHAKING TENT ritual) are among the best documented. The myths of Indian and Inuit populations are unique and significant aspects of Canada's folklore. These often tell about the theft of light and fire, and feature a culture hero who secures various things for his people. Such creation and hero myths include the RAVEN and THUNDERBIRD cycles of the West Coast and the NANABOZO stories of the Algonquian, which form 2 of the most extensive bodies of native Indian myth. Sacred legends, incorporating elements from tribal history, and to a lesser extent fables and wonder tales, are important parts of both Inuit and Indian folklore (*see* NATIVE PEOPLE, RELIGION).

Sung and spoken narrative is the major focus in French Canadian folklore, which includes, in addition to that of Québec, the folklore of Acadian communities in the Maritimes and of French communities in northern Ontario and parts of western Canada. The impact of Roman Catholicism is especially pronounced in many religious legends about the saints of the Middle Ages, miraculous healings and rescues, the creation and the flood. This body of folktale also features international tales of magic, many of which have been traced to pre-Christian sources. Their plots illustrate the features of typical wonder tales: repetition by threes, an emphasis on trials and quests, the triumph of the youngest son, magic objects and supernatural helpers, marvellous transformations and happy endings. In addition to an active inventory of jokes, anecdotes and circular formula tales, the traditional narrative folklore also includes many local legends reflecting lifestyles associated with such traditional occupations as farming, hunting, fishing and lumbering. Common subjects include hidden treasures, will-o'-the-wisps, flying canoes, werewolves, sorcerers and encounters with the devil. Prominent personages in the French Canadian narrative tradition are the popular hero-figure Ti-Jean (Little John), a fabulous hunter named Dalbec, and Jean CADIEUX, a voyageur whose tragic death is the subject of the earliest, distinctly French Canadian folk song (*see* ORAL LITERATURE IN FRENCH).

Anglo-Canadian folklore has not attracted attention equal to that given aboriginal and French Canadian folklore. This has resulted in comparatively few study materials, although much folkloric data can be culled from local histories and related sources (*see* ORAL LITERATURE). Many varieties of folk songs have been well documented, especially those that pertain to children, lumbermen and seamen, including an important category of shipwreck songs from the East Coast and the Great Lakes. Few examples of international tales of magic have been found among Anglo-Canadians, although jokes and anecdotes are widespread and include popular tall tales and ethnic jokes, of which the "Newfie" jokes are especially common. There are some collections of superstitions and supernatural tales, mainly from Nova Scotia. An active dept of folklore at Memorial U of Newfoundland in St John's provides the best documentation of Anglo-Canadian folklore. Especially important are MUMMING, riddles and other forms of folklore that are traced, recorded and studied in Newfoundland, although poorly documented elsewhere in Canada. Square-dance calls, children's autograph verses and legends about the SASQUATCH, OGOPOGO and related monsters of western Canada are also collected. The material folk culture of Anglo-Canadians attracted much interest as a consequence of the 1967 Centennial celebrations. A profusion of attractive coffee-table picture books and albums appeared, devoted to the documentation of Canadian houses, BARNS, LOG HOUSES, fences, churches, LIGHTHOUSES, outhouses, as well as FURNITURE, pottery, QUILTS and hooked RUGS. The reports of the activities of English poltergeists on Canadian soil show the continued influence of "Old Country" folklore. The large number of popular urban tales, in the form of migratory belief legends transmitted by teenagers and bearing such motifs as "Baby-sitter mistakes child for turkey," "Girlfriend's legs cut off" and "The grandfather's liver," reveals the strong impact on Anglo-Canadian folklore of new folkloric patterns from the US.

Canada's folklore composite in the second half of the 20th century has its roots in over 70 different traditions from around the world (*see* MULTICULTURALISM). Preliminary studies show, for example, the existence of a considerable body of folk beliefs and practices associated with folk medicine of the Pennsylvania Germans of southern Ontario; a sizable and varied body of lore among Ukrainians on the Prairies; and Old World narrative patterns among Icelanders in Manitoba and Yiddish-speaking Jews of Montréal. In addition to these groups, folklore studies relating to other ethnic communities in Canada have also appeared among Canadian Poles, Norwegians, Koreans, Danes, Hungarians, Swedes, blacks, Italians, Greeks, Chinese, Doukhobors, Gypsies, Romanians and Finns. In the 1960s, ethnic FOLK FESTIVALS became an especially productive phenomenon from coast to coast and attracted attention to Canada's rich heritage of folk traditions.

Folklore Studies Undergraduate and graduate degree programs in folklore are offered in French (since 1944) at Laval in Québec City and in English (since 1962) at Memorial in St John's, Nfld. Instrumental in organizing and heading these programs in early years were Luc Lacourcière at Laval and Herbert Halpert at Memorial. Both Laval's Archives de folklore and Memorial's MUNFLA (Memorial U of Newfoundland Folklore and Language Archive) have amassed archival materials relating to the folklore of their respective provinces. Other universities offering courses in Canadian folklore include Moncton, Québec at Trois-Rivières, York, Laurentian, Winnipeg, Manitoba, Saskatchewan, Calgary and Alberta. The dept of folklore at Laurentian U in Sudbury, founded by Germain Lemieux, has an extensive collection of Franco-Ontario folklore materials, and the Centre for the Documentation of Traditional Culture at Trois-Rivières, founded in 1970 by Robert-Lionel Séguin and Maurice Carrier, is important for its photographic and documentary archival materials relating to Québec material culture.

The country's leading folklore-research centre is the Canadian Centre for Folk Culture Studies, a unit of the Canadian Museum of Civilization in Ottawa. The centre is important for its holdings relating to French Canada, West Coast and Huron Indians and the country's minority ethnic groups. The Manitoba Museum of Man and Nature in Winnipeg has a program exploring the ethnic character of the non-indigenous people of Manitoba, and its collections reflect the ethnic identities of these people.

The Folk Life program of the Provincial Museum of Alberta was created in 1975 and is responsible for the acquisition, documentation, research and interpretation of material on the cultural life of Alberta's non-indigenous people; its artifact collection contains more than 3000 pieces. In 1964 the Canadian Folk Arts Council was established under government sponsorship and, with its network of affiliated councils, serves as the rallying point for the nation's numerous amateur and semiamateur folk performing groups. The council maintains its head offices in Toronto and Montréal and publishes a quarterly magazine, *Troubadour.* Other national organizations are the Canadian Folk Music Society (est 1957) and the Folklore Studies Assn of Canada (est 1975).

The major pioneering figure in Canadian folklore research in the 20th century is Charles Marius BARBEAU, many of whose publications appeared under the auspices of the Canadian Museum. However, no distinctly Canadian approach has been developed for the study of folklore, and almost all major folklorists in Canada have received much of their formal academic training abroad. By 1980 the country's 3 major folklore study centres had unofficially assumed separate but occasionally overlapping responsibilities for French Canadian folklore (Laval), Anglo-Canadian folklore (Memorial) and minority-language ethnic groups (Ottawa). The most important bibliography in Canadian folklore is the joint compilation of Edith FOWKE and Carole Henderson Carpenter, *A Bibliography of Canadian Folklore in English* (1981). General works include Carpenter's monograph, *Many Voices: A Study of Folklore Activities in Canada and Their Role in Canadian Culture* (1979); K.S. Goldstein's *Canadian Folklore Perspectives* (1978); the only autobiography written by a prominent folklorist, Helen Creighton's *A Life in Folklore* (1975); Magnus Einarsson's multicultural photo-study, *Everyman's Heritage: An Album of Canadian Folk Life* (National Museums, 1978); and Edith Fowke's pioneering anthology, *Folklore of Canada* (1976). In 1972 the journal *Ethnomusicology* (vol 16, no 2), edited by Israel J. Katz, devoted a special issue to Canada. Regional collections include *Folklore of Nova Scotia* by Mary L. Fraser, *Folklore from Nova Scotia* by Arthur Huff Fauset, *Folklore of Lunenburg County, Nova Scotia* by Helen Creighton, *Christmas Mumming in Newfoundland* edited by H. Halpert and G.M. Story, and *Folklore of Waterloo County, Ontario* by W.J. Wintemberg. Among the varied publications on French Canadian folklore, the series *Les Archives de folklore* is internationally significant, as are the many works of C. Marius Barbeau.

Books by Leonard Bloomfield on the Cree, by Franz BOAS on Northwest Coast Indians and by Barbeau on the Huron and West Coast Indians hold special interest in folklore studies of Canada's native peoples. Other researchers include Marie-Françoise Guédon, Diamond JENNESS, Gertrude P. Kurath and Paul Radin. The special issue of *Canadian Ethnic Studies* 7 (1975, ed Robert B. Klymasz) on *Ethnic Folklore in Canada* is particularly valuable for folklore of ethnic groups. The Canadian Museum of Civilization's Canadian Centre for Folk Culture Studies in Ottawa has also released a number of relevant reports in its Mercury Series of publications. In addition to *Les Archives de folklore* and *Troubadour*, 4 other folklore periodicals have been active since the 1970s: *Bulletin of the Folklore Studies Association of Canada* (est 1976), *Canadian Folk Music Journal* (est 1973), *Canadian Folklore Canadien* (est 1979) and *Culture and Tradition* (Memorial and Laval, est 1976).

The field of children's lore in Canada has attracted the attention of such researchers as Barbara Cass-Beggs, Edith Fowke and Kay Stone. Notable publications include a compilation by Peter B. Michalyshyn, *Tic-Tac-Togetherness: A Collection of Intercultural Games for Children* (1979). Study kits and exhibits prepared by several museums across the country alert developers of educational curricula of the richness of Canada's folk heritage. *Oracle*, a bulletin published by the Canadian Museum of Civilization, is also useful for teachers.

Nonprint materials relating to Canadian folklore include several works produced by or available through the National Film Board. Folk arts and crafts are well represented by 3 films, *Maud Lewis, In Praise of Hands* and *Inventors of Thingumajigs*. Three other films, *Pen-Hi Grad, Wedding Day* and *Pleasure Faire*, provide an insight into folk festivals, celebrations and rituals. Folk religion is well documented in the NFB's film *The Hutterites* (*see* HUTTERITES), and in another film about the DOUKHOBORS and their *Living Book*. *The Sunny Munchy Crunchy Natural Food Shop* shows, in humorous fashion, the impact of traditional recipes and ingredients on modern eating habits. *The Songs of Chris Cobb* documents folk singing in a Newfoundland outport, and *Hinchinbrook Diary* and *Bekevar Jubilee* depict the general folklore complex of a particular community. *Canadians Can Dance* reveals the array of current Canadian folk-dance styles and traditions.

Guyasdomo D'Sonogua (1912), watercolour by Emily Carr (*courtesy Provincial Archives of British Columbia*).

Of the many sound recordings produced over the years, the following are of special importance: *Canadian Folk Songs* (ed C. Marius Barbeau and released as vol 8 in the Columbia World Library of Folk and Primitive Music); over 20 titles on the Folkways label; and *Canadian Folk Songs: A Centennial Collection*, 9 records featuring innovative performers (RCA Victor, 1967).

ROBERT B. KLYMASZ

Fonyo, Stephen Charles, "Steve," handicapped runner (b at Montréal 29 June 1965). Despite losing most of his left leg to bone cancer at age 12, Fonyo ran across Canada in a "Journey for Lives" to raise money for cancer research. His remarkable 7924 km run started in St John's 31 Mar 1984, when he dipped his artificial leg into the Atlantic Ocean, and ended 29 May 1985, with a similar dip into the Pacific Ocean in Victoria. Fonyo was inspired by fellow British Columbian Terry FOX, who had attracted world attention with his attempt at a similar run in 1980. Fonyo received less publicity and support at first, but he emerged from Fox's shadow by passing beyond the symbolic point outside Thunder Bay, Ont, where Fox had aborted his run. Thousands lined his route and packed auditoriums to cheer him on and give increasingly larger donations to the fund, which eventually reached approximately $13 million. In 1986, after a period of recuperation, he embarked on another fund-raising run for cancer research, running from the northern to the southern tip of Great Britain. Fonyo completed this run in May 1987, and announced that he planned no further cancer-research marathons.

BARBARA SCHRODT

Food Additives Consumers normally consider that the term "food additive" refers to almost all substances, primarily chemical in nature, added to foods during production, manufacture, packaging or storage. However, as defined under the Canadian Food and Drug Regulations, a "food additive" means any substance, including any source of radiation, the use of which results or may reasonably be expected to result in it or its by-products becoming a part of or affecting the characteristics of food. Based on this definition, the term does not encompass materials such as salt, sugar and starch used as ingredients of food or commonly sold as food products. Certain other substances are excluded from the definition because they fall into categories covered separately under the Food and Drug Regulations and are thus subject to other controls. These ingredients include vitamins, mineral nutrients, amino acids, spices, seasonings and flavouring preparations, as well as agricultural chemicals, food-packaging materials and veterinary drugs.

Food additives are controlled by means of a positive listing system of permitted substances. If an additive is not on this list, it may not be used in a food offered for sale in Canada. The permitted list names the additive and lists the foods in which it may be used and the levels of use. The list encompasses some 380 substances classified into 14 tables based on the function of the additives. Food additives perform a variety of functions in food manufacture. For each function a number of different additives are permitted, to allow manufacturers the choice necessitated by variations in food properties, processing variations and market availability of the additive.

The function of additives and their exact mode of action is complex; however, for the functions noted, the additives do what is implied in the table title. For example, certain food products (eg, salt, dried-powder mixes) tend to absorb moisture from the atmosphere, which causes them to clump or cake. Anticaking agents prevent this from occurring and allow the food product to remain free running. Similarly, firming agents maintain the texture of a number of processed foods, such as fruits and vegetables, which would otherwise go soft as a result of heat treatment during processing.

Dough conditioners modify the strength of flour, improve the handling properties of dough and reduce mixing time, resulting in better texture and volume in bakery products. Colouring agents are added to foods to give them an appetizing and attractive appearance. Emulsifying, gelling, stabilizing and thickening agents modify texture and impart a desired consistency to foods. Such agents may also be used to help keep suspended food particles from separating and settling to the bottom (eg, the chocolate in chocolate milk) and to modify the consistency of products (eg, frozen desserts).

Because food technology is forever changing and new foods are constantly under development, there is a continual demand for new food additives. In Canada, for a new substance to be added to the listing of permitted additives, a submission of information is required, the format of which is outlined under the Food and Drug Regulations. This submission must include a description of the food additive, its method of manufacture, chemical and physical properties, composition and specifications. It must also include data establishing that the additive will have the intended effect and detailed reports of tests made to establish the safety of the additive under the conditions of use recommended.

Additives may be removed from the positive list of substances based upon evidence of possible hazard to the consumer. Examples of substances which are no longer permitted in Canada are nitrogen trichloride (bleaching agent in flour), cobaltous chloride (foam-stabilizing agent in beer), benzyl violet (colour in foods) and saccharin (sweetener in dietetic foods). Food additives have been and continue to be a controversial subject. Although it would be possible to produce and manufacture some foods without using these substances, many of the products currently available would not be possible without them, particularly convenience "ready-to-serve" products and foodstuffs requiring preservation. S.W. GUNNER

Food and Beverage Industries Food and beverage processing or manufacturing is one of Canada's major secondary industries and a vital component of the nation's overall AGRIBUSINESS system. In 1985 the industry had 3554 plants in production and the value of shipments was $38.14 billion. It spent nearly $24.7 billion on materials and supplies.

For statistical purposes, the total agribusiness system can be broken down into 5 sectors: agriculture (and fisheries); food and beverage processing; wholesale trade; retail trade; and institutional feeding (restaurants, etc). Statistics Canada figures indicate that, in 1986, agribusiness employed 1.5 million people or 11.5% of Canada's labour force. Agriculture is the largest employer, with 518 000 people. It is interesting to note that, despite significant improvements in agricultural production, this figure has remained almost unchanged since 1971. In contrast, employment in the restaurant business expanded by an astounding 122% during the same period, from about 200 000 in 1971 to 444 900 in 1986. The third-largest sector, retail, has a work force of 230 500, followed by manufacturing with 220 200 and wholesale with 61 800. In some provinces, employment exceeds the 13.4% national figure: in Sask 26% of the labour force is engaged in agribusiness, in PEI 25%, in Nfld 19%, in Man 17%, in NB 15.8%, in NS 14.6% and in Alta 13.9%. Only Qué (12.5%), Ont (12.2%) and BC (11.6%) fall below the national average.

The food and beverage industries consist of 17 sectors: MEAT-PROCESSING INDUSTRY, with 535 plants in operation in 1985; poultry-processing industry, 96; fish products industry, 390; DAIRY INDUSTRY, 394; CONFECTIONERY INDUSTRY, 121; SUGAR INDUSTRY, 9; FRUIT AND VEGETABLE INDUSTRY, 222; BAKING INDUSTRY, 1473; biscuit industry, 31; miscellaneous food industries, 356; VEGETABLE OIL INDUSTRY, 11; feed industries, 554; flour and breakfast cereal industry, 58; SOFT-DRINK INDUSTRY, 187; DISTILLING INDUSTRY, 30; BREWING INDUSTRY, 41; WINE INDUSTRY, 46. This industrial complex is one of the world's most modern and efficient food and beverage production systems. Statistics Canada data show that, in 1983, Canadians spent only 20.1% of personal disposable income on food and nonalcoholic beverages consumed at or away from home; in 1981, 21.2%; in 1977, 21.3%. The proportions of personal income for food and beverage purchases at stores for home consumption suggest a similar trend: from 14.5% in 1977 to 14% in 1983. Food purchases in restaurants have averaged about 4% of disposable income between 1971 and 1983. The cost of eating was lower in the US (16.1%), France (18.9%) and Switzerland (19.9%). Other developed countries spend considerably more, eg, West Germany, 23.7%, Japan, 24.8%, Italy, 29.1%, and Greece, 35.6%. It has been estimated that consumers in most Soviet Bloc countries spend more than 35% of income on food and beverages.

In contrast, Canadian food and beverage industries have had some of the lowest levels of profitability of all Canadian industries. There has been a steady decline in recent years; however, in 1986, after-tax profit per dollar of sales was 4.6%, a noticeable increase from the decreases of 2.25% in 1980 and 2.63% in 1978. Despite low profits, the food and beverage industries continue to invest heavily in building new plants, expanding and modernizing existing facilities, and purchasing newer, more efficient process and packaging systems.

Paradoxically, food- and beverage-processing companies are high-risk operations in environmental terms because of the wastes they produce. Unlike industrial wastes polluted with toxic chemicals, effluents from food operations are a problem because of their high nutritional value. If such wastes are released untreated to surface waters, a rapid and unacceptable growth of ALGAE and bacteria may occur. In the case of algae, such development depletes the oxygen supply, destroying fish populations. As a result, Environment Canada strictly enforces a set of effluent guidelines for every type of food- and beverage-processing operation; several provinces have even more demanding food-industry waste guidelines. The food and beverage industries are among the most highly regulated industries in Canada, affected by regulations administered by several federal and provincial departments (*see* FOOD LEGISLATION).

Technology The industry employs the most modern processing and packaging techniques. For example, thermal processing of foods and beverages in cans, glass and other forms of rigid packaging permits products to be stored at room temperature for several years without deterioration in product flavour or nutritional quality. Other methods of food preservation used in Canada include freezing, freeze-drying, drying, pasteurization, pickling and fermentation. Canadian companies are often leaders in N America in introducing new processing and packaging methods. A recent example is the use of the retortable pouch (the so-called soft tin can) for the production of shelf-stable products. Aseptic packaging of milk and fruit juices in laminated (paper and plastic) containers, a technique developed in Europe, first appeared in Canada in 1965 and was well established by the late 1980s. One other sophisticated processing technique, food irradiation, is now being used in N America, and Canadian researchers at ATOMIC ENERGY OF CANADA LTD have been prime movers in developing this completely safe approach to food preservation. In 1987 there were over 145 irradiation installations in the world, more than 66% developed and built by AECL. Most of the systems are used to produce sterile medical and drug supplies and packaging materials, but there are 10 which are employed full time and some 30 others part time for food preservation. In 1983 the Health Protection Branch initiated a proposal that irradiation be reclassified as a food-processing method, rather than as an additive. A decision is expected in 1988.

Associations Most sectors of the food and beverage industries are represented by a national association, often supported by provincial counterparts. A major function of these associations is to gain industry consensus on issues affecting their sector and to consult with governments on these problems. They also act as information clearing houses. ROBERT F. BARRATT

Food Banks In Canada, the term "food bank" is often used to describe any cache of food designated for charitable purposes. In its most specific sense, however, the term food bank is used to describe any large-scale food recovery program that redistributes food, free of charge, to the community, usually through existing social service agencies or churches.

Initially developed in the US, the food bank concept was first successfully developed on a large scale in Canada by the Edmonton Gleaners Association. The initial impetus for the development of food banks was the clear evidence of unmet needs in the community, which exist largely because of limitations or failings in social service systems. This provided the primary motivation for churches and agencies to undertake the provision of direct, emergency food services to private homes. Another major function of food banks is the supplementing of institutional feeding or kitchen programs with "salvageable," or "surplus," food collected from manufacturers, grocers, retailers and wholesalers. Public canned-food drives and food purchased through donated funds account for the rest.

Funding for food banks varies greatly from city to city. Some major food banks have accepted government support; however, food banks often decline government funding, preferring to operate on publicly donated funds rather than becoming an established part of a government structure. Others receive support from their local "United Way" fund-raising organizations (eg, Edmonton, Montréal, Ottawa). Food banks, by and large, proclaim themselves to be voluntary, "short-term emergency" responses to the problem of hunger, and call upon governments and other established agencies to develop co-ordinated strategies to deal with the problem in the longer term. Some food banks have played a key role in highlighting major problems and openly advocating improvements. Conferences have been held in Edmonton (1985) and Toronto (1986) with a view to establishing a national association, and some initial development has already occurred.

It is estimated that there are approximately 30 food banks, and hundreds of associated feeding programs, in Canada. BRIAN BECHTEL

Food Legislation Legislation designed to prevent the sale of unsafe or unwholesome food represents one of the oldest forms of governmental or societal intervention in the AGRICULTURE AND FOOD system. One of the earliest references to food adulteration is found in the English Assize of Bread Act, which dates back to about the year 1200 during the reign of King John. This statute began as an economic measure relating to the quantity of bread that bakers were obliged to offer for sale. During the 13th century it was expanded to include ale, fish, meat and various other food commodities. Over the years the statute evolved to include quality of food because it made little sense to purchase a certain quantity of food only to find that it had been watered down or was so unsafe or unwholesome as to be unusable. In 1860 the English Parliament enacted a landmark broad food law, not designed to control specific items but rather aimed at preventing adulteration of all food and drink. This law was amended in 1872 and again in 1875.

In Canada in the latter half of the 19th century, developments were influenced by English initiatives. Although certain food laws were in force before Confederation (1867), the first federal legislation dealing with adulteration of food was enacted in 1874. It is interesting to note that the US did not pass similar legislation until 1906, although before that time various commodity-oriented statutes were in existence which contained elements relating to adulteration and food safety. The 1874 law received its impetus from the large quantities of grossly adulterated liquor being consumed. Parliament was besieged with requests to do something about the situation. In response, early legislators took the position that liquor *per se* should not be banned, only adulterated or unsafe liquor. Hence, on 1 Jan 1875 an Act to Prevent the

Adulteration of Food, Drink and Drugs came into effect. This statute included a penalty of a $100 fine and a month in jail, with or without hard labour, for any manufacturer of liquor adulterating his product with substances such as salt, copper sulphate, opium, tobacco, Indian hemp or salts of lead and zinc. The second offence carried a $400 fine and 3 months in jail. The 1875 Act has been amended and altered many times over the years, and in 1920 it was superseded by the Food and Drugs Act. The most recent revision came into effect in 1954 and is currently in force.

The Food and Drugs Act is considered to be a consumer statute and is intended to protect consumers from health hazards and fraud in the sale and use of food, drugs, cosmetics and medical devices. The Act finds its constitutional authority in that section of the CONSTITUTION ACT, 1982, dealing with criminal law. Its enforcement is one of the responsibilities of the federal minister of national health and welfare. Unlike legislation enforced by the federal ministers of agriculture and fisheries, it is not and never was intended to assist producers, manufacturers or retailers in preparing or marketing foods. Sections 4, 5 and 7 of the Food and Drugs Act are very important because they cover, in a very general way, all major aspects of safety and fraud associated with the sale and consumption of food. Section 4 deals with product safety, integrity and freedom from adulteration. Section 5 deals primarily with aspects of economic fraud and section 7 with production, manufacturing and storage of food under unsanitary conditions.

Section 25 provides authority for the writing and passage of regulations for carrying out the purposes and provisions of the Act. It is through the use of these regulations that specific control is exercised. For example, Division 16 of the regulations lists, in table form, some 380 permitted FOOD ADDITIVES. If a substance does not appear in one of the 15 tables of Division 16, it may not be used as a food additive. Regulations prescribing maximum permissible levels for the occurrence of PESTICIDES and other agricultural chemicals in foods are also tabled on a similar "positive listing" basis. When a substance is found to be toxic and required to be severely restricted or prohibited in the food supply, a "negative listing" principle may be used. This device has been used in section B.01.046 of the regulations to restrict severely or prohibit the presence of some 16 substances with demonstrated toxicity by declaring them to be adulterants. In July 1983 the Dept of National Health and Welfare proposed that food irradiation be regulated as a process rather than a food additive, in accordance with international recommendations endorsed by both the World Health Organization and the Food and Agriculture Organization. This proposal has resulted in considerable controversy and is not expected to be finalized until the autumn of 1988.

In addition to the "positive" and "negative" listing techniques, certain specific regulations have been established to prohibit the presence of pathogenic SALMONELLA bacteria in susceptible products, including chocolate, processed eggs and frog legs. Regulations have also been used as a means of providing a legal identity to groups of foods and of ensuring the nutritional adequacy of certain foods considered critical in the diets of certain individuals or groups of individuals.

The Food and Drugs Act and Regulations may be considered as the basic federal statute dealing with food safety and nutrition in Canada, but there are many other pieces of legislation that have an impact on the sale of foods at both the federal and provincial levels. For example, departments of agriculture and fisheries at both federal and provincial levels have legislation used for the control and marketing of specific commodities. These statutes often deal with product identity and quality in relation to grade standards. The Pest Control Products Act and Regulations are of particular interest, in that the federal minister of agriculture is responsible for registering pesticides for use in Canada, while the minister of national health and welfare acts as principal health adviser in evaluating the safety of pesticide residues and establishing maximum safe limits for these residues in food. Federal and provincial departments of the environment have, in recent years, established regulations respecting discharge into the environment of certain toxic substances which could ultimately contaminate the food chain. All provincial jurisdictions also have public-health Acts and regulations which provide the medical officer at the city, regional, county or municipal level with considerable authority in regulating food-manufacturing and food-service establishments. Regulation of food safety must continue to be a dynamic process reflecting both technological and societal change. In this way, Canadian consumers will continue to enjoy one of the safest food supplies in the world.

B.L. SMITH

Food Poisoning includes intoxication and infection resulting from consumption of foods contaminated by toxins (poisons) produced by specific micro-organisms, or the presence of infectious micro-organisms, heavy-metal contaminants (eg, copper) or natural toxins. Food poisonings are generally characterized by gastrointestinal disorders and occasionally result in death. In Canada, approximately 1000 outbreaks, involving 5000-6000 cases, are reported annually. This figure probably represents 1% of actual cases. Most cases go unreported or are attributed to "24-hour flu." Most outbreaks in Canada are associated with meats and poultry, the principal cause being severe mishandling of food, especially improper cooling and inadequate reheating.

Staphylococcal ("staph") food intoxication is most common. It is caused by a heat-stable toxin produced by some strains of *Staphylococcus aureus* bacteria. Symptoms, including cramps, nausea, vomiting and diarrhea, begin in 1-6 hours and last for 24 hours. Of growing concern is salmonellosis, *Salmonella* food infection, especially associated with poultry and egg products but also with many other foods, from spices to chocolate candy. Symptoms, including cramps, chills, vomiting, diarrhea and fever, begin in 8-24 hours and last 2-3 days or longer. Infected persons often become asymptomatic carriers of SALMONELLA. In the aged, infirm or infants, salmonellosis can result in death. A few outbreaks, involving many cases, of *Clostridium perfringens*, ie, perfringens poisoning or "institutional" food poisoning, occur annually. Symptoms are mild, including abdominal cramps and diarrhea. Food contaminated with *C. botulinum* may contain a neurotoxin that causes the rare but severe form of food poisoning, BOTULISM. Food poisonings associated with *Escherichia coli*, *Yersinia enterocolitica* and other bacteria are uncommon in Canada. Heavy metals account for less than 1% of outbreaks. During the 1970s, *Campylobacter jejuni* was identified as a major cause of human gastroenteritis. *Campylobacter* are frequently found in poultry meat, but thus far outbreaks of campylobacterosis from foods have only been associated with unpasteurized milk and untreated water supplies. Each year outbreaks of trichinosis, ie, infestation by the parasite *Trichinella spiralis*, occur from ingestion of undercooked meats, especially pork, and wild game such as bear meat.

MICHAEL E. STILES

Football For many years, the term football described the practice of kicking an object, usually a round ball, and directing it into a designated goal area. It was not until 1823, a traditional myth says, that William Webb Ellis, a student at the British public school of Rugby, picked up the ball and ran, contrary to the game's conventions. Others naturally took after him to bring him down. A code of rules evolved and the "Rugby game" was taken and played wherever the school's graduates were placed. Thus did RUGBY make its way to Canada, brought by the various immigrants, civil servants, clergy and military personnel who had a Rugby educational background.

By the 1870s a hybrid form of the Rugby game was being played in Montréal among the garrison personnel, citizens and McGill U. In 1874, McGill was invited to Cambridge, Mass, to play a game of "football" with Harvard. It was only upon arrival that the McGill team found that Harvard played a version of the kicking (soccer) game. To solve the dilemma, 2 games were played, each under the other's rules, and thus was the McGill version introduced into the US. Harvard took immediately to the new game and sent to England for the current rugby rules. Within a year of their receipt, Harvard had persuaded other eastern US teams (known as the Ivy League) to adopt the game. Although rugby featured spontaneity of play, the Americans soon made the style of play more organized and subject to planning and design. For example, where rugby called for the ball to be put into play by a scrum, with possession going to whoever won the ball from the scrum, the Americans introduced a "snap back" system and a certain number of attempts to gain a set amount of yardage or give up possession. The continual evolution and development of the American game served to influence the Canadian, more so as British influence waned in Canada.

The present sport of Canadian football closely resembles the American, with some significant differences: the Canadian playing field is much larger (9 m longer, 6 m wider and with end zones 13 m deeper); the Canadian game allows 12 players per side, compared to 11 in the US, and allows much more movement of players before the ball is put into play; only 3 downs, compared to 4 in the US, are allowed for the offensive team to make 10 yards and retain control of the ball; the team receiving a punt must run it back – there is no option to call the ball dead by a "fair catch"; any member of the offensive backfield may be in motion prior to the snap of the ball. Other minor differences exist, eg, there is a 1-yard restraining area between offensive and defensive lines. Partisans of the Canadian version claim it is more exciting and unpredictable than American football.

Football is played at most Canadian universities and its acceptance at high schools has given it advantages over other team sports, such as baseball. There is some regional variation in the rules among Canadian leagues, but the scoring is the same: 6 points for a touchdown (for carrying the ball across the opponent's goal line or catching the ball in the opponent's end zone), 3 for a field goal (placement kick between the goalposts), 2 for a safety touch (tackling a ballcarrier who by his own momentum has entered his own end zone), 1 for a conversion of the touchdown (some leagues allow for 2) and a single point when the ball is kicked through the end zone and out of play or when the ball is downed in the end zone after a punt (formerly called a "rouge") or a missed field goal. These points for kicking are unique to Canadian football.

In Canadian football's formative years, various regional sports governing bodies were responsible for declaring a champion as well as for setting the rules and regulations among member teams. The Québec Rugby Football Union (QRFU) and Canadian Rugby Union (CRU) were formed in

1882; the Ontario Rugby Football Union (ORFU) in 1883; the Canadian Intercollegiate Rugby Football Union (CIRFU) in 1898; and the Interprovincial Rugby Football Union (IRFU) in 1907. The Western Canada Rugby Football Union (WCRFU), encompassing unions from Man, Sask and Alta, was formed in 1911. Each union declared a champion, except for the Canadian, which was to provide a "Dominion Championship" arrangement. Gradually, the prestige associated with the CRU's Dominion title led to more uniformity in rules. The GREY CUP game, first played in 1909, symbolized henceforth the Canadian championship. The first game was played between U of Toronto, representing the CIRFU, and the Toronto Parkdale Canoe Club (ORFU); U of T won 26-6.

Western teams competed for the trophy for the first time in 1921. The game between the EDMONTON ESKIMOS and the TORONTO ARGONAUTS was won by Toronto 23-0. Nevertheless, there was no question that the best football was being played by the university teams during the early years of the Grey Cup. Under Harry Griffith, who was classified as an "honorary coach" (in those days a paid professional coach was not acceptable in a sporting milieu governed by the rules and conventions of amateur sport), and with players such as Smirle "Big Train" Lawson and Hughie Gall, consecutive titles (1909, 1910 and 1911) were won by the U of T team. McGill, coached by Frank Shaughnessy, whose hiring as a "professional coach," the first for such a purpose, created much controversy, was perhaps the best team from 1912 to 1919, but they refused to take time from their studies to pursue the Grey Cup. During 1922, 1923 and 1924, Queen's won 3 consecutive Grey Cups led by Harry "Red" Batstone and Frank "Pep" Leadley. An indication of the strength of the Queen's team coached by Bill Hughes was evident in the score of the 1923 game. Queen's defeated the WCRFU Regina Roughriders (*see* SASKATCHEWAN ROUGHRIDERS) by a score of 54-0!

From 1925 on, the Intercollegiate Union gave way to the stronger city-based teams and unions. Football began to attract large numbers of spectators and teams sought ways to make the game more pleasing to the public. Clubs set out to attract proficient players, and amateurism lost its control. In 1931, when the forward pass was approved for all Canadian leagues (it had long been part of the US game) the Montréal Amateur Athletic Assn (*see* MONTREAL ALOUETTES), known as the "Winged Wheelers," imported Warren Stevens from Syracuse U to play quarterback. The team's success in winning the Grey Cup sparked a more intense search for American talent, especially by western teams, to augment the players on whom they could draw with their smaller population base. The WINNIPEG BLUE BOMBERS' general manager, Joe Ryan, was able to sign 9 Americans for the 1935 season for $7500. The move paid off handsomely as Winnipeg defeated the Hamilton Tigers (*see* HAMILTON TIGER-CATS)18-12, the first Grey Cup victory for a western team. It also heightened the conflict between the CRU and the leagues competing for the Grey Cup. The CRU was interested in maintaining at least a façade of amateurism, while the leagues wanted to field the best teams possible. The friction would continue until 1956 when the CRU was controlled by the leagues representing the 9 strongest teams in Canada. An ORFU team from Sarnia had gained similar success because of sponsorship by an oil firm. The "Imperials," as they were known, were able to augment local talent with players such as "Bummer" Stirling, Norm Perry and the giant Orm Beach. They were the 1934 and 1936 Grey Cup champions.

Canadian Football Chronology

Date	*Event*
1865	The first account of a game of rugby football played in Canada, between English officers and civilians, mainly from McGill U
1867	In Ottawa on Sept 16 a game was played between the Rough Riders and the Senators
1868	The Montreal Football Club was established
1874	Rules of a hybrid game of English rugby devised by McGill were first used in the US in a game at Boston between McGill and Harvard. On May 14, Harvard won 3-0 using Harvard rules. The next day the teams tied 0-0 while playing Canadian rules. Toronto Argonauts were formed
1879	U of Michigan played a game against U of T
1882	The Quebec Rugby Football Union was formed – the first league in Canada. On Oct 21, the Canadian Rugby Football Union was founded
1883	On Jan 4, the Ontario Rugby Football Union was formed. Toronto Argos def Ottawa 9-7 in the first championship game
1884	The first championship game played between the QRFU and the ORFU resulted in a 30-0 victory for Montreal
1886	The ORFU seceded from the CRFU, which then ceased to function
1891	Canadian Rugby Union formed
1892	First CRU championship game played at Toronto; Osgoode Hall def Montreal
1895	Length of game changed to two 40-minute halves. Edmonton, Ft Saskatchewan and Strathcona played the first series of scheduled games on the Prairies
1897	On Nov 24, the Canadian Intercollegiate Rugby Football Union was organized in Kingston, Ont
1898	First intercollegiate game– McGill vs U of Toronto
1902	Games to consist of four 15-minute quarters
1904	Value of try (touchdown) increased from 4 to 5 points
1905	The ORFU reduced teams to 12 men per side; adopted the snapback system of putting the ball into play; required offensive team to make 10 yards on 3 downs
1906	Specifications laid down for size of football: 11" long, 23" in circumference and 13 3/4 ounces in weight. Field goals devalued from 5 to 4 points
1907	The interprovincial Rugby Football Union formed, with Hamilton Tigers, Toronto Argonauts, Ottawa Rough Riders and Montreal
1908	Calgary Tigers formed. Field goals devalued from 4 to 3 points
1909	Lord Earl Grey, the gov gen of Canada, donated a trophy for the football championship of Canada. The first game was played in Toronto on Dec 4; U of T def Parkdale 26-6 before 3807 fans
1910	Regina Roughriders formed
1911	Western Canada Rugby Football Union
1912	Edmonton Eskimos, first Western team to play in a Grey Cup game, lost to Toronto Argonauts 23-0
1925	McGill coach Frank Shaughnessy introduced the "huddle" to Canadian football
1927	CRU adopts limited use of forward pass
1931	CRU approved the forward pass for all leagues.
1935	First time a Western team won the Grey Cup. Winnipeg def Hamilton Tigers
1936	Teams were restricted to a maximum of 5 imports. The Western Interprovincial Football Union (WIFU) formed. College teams stopped competing for the Grey Cup
1945	Calgary Bronks change name to Stampeders
1946	Montreal Alouettes organized. Regina Roughriders change to Saskatchewan Roughriders
1948	Hamilton Tigers rejoin the IRFU ("Big Four"). Calgary Stampeders introduce pageantry to Grey Cup game
1949	Edmonton Eskimos rejoin WIFU
1950	Hamilton Tigers and Hamilton Wildcats amalgamate to form Hamilton Tiger-Cats
1952	First Grey Cup game carried live on TV
1953	Billy Vessels won first Schenley Award
1956	Value of a TD was increased from 5 to 6 points
1960	IRFU ("Big Four") changed name to Eastern Football Conference
1961	WIFU changed name to Western Football Conference. Partial interlocking schedule introduced between conferences
1962	Grey Cup Game stopped by fog, final 9 min and 29 sec played the next day
1965	Canadian Football Players Assn organized
1966	Unlimited blocking on rushing plays is legalized
1970	Artificial turf installed in Vancouver's Empire Stadium
1972	Canadian Football Hall of Fame opens in Hamilton
1974	Eastern Conference adopts 16-game schedule
1975	First Grey Cup final held on the Prairies, in Calgary. 2-point convert introduced
1981	Complete interlocking schedule introduced
1982	Montreal Concordes replace troubled Alouettes. Edmonton extends record to 5 consecutive Grey Cup victories
1987	Montreal Alouettes folded

In an effort to stem the influx of American "imports," the CRU sought to impose a residence rule. It soon became obvious, however, that the member clubs and leagues were not as adamant. The Grey Cup was gaining prestige and acceptance with the public. With the end of WWII and the resumption of the various leagues, the 1946 CRU meeting stipulated that each team could play with 5 American imports. Some teams, notably the Toronto Argonauts, preferred to play with an all-Canadian lineup. The Argos did so until 1950 and in the process won 3 consecutive

Grey Cup championships under coach Teddy Morris (1945, 1946 and 1947). The 1948 Grey Cup game, won by the CALGARY STAMPEDERS 12-7 over the OTTAWA ROUGH RIDERS, was a catalyst in several ways. To be sure, the excitement generated by the westerners turned the final into a national celebration. But just as importantly for the development of football, the 1948 game marked an escalation in the quality of player attracted to play in Canada. Previously, many clubs got much of their import talent from among those with American college football experience. The American Football Conference's disbanding meant that many players would be available to the Canadian game.

It soon became obvious that the smaller centres of the ORFU (Toronto Balmy Beach, Kitchener, Sarnia and Brantford) could not compete. In fact, they seemed to be a hindrance to the Western Interprovincial Football Union (1936) and the eastern teams, known as the "Big Four." The 1954 game between Edmonton and Kitchener (actually a "farm team" for the Eskimos) represented the last time the ORFU was scheduled into the Grey Cup play-downs. By 1956, the Canadian Football Council was formed, becoming the CANADIAN FOOTBALL LEAGUE (CFL) in 1958. The professional league was now in charge of its own operations and proceeded to modify the game according to its perceived needs. The CRU remained in existence but was effectively controlled by the CFL. In 1966, the CRU turned the trusteeship of the Grey Cup over to the CFL and changed its name to the Canadian Amateur Football Assn (CAFA). Since 1966, the CAFA has concerned itself with the game as played outside the CFL and educational institutions. It organizes national championships as well as recreational "touch" leagues, an expanding area for those who wish to enjoy the throwing, kicking, running and catching aspects of the game.

The CFL, in the meantime, increased rosters (35 in 1986), allowed unlimited blocking, introduced a "taxi squad" – officially known as the "reserve list," and made up of players who can practise in order to play in emergency situations – and allowed 15 imports. In addition, prior to the 1987 season, the Montreal Alouettes suspended operations indefinitely. To compensate, the CFL shifted the Winnipeg Blue Bombers to the eastern conference. A controversial regulation, known as "the designated import rule," that permitted 2 imports designated as quarterbacks to play at any time effectively curtailed the development of Canadians at this position after its passage in 1970. This was subsequently changed, in Feb 1986, to allow each team 3 quarterbacks. Since most head coaches and general managers of the 9 CFL teams have been Americans, it is natural that graduates of the American colleges are sought for the critical quarterback position, rather than Canadians with potential who need time to develop. Indeed, since the CFL teams are controlled by Americans, it is not surprising that there is pressure to make Canadian football more akin to the American game because it is the style of play most familiar to the coaches and many players. Because of this some critics say that the football played in the CFL is becoming less and less an expression of Canadian culture. Although Canadians, such as Russ JACKSON, have excelled at the quarterback position, most of the key players on CFL teams are American. It could be said that Canadian football is a game played by Americans for a Canadian championship represented by an Englishman's cup. The play-off system continues to admit 6 of 9 teams to post-season play (though not necessarily the top 3 teams from each of the western and eastern conferences, eg, the 1986 season saw 4 western but only 2 eastern teams qualify for the play-offs), and every team has won the Grey Cup since the mid-1950s. During the 1970s a superb Edmonton team dominated Canadian football, winning an unprecedented 5 consecutive Grey Cups between 1978 and 1982.

Intercollegiate football has developed independently under its own governing body, the Canadian Interuniversity Athletic Union (CIAU). The last representative of the CIAU to challenge for the Grey Cup was the 1932 U of T team. Once the CIAU decided to bypass this challenge, regional unions became the focal point of the growing number of universities. In Nov 1959 the first Canadian college championship game was played at Toronto's Varsity Stadium. The Western Ontario Mustangs defeated the UBC Thunderbirds 33-7 to win the Sir Winston Churchill Trophy, an original sculpture entitled "Onslaught," by R. Tait MCKENZIE. Not until 1965, however, was the college championship played regularly. That year, Governor General Georges VANIER lent his name to a trophy, the VANIER CUP, to be contested annually. For the first 2 years, it was an invitational event, but in 1967 it was declared the national championship of the CIAU. Semifinals are usually played in the Maritimes and western Canada to determine the 2 finalists. The 4 regions eligible are the Western Intercollegiate Football League (WIFL), the Ontario Universities Athletic Assn (OUAA), the Ontario-Québec Intercollegiate Football Conference (OQIFC) and the Atlantic Universities Athletic Assn (AUAA).

The Canadian Football Hall of Fame and Museum (founded 1962) was housed in its present building in Hamilton in Nov 1972. It traces the history of Canadian football over the past century and celebrates leading players and builders of the sport. The museum contains a theatre, video monitors, giftshop and exhibits – notably a series of steel busts of Hall of Famers. The Grey Cup and Schenley Trophy are on permanent display. Members of the Hall of Fame are chosen by a committee composed of reporters and sportscasters (current and retired) along with former players. *See also* BRITISH COLUMBIA LIONS. FRANK COSENTINO

Reading: Frank Cosentino, *Canadian Football: The Grey Cup Years* (1969); G. Currie, *One Hundred Years of Canadian Football* (1968); J. Sullivan, *The Grey Cup Story* (1974).

Foothills, a region of rolling, undulating or hilly terrain lying between an area of plains and a MOUNTAIN RANGE. Generally, foothills are regarded as a transitional relief form combining some of the elements of a lower-elevation, flat landscape with those of mountainous topography, but without extensive or extreme portions of either. Physiographically, the foothills are regarded as part of the mountains. The French word *piedmont* ["at the foot of the mountain"] is sometimes used to describe an area within which foothills lie. In northern Italy the region of Piemonte is a hilly area lying between the wide, flat valley of the River Po and the Italian Alps. In Canada, the foothills of the ROCKY MOUNTAINS occupy an area between the Rockies and the Alberta plains and associated lowlands of northeastern BC. Covering about 60 000 km^2, this region extends from the Canada-US border northwestward, a distance of some 1100 km, to the Peace R region of BC, and averages about 50 km in width. Summit elevations in the foothills average approximately 1800 m; the plains area to the E and the mountains to the W average about 1200 m and 2500 m, respectively. Most of the foothills of the Rockies consist of folded and faulted Mesozoic and Cretaceous sedimentary rocks that were deformed by mountain-building forces (the Columbian and Laramide Orogenies) that occurred during Cretaceous (144-66.4 million years ago) and early Tertiary(66.4 to 36.6 million years ago) times. The foothills were extensively glaciated during the Quaternary (1.6 million years ago to about

Foothills and Rocky Mountains west of High River, Alta (*photo by Richard Harrington*).

10 000 years ago). In the last major ice advance, the Wisconsin, the mountain (Cordilleran) glaciers and the Continental Ice Sheet merged and covered some areas of the foothills while other areas, especially in the Porcupine Hills in southern Alberta, remained ice free. *See also* GLACIATION. IAN CAMPBELL

Footwear Industry, sector of Canada's MANUFACTURING industries that produces footwear to meet various needs, including specialized industrial footwear, functional footwear, cold-weather footwear, slippers, and dress, casual and athletic shoes for men, women and children.

History The footwear industry is one of the oldest in Canada. The name of the first person in Canada to cobble a pair of shoes has not been recorded, but François Byssot of Pointe-Lévy, Qué, built the first tannery in 1668. Byssot was assisted by Jean TALON, who advanced the sum of 3268 livres from the royal coffers. The Compagnie des Indes occidentales contributed another 1500 livres. The first Canadian census (1666) revealed that 20 shoemakers served a population of 3215 inhabitants. The industry was required not only to look after the needs of the colony but also to equip a regiment of soldiers. Like cobblers all over the world, Canadian shoemakers used an awl, a curved knife, a needle and a wooden last. They set up shop in their own homes, employing 4 or 5 workers.

Toward the middle of the 19th century, the introduction of machinery revolutionized the production of footwear. The sewing machine was adapted for stitching footwear components. Other devices were developed for cutting, cementing, nailing and vulcanizing parts of the shoe. Eventually, what had been a cottage craft became a sophisticated, highly mechanized factory industry. The 1871 census reported 4191 footwear-manufacturing establishments in Canada. Most were small shops which also did shoe repairs. With the advent of mechanized shoemaking equipment, many of these small manufacturers were forced out of business by the high capital cost of machinery and plant construction.

The Modern Industry Consolidation has also marked the modern industry. In 1950 the 292 footwear factories in Canada produced 33.9 million pairs of shoes, valued at $111 million. The industry employed 20 785 workers. In 1985 there were 169 factories employing 14 164 persons and producing 43 million pairs of footwear valued at $870 million. The industry is concentrated in Montréal, Québec City, Toronto and the Kitchener-Cambridge, Ont, area. About 90% of the firms are Canadian owned. Successful Canadian shoe manufacturers include Bastien Brothers Inc, St-Émile, Qué, who produce winter boots for the N American market; Santana Inc, Sherbooke, producers of women's winter boots and casual footwear; Greb Industries, producers of Bauer skates, Hush Puppies and Kodiak work and hiking boots; Kaufman Footwear, Kitchener, producers of waterproof footwear, safety boots and Sorel winter footwear; Susan Shoe Industries Ltd, Hamilton, producers of Cougar casual footwear; and Tender Tootsies Ltd, Canada's most successful and largest maker of popularly priced women's footwear, using man-made materials. Bata Ltd, Don Mills, Ont, is the world headquarters of the Bata Shoe Organization, the largest shoe marketing and manufacturing enterprise in the world (operating 192 companies in 61 countries).

In 1968 shoe production reached a peak of 52.9 million pairs, falling to 43 million pairs in 1986, a drop caused chiefly by the influx of footwear imported from low-wage countries in which average earnings are one-tenth those of a Canadian shoe factory worker. Until the early 1960s, imports were not significant in the Canadian market, but they soared from 6.8 million pairs in 1972 to 75 million pairs in 1986, the latter figure representing 63% of the apparent Canadian market for footwear that year. Imports from Asia took over most of the low-price ranges; those from Europe captured much of the market for fashion footwear. The deterioration in the Canadian share of the domestic market caused shoe manufacturers to seek the protection of the federal government against the flood of imports. The industry maintains that the current market share, less than 50%, threatens the survival not only of the Canadian footwear industry but also of related industries (eg, the leather industry) and many suppliers. In response to the shoe manufacturers' briefs, the government instituted protective measures against imports in 1977 by imposing quotas on all footwear coming into Canada. Quotas were to be in effect until Dec 1988. Under their protection, the industry continued to introduce automation and electronic technology, and undertake restructuring programs to help it meet foreign competition. The Canadian industry is also developing export markets and increasing specialization in winter footwear, for which it has already gained a world reputation for excellence.

Although wages have more than doubled in the past decade, they have remained below those for other manufacturing industries. Of every dollar received by manufacturers from footwear sales, half pays for materials and a quarter for labour. The remaining 25% covers administration costs and profits. *See also* APPRENTICESHIP; Thomas J. BATA; LEATHERWORKING.

FRANCES KELLEY

Forage Crops are plants grown primarily for livestock feed; they are consumed either as hay, silage or green feed, or are grazed by animals. The 2 major forage plant groups are LEGUMES and GRASSES.

Legumes All legumes have seed pods and are able to fix nitrogen in their root nodules. Of the 2 commercial ALFALFA species, *Medicago sativa* has been Canada's most valuable forage, producing high yields for hay or silage; *M. falcata* has provided cultivars that succeed under low-moisture PRAIRIE conditions. Red CLOVER (*Trifolium pratense*), a biennial, succeeds better under imperfect drainage than alfalfa does; it is widely grown in Canada, where sufficient rainfall occurs. Alsike clover (*T. hybridum*) has characteristics similar to those of red clover and is grown in mixtures with grasses. White clover (*T. repens*), used in mixtures with grasses for pasture and hay, grows along the ground and has numerous runners. Bird's-foot trefoil (*Lotus corniculatus*) has yellow flowers; its persistent habit of growth makes it valuable for long-term pasture. Sweet clover (genus *Melilotus*) is a tall biennial, most widely grown in western Canada for hay or silage. FABA BEANS, field PEAS and various VETCHES have been used as green feed or hay.

Grasses Grasses have played an important role because of their diversity and ability to grow under a wide range of soil and climate conditions. Timothy (*Phleum pratense*), the most widely grown grass outside dry parts of the Prairie region, grows best on heavy soils with high moisture-retaining capacity. Orchard grass (*Dactylis glomerata*) has a deep, fibrous root system, adapted to open, drier soil types, and responds to fertilizers and irrigation. Bromegrass (*Bromus inermis*), well adapted to open dry soils, has been grown in mixtures with alfalfa in drier areas of eastern Canada and on the Prairies. Reed canary grass (*Phalaris arundinacea*), native to N America, grows in clumps that spread rapidly by stout, creeping rootstalks and does best under high-moisture conditions. Kentucky bluegrass (*Poa pratensis*) is widely distributed, especially in cool, humid areas, where it provides natural pasture in uncultivated areas. Crested wheatgrass (genus *Agropyron*) was introduced from western Siberia. A bunchgrass with a dense, deep root system, it produces leaves from mid-Apr to late June and is adapted to prairie conditions. Intermediate wheatgrass (*A. intermedium*), with a deep root system, is adapted to dry prairie conditions, is easy to establish and provides palatable pasture. Russian wild ryegrass (*Elymus junceus*) is drought and cold tolerant, has a high protein content and is palatable in autumn.

Cultivation In the late 1980s there were 4.4 million ha of improved pasture and 5.1 million ha of forage crops in Canada. Cultivation practices vary with climatic zone, but in general forage crops are established in spring, on fully ploughed land, and are seeded using grain drills, with oats or barley as nurse crops. Recent developments on dairy farms have resulted in direct seeding of alfalfa and grass mixtures; a hay harvest is taken in the first year. In areas where corn silage provides high-energy (ie, high-carbohydrate) feed, alfalfa and alfalfa-grass mixtures provide the high-protein feed, and many farms grow both. Timothy-alfalfa is used on well-drained, heavy soils that have a high moisture-retaining capacity. In imperfect drainage situations, red clover and alsike are mixed with timothy for hay or silage. In the northern clay belt of Ontario and Québec, red clover, alsike and timothy are used to provide hay or silage in support of a cow-calf system. In eastern Québec and the Maritimes, timothy represents over 80% of the forage produced; it is established with oats as a nurse crop. In western Canada, crested wheatgrass is widely used and alfalfa-bromegrass dominates the irrigated regions of Alberta and Saskatchewan for hay and silage. Brome-alfalfa is widely used for hay in Manitoba and on drier soils in Ontario and Québec. In BC, alfalfa, red clover, orchard grass and perennial ryegrass are top forage species.

Variations in soil type, fertilization practices, intensity of farming systems and climatic zones make it difficult to estimate yields. For example, under favourable conditions, timothy may yield 9 t of dry matter per hectare; if moisture is restricted and summer temperatures are high, yields would be only one-third as great. Thus, in southern Ontario yields of timothy approach 12 700 kg/ha; in northern Ontario, 6500 kg/ha. In the prairies, crested wheatgrass and bromegrass would yield 3700 kg/ha under conditions prevailing in central Saskatchewan. The contribution of forage crops to the Gross Domestic Product would parallel closely the value of dairy products, beef and sheep, as over 85% of the feed used on the farm comes from forages, hay, silage and grazing hectarages.

W.R. CHILDERS

Forcier, Marc-André, director (b at Montréal 19 July 1947). His first feature film, a small-scale production called *Le Retour de l'Immaculée Conception* (1971), revealed his original approach to cinema. He developed his style by creating a world composed of eccentric characters who apparently reject the values of the society in which they live but who are nonetheless deeply rooted in that society. Forcier explored that world in *Bar salon* (1973); the film that established his reputation, *L'Eau chaude, l'eau frette* (1976); the extraordinary *Au clair de la lune* (1982); and *Kalamazoo* (1987).

PIERRE VÉRONNEAU

Ford, Robert Arthur Douglas, diplomat, poet (b at Ottawa 8 Jan 1915). Ford joined the Dept of External Affairs in 1940 and in 1946 was second secretary in the Canadian embassy in Moscow, where he spent much of his career in various positions, including ambassador (1964-80). Other postings have included Yugoslavia and the United Arab Republic. He was special adviser to the Canadian government on East-West relations 1980-85. Ford is the author of 4 collections of verse, including translations – *A Window on the North* (Gov Gen's Award, 1956), *The Solitary City* (1969) and *Holes in Space* (1979). All are distinguished by a clinical despair and a precision of language and form. Ford might be said to be, like Lester PEARSON or Charles RITCHIE, in the humanistic tradition of Canadian diplomacy that is now, alas, obsolete. *Needle in the Eye: Poems New and Old* (1983), *Russian Poetry: A Personal Anthology* (1985) and *Doors, Words and Silence* (1985) are his most recent publications.

DOUGLAS FETHERLING

Ford Motor Company of Canada, Limited, with head offices in Oakville, Ont, is a major manufacturer and distributor of automobiles in Canada. First incorporated in Ontario in 1904, the Canadian company was reincorporated in 1911. In the 1960s, following implementation of the CANADA-US AUTOMOTIVE PRODUCTS AGREEMENT, Ford's manufacturing and assembly operations were modified to permit longer production runs of fewer products. The company manufactures automotive safety glass and, in partnership with Essex Manufacturing (formed in 1978), engines and casts. Automobile and truck assembly operations are located in Oakville. The company also imports vehicles from its US parent. In 1986, it had sales or operating revenue of $14.3 billion (ranking 3rd in Canada), assets of $3.1 billion (ranking 34th) and 27 500 employees. Ford Motor Company of Detroit, Mich, holds 94% of the shares.

DEBORAH C. SAWYER

Foreign Aid The modern concept of foreign aid – assistance from rich, industrialized countries to poorer, developing countries – has its roots in post-WWII RECONSTRUCTION. The success of the Marshall Plan in channelling resources from the US to war-torn Europe convinced Western leaders that a similar transfer of resources to newly independent countries in Asia and Africa would likewise lead to rapid development. Canada's aid program began in this period of prevailing optimism. In 1950 Canada joined the COLOMBO PLAN to support the recently independent COMMONWEALTH countries of Asia. During the next 2 decades Canada's program grew steadily, expanding to include the Commonwealth Caribbean (1958), Commonwealth Africa (1960) and francophone Africa (1961). In 1970 the program was extended to Latin America.

Governmental Assistance The foundations for Canada's program for the 1970s were laid in the mid-1960s, when the government undertook to raise levels of aid drastically. In 1968, 3 significant events occurred; first, the CANADIAN INTERNATIONAL

DEVELOPMENT AGENCY was created to administer Canada's aid efforts; second, Pierre Trudeau, a man with an abiding interest in international development, became prime minister; and third, former PM Lester B. Pearson headed an international commission to examine the results of 20 years' development assistance and to propose policies for improvement. The commission's report, *Partners in Development,* called for each donor country to provide foreign aid equal to 0.70% of its Gross Domestic Product. Canada accepted this target in 1970 and has repeatedly reaffirmed its commitment, but by 1986 had achieved only 0.46%. Still, in 1986 Canada distributed more than $2 billion of aid through various channels and covering a vast array of activities. Direct country-to-country (bilateral) aid accounts for almost half of all Canadian aid, supporting more than 90 countries. Most bilateral aid is concentrated on about 30 countries, with India, Pakistan, Bangladesh [E Pakistan] and Sri Lanka [Ceylon] – 4 of Canada's original Colombo Plan recipients – still receiving about one-third. Bilateral aid is normally provided not in cash but in Canadian goods and services, including wheat and flour, railway locomotives and parts, equipment for hydroelectric generation and transmission, fertilizer, seeds and farm implements, and personnel to serve as advisers or instructors.

Multilateral aid, generally in cash, flows from Canada to many international organizations, which undertake their own activities. Most notable are the World Bank and other multilateral development banks, and the specialized agencies of the UNITED NATIONS. These multilateral institutions account for more than one-third of Canada's foreign aid. The balance supports the International Development Research Centre – a public corporation founded in 1970 to fund research on the needs of developing countries – and Canadian nongovernmental organizations in developing countries.

There are few precedents for one state or people accepting some continuing responsibility for the improvement of other states and peoples, without demanding repayment in wealth or power. The very newness of the phenomenon makes it complex and controversial. There is still no completely shared view in donor countries about what aid should do, or how best to do it. Some people still adhere to the ideological or strategic view that the West should aid developing countries in order to maintain friendly relations and dissuade them from aligning themselves with the competing Soviet bloc. Other people view underdevelopment in Third World countries as a product of exploitation by advanced countries, and see generous aid as a kind of reparation. The prevailing motivation for Canadian foreign aid, as revealed in public-opinion surveys and in the statements of political leaders, is a humanitarian concern for the many millions of people who are obviously far poorer than most Canadians. Disparities in living standards are so great and so far beyond the control of poor people that many Canadians now view the obligation to help as one of basic justice rather than of charity. Humanitarianism, however, is never the only motive, particularly for government-to-government aid. When the Canadian government allocates official development assistance, it is also influenced somewhat by commercial interests (developing sales and future markets for Canadian products) and by political interests (the desire to build or maintain good relations with the recipient government).

Even when the primary motive is humanitarianism, there are tensions between the need for short-term assistance to relieve hardship and longer-term help to enable poor people eventually to become more self-sufficient. The latter approach has become more widely accepted, especially with the emphasis since the mid-1970s on "basic human needs" development. But it is proving frustratingly difficult to achieve quick or impressive results with this kind of aid. Many experts are convinced that existing power structures in many developing countries are themselves a major obstacle to improvements for poor people, and that official aid often reinforces these structures, rather than making them more responsive. Observers who are skeptical of government intervention in economic life also raise doubts about the potential effectiveness of official aid, which by necessity is channelled through recipient governments. In most developing countries, aid is a small part of total investment and concentrated where the private sector can rarely take a leading role. Nevertheless, foreign aid is a small but important component in the development process. Its success depends on the domestic efforts of developing countries and the whole range of other links between developed and developing countries.

BERNARD WOOD AND ROGER EHRHARDT

Nongovernmental Assistance In part because of dissatisfaction with the results of government-to-government aid, industrialized countries have over the past decade allocated a substantial and rising share of their foreign aid to nongovernmental organizations (NGOs). Voluntary assistance to developing countries, through churches and other charitable organizations, predated direct government involvement, but it is only over the past 2 decades that governments have begun to fund the work of NGOs. By the mid-1980s, Canadian federal and provincial government funding of NGOs' work amounted to between $200 and $250 million (or 10-12% of total foreign aid), with at least an equivalent amount raised from private sources. At the same time, there has been a tremendous expansion in the number of NGOs – now about 250, including not only the traditional voluntary aid agencies but also colleges and universities, co-operatives, professional associations, and unions.

Early NGO activities stressed emergency relief and welfare activities, including the shipment of food and clothing and the sponsorship of children and families. While such activities remain important (and highly visible), emphasis is now more often placed on longer-term development work, geared to promoting local self-reliance, and often implemented via indigenous Third World NGOs. While most NGO projects remain small and community based, some agencies are beginning to take on larger infrastructures and service-delivery programs. Most NGOs believe that educating Canadians about international development – and their relevance to Canadians – is an integral part of their work. Indeed, a large number of "learner centres" and other agencies are geared solely to educational work.

Supporters of NGOs claim that they possess several advantages over official aid channels — speed, flexibility, low cost, innovativeness and, above all, an ability to reach the poorest effectively. While examples of innovative and successful NGO projects abound, the case for their greater effectiveness remains in large measure unproven. As the scale and complexity of NGO programs increase, so do the expectations of NGO performance and the demands upon them to prove their worth. At the same time, many fear that, as NGOs change from idealistic do-gooders to professional development workers, they may come to ignore their ultimate source of strength: the strengthening of links between Canadians and the citizens of developing countries. *See also* CANADA-THIRD WORLD RELATIONS. BRENT COPLEY

Reading: Canada, *Strategy for International Development Cooperation 1975-1980* (1975); K. Spicer, *A Samaritan State?* (1966).

Foreign Investment in Canada is both *direct* (made to control enterprises) and *portfolio* (made only for the interest or dividends paid or the possible capital gain to be achieved). The amount of both types is very large, with the consequence that a considerable fraction of the Canadian ECONOMY is controlled by foreigners and the annual interest and dividend payments made to them is very large ($18.7 billion in 1986). Total investment income payments, which includes interest and dividend payments as well as miscellaneous income payments, amounted to $23.9 billion in 1986. The degree of foreign ownership and control is especially high – in the neighbourhood of 50% – in 2 major sectors of the economy: manufacturing and resource development (ie, the mining, forest, gas and oil industries). This large foreign presence in the economy, quite unparalleled elsewhere in the world, has deep historic roots. Beginning in the mid-19th century, when Canada was still a British colony, British investors readily supplied capital, chiefly of the portfolio type, for Canadian development. It was this capital that financed much of the construction of Canada's railways and cities in the half century prior to WWI.

Meanwhile, the US was building a huge national economy which would far surpass that of any European country. Its railway network joined all its regions into one immense market, making gigantic industrial plants feasible and profitable. For some of these giant firms it became desirable to set up distant branch establishments, closer to natural resources or where local markets might be more economically served; the railway, the telegraph and later the telephone made it possible to exercise effective control over operations far from headquarters. As natural resources became depleted in the US, American industrial firms sought supplies elsewhere. The first Canadian resource upon which Americans drew heavily was timber, especially that of Québec and Ontario (*see* TIMBER TRADE HISTORY). American lumbermen came to Canada and built large mills to process lumber for sale in the US. These were not branches of US firms, however. The men who established and owned them eventually became Canadians. The first significant branch plants were newsprint mills, built by US papermakers. They would have preferred simply to buy logs to feed their mills in the US, but provincial governments, anxious to secure jobs and economic development, refused to permit the export of logs from forestlands that they controlled, insisting that American companies build local mills. By 1929, Canada accounted for about 65% of world exports of newsprint; 90% of it went to the US.

The discovery of valuable minerals (gold, nickel, zinc and other nonferrous metals) created a mining industry in which US and some British capital soon played a commanding role. Gold, found in river bars and surface deposits, was extracted first by individuals using cheap and simple methods and then by large-scale, capital-intensive methods. Established American mining firms set up branches to carry on this type of activity, furnishing skill, capital and experience. From the beginning, base-metal deposits were exploited chiefly by companies established and controlled by US mining corporations. After WWI, US firms in other industries began to operate branches in Canada on a large scale. Manufacturing companies set up branch plants to serve the Canadian market, thereby avoiding high freight costs and import duties. Also, US-owned branch plants benefited from the fact that products made in Canada were admitted at preferential tariff rates to other British Empire countries. New variety- and grocery-store chains built stores in many cities. By 1930, US direct investment in Canada was more than 5 times that of the United Kingdom.

The 1929 stock market crash and the GREAT DEPRESSION brought practically all forms of foreign investment to a standstill that lasted throughout WWII. In the early 1950s, US investment resumed substantially. American industrial corporations undertook enormous mining projects and, following the discovery of the Leduc oil pool (1947), US firms spent enormous sums on oil and gas exploration, and on pipelines and refineries. The increasing population and its growing affluence made the Canadian market highly attractive to US firms. Manufacturers of consumer products set up branches, as did retail and financial firms and suppliers of equipment and services required by business firms.

Canada was a relatively secure and familiar market for US companies, in which they were able to operate very effectively. Conceivably, goods and services produced in the branch plants of US firms could have been provided by Canadian-owned enterprises, but US firms had the enormous advantage of much greater capital and experience and strongly established, valuable connections. The markets of many US-owned plants in Canadian resource industries were firmly established, as parent plants in the US bought all their products. Many US-manufactured products were already well known in Canada, thanks to the wide circulation here of US publications, in which those products were advertised, and the extensive travel and visitation in the US by Canadians. Branch plants tended to buy equipment and materials from their parent organizations or the US firms that regularly supplied their parents. Canadian-owned firms inevitably had great difficulty in competition against American branch plants that had these advantages.

Presumably the role of US-controlled firms in the economy would not have grown so rapidly if authorities had restricted it or had provided special assistance to Canadian-owned firms, but they were anxious to achieve as much economic development as possible and were unconcerned by the large increase in US participation in the economy. As a matter of principle, they treated US-owned and Canadian-owned firms with absolute impartiality. In a relatively small number of instances, foreign firms licensed Canadian firms to use TECHNOLOGY the former had developed so that goods and services using that technology were produced in Canadian-owned establishments. In addition to setting up branch plants in Canada, US firms bought established Canadian firms, incorporating them into their organizations. Many Canadian businesses were sold to US corporations for considerably more than they would have received from Canadian buyers. As a result of all these considerations, US direct investment – $3.4 billion in 1950 – was nearly 20 times that figure in 1980. Some of this increase was attributable to INFLATION, but a large portion of it reflected increased ownership of physical assets in Canada.

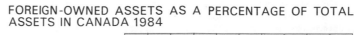

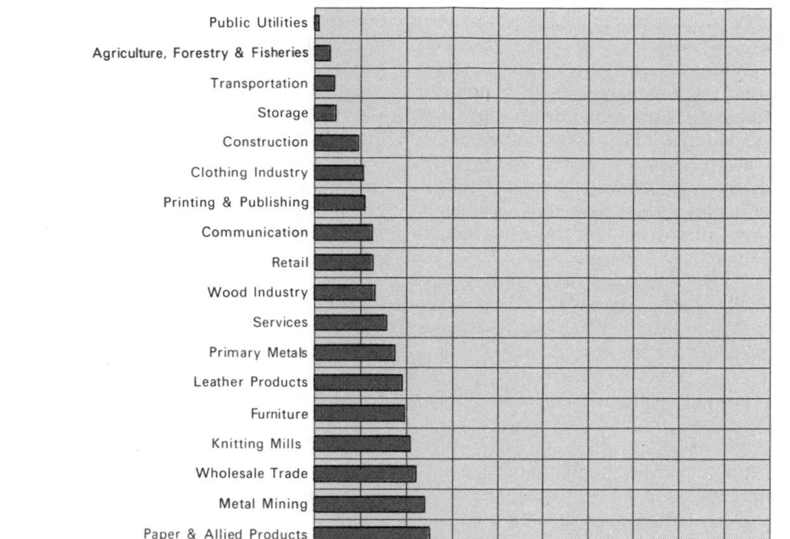

Source: Statistics Canada, Cat 61-210

Although US-owned firms initiated the production here of many novel products and services and provided welcome job opportunities, there have been – and still are – problems caused by their presence. Huge and increasing amounts of money have to be remitted to US owners in the form of dividends on their investment and contributions by branch plants toward head office costs of administration, research, product development and advertising. A large proportion of these payments must be made in US dollars; where payment in US dollars is not required by contract, the investors, receiving payment in Canadian dollars, wish to exchange them for US currency. The consequence is that a very large fraction of the US dollars that Canada earns by its exports must be used to make interest and dividend payments and branch plant remittances to US firms. The amount of our dollar earnings left after these payments are made has often been insufficient to pay for all our imports, obliging Canada to borrow abroad – and thereby increase the amount of interest that will have to be paid to foreigners in the future.

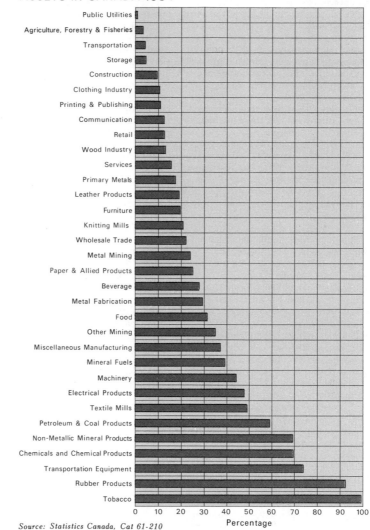

MULTINATIONAL CORPORATIONS carried on their Canadian operations to serve their own best interests, not those of Canada. INDUSTRIAL RESEARCH AND DEVELOPMENT, essential to industrial innovation and growth and providing highly desirable job opportunities, was generally done not in Canadian branch plants but in US facilities. When demand for the products of some international companies fell, they would reduce the scale of operations or close down the Canadian branch while maintaining operations in the parent plant. When an international firm uncovered a cheaper source of supplies or labour in another country, it might close down its Canadian operation. The presence of giant, foreign-owned companies made it difficult for the government to stabilize the economy. Possessing great financial power and having wide international interests, these firms could not be induced or pressured to alter the tempo of their Canadian operations to help keep the economy on an even keel. Being subject to American legislation that forbade US firms and their affiliates to trade with US enemies, plants here could not export their products to some countries with which Canada had normal trade relationships. Corporate strategy frequently had the same consequences; branch plants were generally designed to serve the domestic Canadian market and lacked the resources or mandate necessary to develop and to sell products in export markets.

Aside from economic concerns, many Canadians (*see* COMMITTEE FOR AN INDEPENDENT CANADA; COUNCIL OF CANADIANS) objected on nationalistic

Distribution of Control of Capital in Nonfinancial Industries 1980

(Source: Statistics Canada 67-202, May 1986)

	Total capital employed (Billions$)	*%controlled in Canada*	*%controlled in US*	*%controlled in other countries*
Manufacturing	69.3	49	40	11
Petroleum and natural gas	45.9	50	38	12
Mining and smelting	16.4	59	29	12
Railways	7.0	99	1	—
Other utilities	73.0	97	3	—
Total	264.9	73	21	6

grounds to the scale of FOREIGN OWNERSHIP and control over the economy (*see* ECONOMIC NATIONALISM). The federal government responded in the 1960s with new legislation forbidding foreigners to own radio and television stations (*see* CULTURAL POLICY); and with restrictions on foreigners' rights to set up banks, insurance companies and other financial concerns; to enlarge established firms; to participate in the exploration of oil, gas and mineral deposits or to acquire uranium mines. In 1973 the federal government established the FOREIGN INVESTMENT REVIEW AGENCY (FIRA) to screen investments by nonresidents, approving only those that would clearly be of benefit to Canada.

The federal government also created the CANADA DEVELOPMENT CORPORATION (1971) and PETRO-CANADA (1974), both of which reduced foreign control by buying out a number of large, foreign-owned concerns. The NDP government of Saskatchewan bought out foreign-owned potash firms. In 1980 the Canadian government introduced its NATIONAL ENERGY PROGRAM, under which it accorded special privileges and financial incentives to Canadian-owned and -controlled firms in the oil and gas industry, prompting the takeover by Canadians of a number of foreign-owned firms. By the early 1980s the proportion of manufacturing, mining, oil and gas industries under foreign control was significantly smaller than it had been a decade earlier.

These measures and actions to limit foreign ownership raised controversy. Businesses that profited from dealing with foreign-owned firms objected, and exponents of private enterprise decried the increasing role of the government in the economy. Provincial politicians, anxious for development that would broaden local economies and add to local employment, objected to federal restrictions that prevented such development. The US government protested against Canadian investment policies and threatened retaliatory action against Canadian firms operating in the US.

While FIRA approved about 90% of the foreign-investment proposals that it reviewed, and was not a significant barrier to foreign ownership, it was angrily criticized for its occasional rejections and sometimes lengthily delayed decisions. In response to the criticisms, the Liberal federal government began to loosen the restrictions. The Conservative administration of PM Brian Mulroney, elected Sept 1984, indicated that it planned to extend its reduction of barriers to foreign investment in Canada, and in 1984 it dismantled FIRA, replacing it with INVESTMENT CANADA, an agency that would welcome foreign investment rather than obstruct or delay it.

Just under 50% of the foreign investment in Canada today is American, most of it "direct," reflecting the fact that many American firms insisted on having control over Canadian operations in which they invested, since success depended on effective application of expertise that they had developed. US investment in Canada of the portfolio type is, however, not much less than its direct investment. In 1981, when Americans' direct investment in Canada amounted to $48.7 billion, their portfolio investments – in bonds of governments and private firms and shares of companies controlled by others – totalled $38.2 billion. By 1986 these amounts had increased to $68.3 billion (direct) and $60.3 billion (portfolio).

Other countries have substantially increased their investment in Canada in recent years, with the consequence that by 1986 the aggregate of non-American foreign investment in this country totalled $131 billion, slightly more than the total of US investment. However, while over half of US investment here was direct, only 19% ($25 billion) of non-American investment here was of that type; the rest was portfolio investment, made chiefly in the form of purchase of bonds issued by Canadian governments and private firms.

Foreign ownership of agricultural land and urban real estate is also important. British investors acquired large Canadian holdings in the 19th century and continued to buy and sell Canadian properties in the 20th. Europeans, particularly West Germans and Italians, acquired large amounts of agricultural land in the 1960s and 1970s, prompting provincial governments to pass legislation restricting the acquisition of land by nonresidents. Hong Kong investors acquired a considerable number of urban properties in the 1980s; however, the total value of foreign investment in Canadian real estate is still only a small fraction of their investment in Canadian stocks and bonds.

The flow of investment funds has not been entirely one-way. Canadians have set up branch plants in foreign countries and made portfolio-type investments in foreign stocks and bonds. In 1986 Canada paid out $18.7 billion in interest and dividends to foreigners but we received only $3.4 billion in interest and dividends on Canadian investments abroad. What's more, in no foreign country does Canadian investment play a dominant role. Our largest foreign investment, which is in the US, gives Canadians control over only a minute portion of the US economy, in contrast to the very large fraction of the Canadian that is controlled by American interests.

RUBEN C. BELLAN

Reading: K. Levitt, *Silent Surrender* (1970); W.H. Pope, *The Elephant and the Mouse* (1971); Statistics Canada, *Corporations and Labour Unions Returns Act: Part I* (1985).

Foreign Investment Review Agency (FIRA), federal agency formed by Parliament in 1973 as a result of concerns raised in the Gray Report about foreign domination of the Canadian economy (*see* FOREIGN OWNERSHIP, TASK FORCE ON). The agency began screening foreign acquisitions of Canadian businesses in Apr 1974 and the establishment of new foreign businesses in Oct 1975. The agency advises the government (through the minister of industry, trade and commerce) on what action should be taken, if any. In making its recommendations, FIRA took the following factors into consideration: 1) the effect of the investment on employment and economic activity in Canada; 2) the effect on Canadian productivity, technological development and product variety; 3) the degree of Canadian participation in management; 4) the effect on competition; and 5) the compatibility of the investment with national policies. From the point of view of ECONOMIC NATIONALISM, FIRA was criticized because it approved most of the applications it received.

However, the agency was strongly opposed by many businessmen, and in Dec 1984 Sinclair STEVENS, industrial expansion minister, revised its mandate to promote and facilitate investment in Canada by Canadians and foreigners; to undertake research and analysis; to provide policy advice; and to ensure that significant investment by foreigners created a net benefit to Canadians. There was also a move within the agency to implement special restrictions in cultural industries, eg, book publishing and film production. Appropriately, the name of the agency was changed to Investment Canada in 1985. *See also* FOREIGN INVESTMENT; FOREIGN OWNERSHIP AND THE STRUCTURE OF CANADIAN INVESTMENT, TASK FORCE ON.

Foreign Ownership, Task Force on (Gray Report), was established (1970) under Herb GRAY. Its purpose was to analyse the impact of the high degree of foreign control on the Canadian economy. It also examined policies that would enable Canadians to exercise greater control over their own economic development and to retain and increase Canadian ownership of business where feasible or desirable for economic, social, cultural or other reasons. In the 1960s, foreign control had reached nearly 60% of total Canadian manufacturing, and 90% of industries such as rubber and petroleum.

The task force concluded (1972) that, in a highly qualified way, FOREIGN INVESTMENT had had a moderately favourable effect overall but that problems did exist, eg, "truncated firms" which performed only a narrow range of activities in Canada and were dependent on foreign technology and management. It suggested that some problems could be handled through general economic policies, eg, tariffs, taxes and patents. It concluded that others would be better solved through administrative intervention on all new foreign investment, case by case, and it rejected a major policy shift, such as a "buy-back" strategy, towards increased Canadian ownership.

C.E.S. FRANKS

Foreign Ownership and the Structure of Canadian Investment, Task Force on In 1967 the Liberal government under PM Lester Pearson was prodded by Walter GORDON into appointing a TASK FORCE on foreign ownership. There were 8 economists on the task force and the chairman was Mel Watkins. The Watkins Report (1968) documented the costs and benefits to Canadians of the high level of foreign ownership of the Canadian ECONOMY. Comprehensive recommendations included the setting up of a development corporation to facilitate Canadian ownership and an agency to co-ordinate policies with respect to multinational enterprise. The task force shifted the debate on foreign ownership toward more interventionist policy leading, in due course, to the creation of the CANADA DEVELOPMENT CORPORATION and the FOREIGN INVESTMENT REVIEW AGENCY. *See also* FOREIGN INVESTMENT; FOREIGN INVESTMENT, TASK FORCE ON.

MEL WATKINS

Foreign Policy, White Paper on, a 6-volume review of foreign policy conducted 1968-70 by the Department of External Affairs with the involvement of many other departments and agencies, as well as invited academics, business people and others. The department had its initial overview rejected by Cabinet. A revised version, more in accord with the speeches and writings of PM Trudeau, was accepted. Besides a general paper, there were sector papers on Europe, Latin America, the US, international development and the Pacific. The Paper recommended that foreign policy be related to 6 national interests: economic growth, social justice, quality of life, sovereignty and independence, peace and security, and harmonious natural environment – with emphasis on the first 3. Canada's role in PEACEKEEPING was to be downplayed, there was to be closer contact with Europe and the Third World, FOREIGN AID was to be increased and the People's Republic of China was to be recognized diplomatically – all of which simply affirmed the redirection of foreign policy already initiated by the new Trudeau government. Canadian-American relations were not examined.

C.E.S. FRANKS

Foreign Relations, *see* EXTERNAL RELATIONS.

Foreign Writers on Canada in English Canada has inspired a substantial literary response from foreign as well as native-born and resident authors. Besides writers of travel narratives, which are considered elsewhere (*see* EXPLORATION AND TRAVEL LITERATURE IN ENGLISH), many poets, novelists and even a few dramatists from the 2 major anglophone nations have written about the country. Much of this material belongs to popular culture rather than art, but occasionally an individual author or work has risen to a significant aesthetic level.

The earliest English literary responses to Canada have to do with exploration, settlement and war. Martin Parker's *Englands Honour Revived* (1628) is a broadside ballad celebrating the temporary capture of Québec from the French. Robert Hayman's *Quodlibets, Lately Come over from New Britaniola, Old Newfoundland* (also 1628) is a collection of verse epigrams celebrating the British colony. The Anglo-French wars of the 18th century inspired a number of works, beginning with the closet drama *Liberty Asserted* (1704) by John Dennis. The fall of Québec in 1759 prompted several tributes, including J. Patrick's *Québec: A Poetical Essay in Imitation of the Miltonic Style* (1760) and George Cockings's *The Conquest of Canada; or, The Siege of Qúebec: An Historical Tragedy in Five Acts* (1773). The neoclassical conventions of bombast and structural formality also govern the first republican American literary response to Canada, Hugh Henry Brackenridge's verse drama *The Death of General Montgomery in the Storming of the City of Quebec* (1777).

In the last quarter of the 18th century, American writers were too busy celebrating their own nascent nationalism to pay much attention to the northern colonies, but a few British writers were discovering in Canada new inspiration for prospect poetry and travelogue fiction. Frances BROOKE's epistolary novel *The History of Emily Montague* (1769) is the most literate of these effusions, being a sincere attempt to evoke impressions of the climate, the French-speaking inhabitants and the Indians. George Cartwright's *Labrador: A Poetical Epistle* (1792) is a more fanciful view of the colonies, while J. Mackay's *Quebec Hill: or Canadian Scenery* (1797) and Cornwall Bayley's *Canada: A Descriptive Poem* (1806) are conventional nature poems.

Throughout the 19th century, Canada was a popular setting for the British novel of exploration and immigration. Such works intersperse description with romance and adventure, in the manner of Sir Walter Scott, or such entertainers as Frederick Marryat and Charles Lever. John GALT's *Bogle Corbet* (1831) is the earliest and most realistic of such works, taking a rather bleak view of the pioneer experience and criticizing British immigration policies, but Captain Marryat's *The Settlers in Canada* (1844) celebrates the values of British imperialism while exploiting scenes of hunting, Indian fighting and land clearing. Marryat's model is followed by R.M. Ballantyne in *Snowflakes and Sunbeams* (1856), *Ungava* (1858) and several other novels. The most prolific worker in this genre was William Henry Giles Kingston, whose many novels of immigration propaganda include *The Log House* (1864), *Snow-Shoes and Canoes* (1876) and *The Frontier Fort* (1879).

In the US, Canadian settings were occasionally incorporated into the popular frontier adventure fiction inspired by James Fenimore Cooper, and into other genres. But American writers were interested in themes and images distinct from those that preoccupied the British. Instead of celebrating imperialism, Americans denounced it, along with French Roman Catholicism, northern primitivism, and the general inferiority of the provinces to the republic. In historical romances, such as Harriet Vaughan Cheney's *The Rivals of Acadia* (1827), Catherine Williams's *The Neutral French; or The Acadians of Nova Scotia* (1841) and Mary Catherwood's *The Romance of Dollard* (1889) and her many other novels of New France, the French are often simultaneously praised for their opposition to British tyranny and condemned for their adherence to Roman Catholicism. American antipathy to the French Canadians' religion reached depths of Gothic scurrility in such trashy but popular works as George Bourne's *Lorette: The History of Louise, Daughter of a Canadian Nun* (1833), the anonymous *Awful Disclosures of Maria Monk* (1836) and Benjamin Barker's *Cecilia; or, The White Nun of the Wilderness* (1845).

The superiority of republicanism over colonialism, and the evils of Roman Catholicism, are recurrent themes throughout the 19th century in American works dealing with English as well as French Canada. Travelogue novels such as Jesse Walker's *Fort Niagara* and *Queenston* (both 1845) gloat over the ostensible backwardness of the provinces, while P. Hamilton Myers's more literate *Prisoner of the Border* (1857) condemns the reactionary loyalty of Canadians during the Upper Canada rebellion of 1837-38. R.T.S. Lowell's *The New Priest in Conception Bay* (1858) and Mary Savage's *Miramichi* (1865) criticize the social and religious primitivism of the maritime provinces. These and other American works propagate stereotypes of ethnic inferiority and political instability while celebrating the American way of life. In this morass of clichés and simplifications, only the work of one writer pretends to any degree of sophistication. William Dean Howells's earliest ventures into realist fiction, *Their Wedding Journey* (1872) and *A Chance Acquaintance* (1873) use the popular tourist regions of the St Lawrence as background for thoughtful explorations into the implications of modern life in N America.

By the beginning of the 20th century, both British and American literary responses to Canada were becoming dominated by the romance of northern adventure, a genre governed by the conventions of the "western," and given new impetus by the fiction of Jack London, as well as by a surge of immigrants and foreign travellers into the Northwest. British writer-adventurers of the time include Roger Pocock, author of *Tales of Western Life* (1888), and Ridgwell Cullum, whose many northern romances include *The Hound of the North* (1904), and *The Triumph of John Kars* (1917). The most prolific writer of this kind of fiction was Harold Bindloss, who wrote at least 30 Canadian novels, beginning with *Alton of Somasco* (1906). Most of this fiction celebrates the English adventurer who, by the strength of his arm and the moral superiority of his purpose, brings British values to the outposts of empire. The writers themselves had usually travelled and adventured in the colonies, but their personal experiences seldom show through the clichés of frontier fiction. Probably the most distinguished of these literary exiles is the Gothic novelist Algernon Blackwood, whose wanderings in Canada produced some striking adaptations of Indian legend and pioneer experience, collected in *The Wolves of God and Other Fey Stories* (1921) and other volumes. Another outstanding literary exploitation of the northern adventure tradition is *Sick Heart River* (1941), a haunting study of spiritual introspection by the eminent novelist of empire, and onetime governor general, John BUCHAN.

In the US, Jack London expounded his naive but humanistic version of Spencerian determinism in many short stories and novels of the Klondike, including *The Call of the Wild* (1903) and *White Fang* (1906). But most of London's imitators abandoned any pretense of intellectual sophistication in favour of the conventions of the sentimental romance. The dean of the northern romance was undoubtedly James Oliver Curwood, who made a fortune from such novels as *The Danger Trail* (1910), *The Country Beyond* (1922) and 30 or 40 others. Sinclair Lewis's *Mantrap* (1926), set in Manitoba, is a clever satire on this kind of fiction. Curwood also exploited the historical romance of New France in *The Plains of Abraham* (1928) and other titles, and his example has been followed in works too numerous to survey in detail but generally dominated by such book-club ephemera as Grace Stone's *The Cold Journey* (1934) and Muriel Elwood's *Heritage of the River* (1945). The eminent mid-western author Willa Cather managed a strikingly original adaptation of this genre in *Shadows on the Rock* (1931), which sees pre-Conquest New France as an elusive, Utopian ideal.

In recent decades, both British and American authors have occasionally turned to formats other than the historical romance and adventure fiction to express their impressions of Canada. In general, there is an inclination among some British writers to satirize imperial idealism and Canadian provincialism. Americans, on the other hand, show a tendency to idealize Canada as an alternative to the disappointments of their own country and to reveal the disillusionment that sometimes follows such idealism.

British novelist Margaret Bullard produced an intolerant but witty satire on Canadian urban life in *Wedlock's The Devil* (1951). Wyndham Lewis expressed himself equally disenchanted with Canadian cities, in *Self Condemned* (1954). The satire continues in playwright Simon Gray's early novel *Colmain* (1963), set in Nova Scotia. The American mid-western novelist Wallace Stegner has used Saskatchewan settings in *On a Darkling Plain* (1940), about the spiritual rejuvenation of a war veteran, and in *The Big Rock Candy Mountain* (1943) and *Wolf Willow* (1963), where prairie homesteading is seen in rather disenchanted terms. From the influx of American draft resisters in the late 1960s and 1970s, little memorable imaginative literature emerged; however, John Birmingham's novel *The Vancouver Split* (1973) is an interesting chronicle of some of the eccentricities of that era, and California writer Ishmael Reed combines past and present in *Flight to Canada* (1976), a comic novel about the black American search for refuge in the 19th and 20th centuries.

JAMES DOYLE

Foreign Writers on Canada in French Until the arrival of Haitians fleeing the Duvalier regime, the majority of foreign Francophones writing about Canada were from France. After 1760, communications between France and its former colony were restricted and there is little mention of Canada in French works. The first French writer to come to Canada was Louis-Joseph-Marie QUESNEL, who arrived by chance in 1779, married and settled in Montréal. His comic opera *Colas et Colinette* (published 1808) was the first to be performed in N America and he also wrote poetry and plays. There were, of course, travellers who recorded their impressions, most of them combining a visit to Canada with a trip to the US. Chateaubriand had referred to Canada in his *Voyage en Amérique* (1827) and masterfully described the Niagara Falls in *Atala* (1801), though he probably saw little of what he depicted. Théodore Pavie, who spent a year in the New World (1829-30), was one of the first bona fide travellers to speak of his experiences in his *Souvenirs atlantiques. Voyage aux États-Unis et au Canada* (1851). Xavier Marmier, an erudite globe-trotter, came to Canada in 1849 and commented on what he saw in *Lettres sur l'Amérique, Canada, États-Unis, Rio de la Plata* (1851). He also wrote a novel, *Gazida* (1860), interesting mainly as a repertory of Indian legends and customs. As contacts between France and its former colony grew easier, travellers became more numerous, but usually spent more time in the US than in Canada. Among the most famous who recounted their voyages was Maurice Sand, the son of the famous novelist. He accompanied Prince Napoleon (later Emperor Napoleon III), and on his return to Paris wrote *Six mille lieues à toute vapeur* (1863), prefaced by his illustrious mother. Other noteworthy travellers are Henri de Lamothe, who wrote *Cinq Mois chez les français d'Amérique. Voyage au Canada* (1879), and Gustave de Molinari, who contributed numerous letters about the US and Canada to the *Journal des débats*. These letters were later published in 3 volumes (1876, 1881, 1886).

Both East and West were to be a source of inspiration to novelists. In 1841, only 4 years after the publication of the first French Canadian novel, *Le Courrier des États-Unis* published *La Rebelle*, a brief work by the Baron Philippe-Régis de Trobriand. The author had spent a few weeks in Canada at a time when the wounds of the 1837 rebellion, which inspired the novel, were still fresh. The most prolific French writer connected with Canada was Henri-Émile Chevalier. He came to Montréal in 1852, and during the 8 years he spent there founded *La Ruche littéraire*, was a regular contributor to several papers, and wrote lengthy adventure novels published mainly in *La Ruche* and *Le Moniteur canadien*. Back in France by 1860, he continued to write novels, some 30 of which have Canada as a background. With their insipid characters and preposterous plots, they have little literary merit, but they do contain many social and political comments and a wealth of information about Indian customs. Jules Verne, the greatest French writer of science fiction, spent "192 hours" on the N American continent in 1867, but apart from Niagara Falls saw nothing of Canada. For *Le Pays des fourrures* (1873; tr *The Fur Country: Twenty Degrees Latitude North*), he found his information in books. In *Famille-sans-nom* (1889; tr *Family Without a Name*, (1892), which is his only political novel and has as a background the events of 1837 rebellion, Verne's sympathy lies with the Patriotes.

At the turn of the century, many novelists, who came to Canada as travellers, lecturers or immigrants, found material for one or more books in what they saw. Louis HÉMON wrote the most famous of all Québec land novels, MARIA CHAPDELAINE (1916). Marie Le Franc came to Montréal in 1906 and remained there some 20 years before returning to France. For the rest of her life, she divided her time between her native Brittany and her adopted land, being equally fond of both. Several of her works were inspired by her beloved Laurentians and by Montréal, which she calls "my city." Her novel *Grand-Louis L'innocent* (1925; tr *The Whisper of a Name*, 1928), won the Prix Femina. *La Rivière Solitaire* (1934), which depicts the suffering of city workers sent to clear land in Temiskaming, and *Pêcheurs de Gaspésie* (1938), which draws attention to the plight of Gaspé fishermen, are 2 of the more successful of the dozen or so works inspired by Canada.

None of the French authors lured to the West by the promise of rapid wealth became rich, but they have left us with a vivid picture of life on the prairies. One of the first, Georges Forestier (pseudonym of Georges Schaeffer), spent 7 years in Manitoba. His novel *La Pointe-aux-Rats* (1907) aims at discouraging immigration, at least from the urban middle classes, and *Dans l'Ouest canadien* (1915), a posthumous volume of short stories, is both touching and humorous. Maurice Constantin-Weyer spent 10 years in the West before he left to fight in WWI. Back in France, he produced an imposing body of work (articles, short stories, novels, biographies, essays), the best of which was inspired by his Canadian experience. Fifteen of his books have the West as a background. *Un Homme se penche sur son passé* (1928; tr *A Man Scans His Past*, 1929), won the prestigious Prix Goncourt. The critics praised Constantin-Weyer's gifts as a landscape painter and his masterful depiction of the North in this partly autobiographical novel. In *Manitoba* (1924), *Cinq Éclats de silex* (1927) and *Clairière* (1929; tr *Forest Wild*, 1932), he eloquently describes the fauna of the West and what he calls the "rhythm of Life and Death." Georges BUGNET came to the West in 1905 and lived the rest of his 101 years in Alberta. Whatever leisure time farming left him, he spent writing, his most successful novels being *Nipsya* (1924), the story of a young Métis torn between the Cree and European ways of life, and *La Forêt* (1935; tr *The Forest*, 1976), about a young French couple's useless efforts to farm in Alberta.

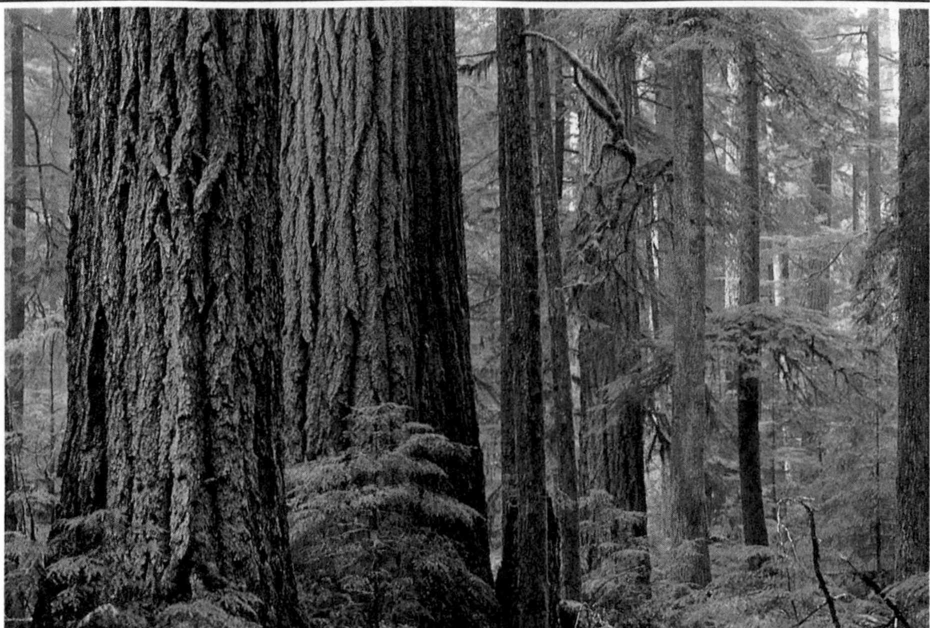

Pacific rain forest (*photo by Tim Fitzharris*).

The best book inspired by the Klondike gold rush is *La bête errante, roman vécu du Grand Nord canadien* (1923) by Louis-Frédéric Rouquette, a jack-of-all-trades who travelled the world. His experiences in the Northwest also inspired *Le Grand Silence blanc, roman vécu d'Alaska* (1921), partly set in Canada, and *L'Epopée blanche* (1926), a moving essay about the work of the Oblate missionaries. Rouquette excels at depicting man's fight against nature and his fellow man. Maurice Genevoix, a member of the French Academy, crossed Canada from east to west in 1939 and vividly described his experiences in *Canada* (1944). *Laframboise et Bellehumeur* (1944) was inspired by 2 trappers he met in eastern Canada, while the subject of *Eva Charlebois* (1944) is the painful adaptation of a young Québécoise to the West. Other less well-known novelists who wrote about Canada are Joseph-Emile Poirier, whose *Les Arpents de neige* (1909) is a novel about the Métis rebellion in Saskatchewan, though the author never set foot in Canada; Victor Forbin, who travelled to Canada several times, once crossing it from coast to coast, and who wrote both novels and essays about the country; and Pierre Hamp, whose subject was manual workers and whose *Hormisdas le Canadien* (1952) was the product of a year spent in Saint-Paul-l'Ermite.

Alexis de Tocqueville made passing references to Canada in his works. Another economist, André Siegfried, spent a year in Canada in 1904 to become acquainted with the political situation. In 1906 he published *Le Canada, les deux races: problèmes politiques contemporains* (tr *The Race Question in Canada*, 1907). After a second trip in 1935, he wrote *Le Canada, puissance internationale* (1937; tr *Canada*, 1939).

In more recent times, no doubt because of the numerous cultural exchanges between Québec and France, Canada has been a source of inspiration to many francophone writers. Chief among these is Bernard Clavel, who won the Prix Goncourt in 1968. This popular and talented novelist has visited Québec many times, spending 2 years there, 1977-79. His *Les Compagnons du Nouveau Monde* (1981) takes place in New France in the 17th century, and he is now writing an epic about settlers in Northern Temiskaming. Five volumes have been published, the first was *Harricana* (1982) and the latest *Amarok* (1987). Angélique, the popular 17th-century heroine of Anne and Serge Golon, often spends time in New France, especially in *Angélique à Québec* (1982). Other contemporary authors who have written about Canada are Michel Desgranges, who never visited the country but whose novel *Manitoba* (1981) was inspired by Riel; Alain Gerber, whose *Le Lapin de lune* (1982) is full of charming fantasy; and Roger Buliard, a priest, whose essays about the Inuit and the work of missionaries make fascinating reading. Other authors of foreign origin, such as novelists Jacques Folch Ribas, Monique Bosco and playwright Robert GURIK, have been writing in Montréal so long that their foreign origin is quite forgotten. PAULETTE COLLET

Reading: Paulette Collet, *Les Romanciers français et le Canada* (1984).

Forest, an ecosystem characterized by a somewhat dense and extensive tree cover. This definition views the forest as more than a simple collection of trees and takes into account shrubs, vines, herbs, mosses, micro-organisms, insects and higher animals which interact among themselves and with their environment. This vastly complex pattern of life is a system in delicate balance. Natural or man-made alterations may trigger far-reaching and sometimes disastrous changes.

Worldwide there are 3 main forest types related directly to climatic zones: equatorial- and tropical-region forests, temperate-zone forests, and forests associated with colder climates. Most of Canada's forest lies within the cold-climate boreal belt extending through Alaska, Siberia, Finland, Sweden and Norway. The boreal forest is composed predominantly of coniferous trees. Temperate-region forests extend into Canada only in milder areas along the Pacific coast and in SW Ontario. In BC the cool, temperate maritime climate supports a forest dominated by CONIFERS; in southern Ontario, under hot, humid summers, a deciduous forest has developed. Between this deciduous forest and the cold-climate boreal forest to the N exists a transitional mixed-wood forest, where coniferous and deciduous trees are about equally represented.

Canada's coniferous trees (34 species) include 9 species of PINE, 5 of SPRUCE, 4 of JUNIPER 3 of HEMLOCK, 3 of LARCH, 4 true FIRS, one DOUGLAS FIR, 2 of CEDAR, 2 of YEW and one CYPRESS. The conifers are variously known as softwoods, evergreens or needle-leaved trees. A mature conifer usually has a straight central trunk and short branches forming a distinctive, columnar crown. With the exception of larches, conifers retain their needlelike leaves for 2 or more years; the leaves are not shed all at once.

There are just over 100 species of deciduous trees in Canada, including 10 of MAPLE, 10 of OAK, 6 of BIRCH, 5 of POPLAR, 5 of hickory, 4 of ASH and 3 of ELM and members of 32 other genera. Deciduous trees, also known as hardwoods or broadleaf trees, vary considerably in form but often exhibit broad, rounded crowns with branches as long or longer than their short, tapered trunks. With the exception of arbutus, deciduous trees shed all their leaves annually.

The first appearance of trees occurred countless centuries before the advent of grasses and the age of dinosaurs. According to paleobotanists, plant life originated in a marine environment more than 3 billion years ago; plants moved onto land only in the late Silurian and early Devonian periods (421-387 million years ago). These first land plants, less than one metre tall, were sporebearers tied to damp environments. In the relatively short Devonian period (408-360 million years ago) the first forests appeared. They were heavily stocked with treelike CLUB MOSSES, having slender trunks and drooping branches. The earliest fossils of gymnosperm seeds date to the late Devonian. Gymnosperms, of which modern coniferous trees are examples, produce seeds that are not enclosed by an ovary.

At the end of the Devonian, extensive, shallow ocean flooding occurred within the N American continent. Rivers poured sediments into this sea, producing great swamps from which eventually sprang the monumental forests of the Carboniferous period (360-286 million years ago). Here, tree-size ancestors of present-day, diminutive HORSETAILS flourished along with FERNS, seed ferns and dominant club mosses, some of which soared over 30 m. At the end of the Carboniferous, these junglelike forests succumbed to major climatic changes and were buried, compressed and ultimately converted into COAL, which has fueled a great part of modern industry. During the Carboniferous, gymnosperms predominated at higher elevations, and the passing of the period set the stage for a major proliferation of gymnosperms, prominent among which were primitive conifers and palmlike cycads. Fern and horsetail numbers decreased.

A still more dramatic advance occurred during the Triassic period (245-208 million years ago), when some plants developed the ability to produce flowers and to encase their seeds inside ovaries or fruits; these were the angiosperms (*see* SEED PLANTS). Many flowering trees (eg, WILLOW, poplar, maple, magnolias) and flowering herbaceous plants appeared. By the end of the Cretaceous period (66.4 million years ago) angiosperms dominated the floral landscape. In parallel with their ascent, a rapidly expanding world of wildlife developed, with insects, birds and mammals drawing upon the forest and helping to sustain and expand it.

Climate soon worked another change upon the N American forest. About 55 million years ago in the "modern" era of the Cenozoic, a long-term cooling trend began; as it intensified, forests that had thrived comfortably within the ARCTIC CIRCLE were pushed southwards. Then, just under 2 million years ago, all but a minute part of Canada was slowly covered by 4 successive, monstrous ice sheets, sometimes as much as 3 km thick. Great glacial tongues also penetrated deeply into the northeastern US (*see* GLACIATION). The advancing ice sheets scoured the forestland, but their slow movement enabled the forest to withdraw each time and find refuge in warmer southern environments. Following the retreat of the last ice sheets (about 10 000 years ago), re-establishment of the forest began. In the vanguard of the northward march were the ALGAE and FUNGI, followed by higher plants, such as mosses, LICHENS and horsetails, capable of living on the cold, wet fringes of the land most recently vacated by ice. Next came the hardy gymnosperms: spruces, firs, pines and larches. Finally, the deciduous trees arrived: the oaks, ashes, maples and other species. These slow-moving belts of vegetation present the essential pattern of Canadian forests today. They may be growing in another interglacial period or may conceivably be in the early phase of a new tropical age. The passage of several centuries may begin to provide answers. *See also* BIOGEOGRAPHY.

C.R. STANTON

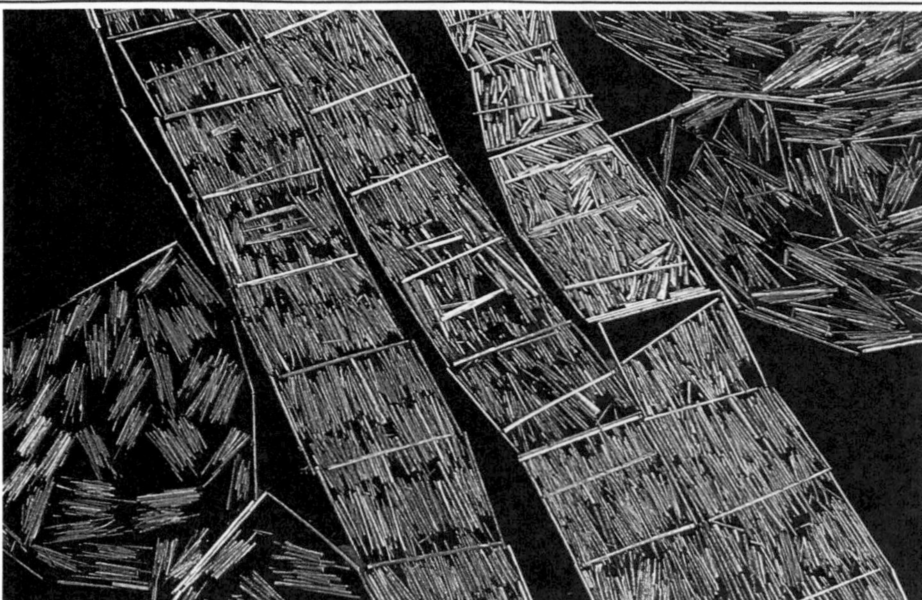

Log booms in Howe Sound, north of Vancouver, BC. Forests cover almost half of Canada's land area (*photo by J.A. Kraulis*).

Forest Economics, the application of economic principles to a wide range of subjects extending from the forest resource through the processing, marketing and consumption of forest products. Forest economics has much in common with AGRICULTURAL ECONOMICS, but although the latter discipline has an established academic history in Canada, no departments of forest economics exist in this country. Forestry students may, however, emphasize economics subjects, supplementing a single forest-economics course with courses in rural sociology, agricultural economics, outdoor-recreation economics, general economics and forest policy. Forest economics courses per se concentrate on the evaluation of the forest resource, on business management principles as applied to the forest and forest-products industries, and on the relation of the forest resource and its exploitation to national economic and social policies. Thus the subject may be seen to address factors affecting the financial viability of a given operation and those affecting the objectives of society as a whole.

Fiscal factors that affect the success of a particular operation include the revenues and costs involved in licensing of public timberland; taxation (in 1986 the provincial and federal governments were expected to receive $4 billion in taxes, timber sale revenues and import duties from the forest industry and its employees); industrial legislation and regulation; costs of inputs and prices of commodities; geographic distribution of customers (as it affects transportation costs); marketing constraints; labour markets; and various federal and provincial policies. The forest economist must also be familiar with technical aspects of forest management and industrial production, and should have at least some knowledge of forest ecology, the processing of timber products, technological innovations and wildlife management.

Forestry resembles agriculture in that both deal with crops, but the differences between them point out some of the constraints that forest economists must consider. For example, agricultural land is usually cropped annually; forests must be managed over several years (the shortest crop cycle, that of hybrid poplar for pulpwood, is approximately 10 years) and failure to do so threatens the long-term viability of an operation, as well as having a negative effect on the ecosystem. This extended perspective also has advantages: it permits the industry to make management decisions, marketing arrangements and other plans for the longer term. Farmers own their land or rent it from private owners; most forestland is publicly owned (the provinces own 67%, the federal government 27%). Thus a real conflict may arise between the industry's desire to "mine" the resource for profit and society's desire to protect public land. This potential conflict is further complicated by the fact that the forest resource base provides several economic and social values that may in some locations conflict with timber harvesting, eg, grazing, HUNTING, recreation, watershed protection. The scale of operation is also a factor: while farms occupy a few square kilometres at most, forests cover almost half of Canada's land area and forest harvesting may affect very large areas.

Thus, while forest economists apply such general economic ideas as supply and demand and other market factors, financial rates of return, capital investment, development, conservation, etc, they must take great care when choosing the analytical framework within which they work. For example, the relative costs and benefits of forest management will differ depending on the length of time under consideration; on whether the calculation involves indirect as well as direct effects; on whether it is done from the perspective of an individual company, a provincial or a national economy, etc. An experienced forest economist can ensure the recognition of economic, social, environmental and political linkages.

One of the most important issues today is the apparent conflict among forestry investment criteria. The traditional approach in professional forestry was to emphasize biological growth. A forest was said to be mature and ready for harvesting when timber of sawlog size was available or when a timber stand ceased to add volume because annual growth was exceeded by disease, decay and mortality. In recent decades, support has grown for the concept of financial rotation, whereby the ideal harvest date is set by its calculated maximum value to the owner. A financial rotation age is based on economic efficiency as measured by market prices and costs. It assumes free competition and the absence of external costs to the ENVIRONMENT, wildlife, etc. This method tends to favour exploitation. As timber supply problems began to emerge worldwide in the past quarter century, the fairness of liquidating forest capital began to be questioned. This change in attitude has resulted in an increasing interest in CONSERVATION criteria that seek to keep the resource base essentially intact over time, a goal with particular appeal to managers of publicly owned land who do not operate by the profit motive and are not expected to apply corporate financial criteria. This approach does not mean a complete break from financial rates of return. Provincial land managers must still use financial methods to allocate funds budgeted for REFORESTATION, and they must choose among sites and silvicultural treatments to achieve the best growth and yield possible with limited funds. Economics aside, the only politically and socially acceptable policy, for public and private forest managers alike, is to replant promptly after harvest. But how much should be spent on more intensive silvicultural activities (eg, thinning and fertilizing)? For provincial foresters the answer is largely political, though it is based on expected long-term economic and social benefits. Private industry and small woodlot owners apply a variety of measures to determine the level of forest management, usually with a shorter time in mind than their public counterparts and with taxes playing a key role. The forest economist can determine the appropriate method of calculating the benefits of forest renewal and protection.

Forest economists also play a crucial role in formulating public policy. Such policy is firmly fixed on the goal of maintaining at least the present harvest in perpetuity. Unfortunately the record of forest-resource management in Canada is well below the level necessary to sustain existing harvest levels, let alone to provide for stable growth. Although Canada does have some of the best forestry performance in the world, it also has far too much that is below an acceptable level. As a result of decades of neglect, timber-supply deficits are emerging in many forest-based communities. In recognition of this threat the provinces and the federal government have begun to formulate new policies and programs that will double or triple spending on forest renewal. Federal government leadership is shown in the adoption of *A Forest Sector Strategy for Canada* in 1981 and 4 follow-up policies in 1982 and 1983. Priorities include increased funding for Canadian forestry faculties; increased research and development; joint programs with the provinces in such areas as replanting, timber-stand improvements, etc; and improved forest-fire suppression (eg, through establishment of a fire co-ordination centre in Winnipeg and a fleet of CANADAIR CL-215 water-bomber aircraft.

The case for forest renewal is based on the need to stabilize existing forest industry employment as well as the estimated 2 indirect jobs associated with each person employed in the woods and mills. It is estimated that 25 000 new jobs could be created in forest renewal alone; an additional 75 000 could be generated through increased output and higher value added in processing. In addition there is the generation of billions of dollars in tax revenue, foreign-exchange earnings, watershed and wildlife protection and the support of a multi-billion recreation and tourism industry. The social costs of neglect are community dislocation, employee relocation and welfare. These costs are probably much higher than those of maintaining timber in scores of threatened forest-based towns.

Other issues for the forest economist are the social and economic impact of ACID RAIN on forests, the pricing of nontimber forest products, the tradeoff between forestry and fishery values, the benefits flowing from forestry science and related new product development, and the national and international sector-development opportunities.

F.L.C. REED

Reading: D. MacKay, *Heritage Lost: The Crisis in Canada's Forests* (1985); R.P. Gillis and T.R. Rouch, *Lost Initiatives: Canada's Forest Industries, Forest Policy and Forest Conservation* (1986); J. Swift, *Cut and Run: The Assault on Canada's Forests* (1983).

Three jumpers work to control a fire in a logging block near Watson Lake, YT. Heavy ground debris made this fire extremely volatile. Over 9000 forest fires occur in Canada each year, 65% of which are caused by human carelessness (*photo by Paul Buitenhuis*).

Forest Fire, a moving combustion reaction, spreading outwards in a band from its ignition source. Rates of advance downwind range up to 6 km/h, but few fires spread faster than 1 km/h, and most move at less than 0.5 km/h. Combustible matter includes leaf litter, dead grass, dry moss or lichen, dead and live brush and live tree foliage. Fires are classed mainly according to whether they remain on the ground surface or rise into the tree crowns. In Canada only CONIFER forests support crown fires; no appreciable part of the live tree trunk burns in this type of fire.

On the average about 9200 forest fires occur annually in Canada. Of these about 65% are caused by humans and 35% by LIGHTNING. Lightning fires account for much more damage on average because they are generally less accessible: each burns an average of 560 ha (compared to 50 ha for a human-caused fire). As of 1986, the 10-year average annual area burned was 2 million ha (0.5% of the entire forest), 85% of which is destroyed by lightning fires. Although 85% of all forest fires affect areas of under 5 ha, occasional single fires exceed 100 000 ha and the largest 2% of fires account for 90% of the area burned. During the period 1977 to 1986 the largest area burned in a single year was 5.4 million ha (1981); the smallest, 289 000 ha (1978). Each year about $250 million is spent in controlling forest fires. About one-fifth of the area burned annually is classified as commercial forest; the remainder is in remote northern areas or in stands having no current industrial potential. The average annual area harvested is about 800 000 ha.

The amount of damage done by a forest fire depends largely on the related factors of size and intensity. Intensity is best measured as the rate of energy output per unit length of moving fire front, expressed in kilowatts per metre (kW/m). Frontal intensities range up to 150 000 kW/m, with flames 50 m or more high, although a slow-moving surface fire may produce only 200 kW/m, with flames no higher than one metre. The immense variation in the behaviour of forest fires depends on the moisture content of the combustible matter, affected by both current and past weather, current wind speed and the kind of forest. Similarly, the great variation in burned area (annually and from region to region within Canada) results primarily from weather variations. Without the efficient and effective action of Canadian fire-control agencies the average burned area would be several times greater. However, when fire weather is critical (strong wind and low humidity after several weeks without rain), it is almost impossible to prevent some fires from becoming very large. A system of forest-fire danger ratings (the Fire Weather Index) is used throughout Canada to measure daily the susceptibility of the forest to fire and to provide fire-control agencies with information on which to base their activities.

Because most forests below 60° N lat are under provincial jurisdiction, fire management is carried out by provincial forestry departments. The Canadian Interagency Forest Fire Centre, established in Winnipeg in 1982, provides information, keeps statistics and co-ordinates interprovincial exchanges of fire-fighting forces and equipment. The federal government's Atmospheric Environment Service (*see* CLIMATE INFORMATION) collects and processes daily weather data and provides fire-danger ratings to provincial fire agencies. The Canadian Forestry Service, in co-operation with several universities, carries out most of the research on forest fires in Canada.

Fire detection in Canada is usually carried out by aerial patrols along standard flight patterns; these patrols have superseded the traditional fire tower. Patrols are backed up by lightning-detection systems that pinpoint probable locations and expected numbers of lightning fires. Fire-control methods include aerial water dropping (sometimes with fire-retardant additives), or control from the ground through portable water pumps with hose lines, tank trucks, bulldozers and hand tools. Burning out from a prepared line to stop an oncoming fire is sometimes feasible. Computerized fire-management systems are increasingly improving control operations.

Fire Ecology and Economics Fire, along with climate and soil, is one of 3 primary physical factors that have shaped the Canadian forest and have kept it from encroaching on grassland. Most of this forest was historically dependent on ecological recycling by periodic fire for its long-term stable existence. The southeastern hardwood forest and the West Coast coniferous rain forest are exceptions to this pattern. In the boreal forest, for example, the main tree species are black SPRUCE, jack PINE, lodgepole pine, trembling ASPEN and white BIRCH, all of which are adapted to regenerate after fire even though all individuals in a large area are killed. In the preindustrial era ignition was by lightning, and perhaps 2-3 times as much forest burned annually as does at present. In the absence of either fire or forest management, deterioration would eventually occur, since these species do not reproduce well without disturbance and it is doubtful that a satisfactory fire-free forest of other desirable tree species would arise in its place. Other prominent species, eg, red and white pine, white spruce and DOUGLAS FIR, require ground that has been prepared by fire for optimum regeneration, but some surviving trees are needed to produce seed. Aspen and POPLAR sucker prolifically from root systems when above-ground trees are killed by fire; other hardwoods sprout from the base of dead trees. Jack and lodgepole pines and black spruce store protected live seeds in their cones for years, only shedding them when the trees are killed. Ecologically then, fire is neither good nor bad, but simply an environmental necessity for the perpetuation of the forest in its natural state.

Economically, fire competes with the forest industry for the annual tree growth on which the industry is based. Some fire-killed timber is salvaged, but salvage is impractical on a large scale. In the ideally managed forest, each stand is regenerated after harvest by silvicultural means, eg, through cultivation and perhaps the use of prescribed fires. Accidental wildfire is excluded. Because it is physically impossible to eliminate all naturally occurring forest fires, an economic compromise is struck. As fire-control efforts are increased, it costs more and more to reduce the average annual burned area. The ideal position is the point at which the cost of further reduction in burned area equals the value of the corresponding potential increase in the harvest (*see* FOREST ECONOMICS). Other recreational and economic forest uses are also taken into consideration, as well as the safety of forest towns.

The ecological realities of fire create a dilemma in large natural parks and other unmanaged, or lightly managed, areas because certain kinds of forest cannot be maintained in perpetuity in the absence of fire. The administrators of Canada's national parks are aware of this problem and are developing policies to cope with it. The interaction of ecological and economic factors complicates forest-fire management and debate about the optimum level of fire control is actively under discussion throughout Canada. The Canadian Forestry Association and its affiliated provincial forestry associations, as well as provincial forestry departments, maintain fire-prevention programs aimed at reducing the number of human-caused fires. Whatever the policy differences of fire management, the rule "do not start forest fires" remains just as valid as ever for the individual citizen. C.E. VAN WAGNER

Forest Harvesting, the process of cutting TREES and delivering them from the forest to sawmills, pulp mills and other wood-products-processing plants. It includes forest engineering, forest-road construction, logging and log transportation.

Forest engineering is the field of engineering that specializes in planning forest harvesting (*see* FORESTRY EDUCATION). A forest engineer working in naturally grown forests must plan and locate permanent roads which meet the long-term goals of forest management and which may later become public-access routes and highways. The logging system best meeting environmental and financial objectives must be chosen; branch-road networks planned; road construction supervised; and logging machines selected. A forest engineer requires knowledge of the principles of FORESTRY, SURVEYING, GEOLOGY and SOIL SCIENCE, and familiarity with available machinery. When developing a harvesting plan, the engineer starts with a long-term forest-management plan, usually prepared by government and industrial foresters in consultation with specialists in fish and wildlife habitat, recreation, water and soil quality. This plan shows the timber area to be cut, the proposed rate of cutting and the special requirements of other forest users.

Forest-Road Construction

The Canadian forest industry builds approximately 15 000 km of logging roads each year, of which over half are temporary winter snow roads and unsurfaced summer roads. Nevertheless, these roads and associated culverts, bridges and other structures constitute huge engineering and construction projects. Bulldozers are used to build roads over dry, sandy soil. In the flat wetlands of the boreal forest in the North, bulldozers and backhoes are used to build up the road from the soil on a wide right-of-way, creating a dike for the road and a deep ditch on either side.

Roads constructed on the BC coast are very costly because of the difficulty of clearing large trees and blasting solid rock encountered in the mountains. All roads are surfaced because the ground is never dry or frozen for predictable periods. Bulldozers and backhoes usually pioneer the subgrades until they encounter rock and require assistance from rock drills. Roads built on steep ground interrupt natural water-drainage patterns and require carefully constructed culverts and bridges to minimize erosion.

Logging

Cutting methods include progressive clear-cutting, patch cutting and individual tree selection. Progressive clear-cutting is commonly practised in natural, undeveloped forests. It requires the least initial road construction, permits loggers to concentrate their operations and enables foresters systematically to prepare sites and engage in REFORESTATION after cutting. Large cutover areas are unpopular with the public and cause potential fire hazards. Logging scattered patches requires more initial road construction and exposes the fringes to wind damage. Patch logging is the usual way to cut successive crops from a forest. Individual tree selection is used to thin an immature forest to increase growth and to cut hardwood species which will grow in shade.

The word "logging" may refer to all harvesting operations or may apply only to the stump-to-roadside activities.

Felling Hand-held chain saws are commonly used for felling (or falling) trees. The faller uses an undercut and wedges to control the direction of fall. Felling is dangerous and requires skill, especially if trees are partly rotten or have intertwined branches. Mechanical felling machines mounted on tractors or excavators, which direct or bunch the tree, are used to fell trees up to 80 cm in diameter. Shears are used to cut pulpwood. Mechanical chain saws, augers and circular saws are used to cut sawlogs where damage to wood from shears is unacceptable. Multi-function tree harvesters are used in stands of small trees (up to 50 cm diameter). They cut, limb and top the trees and move them to the roadside, or perform any combination of these functions. These machines are expensive and operate best where large numbers of trees can be cut in one location.

Skidding involves dragging logs or trees to the roadside with a horse, wheel skidder or tractor. Horses and farm tractors are used on small private woodlots, but articulated, centre-steering wheel skidders (developed in Canada in the 1950s) have replaced horses on most operations. A faller with a hand-held chain saw and a skidder operator often operate as a team: they log "hot," ie, skid each tree soon after it is cut. If mechanical cutters are used, the trees are felled days or weeks before skidding. Trees felled and bunched with a feller buncher are often skidded with a grapple skidder which can pick up the complete bunch. Crawler tractors with bulldozer blades are used for skidding on steep ground where trails are required.

Yarding is the dragging of logs from stump to roadside using cables and yarders (winches). The most common methods are high-lead, in which logs are lifted at one end and dragged across the ground, and skyline, in which the log is transported wholly through the air. Normal yarding distances are up to 300 m, but special systems can yard at distances of 500 m and, in some cases, 700 m. Helicopters are used for logging valuable timber from places inaccessible by road or where roads would cause damage.

Slashing involves cutting the tree into pulpwood bolts, usually 1.25 or 2.5 m long. Roadside slashers are large machines with conveyor systems and circular saws.

Sorting Logs are sorted by species and grade so that they can be manufactured into the most valuable products. Sorting takes place at landings, points of transfer from trucks to secondary transportation, or at mills. Front-end loaders, log stackers and cranes are used for sorting. Frequent communication between forest operations and mill is essential to ensure that specific logs go the correct mill.

Log Transportation

Most trees harvested in Canada are transported from the forest by truck. Front-end loaders, cranes and special log loaders are used to load trucks in the landing. Pulpwood is hauled crossways on flat-deck semitrailers, an efficient system which permits hauling of maximum allowable loads. In eastern Canada, tree lengths are also hauled on flat-deck trailers. In BC, where logs are long enough to span the distance between truck and trailer, pole trailers are used.

Logging railways were common in Canada until the 1950s. Because of high track-maintenance costs and the need to have large volumes of timber available to one route, most have now been replaced by trucks. Commercial railways are still used as secondary transportation for moving logs long-distance.

Water transport is a common form of secondary log transport on lakes and rivers and on the Pacific coast. Most river drives in eastern Canada have been eliminated because of environmental concerns and log losses through sinkage. On the BC coast, logs are transported by truck to the water and then formed into rafts of log bundles for transport to mills. Bundling logs reduces losses from sinkage and escape. Logs from the Queen Charlotte Is and the W coast of Vancouver I are transported through rough seas on barges and log ships. Water transport is cheap and is the only method of transporting logs from isolated islands or coastal inlets. The forest industry in BC supports a large secondary industry of tugs and barges, which move not only logs but pulp, pulp chips, lumber and other products.

Forest Products

Canada's forests produce a variety of commercial products. Higher-grade BIRCH, MAPLE, OAK, DOUGLAS FIR, sitka SPRUCE and western red CEDAR are manufactured into expensive veneers and finished lumber. White spruce, western HEMLOCK and lodgepole PINE are used for construction lumber; black spruce, jack pine and hemlock are excellent for newsprint. Lower grades of all species are made into pulp. In many parts of the world, fuel wood is the major forest product. In Canada the use of wood as fuel has decreased until recently. The ENFOR (energy from the forest) program has stimulated interest in forest waste as a fuel and encouraged the forest industry to produce more of its own energy (*see* BIOMASS ENERGY). The manufacture and sale of forest products is becoming more integrated, to ensure that each log is cut into the most valuable product. In this way, Canada can conserve its remaining stands of quality trees and ensure that maximum benefits are derived from forests. G.V. WELLBURN

Forest Ranger The term ranger probably has its origins in the N American wars of the 18th and 19th centuries, when, because land was heavily forested, armies developed special combat units of woodsmen and marksmen to carry out reconnaissance as well as surprise and diversionary raids. In Canada, similar knowledgeable woodsmen were the fur trappers and COUREURS DE BOIS, who later showed industrialists and government officials the locations of valuable forest stands. Most of these men were capable of withstanding long periods of isolation and had learned from the native people the art of survival in the forest. With the birth of a large-scale FORESTRY industry, supervisors and high-ranking administrators were in many cases drawn from the ranks of self-taught foresters. The need to replace them upon retirement ultimately led, beginning in the 1920s, to the creation in Canada of forest-ranger schools (the first was established in the province of Québec in 1923), which provided specialized training, first at the secondary-school level and later at the technical-school level (*see* FORESTRY EDUCATION). The Maritimes Forest Ranger School, NB, is the only such school still using the term forest ranger.

In the US system of national forests, rangers control administrative units of up to 200 000 ha and manage all renewable resources within the unit. In Canada, as a result of the changing nature and specialization of forestry work, the term has been superseded by more precise designations (eg, forest technician, wildlife manager). Despite the fact that the role and responsibilities of forest rangers or wardens have changed greatly over the years, films and television persist in portraying the ranger as the amiable protector of the forest and its woodland creatures. Young people interested in forestry are encouraged by groups such as the Junior Forest Wardens in western Canada and the 4-H CLUBS in Québec. MARCEL LORTIE

Balsam poplar dominates the southern Boreal Forest Region (*photo by Tim Fitzharris*).

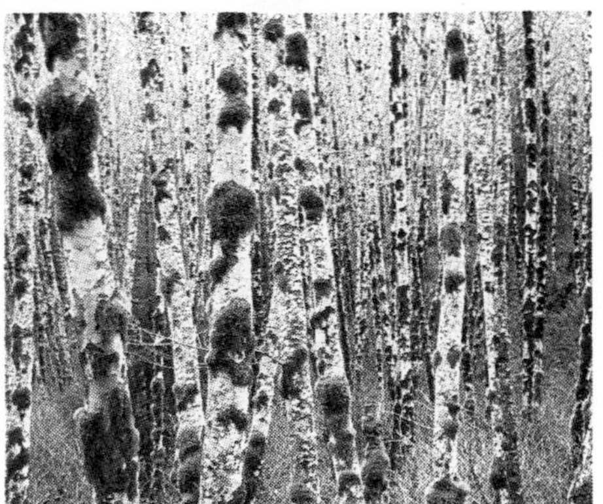

Red alder is a short-lived tree of the forest region of western BC (*photo by Tim Fitzharris*).

Forest Regions Canada's FOREST scientists have mapped its great tracts of forest and divided them into 8 regions. A forest region is defined as a major geographic belt or zone characterized by a broad uniformity both in physiography and in the composition of the dominant tree species. Emphasis is placed on the forest region as an areal entity. The complex effect of climate and other environmental components have not been taken into account in setting boundaries.

Boreal Forest Region Approximately 80% of Canada's forested land is in this immense boreal forest region, which in Canada swings in an arc S from the Mackenzie River Delta and Alaskan border to NE British Columbia, across northern Alberta and Saskatchewan, through Manitoba, Ontario and Québec, terminating in northern Newfoundland on the shores of the Labrador Sea. The northern boreal region consists of open forest with trees growing farther apart and smaller in size as the forest stretches towards the TUNDRA, where only dwarf specimens persist. The southern boreal region presents a denser, closed forest which, at its SW boundary in the Prairie provinces, gives way to a transitional zone dominated by POPLAR. Known as the aspen grove, this part of the forest thins out into open, almost treeless prairie. White and black SPRUCE are the principal species of the predominantly coniferous boreal forest, but other CONIFERS (eg, balsam FIR, jack PINE and especially tamarack) also have a wide distribution. There is a general admixture of broad-leaved trees in the region, including white BIRCH, balsam poplar and the wide-ranging trembling ASPEN.

Great Lakes-St Lawrence Forest Region, less than one-tenth of the size of the boreal forest, is Canada's second-largest forest region. With the exception of a 322 km gap, where the boreal region touches the N shore of Lk Superior, it stretches from SE Manitoba to the Gaspé Peninsula. It is bordered to the S by the deciduous forest region, and is a transitional forest between the coniferous and broad-leaved regions. Characteristic species are eastern white pine, red pine, eastern HEMLOCK and yellow birch. Sugar and red MAPLES, red OAK, basswood and white ELM are also found, as are many boreal species.

Acadian Forest Region Closely related to the Great Lakes-St Lawrence Forest Region, this region is confined to NS, PEI and a large portion of NB. Red spruce, balsam fir, yellow birch and sugar maple are commonly found here. Black spruce, white and grey birch, red oak, white elm, black ASH, red maple, trembling aspen and balsam poplar are widely distributed.

Deciduous Forest Region, Canada's smallest forest region, borders on the SE shore of Lk Huron and the northern shores of Lakes Erie and Ontario. Despite its small size, this region contains the largest number of native tree species of any region. Along with the broad-leaved trees common to the Great Lakes-St Lawrence Forest Region are found the cucumber tree, tulip tree, black gum, blue ash, sassafras and others which are at the northern limits of their range. Conifers occur only as a scattering of eastern white pine, tamarack, eastern red CEDAR and eastern hemlock.

The remaining forest regions are located almost completely within British Columbia.

Coast Forest Region covers the lower seaward slopes of British Columbia's Coast Mts and extends to the coastal islands. Characteristic species are western hemlock, DOUGLAS FIR, western red cedar and Sitka spruce, all renowned for their value as timber-producing trees. By comparison, the region's broad-leaved trees (eg, black cottonwood, red ALDER, big-leaf maple) have a limited distribution and are of minor economic importance.

Subalpine Forest Region, composed of coniferous forests, is situated on the mountain uplands of BC and western Alberta. Characteristic trees are Engelmann spruce, alpine fir and lodgepole pine; occasional species include western LARCH, whitebark pine and limber pine, together with yellow CYPRESS and mountain hemlock on the more westerly ranges. The subalpine region makes an impressive contribution to the scenic splendour of the Canadian CORDILLERA and offers unique features of watershed protection and stream control in high-mountain source areas. The trees at lower elevations are harvested for timber.

Montane Forest Region includes British Columbia's central plateau and several valley pockets adjacent to the Alberta boundary, areas which share a prevailing dry climate. The characteristic tree of this region is the blue Douglas fir, a smaller variety of the coast-region type. Lodgepole pine and trembling aspen are generally present and white spruce is found in cooler, shaded, valley locations. In southern parts of the region's more open forest, ponderosa pine is common. Engelmann spruce and alpine fir from the subalpine region, together with western

Douglas fir forest, characteristic of the Montane Forest Region (*photo by Tim Fitzharris*).

white birch, are important species of this region's northern limits.

Columbia Forest Region lies in SE British Columbia between the Rockies and the central plateau and fingers its way through the subalpine region along river valleys and lakes. The forest of this interior wet belt strongly resembles that of the coast region, although fewer species occur in the interior. Characteristic trees are western red cedar and western hemlock. The blue Douglas fir is widely distributed, and in southern parts western white pine, western larch, grand fir and western YEW are found. Engelmann spruce is found in the upper Fraser Valley and occasionally at higher elevations in the region. C.R. STANTON

Forestiers et voyageurs, a novel by Joseph-Charles Taché (1863), is a unique blend of fact and fancy. It bridges the folktale and the episodic novel, humorously recounting the stories and adventures of "le père Michel," a typical Canadian VOYAGEUR. Realistic descriptions of hunting and fishing, with Indians and with seigneurs, develop into the narrative of Michel's escapades farther afield, helping the NORTH WEST CO defeat the HUDSON'S BAY CO traders. Both locales are nostalgically characterized as the sources of French and aboriginal legends and songs, which form part of the national heritage. Taché's manuscript, containing a wealth of etymological and anthropological lore, was serialized in *Les* SOIRÉES CANADIENNES (1863) and *Le Foyer domestique* (1878-79); it was first published as a book in 1884. MICHÈLE LACOMBE

Forestry can be defined as the science, art and practice of managing and using for human benefit the natural RESOURCES that occur on and in association with forestlands. The forest resource is of major social and economic importance to Canadians. In 1982 the logging, wood, paper and allied industries of Canada directly employed 260 000 people. An analysis of forest-based communities has established that for each individual employed in the woods and mills, one job is created locally and another elsewhere within the national economy; thus the forestry sector alone generates jobs for over 780 000 workers. Expressed another way, approximately 7.4% of Canada's 1982 work force relied upon the forests for their livelihood. Exports of forest products in 1986 were $17.5 billion or about 14.5% of the country's total domestic export values. Forest products' net earnings for 1986 of $16.5 billion contributed more to the positive balance of trade of $9.6 billion than any other major commodity group. Impressive as the economic contributions of forest products may be, they do not fully reflect the importance of the forest resource and its management. Streamflow, soil erosion, sedimentation, fish and wildlife may all be profoundly influenced, depending on how the resource is managed. Forests remain the home of many of Canada's native peoples and provide a domain for camping, hunting, hiking, angling, photography, nature study and sightseeing for all Canadians and visitors. Such activities generate much of the multi-billion-dollar contribution which the recreation and tourism industry makes to the national economy. Forests provide an additional, although intangible, benefit: the opportunity for renewal of the human spirit.

Forest Ownership and Administration

Canada's land area (excluding water) is almost 9.2 million km^2, and of this total about 4.4 million km^2 is forestland. Forest inventories have been completed on 3.4 million km^2, or about 78% of forestlands. Most Canadian forestland is administered by provincial and federal governments. Provincial governments are responsible for about 67% of inventoried forestland; the federal government for 27%; private owners for 6%.

A converted WWII A-26 bomber drops Phoschex, a paintlike liquid used to retard fire spread, allowing ground crews more time to control a forest fire (*photo by Paul Buitenhaus*).

The British North America Act of 1867 assigned "The Management and Sale of the Public Lands belonging to the Province and of the Timber and Wood thereon" to the exclusive jurisdiction of each provincial legislature, regardless of when it joined Confederation. However, the federal government continued to administer the forests of Manitoba, Saskatchewan and Alberta and the 64 km-wide railway belt along the route of the CPR in BC until 1930.

Each province has a forestry agency, usually a branch or service located within a ministry charged with responsibility for natural resources. This agency is normally concerned with a wide range of forestry matters: timber disposal; FOREST FIRE protection and management; protection against insects and diseases; forest inventory; extension and information services; forest management and SILVICULTURE, REFORESTATION and forest research. Forest resources of the YT and the NWT as well as those on federal crown lands (Indian reserves, military bases and national parks) are the responsibility of the federal government. Privately held forestland, 80% of which is located E of Manitoba, is managed by its owners, but provincial governments may subsidize private forest management in some regions and may influence it through taxation policies, protection regulations, etc.

Canada's Major Forest Industries

Based on the 5-year period 1978-82, Canada's estimated average annual roundwood cut amounted to 148.6 million m^3. The 1982 wood harvest reached an estimated 127 million m^3 and the ranking timber-producing provinces of BC, Québec and Ontario were responsible respectively for 44%, 23% and 16% of that total. The timber produced was 91% softwood, 9% hardwood. In 1982 major forest industries (logging, wood, and paper and allied) employed 260 000 workers, who collectively earned almost $6.4 billion in salaries and wages. Canada's total forest-products export income for 1986 was more than $17.5 billion: 74% from the US, 4% from Japan, 4% from the UK and the remainder from numerous other trading partners.

In 1982 Canada's logging industry, which produces logs, bolts, pulpwood, pulpwood chips, poles and piling, employed 40 000 people earning a total of $1 billion. In the same year the industry shipped $4-billion worth of goods, most of which were processed domestically; exports of raw wood materials amounted to only $225 million. Japan, the US and the People's Republic of China were Canada's major customers for logs. All pulpwood chips and most pulpwood exported also went to the US and Japan.

The wood industries of Canada include SAWMILLS and planing mills; shingle mills; veneer and plywood mills; sash, door and millwork plants; wooden-box factories; the coffin and casket industry; and miscellaneous wood industries responsible for producing such commodities as particle board, wafer board and cooperage. In 1982 the 97 000 workers employed in these areas earned $2.1 billion. The value of goods shipped reached $7.2 billion; exports totalled more than $6.3 billion. Lumber accounted for $4.9 billion of export sales, 80% to the US. Japan, the UK, Saudi Arabia, France, Australia, Algeria and West Germany were also important lumber customers. Exports of shakes and shingles earned $268 million, with the US accounting for 99% of the market. The US also bought 82% of veneer exports valued at $116 million. The main plywood importer was the UK, which took 40% of the $122-million market; the US ranked next, followed by Italy and W Germany.

The paper and allied industries include pulp and paper mills, asphalt roofing manufacturers, paper box and paper and plastic bag manufacturers, and miscellaneous paper converters producing such items as waxed paper, facial tissue, toilet paper and stationery. In 1982 the 123 000 people engaged in these occupations earned $3.3 billion. The establishments they worked for shipped goods worth $14.8 billion, and total exports of wood pulp, paper, paperboard and other paper products amounted to $11 billion. The major export items were wood pulp and newsprint, which earned $4.1 and $5.7 billion, respectively in 1986. The US was Canada's principal customer for each of these commodities, purchasing 49% of the wood pulp and almost 82% of the newsprint in 1986. Japan, W Germany, Italy and the UK also imported substantial quantities of Canadian wood pulp, and the UK, Venezuela, Brazil and W Germany were major customers for newsprint.

No reference to Canada's forest industries would be complete without mention of 2 much smaller forest ventures, the Christmas tree and MAPLE SUGAR INDUSTRIES. Canada's main Christmas-tree species are balsam FIR, SPRUCE, Scots PINE, lodgepole pine and DOUGLAS FIR. Some trees occur naturally and others, particularly Scots pine, are plantation grown. No accurate figures are available for Christmas-tree production, but it is estimated that approximately 5 million were cut in 1980. Exports for 1986 amounted to 2.7 million trees valued at $23.5 million. Almost half of the exported trees were grown in NS; the balance largely in Québec, NB, Ontario and BC. The US took 97%, the remainder going largely to Caribbean and Caribbean-rim countries.

The 1985 production of maple syrup amounted to 9870 kL. Just over 90% of this volume was tapped in Québec. Ontario was responsible for most of the balance with minor contributions from Nova Scotia and New Brunswick. The gross value of 1985 production was $45.9 million. Exports for 1986 were valued at $50.6 million, and the main buyer was the US, which purchased 83% of this total.

Forest Enemies

Canada's forests are constantly threatened by forest fires, INSECT PESTS and PLANT DISEASES. Significant research, management and forest protection efforts are directed towards mitigating losses. Between 1972 and 1981, an average of 9160 fires burned just over 2 million ha of forest annually; losses of timber, together with real and personal property, averaged $183 million per year. During the 1982 fire season a total of 8941 fires burned almost 1.7 million ha. Timber and property losses amounted to $196.6 million and fire-fighting costs reached $141.6 million, about 32% over budget. In 1982, 65% of forest fires were caused by people; 32% by LIGHTNING; the remainder were of unknown origin.

During the 1977-81 period, the average annual loss caused by important forest pests has been estimated at 107.4 million m^3 of wood. This loss, 58% attributable to insects and 42% to diseases, represents a combination of tree mortality and growth reduction. By far the most important of the insect pests is the spruce budworm, followed by ASPEN defoliators, mountain pine BEETLE and spruce bark beetle. Decay accounts for just over half of the losses caused by disease; hypoxylon canker and dwarf MISTLETOE are responsible for most of the balance.

Forestry Research

The dominant role in forestry research in Canada is assumed by the federal government, through the Canadian Forestry Service (CFS). The CFS, part of Environment Canada, has its headquarters in the National Capital Region. It operates 6 regional forest research centres across the country and 2 research institutes: the Forest Pest Management Institute at Sault Ste Marie, Ont, and the Petawawa National Forestry Institute at Chalk River, Ont.

Through departments responsible for forestry, the governments of BC, Ontario and Québec support substantial research programs. The remaining provinces generally support smaller programs. Provincial research organizations and industrial research corporations, such as the CENTRE DE RECHERCHE INDUSTRIELLE DU QUÉBEC, the ONTARIO RESEARCH FOUNDATION, BRITISH COLUMBIA RESEARCH COUNCIL, the Pulp and Paper Research Institute of Canada, the Forest Engineering Research Institute of Canada, and FORINTEK Canada Corporation, conduct a wide range of forestry research projects. Major forest-industry companies, along with industrial suppliers, also make significant contributions, especially in the area of pulp and paper research.

Loading pine logs near Smithers, BC (*photo by Tim W. Parkin/Pathfinder*).

University-based forestry research is closely associated with Canada's 6 professional forestry schools located at the universities of New Brunswick, Laval, Toronto, Lakehead, Alberta and British Columbia, but considerable work is also accomplished in other university departments and faculties across the country.

Forest Management

Forest management in Canada is concerned with FOREST HARVESTING, site preparation and improvement, forest regeneration, tending and conversion of timber stands, tree improvement, and protection of the forest from fire, insects and diseases. In a broader context, forest management melds the foregoing activities with the country's economic, social and environmental objectives.

From the birth of the square-timber trade to the present, the emphasis in Canada has been on the exploitation of public forests for their timber values. Notwithstanding forest-management commitments to sustained yield in more recent years, the country now finds itself on the threshold of a serious wood shortage. Timber reserves have been reduced to critical levels by a combination of factors, the most important of which has been neglect of forest renewal. Heavier-than-anticipated losses from fire, insects and diseases, coupled with the establishment of parks and wilderness preserves and environmental constraints placed upon timber harvesting, have also contributed to the problem. Only 4 provinces now have uncommitted softwood reserves, which unfortunately are largely uneconomic to log because of remoteness and other factors. Two provinces appear about in balance; the remaining 4 are in a deficit position. Higher-value hardwood stands in the East have been severely overcut as well, and renewal is virtually nonexistent. More than half the country's hardwood forests consist of poplar species which, for reasons of quality and product suitability, are unattractive commercially.

In light of Canada's economic reliance upon its forest-products industries, the spectre of wood shortages is serious indeed. With substantial increases in world consumption of paper and paperboard, wood-based panels and lumber projected for the period 1980-2000, the urgent need to deal with the country's timber supply problems becomes even more apparent. Wide-ranging consultations involving departments of the federal government, the provinces, the forest industry, the Canadian Council of Resource and Environment Ministers, the Canadian Forestry Advisory Council, forestry schools and non-government organizations have recently taken place. There has been agreement on findings regarding timber supply, market potential, research and manpower needs, the urgency of forest renewal and the formulation of a new forestry strategy. The key elements of this new approach relate to the application of intensive forest management and improved protection against forest fire, insects and diseases.

Intensive forest management means greater effort in such areas as site preparation, the use of genetically superior planting stock, prompt and effective planting after harvest or natural loss, thinning, fertilization, and weed control. Experience suggests that gains of 50-100% in wood volume are possible through application of intensive forest management. Improved protection against fire and pests is believed capable of reducing average annual losses by some 15%. Besides these potential benefits there is a recognized need for a program of timber-stand improvement, and for efforts to rehabilitate some of the inadequately stocked, burned and cutover productive forestland – estimated in 1977 to be close to 30 million ha. Given success in such management measures, there is hope of reaching the target harvest level of 210 million m^3 endorsed by the Canadian Council of Resource and Environment Ministers for the year 2000. Achievement of this goal would mean an increase of 65% over the 1982 harvest level.

Canada is necessarily moving out of an era of forest exploitation into one of intensive sustained renewal. Demands on the forestland base have increased to meet such legitimate developments as wilderness areas, parks, urban expansion, highways and reservoirs. However, if Canada, with a finite area of economically productive forestland, is to remain competitive in forest-products production, these demands cannot continue indefinitely and, more importantly, cannot infringe on land regarded as the best available for forest production.

It is possible to manage forestland for such diverse values as recreation, timber, water, forage, wildlife, fisheries and soil conservation, but it is not easy. A complex host of technical factors contribute to the difficulty, but the principal problems arise because people have not yet fully realized that the days of reaping unlimited, wide-ranging benefits are past. Unquestionably, most forestland belongs to the people of Canada, and it is right that their views and desires respecting its use be considered and accommodated to the point where the most desirable mix of economic, social and environmental goals is attained. Such judgements are ultimately the responsibility of Canada's governments. When these judgements are confirmed as essentially fair, wise and practical, forest management will have become integrated forest-resource management. *See also* TIMBER TRADE HISTORY.

C.R. STANTON

Reading: D. MacKay, *The Lumberjacks* (1978); C.R. Stanton, *Canadian Forestry – The View Beyond the Trees* (1976).

Forestry Education concerns training people in the science or art of managing forestlands and their renewable RESOURCES to ensure continuous production of forest goods and services. It draws on a number of basic disciplines (eg, BIOLOGY, MATHEMATICS, PHYSICS, CHEMISTRY, GEOLOGY, ECONOMICS) as they apply to such areas as the protection, harvesting, renewal, management and use of the forest and its products. Forestry education has 2 principal objectives: to train students at various levels to apply scientific knowledge to forestry problems and to make the general public aware of the importance of forests. Depending on the objective, forestry education involves a variety of groups, including universities, specialized schools and associations.

University Training

Undergraduate Training Canada's first efforts in forestry education were devoted to the university training of professionals. University of Toronto established the country's first faculty of forestry in 1907. By 1987 there were forestry programs also at U of New Brunswick, Laval U, UBC, University of Alberta, Lakehead U and U de Moncton.

Programs offered in Canadian universities were initially influenced by those in the US, which in turn drew upon European sources.

Objectives of Canadian university forestry programs are tailored to the qualifications needed to practise FORESTRY, labour-market requirements, new concepts such as multiple-use forest management, the growth of knowledge and, more recently, the needs of foreign countries. Initially, forestry schools were professional schools, training specialists.

Since training requirements are becoming increasingly complex and difficult to meet, academic experience has led Canadian forestry schools to abandon monolithic programs and to adopt others which meet the specific interests of students, while providing a common basic training that satisfies the profession. This delicate balance is frequently modified to meet new imperatives of the forest industry.

In the late 1980s in Canada, 400-500 men and women graduated in forestry each year. Under normal conditions, this number would be required to meet the country's basic needs, but intensive forestry would require more. Even in optimum economic conditions the Canadian situation is not comparable to that of several other forested countries. The US, with less forested land than Canada, has 10 times as many university forestry schools and graduates, a fact that reflects the status of forestry in the 2 countries. The continued intensive and multiple-use management in the US cannot, however, be compared with Canadian forestry, with its emphasis on forest harvesting. Many observers suggest that if Canadians wish to continue using their forests to advantage, they must soon change their attitudes toward a resource that, though at first judged inexhaustible, is now beginning to show signs of depletion. The movement toward increasingly intensive management should lead to an increased demand for professional foresters, which the Canadian university forestry schools should be able to meet, at least until the year 2000.

Postgraduate Studies are offered in 6 of the 7 Canadian university forestry schools. Nevertheless, despite what could have been a productive experiment, these schools have had trouble achieving their objectives in postgraduate studies. The transformation from professional schools to university faculties concerned with research has proved difficult. The domination of forestry research by the Canadian Forestry Service (CFS) has probably also slowed the growth of university research programs. Some professors, however, have qualified for grants from funding organizations such as the NATURAL SCIENCES AND ENGINEERING RESEARCH COUNCIL (NSERC), or from provincial agencies, eg, the Québec Researcher Training and Research Action Program. In 1981 NSERC created a special program to develop forestry research. Other provincial activities, such as the creation of a forestry research foundation in BC, are now being undertaken. To promote careers in forestry research, the CFS developed a grant program for university forestry schools in the 1960s. However, research positions were rare in the 1970s. Summer employment programs intended to introduce students to research have almost disappeared in the last few years, and candidates interested in careers in research have accepted high-paying jobs in the forest industries. As a consequence of these trends, Canadian universities awarded only 12-15 PhDs and 60-70 MAs each year during the 1970s and 1980s. Many of the graduates are foreign students who return to their own countries upon graduation.

These weaknesses in forestry training are having serious consequences at a time when Canadian forest renewal is beginning. Like the universities, research agencies such as CFS face serious problems in finding trained candidates to carry on the work. The Canadian Forestry Advisory Council indicated that in 1982 the development of postgraduate studies in forestry was the primary concern of forestry education in Canada.

Technical Training

For a long time in Canada, there has existed a level of forestry employment the training requirements of which are of a technical, trade or craft nature. These needs were eventually met by the creation of special programs. Apart from attempts made by U of T in 1918 and UBC in the early 1920s, Québec was the first province to establish a FOREST RANGER school (1923).

Today in Canada, about 20 schools, institutions and regional or community colleges offer courses in forestry techniques through 1-, 2- and 3-year programs. Other schools train forest technicians in programs concentrating on particular aspects of forestry, eg, WILDLIFE CONSERVATION AND MANAGEMENT. In the 1980s, about 800 students graduated annually. In difficult economic times, this number exceeds labour-market demand, but it might not meet requirements generated by recovery in Canada's forest sector.

While the content of technical training programs was being refined, programs dealing with forestry practice also became more specialized, particularly in forest operations (eg, training heavy-machinery operators, scalers) and in SAWMILLS (sawyers, wood graders). These courses (usually one year) are part of, or are run parallel to, the secondary level of technical training. In most technical programs, theoretical training is supplemented by practical work with commonly used equipment.

The need to improve forest production has resulted in increased demand for silvicultural workers to fill over 20 000 new jobs. This specific need is met, at the moment, by intensive on-site courses, especially for introductory and SILVICULTURE training programs which have resulted from government policies concerning private forests. New Brunswick's 1978-82 forest-employment program is a case in point. Programs to train the owners of woodlots are also provided through government advisory services and provincial forestry associations, alone or in conjunction with the Canadian Forestry Association. MARCEL LORTIE

The Forges St-Maurice interpretation centre evokes its predecessor's functions and nature under a protective contemporary structure. The exterior, shown here, attempts to suggest the outlines of vanished architectural features (*courtesy Gauthier, Guité & Roy*).

The Forges St-Maurice historical interpretation centre, interior view. The architects had to choose one version from 150 years of modifications, integrating artifacts among reconstructed forms (*courtesy Gauthier, Guité & Roy*).

Forges Saint-Maurice, Les (St Maurice Forges), Canada's first heavy industry. The St Maurice iron ore deposits near TROIS-RIVIÈRES were developed by the second company endowed with a monopoly grant (25 Mar 1730) and state subsidies, after an earlier company had failed. Iron production began in 1738 and continued more or less uninterruptedly until the forges closed in the late 19th century. Bankruptcy of the company's director, F.E. Cugnet, led to state takeover in 1742, and after the Treaty of PARIS (1763) ownership passed to the British Crown. The ironworks were then run by lessees, the most important being Matthew Bell in the years 1800-45. The most technically advanced ironworks in America in their first 100 years, the forges had long been obsolete when shut down in 1883. The plant employed over 100 specialized craftsmen and 300-400 labourers, and produced forged iron and molded products such as pots, pans and stoves. Experiments with steelmaking and cannon-founding in 1747 were not fruitful. The work force, originally from the iron-producing regions of Burgundy, developed as a distinctive community, living in Canada's first COMPANY TOWN. In 1973 the St Maurice Forges became a national historic park, and archaeological research continues on the site. *See also* IRON AND STEEL. DALE MIQUELON

Forget, Sir Joseph-David-Rodolphe, stockbroker, politician (b at Terrebonne, Canada E 10 Dec 1861; d at Montréal 19 Feb 1919). As a partner in the brokerage firm of his uncle, Louis-Joseph FORGET, Rodolphe Forget became actively involved in the affairs of the Montreal Street Rail-

way Co (later Montreal Tramways), and the Richelieu and Ontario Navigation Co, the Montreal Light, Heat and Power Co, Canada Cement and other companies. After the partnership with his uncle was dissolved (1907), he devoted himself to reorganizing the transportation and utility companies in Québec C, and to controversial attempts to sell the securities of the Quebec Railway, Light and Power Co in France. Although this company was modelled on Montreal Light, Heat and Power, it was far less successful and Forget had to call on government assistance during WWI. He was chairman of the Montreal Stock Exchange, 1908-11, a Conservative MP, 1904-17, and was created a knight bachelor in 1912.
T.D. REGEHR

Forget, Louis-Joseph, stockbroker, politician (b at Terrebonne, Canada E 11 Mar 1853; d at Nice, France 7 Apr 1911). Forget established his own brokerage firm in Montréal in 1873, dealing mainly in transportation and utility company securities. His main business interests included the Richelieu and Ontario Navigation Co, the Montreal Street Railway Co and several Montréal utility companies that were merged to form Montreal Light, Heat and Power Co. In the latter 2 ventures Forget was closely associated with Sir Herbert HOLT. Until 1907 he worked in partnership with his nephew, Joseph-David-Rodolphe FORGET. He was president of the Montreal Stock Exchange, 1895 and 1896, and was appointed to the Senate in 1896.
T.D. REGEHR

Forillon National Park preserves the dramatic coastline of the Gaspé Peninsula (*courtesy Environment Canada, Parks*).

Forillon National Park (est 1970, 238 km²) lies at the outer tip of the GASPÉ PENINSULA. Wild and beautiful, the park is a dramatic product of erosion. Its coastline is framed by soaring limestone cliffs, pebble beaches and rocks sculptured by the pounding sea. Rugged hills and gorges laced with tumbling streams lie inland. The park is covered mainly by boreal forest, but the limestone cliffs are characterized by tundra species. Wildlife includes deer, moose, lynx, black bear and red fox. Whales and seals can be seen from coastal cliffs. An estimated 220 bird species visit annually. Some, such as the herring gull, double-crested cormorant and black-legged kittiwake, nest in cliff-side colonies. The area was a traditional summer hunting and fishing ground for the MICMAC. Jacques CARTIER explored the region in 1534. French and English settlers arrived 200 years later and harvested cod, herring, mackerel and salmon – fish still abundant in surrounding waters. The park offers opportunities for outdoor recreation.
LILLIAN STEWART

Forrestall, Thomas DeVany, painter (b at Middleton, NS 11 Mar 1936). After graduating in 1958 from MOUNT ALLISON (where he studied with Alex COLVILLE), Tom Forrestall was assistant curator at the Beaverbrook Art Gallery in Fredericton (1959), but became a full-time painter the following year. His realistic works, often done in egg tempera, convey his ideas of the East Coast landscape and its dwellings. From the early 1960s, Forrestall experimented with panels shaped from triangles to T-forms, each chosen to fit his painterly ideas. He has also painted a large number of out-of-doors watercolours which express much the same ideas as his egg tempera works, but in a more relaxed and joyous mood. His watercolours, in contrast to his more metaphysical and individual canvases, form one long series and deal with a sense of place. He became an Officer of the Order of Canada in 1986.
JOAN MURRAY

Reading: P. Duval, *High Realism in Canada* (1974).

Forrester, Alexander, clergyman, educator (b in Scot 1804; d at New York C, NY 20 Apr 1869 and buried at Truro, NS). Ordained in the Church of Scotland, Forrester left it in 1843 to help establish the Free Church. In 1848 he immigrated to NS, serving the Free Church in Halifax before being named superintendent of education, and first principal of the Normal School in 1855. Like his predecessor John William DAWSON, he was a strong advocate of compulsory assessment, teacher training and a centralized system of education. Author of *The Object, Benefits and History of Normal Schools* (1855) and *The Teacher's Textbook* (1867), from 1858 to 1860 he edited and published the *Journal of Education*. Many of his proposals were incorporated in the free-school legislation passed by Charles TUPPER's administration in 1864-65. Forrester, an ardent Liberal, was replaced as superintendent, but continued as principal of the Normal School until his death.
WILLIAM B. HAMILTON

Forrester, Maureen, contralto, teacher, consultant (b at Montréal 25 July 1930). She first studied piano and then began singing in Montréal church choirs. At 20 she became a student of Bernard Diamant and at age 21 made a successful professional debut with the Montréal Elgar Choir. Assisted by a scholarship from the Ladies' Morning Musical Club and by J.W. MCCONNELL, who undertook to finance the first 2 years of her career, she made debuts with the Montreal Symphony Orchestra (*see* ORCHESTRE SYMPHONIQUE DE MONTRÉAL), CBC radio and TV, and the TORONTO SYMPHONY, and toured Ontario and Québec for JEUNESSES MUSICALES DU CANADA. Following her New York Town Hall debut in 1956 she became one of N America's most sought-after contraltos and over subsequent years performed with leading symphony orchestras and appeared in recital throughout N America, Europe, Australia, Israel, the USSR, China and Japan. From 1965 to 1974 she sang with Lois MARSHALL in the famous Bach Aria Group. Her operatic career, though successful, has been mostly limited to Canada and the US. Her teaching career included a series of workshops in China, filmed by the National Film Board. A superb musician, Forrester is comfortable in most of the contralto and mezzo literature, particularly the work of German composers, and her darkly rich voice inspired Canadian composer Harry SOMERS to write *Five Songs for Dark Voice* for her. Since 1984 she has been chairman of the Canada Council, an appointment that was an appropriate recognition of her concern for the arts in Canada. In addition to many national and international honours, she was made Companion of the Order of Canada in 1967 and received the Molson Prize in 1971. In May 1986 Forrester became chancellor of Wilfrid Laurier U. Her autobiography, *Out of Character*, appeared in Nov 1986.
MABEL H. LAINE

Maureen Forrester, contralto, photographed during a performance of "Dido's Lament" by Purcell for the CBC television series "The Music of Man" (*courtesy Canapress Photo Service*).

Forsey, Eugene Alfred, intellectual, senator (b at Grand Bank, Nfld 29 May 1904). A Rhodes scholar, Forsey was educated at McGill and Oxford, where he studied philosophy, politics and economics. By the time he became lecturer in the dept of economics and political science at McGill, his constitutional conservatism and social radicalism were firmly established. He worked for the CANADIAN LABOUR CONGRESS and became well known for his socialist politics; paradoxically, he was also close to Conservative Arthur MEIGHEN, whose views on the KING-BYNG AFFAIR Forsey found compatible. He published one influential study, *The Royal Power of Dissolution of Parliament* (1943), but he is best known for his innumerable debates and acerbic articles and letters on public affairs. He twice ran as a CCF candidate, but he refused to join the NEW DEMOCRATIC PARTY because of its policy of DEUX NATIONS. Appointed to the Senate, Forsey sat as a Liberal 1970-79 but left the party in 1982 after disagreements over constitutional amendments. Forsey also published *Trade Unions in Canada: 1812-1902* (1982) and, with J.A. Richardson and G.S. Kealey, *Perspectives on the Atlantic-Canada Labour Movement and the Working Class Experience* (1985). He was named to the Privy Council of Canada in 1985.
ROBERT BOTHWELL

Reading: Eugene Forsey, *Freedom and Order: Collected Essays* (1974).

Forster, John Wycliffe Lowes, portrait and landscape painter, writer (b at Norval, Canada W 31 Dec 1850; d at Toronto 24 Apr 1938). In 1869 he began studying portraiture in Toronto. He travelled to England and Europe in 1875 and 1879 and studied painting in Paris. He returned to Toronto to establish a permanent studio in 1883, and over the next few decades he exhibited locally and internationally.

The successor to G.T. BERTHON, Forster was among the most popular academic portraitists in Toronto during the late 19th and early 20th centuries. His sitters included Alexander Graham Bell, Bliss Carman, Timothy Eaton, and PMs Laurier, Macdonald and Mackenzie, among others. His commissions for the Ontario government included portraits of historical figures: James Wolfe, John Graves Simcoe, Isaac Brock and William Lyon Mackenzie. He is represented in the federal and Ontario parliamentary collections and numerous other public collections. His writings include 2 volumes of autobiography and a survey of early Ontario artists.
ROBERT STACEY

Forsyth, Lionel Avard, lawyer, industrialist (b at Mount Benson, NS 1 Aug 1890; d at Montréal 1 Jan 1957). Forsyth graduated from King's College (Windsor, NS) and attended Harvard before joining the BANK OF NOVA SCOTIA in 1913. After 18 months in Havana, Cuba, he became a professor of modern languages at King's. Forsyth taught himself law and was admitted to the NS Bar in 1918. In 1926 he left a successful Halifax law practice to join Montgomery, McMichael, Common, Howard and Ker in Montréal. There he developed a large corporate clientele and by 1946 was a director of over 40 companies. In 1950 he became president of Dominion Steel and Coal Corp, which employed one-sixth of Nova Scotia's work force. Forsyth rejuvenated the company, developing an ambitious and successful expansion program and establishing harmonious industrial relations. CHRISTOPHER G. CURTIS

Fort Amherst, on the W shore of Charlottetown Harbour, PEI, built in late 1758 by the British. The site had been known previously as Port La Joie, established 1720 as the capital of the French colony of Île Saint-Jean. During the SEVEN YEARS' WAR British troops captured Port La Joie in mid-Aug 1758, following the surrender of LOUISBOURG. With the end of hostilities Ft Amherst soon fell into disrepair, and in 1768 the garrison was permanently withdrawn to Halifax, the centre of maritime defence. Nonetheless, in 1799 a blockhouse and battery were erected near the site, although the major defence works were at Charlottetown. In 1967 Fort Amherst National Historic Park was created. ROBERT S. ALLEN

Fort Anne, situated at the junction of the S bank of the Annapolis R and Basin (Annapolis Royal, NS), was initially the site of the second French (Acadian) community of PORT-ROYAL. Captured by New England and British troops in 1710, the fort and town were renamed Fort Anne and Annapolis Royal after Queen Anne. As one of the oldest continuously occupied sites in N America, this settlement became the first capital of peninsular NS following the Treaty of UTRECHT (1713). For the next 40 years, the British at Fort Anne maintained a precarious position in the Acadian-dominated province and were frequently attacked by French and Indian raiding parties. The status of the fort declined with the founding of Halifax (1749) and the expulsion of the Acadians (1755). In disrepair, Fort Anne was transferred to the National Parks Service in 1917 and became one of Canada's first national historic parks. ROBERT S. ALLEN

Fort Battleford When the settlement of BATTLEFORD, in what is now W-central Saskatchewan, was named the capital of the North-West Territories (1876), the NORTH-WEST MOUNTED POLICE established a post to deal with anticipated native problems. Adjacent to the territorial government complex and a developing townsite, the fort consisted of about 10 buildings, including officers' quarters, a barracks, a storehouse, a workshop and stables. By 1880 a palisade enclosed the buildings in an area 145 by 155 m. During the NORTH-WEST REBELLION in the spring of 1885, the fort became a shelter for white settlers and an operations base for troops, as Métis and native insurgents sacked the Battleford townsite and farmsteads within the region. The post continued as a divisional headquarters and barracks until 1924. In 1951 the site became a national historic park, with many of the buildings restored or reconstructed for public visitation. MARK RASMUSSEN

Reading: A. McPherson, *The Battlefords: A History* (1967).

Fort Beauséjour, on the W bank of the Missaguash R near present-day Sackville, NB, built 1751-55 by the French as a counter to nearby British Ft Lawrence (near Amherst, NS). Ft Beauséjour was in poor condition in June 1755 when an attacking force of Massachusetts volunteers and British regulars laid siege. Within 2 weeks, and after suffering a direct hit on a "bombproof" shelter, French commander Louis Du Pont Duchambon de Vergor capitulated. The British renamed the site Ft Cumberland and strengthened the works. In Nov 1776, during the AMERICAN REVOLUTION, Ft Cumberland, under Lt-Col Joseph Goreham of the Royal Fencible Americans, thwarted an attack by New England colonial rebels. Some repairs were made to the fort at the beginning of the WAR OF 1812, and a military presence remained there until 1833. In 1926 Fort Beauséjour National Historic Park was established. ROBERT S. ALLEN

Fort Calgary, located at the junction of the Bow and Elbow rivers on the site of the present-day city of Calgary, was established in 1875 as a North-West Mounted Police post by Ephrem-A. Brisebois, one of the original officers of the force. Initially called Fort Brisebois, the name was changed to Fort Calgary in June 1876. As one of the most active police posts in S Alberta, Fort Calgary became a district headquarters; but the arrival of the railway in 1883 and the subsequent rapid growth and expansion of Calgary destroyed the post's reason for existing. Fort Calgary is now securely buried under city concrete. ROBERT S. ALLEN

Fort Carlton, situated on the S branch of the North Saskatchewan R near Duck Lake (Sask), was established in 1810 as an HBC fur trade and provision post. Initially called Carlton House, 2 previous posts had been located in the area in 1795 and 1804 before being abandoned permanently for the present location. Until 1882, Fort Carlton remained a particularly important fur-trade depot in western Canada. Near the site, Treaty No 6 (1876) was signed between the Plains and Wood Cree and the Dominion government. In Mar 1885, during the North-West Rebellion, the post was destroyed by fire. At present, the partly reconstructed Fort Carlton is a Saskatchewan provincial historic park. ROBERT S. ALLEN

Fort Chambly, est 1665 as Fort Saint-Louis by the French CARIGNAN-SALIÈRES REGIMENT on the Richelieu R near modern Chambly, Qué. By 1709 strategic considerations demanded that the site be strengthened, and a stone fort replaced the original wooden structure. Chambly subsequently became a warehouse and supply depot for other forts on the Richelieu. In Sept 1760 the crumbling and weakly defended Chambly surrendered to the British without a shot being fired. Early in the AMERICAN REVOLUTION, Chambly was captured by the colonial rebels, but in June 1776 the British reoccupied it, and for the rest of the conflict Chambly was not threatened. In 1813, during the WAR OF 1812, construction of a vast military complex was undertaken. Insufficient maintenance reduced Chambly to a dilapidated condition, and it was abandoned in 1851. Private restoration in 1882-83 preserved the site, which became Fort Chambly National Historic Park in 1921. ROBERT S. ALLEN

Fort Chipewyan, Alta, UP, pop 922 (1986c) 944 (1981c), was established for the NORTH WEST COMPANY in 1788 by Roderick Mackenzie, cousin of Alexander MACKENZIE. Situated at the hub of the Mackenzie R drainage system (Athabasca, Peace and Slave rivers), it became an entrepôt for northern and western exploration and the expanding fur trade. A fur-trade eldorado, Fort Chipewyan was the scene of fierce struggles between the NWC, the XY COMPANY and the HUDSON'S BAY COMPANY, which culminated in the HBC gaining control in 1821. Its significant role in the fur trade declined after the introduction of steamboats (*SS Grahame* was constructed at Fort Chipewyan in 1882-83). The Oblates of Mary Immaculate founded a mission in 1851, followed by the Anglicans in 1874. In 1898 the NWMP established a post, and Treaty No 8 was signed there in 1899. The oldest continuously occupied settlement in Alberta, Fort Chipewyan became a focal point of Peace-Athabasca Delta Project studies after the construction of the W.A.C. Bennett Dam. Inaccessible by road, the local community relies upon seasonal trapping and fishing, supplemented by employment in the nearby oil-sands plants and Wood Buffalo National Park. JAMES M. PARKER

Fort Churchill, *see* PRINCE OF WALES'S FORT; CHURCHILL.

Fort Duquesne, located at the confluence of the Allegheny and Monongahela rivers at the site of present-day Pittsburgh, Pa, was begun by the British in 1753. In Apr 1754 it was captured by the Sieur de Contrecoeur and the French completed construction. In 1755 Gen Edward Braddock and a powerful force were soundly defeated in an attempt to recapture the fort. The British recovered the site in 1758, but the French destroyed the fortifications before withdrawing. The site was renamed Ft Pitt and rebuilt by the British after 1761. It was unsuccessfully attacked by PONTIAC in 1763. JAMES MARSH

Fort Edmonton, was established on the N Sask R in 1795 by the HUDSON'S BAY CO as a fortified trading post next to the rival NORTH WEST CO which had earlier built its own fort nearby. After the amalgamation of the 2 companies in 1821, Fort Edmonton emerged as the leading centre of the Saskatchewan district fur trade. The fort was rebuilt on higher ground in 1830 – after severe flooding – near the present-day Alberta legislature building. From 1826 to 1853 the fort thrived under the management of the colourful John ROWAND and has been painted for posterity by Paul KANE (1846). After the HBC surrendered RUPERT'S LAND (1869-70), the fort gradually fell into decline and was dismantled in 1915. Today Fort Edmonton Park, located in SW Edmonton, features a reconstruction of the fort and, as a living museum, depicts the early development of Edmonton. The park is operated by the City of Edmonton and enjoys a yearly visitation of approximately 170 000. JAN SWITZER

Fort Ellice was a HUDSON'S BAY CO trading post located on Beaver Cr near the confluence of the Assiniboine and Qu'Appelle rivers, just E of the present-day Manitoba-Saskatchewan border. Established in 1831 by C.T. William Todd, the fort was intended to protect claims to HBC lands from venturing American interests, as well as to sell provisions such as pemmican, tools and traps to passing traders. The post was named after Edward ELLICE, an English MP and senior in the HBC's London Committee. In 1862, the modest installation was replaced by a larger and more elaborate structure, approximately 2 km E. This second provisional post, which retained the name of the first, included a large, 2-storey officers' quarters-reception hall, a row of smaller houses, stores and a workshop, all surrounded by a log palisade. After the 1870 Deed of Surrender transferring many HBC rights to the new national government, the fur trade in the West began to give way to general settlement, and this fort like many others became redundant. Today a historical marker stands near the site of this once-vibrant post. MARK RASMUSSEN

Fort Erie, Ont, Town, pop 23 253 (1986c), 24 096 (1981c), inc 1931, located at S entrance to

Peace Bridge across the Niagara R at Fort Erie, Ont, one of the busiest border crossings between Canada and the US (*photo © 1984 Hartill Art Associates, London, Ont*).

the NIAGARA R, opposite Buffalo, NY. Loyalists settled in the area in 1784, followed by German immigrants, but forts had guarded this strategic point since 1764. The village near the British fort of the same name amalgamated with the town of Bridgeburg, a railway centre, and became the town of Fort Erie, in 1931. The town is the site of one of Canada's largest horse-racing tracks; it also includes summer cottages and recreational communities along Lk Erie, eg, Crystal Beach, and is the S entrance to the Niagara R Parkway, as well as the terminus of the QUEEN ELIZABETH WAY from Toronto. Two early forts were destroyed by the powerful Niagara R, and the third was partly destroyed by American soldiers in 1814 – the last foreign troops to occupy Canadian soil. Today the Peace Bridge (1927) soars across the river and the town is one of the busiest border crossings between Canada and the US. JOHN N. JACKSON

Fort Frances, Ont, Town, pop 8870 (1986c), 8906 (1981c), inc 1903, located in northwestern Ontario at the W end of RAINY LAKE, where it drains into Rainy R. The river forms the boundary with the US and Fort Frances is linked by a bridge to International Falls, Minn. Located along the traditional canoe route to the western fur country, it was the site of Ft Saint-Pierre, which was constructed in 1731 by La Jemerais, LA VÉRENDRYE's nephew. The date of the establishment of Fort Lac La Pluie has not been determined, but it was used by the NORTH WEST CO after its establishment in 1776. Subsequently the HBC also established a post, which was named Fort Frances after the wife of the HBC governor, Sir George SIMPSON. As settlers were attracted to the western plains it became a staging post on the Dawson Route, an artery of lakes, rivers and wagon roads linking Lk Superior to Red R, inaugurated 1870. The turbulent falls at the site attracted milling activity and the town became a centre for sawmilling in the late 1800s. A hydroelectric dam was built 1905-10 to provide power for the paper mill. It is also at the hub of popular fishing and hunting country, and tourism is the town's second-largest employer. DANIEL FRANCIS

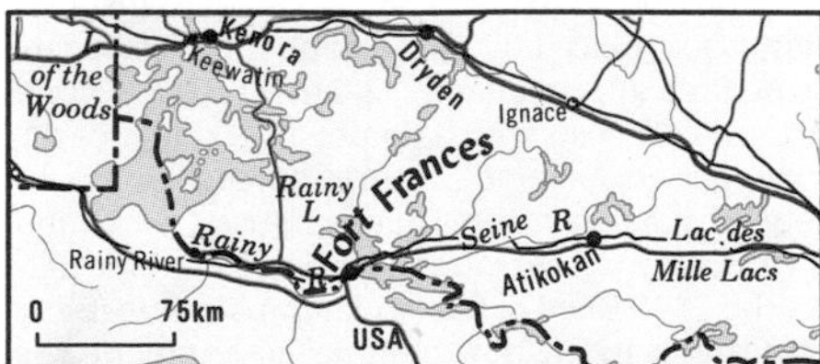

Fort Frances Case (1923) In 1917, under the WAR MEASURES ACT the government fixed the price and quantity of newsprint paper produced; subsequent legislation created the Paper Control Tribunal which set retroactive prices through 1919, although wartime conditions had ceased. In *Fort Frances Pulp and Power Co Ltd* v *Manitoba Free Press Co Ltd*, the JUDICIAL COMMITTEE OF THE PRIVY COUNCIL ruled that Parliament, because of its authority under the PEACE, ORDER AND GOOD GOVERNMENT clause of the CONSTITUTION ACT, 1867, may adopt a measure such as the War Measures Act and authorize the governor-in-council to enact orders-in-council concerning the control and supply of newsprint. The emergency power may outlive the duration of the conflict which gives rise to it; Parliament may adopt measures which normally would fall within provincial jurisdiction. GÉRALD-A. BEAUDOIN

Fort Franklin, NWT, Hamlet, pop 532 (1986c), 521 (1981c), is located about 10 km NE of the head of the Great Bear R, 544 air km NW of Yellowknife. Named after Sir John FRANKLIN, the settlement was a trading post for both the NORTH WEST CO and HUDSON'S BAY CO. The local DENE retained a nomadic life-style until about 1950 when the community became more settled with the establishment of a Catholic mission (tipi-shaped), a school and a store. Today the local residents still subsist mainly on hunting, fishing and trapping. ANNELIES POOL

Fort Frontenac was located at the mouth of the Cataraqui R, at the site of present-day KINGSTON, Ont. Construction began during negotations between Gov FRONTENAC and a delegation of Iroquois in July 1673. Ostensibly the fort, initially known as Ft Cataraqui, was meant to provide protection for Ville-Marie [Montréal], but it was intended as much to further fur-trading interests in the Great Lakes and Ohio Valley areas. After the Iroquois assault on Lachine in 1689, Gov DENONVILLE ordered the fort abandoned. When Frontenac returned to New France he revoked the order and the fort continued to serve French interests on Lake Ontario, acting as a counterpoise to the English Ft Oswego across the lake. In 1756, at the beginning of the SEVEN YEARS' WAR, Ft Frontenac was an arsenal and naval base for French forces on the Great Lakes. Reinforced by troops under François-Charles de Bourlamaque and later MONTCALM, it nevertheless fell to the British under John Bradstreet in Aug 1758. JAMES MARSH

Fort Garry, Lower, built 30 km down the Red R from Ft Garry [Winnipeg] during the 1830s as the HUDSON'S BAY CO's administrative centre for RUPERT'S LAND. It was hoped that the lower fort would be free from the spring flooding that beset the older community, and would house a more respectable class of citizen. But the original settlement was well located at the forks of the Assiniboine and Red rivers and even in the 1830s was developing as the natural centre of the RED RIVER COLONY. Although it never achieved the status originally intended, Lower Fort Garry served in a number of minor roles. During the Oregon crisis (*see* OREGON TREATY) in the 1840s, a British army contingent was stationed at the fort; in 1871 some opponents of Louis RIEL rallied around Stoughton Dennis there; and during the winter of 1873-74 the NORTH-WEST MOUNTED POLICE trained its first recruits at the fort. It later served as the first provincial penitentiary and as an insane asylum. In the early 20th century it was a residence for HBC officials, and thereafter was leased to a country club. In 1951 the HBC gave the property to the federal government. It was designated a national historic park and, after restoration carried out in the 1960s and 1970s, the fort is now one of the major HISTORIC SITES of Parks Canada. C.J. TAYLOR

Fort Garry, Upper, situated at the forks of the Red and Assiniboine rivers in the heart of the RED RIVER COLONY, was a HUDSON'S BAY CO post established in 1822. Previous fur-trade posts had been located periodically in the area. Severe flood damage in 1826 prompted the construction of a new post, Lower Fort Garry, 32 km downriver. In 1836, however, in order to facilitate the general administrative and supply needs of the settlement, the HBC returned to the forks and built a new fort, Upper Fort Garry, near the old site. This fort was seized by Louis Riel during the RED RIVER REBELLION of 1870. With the decline of the fur trade and the growth of Winnipeg, Fort Garry virtually disappeared. ROBERT S. ALLEN

Fort George, situated on the W side of the Niagara R at NIAGARA-ON-THE-LAKE, Ont, was built by the British between 1796 and 1799 as a replacement for FORT NIAGARA across the river, which was evacuated in accordance with the terms of the JAY TREATY. The new post also served as headquarters for the British Indian Department in Upper Canada. During the WAR OF 1812, Fort George fell to an overwhelming American naval and military force on 27 May 1813, after fierce resistance, but was retaken the following December. By the end of the war, with the battered Fort George tumbling into ruins, the British concentrated their defences for the Niagara area at the nearby Fort Mississauga. In the late 1930s, a reconstruction of Fort George was undertaken by the Niagara Parks Commission, and the restoration was officially opened to the public in 1950. Fort George was declared a national historic park in 1969 and receives 125 000 visitors annually. ROBERT S. ALLEN

Fort Good Hope, NWT, Settlement, pop 562 (1986c), 463 (1981c), is situated on the E bank of the MACKENZIE R, 805 air km NW of Yellowknife. Established by the NORTH WEST CO in 1805, it was the oldest fur-trading post in the lower MACKENZIE Valley. The settlement is known for its picturesque and unusual church, Our Lady of Good Hope, which was decorated with murals by a Catholic priest in 1878. In recent years the settlement has become known as the home of many DENE political leaders. The community has a school, and a hotel owned by residents. Most of the residents still trap, hunt and fish for their livelihood. *See also* HARE. ANNELIES POOL

Fort Haldimand, located on the W promontory of Carleton I at the E end of Lake Ontario, about 16 km offshore from Kingston, Ont, was built by the British in 1778 during the American Revolution. Established as a military and commercial base of operations for British forces, and particularly their Indian allies, Fort Haldimand was largely replaced by Oswego to the S in 1782. In the years immediately following the war, British and Loyalist activity in the area shifted to Cataraqui [Kingston], and Fort Haldimand soon fell into disrepair. Nonetheless, a token British presence remained, and 3 veterans surrendered to American troops in the first months of the War of 1812. Carleton I was formally ceded to the US in 1817. ROBERT S. ALLEN

Fort Henry, Kingston, Ont, originally built during the WAR OF 1812 on Pt Henry, beside Lk Ontario, to guard the outlet to the St Lawrence R and the Kingston Navy Yards. The strategic importance of the location increased after the completion of the RIDEAU CANAL, which provided a military supply route between Montréal, Bytown [Ottawa] and Kingston; the fortress was rebuilt in 1836, the better to defend the end of the canal most vulnerable to American attack. It was the principal fortress of UPPER CANADA, garrisoned by troops of the British army until 1870 and then by units of the Canadian Militia until 1890, when the fort was abandoned as a defensive structure. In both world wars it housed PRISONERS OF WAR. During the 1930s it was acquired by the Ontario government, which had it restored as a historic park as part of a Depression works project. Today, Old Ft Henry, a major historic attraction in a city that boasts many fine old buildings, houses a

Fort Henry's sunken, star-shaped pattern was typical of 19th-century fortifications. It was built during the War of 1812 and rebuilt in 1836 to defend the Rideau Canal (*photo by Malak, Ottawa*).

museum of military arms and equipment. During the summer the "Fort Henry Guard" demonstrates precision drill maneuvres. C.J. TAYLOR

Fort Langley, est 1827 on the Fraser R, 32 km E of Vancouver near present-day LANGLEY, BC, was important in the province's development until the post's abandonment in 1886. Part of a network of trading posts established by the HUDSON'S BAY COMPANY on the Pacific slope, it was initially a fur trade post but soon became a provisioning and administrative centre for the company's Columbia District. The old fort was abandoned in 1839 and a new one was built 35 km upstream. After a fire, it was rebuilt in May 1840. The fort operated a large farm, initiated fish packing and became a commercial centre for the colony of British Columbia. By the time it became a national HISTORIC SITE in 1923 its buildings were crumbling. But beginning in 1955 several buildings were reconstructed, and Ft Langley is now an important tourist attraction. C.J. TAYLOR

Fort la Reine is the name used for a series of early French fur-trade posts located W of Winnipeg on the Assiniboine R. The original fort was established in 1738 by Pierre Gaultier de Varennes et de LA VÉRENDRYE and his sons, independent fur traders and explorers. The log fort was the La Vérendrye headquarters for a series of expeditions into the Canadian prairies in quest of the rumoured "Western Sea." It was also a natural portage point from the southern water route of the native people and French traders to Lake Manitoba and the North. While historical records indicate the fort being abandoned, burned and rebuilt at least twice over a few decades, its exact locations and dates are in some question. Although there is evidence that the first post was near the present-day community of Poplar Point, its traditional location is generally acknowledged as being near Portage la Prairie, approximately 25 km SW. In 1928 a federal plaque was erected to commemorate Fort la Reine's history, and a reconstructed post was built just E of Portage la Prairie. MARK RASMUSSEN

Fort Liard, NWT, Settlement, pop 395 (1986c), 405 (1981c), is located on the S bank of the LIARD R, 544 air km SW of Yellowknife and about 25 km N of the BC border. One of the oldest continuously occupied aboriginal sites in the NWT, the area has been used as a fishing camp by Indian cultures for about 9000 years. As late as 1966, most of the DENE residents still lived the traditional life-style and spent winter months away from the settlement and on the trapline. Today, trapping and hunting are combined with a wage economy. The community was isolated until the opening of the LIARD HIGHWAY in 1983. ANNELIES POOL

Fort Macleod, Alta, Town, pop 3132 (1986c), 3139 (1981c), inc 1892, is located on the Oldman R, 165 km S of Calgary. In Oct 1874, 150 North-West Mounted Police established the first police post in present-day Alberta on an island in the Oldman R, and named it after Asst Commissioner James F. MACLEOD. Annual flooding forced the post's move to the present site 10 years later. It was the headquarters of the force 1876-78, a divisional centre to 1919 and thereafter a subdivisional headquarters. The centre from which the whisky trade was wiped out in the southern plains, Fort Macleod was a judicial seat and the scene of several famous trials, including that of CHARCOAL, arrested for the murder of an NWMP sergeant. Even as it declined as a police centre, Fort Macleod continued to function as a regional distribution point for a ranching and farming hinterland. Today, tourism is a major industry. The Fort Museum (a reconstruction of the original fort) and the heritage buildings located on the main street attract 60 000 visitors annually. FRITS PANNEKOEK

Fort McMurray, Alta, City, pop 34 949 (1986c), 31 000 (1981c), inc 1947, as a city 1980, is located near the confluence of the Athabasca and Clearwater rivers in northeastern Alberta. A former NWC post, it was rebuilt in 1870 and named after HBC Factor William McMurray. It functioned primarily as a fur-trade post and transportation centre connecting Edmonton to the Athabasca country. The horse and sternwheeler were critical to its survival until 1922 when the railway reached Draper, 12.8 km S. Several fish plants and a salt-extraction industry developed thereafter. During WWII the town was an important base for the CANOL project. Fort McMurray is located in the 31 000 km^2 oil sands, said to contain an estimated 3.9 billion m^3 of recoverable synthetic crude oil. Experimentation in oil recovery and its impact on the town's economy date from the early 20th century. In 1964 the Great Canadian Oil Sands project was given permission to start construction and modern Fort McMurray was born, growing from 1200 people that year to 10 000 by the mid-1970s. The population had more than tripled by 1987. The Fort McMurray area was hit severely by the slump in world oil prices in 1986. However, although it experienced labour disputes, strikes and lockouts that year, the oil industry still managed to maintain and even better production levels. Having now shed its "boom-town" image, Fort McMurray is a modern, vibrant city, complete with college facilities and a thriving cultural and artistic community. FRITS PANNEKOEK

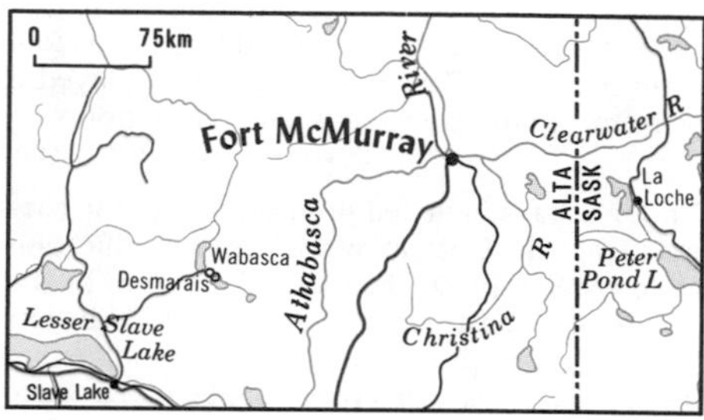

Fort McPherson, NWT, Settlement, pop 760 (1986c), 632 (1981c), is located on the E bank of the Peel R, 1107 air km NW of Yellowknife. Named for an HBC trader, the settlement has been a Loucheux DENE village since 1852, when Dene moved there because the site commands an excellent view of the MACKENZIE R Delta. It is the home of Chief John Tetlichi, who became the first Dene member of the NWT Territorial Council in 1967, and Wally Firth, who was elected in 1972 as the first native MP. Although the community has now been influenced by the construction of the DEMPSTER HIGHWAY and oil exploration, the Loucheux inhabitants maintained an independent bush life-style well into the 1960s. ANNELIES POOL

Fort Malden (Fort Amherstburg), situated on the E side of the Detroit R at AMHERSTBURG, Ont, was built by the British between 1796 and 1799. Initially the post served as a major garrison, naval base and key centre for the British Indian Department in western Upper Canada. During the WAR OF 1812, Fort Malden was headquarters for the Right Division of the British army. The post was abandoned in Sept 1813, owing to the American control of the upper lakes following the Battle of PUT-IN-BAY (Lake Erie). Reoccupied and partly rebuilt by the British after the war, Fort Malden gradually declined in importance, and although there was a brief flurry of activity during the 1837-38 period of political unrest, regular troops were withdrawn in 1851. Declared a national historic park in 1941, Fort Malden receives about 100 000 visitors annually. ROBERT S. ALLEN

Fort Michilimackinac (Mich), refers to 3 distinct military posts at the Straits of Mackinac. French explorers arrived in 1634, establishing a fort on the N shore of the straits in 1690 (St Ignace, Mich). A new stockade was erected on the S shore (Mackinaw City, Mich) about 1715 and held until the arrival of British troops in 1761, during the SEVEN YEARS' WAR. Captured by the Chippewa during the PONTIAC uprising of 1763,

Michilimackinac was reoccupied a year later. The post was moved to nearby and more secure Mackinac I (Mich) during the American Revolution and was ceded to the US in 1796. British forces from FORT ST-JOSEPH, on St Joseph's I (Ont), captured Michilimackinac in 1812, during the WAR OF 1812, thereby gaining control of the North-West until the post was again returned to the US in 1815. Fort Mackinac, as the island post is more commonly called, was a major fur-trading centre until the 1830s and was garrisoned until 1895. Today the second and third forts are open to the public as museums. BRIAN LEIGH DUNNIGAN

Reading: E.O. Wood, *Historic Mackinac* (1918).

Fort Nelson, BC, Village, pop 3729 (1986c), 3724 (1981c), inc 1971, is located in the NE corner of BC, 410 km N of FORT ST JOHN. W.F. Wentzell of the NORTH WEST CO sent George Keith to establish a post here in 1805, and it was re-established by the HBC in 1865. The area has grown rapidly in recent years through new developments in the forest industries and renewed interest in local petroleum and natural-gas resources. Services for the transportation sector are also part of the local economy. Completion of the BC Rail extension from Fort St John in 1971 played a large role in the area's subsequent expansion. ALAN F.J. ARTIBISE

Fort Niagara, situated on the E side of the Niagara R at Lake Ontario, was a French fortification from 1678 to 1759. The site is highlighted by the 1726 stone-constructed "French Castle." The fort surrendered to the British in July 1759 following a siege and the wilderness battle of La Belle Famille. During the American Revolution, Fort Niagara was the major British supply depot for the Loyalist provincial corps, John BUTLER'S Rangers, and Indian allies. Garrisoned by American troops from 1796, Fort Niagara was captured by British and Canadian forces in Dec 1813 during the WAR OF 1812. Returned to the US in 1815, the fort remained a peaceful border post. Old Fort Niagara, restored 1927-34, is a New York state historic site operated by the Old Fort Niagara Assn. About 120 000 people visit annually. ROBERT S. ALLEN

Fort Norman, NWT, Settlement, pop 332 (1986c), 286 (1981c), is located at the junction of the MACKENZIE R and Great Bear R, 624 air km NW of Yellowknife. Because of its location at a river junction, the site has always been of seasonal importance to the Slavey DENE. Sir John FRANKLIN used it as a transportation centre for his explorations into the region. A notable feature is the Anglican church, built of squared logs in the 1860s. The trapping life of the Dene is supplemented by employment in the oil industry at nearby NORMAN WELLS. ANNELIES POOL

Fort Pitt Founded in 1830, Fort Pitt was the major HUDSON'S BAY CO trading post between Forts Edmonton and Carlton (Sask), located at a large bend in the N Saskatchewan R just E of the modern Alberta-Saskatchewan border. It was one of 2 principal points for signing Treaty No 6 in 1876. On 14 and 15 Apr 1885, during the NORTH-WEST REBELLION, Chief BIG BEAR'S Cree band besieged the fort. After a skirmish in which a policeman was killed, the Indians permitted the fort's North-West Mounted Police detachment to flee downriver and then took the civilian occupants prisoner and looted the post. BOB BEAL

Fort Prince of Wales, *see* PRINCE OF WALES'S FORT.

Fort Providence, NWT, Settlement, pop 588 (1986c), 605 (1981c), is located on the NE bank of the MACKENZIE R, 233 air km SW of Yellowknife. Local Slavey DENE were attracted to this community after a Roman Catholic mission was built by Father Grolier in the 1850s. In 1867 the Grey Nuns established a boarding school for Dene children, and an HBC trading post, RCMP and federal government departments followed soon after. Prior to the 1950s, when an all-weather road was built, access was limited to river or air. Today the Yellowknife Highway, between Hay River and Yellowknife, passes within 6 km of the community, which is also the site of a Mackenzie R ferry crossing. The Dene residents still practise the traditional hunting and trapping life-style, combined with a wage economy, and Fort Providence is the centre of a renaissance of traditional crafts, notably moosehair tufting and porcupine quill weaving. ANNELIES POOL

Fort Qu'Appelle, Sask, Town, pop 1915 (1986c), 1827 (1981c), inc 1951, is located 70 km NE of Regina in the scenic Qu'Appelle Valley. Named for the QU'APPELLE R, Fort Qu'Appelle was the hub of several historic trails that traversed the North-West. An Anglican mission was established there in 1854, and 10 years later the HBC erected a provisioning post and district headquarters. The Cree and Saulteaux signed Treaty No 4 at this site in 1874, and a year later a NWMP outpost was established near the present townsite. In 1881 Chief SITTING BULL and a party of Sioux warriors travelled to Fort Qu'Appelle to secure provisions and negotiate with Supt James WALSH. The fort was chosen by General MIDDLETON as a temporary headquarters and base of operations for his troops on the way to BATOCHE during the NORTH-WEST REBELLION (1885). Though it lost out to Regina in a bid to succeed BATTLEFORD as the territorial capital in 1882, the town has prospered through the exploitation of its considerable recreational potential and benefited from the mixed farming that predominates in the area. GARTH PUGH

Fort Reliance, YT, is an abandoned post, established in 1874, located on the E bank of the YUKON R, 13 km downstream from DAWSON. It remained the centre of the FUR TRADE and mining on the upper Yukon R for more than a decade. In 1886 a gold discovery drew miners to the mouth of the Stewart R, and when a new post was built there, the buildings at Ft Reliance were dismantled and used for fuel on riverboats. Many of the creeks and settlements on the Yukon, such as FORTY MILE, were named for their distance from Ft Reliance. H. GUEST

Fort Resolution, NWT, Settlement, pop 447 (1986c), 480 (1981c), is located on the S shore of GREAT SLAVE LK, 153 air km S of Yellowknife. This community, where trapping still provides the livelihood for the majority of DENE and MÉTIS residents, dates back to the establishment of the NORTH WEST CO trading post in 1786. The HBC established a post in 1815, and when the companies united in 1821, the post was called Fort Resolution. The community became an important medical and educational centre when the Oblates and Grey Nuns built a large tuberculosis hospital there in 1938-39. When the responsibility for the care of TB patients was transferred to Edmonton in 1956, Fort Resolution began to decline in importance as a regional centre. The traditional hunting-trapping economy of the community was diversified in 1964 with the construction of a local sawmill; however the nearby Pine Point Mines closed 1986-87. ANNELIES POOL

Fort St James, BC, Village, pop 1983 (1986c), 2284 (1981c), inc 1952, located in central BC 50 km N of Vanderhoof on the SE shore of Stuart Lake. Part of the territory of the Carrier of the DENE people, Fort St James is the oldest, continuously inhabited community in BC. It was founded in 1806 by Simon FRASER as a NORTH WEST CO post. The fort was the administration centre for northern and central BC, then called NEW CALEDONIA, until 1857. The fur trade had declined by the 1880s and 1890s, and Fort St James did not expand substantially until the extension of the BC Railway through the village in the late 1960s. The railway spurred mining and forestry industries in the region, and sawmills are the economic base, along with tourism and some mining. Some of the buildings dating from the 1890s have been preserved as a national historic site (1971). The oldest Catholic church in BC, Our Lady of Good Hope, is situated on Stuart Lake and numerous petroglyphs are to be found in the area. JOHN R. STEWART

Fort St John, BC, City, pop 13 355 (1986c), 13 891 (1981c), inc 1975, is located in northeastern BC, about 500 km N of Prince George. In 1793 Alexander MACKENZIE reached a point on the Peace R south of here. A series of forts were established during the fur-trading era, and over the years the community has moved from one side of the river to the other. Towards the end of WWI and into the 1920s, settlers moved westward to the fertile agricultural lands on both sides of the Peace R. Population increased greatly after completion in 1942 of the Alcan Military Road. The discovery of oil S of the city in 1951 attracted more people and turned the town into a BC oil exploration centre. Fort St John has since become the largest centre in BC north of Prince George, with a trading area population of 26 000. Agriculture, forestry, and the oil and gas industry are the basis of the expanding local and regional economy. Taylor, an incorporated community just S of the city, is the site of a refinery, a sulphur plant, natural gas and oil pumping stations, and a large sawmill. The city's facilities include a campus of Northern Lights Community College. ALAN F.J. ARTIBISE

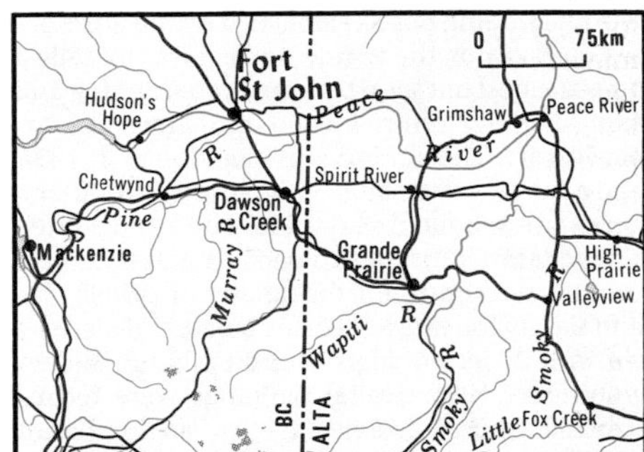

Fort St-Joseph, situated on the SE tip of St-Joseph I at the eastern entrance of the channel linking Lakes Huron and Superior, was established by the British in 1796. The fort was strategically located to preserve both British fur-trade interests and the loyalty of Indian allies in the North-West. In July 1812, during the opening weeks of the WAR OF 1812, the American post at Michilimackinac (Mackinac I) was captured in a surprise attack, spearheaded from Fort St-Joseph. With the British based at Michilimackinac for the duration of the war, the vacated St-Joseph was burned by enemy forces. Following the war, the British did not reoccupy St-Joseph, although the island was not formally evacuated until 1829. An historical archaeological program at Fort St-Joseph has been ongoing since the early 1960s. ROBERT S. ALLEN

Fort Saskatchewan, Alta, City, pop 11 983 (1986c), 12 169 (1981c), inc 1985, is located 30 km NE of EDMONTON on the prairie parklands adjacent to the N Saskatchewan R. While the fur trade flowed through the region as early as the 1790s, and pioneering French Canadians began farming in the area in 1872, the community really started with the establishment of a North-West Mounted Police post in 1875. Inspector W.D. Jarvis was said to have chosen the spot over competing Edmonton because of its gentler banks for a future railway crossing and avoidance of Hudson's Bay Co lands. Although the fort was originally known as Sturgeon Creek Post, it was later renamed Fort Saskatchewan. During the 1880s, extensive surveying took place for both the expanding urban settlement and surrounding river lot farmlands. The CNR line reached the town in 1905 and built the bridge Jarvis had envisaged years earlier. WWI brought on the decline of the Mounted Police post. In 1952, Sheritt Gordon Mines Ltd built the community's first major industry, a multimillion-dollar nickel refinery, and this later gave rise to both a significant fertilizer plant and in 1966 the Sheritt Mint for coins and medallions. Today, these plants, the provincial jail and a thriving service component support one of Alberta's oldest settlements. MARK RASMUSSEN

Reading: P.T. Ream, *The Fort on the Saskatchewan* (1974).

Fort Selkirk, YT, is an abandoned settlement located at the confluence of the YUKON R and Pelly R. Formerly Yukon headquarters of the HBC (established in 1848 by Robert Campbell), and after 1898 of the YUKON FIELD FORCE, it was abandoned permanently after the completion of the Alaska and Klondike highways brought an end to commercial traffic on the Yukon R. H. GUEST

Fort Simpson, NWT, Village, pop 987 (1986c), 980 (1981c), inc 1973, is located on an island at the confluence of the MACKENZIE and LIARD rivers, 378 air km SW of Yellowknife. The original fort, called Fort of the Forks, was built by the NWC in the early 1800s; in 1821 it was named after HBC governor Sir George SIMPSON. The oldest continuously occupied trading post on the Mackenzie, the community in the late 1960s became a base for oil exploration and a NWT government administration centre. It is the terminus of the NWT highway system. The mixed native-white population is employed in government, the transportation industry or traditional hunting and trapping activities. Pope John Paul II visited here 20 Sept 1987, 3 years after his first Canadian visit. ANNELIES POOL

Fort Smith, NWT, Town, pop 2460 (1986c), 2298 (1981c), inc 1966, is located on the SW bank of the SLAVE R near the Alberta-NWT border, 724 air km N of Edmonton. Situated on the river that was an important link between the Prairies and the MACKENZIE R valley, the site was a PORTAGE route around 3 sets of rapids. The HBC established a trading post here in 1874. The post was named in honour of Donald SMITH, later Lord Strathcona, an HBC governor and member of the first NWT Council. The settlement was affected by the Yellowknife GOLD RUSHES when prospectors rushed through the area. Fort Smith was the first administrative centre in the NWT and served as government headquarters until the territorial capital was established in Yellowknife in 1967. Today the town's residents depend on trapping, tourism and government employment for their livelihood. ANNELIES POOL

Fort Steele, BC, UP, pop 118 (1986c), 100 (1983e), is located at the junction of Wild Horse Cr and the Kootenay R, 17 km NE of Cranbrook. The Wild Horse gold rush opened the area to settlement in 1863. An estimated $9 to $20 million was taken out of creeks in the area. Prospectors found a black stallion, giving rise to the original name "Stud Horse Creek." A second rush for gold in 1884 led to friction between miners and Kootenay Indians. Sam STEELE and the North-West Mounted Police were brought in, and they built the post named Fort Steele. After 1904, when the railway bypassed it to make Cranbrook the region's principal centre, Fort Steele became a ghost town. In the 1960s the province made the town a heritage site and reconstructed it on an 1880s theme. Tourism and some ranching are the area's chief enterprises. WILLIAM A. SLOAN

Fort Walsh, in the Cypress Hills of SW Saskatchewan, was constructed in 1875 and played a vital role in preparing the West for peaceful settlement (*photo by Jim Merrithew*).

Fort Ticonderoga (Carillon), a "place between the waters," is strategically situated at the confluence of Lakes Champlain and George in upper New York. Built by the French in 1755 to protect CROWN POINT and the route to Canada, the Battle of Ticonderoga, in which the Marquis de MONTCALM smashed a superior British attacking force, was fought here in July 1758. The French abandoned Ticonderoga the following year. In May 1775, during the early stages of the American Revolution, the fort was taken without a struggle by colonial rebels. The British briefly reoccupied Ticonderoga in 1777 but withdrew later that year after the surrender of Gen John BURGOYNE at Saratoga, NY. Since about 1820, the Pell family has owned and administered Fort Ticonderoga, and it has been generally restored to its 18th-century appearance. ROBERT S. ALLEN

Fort Vancouver A HUDSON'S BAY CO fur-trade post, it was originally constructed in 1825 by Dr. John McLoughlin about 150 km inland on the N bank of the Columbia R, 8 km above the mouth of the Willamette. In 1829, the site was shifted closer to the Columbia, about 2 km W of the old fort. The newer structure is Fort Vancouver, the remains of which were unearthed and are now a historic monument in Vancouver, Wash. Strategically located to protect British interests, it was the company's Columbia district headquarters, and all trading and shipping operations W of the Rockies were directed from it. The fort was enclosed by a large stockade and was self-supporting, with farming, fishing and sawmilling being developed adjacent to it. The OREGON TREATY of 1846, which placed the fort in American territory, forced the company to transfer its depot to FORT VICTORIA in 1849, eventually abandoning the fort in 1860. DENNIS F.K. MADILL

Reading: J.A. Hussey, *The History of Fort Vancouver and its Physical Structure* (1957).

Fort Victoria In 1842, James DOUGLAS of the Hudson's Bay Co selected the Port of Camosack (the harbour where Victoria now stands) as a new fur-trade post – eventually to replace FORT VANCOUVER as the company's Pacific headquarters and to bolster the British claim to Vancouver I. Known first locally as Fort Albert, the original intention was to name the site Fort Adelaide, but on 10 June 1843 it was officially christened Fort Victoria. The OREGON TREATY of 1846 effectively terminated Fort Vancouver as Columbia district headquarters, and in 1849 it was superseded by Fort Victoria. The crown colony of Vancouver I was also established in 1849 and Richard Blanshard, who became its first governor in 1850, resided at Fort Victoria. Victoria townsite was surveyed adjacent to the fort in 1851-52 and during the Fraser gold rush of 1858 its population soared. Fort Victoria eventually became an anachronism and by 1864 its last remnants had disappeared. DENNIS F.K. MADILL

Reading: D. Pethick, *Victoria: The Fort* (1968).

Fort Walsh, located in the CYPRESS HILLS, 170 km SW of present-day Swift Current, Sask, was an early North-West Mounted Police post constructed in 1875 by men under the command of Insp James WALSH, for whom it was named. It became headquarters of the force in the West in 1878, and until it was dismantled and abandoned (1883), Fort Walsh played a vital role in preparing the Canadian West for peaceful settlement. A bustling frontier town sprang up near the fort. Following the Custer massacre (1876), the Mounted Police centered on Fort Walsh were called upon to mediate with refugee Sioux who had followed Chief SITTING BULL across the US border, thereby creating an international incident. With the coming of the railway, the signing of treaties and the return of the Sioux to the US in 1881, Fort Walsh was abandoned. In 1942 the RCMP established a remount ranch to breed and raise horses for the force. In 1968 the property was transferred to Parks Canada and became a national historic park. GARTH PUGH

Fort Whoop-Up, situated at the junction of the Oldman and St Mary rivers, near present-day Lethbridge, Alta, was established in 1869 by John J. Healy and Alfred B. Hamilton of Montana for the sole purpose of gaining a quick profit through an illicit trade in whisky with the native people of the unpoliced southern prairies of western Canada. Initially called Fort Hamilton, which was burned by the Blackfoot after one trading season, a second and larger fort was built in 1870 and named Whoop-Up. This was the most formidable and notorious of the several American whisky posts located in southern Alberta, and the entire area became known as "Whoop-Up country." The whisky posts were abandoned with the arrival of the North-West Mounted Police in 1874. In succeeding years, Fort Whoop-Up served as an outpost for the force. *See also* WHOOP-UP.

ROBERT S. ALLEN

Fort William In 1803 the NORTH WEST COMPANY constructed a new fort at its Lk Superior headquarters, replacing GRAND PORTAGE, which had come under US jurisdiction. At the mouth of the Kaministiquia R some 50 km N of the international boundary, the new depot served until 1821 as the site for the NWC's annual summer rendezvous of Montréal agents and WINTERING PARTNERS, and as its major transshipment point for furs and trade goods. Named in 1807 after NWC chief superintendent William MCGILLIVRAY, Ft William occupied a pivotal place in the company's vast trading network. In 1816-17 Lord SELKIRK occupied Ft William for 10 months as a consequence of the SEVEN OAKS INCIDENT. This occupation, combined with major financial difficulties, led to the NWC merger with the HUDSON'S BAY COMPANY in 1821. With the Montréal transportation system virtually abandoned in favour of the HBC's, Ft William lost its importance in the FUR TRADE. As a post and fishing station of the HBC, it gradually declined until its closure in 1883. In 1902 its last standing structure, the NWC's Stone Store, was demolished to make way for the CPR's expanding grain and freight shipping facilities. The only reminders of Ft William's fur-trade past now at its original site are the local historical society's cairn, unveiled 1916, the Historic Sites and Monuments Board's marker, erected 1981, and neighbouring street signs bearing the names of renowned NWC and HBC fur traders.

Prompted by the community's active interest in Ft William's role as gateway between East and West, and also by the recognized potential of heritage attractions for tourism, the Ontario government decided in 1971 to reconstruct Ft William to the NWC period. Known as Old Fort William, the reconstruction is located in Thunder Bay, Ont, at Point de Meuron, 14 km upriver from the original site. Through its costumed staff, the fort's living historical program depicts the activities of the rendezvous, the annual gathering of Scots traders, French Canadian VOYAGEURS and Indian trappers. It also portrays the fur-trade society and material culture of the early 19th century. Other facilities include an interpretive centre, a resource library, a gift shop, a historic-food outlet and programs for schools and special-interest groups.

JEAN MORRISON

Fort William was constructed in 1803 to replace the NWC post of Grand Portage. Until 1821 it was the pivotal transshipment point for furs and trade goods. The present reconstruction is located in Thunder Bay, Ont, 14 km upriver from the original site (*courtesy Ontario Ministry of Tourism and Recreation*).

Fort William Freight Handlers Strike, by 700 nonunionized immigrants, occurred 9-16 Aug 1909. Greek and Italian strikers engaged Canadian Pacific Railway police in a protracted gun battle on Aug 12, whereupon Col S.B. STEELE restored order using the local militia and the Royal Canadian Mounted Rifles from Winnipeg. A federal conciliation board granted a satisfactory settlement, but in 1910 the CPR fired its 400 southern European employees.

JEAN MORRISON

Fort York [Toronto] was sacked twice by the Americans during the War of 1812 (*courtesy National Archives of Canada/C-40091*).

Fort York, situated on the N shore of Lake Ontario at Toronto, was built in 1793 by the Queen's Rangers under Lt-Col John Graves SIMCOE, first lieutenant-governor of Upper Canada. The fort was to provide for the defence of the naval arsenal and new town of York, which replaced Newark (Niagara-on-the-Lake) as the provincial capital. Attacked twice during the WAR OF 1812 by American amphibious forces, on 27 Apr 1813 and again in Aug, Fort York was left in a ruinous state. In the late 1830s, a new fort was begun just to the W of the original site, the centre of which was the "Stanley Barracks." Yet "Old" Fort York remained active throughout the years, and was eventually restored in 1934 in conjunction with the centennial of the city of Toronto. The site is administered by the Toronto Historical Board and receives about 90 000 visitors annually.

ROBERT S. ALLEN

Forteau, Nfld, Community, pop 580 (1986c), 520 (1981c), inc 1971, is a fishing and services centre on Forteau Bay in southern Labrador, 25 km across the Str of Belle Isle from insular Newfoundland. Its name likely derives from the French *fort* ("strong"), referring to the bay's strong winds. A major site of Maritime Archaic Indian, Montagnais and Inuit habitation from 7000 years ago, Forteau was used by BASQUE whalers, and later by French, English and Newfoundland fishermen from the late 1500s. A garrison fort was erected in Baie Forteau 1710, and the bay was a base for the French migratory fishery; after the British were granted Labrador in 1763, Jersey and British merchant firms took over the fishery. In 1857 the Pointe Amour navigational light, the tallest (33 m) in Newfoundland and Labrador, was built, and remains today. A GRENFELL Mission nursing station opened 1909 and a Grenfell boarding school by 1939. The first high school on the Labrador coast opened there in 1964. The modern town, still dependent upon the fishery, services much of the southern coast of Labrador.

JANET E.M. PITT AND ROBERT D. PITT

Reading: J.A. Tuck, *Newfoundland and Labrador Prehistory* (1976).

Fortier, Paul-André, dancer, choreographer (b at Waterville, Qué 29 Apr 1948). A strong, unsettling presence, Fortier emerged from the cradle of Montréal indépendantiste dance, Groupe nouvelle aire, in the mid-1970s. Given the Jean A. Chalmers Award for choreography in 1981, he founded his own company, now Fortier Danse-Création. His choreographies, ranging from *Derrière la porte un mur* (1978) to *Le mythe décisif* (1987), comment on society, using sex and violence as a metaphor for power. His style oscillates between post-modern minimalism and the hard-edged German expressionism of the 1930s. He taught literature and theatre at Granby 1971-75 and dance at Concordia and UQAM 1981-82.

KATI VITA

Fortification, a barrier thrown up between a defender and his assailant, its sophistication depending mainly upon the skills of the defender and the weapons available to the assailant, and whether the structure is permanent or a temporary defence. The earliest fortifications probably consisted of felled trees, interlaced thornbushes or stones rolled together. Fortifications of this type were built by the Huron and other Iroquoian groups before the arrival of the Europeans. Among Europeans these primitive forms eventually developed into walls of earth, timber, stone or baked brick. Although the barrier posed by these walls was sometimes increased by setting a ditch below their outer faces, fortification did not progress beyond this rather simple conception until the 16th century. The chief reason for the lack of innovation is that the main agent of assault continued to be infantry, to which a good wall was a formidable barrier, while such infantry-support weapons as the battering ram or machines for throwing stones posed relatively little threat to solid walls. The technological breakthrough of the late 15th century was artillery, and the early modern revolution in fortification was a response to this new threat. Gunpowder first appeared in Europe in the 14th century, but it was not until the 15th century that tubes using it to launch projectiles were effective. From the late 15th century, when several Italian fortresses fell to French artillery, defensive designs changed rapidly.

Early modern fortresses used elements of medieval defences but builders covered them against artillery fire by sinking the complexes into the ground. A deep ditch in front of a low wall remained a barrier to infantry while offering a smaller target to artillery. The earth from the excavation was piled on the outer side of the ditch in a long slope which further reduced the target area of the wall and also slowed charging infantry. Although there were refinements, these were the basic elements of the new fortifications, and the star-shaped designs of the central complex allowed every point of the fortified perimeter to be swept by the defenders' guns.

Both medieval and early modern fortification styles were built in Canada, the choice depending upon whether a place would have to face artillery. Artillery was used only by Europeans, and – because of the cumbersome nature of early guns – the only fortifications built for defence against artillery were normally those near water transportation routes accessible to Europeans. Thus, the PORT-ROYAL habitation built by CHAMPLAIN in 1605 in Acadia – the earliest European fortification in America N of the Spanish settlements – is but a few connected buildings huddled around a court, presenting solid blank walls on the outside. However, the small complex is embellished with a little walled battery for light guns facing the water. Champlain built a similar structure at Québec in 1608. The choice of style was determined more by location than by the period during which construction took place: simple palisaded strongpoints were constructed well into the 19th century in the West, whereas LOUISBOURG, built on Cape Breton I in the second quarter of the 18th century, is the most highly developed example of early modern fortification in N America.

In NEW FRANCE most forts were built on the Lake Champlain-Richelieu R invasion route (*see* FORT CHAMBLY), although fortified trading posts were built deep in the interior (*see* FORT DUQUESNE); later, in UPPER CANADA, the focus was on the threatened Niagara frontier (*see* NIAGARA HISTORIC FRONTIER). Around 1800 the British built high, round stone towers to strengthen the ports of Halifax and Saint John (*see* MARTELLO TOWER). In the North-West, simple wooden palisades sufficed except at PRINCE OF WALES'S FORT on Hudson Bay and at Upper and Lower Fort Garry (*see* FORT GARRY, LOWER and FORT GARRY, UPPER) on the Red R, where stone walls were built as protection against attack.

The WAR OF 1812 ended in a stalemate, thanks in part to British naval power on the Atlantic and Lake Ontario, and the RUSH-BAGOT AGREEMENT of 1817 severely limited warships on the Great Lakes and Lake Champlain. Because the US, with a 10-to-one population advantage over British North America, had a greater potential to build ships in the interior, the British government built the RIDEAU CANAL so that gunboats could be rushed from the Atlantic to vital Lake Ontario; and elaborate stone forts in sunken star-shaped patterns were built at Kingston (FORT HENRY) where the Rideau Canal would reach Lake Ontario, at Île-aux-Noix where the Richelieu R flows out of Lake Champlain, at oft-besieged Québec City (*see* QUÉBEC CITADEL) and at Halifax, the Royal Navy's N American base (*see* HALIFAX CITADEL).

View of Louisbourg from a warship, as it would have appeared in 1744. Painting by Lewis Parker (*courtesy Fortress of Louisbourg National Historic Park and Lewis Parker*).

A technological revolution in warfare in the mid-19th century upset long-established assumptions about the relative strengths of attack and defence. Ironclad enemy steamships, firing conical shells from rifled cannon, might suddenly destroy the Royal Navy in its bases. Britain reacted by overstressing coast defences, first at Portsmouth and Plymouth and then in British North America. When the AMERICAN CIVIL WAR briefly renewed the possibility of war with the US, the British government undertook major new forts in Bermuda and Halifax and at Lévis, opposite Québec City.

With a half dozen new batteries, Halifax harbour was fortified on a scale to resist the combined fleets of the world. An example shows the rapid evolution of the fort-maker's art. In the early 1860s the lower (and thus more vulnerable) battery on Georges I was remodelled to give its rifled, muzzle-loading cannon protection behind iron-shielded, stone portholes in thick earthworks. In the late 1880s York Redoubt's guns were remounted in circular concrete pits to permit all-round fire and placed behind gently sloped parapets designed to deflect, rather than to resist, incoming shells. In the early 1890s Halifax began the changeover to breech-loading guns, and a complete rearmament took place 1898-1906.

In 1905-06 the Canadian government took over the British fort at Halifax and a similarly defended one at Esquimalt, BC. As the 20th century progressed, the range of artillery batteries became but one element in an integrated harbour-defence system which included mines, submarine nets and aircraft. During WWII Canada built a new system of modern coastal forts at Esquimalt, Prince Rupert, Vancouver, Halifax, Sydney, Saint John and a number of Newfoundland ports. Since WWII self-propelled missiles and atomic warheads have created a technological revolution necessitating another reappraisal of techniques of defence. *See also* ARMAMENTS.

G.A. ROTHROCK AND C.S. MACKINNON

Reading: L.F. Hannon, *Forts of Canada* (1969).

Rendezvous of the North West Company (1805), engraving by an unknown artist. Fort Kaministiquia (which was renamed Fort William in 1807) was the hub of the NWC's activity. Similar fortified posts were strung out across the North-West (*courtesy National Archives of Canada/C-24733*).

Fortin, Marc-Aurèle, painter, engraver (b at Ste-Rose, Qué 14 Mar 1888; d at Macamic, Qué 2 Mar 1970). Fortin's work, devoted entirely to landscape, demonstrates his love for a rich and bountiful nature. His brush transforms heavy clouds, thick foliage and rising hills into large, free forms, vibrating with colour. Despite studying in the rather conservative setting of the École du Plateau with Ludger LAROSE, the Monument national with Edmond DYONNET (1904-08), and at the Chicago Art Institute (1908-14), he developed a modern view of rural subjects. The Laurentian lowlands, the Montréal suburbs, the Charlevoix region and the Gaspé Peninsula in turn attracted his attention. Only relatively late in life did this solitary painter receive limited recognition: the Jessie Dow Award (Art Assn of Montreal, 1938), associate of the Royal Canadian Academy of Arts (1942) and a retrospective exhibition at the Musée du Québec (1944). Fortin remained unfathomable for most of his contemporaries. His prolific production, experimentation with various media and personal vision of nature have established him as a pioneer of modern art in Québec.

LAURIER LACROIX

Fortin, Maxime, parish priest, editor, Catholic union organizer (b at St-Aubert, Qué 17 Mar 1881; d at St-Jean-Port-Joli, Qué 4 Aug 1957). A dominant figure in Catholic unionism in Québec, Fortin was a founding member and first chaplain (1921-32) of the Canadian Catholic Confederation of Labour (CCCL), chaplain of the Québec City Catholic Labour Council, and a professor at Collège Ste-Anne-de-la-Pocatière. Involved in resolving Québec's social and economic problems, he was director and editor of *L'Action catholique* and l'Association catholique de la jeunesse canadienne française. Fortin established Cercles d'études des ouvriers at Québec to build an elite to propagate the church's SOCIAL DOCTRINE to workers and to organize confessional national unions. He organized workers and helped the CCCL obtain federal government recognition. Fortin pragmatically endorsed strikes, strike funds and closed shops; but he warned that workers were not "docile sheep" and was against class struggle, sweetheart contracts and management's intransigence towards unionization. *See also* CONFEDERATION OF NATIONAL TRADE UNIONS. F.J.K. GRIEZIC

Fortin, Pierre-Étienne, politician, surgeon, conservationist (b at Verchères, LC 14 Dec 1823; d at La Prairie, Qué 15 June 1888). After graduating from the Petit Séminaire de Montréal (1841) and McGill Coll (1845), he practised medicine at GROSSE ÎLE (1847-48). As the first magistrate responsible for protection of fisheries in the Gulf of St Lawrence 1852-67, he initiated early conservation efforts, provided early faunal studies, promoted new marine initiatives, and sought greater rights for Canadian fishermen. He represented Gaspé in the Commons 1867-74 and 1878-87 and in the Québec legislature 1867-78, serving as commissioner of crown lands 1873-74 and Speaker 1875-76. His efforts helped initiate fire protection, forest conservation, the Baie de Chaleurs Ry, and portions of telegraph, postal and lighthouse services for the Gaspé. He was appointed to the Senate in 1887. MARTIN K. MCNICHOLL

Fortune, Nfld, Town, pop 2370 (1986c), inc 1946, is located on the W end of the Burin Pen at the mouth of Fortune Bay. Its name, dating from the early 1500s, probably commemorates some fortunate – or unfortunate – occurrence. Situated near the Grand Banks, it and the nearby harbour of Grand Bank were likely utilized by a series of Portuguese, French and English fishermen throughout the 17th and 18th centuries. When English settlers were forced to leave French Saint-Pierre after the Treaty of PARIS (1763), many settled in the area of Fortune, only 50 km from the island. During the 19th century, the inshore and bank fisheries continued to attract settlers and shipbuilding grew in importance. In this century, furniture manufacturing and wholesale and retail businesses have added to the local economy, which is still primarily based on fishing and fish processing. A regular ferry service operates between Fortune and Saint-Pierre. ROBERT D. PITT

Forty Mile, YT, is an abandoned settlement on the YUKON R named for its distance from FORT RELIANCE. Gold was discovered in the area, and in 1887 A. Harper and L. McQuesten built a store at the mouth of Forty Mile R. William C. BOMPAS opened an Anglican mission the same year, and a rival store opened 1893. The 2 posts formed the nucleus of a thriving community which served several thousand miners until their exodus to the KLONDIKE in 1896. H. GUEST

Forty-ninth Parallel is the line of latitude that forms the boundary between Canada and the US from LAKE OF THE WOODS to the Str of GEORGIA. The section from Lake of the Woods to the summit of the ROCKY MTS was agreed to in the CONVENTION OF 1818, and that from the Rockies to the Str of Georgia in the OREGON TREATY of 1846. As ultimately surveyed and demarcated, the boundary actually consists of several chords drawn between astronomically determined points on the curved parallel. The parallel also forms the first baseline for the Dominion Lands Survey System by which the territory that became the provinces of Manitoba, Saskatchewan and Alberta and some adjacent parts of British Columbia and Ontario was subdivided. It and the baselines every 24 miles (38.6 km) N of it are E-W survey control lines which are run as 6-mile (9.6 km) chords to curved parallels of latitude. N.L. NICHOLSON

Cutting along the 49th Parallel, near the right bank of the Moyie River in southern BC, looking west, 1860-61 (North American Boundary Commission) (*courtesy National Archives of Canada/C-78979*).

Forward, Frank Arthur, engineer, educator, inventor (b at Ottawa 9 Mar 1902; d at Vancouver 6 Aug 1972). Known internationally for his metallurgical-process discoveries, Forward was also a prominent educator and science administrator. Forward taught and conducted research at UBC from 1935 to 1964, serving in WWII as technical director of the War Metals Research Board. In the 1950s he invented and developed a highly successful process for leaching NICKEL and other metals from sulphide ores, an achievement that brought him international recognition and many honours. Director of the Canadian Uranium Research Foundation in the 1960s, Forward was also president of both the Canadian Council of Professional Engineers and the Canadian Institute of Mining and Metallurgy. In 1964 he became the first director of the Science Secretariat of Canada (a Privy Council office) where he helped to formulate a SCIENCE POLICY for Canada. JOHN LUND

Fosheim Peninsula, about 10 230 km^2, on western ELLESMERE I, is bounded S to NE by Bay Fjord, Eureka Sound, Greely and Cañon fjords. The northwestern part is low and undulating, but low mountain ranges in the E reach 1295 m, dotted with small ice fields and glaciers. Protected on all sides by mountain ranges, the peninsula is relatively sheltered and supports a polar semidesert. Arctic hares are periodically abundant; muskoxen are common, but caribou are scarce. The peninsula was sighted by A. Greely of the US Army in 1881, but was first explored in 1899 by the expedition led by Otto SVERDRUP, who named it after a member of his party, Ivar Fosheim. S.C. ZOLTAI

Fossil [Lat *fossilis*, "dug up"], trace of an ancient animal or plant preserved in the Earth's crust. PALEONTOLOGY is the modern, scientific study of fossils, but these curious objects have attracted attention since ancient times. Opinions were divided as to whether they were relics of once-living creatures, or were random results of processes without any particular significance. A few original thinkers deduced that not only were they products of ancient life but that they also recorded the former distribution of land and sea. The Greek scholar Herodotus concluded that the presence of marine shells in the interior of Egypt demonstrated that the area had been inundated in former times. In the 16th century, Leonardo da Vinci not only accepted fossils as relics of former life but also argued, from their presence high in the mountains, that there had been profound changes in the level of the sea. Glimpses of the true meaning of fossils were offered by the 17th-century English physicist Robert Hooke, who suggested that fossils recorded changes in climate and succession of life.

The great breakthrough that established fossils as the chroniclers of GEOLOGICAL HISTORY was made independently, early in the 19th century, by William Smith in England and Georges Cuvier and Alexandre Brongniart in France. They discovered that a distinct succession of fossils exists in stratified layers of SEDIMENTARY ROCKS. They also noted that while deposits of the same age carry the same kinds of fossils, rocks of different ages carry different fossils. Study of the succession of fossils in rock layers (biostratigraphy) provides a basis for establishing a history of the Earth. By 1842, the broad divisions of geological time had been defined for Europe and for N America, and much detail had been worked out on local sequences of rock formations and their fossil contents. L.S. RUSSELL

Fossil Animals The first animals were microscopic in size and left no known FOSSIL remains. The oldest animal fossils occur in sediments deposited under shallow equatorial seas over 600 million years ago. Probably less than 100 species are known, most being jellyfish and leaflike, soft corals. These fed on microscopic organisms filtered from seawater, while less abundant, wormlike animals sifted organic debris from soft sediments on the seafloor. The most important fossil sites in the Western Hemisphere, both for their great age and the relatively deepwater environments they represent, are located on the Avalon Peninsula, Nfld.

By 500 million years ago, primitive jointed-legged animals (eg, TRILOBITES) were abundant in the seas, together with small, shelled animals and primitive, noncoralline, reef-forming organisms. The BURGESS SHALE, a UNITED NATIONS WORLD HERITAGE SITE in Yoho National Park, has yielded superbly preserved fossils of archaic soft-bodied animals, buried in fine-grained mudstones at the base of a tropical algal reef. Approximately 140 species have been identified at this site alone, including antecedents of backboned animals. It is the most diverse fauna known for this time. The nutrient-rich coastal margins of shallow equatorial seas provided a centre of origin for new kinds of marine animals, which usually displaced the more primitive forms toward the ocean basins. Accordingly, about 450 million years ago, the trilobite faunas were displaced by shallow-water communities dominated by primitive corals, lamp shells, sea lilies and straight-shelled MOLLUSCS. Their fossil remains are found in flat-lying marine limestones, shales and sandstones throughout Canada.

An extinction interval occurred approximately 435 million years ago, coinciding with the spread of continental ice sheets over what has become the Sahara Desert, and the withdrawal of shallow seas from the continents. However, representatives of most major groups of marine organisms survived and repopulated the seas. The Hagersville, Ont, site containing large, shallow, marine shellfish is dated at 380 million years old.

A symbiosis between FUNGI and green ALGAE gave rise to the land plants, which spread across fertile deltas and coastal lowlands 410 million years ago. Terrestrial arthropods also appear in the record at this time. About 350 million years ago, a brackish water lagoon near Miguasha, Qué, was the burial site of outstandingly preserved specimens of about 2 dozen species of lungfish and lobe-finned fishes. Among them are the remains of the oldest known amphibians. Another profound extinction of unknown cause occurred shortly thereafter.

By 300 million years ago, the major groups of marine animals were again highly diverse. The oldest, truly terrestrial, backboned animals were lizardlike reptiles, whose skeletons are preserved in still-standing hollow tree trunks, buried in sediments now exposed in the sea cliffs near Joggins, NS. These reptiles fed on arthropods, initiating an ecological relationship between the 2 major groups of terrestrial animals which has continued to the present. Backboned animals did not begin to feed directly on land plants until 20 million years later. From this period on, the number of major groups of terrestrial animals was at least half that of major groups of marine animals. Fossils of primitive, mammallike reptiles estimated to be about 275 million years old are found on ancient semiarid deltas at Charlottetown, PEI.

The greatest recorded mass extinction occurred about 230 million years ago. It has been estimated that 90% of marine animal species disappeared, and major groups were unable to regain their former importance. Land animals were reduced similarly. The extinctions have been linked to the coalescence of continental blocks into a single super-continent, although the brevity of these extinction intervals is seen by some to be incongruent with ponderous continental movements. Marine faunas, hereafter, were characterized by an abundance of molluscs, arthropods and bony fishes; on land, large reptiles close to the ancestry of mammals were replaced by reptiles related to crocodiles. As during other extinctions, small insectivorous, backboned animals did not seem to suffer as greatly as many of their larger relatives. Another, less severe, extinction occurred 195 million years ago. Crocodilelike terrestrial faunas were then replaced by communities dominated by mammals and DINOSAURS. Mammals were small during the period of dinosaurian ascendancy and probably possessed high metabolic rates in relation to their body size. These rates enabled insectivorous mammals to match activity levels sustained by INSECTS as a consequence of their still smaller body size. Primitive BIRDS, descended from small carnivorous dinosaurs, are also presumed to have had high metabolic rates. Conversely, herbivorous dinosaurs became large, in part as a result of economies gained by a relative decrease in the effort required for locomotion and a reduced basal metabolic rate associated with increased body mass. They were energy-efficient browsers of bulk vegetation. The largest and most diverse assemblage of dinosaurs known is represented by skeletons preserved in the badlands of DINOSAUR PROVINCIAL PARK, Alta, another UN World Heritage Site. More than 300 specimens belonging to 31 species have so far been collected. The wealth of fossil materials has served as a basis for studies on dinosaurian ecology of about 75 million years ago.

About 65 million years ago, a mass extinction abruptly eliminated the dinosaurs and an estimated three-quarters of then living species. The extinctions are associated with a chemical anomaly in the sediments of the time which suggests the impact of an asteroid. The Marine molluscs, arthropods and bony fishes soon regained and surpassed their former levels of diversity. By 50 million years ago, Earth had ceased to be predominantly a water world, as many vital substances were captured and retained in terrestrial ecosystems. Birds and mammals diversified on land, their generally smaller body sizes favouring the existence of a larger number of species than was the case in dinosaurian faunas. Fossils of early mammals, turtles and crocodiles in warm, broadleaf forests estimated to be about 50 million years old occur on Ellesmere Island, NWT. In the Cypress Hills, Sask, an abundant and diversified fauna of large, fossil mammals (about 35 million years old) occurs. The ancestors of man appeared in equatorial regions of Africa and Asia about 3 million years ago. In the OLD CROW BASIN, YT, 25 000-30 000-year-old fossils of Ice Age mammals and early man are found in unglaciated terrain.

During the past 400 million years, arthropods have dominated land faunas in number of species and individuals, and in the volume of organic material consumed. This domination is now being challenged by one uniquely successful species of backboned animal, *Homo sapiens*, which has acquired a highly complicated brain giving it an enormous selective advantage.

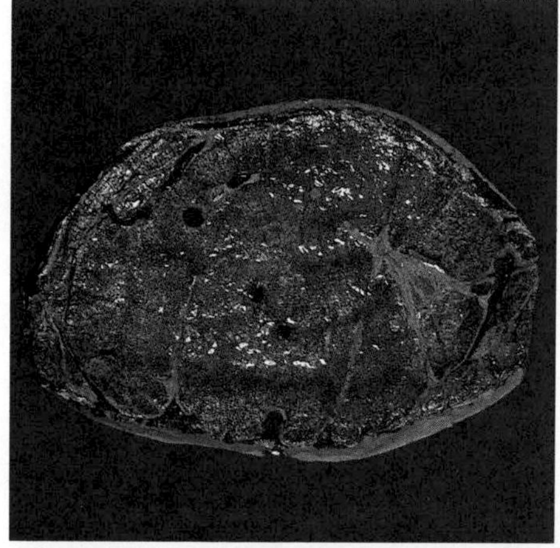

Placenticeras ammonite with bite marks from a mosasaur reptile, from 70 million years ago (Cretaceous), southern Alberta (*courtesy Brian D.E. Chatterton*).

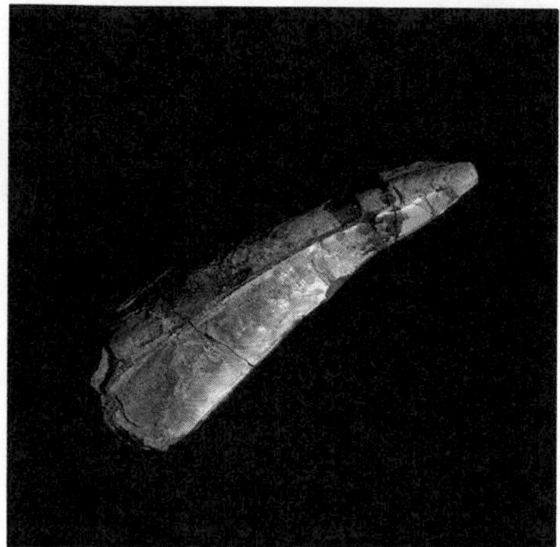

Pinna curvimarginata marine clam, from 70 million years ago (Cretaceous), southern Alberta (*courtesy Brian D.E. Chatterton*).

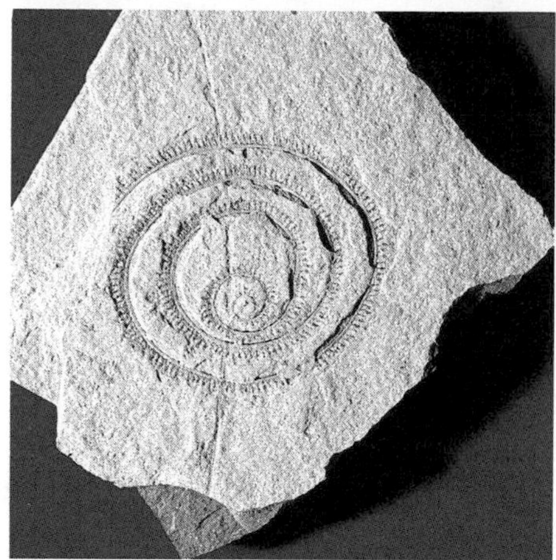

Monograptus spiralis, a marine pelagic graptolite from 428 million years ago (Silurian), the Canadian Arctic (*courtesy Brian D.E. Chatterton*).

Longusorbis cuniculosus, a crab from 75 million years ago (Upper Cretaceous), Vancouver (*courtesy Brian D.E. Chatterton*).

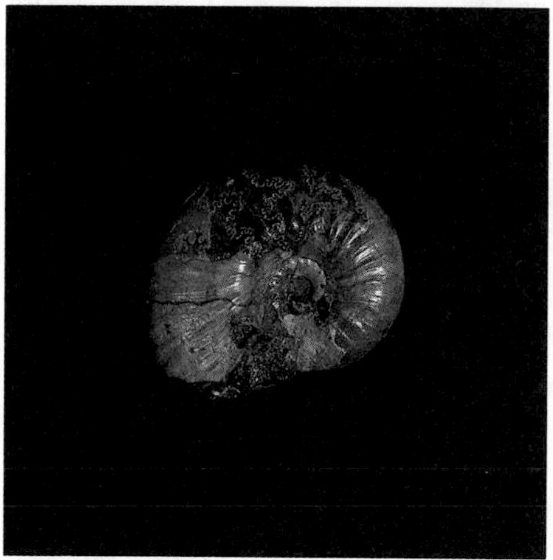

Beaudenticeras, marine ammonite from marine shales of the Cretaceous from 100 million years ago, northern Alberta, Peace River country (*courtesy Brian D.E. Chatterton*).

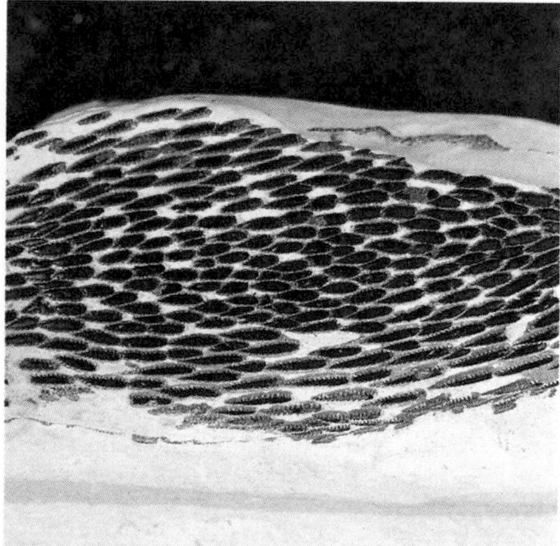

Traquairaspis scales from the head of a marine ostracoderm fish from 420 million years ago (Silurian), Mackenzie Mountains, NWT (*courtesy Brian D.E. Chatterton*).

The fossil record retains an enormous amount of unexplored and interesting information on the EVOLUTION of animal life. It can reveal the physical or biological conditions that will produce evolutionary stagnation or evolutionary acceleration. The record will provide the means to measure the progress of trends such as the differentiation of primitive, segmented worms into more complex organisms such as butterflies and birds; the development of simple communities dominated by archaic jellyfish into the intricate animate realms of modern coral reefs; and the appearance of similar structures in unrelated animals (eg, the brain in an octopus and an owl). The record will also have important implications for the study of the evolution of animate organisms in extraterrestrial worlds. It will show whether mass extinctions stimulate evolution toward higher levels of animal complexity or the converse. The record of animal life on Earth should provide a framework for projecting its evolution into the next few million years. In a general way, the specialization of

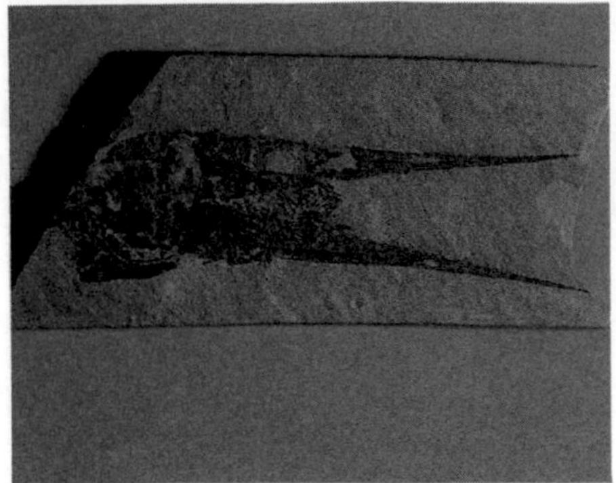

Open jaws of *Saurichthys* with smaller fish stuck in jaws from 235 million years ago (Triassic), eastern BC. Head about 40% of length (*courtesy Brian D.E. Chatterton*).

animal structures and multiplication of animal species have been stimulated by competition in the struggle for existence. Thus the rate at which the number of animal species increased, over periods of tens of millions of years, has been approximately proportional to the number of species in existence. The total number of species present on Earth, accordingly, tends to grow ever more rapidly. In a similar manner, humanity's most valuable competitive asset, its brain, has evolved according to a pattern that suggests that the rate of increase in brain size is proportional to brain size. This implies that competition between individuals of our species generates the selective pressure in brain evolution, and increase in brain size should continue. A long-term trend toward an increase in the variety and complexity in animal life has been interrupted periodically by shorter intervals marked by severe extinctions. The causes of individual mass extinctions may differ. Mankind is clearly implicated in the extinctions that began toward the end of the last ICE AGE (10 000 years ago) and which continue today. After earlier mass extinctions, the few surviving organisms soon differentiated into an array of different species, which developed many modifications of the successful ancestral body plan. Perhaps our species is the primitive stem of a new kind of animal, the intellectual qualities of which will differentiate and expand into another array of different and increasingly complex animals in the history of terrestrial life. DALE A. RUSSELL

Fossil Plants Paleobotany is the study of ancient plant life using FOSSIL evidence. "Plant" refers to familiar land plants, and also to aquatic plants, MOSSES, LIVERWORTS and ALGAE. Although not plants, FUNGI and BACTERIA are often included. The first organisms to evolve on Earth resembled bacteria. They consumed organic molecules from which they themselves originated and molecules formed by the combination of carbon dioxide, water and nitrogen, accumulating since oceans first formed. These organisms reproduced rapidly and, over millions of years, devoured all available food. Greater success required the EVOLUTION of plants – organisms capable of manufacturing their food using sunlight and inorganic molecules. The simplest living photosynthesizers are BLUE-GREEN ALGAE, which now live in nearly every environment and, in some aquatic habitats, produce stromatolites – mounds composed of layers of sediment. The earliest signs of life are 3.5-billion-year-old cells in carbonaceous cherts from western Australia which resemble modern blue-green algae. Stromatolites 3.2 billion years old have been found in Africa. The Canadian SHIELD contains stromatolites more than 2.5 billion years old. On the shores of Lk Superior, near Kakabeka Falls, stromatolites and the microscopic organisms that grew on them 1.9 billion years ago have been preserved in silica; these organisms compare closely with living blue-green algae. Their description, by E.S. Barghoorn and S.A. Tyler in 1965, startled geologists and biologists. Although the presence of life on the early Earth had been hypothesized, proof of its existence had been lacking. These fossils, the first indisputable evidence that life existed at such an unimaginably distant time, initiated investigation of Precambrian algae around the world.

Throughout most Precambrian time, Earth was dominated by blue-green algae and bacteria; complex algae and animals appeared less than 1 billion years ago. Complex life forms appeared so late in part as a result of the chemistry of life. Free oxygen (O_2) is necessary for the aerobic (oxygen-requiring) metabolism common to all living plants and animals (excluding anaerobic blue-green algae and bacteria). Ancient Earth was oxygen-poor, so most modern life forms could not exist. The origin and maintenance of free oxygen on Earth derives from plant photosynthesis. The oxygen produced by early blue-greens quickly reacted with elements (eg, iron, to produce rust). Algae literally had to "rust" Earth for 2 billion years before oxygen began accumulating in the air and oceans. Transition from anaerobic to aerobic conditions occurred near the close of the Precambrian. Evolution then proceeded, fueled by the fires of aerobic metabolism, at a great and seemingly ever-increasing rate. Survival of such ancient organisms as blue-green algae is due to their remarkable adaptability in an ever-changing world, and to the ever-present place in the environment for such small and simple life forms.

The fossil record of higher algae is poor, except for lime-secreting red algae and green algae. Since Cambrian time, these algae have been important in the construction and cementation of reefs. The Leduc, Swan Hills and Rainbow Lk reefs of Alberta form natural reservoirs for some of Canada's oil.

Invasion of land by plants from an aquatic environment occurred late in the Silurian period, about 410 million years ago. Water, of prime importance to living things, is easily available to aquatic organisms, but ancestors to land plants had to develop water-conserving features for survival out of water: cuticle, a waterproof waxy coating; roots or other underground organs for absorbing water; a conducting system for water transport; and watertight reproductive bodies. With life possible on land, a vast, new habitat was available to any algal group overcoming the water barrier. Many must have tried; only 2 succeeded, both evolving from green algae: bryophytes (mosses and liverworts); and vascular plants, with internal woody tissue for support and water movement. Since the initial colonization of land in the Silurian, no new groups of land plants have evolved from algae. Competition with pre-existing, increasingly well-adapted groups became too severe. Bryophytes, bound to a life-style and structure that keep them small, are usually fragile, and seldom occur as fossils. Mosses and liverworts first appear in Devonian rocks. Forty-five-million-year-old fossil mosses from BC are very similar to living mosses, suggesting that many species of bryophytes are ancient and evolve very slowly. Vascular plants have been the dominant land vegetation for over 400 million years and have been continually evolving in response to climatic and environmental change. Evolution of new, extinction of old, and survival of well-adapted forms is the recurrent theme.

The earliest vascular plants, the rhyniophytes, were small, naked, simply branched, without roots or leaves. They gave rise to 2 groups in the early Devonian: zosterophylls, usually covered by soft spines; and trimerophytes, tending to complex branching and a shrubby habit. Well-preserved fossils of all 3 early Devonian groups are found at famous fossil plant localities at Gaspé and Chaleur bays (Qué and NB, respectively) and the Abitibi R near James Bay, Ont. These fossils provide much information about plant structure and evolution. J.W. DAWSON first examined them and recognized their significance. His discovery of these strange, leafless plants was largely ignored; none believed such a world existed. Dawson persevered, however, and is now recognized as the founder of Devonian paleobotany.

Several new groups of land plants evolved in the middle to late Devonian. Zosterophylls gave rise to plants with leaves which evolved from spines: CLUB MOSSES and giant scale trees (Lepidodendrales). The trimerophytes left by far the greatest number of descendant groups: HORSETAILS, with whorled appendages; FERNS, with

Amyzon aggregatum, a freshwater fish from 45 million years ago (Eocene), Horsefly Creek, BC (*courtesy Brian D.E. Chatterton*).

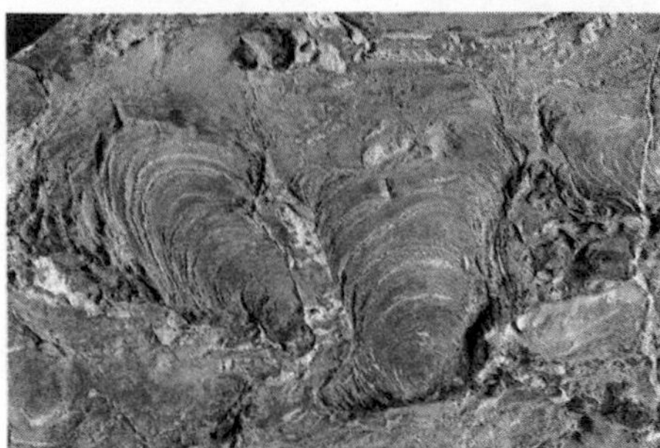

Stromatolites, blue-green algal mounds, Precambrian age, Great Slave Lk, NWT, about 2.5 billion years old. The site contains some of the earliest evidence for life on Earth (*courtesy James Basinger*).

Cercidiphyllum, the Katsura, an early Tertiary angiosperm, about 60 million years old. Katsuras once covered much of Canada, but now survive only in southeast Asia (*courtesy James Basinger*).

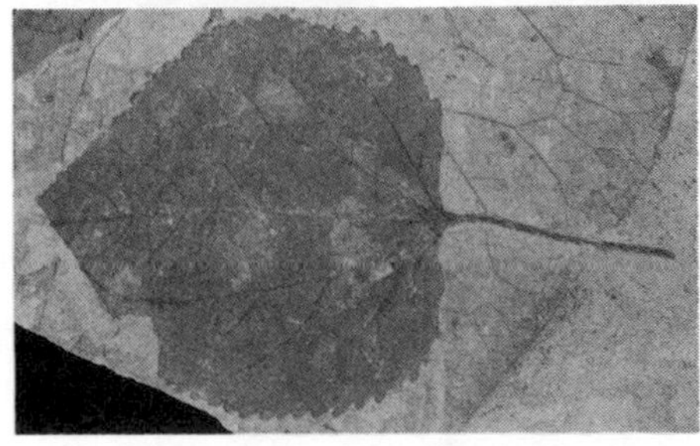

Stromatolite Reef, Great Slave Lake, NWT. These rocks are entirely made up of fossilized stromatolite reefs, some 2 billion years old. Stromatolites were colonies of blue-green algae, one of the earliest forms of life on Earth (*courtesy Ron Redfern, Random House Inc*).

compound leaves evolved from large branching systems; and progymnosperms, woody, free-sporing ancestors to SEED PLANTS, which were of 2 types – those with compound, fernlike leaves (seed fern type), and those with simple leaves evolved from small terminal branches (CONIFER type). Progymnosperms developed thick, woody stems and formed the first extensive forests, some preserved at Escuminac Bay and Gaspé, Qué; Ghost R area, Alta; and Hess Mts, YT.

The early Carboniferous differed markedly from the Devonian, as rising sea levels flooded most of the continent. Few fossil plants are known from this time in Canada. As sea levels fell in the late Carboniferous, great swamps developed on old seafloors. Sydney and Pictou coalfields, NS, and Minto coalfield, NB, are legacies of these coal-age swamps. Late Carboniferous fossils from these coalfields, extensively studied by W.A. Bell, reveal a strange world of scale trees (giant club mosses more than 30 m tall) and calamites (giant horsetails 20 m tall). Calamite twigs, with star-shaped whorls of leaves, are abundant and easily recognized. Cordaites, extinct relatives of conifers, were the only tough, woody plants of the swamps. Ferns and seed ferns, unrelated groups, produced similar types of fernlike foliage. Although the Carboniferous is often called the "Age of Ferns," many types of fernlike leaves actually bore seeds, and therefore only superficially resembled ferns.

Plants that grew in dry uplands of the Pennsylvanian were rarely fossilized. True conifers, hardy ferns, cycads, and seed ferns were evolving in these dry areas. The Permian and Triassic periods brought further lowering of ocean levels, GLACIATION in the Southern Hemisphere, and desert conditions in much of N America. Carboniferous swamp plants became extinct and plants adapted to dry conditions flourished. Triassic forests of conifers, cycads and cycadeoids (seed fern descendants with stubby trunks and stiff, feather-shaped, compound leaves), ferns and seed ferns are preserved in coal-bearing rocks of Axel Heiberg and Ellesmere islands. The "Age of Conifers and Cycads" had begun and continued for over 100 million years, paralleling the "Age of Dinosaurs." When ocean levels rose and moisture increased during the Jurassic and Cretaceous periods, these plants spread to available habitats. Many early Cretaceous fossils are found in western Alberta coalfields (Canmore, Luscar and Grande Cache). In the early Cretaceous, seed ferns became extinct but, before doing so, gave rise to angiosperms, the flowering plants.

The early angiosperms developed advantages over contemporary groups (eg, rapid reproductive cycle), which made them highly efficient plants, well adapted to "weedy" growth. These modifications, including flowers for attraction of insect pollinators, proved advantageous in many habitats. Interaction between plant and pollinator has been a driving force behind the astounding diversification of both flowering plants and insects. Some of the earliest known flowering plants are found in northeastern BC coalfields. Late Cretaceous floras of the Dawson Creek area of BC, and Milk R, Alta, reveal increasing dominance by angiosperms. These fossils, while vaguely resembling living angiosperms, represent archaic, extinct families, and their relationships to living groups remain unclear.

At the end of the Cretaceous, the climate cooled, inland seas covering much of western Canada drained, and DINOSAURS became extinct. With the dawn of the Tertiary, Earth entered the Age of Mammals, and paralleling the rise of mammals is the rise of the "modern" flora, which consists overwhelmingly of flowering plants. Although the climate had cooled, forests grew as far N as Ellesmere I. Early Tertiary (Paleocene) fossils, 55 to 65 million years old, are found over much of Alberta (eg, Red Deer R, Lk Wabamun coalfields, Robb to Coal Valley coalfields) and southern Saskatchewan (eg, Eastend area to Estevan coalfield). These floras reveal a variety of flowering plants, including members of the sycamore, birch and walnut families, but the most abundant fossil plants are the katsuras and the dawn redwood, now native only to southeastern Asia. During the Eocene epoch of the Early Tertiary period, a brief climatic warming coincided with rapid diversification of flowering plants. Eocene fossils in BC (Princeton, Kamloops and Smithers areas) reveal increasing numbers of modern plant families, with extinct species of birch, maple, beech, willow, chestnut, pine and fir.

Exceptionally well-preserved fossil forests found on Axel Heiberg and Ellesmere islands in the Canadian Arctic illustrate clearly the contrast between modern Canadian vegetation and the floras of a much warmer past. These fossil forests, 40 to 60 million years old, consist of large stumps, many over 1 m in diameter, preserved where they grew, still rooted in ancient soil. Thick mats of leafy litter that formed the forest floor reveal the types of plants inhabiting the forests. Lush redwood and cypress swamps covered the lowlands, while the surrounding uplands were dominated by a mixed conifer/hardwood forest resembling that of modern eastern N America. Even accounting for continental drift, these forests grew well above the Arctic Circle, and bear witness to a time in Canada's past when an arctic climatic regime did not exist.

Climate began cooling again in the middle Tertiary, culminating in the glaciation of Canada, which began about 2 million years ago.

Alethopteris, Carboniferous fernlike foliage, about 300 million years old (*courtesy James Basinger*).

Late Tertiary fossil plants are uncommon in Canada, but Miocene peat beds found on Banks and Meighen Is, NWT, which contain spruce, birch, walnut, pine and larch, represent some of the last high arctic forests.

The Pleistocene Glaciation has entirely altered the face of Canada, with the repeated advance and retreat of ice sheets as much as 3 km thick. During interglacial stages, forests returned to colonize the devastated landscape. The well-preserved remains of an interglacial flora are found in the clays exposed in the Don Valley Brickyard of Toronto. The Don flora indicates that during past interglacial stages the climate of Canada has been much milder than that of the interglacial stage in which we now live.

About 10 000 years ago the most recent ice advance ended. Tertiary cooling and glaciation eliminated the old northern forests from Canada. Many plants found refuge in southeastern N America and China, where their descendants still live. Floras in these 2 areas are similar even today. Most modern Canadian plants are recent migrants from unglaciated areas and form quite different assemblages from those of previous ages. The modern world is only the most recent chapter in the long and fascinating history of life. It is fortunate that the rocks of Canada preserve, often in exquisite detail, such a significant part of this history. JAMES BASINGER

Foster, David Walter, musician, writer, arranger, producer (b at Victoria 1 Nov 1949). After piano studies, he moved to England (1966) to pursue a pop music career. He resettled briefly in Toronto (1967), playing with Ronnie HAWKINS, and Edmonton (1969), before returning to Vancouver to form the band Skylark. Following the band's breakup in Los Angeles, he stayed in the US, where his multifaceted career has made him one of the most influential international music figures of the 1980s. Foster's production credits include Chicago, Kenny Rogers, Barbra Streisand and the Broadway-cast album *Dreamgirls*. He has contributed hit songs to numerous recording artists and the films *Urban Cowboy, Footloose, Two of a Kind, Ghostbusters*, *St Elmo's Fire* and *The Secret of My Success*. In 1985, Foster co-wrote and produced "Tears Are Not Enough," performed by Northern Lights, Canada's contribution to African famine relief. He is the producer for Canadian singers Anne MURRAY and Gordon LIGHTFOOT, and he established "The David Foster Song Writing Contest" in Alberta. Between 1979 and 1985, Foster was nominated for 21 (US) Grammy Awards (winning 4), won the 1985 JUNO AWARD for Producer of the Year, and was the 1985 BMI (US) most performed "Songwriter of the Year." In 1987 he won the Juno Award for Instrumental Artist of the Year. BOB HUNKA

Popular music producer and songwriter David Foster (*courtesy Shankman-DeBlasio Inc/David Foster*).

Foster, Edward, policeman, fingerprint pioneer (b near Stittsville, Ont 14 Nov 1863; d at Ottawa 21 Jan 1956). Foster joined the DOMINION POLICE as a constable in 1890. While at the St Louis World's Fair in 1904, his interest was awakened in the controversial science of fingerprint identification. On returning to Canada, Foster advocated the advantages of fingerprinting over the Bertillon system (based upon body measurements), and pressed for a central repository of fingerprints. Promoted to inspector in 1910, his perseverance resulted in the opening of a national fingerprint bureau in Ottawa the following year. Foster continued to head the bureau, after it was absorbed by the RCMP, until his retirement in 1932. S.W. HORRALL

Foster, Sir George Eulas, politician (b in Carleton County, NB 3 Sept 1847; d at Ottawa 30 Dec 1931). Educated at UNB, he became professor of classics there, 1873. Elected to the Commons as member for Kings in 1882, he was appointed minister of marine and fisheries (1885) in the MACDONALD government. In 1888 he took over finance, a portfolio he kept through the succeeding prime ministerships of ABBOTT, THOMPSON, BOWELL and TUPPER. A leading member of the Conservative Opposition, he joined the BORDEN government as minister of trade and commerce, 1911. He was a Canadian delegate to the 1919 peace conference and was appointed to the Senate in 1921. Foster was intelligent, able and hardworking. Borden also found him remarkable for lack of tact, for having an incredibly messy office – where Cabinet papers could disappear – and a penchant for extending his jurisdiction in every direction. Though never greatly loved, Foster was respected for his rigorous administrative abilities. P.B. WAITE

Foster, Harold, artist, author (b at Halifax 16 Aug 1892; d at Spring Hill, Fla 28 July 1982). Father of the adventure comic strip, Foster crossed Halifax harbour on a 12-foot (3.6 m) raft at age 8, skippered a 30-foot (9 m) sloop at 12, and after moving to Winnipeg helped support his family by hunting and fishing. He discovered a million-dollar gold lode near Rice Lk, Sask, and when he lost it to "claim jumpers" he bicycled 1600 kilometres to Chicago, Ill, for formal art training. He twice revolutionized newspaper comics. His *Tarzan* (1929-37) introduced adventure and realistic artistry, and in 1937 he created *Prince Valiant*, an original "illustrated historical novel" with complex, realistic characters, plotting and a literate text. Foster wrote and illustrated *Prince Valiant* for 42 years. His work, based on visits to the locales used and on research into medieval life, has been praised by both historians and teachers. GERALD J. RUBIO

Foster, John Stuart, physicist (b at Clarence, NS 30 May 1890; d at Berkeley, Calif 9 Sept 1964). After receiving a doctorate from Yale, he was appointed assistant professor of physics at McGill in 1924 and did post-doctoral work with Niels Bohr in 1926. A specialist in experimental spectroscopy, he made important contributions to the study of the "Stark effect" (the effect of an electric field applied to an atom), which played a critical role in the transformation of modern PHYSICS. Elected a fellow of the RSC in 1929, he received the Levy Medal of the Franklin Institute in 1930 and in 1935 was elected to the Royal Society of London. During WWII Foster was liaison officer for the NATIONAL RESEARCH COUNCIL at the Radiation Laboratory of MIT, centre of the US effort in radar development. His most important contribution to the war effort was a rapid scanner now known as the Foster scanner. He returned to McGill in 1944 and worked on constructing a proton accelerator (a cyclotron), completed in 1949. In 1964 his laboratory was named after him. YVES GINGRAS

Foster, Walter Edward, businessman, politician, premier of NB 1917-23 (b at St Martins, NB 9 Apr 1873; d at Saint John 14 Nov 1947). Chosen Liberal Opposition leader in 1916 and premier following the Liberal victory in 1917 he sat for Victoria in 1917 and Saint John City in 1920. An advocate of MARITIME RIGHTS, his government established the Dept of Health 1918, enfranchised women (1919) and created the NB Electric Power Commission 1920. Owing to personal financial problems, he resigned in 1923. He was named secretary of state in 1925 but was defeated in a federal election that year. Appointed to the Senate in 1928, Foster acted as Speaker, 1936-40. DELLA M.M. STANLEY

Foster, William Alexander, barrister, essayist (b at Toronto 16 July 1840; d there 1 Nov 1888). He was a leading spokesman for a Toronto-centered group of intellectuals and public men who, in the wake of Confederation (1867), came to believe that without a unifying sense of purpose Canadian nationhood would succumb to American hostility, British indifference, racial animosity and political partisanship. In *Canada First* (1871) he described a Canadian national identity forged out of the process of nation-building, particularly Canadians' continuing confrontation with an inhospitable northern environment. Pride in their accomplishments and a belief in their destiny would give Canadians a sense of purpose before the forces of national disunity and dismemberment. In the wake of the PACIFIC SCANDAL, Foster and his friends launched the Canadian National Assn, to give political expression to the aims of the CANADA FIRST movement in 1874. They intended to enter politics on a platform of pure administration, political reform, protective tariffs and patriotism, but failed to elect a single candidate. DAVID GAGAN

Foster, William Wasborough, military officer, public servant, mountaineer (b at Bristol, Eng 1875; d at Vancouver 2 Dec 1954). Energetic, capable and good-humoured, Foster immigrated to Canada in 1894 to work for the CPR before becoming BC's deputy minister of public works in 1910. A front-line soldier in WWI, he won 15 decorations, a battlefield promotion and a VC recommendation, honours that contributed to his 1935 appointment as Vancouver's chief of police. In WWII, as a maj-gen responsible for the defence of western Canada, he supervised construction of the Canadian portion of the Al-Can Highway. As much mountaineer as militiaman, he participated in the first ascents of Mt ROBSON (1913) and Mt LOGAN (1925). BART ROBINSON

Fotheringham, Allan, columnist, author, humourist (b Murray Allan Scott at Hearne, Sask 31 Aug 1932). As Canada's best-read political columnist, and combining a vivid comic sense with the instincts of a superb reporter, Fotheringham has produced some of the funniest, most penetrating political commentary of his generation. After graduation from UBC in 1954 (where he edited the student newspaper, the *Ubyssey*), he joined the Vancouver *Sun* as a sportswriter. In

1959 he began writing a daily column. At first his beat was City Hall, but his acerbic wit was soon directed at larger targets: provincial politicians and their counterparts in Ottawa and Washington. He left the *Sun* after a dispute with the publisher and joined Southam News Service as Ottawa columnist. In 1984 Fotheringham became Southam's Washington correspondent, but he continued to comment on the Canadian scene in his widely read column in *Maclean's* magazine. He is the author of 3 best-selling books: *Malice in Blunderland* (1982), *Look Ma...No Hands* (1983) and *Capitol Offences: Dr Foth Meets Uncle Sam* (1986). He is a resident panelist of CBC-TV's FRONT PAGE CHALLENGE. *See also* ESSAY IN ENGLISH.

ALEXANDER M. ROSS

Foulis, Robert, civil engineer (b at Glasgow, Scot 5 May 1796; d at Saint John 26 Jan 1866). Foulis studied medicine, engineering and painting in Glasgow and Edinburgh. In 1818 he was painting in Halifax and in 1821 moved to Saint John. He installed the machinery in the second and third steamers to ply the Saint John R, established the Saint John Foundry, lectured in chemistry, established a "School of Arts" and was a founding member of the MECHANICS' INSTITUTE. He presented his plan for a steam fog whistle to the Lighthouse Commissioners in 1853. A steam alarm was installed on Partridge I in 1860 but not until a government report recognized Foulis's earlier contribution did he gain recognition as inventor of the world's first steam-operated fog alarm. He also invented a "Tide Machine" designed to harness the tides of the Bay of Fundy, an "Amphocratic Steam Engine" for use in sawmills, an "Illuminating Gas Apparatus" for making coal and water gas, and a method of telegraphing by means of steam whistles.

HAROLD E. WRIGHT

Foulkes, Charles, army officer (b at Stockton-on-Tees, Eng 3 Jan 1903; d at Ottawa 12 Sept 1969). Educated in London, Ont, Foulkes joined the Canadian Army in 1926, commanding the 2nd Canadian Infantry Division in Normandy before taking over the 1st Canadian Corps in Italy (Nov 1944) and then Northwest Europe (Feb 1945). He accepted the surrender of German forces in Holland in May 1945 and returned to Canada as chief of the general staff. In 1951 he was appointed chairman of the chiefs of staff. An advocate of close military ties with the US, he resigned in 1960 in opposition to the non-nuclear policies of the DIEFENBAKER government. He taught strategic studies at Carleton (1968-69).

STEPHEN HARRIS

Foundations are "non-governmental, non-profit organizations with funds (usually from a single source, either an individual, a family, or a corporation) and program managed by (their) own trustees or directors, established to maintain or aid social, educational, charitable, religious, or other activities serving the common welfare primarily through the making of grants" (F. Emerson Andrews, first president, The Foundation Centre, NY).

The development of charitable foundations in N America has been a phenomenon of the 20th century. Unlike the US, however, it is only in the past 20 years that foundations have assumed a major role in Canadian philanthropy. A study by the Canadian Centre for Philanthropy in 1982 suggests that only about 2% of Canadian foundations existed prior to 1940. In the following decade another 5% were founded, followed by 17% in the 1950s, 29% in the 1960s and 47% in the 1970s. Figures for the 1980s are not available, but new foundations are being established.

Reflecting the minor role of foundations in Canadian society, prior to 1977 the rules governing the establishment and donations practices of foundations were extremely relaxed: a foundation had only to be registered with the Dept of National Revenue if it wished to issue income tax receipts for donations received. In that year, however, major legislation was enacted governing the establishment of foundations and their disbursement practices. The new rules required that all foundations be registered with Revenue Canada to obtain tax-exempt status and that substantial minimum disbursement levels be met on an annual basis. Foundations were required to register as "private" (established by an individual or family) or "public" (where a fixed proportion of board members are not related and funds are from more than one source), and the actual disbursement requirements depended on that classification.

Most foundations found these rules to be equitable, but the federal government apparently perceived that they were open to abuse. The budget proposals of 12 Nov 1981 indicated an intention to effect drastic increases in disbursement requirements that would have eroded foundations' capital so as to effect their eventual disappearance. Following representations from all sectors of the philanthropic community, these proposals were modified in a release from the minister of finance dated 21 Apr 1982. An accompanying statement, indicating the government's support for the idea of foundations, should again ensure growth in this sector.

Role and Responsibilities Foundations occupy a unique place in Canadian philanthropy. Unlike most other granting sources, their incomes are generally constant, sometimes even greater every year. They have relative freedom from outside pressures, which gives them continuity and stability and offers opportunities to provide "venture capital" for innovative programs or support to new or unpopular causes. Generally, however, their support is given to traditional activities. Foundations have played an important role in the maintenance of a pluralistic Canadian society – historically a healthy and productive balance between government measures and private philanthropy. Foundations are also finding it necessary to assume new responsibilities, including a high level of public accountability, the provision of expert or technical advice to charitable organizations, and as "lead" donors for major charitable campaigns.

Facts About Canadian Foundations There are little more than 600 foundations in Canada, compared to over 22 500 in the US, yet the relative impact on philanthropy is greater for Canadian organizations. In Canada it is estimated that foundations account for 8.2% of all charitable giving; in the US they are responsible for only 4.9%. Total assets held by Canadian foundations are nearly $2 billion, and from that base in 1985 grants of more than $166 million were made. They ranged in size from hundreds of thousands of dollars to a single dollar provided for a subsidized rent, charged for the premises in which an Edmonton group runs a shelter for battered women and children. Canada's top 50 foundations now hold 80% of foundation assets and make 65% of all grants.

Regional Analysis Although western Canada has 27.74% of Canada's foundations, Saskatchewan and Manitoba are seriously underrepresented with 0.4% and 3.3%, respectively. Québec with 26.2% lags behind Ontario with 44.68%. NS has 0.98%, NB has 0.4%, and PEI and Newfoundland have none at all. Since many foundations restrict their giving to their own province or regions, the most economically disadvantaged regions of Canada are also those with the least access to foundation support.

Largest Foundations, 1985

Source: Canadian Index to Foundation Grants Database

Foundation	Total assets	Rank by grants	Total grants
1 J.W. McConnell/Griffith	280 806 419	2	11 956 150
2 Vancouver	120 400 000	1	12 240 567
3 CRB [1,3]	100 000 000	36	600 000
4 Hospital for Sick Children	81 989 180	3	9 390 180
5 Donner Canadian	69 000 000	11	2 957 000
6 Kahanoff	60 010 315	10	3 046 156
7 Macdonald Stewart	52 406 221	6	4 834 154
8 Bronfman, The Samuel & Saidye	40 953 075	5	5 447 845
9 Physicians' Services Inc	36 377 112	14	2 410 320
10 RHW	36 379 867	7	4 455 574
11 McLaughlin, R. Samuel	35 853 733	15	2 315 500
12 Bell, Max	35 182 000	9	3 447 000
13 Eldee	32 317 229	12	2 716 059
14 Winnipeg	31 212 447	18	2 170 104
15 Bickell, J.P.	30 346 017	16	2 276 783
16 Morrow, F.K.	28 759 710	13	2 431 200
17 Van Dusen, W.J.	26 718 255	19	1 726 710
18 Assoc. Medical Services Inc [2]	26 156 913	48	9 000
19 Molson Family	23 479 027	21	1 422 500
20 Laidlaw	20 962 076	24	1 201 654
21 Atkinson	20 206 688	29	932 462
22 Kinnear, Henry White	19 863 105	23	1 217 740
23 Counselling	19 417 976	44	347 237
24 McLean	17 480 554	32	782 537
25 Dunn, Sir James	16 111 786	46	209 000
26 Lam, Dorothy & David [1,3]	15 322 881		N/A
27 Beaverbrook Canadian	14 569 754	25	1 116 228
28 Crabtree, Harold	14 569 754	27	1 068 166
29 Windsor	13 916 226	26	1 100 500
30 Ivey, Richard	13 346 044	33	723 400
31 Levesque, J. Louis	13 092 831	38	555 163
32 Jackman	12 754 753	17	2 178 642
33 Birks	11 422 012	39	513 344
34 Lawson	11 091 453	20	1 453 248
35 Woodward's, Mr & Mrs P.A.	10 270 100	34	667 453
36 Tanenbaum, Faye & Joseph	10 176 384	8	3 489 637
37 Greenshields, Elizabeth	9 717 425	43	412 000[4]
38 Nickle	8 990 314	42	417 675
39 Koschitzky	8 976 838	37	562 120
40 Christie, Nat	8 785 742	28	977 213
41 Muttart, Gladys & Merrill	8 540 336	40	443 133
42 Law Foundation of BC	7 647 804	4	6 772 000
43 Richardson, Kathleen M	7 630 271	41	425 775
44 Brawn	7 530 002	47	11 666
45 DeSeve, J.A.	7 507 914	22	1 416 000
46 Hyland, Nelson Arthur	7 275 256	45	293 600
47 Eaton	7 232 550	30	921 210
48 Devonian	6 862 433	31	792 106
49 Sifton, Carolyn	6 379 075	35	618 000
Total	1 518 405 317		108 189 150

[1] Recently established foundation

[2] Funds totalling $944 318 are allocated to the Hannah Institute of Medicine which is involved in direct charitable activity

[3] 1986 financial information

[4] Direct charitable activity.

Foundation Interests Because of the lack of commitment to research on the part of both governments and business in Canada, a multitude of research areas are funded by foundations: aeronautical, agricultural, applied scientific, auditing, behavioural science, biological, communications, education, energy, environment, epidemiology, industrial society, medical research, social science, theological and transportation. In addition, grants are also made to the arts, to educational, health and religious institutions, and to social welfare (*see* EDUCATIONAL FOUNDATIONS).

Types of Foundations Canadian foundations fall into 4 principal categories. *Family Foundations* Most Canadian foundations have been established by an individual, a family or a related group of people: 44 of the country's 50 largest foundations are family foundations, the typical "private" foundation. These foundations are usually established to support causes of interest to the original donor or donors and, even after their deaths, family foundation boards are likely to maintain the general direction established by the founders. *Community Foundations* The funds of community foundations come, most commonly, from bequests of the citizens of the community. These "public" foundations, having a broad, representative board of directors, can provide a continuing source of funds that can be used for innovative or preventive programs within a community that cannot be funded by governments or annual campaigns. In the words of Alan G. Howison, executive director of the Winnipeg Foundation, "The main funders in the social welfare scheme, government and The United Way, have their plates so full of have to do projects that there is little money left for prevention." *Corporate Foundations* Although they provide an excellent opportunity for stabilizing corporate donations programs, corporate foundations have not been widely used by Canadian companies. Through the foundation mechanism, a reserve can be built up in good years so that a consistent donations program can be maintained during economic downturns. In 1985 Canadian corporate foundations listed only $16 million in assets and grants totalled just over $6 million. These figures suggest that corporate foundations are used primarily as a management tool for centralizing the corporate donations program. Recent tax measures have encouraged growth of Canadian corporate foundations to match that of the US, where they are the fastest growing members of the foundation sector. *Special-interest Foundations* are those whose assets have been acquired from various sources, usually for quite specific purposes. The Physicians' Services Incorporated Foundation, founded with money from a private medical insurance plan that was superseded by government, is an example; another, and growing, example is the hospital foundation. ALLAN ARLETT

Reading: Allan Arlett, ed, *The Canadian Directory to Foundations and Granting Agencies* (1982).

Four Seasons Hotels Ltd, with head offices in Toronto, owns and manages hotels and properties. Incorporated in 1968, the company owned and operated Toronto's Inn on the Park hotel. In 1969 the Four Seasons Israel opened and the company launched a joint venture with Sheraton Hotels to open the Four Seasons Sheraton in Toronto. Further international expansion began in 1970 when Four Seasons opened the Inn on the Park in London, Eng. Today the company has 23 hotels in Canada, the US and the UK. In 1986 it had sales or operating revenue of $194.7 million (ranking 340th in Canada), assets of $142.3 million and 8500 employees. Triples Holdings Ltd holds 83% of the shares. DEBORAH C. SAWYER

4-H Clubs The 4-H movement began in the US at the turn of the century; the first similar club in Canada was organized in Roland, Man, in 1913, and the concept quickly swept through the settled agricultural regions of the country. As the movement spread across Canada, national agencies (eg, the railways, the federal Department of Agriculture) became involved, helping, for example, to sponsor a national judging competition in connection with the Royal Winter Fair in Toronto. By 1930 the need for a national organization to help sponsor and co-ordinate the program across Canada became apparent, and in Jan 1931 the Canadian Council on Boys and Girls Clubs was organized. In Canada the name "Boys and Girls Clubs" was used until 1952 when the name 4-H, used in the US and many other countries, was adopted. The Canada 4-H Council combines private and government efforts and resources and offers a forum for national discussion and exchange of information as well as many national programs for 4-H members and for their leaders.

The stated purpose of the early Boys and Girls clubs was to provide rural young people with the opportunity to learn farming and homemaking skills. The 4-H program now emphasizes all aspects of the mental, emotional, social and physical growth of its members. The motto "Learn to Do by Doing" is the basis of all 4-H activities. Members are responsible for developing and executing projects as varied as raising a calf, sewing a dress or learning photography. By helping members acquire a positive attitude toward learning, 4-H helps them increase their knowledge and develop valuable skills. Agricultural Extension Services (*see* AGRICULTURAL EDUCATION) have traditionally provided organizational leadership, while encouraging members actually to run their clubs. Volunteer leaders are vital to the success of the 4-H program. About 13 000 volunteers provide guidance to 48 000 members aged 9 to 19 who regularly recite the 4-H pledge: "I pledge my Head to clearer thinking, my Heart to greater loyalty, my Hands to larger service, and my Health to better living, for my Club, my Community, and my Country." HELGI H. AUSTMAN

Fowke, Edith Margaret, née Fulton, folklorist, collector, writer, teacher (b at Lumsden, Sask 30 Apr 1913). After receiving an MA from U Sask, Fowke moved to Toronto and became interested in Ontario FOLKLORE, collecting and recording on her field trips throughout the southern part of the province many of the folk songs she presented weekly on CBC "Folk Song Time" (1950-63), "Folk Sounds" (1963-74), "Folklore and Folk Music" (1965) and "The Travelling Folk of the British Isles" (1967). In 1971 she began teaching folklore at York U. An avid collector of folk song recordings and a prolific writer on Canadian FOLK MUSIC, Fowke was a founding member of the Canadian Folk Music Society, becoming editor of the *Canadian Folk Music Journal* in 1973. Recent works include, as co-editor, *Explorations in Canadian Folklore* (1985) and *Tales Told in Canada* (1986). In 1985-86 she was president of the Folklore Studies Assn. MABEL H. LAINE

Fowke, Vernon Clifford, economic historian, professor (b at Parry Sound, Ont 5 May 1907; d at San Francisco, Calif 24 Feb 1966). He graduated from U of Sask in 1929, and immediately joined the teaching staff. He continued his graduate studies at U of Chicago and U of Washington, where he received his PhD in 1942. His doctoral thesis, published as *Canadian Agricultural Policy* (1946), remains a key study and established him as the most influential historian of Canadian agriculture. It was supplemented by *The National Policy and the Wheat Economy* (1957) and (with George BRITNELL) *Canadian Agriculture in War and Peace* (1962) and numerous articles. Fowke also advised numerous royal commissions including the Rowell-Sirois Royal Commission on DOMINION-PROVINCIAL RELATIONS and, after 1946, served on the Transportation Advisory Board, where he played a key role in defending the CROW'S NEST PASS AGREEMENT. One of the most influential Canadian economists of his day, he was elected a member of the Royal Soc of Canada in 1954. PAUL PHILLIPS

Fowler, Daniel, painter (b at Champion Hill, Eng 10 Feb 1810; d on Amherst I, Ont 14 Sept 1894). He studied 1831-34 with painter and lithographer J.D. Harding, then spent a year in Europe sketching and painting. In 1843 he came to Canada for health reasons, bought a farm on Amherst I, and did not return to painting until 1857. The slightly mannered style of his European period gave way to an original and lively approach as he worked directly from nature, painting flowers, dead birds and landscapes. He was unique in Canada at that time in exploring broken brushwork, the spatial composition and structure associated with the French impressionists and Cézanne. FRANCES K. SMITH

Reading: Frances K. Smith, *Daniel Fowler of Amherst Island, 1810-1894* (1979).

Fowler, Robert MacLaren, lawyer, executive (b at Peterborough, Ont 7 Dec 1906; d at Hawkesbury; Ont 13 July 1980). Fowler played many roles but was best known for chairing a royal commission and a federal committee on broadcasting. He attended U of T and Osgoode Hall, and built a career as president of the Canadian Pulp and Paper Assn. A friend of Liberal politicians and bureaucrats, Fowler was named to head the Royal Commission on BROADCASTING of 1955. His report, tabled Mar 1957, strongly supported the CBC but called for a new regulatory authority to administer public and private broadcasting. The Conservative DIEFENBAKER government did not accept all the recommendations, and in 1965 Fowler headed a new investigative committee. Widely reported was his comment that in broadcasting all that matters is program content; all the rest is housekeeping. Fowler again recommended changes, and this led to the creation of the Canadian Radio-Television Commission (*see* CANADIAN RADIO-TELEVISION AND TELECOMMUNICATIONS COMMISSION). J.L. GRANATSTEIN

Fox, small, carnivorous mammal of the DOG family. Four species inhabit Canada: red or coloured, grey, arctic and swift foxes (*Vulpes vulpes, Urocyon cinereoargenteus, Alopex lagopus, V. velox*, respectively). Red and arctic foxes have circumpolar distribution; grey foxes are New World foxes; swift foxes are common in the US. Red foxes are largest (2.5-6.5 kg) and may be reddish with a "cross" on the back or, rarely, black or may have silver-tipped hairs. Feet and ear tips are black; tail tip, white. Common in farming and wooded areas, they extend from the US border to the tundra in all provinces, but are absent from coastal BC and southern Alberta-Saskatchewan. They eat rodents, insects, frogs, seeds, fruit, eggs and some poultry. They breed in Jan-Feb; usually 4-5 cubs (1-10) are born 52-54 days later in a den of earth. Both parents feed them. They become independent at about 6 months and breed in their second year. Arctic foxes are smaller, with rounded ears and heavy, white winter fur and dark brownish summer fur. They are normally restricted to the tundra and northern coasts. Diet is similar to that of red foxes, and they scavenge other carnivore kills. Mating is in Feb, with 5-6 (maximum 14) cubs born 50-57 days later. Red and arctic foxes were farmed for their pelts, but artificial furs have destroyed the market. Grey foxes, similar in food habits and size to red foxes, are slimmer, with slightly rounded ears, a black back stripe and speckled, grey sides. Undersides are off-white; neck, back of ears and legs are yellowish buff. They are found in southernmost Manitoba, Ontario and Québec. They prefer wooded or broken country, live in hollow logs or overhangs, often climb trees, enjoy sunning themselves, and are not strictly nocturnal. Mating is in Feb-Mar with litters averaging 4 cubs (1-7), born about 63 days later. Young become independent in autumn and breed the following season. Swift fox, the smallest Canadian fox, may be a subspecies of kit fox (*V. macrotis*). It occurred from southern Alberta to SW Manitoba but was considered extinct in Canada by 1970. Individuals selected from a captive population, bred from animals obtained from Colorado in 1972, have been released since 1980 in the short-grass prairie of southeastern Alberta, near Manyberries and Medicine Hat, and in

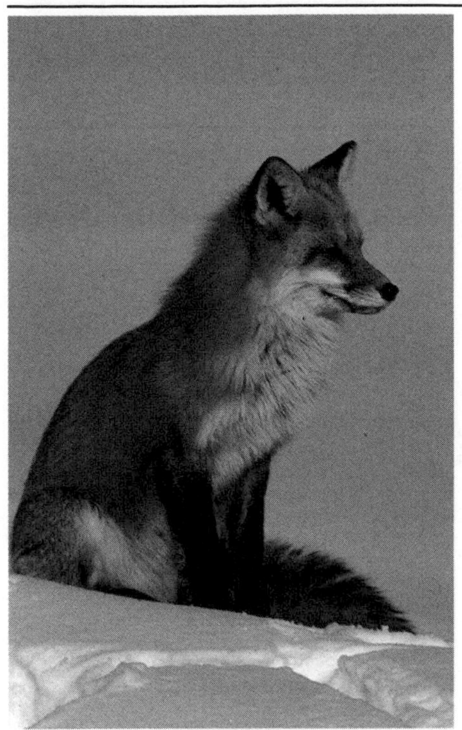

The red fox (*Vulpes vulpes*) is common in farming and wooded areas across Canada, from the US border to the tundra (*photo by Stephen J. Krasemann/DRK Photo*).

southwestern Saskatchewan. Some successful breeding in the wild is recorded. Its habits are essentially the same as those of red foxes. *See also* FUR FARMING. C.S. CHURCHER

Fox, Francis, lawyer, politician (b at Montréal 2 Dec 1939). He was educated at Jean-de-Brébeuf College, U de M (LL.L), Harvard Law School (LL.M) and Oxford (MA). He was called to the Québec Bar in 1963 and worked as a lawyer from 1965 to 1968. In 1972 he was first elected Liberal MP in Montréal. He was re-elected 1974, 1979 and 1980 and was solicitor general of Canada 1976-78, resigning over a controversy. He returned as secretary of state and minister of communications 1980-82 and continued as minister of communications 1982-84. He oversaw a major reorganization of the 2 departments and was instrumental in initiating many new federal cultural policies, including the creation of Telefilm Canada, the broadcast fund and co-production treaties in film and television. After a brief stint as minister of international trade in the Turner Cabinet, he was defeated in the fall election of 1984. He returned to private life as a partner with the law firm Martineau, Walker, and he was also chairman of the board of Young Canada Television (1985). JAMES MARSH

Fox, Gail, poet (b at Willimantic, Conn 5 Feb 1942). Fox immigrated to Canada in 1963 and came to public attention in the late 1960s and early 1970s as part of a group of writers centered at Queen's and led by poets Tom MARSHALL and David HELWIG and associated with the journal *Quarry*, which she later edited. Her collections of intense yet often lyrical poetry include *Dangerous Season* (1969), *The Royal Collector of Dreams* (1970), *Flight of the Pterodactyl* (1973), *The Ringmaster's Circus* (1973), *God's Odd Look* (1976), *Houses of God* (1983) and *Deepening the Colours* (1987).

Fox, Irving Kingsbury, professor, resource planner, conservationist (b at Bolton, Mich 7 Dec 1916). After obtaining a U of Mich MA, Fox served with the US government and in 1955 joined Resources for the Future Inc, as VP, devoting himself to water resources. A period as director of the Water Resources Center at U of Wis preceded his joining UBC as director of Westwater Research and professor of community and regional planning. There, through teaching, research and public activity, he pioneered river basin studies in Canada, integrating social and environmental considerations. In his many publications, which include a monograph on the Yukon and the organization of studies related to the Fraser R estuary, and other ways, Fox has made a remarkable impact upon resource use in Canada. IAN MCTAGGART-COWAN

Fox, John Richard, painter (b at Montréal 26 July 1927). Trained by Goodridge ROBERTS, Fox also worked under John LYMAN at McGill. In 1952 he entered the Slade School of Art, London, Eng, and later spent 2 years in Italy and France before finally returning to Montréal in 1957. In 1964 he completed a mural for Charlottetown's Confederation Centre. Fox was well known for his intimist figure and landscape paintings when in 1972 he began to paint large abstract works influenced more by European and American modernism than by a Québec sensibility. Without the distraction of recognizable imagery, Fox pursued his preoccupation with figure-ground ambiguity and moved through abstract impressionism to collage-inspired symbolic abstraction. He has shown widely in Canada. SANDRA PAIKOWSKY

Fox, Luke, also spelled **Foxe,** explorer (b at Kingston-upon-Hull, Eng 20 Oct 1586; d *c* 15 July 1635). He left for the Arctic in 1631, 2 days after Thomas JAMES left on a rival voyage. He explored the W shore of HUDSON BAY and met James by chance near Cape Henrietta Maria, turned N and was the first to sail beyond Foxe Channel (named for him later by W.E. PARRY), into FOXE BASIN, and along the Foxe Peninsula. His report of impenetrable barriers cancelled the last hope of a NORTHWEST PASSAGE and abated the zeal for arctic exploration for almost 200 years. Fox answered criticism that he had given up too easily with a remarkable book, *North-West Fox* (1635), a rare document of arctic exploration. JAMES MARSH

Fox, Terrance Stanley, "Marathon of Hope" runner (b at Winnipeg 28 July 1958; d at New Westminster, BC 28 June 1981). Terry Fox was a good athlete studying kinesiology when, in 1977, it was discovered he had osteogenic sarcoma, a rare form of bone cancer. It was necessary to amputate most of one leg. While recovering, he developed the idea for a "Marathon of Hope" – a run across Canada to raise money and generate publicity for cancer research. After extensive training, he began his run at St John's on 12 Apr 1980 and ended it on Sept 1 in Thunder Bay, Ont, after cancer was discovered in his lungs. During that period, he had run 5373 km at a pace of nearly 40 km per day. Inspiring millions of people around the world, he drew nationwide attention and raised $1.7 million. Gripped by an outpouring of emotion, Canadians donated an additional $23 million to the fund. For his efforts, he was made a Companion of the Order of Canada and a BC mountain was named after him. Thousands annually participate in a fund-raising run named after him. J. THOMAS WEST

Terry Fox monument, Ottawa (*courtesy National Capital Commission/photo by T. Atkinson*)

Foxe Basin, NWT, is bordered on its eastern and northern sides by the coast of BAFFIN I and in the W by the MELVILLE PEN. Named for 17th-century arctic explorer Luke FOX [Foxe], it is a smaller version of HUDSON BAY, being an enclosed depression in the Canadian SHIELD, with an ancient land surface preserved under limestone sediments beneath its shallow waters. Maximum depths in Foxe Basin only reach 90 m, but much of the basin is shallower, with long, gently shelving shorelines, making navigation hazardous. The basin's shallowness keeps it ice covered for long periods. Grounding of sea ice on the bottom disturbs silt, which is incorporated into the ice, turning it a distinctive brown colour. The basin's shape acts to confine the movement of water, and some of the greatest tidal ranges in arctic waters are found at its outlets, reaching 3.5 m at Fury and Hecla Str and 7 m through Foxe Ch. Because of its shallowness, ice and tidal ranges, Foxe Basin has been bypassed as a route to the Arctic. DOUGLAS FINLAYSON

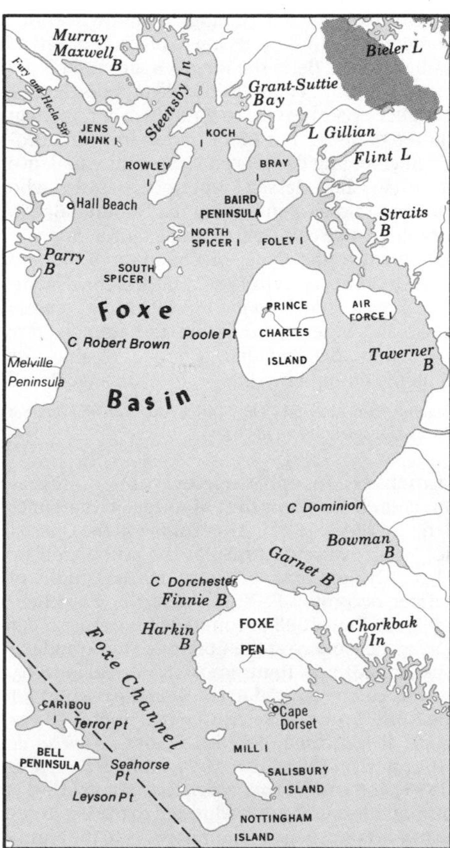

Celia Franca, dancer and founder of the National Ballet of Canada (*courtesy National Ballet Archives*).

Franca, Celia, stage name of Celia Franks, dancer, choreographer, director, teacher (b at London, Eng 25 Jun 1921). As founder of the NATIONAL BALLET OF CANADA, Franca – a strong-willed, dynamic woman – has played a central role in the development of BALLET in Canada. She was trained in England at London's Guildhall School of Music and at the Royal Academy of Dancing. She performed there with various companies, among them the Ballet Rambert and Sadler's Wells Ballet. Her earliest choreography was also created in England. Her artistic and marked organizational gifts caused Franca to be recommended to a group of Toronto ballet-lovers who in 1950 wanted to establish a classical ballet company in Canada. Franca agreed to become founding artistic director of the National Ballet of Canada in 1951 and remained its head until 1974. Despite a lack of adequate financial support and the short supply of well-trained classical dancers, Franca succeeded in developing a well-schooled repertory ballet company that by the early 1970s had gained an international reputation.

Franca continued to dance leading roles until 1959 (she continues to appear in character parts as a guest artist) and choreographed or staged from memory established works in the classical repertory as well as a number of her own works. Sometimes accused of trying to produce a copy of Sadler's Wells (later the Royal) Ballet and of failing to develop Canadian choreographers, Franca did offer opportunities to a number of Canadian choreographers, but more importantly she provided emerging dancers an opportunity to dance the established classical repertoire. Franca, who moved to Ottawa on leaving the National Ballet, remains active as a teacher and lecturer. She was appointed to the Order of Canada in 1967 and made a Companion in 1985. She became a member of the Canada Council in 1983, and among her many other honours are the MOLSON PRIZE 1974 and the Canadian Council of the Arts Diplôme d'honneur 1986. MICHAEL CRABB

Reading: Ken Bell and Celia Franca, *The National Ballet of Canada: A Celebration* (1978).

Franchère, Joseph-Charles, painter, illustrator, church decorator (b at Montréal 4 Mar 1866; d there 12 May 1921). After studies at the Conseil des Arts et Manufactures, at the school run by Abbé Chabert, and a period in the studio of painter-decorator F.-X.-E. Meloche, Franchère left for Paris in 1888 to complete his training. For 2 years he worked at the Colarossi studio and the Académie Julian. Returning to Montréal in 1890, he was commissioned to do 3 large paintings for the Notre-Dame du Sacré-Coeur chapel of NOTRE-DAME. He returned to Paris to paint *La Vierge de l'Apocalypse* (1892), *La Multiplication des pains* (1893) and *Le Christ consolateur des affligés* (1895). During this stay, he was admitted to the École des beaux-arts and began sending works to the annual exhibitions of the Art Assn of Montréal and the ROYAL CANADIAN ACADEMY OF ARTS. Franchère's work was exhibited at the world fairs in Chicago (1893), Buffalo (1901) and St Louis (1904). As well as doing church murals in Québec during these years, he taught at the Conseil des Arts et Manufactures and the Monument National, and illustrated several books, including P.E. Prévost's *Chansons canadiennes* (1907) and Abbé Lionel GROULX's *Les Rapaillages* (1916). Trained in the academic tradition, Franchère specialized in subject pictures idealizing country life, and in works inspired by symbolism. LAURIER LACROIX

Franchise, the right to vote in public ELECTIONS for members of Parliament, provincial legislatures and municipal councils. The Canadian franchise dates from the mid-18th-century colonial period when, as a general rule, restrictions effectively limited the vote to male property holders. Since then the particular voting qualifications and the pace of expanding the categories of eligible voters have differed according to jurisdiction and have reflected changing social values. For the first 50 years after Confederation the federal franchise was manipulated in a blatantly partisan fashion by both national parties. At various times up to 1920 the Dominion franchise was based either on the electoral lists drawn up by the provinces for provincial elections (thereby ensuring that the "national" franchise differed from one province to another) or on a federal list compiled by enumerators appointed by the governing party in Ottawa. From 1867 to 1884 it was based on provincial laws and included a property qualification. The resulting "staggered vote" benefited the Conservative Party. Canada's most controversial franchise legislation was adopted by Parliament during WWI. The WARTIME ELECTIONS ACT and the Military Voters Act of 1917 enfranchised female relatives of men serving with the Canadian or British armed forces as well as all servicemen (including minors and Indians); it disenfranchised conscientious objectors and British subjects naturalized after 1902 who were born in an enemy country or who habitually spoke an enemy language. Not surprisingly, the government of the time openly admitted that the legislation was biased in its favour and the 1917 election results proved it right. Such abuses and shifts in the policies governing the right to vote ended in 1920 with the adoption by Parliament of an Act establishing a standard Dominion-wide franchise.

Although occasional instances were recorded of women voting in pre-Confederation Nova Scotia and LOWER CANADA, between 1809 and 1834, Canadian women were systematically and universally disenfranchised. Apart from their temporary and selective enfranchisement under the Wartime Elections Act, women were first granted the right to vote federally in 1918. Not until 1940 were all Canadian women guaranteed the right to vote provincially. In 1916, Manitoba became the first province to enfranchise women for provincial elections; in 1940, Québec was the last. From the time they first began arriving in the 19th century through much of the first half of the 20th century, most Canadians of oriental ancestry were denied the right to vote in federal and provincial elections. With the extension of the federal franchise to JAPANESE Canadians in 1948, the last statutory disenfranchisement of Asians was removed. Non-status Indians received full voting rights at the provincial level, starting in BC in 1949 and ending with Québec in 1969. The federal franchise was extended to the Inuit in 1950 and to status Indians in 1960.

Canada now has a virtually universal franchise at both the provincial and federal levels. In federal elections all Canadian citizens 18 years of age and older (from 1920 to 1970 the minimum age had been 21) are eligible to vote, except those barred by the provisions of the Canada Elections Act – federal judges, inmates of prisons and mental institutions, and any person disqualified for corrupt or illegal electoral practices. These restrictions may be challenged under the CONSTITUTION ACT, 1982, which stipulates "every citizen of Canada has the right to vote in an election of members of the House of Commons or of a legislative assembly and to be qualified for membership therein." JOHN C. COURTNEY

Franck, Albert Jacques, Albie, painter (b at Middelburg, Holland 2 Apr 1899; d at Toronto 28 Feb 1973). He was long-distance swimming champion of Belgium in 1924, worked as a swimming coach at the central YMCA in Montréal after immigrating to Canada, and then held various jobs in Toronto and Montréal. The turning point in Franck's career came after WWII when he rented a shop on Toronto's Gerrard St, the city's "Greenwich Village," and restored pictures, designed Christmas cards and displayed his paintings. Franck, generous with food and advice, became *paterfamilias* to a considerable group of younger artists.

Franck tried to paint all the seasons of the year, but winter became his subject, and he found his true *métier* in the tumbled houses and the acrid lanes of Toronto neighbourhoods. His work took on a new plastic power, the colour deepened, and detail was reduced in a design that gave freedom to heightened feeling. Franck gradually received critical and financial success as his love of old brick, dirty snow and lane fences spread into the larger texture of Canadian life. He made people see the ordinary that is home. His vision of Toronto was a fulcrum for the simple idea that cities become great by what they preserve. HAROLD B. TOWN

Reading: Harold Town, *Albert Franck* (1974).

Francks, Don Harvey, or Iron Buffalo, actor, jazz musician, environmental activist (b at Burnaby, BC 28 Feb 1932). Talented, international entertainer and honorary Cree, he achieved "failed Broadway star" status 16 Feb 1964 when the musical *Kelly* folded after one night. Other New York stage excursions included *The Flip Side* and *On a Clear Day*. Frequently on CBC radio and TV including "Nero Wolfe" (1982) and "This Land" (from 1979), he won 2 successive ACTRA AWARDS for performances in "Drying Up the Streets" (1980) and "The Phoenix Team" (1981). His American TV series appearances include "Jericho, The Man from U.N.C.L.E." and "Mission Impossible," and he was also featured in such films as *Finian's Rainbow, The Drylanders, Ivy League Killers, The Tomorrow Man, Old Fish Hawk, Labour of Love, Oklahoma Smugglers, Good Times at the Rainbow Bar and Grill* (which also included his daughter Cree Summer and was telecast in 1987) and *The Arm*. DAVID GARDNER

Franco-Americans From the mid-19th century to around 1930, over 900 000 francophone Québecois emigrated to the US. They migrated in waves, especially after the AMERICAN CIVIL WAR and around 1890, managed to feel at home and, in a few generations, adopted the habits and customs of their new surroundings. Their descendants are known as Franco-Americans, though the term did not appear in New England until the end of the 19th century and even today is unknown to the majority, who instead talk about "French Canadians." The approximately 5 million Franco-Americans constitute the largest element within the Québec diaspora in all N America.

The magnitude of the huge migration ("La Grande Hémorragie") shook Québec society and led to a renewal of nativism in New England, where almost half the emigrants settled. Most of the emigrants came from underdeveloped rural areas of Québec. They were looking for financial and job security, especially in textile and shoe factories. Franco-Americans' job skills diversified over time, however, and they gained access to commercial positions and to the liberal professions. Around 1930, when the GREAT DEPRESSION put a stop to emigration, the New England states had gained a significant Franco-American population, most of it in industrial cities like Lowell, Lawrence and New Bedford (Mass), Woonsocket (RI), Manchester and Nashua (NH), and Biddeford and Lewiston (Me).

These French, Catholic Franco-Americans created "little Canadas" in some districts in the major American cities, faithfully reproducing their cultural life and Québecois religious institutions. Until WWII, and despite their Americanization, the descendants of the Québecois emigrants probably managed to preserve their identity better than other ethnic groups. Several major figures in Québec history had Franco-American roots, including journalist Olivar Asselin, writer Honoré Beaugrand, essayist Edmond de Nevers and ultramontane Jules-Paul TARDIVEL. Some Franco-Americans were repatriated to Canada around the beginning of the 20th century and formed the core of numerous francophone settlements in the West (*see* FRENCH IN THE WEST). With time, however, most Franco-Americans succumbed to the attractions of the American way of life and the English language, especially since they lived primarily in heavily urbanized surroundings. Nevertheless, today some Franco-Americans continue – though primarily in English – to take an interest in their historical roots, and preserve their network of ethnic relations and certain folkloric or gastronomic traditions. This mixture of modern and conservative has not prevented some Franco-Americans, eg, writer Jack Kerouac, athlete Napoleon Lajoie, from having a major impact in the US. However, the secularization of Québec society and its profound changes since the QUIET REVOLUTION have caused Franco-Americans and Québecois to have less in common than they once had. PIERRE ANCTIL

Franco-Ontarians are those Canadians whose mother tongue is French and who live in Ontario. In the 1986 census, 475 605 Ontarians (5.5% of the total population) indicated that French is their mother tongue, and an estimated 75% of these use French at home. Four out of 10 Franco-Ontarians live in the eastern part of the province between Ottawa and the Québec border; 33% are spread throughout the cities and towns of northern Ontario, and more than 25% live in major industrial centres and in long-established rural communities to the south.

French have lived in Ontario since the beginning of the French regime. In 1610, Étienne BRÛLÉ, on a reconnaissance mission for Samuel de CHAMPLAIN, was the first white man to set foot in what is now Ontario. French soldiers were later garrisoned in Fort Pontchartrain [Detroit] and FORT FRONTENAC [Kingston], while settlers lived near the forts, and COUREURS DES BOIS, missionaries and VOYAGEURS roamed the province.

The first agricultural settlement was established in the Detroit region in 1710, but French officers and colonial administrators returned to France after the territory was ceded to England. There was no further reinforcement of the small francophone communities until after 1840 when the rapidly growing population of Québec began to spill over into eastern Ontario, then (after 1880) into the Sudbury region, and finally at the turn of the century, into the "clay belts" of the north (Haileybury-Hearst). The industrial cities of the south have been attracting both Québecois and northern Franco-Ontarians for more than 100 years. ACADIANS, as well as Francophones from Belgium, France, Switzerland and North Africa joined many of these communities.

The great majority of Franco-Ontarians sought to recreate in Ontario their traditional cultural institutions – francophone Catholic parishes and French schools, co-operatives, and CAISSES POPULAIRES (a form of credit union developed in Québec). In 1910 they founded the Association canadienne-française de l'Ontario (ACFO) and, 3 years later, the Ottawa daily newspaper, *Le Droit*. Since 1910 Franco-Ontarians have battled, sometimes bitterly, to maintain and encourage school programs taught in French, particularly during the crisis caused by Regulation 17 (*see also* LANGUAGE POLICY; ONTARIO SCHOOLS QUESTION).

Because of their small numbers, Franco-Ontarians do not play a significant collective role in provincial or federal politics, but they wield considerable influence in a few ridings in the north and the east, and can therefore make their voices heard in Toronto and Ottawa. Their political energies are focused on defending their language and affirming their culture through such instruments as the ACFO and various regional and community-based volunteer organizations.

As a group, they are strongly represented in the primary sector (forestry, agriculture, mining), the public sector, and education.

Many Franco-Ontarians still centre their lives around the more than 200 active French Catholic parishes in the province. Dozens of "centres culturels" bring together craftspeople and artists. The 2 cultural areas in which Francophones are most productive are theatre, amateur and professional, and poetry. French radio and television, primarily Radio-Canada and to some extent the Ontario educational television network, serve the Franco-Ontarian community.

Increasingly, Franco-Ontarians are migrating to the large anglophone cities and losing touch with the religion that has constituted a strong bulwark of French culture. Anglo-francophone marriages are now more common than in the past and the home language of such families is usually English. However, a significant number of Franco-Ontarians seem determined to preserve their distinctive culture. The OFFICIAL LANGUAGES ACT of 1969 and the policy of the Ontario government to provide bilingual services to Francophones have provided some support for these efforts.

PIERRE SAVARD

Francophone-Anglophone Relations "Two nations warring in the bosom of a single state" was Lord DURHAM'S assessment of the relationship between LOWER CANADA'S 2 cultural and linguistic communities during the 1830s. Observers of the continuing debate over Québec's role within Confederation might be tempted to believe that Durham's assessment can be applied as a general principle to the entirety of the Canadian experience, but in fact the quality of francophone-anglophone relations over the past 200 years has ebbed and flowed in response to changing socioeconomic, political and ideological factors as well as to the commitment of French Canadians to survival and equality.

Any search for a theme to francophone-anglophone relations must take into account the fact that the francophone community constitutes a cultural minority; today, Francophones comprise only 27% of the Canadian population. Nevertheless, in Québec, Francophones have managed to remain at a constant 80% of the population despite extensive out-migration of Francophones and the continual arrival of non-French-speaking immigrants. Now that the birthrate among Francophones has dropped below the replacement level, contemporary Québecois nationalists feel that their majority position is threatened by an English-speaking minority that constitutes 35% of the population of metropolitan Montréal. Furthermore, when the intellectual and political elites of both communities have proposed and then attempted to reach divergent rather than co-operative social and political goals, the relationship between Francophones and Anglophones has been severely strained.

From 1763 to 1800, the relationship between the British colonial rulers and the traditional clerical and seigneurial leaders of French Canada was tense yet cordial. They shared the same commitment to Ancien Régime values and institutions. Both the QUEBEC ACT of 1774 and the CONSTITUTIONAL ACT, 1791, were deliberate attempts to reinforce the existing colonial social and political structures. However, this social contract began to break down after 1800 when Québec's economy and social structure were altered in fundamental ways. By 1820 Montréal was no longer the centre of the FUR TRADE, and the wheat economy of Lower Canada was in a serious crisis.

The seigneurial class, lacking its traditional access to wealth in the army, in the bureaucracy and in commerce, declined very rapidly after 1800, and the Catholic Church was unprepared at this time to assert control over Québec society (*see* SEIGNEURIAL SYSTEM). It was into this unstable context that a new francophone professional middle class emerged. This ambitious new class used the ideologies of NATIONALISM and political liberalism to gain control over the Assembly of Lower Canada by 1810, and then began to push for full control over the office of governor and the legislative and executive councils. When successive governors, with the support of the Anglo-Scottish merchants, refused to share power in any meaningful way, the francophone middle class, under the banner of the Parti patriote, advocated political reforms that would grant it full control over the appointed councils. When British colonial officials rejected these reform proposals, the Parti patriote attempted (1837-38) to seize power through arms. They intended to create an independent French Canadian republic under the presidency of Louis-Joseph PAPINEAU. The revolt failed because it lacked popular support, strong and courageous leadership, and because of the quick and harsh counteroffensive of well-armed British troops (*see* REBELLIONS OF 1837). The Parti patriote was left in total disarray and the separatist option was discredited for generations.

In the aftermath of the rebellions, the DURHAM REPORT and the ACT OF UNION of 1840 (proclaimed Feb 1841), which united Upper and Lower Canada in the PROVINCE OF CANADA and placed French Canadian society firmly under the control of an anglophone-controlled assembly and executive councils, the francophone professional middle class divided into 2 groups. One group, under the leadership of L.H. LAFONTAINE and E. PARENT, pursued a strategy of maximizing the autonomy of French Canada's cultural, social and religious institutions, hoping thereby to undermine the assimilationist intentions of Lord Durham and the British colonial officials. In order to achieve their goal they co-operated with Upper Canadian reformers in the struggle for and achievement of RESPONSIBLE GOVERNMENT. The second group, comprising remnants of the Parti patriote and a younger generation of nationalists in the INSTITUT CANADIEN and the PARTI ROUGE, rejected the Act of Union and campaigned for its repeal. As committed political nationalists they fought for the creation of a politically autonomous, secular and democratic Québec nation-state. After the achievement of responsible government in 1848, the reform party of LaFontaine and Parent evolved into the PARTI BLEU, which under the leadership of Joseph-Édouard CAUCHON and George-Étienne CARTIER became part of the CONSERVATIVE PARTY.

The Conservative Party, with the full support of a reinvigorated Catholic Church, sought further to enhance the autonomy of French Canada's cultural, social and religious institutions. The party also co-operated with the Anglo-Scottish bourgeoisie, represented by the Liberal-Conservative Party of J.A. MACDONALD, in the pursuit of economic development through the building of railways and the expansion of trade with the US and Great Britain. By 1865 a political deadlock developed in the Assembly because an increasing majority of Upper Canadians, led by George BROWN and his CLEAR GRIT faction, wanted out from under the yoke of a Union dominated by anglophone Montréalers and Cartier's bleus. The deadlock was broken when all members of the Assembly, except those belonging to the *rouge* movement, agreed to pursue the implementation of a federal system for Upper and Lower Canada or for all the British N American colonies.

After a lengthy and at times heated debate in the Assembly of the Canadas in 1865, the Québec resolutions, which called for the creation of a central government and a number of provinces, including Québec, were passed. Members of the *rouge* movement objected to the new constitution because, they claimed, it was too centralist and did not guarantee the survival of the francophone community. A slight majority of Francophones, convinced by the Conservative Party and a very cautious Catholic Church that the new constitution did offer certain guarantees, were willing to face the new risks primarily because of the increased political and cultural autonomy of the new province of Québec. During the 1867 federal and provincial elections the Conservative Party gained 45 of the 65 seats, a clear demonstration of the general support for the new constitutional arrangement. French Canadian secular and clerical leaders were beginning to participate in a small way in the commercial and industrial development of Québec. The modernization of the agricultural sector as well as the industrialization of the province in the last quarter of the century helped the francophone community pursue and achieve some of its cultural, social and political aspirations.

Within 30 years of CONFEDERATION, Québec's French Canadian majority developed a new attitude toward the Canadian federal system, for 2 reasons. First, there was a growing sense of confidence based on economic, cultural and religious renewal and expansion of the French Canadian society in Québec. Second, there was the increasingly difficult plight of the francophone minorities outside the province as evidenced by the 1871 abolition of the informal separate schools used by New Brunswick's Acadians; the RED RIVER REBELLION of 1869-70 and the NORTH-WEST REBELLION of 1885 (which both English- and French-speaking central Canadians interpreted as a struggle between French Catholics and English Protestants over who would determine the character of the West); the 1890 decision of the Manitoba Liberal government to abolish funding for Catholic schools recognized under the MANITOBA ACT of 1870 (*see* MANITOBA SCHOOLS QUESTION); the curtailment of separate schools in the 1905 Act creating the provinces of Alberta and Saskatchewan; and finally, Ontario's Regulation XVII, which undermined an informal system of bilingual separate schools by outlawing the use of French as a language of instruction until the late 1920s (*see* ONTARIO SCHOOLS QUESTION). As a result of these crises, Québec's French Canadian majority increasingly identified with the beleaguered francophone minorities as they came under attack from an aggressive and vocal English-speaking Canadian society determined to create a strong and homogeneous British Canadian national state.

In fact, many French Canadians felt their society was being forced to choose between provincial rights and minority rights, a choice that was simply not acceptable because provincial autonomy was considered the very root of the survival of the French Canadian nationality in Canada. In order to resolve this dilemma, a number of prominent French Canadians, led by Judge T.J.J. LORANGER and the journalist and politician Henri BOURASSA, began to supplement the "compact of provinces" theory with a "compact of nationalities" theory. It was argued that the concept of 2 nations, or 2 founding peoples, constituted the heart of Confederation. Consequently, francophone leaders responded to the minority-rights crises by appealing to the federal government to enforce the Constitution; only the full acceptance of a bilingual and bicultural country could prevent renewed and politically divisive attacks on francophone minorities. PM Wilfrid LAURIER attempted to apply the "two-nation" concept in his 1897 agreement with Premier GREENWAY of Manitoba. The agreement, which provided some restitution for Manitoba's rural Catholics, was abolished in 1916 by the Liberal government of T.C. Norris.

There was even less agreement between French- and English-speaking Canadians over foreign policy, especially the issue of Canada's role in the British Empire. From 1900 to 1920, French Canadian and British Canadian nationalists clashed repeatedly. French Canadian nationalists, led by Henri Bourassa, objected vociferously to Canada's increased participation in imperial schemes, whether economic, political or (especially) military. Bourassa strongly opposed the participation of Canadian troops in the SOUTH AFRICAN WAR on the grounds that all forms of IMPERIALISM were immoral and that the incident would serve as a precedent for future participation in other British imperial wars. Laurier tried to hold the moderates of both communities together by avoiding commitments and by creating, in 1910, a Canadian navy that could be put at the disposal of the Royal Navy in times of war, but this strategy merely aroused the ire of the nationalists on both sides and contributed to Laurier's downfall in the 1911 election. The inevitable clash between the 2 sides reached its climax in the 1917 CONSCRIPTION crisis and was symbolized by the formation of Borden's UNION GOVERNMENT that same year. The conscription issue divided the political parties along ethnic lines, as the vast majority of English-speaking MPs supported conscription and the Union government, while all French Canadian MPs were re-elected as anticonscriptionist Liberals.

The impact of this crisis on anglophone-francophone relations was devastating, especially for the intellectual and political elites of both communities. For the federal Conservative Party it proved a long-term disaster. French Canada's nationalists turned inward, away from Bourassa's laudable goal of achieving a bilingual and bicultural country. Abbé Lionel GROULX and his nationalist colleagues in *l'*ACTION FRANÇAISE focused their attention on protecting the French Canadian society of Québec from the onslaught of rapid industrialization and urbanization. They began to think seriously about the growing economic inferiority of French Canadians as individuals and as a collectivity. The French Canadian professional and commercial middle classes encountered increased competition from English Canadian and American conglomerates. On occasion, out of desperation, Groulx and his colleagues dreamed of an independent, traditional and rural French Canadian nation. Much of their desperation stemmed from the fact that the majority of French Canadians supported the Liberal government's policy of economic expansion through the development of Québec's abundant natural resources, particularly its forests and hydroelectric potential.

With the GREAT DEPRESSION, the serious economic disadvantages of French Canadians as a community and as individuals were made clear to the public. Middle-class French Canadians reacted by advocating socioeconomic and political reforms, eg, the creation of co-operatives, state support for francophone entrepreneurs, nationalization of the anglophone hydroelectric companies, regulation of large corporations and "buy-French-Canadian-made-products" campaigns. These measures, they claimed, would shore up traditional French Canadian society while giving middle-class French Canadians greater control over the economic development of Québec.

The UNION NATIONALE under Maurice DUPLESSIS made up of old-line Conservatives, disenchanted Liberals and traditional nationalists, took advantage of the nationalist reawakening created by the Depression to defeat the LIBERAL PARTY in 1936. Despite English-speaking Canadians' fears, Duplessis, who was essentially a constitutional nationalist, refused to proceed with the economic nationalist reforms championed by the nationalists inside and outside of the party. His party was defeated in the 1939 provincial election, which he chose to contest on the use of conscription, by the direct intervention of the Liberal Party of Mackenzie KING and Ernest LAPOINTE, King's French Canadian lieutenant. Lapointe and his francophone colleagues had threatened to resign and allow the conscriptionist Conservative Party to take over the federal reins if French Canadians refused to turf out the troublesome Duplessis. In return for a promise of no conscription for overseas service, French Canadians reluctantly agreed to Canadian participation in WWII.

With the fall of France in 1940, the demand for conscription from parts of English-speaking Canada intensified. PM King hoped to undermine the conscriptionist movement, especially its Tory leader Arthur MEIGHEN, by holding a plebiscite in which all Canadians would be asked to relieve the federal government of its pledge of no conscription for overseas service. Haunted once again by the threat of conscription, various French Canadian nationalist movements came together in the League for the Defence of Canada to campaign vigorously and successfully for a NO vote in the Apr 1942 plebiscite. Canada was again divided between the 2 communities.

King heeded the message and declared that there would be "conscription if necessary, but not necessarily conscription." His government was able to delay the implementation of conscription until late in 1944, when a vocal Cabinet minority and rebellious military officers forced King to consent to conscript 16 000 of the home-defence forces. French Canadian nationalists were incensed, but the decision had come too late to help their movement, the BLOC POPULAIRE CANADIEN, during the 1944 provincial election. In the 1945 election, French Canadians helped re-elect the Liberal government.

Anglophone-francophone relations had weathered both the depression and the war. Both communities had continued to play by the rules established in 1867, while nevertheless continuing to challenge the interpretation of those rules, especially in the area of social policy. Between 1945 and 1975 this situation changed dramatically as a result of several factors. The most important political factor was Ottawa's postwar decision (which was supported by a new generation of English Canadian nationalists) to forge ahead with the creation of a centralized WELFARE STATE. Ottawa's predominantly anglophone politicians and bureaucrats argued that the federal government needed full control over all forms of direct TAXATION to ensure stable economic development and to defray the cost of programs such as UNEMPLOYMENT INSURANCE, FAMILY ALLOWANCES, OLD-AGE PENSIONS, and hospital and medical-insurance schemes.

While the provinces rejected Ottawa's arguments they were slow to make counter-proposals. In Québec, however, the French Canadian nationalist movement exerted sufficient pressure on the Duplessis government to ensure that it would reject Ottawa's tax-rental scheme and its more audacious measures, such as federal grants to universities. For a younger generation of French Canadian nationalists this defensive strategy was insufficient. These "neo-nationalists," as they came to be called, led by André LAURENDEAU, Gérard FILION and Jean-Marc LÉGER and supported by a new francophone middle class educated in the sciences and social sciences, advocated the creation in Québec of a secular, interventionist, francophone-controlled state which would undertake the development of natural resources by French Canadians for French Canadians. Only an active nationalist state could help create an appropriate environment for the emergence of a strong francophone industrial and financial bourgeoisie. In order to ensure that a sufficient number of French Canadians were prepared to assume control of a modern secular society, the state would proceed with comprehensive modernization of education at all levels, and to ensure that the welfare-state apparatus as it affected Québec was controlled by Francophones, neo-nationalists proposed that all social programs be taken over by the Québec government. This exercise of Québec's constitutional prerogatives, both established and new, would require a significant increase in the province's ability to collect taxes.

The socioeconomic changes in Canada that were caused by growing industrialization and urbanization and the influx into Canada of thousands of immigrants who spoke neither English nor French created new strains on the French Canadian society; at the heart of the tension lay the realization by Francophones that their economic and social future was urban and industrial. The francophone community's search for survival and equality clashed with the postwar national aspirations of English-speaking Canadians, and the stage was set for conflict over available resources and jobs. Moreover, with the rapid secularization of French Canadian society, Catholicism no longer distinguished French Canada from the rest of N America. With the increased assimilation of Francophones outside Québec and the overwhelming integration of all immigrants into Québec's English-speaking community (which comprises nearly 35% of metropolitan Montréal's population), it was inevitable that language would become a dominant issue in contemporary Québec.

The defeat (1960) of the Union Nationale by the Liberal Party of Jean LESAGE ushered in the QUIET REVOLUTION, which signalled the beginning of a dual struggle: one involving the new middle-class' political and socioeconomic battle for greater control over Québec's economic resources, and another involving a bitter and divisive attempt to redefine the role of the francophone society within Canada. Since the early 1960s successive Québec governments have tried to change the socieconomic relationship between that province's francophone majority and its English-speaking minorities. In the first stage of the Quiet Revolution, the Lesage government modernized and expanded the public and parapublic sectors to provide employment for the postwar BABY BOOM generation of highly educated Francophones. For example, private hydroelectric companies were nationalized. As a result, HYDRO-QUÉBEC (est 1944) became one of the largest CROWN CORPORATIONS in Canada. Francophones were able to work entirely in French and to demonstrate their technical, scientific and managerial skills, a process which also occurred in the fields of education, social welfare and health services, and in the government bureaucracy in all departments and at all levels.

French Canada's attempt to redefine its role within Canada has produced vigorous public debates during the past 20 years. In their 1965 royal commission preliminary report on BILINGUALISM AND BICULTURALISM, the commissioners stated that Canada was in the midst of its most serious political crisis since Confederation. Beginning in 1963, several bombs had been set off in Montréal mail boxes, and 2 separatist parties were successfully recruiting francophone university students. By the mid-1960s a wide variety of proposals for restructuring, renewing and even dismantling the Canadian federal system were forthcoming.

Drawing upon the recommendations of the Tremblay Commission Report of 1956, many Québec neo-nationalists advocated the entrenchment, in a renewed Constitution, of "special status" for the province of Québec, while others demanded a form of "associate-state" status. In fact, by 1966 the political parties were leapfrogging one another in a desperate attempt to keep pace with the nationalist momentum sweeping Québec. Daniel JOHNSON, the leader of the Union Nationale, issued an ultimatum to Ottawa entitled *Equality or Independence.* Special or associate-state status would entail very extensive decentralization of what was considered by many Canadians already a far too decentralized federal system. Yet there were also a number of neo-nationalists who argued for the complete political independence of Québec.

By the mid-1960s, the neo-nationalists encountered opposition from all national parties and a number of prominent Francophones such as Jean MARCHAND, Pierre Elliott TRUDEAU and Gérard PELLETIER. These men had been recruited by the Liberal Party of Prime Minister PEARSON to enhance francophone participation in the national government and help Ottawa head off potentially dangerous political clashes with Québec's increasingly separatist-oriented neo-nationalist movement.

The federal forces, under PM Pierre Trudeau, proposed a twofold strategy: to enhance the full participation of Francophones in all national institutions through a policy of official bilingualism and to insert into a renewed Constitution guarantees for all minorities via an entrenched Charter of Rights. While the first goal was met in 1969 with the passing of the OFFICIAL LANGUAGES ACT, the second was not accomplished until 1982 (*see* CONSTITUTION, PATRIATION OF).

Québec presented the major obstacle in the path of a renewed Constitution. The new liberal leader and premier of Québec by 1970, Robert BOURASSA, attempted to secure increased provincial powers in the area of social policy in return for his government's consent to patriate the Constitution and entrench a Charter of Rights. When Bourassa failed to accomplish his goal, neo-nationalist pressures forced him to reject the 1971 Victoria Charter.

In 1976 the PARTI QUÉBÉCOIS, committed to the achievement of political independence for Québec, was elected. The PQ government moved quickly to accomplish its election promises, especially in the highly sensitive area of language legislation. When it had become apparent by the late 1950s that room for expansion in the public sector was not infinite, pressure had begun to build in nationalist circles for language legislation making French the dominant language of work in both the private and public sector. In 1974 the Liberal government of Robert Bourassa implemented BILL 22, under which French became the official language of Québec and enrolment in English-language schools was restricted. While this legislation was too drastic for Québec's anglophone and allophone communities, it did not go far enough for an increasing majority of French Canadians, who felt Bill 22 had too many awkward provisions and did little to ensure that French would become the effective language of work for all Québec's citizens. In response to strong and widespread nationalist pressure inside and outside the party, the assembly passed BILL 101, known as the Charter of the French Language, which made French the only official language of Québec, established a schedule for making French the dominant language of work and stipulated that all immigrants entering Québec from other parts of Canada and the world must enrol their children in French-language schools.

These developments considerably heightened the tension in anglophone-francophone relations, not only in Québec but throughout Canada. The federal Liberal Party, after its re-election to office in 1980, campaigned hard to ensure a defeat of the PQ-sponsored referendum requesting that Quebeckers grant the PQ government a mandate to negotiate SOVEREIGNTY-ASSOCIATION.

The Trudeau government's decision to pursue the patriation of the Constitution with an amendment formula and an entrenched Charter of Rights was prompted by the victory of the federalist forces in the QUÉBEC REFERENDUM campaign. The constitutional agreement was approved by Ottawa and all the provinces except Québec. The tragedy was that, in the process of political maneuvering, Québec had agreed with several other provinces to relinquish its traditional veto over constitutional changes crucial to the survival of the French Canadian nationality. A process of constitutional renewal set in motion largely in response to the new needs of Québec resulted in an agreement which could, under the appropriate set of circumstances, create new tensions and even overt hostility between Canada's 2 linguistic communities.

While the PQ government was re-elected in 1981, it was weakened by internal battles and was soundly defeated by Robert Bourassa's Liberal Party in 1985. Bourassa committed his government to signing the 1982 Constitutional Accord if certain demands were met by Ottawa and the provinces. These 5 minimum demands included the constitutional recognition of Québec as a "distinct society" with the right to protect and promote that distinctiveness; the right to opt-out with full financial compensation of all national programs in areas of provincial jurisdiction; an amendment formula that gives Québec a veto over all major constitutional reforms; a guarantee of increased powers over immigration; and finally, some input into the appointment of judges to the Supreme Court. On 30 Apr 1987, after months of behind-the-scenes negotiations, PM Brian MULRONEY's government announced the MEECH LAKE ACCORD. The Accord was considered acceptable by the NDP and Liberal parties but was stridently denounced by ex-PM Trudeau as diminishing the prerogatives of the national government and hence of national patriotism and setting in motion an irreversible trend toward increased provincial autonomy with "special status" for Québec. To take effect, the Accord must be ratified by all 10 provinces and the House of Commons and the Senate by June 1990. The debate over our constitutional future is just getting started and the implications of this ongoing process for francophone-anglophone relations is difficult to predict with any degree of accuracy. *See also* OCTOBER CRISIS; QUÉBEC SINCE CONFEDERATION. M. D. BEHIELS

Francophonie is a term that emerged in the 1950s and has 2 main meanings. The primary one designates the grouping of peoples and communities throughout the world with French as their maternal or customary language. In its second sense, the term has come to mean an increasingly large and complex network of private and public organizations promoting special ties among all Francophones.

Except for international institutions created and run by France, such as Alliance française (1883), International Francophonie is relatively young. Truly multilateral associations devoted to closer ties between francophone groups began to appear shortly after WWII, eg, la Fédération internationale de la presse de langue française (Paris, 1948), l'Association des universités partiellement ou entièrement de langue française (Montréal, 1961) and l'Institut international de droit d'expression française (1964). These are all private bodies, although they often benefit from government subsidies. The private sector of International Francophonie continues to develop rapidly. There are some 50 international French-language federations, communities, academies, associations and institutes working to increase co-operation in many different fields.

In 1967, elected members of some 20 national parliaments met as delegates in Luxembourg to set up the Association internationale des parlementaires de langue française. Two years later, an international conference in Zaire brought together an equal number of ministers of education, this time officially representing their governments. However, a permanent body was not formed until 1970, when ministerial delegates from 21 countries met in Niamey, Niger, to found l'Agence de coopération culturelle et technique (ACCT), an international organization devoted to multilateral governmental co-operation. The ACCT brings together French-speaking states whose mutual goals include the development of culture, education, science and technology. The first full-fledged meeting of the ACCT was held in Paris 1986. In 1987 delegations from members and nonmembers that met at Québec City were Belgium, Benin, Burkina Faso [Upper Volta] , Burundi, Canada, Central African Republic, Chad, Comoros, Congo, Djibouti, Dominica, Egypt, France, Gabon, Guinea, Guinea-Bissau, Haiti, Ivory Coast, Laos, Lebanon, Luxembourg, Madagascar, Mali, Mauritania, Mauritius, Monaco, Morocco, Niger, Rwanda, St Lucia, Senegal, Seychelles, Switzerland, Togo, Tunisia, Vietnam and Zaire. Two Canadian provinces, Québec and New Brunswick, have the status of participating governments. At this summit, Canada announced a contribution of $17 million to assist new and existing projects in French-speaking Africa and debt forgiveness of $325 million in loans, affecting African nations. The next summit is to be held in Senegal in 1989.

The comparison is often drawn between Francophonie and the COMMONWEALTH. The similarities are evident: each includes developing and developed countries; each consists largely of former colonies, most of which achieved independence after WWII; finally, each has the same general objectives of mutual assistance, co-operation and development in all fields. But Commonwealth structures are very different from those adopted by Francophonie. Despite much discussion of the idea, for example, there is no equivalent in Francophonie of the biannual summit meetings held by the heads of state of Commonwealth countries. Canada has been active in International Francophonie since its beginnings, in both public and private sectors. GÉRARD PELLETIER

Francq, Gustave, typographer, labour leader (b at Brussels, Belgium Mar 1871; d at Montréal 2 Jan 1952). Sometimes considered the father of international unionism in Québec, Francq immigrated to Québec C in 1889 and learned typography. In Montréal, he became an official in the Union typographique Jacques Cartier and in the Conseil des métiers et du travail de Montréal and was VP of the TRADES AND LABOR CONGRESS OF CANADA 1909-11. In *Le Monde ouvrier/The Labour World,* the journal he founded in 1916, he defended the international union movement against criticism by clergy and Catholic unions. In 1908 Francq ran in the provincial election on behalf of the Parti ouvrier. After WWI he grew closer to the LIBERAL PARTY. In 1926 he was appointed the first president of Québec's Minimum Wage Commission. He became honorary life president in the Fédération provinciale du travail du Québec for his outstanding contributions to international unionism in Québec. JACQUES ROUILLARD

Some 74 million tonnes of rock crashed down Turtle Mountain in the disastrous 1903 Frank Slide that killed at least 70 people (*courtesy Elliott and Nicole Bernshaw/ Bernshaw Photography*).

Frank Slide At 4:10 AM on 29 Apr 1903, 74 million t of rock crashed down the E slope of Turtle Mtn in the CROWSNEST PASS region of Alberta, burying a mine entrance and the eastern outskirts of Frank, NWT (Alta), sweeping 1.6 km across the valley and covering roads, railways, houses and farms. After 13 hours of heroic effort, 17 men entombed in the mine, fighting a dwindling air supply, dug a new shaft and emerged to freedom. Twenty-three men, women and children were rescued from the rubble, but at least 70 others died in the sudden disaster. The town was evacuated as a precaution against further slides. When none occurred the residents returned and reopened the mine. A new coal mine was opened north of the mountain. In 1913, the old mine was closed and in 1918 fires closed the entire workings. Turtle Mtn is a naturally unstable slope, and earthquakes, erosion and coal mining combined to cause the rockslide. Turtle Mtn is now monitored daily for any movement. *See also* DISASTERS; ROCKSLIDE. FRANK W. ANDERSON

Reading: Frank W. Anderson, *Turtle Mountain Disaster* (1986).

Franklin, Sir John, naval officer, arctic explorer (b at Spilsby, Eng 16 Apr 1786; d 11 June 1847 aboard HMS *Erebus,* in Victoria Str, NWT). From 1801 to 1804 Franklin developed surveying skills and an interest in natural science, which determined his future as the best-known and perhaps greatest explorer in the British-American Arctic. He owes his fame to the long and much publicized search for him and his lost vessels; he earned it with his exploratory expeditions – westbound from the Atlantic – and by his charting of Canada's arctic seaboard. He has been called discoverer of the NORTHWEST PASSAGE, but not one man lived to report his success, which only became known 9 years after its discovery by Robert MCCLURE had been announced.

In 1818 Franklin was second in command of an abortive voyage into the Spitsbergen ice. In 1819 the British ADMIRALTY appointed him to map N America's unknown arctic seaboard. He was to descend the turbulent and supposedly unnavigable COPPERMINE R and explore eastward by canoe. In 1821 he surveyed about 340 km of intricate, ice-infested shoreline, but through cold and hunger lost about 10 men on the overland homeward trek owing to the inadequacy of canoes in pack ice and his unfamiliarity with traders, VOYAGEURS and northern conditions. In his well-organized second expedition (1825-27), he made the approach in seaworthy boats by the Mackenzie R, and from its mouth sent 2 boats east to map as far as the Coppermine R while he headed west. Hindered by ice and fog he surveyed 640 km of shoreline before turning back from an inlet he named Prudhoe Bay. The eastern detachment completed its assignment and, as prudently arranged by Franklin, made a quick, safe return overland.

Thomas Simpson of the HBC extended these surveys, and to the N ships explored among the islands. In 1845 Franklin was sent with 2 vessels, *Erebus* and *Terror*, to join these discoveries together and sail through the Northwest Passage. He never returned, and after a 12-year search by numerous vessels it was learned that on the brink of success his ships had been frozen in W of King William I. Franklin had died 11 June 1847, and command devolved on Capt Francis Crozier who abandoned ship and with 105 surviving crew trekked southward toward the Back R. All perished, most of them near Victory Point. The fame of Franklin's "mystery" and the many voyages made to solve it have obscured the explorer's solid merits. He had shown boldness and resource in pioneering a new method of discovery in the Arctic and had added more to the coastal map of Canada than any other explorer except George VANCOUVER. *See also* FRANKLIN SEARCH. L.H. NEATBY

Sir John Franklin, arctic explorer, best remembered for the long and much-publicized search for him and his lost vessels. He perished in his icebound ship off King William I (*courtesy National Archives of Canada/C-1352*).

Franklin, Ursula Martius, physicist, educator (b at Munich, Germany 16 Sept 1921). A specialist in the structure of metals and alloys, she pioneered the development of archaeometry, which applies the modern techniques of materials analysis to ARCHAEOLOGY. She was educated at the Technical U of Berlin and did post-doctoral studies at U of T. After working for the Ontario Research Foundation 1952-67, she joined U of T's department of metallurgy and materials science in 1967. Franklin has helped develop science policy through the Science Council of Canada and the Natural Sciences and Engineering Research Council of Canada. She worked on gathering and analysing data on the strontium-90 accumulation in the teeth of children in Canada as a result of fallout from tests of nuclear weapons; the dating of copper, bronze, metal and ceramic artifacts of prehistoric cultures in Canada and elsewhere; and she has tried to educate society and scientists to the impact of science and technology on human survival and quality of life. She is a tireless advocate for Science for Peace. Her work has received worldwide recognition and brought her many honours. These include a Doctor of Science from Queen's (1985) and a Doctor of Humane Letters from Mount Saint Vincent (1985). In 1984 Franklin became the first woman to be named a University Professor at U of T.

ROSE SHEININ

Franklin Search The disappearance of Sir John FRANKLIN and his crew in what is now the Canadian Arctic set off one of the greatest rescue operations in the history of exploration. Franklin's 2 ships had sailed from England on 19 May 1845 and were last sighted in late July heading for Lancaster Sd. A 3-way search was organized in 1848, with Sir James Clark ROSS proceeding through Lancaster Sd, Capt Henry Kellet via Bering Str, and John RAE and Sir John RICHARDSON trekking overland from the Mackenzie R. No definite traces of the expedition were found and in 1850 more search parties were sent out. The Admiralty sent Richard Collinson and Robert MCCLURE via Bering Str, and Horatio Austin and William Penny from the E. The HBC sent its own expedition under Sir John ROSS, and the first American expedition to the North was led by E.J. De Haven. Lady Franklin financed an expedition under Charles Forsyth.

Franklin's 1845-46 winter quarters on Beechey I were found, but his fate remained unknown and Lady Franklin sent another search party out in 1851. The Admiralty sent its last and greatest expedition in 1852 under Sir Edward BELCHER, as concern mounted not only for Franklin but also for McClure and Collinson, who had not been heard from. In Aug 1853 the supply ship BREADALBANE sank in a storm off Beechey I. Belcher returned ignominiously in 1854 after unnecessarily abandoning 4 ships. Though nothing new was learned of Franklin's whereabouts, the expedition had managed to rescue McClure, who with his crew was awarded the Admiralty prize for completing the NORTHWEST PASSAGE. It was John Rae who in 1854 was given the £10 000 reward for settling Franklin's fate: on the basis of Inuit reports and evidence of personal effects belonging to the crew, he concluded that all had perished on or near KING WILLIAM I. Lady Franklin was not convinced, and sent Leopold MCCLINTOCK in 1857. This expedition explored King William I, and in 1859 found additional artifacts, skeletons and the only written record of the disaster. In 1869 American explorer Charles Francis HALL briefly searched the SE region of King William I, and in 1879 another American, Lieutenant Frederick SCHWATKA, made the first summer search of the island and the adjacent mainland.

The graves of 3 Franklin expedition crewmen located on Beechey I, NWT. In the foreground is the grave of 20-year-old petty officer John Torrington (d 1 Jan 1846); the centre grave is that of 25-year-old ablebodied seaman John Hartnell (d 4 Jan 1846), and the third grave is that of 33-year-old Royal Marine private William Braine (d 3 Apr 1846). The original headboards were erected at the time of burial in 1846. These were replaced with replicas during the 1970s by the Canadian government (*photo by Owen Beattie/U of A*).

Searches for the remains of Franklin's expedition continued into the 20th century. In 1930 a Canadian government-sponsored party, led by Major L.T. Burwash and flown by bush pilot Walter Gilbert, found some artifacts on the NW side of King William I, but too few to be of great significance. In 1931 William Gibson of the HBC searched the south coast of King William I, discovering a number of skeletons and artifacts. The 19th- and early 20th-century Franklin searches resulted in a great expansion in the knowledge of numerous islands and various routes through the Northwest Passage. More recent Franklin searches have involved a systematic and scientific approach to the problem. Anthropologists from the U of A discovered the scattered and fragmentary remains of at least 7 unidentified Franklin expedition crew members on King William I during archaeological surveys conducted there in 1981 and 1982. Analysis of the remains identified the presence of SCURVY and the probable occurrence of cannibalism, a controversial and unresolved issue of the Franklin expedition first raised by Rae in 1854. In 1984 and 1986 U of A researchers temporarily exhumed and examined 3 Franklin expedition crew members preserved in permafrost since their burial on Beechey I early in 1846. The results of this research indicate that food quality and preservation problems may have contributed to the disaster.

JAMES MARSH AND OWEN BEATTIE

Reading: R. Amy, R. Bahatnagar, E. Damkjar and Owen Beattie, "Report of a post-mortem exam on a member of the last Franklin Expedition," *Canadian Medical Association Journal* 135 (1986); Owen Beattie, "Elevated bone lead levels in a crewman from the last Arctic Expedition of Sir John Franklin," *The Franklin Era in Canadian Arctic History: 1845-1859* (1985). L.H. Neatby, *The Search for Franklin* (1970).

Franks, Wilbur Rounding, medical researcher, inventor of the "G suit" (b at Weston, Ont 4 Mar 1901; d at Toronto 4 Jan 1986). After graduating in medicine at U of T, Franks trained in cancer research under F.W. BANTING and took charge of wartime RCAF medical research after Banting's death. He invented the pressure suit, which allows pilots to carry out high-speed maneuvres without losing consciousness, used by Allied fighter pilots from 1942 onwards. Astronauts' pressure suits today are mere refinements of Franks's design. For this project, he built in wartime the first Canadian human centrifuge. Franks's wartime laboratory became the RCAF Institute of Aviation Medicine, now the Defence and Civil Institute of Environmental Medicine, Toronto.

DONALD J.C. PHILLIPSON

Franquelin, Jean-Baptiste-Louis, cartographer, royal hydrographer, teacher of navigation (b at Saint-Michel de Villebernin, France 1651; d in France after 1712). The first official cartographer in Canada, Franquelin drew some 50 richly illustrated manuscript maps of New France between 1674 and 1708. Although not published, his maps were important sources for French mapmakers, especially Guillaume Delisle (*Carte du Canada*, 1703). Franquelin came to Canada as a trader in 1671. Recognizing his talents Governor Frontenac recruited him to draw maps (*see* CARTOGRAPHY). Between 1674 and 1684 he recorded the explorations of Louis JOLLIET and Cavalier de LA SALLE, and in 1686 Franquelin was appointed king's hydrographer. In 1692 he went to France to complete a series of maps on the New England coast. His wife and 10 of 13 children were to join him the following year but were drowned in a shipwreck. Although he held his Canadian appointment from 1686 to 1697 and again from 1701 to 1703 he never returned, and from 1694 to 1707 he seems to have been working for Louis XIV's military engineer, Vauban.

C.E. HEIDENREICH

Armand Frappier, outstanding microbiologist (*photo by André Larose, Montréal*).

Frappier, Armand, physician, microbiologist (b at Salaberry-de-Valleyfield, Qué 26 Nov 1904). After receiving his MD (1930) and MSc (1931) from U de M, Frappier won a scholarship from the Rockefeller Foundation (1931-32). He studied tuberculosis and BCG (bacille Calmette-Guérin) vaccine in the US and at the Institut Pasteur in Paris, working in the Calmette, Guérin and Nègre laboratories. He returned to the Institut in 1937 to study applications of immunology and anatoxins.

In 1933 Frappier became chief of the laboratories at Hôpital Saint-Luc and professor of bacteriology at U de M. In 1938 he founded the Institut de microbiologie et d'hygiène de Montréal (renamed INSTITUT ARMAND-FRAPPIER in 1975), with the complementary goals of research, post-academic teaching, certain health services, and services to industry in the production of biological products. In 1945 he founded the first French-language school of hygiene in the world at U de M, and was its dean 1945-65.

Frappier was one of the first N Americans to confirm the safety and efficacy of BCG and to develop original study and utilization methods for the vaccine. With his colleague Paul Lemonde and his daughter, Lise Davignon, he showed for the first time a nonspecific preventative effect of this vaccine in cases of infant leukemia. For years he studied the mechanisms of infection and of resistance (specific or nonspecific) to certain infections. He has encouraged the international study of leprosy at the Institut and helped bring about the establishment there of one of the few laboratories devoted to this work. Frappier, who retired in 1974, remains a consultant and is professor emeritus of U de M. Foreign associate of the Académie nationale de médecine de France, he was president of the BCG committee of the International Union Against Tuberculosis and a member of the experts panel of TB for the World Health Organization. Among other honours, he is a Companion of the Order of Canada and officer of the Order of the British Empire, and holds honorary doctorates from Laval and the universities of Paris, Montréal, Québec and Krakow. CLAUDE VÉZINA

Fraser, Blair, journalist (b at Sydney, NS 17 Apr 1909; d on the Petawawa R, Ont 12 May 1968). Fraser was one of the leading journalists of the 1950s and 1960s, and as Ottawa editor of *Maclean's* 1943-60 he had a unique opportunity to influence a national audience. Educated at Acadia, Fraser worked on Montréal's English dailies 1929-43, and went to *Maclean's* to cover wartime politics. His success was based on his close friendships with politicians and officials; he had unrivalled access to government secrets when the Liberals were in power and only slightly less when the Conservatives were at the helm. When he left Ottawa in 1960, he became editor of *Maclean's* for 2 years and was then the magazine's London correspondent, before returning to Ottawa in 1963. He drowned in a canoeing accident. J.L. GRANATSTEIN

Fraser, Frank Clarke, physician, medical geneticist (b at Norwich, Conn 29 Mar 1920). After graduating from Acadia in biology in 1940, Fraser received an MSc in 1941 and a PhD in 1945 from McGill. Interested in GENETICS as applied to human conditions as well as the genetics of malformations in mice, he entered medical school at McGill and graduated in 1950. He started the first medical genetics clinic in a Canadian hospital at Montréal Children's, was president of the American Soc of Human Genetics (1961-62), of the Teratological Soc (1962-63) and of the Canadian Coll of Medical Geneticists (1980-83), and has served on numerous human-genetics committees. He has been professor emeritus at McGill since 1985 and that same year became an Officer of the Order of Canada. A prolific and valuable contributor to the literature, he has published more than 200 works dealing with the genetics of congenital malformations in mice and humans and has greatly influenced a generation of physicians and geneticists. P.A. BAIRD

Fraser, Graham, industrialist, community leader (b at New Glasgow, NS 12 Aug 1846; d there 25 Dec 1915). Following training in the US, Fraser returned to New Glasgow in 1867 to work in J.W. CARMICHAEL's shipyards. In 1872 he and George Forrest Mackay formed the Hope Iron Works, which became the Nova Scotia Forge Co in 1874. In 1882 Fraser organized the Nova Scotia Steel Co at Trenton. At nearby Ferrona, Fraser built North America's first coal-washing and retort ovens for making coke. Fraser led Scotia's development of iron-ore deposits at BELL ISLAND, Nfld, and coal at SYDNEY MINES, Cape Breton. He resigned in 1903, however, over questions of financial management, and for a short time was director of works for Dominion Iron and Steel. Fraser served New Glasgow variously as town councillor, water commissioner, mayor and director of the Aberdeen Hospital. L.D. MCCANN

Blair Fraser was one of the leading journalists of the 1950s and 1960s. He drowned in a canoeing accident (*courtesy National Archives of Canada/MISA/CBC Coll/ 14057*).

Reading: J.M. Cameron, "The Steelmakers," NS Historical Soc *Collections* 40 (1980), and *Political Pictonians* (1967).

Fraser, John Anderson, journalist (b at Montréal 5 June 1944). After study at several Canadian and British universities Fraser worked as music and dance critic on the Toronto *Telegram* during 1971-72 and at similar duties on the *Globe and Mail* during 1972-77 before being chosen, rather unexpectedly, to be that newspaper's correspondent in Peking. By chance the term of his assignment, 1977-79, coincided with China's "Tiny Democracy Movement," during which the normally strict controls on the Chinese people were briefly relaxed by the authorities, and Fraser was able to report on aspects of the country ordinarily concealed from western correspondents. His reports won a National Newspaper Award (his third) in 1978; and his book, *The Chinese: Portrait of a People* (1980) was a bestseller. His subsequent career, as columnist, editor and European correspondent for the *Globe and Mail*, was less spectacular. In 1987 he was named editor of *Saturday Night* magazine. STANLEY GORDON

Fraser, John Arthur, artist, illustrator, teacher (b at London, Eng 9 Jan 1838; d at New York C, NY 1 Jan 1898). Soon after emigrating from England in 1858, Fraser joined the firm of William NOTMAN in Montréal as a tinter of photographs, and in 1868 he moved to Toronto to establish the partnership of Notman and Fraser. He was the prime mover behind the formation of the Ontario Soc of Artists in 1872 and he taught in its School of Art, founded in 1876. He was also involved in the Royal Canadian Academy (est 1880). A belligerent man of strong opinions, Fraser was frequently embroiled in bitter disputes with fellow artists. During the last 14 years of his life, Fraser lived in the US. His landscapes were praised by reviewers for the artist's photographic realism, observation of detail and use of light and colour. MARY F. WILLIAMSON

Fraser, John James, lawyer, premier (1878-82) and lt-gov (1893-96) of NB (b at Miramichi, NB 1 Aug 1829; d in Italy 24 Nov 1896). An outstanding lawyer, in 1865 Fraser won a seat in the provincial legislature as an anti-Confederation candidate. From 1871 to 1872 he was president of the executive council and from 1872 to 1878 provincial secretary. He was premier and attorney general 1878-82. He was appointed to the Supreme Court of NB in 1882 and from 1893 to 1896 was lt-gov. He was a mild-mannered, popular man who was liked even by his opponents. His colleagues apparently ran his government, however, and his administration did not produce much significant legislation. ARTHUR T. DOYLE

Fraser, Simon, fur trader, explorer (b at Mapletown, near Bennington, Vt 1776; d at St Andrews, Canada W 18 Aug 1862). Fraser was the youngest son of a Loyalist officer, who was captured by revolutionaries and died in prison. His widow brought Simon to Montréal, where his uncle, Judge John Fraser, educated him. In 1792 he joined the NORTH WEST CO as a clerk; in 1799 he was serving in the Athabaska Dept and he became a partner in 1801. Fraser's main achievements occurred between 1805 and 1808. In 1805 he was placed in charge of the company's operations beyond the Rockies, and he founded the earliest settlements in the area he named NEW CALEDONIA (central BC). He established Ft McLeod in 1805, Ft St James and Ft Fraser in 1806, and Ft George (at present PRINCE GEORGE) in 1807. In 1808, he set out to explore the river he thought was the Columbia. Following the stretch explored by Alexander MACKENZIE in 1793, he entered territory unknown to white men and struggled through the perilous stretch now known as the FRASER RIVER CANYON. At the hostile village of Musqueam at the river's mouth, he took bearings and realized he could not be on the Columbia. Greatly disappointed, he turned back. David THOMPSON, who explored the real Columbia, named Simon's river the FRASER R; Simon had already named the THOMPSON R in David's honour.

Fraser wearied of the FUR TRADE and in 1815 sought retirement, but was persuaded to go back to Athabaska. He was one of the NWC officers arrested by Lord SELKIRK at FT WILLIAM in 1816 and charged with complicity in the SEVEN OAKS INCIDENT. Fraser was eventually acquitted; meanwhile he had retired to St Andrews among the Scots of Glengarry County, where he spent the rest of his life uneventfully. The documents relating to his great journey, *The Letters and Journals of Simon Fraser, 1806-08*, were edited by W. Kaye LAMB and finally published in 1960.

GEORGE WOODCOCK

Fraser, William, first Roman Catholic bishop of Halifax (b at Glenn Cannich, Scot 1778 or 1779; d at Antigonish, NS 4 Oct 1851). A missionary by training and preference, he was most effective when serving the spiritual and educational needs of his fellow Highland Scots in eastern NS. A reluctant but sincere prelate, his tenure as vicar apostolic of NS (1824-42) was the focus of unrest between Scottish and Irish elements of the church in NS. His decision not to move to Halifax, after being appointed bishop of Halifax in 1842, soon led to a division of the diocese of NS, with Fraser being appointed bishop of Arichat and William Walsh, an Irishman, becoming bishop of Halifax. Fraser was a pious and devoted priest, and his chief legacy was the establishment of Saint Andrew's Grammar School at Arichat, the precursor of St Francis Xavier U at Antigonish.

DAVID B. FLEMMING

Fraser Institute, a nonprofit group established in 1974 under federal charter and headquartered in Vancouver. The institute, which has been noted for its conservative views, operates as a research and educational organization that supports free enterprise and attempts to influence public policy through publication of studies by staff economists and academics; through representations to governments; placement of materials in schools, universities and churches; media interviews; and speeches and symposia. It is funded by private donations, fees and sales of publications.

GORDON W. STEAD

Fraser River, 1368 km long, with a drainage basin of 233 000 km², rises in the western slopes of the ROCKY MTS near Jasper National Park at an elevation of 1109 m, and flows slowly NW in meandering channels along the flat valley floor of the ROCKY MTN TRENCH to Prince George, BC, where it bends to a southward course. The gravel banks of the Fraser then increase in height to 50-100 m where the river has cut down into the glacial deposits of the central Interior Plateau; the river's velocity of flow increases S of Prince George as it is joined by several tributaries, the largest being the NECHAKO R from the NW.

The Fraser enters FRASER RIVER CANYON S of Quesnel, and where it is joined by the Chilcotin R from the W, the river has cut down 300-600 m into the bedrock of the Interior Plateau. At the southern end of the canyon, near Yale, the river flows between the N end of the CASCADE MTS to its E and the COAST MTS on the W. In this middle section the Fraser is joined by large tributaries such as the Quesnel and THOMPSON rivers from the E and the West Road and Chilcotin rivers from the W. At Hope the Fraser is only about 5 m above sea level, though this height varies seasonally. Its average annual flow here of 269 000 m³/s varies between an average low of 70 800 m³/s in Mar and an average peak flow of 850 000 m³/s in June. The Lower Fraser R bends westward at Hope and its valley broadens into a delta that is about 50 km wide where the river empties into the Str of GEORGIA. The southwestern part of the Fraser delta is in Washington state, US.

The river was named by David THOMPSON after Simon FRASER of the NWC, the first European to follow its course to its mouth in 1808. Little use was made of its central portion, because of its turbulent currents, until the discovery of gold on sandbars N of Yale in 1857. The CARIBOO GOLD RUSH which followed to the N brought the first narrow road (CARIBOO ROAD), carved into the canyon walls, and later the CPR followed the gash of the Thompson-Fraser rivers as the only low-level route through the Coast-Cascade mountain barrier to southwestern BC.

The Fraser R basin is well forested in its central sections, but has grassland vegetation and cattle ranching in the SW along the Chilcotin R and in its dry lower altitudes, as near Ashcroft. Numerous large sawmills and pulp and paper mills are the basis of the urban economies in the largest cities of Kamloops, Prince George and Quesnel. Mining of gold, copper, molybdenum and mercury has flourished at various times and places throughout the basin. The headwaters of the river's many tributaries are the spawning grounds of PACIFIC SALMON, which are caught later off the mouth of the Fraser.

J. LEWIS ROBINSON

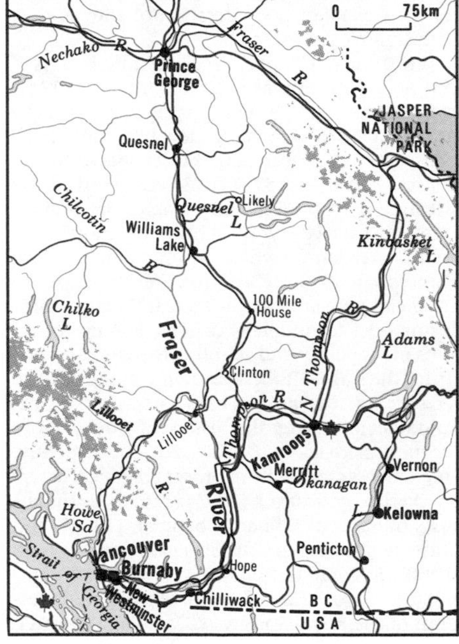

Fraser River Canyon was formed during the Miocene period (23.7-5.3 million years ago) when the river cut down into the uplifting southern part of the Interior Plateau of British Columbia. The canyon characteristics of this middle section of the FRASER R extend about 270 km N of Yale. At HELL'S GATE, S of Lytton, the canyon walls rise about 1000 m above the narrow, rushing river; 2 transcontinental railways and the TRANS-CANADA HWY have been carved into the rocky canyon sides. Fish ladders were built along the river's side to permit migrating PACIFIC SALMON to pass a former rockslide that partially blocked the river.

J. LEWIS ROBINSON

Fraser River Fishermen's Strikes On 8 July 1900, fishermen for 47 salmon canneries that lined the lower Fraser R from New Westminster to the river mouth struck for a season-long, 25-cent, minimum price instead of prices which dropped as catches increased. Whites, Indians and Japanese faced a canners association made desperate by overexpansion and lower selling prices and backed by the provincial government. Calling out first the provincial police and then the militia failed to break the strikers, who were led by Frank Rogers, a longshoreman and socialist activist. Eventually, on July 31, whites and Indians accepted a season's price of 19 cents. The Japanese, however, had accepted slightly less favourable terms on July 23. The following year, a "big" year in the sockeye salmon cycle, a second strike over prices began July 1. When the Japanese started to fish on the canners' terms, while whites and Indians stayed out, the previous season's tensions among ethnic groups erupted into open conflict, with net cutting, marooning of Japanese and the arrest of strike leaders. Finally, a "committee of business men" mediated a return to work on July 21, virtually at the prices offered by the canners. Nevertheless, these strikes established the principle of season-long, minimum prices and created the Grand Lodge of BC Fishermen's Unions, which first set the goal of coast-wide union organization.

H. KEITH RALSTON

Fraser River Lowland is a triangular area in southwestern BC at the mouth of that river. The eastern apex of the triangle is at Hope, about 160 km inland from the Str of GEORGIA, and the lowland broadens to the W to a width of about 50 km. The international boundary between BC and Washington state crosses the southwestern part of the lowland. The COAST MTS form the northern boundary of the delta-lowland. The lowland is the largest area of level land with suitable agricultural soils in coastal BC.

The lowland is formed from both glacial and alluvial deposits laid down more than 10 000 years ago as a delta at the mouth of a much larger postglacial Fraser R. Following postglacial uplift of the land and erosion into the deposits by the modern FRASER R, the older delta deposits are now about 100 m above sea level. Lower-level lowlands, almost at sea level, are the result of recent alluvial deposition along the floodplain of present Fraser R channels and are protected from flooding by dikes. Dairy farming is typical on the alluvial soils of the lowest areas; the poorer soils of the postglacial, raised delta are used for small fruits, berries, poultry farming and forests.

Known locally as the Lower Fraser Valley or the Lower Mainland, the lowland holds more than half of the population of BC, including on its NW edge the city of VANCOUVER. Much of the western section of the delta-lowland has been occupied by the outward spread of residential, commercial and industrial land uses of Metropolitan Vancouver; in other parts of the lowland, agricultural land is protected from urban encroachment by zoning regulations. Indians occupied fishing sites near the mouth of the Fraser for a few thousand years before the establishment of FORT LANGLEY in 1827. Agricultural settlement came after the Fraser (1858) and Cariboo (1862) GOLD RUSHES, but the full agricultural use of the lower lands with better soils had to await improvements in drainage and diking early in the 20th century.

J. LEWIS ROBINSON

Fraser River Railway Strikes broke out on 27 Mar 1912, when railway workers organized by the INDUSTRIAL WORKERS OF THE WORLD (IWW) walked out of construction camps on the Canadian Northern line to protest conditions. By 2 Apr, 8000 men were on strike and work had ceased on 640 km of construction line; later, workers on the Grand Trunk Pacific line joined the strike. Unskilled immigrant workers struck to demand strict enforcement of the Provincial Health Act, a 9-hour day and a minimum wage of

$3 per day. The IWW set up camps to feed and shelter the workers, and picketed employment offices in Vancouver, Seattle, Minneapolis and San Francisco to prevent the hiring of strikebreakers. The Wobbly poet and martyr Joe Hill visited the camp at Yale and wrote several songs, including "Where the Fraser River Flows," still a labour standard. The federal government refused the IWW request for arbitration under the Industrial Disputes Investigation Act, and the provincial government broke the strikes with violence and arrests; by June, more than 300 Wobblies had been arrested and many more driven from the region. Small concessions were won by the workers, but the strikes are more important for showing that unskilled workers could be successfully organized. The Fraser R strikes also mark the peak of IWW organization in Canada.

J. MARK LEIER

Fraud The criminal law of fraud has developed relatively recently. According to traditional English common law, it was generally no offence to defraud someone, particularly if the victim failed to exercise common prudence. Under the Canadian CRIMINAL CODE everyone who by deceit, falsehood or other fraudulent means defrauds the public or any person of any property, money or valuable security is liable to either 10 years imprisonment, if the value of the subject matter is over $200, or up to 2 years if it is not. In addition, the Criminal Code sets out a number of offences involving fraud in special circumstances, eg, in the use of the mails, concerning precious metals, etc. In *Theft and Fraud*, the federal Law Reform Commission recommended that the law of fraud be simplified but that its substance remain essentially unchanged.

LEE PAIKIN

Frazee, Rowland Cardwell, banker (b at Halifax 12 May 1921). From 1979 to 1986, he was chief executive officer with the ROYAL BANK OF CANADA, the largest chartered bank in the country. Initially joining the bank in 1939 in St Stephen, NB, Frazee spent his entire career in its service, with the exception of wartime service with the Canadian Army in Europe and university studies leading to a BComm at Dalhousie U in 1948. A steady rise through the Royal's district and regional operations led in 1970 to his appointment as vice-president. Two years later, Frazee became chief general manager and then in 1977 was appointed president. He served as chief executive officer from 1979 and chairman from 1980 until his retirement in 1986, and will continue as a bank director until 1992. A conventional banker in his career progression, Frazee was unconventional in his willingness to speak out on matters of national importance, such as federal fiscal and monetary policy. He served as chairman of the Business Council on National Issues, a prestigious business lobby group, and as president of the CANADIAN BANKERS' ASSOCIATION. A director of many companies, Frazee is also active as a director of many charities and organizations.

DUNCAN MCDOWALL

Fréchette, Louis-Honoré, poet, playwright (b near Lévis, Qué 16 Nov 1839; d at Montréal 31 May 1908). Fréchette was the most important man of letters in 19th-century Québec. The son of an illiterate contractor, he studied first under the Brothers of the Christian Schools and then in 3 classical colleges: the Petit Séminaire de Québec, Ste-Anne-de-la-Pocatière, and Nicolet. After graduation he studied law at Laval. He was already writing poems and his first play, *Félix Poutré* (1862); his first collection of verse, *Mes loisirs*, appeared in 1863.

After unsuccessful attempts at practising law and founding Liberal newspapers, Fréchette immigrated to Chicago, where he remained for 5 years (1866-71) working for the Illinois Central Ry. While there he launched other newspapers and wrote for the stage, but his manuscripts perished in the Chicago fire of 1871. His only surviving work from this period is a violent verse polemic, *La Voix d'un exilé* (1866-69), denouncing the Canadian Confederation of 1867 and its Conservative sponsors.

Returning to Canada, Fréchette threw himself into politics, sitting as federal member for Lévis from 1874 to 1878. After marrying into a wealthy family in 1876, Fréchette devoted himself increasingly to literature, and his second verse collection, *Pêle-mêle* (1877), was well received. By distributing complimentary copies in France, Fréchette paved the way for his recognition by the French Academy, which awarded him a Prix Montyon in 1880. Henceforth, Fréchette was the unofficial poet laureate of French Canada, composing odes for public occasions, issuing collections of his poetry and adapting the works of others for the stage. His best-known volume of verse is *La Légende d'un peuple* (1887), a series of historical tableaux tracing the history of Québec from Jacques CARTIER to Louis RIEL. Subsequently, Fréchette wrote chiefly in prose: polemical letters on Québec education (1893); replies to the attacks of his rival William Chapman (1894); and Christmas stories in English (1899) and French (1900). Decorated in France and England, honorary doctor of 4 Canadian universities, and president of the Royal Society of Canada (1900-01), Fréchette was the most widely honoured literary figure of his time in Canada.

DAVID M. HAYNE

View of Fredericton from River (1830), watercolour by an anonymous artist. As a Loyalist haven and capital town, Fredericton took on an appropriately aristocratic and genteel flavour (*courtesy Beaverbrook Art Gallery*).

Fredeen, Howard, agricultural research scientist (b at Macrorie, Sask 10 Dec 1921). He received an MSc from U Sask in 1947 and joined the staff of the Lacombe Research Station, Alta, subsequently obtaining a PhD in ANIMAL BREEDING and genetics from Iowa State College (1952). Fredeen spent his entire career with Agriculture Canada's Research Branch, retiring 6 July 1984. With the late J.G. Stothart he was the co-developer of the Lacombe breed of hogs, still renowned for its excellence. Fredeen played a major role in developing Canadian livestock breeding policies and in introducing innovative breeding practices and new techniques for carcass evaluation. As well as writing more than 300 scientific and technical papers, he has established an international reputation by frequently representing Agriculture Canada abroad. He has received numerous honours, including a fellowship in the Agricultural Institute of Canada, the Public Service of Canada Merit Award and the Genetics Society of Canada Award for excellence. Fredeen has edited a history of Lacombe district and has received a Lacombe Citizen of the Year Award.

ADRIANA A. DAVIES

Fredericton, NB, City, pop 44 352 (1986c), 43 723 (1981c), inc 1848, provincial capital, is located in central New Brunswick, just below the head of tide on the SAINT JOHN R, 135 km inland from the Bay of FUNDY.

Settlement The founding of Frederick's Town between 1783 and 1785 was inextricably interwoven with the attempts of the LOYALISTS and their sympathizers to create a new province and a "haven for the King's friends" in British North America. Carefully planned ahead of any permanent settlement, Fredericton (named after Prince Frederick of Osnaburg) was to be their capital and the centrepiece of their new society. Besides assuming the seat of government with the creation of NEW BRUNSWICK in 1784, Fredericton was to become a British military headquarters, a centre of education and culture, and a stronghold for the Anglican Church. The capital was to take on an appropriately "aristocratic flavour" in contrast to the fledgling commercial entrepôt of SAINT JOHN, already distastefully dominated by "men in trade."

Prior to the arrival of the Loyalists, both the advantages and disadvantages of the future site of Frederick's Town had been realized by Indians and Acadians. The MALISEET recognized the value of the scenic alluvial plain that had formed at this central, inland river junction. It marked the terminus of an important portage route from the MIRAMICHI R and for several generations was the site of Maliseet camps and a burial ground. The strategic advantages of St Anne's Point (as it became known) were not fully recognized, however, until 1691 when Gov Joseph Robinau de Villebon decided to establish the capital of ACADIA at the mouth of the Nashwaak R, opposite the alluvial plain. The site afforded a fine deepwater anchorage on the main artery into the region, and it could be defended more easily from the attacks of the British or New Englanders than a location closer to the Bay of Fundy. Yet by 1698 de Villebon abandoned Fort Nashwaak. Eminently secure in wartime, in times of peace the site was too isolated from the main routes of trade, commerce and communication to do well economically. In the 1730s Acadian farmers established a settlement on the rich soils of the plain at St Anne's; but less than 20 years later they were described as "exceeding poor" and had "become half savage

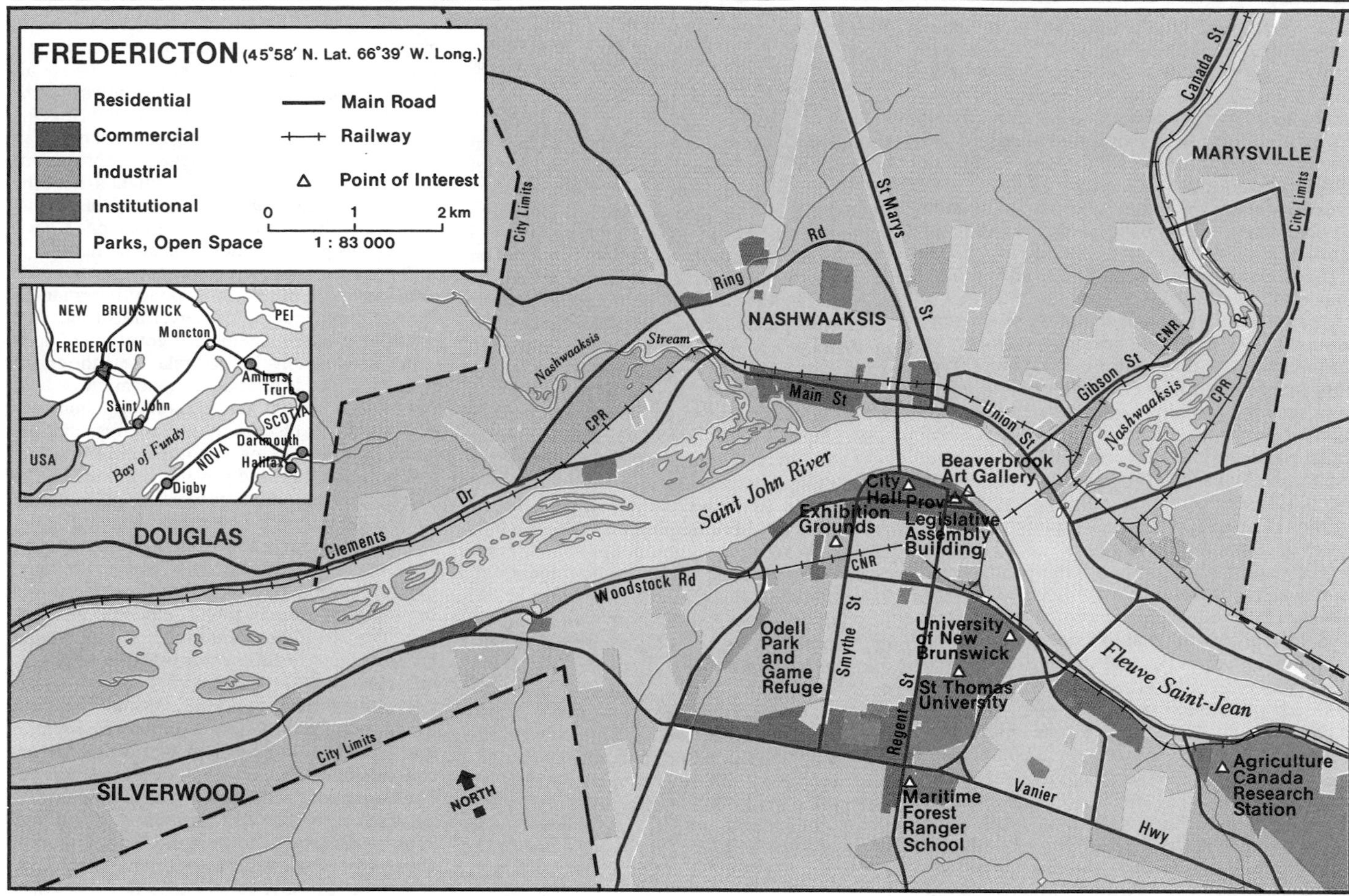

from neglect." The remnants of the settlement were swept aside in 1759, clearing the way for the Loyalists and their "design."

Development In the 200 years following 1783, Fredericton unfolded very much as its founders had hoped. In addition to its role as provincial capital, it became the shire town of York County (1785). Substantial pieces of land on the town plot were set aside for government, for a university, for the Anglican Church and for the military. King's College received a royal charter in 1828 and began to grow "Up the Hill," especially after the construction of a fine stone building that same year. Equally grand stone barracks and a military compound grew up in the centre of the town; and Bishop John MEDLEY's selection of the community as the site for CHRIST CHURCH CATHEDRAL in the newly created Anglican see of NB in 1845 was directly responsible for the elevation of Fredericton to city status in 1848. The magnificent cathedral was constructed from 1846 to 1853.

In time, modifications were made to the Loyalist design. King's College was reorganized into the nondenominational UNIVERSITY OF NEW BRUNSWICK in 1859, as Methodists and other nonconformists from Saint John and all corners of the province assailed Fredericton and its Anglican "establishment." The British garrison left in 1869, shortly after the coming of Canadian Confederation, by which time Irish, Presbyterians and Catholics had altered the demographic and religious base. Lumbering, and to a lesser extent agriculture, plus Fredericton's role as a point of transshipment between the lower and upper Saint John R, brought prosperity throughout the century.

Population The city grew slowly – to only 7117 by 1901. In 1941 it still contained only 10 062 inhabitants. The immigrants brought diversity, divisions and community tensions; an Irish Catholic was killed in "Orange-Green" riots in 1847, and there were less violent political conflicts between the poorer Upper Towners and the more affluent, "established" Lower Towners over town-clock, marketplace and wharf sites. Yet a "gentleman-like" atmosphere prevailed in the city. Fredericton's genteel society was responsible for producing such literary figures as Bliss CARMAN and Sir Charles G.D. ROBERTS. In the 20th century, Max AITKEN donated a fine art gallery (Beaverbrook Art Gallery) and a playhouse was built, both in Lower Town, near the cathedral and provincial assembly.

Cityscape A different kind of society emerged on the N side of the river during the 19th century. In 1862 Alexander "Boss" Gibson began the construction of his industrial empire at Marysville with a lumber mill on the Nashwaak. Before he was done he had constructed one of the largest cotton mills in Canada (1883-85) and an entire community to go with it. He built brick row houses for his workers, detached homes for management, a boarding house, a company store, a magnificent Methodist church and a railway to Chatham. Though Gibson was forced to sell out in 1908 under pressure from a central Canadian cotton consortium that he refused to join, the mill limped on until 1973, and Marysville added another different industrial working-class community to the area.

Overall though, Fredericton continued to be dominated by its government and university functions, and has retained its air of gentility. Industry has come and gone, yet politics and education have expanded substantially since WWII, stimulating the city's largest-ever surge forward in physical and population growth. In the last 30 years it has expanded to an area of 132 km^2 and a population of more than 44 000. Still, Fredericton remains much as its founders would have wished: small, intimate and personal, cultured, refined and with an air of prosperity and importance in the midst of New Brunswick.
ALAN BROOKES

Free Trade A free trade area, as defined by the GENERAL AGREEMENT ON TARIFFS AND TRADE (GATT), is "a group of two or more customs territories in which duties and other restrictive regulations of commerce...are eliminated on substantially all the trade between the constituent territories in products originating in such territories." It is technically distinguishable from a customs union in that the members have the freedom to maintain their own duties or other trade arrangements with third countries that are not members of the free trade area, whereas with a customs union, duties and trade regulations regarding third countries are the same for all members. A common market takes the degree of economic integration one step further – to include the free flow of the factors of production (labour and capital) among the member nations. The trade liberalization discussions of 1986-87 between Canada and the US were generally interpreted to involve the establishment of a free trade area only, rather than a customs union or common market. Yet, students of the Canada-US relationship observed that the degree of integration existing between the 2 nations was in many respects already greater than that between the members of the European Economic Community (EEC) after several decades of integration.

Traditionally, free trade negotiations have focused upon the elimination of tariffs and quantitative restrictions on merchandise trade. With the completion in 1987 of the major tariff reductions negotiated under the GATT Tokyo Round, tariffs were no longer the main focus, particularly for Canadians exporting to or desiring to export to the US. The vast majority of Canadian shipments to that country entered tariff free, and less than 10% of exports faced US tariffs in excess of 5%. The products involved were those such as clothing, textiles and footwear. Some commodities of course continued to face such high tariffs that they were not sold to the US at all. From Canada's viewpoint of trade liberalization, more important objectives than the removal of remaining US tariffs were to obtain secure and stable access to US markets, without constantly having to fight US countervail or other safeguard actions; to agree with the US on what Canadian federal government assistance to industry was countervailable and what was not; and to settle upon a dispute-settlement mechanism that did not rest entirely on decisions made in the US. Canada also wanted exemption from US "Buy America" rules.

The US in turn wanted all trade in services included in any free trade arrangement. Services include the communications and cultural sectors (telecommunications, radio, TV, newspapers and publishing), advertising, transportation, consulting, recreational facilities, and financial services of all types. The US also wanted unhindered access for investment in Canadian industries, particularly the energy sector, without Canadian federal government surveillance or restrictions of any type.

The gains many Canadians expected if negotiating objectives were achieved included the possibility of attaining greater economies of scale and lower costs in manufacturing by having guaranteed access to the huge US market, greater incentives for domestic firms to do more research and development and adopt the latest technology available from abroad, more processing of natural resources in Canada prior to exporting them, greater employment, lower foreign ownership in the long run, and lower prices for consumers because of domestic tariffs being removed and greater productivity of Canadian industry. Disputes occurred within Canada regarding how extensive the gains would be. Some observers felt that they were greatly exaggerated and that the costs of free trade were understated or ignored. The macroeconomic models used to estimate the gains frequently disagreed in their predictions, so that their major contribution was to emphasize how difficult it is to predict the effects of trade liberalization. All parties agreed, however, that a flexible Canadian dollar, vis-à-vis the US dollar, was an important safety valve. If it was artificially pushed much closer to parity with the US dollar because of pressures by US officials, many Canadian industries would find it difficult to compete with US firms in the Canada-US market.

A concern of some Canadians was whether a bilateral free trade arrangement with the US involving all service industries, including many of a cultural nature, relatively unhindered access for US investors to the Canadian economy, and a continental energy policy would erode Canadian economic and political sovereignty irreversibly. A closely related concern was with respect to the overestimate by many Canadians of the net gains from free trade and the hope of the federal Conservative government that a free trade deal would restore its favour with voters. The fear was that these conditions might stimulate Canada to give away too much in the negotiations without gaining its main objective – guaranteed access to the US market through exemption from highly protectionist existing and forthcoming US fair trade or contingency laws. The position taken by most of those concerned was that a multilateral approach to free trade through the Uruguay Round of GATT negotiations may be a more desirable alternative for Canada in the long run. PM Mulroney and President Reagan signed the Free Trade Agreement Jan 1988, though it remained to be ratified in both countries. *See also* ECONOMIC NATIONALISM; ECONOMICS; SOFTWOOD LUMBER DISPUTE.

BRUCE W. WILKINSON

Reading: R.G. Lipsey and M.G. Smith, *Taking the Initiative: Canada's Trade Options in a Turbulent World* (1985); Bruce W. Wilkinson, "Canada-United States Free Trade: Setting the Dimensions," *The Political Economy of Canada-United States Free Trade* (1987).

Freedman, Harry, composer, English-horn player (b at Lodz, Poland 5 Apr 1922). He is one of the first nationally known composers to have trained almost entirely in Canada. Initially disposed to a career as an artist, Freedman attended the Winnipeg School of Art at age 13. After an interest in big band jazz led to clarinet lessons at age 18, he was introduced to the symphonic repertoire by teacher Arthur Hart. Freedman took up the oboe and studied composition with John WEINZWEIG 1945-51. He was with the TORONTO SYMPHONY playing the English horn 1946-71. In 1971 Freedman was appointed the orchestra's first composer-in-residence and dedicated most of his time to composing. Weinzweig's influence is manifest in Freedman's use of various aspects of the 12-tone technique, strictly in *The Tokaido* (1964) for chamber ensemble, more informally in *Tangents* (1967) for orchestra. Several compositions were inspired by Canadian paintings: *Tableau* (1952), *Images* (1958), *Klee Wyck* (1970). Freedman first won critical acclaim for his superb orchestration, a legacy of his symphonic experience, with *Symphony No 1* (premiered 1961). Wit and humour are displayed in *The Explainer* (1976), a satire on the jargon of the music-appreciation lecturer. Freedman has also written music for theatre, television and film, notably Paul ALMOND's *Act of the Heart*. He collaborated with Brian MACDONALD on *Rose Latulippe*, a ROYAL WINNIPEG BALLET commission, and on several other Royal Winnipeg ballets. He was appointed to the Order of Canada in 1985.

ANN SCHAU

Freedom of Information During the 1960s and 1970s citizens, as users of government services, began to feel entitled to certain rights arising out of their relationship with government. Initially, this was manifested in the growth throughout Canada of the institution of the OMBUDSMAN, generally designed as a mechanism to redress government wrongs and reduce the "red tape" characteristic of government bureaucracy.

Government information and its accessibility may be divided into categories, first, that concerned with access to government information concerning oneself stored in government data banks. Federally, this information became accessible to individuals in 1978, with the enactment of so-called PRIVACY legislation. Essentially, the federal government established an index of federal government data banks; individuals could apply to a given data bank contained in the index for access to information concerning themselves. The enabling legislation did, however, provide for a series of exemptions in categories such as national security, FEDERAL-PROVINCIAL RELATIONS, and ongoing law-enforcement investigations and others. If the government invoked a "blanket" exemption, universally eliminating specified data banks from access, or an exemption in respect to an individual application, part or all of the information might be withheld, but individuals did have recourse to a privacy commissioner who could represent the interest of a dissatisfied applicant. If the decision of the particular government department remained unchanged, no further recourse was available. If information was provided and applicants believed it to be erroneous, the privacy commissioner could again come to their assistance; and if there was a refusal to change the information, at the very least it would be noted in the data bank that a request for a change in the information had been made and denied. The legislation was amended in 1982, effective 1 July 1983, to allow a further recourse in the event of either a denial of information through the invocation of an exemption or a refusal to change allegedly incorrect information. If the privacy commissioner does not succeed in convincing the appropriate government department of either an entitlement or a change of allegedly erroneous information or both, there is now a right to have the matter reviewed, *in camera*, by a justice of the Trial Division of the FEDERAL COURT OF CANADA. A decision by this judge is binding on all parties.

The second kind of government information is what might be described as policy information, eg, anything contained in government files that contributes to the making of a government decision, including any decision relating to the enactment of either legislation or regulation or both (*see* OFFICIAL SECRETS ACT). This information may take the form of consultants' reports, internal studies, etc. Following a complex legislative history – which included private members' bills, a federal government GREEN PAPER, draft legislation by one government and subsequent legislation enacted by another government – the ACCESS TO INFORMATION ACT was finally passed in 1982 and took effect on 1 July 1983, chiefly as a result of strenuous lobbying by the Canadian Bar Association. This "freedom of information" law entitles an individual to examine this kind of government information and it provides for the speedy provision of the information at reasonable cost. It establishes an information commissioner, with a role and function similar to that of the privacy commissioner, and also provides for certain exemptions under which some or all of the information may be withheld. Again, an applicant may apply to the Trial Division of the Federal Court of Canada for a review, *in camera*, of the decision by government to invoke an exemption and withhold the information. One of the controversial features of the 1982 law is a section which provides that Cabinet documents, and in effect any other document referring to or flowing from Cabinet documents, fall outside the law. Such documents are not only unavailable but are also not subject to the review procedure.

Section 75 of the 1982 Access to Information Act (as well as s75 of the companion Privacy Act) requires a parliamentary committee to review the provisions and operations of both statutes. As a result of that provision, the Standing Committee on Justice and the solicitor general conducted a major review culminating in a report released Mar 1987. This report contained numerous recommendations addressing, for example, the nature and scope of the existing exemptions, the present exclusion of Cabinet documents from the ambit of the Act, a proposal to widen the accessibility of documents to include those relating to the operations of crown corporations, and a further proposal to shorten the time by which documents must be provided. It is anticipated that several of these and other recommendations will ultimately lead to amendments to the Act, in order to improve public accessibility to federal government documents. Many of the recommendations are in response to criticisms made by users of the Act during its first 3 years.

Some provinces have freedom-of-information laws and others have conducted studies on the subject, but generally provinces have not entered this field as deeply as the federal government.

The main rationale for the enactment of freedom-of-information laws is that an informed citizenry must have access to government information in order to assess, evaluate and select government in an enlightened way. Secondly, presuming that knowledge is power, it is argued that citizens are entitled to share that power with government and are best able to do so with access

Cartoon by Duncan Macpherson (Oct 1978) mocks the attitude of government in preventing access to information *(National Archives of Canada/C-112688/Toronto Star Syndicate)*.

to government data. The users of freedom-of-information laws, judging from the American experience, have tended to be investigative journalists, academics (particularly historians) and defence counsel.

The Act has generated approximately 2500 requests for information per year, many by so-called "information consultants." These are persons and firms who are in the business of – and who have gained considerable expertise in – making applications under the Act on behalf of the various users. G. GALL

Freemasonry is an international, semi-secret, fraternal movement of regionally or nationally federated organizations with about 200 000 Canadian members. Although Freemason mythology traces the group's origins to the construction of King Solomon's Temple, historians identify its origins in English medieval stonemason guilds, which formed among the skilled craftsmen who built cathedrals, castles and other stone structures (the term "Masonic lodge" derives from the working quarters that masons built next to construction sites). Changing economic and religious conditions after the Gothic period brought a decline in majestic building projects, and by the 17th century, lodges could stay alive only by supplementing the membership of working ("operative") masons with nonmasons ("accepted masons"). The latter probably felt attraction to the group because of its lore, intellectual traditions, secrecy and fellowship.

Modern, "speculative" Masonry derives from a fourfold merger of lodges into the Grand Lodge of England (The Moderns) on 24 June 1717. The Grand Lodge of Ireland formed around 1725, the Grand Lodge of Scotland arose in 1736, and a rival Grand Lodge of England (The Ancients), formed in 1751 but merged with The Moderns in 1813. These 4 bodies were the sources for Masonic lodges worldwide, and today lodges also exist in the US, France and other European countries, Latin America and most former British colonies.

While British soldiers serving in what is now Canada sometimes were Masons, the first civilian Masonic lodge was the Annapolis Royal, NS, Lodge, which received warrant from The Moderns Lodge in Boston in June 1738. Other warrants followed for lodges in St John's (1746 and 1766), Halifax (1750 and 1751) and Québec (1764). Unverifiable, but old, claims place Masons in Québec as early as 1721, yet French Freemasonry has not contributed to Canadian Masonic activity. With the division of Québec into Upper and Lower Canada in 1791, only 4 Masonic lodges were operating in Upper Canada (Brockville, Cornwall and 2 at Niagara). Membership increased along with the population, however, until the movement suffered a temporary setback in the aftermath of an 1826 scandal in upstate New York in which Masons were suspected of killing a vocal apostate named William Morgan. Local Masonic lodges formed at later dates in what became other provinces – BC (1859), Manitoba (1864 and 1870), Alberta (1882) and Saskatchewan (1883). Thirty Canada West and Québec lodges banded together in 1855 to form the Grand Lodge of Canada, and Ancient Masonic lodges established their own Grand Lodge 2 years later. The 2 bodies united in 1858, except for a few lodges that maintained allegiance to the Grand Lodges of England, Ireland or Scotland. Québec established its own Grand Lodge in 1869, and other provincial Grand Lodges formed themselves as local situations demanded. In 1887, the Grand Lodge of Canada amended its name to acknowledge the provincial nature of Canadian Freemasonry, henceforth calling itself "The Grand Lodge of Ancient and Accepted Masons of Canada in the Province of Ontario." Headquartered in Hamilton, approximately half the country's Freemasons fall under its care.

An ideological child of the Enlightenment, Masonry incorporated Newtonian ideas about God as "the Great Architect of the Universe" into its rituals and symbology. Candidates for initiation must hold a basic belief in a supreme being, but not necessarily a Christian one. (The secret oaths, anticlericalism, non-Christian borrowings, and competing religious and political overtones led to papal proscriptions in 1751, and more than a dozen further pronouncements have appeared since then.) Members are initiated into the lowest of 3 levels, or degrees, of teaching (called Craft Masonry), but if they progress past the third level (and most do not) they can then enter into further degrees, either through a 6- (or, in Britain, a 7-) level system called the York Rite or a 30-level system called the Scottish Rite. Upward progress requires candidates to study about, and then participate in, rituals believed to propound moral precepts.

Anti-masonic fear has surfaced occasionally in Canadian history, as it has in other countries. Upper Canada's Lt-Gov John Graves SIMCOE feared sedition from Montréal Freemasons in 1794 because of their connections with fellow "craft" members in the then bellicose state of Vermont. Spurious connections between Freemasons and Jews appeared in Alberta Social Credit ideology during the Depression. Nonetheless, Masonry boasts a long list of prominent members, including members of the British royal family; George Washington and many other American presidents; Mozart, Voltaire, Goethe and Winston Churchill. Noteworthy Canadian Masons include Sir Allan N. MACNAB, John R. ROBERTSON, Joseph BRANT, Sir John ROSE, John D. EATON, NS Prem John M. BUCHANAN, 16 Ontario premiers (eg, William G. DAVIS) and 6 prime ministers – Sir John A. MACDONALD, Sir John J.C. ABBOTT, Sir Mackenzie BOWELL, Sir Robert L. BORDEN, Viscount R.B. BENNETT and John G. DIEFENBAKER. *See also* SECRET SOCIETIES. STEPHEN A. KENT

Reading: R.V. Harris, *The Beginnings of Freemasonry in Canada* (1938); M.C. Jacob, *The Radical Enlightenment: Pantheists, Freemasons and Republicans* (1981); S. Knight, *The Brotherhood: The Secret World of the Freemasons* (1984).

Frégault, Guy, historian (b at Montréal 16 June 1918; d at Québec C 13 Dec 1977). Frégault pursued classical studies at Saint-Laurent and Jean-de-Brébeuf colleges in Montréal. He then enrolled in U de M and eventually completed his PhD in history at Loyola U, Chicago, in 1949. In addition to his academic positions as professor of history at U de M, director of the Institut d'histoire and chairman of the history department at U of O, Frégault served as deputy minister of the cultural affairs department (1961-66 and 1970-75) in the Québec government. A member of the ACADÉMIE CANADIENNE-FRANÇAISE and of the Académie des sciences d'outre-mer, he was awarded several prizes for his work on the history of New France, including the Prix Duvernay in 1944, and both the Prix David and the Prix France-Québec in 1969. Frégault's articles on the French regime have appeared in numerous periodicals. Frégault was renowned for his rigorous research and his scientific treatment of his material. His most famous work is *Iberville le Conquérant*. GISÈLE VILLENEUVE

French, David, playwright (b at Coley's Point, Nfld 18 Jan 1939). French moved with his family from Newfoundland to Toronto when he was 6. He studied acting after high school, performing professionally (1960-65) before turning full time to playwriting. His earliest plays were half-hour TV dramas broadcast on CBC, beginning with "Beckons the Dark River" (1963). His first stage play, *Leaving Home* (1972), produced and directed by Bill GLASSCO at Toronto's TARRAGON THEATRE, portrayed with humour and powerful emotion the generational conflict and cultural alienation within a Toronto family of transplanted Newfoundlanders. Its sequel, *Of the Fields, Lately* (1973), won the Jean A. Chalmers Outstanding Play Award and cemented French's position as Canada's foremost stage realist. The third play in what became "the Mercer Trilogy," *Salt-Water Moon* (1984), follows the courtship of the characters who turn up as the parents in the other 2 plays. *Jitters* (1979), a backstage comedy, is one of the most frequently produced plays in the history of Canadian theatre. JERRY WASSERMAN

French, Sir George Arthur, soldier (b at Roscommon, Ire 19 June 1841; d at London, Eng 7 July 1921). A Royal Artillery officer, French established the Canadian Militia gunnery school at Kingston in 1871. As commissioner of the NWMP (1873-76), he organized the force and gave it its military character. A.B. MCCULLOUGH

French Canadian Nationalism, a wide variety of manifestations of the collective will of much of Canada's French-speaking population to live as a distinct cultural community. Its innumerable ramifications have been not only cultural but also political, economic and social. Historians disagree about its beginnings. Guy Frégault suggests that the inhabitants of colonial NEW FRANCE in the early 18th century were sufficiently different from those of France for a distinct national sentiment to exist. Michel Brunet argues that the CONQUEST of 1760, by transforming the French in Canada into a conquered people, triggered a defence mechanism that has endured. Others, such as Fernand OUELLET, are convinced that NATIONALISM had its origin soon after 1800 when social strains and economic crises increased animosity between French and English inhabitants of LOWER CANADA. Political scientist Léon Dion distinguishes 4 types of French Canadian nationalism: conservative (dominant until 1960), liberal (post-1960), social-democrat and socialist (both "challengers" since 1960). Wherever the debate may lead, it is clear that French Canadian nationalism has been present for at least 150 years and that, because of its nature, it will probably endure as long as there are French-speaking Canadians (*see* HISTORIOGRAPHY IN FRENCH).

For over a century, French Canadian nationalism was generally linked to conservative causes and to the perpetuation of a traditional society. For the clerical and professional elite, fidelity to language, culture and religion implied respect for the acceptance of the established social order in which the Roman CATHOLIC Church dominated, agriculture was lauded as society's material and moral foundation, parish and family were the basic social institutions, commercial and industrial pursuits were disdained, and foreign influences were shunned. To what extent was this concept of nationalism shared by the common man? The very insistence with which the clerical elite defended its concept of society betrayed the existence of challenges to the social order, especially when nationalist credos seemed to conflict with conditions for individual material betterment. An agricultural way of life was vigorously defended by the nationalists, but by 1921 half of Québec's population was urban and migration to the cities showed no signs of abating, except during the GREAT DEPRESSION, when industrial jobs were scarce.

Nationalism between the 1840s and the 1940s also had important political aspects. It meant denying the conclusion of the celebrated DURHAM REPORT that the "inferior" French Canadian nation would be absorbed. It also meant struggling against the conditions imposed by the 1840 ACT OF UNION which in 1841 joined Upper and Lower Canada into a single colony. It signified fighting for recognition of French and Catholic rights at CONFEDERATION, notably within Québec, and later in the English-speaking provinces in the face of attempts to abolish French or Roman Catholic schools (*see* MANITOBA SCHOOLS QUESTION). It encompassed Jules-Paul TARDIVEL's efforts to promote an independent French state in N America, a sort of reconstituted New France. It also meant an unrelenting campaign, with considerable popular support, against what was regarded as British imperialism – political, economic and especially military. Henri BOURASSA's nationalist group led this battle, which culminated in the 1917 CONSCRIPTION crisis when French Canada massively refused compulsory military service overseas. This crisis was replayed during WWII, though this time with somewhat less dramatic political consequences.

After 1900 some nationalists became increasingly preoccupied with economic questions. Errol Bouchette argued that French Canadians must take hold of their industry and avoid yielding the province's natural resources cheaply to foreign control. In the 1930s, members of ACTION LIBÉRALE NATIONALE proposed nationalization of certain foreign-owned (ie, non-French Canadian) monopolies, such as the electricity trust. Others, in an effort to promote French Canadian commerce, led "Buy French Canada" campaigns and warned against the patronizing of Jewish establishments.

Following WWII, rapid changes in French Canadian society, characterized by increasing diversity, led to new expressions of nationalism (*see* QUIET REVOLUTION). Economic and political themes became central and, particularly after 1960, the province of Québec became principal supporter of the French Canadian collectivity, or at least of those French Canadians (about 80% of the Canadian total) living within Québec. For example, after the 1962 provincial election, in which nationalist themes predominated, the government nationalized private electric power companies, integrating them with the existing HYDRO-QUÉBEC; in 1986 it ranked as Canada's second-largest crown corporation as judged by assets.

But the major debate centered on the place of Québec and French Canada in Canada. Daniel JOHNSON, Québec premier 1966-68, Claude RYAN, editor of the daily newspaper *Le* DEVOIR, and others favoured a new Canadian constitution that would expand Québec's area of legislative jurisdiction and establish a bilingual and bicultural Canada, ensuring the equality of the 2 founding peoples (*see* DEUX NATIONS). Still others centered their nationalism squarely on Québec and attacked the Canadian dream as unrealistic. For them the solution was political independence. In the early 1960s several parties and movements sprang up, preaching independence within a variety of social frameworks ranging from the extreme left to the extreme right. Of these, the Rassemblement pour l'indépendance nationale and the Ralliement national participated actively in the 1966 provincial election. In 1967 René LÉVESQUE, a former member of Jean LESAGE's Liberal Cabinet, founded the Mouvement souveraineté-association, transformed the following year into the PARTI QUÉBÉCOIS, which was elected in 1976 and again in 1981. In 1977 that government adopted a French Language Charter (*see* BILL 101) which generally responded to nationalist language desires. In May 1980 the government held a provincial referendum in which it asked for a mandate to negotiate SOVEREIGNTY-ASSOCIATION with the rest of Canada. Nearly 60% voted "No," although French-speaking Québecois were split almost evenly.

Canada's new CONSTITUTION, adopted Apr 1982, was vigorously denounced by most Québec nationalists, regardless of political affiliation, since it seemed to end, at least temporarily, their hopes to gain greater power for Québec. Political events since 1980, as well as difficult economic and social conditions within Québec, seriously weakened the government's position and precipitated a dramatic upheaval within the PARTI QUÉBÉCOIS. The PQ was defeated by Robert Bourassa's Liberals Dec 1985, ushering in an era in which Québec nationalists sought to redefine their goals and French-speaking minorities outside Québec continued their struggle for recognition of linguistic rights. The 1987 MEECH LAKE ACCORD raised new questions about Québec's place in the Canadian confederation. RICHARD JONES

Reading: R. Cook, *French Canadian Nationalism* (1969); D.B. Miquelon, *Society and Conquest* (1977); S.M. Trofimenkoff, *The Dream of Nation* (1983) and, ed, *Abbé Groulx* (1973).

French in the West In the 17th century Frenchmen travelled west from Montréal as COUREURS DE BOIS and explorers, searching for furs and an overland route to the MER DE L'OUEST. Pierre RADISSON and Médard Chouart DES GROSEILLIERS, who journeyed to Lk Superior 1659-60, persuaded the English to establish posts on Hudson Bay (*see* HUDSON'S BAY CO), and in 1682 Radisson explored 300 km inland from the bay.

In the 1730s Pierre LA VÉRENDRYE and his sons extended the French fur routes westward, establishing a chain of forts in the Winnipeg Basin. After the CONQUEST (1760), French traders in the West worked for the NORTH WEST CO and the HBC, aiding in the expansion of the FUR TRADE to the shores of the Arctic and Pacific. The first white woman to live in the West was Marie-Anne LAGEMODIÈRE, the wife of a fur trader.

From the earliest times, many French traders married native women. Their children, the MÉTIS, lived throughout the Prairies. Seminomadic, many of them worked as guides and interpreters for the fur-trading companies. At the request of Lord SELKIRK, missionaries were sent from Québec to the North-West; Fathers Joseph Norbert PROVENCHER and Sévère Joseph Nicolas Dumoulin reached the RED RIVER COLONY in 1818. In 1844 the diocese of the Red River became the Apostolic Vicariate of the North-West under Father (later Bishop) Provencher's guidance. Schools were established by the Grey Nuns and the Christian Brothers. The Métis were encouraged to settle on the land. By 1845 Bishop Provencher had persuaded the Oblates in France to send missionaries; one of the first to arrive was Alexandre TACHÉ, who later recruited Father GRANDIN. Grandin, with Father Albert LACOMBE, helped found the Catholic Church in what is now Alberta.

Taché was a witness to the events leading to the formation of Louis RIEL's provisional government in 1870 and he pleaded with John A. MACDONALD for a general amnesty (*see* RED RIVER REBELLION). The Métis rebellion led by Riel was quashed at BATOCHE in 1885, and Riel was hanged for treason in Nov 1885 (*see* NORTH-WEST REBELLION). Riel's execution further divided the new Dominion along ethnic and religious lines.

Under the 1870 MANITOBA ACT both French and English had been granted equal rights, but by 1890 the large influx of English-speaking immigrants had altered the ethnic structure of Manitoba. The Manitoba legislature passed an Act depriving French and Catholics of certain rights (*see* MANITOBA SCHOOLS QUESTION). By 1892 the same situation had developed in the North-West Territories. The French Canadians in Québec, who until that time had considered the West part of their heritage, were now given to understand that a French-speaking western province would not be tolerated and that the constitutional rights of French Canadians regarding religion and language would be disregarded.

In 1976 a French Canadian, Georges Forest of St-Boniface, Man, refused to pay a parking ticket written in English only. The county judge ruled in his favour and after a series of appeals that went to the SUPREME COURT OF CANADA, Manitoba was once more declared a bilingual province. Further attempts to entrench French services for the French-speaking population, made by the PAWLEY government in 1984, met with strong opposition in the legislature and throughout the province. Conservative Opposition tactics prevented a vote from being taken in the House and the Pawley government was forced to withdraw its amendment. The Conservative tactics were severely censured by the federal representatives of all parties, and the French Canadians have once more taken their case to the Supreme Court. In Apr 1987 NDP MLA Leo Piquette tried to use French in the Alberta legislature setting off a controversy unresolved by the end of the year.

Over the years, the western provinces have attracted a variety of French-speaking immigrants. Some have been from Québec, although in the last decades of the 19th century Québec discouraged its inhabitants from moving west; too many people were already leaving the province for the New England states. Nevertheless, French Canadian missionaries promoted francophone settlement in the West, especially between 1880 and 1912. Many of the settlers came from France, while others were from Québec, New England and Belgium (though WWI ended emigration from Belgium and France). Most of them settled in the Prairie provinces. During the GREAT DEPRESSION another group of French-speaking settlers established themselves in the Peace River Lowland. The oil boom in Alberta and the development of the pulp and paper industry in BC have attracted the most recent migrants from Québec to the West. There are now some 320 000 persons of French extraction living in the 4 western provinces, some 160 000 of whom claim French as their mother tongue.

French Canadians have contributed to the economic and political structures of western Canada from earliest times. They sat in the Council of the North-West Territories and in the first legislatures of the western provinces. Men such as Prosper Edmond Lessard, Wilfrid Gariépy, Jean-Léon

CÔTÉ, Aristide Blais, Léonidas Alcide Giroux, Joseph Méville Déchêne, Lamdas Joly, J.W. Beaudry, J.H. Tremblay, Frédéric Villeneuve, Lionel Tellier and Lucien Maynard were actively involved in the Albertan and federal political scene, either as senators or members of Parliament. The list is much longer for Manitoba. Québec established banking institutions in the West; the Banque canadienne nationale (or Banque D'Hochelaga as it was earlier known) helped fund new settlers of all ethnic groups. Hospitals, colleges and convents were founded and financed by Québec religious institutions. Insurance companies such as La Sauvegarde and La Familiale in Saskatchewan offered their services to French Canadians in the West; CAISSES POPULAIRES, founded during the Depression, still prosper.

In business, French Canadians participated in the development of the West and as doctors, lawyers, judges, engineers, architects, etc, have been strongly represented in the professions. French-speaking western Canadians have included outstanding writers in the fields of journalism, history and literature (*see* Gabrielle ROY, Georges BUGNET). A recent publication, *Répertoire littéraire de l'ouest canadien,* lists 84 literary authors who wrote and published in French in western Canada. This anthology is published by Centre d'études franco-canadiennes de l'Ouest (CEFCO) in St-Boniface, Man. ROGER MOTUT

French Language In the early 17th century France founded 2 colonies in N America: ACADIA and NEW FRANCE. Between 1755 and 1763 the English deported more than 10 000 of the approximately 14 000 Acadians. Many of the exiles subsequently returned to settle in New Brunswick, Nova Scotia and PEI. Today, their descendants number more than 350 000, and three-quarters of them still speak French. New France developed slowly; it had a population of less than 13 000 in 1695 and approximately 70 000 in 1763, when it became a British colony. Today, more than 5 million descendants of these early French settlers live in the province of Québec, and almost a million more are scattered W of Québec from Ontario to British Columbia (*see also* FRANCO-AMERICANS).

The early settlers of Acadia and New France came from various localities in Europe (mostly from France), and the forms of language they spoke reflected their different regions of origin. In Acadia, according to records for 1707, 51% of the population came from Poitou, Aunis and Saintonge; 3% from Guyenne and Pays Basque; 11% from Brie, Orléans, Paris, Normandy, Maine and Brittany; 1% from Champagne and Burgundy; in addition, 26% were of unknown French origin, 5% were of English and 4% of other origins. In New France in 1700, 29% had originated in Poitou, Aunis, Saintonge and Angoumois; 5% in Limousin, Périgord and Guyenne; 22% in Normandy and Perche; 15% in Paris and Île-de-France; 13% in Anjou, Touraine, Beauce and Maine; 9% in Brittany, Picardy and Champagne; and 7% in other regions. This distribution reveals that over half of the Acadians came from western France, between the Loire R and the Pyrénées, and that about one-eighth came from N of the Loire. In Canada the reverse was true: well over half came from N of the Loire and about one-third from S of that river. This difference in origins is at the root of the difference between today's 2 closely related dialects, *Acadian* and *Franco-Canadian.*

The colonists who settled in Canada simply reflected the linguistic situation prevailing in France in the 17th and 18th centuries, when dialects flourished. French was spoken only by those from Paris and Île-de-France (administrators, functionaries, members of the church and army officers). Those from elsewhere spoke various *patois,* and true French speakers were rare. Upon arrival in the New World, the patois speakers did not establish linguistically distinct communities; French dominated, and this resulted in the creation of a common Canadian tongue, very close to French, by the end of the 17th century. By mid-18th century the various patois no longer existed in Canada, although their influence on Canadian French could still be heard in isolated words, morphological forms, pronunciation and intonation.

Canadian French Today In the 1986 census, more than 6 million Canadians claimed French as their mother tongue. Dialectologists and sociolinguists have conducted many studies of French, particularly since the 1960s, in the Maritimes, Québec and Ontario, in both rural and urban areas; the 4 western provinces have been virtually neglected.

Acadian and Franco-Canadian speakers understand one another easily. Acadian, spoken in the Maritimes and in parts of Québec (Magdalen Is, southern Gaspé and certain villages on the N Shore of the St Lawrence, including Havre-St-Pierre and Natashquan), is characterized by certain distinctive phonetic features. It is also characterized by numerous words originating from regions S of the Loire, eg, *éparer* (Fr *étendre,* "to hang out [fishing nets] to dry"), *charrette* (*tombereau,* "cart"), *remeuil* (*pis,* "cow's udder"), *coquemar* (*bouilloire de cuisinière,* "kettle"), *lisse* (*perche de clôture,* "fence post"), *amoureux* (*capitules de bardane,* "burdock flowerhead"), *barge* (*meule de foin,* "haystack") and *bargou* (*gruau,* "gruel").

Franco-Canadian, although spoken throughout an extensive region and having certain regional differences in vocabulary (Montréal, Québec City, central Québec, Saguenay-Lac Saint-Jean) is characterized by archaisms, dialectalisms, borrowings from N American Indian languages, and anglicisms. The many archaisms (a feature common to emigrant languages) include such expressions as *mitan* (modern Fr *milieu,* "middle"), *serrer* (*ranger,* "to tidy"), *gager* and *gageure* (*parier* and *pari,* "to bet" and "a bet"), *noirceur* (*obscurité,* "darkness"), *dalle* (*gouttière d'un toit,* "eavestrough") and *menterie* (*mensonge,* "lie"). The several hundred Indian borrowings, which are proof of a long history of contact between Francophones and Canada's indigenous peoples, include *babiche* (*mince lanière de cuir,* "thin strip of leather"), *nigog* ([*variété de*] *harpon,* "[type of] harpoon"), *boucane* (*fumée,* "smoke"), *atoca* (*canneberge,* "cranberry"), *micouenne* (*cuiller en bois,* "wooden spoon"), *sagamité* (*bouillie de maïs,* "cornmeal"), *pimbina* (*viorne trilobée,* "viburnum"), *achigan* ("black bass") and *manitou* ("God").

Canadian French has also been much influenced by English. Anglicisms are used in the language of general administration, justice, business and industry where, not long ago, borrowed English words were very numerous. For example, unilingual francophone forest workers had only English technical words, eg, "cull" (*bois de rebut*), "boom" (*estacade*), "skid" (*longeron*), "skidder" (*débusqueur*) and "cant-hook" (*sapi* or *levier; see* PEAVEY). Since the 1960s the pressure exerted by the English language has been weaker, because of an increased general awareness of French vocabulary on the part of workers and as a result of legislation designed to make French the language of work in Québec.

Spoken and written Canadian French is used at many different levels: the written language of a theatrical play set in a working-class quarter of a large city (*see* JOUAL), for example, is different from the language of a philosophical treatise. In the early 1980s English words were used less than 1% of the time in working-class areas.

Since the early 1960s, and in step with the QUIET REVOLUTION, the general level of college and university education among Francophones has risen greatly, particularly in scientific fields. This fact, together with federal and provincial legislation and pride on the part of French speakers, indicates that the French language in Canada, particularly in Québec, New Brunswick and Ontario, is assured not only of survival but of continued change and growth. *See also* LANGUAGE POLICY.

GASTON DULONG

Reading: M.M. Orkin, *Speaking Canadian French* (1967); S. Robinson and D. Smith, *Practical Handbook of Quebec and Acadian French* (1984).

French River, 290 km long (to head of Sturgeon R), rises in Lake NIPISSING, splits into 2 branches around Eighteen Mile I, reunites and plunges through a narrow channel towards GEORGIAN BAY. Its rocky shores are a maze of channels and bays, and its course follows a complex of natural fissures and faults in the Canadian SHIELD. The river was a swift, one-day run for the VOYAGEURS, and played a part in the FUR TRADE as early as 1615, when it was travelled by CHAMPLAIN. It is still a popular canoe route, and muskellunge, walleye, bass and pike are plentiful. Fur-trade artifacts and native utensils have been recovered from the area; in particular 3 Huron cooking pots in the summer of 1987 that are estimated to be 4 centuries old. Indian rock paintings are visible near Keso Point. JAMES MARSH

French Shore was an area of coastal Newfoundland where French fishermen enjoyed treaty rights granted by the British from 1713 to 1904. Anglo-French rivalry in Newfoundland began in the 1500s, intensified in the 1600s over the establishment of fishing stations and colonies, and was ultimately decided by European wars. In 1713 the Treaty of UTRECHT recognized British sovereignty over all French colonies and fishing territories in Newfoundland, except for the right to use for fishing, but not settlement, the coast westward from CAPE BONAVISTA, around BONAVISTA B, NOTRE DAME B, White Bay and the Great Northern Pen, S to Point Riche, near PORT AU CHOIX. In peace negotiations between Britain and France 1713-1814 the French Shore was usually an issue. The Treaty of PARIS (1763) confirmed the 1713 boundaries but ceded SAINT-PIERRE AND MIQUELON to France. The Treaty of PARIS (1783) altered the French Shore boundaries to the coast between Cape St John on the W side of Notre Dame B, around the Great Northern Pen, and southward along the entire W coast of Newfoundland to Cape Ray, NW of CHANNEL-PORT AUX BASQUES. These terms were confirmed by the 1814 Treaty of Paris.

Between 1815 and 1904 the French Shore ceased to be a wholly Anglo-French issue as Newfoundland gained representative (1832) and responsible (1855) government and began to challenge France's claim to exclusive use of the shore. Settlement radiated W in the 1800s and the colony pressed its claims to a concurrent fishery. Despite numerous conventions and commissions, it was not until the Anglo-French Convention of 1904 that France ceded all fishing rights, except for an equal summer fishery and the islands of Saint-Pierre and Miquelon. Though the French Shore disappeared, its influence is still felt in some areas, in the language, music and folk culture as well as in modern place-names.

JANET E.M. PITT

Reading: F.F. Thompson, *The French Shore Problem in Newfoundland* (1961).

Frenchman's Butte, Battle of On 28 May 1885, during the NORTH-WEST REBELLION, the Al-

berta Field Force under Gen Thomas B. STRANGE fought an indecisive battle against Cree under war chief Wandering Spirit (hanged at Battleford, 27 Nov 1885, for his role in the killings at FROG LAKE) N of a prominent hill called Frenchman's Butte, about 45 km NW of modern Lloydminster. The 2 sides fired at each other across a valley for several hours before they both retreated. None of Strange's force were killed and Cree casualties were light. Today a trail begins to the N of the battlefield. It passes Cree pits in a gully, and then runs along the main Indian position, where a plaque on a large rock commemorates the battle.
BOB BEAL

Frenkel, Vera, artist, independent film and video producer, writer (b at Bratislava, Czech 10 Nov 1938). Recognized internationally as a printmaker and sculptor, Frenkel, since 1974, has been in the forefront of the visual, spatial and narrative uses of video. Her first video work, *String Games: Improvisations for Inter-City Video* (1974), a live-to-tape direct transmission between Toronto and Montréal, investigated questions of language, codes and signs, and the invention of meaning. The video installation, *Signs of a Plot: A Text, True Story & Work of Art* (1978) and a video trilogy, *The Secret Life of Cornelia Lumsden: A Remarkable Story* (1979), written, directed and performed by the artist, are situated at the boundary between documentary and fiction. *The Last Screening Room: A Valentine* (1984) and *Ruling Fictions* (1984) continue her work with the mythic properties of popular culture. Frenkel's stand against censorship is focused in *The Business of Frightened Desires: Or the Making of a Pornographer* (1985), a slide-sound installation. *Attention: Lost Canadian*, a computer work for multiple monitors, and designed for the Canada Pavilion at Expo 86, was later transmitted electronically to the Italian Pavilion at the 1986 Venice Biennale. With *Lost Art: A Cargo Cult Romance* (1986), a new cycle of work began on the attribution of meaning, false messiahs and millennial fantasies. At U of T, 1970-72, and York U since 1972, Frenkel has gained a reputation as an innovative teacher and her essays, fiction and poetry have appeared in several publications.
JOYCE ZEMANS

Freshwater Institute (FWI), one of the world's leading research centres for freshwater fisheries research, is the regional headquarters of the federal Department of Fisheries and Oceans for Ontario, the Prairie provinces and the NWT. The predecessor of the FWI was the Central Fisheries Research Station of the FISHERIES RESEARCH BOARD of Canada. Established in Winnipeg in 1944, the station was moved to London, Ont, in 1957 and then back to Winnipeg as the FWI in 1966. New laboratory and office facilities were opened in 1973. The FWI provides facilities for fisheries and environmental research as well as for the non-research activities of the region, such as fisheries inspection. It is the major federal government centre for freshwater and arctic fisheries research. Scientists at the FWI play a critical role in a number of regional and national issues relative to freshwater, freshwater fisheries, and arctic marine fish and marine mammals, such as the impact of arctic oil and gas development on fish and marine mammals, the impact of hydro development on fish habitats, toxic contaminants, AQUACULTURE development, inland fisheries enhancement and ACID RAIN. Scientific disciplines at the FWI include population biology, limnology, fisheries biology, chemistry and toxicology, marine mammal biology and related fields. Studies are carried out in extensive laboratory facilities at the FWI and at field stations located at various latitudes from the Canada-US border to the arctic islands.
G.B. AYLES

Frezenberg Ridge Princess Patricia's Canadian Light Infantry, composed largely of British-born former regular soldiers, had gone to Flanders in Dec 1914 in advance of 1st Canadian Division, as part of the British 27th Division. When the Germans launched a major attack into the YPRES Salient, over Frezenberg Ridge, on 8 May 1915, the PPCLI held the S shoulder of the breach. Despite incurring 392 casualties out of an initial strength of 546, the battalion held on and prevented the Germans from rolling up the British line S towards Armentières, France. *See also* WORLD WAR I.
BRERETON GREENHOUS

Friedman, Sydney Murray, scientist, scholar, physician (b at Montréal 17 Feb 1916). A 1940 medical graduate of McGill, Friedman served in the RCAF during WWII. He returned to McGill and earned his PhD in anatomy (1946) and thereafter began a distinguished career in academic medicine. He was appointed the first professor and head of the dept of anatomy at UBC (1950-81). His scientific research on the effects of sodium and hormones on blood vessels in hypertension has spanned 40 years. He is known internationally as a scientific author and lecturer. Friedman's many honours include Royal Society of Canada membership, the J.C.B. Grant Award and outstanding service awards from the Heart Foundation and the Ciba Foundation. He is also a founding member of the BC Heart Foundation. Since 1985 he has been professor emeritus at UBC.
C.E. SLONECKER

Friendship Centres, are nongovernment native agencies, funded primarily by the Dept of the Secretary of State but autonomous in running their own affairs. These voluntary associations sponsor activities such as cultural events, dances, sports and recreation, job-training and educational services, and economic co-operatives, and are often located in urban areas. Regardless of their explicit functions, they are small and intimate enough to provide a social environment that is psychologically comfortable, and so function as friendship centres. Individuals help each other cope with the problems and anxieties of racial discrimination, poverty and alienation experienced in urban areas.
RENÉ R. GADACZ

Reading: J.A. Price, *Native Studies* (1978).

Fripp, Thomas William, painter (b at London, Eng 23 Mar 1864; d at Vancouver 30 May 1931). Grandson of the founder of the Royal Watercolour Soc (Nicholas Pocock) and son of George Arthur Fripp, under whom he studied, he also studied at St John's Wood Art School, the Royal Academy Schools (1887), and in France and Italy. Fripp immigrated to BC in 1893. He farmed at first, then moved to Vancouver in 1904 where he worked in a photography studio for 2 years before turning to painting full time. He gained acclaim for his watercolours of the Rocky Mts and Pacific coast landscapes and painted some oils and portraits. A founding member of the BC Art League, Fripp was first president of the BC Society of Fine Arts (1909) and a member of the BC Society of Artists.
PATRICIA E. BOVEY

Fritz, Madeleine Alberta, paleontologist (b at Saint John 3 Nov 1896). She was educated at McGill and U of T and, while a student of William Arthur PARKS (and later as associate director of the Royal Ontario Museum of Paleontology), was a leader in the N American study of Ordovician bryozoa. For many years a professor of geology at U of T, she was the second woman in Canada to be elected a fellow in the Royal Soc of Canada. Her studies on the PALEONTOLOGY and stratigraphy of Toronto and vicinity stand as a definitive work.
JOAN BURKE

Sir Martin Frobisher, Elizabethan mariner, who in his search for a Northwest Passage to Asia ended up in remote Frobisher Bay on SE Baffin I (*courtesy National Archives of Canada/C-11413*).

Frobisher, Benjamin, fur trader (b at Halifax, Eng *c*1742; d at Montréal 14 Apr 1787), brother of Joseph and Thomas FROBISHER. After coming to Québec about 1763, he and his brothers entered the FUR TRADE of the North West. For the most part he managed business affairs in Montréal and England while his brothers traded in the field. The family was an original shareholder in the NORTH WEST CO.
DANIEL FRANCIS

Frobisher, Joseph, fur trader, merchant (b at Halifax, Eng 15 Apr 1740; d at Montréal 12 Sept 1810). In partnership with brothers Benjamin and Thomas FROBISHER he was one of the "pedlars from Quebec" engaged in the FUR TRADE in western Canada after 1770. In 1774-75 he wintered on the Churchill R in an attempt to intercept furs coming downriver to the HBC. This pioneering excursion led a few years later to the penetration by Québec traders into Athabasca Lk country. In 1776 Frobisher settled in Montréal where he became one of the great fur merchants. He was an original partner in the NORTH WEST CO and in 1787 joined Simon MCTAVISH to form McTavish, Frobisher and Co, the NWC's principal outfitter and sales agent. After his retirement in 1798, he lived at his stately home, Beaver Hall.
DANIEL FRANCIS

Frobisher, Sir Martin, mariner (b near Wakefield, Eng 1539; d at Plymouth, Eng 22 Nov 1594). In 1576 he searched W of Greenland for a passage to Asia, discovered FROBISHER BAY, and returned with ore thought to contain gold. He made a second voyage (1577), hauling back more earth. On his last expedition (1578), he commanded a flotilla of 15 vessels. Driven by storms across the entrance to HUDSON STR, he landed at Kodlunarn I, in Warwick's Sound, where his men excavated tonnes of ore which proved worthless. Depressions in the rock where the miners dug and the ruins of a stone house are still visible. His patron, Michael Lok, was ruined, but Frobisher's seafaring career continued. He accompanied DRAKE to the West Indies and was knighted for his heroism against the Spanish Armada (1588). He died of wounds sustained in action against the Spanish at Crozon, near Brest, France.
JAMES MARSH

Frobisher, Thomas, fur trader (b at Halifax (?), Yorkshire, Eng 1744; d at Montréal 12 Sept

1788). After arriving in Québec in 1769, he joined his brothers Joseph and Benjamin FROBISHER in the western FUR TRADE. In 1776 he founded the first trading post at ÎLE-À-LA-CROSSE, a stepping stone to the Athabasca Lk country. DANIEL FRANCIS

Frobisher Bay (community), *see* IQALUIT.

Frobisher Bay is a deep indentation in the extreme SE coastline of BAFFIN I, over 230 km long and 40 km wide at the mouth, narrowing to 20 km towards its head. The configuration of the bay has a funnelling effect, so that the harbour of the settlement of IQALUIT [Frobisher Bay] at the bay's head experiences a twice-daily tidal range of 7-11 m. The bay's general physiography is the result of tectonic events associated with the rifting of the N Atlantic in the early Tertiary, during which time that part of the Precambrian Shield in the Frobisher Bay area was downfaulted and the blocks on either side were uplifted and tilted up to the NE. An abrupt contact between these units is marked by the high cliffs rising from the bay, which because of the tilting are 330 m high on the N shore and twice that height on the S shore. Overdeepening occurred during the Pleistocene glaciation, when the Frobisher Bay trough was filled by a major outlet glacier from ice centered over FOXE BASIN. The bay is named for Sir Martin FROBISHER, who discovered it in 1576. He believed the bay was a strait, and it first appeared on maps as Frobisher Strait. DOUGLAS FINLAYSON

Frog, AMPHIBIAN belonging to order Anura. The adult, typically, has no tail or ribs, longer hindlimbs than forelimbs, well-developed eyes and skin equipped with mucus and venom glands. Frog eggs are usually fertilized externally and develop into the free-swimming larval stage (tadpole or polliwog). The tadpole is transformed into its adult state through metamorphosis. This process involves numerous morphological and physiological changes: loss of tail and gills, limb and lung development, restructuring of the digestive system from vegetarian to carnivore and alteration of sensory receptors to suit a terrestrial lifestyle. Frogs, the largest group of amphibians (about 2700 living species), are found on all continents except Antarctica. They are grouped into about 20 families but this varies according to classification methods. The frogs of the large Bufonidae family, known as TOADS, generally have relatively drier skin and reduced webbing between their toes. Other frogs commonly called toads include the N American spade-foot toad (family Pelobatidae), the Mexican burrowing toad (Rhinophrynidae) and the European midwife toad (Discoglossidae).

Frogs appeared very early in the FOSSIL record. *Triadobatrachus,* found in Triassic deposits (245-208 million years old) in Madagascar, is the earliest known frog. Jurassic deposits (208-144 million years old) in S America contain frogs having a general body plan similar to some present species. Truly amazing adaptations permit frogs to exploit habitats ranging from rain forests to deserts and from the tropics to the Arctic Circle.

Only 21 or 22 species of frogs live in Canada; most are restricted by climatic limitations to extreme southern Canada. The western mountains form an effective east-west barrier restricting such species as red-legged frog to coastal BC, Pacific tree frog and tailed frog to low and high elevations in BC, and western spotted frog to BC and the foothills in western Alberta. The tailed frog lives in mountainous streams in southern BC and has some interesting specializations. Adapted to fast-flowing streams, male tailed frogs use the tail for internal fertilization of eggs. Tadpoles have expanded mouthparts for adhering to rocks. The western toad is cold tolerant enough to live at

Most of the 21 or 22 species of frog native to Canada – such as the leopard frog seen here – live in the extreme southern regions (*photo by Mary W. Ferguson*).

high altitudes in BC and Alberta. The wood frog ranges above the Arctic Circle in the Yukon, where forest extends along river valleys. This species has an extensive Canadian range occurring from coast to coast except in arid areas and on the SW coast. The bullfrog is the largest Canadian frog and, although originally an eastern species, has been introduced in BC. Green frogs have been introduced to the Vancouver area and leopard frogs to Vancouver I. Newfoundland has no native frogs, but green, leopard, wood and chorus frogs, as well as toads, have been introduced and have become established.

Frogs are ecologically important, in that as vegetarian tadpoles they are primary consumers in the food chain and later serve as food for various invertebrates and vertebrates. The carnivorous adults consume insects and are in turn consumed by fish, birds and mammals. Although frogs are a relatively minor food item for humans, they are useful in the biological control of INSECT PESTS and certain large species have been introduced to various parts of the world. Frogs are also used in many fields of research and for anatomical studies in educational institutions. Collection for teaching and research purposes, and harvesting for frogs legs and fish bait, may be factors in the reduction of natural populations of commonly used species, but yearly climatic fluctuations and the increasing drainage of habitat are equally important.

Frogs are frequent subjects of folklore and ritual. In dry regions they are associated with life-giving rain and symbolize fertility. European folklore often features frogs and toads as evil. The nocturnal vocalizations of frogs, usually associated with storms or rains, are considered by some American native peoples to be spiritual outcries. In fact, male vocalizations serve to attract females to favourable breeding sites. In some species, the female perceives only a narrow frequency range, hearing only her own species. The call in some species may also delineate a male's breeding territory. JAMES P. BOGART

Canadian Frogs and Toads

Common Name	*Scientific Name*	*Range*
bullfrog	*Rana catesbeiana*	Ont to NS; introduced BC
green frog	*R. clamitans*	Ont to NS; introduced Nfld, BC
mink frog	*R. septentrionalis*	E Man to NS
pickerel frog	*R. palustris*	Ont to NS
northern leopard frog	*R. pipiens*	coast to coast, N to NWT
wood frog	*R. sylvatica*	coast to coast, N to NWT, YT
western spotted frog	*R. pretiosa*	Alta, BC
red-legged frog	*R. aurora*	Vancouver I and SW mainland
cricket frog	*Acris crepitans*	extreme SW Ont
striped chorus frog	*Pseudacris triseriata*	Ont, SW Qué to northeastern BC, N to NWT
spring peeper	*Hyla crucifer*	Man to NS
tetraploid grey tree frog	*H. versicolor*	E Man to SW Qué, NB
diploid grey tree frog	*H. chrysoscelis*	southern Man
Pacific treefrog	*H. regilla*	southern BC
tailed frog	*Ascaphus truei*	southern BC
American toad	*Bufo americanus*	NWT to NS
Great Plains toad	*B. cognatus*	BC to Ont
western toad	*B. boreas*	BC and W Alta, N to YT
Fowler's toad	*B. fowleri*	SW Ont
plains spadefoot	*Scaphiopus bombifrons*	S Alta to Man
Great Basin spadefoot	*S. intermontanus*	southern BC

Front de libération du Québec (FLQ), a revolutionary movement that used propaganda and TERRORISM to promote the emergence of an independent, socialist Québec. The movement was founded in March 1963, when Québec was undergoing a period of remarkable change (industrial expansion, modernization of the state), but it was also stimulated by international factors such as the decolonization of Algeria. Pierre Vallières, the author of the book NÈGRES BLANCS D'AMÉRIQUE, joined the FLQ in 1965 and is generally considered the "philosopher" behind the organization.

In 1963 underground FLQ activists (some of whom were arrested) placed bombs in mailboxes in 3 federal armories and in Westmount, a wealthy upper-middle-class anglophone area of Montréal. In 1964 another group of FLQ members stole approximately $50 000 in cash and military equipment, and at a holdup at International Firearms the company vice-president was killed by the FLQ and another employee was killed by the police, who mistook him for one of the thieves. From 1965 to 1967, the FLQ associated itself with the activities of striking workers. It was involved in over 200 bombings between 1963 and 1970, and in 1968 it began using larger and more powerful bombs, setting them off at a federal government bookstore, at McGill University, at the residence of Jean DRAPEAU and the provincial Department of Labour, and at the Montreal Stock Exchange, where 27 people were injured. In the fall of 1969, the movement split into 2 distinct cells: the south shore gang (which became the Chenier cell) led by Paul Rose, and the liberation cell, under Jacques Lanctôt. Montréal based, both cells claimed about 12 members.

In the fall of 1970 (*see* OCTOBER CRISIS) the FLQ kidnapped Pierre LAPORTE and British trade commissioner James Cross. Laporte was later murdered. Under the WAR MEASURES ACT, more than 450 people were arrested, including 150 "suspected" FLQ members. Paul Rose and Francis Simard were eventually sentenced to life imprisonment for the murder of Laporte. Bernard Lortie was convicted of kidnapping Laporte, and Jacques Rose was convicted as an accessory. Of the Cross kidnappers, 5 fled to Cuba and then to France, and eventually returned to Canada. One had remained in Montréal but was arrested in 1980 and sentenced in 1981. The movement had ceased activities in 1971. MARC LAURENDEAU

Front Page Challenge, the CBC game-interview TV program, is the longest-running of its kind in N America. Intended as a 13-week summer replacement for The Denny Vaughan Show, FPC first aired 24 June 1957. On 11 Oct 1986 it began its 30th season with a telecast from the National Arts Centre, featuring Governor General Jeanne SAUVÉ as guest panelist. The show's format, created by John Aylesworth and Harvey Hart, requires panelists to identify a mystery challenger, who represents – and is often the central figure in – a major news story. Over the years, challengers have included 6 Canadian prime ministers, most provincial premiers, and such diverse personages as Indira Gandhi, Sir Edmund Hillary, Eleanor Roosevelt, Martin Luther King, Gordie HOWE, Igor GOUZENKO and Mary Pickford. Beyond the impressive guest list, the show offers a distinctively Canadian interpretation of national and international events. Its base in entertainment rather than public affairs programming allows it unusual latitude and has fostered a unique credibility. The regular panelists – for many years Gordon SINCLAIR, Betty Kennedy and Pierre BERTON – built a reputation for intelligence and unedited spontaneity and, along with moderator Fred Davis, became national celebrities (Kennedy succeeded Toby Robins in 1962, while Allan FOTHERINGHAM replaced the deceased Sinclair in 1984). Toronto-based FPC has toured most Canadian cities from St John's to Victoria to Yellowknife, always playing to sold-out houses. MARK D.B. KENNEDY

Reading: A. Barris, *Front Page Challenge* (1981).

Frontenac After William Durant lost control of GENERAL MOTORS for the second time, he started Durant Motors, and a Canadian branch was established in the Toronto suburb of Leaside. This branch was so profitable, despite serious problems at the parent firm, that it went independent, founding Dominion Motors Ltd in 1931. Its cars were named after the comte de FRONTENAC, a governor of New France. The first Frontenac was like the Durant Six, featuring automatic starting (when the ignition was turned on) and freewheeling (engine compression not slowing the car while coasting). Frontenac later added the small, 4-cylinder, US DeVaux and the larger Continental to its range. Eventually, the Great Depression had its effect and production ended in Dec 1933, nearly 2 years after Durant Motors had succumbed. R. PERRY ZAVITZ

Reading: Perry Zavitz, *Canadian Cars 1946-1984* (1985).

Frontenac was the first steamboat launched on the Great Lakes. She was built by American contractors in 1816 at Ernesttown [Bath, Ont] for a company of mainly Kingston (Ont) investors. The following spring she began her regular schedule on Lake Ontario between Kingston, York [Toronto] and Niagara-on-the-Lake. Measuring in all about 700 tons, *Frontenac* was 51.8 m along the deck and 9.1 m across the beam, with a hold 3.5 m deep. Her 50-hp Boulton & Watt steam engine propelled the steamboat at about 10.6 km/h. Costing in excess of £15 000 and operating in a province of only about 100 000 people, *Frontenac* rarely turned a profit. After 8 years, she was sold at auction for £1550 to John Hamilton who, with his brother Robert, operated *Frontenac* for another 2 years. In 1827, she was taken to Niagara where, while being scrapped, she was burned by an arsonist. WALTER LEWIS

Frontenac, Louis de Buade, Comte de, gov gen of New France (b at St-Germain, France 22 May 1622; d at Québec City 28 Nov 1698). This imperious count had been an officer in the French and Venetian armies. In 1672 he obtained the governorship of Canada, in part, to put off his creditors. With the intendant absent 1672-75, he extended his viceregal and military authority to civil matters. His pretensions, such as being the Conseil Souverain's chairman, were resisted by other officials, whom he sometimes exiled or placed in confinement. The clergy were offended by his approval of selling brandy to the Indians. After 1675 he conflicted with Intendant Jacques DUCHESNEAU who had his own faction in the FUR TRADE. The quarrels led to the recall of both officials to France in 1682.

Frontenac gave France a territorial empire acquired in defiance of his instructions. The king and the minister for the colonies told administrators in Canada to confine French settlement to areas with direct maritime links with France, to gather colonists into defensible communities and to occupy settlers in farming and manual trades. The fur trade was blamed for the dispersal of manpower and for the military and economic weakness of New France. Frontenac used his authority to send out exploratory parties and to establish forts – trading posts really – to benefit his confederates in the fur trade. A network of forts appeared on the Great Lks and along the tributaries of the Mississippi. Denial of this territory to the expanding British colonies led inevitably to war and eventually the end of France's N American empire.

Frontenac was reinstated as governor in 1689, when nations of the Iroquois Confederacy were attacking New France. He had orders to seize the Iroquois supply base – the colony of New York. Instead, he sent raiding parties against frontier settlements there and in New England. As a riposte, a seaborne expedition under Sir William PHIPS besieged Québec. When summoned to surrender, Frontenac responded, "I have no reply ... other than from the mouths of my cannon and muskets." Sickness and cold weather forced the invaders to withdraw. Frontenac wrongly believed he could end Iroquois hostility with diplomacy. In 1696, under ministerial orders, he commanded a punitive expedition that destroyed ONEIDA and ONONDAGA villages and crops (*see* IROQUOIS WARS). Though less quarrelsome in his second administration, Frontenac still used his powers to profit from the fur trade, which he was accused of underwriting with military funds. Frontenac might have been dismissed had he not died in 1698. PETER N. MOOGK

Reading: W.J. Eccles, *Frontenac, The Courtier Governor* (1959).

Frontier Thesis was formulated 1893, when American historian Frederick Jackson Turner theorized that the availability of unsettled land throughout much of American history was the most important factor determining national development. Frontier experiences and new opportunities forced old traditions to change, institutions to adapt and society to become more democratic as class distinctions collapsed. The result was a unique American society, distinct from the European societies from which it originated. In Canada the frontier thesis was popular between the world wars with historians such as A.R.M. LOWER and Frank UNDERHILL and sociologist S.D. CLARK, partly because of a new sense of Canada's N American character.

Since WWII the frontier thesis has declined in popularity because of recognition of important social and cultural distinctions between Canada and the US. In its place a "metropolitan school" has developed, emphasizing Canada's much closer historical ties with Europe. Moreover, centres such as Montréal, Toronto and Ottawa had a profound influence on the settlement of the Canadian frontier. Whichever argument is emphasized, however, any realistic conclusion cannot deny that both the frontier and the ties to established centres were formative in Canada's development. *See also* METROPOLITAN-HINTERLAND THESIS.
D.R. OWRAM

Frost, Leslie Miscampbell, lawyer, politician, premier of Ontario 1949-61 (b at Orillia, Ont 20 Sept 1895; d at Lindsay, Ont 4 May 1973). After service in WWI and convalescence from a severe wound, he graduated from Osgoode Hall in 1921. With his brother he purchased a law practice in Lindsay and became an active member of the CONSERVATIVE PARTY. Elected to the legislature in 1937, he was appointed provincial treasurer and minister of mines in the Cabinet of George DREW in 1943. Six years later he became Conservative leader, inheriting the premiership. A genial master of pragmatic politics who personified the values of small-town Ontario, he led his party to 3 sweeping electoral victories. His governments initiated progressive legislation in health, education and human rights, and encouraged growth in the private economic sector through fiscal policy and public investment. He resigned as leader and premier in 1961. ROGER GRAHAM

Reading: J. Manthorpe, *The Power & the Tories* (1974).

Fruit and Vegetable Industry This important sector of Canada's FOOD AND BEVERAGE INDUSTRIES is made up of companies that process fruits and VEGETABLES. Their primary products are canned, frozen or otherwise preserved fruits and vegetables, vegetable and fruit juices, soups, pickles, jams, jellies and marmalades, cider, sauces and vinegar. The industry employs more than 17 300 permanent workers; during the harvesting and processing seasons temporary help expands the work force considerably. In 1985 the industry spent more than $1.3 billion on the purchase of raw agricultural products, packaging and other necessary materials and supplies. It shipped finished products valued at more than $2.4 billion.

The industry began in the late 1880s when George Dunning established the country's first fruit and vegetable canning factory in Prince Edward County, southeastern Ontario. By 1900, 8 canning plants were in production in the county, half of the total in Canada at the time. During the early 1900s, the industry became firmly established in all the major fruit- and vegetable-growing regions of Canada. By 1985, as a result of plant consolidation and reorganization, only 222 fruit and vegetable factories remained in production; this number should change little in coming years. Of the 222 plants in operation in 1985, Nfld had 1; PEI, 3; NS, 11; NB, 4; Qué, 61; Ont, 95; Man, 5; Sask, 2; Alta, 8; and BC, 32.

Prior to the mid-1940s, the primary food-preservation techniques were drying, pickling and high-temperature canning. The last procedure, by far the most important, involves filling metal or glass containers with a partially cooked product, then sealing the container and heating it to high temperature for varying lengths of time. This method completely sterilizes the contents and permits storage at room temperatures for long periods. The first Canadian frozen fruit and vegetable operation was established by William H. Heeney. In 1932 his company, Heeney Frosted Foods Ltd of Ottawa and Montréal, produced the country's first commercial frozen food, a strawberry pack. From a slow beginning the market for frozen fruit and vegetable products has grown in the last 10-15 years. By 1985 there were 35 frozen fruit and vegetable operations in Canada distributed as follows: PEI, 1; NS, 1; NB, 2; Qué, 5; Ont, 14; Man, 2; Alta, 2; and BC, 8. In that year, the value of factory shipments of finished frozen fruits and vegetables was $587 million. Canned fruit and vegetable production still far outweighs frozen, but future production of frozen goods will increase at the expense of canned products.

The industry is subject to many federal, provincial and municipal regulations, but the primary governing body is Agriculture Canada (*see* FOOD LEGISLATION). All Canadian fruit and vegetable processors are federally licensed and must conform to regulations enforced by inspectors from Agriculture Canada's fruit and vegetable inspection branch. It is mandatory for food plants shipping products across provincial or international borders to be federally inspected.

Unlike the processing industries of some other countries, the Canadian industry does not own an extensive amount of land for agricultural production. It does, however, exert considerable control over what crop varieties are grown. In most cases, Canadian farmers contract to grow certain crops for a specific processor or group of processors. Most vegetables destined for canning or freezing are picked by mechanical harvesters, usually owned by the processing companies. Increasingly, fruit crops (eg, Ontario's grape crop) are being harvested mechanically, also with harvesters owned by processing companies. Canned and frozen fruits and vegetables are graded to meet federal government regulations as follows: fancy (top quality), choice (good quality) and standard (bottom quality). Most Canadian canned and frozen fruit and vegetables are of "fancy" or "choice" quality. The processing sector is represented by 2 Ottawa-based national associations and their provincial counterparts: the Canadian Food Processors' Assn and the Canadian Frozen Food Assn. ROBERT F. BARRATT

Fruit Cultivation Most of the fruit species cultivated in Canada belong to the ROSE family, the most important genera being *Malus* (APPLE), *Pyrus* (PEAR), *Prunus* (PEACH, nectarine, PLUM and prune, CHERRY, APRICOT), *Fragaria* (strawberry), *Rubus* (raspberry) and *Vaccinium* (cranberry, blueberry). Other major families having cultivated fruit species are Saxifragaceae, with *Ribes* (currant and gooseberry), and Vitaceae, with *Vitis* (GRAPE). Each fruit species has many cultivars (commercial varieties), developed for various characteristics. For example, in Canada adaptation to a specific climatic factor (eg, cold winters) is important. Breeding and selection programs give priority to these requirements; crop research programs have developed many cultivars.

The FRUIT AND VEGETABLE INDUSTRY is an important part of the agriculture and food distribution sectors of the economy. More than 40% of all foods consumed in Canada are fresh and processed fruits and vegetables. About 30 major fruit and vegetable crops are grown, with an annual farm-gate value of about $850 million. About 37% of this figure is for fruits (*see* BERRIES).

Canadian-grown fruit is marketed fresh or is processed in various ways; eg, 56% of apples are sold fresh (at harvest or later), the remainder being processed into juice, sauce, pie filling, frozen slices and other products. Similarly, about 66% of the "tender" fruit (cherries, peaches, pears, plums, prunes) are sold fresh and the remainder processed. Sweet cherries are processed for brining (for maraschino cherries) or frozen (for ice cream and baking use). Tart cherries are frozen or canned (pie filling, jams, jellies, juices). Most Canadian-grown grapes are processed into WINE and juice. The perishable fruits (strawberry, raspberry, blueberry) are preserved by freezing or canning. Some fruits, particularly apples and pears, are stored at harvest rather than being processed or immediately sold fresh. The fruit continues to live after harvest, using oxygen, giving off carbon dioxide and generating heat. This leads to breakdown of fruit tissues. Refrigeration and controlled-atmosphere storage allow orderly marketing of fresh fruit almost year-round.

Fruit growing is usually restricted to areas where the temperatures do not go much below -20°C. Fruit growing occurs in NS, NB, SW Québec, southwestern Ontario and BC.

Nova Scotia Production is confined to the ANNAPOLIS LOWLANDS, well suited to production of apples, blueberries and strawberries. Winter temperatures often dip to -24°C; hence, peach and cherry growing are marginal.

New Brunswick Severe winter temperatures restrict production to the Saint John R valley. Only apples can withstand severe winter temperatures (often -24°C, but reaching -34°C). Some blueberries and strawberries are grown.

Québec Orchards are located mainly on light soils around the bases of old volcanic hills that rise above the dry loams of the plains, and in the foothills of the Appalachian Mts, near the US border. Low winter temperatures can cause extensive tree damage. For example, in the winter of 1917-18 temperatures of -37°C to -40°C resulted in losses estimated at 50%.

Ontario The moderating influence of lakes Huron, Erie and Ontario, coupled with suitable soils, allows the growing of a complete range of fruit crops in southwestern Ontario. The more tender fruits (eg, peach, cherry, grape, plum, pear) are limited to the Niagara Fruit Belt on the SW shore of Lk Ontario. Apples are grown over much of the southern part of the province, including the S shore of Georgian Bay.

British Columbia Strawberries, raspberries, loganberries and grapes are cultivated in the Lower Mainland area but the fruit-growing region is the OKANAGAN VALLEY. The valley is in the rain-shadow area of the interior; hence, fruit growing is dependent on irrigation. The complete range of fruit crops is grown, but the major crop, apples, accounts for two-thirds of the area. Most orchards are located on the top and sides of terraces along the sides of lakes. Deep, dividing gullies, running from the high slopes down to the water, provide air drainage to prevent frost damage. Winter damage to trees is a recurring problem; eg, low temperatures in the 1949-50 winter caused an estimated loss of 20% of all trees. J.T.A. PROCTOR

Reading: W.H. Upshall, ed, *History of Fruit Growing and Handling in the United States and Canada* (1976).

Fruits of the Earth, novel by Frederick Philip GROVE, was published 1933 in Toronto. To dramatize the tragedy of the pioneer, Grove charts the life of Abe Spalding, a man imbued with an indomitable drive to impose his will on the prairie. Spalding leaves Ontario for Manitoba, where, through years of unrelenting work, he masters his land, builds a mansion and becomes a power in the community. But his triumphs are fleeting: in time he becomes alienated from his family, and the natural world begins to prove itself impervious to human designs. In the end, the pioneer's great dream – to conquer raw nature – does violence to his own human nature. NEIL BESNER

Frum, Barbara, née Rosberg, radio and TV journalist (b at Niagara Falls, NY 8 Sept 1937). Educated at U of T, she wrote for numerous magazines, performed on TV and radio in the late 1960s, and did thoughtful, incisive and often acerbic interviews with international figures on CBC Radio's popular phone-out show "As It Happens," 1971-81. Canada's most respected and best-known interviewer, she has won many journalism awards. Since Jan 1982 she has been a host of "The Journal," CBC TV's nightly current-affairs program. ALLAN M. GOULD

Fry, Frederick Ernest Joseph, aquatic ecologist (b at Woking, Eng 17 Apr 1908). From 1936 to 1974, including 4 years (1941-45) with the RCAF doing research in aviation medicine, Fry was professor of zoology at U of T. Since 1974 he has been professor emeritus and an associate of the Institute for Environmental Studies. A brilliant scientist and influential teacher, he is best known internationally for his work in physiological ecology, which developed a new understanding of the activities of fishes in relation to the physical and chemical environment. His major contribution to population dynamics, "virtual population analysis," remains one of the principal tools used internationally to manage major fisheries. He was awarded an MBE in 1944, elected to the RSC in 1948, and has received many medals and awards. He has been president of the American Soc of Limnology and Oceanography (1951), the American Fisheries Soc (1966), the Canadian Soc of Zoologists (1966) and the American Inst of Fishery Research Biologists (1972). In 1974 the Canadian Soc of Zoologists established the Fry medal in recognition of his contribution to Canadian science. S.R. KERR

Frye, Herman Northrop, literary critic, university professor, editor (b at Sherbrooke, Qué 14 July 1912). A professor of English at Victoria Coll, U of Toronto, since 1939, Frye has achieved international recognition for his literary theories, expounded in his study of William Blake's prophecies, *Fearful Symmetry* (1947), his grammar of mythic form, ANATOMY OF CRITICISM (1957), and his study of the Bible's symbolism, *The Great Code* (1982). These works, particularly the *Anatomy,* have made Frye one of this century's leading literary theorists. Although noted for clarity of style, his writing for the average reader is conceptually difficult and best approached through *The Educated Imagination* (1963).

Raised in Moncton, Frye first came to Toronto to compete in a national typing contest in 1929, in which he won second place in the novice class. Soon after, he enrolled at Victoria Coll and, except for 2 years of study in the late 1930s at Merton Coll, Oxford, he has remained associated with the college, and became chancellor in 1978. While still a graduate student, Frye decided to write a definitive study of Blake's prophetic poems, then considered incoherent, even aberrant. In *Fearful Symmetry,* Frye showed that Blake deliberately used a regular pattern of symbolism based on earlier writers such as Milton and ultimately on the Bible. In *Anatomy of Criticism,* Frye expanded this notion by outlining a verbal universe of repeated archetypes and symbolism and rhetoric that binds all literature together. This universe consists of desired and abhorred worlds, the former expressed by comedy and romance, the latter by tragedy and irony. Frye's own evangelical Methodist upbringing influences his view that there is in human culture an inherent impulse towards affirming the sunnier vision and implementing it in the world. Ironically his own view of Canadian literature, which he has never much admired, is notoriously sunk in gloom. Frye contends that like the poetry of his own mentor, E.J. PRATT, it is the product of a "garrison mentality" of beleaguered settlers who huddled against the glowering, all-consuming nothingness of the wilderness. Its birth lay in a blighted winter, rather than vibrant spring, mentality.

Despite his insistence on the ultimate visionary process of literary studies, Frye has demanded the kind of discipline in study he experienced himself in music, which has an intensely integrated theory. He teaches that literature is not a grab bag of thousands of individual works but an integrated universe of recognizable forms. He has always seen a close association of a disciplined recognition of form with major literary talent, such as that of his own preferred subjects, Spenser, Shakespeare, Milton, Blake, Yeats and Eliot. He has spurned a predominantly evaluative approach to literature because evaluation tends to say more about the critic than the work studied. This has led him into endless international controversy, which has obscured his fundamental purpose in trying to establish an objective and universally accepted terminology for literature studies.

Northrop Frye, literary critic internationally recognized for his study of William Blake and his works on mythic form and biblical symbolism (*photo by Roy Nicholls*).

Frye's enormous influence peaked in the mid-1960s when a new generation of scholars, influenced by the ideas of the *Anatomy,* were attracted by his insistence that literary criticism was not a poor cousin of PHILOSOPHY, PSYCHOLOGY, LINGUISTICS or aesthetics but a symbolically co-ordinated discipline that outlines the shape of the human imagination itself. As such, it has its own authority, which can be useful in the study of other arts and social sciences. Along with many honours and citations, Frye has also received the Royal Bank Award. Among his recent publications are *Northrop Frye on Shakespeare* (1986, Gov Gen's Award for nonfiction) and *On Education* (1987).
JOHN AYRE

Fuca, Juan de, pilot, apocryphal explorer of the NORTHWEST COAST (b at Valeriano, Cephalonia I, Greece; d there *c*1602). Other than what Michael Lok, an English promoter of geographical discovery, reported in 1596, little is known about Fuca. According to his own story, he was a pilot in Spain's Pacific maritime service. He claimed to have led a 1592 voyage of discovery N from Mexico that encountered a passage leading to the "North Sea" (possibly the Arctic Ocean) between 47° and 48° lat. Fuca told Lok that he sailed through the broad passage before retracing his course to Mexico. The discovery much later of the strait now bearing Fuca's name at 48°30′ lat gave credence to his story and suggested the possibility of a 16th-century Spanish voyage to the NW Coast. More likely, Fuca told Lok an exciting tale in order to obtain financial compensation. Spanish archival sources and published works offer no evidence. CHRISTON I. ARCHER

Fuel Cell, device that directly converts the energy potential of fuels into electrical power. (Electrical power is equivalent to work output.) Directly means without first burning the fuel to cause a temperature rise followed by a second-step, which is the conversion of heat into work. It is the heat-to-work step in conventional 'heat engines' that results in the severe efficiency constraints imposed by the second law of thermodynamics. (Just about every technology we now use to convert fuel to power is a heat engine – automobile engines, aeroplane engines, outboard motors and even nuclear-generating stations, but not electric motors which convert electricity to power.) By avoiding the heat-to-work step, fuel cells avoid the efficiency constraint imposed on today's technology for converting fuel to work (power).

The fuel cell concept has been known for more than a century. But modern fuel cell development dates from the late 1930s when F.T. Bacon developed an alkaline electrolyte fuel cell that used hydrogen and oxygen. This development formed the basis of the fuel cells that were used to generate onboard electricity for today's spacecraft. The water waste product from these fuel cells is used as astronaut drinking water. Terrestrial applications, for uses such as locomotives, mining vehicles, submarines and even electric utility stations, are now in stages of planning, design or development. A fuel cell is an electrochemical energy conversion technology — a classification shared with electricity storage batteries (which convert energy, stored within their own material, into electricity) and electrolysis plants (which convert electrical energy into chemical energy stored in hydrogen and oxygen, by splitting water molecules). Looking into the next century, the importance of electrochemical energy conversion technologies will grow perhaps to eclipse today's ubiquitous heat engines. All living things convert their fuel (food) to work (power) by electrochemical processes — for growing, running, swimming or flying. But about 2 centuries ago, when mankind first invented machines to convert fuel to work, the electrochemical way of nature was not followed. Instead, heat engines were invented, of which the first was the steam engine. Electrochemical energy conversion is inherently more efficient, although today it suffers from low power *densities* when compared to heat engines. But with continuing advances in materials and catalysts, power densities could be increased dramatically. This, together with the parallel evolution towards the hydrogen age, will almost certainly make the fuel cell a common feature of everyday life in the 21st century. DAVID S. SCOTT

Fulford, Robert Marshall Blount, editor, essayist, critic (b at Ottawa 13 Feb 1932). Editor of SATURDAY NIGHT magazine 1968-87, Fulford has been a champion of liberalism in somewhat the same tradition as J.W. DAFOE and Frank UNDERHILL. Self-educated, he joined the Toronto GLOBE AND MAIL as a copyboy in 1949 and held reportorial jobs until 1953. He was then an editor and writer on various magazines, notably MACLEAN'S, but it was at the TORONTO STAR, which he joined in 1958, that he became an influential critic, first of books, art and jazz, and finally of ideas. During his tenure at *Saturday Night,* from which he resigned in June 1987 after Conrad BLACK's takeover, he switched from continentalism to nationalism and in the 1980s drifted towards the more conservative end of the liberal spectrum. His attitudes towards popular culture, which he once relished as a sort of democratic kaleidoscope, have also changed, though his books on the subject, including *This was Expo* (1968), *Marshall Delaney at the Movies* (1974) and *An Introduction to the Arts in Canada* (1977), remain valuable and enjoyable for their subtle, even style, informed wit and ability to deal lucidly with elusive notions. In Nov 1987, Fulford became Barker Fairley distinguished visitor in Canadian culture at University College, U of T. He became an Officer of the Order of Canada in 1984.
DOUGLAS FETHERLING

Fuller, Thomas, architect (b at Bath, Eng 8 Mar 1823; d at Ottawa 28 Sept 1898). In 1857 Fuller left England to set up practice in Toronto with Chilion Jones. The firm, with Fuller responsible for design, specialized in Anglican church architecture in a Gothic revival style and won 2 important competitions, the first for the PARLIAMENT BUILDINGS in Ottawa in 1859, and the second for the New York State Capitol in Albany in 1867. In 1881 Fuller was appointed Dominion chief architect and during his 15-year tenure supervised the design of over 140 buildings across the country. Perhaps more than any other architect, he was responsible for defining the character of federal architecture in Canada. His small post offices, executed in a blend of Gothic and Romanesque forms and characterized by their picturesque massing, and accented by stone gables and tall clock towers, provided immediately recognizable symbols of the federal government and established a design that endured into the 1930s.
JANET WRIGHT

Fuller, William Albert, ecologist, conservationist (b at Moosomin, Sask 10 May 1924). He is best known in academic circles for his long-term studies on population fluctuations of small mammals, especially in taiga. After 12 years with the CANADIAN WILDLIFE SERVICE (1947-59), when he studied larger mammals and surveyed several northern areas, he joined U of A's zoology department (1959). During his wildlife-service career, he was the first biologist to see the last remaining natural nesting grounds of the WHOOPING CRANE. Fuller applies ecological principles to conservation problems; he has chaired a subcommittee of the International Biological Program and the National Research Council of Canada's Associate Committee on Ecological Reserves, and serves on the board of the International Union for the Conservation of Nature and Natural Resources.
MARTIN K. MCNICHOLL

Fullerton, Douglas H., economist, financial consultant (b at St John's 3 Sept 1917). As investment manager for the CANADA COUNCIL (1957-68) he placed the council on a sound financial footing, and as chairman of the NATIONAL CAPITAL COMMISSION (1969-73) he led the government's program to redevelop the central area of HULL. He has advised governments on diverse matters, including pension reform, public transit systems, the coal and steel industries in Atlantic Canada, and the nationalization of Québec hydro companies and Saskatchewan potash mines. Fullerton is noted for his populist approach to urban planning, emphasizing that people come first, and he has written a newspaper column on urban affairs. He is author of *The Bond Market in Canada* (1962), *The Capital of Canada: How Should It Be Governed?* (1974), *The Dangerous Delusion: Quebec's Independence Obsession* (1978) and *Graham Towers and his Times* (1986). From 1979 to 1985 he was honorary professor of urbanism at U of Calgary.
WILLIAM T. PERKS

Fulmar, Northern (*Fulmarus glacialis,* family Procellariidae, order Procellariiformes), medium-sized, tube-nosed seabird, about 50 cm long, related to the albatrosses. Birds from warmer parts of the Atlantic are usually white with greyish wings, while those from colder parts are brown all over; the opposite holds in the Pacific. Originally, the northern fulmar was an arctic bird, but around 1820 it began to spread southward into the eastern Atlantic, perhaps scavenging from the fisheries. It reached Atlantic Canada around 1970, and a few pairs now nest in Newfoundland. Most Canadian fulmars, about 400 000 pairs, breed in the eastern Arctic, above 67° N. Alaskan migrants visit BC waters; birds from Greenland and the eastern Atlantic winter off Newfoundland. Fulmars breed on steep cliffs, laying a single, whitish egg on bare ledges. They defend their nests by vomiting a stinking oil over any intruder. R.G.B. BROWN

Fulton, Edmund Davie, lawyer, politician, judge (b at Kamloops, BC 10 Mar 1916). Son of an MP and grandson of a former BC premier, he distinguished himself as a Rhodes scholar, MP, Cabinet minister and judge. First elected to the House in 1945, Fulton ran for the Progressive Conservative Party leadership in 1956. In June 1957, he was appointed minister of justice and was highly regarded in that position. Fulton was involved with patriation of the CONSTITUTION (the Fulton-Favreau formula reflects his views on federal-provincial relations) and the COLUMBIA R TREATY negotiations during this period. In 1963 he was elected leader of the BC Tories, but in 1965 returned to federal politics. He was a justice of the BC Supreme Court from 1973 to 1981. In 1986 he was appointed commissioner of the Canadian section of the International Joint Commission. *See also* Guy FAVREAU. PATRICIA WILLIAMS

Functionalism, a concept of world order developed in the early 20th century by such writers as Leonard Woolf and David Mitrany, who argued that if nations joined in economic and social interdependence, and if national well-being depended upon the maintenance of peace, then war would be less likely. This theory influenced the founders of the UNITED NATIONS, with its specialized functional agencies and its particular organs for security and for economic and social questions. Canadians extended the concept into the theory of functional representation, where membership and influence in the various United Nations bodies would be accorded to those countries with special interests in, and contributions to make to, the specific subject for which the body was responsible. JOHN W. HOLMES

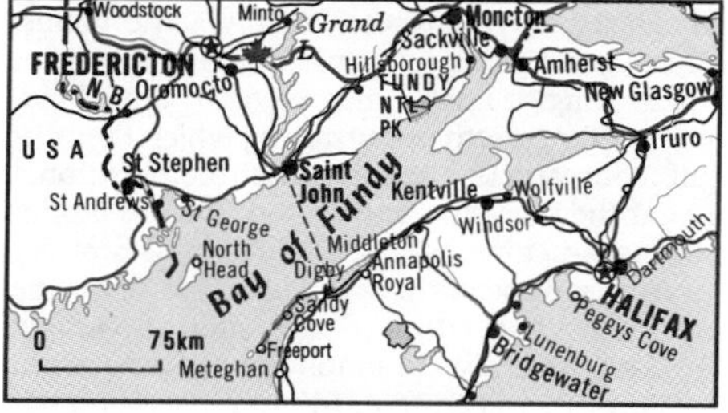

Fundy, Bay of and **Gulf of Maine,** with a total area of about 1.8 x 10^5 km^2 and depths generally less than 200 m, are a part of the Continental Shelf off eastern Canada and New England. The area of the Bay of Fundy alone is about 1.6 x 10^4 km^2. Its name is likely a corruption of the French *fendu* ("split"). It was known for a time as La Baie Françoise.

Between about 15 000 and 10 000 years ago, as the glaciers retreated from the last ice age, parts of GEORGES BANK and other shallow areas were dry land; fragments of trees and mammoth teeth from this era are still found occasionally in fishing trawls. A rising sea level since then not only submerged these offshore banks, but also led to the development of the present tidal regime. The tides of the Bay of Fundy are the world's largest, with a range from low to high tide that can exceed 16 m in MINAS BASIN at the head of the bay. At peak flood tide the flow of water across the edge of the continental shelf into the Gulf of Maine is 25 x 10^6 m^3/s, 2000 times the average discharge of the ST LAWRENCE R. The flow past Cape Split into Minas Basin is 40 times that of the St Lawrence.

The main reason for these large tides is that because of its shape, size and depth, the Bay of Fundy-Gulf of Maine system has a natural period of oscillation of about 13 hrs. As a result, its waters respond vigorously to the push they get every 12.4 hours from the N Atlantic tides – a phenomenon known technically as a near-resonant response. The Reversing Falls at SAINT JOHN, NB, and the tidal bores in rivers near the head of the bay are well-known natural phenomena associated with the tides. The large tides also have dramatic effects on oceanographic conditions throughout the region. Large areas, such as Georges Bank, much of the Bay of Fundy, and the area off SW Nova Scotia, are kept well mixed vertically by the strong tidal currents (with resulting cold surface waters and frequent fog), rather than developing the warm surface layer that occurs in less-well-mixed waters in summer. The tides also contribute to the average circulation patterns in the region.

These effects influence biological productivity, generally favourably, by returning nutrients to surface layers where they can be utilized. Thus the waters off southwestern NS form the summer feeding ground of the Nova Scotia herring, a major stock of several hundred thousand tonnes. Off BRIER and GRAND MANAN islands, where tidal currents interact with the sharp topographic relief, swarms of copepods and euphausiids (or krill) are often found at the surface. This condition attracts fin and humpback whales, along with large flocks of plankton-feeding birds, such as phalaropes, shearwaters and gulls. In the bay's upper reaches the strong tidal currents keep so much mud in suspension that light penetration, and hence biological productivity in the water, are greatly reduced. Most of the biological productivity occurs on the mud flats, which are important feeding grounds in late summer for the vast flocks of migrating shorebirds, particularly semipalmated sandpipers.

The region's fisheries, particularly for scallops and groundfish on Georges Bank, for herring and lobster off southwestern NS and for herring in the Bay of Fundy, are of great importance to many small communities, and indeed to the general economy of NS, NB and the New England states. New developments are largely centered around fisheries and energy. Considerable effort is being devoted to research and international diplomatic activity to permit sensible regulation of the fisheries. The problem has been particularly acute on Georges Bank, where the US and Canada disputed the location of the international boundary and the setting and sharing of quotas for the various fisheries, and where exploratory drilling for oil and gas, with attendant risks to the fisheries, has occurred.

Even with the Oct 1984 boundary decision by the International Court at The Hague, joint management of migratory fish stocks will still be required. A proposed superport and oil refinery at Eastport, Maine, was strongly opposed by Canada, as the area's strong tidal currents and narrow channels make navigation hazardous and would make it very hard to prevent any oil spill from contaminating large sections of coastline.

One major possible development in the upper reaches of the Bay of Fundy is of tidal power. Schemes with a power output equal to that of several nuclear-power stations are technically feasible; a small pilot plant has been built in NS's Annapolis Basin (*see* TIDAL ENERGY). Surprisingly, these large schemes may lead to a slight increase in the tidal range over much of the Bay of Fundy-Gulf of Maine outside the barrage. In the head pond behind the barrage the operation of the plant would lead to a substantial change in low-tide level and to a reduction of the tidal range, and hence of currents, by a factor of about 3. The possible effects of such a change on the extent and biological productivity of the mud flats, and hence on migrating shorebirds, are not yet fully understood. CHRIS GARRETT AND TONY KOSLOW

Fundy National Park (est 1947), renowned for its high tides averaging 10 m, stretches for 17 km along the Bay of FUNDY and extends inland to cover a 207 km^2 area of wooded hills cut by deep valleys and tumbling streams. The park's seaward edge features wave-pounded cliffs and cobble beaches. At low tide sea anemones, barnacles and a host of other marine invertebrates can be found sheltering in small tidal pools or among seaweed. In late summer, flocks of migrating shorebirds congregate on the tidal flats. Inland, the budworm-ravaged forests of spruce and fir are home for white-tailed deer, moose, red fox, black bear, bobcat and, possibly, the rare eastern cougar. Coyote are recent immigrants to the park. In presettlement days MICMAC lived here. More recently, lumbering and shipbuilding were major activities of Irish and English settlers. The park has 5 serviced facilities for outdoor recreation.

LILLIAN STEWART

Funeral Practices consist of customary observances for the dead and arrangements made for disposition of the body. There is a network of social and legal requirements to be met that usually involve the services of various professionals (*see* DEATH AND DYING).

Predeath Protocols Many arrangements can be made prior to death, from wills to donation of body parts, but Canadian laws and customs restrict how a person's wishes are implemented after death. There is a growing tendency, supported by memorial societies and the medical fraternity, to donate body parts for transplant or for research, but an individual's wish to donate may be countermanded if the family has strong views about dismembering the deceased. Religious attitudes and traditions influence these decisions. A person may dictate the nature and type of funeral, the final disposition of the remains, and even arrange the newspaper announcement ahead of time. Prearranged funerals are much more common than they were 30 years ago. Memorial Societies are volunteer, nonprofit consumer-information organizations that are found in most major cities. Their function is to encourage preplanning and to ensure that simple, low-cost funeral options are available from the funeral industry.

For highly placed individuals, or for a member of the armed forces or the police, public protocols regarding funeral arrangements may take precedence over individual or family customs and wishes. In all arrangements, both group values and professional organizations play a significant role.

Preburial Procedures An individual may be pronounced dead if the vital signs are missing or if brain waves are no longer detected. If sudden death is involved or if there is no clear reason for death, the provincial coroner or medical examiner requires an autopsy to be performed. Since health care is a provincial responsibility, the legal requirements are specified in provincial legislation. In all cases, legal requirements take precedence over religious views. Unwritten codes are also observed in announcing a death. Immediate next of kin take precedence over relatives who may be nearer to the scene of death, and it is a breach of etiquette not to notify a close relative about a death. Since nothing can be done until the physician signs the death certificate, hospital protocol requires this step. With Orthodox Jews, there may be a delay in announcing a death (especially just before the beginning of the sabbath) and arrangements for interment have to wait until after the sabbath.

Deaths caused by highly infectious diseases are treated differently from others; for instance, if death is from hepatitis, the body must be sealed in a casket immediately and no embalming can take place. If a body is to be shipped out of the country, the local Board of Health must certify that the body is not the carrier of a communicable disease.

Funeral homes are a service industry in Canada. Some provinces, such as Ontario, require a funeral director, though in most provinces these services are optional. Most funerals in remote places take place in funeral homes. Provincial licensing is required for embalmers, and though embalming the body is not a legal requirement in Canada, it is an accepted practice. Provincial legislation requires embalming or sealing only for bodies that will not reach their place of burial within 72 hours of the death. Educational requirements for embalmers differ throughout Canada, the minimum being a 2-week vocational course, a correspondence course and on-the-job apprenticeship.

Some religious groups, such as Hindus and Sikhs, may require preparation of the body to be done by the eldest son or by a designated individual, but for the majority of Canadians the funeral director prepares the body: washes it, ejects blood from the veins and substitutes embalming fluid (thus removing the discoloration of the skin), cleans and disinfects the chest and abdominal cavity, applies makeup, fixes the hair and dresses the body in clothes provided by the next of kin. Restorative work, if the face has been damaged, may also be done. Muslims are an exception to this practice, since they traditionally bury the dead in a shroud.

Funeral directors have several options regarding cost and services. Some provide a casket and all essential services for a fixed price. This unit pricing system is popular with prearranged funerals and requires less time and decision making for the bereaved. Another option is the functional pricing system, in which the price of the chosen casket and the desired services are added to the basic price. Despite widespread criticism of the industry's costs, little has changed. Elaborate caskets may be purchased and expensive services chosen, sometimes from guilt on the part of survivors, sometimes for the public image of the family. Funeral costs can vary from region to region or from urban to rural areas.

The wake, a vigil held over the body prior to burial, commonly took place at the home of the family of the deceased. Although this custom still occurs, especially in families that have recently come from Europe, wakes are now usually replaced by viewing times at the funeral home, when members of the family will be present to respond to the condolences of visitors. For many years it was customary for close friends and relatives to buy flowers, the size of the floral spray varying according to closeness with the deceased. In recent years a marked trend to request gifts to charities in lieu of flowers has taken place.

Funeral services differ according to religious and cultural practices. For Roman Catholics, Anglicans and Eastern Christians of Orthodox persuasion, as well as for those who were closely connected to a church during their lives, the norm is to have the service at the church with the body present. For some of these faiths, the church is the only sanctified locale in which a mass may be held, but in many communities the church is regarded as the proper place for funerals, no matter what the denomination. In urban settings, the funeral chapel plays a much larger role. Fewer than 5% of the population have no funeral service at all.

A common scene in Canada is the funeral procession, headed by cars containing the chief mourners and followed by the hearse and friends of the family. The lights on the motorcade were traditionally the signal for bystanders to pause in respect to the departed, a custom that has been eroded in contemporary Canada.

Interment Cremation (to reduce to ashes by burning) is becoming more common; the funeral industry's income from cremations grew almost 50% between 1980 and 1984. More recent statistics are not available. Even among Roman Catholics the trend toward cremation is growing, and in 1983 the Pope lifted any prohibition against it. Funeral directors suggest that the mode of disposal is defined culturally, not religiously. Lack of space available for burial use has also encouraged the trend to cremation.

CEMETERIES may be either private or public, though there are legislated restrictions on private cemeteries. A gravesite is regarded by the law as a piece of real estate and a deed is issued for the lot. The "deed" is frequently a form of rental and not a complete transfer of title. Most cemeteries have regulations regarding TOMBSTONES, markers and even flowers. Ethnic and sectarian cemeteries are common in Canada and have restrictions based on memberships. Cemeteries may impose time limits on the use of plots or may reuse a plot for a relative after a specified period of time. The trend away from ostentatious monuments continues, sometimes at cemetery insistence, but also because of high prices for marble. Some memorial parks with special theme areas or ethnic gardens have been established across the country, and costs for their plots include a percentage for perpetual care.

The graveside service with the committal to earth, usually with a symbolic toss of earth on the lowered casket, is the last act of the mourners. Closing the grave is left to the cemetery workers. Disposal of ashes from cremation is left to the family of the deceased, and since there are no laws requiring specific places of deposit, the ashes may be spread anywhere. Some people arrange for them to be placed in an urn, and some cemeteries sell niches in a vault for this purpose.

Postburial Rites No set period is allocated for the bereavement; traditional Jewish law specifies one week of mourning, after which reintegration with the community is enjoined. Widows in some traditions, such as Coptic Christian, are required to wear black clothing for a year, at the end of which a memorial service is held. Some Catholics adhere to the practice of holding a mass on the first anniversary of the death and some have masses said for the deceased, but Protestants have eschewed this remembrance of the dead. Mormons often initiate special rituals designed to elevate to a state of grace the souls of those who have died without being initiated into the faith. Various Orthodox believers have an annual day for remembering the dead, when the names of all the dead from the community are read, and prayers said, after which the family will have a picnic at the gravesite. For most Canadians, the funeral service is the last public occasion for relating to the dead. For those who leave a will, an executor will call the beneficiaries together for its reading, and the memory of the deceased lives on in the disposal of the inheritance. Private grave visitation may serve to bolster the memory but, except for those who follow ancestral traditions, there is little overt link with the dead. EARLE WAUGH

Fung, Donna Lori, gymnast (b at Vancouver 21 Feb 1963). She was western Canadian all-round champion of rhythmic gymnastics in 1981 and finished sixteenth in rope in the world championships that year. Fung was Canadian national all-round champion 1982, 1983, 1984 and 1986 and first all-round in the pre-world championships at Lausanne, Switz, and ninth in the ribbon at the world championships at Strasbourg, France, 1983. She won the first Olympic gold medal in all-round rhythmic gymnastics, at Los Angeles in 1984. In both 1984 and 1986, Fung finished first all-round in the Four Continents championships but finished ninth all-round – after a first place all-round in the world trials – in the 1985 world championships. JAMES MARSH

Fungus, common name for any member of the kingdom Mycota. Fungi share some features with the lower plants and share others with the simpler animals, but are independent of either group. Like plants and animals, they evolved from the protistans. Vegetatively, fungi usually consist of slender filaments (hyphae) massed together in a mycelium which carries on the functions of metabolism and reproduction, but their fruit bodies are often complex. Since all fungi lack chlorophyll and cannot feed themselves through photosynthesis, they are heterotrophs and must use complex organic compounds of nitrogen and carbon for metabolism. Therefore, they commonly exist as parasites, drawing nutrients directly from a host plant or animal which they may injure; or as saprophytes, living on dead or decaying matter. Fungi were long treated as plants and, because of their intimate associations with plants, they continue to be studied chiefly in BOTANY and plant pathology institutions. Mycology, the study of fungi, began in Canada as a result of concern about plant diseases and timber decay. Its history is traced in works on plant pathology.

Classification Advances in BIOCHEMISTRY and electron microscopy have required changes in fungal classification. Acceptance of the kingdom Mycota (as distinct from the kingdom Plantae) entailed changes in rank. Changes are continuing, and the provisional system presented here omits several minor groups. Two divisions are recognized: Myxomycota, mainly slime molds, often considered protistans; and Eumycota or typical fungi. Slime molds have an amoeboid, noncellular growth phase during which they engulf food particles. At the end of the nutritional period they develop varied and often beautiful fruiting structures which produce masses of dry spores that disperse the organisms. They lack true mycelium, but curious and often decorated threads frequently are found among the spores. They are generally studied by mycologists. Eumycota include 5 subdivisions.

Occurrence Fungi grow in almost all environments from tropic to high arctic: in soil, fresh water (including hot springs) and seawater, or in association with many animals and all plant groups. Species attacking man, eg, on the skin (dermatophytes) or in the lungs, are relatively few but are difficult to eradicate.

Associations involving fungi are many and often very important. LICHENS have arisen repeatedly through association of various fungal genera with numerous algae. The importance of a fungal group in Canada does not always correlate with numbers of species, eg, some important pathogens (agents of disease) belong to small groups. Major groups in Canada include wood-rotting Aphyllophorales, more than 800 species; MUSHROOMS (Agaricales), more than 3000 species; ascomycetes and deuteromycetes, *c*5000 species (estimates are doubtful because many have unknown life cycles); rusts (Uredinales), 450 species and well-marked varieties; smuts (Ustilaginales), 140 species; downy mildews (Peronosporales), 100 species. Among important fungal PLANT DISEASES are wheat stem rust (*Puccinia graminis*), which reduced the Canadian crop in 1916 and 1954 by about 2.7 and 4 million tonnes; other cereal rusts (*Puccinia*), which take a continuing toll; white pine blister rust (*Cronartium ribicola*), which nearly eliminated the eastern white pine; cereal smuts (*Tilletia* and *Ustilago*); potato late blight (*Phytophthora infestans*); sunflower downy mildew (*Plasmopara halstedii*); onion downy mildew (*Peronospora destructor*); chestnut

A slime mold (*Myxomycota*), one of the 2 main classes of fungi (*photo by Mary W. Ferguson*).

blight (*Endothia parasitica*), which virtually destroyed the American sweet chestnut; and apple scab (*Venturia inaequalis*), which often causes heavy loss. Another important aspect of fungal activity is the production of serious toxins in moldy grain.

However, many fungal associations do no appreciable harm to the plant and some are highly beneficial. About 95% of SEED PLANTS have MYCORRHIZAE, associations with one or more fungi that assist plant nutrition in most situations. Work in progress at Zürich, Switzerland, shows that healthy tissues of many plants yield numerous fungi, occasionally over 100 from a single plant species. These fungi do no visible harm to the plant and the associations may be mutually beneficial. In nature, symbioses with fungi seem to vary from mildly injurious to strongly beneficial to the plant. Even parasites such as rusts probably supply some nutritional aid to the plant, partly offsetting their damage. Only when large areas are planted to one, often genetically uniform, crop do devastating losses occur. In natural grasslands, several to many GRASS species usually occur in mixed stands. This variety buffers the association against violent change, and rusts, although present, do little harm. In natural FORESTS, decay occurs chiefly in overmature or wind-thrown trees, and fungi speed the recycling of wood and bark into usable nutrients; but when the forest is treated as a crop, decay can be very costly. Trees must be cut while relatively young to reduce loss from decay; slash may stimulate growth of decay fungi; and human activity may damage trees and provide sites for infection. With fungi that are adapted to all trees and various climates, the problem is complex. The breakdown of litter in forests, grasslands and other biomes is as important as tree decay, although less spectacular. In each habitat there is an elaborate sequence of fungi, bacteria and minute animals, which completely reduce tissues to plant nutrients. Fungi are especially important in severe climates (eg, arctic deserts) that have minimal bacterial activity.

Dispersal Most species have airborne spores; some are spread in water or by water splash, and a few are carried chiefly by insects. Spores of some host-limited ascomycetes stick to seeds, fruits or bulbils of the plant and are carried with them. Thus, they may occur at the extreme limit of the host's range. Some pathogens are carried within seeds. Airborne spores may be released passively or discharged forcibly.

Fungi in Human Affairs The fungi best known to city dwellers are conveniently, if inexactly, termed MOLDS. They include the variously coloured growths that occur in damp environments on fruit, bread, cheese, leather and other organic substances, and involve members of several groups of fungi. Some optical glass is etched (and the part ruined) by fungal secretions. Mites carrying spores could enter poorly sealed instruments, die on a lens, and supply nutrient for a mold colony. Damage from fouling in Canadian-built field glasses and riflescopes was greatly reduced by improved packing and storage methods and by redesigning for perfect sealing. Although fouling is mainly a problem of humid tropics, severe damage did occur in a damp depot in Ontario, and some fouling was recorded in a survey instrument on Baffin I.

Edible mushrooms are a popular food (*see* MUSHROOM CULTIVATION) and other fungi also have uses in the various food industries. Industrial mycology was long concerned mainly with the use of YEASTS and a few molds in baking, brewing and wine making, and in flavouring cheeses. Development of antibiotics stimulated the use of more molds and, recently, some bird's nest fungi have yielded a promising antibiotic. Much attention is now being paid to the use of fungi (including some mushrooms and bird's nest fungi) for breaking down wood, straw and other plant debris into alcohol or edible carbohydrates. D.B.O. SAVILE

Fungi grow in almost every environment, from the High Arctic to the tropics (*photo by Tim Fitzharris*).

Reading: Elizabeth Moore-Landecker, *Fundamentals of the Fungi* (1982).

Funk Island, 25 ha, is a flat, 15 m high, wedge-shaped granite island, 800 m by 400 m, lying 60 km off Newfoundland's NE coast, E of FOGO ISLAND. The origin of the name is unknown, though it may have been inspired by the smell of the guano that covers much of the island. The W end is crowned by a 15 m cairn built by past visitors to this nearly barren spot. Jacques CARTIER visited the island, as countless other mariners did, for the abundant eggs and birds found there. Once a favourite hunting ground of coastal residents, both native and European, it was the last known breeding place of the GREAT AUK, *Pinguinis impennis* (extinct from about 1840). Here "factories" were set up and the birds were boiled, their valuable feathers removed, and the bodies discarded. Consequently the island was the source of most of the great auk skeletons preserved in museums around the world. Today, still populated by thousands of murres, terns and puffins, the island is a seabird sanctuary protected by law. ROBERT D. PITT

Fur Farming In Canada, the primary mammal species raised for fur are the MINK (*Mustela vison*) and the FOX (genus *Vulpes*). A limited amount of chinchilla (*Chinchilla laniger*) is also raised. Before 1890, all fur in Canada was taken by trapping; now, however, 40% of Canadian furs come from farming operations.

Mink, a carnivore, has been raised for its fur since the beginning of the century. Mink farming began as an offshoot of fox farming. Canada produces only 6% of the world's pelts, but the "Majestic" mink is widely acclaimed. Today, about 600 Canadians are engaged in mink farming, primarily in Ont, BC, NS and Qué. They belong to the Canada Mink Breeders Assn. In 1985 Canada sold about one million pelts, at an average price of $35.07 and a net profit of just over $5 per pelt.

Selective breeding has produced over 200 shades of fur (in the whites, blacks, browns and blues) among the mink types: Standard, Jet Black, White, Pastel, Pearl, Lavender, Buff, Demi Buff, Aleutian, Silverblu, Sapphire, Violet, etc. Mink are aggressive animals and must be handled with care. A typical mink farm has separate sheds for kits and for breeding adults; each shed holds several rows of individual cages. Establishing a mink fur farm requires an investment of about $275 per breeding female. One worker can care for 500-600 breeding females but vaccination and pelt preparation require extra workers.

The mink is killed by injection, gas or electrocution, and then skinned. The pelt is fleshed and degreased and dried on boards, usually fur side out. Pelts are then sent to a fur centre for classification ("Majestic," "Canada," "Unlabelled") and sale by auction; most pelts are classified and sold by the HUDSON'S BAY CO.

Fox, a carnivorous member of the family Canidae, has been farmed since about 1890. In the past, fox breeding underwent great fluctuations but, in the last decade, market demand and prices have improved. In 1985-86 Canada produced 135 997 fox pelts. In that year, the price of the Canadian fox averaged $127 a pelt; production costs, about $100. In 1985 there were 938 fox farmers in Canada, mostly in Ontario, NS, NB, and PEI. A typical farm has breeding and fur sheds and a service building, but some farmers keep their breeding foxes in outdoor cages. Establishing a fox farm requires about $800-1100 per breeding female. A single worker can look after about 100 breeding females. Fox pelts are prepared in the same way as mink pelts; the skin is always dried fur side out. Classification and sale at auction take place at the same fur centres that handle mink. RENÉ BELZILE

Fur Industry The Canadian fur industry consists of companies that buy raw furs from trappers, dealers or fur-marketing companies (eg, HUDSON'S BAY CO raw-fur auctions), send them to fur dressers and dyers in Toronto, match the skins and cut and sew them into garments. Most manufacturers make coats and most specialize in 2 or 3 types of fur only. Before the coat can be finished, it must go through a fur-cleaning process and some companies do only this. Some cleaners also maintain cold fur-storage vaults to house furs during the summer, but many retail furriers also have their own vaults. Fur factories are generally small, with 279 of the 280 factories employing fewer than 50 people; only one of the 280 operating factories employed more than 100 people in 1986. In that year there were 3700 furriers in the manufacturing work force, with about 2950 in Québec, 675 in Ontario and 75 in Manitoba. Almost all fur companies are Canadian owned; there is some foreign ownership, mainly American, in the retail sector and some Japanese investment in the manufacturing sector.

Fur garments have been made using hand techniques for more than 100 years, although new technologies have been introduced in the last decade. Innovations include cutting machines, an attachment to guide fur through the wheels of the fur-sewing machine, and a German invention for finishing a coat, ie, installing the lining, as well as German and Japanese machines that cut and sew a mink skin into a "let-out" stripe. Almost no research and development is done anywhere except in Germany and Japan, but innovation exists in Canada in dressing, dyeing and cutting.

Canada is known internationally as the producer of the world's finest furs. Jacques CARTIER was met in 1534 on the shores of the St Lawrence R by Indian chiefs wearing the robes of their rank, hand sewn from beaver and bear pelts. Western Europeans wintering in Canada found it essential to tan and sew pelts they had obtained by trapping or barter, although the resulting garments could hardly be called fur coats, since there was no styling. A modest custom-fur business sprang up to meet the demands of voyageurs and traders who wanted better garments. Exported pelts were used mainly for men's hats, but gradually fur fashions began to appeal to women in Europe and Canada.

This demand created a market for custom furriers, who designed, made and maintained fur garments. The Hudson's Bay Co, formed in 1670 to collect pelts from Rupert's Land, slowly developed a garment business as well. From 1880 to 1920, many of the immigrants from Ukraine, Poland and Austria, as well as young men from England and Scotland, had had experience with the needle in Europe and went into Canadian fur stores and workrooms. The early custom furriers were Anglo-Saxon, but by 1930 Jewish immigrants had developed a wholesale manufacturing industry to serve the custom trade and the developing retail trade. In 1933, as the GREAT DEPRESSION created financial chaos, manufacturers formed the Fur Trade Credit Assn of Canada, later the Fur Trade Assn of Canada. Retailers formed the Retail Furriers Guild of Canada. Each May the Fur Trade Assn and Trade Fair Entrepreneurs sponsor great fur fairs and international shows in Toronto and Montréal, where retailers order coats for August fur sales. The 1950s and 1960s brought many trained furriers from Greece, almost all being from the small town of Kastoria which had been totally employed in manufacturing fur items for 2000 years. The Greek furriers

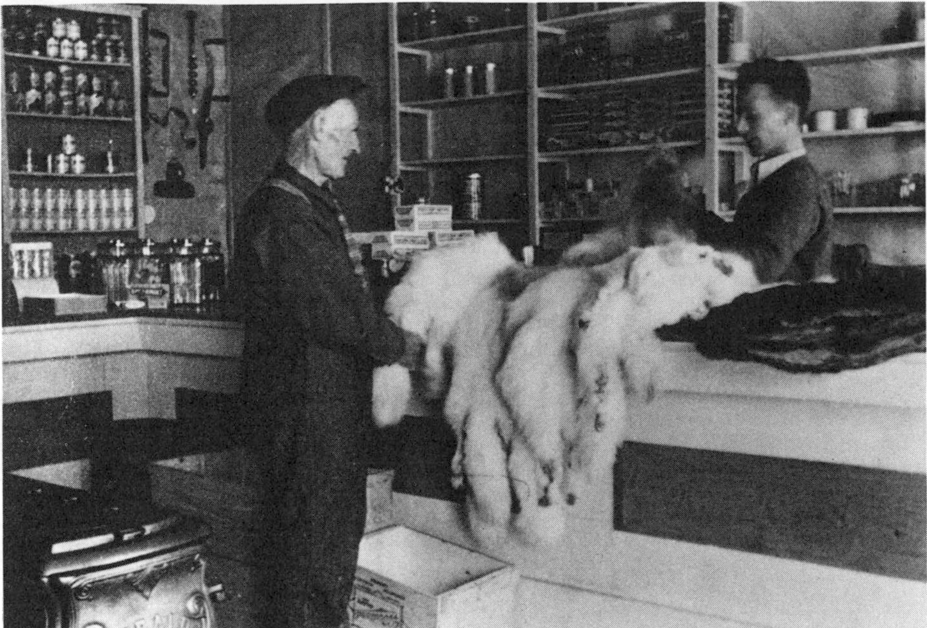

Archie White trading furs for stores from Andy Reid, manager of the HBC post at Cameron Bay, NWT, Aug 1937 (*courtesy National Archives of Canada/C-33945*).

congregated in Montréal, Toronto and New York, and they are becoming a major factor in Canadian fur manufacturing. They have developed their own trade association in Toronto.

Fur-production workers can be trained on the job or at Toronto's George Brown College to become cutters (who cut the pelts to fit the pattern, using a pointed razor-bladed knife), operators (who sew the pieces together), blockers (who tack or staple the sewn sheets of fur to the tracing of the pattern) and finishers (who close the coat and install the lining, buttons, etc). The fur industry consumes relatively little energy because so much of the work is done by hand. Synthetic fur uses much more energy and its manufacture creates chemical pollution.

The Canadian fur industry is a significant exporter of pelts and garments. The largest customers are the US, western Europe and recently Japan, which is a rapidly growing market. According to Statistics Canada, the fur industry has grown from $51 million in wholesale shipments in 1970 to $170 million in 1978 (of which $81 million was exported) and to $421 million in 1986 (of which $207 million was exported). In 1919 there were 107 plants; the peak of 642 plants was reached in 1949, and by 1986 the number had dropped to 280. Between 1949 and 1986 the number of employees decreased from 6700 to 3700. The fur industry receives no tariff protection, but duties into the US are dropping. Raw-fur prices continue to be very high, reaching new records throughout the world.

SIDNEY S. SCHIPPER

Fur Trade in Canada began as an adjunct to the fishing industry. Early in the 16th century fishermen from NW Europe were taking rich catches of COD on the Grand Banks off Newfoundland and in the Gulf of St Lawrence (*see* FISHERIES HISTORY). Drying their fish onshore took several weeks, during which time good relations had to be maintained with the Indians who were eager to obtain metal and cloth goods from the Europeans: iron knives and axes, awls, copper kettles, blankets and trinkets. All they had to offer in exchange were furs and fresh meat. The fishermen found an eager market in Europe for the furs and made high profits. When the wide-brimmed felt hat came into fashion later in the 16th century, the demand for BEAVER PELTS increased tremendously. The best material for hat felt was the soft underfur of the beaver, the strands of which had tiny barbs that made them mat together tightly.

Early in the 17th century French traders established permanent shore bases in ACADIA, a post at TADOUSSAC (Qué) and in 1608 a base at QUÉBEC to exploit the trade more effectively. The following year the Dutch began trading up the Hudson R (NY) and in 1614 established permanent trading posts at Manhattan and upriver at Orange [Albany]. This activity marked the beginning of intense rivalry between 2 incipient commercial empires. During these years the number of traders flooding into the St Lawrence region and cutthroat competition among them greatly reduced profits. In an attempt to impose order the French Crown granted monopolies of the trade to certain individuals. In return, the monopoly holders had to maintain French claims to the new lands and assist in the attempts of the Roman Catholic Church to convert the Indians to CHRISTIANITY.

In 1627 Cardinal Richelieu, first minister of Louis XIII, organized the COMPAGNIE DES CENT-ASSOCIÉS to put French territorial claims and the missionary drive on a firmer footing. Missionaries were sent out: in 1615, 4 Récollets, and in 1625 the first members of the powerful Society of Jesus (Jesuits) arrived at Québec. A mission base, STE MARIE AMONG THE HURONS, was established among the HURON near Georgian Bay, but the Huron were more interested in the trade goods of the French than in their religion. Yet it was fur-trade profits that sustained the missionaries and allowed the company to send hundreds of settlers to the colony. In 1642 VILLE-MARIE [Montréal] was founded as a mission centre. In 1645 the company ceded control of the fur trade and the colony's administration to the colonists (*see* COMMUNAUTÉ DES HABITANTS). Unfortunately, they proved to be inept administrators, and fur-trade returns fluctuated wildly as a result of an IROQUOIS blockade of the Ottawa R route to the West. Finally, after a desperate appeal by the colonial authorities to Louis XIV, in 1663 the Crown took over the colony.

The main staple of the trade was still BEAVER for the hat industry. The Ministry of Marine (*see* MINISTÈRE DE LA MARINE), responsible for colonial affairs, leased the West Indies trade, the African slave trade and the marketing of Canadian beaver and moose hides to the newly formed COMPAGNIE DES INDES OCCIDENTALES, in reality a crown corporation. All permanent residents of the colony were permitted to trade for furs with the Indians but they had to sell the beaver and moose hides to the company at prices fixed by the Ministry of Marine. All other furs were traded on a free market; thus the trade was not a monopoly, but the law of supply and demand had been suspended for beaver and moose hides.

Jean-Baptiste Colbert, the French minister of marine, hoped to see the Canadian economy diversified to produce raw materials for French industry, particularly timber, and minerals and foodstuffs for the West Indies plantations. Thousands of emigrants were shipped to Canada at the Crown's expense to bring the land into production. Colbert discovered that a sizable proportion of the young men did not remain on the land but disappeared for years to trade with the Indians in their distant villages (*see* COUREURS DE BOIS). The main reasons for this phenomenon were the assured profits in the trade and the imbalance of the sexes, which was so great that until about 1710 only about one man in 7 could hope to find a wife – a necessity on a farm. In the interior, however, the traders quickly formed alliances with Indian women, whose economic skills facilitated adaptation by the French to wilderness life. By 1681 Colbert was forced to acknowledge the pull of the fur trade, and he inaugurated the *congé* system. Each year up to 25 congés (licences to trade) were to be issued by the governor and the intendant. Each congé allowed 3 men with one canoe to trade in the West. It was fondly hoped that the Canadians would wait their turn for a congé, thus leaving the colony only 75 men short each year.

The new system did little to reduce the number of men away from the settlements (most of them illegally), and the amount of beaver pouring into Montréal continued to increase astronomically. By the 1690s the Domaine de l'Occident (Company of the Farm), which had been obliged to take over the beaver trade in 1674 from the defunct Compagnie des Indes Occidentales, was complaining of a huge glut. In 1696, in desperation, the minister of marine gave orders to suspend the beaver trade, to stop the issuing of congés and to abandon all the French posts in the West, except Saint-Louis-des-Illinois. This occurred while England and France were at war and the Canadians were engaged in a desperate struggle with the English colonies and their Iroquois allies. The governor and intendant at Québec protested vigorously, declaring that to abandon the posts meant abandoning the Indian allies, who would then go over to the English. New France would be doomed. In addition, the English had been established since 1670 at posts on Hudson Bay (*see* HUDSON'S BAY COMPANY), and the western posts were essential to fend off that competition. The Canadian COMPAGNIE DU NORD had been founded in 1682 to challenge the HBC on its own ground, but it was a failure. The minister of marine was obliged to rescind his drastic orders and the beaver trade was resumed, for purely political reasons.

In 1700, on the eve of new hostilities, Louis XIV ordered the establishment of the new colony of Louisiana on the lower Mississippi R, settlements in the Illinois country and a garrisoned post at Detroit. The aim was to hem in the English colonies between the Allegheny Mts and the Atlantic. This imperialist policy depended on the support of the Indian nations; and the fur trade was used to maintain their alliance.

In 1715 it was discovered that rodents and insects had consumed the glut of beaver fur in French warehouses. The market immediately revived. As an item on the balance sheet of French external trade, furs were minuscule, and their share was shrinking proportionately as trade in tropical produce and manufactured goods increased; but it was the backbone of the Canadian economy.

Oxford House, a Hudson Bay Co trading post on Oxford (Holy) Lake, *c*1837. When the Indians came to trade they camped close to the post in an area called the "plantation" (*courtesy National Archives of Canada/C-41646*).

Unlike the HBC with its monolithic structure, staffed by paid servants, in New France down to the early years of the 18th century the trade was carried on by scores of small partnerships. As the 18th century wore on and costs rose with distance, the trade came to be controlled by a small number of BOURGEOIS, who hired hundreds of wage-earning VOYAGEURS. Most companies consisted of 3 or 4 men who obtained from the authorities the lease on the trade at a specific post for 3 years; all members shared profits or losses proportional to the capital subscribed. Trade goods were usually obtained on credit, at 30% interest, from a small number of Montréal merchants who also marketed the furs through their agents in France. The voyageurs' wages varied from 200 to 500 *livres* if they wintered in the West. For those who paddled the canoes westward in the spring and returned with the autumn convoy, the usual wage was 100-200 *livres* plus their keep (about double what a labourer or artisan would earn in the colony).

Between 1715 and the SEVEN YEARS' WAR (1756-63) the fur trade expanded greatly and served a variety of purposes – economic, political and scientific. Educated Frenchmen were keenly interested in scientific inquiry, and government members, eager to discover the extent of N America, wished a Frenchman to be the first to find an overland route to the western sea (*see* NORTHWEST PASSAGE). Commissions were granted to senior Canadian officers, such as Gaultier de LA VÉRENDRYE, to discover that route. They were given command of vast western regions (some of which overlapped territory claimed by the British), with sole right to the fur trade. Out of their profits they had to pay the expenses of maintaining their posts and sending exploration parties west along the Missouri and Saskatchewan rivers. The Crown thereby made the fur trade pay the costs of its pursuit of science, and also maintained control over its subjects in the wilderness and its alliances with the Indian nations to exclude the English. By 1756, when war with England put a stop to EXPLORATION, the French had reached the foothills of the Rocky Mts. Warfare between the BLACKFOOT and CREE prevented further advances.

Throughout this period there was keen competition between the Canadian traders and the HBC, with the Canadians taking the lion's share of the trade. They had many advantages: they controlled the main waterways throughout the West; they had a sure supply of the birch bark needed for canoes (something that the Anglo-Americans and the HBC men both lacked); many of their trade goods were preferred by the Indians; and they had good relations with the Indians, with whom they had developed extensive kinship ties. Attempts by the English of the Thirteen Colonies to obtain more land for settlement by any means angered the Indians. The French did not covet Indian lands, but were determined to deny them to the English.

HBC traders made no real attempt to push their trade inland. Instead, they waited in their posts for the Indians to come to them. The Indians were astute enough to play the English and French off against each other by trading with both. The French dared not try to prevent Indians from taking some furs to the bay but made sure to obtain the choice furs, leaving only the bulky, poor-quality ones to their rivals. In the St Lawrence region, New York and Pennsylvania traders made little attempt to compete with the Canadians. Instead, they purchased furs clandestinely from the Montréal merchants. In this way the Canadians obtained a good supply of strouds (coarse English woollen cloth), a favourite English trade item. The illicit trade between Montréal and Albany also removed any incentive the New York traders might have had to compete with the Canadians in the West.

When the Seven Years' War began, the fur trade continued out of Montréal. The Indian nations had to be kept supplied, but the volume of exported furs steadily declined. Within a year of the French capitulation at Montréal in Sept 1760, the trade began to revive, largely supported by British capital and Canadian labour.

W.J. ECCLES

Fur Trade After 1760

At the time of the CONQUEST, 1759-60, 2 systems dominated the commercial fur trade of the northern half of the continent: the St Lawrence-Great Lakes system, based at Montréal and extending to the upper reaches of the Mississippi R and its major northern tributaries, as well as to the prairies and the southern portion of the Canadian Shield; and the Rupert's Land system, which theoretically covered the whole region draining into Hudson and James bays. The St Lawrence-Great Lakes system, developed by the French, had come to be served by the *en dérouine* (itinerant peddling) pattern of trade, ie, a pattern in which the trade, dominated by many small partnerships, was conducted by parties of a few men sent out to do business with the Indians in their own territory. The Rupert's Land trading system, by contrast, had not evolved in the same manner; in 1760 the HBC's employees still followed the practice of remaining in their coastal "factories" (major trading posts), awaiting the arrival of Indians to trade.

After the Conquest, Anglo-Americans (Yankees, or *Bastonnais)*, English and Highland Scots merchants supplanted the Canadian bourgeois and the agents of French merchants at Montréal. The new "pedlars" forged a new commercial link with London. The upsurge in activity in Montréal disturbed the HBC's "sleep by the frozen sea": the success of its new rivals forced the company to alter its coast-factory trading policy, and in 1774 the HBC penetrated inland from the bay to found CUMBERLAND HOUSE, close to the Saskatchewan R. For their part, the pedlars learned that co-operation among themselves, rather than competition, was the road to commercial success. The resulting NORTH WEST COMPANY rose rapidly to a position of dominance in the trade by gaining a *de facto* monopoly of the trade in the fur-rich area around Lk ATHABASCA. Staple fur (beaver) and fancy furs (mink, marten, fisher, etc), unsurpassed in quality and number, assured handsome profits in spite of the high costs of the necessarily labour-intensive transportation system, the canoe brigade. The annual dash of brigades from Fort Chipewyan to GRAND PORTAGE (later to FORT WILLIAM) on Lk Superior created much of the romantic image of the fur trade. To maintain its Athabasca monopoly the NWC competed, at a loss if necessary, with its opponents on the Saskatchewan R, around Lk Winnipeg and N of the Great Lakes. On the N Saskatchewan R, the rival companies leapfrogged westward past each other's posts in an attempt to gain a commercial advantage with the Indians. In all regions, small trading parties travelled *en dérouine* to waylay Indians travelling to rivals' posts and, when necessary, to force them to trade. In this competition the HBC appeared disadvantaged in spite of its having a major entrepôt, YORK FACTORY on Hudson Bay, much closer to the fur-gathering areas than was the NWC's transshipment point of Montréal. The HBC lacked personnel and equipment equal to the tasks of inland travel and trade. Not until the 1790s did the HBC evolve the YORK BOAT brigade as an answer to its rival's *canot de maître* and *canot du nord.* Even then, improved equipment and personnel were not sufficient to turn the commercial tide in the company's favour.

Montréal agents such as Simon "The Marquis" MCTAVISH and his nephew and successor William MCGILLIVRAY shrewdly directed the NWC's affairs, but much of the company's success was due to the élan of its officers and employees (*engagés*). WINTERING PARTNERS participated in decision making and enjoyed the profits of the trade. Unlike the HBC, the NWC permitted all ranks to take Indian wives *à la façon du pays,* a policy that resulted in a certain stability and a sizable MÉTIS population by the early 19th century. In 1789 Alexander MACKENZIE carried the company's flag to the Arctic Ocean, and in 1793 he reached the Pacific Ocean overland. Later explorers such as Simon FRASER and David THOMPSON opened up the fur lands west of the Rocky Mts. The signing of JAY'S TREATY in 1794 ended the southwest trade, and a new rival, the XY COMPANY, appeared in 1798. But the NWC met its challenge and in 1804 absorbed this upstart.

It was the revitalization of the HBC, beginning in 1810, that ultimately defeated the NWC. That year, the earl of SELKIRK's decision to establish a settlement in HBC territory led him to purchase sufficient stock to place 4 friends (2 of them kinsmen) on the HBC's 7-man governing committee. These men, new to the company, emphasized efficiency in the trading process as the means to reduce costs and turn from loss to profit. Success in this endeavour led the company to attempt to invade the Athabasca country in 1815. Poor planning by the expedition's leader and the NWC's influence with the Indians in the region caused as many as 15 men to die of starvation. But the HBC, undaunted, returned a few months later and successfully challenged the NWC monopoly.

The governing committee gave Selkirk's RED RIVER COLONY assistance and co-operation, although officers in the region were unenthusiastic. The NWC saw the settlers as supporters of their newly revitalized commercial rival, and convinced the local Métis, who had settled the region earlier, that their lands were threatened. Commercial conflict erupted in violence when the colony's governor and some 20 other settlers and HBC servants died in the SEVEN OAKS INCIDENT on 19 June 1816; the Métis lost only one man. Such occurrences led the British government to demand that the competing fur companies resolve their differences. To this end the government passed legislation enabling it to offer an exclusive licence to trade for 21 years in those areas of British North America beyond settlement and outside Rupert's Land. In 1821 the 2 companies

Crew pulling their boats against the current ("tracking") on the Athabasca R (*courtesy Provincial Archives of Alberta/E. Brown Coll/B2872*).

created the "Deed Poll," a document which outlined the terms of a coalition between them, detailed the sharing of the profits of the trade between the shareholders and individual officers in the field, and explained their relationship in the management of the trade. It was in this manner as well as in the sharing of profits that elements of the NWC survived in the new HBC, although what was a coalition in name became absorption by the HBC in fact when, in 1824, the board of management was eliminated. A majority of officers in the HBC after 1821 were former Nor'Westers.

Commercial agreements between 2 separate companies and the support given by government legislation and proclamation could not hide the NWC's defeat. The victorious HBC once again sought to increase its efficiency. Under the direction of Gov George SIMPSON, the "Little Emperor," the HBC achieved undreamed-of profits. But such profits required a constant monitoring of costs and a constant search for savings, as well as a policy of sharp competition with rivals in border areas. Through the company's policies and the actions of its personnel, the inhabitants of the old North-West had their initial exposure to the influence of changes wrought in Britain by the Industrial Revolution.

In monitoring the costs of the trade, Simpson clearly saw the importance of providing support to Indians hunting and trapping. In times of adversity the company offered medical services and sufficient supplies and provisions for the trapper and his family to survive. Yet in systematizing these services Simpson's policies led the Indians into an increasingly dependent relationship with the HBC. The Plains Indians, while the BUFFALO HUNT was still possible, could be independent of the company's services, but for others the new reality was increasingly economic dependence. Simpson's reforms, however, allowed HBC expansion along the Pacific coast, northward to the Arctic and into the interior of previously largely ignored Labrador. Such a vast fur domain attracted rivals.

Simpson's fundamental strategy was to meet competition in the frontier areas to preserve the trade of the interior. On the Pacific coast he reached an agreement with the Russian Fur Company permitting the HBC to pursue the maritime trade and successfully challenge the pre-eminence of the Americans. South and east of the Columbia R he encouraged expeditions to trap the region clean in a "scorched-earth" policy that left no animals to attract American "mountain men" or trappers. In the Great Lakes area he licensed small traders to carry competition to the territory of the American Fur Company, eventually causing it to abandon the field for an annual payment of £300. Farther east, the opponents were more difficult to dislodge. The KING'S POSTS, a series of posts N of the St Lawrence originally belonging to the French king, had been granted in 1822 to a Mr Goudie of Québec City, and along the Ottawa R lumbering provided bases for competition to arise. Yet the company vigorously pursued its competitors in all the frontier areas, sustaining its monopoly of the trade in Rupert's Land and in the licensed territories to the N and W. Even when, in the 1830s, silk replaced felt as the favoured raw material in the manufacture of hats and beaver lost its value as a staple fur, the company maintained a profitable trade emphasizing fancy fur. Settlement, not commercial rivals, finally successfully challenged the company.

West of the Rocky Mts, American settlers succeeded where their predecessors, the mountain men and the ships' captains, had failed. As a result of the OREGON TREATY of 1846 the HBC retreated N of the 49th parallel of latitude. To the E, at Red River, the HBC met the challenge of free traders by charging Guillaume Sayer and 3 other Métis in 1849 with violation of the HBC monopoly. Although the company won a legal victory in the courtroom, the community believed that the free traders had been exonerated. Henceforth the company would meet the free traders with the techniques of competition learned elsewhere in its domain to slow the assault on the fur resources to the W and N. In Lower Canada the company had acquired the lease for the King's Posts in 1832, but the northward march of lumbermen signalled the lessening importance of the fur trade in this region. Simpson countered brilliantly by making his company an important supplier of goods needed by the lumbermen.

When the geographical isolation of the West was breached in the 1840s, metropolitan institutions other than the fur interests became involved in opening the "Great Lone Land." Roman Catholic and Anglican missionaries who had appeared earlier now penetrated to the heart of the continent. They were followed by adventurers and government expeditions (eg, the PALLISER EXPEDITION) seeking resources other than fur. Simpson's death in 1860 and the sale in 1863 of the HBC to the International Financial Society, a British investment group that saw settlement as a source of profits, marked the beginning of the end of the historic fur trade. In 1870 the HBC's vast territory in the West was transferred to Canada, and what had been a trickle of settlers coming from Ontario became a flood. As settlement spread N and W, the HBC and rival free traders intensified the northward push of the trade, and eventually established enduring trading contacts with the Inuit.

In the face of competition and the presence of the Canadian government, the HBC reduced the support services that had been a part of its trading relationship with the Indians and had buffered the Indians against the swings of fur-market demands in western Europe. In the 20th century, fortunes in the fur trade came to reflect the swings of the market and the advent of FUR FARMING (*see* FUR INDUSTRY). Increasingly the Indians looked to the missions and even more to the government for support in times of adversity. This shift culminated in the granting of family allowance, schooling and pensions after WWII, and marked the end of the historic fur trade. FUR TRAPPING continues as a cash crop in frontier areas, but as a way of life it is confined to a few northern areas.

Historically, however, the fur trade played a formative role in the creation of Canada. It provided the motive for the exploration of much of the country and remained the economic foundation for western Canada until about 1870. The fur trade also determined the relatively peaceful patterns of Indian-white relations in Canada. A central social aspect of this economic enterprise was extensive intermarriage between traders and native women, which gave rise to an indigenous fur-trade society that blended Indian and European customs and attitudes. JOHN E. FOSTER

Reading: W.J. Eccles, *The Canadian Frontier 1524-1760* (rev ed, 1983) and *Canadian Society During the French Regime* (1968); D. Francis, *Battle for the West* (1982); C. Gilman, *Where Two Worlds Meet* (1982); R. Glover, "Introduction" in E.E. Rich, ed, *Andrew Graham's Observations on Hudson's Bay 1767-91* (1969); H. Innis, *The Fur Trade in Canada* (1930); G.L. Nute, *The Voyageur* (1931); A.J. Ray, *Indians in the Fur Trade* (1974); E.E. Rich, *The Fur Trade and the Northwest to 1857* (1967); Sylvia Van Kirk, *"Many Tender Ties"* (1980).

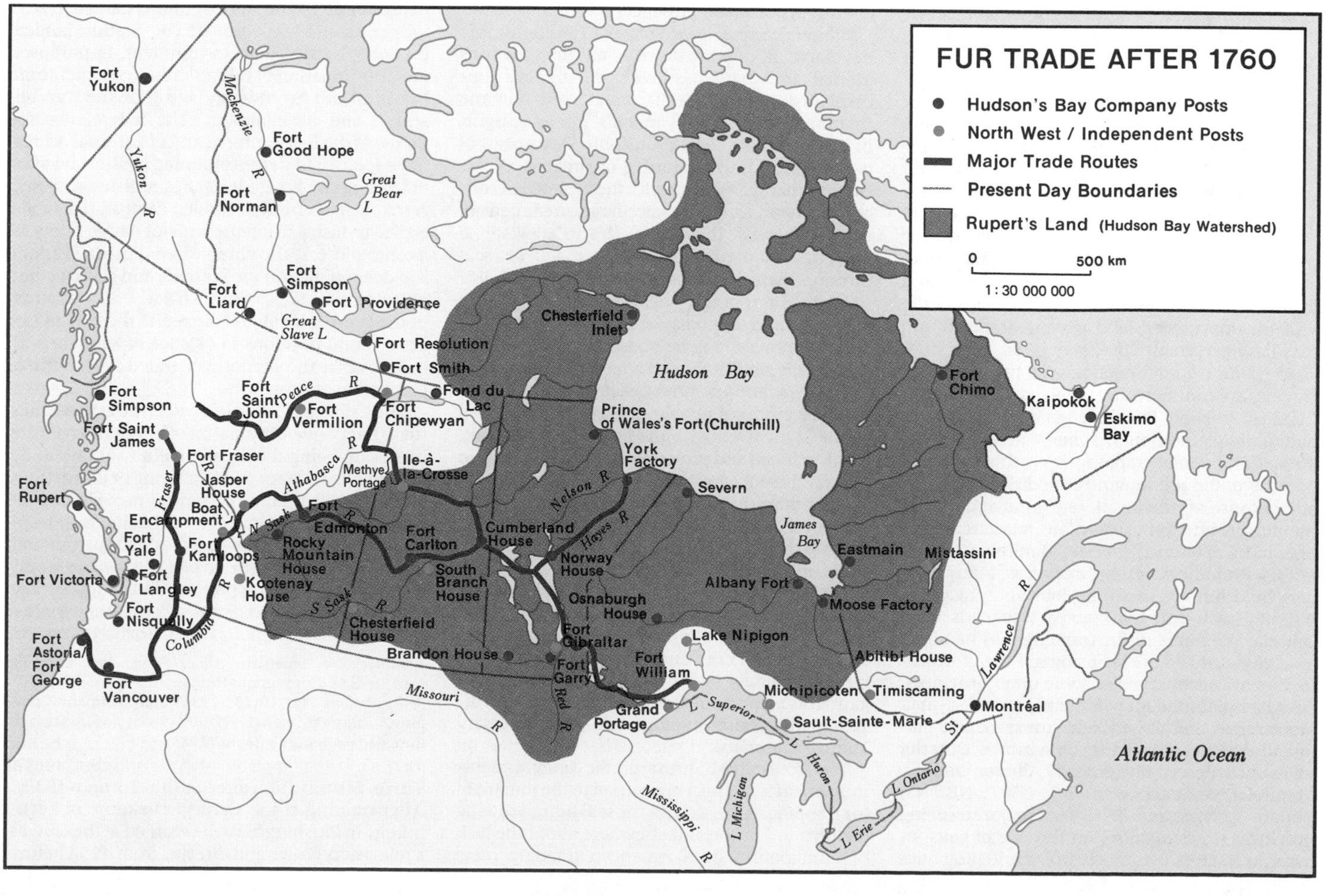

Fur Trade Routes Throughout the period of the historical fur trade, water routes were the natural "highways," and canoes (later boats – principally York boats) the vehicles. The placement of trading posts depended on the presence of numbers of Indians willing and able to trade, and on the ease of transportation to and from them. In the Atlantic region, the absence of a dominant river system resulted in only a localized traffic in furs; but the French tapped a vastly greater potential via the St Lawrence R and its tributaries. At posts at Tadoussac, Québec and Montréal they received furs from the Montagnais, ALGONQUIN, HURON and OTTAWA, who travelled various rivers from the King's Domain, or came down the Ottawa R from Lk Timiskaming and beyond. But most important to the later trade was the route the French themselves developed to the west via the St Lawrence, Ottawa and French rivers; by the 1740s they had extended it to the head of Lk Superior and thence to the prairies. After the CONQUEST of 1759-60 this

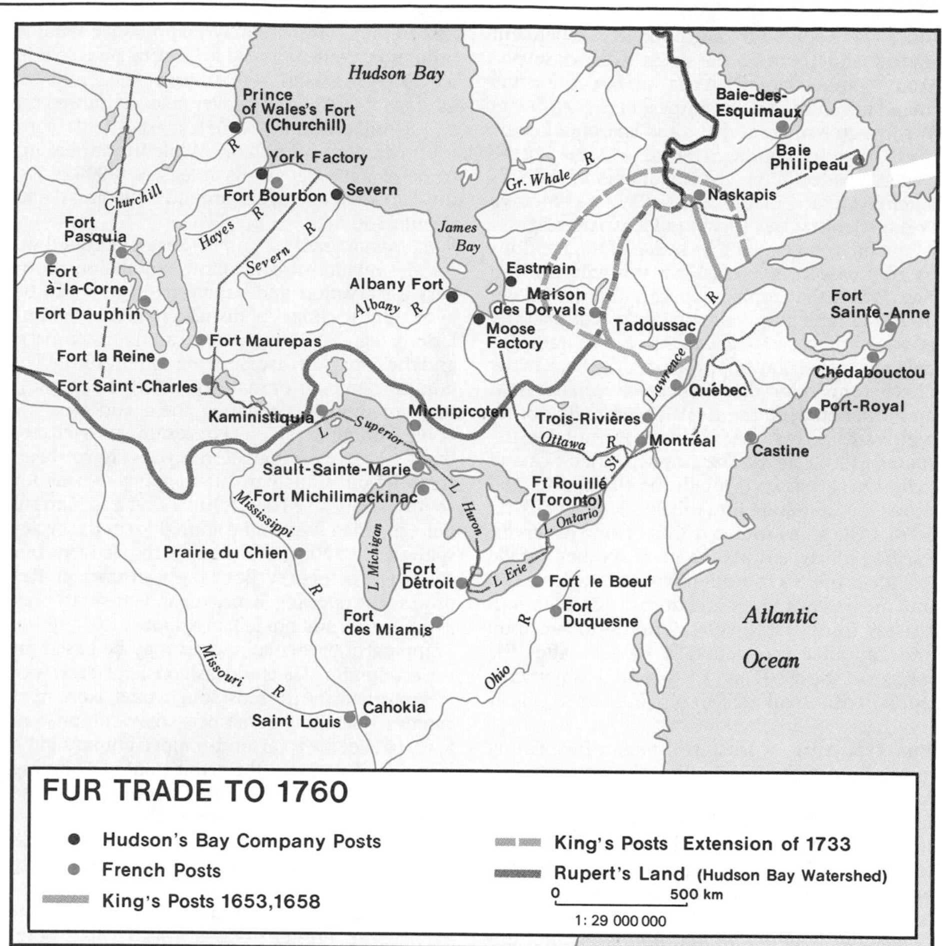

route was adopted by anglophone independent traders and then by the NORTH WEST COMPANY. From Kaministiquia (later FT WILLIAM) the route inland began at GRAND PORTAGE and twisted N and W through a series of rivers and lakes marked by over 50 tortuous portages. From Lk Winnipeg the traders headed W via the 2 branches of the Saskatchewan R; many went NW via Methye Portage [PORTAGE LA LOCHE] to Lk ATHABASCA.

The other major route was that of the London-based HUDSON'S BAY COMPANY through Hudson Bay. When that company began to move inland in 1774, with the construction of CUMBERLAND HOUSE on the Saskatchewan, most of its traffic inland was by the Hayes R from YORK FACTORY. In the direct competition that ensued between the HBC and other traders, the rivals paced one another westward across the prairies. Eventually the routes proceeded via the Howse, Athabasca and Yellowhead passes through the Rocky Mts and down the Columbia R to the Pacific region. After 1814 HBC ships rounded Cape Horn to service Pacific posts by sea. As the more southerly trade declined, traders moved down the Mackenzie R into the western Arctic and from the East Main (E coast of Hudson Bay) inland. Access to Ft Chimo and Labrador was generally by sea. After the merger of the NWC and HBC in 1821, shipments through Montréal ceased. JAMES A. OGILVY

Fur Trapping At least 3-5 million fur-bearing animals are trapped annually in Canada, primarily for their skins (pelts), although occasionally for bait and for human, dog and wild animal food. Because of its economic and cultural importance to those who make their living by trapping, and because of the concern for the suffering of the animals, trapping has become a contentious issue.

Traditional and Cultural Aspects Before Europeans came to N America, trapping was an integral part of the aboriginal way of life, providing food, clothing and shelter. The subsequent development of the FUR TRADE, however, profoundly altered the native economy. Trapping became an end in itself, to the point that some species were put in jeopardy. The decline in the FUR INDUSTRY over the last century and the application of a new set of values focusing on the suffering of the animals have not only caused some economic and social hardships among native groups but also seem to some people to threaten their very way of life. Nevertheless, under the ROYAL PROCLAMATION OF 1763 (and other subsequent constitutional amendments), aboriginal hunting, trapping and fishing rights to obtain food at all seasons of the year on unoccupied land were guaranteed and may have precedence over provincial game laws.

Economics About 80 000 people, predominantly male, are commercially involved in trapping in Canada. Probably less than 15-30% of these are native people, although some sources estimate 50%. Commercial trapping is seasonally based because of the prime winter condition of the fur and because of provincial, territorial and federal trapping restrictions. There are registered traplines in BC, Yukon T, Alberta, Manitoba and Ontario, with some covering large areas. Many trappers hold full- or part-time jobs and engage in trapping in off-duty hours and at weekends. Educational programs in fur trapping and handling are mandatory before licensing in BC and Ontario, and are encouraged in some other provinces, eg, Alberta. Canadian wild fur represents a small percentage of total worldwide fur sales. The major fur-producing trapping province is Ontario, followed in descending order by Alberta, Québec, Manitoba, Saskatchewan, BC, NWT, NB, NS, Yukon T, Nfld and PEI. The major trapping provinces exact royalties on the sale of pelts: as much as $750 000 annually in Ontario. Royalties and trapping licences may help finance wildlife programs. Canadian wild furbearing pelts sold in the 1985-86 season were valued at $50.2 million. Of this total, 423 198 beaver pelts accounted for $14.8 million, and 182 088 marten pelts contributed nearly $9 million. While the annual income of some trappers is at least $20 000 gross, the Canadian average is around $700 gross, and about $350 net.

Biological Needs for Trapping are predicated on the desirability of controlling population numbers if starvation and habitat damage are to be avoided: the danger of diseases in wildlife populations (eg, sarcoptic mange, canine distemper), and the danger of disease being communicated to domestic animals or man (eg, rabies, tularemia). Any attempt at alleviating these concerns involves imponderables. For example, well-defined, 10-year population cycles have been shown from Canadian fur-trapping returns for coyote, snowshoe hare, mink, fisher and marten. For Canadian lynx and coloured foxes the cycles span the past 200 and 100 years, respectively, but the causes of these cyclic changes are unclear. Reproductive rates (eg, in beaver and muskrat) may actually rise, and not fall, in response to trapping. Trapping of particular species may be based on the economics of fads and fashions; the rarest species may become the most sought after. Nontarget catches (including some pets) may comprise at least 10% of the total land-trapped animals but a lesser percentage of the semiaquatics. Thinning out a population may or may not reduce disease incidence. In some areas where the leg-hold trap has been banned, there have been no observable increases in diseases. Species most commonly trapped include the following (depending on regional differences): badger, beaver, bobcat, cougar, coyote, ermine (weasel), fisher, fox, hare, lynx, marten, mink, muskrat, otter, rabbit, raccoon, skunk, squirrel, wolf and wolverine. Bears are trapped in some provinces.

Ethical Concerns about Trapping The continuing development of more humane attitudes towards animals in Canada has involved 2 areas of concern: first, animals' welfare and their humane treatment, and, second, animals' interests, rights of liberation and legal protection. One group of people (including supporting organizations) has been primarily involved with the first area of concern. When faced with specific mistreatment of certain animals, this group tries to alleviate or prevent that particular inhumane act: eg, seal hunting (which has sometimes involved live skinning); trapping (where animals may suffer for prolonged periods); and the food industry (where animals may be housed in cramped and inhumane conditions, and where their slaughtering may induce fear, stress, suffering and panic). Another group of people, while being informed about or involved with the first area of concern, has developed and projected some consistent and broadly based moral and ethical positions that suggest ways in which man should behave towards all animals, so that, whenever possible, none of them are needlessly abused or exploited. Such philosophies generally govern one's own behaviour and can act as a conceptual guide to others. The concepts of animal protection, rights, interests and liberation are encouraging an increasing number of Canadians to refuse to participate knowingly in the use of products, such as garments made from fur trapping, which have involved the abuse, exploitation or unnecessary killing of animals.

The conceptual thrust of the animal rights movement is in direct opposition to the pursuit of fur trapping. Also, as with the seal hunt, growing concern in Europe and elsewhere about the lack of humaneness in N American trapping may, considering Canada's heavy dependence on the export market, decisively influence the continuance of Canadian fur trapping.

Traps are for holding (eg, foot snare, leg-hold, box), or killing (eg, deadfall, neck snare, Conibear, submarine trap). Box holding traps are cumbersome to transport and may cause stress, but they are normally noninjurious. Some species caught in a leg-hold may bite off a limb or limbs ("wring-off") to escape – unless the trap has a "stop-loss" device. Steel-toothed, leg-hold traps are still manufactured (1986) in the US but are banned in BC, Alberta, Ontario and NS. The neck snare may slowly choke the animal to death, as it struggles to escape, or catch around other parts of the body – it can cause gross injuries and protracted suffering. The Conibear trap may not kill quickly if the animal enters it incorrectly or if the closing impact is insufficient. If traps are not visited regularly, animals may suffer from exposure, stress, thirst, starvation, gangrene and predation. Only BC, Ontario, Alberta, NB and PEI require visitation every one to 3 days. To avoid bullet holes in the pelt, a trapper dispatches an animal by clubbing its head, by using a snare on a handle to choke it, or by stamping on its chest.

The Association for the Protection of Fur-bearing Animals (APFA) and the Canadian Association for Humane Trapping (CAHT) have been influential in informing the public and also governmental officials about the ethical issues and suffering involved in trapping (including the presentation of films); in sponsoring research on the development of more humane traps; and in advocating the withdrawal of inhumane traps (leg-hold traps are now banned as land sets for a number of species in BC and Ontario). CAHT joined with the Canadian Federation of Humane Societies to form the Humane Trap Development Committee (HTDC). The HTDC definition of a humane death is that the animal suffers neither panic nor pain. The Fur Institute of Canada (FIC), formed in 1983, is a private corporation funded primarily by the federal government. Its purposes are dissemination of information to the public on behalf of the fur industry and humane trap research and development. The federal departments of the Environment and of External Affairs have sponsored papers outlining possible ways of defending the fur trade against anti-fur activists. A strong, government-funded campaign defended the industry using the issue of native rights as a centrepiece. It also emphasized Canada's historical dependence on the fur trade and claimed that trapping maintains nature's balance. The attempt of the pro-fur lobby to "discredit" those who express moral positions in defence of animals is illustrative of the friction generated between the conflicting groups.

The Criminal Code of Canada (s402(1)a) states that "Every one commits an offence who wilfully causes or, being the owner, wilfully allows to be caused unnecessary pain, suffering or injury to an animal or bird"; but there is no precedent for it being applied on behalf of wild animals in trapping. A private member's Bill (C-208) to amend the Criminal Code (in favour of humane traps) led to evidence being presented in 1977, but the Bill was not adopted. *See also* FUR FARMING; FUR INDUSTRY; FUR TRADE. BRUCE GORDON CUMMING

Reading: J.A. Bateman, *Animal Traps and Trapping* (1973); B.G. Cumming, "Human and Animal Rights," *Policy Options* 7(7):19-23 (1986) and "Humane Trapping," *Policy Options* 8(1):27-30 (1987); Fur Institute of Canada, *On Nature's Terms* (1985).

Furie, Sidney, film director (b at Toronto 1933). After training at the Carnegie Institute of Technology in Pittsburgh, Pa, he worked at the CBC as a television writer and director from 1954 before striking off as an independent filmmaker with 2 low-budget features, *A Dangerous Age* (1957) and *A Cool Sound from Hell* (1958). These gritty dramas of adolescent angst were praised abroad but failed to get Canadian distribution, and Furie thereupon left for greener pastures in Britain, where he coincided briefly with kitchen-sink realism in *The Leather Boys* (1964) and then had a big hit with the aggressively stylized *Ipcress File* (1965). This success drew him to Hollywood, where he has since directed many films. There, his initially flashy visual style eventually gave way to a rather more sedate approach to big-budget commercial productions. His notable American movies include *The Appaloosa* (1966), *Lady Sings the Blues* (1972), *Gable and Lombard* (1976), *The Entity* (1982) and *Night Magic* (1985). WILLIAM BEARD

Furniture, Country In studies of antiques or material history, "country" (ie, traditional, provincial or folk) styles are contrasted with stylized or formal ones. What one individual calls country and admires perhaps for its decoration or painted finish, another may reject as crude and primitive. Although some may expect formal furniture to be constructed of finer hardwoods (eg, walnut, cherry, mahogany) and country furniture of softwood (eg, pine), an understanding of the difference between country and formal furniture goes beyond methods and mediums of construction, forcing consideration of other factors, including where and when the furniture was produced. Country furniture is probably best understood as material produced after or similar to the mainstream of influences or period styles (eg, Chippendale, Hepplewhite, Sheraton), using local woods and influenced by the limitations of the cabinetmaker's tool chest, imagination and level of workmanship. Country furniture includes all types found in formal furniture (eg, tables, chairs, cupboards, chests) as well as additional forms.

Maritime Provinces

Settlement in the Maritimes (comprising NS, NB and PEI) was essentially a rural experience. Although port cities, such as Halifax and Saint John, were important as political, social and economic centres, most people lived in small farming and fishing communities. Because of distances, lack of adequate roads and unreliable methods of transportation and communication, contact between the regions was limited and rural areas were isolated from urban centres and mainstreams of fashion and taste.

After the expulsion of the ACADIANS (1755-63), the first influx of immigrants began with the arrival of the PLANTERS from New England, followed by the LOYALISTS in 1783-84 and a substantial Scottish migration in the early 19th century. Although many of these settlers brought or imported their domestic furnishings, the migration included cabinetmakers, carpenters and joiners whose arrival and settlement quickly led to the establishment and production of indigenous Maritime-Canadian furniture, based on English and American styles familiar to the craftsman. Because cabinetmaking was essentially a conservative craft, based on an established APPRENTICESHIP system, and because furniture styles have a tendency to persist over long periods of time, the country furniture produced in the Maritime provinces from about 1770 to 1850 reflected the continuation of earlier styles such as Chippendale. Only in cities, which were open to the influx of new fashions, would one expect furniture styles to attempt to keep pace with new developments and trends in taste. The rural character of Maritime society also influenced the choice of construction materials. Except in urban centres, particularly port cities, where exotic woods (eg, mahogany) were available to local craftsmen, most furniture was constructed of immediately available woods (eg, pine, birch, maple). Figured hardwoods (eg, birch, maple) were commonly used in both formal and country furniture because of their decorative grain. Country furniture (particularly that produced in pine) was often painted to represent more formal furnishings in exotic wood. In some cases, these painted finishes, which are often very vibrant and colourful, are the most important distinguishing feature of country furniture.

Thomas Nisbet table, *c*1830, from Saint John, NB (*courtesy Royal Ontario Museum*).

French (Acadian), English, Irish, Scottish and German influences are evident in the country furniture styles of the Maritimes. All ethnic groups used similar types of domestic furnishings, including blanket boxes, chests of drawers, tables of various sizes with and without drawers, chairs with and without arms, and corner and flat-to-the-wall cupboards. Not all groups, however, are represented in all 3 provinces, and some groups lavished more attention and detail on certain types of furniture than on others.

Prince Edward Island The flat-to-the-wall kitchen cupboard, usually with an open top, seems to have been the focal point of furnishings of Scottish and Irish homes during the 19th century. Although most of these cupboards were made by unknown craftsmen, PEI is rich in examples of furniture signed or in some way identified by its makers. Such cabinet and chair makers include Benjamin Chappell, a wheelwright from London who arrived in 1774, and Samuel Bagnall, a Loyalist who arrived from Philadelphia in 1787. Both are well known for their chairs, examples of which exist in both public and private collections.

New Brunswick is also rich in furniture by known makers, particularly in Saint John, which was the most important centre of cabinetmaking. Known cabinetmakers working before 1800 include Robert Chillas, who arrived from New York in 1783; Daniel Fowler, who settled in 1785; and Nathan Oaks and Robert Blackwood, who took out Freeman papers (received upon payment of a registration fee and the swearing of an oath of allegiance in order to operate a business in Saint John) in 1795 and 1796.

Nova Scotia Like Saint John, Halifax was an important centre of cabinetmaking. NS saw the largest immigration of "Foreign Protestants" in the Maritimes. LUNENBURG was settled by German-speaking immigrants in 1753. Although the initial migration numbered less than 2000, the Germans gave Lunenburg county a distinctive tradition and culture which still survives. One of the early Lunenburg town furniture makers, listed in 1794 as a turner and wheelwright, was Casper Jung, who later anglicized his name to Young. In Halifax many signed examples of Windsor chairs are known by such makers as James Cole (about 1817), who came to Halifax from the US; George Gammon (about 1838), who worked in Cole Harbour, Halifax County; and Joy Humeston (about 1805), who made Windsor-style bamboo chairs and settees in Halifax. The Sibley family of Colchester County made other types of furniture but their chair, with its distinctive, shaped back slats and mushroom finials, is best known. Beginning with Joseph Sibley (born 1790), who was known locally as the "chair maker," the Sibleys continued in operation until 1900.

Of the Maritime provinces, NB and NS saw the largest influx of French-Acadian immigrants, beginning with the establishment of PORT-ROYAL in 1605. Expulsion of these Acadians was accompanied by the confiscation or destruction of such of their belongings as they could not carry with them. Therefore, much of the furniture identified today as "Acadian" actually dates from the post-expulsion period when, beginning in 1764, the French-Acadians returned to the region.

By the middle of the 19th century the craft tradition of furniture manufacture was rapidly being replaced by mechanization and factory production. Although in certain rural areas, such as parts of PEI, earlier furniture styles persisted well into the late 19th century, the cabinetmaking-apprenticeship tradition slowly disappeared as the Maritimes moved into the industrial age.

RICHARD HENNING FIELD

Newfoundland

No furniture is known from Newfoundland which can be dated earlier than 1810-20, when restrictions on land granting were lifted and local development encouraged. The first British-trained cabinetmakers, Mark Green and George Hancock, arrived in St John's in 1815 to serve its growing population. Samuel Creed came from Halifax about 1833 and his surviving work suggests a conservative approach to current furniture styles. The fact that W. Gammon produced Windsor chairs in both Halifax and St John's, and that similar comb-back Windsors are found both in NS and Newfoundland, suggests an early, strong craft connection in the Atlantic region.

Although some cabinetmakers worked in major outports such as HARBOUR GRACE, most were in St John's, the economic and political capital. That city had 6 cabinetmakers in the 1840s, 10 in the 1870s. Matthew Pope's furniture factory, opened in 1859, was one of a number that produced household and institutional furniture. What is known of the work of these individuals and factories suggests that their work was not imaginative; they were content to copy pattern-book styles to the limit of their abilities and equipment. There were exceptions, for example, H.W. Winter's workshop at Clarke's Beach, Conception Bay.

Real imagination can be found in outport furniture, whether homemade or made by a local carpenter. In such pieces as washstands and benches the whole repertoire of decorative treatments, eg, chip carving, applied motifs, spindles, chamfers, moldings and arches, was exploited in inventive combinations augmented by strong colours in the paintwork. Where a particular skill was required, eg, with chairs requiring joinery, conservatism crept in. Old styles survived and new ones were adapted to the limitations of the craftsman and his tools. A form of chair generally considered 17th century, the Carver chair, was made until the end of the 19th century. Sheraton chairs are not uncommon (Chippendale are rare) but never have the turned leg (which requires a lathe) associated with the style; rather, they have the square-tapered Hepplewhite leg, which was easier to

Rope bed and cradle (*courtesy Metropolitan Toronto and Region Conservation Authority/Black Creek Pioneer Village*).

make. Similarly, because of the difficulty of producing them, no chairs with the Hepplewhite shield-back or Victorian balloon-back are found. This interaction of professionalism and conservatism can also be found in kitchen dressers of the 1810-20 period. These pieces were probably the work of housewrights, because they were generally part of the whole architectural treatment of the kitchen. Because the housewrights were not constructing for themselves, they could not indulge their imaginations and had to construct something which spoke of the owner's standing in the community, a situation which inspired conservatism.

At the end of the 19th century, the appearance of factory-made furniture, the availability of mail-order catalogues (the ordinary man's pattern book) and the more widespread use of woodworking equipment had their first effect on outport furniture. Chairs and settees in what must be called "Catalogue Style," with thin frames and applied decoration, replaced an earlier factory form, Eastlake, with machine-gouged decoration. Furniture imitating these forms is generally found outside St John's, where it was difficult to get "bought" furniture. It has an element of expediency, making use as it did of salvaged wood from packing cases or houses as well as of whole elements (eg, legs) from discarded furniture. Such curious combinations reflect an economy that discouraged waste.

Because of Newfoundland's location on the periphery of N America and its marginal economy, the island's furniture, like many of its other CRAFTS, never entered the mainstream of the other Atlantic nations. As a consequence, Newfoundland retained earlier forms and construction techniques but applied to those forms a range of decorative treatments that speak of a strong and vigorous visual imagination. SHANE O'DEA

Ontario

The phrase "country furniture" aptly describes most surviving antique Ontario furniture, held privately and in museum collections. Settlement began after the AMERICAN REVOLUTION and intensified during the 19th century. In those first years, the pressures of pioneering life ensured that most families had little time or money for high-style furniture, let alone access to it. Ontario country furniture was fashioned of native woods (eg, walnut, maple, cherry, birch, oak, basswood, pine), by hand, usually with some skill. It can be divided into 3 categories: copies of high-style furniture of British and American derivation; furniture with form and decoration of French, German and other European ethnic origin; and sturdy utilitarian furniture that was used almost universally in town and country and in the less important rooms of city homes. All of the Georgian, Empire and Victorian styles were reproduced, alone or in combination, with varying degrees of success. Ontario cherry and figured maple provided excellent substitutes for imported mahogany and satinwood. Stain and paint were employed to simulate costly woods, veneers, inlay and carving, when cost or lack of skill or tools forbade such embellishments. Especially during the early years, cabinetmakers were more likely to use hardware (ie, hinges, handles, etc) that was readily available rather than what matched the style of the furniture. Decorative motifs such as the German 6-sided star and French diamond-shaped panels sometimes were used on country furniture that was British or American in form and style. Relatively few tools were needed to construct utilitarian furniture so it could be undertaken by most carpenters as well as joiners and cabinetmakers. Dual-purpose, space-saving forms included a chair with a back that could be lowered to form a table top, and a bench with a seat that unfolded to a full bed.

Country chairs fall into 3 groups: slat-backs, Windsors and Fancy chairs. Slat-back chairs had 4 turned legs, the rear ones extended and joined by several slats at the top to form a ladder back. A variation, the banister-back, had 2 slats, pierced by several vertical spindles. Woven ash splints or elm bark formed the seats. The Windsor, a chair of English derivation, was constructed like a stool with a back attached to the seat. Such chairs were named according to either the style or the shape of the back, eg, Sheraton, loop- or bow-back, arrow-back, low-back or Captain's, comb-back, spindle-back, short spindle-back or chicken coop, and gunstock. Slat-backs and Windsors were made as side chairs, armchairs and rockers; most were painted. Fancy chairs were side chairs with back, seat and leg patterns derived, at least in part, from Georgian and Victorian styles. Decorative, figured wood often was used; the seats were made of cane or rush. Many Windsors and Fancy chairs also were produced in early Ontario furniture factories.

The high, heavy, 4-post, rope-spring bedstead and accompanying trundle bed were succeeded by a lower, lighter spool-turned bed with slats. Hired-man cots, with spool-turned ends, became country settees when spooled or solid backs were added. Tables and stands of all sizes and for all purposes had tops that tilted, lifted, pivoted or were detachable, and leaves that could be dropped, drawn out or detached. Country schoolmaster desks with slanted lift tops might be attached to or detachable from a long- or short-legged frame below and a postmaster cupboard with pigeonholes above. Drop-front desks were composed of a cupboard front that dropped to form a writing surface, supported by a table or a lower cupboard. Country cupboards of one or 2 pieces, with glazed, solid, or no doors, some having a pie shelf sandwiched between the upper and lower parts, were built into corners or walls or were free standing. They were made in many sizes and shapes for storage of food or dishes and as dry sinks. Linen presses and wardrobes were constructed with fixed parts or, for ease of relocation, detachable ones. Most cupboards were painted or stained dark. Lift-top box chests, the earliest and best made of 6 dovetailed boards, were numerous and even incorporated into the top part of early chests of drawers. ELIZABETH INGOLFSRUD

Manitoba–Red River

With the arrival of the SELKIRK settlers in 1812 and the subsequent construction of permanent establishments by the HUDSON'S BAY COMPANY (HBC) and NORTH WEST COMPANY (NWC), domestic residences and a tradition of country furniture were introduced in the Red River valley. From the outset, the geographic isolation of the RED RIVER COLONY and the logistic difficulties inherent in transport worked against the importation of furniture. Furniture sent out by the London-based HBC had to be transported by the annual ship to York Factory, transferred to the York Boat brigades and carried the 1300 km inland to Red R. Aside from company officers, who imported fine furniture, employees were limited to the quantity of household goods they could transport in small wooden trunks or cassettes. The early settlers in Red R confronted these transportation difficulties by producing their own furniture on a modest scale. Settlers and company personnel who had the tools fashioned tables, chairs (eg, the Red River chair, a sturdy pine chair with a plank seat), storage chests and beds that put utility and structure ahead of ornament. Consequently, furnishings in even the centrally located fur-trade posts at Red R were characterized by simplicity, even austerity. Because the Red R community was primarily French, Scottish and English in cultural antecedents, no single, distinctive furniture tradition emerged.

Examples of surviving country furniture (chairs, chests, cradles, sofas, sideboards) are housed in private collections or museums and historic parks such as St-Boniface Museum or Lower Fort Garry. The principal woods used were oak, pine and ash, which were readily available in the area. After frames were carefully cut and fitted, joints were firmly fastened by wooden dowels, varying in diameter from one-quarter inch (about 0.5 cm) in the HBC "board room" chairs to one-half inch (about 1 cm) in beds and sofas. Generally, the furniture was left in its natural state until the 1870s, when many pieces were stained, waxed and ornamented with carvings of flowers or other designs. By the 1860s improvements in transportation through the St Paul route and the arrival of professional cabinetmakers spelled the decline of country-made furniture in the Red River valley. GREGORY THOMAS

Furniture, English, Scottish and American

It is a common misconception that early Canadian furniture consists only of pieces (eg, chairs, tables) roughly hewn from pine. In fact, much "fine" or formal furniture intended for the drawing room, parlour, dining room, etc, was made, following European models, by craftsmen well versed in their craft. ENGLISH, Scottish and LOYALIST influences are apparent in much surviving Canadian-made furniture, in specific details and characteristics unique to particular areas.

Georgian Period

During the earliest period of English settlement in Canada (in NS from 1713 to 1783) domestic furnishings were either imported or homemade. A few cabinetmakers, notably Edward Draper, are recorded as working in Halifax after 1749. No known Canadian-made furniture survives from this period. The Loyalists, who arrived in 1783-84, comprised the first substantial English-language population and were followed by an influx of Scottish settlers. Both groups included a great variety of specialized craftsmen, cabinetmakers among them.

The earliest known English Canadian formal or stylized furniture dates from about 1785 and follows then fashionable English styles. The so-called Chippendale style, in vogue in England until the 1780s, was followed by the Hepplewhite, Sheraton, classical-revival and regency forms into the early 19th century. While the cabinetmakers produced what their markets demanded, they were also products of their conservative training. As in most CRAFTS, training in cabinetmaking was through the APPRENTICESHIP system, so that cabinetmakers had a strong tendency to build furniture in the same styles and the same manner as had their teachers and masters. Changes in style and fashion most rapidly affected the larger cities. In outlying areas, particular styles in furniture, notably the Chippendale, were produced long after their periods of actual fashion had ended (*see* FURNITURE, COUNTRY). One notable craftsman, James Waddell of Truro, NS, made Chippendale chairs as late as 1825. Canadian furniture also includes examples of "throwback" pieces, ie, items produced from observation or memory in styles long out of fashion. Although derived from English forms, Canadian-made formal furniture was far simpler. It was also relatively unornamented, compared to its English or American colonial counterparts; inlay work and carving were rare.

The earliest centres of sophisticated cabinetmaking and production were Halifax and Montréal. Many examples of Chippendale furniture of the 1780s and 1790s survive from these centres. Montréal furniture of the late 18th and 19th centuries was, by all accounts, the finest produced. Some Montréal examples are well veneered with exotic woods and include complex inlaid stringing and banding. Halifax furniture was far simpler. Although Québec was a smaller city than Montréal, specialized cabinetmakers were in operation there as early as the 1780s, producing very fine work. Most notable perhaps are clock cases by the Loyalist James Orkney. The Bellerose brothers, who operated in Trois-Rivières before 1800, are also known for fine clock cases. Cabinetmaking in NB developed in the 1780s and 1790s in Saint John and the Saint John R valley, but no NB furniture predating 1800 is known, nor has any NB Chippendale furniture been found; all pieces are in the later styles of the early 19th century. In Upper Canada in the first generation of settlement, furnishings also seem to have been imported or homemade. A few cabinetmakers are known to have operated before 1800, but again no formal furniture survives which can definitely be dated to before 1800.

While Canadian formal furniture can generally be identified as Canadian and often be ascribed to a particular region, it can rarely be attributed to a specific maker. Before the industrial period of the 1840s and 1850s, very few cabinetmakers marked or labelled their furniture. Before 1825 only 3 cabinetmakers are known to have used paper labels: the firm of Tulles, Pallister and McDonald of Halifax (1810-11); Daniel Green of Saint John, NB (before 1820); and Thomas Nisbet of Saint John (1813-48). Occasional pencil or ink markings found are often the signatures of owners rather than of makers.

Imported West Indian mahogany was the favoured cabinet wood, as in Britain and the US. Mahogany logs were relatively inexpensive to transport by sea, as ballast cargo. Mahogany was available, however, only to cabinetmakers in port cities: Halifax, Amherst, Saint John, Québec City, Trois-Rivières and Montréal. Transporting the heavy wood overland was so impractical that cabinetmakers even slightly removed from the ports depended instead on native woods. In the Maritimes, birch, stained to a dark colour and known as "poor man's mahogany," was a widely used cabinet wood. In simple inlays, or segments such as drawer fronts, birch was often mixed with maple. In Québec butternut and maple were quite widely used in areas where mahogany was not available. Upper Canada, inaccessible to imports of mahogany until about 1830, depended for finer furniture on cherry, walnut and figured maple. The secondary or structural wood of virtually all Canadian furniture was pine, although exteriors were made of hardwoods. Mahogany was the only imported wood available before about 1810. Especially after the WAR OF 1812, satinwood and rosewood began to appear in Canadian furniture, usually in small segments and as veneers or inlays. Except for simple iron hinges, all hardware (ie, drawer pulls, casters and small knobs, typically of brass) was imported. As well as typically being of mixed woods, Canadian stylized furniture is often of mixed styles: characteristics of 2 or more design forms are often evident in a single piece of furniture.

With the coming of canals, steamships and finally railways, the increasing mobility of people led to an increasing homogenization of style and design forms. Identifiable regional characteristics began to disappear slowly by 1830 and were entirely gone by 1860. New technologies also had an impact on the style and craft of cabinetmaking. The development of the circular saw after 1820, followed by the veneer mill in the 1830s, made veneers far less expensive to use than had been the case in the earlier period of hand carving. The screw-thread lathe led, in the 1820s, to a fashion for round, rope-turned legs on tables and case pieces. Again, these details were inexpensive because of mechanical production. Elaborate carving machines followed, making possible the decorative excesses of the Victorian period.

Beginning in the 1830s, furniture styles were increasingly adapted for component manufacture by machinery. The growth of the factory system after the 1830s led to a complete homogenization of design throughout N America and, by the 1860s, to a decline in the craft of cabinetmaking. Although there were many changes of style and fashion in the mid-19th century, furniture itself more and more became the product of factories and mechanization, and less and less the product of individual skills. D.B. WEBSTER

Empire and Victorian Furniture

During the Empire and Victorian periods, furniture design largely abandoned the restrained geometry of Hepplewhite, Sheraton and Adam in favour of picturesque outlines and historical revivals more in keeping with the eclectic ARCHITECTURE of the time. In addition, factory production and new forms of woodworking machinery began to replace the traditional methods of the furniture craftsman.

Empire refers to styles which first gained popularity in France during the reign of Emperor Napoleon I, in the first 2 decades of the 19th century. This period corresponds roughly with the time of the English regency. Fashionable furniture of the time was inspired by ancient Roman, Greek and Egyptian designs, popularized through publications such as Thomas Hope's *Household Furniture and Interior Decoration* (1807). Classical styles continued to dominate through the 1830s and 1840s. In Canada, "Empire" sometimes is used to describe the later manifestations of this style, which tended to follow American precedents; "regency" is the preferred term for earlier work.

Chairs from this period often followed the Greek *klismos* form, with sabre-shaped legs and a broad crest rail (ie, horizontal member at the top of the back). Armchairs had scroll-curved arms left open below. Sofas also tended to have scrolled arms, upholstered and often fitted with cylindrical cushions where they met the seat. The scrolled arms of Empire sofas found their counterpart in the high, curved headboards and footboards of "French bedsteads" (now commonly called sleigh beds). Tables often were supported on heavy pedestals set on wide bases with scrolled feet. Case pieces (eg, chests of drawers, sideboards) often had overhanging top drawers with columnar supports. Mahogany veneer over pine was commonly used.

Victorian By the mid-19th century, a wide variety of styles was replacing the classically derived Empire. The Victorian period (1837-1901) first saw the development of the rococo-revival or "modern French" style, which brought a return to rounded curves and naturalistic carving. The balloon-back side chair with its rounded open back and cabriole (S-shaped) legs was popular. The introduction of coil springs and factory-made upholstery materials in plush and horsehair brought a new era of comfort. Almost all lines were rounded; frames and cases were ornamented with carving in the forms of fruit, leaves and flowers.

At the same time, Gothic-revival furniture was coming into vogue, making use of architectural elements such as pointed arches, finials (eg, decorative knobs) and tracery. It was deemed most suitable for the library or entrance hall, where Gothic-revival chairs and benches often were the only unupholstered seating furniture in the house. "Elizabethan" was another popular mid-century style, although its characteristic ball or spool turnings had little to do with what actually had been used during the reign of Elizabeth I. All of these styles and their variants could be found in such popular handbooks as A.J. Downing's *The Architecture of Country Houses* (1850) or Blackie and Son's *The Victorian Cabinet Maker's Assistant* (1855).

By the late 1860s, some began to question the widespread use of revival styles, applied ornament and the trend toward factory production. In 1868, the English designer C.L. Eastlake published *Hints on Household Taste in Furniture, Upholstery and Other Details,* which advocated what he believed to be a return to simple, sturdy craftsmanship. The furniture he illustrated was invariably solid and geometrical in outline, eschewing the rounded curves of the rococo revival. It was ornamented with incised decoration in geometrical patterns, simple turnings and pierced decoration. Details of construction often were made visible through exposed pegs and joints. Eastlake's ideas found their counterparts in the Arts and Crafts Movement and the development of

This style of chair, with a Sheraton-style back, Chippendale arms and tapered legs, was common in the Scottish settlements of eastern Ontario (*courtesy National Museums of Canada/Canadian Museum of Civilization*).

"mission" furniture. Much to the chagrin of the reformers, however, factories began taking up the name "Eastlake" and applying it to mass-produced furniture of simple, squarish outline. The Victorian period saw the introduction of a wide range of woodworking machinery which, combined with the development of steam power, the growth of markets and improved transportation, brought an end to the small, independent craftsman's shop.

Among the largest Canadian furniture factories was that of Jacques and Hay in Toronto, which produced such large quantities of furniture (from school desks to parlour suites) that often all Canadian Victorian furniture is erroneously called "Jacques and Hay." Proximity to the US also influenced furniture making in Canada. From an early date, Canadians purchased furniture, at both wholesale and retail levels, from American suppliers.

Interest in revival styles continued to dominate the furniture trade. Among the most influential by the 1870s was the renaissance-revival style, characterized by the use of bold cornices, pediments and pilasters, high-relief carving, classical anthemia (ie, floral or foliated ornaments) and a multitude of finials and drops. Bedsteads, sideboards and dressing bureaus with attached plate glass mirrors grew to astonishing heights. Marble tops became increasingly popular. Chair and sofa frames took on an often spiked, attenuated look; legs often were tapered, with either turned or panelled decoration.

The last years of Victoria's reign saw revivals of nearly every preceding style. Reproductions might be faithful to the original form or might be creative revivals influenced by the sinuous curves and sometimes bizarre shapes of art nouveau. The use of upholstery reached its height, the frame often covered entirely with several types or colours of fabric and fringed with tassels. New materials became popular, particularly wicker, iron, brass and bentwood. Oak replaced black walnut as the preferred wood for most furniture. Mail-order houses such as The T. EATON COMPANY offered to ship furniture anywhere by rail.

W. JOHN MCINTYRE

Reading: H. Dobson and B. Dobson, *The Early Furniture of Ontario and the Atlantic Provinces* (1974); H. Pain, *The Heritage of Upper Canadian Furniture* (1978).

Furniture, French Canadian furniture of French derivation was made between 1650 and 1820. It is of the traditional or regional type, ie, made of solid, jointed wood. This furniture was distinct from the grand style that emanated from the French court but was influenced by it, borrowing technical and artistic features, while retaining a peasant flavour. Some furniture was made by unskilled hands for a family's own use; most was made by skilled carpenters, who had come from France to meet the demands for churches, dwellings and furniture for the agricultural society that had replaced that of the fur traders. These men were artisans trained in the rigorous traditions of French *menuisiers,* ie, joiners. They were not *ébénistes,* cabinetmakers, whose specialty was marquetry and veneer. In the towns and villages of NEW FRANCE, professional woodworkers had their own shops, but sometimes worked directly in churches and dwellings where a particular piece was to be installed. There were also itinerant woodworkers who roamed the countryside and often spent weeks at a time making an armoire for a family, a convent or a seigneur.

The design and details of this furniture reflect regional origins from many French provinces, mainly Normandy, Picardy, Île de France, Brittany, Poitou, Aunis and Saintonge. The carved decorations particular to these regions are distinguished by traditional folk motifs: stylized flowers, leaves, rosettes, trees, stars and crosses of every kind of the Haute Bretagne; chip-carved circles, discs, lozenges, shells and hearts of the Loire Atlantique; in fact, whatever might spring from a pair of compasses and ruler or be drawn freehand. With time, these motifs became less varied than in Europe, until they evolved into entirely indigenous designs.

As in the French provinces, styles evolved slowly and period influences showed in furniture made long after the historical eras for which they were named. Between 1650 and 1750, the predominant inspiration was the Henry IV and Louis XIII style, featuring rectilinear lines and geometrical ornamentation with broad surfaces, pediments, multiple panels, lozenges, high and low diamond points and wood turnings with chamfered (ie, bevelled) cubes or in a spiral twist. The flowing lines, graceful shapes and often asymmetrical decoration of the *régence* and Louis XV styles appeared between 1740 and 1760 and became very popular. In New France, as in the country districts of France, the heavily ornate Louis XIV styles had little impact. Whatever the period, there was no ormolu, marble or veneer, and little lacquer or marquetry; however, the furniture was liberally ornamented, particularly after 1785, both in the shaping of integral parts (eg, door panels, rails, aprons, legs, rungs) and with increasingly profuse and ebullient surface carving. The woodworkers were less inhibited than their counterparts in France; embellishment beyond the traditional motifs appeared earlier and sometimes included features never seen in France.

The *Rocaille* style, reminiscent of 18th-century gardens, flourished in the Louis XV period and was the last direct influence from France. Its principal motif was crosiered branches entwining leaves, flowers and shells. After the SEVEN YEARS' WAR, this style exerted a powerful influence on the traditional furniture of French Canada, which reached its peak of refinement in technique and design between 1785 and 1820. In this period, features of English and American designs began to appear in combination with the traditional French features, sometimes with harmonious effect, sometimes without.

The woods available or appropriate for furniture were unfamiliar to the early immigrant craftsmen. White pine, butternut and yellow birch, none of which was known in France, were the most widely used between 1650 and 1750. White and sugar maple were at first used as firewood and considered too difficult to work, but became popular at the end of the 18th century, particularly if the grain was wavy or curly. Ash and basswood were little used until the mid-19th century. Imported mahogany was introduced with English and American styles. Between 1650 and 1750, most furniture was stained a dark maroon, but after that period, almost all was painted, using powdered colours mixed with glue, linseed oil or skimmed milk, to seal the wood against dirt and grease. The colours were chiefly blue, green, pale or dark blue-green and white (tinted with yellow ochre or red ochre, very popular between 1785 and 1820). Iron and brass escutcheons, latches, handles, drawer pulls and fische hinges, often artistically designed, were made locally, usually on French patterns. The rattail or devil-tail hinge may have been adopted from England or New England, but was also current in Lorraine and Alsace.

Chests, the earliest and most basic form of storage, were of 2 types, flat topped (*coffres*) or dome topped (*bahuts*). They are simple, sturdy and generally made of pine, with corner posts and tongue-and-groove boards, the mortice-and-tenon joints secured with dowels. There may be panelling or geometric decoration. The lids are attached with strong hinges and close at the front with heavy locks, for everything was kept under lock and key.

Armoires and Buffets evolved naturally from the chest. Buffets, for storing food and dishes, were often 2 tiered, like 2 chests, one on top of the other, with doors instead of horizontal lids. Armoires, vertically extended buffets, are the most interesting of all rural furniture, for they lend themselves to the widest variety of style and decoration. They may have 1, 2 or 4 doors, most commonly 2 doors. Louis XIII designs (eg, lozenge panels) are typical in the early period. These motifs were followed but not entirely supplanted by Louis XV styles (eg, diamond points). Between 1785 and 1820, shaped and carved decoration of *rocaille* and every other inspiration abounded. Such decoration was particularly exuberant in the Montréal region, where most of the prosperous merchants lived. Elements of English design, notably of Adam inspiration, were sometimes pleasingly blended with French designs. All armoires were assembled with mortice-and-tenon joints, without glue. Large pieces could therefore be dismantled for moving. Variations include dressers, glazed buffets and corner cupboards. Food lockers with ventilation to keep food fresh tend to be primitive, as are bucket benches and most dough boxes.

Commodes In Canada the commode, which also evolved from the chest, was rare in 1750 but rapidly gained popularity. It was found mostly in the homes of the rich but also in rural houses. The early models were sturdy pieces with 3 or 4 drawers. Later, there were more refined models with rounded corners and shaped fronts, the most popular being the *arbalète* (crossbow) style, a serpentine outline with a recessed, flat plane in the centre. The corner uprights of these commodes were cut from a single massive piece of wood; the drawer fronts, from immensely thick boards shaped only on the outside. The inside was left flat, contrary to the practice in France. The draw-

Late 18th-century serpentine-fronted Québec commode, made of butternut in the Louis XV rococo style (*courtesy Royal Ontario Museum*).

ers were assembled with a huge dovetail on each side, as in France, and secured by a large, hand-forged nail. The feet are often of Louis XV cabriole style; however, after 1775, a popular design was the claw-and-ball foot of Chippendale inspiration. A very popular example of melded French and English design is the *arbalète* front combined with the claw-and-ball feet. Canadian commodes were always smaller than their French counterparts.

Beds in the early period were designed for privacy and protection from draughts. The *cabane* was a closed wooden box, lined with woolen cloth and with a straw mattress laid on planks. Four-poster beds with spiralled, turned or tapered columns were hung with curtains. In the early 19th century, as larger stoves were introduced, curtains were abandoned, the posts became shorter, and eventually spindle beds and sleigh beds appeared, as did folding and movable beds.

Tables usually have pine tops and hardwood legs and stretchers which, in fine pieces of the early period, are turned in the Louis XIII manner, often with finials (ie, decorative knobs). Many later pieces have cabriole legs. Aprons are often shaped and carved, and many have a drawer. Half-moon tables were common, but console tables were found only in churches and wealthy homes.

Desks were owned by the elite. The most common type was the slat-top *secrétaire,* although the earliest in existence is a knee-hole desk in the Louis XIII manner.

Chairs with backs were rare in the 17th- and 18th-century peasant homes in France, but were quite common in New France. The distinctive Île d'Orléans chair, jointed and usually with an open-frame back, was found in every house in the region of Île d'Orléans and Côte de Beaupré and was inspired by the Lorraine chair in France. Chairs termed "à-la-capucine" were found everywhere. They have high backs, straight or turned legs and shaped, ladder-back rails, dowelled firmly into the uprights. Armchairs appeared in the latter part of the 17th century in Louis XIII styles, often upholstered. With the popular "os-de-mouton" armchair of the 18th century, graceful curves succeeded the earlier straight lines. Many other armchairs demonstrate originality and inventiveness. Chair seats were made of twisted straw or marsh grass woven in a diamond-point pattern; plaited elm bark woven in a basket-weave pattern; or rawhide, popular in the Montréal region. Upholstery was covered in serge, tapestry, needlepoint, painted linen or moquette (a woolen pile fabric); cushions were widely used on chairs, attached by ribbons. The rocking chair came to Canada in the 19th century through American chairmakers and won instant popularity. French Canadian woodworkers created an infinite variety and decorated them with motifs of every inspiration.

These were the last innovations to enrich Canadian furniture of French derivation. After the 1820s, furniture in French styles soon ceased to be made. The thread of tradition and aesthetics was lost with the last generation of woodworkers trained in the French tradition, and the heritage was forgotten. It was brought to light about 1925 by a few discerning collectors, but it was not generally recognized until after the Second World War JEAN PALARDY

Québec pine armoire, in Burgundian style, late 18th or early 19th century (*courtesy Royal Ontario Museum*).

Furniture, German Furniture of Germanic derivation occurs in Canada as a result of emigration from Germany and from Pennsylvania (*see* GERMANS). Traditional German furniture in Europe evolved over several centuries to serve the needs of ordinary, primarily rural, people. The basic forms changed little through the years, although stylistic influences were adopted from fashionable furniture designs from time to time. The most important of these influences and, in fact, the dominant style of traditional German furniture in the 18th and 19th centuries was the baroque style, which inspired the complex intersecting curves in the design profiles and a profusion of decorative elements in surface treatment.

Traditional German furniture makers were excellent craftsmen, and even the most commonplace objects were carefully made, with well-fitted dovetail joints, crisp moldings, neat cutouts and pleasing proportions. The more ambitious and formal examples display excellent carving and inlay work. There were numerous centres of German settlement in early Canada, where skilled immigrant craftsmen made furniture in the traditional styles of the homeland. In NS, Germans arrived as early as 1749, and throughout the 19th century, thousands came to Ontario from the continent and from Pennsylvania. As the Prairie provinces developed, groups of MENNONITES and HUTTERITES found refuge there. The German settlements included members with a wide range of traditional skills; thus, the old traditions survived in many centres with little influence from the outside. Germanic furniture made in Canada includes a range of traditional forms which reflect several centuries of style and many regional characteristics. These traditional elements may be seen in combination with ideas adopted from the English-speaking community, especially in Pennsylvania-German furniture made in Ontario. The Pennsylvania Germans brought a furniture tradition which had been substantially altered as a result of their American experience. In particular, they had adopted the English Chippendale style in more formal furniture forms such as writing desks, chests of drawers and tall case clocks. Continental styles were retained in tables, benches, storage chests, cradles and other utilitarian furnishings. Similarly, the traditional German styles occurred, with various modifying influences, in other Canadian centres until mass-produced furniture largely replaced that of the local craftsman in the early 20th century. The most common forms in the German tradition are storage chests, tables, benches, chairs, cradles, beds, dish dressers, cupboards and *schrank*.

Storage Chests are, typically, simple rectangular forms. They may be plain or enriched by panels, moldings or turned details arranged in a geometric design. The base is sometimes intricately shaped or the chest might sit on bulbous turned feet.

Tables The most common design in dining tables was the sawbuck type, which has X-shaped trestles and a central stretcher supporting the tabletop. Most German country tables have a shaped cleat under the tabletop at each end, through which wooden pins are inserted to secure the top to the base; the top can be easily removed for cleaning.

Benches, the traditional seating form at these tables, were of simple plank construction on shaped trestles. The most popular type of chair was also of plank construction, with a shaped, often carved, back. The seat is a solid plank; the simple legs,

Dry sink, common in Pennsylvania German homes in Upper Canada during the early 19th century and until much later periods (*courtesy National Museums of Canada/Canadian Museum of Civilization*).

inserted into cleats under the seat, lack the stretchers (to strengthen the chair base) found in many country chair designs.

Beds and Cradles are often of panelled construction, or the profiles may be a complex arrangement of intersecting curves. Many German cradles feature distinctive heart-shaped cutouts at the head and foot, decorative elements that also serve as handles.

Dish Dressers with open shelves above and drawers and doors below were popular in country kitchens; wall cupboards and corner cupboards with glazed doors were used in the better rooms, particularly in urban houses. The recurring baroque influence is often apparent in these pieces in the complex curves and arches in the design of cornices and door panels.

Schrank, a large storage cupboard or wardrobe, is the most important form in the German furniture tradition and provided the craftsman with an opportunity to display his finest skills in creating elaborate panels, moldings and various surface treatments. The traditional schrank had 2 large doors, possibly 2 or more drawers below and different interior arrangements of hangers, shelves or drawers for storing clothing, linens, utensils, food or other household items. Because of its great size, the schrank was usually made in sections which could be separated for moving. Those used in the kitchen for food (*milchschrank*) have open grillwork in the doors for ventilation.

An attractive aspect of German traditional furniture, and further evidence of the baroque influence, is the extensive use of surface decoration employing various motifs including flowers, leaves, birds, stars, whorls, hearts and geometric designs, as well as names and dates in a calligraphic style. Often, the decoration commemorates a family event such as a wedding, anniversary or birth. These decorations may be painted in different polychrome techniques, carved into the surface or inlaid in contrasting wood tones. Furniture with painted decoration was usually made of softwood (eg, pine); inlaid or carved pieces were fashioned in hardwoods and were likely to be more sophisticated in style and execution. *See also* GERMANIC FRAKTUR. HOWARD PAIN

Furniture and Fixture Industry Canadian furniture originated with the first settlers and consisted of simple, handmade, utilitarian products. Later, local carpenters made furniture for others. The first Canadian furniture company was established in Berlin [Kitchener], Ont, in 1830; the next, in Toronto in 1834. The industry developed considerably in the last half of the 19th century, mainly in Ontario. There were a few factories in Québec before 1900, but the industry, particularly in the medium to low price ranges, developed there primarily after WWII.

Furniture is considered, in economic terms, an "elastic commodity," ie, very sensitive to economic changes. This sensitivity was obvious in the 1930s, when production fell by two-thirds between 1930 and 1933. In 1985 shipments totalled $3.4 billion, of which 55% was produced in Ontario, 30.3% in Québec, 8.5% in the Prairie provinces, 3.5% in BC and 1% in the Atlantic provinces.

Today the Canadian furniture industry is divided into 3 subsectors: household furniture, office furniture and miscellaneous furniture (ie, for restaurants, churches, schools, etc, and box springs and mattresses). The industry operates at 3 levels (manufacturers, distributors, retailers). Manufacturers transform raw materials into finished products. Distributors are agents or sales representatives who sell the finished product to the retailer. Because few manufacturers have large enough sales volumes in a region to justify full-time sales staff, sales representatives are usually free-lance agents representing several product lines. Retailers sell furniture to consumers.

The Modern Industry

The Canadian furniture industry is 97% Canadian owned and consists mainly of small or medium-sized family-owned and -operated firms. Automation strongly affected the industry in the early 1970s and was partly responsible for the decline in employment at that time. A small percentage of the industry's production remains at the "craftsman" stage.

In 1985 the industry employed nearly 50 000 people, with a total payroll of almost $969 million. Work-force numbers include more than 42 600 production workers, 7300 working owners and clerical and administrative employees. The average wage for production workers was about $8.11 an hour in 1985. The industry is largely unionized, particularly in the case-goods (ie, wooden) subsector.

In 1985 there were 1727 furniture plants in Canada: 714 in Ontario, 669 in Québec, 159 in the Prairie provinces, 143 in BC and 39 in the Atlantic provinces. Nearly 50% of the major manufacturers are located in rural areas. In 1985 the industry consumed over $1.6 billion in supplies and materials (ie, nearly 46% of the value of Canadian furniture sales) and some $48 million in fuel and electricity. Raw materials included wood in all forms (over 30% of materials used in furniture manufacturing), furniture frames, rubber and plastics, textiles, plastified fabrics, steel and metal, paints, lacquers, sealers and varnishes, and miscellaneous materials (eg, mirrors, packaging, hardware).

In 1985 factory shipments of furniture and fixtures totalled $3.4 billion: the household sector accounted for $11.5 billion; office sector, $846 million; miscellaneous furniture, $1.1 billion. The type of production varies among regions. Québec accounts for almost 50% of case-goods production; Ontario produces much upholstered and office furniture. Exports of household, office and miscellaneous furniture and fixtures combined totalled $668 million, while imports totalled $432 million. In the household furniture sector, however, exports in 1985 totalled a mere $182 million while imports came to $312 million. Thus the household-furniture subsector accounts for approximately 72% of imports and 27% of exports in all categories. Canada's total furniture production in 1985 accounted for 0.72% of the Canadian Gross Domestic Product ($476 361 million in current dollars).

The industry is affected by federal pollution-control legislation. Air pollution from paint and lacquer fumes is the most frequently cited environmental problem. Safety-related legislation has been passed on mattress flammability, light fixtures and children's furniture (eg, lead content in paint, sharp edges).

The industry has received federal and provincial aid (eg, for expansion programs, development of microprocessor data, industrial renewal, energy conservation, market development), but none of these measures are specific to the furniture industry. As a result of the FREE TRADE agreement signed between Canada and the US in Oct 1987, total tariff reductions on furniture will span a 5-year period, commencing 1 Jan 1989.

The Canadian furniture industry often finds it difficult to compete with other countries. Labour costs are much higher than in most competing countries – particularly the US, the source of most furniture imports. Canadian companies also have high transportation costs: it has been estimated that in 1978 Canadian furniture transportation costs exceeded US costs by as much as 40%. Because of the decreasing value of the Canadian dollar, imports to Canada of certain raw materials (eg, textiles, exotic woods) have increased dramatically. Finally, Canada's mostly small- and medium-sized companies have difficulty competing with American firms that have a much larger production capacity and thus can achieve economies of scale.

Two colleges offer courses on furniture production: l'École québécoise du meuble et du bois ouvré in Victoriaville, and Conestoga College in Ontario. Several colleges and universities offer courses or programs in INDUSTRIAL DESIGN and some in woodworking. There are 3 industry associations: the Québec Furniture Manufacturers' Assn Inc (Québec and the Maritimes); the Ontario Furniture Manufacturers' Assn Inc (Ont); Furniture West Inc (Prairie provinces and BC). These trade associations have formed the Canadian Council of Furniture Manufacturers to represent the interests of the industry nationally. There are 4 major Canadian furniture trade magazines: *Canada's Furniture Magazine* (Victor Publishing Co Ltd) and *Home Goods Retailing* (MACLEAN HUNTER LTD) for household furnishings; *Canada's Contract Magazine* (Victor Publishing Co Ltd) and *Canadian Interiors* (Maclean Hunter Ltd) for office and contract furnishings. LISE BUISSON

Fury and Hecla Strait is located at the northern end of FOXE BASIN, connecting the basin with the Gulf of BOOTHIA, and separating Melville Peninsula on the mainland and Baffin Island to the N. It is 190 km long and as it is only about 50 km wide it is very often jammed with ice. The strait was discovered in July 1822 by William Parry and it naturally aroused interest as a possible link in the NORTHWEST PASSAGE; Parry's way was blocked by ice but a land reconnaissance confirmed that the strait led to open water. Parry named the strait for his ships, HMS *Fury* and HMS *Hecla*. Joseph Bernier attempted to traverse the strait in 1911, but was also prevented by heavy ice.

JAMES MARSH

Gaboury, Étienne-Joseph, architect (b at Swan Lake, Man 24 Apr 1930). Gaboury's strong links to the prairie landscape and the Franco-Manitobain community of his youth are reflected in his architecture. He was educated at St-Boniface Coll, U Man (B Arch, 1958) and the École des beaux-arts, Paris (where the late work of Le Corbusier influenced him strongly). After apprenticing in Manitoba, Gaboury formed a partnership with Denis Lussier and Frank Sigurdson, and since 1976 has been principal of his own Winnipeg-based firm. An important early building was the 1968 Precious Blood Church, St-Boniface, a strikingly mystical church notable for its double helix of beams spiralling above the altar. Gaboury has worked in a variety of other idioms, including the high-tech Royal Canadian Mint near Winnipeg (1978) and the hybrid Canadian-Mexican regionalism of the Canadian Embassy in Mexico City (1982). Gaboury's designs are linked by a concern with landscape, texture and cultural identity, and the manipulation and celebration of sunlight. TREVOR BODDY

Gage, Thomas, army officer (b in Eng 1719 or 1720; d at London, Eng 2 Apr 1787). He served during the SEVEN YEARS' WAR in N America from 1755 and was present during several of the operations preceding the CONQUEST in 1760. He was then installed as military governor of Montréal, where, like fellow governors James MURRAY and Ralph BURTON, he attempted to reconcile the Canadians to British rule by retaining existing customs as much as possible and by introducing useful innovations such as his use of captains of militia in the administration of justice. In 1763 Gage replaced Jeffery AMHERST as commander-in-chief at New York City, where he was primarily concerned with growing tensions in the Thirteen Colonies. In 1774 he also became governor of Massachusetts, but his initial optimism faded as he recognized the strength of opposition to British policies. His increasingly gloomy reports caused his recall soon after the outbreak of hostilities in 1775. STUART R.J. SUTHERLAND

Gagetown, NB, Village, pop 635 (1986c), 618 (1981c), is situated on Gagetown Creek, adjacent to the SAINT JOHN R and opposite the mouth of the Jemseg R. English settlement began soon after Robert MONCKTON'S expedition cleared the French from the lower Saint John Valley in 1758. By the time the LOYALISTS arrived in 1783 Grimross, as it was then known, had a population of some 200. It was laid out in grid pattern as a possible site for the provincial capital, but Gov Carleton chose St Anne's [Fredericton] and Gagetown became the shire-town of Queens County. During the 19th century it was the most important centre between Fredericton and SAINT JOHN and a prosperous farming and lumbering community. The establishment of GAGETOWN CFB after WWII stripped the village of its hinterland, and the abolition of county government in the 1960s deprived it of its importance as the shire-town. Although the village now lacks an important industry, it remains a viable community. JAMES K. CHAPMAN

Gagetown CFB functions primarily as the combat-training centre for the Canadian Army and comprises 111 000 ha between Fredericton and Saint John, NB, west of the Saint John R. Named after a nearby town, it is roughly egg shaped, with the permanent campsite at the northern tip. About 3000 soldiers are posted at the base, but the number of additional, temporary postings for combined arms (infantry, armour, artillery, air support) combat training varies greatly. The base was constructed in the early 1950s when Canada's NATO commitments required a location large enough for training an entire division. The federal

government chose this site partly to provide needed economic stimulus to central NB and because fewer than 3000 people would be displaced in expropriating the land. Militarily it offered nearness to an all-weather Atlantic port and a varied terrain – including open lands similar to northern Europe, swamps, dense forest and high hills. American and British forces have also used the base. BILL SMITH

Gagnon, André, pianist, composer, conductor, arranger (b at St-Pacôme-de-Kamouraska, Qué 2 Aug 1942). Despite the eclecticism of his compositions and interpretations, Gagnon has created for himself an easily identifiable style, a mixture of light and classical music. He studied with Léon Destroismaisons (theory), Germaine Malépart (piano), Clermont PÉPIN (composition) and, in Paris, with Yvonne Loriod (piano). Early in his career, he worked as accompanist, conductor or arranger for such artists as Claude LÉVEILLÉE, Pauline JULIEN, Renée CLAUDE and Monique LEYRAC. After 1969 he concentrated on composition, arrangements and his career as a soloist. He won Juno awards for his records *Saga* (1974) and *Neiges* (1975) and as best instrumentalist (1977). His *Petit concerto pour Carignan et orchestre* (1976) has been performed by Yehudi Menuhin and Jean Carignan. He composed *Mad Shadows* (1977) for the National Ballet, after a novel by Marie-Claire Blais; it has been performed at Covent Garden and the Metropolitan among other places. In 1979 his record *Le Saint-Laurent* was chosen the best instrumental record of the year during the ADISQ gala. He toured Australia and Japan in 1987. HÉLÈNE PLOUFFE

Gagnon, Charles, painter, photographer, filmmaker (b at Montréal 23 May 1934). He spent the years 1955-60 in New York studying, painting in an abstract expressionist style, and photographing neglected or abandoned parts of the city. He returned to Montréal in 1960. He made his first films in the mid-1960s and has continued to work in a range of media. He undertook a large commission for the Christian Pavilion at EXPO 67, as well as a mural for the Lester B. Pearson Building in Ottawa. The latter, titled *Screenspace,* is a text painting based on the late prime minister's writings. DAVID BURNETT

Reading: Philip Fry, *Charles Gagnon* (1978).

Gagnon, Clarence, engraver, painter (b at Montréal 8 Nov 1881; d there 5 Jan 1942). After studying at the École normale du Plateau in Montréal, he received his artistic training from the painter William BRYMNER at the Art Assn of Montreal 1897-1900. The generosity of art patron James Morgan allowed him to go to Paris and study in the studio of painter Jean-Paul Laurens. Gagnon distinguished himself early in his career by the quality of his engravings, and won a gold medal at the St Louis Exhibition in 1904 and an honourable mention the following year at the Salon des artistes français in Paris. Returning to Canada 1909, he divided his time between Montréal and Baie-St-Paul. He became a member of the Royal Society of Canada and later he was elected associate of the Royal Canadian Academy of Arts and, in 1923, received the Trevor Prize of the Salmagundi Club of New York. He illustrated *Le Grand Silence blanc* (1929) and the deluxe edition of Louis Hémon's *Maria Chapdelaine* (1933). Upon his return from a second stay in France, 1922-36, U de Montréal awarded him an honorary doctorate. MICHEL CHAMPAGNE

Gagnon, Ernest, folklorist, organist (b Frédéric-Ernest-Amédée at Rivière-du-Loup [Louiseville], Qué 7 Nov 1834; d at Québec City 15 Sept 1915). Member of a prominent Québec City musical family, Gagnon is most noted for his work as a collector of French Canadian FOLK MUSIC. His song transcriptions, published 1865-67 as *Chansons populaires du Canada,* not only helped conserve a rich heritage, but alerted the musical world to the dignity and beauty of Québec's oral song tradition. Gagnon was also an expert plainsong accompanist and virtuoso organist at St-Jean-Baptiste Church 1853-64 and at the Québec Basilica 1864-76. BARCLAY MCMILLAN

Gagnon, Jean-Louis, journalist, writer, political activist, civil servant (b at Québec C 21 Feb 1913). He had a classical education at the colleges of Sainte-Marie and Brébeuf in Montréal and at U of Ottawa. As a journalist during the 1930s he propounded anti-clerical ideas, then right-wing separatism in Paul Bouchard's *La Nation*, followed by international socialism. The war, however, turned Gagnon into a lifelong liberal-democrat and a strong Canadian federalist. He favoured Canada's participation in WWII and was a supporter of CONSCRIPTION during the 1942 plebiscite. He was in Ghana 1942-43 as a journalist, from 1943 to 1946 was head of the news agency France-Afrique in Montréal and then followed 3 years in Rio de Janeiro.

Returning to Canada in 1949, Gagnon worked for CKAC radio, where he organized a union local for journalists and established ties with the Québec Liberal Party. He was one of the founding members of the Fédération libérale provinciale, created in 1955 to democratize the structure of the provincial Liberal Party and to allow the modernization of party policy. In 1958 Gagnon accepted an offer to become editor-in-chief of Montréal's largest francophone daily, *La Presse*. He assembled a dynamic editorial team, whose support of the modernization of Québec society contributed to the narrow victory of Jean LESAGE's Liberal Party in June 1960, a victory which ushered in the QUIET REVOLUTION.

Fearful of the rise of separatism, Gagnon agreed in 1963 to become a member of the Royal Commission on BILINGUALISM AND BICULTURALISM, and when André Laurendeau died prematurely in June 1968, Gagnon replaced him as co-president. In 1970 Gagnon was appointed director general of Information Canada, which had been created to lead the struggle for the preservation of Canadian unity. Between 1972 and 1976 he was Canada's ambassador and permanent delegate at UNESCO in Paris, and he ended his career as a member of the Canadian Radio-television and Telecommunications Commission 1976-83. Gagnon received many awards, acknowledging his many journalistic achievements and his avid support for the arts, and was made a fellow of the Royal Society of Canada (1971) and an Officer of the Order of Canada (1980). The first volume of his memoirs, *Les Apostasies: Les Coqs de village*, appeared in 1985. M.D. BEHIELS

Gagnon, Wilfrid, businessman (b at Montréal 15 Sept 1898; d there 10 June 1963). A graduate of Montréal's Collège Sainte-Marie, Gagnon joined his family's shoe-manufacturing firm, Aird and Son Ltd, becoming president in 1926. In 1936 he was minister of commerce and industry in Premier GODBOUT's Liberal government. During WWII he became a DOLLAR-A-YEAR-MAN in Ottawa's Department of Munitions and Supply, playing an important role in industrial mobilization. He was created a CBE in 1948. Building on his business experience and wartime acquaintance with E.P. TAYLOR, Gagnon assumed senior positions in over 25 financial, manufacturing, retail and natural-resource enterprises. He was chairman of Banque canadienne nationale, Dow Brewery Ltd and Canadian Aviation Electronics; president of Narwil Shoes Ltd and Wilmont Shoes Ltd; director of, among others, the CNR, Trans-Canada Airlines and Argus Corp; and governor of the U de Montréal. J. LINDSEY

Galaxy Stars are not distributed uniformly throughout the universe but are usually found in giant aggregations, known as galaxies, that are classified, according to their shapes, as spiral, elliptical or irregular. Earth's own galaxy is a large and probably typical spiral. Its most obvious component is an immense, flat rotating system of stars estimated to be about 100 000 light-years (some 10^{18} km) across. Serious attempts to estimate the size of the galaxy began in the 19th century. The early pioneers failed to appreciate its true immensity, partly because they did not recognize the existence of dust and gas between the STARS, which absorb starlight on its way to Earth and prevent us from seeing the farthest reaches of our own galaxy. The application of photography to ASTRONOMY made it possible to accumulate data about apparent changes in the relative positions of stars (ie, proper motions) much more rapidly, and SPECTROSCOPY enabled astronomers to study velocities of stars along the line of sight (radial velocities). Thus, it became possible to study not only the structure of the galaxy but also its dynamics. A classic study was made by J.S. PLASKETT and J.A. PEARCE at the Dominion Astrophysical Observatory, Victoria. The results, published in 1935, gave the best available idea of the size, structure and rotation of the galaxy until the advent of radio astronomy after WWII (*see* OBSERVATORY). The explosive development of astronomical knowledge in the last 2 decades inevitably led to revisions. This study also helped astronomer C.S. BEALS to develop greater understanding of interstellar matter.

There are estimated to be about 100 million galaxies in the observable universe. Many are powerful emitters of radio waves and study of their emissions has increased our knowledge of the universe. Most powerful and puzzling of all are the quasars, now generally believed to be very distant extragalactic objects, but the real nature of which is not yet understood. *See also* BLACK HOLE.

Galbraith, John Kenneth, economist, writer (b at Iona Station, Ont, 15 Oct 1908). Having graduated from Ontario Agricultural Coll (Guelph) in 1931, Galbraith received a doctorate in agricultural economics at U of Calif, Berkeley. Most of his active life was spent connected with Harvard, where postdoctoral work at Cambridge, Eng, had fitted him to replace Robert BRYCE as resident Keynesian. An activist liberal, Galbraith was personal adviser to every Democratic candidate for the US presidency from F.D. Roosevelt to L.B. Johnson and thus held a number of public positions including controller of prices in WWII and US ambassador to India (1961-63). He was active in Americans for Democratic Action, a group of eminent liberal intellectuals, particularly during its opposition to the Vietnam War.

John Kenneth Galbraith, one of the world's best-known economists, wrote an entertaining account of his boyhood in southern Ontario (*courtesy Canapress Photo Service*).

Galbraith's contribution to social science is an alternative to the established, neoclassical concept of capitalism. In a number of books, including *American Capitalism* (1952), *The Affluent Society* (1958) and *The New Industrial State* (1967), he established a basis for liberal policy on the ideas of "countervailing power," "conventional wisdom," the "technostructure" and the institutional "convergence" of communist and capitalist systems. In 1956 he testified before the Royal Commission on CANADA'S ECONOMIC PROSPECTS and, at the request of CANADIAN PACIFIC, he watched over the production of R.E. Caves and R.H. Holton on *Canadian Economy: Prospect and Retrospect* (1959). *The Scotch*, Galbraith's entertaining account of his boyhood environment in southern Ontario, was published in 1964. His *Age of Uncertainty* (1977) was televised in a series on BBC. He is the author of *Anatomy of Power* and *A View from the Stands: Of People, Military Power and the Arts* (1986). ROBIN F. NEILL

Reading: J.K. Galbraith, *A Life in Our Times* (1981).

Galiano Island, 5787 ha, is one of BC's GULF IS, named for Spanish navy commander Dionisio Galiano, who explored the area 1792. It has the driest climate of the islands. Shell middens at Montague Harbour suggest that Salish have used the island for several thousand years. Settled by immigrants during the 1858 BC gold rush, the island became known as "Little England" because British families sent sons there to learn farming. Most settled at the S end; much of its narrow length was set aside for timber production. The island is now best known for its colony of writers, craftsmen and artists. PETER GRANT

Gallagher, John Patrick, "Jack," geologist, industrialist (b at Winnipeg 16 July 1916). After working as a student geologist in the NWT and graduating from U of Man, he spent 11 years, starting 1938, as a petroleum geologist exploring for oil for Shell Oil, Standard Oil of New Jersey and Imperial Oil, in California, Egypt, S America and western Canada. In 1950 he established a firm that later became DOME PETROLEUM, with initial financing of $250 000 in equity and $7.7 million in loans, backed by Dome Mines and the endowment funds of several American universities. Dome made promising discoveries of oil at Drumheller and gas in the Provost field in Alberta, but Gallagher's real interest was in the Canadian Arctic, where, with its partners, Dome spent hundreds of millions of dollars drilling in the BEAUFORT SEA, finding several deposits of oil and gas that would, however, require billions of dollars to be brought into production. In the late 1970s Dome began unprecedented expansion and, after accumulating debts of some $7 billion, was forced to sell many of its assets. The sale of Dome itself was under negotiation late in 1987. Gallagher resigned as chairman of the board and CEO in 1983. Since 1984 he has been chairman of Parma Petroleum Ltd. EARLE GRAY

Gallant, Mavis Leslie, née Young, writer (b at Montréal 11 Aug 1922). An only child of mismatched parents, Gallant was raised virtually as an orphan. From the age of 4 she attended 17 different schools – public, convent and boarding – and her formative years were characterized by upheaval and the trauma of rejection. Her father died while she was a youngster, and her mother rapidly remarried; subsequently, Gallant was sent to live with a guardian in the eastern US. On completing her education she returned to Canada, where she did a brief stint in the cutting room of the National Film Board before becoming a feature reporter for the *Montreal Standard* in 1944. While a journalist, she married John Gallant, a musician from Winnipeg, but they soon divorced. Gallant began writing fiction in Canada, publishing stories in *Preview* (1944), the *Standard Magazine* (1946) and *Northern Review* (1950). But in 1950, determined to write fiction full time, she courageously departed for Europe, finally settling in Paris, where she still resides. Gallant achieved her ambition quickly; since 1951, she has published more than 100 stories, most of which first appeared in the *New Yorker* magazine, where she continues to publish; they are collected, along with several novellas, in *The Other Paris* (1956), *My Heart Is Broken* (1964), *The Pegnitz Junction* (1973), *The End of the World and Other Stories* (1974) and *From the Fifteenth District: A Novella and Eight Stories* (1979).

Gallant's vibrant, flawless prose, often presented in a detached ironic tone, carries a highly visual quality, and her sharply delineated characters are routinely set within a truthfully rendered specific time and place. While it is difficult to generalize about her prodigious output, it seems that, perhaps because of her own troubled childhood, she is frequently drawn to the plight of frightened, lonely children and adolescents, and writes compassionately of their anguish. Another recurring focus is on expatriates – English, American or Canadian – who have been displaced from their cultural milieu through choice or circumstance; lacking a clear sense of direction, they are adrift as permanent tourists, eking out miserable lives in run-down European hotels and *pensions*. In her 2 novels, *Green Water, Green Sky* (1959) and *A Fairly Good Time* (1970), similar patterns are evoked, with characters perpetually in transit. Always fascinated by varieties of exile and intensely interested in politics, Gallant has also written compelling stories about Germans who found themselves strangers in their homeland after WWII.

Neglected for a long time in Canada, Gallant has finally gained recognition here. In 1981 she was appointed an Officer of the Order of Canada, and in 1982 Toronto's Tarragon Theatre premiered her first play, *What Is To Be Done?* In the same year, *Home Truths: Selected Canadian Stories* (1981) won the Governor General's Award. This collection of stories about young Canadians at home and abroad concludes with the 6 linked "Montréal Stories," which are as close as Gallant has come to a precise evocation of her childhood and her youthful wartime experiences during Montréal's "two solitudes." In 1983-84, Gallant returned to Canada to take up the post as writer-in-residence at U of Toronto, and in 1984 she received the Canada-Australia literary prize.

Mavis Gallant, Canadian expatriate writer, in May 1946 (*courtesy National Archives of Canada/PA-115248/G. Scorras*).

Gallant also speaks with an authoritative voice about her adopted homeland. In the collection *Overhead in a Balloon: Stories of Paris* (1985) she depicts French life in the postwar period. Displaying a great gift for nonfiction, she has also written an impressive body of reviews and essays on French culture and society, most notably a lucid, sympathetic introduction to *The Affair of Gabrielle Russier* (1971) and a graphic, eyewitness account of the 1968 Paris student riots. These latter works of nonfiction, initially published in the *New Yorker*, are now collected in *Paris Notebooks: Essays and Reviews* (1986). Since the early 1970s Gallant has been working on a biography of Alfred Dreyfus.

DONNA COATES

Reading: The entire issue of *Canadian Fiction Magazine* 28 (1978) is devoted to Gallant.

Gallicanism, primarily a theory about the proper relationship between church and state. In NEW FRANCE this relationship was governed by a web of traditions and usages that defined the status of the French church, both within the secular kingdom and within the universal church. Gallicanism's major characteristics included a certain defiance of the papacy, the defence of Gallic freedoms (which discounted the idea of absolute papal authority, in temporal or spiritual matters, over the French king and church), and the desire to ensure the Crown's full power even in the spiritual domain. After the CONQUEST, and especially in the 19th century, Gallicanism became a theory with 2 groups of supporters: those who did not believe in papal infallibility or saw no need to accept it as dogma; and those who halfheartedly accepted a degree of state intervention in traditionally church-controlled domains such as education, marriage and the keeping of registries.

Gallicanism flourished in New France in the latter part of the 17th century, when Intendant Jean TALON and Gov FRONTENAC sought to reduce overwhelming religious influence and make the church obey the state. A modus vivendi was quickly reached, guaranteeing a certain autonomy to the church while permitting some state intervention, even in such purely religious questions as the life of religious communities. However, after 1760, having assured its survival and won for itself a degree of freedom, Canadian CATHOLICISM rethought the division of religious and civil power. Two tendencies appeared after 1840. On the one hand, ULTRAMONTANES supported the supremacy of the church and its prior right in education, the legislation of marriage, and all joint domains. On the other, those who modified these claims to any degree or defended the rights of the state were called Gallicans – a title that included groups such as the Sulpicians; lawyers such as George-Étienne CARTIER, Rodolphe Laflamme and Joseph DOUTRE; and Université Laval professors such as Jacques Crémazie and Charles-François Langelier. Soon, however, extreme ultramontanes threw the epithet "Gallican" at anyone who did not think the way they did; Gallicanism as such existed to some degree but merged with Catholic liberalism, which was similarly denounced until the end of the 19th century.

NIVE VOISINE

Gallie, William Edward, surgeon, educator (born at Barrie, Ont 29 Jan 1882; d at Toronto 25 Sept 1959). He matriculated from Barrie Collegiate Institute in 1899 and received his MD from U of T in 1903. He spent the next 2 years interning in Toronto at the Hospital for Sick Children and Toronto General Hospital. A third year was spent at the Hospital for the Ruptured and Crippled in New York. Dr. Gallie and his associates made widely accepted contributions in the areas of tendon fixation, repair of bone and the transplantation of tissue as "living sutures." He held appointments at the Hospital for Sick Children and Toronto General Hospital, advancing to being surgeon-in-chief at both these institutions. He served as chairman of the department of surgery (1929-47) and as dean of medicine (1936-46) at U of T. As chairman of surgery at U of T, he instituted in 1931 an organized training program for surgeons in Canada, which became known as the Gallie Course in Surgery.

DONALD R. WILSON

The common gallinule (*Gallinula chloropus*), also called moorhen (*artwork by Claire Tremblay*).

Gallinule, common name for some marsh-dwelling birds of the RAIL family (Rallidae), now also known as moorhens. Six genera, with around 14 species, occur worldwide. Several island-dwelling species are becoming rare. The common gallinule or common moorhen (*Gallinula chloropus*) breeds in a small area in southeastern Ontario and nearby Québec and has occurred in Manitoba. It resembles the COOT but has a bright red bill and forehead, green legs and lobeless toes. Like the coot, it pumps its head when swimming. Like coots, gallinules are often colonial; their nests are similar. The gallinule lays 9-12 buff eggs, spotted with dark brown. Common gallinules often betray their presence by loud, henlike cackling. The purple gallinule (*Porphyrula martinica*) breeds in southeastern US southward; its occurrence in eastern Canada is only casual.

E. KUYT

Post office, Galt [now Cambridge], Ont (*courtesy National Archives of Canada/PA-31834*).

Galt, Ont, City, inc 1915, located on the Grand R 90 km W of Toronto. It was established around 1817 by William Dickson, a lawyer and merchant from Niagara-on-the-Lake. He engaged Absalom Shade, a Pennsylvanian Dutch carpenter, to build the townsite and mill and so it became known as Shade's Mill. In 1827 it was renamed Galt after John GALT, the Scottish novelist and colonizer who founded the CANADA CO. It was a centre of Scottish settlement in Upper Canada. The first macadamized road in UC linked it to Hamilton in 1837. The Grand R provided abundant water power and during the 19th century Galt was a significant manufacturing centre. In 1973 it formed part of the new city of CAMBRIDGE.

DANIEL FRANCIS

Galt, Sir Alexander Tilloch, politician, promoter (b at London, Eng 6 Sept 1817; d at Montréal 19 Sept 1893). Galt emigrated to Canada in 1835 to work for the British American Land Co, which was opening land for settlement in Québec's Eastern Townships. As he rose in the company, Galt saw the advantages for the area of a railway link to the ocean, and he became president of the ST LAWRENCE AND ATLANTIC RAILROAD in 1849. Galt was no exception to the rule that railway promoters — in search of state subsidies and bond guarantees — often entered politics, and he represented Sherbrooke in the legislature of the PROVINCE OF CANADA (1849-50, 1853-67). A Liberal, Galt voted against the REBELLION LOSSES BILL and supported the demand for ANNEXATION to the US (1849). In 1858 he introduced a resolution calling for a federal union of all the British N American colonies, and he joined the reconstructed Cartier-Macdonald ministry of DOUBLE-SHUFFLE fame that year as finance minister after being promised support for his union proposal. His revenue tariff of 1859, which provided "incidental" protection to Canadian manufacturers aroused protest from British manufacturers, but Galt argued that without the right to set its own tariffs, a colony did not enjoy self-government. Galt, a member of the GREAT COALITION Cabinet, attended the QUÉBEC CONFERENCE in 1864 and was a Canadian delegate to England in 1865 and 1866. He resigned from the Cabinet in 1866 when he failed to obtain the education guarantees he had promised to Québec Protestants. After Confederation he joined the first federal Cabinet as minister of finance, but was forced to resign in Nov 1867 over the failure of the Commercial Bank of Kingston.

He retired from Parliament in 1871, having opposed the Conservatives but being unwilling to support the Liberals. Galt was knighted for his services on the commission to settle the question of American payment for access to Canadian fisheries, as arranged by the Treaty of WASHINGTON. He was the first high commissioner of Canada in London 1880-83, appointed to promote interest in financing Canadian railways, buying Canadian products, and emigration to the Canadian North-West. While in London, Galt furthered his own plans to develop coal fields that his son Elliott had discovered in southern Alberta while serving as assistant Indian commissioner. With the backing of London businessmen and federal land grants, Galt incorporated the North Western Coal and Navigation Co, and began operations near Lethbridge. The successful business was sold to the CANADIAN PACIFIC RAILWAY in 1910. Truly, "the life of Alexander Galt is a history of Canada in the 19th century." MARGARET E. MCCALLUM

Galt, John, novelist, colonial promoter (b at Irvine, Scot 2 May 1779; d at Greenock, Scot 11 Apr 1839). While struggling to survive as a man of letters, Galt became involved with Canadian affairs, first as agent for those claiming losses in the WAR OF 1812, and subsequently (1824) as secretary of the board of directors of the CANADA CO. He came to Upper Canada on several occasions, remaining 1826-29 as company superintendent and founding the town of GUELPH in 1827; the town of Galt (now CAMBRIDGE) was named after him. He had continual conflict with the directors and was eventually recalled and spent his last years in impoverished ill health. Galt's best-known fiction deals mainly with Scottish life, and his writings, except for his *Autobiography* (1833) and *Literary Life* (1834), show only a limited influence of his Canadian involvements. Two of his novels embody his idea of emigrants best suited to the US (*Lawrie Todd,* 1830) and Canada (*Bogle Corbet,* 1831). J.M. BUMSTED

Gamache, Louis-Olivier, an inhabitant of Île d'ANTICOSTI who had a reputation as a man who sold his soul to the devil and had supernatural powers. He was referred to as a pirate and it was said that, when pursued, he escaped by causing his ship to turn into a ball of fire. NANCY SCHMITZ

Gambling is the betting of something of value on the outcome of a contingency or event, the result of which is uncertain and may be determined by chance, skill, a combination of chance and skill, or a contest. Long before John Cabot's voyage to Canada in 1497, gambling was popular among native people. While many of the native games from the past are now recalled only as a part of cultural history, native people used gaming sticks for centuries before the arrival of the Europeans and the decks of playing cards they brought with them.

For the past century or so the most popular gambling games have been the card games of poker, stook and blackjack, and the dice games of craps and barbotte. During the KLONDIKE GOLD RUSH, the game of Faro, played with a regular deck of cards, was popular. The origins of Faro can be traced to the German game of "landsquenet," which was played as early as 1400. Faro was introduced by American gamblers in areas such as Dawson City, Yukon, where fortunes were won and lost on the turn of a card. When the gold rush ended, so did the popularity of Faro in Canada, although its popularity has survived in the US. (The name has also survived in the name of the town of FARO, YT.) Since its original enactment in 1892, the Canadian CRIMINAL CODE, following the English common law, has tolerated gambling under certain conditions. A 1910 amendment allowed pari-mutuel (from "Paris mutuel") betting. This form of betting, in which winners divide losers' stakes and a cut of the bet goes to the track, to the horsemen and the state, became the official and legal form of betting in France in 1894. The amendment also allowed occasional games of chance where profits were used for charitable or religious purposes. A few games were also permitted at agricultural fairs and exhibitions.

Gambling laws, although amended from time to time, remained relatively unchanged until 1970, when sweeping changes to the Criminal Code gave the provinces the authority to license and regulate gambling, with a few exceptions. Some forms of gambling are now operated in some provinces. Casinos operate in Calgary and Edmonton under licence, with proceeds going to charity. The Manitoba Lotteries Foundation, a crown agency, operates casinos in that province which, in addition to offering blackjack and roulette, also offer the only Pai Gou games in Canada, along with several other casino games. Other provinces are studying regulated versus government-operated casino models. The 1970 changes have resulted in the creation of a multi-billion-dollar gambling industry throughout Canada. The provincial governments are now actively involved in operating LOTTERIES. A large number of charitable and religious groups have come to rely upon gaming revenues for annual budgetary obligations. Agricultural Exhibitions and fairs derive substantial profits from gambling activity during annual celebrations. Pari-mutuel racetrack betting has long been a popular pastime; in 1984 Canadians bet $1.64 billion at racetracks across Canada (*see* THOROUGHBRED RACING).

Sports betting, by far the most popular form of illegal gambling, generates large profits for the bookmakers, and is the largest source of gambling revenue of ORGANIZED CRIME. Illegal private gaming houses can be found in every major Canadian city. Swindlers, using a variety of cheating techniques, are common in gaming houses and are also active in legally operated private gambling establishments but almost never attract the attention of law enforcement. Illegal gambling is generally perceived as a "victimless crime" and is not one for which the police receive many complaints. Unlike other crimes, modern illegal gambling is tolerated, and there is no public pressure exerted to control it. Its existence and continual growth has seemingly had no effect on the legal gambling market. At the same time, liberalization of legal gambling activities since 1970 appears to have had no effect on illegal gambling.

During the past 80 years gambling in Canada has evolved from an activity socially tolerated only within narrow restraints to a broadly acceptable leisure-time activity. The social, legal and economic consequences of these activities have yet to be chronicled. R. RONALD SHEPPARD

Reading: W. Fadington, ed, *Gambling and Society* (1976); R. Herman, *Gamblers and Gambling* (1976); A. Waller, *The Gamblers* (1976).

Gambo, Nfld, Town, pop 2723 (1986c), inc 1980, is an amalgamation of 3 communities – Dark Cove, Middle Brook and Gambo (inc 1963) – stretching along the shore at the end of Freshwater Bay, a long indraft of Bonavista Bay. Gambo, whose name is from the Portuguese *gama*, doe, or more likely from "gambo," a sledge to haul timber, first appears in the 1857 census and thereafter grew as a major lumbering, sawmilling and salmon-fishing centre. In the 1860s David Smallwood (grandfather of Joseph SMALLWOOD) began a sizable sawmill which became the first in Newfoundland powered by steam. After the trans-insular railway reached Gambo in the 1890s, the town became a link between coastal boats and the rail line. Residents continued to be employed cutting or processing timber products for other local mills and for large paper companies until a series of forest fires (especially in 1961) consumed most of the remaining stands. On the route of the Trans-Canada Highway and the railway, and at the start of the highway to northern Bonavista Bay, it continues to be a major regional service centre. ROBERT D. PITT

Game Bird, any bird that is hunted, excluding WATERFOWL; 25 species now occur in Canada. Game birds are hunted because they are good to eat and are challenging to the hunter. Most are shot by walking hunters, who sometimes use pointing or retrieving dogs. Sandhill CRANES, band-tailed PIGEONS and mourning doves may be shot from blinds. The wild turkey (family Meleagrididae) disappeared from Ont around 1902 but has been introduced locally in Ont, Man, Sask and Alta. Eight members of the GROUSE family are found in Canada: spruce grouse in coniferous forest everywhere except PEI, introduced to Nfld; blue grouse in coniferous forest and savannah in Alta, BC, YT and southwestern NWT; sage grouse in southern Alta and Sask and formerly BC on sagebrush range; ruffed grouse everywhere in deciduous forests, introduced into Nfld; sharp-tailed grouse in open and brushy habitat in muskeg and grassland W of the James Bay region, Que, to BC; white-tailed PTARMIGAN in alpine areas of the West; rock ptarmigan in tundra and alpine habitats in BC, YT, NWT, Qué and Nfld; willow ptarmigan in tundra, shrub-tundra and alpine habitats in BC, YT, NWT, Man, Ont, Qué, Nfld and, in winter, in northern Alta and Sask; introduced to NS. The greater prairie chicken, formerly found on the prairies and in Ont, has almost disappeared.

The only native PHEASANT is northern bobwhite, found in bushy and agricultural land in Ont. It has been introduced successfully to BC and unsuccessfully to Man and Alta. California and mountain quail, introduced to southern BC from the US, occupy wooded and brushy range. From Europe and Asia came the ring-necked pheasant and the gray (Hungarian) partridge, now established on agricultural land locally in all provinces but Nfld, and the chukar, established in the dry interior of BC and in southern Alta. The sandhill crane breeds on tundra and muskeg from Baffin I and the James Bay area of Qué to Siberia and locally on prairie. It migrates through western Ont, the prairies and BC. Of the RAIL family, the American coot (west of NB) and the common moorhen (southern Ont and Qué) are most commonly hunted in marshes. The smaller king rail (southern Ont) and Virginia and sora rails (all provinces) are rarely taken. The only members of the SANDPIPER family now hunted are the American WOODCOCK (from southern Man to Nfld) in woodland and the common SNIPE (throughout Canada) in marshland and wet pastures. Two members of the pigeon family are hunted: the band-tailed pigeon in forested western BC and the mourning dove, which occurs in agricultural land in all provinces except Nfld and PEI but is hunted only in certain provinces. Both species winter in the US. The once plentiful PASSENGER PIGEON is extinct.

The harvest of game birds is controlled by bag limits and by length and timing of seasons. Not all species are legally hunted wherever they occur. Provinces and territories have the authority to set hunting regulations for turkey, grouse, pheasant, partridges and quail. These are considered non-migratory, although some grouse populations may migrate long distances. The migratory game birds, including sandhill crane, American coot, common moorhen (gallinule), rails, American woodcock, common snipe, band-tailed pigeon and mourning dove, are regulated by the federal government under the Migratory Birds Convention Act (1917). The annual Canadian harvest of these birds probably exceeds 2.8 million.

H.G. LUMSDEN

Games are distinguishable from other forms of play in that they are contests in which all players start out with equal chances of winning; they end

Some of the 25 species of game birds hunted in Canada (left to right), American coot, common snipe, willow ptarmigan, ruffed grouse, ring-necked pheasant (*artwork by Claire Tremblay*).

when a winner or loser is determined; and although the play may appear spontaneous or unsupervised, it is in fact guided by rigid rules and procedures. Although many games are played without objects, the term "game" is often associated with a visible item.

History of Games in Canada

Children's Outdoor and Group Games Many games have their roots in Europe and the US. Games have been played for centuries with little change as they came down through the years, passed from one child to another. The development of public education systems in Canada, featuring schools with playgrounds, fostered the spread of traditional group games and also served as a setting for the creation of new games. Forms of most of these traditional games, such as hopscotch and tag, are still popular with children today. In the 19th century, boys and girls everywhere played games such as hide-and-go-seek, tag, blindman's buff, skipping, leap frog, hopscotch, red rover and puss-in-the-corner (the latter, known today as four square, is a game in which 5 children compete to occupy 4 places on the corners of a square). Even games such as "I spy" and the sidewalk game of "Step on a crack, you'll break your mother's back, step on a nail, you'll put your father in jail" (inspired by the introduction of wooden sidewalks) are known to have been played by Canadian children a century ago.

Like children everywhere, Canadian children played games with an assortment of ephemeral objects, such as sticks, stones and "junk." Since many families did not have money to spend on children's playthings, most game objects were made of "found" or inexpensive materials. These included knucklebones (small bones in the hind legs of a sheep) used as dice or in games like jacks. Hoops from discarded barrels, or rims of wheels, were trundled with sticks in races along roads and pathways. Marbles, which were played mainly by boys, were generally made of clay and could be homemade. Manufactured clay, glass, ceramic and agate marbles were imported from Germany until the early 20th century, when the US began mass manufacturing glass marbles. Marbles were used in games such as ring taw and conkers. Boys also played with tops. Again, these could be homemade, using a spool and dowel, or could be purchased from local stores. They came in many forms, including whipping tops, peg tops and hand spinners. Also popular was bilboquet, a game in which a ball is attached by a string to a handle with a cup-shaped end. The object of the game is to hold onto the handle, swing the ball up and try to catch it in the cup. Children played with balls and kites, and these too could be homemade.

Commercially Manufactured Board and Table Games for Children The second half of the 19th century witnessed the rapid growth of an educated urban middle class, which for the first time provided a market for the establishment of a commercial game industry. This industry not only produced copies of traditional and classic games but developed new games and game materials for a growing child market. Eventually, these materials filtered into children's game playing, but, although they were heavily advertised by the 1870s and 1880s, it is not known to what degree mass-manufactured games were played compared to homemade or locally produced items.

During the first half of the 19th century, Britain, Germany, France and the US started producing game boards for children, but most were expensive since they were handpainted on linen. By the time of Confederation cheaper wood or cardboard games were available in most Canadian urban centres. Some were traditional games that had been played for hundreds of years in Europe, the US and Canada, eg, CHESS, chequers, backgammon, fox and geese, and 9-men's morris. Other games were newly designed for children's use and featured moral or educational themes to make them more attractive to parents. By the 1880s, the children's game industry was actively producing and selling a number of board games which were for children's amusement only and which dealt with popular themes (such as "The Little Shoppers Game") rather than moral concerns. These games were mainly produced by American and some British companies, and it was not until 1886 that the Canada Games Co was formed. This firm was a branch of the British Copp Clark Co and never fared very well; most of its games were cheaply made and less attractive than the American or European products. Nevertheless, it did produce some "Canadianized" versions of standard games, such as Toboggans and Stairs which was based on the traditional Snakes and Ladders. Children's games were frequently manufactured by book publishers and were sold through mail order catalogues such as Eaton's (beginning in the 1880s) and in local bookshops.

In addition to the games mentioned, late-19th-century manufacturers offered games of physical dexterity, such as parlour (table) versions of tennis, croquet and tiddly-winks. Fort and bagatelle were wooden table games with marbles as projectiles to hit targets. Fort stopped being manufactured in the 1920s and has never been revived, while bagatelle evolved into pinball. Because these 2 games were constructed of wood, they were also made locally by furniture and barrel manufacturers. Although the Canadian industry and market for children's games became stronger after WWI, Canadian game producers faced heavy competition from their American counterparts, who continued to develop blockbusters such as Monopoly, Clue and Scrabble.

Throughout Canada's history, popular culture and technology have affected game playing. Group games such as tag were often renamed according to popular themes, for example, as "cowboys and Indians" during the 1940s and 1950s when children's radio and television programming featured western themes. Lately, these games are more likely to have "space invader" themes. With the advent of movies, radio and television, many children's board games took on popular personalities such as the 1957 Leave It To Beaver Game, and this continues up to the present. J.R.R. Tolkien's *The Hobbit* and his *The Lord of the Rings* trilogy influenced the development during the late 1970s and early 1980s of a series of fantasy role-playing games, such as Dungeons and Dragons. Combining the elements of chance and strategy within player-designed fantasy plots, these games usually feature exaggerated bravado and sex stereotyping in comic book fashion. Because of these elements their appeal is generally limited to adolescent males, and the engrossing nature of play has worried some parents. The recent popularity of fantasy role-playing games is evident in the growth of players' organizations and stores selling gaming equipment.

The introduction of computer technology into the sphere of game playing witnessed a temporary boom of television and hand-held electronic games for children in the late 1970s and early 1980s. Some of these games were designed as educational materials; others were based on traditional sports. A corresponding development has been the gradual replacement of traditional pinball machines with video games, whose popularity has led to the development of video arcades.

Games Played by Adults Like children's games during the 19th century, most adult games in Canada were traditional and required few purchased materials. Comparative lack of leisure time was probably the significant factor limiting game playing for most adults. Traditional European board games such as chequers, chess, backgammon and 9-men's morris were often handmade (9-men's morris is a strategy game based on a 3-in-a-row design and is little known to contemporary Canadians). In Québec, chequers, which was known as "jeu de dames," was often played on a board of 12 x 12 squares (in contrast to the regulation chequers/chess board of 8 x 8 squares). Today all such handmade boards are considered "folk art" collectibles.

Game producers manufacturing materials for children in the second half of the 19th century also produced games for family participation. Parlour games such as "authors" (a card game in which you had to match an author with a quotation) and "lost heir" (a matching card game) were extremely popular. "Conversation cards" were question-and-answer card games designed to break the ice in mixed company in Victorian parlours. They were advertised as a blessing to bashful people and sometimes as "leading to the gates of matrimony." Cards continued to be probably the most popular game items for adults. Playing at cards tended to be an urban adult activity, euchre and whist being the most popular in English-speaking Canada. Whist is an old European card game for 4 people, involving a trump suit and the taking of tricks, and was the precursor of BRIDGE, which became popular in the 1920s. In the 1930s games such as Monopoly and Scrabble were released for adults, and as major sellers they were only recently outsold by the popular Canadian-produced game, Trivial Pursuit. Marketed first in the early 1980s, Trivial Pursuit is a board game that involves answering questions provided on cards. Its success has been phenomenal, and in a complete role reversal, Canadian game inventors have provided a prototype that has been copied by American and European companies. An offshoot of the demand for this game has been the unprecedented flourishing of game invention in Canada by others hoping to achieve similar success. This interest has also sparked the revival of existing game firms in Canada, including the Canada Games Co. Their successful adult "word and idea" games such as Balderdash, and QWR (Quick Wit and Repartee) and Waddington and Sanders Whatzit and Slang Teasers address a growing urban literate adult market first successfully identified in the 1980s by the makers of Trivial Pursuit. Other popular contemporary Canadian-made games for adults include Scruples (High Game Enterprises). The popularity of murder-mystery dramas involving audience participation has fostered the production of An Evening of Murder (Waddington-Sanders) games.

While the Canadian game industry is most noted today for Trivial Pursuit, it has had past successes, such as the Munro 6-Man Table Top Hockey Game (*see* TOYS). The Munro company operated as a family cottage industry in Ontario from the 1930s to the 1950s and was then the biggest manufacturer of table top hockey games in the world; its games are easily identified by a wooden sloped rink, bent wire players and hand-crocheted nets. Each year hundreds of new games are introduced to the Canadian market from an international industry. Some, like the puzzle cube created by Hungarian architect Rubik, have instant but short-lived popularity, while other more enduring games, such as Scrabble, have earned a "classic" status. In Canada, the major centre for the study of games is the Museum and Archive of Games, at U of Waterloo. MARY TIVY

The northern gannet (*Sula bassanus*) breeds in dense colonies on steep sea cliffs or cliff tops (*photo by Tim Fitzharris*).

Gananoque, Ont, Town, pop 4939 (1986c), 4863 (1981c), inc 1890, located at the confluence of the St Lawrence and Gananoque rivers, 29 km E of Kingston. The site was known in French times but was not surveyed until 1784. LOYALISTS John Johnson and Joel Stone were granted land in the area but quarrelled over the site. A compromise in 1789 gave Johnson the best land E of the Gananoque R, but Stone remained a resident, built a sawmill and with the McDonald family developed the site. It was raided by American forces under Benjamin Forsyth, Sept 1812. From the 1830s metal industries have been important. As "Gateway to the Thousand Islands," it is a major tourist centre. There is a bridge to the US at Ivy Lea. K.L. MORRISON

Gander, Nfld, Town, pop 10 207 (1986c), 10 404 (1981c), inc 1954, is located on Gander Lake in east-central Newfoundland. Both the town and lake are named after the GANDER R. This fog-free site was selected by the British and Canadian governments in 1935 to accommodate such flights as the regular transatlantic air service that had developed in the 1930s. By 1938 construction of what was then one of the world's largest airports had been completed and the community of Gander begun. During WWII Gander was a strategic link in the N American chain of defence, and in the RAF Transport Command's vital Atlantic FERRY COMMAND. The RCAF established a base here in 1940, which was also used by the USAF. The civilian use and enlargement of facilities after the war attracted a population of about 3000 by 1951, and by 1954 construction of a planned townsite began. Although Gander's importance as a refueling point has diminished, it has continued to attract many international flights, particularly from eastern Europe, and thus records many of the defections from communist countries that occur in Canada. Air Traffic Control (ATC) at Gander, the only oceanic unit in Canada, has jurisdiction over international and domestic airspace from W of Nfld to the mid-Atlantic and N to Greenland. In recent years the town has also become a major service centre. In Dec 1985 Gander was the focus of worldwide attention when a DC-8 carrying 256 passengers, 248 of them US soldiers returning from the Middle East, crashed after takeoff. All passengers and crew were killed in the worst DISASTER over Canadian soil. JANET E.M. PITT AND ROBERT D. PITT

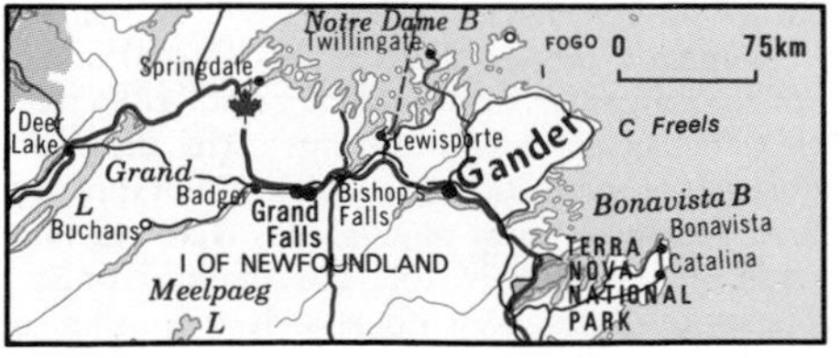

Gander River, 175 km long, drainage basin 6400 km², is the principal river of NE Newfoundland, emptying into Gander B. Named for its abundant geese, it rises in the central plateau and eventually falls 427 m to the Atlantic. The NW Gander flows 97 km into the W end of Gander Lk where it is joined by the 77 km long SW Gander R. The main river begins on the N side of the lake and twists NE 44 km to the sea. A waterway of the BEOTHUK, it has been fished for salmon by Europeans since 1725. It reaches into excellent stands of timber and has long been a route for lumbering. ROBERT D. PITT

Ganges, BC, UP pop 1133 (1986c), 1118 (1981c), is the major community centre of Saltspring I, the largest island in the southern GULF IS chain. Named after HMS *Ganges*, flagship on the Pacific Station 1857-60, it is located at the head of a long harbour and was first settled in 1859. In summer it is a favourite stopover for boating enthusiasts. Besides marina and commercial facilities, there are provincial government offices, a high school and a hospital which serve the outer Gulf Is. MARIE ELLIOTT

Gannet, or northern gannet (*Sula bassanus*), large, long-winged SEABIRD, white except for conspicuous black wing tips and yellowish tinged head. It weighs about 3100 g and is up to 100 cm long. Nine species of gannets and boobies comprise the predominantly tropical family Sulidae. All have a stout appearance, thick, sharply pointed bills, fairly short necks and legs, and wedge-shaped tails. They feed on fish caught by plunge-diving, often from heights of 20-30 m. Northern gannets are confined to the N Atlantic. They breed in dense colonies (6 in Canada) on steep sea cliffs or cliff tops, mainly on islands. Gannets first breed when 5-6 years old. Each pair produces a single, whitish egg. Incubation takes about 44 days and the chick is fed by its parent for about 90 days. Adults and immatures are common inshore in autumn, moving offshore in winter. About 70% of the N American population of 41 100 breeding pairs nest at 3 sites in the Gulf of St Lawrence; the remainder on the southeastern coast of Newfoundland. The largest colony, at Bonaventure I, Qué, is a federal migratory bird sanctuary and a provincial park. D.N. NETTLESHIP

Ganong, Gilbert White, confectionery manufacturer, politician, lt-gov of NB 1917 (b at Springfield, NB 22 May 1851; d at St Stephen, NB 31 Oct 1917). Persuaded by his brother, James Harvey Ganong, to give up teaching for commerce, he came to St Stephen in 1873 and opened a grocery and commission business, which was shortly expanded into a bakery and confectionery manufactory. In 1878 the brothers opened a soap factory as well. Their staple, Surprise Soap, sold nationally until 1946 when the factory was closed by Lever Brothers Ltd, its owners since 1913. Their confectionery business developed into Ganong Bros, Ltd, still a Canadian-owned confectionery company. In 1889 Gilbert White Ganong invented and patented a process for printing the company name on the bottom of chocolates and for years used the advertising slogan "The Maker's Mark on Every Piece." In 1896 Ganong was elected MP for Charlotte County; he was re-elected twice and in 1917 was appointed lieutenant-governor of NB. MARGARET E. MCCALLUM

Ganong, William Francis, regional historian, cartographer, botanist, linguist (b at Carleton, NB 19 Feb 1864; d at Saint John 7 Sept 1941). A passionate lover of New Brunswick, Ganong devoted his life to its study. After attending U of New Brunswick (BA, 1884; MA, 1886), Harvard (BA, 1887) and Munich (PhD, 1894), he taught botany at Smith College, Northampton, Mass, a position he held until his appointment as professor emeritus on his retirement in 1932. His summers were spent canoeing through NB, mapping the province's waterways and recording the stories of the Micmac and Maliseet, whose language he learned. He published over 150 papers and standard texts, and worked to revitalize the New Brunswick Museum in Saint John, to which he donated his papers. Honours included life membership in the Natural History Society of New Brunswick (1915), the Royal Society of Canada's Tyrrell Medal (1931), and a PhD (1898) and LLD (1920) from UNB. From 1918 to 1939 he was an active director of Ganong Bros, Ltd, the family-owned confectionery firm founded by his father, James Harvey Ganong, and uncle, Gilbert White GANONG. MARGARET E. MCCALLUM

Gar, large, slender, thick-scaled, predatory fish of family Lepisosteidae, order Semionotiformes, class Osteichthyes. Gars are found in fresh waters of eastern N America, Central America and Cuba, occasionally in brackish water and, rarely, in the sea. The 7 living species are divided into 2 genera (*Lepisosteus* and *Atractosteus*) by some ichthyologists; others consider them all as *Lepisosteus*. In Canada, 2 species, the rare spotted gar (*L. oculatus*) and the more familiar longnose gar (*L. osseus*), reach their northern limit in the Great Lakes drainage basin. Gars are characterized by diamond-shaped scales and a long snout with needlelike teeth. The gas-bladder, cellular and richly supplied with blood vessels, acts as a lung, enabling gars to breath air in stagnant waters. Gars may reach 183 cm long and 22 years of age. They feed principally on other fishes, which they seize by a darting movement from cover of vegetation. A sideways swipe of the snout impales prey crosswise on their teeth. Gar flesh is edible but not attractive. The eggs are poisonous to mammals and birds. The importance of gars as predators of economically important fishes is uncertain, but large gars can destroy gear set for other fishes. BRIAN W. COAD

Garant, Serge, composer, conductor, pianist, teacher, critic (b at Québec City 22 Sept 1929; d at Sherbrooke, Qué 1 Nov 1986). A daring and innovative musician, Garant was known for his promotion of 20th-century music, especially that of Canada. He studied in Montréal with Yvonne Hubert (piano) and Claude CHAMPAGNE (composition), and in Paris with Olivier Messiaen and Andrée Vaurabourg-Honegger. Returning to Montréal, he worked in counterpoint with Jocelyne Binet, and later took summer courses with Boulez in Switzerland. By combining recording tapes and instruments in *Nucléogame* (1955) and by using the aleatory technique in his *Trois Pièces* for string quartet (1958), Garant introduced 2 innovative procedures into Canadian music. However, it was *Anerca*, premiered in 1961 by Mauricio Kagel, that gained him recognition as a leading Canadian musician. Garant worked for CBC Radio as an arranger, accompanist, conductor and critic. He was also musical director of the Société de musique contemporaine du Québec, co-president of the national committee of the Société internationale pour la musique contemporaine and a professor at U de M. He was awarded the Canadian Music Council Medal (1971), the Harold Moon trophy from the Performing Rights Organization of Canada Ltd (1978), the 1979 Prix de musique Calixa-Lavallée, and the Canada Council prize for music (1984). He was made a Member of the Royal Society of Canada in 1986. HÉLÈNE PLOUFFE

Garapick, Nancy Ellen, swimmer (b at Halifax 24 Sept 1961). Although proficient in backstroke, butterfly, freestyle and individual medley, she enjoyed possibly her greatest success in the backstroke, setting a world record of 2:16.33 for the 200 m (1975) and a Canadian and Olympic mark of 1:03.28 for the 100 m (1976). Displaying her skills throughout the world with Canada's national aquatic team, Garapick collected an impressive array of honours and records. She represented Canada in the 1976 Montréal Olympics, claiming 2 bronze medals, and was named to the Canadian team for the boycotted 1980 Moscow Olympics. At age 14, in 1975, she was named Canada's female athlete of the year. BOB FERGUSON

Garbage, *see* SOLID WASTE; WASTE DISPOSAL.

Garden Island Rafting and Shipbuilding Enterprises Dileno Dexter Calvin (1798-1884), a timber merchant from Clayton, NY, relocated his business on Garden I (26.3 ha at the E end of Lk Ontario) in 1836. By 1880 he owned the island; today it remains the exclusive property of his descendants. The core of Calvin's business was rafting timber, primarily pine and oak, which was collected by ship throughout the entire Great Lakes basin, and delivering it to Québec City where it was transshipped to Britain. From Garden I, Calvin, who quickly became a Tory and a monarchist, was able to operate within the British trading system. Calvin's firm employed as many as 700 men to operate the rafting enterprise and build ships. In 1865 among other years, Calvin's was the largest timber operation in Québec City. His TIMBER RAFTS could be nearly a km long and include 165 000 cubic feet of timber: they were among the largest man-made structures in the 19th century. Calvin built ships in the winters to keep his work force together. The policy was to build a ship a year. At least one, *Garden Island*, a barque, was built for ocean commerce. Rafting and shipbuilding ended with the onset of WWI. Garden I, complete with many 19th-century frame buildings, survives as an evocative relic from the timbering days for some 20 families of cottagers. DONALD SWAINSON

Gardiner, Frederick Goldwin, lawyer, politician (b at Toronto 21 Jan 1895; d there 22 Aug 1983). A law graduate of Osgoode Hall (1920), Gardiner began his political career in 1936 as deputy reeve of Forest Hill, a suburban village in N Toronto. An ardent proponent of municipal amalgamation, he was persuaded to become first chairman of Metropolitan Toronto in 1953. Nicknamed "Big Daddy," he dominated municipal politics during a period in which Toronto "shrunk at the core and burst at the seams." He retired as chairman in 1961 and was appointed a Toronto Hydro commissioner in 1965, serving until 1979. A sharp debater and colourful speaker, he was also influential in the provincial and federal Conservative Party, and held several directorships of major corporations. JAMES MARSH

Gardiner, James Garfield, "Jimmy," teacher, farmer, politician, premier of Saskatchewan (b in Hibbert Township, Ont 30 Nov 1883; d at Lemberg, Sask 2 Jan 1962). Of Scots descent, Gardiner left Ontario for the North-West Territories and in 1905 witnessed the creation of Saskatchewan, where he remained to champion Prairie interests. As MLA (1914-35), Cabinet minister (1922-26), premier (1926-29, 1934-35), and leader of the Opposition (1929-34), he tirelessly pursued Liberal policies. He served as federal minister of agriculture 1935-57 (a record length of time for any Canadian to hold one portfolio) and was so single-minded in espousing western affairs that he frequently exasperated his colleagues. His PRAIRIE FARM REHABILITATION ADMINISTRATION was designed to assist drought-stricken prairie farmers. He was also minister of national war services in 1940-41. He sought his party's national leadership unsuccessfully in 1948. Gardiner's role as a western tribune was influenced by early poverty and a doctrinaire training in liberalism at Manitoba Coll. His faith in individual effort and in limited government as the servant of individuals never wavered, and he consistently applied his ideas to building his province and helping its citizens in turn through depression, war and reconstruction. Notably partisan, he held that a minister should be fully responsible and he believed frankly in patronage. NORMAN WARD

Gardiner Dam, located 100 km S of SASKATOON, is a 4 km long earth-fill structure towering 64 m above the S Saskatchewan riverbed. A dam near the "elbow" of the river (*see* ELBOW) had first been suggested in 1858 by Henry HIND, but construction did not begin until 1958 when a cost-sharing agreement was signed by the DIEFENBAKER (federal) and Douglas (provincial) governments. The dam is named after J.G. GARDINER, former Saskatchewan premier. The body of water behind the dam is named DIEFENBAKER LAKE after the man who, as prime minister, put the plan in motion (though Diefenbaker and Gardiner were arch-opponents). The dam was created to utilize better the water resources of the S Saskatchewan R for irrigation, recreation, urban water supply and electrical power. It was officially opened in 1967. DON HERPERGER

Garibaldi Provincial Park (est 1920), 1950 km^2 mountain wilderness located some 60 km N of Vancouver, normally reached by a short trail from Highway 99, N of Squamish. The mountains, which dominate the park and rise to 2678 m at Mt Garibaldi, are of recent volcanic origin. Lava from Price Mtn created a dam allowing 3000 m deep Lk Garibaldi to form. Subsequent erosion, especially by glaciers which still persist at higher altitudes, has sculpted the peaks, notably Black Tusk, and gouged the valleys, leaving a landscape of spectacular rugged beauty. Below 1500 m is a dense forest of Douglas fir, western red cedar and western hemlock; above, more scattered growth of mountain hemlock, yellow cedar, alpine fir and white bark pine. The alpine regions feature heather, numerous wildflowers and perpetual snow. Large mammals are scarce; more noticeable are marmots, squirrels, ptarmigans, Canada jays and golden eagles.

Mt Garibaldi was named in 1860 by Royal Navy Captain George Richards after Italian revolutionary Giuseppe Garibaldi. Difficulties of access inhibited human exploitation of the area. Today, some 17 600 ha around Black Tusk are afforded special protection in a Nature Conservancy Area. Adjacent to the NW boundary is the Whistler Mtn ski resort. JOHN S. MARSH

Garneau, François-Xavier, notary, civil servant, poet, historian (b at Québec City 15 June 1809; d there 3 Feb 1866). The greatest writer of 19th-century French Canada and its most important historian, he had a major influence on the thinking and letters of his time.

The son of an unschooled, poor father, young François-Xavier was soon known for his keen intelligence. He excelled in primary school, but lack of money apparently barred his way to a classical education. His self-education and natural reserve explain the "proud independence" which impressed his contemporaries. Having decided in 1825 to become a notary, he spent 5 years clerking for Archibald Campbell. The latter had an outstanding library and encouraged Garneau to study both English and French history and letters. He also helped him make a trip to the US, where Garneau discovered American-style democracy and confirmed his sense of identity as a North American. In 1831 the young notary went to London for 2 years as secretary to Denis-Benjamin Viger, sent to defend the rights of French Canadians. Garneau learned much about British politics and society and visited Paris twice. Back in Québec in 1833, he halfheartedly exercised his profession, wrote poems, started a cultural magazine and eagerly followed the debates in the House of Assembly and the Legislative Council, dominated respectively by French Canadian nationalists and the Anglo-Canadian establishment.

Garneau began his work as a historian in the late 1830s. He worked, above all, on a vast synthesis of French Canadian history, the 3-volume HISTOIRE DU CANADA, which appeared between 1845 and 1848. A supplement published in 1852 brought the account up to 1840. Garneau presented the history of French Canadians as a struggle for survival – against the Indians and Anglo-Americans on the battlefield, and then against the English-Canadian oligarchy in the parliamentary arena. The work was hugely successful and caused Garneau, while still alive, to be hailed "national historian." For over a century, novelists, poets and political thinkers borrowed from his documentation and interpretations. His spirited and passionate style assured the *Histoire* lasting success. After 1845 the clergy began to show concern regarding certain Gallican and liberal aspects in the work, and Garneau then developed a more conservative nationalism in religious matters. For 100 years the historiographical interpretation of French Canada was a synthesis of Garneau's political interpretation and the religious one of Catholic historians such as Abbé Ferland.

Garneau lived a quiet life first as a notary and, later, from 1844 to 1864 as city clerk. He was peace loving, even timid, but held firmly to his opinions. His capacity for work was legendary. Though impassioned by politics, he never entered political life. In his view, the church should either be subordinate to the state or uninvolved in sociopolitical affairs, yet he viewed Catholicism as integral to the national identity of French Canadians. In his nationalist interpretation of history and love of his native land which pervaded his style, Garneau remains a major figure in French Canadian literature. PIERRE SAVARD

François-Xavier Garneau, the greatest writer of 19th-century French Canada and its most important historian (*courtesy National Archives of Canada/C-6721*).

Garneau, Hector de Saint-Denys, poet (b at Montréal 13 June 1912; d at Ste-Catherine-de-Fossambault, Qué 24 Oct 1943). Saint-Denys Garneau's writing marks a turning point in the history of Québec poetry. Great-grandson of the historian François-Xavier GARNEAU and grandson of the poet Alfred Garneau, Saint-Denys Garneau was the son of a comfortable middle-class family and cousin of the poet and novelist Anne HÉBERT. While taking his classical secondary course at the Jesuit colleges Sainte-Marie, Loyola and Jean de Brébeuf, he also attended art classes at the École des beaux-arts in Montréal, but in 1934 his studies were interrupted by a rheumatic heart condition. Devoting himself to poetry, painting and music, he was associated for the next 3 years with the young Catholic intellectuals responsible for the magazine *La Relève*. During the 1930s also he kept his *Journal* (posthumously published in 1954 and translated into English by John Glassco in 1962) and composed the poems to appear in his only collection of verse, *Regards et jeux dans l'espace* (1937). Disillusioned by the volume's reception, Saint-Denys Garneau withdrew to the seclusion of the family manor house at Ste-Catherine-de-Fossambault near Québec City, where he died in 1943, apparently of a heart attack, while canoeing alone.

Radical in its form, with its unrhymed lines of various lengths, its lack of punctuation and its broken syntax, Saint-Denys Garneau's poetry was equally original in its themes (the spiritual adventure of the poet, the nature of artistic creation, the search for purity) and in its ironic distance. His hermetic poems, his cerebral correspondence and the restless searching of his diary make of Saint-Denys Garneau a unique figure in the intellectual history of Québec and its first truly modern poet. DAVID M. HAYNE

Garneau, Marc (b at Québec C 23 Feb 1949), first Canadian ASTRONAUT to enter space, during the 41-G mission of the American space shuttle Challenger, 5-13 Oct 1984. He received his training in Canadian military colleges, at St-Jean (Qué) and Kingston (Ont), and at Imperial College of Science and Technology, London, Eng, where he received a PhD in electrical engineering. A naval officer with the Canadian Armed Forces, he spent 10 years as a combat systems engineer, during which time he designed a simulator for training officers in the use of missile systems aboard "Tribal" class destroyers. Member of the

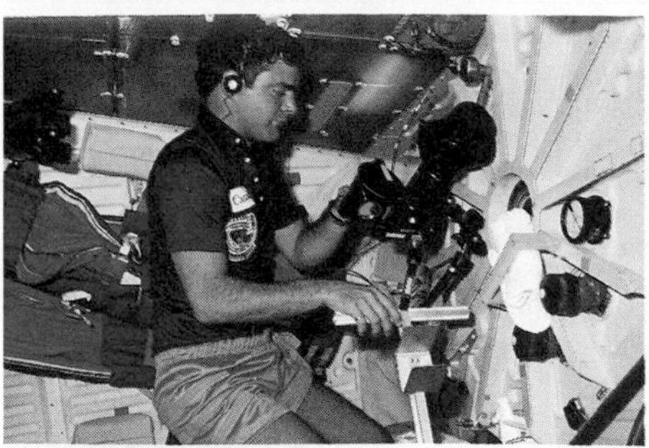

Canadian astronaut Marc Garneau with equipment in the Space Shuttle (*courtesy SSC Photocentre*).

first team of 6 Canadian astronauts from Feb 1984 on, he was released from his National Defence work in order to take on new duties with the space program of the National Research Council. During his 8-day space mission, he carried out 2 types of experiments, the first being in space science, in particular testing the space vision system developed by the NRC, and the second concerning life in space, specifically problems of space-induced nausea. He is an Officer of the Order of Canada. FRANÇOISE CÔTÉ

Garneau, Raymond, politician (b at Plessisville, Qué 3 Jan 1935). Usually seen as one of the bright lights of the Liberal Party, Garneau made his reputation as finance minister in Québec, 1970 to 1976. Trained at U Laval and at Université de Genève in economics, he became executive assistant to Prem Jean LESAGE in 1965 and remained with him until 1970. In that year he was elected to the National Assembly and was immediately named minister of finance and president of the Treasury Board by Robert BOURASSA. Garneau held these posts (as well as the education portfolio from 1975 to 1976) until the defeat of the Bourassa government in 1976, providing successful stewardship in a difficult period. He then worked in business with the Laurentian Group and the Montreal City and District Savings Bank until he ran federally in 1984 – securing election in Laval des Rapides – against the *bleu* tide. In Parliament Garneau has served quietly but with distinction as Opposition financial critic and as president of the Québec Liberal caucus, in effect the Québec leader. In July 1987 Liberal leader John Turner named Garneau his Québec lieutenant. J.L. GRANATSTEIN

Garner, Hugh, writer (b at Batley, Eng 22 Feb 1913; d at Toronto 30 June 1979). Garner's parents immigrated to Canada in 1919 and his father abandoned the family soon after. Garner spent his youth in the poorer neighbourhoods of downtown Toronto and entered the publishing world as a newspaper copyboy. He rode the rails during the Depression and fought in the Spanish Civil War and WWII. Garner's poor, urban and Protestant background was a rare one for a Canadian writer and pervades his work. His focus is working-class Ontario and his preferred genre, the realistic novel; the best-known example is *Cabbagetown* (1950). Frequently, his theme is the victimization of the worker, reflecting his early association with radical socialism. The legend of Garner grew out of a hard-living life-style that fed his writing. To the end he smoked and drank, and was outspoken, abrasive and always unfashionable. His extensive literary output – 100 short stories, 17 books, hundreds of articles and radio and TV scripts – has been criticized for banality and flawed characterization, but he loved telling stories and was genuine in his talent and determination. In 1963 a collection of his short stories won the Gov Gen's Award. MARLENE ALT

Garratt, Phillip Clarke, aviator (b at Toronto 13 July 1894; d there 16 Nov 1975). He served in WWI with the Royal Flying Corps, flew as a commercial pilot and joined DE HAVILLAND AIRCRAFT in 1936 where he directed the development of aircraft to operate in the Canadian North (*see* BUSH FLYING). After WWII, he fostered development of the Chipmunk trainer and a series of successful STOL aircraft, including the BEAVER and OTTER. He was awarded the MCKEE TROPHY in 1951 and 1966.
JAMES MARSH

Garrett, Christopher John Raymond, physical oceanographer (b at Bude, Eng 30 July 1943). Educated at Cambridge, he joined the department of oceanography at Dalhousie University in 1971. Known for his early work with W.H. Munk on the description of internal wave characteristics, he is also respected for his research on frontal processes, ocean mixing and shelf dynamics, and in Canada for his explanation of the high tides of the Bay of Fundy. He has also worked on various practical issues, including iceberg trajectory prediction and the problem of radioactive waste disposal in the deep ocean. In 1982 he won the A.G. HUNTSMAN award in physical oceanography. A.J. BOWEN

Garrison Towns, places where troops are stationed, usually for defence but sometimes for prestige reasons, as in CAPITAL CITIES where they form part of the governor's entourage. The first garrison towns were Placentia and St John's (Nfld), Port-Royal and Canso (NS), and Québec City. By the 18th century, LOUISBOURG, Halifax and Montréal were added to the number. Small bodies of troops periodically garrisoned lesser centres such as Saint John. In some cases a town grew up around a fort or barracks, and troops continued to be posted there even after the fortifications had sunk into ruin. Montréal and Kingston were in this category by 1870 when imperial garrisons were withdrawn from Canada, leaving only Halifax and Esquimalt with small contingents.

In 1662 Placentia had a garrison of 25 French soldiers. Its growing importance as the centre of the French fishing fleet meant an increase of its garrison to about 150 by 1704. It was fear of this garrison town that provoked the first British garrison at St John's in 1696. Troops and fishermen from Placentia formed the nucleus of the first garrison and townsmen of Louisbourg in 1713. By then Québec City had become the predominant garrison town in Canada, following the arrival of some 1100 troops of the CARIGNAN-SALIÈRES REGIMENT in 1665. Their successors at Québec City were the TROUPES DE LA MARINE, who also served in Acadia. The growth of Louisbourg as a garrison town both within and without the fortress eventually led to the founding of Halifax as a counterpoise British garrison town in 1749.

View of the Champ de Mars, Montreal, by Robert A. Sproule. Montréal was one of the main British garrison towns that emerged after 1760 (*courtesy National Archives of Canada/C-2640*).

Six species of garter snake occur in Canada in a variety of habitats, from the NWT to urban environments of the south (*artwork by Claire Tremblay*).

The major British garrison towns that emerged after 1760 and multiplied after the AMERICAN REVOLUTION were Québec City, Montréal, Kingston, Niagara, York, London and Amherstburg. Together with St John's, Halifax and Fredericton, they usually had about 7000 troops, their number kept roughly equal to the standing peacetime army of the US, perceived as Canada's potential enemy until 1871. Not only did the garrison towns attract farmers, merchants and professionals to service the garrison, but imperial troops left their mark upon such towns. There was the welcome largesse of the military chests which sometimes even surpassed the provincial government's annual revenue. This military outlay went for food, fuel, fortifications, canal building, drink and other amenities for the troops. There was also the myriad activities of the officers and men in cultural, religious and fraternal relations with townsmen. In Montréal, for instance, it was soldiers of the garrison who introduced rowing on the St Lawrence. They encouraged fencing, curling, cricket, hockey and the steeplechase. They patronized Masonic and Orange lodges, built the first Presbyterian and Anglican churches in the city, and helped develop the early Montréal police force. ELINOR KYTE SENIOR

Garson, Man, Village, pop 313 (1986c), 318 (1981c), inc 1915 as the village of Lyall, is located 37 km NE of Winnipeg. In 1927 it reverted to its original name – after William Garson, an early quarrier of the area's mottled Tyndall limestone, used in many prominent Canadian buildings. (The interior walls of the Centre Block of the Parliament Buildings are constructed of Tyndall limestone from Garson.) Mixed farming by Ukrainian, German, Polish and Anglo-Saxon settlers began in the region in the 1880s. Garson operated the first of 5 limestone quarries which attracted a cosmopolitan mix of skilled workers from the turn of the century onward. Only one quarry operation remains today. The village's residents primarily commute to nearby centres to work. D.M. LYON

Garson, Stuart Sinclair, lawyer, politician, premier of Man (b at St Catharines, Ont 1 Dec 1898; d at Winnipeg 5 May 1977). After moving to Winnipeg as a child, he attended the Manitoba Law School, was called to the bar in 1919 and practised law at Ashern and Eriksdale, Man, until 1936. A Liberal-Progressive MLA for Fairford 1927-48, he held office as provincial treasurer 1936-48 and premier 1943-48. In 1937 he was instrumental in securing the appointment of the Royal Commission on DOMINION-PROVINCIAL RELATIONS; the greatest achievement of his premiership was the inauguration of an effective program of rapid rural electrification. From 1948 to 1957 he served as federal minister of justice and attorney general and as Liberal MP for Marquette. He then left politics to practise law until his retirement in 1965. He was named a Companion of the Order of Canada in 1971. DONALD SWAINSON

Garter Snake, common name for 30 species of harmless colubrid snakes of the genus *Thamnophis,* found from NWT to Costa Rica. Most have a prominent, longitudinal stripe down the back. Six species occur in Canada, including the common garter snake, which has the widest range of any N American snake. Garter snakes are often abundant and occupy a wide variety of habitats, including urban settings. Diets vary among species but include slugs, earthworms, fish and amphibians. Mammals are eaten occasionally, especially by the western terrestrial garter snake, which restrains such prey by a primitive coiling behaviour. All are live-bearing and normally produce 10-20 young by late summer to early fall. PATRICK T. GREGORY

Gascon, Jean, actor, director (b at Montréal 21 Dec 1921). While studying at the Collège Sainte-Marie, he attracted attention for his performance in several plays with Jean-Louis ROUX. In 1942 they both appeared in *L'Échange* directed by Ludmilla Pitöeff for the Compagnons de Saint-Laurent. Gascon enrolled in medicine but continued his acting career with the Compagnons. When Pitöeff returned to Montréal with her company in 1946, Gascon and Roux appeared with her in *Phèdre* and *Le Pain dur*, and the following year Gascon followed Roux to France to perfect his craft. Gascon remained there several years, working especially at Copeau's École du vieux-colombier. When he returned to Canada, he, Roux, Éloi GRAMMONT and several others began the THÉÂTRE DU NOUVEAU MONDE, with Gascon serving as director. Early in 1952 they founded the École du TNM, which was replaced in 1956 by the National Theatre School. Gascon managed the TNM until 1966, as well as taking roles in plays such as

L'Avare, *Don Juan* and *Richard II* and directing productions including *La Tartuffe*, *Venise sauvée*, *L'Opera de quat'sous* and *Klondyke*. Under him the company took part in several international festivals and in 1958 toured Europe, the US and Canada. Gascon appeared in 1956 in *Henry V* at the STRATFORD FESTIVAL and returned there to direct *Othello* in 1959 and *The Comedy of Errors* in 1964. He succeeded Michael Langham as artistic director (1968-74) at Stratford. After leaving Stratford, he took charge of theatre at the NATIONAL ARTS CENTRE in Ottawa in 1977. He was stage director of *The Barber of Seville* at the Opéra de Montréal in 1986. Gascon's many honours include the Prix Victor-Morin, the Royal Bank Award and the MOLSON PRIZE; he is a Companion of the Order of Canada. ANDRÉ G. BOURASSA

Gaspé, Qué, City, pop 17 350 (1986c), 17 261 (1981c), inc 1874, is located on the bay bearing the same name, 650 km NE of Québec City. The name, whose origin and meaning are disputed, extends to an entire region, the GASPÉ PENINSULA. Following the amalgamation of 12 neighbouring localities between Anse-à-Valleau and Pointe-St-Pierre in 1970, Gaspé is now one of Québec's largest municipalities. It is one of the oldest settlements in N America: on 24 July 1534, Jacques CARTIER took possession of Canada on behalf of the king of France and placed a cross at this location, which very soon became a fishing port and supply centre for NEW FRANCE. Between 1628 and 1760, Gaspé was the scene of several incidents between the French and English. Sir William PHIPS's troops burned the village in 1690 and the English built a fort there just before the Conquest. After the American Revolution, many LOYALISTS settled in the area. Since then the population has been largely English speaking. Cod and salmon fishing dominated the economy for many years, but today other activities such as forestry, trade and tourism play a key role. A regional history and folklore museum opened in 1976; a nearby monument commemorates the arrival of Cartier. ANTONIO LECHASSEUR

Gaspé Peninsula, a large peninsula in eastern Québec, comprises 5 counties (Bonaventure, Gaspé-Est, Gaspé-Ouest, Matane and Rimouski) with a population of 196 881 (1986c). Except for the copper-mining town of Murdochville, most of the population lives along the lengthy coastline within a few km of the St Lawrence R, the Gulf of St Lawrence and Chaleur Bay. Principal towns include RIMOUSKI, GASPÉ and Matane.

The name Gaspé probably derives from a MICMAC word meaning "land's end." When Jacques CARTIER landed in Gaspé Bay in 1534 to plant a cross and claim the land for the king of France, he found the area occupied by Iroquoian-speaking Indians. By the beginning of the 17th century, when Samuel de CHAMPLAIN sailed along its coasts, the peninsula was inhabited by Micmac. Although never probably numbering more than a few hundred, they have continued to live there since. They were Christianized by French missionaries in the 17th century. The rich supplies of codfish, found in great numbers only a few km from shore, have long been the focus of the Gaspé economy; every year, for centuries, hundreds of tonnes of fish have been shipped to Europe, S America and the US. The wide, stony beaches and reliable sun and winds of Gaspé were perfect for dry-curing the cod; until refrigeration arrived in the 20th century, this was the only means to ensure that the fish would endure the long voyages to market without spoiling.

In the French period only a few fishermen settled in Gaspé permanently. When James WOLFE and his forces arrived in 1758 they found about 400 permanent residents on the coast. He destroyed their homes and possessions and sent most of them back to France. Still, a few managed to hide in the woods, continuing to live in Gaspé after it became British territory in 1763. They were joined by several families of ACADIANS who had avoided the British deportation campaign in NS. In 1784 about 400 English-speaking LOYALISTS, refugees from the American Revolution, came to settle in Gaspé. Thereafter, few immigrants arrived, though the population grew vigorously by natural means.

It was a long time before the people of Gaspé escaped dependence on the fishing industry. A little mixed farming was practised in Bonaventure County, but it was not until the 20th century that the forest and mineral resources of the interior were seriously exploited. Construction of a railway connection only began in the 1890s. In recent years tourism has become an important source of employment as thousands of visitors come to see the famous PERCÉ ROCK, the great bird colonies of Île de BONAVENTURE, Gaspésie Provincial Park in the rugged interior and FORILLON NATIONAL PARK. DAVID LEE

Gatineau, Qué, City, pop 81 244 (1986c), 74 988 (1981c), inc 1975, is located at the junction of the R Gatineau and OTTAWA R, adjoining HULL, Qué. It was created through the merger of 7 municipalities situated E of the Gatineau R (Pointe-Gatineau, Touraine, East Templeton, East part of East Templeton, West Templeton, village of Templeton and Gatineau), and is the largest French-speaking municipality of the National Capital Region and sixth-largest city in Québec. It is named for Nicolas Gastineau who was active in the fur trade of the area in the 17th century. Gatineau has experienced impressive growth in the last 15 years, including such developments as a shopping centre (Les Promenades de l'Outaouais), a hotel (l'Auberge des Gouverneurs), hospital facilities, an airport coupled with a large industrial park, and a superhighway. Spread over 272 km^2, it is inhabited by a population whose mother tongue is predominantly French. PIERRE-LOUIS LAPOINTE

Gaucher, Yves, painter, printmaker (b at Montréal 3 Jan 1934). One of Montréal's most important abstract artists during the 1960s, he made his initial mark as a printmaker. His first purely abstract work is a suite of prints, *En Hommage à Webern* (1963), inspired by a Paris visit during which he realized that his artistic affinities were with New York, not Europe. Though his work developed parallel to American colour-field painting, he made formal choices closer to contemporary Montréal developments. His shapes and surfaces are anonymous and hard-edged, and he continues to be challenged by "relational" painting – balancing off structural components (since 1973 coloured planes of unequal weight and energy) to achieve a taut surface equilibrium. Gaucher's Apr 1986 show at the Olga Korper Gallery in Toronto indicated a shift from the controlled balance of earlier work. Gaucher sees formal problems as metaphors for existential ones, and reconfirms abstract painting's tradition of moral and spiritual enquiry. ROALD NASGAARD

Gaudard, Pierre, photojournalist (b at Marvelise, France 6 Oct 1927). Gaudard moved to Montréal in 1952 and gained national recognition in the late 1960s with an extended photo-essay, about blue-collar workers, exhibited and published by the National Film Board. In 1972 he joined the short-lived Groupe d'action photographique (GAP), which recorded urban and rural Quebecers' lives. A commission from *Time* (Canada) to illustrate a cover story on the Canadian penal system in 1974 led to a Canada Council Senior Arts Award and a travelling exhibition in 1977 by the NFB. In 1980 Gaudard spent a year photographing in his native France. The resultant images, characterized by gentle humour and irony, were exhibited by the NFB in different parts of Canada. In 1984 Gaudard published *Retours en France* and in 1985 he had an exhibition of his work at the Centre international d'art contemporain in Paris. LOUISE ABBOTT

Gaudaur, Jacob Gill, Jr, "Jake," football player, executive, commissioner (b at Orillia, Ont 5 Oct 1920). An all-round athlete, he was a prominent oarsman and an accomplished lacrosse player in his youth. He joined the RCAF and played football with the champion Toronto RCAF-Hurricanes (1942). He continued playing after WWII, finally joining the Hamilton Tigers in 1948. He was captain of the club from 1950 and centre on the 1953 Hamilton Tiger-Cats Grey Cup championship team. From 1954 to 1968, he was president and general manager of the Tiger-Cats. He also played an unofficial role for the CANADIAN FOOTBALL LEAGUE, selling TV rights and negotiating an agreement with the US National Football League to honour each league's contracts. In Apr 1968 he was appointed commissioner of the CFL, a position he held to 1984. He is an Officer of the Order of Canada. FRANK COSENTINO

Gaudreault, Laure, teacher, unionist, journalist (b at La Malbaie, Qué 25 Oct 1889; d at Clermont, Qué 19 Jan 1975). Gaudreault attended the École normale Laval and then taught in Québec village grade schools. She wrote for various papers, analysing the position of women and, from 1930 on, tried to awaken her readers to the harsh working conditions of female rural school teachers. In 1936 she did the groundwork for the Association catholique des institutrices rurales and, in 1937, the Fédération catholique des institutrices rurales. She then organized female rural teachers to win improvements in salaries and pension programs; published *La Petite Feuille* and became a union organizer; was part of the 1946 fusion of various teachers' unions into the Corporation générale des instituteurs et des institutrices catholiques du Québec (CIC), the precursor of today's Centrale de l'enseignement du Québec. As vice-president of the CIC, 1946-65, she participated in the major union battles of Québec teachers. MICHELINE DUMONT

Gauld, Bella Hall, labour educator, political activist (b at Lindsay, Ont 31 Dec 1878; d at Montréal 21 Aug 1961). Raised on a farm in Manitoba, Gauld qualified as a teacher before studying piano in Germany. Back in Canada (1905), she worked with German immigrants near Brandon and then joined J.S. WOODSWORTH's All People's Mission in Winnipeg (1911). On his recommendation, she was hired as first director of the Montréal University Settlement (1914). She studied at the Rand School of Social Science (1919) and returned to Montréal to establish the Labour College (1920). On its demise (1924), she worked for the Women's Labour League which sponsored camps for poor children. Gauld joined the COMMUNIST PARTY OF CANADA (1922), becoming president of the Montréal branch of the Friends of the Soviet Union (1926-39). In the 1930s she operated a soup kitchen and played piano at fund raisers for various ethnic communities. During WWII, she was a frequent soloist at Navy League concerts for servicemen. She remained active in the Party until her death. MARGARET E. MCCALLUM

Gault, Andrew Hamilton, army officer (b in Eng 18 Aug 1882; d at Montréal 28 Nov 1958). Of Canadian parents, he attended McGill U. Commissioned in the 2nd Canadian Mounted Rifles, he served in the SOUTH AFRICAN WAR and joined the Canadian Militia on return to Canada. On the eve of WWI he offered the Canadian government $100 000 to help raise and equip an infantry battalion for overseas duty, leading to the formation in 1914 of the Princess Patricia's Canadian Light Infantry regiment. Gault accompanied the regiment overseas as second-in-command, fighting until the loss of his left leg. On retirement (1920), he took up residence in England and was elected Conservative MP for Taunton (1924-35). Recalled to active duty in WWII, he served on staff with the Canadian Army in England (colonel, 1940; brigadier, 1942) and returned to Canada in 1945. Appointed honorary colonel (1948) and colonel (1958) of his regiment, he showed a keen interest in it until his death. JEAN PARISEAU

Gaultier, Jean-François, king's physician, naturalist (b at La Croix-Avranchin, France 6 Oct 1708; d at Québec C 10 July 1756). Appointed king's physician of New France, he arrived in Québec in 1742. There he took over M. SARRAZIN's medical and scientific duties, and became a corresponding member of the Académie royale des sciences in 1745. In 1747, encouraged by LA GALISSONIÈRE, he arranged for the post commandants to collect plant specimens for him. In 1749 Gaultier and Pehr KALM botanized around Québec City and east to Les Éboulements, and Kalm named for him the genus *Gaultheria,* or WINTERGREEN. Gaultier shipped plants to France each year. His 1749 manuscript lists 134 species, 61 first described by Sarrazin to which he added detail and 73 not mentioned by Sarrazin. Gaultier concentrated on the ligneous plants in his work and differentiated between 4 species of pines. He set up the first meteorological station in Canada and kept a log 1742-56, as well as sending minerals and preserved specimens of animals to France. But botany, including the medical properties of plants, was his great interest. His history of MAPLE SUGAR was published in the memoirs of the Académie. BERNARD BOIVIN

Gauthier, Eva, mezzo-soprano, teacher (b at Ottawa 20 Sept 1885; d at New York C, NY 26 Dec 1958). In 1901, 5 years after taking part in the farewell tour of Emma ALBANI, she made her debut in Ottawa. In 1902 she left for Europe, where she studied elocution with Sarah Bernhardt and sang in concert with Enrico Caruso. She left the stage after 1910 and thereafter appeared only in concert or recital, giving the premiere performance of more than 700 songs and helping to introduce George Gershwin to a wider audience in 1923. Eastern music, which she had studied in the Orient where her husband owned plantations, was also part of her varied repertoire. HÉLÈNE PLOUFFE

Gauvin, William Henry, engineer, educator, science policy planner (b at Paris, France 30 Mar 1913). A graduate of McGill (PhD, 1945), he has continued his association with that university (associate professor of chemical engineering, 1947-62; research associate, 1961). He has been a member of McGill's board of governors, the National Research Council (1964-70) and the Science Council of Canada (1966-70), and a frequent adviser to both the federal and Québec governments. A man of boundless energy and enthusiasm, Gauvin was consultant and then head of the chemical engineering division, Pulp and Paper Research Inst of Canada (1951-61); and his research work with Noranda Research Centre (1961-83) was a source of inspiration to many. His publications include more than 150 papers on electrochemistry, high-temperature heat and mass transfer, fluid mechanics and plasma technology. Additionally, he has made generous contributions to the development of the chemical engineering profession in his roles as member and chairman of professional associations in Canada and beyond. He was made a Companion of the Order of Canada in 1975 and was awarded the Thomas W. Eadie Medal of the Royal Society of Canada in 1986.

Gauvreau, Claude, writer, artist (b at Montréal 19 Aug 1925, d there 9 July 1971). Gauvreau studied at the Collège Sainte-Marie in Montréal but was expelled in his last months of study for having maintained publicly that the idea of hell was absurd. He later earned a BPL from U de M. During this period he published remarkable articles in several student and left-wing papers. Gauvreau was especially influenced by the painter Paul-Émile BORDUAS and from 1942 on followed the activities of the AUTOMATISTES. His main contribution to the group's activities was as a writer, first (by 1943) as a critic and then (by 1944) as a playwright and poet. The performance of *Bien-être* in May 1947 and the 1948 publication of this "dramatic object" in the collective REFUS GLOBAL were among the first signs of modernism in Québec theatre. His "amour fou" for certain great artists, especially actress Muriel Guilbault, is one of the principal themes of his work. Only one of his works was published in its entirety during his lifetime – a collection of poetry entitled *Brochuges. Oeuvres créatrices complètes* did not appear until 1977. ANDRÉ G. BOURASSA

Gauvreau, Pierre, painter (b at Montréal 23 Aug 1922). In 1941, while a student at Montréal's École des beaux-arts, he discovered French modernism through magazine reproductions. His works made under this influence attracted Paul-Émile BORDUAS, who invited Gauvreau to join the radical young artists and intellectuals who met informally in his studio. Like them, Gauvreau and his poet brother (Claude GAUVREAU) became interested in the surrealist idea of automatism as a way of releasing creativity. In 1943 Gauvreau and others were invited to exhibit with the Contemporary Art Society, which fostered Québec's most adventurous art. Gauvreau remained associated with this circle, and became part of the group known as the AUTOMATISTES, who with others produced the 1948 manifesto REFUS GLOBAL. By the mid-1950s, Gauvreau was using looser, more gestural imagery in his work, and was also working for the new medium of TV, as a writer, director and producer. He stopped painting in the early 1960s and did not start again until 1975. His recent work continues his exploration of gesture and calligraphy. KAREN WILKIN

Gavazzi Riots On 6 June 1853, Alessandro Gavazzi, a recently arrived Italian patriot, gave a speech in Québec City at the Free Presbyterian Church. A riot resulted, the principal participants being Irish Catholics who reacted violently to Gavazzi's anti-Catholic sentiments. Gavazzi attributed the failure of the Italian national movement of 1848-49 to the defection of Pope Pius IX from the cause, and therefore rejected Catholicism. On June 9 he repeated his diatribe at Montréal's Zion Church. In the following riot, the police lost control and Mayor Charles Wilson apparently called out a detachment from the local garrison. The soldiers opened fire, killing 10 and wounding 50. The riots caused by Gavazzi's incendiary preaching in Québec and Montréal illustrate the instances of religious fanaticism that occurred frequently throughout the 19th century. PHILIPPE SYLVAIN

Gayford, Thomas, equestrian (b at Toronto, Ont 21 Nov 1928). An outstanding international competitor, Gayford was a member of the Canadian jumping team from the late 1940s until the early 1970s; he then became team coach. He first represented Canada at the 1952 Helsinki Olympics in the 3-day event and in 1959 helped win the 3-day event Pan-American Games gold medal. With James DAY and James ELDER he formed the gold-medal show-jumping team at the 1968 Mexico City Olympics. This team went on to win several international events. Gayford also captained the 1971 champion Pan-American Games team. He was 3 times individual high-jumping champion at the NY National Horse Show and jumping champion at the National Horse Show (1972). Since 1978 he has served as chef d'equip of the national jumping team. BARBARA SCHRODT

Geddie, John, Presbyterian missionary (b at Banff, Scot 19 Apr 1815; d at Geelong, Australia 14 Dec 1872). Geddie came with his family to Pictou, NS, in 1816 and after studying theology with Thomas MCCULLOCH became a minister in PEI. In 1848 the Presbyterian Secession Synod of NS sent him to the New Hebrides Is in the S Pacific. Although 3 workers were murdered and several died of tropical diseases, Geddie persisted with his work until infanticide and polygamy were eliminated. His epitaph reads: "When he landed in 1848, there were no Christians here, and when he left, in 1872, there were no heathen." JOHN S. MOIR

Gee, Fred Melsom Edward, impresario (b at Cardiff, Wales 21 July 1882; d at Winnipeg 8 June 1947). Active primarily as a church organist, accompanist and teacher in Winnipeg after immigrating to Canada in 1902, Gee's success in presenting occasional concerts by famous musicians encouraged him to become a full-time impresario. In 1927 he established the Celebrity Concert Series, which, during the remainder of Gee's life, delighted large Winnipeg audiences with its steady parade of stellar performers. In 1938 the series had 3500 subscribers and was thought the largest in N America. Gee expanded his enterprise to Brandon, Regina, Saskatoon, Calgary and Edmonton. After his death, A. (Arthur) K. Gee, his eldest son, continued in concert management until 1968. BARCLAY MCMILLAN

Gélinas, Gratien, man of the theatre (b at St-Tite, Qué 8 Dec 1909). The multiple activities of Gélinas – actor, director, producer, playwright – laid the base for contemporary Québec theatre. In 1937 Gélinas created the radio character Fridolin – a naïve, resourceful, softhearted but cynical young Montréaler. Fridolin became, in monologue form, the central character in annual theatrical revues, the *Fridolinons* or *Fridolinades* (1938-46), which were a spirited, popular and professional mixture of musical comedy, dance, mime and song, romantic sketches, satires and scenes of contemporary mores and trends. *Les Fridolinades* did not begin to appear in written form until 1980. Besides being a commentary on the social, political and cultural scene, they were a revue of theatrical styles and genres, from burlesque to melodrama, from the radio series to official speeches.

Tit-Coq, created in 1948, grew out of Fridolin. The drama of the bastard who did not want to leave bastards behind him, the unemployed conscript, the soldier sent to England who never really came home, contrasted in the play with vivid, moving tableaux of traditional family life. *Tit-Coq* triumphed in Canada (though it failed on Broadway) and inspired other playwrights. It dominated Gélinas's life for several years – revivals, tours, translations, films – but he worked briefly for TV, appeared in plays at the STRATFORD FESTIVAL and in 1957 founded La COMÉDIE-CANADIENNE, which he directed until 1972. Gélinas's second play,

Gratien Gélinas's puppet character Fridolin was the central character in the annual revue *Fridolinons*; 1945 photo (*courtesy National Archives of Canada/PA-122724/ NFB/Ronny Jacques*).

Bousille et les justes (1959), is stronger and tougher than *Tit-Coq*. Another orphan, Bousille, is servant and scapegoat to a hypocritical and evil family of entrepreneurs, typical representatives of the class that rose to prominence during the Maurice DUPLESSIS regime. *Hier, les enfants dansaient* (1966) is a more conventional study of family tensions arising from Québec/Ottawa political tensions. Gélinas was chairman of the CANADIAN FILM DEVELOPMENT CORPORATION 1969-78 and was co-president of the Groupe de travail sur le statut de l'artiste, created by the federal minister of communications in 1986.

In 1969 he was the translator-adapter for George RYGA's *Rita Joe*, a remarkable film director of his own shows from the 1940s on, and a born writer for and about the theatre. Gélinas has worked within a popular cultural tradition and transformed it. LAURENT MAILHOT

Gellman, Steven, composer, pianist (b at Toronto 16 Sept 1947). After early studies with Samuel Dolin in Toronto, he attracted attention in 1964 as soloist in his piano concerto, with the CBC Symphony Orchestra, and as first Canadian recipient of a BMI Award for student composers. Further studies were with Berio, Persichetti and Sessions at the Juilliard School (1965-68), Milhaud at Aspen, Colo (1965-66), and Messiaen at the Conservatoire de Paris (1973-76). Since 1976 he has taught at the U of Ottawa. Gellman's music is one of evocative, colourful sonorities, sometimes in an oriental-inspired contemplative mood, "in praise of the transcendental." Among his works are commissions from the Stratford Music Festival (*Mythos II*, 1968), CBC (*Symphony in Two Movements*, 1971; *Symphony II*, 1972; *Chori*, 1974), Hamilton Philharmonic (*Odyssey*, 1971; *The Bride's Reception*, 1983), Besançon Festival (*Deux tapisseries*, 1978), McGill U (*Trikaya*, 1981) and Toronto Symphony (*Awakening*, 1982, and *Universe Symphony*, 1985).

PATRICK CARDY

Gellner, John, author, journalist (b at Trieste, Italy 18 May 1907). A graduate of Masaryk U in Brno, Czech, where he practised law until 1939, Gellner served in the RCAF from 1940 until he retired with the rank of wing commander in 1958 to become a free-lance journalist. The bitter memory of WWII turned Gellner to the study of history and international power relationships and to the belief that only strength had ever preserved nations from war. He was also an influential force behind Liberal defence policy in the early 1960s. Among his publications are *The Czechs and Slovaks in Canada* (1968), *Canada in NATO* (1970) and *Bayonets in the Streets* (1974), along with hundreds of articles on defence and international relations. He was a professor of political science at York, 1972-82 and editor of the *Canadian Defence Quarterly* 1971-87. NORMAN HILLMER

Gemstone, MINERAL, rock or organic material used for personal adornment or for decorative purposes. A gem is the cut and polished finished product. Most gemstones are minerals: about 100 of the nearly 3000 mineral species known have gem varieties, but only about 25 are commonly marketed. The essential attributes of gemstones are beauty, derived from colour, brilliance, pattern, texture or light-reflecting qualities; durability, ie, sufficient hardness to resist abrasion, breakage or decomposition; and rarity, a quality that enhances their desirability and value.

Canada's most important gemstone, nephrite jade, was used extensively in British Columbia's Northwest Coast as early as 3000 years ago. The INUIT of Ellesmere I, 500-700 years ago, chipped, shaped and drilled nodules of amber to form round and oval beads. They selected the clearer, gem-grade material, believed to have weathered from Tertiary coal beds (66.4-1.6 million years old) along the shore of Hazen Lk, where amber is still found today. They also fashioned ivory into beads and artifacts. Ivory was used for tools earlier (7500 years ago) by the Maritime Archaic peoples in coastal Labrador. The first gemstone exported from Canada is believed to be amethyst from NS. Crystals were presented to Henri IV of France by Sieur de Monts when he was governor of Acadia, and one became part of the French crown jewels.

Modern use of Canada's gemstones began in the 19th century. As geological explorations disclosed gemstone occurrences, amateur lapidaries cut or carved and then polished the rough material, releasing its beauty and transforming it for gem or ornamental use. While lacking deposits of traditional gemstones (eg, diamond, ruby, emerald, sapphire), Canada can claim a varied assortment of lesser known but appealing gemstones. Their intrinsic value is relatively low but, in the hands of an expert artisan or creative designer-jeweller, their inherent beauty can be captured and their value enhanced.

Extraction of Canada's gemstones is both hobby oriented and a commercial enterprise. The amateur lapidary, individually or in lapidary club excursions, selects raw materials from outcropping rocks or from old pits and mines (*see* ROCK AND MINERAL COLLECTING). In some cases, as in the Cassiar asbestos mine in BC, the Jeffrey asbestos mine in Asbestos, Qué, and the Geco base-metal mine in Manitouwadge, Ont, interested miners or geologists rescued the gemstones (nephrite jade, hessonite garnet and iolite, respectively) from large-scale mining operations. From Yukon placer operations, the larger gold nuggets are set aside for use in JEWELLERY.

Commercial mining solely for gem material is small scale, often a one-person operation, and sporadic, responding to a fluctuating demand. The largest and most important commercial operations are for nephrite jade recovered from alluvial boulders and bedrock deposits. Production in recent years came from the Mt Sidney Williams, Mt Ogden, Cry Lk and Dease Lk areas of BC and from the Frances Lk area in the YT. Most of the jade was exported to cutting centres in the Far East. The 1985 total BC production of 98 931 kg was valued at $706 010, a drop from the 1978 all-time high of $1.42 million in 1978, which reflects a depressed world demand. Canada is the world's leading producer of nephrite jade. Smaller commercial operations are conducted intermittently for amethyst near Thunder Bay; sodalite and rose quartz near Bancroft, Ont; labradorite on Tabor I, Lab; amazonite (microcline) near Eganville, Ont, and Lac St-Jean, Qué; and rhodonite at Saltspring I, BC. The output is exported to suppliers in the US and to cutting centres in the Orient and Europe. A small proportion is distributed domestically to amateur lapidaries and to some of 211-odd mineral/lapidary dealers in Canada. The exported material often returns to suppliers and retailers as unmounted cut stones and beads, jewellery or ornamental objects, their origin recognized only by geologists or connoisseurs of Canadian gemstones. One gemstone, ammolite, from Lethbridge, Alta, is an exception in that it is extracted and processed into jewellery-ready stones in an integrated operation. Canada's newest gemstone, it was introduced in the late 1970s and is derived from the iridescent shell of the Cretaceous (144-66.4 million years ago) ammonite fossil, *Cephalopoda ammonoidea*. The finished stone, an opallike mosaic of brilliant colours, is sold mainly to manufacturers and jewellers in Japan, Canada and the US. It is also known by the trade names "calcentine" and "korite."

Ammolite from Lethbridge, Alta (*courtesy Geological Survey of Canada*).

Domestic use of commercial gemstone production is by hobbyists or custom lapidaries and designer-jewellers. Techniques used for cutting, shaping and polishing the rough material are essentially the same as those in use the world over for about 500 years. Transparent gemstones are faceted, ie, cut with flat faces (facets) as in a diamond; translucent and opaque material is cut in the cabochon style, with domed top and flat base. Nongem-grade material is carved into sculptures and ornaments (*see* INUIT ART).

Noncommercial extraction is by amateur lapidaries who process their own material. These gemstones are regarded as collectors' stones. The most common and popular are the quartz gemstones, agate and jasper, from localities in BC, Alta, Man, the Lk Superior region, Gaspé and the Bay of Fundy; amethyst from NS; and petrified wood from BC and Alta. Less common collectors' gemstones include Alberta amber, British Columbia idocrase, Ontario feldspars (perthite and the moonstonelike peristerite), Québec scapolite, Newfoundland xonotlite and ivory, and soapstone and lapis lazuli from the territories. These collectors' stones are generally seen as unmounted cut stones, set in jewellery or as carvings at craft shows or gem and mineral shows staged annually by some of the 117 lapidary and mineral clubs in Canada. Jewellery and sculptures fashioned by native peoples are often sold through co-operatives. Canada's gemstone industry is modest in terms of production. It does, however, support domestic lapidary interests and a tourist industry; most of the deposits are open to visitors, both Canadian and foreign. ANN P. SABINA

Genealogy is the study of family history, and usually involves the preparation of a pedigree (family "tree") and an accompanying narrative. Traditionally, genealogy and HERALDRY have been the preserve of the educated, the leisured and the high-born, but since the 1960s there has been a phenomenal expansion of the hobby. Many people believe that Alex Haley's popular book *Roots* (1976), which was made into a TV drama, sparked the explosion of interest; however, Canadian genealogical pioneers such as Cyprien Tanguay (1819-1902), Edward Marion Chadwick (1840-1921), Placide Gaudet (1850-1930), Pierre-Georges Roy (1870-1953) and William D. Reid (1905-69) were busy compiling studies of our forebears long before the pursuit became popular. Today, increasing numbers of Canadians have the spare time and the means to embark on this personal journey into the past.

A genealogical study begins with the researcher recording everything he knows about his immediate family. This information can be supplemented by oral tradition from elderly relatives. Family papers, such as letters, deeds and diaries, can help verify these recollections, as can old photographs. When such sources are exhausted, the researcher must turn to the public holdings of archives, libraries, government agencies and other institutions. These repositories contain a surprising wealth of data in church registers, newspapers, cemetery transcriptions, censuses, assessment rolls, wills, historical journals and monographs, passenger lists, petitions, maps and atlases, vital statistics, naturalization papers, Indian land claims, etc.

Guidance for the novice is available in numerous genealogical handbooks, journals and newsletters. An excellent beginner's manual is *Tracing Your Ancestors in Canada* (9th ed, 1988, rev by Janine Roy), available from the NATIONAL ARCHIVES OF CANADA. Each province has at least one genealogical society. These organizations offer publications, lectures, workshops and conferences on finding one's "roots." More specialized associations can also sometimes furnish useful information. The reluctant researcher has the option of commissioning a professional genealogist. At some point the amateur genealogist may need to hire an expert in Canada or abroad, to overcome a particular difficulty (eg, a search of records in an unfamiliar language), but most family historians find it more satisfying to discover their lineage firsthand. Research need not involve costly commissions and extensive travel. Local public libraries can often borrow required books and microfilms from other libraries and archives. Additional resources can be found in university libraries and branch libraries of the Mormon Church; at the latter one can examine microfilmed records from the world's largest genealogical collection in Salt Lake City, Utah.

After the gathering of information, it is important to preserve the findings for posterity. Ideally a genealogy should include not only pedigree charts but also a documented, written history of the family. Some genealogists add illustrations and others even publish their work. However modest the findings or the format may be, it is worthwhile to distribute copies to relatives, libraries and archives, so that fellow researchers may benefit from the findings and reciprocate.

Genealogy is an absorbing, lifelong pastime. Every search, every family has its own story. Although detective skills and patience are often tested, the curious and imaginative genealogist is seldom disappointed. Along the way each family historian acquires a personal link with the past and a greater sense of self-identity.

JOHN D. BLACKWELL AND LAURIE C.C. STANLEY

Reading: Research in Canada: Angus Baxter, *In Search of Your Roots* (rev ed, 1984); Eric Jonasson, *The Canadian Genealogical Handbook* (2nd ed, 1978); M. Langlois, *Cherchons nos ancêtres* (*c* 1980); K. Mennie-de-Varennes, comp, *Annotated Bibliography of Genealogical Works in Canada* (6 vols, 1986-88); Research Outside of Canada: Angus Baxter, *In Search of Your British & Irish Roots* (1982) and *In Search of Your European Roots* (1985); Noel Currer-Briggs, *Worldwide Family History* (1982); P.W. Filby, comp, *American & British Genealogy & Heraldry* (3rd ed, 1983) and *1982-1985 Supplement* (1987) and *American Directory of Libraries with Genealogical and Local History Collections* (1988); and *Passenger and Immigration Lists Bibliography* (1988); R.R. Hilborn, *Hilborn's Family Newsletter Directory* (3rd ed, 1984); K.A. Johnson et al, eds, *Genealogical Research Directory* (1988).

General Agreement on Tariffs and Trade (GATT) est 1948. During WWII it became evident to the allies that after hostilities ceased it would be desirable to have a multilateral institutional framework within which world trade could be conducted and progressively liberalized, consultation on trade problems among member nations could take place and be resolved, and data on world trade characteristics and trends could be collected and disseminated. Accordingly, after several preparatory sessions, Canada and 22 other nations signed the General Agreement on Tariffs and Trade on 20 Oct 1947. The agreement came into effect 1 Jan 1948. As part of the preparation for this agreement the 23 signing nations carried out negotiations among themselves to reduce some tariffs and other barriers to trade. Canada negotiated with 7 of the countries. Its discussions with the US were the most extensive of any that took place at that time. Canada had negotiated trade agreements with the US in 1935 and 1938, but once both nations signed GATT it became the basic agreement governing trade relations between them, superseding the 1938 agreement. GATT rules (Article I) require that any member country must give all other members the same privileges regarding tariffs or other commercial policy measures that it gives to the most favoured nation with which it negotiates – the most-favoured-nation principle (MFN). Some exceptions are permitted, and Canada has been a beneficiary of several of them. Article I allows for preferences which existed prior to GATT, such as the British Commonwealth preferences, to be retained. The US received a waiver from the MFN rules to enter the CANADA-US AUTOMOTIVE AGREEMENT in 1965 (Autopact). Canada, like other developed countries, also received waivers to grant tariff preferences to developing countries on a range of products. It is also a party to the Multifibre Agreement (MFA) which allows a number of developed countries to impose quantitative import restrictions on textile imports from developing countries; finally, FREE-TRADE arrangements among countries are expressly allowed under Article XXIV of GATT.

Quantitative limits on imports are generally prohibited by GATT (Article XI), but exceptions are allowed in certain circumstances, such as when a nation is suffering major BALANCE-OF-PAYMENTS problems (Article XII) or desires to prevent major injury to domestic producers (Article XIX) or finds it necessary to restrict imports for health, morality, security or other specific reasons (Articles XX and XXI). The 2 most important exceptions for Canada, however, are the MFA and the arrangements for agricultural products. These latter products were excluded from the trade liberalization framework of GATT, primarily because of US insistence. Canada and other major agricultural exporters vigorously objected. Canada also subsequently objected to the special waiver which the US received in 1955 to enable it to restrict imports of dairy products, even though it had no domestic production controls. Subsequently, Germany and Switzerland, after much controversy, got other waivers to restrict agricultural imports. These exclusions and waivers from GATT have produced the maze of restrictions on agricultural imports and export subsidies that exist today. Canada now has its own share of restrictions on imports of grains and of dairy and poultry products, as well as export subsidies of some dairy products and eggs to dispose of surpluses.

GATT prohibits export subsidies, except on agricultural goods (Article XVI), and condemns dumping – selling products abroad for less than they are sold domestically (Article VI). Countervailing duties and anti-dumping duties respectively can be applied against countries that engage in these practices if material injury to domestic industry occurs or is threatened, or if a domestic industry cannot be established because of them. The particularly energetic way in which the US has applied the countervailing rules in recent years has made it difficult for some Canadian producers who sell to the US.

Seven rounds of GATT negotiations have taken place, of which the most important was the Tokyo Round, concluded in July 1979. Average tariff reductions were about 35%, to be completed in stages by 1987, by which time duties by the major industrialized countries averaged 6-7% on finished manufactures, about 4% on semi-manufactured goods, and 0-0.5% on raw materials. The Tokyo Round also saw the adoption of 5 "codes" on nontariff measures. These related to government procurement, technical barriers to trade (such as product standards), import licensing, customs valuation and, most important of all from Canada's viewpoint, subsidies and countervailing duties. As a consequence of this new code, the US finally amended its legislation on countervailing duties to bring it into line with the GATT rules requiring evidence of "material injury" before such duties could be levied. Another code adopted by the majority of developed countries provided for the removal of all tariffs and import restrictions on civil aircraft and parts.

Today over 90 countries are members of GATT. The eighth round of GATT negotiations, the Uruguay Round which began Sept 1986, promises to be the most ambitious of all. The initial Ministerial Declaration provided for negotiations to reduce or eliminate not only tariffs but also nontariff measures. Other items to be considered include ways of integrating the textile and clothing sector into GATT, the reduction of subsidies as well as import barriers on agricultural products, safeguard provisions, dispute settlement mechanisms, intellectual property rights and trade-related investment measures. Liberalization of trade in services of all types is also to be negotiated. The declaration called for the negotiations to be completed in 4 years. BRUCE W. WILKINSON

General Motors of Canada Limited, with headquarters in OSHAWA, Ont, is a major manufacturer and distributor of cars and trucks. It was formed in 1918 by the merger of the McLaughlin Motor Company, Ltd, and the Chevrolet Motor Company of Canada Ltd, and was incorporated as a wholly owned subsidiary of the American-owned General Motors Corporation. By 1921 the company was making Buicks, Oldsmobiles and Oaklands. Since then, GM has grown through various acquisitions and expansions. From 1942 until the end of WWII civilian AUTOMOBILE production was suspended so that the company could manufacture tanks, machine guns and other military equipment. In 1986 GM had sales of $18.5 billion (ranking 1st in Canada), assets of $4.7 billion and 45 994 employees. General Motors Corp of Detroit holds 100% of the shares.

DEBORAH C. SAWYER

Genereux, George Patrick, trapshooter, physician (b at Saskatoon 1 Mar 1935). At 13 Genereux claimed Midwestern International handicap honours, followed by 3 successive Manitoba-Saskatchewan junior titles. He also won the N American junior crown at Vandalia, Ohio, and tied for 2nd in world championship competition at Oslo. This tall 17-year-old with cool nerves and a keen eye reached the pinnacle of his shooting career in Helsinki in 1952 when he emerged with an Olympic gold medal. He was recognized as Canada's male athlete of that year. In 1960 he received his medical degree from McGill.

BOB FERGUSON

Genest, Jacques, physician, medical researcher (b at Montréal 29 May 1919), founder of the Institut de recherches cliniques in Montréal. Genest studied at Coll Jean-de-Brébeuf and did his medicine at U de M before specializing in surgical anatomy and physiology at Harvard Medical School. He spent 6 years in the US, first at Harvard and then at the Rockefeller Institute, NY. On his return to Québec, the provincial government had him carry out a study of European research centres. In 1952 he began to practise medicine at Hôtel-Dieu and there established his first laboratory. Ten years later, with a research team which had felt cramped at the hospital, he carried out his dream of establishing his own institute, the Institut de recherches cliniques. Thanks to his interdisciplinary approach, the institute became an almost unparalleled example of the direct application of molecular biology to the study of clinical medical problems. One of the institute's teams, led by Dr Marc Cantin, identified the heart hormone, or ANF (atrial natriuretic factor), secreted by granules found inside certain cells of the auricles of the heart. This hormone plays an essential role in the control of the volume and pressure of the blood. Among other honours he has received the Royal Bank Award (1980) and the Killam Memorial Prize (1986). In Dec 1987 he was named honorary professor of the Academy of Medical Sciences of China in Beijing.

FRANÇOISE CÔTÉ

Genetic Diseases result from chromosome abnormalities or mutant genes showing a specific pattern of inheritance. In addition, genetic factors are involved in susceptibility to some nongenetic DISEASES. As progress has been made in eliminating infectious diseases, genetic disease has come to represent an increasingly larger proportion of all disease. Genetic diseases among animals, particularly domestic species, have sometimes provided useful information about human counterpart disorders. In Canada the earliest studies of human genetic disease were carried out by Norma Ford WALKER (Toronto), Madge Macklin (London, Ont) and F. Clarke FRASER (Montréal). Recent advances in the study of DNA, the chemical basis of genes, are making possible the identification of the basic defect in many diseases and will increase the possibility for understanding and controlling human genetic disease. A complete knowledge of disease at the gene level may make possible the replacement of faulty genes through GENETIC ENGINEERING. Information on specific diseases is available through genetic counselling services associated with medical schools and affiliated hospitals. Prenatal testing, frequently using DNA technology, is available for a number of genetic disorders.

Chromosome Abnormalities

Humans have 46 chromosomes, ie, 22 pairs of autosomes (responsible, among other features, for reproduction, ie, XX in females, XY in males). Extra or missing chromosomal material usually results in pregnancy loss. About 15% of pregnancies end in spontaneous abortion (miscarriage) during the first 3 months; 40-50% of aborted fetuses have a chromosome abnormality. The most common type of chromosome abnormality among live-born infants is Down syndrome, also called trisomy 21, in which affected individuals have 3 (instead of 2) of the chromosome designated 21. This condition occurs in about 1 in 700 pregnancies (1 in about 40 for mothers over 40 years of age). Affected individuals have multiple physical abnormalities and mental retardation. Abnormalities of a single sex chromosome are usually less severe than those in autosomes. Loss of an X chromosome results in Turner syndrome, found in approximately 20% of all spontaneously aborted fetuses and 0.0005% of newborns; normal mental development, short stature and infertility are characteristic. In Kleinfelter syndrome (XXY), affected individuals are tall, often mentally retarded and have poorly developed secondary sexual characteristics. Chromosome abnormalities are rarely inherited.

Single Gene Disorders

Most genetic diseases result from inheritance of a single disease-controlling gene.

Autosomal Recessive Inheritance Disease is inherited in a recessive manner when the clinically recognized characteristic is hidden in heterozygotes, ie, individuals who inherited the disease gene from only one parent. Only homozygotes, ie, individuals who have received the disease gene from each parent, are clinically affected. Partial abnormalities frequently can be found in heterozygotes. Often the gene involved normally produces an enzyme which is absent in an affected homozygote. These enzyme defects, termed inborn errors of metabolism, can occur in a wide range of biochemical pathways.

Typically, specific genetic diseases occur in all racial groups, although the frequencies are markedly different between groups. Cystic fibrosis is the most common autosomal recessive disease in white children. Affected individuals suffer abnormalities of secretion of pancreatic and digestive tract enzymes; thick mucus can block the small airways of the lung. In phenylketonuria, affected infants lack an enzyme that metabolizes the amino acid phenylalanine (present in milk). The result is an accumulation of abnormal toxic products that cause mental retardation. Many provinces have screening tests so that those affected (about 1 in 10 000 newborns) can be diagnosed and immediately placed on a diet with low levels of phenylalanine. Tay-Sach's disease occurs more frequently (1 in 1600 births) in Ashkenazi Jews than in other racial groups. The absence of an enzyme leads to neurological deterioration and eventual death (at 2-4 years). Recessively inherited anemias can be caused by one of a number of abnormal hemoglobins. Sickle-cell hemoglobin, the most common abnormal type, produces sickle-cell disease in homozygotes; about 1 in 400 N American Blacks are affected. Affected individuals are severely anemic and suffer from arthritislike pain in joints and muscles.

Autosomal Dominant Inheritance Individuals can be clinically affected, regardless of sex, when they carry one normal and one disease gene. Affected individuals pass the disease to 50% of their offspring. Typically, dominant conditions show variable penetrance, ie, some individuals are severely affected while others show few or no effects. Variable penetrance is typical in osteogenesis imperfecta, which results in abnormally brittle bones. Variable age of onset (from about 16 to over 50 years) is characteristic of Huntington disease, which leads to jerking movements of limbs and mental illness.

X-Linked Inheritance A disease gene on the X chromosome can be recessive or dominant; however, as for autosomal traits, recessive conditions are more common. Females, having a normal gene on the other X chromosome, do not express the disease; males are affected. Hemophilia, a bleeding disorder that occurs in 1 in 10 000 males, is such a trait. Queen Victoria was a carrier and some of her male descendants were affected. Muscular dystrophy, which involves progressive deterioration of muscle, is another such disease.

Multifactorial Diseases

Many of the common congenital abnormalities (ie, those present at birth) are multifactorial traits for which both environment and genetic factors are responsible. Cleft lip and palate, pyloric stenosis (blockage of the stomach) and neural tube defects (spina bifida and anencephaly) are common abnormalities of this type. Risks for recurrence in brothers, sisters or offspring are usually about 3-5%, varying with sex of the affected child. Neural tube defects can be detected prenatally. For most such abnormalities, the specific environmental and genetic factors have not been identified; however, it is known that HLA types (ie, markers on the surface of human white blood cells), which can now be identified by DNA methods, influence the susceptibility to diseases involving the immune system.

DIANE WILSON COX

Genetic Engineering is the artificial alteration of the genetic composition (the "genome") of cells or organisms. Since the genome is transmitted to descendants, the alteration is self-perpetuating; because the genome controls biological activities, its manipulation may significantly alter biological function. The broadest definition of genetic engineering includes artificial selection of plants and animals, practiced consciously or inadvertently in the development of domesticated varieties since prehistory. Conscious artificial selection of man (Eugenics) has generally found disfavour, for a variety of sociological, ethical and biological reasons.

As our knowledge of the workings of inheritance and genetic organization increased, so did the possibilities for genetic engineering. The term itself was introduced only when general means to move genes (hereditary factors, segments of DNA) between remotely related species developed in the mid-1970s. Interspecies gene transfer has its parallel in nature; rare natural hybrids lead to novel species with genetic components of both pre-existing species. Interspecies hybridization, arising either naturally or artificially, played an important role in the development of many domesticated plants. The methods of genetic engineering extend the possibilities of gene transfer beyond the limits of sexual compatibility.

The development of modern genetic engineering depended upon a number of major technical advances: cloning, cell fusion, nuclear transplantation, gene cloning and transfection.

Cloning is the production of groups of genetically identical cells or individuals from a single starting cell; all members of a clone are formally identical, genetically. All micro-organisms, many plants and a few multi-cellular animals frequently form clones as a means of reproduction – "asexual" reproduction. In man, identical twins are clones, developing after separation of the earliest cells formed from a single fertilized egg. In combination with test-tube fertilization and embryo transplants, Alta Genetics of Calgary is a world leader in the use of artificial twinning as a tool in genetic engineering of cattle. Manipulating plant hormones in plant cell cultures can yield clones consisting of millions of plantlets, which may be packageable to form artificial seed.

Cloning is not strictly genetic engineering, since the genome normally remains unaltered; but it is a practical means to propagate engineered organisms. Further, under some conditions, for unknown reasons, plants produced as clones exhibit inheritable "somaclonal" variation, which contributes significantly to plant breeding resources.

Cell Fusion Cells and nuclei of both plants and animals can be caused to fuse, producing hybrid cells. Under favourable circumstances, a viable, hybrid cell-line may arise. Cultured hybrid plant cells can regenerate whole plants, so cell fusion allows crosses of sexually incompatible species. Most mammalian cells cannot regenerate whole individuals; however, the fusion of antibody-forming cells (which are difficult to culture) and "transformed" (cancerlike) cells, gives rise to immortal cellular clones, each producing one particular antibody, so-called monoclonal antibodies. These cell-lines can be used for commercial production of diagnostic and antidisease antibody preparations. Fusions involving human cells played a major role in investigations of human heredity and GENETIC DISEASE.

Nuclear Transplantation Microsurgery allows removal and reimplantation of cell nuclei. Cells with transplanted nuclei may give rise to whole organisms; for example, clones of frogs have been produced by transplantation of identical nuclei from a young embryo, each to a different anucleate frog egg. The technique has not yet found practical application, but has been of great importance in studies on vertebrate (including mammalian) development. There is no known instance of human cloning by this (or other) means. Nonetheless, frequent calls for regulation of human cloning and genetic engineering occur, stemming from similar considerations which lead most commentators to reject Eugenics.

Gene Cloning is fundamental to genetic engineering. A segment of DNA from any donor organism is joined, in the test-tube, to a second DNA molecule, known as a vector, to form a "recombinant DNA molecule." As a result of vector design, recombinant DNA can enter (transfect) some particular organism, often the enteric bacterium, *Escherichia coli*. There, it engages the cellular machinery for DNA replication, so that the donor DNA is propagated and may impose upon the host hereditary features from the donor. Production of recombinant DNA molecules is now technologically routine. However, each new gene to be "cloned" presents a puzzle as to how to identify it, among the hundreds of thousands of clones potentially produced from a given donor genome.

Gene cloning in microbes has reached commercial application, notably with the marketing of human INSULIN produced by bacteria. Many similar products are under development, including growth hormones, blood-clotting factors and anti-viral interferons. Gene cloning has revolutionized understanding of genes, cells and diseases. It has raised diagnosis of hereditary disease to high science and contributed precise diagnostic tools for infectious disease.

Transfection (=transformation=transvection) is the uptake of a recombinant DNA molecule by a cell. Vector design is, in large part, dedicated to promoting transfection. Each kind of cell is best transfected with different vectors. For bacteria, vectors are based on DNA molecules that naturally move between cells – bacterial viruses and plasmids. Mammalian vectors usually derive from mammalian viruses. In higher plants, the favoured system is the infectious agent of crown-gall tumours. Most important are "shuttle" vectors, which transfect several types of cell, facilitating rapid gene transfer between different organisms.

To avoid potential "biohazards," even bacterial transfection is publicly regulated in Canada and the US by the scientific granting agencies and by law in some other countries. Biological containment, the deliberate hereditary debilitation of host cells and vectors, is required. In using mammals and higher plants, especially strict regulations apply, requiring physical isolation.

A great deal remains, both in development of techniques and in acquisition of fundamental knowledge needed to apply them appropriately. Nonetheless, genetic engineering promises a world of tailor-made crop-plants and farm animals; cures for hereditary disease by gene replacement therapy; an analytical understanding of CANCER and its treatment; and a world in which much of our present-day, harsh, chemical technology is replaced by milder, organism-dependent, fermentation processing.

In Canada, genetic engineering research is taking place in laboratories of universities, industries, and federal and provincial research organizations. For example, in the industrial sector, RDT research for medical applications is occurring at Ayerst Laboratories, Montréal, CONNAUGHT LABORATORIES, Toronto, and INSTITUT ARMAND-FRAPPIER, Laval-des-Rapides, Qué. Inco is applying RDT research to mining and metallurgy, and Labatt's Breweries is using recombinant techniques in yeast genetics experiments. The Veterinary Infectious Disease Organization, based at U of Saskatchewan, is using genetic engineering technology for production of new vaccines for livestock diseases. *See also* ANIMAL BREEDING; PLANT BREEDING; BIOTECHNOLOGY; TRANSPLANTATION.

B.H. LESSER AND DAVID NASH

Genetics is that subdiscipline of biology devoted to the study of heredity, the phenomenon by which organisms pass on their characteristics to their offspring. Although humankind has always shown an interest in heredity, the practice of the science is usually considered to have begun in 1865 with Gregor Mendel, an Austrian monk. Through a study of pea plants, Mendel worked out the simple patterns of inheritance that apply to most inheritable characteristics of living things (eg, height, shape, colour, hairiness, smell, behaviour, disease resistance). Mendel formulated the concept of the gene to define the fundamental units of heredity that determine such properties. Today the molecular structure and function of genes is quite well understood.

Modern genetics may be conveniently divided into 3 areas of study: transmission genetics, population genetics and molecular genetics. Transmission genetics is concerned with identifying genes affecting a particular characteristic and the patterns by which these genes are transmitted from generation to generation, and from cell to cell. Population genetics analyses the pattern of distribution of such genes in populations of organisms. Molecular genetics focuses on the structure and function of the genetic units, ie, the chemical composition of genes and their expression in structural proteins and enzyme proteins, important functional components of cells.

Transmission Genetics The total genetic complement of a cell or organism is defined as the genotype. Its physiological expression is called its phenotype. Genes can be identified only if some variation is visible in the phenotype. Phenotypic variation can be discontinuous (eg, yellow versus green seeds) or may occur as a range (eg, very short to very tall). Discontinuous variation can usually be explained by a simple (often single) gene difference. Continuous variation usually involves a larger number of interacting genes (polygenes); the greater the number of genes involved, the greater the possible range of variation. Mendel's classic experiments dealt with the inheritance of discontinuous traits.

Molecular Genetics Genes are organized into structures called chromosomes (humans have 2 sets of 23 chromosomes, each parent contributing a set, for a total of 46). Each chromosome contains a 50 mm length of a threadlike chemical called DNA (deoxyribonucleic acid); however, as each chromosome is less than 0.005 mm long, the DNA is very efficiently packed through coiling and supercoiling. A gene is simply a segment on the thread with a specific function. It embodies a coded message, in the form of a sequence of "building blocks" (nucleotides), that dictates the sequence of amino acids produced to make up a specific protein molecule. The proteins control chemical reactions taking place in cells, or are important structural components of cells.

Prokaryotes, ie, organisms composed of a single cell that lacks a membrane-bound nucleus (eg, bacteria), carry a single chromosome that undergoes replication during one cycle of cell duplication. The cell divides by binary fission to yield 2 daughter cells, each of which carries a daughter chromosome. Eukaryotic organisms, ie, those composed of one or more cells having membrane-bound nuclei (all "higher" organisms), contain 2 kinds of cells with different genetic potential. Somatic (or body) cells carry 2 copies of each of their chromosomes and are called diploid cells. Gametes or germ cells (eg, sperm, egg) carry one copy only of the gene complement and are haploid. In eukaryotes, 2 haploid germ cells unite at fertilization. The resulting zygote undergoes cell division and differentiation, eventually producing the adult organism. Cells that derive from division of prokaryotic cells or somatic cells will be exact genetic copies of their parents. In contrast, every haploid gamete is different, representing a unique combination of the parental genes: this results in genetic diversity in progeny.

Living things can duplicate their genetic material exactly, an ability that results from the replicative ability of the DNA sequence. Infrequently, this DNA undergoes a change, termed a mutation, that alters both genotype and phenotype and results in genetic variation. Mutations without obvious cause are referred to as spontaneous mutations; induced mutations result mainly from damage to genes caused by environmental chemicals and radiation. Mutations are the material on which the environment acts to produce evolution; thus, a mutation that gives an organism an advantage may permit it to survive longer and produce more offspring which, in turn, contain the mutated gene. Over time, an entire population may change. Of particular concern to human populations is environmental mutagenesis, the development of mutations caused by environmental changes. Increasing levels of chemicals and radiation in the environment may cause mutations in germ cells that over time would result in increased heritable genetic disease, or mutations in somatic cells resulting in CANCER.

Canadian Contributions

Genetics has had a major impact on medicine, agriculture and forestry. It is now recognized that health and illness are strongly influenced by genetics; in fact, many diseases are known to be genetic in origin, resulting from a mutation. Well-known examples of such genetic diseases are hemophilia, phenylketonuria (PKU) and cystic fibrosis. Important work on genetic diseases has been or is being done by F. Clarke FRASER (McGill University), who worked on the genetics of abnormal development in mammals; Howard NEWCOMBE (Atomic Energy of Canada, Chalk River, Ont), who studied bacterial population genetics, mutagenesis, radiation genetics and human population genetics; Charles SCRIVER (McGill) for contributions on human genetic diseases. The recent establishment of somatic cell genetics in Canada owes much to L. SIMINOVITCH (U of T).

Genetics has been applied to plant breeding and ANIMAL BREEDING. Canadian researchers have produced outstanding examples of improvement by genetic manipulation, the earliest being Marquis winter WHEAT, produced early in the 20th century by Charles E. SAUNDERS to withstand the severe prairie climate. More recently, Canadian geneticists have produced strains of wheat resistant to rusts (destructive parasitic FUNGI). Triticale, a new cereal crop, was developed by Leonard H. Shebeski and Edward N. Larter at University of Manitoba. The development of CANOLA, ie, improved varieties of rape plants for production of a vegetable oil, was undertaken by research groups headed by R.K. DOWNEY (Agriculture Canada, Saskatoon) and Baldur STEFANSSON (University of Manitoba).

In 1944 Canadian biochemist Oswald Avery demonstrated that DNA is the hereditary material of the cell, a discovery that made possible the clarification of DNA structure by James Watson and Francis Crick in 1953. Other Canadian geneticists whose work has made major contributions to the international body of genetic knowledge include Howard FREDEEN (Agriculture Canada RESEARCH STATION, Lacombe, Alta), who developed the industrially important Lacombe hog; Leonard H. Butler (U of T), who studied tomato genetics; Clayton O. PERSON (University of British Columbia), for his work on the genetic basis for host-parasite relationships; Jack Von Borstel (University of Alberta), for his work on the genetics of YEAST; Bruce Chown (Winnipeg) for his work on human genetics; Peter Moens (York) for his work on cytogenetics; Allen P. James (NRC, Ottawa) for his work on yeast genetics; Etta Käfer (McGill) for her work on the genetics of the fungi *Aspergillus* and *Neuspora*; and Michael Smith (UBC) for his work on site-directed mutagenesis. David T. SUZUKI (UBC) achieved worldwide recognition for his work on the genetics of the fruit fly (*Drosophila melanogaster*).

The most recent revolution in biological science has come as a result of the evolution of recombinant DNA technology. These biochemical techniques permit genes to be removed from their original organism and spliced into the chromosomes of simple organisms (eg, bacteria, fungi); thus, they are far more amenable to study. Furthermore the cloned genes can be put to use to make their normal gene product in a new host that can be grown in large batches. Already such GENETIC ENGINEERING has found application in biotechnology. For example, new strains of bacteria have been developed with major importance in industry, agriculture and medicine (eg, useful in production of insulin, human growth hormones, interferon for the treatment of viral-induced diseases and oil- and wood-degrading enzymes). In other approaches, useful novel genes, such as those for herbicide resistance, are being introduced into plants, and others into mammalian cells (a technique possibly leading to human gene therapy).

Education and Societies in Canada

Professional training for a career as a geneticist or medical geneticist can be obtained in universities or medical schools. At the undergraduate level students obtain a BSc degree in biology, genetics, microbiology, biochemistry or molecular biology. Graduate studies lead to MSc or PhD degrees. The MSc qualifies an individual for work in a research facility in a subordinate position and to teach; the PhD permits work as an independent genetic researcher in a university department or other research institution. Physicians may take specialized genetics training through the Canadian College of Medical Geneticists (headquartered at the Alberta Children's Hospital, Calgary), the world's first such institution. A candidate desiring to pursue a career in clinical genetics (eg, genetic counselling) must pass the examination of the CCMG.

In Canada, research is proceeding in all areas of modern genetics. Most work is taking place at the universities and is funded mainly through federal grants. The federal government also sponsors research directly through its own administrative structure (eg, the many research branches of Agriculture Canada). Industry, especially companies producing agricultural or medical products, are becoming increasingly involved in genetics research. Medical genetics studies are undertaken at universities and hospitals. In this area, the BC Health Surveillance Registry has compiled a complete record of all birth defects in the province since 1952, a record almost unique in the world. These data permit research into risk estimates for various genetic conditions and of population trends in genetic disease

Geneticists make a major contribution to Canadian life in a variety of professional situations, eg, as research scientists at university, government or industrial laboratories and as genetic counsellors in hospitals. The Genetics Society of Canada, headquartered in Ottawa, is the professional association of Canadian geneticists. It holds annual meetings and publishes a journal, *Genome*, with international distribution. A.J.F. GRIFFITHS

Gentian, common name for several plants of family Gentianaceae, primarily in genus *Gentiana*. The genus contains about 400 species of herbaceous perennials, some weedy, others with large, attractive, trumpet-shaped, usually blue flowers. Found chiefly in northern temperate and arctic zones, the genus is best developed in the mountains of Europe and Asia, where many excellent garden plants originated. At least 16 species occur in Canada, primarily in damp soils. Most are found W of Ontario; some are arctic; none have been reported from PEI or NS. The root of European yellow gentian (*G. lutea*) was used extensively as a tonic to promote digestion and aid appetite; closed gentian (G. *andrewsii*), native to eastern Canada, is said to have identical properties. N American Indians and European settlers used any species for a bitter tonic that was prepared by pouring boiling water over leafy tops and roots. Settlers improved on the infusion by adding a generous quantity of brandy.
GILLIAN FORD

Geoffrion, Joseph André Bernard, "Boom Boom," hockey player (b at Montréal 16 Feb 1931). He joined the MONTREAL CANADIENS in 1950, playing with them 14 years. His perseverance, thundering shot and spirited play made him one of the highest scorers in hockey history. He won the CALDER TROPHY (1951-52), the ART ROSS TROPHY (1954-55, 1960-61) and the HART TROPHY (1960-61). In 1961 he became the second player (after Maurice RICHARD) to score 50 goals in a season. He retired briefly then joined New York Rangers 1966-68. He scored 393 goals, 429 assists in regular season play, and 58 goals, 60 assists in playoffs. JAMES MARSH

Geographical Information Systems (GIS) are systems designed to store and manipulate data relating to locations on the Earth's surface. Common applications are land inventories, the census, urban planning, and so on, where the data banks contain locational references such as a county, or the actual boundaries of land parcels. Equivalent terms for such information are "spatial" and "geo-coded" data. Because of the need to manipulate extremely large quantities of data, most modern GIS now employ computer technology.

Canada has been a pioneer in the development of GIS. The Canada Geographic Information System (CGIS), initiated in 1963 by the Agriculture Rehabilitation and Development Agency, was the first operational land resource GIS. Now operating under Environment Canada, CGIS holds the world's largest land resource data bank. Another early system was the Geographically Referenced Data Retrieval System of Statistics Canada, started around 1965. Many of the concepts and methods developed for these systems are now routinely incorporated into new systems. Large GIS are still predominantly operated by federal and provincial agencies such as the CGIS and the Canada Soil Information System of Agriculture Canada, but there is growing application of GIS in urban planning, forest and petroleum industries, utilities, transportation systems, etc. It is expected that usage of the GIS will continue to expand.
THOMAS K. POIKER AND IAN K. CRAIN

Geography A core of geography deals with the description and analysis of physical environmental phenomena and their interrelationships, and with distribution patterns of human POPULATIONS and their activities as they affect the Earth. As history interprets temporal sequences, so geography interprets spatial associations. Geography is broken into subfields with varying emphases. PHYSICAL GEOGRAPHY is less directly concerned with people than is human geography. It describes and analyses the distribution and process relationships among elements in the physical environment, eg, landforms, CLIMATE, VEGETATION, SOILS and DRAINAGE. Some of its subfields are GEOMORPHOLOGY, CLIMATOLOGY, HYDROLOGY and BIOGEOGRAPHY. Human geography places more emphasis on people and is concerned with the reasons for the location of human activities. Some of its subfields are cultural, historical, economic, political and urban geography. Geography serves as a link between the physical and SOCIAL SCIENCES. The discipline is taught "topically," ie, as subfields (geomorphology, economic geography, etc) and "regionally," ie, by studying distribution patterns within defined areas.

Geography is one of the oldest studies, originating with Greek scholars 2000 years ago [*geo*, "earth"; *graphos*, "to write"]. The concepts of modern geography were developed in Germany in the last half of the 19th century, and the subject was well known in France and Britain early in the 20th century. Geography was mainly an academic discipline in most countries until about 1940. The application of knowledge about the world's physical environments and resources became significant during WWII, and applied geography became a career possibility after 1945. Much of the philosophy and methods of modern geography came to Canada through Canadians trained in geography departments in American universities during the 1950s and 1960s. Other geographers came from Britain and France.

In 1922 UBC became the first Canadian university to have a partial geography department, when a dept of geology and geography was established. Courses were taught by professors trained in geology. The first academic geographers came from France in the mid-1920s and lectured at Université de Montréal. The first full dept of geography was established at University of Toronto in 1935, headed by T. Griffith TAYLOR, a British geographer who had lectured in Australia. Most large Canadian universities established geography departments during the 1950s; 37 universities had geography departments or geography programs in 1985.

Although the term "geographer" was used by provincial and federal governments before 1940, it usually referred to a person engaged in map production (*see* CARTOGRAPHY) and often trained in drafting or SURVEYING. The federal government engaged its first professional geographer, J. Lewis Robinson, in 1943, and geographers were carrying on studies in RESOURCE USE and planning in most provincial governments by the 1950s. The Canadian Assn of Geographers was formed in 1951 when about 50 geographers, mainly from Ontario and Québec, met at McGill in Montréal. The first president was Donald PUTNAM of U of T. Members have an academic degree or professional experience in geography. The association publishes a quarterly periodical, *The Canadian Geographer.* Geographical societies which are not professional organizations but are open to the public operate in some parts of Canada. The oldest is the Québec Geographical Soc (founded 1877); the largest, the Royal Canadian Geographical Soc, which publishes the popular CANADIAN GEOGRAPHIC.

Geographers are employed in diverse occupations. Most students at the bachelor level do not become professional geographers. For many of these, geography is part of a general education which permits them to become involved in matters such as people's use of the natural environment and natural-resource analysis, or to study about people and their activities in cities or in large regions. Many students continue into fields such as planning (environmental, urban, etc), architecture, law, commerce, public administration and especially teaching. By the mid-1970s increasing numbers of geography students were finding employment in business and industry. Others work where their technical skills in the design, preparation and reading of maps are useful, and where knowledge of air and satellite photos, or statistical methods, are required.

During the 1980s Canadian universities granted about 200 master's degrees in geography each year. Most of these geographers became lecturers in community colleges; planners, research scientists and administrators in consulting firms or governments; or applied geographers in business and industry. During the 1980s doctoral degrees in geography were awarded each year to 25-35 people, most of whom became university professors.

J. LEWIS ROBINSON

Geological Dating For centuries people have argued about the age of the Earth; only recently has it been possible to come close to achieving reliable estimates. In the 19th century some geologists realized that the vast thicknesses of sedimentary rocks meant that the Earth must be at least hundreds of millions of years old. Charles Darwin reinforced this idea by pointing to the time that must have been required for the EVOLUTION of advanced life from primitive forms. On the other hand, the great physicist Lord Kelvin vehemently objected and suggested that the Earth might only be a few tens of millions of years old, based on his calculations of its cooling history. These discussions were rendered obsolete by the discovery of radioactivity in 1896 by the French physicist Henri Becquerel. The existence of radioactivities of various kinds in rocks has enabled earth scientists to determine the age of the Earth, the moon, meteorites, mountain chains and ocean basins, and to draw up a reasonably accurate time scale of evolution. It has even been possible to work out a time scale of the reversals of the Earth's magnetic field. This "radiometric" approach has superseded all other techniques for determining absolute ages.

Radioactive Clock The vast majority of atoms (each composed of a nucleus surrounded by electrons) are stable. Essentially, they will exist forever. A critical few, however, are unstable. Their nuclei tend to emit particles spontaneously, ie, they are radioactive. Because of this particle emission, the original radioactive parent atom changes its identity, becoming a different, stable daughter atom. This change takes place at a known rate determined by the half-life, ie, the time required for one half of the original number of radioactive atoms to convert to the stable daughter product. The remaining number of radioactive atoms is halved every half-life. Radioactive elements of use in geological dating have relatively long half-lives. A good example is rubidium-87 which changes to strontium-87 at a rate of one-half every 50 billion years. Therefore, a rock can be dated by measuring how much of its original rubidium content has changed into strontium. The other key dating techniques involve uranium-235 transforming to lead-207 at a rate of one-half every 713 million years, uranium-238 becoming lead-206 at one-half every 4.5 billion years, potassium changing to argon (and calcium) at one-half every 1.3 billion years and samarium-147 becoming neodymium-143 at one-half every 1.06 billion years. These radioactive processes present a set of natural clocks which reveal when the rock was formed, or when it was last heated severely. The well-known carbon-14 method involves the conversion of radioactive carbon-14 to stable nitrogen, at a rate of one-half about every 5700 years. It can only be used to date organic matter, and is accurate only for materials younger than about 70 000 years (*see* ARCHAEOLOGY; GLACIATION).

Since 1950, radiometric methods have been developed to a very sophisticated level in several countries, including Canada. It has been demonstrated that when rocks which have led an undisturbed history are analysed, all methods reveal the same age. This uniformity demonstrates that the principle is reliable. When disturbed rocks are studied, the different techniques may give different readings and much research has been carried out on how to interpret such results. It often proves possible to date even severely disturbed rocks.

Age of the Earth To date the time of formation of a planet 12 640 km in diameter and 70.8% covered by water is not easy. Only the tiniest fraction of the Earth, the crust, is accessible. Those rocks available for analysis (ie, the oldest ones) have been heated and squeezed many times in their GEOLOGICAL HISTORY, because for billions of years continents have been drifting over the Earth's surface, colliding and producing mountains and new ocean floors. Two approaches have been developed to circumvent these problems. The first involves sampling as much of the Earth's crust as possible and dating these rocks. The Earth certainly must be older than the oldest terrestrial rocks found. Stephen Moorbath and his colleagues at Oxford have shown that rocks near Godthaab in SW Greenland either formed or were in existence approximately 3.8 billion years ago. These results have been confirmed and agreement has been found among the rubidium-strontium, uranium-lead and samarium-neodymium methods. Rocks of almost this age have also been identified in other localities, including Labrador, Minnesota, Africa and India. Therefore, it is clear that the Earth is over 3.8 billion years old. Many scientists are searching for rocks older than these, and in 1983 Australian scientists claimed to have discovered minute zircon crystals 4.2 billion years old.

The second approach, which is more indirect but gives an answer currently believed correct, involves a comparison of the Earth with meteorites. They have clearly fallen to Earth from outside, often gouging out huge craters such as that called New Québec (61°17′ N, 73°41′ W). Rubidium-strontium, potassium-argon, uranium-lead and samarium-neodymium dating all show that the meteorites formed about 4.6 billion years ago. But detailed studies of lead isotopes in meteorites and terrestrial rocks strongly indicate that the Earth and meteorites formed at the same time. Therefore, since the meteorites are very accurately dated at 4.6 billion years old, the Earth is also considered to be the same age. Dating of the lunar samples collected by the Apollo missions strongly indicates that the moon is of the same age. If the Earth, the moon and meteorites are all 4.6 billion years old, then so very probably is the whole solar system.

Age of Canadian Shield The most ancient rocks of Canada comprise the Canadian Shield (*see* GEOLOGICAL REGIONS). Many Canadian scientists, and others, have examined these rocks to work out the region's history. The Shield is made up of areas of rocks of distinctive ages. The oldest, found in Saglek Bay and near Hebron Fjord in Labrador, are about 3.6 billion years old. Other massive slabs are dated at 2.9-2.5 billion years, 1.8-1.7 billion years and 1.3-0.9 billion years. Some of these areas represent the roots of what were ancient mountain chains, the upper parts of which were long ago removed by EROSION. Others represent volcanic belts, many of which have never been very deeply buried. Scientists are studying whether these portions of different age and geological history were always close together or were far apart until gathered together by continental drifting and PLATE TECTONICS. Although the igneous rocks of the Shield are very ancient, the formation of igneous rocks has been a continuing process in Canada. The rocks formed by the Aiyansh lava flow in BC are thought to be 90 to 350 years old, confirming legends of the Tsimshian people of Nass R describing volcanic activity.

Time Scale of Biological Evolution It seems probable that life has existed on the Earth for well over 3 billion years. FOSSIL bacteria have been tentatively identified in the Fig-Tree Sediments in South Africa. Volcanic rocks associated with these have been dated at 3.5 billion years by the samarium-neodymium method by scientists at Columbia U and by the potassium-argon method at U of Toronto. Probably the oldest fossils in Canada (2.5 billion years old) are the stromatolite formations at Steep Rock Lk, Ont. An indisputably biogenic, highly diverse microfossil assemblage is present in the approximately 1.9-billion-year-old Gunflint cherts of southern Ontario. However, the fossil record is well documented only for the last 570 million years, for only during that period did organisms exist with the hard phosphate or calcium-carbonate components which make for good fossil preservation. The final 570 million years of evolution have been divided by paleontologists into 3 eras: Paleozoic (ancient life), Mesozoic (middle life) and Cenozoic (present life). The eras are subdivided into periods. The numerical estimates of the time occupied by these periods were made mostly with the aid of potassium-argon and rubidium-strontium dating of rocks which could be correlated with the time

The McDonald Fault, Great Slave Lake, NWT. The fault was active more than 2 billion years ago, when the Great Slave Plate and the Churchill Plate were moving in opposite directions. The raised escarpment at the left is made up of rocks of the Churchill Province (*courtesy Ron Redfern, Random House Inc*).

scale. Humans are creatures of only the last few million years. Fossils of apelike, upright-walking, potential human ancestors were found in 1981 in Ethiopia by an international expedition led by Desmond Clark of U of California at Berkeley. A volcanic ash associated with these fossils has been dated at U of T at about 4 million years old, showing that creatures even remotely resembling modern humans have been on the Earth for less than one-tenth of 1% of our planet's history. DEREK YORK

Reading: Derek York, *Planet Earth* (1976).

Geological History Fundamental to all ordering of events of the Earth's history is the principle of the positional relationships of rock and MINERAL bodies. For example, in any stratified rock sequence, younger rocks overlie older ones. Similarly, stratified SEDIMENTARY ROCKS intruded by formerly molten IGNEOUS ROCKS are clearly older than the igneous rocks. Study of positional relationships allows the geologist to establish a relative sequence of events. Positional relationships underlie all attempts to decipher geological history, and they allowed the development in the 19th century of a relative time scale based on the sequences of fossil assemblages which also provided evidence for the theory of EVOLUTION.

At the end of the 18th century, James Hutton formulated another major contribution to the understanding of the rock record, the principle of uniformitarianism, which states that the same geological processes now operating also acted in the past, producing similar results. This principle underlies the use of modern geological processes, rates and products as guides in interpreting and explaining the rock record. On a broad scale, 3 geological phenomena exhibit systematic changes which are essential to the construction and continued refinement of the geological time scale: the evolution of life, the radioactive decay of unstable isotopes and the paleomagnetic signature of rock and mineral bodies.

Whereas earlier attempts to understand the Earth's history focused on specific kinds of rocks, with crystalline igneous rocks considered oldest and sedimentary rocks progressively younger, the recognition of distinctive FOSSILS within the younger part of the rock record led to rapid progress. Most major divisions of the Phanerozoic [Gk, "visible life"] part of the geological time scale, the last 570 million years, were established in the 19th century, based on their distinctive fossil content. Cambrian, Permian, Triassic and most other names of the Phanerozoic systems were in common use before 1900 to refer to the rocks and time periods in which particular organisms were abundant. Recognition of the geological periods and eras permitted relative dating of rocks to move from local divisions, based on positional relationships, to regional and international dating; however, the time scale remained relative.

Calibration of the 19th-century geological time scale had to await 2 major advances of 20th-century earth science: discovery of natural radioactivity and development of tools to measure this radioactivity accurately (*see* GEOLOGICAL DATING). Radiometric dating techniques have permitted calibration of the geological time scale and are essential to subdivision of the vast Precambrian part of the rock record which lacks hard-shelled fossils.

Geological Eras About five-sixths of geological time is assigned to the Precambrian, which ended about 570 million years ago. Less is known about it than about the Phanerozoic (the most recent 570 million years) because more of the Phanerozoic is preserved and exposed, and because it contains most of the fossil record. The concept of geological eras came from the Phanerozoic part of the rock record, and the names of its 3 eras – Paleozoic (ancient life), Mesozoic (middle life) and Cenozoic (modern life) – are based on how closely the fossils resemble living forms. Each era had its own most characteristic organisms, and these and others are used to identify Phanerozoic rocks around the world. The hard-shelled arthropods and corals of the Paleozoic oceans gave way to the reptiles of the Mesozoic oceans and, in particular, to the land-dwelling DINOSAURS. These, in turn, were replaced by the more adaptable, warm-blooded mammals of the Cenozoic. Canada has world-famous exposures of Lower and Middle Paleozoic sedimentary rocks in the Rocky Mts (*see* BURGESS SHALE); of classic, Upper Paleozoic rocks in the high arctic islands; and abundant, widespread Mesozoic and Cenozoic successions in the sedimentary basin of the prairies (*see* BADLANDS; DINOSAUR HUNTING IN WESTERN CANADA), in the northern arctic islands and on the Continental Shelf off the Atlantic provinces.

The great age of Precambrian rocks and the general lack of fossils precludes fine-scale subdivision of this part of the rock record. Nevertheless, there are major global changes in the nature of these rocks through time. Archean rocks, those older than about 2.5 billion years, commonly consist of belts of volcanic rocks (greenstone belts) surrounded by masses of granitic rock. The Superior Province of the Canadian SHIELD is the largest and among the best-known bodies of exposed Archean rocks in the world. Proterozoic rocks, also abundant in the Shield, are about 570 million to 2.5 billion years old. These rocks begin to have a modern look: large sequences of shallow marine and continental sedimentary rocks can be distinguished, as can mountain belts similar to modern, continental-margin, mountain belts. There is no agreement on whether plate-tectonic processes operated in Archean time, but there is reasonable evidence that some lithospheric plates were established by Proterozoic time. This evidence is provided largely by the strong similarity between the Proterozoic Wopmay mountain belt in the Slave Province of the Canadian Shield and modern mountain belts.

Since the 1960s, the advent and acceptance of plate-tectonic concepts has resulted in great interest in detailed reconstruction of the Earth's crust and surface in past geological times. Canadian earth scientists are leaders in this work because of the long emphasis on regional geological studies in Canada and because of the diversity and complexity of the country – with its enormous Precambrian-Shield core, its widespread interior-platform sediments, its continent-bounding mountain belts on east, west and north sides, and its well-developed, continental-margin sedimentary sequences. This work depends fundamentally on continued refinement of subdivisions and methods of dating the rock record, through paleontological studies, radiometric dating, magnetic reversal chronology and other methods. The selection of suitable field localities as standards or references for geological systems (such as the Devonian), is a vital part of this work. Government earth scientists, especially those of the GEOLOGICAL SURVEY OF CANADA, play a key role in regional geological studies, particularly in remote areas of northern Canada (*see also* GEOLOGICAL REGIONS; PLATE TECTONICS).

R.W. MACQUEEN

Geological Regions Canada consists of 6 geological regions. Five of them are of Phanerozoic age (less than 570 million years old) and are arranged roughly concentrically around and partly on the sixth, the Canadian SHIELD (of Precambrian age, more than 570 million years old). The Phanerozoic regions, which overlap in age, are the Innuitian Orogen, the Appalachian Orogen, the Interior Platform, the Canadian Cordillera and the continental shelves. Each region has a distinctive architecture and is composed of building blocks of characteristic types and sequences of rocks (tectonic assemblages) that record its development (*see also* PLATE TECTONICS). Probably the most important developmental events in GEOLOGICAL HISTORY were the orogenies, periods during which compressive deformation,

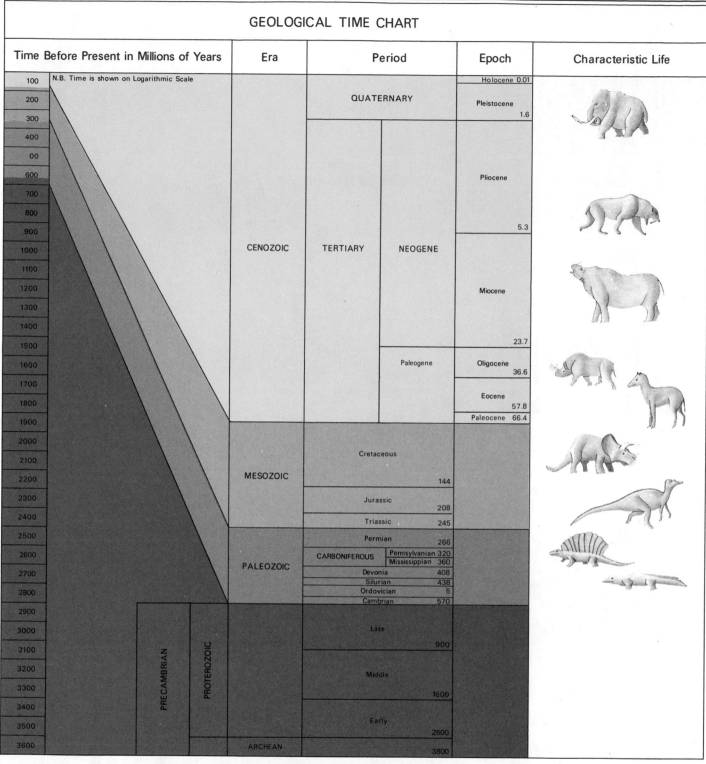

GEOLOGICAL TIME CHART

Time Before Present in Millions of Years: 100, 200, 300, 400, 00, 600, 700, 800, 900, 1000, 1100, 1200, 1300, 1400, 1500, 1600, 1700, 1800, 1900, 2000, 2100, 2200, 2300, 2400, 2500, 2600, 2700, 2800, 2900, 3000, 3100, 3200, 3300, 3400, 3500, 3600

N.B. Time is shown on Logarithmic Scale

Era	Period		Epoch	Characteristic Life
CENOZOIC	QUATERNARY		Holocene 0.01	
			Pleistocene 1.6	
	TERTIARY	NEOGENE	Pliocene 5.3	
			Miocene 23.7	
		Paleogene	Oligocene 36.6	
			Eocene 57.8	
			Paleocene 66.4	
MESOZOIC	Cretaceous 144			
	Jurassic 208			
	Triassic 245			
PALEOZOIC	Permian 266			
	CARBONIFEROUS	Pennsylvanian 320		
		Mississippian 360		
	Devonia 408			
	Silurian 438			
	Ordovician 5			
	Cambrian 570			
PRECAMBRIAN / PROTEROZOIC	Late 900			
	Middle 1600			
	Early 2500			
ARCHEAN	3800			

metamorphism, granitic intrusion and other processes formed MOUNTAIN RANGES.

Canadian Shield

The Canadian Shield is a mosaic of geological provinces in which those of Archean age (more than 2.5 billion years old) are surrounded by a matrix of Proterozoic rocks (2.5-0.57 billion years old). The Archean provinces (Superior, Slave, Kaminak and Nutak) were cratons (ie, stable, low-lying continental parts of the Earth's crust) by the end of the Kenoran Orogeny (2.5 billion years ago); now they are mainly metamorphic and granitic rocks with irregular belts of turbidites and "greenstone" (metamorphic basic volcanics) 18 km in thickness. The Proterozoic provinces (Bear, Churchill, Labrador and Southern) are marked by orogenic trends developed during the Hudsonian Orogeny (1.9-1.8 billion years ago). The Shield was finally completed on the SE by the addition of Grenville Province about 1 billion years ago.

Superior Province is the largest Archean province. Its southern part comprises easterly trending belts, alternating between gneisses and greenstone. Some 3.8-billion-year-old gneisses occur in the extensions of Superior Province into Minnesota and of Nutak into Greenland. Slave and Kaminak cratons resemble Superior craton in overall aspect, age of contained rocks, and nature and timing of structural development. In Slave craton, however, weakly metamorphosed turbidites (ie, SEDIMENTARY ROCKS formed in water) predominate.

Churchill Province, the largest of the Lower Proterozoic provinces, includes the sinuous, intensely deformed, metamorphosed and intruded "Reindeer-Circum-Ungava" belt and the reworked fragments and edges of Archean cratons in "Northwest Churchill" domain. The southern margin of "Circum-Ungava" belt contains 6-10 km of Lower Proterozoic layered rocks overlying the Archean basement rocks of Superior Province. This rock succession, reflecting the separation of parts of Superior Province, comprises local clastic-volcanic rift assemblages, overlain by a clastic-carbonate shelf assemblage, succeeded by iron formation (*see* MINERAL RESOURCES). The shelf sediments pass outward into oceanic basalt with some ultramafic lava (ie, lava rich in iron and magnesium).

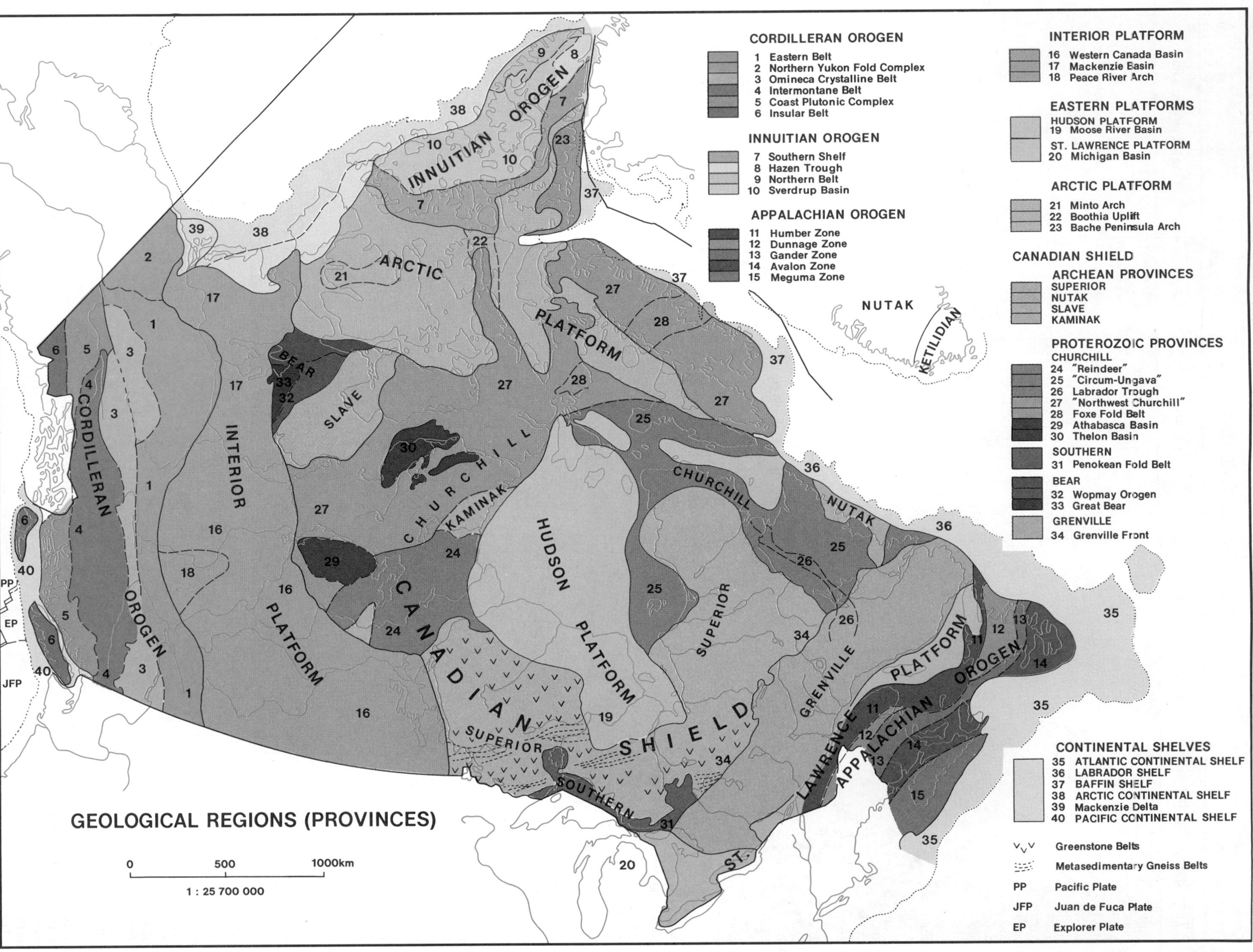
GEOLOGICAL REGIONS (PROVINCES)
0 500 1000km
1 : 25 700 000
CORDILLERAN OROGEN
1 Eastern Belt
2 Northern Yukon Fold Complex
3 Omineca Crystalline Belt
4 Intermontane Belt
5 Coast Plutonic Complex
6 Insular Belt
INNUITIAN OROGEN
7 Southern Shelf
8 Hazen Trough
9 Northern Belt
10 Sverdrup Basin
APPALACHIAN OROGEN
11 Humber Zone
12 Dunnage Zone
13 Gander Zone
14 Avalon Zone
15 Meguma Zone
INTERIOR PLATFORM
16 Western Canada Basin
17 Mackenzie Basin
18 Peace River Arch
EASTERN PLATFORMS
HUDSON PLATFORM
19 Moose River Basin
ST. LAWRENCE PLATFORM
20 Michigan Basin
ARCTIC PLATFORM
21 Minto Arch
22 Boothia Uplift
23 Bache Peninsula Arch
CANADIAN SHIELD
ARCHEAN PROVINCES
SUPERIOR
NUTAK
SLAVE
KAMINAK
PROTEROZOIC PROVINCES
CHURCHILL
24 "Reindeer"
25 "Circum-Ungava"
26 Labrador Trough
27 "Northwest Churchill"
28 Foxe Fold Belt
29 Athabasca Basin
30 Thelon Basin
SOUTHERN
31 Penokean Fold Belt
BEAR
32 Wopmay Orogen
33 Great Bear
GRENVILLE
34 Grenville Front
CONTINENTAL SHELVES
35 ATLANTIC CONTINENTAL SHELF
36 LABRADOR SHELF
37 BAFFIN SHELF
38 ARCTIC CONTINENTAL SHELF
39 Mackenzie Delta
40 PACIFIC CONTINENTAL SHELF
Greenstone Belts
Metasedimentary Gneiss Belts
PP Pacific Plate
JFP Juan de Fuca Plate
EP Explorer Plate
CORDILLERAN OROGEN
INTERIOR PLATFORM
INNUITIAN OROGEN
ARCTIC PLATFORM
BEAR
SLAVE
CHURCHILL
KAMINAK
CANADIAN SHIELD
HUDSON PLATFORM
SUPERIOR
SOUTHERN
NUTAK
GRENVILLE
ST. LAWRENCE PLATFORM
APPALACHIAN OROGEN
KETILIDIAN

Convergence and orogeny are manifested along the southern margin of the "Circum-Ungava" belt by folds and thrust faults. The northern margin of the belt is a rough mirror image of the southern margin.

"Reindeer" belt is a region of complexly deformed metamorphic rocks that includes the Flin Flon and Lynn Lk volcanic arcs separated by a turbidite basin. The NW margin contains metamorphosed remnants of shelf sediments interfolded with Archean basement that extends into the later was probably a semi-stable extension of Slave Craton that was variably affected by the Kenoran and Hudsonian orogenies. It contains remnants of a thin veneer of Lower Proterozoic rocks consisting of 1.5 km of quartz-rich clastics, deposited in restricted basins, succeeded by a more extensive, 3 km thick, platformal assemblage of quartz-rich sandstone, carbonate, local clastics and volcanics. Much of the domain is characterized by the jostling of large blocks of Archean basement, brought together along major faults. In the Foxe Fold Belt, Archean basement and the overlying Proterozoic sediments are tightly folded together; elsewhere they are more broadly folded.

Southern Province contains a southeasterly thickening wedge of Lower Proterozoic, quartz-rich, shelf clastic sediments and subordinate mixed volcanics (7-11 km thick). The wedge accumulated along the southern edge of Superior Province. Its lowest part includes uranium-bearing conglomerate; its upper (NE) part contains sediments deposited during an ancient ICE AGE. The SE part of the wedge was variably metamorphosed and deformed by folds and thrust faults, pushed N to form the Penokean Fold Belt. The intensity of metamorphism and deformation increases southward, reflecting the convergence of a 3.5-billion-year-old Archean cratonic block northward against Superior Craton (2.2-1.7 billion years ago). Sudbury Basin and its associated nickel-rich intrusion may have resulted from meteorite impact about 1.85 billion years ago (*see* METEOR).

Bear Province consists of the northerly trending Wopmay Orogen overlapped (in the N) by younger Proterozoic rocks. Westward from Slave Craton the orogen comprises 4 zones, all cut by northeast-trending strike-slip faults. The first zone is a thin veneer of platform carbonate and sandstone superimposed by the outer part of a westerly derived clastic wedge. An eastward thrust and folded assemblage (5 km thick) of shelf clastics and carbonate is overlain by the wedge. A clastic-volcanic rift assemblage (10 km thick) overlain by fine-grained off-shelf clastics, then by early clastic wedge rocks, was deformed, metamorphosed and intruded by 1.89-billion-year-old granites. Finally, in Great Bear Belt, 1.87-billion-year-old arc volcanics (8 km thick) were deposited on 1.92-billion-year-old basement and are overlapped by younger, more extensive arc volcanics. The orogen began its complex evolution 2.1 billion years ago with the splitting of Slave Craton along northerly and east-northeasterly trending rifts. This led to the deposition of a continental margin assemblage along the W edge of Slave Craton. The assemblage was deformed, metamorphosed and intruded by granites 1.9 billion years ago in response to the collision of a microcontinent from the west. Subsequently, east-sloping subduction led to arc volcanism which extended onto the continent. A second collision farther W generated northeast- and southeast-trending strike-slip faults across the entire orogen. The indentation of Churchill Province by the rigid Slave Craton cracked the Churchill crust and possibly gave rise to 1.8-billion-year-old alkaline volcanics in the Thelon Basin.

The middle and late Proterozoic record is fragmentary but nevertheless indicates stability of the Canadian Shield from 1.8-0.57 billion years ago. In Middle Proterozoic time, an extensive 1.5-billion-year-old continental and marine sandstone-carbonate assemblage (preserved in separate, partly fault-bounded basins, eg, Athabasca Basin) was deposited over much of the Shield, overlapping 1.8-billion-year-old alkaline volcanics. Concurrently, from Labrador SW into Grenville Province, huge masses of anorthosite (composed almost entirely of plagioclase feldspar) and related granitic rocks were intruded. Concurrent and later widespread stretching across much of the Shield resulted in rifting, dike intrusion and volcanism. About 1.3 billion years ago, rifting, accompanied by basaltic volcanism and intrusion of alkaline rocks, began in Labrador parallel to Grenville Front. Enormous amounts of basalt were extruded in the Lake Superior region, accompanied by alkaline intrusions nearby, during the formation of a major continental rift that extended NE from central Kansas to Lk Superior and SE into Michigan (1-1.3 billion years ago). Depression of the crust from the weight of the volcanics created a basin in which clastic sediments were deposited until the end of Precambrian time. Concurrently, swarms of basic dikes, 1.2 billion years old, were intruded along northwesterly and northeasterly trends across much of the Shield; related basalts were extruded into parallel northwesterly trending sediment-filled rifts on Baffin I and as lava plateaus in northern Bear Province.

Grenville Province The convergence of Grenville Province against the adjacent provinces to the NW completed assembly of the Canadian Shield (0.9-1.2 billion years ago). Near Grenville Front this resulted in thickened crust and northeasterly trending structures pushed towards the northwest. Subsequent uplift and erosion reveals widespread metamorphic rocks.

Interior and Related Platforms

At the end of Precambrian time (0.57 billion years ago), the Canadian Shield was a stable craton of low relief forming the foundation of the N American continent. In early Paleozoic time the Shield was depressed slightly, and much of it was gradually covered by warm, shallow seas. This inundation resulted in deposition of interrupted platformal sequences (1-3 km thick), now preserved in the Interior, Arctic, Hudson and St Lawrence platforms. These sequences generally consist of quartz-rich sandstone, overlain by interbedded carbonate and shale. By mid-Paleozoic time, differential uplift and subsidence across the Shield had created a network of arches and intervening basins which led to interruptions in the depositional sequences. The uneven relief, together with the growth of carbonate reefs, produced enclosed basins in the central Interior Platform, in Hudson Platform and in Michigan Basin where evaporites (eg, salt, potash) accumulated.

Platformal sequences of the Interior Platform, containing rocks from Cambrian to Jurassic age, are overlain by a foreland basin which migrated eastward and covered much of the platform ahead of advancing pulses of deformation and uplift in the Cordillera. Sandstone, conglomerate, shale and coal accumulated in 2 major clastic wedges of late Jurassic-early Cretaceous and late Cretaceous-Paleocene age, respectively. The lower wedge reflects several lesser, northward-migrating pulses. The 2 major wedges are separated by mid-Cretaceous marine shales deposited in a shallow sea that covered Interior Platform. A clastic wedge in Mackenzie Basin accumulated in pulses from early Cretaceous to Eocene time. Lower Cretaceous coal-bearing clastics were deposited in Moose River Basin on Hudson Platform.

Appalachian Orogen

The Appalachian Orogen records the latest Precambrian rifting of the ancestral Canadian Shield, the earliest Paleozoic opening of the Iapetus Ocean to the E, its mid-Ordovician closing and related deformation, and mid- and late-Paleozoic folding and faulting. The orogen consists of several zones of which only the innermost, Humber Zone, was deposited directly on ancestral N America. There, Grenville Province basement is overlain by Upper Proterozoic rift clastics and volcanics covered by a more extensive Cambrian-Ordovician sandstone-carbonate shelf assemblage. Succeeding clastics were derived from the SE, heralding the early Paleozoic arrival of a slice of off-shelf assemblage and higher slices of Ordovician oceanic crust thrust northwestward from Dunnage Zone and now stacked above the clastics.

Dunnage Zone consists of rock complexes which floored the Iapetus Ocean: pieces of upper mantle-oceanic crustal sequences overlain by Lower Ordovician arc volcanics, related clastics and local masses of jumbled blocks of volcanics and clastic rocks surrounded by Ordovician shale. The ocean's eastern margin may be represented in Gander Zone by pre-Middle Ordovician clastics, associated with gneisses in Newfoundland and overlain by arc volcanics in NB. Zonal boundaries are straddled by overlying Upper Ordovician-Silurian marine and continental sediments and volcanics indicating that Dunnage and Gander zones were accreted to N America during the mid-Ordovician Taconian Orogeny.

Avalon Zone is a foreign fragment composed of Proterozoic partly glacial sediments and volcanics, overlain by Cambrian sediments containing FOSSILS different from those in Humber Zone and St Lawrence Platform, and capped by Ordovician clastics with iron formation. Avalon Zone accreted to Gander Zone during mid-Paleozoic Acadian Orogeny, resulting in steeply inclined folds and faults and extensive granitic intrusion across the entire orogen, and disruption along steep faults in nearby platforms.

Meguma Zone is also foreign because it includes folded Cambrian-Ordovician turbidites, derived from an unknown source to the SE, and distinctive granites of Devonian age unlike those associated with Acadian Orogeny. Meguma Zone was accreted to Avalon Zone along steep faults with horizontal slip before both zones were partly covered by continental, coal-bearing Carboniferous clastics. The region contains evidence recording the final assembly of the supercontinent Pangea. The development of rifts in Triassic time (245-208 million years ago), the deposition in them of rift clastics and basalt and the intrusion of alkaline rocks in the Cretaceous are associated with the breakup of Pangea and the subsequent opening of the Atlantic Ocean in the Mesozoic.

Innuitian Orogen

The Innuitian Orogen began with earliest Paleozoic rifting of northern ancestral N America, followed by early Paleozoic deposition of shelf and off-shelf sediments, the latter in a deep trough bounded on the N by foreign continental fragments. A younger, overlapping clastic wedge was deformed in the mid-Paleozoic and, finally, the orogen was partly superimposed by a mainly Mesozoic clastic basin, which was itself deformed in latest Mesozoic and early Tertiary time.

The Arctic Platform merges northward into a Cambrian-Lower Devonian southern shelf assemblage of 5 km of carbonate, shale and evaporite. It is adjoined by Hazen Trough, containing Lower Cambrian rift clastics overlain by deep-water shale and 3 km of turbidites. Hazen Trough is bounded on the N by the Northern Belt which comprises continental fragments (largely volcanics and granites). Northerly derived turbidites indicate that the Northern Belt was uplifted, following the collision (along a zone marked by oceanic ultramafic rocks) of Proterozoic and Middle Ordovician fragments in mid-Ordovician time. This collision ended arc volcanism in the Northern Belt. It was followed by pulses of folding and uplift in Silurian and Devonian times and by granitic intrusion in the Devonian. Uplifts in northeastern and eastern parts of the orogen shed detritus to a southeastward-advancing Middle and Upper Devonian clastic wedge. It was compressively folded during the Ellesmerian Orogeny (about 345 million years ago) which migrated from the Northern Belt to the Southern Shelf. Subsequently, stretching and subsidence led to the deposition of 12 km of sediments in Sverdrup Basin, mainly of Mesozoic rift clastics and basaltic lava and intrusion, and some Upper Paleozoic evaporites that were locally squeezed upward into overlying sediments. The latest Cretaceous uplift in the eastern Sverdrup Basin shed a clastic wedge across the basin to the continental margin. This was succeeded by the Eurekan Orogeny (about 65 million years ago) which created broad folds and thrust faults directed south and east. At the same time, more than 3 km of clastics accumulated in local basins on land and in narrow, marine fault-troughs. Late Cenozoic vertical faulting produced the present topography.

Canadian Cordillera

In the Canadian Cordillera rifting and continental shelf development took place from Proterozoic to mid-Mesozoic time in the Eastern Belt. Elsewhere, foreign fragments were accreted successively to western N America in mid- and late-Mesozoic time. Each accretion was followed by orogeny and deposition of a clastic wedge; related metamorphism and granitic intrusion were restricted mainly to zones straddling the boundaries of accreting blocks. Since the late Mesozoic, the Pacific Ocean Basin has slid under and horizontally past the Cordillera along northwest-trending transform faults.

A long-lived phase of continental margin sedimentation from Proterozoic to Jurassic time (2.5 billion-144 million years ago) is recorded in the Eastern Belt in at least 3 rift and shelf assemblages, totalling 25 km in thickness. The 2 Middle Proterozoic assemblages reflect continental rifting and separation 1.5 billion years ago, and deposition of 2 clastic-carbonate shelf sequences, the first of which was deformed 1.35 billion years ago. They were accompanied by development of connecting, easterly trending fault-troughs that protruded into the continent. The third assemblage comprises partly glacial Upper Proterozoic rift clastic overlain by Cambrian to Jurassic shelf sequences continuous with thinner sequences in Interior Platform but passing westward off the shelf to shale and turbidites. Northern Yukon underwent Devonian-Mississippian folding, granitic intrusion and uplift. This and other northern Cordilleran uplifted areas shed clastics SE across the continental margin.

An accretionary phase in late Jurassic to Cretaceous time resulted from the westward drift of N America and its collision with several northward-moving Pacific plates. Several foreign blocks were amalgamated into 2 large composite fragments (Intermontane and Insular belts) which, as a result of this collision, were then accreted successively to N America. The foreign blocks show fossil and other evidence of displacement through 30° or more of latitude.

The Intermontane Belt consists of 2 extensive Upper Triassic-Middle Jurassic volcanic arcs, each

Big Muddy Valley, Alta (*top*); Baffin Island, NWT (*centre*); and Shield near Flin Flon, Man, display the enormous variety among Canada's geological regions (*photos by Richard Vroom/Miller Services Ltd*).

built largely on an Upper Paleozoic foundation. They are separated by an oceanic terrane which includes subduction complexes of repetitively stacked accretionary wedges and of jumbled blocks of basalt, ultramafic, chert and blueschist. The eastern arc is bounded on the E by a region of Upper Paleozoic oceanic crust, telescoped over a small Paleozoic terrane that was deformed before Mississippian time.

The Omineca Crystalline Belt embraces the region where the Intermontane composite fragment collided with and partly overrode the Eastern Belt. This mid-Jurassic collision gave rise to the Columbian Orogeny. Rocks of the outer part of the continental margin and the adjacent Intermontane fragment were compressed, metamorphosed and displaced into stacked sheets transported mainly eastward, but also partly westward, from a central metamorphic core zone. From the resulting uplift, clastics were shed mainly eastward into a foredeep and partly westward into a backdeep. Eastward displacement over the Canadian Shield resulted, in effect, in a westward subduction of continental crust which, when partially melted, gave rise to mid-Cretaceous granites in eastern Intermontane and Eastern belts.

Insular Belt comprises 2 large terranes amalgamated in late Jurassic time. One is mainly of Paleozoic sediments and volcanics; the other a Triassic to mid-Jurassic sequence of basalt, carbonate and arc volcanics, overlying an Upper Paleozoic basement. The outer margins of the belt contain remnants of Upper Mesozoic and Cenozoic subduction complexes, suggesting prolonged east-sloping subduction of oceanic crust beneath the Insular Belt. In late Cretaceous time an Insular composite fragment collided with and accreted to the Intermontane Belt which was by then part of N America. This process created the Coast Plutonic Complex, a belt, uplifted in Cenozoic time, consisting of extensive granitic plutons and of medium-grade metamorphic rocks that straddle the boundary between these composite belts. Contemporaneously, arc volcanism and related intrusions of granitic plugs took place in the Intermontane Belt while in the Eastern Belt further thrust faulting and uplift during Laramide Orogeny completed the building of the Rocky Mountains. A related clastic wedge was deposited in a foredeep extending into the western Interior Platform. In the late Cenozoic, extensive crustal stretching resulted in extrusion of widespread sheets of fluid basalt over much of the Intermontane Belt and of local rift and arc volcanics in its western part.

Continental Shelves

The Canadian continental shelves are the youngest additions to Canada's landmass. The arctic and eastern shelves developed along continental margins adjacent to opening oceans; the Pacific Shelf formed along a continental margin that slides over or horizontally past oceanic crust. The shelves form submarine terraces, 5-700 km wide and up to 300 m deep. With the exception of the Pacific Shelf, they are underlain by relatively undeformed Mesozoic and Cenozoic prisms of sedimentary rocks (3-13 km thick), composed of materials eroded from the continent, draped over older rocks along its margin.

The Arctic Shelf evolved following opening of the Arctic Ocean basin, possibly from the counterclockwise rotation of Alaska 120 million years ago. Subsequently, 4 km of shelf sediments were superimposed by 9 km of Upper Cretaceous-Cenozoic clastics of the Mackenzie Delta which progressively expanded northward. The eastern shelves built outward as the Atlantic Ocean basin opened and as N America separated from Africa 165 million years ago, from Europe 100-90 million years ago, and from Greenland 70-60 million years ago. Eastern shelves comprise 2 or 3 tectonic assemblages: a lower rift assemblage in fault troughs containing clastics, evaporites and volcanics lying on Precambrian and Paleozoic rocks; an upper, more extensive clastic-carbonate shelf assemblage deposited during a continental drifting phase after the continents separated; and a final capping of Pleistocene glacial deposits. Continental crust is 35 km thick under the inner shelf, thinning to 15-20 km under the outer shelf.

The narrow Pacific Shelf lies along an active margin marked by numerous EARTHQUAKES. West of Vancouver I, the oceanic Juan de Fuca and Explorer plates are descending beneath the continent along a northeasterly sloping subduction zone. This has resulted in 2 modern assemblages: an active volcanic arc 300 km NE of the foot of the Pacific Shelf, where the subduction zone emerges; and Upper Mesozoic and Cenozoic accretionary prisms of clastics and oceanic volcanics scraped off the descending plate and stacked in easterly tilted wedges beneath the narrow shelf. Northwest of Vancouver I, however, oceanic crust of the Pacific Plate is sliding horizontally NW past the continent along a transform fault. J.O. WHEELER

Reading: R.J.W. Douglas, ed, *Geology and Economic Minerals of Canada* (2 vols, 1970).

Geological Survey of Canada, one of Canada's oldest scientific agencies, was founded in 1842 to assist in developing a viable MINERAL industry by establishing the general geological base on which the industry could plan further, detailed investigations. Originally limited to the Province of Canada, the GSC is now involved in earth-science studies throughout Canada, especially in the YT and the NWT. On 10 Sept 1841, £1500 was set aside to establish a geological survey, and the GSC began work in a warehouse in Montréal. The first director, geologist William Edmond LOGAN, was appointed in Apr 1842. His first project, a simple questionnaire sent to landowners, doctors, etc, from Niagara to Gaspé, provided the first overview of the GEOLOGY of the area. Logan's one assistant, Alexander Murray, was a topographer. Later, T.S. HUNT and Elkanah BILLINGS joined the GSC as mineralogist and paleontologist, respectively. In the next decade the GSC participated in several international exhibitions (eg, London, 1851; Paris, 1855) at which elegant displays advertised Canada's potential MINERAL RESOURCES. The first comprehensive report of the geology of the United Province, Logan's *Geology of Canada,* was published in 1863, and the first large-scale maps appeared in the same decade (*see* CARTOGRAPHY). Confederation increased tenfold the area for which the GSC was responsible. Emphasis was given to economic geology, especially to assist the government in making railway land grants. The value of the GSC to the economic growth of Canada became obvious during the mid-19th century. The organization, funded initially by two 5-year parliamentary grants, was a branch of the Dept of the Interior in 1877-90, moving to Ottawa in 1881. Between 1890 and 1907 it formed a separate department. Then began the change of titles reflecting the growth of parts of the original GSC: Mines (1907), Mines and Resources (1936), Mines and Technical Surveys (1950) and finally Energy, Mines and Resources (1966). The National Museums of Canada, the Topographic Survey and the Canada Centre for Mineral and Energy Technology (formerly the Mines Branch), all originated in the GSC.

Early geologists were also explorers, geographers, botanists, zoologists and anthropologists who played a large role in opening up the West and later the Arctic. Notable names include G.M. DAWSON, third director, who carried out extensive reconnaissance mapping in BC, prepared a comprehensive report on the Haida, and mapped in the YT a decade before the KLONDIKE GOLD RUSH; Robert BELL, who for 34 years explored the North and West, including the coasts of Hudson Str and Hudson Bay; A.P. LOW, whose work in central Labrador and Ungava included recognition of the potential of the region's vast iron resources and who, in 1903-04, commanded the government expedition to northern waters in the *Neptune*, in a voyage that was Canada's first clear exercise of authority over the ARCTIC ARCHIPELAGO; J.B. TYRRELL, whose epic trips across the Barrens in 1893 and 1894 filled large blanks on the map; and J. Mackintosh Bell, whose surveys from Lk Athabasca to Great Bear Lk in 1900 resulted in observations that 30 years later led Gilbert LABINE to the discovery of URANIUM deposits at Port Radium.

Studies having a strong economic focus were emphasized during the 1930s and WWII, but by 1950 the need for the earth sciences to benefit from rapid advances in technology became apparent. The GSC again became research oriented and experienced a considerable expansion in staff and resources. To facilitate its coast-to-coast activities and provide closer liaison with its users, several small regional offices were expanded and a new headquarters was opened in Ottawa (1959).

To provide basic earth-science information, the GSC has always depended on field studies. The introduction of light-weight helicopters in the 1950s provided a tool that allowed the geologist to spend most of the working day making observations, instead of slogging through bush, climbing mountains or portaging a canoe. By 1973, all of Canada had been examined at a reconnaissance scale and more detailed studies had begun.

Technological developments in the field of airborne geophysics have made major programs possible, such as the GSC's national aeromagnetic survey. By 1987, more than 10 million line-kilometres had been flown, and 9000 aeromagnetic maps portraying data of great interest to the mining industry had been published. The expertise of the GSC's in the fields of airborne geophysics and GEOCHEMISTRY has also allowed significant contributions to be made to developing countries, especially in Africa, through the Canadian International Development Agency (CIDA).

On 1 Apr 1986 EMR's Earth Physics Branch was amalgamated with the GSC, thereby adding expertise in seismology, terrestrial magnetism, gravity and geodynamics. The reorganization was made in response to recommendations contained in a report of the Task Force on Program Review chaired by the deputy prime minister.

A further reorganization took place in Apr 1987 when the GSC became a sector of EMR headed by an assistant deputy minister and comprising 4 branches. Responsibility for the Polar Continental Shelf Project was also transferred to the GSC at that time.

The role of the Geological Survey is to ensure that geological, geophysical and geochemical knowledge, technology and expertise are available concerning Canada's landmass and offshore areas, including knowledge about mineral and energy resources and the conditions affecting land and seabed use. Such information is required for effective exploitation of mineral and energy resources, estimation of Canada's resources, use of land and related issues of public safety and security, and to aid various levels of government in formulating policies.

In 1987-88 the GSC had a budget of over $100 million, a coast-to-coast staff of nearly 1000, and was organized into 4 branches and 8 Divisions. About 40% of the budget reflects the impact of shared federal provincial programs or short-term, special initiatives.

Robert Bell's geological survey party, Lake of the Woods, 1883. Bell (4th from right, standing) explored the North and West for 34 years on behalf of the GSC (*courtesy National Archives of Canada/C-18874*).

The Office of the Chief Scientist; Programs, Planning and Services Branch is composed of the Geoscience Information Division, Ottawa, which ensures that results of branch scientific programs are made available to users in a timely and cost-effective manner; maintains the GSC Library as the geoscience component of the National Library; manages GEOSCAN, the federal/provincial/industry geoscience bibliographic database; co-ordinates branch informatics applications and provides advice on data systems; the Administrative Services Division; the Frontier Geoscience Program Office; the Mineral Development Agreements Program Office; and the Program Planning and Co-ordination Division, which provides project management, analysis and evaluation.

The Continental Geoscience and Mineral Resources Branch is composed of 2 divisions. The Mineral Resources Division, Ottawa and Vancouver, is responsible for research on the formation of mineral deposits and their relationships to Canada's principal geological regions; development of guidelines to assist mineral exploration and resource management and land use planning; provision of analytical and mineralogical services to support branch programs; curation of national mineral and ore research collections; research on geochemical processes and the development, application and evaluation of methods to assist in the mineral exploration and resource assessments; development and application of mathematical and statistical methods for geoscience data; development, application and evaluation of geophysical methods to assist in mineral exploration and geological mapping. The Lithosphere and Canadian Shield Division, Ottawa, is responsible for the composition, structure and evolution of the Canadian lithosphere as exposed in the Canadian Shield and represented in the subsurface beneath the sedimentary rocks; geochronology; paleomagnetism; igneous and metamorphic petrology.

The Geophysical Surveys, Hazards and Terrain Sciences Branch also has 2 divisions. The Terrain Sciences Division, Ottawa, Calgary and Vancouver, is responsible for providing geoscientific data and interpretive information on the surficial geology and geomorphic processes of the Canadian landmass and for geotechnical aspects of surficial and bedrock materials that have a bearing on the use of the terrain. The Geophysics Division, Ottawa, is responsible for the physics of the solid earth with special reference to the large-scale structure of the lithosphere-asthenosphere system in Canada; seismicity and seismic risk; national seismological geomagnetic and geodynamic observatory networks; national gravity and aeromagnetic mapping programs; national geophysical databases and methodology for manipulation and display.

The Sedimentary and Marine Geoscience Branch has 4 divisions. The Institute of Sedimentary and Petroleum Geology, Calgary and Ottawa is responsible for conduct of mapping and topical studies to establish the geoscience base for the sedimentary basins of western and arctic Canada; and evaluation programs for petroleum and coal resources. The Cordilleran and Pacific Margin Division, Vancouver and Sidney, BC, is responsible for seismology of cordilleran and offshore regions to assist in identification, elucidation and mitigation of earthquake hazards; studies in neotectonics; nature, origin and evolution of the lithosphere of the cordilleran and offshore regions and their mineral and hydrocarbon resources; assessment of volcanic and terrain hazards to facilitate land use planning and development.

The Atlantic Geoscience Centre, Dartmouth, NS, is responsible for geological, geophysical and geochemical studies in the Atlantic and Arctic offshore areas to assist in the search for hydrocarbon resources and in resource evaluations, in protection of the marine environment, and in improving the safety of coastal and offshore engineering structures. Finally, the Polar Continental Shelf Project at Resolute and Tuktoyaktuk, NWT, is responsible for providing logistics sup-port and advice to facilitate effective conduct of scientific activities by government agencies and universities in the Arctic Islands and Arctic Ocean areas.

R.G. BLACKADAR

Reading: Morris Zaslow, *Reading the Rocks* (1975).

Geology Every day of our lives we interact with the planet we live on. Normally, the interaction is quiet and unobtrusive and we take a stable ENVIRONMENT for granted. But, at times, we are reminded that this planet changes: a VOLCANO erupts in a remote country and its dust reduces sunlight by 5% for a few years; an EARTHQUAKE leaves thousands dead or homeless. We have been forced to become aware of the limitations and fragility of the Earth, and of problems such as acid rain and toxic-waste pollution. Geology deals primarily with the study of the planet Earth. Significant questions involve the size, shape and chemical makeup of the Earth, now and throughout geological time. Of equal importance are questions about the origin and evolution of life, and about resources and the possible effects of resource limitations on human development and survival.

Earth is 70.8% covered by water but only with the development of sonar techniques has it become possible to describe the solid earth below the oceans. With increasingly sophisticated satellite observations, relatively fine structural details (eg, areas of volcanic activity) can be seen. With modern techniques geologists can observe on almost all appropriate scales: we can "see" the entire planet on a scale of 10^7 m and, with electron microscopes, we can see atoms of $1/10^{10}$ m diameter.

Geological Sciences in Canada

Canada has the second largest land area (after the USSR) and the largest coastline of any nation, as well as a vast area of continental shelf. Its population is small; the natural resources vast. Geology in Canada may have begun with Jacques CARTIER when, in the 1530s, he returned to France with a load of worthless crystals he thought were diamonds. Martin FROBISHER made the same error in the 1570s, mining quantities of useless ore on Baffin Island. In the early 1800s, systematic geological mapping in Europe was becoming a science. The Industrial Revolution demanded coal, iron ore and other minerals, and early hit-and-miss PROSPECTING techniques were proving costly. Public interest in geology broadened as the study of rocks accelerated and, inevitably, as dogmas concerning time and life came under fire. In Canada, the systematic study of geology can be said to have begun in 1842 with the founding of the GEOLOGICAL SURVEY OF CANADA.

Early geologists in Canada went far beyond the massive task of describing the stratigraphy and producing accurate maps; they were true natural scientists who described every aspect of the natural and human environment. The great traditions established at that time have continued, and the present GSC remains a world leader. The mineral industry was slow in attaining worldwide importance. It was not until after 1945 that the steel, oil and gas industries began accelerated development; Canada first exported oil in 1949. The community of geologists grew with the mineral and oil boom. Canada became a leader in techniques for REMOTE SENSING, for geophysical techniques based on gravity, and for seismic, magnetic and electrical methods of mapping. As detailed maps improved, the most favourable rocks for particular resources became better understood. Canada perhaps still leads the world in modern prospecting technology, and Canadian geologists are sought in developing countries to assist in exploration programs. As the resource industries became increasingly important, the provinces began to build their own more specialized surveys, which have come to assist and amplify the task of the GSC. The membership patterns of the various specialized societies (involving government, university and industry representatives) illustrate the strength of the geological community.

Abbé Jean Holmes began geology instruction in Canada early in the 19th century at the SEMINAIRE DE QUÉBEC (later U Laval). The first geology department was established at University of Toronto in 1853. To provide for the training of young geologists, William LOGAN endowed a professorship of geology and paleontology at McGill University. In 1855, J.W. DAWSON became principal of McGill and first incumbent of that chair. By the end of the 19th century there were 6 geology departments in Canadian universities. The most impressive growth occurred 1949-70, when the number increased from 15 to 30. Earth science instruction also takes place in departments of geography, physics, mineral and mining engineering, civil engineering (geotechnique) and soil science. Geochemistry and geomorphology are also geological subjects.

Relation to Other Sciences and Society

To many, the most important justification for the study of geology is the necessity of providing raw materials. In Canada, the economic aspect of the science is large: in 1986 minerals were estimated to provide one-quarter of exports and, overall, about one-tenth of Canada's economy is directly involved in the mineral industry. Today, the impact of earth sciences goes much further than mineral and energy production. Geochemists are skilled in the analysis of trace quantities of metals and hence are in demand for the study of environmental aspects of inorganic pollution (eg, heavy

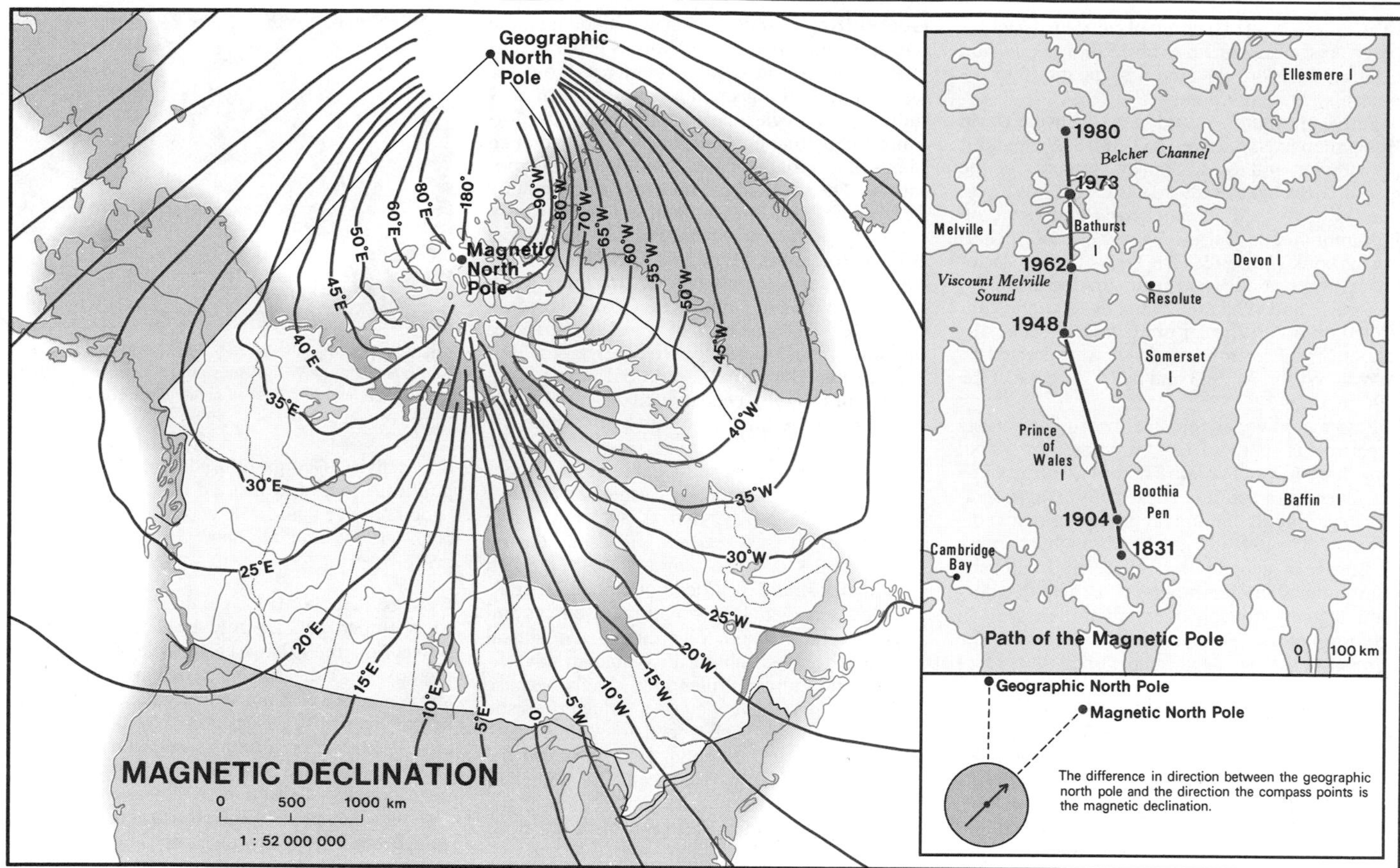

metals). Geologists are needed when dams, highways, airports, nuclear power plants, urban expansion or even agricultural developments are planned. Earth scientists are involved in any problem focusing on human impact on the environment.

The earth sciences have always had close links to other sciences. Thus, the solid-state physics of materials under extreme pressure and temperature is closely related to studies of the deep Earth and of objects in space. Views on nuclide synthesis in stars draw heavily on data from geochemistry. For biology, studies of fossil organic matter in rocks make a vital contribution to an understanding of the origin of life and its tolerance to environmental change. Modern geologists require knowledge from many related sciences, for example, the paleontologist needs biology; the geophysicist, physics and applied mathematics; the structural geologist, a background in solids mechanics and fluid dynamics.

Canadian Institutions

Federal and provincial geological surveys still remain the key organizations for a continued understanding and improvement in knowledge of Canadian geology. From their work come essential geological and geophysical maps. University geologists have made large contributions to understanding the fundamental processes of geology. The main earth science societies and their publications include Assn of Exploration Geochemists, *Journal of Geochemical Exploration;* Canadian Assn of Geographers, *Canadian Geographer;* Canadian Exploration Geophysical Soc, Canadian Geophysical Union, *Canadian Geophysical Bulletin;* Canadian Geotechnical Soc, *Canadian Geotechnical Journal;* Canadian Institute of Mining and Metallurgy, *Canadian Mining and Metallurgical Bulletin, Journal of Canadian Petroleum Technology, Canadian Metallurgical Quarterly;* Canadian Quaternary Assn; Canadian Soc of Exploration Geophysicists, *Journal of the Canadian Soc of Exploration Geophysicists;* Canadian Soc of Petroleum Geologists, *Bulletin of Canadian Petroleum Geology* and *Reservoir;* Canadian Soc of Soil Science, *Canadian Journal of Soil Science;* Canadian Well Logging Soc, *The CWLS Journal;* Geological Assn of Canada, *Geoscience Canada, Canadian Journal of Earth Sciences, Geolog;* International Assn of Hydrogeologists/Canadian Chapter; Mineralogical Assn of Canada, *Canadian Mineralogist.*

The Canadian Geoscience Council, a group whose membership consists of the societies listed above, co-ordinates information from all subdisciplines. It also publishes special studies (eg, a recent pamphlet on careers in geoscience). The Geological Survey of Canada and the various provincial surveys publish bulletins and maps and supply information of local and general geological significance. W.S. FYFE

Reading: R.J.W. Douglas, ed, *Geology and Economic Minerals of Canada* (1970); F. Press and R. Siever, *Earth* (1982).

Geomagnetic Pole The Earth behaves like a magnetised sphere with its magnetic poles near, but not identical to, its poles of rotation. In 1831 James Clark Ross located the N magnetic pole on KING WILLIAM ISLAND in the Canadian Arctic where his compass dipped vertically downwards. This pole probably moves continuously and it is now N of BATHURST ISLAND. Convection currents flowing in the white-hot liquid iron of the Earth's outer core are thought to generate the main magnetic field; secondary effects from the sun (eg, magnetic storms, solar winds) continuously agitate the field and its poles (*see* NORTHERN LIGHTS). An investigator in space would see that the field is distorted. The average of the whole field would have a pole (ie, north geomagnetic pole) over Baffin Bay near NW Greenland. The south magnetic pole is in Antarctica. Irregularities in the core's convection currents are believed to cause the magnetic poles to wander about the poles of rotation and to change in intensity so that the field dies away and returns with reversed polarity at intervals of thousands of years. This property is useful in archaeology, in dating magnetic rocks and in measuring the rates of seafloor spreading. J. TUZO WILSON

Geomorphology is concerned with the form of the Earth's surface. It includes the description, classification, internal structure and GEOLOGICAL HISTORY of surface features resulting from erosion and deposition by rivers, glaciers, ocean waves, wind, gravitational movement of material down slopes and weathering. Faulting of the Earth's crust and volcanism are also included. Most of Canada was covered by continental glaciers several times; therefore, glacial GEOLOGY receives most attention from Canadian geomorphologists. Arctic geomorphology and coastal geomorphology are also important. Most geomorphic processes result from the CLIMATE; hence, CLIMATE CHANGE is a uniting theme, especially in the closely related field of Quaternary geology, which deals with the last 2 million years.

Geomorphological accounts occur in most reports of exploration since the 1850s and surface deposits have been described by the GEOLOGICAL SURVEY OF CANADA (GSC) since its creation in 1842. Early discussions focused on whether erratic boulders were transported by floating ice or by continental glaciers. By about 1875 the glacial theory was widely accepted, except by J.W. DAWSON of McGill, author of *The Canadian Ice Age* (1894). His son, G.M. DAWSON, explored much of western Canada and published the first comprehensive work on Canada's physiography (1884). Before 1850 most geomorphology reports were minor sections within reports on bedrock, but several geologists with the GSC made more definitive contributions: Robert Chalmers in southern Québec and NB; J.B. TYRRELL in northern Manitoba; W.A. Johnston in Ontario, the eastern prairies and BC; J.W. Goldthwait in the St Lawrence Valley and NS; and E.M. Kindle studying recent sedimentation processes. After WWII the GSC established a group of a dozen glacial geology specialists, which evolved into the Terrain Sciences Division, the largest single group of geomorphologists in Canada.

Early contributors outside the GSC were David Honeyman in NS (active 1862-88); J.W. Spencer, F.B. Taylor and G.M. Stanley, students of the glacial Great Lakes (1894-1945); and A.P. Coleman who worked across Canada and wrote on Precambrian and Pleistocene GLACIATIONS, including his book *The Last Million Years* (1941). Glaciological observations were begun in Alberta and BC by George and William S. Vaux in 1899 and continued by A.O. Wheeler until 1931. Erosion surfaces of the Precambrian SHIELD were treated by A.W.G. Wilson in 1903 and by H.C. Cooke of the GSC in 1929-33.

Physiography took root in university GEOGRAPHY departments in the 1930s, promoted by Raoul Blanchard in Québec and Thomas Griffith TAYLOR at University of Toronto. The expansion of geography departments offering programs in PHYSICAL GEOGRAPHY (3 in 1947, 38 in 1986) brought an influx of European geographers. In 1986, 25 departments offered masters programs; 17 awarded doctoral degrees. Probably over half of these were in geomorphology. Similar growth increased the number of geology departments from 15 to 33, of which 23 gave graduate instruction in geomorphology and 14 offered advanced degrees in geomorphology or Quaternary geology. The Geographical Branch, a federal agency parallel to the GSC, was created in 1947 and emphasized arctic geomorphology. It was dissolved in 1967; its journal *Geographical Bulletin* ceased publication and most staff members joined other units. An explosive increase in the number of geomorphological publications took place between 1950 and 1970. Regional monographs appeared on the Canadian CORDILLERA by H.S. Bostock (1948), on southern Ontario by L.J. Chapman and D.F. PUTNAM (1951), on BC by S.S. Holland (1964), on the Arctic by J.B. Bird (1967) and on Canada as a whole by Bird (1972).

Applications Geomorphology is applied in soil research; in engineering geology and civil engineering projects such as route location, foundation problems, construction materials, slope stability and geological hazards; and in environmental and groundwater studies. The tracing of transported indicators is an important technique in mineral prospecting. REMOTE SENSING requires some knowledge of geomorphology. In Canada great effort is expended in mapping surficial geology, terrain characteristics and resources such as sand and gravel (*see* CARTOGRAPHY). Much applied research is done on the behaviour of frozen ground and on slope stability (*see* LANDSLIDES). The federal and most provincial governments have geomorphologically oriented agencies. The GSC was responsible for about a third of the projects in Canada: Environment Canada, the Alberta Research Council and the Ontario Geological Survey had roughly 6% each. Among academic institutions, University of Alberta (Geology) leads with 10%.

Societies and Journals Many Canadian geological geomorphologists are members of the Geological Soc of America and publish in its monthlies, *Bulletin* and *Geology*. The Geological Assn of Canada with the *Canadian Jnl of Earth Sciences* is a major forum. The *Canadian Geographer* of the Canadian Assn of Geographers contains some geomorphology and L'Association Québecoise pour l'étude Quaternaire and the Canadian Quaternary Assn sponsor the journal *Géographie physique et Quaternaire*. In 1987 the geomorphological community in Canada was host to the 12th International Congress of the International Union for Quaternary Research which met in Ottawa for 10 days.

J.A. ELSON

Geopolitics, a strategy for national identity and development based on a country's geographical characteristics and natural resources. From the development of a geopolitical strategy can flow industrial strategies, defence policies and a formula for permanent control over local branch plants of externally owned, multinational corporations. The study of the influence of geography on national and international politics began in the early 20th century. In 1919 an influential British geographer, Sir Halford J. Mackinder, theorized that the domination of the Euro-Asian "heartland" by one country, eg, Germany, would upset the world's balance of power. German geographers used Mackinder's theories to provide a justification for Nazi territorial expansion. Geopolitics has also been used to explain the idea of "Manifest Destiny" espoused by the US in the 19th century.

Canada is an outstanding example of a "geostrategic region," identified by American political geographer Saul B. Cohen as a region "large enough to possess certain globe-influencing characteristics and functions." In 1937 French geographer André Siegfried noted that Canada's 2 basic assets were its vast natural resources and its geographic position. Nevertheless, geopolitical thinking has been absent in Canadian governmental and industrial planning, chiefly because policy planners have viewed it as deterministic and authoritarian. Such federal government programs as the 1961 National Oil Policy and the 1980 National Energy Policy could be defined as "geopolitical": both policies represented efforts towards the "Canadianization" of our strategically situated but largely foreign-owned oil and natural gas industries. The long search for a national industrial strategy has failed partly because Canadians have not developed a prior and overall geopolitical view of Canada. Though Canada's planning for the development of the arctic regions remains piecemeal, for the first time since the 1940s Canada is planning a geopolitical strategy for defence. The White Paper on Defence, announced 5 July 1987, proposes 10 to 12 unarmed nuclear-powered submarines which would guarantee a Canadian naval presence in the Arctic, Atlantic and Pacific Oceans.

By comparison, other large nations, including the US, USSR and Brazil, with great potential in their natural resources and dominant geographical positions in their regions, have already defined themselves geopolitically. Their well-developed geopolitical positions have resulted in the growth and use of their military and commercial sea power, the control of their natural resources, and the direction of management and labour toward national goals.

JOHN D. HARBRON

George, Dan, or Teswahno, actor, public speaker (b on Burrard Indian Reserve No 3, BC 24 July 1899; d at Vancouver 12 Sept 1981). By his film roles and personal appearances Dan George helped improve the popular image of Indian people, often represented as bad characters. Until age 60, he worked as longshoreman, logger and itinerant musician, and was chief of the Squamish Band of Burrard Inlet, BC, 1951-63. He was discovered in 1959 and acted a succession of roles as gentle Indian elder on Canadian television and stage, including CBC's "Cariboo Country" (1961) and the original production of George RYGA's *The Ecstasy of Rita Joe* (1967, publ 1970). He recited his much-publicized "Lament for Confederation" on Indian defeat and resurgence at Vancouver's Canadian Centennial celebrations in 1967. During his Hollywood career his roles included at least 8 feature films, among which are *Smith* (1969), *Little Big Man* (1970), *Harry and Tonto* (1974) and *The Outlaw Josey Wales* (1975). A non-activist, George refused to endorse Indian political causes but insisted on portraying only "good" native figures. He was author of *My Heart Soars* (1974) and *My Spirit Soars* (1982), both prose-poetry.

BENNETT MCCARDLE

Chief Dan George shown here with another Canadian, Glenn Ford, in the Walt Disney production *Smith* (1968) (*courtesy National Archives of Canada/MISA/12751*).

George, Gloria Mary, politician, public servant (b at Hubert, BC 24 July 1942 into the Wet'-Suwet'En – the Athapaskan people of the Skeena region). Her father having signed away his status, she was raised as a nonstatus Indian. Among the first to join the BC Association of Non-Status Indians, 1969, she became its secretary-treasurer in 1971. She became secretary-treasurer of the Native Council of Canada in 1972, was elected NCC vice-president in 1974 and president the following year, becoming the first and so far the only woman to lead a major aboriginal political organization. As president 1975-76, she attained greater government recognition of the NCC and advocated programs to make police and others in the justice system aware of the needs of native people. She was a member of the Canadian Human Rights Com-

The George Cross has been awarded to 8 Canadians (*courtesy National Museums of Canada/Canadian Museum of Civilization/K71-96*).

mission (1978-80) and the BC Human Rights Commission (1980-82). PAUL TENNANT

George Cross The aerial bombing of centres of civilian population in Britain early in WWII gave rise to numerous acts of the most conspicuous bravery. In response, King George VI instituted a major decoration in 1940 for which civilians and members of the armed forces are eligible. The George Cross ranks immediately after the VICTORIA CROSS in the scale of Commonwealth HONOURS. Recipients have included 8 Canadians and one non-Canadian serving in a Canadian military unit. The decoration is in the form of a plain silver cross with, at its centre, a representation of St George slaying the dragon encircled by the words "For Gallantry." The ribbon is "garter" blue. CARL LOCHNAN

George Rivière, 560 km long, in northern Québec, drains N into the E side of UNGAVA BAY. Its southern and eastern divides, along with those of tributary rivers Ford and De Pas, extend along much of the Québec-Newfoundland and Labrador border. The river's 41 700 km^2 basin includes Lac de la Hutte-Sauvage (Indian House) and Lac aux Goélands (Whitegull) among many lakes that provide a mean discharge of 881 m^3/s. Over granitic gneiss of the Churchill geological area, the vegetation is transitional – from boreal forest in the S and W to tundra in the E and N. The river has supported a salmon sport fishery and the basin makes up much of the range of the George River CARIBOU herd. Native occupation of the area is by MONTAGNAIS-NASKAPI Indian and LABRADOR INUIT. Moravian missionaries named the river for George III in 1811, but European exploration of the extent of the river was not made until John MCLEAN'S attempt to establish a transportation route for the HBC from Fort Chimo to Lk MELVILLE. McLean first crossed the area in 1838, on the exploratory journey on which he discovered CHURCHILL FALLS. IAN MACCALLUM

George Weston Limited, with head offices in Toronto, is a Canadian food company incorporated in 1928 to acquire the business and assets of a predecessor of the same name, which was incorporated in 1910. The company grew between 1938 and 1980 by acquiring various assets in the food industry, including Loblaw Groceterias Co Ltd and Donlands Dairy Ltd. Today, George Weston Limited is engaged in the wholesale and retail distribution of food and other products; it manufactures bakery, confectionery and dairy products and operates subsidiaries in Canada and the US. Its Loblaw Companies Limited division currently operates supermarkets in Canada and the US. In 1986 it had annual sales of $10 billion (ranking 5th in Canada), assets of $3.2 billion (ranking 32nd) and 54 000 employees. Wittington Investments (WESTON family) owns 58%. DEBORAH C. SAWYER

Georges Bank is a large submarine bank (250 km by 150 km) at the edge of the Atlantic continental shelf between Cape Cod and Nova Scotia. Typical water depths are 50-80 m, but in some areas the water shoals to 10 m and less. Georges Bank is within the Bay of FUNDY-Gulf of Maine tidal system, and strong oscillatory tidal currents, typically 80-100 cm/s (1.6-2.0 knots), pass across the top of the bank, keeping the water column there well mixed even in summer. The average currents follow the contours of the bank, however, forming a clockwise gyre, and water on top of the bank remains there on average for several months during the summer. Georges Bank is one of the most biologically productive regions in the world's oceans, largely owing to the tidal mixing, which brings to the surface a continuous supply of regenerated nutrients from the sediments. The combination of high primary productivity and prolonged residence of the water leads to the buildup of high concentrations of plankton on the bank. As a result, Georges Bank sustains large stocks of fish, such as herring, haddock and cod, as well as SCALLOPS.

The scenery of Georgian Bay makes it one of Ontario's favourite recreation areas *(photo by Mary W. Ferguson)*.

Georges Bank has traditionally been fished by Canadian and American fishermen; properly managed, Georges Bank can sustain estimated annual fishery yields of about 420 000 t. In recent decades it was severely overfished by distant water trawling fleets, primarily from the Soviet Union and Poland. The Georges Bank herring, one of the world's largest herring stocks, with a biomass of approximately one million tonnes, virtually disappeared during this period. A boundary decision in Oct 1984 by the International Court at The Hague allocated five-sixths of the bank to the US. The easternmost sixth, awarded to Canada, is rich in groundfish and scallops. Joint management by the US and Canada of migratory fish stocks will still be required, however. Between 1976 and 1984, 10 wells were drilled on the American part of the Georges Bank, and oil companies in the late 1980s still express interest in drilling on both sides. However, the size and value of the oil and gas reserves are not yet known, and the impact on the fisheries of exploiting these resources is not well understood. CHRIS GARRETT AND TONY KOSLOW

Georgetown, PEI, Town, pop 729 (1986c), 737 (1981c), inc 1912, the capital of Kings County, is on the province's eastern coast, 50 km SE of Charlottetown. Named for King George III, it is the site of an excellent harbour, in proximity to both the Gulf of ST LAWRENCE and NORTHUMBERLAND STR. In the 19th century, Georgetown became a principal Island shipbuilding and commercial centre. However, the town's economy was debilitated by the late 19th-century collapse of the shipbuilding industry. When railway and then highway construction increased Georgetown's coastal isolation, the centrally located community of MONTAGUE became the commercial centre of southern Kings. In this century Georgetown's story has been one of further decline. Georgetown Seafoods and the modern shipyard are the principal sources of employment. W.S. KEIZER

Georgia, Strait of, body of water separating VANCOUVER I and mainland British Columbia S of QUADRA I. Part of a basin between 2 mountain ranges, the floor of the strait was deepened in the ice age by south-flowing glaciers. Coastal Salish have used sites on the strait for between 5000 and 10 000 years. In 1791, 2 Spanish navy ships under Francisco Eliza explored its coast. Capt George VANCOUVER followed in 1792, naming it the Gulf of Georgia, after George III, the British monarch. "Gulf" was changed to "strait" in 1865. Most of BC's population has clustered around the Strait of Georgia, especially in metropolitan Vancouver. It has year-round deep-sea shipping ports in Burrard Inlet, on the Fraser R estuary, at Roberts Bank, on Vancouver I's E coast, on Howe Sound and at Powell River. These are typically linked with railheads, and with forest-products mills or other manufacturing plants. The strait is also the main centre of the PACIFIC SALMON fishery, and its mild, rain-shadow climate makes it a popular marine recreation area in summer. PETER GRANT

Georgian Bay, NE arm of Lake HURON in S-central Ontario. It is shielded from the lake by the limestone spine of the NIAGARA ESCARPMENT, which extends in a great arc NW up the BRUCE PENINSULA. The bay is fed from Lk Superior via the North Channel, between Manitoulin I and the N shore, and independently by the Mississagi, Spanish, French, Magnetawan, Muskoka, Severn and Nottawasaga rivers. The strait between the Bruce Peninsula and MANITOULIN I is called Main Channel (25 km wide). In contrast to the soft, white limestone cliffs of the W shore, the E shore is cut into the hard edge of the Canadian Shield, fractured into myriad bays, inlets and sounds, with thousands of islands strewn along the coasts. On the inner, SW curve of Nottawasaga Bay are numerous sandy beaches, the longest of which is Wasaga. Located around the bay (from SW to NE) are OWEN SOUND, COLLINGWOOD, Wasaga Beach, MIDLAND, Pt McNicoll, Victoria Harbour and PARRY SOUND; in summer local residents are greatly outnumbered by tourists.

BRÛLÉ was the first European to see the bay (perhaps as early as 1610) and CHAMPLAIN came via the FRENCH R (1615) to visit the Huron, who lived on a small peninsula along the SE shore (*see* HURONIA). Jesuit missionaries came to the area in the 1620s and BRÉBEUF was entrusted with founding a permanent mission in the area in 1634 (STE

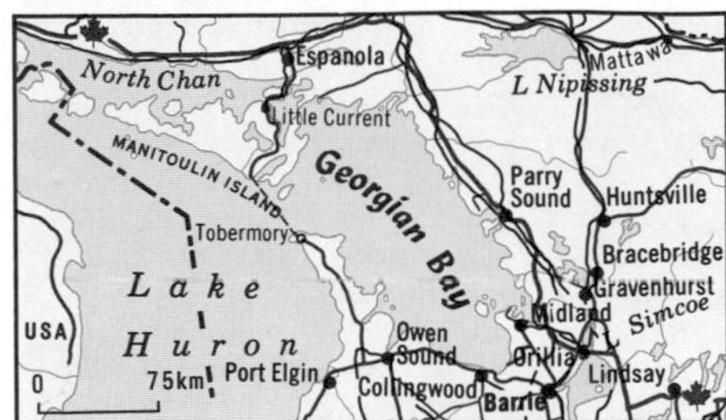

MARIE AMONG THE HURONS). The bay also has a natural water connection, sometimes called the Toronto Passage, to Lk Ontario via Lk Simcoe and the Nottawasaga R. It was used by the Indians and later during the War of 1812, when a military base was opened at Penetanguishene. Settlement followed the building of a railway from Barrie to Collingwood in 1855. Free land grants opened the area in 1868, but the soil is generally unfavourable to farming. The key industry of the late 19th century was logging; in 1890 Midland was second in production only to Ottawa. By 1900 most of the original forests had disappeared; the lumber industry died, leaving behind slashed-over terrain and a few local mills. The fishing industry lasted longer. Immense quantities of whitefish, trout and pickerel were shipped out by rail until the 1950s. By 1960 the industry was virtually ruined by the LAMPREY. Today there is a variety of secondary industry around the bay – textiles, cameras, shipbuilding. But the once-profitable grain-handling business diminished rapidly after the ST LAWRENCE SEAWAY opened. Tourism, based on the natural splendour of the Georgian Bay area, began in the 1850s with the arrival of the railway and is now the main industry. Summer homes were built along the N shore in the 1880s, and thousands came after 1900 by train to Parry Sound and Midland, thence by boat to the islands to fish, sail and pitch tents – a pattern of vacationing repeated every year. The best-known areas are the N shore islands, the "Thirty Thousand Islands" on the E shore, Manitoulin I, the amusement-park atmosphere of Wasaga Beach, the yacht harbour at Tobermory and the Martyrs' Shrine and reconstructions of Ste Marie and a Huron village near Midland.

Called Lk Manitoulin by Capt William Fitzwilliam Owen, who charted the area 1815, the bay was later decreed part of Lk Huron and named for King George IV by Capt H.W. Bayfield's Admiralty Survey 1819-22. Nearly as large as Lk Ontario, it is one of the world's great bodies of fresh water. JAMES MARSH

Reading: J. Barry, *Georgian Bay: The Sixth Great Lake (1968)*.

Georgian Bay Islands National Park (est 1929) comprises 59 islands located off the SE coast of GEORGIAN BAY. Two other islands, Flowerpot and Cove, situated farther W off the tip of the BRUCE PENINSULA, are part of the recently created Fathom Fire National Marine Park. The Precambrian granite islands of the E, which inspired many GROUP OF SEVEN paintings, are a stark contrast to the eroded limestone islands to the W, with their caves, "flowerpot" formations and rich maple-beech forests. Although small (24.1 km^2), the park protects several unusual species. Beausoleil I, the largest park island, is one of the last strongholds of the Massassauga rattlesnake, eastern Canada's only venomous snake. Other noteworthy species protected include the eastern fox snake, hognose snake, spotted turtle, calypso orchid and squawroot. The park has recreational facilities. Scuba diving is popular and the area has long been famous as a boating mecca. LILLIAN STEWART

Geothermal Energy is the exploitable heat within the Earth. The interior of the planet is maintained at a high temperature by a vast store of heat, of which part remains from the formation of the Earth and part is continually generated by the decay of radioactive elements. Heat generated is roughly balanced by heat escaping through conduction to the surface, geysers and hot SPRINGS, and volcanic action. Some of this ENERGY becomes concentrated in deposits that can be tapped; research into geothermal energy seeks to discover new deposits of heat and to improve exploration and exploitation technology. Geothermal energy involves a relatively new technology compared to that developed for fuels such as oil or gas, but as these finite resources are used and become more expensive geothermal energy will grow in importance.

Most geothermal deposits involve a coincidence of water and heat. Surface water sinks into the ground, some of it penetrating deep into cracks or porous rocks where it may become trapped in large reservoirs for long periods. In stable, nonvolcanic parts of the Earth's crust, temperature increases in a downward direction at an average rate of about 25°C/km, and hot reservoirs are found only where porous rocks extend to depths that are hot under normal conditions. These are usually in large sedimentary basins, in the rocks that sometimes hold petroleum deposits. In volcanic areas, water becomes intensely heated at shallow depth and some reservoirs become large deposits of exploitable energy. A few reservoirs, eg, Larderello in Italy, contain steam at about 235°C, but most contain water under high pressure at temperatures up to 400°C. When temperatures are higher than 200°C, reservoirs can be drilled for steam to drive turbines for production of electricity. Geothermal waters at lower temperatures can be used for many direct applications (eg, heating buildings, drying crops). Some hot rocks do not have a convenient water stream to extract their heat and an artificial circulation system must be created. Such a system is being developed in the US at Los Alamos, where a pair of holes have been drilled, the rock between has been fractured to complete the circulation path, and electric power has been generated.

In Canada geothermal potential is found in the sedimentary rocks of the prairies and in a broad band bordering the oceans. The central area of the Canadian landmass, the SHIELD, is too old and cool to yield useful heat. The total potentially usable heat in hot water in the sediments of the prairies is equivalent to 300 times Canada's total energy needs in 1987, but only a small fraction of this heat is readily exploitable at current energy prices and with current technology. British Columbia's mountains contain about a dozen volcanic centres that may have geothermal deposits capable of producing electric power. There are also hot dry-rock deposits in volcanic centres and more widespread zones of intrusive rocks, and in small sedimentary basins that may be abnormally warm. One of the volcanic centres, Mt Meager, has been drilled by BC HYDRO for geothermal steam. Temperatures of about 250°C were encountered, but the project to build a 50 Mw plant has been abandoned, pending future energy shortages. In the arctic islands, the Sverdrup Basin probably holds a large geothermal resource, but opportunities for using it are few. There is a deep sedimentary basin under PEI and the Gulf of St Lawrence, but little is known about its temperature and water content. The Atlantic margin of Canada also contains large granitic bodies, some with sufficient heat production from radioactivity to give high temperature at a depth of about 3 km.

The US, USSR, Italy, NZ, Iceland, France, Hungary and several other countries are already using geothermal energy for electric-power generation, residential and commercial heating, and agricultural and industrial processes. In volcanic areas, geothermal energy seems to be renewable, provided that extraction rates are carefully controlled. In sedimentary basins it is not renewable at a reasonable rate and parts of the reservoir can be cooled to a level from which it will recover only after a few hundred years. Harmful environmental effects are few – usually the result of failing to reinject cooled water. ALAN M. JESSOP

Reading: L. Rybach, *Geothermal Systems* (1981).

Geraldton, Ont, Town, pop 2882 (1986c), 2965 (1981c), inc 1937, is situated in NW Ontario on the CNR, 282 km NE of Thunder Bay. Established in the early 1930s as a consequence of the Little Long Lac gold rush, the town derived its name from its 2 co-founders, mining entrepreneurs J.S. FitzGerald and Joseph Errington. At the height of the boom in the later 1930s, Geraldton acted as a service centre to a dozen gold-mining camps as well as to the developing pulpwood industry in the area. The major mine was the Macleod-Cockshutt, which in its nearly 30-year existence extracted more than $49 million of gold. Its closure in the late 1960s contributed to the gradual decline in Geraldton's population from a high of 3588 in 1965. MATT BRAY

Geranium, annual, biennial or perennial plant of genus *Geranium*, family Geraniaceae [Gk geranos, "crane"], with opposite, palmate and often divided leaves. Flowers have all parts in fives: 5 green sepals; 5 pink or purple, rarely white, petals; 10 stamens, etc. Its common name, "cranesbill," is derived from characteristic, beaked fruit, which explodes, when ripe, into 5 one-seeded parts which remain attached to a central column. About 275 species are known worldwide; in Canada, 7 species are native, 5 or 6 have been introduced. Bicknell's cranesbill (*G. bicknellii*), widespread across Canada in open woods and disturbed soils, is a dainty plant, 10-50 cm high, with small, paired, rose-coloured flowers. Spotted cranesbill (*G. maculatum*), a perennial plant, 20-60 cm tall, is found in woods, thickets and meadows in Ontario and Québec. It is quite showy with palmate leaves and large, rose-purple flowers. The underground stem (rhizome) is rich in tannin and gallic acid and produces an astringent, hence the common name alum root. Indians used the rhizome for diarrhea, dysentery, internal and external bleeding, mouth ulcers and sore throats. White geranium (*G. richardsonii*), distinguished by white flowers with purplish veins, grows to 40-80 cm and occupies moist open woods, thickets and alpine meadows from the YT to BC, east to Saskatchewan. Sticky purple geranium (*G. viscosissimum*), a showy, glandular plant with large, divided leaves and large, reddish purple flowers, grows up to 60 cm and is found in moist meadows in mountains and foothills and moist fescue prairie of BC, Alta and Sask. The familiar garden form is not a true geranium but belongs to genus *Pelargonium*, family Geraniaceae, and is native to S Africa. BERYL HALLWORTH

Gérin, Léon, lawyer, farmer, federal civil servant, sociologist (b at Québec C 17 May 1863; d at Montréal 15 Jan 1951). The founder of empirical SOCIAL SCIENCES in French Canada, Gérin had an outstanding reputation because of his numerous well-documented studies of Québec's rural society. After graduation from law school at U de M (1885), Gérin went to Paris, where he registered at the Museum of Natural History. After meeting Edmond Demolins and the Rev de Tourville, both disciples of Frédéric Le Play, Gérin left the museum and spent 6 months at the École de science sociale. Returning to Canada in 1887, Gérin bought a farm and joined the Ottawa civil service. He soon became, through numerous and meticulous publications about rural Québec, a prestigious and prolific writer. He became a fellow of the RSC in 1898 and president of the French section in 1900. He was elected RSC president in 1933 and was awarded the Lorne Pierce Medal in 1941. MARC-ADÉLARD TREMBLAY

Gérin-Lajoie, Antoine, journalist, lawyer (1848), public servant, writer (b at Yamachiche, LC 4 Aug 1824; d at Ottawa Aug 4 1882). As a student at Nicolet College, he wrote the poem "Un Canadien errant" (1842) and *Le Jeune Latour* (1844), the first Canadian tragedy. He was a founding member and president of the INSTITUT CANADIEN and one of its highly respected lecturers, a journalist for *La Minerve* (1845-47), the author of a very useful *Catéchisme politique* (1851) and a public servant. After being translator to the Assembly of the Province of Canada, he was assistant librarian at the Library of Parliament 1856-80 and chief compiler of its *Catalogue* (2 vols, 1857-58). He helped found Les SOIRÉES CANADIENNES and *Le Foyer canadien*, of which he was the leading figure (1862-65). His most famous work is a 2-part novel: *Jean Rivard, le défricheur* (1862) and *Jean Rivard, économiste* (1864), which extols the virtue of clearing uncultivated land in Québec as a means of ensuring survival of the French Canadian nation. Part of his *Mémoires* (1885) and an historical work, *Dix ans au Canada, de 1840 à 1850* (1888-91), were published posthumously.
RENÉ DIONNE

Gérin-Lajoie, Marie, née Lacoste, author, educator, organizer (b at Montréal 19 Oct 1867; d there 1 Nov 1945). Gérin-Lajoie combined Catholicism and family life with reform work, developing a concern for women's rights after she discovered women's legal disabilities from reading her father's law books. A founder of the Fédération nationale St-Jean-Baptiste (1907), bringing together francophone women from charitable and professional associations, she directed its activities for the next 20 years, working closely with local branches of the National Council of Women of Canada. She was a lecturer at U de Montréal and wrote *Traité de droit usuel* (1902) and *La Femme et le code civil* (1929). Although Gérin-Lajoie gave up her position as head of the francophone section of the Provincial Franchise Committee when the bishop of Montréal expressed disapproval of women voters (1922), she continued to agitate for women's rights. She testified before the Dorion Commission (1929) whose recommendations led to amendments to the Québec Civil Code. MARGARET E. MCCALLUM

Gérin-Lajoie, Paul, lawyer, politician (b at Montréal 23 Feb 1920). Gérin-Lajoie was one of the leading political figures in Québec's QUIET REVOLUTION: minister of youth (1960-64) and of education (1964-66) of the Liberal regime of Jean LESAGE. A cultivated Rhodes scholar with an Oxford doctorate, and an eminent international and constitutional lawyer, Gérin-Lajoie was well equipped to battle Ottawa in the frequent federal-provincial squabbles of the time. As Québec's first minister of education, he dismantled the old church-dominated system and built a secular, centralized administration emphasizing post-secondary schooling. He was subsequently an independent-minded, highly visible and controversial president of the federal CANADIAN INTERNATIONAL DEVELOPMENT AGENCY 1970-77. NORMAN HILLMER

Germain, Jean-Claude, writer, theatre producer (b at Montréal 18 June 1939). While attending U de M (1957-59), he established the Théâtre Antonin-Artaud in 1958 and began work on a production of *Ubu roi* that had to be cancelled for lack of funds. In 1969 he established the experimental Théâtre du même nom (TMN) where he clearly demonstrated his distance from the theories of the "Cartel" espoused by the THÉÂTRE DU NOUVEAU MONDE (TNM). The actors of Germain's company, known popularly as the Enfants de Chénier (1969-71) and later P'tits Enfants Laliberté (1971-73), combined with André Brassard's group (Théâtre de Montréal) and Jean-Pierre Saulnier's company (Apprentis-Sorciers) to form the Centre du théâtre d'aujourd'hui, of which Germain was general manager 1972-82. Since 1969, Germain has produced some 15 collective creations, made 4 adaptations and, since 1973, produced 8 of his own texts. He has published poetry in *L'Action nationale* (1966-67), 3 outlines for collective plays, 2 adaptations and a dozen of his own plays. He has published short essays on theatre in *Pays théâtral* (1977-80) and, since 1973, has taught at the National Theatre School. ANDRÉ G. BOURASSA

German Writing German Canadians, Canada's third-largest ethnic group, hail from a variety of national and cultural backgrounds: GERMAN, Austrian, SWISS, MENNONITE and others. Common to them are their language (High or Low German, or a variety of dialects), the experience of leaving the Old World and finding roots in the New World, and that of learning the new language(s) and adapting to new customs. Reflecting their experience, first-generation writers generally perceive and portray the new country from their perspective of the old, and in their native tongue; the next generation, having acquired the new cultural traditions and at least one of the official languages, contributes to one of Canada's mainstream literatures, usually English Canadian.

Chronology and locations of developing literary activity are related to settlement. In 1750 the first Germans arrived in Nova Scotia and established LUNENBURG. At the time of the American Revolution the Loyalists – among them some of German origin – moved N. During the 1830s many Mennonites from Pennsylvania settled in the Berlin [Kitchener, Ont] area. Large waves of German immigration came from Europe to Ontario, 1830-80, and to western Canada, 1880-1910. The most significant influxes followed the 2 world wars, and during the same periods many Mennonites came, mainly to Manitoba.

The pioneers had little time for literature, but newspapers and periodicals provided an early forum for creative writing. One of the earliest publications, *Der Neu-Schottländische Calender* (1788-1801), featured anonymous poems and short prose. Among the numerous German-language newspapers, the *Berliner Journal* (Waterloo) is of special interest for its humorous and entertaining dialect letters to the editor by John A. Rittinger. Spiritual leaders published religiously oriented didactic literature in early church bulletins, such as the *Kirchenblatt der Evangelisch-Lutherischen Synode von Canada* (1869-1909) and *Der Deutsche Lutheraner* (1920-22); samples from 14 contributors are contained in the collection *Hier laßt uns Hütten bauen. Deutsche Gedichte Lutherischer Pfarrer in Ontario (1869-1930)* (Gerhard Friesen, ed, 1984). These poems, along with book-length publications by Father Eugen Funcken (1831-88) and Heinrich Rembe (1858-1927), for example, reflect strong influences of German classicism and romanticism, as does early Canadian Mennonite devotional didactic literature, which was written in Low German for a Mennonite audience. A significant departure in Mennonite literature is the recording of the experience of being uprooted from Russia, migrating to Canada and starting anew. Dietrich Neufeld's diary, *Ein Tagebuch aus dem Reiche des Totentanzes* (1921), and Hans Harder's *In Wologdas weissen Wäldern* (1934; tr *A Russian Dance of Death*, 1977, and *No Strangers in Exile*, 1979, respectively), and the novels of Gerhard Toews (pseud Georg de Brecht) deal with these chaotic times and events. Other important works are Arnold B. Dyck's educational, autobiographical novel *Verloren in der Steppe* (1944; tr *Lost in the Steppes*, 1974) and the vivid poetry of Gerhard Friesen (pseud Fritz Senn). Beginning in 1935, the periodical *Die Mennonitische Warte* encouraged literary activity. The anthologies *Harvest* (ed William de Fehr et al, 1974) and *Unter dem Nordlicht* (ed G.K. Epp, 1977) feature poetry and short prose in High and Low German and in English by more than 40 Mennonite contributors. Most significant in contemporary Mennonite literature is a new generation of writers born in Canada and writing in English, including Rudy WIEBE, Clint Toews, David Waltner-Toews, Menno Wiebe and Patrick Friesen.

Writers who had made their debut in German-speaking Europe continued to publish there. Else Seel (1894-1974) came from Berlin in 1927 to the BC wilderness, where she wrote poetry, short prose and a diary reminiscent of the work of Catharine Parr TRAILL and Susanna MOODIE. Walter Bauer (1904-76), well known as an author in Germany, came to Canada in 1952. His books on Canadian themes reflect his European view of Canada. A small part of his work is available in English translation: *The Price of Morning* (1968) and *A Different Sun* (1976; both tr Henry Beissel) and *A Slight Trace of Ash* (1976, tr H. Milnes). Swiss-born Hermann Böschenstein (1900-82), author of expressionist prose, wrote, besides scholarly publications on German literature, short stories and a novel dealing perceptively with the immigrant experience. Some writers who were at home in both German and English made their mark in English Canadian literature: Felix Paul Greve, under his adopted name Frederick Philip GROVE, became one of Canada's most important realists; his work is deeply rooted in the literary traditions of German naturalism and neo-romanticism.

Three writers came to Canada during WWII via internment in England: Carl Weiselberger (1900-70), already known in Vienna, served as the art and music critic of the *Ottawa Citizen* after his internment, and wrote short stories and newspaper articles reflecting a refreshing enthusiasm for his new homeland. Henry KREISEL, born in Vienna, Austria has written short stories and 2 novels, *The Rich Man* (1948) and *The Betrayal* (1964), with themes concerning Europe and Canada. Charles Wassermann (1924-78), reporter, broadcaster and writer, became an important intermediary between the Old World and the New.

The writers who came to Canada at an early age were most successful in adopting English as their creative medium: Henry Beissel, born in 1929 in Cologne, Germany, came to Canada in 1951 via England. His work dealing with Indian and Inuit themes, his epic *Cantos North* (1982) and his subjective *Kanada, Romantik und Wirklichkeit* (1981) are sensitive statements about the Canadian experience. Derk Wynand, born in 1944 in Bad Suderode, Germany, came to Canada in 1952 and became known as the translator of H.C. Artmann and as an author of modernist poetry and short prose in English. Andreas Schroeder, born in Hoheneggelsen, Germany, in 1946, was educated in Canada and is known as an editor and translator from German and an author of prose and poetry in English. Ulrich Schaffer, born in 1942 in Germany, came to Canada in 1953. Though he writes in both English and German, his audience is primarily in German-speaking western Europe. His writing, often inspired by the Canadian landscape, is sometimes reminiscent of Kafka. Those writers who continue to write in German well after their arrival in Canada invariably have to contend with the problems of both publication in a minority language and reaching an audience. Rolf Windthorst, born in 1909 in Dortmund, Germany, and living in Alberta since 1956, and Valentin Sawatsky, born in Ukraine in 1914 and living in Ontario since 1950 – to name but 2 of the more prolific writers – have not been able to find the readership their works may deserve.

The anthologies edited by Friesen as well as *Ahornblätter* (comp Heinz Kloss and Arnold B. Dyck, 1961) and *Nachrichten aus Ontario* (ed Hartmut Fröschle, 1981) feature samples of work by over 60 authors. The latter also contains a comprehensive introduction to German Canadian literature, a useful "Who's Who" and a selected bibliography. Critical attention to the writing of German Canadians is recent. The most important forums are the *German-Canadian Yearbook* (ed Hartmut Fröschle, 1973-), the proceedings of symposia on German Canadian studies and 2 series of critical editions and studies of German Canadiana. WALTER E. RIEDEL

Reading: K. Gürttler, ed, *Symposium* (6 vols, 1976-); H. Loewen, ed, *Mennonite Images* (1980); W.E. Riedel, ed, *The Old World and the New* (1984).

Germanic Fraktur and Calligraphy Handwriting has served the needs of communication and recording in every literate culture and has been regarded as an essential tool of civilization. Frequently, however, lettering has been developed beyond the utilitarian level to an artistic form. The artistic CALLIGRAPHY that flourished after the 17th century among the peoples of southern Germany, Alsace and Switzerland is known as *fraktur*. Related to the English word "fracture," the term suggests a lettering form with fractures or breaks in the script, which give an ornamental or decorative effect.

MENNONITES migrating from Pennsylvania to Ontario between the 1780s and 1830s brought along this art form. It flourished chiefly in 3 areas of early Ontario: the Niagara Pen (Lincoln and Welland counties), upper York County (especially Markham and Vaughan townships) and Waterloo County. Beautifully decorated fraktur songbooks, as well as drawings and exercises, were made by Samuel Moyer and other Mennonite teachers at Vineland in Lincoln County during the early 1800s. In the Markham area of York County one interesting artist, Christian L. Hoover, took up the activity during a year of severe illness, making hand-lettered and decorated birth records for relatives and friends. The largest output occurred from the 1820s to the 1890s in the sizable Mennonite community of Waterloo County, where several artists produced colourful fraktur drawings and texts. Anna Weber, one of the few women to practise the art, appears to have been a lonely individual, suffering from poor health, who made delightful drawings of birds, trees and animals for friends and visitors and for children of families who looked after her in her later years.

Anna Weber, *Birds and Checkered Sheep* (1875) (*private collection*).

The art has revived somewhat in recent years with its reintroduction into some Old Order Mennonite schools in the Waterloo area of southern Ontario, and with a growing interest by the public at large in relearning lost artistic forms. During its high point, in 19th-century Ontario, fraktur was one of Canada's most exuberant folk-art traditions. MICHAEL S. BIRD

Reading: Michael S. Bird and Terry Kobayashi, *A Splendid Harvest: Germanic Folk and Decorative Arts in Canada* (1981).

Germans Few Canadians of German-speaking origin are *Reichsdeutsche* (from Germany); most are *Auslandsdeutsche* (from other lands), and may include Roman Catholics, Jews, Mennonites, Lutherans or others, who originate from Estonia in the N to the Black Sea in the S, from Alsace in the W to the Caspian Sea in the E.

Preliminary data from the 1986 census showed almost 900 000 Canadians of German origin, but other estimates show numbers as high as 1.7 million if all Canadians of German-language descent are counted.

Migration and Settlement The Thirty Years War, 1618-48, upset the balance of the German population and caused the first wave of migrants to the New World. Later, a small number of settlers of German origin, including some demobilized soldiers who had served under the French king at Port-Royal, Louisbourg and Québec, established themselves in New France; in 1664 Hans Bernard, the first recorded German settler, purchased land near Québec. Between 1664 and 1700 the migration of civilians was overshadowed by the settlement of soldiers from the garrisons of New France. Between 1750 and 1752 about 2000 German newcomers landed at Halifax. They were Protestants and represented the first organized attempt to settle Germans in Canada. They had been recruited by the British government from principalities suffering from severe economic problems, religious persecution or war. In 1753 some 1453 of the immigrants were moved to Merligash (renamed LUNENBURG) where they became fishermen and boat builders.

Between 1760 and 1770 Germans from Europe and Pennsylvania settled in Annapolis County (NS) and in several other areas that later became part of New Brunswick. During and after the American Revolution, among the thousands of United Empire Loyalists who journeyed to British N America, were many persons of German origin who had settled earlier in Pennsylvania, New York and even Georgia. Some formed part of the group who sailed from New York to Halifax in 1783, the others either moved up the Hudson River Valley by Lk Champlain and down to Sorel or made their way over the Niagara frontier. These groups included ordinary civilians as well as members of militia regiments and German regiments who had fought for the British Crown. Of some 1200 discharged German soldiers of Brunswick regiments recruited in German principalities and sent to Canada to defend it against American invasion, several hundred settled in Lower and Upper Canada, New Brunswick and Nova Scotia, where they founded the Hessian Line and Waldeck Line settlements.

In 1792, after John Graves SIMCOE became lieutenant-governor of Upper Canada, native Americans who still sympathized with Great Britain were invited to take up free land in the new province, and many settlers of German origin did so. Between 1792 and 1837 German settlers also arrived in Canada from New Jersey and Pennsylvania. They were not of Dutch origin but nevertheless were known as "Pennsylvania Dutch." The majority were MENNONITES who sought not only free land but religious freedom and exemption from military service. Americans regarded Mennonites and other "plain folks" Germans with great suspicion because they had been conscientious objectors and had not been involved in the war. For these migrants the "German Company" purchased land in the Grand River Valley of Ontario, and Waterloo County became the centre of German settlement. Berlin (now KITCHENER) was the principal community. Settlers of German LUTHERAN and Catholic origin also settled in this area and Mennonites founded communities in the Niagara district and in York County, at Whitchurch. Settlers travelled from the US in their Conestoga wagons, which were antecedents of the prairie schooners of the North American West.

After 1830 many German Catholics and Amish people arrived directly from Europe, settling in Perth, Huron, Bruce and Grey counties. Others, chiefly from Prussia, settled along the Ottawa R in Renfrew County and in Québec's Pontiac County. By the time of Confederation, about 200 000 people of German origin had settled in Canada, mostly in Ontario. About 1500 lived in Québec (mainly Montréal) and 47 000 in the Maritimes, including 20 000 in Lunenburg County (NS). The immigration from Germany, which continued until the 1870s, changed drastically with the prosperity of the newly established German Empire; it was replaced by large numbers of German-speaking Mennonites from Ukraine who helped pioneer settlements on the prairies. After Canada acquired land from the Hudson's Bay Company the township system of settlement was adopted in 1871 and the Dominion Lands Act of 1872 facilitated homesteading. From 1872 onward, William Hespeler, an immigrant himself and a colonizer, contacted Mennonites and HUTTERITES who were intent upon leaving southern Ukraine because of changing Russian policies towards minorities. He persuaded a group of leaders to come and search for suitable land in Manitoba. The leaders received freedom from military service for their members, the right to educate their children and other concessions that led them to endorse migration to Canada. About 7000 Mennonites immigrated to Manitoba between 1874 and 1880, settling in the East Reserve – E of Niverville, W of STEINBACH – and the West Reserve – E of Morden and W of Rosenfeld. Eastern Canadian settlers had doubted that the prairies could be settled, but the Mennonites confirmed that prairie soil was indeed fertile, and many of the colonizers prospered. From 1880 to 1900, thousands of settlers of German origin (many from Eastern and Southeastern Europe) settled in Manitoba, Saskatchewan and Alberta. Most settlements were along denominational lines. Mennonites lived in Swift Current and Rosthern, Lutherans in central Saskatchewan and Roman Catholics, after 1903, in the St Peters Colony, near Humboldt, and in the St Josephs Colony, near Tramping Lake. By 1914 about 35 000 Germans had settled in Manitoba, comprising 7.5% of the population; in Saskatchewan the number of immigrants with German origins jumped from under 5000 in 1901 to 100 000 in 1911, and German communities in Alberta, including the Josephsburg Colony (also called Medicine Hat) and those along the Calgary and Edmonton Railway had, by 1911, reached a population of about 41 000 people.

Although a small number of German settlers moved to BC under the auspices of the HBC, any sizable settlement dates from the Fraser River Valley gold rush of 1858 and a later one in the Cariboo Mts. Most of these Germans made comfortable livings as grocers, farmers, craftsmen, shopkeepers and brewers. By 1911 there were about 11 800 German-speaking persons in BC but a slump beginning in 1912 and WWI curbed German immigration.

WWI had a profound impact upon German Canadians. Until then, they were considered preferred immigrants, but with the outbreak of war the Canadian government restricted immigration. As a result of the war against Germany, Germans and other Europeans were vilified, arbitrarily interned, their properties confiscated and never accounted for and the use of their language restricted or banned altogether (*see* PREJUDICE AND DISCRIMINATION). Because Mennonites became one of the special targets of this new policy, about 6000 Old Colony Mennonites from Manitoba and Saskatchewan left Canada in the 1920s and settled in Chihuahua, Mexico, but retained their Canadian citizenship.

In 1918 a party of about 50 German-speaking Hutterites did immigrate to Canada from Dakota, settling in Manitoba and Alberta where their communal way of life often sparked conflict between their community and the government and local people. Germany did not acquire "favoured nation" status until 1927, but between 1919 and 1935 some 97 000 German-speaking immigrants arrived in Canada from Poland, Austria, Czechoslovakia and parts of Germany (including, for example, Baltic Germans who only began to arrive in Canada after WWI when Baltic German estates were expropriated). Some of the newcomers were artisans, shopkeepers and labourers; many were young men and unattached workers, who as nonpreferred migrants had to work on farms for an initial period of time. After a few years, these men drifted into the towns and cities in search of urban employment that would allow them to raise passage money to bring over their families. Some succeeded but the majority, because of the Great Depression, were unable to do so. Migration came to a virtual standstill during the 1930s and many migrants decided to go home. In the late 1930s there was a small flow of Sudeten Germans, who because of their Social Democratic political affiliation emigrated to escape Nazi persecution. Otherwise, Canada closed its doors to thousands of JEWS seeking refuge from Nazi rule (*see also* IMMIGRATION). After the British evacuation of Dunkirk, people of German or Austrian origin living in the UK were classified as "friendly aliens" and 6700 were sent to Canada for detention. By 1943 they had been released and 5200 remained in Canada.

The treatment of German Canadians during WWII was remarkably mild. While known Nazi sympathizers were interned for prolonged periods, other German Canadians were left alone. Only the property of German nationals was confiscated. Between 1947 and 1950 immigration to Canada by Germans included many German-speaking refugees from Eastern Europe (ethnic Germans or *Volksdeutsche*), from Romania, Yugoslavia and the former Austria-Hungary. In 1950 a ban on immigration of German nationals was lifted. Between 1951 and 1960 about 250 000 German immigrants arrived in Canada, about 60% of whom remained in Canada permanently. In 1958 new immigration regulations, designed to maintain a lower level of immigration of any kind into Canada, were implemented. Since the 1970s the Old Colony Mennonites have slowly returned from Mexico and Latin America and an increased migration of German industrialists and investors has begun.

Social and Cultural Life The majority of German Canadians have acculturated in a selective fashion, retaining some of their ethnic traits but discarding others in favour of Canadian patterns. There is no unified German culture in Canada; instead there is religious and cultural pluralism. Most Canadians of German origin belong to the Protestant churches, but about 25% are Roman Catholic and 9% are Mennonites or Hutterites. The life of the early settlements revolved around the churches, which were responsible for language schools, care of the needy and recreational facilities.

The German Benevolent Society (est 1835 in Montréal) and the Germania Club (est 1864 in Hamilton) are the oldest surviving German Canadian clubs. After WWII new clubs were organized to help recently arrived immigrants or to promote cultural interests. One of the oldest Canadian musical societies, the Québec Harmonic Society (est 1820), was founded by the German Frederick Glackemeyer, and many choir groups were formed before Confederation.

The national umbrella organization for German Canadians is the German-Canadian Congress, fd 1984, which represents the many diverse religious groups and countries of origin of German-speaking immigrants. Preservation of cultural heritage of German-speaking Canadians and articulation of group interests within the framework of multiculturalism are objectives of the congress. Festivals and celebrations are popular among Germans. The largest festival is Oktoberfest, now held in Kitchener. Christmas is also a major celebration. The custom of a lighted evergreen tree, which originated in Germany in the 16th century, was introduced into Canada in 1781 by Baroness von Riedesel.

The first German-language publication, *Halifax Zeitung*, appeared in the 1780s. By the late 1980s the weekly *Kanada Kurier* was the largest German-language newspaper. German-language broadcasting is conducted on privately operated radio stations.

One governor general (Edward SCHREYER), one prime minister (John DIEFENBAKER) and members of the federal and provincial governments have been German in origin, but considering the numbers of German immigrants to Canada, Germans have not been proportionately represented in politics.

Economic Life Economically German Canadians are generally prosperous. They have retained the management of German-owned companies and are prominent in technical and professional occupations. Germans are also overrepresented in skilled trades and machine-working occupations and farming. German farmers began grape growing in the Niagara Peninsula. Canadians of German origin are underrepresented in public service, however, where the German component is slightly over 3%. R.A. HELLING

Reading: W.R. Bell, *The Foreign Protestants and the Settlement of Nova Scotia* (1961); F.H. Epp, *Mennonites in Canada, 1786-1920* (1974); H. Froeschle, *German-Canadian Yearbook/DeutschKanadisches Jahrbuch* (1973*ff*); O. Gingerich, *The Amish of Canada* (1972); G.E. Reaman, *The Trail of the Black Walnut* (1957) H. Troper and I. Abella, *None Is Too Many* (1982).

Gerontology, the scientific study of AGING and its consequences, eg, social and economic problems precipitated by growing numbers of elderly in a population; psychological aspects of aging; physiological bases of aging; and general biological aspects of aging in all animal species.

Systematic Canadian research began in 1944 with the founding of the Gerontologic Research Unit at McGill University. During the 1950s the Canadian Welfare Council formed the Committee on Aging, which began research in social gerontology that continues under its successor, the Canadian Council on Social Development. The Ontario Geriatrics Research Society became the Canadian Geriatrics Research Society in 1975. Research was stimulated by provincial conferences on aging held in several provinces beginning in 1957 and continued through the early 1960s. In 1966 the final report of the Senate's Special Committee on Aging was published, the first provincial office on aging, in Ontario, was created and the Canadian Conference on Aging was held. Increasing participation of Canadian gerontologists in international gerontology associations led to the establishment of the Canadian Association on Gerontology/Association canadienne de gérontologie (CAG/ACG) in 1971. By 1987 it had grown to about 1500 members in 5 divisions, representing subspecialty interests in social sciences, psychology, biology, health sciences and social welfare. The CAG/ACG is the major forum for gerontological research in Canada through its annual conferences and its *Canadian Journal on Aging*, est 1982. In addition, all provinces have provincial associations, 8 of which are affiliated with the CAG/ACG. Québec has 2 nonaffiliated organizations. Several related organizations with gerontological activities exist in many provinces and some of these, such as the Ontario Psychogeriatric Association, are actively involved in research.

Since the late 1970s, extensive research support has been provided for social gerontology by the Social Sciences and Humanities Research Council of Canada through its Strategic Grants Program in Population Aging. Health-related research, both geriatric and social, has received increased funding support in Ontario by the Gerontology Research Council of Ontario, est 1980. Significant in-house or contractual research concerned with income security and health-provision issues associated with the aging of the population has been generated by federal and provincial task forces and committees and by the Economic Council of Canada.

The need for research in gerontology has been most evident in relation to the economic aspects of population aging, especially PENSIONS policy and because older people use health services more extensively than do the young. Because age is a major basis on which we establish rights and obligations as well as informal expectations for behaviour, population aging will necessitate the adaptation of many social institutions, from the design of cities and transportation systems to reforms in FAMILY LAW. The expectation of a long life challenges the old and the young with whom they share familial and social relations. For these reasons, general interest in aging and research in gerontology has grown significantly over the past 50 years. VICTOR W. MARSHALL

Gerussi, Bruno, actor (b at Medicine Hat, Alta 1928). He is well known as Nick Adonidas on "The Beachcombers," one of the longest-running and most successful series in CBC television history. Before joining The "Beachcombers" in 1972, he hosted "Gerussi!" on CBC radio for 4 years. His early childhood was spent in Exshaw, Alta, and New Westminster, BC. A scholarship to the Banff School of Fine Arts was important in preparing him for a career as an actor. In 1954 he joined the Stratford Festival in its second season and appeared in *The Taming of the Shrew* and *Oedipus Rex*, both directed by Tyrone GUTHRIE, and *Measure for Measure*. He became one of the leading actors in the Stratford company playing Romeo to Julie Harris's Juliet in 1960, Ariel in *The Tempest* in 1962, and Mark Antony in *Julius Caesar* in 1965. His Feste in the 1957 production of *Twelfth Night* was highly praised by Robertson DAVIES as "a masterly performance which broods over the whole play and sets its tone." Gerussi made his New York debut as Launce in *Two Gentlemen of Verona*. The next season he toured the US with the National Phoenix Theatre as Sir Edward Mortimer in *Mary Stuart*. In addition to his continuing role as Nick, other television appearances include an Italian immigrant in "The Newcomers 1978" (1980) and in Bernard Slade's "Moving Day" (1987). JAMES DEFELICE

Gesner, Abraham, geologist, author, chemist, inventor (b near Cornwallis, NS 2 May 1797; d at Halifax 29 Apr 1864). Gesner invented kerosene oil and, because of his patents for distilling bituminous material, was a founder of the modern petroleum industry. He studied, described and mapped the distribution of rock formations in NS, NB and PEI. His father, Col Henry Gesner, was exiled from a large farm in NY state and moved to the Annapolis Valley. After elementary schooling in NS, Abraham enrolled as a medical student in London, Eng, in 1825, and graduated as a physician and surgeon. He returned to Parrsboro, NS, and began a medical practice and also continued to explore NS by boat, on horseback and on foot. He moved to Saint John, NB, 1838, and his 5 annual reports on the geology of NB (1839-43) established him as the first government geologist in a British colony. During this time he rediscovered the veins of solid bitumen in Albert County, which he used in experiments in distillation. He used his field collections to start the first natural history museum in Canada at the Mechanics' Institute, Saint John, NB, 1842, before returning to NS in 1843. Beginning about 1846 he developed experiments for distilling "coal oil" from solid hydrocarbons and coined the name kerosene for the lamp oil that he had perfected by 1853. He obtained patents in 1854 and a factory was set up under his guidance on Long Island, NY, to manufacture kerosene, which became standard lighting fuel in homes. In 1863 he sold his patents and returned to Halifax where he was appointed professor at Dalhousie. Gesner wrote numerous scientific papers and reports and several books, the most important of which was *A Practical Treatise on Coal, Petroleum and Other Distilled Oils* (1861). His other inventions include one of the first effective wood preservatives, a process of asphalt paving for highways, briquettes made from compressed coal dust, and a machine for insulating electric wire. Imperial Oil has provided a tribute at his grave in Halifax for he did "give the world a better light." L.M. CUMMING

Getty, Donald Ross, athlete, businessman, premier of Alberta (b at Westmount, Qué 30 Aug 1933). He graduated in 1955 from Western with a degree in business administration before joining the EDMONTON ESKIMOS football team, for whom he played quarterback. He was named "Outstanding Canadian" in the Western CFL in 1959. He joined Imperial Oil in 1955 and became a manager at Midwestern Industrial Gas in 1961. In 1964 he formed Baldonnel Oil and Gas and in 1967 became a partner of the investment firm Doherty, Roadhouse and McCuaig. He was among the original 6 Conservative members elected with Peter LOUGHEED in 1967 and in 1971 was appointed minister of intergovernmental affairs. He was reelected in 1975 and reappointed to the Cabinet as minister of energy and natural resources. He left

Don Getty became premier of Alberta in 1985 (*courtesy Office of the Premier*).

politics in 1979 and became president of D. Getty Investments Ltd. He also served on the boards of several companies, including Brinco, NOVA and the Royal Bank. In 1985 he successfully contested the leadership of the provincial Conservative Party and was sworn in as premier 1 Nov 1985, winning a seat in a by-election in Dec. In a worsening economic climate, he saw the Conservative majority reduced from 75 of 79 seats to 61 of 79 in the election on 8 May 1986 and faced a difficult stewardship as falling resource prices drastically reduced provincial revenues. He is a strong proponent of a FREE TRADE agreement with the US.

Ghent, Treaty of, signed in Ghent, Belgium, on Christmas Eve 1814 by Great Britain and the US to end the WAR OF 1812. The military situation was so balanced that neither side had achieved its war aims. Consequently, none of the issues over which the nations fought was included in the treaty. It was simply agreed to return to the *status quo ante bellum:* there was nothing on neutral rights or IMPRESSMENT, no mention of the question of Indian lands in the Midwest, and all captured territory was returned. Because communications were slow, a major battle – the American victory at New Orleans – took place 2 weeks after the signing. Issues not covered by the treaty, such as disputed boundaries between the US and parts of what is now Canada, were later decided by joint commissions, and since then Britain and the US have settled their differences peacefully. CARL A. CHRISTIE

Ghiz, Joseph A., premier of PEI (b at Charlottetown 27 Jan 1945). Ghiz received his early education in Charlottetown before studying at Dalhousie (BComm 1966, LLB, 1969) and Harvard (LLM, 1981). In 1970, he passed the bar and became a participant in the Liberal Party. He was crown prosecutor 1970-72; a sessional lecturer in business law at UPEI 1969-72; a senior partner of Scales, Ghiz, Jenkins and McQuaid, and president of the PEI branch of the Canadian Bar Association. Ghiz was elected president of the PEI Liberals in 1977 and became their leader in 1981. His inexperience was a factor in the Liberal's unsuccessful bid for power in the 1982 election. As an MLA, Ghiz developed into an effective opposition and party leader, and by the 1986 election the Liberals were well organized. They accused the Conservative government of making poor financial decisions and of not defending Islanders' rights before their federal allies, and in the election they received a 22-10 seat majority. After much doubt and controversy concerning the willingness of Islanders to vote for a leader of Lebanese extraction, the matter was put to rest when Ghiz was sworn in as premier on 2 May 1986. His support of the MEECH LAKE ACCORD and opposition to FREE TRADE kept him in the public eye through 1987. W.S. KEIZER and DAVID A. MILNE

Gibb, Charles, horticulturist (b at Montréal 29 July 1845; d at Cairo, Egypt 8 Mar 1890). Poor health led Gibb to seek an outdoor occupation and in 1872 he established extensive orchards at Abbotsford, Qué, to study fruit culture and arboriculture, and to test plant material from abroad. He was a leading figure in the Montreal Horticultural Soc and Fruit Growers' Assn, besides being a patron of the Art Assn of Montreal and a benefactor of McGill U. In 1882 he travelled through northern Europe and Russia collecting seeds and plants on his first foreign exploration in search of fruit varieties which could be used in improving Canadian strains. The Russian apple seeds he collected were given to the Central Experimental Farm, Ottawa, and became the foundation of its apple-breeding program. These strains were of great importance in apple-hybridizing programs in Manitoba and Saskatchewan after WWI. In addition to his practical work, Gibb published a number of articles on fruit growing, the introduction of Russian apple strains into our fledgling breeding programs, and the results of his own Abbotsford trials of exotic ornamentals and fruits. EDWINNA VON BAEYER

Gibbon, John Murray, writer and cultural promoter (b in Ceylon 12 Apr 1875; d at Montréal 2 July 1952). Educated at Aberdeen, Oxford and Göttingen universities, Gibbon came to Canada in 1913 as publicity manager for the CPR. Founding president of the CANADIAN AUTHORS ASSOCIATION in 1921, he was an enthusiast of folk culture and organized a series of folk and handicraft festivals, beginning 1927. With Sir Ernest MACMILLAN he published the 4-volume *French Canadian Folk Songs* (1928) and a number of other collections. His historical books include *Scots in Canada* (1911), *Steel of Empire: The Romantic History of the Canadian Pacific* (1935), *Canadian Mosaic* (1938), several novels and 2 histories of nursing. Apparently forgotten by folklore scholars today, Gibbon was an important figure in the evolution of a bilingual, multicultural, national culture. DONALD J.C. PHILLIPSON

Gibson, George, "Mooney," baseball player (b at London, Ont 22 July 1880; d there 25 Jan 1967). Gibson signed a pro contract in 1903 and joined the Pittsburgh Pirates 2 years later. He had a strong throwing arm and led National League catchers in fielding percentage several times. He was a member of Pittsburgh's 1909 World Series champions and played in the majors until 1918. Known as a developer of young pitchers, Gibson later managed the Pirates (1920-22, 1932-34) and the Chicago Cubs (1925). He was named Canada's baseball player of the half century and in 1958 was the first baseball player elected to Canada's Sports Hall of Fame. WILLIAM HUMBER

Gibson, Graeme, writer, cultural activist, teacher (b at London, Ont 9 Aug 1934). Although best known for his 3 novels, Gibson has also made national contributions through organizational initiatives. Educated at Western, in 1961 he began an 8-year career teaching English at Ryerson. He was instrumental in forming the WRITERS' UNION OF CANADA, which he chaired 1974-75. In 1973 he began work on a literary resources guide and was concurrently developing the Book and Periodical Development Council. The Writers' Development Trust was another group Gibson helped launch. His novels include *Five Legs* (1969), *Communion* (1971) and *Perpetual Motion* (1982). In 1971 he wrote a film script of Sinclair ROSS'S AS FOR ME AND MY HOUSE. He has also written travel articles, a book of interviews entitled *Eleven Canadian Novelists* (1973), was awarded the Writers Exchange Fellowship to Scotland (1978) and has been writer-in-residence at U Waterloo and U Ottawa (1985). MARLENE ALT

Gibson, Sir John Morison, businessman, lawyer, politician, lt-gov of Ont (b at Toronto 1 Jan 1842; d at Hamilton, Ont 3 June 1929). A Liberal provincial politician known for his reformist views, Gibson was responsible for the 1893 Act for the prevention of cruelty to children, which led to the creation of Children's Aid societies in Ontario. His Hamilton-centered business interests encompassed industrial promotion, real-estate development, the provision of urban services such as utilities and streetcars, and the organization and operation of interurban electric railways. In the early 20th century, companies in which he was a principal dominated the hydroelectricity supply system and radial railway network of the Hamilton-Niagara region. A renowned rifleman and militia supporter, Gibson served as first president of the Canadian Red Cross 1896-1910 and was lt-gov of Ontario 1908-14. CAROLYN GRAY

Gibson, Tom, painter, photographer (b at Edinburgh, Scot 11 Dec 1930). He documents, in a highly personal way, what he sees in the streets, his images revealing both the amusing and the alienating sides of urban life. Gibson settled in Toronto in 1952, enrolled at the Ontario Coll of Art and became part of a circle of artists including Graham COUGHTRY, William RONALD and Michael SNOW. By the mid-1960s he had left painting for photography. He moved to Montréal in the mid-1970s and began to teach photography at Concordia. Gibson's black-and-white photographs have been shown nationally and internationally and have appeared in magazines and books, including *Tom Gibson Signature 1* (National Film Board, 1975). LOUISE ABBOTT

Gibson, William Wallace, aircraft inventor (b at Dalmellington, Scot 1876; d at San Francisco, Calif Dec 1965). After making a fortune in mining, Gibson built the first successful Canadian aircraft engine, and then the Twin-Plane aircraft, which first flew Sept 1910 near Victoria, BC, with a 60-hp gasoline engine. A second aircraft, the Multi-Plane (with 4 narrow sprucewood wings) is reported to have flown successfully the following year near Calgary before being wrecked in a crash. Broke, Gibson returned to mining and later moved to San Francisco. DONALD J.C. PHILLIPSON

Gibsons, BC, Town, pop 2675 (1986c), 2594 (1981c), located just N of Vancouver at the northern entrance to Howe Sound, reached from Vancouver by car ferry from Horseshoe Bay. The Chekwelp band of Squamish Indians lived in the area until relocated to Squamish in the 1890s. The town is named after George William Gibson, who arrived in BC in the 1850s and settled just inside Howe Sound in 1886. Originally (and still colloquially) it was called Gibsons Landing, but the post office shortened the name to Gibsons in 1947. Logging and fishing began late in the 19th century. A large influx of Finnish settlers in 1905 led to the establishment of the community's first store and post office. A jam-canning industry was important in the 1920s and 1930s. Today the forest industry, a pulp mill at Port Mellon, commercial fishing and tourism are the main stay of the economy. In recent years Gibsons has become well known as the locale for the CBC television series "The Beachcombers." JOHN STEWART

Giguère, Roland, poet, painter, publisher (b at Montréal 4 May 1929). Recipient of the Paul-Émile Borduas Award in Visual Arts (1982) and a nominee for the coveted Prix David in literature that year, Giguère has, with the foundation of the Éditions Erta (1949), played a major role in the development of Québec's artistic life.

It was not until publication of his first collected volume of poems, *L'Age de la parole* (1965), that he gained recognition, being awarded the Prix France-Québec and the Grand Prix littéraire de la ville de Montréal. For political reasons Giguère refused in 1974 the Gov Gen's Award for *La Main au feu* (1973). His most recent collection is *Forêt vierge folle* (1978). Influenced by the surrealists, Giguère has always refused to equate poetry and the written word. To him, poetry is a way of life, a perpetual revolt in which the exterior world is invaded by the artist's interior world.

JEAN-MARCEL DUCIAUME

Gilbert, Sir Humphrey, explorer (b near Dartmouth, Eng *c*1537; d at sea 9 Sept 1583). Gilbert was an early publicist for the idea of a NORTHWEST PASSAGE, compiling an influential *Discourse* (1576) on the subject, and his experience in colonizing Ireland suggested similar ventures farther afield. He received letters patent 11 June 1578 from Queen Elizabeth authorizing him to colonize the coast of N America. His first attempt, in 1578, was frustrated by poor organization, desertion and storms. Undaunted, he regrouped and set out again 11 June 1583 with 5 vessels (*Delight, Raleigh, Golden Hind, Swallow* and *Squirrel*); the queen tried to persuade Gilbert to stay behind, noting he was a man "of not good happ by sea." The *Raleigh* turned back, but the other 4 ships arrived off St John's Aug 3. Brandishing his letters patent (known as "Gilbert's Charter"), he entered the harbour Aug 5 and formally took possession of Newfoundland. He dispatched *Swallow* to England with the sick and malcontents and left St John's Aug 20, losing *Delight* in shoals off Sable I, and turned homeward in heavy seas. On the evening of Sept 9 Gilbert reportedly sat astern of *Squirrel* repeatedly calling out, "We are as neare to Heaven by sea as by land." Near midnight he and the *Squirrel* were "devoured and swallowed up of the Sea." The *Golden Hind* reached Dartmouth Sept 22.

Vain, tempestuous, even cruel, Gilbert was typical of the early adventurers who became obsessed with America. His own exploits were failures but his persuasive, if faulty, advocacy of a Northwest Passage spurred a lasting fascination, and although his seizure of Newfoundland seemed a formality, it was not seriously disputed and the colony became the first English possession in the New World. JAMES MARSH

Sir Humphrey Gilbert, Elizabethan explorer who took possession of Newfoundland for England Aug 1583 (*courtesy National Archives of Canada/C-4725*).

Gilbert, Kenneth, harpsichordist, organist, musicologist (b at Montréal 16 Dec 1931). After winning the Québec government's Prix d'Europe for organ in 1953, he moved to the forefront of virtuosity and scholarship. His new editions of early keyboard music (notably of Couperin's and Rameau's complete harpsichord works, and Scarlatti's sonatas) have won the admiration of musicologists worldwide. A strong advocate of classical organ design, he spearheaded the return to mechanical action in many new installations across Canada. Since 1965 Gilbert has performed almost exclusively on the harpsichord, appearing in N America and Europe as soloist, chamber musician and recitalist. International critics have praised highly his many records, among them the complete harpsichord works of Couperin (1970-71) and Rameau (1976), and J.S. Bach's *Goldberg Variations* (1987). BARCLAY MCMILLAN

Gill, Charles, painter, teacher (b at Sorel, Qué 21 Oct 1871; d at Montréal 16 Oct 1918). He began to study design in Nicolet with Abbé Thomas Maurault and continued his art studies in Montréal with William Raphael and then William BRYMNER. Encouraged by American painter George de Forest Brush, he studied at the École des beaux-arts in Paris and frequented the literary circles of Montmartre and the Latin Quarter, making friends with Alphonse Allais and Paul Verlaine. In 1892 he came home to win the contract for a large canvas, *La Visitation*, intended for the Sacré-Coeur Chapel of Notre-Dame de Montréal. He became professor of design at the École normale Jacques-Cartier, teaching concurrently at the Monument National and the École des arts et metiers. Around 1895 Gill helped found the École littéraire de Montréal, with Louvigny de Montigny, and soon became a brilliant writer, regularly publishing his stories, poems, and art critiques and commentaries. He died a victim of the 1918 influenza epidemic. His sister Marie published his poetry in 2 volumes – *Le Cap éternité* and *Les Étoiles filantes*.

MICHEL CHAMPAGNE

Gill, Robert, theatre director, teacher (b at Spokane, Wash 19 July 1911; d at Toronto 10 Aug 1974). He studied and later taught at Pittsburgh's Carnegie Tech and was active with Pittsburgh Playhouse and Opera Soc, and Woodstock (NY) Playhouse. He was Hart House Theatre director, U of T, from 1945 to 1965, and trained a generation of actors and directors that helped launch Canada's professional theatre, including William HUTT, Kate REID, Charmion King, Donald SUTHERLAND and Barbara Hamilton. He was instrumental in founding the Straw Hat Players in Muskoka (1947) and Toronto's Crest Theatre (1954). He also taught at the Royal Conservatory of Music, Toronto, the Banff School of Fine Arts, Banff, Alta, and at UBC. DAVID GARDNER

Gilmour, Allan, shipbuilder, timber merchant (b at Craigton, Mearns [Strathclyde], Scot 29 Sept 1805; d at Glasgow, Scot 18 Nov 1884). Through his uncle, the key partner in the timber-importing firm of Pollok, Gilmour and Co of Glasgow, he obtained a clerk's position in 1819, rapidly securing promotion to the booming Miramichi branch and then returning to Scotland for a year of learning the shipbuilding trade, which he practised for Pollok, Gilmour in several of its thriving Canadian branches. Several very large vessels were designed and built by him as timber carriers, and these made gigantic profits for the company in the 1830s and 1840s. He gave important evidence to parliamentary committees on the navigation laws and the measurement of ships. He retained his partnerships in the various Pollok, Gilmour branch firms until his death. DAVID S. MACMILLAN

Gilmour, Clyde, broadcaster, critic (b at Calgary 8 June 1912). An influential film and record columnist who has written for a number of newspapers and magazines, Gilmour is best known as a radio personality. He was named a Member of the Order of Canada in 1975 in recognition of the national appeal of "Gilmour's Albums," which in Oct 1986 marked its 30th anniversary. It was the longest running 1-person show in CBC history and the 3rd-longest running program still on the air, surpassed only by the Metropolitan Opera and NHL broadcasts. BARCLAY MCMILLAN

Gimli, Man, Town, pop 1681 (1986c), 1550 (1981c), inc 1947, is located on the W shore of Lk WINNIPEG, 85 km N of Winnipeg. The mother colony of several N American Icelandic settlements, Gimli developed after a series of natural disasters forced ICELANDERS to leave their island 1874-76. Some 200 arrived near Gimli in October 1875 to settle New Iceland, a tract of land outside the boundaries of Manitoba reserved for their use by the Dominion government. The settlers experienced extreme hardships – smallpox, flooding, religious differences – which led to out-migrations, but they also developed schools, a newspaper, a fishing industry and a self-governing colony with a sophisticated constitution. New Iceland came under Manitoba's jurisdiction 1881, and by the late 1890s the area was receiving Ukrainian, Polish, German and Hungarian immigrants.

Farming, fishing and mink ranching shaped Gimli's early economy, but an air-force base established during WWII was a major boost. When the base closed in 1971 an industrial park was formed and the town's recreation resources were revitalized to offset the loss. The CN Transportation Training Centre, established at the industrial park in June 1972, trains engineers, dispatchers, supervisors and other CN employees from all over Canada. The Seagram Co is a major employer in the area. Its distillery, warehouses and bottling plant (opened 1968) is situated on a 120 ha site 3 km NW of Gimli and employs about 135 people. On 23 July 1983 Gimli Airport was the landing site for the "Gimli glider," an Air Canada 767 en route from Montréal to Edmonton, which ran out of fuel over Red Lake, Ont, and glided to a safe landing at Gimli. D.M. LYON

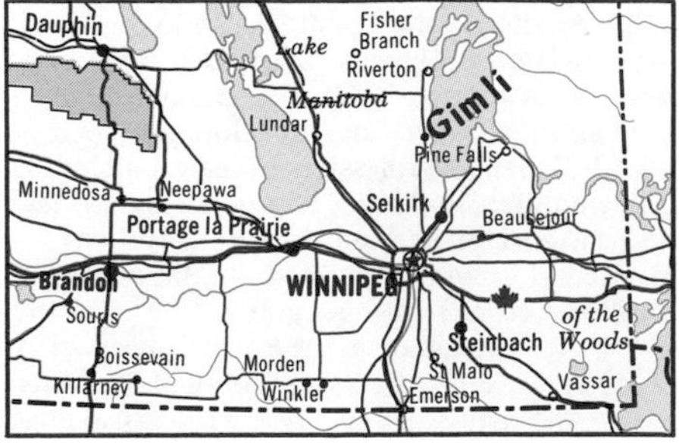

Ginger Group, an independent group of members of Parliament who in 1924 split from the PROGRESSIVE PARTY because they did not support a party structure that inhibited an MP's ability to act solely as the representative of his constituents. The group, named after the Tory MPs who in 1917 opposed the MILITARY SERVICE ACT, was initially composed of UNITED FARMERS OF ALBERTA representatives G.C. Coote, Robert Gardiner, E.J. Garland, D.M. Kennedy and Henry Spencer, and UNITED FARMERS OF ONTARIO representative Agnes MACPHAIL. Later, working with Labour MPs J.S. WOODSWORTH, William IRVINE, A.A. HEAPS and Angus MacInnis, it included Ontario MPs W.C. GOOD and Preston Elliott, Alberta Independent Joseph Shaw, Milton Campbell from Saskatchewan and W.J. Ward from Manitoba. The Ginger Group declined along with the Progressive Party; some members later helped found the CO-OPERATIVE COMMONWEALTH FEDERATION.

Ginseng, herbaceous perennial plant of genus *Panax*, ginseng family (Araliaceae), discovered in N America by Joseph-François LAFITAU. Six species are known, 2 from N America, 4 from E Asia. Plants grow to 30 cm and have a large, fleshy, often forked root. Although there seems to be no scientific evidence of medicinal value, ginseng has a long history of medical use, continuing today. The Chinese, in particular, considered its dried root immensely valuable in prolonging life, vitality and sexual potency. American ginseng (*P. quinquefolius*) occurs in woods of central and eastern N America; however, local demand has resulted in its becoming very rare in the wild. It was once exported to China, but the Chinese found it inferior to their own product. Dwarf ginseng (*P. trifolius*) grows in moist woods from Ontario to the Maritimes. Ginseng (*P. pseudo ginseng*), native to Korea and Manchuria, is now cultivated quite extensively in eastern Canada. GILLIAN FORD

Girard, Marc-Amable, notary, politician, premier of Manitoba (b at Varennes, LC 25 Apr 1822; d at St-Boniface, Man 12 Sept 1892). A Conservative and disciple of George-Étienne CARTIER, Girard came to Manitoba 1870 to uphold French language, religious and political rights as guaranteed by the Manitoba Act. He served on the Executive Council 1870-72 and in the Assembly 1870-83. In 1871 he was appointed to the Canadian Senate. Girard became premier of Manitoba June 1874, the first French Canadian to hold that post, but resigned later that year. He served in John NORQUAY'S Cabinet 1879-83. Girard was a man of compromise, respected for his personal charm and integrity, but he lacked the leadership necessary to promote French Canadian political interests during a critical transition. DIANE PAYMENT

Girl Guides Official operation in Canada dates from Jan 1910 when the 1st St Catharines Co was registered by the Girl Guide Organization founded in Great Britain in 1909 by Lord Baden-Powell. Canadian headquarters were established in Toronto in 1912; 5 years later a Canadian Council was federally incorporated and in 1961 the organization became known as Girl Guides of Canada/Guides du Canada. In 1986, 211 172 girls across Canada between the ages of 6 and 17 were enrolled in Guides' various branches under the direction of 44 172 volunteer leaders.

The philosophy of the organization is expressed in the promise that Guides have made since 1909 to do their duty to God, monarch and country, to help others at all times and to obey the Guide law. This 10-point law and the motto "Be Prepared" reflect the organization's aim of training girls to fulfil their roles as responsible citizens and family members. The guiding program requires girls at different levels to pass a series of tests and to earn badges in a wide variety of fields. Camping and nature activities have always been an important element of guiding.

Membership is open to all girls who accept the principles of the Guide promise and law. Canada's involvement in the World Assn of Girl Guides and Girl Scouts brings Canadian Guides into contact with girls throughout the world and opens up avenues of international exchange. National headquarters and archives are located in Toronto. PATRICIA G. DIRKS

Girouard, Sir Édouard Percy Cranwill, railway builder, governor (b at Montréal 26 Jan 1867; d at London, Eng 26 Sept 1932). A graduate of the Royal Military College, Kingston (1886), he was commissioned in the Royal Engineers in 1888 and was in charge of the Sudan railways 1896-98. His construction of a line bypassing the Nile cataracts in the Sudan made possible Kitchener's victory at Omdurman. He then ran railways in S Africa, 1899-1904. Girouard served as high commissioner and then governor of northern Nigeria, 1907-09, and governor of the British East Africa Protectorate (Kenya), 1909-12. In Nigeria, the effects of his policies created a major impediment to Nigerian unity. In Kenya, his views on land alienation conflicted with those of the British government, and he resigned under a cloud. Except for a brief period of munitions procurement and railway organization in Belgium during the war, he was a director of the armaments firm Armstrong Whitworth 1913-32. RICHARD STUART

Girty, Simon, frontiersman, LOYALIST, Indian agent (b near Harrisburg, Pa 1741; d at Malden, UC 18 Feb 1818). The legendary "white savage" of American frontier lore, he was an early Loyalist settler in Upper Canada. Girty lived several years in Indian captivity as a boy, and later became a scout and interpreter. During the AMERICAN REVOLUTION he joined the British Indian Department at Detroit and accompanied Indian raiding parties south. He was greatly feared by American pioneers but stories of his cruelty are exaggerated. In 1784 Girty settled on a farm at Malden. He continued to support Indian resistance against American expansion in the Ohio Valley until 1796 when the US took possession of Detroit. He is portrayed as a villain in romantic American novels and in Stephen Vincent Benét's "The Devil and Daniel Webster" (1937). He was the model for Sampson Gattrie in John RICHARDSON'S novel *The Canadian Brothers* (1840). EDWARD BUTTS

Gisborne, Frederick Newton, telegraph engineer (b at Broughton, Eng 8 Mar 1824; d at Ottawa 30 Aug 1892). At the age of 32, Gisborne completed the first submarine telegraph line in N America, joining Newfoundland across the Cabot Str with the mainland. Gisborne immigrated to Canada in 1845, became a telegraph operator and soon manager of the NS Telegraph Co. He created a company to link St John's with NB. Though nearly ruined in 1853 by the cost of building a land line across 640 km of Newfoundland wilderness, he was refinanced by Cyrus Field, the American industrialist. Together they completed the Nfld telegraph, from Cape Ray to Cape Breton, in 1856. Field went on to tackle the N Atlantic, succeeding in 1866 after 3 earlier cables broke. Gisborne became superintendent of the Canadian goverment telegraph service in 1879. He was a charter member of the RSC in 1882 and held many patents for his own inventions. DONALD J.C. PHILLIPSON

Gitksan ("people of the Skeena") live along the Skeena R of northwestern BC in 6 villages: Hazelton, Kispiox and Glen Vowell (the Eastern Gitksan bands) and Kitwanga, Kitwankool and Kitsegukla (the Western Gitksans). Their language, forms of Nass-Gitksan, is related within the TSIMSHIAN Language Family to Coast Tsimshian and probably also to the Penutian tongues of California and Oregon. A matrilineal people, Gitksans are born into one of 4 lineages or phratries (to which their mate, when they marry, may not belong). Contemporary Gitksan life is still centered around the obligations and privileges of the POTLATCH and community feasts. The Gitksan language is being replaced in use by English, and Gitksans no longer burn the bodies of their dead, a cultural trait which they shared with their Carrier neighbours but not with related Tsimshian or Nishga (Nisga'a) groups. They are now most noted for their traditional art, which ranges from the complex Chilkat blankets and intricately wrought mountain-sheep horn spoons to the totem poles which the heirs of chiefs were obligated to raise as memorials. These traditional crafts are encouraged by programs of Ksan (the reconstructed Gitksan village which serves a cultural centre), the band councils and band-operated schools, and the Gitksan-Wet'suwet'en (previously Gitksan-Carrier) Tribal Council. This vocal organization, dedicated to document and foster the traditions of both the Gitksan and the Carrier Indians of the Bulkley R valley, is engaged in land claims litigation with the province of BC on behalf of the chiefs of the 2 groups.

J.V. POWELL AND VICKIE D. JENSEN

Gjoa Haven, NWT, Hamlet, pop 650 (1986c), 523 (1981c), is located on the SE coast of KING WILLIAM I, off the mainland Arctic coast, 1062 air km NE of Yellowknife. The area is the traditional territory of the NETSILIK INUIT. It derived its name from Roald AMUNDSEN, the first person to navigate the NORTHWEST PASSAGE. He wintered there and called the site after his ship, *Gjoa*. Trapping, hunting and carving are the sources of livelihood of the mostly Inuit population. The community is noted for its production of distinctive Inuit wall hangings. Channels and bays in the area are icebound for most of the year. ANNELIES POOL

Glace Bay, NS, Town, pop 20 467 (1986c), 21 466 (1981c), inc 1901, is located on the E coast of CAPE BRETON I. Facing into the sun and the Atlantic Ocean, the location was known to the Micmac as *Wasokusegwom* ("bright home") and to the French, who mined coal for LOUISBOURG from the cliffs, as "Baie de Glace," a reference to annual drift ice from the Gulf of St Lawrence. The Dominion Coal Co (1893) made Glace Bay a boom town, and the municipality emerged from the smaller 19th-century colliery settlements. Immigrant workers came from Britain and Europe, but most of the population was drawn from rural Cape Breton, the Maritimes and Newfoundland. To exploit the rich bituminous coal seams underlying the district and dipping under the ocean floor, Dominion Coal operated 11 collieries within the town, including some of the largest and most productive coal mines in N America. Although the coal company dominated the local economy, by the 1920s Glace Bay was a union stronghold: the coal miners had a powerful influence on community life, and "company town" gave way to "labour town." The declining economic importance of coal led to Dominion Coal's withdrawal in 1967; the publicly owned Cape Breton Development Corp operated the town's one remaining colliery until 1984. Despite high unemployment and out-migration, and costly disappointments such as the heavy-water plant constructed in the 1970s, Glace Bay stands fast, proud of past achievements and hopeful of a change in its fortunes. The Miners' Memorial Museum is a tribute to the people of Glace Bay and the surrounding coal towns. DAVID FRANK

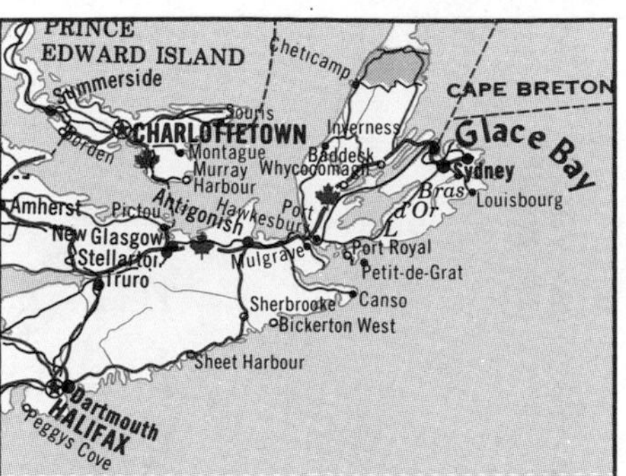

Glaciation is defined as the formation, movement and recession of GLACIERS. At present glaciers cover about 10% of the world's land area (14.9 million km^2). Most of this area is under the Antarctic and Greenland ice sheets; only about 700 000 km^2 is covered by the thousands of glaciers in the remainder of the world. Glaciation has been much more extensive in the past than it is today, occurring mostly as large, continental ice sheets. During expansion and recession of glaciers, the processes of EROSION and deposition may occur. Erosion by glaciers takes place mainly by abrasion and quarrying. Abrasion occurs when fine particles and fragments held in the ice, at or near the base of a glacier, move across the underlying material, commonly bedrock. This process can striate and polish fragments in the ice and the underlying bedrock. In addition, abrasion may form elongated, gutterlike channels (flutings) in the bedrock. Quarrying, the removal of blocks of bedrock by overriding ice, usually occurs where the bedrock is easily fractured, or where planes of weakness, such as joints, are present. *Roches moutonnées*, large, knoblike bedrock features with streamlined sides tapering upglacier, and steep, abruptly broken sides downglacier, result from abrasion and quarrying. Relatively more erosion and removal of material takes place in valley glaciers, where the ice is confined by topography, than in the less constrained ICE CAPS and ice sheets. U-shaped valleys, such as the Bow Valley in the Rocky Mts, are formed where glacial erosion has deepened and widened pre-existing river valleys.

As erosion takes place in one area, deposition may occur in another. Forms such as DRUMLINS (streamlined, oval mounds commonly 15-25 m high and about 1500 m long) and certain kinds of ground MORAINE (low-relief, undulating terrain commonly up to 6 m high) can form under moving ice. However, most glacier deposition takes place near the terminus (boundary) during retreat of the ice. Features which can occur include hummocky moraine, high-relief forms up to about 10 m high, consisting of mounds, ridges and doughnut-shaped knobs; series of arcuate (bow-shaped) ridges of varying heights and lengths, named (according to their form, origin and position) cross-valley, ribbed, washboard, De Geer, push, ice-thrusted and recessional moraines; single, prominent ridges marking the limit of a glacial advance, called end or terminal moraines; and ground moraine. Most of these features contain a high percentage of glacial till. Till, in the strictest sense, is unstratified, unsorted material deposited directly from a glacier. It usually consists of a heterogeneous mixture of clay, silt, sand, pebbles, cobbles and boulders, with most constituents closely reflecting the composition of local bedrock. Commonly, larger particles are angular to well-rounded, striated, and show a preferred orientation. Till can be subdivided into several types depending on the location of debris in the ice and how it was deposited.

Glaciers are also directly or indirectly responsible for various other deposits. Meltwater, originating on the surface, inside a glacier, or at its base, may form braided streams beyond the glacier margin. These streams display an interconnecting network of shallow channels which carry and deposit gravel and sand. Gravel is an important industrial resource in Canada, and some of the largest deposits have resulted from glacier-derived braided streams. An outstanding modern example is the Donjek R, YT, fed from the Donjek Glacier in the St Elias Range. Kames and ESKERS (knoblike features and sinuous ridges, respectively) result from the deposition of SAND AND GRAVEL by glacial streams. Glacially associated lake deposits form large plains that cover wide areas of Canada. The lakes were formed by direct damming by the glacier or by impedances to preexisting drainage. Manitoba's glacial Lake AGASSIZ is an outstanding example of a glacially dammed lake. Most sediments deposited in glacial lakes consist of silt and clay, which commonly form varves, ie, pairs of coarse and fine layers deposited in one year. Beach ridges composed of gravel and sand occur along the margins of some former glacial lakes. The absence of vegetation in recently deglaciated areas and the exposure of unconsolidated sand and silt (such as occurs in interchannel areas of braided rivers and former lake beds) allow wind to form sand dunes and deposit loess. Dunes are formed by the shifting of sand by saltation and traction; loess deposits, consisting of fine sand and silt, originate from suspended material that may have been carried hundreds of kilometres (*see* AEOLIAN LANDFORM).

The areal extent and succession of glacial deposits indicate how far and how often glaciers expanded in the past. Most is known about glacial activity of the past 2-3 million years, although evidence indicates that glaciation took place several times during GEOLOGICAL HISTORY. During the Pleistocene ICE AGE, as much as 30% of the Earth was covered by glaciers. Glaciers formed and expanded in mountainous regions throughout the world. In northern latitudes (eg, Canada and northern Europe) ice caps developed, expanding to ice sheets. About 97% of Canada was covered; hence, this country contains more glaciated terrain than any other.

The number of major glaciations that occurred during the Ice Age is open to question. Traditionally, 4 glaciations were recognized, each lasting approximately 100 000 years, separated by long, warmer periods. From oldest to youngest, these are known in N America as Nebraskan, Kansan, Illinoian and Wisconsinan. Within these major glaciations, minor glacier retreats and advances are recognized. New evidence and reinterpretation of old data suggest that ice did expand and retreat many times, but the complexity of the data is such that it is not even possible to say with certainty that there actually were 4 major glaciations. Much is known about the Wisconsinan, less about previous glaciations. Since the Wisconsinan was the latest glaciation, evidence (eg, moraines) is relatively well preserved. In addition, the time of the Wisconsinan glaciation can be estimated, mainly through radiocarbon dating of organic matter from below, within and above Wisconsinan glacial deposits (*see* GEOLOGICAL DATING). Although radiocarbon dating is by far the most important method for determining when glaciers expanded, it is useful only for material less than about 70 000 years old.

The farthest limits of glaciation in Canada took place mostly before the late Wisconsinan. It is not known whether this was during an early portion

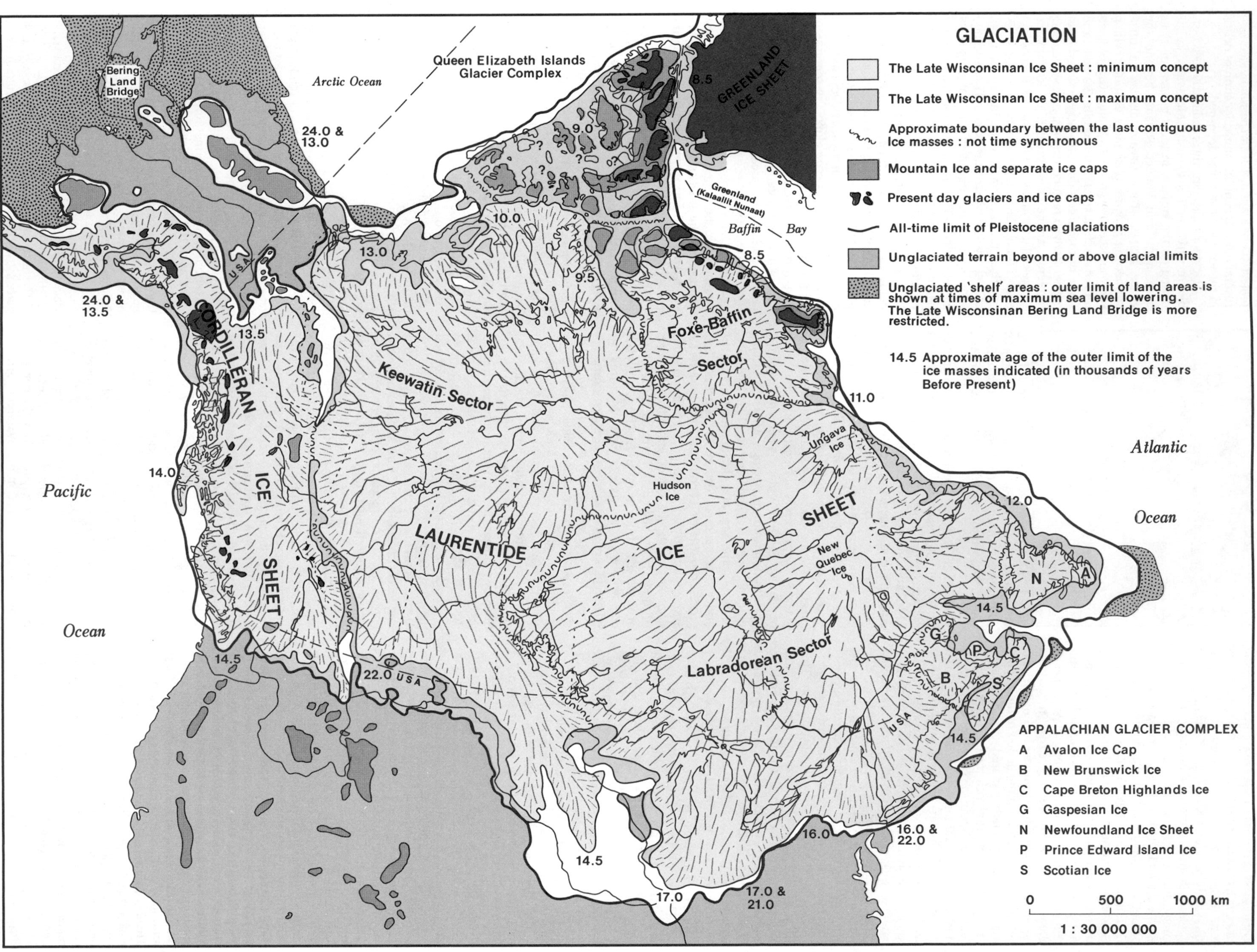
GLACIATION
The Late Wisconsinan Ice Sheet : minimum concept
The Late Wisconsinan Ice Sheet : maximum concept
Approximate boundary between the last contiguous Ice masses : not time synchronous
Mountain Ice and separate ice caps
Present day glaciers and ice caps
All-time limit of Pleistocene glaciations
Unglaciated terrain beyond or above glacial limits
Unglaciated 'shelf' areas : outer limit of land areas is shown at times of maximum sea level lowering. The Late Wisconsinan Bering Land Bridge is more restricted.
14.5 Approximate age of the outer limit of the ice masses indicated (in thousands of years Before Present)
APPALACHIAN GLACIER COMPLEX
A Avalon Ice Cap
B New Brunswick Ice
C Cape Breton Highlands Ice
G Gaspesian Ice
N Newfoundland Ice Sheet
P Prince Edward Island Ice
S Scotian Ice
0 500 1000 km
1 : 30 000 000
Bering Land Bridge
Arctic Ocean
Queen Elizabeth Islands Glacier Complex
GREENLAND ICE SHEET
Greenland (Kalaallit Nunaat)
Baffin Bay
Pacific
Ocean
Atlantic
Ocean
CORDILLERAN ICE SHEET
LAURENTIDE ICE SHEET
Keewatin Sector
Foxe-Baffin Sector
Labradorean Sector
Hudson Ice
Ungava Ice
New Quebec Ice
USA
24.0 & 13.0
24.0 & 13.5
13.5
13.0
10.0
9.0
9.5
8.5
11.0
12.0
14.0
14.5
22.0
16.0
16.0 & 22.0
17.0
17.0 & 21.0

Head of the Lillooet Glacier (*courtesy Colour Library Books*).

of the Wisconsinan or if it represented an earlier major glaciation such as the Illinoian. It is evident, however, that during the Pleistocene, ice never flowed far beyond the late Wisconsinan limits and, in general, conformed roughly with the configuration of the latest glaciation. Glaciers never extended into the northern YT and parts of the western NWT. In addition, the highest peaks of western Canada and the higher hills on the prairies (eg, the CYPRESS HILLS) have never been glaciated (*see* NUNATAK). Although the climate was severe enough to support glaciers, there was not enough moisture to nourish their expansion.

Enough information is available from glacial and associated deposits and from radiocarbon-dated organic samples to give a reasonable account of the Wisconsinan glacier complex in Canada. Sometime after about 100 000 years ago, ice caps formed and expanded in several parts of Canada. Major areas of accumulation included the Keewatin Sector, the Labradorian Sector and the Foxe-Baffin Sector. Minor ice caps formed in the Atlantic provinces and the arctic islands. In time, these ice caps coalesced, forming the Laurentide Ice Sheet. Apparently, at about the same time, valley glaciers expanded in the western mountains and, in time, formed the Cordilleran Ice Sheet. There is conflicting evidence about how far the ice sheets expanded initially. At least one retreat occurred before the final onslaught which probably began about 25 000 years ago and reached the areas illustrated on the map. The maximum limit reached by the late Wisconsinan ice sheets is under debate. In addition, there is evidence that the time of maximum expansion of the ice sheets varied from region to region. The Laurentide Ice Sheet probably had a maximum ice thickness close to 4000 m; that of the Cordilleran Ice Sheet may have been close to 2000 m.

As recession of the ice sheets took place, most of the glacial landforms seen today across Canada were formed. There were minor readvances during the overall retreat, but in general the retreat was relatively rapid, with ice withdrawn from most of Canada by 10 000 years ago. Since that time, glacial and other landforms have been modified by various agents such as water and wind. However, these changes have been minor, and the preservation of the present glacial landscape is ensured for thousands of years to come.

N.W. RUTTER

Glacier, a large mass of ice, formed at least in part on land, which shows evidence of present or former movement. It is formed by the compaction and recrystallization of snow into ice crystals and commonly also contains air, water and rock debris. Movement is downslope or outward in all directions, caused by the glacier's stress system. Internal deformation and basal slippage of ice is common. Glaciers may end on land, in the ocean (as an ice shelf) or in a lake. The 2 principal types are valley glaciers and ice caps. Movement of valley glaciers is controlled by topography. Although velocity varies, most average less than a metre per day. However, some valley glaciers, called surging glaciers, can achieve daily speeds in excess of 60 m. Tens of thousands of valley glaciers now exist worldwide. In Canada they are found mainly at higher elevations of the western mountain systems and in the mountains and highlands of the arctic islands, eg, AXEL HEIBERG, ELLESMERE, DEVON and BAFFIN. Many are less than a kilometre long. Others are much longer, eg, the Hubbard Glacier in the YT and Alaska, which is over 100 km long. Ice caps or ice sheets (if they are over 50 000 km^2) are dome shaped and not greatly impeded by topography; thus, they are able to move outward in all directions. Generally, velocities of ice caps and ice sheets are lower than those of valley glaciers. Canada has several ice caps, located in the Cordillera and arctic islands (*see* ICE CAP).

Many features commonly produced by glaciers can be observed on or near the Athabasca Glacier in the Rocky Mountains of JASPER NATIONAL PARK. This glacier, fed by the COLUMBIA ICEFIELD, has been retreating for several years. Various features can be observed on the glacier surface, including crevasses, fissures that form from tensile stress in the glacier surface; icefalls, resulting from crevasses formed where the glacier hangs over a bedrock protuberance; and a medial MORAINE, composed of debris and ice, which is formed where 2 valley glaciers coalesce.

Other features that were formed during the retreat of the glacier (and can be seen nearby) include lateral moraines, formed by debris deposited along the glacier terminus. In addition, glacier meltwater carries and deposits debris, forming such features as deltas and glacial-outwash plains composed of sand and gravel. *See also* GLACIATION.

N.W. RUTTER

Reading: J.T. Teller, et al, *Glacial Lake Agassiz* (1983).

Athabasca Glacier (*photo by J.A. Kraulis/First Light*).

Glacier National Park (est 1886, 1350 km²) was carved from the rugged Selkirk and Purcell mountains of BC by more than 400 GLACIERS. Its sheer valley walls have been scarred by countless AVALANCHES caused by heavy snowfalls. Underground rivers have created unique CAVE systems. Half of the park is alpine TUNDRA, where meadows burst into flower only for a few short weeks each year. Below the meadows, stands of Engelmann spruce and alpine fir descend to the interior rain forest of western red cedar and western hemlock. High mountains, deep snow and long winters make a harsh environment for wildlife. Some species, eg, mountain goat, are able to withstand the rigorous conditions year-round. Others, eg, hoary marmot, hibernate in winter. Glacier is famous for its black and grizzly bears, which find abundant forage on the park's slopes. The rugged Selkirk Mts were a barrier to travellers until the discovery of ROGERS PASS in 1881. Development of the pass as a link in the building of the first transcontinental railway and, in later years, the Trans-Canada Hwy has played a major role in the park's history. The mountains offer a dramatic backdrop for campers and a challenge for hikers and climbers. LILLIAN STEWART

Gladstone, Man, Town, pop 951 (1986c), 964 (1981c), inc 1882, is located on the Whitemud R, 138 km NW of Winnipeg and 30 km W of the southern tip of Lake Manitoba. Ontario farmers seeking new land settled in 1871 at the Third Crossing where the North Saskatchewan Trail crossed the Whitemud for the third time. The community – known first as Palestine and later as Gladstone after the noted British PM – was on the fringe of prairie settlement, and became a takeoff point for pioneers travelling farther W. A population and land boom occurred, sparked by construction of a railway link with Portage la Prairie, but soon collapsed, leaving the town in debt. Today, Gladstone serves the surrounding mixed farming district and has an important cattle-auction mart. D.M. LYON

Gladstone, James, or Akay-na-muka, meaning "Many guns," Canada's first native senator (b at Mountain Hill, North-West Territories 21 May 1887; d at Fernie, BC 4 Sept 1971). Gladstone, a member of the BLOOD tribe, devoted most of his life to the betterment of Canadian Indians. He was president of the Indian Assn of Alta (IAA) and 3 times was a delegate to Ottawa to discuss proposed changes in the INDIAN ACT. He played a prominent part in the fight for better education, greater respect for treaty rights, and participation of Indians in their own administration. On 1 Feb 1958 he was appointed to the Senate of Canada and in his maiden speech he spoke in Blackfoot "to place in the official debates a few words in the language of my people, the Blackfoot Indians, as a recognition of the first Canadians." In the Senate, Gladstone spoke strongly on issues that affected natives; he sat on the 1959 joint committee to investigate Indian affairs. JAMES DEMPSEY

Reading: Hugh A. Dempsey, *The Gentle Persuader* (1987).

Glass The first known Canadian glass factory or glasshouse, the Mallorytown Glass Works in Upper Canada, began operation in 1839 and closed in 1840. Glassmaking involved a large investment in raw materials, equipment and salaries. The smallest glasshouses employed 15-20 men producing glass from a 5-pot furnace; additional workers were needed to perform ancillary functions (eg, cutting firewood, unpacking raw materials, packing finished products). Thus, it is not surprising that the early period of glassmaking in Canada (1839-80) was one of changing partnerships and of firms going into and out of business. Throughout the 19th century imported glass set the fashion and competitive standard. Between 1840 and 1860, 5 Canadian glass factories manufactured the most useful glass products – common green window glass and bottles.

Soda water bottle (left) and fruit jar (right) from the Hamilton Glass Works, 1865-96 (*courtesy Royal Ontario Museum*).

Manufactured and Pattern Glass The Canada Glass Works at St Jean, Canada E (now Québec), 1845-51, and the Ottawa Glass Works at Como, 1847-57, were window-glass factories located on water routes leading to Montréal. From this distribution centre, sales were advertised as far away as Hamilton. Window glass was made by blowing an elongated, hollow tube. Both ends were cut off and the tube was slit lengthwise and opened out into a flat sheet which was cut into various pane sizes. The largest windowpane available measured about 76 by 102 cm.

Bottles might be free blown but, more often, were mold blown, using iron molds. A general line of bottles, made after 1851 by the Como factory and the Foster Brothers Glass Works, St Jean (about 1855-58), would include aquamarine medicine bottles, soda or mineral water-bottles, whisky flasks, ale and wine bottles, square, tapered case bottles to fit travelling cases, and large demijohns for storing liquids, made in black (really a very dark green) glass.

The 4 major companies operating between 1860 and 1880 made bottles, jars and lamp chimneys as staple products. All were located near shipping facilities or the railway lines laid down in the 1850s. The Canada Glass Works, Hudson, Qué, 1864-72, and the Hamilton Glass Co, Hamilton, Ont, 1865-96, were "green" glasshouses. Green glass, used for window glass and bottles, ranges in colour from aquamarine through green, olive green and amber. The colour results from iron impurities in the sand, the major raw ingredient used in glassmaking. The St Lawrence Glass Co, Montréal, 1867-73, and the Burlington Glass Co, Hamilton, Ont, 1874-98, were flint houses. "Flint," or colourless glass, used for finer glass lamps and tablewares, is made by adding a decolorizing agent that masks out the natural green colour. After 1864, an improved soda-lime formula for a good-quality colourless glass reduced the costs of raw materials to one-third of the costs of the lead glass formula then in use. This development opened the druggists' bottle trade to flint glasshouses. It also greatly expanded the market for cheaper, pressed flint-glass lamps and tablewares.

Druggists' bottles were mold blown in green, amber and flint glass in sizes ranging from individual doses of 1 or 2 ounces (28 or 56 mL) to a 16-ounce (about 450 mL) size. By the mid-1870s all N American druggists'-ware manufacturers were making round, oval, square and rectangular mold shapes. On special orders, bottle molds would be lettered with the name of the retail druggist or the patent medicine. A cheaper method used a letter plate that could be inserted into a standard mold shape.

At first, soda-water bottles were egg shaped, a style introduced in England as early as 1814. In 1870 a modified version with a flat bottom was patented and, beginning in the early 1870s, a cylindrical bottle was also made with rounded shoulders and base or with a small flattened base, allowing the bottle to stand upright. These bottles were used by the growing number of late-19th-century bottlers of sweetened SOFT DRINKS and ginger beer. Whisky flasks and bottles were made up for distilleries. The BREWING INDUSTRY required cylindrical, mold-blown black or amber bottles for its ale, beer and porter. Although some custom-lettered molds were made up for Canadian breweries, most used plain bottles identified with paper labels bearing trademarked designs and names.

A mold-blown glass preserve jar was first patented by John Mason in the US in 1858. It had a wide mouth with spiral threading blown into the glass at the neck that created a tight seal with a metal screw-cap lid. This improvement over pottery jars and the advantage of visible contents encouraged home canning. The 2 Hamilton factories and the one at Hudson, Qué, all marketed one or 2 jar styles; the Hamilton ones were identified by the glass-company name blown into the glass.

The 2 flint factories (St Lawrence Glass Co and Burlington Glass Co) made lamps and lamp chimneys, as did the Hudson factory. The fragility of the chimneys, which required a daily washing, created a high-volume trade. The St Lawrence Co also made pressed flint-glass tablewares. The molten glass was pressed into patterned molds by a plunger that forced the glass into all parts of the mold. This process produced identical pieces very quickly and cheaply. By the 1860s heavy geometric designs, imitating cut glass, were in favour. Tableware sets included covered compotes and bowls, nappies, sugar and cream sets, spoon holders, tumblers, goblets, water pitchers, salt cellars and casters.

During the period 1880-1900, bottles, jars and chimneys continued to be staple products of the green and flint Hamilton factories, of several smaller firms established in the 1890s and of the 3 major new factories: the green and flint glassworks of the North American Glass Co (later Diamond, Diamond Flint, Dominion, Domglas), Montréal, 1880 to the present; the flint factory of the Nova Scotia Glass Co, New Glasgow, NS, 1881-92; and the Sydenham Glass Co, Wallaceburg, Ont, 1894-1913.

In druggists' bottles, some Canadian shapes were probably introduced in the 1890s. They were named for the city in which the factory was located or for the glass company. Jars were lettered with the glass-company name or with a trademarked name suggesting quality, eg, "Crown" or "Best." By the 1880s the number of pieces offered in a tableware set had expanded and commonly included several sizes of plate, bread plate, footed cake plate or salver, butter dish, mug, celery vase, relish dish, and quart and

Cut-glass rose bowl from the Gundy-Clapperton Co Ltd, Toronto, *c*1905-20 (*courtesy Royal Ontario Museum*).

half-gallon jugs. The new designs of the 1880s were delicately molded flowers, birds, berries, leaves, crests, scrolls, commemorative events and fine, shallow-pressed geometric patterns made by the flint factories. By the 1890s patterns were more deeply pressed, imitating the current fashions in cut glass, or with bolder patterns of leaf or fruit. Panelled patterns were also popular. After the mid-1890s, pressed emerald green glass and white and blue (pale turquoise) opal pressed glass became popular. By 1900 Canadian firms supplied half of the Canadian market of 5.5 million people with bottles, lamps and tablewares.

From 1900 to 1932 pressed glass patterns continued to imitate the pinwheels, stars and floral designs of cut glass. They were made by the Diamond Flint/Dominion Glass Co, Montréal, and by that company's tableware and illuminating plant in Toronto, the Jefferson Glass Co, from 1913-25. By the mid-1920s imitation cut patterns were becoming less popular, as new, delicately molded floral designs in pale pink, green, yellow and blue glass replaced them. By 1932, the Dominion Glass Co phased out production of most of its earlier tablewares, concentrating on hotel wares and on several simple, geometric patterns in the new pastel shades. As in the 19th century, bottles and jars were a staple and, after 1932, became the major production line of both the Dominion Glass Co (with plants in Montréal, Qué; Toronto, Hamilton, Wallaceburg, Ont; Winnipeg, Man; Redcliff, Alta; and Burnaby, BC) and the Consumers Glass Co, Toronto (est in Montréal in 1917 and now Consumers Packaging, Inc, with glass plants in Ville St-Pierre and Candiac, Qué; Toronto and Milton, Ont; and Lavington, BC). After 1907 large orders were produced by the newly introduced automatic bottle-blowing machinery.

Cut Glass Between 1867 and 1900, the 5 Canadian flint-glass manufacturers concentrated on making the cheaper grades of glass bottles, lamp chimneys and pressed tablewares. All of them employed cutters to decorate their wares. From surviving examples, this earliest cut glass was engraved. The engraver used fine copper wheels and abrasives to cut minute, shallow lines in the glass. Usually, no final polishing was done and the designs appear with the opaque, greyish surface made by the engraving wheel. This technique was used for adding monograms to goblets and special presentation pitchers, or decoration to tableware sets, lamp chimneys and door lights. Fern fronds, wreaths of leaves, and sometimes grape vines and flowers, all reduced to a stylized simple form, were the most common decorative motifs.

The making of the more expensive and more deeply cut glass tablewares began in Canada about 1895. Between 1900 and 1930, 4 major firms made cut glass: George Phillips, Montréal, 1904-71; Gowans, Kent & Co, Toronto, about 1900-18; Gundy-Clapperton, 1905-20, later Clapperton, 1920-72; and Roden Bros, Toronto, about 1907-54. One of the largest, the Gundy-Clapperton firm, employed 50 cutters in 1912. In addition, some 15 other glass-cutting firms were in operation during the period. They were concentrated in Toronto and Montréal, or located in Ontario centres (eg, Ottawa, Lakefield, Wallaceburg, Waterford) and in Winnipeg, Calgary and Vancouver. Some of these operations were one- or 2-man cutting shops. Many of the highly skilled glass cutters, including George Phillips and Harry Clapperton, came from the US.

High-quality lead-glass blanks, ie, the undecorated pieces for cutting, were imported from the Val St Lambert factory in Belgium; the Baccarat firm in France; Libbey Glass Co, Toledo, Ohio; O.C. Dorflinger & Sons, White Mills, Pa; and Mt Washington Glass Co, New Bedford, Mass.

In the larger cutting shops, cut glass was usually produced by a team of cutters, each with his specialty. The "rougher," using a stone wheel and a fine abrasive, followed the designer's marks that outlined the decoration and made the first deep cuts in the glass. At this stage, there was always the danger of cutting too deeply and ruining the piece. The work was then passed on to a "smoother," who also used a stone wheel to smooth the first deep cuts and added the shallower lines of the design. Cutting gave the cut areas a dull, opaque surface. By the time the Canadian firms were in operation, the final polishing was no longer done with a wooden wheel and fine pumice. Instead, the glass was dipped in a bath of sulphuric and hydrofluoric acid, which returned a clear, sparkling finish to the cut areas. The process had been invented in the 1890s and helped cut production costs. In smaller shops, the whole cutting process would be carried out by one man.

The Canadian firms used the hob stars, pinwheels and stars that became popular in the American industry in the late 1880s and 1890s, and the more recent stylized flower and leaf patterns. They created many of their own designs of a brilliant beauty, with such names as Primrose, Oak, Tulip (Gundy-Clapperton); Cornflower, Poppy and Sunflower (Roden Bros); Maple Leaf (Gowans, Kent); as well as many geometric patterns. The Toronto firms marked many of their pieces permanently with an acid-etched trademark: Gundy-Clapperton with "GCCO" in the leaves of a cloverleaf; Clapperton with a "C" in a cloverleaf; Roden Bros with an Old English "R" flanked by lions; and Gowans, Kent with the word "ELITE" in a maple leaf in a circle.

By about 1930 the smaller glass-cutting shops in Canada had vanished. They faced stiff competition from the larger firms, and their disappearance coincided with a decline in the demand for elaborately cut glass. A new style of lighter blown glass with highly polished, shallow-cut delicate floral and leaf patterns found favour in the market. From 1930 to 1972 firms such as Phillips and Clapperton followed much simpler geometric designs in cutting. One firm, W.J. Hughes, Toronto, specialized in cutting one pattern, Cornflower, which they first made in 1914 and still produce. Other new firms, such as the Mayfair Glass Co, Montréal, and the Crystal Glass Co and Monogram Glass Co, both of Toronto, produced the new light cut wares in patterns such as Carnation, Laurel and Grapes, Marguerite and Comet.

JANET HOLMES

Rainbow's Edge, by Lutz Haufschild, bevelled glass, 1986; executed with Kitsilano Glass, Vancouver. Since the 1960s a number of Canadian artists have turned to stained glass as a medium of artistic expression (*courtesy Lutz Haufschild*).

Glass, Stained Despite a number of technical developments, Canadian 20th-century stained-glass craftspeople have continued largely with the traditional technique of hand-made glass set and soldered in a matrix of lead strips (cames). However, *dalle-de-verre*, or cast slab glass, silicon adhesives and epoxy resins, sandblasting devices and a range of new tools and machinery have reduced fabrication time and extended the range of technical and aesthetic possibilities. Stained glass in Canada is of 4 major types. The oldest type, dating from the 1850s in this country, involves production of memorial windows in the Gothic-revival style by companies belonging to the religious art industry. A second type, also influenced by historical styles, is the work of studios devoted to recreating or restoring art nouveau, Edwardian or art deco windows for period houses, restaurants or bars. More recent directions (from the early 1970s) include the development of the stained-glass hobbyist and the emergence of the artist-craftsman of the studio-glass movement.

Of particular benefit to the hobbyist has been the development of a comprehensive Canada-wide distribution network for stained-glass tools and supplies. Courses, mostly at the elementary level, have become widely available through schools, colleges, youth organizations and studios. Accordingly, stained glass has become an inexpensive, accessible part-time leisure activity for thousands of Canadians.

Influenced by postwar developments in stained-glass design in Germany and England, and encouraged by the energy of the stained-glass renaissance in the US in the late 1960s, a number of Canadian artists have turned to stained glass as a medium for contemporary artistic expression. Although primarily concerned with architectural applications, many of these artist-craftsmen (so-called because they both design and fabricate) also began to produce autonomous works that could be exhibited independent of an architectural setting. Thus, exhibitions of stained glass, once a rarity in Canada, now occur frequently. In 1976, Canada's first association of stained-glass artists and craftsmen was founded in Toronto. Supported by some 150 (1987) members from all parts of the country, Artists In Stained Glass encourages the development of stained glass as a contemporary ART form.

ROBERT JEKYLL

Glassco, John, poet, translator (b at Montréal 19 Dec 1909; d there 29 Jan 1981). Glassco will be remembered for his brilliant autobiography, his elegant, classical poems and for his translations. He came from a respectable Montréal family but escaped at 20 to Paris, where he lived for 3 wild, exhilarating years. This period is recalled in MEMOIRS OF MONTPARNASSE, written well after his return to Canada in 1932 with a near-fatal illness, and not published until 1970. It is a dazzling book: elegant, witty, precocious, outrageous, combining a supreme evocation of Paris in the 1920s with a profound examination of the author's own fascinating character. Glassco's later years were spent mostly in Montréal and rural Québec. He wrote poetry (his *Selected Poems* won the Gov Gen's Award in 1971) and some fiction, collected in *The Fatal Woman* (1974). He also wrote, with customary elegance and wit, what he himself called "aphrodisiac works ... as an article of commerce." His translations of French Canadian poetry are, along with F.R. SCOTT's, the finest yet to appear – his greatest achievement being the *Complete Poems of Saint-Denys-Garneau* (1975).

STEPHEN SCOBIE

Glassco, William Grant, director, producer (b at Québec City 30 Aug 1935). As artistic director of TARRAGON THEATRE in Toronto (1971-82), Bill Glassco contributed to the development of Canadian theatre and drama by producing the works of numerous Canadian playwrights. Besides premiering plays by established writers such as James REANEY (*The Donnellys* trilogy), Glassco worked closely with emerging playwrights to develop their dramatic texts and employed leading Canadian actors to premiere new scripts. The works of playwrights such as David FREEMAN and David FRENCH were first staged at Tarragon. Glassco also introduced the works of leading Québec playwrights, particularly Michel TREMBLAY, at the Tarragon. In 1985 Glassco became director of CentreStage, re-establishing it as one of Toronto's leading companies. ANTON WAGNER

Glenbow Museum, founded in Calgary in 1954, is one of Canada's foremost museums of art and western history. It was created by oilman and philanthropist Eric L. HARVIE as an outgrowth of his personal interest in collecting memorabilia. In 1966 its assets were donated to the people of Alberta and the Glenbow-Alberta Institute was formed to administer the huge collections of artifacts, paintings, books and documents. In 1976 the government of Alberta constructed a large 8-storey structure in downtown Calgary, providing 8361 m^2 of exhibition space. This has permitted the displaying of world-class exhibitions as well as its own unique collections dealing with western Canadian history, native peoples and other related topics. The Glenbow's holdings are among the largest in Canada. It has some 24 000 works of art, the largest nongovernment collection of western Canadiana books and manuscripts in existence, and major holdings of pioneer, ethnic, military, and Indian artifacts. Included in its art collections are works by such well known figures as Paul KANE, Carl Rungius, Belmore Browne, W.J. PHILLIPS, F.A. VERNER, Albert Bierstadt and A.F. KENDERDINE.

With its reputation as a lively and active institution, the Glenbow has carried out an extensive publishing program producing many books and catalogues on subjects of western Canadian art and history. During the 1988 Winter Olympics, the museum's exhibit "The Spirit Sings: Artistic Traditions of Canada's First Peoples" became the focal point of a protest by the Lubicon tribe against the federal government's native land-claims policy. DONNA LIVINGSTONE

Glengarry School Days: A Story of the Early Days in Glengarry, by Ralph Connor (Charles William GORDON), was published in Toronto, New York and London, 1902. Connor's schoolboys come under the influence, first, of the universally loved and respected Archie Munro, and then of John Craven, who, through his contact with the minister's wife, is transformed from a talented but disreputable young teacher into a man filled with faith and bound for the ministry. *Glengarry School Days* sets out, with energy and good will, a clear design of moral and religious imperatives for the formation of good character; Connor's stories celebrate his SCOTS figures' hardy self-reliance, their deep respect for what they understand as God's law, and the ordered vigour of the lives they make in the light of their faith. NEIL BESNER

Glenie, James, army officer, politician (b at Fife, Scot 1750; d at London, Eng 23 Nov 1817). After service in Québec during the AMERICAN REVOLUTION Glenie resigned his army commission and settled in New Brunswick (1787). Already he had a reputation as an opinionated and prickly officer, yet blessed with intellectual ability and engineering talent. His involvement in the masting trade and frustration over several land schemes brought him into conflict with Lt-Gov Thomas CARLETON and the LOYALIST élite. First elected to the NB Assembly in 1789, Glenie, part of the Assembly rights faction, became an outspoken critic of the governor and Council, and contributed substantially to the political deadlock of 1795 to 1799. While Glenie's attacks did make the Loyalist political culture more accommodating, his abrasive and relentless opposition alienated friends as well as foes. By the early 1800s moderate assemblymen had come to terms with Carleton and the Council but Glenie's criticisms continued, although frequently lacking majority support in the Assembly. By 1805 Glenie withdrew to England to eke out a living through various appointments and then by employing his considerable talents as a mathematician, but he died in poverty. WILLIAM G. GODFREY

Global Communications Limited, est 1970, owns and operates Global Television Network and is based in Toronto. The CRTC granted the company a broadcast licence for operations in southern Ontario 21 July 1972. Insufficient viewers and revenues brought about reorganization and new ownership by Global Ventures Western Ltd and IWC Communications Ltd in 1974; Ventures bought out IWC in 1976. In 1978 Global acquired Tee Vee Records Inc, primarily a retail record distribution operation, as well as control of Prosoccer Ltd, which operated the now-defunct soccer team, Toronto Blizzard. Each lost money and was subsequently sold off. The television operation continued to grow and now generates more than $50 million in revenues from air-time sales alone and another $12 million from production and syndication. By 1986 the company had established itself as a major producer. Global Television Network covers approximately 94% of Ontario, reaching approximately 3 million households and 8.5 million people.

Globe and Mail, Toronto, was founded in 1936 when George McCullagh united 2 influential and historically important dailies, the *Globe* and the *Mail and Empire*. From the beginning, the new newspaper took on the character of the old *Globe*. George BROWN launched the *Globe* in 1844 with the support of a group of Reformers. Although at first a party journal, the *Globe* quickly became required reading for the educated and business community in Toronto and the surrounding countryside through a shrewd mixture of news, features, forceful editorials and technological innovation. By 1853 the 4-page paper had become a daily, with a weekly edition for out-of-town subscribers; in 1876 Brown commissioned early morning trains to Hamilton and later London, and absorbed mailing costs for the daily *Globe*. As new presses and cheap paper enabled the journal to expand in size, the first women's section was added in 1882 and, within a decade, drawings and photoengravings. By 1900 the *Globe* was established as a quality paper attractive to advertisers, and with a combined circulation for all editions of 69 545. Just after the turn of the century it added the words "Canada's National Newspaper" to its masthead and began its pursuit of readers in all parts of the country. Meanwhile, the *Mail* had been established as a Conservative party organ in 1872 and, in 1895, absorbed another Tory paper, the *Empire*. In 1900 the *Mail and Empire* boasted a circulation of 61 720.

The *Globe and Mail* became the flagship of FP Publications' chain of NEWSPAPERS in 1965 and, in 1980, was bought by the THOMSON GROUP. It has become a journal of record as well as of the business, political and cultural communities. As a "writer's newspaper," the *Globe and Mail* has given skilled journalists such as Jeffrey Simpson and John Fraser the opportunity to practise their craft. In 1987 circulation stood at about 320 000. The national edition is beamed by satellite to printing facilities across the country. Three regular magazines are produced, a quarterly travel magazine, *Destinations*, a monthly *Report on Business* and an annual *Report on Business 1000*. Staff reporters are based in 8 Canadian cities and abroad in Harare, London, Mexico City, New Delhi, New York City, Moscow, Tokyo and Washington. RICHARD J. DOYLE

Globe Theatre, Regina, was founded by Ken and Sue Kramer in Aug 1966 with assistance from the CANADA COUNCIL and various provincial boards. Canada's first professional children's theatre, it travelled to schools across the province presenting a variety of programs. In 1986 their 30 week tour was attended by 95 000 school children. Parental response to the plays was so enthusiastic that in 1967 the Kramers established an adult theatre in Regina. After many moves, in 1980 the Globe acquired a 400-seat facility in a renovated downtown historic building. Unique among Canadian theatrical companies, the Globe has a writer-in-residence, Rex DEVERELL, whose plays, such as *Black Powder* and *Medicare*, deal with regional political issues and history. Plays by George RYGA, James REANEY, Rick SALUTIN and W.O. MITCHELL have also been performed. In 1983-84 the Globe, still under the artistic directorship of Ken Kramer, presented a season that included Shakespeare, Shaw, Alan Ayckbourn, Molière and *Mandarin Oranges* by Deverell. In 1986 some 40 000 patrons attended performances at the Main Stage.

CHARLOTTE STEVENSON

Glooscap, the culture hero, transformer of the Eastern Woodlands Indians. Huge in size and powers, Glooscap is said to have created natural features such as the Annapolis Valley, in the process often having to overcome his evil twin brother who wanted rivers to be crooked and mountains impassable. Glooscap slept across NS, using as his pillow PEI, known to the natives as Abegweit, meaning "Cradled on the Waves."

CAROLE H. CARPENTER

Glyde, Henry George, painter, art educator (b at Luton, Eng 18 June 1906). Glyde was trained at the Royal Coll of Art, London (1926-30). He came to Canada in 1935 to teach drawing in Calgary at the Provincial Institute of Technology and Art and in 1936 became head of the art department. He was also head of the painting division of the Banff School of Fine Arts (1936-66), and in 1937 began teaching community art classes with the Dept of Extension, U of A. Glyde's most significant works are oils and murals depicting a type of social realism. These works are a valuable documentary of urban and rural prairie life. His murals are classical, the colours sombre, and the figure groupings mythological and symbolic in mood and content. The emphasis on structural realities has carried over to his interpretation of the Alberta landscape and to his portrayal of the BC coast. A major retrospective exhibition was produced by the Glenbow Museum in 1987.

KATHLEEN LAVERTY

Gnatcatcher, Blue-Gray (*Polioptila caerulea*, family Muscicapidae, subfamily Sylviinae), tiny, migratory, insectivorous songbird, the sole representative in Canada of the tropical New World tribe, Polioptilini (13 species). It is slender-bodied, blue-grey above, whitish below, with a long, black tail. It is rare in Canada, breeding only in southern Ontario in open, broad-leaved deciduous woodland with brushy undergrowth. Nesting occurs late May to mid July. Clutch includes 4-5 eggs. Song is high-pitched and squeaky; more commonly heard is a buzzy call note.

J.C. BARLOW

Goat Farming Goats (family Bovidae, genus *Capra)*, ruminant mammals with backwardly arching hollow horns, short tail and usually straight hair, are related to SHEEP but are of slighter build. Goats were domesticated as early as 7000 BC and have provided humans with food (milk, cheese, butter), leather and mohair. They were probably introduced with sheep by early settlers in New France. Goats are now raised in every province except Newfoundland, but are most popular in Ontario (about 45% of the goats registered in 1986 were in that province), BC (16%) and Québec (18%).

There are 4 kinds of breeding operations: for industrial milk production (milk is sold to processing plants for cheese making), for farm cheese production (sold by the producer), for meat production (meat is a by-product for milk producers but some breeders specialize in the production of slaughter goats) and for mohair wool production. Goats fall into 3 categories: nonregistered (grade) goat, the pedigree is either unknown or unregistered, or its parents are not registered; registered goat (Canadian), the mother's pedigree is unknown or unregistered but the father's pedigree is registered; registered goat, the pedigree can be traced back to the first goats imported to Canada. Five milk breeds are important in Canada: Alpine (of the 48 343 goats registered in Canada to 31 Dec 1986, 1842 were Alpine), Nubian or Anglo-Nubian (948), Saanen (441), Toggenburg (409) and La Mancha (54). Two breeds, Angora and Cashmere, are raised mainly for wool. In goat breeding, each animal is identified and a register is kept of its birth date, breed and sex, identification number, breeding, kidding and weaning dates, vaccinations, antivermin treatments and milk-control reports.

The doe matures at 3 months but must not be bred before it is 7-9 months old; it reproduces once a year. Artificial insemination enables a large number of females to be impregnated with the sperm of a highly bred buck. The average gestation period is 5 months (153 days). The doe has 2 mammary glands. Diet, lactation stage, number of lactations, health and herd management are the major factors influencing milk production. Genetic improvement of the goat population is essential. Selection involves eliminating imperfect animals and keeping well-formed ones (body, hooves, pelvis, limbs, udders). A table for classifying the physical conformation of goats has been developed by the Canadian Goat Society, Fergus, Ont. Genetic selection also includes breeding characteristics (eating habits, fertility, prolificness) and milk-production characteristics, both quantitative and qualitative. Quantitatively, production increases 200 kg between the first and third lactations; this level is maintained between the third and seventh lactations and then declines. Qualitative aspects involve the levels of nitrogen and bytyrin in the milk.

Goats are fed twice daily; fodder makes up 72% of the daily intake of dry feed. Goats are very selective and like leaves and young sprouts. They prefer rolled cereals or concentrated nutrients in tablet form over finely ground grains. Like other ruminants they can digest foods rich in cellulose and then metabolize the volatile fatty acids. The Canadian Goat Society, founded in 1917, is the registry agency.

JEAN-PAUL LEMAY

Godbout, Jacques, novelist, essayist, filmmaker, poet (b at Montréal 27 Nov 1933). One of the most important writers of his generation, Godbout strongly influenced post-1960 Québec intellectual life. After studies at Coll Brébeuf and U de M, he taught French in Ethiopia. He joined the NATIONAL FILM BOARD (1958) as producer and scriptwriter. Co-founder of *Liberté* (1959), the Mouvement laique de la langue française (1962) and the Union des écrivains québecois (1977), Godbout was active in the QUIET REVOLUTION, constantly analysing society through contributions to various periodicals. His most important essays, demonstrating his penetrating mind and concern for democratic values, were collected in *Le Réformiste* (1975) and *Le Murmure marchand* (1984). Godbout's films include 4 full-length features (*Yul 871, Kid Sentiment, Ixe 13, La Gammik*) and more than 15 documentaries. He has written 7 novels: *L'Aquarium* (1962), *Le Couteau sur la table* (1965; tr *Knife on the Table*, 1968), *Salut Galarneau!* (1967; trans *Hail Galarneau!*, 1970), *D'amour, P.Q.* (1972), *L'Isle au dragon* (1976), *Les Têtes à Papineau* (1981) and *Une Histoire américaine* (1986).

ANDRÉ SMITH

Godbout, Joseph-Adélard, agronomist, professor, premier of Québec (b at St-Éloi, Qué 24 Sept 1892; d at Montréal 18 Sept 1956). He was educated at Ste-Anne-de-la-Pocatière and the Massachusetts Agricultural Coll and taught agriculture at Ste-Anne-de-la-Pocatière 1918-30. Elected Liberal MNA for L'Islet in 1929, he was minister of agriculture in the L.A. TASCHEREAU administration 1930-36. He became premier in Aug 1936 upon the unexpected resignation of Taschereau under the violent attacks of the new Union Nationale leader Maurice DUPLESSIS. His party was defeated in the 1936 elections, but despite his own defeat he remained Liberal Party leader thanks to the assistance of federal Liberal minister Ernest LAPOINTE. Heavy support from the federal Liberal Party enabled him to regain power in the 1939 elections. Because of his close ties with the federal party, Godbout did not strongly oppose the military CONSCRIPTION imposed in 1944 following a Canada-wide referendum. He also accepted the federal government's appropriation of various revenue sources that until then had belonged to the provinces. Despite some socially progressive bills, including one granting women the right to vote in Québec provincial elections (1940), Godbout's party was defeated in 1944; he lost his own seat in 1948. The next year he was made senator for Montarville.

DANIEL LATOUCHE

Goderich, Ont, Town, pop 7352 (1986c), 7322 (1981c), seat of Huron County, inc 1850, located on a bluff above Lk Huron at the mouth of the Maitland R, 130 km NE of SARNIA. The site, with its small natural harbour, was discovered 1827 by the CANADA CO'S William "Tiger" DUNLOP. It was named for Lord Goderich, British PM 1827-28. A trail chopped 97 km through the bush provided access in 1828. The townsite was laid out 1829 with the idea that Goderich would become the entrepôt for the Canada Co's 400 000 ha Huron Tract.

Goderich, Ont. The townsite, laid out in 1829, has wide, tree-lined streets radiating from a central octagonal square (*photo by John deVisser/Masterfile*).

The town has wide, tree-lined streets which radiate from a central octagonal square like the spokes of a wheel. Development fell short of expectations, and while the town became the terminus of a railway from Buffalo in 1858, it commanded only local trade. In 1866 the discovery of salt by a company drilling for oil gave Goderich a major industry. Since the 1870s it has remained stable, growing slightly with the development of the resort industry. The massive stones of the historic HURON COUNTY JAIL (1839-42) contrast with its graceful design; the exercise yards are enclosed by an octagonal wall.

HUGH JOHNSTON

Godfrey, Dave, writer, publisher, academic (b at Winnipeg 9 Aug 1938). Godfrey's books include *The New Ancestors* (Governor General's Award 1970), a powerful and complex novel set in Africa, where the author served with CUSO, and several collections of highly stylized short stories. An activist in Canadian cultural politics beginning in the late 1960s, he was co-founder of both the HOUSE OF ANANSI and New Press, and at present runs Press Porcépic with his wife, writer Ellen Godfrey. He is also co-owner of Softwords, part of Press Porcépic, which produces educational software. He studied at U of T, Iowa and Stanford, and currently teaches creative writing and publishing at U of Victoria.

JOHN MOSS

Godfrey, John Ferguson, academic, editor (b at Toronto 19 Dec 1942). A surprising choice to become editor of the *Financial Post* in 1987, Godfrey was educated at University of Toronto and Oxford where he studied French history. He taught at Dalhousie U from 1970 and in 1977 became president of the tiny U of King's College, located on Dalhousie campus. As president, Godfrey was enormously successful in attracting publicity to his institution and himself, and he also worked for many good causes, most notably the Ethiopian airlift which he began in an effort to alleviate the terrible famine there.

J.L. GRANATSTEIN

Goforth, Jonathan, Presbyterian missionary (b at Thorndale, Canada W 10 Feb 1859; d at Wallaceburg, Ont 8 Oct 1936). Inspired by G.L. MACKAY'S work in Formosa [Taiwan], Goforth left farming to study at Knox College, U of T, graduating in 1886. The following year he was sent to

Henan Province, China. Thanks to his policy of identifying with Chinese culture, friendly officials helped the 14 Canadian missionaries and dependants in Henan escape during the Boxer Rebellion. After the uprising the mission grew rapidly. Goforth refused to join the UNITED CHURCH OF CANADA in 1925 and started a mission in Manchuria. JOHN S. MOIR

Goggin, David James, educator (b in Cartwright Twp, Durham County, Canada W 25 Nov 1849; d at Toronto 18 Dec 1935). Generally regarded as the founder of the centralized, fully professional school systems of Alberta and Saskatchewan, Goggin generated controversy during his term as superintendent of education in the North-West Territories (1893-1902) when he set out, with the full support of the government, to make the schools the principal engine for assimilating the immigrant population to the dominant British Ontarian Protestant norm. By requiring that only English be used in the classroom, and by emphasizing training in citizenship rather than intellectual development, he hoped to advance national unity by imposing cultural uniformity and a sense of social responsibility upon his students. Some francophone Catholics objected; and the NORTH-WEST SCHOOLS QUESTION of 1905 resulted from their abortive attempt to overturn his system. STANLEY GORDON

Golab, Anthony Charles, Tony, "Golden Boy," football player (b at Windsor, Ont 17 Jan 1919). Golab was a hard-charging, versatile player with the OTTAWA ROUGH RIDERS. He joined the Sarnia Imperials (ORFU) in 1938 and the Ottawa Rough Riders in 1939, where he won the Jeff Russell Trophy as most valuable player in 1941. As an RCAF flight lieutenant and pilot during WWII he was shot down and wounded. He returned to Ottawa to play until 1949, his spirited style making him a fan favourite. Golab, who played offence and defence, appeared in 4 GREY CUP games. FRANK COSENTINO

Gold (Au) is a bright, shiny, yellow metal, notable for its high density (19.3 times the weight of an equal volume of water) and valued for its extreme ductility, strong resistance to corrosion, lustrous beauty, and scarcity. Pyrite, or fool's gold as it is sometimes known, can be distinguished from real gold by its brittleness and hardness as well as that it appears black in powder form. As it is the least chemically active of all metals, gold usually occurs in a free or uncombined state. It is found as nuggets, flakes or dust in gravel and sand deposits along creeks and rivers, but more often gold is recovered from veins (called lodes) in bedrock. Gold is also produced as a by-product of base-metal mines; about one-fifth of Canada's gold production comes from this source.

There are various ways to separate and recover gold, depending upon the nature of the ore. When gold occurs in a relatively coarse, free state, it can be recovered by mechanical means such as gravity traps and shaking tables, where the gold separates out because of its high specific gravity. Cyanidation is a chemical process used to recover gold that is very finely distributed in the ore. The process is complex but basically involves a cyanide solution being added to finely ground ore and then being agitated in the presence of air to dissolve the gold. After a variety of treatment steps, the solution containing the gold is clarified and the gold is precipitated by the addition of zinc dust to the solution. Recent refinements to this process include the carbon-in-pulp process, which uses activated carbon to collect the gold without having to filter the ground ore slurry. The activated carbon is stripped of its gold in an acid bath and then recycled. Once the gold is separated from the ore and is in the form of an impure precipitate, it is placed, along with a fluxing agent, into a high-temperature furnace. A chemical reaction takes place, in which the flux and the impurities combine to form a slag and the molten gold sinks to the bottom of the furnace where it is drawn off and poured into molds to form doré bars, which contain the gold and any silver that may have been present in the original ore.

Gold has been one of the ultimate symbols of wealth from the earliest civilizations to the present. Even though it is too soft for weapons or tools, people have treasured gold for its decorative and monetary value. Gold has several industrial uses. Being chemically inert, it has long been popular in dentistry for crowns and caps. Resistance to corrosion, along with electrical conductivity, make it useful in precision electronic equipment. When a thin film of gold is applied to window glass, a building's thermal properties are improved dramatically, reducing the amount of heat gain in the summer and heat loss in the winter, eg, the ROYAL BANK building in Toronto.

Gold was first discovered in Canada in 1823 along the shores of the Chaudière R in the Eastern Townships of Québec. In 1858, following the famous rushes in California and Australia, gold was discovered in the sands of the Fraser R in the interior of BC and this started the CARIBOO GOLD RUSH. Almost 40 years later, the legendary KLONDIKE GOLD RUSH in the Yukon marked the beginning of one of the most productive periods in Canadian gold-mining history. The early 1900s saw the establishment of several major gold-mining camps in N Ontario such as Porcupine, Timmins, Larder Lk, Kirkland Lk and Red Lk. The gold excitement then swept across the provincial boundary into N Québec and gold was discovered at Bourlamaque, Val D'or, Chibougamau and Malartic. At the outbreak of WWII, Canada's gold-producing capacity was expanded in order to help meet wartime expenditures. Production reached an all-time high of 166 t in 1941 but then declined dramatically owing to wartime conditions.

By 1970, rising production costs had forced the closure of many gold mines in Canada and production dropped to one-third of peak levels. Changes in international monetary policies led to a startling increase in gold prices in the late 1970s (*see* GOLD STANDARD) which, in turn, encouraged increased activity in gold exploration and new mine development. The 1981 discovery and subsequent development of the large Hemlo gold deposit in N Ontario, followed by other discoveries and developments in each of Canada's provinces and territories, has resulted in increased production and a renewed importance of gold to the Canadian economy. In 1986, Canada was the world's third-largest gold producer behind South Africa and the USSR, and accounted for 10% of production in the Western world. Canadian production was 104.7 t valued at $1.7 billion. This output will probably increase in 1988 when several new mines come into production.

DON LAW-WEST

Gold Rushes Hardrock GOLD deposits have been found throughout the world and have always required specialized skills and complex, expensive equipment to exploit. It was the discoveries of free (or placer) gold, which could be worked cheaply by amateurs, that sparked excitement and publicity, and hence gold "rushes." Placer gold was found in commercial quantities mainly in the western cordillera region, from California to Alaska, where a series of gold rushes occurred in the mid-to-late 19th century. Gold rushes could not exist before the era of the telegraph, mass circulation newspapers and steamboats, and after 1900 no substantive alluvial goldfields remained undiscovered. In the same period there were side rushes to other Pacific Rim countries; minor rushes also occurred elsewhere in British N America (in Nova Scotia, SE Ontario and SW Québec), but no significant placer mining occurred in these regions.

The "rush" phenomenon involved a brief period of discovery – accidental or by roving prospectors – of free gold in paying quantities; word of this spread, first locally, attracting other prospectors (who abandoned lesser-paying "digs") and their suppliers. Then, depending on the richness and extent of the goldfields, word was carried farther afield by outbound prospectors and through the commercial press, resulting in an even greater influx of goldseekers and adventurers into the gold-bearing territory. The search for free gold in the gold rush era followed a roughly northward drive from California, where an accidental discovery on Sutter's Creek in 1848 resulted in a massive rush to the area in 1849 and into Oregon, Washington and British Columbia territory in the next decade.

In BC, excitement over discoveries of free gold in the Queen Charlotte Is (1851) led to extensive prospecting throughout the coastal islands and the lower mainland, where gold discoveries in the lower and middle Fraser R areas led to a small rush to the Yale area in 1858 (the Fraser R gold rush). From there prospectors fanned out to the east, where small gold rushes occurred in the Boundary (Rock Creek), Similkameen (Wild Horse Creek) and Thompson R (Big Bend) districts; and to the N into Cariboo country, where a major boom occurred between 1860 and 1866 (*see* CARIBOO GOLD RUSH). Meantime, other prospectors had been searching the territory in the Edmonton region, along the Bow, Red Deer, N Saskatchewan and McLeod rivers, where short-lived, fairly localized rushes occurred. Fired by the Cariboo finds, prospectors began a serious assault on the northern cordillera region. To the E, they panned their way along the Finlay and Parsnip rivers and down the Peace R to the Fort St John region; to the W, they worked up the Omineca R, where a minor rush into Omineca country occurred in 1868. They then entered the difficult territory N of it, approaching the Cassiar Mts via both the Liard and Stikine rivers. At Dease Lake, a major strike led to a rush to the heart of Cassiar country in 1872.

Closing in on what they believed to be the single, massive source of the other placer goldfields, the "mother lode," prospectors moved into central Alaska-Yukon, panning their way up the Yukon R. Worldwide publicity given to the discovery of large nuggets on Bonanza Creek on the Klondike R, in 1896, led to the most famous rush of them all, the KLONDIKE GOLD RUSH (1897-98), and there followed smaller rushes to Nome, Alaska, and to Atlin in the NW corner of BC.

The majority of prospectors and miners, as well as many of the speculators, merchants, craftsmen, entertainers and adventurers who participated in each of the gold rushes, were from the Pacific coast region, especially from California, and there were numerous CHINESE as well as local native people who participated in guiding, freighting and prospecting. But men (and some women) from the more settled parts of N America and other parts of the world participated as well, especially if deep placers were discovered.

Placer mining technology involved the recovery of auriferous deposits and the separation of the gold (washing) from the detritus; most of the methodology was worked out in the California goldfields and spread from there. The discovery and early gold-rush phase for any placer goldfield involved PROSPECTING, panning and surface sluicing. The surface sandbars and gravels could be

The Neversweat Company tunnel, Williams Creek in the Cariboo country, 1868 (*courtesy National Archives of Canada/C-173/F. Dally*).

worked by individuals with little capital. These usually yielded only fine gold. Once the most accessible deposits were exhausted, and if no subsurface placers were uncovered, the area was soon abandoned. Coarse gold (or nuggets), which was more valuable than fine gold, was situated in deep placers. If there were "underground pay streaks" to be exploited, a second phase of developments occurred. Miners used picks and shovels to open small holes and pits; they then sank shafts into the beaches and hillsides, and processed the gravel and muck in a complex arrangement of sluices. This involved the use of more labour, and more complex and expensive technology – much of it factory-made – and increasingly greater supplies of water and wood; and this in turn required the formation of partnerships and limited companies, and the establishment of more permanent living, supply and administrative centres. This phase, too, was short-lived. In a few cases where significant alluvial deposits were exceptionally rich, as was the case in the Klondike and to a lesser extent the Cariboo fields, much more capital-intensive hydraulic or steam-dredging operations were eventually undertaken; these required not only sophisticated, capital-intensive mining technology but also separate, highly organized systems for water supply and control, for which the organization of large companies was required.

Gold rushes did little to increase the world supply of gold, and unless they were exceptionally rich and possessing workable quartz veins, most made no permanent contribution to mining. On the other hand, placer gold often lured people into a mineral-bearing territory, thus opening it up to other mineral development. The gold rushes also served to open large territories to permanent settlement, for the goldfields offered the unsuccessful goldseeker at least the possibility of farming or ranching. Although the Klondike goldfield offered no such possibilities for agricultural settlement, its popularity was exploited extensively by Canadian immigration officials and western commercial interests to advertise the potential of the Canadian Northwest as a place to settle. For the native population of BC and the Yukon, this intense scramble for gold and the rapid mining and agricultural settlement that followed in its wake brought about the swift imposition of systems of authority which were essentially alien to their own.

The gold rushes had an impact even on those who were not directly involved, for they provided a popular theme for so much writing in the 19th and early 20th centuries, particularly in the US. The gold rush theme was included in everything from dime novels to the classic works of fiction by Jack London, the poetry of Robert SERVICE and early motion pictures, such as Charlie Chaplin's *Gold Rush*. The more recent literature on gold rushes is more along the lines of historical narratives (*see* Pierre BERTON) and personal reminiscences which employ a less dramatic perspective. Barkerville, BC, Dawson City and Whitehorse, YK, and Edmonton each hosts annual celebrations of the gold rush days. DIANNE NEWELL

Reading: W.P. Morrell, *The Gold Rushes*, (1941); W.J. Trimble, *The Mining Advance into the Inland Empire*, (1944).

Gold Standard, monetary system in which a currency unit (the Canadian dollar, for example) is defined in relation to a certain quantity of gold, and in which the monetary authority (central bank) agrees to buy and sell gold freely at this price. International gold flows are unrestricted and international payments are balanced by gold movements. Canada was officially on the gold standard after 1851, but followed most other nations in abandoning it in 1914. A version of the standard was re-established in 1926 but permanently abandoned in 1931. The gold standard restrained governments from expanding credit, keeping international creditors happy, but it also meant that economic instability in one country was transmitted to others by gold movements. Modern nations have been loath to subjugate their domestic economies to the vagaries of world economic conditions, although a return to the gold standard has been advocated in the US and elsewhere as a means of disciplining monetary authorities. JAMES MELVIN

Goldbloom, Alton, pediatrician, educator, author (b at Montréal 23 Sept 1890; d there 3 Feb 1968). A 1916 McGill medical graduate, Goldbloom pioneered modern pediatrics in Québec and eastern Canada. Following internships, including 2 years in New York, he began to practise in Montréal (1920). He played a leading role in developing the Montréal Children's Hospital and the Dept of Pediatrics at McGill. His book, *The Care of the Child* (1928), was translated into French and Dutch. In 1959 *Small Patients: The Autobiography of a Children's Doctor* was published. Goldbloom's wit and encyclopedic knowledge made him a popular lecturer. HAROLD SEGALL

Golden, BC, Town, pop 3584 (1986c), 3476 (1982c), inc 1957, is located on the COLUMBIA R and Trans-Canada Hwy, 260 km W of Calgary, Alta. It is situated between the Selkirk Mt Range and Glacier National Park on the W and between the Rocky Mts and Yoho National Park on the E. In the 19th century the area was known as the Cache, or Kicking Horse Flats, but in 1883, during construction of the CPR, the community was named Golden City as a counterpart to Silver City (Castle Mtn, Alta). The town owes its start to the railway, still its principal employer. The region around Golden also supports several sawmills and plywood plants and some mining. Before construction of the Rogers Pass section of the Trans-Canada Hwy in the early 1960s, Golden was the eastern end of the Big Bend Hwy which followed the big bend of the Columbia between Revelstoke and Golden. Tourist traffic on the Trans-Canada Hwy is also important to the economy. JOHN R. STEWART

Golden Boy, gilded 4 m statue atop the dome of the Manitoba Legislative Building. It was sculpted by Charles Gardet of Paris and cast in 1918 at the Barbidienne foundry in France. The figure was in place when the building was officially opened in 1929, and in 1970, on Manitoba's centenary, the torch was electrically lit. The boy is a runner, like the messengers in Greek mythology. He carries a sheaf of golden grain in his left arm, while his right hand holds high a torch. Golden Boy is said to embody the spirit of enterprise and youth, and he faces north, where the future promise of his province lies.

Close-up of Golden Boy statue on the top of the dome of the Manitoba Legislative Building, Winnipeg (*courtesy SSC Photocentre/photo by Jim Merrithew*).

Golden Dog (*le chien d'or*), stone bas-relief bearing the figure of a dog gnawing a bone, with the inscription: "Je suis un chien qui ronge lo [l'os]/ En le rongeant je prend mon repos/Un tems viendra qui nest pas venu/Que je morderay qui maura mordu" ("I am a dog that gnaws a bone/In gnawing it I take my rest/A time will come which is not yet/When I shall bite him who has bitten me"). The stone was built into a house erected by Timothée Roussel in Québec City in 1688. It may have been set there by Roussel or by Nicholas Philibert, who bought the house in 1734 and may have used the image to protest the corrupt practices of Intendant François BIGOT. In 1871 the house was destroyed to make way for a post office, and the stone was moved to the new building's portico. The many legends connected with the Golden Dog all turn on revenge and end in tragedy. One version was the basis for William KIRBY'S GOLDEN DOG.

Golden Dog (Le Chien d'Or), A Legend of Quebec, The, by William KIRBY, appeared in New York and Montréal, 1877. The first edition contained many errors, and the supposedly "authorized" edition, *The Golden Dog (Le Chien d'Or), A Romance of the Days of Louis Quinze in Quebec* (Boston, 1897), was, according to Kirby, "a poor mutilated thing." The many other editions and abridgements are also textually unreliable. The novel's action takes place just before the fall of New France, when the supporters of the popular Chien d'Or trading house, headed by the bourgeois Philibert, struggle against the decadent and corrupt Grand Company of the Intendant BIGOT. Two ill-fated romances are interwoven: that of Amélie de Repentigny with Philibert's son, Pierre; and that of Le Gardeur (Amélie's brother) with the self-seeking Angélique des Meloises, who eventually persuades him to kill Philibert. This action precipitates the collapse of the colony. The novel mixes Gothic and historical romance with Québecois history and legend; it also provides insight into 19th-century English Canadian perceptions of French Canada's past. *The Golden Dog* was translated into French by Léon-Pamphile Le May as *Le Chien d'Or: légende canadienne* (Montréal, 1884; rev 1926). NEIL BESNER

Golden Hinde, elev 2200 m, is the highest mountain on VANCOUVER I, located near the Island's centre in Strathcona Pk. The peak was known as Rooster's Comb until R.P. Bishop submitted to the Geographic Board of Canada (confirmed 1939) the present name (after the ship of Sir Francis DRAKE, who may have reached this latitude and sighted the mountain). It was possibly discovered in July 1896 during the Bolton-Laing survey of the Island. GLEN BOLES

Goldenrod, genus *Solidago*, showy, perennial, herbaceous plant of the Compositae or Asteraceae family. Nearly 100 species have been described, chiefly from N America. Thirty-two species occur in Canada, 6 of which are distributed transcontinentally. Eastern Canada (Ontario to NS) has 11 species, with an additional 6 species found only in southern Ontario (the richest part of Canada for varieties of goldenrod). Goldenrods grow in dry, sterile to moist, rich soils, in prairie and wooded locations, and from the brackish seashore to high mountain elevations. The stems are usually simple, bearing distinctly toothed or lobed leaves. The flower cluster is usually a large, loose plume of several hundred heads, each a small "daisy" – a central mass of small, tubular florets surrounded by radiating, strap-shaped florets. The flowers are yellow and bloom in mid-to-late summer and autumn. The calyx tube, firmly attached to the ovary of individual florets, is crowned by fine hairs that form a parachute at the top of the tiny, dry, ripened fruit and aid in wind dispersal. Goldenrod is wrongly blamed for hay fever caused by RAGWEED pollen. *See also* PLANTS, NATIVE USES.

Goldhamer, Charles, painter (b at Philadelphia, Pa 21 Aug 1903; d at Toronto 27 Jan 1985). He was commissioned as one of Canada's official war artists, and his candidly observed charcoal drawings of burned Canadian airmen in an English hospital are some of the most horrific images of WWII. After the war, for a time, he was married to British comedienne Anna Russell. For 42 years he was in the art department of Toronto's Central Technical School (he retired as chairman 1969). His use of demonstrations and working directly are a style of teaching he learned from Arthur LISMER, his own teacher at the ONTARIO COLLEGE OF ART (1922-26). Like other painters in the 1930s, especially his friend Fritz BRANDTNER, Goldhamer found a base in Baie-St-Paul, painting habitants in Charlevoix County. His work in Québec, often in watercolour, was the start of his reputation. Fresh and sparkling, it recorded the area's rolling terrain. Sometimes his watercolours – like those of Carl SCHAEFER and Charles COMFORT – recall the work of American artists Charles Burchfield and Charles Sheeler. JOAN MURRAY

Goldsmith, Oliver, poet, civil servant (b at St Andrews, NB 6 July 1794; d at Liverpool, Eng 23 June 1861). The son of Loyalists and grand-nephew of Irish poet Oliver Goldsmith, he was employed for most of his life in the commissariat of the British army at Halifax. His long poem, *The Rising Village,* originally published in England (1825) and later revised in Canada (1834), was the first book-length poem published by an English Canadian. In heroic couplets, Goldsmith depicts the progress of settlement and civilization in a Maritime community, but subtly cautions that the settlers must remain vigilant and loyal to Britain – lest the wilderness reassert its chaos and the lawless youth rebel in a (perhaps) American revolutionary spirit. *The Autobiography of Oliver Goldsmith*, discovered by W.E. Myatt, was published with his notes in 1943. GERALD LYNCH

Golf is an outdoor game played with a small hard ball and a set of clubs with iron or wooden heads. The object of the game is to make one's way round a specially laid out course in as few strokes as possible, hitting the ball from certain starting points, or tees, to specific targets, which are holes set in the ground. Most golf courses have 18 holes. The name "golf" probably derives from the German *kolbe*, meaning "club." The game's ancestry is obscure, but golf as we know it was first played in Scotland in the last half of the 15th century, although the Scottish Parliament by 1491 had passed 3 edicts ordering that it be banned, reasoning that interest in it kept people from more practical pursuits and interfered with military activities. Golf spread, nonetheless, and when native Scots emigrated to Canada, they took what came to be known as the "Royal and Ancient Game" with them.

The first golf club in Canada was the Montreal Golf Club, founded in Nov 1873 by Scotsman Alexander Dennistoun; he was also the first president and the captain of the club. He was joined in his efforts by John G. and David D. Sidey, Scottish brothers who had immigrated to Canada. The first course for the Montréal club was over property called Fletcher's Field, owned by the city of Montréal. In 1884, Queen Victoria, through the earl of Derby, bestowed upon the club the "Royal" prefix. The Quebec Golf Club (now Royal Quebec Golf Club) was founded in 1874. Play was over Cove Field between the Citadel and the Plains of Abraham. Canada's third course belonged to the Toronto Golf Club, founded in 1876. The fourth was the Brantford (Ont) Golf Club, begun in 1879. One of its members, Ralph H. Reville, began Canada's first golf magazine, *Canadian Golfer*, in 1915. The magazine continued under Reville's direction through 1932 and became the primary source for early Canadian golf history. Canada's first 18-hole course was the Victoria Golf Club, started in 1893; until then golfers had played over 9 holes. In 1894 the Winnipeg Golf Club was founded, followed by the Calgary Golf Club in 1895 and the Halifax Golf Club and the Edmonton Country Club in 1896. By the turn of the century, golf was firmly established in Canada. The first municipally owned and operated golf course was opened by the city of Edmonton in 1912, and within a short time there was hardly a town in Canada that did not have a golf course. Today, Canada has numerous outstanding courses, with the National Golf Club in Woodbridge, Ont, and Glen Abbey Golf Club in Oakville, Ont, generally considered the best championship courses.

Seeking competition and camaraderie, club members began to play against one another. The first interclub match was held on Cove Field in Québec City in 1876 and the host team defeated Montréal by 12 holes. The first interprovincial match took place in 1882 when Québec played Ottawa at Montréal. The Canadian Golf Assn, later to become the Royal Canadian Golf Assn (RCGA), was formed in 1895, spurred on by the efforts of A. Simpson, secretary to the Royal Ottawa (formerly Ottawa) Golf Club. The RCGA aimed to promote and develop golf in Canada, to protect the mutual interests of its members, establish consistency in the handicapping, or rating, of golfers, and to conduct national championships. In 1895 it conducted the first Canadian amateur championship, at the Royal Ottawa course. The winner was Tom Harley, a Scotsman who had moved to Kingston, Ont.

At first, the RCGA conducted national championships for men and women. The first Ladies' Championship of Canada was held in 1901 at Royal Montreal and was won by member Lily Young. In 1913, Florence Harvey, a member of the Hamilton (Ont) Golf Club, founded the Canadian Ladies' Golf Union. She had recently competed in England and, observing the good work of the Ladies' Golf Union there, saw no reason why a similar organization could not exist in Canada. By 1924 the CLGU, now the Canadian Ladies' Golf Assn, was ready to take over its own championship and the RCGA relinquished control. The CLGA adopted similar objectives in women's golf to those of the RCGA in men's.

As more novice golfers joined clubs across Canada, the need for instructors was met by the many Scots who had been working at Canadian clubs and were adept at golf. They brought a knowledge of the game's principles and transmitted them to their members. By 1911 there were so many club professionals that they formed the Canadian Professional Golfers' Assn. Their inaugural championship was held in 1912 at the Mississauga Golf Club, near Toronto. Earlier, the first Canadian Open had been conducted by the RCGA in 1904. It was won by J.H. Oke, an Englishman who had spent some time in Canada, but 8 of the next 10 Opens were taken by professionals firmly ensconced at Canadian clubs. George Cumming, professional to the Toronto Golf Club 1900-50, brothers Charles and Albert Murray of the Royal Montreal and Outremont (Qué) clubs, and Karl Keffer of Royal Ottawa starred in that decade of tournaments. It became obvious that professionals could both teach and play golf. Eventually these roles were divided, as memberships swelled and competition became so fierce that anybody who wanted to play for a living had to be devoted to practice and competition.

At the same time, Canadian amateurs were also busily engaged in their sport. George S. LYON, a former cricketer who played golf at the Rosedale and Lambton clubs in Toronto, won the Canadian amateur title 8 times between 1898 and 1914, as well as the 1904 Olympic golf event. C. Ross (Sandy) Somerville of the London Hunt Club won it 6 times 1926-37; and Ada MACKENZIE, founder of the Ladies' Golf and Tennis Club in Thornhill, Ont, won the Canadian ladies' amateur title 5 times 1919-35. They were later joined

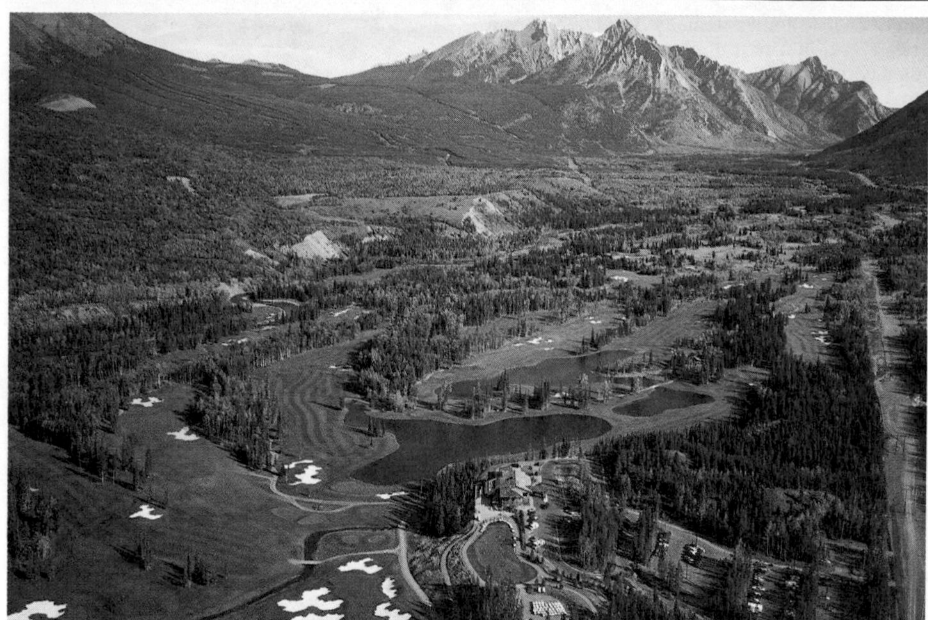

Spectacular Kananaskis Country has 2 championship 18-hole golf courses (*courtesy Kananaskis Country*).

as top amateurs by Marlene Stewart STREIT, 11-time ladies' amateur champion, ladies' British Open amateur champion (1953) and US women's amateur champion (1956); and Gary Cowan of Kitchener, Ont, winner of the US men's amateur in 1966 and 1971. During Somerville's tenure as Canada's top amateur (he also won the US men's amateur in 1932), the interprovincial team matches for the Willingdon Cup had been inaugurated in conjunction with the Canadian amateur. The matches began in 1927 when Governor General Viscount Willingdon presented the cup to the RCGA. Four-man teams have competed annually for the trophy after emerging from provincial playdowns. As the top golfers edged into middle age, senior championships arose to fill the need for competition and Lyon himself took the first 6 events held by the Canadian Senior Golf Assn from 1918 to 1923.

On the professional side, the Canadian Open became one of the most sought-after titles in golf as players from Canada, the US and around the world competed for prizes that rose to $850 000 by 1987. From 1920 to 1935 the Open was played for the Rivermead Cup; from 1936 to 1970 the Seagram Gold Cup was at stake; and after 1971 competition was for the Peter Jackson Trophy. On the US men's pro tour, Canadian Stan LEONARD won 3 events 1957-60, while George KNUDSON had won 8 by the time he turned to teaching in the late 1970s; he had also won the 1968 World Cup with Al Balding. On the women's tour, Sandra POST of Oakville, Ont, won the Ladies Professional Golf Assn championship on her first year on the tour and won more money than any Canadian professional, male or female. In 1980 Dan HALLDORSON and Jim Nelford won the World Cup of professional golf for Canada; that same year Halldorson won on the US tour and in 1981 Dave BARR of Kelowna, BC, did the same. In 1984 Nelford, Halldorson and Barr were all among the top 100 money winners on the US tour.

More than 1300 clubs belonged to the RCGA by the 1980s. Junior golf had been strong since the first Canadian junior was held in 1938. The best junior women golfers had competed for the Canadian junior girls' championship since 1955. Stimulated by the prize money available in golf around the world and encouraged by the RCGA, the CLGA, and provincial golf associations, junior golfers began to look to golf as a career and to attend college on golf scholarships. In 1979 the Canadian Golf Foundation, an arm of the RCGA, was founded to act as a clearing house for Canadian golf information. In 1982 the foundation offered scholarships for eligible Canadians to attend college.

The long tradition of golf as a participant sport, the pleasant environment in which it is played, and the long life of the sport for individuals ensure that it will remain a popular hobby. There is something in golf that keeps people interested – perhaps the personal test of ability – and despite severely increasing land costs, escalating fees for play, and the undeserved reputation of the game as a sport exclusive to the leisured and moneyed class, golf has endured for centuries.

LORNE RUBENSTEIN

Golf Courses are specially designed pieces of land of variable dimensions and topography that are used for the playing of golf. They are usually divided into 18 segments, each consisting of a starting point, or tee, from which a player strikes a ball towards his ultimate target. This target is a hole 11 cm in diameter that is located on a closely mown portion of grass, known as a green. There are also 9-hole golf courses. A well-designed course will challenge the skilled player while still offering pleasure to the lesser golfer.

Canada's first formal course opened in 1873 and belonged to the Montreal Golf Club. It was located on Fletcher's Field, part of the city-owned Mount Royal Park in Montréal. As the game became more popular and as the club attracted more members, more property was needed. Today the privately owned Royal Montreal Golf Club is located on Île Bizard, Qué, some 30 km from Fletcher's Field. Typically, golf courses have moved outwards from the city centre as cities have grown. Canada's first municipal course opened in Edmonton in 1912. The private Edmonton Golf Club had a course on the Hudson's Bay Flats below the Legislature Building. That year the city bought the property and kept the course as part of Victoria Park.

As of 1985 there were 1561 (9-hole and 18-hole) courses in Canada. They fit into 5 categories: privately owned and restricted to members; semi-private, offering memberships but open to nonmembers on payment of a daily green fee; public, open to all golfers on payment of a daily green fee; municipal, owned by a city, township or municipality; and resort. A list of the finest courses is always arbitrary, but most golfers agree that the National Golf Club in Woodbridge, Ont, and the Glen Abbey Golf Club in Oakville, Ont, are the most difficult courses in Canada. Kananaskis Country has 2 spectacular 18-hole courses; other equally scenic courses are in Banff and Jasper and the Capilano Club in Vancouver. The Canadian Open is held annually at Glen Abbey under the auspices of the Royal Canadian Golf Assn, which owns the course.

LORNE RUBENSTEIN

Good, William Charles, farmer, co-operative and agrarian leader (b near Brantford, Ont 24 Feb 1876; d at Paris, Ont 16 Nov 1967). A student of social and religious issues and a member of a family long involved in farm organizations, Good was on the executive of the Farmers' Assn in 1904. In 1907 he helped amalgamate the association with the Dominion Grange and became president of the new organization in 1912. A proponent of the need for farmer unity, Good, with E.A. PARTRIDGE and E.C. DRURY, drafted the constitution of the Canadian Council of Agriculture in 1909. In 1914 he helped organize the United Farmers of Ontario and the United Farmers' Co-operative. Good was a leader of the PROGRESSIVE PARTY and sat as an Independent-Progressive in the Commons 1921-25, where he advocated electoral reform, banking reform, temperance and tariff reform. Elected president of the Co-operative Union of Canada in 1921, he held that post until 1945. Philosophically committed to a co-operative world view, he encouraged all forms of co-operative organizations (*see* CO-OPERATIVE MOVEMENT). IAN MACPHERSON

Gooderham, William, distiller, businessman, banker (b at Scole, Eng 29 Aug 1790; d at Toronto 20 Aug 1881). Migrating to Canada in 1832, Gooderham became involved in the Toronto milling trade with his brother-in-law James Worts, who died in 1834. From a small distillery built in 1837 to handle surplus grain from his flour mill, Gooderham and his nephew, James Gooderham Worts, constructed Canada W's largest distillery in 1859, and by 1875 they were producing one-third of all proof spirits distilled in Canada and were one of Canada's most successful distilling firms. Gooderham was also president of the Bank of Toronto from 1864 until his death, a promoter of the Toronto and Nipissing Railway, and one of Toronto's most prominent businessmen. The Gooderham and Worts empire encompassed not only distilling and railways but lake transportation, livestock yards, retailing, woollen mills and banking. Gooderham prospered by embracing new techniques and new markets, thereby spreading his risk in an economy subject to sharp fluctuations.

The Gooderhams have remained prominent in Toronto business and philanthropy. **William Jr** (1824-89) pursued a less successful commercial career but was influential in philanthropy and Methodism. Another son, **George** (1820-1905), served as president of the Bank of Toronto and of Gooderham and Worts. His son **Sir Albert Edward** (1861-1935) helped manage the family business while pursuing philanthropic interests, notably the establishment of Connaught Laboratories.

DUNCAN MCDOWALL AND DON SPENCER

Goodridge, Augustus Frederick, businessman, politician (b at Paignton, Eng 1839; d at St John's 16 Feb 1920). First elected as a Conservative in 1880, Goodridge moved into Opposition in the mid-1880s and became leader in 1884-85. He was a member of the Reform Party government led by Sir Robert THORBURN 1885-89. He became premier of Newfoundland in Apr 1894 when

William WHITEWAY's government resigned after petitions alleging corrupt electoral practices against a majority of its members had been filed in the Supreme Court. Goodridge's Tory government clung to power for 8 months amidst growing political and financial chaos, resigning on Dec 12 after the collapse of the 2 local banks.

ROBERT D. PITT AND J.K. HILLER

Goodwin, Albert, "Ginger," labour leader, socialist (b at Barnsley, Eng 10 May 1887; d at Willemar Lake, Vancouver I 27 July 1918). A resident of Cumberland, BC, he participated in the 1912-14 Vancouver I coal miners' strike. In 1917 he was elected to the executive of the BC Federation of Labour and to the presidency of District 6 of the International Union of Mine, Mill and Smelter Workers in the Kootenays. After falling out with that union, he organized the Trail Trades and Labour Council, which he led in a strike for the extension of the 8-hour day.

When conscription became law in 1917, Goodwin was classified as fit for military service even though tuberculosis had previously rendered him unfit. By then he had enemies not only in management and the government but also in the union of which he had been president. After twice vainly appealing his reclassification, he and several other draft evaders hid in the bush near Cumberland, where they were provided with supplies by people from the town. Police Constable Dan Campbell tracked him down and killed him. Campbell was charged with manslaughter but was exonerated before a grand jury, meeting *in camera*. Goodwin's friends, both then and in the years since, have pointed out many discrepancies in the official record. On the day of his funeral, Aug 2, the Trades and Labor and Metal Trades Council of Vancouver called all members out for 24 hours to protest "the shooting of Brother A. Goodwin." The overwhelming response gave BC its first general strike.

LYNNE BOWEN

Goose, member of a widespread group of WATERFOWL ranging in size from the giant Canada goose (*Branta canadensis maximus*) to the diminutive cackling goose (*B.c. minima*). The term goose is applied to many species of waterfowl in the Southern Hemisphere, but the only true geese are found in N America, Europe and Asia. Geese belong to 2 main groups, true geese (genus *Anser*) and Brant geese (*Branta*). Some taxonomists subdivide geese into additional groups, eg, Hawaiian goose or nene (*Nesochen*), emperor goose (*Philacte*) of Alaska, bar-headed goose (*Eulabia*) of Tibet and India, or snow geese (*Chen*). Their taxonomy at the specific and subspecific level is very complicated, especially in the races of the Canada goose and bean goose (*Anser fabilis*). There are 7 species of geese in N America, most of which breed in the boreal forest and TUNDRA. The Canada goose may have as many as 50 distinct races and variations, ranging in size from the cackling goose of Alaska (1 kg) to the Canada goose of Manitoba (10 kg); all have the same general pattern of black neck and head with a white throat patch. Brant geese (*B. bernicla*) are divided into 4 populations: those from the eastern QUEEN ELIZABETH IS winter in Ireland; those from the western Queen Elizabeth Is in Puget Sound and the lower BC mainland; those on the coastal tundra of the NWT in Baja, California; and those from FOXE BASIN off the coast of New Jersey. The lesser and greater white-fronted geese (*A. erythropus* and *A. albifrons*, respectively) are circumpolar, breeding in the arctic tundra. Snow geese (*Chen caerulescens*) breed in the High Arctic and Ross's geese (*C. rossii*) in the Low Arctic. Geese in Canada are intermediate in size between swans and ducks. Males are called ganders; juveniles, goslings. Geese are believed to mate for life. Members of various species may nest singly or in colonies. Usually 3-6 eggs are laid (range 2-9) in a nest of plant debris, moss, etc, lined with down. Both parents care for young.

F.G. COOCH

Gordon, Andrew Robertson, physical chemist, educator (b at Toronto June 26 1896; d there 29 July 1967). He was an officer in the Canadian Field Artillery in WWI and was appointed to the department of chemistry of U of T in 1925. He was widely recognized for his pioneering research on the calculation of chemical properties by quantum statistical mechanics and in 1946 received an OBE for research and advice during WWII. He made significant contributions to the theory of electrolytic solutions. Head of the department of chemistry 1946-60, he was a founding member of the Defence Research Board and founding director of ATOMIC ENERGY OF CANADA LTD. He greatly improved the stature of graduate studies as dean of graduate studies, University of Toronto, 1953-64.

D.J. LE ROY

Gordon, Sir Charles Blair, banker, manufacturer (b at Montréal 22 Nov 1867; d there 30 July 1939). Five years after beginning work in a dry-goods store, Gordon formed the Standard Shirt Co and in 1904 oversaw the organization of Dominion Textiles. He became company president 1909 and was a founder and president of Dominion Glass. Recognized as a consummate organizer and a shrewd financier, Gordon's career paralleled the consolidation of Canadian business and the rise of Montréal as Canada's banking centre. His long-standing association with the BANK OF MONTREAL was marked by his appointment as a director 1913 and president 1927. During WWI, Gordon served on the IMPERIAL MUNITIONS BOARD in Ottawa and with the British War Mission in Washington. He received a knighthood for his contributions.

PETER E. RIDER

Gordon, Charles William, pen name Ralph Connor, clergyman, novelist (b in Glengarry Cy, Canada W 13 Sept 1860; d at Winnipeg 31 Oct 1937). The most successful Canadian novelist in the early 20th century, Gordon used literature as a pulpit to preach his energetic branch of "red-blooded Christianity." Educated at U of T and Edinburgh, he was ordained a Presbyterian minister in 1890 and undertook mission work for 3 years in the Banff, Alta, area before becoming a pastor in Winnipeg. In 1897, as a fund-raising effort, he published some short stories about mission work in the West, and with their success he began producing best-selling western novels such as *The Sky Pilot* (1899) and *The Prospector* (1904). These early novels are fast-paced, sentimental melodramas, with stereotyped characters dramatizing the conflict between good and evil in frontier settings presided over by exemplary churchmen. The greatest influence on Gordon after his mother was Dr James ROBERTSON, the Presbyterian superintendent of missions in the West, whose biography Gordon wrote in 1908. Gordon also published several novels set in Glengarry County, including GLENGARRY SCHOOL DAYS (1902), in which he recreated the history of settlement there.

During WWI, after serving in France as chaplain to the Canadian forces, Major Gordon toured the US speaking in favour of American participation in the war. His novels then and afterwards were broader in scope and setting, more bluntly didactic in applying theology to modern society, and less popular than his westerns. Returning to Winnipeg, he chaired the Manitoba Council of Industry for 4 years after the 1919 WINNIPEG GENERAL STRIKE and negotiated in numerous labour disputes. In 1921 he became moderator of the Presbyterian Church in Canada and helped form the

Charles W. Gordon, who wrote under the pen name Ralph Connor, served as chaplain to the 43rd Cameron Highlanders of Canada (*courtesy National Archives of Canada/C-19115*).

UNITED CHURCH in 1925. His autobiography, *Postscript to Adventure*, was published posthumously in 1938.

TERRENCE CRAIG

Reading: Ralph Connor, *The Man from Glengarry* (2nd ed, 1960) and *The Prospector* (1904).

Gordon, Crawford, business executive, public servant (b at Winnipeg 26 Dec 1914; d at New York City, NY 26 Jan 1967). Educated at private schools and McGill, Gordon worked in the Dept of Munitions and Supply during WWII. At the end of the war he became C.D. HOWE's director of industrial reconversion. After a stint in private industry Gordon returned to government service in 1951 as co-ordinator of production for the Dept of Defence. Sent to the A.V. Roe aircraft plant at Malton, Ont, to improve production of the AVRO CF-100 fighter, Gordon was president and general manager of the company 1951-59. He presided over the development of the CF-105 (AVRO ARROW), cancelled by the government in 1959.

ROBERT BOTHWELL

Gordon, Donald, banker, business executive (b at Old Meldrum, Scot 11 Dec 1901; d at Montréal 2 May 1969). Gordon left Scotland when young and joined the Bank of Nova Scotia, working up through the ranks while attending night school. He was rewarded with promotions to head office and eventually to the Toronto branch. In 1935 he was recruited as secretary of the new Bank of Canada and in 1938 became deputy governor. When war broke out Gordon was assigned to the Foreign Exchange Control Board and in 1941 was made chairman of the WARTIME PRICES AND TRADE BOARD, a job at which he was highly successful. In 1947 he returned to the Bank of Canada, leaving again in 1950 to become president and chairman of the CNR. Gordon presided over a difficult period of labour troubles, a declining share of passenger traffic, the expense of modernization and demands to appoint more French Canadians to senior management. He claimed that he had done all that he could with what was available and in response was burned in effigy in

Montréal. Gordon retired in 1967 to become president of Brinco and chairman of the CHURCHILL FALLS power project. ROBERT BOTHWELL

Gordon, John King (b at Winnipeg 6 Dec 1900), son of Charles GORDON (pen name Ralph Connor). After studying at U of Manitoba, Oxford and Union Theological Seminary, Gordon taught at United Theological College in Montréal. His departure from the college because of his socialist views provoked a notable debate on ACADEMIC FREEDOM. He was a founding member of the Fellowship for a Christian Social Order, the LEAGUE FOR SOCIAL RECONSTRUCTION and the CO-OPERATIVE COMMONWEALTH FEDERATION. In New York C he was managing editor of *The Nation* (1944-47) and joined the staff of the UN, serving it in critical times in Korea, the Middle East and the Congo. After 1962 he taught international relations at the universities of Alberta and Ottawa, was chairman of CUSO, president of the United Nations Assn and an adviser to the International Development Research Centre. JOHN W. HOLMES

Gordon, Walter Lockhart, public servant, politician, author (b at Toronto 27 Jan 1906; d there 25 Mar 1987). Gordon was educated at Upper Canada College and RMC, becoming a partner in the accounting firm Clarkson, Gordon and Co in 1935. During WWII he served in the Bank of Canada and the Ministry of Finance; in 1946 he chaired the Royal Commission on Administrative Classifications in the Public Service, and 1955-57 the Royal Commission on CANADA'S ECONOMIC PROSPECTS. Gordon's concern for Canadian economic independence led him into the Liberal Party after L.B. PEARSON became leader in 1958; in May 1963 Gordon became minister of finance in the Pearson government. His 1963 budget proposal for a tax on takeovers of Canadian firms was withdrawn under pressure, and his influence in Cabinet waned until his resignation after general election of Nov 1965. He returned to Cabinet as president of the privy council in 1967 to oversee the Watkins task force on the structure of Canadian industry, and resigned after completion of the report in 1968. In the 1970s he inspired the COMMITTEE FOR AN INDEPENDENT CANADA; in the 1980s he gave leadership to the movement for nuclear arms control and disarmament. DENIS SMITH

Reading: Walter Gordon, *A Political Memoir* (1977); Denis Smith, *Gentle Patriot* (1973).

Gore, Francis, colonial administrator (b at Blackheath [London], Eng 1769; d at Brighton, Eng 3 Nov 1852). The third lt-gov of Upper Canada, he came to the colony after a brief career in the army and as lt-gov of Bermuda. His first term (1806-11) was marred by bitter quarrels with Judge Robert Thorpe and Surveyor General Charles B. Wyatt, which ended in their suspension from office. He was absent on leave during the War of 1812. His second term (1815-17) closed with his prorogation of the Assembly, which had objected to his ban on the issuing of land patents to American immigrants, was impatient with delays in obtaining compensation for wartime damage to private property and was dissatisfied with his slow administration. Before that, he had got on well with the Assembly and had secured bills to build roads, reorganize the militia and found schools. He returned to England to become a deputy teller of the Exchequer. S.R. MEALING

Gorman, Charles, speed skater (b at Saint John 6 July 1897; d at St Martins, NB 11 Feb 1940). Despite suffering a shrapnel wound in one leg during WWI, Charlie Gorman's international success earned him the title of "the man with the million dollar legs." Developing a long, sweeping stride, he won the 1924 US amateur title and the world championship 2 weeks later. He lost both in 1925 but defeated Clas Thunberg, the 1924 Olympic champion, to reclaim his world title the next year. On his retirement in 1928 he held 7 world records. J. THOMAS WEST

Gosford, Archibald Acheson, 2nd Earl of, colonial administrator (b in Ire 1 Aug 1776; d at Markethill, Ire 27 Mar 1849). Scion of a prominent Anglo-Irish family, he was an outspoken opponent of the ORANGE ORDER and strongly supported a policy of conciliation in Ireland. After a parliamentary career he was appointed gov gen of British N America in 1835 and placed in charge of a commission of inquiry into the crisis in LOWER CANADA. A number of its recommendations were embodied in the Russell Resolutions in 1837. From 1835 to 1837 Gosford vainly sought to satisfy the Assembly of LC without alienating the colony's anglophone minority, but his efforts at conciliation did divide the PATRIOTE Party and helped limit the support given the REBELLIONS OF 1837. He resigned in Nov 1837, after violence began, and finally left Canada for England in Feb the following year. His tragedy was that he had been sent to govern Lower Canada at a time when a peaceful solution to the crisis there was no longer possible. P.A. BUCKNER

Gosling, William Gilbert, merchant, politician, author (b at Paget, Bermuda 8 Sept 1863; d there 5 Nov 1930). Gosling came to Newfoundland in 1881 as a clerk with a fish-exporting firm. Known for his literary interests, Gosling organized an urban-reform movement in St John's in 1913. As a result the city's elective council was replaced by a 12-man commission which drafted a new municipal charter under Gosling's chairmanship. Although the legislature initially refused to pass the charter, Gosling was elected mayor in June 1916. During his tenure he promoted public housing, tax reforms and the formation of the Child Welfare Assn. He finally got the legislature to pass the charter in 1921 – the basis of present municipal government in St John's – and withdrew from public life. He wrote *A History of Labrador* (1910) and a biography of Sir Humphrey GILBERT (1911). His extensive collection of books formed the basis of the city's first public library. MELVIN BAKER

Goss, William Arthur Scott, civic employee and photographer (b at London, Ont 4 Mar 1881; d at Toronto 1 June 1940). As official photographer for Toronto 1911-40, he produced over 30 000 photographs documenting a period of dramatic expansion in the city's history. These photographs are characterized by their realism and technical brilliance. An exponent of "pictorialism," in which photography was employed for artistic ends, Goss came into contact with many Canadian artists, and his soft-lens portraits and landscapes received critical acclaim in Canada and abroad. VICTOR RUSSELL

Gosse, Philip Henry, naturalist, religious writer (b at Worcester, Eng 6 Apr 1810; d at St Mary Church, near Torquay, Eng 23 Aug 1888). The foremost popularizer of natural history in mid-Victorian England and leader of a Brethren community in Devonshire, he made his decision to devote his life to the study of nature and the practice of evangelical Christianity during years spent in Canada. Gosse left Poole, Eng, in 1827 to work for 8 years as a clerk in a merchant's counting-house at Carbonear, Nfld. Then in 1835 he attempted to farm just N of Compton in Lower Canada. The experiment proved a failure and he left Canada in 1838. Although Gosse's sojourn did not influence significantly his achievements, he has a place in the history of Canadian science. He was the first person to investigate systematically and record the entomology of Newfoundland. *The Canadian Naturalist* (1840; repr 1971) was Gosse's popular book on the flora and fauna of the Eastern Townships. Characteristically accurate and original in its ecological descriptions, though weak in taxonomy, the work provided first lessons for later generations of Canadian naturalists. DOUGLAS WERTHEIMER

Gotlieb, Allan Ezra, public servant (b at Winnipeg 28 Feb 1928). A Rhodes scholar and international lawyer with a reputation for intellectual toughness, Gotlieb joined the Dept of External Affairs in 1957, and was assistant undersecretary and legal adviser 1967-68. A member of P.E. TRUDEAU's inner circle, he was deputy minister of the new Dept of Communications 1968-73 and of Manpower and Immigration 1973-76. He returned to External Affairs as undersecretary 1977-81 and has since been ambassador to Washington where he played a highly visible role under both Liberal and Conservative prime ministers. He is the author of *Disarmament and International Law* (1965), *Canadian Treaty-Making* (1968) and *Impact of Technology on International Law* (1982). He is a Companion of the Order of Canada and is married to Sondra GOTLIEB.

ANNE HILLMER AND NORMAN HILLMER

Gotlieb, Calvin Carl, "Kelly," professor emeritus of computer science (b at Toronto 27 Mar 1921). A pioneer in the computer industry, Gotlieb received a PhD in physics from U of T in 1947. A founding member of the university's computation centre in 1948, he began teaching computer science in 1951. In time his interest shifted from hardware to computer applications and software, and eventually to the socioeconomic implications of computer technology. He was instrumental in founding the Computing and Data Processing Assn of Canada (now the Canadian Information Processing Soc) in 1958. An expert in mathematical, business and scientific applications, he has been consulted on social issues, timetables, graph theory, international development, and seaway calculations since 1950. His publications include *Social Issues in Computing* (co-author, 1973) and *Economics of Computers* (1985). J. KNELMAN

Gotlieb, Phyllis Fay, née Bloom, author (b at Toronto 25 May 1926). Raised and educated in Toronto, Gotlieb received her BA (1948) and MA (1950) from U of T. She has published 4 volumes of poetry: *Within the Zodiac* (1964), *Ordinary Moving* (1969), *Doctor Umlaut's Earthly Kingdom* (1974) and *The Works* (1978); her novel *Why Should I Have All the Grief?* (1969) explored her Jewish roots. She began writing science fiction in the 1960s and has published 5 sci-fi novels: *Sunburst* (1964), *O Master Caliban* (1976), *A Judgement of Dragons* (1980), *Emperor, Swords, Pentacles* (1982) and *The Kingdom of Cats* (1985). *Sunburst* has been translated into Dutch, French, Norwegian and German; *O Master Caliban* into Japanese, German and Italian. Gotlieb has also written numerous short stories in the sci-fi genre, which have been anthologized in collections, and has published one volume of her own short stories, *Sun of the Morning* (1983). Her poetry, blending fantasy and metaphysics, predicts her subsequent development as a science-fiction writer. She has distinguished herself as world-class in this genre. She is also the author of "Hasidic Influences in the Work of A.M. Klein" (Klein symposium, U of Ottawa, 1974), an in-depth analysis of this aspect of Klein's writing. SHARON DRACHE

Gotlieb, Sondra, author (b at Winnipeg 30 Dec 1936). Educated in Winnipeg, she has published 2 novels: *True Confections* (1978), subtitled *Or*

How My family Arranged My Marriage, which won the Stephen Leacock Medal for Humour, and *First Lady, Last Lady* (1981), a lively tale of diplomatic life. Gotlieb also writes nonfiction: *The Gourmet's Canada* (1972), *Cross Canada Cooking* (1976), and has written articles for *Saturday Night, Maclean's, Chatelaine* and the *New York Times*. In 1985 she published *"Wife of...,"* a collection of her bimonthly columns in the *Washington Post*. This irreverent account of life in US Powertown is a universal undressing of public personalities, written with characteristic wit.

Goudge, Thomas Anderson, philosopher (b at Halifax 19 Jan 1910). A student of G.S. BRETT at Toronto (PhD 1937), he spent a year at Harvard during a time of intense interest in mathematical logic and philosophy of science there. Appointed to U of T (1938-76), he introduced these subjects into a curriculum focused on the history of philosophy. While chairman, expanding enrolment allowed him to appoint people to work in these and other areas of contemporary interest. His publications include a study of *The Thought of C.S. Peirce* (1950), a logician, philosopher of science and early pragmatist, and *The Ascent of Life* (1961), which maintains that evolutionary biology explains the world in a manner unlike, for example, that of physics. He is a fellow of the Royal Society of Canada (1955). THOMAS MATHIEN

Goudie, Elizabeth, née Blake, writer (b at Mud Lake, Lab 20 Apr 1902; d at Happy Valley, Lab 10 June 1982). Of Inuit, Indian, French and English ancestry, she married Jim Goudie, a Labrador trapper, in 1920. For 40 years she raised her family and lived the difficult life of a trapper's wife. Her husband died in 1963 and Goudie wrote her autobiography, *Woman of Labrador* (1973). The book combined a history of Labrador with a moving story of Goudie's life. The first recorded story of a trapper and his family in the Labrador wilds, it drew warm praise from the critics and she became internationally known. JOHN PARSONS

Gouin, Sir Jean-Lomer, lawyer, politician, premier of Québec (b at Grondines, Canada E 19 Mar 1861; d at Québec City 28 Mar 1929), was the father of Paul GOUIN, founder and leader of the ACTION LIBÉRALE NATIONALE. Of modest origins but well connected following his marriage to the daughter of Prem Honoré MERCIER, Gouin began his career in Montréal civic politics, joining the provincial Cabinet in 1900. He became premier in 1905, continuing and defending his predecessor S.N. PARENT's policy of industrial development against a concerted attack by Henri BOURASSA. Although welcoming foreign investment to develop Québec's resources, Gouin was anxious that French Canadians should share the benefits of industrialization. He became a committed educational reformer, eventually serving as president of Université de Montréal and chairman of 2 enquiries into public education in the 1920s.

Like other Québec Liberals, Gouin felt betrayed when the federal government imposed CONSCRIPTION in WWI but reaffirmed his commitment to Confederation in the "Francoeur Debate" of 1918 and ran for Parliament in 1921, having resigned from the premiership in July 1920. Minister of justice 1921-24 in Mackenzie KING's Cabinet, he functioned primarily as spokesman for tariff-protected industries, contributing to an impression that he had become a tool of powerful financial interests. Disillusioned, the author of Québec's dramatic emergence as an industrialized province soon retired from politics. He became lt-gov of Québec in 1929, but died after less than 3 months in office. BERNARD L. VIGOD

Gouin, Paul, lawyer, politician (b at Montréal 20 May 1898; d there 4 Dec 1976), son of Lomer GOUIN and grandson of Honoré MERCIER, both former prime ministers of Québec. In 1934 Gouin established the ACTION LIBÉRALE NATIONALE which attracted reform-minded Liberals and nationalists opposed to the policies of the TASCHEREAU administration. Prior to the 1935 elections, Gouin formed an alliance with Conservative Party leader Maurice DUPLESSIS; he soon became disenchanted with Duplessis, however, and left the coalition before the 1936 elections which Duplessis's UNION NATIONALE won handily. Most of Gouin's followers abandoned him to follow Duplessis. After the demise of the ALN, Gouin contributed to the foundation of the BLOC POPULAIRE CANADIEN in 1942. RICHARD JONES

Gouin, Réservoir, 1570 km^2, elev 404 m, max length 102 km, average depth 5 m, third-largest "lake" (really a collection of hundreds of small lakes containing innumerable islands) in Québec, is located in S-central Québec, equidistant from Ottawa, Montréal and Québec City. It was created in 1918 at the upper reaches of Rivière ST-MAURICE by the Québec Streams Commission to facilitate power developments on the St-Maurice R by controlling the flow of water. The reservoir was named after Sir Jean-Lomer GOUIN, premier of Québec 1905-20. DAVID EVANS

Gould, Glenn Herbert, pianist, writer, broadcast and recording artist (b at Toronto 25 Sept 1932; d there 4 Oct 1982). Dissatisfied with the concert medium, he abandoned a thriving international concert career for performances using recorded-sound technology. His work had a unique importance in music and communications. Gould received his musical education at the ROYAL CONSERVATORY OF MUSIC, where his piano teacher was Alberto Guerrero. He was concerto soloist with the Toronto Symphony at age 14. Solo concerts, appearances with many Canadian orchestras, and CBC network broadcasts, as well as his championing of nonstandard piano fare (Bach, the 16th-century English keyboardists, moderns such as Hindemith and Schoenberg) placed him among Canada's leading musical performers when still in his early twenties. Debuts in Washington, DC, and in New York C in Jan 1955, and his first US recording later that year (Bach's *Goldberg Variations*), brought immediate international attention. Concerts and orchestral engagements in the US, England, Austria, Germany, Israel and the USSR (where he was one of the first Canadians to tour) followed, along with regular recordings. He was summer music co-director at the STRATFORD FESTIVAL 1961-64.

Glenn Gould, one of the most brilliant pianists of his generation, in rehearsal, Toronto, 1974 *(courtesy National Archives of Canada/PA-137052/Walter Curtin)*.

Then in 1964 Gould retired from the concert stage, preferring the possibilities inherent in recording technology over "live" performance with what he called its "non-take-two" limitations and frequent sports-arena atmosphere. It was an unprecedented – and rigidly kept – resolve, but not a surprising one for this exceptional and unorthodox figure. Gould's pianism was marked by uncanny linear detail and strong drive. His classical realizations were often provocative, and occasionally eccentric, in tempo and articulation. The music's contrapuntal fabric held for him far more importance than its sensuous appeal. His recorded repertoire includes virtually all the Bach and Beethoven keyboard works, much Mozart, much early-to-middle 20th-century music, but few 19th-century piano staples.

His later personal appearances in public were rare, but his career expanded into TV and radio documentaries (on both musical subjects – eg, the conductor Stokowski, one of his idols – and nonmusical ones – eg, *The Idea of North*, prompted by a train trip to Churchill, Man). His literary flair, already familiar from radio scripts and record sleeve notes, broadened in significant articles and reviews (*Globe and Mail, New York Times Magazine, High Fidelity, Piano Quarterly)* on everything from concert life and technology to admired popular stars (Barbra Streisand, Petula Clark). He also created backgrounds for several US and Canadian films. He received the Harriet Cohen Bach Medal (1959) and the Molson Prize (1969). Geoffrey Payzant's *Glenn Gould: Music and Mind* (1978) is an in-depth account of Gould's singular views on musical aesthetics.

In 1981 Gould recorded the Bach "Goldbergs" a second time, announcing this as his farewell to piano-solo recordings. He began experimental taping sessions as conductor with small ensembles, intending to make this his new concentration. The day after his 50th birthday he suffered a severe stroke from which he never recovered. In his honour the Glenn Gould Foundation was established to commemorate the work of celebrated Canadian musicians. JOHN BECKWITH

Goulden, Cyril Harold, geneticist (b at Bridgend, Wales 2 June 1897; d at Ottawa 4 Feb 1981). Son of a homesteader, Goulden took the course for farmers at U of Sask and went on to a PhD in plant breeding before becoming chief cereal breeder at the Dominion Rust Research Laboratory, Winnipeg, in 1925 (*see* J.H. CRAIGIE). He succeeded L.H. NEWMAN as Dominion cerealist in 1948 and later became assistant deputy minister for research in the Dept of Agriculture. Contrary to early genetic theory, wheat resistance to rust diseases was controlled not by a single gene but by the interaction of several – which made both plant genetics and its application to farming much more difficult. A natural mathematician, Goulden took up the new specialty of biostatistics (and wrote the first N American textbook on the subject in 1937 for the students he taught at U of Man). As head of cereal breeding at Winnipeg for 23 years, Goulden was responsible for the creation of Renown, Regent and Redman wheats, suitable for the Canadian climate and possessing various rust-resistant qualities. He also developed 6 varieties of rust-resistant oats.
DONALD J.C. PHILLIPSON

Goulding, George Henry, track and field athlete (b at Hull, Eng Nov 1885; d at Toronto 3 Feb 1966). Originally attracted to marathon racing with the Toronto Central YMCA, he began "heel-and-toe" (walk) racing on a whim, first appearing internationally at the 1908 London Olympics; he placed 4th in the 3500 m walk. At the 1912 Stockholm Olympics he won gold in the 10 000 m walk. Turning to invitational track meets in Canada, Britain and the US, he won 300 races at distances from 1 to 40 miles. He competed in many stunt races, winning against a man driving a horse and buggy and against a 4-man US relay team, and attracted thousands of spectators wherever he competed. TED BARRIS

Goulds, Nfld, Town, pop 4688 (1986c), inc 1971, is an inland agricultural and residential community 12 km S of St John's. Its name may be derived from "golds," which described yellow flowers abundant in the area. Its first settlers, by 1857, were farmers and the area continues to be one of the few good agricultural regions on the Avalon Peninsula. In this century Goulds became predominantly a residential suburb of St John's and until incorporation was under the jurisdiction of the St John's Metropolitan Area Board. Because of the scarcity of fertile land, its farmland is protected by legislation and development has been restricted to nonarable areas.
ROBERT D. PITT

Goulet, Robert Gerard, baritone, actor (b at Lawrence, Mass 26 Nov 1933). His rich voice and expert showmanship have gained him critical acclaim and popularity in Canada and the US. After training in Edmonton and Toronto, Goulet sang minor roles in the CANADIAN OPERA CO and made his CBC TV debut in 1954. Appearances with CBC, "Theatre Under The Stars," and STRATFORD FESTIVAL followed. Goulet's realization of the role of Sir Lancelot in Lerner and Loewe's *Camelot* (Toronto and New York, 1960) was an immediate triumph and led to a successful career in the US in the 1970s, mostly as a nightclub entertainer.
ANN SCHAU

Gourlay, Robert Fleming, polemicist, reformer (b at Craigrothie, Scot 24 Mar 1778; d at Edinburgh, Scot 1 Aug 1863). A successful farmer and writer who fell into financial difficulties, he came to UPPER CANADA in 1817 to take up land he owned in Dereham Township and to write an immigrant's guide. The questionnaire and township meetings that he arranged to get information being thought radical, he was refused the grant of land on which he had planned to settle families from Scotland. He attacked the FAMILY COMPACT and became its most celebrated victim. Twice acquitted of libel, he was banished for sedition in 1819 after a trial in which it became clear that his mental health had failed. He published more than 80 titles, most of them vituperative defences of his own conduct. His 2-vol *Statistical Account of Upper Canada* (1822) is the most systematic contemporary survey of the province. In the introduction he condemned the government of Upper Canada, especially John STRACHAN. He thought that general ownership of land was the only sound basis for society and proposed a land tax to fund immigrants. His later advocacy of a union of British N America was written from an asylum in England. In the US in 1837 he condemned W.L. MACKENZIE's rebellions. He believed in petitioning and withholding supply as constitutional methods of achieving reform. His banishment was rescinded in 1839, and he returned to Upper Canada in 1856. After failing to be elected in 1858, he went back to Scotland. S.R. MEALING

Reading: R.F. Gourlay, *Statistical Account of Upper Canada*, ed S.R. Mealing (1974); L.D. Milani, *Robert Gourlay, Gadfly* (1971).

Gouverneur (governor), the French monarch's official representative in NEW FRANCE. The office, created before a complete system of government had been established, was always granted to a member of the nobility by royal commission, and the appointment could be withdrawn at any time. The governor had to account for his administration annually to the minister of marine (*see* MINISTÈRE DE LA MARINE), who was responsible for the colonies. The governor had far-reaching powers, most importantly external affairs (relations with the native nations and with the British colonies) and military matters. As commander in chief of the army, he determined peace or war. He and the INTENDANT jointly supervised the colony's development, handled SEIGNEURIAL land grants and controlled the FUR TRADE. Through his prestige, power and advice, the governor played a major political and social role. Samuel de CHAMPLAIN has often been considered New France's first governor; celebrated ones of later years were FRONTENAC, Philippe de Rigaud de VAUDREUIL, and his son Pierre de Rigaud de VAUDREUIL. *See also* GOVERNOR GENERAL.
JACQUES MATHIEU

Gouzenko, Igor Sergeievich, intelligence officer, author (b at Rogachov, USSR 13 Jan 1919; d near Toronto late June 1982). At the beginning of WWII Gouzenko took intelligence training and in 1943 was appointed cipher clerk at the Soviet legation in Ottawa, where he learned that Soviet intelligence operated several spy networks in Canada. Disenchanted with Soviet life and politics, he decided to defect when he learned in 1945 that he and his family were to be sent home. On Sept 5 Gouzenko left the embassy with documents illustrating Soviet espionage activities. Initially, no one in Ottawa took him seriously; only on Sept 7, following an abortive Soviet attempt to recapture him, were he and his family given protective custody. When it became evident that a widespread espionage network was operating, Mackenzie KING's government authorized the arrest of 12 suspects. After interrogation, they were brought before a royal commission. Gouzenko's testimony and documents impressed the commissioners, who confirmed in July 1946 that a spy ring had been operating in Canada, aimed at, among other things, the secrets of the atomic bomb. A number of suspects were subsequently convicted and imprisoned.

Igor Gouzenko, a cipher clerk at the Soviet embassy in Ottawa, defected in 1945. His life was surrounded in secrecy although he emerged from time to time, wearing a mask (*courtesy National Archives of Canada/PA-129625/Montreal Star*).

Gouzenko was given a new identity, and for the rest of his life he and his family had police protection. He produced a memoir, *This Was My Choice* (1948), and a novel, *The Fall of a Titan*, which received the Gov Gen's Award (1954). From time to time he emerged from the shadows, always wearing a protective mask, which for most Canadians became his trademark. Even his death, apparently from natural causes, was surrounded in secrecy. ROBERT BOTHWELL

Government in its narrow sense may refer to the group of ministers comprising the CABINET, as in "the Mulroney government" or "the Getty government." It may mean the whole STATE apparatus including the Cabinet, the legislature, the courts, the civil service, the armed forces and so on, as in "Why doesn't the government do something about it?" or "Too much government in our lives." A third meaning has to do with the achievement and exercise of power. A government is different from other organizations in society because of its ability to make rules for the whole society. This results from its control of the police and the army, but also from a recognition by the citizens of the government's legitimacy.

Organization of Government In Canada the government's legitimacy derives from the CONSTITUTION. Powers of government are divided among its branches – legislature, executive and JUDICIARY. In the legislature elected representatives adopt laws and vote on taxes and other revenues. The executive proposes legislation, presents budgets to the legislature and implements laws. The judiciary is the final interpreter of the laws.

In a democracy it is not sufficient that the legislature members be elected (the SENATE is an exception to this rule); in the parliamentary tradition inherited from Great Britain the ministers of the executive must resign when they fail to retain the confidence of the majority of the members of the legislature. The courts must be free to interpret the laws without interference from Cabinet ministers or members of the legislature. In recent decades this balance has been threatened by the growth of the executive, partly the result of the complexities of expanding state power. Federally and provincially the executive has 3 separate parts. The head of state is the Queen's representative: federally, the GOVERNOR GENERAL; provincially, the LIEUTENANT-GOVERNORS. He or she must approve laws and important executive decisions before they come into effect. However, by convention, if the Cabinet has the support of a majority of the legislature the head of state's role is purely formal. The second part of the executive is the Cabinet, comprising the prime minister (leader of the majority party) and ministers chosen by him from among the leading members of his party in the legislature. Most ministers will be appointed to head a government department, but some will be given co-ordinating posts and others will have special duties, eg, government leader in the legislature. The third and largest part of the executive is the administration – the government departments, armed forces and various autonomous bodies. While departments are the basic organs of administration, answering through their minister to the legislature, the autonomous bodies, eg, CROWN CORPORATIONS and regulatory commissions, have more limited roles. Other boards run government insurance and loan schemes; ADMINISTRATIVE TRIBUNALS are used in areas such as income tax, immigration and social services.

Levels of Government, Centralization and Decentralization Although national, provincial and municipal levels of government exist in Canada, only the first 2 have clear powers which other levels cannot usurp (*see* DISTRIBUTION OF POWERS). MUNICIPAL GOVERNMENTS have only those powers that are granted to them by their provincial governments; one of the important changes in Canadian government since 1867 has been the assumption by the national and provincial governments of functions once belonging to municipalities. (Centralization is the concentration of decision-making authority in a national or higher-level government, while DECENTRALIZATION, on the other hand, is the distribution of such authority to regional or local governments.)

Changing Role of Government In 1867 the BRITISH NORTH AMERICA ACT assigned to the federal government authority or jurisdiction over defence and external affairs, criminal law, money and banking, trade, transportation, citizenship and Indian affairs. The provinces were to be responsible for education, civil law (including property and civil rights), health and welfare, natural resources and local government. The 2 levels of government were assigned joint jurisdiction over agriculture and immigration and, as it evolved, over most revenue sources. Changing social and economic conditions and ideas about the proper role of government have brought one level and then the other into prominence. In the 19th century, although the predominant philosophy was laissez-faire or nonintervention by government in economic life, the federal government used its control of the tariff to encourage industry in the East and used a combination of land and money grants to private companies to build railways, first the INTERCOLONIAL to the Maritimes, then the CANADIAN PACIFIC to the West. The provinces also plunged into support for railway building, but they were engaged in an almost constant struggle with the federal government to establish their claim to adequate powers and revenues. From 1900 to 1930 (excepting WWI), the provinces dominated as prosperity brought rising revenues to their governments. They built dams and highways and extended school and health services. The new urban, industrial and commercial life led to government regulation of health and safety, trade practices, highway traffic, etc – all provincial responsibilities. War and depression, however, brought the federal government again to the fore. In both world wars it not only directed the defence effort but used the powers given to the cabinet by the WAR MEASURES ACT to direct the economy. It took the leading part in organizing relief measures during the Great Depression. Various joint federal-provincial programs were created for public works and "back to the land" projects, as well as for the provision of direct relief.

Following the Royal Commission on DOMINION-PROVINCIAL RELATIONS (1937-40) the federal government proposed that it assume direct responsibility for regulating the economy and for the most important social insurance programs in exchange for the lion's share of government revenues. The provinces rejected this proposal at a conference in 1941, but many of the ideas were introduced piecemeal. By constitutional amendment, with the consent of the provinces, the federal government was given responsibility for unemployment insurance in 1940 and old-age pensions in 1951. Also with provincial consent, family allowances were created by federal law in 1944 and the CANADA PENSION PLAN in 1965 (introduced 1966). Conditional financial grants (or shared-cost programs) were used increasingly in the postwar period by the federal government to prod the provinces to action in fields such as highway construction (the Trans-Canada Highway), post-secondary and university education, unemployment assistance, hospital insurance and health insurance.

Because of these initiatives and because of international tension after WWII, the provinces did not achieve until the 1960s the kind of primacy they enjoyed in the 1920s. While many foreign observers find Canada a very decentralized state with strong powers vested in the provinces, the latter continue to feel that the federal government interferes in the discharge of their responsibilities. For its part, as costs soared in the late 1970s, the federal government tried to find ways to limit its expenses, especially in health and higher education programs.

Controlling the Administrative State With the growth of the WELFARE STATE and increasing government management of the economy, the administrations of all levels of government have expanded and become increasingly difficult to control. The number of people working directly or indirectly for one level of government or another represents about 18% of the labour force. The size and complexity of government departments have challenged the principle of ministerial responsibility. Members of Parliament have a full-time job trying to oversee the activities of the government and the administration. The role of the courts is being taken over in many cases by administrative tribunals.

Since the mid-1960s different solutions to these difficulties have been suggested. Cabinets have created their own planning and co-ordinating staffs, usually grouped around the prime minister or the TREASURY BOARD. The Cabinet has often developed a specialized committee structure to do the detailed work, leaving only broad questions of policy for plenary sessions. The legislatures have also created committees whose members specialize in the affairs of one or 2 departments. They have streamlined their procedures and introduced small research budgets to allow Opposition parties to conduct their own studies. The measures taken to control government power include the establishment of OMBUDSMEN. FREEDOM OF INFORMATION laws have made some government information open to public scrutiny, and the CANADIAN CHARTER OF RIGHTS AND FREEDOMS has enabled the courts to invalidate laws or administrative actions infringing on basic personal freedoms or rights.

Disillusion with the welfare state has led others to propose more radical solutions, involving some reduction or "downsizing" of governments. Most new governments these days will have on their agenda proposals involving one or more of the following: having private companies do work that has traditionally been done by civil servants ("contracting out"); selling off certain crown corporations ("privatization"); reducing government regulation of private enterprises ("deregulation"). J.I. Gow

Reading: Audrey D. Doerr, *The Machinery of Government in Canada* (1981); J. McMenemy, *The Language of Canadian Politics* (1980); J.R. Mallory, *The Structure of Canadian Government* (rev ed, 1984).

Government Building Government has always been the most important patron of ARCHITECTURE in Canada, and this role has increased rapidly over the past few decades. As its duties and responsibilities expand, so do its building needs. Today all levels of government contribute to all aspects of our built environment. Courthouses, schools, hospitals, military buildings, firehalls, market halls, factories, theatres, museums, police stations, recreational buildings and housing are required for the varied functions of government. The buildings most readily identified with gov-

Early government buildings, such as Government House, Fredericton, NB, drew upon 18th-century Palladian traditions, a classical mode of building. These impressive buildings reinforced the presence of British rule (*courtesy National Archives of Canada/C-3558*).

ernment are those housing the central legislative and administrative portions of the political system. On the municipal level, government is identified with city hall and on the provincial level with buildings housing the legislature. The federal government is identified by the federal buildings in Ottawa and by hundreds of post offices, customs houses and office buildings in all parts of the country.

Design of government buildings varies according to the changing institutions and functions of the state as well as the changing architectural tastes. Despite this diversity, common themes or characteristics can be identified regardless of the date of construction. Government buildings tend to be constructed of enduring materials, commonly stone or brick, which impart a sense of weight, permanence and stability. Scale varies according to function, but generally government buildings are designed to dominate their surroundings, thereby visually establishing their central role in the community. Only in Québec was this position of dominance challenged by the church. In style, government buildings conform to current tastes in design, but government architecture has traditionally incorporated symmetrical elevations and balanced compositions. These aesthetic qualities reinforce values of order, reason and balance considered appropriate to the state. More significantly, government buildings are not generally noted for their architectural daring. As a symbol of the established state and its political traditions, governments prefer architecture that is contemporary but also reflects accepted standards.

The earliest government buildings in Canada were erected in the early 17th century for the French settlements in New France and Acadia. A legislative council building, called the Senéchaussée, was built in Québec in the mid-17th century, but the most important government building was the Château Saint-Louis, the residence of the governor. Typical of the initial phases of settlement, the first Château Saint-Louis was a simple, unpretentious structure. Located within the military compound on top of Cap-Diamant, it differed little in design from the surrounding military buildings. Only its larger scale and prominent setting overlooking the cliffs visually distinguished it from its immediate surroundings.

In 1663 New France was named a province of France, and the local government became directly responsible to the Crown. This new status marked the colony's transition from a rough military and commercial outpost of empire into a permanent centre of French culture and society. This growing maturity was soon reflected in its major government buildings. In 1692 plans were drawn up for a new Château Saint-Louis. Built of stone, 2 storeys in height with a steeply pitched roof, symmetrical plan and impressive central frontispiece, it resembled French palaces of the 17th century. The palatial quality of key government buildings in New France was equally evident in the 1715 design of the palace of the intendant. Like the Château Saint-Louis it was a 2-storey, dressed-stone building with a mansard roof, a U-shaped plan with a projecting frontispiece and 2 end pavilions. The palace contained a large assembly room for the meetings of the legislative council as well as numerous private apartments, a chapel, stables and beautifully landscaped gardens.

After the fall of New France the influx of United Empire Loyalists following the American Revolution greatly consolidated the British presence. At the end of the 18th century, centres of colonial government had been established in St John's, Halifax, Fredericton, Charlottetown, Québec City and York [Toronto]. The major government buildings were the residence of the governor, and the legislative buildings which housed both the legislative council and the legislative assembly.

The first 4 decades of the 19th century were a period of growth and stabilization for these British settlements. In the Atlantic colonies this change was reflected in the construction of a number of imposing public edifices, including new governors' residences in Halifax (1800-05), Fredericton (1826-28) and St John's (1827-31), and a series of legislative buildings or province houses in Halifax (1811-18), Charlottetown (1839-48) and St John's (1847-50). These buildings have much in common. All were designed by architects or builders trained in Britain either as civilians or as officers of the Royal Engineers. They drew upon the well-established, 18th-century, British Palladian tradition, a classically inspired mode of building which featured a symmetrical plan, often with flanking wings or projecting pavilions, and a large central portico set upon a rusticated or arcaded base. The imposing visual impact of these dignified classical buildings was greatly enhanced by their use of finely dressed stone. Their weight and mass set them apart from the surrounding buildings, which were predominantly of wood, and reinforced the idea of these buildings as the keystones of British rule.

During the same period Upper and Lower Canada were reluctant to spend large sums on lavish architecture, although several plans had been submitted for public buildings. Because the Canadas were so vulnerable to attack from the US, budgetary priority was given to military works in the form of canal systems and fortifications. The government institutions of Upper Canada were first housed in a long range of military buildings on the lakefront, and later in a slightly more refined but still fairly modest one-storey brick structure (1831) situated on Front Street in York. In Lower Canada, the legislature met in the old episcopal palace of the French regime (Québec), which had been refurbished in a more anglicized style in 1831. The construction of permanent government buildings was further delayed by the union of the Canadas in 1841 and by the failure of the new government to choose a permanent site as the capital.

In 1857 Ottawa was selected as the seat of government for the united Canadas and work then began on the construction of an appropriate home for the colonial parliament. A fanciful Gothic design for a Parliament building and 2 departmental blocks in the same style was selected in 1859. The picturesque design, with its irregular skyline, rich textures, polychromatic stonework and intricate medieval detailing, differed substantially from the cold, reserved classicism of the earlier legislature buildings in the Atlantic colonies; but in many respects the Ottawa buildings share a common visual language consistent with other government architecture in Canada. The use of stone and the grand scale visually dominated and overpowered the town that surrounded it. Despite the fanciful quality of the detail, the architects consciously avoided the usual asymmetry of the Gothic style and imposed a formal, symmetrical composition on the overall plan and elevation. Like the earlier legislature buildings, the design of the Ottawa PARLIAMENT BUILDINGS was self-consciously British. Inspired by the example of the new Parliament Buildings in London, begun in 1836, and by the prevailing perception of the Gothic style as being the only truly British style, a Gothic design for the Ottawa buildings reconfirmed the cultural and political bonds with Britain that set Canada apart from the American republic.

The establishment of a federal government in 1867 created a demand for public buildings across the country. Although many existing post offices and customs houses had been inherited from the old colonial institutions, the new government recognized the need to project a fresh and dynamic image by constructing substantial public buildings. This initial federal building program was dominated by the Second Empire style, characterized by a high mansard roof and by ornately carved classical ornamentation. It was a rich style, evocative of wealth, confidence and a sense of grandeur. This style was applied to some 24 post offices and customs houses erected under the direction of the Dept of Public Works in the 15 years following Confederation, thereby imposing a unified architectural theme on federal buildings across the country.

From Confederation to the end of WWI the appearance of federal architecture changed with

The Saskatchewan Legislative Building, Regina, like all legislature buildings of the 3 Prairie provinces, was designed in the grand classical manner, at the height of the Beaux-Arts fashion (*photo by Jim Merrithew*).

changing architectural fashions. In the early 1880s the now outdated Second Empire style gave way to a late Victorian Romanesque vocabulary with its heavy stonework, round arches and massive, off-centre clock towers. This general profile of public building became so strongly associated with the federal government that it persisted into the 1920s and even into the early 1930s. Gradually, however, this type was replaced by the Beaux-Arts style of the 1910s and 1920s. But despite these changes in style, federal buildings continued to be visually consistent. Their solid stone or brick construction and their prominent setting established an imposing presence in the community and the repetition of related design types across the country created recognizable symbols of the federal government.

The 1930s marked a transitional phase in federal architecture. Stylistically, this era was characterized by an aesthetic compromise between traditional classicism and the modern movement. Federal buildings retained the formal, symmetrical composition and the sense of mass and weight; but in place of the traditional decorative vocabulary a modernistic language was used featuring austere stylized forms, clean crisp lines and sculptural motifs based on contemporary iconography. In the 1930s a new type of federal building was introduced. Whereas previously the regional departments of the federal government consisted primarily of the post office, customs house and perhaps the Inland Revenue Department, during the Depression the regional activities of the federal government expanded. In large urban centres, such as Halifax, Toronto, Winnipeg and Regina, the government constructed a number of "Dominion" or "Federal" buildings which were large, multistoried buildings housing a variety of federal offices under one roof.

Confederation had also created the secondary, provincial level of government, but the provinces were slower to express themselves architecturally. In the established eastern provinces most legislatures continued to use existing colonial buildings, and the provinces of NS and PEI continue to do so today. In the late 1870s Québec and NB were the first to construct new legislature buildings, both of which imitated the federal example by employing the mansarded Second Empire style. The newly founded province of Manitoba also received a fairly substantial legislature building, built by the federal government as part of the Confederation agreement. It was later replaced by a legislature building of the province's own design.

At Confederation the western regions were still relatively undeveloped. This was evident in their unassuming government architecture. Only BC, whose origins as a colony dated from the mid-19th century, had a sizable legislature building. This curious structure, known locally as the "Birdcage," was built 1859-64. It consisted of a series of separate structures grouped in an ordered symmetrical composition which imposed the sense of visual formality characteristic of government architecture; but its light, rather exotic design with an intricate pattern of half-timbering, ornate eave brackets and bellcast roof lacked dignity and decorum. The "Birdcage" was replaced in 1898 and destroyed by fire in 1957.

The second phase of provincial architecture dates from the turn of the 20th century when both the provinces of Ontario and BC constructed their own lavish legislature buildings which reflected the eclectic tastes of the late Victorian era. The picturesque synthesis of Romanesque, medieval and classical motifs of the BC Legislature Buildings represents the extravagant example of this period. The Prairie provinces adopted a very different style of building. Constructed during the

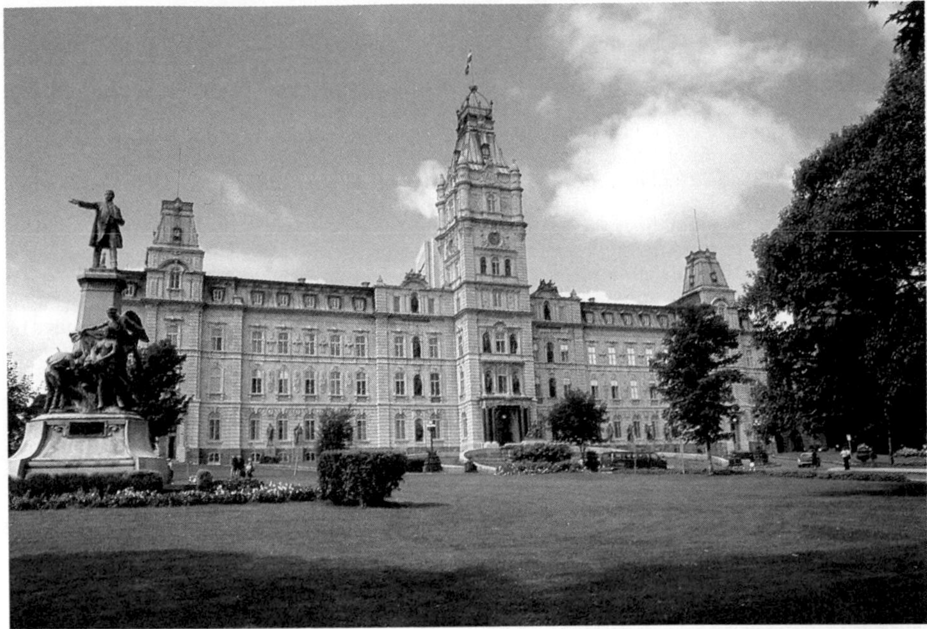

Québec National Assembly, Québec City (*courtesy Environment Canada, Parks/Heritage Recording Services*).

height of the Beaux-Arts fashion, all 3 legislature buildings (Edmonton 1908-12, Regina 1908-12, Winnipeg 1913-29) were designed in the grand classical manner, with monumental porticos, crisp stonework and massive central domes. The strong association between provincial architecture and an austere classicism continued well into the post-WWII period. In 1959 Newfoundland constructed a new provincial legislature building. Although modernistic in its absence of historical details and its vertical strip windows, its symmetrical plan recalls the classical formalism of the earlier provincial buildings.

After WWII conventional architecture gave way to the modern age and a new language of bold geometric masses formed of steel, concrete and glass. Since that time there have been no new legislature buildings, with the exception of Newfoundland, but governments have been actively building. The expansion of government activities led to the need for a range of building types more specialized in function. Often these buildings have a lower profile than previous government architecture. For example, over the past 30 years the federal post office has gradually moved out of its old buildings, which had formed the visual core of so many towns, into small, open structures that quietly merge into the streetscape rather than control it. In the provincial and federal capitals the public service has grown at a rapid pace, creating a vast demand for new office accommodation. The buildings constructed to meet this need often lack the sense of monumentality and grandeur that sets them apart from surrounding structures. Governments now occupy glass and concrete office towers that are indistinguishable from those of any other large corporation, as the new federal office buildings in Hull, Qué, exemplify.

High-profile architecture represents the smallest but most prominent category of government building: monumental architecture whose scale, materials and setting distinguish it from its surroundings. The courthouse in Vancouver, designed by Arthur ERICKSON, with the daring and dramatic slope of its glass wall, or the 1964 Confederation Centre in Charlottetown, featuring a monolithic, almost primitive form of stone slab construction, are both high profile, as is Canada Place, an enormous glass structure built for the federal government in Edmonton (scheduled completion 1988). Though the language of architecture has changed substantially from the early 19th century, these modern buildings still serve as visual anchors to the community and as symbols of provincial and national pride. JANET WRIGHT

Government Organization, Royal Commission on (Glassco Commission), was appointed in 1960 under J. Grant Glassco, a prominent businessman and chartered accountant, to inquire into the organization and methods of the departments and agencies of the federal government. It investigated 23 departments, the armed forces, 21 statutory boards and 42 corporations. The commissioners also visited the UK and the US. Taking testimony from former US president Herbert Hoover the commissioners earned themselves the sobriquet "the Canadian Hoover commission," after the aggressive inquiries conducted by Hoover into the American administrative structure. The 5-volume commission report (released 1962-63) recommended that government should "let the managers manage"; that departments should be free of inappropriate central control and should be allowed to devise management methods suited to their needs; that TREASURY BOARD should be reorganized to control and harmonize government operations; and that senior officials should rotate from department to department. A special Bureau of Government Organization was created to implement the recommendations, many of which were put into practice through the Transfer of Duties Act and later consolidated in the Government Organization Act (1966). Most observers acknowledge that the Glassco reforms did not work, particularly regarding the role of Treasury Board; that the commission did not address the operations of the executive and Parliament; and that the result was a growth of CENTRAL AGENCIES lacking effective control and unity. S.L. SUTHERLAND

Governor General Without interruption since the beginning of European settlement in Canada, a governor or governor general has been at the head of the country as the resident representative of the CROWN. Although the modern office is usually regarded as descended from the British institution, the present governor general, the Rt Hon Jeanne SAUVÉ, is in fact the sixtieth successor to Champlain, who became governor in 1627; she is the twenty-third since Lord MONCK was sworn in

Governors General

French Regime	
Samuel de Champlain	1612-29; 1533-35
Charles de Montmagny	1636-48
Louis d'Ailleboust de Coulonge	1648-51
Jean de Lauson	1651-56
Vicomte d'Argenson	1658-61
Baron Davaugour	1661-63
Sieur de Mézy	1663-65
Sieur de Courcelle	1665-72
Comte de Frontenac	1672-82
Joseph de La Barre	1682-85
Marquis de Denonville	1685-89
Comte de Frontenac	1689-98
Louis de Callière	1699-1705
Marquis de Vaudreuil (Philippe)	1705-25
Marquis de Beauharnois	1726-47
Marquis de La Jonquière	1749-52
Marquis Duquesne de Menneville	1752-55
Marquis de Vaudreuil-Cavagnal (Pierre)	1755-60
British Regime	
James Murray	1764-68
Sir Guy Carleton (Baron Dorchester)	1768-78
Sir Frederick Haldimand	1778-86
Baron Dorchester	1786-96
Robert Prescott	1797-1807
Sir James Craig	1807-11
Sir George Prevost	1811-15
Sir John Sherbrooke	1816-18
Duke of Richmond	1818-19
Earl of Dalhousie	1820-28
Baron Aylmer	1831-35
Earl Amherst	1835
Earl of Gosford	1835-37
Earl of Durham	1938
Sir John Colborne	1839
Charles Poulett Thomson (Baron Sydenham)	1839-41
Sir Charles Bagot	1841-43
Sir Charles Metcalfe	1843-45
Earl Cathcart	1846-47
Earl of Elgin	1847-54
Sir Edmund Head	1854-61
Viscount Monck	1861-67
Post Confederation	
Viscount Monck	1867-68
Sir John Young (Baron Lisgar)	1869-72
Earl of Dufferin	1872-78
Marquess of Lorne	1878-83
Marquess of Landsdowne	1883-88
Baron Stanley of Preston	1888-93
Earl of Aberdeen	1893-98
Earl of Minto	1898-1904
Earl Grey	1904-11
Duke of Connaught	1911-16
Duke of Devonshire	1916-21
Lord Byng	1921-26
Viscount Willingdon	1926-31
Earl of Bessborough	1931-35
Lord Tweedsmuir	1935-40
Earl of Athlone	1940-46
Viscount Alexander of Tunis	1946-52
Vincent Massey	1952-59
Georges Vanier	1959-67
Roland Michener	1967-74
Jules Léger	1974-79
Edward Schreyer	1979-84
Jeanne Sauvé	1984-

at CONFEDERATION on 1 July 1867; and she is the first woman to be appointed to the office. The office has developed with Canada's evolution from colony to nation. At first, governors general represented imperial governments and were responsible to various colonial ministers. After Confederation they were empowered to govern according to the wishes of the Canadian PRIME MINISTER in all internal issues, but until WWI they were still obliged to acknowledge British policy in EXTERNAL RELATIONS. After the STATUTE OF WESTMINSTER of 1931, they became the SOVEREIGN'S personal representatives. Finally, on 1 Oct 1947, George VI formally delegated to the governor general all the sovereign's authority in Canada. In 1952 Vincent MASSEY became the first Canadian to be appointed governor general. Since then, a tradition of alternating anglophone and francophone governors general has emerged.

Earl of Minto, governor general of Canada 1898-1904 (*courtesy National Archives of Canada/C-8465*).

In Canada, as in many constitutional monarchies, there is a clear division between the office of the head of state and that of the head of government. The latter is occupied by the prime minister, an elected political leader. The former is held by the governor general who, like the sovereign, stands above politics. Appointed by the sovereign on the prime minister's recommendation, the governor general usually holds office for at least 5 years. Whereas the prime minister speaks for the political majority, the governor general represents the whole country.

On taking office (at a ceremony usually held in the Senate Chamber), a governor general is accorded the title "Right Honourable" for life and "His Excellency" or "Her Excellency" for the period in office. Two official residences are provided: RIDEAU HALL, which forms part of a 36 ha estate on the Ottawa R, and the Governor's Wing at the QUÉBEC CITADEL. The salary was fixed, in s105 of the BRITISH NORTH AMERICA ACT, at £10 000, an amount corresponding to the 10 000 *livres* set as the salary of the governor of New France in the 1660s. In 1970 this was converted as $48 666.63. The governor general's personal standard flies wherever he or she is in residence and takes precedence over all other flags in Canada except the monarch's. It is dark blue with, at the centre, the gold Canadian crest: a crowned lion carrying a red, stylized maple leaf in his right paw.

Gov Gen Jeanne Sauvé's coat of arms. The gold mace represents her tenure as speaker, the fleur de lis her French Canadian heritage. The motto translates "Strength and Tolerance" (*courtesy Government House, Ottawa*).

Parliament has 3 elements: the SENATE, the HOUSE OF COMMONS and the queen. As the queen's representative, the governor general summons, prorogues and dissolves Parliament, authorizes treaties, receives and sends ambassadors, commissions officers in the armed forces and gives royal assent to bills that have passed both the House of Commons and the Senate, thereby giving them the force of law. By constitutional convention, the governor general exercises these prerogatives only in accordance with ministerial advice. But by the same conventions, he or she retains special personal authority in times of emergency or in exceptional circumstances; in such cases, he or she may appoint or dismiss a prime minister and may dissolve Parliament. On at least 2 occasions since Confederation (1891, 1893) governors general (Lords STANLEY and ABERDEEN) had to designate a prime minister, but they have never had to dismiss one. At least once (1926) a governor general (Viscount BYNG) refused a prime minister's advice to dissolve Parliament (*see* KING-BYNG AFFAIR).

The governor general also holds the constitutional rights of the head of state: "the right to be consulted, the right to encourage, the right to warn." These are usually exercised by the receipt of Cabinet minutes and through regular visits from the prime minister and government officials. The governor general is the executive power of the governor-in-council, receiving advice from the Canadian PRIVY COUNCIL (the most important part of which is the CABINET) and signing ORDERS-IN-COUNCIL.

The governor general is designated by law as commander in chief of the Armed Forces, is charged with swearing in Cabinet ministers and commissioning high officials of state. He or she is chancellor of the Order of Canada and the Order of Military Merit, and is responsible for the administration of the whole Canadian system of HONOURS. The governor general is official host to visiting heads of state and can represent Canada abroad.

Extensive hospitality and travel within Canada make the governor general more familiar with the country, the people and the issues than most others can be. The office of governor general is also charged with symbolizing national community and continuity. It is a subtle presence above divisions and differences, affirming community, an acceptance of inherited loyalties and permanent ideals. *See also* GOUVERNEUR.

JACQUES MONET, S.J.

Reading: Jacques Monet S.J., *The Canadian Crown* (1979).

Governor General's Literary Awards were first presented in 1936 by the CANADIAN AUTHORS ASSN. The CAA did the judging itself until 1944, when an independent Awards Board was established. In 1959 the CANADA COUNCIL undertook to administer the awards and to provide at least 6 prizes of $1000 each for fiction, nonfiction, and

Recent Governor General's Award Winners

Year	Fiction	Poetry and Drama	Nonfiction
1982	G. Vanderhaeghe, *Man Descending*	P. Webb, *The Vision Tree*	C. Moore, *Louisburg Portraits*
	R. Fournier, *Le Cercle des Arènes*	M. Savard, *Forages*	M. Lagueux, *Le Marxisme des annés soixante*
1983	L. Rooke, *Shakespeare's Dog*	D. Donnell, *Settlements*	J. Williams, *Byng of Vimy*
	S. Jacob, *Laura Laur*	S. Paradis, *Un goût de sel*	M. Cusson, *Le contrôle social du crime*
1984	Josef Škvorecký, *The Engineer of Human Souls*	Paulette Jiles, *Celestial Navigation*	Sandra Gwyn, *The Private Capital: Ambition and Love in the Age of Macdonald and Laurier*
	Jacques Brault, *Agonie*	Nicole Brossard, *Double Impression*	Jean Hamelin and Nicole Gagnon, *Le XXe siècle: Histoire du cumolisme québécois*
		Judith Thompson, *White Biting Dog*	
		René-Daniel Dubois *Ne blâmez jamais les Bédoins*	
1985	Margaret Atwood, *The Handmaid's Tale*	Fred Wah, *Waiting for Saskatchewan*	Ramsay Cook, *The Regenerators: Social Criticism in Late Victorian English Canada*
	Fernand Ouellette, *Lucie ou un midi en novembre*	André Roy, *Action Writing*	François Ricard, *La Littérature contre elle-même*
		George F. Walker, *Criminals in Love*	
		Maryse Pelletier, *Duo pour voix obstiñees*	
1986	Alice Munro, *The Progress of Love*	Al Purdy, *The Collected Poems of Al Purdy*	Northrop Frye, *Northrop Frye on Shakespeare*
	Yvon Rivard, *Les silences du corbeau*	Cécile Coutier, *L'écouté*	Rejean Robin, *Le réalisme socialiste: une esthetique impossiblé*
		Sharon Pollock, *Doc*	
		Anne Légault, *La visite des sauvages*	

drama or poetry in English and French (previous awards had been for works in English only). That year the category of juvenile literature, which had been established in 1948, was dropped. In 1971 the council assumed responsibility for appointing two 9-member juries – one anglophone and one francophone – drawn from among experienced writers, academics and literary critics. The cash award was raised to $5000 in 1975, and the separate category of drama was added in 1981.

Like any prize, the Gov Gen's Awards are controversial from time to time; contemporary judgements do not always stand the test of time. There is a general complaint that writers have not always won for their best work, and there are specific criticisms (eg, the failure of Northrop FRYE's *The Great Code* to win an award in 1983). Some winners have refused to accept the award for political reasons. Nevertheless the Gov Gen's Awards are the pre-eminent LITERARY PRIZE offered for single works in Canada, and they serve to reward Canadian writers, as well as to publicize Canadian writing through the ceremonies held in various centres across the country. The 1986 awards were presented by Gov Gen Sauvé in Toronto 27 May 1987.

Gowan, Sir James Robert, lawyer, jurist, senator (b at Cahore, County Wexford, Ire 22 Dec 1815; d at Barrie, Ont 18 Mar 1909). At 27, Gowan was the youngest judge appointed in Canada W, and he sat on the bench 1843-83. He organized the judicial system in the newly created district of Simcoe, the largest jurisdiction in the colony. Gowan also served as Sir John A. MACDONALD's unofficial legal draftsman and sat on several royal commissions. These included every committee struck to revise the statute law of Canada W, Ontario and post-1867 Canada, and the commission that investigated the PACIFIC SCANDAL in 1873. Gowan also chaired several academic boards and, in 1855, founded the first legal periodical in Canada W, *The Upper Canada Law Journal*, which survives as the *Canadian Bar Review*. In 1885 he was appointed to the Senate.
D.H. BROWN

Grace, Nathaniel Hew, chemist (b at Allahabad, India 10 Nov 1902; d at Rochester, Alta 13 Nov 1961). The son of a missionary, Grace attended schools in California and Saskatchewan. He graduated from U of Sask (1925) and completed his PhD in physical chemistry at McGill (1931). He spent the next 20 years with the NATIONAL RESEARCH COUNCIL in Ottawa, where his diverse contributions included pioneering work on plant growth regulators. He was appointed an MBE in 1946 for research related to wartime shortages of raw materials. In 1951 Grace joined the ALBERTA RESEARCH COUNCIL as its first full-time director of research. Under his guidance, the council initiated important new areas of activity, notably groundwater and hailstorm research. Grace's dedication to research of social significance and high scientific quality laid the foundation for the research council's important role in the development of Alberta.
E.J. WIGGINS

Grackle, *see* BLACKBIRD.

Gradus, Lawrence, choreographer (b at Brooklyn, NY 30 Oct 1936). Trained in New York C, he first performed with the American Ballet Theatre in 1951, rising from corps member to soloist. He joined Les GRANDS BALLETS CANADIENS in 1968 and co-founded with Ludmilla CHIRIAEFF Les Compagnons de la danse, an educational touring group. Gradus formed his own company, Entre-six (1974), and the following year received the Jean A. Chalmers Choreographic Award. He moved to Ottawa as artistic director of the THEATRE BALLET OF CANADA in 1980. The company performs primarily his creative work in which ballet and modern dance flow easily together.
JILLIAN M. OFFICER

Graham, Andrew, fur trader (b probably near Edinburgh, Scot *c*1733; d at Prestonpans, Scot 8 Sept 1815). Graham worked for the HUDSON'S BAY COMPANY at Churchill, YORK FACTORY and Ft Severn (1749-75). One fish and 4 birds sent by him from Ft Severn in 1771 were immortalized as "type specimens" when given Latin names by Johann Reinhold Forster in England. At York Factory in 1771-72, closely associated with surgeon Thomas Hutchins, Graham wrote important accounts of the native peoples, birds and mammals of HUDSON BAY, including the first description of the "plunge-holes" made by the great gray OWL, in catching mice beneath deep snow. Graham described 111 bird species and Hutchins added another 12. The contributions of the 2 men were sorted out nearly 200 years later by Glyndwr Williams and published in 1979 as *Andrew Graham's Observations on Hudson Bay, 1767-1791.*
C. STUART HOUSTON

Graham, Howard Douglas, lawyer, army officer (b at Buffalo, NY 15 July 1898; d at Oakville, Ont 28 Sept 1986). A WWI veteran, having enlisted at age 17, Graham rose to become chief of the general staff 1955-58. He practised law in Trenton, Ont, 1922-39, and was mayor in 1933. He was a militia officer between the wars and went overseas as second-in-command of the Hastings and Prince Edward Regiment in late 1939 and commanded the regiment 1940-42. As commander of 1st Canadian Infantry Brigade 1943-44, he served in Sicily and Italy. He remained in the army after WWII, becoming the only army chief who had not devoted the bulk of his career to professional soldiering. After retirement he was president of the Toronto Stock Exchange 1961-66. His memoirs, *Citizen and Soldier* (1987) appeared shortly after his death.
NORMAN HILLMER AND WILLIAM JOHNSTON

Graham, Hugh, Baron Atholstan, newspaper publisher (b at Atholstan, Canada E 18 July 1848; d at Montréal 28 Jan 1938). In 1863 Graham went to work on the Montréal *Daily Telegraph* and by 1869 became a partner in the new evening paper, the *Star*. He transformed the *Star* into Canada's largest and most profitable daily, partly through technical innovations such as its overseas cable service and especially through its loyalty to the British imperialist ideal. Partly owing to the *Star*'s pressure, the LAURIER government decided to commit Canadian troops to the SOUTH AFRICAN WAR. For his crusades during WWI (when his home was dynamited by anticonscriptionists), Graham was elevated to the peerage in 1917 as Baron Atholstan of Huntingdon, Qué, and Edinburgh, Scot.
DOUGLAS FETHERLING

Graham, Laurie, alpine skier (b at Orangeville, Ont 30 Mar 1960). A skier from the age of 5, she began competing in the Nancy Greene Ski League at 10 and reached the international circuit at 17, winning the Nor-Am downhill championship in her first year. Over the decade since her debut on the World Cup circuit in 1977, she has become one of its best known and accomplished skiers, winning 6 races including the first World Cup downhill held in Canada at Mt Tremblant, Qué, in 1983. As a downhill specialist known for her technical skill, she also demonstrated great versatility at Puy St Vincent, France, in 1984 by becoming the first Canadian to win a World Cup Super Giant Slalom.
MURRAY SHAW

Graham, Stuart, aviator (b at Boston, Mass 2 Sept 1896; d at Port Charlotte, Fla 16 July 1976).

Raised and educated in NS, he served in the Royal Naval Air Service, patrolling shipping lanes in flying boats. He was Canada's first professional peacetime pilot and his forestry patrol near Grand-Mère is regarded as the beginning of BUSH FLYING in Canada. He was decorated by Emperor Haile Selassie for organizing civil aviation in Ethiopia. JAMES MARSH

Grain Elevators provide for the storage, cleaning and weighing of grain and for its loading from elevator bins into railway cars and trucks or from port elevators into ships. The name is derived from its essential mechanical feature, the elevator proper or "leg" – an endless belt carrying a succession of buckets, which lift the grain from a low-level pit (into which it has been delivered) to the top of chutes, which lead to the storage or cleaning bins.

Both concrete and timber elevators are familiar Canadian landmarks, the latter perhaps being the most distinctive architectural symbol of the Prairies. Elevators spread with the CANADIAN PACIFIC RY across the Canadian West in the 1880s; after 1900 a second wave of construction followed the building of the CANADIAN NORTHERN RAILWAY. By the 1930s there were nearly 6000, though the number has declined as farming and transportation have grown more efficient. Because elevators are essential to the movement and marketing of grain, their history is intertwined with economics and politics, especially the development of the CO-OPERATIVE MOVEMENT and the wheat pools. The familiar rectangular, pitched-roof country elevators appeared from 1881 when the first was built by the Ogilvie Milling Co in Gretna, Man (a circular wooden elevator was built at Niverville, Man, in 1879). Many more were soon built at railway sidings across the Prairies, within easy reach of the farms. From them, grain was moved by rail to much larger terminal elevators at port cities, where it was loaded for shipping to the East and overseas. The first Canadian terminal elevator was completed by the CPR in 1884 at Port Arthur [Thunder Bay], and others rapidly followed. A third type, transfer elevators, were built at such inland centres as Calgary, Edmonton, Saskatoon and Moose Jaw for the collection of grain and its distribution to regional markets.

Country elevators and the earliest terminal elevators were built of timber, though frequently covered with sheet metal. The construction of walls and bins was of "crib": 2 x 6- or 2 x 4-inch timbers laid one above another on the flat and spiked together, with the ends alternately overlapping at the corners. A typical elevator might be 9-10.5 m on side in plan, rising 23 m or more above massive concrete foundations to the ridge of the narrower top section or cupola. Such an elevator held 35 000 to 40 000 bushels of grain. While wood has remained the most economical material for country elevators, from the 1900s slip-formed cylindrical concrete bins became the standard for the larger transfer and terminal elevators. The first was built at Minneapolis, Minn, in 1901, using recent European innovations in the reinforcing and forming of concrete silos. Canadian examples followed, and reinforced concrete was used at Port Arthur around 1903. Port of Montréal Elevator No 2 (completed 1912; demolished 1978) was one of the earliest all-concrete structures, "at the time probably the largest and highest concrete building in existence," according to its designers, the John S. Metcalf Co. Founded in Chicago, Ill, in 1887 by John S. Metcalf of Sherbrooke, Qué, the company built huge elevator complexes across the US and Canada, and in Europe, S Africa, Argentina and Australia from its offices in Montréal, Vancouver, Chicago and London, Eng. Another major grain-elevator engineering firm, founded by C.D. HOWE, was responsible for the SASKATCHEWAN WHEAT POOL'S North Vancouver Terminal (1966-81). These structures were not only impressive engineering feats but were an inspiration to pioneering European architects. Photographs of elevators at Calgary and Montréal were given by Walter Gropius to Le Corbusier and published in his *Vers une architecture* (1923).

Recent innovations include the sloped-bin concrete "Buffalo" and the diamond-shaped "Buffalo 2000" elevators designed for the Alberta Wheat Pool by K.U. Driedger of A.B.L. Engineering Ltd. The first such country elevator was built at Magrath, Alta, in 1980 and by 1987, 6 had been completed. Though more expensive than timber elevators, the new designs are fireproof, more efficient and more durable. The technology has been sold to Brazil. MICHAEL MCMORDIE

Grain elevators, like these in southern Alberta, are familiar landmarks across the western prairies (*photo by Richard Harrington*).

Grain Growers' Associations, a group of farm organizations formed on the Prairies in the early 20th century. They developed in the wake of the Manitoba Grain Act (July 1900), which regulated railways and grain elevators in the interests of grain growers. This Act, the result of considerable agitation in rural areas since the late 1880s, was regarded by farmers as a major victory. But dissatisfaction with the handling of the 1901 bumper crop led farmers at Indian Head (in present-day Saskatchewan) to convene a meeting in Dec 1901, at which the Territorial Grain Growers' Assn was formed. The Manitoba Grain Growers' Assn, established 1903 at Virden, followed. In 1906 the Territorial Grain Growers' Assn was divided into the Saskatchewan Grain Growers' Assn and the Alberta Farmers' Assn. The latter joined with the Canadian Society of Equity to create the UNITED FARMERS OF ALBERTA in 1909. In 1920 the Manitoba Grain Growers' Assn was reorganized as the UNITED FARMERS OF MANITOBA in an attempt to gain the support of all farmers and to proclaim an intention to enter politics. The Saskatchewan Grain Growers' Assn amalgamated with the Farmers' Union of Canada in 1926 to create the militant UNITED FARMERS OF CANADA (Saskatchewan Section).

Grain growers' associations were powerful spokesmen for the Prairies and Canadian agriculture generally. They lobbied provincial and federal governments for reform of the grain-marketing system and improvement of rural life. They sponsored the development of 3 large farmer-owned grain-marketing organizations, the Grain Growers' Grain Co (1906), the Saskatchewan Co-operative Elevator Co (1911) and the Alberta Farmers' Co-operative Elevator Co (1913). They published the GRAIN GROWERS' GUIDE 1908-28, which was the main voice of western agriculture until the mid-1920s. The associations agitated for better roads, schools and medical care for the countryside. Particularly responsive to the plight of rural women, they embraced WOMEN'S SUFFRAGE and helped to win the vote for women on the Prairies during WWI. Technically, the associations were politically neutral, but some early leaders, such as Liberals C.A. DUNNING, M.A. MOTHERWELL and T.A. CRERAR, achieved national political prominence. Politics, however, was a vexing issue for the associations and was one of the reasons they disappeared after farmers began to assert themselves and demand a more direct voice in the political process. IAN MACPHERSON

Reading: W. Irvine, *The Farmers in Politics* (1920).

Grain Growers' Guide, journal published 1908-28 for Prairie grain growers' associations. In 1928 it became the *Country Guide*, which is still published by the United Grain Growers in Winnipeg. Editors included E.A. PARTRIDGE, Roderick McKenzie and (1911-35) George Chipman. The *Guide* advocated educational reform to make rural schools more responsive to change, and it supported the TEMPERANCE MOVEMENT, the CO-OPERATIVE MOVEMENT and the SOCIAL GOSPEL. Its commentators included Nellie MCCLUNG, Irene PARLBY and Violet MCNAUGHTON, prominent leaders of the women's movement. Its commitment to reform made the *Guide* a major spokesman for the PROGRESSIVE PARTY. During the early 1920s, as the Progressive movement declined, the *Guide*'s commitment to reform waned, and by 1928 it was devoted to rural life, advising farmers on technical problems and providing amusement for rural families. In its day the *Guide* articulated a western rural view with vigour, style and effectiveness.
IAN MACPHERSON

Grain Handling and Marketing There are approximately 120 000 grain-producing farms in Canada. Yearly production varies substantially, depending on climatic conditions. In 1985-86 approximately 32 million t of grain were marketed, wheat accounting for over 67% of this total. Harvested in the late summer and early fall, grain is trucked from the combine to storage bins located on the farm. Storage time on the farm varies, depending upon delivery opportunities at primary grain elevators as determined by the CANADIAN WHEAT BOARD (CWB). Some grain does not enter the commercial grain-handling system, but is retained as seed or consumed locally as livestock feed.

The CWB is the agricultural marketing board responsible for the marketing of western Canadian grains (WHEAT, OATS, BARLEY) intended for human consumption or export. Feed grains may be sold to the CWB at the farmer's discretion; however, sale of OILSEEDS and most feed and industrial grains is privately controlled. In addition to marketing as much grain as possible at the best possible prices, the CWB aims to provide price stability and ensure that each producer gets a fair market share each crop year. The CWB periodically issues delivery quotas, which tell farmers that the board is willing to accept a certain volume of a specified grain from each farmer at primary elevators in a defined geographic region. Quotas, based on the board's sales commitments and stocks on hand in the elevator system, are issued so as to maintain a relatively even flow of grain from farms through the primary elevator system. Before making export commitments, the board is required to ensure that the domestic market is adequately supplied for both feed and industrial uses. The board may sell directly to foreign government buying agencies (eg, the USSR, the People's Republic of China), to commercial interests in foreign countries (eg, Peru, the Philippines) or to private trading companies, which then resell to foreign buyers.

As delivery opportunities arise, the grain is moved off the farm by the farmer's own truck or that of a hired commercial trucker. Farm trucks vary in carrying capacity from 3 to 20 t, the average being about 8 t. Grain may be trucked up to

125 km, but the average distance is about 20 km. Most grain is delivered to primary or country elevators but some is taken directly to feed mills or processing plants.

The primary elevator accumulates small lots of grain (sorted by species and grade) from individual farmers until there is enough to fill railcars. The primary elevator system consists of about 1900 elevators located at 1100 railway shipping points, with a total storage capacity of 7.7 million t. During the past decade the number of primary elevators has decreased by almost 55%; the decrease in storage capacity has been nearly 20%. Primary elevators, each employing a manager, are operated by grain companies, either farmer-owned co-operatives or privately owned companies. Six companies now own over 95% of all primary elevators. The largest grain-handling company is the SASKATCHEWAN WHEAT POOL, a farmer-owned co-operative with approximately one-third of the primary elevators on the prairies.

When grain is delivered to the elevator, the manager weighs and samples it, assigns a grade and issues a negotiable cash ticket to the farmer. If the wheat, oats or barley is destined for export, it becomes the property of the CWB and the primary elevator company acts as an agent of the board. In the case of flaxseed and CANOLA the primary elevator company assumes ownership; feed grains destined for domestic use may be sold either to the CWB or to the primary elevator company. Grain companies recover their elevator costs from the farmer through handling and storage charges. Maximum allowable charges are specified by the Canadian Grain Commission, and grain companies establish their charges within these limits.

The Canadian Grain Commission, answerable to the minister of agriculture under the Canada Grain Act, is responsible for establishing and maintaining standards of quality for Canadian grain and regulating grain handling in Canada to ensure a dependable commodity for domestic and export markets. Specific responsibilities include establishing grain grades and standards; official inspection of grain for export; licensing all types of grain elevators; supervision of treatment or fumigation of grain; setting of maximum fees chargeable by elevators for services (eg, receiving, cleaning, drying, shipping); inspection of elevators for compliance with operating procedures as detailed by the Canada Grain Act; and operation of the Grain Research Laboratory, which conducts research on the quality of cereal grains and oilseeds.

Grain is moved from the primary elevator system to port and other terminals by rail, using approximately 11 000 boxcars and 14 700 hopper cars. The capacity of a standard boxcar is about 54 t; of an average hopper car about 91 t. During peak movements, about 500 trains per week place empty cars at primary elevator points and take loaded cars to their destinations. The primary elevators are located at some 1100 points along approximately 30 000 km of rail lines, about 85% of which are branch lines with various carrying capacities. The average distance from a primary elevator to a port-terminal elevator is 1400 km; the average round-trip time is slightly under 3 weeks.

Grain moves from primary elevators to port terminals on Canada's West Coast (VANCOUVER and PRINCE RUPERT), on the Great Lakes (THUNDER BAY) and on the shores of Hudson Bay (CHURCHILL). The port-terminal elevators receive, store, process and ship grain. Processing includes cleaning of grain to export standards, drying, destoning and fumigating when necessary.

On the West Coast the total storage capacity is 1 212 000 t, most of which is at 5 terminals in

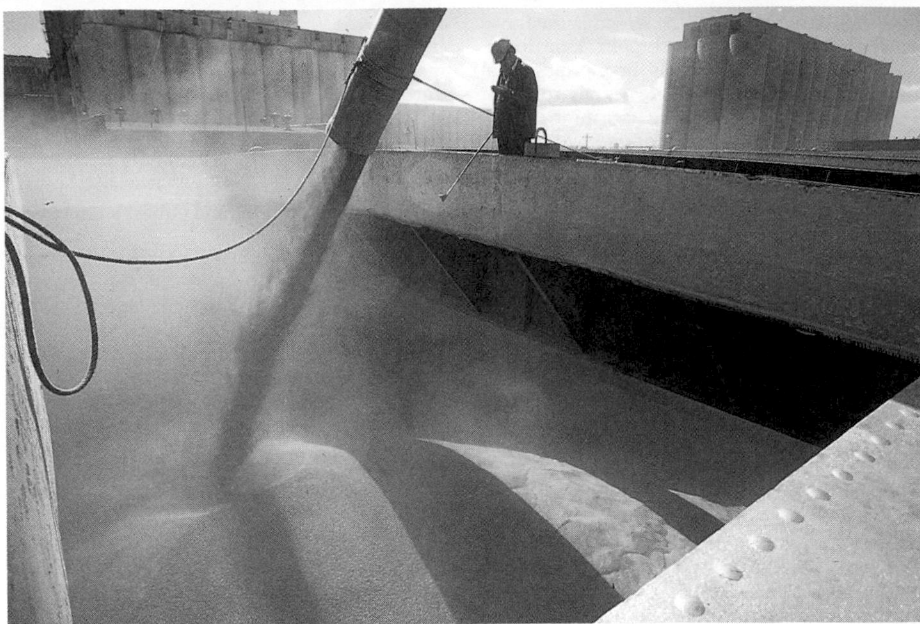

Workers loading barley into the holds of a grain ship at Thunder Bay, Ont (*courtesy SSC Photocentre*).

Vancouver. West Coast terminals operate on a year-round basis. The terminal at Churchill, with a storage capacity of 140 000 t, has a very limited shipping season (less than 3 months per year).

Thunder Bay has 12 terminal elevators with a combined storage capacity of approximately 2 million t; these terminals ship grain for approximately 8 months of the year. Grain loaded onto ships at Vancouver, Prince Rupert and Churchill moves directly to export destinations. In the case of Thunder Bay, only about 10% is loaded directly onto oceangoing ships; the remainder is carried by lake vessels to transfer elevators situated along the waterway between Thunder Bay and the seaboard. There are 27 transfer elevators with a capacity of 3.4 million t.

Grain received at transfer elevators is either loaded onto oceangoing ships or is stored for future export shipment or for domestic distribution in eastern Canada. In addition to terminal and transfer elevators, there are 28 process elevators with a capacity of 468 000 t, located mostly in the prairies. Their function is to receive and store grain for direct manufacture or processing into other products.

The WINNIPEG COMMODITY EXCHANGE is a voluntary association of representatives of practically all firms and agencies involved in marketing western Canadian grain. Members are from private and co-operative elevator companies, shippers, millers, the CWB, banks, railways and foreign grain companies. The exchange provides facilities for trading in both cash and future contracts and establishes the conditions under which grain trading shall be conducted.

E.W. TYRCHNIEWICZ

Reading: T. Veeman and M. Veeman, *The Future of Grain: Canada's Prospects for Grains, Oilseeds and Related Industries* (1984).

Grammont, Joseph-Éloi-Augustin, dit de Grandmont, writer, director (b at Baie-du-Febre, Qué 17 Apr 1921; d at Montréal 25 Nov 1970). He studied at the Séminaire de Nicolet and Montréal's École des beaux-arts, where he was a leading opponent of the conservative director, Charles Maillard, a proponent of naturalism. He later spent 1946-48 studying at the Sorbonne and the École du Louvre. During 1944 to1946 he was an arts critic for *Le Devoir*; in 1946 he directed the series "Les Cahiers de la file indienne" and wrote the first collection of poetry in this series: *Le Voyage d'Arlequin*, illustrated by his former teacher, Alfred PELLAN.

Upon his return from Europe, he wrote screenplays for Renaissance Film, as well as about 30 short stories for Radio-Canada, most of which were produced by Guy BEAULNE (1950-52). In 1949 he co-founded, with Jean-Louis ROUX, the Théâtre d'essai which opened with one of his plays, *Un fils à tuer*.

This theatre was replaced in 1951 by the Théâtre du nouveau-monde, which he directed for 3 years. Between 1954 and 1964, Radio-Canada broadcast a novel for radio by him (over $1\frac{1}{2}$ years), 4 radio plays in the "Nou- veautés dramatiques" series and 4 humorous weekly or daily serials. He authored an excellent adaptation of *My Fair Lady* and died only a few months after his appointment as professor at U de M's School of Translation.

ANDRÉ G. BOURASSA

Granby, Qué, City, pop 38 508 (1986c), 38 069 (1981c), inc 1916, located on the N Yamaska R, is an industrial crossroad of Québec's EASTERN TOWNSHIPS. First settled by British colonists and Loyalists, it was named for an English village. The city's present population is predominantly French Canadian. Situated 84 km SE of Montréal and about 40 km from the US border, Granby remained a modest agricultural centre until the 1940s. Subsequently, municipal annexation and an ambitious economic promotion program by the city administration has resulted in large-scale industrial diversification and population growth. Forty-three of its 201 industrial plants are based in western Europe and the US. Major employers include producers of textile and knitted goods, consumer and rubber clothing, precision metal, plastic and electronic products, printed paper and publications, and food products. Smaller firms are part of the high-technology sector. Regional services, including CEGEP Granby (a college), and provincial offices employ a large professional work force. Granby's tourist industry links the

city's rural surroundings with its industrial base. Granby Zoo, one of the largest in Canada, and nearby Mt Yamaska are complemented by an ecological centre and a gastronomical festival.

PAULA KESTELMAN

Grand Bank, Nfld, Town, pop 3732 (1986c), inc 1943, is located in Fortune Bay on the W side of the Burin Pen. Likely used by the French as a fishing port from the 1600s, it first reported permanent English settlers after the Treaty of UTRECHT (1713), and like nearby Fortune, its population grew after the Treaty of PARIS (1763). During the 19th century it continued to be the largest community in the region and developed as a major Grand Banks fishing centre and shipbuilding town. It had the benefit of schools and a doctor by the mid-1800s and a hospital by the end of the century. Today it is still a major fishing and fish-processing centre, a service centre for communities on the peninsula and in Fortune Bay, and is the site of the Southern Newfoundland Fishermen's Museum.

ROBERT D. PITT

Grand Banks, part of Canada's continental shelf, lying SE of Newfoundland, consist of several separate banks, foremost of which are Grand, Green and St Pierre; their area (for water depths shallower than 200 m) is 282 500 km^2. Water depths over the banks are generally less than 100 m.

The banks are an internationally known fishing ground most noted for cod, but haddock, redfish, flatfish (including halibut), mackerel and herring are also caught. This abundant fish resource was first noted by John CABOT in 1497 and shortly thereafter began to attract numerous European fishermen. The first settlements on Newfoundland were established as bases for drying and salting fish for transport back to Europe. In this century, European, American and Canadian boats have continued to fish on the banks, being joined in the mid-1950s by large Soviet and Japanese vessels. Since 1977, when Canada extended its offshore jurisdiction to include most of the Grand Banks, foreign fishing has been greatly reduced.

The water over the banks is mainly supplied by the southward-flowing cold Labrador Current, and, to a lesser extent, the eastward-flowing warm Gulf Stream. The Labrador Current splits as it approaches the Grand Bank, with one branch moving S along the coast of Newfoundland through Avalon Channel to St Pierre Bank. The other branch circulates clockwise around the Grand Bank, concentrated at its outer edge. The warm Gulf Stream waters are generally located S of the Grand Banks, but do on occasion move N onto their southern edge. Warm air masses moving from the Gulf Stream over the colder Labrador Current water produce heavy fog, especially in spring, when the air-sea temperature differences are greatest. Icebergs, carried along the edge of the banks by the Labrador Current, are also most numerous in spring.

Oil drilling, which began on the banks in the late 1970s, gained public attention with the disastrous loss of the OCEAN RANGER rig, 15 Feb 1982. Test wells have been promising and there are expectations that oil production will begin in the near future.

KEN DRINKWATER AND ALLYN CLARKE

Grand Bay, NB, Village, pop 3319 (1986c), inc 1972, located on the northern boundary of Saint John about 12 km from the city centre, named for the bay of the same name. The bay was named by the French in the 17th century for the shape of the Saint John R at that point. A rural area, it was developed as a summer community early in the 20th century, and after WWII it began to attract people from Saint John as permanent residents.

BURTON GLENDENNING

Grand Falls, Nfld, Town, pop 9121 (1986c), 8765 (1981c), inc 1961, is located in central Newfoundland on the EXPLOITS R. The pulp and paper town is named after the river's spectacular falls. In 1905 the Anglo-Newfoundland Development Co acquired a 99-year lease to 10 360 km^2 of timber land and its minerals. The construction of the pulp and paper mill, supplied with power from the falls, on the route of the trans-insular railway, and with access to the seaport of Botwood (35 km NE), was completed 1909, as was the first phase of the well-planned town, which continued to be company built and administered until 1961. It then incorporated as a municipality. The mill was acquired in 1961 by Price Brothers, which later became a division of ABITIBI-PRICE; it remains the town's largest employer. The position of Grand Falls on major water and overland routes has made it an important regional centre.

ROBERT D. PITT

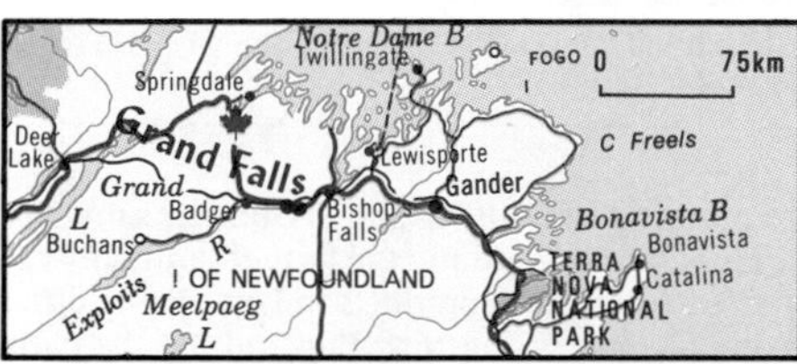

Grand Falls, NB, Town, pop 6209 (1986c), 6203 (1981c), inc 1890, is located 228 km up the SAINT JOHN R from Fredericton at the point where the Canada-US boundary begins to be designated by the river. The cataract from which the town's name originates was the site of overnight encampments from the time of the MALISEET. Grand Falls had a brief stint as a military post at the time of the boundary dispute, but the initial surge of settlement came through the entrepreneurial efforts of Sir John Caldwell, who brought settlers in to run his around-the-clock sawmill operation in the late 1830s. The surrounding area was settled by farmers in the ensuing decades, and with the completion of railway links in the 1870s the town embarked on an era of being a tourist and resort attraction in the vein of Niagara Falls. In the 1920s a dam and electrical-generating station changed the effect of the falls, and Grand Falls's post-WWII prosperity has depended almost entirely on potato production and export.

FRED FARRELL

Grand Forks, BC, City, pop 3282 (1986c), inc 1897, is at the junction of the Kettle and Granby rivers, 124 km E of Osoyoos and 140 km W of Nelson. Like many other towns originally based on mineral extraction, Grand Forks has a history of boom and bust. A few ranchers settled in the 1880s, but the town was established as a result of the discovery of copper at nearby Deadwood and Phoenix. In 1900 the Granby Co opened its smelter at Grand Forks. At its height this employed 400 men and had a capacity of about 3500 tonnes of ore per day, but after WWI the price of copper dropped and in 1919 the smelter closed. By this time the fertile valleys surrounding the town had been settled, many of the settlers being DOUKHOBORS who began arriving from Saskatchewan in 1909. Fruit production is now declining as emphasis has shifted towards mixed farming and beef cattle.

DAVID DENDY

Grand Lake, 539 km^2, elev 87 m, max length 91 km, average depth 110 m, largest lake in Newfoundland, is located on the W side of the Island, 24 km SE of CORNER BROOK. Fed by numerous small streams and brooks, it drains into Deer Lk, via the Newfoundland Canal, and then, via the HUMBER R and Humber Arm, into the Bay of Islands. The lake contains the uninhabited Glover I (200 km^2), and to the NE, together with Sandy and Birchy lakes, forms a 145 km waterway much used by canoeists.

DAVID EVANS

Grand Manan Island, NB, 142 km^2, is the largest and most remote of the 3 major islands at the entrance to the Bay of Fundy (the other 2 being DEER and CAMPOBELLO IS). It is 24 km long and 10 km at its widest point. Accessible year-round by ferry from Blacks Harbour, it is 27 km from the NB mainland, 13 km from the Maine coast. Its name is part-French, part-Passamoquoddy (*munanook*, meaning "island") in origin. With a population of about 2500 – chiefly in the villages of North Head, Grand Harbour and Seal Cove – its chief industries are fishing (sardines, herring, lobster), forestry (spruce, balsam, birch, poplar), dulse (seaweed) gathering and tourism. Steep cliffs rise to 125 m on the N and W showing 7 different strata of the Earth's crust, including 900-million-year-old sedimentary rock. Mixed in as well is 16-million-year-old volcanic rock.

Grand Manan is on the eastern flyway for migratory birds, and more than 400 species have been counted at the E coast sanctuary between Grand Harbour and Seal Cove. The island is a

Grand Manan I, in the Bay of Fundy, is on the eastern flyway for more than 400 species of migratory birds (*photo by Freeman Patterson/Masterfile*).

convenient spot for whale watching, as several species, including N American humpback, minke, finback, pothead and the nearly extinct right whale, inhabit the surrounding waters. Seals and whitesided dolphins are seen as well. The first recorded visit by Europeans was made in 1604 by Samuel de CHAMPLAIN and the Sieur de MONTS, though the Norse may have visited earlier. The island was a French seigneury for many years, but most inhabitants are descended from Loyalists who settled here following the American Revolutionary War. Among the first to arrive (1784) was Moses Gerrish, whose Grand Harbour home is now the Grand Manan Museum.

HENRY F. HEALD

Grand-Mère, Qué, City, pop 14 582 (1986c), inc 1898, located on the ST-MAURICE R, 35 km N of Trois-Rivières. Grand-Mère is an important railway and river transportation centre serving the lumber, pulp and paper, hydroelectric and textile industries operating in and around the municipality. It is also a major supplier of service industries. The city takes its name from a large stone – bearing a startling resemblance to an old woman – which used to protrude in the middle of a nearby waterfall. In 1916, the stone was moved to the centre of town and is now a tourist attraction. The first French missionary contact with the indigenous people, the Montagnais, took place in 1651, but the region remained virtually unsettled for nearly 200 years. In the 1830s some lumbermen began to work the area, and for the next half-century some small-scale trapping and logging on the St-Maurice constituted the only economic activity. Grand-Mère owes its existence to the building in 1890 of a hydroelectric power station on the site of Grand-Mère Falls by Montréal businessman John Forman. This attracted many industries which are still active in the city. Grand-Mère has grown significantly since 1945, and it experienced an economic boom when a dam was built there in the mid-1970s, temporarily swelling the population to nearly 20 000. SERGE DURFLINGER

Grand Portage, fur-trade depot and route of the VOYAGEURS at the western extremity of Lk Superior. It was the first and most strenuous of the 29 PORTAGES from Lk Superior to Lac La Croix, requiring that each voyageur carry 4 loads of 80 kg over some 14 km of rocky trails around the cascades of the Pigeon R. The Pigeon R route had long been used by Indians and was opened to the FUR TRADE by Pierre Gaultier de Varennes et de LA VÉRENDRYE. The NORTH WEST CO established an extensive post at the mouth of the river, which by 1784 was the wilderness capital of the fur trade, providing a meeting place for the voyageurs bringing supplies from Montréal (PORKEATERS) and the traders bringing furs from the North West (WINTERERS). Within the post, which was protected by a 5 m high palisade, reinforced with a bastion and a heavy gate, were the Great Hall, living quarters, shops, warehouses and a stone powder magazine. Because the settling of the Canada-US boundary left the post in American territory, the post was abandoned in 1802 and NWC activities were relocated at FORT WILLIAM at the mouth of the Kaministiquia R. This route, which had been travelled by de Noyon in 1688, was more arduous than Grand Portage, requiring a portage of Kakabeka Falls and a gruelling haul over the height of land to the Savanne R. JAMES MARSH

Grand Pré, NS, UP, 83 km NW of HALIFAX. Founded by ACADIANS shortly before 1680, the name refers to the 1000 ha "Great Meadow" of fertile marshland that drew settlers eastward from PORT-ROYAL to farm on the shores of MINAS BASIN. Using traditional French diking techniques to protect the low-lying marsh from the saltwater tides of the basin, Grand Pré farmers annually exported agricultural products to Port-Royal, other French colonies and New England. By the early 18th century, Grand Pré was the focus of Les Mines (Minas), the most populated of 3 Acadian districts. In the 1740s it consisted of 150 houses that stretched in a line some 4 km long. On 11 Feb 1747, it was the scene of the Battle of Grand Pré, a surprise attack by French and Indians on British troops during the WAR OF THE AUSTRIAN SUCCESSION. Longfellow's romantic poem *Evangeline* portrayed the tragic events of the Acadian deportation at Grand Pré (1755). In 1917 property near the centre of the village was set aside to develop as a tourist attraction. A bronze statue of Evangeline was unveiled in 1920, and a memorial chapel in the style of mid-18th-century French architecture opened in 1930. The area is now a historic site – Grand Pré National Historic Park.

DEBRA MCNABB

Church and statue of Evangeline at Grand Pré, NS (*photo by Malak, Ottawa*).

Grand Theatre The original Grand Opera House opened amid a strong amateur and professional theatrical tradition on 8 Sept 1881 in the upper floors of the Masonic Temple at London, Ont. At its peak in the 1890s, the 2070-seat Grand was host to 100 companies and 300 performances annually. World-renowned artists, including Sarah Bernhardt, Lily Langtry and Ellen Terry and Canadians Clara MORRIS, Emma ALBANI and Henry MILLER, performed in the classical melodramas of the time. When this theatre, part of a Michigan-Ohio-Ontario circuit, burned in 1900, C.J. Whitney, the original lessee, and Ambrose Small, a Canadian impresario, rebuilt and relocated the Grand. Although the capacity was reduced to 1850, the proscenium was larger. In 1924 the building was sold to Famous Players. The Grand regained its legitimacy in 1945 when it was purchased by London Little Theatre, an active amateur group that won many Dominion Drama awards. In 1971 this group was replaced by a professional company. Major structural renovations in 1977-78 reduced capacity to 829. In 1983 the company, renamed The Grand Company under artistic director Robin PHILLIPS, announced an ambitious season of 9 plays, but the repertory system was terminated after one year.

KATHLEEN D.J. FRASER

Proscenium arch of the Grand Opera House, London, Ont, which opened in 1881 and later housed the Grand Theatre Co (*courtesy the Grand Theatre*).

Grand Trunk Pacific Railway was a 4800 km system whose main line ran from Winnipeg via Melville and Edmonton to Prince Rupert, BC. Incorporated in 1903, it was built between 1906 and 1914 to provide the GRAND TRUNK RY with western connections. It was to have assumed responsibility for the government-built National Transcontinental Ry, but financial difficulties prevented this from happening. The Grand Trunk Pacific faced severe competition from the CANADIAN PACIFIC RY and the CANADIAN NORTHERN RY, both of which had excellent branch and feeder lines on the prairies. Construction costs, the exigencies of wartime financing, and the lack of a viable system of branch lines brought the Grand Trunk Pacific into receivership. The Grand Trunk, which had guaranteed Grand Trunk Pacific securities, tried to escape its obligations, but eventually the western road also dragged the Grand Trunk into default and NATIONALIZATION. The federal government decided in 1919 to acquire both the Grand Trunk Pacific and the Grand Trunk at a price to be established by arbitration, and in 1923 the operations of the Grand Trunk, the Grand Trunk Pacific and the National Transcontinental merged with those of the recently nationalized Canadian Northern Railway to form the new CANADIAN NATIONAL RAILWAYS system. T.D. REGEHR

Grand Trunk Railway of Canada was built to provide a main trunk line "throughout the entire length of the Province of Canada, and from the eastern frontier thereof...to the city and port of Halifax." Under the sponsorship of Sir Francis HINCKS, the GTR was formally incorporated in 1852 to build a railway from Toronto to Montréal. In 1853 it amalgamated with 5 other railway companies, a method of operating which was to characterize its major expansion periods and supplement the construction of new track. Much of the financing had to be raised in England, and the English construction firm of Peto, Brassey, Jackson and Betts received the contract to build the Montréal-to-Toronto section in return for agreeing to promote the company. Gzowski & Company received the contract for the Toronto-to-Sarnia section. Brassey claimed his company suffered heavy losses on its contract, while Casimir GZOWSKI, more familiar with Canadian conditions, made a fortune. Hincks's enemies claimed that he, too, made a fortune – at the expense of the railway.

Work proceeded vigorously from town to town. Navvies from England swelled the labour force – at one time 14 000 men and 2000 horses were employed in Canada W alone. The line did not face challenges such as those of the CANADIAN PACIFIC RAILWAY in the mountains but achieved at least one notable engineering feat in construction of the tubular Victoria Bridge across the St Lawrence R at Montréal. The 2009 m long iron tube rested on 2 abutments and 24 piers designed to resist the crushing ice of the river; it was opened to traffic in Dec 1859. Despite financial difficulties, the GTR expanded steadily, often leasing

Grand Trunk Railway Chronology

	Amalgamations
1 July 1853	The Grand Junction Railroad Co
	The Grand Trunk Railway Co of Canada East
	The Quebec and Richmond Railroad Co
	The St Lawrence and Atlantic Railroad Co
	The Toronto and Guelph Railway Co
1 Oct 1857	London and Grand Trunk Junction Railway Co
12 Aug 1882	The Great Western Railway Co
24 Feb 1888	The Hamilton and North-Western Railway Co
	The Northern Railway Co of Canada
10 May 1892	The Northern and Pacific Junction Railway Co
1 Apr 1893	The Beauharnois Junction Railway Co
	The Brantford, Norfolk and Port Burwell Railway Co
	The Cobourg, Blairton and Marmora Railway and Mining Co
	The Galt and Guelph Railway Co
	Grand Trunk, Georgian Bay and Lake Erie Railway Co
	The Jacques Cartier Union Railway Co
	The Lake Simcoe Junction Railway Co
	The London, Huron and Bruce Railway Co
	The Midland Railway of Canada
	The Montreal and Champlain Junction Railway Co
	The North Simcoe Railway Co
	The Peterborough and Chemong Lake Railway Co
	Waterloo Junction Railway Co
	Wellington, Grey and Bruce Railway Co
29 Jul 1914	Canada Atlantic Railway Co
	Purchases
14 Nov 1865	Preston and Berlin Railway property
14 June 1872	Montreal and Champlain Railroad
19 Apr 1884	The Welland Railway property

existing railways as a means of expansion. It eliminated its main competitor and added another 1450 km of track with the takeover of the GREAT WESTERN RAILWAY in 1882. Additional links to the US rail system were established with the International Bridge across the Niagara R, and the impressive St Clair Tunnel beneath the St Clair R. At Confederation the GTR was the largest railway system in the world, with 2055 km of track; by the late 1880s it had grown to over 700 locomotives, 578 cars, 60 post-office cars, 131 baggage cars, 18 000 freight cars and 49 snowplows. The GTR ran unbroken from Sarnia to Portland, Maine.

Cost of construction, absentee management (the head office was in London, Eng) and failure to generate anticipated levels of traffic left the company debt ridden and unable to upgrade its equipment. It suffered bad publicity with several accidents; on 29 June 1864 a GTR train plunged off the Beloeil Bridge into the Richelieu R, killing 99 people. Another incident made headlines around the world when, on 15 Sept 1885, a GTR train was charged by Jumbo, the famous circus elephant, near St Thomas, Ont. The elephant was killed. From the mid-1890s until WWI the GTR undertook a massive betterment program on its property. This included double-tracking of the main line from Montréal to Sarnia, reducing curves and grades to improve operating efficiency, and reconstruction of bridges, buildings and yards. Subsequent rebuilding of the system was not required until after WWII.

Envious of the CPR thrust into the West, the GTR set up a subsidiary, the GRAND TRUNK PACIFIC, to build a transcontinental line. Completed in 1914, the railway was a financial disaster and was largely responsible for the bankruptcy of the GTR in 1919. The federal government, which had already given the GTR some $28 million in subsidies and loans, took over the railway on 10 Oct 1919. It was placed under the management of the CANADIAN NATIONAL RAILWAYS on 30 Jan 1923. JAMES MARSH

Reading: A.W. Currie, *The Grand Trunk Railway of Canada* (1957).

Grand Valley, Man, is a provincial recreation park 10 km W of Brandon on the Trans-Canada Hwy. Once a community on the N bank of the Assiniboine R, Grand Valley died when BRANDON, 3 km W on the S bank of the Assiniboine, was created in 1881 as the CPR's divisional headquarters. Settlers from Nova Scotia and Québec homesteaded here 1877-79. Population, stores and services grew. Several attempts were made to entice the CPR to locate at Grand Valley but the rivalries involved, combined with spring flooding in 1881, caused the higher site of Brandon to be chosen. Homesteaders moved across the river; businessmen moved to Chater or Brandon. By 1884 only a few houses remained, and the townsite eventually reverted to a homestead. D.M. LYON

Grandbois, Alain, poet (b at St-Casimir, Qué 25 May 1900; d at Québec City 18 Mar 1975). He is considered the first great modern Québec poet. He travelled the world 1918-39 and shared the hopes and problems of contemporary man. His work closely integrates the themes of exploring the secrets of the world and studying human destiny, each one reinforcing the other. His writing and subject matter thus had a depth and breadth previously unknown in Québec, making them a model for various young poets of the 1950s. *Né à Québec: Louis Jolliet* (1933), *Les Voyages de Marco Polo* (1941), *Avant le chaos* (1945) and *Visages du monde* (1971) all demonstrate his knowledge of the world. The confrontation with destiny (adventure, glory, love, liberty, death) occurs in precise locations, through specific characters. His poetry – *Îles de la nuit* (1944), *Rivages de l'homme* (1948), *L'Étoile pourpre* (1957), *Poèmes épars* – develops these topics within a single character, the man of the "long voyage insolite/A travers l'incantation du temps." The poetry is metaphysical, its scope being that of destiny explored, through exploratory words, and with its developed rhetorical structure it speaks for all in an intimate and personal tone. YVES BOLDUC

Reading: Yves Bolduc, *Alain Grandbois: le douloureux destin* (1982).

Grande Cache, Alta, Town, pop 3646 (1986c), 4523 (1981c), inc 1966, located 430 km NW of Edmonton, was created 1966 to mine coking coal. The coal's location had been known for years but awaited development of a market in Japan's blast furnaces and completion of the Alberta Resources Ry N from the CNR main line. Named for a "grande cache" of furs said to have been left there by Ignace Giasson (1820), it is a neatly laid-out model town. Nearby Willmore Wilderness Prov Pk promises the development of tourism. The *Grande Cache Mountaineer* is the weekly newspaper. ERIC J. HOLMGREN

Grande Entrée, Île de, Qué, pop 787 (1986c), 867 (1981c), situated almost in the middle of the Gulf of ST LAWRENCE and flanked in the N by Île d'ANTICOSTI, in the S by PRINCE EDWARD I and on the E by CABOT STR, is one of the 16 islands comprising Îles de la MADELEINE. The island group was discovered by Jacques CARTIER (1534) and was later explored by Samuel de CHAMPLAIN. Grande Entrée was leased to Nicolas DENYS in 1653 by the COMPAGNIE DES CENT-ASSOCIÉS. After 1787 it became part of the holdings of Capt Isaac Coffin (Coffin is the island's English name today) of the Royal Marines as a reward for services to the English Crown. A Canadian corporation, the Magdalen Island Co, bought all the islands from the absentee Coffin family in 1903. Grande Entrée is joined to the other islands by lagoon-forming sandbars, and is characterized by rapidly eroding red sandstone cliffs. A constant hazard to shipping, the island group is noted for fishing, sealing and its spectacular colonies of seabirds. During the summer, the entire archipelago attracts many tourists. DAVID EVANS

Grande Prairie, Alta, City, pop 26 471 (1986c), 24 263 (1981c), inc 1958, is located 460 km NW of Edmonton. Surrounded by rich agricultural land, it is the business and transportation centre of the PEACE RIVER region.

History Although the area had been the domain of fur traders since Alexander MACKENZIE ascended the Peace R (1792-93), the present townsite was not settled until 1881, when Tom Kerr erected an HBC trading post. Shortly thereafter, Louie Callihou, a part-Iroquois farmer who sowed grain, constructed the first barn and corral. The community received its name from Father Grouard, an RC missionary who labelled the gently undulating wilderness "la grande prairie." After 1900 a trickle of pioneers traversed the Edson Trail and ATHABASCA LANDING TRAIL and took up homesteads here. Growth continued with completion of the Edmonton, Dunvegan and BC Ry extension line in 1916.

Economy Historically, Grande Prairie has evolved around agriculture. With demobilization following WWI, soldier settlement schemes, continued high wheat prices and publicity for the Peace R district as Canada's new agrarian mecca, migration increased throughout the 1920s. Strategically situated with a vast expanse of fertile land N, E and W, Grande Prairie by the 1930s served as the wholesale centre for the region. Although its population was only 1464 (1931c), its retail business in 1929-30 surpassed $2 million. In recent years the city's economy has become diversified, with the forestry and petroleum industries augmenting agri-business. The major employer is Procter and Gamble (which completed an $80-million pulp mill 1973) followed by North Canadian Forest Industries. Grande Prairie experienced an unprecedented boom 1978-80 due largely to the discovery of the Elmworth "deep-basin," a major gas field near the city. Extensive gas and oil activity with its concomitant impetus to the commercial and service industries resulted in a large population increase 1979-80. Between 1981 and 1987 the growth in population slowed as a result of the economic stagnation. By 1987, however, increased activity in the oil and gas industry and in forestry brought renewed interest in the area.

Cityscape The city contains beautiful parkland surrounding a man-made reservoir in its centre. Cultural life is focused on the regional college (designed by Douglas CARDINAL), which provides not

The cultural life of Grande Prairie is focused on the regional college (*photo by J.A. Kraulis*).

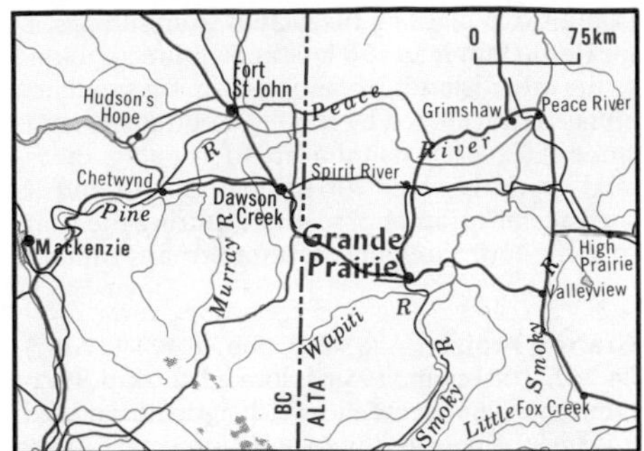

only diverse educational opportunities, but possesses one of the finest auditoriums in western Canada. J. PETRYSHYN

Reading: I.M. Campbell, *Grande Prairie: Capital of the Peace* (1968); C.A. Dawson, *The Settlement of the Peace Country* (1934).

Grande Société, contemporary name for war profiteers charged with providing food for Canada and the French troops stationed there during the SEVEN YEARS' WAR. The official supplier received only one-fifth of the société's profits, and silent partners almost certainly shared their three-fifths with Canada's last intendant and possibly with the governor. The other one-fifth was divided among those who looked after the Québec and Montréal operations. Intendant BIGOT wielded extensive power over Crown expenditures in the colony, so the société was in the enviable position of buying supplies from itself with the king's money. Since supplying the FUR-TRADE posts was most remunerative, the société shipped much-needed foodstuffs westward. Much of the money seems to have found its way back to France; some was even returned to the royal treasury in the late 1760s after conviction of those involved. Embezzlement, common under the Ancien Régime, was all the more tempting in Canada because of the enormous expenditures incurred by the Crown in order to save its colony from the British. TOM WIEN

Grandin, Vital-Justin, Roman Catholic bishop of St Albert, b at St Pierre-la-Cour, France 8 Feb 1829; d at St Albert, Alta 3 June 1902). As a pioneering Oblate missionary of the Canadian West, he became the first bishop of the then vast and newly created diocese of St Albert in 1871. Wholly dedicated to bringing Roman Catholicism to the Indians and the Métis, he worked despite great hardships to develop the missions. In 1875 he lobbied the Canadian government for funding to aid agriculture, education and health care. During the 1885 NORTH-WEST REBELLION he advocated moderation and "obedience" to the Canadian authorities. His cause for sainthood was introduced at Rome in 1937. LOUISE ZUK

Grands Ballets canadiens, Les, of Montréal, was founded by Ludmilla CHIRIAEFF in 1958 as a troupe of 16 dancers. It was the natural outgrowth of Mme Chiriaeff's earlier activities in Montréal, where she had settled after emigrating from Europe in 1952. Her first ballets were created for the acclaimed CBC French Network TV program, "L'Heure du concert." Her company, Les Ballets Chiriaeff, began giving live public performances in 1954, despite opposition from the then highly conservative Catholic Church in Québec. Mme Chiriaeff had established her first school in 1952 and, in 1958, the Académie des grands ballets canadiens was established to prepare dancers for the emerging company. In 1970, the Ecole supérieure de danse du Québec was founded to provide professional training for advanced students. Since relinquishing her position as artistic director in 1974, Mme Chiriaeff has focused her attentions on the schools, where she has been able to provide ballet training for talented children from all parts of Québec.

Throughout its existence, Les Grands Ballets (now about 38 dancers) has been distinguished by its commitment to Canadian choreographers, composers and designers. In the early years, Mme Chiriaeff choreographed many ballets. Since then other important contributions to the repertoire have been made by such Canadian choreographers as Fernand NAULT, Brydon PAIGE and Brian MACDONALD. The company has also accumulated a diverse repertoire representative of the best in traditional and contemporary ballet and modern dance, performing works by such renowned choreographers as George Balanchine, John Butler, Lar Lubovitch and Paul Taylor. It also continues to present the works of a younger generation of Canadian choreographers, including among others James KUDELKA, Judith MARCUSE and Linda Rabin.

Les Grands Ballets has travelled extensively across Canada. It made its first US appearance in 1959, visited Europe in 1969, 1974, 1982 and 1984, and has appeared in Latin America and Asia. From 1970 to 1972 it became internationally known for its popular dance adaptation, by Fernand Nault, of the rock opera *Tommy*, composed by the British group, The Who. In the early 1980s the artistic direction of the company was provided by a committee consisting of ballet mistress Linda Stearns, répétiteur Daniel Jackson, and director general Colin McIntyre. Jeanne Renaud joined Linda Stearns as co-artistic director in 1985 but left in Dec 1987. Linda Stearns remained as sole artistic director. Both administrations have succeeded in maintaining a high profile for Les Grands Ballets as a versatile, creatively vital company. MICHAEL CRABB

Jardin aux Lilas was staged in 1981 by Les Grands Ballets canadiens (*courtesy Les Grands Ballets canadiens/photo by Andrew Oxenham*).

Grandview, Man, Town, pop 941 (1986c), 1013 (1981c), inc 1909 (Village, 1906), nestles between Riding and Duck Mts on the Valley R, 360 km NW of Winnipeg. As a service centre, Grandview relies on surrounding grain, livestock and dairy farms, and winter logging. Tourism has been encouraged by improved accessibility and amenities in Duck Mountain Provincial Park, the site of Baldy Mtn, the highest peak in Manitoba (832 m). Early agricultural settlement began in the 1880s, but the area was not formally opened to homesteading until the 1890s. British and Ontario farmers, some moving from southern Manitoba, were followed 1900-10 by Ukrainian families. The Grandview townsite was established in 1900 in association with the planned extension of the Canadian Northern Ry west of Dauphin. D.M. LYON

Grange, The Throughout its history this elegant brick building, constructed about 1817 on a 40 ha property stretching from Queen to Bloor streets, has been linked to the social, intellectual and political life of Toronto. Built for D'Arcy Boulton, Jr, it subsequently became home to Goldwin SMITH. Acquired in 1911 by the Art Museum of Toronto (now ART GALLERY OF ONTARIO), the building was restored to its appearance of the years 1835-40. The composition of its facade, with a slightly projecting section topped by a pediment, shows the influence of 18th-century British classical architecture as it was expressed in several grand colonial homes in the early 19th century. NATHALIE CLERK

Granisle, BC, Village, pop 646 (1986c), located in central BC on the west shore of Babine Lake, the largest natural lake in the province. The economy is based on the 2 large copper mines adjacent to the community. The village was founded in 1965 by the Zapata Granby Mining Co when it opened the Granisle open-pit copper mine on Sterret I in Babine Lake. In 1972 Noranda Mines opened the Bell Copper Mine on the nearby Babine Pen. Noranda took over the original Granisle Mine in 1981. The major Skeena R salmon run is aided by the salmon hatcheries near Granisle. JOHN R. STEWART

Grant, Charles, "Charlie," salesman, human rights activist, (b at Toronto 22 Oct 1902; d there 28 May 1980). Of Scots Presbyterian background, Grant left home at an early age to travel the world. After many adventures in western Canada and the Orient, he settled in Vienna and became a diamond broker. In 1938 he was arrested by the Nazis for "currency speculation" and was sentenced to several months in jail – but ended up spending the entire war in internment camps. On his return home, he attempted unsuccessfully to create an organization to bring to Canada large numbers of young orphans from Europe. He spent the last 3 decades of his life as a human-rights activist. A largely fictional account of his life, "Charlie Grant's War," was telecast on CBC in 1985. With no corroborating evidence, it claimed that Grant saved 647 Viennese Jews by providing them with stolen visas. True or not, Grant should be remembered less for what he did during the war than after it – fighting ANTI-SEMITISM, RACISM and bigotry in Canada. IRVING ABELLA

Grant, Cuthbert, fur trader, Métis leader, captain of the Métis at SEVEN OAKS (b at Fort de la Rivière Tremblante [Sask] *c*1793; d at White Horse Plains [St-François-Xavier, Man] 15 July 1854). Grant, his reputation tarnished by the events at Seven Oaks, overshadowed in history by RIEL, has not been given due credit for his leadership of the MÉTIS. Of Scottish and Cree or Assiniboine background and educated apparently in Montréal, Grant came back to the North West as a trader-bourgeois of the NORTH WEST CO in 1815. In 1816 he led the Métis to victory at Seven Oaks, an unplanned clash of Métis and Selkirk settlers. Three years after the amalgamation of the NWC and HUDSON'S BAY CO, in the spring of 1824, Grant led 80 to 100 Métis families to settle and farm at White Horse Plains (Grantown, later St-François-Xavier). In 1828 he was appointed warden of the Plains by HBC Governor George SIMPSON, and for at least 25 years his followers served as providers and protectors of the RED RIVER COLONY. Grant was a founder of the Métis Nation, but ironically, it was a younger generation of Métis nationalists who, by defying his attempts to uphold the HBC monopoly at the Sayer trial in 1849, brought his career as warden and sheriff of ASSINIBOIA to an end. EMMA LAROCQUE

George P. Grant's *Lament for a Nation* (1965) attracted wide attention for its sombre conclusion that Canada was doomed to disappear in the American empire of modern liberalism (*courtesy Canapress Photo Service*).

Grant, George Monro, Presbyterian minister, educator (b at Albion Mines, NS 22 Dec 1835; d at Kingston, Ont 10 May 1902). Educated at Pictou Academy and West River Seminary in Nova Scotia, Grant attended Glasgow U (MA 1857) and was ordained in the Church of Scotland in 1860. After spending 3 years in different Maritime locations as a missionary, he was offered the pulpit of St Matthew's Church, Halifax, in 1863, a position he held until he accepted the principalship of Queen's U, Kingston, in 1877. He was principal of Queen's until his death and was the author of several books, including *Ocean to Ocean* (1873), an account of his journey overland to the Pacific with Sandford FLEMING'S expedition in 1872, and *The Religions of the World* (1894).

Grant inherited a small and financially unstable denominational college and spent much of his indomitable energy thereafter in raising an endowment fund and acquiring (and retaining) major scholars, especially in the humanities. He was also fully aware, however, of the necessity of strong faculties of science (pure and applied) if Queen's was to acquire a truly national stature. By the time of his death few denied that his goal had been realized.

Principal Grant was an almost archetypal "muscular Christian," greatly admiring Thomas Arnold of Rugby as well as Victorian social reformers. While not a systematic scholar, he read widely and his thought and conduct were practical applications of the philosophical idealism given voice by his colleague at Queen's, John WATSON. He believed that the knowledge and ideals acquired at university should be actively used in professional public life for the social good, and the power of his example encouraged commitment of students to a SOCIAL GOSPEL. To this organic view of society he added a firm commitment not only to the Canadian nation but also to its place within the British Empire. A leader in the Presbyterian Church in Canada (he was moderator in 1889), he was nevertheless a major spokesman for ecumenicism. He left behind him no great body of scholarship but at his death the phrase "Principal Grant" had become one of legendary significance. A.B. MCKILLOP

Grant, George Parkin, social philosopher, university professor (b at Toronto 13 Nov 1918), son of William Lawson Grant and grandson of George Monro GRANT and Sir George PARKIN. A brooding philosopher of apparently implacable pessimism, Grant is one of the most influential Canadian thinkers of his era, having evolved from a nationalist and "Red Tory" position to a concern with the fate of the entire Western world. Educated at Queen's and Oxford, Grant taught philosophy at Dalhousie 1947-60, then became chairman of the department of religion at McMaster. In 1980 he returned to Dalhousie as a professor of political science and classics. In *Philosophy in the Mass Age* (1959), he began to wrestle with the conflict between Western moral traditions and the new religion of technological progress. LAMENT FOR A NATION (1965), a meditation on the implications of the DIEFENBAKER period, attracted wide attention for its sombre conclusion that Canada – a nation with conservative roots – was doomed to disappear in the American-led empire of modern liberalism, which for Grant is an inexorable force leading to a universal and homogenous state of almost certain tyranny. Similar concerns dominate *Technology and Empire* (1969), in which Grant saw the Vietnam War as an evil and exemplary product of Western ideology.

Using contemporary issues as a springboard for his speculations, Grant has attracted a large following among younger writers and nationalists, most of whom see his pessimism less as an irrevocable verdict than as an invigorating challenge to unite the achievements of modern science and classical philosophy. This challenge was maintained in *English-Speaking Justice* (1974, repr 1978 and 1985), in which Grant concludes that traditional concepts of freedom and justice have been transcended by the doctrine of technological progress, with an implication that the entire Western experience has been some sort of gigantic error. *Technology and Justice* (1986) explores this topic further.
CHARLES TAYLOR

Reading: Charles Taylor, *Radical Tories: The Conservative Tradition in Canada* (1982); L. Schmidt, ed, *George Grant in Process* (1978).

Grant, Sir James Alexander, physician, politician (b at Inverness, Scot 11 Aug 1831; d at Ottawa 5 Feb 1920). A graduate of Queen's and McGill, he practised medicine for all of his professional life in Ottawa. He was personal physician to the first 8 governors general (1867-1905). Successful care of Princess Louise, Marchioness of Lorne, earned him a KCMG in 1887 and Queen Victoria's motherly thanks. His professional eminence led to election as president of the CANADIAN MEDICAL ASSN and the Royal Soc of Canada. Grant sat in Parliament for Russell County 1867-73 and Ottawa 1893-96 and gained distinction by introducing the original CANADIAN PACIFIC RY Bill in 1872, using an appropriate medical metaphor, when he said Canada would become one great country by "placing an iron splint on these provinces to strengthen the union and develop trade." A.A. TRAVILL

Grant, John Charles Boileau, anatomist (b at Loanhead, Scot 6 Feb 1886; d at Toronto 14 Aug 1973). After service as a medical officer in the imperial forces in WWI, Grant became professor and head of the dept of anatomy, U of Man (1919-30), of U of T (1930-56), professor emeritus, U of T (1956-73), and visiting professor of anatomy, U of Calif, Los Angeles (1961-69). Author of *A Method of Anatomy, An Atlas of Anatomy* and *A Dissector of Anatomy,* Grant was also a contributor to Gray's *Anatomy* 18th and 20th editions; Morris's *Anatomy, Myology,* 10th and 11th editions; Cuningham's *Anatomy, Respiratory System,* 9th and 10th editions; and *Anthropometry of the Saulteaux, Cree, and Chipewyan Indians.* Grant was a stimulating teacher of human anatomy and his influence through his textbooks was worldwide. During the Great Depression he provided encouragement and monetary assistance to dozens of unemployed.
ROSS G. MACKENZIE

Grant, John Webster, UNITED CHURCH clergyman, church historian (b at Truro, NS 27 June 1919). He attended Dalhousie, Princeton and Oxford universities (Rhodes scholar 1941), graduated in theology from Pine Hill Divinity Hall, Halifax, and served as a wartime chaplain in the RCN. He taught church history at Union Coll, Vancouver, 1949-59, except for one year as a visiting professor in India. In 1959 he joined RYERSON PRESS and a year later became its editor in chief. From 1963 until retirement in 1984 he was professor of church history at Emmanuel Coll, Toronto. Besides numerous scholarly articles, he has written more than a dozen books on church history, particularly Canadian. He has been active in several academic and religious organizations, including the United Church's commission on union with the Anglicans, where he was chairman of the executive committee 1967-71. He is the recipient of 4 honorary degrees. JOHN S. MOIR

Grape, common name for a family (Vitaceae) of woody, climbing vines and the fruit clusters they produce. The genus *Vitis* includes 30-50 species. The Old World species *V. vinifera* has been cultivated for at least 5000 to 6000 years. Many different grape species exist from Canada to Mexico. *V. labrusca* and *V. riparia* are the 2 main northern species. As early as 1616 attempts were made to grow *V. vinifera* in eastern N America. Cultivation of this species has continued but remains economically unsuccessful in Canada, although small quantities are grown for special wines. However, *V. vinifera* has been used extensively in hybridization of many important cultivated varieties. There are 2 main grape-growing areas in Canada, the NIAGARA PENINSULA, Ont (over 80% of plantings), and the OKANAGAN VALLEY, BC, with some plantings in SW Ontario and NS. Some 76 617 t of grapes were grown in Canada in 1985, with a value of over $36 million. The Niagara region has 177 frost-free days and an average rainfall of 678 mm. The 2335 heat units (above 5°C) are adequate for crop maturity. In BC, irrigation is required to supplement rainfall. Some cultivation is necessary for best results in vineyards. Chemicals are used for weed control, except on young vines. Green-manure crops are sown in midsummer and fertilizers are applied as needed. Common insect pests include leafhoppers, flea beetles, berry moth and phylloxera. The main plant diseases are powdery mildew, downy mildew, black rot, botrytis and dead arm. Most of the grapes produced in Canada are used by processors to make WINE and juice. Small quantities are sold for home winemaking and dessert purposes. The main varieties grown are Concord, De Chaunac, Niagara, Elvira and Foch. About 45 varieties are used by the wineries. Agriculture Canada and Ontario Ministry of Agriculture and Food scientists, working at RESEARCH STATIONS in Summerland, BC, and Vineland, Ont, respectively, have aided local wineries by breeding new hybrid vines and evaluating wines. *See also* CROP RESEARCH.
O.A. BRADT

Graphic Art and Design are 2 branches of verbal/visual communications which include the related callings of commercial art, book and periodical illustration, typography and type design. They come under the title of "applied arts" as opposed to the so-called "fine arts" (including PRINTMAKING) because of their subservience to the message to be conveyed, the object to be sold, or the service to be advertised. In this sense they are first cousins to INDUSTRIAL DESIGN.

Until the 1870s and 1880s, most art training in Canada was of a severely practical nature, with subjects being limited to technical drawing and watercolour painting for the benefit of draughtsmen, artisans, builders and schoolteachers. The introduction of commercial art, lithography, engraving, lettering and illustration classes to the curricula of the fine-art colleges founded in Halifax, Québec, Montréal, Toronto, Winnipeg, Vancouver and other larger centres after Confederation answered a demand from printers, newspaper and magazine publishers, and advertising agencies (the first of which was established in Montréal in 1889) for trained artists who could work with typesetters, copywriters and editors in the preparation of a variety of graphic materials involving the use of drawn or painted images and hand-lettered or typeset texts.

At first such functions had been performed by anonymous craftsmen for such formats as the inn sign, the stagecoach and steamship advertisement, the shop-window showcard, the product label, the auction broadside and the agricultural fair poster. These freelancers, who came to be known by the generic term "graphic artists," had to adapt their often self-taught aptitudes to keep pace with the changes that began to take place in the Canadian printing, engraving and papermaking industries when the waves of the European Industrial Revolution reached these shores. Lithography, invented by Senefelder in 1796, was brought to York [Toronto] by Samuel Tazewell in 1832, and was reintroduced more successfully by Hugh Scobie in 1843. This medium opened new possibilities for book, map and atlas publishers and for the manufacturers of commodities and the promoters of entertainments, as it allowed for the reproduction of highly detailed and lifelike scenes and objects, as well as for the more artistic integration of written and pictorial components, than did the standard combination of wood-engraving and wooden or metal type.

Such subsequent improvements as the chromolithograph (an innovation of the 1840s) and the steam-driven rotary press made a once-cumbersome and expensive technology competitive with wood- and steel-engraving and their successor, the photographic line and halftone plate. Montréal's William Leggo (1830-1915) put Canada at the forefront of reprographic technology with his invention of Leggotype, patented in 1865 as a photoengraving process used to reproduce line drawings and copy engravings. Later extended to cross-line screen work, Leggotype was applied in the reproduction of the world's first magazine halftones, which appeared in the inaugural edition of Desbarat's *Canadian Illustrated News* in 1869.

At first, Canada's commercial lithographers tended to come from Germany (Bavaria being the home of the porous limestone whence the process's name – literally, "drawing on stone" – is based), whereas line engravers were largely British in origin. Most notable among the latter were John Allanson (1800-59), a student of master wood-engraver Thomas Bewick who arrived in Toronto in 1849, and Frederick Brigden Sr (1841-1917), who served his apprenticeship in London under Bewick's disciple, W.J. Linton, and immigrated to Canada around 1873. His company, the Toronto Engraving Co, changed its name to Brigden's Ltd, and under the directorship of Fred Brigden Jr attracted the services of many talented Toronto artists who contributed drawings to be engraved on boxwood or photoengraved on metal plates by Brigden employees. (The Winnipeg branch of the firm, headed by Arnold Brigden, employed a number of important figures who went on to careers as painters

CANADIAN OPERA 1977
DON CARLOS • THE MAGIC FLUTE
DAUGHTER OF THE REGIMENT • WOZZECK
O'KEEFE CENTRE, TORONTO, SEPTEMBER 14TH TO OCTOBER 29TH

The Canadian Opera Company season poster. The painting, by artist Heather Cooper, 1977, was commissioned to portray the essence of opera (*courtesy Heather Cooper*).

and teachers – among them Charles COMFORT, Fritz BRANDTNER and W.J. Phillips.)

The importation of skilled engravers and the establishment of domestic firms such as Brigden's, Alexander and Cable, Barclay, Clark and Co, the Canadian Photo-Engraving Co and the Thomson Engraving Co, encouraged newspaper and magazine publishers, and the advertisers on whom they had come increasingly to depend to supplement their subscription revenues, to experiment first with small illustrations, cartoons, decorative headings and vignettes, then with larger and more elaborate ones. The addition of the artist-reporter to the newspaper staff soon followed, the first practitioners of this new profession – the immediate predecessor of the photo-journalist – usually stepping into their roles from the in-house plate-engraving and layout department. The leader in this diversification process was the art department of the Toronto *Globe*, which joined forces with the Toronto Lithographing Co, Canada's largest and most advanced litho company, in the 1880s to produce advertising posters and such specialty publications as *The Canadian War News* (issued weekly to report on the events of the 1885 North-West Rebellion). Prominent Toronto Litho Co employees included W.D. Blatchly, Henri JULIEN, J.D. Kelly, C.W. JEFFERYS and William Bengough, younger brother of the brilliant political caricaturist J.W. BENGOUGH, who founded the satirical periodical *Grip* in 1872. Out of this magazine came the commercial-art firm of Grip Ltd, which in the 1900s and 1910s boasted a staff of designer-illustrators who played a key role in the creation of a national school of landscape painting, among them C.W. Jefferys, Tom THOMSON and future members of the GROUP OF SEVEN. Several of these artists followed Grip's inspired art director, A.H. Robson, to Rous and Mann Press Ltd, which specialized in fine commercial typography and presswork, while Franklin CARMICHAEL and A.J. CASSON moved on to the first Canadian silkscreen printing firm, Sampson, Matthews Ltd, founded by artist J.E. Sampson and businessman C.A.G. Matthews.

Toronto Litho Co's leading Toronto rival was the English-born watercolourist J.T. Rolph's engraving and lithography concern. Rolph, Smith and Co merged with Stone Ltd to form Rolph-Clark-Stone in 1917; Grip, meanwhile, evolved into Rapid Grip and Batten, now Bomac Batten.

Montréal lagged behind Toronto as a printing and commercial art centre, and such litho and engraving houses as it supported – eg, A. Sabiston and Co – were run by Anglophones who rarely employed French Canadian illustrators or designers. By the turn of the century most medium-sized Canadian cities had their own graphic art establishments, usually connected to a printing company, department store, newspaper or magazine. The separation of forces into commercial art studio, advertising agency, engraver and lithographer came later.

The stodginess and overdecorativeness that marred Canadian graphic art and design were the targets of the younger illustrators who looked to Europe and the US for inspiration. Grip Ltd's F.H. VARLEY and Arthur LISMER had received their training at the Sheffield School of Art and, like J.E.H. MACDONALD, were steeped in the Arts and Crafts and Art Nouveau design conventions of the era. MacDonald had immersed himself in the principles of William Morris while working in London for Carlton Studios, which had been set up in 1902 by 3 ex-Grip employees (A.A. Martin, T.G. Greene and Norman Price) who would go on to claim that they had introduced the "studio idea" to Great Britain. So successful were they in exporting this Toronto-born concept that by the 1920s they were listed as being the largest such concern in the world.

Colour lithographic posters were first used to fight a federal election campaign in 1891, when the Industrial League hired Toronto Litho Co to produce a series of 4-colour and black-and-white cartoons to support Sir John A. Macdonald's Conservative Party. This established a precedent for the collaboration of governmental and quasi-governmental bodies with advertising and graphic art houses in the production of official propaganda. In the 1890s and 1900s, Sir Clifford SIFTON's Dept of the Interior, for instance, issued posters in conjunction with the CPR to populate the "Last, Best West," a relationship that persisted into the 1920s. Other transportation companies, such as the CNR and Canada Steamship Lines, were also quick to get into the act.

Canada's entry into WWI brought with it a need to co-ordinate recruitment, Victory Bond, "home front" and other campaigns, which resulted in the formation of the War Poster Service, responsible for publishing material for national distribution. Private printing and graphic art firms, such as Toronto's Rous and Mann Press and Montréal's Mortimer Co Ltd, benefited from this work, which generally involved the designing and printing of colour lithographic posters, billboards and press advertisements. Similarly, during WWII, the National War Financing Board was set up to sell Victory Bonds; the director of Public Information cautioned that loose lips sink ships; and the National Film Board issued striking posters (many designed by "Mayo," as Montréal's Harry Mayerovitch signed himself) to advertise the documentaries it produced for the Wartime Information Board, successor to the DPI. Among the Canadian designers and illustrators who lent their talents to these intensive campaigns were Leslie Trevor, A.J. Casson, Eric Aldwinckle, Albert Cloutier, William Winter, Alex Colville, Philip Surrey, Rex Woods, J.S. Hallam, A. Bruce Stapleton and Henry Eveleigh.

The tradition of the painter turning to commercial art, illustration or typographic design to finance his or her fine-art career continued with

Bertram Brooker, Carl Schaefer, Clare Bice, Fred J. Finlay, Jack McLaren, John A. Hall, Jack Bush, Oscar Cahén, Harold Town and, into the early 1960s, Joyce Wieland, Michael Snow and Louis de Niverville. Graphic designers, commercial and editorial illustrators and art directors by day, painters by night, by weekend and holiday, these were the anglophone counterparts of the québecois artists whose livelihoods were provided by church commissions and teaching jobs in art colleges. This splitting of energies prevailed in Canada at least up to the 1960s, when the CANADA COUNCIL and the provincial arts councils introduced the grant system, which released artists from their servitude to applied art. In their place arose a class of professionals for whom design was not a begrudged avocation but a full-time occupation.

Although there were a few forward-looking commercial-art and illustration specialists in Canada before WWII, their efforts to impose international standards were usually thwarted by the innate conservatism of advertisers and the agencies that served their needs. Toronto's Eric Aldwinckle and Montréal's Raoul Bonin and Allan Harrison were among the first of their breed to try to apply the *art moderne* theories and practice of E. McKnight Kauffer, Jean Carlú and A.M. Cassandre to the poster in the 1940s, but their form-follows-functionalism did not find many exponents until the 1950s when a new generation of graphic and industrial designers took over the industry in Canada. Their contemporaries Henry Eveleigh and Carl Dair formed a partnership in Montréal in 1947, which, though it was dissolved in 1951, offered a model for other such collaborations. Dair went on to design "Cartier," Canada's first and only domestically produced typeface, as a Centennial project in 1967.

The rate of change was accelerated with the influx of immigrants from war-devastated Europe, who brought with them the advanced styles and techniques they had developed alongside such modernist art movements as De Stijl and Purism: the asymmetric typography pioneered by Jan Tischold, the grid system and the *sans serif* typography preferred by the Swiss and German leaders of the field. The 1950s, 1960s and early 1970s were dominated by these émigrés and their disciples – among them Rolf Harder, Ernst Roch, Fritz Gottschalk, Gerhard Dorrié, Walter Jungkind and Walter Jule – to the point that Canada's finest homegrown designer, Allan Fleming, could complain that the mechanical sterility of "Futura," the favoured typeface of the period, had stripped the country's design of any recognizable identity.

The imported modes arrived first, and persisted longest, in Montréal, where the Swiss training and Bauhaus aesthetics of Georges Beaupré and Laurent Marquart could also be found in the work of their coevals Pierre-Yves Pelletier and Jean Morin. In Toronto the less doctrinaire British typographical heritage informed the contributions of Clair Stewart, Allan Fleming, Leslie Smart, Paul Arthur, Carl Brett and John Gibson. Fleming's work at Cooper and Beatty and later at U of T Press set a standard which inspired his colleagues and successors at the press, Will Rueter and Laurie Lewis, to similar heights, while Frank Newfeld and V. John Lee at McClelland and Stewart, Peter Dorn at Queen's U Press and Robert Reid and Ib Kristensen at McGill U Press also encouraged academic and commercial publishers to take an interest in "the look of the book." Fleming, who also set his stamp on the national psyche with his elegant logotype for CNR, argued for a more humane, graceful and historically aware style than was the internationalist norm.

"La Nouvelle Année" in *Le Monde Illustré*, 5 Jan 1901 (*courtesy National Archives of Canada/C-105550*).

The 2 events that brought Canadian graphic design into the second half of the 20th century were EXPO 67 and the 1976 Montréal Olympics. In charge of La Compagnie de l'Exposition de 1967's graphics and signage program was Montréal's Georges Huel, who designed the official Expo poster, while Guy Lalumière was responsible for the posters for the cultural pavilions. Other designers employed by the Canadian Government Expositions commission included Burton Kramer, Frank Mayrs and Neville Smith, the latter 2 of whom also worked on the interior of the Canadian Pavilion at the 1970 Osaka World's Fair. The unfortunate decision to use Adrian Frutiger's impersonal "Univers" typeface for all of Expo's posters and signage resulted in a sterile uniformity that also marred the graphics program of the XXI Olympiad. Georges Huel, director-general of graphics and design for Le Commité de l'Organisation des Jeux Olympiques (COJO), hoped to use the occasion to "show ... that with good planning, the right people involved in design can really contribute to an event like our Games." The "right people" turned out, to the dismay of the rest of Canada's designers, illustrators and photographers, to be Montréal's advertising and design establishment: Huel took care of signage, furniture designs, uniforms, etc, P.Y. Pelletier acted as deputy-director in charge of all printed material, and Fritz Gottschalk headed the Design and Quality Control Office. In all, COJO commissioned the services of 8 permanent designers and over 100 freelancers. If nothing else, Expo and the Olympics brought into prominence Québec's graphic design talent-bank, as represented by the likes of Pierre Ayot, Raymond Bellemare, Yvon Laroche and Guy St-Arnaud, in addition to the Italian-born maverick Vittorio Florucci, who silkscreened his own posters when his designs were rejected by COJO.

The 1970s were also marked by the formation of a number of influential graphic design partnerships: for instance, Rolf Harder's and Ernst Roch's Design Collaborative, Penthouse Studio and Studio 2+2, in Montréal; Gottschalk and Ash, Graafiko, Fleming and Donoahue, Burns and Cooper and Eskind-Waddell, in Toronto; and MacDonald, Michaleski and Associates, in Winnipeg. While most of these companies have broken up, new affiliations have since been established, though the trend of the 1980s has been to smaller, more flexible, less agency-like houses that allow designers to make personal statements. Increased specialization is also a characteristic of the last 2 decades, with more and more firms concentrating on such esoteric disciplines as corporate design and signage, logotypes and, most recently, computer graphics, which, alongside computer typesetting and laser printing, are revolutionizing the profession.

The growing reliance of designers on typographic and photographic components and the reduction of the importance of commissioned illustrations in the immediate postwar period was marked by the formation of the Society of Typographic Designers of Canada in 1956. The emergence of such bodies was a feature of a phase of expansion and consolidation, which culminated with the establishment of the Society of Graphic Designers of Canada (SGDC) at a meeting of representatives from across the country in Ottawa in 1974. The SGDC received its federal charter in 1976, and went on to form a number of autonomous chapters, but its influence waned in the 1980s as designers reacted to the tendency of such top-heavy organizations to become powerbases for the promotion of individual reputations.

The independent Société des graphistes du Québec, founded in 1972, is more tightly knit than its anglophone counterpart, in reflection of the relative size and cohesiveness of the province's French Canadian design community, but it, too, shows the effects of recent events such as the failure of the *séparatiste* cause. While many of the younger designers supported this nationalist movement, senior voices cautioned that Sovereignty-Association would mean the loss of the lucrative federal government contracts on which the industry, as elsewhere in Canada, was heavily dependent.

Ottawa's attempts to raise public consciousness of all forms of design excellence in the 1970s, through such agencies as Information Canada and Design Canada, were doomed by cutbacks, official indifference or opposition to what was considered a "frill," as well as internal strife. However, Ulrich Wodicka and his team were able to impose a standard signage and identity program on all federal departments through their work with Information Canada and the Treasury Board. Such activities led to the emergence of the "official" designer, a bureaucrat often suspected of being unable to function in the harsh realities of the world beyond the confines of the capital.

Paralleling the professional societies and support agencies were the art directors' clubs that grew up in Montréal, Toronto, Winnipeg and Vancouver to reward innovation and quality through annual exhibitions and publications and the draughting of codes of ethics and standards. Their pursuits augmented those of the art schools and community colleges across Canada, which began to upgrade their programs in the 1960s to meet the demands of an ever-more exacting marketplace. These departments, such as the one headed at the NOVA SCOTIA COLLEGE OF ART AND DESIGN by Anthony Mann, acted as catalysts within their respective environs, bringing word of international developments and sparking creative responses. Thus both the West and the Maritimes were able to compete in excellence with anything Toronto and Montréal could offer – witness the posters designed by Bernard Michaleski for Winnipeg's Manitoba Theatre Centre, or Stefan Czernecki for Theatre Calgary – though recessions have repeatedly driven the ability as well as the money back to the major central cities.

Today, there is no one identifiable "Canadian" graphic design style. Eclecticism and diversity are the rule here, as they are in the political, social, ethnic and cultural makeup of the nation as a whole. If any one pattern has emerged in the post-modernist 1970s and 1980s, it is the revival of illustration and the use of classic typefaces as serious competitors with photography for the affections of art directors and editors, especially those of high-quality magazines, and of promoters of cultural events. Thus encouraged, increasing numbers of Canadian illustrators are penetrating the formerly exclusive British and American publishing markets, while our book designers and graphic designers are carrying away their share of international awards.

Canada has been the site of several important design and design education conferences, the first of which took place at U of Alberta in 1975 under the sponsorship of the SGDC and the SGC, the National Design Council and the Canada Council. An International Design Symposium was held at U du Québec à Montréal in 1980, and teacher and designer Andy Tomcik, organized a major Alliance graphique internationale conference at York U in 1982. These events have helped to raise Canada's design profile beyond its borders and to give a sense of national purpose and direction within them. So too has the appearance of special issues of international design periodicals devoted to Canadian graphic art and illustration.

Public awareness of Canada's contributions to these fields lags behind that of other aspects of our cultural makeup. Because graphic art and design are all around us, they tend to be ignored – to become invisible. They can only improve and progress if there is a continuing demand for universally recognized standards of excellence that do not compromise our need to express ourselves as a confederation of peoples and places through the applied as well as the fine arts. *See also* ONTARIO COLLEGE OF ART; PRIVATE PRESSES. ROBERT STACEY

Reading: C. Dair, *Design with Type* (1967); J. Gibson and L. Lewis, eds, *Sticks and Stones: Some Aspects of Canadian Printing History* (1980); Robert Stacey, *The Canadian Poster Book* (1979).

Graphic Publishers Limited (1925-32), also referred to as Graphic Press, was established by Henry C. Miller, a printer in Ottawa, who was determined to create a Canadian publishing house with an exclusive commitment to Canadian authors and "Well-Made Canadian Literature." The press had a tangled corporate history, partly because of the great financial difficulties it experienced from undercapitalization and also because of the Depression, which overtook the latter period of its history. However, it managed to publish some 71 titles under its imprint, in addition to an associated vanity list called RU-MI-LOU publications. Although there does not appear to have been a consistent editorial policy, Graphic produced fiction and poetry as well as some history and criticism. Frederick Philip GROVE, who served briefly as its editor from late 1929 to early 1931, was one of a number of well-known Canadian literary personalities connected with Graphic. Others included Lawrence J. BURPEE, William Arthur DEACON, Raymond KNISTER who won the First Prize Award in the Graphic Novel Contest with his manuscript of *My Star Predominant* (later published by Ryerson) and Madge MacBeth, Graphic's most prominent author, who helped to launch the press by providing it with its first book and who wrote under her own name and the pseudonyms of Gilbert Knox and W.S. Dill. Alan B. Beddoe, an Ottawa artist, did much of the designing for Graphic and created its distinctive thunderbird logo which appears on the title pages and the spines of Graphic books. Graphic published both in a hardcover and a paperback format. MICHAEL GNAROWSKI

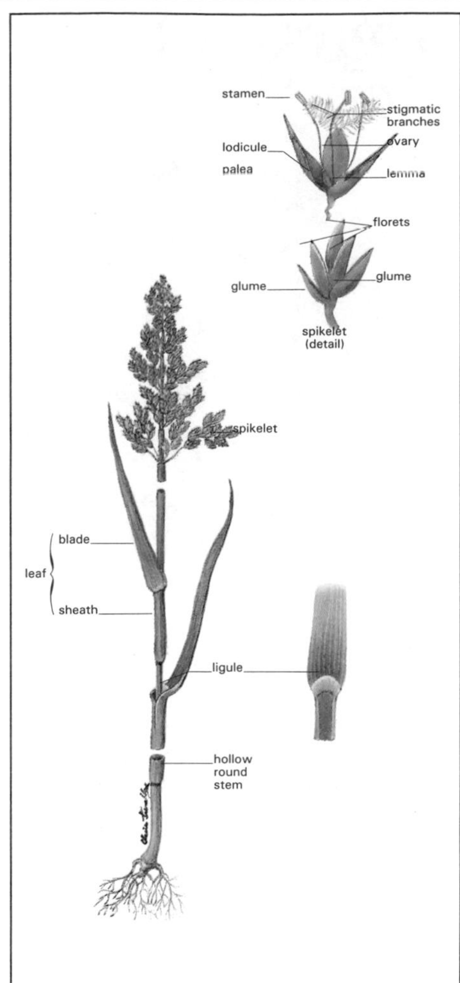

Grass (*artwork by Claire Tremblay*).

Grasses are among the most familiar and important flowering plants. They are used primarily as foodstuffs. Humans consume grasses directly as CEREALS (eg, wheat, corn, barley, rye, oats) or as sweetening (eg, sugar from sugar cane, molasses from sorghum). Most meat and dairy products are derived from grass-eating domesticated animals. Many wild animals are also grass eaters. Grasses contribute to the aesthetic environment as turfs gracing playing fields, golf courses and lawns, and as ornamental garden grasses. They stabilize soil and prevent erosion. Grasslands began to appear about 25 million years ago, changing the face of much of the world and providing food for grazing animals. Grasses and grazers evolved together. Grasses benefit because grazers control the growth of competing species and provide fertilizers. Grasses owe their success largely to peculiarities of their structure. They consist of vegetative structures (roots, stems and leaves) and reproductive structures (flowers and associated modified leaves). Although most grass parts are like those of other flowering plants, certain structures are unique. Usually, the stems (culms) are hollow, except at points (nodes) where leaves are attached. However, some well-known grasses do not have hollow internodes, eg, corn (*Zea mays*) and big bluestem (*Andropogon gerardii*) of the Canadian prairies. The characteristic grass leaf consists of a sheath (basal portion of the leaf) surrounding the stem for some distance above the node. The part of the leaf that diverges away from the stem is the blade. At the junction of sheath and blade, there is often a small structure (ligule) forming a continuation of the sheath. Sheaths of grass leaves may be open (with edges overlapping but not fused) or closed (with fused edges). Closed sheaths are less common but are found in the widespread bluegrasses (*Poa*) and bromegrasses (*Bromus*).

Grasses range in size from 3 cm (eg, *Aira praecox* of Vancouver I) to 2 m (eg, *Elymus cinereus* of BC and Alberta). Their life cycle may be completed in a single year, as in many annual crop plants, or they may survive for hundreds of years, as do native prairie perennials. Canadians usually associate grasses with prairie vegetation, although they occur in all habitats except in the densest woods. Some grasses (eg, 3-awn grass, *Aristida longiseta*) are found in arid regions of British Columbia, others (eg, wild rice, *Zizania aquatica*) in eastern Canadian lakes. Certain genera (eg, *Arctagrostis* and *Arctophila*) are native to the Canadian Arctic.

Turf grasses are developed from species that show desirable characteristics, eg, density of growth, fast growth after seeding, ability to remain green, etc. In Canada cold hardiness and frequently drought resistance are also important. Popular Canadian lawn grass mixtures often include species of *Poa* (eg, Kentucky bluegrass, roughstalk bluegrass) and *Festuca* (especially creeping red fescue, chewing fescue), although other useful species have been developed.

JACK MAZE

Reading: A. Arber, *The Gramineae* (1959).

Grasshopper, common name for straight-winged insects which, together with locusts, make up the order Orthoptera. Over 12 000 species are known worldwide; about 140 in Canada, ranging in length from 2-12 cm. All provinces have grasshoppers; most species occur in the western grasslands, but some live in forest clearings and on trees in river valleys north to YT. Grasshoppers are herbivorous and diurnal. Most have wings; many are strong fliers. Unlike locusts, grasshoppers are usually nonmigratory. Usually one generation is produced annually, from eggs that have overwintered. Some grassland species overwinter as immature nymphs; a few, in the interior of BC, require 2 years to mature. Females lay several clutches (egg pods), each containing 10-90 eggs, depending on species. Under favourable, late summer conditions, large numbers of egg pods are deposited by pest species in densely packed egg beds or distributed through cultivated fields. In spring, many nymphs hatch and attack seedling cereal crops. Damage can be extensive: in outbreak years 5-10% of cereal crops may be lost to grasshoppers. Several species, especially the Rocky Mountain locust (*Melanoplus spretus*), extinct since 1902, discouraged, for a time, settlement of western Canada. Winged adults, flying downwind, can emigrate to invade ripening crops many kilometres distant. Five species are important insect pests: 4 species of genus *Melanoplus* and the clear-winged grasshopper, *Camnula pellucida*. All damage cereal crops; the latter devastates BC rangeland grasses. Several other species compete with cattle for forage. Hot, dry weather favours population growth; cool, damp weather retards growth and encourages fungi and bacteria that can wipe out large grasshopper populations. Birds, small mammals, and other insects prey on grasshoppers; small worms and maggots are internal parasites. Although weather and natural control agents are most effective in keeping numbers down, chemical control during an outbreak is still required for crop protection. The so-called long-horned grasshoppers are not true grasshoppers. They are more closely related to CRICKETS.

P.W. RIEGERT

Grasslands National Park (est 1981, 920 km^2 – proposed) situated in the SW Saskatchewan PRAIRIES on the Canada/US border. At first glance, the park area appears empty: a gently undulating expanse of sun-scorched plains. But hidden from view are BADLANDS, meandering rivers and fertile sloughs. The hot, dry summers and cold winters produce an environment that supports a unique flora and fauna, including several species of rare herbs, 2 rare grasses and Canada's only black-tailed prairie dogs. Among its grasses the park also supports pronghorn, coyote, red fox, mule deer and numerous small mammals. Species of reptiles and amphibians, rare elsewhere in Canada, can be found along the Frenchman R valley. Until the 1850s the park area was inhabited only by nomadic Indians who hunted throughout the territory. At that time, rapid settlement led to the growth of ranching. As of early 1988, the park had still not been established because of a dispute over potential resource development.

LILLIAN STEWART

Grassy Narrows, Ont, IR, Kenora Dist, pop 740 (1986c), is situated on the English-Wabigoon river system 89 km NE of Kenora. In 1970 two Ojibwa bands in NW Ontario, the Grassy Narrows band and the Islington band on the Whitedog Reserve, came to public attention when it was revealed that an alarming number of their members were displaying symptoms of the debilitating Minamata disease, a form of MERCURY poisoning named after the Japanese fishing village where it was first diagnosed in 1956. Studies determined that the fish eaten by these people contained excessively high mercury levels. The source of the pollution proved to be the chemical plant operated by Reed Paper Ltd as part of its pulp and paper operations at Dryden, upstream from the reserves. From 1962 to 1970 between 4 and 9 kg of mercury per day had been dumped into the Wabigoon R. The provincial government reacted to these findings by ordering Reed to cut its disposal of mercury; in fact, only after Reed ceased using mercury in its operations in Nov 1975 did the river systems begin to clear up.

The economic and social impact of the remedy to the mercury pollution proved nearly as devastating to the Grassy Narrows and Islington bands as the problem itself. The decline of tourism and the loss of traditional ways of life created social problems. Alcohol and drug abuse, family violence, suicides and depression became all too common in the late 1970s. With the 1980s the situation began to change, largely because of the efforts of the people themselves. In 1986 these efforts were greatly enhanced when a long-awaited settlement was reached with Reed, its successor company Great Lakes Forest Products, and the federal and provincial governments, which provided $16.7 million compensation to the 2 bands.

MATT BRAY

Gravelbourg, Sask, Town, pop 1305 (1986c), 1338 (1981c), inc 1916, is located on a CPR branch, 119 km SW of Moose Jaw. It was named after Father Louis-Joseph-Pierre Gravel (1868-1926), a missionary colonizer, who settled there with 5 brothers and a sister in 1906. Gravel sought fellow immigrants among Québec and New England Francophones, hoping to establish a number of French settlements in the same general area. In 1918 a convent was built in the town as well as a college, which was affiliated with U of Ottawa; other Catholic buildings followed: a Romanesque cathedral (1919), a monastery (1926) and a hospital. With the creation of the Diocese of Gravelbourg (1930) and the appointment of a francophone bishop, the town became known as the mecca of Saskatchewan's French inhabitants. In recent years, its importance for French Canadian culture has continued. Its college has become a residential, co-educational, French-language high school. The Centre Culturel Maillard (constructed 1984-85) houses a museum and is the house and meeting place of several francophone associations. It has the only professional French Canadian dance ensemble in the province.

MARGARET BAERWALDT

Gravenhurst, Ont, Town, pop 8926 (1986c), 8532 (1981c), inc 1887, located at S end of Lk Muskoka, 170 km N of Toronto. The name was arbitrarily assigned by the federal government, perhaps after a place in Washington Irving's novel *Bracebridge Hall.* In the 19th century it was a sawmilling centre, but as logging declined tourism became the most important activity. The Muskoka district, with its many wooded islands set among the crystal waters of a series of interconnected lakes, developed into a popular cottage and tourist resort area, earning Gravenhurst its nickname "Gateway to the MUSKOKA LAKES." The town was long a base for steamer service for the Muskoka Lks, and the paddle steamer *Segwun* has been restored to its original (1887) condition. The birthplace of native son Norman BETHUNE has been restored as a museum and national historic site.

DANIEL FRANCIS

Gravity, the fundamental physical property of attraction between all bodies, is here considered mainly as it relates to the study of the Earth. Measurements of the acceleration resulting from gravity are used in physical geodesy, which studies the size and shape of the Earth, and in geophysics in determinations of the distribution and structure of masses beneath the Earth's surface. Gravitational acceleration is measured in "gals" (after Galileo): 1 gal = 0.01 m per second per second. At the Earth's surface, the acceleration is approximately 980 gals and varies with latitude and elevation through a range of about 7 gals. Absolute measurements, accurate to the order of 0.01 milligal, are now being made using LASERS and advanced ELECTRONICS for direct observations of the acceleration of freely falling bodies. Relative measurements, accurate to 0.05 milligal or better, are routinely made using easily portable gravity meters (gravimeters), which measure differences of attraction with a delicate spring mechanism. Such instruments have been adapted for use on the seafloor, on ice surfaces or in moving ships and aircraft. Gravity fields have also been calculated from the precise tracking of SATELLITES around the Earth, the moon, Mars and other planetary bodies.

Gravity measurements are compared to an internationally adopted theoretical formula determined from basic parameters defining the shape of the Earth. Differences between measured and theoretical values are calculated to give the free-air gravity anomaly, ie, the value the measurement would have if the point of observation were at sea level; or the Bouguer gravity anomaly, which is calculated assuming that there is a slab of rock of uniform density (commonly 2.67 megagrams/m^3) between the point of observation and sea level. In mountainous regions, the effect of rugged terrain must also be calculated.

Gravity maps are produced by drawing contours joining points of equal gravity anomaly, or by assigning colours to the average gravity anomaly in a pixel or unit cell to produce a solid colour map using a modern automated plotter. Regions of relatively positive anomaly (gravity "highs") and relatively negative anomaly (gravity "lows") correspond to mass excesses and deficiencies beneath the surface. The Gravity Anomaly Map of Canada 1987 combines Bouguer anomalies on land and free-air anomalies offshore, showing coverage of approximately 80% of Canada and adjacent oceans by observations 12 km apart or closer. The pattern of anomalies over Canada reflects its geologic history of ancient mountain-building episodes, volcanic activity, deposition of sediments and other GEOLOGICAL PROCESSES.

Gravity measurements are used by exploration companies in determining the most promising region for economic exploitation of oil, gas and mineral resources. For example, in the Beaufort Sea, the Arctic Archipelago and the seafloor off Nova Scotia and Newfoundland, analysis of gravity anomaly patterns has been a significant part of the search for oil-bearing and gas-bearing formations. In Canada gravity anomalies have also been used to trace the extent of mineral provinces. A good example is the Manitoba Nickel Belt, where ore bodies are distributed along the axis of a negative gravity anomaly. Other mineral provinces so examined include the iron ranges of Labrador, the Sudbury Basin, the Abitibi-Timmins belt and the copper-bearing rocks of the western cordillera. Although few ore bodies are discovered directly by reconnaissance gravity mapping, detailed gravity surveys are often used to define the extent of ores and estimate reserves. Tonnages of massive sulphide deposits in the Northwest Territories and northern Ontario and salt volumes in Nova Scotia have been determined in this way.

Gravity measurements are also used in studies of movements of the Earth's surface associated with large EARTHQUAKES, VOLCANOES or the motions of the continents; or the uplift of regions such as Hudson Bay, which is still rising at a rate of about 2 cm per year after being depressed by the last continental GLACIATION more than 10 000 years ago.

M.R. DENCE AND R.A. GIBB

Gray, George R., track and field athlete (b at Coldwater, Canada W 4 May 1865; d at Sault Ste Marie, Ont 7 Jan 1933). After high school he competed for 17 years at his specialty, putting the shot, without being defeated. At age 20 in 1885, at the Canadian Amateur Athletic Assn meet in Toronto, he defeated champions from other countries with his first put of 41′ 5.5″ (12.64 m) and was acclaimed world champion. From 1887 he competed for the famous NY Athletic Club, which paid his expenses, while continuing his Canadian career in the lumber business. He held and broke the world shotput record several times, competing throughout N America and in Britain. By retirement he had won 188 first-place medals and trophies.

GERALD REDMOND

Gray, Herbert Eser, politician (b at Windsor, Ont 25 May 1931). He graduated from the School of Commerce of McGill U and Osgoode Law School, Toronto, and is a member of the Ontario Bar. He has represented a Windsor constituency in Parliament since 1962. A prominent Liberal nationalist, in 1969 he was the first Jew to be appointed to Cabinet. He gained attention through his report on FOREIGN OWNERSHIP tabled in 1972 when he was minister of national revenue. Though not reappointed to Cabinet after the 1974 election, he became minister of industry, trade and commerce in 1980 and was president of the Treasury Board until the defeat of the Liberal government in 1984. Since then he has been Opposition House Leader and a vocal critic of establishing freer trade links with the US. JOHN ENGLISH

Gray, James Henry, journalist, social historian (b at Whitemouth, Man 31 Aug 1906). Gray grew up in Winnipeg, left school to help support his family, and after a series of jobs went on relief during the Depression. He worked for the *Winnipeg Free Press* 1935-47, first as a reporter and later as an editorial writer. He edited Calgary's *Farm and Ranch Review* 1947-55, introducing unaccustomed topics such as farmers' subsoil rights, and the *Western Oil Examiner* 1955-58, where he championed the unpopular notion that independent Canadian oil producers should take precedence over American multinationals. Later, he moved to the Home Oil Co to promote the building of a Canadian pipeline to the East. Gray's books, written after his retirement, draw on personal experience and original research. Lively and detailed, they investigate such facets of prairie life as the fight against the dustbowl, the Depression, prostitution, prohibition, the Calgary Stampede and the legal profession in Alberta. JEAN O'GRADY

Reading: J.H. Gray, *The Winter Years* (1966), *The Boy from Winnipeg* (1970), *Booze* (1972), *Troublemaker!* (1978), *A Brand of its Own* (1985) and *Talk to My Lawyer* (1987).

Gray, Jessie Catherine, surgeon, lecturer, researcher (b at Augusta, Georgia 26 Aug 1910; d at Toronto 16 Oct 1978). Canada's "first lady of surgery," and one of the 4 leading cancer surgeons in N America, Gray earned a formidable succession of firsts: first woman gold medalist in medicine at U of T (1934); first woman to obtain the master of surgery degree (1939); first woman resident surgeon at the Toronto General Hospital; first woman fellow of the Royal Coll of Surgeons (Canada, 1941); first woman member of the Central Surgical Society of N America; first woman elected to the Science Council of Canada (1966). She was appointed associate surgeon in chief at Women's College Hospital, Toronto, in 1941, and held the post of surgeon in chief from 1945 to her retirement in 1965. DONNA YAVORSKY RONISH

Gray, John Hamilton, lawyer, politician, judge, premier of NB (b at St George, Bermuda 1814; d at Victoria 5 June 1889). Remembered as a FATHER OF CONFEDERATION, Gray, a brilliant orator, used his skill in the courtroom, as lieutenant-colonel in the militia, on the stump, in the NB Assembly, in the Canadian House of Commons and on the BC Supreme Court. A "Conservative of the old school ... gentlemanly ... forgiving," he was considered somewhat shallow, shifting to any wind. His premiership of New Brunswick 1856-57 was tarnished by imperial influence, and his support of CONFEDERATION saw him abandon his colleagues for the Liberal S.L. TILLEY. He had, however, advocated union as early as 1849. His reward was the puisne judgeship of British Columbia's Supreme Court in 1873. Though resented by some in BC as an "empty-headed favourite," Gray's reputation as a jurist and arbitrator grew. He stood against the majority in his defence of the rights of the CHINESE, and became an expert on Canadian-American boundary negotiations. CARL M. WALLACE

Gray, John Hamilton, soldier, premier of PEI (b at Charlottetown 14 June 1811; d there 13 Aug 1887). Educated in England, Gray served for many years in South Africa and India with the 7th Dragoon Guards, retiring permanently to PEI in 1856. Elected to the Legislative Assembly in 1858 and 1859, Gray supported Bible reading in the schools and a commission to settle the LAND QUESTION. He became premier on 2 March 1863, supporting Maritime union and, after the CHARLOTTETOWN CONFERENCE, which he hosted, CONFEDERATION. When the Islanders rejected the union of British North America after the QUÉBEC CONFERENCE, Gray suddenly resigned as premier on 20 Dec 1864, perhaps influenced by his wife's illness. He became increasingly involved in the military affairs of the Island and later the Dominion. J.M. BUMSTED

Gray, John Howard, playwright (b at Ottawa 26 Sept 1946). Raised in Truro, NS, and educated at Mount Allison and UBC, Gray was a founder of Vancouver's Tamahnous Theatre. His celebrated play, *Billy Bishop Goes To War* (1978), is a 2-man musical which scrutinizes W.A. BISHOP's rise to heroic stature. After touring Canada, *Bishop* opened on Broadway in 1980. It won a Gov Gen's Award for drama in 1983. Gray has also written the plays *18 Wheels* (1977) and *Rock and Roll* (1981), and the novel *Dazzled* (1984). He is an outspoken nationalist on cultural matters. NEIL BESNER

Gray, Joseph Alexander, physicist (b at Melbourne, Australia 7 Feb 1884; d at London, Eng 5 Mar 1966). After graduating from Melbourne U in 1907, Gray worked in Sir Ernest RUTHERFORD's laboratory in Manchester, Eng, concentrating on the study of the interaction of electrons and X rays with atoms. In 1912 he went to McGill to conduct further research. On the Western Front in WWI, he was in charge of locating enemy batteries by sound ranging. Awarded an OBE, Gray returned to McGill in 1919. From 1924 until his retirement in 1952, he was research professor at Queen's. His discoveries regarding the breadth of the energy spectrum of electrons and the scattering of X rays were important contributions to the development of the new theory of the atom. The Royal Society of London, to which he was appointed in 1932, credited his work as "clearly foreshadowing what is known as the Compton effect" (for which A.H. Compton received the Nobel Prize). He was elected to the RSC in 1922 and received the first gold medal of the Canadian Association of Physicists in 1956. YVES GINGRAS

Gray, Robert, sea captain, fur trader (b at Tiverton, RI 10 May 1755; d probably at sea 1806). He made 2 voyages to the NORTHWEST COAST for Boston merchants investing in the sea-otter fur trade. The first, 1787-90, was under the command of John Kendrick with 2 ships: the *Columbia Rediviva* (the *Columbia*) and its tender the *Lady Washington*, which was commanded by Gray. On trading voyages Gray proved the insularity of the Queen Charlotte Is. He sailed the *Columbia* back to Boston via the Orient, making it the first American ship to sail around the world. On his second voyage, 1790-93, he captained the *Columbia*, wintered on Meares I (1791-92) where he built Ft Defiance and a trading sloop, the *Adventure*, and in 1792 discovered the Columbia River, which was named for his ship. This discovery later supported the US claim to the Oregon Territory. JOHN DEWHIRST

Reading: F.W. Howay, ed, *Voyages of the "Columbia" to the Northwest Coast* (1941).

Gray, Robert Hampton, aviator (b at Trail, BC 2 Nov 1917; d in Onagawa Wan, Honshu I, Japan 9 Aug 1944). During WWII he served aboard the RN aircraft carrier HMS *Formidable*. He was awarded the VICTORIA CROSS for a valiant dive-bombing attack on a Japanese destroyer. Though he was wounded and his aircraft in flames, he sank the ship with a direct hit. He was killed when his plane crashed.

Gray Burial Site, N of Swift Current, Sask, lies on a sandy hillside to the W of an ancient glacial outwash channel. Excavations between 1970 and 1974 showed that it was used as a traditional burial ground by a small band of hunters who roamed the region between 3500 and 1000 BC. With a mobility based on the use of pack dogs, they followed the seasonal wandering of the bison herds. They supplemented their diet with berries, other mammals such as deer and pronghorn, and smaller animals including birds and their own dogs. During their seasonal travels they are thought to have accumulated the bones of their dead, returning periodically to the location of the Gray Site for formal burial ceremonies. The bones were interred in composite groups, including those of a number of children and one or more adult crania. The associated artifacts and the character of the burial remains reveal the antiquity of the ritual and ceremonialism that was typical of the Plains Indians of the historic period. *See also* ARCHAEOLOGY; PREHISTORY. JAMES F.V. MILLAR

Grayling, common name for freshwater fishes of class Osteichthyes, family Salmonidae (SALMON), subfamily Thymallinae (sometimes elevated to family rank). Graylings are most easily identified by their very large dorsal fins. Arctic grayling (*Thymallus arcticus*), the only species in Canada, is one of 4 species widely distributed throughout the Northern Hemisphere. In Canada, it is confined to areas W of Hudson Bay, including northern portions of Manitoba, Saskatchewan, Alberta and BC, as well as the YT and the NWT, exclusive of the arctic islands. It also has a limited distribution in the Flathead R in southeastern BC and the Belly R in southeastern Alberta. Grayling occupy a wide variety of freshwater habitats but, although they sometimes enter brackish waters of coastal lagoons, they are generally intolerant of marine water.

Typically, adults spawn and young are reared in small, warm streams. They leave in fall to overwinter in larger streams or lakes or in the vicinity of perennial springs. Some populations are highly migratory, eg, some individuals of a population spawning in the upper reaches of the Donnelly R, NWT, overwinter in Great Bear Lk, over 350 km away. During the short northern summer, grayling feed voraciously on a wide variety of foods. They grow relatively rapidly until they reach maturity. Thereafter, growth slows as much of their energy intake is committed to reproduction. In the Far North, grayling sometimes live for 20 years. Grayling spawn in spring, often migrating under ice to reach spawning locations as early as possible. No nest is prepared. Eggs may fall among cracks between large rocks or the vigorous quivering of the spawning fish may deposit fine materials over them. Graylings are a prized sport fish, easily taken by fly-fishing or spinning gear, but are highly susceptible to overfishing. In some areas, populations have declined dramatically because of excessive angling. Although sometimes taken by native fishermen, grayling are not especially sought after. PETER J. MCCART

Great Auk (*Pinguinus impennis*), largest and only flightless AUK, is now extinct. All auks are expert divers which swim underwater using their wings, but the great auk had flipperlike wings, too short for flight. It was the original penguin (true penguins are unrelated birds native to the Southern Hemisphere). Great auks bred in large colonies at a few offshore islands in low arctic and boreal waters of the N Atlantic, from the Bird Rocks in the Gulf of St Lawrence to northern Britain. They laid a single, large egg on bare rock and the breeding cycle was completed in about 7 weeks. Their pattern of incubation and chick-rearing may have resembled that of the RAZORBILL, their closest living relative. The main food was probably fish. In winter, birds ranged offshore from southern Greenland to southern Spain and Florida. They were especially numerous on the GRAND BANKS. The great auk was destroyed by man. Flightless, and colonial when breeding, it was heavily exploited by early explorers for fresh food, by fishermen for bait and, in the late 1700s, by commercial hunters for feathers. The largest and best-documented colony, on FUNK I, Nfld, had been destroyed by about 1800. The last known breeding pair was collected (3 June 1844) on Eldey Rock off SW Iceland. D.N. NETTLESHIP

Great Awakening, New England-based movement of religious revivalism and evangelical pietism which came to Nova Scotia in 1775 with Henry ALLINE'S decision to preach; it subsequently spread across the Maritimes. The religious currents which produced it were international and at least a century old. Evangelical pietism had begun among LUTHERANS in Germany at the close of the 17th century, spread to England to influence the growth of METHODISM, and contributed to a major religious outpouring in colonial America between 1720 and 1745. From New England, the centre of American revivalism and the source of most early British settlement in Nova Scotia, beliefs and experiences familiar to those acquainted with revival and pietism came to the Maritimes. But the Canadian Awakening was also an indigenous response to peculiarly local conditions. In their scattered wilderness settlements Maritimers teetered on the brink of economic disaster, and with the outbreak of the American Revolution – which the isolated settlers did not really understand – there was a crisis of identity which a movement emphasizing personal salvation could allay, if not resolve.

Alline was soon joined by others. Some, such as John Payzant, were converts through Alline's preachings, but others, such as William BLACK and his Methodist colleagues, apparently arrived at a similar point independently of Alline's "New Light" movement. Alline and his immediate followers accepted infant baptism, but many of those later involved rejected the concept as incompatible with the crisis conversion experience of being "born again." By the 1790s, when the movement had spread beyond NS into NB and PEI and even to the US, the main competition was between Methodists and BAPTISTS. The Great Awakening contributed to religious fragmentation in the Maritimes, and helped establish a regional inclination toward EVANGELICAL churches which remains characteristic. The revival never really ended, but ebbed and flowed throughout much of the 19th century as settlement spread. J.M. BUMSTED

Great Bear Lake, 31 300 km², elev 156 m, lies astride the Arctic Circle in the northwestern NWT, about 200 km S of the Arctic Ocean. It is the eighth-largest lake in the world, fourth in N America and the largest lying entirely within Canada. It is 320 km long, up to 175 km wide

Great Bear Lake, NWT, the largest lake entirely in Canada and the 8th-largest lake in the world. Port Radium (now Echo Bay) is shown (*photo by John deVisser*).

and very deep – 413 m at one point. Dotted with numerous small islands, it is shaped like a giant amoeba with 5 great arms – Keith, McVicar, McTavish, Dease and Smith – which meet in a common centre. Great Bear R (120 km) drains the cold waters SW to the MACKENZIE R at Ft Norman. A string of interconnected lakes to the S – Hottah, Hardisty, Rae, Faber – are drained by the Camsell R into Conjuror Bay. Great Bear Lk lies in a vast wilderness, with the S and W arms reaching into the tundra and the E shore lapping the hard rock edge of the Canadian shield. The S and W shores are wooded, mostly with stunted spruce. The lake is icebound for 8 months of the year, often into July, and is served by tugs and steamers when free.

Europeans only slowly became aware of the location and immensity of the lake. Peter POND learned of its general location in 1783-84, and the FUR TRADE came to the area around 1800. John FRANKLIN'S expedition established Ft Franklin on Keith Arm 1825-26, while John RICHARDSON surveyed the N shore. P.W. DEASE spent the winter of 1837-38 at Ft Confidence, and a geological survey was carried out by Robert BELL 1900. Settlement was transient until pitchblende (an ore containing radium and uranium) was discovered in 1930, and Port Radium (now Echo Bay) was established at the E end of McTavish Arm 1933. Exploration and servicing were made possible by BUSH FLYING. Some of the ore used to make the atomic bombs used by the US in WWII was mined here. Exhaustive mining depleted the reserves and the mines have been abandoned. The lake is well stocked with fish, including relic species thought to have moved S from the Arctic Ocean ahead of the glaciers. Commercial fishing is not allowed because of the slow regeneration of the fish in the ice-cold water. The lake's name, adopted 1902, likely refers to the bears in the area and to the size of the lake. A more poetic explanation is that it was named for the northern constellation of stars, called Great Bear, which is reflected in its waters. JAMES MARSH

Great Coalition, 1864-67 The politics of the PROVINCE OF CANADA in the early 1860s were marked by instability and deadlock. The external dangers posed by the American Civil War combined with a legislative impasse to make drastic action necessary. The union of the Canadas had clearly failed, and its political leaders were ready to forget old political feuds to create a new political order. REFORM MOVEMENT leader George BROWN proposed that a parliamentary committee with members from all groups investigate how the impasse might be broken. This committee quickly concluded that the best solution was confederation of BRITISH NORTH AMERICA or the federal union of the Canadas. Brown quickly responded to the report by joining a coalition with the Conservatives with the intention of creating a new union. (It was announced to Parliament on 22 June 1864.) Thus the Great Coalition was formed under the leadership of Brown, George-Étienne CARTIER and, above all, John A. MACDONALD. The broadly based coalition was remarkably successful in meeting its major aims: the ending of political deadlock and the creation of a new political entity. It remained largely intact as the government of the Province of Canada until CONFEDERATION. JOHN ENGLISH

Great Depression Few countries were affected as severely as Canada by the worldwide Depression of the 1930s. It is estimated that between 1929 and 1933 Gross National Expenditure declined by 42%, by the latter year 30% of the LABOUR FORCE was unemployed, and 1 in 5 Canadians became dependent upon government relief for survival. Until WWII the UNEMPLOYMENT rate never declined below 12%. The Depression's severity was aggravated by its uneven impact, a rudimentary social-welfare structure and misguided government policy. Because 33% of its Gross National Income derived from exports, Canada was particularly affected by the collapse in world trade. The 4 western provinces, which depended almost exclusively on primary-product exports, were the most affected. In Saskatchewan, plagued by crop failures and the lowest price for wheat in recorded history, total provincial income plummeted by 90% within 2 years, forcing 66% of the rural population onto relief. The other western provinces were technically bankrupt from 1932 onwards. Although Ontario and Québec experienced heavy unemployment, they were less severely afflicted because of their more diversified industrial economies, which produced for the protected domestic market. The Maritimes had entered into severe economic decline in the 1920s and had less distance to fall.

The burden of the Depression was also unequally distributed between classes. Although wages dropped throughout the 1930s, prices declined even faster. As a result, the standard of living of property owners and those with jobs increased. Farmers, young people, small businessmen and the unemployed bore the brunt of economic hardship.

Demographic changes were a revealing index of hardship. POPULATION growth throughout the 1930s reached the lowest point since the 1880s through a combination of plummeting IMMIGRATION and birthrates. The number of immigrants accepted into Canada dropped from 169 000 in 1929 to fewer than 12 000 by 1935 and never rose above 17 000 for the remainder of the decade. During that time European JEWS fleeing Nazi Germany were denied a sanctuary in Canada (*see* REFUGEES). The number of Canada's deportations,

En route to Ottawa, some 1800 unemployed men stopped at Regina, Sask, June 1935 (*courtesy National Archives of Canada/C-24840*).

however, rose from fewer than 2000 in 1929 to more than 7600 just 3 years later. Almost 30 000 immigrants were forcibly returned to their countries of origin over the course of the decade, primarily because of illness or unemployment.

Canada's birthrate dropped from 13.1 live births per 1000 in 1930 to only 9.7 by 1937, the lowest ratio until the 1960s. During the 1930s, 50 years of urbanizing momentum were reversed as Canada's rural population (outside of Saskatchewan) grew more rapidly than its urban population. For many of the unemployed "going back to the land" was preferable to a miserable existence on urban relief.

With almost 33% of its gainfully employed still engaged in agriculture in 1931, Canada did not have an adequate system of dispensing welfare to the jobless. Although unemployment was a national problem, federal administrations led by the Conservative R.B. BENNETT (1930-35) and the Liberal W.L. Mackenzie KING (from 1935 onwards) refused, for the most part, to provide work for the jobless and insisted that their care was primarily a local and provincial responsibility. The result was fiscal collapse for the 4 western provinces and hundreds of municipalities and haphazard, degrading standards of care for the jobless. Monthly relief rates for a family of 5 varied from $60 in Calgary to $19 in Halifax. Although there were no official accounts of starvation, reports by medical authorities of scurvy and other diet deficiency diseases were common throughout the decade. Because local governments refused to aid single, homeless men, between 1932 and 1936 the federal government established UNEMPLOYMENT RELIEF CAMPS. Run by the Dept of Defence, the camps paid the men 20 cents a day for construction work in the bush. In 1935 a protest against conditions in the camps culminated in the Regina Riot – the most violent episode of the 1930s, in which one policeman was killed, dozens of men were injured and 130 arrested (*see* ON TO OTTAWA TREK).

The Depression altered established perceptions of the economy and the role of the state. The faith shared by both the Bennett and King governments and most economists that a balanced budget, a sound dollar and changes in the tariff would allow the private marketplace to bring about recovery was misplaced. The Depression spawned a variety of political reform movements, particularly at the provincial level, which advocated the use of the state to initiate recovery. The reforms included the inflationary SOCIAL CREDIT theories of Alberta Premier William ABERHART, the "Work and Wages" program of BC Premier T. Dufferin PATTULLO, and the democratic socialism of J.S. WOODSWORTH and the CO-OPERATIVE COMMONWEALTH FEDERATION. The UNION NATIONALE in Québec, led by Maurice DUPLESSIS, H.H. STEVENS's Reconstruction Party and the New Democracy movement of W.D. HERRIDGE were also spawned by the Depression. The COMMUNIST PARTY OF CANADA was virtually outlawed from 1931 (when 9 of its leaders were arrested and convicted under s98 of the Criminal Code for being members of an "unlawful association") until 1936, and banned when war was declared in 1939, although affiliated groups such as the Workers' Unity League, the Relief Camp Workers Union and the National Unemployed Workers Association played a significant role in organizing the unskilled and the unemployed in protest marches and demonstrations.

Although the national impact of these organizations was minimal, the Depression did ultimately result in an expansion of state responsibility for the economy and for social welfare. In 1934 Bennett's government created legislation to establish the BANK OF CANADA to regulate MONETARY POLICY; in 1935 the CANADIAN WHEAT BOARD was created to market and establish a minimum floor price for wheat; and in 1940 the federal government assumed responsibility for the unemployed by introducing a national UNEMPLOYMENT INSURANCE scheme and employment service. The Depression also legitimized the economic theories of British economist John Maynard Keynes, who argued that, if private investment failed to produce full employment, the state must initiate public investment through deficit spending to create jobs. Keynes's ideas influenced the National Employment Commission report (1938) and the report of the Royal Commission on DOMINION-PROVINCIAL RELATIONS (1940). The latter was important in generating the idea of EQUALIZATION PAYMENTS. Not until war broke out in 1939, however, did KEYNESIAN ECONOMICS become a deliberate part of government policy, and it was the massive state expenditures necessitated by the war that finally reduced unemployment to minimal levels by 1942. *See also* HISTORY SINCE CONFEDERATION; BUSINESS CYCLES; BENNETT'S NEW DEAL. JAMES STRUTHERS

Reading: J.L. Granatstein et al, *Twentieth Century Canada* (1983); M. Horn, ed, *The Dirty Thirties: Canadians in the Great Depression* (1972); H.B. Neatby, *The Politics of Chaos: Canada in the Thirties* (1972); B. Palmer, *Working-Class Experience: The Rise and Reconstitution of Canadian Labour 1800-1980* (1983); James Struthers, *No Fault of Their Own: Unemployment and the Canadian Welfare State, 1914-1941* (1984).

Great Divide Trail is a long-distance hiking trail, paralleling where possible the CONTINENTAL DIVIDE of Canada's Rocky Mts range. Some 560 km of the trail lies within the boundaries of Banff, Kootenay, Yoho and Jasper national parks, extending from Palliser Pass in the S to Mt ROBSON in the N. A series of high alpine trails combine to form a "Great Divide Route" which, if followed in its entirety, brings the hiker to elevations of just below 3000 m and gives a perspective of the entire Rockies landscape. In the mid-1970s the Great Divide Trail Assn of Calgary began work to extend the trail S from Banff National Pk along the BC-Alberta border to Waterton Lks National Pk. This section would follow some of the most spectacular scenery of the southern Rockies, adding about 700 km to the overall trail length and making it the longest hiking trail in Canada. BART DEEG

Great Lakes are the largest group in a chain of large lakes (including Winnipeg, Athabasca, Great Slave and Great Bear) that lies along the southern boundary of the Canadian Shield. From W to E the Great Lakes comprise Lakes SUPERIOR, Michigan (entirely in the US), HURON, ST CLAIR, ERIE and ONTARIO. They have a total area of approximately 246 050 km^2 and drop from 183 m above sea level at Lk Superior to 74 m at Lk Ontario – the most dramatic drop occurring at NIAGARA FALLS. Lake St Clair, while not properly a "great lake," is considered part of this Laurentian chain. After withdrawal of the Paleozoic seas, which had spread across most of the continent, there is little record of geological events in the Great Lks area between the end of the Pennsylvanian and late Tertiary periods. Although broad river valleys likely crossed the area, remnants of Tertiary erosion surfaces in Illinois and Wisconsin cannot be traced across the Great Lks, and reconstructions of preglacial drainage are uncertain. The Great Lks lie near the intersection of the Hudson Bay, Mississippi R and St Lawrence R drainage basins; because of progressive headwater capture by the Mississippi, that watershed now lies only about 10 km from parts of the southern shores of Lks Erie and Michigan, and only about 20 km from the western end of Lk Superior. Postglacial isostatic uplift continues to raise the northern shorelines of the Great Lks by about 0.4 m per century, relative to the southern shores of Lks Erie and Michigan.

The Great Lks occupy bedrock depressions that have been differentially eroded by glacial ice, and their form and location are largely controlled by structural geology. The arcuate forms of Lks Huron and Michigan have developed around the periphery of the Michigan structural basin, and the more resistant Silurian limestones and dolomites (NIAGARA ESCARPMENT) separate GEORGIAN BAY and Green Bay from the main lakes. The form of Lk Superior is largely controlled by Precambrian geology; that of Lks Erie and Ontario by trends in the underlying Appalachian geosyncline.

During the last glacial period (which lasted more than a million years) there were 4 glacial stages and, with each, the lake basins were progressively enlarged. Towards the end of the last glaciation (Wisconsin), lakes formed in front of retreating ice margins, first in the Erie and Michigan basins, and drained S to the Mississippi more than 14 000 years ago. Subsequently, a lake formed in the southern part of the Huron basin and drainage between Erie, Huron and Michigan was linked. There was also an outlet to the Hudson R (S of the

Ontario basin). The Ontario basin became ice free about 12 000 years ago; Lk Superior and Georgian Bay later. The presence of ice margins caused many early lakes to form at very high levels. At one time, a single huge lake covered much of the upper Great Lks area (Superior, Michigan and Huron). As the ice melted away from the natural outlets, lake levels often dropped quickly and to extremely low levels, for example, about a 150 m drop in the Ontario basin, with the opening of the St Lawrence Valley (12 000-11 500 years ago). As a result of continued uplift during the past 10 000 years, upper lakes drainage was fully transferred (through Lks St Clair and Erie) to Lk Ontario only 4000-5000 years ago, when the Chicago outlet (Lk Michigan) closed.

The Great Lakes have, since the days of the early fur trade, provided an important transportation route to the interior of the continent, and with the opening of the ST LAWRENCE SEAWAY (1959) they became a truly international waterway. P.G. SLY

Great Lone Land: A Narrative of Travel and Adventure in the North-West of America, The, by William Francis BUTLER, appeared 1872 in London. Butler's accounts of his adventures are the most poetic and the most personable of the 19th-century Canadian travel narratives. His lyrical descriptions of landscape, climate and seasonal change testify to his deep admiration for the sheer, unpopulated expanse and beauty of the Canadian West. Sent by the English in 1870 to gather intelligence about the RED RIVER REBELLION, Butler actually met with Louis RIEL at Ft Garry; his description of the encounter remains one of the most vivid portraits of Riel in our literature. *The Great Lone Land* was reprinted (Edmonton, 1968) with an introduction by Edward McCourt. NEIL BESNER

Rubber impression of Great Seal of Canada, Queen Elizabeth II (*courtesy National Archives of Canada/C-33866*).

Great Seal of Canada With the creation of the new state of Canada in 1867 a seal was needed for purposes of government. Accordingly, a temporary seal was readied. The intricate work of engraving a permanent seal was completed in England in 1869 and delivered to the governor general. It was single sided and showed Queen Victoria seated beneath a gothic canopy. Following custom, new seals were prepared with the accession of each new monarch: Edward VII, George V, George VI (because of his abdication, no great seal for Edward VIII was put into use) and Elizabeth II. That for the new queen was made at the Royal Canadian Mint in Ottawa. It was designed by Canadian artist Eric Aldwinckle and depicts the queen and the royal armorial bearings of Canada. It was authorized for use 14 Nov 1955. The governor general is the official keeper of the great seal; the registrar general has the day-to-day custody.

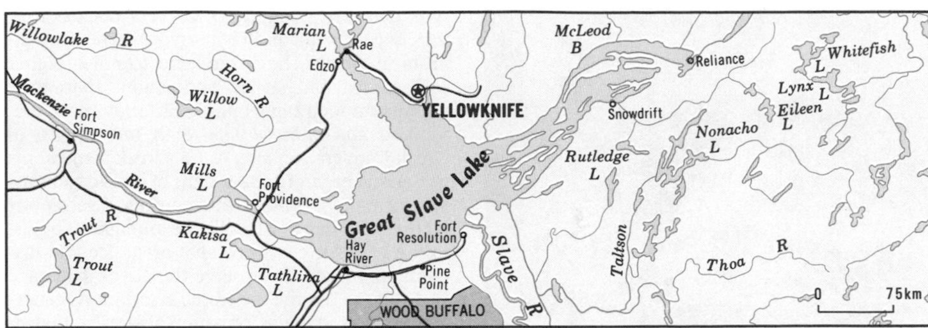

The great seal is usually impressed directly onto the surface of a document (*see,* for example, the photo of the constitution document accompanying the CONSTITUTION entry).

Great Slave Lake, 28 600 km², elev 156 m, fifth-largest lake in N America, tenth in the world, located in S-central NWT. It was named by Samuel HEARNE after the SLAVEY Indians. Great Slave, along with GREAT BEAR, ATHABASCA and a tangled chain of lakes between, are remnants of a single postglacial pool. Its S and E shores cut into the granite edge of the Canadian Shield; to the N and W lie the Barren Lands. Cold, very deep (614 m) and frozen 8 months of the year, Great Slave is a vast reservoir for numerous rivers and streams which spill over the crest of the Shield. Among these are the Yellowknife, Snare, Emile, Beaulieu, Snowdrift, Taltson and HAY; the Slave R carries the waters of the PEACE R past thick forest into the flat, grassy marshes of the delta on the S shore of the lake. The great MACKENZIE R issues from the extreme W end. Alexander MACKENZIE found the outlet in 1789, but the lake was first crossed by Hearne in the winter of 1771.

The CHIPEWYAN of the area carried furs to Hudson Bay as early as the 1730s, and the fur trade dominated the economy almost to WWII. The earliest settlements in the area were HBC posts: FORT RESOLUTION, Fort Rae (now RAE-EDZO), FORT PROVIDENCE and FORT RELIANCE. Robert BELL conducted the first survey (1899) and described the area's mineral potential. Klondike-bound travellers prospected in the area, but the gold rush came in 1934, when gold was discovered in the volcanic rock W of Yellowknife Bay. Next year the town of YELLOWKNIFE was established. The mining of the huge lead-zinc deposits SW of the lake began 1964 after completion of the Great Slave Lake Ry to HAY RIVER and PINE POINT and the construction of a hydroelectric plant on Taltson R. A prosperous commercial fishery centered on Hay River dates from 1945; the chief catches are whitefish and lake trout. The all-weather MACKENZIE HIGHWAY, begun in 1945, goes to Hay River and Yellowknife; it was constructed primarily to serve the fishery but also reaches communities hitherto isolated by the winter freeze. Great Slave has long been part of the Peace-Mackenzie waterway, and tugs and barges still ply the lake, though it is susceptible to savage storms. JAMES MARSH

Cold and deep, and frozen 8 months of the year, Great Slave Lake is the 2nd-largest lake lying entirely in Canada and the 10th-largest lake in the world (*photo by Hälle Flygare*).

Great Western Railway The London and Gore Railroad Co, incorporated 6 May 1834, changed its name to the Great Western Rail Road Co in 1845 and to the Great Western Railway in 1853. Promoted by lawyer-politician Allan Napier MACNAB and more significantly by Hamilton merchants Isaac and Peter Buchanan, R.W. Harris and John Young, and aided by government guarantees, the railway attracted sufficient American and British capital to open its main line (Niagara Falls-Hamilton-London-Windsor) in Jan 1854. By 1882 it operated 1280 km of track throughout SW Ontario and 288 km in Michigan.

Under Charles John Brydges's aggressive management, the railway enjoyed initial financial success, but following the depression of 1857 it suffered as a result of careless construction, rapid expansion, increased local competition and protracted internal managerial conflict. While the railway helped to stimulate and integrate the local economy, it also relied for 40-60% of its gross revenue on through American traffic between New York and Michigan states. As American competitors consolidated lines, through rates fell and the Great Western and its chief local rival, the GRAND TRUNK RAILWAY, suffered. In 1882, after decades of disastrous competition, the 2 railways merged forces in order to compete more effectively with rival American railroads. PETER BASKERVILLE

Grebe, common name for members of the family Podicipedidae, aquatic birds with almost worldwide distribution. Grebes have pointed bills and very short tails. Adults are black, grey or reddish above, white below. Grebes use their feet and wings to propel themselves under water where all species obtain most of their food. Their legs, lobed toes and nails are flattened for efficient use under water, but because the legs are set far back under the body, movement on land is difficult. Wings are small and flight inefficient; some species found outside Canada are flightless. About 20 species are known, including the recently described hooded grebe (*Podiceps gallardoi),* discovered in 1974 in southern Argentina. Five species occur in Canada: pied-billed, horned, rednecked, eared and western grebes (*Podilymbus podiceps, Podiceps auritus, Podiceps grisegena, P. podiceps nigricollis* and *Aechmophorus occidentalis,* respectively). Grebes spend most of their lives in the water and build nests with aquatic vegetation. These nests float, anchored to emergent water plants, or are built up from the bottom of a pond or lake. They are usually surrounded by water plants protecting them from waves and predators.

Five species of grebe occur in Canada, including the eared grebe (*P. podiceps nigricollis*), nesting as far north as the treeline (*photo by Tim Fitzharris*).

Some species nest in large colonies; others are solitary, nesting as isolated pairs. Courtship behaviour involves complex vocal and visual displays. In Canada clutches contain 3-7 eggs (range 1-10). Parents take turns incubating. Both adults care for young, which leave the nest sometimes within minutes of hatching. Hatchlings ride on their parents' backs; after 1 or 2 weeks chicks swim by themselves. Canadian grebes range in size from the 287 g eared grebe to the 1.5 kg western grebe. Larger grebes eat mostly fish; smaller ones generally eat insects, crustaceans, snails and small fish. In Canada they nest from NS and PEI to central BC, and N along the treeline to the YT and western NWT. Grebes migrate at night, wintering in salt water along both coasts of N America and also in fresh water in the US. Grebes are thought to be most closely related to LOONS. SPENCER SEALY

Greeks Greek immigration to Canada began early in the 19th century. Greeks from the islands (eg, Crete, Syros and Skopelos) and from the Peloponessus, especially the poor villages of the provinces of Arcadia and Laconia, settled in Montréal as early as 1843. However, in 1871 only 39 persons of Greek origin were known to be living in Canada. Greek immigration, sporadic prior to 1900, increased considerably in the early 20th century as a result of poverty, wars and political upheavals at home. The 1981 census recorded 250 000 people of Greek origin in Canada; the 1986 census, only 143 000. But other estimates claim up to 350 000.

Migration and Settlement In 1901, 213 Greek immigrants resided throughout Canada; in 1911 the number was 2640; in 1931, 5580 and in 1941, 5871. Immigration was halted during WWII, but from 1946 to 1981 about 116 300 Greek immigrants entered Canada. By 1981, 80% of Greek Canadians lived in the cities of Montréal, Toronto and Vancouver, many in patterns of residential clustering.

Economic Life Generally the pre-WWII immigrants had little formal education, yet some of them are now among the wealthiest members of the Greek community, in which they are very active. Post-WWII immigrants were overrepresented in the unskilled occupational categories. In time many of them moved up the social scale by establishing their own small businesses. Immigrant entrepreneurs are actively involved in the restaurant business, the FUR INDUSTRY, fruit and grocery wholesale and retail firms, travel agencies, etc. Those Greek immigrants who are professionals typically work as engineers, lawyers, doctors, university professors and civil servants. The Canadian-born Greeks, however, tend to enter higher professional and skilled occupations than their parents through higher academic attainment.

Social and Cultural Life With the growth of Greek immigration after 1905, Greek settlements in Canada began to show signs of ethnic community formation. Cultural and patriotic associations were established first to help the immigrants adjust to the new society, to combat prejudice and discrimination and to preserve the Greek language and culture. In time the ethnic associations generated an interest in the formation of parish communities to perform both religious and cultural functions. The establishment of the first Greek ORTHODOX CHURCHES in Montréal (1906) and in Toronto (1909) signified the beginning of Greek parish communities in Canada. Approximately 95% of Greek Canadians belong to the Greek Orthodox Church, headquartered in Toronto. The church has contributed significantly to the preservation of Greek identity through the use of the Greek language in religious services and through its devotion to Greek ideals. The leader of the Greek parish communities is the Metropolitan Bishop of Canada, through whom the church is associated with the Greek Orthodox diocese of N and S America.

Major Greek organizations include the American Hellenic Educational and Progressive Association (AHEPA) introduced into Canada from the US in 1928, the Greek Orthodox Youth of America, the Hellenic Canadian Federation of Ontario, the Hellenic Canadian Federation of Québec and the Hellenic Canadian Congress. The congress was organized in 1986 to function as an umbrella organization for all Greek Canadians and to provide them with a united voice on the ethnocultural affairs at the federal governmental level. Many regional, philanthropic and social societies have been established to help newcomers and the regions from which they emigrated, and to promote understanding of Greek culture.

In the early 1980s a secular model of Greek community organizations appeared in various cities, including London, Sarnia and Markham in Ontario, and Edmonton, as an alternative to the traditional parish community structure. This type of organization constitutes an ethnocultural community without any religious functions of church affiliation. Greek Canadians are eligible for membership regardless of their religious background. The establishment of secular community structures are inevitable consequences of post-WWII demographic changes within Greek communities.

Several Greek Canadian newspapers, eg, *Hellenic Tribune, Greek Canadian Weekly, Greek Courier*, as well as magazines, have helped Greeks integrate into Canadian life while keeping them informed of events in Greece. Customs and traditions include celebrations of Greek national holidays (particularly March 25, Greek Independence Day), religious festivities and holidays, as well as annual dances and picnics.

Group Maintenance The Greek family plays an important role in teaching children the Greek language and values, and providing them with some sense of identity with Greek culture. Since the 1960s Greek language schools have grown in variety and enrolment. Overall, Greek immigrants are not highly integrated into Canadian society, because of low academic attainment in the homeland, short length of residence in Canada, and unfavourable employment conditions for many new immigrants in the early years. This situation is changing, however, as the second and third generations of Greek Canadians take their place in Canadian society. As active participants in the Canadian mosaic, Greek Canadians will continue to make important contributions to the economic and cultural growth of Canadian society.

PETER D. CHIMBOS

Reading: Peter D. Chimbos, *The Canadian Odyssey: The Greek Experience in Canada* (1980) and "The Changing Organization of Greek Canadian Communities," in *International Journal of Comparative Sociology* (1987); George Vlassis, *The Greeks in Canada* (1953).

Green, Blankstein, Russell (GBR), prominent architectural firm in Winnipeg, founded 1932 by L.J. Green (1899-1969) and Cecil N. Blankstein (b 1908), who were joined 1934 by G.L. Russell (1901-77) and Ralph C. Ham (d 1940). All were graduates of the School (later Faculty) of Architecture at University of Manitoba. In the 1930s the firm's most notable work was a series of housing proposals for the city of Winnipeg that eventually bore fruit with the design of Wildwood Park 1946. Based on the plan of Radburn, NJ, it was the first residential garden suburb on the Prairies. The 1950s saw GBR do buildings at U of Manitoba, the Winnipeg Post Office, Norquay office building, and Polo Park Shopping Centre. In the next decade it won competitions for Winnipeg's city hall and international airport. Throughout 3 decades, GBR helped bring modernist architecture to Manitoba.

WILLIAM P. THOMPSON

Green, Howard Charles, lawyer, politician (b at Kaslo, BC 5 Nov 1895). Appointed minister of public works in the first DIEFENBAKER government, Green assumed the Dept of External Affairs portfolio in 1959 after Sidney SMITH's sudden death. Green was a strong supporter of the COMMONWEALTH, a position he shared with his prime minister. During his tenure in external affairs, Green was an advocate of nuclear disarmament and sponsored UN resolutions that furthered that goal. He took an active role for Canada in various international discussions that contributed to a higher profile internationally. First elected to the House in 1935, Green served until his defeat in the 1963 general election. PATRICIA WILLIAMS

Green Fishery, the COD fishery carried out in Newfoundland and Labrador in which the product is preserved in salt on board the fishing ship to be dried later. The green fishery was undertaken by fishermen on fishing grounds too far from suitable or convenient land sites where the fish could be dried. It required the use of much more salt than did the DRY FISHERY, but it had the advantages of less handling time during the fishing season and less dependence on variable curing weather near the fishing grounds. The green fishery made ships less dependent on shore facilities and therefore was not tied to one geographical area. *See also* FISHERIES HISTORY. ROBERT D. PITT

Green Paper, a statement by the government, not of policy already determined, but of propositions put before the whole nation for discussion. Like a WHITE PAPER it is an official document sponsored by the Crown. It is produced early in the policymaking process, while ministerial proposals are still being formulated. Many so-called White Papers in Canada have been, in effect, Green Papers, while at least one Green Paper – that on immigration and population in 1975 – was released for public debate after the government had already drafted legislation.

C.E.S. FRANKS

Greene, Daniel Joseph, lawyer, politician, Liberal prime minister of Nfld 1894-95 (b at St John's 1850; d there 12 Dec 1911). He became prime minister of Newfoundland 13 Dec 1894 in the wake of the legal and political turmoil surrounding the 1893 elections. Educated in law at Laval, he began his 22-year political career in 1875, became leader of the Opposition in 1887 and in 1890 was part of a delegation to Ottawa protesting French fishing rights in Newfoundland (*see* FRENCH SHORE). Greene's most pressing problems upon succeeding Augustus GOODRIDGE's brief Conservative administration were the consequences of the collapse of 2 major Newfoundland financial institutions on Dec 10, but the most significant legislation passed during his 58-day tenure was the Disabilities Removal Act. This allowed candidates who had been disqualified because of election irregularities in 1893 to seek election again. This Act, and Greene's resignation on 8 Feb 1895, allowed William WHITEWAY to resume the prime ministership. ROBERT D. PITT

Greene, Lorne Hyman entertainer (b at Ottawa 12 Feb 1915; d at Santa Monica, Calif 11 Sept 1987). While taking chemical engineering at Queen's, he became involved in amateur theatrics and after graduation spent 2 years in New York studying drama. Settling in Toronto, he became active in radio, eventually as chief news broadcaster for the CBC 1939-42. Following service in WWII, he returned to radio in Toronto, was co-founder of the Jupiter Theatre there and established and taught at the Academy of Radio Arts. In 1953, like many of his talented contemporaries, he headed south and for 5 years appeared in Broadway plays, Then for 14 years, beginning in 1959, he was Ben Cartwright on the highly successful TV series "Bonanza." Thereafter, he continued to appear on television, including stints in several other series such as "Battlestar Galactica." In the 1980s his energy was mainly directed at wildlife and environment preservation, notably through his television series "Lorne Greene's New Wilderness." At the 1987 Geminis he was posthumously awarded the Earl Grey Award. CHARLES DOUGALL

Greene, Nancy, alpine skier (b at Ottawa 11 May 1943). Raised in Rossland, BC, she only began serious racing at age 14. Outstanding ability led to her selection to the 1960 Olympic team after only 2 years of racing. Finishing twenty-second in the Olympic giant slalom, she became determined to match her roommate Anne HEGGTVEIT's victory. During the early 1960s she had several major US and European victories, but was inconsistent. Her aggressive style caused several injuries, including torn ligaments in the 1966 world championships. Resolving to try for more control she achieved remarkable results, concluding the 1967 season with 3 straight victories to win the World Cup. In 1968 she continued her domination of the sport, winning an Olympic gold medal in the giant slalom, a silver in the slalom, and 9 straight victories to clinch her second World Cup. She was Canada's Athlete of the Year in 1968. MURRAY SHAW

Nancy Greene dominated World Cup skiing in 1967 and 1968, culminating in Olympic gold and silver medals (*courtesy Canada's Sports Hall of Fame*).

Greenfield, Herbert, farmer, politician, businessman, premier of Alberta 1921-25 (b at Winchester, Eng 25 Nov 1867; d at Calgary 23 Aug 1949). Greenfield migrated to Canada in 1892 and established a homestead N of Edmonton in 1906. By 1921 he was president of the Alberta Assn of Municipal Districts and an interim VP of the UNITED FARMERS OF ALBERTA. Though not initially a candidate when the UFA entered the 1921 provincial election campaign, he was asked to accept the position of premier after it was refused by Henry Wise WOOD. Sworn in as premier, provincial secretary and provincial treasurer on 13 Aug 1921, Greenfield led the novice UFA government in its response to drought and credit problems of Alberta farmers and its assistance in establishing a voluntary wheat pool and other commodity marketing pools. Often ill and absent during 1923, and increasingly regarded as ineffective thereafter (although he maintained his personal popularity), Greenfield resigned on 23 Nov 1925 in favour of John Edward BROWNLEE. CARL BETKE

Greenhouse Crops The cultivation of greenhouse crops is the most intensive form of agricultural production. Investment and labour costs are greater in this sector than in any other; however, the yield and value of crops are correspondingly high. The greenhouse essentially provides a controlled climate which, in adverse conditions, may be adapted to the needs of particular crops. For example, in northern countries such as Canada, where outdoor cultivation is possible for only about 5 months of the year, greenhouses provide a temperature-controlled environment which also shelters plants from heavy rain, strong winds, insects and other pests. Although greenhouses are used by amateur gardeners and by training and research institutions, highly specialized growers of ORNAMENTAL plants and market-garden produce form the most important group in Canada's greenhouse-crop industry. The overall objective of this industry is to provide Canadian consumers with fresh produce for as much of the year as possible.

The major producers of greenhouse crops are located in Ontario, Québec and BC, which had 3 000 759 m², 664 366 m² and 653 000 m², respectively, of greenhouse space in 1985. About 60% of the Canadian greenhouse industry is located in Ontario, the largest production centre being Leamington, Essex County; Kent County is also very important. Both regions are at the most southerly point of Canada and have favourable climates. In other provinces, the major production areas are located near large cities (eg, Montréal, Vancouver). Although much of the total greenhouse area in Canada is devoted to market produce (tomatoes, cucumbers, etc), the market value of greenhouse-grown ornamentals is generally about 7 times greater, and was worth over $314 million in 1985. Tomatoes represent over half of vegetable sales; cucumbers, 45%. The major species of greenhouse-grown FLOWERS are ROSES, chrysanthemums and carnations; green-leaved tropical plants are also popular. The major challenge for the greenhouse sector in future is to maintain industry profits by reducing energy costs and increasing production. A great deal of engineering and horticultural research is devoted to ensuring the survival of one of the most important sectors of Canada's horticulture system. MARC J. TRUDEL

Greenland (Kalaallit Nunaat), Canada's northeasterly neighbour, is the world's largest island. It is under Danish sovereignty. Vikings from Greenland were among those who explored and settled Vinland *c*1000 AD (*see* NORSE VOYAGES). During the 1920s Canadian authorities became alarmed as Greenlandic Inuit hunted muskoxen on Ellesmere I, and consequently they were hesitant about allowing Knud Rasmussen, nowadays Greenland's foremost hero, to make his fact-finding trip across the Canadian Arctic lest he threaten Canadian sovereignty. In WWII, when Nazi Germany overran Denmark, Canada established a consulate in Greenland. Canadian and US suppliers replaced traditional Danish ones, and the Aluminium Co of Canada purchased cryolite from Ivigtut for production of Allied aircraft. Since Greenland attained internal self-government in 1979, commercial airlines have linked its capital, Nuuk [Godthaab], with IQALUIT [Frobisher Bay], thereby facilitating trade and tourism. Greenlanders have protested Canadian plans to transport fossil fuels from the Beaufort Sea through the Davis Strait, and Canada and Greenland dispute ownership of Hans I. GRAEME S. MOUNT

Gail Greenough and Mr T at the world show jumping championships in Aachen, W Germany, July 1986 (*photo by Jayne Huddleston*).

Greenough, Gail, equestrian (b at Edmonton 7 Mar 1960). On 13 July 1986 at Aachen, W Germany, she became the first Canadian and first woman to win the world show jumping championship. Although she had taken up equestrian sports at the age of 11, Greenough was a relatively inexperienced rider at the world championship; she had been on the Canadian equestrian team since 1983 and had competed at few World Cup events. However, over 5 days of competition she and her horse, Mr T, produced several clean rounds. In the final, she had to ride 3 of the 4 rounds using her competitors' horses. Incurring no penalty points, she took the title and the $23 000 first prize. In June 1987 her victory in the Loblaws Showjumping Classic qualified her for competition in the Aug 1987 Pan-Am Games and the World Cup competition. J. THOMAS WEST

Greenpeace, originated in Vancouver (1970) as a small group opposed to nuclear testing in the

Pacific, and has blossomed into one of the largest and best-known environmental organizations in the world, addressing itself to a wide range of international and local issues. Through nonviolent confrontation it attempts to draw attention to violations of ecological principles, such as the equal rights of all species to exist and flourish. No longer based in Canada, Greenpeace maintains relatively autonomous offices throughout the world, coordinated by the Greenpeace Council in Amsterdam. Total membership is difficult to estimate as it fluctuates according to interest in current issues, but over $2 million is raised yearly in N America alone through membership fees, donations and the sale of promotional items.

In the hope that public pressure will help change policies, Greenpeace aims for maximum publicity for its activities. In its most publicized campaigns, against nuclear testing and SEALING and WHALING policies, the environmentalists have intervened directly and exposed themselves to risk. One Greenpeace member was killed on 10 July 1985 when French agents placed underwater bombs on the Greenpeace flagship *Rainbow Warrior* in Auckland, New Zealand. The ship had been about to embark as part of a "peace flotilla" to Mururoa Atoll, the French nuclear test site in French Polynesia. The success of Greenpeace tactics is difficult to measure, but certainly they have brought various issues to public attention. The public's response to Greenpeace has varied widely from apparently almost unanimous support of antinuclear testing and "Save the Whales" campaigns to very strong opposition to some of the tactics the group employs, often on more local issues. P. DEARDEN

Reading: R. Hunter, *Warriors of the Rainbow* (1979).

Greenstone, general term for dark green, compact metamorphic rocks formed by the alteration of dark-coloured IGNEOUS ROCKS. Basalt, a common example, is a major component of the greenstone belts of the Canadian SHIELD. These belts contain the Shield's principal gold and base-metal mines. The term greenstone is also used for green ornamental materials used for sculpture and gems, such as nephrite jade, serpentine, fuchsite (a chrome-mica rock) and chlorastrolite (a tortoiseshell-like GEMSTONE composed of pumpellyite needles). ANN P. SABINA

Greenway, Thomas, merchant, farmer, land speculator, politician, premier of Manitoba (b at Kilkhampton, Eng 25 Mar 1838; d at Ottawa 30 Oct 1908). Instrumental in the formation of the Liberal Party of Manitoba, Greenway was its first leader and premier of Manitoba 1888-1900. In 1844 the Greenways immigrated to Huron County, Canada W. Thomas eventually became an independent supporter of Sir John A. MACDONALD's Liberal-Conservative Party and MP for South Huron, 1875-78. However, he broke with Macdonald on the NATIONAL POLICY tariff and became a Liberal. In 1879 he moved to Manitoba and was elected MLA that year; by 1882 he led a provincial rights opposition which became the Liberal Party. As premier he ended federal disallowance of Manitoba railway legislation and the CPR monopoly, bringing the Northern Pacific into the province to induce competition in freight rates. He is remembered, however, for the elimination of minority educational rights for Roman Catholics; the MANITOBA SCHOOLS QUESTION dominated provincial and federal politics during his years as premier. He remained leader of the provincial Liberals until his election as MP for Lisgar in 1904. DAVID J. HALL

Greenwich, Sonny, né Herbert Lawrence Greenidge, guitarist (b at Hamilton, Ont 1 Jan 1936). This most intriguing of Canada's jazzmen has divided his life between musical and spiritual pursuits, thus turning away from a potentially major career. Emulating jazz saxophonists, he developed a highly personal music and original guitar style, which left him working largely in isolation. He has performed only sporadically, beginning about 1958 with small ensembles in Toronto and Montréal and reaching a wider audience through brief liaisons with other musicians (eg, John Handy, 1966-67), through his 1970s recordings, *The Old Man and the Child, Sun Song* and *Evolution, Love's Reverse* and more recently *Bird of Paradise* (1986). MARK MILLER

Reading: Mark Miller, *Jazz in Canada: Fourteen Lives* (1982) and *Boogie, Pete and the Senator* (1987).

Greenwood, BC, City, pop 767 (1986c), inc 1897, is located 27 km W of GRAND FORKS on Hwy 3. It grew on the mining boom in the boundary district in the 1890s and nearly died when the boom ended. Prospectors staked outcroppings of copper ore in the area from 1886 onwards, and in 1891 the famous Mother Lode mine at Deadwood, 3 km W of Greenwood, was discovered. The townsite, named after Greenwood mining camp in Colorado, was laid out in 1895 and by 1899 the population reached 3000. The BC Copper Co opened a smelter in 1901 to treat the ore from the Mother Lode mine and employed up to 450 men in its mine and smelter. After WWI, however, a drastic fall in copper prices caused the closure of both operations, and Greenwood became little more than a ghost town. It was revived in 1942 when 1200 Japanese Canadians were interned there. Some of them remained after the camp was closed in 1946, and about 25% of local residents are of Japanese origin. Logging and sawmills are the major employers. Visitors are reminded of the boom years by the gaunt smokestack of the old smelter and the old courthouse, preserved nearly unchanged. DAVID DENDY

Gregg, Milton Fowler, diplomat, politician, soldier, educator (b at Snider Mountain, NB 10 Apr 1892; d at Fredericton 13 Mar 1978). He attended NB Provincial Normal School and Acadia U and during WWI served in France as a stretcher bearer and was recruited to officer training while in an English hospital recovering from his second wound. As a lieutenant with the Royal Canadian Regiment, he was again wounded and was awarded the MILITARY CROSS and Bar and the VICTORIA CROSS. Between the wars he worked for the Soldiers Settlement Board and the *Halifax Herald*, and was sergeant-at-arms of the House of Commons 1934-39. In WWII he served overseas as second-in-command of the RCR and as c/o of the West Nova Scotia Regiment; then as commandant of officer training schools in Vernon, BC, Brockville, Ont, and Sussex, NB. Retired as a brigadier-general, he was president of UNB 1944-47, responsible for integrating returning soldiers into the university through Alexander College. He was elected an MP in 1947 and served as minister of fisheries (1947-48), veterans affairs (1948-50) and labour (1950-57). He was the representative of the UN in Iraq (1958-59), of UNICEF in Indonesia (1960-63) and of Canada to the UN (1963), then Canadian commissioner and high commissioner to British Guiana and Guyana (1964-67) and president of the Canadian Council for International Cooperation (1968). BURTON GLENDENNING

Grenfell, Sir Wilfred Thomason, medical missionary (b at Parkgate, Eng 28 Feb 1865; d at Charlotte, Vt 9 Oct 1940). Grenfell entered the London Medical School in 1883 and 2 years later was converted to active CHRISTIANITY at a tent meeting of American evangelist Dwight L. Moody. In 1888 he followed the suggestion of one of his teachers, Sir Frederick Treves, that he join the Royal National Mission to Deep Sea Fishermen. He was made superintendent in 1889 and for 3 months in 1892, at the mission's request, cruised the Newfoundland and Labrador coast where 30 000 stationers, 3300 "livyers" (permanent settlers) and 1700 Inuit received only an annual visit from one government doctor. Grenfell treated 900 patients and saw a great opportunity for medical and missionary work. He raised funds to open the first hospital at Battle Harbour in 1893. Grenfell was a forceful speaker and easily gained the friendship of influential men. His medical mission grew rapidly with hospital, orphanage and nursing stations and the first co-operatives in Newfoundland. Grenfell did not winter in the North until 1899 and spent comparatively few winters there, establishing his headquarters at ST ANTHONY, Nfld. A prolific writer and forceful publicist, he often used artistic licence in accounts of life on the northern coasts. His main financial support came from the US. In 1909 he married a Chicago heiress, Anne MacClanahan, who took him away from life on the coast. Growing friction with the mission eventually led to a split, and the International Grenfell Assn was incorporated in 1912. The practical medical work of the IGA was carried on by dedicated if autocratic doctors, while Grenfell became increasingly involved in fund raising. He was made CMG in 1906 and KCMG in 1927, the year in which he retired to Vermont. Famous in his lifetime, he is now largely forgotten; his papers are in the Yale medical history library. TERENCE MACARTNEY-FILGATE

Wilfred T. Grenfell built hospitals, an orphanage and nursing stations to serve the people of the Newfoundland and Labrador coasts (*courtesy National Archives of Canada/C-68717*).

Gretzky, Wayne, hockey player (b at Brantford, Ont 26 Jan 1961). He was a hockey prodigy who, with his father's guidance, mastered the skills of the sport on a backyard rink. He played junior hockey for Sault Ste Marie Greyhounds and in 1978 turned professional with WHL Indianapolis Racers and EDMONTON OILERS. At age 17 he was the youngest athlete playing a major-league sport in N America. He tied for the scoring lead in Edmonton's first season in the NHL (1979-80), won the HART TROPHY as the league's "most valuable player" and the LADY BYNG TROPHY, and began an assault on scoring records that is likely unprecedented in any sport. In his second NHL season (1980-81) he scored 164 points, breaking Phil ESPOSITO's single-season record of 152 points and surpassing Bobby ORR's assist record of 102 with 109. The following year he scored 212 points, including 92 goals – shattering Esposito's previous record of 76 goals. He has won the Hart Trophy in all 8 of his NHL seasons, the ART ROSS TROPHY 7

Captain Wayne Gretzky holds aloft the Edmonton Oilers' first Stanley Cup, 1984 (*photo by Mike Pinder/Edmonton Journal*).

times, and at the end of the 1986-87 season he held 44 individual records, including a consecutive-game point streak of 51 games (1983-84). After only 8 NHL seasons, Gretzky's 543 goals placed him 8th among all-time players, his 977 assists placed him 3rd and his 1520 points 4th. He has also been the leading scorer in all 5 international tournaments in which he has played, including the 1987 CANADA CUP.

Gretzky's mastery of his sport owes much to his agility, speed and accurate shot, and he is undoubtedly the greatest passer in hockey history. But it is his instinctive grasp of the flow of play – his sense of how opposing players and teammates will react to each situation – that makes him such a creative player. His personal charm as well as his scoring feats have endeared him to the N American sporting public. JAMES MARSH

Grey, Albert Henry George Grey, 4th Earl, governor general of Canada, 1904-11 (b at St James's Palace, London, Eng 28 Nov 1851; d at Howick, Eng 29 Aug 1917). A keen imperialist, Grey saw his appointment as governor general as an opportunity to forge stronger links of empire. In public speeches in Canada he tried to foster imperial pride and in private he urged PM Wilfrid LAURIER to respond favourably to proposals for closer defence ties. He devoted much of his time to Canadian-American relations, working closely with the British ambassador to the US and acting as mediator when Britain and the US seemed to misunderstand Canada's position. Despite vigorous effort, he was unable to achieve the entry of Newfoundland into the Canadian federation. Perhaps best remembered as the donor of the GREY CUP for football supremacy, Grey himself was more interested in the music and drama festivals he inaugurated. It was fortunate for Canada and Britain that in this difficult transition period in imperial relations a governor general of Grey's energy and charm was associated with a prime minister of Laurier's strength and patience.

M.E. HALLETT

Grey Cup, trophy produced by Birks Jewellers that has been part of Canadian sports since 1909, when it was donated by Governor General Earl GREY for the Canadian FOOTBALL championship. The original conditions stated that the "cup must remain always under purely amateur conditions," although there is good reason to believe that this was at the urging of P.D. Ross of the Ottawa *Journal* rather than Lord Grey. Until 1966, the cup was presented to the Canadian champion by various trustees, including, from 1921, the Canadian Rugby Union (CRU). In 1966, the CRU named the Canadian Football League (CFL) trustee. In the early years (1909-24) the university teams were invariably the Grey Cup champions. From 1925 to 1945 the representatives from senior city leagues were supreme, and they continued to contest the cup until the early 1950s, when the professional teams that later comprised the CANADIAN FOOTBALL LEAGUE began to dominate.

In 1948 the CALGARY STAMPEDERS and their supporters transformed the Grey Cup game into a week-long carnival of festivities, a national celebration, and the most watched sporting event in Canada. In 1962, hailing the game as an instrument of national unity, Parliament decreed that both major Canadian television networks must make the television transmission of the game available to the other so that all regions could see it. FRANK COSENTINO

Grey Cup Champions 1945-1987

1945	Toronto Argonauts
1946	Toronto Argonauts
1947	Toronto Argonauts
1948	Calgary Stampeders
1949	Montreal Alouettes
1950	Toronto Argonauts
1951	Ottawa Rough Riders
1952	Toronto Argonauts
1953	Hamilton Tiger-Cats
1954	Edmonton Eskimos
1955	Edmonton Eskimos
1956	Edmonton Eskimos
1957	Hamilton Tiger-Cats
1958	Winnipeg Blue Bombers
1959	Winnipeg Blue Bombers
1960	Ottawa Rough Riders
1961	Winnipeg Blue Bombers
1962	Winnipeg Blue Bombers
1963	Hamilton Tiger-Cats
1964	British Columbia Lions
1965	Hamilton Tiger-Cats
1966	Saskatchewan Roughriders
1967	Hamilton Tiger-Cats
1968	Ottawa Rough Riders
1969	Ottawa Rough Riders
1970	Montreal Alouettes
1971	Calgary Stampeders
1972	Hamilton Tiger-Cats
1973	Ottawa Rough Riders
1974	Montreal Alouettes
1975	Edmonton Eskimos
1976	Ottawa Rough Riders
1977	Montreal Alouettes
1978	Edmonton Eskimos
1979	Edmonton Eskimos
1980	Edmonton Eskimos
1981	Edmonton Eskimos
1982	Edmonton Eskimos
1983	Toronto Argonauts
1984	Winnipeg Blue Bombers
1985	British Columbia Lions
1986	Hamilton Tiger-Cats
1987	Edmonton Eskimos

Grey Nuns, name commonly given to 5 distinct Roman Catholic religious communities of women, all springing from the original foundation, the Sisters of Charity of the Hôpital Général, in Montréal. There, in 1737, a young widow, Madame d'YOUVILLE, formed a charitable lay association which opened a house for the poor. Ten years later they took on the direction of the Hôpital Général of Montréal. The brothers who had been running the hospital had been very popular and those who resented the change mocked the sisters as "*les grises*," that is, "tipsy women." In 1755, when their religious community was finally officially recognized, they took a grey habit in deliberate reference to the derisive title. It was not until the 1840s that the question of expansion to other houses arose. They decided at first to follow the pattern of cloistered communities by having each foundation independent. Thus in 1840 they took on a hospital in St-Hyacinthe, in 1843 ventured much farther afield to St-Boniface on the Red R, in 1845 undertook the work of teaching in Bytown [Ottawa] and in 1849 opened an orphanage in Québec. These foundations, except for St-Boniface which needed the support of the Montréal community, became centres of distinct congregations, sharing traditions but developing different works and spiritualities of their own as well. A later development saw an English-speaking offshoot of the Ottawa community establish another separate congregation in 1926 in Pembroke, Ont. All of the communities flourished. By the mid-1960s there were about 7000 Grey Nuns in Canada, but the general decline in vocations diminished their numbers to just over 4000 by the mid-1980s; the Montréal, Ottawa and Québec congregations each have about 1200, while St-Hyacinthe has just under 200 and Pembroke just over 200. REV JAMES HANRAHAN

Grey Owl, *see* BELANEY, ARCHIBALD STANSFELD.

Grierson, John, film producer (b at Deanston, Scot 26 Apr 1898; d at Bath, Eng 19 Feb 1972). Grierson is best known as the father of documentary cinema and the man who created the NATIONAL FILM BOARD of Canada. In 1938, after some 10 years' involvement in government filmmaking in England, he was invited to Canada to study the Canadian government's use of film. His report led directly to the creation of the NFB in May 1939. Shortly after the outbreak of war, he was appointed government film commissioner in Canada, a post he held until 1945. Under his direction the NFB grew to be a large organization, producing both regular series of theatrical shorts (*Canada Carries On* and *The World in Action*), which were shown monthly in Canadian and US cinemas, and hundreds of nontheatrical films shown across Canada in a network of industrial, rural and trade-union circuits.

Grierson activated the Canadian film industry almost single-handedly. He had enormous energy, a deep-seated vision of what he wanted to accomplish, an excellent eye for talent and got

Under John Grierson's leadership, the NFB achieved international recognition (*courtesy National Archives of Canada/MISA/7633*).

the best out of the people who worked with him. His belief in the documentary film – a term he coined in a review in 1926 – influenced a generation of filmmakers, and his thinking governed the evolution of the dominant aesthetic of Canadian cinema, strongly rooted in reality. He provided a rationale and a purpose for the NFB that turned it into one of the most creative film organizations in the world.

Grierson left Canada in 1945 to form a film company in New York, but he was implicated in the communist scare that followed the defection of Igor GOUZENKO and this effectively ended his career in N America. In 1947 he was named director of mass communications at UNESCO in Paris. After 3 years he joined Group 3, an unsuccessful experiment in feature filmmaking established in England 1950. Grierson then hosted a popular TV program based in Scotland, "This Wonderful World," for 10 years, and spent the last period of his life travelling and teaching, including lecturing at McGill. PIERS HANDLING

Griffon, first ship to sail the Upper Great Lakes, launched at Cayuga Creek, on the Niagara R, 7 Aug 1679. A small barque, armed with 7 cannon, it sailed under the command of LA SALLE to Michilimackinac and Green Bay. Loaded with furs, the *Griffon* was lost on the return voyage, likely in the storms of Lk Michigan. J. MARSH

Grignon, Claude-Henri, journalist, critic, novelist, author of radio and TV serials (b at Ste-Adèle, Qué 8 July 1894; d there 3 Apr 1976). Grignon is known primarily for his novel *Un Homme et son péché* (1933), whose hero, the miserly Séraphin Poudrier, became the central figure in adaptations for radio, TV and 2 films. This original, powerful novel broke with the convention of extolling rural life and won Québec's Prix David (1935). Some 100 000 copies of the book have been printed, and it has been adapted as a series on radio and TV. Grignon, who has other publications to his credit, also became well known as a virulent critic, thanks to *Les Pamphlets de Valdombre* (1936-43). In 1962 he became a member of the RSC. *Un Homme et son péché* was translated into English as *The Woman and the Miser* (1978). ANTOINE SIROIS

Grimsby, Ont, Town, pop 16 956 (1986c), 15 797 (1981c), inc 1876, is situated in the Niagara Peninsula to the E of Hamilton. The first European settlers, primarily Loyalists, arrived in the 1780s after the American Revolution. Originally called The Forty, it was named for Grimsby, Eng. Following the clearing of the land for mixed-farming practices, Grimsby grew as an agricultural service centre. In the late 19th century, 2 developments aided its growth. The large-scale expansion of orchards and vineyards in the area resulted in several packing and canning plants and a winery. For a while the town was popular as a lakeside resort, with steamboat services from Toronto. More recently, it has attracted a variety of light industries. Good communications with Hamilton, first by interurban electric railway and later by the QUEEN ELIZABETH WAY, have fostered the growth of a dormitory community. The Manor, a gracious Loyalist residence (1798), is one of Ontario's few remaining 18th-century buildings. H.J. GAYLER

Reading: P. Dechman, ed, *Once Upon a Little Town* (1979).

Grisdale, Joseph Hiram, agronomist (b at Ste-Marthe, Qué 18 Feb 1870; d at Iroquois, Ont 24 Aug 1939). Son of a farmer, trained at OAC and Iowa State Coll, Grisdale joined the staff of the Central Experimental Farm, Ottawa, in 1899, and in 1911 succeeded William SAUNDERS as director. He became deputy minister of agriculture, the first agronomist in this post, in 1918, and was a powerful figure in Ottawa, sitting on the National Research Council and leading the Canadian delegations at the 1926 and 1928 imperial conferences on co-ordinating research. He retired owing to ill health in 1932, was shipwrecked 4 days later on a Bermuda cruise ship, and survived to breed Jersey cattle and apples on his own farm. DONALD J.C. PHILLIPSON

Grise Fiord, NWT, Settlement, pop 114 (1986c), 106 (1981c), is located on the S coast of ELLESMERE I. Canada's most northerly INUIT community, it is situated in game-rich country from which the residents derive their living. The settlement is the result of federal government efforts to alleviate poor economic conditions among the Inuit and to establish Canadian sovereignty over the arctic islands. Inuit families from other areas of the North were settled in the area by 1953. Grise Fiord means "Pig Fiord" in Norwegian. Many NWT residents consider the community setting the most beautiful in the North. ANNELIES POOL

Grise Fiord, NWT, Canada's most northerly Inuit settlement (*photo by Karl-Heinz Raach*).

Grit, a popular reference to a member of the LIBERAL PARTY of Canada. The nickname derives from grit, fine sand or gravel, which is often valued for its abrasive quality, and from an American slang term implying firmness of character, as used in the phrase "true grit." Canadian political usage of the word dates from 1849, when progressive members of the Upper Canada Reform Party were dubbed CLEAR GRITS and characterized as being "all sand and no dirt, clear grit all the way through." Led by George BROWN of the *Globe*, in the early 1870s the progressive members joined with Lower Canada reformers to create the Liberal Party, and the description of the few was applied to the many. JOHN ROBERT COLOMBO

Grizzly Bear (*Ursus arctos horribilis*), large mammal of the order Carnivora. It differs from other N American carnivores in that it eats primarily plant matter. Grizzlies opportunistically kill or scavenge animals, especially ungulates, ground squirrels and insects. They are also attracted to edible garbage. In fall they dig dens and begin a 4-7-month dormant period during which they usually do not eat, urinate or defecate. Courtship and copulation occur mid-May through early July; embryo implantation is delayed until fall. In delayed implantation the fertilized egg develops slowly, while floating in the uterus. Eventually, it becomes attached to the wall of the uterus and development continues normally until birth. Young are born Jan-Feb. Newborns weigh about 0.5 kg, are very immature, and are nursed inside dens for up to 3 months. Litters average 2 young (range 1-4). Females breed about once every 3 years (range 2-5 years). Grizzlies thus have few young and hunting must be carefully regulated to maintain a population. In the wild most die before reaching adulthood and 15-25 years is considered old. Grizzlies have longer front claws and are larger than black BEARS. Large males may weigh 250-400 kg; large females, 150-200 kg. Grizzlies have a hump on the back and a dish-shaped facial profile. They range from black through brown to blond. Often the ends of hair on the flanks, back and shoulders are grizzled (ie, have white or grey flecks). Mothers may defend their young and males may fight, especially during breeding season. Occasionally, aggression is directed toward humans: in Canada's national parks, about one visitor in 2 million is injured by a grizzly. Grizzlies may stand on their hind legs when sensing their environment. They typically charge on 4 legs and can run at least 50 km/h. They prefer semiopen habitats; an adult male may have a home range of 1000-1500 km^2. As human populations have expanded, grizzly bear numbers have declined. They were extirpated from the prairies by about 1900. Today, they are found in Alberta (estimated population 800), BC (16 000), the NWT (4000-5000) and the YT (5000-9000). Grizzlies were sacred, yet fearsome, animals to most native people. STEPHEN HERRERO

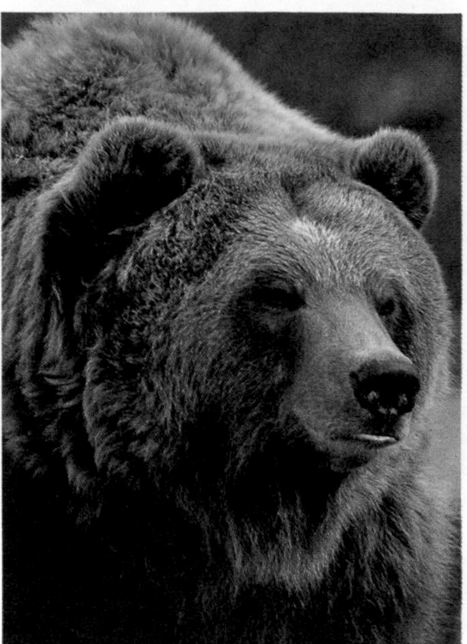

Grizzly bear (*Ursus arctos horribilis*), so-called for the grizzled (ie, flecked) hair on its flanks, back and shoulders (*photo by Stephen J. Krasemann/DRK Photo*).

Gros-Louis, Max, or Oné-Onti, politician, businessman (b at Huron Village IR, Loretteville, Qué 6 Aug 1931). After working as a surveyor's labourer and travelling salesman, he became a producer of pan-Indian handicrafts and manager of a Huron dance troupe. First elected chief of the Huron of Lorette in 1964, he was involved in the Indians of Canada pavilion at Expo 67, in the foundation of the Indians of Quebec Association (secretary and spokesman, 1966-73), and in the National Indian Brotherhood (Québec representative, 1970). As a publicist claiming to speak for Québec Indians, and as a community leader advocating individualist approaches to economic and social problems, he has differed with native and other groups over LAND CLAIMS and relations with non-Indian governments. His autobiography, *First Among the Huron*, was published in 1973. BENNETT MCCARDLE

Gros Morne National Park (est 1970) covers 2000 km^2 on the W coast of Nfld. The spectacular landscape was created by the grinding action of glaciers on the ancient Long Range Mts. Barren rocky ridges and tundralike slopes contrast with forested foothills and boggy coastal plains, where mosses and pitcher plants thrive. The presence of caribou and arctic hare reflect the northern character of the park. Pine marten inhabit dense forest areas while moose and snowshoe hare, although not native, are frequently observed. Terns and gulls abound along the coast; ptarmigan typify the bird life of the heathlands and barrens. Pre-European culture in the area dates from 2500 BC when the Maritime Archaic Indians inhabited the area. DORSET and BEOTHUK cultures followed. European contact was established with the arrival of Jacques Cartier in the adjacent Gulf of St Lawrence (1534); however, European settlement did not occur until the late 1800s. The park has facilities for tent and recreational-vehicle camping and for primitive winter camping. In summer, hiking, fishing and cool saltwater swims are popular. Visitors in winter can cross-country ski, snowshoe and snowmobile. LILLIAN STEWART

Grosbeak, common name for large members of 2 families of birds, Emberizidae (SPARROW, BUNTING) and Fringillidae (FINCH), with large, deep bills adapted for cracking hard-coated seeds. In Canada, 4 breeding species occur. Another species, blue grosbeak (*Guiraca caerulea*), is a rare straggler to southern Ontario. Rose-breasted grosbeaks (*Pheucticus ludovicianus*) are common in deciduous forests from NS to northern BC. Males have striking plumage: black heads; black and white backs, wings and tails; white underparts; rose red, triangular patch on the breast; and white bill. Females are brown with dark streaks but have the characteristic large, white bill. The black-headed grosbeak (*P. melanocephalus*), occurring in wooded valleys from southern BC to southwestern Saskatchewan and rarely Manitoba, is distinguished by its yellow-brown underparts and brownish collar and rump. These 2 species are similar in size; females of both are easily confused; and males have similar songs. Hybrids have been found where ranges overlap. Evening grosbeaks (*Coccothraustes vespertinus*) are familiar winter birds and readily attracted to feeders with sunflower seeds. Males have lemon yellow bodies; brown crowns, necks and upper backs; black tails and wings with large, white wing patches; and large, greenish yellow bills. Plumage of females is duller. Their summer distribution is incompletely known; they are known to occur from BC across the coniferous forests to the Maritimes (recent arrivals). Pine grosbeak (*Pinicola enucleator*), the largest grosbeak in Canada, breeds across northern Canada from YT to NB, and S along the Rocky Mts in BC and Alberta. Males are predominantly pinkish red, with 2 white bars on grey wings. Females and immatures are grey, with wings similar to males, and head and rump tinged with yellow. They prefer pine and spruce trees, extracting seeds from cones. In fall and winter they also feed on fruit and berry seeds. Their call notes of usually 3 tuneful whistles are extended to form a song.

RICHARD W. KNAPTON

Pine grosbeak (*Pinicola enucleator*) breeds across northern Canada (*artwork by Claire Tremblay*).

Gross National Product (GNP, since 1986 **Gross Domestic Product**) refers to the money value of all goods and services produced in a nation during a stated period of time, usually a year. Despite its limitations GNP is the best overall measure of economic performance; it is often used to calculate changes in the welfare of a country's residents. Its principal components are wages, salaries and supplementary labour income; military pay and allowances; corporation profits before taxes (minus dividends paid to nonresidents); interest and investment income (except for interest on consumer loans and government income from crown corporations); net income (pretax profits) of farm operators; net income from businesses and of professionals, eg, doctors; and rental income; and an adjustment for changes in the value of inventories because of price changes. Together these items comprise net NATIONAL INCOME at factor costs, or the earnings of various factors of production. GNP is measured by including as well indirect taxes less subsidiaries, eg, manufacturers' sales taxes, business property taxes and other taxes levied on businesses but paid by (or "shifted to") consumers; capital-cost allowances and miscellaneous adjustments for depreciation of business assets; and a residual error of estimate, a small statistical balancing of figures. Another measure, that of gross national expenditure (total level of demand in the economy for goods and services), reveals how GNP is consumed through consumer spending, investment and government spending.

In 1986, StatsCan switched to GDP in their calculations of national production to facilitate comparisons with other statistics, such as provincial employment and productivity stats. Although GDP is not used by the US, it is more closely aligned with international practice as recommended in the UN System of National Accounts. The Organization for Economic Co-operation and Development also uses GDP as a basis for economic comparisons; in 1987 OECD estimated Canada's 1985 per capita GDP to be $13 635 US, compared to $16 494 for the US, $12 006 for Sweden and $7943 for the UK.

Grosse Île, or Quarantine I, 2.9 km long by 1 km wide, 46 km downstream from Québec City in the ST LAWRENCE R estuary. The island is a wooded Appalachian ridge sculpted by coves and capes. In 1646 the Île de Grâce was ceded to Gov Charles Huault de MONTMAGNY. Usage transformed the name from Grace I to Grosse Île. In 1832 the deserted island became a quarantine station where 51 146 IRISH and ENGLISH immigrants were examined (of the total of 61 800 received in Canada). In 1833 the station received 21 732 immigrants; in 1834, 30 945. Some died of CHOLERA. In 1847 the Irish famine sparked emigration despite a typhus EPIDEMIC. Irish immigrants endured 6-12 weeks of inhuman conditions in 221 ships to reach Canada – 8000 were buried at sea. At the Grosse Île quarantine station medical superintendent Dr George Mellis Douglas and his team removed some 4500 corpses from the ships and examined 68 106 immigrants, of whom 5424 died. Ships had to be sent to Pointe Saint-Charles, Montréal, where 6000 Irish immigrants died and are buried. Several doctors, priests and nuns died, and many orphans were adopted by French Canadian families. In 1937 the station was closed. Since secret bacteriological research began there in 1947, access to the island has been forbidden.

SERGE OCCHIETTI

Grossman, Daniel Williams, dancer, choreographer (b at San Francisco, Calif 13 Sept 1942). A compelling performer of contemporary dance, Grossman was a member of the renowned Paul Taylor Dance Co 1963-73, after which he joined TORONTO DANCE THEATRE. In 1975 he formed the DANNY GROSSMAN DANCE CO as a vehicle for his own compositions. Grossman's works are remarkable for their inventive exploration of grotesque but appealing movement and for their humour, compassion and sometimes alarming virtuosity. He won the Jean A. Chalmers Choreographic Award in 1978, and he and his company (14 members in 1987) have earned an enviable international reputation. PENELOPE DOOB

Groulx, Gilles, film director (b at Montréal 30 Aug 1931). In 1956 he joined the NFB as a film editor and co-directed with Michel BRAULT the celebrated documentary *Les Raquetteurs* (1958). After directing numerous documentaries, he turned to feature films and produced the now classic *Le Chat dans le sac* (1964). He pursued his interest in cinema, politics and aesthetics with energy, directing 3 feature films in the next 3 years. *24 Heures ou plus* (1972) was deemed too politically controversial and was suppressed for 5 years. Groulx left the NFB during that period but returned in 1977. In 1980 he began production of the film opera, *Au pays de Zom*, but because he was in a serious automobile accident, it was not completed until 1983.

PIERRE VÉRONNEAU

Groulx, Lionel-Adolphe, historian, priest, nationalist spokesman (b at Vaudreuil, Qué 13 Jan 1878; d there 23 May 1967). Commemorated by Claude RYAN as the spiritual father of modern Québec, Groulx was French Canada's foremost historian until the 1960s and, after Henri BOURASSA, Québec's most prominent nationalist spokesman. Through his teaching and writing, his sermons and his direction of nationalist organizations, Groulx was a controversial figure, inspiring thousands of young people with a pride in French Canada's past and a confidence in Québec's future.

Born of rural parentage, Groulx had rudimentary village schooling and then classical college training in the seminary in Ste-Thérèse. The intense religious atmosphere of his upbringing and school life led him towards the priesthood and teaching. As a student and then ordained priest he taught literature and history at the college in Valleyfield from 1900 until 1915 with a 3-year interruption for graduate theological and linguistic study in Europe 1906-09. During his early teaching days, Groulx developed his 2 lifelong passions: a commitment to young people and to the study of history. He initiated the Association catholique de la jeunesse canadienne-française, a province-wide student body, inspiring its members to develop high religious and social ideals and to put them into practice throughout their lives. Groulx gleaned illustrations for the students from the past as he trained himself to be an historian. The effort entailed creating a course and a text in Canadian history virtually from scratch. He developed François-Xavier GARNEAU's view of the CONQUEST as a disaster and his

Lionel-Adolphe Groulx, who urged French Canadians to draw their inspiration from their religion and their past (*courtesy National Archives of Canada/C-16657*).

idea of history as a struggle by examining the post-Conquest period (*see* HISTORIOGRAPHY). The novelty of that approach is hard to imagine because Groulx was so successful in undermining the common assumption that the British presence in Québec was beneficial and that French Canadian subordination was natural. In 1915 Groulx was appointed to the first chair in Canadian history at U de M, a position he held until 1949.

Groulx saw politics through the eyes of Henri Bourassa, embittered and unhappy over the ONTARIO SCHOOLS QUESTION and Canada's participation in WWI. With friends in the Ligue des droits du français he worried over the diminishing stature of the French language in the burgeoning world of commerce and industry. His history lectures, published annually 1916-21, continued their assault on the unknown and the commonplace. During 1917, the year of CONSCRIPTION, Groulx's history lessons threw a dash of cold water on Confederation itself. From 1920 to 1928 he edited a monthly journal ACTION FRANÇAISE and animated a nationalist organization of the same name. In the journal Groulx kept posing the worrisome question of French and Catholic survival in an urban, industrial, Anglo-Saxon environment, and he toyed with the idea of an autonomous state for French Canada. He carefully avoided the word SEPARATISM and denied all his life any advocacy of it. But still the thought was there if only as an ideal. Perhaps French Canadians *could* organize their social, economic and political existence in their own way, drawing their inspiration and their genius from their religion, their past and their French culture.

Groulx maintained that ideal through some of the darkest episodes in modern Québec history. The Depression of the 1930s found him involved with yet another nationalist organization, ACTION NATIONALE, which interpreted the Depression as the result of excess industrialization fostered by American capitalists and abetted by an overly generous provincial government. During WWII Groulx bluntly blamed English-speaking Canadians for the division over conscription. Usually Groulx was more severe with his fellow French Canadians: they must insist on their equal place in Canada. In the 1950s Groulx chastised a new generation for sloughing off their religious heritage. In an increasingly secular society, Groulx emphasized that heritage in his major work *Histoire du Canada français* (1950-51) and in the historical journal he founded in 1947 and edited for 20 years: REVUE D'HISTOIRE DE L'AMÉRIQUE FRANÇAISE. What he did share with the younger generation was a distaste for Maurice DUPLESSIS and great excitement over the beginnings of the QUIET REVOLUTION. Indeed Groulx cast off his clerical prudence momentarily to vote in the election of 1962 when nationalization of hydro was at stake. Finally, the *petit peuple* were taking part of their destiny into their own hands.

Groulx maintained his ardour to the day he died. Just 2 weeks before, he was discussing history at the Youth Pavilion at Expo 67, and on the very last day of his life the last of his more than 30 books was launched, significantly entitled *Constantes de vie.* SUSAN MANN TROFIMENKOFF

Reading: Lionel Groulx, *Mes mémoires* (1970-74), and *Abbé Groulx: Variations on a Nationalist Theme,* ed Susan Mann Trofimenkoff (1973); Susan Mann Trofimenkoff, *Action française: French Canadian Nationalism in the 1920s* (1975), and *Dream of Nation: A Social and Intellectual History of Québec* (1982).

Groundhog, *see* MARMOT.

Groundsel, or ragwort, common names for plants of genus *Senecio,* family Compositae or Asteraceae. The genus, one of the largest plant genera (1000-2000 species), occurs worldwide and is very diverse, including small trees, shrubs, annual and perennial herbaceous plants and succulents (ie, plants with fleshy tissues for conserving moisture). About 30 species are native to Canada, growing in habitats ranging from ponds to prairie grasslands; from moist woods to mountain tops; and in the Arctic. Exact species numbers are difficult to determine because of the hybridization and complex variation patterns found in some groundsels. Flower heads are mostly yellow, and usually have both ray and disc florets, although the former are lacking in the ubiquitous, introduced weed *S. vulgaris,* common groundsel. The leaves (bracts) below the heads are typically arranged in a single, circular row. The fruit, a small, dry, one-seeded achene, bears a crown of white bristles. Golden ragwort or squaw-weed (*S. aureus*), found from Manitoba eastwards, was used by native peoples to heal wounds and for birth control. *S. cineraria,* "dusty miller" or "cineraria," is a widely grown ornamental; *S. cruentus* is a greenhouse favourite.

Groundwater, the water filling the pores and fissures of soils and rocks beneath the land surface. Although not as widely used as river or lake water, groundwater is a valuable water source because of its clarity, purity and consistent, cool temperature, and because it usually provides a reliable, continuous supply, even in dry seasons and droughts. Groundwater has also played an important role over geologic time in creating some of Canada's best-known resort attractions. For example, groundwater can dissolve soluble rocks and its circulation is responsible for formation of CAVES in limestone terrain (*see* KARST LANDFORM). Groundwater, heated at depth, often rises to the surface to form hot SPRINGS like those at Banff and Jasper, Alta, and Radium and Fairmont, BC.

Group of Seven was founded in 1920 as an organization of self-proclaimed modern artists. The original members – Franklin CARMICHAEL, Lawren HARRIS, A.Y. JACKSON, Franz JOHNSTON, Arthur LISMER, J.E.H. MACDONALD and F.H. VARLEY – befriended each other in Toronto between 1911 and 1913. All except Harris, who was independently wealthy, made their living as commercial artists, and several of them even worked together in the same shop. Tom THOMSON, another commercial artist, was included in this circle of friends, but since he died in 1917 he never became a member of the Group. He was important to the other artists, however, for he was an avid outdoorsman and awakened their interest in painting the rugged northern Ontario landscape.

The Group were not exclusively landscape painters, and it was only after their first exhibition at the Art Gallery of Toronto in 1920 that they began to identify themselves as a landscape school. They were initially drawn together by a common sense of frustration with the conservative and imitative quality of most Canadian art. Romantic, with mystical leanings, the Group and their spokesmen zealously, and sometimes contentiously, presented themselves as Canada's national school of painters. This provoked the ire of the artistic establishment, which seems to have hated their rhetoric even more than their paintings. Eric Brown, director of the National Gallery of Canada, always stood by them. He began buying their paintings for the gallery's collection several years before the Group was formally established, and in 1924 and 1925 he made sure they were well represented in the Canadian art shows that went to the prestigious Wembley exhibition in England. This enraged many members of the Royal Canadian Academy, who felt that the Group were given an unfair advantage, but British press reports were so favourable that both Brown and the Group felt vindicated.

Like the European *fin de siècle* symbolists and postimpressionists from whom their aesthetic largely derived, the Group rebelled against the constraints of 19th-century naturalism and tried to establish a more equitable and independent relationship between art and nature. They shifted emphasis away from similitude – the imitation of natural effects – towards the expression of their feelings for their subjects. As they often painted together, both in the bush and in the studio, their paintings developed along somewhat similar lines. The canvases exhibited in their early shows usually have heavy impasto and bright colours, and are boldly summarized with attention drawn to surface patterning. This is as true of the portraits of Harris and Varley as of the landscapes. In 1922 MacDonald began using thinner paint and more stylized designs, and Harris, Carmichael and Varley soon began heading in the same direction. Harris went further than the others, however, and by the mid-1920s he had reduced his paintings to a few simplified and nearly monochromatic forms. Ten years later he became the only member of the Group, and one of the first Canadian artists, to turn to abstraction.

Through self-promotion and through friends at the Arts and Letters Club and the *Canadian Forum,* as well as with the support of the National Gallery, the Group's influence steadily spread during the 1920s. In 1926, after Franz Johnston's resignation, A.J. CASSON was appointed a member. The Group realized they could hardly call themselves a national school of painters as long as they all lived in Toronto, so they invited other artists to join them: in 1930 Edwin HOLGATE from Montréal and in 1932 L.L. FITZGERALD from Winnipeg were admitted to give the organization a wider geographic base.

Harris and Jackson influenced and encouraged the next generation of Canadian artists, and Lismer, MacDonald and Varley all became distinguished and influential teachers. Disbanded in

Terre Sauvage (The Northland), 1913, oil on canvas, by A.Y. Jackson (*courtesy National Gallery of Canada, ©Dr Naomi Jackson Groves*).

1933, the Group had become as entrenched, and in some ways as conservative, as the art establishment it had overthrown. Its influence has therefore been a mixed blessing, and it is not surprising that it was in Montréal, which did not respond to the Group's call, that the next generation of significant Canadian painters emerged. Paintings by members of the Group of Seven can be found in most Canadian public art galleries.

CHRISTOPHER VARLEY

Reading: J. Russell Harper, *Painting in Canada* (1977); D. Reid, *A Concise History of Canadian Painting* (1973) and *The Group of Seven* (1970).

Groupe de la Place Royale, Le, integrates theatre, dance, voice, technology and music in ways that make it Canada's most consistently innovative modern-dance company. It was formed in Montréal (1966) by Jeanne Renaud with Peter Boneham as assistant artistic editor. Renaud, a French Canadian who had studied in New York with Hanya Holm and Mary Anthony, was noted for very abstract and unemotional choreography. Boneham, originally trained in ballet, served as artistic codirector, dancer, choreographer and teacher for the company. Renaud left the company in 1971 and it came under the joint direction of Boneham and Jean-Pierre PERRAULT the following year. Boneham has been sole director since 1980. Davida Monk became the assistant director in 1987. Le Groupe moved to Ottawa in 1977. The company now performs at the NATIONAL ARTS CENTRE and tours across Canada. CAROL BISHOP

Grouse (Tetraoninae), small subfamily (18 species) of chickenlike birds with circumpolar distribution above lat 26° N. It includes PTARMIGANS as well as those birds commonly called grouse. Members of the largest species can weigh up to 6360 g; the smallest, 340 g. Of the 10 N American species, 9 occur in Canada (6 grouse, 3 ptarmigans). Grouse species are blue (*Dendragapus obscurus*), spruce (*D. canadensis*), ruffed (*Bonasa umbellus*), sharp-tailed (*Tympanuchus phasianellus*) and sage grouse (*Centrocercus urophasianus*). The greater prairie chicken (*T. cupido*) has virtually disappeared in Canada. Grouse inhabit woodlands, tundra and, in N America, grasslands. Adult plumages are cryptic patterns of brown, grey and black with paler or white underparts. There are many plumage modifications associated with displays, eg, pointed or curved tail feathers, elongate neck feathers, neck ruffs and pointed primaries. All species have completely or partially feathered legs; when toes are not feathered, they grow 2 rows of narrow scales, like the teeth of a comb, as "snowshoes." Nostrils are covered by feathers. In breeding season, males give elaborate displays alone or in groups (leks) involving strutting, whirring of wings and sometimes vocal accompaniment. Some have red or yellow erectile combs above the eyes, and colourful neck patches of bare skin which are made prominent by the inflated esophagus. As a group, grouse are important GAME BIRDS attracting over 10 million hunters annually. Ruffed grouse are the most sought-after species. S.D. MACDONALD

Grove, Frederick Philip, author, teacher, translator (b Felix Paul Berthold Friedrich Greve at Randomno, Germany 2 Feb 1879; d at Simcoe, Ont 19 Aug 1948). Grove was raised in Hamburg, attended university at Bonn and Munich, but left to become a poet, associated briefly with Stefan George and the neoimpressionists. The volume of poems *Wanderungen* (1902) was his first book. He made a precarious living translating English and French authors into German, was in debt and briefly in prison. He left Germany in 1909 and under his new name in 1913 began a new life as a schoolteacher in Manitoba.

Encouraged by the publication of *Over Prairie Trails* (1922) and *Turn of the Year* (1923), Grove gave up teaching after 1923 and devoted his life to writing, publishing one volume of essays, one volume of short stories (posthumously), a satire, 7 novels and a fictionalized autobiography, IN SEARCH OF MYSELF (1946), which won a Gov Gen's Award. *Settlers of the Marsh* (1925), a harsh yet romantic story of a settler's ambition betrayed by sexuality, is said to have introduced realism to Canadian fiction. With *Our Daily Bread* (1928), *The Yoke of Life* (1930) and FRUITS OF THE EARTH (1933), it records the high ambitions, personal failures and belated self-knowledge of its aloof and strongly individual protagonist. Something of a dandy in his youth, the later, austere Grove is reflected in these uncompromising pioneers. *A Search for America* (1927) is Grove's most successful book. Failure, and a kind of triumph, inform the 3 late works: THE MASTER OF THE MILL (1944), *In Search of Myself* and *Consider Her Ways* (1947). *The Master of the Mill* is the first Canadian novel to explore the social effects of monopoly capitalism. Its protagonist, like the narrator of the autobiography, tries to account for his own, and mankind's, failure to realize his potential greatness.

Neglected in his lifetime, Grove has been studied in 6 books and numerous articles and theses. Desmond Pacey's *Frederick Philip Grove* (1945) was the first, but Pacey mistakenly accepted the autobiography as fact. D.O. Spettigue's *FPG: The European Years* (1973) brought the German and Canadian careers together. Margaret Stobie's *Frederick Philip Grove* (1972) examined his life

Nine species of grouse occur in Canada, including the ruffed grouse (*Bonasa umbellus*) shown here – the most sought-after game bird (*artwork by Claire Tremblay*).

and work in Canada. The principal German works are becoming available in translation. Unpublished novels, essays and poems, mostly in the Grove collection at U Man, are being published. The *Letters* were edited by Desmond Pacey (1976). D.O. SPETTIGUE

Groves, Abraham, physician (b at Peterborough, Canada W 8 Sept 1847; d at Fergus, Ont 12 May 1935). After graduating from the Toronto School of Medicine in 1871, Groves practised in Fergus for 60 years. He performed the first successful appendectomy in N America (10 May 1883) and was as skillful in a farm kitchen as in a hospital operating room – sterilizing his instruments before it became standard practice. In 1902 he established the Fergus Royal Alexandra Hospital, later renamed the Groves Memorial Hospital, and in 1934 his *All in the Day's Work: Leaves from a Doctor's Case-Book* was published.

J.T.H. CONNOR

Guarantee Act, 1849, conceived by Francis HINCKS and carried in the Legislative Assembly of the Province of Canada, established the principle of government assistance to railways. Under the terms of the Act, any railway more than 75 mi (120 km) long was eligible for a government guarantee on the interest of half its bonds as soon as half the line had been completed. Several railways received assistance under this Act, most notably the GREAT WESTERN, the ST LAWRENCE AND ATLANTIC, and the Ontario, Simcoe and Huron. Indeed, with the incentive of the Guarantee Act, as well as with the aid provided by the 1852 Municipal Loan Act, railway building became a mania in the Canadas, the amount of track increasing from 106 km in 1850 to more than 3200 km in 1860. The darker side of this policy was the economic recklessness that government assistance encouraged: by 1860 railways in the Canadas were suffering severe financial problems, and many municipalities had so overextended themselves that they were having difficulty meeting their obligations to the MUNICIPAL LOAN FUND.

CURTIS FAHEY

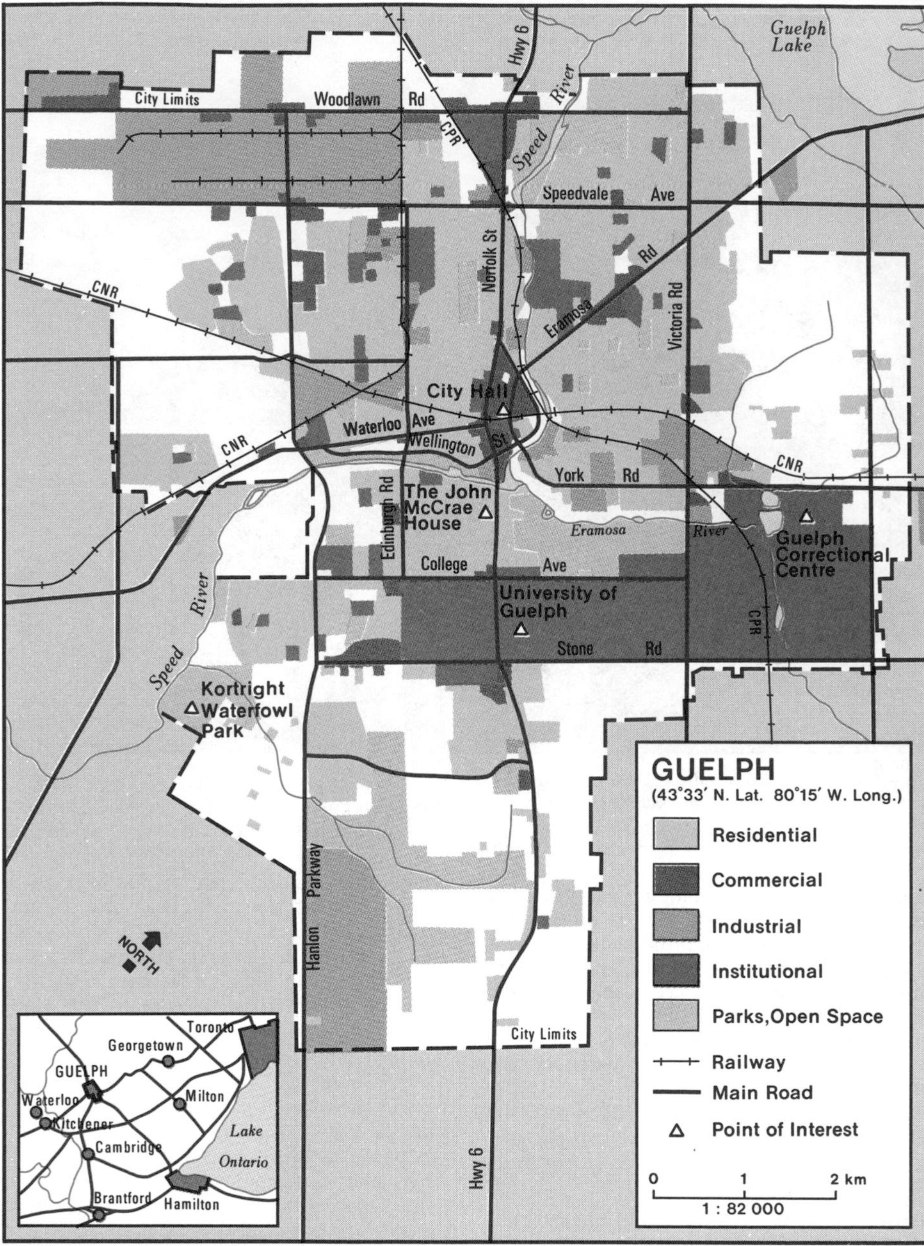

Guelph, Ont, City, 78 235 (1986c), 71 207 (1981c), inc 1851 as a village, 1856 as a town and 1879 as a city. The seat of Wellington County, it is located on the Speed R in south-central Ontario, 96 km west of Toronto and 28 km east of Kitchener-Waterloo. It has a land area of 68 km^2 and an elevation of 300-360 m above sea level. This industrial and educational centre is set in the heart of an attractive and highly productive agricultural region.

Settlement and Development Guelph was founded as a planned town in 1827 by John GALT, a Scottish novelist, who was superintendent of the CANADA COMPANY, a land company based in London, England. Galt effectively used the concept of planning towns in advance of general settlement in order to stimulate sales of agricultural land. To this end he laid out an imaginative town plan, with streets radiating from a focal point, based on American precedents such as Buffalo. The original design is still discernible in the present business core. Galt chose the town's name to honour Britain's royal family, the Hanoverians, who were descended from the Guelfs, one the great political factions in late medieval Germany and Italy. The waterpower potential at the townsite attracted a number of large mills during the 19th century; the most important of these were owned by William Allan and James Goldie. From the 1860s, several local industries established a worldwide reputation, based on technological innovation; these included the Raymond Sewing Machine Co and the Bell Organ Co.

Economy The economic base of the community has continued to be diversified manufacturing, which employs about 40% of the local work force. Major firms include Transelectrix Technical Inc (formerly part of CGE), Canadian General Electric – Magnet Wire Production Section, Hammond Manufacturing Co Ltd (electrical), IT-Telegraph Canada Ltd, Imperial Tobacco, W.C. Wood (freezers), Omark Canada Ltd and Fiberglas Canada Inc. The city has been a pioneer in the trend to municipal ownership of utilities. In the 1880s it built its own railway, the Guelph Junction, which it still owns. After the turn of the century, led by its major businessmen through the Board of Trade, the city took over the water, gas, electricity and streetcar systems.

Education The UNIVERSITY OF GUELPH was established in 1964, but it represents an amalgamation of several colleges whose traditions go back more than a century. The Ontario Agricultural Coll was founded in 1874 on a 200 ha experimental farm S of the townsite. It has been an important force in agricultural research throughout the world. Among its noted graduates is the economist John Kenneth GALBRAITH. A second college, the Macdonald Institute, was built in 1903, at the instigation of Adelaide HOODLESS, to teach household science. In 1922 the Ontario Veterinary Coll was moved to the Guelph campus. The present university's full spectrum of programs attracts about 11 500 undergraduates; its research has won international recognition in a wide variety of fields, especially for helping to solve the complex agricultural problems of developing countries.

Cityscape Much of the city's 19th-century townscape still exists. The wide use of a warm-hued, locally quarried limestone, easily worked by stone carvers, has given a visual unity to much of the community. This is especially evident on major downtown streets such as Wyndham where architects used almost continuous cornice heights and consistent window spacings with neighbouring buildings. Particularly significant structures include the Renaissance Revival-style City Hall (1856), designed by William THOMAS, and Joseph Connolly's Church of Our Lady (1877-88), which still dominates the city.

Population The population of Guelph has always been highly British in ethnic origin, with those of English background dominating (92% British, 1880; 87%, 1921). More recently (1971) the British proportion had dropped to 67%. The most important new group, those of Italian origin, stands at about 10%.

Culture The city and district are home to a

number of well-known artists, such as Ken DANBY. Major support for artistic activity is provided by the new Macdonald-Stewart Art Gallery on the university campus. Guelph's cultural heritage, however, is primarily musical. Edward JOHNSON (1878-1959), the world-famous operatic tenor and manager of New York's Metropolitan Opera, was born and educated here. His tradition is carried on by the Edward Johnson Music Foundation, which annually sponsors the highly acclaimed Guelph Spring Festival, a 2-week presentation of concerts, operas, films and plays. G.A. STELTER

Reading: L. Johnson, *History of Guelph, 1827-1927* (1977).

Guerre, Yes Sir!, La (1968), Roch CARRIER's first and best-known novel, is a surrealist fable set in rural Québec during WWI. Carrier uses the CONSCRIPTION crisis to allegorize the tragedy of fear and hatred governing French-English relations. The novel is dominated by the wake and funeral of the war hero Corriveau. Corriveau's friend Bérubé beats his bride Molly, a Newfoundland whore, while his officers, the "English" soldiers who delivered the corpse, are attacked by the villagers. Other vignettes reflect violence literally and linguistically: Joseph chops off his hand in order to avoid conscription, while Amélie rules over her deserter husband and the draft-dodging Arthur, loving both cowards. Carrier's nightmare vision portrays the peasant and his language realistically but sympathetically. The novel was translated by Sheila Fischman (1970) and adapted for the stage in French (1970) and English (1972). MICHÈLE LACOMBE

Guess Who, leading Canadian rock band (1968-75), formed in Winnipeg (1965) as Chad Allen and the Expressions. Personnel changed frequently. Singer Burton CUMMINGS and drummer Garry Peterson were constants; guitarist Randy Bachman was an important member until 1970 (*see* BTO). The band had many international hit singles and albums, and toured worldwide. Cummings pursued a successful solo career after 1975. A reconstituted Guess Who was active after 1978. In 1983 the Guess Who reassembled for a Reunion Tour which resulted in a concert video and a live album. MARK MILLER

Guèvremont, Germaine, née Marianne-Germaine Grignon, writer (b at St-Jérôme, Qué 16 Apr 1893; d at Montréal 21 Aug 1968). After studies in Ste-Scholastique, St-Jérôme, Lachine and Toronto (Loretto Abbey), Guèvremont worked at Ste-Scholastique courthouse. In 1916 she married Hyacinthe Guèvremont, an Ottawa civil servant. In 1920 the family moved to Sorel where they lived until 1935, when they moved to Montréal. Guèvremont took up journalism in Sorel, writing for the *Montreal Gazette, Le Courrier de Sorel, Paysana* and *L'Oeil*. In 1942 she published her first book, a collection of stories called *En pleine terre,* and began editing her major work, *Le* SURVENANT, 2 chapters of which appeared in *Gants du ciel* in 1943. *Le Survenant,* for which she won the Prix Duvernay, Prix David and Prix Sully-Olivier de Serres, was published by Beauchemin (1945) and in Paris by Plon (1946). *Marie-Didace,* the second instalment of *Le Survenant,* appeared in 1947. It was a triumph, winning her election to the Académie canadienne-française in 1948, the Gov Gen's Award for the English translation (*The Outlander*) in 1950, honorary doctorates, popular acclaim with radio (1951) and TV adaptations (1954-60), and election to the RSC in 1962. YVAN G. LEPAGE

Guggisberg, Sir Frederick Gordon, soldier, governor (b at Galt, Ont 20 July 1869; d at Bexhill, Eng 21 Apr 1930). Commissioned in the Royal Engineers in 1889, he served first in Singapore, then at the Royal Arsenal, Woolwich, and as a surveyor in West Africa 1902-14. After distinguishing himself in WWI, he was governor of the Gold Coast (Ghana) 1919-27, where he implemented a 10-year development plan to provide an economic and social infrastructure. He constructed a harbour, college and hospital, improved transportation and encouraged agriculture. He pushed for African advancement in the colonial service, but conceded little to national political demands. He later served as governor of British Guiana. Gold Coast chiefs placed a memorial over his grave, and in 1974 Ghana erected a statue of him in the capital city of Accra. RICHARD STUART

Guibord Affair One of the most dramatic incidents in the conflict between Catholicism and liberalism in Québec was the suppression by the bishop of Montréal of the INSTITUT CANADIEN. Founded in 1844, it possessed a library for the use of the members containing many books prohibited by the Roman Catholic Index of forbidden books. Bishop Ignace BOURGET regarded the activities of the society as dangerous to the faith of the French Canadians and its very existence as a challenge to the authority of the church. In July 1869 the bishop, supported by Rome, placed the Institut under an interdict. In Nov 1869 Joseph Guibord, who explicitly refused to renounce his membership in the Institut, died, and Bourget denied him burial in consecrated ground. That action opened more than 5 years of violent argument. A suit was brought against the bishop by Guibord's widow Henriette, and in 1874, after a series of appeals, the Judicial Committee of the Privy Council ordered that Bourget's decision be reversed. Guibord's body meanwhile had been placed in a Protestant cemetery. But because of outraged feelings among Catholics in Montréal, an attempt at interment in the Roman Catholic cemetery on 2 Sept 1875 failed. It was finally accomplished on Nov 16 with an armed military escort. Even then Bourget had the last word. After the burial, he immediately deconsecrated the plot of ground where Guibord's body lay. The Institut canadien did not survive the affair. With only a handful of members remaining, it soon disappeared from public life. H. TURNER

Guillaume-Delisle, Lake, 702 km², is a large, triangular, saltwater lake in northern Québec, connected to the E shore of HUDSON BAY by a long, narrow channel. The TREELINE begins a few km N and the many islands that litter the southern portion of the lake are wooded. The area was visited seasonally by INUIT and Naskapi, especially at the 2 Whale rivers, a short distance to the S, where beluga whales congregate in the summer. The lake was originally called Richmond Gulf by the HBC, which operated a trading post on the S shore in the 1750s. DANIEL FRANCIS

Guimond, Olivier, actor, mime (b at Montréal 1914; d 1971). The son of vaudeville artists Effie MacDonald and Olivier Guimond (Ti-Zoune), he was placed at age 7 in Mont-Saint-Louis in Montréal, where he stayed until he was 16. He quickly made his mark in Montréal cabaret, but it was not until 1958 that television made him Québec's number-one comic. That year producer Noël Gauvin hired him as the star of the popular variety show *Music-Hall* (Radio-Canada). From the opening of Télé-Métropole (1961), he played the title role in the TV series *Cré Basile*. Other TV series followed (*Le Zoo du capitaine Bonhomme, La Branche d'Olivier, Smash*) and operettas (*Les Trois Valses, La Vie parisienne*). His innate comic sense and extraordinarily supple body prompted comparison to Charlie Chaplin. CARMEN LANGLOIS

Guitar With its small body and 6 nylon strings, the classical guitar is played on a wide fingerboard, allowing for simultaneous control of melody and harmony. It is responsive to a considerable degree of musical expression, on par with the violin and other concert instruments. The guitar can be traced back to harp and lyre-like instruments found in the ruins of the ancient Sumerian city of Ur (2500 BC). The course of guitar evolution led circuitously to the 15th- and 16th-century, 4- and 5-string guitar which however, did not gain much recognition until the 17th century in the French court of Louis XIV. The 19th century saw the classical guitar as we know it today develop in construction, performance, pedagogy, repertoire and popularity; and the 20th century brought it worldwide popularity, almost solely through the efforts of its master performer Andres Segovia. The electric guitar was introduced in the US in the 1930s and became extremely popular in JAZZ, and later in POPULAR MUSIC.

Although the guitar was brought to Canada as early as the mid-17th century, it had limited use. There were few if any classical guitarists in Canada even in the 1950s, although the influential guitarist and teacher Eli Kassner came to Toronto in 1951 from Austria. Composer Harry SOMERS took guitar lessons from Kassner in 1957 and his "Sonata for Solo Guitar" (completed 1959 and premiered 1964) was the first major Canadian work written for the classical guitar. Though pieces were written by composers John BECKWITH, Walter Buczynski and others, there were few Canadian guitarists to perform them until the 1970s and 1980s, when a number of superb professionals emerged, including Pierre Augé, Liona BOYD, Philip Candelaria, Lynne Gangbar, Paul-André Gagnon, Davis Joachim, Norbert KRAFT, Michael Laucke, Peter McCutcheon, Gordon O'Brien, Alan Torok, Jean Vallières, the Wilson-McCallister Duo, Tom and Lynn West and the Laval Trio. Guitarists Michael Shutt (from the UK) and Paul Gerrits (from the Netherlands) immigrated to Canada. Well-known professional pop and folk guitarists in Canada have included Randy Bachman (*see* BTO), Bruce COCKBURN, Robbie Robertson and Dom Troiano; jazz guitarists have included Ed BICKERT, Sonny GREENWICH, Nelson Symonds and Lenny BREAU.

Guitar making has spread to several centres, mostly at the craft level; Richard Berg, Marshall Dun, Oscar Graff, Neil Herbert, Robert Holroyd, Pat Lister and Michael Shriner are a few of the excellent luthiers across Canada.

Canadian works composed for the classical guitar have had a corresponding increase, and Boyd, Kraft and Laucke, among others, have launched successful recording careers. Amateur playing, competitions and workshops have been encouraged by the Classical Guitar Soc of Toronto (est 1956) and similar organizations across Canada. Formal instruction is offered by the ROYAL CONSERVATORY OF MUSIC OF TORONTO, the BANFF CENTRE FOR CONTINUING EDUCATION and the Orford Art Centre (JEUNESSES MUSICALES DU CANADA). Canada's first international guitar festival, Guitar '75, was held in Toronto and has been held every 3 years since. Under Kassner's direction, the festival has commissioned new works and has become the most important event of its kind in the world. Guitar '84 featured new concertos by Stephen Dodgson (UK), Leo Brouwer (Cuba) and Harry Somers. Guitar '87 featured the new "Toronto Concerto" by Leo Brouwer, played by John Williams and the Toronto Symphony under Brouwer's direction. D'ARCY GREAVES

Gulf Canada Resources Limited was incorporated in 1906 as the British American Oil Company Limited. In 1969 Gulf Oil Corp of the US bought BA, which became Gulf Oil Canada Limited. The name, Gulf Canada Ltd, was adopted in 1978 and in July 1987 the company became Gulf

Canada Resources Limited. In May 1985, in the second-largest takeover in Canadian history, the Reichmann brothers, through Olympia and York Developments Ltd of Toronto, acquired San Francisco-based Chevron Corp's 60% interest in Gulf. In 1985 Gulf acquired majority interest in Abitibi-Price Inc and by mid-1987 had 83%. In Oct 1986 it acquired Hiram Walker Resources Inc; by mid 1987 it had 49%. Today Gulf has diverse interests: forest products, natural gas distribution, distilled spirits and pipelines. It has consolidated its interests in Consumers Gas Co, Hiram Walker-Gooderham Worts and Interprovincial Pipe Line into GW Utilities. O&Y now owns 79% of Gulf, which in 1986 had sales of $4 billion (ranking 20th in Canada), assets of $6.7 billion (ranking 12th) and 172 500 employees. DEBORAH C. SAWYER

Gulf Islands are a cluster of 225 islands and islets in the Str (originally Gulf) of GEORGIA E of VANCOUVER I, BC. SALTSPRING is the largest and most populated, and is linked with GALIANO, N and S Pender, MAYNE and Saturna islands by car ferry. VALDES, Thetis, Kuper and Gabriola islands have similar physical and climatic features. Glacial movement created distinctive oceanside and hill-and-valley landscapes on the larger islands, eroding folded sedimentary rock into ridges of sandstone and conglomerate and narrow valleys of softer rock. Exposed bedrock on the islands' numerous points and coves forms interesting stacks, fretworks and galleries. A smooth-barked leafy evergreen, the arbutus tree, occupies exposed rocky sites overlooking the water, and the Garry oak grows on parkland on the islands' sunny sides. Their bucolic charm, calm waters, rich bird and marine life and mild climate, in the driest zone on Canada's Pacific coast, have attracted homesteaders and cottagers since about 1859. Stands of tall timber growing in deep soil were logged early in this century. With improved ferry service since the 1960s, tourism has challenged farming as the islands' most productive industry. The resident population has burgeoned, mostly from an influx of retired people, but also artists such as Robert Bateman and craftspeople. A number of West Coast artists, craftsmen and writers have also settled here. Preserving the Gulf Islands' character in the face of development pressure is a local political issue. PETER GRANT

Gull (Laridae), family of long-winged, web-footed birds containing 2 subfamilies: Larinae (true gulls and kittiwakes, about 44 species) and Sterninae (TERNS, about 40 species). Larinae are distributed worldwide; in Canada 22 species of gulls and kittiwakes have been recorded, 18 as breeding. All but one species of Larinae have a squared-off tail. Most adults are white with grey back and wings, and black wing tips. Most have white heads, but some smaller species have black heads. Nearly all juveniles are brownish, becoming white adults in 2-3 years. They are relatively long-lived (banding records show 20-30 years), breeding from 3 to at least 12 years of age. On the West Coast, the glaucous-winged gull (*Larus glaucescens*) is the common nesting gull. Herring, ring-billed, California and Franklin's gulls (*L. argentatus, L. delawarensis, L. californicus, L. pipixcan,* respectively) nest on the prairies. Herring gulls and ring-billed gulls also nest on the Great Lakes. They are joined, in the St Lawrence R and Maritimes, by great black-backed gulls (*L. marinus*) and, in the Maritimes, by black-legged kittiwakes (*Rissa tridactyla*). Bonaparte's and mew gulls (*L. philadelphia* and *L. canus*) and herring gulls nest in the boreal forest region of Canada. Glaucous, Iceland, Thayer's, ivory, Sabine's and Ross's gulls (*L. hyperboreus, L. glaucoides, L. thayeri, Pagophila eburnea, Xema sabini, Rhodostethia rosea*, respectively) nest in arctic Canada.

Gulls frequent coastal and freshwater shores. Although omnivorous, gulls feed primarily on fish. Most nest on the ground, on islands or peninsulas in wild, rural or urban settings. Franklin's and Ross's gulls nest in marshes; Bonaparte's and less frequently mew gulls nest in trees. In southern Canada, nesting begins mid-late Apr, progressively later to the N. Most Canadian species lay 3 olive green, brown-splotched eggs. Nests range from small accumulations of vegetation and debris to large (46 cm diameter), well-made structures with well-maintained nest bowls. Eggs hatch in 3-4 weeks; down-covered young have open eyes, and can walk hours after hatching. Adult gulls swallow their food whole, then fly to the nest to regurgitate it for young. Young gulls fly about 6 weeks after hatching. A pair of adults may raise 1-2 young from 3 eggs. Young gulls die from exposure, toxic chemicals passed into the egg from the female, starvation, or attacks from adult gulls or predators. Deaths often result because young are unskilled at competing for food. Most gulls in Canada migrate to areas of open water. Generally, gulls breeding from Manitoba westward migrate to the Pacific coast and southward; those nesting E of Manitoba go to the Atlantic coast and southward. Franklin's gull, which winters in S America, has one of the longest MIGRATION routes of any gull in Canada. D.V. WESELOH

Gun Control laws seek to limit access to firearms by the potentially dangerous, irresponsible or criminal and to encourage the responsible handling, storage and use of firearms. The Criminal Code, amended in 1977 to strengthen its provisions relating to gun control, defines a firearm as any barrelled weapon from which a bullet may be discharged and which is capable of causing serious bodily injury or death to a person. It defines a prohibited weapon as one that is capable of firing bullets in rapid succession during one pressure of the trigger.

In order to acquire and use firearms, individuals must register for a permit and meet criteria set out in the Code. The issuance of registration certificates is controlled, and businesses are required to maintain inventory and transaction records.

The Code also provides for the enforcement of gun-control laws. It authorizes a peace officer to search for and seize a firearm without a warrant, whether on a person, in a vehicle, or in a place, and provides for penalties for the criminal use of firearms and the use of prohibited weapons; it prohibits the improper storage and transportation of firearms, the pointing of a firearm, the carrying of a concealed weapon without permit, and the gift of a weapon to an intoxicated person, or a person of unsound mind.

The Code does allow for certain uses of firearms by gun clubs and collectors (eg, for sporting activities), by those who need them for hunting, and for those who require them in their employment (eg, peace officers, customs officers). Even these exceptions are subject to the provision, however, that anyone may be prohibited by a court from possession of a firearm for a period of time if the court considers such prohibition desirable in the interests of public safety. VINCENT M. DEL BUONO

Gunanoot, Simon Peter, also Simon Peter Johnson, GITKSAN businessman, outlaw (b at Kispiox, BC *c*1874; d of pneumonia NE of Stewart, BC Oct 1933). Gunanoot owned a store at Kispiox and ran a ranch and packtrain near Hazelton, and a trapline. On 19 June 1906, near Hazelton, Alexander MacIntosh and Max Leclair were killed by single shots in the back. Because Gunanoot had threatened to kill MacIntosh earlier, during a drunken brawl, the BC Provincial Police charged him with the murder of MacIntosh and, along with his brother-in-law Peter Himadam, with the murder of Leclair. Taking family members with them, the suspects escaped into the wilderness. For 13 years Gunanoot evaded capture, travelling on foot with his family and sometimes alone. He ranged from Bear Lake to Telegraph Creek to McDames, selling furs whenever he could. Although a $2000 reward was offered for information leading to his arrest, and many northerners who believed Gunanoot to be guilty actually saw him, none betrayed him. In June 1919, with the aid of rancher George Beirnes and noted defence lawyer Stuart Henderson, Gunanoot surrendered. In Oct an Assize Court jury in Vancouver found him not guilty of murdering MacIntosh, but the Crown stayed the Leclair murder charge. Himadam surrendered in 1920 and was discharged at the preliminary hearing. GEORGIANA BALL

Reading: D.R. Williams, *Simon Peter Gunanoot: Trapline Outlaw* (1982).

Gundy, James Henry, investment dealer (b at Harriston, Ont 22 Mar 1880; d at Toronto 10 Nov 1951). After working for the Central Canada Loan and Savings Co and Dominion Securities Corp, in 1905 Gundy organized the firm of WOOD, GUNDY and Co, which within several years became Canada's largest investment firm. During WWI he was chairman of the special subscriptions committee of several victory loans and later president of the Investment Bankers' Assn of Canada. As an investment dealer he was active in the merger wave of 1923-30 in Canada, mainly in the financial reorganization of companies such as Simpsons, Canada Power and Paper, Dominion Steel and Coal Corp and Massey-Harris. He was a member of the boards of directors of dozens of Canadian companies, including British Columbia Power Corp, Halifax Shipyards, Dominion Life Assurance Co, London Canadian Investment Corp, North American Life Assurance Co and Canada Cement. JORGE NIOSI

Gunn, William Walker Hamilton, ornithologist, ecologist (b at Toronto 18 Mar 1913; d at Lindsay, Ont 15 Oct 1984). His research on bird migration and behaviour has been applied effectively to ecological management and public education. He was the first executive director of the Federation of Ontario Naturalists 1952-55 and helped found several naturalist and professional biologist organizations. His research into conflicts between birds and aircraft in the 1960s helped develop a warning system still in use by Canadian officials. He was a founder, first president (1971-80) and chairman (1980-84) of LGL Ltd, an early environmental consulting firm. He also pioneered the recording of bird songs, and in 1963 became associated with the CBC as consultant and sound recordist, especially for "The Nature of Things" series. His research, conservation efforts and educational endeavours have been recognized by awards and appointments to several naturalist organizations. MARTIN K. MCNICHOLL

Gunning, Harry Emmett, scientist, administrator (b at Toronto 16 Dec 1916). After obtaining an MA in English and a PhD in chemistry at U of T (1942), he was a research fellow at Harvard and NRC; professor at U of Rochester (1946) and Illinois Inst of Technology (1948); professor and head of chemistry at University of Alberta (1957), president there 1974-79 and professor emeritus (1981). He made major contributions to science, publishing 175 research articles on photochemistry, free radical reactions, chemical kinetics and mechanisms of energy transfer. He pioneered research on the chemistry of sulphur atoms and was among the first to investigate photochemical methods for separating isotopes. Former council member of NRC and president of the Chemical Inst of Canada, and current board member of the Alberta Oil Sands Technology and Research Authority, he introduced many innovations in science policy and administration, and promoted the interaction of academia with industry and government. He played an important role in promoting research and development for the exploitation of the vast oil sand resources of Alberta; in high technology, establishing Chembiomed Ltd; and in bringing into existence the Edmonton Research and Development Park.

OTTO P. STRAUSZ

Gurik, Robert, dramatist (b at Paris, France 16 Nov 1932). He immigrated to Canada in 1951 and qualified as an engineer before deciding to devote himself to theatre. His plays treat a variety of themes, from the one-act satire *Le Chant du poète* (1963) to the science fiction of *Api 2967* (1966) and the Kafkaesque *Le Procès de Jean-Baptiste M.* (1972), the latter depicting an average Québecois who out of frustration turns to violence and revenge against society. Apart from *Le Pendu* (1967), Gurik's best-known plays have strong political content, especially his parody of contemporary Canadian politicians, *Hamlet, prince du Québec* (1968), *Play Ball* (1974) and *La Baie des Jacques* (1978). He is the author of 2 novels, *Spirales* (1966) and *Jeune Délinquant* (1980).

L.E. DOUCETTE

Gustafson, Ralph, poet, professor (b at Lime Ridge, Qué 16 Aug 1909). Gustafson has written more than 20 books of poetry and edited several important anthologies of Canadian verse; he has also published 2 books of short stories. He was raised in Sherbrooke, Qué, and educated at Bishop's U and Oxford. He taught at Bishop's from 1963 until his retirement in 1979. His poetry, which is widely celebrated for its exquisite craft, its erudition and its passionate simplicity, often evokes 2 strong currents in Canadian literature: the colonial impulse to look back to European history and culture; and then the urgent post-colonial need to survey and celebrate Canadian geography, to define and create a Canadian sense of place. Gustafson has worked for many years as a music critic and was a correspondent with the British Information Services during WWII. Widely travelled, he has often written poetry with political import extending beyond the Canadian scene. Among his many awards is the Governor General's Award for his 1974 book of poems, *Fire on Stone*. *Collected Poems* (2 vols) and *Winter Prophecies* were published in 1987. NEIL BESNER

Reading: Wendy Keltner, *Ralph Gustafson* (1979).

Gutenberg Galaxy: The Making of Typographical Man, The, by Marshall MCLUHAN (Toronto 1962), is a brilliantly eclectic analysis in which McLuhan claims that print technology has modified the form of our perception, shifting and concentrating perceptual emphasis from the ear to the eye, with tremendous consequences for individuals and cultures. McLuhan describes the condition of "typographic man" at the historic moment when electronic media meet with print media, an encounter McLuhan studies in his next major work, *Understanding Media* (1964). *The Gutenberg Galaxy* established McLuhan as one of the Western world's most influential and controversial writers in the redefined field of communications; the implications of his often-quoted watchwords, phrases and syntheses continue to fascinate and disturb the post-modern imagination. *The Gutenberg Galaxy* has been translated into French (Paris, Montréal, 1967), as *La Galaxie Gutenberg: la genèse de l'homme typographique,* by Jean Paré. NEIL BESNER

Guthrie, Sir William Tyrone, stage director, producer (b at Tunbridge Wells, Eng 2 July 1900; d at Newbliss, County Monaghan, Ire 15 May 1971). The great-grandson of the 19th-century actor Tyrone Power, he made his stage debut as a performer at Oxford in 1919. A frustrated singer, actor and playwright (*Top of the Ladder,* 1950), he pioneered radio drama production in Belfast (1924-26) for the BBC, a phenomenon he repeated in Canada in 1931 for the fledgling CNR radio network. His career as a renowned stage director began in Glasgow (1926-28), proceeded to Cambridge (1929-30) and London (1931). As the resident producer-director of London's Old Vic and Sadler's Wells companies (1933-47), he developed his special interests in Shakespearean production and opera. In 1953 he became the founding director of Canada's STRATFORD FESTIVAL, reintroducing Shakespeare's thrust stage, a design concept to be echoed in theatres around the world. He was knighted in 1961 and 2 years later guided the theatre in Minneapolis that bears his name. His books include *A Life in the Theatre* (1959), *A New Theatre* (1964) and *Tyrone Guthrie on Acting* (1971). DAVID GARDNER

Reading: James Forsyth, *Tyrone Guthrie* (1976).

Gutteridge, Helena Rose, feminist, trade unionist, socialist politician (b at London, Eng 1879 or 1880; d at Vancouver 3 Oct 1960). Gutteridge immigrated to BC in 1911 and organized the BC Women's Suffrage League. Her interest in working-class women contributed to her participation in trade-union activities, and before long she took a leading role on the Vancouver Trades and Labor Council. Her responsibilities there kindled a turn to socialist politics and membership in the CO-OPERATIVE COMMONWEALTH FEDERATION. In Mar 1937 she was elected as a CCF representative to Vancouver City Council, becoming its first woman member. SUSAN WALSH

Reading: B. Latham and C. Kess, eds, *In Her Own Right* (1980).

Guy, John, merchant venturer, colonizer, governor of the first English colony in NEWFOUNDLAND (d Mar 1629, monument at Bristol, Eng). Guy, an early advocate of colonizing Newfoundland, was appointed governor of the colony created by the London and Bristol Co in 1610. He selected Cupers Cove (now CUPIDS) as the site of the settlement; from 39 members in its first year the colony increased to over 60 under his leadership. After 5 years he returned to England but remained a strong supporter of the Newfoundland plantation against English migratory-fishing interests, economic difficulties and war. G.M. STORY

Guyon, Jean, priest, artist (b at Château-Richer, Qué 5 Oct 1659; d at Paris, France 10 Jan 1687). Bishop LAVAL had great hopes for this young Canadian priest, who died before he could create any significant body of work. The lovely oil portrait of Mother Jeanne-Françoise Juchereau, *dite* de Saint-Ignace, in the Hôtel-Dieu in Québec C, is attributed to him. In addition the Séminaire de Québec at one time had some of his watercolour studies of the flora of Québec. At his death his effects included some oil paints and sculptor's tools, evidence that he intended to help decorate the religious buildings constructed under Laval.

FRANÇOIS-MARC GAGNON

Guysborough, shire town, Guys Co, NS, Village, located on the E shore, 51 km from Canso Causeway. It was originally called Chedabucto, from the Micmac *Sedabooktook* (harbour running far back) and is believed to be the "sweet water bay" entered by the Portuguese FAGUNDES (1520). Nicolas DENYS's fishing station (fd 1654) employed 120 men by 1657. Bergier, a Huguenot merchant, expanded and built a fortified trading post (1682). Fortunes fluctuated with feuds between competing Frenchmen, and wars with England, as when Sir William PHIPS captured Chedabucto (1690). 700 Acadians were still living here when 9 English families settled (1768). After 1784, LOYALISTS, their former slaves and disbanded troops moved in, renaming Chedabucto after Sir Guy CARLETON. Almost destroyed in the great gale Oct 1811, Guysborough was rebuilt, prospering during the 1800s in lumber and shipbuilding. Today, the village administers the surrounding municipal district (pop 7294, 1986c). JUDITH HOEGG RYAN

Gwatkin, Sir Willoughby Garnons, soldier (b in Eng 11 Aug 1859; d at Twickenham, Eng 2 Feb 1925). Educated at King's College, Cambridge, and commissioned in the British army in 1882, Gwatkin was permanently seconded to Canada in 1911. As chief of the general staff, Canadian militia, 1913-19, Gwatkin had the key responsibility for implementing Canada's military policies during WWI. An able and scholarly administrator who found diversion in writing Latin verse, Gwatkin also guided the formation of a postwar Canadian air force and was a pioneer in promoting the development of military and civil AVIATION. He was KCMG and CB. W.J. MCANDREW

Gwyn, Richard John Philip Jermy, journalist, author (b at Bury St Edmunds, Eng 26 May 1934). A graduate of Sandhurst, Gwyn immigrated to Canada in 1954, and from 1956 to 1967 pursued a career in journalism, primarily as a parliamentary correspondent. In 1968 he abandoned journalism to become executive assistant to Eric KIERANS, then minister of communications at Ottawa, and 2 years later was appointed director-general of social and economic planning in the Dept of Communications. In 1973 Gwyn resumed his journalistic career, now as syndicated national affairs columnist for the *Toronto Star*. By his commentary there and on frequent appearances on radio and television public affairs programs he quickly established himself as one of the country's pre-eminent political analysts. He has published several books, including biographies of Joey Smallwood and Pierre Trudeau and, more recently, *The 49th Paradox* (1985). In 1985 he was transferred to London to serve as European correspondent. STANLEY GORDON

Gwynne, Horace, "Lefty," boxer (b at Toronto 5 Oct 1912). Gwynne left school after grade 8, weighing 65 lb (29.5 kg). When he started to grow, he began working out in Stokley's Gym in Toronto to lose weight in order to become a jockey. At 19 he won the Canadian amateur flyweight championship in London, Ont. He entered the 1932 Olympic trials as a bantamweight, a class permitting up to 118 lb (53.5 kg); he weighed 116. He won the Canadian amateur bantamweight title, which sent him to the 1932 Olympic Games in Los Angeles, despite his having fought only 15 bouts. He won the Olympic gold medal match against the German, Hans Ziglarski, knocking him down in the second round. Immediately after the Olympics he turned professional. He won the Canadian professional bantamweight title in 1935 and held it until 1939, retiring undefeated. He has been inducted into the Canadian Boxing Hall of Fame and the Canadian Sports Hall of Fame. A.J. "SANDY" YOUNG

Gymnastics This sport is performed in many different formats: women on the vaulting horse, uneven bars, balance beam and in floor exercises; men on the vaulting horse, pommel horse, rings, parallel bars, horizontal bar and in floor exercises. It is participated in by all ages for fun, fitness, competition and social relaxation, and is included in modern-day school curriculums across

Elfi Schlegel, the first Canadian to win a medal in an international gymnastics meet – a bronze in vaulting at the 1980 World Cup (*photo by Ron Watts/First Light*).

Canada. One of the oldest and most fundamental sports, it originated in ancient Greece. Modern-day artistic gymnastics developed in Germany in the early 1800s. The first Olympic Gymnasium opened in Montréal in 1843, followed by others in Québec City, Toronto, Hamilton, Ottawa, Halifax and Victoria. The inspiration for these clubs came mostly from immigrants from Germany and Czechoslovakia; an Englishman, F. Barnjum, was responsible for developments in the most active centre at that time, Montréal. The sport was introduced into school curriculums in the 1800s under the advisement of Egerton RYERSON, and in 1899 Canada became the fourteenth country to join the International Gymnastics Federation.

Competitively, individuals such as Lou Sievert, Alan Keith and Orville Elliott represented Canada at the 1904 and 1908 Olympic Games. In 1956 Ernestine Russell was Canada's first woman Olympic competitor. She placed first all-round at the 3rd Pan-American Games in Chicago (1959), making her the first Canadian medal winner in international gymnastic competition. Susan McDonnell won the women's uneven bars event at the 5th Pan-Am Games in Winnipeg (1967). Canada entered full teams (men and women) in the 1962 world championships in Prague and in the 1968 Mexico City Olympics. By 1976 Canada's women's team was ranked in the top 10 in the world; by 1979 the men ranked in the top 15. The first national championship was held in 1923 at the Canadian National Exhibition in Toronto. The CNE donated all awards and for 11 consecutive years hosted this event for men. Women entered the championships for the first time in 1954. Canada has hosted many teams, the first being the Japanese in 1962, and was the host country of the 1980 World Cup in gymnastics. In 1985, the 23rd world championships was hosted in Montréal; Canada's women's team placed 9th and the men's team 11th.

Canadian gymnastics now has an organization with a full-time staff, sophisticated national programs, a registered membership of over 150 000, over 500 active coaches and many thousands of dedicated supporters. Recent outstanding Canadian gymnasts include Philip Delesalle, whose best career performance was 12th all round at the 1979 world championships in Fort Worth, US; Elfi Schlegel, the first Canadian medal winner in a World Cup (bronze in vaulting); and Brad Peters (14th all round in the world from his performance at the world championships in 1985). In the 1983 World University Games at Edmonton, Canada won 4 medals in gymnastics, including a gold by Phillipe Chartrand. In the 1984 Los Angeles Olympics, the women's team placed 5th overall; Kelly Brown was 6th in the vault. The men's team placed 8th. Chartrand won a gold medal on the high bar at the 1986 Leningrad invitational, attended by over 80 gymnasts from 36 countries. In the 1987 Pan-Am Games Canada's men's team placed 5th and its injury-plagued women's team won a bronze. In rhythmic gymnastics, 13-year-old Mary Fuzesi won a silver and 3 bronze and Susan Cashman won a bronze. The Canadian Gymnastics Federation boasts fine development programs for all ages. CAROL ANNE LETHEREN

Gypsum, mineral consisting of water-containing calcium sulphate ($CaSO_4.2H_2O$). When calcined (roasted) at temperatures of 120-250°C, gypsum releases 75% of its water. The resulting plaster of paris, when mixed with water, can be molded, shaped or spread, then dried or set to form hard plaster. Gypsum was used by the builders of the pyramids as a construction material and earlier by artisans producing decorative objects. Nova Scotia gypsum was shipped to the eastern US in the 1780s for use as land plaster. The popularity of gypsum as a building material grew from the mid-1880s as methods of controlling setting time were developed. Crude gypsum is pulverized and heated to form stucco, which is mixed with water and aggregate (sand, vermiculite or expanded perlite) and applied over wood, metal or gypsum lath to form interior wall finishes. Gypsum board, lath and sheathing are formed by introducing a slurry of stucco, water, foam, pulp and starch between 2 unwinding rolls of absorbent paper, resulting in a continuous sandwich of wet board. Gypsum is also used as a filler in paint and paper manufacture, as a substitute for salt cake in glass manufacture and as a soil conditioner. Canada ranks second among world producers of crude gypsum, after the US. Over 80% of Canadian production comes from the Atlantic provinces, about 70% of this being shipped to American wallboard plants. Other major sources are in Ontario, Manitoba and BC. Crude gypsum is a low-cost, high-bulk mineral commodity and contributes only marginally to the Canadian GDP (about 0.016% in 1985). The gypsum products industry contributes considerably more (about 0.084% in 1985). D.H. STONEHOUSE

Gzowski, Sir Casimir Stanislaus, engineer (b at St Petersburg [Leningrad], Russia 5 Mar 1813; d at Toronto 24 Aug 1898). He began his ENGINEERING career in Canada in 1842. As a superintendent of public works of the Province of Canada, he improved waterways and canals and constructed roads, harbours and bridges. Later he built the Canadian portion of the ST LAWRENCE AND ATLANTIC RAILROAD (1846-53) and constructed the GRAND TRUNK RAILWAY line from Toronto to Sarnia (1852-60). He designed and built the international bridge between Fort Erie and Buffalo, NY (1870-73), a difficult job because of strong currents, ice and winds. At the same time he served on a commission to study inland waters from the Atlantic to Lk Superior; its report of 1871 anticipates the system now known as the St Lawrence Seaway. Gzowski was the first chairman of the Niagara Parks Commission and planned the park system along the Canadian bank of the river. Together with several other engineers he formed the Canadian Soc of Civil Engineers and later served as president (1889-91). Established during his term of office, the gold Gzowski Medal has been awarded annually for outstanding written contributions to engineering. Keenly concerned over the defence of Canada, Gzowski fought for the strengthening of the Canadian militia and served in it as lieutenant-colonel and colonel. Appointed aide-de-camp to Queen Victoria (1879), he was awarded a KCMG (1890) in recognition of his services in the military and engineering fields. PHYLLIS ROSE

Sir Casimir Gzowski began his career in Canada as a superintendent of public works of the Province of Canada (*courtesy National Archives of Canada/C-8620*).

Broadcaster and writer Peter Gzowski (*CBC Photo by Fred Phipps*).

Gzowski, Peter, broadcaster, editor, writer (b at Toronto 13 July 1934). Great-grandson of the engineer Sir Casimir GZOWSKI, he grew up in the small town of Galt, Ont, and was shaped by the disciplined traditions of Ridley College. At U of T he edited *The Varsity* and acquired the passion for journalism which took him to jobs in Timmins, Moose Jaw and Chatham. In 1958 his mentor Ralph Allen invited him to join *Maclean's*, where he became managing editor in 1962. A restless, versatile man, Gzowski also worked as entertainment editor of the *Toronto Star*, as editor of the *Star Weekly*, and (briefly in 1970) as editor of *Maclean's*. He became a household name as the host of CBC radio's lively, eclectic "This Country in the Morning" (1971-74), but his subsequent talk show on CBC-TV, "90 Minutes Live" (1976-78), was a failure. He wrote several nonfiction books, notably *The Sacrament* (1980) and *The Game of Our Lives* (1981), before returning to CBC radio as host of "Morningside" in 1982. His curiosity, sensitivity and wit, combined with his patriotism and ability to project personal warmth, made him one of the best (and best-loved) broadcasters in Canada. *The New Morningside Papers* was published in 1987. MARK ABLEY

Habitant (inhabitant) In NEW FRANCE, habitants were free proprietors who were differentiated from indentured servants and those whose stay was perceived to be temporary. By the late 17th century, "habitant" came to mean peasant proprietor, as opposed to seigneur or town resident. Finally, in the waning years of the 18th century, when landless peasants had become common, all those who earned their living from agricultural labour were known as habitants. *See also* SEIGNEURIAL SYSTEM. TOM WIEN

Hachey, Henry Benedict, oceanographer (b at West Bathurst, NB 7 June 1901; d at St Andrews, NB 24 June 1985). Educated at St Thomas U, Saint Francis Xavier, McGill and U of T, he was professor of physics at UNB before joining the Biological Board of Canada (later the Fisheries Research Board) at St Andrews, NB, in 1928. In 1930 he was appointed officer in charge of the Hudson Bay Fisheries Expedition. His service with the armed forces (1940-46) included operational research and antisubmarine duties. As chief oceanographer of Canada (1946-64), he co-ordinated the work of various government agencies in developing Canadian OCEANOGRAPHY. As head of the Atlantic Oceanographic Group of the FRB he established the course of oceanographic studies on the East Coast and Arctic now largely sustained by the BEDFORD INSTITUTE OF OCEANOGRAPHY. He was the first Canadian to use mathematical techniques to calculate ocean currents. His outstanding scientific contributions to oceanography have been widely recognized. NEIL J. CAMPBELL

Hackett, James Keteltas, expatriate actor (b at Wolfe I, Ont 6 Sept 1869; d at Paris, France 8 Nov 1926). A handsome, swashbuckling, matinee idol, he made his name as the romantic hero of such 1890s' hits as *The Prisoner of Zenda* and *Rupert of Hentzau*. He made his professional debut in 1892 in Philadelphia where he was amateur duelling champion. He toured to Halifax and Saint John in 1893 and opened his own theatre in New York in 1905. Aspiring to serious roles, he mounted with an inherited fortune New York productions of *Othello* (1914) and *Macbeth* (1916), remembered for their advanced scenic design. In 1920 *Macbeth* was taken successfully to London and Paris. He was awarded the French Legion of Honour. DAVID GARDNER

Haddock, *see* COD.

Haendel, Ida, violinist (b at Chelm, Poland 15 Dec 1924). Celebrated for flawless technique and beauty of tone, Haendel has enjoyed great demand as a soloist, recitalist and recording artist, performing a large repertoire ranging from Bach to Bartók through a lengthy international career. A child prodigy in her native Poland, she immigrated to England prior to WWII. She gave recitals for British servicemen and appeared as soloist in concertos with many well-known British and European conductors. Haendel immigrated to Canada in 1952 and settled in Montréal. She has given recitals in Canada and performed with major orchestras, among them the Montréal, Toronto and Vancouver symphonies. In 1977, with a CBC orchestra conducted by Franz-Paul Decker, she gave the Canadian premiere of Benjamin Britten's *Concerto*. BARCLAY MCMILLAN

Hagerman, Christopher Alexander, lawyer, politician, judge (b at Adolphustown, UC 28 Mar 1792; d at Toronto 14 May 1847). "Handsome Kit" grew up outside the charmed circle of pupils educated by John STRACHAN. Rising spectacularly by dint of his service during the War of 1812, he was appointed to the lucrative collectorship of customs at Kingston. He was called to the Bar in 1815 and proved a brilliant lawyer and eloquent orator. This latter gift served him well as an assemblyman and leading conservative spokesman in 4 parliaments. A large, powerfully built man, he was bumptious and aggressive: on one occasion, he horsewhipped Robert GOURLAY. His impulsive actions at times had disastrous political results, notably his role in handling the ALIEN QUESTION and the expulsion of William Lyon MACKENZIE from the assembly. His bellicose personal traits, natural abilities and ardent defence of toryism in successive administrations made Hagerman a *bête noire* of the Opposition. He was a particular favourite of Lt-Gov COLBORNE and served as solicitor general 1829-33 and attorney general 1837-40 when like others of the so-called FAMILY COMPACT he was appointed to the Court of Queen's Bench, a position he held until his death. ROBERT L. FRASER

Haida village on the Queen Charlotte Is, BC, with totem poles depicting stories and family crests, 1878 (*courtesy Geological Survey of Canada/250*).

Hagfish, group of primitive VERTEBRATES which together with LAMPREYS and various extinct forms comprise the fish class Agnatha. Hagfishes have an eellike body with a cartilaginous skeleton which permits a degree of flexibility unique among vertebrates. The mouth is a fleshy tunnel with an eversible tongue carrying 2 rows of horny teeth; a single tooth occurs on the palate. Hagfishes have 6-8 barbels (whiskerlike tactile organs) around the mouth and a single nostril. The eyes lack a lens. External gill openings (1-16 pairs) occur on each side. Scales and paired fins are absent; a single fin extends around the posterior profile. A well-marked series of mucous pores occurs along the sides; when handled or disturbed, hagfishes produce large amounts of mucus. Hagfishes are hermaphroditic and lack a larval stage. A few large (30 x 10 mm) keratinized eggs are laid. Unlike lampreys, hagfishes do not shrink in size at spawning. All species live only in salt water, sometimes at great depths. They feed on dead or dying fish by boring into the body cavity, and may be damaging to FISHERIES. In Canada, one species, *Myxine glutinosa*, is found in the Atlantic; 2 species of genus *Eptatretus* in the Pacific. VADIM D. VLADYKOV

Haida live along the coastal bays and inlets of the QUEEN CHARLOTTE IS, BC. Archaeological evidence confirms continual habitation on the islands for at least 6000-8000 years (*see* PREHISTORY). A few hundred years ago a small group of Haida migrated N to the southernmost islands of the Alaskan "panhandle," where their descendants live in the village of Hydaburg. The Haida language is an isolate with 2 dialects – Masset is spoken in the northern islands and Skidegate in the S. Haida culture and art are distinctive within Northwest Coast traditions, though there are cultural similarities to the neighbouring TSIMSHIAN and TLINGIT.

Traditionally, each village was an independent political unit, and to a great extent each family in a village was an independent entity. All Haida, however, belonged to one of 2 clans – the Eagle or the Raven. A Haida always married a member of the opposite CLAN, and clan membership was inherited from the mother. Individuals publicly proclaimed clan membership through an elaborate display of inherited family crests, carved on TOTEM POLES erected in front of houses and carved or painted on great war CANOES, cedar boxes, MASKS, and utilitarian and decorative objects. Large ceremonial feasts (*see* POTLATCH) were a focus of Haida life, a means of reinforcing the social and economic organization and the interdependence of clans, lineages and villages.

The first recorded European contact (1774) was with the Spanish explorer Juan PÉREZ. British

Capt George Dixon initiated trade (1787) with the Haida for sea-otter pelts, and the Haida remained at the centre of the lucrative China sea-otter trade until the mid-1800s.

European settlers did not significantly populate the Queen Charlotte Is until almost 1900. Mainland fur traders estimated a Haida population before 1850 of 6000-8000. By 1915 the population had declined to 588 people, mainly because of smallpox and other diseases. Though the Haida were traditionally a warlike people, their large seagoing canoes carrying them on raiding expeditions as far S as Washington state, incidents of violent confrontation with Europeans were few. In 1986 the Haida population on the Queen Charlotte Islands was approximately 2000.

Contemporary Haida are famous for their fine art (*see* NORTHWEST COAST INDIAN ART), and many work as prosperous commercial fishermen, loggers and artists. *See also* NATIVE PEOPLE: NORTHWEST COAST and general articles under NATIVE PEOPLE.

TRISHA GESSLER

Reading: J.R. Swanton, "Contributions to the Ethnology of the Haida," *The Jesup North Pacific Expedition*, Vol 5, Part 1 (1901).

Haida, a powerful WWII "Tribal" Class destroyer, commissioned 30 Aug 1943, built in England for the Royal Canadian Navy. From Jan 1944 to Jan 1945 it patrolled the English Channel and the Bay of Biscay, and it was present at the NORMANDY INVASION, 6 June 1944. *Haida* became famous for participating in the destruction of several German ships. After peacetime service, 1947-50, it received modern armament and from 1952 to 1954 served with UN forces in Korea. It remained in service with the RCN until 11 Oct 1963. The next year friends and admirers bought it, and in 1970 it was taken over by the Ontario government and moved permanently to Ontario Place, Toronto, as a memorial.

ROGER SARTY

Haig-Brown, Roderick, author, conservationist (b at Lancing, Eng 21 Feb 1908; d at Campbell River, BC 19 Oct 1976). Haig-Brown's early appreciation of nature greatly influenced his later life. A 1926 visit to the American West impressed him with the hunting and fishing opportunities of the Pacific coast, and he immigrated to Vancouver I in 1931, eventually settling at Campbell River. He made his living by logging, trapping, guiding and increasingly by writing. His early stories fictionalized various types of wildlife, including cougars (*Panther*, 1934) and Atlantic and Pacific salmon (*Return to the River*, 1941; *Silver*, 1931). Although his later adult novels were moderately successful, he is perhaps best known as an author of children's literature. *Starbuck Valley Winter* (1943) and its sequel *Saltwater Summer* (1948) received much acclaim, the latter winning a Gov Gen's Award. His essays on sportfishing (*A River Never Sleeps*, 1946; *Measure of the Year*, 1950) have considerable literary merit and wide popular readership. His *A Primer of Fly Fishing* (1964) is considered a standard work on the subject. A committed conservationist, Haig-Brown eloquently condemned the rank exploitation that has characterized much of the development of the West.

C.J. TAYLOR

Hail, precipitation consisting of lumps of ICE, 5 mm to 10 cm in diameter and about 0.1 g to 1 kg in weight. A 290 g hailstone that fell near Cedoux, Sask, is one of the largest recorded in Canada. A hailstone begins as a frozen RAIN droplet or snow pellet, falling through a CLOUD which has a temperature below 0°C. The embryo hailstone collects water by collision with super-cooled (unfrozen) cloud droplets. Vertical air currents of 10-50 m per second help keep it in the cloud as it grows. Some of the accreted water freezes, yielding ice which may be bubbly or clear, depending on the cloud liquid-water concentration, air temperature and hailstone size. Variations of these parameters during the hailstone's growth lead to an onionlike appearance, consisting of alternating layers of clear and bubbly ice. These layers, clues to the hailstone's history, can be seen by cutting the hailstone in half, or by examining a thin slice between crossed, polarizing filters.

Although hail occurs in all provinces, it is most frequent and severe in Saskatchewan and Alberta, where farms have been hit up to 10 times in one year. Here, hail comes mostly from late-afternoon, summer THUNDERSTORMS, which can grow to heights of almost 20 km. Severe hailstorms may last for several hours and leave a hail swath up to 50 km wide in places and hundreds of kilometres long. Large hailstones damage crops, buildings and automobiles. Very big ones have as much energy as a bullet and can injure or kill animals and people. A hailstorm in Calgary on 28 July 1981 caused $100 million of damage to property. The total annual loss to crops and property in Canada may exceed twice that amount. In Alberta attempts to reduce hail damage, through cloud seeding with silver iodide, have been undertaken since 1956. Although some evidence appears to indicate benefits from this practice, hail suppression remains controversial.

E.P. LOZOWSKI

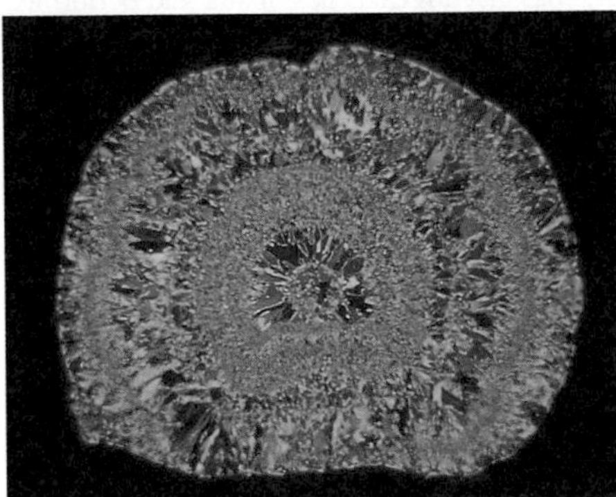

This hailstone, 7 cm across, fell near Cedoux, Sask, on 27 Aug 1984. A thin slice reveals colourful ice-crystal layers, which provide clues to how the stone was formed. A hailstone begins as a frozen rain droplet or snow pellet (*courtesy Edward Lozowski/Tony Kot*).

Hailey, Arthur, author (b at Luton, Eng 5 Apr 1920). He served in the RAF 1939-47 as a flight lieutenant and immigrated to Canada in 1947. He has become a successful writer of POPULAR LITERATURE, and his forte lies in his practice of writing novels – dealing with fashionable subjects – that have been well researched. His literary career has spanned a quarter of a century. After collaborating on adventure novels in the 1950s, he produced a string of BEST-SELLERS, including *The Final Diagnosis* (1959), *In High Places*, dealing with the Ottawa political scene (1962), *Hotel* (1965), *Airport* (1968), *Wheels* (1971), *The Moneychangers* (1975), *Overload* (1979) and *Strong Medicine* (1984). He has written scripts for a number of movies, including *Hotel* (1966), *Airport* (1970) and *Strong Medicine* (1986) and numerous television plays. He now lives in the Bahamas.

DAVID EVANS

Haileybury, Ont, Town, pop 4820 (1986c), 4925 (1981c), inc 1904, located on NW shore of Lk TIMISKAMING, 150 km N of North Bay. Haileybury was established and named (after his English *alma mater*, Haileybury College) by C.C. Farr, who came to the area as an employee of HBC in 1883. Because of its readily accessible port facilities on Lk Timiskaming and its proximity to the silver mines of COBALT and to the agricultural region known as Little Clay Belt, Haileybury developed as a residential, mercantile and service centre for the whole vicinity. Famous for its devastation by several forest fires, most notably the Great Fire of 1922 which dispossessed over 2900 people, the town has since maintained and strengthened its role as a commercial entrepôt, and has taken on new functions as seat of the District of Timiskaming and site of a campus of the Northern College of Applied Arts and Technology (School of Mines).

MATT BRAY

Haines Junction, YT, Village, pop 340 (1986c), 366 (1981c), is located at the junction of the ALASKA HWY and the Haines Hwy, built to the port of Haines, Alaska, by US Army engineers 1942-45. Army barracks and shops were the first buildings on the site, and a Canadian customs office and RCMP station followed completion of the road. As headquarters of KLUANE NATIONAL PARK, Haines Junction offers facilities for trail riding, mountain climbing and photographic expeditions.

H. GUEST

Hainsworth, George, hockey player (b at Toronto 26 June 1895; d near Gravenhurst, Ont 9 Oct 1950). He joined the MONTREAL CANADIENS in 1926 as a replacement for Georges VÉZINA and was traded to the TORONTO MAPLE LEAFS in 1933, playing 3 ½ years before returning briefly to Montréal. He won the VÉZINA TROPHY the first 3 years it was awarded and recorded 22 shutouts in 44 games in 1928-29 and 94 shutouts in 464 NHL games. He was killed in a car crash.

JAMES MARSH

Haldimand, Ont, Town, pop 17 701 (1986c), est 1974 from the town of Caledonia, the townships of Oneida, Seneca, North Cayuga, South Cayuga, Rainham and Walpole (part), and the villages of Cayuga and Hagersville in the county of Haldimand. It is situated between the cities of Hamilton and Nanticoke, W of Dunnville. The land was ceded by the Six Nations in the 1850s and settled by British immigrants. It is undulating terrain, level along the river valleys, and primarily agricultural. There are summer cottages along Lk Erie, former gypsum mines and natural gas wells. Small centres include Canfield, Hagersville and Fisherville, then Cayuga and Caledonia on the Grand R. The town offices are in Cayuga.

JOHN N. JACKSON

Haldimand, Sir Frederick, army officer, governor (b at Yverdon, Swit 11 Aug 1718; d there 5 June 1791). As governor of Québec, Haldimand concentrated on defending the province militarily and the status quo politically. After service in Prussia and Holland, he transferred to the British army in 1756. He served in N America during the SEVEN YEARS' WAR, and after the CONQUEST of Canada he was twice military governor of Trois-Rivières. He was named Guy CARLETON's successor as governor of Québec in 1777, although Carleton remained in office until June 1778 when Haldimand finally arrived to take over. Haldimand's appointment lasted until 1786 but he was in the province only until 1784. He attempted to improve the province's defences and sent raiding parties against the American frontier. Politically, Haldimand agreed with the French party that the QUEBEC ACT represented the charter of government and rejected the English-speaking community's demands for English institutions. As the AMERICAN REVOLUTION ended, he was responsible for establishing the LOYALIST refugees in what is now Ontario, a task he carried

Portrait of Gov Frederick Haldimand, from the studio of Sir Joshua Reynolds, London, *c*1778 (*courtesy National Portrait Gallery, London*).

out efficiently, and for reconciling the Six Nations to their resettlement in Canada.

STUART R.J. SUTHERLAND

Haliburton, Thomas Chandler, author, judge, politician (b at Windsor, NS 17 Dec 1796; d at Isleworth, Eng 27 Aug 1865). Haliburton was a born Tory, whose father and grandfather had been lawyers and judges. An Anglican, he was educated at King's Collegiate School and King's College, Windsor, NS. Following graduation in 1815 he studied law and was admitted to the bar in 1820. Gregarious and ambitious, he soon founded a law practice in Annapolis Royal and established a sufficient local reputation to become an MLA in 1826. Three years later he was elevated to the bench. In 1854 he was appointed to the NS Supreme Court but retired 2 years later because of ill health. While a judge, and in addition to his family and social life and his writing, Haliburton was an active businessman. He relinquished direct participation in his business endeavours when he moved to England following his retirement from the bench. There Haliburton settled at Isleworth and in 1859 became the Tory MP for Launceston. He retired from politics in England in 1865.

Thomas Chandler Haliburton, lithograph by E.V. Eddie. Haliburton's book, *The Clockmaker*, made him the first Canadian writer to gain an international reputation (*courtesy National Archives of Canada/C-6087*).

Haliburton's reputation lies in the many substantial works in provincial history, political pamphlets and fiction that he wrote from 1823 to 1860. His first book was published in 1823 when he was 27. *A General Description of Nova Scotia* (1823) was followed by a more ambitious, 2-volume work, *An Historical and Statistical Account of Nova Scotia* (1829). His other historical writings include *The English in America* (1851) and *Rule and Misrule of the English in America* (1851). Two political works also demonstrate Haliburton's lifelong interest in Canadian affairs: *The Bubbles of Canada* (1839) and a shorter pamphlet, *A Reply to the Report of the Earl of Durham* (1839). It was *The Clockmaker; or the Sayings and Doings of Sam Slick of Slickville* that made Haliburton the first Canadian writer to gain an international reputation. Twenty-two instalments of *The Clockmaker* appeared in the newspaper *Novascotian* before it was first published in book form by Joseph HOWE in 1836. There soon followed *The Clockmaker*, 2nd series (1838), and in 1840 the 3rd series. It is estimated that as many as 80 editions of *The Clockmaker* appeared during the 19th century.

Perhaps Haliburton's finest and most enduring work is *The Old Judge; or Life in a Colony* (1849). This work reveals Haliburton in a more sombre and reflective mood as he states with genuine feeling his farewell to Nova Scotia. *The Old Judge* lacks the wisecracking observations that made the adventures of Sam Slick so readable, but it is balanced and marked by a maturity not always present in Haliburton's other writings.

Like his fellow Nova Scotians, Thomas MCCULLOCH and John YOUNG ("Agricola"), Haliburton provoked Nova Scotians to better themselves in agriculture and business to combat the depression of the 1820s. Despite his initial debt to McCulloch, he extended his writings to fight the political situation both at home and in England. *The Clockmaker* has been described as "a series of moral essays pointed by satire." There can be no doubt about Haliburton's extraordinary ability as a writer of social satire, which was heightened by his ear for local idiom, dialect and anecdote. No full bibliographical study of Haliburton's career has yet been made, nor is there a book-length biography.

DOUGLAS LOCHHEAD

Halibut, *see* FLATFISH.

Halibut Treaty, 2 Mar 1923, a Canadian-American agreement concerning fishing rights in the N Pacific Ocean; the first treaty independently negotiated and signed by the Canadian government. Although Canada's right to negotiate commercial treaties was well established, the British wished to sign the convention along with Canada, as they always had. PM Mackenzie KING argued that the matter was solely the concern of Canada and the US; he threatened separate Canadian representation in Washington, and the British acquiesced. The Halibut precedent, confirmed by the Imperial Conference of 1923, was an important step towards establishment of Canada's right to separate diplomatic action. *See also* EXTERNAL RELATIONS.

NORMAN HILLMER

Halifax, capital of Nova Scotia and largest city in Atlantic Canada, occupies a strategic and central location on the province's E coast. With neighbouring Bedford and DARTMOUTH, it surrounds one of the world's largest harbours. Sometimes called "Warden of the North" for its historic military role, today it is a major regional centre for Atlantic Canada's economy. Founded in 1749 and first named Chebucto, it was renamed shortly after as Halifax in honour of George Dunk, earl of Halifax and chief lord of trade and plantations, who masterminded its settlement.

Settlement MICMAC occupied various harbour sites, as did French forces temporarily as late as 1746. To counter the French presence at LOUISBOURG, but ultimately and more importantly to exploit the rich cod fishery, the British government sponsored a settlement plan for Nova Scotia focused on Halifax. Some 2500 settlers, recruited mainly from England and led by Col Edward CORNWALLIS, established a new town in the summer of 1749. The gridlike plan, with a central square, was later copied throughout the region. Settlers drew free building lots, but few completed houses before winter, when half the population fled to the American colonies. Dartmouth was first settled in 1750, but the Indian threat and isolation from Halifax's defences restricted growth.

Development Halifax functions on the margin of the Canadian and N Atlantic trading world. This "tyranny of location" makes it less favoured for growth than other Canadian cities. Exports of fish and forest staples were comparatively small and mercantile activity risky until the early 19th century. Wartime activity buoyed the local economy during the Napoleonic Wars (1793-1815). Economic growth based on trade to the West Indies and international shipping expanded wealth and population, culminating in a "golden age" of prosperity at mid-century. Enos COLLINS established the Halifax Banking Co; Samuel CUNARD earned his early fortune in the city. The age of sail was surpassed by railway building after 1850 and the new industrialism of the 1870s, both linking Halifax to the continental economy. But the industrial spurt in Halifax and Dartmouth, including a cotton factory, 2 sugar refineries, a ropework and railcar plant, was short-lived. Some of these businesses were destroyed during the HALIFAX EXPLOSION (1917). Distance to markets, lack of local resources, and central Canadian

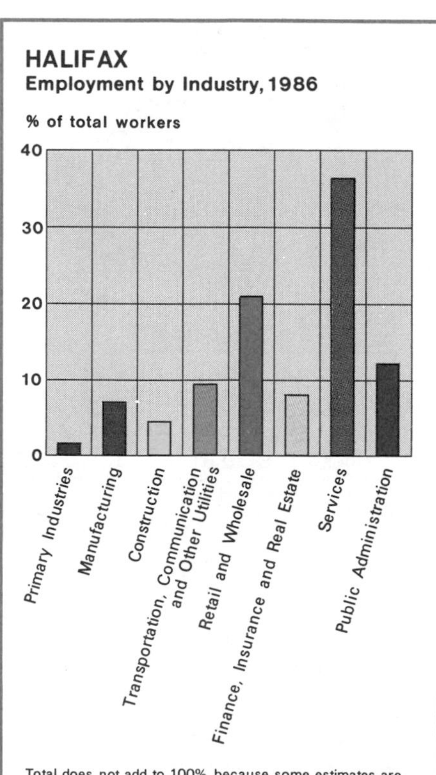

Total does not add to 100% because some estimates are not available and some workers are unclassified
Source: Household Surveys Div, Statistics Canada

Population: 113 577 (1986c), 114 594 (1981c); 295 990 (CMA, 1986c), 277 727 (CMA, 1981c)
Rate of Increase (1981-86): (City) -0.9%; (CMA) 6.6%
Rank in Canada: Thirteenth (by CMA)
Date of Incorporation: 1841
Land Area: City 62 km²; 691 km² (CMA)
Elevation: 32 m
Climate: Average daily temp, July 18.2°C; Jan -3.1°C; Yearly precip 1282 mm; Hours of sunshine 1872 per year

competition limited further manufacturing expansion.

By WWI, the BANK OF NOVA SCOTIA and the Merchants Bank of Halifax (ROYAL BANK) had relocated in Toronto and Montréal. Halifax strengthened only its transportation function. The large-scale ocean terminals were initiated in 1912. Wartime activity (1914-18 and 1940-45) heightened Halifax's enduring strategic role, but steady development from the 1950s stems from wholesale distribution, transportation, government services, and specialized functions such as the internationally famous BEDFORD INSTITUTE OF OCEANOGRAPHY. Offshore oil discoveries promise additional growth. Halifax's economic base is largely determined by its maritime, but nonetheless peripheral, location in Canada.

Cityscape Early Halifax stretched N and S for several kilometres along the harbour, flanked to the W by the HALIFAX CITADEL and the Common. The Naval Dockyard (1758) occupied a site in the North Suburbs, a working-class district even today. The South Suburbs and large estates on the Northwest Arm were preserves of the upper classes. St Paul's, Canada's oldest Anglican church (1750), PROVINCE HOUSE (1818), Government House (1827) and other important institutional and residential buildings attest to Halifax's rich architectural heritage. Like Vancouver's Stanley Park, Halifax's Point Pleasant Park (1866) was once a military reserve. By the 1950s, much of peninsular Halifax was built up. In Dartmouth, locks of the Shubenacadie Canal and waterfront manufacturing tell of 19th-century industries. With the recent spanning of Halifax Harbour by the Angus L. MacDonald (1954) and A. Murray MacKay (1970) bridges, Dartmouth's residential importance grew rapidly. Suburban Bedford and the Sackville district now share this growth. Central Halifax has been revitalized by extensive redevelopment around the original central square and waterfront. Projects include Scotia Square, Historic Properties, the Maritime Museum and a courthouse. Dartmouth's historic core has been similarly restored.

Population Until recently, Halifax has been overwhelmingly British; people of British origin now make up about 80% of the population. Most are either ENGLISH or IRISH; Scots number fewer. These groups were present at Halifax's founding and were soon joined by GERMANS ("Foreign Protestants") and Americans. The Irish gained the majority through the early 19th century. Late 19th-century immigration bypassed Halifax for Ontario and the West. Growth was therefore slow, dependent on natural increase and on migrants from rural NS. Expansion of the city boundaries westward in 1969 boosted population considerably. Summer brought additional army and navy personnel (as did war); winter, extra dockworkers. Today, many newcomers to Halifax-Dartmouth are transients, employees of the armed forces, national corporations, research institutes and the federal government.

Economy and Labour Force The strength of the metropolitan area economy rests on Halifax's defence and port functions, and on the service sector. Manufacturing employs few people; fishing is unimportant. Regional prominence in government administration, health services, university education, research activities, as well as the traditional functions of trade, distribution, transportation and finance all sustain Atlantic Canada's most dynamic urban economy. In fact, considerable disparities distinguish the well-being of Halifax-Dartmouth from most of the Maritimes. Despite success, control of the economy lies beyond the city; branch businesses are the major employers.

Transportation Halifax is the principal port in the Maritimes. Two large container terminals, recently built, serve all Canada. Containers travel

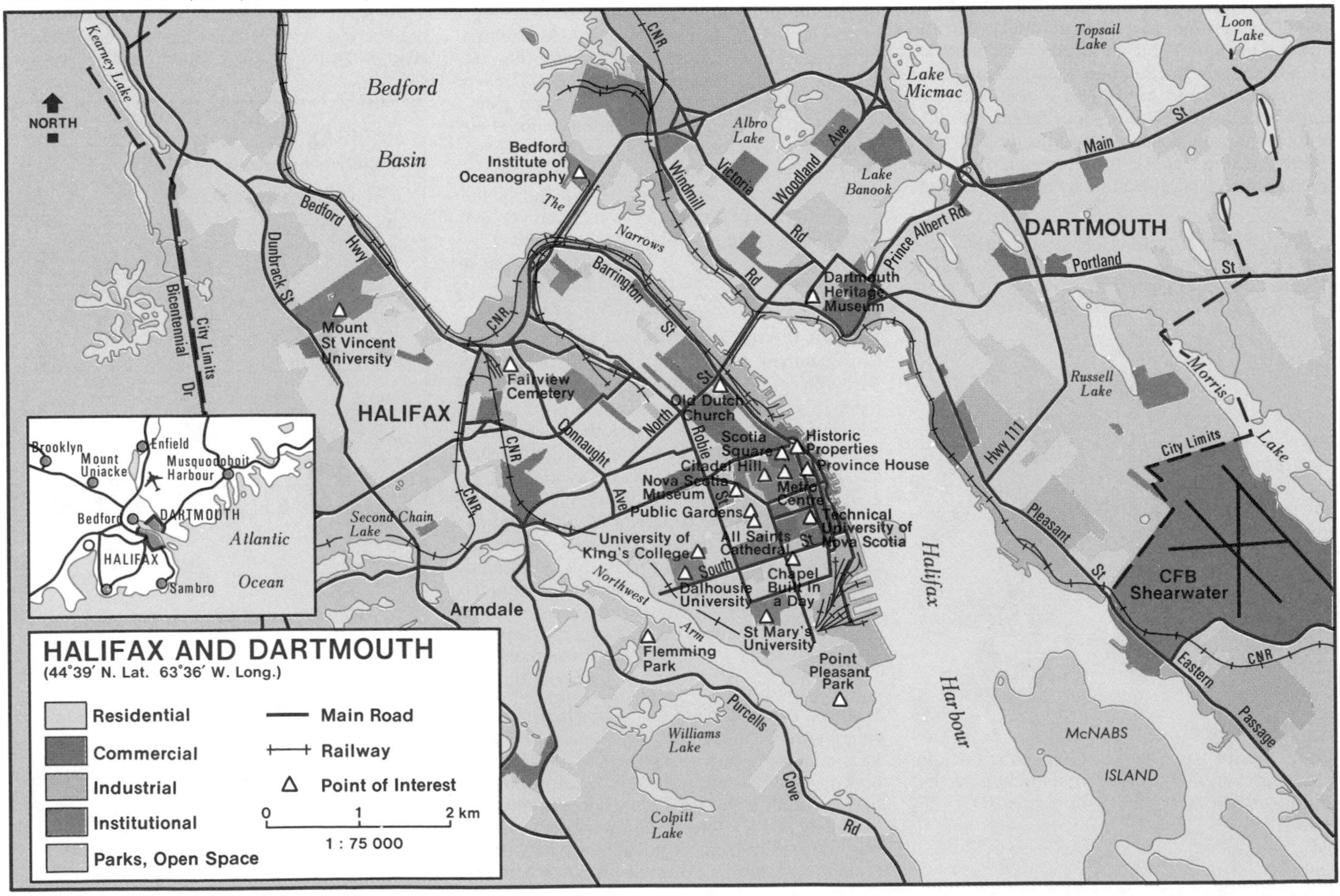

Halifax, with the Old Town Clock and fortified Citadel Hill behind the high-rise buildings of the city centre (*courtesy Colour Library Books*).

HALIFAX AND DARTMOUTH
(44°39′ N. Lat. 63°36′ W. Long.)

Residential — Commercial — Industrial — Institutional — Parks, Open Space
Main Road — Railway — Point of Interest
0 1 2 km — 1 : 75 000

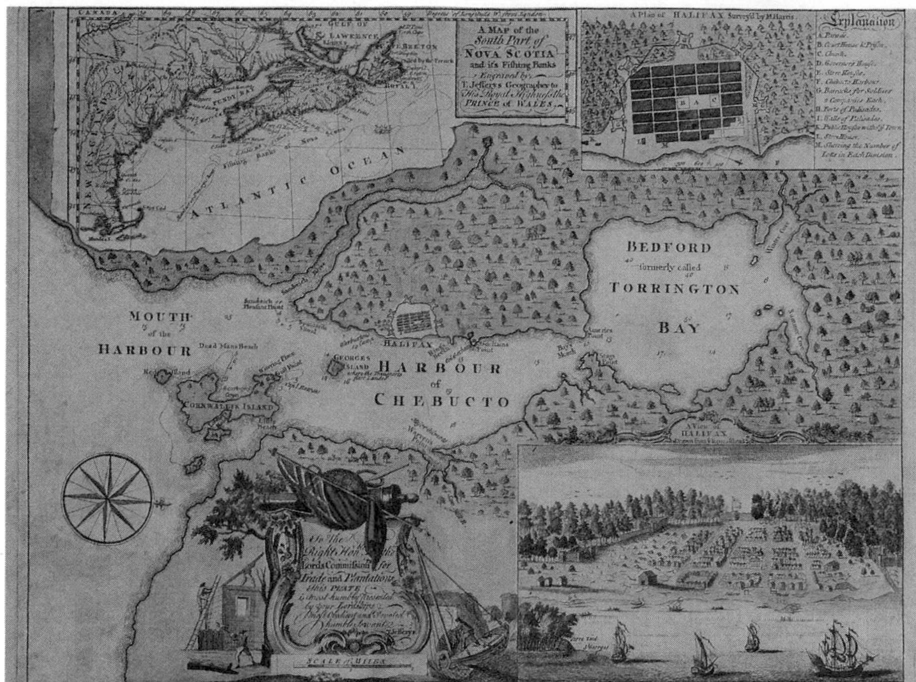

Chart and drawing of Halifax in 1750. The city was founded a year earlier on a gridlike plan with a central square (*courtesy National Archives of Canada*).

over the CNR, the successor to the INTERCOLONIAL RY, which was once headquartered briefly in Halifax (1872). The CPR's Dominion Atlantic Ry runs to the Annapolis Valley and by car ferry across the Bay of Fundy to SAINT JOHN. Other lines along the southwestern and eastern shores now stand idle. Halifax merchants once owned many ships and they dominated the province's shipping industry throughout the 19th century, a prominence not sustained in the steamship era; major steamship companies were owned by outsiders. The Halifax International Airport is now home field to Eastern Provincial Airways and is served by Air Canada and Canadian Airlines International. Water, rail and air facilities will expand with offshore oil development.

Government and Politics Continuity and accommodation mark Halifax politics, but significant reforms have occurred through the city's history. Until incorporation as a town in 1841, local affairs were governed by an appointed "clique of magistrates." Joseph HOWE promoted reform, and with Halifax's incorporation, an elected mayor and council of aldermen representing city wards managed urban affairs. This system still exists. Through RESPONSIBLE GOVERNMENT, established in NS in 1848, Halifax lost dominance over provincial politics. Since 1967, however, when more legislative seats were created, metropolitan Halifax has reasserted a prominent position in provincial politics. Other changes include a short-lived board of control, established at the time of WWI during the Urban Reform era, and the introduction of a city manager in 1951 to administer day-to-day business affairs. Partisan politics play little role in local government, despite significant class and religious divisions. A "dual" school system, introduced in the 1860s, operates Catholic and other "public" (nonsectarian) schools, but the 1969 annexation of suburban districts from the County of Halifax and school closures in central Halifax have weakened this system. A century-old "gentleman's agreement" of alternating Catholic and Protestant mayors ended in 1968 when incumbent Allan O'Brien, a Protestant, won re-election against another Protestant. Metropolitan government for Halifax, Dartmouth, Bedford and neighbouring communities does not yet exist, but several metropolitan agencies provide region-wide planning, sanitary and transit service.

Cultural Life Halifax is the cultural centre of Nova Scotia. From its founding, music, art and the theatre have been central attractions. When it was a garrison town, many officers both supported and participated in these activities. The NEPTUNE THEATRE, the NOVA SCOTIA COLLEGE OF ART AND DESIGN, and the Atlantic Symphony today continue these traditions. Well-known writers associated with the capital are Thomas Chandler HALIBURTON, Thomas MCCULLOCH, Thomas RADDALL, Hugh MACLENNAN and Charles RITCHIE. MacLennan's *Barometer Rising* details the drama surrounding the Halifax Explosion of 1917. The Halifax *Gazette* (1752), Canada's first newspaper, and the *Novascotian*, once a forum for Joseph Howe's reform politics, are no longer published; remaining are the *Chronicle-Herald*, the *Mail-Star*, the (Sackville) *Daily News* and Dartmouth's weekly *Free Press*.

The NS Museum and the Maritime Museum exhibit the historic past, which is also recorded by the Public Archives of NS. Traditions are further upheld by long-established ethnic organizations such as the Charitable Irish Soc (1786) and the North British Soc (1761). There are several universities in Halifax, most with religious affiliations. DALHOUSIE (founded 1818) was the first. SAINT MARY'S (chartered 1841) is the oldest English-speaking Roman Catholic university in Canada. King's Coll U, founded 1789 at Windsor, moved to Halifax in 1929. MOUNT SAINT VINCENT, a university since 1966, was founded in 1873 by the Sisters of Charity as a residential school for young ladies and received degree-granting status in 1925. The TECHNICAL UNIVERSITY OF NOVA SCOTIA, the NS Institute of Technology, and the NS College of Art and Design offer specialized programs. Amateur rather than professional sports characterize the metropolitan area. The Wanderers' Amateur Athletic Assn (1882) is most renowned. Yachting, rowing, canoeing, curling, swimming and other sports have produced national champions. L.D. MCCANN

Reading: M.J. Bird, *The Town That Died* (1962); Phyllis Blakeley, *Glimpses of Halifax* (1973); Thomas Raddall, *Halifax: Warden of the North* (1965).

Halifax Citadel The present citadel, located on an imposing elevation overlooking the original town and harbour of the capital of Nova Scotia, is actually the fourth fortification built on the site. Earlier works were built in 1749-50, 1776-81 and 1795-1800. Plans and estimates for the present fort were submitted in Dec 1825. Three years later the British government granted the necessary funds and work began in Sept 1828. The men most responsible for the construction were Sir James Carmichael Smyth and Col Gustavus Nicolls, both Royal Engineers officers. Construction was plagued with design and structural problems and took almost 30 years. The fort, finally completed 1855-56, cost £242 122. The general introduction of rifled artillery (with greater range and accuracy than earlier guns) shortly after completion of the Citadel rendered the costly installation obsolescent. It was partially rearmed in the 1860s and 1870s, and continued in use as a barracks into the 20th century. Upon departure of the British garrison in 1906, it was handed over to the Canadian militia. In May 1951 it was transferred to the Dept of Resources and Development; and finally, in July 1956, the site was declared a national historic park. About 1 million people visit the site annually. ROBERT ALLEN

The Tandem Club, an association of the urban gentry that met in Halifax in the winter months (*courtesy National Archives of Canada/C-13362*).

The Halifax Citadel, completed 1855-56, took almost 30 years to build and is the fourth fortification on the site. It continued in use as a barracks into the 20th century (*photo by Sherman Hines/Masterfile*).

Halifax Explosion At 8:45 AM, 6 Dec 1917, at the height of WWI, the Belgian Relief vessel *Imo*, through human error and negligence, collided with the French munitions carrier *Mont Blanc* in the narrowest part of Halifax harbour. Sparks generated by the collision ignited benzol stored on *Mont Blanc*'s deck; the burning liquid then seeped into the holds, where it lit 2766 t of picric acid, TNT and guncotton. At 9:06 the munitions ship blew a mile high in the world's greatest man-made explosion before Hiroshima.

Over 2.5 km^2 of Halifax's industrial N end was totally levelled, either by the blast, the subsequent tidal wave or the raging fire caused when structures collapsed inward on roaring stoves and furnaces. Homes, offices, churches, factories, vessels, the railway station and freight yards – all were obliterated. Farther from the epicentre, Citadel Hill deflected shock waves away from S and W Halifax, where shattered windows and doors were the predominant damage. Across the harbour, Dartmouth suffered devastation to a lesser degree, since its N section was sparsely developed. The blast shattered windows in Truro, 100 km away, and was heard in Prince Edward Island.

Out of a population of less than 50 000, over 1600 people died and 9000 were injured, including 200 blinded by flying glass. Sixteen hundred buildings were destroyed and 12 000 damaged; 6000 people were homeless and 20 000 lacked adequate shelter. Total damage amounted to $35 million. The misery was compounded by a forced evacuation of the city, necessitated by fire threatening the main dockyard magazine, and by appalling weather conditions in the days immediately following the explosion.

Relief assistance was immediate and extensive. Trains from throughout the Maritimes and from central Canada and New England brought medical aid, food, clothing, building materials and skilled labourers. The continuing assistance provided by the Massachusetts Relief Committee was particularly noteworthy. Money donated by government, industry and individuals worldwide eventually totalled some $30 million, and was administered 1918-76 by the HALIFAX RELIEF COMMISSION. LOIS KERNAGHAN

Reading: M.J. Bird, *The Town that Died* (1962); G. Metson, *The Halifax Explosion* (1978); Hugh MacLennan, *Barometer Rising* (1941).

View of the heart of the devastated area near Halifax after the explosion, showing the ruins of the Grove Church (*courtesy National Archives of Canada/C-3625*).

Halifax Relief Commission began 6 Dec 1917 as an emergency committee to provide immediate relief after the HALIFAX EXPLOSION. In Apr 1918, a 3-man commission was incorporated by provincial statute to administer a $30-million fund for medical care, social welfare, compensation and reconstruction. Total destruction and lingering human misery encouraged the rapid implementation of various innovative civic-planning and social-rehabilitation schemes, including a master town plan in 1921 and Canada's first public-housing project, the Hydrostone development, built in the devastated area and administered by the commission. By 1948 the commission's priorities had changed and it became a pension board. In 1976, with $1.5 million remaining and with 65 disabled dependants, the Halifax Relief Commission was terminated and its responsibilities transferred to the Canada Pension Commission.
LOIS KERNAGHAN

Hall, Charles Francis, Arctic explorer (b in Vermont 1821; d in Greenland 8 Nov 1871). An engraver by trade, Hall was fascinated by accounts of the search for Sir John FRANKLIN and in 1860, as a private citizen, he went by whaling ship to Baffin I. For 2 years he learned Inuit travel techniques and collected oral traditions, and he found material evidence of Sir Martin FROBISHER's excavations. He then published *Life with the Esquimaux* and secured Henry Grinnell's financing for a new expedition. In 1864 Hall and his Inuit friends, Joe and Hannah, were transported by a whaler to northwestern Hudson Bay. After frustrating years near Repulse Bay and Igloolik, they reached King William I in 1869, where Hall interviewed witnesses of the Franklin disaster and collected a skeleton. Later that year the US government appointed him to command a scientific polar expedition in the *Polaris*; on this expedition, by ship and sled, he achieved a new record of 82°N. He died, perhaps from poison, while overwintering in the ship. *See also* ARCTIC EXPLORATION. C.S. MACKINNON

Reading: C.C. Loomis, *Weird and Tragic Shores* (1971).

Hall, Emmett Matthew, lawyer, judge (b at St-Colomban, Qué 9 Nov 1898). In 1910 Hall moved to Saskatoon with his family. A classmate of John G. DIEFENBAKER, he graduated in law from U of Sask in 1919 and was appointed chief justice Court of Queen's Bench for Saskatchewan in 1957. He became chief justice of Saskatchewan in 1961 and was elevated to the Supreme Court of Canada in 1962, retiring in 1973. He has reported on a national health scheme for Canada (1964), the Ontario primary- and secondary-school programs (1968), railway arbitration (1973), provincial court structure in Saskatchewan (1974) and grain handling and transportation in western Canada (1977). He received the only honorary medical degree ever awarded (U of O), and was chancellor of U Sask 1980-86.
FREDERICK VAUGHAN

Hall, Glenn Henry, hockey player (b at Humbolt, Sask 3 Oct 1931). He turned pro with Indianapolis of the AHL and played for Edmonton of the WHL before joining Detroit Red Wings of the NHL in 1955-56. Despite winning the Calder Trophy (best rookie), he was traded to Chicago Black Hawks the next year. He was drafted by the St Louis Blues in the expansion draft 1967. He won the VÉZINA TROPHY 1963, 1967 (shared) and 1969 (shared), and the CONN SMYTHE TROPHY (most outstanding player in the playoffs) for his spectacular performance in the 1968 playoffs. He was first all-star goalie 7 times and, despite his notorious bout of nerves before each game, played more games than any other goalie except Terry SAWCHUK, 502 of them in a row; he still ranks 3rd in shutouts. Over 16 NHL seasons he played 906 games, with a 2.51 goals against average and 84 shutouts, and a 2.79 average in 115 playoff games.
JAMES MARSH

Hall, John Scott, painter (b at Edmonton 17 Jan 1943). Hall studied at the Alberta College of Art, Calgary (1960-65) and Instituto Allende in Mexico (1965-66) and has taught at Ohio Wesleyan U, Delaware, Ohio (1969-70), Alberta College of Art (1970-71) and U of Calgary (1971-). He rose to national prominence during the 1970s with his large hyper-realist still-life paintings of common objects that he selected intuitively, then carefully arranged in glass-covered boxes. More recently he has painted from photographs of similar still-life arrangements of toys and souvenirs. His painstaking enlargements of these objects on canvas add to their implied importance, but the paintings are so cool and detached that they are impossible to interpret literally. In 1985 an exhibition of paintings done 1983-85 was held at Toronto's Wynick-Tuck Gallery.

CHRISTOPHER VARLEY

Halldorson, Daniel Albert, golfer (b at Winnipeg 2 Apr 1952). Halldorson grew up in Shilo, Man. He first golfed at the Sandy Hook Golf Club across the road from his house. After turning professional in 1971, he eventually found his way to the US tour in 1979. He won the 1980 Pensacola Open and with Jim NELFORD of Burnaby, BC, took the team title in the 1980 World Cup in Bogota, Colombia. Skin ailments interfered with his play from 1982 until 1985, by which time he had fully recovered. That year he and Dave BARR of Kelowna, BC, won the team title in the World Cup in La Quinta, Calif. Halldorson plays the US tour full time, but as a strong supporter of Canadian golf he often plays Canadian events as well.

LORNE RUBENSTEIN

Halliburton, Sir Brenton, army officer, lawyer, politician (bap at Newport, RI 27 Dec 1774; d at Halifax 16 July 1860). By relationship and marriage an integral part of Nova Scotia's elite, he advanced rapidly: was admitted to the NS Bar, 1803, appointed a supreme court judge 1807, member of the COUNCIL OF TWELVE 1815 and chief justice 1833. Though generally moderate in religious matters, politically he was an out-and-out Tory, and this raised suspicions that his ideology might colour his judicial conduct. Presiding over Joseph HOWE's trial for criminal libel in 1835, he expressed the opinion that Howe was guilty which, although right in law, the jury refused to accept. Not brilliant as a judge, he was at least highly competent and in 1851 even Howe called him a "capital judge." His last honour was a knighthood conferred in 1859. Taking it for granted that the chief justiceship was a lifetime position, he died still in office in his 87th year.

J. MURRAY BECK

Halpenny, Francess Georgina, editor (b at Ottawa 27 May 1919). After studies in English at U of T, she began in 1941 her long association with U of T Press, interrupted only by service in the RCAF 1942-45. She headed the editorial department of UTP 1957-69 and then became general editor of the DICTIONARY OF CANADIAN BIOGRAPHY, a joint UTP-Presses de l'U Laval project. While continuing as general editor, she was dean of the Faculty of Library Science at U of T 1972-78 and was appointed to the National Library Advisory Board in 1977, a board she chaired 1979-82. She was associate director (academic) of UTP 1978-84. Through these years she continued an interest in theatre as an actor and writer. Indefatigable and unfailingly optimistic, she has encouraged scholarly publishing in Canada over 40 years by her teaching, writing, editorship of the *DCB*, and dedicated committee work at the national level. A member of the Royal Soc of Canada, she was awarded the MOLSON PRIZE in 1983 and made a Companion of the Order of Canada in 1984. Other honours include the U of T Faculty Award (1985) and the UBC Medal for Canadian Biography (1986). Since 1985 she has been associate editor of *Scholarly Publishing*.

MARY MCDOUGALL MAUDE

Halton, Matthew Henry, journalist (b at Pincher Creek, Alta 7 Sept 1904; d at London, Eng 3 Dec 1956). One of Canada's most distinguished journalists, and one of the finest reporters to establish a national reputation as a radio broadcaster, Halton attended U of Alberta (BA, 1929) and U of London before joining the *Toronto Star* in 1931. In 1932 he became the *Star*'s European correspondent, and thereafter his career was spent in Europe. In addition to interviewing the major personages of the time, he served with distinction as a war correspondent during the Spanish Civil War (1936), the Russo-Finnish War (1939-40) and in the Middle East in 1941-42. He was the senior war correspondent for the CBC during the campaigns in Sicily, Italy and North-West Europe. Awarded the OBE in 1945, he served as the CBC's European correspondent from 1945 until his death.

STANLEY GORDON

Halton Hills, Ont, Town, pop 35 570 (1986c). Halton Regional Mun, 20 km W of Metro Toronto, was created 1974 by amalgamation of Acton, Georgetown and Esquising township. Acton was settled about 1820, first being called Adamsville after a pioneer family, then Acton after the English town of that name. It was incorporated as a village in 1873. A tannery, which opened that year, remained the dominant industry until its closure in 1986. Georgetown was settled by the Kennedys, a Loyalist family, and was named for either George Kennedy or George III. It was incorporated as a village in 1864 and as a town in 1922. In 1873 the Barber family established woolen mills and later, more celebrated paper mills. They were pioneers in the use of electric power. The Grand Trunk Railway came in 1856. Today the region's main products are paper products, electric wiring devices, weather stripping and microwave components. The newspapers are the *Acton Free Press*, *Halton Hills Herald* and *Georgetown Independent*.

K.L. MORRISON

Hambraeus, Bengt, composer, organist, musicologist (b at Stockholm, Sweden 29 Jan 1928). After studies with organist Alf Linder (1944-48) and musicologist Carl-Allan Moberg (1947-56) and attendance at the Darmstadt summer courses (1951-55), he received a doctorate in musicology from Uppsala U in 1956. He joined the Music Dept of the Swedish Broadcasting Corp in 1957, eventually becoming head of production, and joined McGill U's Faculty of Music in 1972. Internationally recognized as a composer, organist, scholar and lecturer, he was awarded Sweden's highest honour, the Royal Medal "Litteris et Artibus," in 1986. Hambraeus's music – stimulated by his investigations of early music, acoustics and electronic studio techniques and by non-Western music and avant-garde techniques – displays a penchant for timbre explorations (especially bell sounds) and collage/quotation effects. His more than 80 compositions are often grouped into "families" of conceptually similar pieces, such as the *Transit, Rota* and *Constellations* series. They include *Transfiguration* (1963) for orchestra; the organ concerto *Continuo – a partire de Pachelbel* (1975); the broadcast opera *Sagan* (1977-79); *Livre d'orgue* (1980-81); the opera *L'Oui-dire* (1984-86); and *Symphonia Sacra in Tempore Passionis* (1985-86) for combined voices and chamber ensemble.

PATRICK CARDY

Hamel, Théophile, painter (b at Ste-Foy, LC 8 Nov 1817; d at Québec City 23 Dec 1870). Appointed official portrait painter in 1853, Hamel was referred to as the national painter by contemporary journalists, and was throughout his career one of the most popular painters with notables and clergy alike. From age 16 to 22, Hamel apprenticed with Antoine PLAMONDON in Québec C. He travelled to Europe in 1843, studying in Rome and visiting France and Belgium. He returned to Québec in 1846, and opened a studio. He moved to Montréal in 1847 for $2\frac{1}{2}$ years before establishing his permanent residence in Québec.

Four Children and a Dog, oil on canvas. Hamel created an interesting gallery of official portraits and of the aspiring members of the liberal professions and their families (*courtesy Musée du Québec/photo by Patrick Altman*).

Given the poorly developed communications of the 19th century, the upper classes used artists to make themselves known and spread their influence over either their flock (clergymen), or voters (politicians) or their social circle (professionals). Inspired by Titian, Hamel developed a style perfectly suited to the aspirations of members of the liberal professions. With Plamondon he had developed the technical mastery needed to paint faithful portraits and learned to handle daring chromatic effects, reflections and the rendition of beautiful fabrics.

Hamel refined his sober art during a stay in Italy 1843-46, studying the works of his mentor, Titian. Hamel created an interesting gallery of historical figures, including Jacques Cartier, Champlain and General James Murray. He did official portraits of the Province of Canada politicians, now housed in the Parliament Buildings in Ottawa, and many other portraits of politicians in Québec C, Kingston, Montréal and Toronto. Catholic and Protestant bishops, grand vicars, priests and founders of religious communities all posed for Hamel. Several notaries, doctors and merchants had themselves painted, with their wives and children on 2 separate panels. Except for children, Hamel generally showed only one figure in a given composition.

Hamel's talent allowed him to move in a few years from a farming background to the liberal professions; his brothers could only reach the level of commerce. Hamel possessed a handsome fortune, was captain of the militia and a member of the INSTITUT CANADIEN; he regularly met with the leading personalities of the day, such as F.X. GARNEAU, P.J.O. CHAUVEAU and Octave CRÉMAZIE. His magnificent, lifelike, austere and dignified portraits helped popularize Titian's style. Hamel also taught other artists, including Napoléon BOURASSA, one of the best Canadian artists of the 19th century. Besides its artistic value, his work allows us to study a section of Canadian society in the mid-19th century. Some of the people he painted left no photographs of themselves or their families. Each portrait shows us what a member of the ruling class thought of himself and how he wished the population to view him.

RAYMOND VÉZINA

Reading: Raymond Vézina, *Théophile Hamel* (1975-76).

Hamilton, Ont, City, centre of the Regional Municipality of Hamilton-Wentworth, situated at the W end of Lk ONTARIO, on Burlington Bay, 68 km SW of Toronto and 66 km W of Niagara Falls and the American border. It is Canada's largest steel producer and ranks high in industrial production. The Regional Municipality of Hamilton-Wentworth (pop 423 398, 1986c) also includes Ancaster, Dundas and Stony Creek, among others.

Population: 306 728 (1986c), 306 434 (1981c); 557 029 (CMA, 1986c), 542 095 (CMA, 1981c)
Rate of Increase (1981-86): (City) -0.1%; (CMA) 2.8%
Rank in Canada: Ninth (by CMA)
Date of Incorporation: Police Village 1833; City 1846
Land Area: 127.9 km^2
Elevation: 76.2 m; 198 m (mountain)
Climate: Average daily temp, July 20.5°C, Jan -6.4°C; Yearly precip 824 mm; Hours of sunshine 2044.6 per year

Settlement The earliest references to habitation in the Hamilton area come from 17th-century French accounts referring to the NEUTRAL nation. French adventurer Étienne BRÛLÉ had visited the Neutral 1616 and again 1624, and Jesuit missionary Jean de BRÉBEUF in 1641. LOYALISTS from the Niagara region – including John Depew (1786) and Richard Beasley (1790-91) – began to settle on and develop the land around Burlington B. In Jan 1815, George HAMILTON, son of Robert HAMILTON (one of the wealthiest and most influential men in Upper Canada), purchased 104 ha of land in Barton Township, laid out a townsite and successfully promoted its selection as the seat of administration for the newly created Gore Dist (1816). Because of the concentration of streams descending the NIAGARA ESCARPMENT and the area's location at the head of navigation on Lk Ontario, it had been developed as a milling and transportation centre even before the establishment of Hamilton.

Development Hamilton's townsite grew slowly until the late 1820s when a newly constructed canal through Burlington Beach permitted schooners and steamers entry into Burlington B. With the access points for roads ascending the Niagara Escarpment, the canal transformed the fledgling community into a significant transshipment point. With enormous migration from the UK during the 1830s, its fortunes grew; its situation made it an ideal location for mercantile houses and manufacturing establishments that could serve the surrounding region. Plans were made for a steamboat company, a bank and a railway to London. An economic panic and the Rebellion of 1837 delayed the railway's construction until the early 1850s. Led by land agent and lawyer Sir Allan MACNAB and others, the city bought into the GREAT WESTERN RY and other lines. Though the railway boom collapsed in 1857, it had attracted stove and farm-implement foundries. Ready-made clothing and sewing-machine manufacture developed during the American Civil War.

Aerial view of Hamilton, Ont. The city's older industries are clustered along the waterfront (*courtesy SSC Photocentre/photo by Bob Anderson*).

The city's industries prospered from the mid-1880s to the early 1890s. In the early 1900s, national railway construction and American branch plants serving the prairie market touched off a factory and residential construction boom that lasted until 1913. The Hamilton Blast Furnace Co began to produce pig iron in the 1890s. During both world wars, Hamilton industries concentrated on the production of war material, converting successfully after 1945 to serve the strong market for appliances, automobiles and houses. With the closing of textile mills and knit-wear plants in the 1950s and 1960s, Hamilton became increasingly dependent on steel. Curtailing of operations at International Harvester, the 1985 closing of Slater Steel and the pull out of Firestone in 1988 demonstrate the erosion of the old industrial mix. In its place there has been an increase of financial services.

Cityscape Hamilton Harbour (Burlington B) extends 8 km W from the channel at Burlington Beach to the steep embankment of Burlington Heights. Until the end of WWII, the harbour and escarpment squeezed urban development along an E-W axis and the 100 m limestone face of the escarpment posed a considerable transportation obstacle to suburban development. Though a series of expressways were constructed during the 1960s and 1970s, the division between the "mountain," as the escarpment is known locally, and the older city below plagues planning. The city's older industries are clustered along the waterfront and CNR tracks. Laboratories, parts distribution centres and light industries have been locating outside the city and along the highway corridors for the past 20 years. The cultural, financial and administrative core has remained near the corner of James and King at Gore Park, extending recently to the W. Residential areas include the old elite Durand District between James and Queen; the innovative west-end middle-class community of Westdale; and extensive working-class areas to the E and NE. Ethnic neighbourhoods abound, usually in association with parish churches and small-business districts.

During the 1960s and 1970s, the skyline changed radically, as high-rise dwellings began to appear near the city's core and spread to adjacent areas. Comparatively few office towers were constructed, reflecting Toronto's proximity and

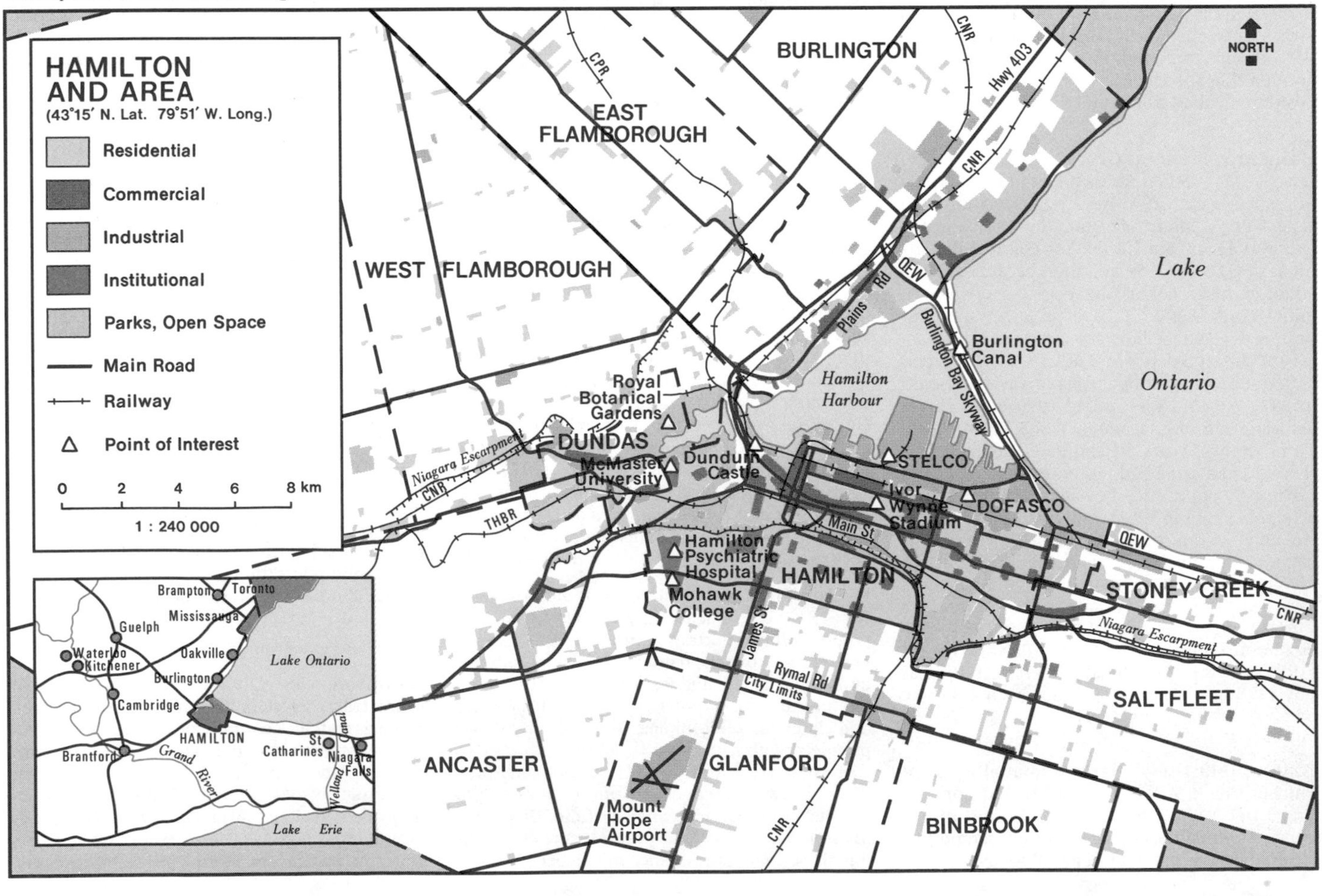

HAMILTON AND AREA
(43°15′ N. Lat. 79°51′ W. Long.)
Residential
Commercial
Industrial
Institutional
Parks, Open Space
Main Road
Railway
Point of Interest
0 2 4 6 8 km
1 : 240 000

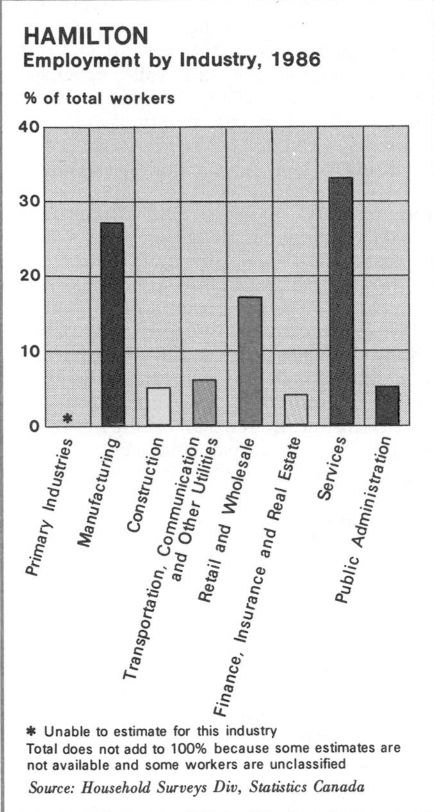

Hamilton's industrial emphasis. The IBM, Stelco, Century 21 and Government of Ontario buildings have been notable exceptions. Though many handsome stone structures were lost in the construction boom, 19th-century structures such as the Commercial Block (1858), residential Sandyford Place (1858) and the renowned St Paul's Church (1857) remain. The city operates an extensive park system, the famous Royal BOTANICAL GARDENS and, through the Hamilton Historical Board, Dundurn Castle (1835), Whitehern (1848), a military museum and a children's museum.

Population The city's population growth has paralleled its economic cycles. After the Great Western Ry plan failed, Hamilton is estimated to have lost 20-25% of its population 1857-64. Immigration from the UK brought increases to 1900. The phenomenal industrial expansion 1900-13 led to territory annexations and attracted industrial and construction workers from the UK, US, Italy and Poland. Refugees from central Europe and the Baltic states arrived during the 1920s. Natural increase was blunted by the economic hardship of the 1930s. During WWII, workers from Québec, the Maritimes and the West came to labour in the war industries. After the war, immigration (Dutch, German, Italian, Polish) reached a peak in 1954. Portuguese, S Asian and W Indian immigrants arrived during the 1960s and 1970s. Industrial uncertainties and the expansion of Ancaster and Dundas have decreased the population of the city proper 0.9% (1971-81); in 1986 it saw a nominal increase of 0.1% over 1981.

Economy and Labour Force Two of Canada's 4 largest steel firms (STELCO and DOFASCO) are located in Hamilton. The 1968 move of Stelco's head office to Toronto and construction of a new mill outside the city at Nanticoke shook civic optimism. Westinghouse, International Harvester, Firestone, Dominion Glass, Otis Elevator, National Steel Car, Canada Canners and Procter and Gamble also have large plants here. Most Hamilton industries have suffered from increased energy costs and economic recessions of the 1970s and 1980s. Hamilton is thought of as a workingman's city, highly unionized. The NINE-HOUR MOVEMENT began in Hamilton in 1872 and the KNIGHTS OF LABOR and AFL actively recruited in the late 19th and early 20th centuries. The CIO campaigned in the 1930s and 1940s for unions that would represent all men in a plant and after serious strikes at 3 major plants in 1946 concluded agreements ensuring higher pay and increased benefits. Another major strike occurred at Stelco in 1981.

Transportation Hamilton's unique location has ensured a significant transportation function for the city. During the middle decades of the 19th century it was an important wholesale and immigrant distribution centre. In the 20th, its transportation pattern has been shaped by industrial giants, such as International Harvester and Stelco, which retain considerable private interest in waterfront development. In tonnage, the port ranks 4th in Canada, ahead of all Atlantic ports and Toronto. The CNR maintains industrial freight facilities and a limited passenger service to Toronto and Niagara Falls. The Toronto, Hamilton and Buffalo Ry, now merged with the CPR, primarily maintains business loops within the city. Intercity bus service has expanded in recent years with the growth of the Ontario government's fleet between Hamilton and Toronto. An Ontario rail commuter service also operates between Burlington and Toronto. Tempus Air connects Hamilton by direct flights with Ottawa and Montréal and Allegheny Commuter to Pittsburgh.

General view of Hamilton (1853), by Robert Reginald Whale, oil on canvas (*courtesy National Gallery of Canada*).

Government and Politics From incorporation as a city (1846), Hamilton has had a council-committee form of government: aldermen elected by wards conduct general business together and meet in committees. As of Jan 1974, 17 council members assumed additional duties on the council of the new Regional Municipality of Hamilton-Wentworth, joined by officials from other jurisdictions. The regional government planning authority manages social services, police protection and water and sewage facilities. Certain local responsibilities are still managed by special commissions, some with regional or federal connections. Elected trustees constitute the public and separate school boards. Since WWII, Hamilton's mayors have served long terms. Party machines with federal and provincial party connections have remained an important aspect of local elections. Though organized labour has endorsed a few candidates, unions and the parties of the left have not always had a forceful presence on city council.

Cultural Life MCMASTER UNIVERSITY, with an enrolment of over 11 000 full-time and 3800 part-time degree students, has been an important city institution since 1930. Hamilton's central library was opened atop the new civic market in 1980. Its substantial Art Gallery includes works by Cornelius KRIEGHOFF and William KURELEK. The Hamilton Philharmonic Orchestra, Mohawk College Singers, McMaster Chamber Orchestra and Opera Hamilton continue the city's music traditions. Unfortunately, the Royal Hamilton Conservatory of Music ceased operations in 1981 for want of funding. Theatre Aquarius and dramatic productions at McMaster and by small theatre groups maintain long association with the stage. Touring companies perform in the attractive Hamilton Place complex. The Hamilton *Spectator*, the SOUTHAM chain's first newspaper (1846) and various ethnic and weekly suburban journals provide newspaper communications. TV station CHCH is one of the country's few independent and unaffiliated television operations. Several ethnic clubs have co-operated to establish the Hamilton Multi-Cultural Centre. In sports, the city has shown a special interest in running, with the annual race around the bay and regular track meets. In professional sport, the city has one team – its beloved HAMILTON TIGER-CATS – and is home to the Canadian Football Hall of Fame. JOHN C. WEAVER

Reading: M. Katz, *The People of Hamilton, Canada West* (1975); John C. Weaver, *Hamilton: An Illustrated History* (1982).

Hamilton, Francis Alvin George, teacher, politician (b at Kenora, Ont 30 Mar 1912). An enthusiastic supporter of the DIEFENBAKER government's "Northern Vision" and an idea man in Cabinet, Hamilton was also a spokesman for western agriculture. After numerous defeats, he was elected to Parliament for Qu'Appelle in 1957; he had been leader of the Saskatchewan Tories since 1949. Appointed minister of northern affairs and natural resources in 1957, he promoted the "Roads to Resources" concept and northern development. In 1960 he became minister of agriculture. The moving force behind the Agricultural Rehabilitation and Development Agency, he engineered several wheat sales to China that gave a much needed boost to western agriculture. He was re-elected MP for Qu'Appelle-Moose Mountain in Sept 1984. PATRICIA WILLIAMS

Hamilton, George, lumberman and merchant (b at Hamwood, Co Meath, Ire 13 Apr 1781; d at Hawkesbury, UC 7 Jan 1839). He was one of the most successful entrepreneurs in the early timber trade in the Ottawa Valley. An Anglican and a Tory, and an outspoken political power in both Upper and Lower Canada, he served both as judge of the district court and as lt-col of the militia.

The family had been involved in the Baltic timber trade but transferred operations to Québec C after Napoleon's continental decrees in 1807. Obtaining Admiralty contracts, the firm of George and William Hamilton developed both as timber exporters and general merchants. In 1812 the Hamiltons foreclosed on a deal mill at Hawkesbury, UC, to which they had lent money, and entered the upcountry trade. George remained the firm's Québec agent until 1816, when on his brother William's retirement he took over the Hawkesbury operations. There, through much economic adversity which saw the firm near bankruptcy several times, George Hamilton displayed the shrewd entrepreneurship that built a lumbering empire which stretched upriver along the Rouge, Rideau and Gatineau rivers and downstream to the company's cove, New Liverpool, Québec C, and from there to Liverpool, Eng. After 1830 Hamilton took on as a partner Charles A. Low, a long-time employee, and by 1835 the firm was valued at £30 000 and cut about 7 million board feet of timber annually.

Much of the timber trade was illegal until 1826, since only wood cut under Admiralty contract was to be taken on public lands. Lumbermen freely practised trespass and intimidation of both government officials and competitors, and Hamilton took an active part in this violence in his efforts to maintain and expand his business operations. But by the mid-1820s he had become an advocate of government regulation to bring order to the trade and to secure the rights of larger operators like himself. After 1828 he lobbied successfully with Gov Gen Aylmer to obtain a licensing system favourable to the bigger businesses in exchange for the payment of revenues to the Crown; and in the early 1830s he was instrumental in obtaining the Gatineau Privilege, which guaranteed the timber on the most important tributary of the Ottawa to timber barons like himself on a noncompetitive basis. PETER GILLIS

Reading: R. Peter Gillis and Tom Roach, *Lost Initiatives: A History of Canadian Forest Industries: Forest Policy and Conservation* (1986).

Hamilton, Robert, businessman, politician (b at Bolton, Scot 14 Sept 1753; d at Queenston, UC 8 Mar 1809). Hamilton was one of the richest men and the chief land speculator in early Upper Canada. Coming to Montréal in 1779, he engaged in trade along the Great Lakes. He built on contacts he had made during the Revolutionary War to enter into the portaging of goods around Niagara Falls, the supply of the army garrisons and general merchandizing, and invested his profits in land speculation. Appointed a judge in 1788, he was made a member of the legislative council of UC in 1792. Hamilton became embroiled in political controversy with Lt-Gov SIMCOE over such matters as regulation of landholding, debt and army provisioning. He controlled much local patronage and brought a number of his Scots relatives to the province, including Thomas Clark and Robert Dickson. His son George founded Hamilton, Ont. BRUCE WILSON

Hamilton Inlet, together with Lk MELVILLE, forms the largest estuary, over 250 km long, 40 km wide (at the western end) and 150 m deep, on the Labrador coast. The 2 are separated, 90 km from the sea, by a narrow passage, 2 km wide and 30 m deep, at Rigolet. Four major rivers, the CHURCHILL, North West (an extension of the Nauskapi R), Kenamu and Goose, draining a substantial portion of the UNGAVA PENINSULA, enter the system. Hydroelectric development at CHURCHILL FALLS constitutes a major industrial benefit to the region. The existing generating station, with an installed generating capacity (5225 MW) more than 10 times that of a conventional station, was completed in the early 1960s. Further developments on the Churchill at Gull Island (1700 MW) and Muskrat Falls (600 MW) are under consideration. The region was first visited by John DAVIS in 1586 and provided sites for French and English traders in the 18th century. The inlet was named for Charles Hamilton, governor of Newfoundland 1818-24. Rigolet was founded by the HBC in 1837. The estuary was surveyed 1949-53 as part of the Blue Dolphin expedition sponsored by the Arctic Institute of N America. There are no major commercial fisheries at present within the inlet, but Hamilton Bank just offshore is the centre for a large international cod fishery.

P.C. SMITH AND R.J. CONOVER

Hamilton Tiger-Cats, FOOTBALL team formed through a 1950 merger between the Hamilton Tigers, who had won 2 Canadian Rugby Union Championships (1906, 1908) and 5 GREY CUPS (1913, 1915, 1928, 1929, 1932) competing as one of the Big Four (Interprovincial Football Union), and the Hamilton Flying Wildcats, who were formed as a service club during WWII, won the 1943 Grey Cup and remained in the Ontario Rugby Football Union after the war. Future CFL Commissioner Jake GAUDAUR played on the new team, which won the 1953 Grey Cup. Beginning in 1957 under coach Jim Trimble (who retired after 1962), the Tiger-Cats played in every national final through 1967, except for those of 1960 and 1966, winning 4 Cups (1957, 1963, 1965 and 1967). Tiger-Cat teams have always been characterized by tough defence. Another Grey Cup victory came in 1972 when the Tiger-Cats played before many Hamilton fans at Ivor Wynne Stadium. Their most recent Grey Cup victory was in 1986 when they upset the Edmonton Eskimos 39-15 at the BC Place stadium in Vancouver. The Tiger-Cats are owned by Harold Ballard who purchased the club in 1978.

DEREK DRAGER

Hampton, NB, Village, pop 3405 (1986c), inc 1966, situated 23 km NE of Saint John on the Kennebecasis R. At incorporation it amalgamated the former communities of Hampton and Hampton Station. The area was part of the seigneury granted to Charles de LA TOUR in 1635 and was also the site of Indian camps, but permanent settlement did not take place until the Loyalists arrived after 1784. Even then it was not until the 1850s, with the construction of the European and North American Ry, that a village called Ossekeag (Hampton Station) developed; the name was taken from Ossekeag Creek and is derived from the Maliseet word meaning "marshy brook." The current name is variously said to be for Hampton near London, Eng, Hampton, NY, and Abner Hampton, a local ferry operator. The shire town for the county was moved to Hampton in 1871, complete with the large stone jail noted prominently in the memoirs of Henry More Smith, *The Mysterious Stranger* (1817). This agricultural community at the western end of the Kennebecasis and Petitcodiac valley system is on the main Moncton to Saint John rail line and is a Saint John dormitory community. The village has a museum, a restored jail and hosts the summer festival of Ossekeag Days. BURTON GLENDENNING

Han territory straddled the Yukon-Alaska boundary, extending along the YUKON R from a few km S of Dawson northward to about 50 km S of Circle, Alaska. Before the KLONDIKE GOLD RUSH there were 3 Han BAND communities along the Yukon R: Nuclako-Ft Reliance near Dawson, Johnny's Village near Eagle and Charley's Village in Alaska, though the Han ranged far up the Klondike, Forty Mile and other rivers. Han speech is distinct from neighbouring Athapaskan languages, but there was interaction with surrounding groups. Out of a Han population of a few hundred, only *c* 10% speaks the language.

In the spring, families moved to camps along the Yukon R where they prepared their equipment, caught whitefish and pike, and hunted moose, caribou and other game. After breakup, at the beginning of summer, they joined other band members at fish camps to catch and dry king and chum salmon. Large summer communities served as points for band and intertribal festivities and for salmon fishing. As fall approached, the Han left the river to hunt, repair their caribou surrounds, and fish in smaller rivers. In late autumn they returned to the Yukon and, during the winter, intermittently left the river to hunt and operate their caribou surrounds.

Han society was divided into 3 exogamous matrilineal clans. Clan membership carried responsibilities such as hospitality and protection to clan mates, and ceremonial obligations to those in opposite clans, such as cremating their dead. There was no formal tribe organization and status and band leadership were attained through individual ability and achievement. The primary social unit was the nuclear family, which often worked in partnership with a closely related family. Cross-cousins were encouraged to marry; a young man usually lived at first with his wife's parents, then established his own residence and, wealth permitting, obtained additional wives. Polyandry also was known.

Han ideology was similar to that of other Athapaskan groups of the Yukon. Shamanism was practised by both men and women to predict the outcome of the hunt, cure illness and destroy enemies. Artistic endeavours were manifested primarily by decorations on clothing and accessories and in songs.

Indirect European influence, principally from coastal Alaska, did not reach the Han until the end of the 18th century. After 1847 the Han dealt directly with HUDSON'S BAY COMPANY traders at Ft Yukon, but the first white settlers were American traders at Ft Reliance and Ft Eagle, 1874-80. By 1885 the focus of trade had changed from the native FUR TRADE to servicing the fledgling placer mining industry. Thereafter, the Han obtained a relatively complete line of Euro-American hardware, clothing and food staples from the trading posts. Gold strikes on the Fortymile R late in 1886 opened the isolated area to outside settlement, and within 10 years Han life style was completely disrupted by the Klondike Gold Rush. Today, many of their highly acculturated descendants live in their original homeland at Dawson and Eagle. *See also* NATIVE PEOPLE: SUBARCTIC and general articles under NATIVE PEOPLE. A. MCFADYEN CLARK

Reading: J. Helm, ed, *Handbook of North American Indians*, vol 6: *Subarctic* (1981); C. Osgood, *The Han Indians* (1971).

Handball is one of the oldest of all games played with a ball. It is recorded as being played in Ireland in the pre-Christian era and is believed to have spread from there. Homer made reference to a Greek lady who was an expert ball player. The English played "Fives," the Spanish "Pelota" and the French "Palm Play," all similar to handball. The modern game is played on a court having 1, 3 or 4 walls, with 2, 3 or 4 players, or 2 teams of 2 participating. The 4-wall game is most popular today. The ball is struck with gloved hands and must strike the front wall of the court during each volley. Returns are made so as to make it difficult for the opponent to return the ball to the front wall. A game is won when one player or team scores 21 points. Points are only scored when serving. In 1863 handball matches were reported in Victoria, BC, and Saint John, NB. World championships have been held on 4 occasions, and the world singles championship has twice been won by players representing Canada: Joey Maher of Toronto (1967) and Merv Deckert of Winnipeg (1984). In the 1987 Pan-Am Games Canada's first international medal (a silver) was won by the women's team, but a loss in the final cost Canada a berth in the 1988 Olympics. In Canada the sport is governed by the Canadian Handball Assn.

STAN C. FISHER AND DON R. BROWNWELL

Handsome Lake Religion is the religion practised by some IROQUOIS communities in Canada and the US. Its adherents are known as "the Longhouse people" because ceremonies are held in a building called the LONGHOUSE. Its beliefs and practices are a blend of ancient Indian traditions and innovations introduced by the SENECA prophet Handsome Lake between 1799 and 1815. In Canada it is represented on Indian reserves at Caughnawaga (near Montréal), Grand River (near Brantford), Oneida (on the Thames R) and St Regis (near Cornwall).

Short versions of the *Gaiwiio*, "the good words" or the Code of Handsome Lake, are recited at the Green Corn Festival in late August or early September and at the Midwinter Ceremonial in January or February. In the autumns of alternate years the *Gaiwiio* is recited in full at a solemn convocation of the Six Nations by designated speakers. Each speaker holds a bundle of WAMPUM strings as his credentials, regalia acquired from his predecessors in office who taught him the *Gaiwiio*. Other rites such as the Great Feather Dance, the drinking of strawberry juice, commentaries on the *Gaiwiio*, and public confessions of moral lapses are performed. Members may also attend other Indian religious rites and Christian churches. The teachings of Handsome Lake played an important role in reconstructing Iroquois society after an almost complete collapse of the social and cultural order in the late 1700s. *See also* NATIVE PEOPLE, RELIGION.

DEREK G. SMITH

Reading: A.F.C. Wallace, *The Death and Rebirth of the Seneca* (1972).

Haney, BC, UP, part of the Dist of Maple Ridge, is situated 18 km E of Vancouver, bounded on the south by the Fraser R and the CPR, and on the north by the Lougheed Hwy. The community was originally named Port Haney after Mr and Mrs Thomas Haney, who homesteaded there in 1876. Early industries were brickmaking and mixed farming. The community developed into the main business centre and seat of government for all of Maple Ridge and because of its proximity is now a "bedroom suburb" of Vancouver. The Haney post office was renamed Maple Ridge in 1970.

MARIE ELLIOTT

Hanington, Daniel Lionel, lawyer, politician, premier of NB (b at Shediac, NB 27 June 1835; d at Dorchester, NB 5 May 1909). Clerk of circuits 1867-70 and a school trustee, he first sat as a Liberal-Conservative MLA for Westmorland in 1870. He was defeated in 1874 for opposing the Common Schools legislation, but was re-elected in 1878 and sat as minister without portfolio until 1882 when he was named premier upon J.J. FRASER's resignation. Sympathetic to the Acadians, he named P.A. LANDRY his provincial secretary. Defeated by a non-confidence vote introduced by A.G. BLAIR in 1883, his government resigned. His forces were defeated again in 1886, but he continued to sit for Westmorland until 1892 when he was appointed puisne judge of the NB Supreme Court.

DELLA M.M. STANLEY

Hanlan, Edward, "Ned," oarsman (b at Toronto 12 July 1855; d there 4 Jan 1908). Hanlan learned to row in Toronto harbour on a makeshift shell fashioned from a wooden plank. He proved himself to be the best sculler in Ontario in a series of races between 1873 and 1876. In 1877 he won the Canadian championship on Toronto Bay and in 1878 took the US title on the Allegheny R. He defeated all challengers and by 1879 was the unquestioned master of rowing in N America. In May 1879 Hanlan beat the English champion on the Tyne R, Eng, by an astonishing 11 lengths. He became world champion in 1880, defeating the world professional champion E.A. Trickett of Australia. After defending his world crown 6 times he lost it to William Beach in 1884. Hanlan was Canada's first athlete to gain international recognition and its first world champion. During a time when rowing was immensely popular all over the world, Hanlan was celebrated and showered with gifts wherever he went. Though lectured sternly by the English press for his flamboyance, he was appreciated for his fine rowing style, with its long, smooth strokes and sharp, clean "catch." He continued to row in the 1890s, winning more than 300 races.

JAMES MARSH

World rowing champion Ned Hanlan was the first Canadian athlete to gain international recognition (*courtesy National Archives of Canada/C-25324*).

Hanna, Alta, Town, pop 3017 (1986), inc 1914, situated 219 km NE of Calgary, was named after D.B. HANNA, 3rd vice-president of the Canadian Northern Railway, and was first settled in 1912. As a Canadian Northern divisional point, it had a 10-stall roundhouse, built in 1913, and excellent connections to Saskatoon and Calgary. Wheat, subject to the booms of the 1910s and late 1920s and the busts of the mid-1920s and 1930s, and cattle have made Hanna the main service centre for the shortgrass country of Alberta. Today's resources include thermo-coal, clay, sand/gravel, petroleum, natural gas and bentonite. Hanna is the subject of the 1946 sociological study by Jean Burnet, *Next-Year Country: A Study of Rural Social Organization in Alberta* (1951).

F. PANNEKOEK

Hanna, David Blythe, accountant, railway director (b at Thornliebank, Scot 20 Dec 1858; d at Toronto 1 Dec 1938). He came to Canada in 1882 to work with the GRAND TRUNK RY and worked with several other railway companies before joining William MACKENZIE and Donald MANN on the CANADIAN NORTHERN RY in 1896. When the Canadian government purchased Canadian Northern he resigned but was appointed first president of the board of directors of the newly formed CANADIAN NATIONAL RY. He retired 1922, but was briefly first chairman (1927-28) of the Liquor Control Board of Ont. He recounted his career in *Trains of Recollection* (1924). The town of HANNA, Alta, is named for him.

ERIC J. HOLMGREN

Hannam, Herbert Henry, educator, farm leader (b at Swinton Park, Grey County, Ont 27 Sept 1898; d at Ottawa 12 July 1963). After attending Ontario Agricultural Coll, Herb Hannam taught school and was livestock editor of *The Canadian Countryman.* He joined the UNITED FARMERS OF ONTARIO as educational secretary in 1928, becoming its secretary-treasurer in 1933 and secretary of its sister organization, the United Farmers' Co-operative Co, in 1936. He wrote *Co-operation: The Plan for Tomorrow which Works Today* (1938) and *Pulling Together for Twenty Five Years* (1940), 2 pamphlets widely used in co-operative and agrarian circles. He helped organize the Ontario Federation of Agriculture and the Canadian Chamber of Agriculture (later Canadian Federation of Agriculture) during the mid-1930s. In 1939 he was elected to the latter's presidency, which became a full-time, paid position in 1943. Hannam was an effective spokesman for Canadian agriculture. He was also a strong supporter of FARM RADIO FORUM which he helped start. Following WWII, Hannam was one of the first to see the importance of food production and marketing in a world with a rapidly growing population.

IAN MACPHERSON

Hanover, Man, Rural Municipality, pop 8033 (1986c), 7428 (1981c), area 71 886 ha, inc 1881, located SE of Winnipeg, encompasses the communities of Blumenort, Grunthal, Kleefeld, Mitchell, New Bothwell, Randolph and Sarto. The town of STEINBACH is no longer part of the RM although the municipal office is located there. Hanover includes land set aside in 1873 as the East Reserve for MENNONITES from southern Russia. Several hundred families arrived in the 1870s and organized self-governing agricultural villages. A second influx in the 1920s followed the Russian Revolution. Difficult farming conditions, disagreements with provincial education policies, and secular influences on the Mennonite way of life caused some of these settlers to move away. Anglo-Saxon, French Canadian, German Lutheran, Ukrainian and Polish settlers also helped build the RM's communities.

Soil and drainage conditions encouraged a diversified agriculture – special crops, livestock, poultry, dairying and cereal grains. Blumenort is a Manitoba poultry centre; Grunthal, a dairy and milk products centre. Kleefeld is known for its beekeeping; New Bothwell for its cheddar cheese; the Steinbach area for cash crops and poultry. Business in the RM mostly serves local markets. Of late several Hanover communities have become locales for commuters who wished to combine urban employment with rural homes and life-styles. D.M. Lyon

Reading: L. Penner, *Hanover: One Hundred Years* (1982).

Hans Island, a tiny unpopulated island S of the 81st parallel in the Kennedy Channel, almost equidistant between Ellesmere I and Greenland, is the only land claimed by Canada still in dispute. Denmark's claim is based on the fact that a Danish expedition discovered and named Hans I (1873), that geologically the island is part of Greenland, and that it is slightly closer to the Greenlandic mainland than to Ellesmere I. Canada maintains that these claims have lapsed because Denmark failed to enforce its sovereignty. Canadian cartographers depict the island as Canadian, and after WWII Canadians operated a temporary scientific station there. More recently Dome Petroleum was active on Hans I. In 1973 Canadian and Danish negotiators failed to resolve the dispute. In 1983 Danish aircraft flew over Hans I; and when Tom Hoeyem, Denmark's minister of Greenlandic affairs, personally planted a Danish flag on the island 28 July 1984, the Canadian government protested. Graeme S. Mount

Hansard is the unofficial name of the record of parliamentary debates. The name comes from T.C. Hansard, who printed the British debates 1812-92. It provides a statement in both official languages of spoken proceedings in both Houses of Parliament, partly for the immediate convenience of legislators but also as an indispensable historical archive. In its present form Hansard dates from 1880, when an official debates reporting branch, which now has its own director, was added to the parliamentary staff. Before that, from 1875 to 1879, a record was provided, though not by regular staff. Before 1875 somewhat haphazard collections were preserved, some of them known as Scrapbook Hansards, based on contemporary newspaper reports which covered Parliament in detail. Several of the colonies kept Hansards irregularly before Confederation, the earliest being NS in the 1820s.

The modern Hansard is an efficient enterprise which, during the session, produces a copy of each previous parliamentary day's debates by 9:00 AM. The printed copies come from shorthand reports taken on the floor of the House by reporters working 10-minute shifts. Each reporter then dictates his notes to a second person, and today electronic records supplement the printed material. The House of Commons has a Broadcast Branch which keeps a complete audio and video record. Hansard is published by the Queen's Printer and, in addition to the daily editions, is issued regularly in bound, well-indexed volumes readily available in libraries.

Provincial debates, not all of which are referred to as Hansards, are published in a variety of ways. In 1986 only New Brunswick and Manitoba provided bilingual services comparable to Parliament's, and only Newfoundland, Nova Scotia and British Columbia used governmental services for the printing of debates (the other 7 provinces and the territories employed commercial firms). PEI alone had no Hansard, though proceedings there were taped and transcripts could be obtained. Saskatchewan was the only province with complete television recording, though other provinces were moving towards it. Unofficial electronic Hansards were possible in Ontario, Québec and the Yukon, where private stations had unlimited access to the legislative chamber. In other jurisdictions film records were permitted for special occasions such as the annual budget. Norman Ward

Hansen, Rick, wheelchair athlete (b at Port Alberni, BC 26 Aug 1957). Inspired by the example of his friend, Terry Fox, Hansen left Vancouver 21 Mar 1985 to travel, in a wheelchair, the equivalent of the distance around the world. With the goal of seeking to increase public support and awareness of the capabilities of the physically disabled, his "Man in Motion" tour raised $20 million which is to be directed to spinal cord research, rehabilitation and wheelchair sports. Before his return to Vancouver 22 May 1987, Hansen travelled through 34 countries, including the US, the UK, China, the USSR and Australia, before starting across Canada. His odyssey lasted 792 days, 467 of which were spent on the road. He wore out 117 tires and 11 pairs of gloves. A world-class competitor in wheelchair sports, he shared athlete of the year honours with Wayne Gretzky in 1983. His story is recounted in *Man in Motion* (1987). In 1987 he became a Companion of the Order of Canada. Hansen is the commissioner general for the Canadian Pavilion for the 1990 Expo in Australia. J. Thomas West

Rick Hansen traversing the Great Wall of China (*courtesy Man in Motion World Tour*).

Hanson, Melvin, "Fritzie," football player (b at Perham, Minn 13 July 1912). Hanson joined the Winnipeg Football Club in 1935, during an era of massive importing of American talent in the Western Conference. In his 7 years with Winnipeg, the most important was the first (1935), when Hanson ran around and between Hamilton Tiger players, including over 300 yards on 7 punt returns alone, to lead Winnipeg and the West to their first Grey Cup win. Hanson's Bombers became the football power in western Canada and reached the championship game again in 1937, 1938, 1939 and 1941, winning in 1939 and 1941. Hanson finished his career, after a brief retirement, by playing 2 seasons (1947 and 1948) with the Calgary Stampeders, who went undefeated to a Grey Cup victory in 1948. Hanson was a 5-time Western all-star, 1937-41, and won the league scoring championship in 1938. He was made a charter member of the Canadian Football Hall of Fame in 1963. Peter Wons

Hantzsch, Bernhard Adolf, explorer, ornithologist (d near the mouth of Hantzsch R, NWT June 1911). Hantzsch sailed with a German ornithological expedition to the eastern Arctic in 1906 and during that summer explored and collected specimens along the coast of Ungava Bay and northern Labrador. From 1909 to 1911, he was part of a larger expedition, sponsored by the Geographical Soc of Dresden. On the way to Cumberland Sd his ship was wrecked and most of his supplies were lost. He made his way to a whaling station on Blacklead I, then to one at Kekerten. He crossed Baffin I on foot, making ornithological and ethnological observations, and in 1910 travelled with a party of Inuit to Foxe Basin where he continued his observations. On his death, which was probably of trichinosis, he was buried by the Inuit, who returned to Cumberland Sd with his journals. W.R. Morrison

Happy Valley-Goose Bay, Nfld, Town, pop 7248 (1986c), 7103 (1981c), inc 1955, is the result of the amalgamation of 2 towns situated at the western end of Hamilton Inlet, Labrador. Happy Valley was a townsite chosen by people relocated from Otter Cr by the Government of Canada in 1941, when it was decided to build an airport at nearby Goose Bay. By June 1943 the airport was the world's largest, used by the RCAF, the USAF and the Canadian Army. As construction accelerated, Happy Valley grew, as over 3000 were employed on the project. The town continued as a small civilian community servicing the base, which remained a permanent airport after the war. In 1974 Happy Valley amalgamated with Goose Bay. The base functions as a refueling and support installation for Military Airlift Command (USAF) and as a training base for fighter pilots of the USAF, RAF, Luftwaffe and Royal Netherlands Air Force. Janet E.M. Pitt and Robert D. Pitt

Grand L
North West River
L Melville
Hamilton In
Churchill
River
Happy Valley-Goose Bay
Eagle R
0 75km

Harbour Breton, Nfld, Town, pop 2432 (1986c), inc 1952, is situated around a protected harbour near the mouth of Fortune B on Newfoundland's S coast. Probably first used by Breton fishermen (the likely source of its name, although it is recorded first as Havre Bertrand) during the 1600s, it was used and then settled by English fishermen in the 18th and 19th centuries. Because of its superior harbour and its proximity to good fishing grounds, including the Grand Banks, it grew as one of the major service and commercial centres on the coast with representatives of several principal local and English fish merchants maintaining premises there over the years, most notably the Newman and Hunt Co. Today Harbour Breton remains an important regional centre, the site of fishing and fish-processing facilities. Robert D. Pitt

Harbour Grace, Nfld, Town, pop 3053 (1986c), 2988 (1981c), inc 1945, with a commodious harbour in western Conception Bay, named for the French *Havre de grâce.* A base of pirate Peter Easton, 1610-13, its settlement was begun about 1618, perhaps by former settlers of the Cupids colony. Until 1923 it had the second-largest population in Newfoundland. Prospering from the Labrador cod and seal fisheries, the Anglo-Irish community was by the 19th century the location of one of Newfoundland's earliest denominational schools (1843). In 1859 it was the site of sectarian riots during the general election, and in 1883 of bitter sectarian violence resulting in 5 deaths. Also, the Methodist movement was introduced to British N America from Harbour Grace in 1765 or

1766 by Rev Laurence COUGHLAN, a convert of John Wesley. Several pioneering attempts at transatlantic and round-the-world flights were made from here 1919-32. In 1932 Amelia Earhart, leaving Harbour Grace, was the first woman to pilot a plane over the Atlantic. The community is today a fish-processing and service centre and supports several small industries.
JANET E.M. PITT AND ROBERT D. PITT

Harding, Victor John, professor of pathological chemistry (b in Eng 23 Oct 1885; d at Toronto 3 July 1934). Graduating in chemistry from Owen's Coll, Manchester (DSc, 1912), Harding began an association with McGill in 1910. He became associate professor of physiological chemistry in 1917. In 1920 he left McGill to become professor of pathological chemistry at U of T. His research was initially on analytical methods in organic chemistry, including amino acids and the chemistry of the ninhydrin reaction. He became recognized primarily for his investigations on carbohydrate metabolism in pregnancy and on toxemias associated with pregnancy. He trained many graduate students, some of whom became prominent biochemists in Canada and the US.
DAVID B. SMITH

Hardisty, Richard Charles, fur trader, senator (b at Ft Mistassini, near James Bay 3 Mar 1831; d at Winnipeg 15 Oct 1889). The mixed-blood son and grandson of chief factors of the HBC and one of 6 brothers in the company's service, Hardisty was educated at Red River Academy (later St John's College, Winnipeg) before joining the HBC as an apprentice postmaster in the Red River Dist. His advancement was steady, and in 1872 he was appointed chief factor at Fort Edmonton, administering a vast district that covered much of present-day Saskatchewan and Alberta. He ran as an Independent candidate for the Dist of Alberta in the federal elections of 1887 but was defeated; the following year he was named to the Senate.
STANLEY GORDON

Hardy, Arthur Sturgis, lawyer and politician, premier of Ontario 1896-99 (b at Mount Pleasant, near Brantford, Ont 14 Dec 1837; d at Toronto 13 June 1901). After a promising early career as a lawyer and city solicitor in Brantford, Hardy was elected liberal MPP for S Brant in 1873. Bills he introduced as provincial secretary (1877-79) touched on social issues and on the administration of justice, while as commissioner of crown lands (1889-96) he was responsible for important timber and mining legislation and for the establishment of ALGONQUIN PROVINCIAL PARK. He succeeded Sir Oliver MOWAT as premier and attorney general in July 1896. Following a narrow electoral victory in 1898, Hardy resigned for reasons of health in 1899.
WENDY CAMERON

Hardy, Elias, lawyer, politician (b at Farnham, Surrey, Eng *c*1744; d at Saint John 25 Dec 1798). Hardy immigrated to Virginia in 1775; like most LOYALISTS he sympathized with America in its quarrel with Britain but opposed the ultimate solution of colonial independence. He became one of thousands who migrated northward to Saint John (then part of NS) in 1783. As leader of the bitter agitation for speedy and equitable land distribution, he allied politically with NS governor John PARR in his futile efforts to prevent the separation of NB in 1784. When the new colony had its first election (1785), Hardy skilfully channelled popular discontent into opposition to the lt-gov of NB, Thomas CARLETON. Hardy was elected to the assembly, though the remainder of his political career (1786-95) was relatively uneventful. Meanwhile, he quickly established himself as NB's leading lawyer.
D.G. BELL

Reading: D.G. Bell, *Early Loyalist Saint John* (1983).

Hardy, Hagood, pop musician (b at Angola, Indiana 26 Feb 1937). He is a major figure in the Canadian recording industry. Raised in Oakville, Ont, Hardy began his career as a vibraphonist in Toronto jazz clubs, travelled (1961-67) with US jazzmen, including Herbie Mann and George Shearing, and then turned to pop music. He led The Montage until 1974 and thereafter worked in Toronto recording studios as a composer of music for jingles and for radio, TV and many films (*Second Wind, Rituals, Anatomy of a Seduction,* etc). His Salada Tea jingle, revised and recorded as *The Homecoming* (1975), was an international hit, and his score for the CBC production of "Anne of Green Gables" (1986) won Emmy and Gemini awards. In 1987 he completed the scoring for 52 half-hour episodes and 4 ninety-minute specials of cartoons based on *The Wizard of Oz.*
MARK MILLER

Hare, a group of Athapaskan-speaking people whose ancestors lived in small, nomadic bands along the lower Mackenzie R valley of the NWT, had a precontact population of 700-800. They pursued a hunting, fishing and gathering way of life centered on caribou, moose, freshwater fish, small game and berries, and exploited a territory from the Yukon border to forested zones W and NW of Great Bear Lake. Several cultural features distinguished the Hare from neighbouring KUTCHIN, MOUNTAIN, SLAVEY and DOGRIB. They spoke their own dialect of Athapaskan and were noted for their timid relations with other native groups. The name Hare, given by early Europeans, reflected their heavy dependence on the snowshoe hare for food and clothing. Since the hare goes through a population cycle every 7 to 10 years, these Indians periodically experienced devastating starvation (*see* RABBIT STARVATION).

The Hare traditionally viewed their world in animistic terms. They observed many taboos to insure good hunting, and relied on SHAMANS to cure illness, protect them against enemies and intercede with the spirits. They had a rich oral FOLKLORE, and participated in drum dances and competitive gambling. Their communities were held together by kinship ties on both the father's and the mother's side. Though the Hare lacked formal leaders, outstanding hunters and shamans had considerable influence. The Hare were governed by an ethic that balanced sharing and interdependence with autonomy and freedom. There was no concept of individual ownership of land, and people were free to hunt and fish in any part of their territory.

First recorded contact with Europeans came during the explorations of Alexander MACKENZIE in 1789. Early in the 19th century the Hare were drawn into the FUR TRADE as forts spread N along the Mackenzie R. Their trading activities were centered on Ft Good Hope and also on Fts Norman and Franklin. A Roman Catholic mission was established in 1859 at Ft Good Hope, and the people's conversion to Christianity began. For much of the 19th century and until the decline of fur prices after WWII, most of the Hare combined trapping with subsistence hunting.

In recent decades the Hare have had to contend with a growing dependence on a wage-labour economy and the effects of alcohol, tuberculosis and other diseases. Although they gave up title to their ancestral lands in a 1921 treaty with the federal government, they have retained the right to hunt, fish and trap in their traditional territory (*see* INDIAN TREATIES). Nevertheless, many have been attracted to the amenities of a settled life in larger towns. A notable exception to this trend was the creation, in the early 1960s, of a new village at Colville Lk, 142 km NE of Ft Good Hope, in an area rich with game and fish. Ft Good Hope and Ft Franklin, with a combined population of 1094 in 1986, are now the major population centres of the Hare people. *See also* NATIVE PEOPLE: SUBARCTIC and general articles under NATIVE PEOPLE.
JOEL S. SAVISHINSKY

Reading: Hiroko Sue Hara, *Hare Indians and Their World* (1980); J. Helm, ed, *Handbook of North American Indians,* vol 6: *Subarctic* (1981); Joel S. Savishinsky, *The Trail of the Hare* (1978).

Hare, term applied to those members of order LAGOMORPHA whose young are born fully haired, with eyes open, and able to run about a few minutes after birth. All N American hares belong to genus *Lepus;* 3 species are native to Canada, one has been introduced. The northernmost species, arctic hare (*L. arcticus*), found in the tundra zone beyond treeline, is the largest Canadian species, with adults weighing 3.2-5.4 kg. Snowshoe or varying hare (*L. americanus*) is widespread throughout Canadian forested areas and provides meat to humans in remote communities. Snowshoe hares exhibit enormous population fluctuations, peaking every 9-10 years. Numbers vary from approximately 1 hare per 50 ha to upwards of 200 per ha. The remaining native species, white-tailed jackrabbit (*L. townsendii*), largely nocturnal and solitary, is found throughout the prairies. In 1912 the European or Cape hare (*L. europaeus*) was introduced to Ontario as a game animal. Restricted to Ontario, it is sometimes a garden pest. Unlike native species, it does not turn white in winter. Young hares (leverets) are born in the open and are weaned after 2-3 weeks (5-6 in white-tailed jackrabbits). Gestation averages 36 days and, depending on the species, a litter contains 1-7 young, with up to 4 litters over a summer. Female hares are usually larger than males; hares are larger than RABBITS.
M.L. WESTON

The snowshoe hare (*L. americanus*) is widespread throughout Canada's forests (*artwork by Claire Tremblay*).

Hare, Frederick Kenneth, environmental scientist, professor, administrator (b at Wylye, Eng 5 Feb 1919). A U of London graduate and wartime meteorologist with the British Air Ministry, Hare came to Canada in 1945 as a geography professor at McGill. He earned his PhD (U de Montréal) studying arctic CLIMATOLOGY and BIOGEOGRAPHY. He has served as dean of arts and science at McGill, master of Birkbeck Coll, London, and president of UBC. A professor of geography and physics at U of T since 1969, he was the first director of the Institute for Environmental Studies there 1974-79, became provost of Trinity Coll, U of T, in 1979 and was appointed U of T professor emeritus (geography) in 1984. His research interests include world climate, notably atmospheric carbon dioxide, CLIMATE CHANGE and arid-zone climates. Long active in movements to protect and conserve the natural environment, Hare led a federal study on nuclear-waste management in Canada and a similar program for the UN Environment Programme. For the Royal Society of Canada he was chairman for studies on the long-range transport of airborne pollutants, on the nuclear winter phenomenon and on lead in the environment. He has also served as director of the Washington-based energy-research group, Resources for the Future. In 1984 he was chairman of the Climate Planning Board in Canada and in 1986-87 was president of Sigma Xi, the Scientific Research Society. A frequent spokesman on the atmospheric greenhouse effect, Hare believes that the main environmental issue confronting Canada in the next 70 years will arise from climatic change induced by fossil-fuel consumption. He has written 180 books and articles, including *The Restless Atmosphere* (1953) and, with Morley K. Thomas, *Climate Canada* (1974). In 1987 he became a Companion of the Order of Canada. DAVID W. PHILLIPS

Harkin, James Bernard, environmentalist (b at Vankleek Hill, Ont 30 Jan 1875; d at Ottawa 27 Jan 1955). He worked in Ottawa as a newspaperman 1893-1901 and then served as secretary to Clifford SIFTON and Frank OLIVER, successive ministers of the interior. When a distinct parks branch was established by the ministry in 1911, Harkin became its first commissioner. With skilful eloquence he promoted the concept of unspoiled but publicly accessible wilderness, believing that parks represented the moral value of outdoor recreation, a haven from degenerate cities. His boundless energy pushed the parks system into 25 years of expansion. An acknowledged leader in wildlife conservation, he was instrumental in framing the Migratory Birds Convention Act 1917. MAXWELL SUTHERLAND

Harkness, Douglas Scott, teacher, farmer, politician (b at Toronto 29 Mar 1903). A schoolteacher, farmer and war hero, Harkness was first elected to the House of Commons for Calgary East in 1945; he subsequently represented Calgary North and Calgary Centre. Tory critic for northern affairs and natural resources between 1945 and 1957, he became minister of agriculture in 1957 and was especially interested in crop insurance and debt adjustment. Appointed minister of defence in Oct 1960, Harkness advocated nuclear weapons for Canada and was soon in conflict with John DIEFENBAKER. He resigned from the government in Feb 1963 over the issue, but sat in the House until 1972.

PATRICIA WILLIAMS

Harlequin Enterprises, the world's largest publisher of romance fiction, was founded in Winnipeg by Richard H.G. Bonnycastle. The company originally published westerns, thrillers, cookbooks, etc, but by 1964 was exclusively publishing romances because they were the strongest sellers. In 1968 the company went public and in 1969 headquarters were moved to Toronto. In 1975 the company was purchased by TORSTAR. In Sept 1984 Harlequin acquired Silhouette, a major US publisher of romance fiction formerly owned by Simon & Schuster. Sales soared from 19 million in 1970 to more than 206 million in 1986; Harlequin publishes in more than 100 countries and in 17 languages.

Harlow, Robert, novelist, teacher (b at Prince Rupert, BC 19 Nov 1923). During WWII Harlow flew as a bomber pilot and was awarded the DFC, retiring at 21. He was a graduate of UBC (1948) and U of Iowa (1951) and worked for the CBC, 1951-65 (director of radio for the BC region 1954-65). In 1965 he became head of UBC's creative writing dept, where he encouraged and influenced several prominent Canadian writers early in their careers. Harlow's novels include *Royal Murdoch* (1962), *A Gift of Echoes* (1965) and his best-known and finest work, *Scann* (1972), which make up the Linden trilogy, named after the imaginary northern BC town that figures in the settings of all 3 books. Later works are *Making Arrangements* (1978), *Paul Nolan* (1983) and *Felice: A Travelogue* (1985). NEIL BESNER

Harness Racing, or trotting, is the competition for purse money between horses bred and trained to "trot" or "pace," driven by a driver in coloured silks who is mounted on a 2-wheeled cart called a "sulky." The horses are called standardbreds and have long pedigrees. As a rural pastime, Canadians raced horses on ice before the advent of pioneer roads. The modern sport consistently records the highest annual attendance of any professional sport in Canada or the US, and is conducted in all 10 provinces. Pari-mutuel betting on races is permitted under the supervision of Agriculture Canada. Racing conduct, rules and licensing are under the jurisdiction of provincial racing commissions and the Canadian Trotting Assn; registration and identification of the Canadian Standardbred Horse Society.

Horses are owned, bred, trained and raced for pleasure and profit by individuals from all walks of life and by corporations, syndicates, breeding farms and partnerships. Familiar as the gentle, tractable "working horse" of our agricultural heritage, harness horses are close to the people who work with them while fans greet their favourites as old friends. Classes of racing are arranged on the basis of age for many stakes, derbies and futurities and also by sex; by money earnings so that the horses are in competitive groups; or by claiming price, when the owner in effect puts a price tag on his horse. Claiming races enable the horses' interests to classify their own horses so that they can be competitive at whatever level they are priced. Thus, the opportunity to do well is offered to horses from superstars to the slower performers. Many thousands are employed full time or part time, or participate for recreation. Racetracks are operated by private owners, by exhibition and fair associations, and even by fraternal and charitable organizations.

Canadians are expert horsemen and hold numerous records in the sport. Consistently more than half of the top 10 N American drivers have been native Canadians. Dave McClary of London, Ont, drove the first 2-minute mile (1.6 km) with a standardbred (1898), while John Campbell of Alisa, Ont, has accomplished more 2-minute miles than any other driver in the history of the sport. Ben White of Whitevale, Ont, was the first to win the Hambletonian Stakes 4 times. In 1981 William O'Donnell of Springhill, NS, became the first to exceed $4 million in yearly winnings. Hervé FILION of Angers, Qué, has won more harness races than any other driver. Michael Lachance of St.-Augustine, Qué, has won more races in a single season (770) than anyone else, eclipsing in 1986 the old record held by Hervé Filion, who became the first to go over the 400 mark. That was Lachance's third straight year to win the N American title. Among the top breeders in Canada with international reputations are Armstrong Brothers of Brampton, Ont; Sky West Farms of Okotoks, Alta; Cantario Farms of Campbellville, Ont; Shadowland Farms of Vienna, Ont; and Seelster Farms of Lucan, Ont.

Great Canadian-bred horses include Tacony, the first Canadian-bred world champion (1853); Gratton Bars, the first to win the top 3 pacing stakes in North America – all in one 3-week period of 1928; Jade Prince, the first 2-year-old world champion pacer (1976); Cam Fella, who closed out a sensational career with 28 straight victories (1983); Niatross, the fastest standardbred of all time with a 1:49.1 time trial, followed by his son Nihilator's fastest-ever race time of 1:49.3.

The Canadian Trotting Assn, formed 1939, is the first to link all tracks under its jurisdiction in a computer network supplying instant results and information. The CTA represents all Canadian provinces except those in the Maritimes, which are now associated with the US but expected soon to join their sister provinces. MARGARET NEAL

Harnoy, Ofra, cellist (b at Hadera, Israel 31 Jan 1965). Prodigious technique, profound musicality and deeply emotional expressiveness combine with personal charm to make Harnoy one of the most exciting young artists in the musical world. Early cello studies begun with her father before immigrating to Canada in 1972 were continued principally with William Pleeth in London and Vladimir Orloff in Toronto. Since her professional debut as soloist with the Boyd Neel Orchestra at age 10, she has appeared throughout the world in recitals and orchestral engagements as well as in radio and television performances. Harnoy's solo recordings and her sensitive performances of chamber music round out the picture of an accomplished young artist of exceptional maturity, versatility and brilliance. In 1987 she received a Juno Award for Best Cassical Album: solo.

BARCLAY MCMILLAN

Harper, J. Russell, art historian (b at Caledonia, Ont 13 Apr 1914; d at Cornwall, Ont 17 Nov 1983). Harper studied at the Ontario College of Art 1938-40, served with the RCAF as radar mechanic 1941-45 in Canada and in England (visiting museums and galleries constantly) and received a BA (1948) and MA (1950) in Art and Archaeology from the U of T. During the 1950s he was on the staff of the Royal Ontario Museum and the New Brunswick Museum, also engaging in archaeological work and research on social history for Ontario and New Brunswick. In 1959 he prepared a report on the potential for restoration of Louisbourg fortress for the Department of Indian and Northern Affairs. He was appointed Curator of Canadian art, National Gallery of Canada (1959-63); chief curator, McCord Museum, McGill U (1965-68); professor of art history, Concordia U (1965-79) and member of the advisory board, *Journal of Canadian Art History* (1974-83). His honours include D Litt, U of Guelph 1972; fellow, Royal Society of Canada 1974; Officer, Order of Canada 1974; Doctor of Fine Arts, Nova Scotia College of Art and Design 1982.

A determined pioneer in the history of art in Canada, he constantly stressed its need for careful, detailed knowledge of artists, their works, and their cultural setting as a means of full understanding of Canadian traditions. He produced essential aids in his *Historical Directory of New Brunswick Newspapers and Periodicals* (1961) and *Early Painters and Engravers in Canada* (1970). *Painting in Canada: A History* (1966) was the first comprehensive study in its field and the first important art book entirely produced in Canada; a revised edition appeared in 1977. His bent for inquiry and his sensitivity to creative expression combined in *Paul Kane's Frontier* (1971) which studied Kane's biography and writings in relation to the sketches and paintings documenting his travels. The same skills made his *Krieghoff* (1979) a definitive study. In his later years Harper had 2 chief interests. One was the development of the first graduate program in Canadian art history, which led into the research *Journal*. The other was the study of FOLK ART in Canada: the result was a seminal touring exhibition in 1973 for the National Gallery and *A People's Art* (1974).

FRANCESS G. HALPENNY

Harper, Vern, or Asini, meaning "stone" in Cree, native dissident, native way teacher (b at Toronto 17 June 1936). Harper is a representative of the more radical wing of the native movement of the 1970s. After a troubled early life, he became politically active as VP of the Ontario Métis and Non-Status Indian Assn (1972-74). With his wife Pauline Shirt Harper (b at Saddle Lk, Alta, 13 July 1943) he organized the Native People's Caravan, a cross-Canada trek ending in a lengthy encampment in Ottawa (1974-75) which succeeded in bringing together native organizations to publicize native grievances. The ideology of the demonstration had strong traditionalist and spiritual elements which reappeared in the Wandering Spirit Survival School of Toronto, founded by Pauline and Vern Harper in 1976. He is author of *Following the Red Path: The Native Peoples' Caravan, 1974* (1979). BENNETT MCCARDLE

Harper, William Edmund, astronomer (b at Dobbinton, Ont 20 Mar 1878; d at Victoria 4 June 1940). After graduating from U of T in 1906, Harper joined the Dominion Observatory, Ottawa, and later conducted a national search for a site for a proposed new observatory. In 1918 he transferred to the new institution, the Dominion Astrophysical Observatory in Victoria, becoming its second director in 1936. His field was the measurement of distances and motions of stars, and especially the study of spectroscopic binaries. He is said to have computed more orbits for these systems than anyone else and, such was his industry, it is likely that he did, at least until the advent of electronic computers. He was an active popularizer of astronomy and was awarded an honorary doctorate by U of T in 1935. A.H. BATTEN

Harrington, Gordon Sidney, lawyer, politician, premier of NS (b at Halifax 7 Aug 1883; d there 4 July 1943). Educated at Dalhousie (LLB, 1904), Harrington practised law in Glace Bay. After serving in the CEF, 1915-20, he became MLA for Cape Breton Centre 1925-33 and Cape Breton S 1933-37. His support from the miners contributed to the Conservatives' victory in the 1925 election and led to his appointment as minister of labour in the E.N. RHODES government. He succeeded Rhodes as premier in 1930. An effective, though sometimes caustic, speaker and a skilful administrator, Harrington followed the orthodox policies of the day in a politically hopeless battle against the Great Depression. Attempts to manipulate the voting lists in the election defeat of 1933 tarnished the record of a competent administration. ERNEST R. FORBES

Harrington, Richard, photographer-writer (b at Hamburg, Ger 24 Feb 1911). Harrington began photography in 1940 when he was working as an X-ray technician in Toronto and was asked to make slides for doctors. A few years later he became a full-time freelance photographer-writer. Often working in collaboration with his author wife Lyn, he has travelled extensively, from the Arctic to the Antarctic, from Albania to Zaire. He has long had a special interest in aboriginal peoples, and probably his best-known and most moving photo essay was done in the Arctic in the late 1940s, documenting a band of nomadic Inuit and their struggle for survival after the annual caribou migration changed course and bypassed them. Harrington has published upwards of 2400 photo stories, and his work has appeared in more than 24 books, including *The Family of Man* (1955), *The Inuit: Life As It Was* (1981), *Richard Harrington's Yukon* (1974) and *River Rafting in Canada* (1984). His photographs have been purchased by the National Archives of Canada, the Smithsonian Institution and the Museum of Modern Art (New York C). LOUISE ABBOTT

Harris, Alanson, manufacturer (b near Ingersoll, UC 1 Apr 1816; d at Brantford, Ont 3 Oct 1894). A sawmill operator in Brant County, Harris bought a foundry in Beamsville in 1857 and began manufacturing farm implements. His firm prospered by aggressive marketing practices and by technological leadership secured through the acquisition of Canadian rights to American patents, and later through the development of its own machinery designs. In 1872 he moved to Brantford and in 1879 began marketing his products in western Canada. His firm, A. Harris, Son and Co Ltd, merged in 1891 with its major competitor, the Massey Manufacturing Co, to form Massey-Harris Co Ltd (later MASSEY-FERGUSON LIMITED, now Varity Corp), Canada's largest farm-implement manufacturer. JOSEPH LINDSEY

Harris, Carrol Wayne, football player (b at Hampton, Ark 4 May 1938). Many regard Harris as the greatest ever to have played the position of centre linebacker in the CFL. The anchor of the CALGARY STAMPEDER defence, he won 4 SCHENLEY AWARDS (1965, 1966, 1970, 1971), the most ever for a defensive player, and was selected to 11 Western all-star and 9 all-Canadian teams. He led the team to 3 GREY CUP appearances, culminating in a win in the 1971 game, in which he was named the outstanding player. His career ended midway in the 1972 season when he sustained a serious neck injury. PETER WONS

Harris, Christie, neé Lucy Christie Irwin, author (b at Newark, NJ 21 Nov 1907). Winner of 4 major children's book awards, Harris grew up on a BC homestead and taught school until her marriage in 1932, when she turned to writing essays and radio scripts. At 50 she began to write children's books. Of her many works, the most outstanding are *Raven's Cry* (1966), a powerful novel tracing the destruction of the Haida nation, and 7 volumes of Northwest Coast Indian tales. Following European fairy-tale conventions, she structured her best works, the Mouse Woman books and *The Trouble with Princesses* (1980), to present her primary theme, the need to respect nature and its balance. RAYMOND E. JONES

Harris, Lawren Stewart, painter (b at Brantford, Ont 23 Oct 1885; d at Vancouver 29 Jan 1970). Catalyst and leader in the creation of the GROUP OF SEVEN, founding member and first president of the Canadian Group of Painters, and the painter who influenced Jock MACDONALD, and through him other Toronto painters, to paint abstractly. Harris had a profound influence on 3 generations of art in Canada. Harris's father was Thomas Morgan Harris, the secretary of the A. Harris, Son and Co Ltd, a manufacturer of farm machinery which in 1891 amalgamated with Massey to form the Massey-Harris Co Ltd: Lawren Harris was thus a rich man. After attending Toronto's St Andrews College, Harris went to U of Toronto where he was encouraged by his mathematics professor to study art in Berlin. After 4 years of study (1904-08), Harris returned to Canada. In 1908 he went on a sketching trip to the Laurentians; in 1909, with J.W. Beatty, he sketched in Haliburton. That fall he went to Lac-Memphrémagog, Qué. At the same time, he drew and painted houses in downtown Toronto; by the winter of 1911-12, he was sketching with J.E.H. MACDONALD and had become friendly with Tom THOMSON. In 1913, Harris and MacDonald visited and were inspired by an exhibition of Contemporary Scandinavian Art at the Albright Art Gallery (now the Albright-Knox) in Buffalo.

By the early 1920s, when the Group of Seven was formed, Harris had developed into a magnificent landscape painter, transforming the powerful forms of nature into works of force and elegance such as *Above Lake Superior* (*c*1924) and *Maligne Lake* (1924). In these and other paintings he reduced the shapes of mountains, shoreline, trees, lakes and clouds, always parallel to the picture plane, to their essentials for an austere, monumental effect. He painted for 5 successive autumns in Algoma and Lake Superior (1917-22), in the Rockies from 1924 on, and in the Arctic in 1930. As artist-in-residence at Darmouth Coll, NH, he moved progressively through drawing into nonobjective art. In Santa Fe, NM, he worked with Dr Emil Bisttram, leader of the Transcendental Group of Painters, which Harris also helped found in 1939. His Vancouver work (1940-70)

Lawren Harris's *Above Lake Superior* (*c*1924) (*courtesy Art Gallery of Canada/gift from the Reuben and Kate Leonard Canadian Fund, 1929*).

continued to explore abstraction inspired by the rhythms of nature. Harris's belief in theosophy is intimately linked to his development as a nonobjective artist. Through abstract paintings, such as *Abstract Painting No 20,* many of which use forms from landscape, he sought to portray a binding and healing conception of the universe – to make the sublime visual. His paintings have been criticized as being cold, but in fact they reflect the depth of his spiritual involvement. His world view makes him unique among Canadian painters, although his philosophy kept him aloof from spontaneously created art – a crucial factor in later painters' abstraction. Nevertheless, his landscape paintings, such as *Lake and Mountains* (1927-28) and some of his abstractions, are among the icons of Canadian art.

In his own lifetime Harris was the subject of 2 retrospectives, in 1948 and 1963. In 1978 the Art Gallery of Ontario held an exhibition, *Urban Scenes and Wilderness Landscapes, 1906-1930.* In 1982-83 a national travelling exhibition of his drawings was held. The bulk of his work is found in the National Gallery of Canada, Art Gallery of Ontario, and the McMichael Canadian Collection, Kleinburg, Ont. In Nov 1987, a 1929 sketch for *Mountains in Snow: Rocky Mountain Paintings, No. VII* sold for $150 000, a record for a Canadian sketch. JOAN MURRAY

Reading: B. Harris and R.G.P. Colgrove, eds, *Lawren Harris* (1969); Joan Murray and Robert Fulford, *The Beginning of Vision* (1982).

Harris, Robert, artist (b at Vale of Conway, Wales 18 Sept 1849; d at Montréal 27 Feb 1919). He is best known for his painting *The Fathers of Confederation,* which was burned in the fire that destroyed the Parliament Buildings in Ottawa in 1916. He immigrated to PEI with his family in 1856, including his brother William Critchlow HARRIS. He studied in Boston, Paris and Rome and travelled extensively in Europe, Canada and the US. He did illustrations for publications in Boston, Halifax, Montréal and Toronto, and was commissioned by Gordon Brown of the *Globe* in 1880 to go to Lucan to sketch the prisoners accused of murdering the DONNELLYS. A distinguished portrait painter, Harris portrayed over 200 of the leading personalities of the day, including Sir John A. MACDONALD, George Monro GRANT and Lord ABERDEEN. He lived much of his life in Montréal teaching at the Art Assn there. He was a founding member of the Royal Canadian Academy in 1880 and of the Pen and Pencil Club in 1890. Elected president of the RCA in 1893, he worked for 13 years to promote young Canadian artists by having them represented at all major international exhibitions of the period. Two of his most popular paintings, *A Meeting of the School Trustees* and *Harmony,* are in the National Gallery of Canada. In 1928 his widow built the Robert Harris Memorial Gallery and Library in Charlottetown, PEI. This building was replaced in 1964 by the Confederation Centre and its gallery houses an extensive collection of Harris's works.

MONCRIEFF WILLIAMSON

Reading: Moncrieff Williamson, *Robert Harris* (1971).

Robert Harris, *Ruth Harris,* oil on canvas (*private coll*).

Harris, Walter, Tsimshian artist (b at Kispiox, BC 10 June 1931). A hereditary chief of the Gitksan village of Kispiox, Harris is a senior artist at the Gitanmaax School of NORTHWEST COAST INDIAN ART at KSAN, Hazelton, BC. Versed in the culture of the Skeena River people, he helped to erect the traditional plank-and-beam woodcarving building at the school; later he taught in that building while fulfilling major commissions. Though a competent and prolific printmaker, Harris is primarily noted as a carver. His impressive "Mother of Grouse" pole at Kispiox commemorates his family's crests, replicating one that disappeared from his home village long ago. CAROL SHEEHAN

Harris, Walter Edgar, analytical chemist, professor (b at Wetaskiwin, Alta 9 June 1915). A recognized leader in the development of teaching and research in analytical chemistry in Canada, Harris studied chemistry at U of Alberta and Minnesota. He joined the dept of chemistry at Alberta in 1946, teaching and carrying on research in polarography, gas chromatography and theories of chemical separation, and developed a vigorous analytical chemistry division. A consultant in analytical education at universities throughout N America, he was also a government adviser on disposal of hazardous wastes. His books include (with H.W. Habgood) *Programmed Temperature Gas Chromatography* (1966), (with H.A. Leitinen) *Chemical Analysis* (1975), (with B. Kratochvil) *Chemical Separations and Measurements* (1974) and *An Introduction to Chemical Analysis* (1981). In 1986 he received an honorary DSc from U of Waterloo. W.F. ALLEN

Harris, William Critchlow, architect (b at Bootle, near Liverpool, Eng 30 Apr 1854; d at Halifax 16 July 1913), brother of painter Robert HARRIS. Brought to Charlottetown as a child, he attended Prince of Wales College and in 1870 joined architect David STIRLING in Halifax. In 1875 he established his own practice in Charlottetown. His buildings reflect a talented and original approach to the High Victorian Gothic style. Over 90 are extant in PEI, NS and NB. They include St James Anglican Church, Mahone Bay, NS (1886); All Souls' Chapel, Charlottetown (1888); and his masterwork, St Paul's Anglican Church, Charlottetown (1895).

GRANT WANZEL AND KAREN KALLWEIT

Harrison, David Howard, physician, politician, farmer, businessman, premier of Manitoba (b at London, Canada W 1 June 1843; d at Vancouver 8 Sept 1905). Educated at U of T and McGill, he practised medicine in St Marys, Ont, until 1882, when he settled in Manitoba and carried on extensive farming operations. Elected an MLA for Minnedosa in 1883, he was appointed minister of agriculture in John NORQUAY's government on 27 Aug 1886. Harrison became premier of Manitoba on 26 Dec 1887, but when the legislature met on 12 Jan 1888 his lack of support was apparent and his ministry resigned on 19 Jan 1888. LOVELL C. CLARK

Harrison, Edward, "Ted," artist, children's book author and illustrator (b at Wingate, County Durham, Eng 28 Aug 1926). The best known of the Yukon painters, Harrison has won international recognition for his painting as well as for his children's stories and illustrations (*The Last Horizon,* 1980; *The Cremation of Sam McGee,* 1986). He studied art at the Hartlepool College of Art in England and later earned an art teacher's diploma. During his schoolteacher days in Carcross, YT, in late 1968, his work underwent a dramatic transformation. He simplified his forms almost to a childlike form and introduced sweeping rhythms and lush colours. His trademark paintings often depict faceless people, with the odd dog or raven, standing in front of sunken houses. The backdrop is always composed of colourful lakes, brilliant skies, and mountains that seem to blend into one another. Harrison was the first Canadian artist-illustrator to be shown at the International Children's Book Exhibition in Bologna, Italy, and at the Otani Memorial Museum of Art in Nishinomiya, Japan. He became a Member of the Order of Canada in 1987. EDWARD STRUZIK

Harrison River, 15 km long, flows SW from Harrison Lk to join the FRASER R about 100 km upriver from Vancouver in southern BC. A famed holiday resort, Harrison Hot Springs, is located where the river leaves the lake. It is named after Benjamin Harrison, deputy governor of the HBC 1835-39. DANIEL FRANCIS

Harriss, Charles Albert Edwin, composer, impresario, educator, organist-choirmaster, conductor (b at London, Eng 16 Dec 1862; d at Ottawa 31 July 1929). Trained as organist and choirmaster in English cathedrals, in 1882 Harriss was appointed to St Alban's, Ottawa, and then to Christ Church Cathedral, Montréal, returning to Ottawa in 1900. Honorary director of examinations of the Royal Schools of Music, first director of the McGill Conservatorium, Harriss also arranged many concerts and festivals, bringing outstanding British artists to Canada, and organized massive choirs. In 1924 he became music director of the British Empire Exhibition in Wembley (London, Eng). His numerous works were performed throughout the British Empire. He received an honorary fellowship from the Royal Academy of Music and the Lambeth doctorate from the archbishop of Canterbury.

MABEL H. LAINE

Harron, Donald, actor, writer, broadcaster (b at Toronto 19 Sept 1924). While studying at U of T, he performed for CBC Radio and the New Play Soc. He had major roles at the STRATFORD FESTIVAL in the early 1950s and then for over a dozen years worked on stage, TV and in films in England, New York and Los Angeles. As the ill-dressed, malapropish farmer from Parry Sound, Charlie Farquharson, and as Toronto matron Valerie Rosedale, he has performed on Canadian radio and American TV, and written such best-selling books as *Histry of Canada* and *Jogfree of Canada,* offering social and political satire while entertaining. Harron also wrote the libretto for *Anne of Green Gables,* Canada's longest-running stage musical, and hosted CBC Radio's "Morningside" 1977-82 and the "Don Harron Show" on CTV 1983-85. A warm, intelligent and thoughtful entertainer, he is notorious for his witty manipulation of language. He published *Debunk's Illustrated Guide to the Canadian Establishment* in 1984 and *Cum Buy the Farm* in 1987. ALLAN M. GOULD

Hart, Benjamin, businessman (b at Montréal 10 Aug 1779; d at New York, NY 27 Feb 1855). Brother of Moses HART and son of Aaron Hart, a prominent Trois-Rivières merchant, Benjamin followed his father's occupation, first at Trois-Rivières and Montréal, then almost exclusively in Montréal. A persistent advocate of Jewish civil liberties, in 1833 he was offered an appointment as a Montréal justice of the peace, as were Samuel B. Hart and Moses Hayes; he and Hayes refused the appointment until 1837 when legislation was passed enabling Jews to take an oath of office which was not repugnant to their religion. Benjamin Hart was also a leading advocate of the revival and restoration of Montréal's Shearith Israel Synagogue. A wealthy merchant, a generous patron of charitable organizations, an outspoken opponent of the Patriote cause and a member of the militia, in 1849 Hart signed the ANNEXATION Manifesto. Shortly thereafter he moved to New York. CARMAN MILLER

Hart, Corey Mitchell, singer, songwriter (b at Montréal 31 May 1961). Hart rocketed onto the music scene with the release of the international hit "Sunglasses at Night" in 1983. His song "Never Surrender" won the 1985 Juno Award for single of the year. In 1985 Hart released *Boy in the Box* on Aquarius Records. The album became the quickest Canadian million-seller in history 7 months after its release. In 1986 he released his third album, *Fields of Fire,* which included songs such as "Can't Help Falling in Love," "Angry Young Man" and "I Am by Your Side."

JOHN GEIGER

Hart, Evelyn Anne, ballerina (b at Toronto 4 Apr 1956). Her distinctive physique, dramatic intensity and sublimely lyrical dancing have made her one of the most compelling stage personalities in Canada. By common standards a late starter, Hart trained briefly at the NATIONAL BALLET SCHOOL, with teachers in London, Ont, and principally at the school of the ROYAL WINNIPEG BALLET, entering the company in 1976. She became a soloist in 1978 and a principal dancer in 1979. In 1980 Hart won the gold medal for best female soloist at the International Ballet Competition in Varna, Bulgaria. She has appeared around the world as a guest artist as well as with other Canadian companies. In 1987 she danced with the Odessa State Ballet, the first time before an eastern European audience since her 1980 performance at Varna.

MICHAEL CRABB

Hart, John, financier, politician, premier of BC (b at Mohill, Ire 31 Mar 1879; d at Victoria 7 Apr 1957). Arriving in Victoria in 1898, Hart worked in a financial firm before founding his own business, Gillespie, Hart and Co, in 1909. Elected a Liberal MLA for Victoria in 1916, and never defeated, he served as "almost a perpetual finance minister" from 1917 until 1949, except for the years 1924-33 when he retired from politics for business reasons. In Dec 1941 Hart became Liberal premier of a coalition government, a position he held until he retired in 1947. Under him the BC Power Commission was established to undertake rural electrification and a program of highway construction was begun, including the Hart Hwy from Prince George to Dawson Creek.

PATRICIA E. ROY

Hart, Julia Catherine, née Beckwith (b at Fredericton 10 Mar 1796; d there 28 Nov 1867). Hart wrote the first work of fiction by a native-born Canadian to be published in Canada. Her novel *St Ursula's Convent; or, The Nun of Canada, Containing Scenes from Real Life,* although published in 1824, was written when she was 17 and it is a sentimental, moralistic melodrama. As a young girl she experienced both the English and French cultures – a dual heritage reflected in her novel. Her second novel, *Tonnewonte* (1825), is set in the US. In this work she wrote to entertain and to set forth her idealism about the freedom and serenity of western frontier life. DOUGLAS LOCHHEAD

Hart, Moses, businessman, landowner (b at Trois-Rivières 26 Nov 1768; d there 15 Oct 1852), brother of Benjamin HART. An eccentric but adept businessman, Hart began his career in Sorel by running a general store and then extended into the import-export business. His most prominent business ventures later included steam navigation and banking, and he was one of the first shareholders of the Bank of Montreal and the Bank of Canada. His desire for a political career was never satisfied, as he repeatedly failed to be elected to the House of Assembly. He nevertheless made his mark as a landed proprietor, owning many properties on the south shore of the St Lawrence as well as around Trois-Rivières.

GISÈLE VILLENEUVE

Hart House, on UNIVERSITY OF TORONTO campus, was designed by the architectural firm of SPROATT AND ROLPH and was built 1911-19. Soldier's Tower, a memorial to the university's WWI dead, was added in 1924. Endowed by the Massey family, and named for Hart MASSEY, Hart House is a large multi-functional student centre with a swimming pool, track, squash courts, theatre, library and dining room, all contained in a building of remarkable architectural coherence. Designed in the Collegiate Gothic style, which was then very popular for educational structures, the stone building features 4 distinct wings surrounding a quadrangle, and such details as mullioned oriel and pointed arch windows, all of which are inspired by the medieval colleges of Oxford and Cambridge. The building's key location and appealing design have ensured its continued prominence on the university campus. SALLY COUTTS

Hart House String Quartet was formed in Toronto in 1923 when Geza de Kresz, violinist, Milton Blackstone, violist, Boris Hambourg, cellist and, a short time later, Harry ADASKIN, violinist, began rehearsing together. The ensemble gave its first concert in the Hart House Theatre in 1924 before an invited audience. So successful was this concert that the Massey Foundation undertook to establish the group permanently by guaranteeing the players' salaries, and as a result the Hart House String Quartet began an internationally respected career lasting until 1946. Hambourg remained with the quartet throughout its career but the other members changed. De Kresz withdrew in 1935 and was replaced by James Levey. Adaskin left in 1938 and was succeeded by Adolph Koldofsky, followed in 1942 by Henry Milligan. Blackstone left in 1941 and was replaced by Allard de Ridder, followed by Cyril Glyde in 1944. The quartet gave 10 annual concerts at Hart House and 10 at Convocation Hall, U of T. It made numerous Canadian tours, gave many concerts in the US and toured Britain and Europe twice. In the early days of broadcasting it was contracted by the CNR, and continued radio engagements into the late 1930s and early 1940s for the CBC. Its repertoire included music from classic, romantic and modern composers. It gave several first Canadian performances and several premieres of the works of Canadian composers. Occasionally the quartet performed with an outstanding guest artist, such as Maurice Ravel, Sir Ernest MACMILLAN and Ernest Seitz. It was internationally acclaimed for its sensitive and skilful playing. Its Victor recordings are treasured by knowledgeable collectors and fortunate owners.

MABEL H. LAINE

Hart Trophy is awarded annually to the player chosen by hockey writers as being "most valuable" to his NATIONAL HOCKEY LEAGUE team. It was donated to the NHL in 1923 by Dr David A. Hart, father of Cecil Hart, former manager of the Montréal Canadiens. The oldest and most prestigious individual award in hockey, it was retired to the HOCKEY HALL OF FAME in 1960 and replaced by the Hart Memorial Trophy. Gordie HOWE won it 6 times, Eddie SHORE 4, Howie MORENZ 3 and Bobby ORR 3. By 1987, Wayne GRETZKY had won the trophy an unprecedented 8 consecutive times.

Hartland, NB, Town, pop 917 (1986c), 846 (1981c), inc 1918, is located at the mouth of the Becaguimec Stream, 124 km upriver from Fredericton on the SAINT JOHN R. First settled by William Orser, a New York Loyalist, the community developed in the 19th century from being the commercial centre for the surrounding farms to being the site of many small manufactures. This varied economic base shifted towards specialization in the 20th century with the development of potato-chip production (Humpty Dumpty Ltd) and trucking (Day and Ross Ltd, one of the 10 largest transport companies in Canada). Although the town's main street has been considerably altered by fire and flood in the last few decades, Hartland is steeped in history. Three New Brunswick premiers have hailed from here. The 391 m Hartland Covered Bridge attracts visitors from around the world. FRED FARRELL

Hartman, Barney, skeet shooter (b at Swan River, Man 2 Nov 1916). Judged by his peers the greatest skeet shooter in the world, Hartman was 10 times captain of the National Skeet Shooting Assn all-American team and 4 times recorded perfect 100x100 with the 410 gauge. He claimed nearly 30 world titles in 12, 20, 28, 410 gauge and all-round categories. He once broke a string of 2002 clay targets without a miss and he frequently shattered records. He won a silver and 4 bronze medals in world competition and for 9 of 12 years as amateur and professional boasted the world's best average. BOB FERGUSON

Hartman, Grace, labour leader (b at Toronto 14 July 1918). Hartman was the first female unionist to hold the top position in a Canadian union. In 1954 she joined the National Union of Public Employees (TLC), where she held several local and provincial positions. When the CANADIAN UNION OF PUBLIC EMPLOYEES (CUPE) was formed in 1963, by a merger of her union with the National Union of Public Service Employees (CCL), she was elected to its national executive as a regional VP for Ontario. Hartman successfully campaigned for full collective-bargaining rights for municipal and school-board employees. She promoted women's rights inside and outside of the labour movement. In 1981 she was jailed for counselling an illegal strike; she insisted that hospital workers, legally barred from striking, must have full collective-bargaining rights. In 1965 Hartman was elected one of CUPE's 5 general VPs; in 1967 she became the national secretary-treasurer, in 1975 the national president, and in 1976 Canadian Labour Congress general VP. She retired in 1983 but remains active in many public-interest groups. LAUREL SEFTON MACDOWELL

Harvest Excursions Before the introduction of the combine, prairie harvests required large numbers of labourers for short periods of time. Harvest excursion trains, 1890-1930, brought workers west – about 14 000 in 1908. Railways offered harvest tickets from any station as far away as the Maritimes to Winnipeg for $15, and a return fare of $20. Excursion trains provided crude accommodation: packed 4 per compartment, passengers slept on slatted wooden seats. Delays, crowd-

A 1911 advertisement for men needed to harvest grain in western Canada. Excursion trains brought workers from as far east as Halifax (*courtesy National Archives of Canada/C-56088*).

ing and drunkenness on occasion led to riots. In the 1920s railways demanded and got RCMP detachments on the trains to keep order. The harvesting work paid $1.75-2.25 for a 10-12-hour day with board, and usually lasted 15 days. A threshing crew of perhaps 2 dozen was paid $2-3.25 each a day with board. Although the journey was rough and the work was gruelling, the excursions introduced Canadians and Britons to the Prairies. Many decided to return permanently to HOMESTEAD. The collapse of the wheat economy in 1930 and changing farm technology ended the era of the harvest excursion. PETER A. RUSSELL

Harvey, Douglas, hockey player (b at Montréal 19 Dec 1924). He rejected offers from major-league football and baseball teams and played amateur senior hockey for Montreal Royals before joining MONTREAL CANADIENS in 1947-48. He was the greatest defenceman of his era, controlling the tempo of the game with pinpoint passing, subtle playmaking and dramatic rushes. He was the defensive leader of the powerful Canadien team that won 5 consecutive Stanley Cup victories 1956-60. He won the JAMES NORRIS TROPHY for outstanding defenceman 7 times, was first all-star 10 times and scored 88 goals and 452 assists in 1113 regular-season games and 8 goals and 64 assists in 137 playoff games. His career in Montréal ended when he became active in the NHL players association and he was traded in 1961 to New York Rangers where he was player-coach for a year. He played for several teams in the minors before returning to the NHL with Detroit and St Louis. He was briefly coach of LA Kings (1970). JAMES MARSH

Harvey, Jean-Charles, journalist, writer, lecturer (b at La Malbaie, Qué 10 Nov 1891; d at Montréal 3 Jan 1967). A lively and outspoken thinker, Harvey was at the heart of almost every cultural, political and social debate of his time. After working as a reporter for *La Patrie* and *La Presse,* Harvey took an advertising position with a Montmagny company. The firm's bankruptcy inspired his first novel, *Marcel Faure* (1922). In Feb 1922 he joined *Le Soleil,* where in 1927 he became editor in chief. He lost his job when his novel *Les Demi-civilisés* (1934) was placed on the Roman Catholic index of prohibited books by Cardinal VILLENEUVE on 26 Apr 1934. He continued to publish and founded the weekly *Le Jour* (1937-46). In 1952 Harvey became a radio news commentator. A year later he moved to *Le Petit Journal,* where he was technical director (1956-66). He published numerous works, lectured across Canada and gave regular radio broadcasts. Faithful to his principles and with independence of spirit, humanitarian ideals and attachment to nature, Harvey was one of the great French Canadian journalists. GUILDO ROUSSEAU

Harvey, Sir John, soldier, colonial administrator, lt-gov of PEI, Nfld and NS (b in Eng 23 Apr 1778; d at Halifax 22 Mar 1852). Of humble birth, he received a commission at the age of 16 in the British army and rose through his own merits to the rank of lt-gen. He served in Flanders and off the coast of France and then in India during the Napoleonic Wars, but he achieved his greatest fame as deputy adjutant general in Upper Canada during the War of 1812, particularly at the Battle of STONEY CREEK on 6 June 1813 when he drove back a much superior American force and saved the whole of the Niagara peninsula from capture. After serving for a decade in Lower Canada after the war he became one of the 4 inspectors general of the Irish Constabulary in 1828.

In 1836 he was appointed lt-gov of PEI, where he acted as a conciliator between the absentee landlords and their tenants and prevented their disputes from erupting into violence. In 1837 he was transferred to NB in order to put an end to the disputes between the Assembly and the executive and he successfully negotiated a settlement with the Reform Party, which ushered in an "age of harmony," albeit at the cost of giving the Reformers a dominant position in both the Legislative and Executive Councils. DURHAM approved of Harvey's activities and SYDENHAM hailed him as "the Pearl of Civil Governors." Harvey successfully negotiated with the governor of Maine to prevent the dispute over the Maine-NB boundary from leading to a war, but he exceeded his authority and was dismissed in early 1841, ironically at Sydenham's request. Fortunately for Harvey, who was chronically in debt, a position was found for him as lt-gov of Newfoundland, where he again acted as a conciliator, this time between the largely English and Protestant merchant class resident in St John's and the largely Irish and Catholic population of the outports. He even reconciled many Reformers to the temporary and abortive constitutional experiment of uniting both elected and appointed members in one legislative body. He was rewarded by promotion in 1846 to the office of lt-gov of Nova Scotia, where he presided over the creation of the first truly RESPONSIBLE GOVERNMENT in N America, winning warm praise from Reformers such as Joseph HOWE and equally warm abuse from the provincial Conservatives. He thus served in all of the BNA provinces and was perhaps the most successful governor of his day. P.A. BUCKNER

Harvey, Moses, clergyman, essayist, naturalist (b at Armagh, Ire 21 Mar 1820; d at St John's 3 Sept 1901). He was of Scottish descent and was ordained a Presbyterian minister in 1844. After serving in Maryport, Eng, he immigrated to Newfoundland in 1852. His ministry at St Andrew's Free Presbyterian Church in St John's was long and successful, but he is best known as a champion of Newfoundland and prolific writer of hundreds of publications. He contributed over 600 articles to the Montréal *Gazette,* some under the pen name "Delta." Elected to the Royal Soc of Canada in 1892, he served with distinction as secretary to the Newfoundland Fisheries Commission, calling for the establishment of a "world class marine sciences research laboratory in Newfoundland." His name is associated with early specimens of the giant squid *Architeuthis* from the 1870s. Truly a Victorian savant and an outstanding man of letters, Harvey was author of *Across Newfoundland with the Governor* (1879), *Text-Book of Newfoundland History* (1885) and *A Short History of Newfoundland: England's Oldest Colony* (1890). F.A. ALDRICH

Harvey, Pierre, cross-country skier (b at Rimouski, Qué 24 Mar 1957). An exceptionally versatile athlete, he began serious competition at age 12 as a swimmer, switching to cycling at 16. On his way to a Québec championship (1975), a Canadian championship (150 km, 1976) and Canada's best 1976 Olympic cycling performance (24th, 180 km), he took up cross-country skiing as winter training. In 1984 he became the first Canadian male athlete to participate in both Olympics in the same year, but he had already begun the concentration on cross-country skiing which was to make him the sport's all-time greatest Canadian champion. His impressive string of achievements so far includes first winner of all 4 gold medals at one Canadian championship (1986 and again in 1987), first Canadian winner of a World Cup Race (Falun, Sweden, 1987, 30 km free technique), and first Canadian Worldloppet winner (Birkebeiner, Norway, 1987). MURRAY C. SHAW

Harvie, Eric Lafferty, oilman, philanthropist (b at Orillia, Ont 2 Apr 1892; d at Calgary 11 Jan 1975). Harvie was called to the Alberta Bar in 1915. He served overseas in WWI, was wounded in France and achieved the rank of captain. As a Calgary lawyer, he was involved in the oil business and in 1944 purchased the mineral rights held by British Dominions Land Settlement Co. With these he formed Western Leaseholds, Ltd, and Western Minerals, Ltd; in 1947-48, when oil was discovered on several of his leases in the Leduc and Redwater fields, he became wealthy. In 1955 he turned to philanthropic endeavours. His major achievement was forming the Glenbow Foundation in Calgary and later overseeing the creation of Heritage Pk. A modest man, he kept most of his good works secret, but he was known for his assistance to the Calgary Zoological Soc, BANFF CENTRE School of Fine Arts and Luxton Museum. He was a founding officer of the Canada Council. HUGH A. DEMPSEY

Harwood, Vanessa, ballet dancer (b at Cheltenham, Eng 14 June 1947). One of Betty OLIPHANT's first pupils in Canada, Harwood attended the NATIONAL BALLET SCHOOL, graduated into the NATIONAL BALLET OF CANADA in 1965, and became a soloist in 1967 and a principal dancer in 1970. Known for her interpretation of *Swan Lake* and *The Dying Swan,* Harwood is admired for her virtuosity and her seductive stage presence. She was actress and dancer at the Canadian Pavilion, Expo 86, and has made numerous guest appearances in the US, Australia and Europe. She became an Officer of the Order of Canada in 1984. PENELOPE DOOB

Hastings, Charles John Colwell Orr, obstetrician, medical officer of health (b in Markham Township, Canada W 23 Aug 1858; d at Toronto 17 Jan 1931). Educated at Victoria Coll Medical School in Toronto with postgraduate training in Great Britain, Hastings was one of the first full-time obstetricians to practise in Toronto. As Toronto's MOH 1910-29, he purified the water supply and established an internationally recognized public-health nursing system. He was a leading pioneer of health education programs, medical and dental inspection in public schools, and neighbourhood baby clinics in Canada. These innovations lowered Toronto's death rate from communicable diseases (from 15.3 per 1000 in 1909 to 10.3 per 1000 in 1925) and made the city a cleaner and healthier place to live. Hastings's accomplishments were recognized with his election as president of the Canadian Public Health Assn in 1916 and the American Public Health Assn in 1918. Through his efforts, Toronto's health department became internationally renowned for its achievements in preventive medicine. HEATHER MACDOUGALL

Haszard, Francis Longworth, lawyer, politician, premier of PEI, judge (b at Bellevue, PEI 20 Nov 1849; d at Charlottetown 25 July 1938). Elected to the Legislative Assembly in 1904, Haszard became premier in 1908, serving until 1911 when he was appointed master of the rolls and judge of the Supreme Court. He retired from the bench in 1930. NICOLAS J. DE JONG

Hatfield, Richard Bennett, politician, premier of NB (b at Woodstock, NB 9 Apr 1931). The longest-serving premier of New Brunswick, he promoted national unity and linguistic equality and worked for the patriation of the CONSTITUTION and a CANADIAN CHARTER OF RIGHTS AND FREEDOMS as well as a constitutional accord in 1987. Educated at Acadia and Dalhousie Law School, he practised law briefly and was sales manager of Hatfield Industries, the family potato chip business 1958-65. In 1961 he was elected Conservative MLA for Carleton County. Unsuccessful in his 1966 bid for the party leadership, he was named House leader in 1968 and elected party leader in 1969. The next year he led his party to victory over L.J. ROBICHAUD.

Hatfield's government consolidated the Liberal program of Equal Opportunity and implemented the Official Languages Act. Political reforms included the Political Process Financing Act and single-member electoral districts, both part of plans to reorganize government structure and responsibility. In spite of controversy over the Bricklin car venture, Point Lepreau nuclear power plant, spruce-budworm spraying and party fund-raising activities, Hatfield's Conservatives were re-elected 1974, 1978 and 1982, and he succeeded in expanding Conservative support in the francophone regions. Nevertheless, his reputation was tarnished by persistent questions about his personal behavior. His leadership was challenged and his party lost every seat in the 1987 election. Hatfield resigned the leadership immediately after. DELLA M.M. STANLEY

As premier of New Brunswick for 17 years Richard Hatfield promoted his province as a microcosm of Canada (*courtesy Canapress Photo Service*).

Hatheway, George Luther, farmer, lumberman, politician, premier of NB (b at Musquash, NB 4 Aug 1813; d at Fredericton 5 July 1872). Elected in 1850 as Reform MLA for York and defeated in 1857, he was re-elected in 1861 and named chief commissioner of public works by S.L. TILLEY. Opposed to the Québec Resolutions, Hatheway left Tilley's pro-Confederation government and was elected in 1865 as an anti-confederate. He declined to lead the government, preferring to be commissioner of public works for A.J. SMITH, and retired in 1866. On accepting the reality of Confederation, he was re-elected in 1870 and in 1871 agreed to form a coalition government. As premier and provincial secretary (1871-72), he and G.E. KING passed the Common Schools Act, thereby introducing a free, tax-supported, non-sectarian school system. DELLA M.M. STANLEY

Haukaness, Lars Jonson, painter, art educator (b at Folkedal, Norway 1862; d at Lake Louise, Alta 4 Sept 1929). Haukaness studied in Kristiania [Oslo] at the Royal Academy of Art (1882-85). He immigrated to the US in 1888, exhibiting at the Chicago Art Museum (1894) and establishing himself as portrait painter in Madison. He returned to Norway 1909-13 and then exhibited 44 canvases in Chicago and Madison (1913). In 1920 he moved to Winnipeg where he exhibited at the Winnipeg Art Gallery (1920) and taught at Winnipeg School of Art (1920-24), and was a friend of LeMoine FITZGERALD and Franz JOHNSTON. In 1923 he was awarded a $50 prize at the Chicago-Norwegian Exhibition for *March Thaw*. He moved to Calgary in 1926 and began evening art classes at the Provincial Institute of Technology and Art (later the Alberta College of Art). In the fall of 1927, Haukaness taught the first day classes in fine art. He was the first teacher of Maxwell BATES and W.L. Stevenson. Haukaness was an impressionist painter particularly interested in mountain landscape, and he regularly spent summers alone in the Rockies painting. He died of a heart attack while on such a painting trip. A large memorial exhibition was held in Calgary in 1931. HELEN COLLINSON

Haultain, Sir Frederick William Alpin Gordon, lawyer, politician (b at Woolwich, Eng 25 Nov 1857; d at Montréal 30 Jan 1942). After qualifying as a lawyer in Ontario, in 1884 Haultain moved to Fort Macleod in what was then the North-West Territories, where he resumed the practice of law. Elected to the Territorial Assembly in 1888, he quickly emerged as leader of the faction demanding RESPONSIBLE GOVERNMENT for the Territories, and after this was won in 1896 he served as first minister of a nonpartisan administration until 1905. A man of the centre, equally popular among both Liberals and Conservatives, he strongly deplored the influence of partyism in politics and always insisted that it had no place in the West. Nevertheless, his disillusionment with Laurier's government during extended negotiations to win provincial status gradually forced him to acknowledge his Conservative allegiance, and he campaigned for that party in the 1904 federal election.

When Laurier was returned to power and provincial status was granted, Haultain was ignored when the new Alberta and Saskatchewan governments were appointed. Subsequently he sat in the Saskatchewan legislature as leader of the opposition Provincial Rights Party from 1905 to 1912, when he retired to the bench as chief justice of the Superior Court of Saskatchewan. Knighted (1916) and named chancellor of University of Saskatchewan and chief justice of the Saskatchewan Court of Appeal (1917), he retired in 1938. STANLEY GORDON

Haultain, Herbert Edward Terrick, mining engineer, educator (b at Brighton, Eng 9 Aug 1869; d at Toronto 19 Sept 1961). A graduate of U of T who acquired practical mining experience in Europe, he returned to Canada in 1905 as professor of mining and engineering at U of T. He remained in that position for more than 30 years. He developed the "Ceremony of the Calling of the Engineer," a private ritual for engineers graduating from Canadian universities, and was instrumental in founding the Technical Service Council, formed for the initial purpose of keeping engineers in Canada. He also designed and built the Superpanner and Infrasizer, instruments used in dressing ore. PHYLLIS ROSE

Haven, Jens, founder of the Moravian mission in LABRADOR (b at Wust, Jutland, Denmark 23 June 1724; d at Herrnhut, Saxony [E Germany] 16 Apr 1796). After 10 years at the Moravian settlement at Herrnhut (1748-58), he was sent to the Inuit Mission in Greenland. In 1764 he went to Labrador, hoping to found a mission for the LABRADOR INUIT. An earlier attempt (1752) had failed. Newfoundland's new governor, Hugh PALLISER, whose jurisdiction included Labrador, supported Haven in the hope that the Moravians could help resolve conflicts between the Inuit and white people. In May 1769, 40 470 ha of land in Labrador were granted to the Moravian Church, and in Aug 1771 Haven and his followers established the first Moravian Mission at NAIN on the northern coast. During Haven's 13 years in Labrador other missions were established at Okak and Hopedale. In 1784 he returned to Herrnhut. A strong-minded man, he believed it was his destiny to work among the Inuit of Labrador, a people he loved. JOHN PARSONS

Reading: John Parsons, *Labrador* (1970).

Ferruginous hawk (*B. regalis*) (*photo by Tim Fitzharris*).

Hawk, common name for several species of diurnal BIRDS OF PREY from widely separate families. These birds are superficially alike, being smaller than EAGLES and having large, keen eyes, hooked bills and sharp, curved talons. True hawks belong to the family Accipitridae, which also includes eagles and Old World vultures and contains over 200 species worldwide. Females of all species are considerably larger than males. Ten species of true hawk breed in Canada. Buteos are the large hawks commonly seen, in spring and summer, soaring over open areas or perched on dead trees or telephone poles. The most common species across southern Canada is the red-tailed hawk (*Buteo jamaicensis*). All 6 Canadian species build their own nests and most nest in trees or on the sides of cliffs. Ferruginous and rough-legged hawks (*B. regalis, B. lagopus,* respectively) have adapted to ground nesting in open, treeless prairie or arctic tundra. Buteos feed largely on rodents and are considered beneficial to humans. Those that breed in Canada normally migrate S in winter, most moving to the southern and central US. Swainson's and broad-winged hawks (*B. swainsoni, B. platypterus*) winter in S America. Of

Hawthorn (*Crataegus*), with flowers and fruit (berries) (*artwork by Claire Tremblay*).

the accipiters (forest hawks), sharp-shinned and Cooper's hawks and northern goshawks (*Accipiter striatus, A. cooperii* and *A. gentilis*) breed across Canada in forested areas. They tend to use different prey species and may be found nesting in close proximity in mixed woodland. Sharp-shinned and Cooper's hawks feed almost exclusively on small birds. Goshawks feed heavily on hares, squirrels and grouse. Although secretive by nature, all 3 species are bold hunters and will protect their nests against all intruders. The marsh hawk or northern harrier (*Circus cyaneus*) breeds across Canada. A slow-flying, open-country hawk, it is most often observed over marshes and meadows hunting for mice and small birds. R.W. FYFE

Hawkesbury, Ont, Town, pop 9710 (1986c), 9877 (1981c), inc 1896, located on the Ottawa R, 100 km NW of Montréal and 95 km E of Ottawa. Founded in 1798, the town was eventually named for Charles Jenkinson, Baron Hawkesbury. Thomas Mears built the first gristmills and sawmills, and the *Union*, the Ottawa R's first steamer. Demand for timber during the Napoleonic Wars created a boom. Timber and pulp-and-paper industries have been supplanted by textiles, synthetic fibres, metal extrusions, steel, glass and plastics. The Grenville Canal on the Québec side of the Ottawa R opposite Hawkesbury is an important link in the river's transportation system. The only interprovincial bridge between Ottawa and Montréal is located at Hawkesbury. Part of Hawkesbury was submerged by a Hydro-Québec dam built 1950-62. K.L. MORRISON

Hawkins, Ronald, "Rompin' Ronnie," rock singer (b at Huntsville, Ark 10 Jan 1935). "The Hawk," a father figure in Canadian rock music, was a rockabilly performer when he first toured Ontario in 1958. He settled in Toronto, despite the international success of such early recordings as "Mary Lou," "40 Days" and the classic "Who Do You Love?" Some of his bands in the 1960s (eg, The BAND, Crowbar) had major careers of their own, as did individually many former Hawkins musicians. He made several comebacks in the 1970s and in 1982 starred on CTV's "Honky Tonk." In 1982 as well he won a Juno Award for country male vocalist of the year. In 1984 he produced an album, *Making It Again*, and made a concert appearance at Expo 86. MARK MILLER

Hawley, Sanford Desmond, jockey (b at Oshawa, Ont 16 Apr 1949). Riding professionally since 1968, Hawley has been one of N America's most successful jockeys. He has won 25% of the races he has entered, the highest winning percentage among N American jockeys; he was Canada's leading jockey in 1969 and won the N American title in 1970, 1972 and 1973. In 1973 he became the first rider to win over 500 races in a single year and, in 1980, won his 4000th career race, the youngest jockey to reach this plateau. Hawley has twice won the LOU MARSH TROPHY, awarded annually to Canada's outstanding athlete. He has also been honoured in the US, winning the prestigious Eclipse Award for his racetrack performances. He rode winners in the QUEEN'S PLATE 4 times. By 1986, the year he was inducted into the Canadian Racing Hall of Fame, he had ridden more than 5000 winners. J. THOMAS WEST

Hawthorn, small, deciduous tree or shrub of genus *Crataegus*, family Rosaceae (rose). Hawthorns are normally armed with strong thorns (modified branches), and have fragrant, insect-pollinated, white, pink or, occasionally, red flowers in showy clusters. The leaves are serrate or lobed and brilliantly coloured in autumn. The red, applelike fruit is fleshy and has 1-5 bony seeds. Most species occur in the north temperate zone. Because of the differing treatment of the many hybrids and asexual clones found in nature, the number of species is variously estimated from 100 to 1100, although the lower numbers appear more realistic. In eastern Canada, hawthorns are very common and are represented by many species; in the West, they are less common. The berries were eaten and used medicinally by Canadian Indians and early settlers, who also made hawthorn wine. Hawthorns are ORNAMENTALS, used in landscaping as trees or in hedges. *See also* PLANTS, NATIVE USES.

Hay River, NWT, Town, pop 2964 (1986c), 2863 (1981c), inc 1963, is located on the S shore of GREAT SLAVE LK at the mouth of the Hay R, 201 air km SW of Yellowknife. The original homeland of the Slavey DENE, Hay River first became settled in the late 1800s with an HBC trading post and Anglican and Catholic missions. The present community dates back to the postwar construction of the MACKENZIE HWY. The community became an important transportation and communications centre. It is the staging point for the shipping industry up the MACKENZIE R and also the centre of the Great Slave Lk commercial fishery. In 1963 a serious flood at the old townsite required the evacuation of the entire population to a safer area upriver. In 1964 the community's economy was stimulated by the completion of a CNR railway link. Today, Hay River remains one of the few NWT communities that is largely dependent on private enterprise. ANNELIES POOL

Hay River Reserve, NWT, IR, pop 180 (1986c), is located on the E bank of the E channel of the Hay R, 201 air km SW of Yellowknife. It is the only Indian reserve in the NWT and was created in 1974 when local DENE residents requested protection of their traditional life-style and lands. In the summer of 1981, forests immediately S were heavily damaged by fire and this affected trapping, a major source of income for local residents. Today, many of those who live on the reserve work in the shipping industry in the nearby town of HAY RIVER. ANNELIES POOL

Hayden, Melissa, stage name of Mildred Herman, ballet dancer and teacher (b at Toronto 25 Apr 1923). During her long performing career she became internationally known as a ballerina of dazzling virtuosity and dramatic intensity. Hayden trained first in Toronto with Boris VOLKOFF before leaving at age 16 for further studies in New York. There she danced with Ballet Theatre (later the American Ballet Theatre) and other companies. In 1950 she joined the New York City Ballet where, except for a return to ABT in the mid-1950s and other brief guest engagements, she danced until her retirement in 1973. Until 1983 Hayden had her own teaching studio in New York and she continues to travel widely to teach and stage Balanchine ballets. MICHAEL CRABB

Hayden, Michael, sculptor (b at Vancouver 15 Jan 1943). Hayden studied at the Ontario College

Michael Hayden, *Arc-en-ciel* (1978), neon lightwork sculpture installed in the vaulted atrium ceiling of Toronto's Yorkdale subway station (*photo by Michel Proulx/Keltia Canada*).

of Art and is a sculptor in light. His work utilizes electronic and computer technology to produce pieces of extraordinary colour and scale to complement the vast spaces of contemporary urban architecture.

One of his pieces, *Arc-en-ciel* (1978), was created for the vaulted atrium ceiling of the Yorkdale (Toronto) subway station, designed by Arthur ERICKSON and Associates. The piece can be viewed from outside the station and the most spectacular perspective is from the air. It is widely recognized as a model of the successful integration of sculpture and architecture. Hayden lives in Los Angeles and has had over 30 solo exhibitions in Canada, the US and Europe. In 1985 *Totem (Homage to Brancusi)* was commissioned for the lobby of the Max Bell Theatre in Calgary.

KARYN ELIZABETH ALLEN

Hayes, Frederick Ronald, biologist, science administrator (b at Parrsboro, NS 29 Apr 1904; d at Halifax 6 Sept 1982). As chairman of the FISHERIES RESEARCH BOARD 1964-69, Hayes guided its expansion and increased links with the universities through grants and research collaboration. His book *The Chaining of Prometheus* (1973) wittily and perceptively explored the subordination of Canadian science to governmental administration. Trained as a zoologist and chemical embryologist at Dalhousie and Liverpool universities (1922-29), he was associate, then full, professor, of zoology at Dalhousie (1930-64), founder and first director of its Institute of Oceanography (1959-64) and vice-president, academic (1963-64). His research using radioisotopes to study lake processes influenced many students. Hayes returned to Dalhousie as Killam research professor in 1969, founding its Institute of Environmental Studies in 1974.

ERIC L. MILLS

Hayes, Kate Simpson, pen name Mary Markwell, writer, journalist (b Katherine Hayes at Dalhousie, NB 1856; d on Vancouver I 15 Jan 1945). Hayes moved to Prince Albert, North-West Territories, in 1879, then after a short-lived marriage settled in 1885 with her 2 children in Regina where she founded a literary and musical society. She wrote for the Regina *Leader*, was territorial legislative librarian, and as Mary Markwell published numerous plays, sketches, short stories, songs and verses. Her *Prairie Pot-pourri* (1895) was the first literary work published in the Territories. Her strong suffrage convictions led her longtime companion and father of 2 of her children, Nicholas Flood DAVIN, to introduce a motion in Parliament (8 May 1895) in favour of women's suffrage. In 1899 she joined the *Manitoba Free Press*, becoming women's editor; she was one of the founders of the Canadian Women's Press Club (1904). In 1906 and after she travelled widely in Britain and Europe encouraging women's immigration to Canada; she was president of the CANADIAN WOMEN'S PRESS CLUB 1906-07 and later women's editor of the *Ottawa Free Press*.

SUSAN JACKEL

Hayes River, 483 km long, rises in Molson Lk (399 km^2) NE of Lk Winnipeg, flows NE to Oxford Lk (401 km^2) and Knee Lk, through the rock and bush of the Canadian Shield, across the clay flats of the Hudson Bay Lowlands and into the bay at YORK FACTORY. It has a DRAINAGE BASIN of 108 000 km^2 and a mean discharge of 694 m^3/s. Its main tributaries, the Fox and Gods rivers, drain numerous lakes N and S of its course. The river, named for Sir James Hayes, a charter member of the HBC, was the chief FUR-TRADE route between Lk Winnipeg and York Factory for nearly 200 years. Though swift and rough in places, it was easier to travel than the turbulent Nelson, which the traders joined, via the shallow Echimamish R, at Cross Lk.

JAMES MARSH

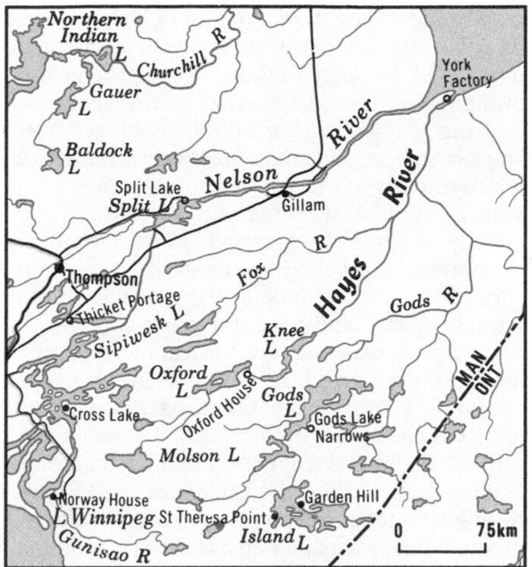

Haynes, Douglas Hector, abstract painter, teacher (b at Regina 1 Jan 1936). He graduated from the art dept of the Provincial Institute of Technology and Art (now Alberta Coll of Art) in 1958, studied at the Royal Academy of Fine Arts, The Hague (1960-61), and travelled widely throughout Europe (1967-68). He first became known for his painted constructions done on burlap, string and other materials (1963-69). In 1970 he visited New York C, renewed an interest in the work of A. Gottlieb and R. Motherwell and shifted his attention to painting. Around 1977, stimulated by Jack BUSH, his work became more personal and accomplished. Elected a member of the Royal Canadian Academy in 1974, Haynes was chairman of the dept of art and design at U of A (1976-80). An exhibition of his work, entitled Cubism Revisited, was held in 1984.

KEN CARPENTER

Hays, Charles Melville, railway president (b at Rock I, Ill 16 May 1856; d in the N Atlantic 15 Apr 1912). At 17 Hays entered the passenger department of the Atlantic & Pacific Ry at St Louis, Mo. His railway career advanced rapidly, and in 1889 he became general manager of the Wabash, St Louis and Pacific Railroad. He came to Canada in 1896 as general manager of the GRAND TRUNK RY, becoming president in 1909. The GRAND TRUNK PACIFIC RY, of which he became president in 1905, was largely his creation. Under his directorship the GTR suffered intense labour strife, and one of Wilfrid Laurier's ministers described Hays as heartless, cruel and tyrannical. He went down in the TITANIC.

ERIC J. HOLMGREN

Hays, Harry William, farmer, rancher, businessman, politician (b at Carstairs, Alta 25 Dec 1909; d at Ottawa 4 May 1982). He was mayor of Calgary 1959-63, federal minister of agriculture 1963-65 and senator 1966-82. He was a director of numerous companies and president and life member of many agricultural organizations. A master Holstein breeder, he was originator of the Hays Converter breed of beef cattle, the first to be recognized for registry. In a lifetime devoted to agriculture, Hays can best be described as an innovator. He instituted the export of cattle by air. As federal minister of agriculture (1963-65) he instituted the Veterinary College at Saskatoon and the Canadian Dairy Commission, expanded the crop insurance system, a national farm accounting system, established new fairs and exhibition classifications, and the importation of exotic breeds of cattle, the Showcase Herds. As senator, he was co-chairman of the Special Joint Committee of the Senate and of the House of Commons on the Constitution.

S.B. WILLIAMS

Hazardous Wastes Waste may be defined as any substance for which the generator or owner has no further use. Hazardous wastes are waste substances whose disposal in the environment could potentially pose hazards to human health, jeopardize natural or agricultural resources, or interfere with other amenities. Disposal of hazardous wastes should be carried out in such a manner that the associated threats to people, resources and amenities are acceptable and minimal.

Terrestrial Environment In the 19th century it was realized that WASTE DISPOSAL must take place in a well-regulated and safe manner, if only to control the spread of disease. The ever-increasing variety of consumer goods generates wastes that are becoming increasingly hazardous. It has been estimated that a million people produce 50 000 to 250 000 t of hazardous wastes each year. Standard sanitary landfills and sewage treatment facilities are inadequate for the disposal of many hazardous wastes, particularly those derived from industrial practices. The dumping of untreated hazardous chemicals can have far-reaching effects. The discharge of inadequately treated liquid waste to rivers and streams has created problems for communities downstream, and landfill dumps of waste chemicals have created significant health hazards to people living in their vicinity. Buried chemicals can produce vapours which can escape to the atmosphere, while liquids, if inadequately contained, can seep into the earth, enter GROUNDWATER and affect drinking water supplies far from the dumpsite. Furthermore, a variety of products and degradation products remain in the environment to enter the hydrologic cycle and be transported through it.

The insidious nature of the effects of low levels of some chemicals in the environment makes it difficult to set safe levels of human exposure. The effects of carcinogenic and mutagenic chemicals may not show up for many years, and often the health defects that do occur cannot be related to a specific cause. However, many hazardous wastes can be treated to render them relatively harmless to humans or to the environment. Such treatments include recycling, physical or chemical reactions, incineration (high-temperature degradation), biological degradation, solidification, deep emplacement and long-term recoverable storage. Recycling, by far the preferred method for recoverable chemicals (eg, waste oil, solvents), provides viable industries in many countries, including Canada. Some chemicals can be treated chemically to form stable, nontoxic materials, eg, some acids can be neutralized to less hazardous brine or precipitated as insoluble salts which can be landfilled. Organic chemical wastes can be incinerated in properly designed furnaces equipped with scrubbers so that only carbon dioxide and water vapour reach the air in appreciable quantities. Thus, even persistent chemicals such as polychlorinated biphenyls (*see* PCBs) can be safely destroyed in well-regulated installations if the incineration time and temperature are adequate for total decomposition and if adequate checks are made on the formation and emission of recombinant products. Other hazardous chemicals normally emitted from chimneys (eg, flyash, other fine particles, acids and alkalis) can be electrostatically precipitated or scrubbed out. Many industries treat biodegradable liquid wastes with bacteria before discharge to surface waters. Heavy metal wastes (eg, electroplating liquors) can be incorporated into a concretelike mass which resists leaching from burial sites. In some areas, waste liquids (eg, brine) can be ejected into permeable underground formations overlain by impermeable rock (deep-well injection). There is a distinct worldwide shortage of proper hazardous waste treatment facilities. In Canada, a milestone was reached 11 Sept 1987 when N America's first comprehensive, integrated hazardous waste treatment facility was opened near Swan Hills, Alta, with the full support of the local people. It is a state-of-the-art facility, capable of treating and safely disposing of all hazardous waste produced in the province. Other provinces are attempting to set up additional facilities to handle the estimated 3.3 million t of hazardous waste generated in Canada each year.

No practical detoxification methods are yet available for some kinds of hazardous wastes such as radioactive material. However, low-level radioactive wastes can often be disposed of safely in shallow trenches on land or can be dumped in the ocean. High-level radioactive wastes such as spent fuel rods are not amenable to such disposal and can either be stored temporarily for future treatment (eg, reprocessing for the recovery of fissionable plutonium) or placed in permanent underground repositories, as is likely to be the case for spent nuclear fuel from Canadian reactors. Sites for such repositories must be selected with the utmost care, taking into account all potential pathways of leakage which might result in human exposure and all potential disturbances to sites which might threaten their integrity, such as tectonic activity.

Although most wastes can be treated for safe disposal, many are not currently so treated (because of short-term economic considerations) where regulatory controls are not adequately restrictive. The costs of proper waste treatment are seldom included in the costs of production unless regulatory constraints are applied. However, unless such restrictions are applied on an international basis, countries introducing more stringent environmental protection regulations will be placed at an economic disadvantage in export markets. Even where legislation to eliminate unsafe practices exists, illegal disposal can still remain a problem, and increased attention to the enforcement of regulations is essential.

A more comprehensive approach to waste disposal needs to be engendered with the purpose of ensuring that there are net benefits to investment in a particular industry, that limits to human exposure to hazardous materials are set and adhered to, and that the hazards to human health and the environment are minimized. The first of these requires that the benefits of the potential production and use of some new substance are assessed against the detriments (eg, the risks to human health and the risk of environmental damage) in order to determine that there is an overall net benefit to be gained from investment in the industry. Second, safe limits to the exposure of humans to the products and wastes disseminated from the industry need to be established and regulatory action adopted to ensure that releases of hazardous materials to the environment do not violate these limits irrespective of the route of exposure. Finally, all alternative options for the production, transport, dissemination and disposal of hazardous products and wastes should be evaluated to ensure the selection of those that minimize the exposures (below the dose limits) to the extent justified by technical, economic and sociopolitical conditions. In the field of radiation protection these 3 principles are referred to respectively as justification, compliance with dose limits and optimization.

Marine Environment The oceans have long been used, both deliberately and accidentally, for the disposal of human and industrial wastes. Potentially deleterious effects of hazardous wastes disposed of into the marine environment include hazards to human health (eg, exposure of bathers to pathogens), hindrance with legitimate uses of the sea (eg, fishing), degradation of the quality of sea water, making it less suitable for recreation, desalination or other uses, and less tangible reductions in the aesthetic attractiveness of the ocean environment. The main types of deliberate waste disposal into the ocean include direct discharge from land through outfalls or other pipelines, dumping from ships and other marine platforms, and incineration on, or liquid discharges from, ships or marine and coastal platforms. Waste materials discharged on land or into freshwater reservoirs (rivers and lakes) may also reach the sea, indirectly through land runoff. Wastes routinely discharged by pipeline or outfall into the coastal zone in Canada include sewage, metal refining wastes, animal and foodstuff processing wastes, and pulp and paper wastes. Nuclear fuel reprocessing wastes can be added to the list in some other countries. In Canada and other coastal states, heat is also discharged to the sea in cooling water from power utilities and from other industrial facilities. Wastes dumped into the Canadian coastal environment predominantly comprise sediments dredged from nearshore areas for navigation purposes, though agricultural and industrial wastes are also dumped occasionally. Some countries have used (or propose to use) incineration at sea for the disposal of persistent organic substances such as PCBs. Ships and other offshore platforms discharge bilge wastes, tank washings, drilling muds, ballast and oily wastes, sometimes illegally.

Another source of waste materials found in the ocean is the atmosphere. Volatile substances, or substances with significant vapour pressures, derived from terrestrial activities can enter the atmosphere and be subjected to long-distance transport, which results in ubiquitous atmospheric fallout of contaminants. This is analogous to the global dissemination of radioactive fallout following nuclear weapons explosions in the atmosphere in the 1950s and 1960s.

Deliberate dumping of material into the marine environment is generally governed by the 1972 International Convention for the Prevention of Marine Pollution by Dumping of Wastes and Other Matter, commonly referred to as the London Dumping Convention. The convention specifies a "black list" of substances (eg, organohalogen, mercury and cadmium compounds, persistent plastics, oils and high-level radioactive wastes) which may not be dumped into the marine environment except as trace quantities in other materials. A further "grey list" defines potentially hazardous substances (eg, arsenic, lead, copper and zinc compounds, cyanides, fluorides and pesticides not included in the black list) which require special precautions in evaluating their suitability for dumping and in the procedures used for dumping. The convention also specifies the procedures and criteria by which national authorities may determine the suitability of all other substances for sea disposal and the locations and methods of dumping. Contracting parties to the convention (signatory nation states) are required to establish and administer appropriate national legislation adhering to its provisions. In Canada, this legislation is the Ocean Dumping Control Act, and permits for ocean dumping are issued under its provisions.

There has been a major shift in global concerns regarding contamination of the ocean, ranging from the effects of large oil-tanker spills, and more insidious releases of oil, to the disposal of low-level radioactive wastes in the ocean through deliberate dumping. Since WWII a number of countries, including the US and several western European nations, have carried out such dumping as a means of disposing of radioactive wastes. However, in 1983 the London Dumping Convention agreed on a moratorium on radioactive waste dumping. Before then, the major continuing disposal of this type was carried out in the eastern N Atlantic by 4 European countries under the auspices of the Nuclear Energy Agency of OECD. In Canada the only deliberate introduction of radioactive material into the ocean has been through routine discharges from the Point Lepreau Nuclear Generating Station (these being extremely small and well regulated within safe limits) and through the use of small quantities of single radioisotopes for sediment transport investigations in coastal areas.

Indirect (ie, by way of freshwater discharges) and direct releases of chemical wastes to coastal waters have resulted in several instances of metallic and organic chemical contamination of nearshore areas, particularly within embayments that have restricted water exchange with offshore areas. Various Canadian East Coast, West Coast and Arctic bays and fjords have been affected in this way. Large-scale contamination is difficult to detect because of the great assimilative capacity of the ocean itself and because of large marginal sea areas (eg, the Gulf of ST LAWRENCE; Bay of FUNDY.) Land runoff is, however, by far the largest source of anthropogenically mobilized (ie, made or moved by humans) material entering the ocean. The cumulative effects of these discharges and of the atmospheric precipitation of chemicals are evident in the oceanic incidence and distribution of some heavy metals, radionuclides and artificial organic compounds such as PCBs.

Until very recently, land discharges into the ocean were not governed by international agreement in the same way as ocean dumping. The major regional convention covering discharges of waste materials from land is the Paris Convention, to which most western European countries are signatories. Canadian legislation governing discharges of material from land includes the Fisheries Act, the Environmental Contaminants Act, the Navigable Waters Protection Act and the Arctic Waters Pollution Prevention Act (*see* ENVIRONMENTAL LAW). In 1985 a major step was taken in formulating international agreement on the marine pollution prevention from land-based discharges with the formulation, under the aegis of the United Nations Environment Programme, of an Agreement for the Protection of the Marine Environment Against Pollution from Land-Based Sources. This agreement is commonly referred to as the Montréal Guidelines, after the city in which it was finalized. Adherence to it will probably require the formulation of new national legislation to regulate land discharges in Canada.

Various views are held on the use of the ocean as a receptacle for wastes. Some regard the ocean as "waste space" that could be put to better use on a waste-receiving environment because its capacity to assimilate wastes, without deleterious effects, is very large. Others feel strongly that the ocean environment should be preserved in as pristine a state as possible, since any major disturbance of the vast and complex oceanic ecosystem will be very difficult to reverse. J.M. BEWERS

Hazelton, BC, Village, pop 436 (1986c), 393 (1981c), inc 1956, is situated at the confluence of the Skeena and Bulkley rivers. The townsite was laid out by Edgar DEWDNEY in 1871 next to the Gitksan village of Gitanmaax. The town flourished in the early years of the 20th century, but went into decline after the completion of the Grand Trunk Pacific Ry in 1914, being on the opposite side of the river from the tracks. Recently Hazelton has regained some of its importance as a regional centre for many small communities nearby. The reconstructed native village of KSAN is a major tourist attraction.The steelhead and salmon fishing in the region is world renowned.
MAUREEN CASSIDY

Hazen, Sir John Douglas, lawyer, politician, judge (b at Oromocto, NB 5 June 1860; d at Saint John 27 Dec 1937). A Fredericton alderman,

1885-88, he was elected mayor in 1888 and MP for Saint John in 1891. Defeated in 1896 when LAURIER came to power, he was elected MLA for Sunbury in 1899 and named leader of the Opposition. Under his leadership the modern Conservative Party emerged as an effective political force in NB, winning power in 1908 and leading battles against political corruption and federal efforts to reduce Maritime parliamentary representation. In 1911 he entered PM BORDEN'S Cabinet as minister of marine and fisheries, minister of naval affairs and MP for Saint John. A member of the Imperial War Cabinet and the International Fisheries Commission, Hazen was appointed chief justice of NB in 1917. DELLA M.M. STANLEY

Head, Sir Edmund Walker, 8th Baronet, scholar, public servant, lieutenant-governor of NB 1848-54, governor general of British N America 1854-61, governor of the HUDSON'S BAY CO 1863-68 (b at Wiarton Place, near Maidstone, Eng 16 Feb 1805; d at London, Eng 28 Jan 1868). He was educated at Oxford, where he took first-class honours in classics at Oriel College and was elected a fellow of Merton. An author, editor and translator, Head wrote articles on law, government, language and philology as well as ballads and poems. He served on the Poor Law commission 1836-47 and was appointed lieutenant-governor of NB in 1848. An able administrator, Head helped to prepare NB for full RESPONSIBLE GOVERNMENT. His interest in defence, railways and a larger British N American federation made him a logical choice for the post of governor general of BNA in 1854. Head's refusal to grant George BROWN dissolution of the House during the DOUBLE SHUFFLE of 1858 caused considerable controversy. As the visitor to King's College (UNB) and McGill, Head contributed to their mid-century reorganization. CARMAN MILLER

Reading: D.G.G. Kerr, *Sir Edmund Head* (1954).

Portrait of Sir Edmund Head (1805-68), gov gen of BNA, by Théophile Hamel (*courtesy House of Commons, Speaker's Office/National Archives of Canada/C-119676*).

Head, Sir Francis Bond, soldier, author, colonial administrator (b at Higham, Eng 1 Jan 1793; d at Croydon, Eng 20 July 1875). Descended from the minor gentry, Head served in the Royal Engineers. Retiring as a major (1825), he became a mining supervisor in S America and earned the nickname "Galloping Head" for his rides across the Andes. The author of several popular travel books, he was appointed an assistant Poor Law commissioner in 1834 and then lieutenant-governor of Upper Canada in 1835. When he arrived at Toronto in Jan 1836, he was welcomed by the Reformers and appointed several moderate Reformers – including Robert BALDWIN – to the Executive Council, but he rarely consulted the councillors, who resigned in a few months. The Reform-dominated Assembly censured him and he dissolved the House and won an overwhelming victory at the polls in 1836 by using the loyalty cry, although his widespread support among moderates quickly dissipated when he engaged in a bitter vendetta against all Reformers. Head cannot be held primarily responsible for the REBELLION OF 1837 in Upper Canada but his unprecedented interference in the election and his uncompromising hostility to the Reformers encouraged extremists, as did his decision to denude the colony of British troops. His excesses led to his recall early in 1838 and he never held office again. PHILLIP A. BUCKNER

Head, Ivan Leigh, public servant (b at Calgary 28 July 1930). A law graduate of U of A, Head taught law there 1963-67 after stints in private practice and the Dept of External Affairs. In 1967 he served as a constitutional adviser to P.E. TRUDEAU, staying on as special assistant after Trudeau became PM the next year. Combative, strong-willed and idealistic, Head quickly became one of the PM's inner circle, and his key external affairs functionary. Head was a strong force behind Trudeau's call for a "north-south dialogue" to aid developing countries, and since 1978 he has been president and governor of the INTERNATIONAL DEVELOPMENT RESEARCH CENTRE. NORMAN HILLMER

Head-Smashed-In Buffalo Jump, archaeological site located on the southern end of the Porcupine Hills in SW Alberta. Beginning nearly 6000 years ago and continuing until as recently as 150 years ago, native people of the Northwest Plains used Head-Smashed-In as one of the many ingenious traps designed to kill large numbers of buffalo. They used skillful decoy techniques to round up herds of buffalo and stampeded them across the Porcupine Hills and over a 10 m-high cliff. Hunters waiting below the cliff killed and butchered the animals, obtaining great quantities of meat, hide and bone. Deposits of butchered bone and stone tools extend to a depth of over 11 m at the base of the cliff. Head-Smashed-In has been designated an Alberta Historical Resource Site, and is on the prestigious list of UNESCO WORLD HERITAGE SITES. An interpretive centre was officially opened by their Royal Highnesses the Duke and Duchess of York on 23 July 1987. *See also* ARCHAEOLOGY; BUFFALO HUNT; PREHISTORY. JACK BRINK

Heagerty, John Joseph, physician, public-health official, historian (b at Montréal 26 Dec 1879; d at Ottawa 7 Feb 1946). Entering federal service as a bacteriologist in 1911, Heagerty joined the new Dept of Health in 1919 and became director of public-health services in 1938. He was noted for his work in Canada's campaign against venereal disease in the 1920s and his proposals for national health insurance in 1943. He also broadcast lectures on Canadian medical history and wrote the 2-vol *Four Centuries of Medical History in Canada* (1928) and *The Romance of Medicine in Canada* (1940). JANICE DICKIN MCGINNIS

Health Policy Canada's national health-insurance program (also called medicare) is designed to ensure that every resident of Canada receives medical care and hospital treatment, the cost of which is paid through general taxes or through compulsory health-insurance premiums. Medicare developed in 2 stages. The first was the Hospital Insurance and Diagnostic Act of 1957, which gave the Canadian government authority to enter into an agreement with the provinces to establish a comprehensive, universal plan covering acute hospital care and laboratory and radiology diagnostic services. Nine years later, the Medical Care Act of 1966 extended health insurance to cover doctors' services. While the basic principles of medicare are determined by federal legislation, responsibility for health under the Constitution falls under provincial jurisdiction. Therefore, there are certain variations in the plan from province to province. However, to be eligible for federal cost sharing, the provinces must meet, in their health policies, criteria of accessibility, universality, comprehensiveness, portability and administration.

Until 1977, federal contributions to acute hospital care and doctors' services matched (approximately), dollar for dollar, provincial spending. At that time, unhappy that its share of health costs was in effect under provincial control, the federal government altered the arrangement by passing the Federal-Provincial Fiscal Arrangements and Established Programs Financing Act. Instead of 50-50 cost sharing, the federal government transferred to the provinces a lump sum based on a 3-year moving average of the Gross National Product (GNP) and per capita cash payment.

The new arrangement allowed the provinces more flexibility, in that they were not limited to using federal funds only for insured hospital and medical services; federal money could now be applied to programs such as extended health care in nursing homes or drug-benefit plans not included in medicare. At this time, however, hospital costs were rising at a rate far exceeding general inflation, leaving the provinces with a heavier share of the health-cost burden. Matters worsened when, beginning in 1982, the federal government further restricted TRANSFER PAYMENTS.

History of Health Policy Prior to Confederation in 1867, there was little organized health care. Local communities had authority to set up their own health boards, and some did so in response to EPIDEMICS such as the cholera outbreak of 1832. The formal legislation authorizing such boards was passed by the Parliament of Upper Canada in 1834, but it was not until 50 years later that the PUBLIC HEALTH Act compelled local governments to set up health boards and impose sanitary regulations. At meetings of the CANADIAN MEDICAL ASSOCIATION, an organization created the same year as Confederation, doctors called for public-health measures, safe water and the reporting of contagious diseases. Not until 1882 did Ontario legislation establish a provincial board of health. Three years later, with a smallpox epidemic raging in Québec, Ontario put public-health doctors on trains crossing the border into Ontario to inspect passengers; the doctors were empowered to arrest anybody who refused to be vaccinated.

Dental Care Until the late 1800s there was a scarcity of dentists in Canada. Tooth decay among children was so prevalent that one Toronto dentist estimated that 50% of the schoolchildren at the turn of the century had rotten teeth. Today, provincial health-insurance plans provide some dental coverage, although such coverage varies from province to province, being generally limited to dental care in hospitals. Some provinces, eg, Nova Scotia and Newfoundland, cover dental care for children, while Alberta provides coverage for citizens over 65. PEI has launched mobile child DENTISTRY units staffed by salaried dentists. A study conducted in 1976 estimated that 18% of the population of Canada (ranging from a low of 3% in the Maritime provinces to 43% in BC) had some form of dental care provided through private insurers.

Mental Health Under the CONSTITUTION ACT, 1867, the provinces were made responsible for asylums for the mentally ill (*see* MENTAL HEALTH). At that time, almost everywhere in the world the insane were kept at home or brutally treated. In Toronto, when a new and better jail was built in 1800, the old jail became an asylum. The Canadian National Committee for Mental Hygiene was founded in 1918, largely due to the efforts of Dr Clarence M. HINCKS, who with the help of leading Canadians raised funds for a survey of conditions in asylums across Canada. These institutions were generally disgraceful, dirty and overcrowded. The committee brought this to the attention of the public, and the provinces soon began to spend more money on institutions for the mentally ill. By the 1950s, discoveries of drugs that could help control the behaviour of mental patients led to a new trend in care. Many patients from psychiatric hospitals were returned to the community. Prior to medicare, the only treatment available to the less affluent was in provincially owned psychiatric hospitals. Although the psychiatric care provided in general hospitals has greatly improved, the gaps in the continuum of care for the mentally ill are only beginning to be closed.

Health Insurance The idea of health insurance had emerged in Germany in the late 1880s and spread throughout Europe, but SOCIAL SECURITY programs were scarcely a priority in infant Canada. By WWI, Saskatchewan had created a plan under which municipalities could tax the population to build hospitals, hire doctors and pay for hospital care. In 1919 the federal Liberal Party made a health plan a plank in its election campaign, but nothing came of it. During the Great Depression, the push for government assistance in meeting health-care costs gained momentum. People could not pay doctors' bills; indigents flooded the hospitals; municipalities, especially those on the Prairies, were bankrupt.

Prior to the enactment of a national hospital-insurance scheme, BC and Saskatchewan operated public, universal hospital-insurance plans. Alberta and Newfoundland had plans that provided partial coverage. By 1956, 50% of Canadians were covered by voluntary private or nonprofit prepayment plans, but public pressure for a nationwide program to protect people from catastrophic health-care costs was growing. This led to a federal government offer to share, on a grant-in-aid basis, the costs of a Canada-wide plan, on condition that the majority of provinces take part and a majority of the population be covered. By mid-1957, 8 provinces indicated that they would join in such a proposal. By 1961 all provinces had hospital plans in operation and 99% of the population was covered. This included coverage for all standard-ward hospital care.

Medical-services insurance was born, with considerable difficulty, in Saskatchewan in 1962. The Saskatchewan medical profession fiercely opposed the intentions of T.C. DOUGLAS's provincial government to require doctors to collect their fees solely from the government plan. On July 1, 90% of the doctors closed their offices in protest (*see* SASKATCHEWAN DOCTORS' STRIKE).The doctors won the right to bill patients if they so chose and to charge more than would be reimbursed to the patients under the provincial plan.

A year before the Saskatchewan battle, PM John Diefenbaker had appointed Justice Emmett HALL chairman of a royal commission on health services. In a 2-vol report (1964-65), Hall recommended medicare for all of Canada. In 1980 he was again asked to review the system, at which time he claimed it was, despite its problems, "by world standards one of the very best health services today." Following the 1964 report, PM Lester Pearson promised that Canada would have a federal medicare program by 1967, and the necessary legislation was passed before the close of 1966. Not all provinces were eager to join the plan. A majority of Canadians were already insured under a variety of private or nonprofit plans, including a major one, Physicians Services Incorporated (PSI), run by doctors in Ontario. Nevertheless, by 1972 all the provinces and the territories had joined in.

Contrary to a widely held belief that doctors oppose medicare, the plan is supported by the Canadian Medical Assn. Indeed the association itself proposed a national insurance plan in the 1940s. However, within the limits established by the federal Acts, each province has its own version of the plan. Some, such as BC and Ontario, pay to a limited extent for chiropractic services, optometry and physiotherapy, whereas Nova Scotia and Newfoundland do not. Saskatchewan and Manitoba pay for their plans from general revenues, whereas Alberta and Ontario charge insurance premiums for those who can pay. Some provinces also cover prescription-drug costs for senior citizens and social-assistance recipients.

Nevertheless, implementation of medicare by the provinces led to considerable tension between the provincial governments and provincial medical associations. Doctors feared, and still do, that medicare would become "state medicine," with governments the sole paymaster and doctors virtually civil servants. In 1986 the Ontario Medical Assn opposed legislation (Bill 94) banning extra-billing by staging a 25-day strike, beginning June 12. Support for the strike action was not 100% within the medical profession itself and was almost nonexistent in the general population, and the doctors lost. The association called an end to the strike on July 6. With extra-billing ended, Ontario recovered $106 million in federal funds, an amount equal to the sum doctors had billed patients directly in the preceding 2 years. The Ontario strike was the only major disruption of medical services in Canada since the Saskatchewan strike 24 years earlier, although medical specialists in Québec did withdraw their services for a short time when Québec implemented its plan in 1970. The Québec plan is unique in that under it patients are not entitled to be reimbursed if they see doctors who bill patients directly. Thus, virtually all Québec doctors bill the plan and there is no extra billing. In Aug 1986 Alberta reached an agreement with its medical association to end extra-billing in that province, as did doctors in New Brunswick, without strikes.

Among Canadian doctors fears of state medicine escalated in the wake of the Hall Commission's 1980 report. The report cautioned that extra charges to patients (by 1984 Canadians were paying $70 million to physicians who extra billed) constituted a barrier to accessibility to medical care that was contrary to the principle and spirit of medicare and that charges by doctors or hospitals would lead to a 2-tier health system, with different standards of care for those who could pay and those who could not.

Conflict among the various protagonists – the federal government, the provinces and the Canadian Medical Association (which represents the majority of Canada's 55 000 doctors) – was inevitable. The federal government claims that it contributes more than 50% ($12.2 billion) of medicare's costs by block grants to provinces and has sought to abolish extra charges to patients for insured services. In 1983 it unveiled provisions designed to curb barriers to access and to eliminate extra billing. It requires that 100% of residents be entitled to insured health services, compared with 95% in previous legislation. The Canada Health Act provides for a reduction of the federal contribution to any province that does permit such patient charges by an amount equal, dollar for dollar, to the amount patients paid. The allied provincial and territorial health ministers deny that extra charges threaten medicare, claiming that the extra revenue is needed to supplement health funds in the face of rising costs and shrinking federal cost sharing. Each province allots roughly 33% of its budget to health.

The Canadian Medical Association claims that medicare is underfunded and that this has resulted in overcrowded hospitals, outdated equipment and waiting lists of patients requiring nonurgent surgery. The CMA estimated that 150 000 patients were on waiting lists in mid-1983 and the number has continued to increase. However, by 1986-87 there was a trend toward providing in the community and in patients' own homes medical care previously obtained in the hospital. New Brunswick, eg, pioneered a "hospital without walls" program. Treatments that once required patients be admitted to hospitals were provided in day-surgery units or out-patient clinics, reducing the need for more hospital beds.

Canada's medicare system compares well with health systems elsewhere in the world. Health-insurance administration costs in Canada were between 5% and 10% of expenditures, compared with over 10% in the US. MARILYN DUNLOP

Heaps, Abraham Albert, labour politician (b at Leeds, Eng 24 Dec 1885; d at Bournemouth, Eng 4 Apr 1954). An impoverished English Jew who immigrated to Canada 1911, Heaps, an upholsterer, became a distinguished parliamentarian as member for Winnipeg N 1925-40. He first gained prominence in Winnipeg as a self-taught statistician for the local Trades and Labor Council, a labour alderman and a leader of the WINNIPEG GENERAL STRIKE. Arrested and charged with seditious conspiracy in June 1919, he cleared himself after a 10-month ordeal in jail and court proceedings. Though an independent Labour (later CCF) MP and a class-conscious socialist, Heaps developed personal and political relationships with PMs Mackenzie KING and R.B. BENNETT. His wit and deep humanism earned him few real enemies, but they included Arthur MEIGHEN, whose prime ministership in 1926 Heaps gladly helped bring to an abrupt end, and Tim BUCK, who tried to wrest away his north-end seat (where there was substantial communist support) in the federal election of 1935. Heaps's tireless efforts as the most credible economic critic in the Commons during the 1920s and 1930s contributed to the passage of vital though limited social legislation by Liberal and Conservative governments. His most keenly felt failures were his unheeded warnings in the 1930s about the dangers of fascism and his desperate lobbying on behalf of anti-Nazi refugees. Ironically, spurious charges of pacifism and disloyalty played the key role in the defeat that ended his political career in the 1940 election. Heaps retired to private life in Montréal and died while on a visit to England. ALLEN SEAGER

Hear Us O Lord from Heaven Thy Dwelling Place, by Malcolm LOWRY (1961), and published posthumously, won the 1961 Gov Gen's Award. It is a collection of 7 interrelated stories and novellas, forming a shared thematic structure and unity of movement. Set in British Columbia, the stories feature 5 protagonists with different names and nationalities, but these characters are primarily aspects of one personality, a man who is undergoing a journey of self-discovery. These central characters are estranged from nature, tyrannized by the past, concerned about the ugly encroachment of civilization, and occasionally misanthropic. However, the final story becomes a lyrical affirmation of the joy of living, as the narrator achieves harmony and balance through his acceptance of the world around him. DONNA COATES

Heard, Robert Donald Hoskin, chemist, biochemist (b at St Thomas, Ont 13 Feb 1908; d at Montréal 8 Sept 1957). Well known for research on the biochemistry of steroid hormones, Heard was largely responsible for the 1944 choice of a Canadian site for the annual prestigious Laurentian Hormone Conference. He was a BA and MA (1930) of U of T and as an 1851 Exhibition Scholar received his PhD from U of Manchester (1932). After a year at Oxford, he returned to U of T as a Banting Research Foundation grantee. His university appointments in biochemistry, at Dalhousie in 1937 and McGill in 1942, enabled him to continue his outstanding teaching and research career until his early death. Author of many scientific papers with his students and collaborators, Heard was noted for developing methods for labelling steroid hormones with radioactivity and for using these "tracers" to reveal the pathways of formation and interconversion of ovarian and adrenal hormones. J.L. WEBB

Hearn, Richard Lankaster, civil engineer, administrator, nuclear power pioneer (b at Toronto 18 May 1890; d there 24 May 1987). On graduating from U of T in civil engineering (1913), he was one of the earliest engineers to join the staff of the fledgling ONTARIO HYDRO, becoming assistant engineer of construction in 1918. From 1921 to 1930 he gained further experience as assistant chief engineer of the Washington Water Power Co, Spokane, but he returned to Canada to join Dr H.G. Acres as chief engineer of his newly formed consultancy. From 1934 to 1942 he carried out notable works as chief engineer of the Dominion Construction Co. Returning to Ontario Hydro in 1942, he was almost immediately loaned to be chief engineer for the building of the Polymer synthetic rubber plant at Sarnia, Ont. In operation in less than 12 months, this was one of Canada's greatest construction achievements. Hearn's work with Ontario Hydro continued until his retirement in 1956, successively as chief engineer (1945), general manager and chief engineer (1947) and chairman (1955). He thus guided Ontario Hydro through its most dramatic expansion, directed the complex conversion of its whole system to 60 cycles and fostered its first venture into the development of nuclear power.

ROBERT F. LEGGET

Hearne, Samuel, explorer, fur trader (b at London, Eng 1745; d there Nov 1792). He joined the HBC in 1766 and was chosen to search for a western passage, by river or sea, across the Barren Lands. His first 2 attempts ended ingloriously, as he was bullied, robbed and deserted by his Indian guides. He left PRINCE OF WALES'S FT again, 7 Dec 1770, with MATONABBEE, a skilful leader of great prestige among the Chipewyan. They walked across trackless wastes, cold, wet and hungry, patiently following the seasonal migrations of the caribou. They travelled W, likely to Alcantara Lk, and then N to the COPPERMINE R. Hearne followed the shallow river to the Arctic Ocean, realizing that it was useless as a trade route. Furthermore, an intensive search yielded only a single lump of copper. Hearne earned the contempt of his companions when he refused to join them in the massacre of a helpless party of Inuit, the traditional enemies of the Chipewyan, at a place he called Bloody Falls. The exhausted Hearne followed his guides as they hurried S, impatient to meet their wives. They crossed GREAT SLAVE LK Dec 24, and Hearne suffered from the extreme cold, losing his toenails to frostbite. Wintering in the forest, where they could hunt and build canoes, Matonabbee's band brought Hearne to base 30 June 1772.

Hearne admitted that his expedition brought no material advantage to the HBC. He tried to

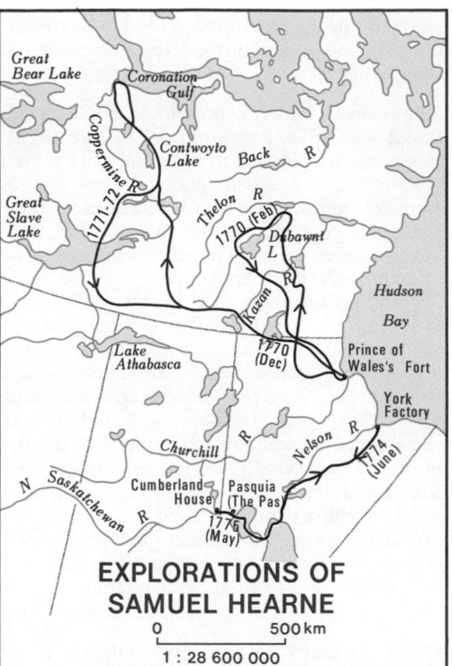

meet competition from Canadian pedlars by building the HBC's first inland post. He was taken up the Grass R to Cranberry Portage, across Lk Athapapusko, down Goose R to Goose Lk, and finally to the Saskatchewan where he began CUMBERLAND HOUSE in 1774. In 1776, he was appointed chief at Prince of Wales's Ft, which he surrendered to the French in 1782. He retired 1787, criticized for his timidity and in failing health, and spent the last few years of his life writing and speaking about his remarkable adventure. The literary artistry of *A Journey from Prince of Wales's Fort in Hudson's Bay to the Northern Ocean*, published 3 years after Hearne's death, secured his fame in letters as well as exploration. He left a dramatic description of his own sufferings and a vivid portrait of Matonabbee and his resourceful people. JAMES MARSH

Hearst, Ont, Town, Cochrane Dist, pop 5559 (1986c), 5535 (1981c), inc 1922, is situated in NE Ontario on the Mattawishkwia R, 318 km NW of Timmins at the western extremity of the Great Clay Belt. Now based on agriculture, lumbering, and pulp and paper, Hearst owed its founding to the construction of the NATIONAL TRANSCONTINENTAL (later Canadian National) Railway, completed 1913. First called Grant, its name was changed to honour Sir William HEARST, the only premier from northern Ontario in the province's history, who promoted the community by establishing an experimental farm there in 1917. Because a significant percentage of its population was drawn from Québec, in 1939 the town was designated the seat of the Roman Catholic bishopric of Hearst. In 1953 Hearst became the centre of French-language higher education in the area with the establishment of the Collège de Hearst, which since 1963 has been an affiliate of Laurentian U at Sudbury. MATT BRAY

Hearst, Sir William Howard, lawyer, politician, premier of Ontario (b in Arran Twp, Canada W 15 Feb 1864; d at Toronto 29 Sept 1941). A lawyer in Sault Ste Marie, he was elected a Conservative MPP in 1908. A leading spokesman for northern Ontario, he entered the Cabinet of Sir James P. WHITNEY as minister of lands, forests and mines in 1911. He played an important role in the negotiations that in 1912 added the Keewatin Terr to Ontario, increasing the province's size by 56%, and succeeded to the premiership in 1914. A strong supporter of the war effort (he was knighted for his contribution in 1917), he also enfranchised women, enacted prohibition, established a department of labour and authorized construction of the Queenston hydroelectric plant, the largest in the world when it opened in 1921, establishing ONTARIO HYDRO as the province's primary producer of electricity. When his government was defeated in 1919, he resumed his law practice. He served on the INTERNATIONAL JOINT COMMISSION 1920-40.

BRIAN D. TENNYSON

Heart Disease In industrial countries more people die from diseases of the heart and blood vessels than from any other single cause. Over the last 30 years, extensive cardiovascular research has resulted in such revolutionary techniques as cardiac catheterization, heart-lung machines, artificial valves, cardiac pacemakers, echocardiography (a machine that uses ultrasound to produce a picture of the heart) and nuclear diagnostic technology. In addition, the management of heart disease by drugs has also improved with the discovery of new agents capable of controlling the force of cardiac contraction. These drugs include inotropic agents, beta blockers (which reduce the amount of work the heart must do) and calcium antagonists.

Coronary artery disease, the most common type of heart disease and the leading cause of death in N America, is almost always the result of atherosclerosis, the clinical name for hardening of the coronary arteries. Atherosclerosis is characterized by the accumulation of fatty deposits and the formation of fibrous tissue in the walls of arteries which then become narrow, thus diminishing the flow of blood and oxygen to the heart muscle. Although atherosclerosis develops quite early in life as the result of a diet rich in animal fat, cigarette smoking and the leading of a sedentary life, symptoms usually develop in the fourth or fifth decade of life. The disease may result in a sudden death in approximately 50% of the patients who have coronary artery disease without knowing it. The average age of death due to coronary artery disease is 52 years. In the remaining 50% of patients the disease may produce attacks of crushing pain (angina pectoris) in the central chest. The surgical management of coronary artery disease enjoys unprecedented popularity because of very low operative mortality (1 to 3%) and because relief of pain is obtained in about 90% of cases. Some 200 000 such operations are performed annually in N America.

Another form of heart disease is that associated with the heart valves. They can be damaged by rheumatic fever, bacterial infections or other disease processes. A defective valve fails to close completely or cannot open fully, thus disturbing the smooth unidirectional flow of blood required for normal functioning of the body. Some malfunctioning valves can be repaired through surgical techniques, but in some cases the valve is so severely damaged that it must be replaced with an artificial (prosthetic) one. The outlook for patients with valvular heart disease has changed dramatically with the introduction of prosthetic valves some 25 years ago. Despite occasional malfunction, clot formation and infection which occur with valve prostheses, a high percentage of patients can now live normal lives.

The heart is a pump made of special muscle whose contractions are triggered and synchronized by electrical impulses produced by its own natural pacemaker. When the natural pacemaker falters, an artificial pacemaker, using batteries and timers, can be used to produce electrical impulses which are transmitted along tiny wires secured to the heart. The pacemaker is a small battery-powered unit usually implanted under the skin and wired to the heart to control its rate and rhythm of contraction. These devices are now very small and durable.

One baby in about a hundred is born with an abnormality of the cardiovascular system. In general, such congenital defects include incorrectly formed valves, holes in the walls (septa) that separate the 2 sides of the heart, and abnormalities in the blood vessels leading in and out of the heart. These fall into 2 broad categories: conditions in which the baby is "blue" (cyanotic heart disease) and those in which the baby's color is normal (acyanotic heart disease). Most congenital heart defects can be corrected surgically in infancy or early childhood. The surgical risk is relatively low (about 5%) and the long-term results are generally excellent.

The last 30 years have witnessed remarkable achievements in cardiovascular medicine and surgery. Some of these achievements have been made by Canadians. Dr W.G. BIGELOW of Toronto, along with Dr J.C. Callaghan of Edmonton, pioneered the work on total body hypothermia (cooling off the body to reduce oxygen requirements during surgery) and laid the foundations for modern cardiac pacemakers. Dr Callaghan was also the first to use successfully the heart-lung machine for open-heart surgery, in Canada in 1956 and the first to insert an artificial valve and correct the tetralogy of Fallot. Dr W. Mustard of Toronto's Hospital for Sick Children pioneered techniques in pediatric cardiovascular surgery, and the "Mustard Repair" for transposition of the great vessels in children has gained international acceptance. Dr. A.M. Vineberg of Montréal studied myocardial revascularization for many years and developed an implantation procedure that was widely used before the introduction of coronary artery bypass procedures and is still sometimes used. J.C. CALLAGHAN

Heart Transplantation, *see* TRANSPLANTATION.

Heart's Content, Nfld, Town, pop 620 (1986c), 625 (1981c), inc 1967, is a fishing town on a protected, urn-shaped harbour in eastern TRINITY BAY. Besides being one of Newfoundland's oldest enduring fishing settlements, it is prominent in the history of international communications. Originally a summer fishing station, by the late 1600s it was a year-round settlement populated mainly by English West Country fishermen who also later developed a shipbuilding industry. In July 1866 the *Great Eastern*, the largest steamship then afloat, made the first successful landing of a transatlantic submarine telegraph cable at Heart's Content. Subsequently, the Anglo-American Telegraph Co established a cable station, which brought an influx of company employees and services. The station closed 1965, mainly because of new technological developments, but the station building was restored as a communications museum. JANET E.M. PITT AND ROBERT D. PITT

Heath, David, photographer (b at Philadelphia, Pa 27 June 1931). He first gained recognition in 1965 with the publication of *A Dialogue with Solitude*, a subjective and moving portfolio of black-and-white photographs exposing the troubled facets of N American society. Abandoned by his parents at age 4, Heath became interested in PHOTOGRAPHY as a teenager and continued to pursue it while serving in the infantry in Korea. In the late 1950s, he moved to New York C, where he worked as an assistant in fashion photography and as a magazine photographer, and was influenced by photo-essayist Eugene Smith. He won a Guggenheim Fellowship in 1963, and taught at various colleges and universities before moving to Toronto and Ryerson in 1970. In addition to teaching, he has mounted several solo exhibitions, including a retrospective at the National Gallery in Ottawa in 1981. LOUISE ABBOTT

Heavysege, Charles, poet (b at Huddersfield, Eng 2 May 1816; d at Montréal 14 July 1876). Heavysege immigrated to Montréal in 1853 as a woodcarver. In 1860 he became a reporter for *Montreal Transcript* and later for the *Montreal Daily Witness*. A quintessential pious Victorian, he published a series of long religious poems under the influence of Milton, Shakespeare and the Bible: *The Revolt of Tartarus* (1852), *Jephthah's Daughter* (1865) and "Jezebel, A Poem in Three Cantos" (1868). His Old Testament spirit also found expression in 2 dramatic works, the famous *Saul: A Drama in Three Parts* (1857; 1859) and *Count Filippo; or, The Unequal Marriage* (1860), an Italianate verse tragedy of adultery and retribution. His one novel, *The Advocate* (1865), was unsuccessful. *Saul* found many admirers, among them Henry W. Longfellow and Sir John A. MACDONALD. Coventry Patmore's praise in the influential *North British Review* was particularly positive. The play was premiered in a CBC radio adaptation in 1974. ROTA HERZBERG LISTER

Hebb, Donald Olding, psychologist (b at Chester, NS 22 July 1904; d at Halifax, 20 Aug 1985). He was a brilliant pupil who completed grades 1 to 4 in one year and 5 to 6 the next. But school proved too easy and when he graduated from Dalhousie, his record was undistinguished. A book by Freud stimulated him to go back to university and he earned an MA in psychology from McGill (1932) and a PhD from Harvard (1936). At that time, the brain was regarded as a relay station to process incoming and outgoing impulses; behaviour was just stimulus and response. Hebb believed more went on in the brain. He worked with Wilder PENFIELD 1937-39 and noted that loss of large parts of the brain did not necessarily diminish intelligence. He studied the development of behaviour in rats, primates and infants. He was convinced that neural circuits linking incoming and outgoing neurons were the loci for thought and emotions. In 1949 he published *The Organization of Behaviour*, which revolutionized psychology by putting "mind" back into the brain. His studies of development showed the importance of environmental stimulation in early childhood that led to the US adoption of Operation Headstart, a program to help children in disadvantaged families. He showed the requirement of constant input for normal brain activity by the abnormal response of subjects to sensory deprivation. DAVID T. SUZUKI

Hébert, Anne, poet, playwright, novelist (b at Sainte-Catherine-de-Fossambault, Qué 1 Aug 1916). Hébert's father Maurice, a provincial civil servant and writer, guided her in the early stages of her literary career. Through her mother, Hébert is a descendant of 19th-century historian François-Xavier GARNEAU and has carried on the family's literary tradition spectacularly. She was also cousin and friend of Hector de Saint-Denys GARNEAU, whose poetry affected her deeply and whose lonely death in late 1943 strongly influenced her. From that point, she felt impelled to open revolt, as her subsequent writings demonstrate. She grew up, studied and lived in Québec C until her mid-thirties. From 1950 to 1954, she worked on Radio-Canada broadcasts and wrote scripts for the NFB. She then went to Paris on a scholarship where, with frequent visits to Québec, she has lived for the past 30 years.

Hébert's road to maturity as a poet had 3 stages. In 1942 she published her first collection, *Les Songes en équilibre*, which portrays herself as existing in a dreamlike torpor. In 1953 appeared *Le Tombeau des rois*, where the self triumphs over the powerful dead who rule the dreams. Finally, in 1960 (when Québec was in the spring of the QUIET REVOLUTION), the powerful verse of *Mystère de la parole* reveals the liberated self. Her first volume of prose, *Le Torrent*, a collection of tales which appeared in 1950, shocked the reading public but has become a classic. Her first novel, *Les Chambres de bois* (1958), contained particularly original imagery, though it was not until 1970 that Hébert convincingly demonstrated her virtuosity in the great novel, *Kamouraska*. Here she skilfully combines 2 plots in a 19th-century Québec setting. The writing has a breathless, anguished and romantic rhythm that underlines well-controlled suspense. The novel earned her France's Prix des Libraires and was made into a film by Claude JUTRA. Like almost all of Hébert's works, *Kamouraska* has been translated into English. In *Les Enfants du sabbat* (1975), Hébert tells a tale of sorcery in Québec. *Héloïse* (1980) is about ghost-vampires in the Paris subway. *Les Fous de Bassan* (1982, Prix Fémina, and filmed by Yves Simoneau, 1986) is set in Gaspé, where 2 teenagers from an Anglo-Protestant village are killed. Hébert has written several plays, published as *Le Temps sauvage*; in the play of that name a mother vainly attempts to shield her children from the outside world.

Poet Anne Hébert writing in LaFontaine Park, Montréal, Qué (*courtesy SSC Photocentre*).

Anne Hébert's career, studded with literary honours and awards (including the MOLSON PRIZE in 1967 and election to the RSC 1960 and a Gov Gen's Award, 1975), is founded on a disciplined life that has always been devoted to writing. Her poetry and prose have become models for other writers and have been analysed in hundreds of studies, particularly in Québec, but also in France and English Canada. PIERRE H. LEMIEUX

Hébert, Henri, sculptor (b at Montréal 3 Apr 1884; d there 11 May 1950). The son of sculptor Louis-Philippe HÉBERT, he studied at the Monument national de Montréal under painter Edmond DYONNET and at the Art Assn with William BRYMNER. He twice went with his parents to Paris, studying under Thomas and Injalbert. He taught several years at McGill while sculpting many busts, and has left some 20 monuments, the most famous being of Louis-Hippolyte LAFONTAINE (in both Québec C and Montréal), *Évangeline* (Grand Pré, NS) in collaboration with his father, the *Monument aux Morts* (Montréal) and *Jacques de Lesseps* (Gaspé). MICHEL CHAMPAGNE

Hébert, Jacques, writer, publisher, senator (b at Montréal 21 June 1923). He studied at Coll Ste-Marie, at St Dunstan's Coll, Charlottetown, and at the École des hautes études commerciales de Montréal. Hébert has published some 20 works (accounts of his adventures, stories, novels, studies), the best known being *Coffin était innocent* (1958) and *Deux innocents en Chine rouge* (with Pierre E. Trudeau, 1960). Hébert worked for *Le* DEVOIR 1951-53 and in 1954 founded the weekly *Vrai*, which he ran until 1959. Meanwhile, he joined the brilliant CITÉ LIBRE team as editorial secretary and administrator. He was then host and scriptwriter for public affairs programs at Radio-Canada (1962-70), then president and general manager of Éditions du Jour until 1974.

In 1980-82 Hébert was co-chairman (with Louis APPLEBAUM) of the Federal Cultural Policy Review Committee. Named a senator in 1983, he brought to this new task the experience of a communicator whose previous activities demonstrated his concern for justice and generosity. A founding member and former president of the Civil Liberties Union (Qué) and founding president of both Canada World Youth and Katimavik, he responded eagerly when called upon to preside over the Special Senate Committee on Youth. Firm in his convictions, he staged a hunger strike in the Senate lobby when Katimavik's survival was threatened in 1986. MARTHE LEGAULT

Hébert, Louis, apothecary, colonist (b at Paris *c*1575; d at Québec Jan 1627). Hébert visited Canada 3 times between 1604 and 1613 with the expeditions of de MONTS, CHAMPLAIN, and Jean de BIENCOURT de Poutrincourt. In 1617 he decided to settle in Québec C with his wife and 3 children. He was ceded 10 arpents of land near the site of the present cathedral of Québec, and his family is renowned for having been the first to cultivate land in Canada. His wife, Marie Rollet, was the first Frenchwoman to scratch the soil of New France. It is said that, thanks to his medical knowledge among other reasons, Hébert was on good terms with the Indians. JACQUES BERNIER

Hébert, Louis-Philippe, sculptor (b at Ste-Sophie de Mégantic, Qué 27 Jan 1850; d at Montréal 13 June 1917). Around 1869 he left the family farm to join the army of pontifical ZOUAVES destined for Rome and Tripoli. The wealth of art he then discovered stunned and stimulated him.

Saint Barthélemy, one of a series of 12 statues representing Christ and the apostles, by Louis-Philippe Hébert (*courtesy Musée du Québec/photo by Patrick Altman*).

Once home, he worked in the studio of painter Napoléon BOURASSA, and over 6 years learned the craft of sculptor. Thereafter he received increasingly important commissions, finally becoming the principal Québec sculptor of his generation. He was the first Canadian-born commemorative sculptor, and his 40 monuments include *Queen Victoria* (Ottawa); *Maisonneuve, Jeanne Mance, Mgr Bourget* and *Edward VII* (Montréal); *Mgr de Laval* (Québec); and 6 sculptures in front of the Québec parliament, Québec City. He also sculpted busts, commemorative medals and numerous statues in wood, bronze and terra-cotta. For many years he taught at Montréal's Conseil des arts et manufactures.

A member of the Royal Canadian Academy of Arts (1880), Hébert was awarded the Medal of Confederation (1894), made a chevalier of France's Legion of Honour (1901), and Companion of St Michael and St George (Great Britain, 1903). In 1971, the St-Jean-Baptiste Soc of Montréal honoured his memory with the Prix Philippe-Hébert, given to an artist of outstanding ability and stature in Québec arts.

MICHEL CHAMPAGNE

Reading: Bruno Hébert, *Philippe Hébert, sculpteur* (1973).

Hébert, Pierre, director of animated films, engraver (b at Montréal 19 Jan 1944). Stimulated by Norman MCLAREN, Hébert experimented with scratching directly on film early in his career and directed films dominated by effects made possible through optical printing: *Opus I* (1964), *Op hop hop op* (1965) and *Autour de la perception* (1968). Later he was attracted to a more political and profound type of animation and, using simple techniques, produced 2 original works, *Père Noël, Père Noël* (1974) and *Entre chiens et loup* (1977). Hébert's latest films – *Souvenirs de guerre* (1982), *Étienne et Sara* (1984), *Chants et danses du monde inanimé – le métro* (1984), *Ô Picasso (Tableau d'une surexposition)* (1985) and *Adieu bipède* (1986) – are a synthesis of his previous work and open to a new use of music in animation.

PIERRE VÉRONNEAU

Hébert, Yves, pen name Yves Sauvageau, actor, playwright (b at Waterloo, Qué 17 May 1946; d at Granby, Qué 12 Oct 1970). After studies in education at the École normale de Sherbrooke (1963-65), he enrolled in the National Theatre School (1965-68). He had previously founded a theatre company in Waterloo called La Lanterne (1962-63) and had performed with the Atelier and the Union théâtrale de Sherbrooke. When he left the National Theatre School he toured Canada with the Jeunes comédiens of the THÉÂTRE DU NOUVEAU MONDE (1968-69). Later he joined the Enfants de Chénier (1969-70), directed by Jean-Claude GERMAIN at the Théâtre du même nom. He won 2 awards in Radio-Canada's Jeunes Auteurs competition (1966) for 2 short plays which were published under his pseudonym. His major plays were published and produced posthumously. ANDRÉ G. BOURASSA

Hec Crighton Trophy was presented to the Canadian Interuniversity Athletic Union in 1967 by the board of directors of the Canadian College Bowl, to be awarded annually to the athlete deemed to be the most outstanding university football player in Canada. The trophy is named after the late Hec Crighton, who was a coach, referee and teacher, and author of the *CIAU Rule Book* and the *Official Football Rule Book*. The first recipient of the Hec Crighton Trophy in Canada's Centennial Year of 1967 was Mike Eben of the U of T. Like Eben, most winners have gone on to professional careers in the Canadian Football League. The 1987 winner was Jordan Gagner of the UBC Thunderbirds. GERALD REDMOND

Hecate Strait is a body of water 48-140 km wide, underlain by a shallow basin (less than 45 m at the N end), separating the QUEEN CHARLOTTE IS from mainland BC. Marine weather conditions are severe: winter storms originating in the Gulf of Alaska bring high waves through the strait and winds persistently higher than 40 km/h off the S end of Moresby I. The open strait and numerous sheltered inlets are rich in marine life. Halibut, groundfish, herring, shellfish and salmon fisheries are centered around PRINCE RUPERT. Hecate Str was navigated for trade and plunder by the HAIDA, whose water-based settlements on the E coast of the Charlottes date from 6000-8000 years ago. Spanish explorer Jacinto Caamaño (1792) was the first European into the waters of the strait, although its name is that of a British paddlewheel sloop that surveyed the N Pacific coast 1860-63. Offshore oil drilling under the southern strait began in the 1950s but was halted in 1972.

PETER GRANT

Hecla, Man, an Icelandic fishing hamlet on Lk WINNIPEG's largest island, is part of Hecla Provincial Park, a 86 350 ha marine park 176 km N of Winnipeg, which includes several islands. Hecla is joined to the mainland by a causeway. Icelandic immigrants opened homesteads on the island beginning 1876. Isolated for many years, they built a self-sufficient community based mainly on fishing for food and export, but including farming, lumbering, lake transport, trapping and quarrying. In the 1890s Winnipeggers began building cottages here. Roads, electricity and a ferry service came only after WWII. In the early 1950s the fishery began to decline and young islanders moved to opportunities elsewhere. Proposals to establish a park and restore the hamlet of Hecla were welcomed initially, but land expropriation and relocation policies caused controversy. Hecla park has several year-round facilities, including a hotel-convention complex. Black I has the greatest geological and biological diversity in Manitoba and is the site of high-grade-silica sandstone quarrying. *See also* ICELANDERS. D.M. LYON

Hector, the brig which carried 178 Scottish immigrants to the PICTOU area of northern Nova Scotia in 1773. Pictou was located on the "Philadelphia Plantation," an 81000 ha tract granted to 14 Scots proprietors and settled desultorily since 1767. Active promotion of the land began in Sept 1772 when John Pagan of Glasgow and John Witherspoon, principal of Princeton College, New Jersey, advertised for settlers in Scottish newspapers, offering land on easy terms and passage to America at £3 5s per adult passenger. Most who accepted this offer came from Loch Broom in Ross and adjacent areas of Sutherland, principally from lands administered by the Board of Forfeited Estates. They were tenants fleeing high rents and bad harvests rather than clearance for sheep, and were not by Highland standards poor.

With a piper, the party left Loch Broom in early July 1773, collecting a few people on Clydeside along the way. The voyage was difficult: 18 children were buried at sea before the passengers stepped ashore into the Nova Scotia wilderness on Sept 15. Complaining about the location of their lands, the settlers were denied provisioning unless they accepted the land offered. They seized the provisions by force, and many left the settlement. The 78 who remained were producing crops by 1774 and within a few years were welcoming other immigrants. Although the *Hector* is popularly regarded as the first vessel to bring Highland immigrants to what is now Canada, several other ships (including the *Falmouth* and the *Alexander*) had previously carried Highlanders to the Island of St John [PEI]. Nevertheless, the *Hector*'s voyage remains the most celebrated in the stories of early Highland settlement in BRITISH NORTH AMERICA. J.M. BUMSTED

Hector, Sir James, geologist, naturalist (b at Edinburgh, Scot 16 Mar 1834; d at Wellington, NZ 5 Nov 1907). As surgeon and geologist to the PALLISER EXPEDITION (1857-60), Hector explored the country from the Red R settlement (Winnipeg) to Vancouver I. In the plains he recognized 3 topographic levels; in 1857 measured the first stratigraphic section including coal layers; attempted to subdivide Cretaceous and Tertiary strata on a geological map published in 1861; and recognized erratics as evidence of extensive former glaciation. He described and sketched the general structure of the Rocky Mts. KICKING HORSE PASS and River were named to commemorate an accident Hector had with his horse. On Vancouver I he studied coal deposits at Nanaimo. In 1861 Hector settled in New Zealand, where he became director of the geological survey. He travelled in BC for a few months after his retirement in 1903, his second and only other visit to Canada. W.O. KUPSCH

Hedley, BC, Improvement District, pop 274 (1986), 426 (1981c), is a pioneer mining community situated on Hwy 3, the major southern transprovincial highway, 39 km E of Princeton in the Similkameen Valley. The first mining claim was staked on nearby Nickel Plate Mountain in 1894, and the community is named for Robert Hedley of Nelson who grubstaked one of the first prospectors. When the mines closed in 1955 they had yielded $47 million in gold, silver and copper. MARIE ELLIOTT

Heeney, Arnold Danford Patrick, public servant, diplomat (b at Montréal 5 Apr 1902; d at Ottawa 20 Dec 1970). A clergyman's son, he was educated at U of Manitoba and Oxford. A successful lawyer in Montréal, he was invited to become principal secretary to PM Mackenzie KING in 1938. Two years later he was named clerk of the Privy Council and secretary to the Cabinet. He organized the work of the Cabinet War Committee, the key ministers, and made his office a clearing point for information and advice. In 1949 he became undersecretary of state for external affairs. He then served as ambassador to NATO, twice in Washington and as chairman of the Civil Service Commission. Until shortly before his death, he was Canadian head of the INTERNATIONAL JOINT COMMISSION and the PERMANENT JOINT BOARD ON DEFENCE. J.L. GRANATSTEIN

Hees, George Harris, politician (b at Toronto 17 June 1910). One of the DIEFENBAKER ministers who resigned during the Feb 1963 crisis, Hees was an able and energetic promoter of Canada. A businessman and athlete, he was elected to Parliament as MP for Broadview (Toronto) in 1950, and held the seat until 1963. Contrary to the wishes of the Tory establishment, who saw him as a brash playboy, he was elected national party president in 1953; his successful tenure was marked by visits and speeches in all parts of the country. Appointed minister of transport in 1957, he was an able administrator; in 1960 he became minister of trade and commerce and immediately organized a successful export drive. Hees did not stand for election in 1963, but was returned for Northumberland in 1965. He ran unsuccessfully for the Tory leadership in 1967. He was appointed minister of veterans affairs by Brian MULRONEY in 1984 and in mid-1987 received an additional portfolio as minister of state for senior citizens. PATRICIA WILLIAMS

Heggtveit, Anne, alpine skier (b at Ottawa 11 Jan 1939). She started skiing at age 2 and by 7 was senior ladies combined champion at Camp Fortune. In 1954, at age 15, she became the youngest-ever winner in the half-century history of the Holmenkollen giant slalom in Norway. In 1960 she won Canada's first Olympic skiing gold medal in the slalom as well as the world slalom and alpine combined titles. MURRAY SHAW

Height of Land, a region of high ground that may act as a watershed. Heights of land were important in the historic FUR TRADE for their influence on the determination of routes and PORTAGES, and they have affected many transportation routes since then. Heights of land were important to native people in demarcating territoriality, as they were later to European colonists. A political boundary, like the boundary between Labrador and Québec, may correspond to a height of land. JOHN ROBERT COLOMBO

Heiltsuk, *see* BELLA BELLA.

Heintzman & Co Ltd, a Canadian piano manufacturing firm established in Toronto by German immigrant Theodore August Heintzman in 1866, is renowned for high-quality craftsmanship. By the beginning of the 20th century the firm had opened branches in other Canadian cities and developed an export trade. Heintzman built its first grand pianos about 1886, and player pianos were produced for several years until their popularity waned in the 1920s. By the early 1960s the firm manufactured about 1500 upright and grand pianos each year. The bulk of production was moved to a new factory built in Hanover, Ont, in 1962, followed by grand-piano manufacturing when the Heintzman firm merged with the Sherlock-Manning Piano Co in 1978. The new company, sold in 1981 to Canadian furniture firm Sklar Manufacturing Ltd, discontinued producing the Heintzman piano in 1987. Early Heintzmans are in the Glenbow Museum in Calgary and the Western Development Museum in Yorkton, Sask. FLORENCE HAYES

Helava, Uno Vilho, inventor (b at Kokemäki, Finland 1 Mar 1923). He invented the analytical plotter for automatically drawing maps from photographs. Helava trained as a surveying engineer and came to Canada in 1953 as a research fellow in photogrammetry at the NATIONAL RESEARCH COUNCIL. By 1957 he had patented a method of using computers to produce maps from aerial photographs, automatically corrected for the curvature of the Earth and atmospheric distortion. The first prototype was built in 1963, using the analogue computer then available, and Helava left Canada to promote his invention. About 70 plotters were built by an Italian-American partnership, chiefly for military clients. In the late 1970s (digital) microcomputers made the Helava system much cheaper, and several hundred plotters have been built. Because of its affinity with other technologies (eg, digital transmission of photographs from orbiting satellites), the Helava system is expected to become the world's standard method of making maps by the end of the century. DONALD J.C. PHILLIPSON

Helders, Johan (John) Anton Joseph, internationally acclaimed amateur pictorial photographer (b at Rhenen, Netherlands 3 May 1888; d at Homestead, Fla 4 Feb 1956). Helders arrived in Canada from the Dutch East Indies in 1924, first settling in Vancouver where his interest in photography was nurtured by John VANDERPANT. Two years later, Helders became maître d'hôtel of the Château Laurier, Ottawa. For the next decade, he was one of Canada's leading fine-art photographers. His prints won awards at salons all over the world and were published in the leading photographic periodicals. A fellow of the Royal Photographic Soc of Great Britain, he served as director for Canada of the Photographic Soc of America. Helders's salon photography diminished after he moved back to Vancouver in 1939. JOAN M. SCHWARTZ

Helicopter, an aircraft that derives its lift and propulsive force from horizontally rotating rotors or blades and is capable of ascending and descending vertically. The torque generated by the blades is balanced either by a vertical tail rotor or by having 2 sets of blades rotating in opposite directions. The helicopter originated as a toy centuries ago, a feathered top which rose in the air when spun between the hand or by means of a string. In the 19th century a few powered helicopter models were made, and the advent of the internal-combustion engine brought a spate of unsuccessful helicopter prototypes in many countries; but the first man to get airborne and descend safely was Paul Cornu of France on 13 Nov 1907. Control was the problem, and the men who showed the way to the practical helicopter were Juan de la Cierva of Spain, with his autogyros, Heinrich Rocke of Germany, and Igor Ivanovich Sikorsky of Russia and the US. The persistence and ingenuity of the many contributors has produced a truly versatile machine, suited to war and peace, and capable of performing tasks beyond the capability of other vehicles.

In Canada, the Froebe brothers of Homewood, Man, designed and built a helicopter, which flew in 1938. Mechanical problems were encountered and the project was abandoned, but the helicopter survived and is now in the Western Canada Aviation Museum in Winnipeg. The SG-IV-C helicopter was designed and built in Montréal by Bernard Sznycer and Selma Gottlieb, and flew on 9 July 1947. After successful completion of the initiated test program, the SG-N-D Grey Gull, the first production machine, was produced, flown on 6 Feb 1948, and granted a Certificate of Airworthiness on 15 Mar 1951. However, financial backing was withdrawn in 1954. There have been no more Canadian designs, and all helicopters used in Canada are of foreign origin. Military use of helicopters started in the RCAF in 1947, with the RCN and army following later. Air-force operations have been mainly concerned with search, rescue and mercy mission, and with heavy lift capability; the navy has been concerned with antisubmarine operations and has developed aids to permit operation from small ships in rough weather, notably the haul-down recovery system; and the army with battlefield operations. The RCAF was heavily involved in the construction of the Mid-Canada Line, and Squadron Leader R.T. Heaslip was awarded the MCKEE TROPHY in 1956 for his contribution to the success of these operations.

Helicopters have been used for forestry protection, crop dusting, surveying, exploration, commuter services, and the support of other industries such as building and off-shore oil. The brilliant pioneer Carl AGAR imported several Bell 47 helicopters in 1947 for spraying the rugged terrain of the Okanagan Valley, and later for oil exploration. Agar's company became one of the world's major helicopter companies. In 1985 nearly 750 helicopters were used commercially in Canada. PHILIP MARKHAM

Hell's Gate is a rocky gorge of the FRASER RIVER CANYON S of Boston Bar, BC. Explorer Simon FRASER recorded a difficult portage (1808) around Hell's Gate. Its name is associated with the disastrous impact of CNR construction on the river's salmon resources. After landslides (1913-14) blocked much of the sockeye run, the catch from the river's stocks plummeted and has never fully recovered. Fishways were constructed here in 1944 to permit spawning fish to pass the rapids. Hell's Gate now has an aerial tram ride and highway tourist facility. PETER GRANT

Hellyer, Paul Theodore, politician, journalist (b at Waterford, Ont 6 Aug 1923). A successful businessman, Hellyer sat in the House of Commons 1949-57 and was re-elected in a by-election Dec 1958. From 1958 until 1963, when the Liberals gained power, Hellyer was instrumental in developing the party's defence policy and urged Lester PEARSON to accept nuclear weapons. After the election victory, Pearson appointed him minister of national defence, and under Hellyer's direction, the Canadian ARMED FORCES were unified. The controversy surrounding the unification likely did not help his political career and in 1967 Hellyer was moved to the Ministry of Transport. In 1968 he ran unsuccessfully for the Liberal leadership. The victor, Pierre TRUDEAU, gave him the additional responsibility for housing policy. After the report of his Task Force on Housing and Urban Development did not win Cabinet approval in 1969, Hellyer resigned from the Cabinet and later from the Liberal Party. He tried to form a new political movement in 1976, Action Canada. When it faltered, he drifted towards the Conservative Party, winning re-election under that banner in 1972 before losing his seat in 1974. Hellyer then unsuccessfully ran for the leadership in 1976. He has not re-entered the House of Commons since, but has voiced political views through a syndicated column he wrote 1974-84 and through several books. JOHN ENGLISH

Helmcken, John Sebastian, surgeon, politician (b at London, Eng 5 June 1824; d at Victoria 1 Sept 1920). In 1847 Helmcken sailed to York Factory and back as surgeon on the HBC supply ship *Prince Rupert* and in 1848-50 was appointed surgeon and clerk to the HBC at Fort Rupert and then at Fort Victoria. Son-in-law of James DOUGLAS, he was Speaker of the Legislative Assembly of Vancouver I 1856-66 when he was elected to the Legislative Council of BC. In 1870 he was one of 3 CONFEDERATION delegates to Ottawa from BC. When BC entered Confederation in 1871, Helmcken retired from politics and devoted himself to medicine and his reminiscences. In 1885 he became first president of the BC Medical Society. ERIC J. HOLMGREN

Reading: D. Blakey Smith, ed, *The Reminiscences of Doctor John Sebastian Helmcken* (1975).

The Hon John Sebastian Helmcken, 1917. He was one of 3 Confederation delegates sent to Ottawa from BC in 1870 (*by permission of the British Library*).

Helmcken Falls, located on the Murtle R in BC's Wells Gray Provincial Park, is the 5th-highest waterfall in Canada (*photo by Valerie J. May*).

Helmcken Falls, located on the Murtle R at the entrance to BC's Wells Gray Provincial Park, an area noted for its many waterfalls, is the highest in the park and fifth highest in Canada. Situated in the SW corner (about 270 km SE of PRINCE GEORGE), a region characterized by volcanic upheavals, the lava-layered falls have a 137 m vertical drop. They were named after the prominent BC physician John Sebastian HELMCKEN in 1913 by Premier Sir Richard MCBRIDE. DAVID EVANS

Helwig, David Gordon, author (b at Toronto 5 Apr 1938). First publishing as a poet, he moved on to drama and fiction, including a series of 4 novels focusing on characters living in Kingston, where Helwig teaches at Queen's U. He has also taught at the penitentiary near Kingston, an experience which led to his nonfiction work, *A Book About Billie* (1972), an assemblage of prose derived from his interviews with a convict. Increasingly his poetry has moved from lyrics to longer narratives, starting with *Atlantic Crossing* (1974), 4 poems about ocean voyagers, and continuing with *A Book of the Hours* (1979), the central poem of which deals with Thomas Bullfinch and his ward, and *Catchpenny Poems* (1984), a series of poetic meditations arising from 19th-century prints. His most recent work is *The Bishop* (1986). PETER STEVENS

Hemlock, evergreen CONIFER, genus *Tsuga*, PINE family (Pinaceae). Early settlers named the hemlock after a European flowering weed because the odour was similar when needles were crushed. Ten species are recognized: 6 in eastern Asia, Japan and Taiwan, and 4 in N America. Of the latter, 3 occur in Canada: eastern hemlock (*T. canadensis*), in southern Ontario, Québec and the Maritimes; western hemlock (*T. heterophylla*) and mountain hemlock (*T. mertensiana*), on the West Coast from Alaska to northern California. Hemlocks are tall, stately trees with slender, usually drooping, leader and branches. Leaves are needlelike but blunt. Cones are nonwoody and small, about 2 cm long (up to 7 cm in mountain hemlock). Pollination occurs in spring and winged seeds are shed in late summer or fall. The root system is shallow and wide-spreading. Hemlock wood is fairly hard, and these trees are harvested extensively for pulp, paper and lumber. JOHN N. OWENS

Hémon, Louis, writer (b at Brest, France 12 Oct 1880; d at Chapleau, Ont 8 July 1913). Hémon immigrated to Canada in 1911. After working (1911-12) as a bilingual stenographer with a Montréal life insurance company, he went to the Lac Saint-Jean region. There he wrote *Maria Chapdelaine: récit du Canada français*, the novel that gave him worldwide success. Unfortunately, Hémon never knew of his fame, for he died in an accident. MARIA CHAPDELAINE was serialized first in Paris in 1914 and 2 years later appeared in Montréal in book form. But it was only after its 1921 French publication that the novel became a success. Today, this account of Québec peasant life is often seen as a symbol of individual and collective alienation. At the time, the novel was used to support a nationalist ideology of fidelity to the past and its traditions. Other works by Hémon are *La Belle que voilà* (1923), *Colin-Maillard* (1924), *Battling Malone* (1925), *Monsieur Ripois et la némésis* (1950), *Lettres à sa famille* (1968) and *Récits sportifs* (1982). JACQUES COTNAM

Hénault, Gilles, writer (b at St-Majoric, Qué 1 Aug 1920). After studying at Collège Mont Saint-Louis, he began a program of self-directed reading and writing, and published several poems. Turning to journalism, he became friendly with various literary figures including Jean-Aubert LORANGER and in particular Éloi GRAMMONT, *dit* de Grandmont, with whom he cofounded the "Cahiers de la file indienne" (1946), a journal they intended to devote to experiments in automatic writing. His decision to join the Communist newspaper *Combat* with Pierre Gélinas (the newspaper was closed down in 1947 by Maurice DUPLESSIS'S PADLOCK ACT) temporarily shut other journalistic doors against him. Hénault then worked as a union organizer in a Sudbury nickel mine and published a number of dissident poems.

Hénault returned to Montréal in 1953 and worked in radio, TV and film as journalist, scriptwriter and host. In 1959 he became literary and artistic editor for *Le* DEVOIR and was director 1966-71 of the Musée d'art contemporain de Montréal. He received awards for his poems and translations in 1962, 1972 and 1979. He was writer-in-residence at U of O in 1975-76 and was in charge of the plastic-art department of UQAM in 1983-84. ANDRÉ G. BOURASSA

Henday, Anthony, explorer (probably b on the Isle of Wight, Eng; *fl* 1750-62). Henday travelled farther into western Canada than any white person had before him, and his journal contains important glimpses of how the native population lived at that time. A labourer for the HBC at York Fort [YORK FACTORY], Man, he volunteered for a mission to encourage distant tribes of Indians to come and trade. Travelling with some Cree, he set out in June 1754 via the Hayes R. The party paddled up the Saskatchewan and then proceeded on foot, apparently along the Battle R valley, meeting many Assiniboine en route. In the autumn they seem to have been southeast of present-day Red Deer, Alta, when they found a great camp of "Archithinues" (Blackfoot or Gros Ventre). Henday and some of the Cree spent part of the winter nearby. In the spring they descended the N Saskatchewan. Middlemen in the fur trade, the Cree collected furs from other Indians as they travelled eastward. The best were sold at French posts conveniently located on the lower Saskatchewan. The remainder were taken to York, where the party arrived in June 1755. In 1759 Henday went west again for a year, this time with some "Archithinues." He left the HUDSON'S BAY COMPANY's service in 1762 and probably returned to England. Described by Andrew GRAHAM as a "bold, enterprising" man, he felt ill rewarded for his great hardships. *See also* EXPLORATION.

JANE E. GRAHAM

Reading: A.J. Ray, *Indians in the Fur Trade* (1974); Glyndwr Williams, "The puzzle of Anthony Henday's journal, 1754-55," *The Beaver* (winter 1978).

Henderson, Alexander, photographer (b at Edinburgh, Scot 1831; d at Montréal Mar 1913). Soon after his 1855 marriage, Henderson immigrated to Canada with his wife and settled in Montréal where he worked in accounting for several years. Taking up photography as a hobby, he made it his profession in 1866. He first did portraits, but attained an international reputation with his landscape photography, receiving medals in London, Dublin, Paris and New York. He documented the principal cities and resort areas of Québec and Ontario, and many Québec villages. Especially fond of the wilderness, he made many photographic trips by canoe to the Blanche, the Rouge and other eastern rivers. In 1872 he began a series on the construction of the INTERCOLONIAL RAILWAY. He made his first trip to the West for the CPR in 1885 and was eventually hired by the CPR in 1892 to set up a new photographic department, his duties including 4 months spent in the field each year. He retired in 1897. STANLEY TRIGGS

Henderson, Alexander, lawyer, politician, commissioner of YT (b at Oshawa, Ont 13 Mar 1861; d at Vancouver 13 Dec 1940). Educated at Osgoode Hall, U of T, Henderson was called to the Ontario Bar in 1899 and the BC Bar in 1891. A Liberal, he represented New Westminster in the BC legislature (1898-1900) and was attorney-general in the SEMLIN administration. Appointed a judge of the Vancouver county court in 1901, he resigned to run in the provincial election of 1906 but was defeated. He served as commissioner of the Yukon Territory 1908-11, a period which coincided with the transition to capital-intensive mining operations in the Klondike goldfields. A quiet and capable administrator, Henderson presided over the first wholly elected Yukon council. H. GUEST

Henderson, John Tasker, radio-physicist (b at Montréal 9 Dec 1905; d at Perth, Ont 2 Jan 1983). Educated at McGill and London, Henderson joined the NATIONAL RESEARCH COUNCIL (1933) in charge of its radio section, where he worked on "atmospherics" (later discovered to be the effect of the ionosphere on radio signals) and built the Cathode Ray Direction Finder invented by A.G.L. MCNAUGHTON and W.A. STEEL. In 1939 he was secretly informed about British advances in RADAR and, in the next few months, Henderson laid the foundations for radar research and manufacture in Canada. He returned to the NRC after RCAF and diplomatic service 1942-47 and became head of its electricity section, which built several cesium atomic clocks (accepted in 1968 as the international timekeeping standard).

DONALD J.C. PHILLIPSON

Hendry, Thomas Best, playwright, theatre administrator, arts consultant (b at Winnipeg 7 June 1929). Tom Hendry began acting and writing for the CBC in Winnipeg in the early 1950s. With John HIRSCH in 1957 he founded Theatre 77, which merged with the Winnipeg Little Theatre in 1958 to become the MANITOBA THEATRE CENTRE, English Canada's first regional theatre. He was administrator of MTC 1958-63, producer of Winnipeg's Rainbow Stage 1958-61, secretary general of the Canadian Theatre Centre 1964-69 and literary manager of the STRATFORD FESTIVAL in 1969. Hendry has fostered Canadian playwriting as a founder of the Playwrights Co-op and Toronto Free Theatre (1971) and the Playwrights Colony at the BANFF CENTRE FOR CONTINUING EDUCATION (1974). Since 1985 he has been policy director, Toronto Arts Council. In 1986 he chaired the Task Force on the National Arts Council and was Barker Fairley Distinguished Visitor in Canadian Culture at U of T. His most important dramas include *Fifteen Miles of Broken Glass* (first produced in 1966), *Satyricon* (1969), *Gravediggers of 1942* (1973), *Byron* (1976) and *Hogtown: Toronto the Good* (1981). ANTON WAGNER

Hennepin, Louis, Récollet missionary, explorer (b at Ath, Belgium 12 May 1626; d *c*1705). In 1675 Hennepin was sent to Canada with René-Robert Cavelier de LA SALLE, commandant of Ft Frontenac, where Hennepin was chaplain 1676-77. In 1678 he was asked to join La Salle's expedition through the Great Lks and, in 1680, with 2 others was sent ahead to explore the upper Mississippi. His journal was the source for *Description de la Louisiane* published in 1683, a year after his return to France. It described the places visited, notably NIAGARA FALLS, and the Iroquois and the Sioux who held the travellers in captivity for 6 months. Hennepin was vainglorious and rebelled against church discipline; he seldom held a position for long. In 1697 he published *Nouvelle Découverte d'un très grand pays* and in 1698 *Nouveau Voyage d'un pais plus grand que l'Europe* in which he claimed he had travelled to the Mississippi's mouth. This attempt to appropriate La Salle's discovery was another self-serving embellishment to justify retelling the 1683 narrative. Hennepin's books were enormously popular in Europe, but he was excluded from Canada and passed into obscurity. PETER N. MOOGK

Reading: Louis Hennepin, *A New Discovery of a Vast Country in America* (1698/1903).

Henry, Alexander, fur trader (b in New Jersey Aug 1739; d at Montréal 4 Apr 1824). He was one of the first English traders, known as the "pedlars from Quebec," to do business in the North-West following 1763. He came to Québec as a young merchant supplying the British army. Travelling to Michilimackinac, the fur-trade entrepôt, he was present at the 1763 Indian attack there, was taken prisoner and lived with the Indians for a year. For several years he traded on Lk Superior, but by 1775 he was on the Saskatchewan R. By 1781 he had retired to Montréal as a general merchant. He joined the NWC but sold his interest in 1796. His memoir, TRAVELS AND ADVENTURES IN CANADA AND THE INDIAN TERRITORIES (1809), is a classic of Canadian travel literature. *See also* EXPLORATION AND TRAVEL LITERATURE IN ENGLISH. DANIEL FRANCIS

Henry, Alexander, "the Younger," fur trader (d at Fort George [Astoria, Ore] 22 May 1814), nephew of Alexander Henry, "the Elder." After entering the fur trade in 1791 he served the NORTH WEST COMPANY for 23 years at posts ranging from Lk Superior to the Pacific Ocean. His journals are among the finest accounts of the western trade and are interesting for their comments on native languages and cultures. DANIEL FRANCIS

Henry, George, or Maungwudaus, meaning "the great hero," or "courageous," Mississauga (Ojibwa) interpreter, Methodist mission worker, performer (b on the NW shore of Lk Ontario *c*1807; d after 1851). Educated in Methodist mission schools, George Henry seemed designed for a role in the church as interpreter and translator. A more exciting career, however, attracted him. In 1844 he organized an Indian troupe which toured Britain and the continent, 1845-48, putting on Indian dances and exhibitions. After his return from Europe Maungwudaus performed for several years in Canada and the US, and later became a well-known Indian herbalist. He wrote a pamphlet, *An Account of the Chippewa Indians, who have been travelling among the Whites, in the United States, England, Ireland, Scotland, France and Belgium* (1848), excerpts from which are found in P. Petrone, *First People, First Voices* (1983).

DONALD B. SMITH

Henry, George Stewart, farmer, businessman, Conservative politician, premier of Ontario (b in King Twp, Ont 16 July 1871; d near Toronto 2 Sept 1953). As Ontario entered the automobile age, he provided the province with its first highway system, but he has been remembered as the dour premier of Depression days. Serving in the legislature for 30 years (1913-43), as minister of public works and highways 1923-30 and then as premier 1930-34, he was dedicated to building good roads. Paved highways were extended from 670 to 3888 km and Canada's first concrete bridge was constructed. With less success he tried to promote a metropolitan Toronto area to plan development. But "Honest George" was drab and prosperous and in 1934 was no match for populist Mitch HEPBURN. BARBARA A. MCKENNA

Henry, Martha, actress (b at Detroit, Mich 17 Feb 1938). Henry has long been associated with the STRATFORD FESTIVAL; since her auspicious debut as Miranda in *The Tempest* in 1962, she has played most of Shakespeare's major roles. Her important non-Shakespearean roles at Stratford include Sister Jeanne in *The Devils*, Mrs Procter in *The Crucible* and Olga in *The Three Sisters*. Henry studied acting at Carnegie Tech in Pittsburgh and after graduation came to Canada to audition for Toronto's Crest Theatre. She played several roles at the Crest but was urged by actor and teacher Powys Thomas to resume her training at the National Theatre School. The directors John HIRSCH and Robin PHILLIPS have been influential in her development. Phillips directed her highly praised performance of Isabella in *Measure for Measure* in 1975 as well as in *Farther West* by John Murrell at Theatre Calgary in 1982 and in the film adaptation of Timothy Findley's *The Wars*, for which she won a Genie at the 1984 Canadian Film Awards. In 1980 she won her first Genie as best actress for her performance in *The Newcomers 1978*. She was also named best actress at the 1986 Genie awards for her performance as Edna in *Dancing in the Dark*. Her other honours include a Theatre World Award in 1971 for her work with the Repertory Company at Lincoln Center, NY.

JAMES DEFELICE

Henry, Robert Alexander Cecil, "Red," businessman, public servant (b at Montréal 20 Sept 1884; d at St Petersburg, Fla 1 Jan 1962). Educated at McGill, Henry worked for the CPR before entering the federal public service in 1908. He worked in the departments of the Interior and Railways and Canals until 1923 and then headed the economics bureau of the CNR 1923-28. In 1929 he became deputy minister of railways and canals, but left in 1930 to become general manager of Beauharnois Light, Heat and Power Co in Montréal. Beauharnois's relations with KING'S government were called into public question 1931-33, but there was no proof of misconduct on Henry's part. In 1939 Henry joined the War Supply Board and, as a member of the executive committee of the Dept of Munitions and Supply, was C.D. HOWE's right-hand man and troubleshooter. After ill health 1941-44, Henry returned to full duty as deputy minister of reconstruction 1944-45. In later years he was a consultant on the development of the St Lawrence Seaway. ROBERT BOTHWELL

Henry, William Alexander, lawyer, politician, judge (b at Halifax 30 Dec 1816; d at Ottawa 3 May 1888). Henry achieved a solid legal and political reputation, cemented by his role as a FATHER OF CONFEDERATION. First elected in 1840 for Antigonish, he rose to provincial Cabinet rank in 1852, but broke with the Liberals (1857) and thereafter served as a minister under Conservative governments. Henry attended the 3 Confederation conferences as Nova Scotia's attorney general and enthusiastically promoted the movement at home; he reputedly helped draft the BNA Act in London. Defeated in the 1867 federal election, he was politically rewarded in 1875 with appointment to the Supreme Court of Canada, where his service was able, but not brilliant.
LOIS KERNAGHAN

Hensley, Sophia Margaretta, née Almon, author, lecturer (b at Bridgetown, NS 31 May 1866; d at Windsor, NS 10 Feb 1946). An early protégé of Sir Charles G.D. ROBERTS, Hensley published articles, poetry and fiction that reflected her interest in women's issues and social tolerance. Active in literary and philanthropic circles, she studied or lived in England, France and the US but always maintained a summer residence in Barton, NS. She was living on the Isle of Jersey at the outbreak of WWII, returning to Canada in 1939. In addition to writing 10 books and periodical contributions under her own name, she used the pseudonyms Gordon Hart, J. Try-Davies and Almon Hensley. Like Roberts, Bliss CARMAN and many other Canadian literary contemporaries of her generation, she published internationally while always describing herself as "a Canadian in thought, feeling and expression."
GWENDOLYN DAVIES

Henson, Josiah, founder of the BLACK settlement at Dawn, UC (b at Charles Co, Md 15 June 1789; d at Dresden, Ont 5 May 1883). Born a slave, Henson escaped to Canada in 1830. Four years later he founded the Dawn community near Dresden, UC, for American fugitive slaves. Aided by a white American missionary, Hiram Wilson, he and his associates organized a manual-labour school, the British-American Institute. He was active on the executive committee until the institute closed in 1868. Although a poor administrator, constantly engaged in disputes over finance and management, Henson served as Dawn's spiritual leader and patriarch and made numerous fund-raising trips in the US and England. He published his autobiography in 1849, and he was allegedly Harriet Beecher Stowe's model for the leading character in *Uncle Tom's Cabin.*
JANE H. PEASE AND WILLIAM H. PEASE

Reading: Josiah Henson, *An Autobiography of the Rev. Josiah Henson ("Uncle Tom") from 1789 to 1881,* ed John Lobb (rev ed 1881; repr 1969).

Hepburn, Douglas, weightlifter (b at Vancouver 16 Sept 1927). Hepburn's birth was difficult, and he has suffered from a club foot and a withered leg all his life. These infirmities did not deter him from training with weights nor did they lessen his determination to excel. Competing in the heavyweight category (over 90 kg) at the 1953 World Weightlifting Championships in Stockholm, Sweden, Hepburn defeated the 1952 Olympic champion by a total of 10 kg. In 1954 he won the heavyweight title at the British Empire and Commonwealth Games held in Vancouver. He then turned to professional wrestling and business. RICHARD CAMPION

Hepburn, Mitchell Frederick, politician, premier of Ontario 1934-42 (b at St Thomas, Ont 12 Aug 1896; d there 5 Jan 1953). Confident and affable, "Mitch" was a popular farmer who won a narrow victory in Elgin W in the 1926 federal election and was re-elected with a healthy majority in 1930. That year he was elected leader of the provincial Liberal Party and broadened its base by allying with the Progressives, conciliating the liberal and labour left, and trying to resolve the split over the Roman Catholic school question and prohibition. His speeches on behalf of Ontario farmers and for freer trade were noted more for their wit than for economic insight. Aided by the Depression, the ineptness of Conservative Premier George HENRY, and funding from business and mining interests, Hepburn won an overwhelming victory in the 1934 provincial election. In office, Hepburn implemented a number of populist measures – the auction of government limousines and the closing of the lieutenant-governor's residence. He cancelled power contracts with 4 Québec companies, tried to bring order to provincial finances, improved labour legislation and aided the iron-ore industry. He regarded the compulsory pasteurization of milk as his greatest accomplishment. Less successful was his attempt to aid parochial schools.

The most celebrated event of his first administration was the strike at General Motors in Oshawa in 1937 (*see* OSHAWA STRIKE). Hepburn, while sympathetic to the unemployed, was opposed to unionization and to letting the Committee for Industrial Organization (later the Congress of Industrial Organizations) into Canada. He supported GM in its refusal to negotiate with the CIO organizers, and when Ottawa refused to dispatch a unit of the RCMP, he organized his own volunteers – Hepburn's Hussars. Ultimately, the strike was settled with what amounted to an acceptance of the union. The strike ruptured Hepburn's relationship with PM KING (which had never been close), and in Jan 1940 he passed a resolution in the Ontario legislature critical of King's war effort. King thereupon called an election, which he won handily. Hepburn's day was over; he helped to scuttle the 1941 federal-provincial conference and supported A. MEIGHEN in the S York by-election of 1942, but his struggle with King ruined his party and destroyed his health. In 1942 he resigned as premier and in 1943 as provincial treasurer. The Liberals asked him to lead the party in the 1945 election, but the party was routed and Hepburn lost his seat. JOHN SAYWELL

Reading: N. McKenty, *Mitch Hepburn* (1967).

Mackenzie King and Mitchell Hepburn in Hepburn's office, Toronto, 1934, the year Hepburn became premier. The two later became bitter political enemies (*courtesy National Archives of Canada/C-87863*).

Royal Arms of France taken from one of the gates of the city of Québec by the British troops in 1759, wood engraving (*courtesy National Archives of Canada/C-4298*).

Heraldry, the creation or study of armorial bearings. Signs and symbols both convey messages, and symbols also play on our emotions. An arrow showing direction elicits no emotional response, but grasping the symbolic value of a flag requires emotional involvement: pride, devotion, patriotism or admiration. An EMBLEM is a sign with a conventionally accepted meaning. The parliamentary mace had its probable origin as an instrument of physical discipline in assemblies, but today it is accepted by convention as an emblem of authority, and as a symbol it arouses respect in viewers. Symbols are found in religion, in the arts and in customs. Coats of arms are visual symbols which reflect the beliefs, aspirations and history of individuals or of groups.

During the Crusades (11th-13th centuries), the European nations felt the need to identify themselves with crosses of various colours, and at the same time to reduce casualties with improved armour. The knight, whose head was entirely covered by a helmet, adopted for recognition a personal symbol which he displayed on his surcoat, shield and banner. Such symbols became the main components of a coat of arms (of which a crest is only a part). Coats of arms, or arms, have survived because they became hereditary within families and their use was extended to corporate and civic entities.

In 1407 a college of arms was created in France by Charles VI, and the granting of arms continued until 1790. The first known heraldic instance in Canada occurred 24 July 1534, when Jacques CARTIER planted at Gaspé a large cross bearing the royal arms of France. The royal arms, 3 gold fleurs-de-lis on a blue field, continued to represent the king of France in the New World. One did not have to be of nobility to bear arms, but in practice most of the armigers (bearers of arms) in New France – government officials, military officers, clergymen and merchants – were nobles. A number of men received letters of nobility and subsequently grants of arms for their services to the sovereign, eg, Charles Le Moyne de LONGUEUIL (1668), Nicolas Juchereau de Saint-Denis (published posthumously, 1697) and Joseph-François HERTEL DE LA FRESNIÈRE (1716).

With the fall of New France, the officers of the British sovereign, the College of Arms in England and the Court of the Lord Lyon in Scotland became the granting authorities in Canada. Few Canadians of French origin have had recourse to British institutions to have their arms legitimized

Coat of arms of Simon McGillivray, watercolour on parchment (*courtesy National Archives of Canada*).

or to have new ones granted. One early exception, Gaspard-Joseph CHAUSSEGROS DE LÉRY, recorded his father's arms and cross of Saint Louis at the College of Arms in June 1763. The first known grant to a Canadian after 1763 was made to James Cuthbert in 1778. The next known grant was to William MCGILLIVRAY in 1801. Early grants were not numerous, in part because Canadians were busy building a country and had little time or money for the niceties of life. A number of cities and institutions took an interest in heraldry, but few had their arms officially recorded. This gave rise to a rather naive style of heraldry, with representations of steamboats, locomotives, grain elevators, factories and forests.

Today there is a revival of heraldry, probably because people are seeking special expressions of their own identities, but also because the importance of symbolism has been recognized in art, religion, psychology and the social sciences. The HERALDRY SOCIETY OF CANADA has done much to foster a knowledge of heraldry and to induce cities, corporations, institutions and individuals to obtain grants of arms. Canadians who have become armigers include Gov Gen Georges P. VANIER, Lord Beaverbrook (*see* Max AITKEN) and Lt-Gov George F.G. STANLEY. The number of municipalities with grants has considerably increased, and now includes Fredericton, Hamilton-Wentworth, Peace River (Alta), Esquimalt (BC) and Grand Falls (Nfld). Among the many corporate or civic bodies bearing arms are the ROYAL SOCIETY OF CANADA, the HUDSON'S BAY COMPANY, the GREY NUNS and numerous universities. Bishops and dioceses usually have arms, as do some counties.

Coat of arms of the 4th Earl of Minto, governor general of Canada, polychrome wood carving (*courtesy National Archives of Canada/C-111471*).

A description in heraldic language is a blazon; the pictorial rendering is the emblazonment. Forms are stylized to bring out the salient points; proportions and the tonality of the colours are important. A good heraldic artist strives for individual style and avoids stereotypes. Without a Canadian heraldic authority, Canadians have been confused in heraldic matters, and designs on the whole have been poor. Canadians should be wary of anyone trying to sell them arms. The arms could be the property of an entirely different family branch with the same name. In most European countries and in Canada, arms are granted to an individual and his descendants; not every family has a coat of arms.

The National Archives of Canada (formerly Public Archives of Canada) responds to inquiries and, within reasonable limits, offers guidance to researchers or designers. It co-operates with museums and individuals to identify coats of arms on artifacts. With the help of heraldic artist and scholar Hans D. Birk, the arms of families from countries other than France and Britain now living in Canada are being documented and painted in colour. The main threat to heraldry today appears to be the LOGO, although heraldists warn that logos may be a passing form which, unlike heraldry, will not endure the test of time. AUGUSTE VACHON

Reading: C. Swan, *Canada: Symbols of Sovereignty* (1977).

Heraldry Society of Canada, headquartered in Ottawa, est 1966 to encourage interest in the history and practice of HERALDRY in Canada. A quarterly illustrated journal issued since 1967, *Heraldry in Canada*, is now the largest single published source relating to historical and contemporary Canadian heraldry. Society activities also include sponsorship of the annual George M. Beley Lecture on Canadian heraldry and the development of a roll of Canadian arms. In 1981 the HSC published a landmark reference text, *Canadian Heraldry*, based on a manuscript by founder Alan B. Beddoe (1893-1975). The society has promoted the establishment of a national authority to grant and regulate the use of arms, with key representations being made to the Special Joint Committee of the Senate and of the House of Commons on the Constitution in 1971 and to the Federal Cultural Policy Review Committee a decade later. Since 1976 those who have given outstanding service to the society have been recognized by appointment to a faculty of Fellows of the Heraldry Society of Canada.

ROBERT D. WATT

Herbarium [Lat *herba*, "herb," formerly any medicinal plant], collection of dried specimens of plants, mounted on sheets of heavy paper and stored in cabinets or bound in book form, and the building that houses such a collection. The term replaced *hortus siccus* [Lat, "dried garden"], which was used until 200 years ago. Herbaria originated in Europe in the 16th century. The largest, in Paris, has over 10.5 million specimens. In 1987, the total holdings of more than 250 institutional and private herbaria in Canada were estimated at 5.5 million. The largest Canadian herbaria are as follows: Biosystematics Research Institute, Agriculture Canada, Ottawa; National Herbarium of Canada, National Museum of Natural Sciences, Ottawa; Herbier Marie-Victorin, Institut Botanique Université de Montréal; University of British Columbia, Vancouver; University of Toronto. The largest private herbarium in Canada was that of Frère MARIE-VICTORIN, which forms the basis of the herbarium which now bears his name.

Reading: F.A. Stafleu, *Index Herbariorum* (1981).

Herbs, technically, are nonwoody, vascular plants, ie, relatively soft plants with specialized systems of vessels for conducting water and nutrients. More commonly, the word refers to various, often aromatic, plants used especially in medicine or as seasoning. Here, "herb" is used in its less technical sense. Herbs and spices differ largely by usage. Spices are normally more aromatic than herbs, and are often of tropical origin. They may consist of seeds, bark, flower buds, fruits, etc. Herbs are usually leafy and locally grown, and their use extends far back into history. Culinary herbs are still of great importance as flavouring; before refrigeration, they were essential as preservatives and to disguise the flavour of bad meat. "Pot herbs" were almost any young, green growth that could be eaten early in spring to supply needed minerals and vitamins after the privations of winter. Various herbal teas, filling the same need, were very important to the inhabitants of the New and Old worlds.

North American Indians were very conversant with the use of herbs for health, healing and spiritual needs. In many cases, discoveries paralleled those of Europe; eg, willow (*Salix*) and poplar (*Populus*), each containing salicylic acid (as does aspirin), were used by both Europeans and Indians for relief of pain and rheumatic complaints. Rose hips (containing vitamin C) were important on both sides of the Atlantic, as were yarrow, sorrel, mint and nettles. Indians introduced European settlers to medicinal herbs which they could substitute for those left at home. Particularly noteworthy were the effective cures for scurvy, chief of which, available even in winter, were teas made of spruce (*Picea*) or cedar (*Thuja*) needles.

Many favourite herbs come from the Mediterranean area and their position in northern gardens must be planned accordingly. A sunny spot, with a light sandy soil that warms up quickly in spring, is ideal. For maximum flavour, herbs should not be given too much water or nitrogen. Luckily, many herbs are annuals or can be grown as such; therefore, they present no problem in any part of Canada. Seed should be sown outside as soon as the soil is warm, or started indoors and transplanted when all danger of frost is past. Dill (*Anethum graveolens*), summer savory (*Satureia hortensis*), sweet basil (*Ocimum basilicum*), chervil (*Anthriscus cerefolium*) and sweet marjoram (*Majorana hortensis*) are annuals that may be grown this way. Parsley (*Petroselinum crispum*) and sage (*Salvia officinalis*) are perennial only in warmer parts of the country, but may be successfully grown as annuals.

Woody perennials such as rosemary (*Rosmarinus officinalis*) and lavender (*Lavandula officinalis*) will not generally overwinter outside. Thyme (*Thymus vulgaris*) is not very hardy, but creeping thyme (*T. serpyllum*) may be used as a substitute. Two popular herbs require somewhat different conditions. Chives (*Allium schoenoprasum*) are easy perennials in any good garden soil and should be divided and replanted every few years. Mint (*Mentha*) is a vigorous perennial, spreading rapidly in moist soil by means of underground stolons (horizontal branches); in dry prairie conditions, it may die out unless moved to new ground frequently.

The medicinal use of plants has a long and honourable history. The Greek Theophrastus (*c*371-286 BC) was the first botanist/physician to write about plants, their identification and uses. Medical knowledge was kept alive in the monasteries during the Middle Ages, and emerged during the 16th century, hand in hand with botany, when schools of medicine and BOTANIC GARDENS were first established. Meanwhile, the local herbalist, wise woman, or shaman continued to minister to the sick, often in competition with the professional doctors. Herbal specialists were sometimes revered, sometimes burned as witches. Because much ancient herbal lore relied on psychological as well as physical methods of curing, the use of herbal medicine fell into disrepute with the advent of "scientific" methods. Herbs, however, are the bases of modern medicines, some of which (eg, digitalis, belladonna and the many opium derivatives) are still obtainable only as plant extracts. Others, first discovered as plant ingredients, are now being manufactured synthetically. Many scientists are now looking at old remedies, and interest in herbal lore has revived as people seek alternatives or supplements to modern medicine. However, the use of herbal medicine is an exacting science in its own right, involving the correct identification and use of what may be highly toxic plants. The use even of simple home remedies and herbal teas should be attempted only by those familiar with plant identification. *See also* individual species entries; PLANTS, NATIVE USES; POISONOUS PLANTS. GILLIAN FORD

Reading: Malcolm Stuart, *The Encyclopedia of Herbs and Herbalism* (1979).

Herchmer, Lawrence William, Indian agent, police commissioner (b at Shipton on Cherwell, Eng 25 Apr 1840; d at Vancouver 17 Feb 1915). He served briefly in the British army and as supply officer for the British Boundary Commission (1872-74) before being appointed an Indian agent in Manitoba in 1876; in 1886 he was made commissioner of the NWMP. A capable administrator, Herchmer reorganized the force into an efficient police service. He greatly improved living conditions, benefits and training for the men, but his quick temper and overbearing nature created many enemies. He was publicly charged with mismanagement and tyrannical conduct. Although a judicial inquiry (1892) cleared him of serious wrongdoing, he was replaced as commissioner in 1900 while serving with the Canadian Mounted Rifles in South Africa, an injustice he protested until his death. S.W. HORRALL

Heriot, George, artist, public official, writer (b at Haddington, Scot 1759; d at London, Eng 1839). His chief importance to Canada resides in his art. He developed his drawing skills at an early age, encouraged by the Scottish Maecenas, Sir James Grant of Grant. In 1777 Heriot sailed for the West Indies where he drew, and composed *A Descriptive Poem, written in the West Indies* (1781). On his return to Britain (in 1781) he attended the Royal Military Academy, Woolwich, receiving instructions in topographical drawing from the illustrious drawing master, Paul Sandby, from whom he likely learned the principles of the Picturesque, an aesthetic system that determined his approach both to descriptive writing and to art. In 1792 he arrived in Canada employed as a clerk in the Quebec Ordinance Department; in 1799 he was appointed head of the Canadian post office. During his long Canadian sojourn (1792-1816) he returned to Britain twice on leaves of absence – in 1796 and in 1806. On the first return visit he seems to have been deeply impressed by the simplicity and monumentality of recent British watercolours and prints. It was also on this visit that his watercolours were accepted for exhibition at the Royal Academy.

Though talented as an administrator, Heriot lacked the diplomatic skills that would have led to

*Lake St Charles Near Quebec, c*1801, watercolour over graphite on laid paper, by George Heriot (*courtesy National Gallery of Canada*).

his promotion and to more power in the colony. However, he often found refuge from the tensions of his duties in travelling, writing, and painting. He wrote *The History of Canada from its first discovery* (1804) and *Travels through the Canadas* (1807), this latter work is illustrated with mainly aquatint plates of landscape, Indian and habitant subjects based on his own watercolour designs. In 1816 he resigned from the post office (owing to increasing difficulties with the colonial administration) and returned to Britain. GERALD FINLEY

Reading: Gerald Finley, *George Heriot: Postmaster-Painter of the Canadas* (1983).

Heritage Canada Foundation, est 28 Mar 1973 under executive director R.A.J. Phillips and chairman Hart McDougall, with a one-time government grant of $12 million, as a private non-profit trust for the "preservation and demonstration of the nationally significant historical, architectural, natural and scenic heritage of Canada." With existing organizations already concerned with the natural landscape, the foundation has concentrated on the built-up environment. In 1987 it had some 20 000 members and a staff of 30 in its Ottawa headquarters. Its executive has included Jacques Dalibard, Pierre Berton and J.P.S. MacKenzie. An elected board of 14 governors, chosen by regions at an annual convention, and 2 government appointees meet 3 times a year to set the foundation's goals.

The foundation's accomplishments in its first decade include establishment of heritage legislation in all provinces; demonstration projects in conservation areas in St John's; Charlottetown; St Andrews, NB; Halifax; Annapolis Royal, NS; Saint John; Quebec City; Ottawa; Winnipeg; Edmonton; Vancouver; and Dawson, YT; establishment of an educational- and technical-services department; publication of a bimonthly magazine, *Canadian Heritage*, together with books, pamphlets and technical manuals; an awards program for excellence in heritage preservation; and a public campaign for heritage awareness, including the establishment of National Heritage Day on the third Monday in Feb.

The foundation has concentrated on preserving main streets of small towns. The foundation is lobbying the federal government to preserve heritage railway stations and to reform the tax system in order to contribute to the preservation of early commercial and industrial structures. In 1987 the Preservation Planning Institute was established to provide an endowment fund and a chair for educators of heritage preservation. The foundation honours lifetime promoters of heritage preservation with the Heritage Canada Awards, and private-sector building renovations with the Montreal Trust/Credit Foncier Award. The latter was awarded to the Monastère du Bon Pasteur complex in Montréal in 1987 and to the Burns Building in Calgary in 1986. The foundation does not give grants, nor does it purchase property except for demonstration purposes. It has also expanded the original definition of "heritage" to include the entire built environment, the great number of buildings which give our communities their special character. A heritage building has been defined as one that is structurally sound and for which a viable use can be found. *See also* HISTORIC SITE. PIERRE BERTON

Heritage Conservation is the understanding, appreciation and preservation of things that are important in our culture and history. Heritage can be a tangible object, such as a building (church, post office, railway station), or it can be an artifact, such as a RED RIVER CART or a NW Coast Indian TOTEM POLE. Heritage can also be intangible, as in FOLKLORE, customs, language, dialect, songs and legends. The term "conservation" means protection from any agent (be it climate or man) that threatens to destroy heritage; it also means increasing our understanding and awareness of heritage. The practice of heritage conservation in Canada usually refers to protecting the built environment, ie, the preservation of buildings, streetscapes, hamlets, neighbourhoods and rural landscapes that have been created in the development of Canada.

Concern for monuments has existed for some time. When the original PARLIAMENT BUILDINGS burned in 1916, the new buildings (completed in 1920) were built in a Gothic revival style to complement the earlier East and West blocks that remained on the site. However, attention to everyday buildings and their protection has developed only recently. It is now common to see communities and individuals protecting, restoring, recycling and conserving shops, banks, houses and industrial buildings. Privateer's Wharf in Halifax, a grouping of early 19th-century buildings, has been restored for commercial uses; the residential neighbourhood centering on the corners of Milton and Park avenues in Montréal has been rehabilitated and is the locus of a number of housing co-operatives; and the Orpheum Theatre in Vancouver has been restored and adopted as the home of the Vancouver Symphony Orchestra. Before WWII interest in conservation had been limited to the protection of sites of national historic importance or scenic beauty. The earliest legislation in Canada to protect a site was the Rocky Mountains Parks Act of 1887. The Historic Sites and Monuments Board of Canada was formed in 1919 to advise the government on sites worthy of official recognition, and the National Parks Act was passed in 1930. Provincial historical associations, particularly in the Maritimes, Québec and Ontario, had been pressuring their governments since the early 20th century for the preservation of sites. These developments determined the nature of government intervention in heritage conservation; federal involvement is limited to the identification and protection of sites of national historic and architectural value, and to the development of programs of research in history, architecture and archaeology which relate to the national interest. Canada has signed international treaties on this subject. Under the Constitution Act, 1982, matters pertaining to property and civil rights are an exclusive concern of the provinces; thus, except for sites of clearly national significance, heritage conservation is primarily a matter of provincial policy.

In recent years, 2 events have fostered concern for retaining built heritage — the Canadian CENTENNIAL of 1967 and the ecology movement which began in the late 1960s. During the Centennial, local events commemorating the past drew attention to the wealth of Canada's architectural heritage and encouraged its preservation. At the national level, events such as EXPO 67 and the Voyageur Canoe Pageant drew Canadians together in a celebration of the past and future. The ecology movement gained momentum from public reaction to projects such as the ST LAWRENCE SEAWAY, which destroyed entire communities and a rich architectural heritage. Earth Day in 1970 was a celebration of the unity of the planet, and the energy crisis has drawn attention since 1973 to the limits of natural resources. Thus, both the philosophy of CONSERVATION and awareness and pride in Canadian history have fostered the growth of the heritage conservation movement in Canada.

In the early 1970s the federal government, through Parks Canada, began to record and interpret architectural history in the Canadian Inventory of Historic Building, a nationwide survey of buildings constructed before 1914. The HERITAGE CANADA FOUNDATION and the Society for the Study of Architecture in Canada were established to lobby for building conservation and to research specific areas of architecture and its history. Today, every province has some form of heritage conservation legislation, which usually concerns itself with specific issues such as individual building protection, area conservation, archaeology and the establishment of a provincial body to encourage heritage conservation publicly and privately. Some provinces have also included museums and archives in their legislation.

Heritage conservation involves the protection of objects and materials of interest in the interpretation of history. This is done mostly by ART GALLERIES AND MUSEUMS and ARCHIVES which collect, identify, preserve and interpret objects taken from their everyday setting. These objects may be small and discrete, such as projectile points or farm implements, or large and interconnected, such as buildings or building groupings. The collections of local museums and heritage villages are examples of this approach.

Heritage conservation also means the commemoration of an event, person, building or site of historical importance. Thus, plaques are erected to note HISTORIC SITES. In many cases, marking a site is not enough, as demolition and destruction have occurred even on marked buildings. For example, the Provincial Lunatic Asylum at 999 Queen Street West in Toronto (architect J.G. HOWARD) was demolished in 1976 by the provincial government, despite opposition from the Toronto Historical Board and the Ontario Heritage Foundation. Protection of a heritage building by a government can occur in 2 ways: by outright purchase or by legislation. As purchase can be costly, preference is often given to legislative means, such as heritage designation. By means of designation, a provincial or municipal government declares that a building must not be altered from the state that makes it a heritage building.

Heritage conservation may be included in land-use planning and development. In some places, heritage conservation is becoming as important in local planning as the provision of social services and community development. Several provinces have tied heritage legislation to environmental legislation and have developed procedures to ensure assessment of the impact of government expenditures or private developments on heritage. The results of a growth in heritage consciousness can be seen across Canada, as areas are protected, buildings are restored, museums are expanded, and long-range plans for the protection of the built environment are implemented. There are still many threats to heritage resources. Willful neglect of important buildings, a public that is not appreciative of heritage, inappropriate conservation of sites and buildings, tax laws that fail to encourage renovation, and zoning that does not consider heritage all threaten conservation.

The key to success is a growing appreciation by all Canadians of the contribution which this heritage can make to our quality of life, and a consensus to use economic and legal measures to capitalize on it. That consensus is still in the formative stage. GEORGE KAPELOS

Heritage conservation includes the protection of historically important buildings such as those in Bonsecours Market in Old Montréal (*photo by Harold V. Green/ Valan*).

Reading: M.C. Denhez, *Heritage Fights Back* (1978) and *Protecting the Built Environment* (1978).

Heritage Trail, route along which selected features of history or natural history are explained for the general public. The earliest interpreted trails, some 60 years ago, dealt only with natural history and were called nature trails. Originally, a typical nature trail was an existing path through a natural area, interpreted by means of signs or a booklet. The first interpreted nature trails in Canada were probably those developed in BANFF NATIONAL PARK in 1959 at the Hoodoos and Bow Summit. Hundreds of trails are now found from coast to coast in Canada, installed and run by national and provincial parks, the Canadian Wildlife Service, tourist departments, conservation authorities, museums, universities, schools, BOTANICAL GARDENS and private agencies.

Visitor numbers are often counted to measure use; however, few trails are systematically evaluated, although the Wye Marsh Centre now uses microcomputers to encourage visitors to evaluate all aspects of their visits. Trails can be expected to increase and diversify, and to become more sophisticated as interpreters and audiences use them more extensively. The following is a short list of selected nature trails in Canada:

Alberta: DINOSAUR PROVINCIAL PARK – Dead Lodge Canyon Nature Trail; ELK ISLAND NATIONAL PARK – Lakeview Trail; WATERTON LAKES NATIONAL PARK – Bertha Falls Trail; WOOD BUFFALO NATIONAL PARK – Lane Lake Trail, Salt River Trail.

British Columbia: GLACIER NATIONAL PARK – Abandoned Rails Trail, Loop Trail, Trestle Trail; MOUNT REVELSTOKE NATIONAL PARK – Inspiration Woods, Giant Cedars, Mountain Meadows.

Manitoba: RIDING MOUNTAIN NATIONAL PARK – Arrowhead, Burls and Bittersweet, Brûlé, Ma-ugun, Oninimik, Loon's Island and Grey Owl trails.

New Brunswick: Various trails at Anchorage Provincial Park, FUNDY NATIONAL PARK, Grand Falls, Hartland, Les Jardins de la République Provincial Park, Mactaquac Provincial Park, North Lake Provincial Park.

Newfoundland: GROS MORNE NATIONAL PARK – Berry Head Pond, Green Gardens, Berry Hill, Lobster Cove Head, Southeast Brook Falls and Stanleyville trails.

Northwest Territories: NAHANNI NATIONAL PARK – South Nahanni River canoe trail.

Nova Scotia: KEJIMKUJIK NATIONAL PARK – Mersey Meadow Trail, Mill Falls Trail; Lake Echo – Echo Look Out Trail; Cabot Trail; Evangeline Trail.

Ontario: Bellevue House National Historic Park; Fort Wellington National Historic Park; GEORGIAN BAY ISLANDS NATIONAL PARK – Beausoleil Island, Bobbies Trail, Flowerpot Island Trail; PUKASKWA NATIONAL PARK – Coastal Hiking Trail; Queenston Heights; Rideau Canal – Merrickvale Lockstation walking tour, Ecotour; Woodside National Historic Park.

Prince Edward Island: Prince Edward Island National Park – Balsam Hollow, Bubbling Springs, and Reeds and Rushes trails.

Québec: FORILLON NATIONAL PARK – Grande-Greve; Lachine Canal; LA MAURICIE NATIONAL PARK – Cascades Trail, Falaises Trail; ST LAWRENCE SEAWAY.

Saskatchewan: Meadow Lake; Prairie Wildlife Interpretation Centre – Swift Current Trail; PRINCE ALBERT NATIONAL PARK – Boundary Bog Trail, Mud Creek Trail.

Yukon Territory: Chilkoot Pass Trail; KLUANE NATIONAL PARK – various trails. DAVID SPALDING

Heron (Ardeidae), family of birds comprising 60 species worldwide, 12 in Canada (including true herons, egrets, night herons and bitterns). Most are long-legged, long-necked wading birds which look for food (tiny fish, crustaceans, insects, amphibians and reptiles) in shallow fresh or salt water. They have long, rounded, rather broad wings and relatively short tails. They are distinguished from CRANES by their position in flight, necks bent and heads supported between their shoulders. All have straight, rather long bills that distinguish them from ibises, which are similar in appearance but have long, curved bills. The sexes vary little in appearance. Plumage is generally dull, but certain species have crests and ornamental plumage during breeding season. Under flank plumage, the bird has layers of powder down, used to rid feathers of oil, grease and mud. The powder is applied by the claw of the middle toe, which has comblike teeth on its inner surface. Once the feathers are preened, the bird waterproofs them with oil from its uropygial glands.

Most herons and egrets nest in colonies, sometimes in mixed-species groups. Nests of small branches are built, sometimes high in trees, usually in wooded areas out of reach of predators. Bitterns nest closer to the ground, usually in freshwater marshes among clumps of reeds. Most species lay 3-5 (usually 4) pale blue or bluish green eggs. The great blue heron (*Ardea herodias*), the largest and most common heron in Canada, stands over 1 m tall. It frequents river banks and tidal bays, where it wades deep into the water to fish. It is found from Nova Scotia to Alberta, and on the British Columbia coast and islands. The black-crowned night heron (*Nycticorax nycticorax*) is a squat, short-toed bird of NS, the Great Lakes-St Lawrence R area, and southern Manitoba and Saskatchewan. It is usually found at river mouths and is especially active at dusk. Its vernacular name, night squawk, results from its cry in flight. The guttural cries of American bittern (*Botaurus lentiginosus*) may be heard in marshlands throughout southern Canada and up to Great Slave Lake, Northwest Territories. The bird blends perfectly with surrounding vegetation. Other breeding species include green-backed heron (*Butorides striatus*), in the Niagara region, southern Québec, part of New Brunswick and possibly Nova Scotia; cattle egret (*Bubulcus ibis*), recently and very locally in Ontario; great egret (*Casmerodius albus*), very locally in southern Ontario and rarely in southeastern Saskatchewan

The great blue heron is the largest and most common heron in Canada (*artwork by John Crosby*).

and Manitoba; yellow-crowned night heron (*Nycticorax violaceus*), only at East Sister I, Ont; least bittern (*Ixobrychus exilis)*, locally in southern Manitoba and NB, and in Niagara region.

JEAN-LUC DESGRANGES

Héroux, Denis, film director, producer (b at Montréal 15 July 1940). Héroux established himself in 1968 with *Valérie*, the first porno-erotic film made in Québec. After several erotic films, Héroux tried historical melodrama in *Quelques arpents de neige* (1972) and light comedy in *J'ai mon voyage* (1973) and *Pousse mais pousse égal* (1974). In the 1970s he became one of Canada's major producers of international co-productions. He directed a few films but abandoned directing for producing. His international reputation has enabled him to work with other celebrated directors: Claude Chabrol, *Violette Nozière* (1977), *Blood Relatives* (1978) and *The Blood of Others* (1984); Claude Lelouch, *A nous deux* (1979); Claude Pinoteau, *L'Homme en colère* (1979); Louis Malle, *Atlantic City* (1980); Jean-Jacques Annaud, *Quest for Fire* (1981); and Alexandre Arcady, *Hold-Up* (1985). Despite his dominant position in the private industry and his commercial success, Héroux's views on the Québec film industry and on national cinema have placed him at odds with his colleagues. He silenced criticism in part by producing Gilles CARLE's *Les Plouffe* (1981) and repeated this success with *Le Crime d'Ovide Plouffe* (1984) and *Le Matou* (1985). Héroux has also been a film critic and was a member of the 1982 Applebaum-Hébert FEDERAL CULTURAL POLICY REVIEW COMMITTEE.

PIERRE VÉRONNEAU

Herridge, William Duncan, lawyer (b at Ottawa 18 Sept 1888; d there 21 Sept 1961). Herridge was the brother-in-law of PM R.B. BENNETT, his minister to the US, 1931-35, and one of his key advisers. He served with distinction in WWI, winning both the DSO and MC. He came to political prominence during the election of 1930, when he wrote speeches for Bennett and helped formulate Conservative strategy. While in Washington he was impressed by F.D. Roosevelt's activist philosophy of government, and he played a prominent role in convincing Bennett to bring a version of the New Deal to Canada in 1935 (*see* BENNETT'S NEW DEAL). In 1939 the mercurial Herridge launched New Democracy, a short-lived political movement advocating monetary reforms and far-reaching government intervention in the economy.

NORMAN HILLMER

Herring, common name for fish of the widely distributed family Clupeidae. The true herring (*Clupea harengus*), a relatively small, bony, soft-rayed fish with an elongate, laterally compressed body, is silvery in colour, shading to bluish or bluish green on the back. Perhaps the most abundant of fishes, it is widely distributed throughout temperate and subarctic waters of the Northern Hemisphere, and is the only member of the genus found in Canadian waters. Adults move in vast schools, often many kilometres long, and migrate annually to spawning grounds in shallower waters. Herring feed on larger ZOOPLANKTON, abundant on or at the edge of the Continental Shelf. They are a major food of larger fishes (eg, COD, SALMON, TUNA, HALIBUT), marine mammals and sea birds.

Herring, abundant on Pacific and Atlantic coasts, also occur occasionally in Arctic waters. The Pacific subspecies (*C. h. pallasi*) differs from the Atlantic form (*C. h. harengus*) in several respects. Pacific herring spawn in spring, directly onto vegetation in intertidal and subtidal waters. They mature in their third year and seldom live more than 8 years. Their maximum standard length is about 26 cm. Atlantic herring spawn either in spring or autumn, usually over a gravel bottom. They mature in their fourth or fifth year, live 18 years or more and attain lengths of 35 cm or over. Herring have supported major commercial FISHERIES on both coasts. Both subspecies experience major population fluctuations caused by differences in brood survival. Prior to the mid-1900s, catches were limited by markets or catching capacities of fishing fleets. The development of an almost unlimited world market for herring meal and oil, plus major advances in fishing technology, led to overfishing of Pacific stocks 1956-66, when annual catches usually exceeded 200 000 t, and of Atlantic stocks 1968-71, when Canadian catches exceeded 400 000 t annually. Both fisheries have since been strictly regulated. Pacific fishermen using mainly purse seines and gillnets, took about 50 000 t annually during the late 1970s; this was further reduced to an average of 34 000 t between 1981 and 1984 and to 16 300 in 1986. However, the value of the catch was much higher than before because of the prime price fetched on the Japanese market for quality herring roe. Catches of Atlantic herring averaged about 235 000 t during the late 1970s, taken primarily by purse seine and mid-water trawl for sale to European processors. Abundance declined on the East Coast also during the early 1980s, with catches declining from 260 000 t in 1980 to about 177 500 t in 1986. A traditional weir fishery for young herring, for canning as sardines, operates in NB.

Six other members of the family are found in Canadian waters. Atlantic round herring (*Etrumeus sadina*), Atlantic menhaden (*Brevoortia tyrannus*) and Pacific sardine or pilchard (*Sardinops sagax*) are ocean spawners most abundant in southern US waters. They are now rare and of no commercial importance in Canada, although Pacific sardines supported a major fishery in BC during a period of high abundance (mid-1920s to 1940s). Alewife or glut herring (*Alosa pseudoharengus*), American shad (*A. sapidissima*) and blueback herring (*A. aestivalis*) are anadromous (ie, live in the sea but spawn in fresh water) on the Atlantic coast. They are also most abundant in the south, but alewife and American shad are relatively common in Canadian coastal waters, where they are fished commercially. American shad, introduced on the Pacific coast in 1871, is now found in the Fraser R and Rivers Inlet. A landlocked form of alewife is plentiful in the Great Lakes; many of its local names include the word herring. At least 4 other freshwater fishes (2 ciscos, goldeye and mooneye) are also known by names sometimes containing the word herring.

A.S. HOURSTON

Herschel Island, 100 km^2, lies in the Beaufort Sea off the N coast of the Yukon Territory. Named in 1826 by John FRANKLIN after the English astronomer Sir William Herschel, its geographical features were named in 1889 by Cdr C.H. Stockton of USS *Thetis*. Beginning in 1890-91, the island was used as a wintering station by American WHALING ships. In response to complaints that the local Inuit were being abused, an Anglican missionary reached the island in 1893; a NWMP detachment was set up in 1903. By 1914 the whaling industry was dead, but the Mounted Police remained to demonstrate Canadian sovereignty in the western Arctic. In Feb 1924 ALIKOMIAK AND TÁTIMAGANA were hanged at the island for murder, the first Inuit to be executed under Canadian law. By the late 1960s the island had no permanent population.

WILLIAM R. MORRISON

Hertel, François, pseudonym of Rodolphe Dubé (b at Rivière-Ouelle, Qué 31 May 1905; d at Montréal 4 Oct 1985). At 20 he entered the Jesuits and he was ordained in 1938. Professor of literature, philosophy and history, he taught at the colleges of Jean-de-Brébeuf, Ste-Marie and André-Grasset, as well as at the Jesuit college in Sudbury. In 1946 he left the order to become a secular priest in Montréal but asked to be laicized the following year. Meanwhile, he contributed articles to several periodicals, including to the review AMÉRIQUE FRANÇAISE until 1947. In 1949 he moved to France, where he gave conferences, founded an art review (*Rythmes et couleurs*, later *Fer de lance*) and ran a publishing firm, Diaspora française. After 37 years of self-imposed exile he returned to Montréal. The writings of this polymath, a member of the ACADÉMIE CANADIENNE-FRANÇAISE, include almost 40 titles. They trace the intellectual development of the mystical poet (*Les Voix de mon rêve*, 1934) and the classical poet (*Axes et parallaxes*, 1946), a man who was also a concerned educator (*Leur inquiétude*, 1936), a baroque storyteller (*Anatole Laplante, curieux homme*, 1944), a provocative essayist (*Cent ans d'injustice?* 1967), a memorialist sensitive to the world of the imagination (*Louis Préfontaine,* *apostat*, 1967) and, lastly, an agnostic philosopher (*Vers une sagesse, Mystère cosmique et condition humaine*, 1975). KENNETH LANDRY

Hertel de La Fresnière, Joseph-François, soldier (bap at Trois-Rivières, New France 3 July 1642; buried at Boucherville, New France 22 May 1722). As a youth, he was captured and adopted by the Iroquois (1661), escaped, and took part in retaliatory raids, accompanying FRONTENAC to Lk Ontario (1673). Though he was fined and briefly jailed for illegal fur-trading activities, his knowledge of Indian languages and warfare was valuable. Under Frontenac's orders, Hertel led numerous expeditions using the Indian method of rapid movement and ambush, including a devastating raid on the New England town of Salmon Falls in which the French claimed 43 Englishmen were killed. Hertel was called "the Hero," the "terror of the English." He commanded FT FRONTENAC 1709-12 and, by marriage with Marguerite de Thavenet, inherited the Chambly seigneury. After long delays owing to his humble birth, he was granted letters of nobility in 1716. JAMES MARSH

Herzberg, Gerhard, physicist, Nobel laureate (b at Hamburg, Germany 25 Dec 1904). He began an academic career at Darmstadt Technical U after earning his doctorate in engineering there and left Nazi Germany in 1935. Herzberg taught at U of Sask 1935-45, coming to Canada on the initiative of J.W.T. SPINKS, who had worked at his Darmstadt laboratory 1933-34. He went to the Yerkes Observatory, Chicago, in 1945, seeking better opportunities for research, and returned to Canada in 1948 to join the staff of the NATIONAL RESEARCH COUNCIL. As director of physics 1949-69, Herzberg and NRC president E.W.R. STEACIE laid the foundations of the NRC's postwar reputation as a scientific "centre of excellence."

Herzberg's own research field was molecular SPECTROSCOPY, the analysis of the spectra of molecules in order to determine their structure. He specialized in free radicals, important intermediates of chemical reactions that have very short lifetimes (microseconds) under laboratory conditions. Free radicals are also found in interstellar space, where they can last for long periods, and their spectra can thus be recorded by special instruments. Herzberg and his associates developed new methods for their spectroscopic analysis. His career included more than 200 scientific publications and he earned many honours, such as fellowship in the Royal Soc of London (1951), the Order of Canada and the Nobel Prize for chemistry in 1971. He was also a vigorous participant in the SCIENCE POLICY debate following the Lamontagne report of 1970. The NRC created its highest grade, Distinguished Research Officer, especially to allow Herzberg to continue personal research after he reached retirement age in 1969 (he continued to hold the post in 1987). In 1975 the NRC's astronomy and spectroscopy units were reorganized as the Herzberg Institute of Astrophysics, and in Sept 1987 Minor Planet No 3316, discovered Feb 1984, was named after him. DONALD J.C. PHILLIPSON

Gerhard Herzberg, winner of the Nobel Prize in 1971 (*courtesy National Research Council*).

Hespeler, Ont, Town, inc 1901, located in SW Ontario, 14 km S of GUELPH. It was first settled by Swiss Germans from Pennsylvania, and originally called Bergytown after an early resident, Michael Bergy. Subsequently the name became New Hope, then Hespeler (1858), after Jacob Hespeler, an operator of mills and small manufactories who moved to the community 1844. His enterprises formed the core of the local economy for most of the 19th century and he was the first reeve of the village. In 1973 Hespeler amalgamated with Preston and GALT to form the new city of CAMBRIDGE. DANIEL FRANCIS

Hesquiaht, a NOOTKA tribe on the W coast of Vancouver I. Their traditional territories include Hesquiat Harbour and the Hesquiat Peninsula. Archaeological investigations have found that Hesquiat Harbour has been occupied by native people for at least 2000 years. The Hesquiaht formerly consisted of several independent small groups, each with its own villages and territory. Some of these groups were the first Nootka people to have contact with Europeans, having met and traded with Juan PÉREZ HERNÁNDEZ off the W coast of the Hesquiat Peninsula in 1774. Warfare with other Nootka and decimation from European-introduced diseases gradually brought about the amalgamation of the Hesquiaht groups into a tribe in the 19th century. In 1875 Rev A.J. Brabant established the first Roman Catholic mission among the Nootka at Hesquiat, the tribal village of the Hesquiaht. In 1964 a tidal wave destroyed Hesquiat, and the Hesquiaht dispersed, largely to Port Alberni and Victoria. Today, they also live at Refuge Cove. JOHN DEWHIRST

Hetu, Pierre, conductor (born at Montréal 22 Apr 1936). He graduated in music from the Conservatoire of the province of Québec and from the Music Dept of U de Montréal. He studied conducting in Paris, Vienna, Siena, Italy, and Dusseldorf, Germany, and with Charles Munch at the Tanglewood Festival. In 1961 he won first prize in the International Competition for Young Conductors in Besançon, France. He was assistant conductor of the Montreal Symphony Orchestra (1963-68), music director in Kalamazoo, Mich (1963-73) and associate conductor of the Detroit Symphony Orchestra (1970-73) and music director of the Edmonton Symphony Orchestra (1973-80). He is a frequent guest conductor with major Canadian orchestras and opera houses, CBC radio and television, and US orchestras. He has conducted in France, Belgium and Switzerland, and in 1976 he led the World Orchestra of "Jeunesses Musicales" in the opening concert and ceremonies of the Montreal Olympics. His conducting of Strauss's *Salome* with the Edmonton Symphony Orchestra brought him the Canadian Music Council Award. HÉLÈNE PLOUFFE

Heward, Efa Prudence, painter (b at Montréal 2 July 1896; d at Los Angeles, Calif 19 Mar 1947). A figure painter of distinction when landscape painting was uppermost, Heward studied in Montréal and Paris. She was a founding member of the Canadian Group of Painters (1933), and joined the Contemporary Arts Soc (1939), differing from her women contemporaries by a strong, individualistic approach to figure painting. Brilliant acid colours, sculptural treatment and an intense brooding quality pervade her pictures, whatever the subject. In her determination that structure would win over pretty landscape, she sometimes isolated the figure against a backdrop of complex, modelled shapes. ANNE MCDOUGALL

Hewitt, Angela Mary, pianist (b at Ottawa 26 July 1958). Among the rising generation of young Canadian musicians on the international scene, Hewitt is one of the very best. Nurtured in a musical family, her piano studies led to U of Ottawa, the teaching of Jean-Paul Sévilla, and the BMus degree at age 18. Hewitt's early promise – acknowledged by many prestigious awards and by orchestral appearances in Canada and abroad – was crowned at the 1985 International Bach Competition in Toronto where she won first prize. Through Angela Hewitt's recitals, orchestral engagements, records, and radio and television appearances, audiences in Europe, Canada, and the US are making ever-wider acquaintance with a mature artist possessed of exceptional authority, polished technique and deeply expressive musicality. BARCLAY MCMILLAN

Hewitt, Charles Gordon, administrator, economic entomologist, conservationist (b at Macclesfield, Eng 23 Feb 1885; d at Ottawa 29 Feb 1920). Hewitt received a doctorate from Manchester U where he also lectured in economic zoology. He was appointed Canada's second Dominion entomologist in 1909. He was instrumental in the passing of the Destructive Insect and Pest Act in 1910 and expanded entomological services of the federal Dept of Agriculture by creating separate units, each headed by an entomologist, to deal specifically with field-crop, garden, forest and stored-product insects. Regional laboratories were established to study insect pests and devise controls. He was also successful in furthering the Canada-US treaty for the protection of migratory birds. A book on the protection of wildlife (1919), one on the housefly, annual entomological reports (1910-16) and many circulars and bulletins are part of his legacy. P.W. RIEGERT

Hewitt, Foster William, broadcaster (b at Toronto 21 Nov 1902; d at Scarborough 21 Apr 1985). He worked briefly as a sportswriter for the Toronto *Daily Star* before switching to the new radio desk. On 22 Mar 1923, using an upright telephone, he made one of the first radio broadcasts of a HOCKEY game (a Senior League match between Toronto Parkdale and Kitchener). Although this success led him to try his hand at broadcasting a wide variety of sports and public-affairs events, his name is most indelibly associated with hockey. He broadcasted the first game from Maple Leaf Gardens when it opened in 1931 and, from that time, his play-by-play descriptions became familiar to fans from coast to coast. His high-pitched voice would rise to a crescendo with his famous phrase, "He shoots! He scores!" He probably did more to popularize hockey in N America than any other person. In 1933 he participated in Canada's first experiment with TV, and when that medium came of age in the 1950s, he readily adapted to it. He was a TV commentator for 15 years and many people remember him in connection with Hockey Night in Canada. J. THOMAS WEST

Hewitt, John, cooper, labour leader, editor (*fl* 1860s-90s). After extensive experience in American labour reform, Hewitt became a major Toronto labour leader. He helped found the Toronto Trades Assembly, led the NINE-HOUR MOVEMENT, and backed the labour paper, the *Ontario Workman*. He was elected first secretary of the Canadian Labor Union (1873). He resigned as secretary of the Toronto Trades Assembly to take a Tory patronage job at the Toronto Water Works, and later was an editor of the *Sentinel,* the Orange Order's weekly. Hewitt's Toryism stemmed from his belief in a coalition of labour and small producing employers. While an anomaly from today's perspective, he represents the radical Tory workingman of his day. G.S. KEALEY

Hewton, Randolph Stanley, painter (b at Maple-Grove, Qué 12 June 1888; d at Belleville, Ont 17 Mar 1960). He studied under William BRYMNER in Montréal (1903) and at the Académie Julian in Paris (1908-13). In Paris he met A.Y. JACKSON (1912), whose influence on his style would be considerable. This influence and the impressionism to which he was exposed in Paris can be seen in his early Canadian landscapes. His interpretation was sympathetic to that of the GROUP OF SEVEN but was not initially well received in his native Québec (1913). Perhaps his strongest development was in figure painting and portraiture, in which he successfully combined the traditional fundamentals with contemporary influences, as in *Sleeping Woman* (1929). He was a founding member of the Canadian Group of Painters (1933) and was elected to the Royal Canadian Academy of Arts in 1934. ERIK J. PETERS

Hibernia Case (*Newfoundland Reference Re Continental Shelf*) On 19 May 1982 the governor-in-council asked the Supreme Court of Canada whether Canada (the federal government) or Newfoundland has the right to explore and exploit the mineral and other natural resources of the seabed and subsoil of the Continental Shelf in the area offshore Newfoundland, approximately 320 km ESE of St John's, and whether Canada or Newfoundland has legislative jurisdiction to make laws in relation to such exploration and exploitation (*see* RESOURCE RIGHTS). The Court held, in March 1984, that Continental Shelf rights are an extraterritorial manifestation of external sovereignty, and hence these rights fall under the jurisdiction of the federal government. The Court held also that the federal government has legislative jurisdiction in relation to the right to explore and exploit in the Continental Shelf by virtue of the PEACE, ORDER AND GOOD GOVERNMENT power in its residual capacity. GÉRALD-A. BEAUDOIN

Hickman, Albert Edgar, businessman, politician (b at Grand Bank, Nfld 2 Aug 1875; d at St John's 9 Feb 1943). Newfoundland's seventeenth prime minister, he held that office for just 33 days from 10 May to 11 June 1924, the shortest administration in Newfoundland's history. He was a prominent St John's businessman when he entered politics in 1913 and became a minister in several Cabinets. He succeeded William WARREN as prime minister when Warren resigned but was soon defeated in a general election by Walter MONROE. Hickman continued as leader of the Opposition until he retired from politics in 1928. ROBERT D. PITT

Hicks, Henry Davies, lawyer, politician, university president, philatelist, premier of NS 1954-56 (b at Bridgetown, NS 5 Mar 1915). Educated at Mount Allison, Dalhousie and Oxford (where he was a Rhodes scholar) and an officer of the Royal Canadian Artillery 1941-45, Hicks, a Liberal, was elected to the NS legislature in 1945. Minister of education 1949-55, he implemented a system of regional and vocational schools. In 1954, after the death of Prem Angus L. MACDONALD and a brief period with H.J. CONNOLLY as premier, Hicks was elected premier by a badly split party. He became leader of the Opposition in 1956. Resigning from the legislature in 1960 to become dean at Dalhousie, he was president 1963-80; since then he has been president emeritus. President of the Canadian Commission to UNESCO 1963-67 and member of the Canada Council 1963-67, he was appointed to the Senate in 1972. M. CONRAD

Hide, Peter Nicholas, sculptor (b in Surrey, Eng 15 Dec 1944). Hide studied under British sculptor Anthony Caro at St Martins School of Art, London, 1964-67, then was instrumental in establishing studios and annual exhibitions for painters and sculptors at Stockwell Depot in S London. He accepted a teaching post at U of A, Edmonton, in 1977 and has since divided his time between Canada and England, where he works at Stockwell Depot for brief periods each summer. Like many sculptors today, Hide works in welded steel. He is one of the few to have broken away from the overpowering influence of Caro, whose art tends to sprawl and spread through space; Hide's tends to be compact and upright. As such, it looks back to the monolithic sculpture of the past, though fully abstract. Composed of rhythmic folds, pleats and projections, his sculptures are often more than 2 m high and have a unique presence. Though influential in Edmonton and London, Eng, his work has unfortunately seldom been exhibited outside those 2 centres. TERRY FENTON

Hiebert, Paul, humorist, professor (b at Pilot Mound, Man 17 July 1892; d at Carman, Man 7 Sept 1987). After completing his education at the universities of Manitoba, Toronto and McGill, Hiebert taught chemistry for many years at U Man; but he won enduring national recognition and affection in 1947 with the publication of SARAH BINKS, a book which has immortalized the fictional poetic exploits of Sarah – Hiebert's "Sweet Songstress of Saskatchewan" – for generations of Canadians. Hiebert extended the range of his warm but wryly hyperbolic commentary on Canadiana (and Binksiana) with *Willows Revisited* (1967) and *For the Birds* (1980), but his best-loved portrait, drawn with gentle mockery, remains that of the legendary Sarah. He was honoured both for his academic achievements (Gov Gen's Award for Science, 1924) and for *Sarah Binks*, which won him the Leacock Medal for Humour in 1947 and has been reprinted several times since. NEIL BESNER

High Arctic Weather Stations (HAWS), managed by the Atmospheric Environment Service of Canada, began as the Joint Arctic Weather Stations (JAWS). Between 1947 and 1950, 5 sites were selected and built jointly by Canada and the US (at Eureka, Resolute, Mould Bay, Isachsen and Alert) to provide the data required for the understanding and prediction of meteorological phenomena on a hemispheric scale and, more specifically, to improve weather predictions for N America. The meteorological data collected is also used by forecasting offices, airlines, climatology studies and research. Each station collects its data primarily from hydrogen-gas weather balloons, which are launched every 12 hours with an attached radiosonde instrument that transmits temperature, pressure and humidity information through a cross-section of the lower 30 km of atmosphere; the radiosonde is electronically tracked to determine wind speed and direction as the instrument rises aloft. In addition, hourly surface weather observations are recorded. Sea-ice thickness and snow depth measurements are taken bi-weekly nearly year-round. Aircraft runways are maintained for resupply and to provide emergency landing for polar flights. The stations have greatly increased our knowledge of the circulation of the Earth's atmosphere and have thus extended the period of reliability of weather forecasts.

Eureka Weather Station, Ellesmere I, was established 7 Apr 1947 by a small force of Canadians and Americans who landed on the sea ice of Slidre Fiord. Since the early 1950s the Canadian officer-in-charge has been appointed ex-officio customs and excise officer, immigration officer, game officer and postmaster. (Philatelists around the world enjoy the unique stamp cachets from these High Arctic post offices.) The station became a solely Canadian operation when the Americans withdrew 2 July 1972. Eureka is the last staging point for many adventurers travelling to the North Pole each spring.

Resolute Weather Station, Cornwallis I, was established in Aug 1947, followed by the RCAF developing an airbase and maintaining facilities until 1 Apr 1964 when operations were transferred to Transport Canada. The last Americans withdrew on 27 Aug 1972.

Mould Bay Weather Station, Prince Patrick I. Here the initial landing was made by US air support on 11 Apr 1948 with 3 station personnel and basic supplies. The airlift was staged from Resolute. The Americans withdrew 2 Nov 1971. This station is the loneliest outpost and can only be resupplied by air, since the ice conditions prevent icebreakers from reaching Mould Bay (although the new Polar Class 8 design might make the first sealift a reality by 1992).

Isachsen Weather Station, Ellef Ringnes I. The first 3 station personnel were flown in to Isachsen from Resolute with US air support on 3 Apr 1948. The Americans withdrew 31 Oct 1971, and budgetary restraints and reductions caused the decommissioning of Isachsen 19 Sept 1978.

Alert Weather Station, Ellesmere I. The initial landing by Canadian and US air forces took place 9 Apr 1950 from Thule, Greenland, although some supplies such as fuel, emergency rations, temporary shelters and a small tractor were left on Cape Belknap in Aug 1948 by the USS *Edisto* icebreaker. The Americans withdrew 31 Oct 1970. Alert is the most northerly permanent research station in the world. In 1986 Canada's first Background Air Pollution Monitoring (BAPMON) Laboratory was inaugurated there. This High Arctic research laboratory will permit scientists from the Atmospheric Environment Service to track changes in the chemical (carbon dioxide, methane, aerosols) and physical composition of the Arctic atmosphere over the next many decades because of the potential impact on world climates and the Arctic ecosystems. It is hoped that scientists will be able to identify major routes of toxic substances in the Arctic. OZONE observations will also be conducted to help resolve the mystery of the breakdown of the polar vortex and discontinuity of ozone levels in the Arctic atmosphere. D.L. STOSSEL

High Level, Alta, Town, pop 3004 (1986c), 2194 (1981c), inc 1965, is located 300 km N of the town of Peace River. It began as a stopping point on the Mackenzie Hwy and later the Great Slave Lake Ry (1963). It is a shipping centre for timber and grain and serves numerous oil rigs at Rainbow Lk to the W. The town is named for its location at the height of land separating the HAY R system from the PEACE R. The weekly newspaper is the *High Level Echo.* ERIC J. HOLMGREN

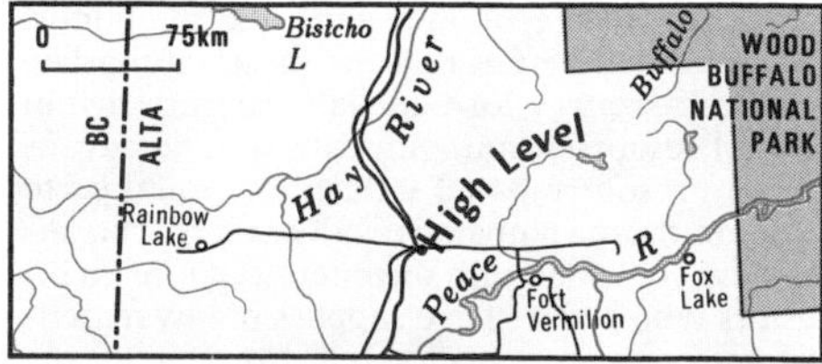

High River, Alta, Town, pop 5096 (1986c), 4792 (1981c), inc 1906, is located 55 km S of Calgary, and was named for the nearby Highwood R, known to the Blackfoot as *ispitsi*, "tall trees." Traces of Indian hunting villages have been found throughout the area, which was opened to ranching in the 1880s. In 1892 the CPR arrived in High River and it became an important shipping point for cattle. Today ranching and wheat growing are the mainstays of the local economy. The ranching past and the life of the homesteaders is preserved in the Museum of the Highwood. W.O. MITCHELL set the scene of many of his stories in the area. The town is the birthplace of Rt Hon Joseph CLARK, prime minister of Canada 1979-80.

ERIC J. HOLMGREN

High School, the term usually applied to the school grades following those of the elementary school. Because the elementary grades have varied from province to province over the decades, high schools have included grades 7, 8 or 9 to 12 or 13. These schools vary in type (academic, vocational, technical, composite) and may be public (free) or private (fee-charging). Originally tending to be somewhat elitist, public high schools have become open and free to all children who have completed elementary schooling. As a result, the number of courses offered has increased markedly. *See also* SECONDARY SCHOOL.

WILLARD BREHAUT

High Technology Technology, along with labour, capital, resources and management, is one of the essential components of industrial production. Most classes of INDUSTRY require some technological input but the amount varies widely among industrial sectors. Some sectors, eg, AEROSPACE, computers, TELECOMMUNICATIONS and PHARMACEUTICALS, are particularly dependent upon advanced TECHNOLOGY (ie, technology that rests on advanced scientific and ENGINEERING knowledge) and are referred to as "high-technology" industries.

Success in high technology depends upon the interaction of highly skilled engineers, scientists, technologists and business managers, operating in an environment which is receptive to new products, processes and services. Thus, high-technology industries flourish in countries with advanced economies, well-developed educational systems and sophisticated markets. High-technology industries form an important component in the economies of most major Western industrial countries, particularly the US, West Germany, Japan, France and Great Britain. Within these countries, the managerial and design headquarters of high-technology firms tend to concentrate in particular regions, usually regions served by strong universities with scientific and technological orientation.

There has been a long-standing debate on the importance of high-technology industry to Canada's economic development. One view is that Canada, as an advanced industrial country with a highly educated work force, should seek to become a major player in international markets for high-technology products. Proponents of this view believe that high technology offers the best growth potential, that it corresponds most closely with the aspirations of individual Canadians and that it is essential if this country is to keep open the widest choice of economic and political options. The opposing view is that the most appropriate economic strategy for Canada, a country rich in natural resources and with comparative advantages in resource-based industries, would be to build on those comparative advantages. The latter view coincides with the interest of foreign investors who seek reliable supplies of raw materials and semiprocessed goods from politically stable resources.

In practice, Canadian policy has been to encourage simultaneously both high-technology and resource-based industries. Hence, Canada has demonstrated less national commitment to high technology than most of its industrial trading partners have. The federal government has shown the greatest interest in high-technology industries; provincial governments have held policies generally more favourable to resource development. The aggregate impact of these mixed policies, combined with a high degree of FOREIGN INVESTMENT and the natural economic forces stemming from Canada's rich resource base, has produced an industrial structure that is oriented towards resources far more than towards high technology. Since the end of WWII Canada has consistently been in a growing net deficit position in its trade in high-technology products, while it has enjoyed a favourable trade position in natural resources and resource-based industries. Many Canadians see this as increasingly poor performance and a major national concern, not only because of its immediate impact on economic growth and employment but also because of the constraints that it may place on Canada's future economic, social and political development.

Man with high-tech products (*photo by Ken Davies/Masterfile*).

Despite the disappointing overall performance of Canadian high-technology industries, certain individual firms have been highly successful. Northern Telecom, now a world-scale technology-based company, had annual sales that rose from $608 million in 1973 to more than $6 billion in 1986. Other high-technology companies' growth rates have been similar but, although in the mid to late 1980s such companies can and do experience difficulties, these firms demonstrate that Canada can be a fertile ground for high-technology industry and that overall performance could improve rapidly, given the right conditions. *See also* ROBOTICS; SCIENCE POLICY; SCIENTIFIC RESEARCH AND DEVELOPMENT; SCIENCE AND SOCIETY.

P.L. BOURGAULT

High Wines, liquor adulterated for use in the FUR TRADE. Fur traders who supplied liquor to the Indians often diluted their brandy, rum, whisky, etc, with flavoured water. The term "high wines" is a misnomer, for the trade goods are not wines but spirits. Trade liquor, whether diluted or not, was also known as "Indian liquor" or "fire-water."

JOHN ROBERT COLOMBO

Higher Criticism involves the application of critical scholarly methods to the study of the origins, textual integrity and interpretation of the biblical record. It began in 18th-century Europe, particularly Germany, and was an attempt to understand events previously held to be of divine inspiration in terms consistent with the secular historical experience. It was often received with suspicion by religious authorities, since it appeared to cast doubt on the inspirational basis and prophetic nature of the Christian revelation.

Canada produced no major exponent of the higher criticism, but several advocates of the approach taught at English Canadian universities between 1890 and 1930, and some ran into major difficulties with university authorities. At the Methodist-controlled Victoria College, for example, the Rev George Coulson Workman (in the 1890s) and the Rev George Jackson (between 1910 and 1913) found strong opposition. Workman was dismissed from his post for challenging the accepted view of messianic prophecy. Even in the 1920s scholars who voiced such views at the University of Toronto faced public criticism in the daily press and uncertain support from their administrative superiors. Because of this, higher criticism in Canada is best studied in the context of ACADEMIC FREEDOM rather than theology.

A. BRIAN MCKILLOP

Highland Games originated among the Scots' Celtic ancestors and became a customary part of their life. Events such as tossing the caber and putting the stone, and competitions in playing bagpipes and Highland dancing formed the core of the festivities, along with footraces, wrestling and tug-o'-war, and novelty events such as three-legged races or the Best-Dressed Highlander competition. Emigration from Scotland dispersed the Highland Games and brought them to N America (where they are often referred to as the Caledonian Games). Given the influence of SCOTS in Canadian history, it is not surprising that their Highland Games have flourished.

A Highland Society was organized in Glengarry, Ont, in 1819 but lapsed after "many successful gatherings." More permanent games were established by the Caledonian Club of PEI in 1838. Similar games followed in Lancaster, Toronto, Cape Breton, Montréal and Zorra, and by Confederation in Halifax, Antigonish, Chatham, Ottawa and Vancouver. Within a few years, they were established in many Ontario townships and in Fredericton, Québec City and Victoria. In 1880, the St Andrew's Society of Winnipeg held the first of its many successful Dominion Day Games at Dufferin Park. The marquis of LORNE patronized these games and others, as did other governors general and many famous Scottish political figures, among them George BROWN and Sir John A. MACDONALD. Former PM John DIEFENBAKER carried on the tradition when he visited the 1975 Glengarry Games, appropriately dressed in a kilt.

It has become customary to hold provincial track and field championships in conjunction with the Highland Games. The festival has thus undoubtedly helped to produce some of Canada's greatest athletes – eg, Duncan Bowie, George GRAY and Walter KNOX – who have won international renown. More significantly, perhaps, it has thoroughly permeated Canadian culture (for example, the novels of Ralph Connor – C.W. GORDON), and Canada is now said to have more bagpipes and Highland dancers than even Scotland itself. Canadian Highland Games remain a vivid reflection of the Scottish tradition in Canadian life.

GERALD REDMOND

Reading: Gerald Redmond, *The Sporting Scots of Nineteenth-Century Canada* (1982).

Higson, Allison, swimmer (b at Mississauga, Ont 13 Mar 1973). This young breaststroke swimmer, coached by Paul Bergen, holds 30 age-group records and established 11 of them at a single meet in Dec 1985. In 1986, at the age of 13, she won 2 golds and a silver relay medal at the Commonwealth Games and then became the youngest medalist ever at the world championships by winning a bronze medal in the 200 m breaststroke. Higson was named Canadian Amateur Swimming Association Female Athlete of the Year 1986 (as well as CASA Junior Athlete

1986) and is one of Canada's outstanding prospects for future international success.

GERALD REDMOND

Hiking can be defined as walking over long distances (preferably in a scenic, natural setting), for pleasure or exercise. For many people, hiking means backpacking; others prefer simply to go rambling. Whatever the definition, more and more Canadians are participating in the activity. In 1976 about 1% of the population 14 years and over had participated. A 1981 survey, scheduled to be carried out again in 1988, showed that this figure had grown to about 5%. About 50% of Canadians walk for pleasure, an activity that includes nature walks, which may or may not involve carrying a pack. Hiking's increase in popularity has resulted in part from a more urbanized population that is interested in the outdoors, in part from increased concern for physical fitness, and in part from easier access to wilderness or park areas. Although one can go hiking almost anywhere, the most likely site is in a park or open-space setting – whether an urban park (High Park, Toronto, or Capital City Park, Edmonton) or a true wilderness setting such as the Canadian Rockies or ALGONQUIN PROVINCIAL PARK. Hiking today is no longer only an activity for the serious nature lover or outdoor enthusiast seeking solitude in nature, although most participants tend to be in the 20-35 age bracket. The sport has also become a group or family activity.

Many people pursue hiking by becoming members of a hiking club or association such as the Bruce Trail Assn, Ontario Federation of Naturalists or Waskahegan Trail Assn. Many clubs were formed to promote the development and use of a particular hiking trail. There is even a newly formed National Trail Assn of Canada promoting the development of a long-distance hiking trail across the entire country from coast to coast. These trails may represent an historic aspect of Canada's heritage or simply provide access through a scenic environment, for example, the Cabot Trail and BRUCE TRAIL. Many are considered long-distance trails, extending for many kilometres and requiring the hiker to "overnight" along the route before completing the hike. Trails exist at all levels of difficulty, from the easy-to-walk rural trails (WASKAHEGAN TRAIL, Alberta) to the more stamina-testing and rugged ones such as WEST COAST TRAIL, Vancouver I. *See also* HERITAGE TRAILS.

BART F. DEEG

Hikers' camp in the Purcell Mountains, BC (*photo by J.A. Kraulis*).

Hill, Daniel Grafton, human rights specialist, historian, public servant (b at Independence, Mo 23 Nov 1923). Following WWII, Canada experienced a concerted effort to overturn the legacy of discrimination suffered by racial minorities. Few were more prominent in this movement than Hill, who came to Canada for graduate studies but committed himself to the quest for justice in his adopted land. As an activist in the 1950s, his touch was always scholarly, using research and public awareness as tools to combat imbedded prejudices. With a PhD in sociology from U of T and a decade's experience with social causes, he was first director of the Ontario Human Rights Commission 1962-71. Under his management the commission evolved innovative tactics, widely copied in Canada and other countries. In 1971 he became the first full-time chairman of OHRC and in 1973 established a consulting firm in human rights with an international clientele. His publications on human rights and black history include *Human Rights in Canada: A Focus on Racism* (1977, 1986) and *The Freedom Seekers: Blacks in Early Canada* (1981). Provincial Ombudsman since 1984, Hill has striven to make that office reflect the "new Ontario" with a forceful outreach program towards traditionally excluded groups and in particular to Canada's aboriginal people.

JAMES W.ST.G. WALKER

Hill, James Jerome, pioneer transportation official, railway magnate (b at Rockwood, UC 16 Sept 1838; d at St Paul, Minn 29 May 1916). In 1856 Hill settled in St Paul. His many business ventures there included the Red River Transportation Co, which had a monopoly of the steamboat business on the Red R. With George STEPHEN and others he acquired the St Paul and Pacific Railroad in 1873-74 (reorganized as the St Paul, Minneapolis and Manitoba Railroad in 1879) and became its president a few years later. Although an original director of the CANADIAN PACIFIC RY, he resigned in 1883 to protest the decision to build the main line N of Lk Superior. He later expanded the St Paul line into the Great Northern Ry, of which he was president from 1893.

JOHN A. EAGLE

Reading: A. Martin, *James J. Hill and the Opening of the Northwest* (1976).

Hill, Philip Carteret, lawyer, politician, premier of NS (b at Halifax 13 Aug 1821; d at Tunbridge Wells, Eng 14 Sept 1894). Called to the bar in 1844, he began his political career as mayor of Halifax 1861-64. In 1867 he was nominated provincial secretary in the first Cabinet under Confederation, but had to resign following the ministry's defeat at the polls. He was returned in 1870 as Reform (Liberal) member for Halifax County. Reappointed provincial secretary in a new Reform administration in 1874, he replaced William ANNAND as premier in 1875. Hill retained both offices until his administration was defeated 1878. He retired to England 1882 where he published several pamphlets, chiefly theological in nature.

LOIS KERNAGHAN

Hill-Tout, Charles, anthropologist (b at Buckland, Eng 28 Sept 1858; d at Vancouver 30 June 1944). After studying theology, Hill-Tout immigrated to Canada and in 1891 became headmaster of a boys' school in Vancouver. He bought land in the Fraser Valley and eventually moved out to farm it and carry on field studies among the Indians. Hill-Tout became perhaps Canada's most important amateur anthropologist, largely through his friendships with the SALISH people. He became president of the anthropological section of the RSC, to which he was elected in 1913, and a fellow of the Royal Anthropological Institute of Great Britain. He published *The Native Races of British North America: The Far West* (1907), but his most important work appears in the field reports collected by Ralph Maud in the 4-vol *The Salish People* (1978).

GEORGE WOODCOCK

Hill 70 The storming of Hill 70 (70 m above sea level) just N of Lens, France, on 15 Aug 1917 was the first major action fought by the Canadian Corps under a Canadian commander, Lt-Gen Sir Arthur CURRIE, who had succeeded Lt-Gen Sir Julian BYNG on June 6. It was entirely successful, and despite intense German counterattacks (Aug 16-18) the Canadians held their ground and subsequently (Aug 21-25) occupied part of Lens. Following on the capture of VIMY RIDGE, it confirmed the combat capabilities of Canadian troops. *See also* WORLD WAR I.

BRERETON GREENHOUS

Hiller, Arthur Garfin, film director (b at Edmonton 22 Nov 1923). He has represented since the 1960s the beau ideal of the successful Canadian filmmaker in Hollywood. He began at CBC radio in 1949, moving to CBC-TV 1953-54 and then to American network TV. His films display an admirable slickness and ease, though arguments over their ultimate artistic value remain unresolved. They include *The Wheeler Dealers* (1963), *The Americanization of Emily* (1964), *Tobruk* (1967), *Popi* (1969), *The Out-of-Towners* (1970), *Love Story* (1970, Academy Award nomination for direction), *Plaza Suite* (1971), *Man of La Mancha* (1972), *The Man in the Glass Booth* (1975), *Silver Streak* (1976) and *The In-Laws* (1979).

WILLIAM BEARD

Hilliard, Anna Marion, physician (b at Morrisburg, Ont 17 June 1902; d at Toronto 15 July 1958). She studied at U of T (BA, MB), did postgraduate work in Britain and in 1928 joined the staff of Women's College Hospital, Toronto, where she headed the dept of obstetrics and gynaecology 1947-57. In 1947 she helped devise a simplified Pap test, which she introduced the following year at WCH's newly formed Cancer Detection Clinic, and she was the driving force in getting WCH accepted as a U of T teaching hospital (1956). Her commonsense approach to women's problems, especially those connected with childbirth, brought her many devoted admirers and led to a series of articles which were the basis of her book, *A Woman Doctor Looks at Love and Life* (1957). She was also the author of *Women and Fatigue*, published posthumously in 1960.

CARLOTTA HACKER

Reading: Marion O. Robinson, *Give My Heart: The Dr. Marion Hilliard Story* (1964).

Hills, George, Anglican bishop of BC 1859-95 (b at Eythorne, Eng 21 June 1816; d 10 Dec 1895). An early graduate of Durham University, Hills was influenced by the Tractarians, serving under Dr Hook at Leeds parish church (1841-48). In 1848 Hills became vicar of Great Yarmouth and in 1859 was appointed to the new colonial bishopric of BC. By nature authoritarian, he came into conflict with the older colonial society, bringing about one of the few splits in the Anglican community in 1874 when his dean, the Rev E. Cridge, withdrew to establish a congregation of the Reformed Episcopal Church. This dispute, based both on doctrinal grounds and on social and personal differences, was fought in ecclesiastical and civil courts, and divided the society of the new Pacific province. Hills's great energies were otherwise devoted to increasing his clergy, travelling through his large diocese, initiating Indian missions, acquiring land and creating churches and schools that were often beyond the financial capacities of his laity. He undoubtedly established the foundation for the predominance of the Church of England in British Columbia.

JEAN FRIESEN

Hilton, Matthew Stewart, boxer (b at Cooksville, Ont 27 Dec 1965). He was one of 7 children, 6 of whom were boys who all boxed because their father had never been defeated during his 8 years as Canadian Welterweight Champion. The Hiltons have won more BOXING matches than any family of boxers in Canadian history. To date, only Matthew is a world champion. As an amateur, he won championships at several weight classifications, as he grew to be a middleweight. As an amateur, he won 106 fights and lost none. On 27 June 1987 he fought Philadelphia's Buster Drayton for the world middleweight title and became the first Canadian to win a boxing world title since Jackie Callura won the featherweight championship in 1943. Undefeated in 27 pro fights, Hilton lists among the great fighters he has beaten Francisco De Jesus, Nino Gonzales and ex-world champion Wilfred Benetez.

A.J. "SANDY" YOUNG

Hime, Humphrey Lloyd, photographer, surveyor, businessman, financier (b at Moy, Ire 17 Sept 1833; d at Toronto 31 Oct 1903). Noted as a pioneer photographer on the Canadian prairies, Hime was photographer and surveyor on the Canadian government's 1858 Assiniboine and Saskatchewan exploring expedition led by Henry Youle HIND. Hime's photographs include views and portraits taken along the route and in the Red River settlements, various HBC forts and native encampments. A portfolio of prints was published in 1860. Hime's subsequent career included mining, business and presidency of the Toronto Stock Exchange. RICHARD J. HUYDA

Reading: H.L. Hime and Richard J. Huyda, *Camera in the Interior: 1858* (1976).

Hincks, Clarence Meredith, physician, mental-health reformer (b at St Marys, Ont 8 Apr 1885; d at Toronto 17 Dec 1964). He received his MD from U of T in 1907 and, finding general practice unsuitable, obtained a part-time post as medical inspector for Toronto schools. In this capacity he was the first to introduce the newly developed Binet-Simon tests for intelligence into Canada. In 1917 he met Clifford W. Beers, founder of the US National Committee for Mental Hygiene, an organization dedicated to improving conditions in America's insane asylums and to promoting sound mental health. With Dr C.K. CLARKE, Hincks founded the Canadian National Committee for Mental Hygiene in 1918, serving first as secretary and then as general director. In 1930 he was also appointed director of the US National Committee, a post he retained until 1939. He remained director of the renamed Canadian Mental Health Assn until his retirement in 1952.

THOMAS E. BROWN

Hincks, Sir Francis, politician, colonial administrator (b at Cork, Ire 14 Dec 1807; d at Montréal 18 Aug 1885). He established the Toronto *Examiner* 1838 and the Montreal *Pilot* 1844. Convinced of the need for an English-French partnership in the United Province of Canada, Hincks and Robert BALDWIN joined with L.H. LAFONTAINE in 1841 to create a Reform Party. The 3 entered the executive of Gov Gen BAGOT in 1842 but resigned over control of patronage in 1843. Hincks became inspector general in the Baldwin-LaFontaine ministry 1848, restoring provincial credit and promoting railway construction, and replaced Baldwin as leader in 1851. Unable to deal with growing sectional feeling and tainted by railway corruption, Hincks's ministry was defeated in 1854. He was governor of 2 Caribbean colonies 1856-69. On his return to Canada in 1869, he became federal minister of finance in Sir John A. MACDONALD's government and concentrated on banking and currency regulation. He left politics for business in 1874. His writings include his *Reminiscences* (1884). DAVID MILLS

Hind, Ella Cora, journalist, women's rights activist (b at Toronto 18 Sept 1861; d at Winnipeg 6 Oct 1942). Denied a position on the *Free Press* upon arriving in Winnipeg in 1882, Hind learned to use the recently introduced typewriter and worked as a secretary, in 1897 becoming a public stenographer even while submitting articles on agriculture. She became agricultural editor of the *Free Press* in 1901, often accurately predicting the western Canadian wheat crop yield, thus achieving renown among grain speculators. The first western female journalist, Hind became president of the Canadian Women's Press Club in 1904. In 1914 she participated in Manitoba's Mock Parliament, in which women sardonically defeated a motion to permit men the vote. Often rebuffed because of her gender, she agitated for WOMEN'S SUFFRAGE, a concern she combined with interest in the WOMAN'S CHRISTIAN TEMPERANCE UNION. At 75 she travelled around the world to observe agricultural methods, writing *Seeing for Myself* (1937). She was awarded an honorary LLD by U Man.

ELIANE LESLAU SILVERMAN

W.G.R. Hind, *The Third Rapid on the Moisie,* produced from sketches made on an expedition with his brother, Henry Youle Hind in 1861 (*courtesy National Archives of Canada/C-13979*).

Hind, Henry Youle, geologist, naturalist (b at Nottingham, Eng 1 June 1823; d at Windsor, NS 8 Aug 1908). Hind was educated at the Nottingham Free Grammar School, a Leipzig commercial college, and Caius College, Cambridge, but graduated from neither of the latter. In 1846 he immigrated to Canada to become in Oct 1847 second master of science and mathematics at the Normal School at Toronto and 1851-63 professor of chemistry at Trinity College. He then supported himself as a consulting geologist in the Maritimes. Hind was closely associated with the establishment of the Canadian Institute, a loose association of engineers and surveyors, and acted as editor of the Institute's journal, the *Canadian Journal* 1852-57. It reflected the growing nationalist spirit, as did Hind's other work. He was a prolific author of popular scientific and exploration materials, producing 4 major government reports on the North-West and Labrador, and 6 books, 25 pamphlets and 22 articles ranging from railway policy to geology to spectrum analysis. The high points of his career were the 2 expeditions into the Red R, Assiniboine and Saskatchewan countries in 1857 and 1858, for which Hind was the scientific observer, naturalist and geologist. These expeditions did much to effect an awareness of the potential of the great North-West in the Canadas. The most important work resulting from these explorations is the 2-vol *Narrative of the Canadian Red River Exploring Expedition of 1857 and of the Assiniboine and Saskatchewan Exploring Expeditions of 1858* (1860).

FRITS PANNEKOEK

Reading: W.L. Morton, *Henry Youle Hind* (1980).

Hind, William George Richardson, artist (b at Nottingham, Eng 12 June 1833; d at Sussex, NB 18 Nov 1889). His older brother Henry Youle HIND arrived in Toronto in 1846 and William seems to have followed in 1852. He set up an art studio but returned to England 8 years later where he was influenced by the paintings of Millais, Hunt and Rossetti, with their attention to minute detail. He joined his brother's expedition to the Moisie R in 1861 and produced over 100 pencil, watercolour and oil studies of the wilderness and native people, as well as sentimental flights of imagination. In 1862 he set off with the OVERLANDERS, completing over 160 sketches and paintings of the journey from Ft Garry to Victoria. Among his best-known works are scenes of farm life and *Oxen With Red River Cart* (1870) from the Red River Colony, and *Bar in a Mining Camp* (1865) and studies of Lillooet miners during the Cariboo gold rush. By 1870 Hind was living in NB and NS and working for the Intercolonial Ry. JAMES MARSH

Hindenburg Line (*Siegfried-Stellung*), a system of fortified and entrenched reserve positions stretching 80 km SE from Arras to Soissons, France, built by the Germans in the winter of 1916-17. On 2-3 Sept 1918 the Canadian Corps broke open its northern hinge (the Drocourt-Quéant switch, or *Wotan-Stellung*) and compelled those German units west of the line to withdraw to it. At the end of the month another Canadian assault forced a crossing of the Canal du Nord, near Cambrai. Again outflanked, the Germans abandoned the line and continued their retreat to the east. BRERETON GREENHOUS

Hinduism, the religion of about 400 million people in India, Africa, Indonesia and the West Indies. Immigration from these countries (principally India) to Canada has provided the base for a Canadian population of about 69 500 Hindus (1981c, the last figures available). Evidence of the existence of Hinduism dates back 4000 years. It reached a stage of high philosophical, religious and psychological development by 1500 BC and has sustained it to the present. Hinduism has maintained its supremacy in India despite numerous migrations into the country and attempts at evangelization by other religions, notably BUDDHISM, ISLAM and CHRISTIANITY. Hindu culture and religion possess a unique vitality which has enabled Hinduism to become the foundation of the religions practised by over half the world's population. People in China, Japan, Tibet, Burma and Ceylon all look to India as their ancestral spiritual home.

For the Hindu, God is the one supreme universal spirit that underlies all human, animal and material life, and towards which all religious feelings and theology strive. To Hindus each religion's and every devotee's particular picture of God represents a true aspect of God. But the uniqueness of the Hindu world view centres on 4 important concepts: *anadi* (beginninglessness), *karma* (the moral law of life), *samsara* (rebirth) and *moksha* (freedom or release). The basic Indian world view assumes a cycle of birth, death and rebirth leading the believer to the desire for release from this endless round of suffering – "suffering," because life in this world implies separation from the divine.

Hindu thought has no concept for the creation of the universe, assuming that everything – the universe, God, scripture and humanity – has existed without beginning. Within this view is the idea of cycles of creation with relative beginnings. Each cycle begins from a pre-existent seed state, grows, flowers, withers and dies. But, just as a dying flower leaves seeds for its own propagation, each cycle drops a seed which begins the next state. In Hindu belief, the universe we are now experiencing is in one such relative cycle of creation. A consequence of this view is typified in the term "karma." Each person is responsible for his or her own destiny. If one performs good actions and thinks good thoughts, this will establish the probability of a good future even in the next cycle of creation. The doctrine of karma teaches that when a person acts or thinks, a memory trace or seed laid in the unconscious will predispose the individual to that same kind of action or thought in the future. Each person is reborn (reincarnated) again and again, according to his or her karma. Many of the thoughts and desires we find when we analyse our unconscious impulses come from thoughts and actions of previous lives. What we experience in this life is in part a consequence of all the good and bad actions and thoughts of previous lives. The doctrine of reincarnation is manifested in society by the caste system, which has 4 levels at which an individual may be reborn, according to the karmic merit accumulated: *brahman* (priest or teacher), *kshatriya* (warrior or politician), *vaishya* (merchant or professional) and *sudra* (servant or labourer). Long after these categories were established some sudras became known as untouchables, or "outcastes."

The karmic balance in the unconscious at the time of death determines the state or level at which a person will be reborn. Through countless lives one can spiral upwards, finally to reach the level of the gods. There the individual experiences the honour of sitting in the place of a deity, exercising the deity's cosmic function until the good merit is exhausted. If through evil living one is reborn as an animal, he will simply follow his instincts and experience the suffering that such instincts produce. Such is the cycle of rebirth, "samsara." How to find a way out of this cycle is an important question in Hinduism and Buddhism. The Hindu answer is called "moksha."

Moksha is release from the merry-go-round of birth, death and rebirth. The 3 ways of obtaining release are the yoga of knowledge, the yoga of action and the yoga of devotion. The yoga of knowledge involves intellectual and psychological techniques developed by Hindu holy men to control their actions and analyse their unconscious. They remove the karmic obstructions of previous lives, recovering the nature of their true selves. The true self is shown to be nothing other than Brahman, or God. The goal of all knowledge, therefore, is the experience of union with the divine. The yoga of action requires that duty be done with no thought for oneself or for the benefit or suffering that one experiences in fulfilling it. Through the performance of one's duty as a dedication to the Lord, a kind of inner purification takes place, resulting in divine union. The yoga of devotion, the most common path, requires that prayers, the chanting of scripture and meditation on the image of the Lord be undertaken with such intensity that inner karmic obstructions are burned up and the Lord is revealed within consciousness. All that is required is willingness to surrender oneself completely in devotion to God. Regardless of which path is followed, the end is the same: the discovery of the true nature within oneself of a spiritual soul (*atman*) which is at one with God.

Hinduism in Canada Immigration to Canada of people from India or of Indian origin began in 1903-04 (*see* SOUTH ASIANS). The census records of 1911 list Hindus and Sikhs together, for a total of 1758. Most of Canada's East Indian community of the first half of this century was of the SIKH faith, and extensive Hindu immigration started only in the 1960s. In Canada, as elsewhere in the Hindu diaspora, the structure of religious life has undergone a marked change. The practice of caste generally follows that in India, with marriages usually made along caste lines; nevertheless the practice is tempered by the egalitarianism of Canadian society. The traditional roles of temple, home altar, village festival and PILGRIMAGE to sacred sites have largely given way to a development in which temples function as the local church does for Christianity. Temples have been built in major Canadian cities from Halifax to Vancouver. A regular pattern of Sunday worship services is cultivated. These services often make reference to the Hindu sacred calendar, commemorating saints and marking seasonal or religious festivals; but the celebrations are conducted on convenient Sundays, since it is often difficult to meet during the work week. Where the Indian community is large enough several temples develop along cultural or ethnic lines. One of the older temples in Toronto (fd 1976) serves a largely West Indian Hindu community, while the Indians from Africa and India attend other temples. Informal *satsangs* (devotional meetings) take place throughout the community, bringing together people of similar cultural and linguistic background or those devoted to a specific spiritual path, such as Vedanta, or a particular *guru* (teacher), such as Sai Baba or Aurobindo.

In cities other than Toronto and Vancouver where there is a single temple it is under the influence of either the Arya Samaj or the Sanatanist tradition. Both use the *Vedas*, the ancient Hindu scriptures, as the source of their rituals. Arya Samaj worship is conducted through the Agnihotra, a ritual involving a series of purifications, the chanting of *mantras* (incantations) and scriptures, along with offerings to Agni, the god-fire who bears all sacrifices to God. Although Hindu art is noted for its magnificent depictions of the gods, Arya Samaj groups do not use images of the various Hindu deities in the act of worship. Sanatanists construct worship around a similar set of purifications, chants and offerings. However, there are lengthy oblations made to various deities through the use of their images. The gods most often called upon are Ganesa, Visnu, Siva, Suryanarayan and Devi. The services are several hours in length, requiring a knowledgeable priest familiar with the complexities of the formal ritual pattern. Both Arya Samaj and Sanatanist forms of worship are structured to make allowances for the Canadian setting and for the diversity of belief among Canada's Hindus.

Most temples in Canada are run by boards along "congregational" lines and are served by one or 2 lay priests. Trained and initiated priests, called *pundits*, serve a Sanatanist temple in Toronto and a Samajes temple in Vancouver. A number of language programs are sponsored by temples across Canada. In some communities children gain a cursory knowledge of Sanskrit, the ancient language of Hindu scripture and ritual, and of languages such as Hindi, Punjabi, Gujarati and Tamil, in which myths and legends are told and devotional hymns sung. Traditional practice requires a series of 12 initiation rites (*samskaras*) or personal religious ceremonies. This cycle has been modified dramatically in the Canadian setting, although most Canadian Hindus are married and cremated according to tradition. Some of them practise rites associated with conception, birth, the first haircut and the initiation of boys into full caste membership (the *upanayana*, or "sacred thread," ceremony).

Hindu communities in the diaspora are visited regularly by various gurus and *swamis* (monks). These may be formally associated with an institution or movement in N America such as the Ramakrishna Mission, or may hail from one of the great *ashrams* (religious communities) of India. The Sri Ramakrishna Mission actively circulates swamis throughout the Vedanta societies in Canada. Although Hindu religious life in Canada is circumscribed by a shortage of priests, a lack of sacred sites and a new set of cultural norms, numerous Hindus remain in contact with gurus who guide their personal religious paths.

DAVID J. GOA AND HAROLD G. COWARD

Reading: David J. Goa, ed, *Traditions in Transition* (1982); S.K. Jain, *East Indians in Canada* (n.d.); T.J. Hopkins, *The Hindu Religious Tradition* (1971); I.M. Muthanna, *People of India in North America* (vol 1, 1975); K.V. Ujimoto and Gordon Hirabayashi, eds, *Visible Minorities and Multiculturalism* (1980).

Hinton, Alta, Town, pop 8629 (1986c), 8342 (1981c), inc 1958, is located in the Alberta foothills, 285 km W of Edmonton. It began as a coal-mining town and was named for the manager of the GRAND TRUNK PACIFIC RY, W.D. Hinton. In 1956, North West Pulp and Power Ltd – now Champion Forest Products (Alberta) Ltd – opened Alberta's first pulp mill in Hinton, and a new town blossomed. It has become the centre for 3 coal mines. There is a championship cross-country ski trail nearby and a new olympic-size luge course. In Feb 1986, 23 people died in a collision between a passenger train and a freight train here. ERIC J. HOLMGREN

Hippies, a term (possibly a variation of "hipster") coined in the mid-1960s to describe the adherents of a subculture (or counterculture) associated with the political and social protest movements of that decade. Although the hippy culture originated in Greenwich Village, New York, and in San Francisco, California, it spread throughout N America. In Canada hippies congregated primarily in the Kitsilano district of Vancouver and around Yorkville Ave in Toronto. They were characterized by long hair, beards and unconventional clothing, by their celebration of drugs (in particular LSD and marijuana) and rock 'n roll, by their affinity to non-Occidental religions (*see* NEW RELIGIOUS MOVEMENTS) and the cultivation of "self-awareness," by sexual experimentation, by their language ("trips," "acid,""flower power"), by economic marginalism and by their youthfulness and middle-class origins. Although they were widely disparaged and ridiculed, their ideals corresponded to the effort of the New Left in general to propose political and cultural alternatives to the institutions of capitalist society; they upheld PACIFISM, communal life, egalitarianism, self-help and the inviolability of the person, and were hostile to private property, bureaucracies and technology. Many of their ideas were inspired by Marshall MCLUHAN and his notions of the postliterate tribal society. In Vancouver, hippie culture was associated with the Easter "be-ins" at Stanley Park, with the underground newspaper *Georgia Straight* and, briefly, in a cross-fertilization with political activism, with the Vancouver Liberation Front. In Toronto, hippies gathered at "love-ins" in Queen's Park, Digger House, Rochdale College (an experiment in "free education") and a mass sit-in on Yorkville Ave. As a mass phenomenon the hippies were short-lived. The Festival Express, a coast-to-coast rock 'n roll festival on board a train in 1970, was probably the last major hippie event. In the end, hippies were unable to devise a strategy that linked the forms of cultural protest to those of mass political action, and they faded into solipsism, anti-intellectualism and varieties of personal therapy. Some of their ideas were subsequently taken up by the ecology movement and community-based urban-action groups of the 1970s. MYRNA KOSTASH

Reading: Myrna Kostash, *Long Way from Home: The Story of the Sixties Generation in Canada* (1980).

Hiram Walker Resources Ltd, with head offices in Toronto, was a Canadian holding company with diverse interests. The company was incorporated as the Consumers' Gas Co in 1848 in the Province of Canada. In 1979 shareholders of Cygnus Corporation Ltd and Home Oil Co Ltd approved their own joint merger, and subsequently one with Consumers' Gas. A year later, stockholders approved the merger of distiller Hiram Walker-Gooderham & Worts Ltd with the company and its wholly owned subsidiary, Home Oil Co Ltd. The name change to Hiram Walker Resources Ltd followed. In a complex series of transactions, major interests in the company were acquired by Gulf Canada Corp (controlled by the REICHMANN's) and the British firm Allied-Lyons in 1987. Later that year Gulf's interests were transferred to another Reichmann controlled company, GW Utilities of Toronto and HWR ceased to exist.
DEBORAH C. SAWYER

Hirsch, John Stephen, theatre director, administrator (b at Siófok, Hungary 1 May 1930). He immigrated to Winnipeg in 1947 and after graduating from U of Man established the Muddiwater Puppets and a troupe for children. In 1957 he and Tom HENDRY cofounded Theatre 77, which they combined with the Winnipeg Little Theatre in 1958 to form the MANITOBA THEATRE CENTRE (with Hirsch as artistic director); it was destined to be the model for a chain of regional stock companies across Canada. From 1967 to 1969 he was co-director of the STRATFORD FESTIVAL and from 1974 to 1978 head of television drama for the CBC. From 1981 to 1985 he was sole artistic director at Stratford, sustaining the theatre in a period when its existence was threatened. Between appointments he has guided productions for Ottawa's National Arts Centre, Toronto Arts Productions, Young People's Theatre and the SHAW FESTIVAL, as well as elsewhere in Canada and abroad. Several of his American productions have been honoured. He won the Outer Circle Critics' Award for *Saint Joan* at the Lincoln Center, New York, an Obie Award for *AC-DC* at the Chelsea Theater, Off-Broadway, and the Drama Critics' Award for *The Dybbuk* at the Mark Taper Forum, Los Angeles (1975), a play he translated and adapted. His work has been seen, as well, at the Tyrone Guthrie Theater in Minneapolis, the Seattle Repertory Theater and the Habimah Theatre in Tel Aviv. Following his tenure at Stratford, Hirsch taught theatre at Yale, was a visiting professor at U of California and launched into film as both an actor (*Sword of Gideon*, 1986) and filmmaker. DAVID GARDNER

John Hirsch, founder of the Manitoba Theatre Centre, was co-director of the Stratford Festival 1967-69 and sole artistic director 1980-85 (*courtesy Canapress Photo Service*).

Hirshhorn, Joseph Herman, mining promoter, art collector (b at Mitau, Latvia 11 Aug 1900; d at Washington, DC 31 Aug 1981). Hirshhorn immigrated at an early age to the US, rising from office boy to stockbroker to entrepreneur. In 1933 he opened an office in Toronto. His reputation in mining circles was mixed; during the war he was arrested as a currency speculator. In the early 1950s Hirshhorn formed a partnership with Franc Joubin, a geologist; together they made the greatest URANIUM strike in Canadian history near Blind River, Ont, and staked it in April and May 1953. The result was the Pronto and Algom mines, which were later consolidated in Rio Algom, a subsidiary of the British firm, Rio Tinto. Hirshhorn's great collection of contemporary art is held in the Hirshhorn Gallery in Washington, DC. ROBERT BOTHWELL

Histoire des Canadiens-français 1608-1880 by Benjamin Sulte (8 vols, 1882-84), proclaims in its own subtitle its significance as a comprehensive study of the French Canadian people (complete with statistics): it examines their "origins; history; religion; wars; discoveries; colonization; customs; domestic, social and political life; development and future." An eccentric "liberal" history, it met with the church's approval – despite its denunciation of the JESUIT RELATIONS – because of its outspoken critique of colonialism and MERCANTILISM and its nationalist concept of the French Canadians as a race. Unlike François-Xavier GARNEAU'S HISTOIRE DU CANADA, which was out of favour in the ULTRAMONTANE climate of the 1880s, Sulte's history defends the habitant as the forgotten hero of his tale and views the old SEIGNEURIAL SYSTEM with nostalgia. Sulte greeted Confederation with qualified approval, stressing the need for provincial autonomy within a structure that ensures a voice for French Canadians. Sulte's *Histoire*, very popular in his day, has not been translated or reprinted. MICHÈLE LACOMBE

Histoire du Canada depuis sa découverte jusqu'à nos jours, a Canadian classic by François-Xavier GARNEAU, appeared in 4 volumes, 1845-52, tracing French Canada's development from Champlain's voyages of discovery to 1840. A vindication of the French Canadian nation in the face of Lord DURHAM's assimilationist policies, it was read as a national epic and a monument to "la survivance." Garneau was first among French Canadians to treat history as a science. He was strongly influenced by French historians, taking up their liberal ideals and romantic style, and adopting Augustin Thierry's theory that interracial antagonism is the prime mover of all history. Garneau's evident patriotism and his status as a national hero tempered criticism of his liberal ideas, which included suggestions of clerical mismanagement in the colony's early history. Garneau revised his text for the second and third editions of 1852 and 1859; Andrew Bell's translation (1860) somewhat misrepresents the text. The standard, indexed edition was the eighth (9 volumes, 1944-46). MICHÈLE LACOMBE

Historic Site, a place designated as having some tangible link with the past through an event, person or building. It is sometimes identified by an associated building or archaeological remains, although often merely by the presence of a statue, cairn or plaque put up more recently. A confusing term associated with historic sites is MONUMENT, which can refer to either a historic building or a commemorative structure.

To be designated a historic site, a place must have more than intrinsic significance from the past; it must be recognized later as having meaning within a larger historical context. This qualification poses a problem of definition because it is sometimes difficult to distinguish between the historical time from which the site derives its significance and its later period of commemoration. War memorials, for instance, are not usually thought of as having intrinsic historical significance, yet with the passage of time some of these have assumed the characteristics of historic sites, eg, the Nelson column erected in Montréal in 1809, the 1854 BROCK memorial at QUEENSTON HEIGHTS (destroyed 1840 and replaced 1853), and the monument erected in honour of MONTCALM and WOLFE in Québec City in 1827, in possibly the earliest commemoration in Canada of an historic event. Another problem that makes defining historic sites difficult is the changing of criteria for their selection. In the late 19th and early 20th centuries, sites were often chosen to commemorate important battles, great men and political events, eg, BATOCHE; CRYSLER'S FARM. Today, greater concern is shown for the history of the common person, ethnic groups and industrial developments, eg, Old FORT WILLIAM; CANNINGTON MANOR; FORGES SAINT-MAURICE; MOTHERWELL HOMESTEAD.

Interest in creating historic sites became fairly widespread in eastern Canada with the rise of nationalist sentiment at the end of the 19th century. Local patriotic and historical associations endeavoured to preserve and mark places important to the historic identity of their particular regions and some argued that their sites were important also to Canada's history. It was realized, too, that historic sites could be popular tourist attractions, especially if occupied by picturesque ruins, although efforts at development were usually limited unless supported by government funding. Following initiatives by Québec organizations in 1907, the federal government created the Québec (later National) Battlefields Commission to develop and preserve the site of the 1759 Battle of the PLAINS OF ABRAHAM. With no structures of the period to work with, the commission planned a landscape park with commemorative monuments. In 1919 the federal government created the Historic Sites and Monuments Board of Canada to advise it on implementing a national program of commemoration and preservation of historic sites, and subsequently most provincial governments appointed similar bodies to advise them on the creation of provincial historic sites.

Until the 1930s efforts at developing historic

sites were largely confined to interpretive plaques. If historic ruins were present they were usually left unimproved, with minimal effort made to prevent further deterioration. The prevailing preservation philosophy in the early 20th century held that reconstruction or major restoration harmed the historical integrity of a site, and the scarcity of funds for expensive restoration projects no doubt encouraged this approach. Nevertheless, some efforts were made to preserve historic buildings. A number of old forts formerly controlled by the British army were transferred to the National Parks Branch of the Dept of the Interior. Ft Anne, Annapolis Royal, NS, was made a national historic park in 1917, FORT BEAUSÉJOUR, NB, in 1926, FORT CHAMBLY, Qué, in 1921 and Ft Wellington, Ont, in 1923. Other military properties were preserved as national historic sites until 1940, when they were designated national historic parks. In Québec and Ontario local groups successfully preserved some important historical buildings. The Montréal Antiquarian and Numismatic Society acquired the Château de Ramezay for a museum building in 1895 and Toronto historical groups fought successfully to save old Ft York from destruction. On the whole, however, preservation projects were rare.

The success of large restoration projects in the US, particularly the reconstruction of Colonial Williamsburg in the 1920s, was largely responsible for changing this attitude. Increased spending on public works during the Great Depression provided further stimulation. In the 1930s the Niagara Parks Commission, an agency of the Ontario government, undertook 4 significant historic projects, 2 of which – Ft George at Niagara-on-the-Lake and Ft Erie (*see* NIAGARA HISTORIC FRONTIER) – involved reconstructing nonexistent FORTIFICATIONS. Subsequently the provincial and federal governments undertook the restoration of FORT HENRY at Kingston. Although in this latter case much of the original fort remained intact, the restoration went beyond structural repairs: interiors were refurbished and furnished with period reproductions and historic artifacts. The largest reconstruction project undertaken is Fortress of LOUISBOURG National Historic Park in Nova Scotia. In 1961 Parks Canada began to rebuild part of the former French fortress demolished by the British in 1758. This involved reconstructing part of the old town as well as the fortifications; interiors have been replicated and the site is interpreted by costumed guides who explain aspects of 18th-century life at Louisbourg.

Related to the reconstruction of buildings is the artificial creation of a historic community using historic buildings moved to the site. Although in a sense not historic sites because the properties lack inherent significance, artificial pioneer communities such as KINGS LANDING, NB, and UPPER CANADA VILLAGE, Ont, are an important aspect of historic preservation in Canada.

More recently, efforts have been directed at preserving historic buildings in their natural settings, retaining the original, or at least some practical, function. Examples of commercial or domestic architecture preserved as historic sites can be found across Canada. They pose special problems for preservation because they usually remain under private control and are vulnerable to destruction or improper renovation. Buildings designated national historic sites, for instance, although marked by distinctive plaques, are not usually protected by federal legislation. Gradually provincial governments are enacting heritage legislation to protect designated buildings. In some provinces, municipalities have been empowered to designate historic resources, which then fall under the protection of the provincial heritage Act. Agencies such as HERITAGE CANADA, along with provincial and local heritage groups, have endeavoured to raise funds for the preservation and proper restoration of privately owned historic buildings. *See also* PARKS; HERITAGE CONSERVATION. C.J. TAYLOR

Historical Geography includes the study both of the geographies of the past and of changes in geographical patterns through time; historical geographers study some aspect or aspects of the GEOGRAPHY of a region, such as population or land use, at a selected period in the past (the cross-section or horizontal approach), or some element or aspect of the evolution of a region (the vertical approach). The horizontal approach reveals the interrelationship of numerous elements of a place at a particular period and also studies the life of an area at a particular time. The vertical approach emphasizes processes and the human thought and activities underlying changes in geographical patterns.

Historical geography was not recognized as a distinct field of university teaching and research in Canada until the 1950s. However, the term geographical history was used in 1749 in a British pamphlet describing NS, although the first major historical geographical study of Canada was by J.D. Rogers, *A Historical Geography of the British Colonies - Canada - Part III Geographical* (1911) – a description and analysis of the settling of Canada, published in England. In 1936 Carl Schott, a German geographer, analysed agricultural settlement in southern Ontario. In the 1950s and 1960s geography departments in Canadian universities expanded as young historical geographers established courses and published research. A distinct area of specialization developed, stimulated by the work of Canadian historians and economic historians, eg, H.A. INNIS. However, the emphasis that geographers place on the spatial patterns of the Earth and how they evolve distinguishes their work from that of historians. A considerable number of historical geographers received graduate training in the US. Andrew H. CLARK (born in Canada and influenced by Innis) of University of Wisconsin was particularly important. Others trained in British universities.

Canadian historical geographers concentrate on their country but a few specialize on other parts of the world and have published research on China, Europe, Latin America, the USSR, South Africa and the US. Within Canada a few scholars have adopted the cross-section approach and have reconstructed the geography of a region at a particular time, but most research is concerned with geographical change through time. Topics include the cultural historical geography of native peoples and their relationship to the FUR-TRADE economy; spatial patterns of IMMIGRATION and the transfer of culture from the Old World to the New; rural settlement; land-use and settlement patterns as they relate to primary-resource development; the founding of urban settlements and their functional development and evolution in relationship to staples and corridors of movement; and the origins and evolution of distinctive rural and urban landscapes, including buildings. Although culture is increasingly recognized as an important factor in determining geographical development, research has just begun on attitudes to and influences on the environment, and the historical geography of manufacturing is barely developed. The history of the mapping of Canada is studied, and facsimile atlases have been prepared showing how maps can be used to interpret the evolving geography of an area. In the late 1970s and early 1980s historical geographers, cartographers and others were preparing a massive 3-vol historical atlas of Canada from the Ice Age to the mid-20th century, the first volume of which was published in 1987.

Specialists are not responsible for all research in historical geography. Geographers who normally work on contemporary geographical problems may adopt an historical geographical approach for a particular research topic. Historical geographers in their turn may occasionally work on contemporary problems, but they usually concentrate on the past and are thoroughly familiar with the archival and field sources and the scholarly literature related to a particular area and period. J. WARKENTIN

Reading: R.C. Harris and J. Warkentin, *Canada Before Confederation* (1974); R.C. Harris, ed, *Historical Atlas of Canada: From the Beginning to 1800* (1987).

Historical Societies in Canada have as their primary purpose the study and promotion of the Canadian historical experience. Through publication of scholarly and amateur works, public education programs, assistance to and co-operation with archives, museums, heritage groups and other similar organizations, hundreds of historical associations provide a valuable service to Canadian life. The first such association, the LITERARY AND HISTORICAL SOCIETY OF QUEBEC, was established in 1824. The Nova Scotia Historical Society began in 1878 and its publication, *Report and Collections of the Nova Scotia Historical Society*, started the following year. The Ontario Historical Society traces its roots back to 1888 with its journal, *Ontario History*, beginning in 1899. Historians in most other provinces have since established similar organizations.

On the national level the CANADIAN HISTORICAL ASSOCIATION, fd 1922, was an outgrowth of the Historic Landmarks Assn of Canada. The latter, established in 1907, had as its main objectives the planning for the 1908 Québec tercentenary and the appropriate recognition of Canada's HISTORIC SITES. The CHA now boasts over 2100 general and student members (1987) and serves the interests of both professional and amateur historians through an active publications program and an annual conference.

Recent years, particularly since Canada's centennial celebrations in 1967, have witnessed a tremendous growth in regional and local historical associations. Societies large and small operate almost exclusively on volunteer assistance. Their activities have increased the awareness among Canadians of the richness of their own history and have encouraged many others to examine their past through local history studies, GENEALOGICAL research and other research projects.

CARMAN V. CARROLL

Historiography, the published product of the historian's declared interest in the past; the writing of history. It is not by itself "history," but is by necessity part of the historical record. The serious study of history therefore also requires an awareness of the historical conditions and social assumptions that give rise to different forms of historiographical interpretation. The Canadian historiographic corpus has developed separately in English Canada and French Canada, but similarities exist. History, once the amateur's preserve, has come to be written principally by professional scholars, both anglophone and francophone. The establishment of such national agencies as the NATIONAL ARCHIVES OF CANADA (NAC) and such bodies as the ROYAL SOCIETY OF CANADA was of benefit to both. Approaches to the recording of history still differ, as do preoccupations in the choice of subject matter; but conferences and journals now provide forums for the sharing of historiographic materials, knowledge and methodology.

Historiography in French

Various descriptive works and narratives dealing with Canada and published in France during the 17th and 18th centuries were entitled "histoires." Although written by Frenchmen who in many cases had only visited NEW FRANCE, these publications profoundly influenced French Canadian historiography. They provided later historians with otherwise unattainable information about events witnessed by their authors, as well as valuable descriptions of the daily lives of colonists and Indians. One historiographic work of this period stands out from the rest: *Histoire et description générale de la Nouvelle France*, by the Jesuit P.F.X. CHARLEVOIX (Paris, 1744). Already a published historian, the author stayed in New France 1705-09 and returned 1720-22, when he travelled from Québec down the Mississippi Valley to New Orleans. His abundantly documented *Histoire* gives a faithful account of political, military and religious events from the early 16th century to 1736. For a century it remained the best history of the French colony.

The Canadiens paid little attention to the historical genre until the early 19th century, when a feeling of FRENCH CANADIAN NATIONALISM developed. The versatile Montréal writer Michel Bibaud brought out *Histoire du Canada* (3 vols, 1837-78) which had some documentary and literary merit. This conservative author criticized French Canadian nationalists, L.J. Papineau in particular. The first volume of François-Xavier GARNEAU'S HISTOIRE DU CANADA, the most important historiographical work ever published in French in Canada, appeared in Québec City in 1845. Two more volumes followed in 1846 and 1848, and the work went through 8 printings in a century. Garneau voiced the ideals that guided French Canadian nationalists until the mid-20th century. He painted vivid accounts of the saga of New France, including the exploits of the explorers and COUREURS DE BOIS and the work of French missionaries. He celebrated the military deeds of Frenchmen and Canadiens who defended their land against the British and, later, the Americans. For the Canadiens, the conflict did not end with the CONQUEST; after 1791 it simply moved indoors to the Parliament. Garneau's vision of a perpetual struggle for survival as the central element of Canadian history has marked all French Canadian historiography until the present day. Garneau disapproved of the REBELLIONS OF 1837 but strongly criticized British policies toward Canadiens. He vigorously denounced the ACT OF UNION as an attempt to destroy the French Canadian nation. A self-taught historian, Garneau made judicious use of official sources and existing publications, and modelled his *Histoire* on the works of his favourite author, French historian Augustin Thierry, who held that racial antagonism was the driving force of history.

Garneau showed French Canadians the power of history as an element of national identity. Those who came after him, proponents of the conservative ideology that dominated Québec from the mid-19th century to the 1960s, produced a host of historical works exalting the national and religious past of the people. In their syntheses and monographs, priest-historians Jean-Baptiste-Antoine Ferland, Étienne-Michel Faillon and Henri-Raymond CASGRAIN stressed the role of the great religious figures of New France. Such accounts complemented Garneau's works which, in the opinion of the clergy, had been unduly secular. Several works stand out in the abundant historical literature of the last half of the 19th century, among them Joseph-Edmond Roy's *Histoire de la seigneurie de Lauzon* (5 vols, 1897-1904), which is still instructive reading.

Two historians dominated the first half of the 20th century: Thomas Chapais and Abbé Lionel GROULX. Chapais established himself with biographies of key figures in New France – Intendant TALON and Gen MONTCALM. But his greatest work was *Cours d'histoire du Canada* (8 vols, 1919-34). The *Cours*, originally given as a series of public lectures at Université Laval, covered the period from the Conquest to Confederation. Chapais took up Garneau's *Histoire* in more rigorous fashion, and had the advantage of fuller documentation. He and his contemporaries benefited from the creation of the National Archives in Ottawa. Chapais's *Cours* is still a mandatory reference work for any student of political and parliamentary history of that era. Other writers, the most famous being Groulx, opposed his criticism of the PATRIOTES and his sympathy for British policies.

In 1915 Groulx inaugurated the chair in Canadian history at the Montréal campus of Université Laval (later U de Montréal). In a few years he became the leading historian of French Canada, the only one whose name could rival Garneau's. Each of his books sparked passionate discussion in French Canadian intellectual circles. His synthesis of Garneau's nationalist ideal with traditional Catholic ideology has never been bettered. *Histoire du Canada français depuis la découverte* (4 vols, 1950-52) is an excellent summary of Groulx's work. Gustave Lanctot, a career archivist with the NAC, was a less outstanding writer than Groulx, but still admirable for his time. His most important work was a 3-volume study of the French regime, *Histoire du Canada* (1959-64). The most prolific French Canadian historian was Robert RUMILLY, primarily known for his monumental 41-volume account of the years between 1867 and 1945, *Histoire de la Province du Québec* (1940-69). Anecdotal, written in popular style and drawn largely from printed primary sources such as newspapers, Rumilly's *Histoire* is still the starting point for any study of the period. Rumilly was also interested in the history of the ACADIANS and the FRANCO-AMERICANS.

French Canadian historiography took a new direction after WWII. In 1947 departments of history were created at the universities of Laval and Montréal, modelled on history departments in European and American universities and staffed by professors trained in the methods of professional historiography: Guy Frégault and Michel Brunet in Montréal, and Marcel Trudel in Québec City. Large numbers of students entered history departments in the 1960s, a movement that resulted in more professors, more graduate theses and more publications. The 1970s saw the creation or further expansion of departments of history at U of Ottawa, U of Sherbrooke, and U du Québec in Chicoutimi, Trois-Rivières, Rimouski and Montréal. History, which had been the preserve of amateurs and a very few university trained scholars before 1945, had in a quarter-century become a major discipline in universities and research institutes. The vitality of the profession in Québec is reflected in the conferences of the Institut d'histoire de l'Amérique française (fd 1947), a gathering of historians whose specialty is the history either of Québec or of Francophones originating there. These annual conferences constitute the province's best forum for Québec historiography, and their methodological and ideological horizons are constantly being enlarged. The Institut publishes the REVUE D'HISTOIRE DE L'AMÉRIQUE FRANÇAISE, which has become the most notable journal for scholarly publications on the history of Québec and French Canada. Other periodicals, such as *Histoire sociale/Social History* (fd 1968 in Ottawa), also publish articles by historians who are studying Québec with new methodologies developed in France, Britain or the US.

Several works stand out from the mass of material that has been published since 1945. Groulx's disciples, unconcerned with religious ideology, developed strong political positions in their historical works: the writings and teachings of Maurice Séguin and Michel Brunet, for example, largely shaped the thinking of the sovereignty movement of the 1960s. The appearance of history as a university discipline led to greater critical rigour in historical works; the abundant and methodical writings and teachings of Marcel Trudel illustrate this development. But the impact of the social sciences on historiography since the 1960s has been especially fruitful. Fernand OUELLET'S *Histoire économique et sociale du Québec, 1760-1850* (1966) was a major event in Québec intellectual life. Ouellet integrated economic and social factors much more firmly than did anyone before him, and drew perceptive conclusions which played down the Conquest as an explanation for French Canadian economic inferiority. He subsequently refined his model, provoking fruitful debates with fellow historians such as Jean-Pierre Wallot. Louise Dechêne's *Habitants et marchands de Montréal au XVII siècle* (1974) is another example of historical work based on today's best historiographical methods. PIERRE SAVARD

Since 1970 French Canadian historiography since 1970 has found itself both continuing and breaking with what has gone before. Earlier gains have remained important, but at the same time – undoubtedly reflecting the changes in contemporary Québec – historiography now presents a new image of Québec. While formerly the unique nature of the Québec historical experience (especially the French Canadian experience) was emphasized, the most recent works show a clear tendency to emphasize similarities between Québec's evolution and those of other societies. Thanks to social history pioneers, the political and nationalist preoccupations which characterized most earlier historical works have now been joined by economic, social and cultural considerations. The history of a nation which used to be described in terms of harmony, continuity and homogeneity is gradually evolving into a history of a more diversified and conflictual community which, with varying degrees of ease, welcomes change.

The extension of the university network has caused an explosion in the number of professional historians. Many people working in other social science disciplines now write history as well. Historians have been enriched by their involvement with geographers, sociologists, economists, political scientists, anthropologists and demographers. It should also be noted that the research and teaching of history is now very largely in the hands of lay people. Today the practice of history is characterized by group effort. Some major studies have been undertaken by multidisciplinary research teams, such as the one studying the history of the Saguenay region. Similarly, specialist teams are studying the history of the Mauricie, of women, of workers and the business world, and of books and printing, just to give a few examples. The publication of collective works is common, and many articles and books are jointly signed by 2 or 3 authors.

The production of francophone Canadianist historians remains largely centered in Québec or in French Canada, while English Canadian historians take more interest in the history of Québec. Nevertheless, there is now more contact between the 2 historiographies than there used to be, and more interest in recent periods.

Recent historiography parallels the greater pluralism of present-day Québec by offering a range of ideological points of view. Professional history is now marked also by its desire to understand the historic evolution of society as a whole. Social history is being energetically pursued, especially in new fields of study such as the history of women, the history of labour, demographic history, and rural, urban and regional histories. Social history is also revitalizing the older fields of study: economic history now stresses socioeconomics; the history of ideas has become the history of ideologies; and political history spends less time on the lives of outstanding politicians in order to concentrate on how they relate to their parties, to the state and to society.

These changes are being accommodated even in the most venerable of the specialized historical reviews, such as the *Canadian Historical Review* and the *Revue d'histoire de l'Amérique francaise*, as well as in new ones such as *Social History/Histoire sociale*, *Labour/Le Travailleur* (fd 1976) and *Urban History Review/Revue d'histoire urbaine*. Masters' papers and doctoral theses are more numerous than ever; the annual meetings of the Learned Societies and various conferences spread word of the new studies. With new and age-old topics of study, new questions and improved methodologies, French Canadian historiography is in full ferment. However, this often exciting history is still young. As always, some poorer works are appearing along with the superior ones. Yet the most striking fact remains that unlike earlier periods, it becomes harder and harder to identify particular leaders. Or perhaps it is just that Québec now has dozens of good historians.

FERNANDE ROY

Historiography in English

Canadian historiography in the English language began virtually with British settlement in America. By necessity, it developed regionally, and it was practised by enthusiastic amateurs. Its *raison d'être* was less to examine the past for its own sake (for in the prevailing Eurocentric view Canada had little "real" history) than to depict the physical features of the land, compile social and economic statistics, and chronicle political advances in a way that encouraged further settlement and investment. It is best regarded as a literary genre aimed at promotion, descriptive rather than analytic. The first example appeared in 1749, with the anonymous publication in London of *A Geographical History of Nova Scotia.* Other such accounts followed, culminating with T.C. HALIBURTON'S *An Historical and Statistical Account of Nova Scotia* (1829), a tract intended to encourage a continued imperial connection.

Other British North American colonies and regions also contributed to this promotional literature during their formative stages. With the opening of the PRAIRIE WEST to European settlement in the 1870s, there appeared such works as Joseph James Hargrave's *Red River* (1871) and George Bryce's *Manitoba* (1882), tracts equally promotional but also reflecting an embryonic regional consciousness. In part this insistence on a distinctive western past was a reaction to the growing historiography produced by Ontarians in the 19th century. In what is now Ontario, the first counterpoint to François-Xavier Garneau's *Histoire du Canada* was John Mercier McMullen's *The History of Canada from Its First Discovery to the Present Time* (1855). Unlike Garneau, McMullen stressed the "positive" implications of the DURHAM REPORT of 1839: the necessity and goodness of material progress, commercial expansion, British parliamentary institutions and colonial self-government. In this view Canada West (Ontario) was seen as both harbinger and guardian of such virtues; other regions were shunted to the periphery, regarded (as with Québec) either as impedimenta or (as with the West) as soil for possible Ontario-based expansion. The Maritime colonies were largely ignored.

The progress of Ontario in the latter 19th century lent an aura of legitimacy to this central Canadian view. CONFEDERATION in 1867 helped forge an equation of Ontario's past with the nation's past. Historical writing in Ontario, obsessed with material progress, preservation of the British connection and the achievement of RESPONSIBLE GOVERNMENT, remained promotional, but now was cast in the language of national destiny. By the mid-1880s journalist John Charles DENT had produced 2 major paeans to progress through political moderation: *The Last Forty Years* (1881) and *The Story of the Upper Canadian Rebellion* (1885). In the next decade another dedicated amateur, engineer William Kingsford, produced the massive 10-volume *History of Canada* (1887-98), stressing the growth of local self-government out of the structures of imperial authority. At the end of the century the writing of Canadian history still remained largely the preserve of literary enthusiasts such as William KIRBY (*The Golden Dog,* 1877), Charles MAIR (*Tecumseh, A Drama,* 1886) and Charles G.D. ROBERTS (*History of Canada,* 1897).

Overlapping with this romantic approach to historical writing, however, was the growth of institutions that provided for gradual professionalization. This resulted ultimately in a profound shift from an emphasis on literary skill to an emphasis on professional discipline. In 1882 the formation of the Royal Society of Canada gave members their first national outlet for reading and publishing scholarly papers for an audience of peers. A second source of professionalization was the rapid expansion of English Canadian university curricula between 1880 and 1920. In 1880 McGill University principal J.W. DAWSON could write that an educated man could gain a general knowledge of history "in an easy and delightful manner by his own reading." A specialized approach, it was thought, could be made simply by gaining a more thorough acquaintance with language and literature, not necessarily with historical documents. But by 1900 the study of history had achieved independence from classics, English literature and political economy, with which it had earlier been associated. By the 1890s chairs of Canadian history existed at U of Toronto and Queen's U, and the subject was also taught by professors of history elsewhere, including U of Manitoba and Dalhousie U. By then, too, the historical romances of American historian Francis Parkman (eg, *Montcalm and Wolfe,* 2 vols, 1884) and the historical criticism of Goldwin SMITH (*Canada and the Canadian Question,* 1891) had shown that Canada's history was not necessarily parochial or lacking in significance. At U of T, George WRONG combined moralistic narrative with a serious attempt to examine original sources, especially in *A Canadian Manor and its Seigneurs* (1908). George Bryce at Manitoba did likewise in his *Remarkable History of the Hudson's Bay Company* (1900).

Perhaps as important were the continuous efforts made by Wrong and Bryce to divorce the writing of history from mere antiquarianism. Bryce was active in the Historical and Scientific Society of Manitoba (fd 1879), and by 1897 Wrong had founded the *Review of Historical Publications Relating to Canada* at U of T. The energies of both men were directed at introducing principles of historical criticism into Canadian historiography. Kingsford's approach was now deemed fundamentally inadequate because of its weak citation of archival sources and its insubstantial interpretive perspective. With the creation in 1872 of the Public Archives of Canada (*see* NATIONAL ARCHIVES OF CANADA) under Douglas Brymner, there was increasingly little excuse for failing to consult basic manuscript and public records. The new preoccupation with empirical verification was also expressed in the writings of Adam SHORTT, who taught Canadian history at Queen's from the early 1890s to 1907. First in a series of studies of Canadian economic and financial institutions, and later in CANADA AND ITS PROVINCES (23 vols, 1913-17) which he conceived and edited with Arthur DOUGHTY, Brymner's successor as Dominion Archivist, Shortt refused to engage in the nationalistic moralizing which was characteristic of Bryce and Wrong. Moreover, *Canada and Its Provinces*, focusing on the growth of Canada as a nation-state, nevertheless remained sensitive to regional distinctiveness and "provincial history." Like the idealist philosophers under whom he had studied while a student at Queen's, Shortt sought to reconcile multiplicity and unity while undermining the significance of neither.

The new academic historians' commitment to empirical verification and "objective" judgement in the first 2 decades of the 20th century did not, however, mean the death of the earlier literary and romantic approach. Instead, "men of letters" turned to BIOGRAPHY, greatly aided by the decision of Toronto publisher George Morang to create a multivolume biographical MAKERS OF CANADA SERIES. The original series and an index, published 1903-11, were written by academics and laymen and marked the apogee of Carlylean hero worship and whiggish progressivism. All subjects were, in some manner, Canada's "Founding Fathers," usually in politics. They were portrayed as "makers" of Canada's national and independent future, not as contributors to its colonial past. Egerton RYERSON was therefore suitable for inclusion; Bishop John STRACHAN was not. Nor was serious criticism of these "makers" to be brooked. When William Dawson LESUEUR, an editor of the series, submitted a manuscript on William Lyon MACKENZIE that was critical of the rebel, his volume was unceremoniously rejected. It was 71 years before this first "modern" Canadian historical biography was published as *William Lyon Mackenzie: A Reinterpretation* (1979).

In spite of the broad emotional appeal of the Makers of Canada series, by 1920 biographical history as represented by the series no longer represented the work being done by the historical profession, increasingly trained at British and American graduate schools. In 1922 the CANADIAN HISTORICAL ASSOCIATION was founded, its publishing vehicle the CANADIAN HISTORICAL REVIEW (which supplanted Wrong's *Review of Historical Publications*). English Canadians had emerged from WWI with a new sense of psychological distance from the British Empire. An emotional attachment still existed, but there was a sense that soon Canada must declare full independence, except in allegiance to the British monarch. The relationship between empire and nation was to preoccupy the next generation and more of English Canadian professional historians. As a consequence, the interwar years witnessed the publication of several major attempts at understanding Canada's complex international status. Most notable among these were W.P.M. KENNEDY'S *The Constitution of Canada* (1922) and Chester Martin's *Empire and Commonwealth* (1929).

One legacy of the Great War had been an increase in autonomist forms of nationalism and an acceptance of the US as a genuine world power. Accordingly, some historians began to study CANADIAN-AMERICAN RELATIONS. Young Canadian historians such as Arthur LOWER and F.H. UNDERHILL, influenced by American progressive historians such as Frederick Jackson Turner and Charles A. Beard, began to stress common geographical, political and economic attributes of 2 nations sharing a continent. This view gained further legitimacy from the growing interdependence of the Canadian and US economies and cultures. Books internationalist in scope and comparative in structure began to appear, most notably by John Bartlet BREBNER: *New England's Outpost* (1927), *The Explorers of North America, 1492-1806* (1933) and *The Neutral Yankees of Nova Scotia* (1937). The search for continental links found popular expression in journalist J.W. DAFOE's series of essays, *Canada: An American Nation* (1935). Increasingly, the categories of American historical analysis were used to give new meaning to Canada's past. This tendency increased as American scholars turned to the study of American-Canadian relations. One massive expression of this CONTINENTALISM was the Carnegie series on Canadian-American relations, 25 volumes by scholars from both countries under the editorship of James T. Shotwell and published 1936-45. In 1945 appeared Brebner's summary volume for the series: *The North Atlantic Triangle.*

English Canadian historical scholarship between the wars was dominated by a concern for establishing the environmental determinants of Canadian history. Underhill, for example, stressed north-south political and economic continental links much as had his intellectual mentor, Goldwin Smith. A different form of environmental determinism was set forth by U of T political economist Harold INNIS. In a series of comprehensive studies of Canadian economic history (especially *The Fur Trade in Canada,* 1930) Innis articulated what came to be known as the STAPLE THESIS. This complex argument, made with great attention to historical detail, stressed that the fundamental material and economic determinants of Canadian history were ones that linked the hinterland economy of Canada to the metropolitan centres of Europe, particularly Britain (*see* METROPOLITAN-HINTERLAND THESIS). The reciprocal relationship between the exploitation of Canadian products and the demands of Europe forged a transatlantic east-west economic axis that transcended north-south continental imperatives. Other aspects of historical development, such as cultural, political and urban growth, were in his view of secondary importance.

Innis's interpretation provided an important means for Canadian historians dissatisfied with continentalist views to remain environmentalists while stressing European, especially British, economic and cultural ties. This was particularly true of Donald CREIGHTON, whose *The* COMMERCIAL EMPIRE OF THE ST. LAWRENCE appeared in 1937. This seminal book owed much to Innis's focus on the transatlantic nature of staple development, but concentrated on the centrality of the ST LAWRENCE RIVER system and the colonial merchants who, after the Conquest, shaped a transcontinental economy. Thus was born the LAURENTIAN THESIS, the dominant interpretation of Canadian history until the 1960s. Creighton himself expanded upon it, most notably in his magisterial biography, *John A. Macdonald* (2 vols, 1952-55), in which Macdonald became the personification of national will, and his great achievement, the construction of the CANADIAN PACIFIC RAILWAY, marked the transcontinental extension of the empire of the St Lawrence to the Pacific. Much of Creighton's great appeal in the 1940s and 1950s was due to the way his works artfully combined initiative and will with social and economic factors, in his words "Character" with "Circumstance."

The effect of Creighton on his generation was profound. His *Dominion of the North* (1944), *Canada's First Century* (1970) and other works kept the Laurentian thesis at the forefront of interpretations of nation-building in Canada, and his biography of Macdonald helped rehabilitate biography as a genre of history. Other scholars produced major studies of neglected figures, most notably J.M.S. CARELESS (*Brown of The Globe,* 2 vols, 1959-63) and Roger Graham (*Arthur Meighen,* 3 vols, 1960-65). By 1960, in fact, political biography had become the dominant form of historical writing in English Canada, in part because of the extraordinary literary power of Creighton's *Macdonald* and in part because of the post-1945 generation's reaction to the rigidities and restrictiveness of economic determinism in the social sciences. At mid-century, the practice of Canadian history was still very much part of the humanist's domain. The "Laurentian school" was not without its critics, most notably W.L. MORTON, whose 1946 essay "Clio in Canada: the Interpretation of Canadian History" had been a major indictment of the hegemonic and exploitative implications of Laurentianism for regions other than central Canada. In his own writings, including *The Progressive Party in Canada* (1950) and *Manitoba* (1957), Morton had made major contributions to the history of a region neglected (except in its role as hinterland) by Laurentian historians, just as G.F.G. STANLEY had done earlier in *The Birth of Western Canada* (1936). But in the 1960s the assumptions of the Laurentian school began to be codified for a new generation in the Canadian Centenary Series, a projected 18-volume comprehensive history of Canada edited by Morton and Creighton. Most volumes in the series (expanded to 20) have now been published.

The exponential growth of Canadian universities, especially graduate schools, in the 1960s and early 1970s, fundamentally altered the direction of Canadian historiography. The financial support of the CANADA COUNCIL (and later the SOCIAL SCIENCES AND HUMANITIES RESEARCH COUNCIL) greatly facilitated scholarly research, writing and publication. Graduates from "regional" universities turned increasingly to studies of urban, ethnic, working class and feminist historiography, often within regional settings. International scholarship, especially the "New Social History" of the 1960s, markedly influenced such scholars, and major works were often set within a framework critical of capitalist social and economic relations. Specialized journals, such as *Acadiensis, B.C. Studies, Labour/Le Travailleur* and *Urban History Review/Revue d'histoire urbaine,* met with an enthusiastic response from the scholarly community. By the late 1970s the earlier attempts at a "national synthesis" had become the subject of much criticism for their failures to account for forms of regional distinctiveness and their singular emphasis upon members of the English and French middle class and their political representatives. Carl Berger's study of the national historians, *The Writing of Canadian History* (1976), was an eloquent capstone to this earlier historiography. Since the mid-1970s historians have pursued the many "limited identities" to which J.M.S. Careless and Ramsay Cook had earlier called attention. The historiography of regions, gender, social class, cities and ethnicity, among others, continued to flourish. That of the nation, whatever that now meant to historians, was largely ignored. Little "national" political or constitutional history was written, and topics such as "Confederation," staple items of the profession in the 1950s and 1960s, failed to find major historical interpreters. The results were ambiguous and ironic. Students of Canadian history knew much more about the particularities of their collective pasts, but the absence of any major new synthesis of that important scholarship meant that the academic pursuit of "limited identities" had at times produced "limited perspectives" for readers of Canadian history. By the late 1980s academic historians had been accused by "popularizers" such as Pierre Berton and Peter C. Newman of having abandoned their public readership in their quest for the esoteric. Academic historians responded with equally acrimonious accusations of the "popu-larizers" that their attempts to sell books by focusing on the elusive national identity had led them to reductionist and stereotyped interpretations of Canada's past. A.B. McKILLOP

History Since Confederation The years from 1867 to 1919 were the formative period for the transcontinental nation-state and its maturing economy. A dependent colonial existence gave way to a semiautonomous nationhood rooted in dynamic growth at home and then manifested in impressive wartime achievements. Yet the rapid growth also brought urban slums, rising labour discontent and social disharmony, as well as an acceleration of linguistic, ethnic and religious divisions. And the military glory of WWI came at a heavy price in blood and national division.

The new state of 1867 – 4 provinces on the Atlantic and along the Laurentian Basin – expanded extraordinarily in less than a decade to stretch from sea to sea. RUPERT'S LAND, from Ontario to the Rockies and N to the Arctic, was purchased from the HUDSON'S BAY COMPANY in 1869-70. From it were carved Manitoba and the North-West Territories in 1870. A year later, British Columbia on the Pacific entered CONFEDERATION on the promise of a transcontinental railway. Prince Edward Island was added in 1873. In 1905, after mass immigration at the turn of the century began to fill the vast PRAIRIE WEST, Alberta and Saskatchewan won provincial status (*see* TERRITORIAL EVOLUTION).

Under the leadership of the first federal prime minister, Sir John A. MACDONALD, and his chief Québec colleague, Sir George-Étienne CARTIER, the CONSERVATIVE PARTY – almost permanently in office until 1896 – committed itself to the expansionist NATIONAL POLICY. It showered the Canadian Pacific Ry with cash and land grants, achieving its completion in 1885. The government erected a high, protective customs-tariff wall to shield developing Canadian industrialism from foreign, especially American, competition. The third objective, mass settlement of the West, largely eluded them, but success came under their LIBERAL successors after 1896. Throughout this period there were detractors who resented the CPR's monopoly or felt, as did many westerners, that the high tariff principally benefited central Canada. Yet the tariff had strong support in some parts of the Maritimes.

The earliest post-Confederation years saw the flowering of 2 significant movements of intense emotional NATIONALISM. In English Canada the very majesty of the great land, the ambitions and idealism of the educated young and an understanding that absorption by the US threatened a too-timid Canada, spurred the growth of the Anglo-Protestant CANADA FIRST movement in literature and politics. Existing political parties, however, were quick to strangle potential competition, and the materialistic ethos of the age largely overrode idealistic reformism. There was also an incompleteness about the Canada Firsters' confusing, nationalist-imperialist vision of grandeur for their country: their vision did not admit of the distinctiveness of the French, Roman Catholic culture that was a part of the nation's makeup.

Their counterparts in Québec, the ULTRAMONTANES, believed in papal supremacy, in the Roman Catholic Church and in the clerical domination of society. Their movement had its roots in the European counterrevolution of the mid-19th century, and it found fertile soil in a French Canada resentful at reconquest by the British after the abortive REBELLIONS OF 1837-38 and distrustful of N American secular democracy. The coming of RESPONSIBLE GOVERNMENT in the PROVINCE OF CANADA by 1850 and of federalism in the new Confederation encouraged these clericalist zealots to try to "purify" Québec politics and society on conservative Catholic lines. The bulwark of Catholicism and of Canadien distinctiveness was to be the French language. Confederation was a necessary evil, the least objectionable non-Catholic association for their cultural nation. Separatism was dismissed as unthinkable and impractical, in the face of the threats posed by American secularism and materialism. But a pan-Canadian national vision was no part of their view of the future.

These 2 extreme, antithetical views of Canada could co-exist so long as the English-speaking and French-speaking populations remained separate and little social or economic interchange was required. But as the peopling of border and frontier areas in Ontario and the West continued, and as the industrialization of Québec accelerated, conflicts multiplied. The harsh ultramontane attacks on rouge radicalism, liberal Catholicism and freedom of thought in Québec alarmed Protestant opinion in English Canada, while the lack of toleration of Catholic minority school rights and of the French language outside Québec infuriated the Québecois (*see* MANITOBA SCHOOLS QUESTION). Increasing social and economic domination of Québec by anglophone Canadians exacerbated the feeling.

Economic growth was slow at first and varied widely from region to region. Industrial development steadily benefited southern Ontario, the upper St Lawrence Valley and parts of the Maritimes. But rural Ontario W of Toronto and most of backcountry Québec steadily lost population as modern farming techniques, soil depletion and steep increases in American agricultural tariffs permitted fewer farmers to make their living on the land. Emigration from the Maritimes was prompted by a decline of the traditional forest and shipbuilding industries, among other factors. Nationwide, from the 1870s through the 1890s, 1.5 million Canadians left the country, mostly for the US (*see* POPULATION).

Fortunately, prosperous times came at last, with a rising tide of IMMIGRATION – from just over 50 000 in 1901 to 8 times that figure 12 years later. A country of 4.8 million in 1891 swelled to 7.2 million in 1911. The prairie "wheat boom" was a major component of the national success. Wheat production shot up from 8 million bushels in 1896 to 231 million bushels in 1911. Prairie population rose as dramatically, necessitating the creation of the provinces of Alberta and Saskatchewan in 1905 and the completion of 2 new cross-Canada railways – the GRAND TRUNK PACIFIC and the CANADIAN NORTHERN. Western cities, especially Winnipeg and Vancouver, experienced breakaway expansion as entrepôts. Nearly 30% of the new immigration went to Ontario, with Toronto taking the lion's share for its factories, stockyards, stores and construction gangs. Both Toronto and Montréal more than doubled their population in the 20 years before 1914.

As Canada increasingly became an urban and industrial mass society, the self-help and family-related social-assistance practices of earlier times were outmoded. The vigorous SOCIAL GOSPEL movement among Protestants and the multiplication of social-assistance activities by Roman Catholic orders and agencies constituted impressive responses, however inadequate. Governments, especially at the provincial level, expanded their roles in education, labour and welfare. An increasingly significant presence in social reform work was that of women, who also began to exert pressure for the vote.

Through the new immigration, Canada was becoming a multicultural society, at least in the West and in the major, growing industrial cities. Roughly one-third of the immigrants came from non-English-speaking Europe. Ukrainians, Russian Jews, Poles, Germans, Italians, Dutch and Scandinavians were the principal groups. In BC there were small but increasing populations of Chinese, Japanese and East Indians. There were growing signs of uneasiness among both English and French Canadians about the presence of so many "strangers," but the old social makeup of Canada had been altered forever.

Sir Wilfrid Laurier at a nighttime rally in Montréal on 27 Sept 1916. Laurier's rule was bedeviled by difficulties with Britain and the US (*by permission of the British Library*).

There was a reduction in the extent of territories controlled by NATIVE PEOPLES and in their degree of self-determination. In the Arctic the Inuit remained largely undisturbed, but most western Indians and Métis lost their way of life as white settlement encroached on much of their hunting lands. In 1869-70 in the Red River region and in 1885 at Batoche in the Saskatchewan country there were unsuccessful armed Métis rebellions led by Louis RIEL (*see* RED RIVER REBELLION; NORTH-WEST REBELLION). During the second rising some Indians were directly involved. Otherwise the "pacification" of the West was generally peaceful, by purchase in exchange for treaty and reservation rights for the Indians, and through land grants to the Métis. Order was kept by the NORTH-WEST MOUNTED POLICE.

In 1896 the prime ministership of Canada passed to the Québecois Liberal Roman Catholic Sir Wilfrid LAURIER. He presided over the greatest prosperity Canadians had yet seen, but his 15 years of power were bedeviled and then ended by difficult problems in Canada's relationships with Britain and the US. During Laurier's tenure as prime minister, Britain's interest in a united and powerful empire intensified. Many English Canadians joined pan-Britannic emotion to Canadian nationalist ambition to call for an enlarged imperial role for Canada. They forced the Laurier government to send troops to aid Britain in the SOUTH AFRICAN WAR, 1899-1902, and to begin a Canadian navy in 1910. In the same spirit came a massive Canadian contribution of men and money to the British cause in WORLD WAR I.

By then the Laurier administration had been defeated, in part because too many English Canadian imperialists thought it was "not British enough," and because the growing *nationaliste* movement in Québec, led by Henri BOURASSA, was sure that it was "too British" and would involve young Québec boys in foreign wars of no particular concern to Canada. But the chief cause of Laurier's defeat in the general election of 1911 was his proposed RECIPROCITY trade agreement with the US, which would have led to the reciprocal removal or lowering of duties on the so-called "natural" products of farms, forests and fisheries. The captains of Canadian finance, manufacturing and transport excited the naturally strong Canadian suspicions of American economic intentions and, with their support, the Conservative Opposition under Robert BORDEN convinced the electorate that Canada's separate national economy and imperial trading possibilities were about to be thrown away for economic, and possibly political, absorption by the US.

The new Borden government faced the terrible decisions and divisions of WWI. There was extraordinary voluntary participation on land, at sea and in the air by Canadians (*see* WARTIME HOME FRONT). But in 1917 the country was split severely over the question of CONSCRIPTION, or compulsory military service. The question arose as a result of a severe shortage of Allied manpower on the Western Front in Europe. The subsequent election of a proconscription UNION GOVERNMENT of English Canadian Liberals and Conservatives under Borden, over Laurier's Liberal anticonscriptionist rump with its support drawn largely from French Canadians, non-British immigrants and radical labour elements, dramatized the national split.

Yet the war also had a positive impact on Canada. Industrial productivity and efficiency had been stimulated. A new international status – as a separate signatory to the Treaty of VERSAILLES and as a charter member of the new LEAGUE OF NATIONS – had been won. And the place of women in Canadian life had been upgraded dramatically. They had received the vote federally, primarily for partisan political reasons. But their stellar war service, often in difficult and dirty jobs hitherto thought unfeminine, had won them a measure of respect; they had also gained a taste for fuller participation in the work world. Canadian men and women, on a much broadened social scale, had been drawn into the mainstream of a Western consumer civilization.

Yet the attempted shift to a peacetime economy was soon clouded by high INFLATION and UNEMPLOYMENT, as well as disastrously low world grain prices. Labour unrest increased radically, farmer protests toppled governments in the West and

Ontario, and the economy of the Maritimes collapsed. Resentment over conscription remained intense in Québec. The early national period of Canadian innocence was over.

RICHARD T. CLIPPINGDALE

The Interwar Years

Canada's population between the world wars rose from 8 to 11 million; the urban population increased at a more rapid rate from 4 to 6 million. WWI created expectations for a brave new Canada, but peace brought disillusionment and social unrest. Enlistment in the ARMED FORCES and the expansion of the munitions industry had created a manpower shortage during the war, which in turn had facilitated collective bargaining by industrial workers. There had been no dearth of grievances about wages or working conditions, but the demands of patriotism had usually restrained the militant. Trade-union membership grew from a low of 143 000 in 1915 to a high of 379 000 in 1919, and with the end of the war the demands for social justice were no longer held in check. Even unorganized workers expected peace to bring them substantial economic benefits.

Employers had a different perspective. Munitions contracts were abruptly cancelled and factories had to retool for domestic production. The returning veterans added to the disruption by flooding the LABOUR MARKET. Some entrepreneurs and some political leaders were also disturbed by the implications of the 1917 Russian Revolution and were quick to interpret labour demands, especially when couched in militant terms, as a threat to the established order. The result was the bitterest industrial strife in Canadian history. In 1919, with a labour force of some 3 million, almost 4 million working days were lost because of STRIKES AND LOCKOUTS. The best-known of that year, the WINNIPEG GENERAL STRIKE, has a symbolic significance: it began as a strike by construction unions for union recognition and higher wages, but quickly broadened to a sympathy strike by organized and unorganized workers in the city. Businessmen and politicians at all levels of government feared a revolution. Ten strike leaders were arrested and a demonstration was broken up by mounted policemen. After 5 weeks the strikers accepted a token settlement, but the strike was effectively broken.

Industrial strife continued, with average annual losses of a million working days until the mid-1920s. By then the postwar recession had been reversed and wages and employment levels were at record highs for the rest of the decade. Some labour militants turned from the economic to the political sphere; some labour candidates were successful early in the decade in provincial elections in Nova Scotia, Ontario and the 4 western provinces, and J.S. WOODSWORTH was elected in N Winnipeg in the 1921 federal election.

The war also left a heritage of grievances in RURAL SOCIETY. Rural depopulation had accelerated during the war, but the farmers' frustration was directed against the UNION GOVERNMENT of Sir Robert Borden, which had first promised exemptions and then conscripted farm workers. A sudden drop in prices for farm produce increased their bitterness. In postwar provincial elections, farmers' parties formed governments in Ontario, Manitoba and Alberta, and in the federal election of 1921, won by W.L.M. KING's Liberals, the PROGRESSIVE PARTY won an astonishing 65 seats on a platform of lower tariffs, lower freight rates and government marketing of farm products.

These social protests declined by the end of the decade. Industrial expansion, financed largely by American investment, provided work in the AUTOMOTIVE INDUSTRY, in PULP AND PAPER and in MINING. Farm incomes rose after the postwar recession, reaching a high of over $1 billion in 1927. The political system also offered some accommodation. Most provincial governments introduced MINIMUM WAGES shortly after the war, and the federal government reduced tariffs and freight rates and introduced OLD AGE PENSIONS. By the end of the decade the impetus for social change had dissipated. Even wartime PROHIBITION experiments had given way to the lucrative selling of liquor by provincial boards.

The GREAT DEPRESSION of the 1930s followed. For wheat farmers it began in 1930 when the price of wheat dropped below $1 a bushel. Three years later it was down to about 40 cents and the price of other farm products had dropped as precipitously. Prairie farmers were the hardest hit because they relied on cash crops, and because the depressed prices happened to coincide with a cyclical period of drought, which meant crop failures and a lack of feed for livestock. Cash income for prairie farmers dropped from a high of $620 million in 1928 to a low of $177 million in 1931 and did not reach $300 million until 1939. Disaster also struck those industrial workers who lost their jobs. UNEMPLOYMENT statistics are not reliable partly because there was no unemployment insurance and so no bookkeeping records, but it is estimated that unemployment rose from 3% of the labour force in 1929 to 20% in 1933. It was still 11% by the end of the decade. Even these figures are misleading: the labour force included only those who were employed or looking for work, excluding most women. Those who were identified as unemployed were often the only breadwinners in the family.

Voters turned to governments for an economic security that the economic system could not provide. Most governments were slow or unable to respond and were replaced by others at the first opportunity. King's Liberals, elected in 1926 after a brief period of Conservative rule, were again rejected in 1930, this time in favour of a Conservative government under R.B. BENNETT. New political parties contested the 1935 federal election – the CO-OPERATIVE COMMONWEALTH FEDERATION (CCF), SOCIAL CREDIT and the short-lived Reconstruction Party – with promises to regulate credit and business. Even Conservative leader Bennett promised improvements (*see* BENNETT'S NEW DEAL), and Mackenzie King and the Liberals, who won the election, spoke vaguely of reform. At the provincial level, the UNION NATIONALE was elected in Québec under Maurice DUPLESSIS and Social Credit in Alberta under William ABERHART, with the older parties in other provinces often turning to new and more dynamic leaders who promised active intervention on behalf of the less privileged.

Governments tried to provide emergency relief, but they too soon needed help. Prairie farmers needed relief in the form of food, fuel and clothing, but they also needed money for seed grain, livestock forage and machinery repairs. Neither municipal nor provincial governments could meet these demands for assistance; in the drought year of 1937 almost two-thirds of Saskatchewan's population required some relief. Other provinces had declining revenues but were not as close to bankruptcy, with the possible exception of Alberta. Inevitably, as the Depression continued, the federal government had to contribute to relief costs.

The role of governments changed, but not dramatically. Most governments would have preferred to provide jobs by undertaking major public-works projects, but with declining revenues and limited credit the cost of materials and equipment was prohibitive. Direct relief was cheaper in the short run. Governments did become more involved in the regulation of business: mortgages and interest payments were scaled down by legislation, and new regulatory institutions such as the BANK OF CANADA and the CANADIAN WHEAT BOARD were established. The major expansion of the bureaucracy, however, would come only after the outbreak of WORLD WAR II in 1939. Trade-union activity revived with the beginning of industrial recovery: by 1937 trade-union membership was back to the 1919 level. Canadian auto workers and miners followed the American lead and formed INDUSTRIAL UNIONS. Their effectiveness was limited by the opposition of Mitchell HEPBURN in Ontario and Duplessis in Québec, and the significant gains, once again, would come only during the war.

In the years between the wars, 2 machines may have done more than the BUSINESS CYCLE to alter the Canadian way of life: the automobile and the radio. The 1920s were the decade of the automobile; in 1919 there was one car in Canada for every 40 Canadians and 10 years later it was one car for every 10. The car created Canadian suburbs and altered the social patterns of the young. In the 1930s it was the radio: there were half a million receiving sets in 1930 and over a million by 1939, bringing news and entertainment into most Canadian homes. The changes brought about by mass production and popular entertainment posed problems for Canadian identity. The tariff (*see* PROTECTIONISM) provided Canadian jobs by ensuring that cars and radios would be assembled in Canada. There was little concern at the time for this expansion of a branch-plant pattern, but there was concern for the BROADCASTING of American programs by Canadian radio stations. The result was the CANADIAN BROADCASTING CORPORATION, with French and English networks broadcasting a combination of Canadian and popular American programs. By 1939 Canadians looked to governments to provide cautious assistance to maintain a Canadian way of life.

H. BLAIR NEATBY

History Since 1945

Canada's political landscape had been fundamentally changed by WWI. During WWII many Canadians predicted another transformation. In 1943 the CCF, a product of 1930s political discontent, stood highest in new public opinion polls. It became the official Opposition in Ontario in 1943 and in 1944 won decisively in Saskatchewan. In Québec, Maurice Duplessis's Union Nationale recaptured power. Federally, Québec's BLOC POPULAIRE retaliated against conscription in 1944. Once again it seemed that the Canadian party system would become a casualty of a European war.

In the federal election of 11 June 1945, held while thousands of veterans were just beginning to come home, Canadians returned the LIBERAL PARTY to office. Mackenzie King's majority was very small, but his survival is nevertheless remarkable: among Allied wartime leaders, only Stalin and he led through both the war and the peacemaking. In 1945 the Liberals added a new commitment to social welfare and Keynesian management of the economy (*see* KEYNESIAN ECONOMICS). Liberal welfare policies – not least among them the FAMILY ALLOWANCE, begun in 1944, and UNEMPLOYMENT INSURANCE, begun in 1940 – attracted many workers and farmers, and rebuffed the challenges from the CCF on the left and the Conservatives on the right. Although the national Liberals continued to enjoy some support in all regions and from all economic groups, CCF and Social Credit held, respectively, Saskatchewan and Alberta throughout the 1950s

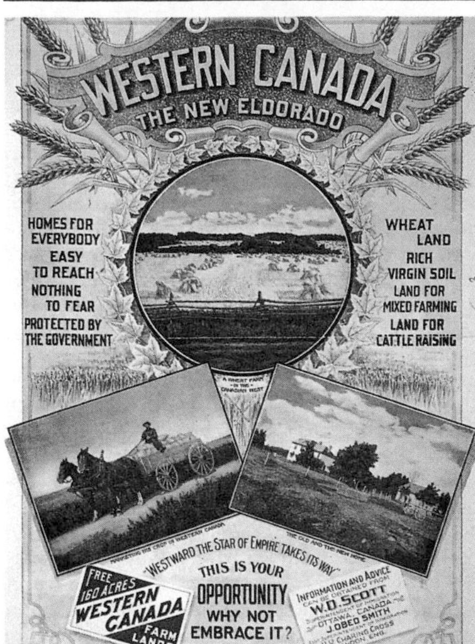

Federal government poster promoting western Canada, "The New Eldorado" (*courtesy National Archives of Canada/C-85854*).

and into the 1960s, and Social Credit governed BC from 1952 to 1972. Historians have attributed Liberal success to the period's unparalleled prosperity, to consensus on foreign policy arising from COLD WAR fears (few had objected when Canada joined the UNITED NATIONS in 1945 or, 4 years later, signed the North Atlantic Treaty and then followed this by sending troops to Europe in 1951), to the nation's need for stability after depression and war, and to a highly competent Cabinet and bureaucracy.

After 1954 these advantages began to disappear. There was a sharp economic slump in 1954, followed by worries that Canada's postwar boom was too dependent upon (mainly American) FOREIGN INVESTMENT. The Cabinet's competency obviously weakened in 1954 when 3 prominent ministers, Douglas Abbott, Lionel Chevrier and Brooke CLAXTON, resigned. In 1956 the PIPELINE DEBATE revealed apparent Liberal arrogance and political clumsiness. Western allies divided during the SUEZ CRISIS when France, Britain and Israel attacked Egypt, and the US and Canada did not support them.

On 10 June 1957 the Conservative Party was elected. Probably most significant in explaining the victory is the Conservatives' choice of John DIEFENBAKER as leader. He brought a flamboyance and a populist appeal that his predecessor, George DREW, completely lacked. He was also a western Canadian who understood and shared the area's grievances against Ottawa. Diefenbaker's brief first term saw taxes cut and pensions raised. The new government also took Canada into the NORAD agreement with the US, and 2 years later scrapped the AVRO ARROW interceptor and purchased BOMARC MISSILES, effective only with nuclear warheads. Seeking escape from the confines of a minority government, Diefenbaker called an election for 31 Mar 1958. Although the Liberals had Lester PEARSON as leader, Diefenbaker won 208 of 265 seats on the strength of his charisma, his "vision" of a new Canada and his policy of northern development. His support was well distributed, except in Newfoundland (which had become the 10th province in 1949).

No one had predicted the extent of the Conservative triumph, but that did not prevent many commentators at the time forecasting a Conservative dynasty and a return to the 2-party system. Historians and political scientists tend to consider the 1958 election as an aberration that neither reflected nor affected the fundamental character of Canadian politics. Yet closer scrutiny reveals a lasting imprint. Since 1958 Conservatives have commanded western Canadian federal politics, and Liberals have found western seats increasingly difficult to obtain. On the other hand, Conservatives, who won 50 seats in Québec in 1958, did not recover from Diefenbaker's failure to build upon his victory there for more than 25 years.

The CCF and the Liberals began rebuilding almost immediately, the Liberals by appealing to urban Canadians and Francophones, and the CCF by strengthening its links with organized labour. Provincial bases were important in this reconstruction. Social Credit governments in Alberta and, to a much lesser extent, BC assisted the Liberals. Within 5 days in June 1960 the party was elected in Québec and NB. In Québec Jean LESAGE modernized Québec Liberal traditions and introduced the QUIET REVOLUTION. In Saskatchewan the CCF sacrificed most for its federal counterpart. Longtime Saskatchewan Prem Tommy DOUGLAS went to Ottawa to lead the CCF's heir, the NEW DEMOCRATIC PARTY, whose formation was an explicit attempt to create a closer link with the labour movement. Without Douglas, the NDP in Saskatchewan bravely introduced medicare in 1962 and, under the lash of a scare campaign, lost the next election to the Liberals. Medicare, however, proved successful and soon became a popular national program.

By 1962 Diefenbaker's 1958 "vision" of Canada had become a nightmare to some and a joke to others. There had been postwar peaks in unemployment, record budget deficits and, in May 1962, a devaluation of the dollar. But neither Pearson nor Douglas made much impact as leaders before the election of 18 June 1962; the Conservatives stayed in power as a MINORITY GOVERNMENT. By early 1963 the Cabinet began to bicker, members resigned ostensibly on the issue of Canadian defence policy, and finally the government collapsed. In a bitter 1963 election campaign Diefenbaker charged that the US, which had openly criticized his refusal to accept nuclear weapons, was colluding with the Liberals to defeat him. The Liberals brushed off the attack and excoriated Diefenbaker for alleged incompetence. The NDP declared a pox upon all who stayed outside its camp. On 8 Apr 1963 the Liberals won a minority government.

The campaign left its mark on subsequent parliaments. The Pearson government sought to be innovative, and in many ways it was – the armed forces were unified and social welfare was extended; but the foul atmosphere obscured its merits. The party became ever more identified with the "politics of national unity," dedicated to containing Québec's aspirations through "co-operative federalism." The NDP argued that this focus distorted the voters' view of their economic circumstances. The Conservatives held that the Liberal approach to national unity was concerned too much with Québec and too little with problems elsewhere. In reality all parties shared a commitment to reform and to the need to deal with Québec's demands for changes in Canada's federal system. Hence, these years were marked by personality quarrels and numerous political scandals, especially the MUNSINGER AFFAIR. They were also notable for the establishment of the CANADA PENSION PLAN and the signing of the CANADA-US AUTOMOTIVE PRODUCTS AGREEMENT, a treaty intended to give Canada a larger share of the continental auto market. Desperate to escape from the minority straitjacket, Pearson called an election for 8 Nov 1965. He won only 2 more seats, remaining 2 short of a majority. Diefenbaker ran a stirring campaign, picking up strength in Atlantic Canada, and took 46 of the 72 western seats. Regional voting patterns persisted as the Liberals took 56 seats in Québec.

In 1967 the Conservatives replaced Diefenbaker with Nova Scotia Prem Robert STANFIELD. Pearson resigned at the end of 1967, to be succeeded by Pierre TRUDEAU, who largely restored party unity. The choice of Trudeau emphasized the Liberals' commitment to finding a solution to the "Québec problem." Trudeau's vigorous opposition to Québec nationalism (*see* FRENCH CANADIAN NATIONALISM) and to "special status" won support in English Canada, while his promise to make the French fact important in Ottawa appealed to his fellow Francophones. Conservatives and the NDP found difficulty in developing a similarly appealing platform, not least because both lacked support in Québec. In 1968, Québec's place in Confederation and Trudeau's personality dominated federal political debate. This dominance endured almost uninterrupted into the 1980s.

In 1968 Trudeau won a majority, appealing across class lines and even across regional barriers. The Liberals won more seats W of Ontario than since 1953. Trudeau's harsh response to terrorism in Québec during the 1970 OCTOBER CRISIS, the growth of leftist sentiment in the NDP and Conservative leadership bickering strengthened Trudeau's position. However, when he called an election for 30 Oct 1972, the Liberals' position was considerably weaker. Their emphasis on BICULTURALISM angered many English Canadians who feared fundamental changes in their lives and their nation; many were also unhappy with the cuts in defence and particularly in the forces dedicated to NATO. The Liberals won only 109 seats, Conservatives 107. The NDP held the balance of power with 31, their highest number to that point. Believing that a Liberal defeat in Parliament would bring a Conservative election victory, NDP leader David LEWIS backed the Liberals. Trudeau took his government towards the left to guarantee NDP support. The Liberals benefited from this political minuet, where the partners pirouetted but never embraced.

In the 1974 election Trudeau's reformist legislation and his opposition to the Conservative policy of WAGE AND PRICE CONTROLS brought many working-class voters to his side, especially in BC and Ontario. The Liberals won 141 seats, the Conservatives 95 and the NDP 16. Political scientists have identified how the 1974 election reflected continuing trends. The regional pattern of support persisted even when economic rather than bicultural issues dominated the campaign. Liberals depended upon Québec to win elections and upon urban Ontario for majorities. Similarly, Conservatives were strongly western oriented in opposition, and they too depended upon Ontario for majorities. New Democrat strength has grown among unskilled workers but dropped among skilled. Nevertheless the NDP percentage of the popular vote has grown, albeit intermittently, since the 1950s. Research indicates that fewer voters remain committed to a single party than was true earlier. Bloc voting is still a characteristic of several ethnic groups and leadership has become much more significant than before. Trudeau's political success is perhaps best explained by the voters' perception that Conservative leaders Robert Stanfield and Joe CLARK were ineffective.

After 1974 Trudeau gave indecisive leadership. Personal problems, weakness in the Cabinet and intractable economic difficulties plagued his government between 1974 and 1979. He surged forward in 1976-77 when René LÉ-

VESQUE'S PARTI QUÉBÉCOIS gained power in Québec; the Liberals clearly benefit most when Canadians focus upon their bicultural nature. When Canada did not collapse within 2 years of Lévesque's win, voters began to worry more about slow economic growth. In May 1979 Clark defeated Trudeau, sweeping English Canada. Although Liberals gained in Québec, Clark was only 4 seats short of a majority.

The Liberal situation seemed more desperate than in 1958. Provincially, especially in the West, they were pathetically weak. Their Québec base might be threatened if an Anglophone replaced Trudeau. Moreover, leadership material was thin, and the successor might face internal party acrimony. But Clark remained personally unpopular, and his party, dependent upon support from the resource-rich western provinces, could not develop an economic or energy strategy that satisfied central Canada, where rapidly rising oil prices were unpopular.

In Dec 1979 the government presented a tough budget and lost a subsequent nonconfidence motion, and an election was called for Feb 1980. Cleverly manipulating the Conservatives' internal differences, the Liberals under Trudeau (who had resigned and then returned) regained their majority in an election in which Ontario swung strongly behind the Liberals, whose policies on resource pricing they favoured and the West abhorred. The Liberals won no seat W of Manitoba and only 2 there. Deep regional divisions in Canadian politics resulted from economic strategies marking a fragmented party system, which mirrored a fragmented nation.

After 1980 Trudeau's government followed a nationalist course for a time. The National Energy Program (soon to be modified) offered great incentives to encourage domestic ownership in the PETROLEUM INDUSTRY. There was a more independent direction taken with respect to the US. After Trudeau had been instrumental in preventing Québec SEPARATISM in a 1980 Québec referendum, the Canadian CONSTITUTION, in which was entrenched the CANADIAN CHARTER OF RIGHTS AND FREEDOMS, was "patriated" to Canada. But the prime minister became ever more unpopular as inflation, interest rates and unemployment rose. In 1984 the Liberals paid the price for alienating the electorate. The Conservatives had replaced Clark with a bilingual Quebecker, Brian MULRONEY, in 1983. The Liberals chose John TURNER as Trudeau's successor a year later. Turner quickly called an election. The result was an overwhelming Conservative victory, as the Tory strength in the West endured while the Liberal fortress of Québec crumbled. Mulroney won 211 seats, 58 of them in Québec; the Liberals retained only 40. The Mulroney government quickly became unpopular, falling into third place in the polls. This unpopularity, however, encouraged the government to be bolder and in 1987 2 initiatives, the so-called MEECH LAKE constitutional accord and the FREE TRADE agreement with the US, gave the government 2 strong issues on which to face the people. Whether the Mulroney government would survive the next election remained unclear; the impact of the government on Canadian policies would endure. JOHN ENGLISH

Reading: I. Abella, *Nationalism, Communism and Canadian Labour* (1973); D.J. Bercuson, *Fools and Wise Men* (1978); Robert Bothwell et al, *Canada Since 1945* (1981) and *Canada 1900-1945* (1987); R.C. Brown and Ramsay Cook, *Canada 1896-1921* (1974); J.M.S. Careless and R.C. Brown, eds, *The Canadians 1867-1967* (1967); Donald Creighton, *Canada's First Century* (1970) and *The Forked Road: Canada 1939-1957* (1976); R.M. Dawson and H. Blair Neatby, *William Lyon Mackenzie King* (3 vols, 1958-76); J.L. Granatstein, *Canada 1957-1967: The Years of Uncertainty and Innovation* (1986); M. Horn, ed, *The Dirty Thirties* (1972); W.L. Marr and D.G. Paterson, *Canada: An Economic History* (1980); A.E. Safarian, *The Canadian Economy in the Great Depression* (1959); J.H. Thompson and A. Seager, *Canada 1922-1939: Decades of Discord* (1985); P.B. Waite, *Canada 1874-1896* (1971).

Hnatyshyn, Ramon John, "Ray," politician (b at Saskatoon 16 Mar 1934). The son of a senator, Hnatyshyn was educated at U of Sask and worked for the government leader in the Senate, 1958-60. He was called to the Saskatchewan Bar in 1957 and practised law in Saskatoon 1956-58 and 1960-74. Elected a Conservative MP for Saskatoon in the 1974 general election, he was minister of energy in the Clark government 1979-80. The moderate, well-liked Hnatyshyn was named House leader in 1984 and after the general election in Sept, served as government leader in the Commons 1984-86 before being named minister of justice. NORMAN HILLMER

Hobson, Joseph, civil engineer (b near Guelph, UC 4 Mar 1834; d at Hamilton 19 Dec 1914). Trained in land surveying and engineering, Hobson served as engineer to Waterloo County and then worked on the building of the GRAND TRUNK RY. In 1875 he became chief engineer of the GREAT WESTERN RY and then of the Grand Trunk Ry. His outstanding works included the tunnel under the St Clair R at Sarnia (the first underwater railway tunnel in N America) and the replacement of the superstructure of the Victoria Bridge over the St Lawrence at Montréal, without interrupting traffic. A brilliant engineer, but an unduly modest man, he left no written record of his notable works. R.F. LEGGET

Hobson, Robert, industrialist (b at Berlin [Kitchener], Canada W 13 Aug 1861; d at Hamilton, Ont 25 Feb 1926). Hobson worked first for the Grand Trunk Ry and in 1896 he became secretary-treasurer of the Hamilton Blast Furnace Co. His executive abilities soon brought him to the top of a firm that before his death became Canada's leading steel producer. In 1899 he became general manager of the Hamilton Steel and Iron Co, and in 1910 VP and general manager of the new Steel Co of Canada (STELCO). By 1916 he was president. During these years he presided over a massive expansion and modernization of the corporation's steel plants and helped to build a secure base for it in widely diversified markets. Simultaneously, his influence in the business community grew enormously, as his directorships proliferated. By the 1920s he was in the front ranks of Canada's "captains of industry." CRAIG HERON

Hochelaga, native village located at the present site of MONTRÉAL. The arrival of Jacques CARTIER at the village in Oct 1535, where he read the Gospel to the Indians and climbed Mt Royal to survey the new world, has become part of Canadian lore. The local inhabitants were IROQUOIS, who lived in palisaded settlements and engaged in agriculture. They likely numbered about 1500. The French offended the Hochelagans by refusing to participate in a feast prepared in their honour and by their abrupt departure. On Cartier's third voyage (1541-42), he skirted the village and followed a trail to the Lachine Rapids. When the French returned in 1603, the Hochelagans had vanished. *See also* STADACONA. JAMES MARSH

Hockey, Ice Hockey is Canada's national game and its greatest contribution to world sport. A major winter preoccupation of Canada's male youth for almost 100 years, ice hockey is now played seriously in 20 countries. Stick and ball games were likely first played on ice in northern England, and British soldiers brought the tradition to Canada early in the 19th century. Variations of the games bandy and shinty were played on ice by British troops garrisoned in Halifax and Kingston in the 1850s, or earlier. The work "hockey" is probably derived from the French *hoquet* ("shepherd's crook"), referring to the shape of the stick, and the nickname "shinny" for informal hockey doubtless comes from the game's origins in shinty. There is evidence that New York Dutch and New Englanders also played a game similar to hockey during colonial times. But these were formless affairs, and ice hockey as we know it was first played in Montréal in 1875, with a set of rules formalized by J.G.A. Creighton, a McGill student. Substitution of a flat, wooden disc (puck) for a ball gave the players more control.

In 1879 the first organized team, the McGill University Hockey Club, was formed, and with the advent of a basic set of rules the sport quickly spread across Canada. The first "world championship" was held in 1883 at the Montréal Ice Carnival and was won by McGill. The first national association, known as the Amateur Hockey Assn of Canada, was formed in 1886, with representatives from Québec City, Montréal and Ottawa. A group of colleges, universities and military and athletic clubs formed the Ontario Hockey Assn in 1890. Gov Gen Lord STANLEY donated a trophy in 1893 for the national championship, and the first STANLEY CUP game was played 22 Mar 1893, with Montreal AAA victorious before a crowd of 5000.

Early hockey was played in rudimentary conditions, mostly outdoors on patches of natural ice, with snowbanks for boards and wooden posts for goals. There were 9 players per side on the ice, and the puck could not be passed forward. The onside rule and primitive face-off ("bully") were adapted from RUGBY. With speed and rough play the game had immediate attraction, and strong local rivalries developed. The sport spread to US universities, beginning with Yale in 1893. Europe's hockey origins date to Vienna in 1885. Belgium, Bohemia, France, Great Britain and Switzerland formed the International Ice Hockey Federation in 1908 and Germany joined 1909. Winnipeg Falcons won the first international world championship, held at the Winter Olympics, Antwerp, 1920. Toronto Granites overwhelmed all opposition to win the 1924 Winter Olympics and U of T Grads won again for Canada in 1928.

The development of hockey in Canada was profoundly changed by the growth and final ascendancy of professionalism. In the prevailing climate of the late 19th century, playing for money was considered immoral, but many players accepted money secretly. The first overtly professional league was formed in 1903 with teams from Pittsburgh, Pa; Sault Ste Marie, Ont; and Houghton, Calumet and Sault Ste Marie, Mich. Most of the best players were Canadian; they commanded extravagant salaries, lived nomadically from one season to the next and played for the highest bidder. At one time, Fred "Cyclone" TAYLOR was the highest-paid athlete in N America. The Ontario Professional League, organized for the 1908 season, was the first openly professional league in Canada. The Eastern Canada Hockey Assn turned professional in Nov 1908. The rival National Hockey Assn was formed 1909 and was reorganized 1917 as the NATIONAL HOCKEY LEAGUE. Professional hockey soon required indoor stadiums, artificial ice and large payrolls. Successful teams in smaller centres, such as Renfrew Millionaires, disappeared; the NHL teams were all in larger cities: MONTREAL CANADIENS, Montreal Wanderers, Ottawa Senators, Toronto St Pats and, briefly, Quebec Bulldogs and Hamilton Tigers.

The Montreal Maroons entered the NHL in 1924 and the league successfully moved into the lucrative urban market of the US, adding Boston

Bruins (1924), New York Americans (1925), Pittsburgh Pirates (1925), New York Rangers (1926), Chicago Black Hawks (1926) and Detroit Cougars (1926). However, almost every one of the players came from Canada. The NHL dominated hockey, monopolized players and controlled salaries and player movement. A few exceptional players were paid up to $10 000 per season, but in the 1920s the average salary had dropped to $900, despite player protests and a threatened strike. After 1945 the controversial C-Form gave NHL teams exclusive control over the future careers of boys from age 15. The sole purpose of amateur junior hockey became the development of players for the NHL – not to win titles, or to represent a community, but to identify individual prospects.

The present form of the sport took shape in the professional leagues, the NHL and the Pacific Coast League. Key innovations were 3 twenty-minute periods (1910), 6 players (1911) and a gradual relaxation of the stricture against the forward pass: allowed between blue lines (1918), within any of the 3 zones (1929-30), and across blue lines (1930-31). The red line was added 1943-44. The result was a faster game and more team play. Although competition remained keen in smaller centres for the amateur trophies, the Allan Cup and Memorial Cup, the focus remained on the NHL, though the number of teams dwindled to 6, with only TORONTO MAPLE LEAFS and Montreal Canadiens in Canada. The Ottawa Senators dominated the 1920s, with 4 league titles and 4 Stanley Cup victories, but folded in 1934. Some early exploits live on: Joe MALONE scored 7 goals in 1 game in 1920. George HAINSWORTH won the VÉZINA TROPHY in its first 3 years. In Mar 1923 Foster HEWITT broadcast a game on radio for the first time. Outstanding players of the era included Frank "King" CLANCY, Charlie CONACHER, Bill COOK, Aurèle JOLIAT, Lester PATRICK and Nels STEWART. Howie MORENZ was the flashiest player, and Eddie SHORE the premier defenceman.

The schedule continued to increase, to 48 games in the 1930s and 70 games in 1949-50. The Toronto Maple Leafs, led by Walter "Turk" BRODA, Syl APPS, Ted KENNEDY and Max BENTLEY, were the dominant team of the 1940s, winning the Stanley Cup 6 times in 10 years. But Maurice "Rocket" RICHARD of the Canadiens was clearly the outstanding offensive player, scoring 50 goals in 50 games in 1944-45, including 5 goals and 3 assists in 1 game.

The outstanding team of the early 1950s was Detroit Red Wings, led by Gordie HOWE (who won the scoring championship 5 times and the HART TROPHY 4 times in the decade), Red KELLY, Ted LINDSAY and Terry SAWCHUK. In the mid-1950s the Montreal Canadiens built possibly the most powerful team in NHL history, with Maurice and Henri Richard, Bernie GEOFFRION, Jean BELIVEAU, Jacques PLANTE, Dickie Moore, Doug HARVEY and others. The Canadiens won the Stanley Cup 6 times, including a record 5 straight.

The NHL expanded into 6 American centres in 1967: Los Angeles, Oakland, St Louis, Minnesota, Pittsburgh and Philadelphia. VANCOUVER CANUCKS were added 1970-71, with Buffalo. Toronto won the Stanley Cup 4 more times before expansion, and Montréal began another string. Chicago managed its first Stanley Cup victory in 23 years in 1960-61, led by the brilliant Bobby HULL, Stan MIKITA and Glenn HALL. Scoring increased in the diluted league, and Phil ESPOSITO of the Boston Bruins set new records for goals (76) in a season and points (152), while defenceman Bobby ORR revolutionized his position, becoming the first defenceman to win the scoring championship. The offensive emphasis of the sport was typified in the 1980s by the incredible scoring feats of Wayne GRETZKY, which are perhaps unmatched in any sport.

Canada defeated the Soviet Union in a thrilling 3-game final series to win the 1987 Canada Cup. With less than $1\frac{1}{2}$ minutes to go in the third period, Mario Lemieux (No 66) scored to lift Team Canada to a 6-5 victory (*photo by Dan Hamilton*).

The NHL's monopoly of professional hockey was broken in 1971 when the WORLD HOCKEY ASSN (WHA) was organized, signing more than 70 players from the NHL, including Bobby Hull. It began with 12 teams and grew to 14 before rising expenses and dwindling crowds reduced it to 7. Fighting had always been tolerated in Canadian hockey, but with the dilution of talent, the increased brawling severely tarnished the sport. A number of well-publicized incidents even brought players into court. In 1979 the feud between the rival leagues ended with a merger, as WINNIPEG JETS, EDMONTON OILERS, QUEBEC NORDIQUES and Hartford Whalers were assimilated by the NHL. The competition for players had substantially raised salaries and finally brought NHL teams to more Canadian cities. In 1980 a team was moved from Atlanta, Ga, to become the CALGARY FLAMES. In 1983-84 Edmonton became the first of the ex-WHA teams to win the Stanley Cup, ending a 4-year reign by the New York Islanders; the high-scoring Oilers captured the cup again in 1984-85 and 1986-87.

Canadian dominance of hockey continued into the 1950s, and senior amateur teams were usually good enough to win international competitions. However, hockey spread rapidly in Europe, particularly in the Soviet Union after WWII, and Soviet teams won the world championship in 1954 and the Olympic gold medal at Cortina, Italy, 1956. From 1963 to 1973, the Soviets won 11 of 12 Olympic and world championships, but Canadians clung to the belief that the Soviets would collapse in competition with professionals. Finally an NHL all-star team met the Soviet "amateurs" in the 1972 CANADA-SOVIET HOCKEY SERIES, perhaps the most dramatic sports event in Canadian history. Canada won 4 games, lost 3 and tied 1, but the shattering of the myth of Canadian hockey supremacy was tantamount to a national identity crisis. Canada has managed to win the CANADA CUP, an international competition held every 3 or 4 years in which Canada can use professionals, in 1976, 1984 and 1987 (losing in 1980), but the Soviets continue to dominate the world championships, the Olympics and encounters with individual NHL teams. The spread and growing proficiency of hockey in Sweden, Finland, Czechoslovakia and the US is reflected in the increasing number of players from these countries in the NHL.

While the Soviet style, which emphasizes speed, passing and teamwork, has reinvigorated the Canadian game, Canadians continue to value the individuality and ruggedness characteristic of the tradition of the sport in their country.

JAMES MARSH

Reading: Ken Dryden, *The Game* (1983); Peter Gzowski, *The Game of Our Lives* (1981); Jim Coleman, *Hockey is Our Game* (1987).

Hockey Hall of Fame, founded in 1943, was the result of meetings of the NATIONAL HOCKEY LEAGUE and Canadian Amateur Hockey Association. The present buildings at Exhibition Place, Toronto, were officially opened in 1961 by PM John G. Diefenbaker and United States Ambassador Livingston T. Merchant. A governing committee comprising representatives from the NHL, CAHA, Metro Toronto and the Canadian National Exhibition Association administers operations, as well as electing builder members. A selection committee, composed of knowledgeable persons from the game and the media, considers player candidates. A maximum of 3 player members may be elected annually, with consideration based on playing ability, integrity, character and contributions to team play and to the game of HOCKEY. Membership at the end of 1987 was 261 – 182 players, 69 builders and 10 on-ice officials.

The Hall is open year-round to the public and has outstanding memorabilia: goaltenders' masks and equipment; players' sticks, skates and pucks; major trophy collections (including the STANLEY CUP); hockey art, geography, international sweaters and assorted other items of interest to hockey fans. M.H. REID

Hocquart, Gilles, intendant of New France (b at Mortagne-au-Perche, France 1694; d at Paris 1 Apr 1783). He followed his father into the marine service and was posted to Rochefort from 1722 until 1729 when he was appointed to New France as financial commissary and acting intendant. He was promoted intendant in 1731. Instructed to expand trade to benefit France while curbing government expenditures, Hocquart was expected to develop the colony's possibilities. To do so, he tried to encourage every kind of Canadian undertaking, such as the FORGES SAINT-MAURICE and shipbuilding.

He eventually succeeded in getting government funds to assist both endeavours. He also promoted agriculture and to assist trade had roads built between Québec C and Montréal and from the latter to Lk Champlain. By 1740 he could claim considerable success in improving New France's economic situation, but the collapse of the underfinanced Saint-Maurice ironworks, the bad harvests of 1741-43 and war between France and Britain in N America 1744-48 destroyed his attempts to stimulate private economic efforts and caused a large deficit in crown expenditures. Replaced in Canada by François BIGOT in 1748, Hocquart was intendant at Brest until retiring in 1764. MARY MCDOUGALL MAUDE

Hodgetts, Charles Alfred, physician, public-health official, teacher, administrator (b at Toronto 23 Aug 1859; d at London, Ont 3 Apr 1952). Hodgetts was medical inspector and later secretary and chief officer of the Ontario Provincial Board of Health and medical adviser 1910-20 to the federal Commission of Conservation. An advocate of PUBLIC HEALTH and dispenser of practical medicine, he emphasized prevention of disease. Public-health officials in the late 19th and early 20th centuries were investigating specific diseases and how to control them, and Hodgetts in particular perceived improved housing and town planning to be important. He considered quick treatment in the case of accident or sudden illness essential, and between 1896 and 1910 devoted much of his time to the RED CROSS SOCIETY, being commissioner overseas 1914-18. He worked tirelessly for the St John Ambulance Assn 1910-32 and was chief officer 1921-32.

GODFREY L. SPRAGGE

Hodgetts, John Edwin, Ted, political scientist, educator (b at Omemee, Ont 28 May 1917). Educated at U of T and Chicago, he is the recipient of many academic honours, awards and fellowships (gold medalist, U of T; Rhodes scholar; FRSC). He taught at Queen's (1945-65) and Toronto (1965-82), and was head of the dept of political studies at Queen's, principal of Victoria Coll (1967-70) and president of Victoria U (at the U of T), 1970-72. His first major research study, *Pioneer Public Service: An Administrative History of the United Canadas* (1956), set the tone for other case studies on administrative histories, culminating in his later book (jointly) *The Biography of an Institution: The Civil Service Commission of Canada – 1908-1967*. Other books include *Canadian Public Service* (co-edited, 1960) and his magnum opus, *Canadian Public Administration* (1973). He brought rare insights to the administrative process through his experience first as editorial director of the Royal Commission on Government Organization (1960-62), and then as a commissioner on the Royal Commission on Financial Management and Accountability (1976-79). In 1981, the Institute of Public Administration of Canada awarded him the Vanier Gold Medal for a lasting and significant contribution to Canadian public administration. A generation of students of public administration, particularly those in the 1960s and 1970s, was shaped at least in part by their exposure to Hodgetts. His lifelong concern about the accountability of the public service, his interest in those administrative values and assumptions which infuse and inspire the Canadian administrative culture, and his role as the foremost interpreter of the administrative history of Canada, stand as his seminal contributions to the field of public administration in Canada. His insights, ideas and probing questions have been reference points for countless professionals, students and scholars interested in public administration as a field of inquiry and practice. Though now retired, in 1987 Hodgetts still continued to edit, research and write, guide students and colleagues and enrich the community of public policy and administration in Canada. A volume of essays in honour of J.E. Hodgetts, *The Administrative in Canada*, was published 1982. O.P. DWIVEDI

Hodgins, Jack Stanley, novelist, short story writer (b at Comox, BC 3 Oct 1938). His fiction, while sometimes experimental, displays a love of narrative. *Spit Delaney's Island* (1976), *The Invention of the World* (1977), *The* RESURRECTION OF JOSEPH BOURNE (1979, Gov Gen's Award) and *The Barclay Family Theatre* (1981) all deal with characters (often the same ones from book to book) reconstructed from the author's Vancouver I childhood. In his hands, they are eccentric but realistic characters, deployed with stylistic suppleness in life-affirming situations. *The Honorary Patron*, published in 1987, was set on Vancouver I as well. He has received a number of awards, including the Canada-Australia Award (1986).

Hodgson, George Ritchie, swimmer (b at Montréal 12 Oct 1893; d there 1 May 1983). Hodgson was Canada's first Olympic swimming champion. He received little formal training as a swimmer but practised summers at his family's cottage in the Laurentians and swam daily in winter at the Montreal Amateur Athletic Assn pool. Representing Canada at the 1911 Festival of the Empire Games, he defeated the world record holder over the 1-mile (1.6 km) distance. At the 1912 Stockholm Olympics he won gold medals in the 400 m freestyle and 1500 m freestyle, setting world records in both. They were not broken until 1924, by the famous American swimmer, John Weissmuller. Hodgson attended McGill and served with distinction in the RAF in WWI. Competing without success in the 1920 Antwerp Olympics, he retired to form an investment brokerage firm. J. THOMAS WEST

Hodgson, Stuart Milton, public administrator, labour leader (b at Vancouver 1 Apr 1924). Hodgson left school in 1940 to work for H.R. MACMILLAN's plywoods division. In 1942 he joined the RCN and was discharged in 1945 after serving on the Murmansk run. Hodgson then returned to the BC lumber industry, joining the International Woodworkers of America in 1946. In 1948 he was elected financial secretary of his local and in 1955 attended the ILO Geneva Conference as the Canadian Congress of Labour delegate. He was appointed to the NWT Council 1964 and served as deputy commissioner 1965-67 and commissioner 1967-79. For his service he was presented the public service's Outstanding Achievement Award in 1976. Canadian co-chairman of the INTERNATIONAL JOINT COMMISSION 1979-81, he was appointed chairman and chief executive officer of the BC Transit Corporation in 1985. ROD MORRISON

Hoedeman, Jacobus, "Co," director of animated films (b at Amsterdam, Holland 1 Aug 1940). Trained in photography, Hoedeman made his first animated film 1956. He immigrated to Canada in 1965 and soon joined the NFB. Two years later he directed his first film. While studying in Czechoslovakia in 1971, he learned the technique of animating puppets, an art in which he has since become a master. Later he animated several Inuit legends. In 1977 Hoedeman produced *Le Château de sable*, for which he won an Oscar. He revived the characters from this film in *Le Trésor des Grotocéans* (1980). His latest film is *Charles et François* (1987). PIERRE VÉRONNEAU

Hoffman, Abigail, track and field athlete, sport administrator (b at Toronto 11 Feb 1947). As a 9-year-old hockey player, she unwittingly caused controversy by entering a male-dominated sport; she later joined the Toronto Olympic Club, winning her first national championship in the 880-yard (806 m) race at the age of 15. She competed internationally from 1962 to 1976 in 4 Olympics, 4 Pan-American Games (2 gold medals) and 2 Commonwealth Games (1 gold). In Ontario, and then as director of Sport Canada (the federal amateur-sport administration), Hoffman is recognized as a campaigner for athletes' rights and women in sport. TED BARRIS

Hoffmeister, Bertram Meryl, soldier, businessman (b at Vancouver 15 May 1907). Hoffmeister commanded the Seaforth Highlanders in Sicily, the 2nd Infantry Brigade at Ortona (1943) and the 5th Canadian Armoured Division, which distinguished itself under his courageous leadership. One of a very few nonregular officers to command a division, he was appointed to take the 6th Division to the Pacific theatre (1945). When the Japanese war ended, Hoffmeister resumed his career in the BC forest industry and was president and chairman of MACMILLAN BLOEDEL LTD, BC's agent general in London and president of the Council of Forest Industries of BC. He was made an Officer of the Order of Canada in 1982. W.J. MCANDREW

Hog Farming Swine (family Suidae) were first brought to what is now Canada in 1598 by the Marquis de La Roche-Mesgouez as part of his unsuccessful venture on SABLE ISLAND. Apart from wild game, pork was the most popular meat of early settlers. It could be preserved in heavy brine and was available as a meat source during the long winters. Today, there are about 10 million hogs on Canadian farms (about 55 million are in the US and 305 million in the People's Republic of China). The terms "pig," "swine" and "hog" are generally interchangeable, although some farmers reserve "hog" to refer specifically to swine raised for market.

In 1986 about 14.4 million hogs were sent to market, about 1.4 million more than in 1983. In 1986 marketed hogs yielded about $2.1 billion in farm cash receipts, about 10% of the national total. The hog industry is more important in some provinces than others: in 1986 it provided 20.8% of agricultural income in Québec, 2.6% in Saskatchewan. In that year, BC produced 2.2% of the national total; Alta, 14.8%; Sask, 6.2%; Man, 11.0%; Ont, 32.0%; Qué, 30.1%; NB, 1.0%; NS, 1.4%; PEI, 1.2%. There are 41 564 hog producers in Canada. Hog farms vary from large, specialized operations, which market several thousand hogs annually, to small mixed farms marketing 100 hogs or less. There are 5 main swine breeds in Canada. Cross-breeding programs are recommended because they result in larger litters of more vigorous pigs, and yield market animals that grow faster and more efficiently.

Yorkshire Hogs originated in England and are all white with erect ears. The most numerous breed in Canada, it is noted for vigour, prolificacy and efficient feed conversion. Yorkshire sows commonly farrow over 10 pigs per litter.

Landrace Hogs originated in Scandinavia and are noted for prolificacy, good mothering ability and a lean carcass with a high proportion of ham. They are commonly crossed with other breeds, yielding hybrid vigour in the young.

Lacombe Hogs are the first livestock breed developed in Canada, a hybrid of Landrace, Berkshire and Chester White. Developed at the Agriculture Canada RESEARCH STATION in Lacombe, Alta, the breed was first licensed in 1957 and is propagated in 24 countries. Hogs are all white with drooping ears and have a slightly heavier bone structure than the Landrace. Rapid growth rate and high lean content characterize progeny of crosses between Lacombe and other breeds.

Duroc Hogs originated in the US, are all red (golden to mahogany), with drooping ears, and have a good carcass and feed efficiency. The Duroc is a hardy breed, noted for large litters.

Hampshire Hogs originated in Kentucky and are black with a white belt around the shoulders. They are exceptionally well muscled, but are somewhat shorter than the Yorkshire and produce smaller litters. When used correctly in a cross-breeding program, Hampshires yield superior carcass quality in offspring. A breeding sow or boar requires about 1 t of feed annually. The market hog converts feed to gain with an efficiency of about 3:1, ie, more efficiently than beef cattle but less efficiently than broiler chickens. The market animal (100 kg) typically yields about 78 kg of trimmed carcass, following slaughter and evisceration. Carcass quality and price paid to the producer is determined by an index, measured by a government grader, which reflects lean meat yield. Slaughtered animals must be disease free and are inspected by government veterinarians. Canadian pork is produced under a high-standard national Health of Animals program (*see* COMMODITY INSPECTION AND GRADING; FOOD LEGISLATION; VETERINARY MEDICINE). As a result, Canada is free of serious livestock diseases (eg, foot-and-mouth disease, swine fever). Since 1937 the industry has had access to a uniform national testing system, the National Record of Performance Swine Testing Program, which provides breeders with a basis for assessing their breeding stock. The Canadian Pork Council (est 1966) represents hog producers. Hog processing provides more jobs than cattle processing, since two-thirds of the meat is sold in processed rather than fresh form. The average Canadian consumed 27.63 kg of hog meat (pork, bacon, ham, sausages, etc) in 1986. About 196 460 t were available for export.

R. BLAIR

Hogan, John Sheridan, journalist, politician (b near Dublin, Ire 1815?; d at Toronto 1 Dec 1859). A contributor to numerous newspapers and magazines, including *Blackwood's*, Hogan founded his own weekly, *The United Empire*, and in 1855 became editor of Toronto's *British Colonist*. That same year he wrote a prize-winning essay on Canada for the Canadian committee of the Paris Exposition. In 1857 he was elected to the Assembly as a Reformer; he was considered one of the rising stars of the Reform Party, but on the night of 1 Dec 1859 he disappeared. His body was found in the Don R 30 Mar 1861, and police investigation revealed that he had been robbed and murdered by thieves known as the Brook's Bush gang. In one of Toronto's most spectacular murder cases, several people were charged and tried but only one, James Brown, was convicted. Brown's execution on 10 Mar 1862 was Toronto's last public hanging. EDWARD BUTTS

Reading: Edward Butts and H. Horwood, *Bandits and Privateers: Canada in the Age of Gunpowder* (1987); W. Stewart Wallace, *Murders & Mysteries* (1931).

Hogg, Frank Scott, astrophysicist (b at Preston, Ont 26 July 1904; d at Richmond Hill, Ont 1 Jan 1951). In 1929 Hogg received the first doctorate in ASTRONOMY awarded by Harvard, where he pioneered in the spectrophotometry of stars and in the study of the spectra of comets. He was assistant editor of the journal of the Royal Astronomical Soc of Canada from 1937. During WWII he developed a 2-star sextant for air navigation. Head of the dept of astronomy at U of T and director of the David Dunlap Observatory from 1946 until his death, Hogg continued its major research program, a study of the motions of faint stars in the line of sight. PETER M. MILLMAN

Hogg-Priestley, Helen Battles, née Sawyer, astronomer (b at Lowell, Mass 1 Aug 1905). In 1930 she married Dr. F.S. HOGG (d 1951) and in 1985 married Prof F.E.L. Priestley. She began her research in the field of globular star clusters and their variable stars in graduate school and in 1931 received a doctorate in ASTRONOMY at Radcliffe. She joined the teaching staff of U of T in 1936 and was appointed professor emeritus in 1976. Making use of the major telescopes at Victoria, BC, Tucson, Ariz, and Richmond Hill, Ont, Hogg became a leading world expert in her field of specialization and has received numerous honours, including Companion of the Order of Canada, the Annie J. Cannon Prize of the American Astronomical Society (1949) and the Rittenhouse Silver Medal (1967). In 1985 she received the Award of Merit, City of Toronto, and the Sandford Fleming Medal, Royal Canadian Institute. Well known for the clarity of her discourses in lectures and on radio or television, Hogg has published numerous scholarly articles and the popular book *The Stars Belong to Everyone* (1976); for 30 years she wrote a weekly column for the Toronto *Star*. In recognition of her contribution to the public's understanding of astronomy, she was the first Canadian to be awarded the Klumpke-Roberts Award (1983). Minor Planet No 2917 has been named Sawyer Hogg.

PETER M. MILLMAN

Helen Hogg-Priestley, a leading world astronomer in the field of star clusters. Minor Planet No 2917 is named Sawyer Hogg for her (*courtesy SSC Photocentre*).

Holgate, Edwin, painter, engraver (b at Allandale, Ont 19 Aug 1892; d at Montréal 21 May 1977). In 1895 the Holgate family moved to Jamaica where Edwin's father was an engineer. Around 1897 Edwin returned to Toronto to study and in 1901 the Holgates settled in Montréal. Edwin became a part-time student *c*1905 at the Art Assn of Montreal under William BRYMNER and *c*1910 took a summer course with Maurice CULLEN. In 1912, during a trip to Paris, he enrolled in the Grande Chaumière. He also travelled in Ukraine and Japan. He came home in 1915 and his first exhibition was at the Arts Club of Montreal in 1922. He taught engraving at Montréal's École des beaux-arts 1928-34, and about 1930 was invited to join the GROUP OF SEVEN. He was known primarily as a portraitist and painted an unusual series of female nudes in outdoor settings during the 1930s. In 1935 he was elected associate of the Royal Canadian Academy of Arts. The National Gallery of Canada held a retrospective of his work in 1975-76.

MICHEL CHAMPAGNE

Holiness Churches, a loose family of some 20 Protestant denominations in Canada that are in general biblically conservative if not fundamentalist, Arminian in theology (ie, rejecting CALVINIST predestination and holding out hope of salvation for all), and advocates of austerity and discipline in life-style. The term "holiness" derives from a commitment to the individual pursuit of "Christian perfection," also termed "second blessing," "sanctification" or "holiness." This state, whether achieved instantaneously or gradually, comes through the action of God's Spirit following EVANGELICAL conversion. A variety of sources in METHODISM, German pietism and American revivalism help explain a number of secondary differences in belief and practice. Holiness was a central concern of early Methodism in both Britain and the US; and some groups (SALVATION ARMY, Free Methodists and Wesleyan Methodists) stem from schismatic Methodist attempts to recover elements of this tradition. Other bodies originated in revival movements among German-speaking settlers in Pennsylvania. Thus the practices of foot-washing and adult baptism by immersion, as well as a tradition of Christian PACIFISM, reflect MENNONITE, Tunker or BAPTIST roots of groups such as BRETHREN IN CHRIST and Church of God.

The holiness revival of the latter half of the 19th century – which gave rise to several groups, notably the Church of the Nazarene – influenced all holiness groups to some degree. Camp meetings and manifestations of religious fervour characteristic of them found renewed vigour when these were falling into disrepute in mainstream Methodism. Like other evangelicals of the period, holiness churches founded BIBLE SCHOOLS that inculcated denominational tradition along with secondary schooling; they established and supported extensive missionary endeavours outside Canada; a number joined in the evangelical crusade for Sunday observance and PROHIBITION. The authority of individual religious experience prompted a larger leadership role for women, and a few of the churches were ordaining women ministers by the beginning of this century. Modern PENTECOSTALISM originated in American holiness circles about 1900; the ensuing controversy over the Pentecostals' belief in a further blessing, "baptism of the Holy Spirit," brought schism in several bodies. This history, as much as theological divergence, explains a continuing holiness reticence towards neo-Pentecostalism, despite obvious similarities in the 2 traditions. Worship in all groups has emphasized the exposition of the Bible; with congregational participation encouraged in singing, exhortation ("testimonies") and free prayer.

Historically, holiness groups were concentrated in southwestern and eastern Ontario and the Prairie provinces; recent statistics confirm this pattern, although churches are found in all regions of Canada. The movement has been traditionally prone to schism. The period since WWII, however, has seen numerous unions. Today, denominations range in size from the Salvation Army (*c*30 000 adult members), the Church of the Nazarene (*c*10 500) and the Free Methodist Church (*c*7400) to groups with a membership of a few hundred. As with other evangelicals, these statistics would be considerably augmented by the inclusion of active adherents. Educational institutions have undergone upgrading, in keeping with a trend towards a more learned ministry. Distinctive standards of dress and deportment have been significantly attenuated. Holiness teaching now tends to emphasize the concept of growth toward sanctification, at the expense of the notion of instantaneous acquisition. A significant element within several denominations (in particular the Missionary Church and the Christian and Missionary Alliance) would question the validity of their classification today as holiness, despite their origins and earlier history.

The following are the most significant members of this family in Canada. Groups German-speaking in origin include Brethren in Christ, formerly Tunkers or River Brethren, who entered Canada 1788; the Church of God (Anderson, Indiana); the Evangelical Association or Evangelical Church and the United Brethren in Christ, which united 1946 to form the Evangelical United Brethren. In 1968 the EUB's Ontario section entered the UNITED CHURCH; the Western Conference remained independent as the Evangelical Church in Canada and, after its 1982 merger with the Evangelical Church of N America, became known as the Evangelical Church.

Two Ontario Methodist ministers, Nelson Burns and Ralph Cecil HORNER, actively promoted holiness within their denomination through the organization of autonomous Holiness Associations before their deposition from the Methodist ministry (1894 and 1895 respectively). Through Horner's subsequent work 4 uniquely Canadian bodies came into existence: Holiness Movement Church (1897); Standard Church of America (the result of a 1916 schism in the HMC); the Gospel Workers Church, fd about 1902 by Frank Delaney Goff, a Horner convert; and the Bible Holiness Movement (1949). Among bodies of American origin, the Free Methodist Church and the Church of the Nazarene have enjoyed considerable success since their entry into Canada (1880 and 1908 respectively). In 1958 the Holiness Movement Church merged with the Free Methodist Church. That year most of the Gospel Workers joined the Church of the Nazarene.

Unlike all the foregoing, the Reformed Baptist Alliance, the result in 1888 of holiness schism within the Free Baptist Church, was centered primarily in NB and NS. In 1966 it united with the Wesleyan Methodist Church of America; in 1968 these were joined by the Pilgrim Holiness Church to form the Wesleyan Church. Since 1943 most holiness denominations have been loosely associated in the Canadian Holiness Federation and at present most are ecumenically committed through membership in the EVANGELICAL FELLOWSHIP OF CANADA. The Free Methodist and the Wesleyan churches are also members of the World Methodist Council.

R. GERALD HOBBS AND HELEN HOBBS

Reading: S.D. Clark, *Church and Sect in Canada* (1948); Melvin E. Dieter, *The Holiness Revival of the Nineteenth Century* (1980); Charles Edwin Jones, *A Guide to the Study of the Holiness Movement* (1974) and *Perfectionist Persuasion* (1974).

Holland, Samuel Johannes, surveyor, cartographer, military engineer (b at Nijmegen, Netherlands 1728; d at Québec C, LC 28 Dec 1801). Holland took part in the sieges of LOUISBOURG (1758) and Québec (1759) and the Battle of STE-FOY (1760), surveyed PEI and Cape Breton I, and founded a system of township surveys in Lower and Upper Canada. Prior to and during his service in the Dutch and British armies 1745-60, he apparently mastered the skills of an artillery officer, a military engineer, cartographer and surveyor – as well as displaying exemplary courage under fire. In 1764 he was appointed surveyor general of Québec and of the northern district of N America. After 1783, the massive influx of LOYALIST settlers following the American Revolution offered him a new challenge in Québec. Holland's system of rapid surveys to create new townships was effective and imaginative, and has proven accurate. From his vantage point on Council as surveyor general, he was able to get the colonial legislature to enact professional standards for surveyors.

F.J. THORPE

Holland, William Lancelot, Asian scholar (b in New Zealand 26 Dec 1907). He was a leader in development of the international Institute of Pacific Relations, serving in New York as research director 1933-44 and then, after wartime service with the US Office of War Information in China, as secretary-general of the IPR 1948-60. When the IPR fell foul of the McCarthyites in the 1950s, Holland accepted an invitation from UBC to become head of its department of Asian studies and bring with him the IPR's journal, *Pacific Affairs*, which he edited from Vancouver. Since 1972 he has been emeritus professor of Asian studies.

JOHN W. HOLMES

Holland Marsh, 2900 ha of organic (muck) soil, is located near Bradford, Ont, 50 km N of Toronto. Draining to the NE by the Holland R (which empties into Cook's Bay, an arm of Lk SIMCOE), the marsh is a flat, level area lying in a shallow basin (oriented in a NE-SW direction) that was an arm of glacial Lk Algonquin. As the lake level dropped and the land rebounded when the glaciers receded, a marsh was formed containing sedges, bullrushes, various marsh grasses and some trees. Dead vegetation accumulated at about 30 cm per 500 years, forming a layer of organic material overlying a clay pan in the basin. In this natural state the marsh and river were home to many species of fish, small animals and birds. The first human use of the marsh was by local Indians (latterly the Huron) as a source of food. Early European settlers (about 1825) also fished and hunted here. Around 1900 the Bradford Mattress Factory used marsh grasses as stuffing for mattresses. The marsh takes its name from the Holland R, which was named after the surveyor Samuel HOLLAND.

In 1904 W.D. Watson, a Bradford grocer, persuaded W.H. Day, professor of physics at the Ontario Agricultural College, Guelph, to investigate the possibility of draining the marsh. Day tested the soil and experimented successfully in growing vegetables. In 1925 drainage operations began and a canal and dikes 28 km long and 2 m deep were constructed around the marsh to divert the Holland R. Pumps were installed to control the water table within the dikes. The project was completed 1930. In 1931 and 1934, 18 Dutch families came to the marsh and formed the nucleus of an expanding and prosperous agricultural community. After WWII, more immigrants from Holland, as well as from other European countries and Asia, settled here. The marsh today is a market garden for the Ontario and foreign markets, producing carrots and onions in particular, as well as lettuce, potatoes, celery, parsnips, cabbage, cauliflower and beets. There are some greenhouses in which tomatoes, cucumbers and commercial flowers are produced. *See also* SWAMP, MARSH AND BOG.

A.M. BLAIR

Hollick-Kenyon, Herbert, aviator (b at London, Eng 17 Apr 1897; d at Vancouver 30 July 1975). He immigrated with his family in 1909 to Ewing's Landing, BC, and joined the Canadian Army in 1914. Twice wounded in France, he was invalided home and in 1917 joined the Royal Flying Corps. He returned to Canada in 1928 and, based in Manitoba, was staff pilot for a commercial airline. In 1935 he joined the Lincoln Ellsworth Antarctic Expedition and was pilot for the first transantarctic flight. He and Ellsworth covered 3 500 km but ran out of fuel and landed about 25 km short of their destination; they were stranded for 2 months until they were picked up by a British ship. In 1937-38, Hollick-Kenyon piloted an aircraft commissioned by the Soviet government in a vain attempt to find a crew of 6 missing on a transarctic flight, a search that covered thousands of sq km of the Canadian Arctic. He flew for Trans-Canada Airlines until 1942, when he joined Canadian Pacific Airlines, where he became CPA's first chief pilot. He retired in 1962 and was named to Canada's Aviation Hall of Fame in 1973.

DEAN BEEBY

Holling, Crawford Stanley,"Buzz," ecologist (b at Theresa, NY 6 Dec 1930 of Canadian parents). One of the best-known Canadian forest entomologists, Holling has gained international recognition for his work in the management of natural resources. He was educated at U of T and UBC. He was known to his scientific colleagues for his research in forest entomology with the Canada Dept of Forestry 1952-64 at Sault Ste Marie, and 1965-67 at Victoria, but his public prominence dates from his subsequent work at UBC, where he became professor of zoology in 1967 and was director of the Institute of Animal Resource Ecology 1969-73. Addressing a variety of resource management problems using a workshop technique, Holling and his colleagues developed a worldwide reputation for incisive and perceptive analysis and their advocacy of "adaptive management policies." Holling was director of the International Institute of Applied Systems Analysis in Vienna 1981-84 and now is a professor at UBC.

PETER LARKIN

Hollingsworth, Margaret, playwright (b at London, Eng 5 June 1939). Emigrating from Britain in 1968, Hollingsworth settled in Thunder Bay, where she gained a BA in psychology from Lakehead U, then moved to Vancouver for an MFA in theatre and creative writing at UBC. Her plays tend to focus on the relationships of women to one another or to their men, exploring the characters' responses to their environment through revelations of their inner lives. Pairs or triads of women alone occupy her one-act stage plays, *Operators* (1974), *Alli Alli Oh* (1977) and its sequel *Islands* (1983). Her full-length plays, *Mother Country* (1980) and *Ever Loving* (1980), concern 3 daughters and 3 war brides respectively, while the character whose perspective dominates her most powerful work, *War Babies* (1984), is a female writer. Five of her plays are collected under the title *Willful Acts* (1985).

JERRY WASSERMAN

Holly, common name for shrub of the holly family, Aquifoliaceae. The true hollies belong to genus *Ilex*, comprising some 400 species worldwide, mostly in Central and S America. Two species occur in Canada. Although well-known for their spiny leaves and red berries, many hollies are nonspiny with black berries. Inkberry (*I. glabra*) has black berries and shiny, evergreen leaves; black alder (*I. verticillata*) has bright red berries and dull green, deciduous leaves. The closely related mountain holly (*Nemopanthus mucronata*) is deciduous and red berried. All 3 inhabit wet woods and swamps in eastern Canada. Numerous cultivars exist, selected for their ORNAMENTAL qualities (eg, leaf variegation) and their compact growth. The name "holly" (from holy) suggests its long association with folklore and religion. The druid ritual of bringing sprigs of the plant indoors to provide winter refuge for woodland spirits continues today at Christmastime. The hard, white wood is used by cabinetmakers. Various parts of the holly plant were used to make a tonic in Europe and N America, and species like *I. paraguariensis* (yerba maté) provide a caffeine tea in Central and S America and Asia.

ROGER VICK

Holman, NWT, UP, pop 303 (1986c), 300 (1981c), is located on the W coast of VICTORIA I, on inlets of Amundsen Gulf, 925 air km N of Yellowknife. The area is the ancestral homeland of the COPPER INUIT. First established 1940 as an HBC trading post, it takes its name from nearby Holman I, which in turn was named for J.R. Holman, a member of the Inglefield arctic expedition (1853-54). It is famous for the Holman Eskimo Co-operative which sells Inuit prints around the world. The Inuit were first taught to make prints by Rev Henri Tardi, an Oblate who settled in the area in 1939. Although the Inuit residents trap, hunt and seal, PRINTMAKING has become the major source of income.

ANNELIES POOL

Holmes, John Wendell, diplomat and scholar (b at London, Ont 18 June 1910). He studied at the universities of Western Ontario and Toronto, and did graduate studies at U of London. In 1943 he joined the Department of External Affairs and served in London, Moscow and New York and held other important positions. He left the public service in 1960 to go to the Canadian Institute of International Relations, as president then director general and, since 1973, as counsellor. He has published works on Canada's external relations policies and practices, particularly in 3 volumes authored by him, which are recognized as indispensable guides to the history of Canada's foreign policy: *Life with Uncle: The Canadian-American Experience*, which analyses Canada's uneasy relationship with the US; the 2 volumes of *The Shaping of Peace: Canada and the Search for World Order* (1979-82) which recounts Canada's role on the world stage. He has written countless valuable articles in popular and specialized publications, many of which have been collected in *The Better Part of Valour* (1970) and *Canada: A Middle-Aged Power* (1976). Holmes has brought a combination of realism and tolerance, with a graceful mixture of elegance and humour, to the study of foreign affairs. He was awarded the Tyrrell Medal of the Royal Society of Canada in 1986.

NORMAN HILLMER

Holmes, Simon Hugh, lawyer, publisher, politician, premier of NS (b at East R, NS 30 July 1831; d at Halifax 14 Oct 1919). One of the most prominent political figures in NS immediately after Confederation, he was influential in the development of provincial mines and railways. He began his career in 1862 as editor-proprietor of the Pictou *Colonial Standard* and was admitted to the bar in 1864. In 1871 he was elected to the legislature as Liberal/Conservative member for Pictou County, and in 1874 he was named leader of the Opposition. A Tory administration was returned in 1878, and Holmes served as premier and provincial secretary until 1882, when he retired from politics and publishing to become crown clerk for Halifax County. LOIS KERNAGHAN

Holt, Sir Herbert Samuel, capitalist (b at Geashill, King's County, Ire 12 Feb 1856; d at Montréal 28 Sept 1941). Holt immigrated to Canada in 1873 and worked as an engineer and contractor on railway construction projects, including the mountain section of the main line of the CPR. He became prominent in the Montréal business community following the merger of several utility companies into Montreal Light, Heat and Power Co in 1902. Under Holt's direction, the company acquired a monopoly over the distribution of hydroelectric power in Montréal and a large share of the generation and transmission of power from various sites in Québec. He was briefly president of the Sovereign Bank of Canada and in 1908 was elected president of the ROYAL BANK OF CANADA, a position he held until 1934. During his presidency the Royal Bank absorbed a number of smaller banks and extended its operations to become the largest institution of its kind in Canada and the third largest in N America. In the late 1920s Holt, with J.H. GUNDY, was active in company mergers in the pulp and paper, textiles, utilities, coal and steel industries. He was created a KB in 1915. T.D. REGEHR

Home Economics describes an area of study and a group of related professional occupations, both of which aim at improving the quality of life of individuals and families by encouraging the effective management of personal resources, eg, time, money and consumer goods.

The study of home economics, which is based on both social and physical sciences, originated at the turn of the century in the US at a series of meetings of academics and national leaders in Lake Placid, NY, who were seeking remedies for the social ills of the day. Ellen Richards, who advocated the idea of "applying science for use in everyday life" is considered by many to be the founder of the field. At the Fourth Lake Placid Conference in 1902 a committee developed the first and often quoted definition of home economics: "the study of the laws, conditions, principles and ideals concerned with man's immediate physical environment and his nature as a social being and specially the relation between those two factors." One of the members of this committee was a Canadian, Alice A. CHOWN of Kingston, Ont.

At the same time, in Canada, Adelaide HOODLESS was promoting the establishment of what was then called domestic science. She headed the first program at U of T and was founder of the Women's Institute (*see* FEDERATED WOMEN'S INSTITUTE OF CANADA) an organization that had a close association with home economics in its earlier days.

The Macdonald Institute, founded at Guelph in 1903, offered was what called "the diamond ring course" because it was seen and promoted as a means of obtaining a husband. There was a 3-month practical program, which included courses in millinery, dairying and poultry raising with strong emphasis on home production, and a 2-year program for teachers who spread theories and practices of household science to rural communities via schools. In the 1960s the institute revised its curriculum in recognition of an increasing need in society for consumer education. It was also evident that the needs of the food industry would be better met through the study of the behavioural aspect of nutrition, eg, product development, consumer acceptance and institutional food-service management. Instructors were imported from other areas (eg, anthropology) to fill out the new specializations. In 1969 the Macdonald Institute dissolved. The university then created the College of Family and Consumer Studies which awards Bachelor of Applied Science and Bachelor of Commerce degrees. The enrollment in these programs in 1987 totalled 12 425 students.

In high schools in some Canadian provinces the study of home economics is now called FAMILY STUDIES, reflecting an emphasis on the study of family living and family relationships. The 2 largest university programs in home economics are offered at U of Man and U of Guelph. A new undergraduate program introduced at Manitoba in 1980 offered courses in textiles, family studies and food and nutrition. Enrolment increased from 120 to 674 by 1987-88. At U of A, the next largest home economics training institute, the options offered to graduates now include dietetics, consumer education, merchandising of textiles, etc. At McGill the School of Household Science became in 1968 the School of Food Science, and the home economics major was shifted to the Faculty of Education. The U of T Faculty of Household Science was replaced by the department of nutritional sciences in the Faculty of Medicine. In 1972, Ryerson developed a 4-year degree program in nutrition, and consumer and family studies. At Laval and U Moncton the home economics departments are known as Institut d'economie familiale.

Graduates of 4-year degree programs in home economics (or equivalent programs) are eligible to join the national professional organization, the Canadian Home Economics Assn, and to work as home economists. Many graduates also join provincial and local organizations. The graduates are usually employed in professional or in business situations, eg, food companies, utility companies, supermarkets, home-equipment manufacturers, etc. Some home economists free-lance; others work in the media and in advertising, product promotion and testing.

A large number of home economists teach in high schools and work in agriculture-related activities. In addition many work as credit and family counsellors. MAY MASKOW

Home Truths, by Mavis GALLANT (Toronto, 1981; repr 1982), winner of the Gov Gen's Award, is a collection of 16 previously published stories about Canada and Canadians. Prefaced by an introduction in which Gallant defends her status as an expatriate writer, the chronologically arranged stories simultaneously depict her precocious talent as a writer of flawless prose and her attempts to come to terms with her past and her country. Each of the book's 3 sections presents recurring Gallant motifs: the first examines the tortured relationships between parents and children; the second features young Canadians abroad in varieties of exile; and the final, the best in the collection, deals with memory. While the latter stories are not purely autobiographical, they are as close as Gallant has come to a precise evocation of her Montréal childhood and the wartime experiences of her youth. Occasionally finding us conservative, reticent and single-minded, Gallant nonetheless looks homeward with humour, compassion and grace.

DONNA COATES

Homesteading, a late 19th- and early 20th-century phenomenon, in which immigrants were attracted to the Canadian West by government advertisements of "free" land.

Under the DOMINION LANDS POLICY, 160 acres cost only $10, but the homesteader had to build a house, often of log or sod, and cultivate a specified area within 3 years. A new homesteader required basic agricultural implements, and since horses were expensive, most used oxen to clear and break the land. A fireguard to protect farm buildings had to be ploughed, and a vegetable garden planted and game hunted to supplement the food supply. If the water was of poor quality, homesteaders had to collect rainwater or melt snow. In many areas a homestead had to be within 15 km of a railway to be farmed economically; the reservation of land for the HBC or railways within this belt was a source of frustration, for the poor or latecomers were forced to settle away from markets and towns. The railroads did provide employment for homesteaders until their farms began producing.

Homesteaders and their families were often separated from friends and relatives, and many suffered years of hardship and loneliness. One of the greatest difficulties was the absence of roads and bridges. Most trails were impassable when wet. In the autumn homesteaders waited until the ground was frozen before transporting their produce to the railhead. Farm accidents often resulted in permanent injury or, because doctors were rare, death. Drought ruined those who settled in the arid Palliser Triangle. For many the price of homesteading was too high; they can-

Homesteaders' shack, 1918. Homesteaders were required to build a dwelling within 3 years (*courtesy Provincial Archives of Alberta/H. Pollard Coll*).

celled their claims and moved away. Adversities, however, bound homesteaders together. Prejudices were lessened as people helped one another. Building and quilting bees were common (*see* QUILTS). Doors were kept unlatched and lanterns hung at night to guide travellers. At first, recreation was confined to the lonely homestead, but as communities grew there were sport days and a variety of entertainment at the community halls. Homesteading on the Prairies declined after WWI as IMMIGRATION fell off and movement toward the cities increased. *See also* LOG HOUSES; PIONEER LIFE; SOD HOUSES. JANE MCCRACKEN

Homicide Canadian law recognizes 3 types of culpable homicide: murder (1st and 2nd degree), manslaughter and infanticide. Murder is the killing of one human being by another with malice aforethought; infanticide is the killing of a newborn child by its mother; and manslaughter, which includes the lesser offence of criminal negligence, is any homicide that is neither murder nor infanticide. First degree murder now consists of 4 forms of homicide: murders that are planned and deliberate, murders of police or custodial officers killed in the line of duty, murders committed in the course of specified criminal acts (hijacking, sexual offences or kidnapping) or murders committed by a person who has been convicted of first or second degree murder. Second degree murder now constitutes all other murders. International homicide statistics are generally unreliable and always outdated, but Canada ranked seventh in a list of 14 selected countries in a 1987 study prepared by the Canadian Centre for Justice Statistics. The study showed that for 1975-79 Canada's homicide rate per 100 000 population was 2.87; at the top of the list was the US (with 8.49 per 100 000 population) and at the bottom was Belgium (with 1.03). The Canadian homicide rate has fluctuated since the late 1960s when an increase was noted. In 1975 rates began to decline an average of 5% annually until 1981, when they began to climb again. Preliminary estimates for 1986 indicate that homicide offences dropped an unprecedented 25% from their 1985 level and that provinces or territories with the highest homicide rates per 100 000 population were NWT (27.5), YT (13.1) and Manitoba (4.36). PEI (0.00) and Nfld (0.69) had the lowest rates, followed by Ont (1.51), NB (1.66), NS (1.70), Qué (2.29), Sask (2.45), Alta (2.64) and BC (2.99). From 1962 to 1985, 20% of all murders were committed during another criminal act. In 1985, of the 651 total murders committed, 32.7% were shootings, 15.5% were beatings, 34.1% were stabbings and 16.9% are classified as "other," which includes strangulation, suffocation, drowning, etc. In 1985, over 63% of the murder victims were male, and over half of all victims were between the ages of 20 and 39. Nearly half of the victims were single; 22.7% were married and 12.1% lived in common law arrangements (the rest were separated, widowed, divorced or marital status unknown). By far the largest number of murder incidents involved only one victim, but 27 involved 2 victims, 4 involved 3 victims and 5 involved 4 victims.

Of the 588 murder suspects in 1985, 521 were male. Over half of the suspects (399) were between the ages of 20 and 39. Total solved murders in 1985 numbered 514. Thirty-nine percent of the solved murders involved domestic relationships between the victim and the killer, and 34.5% were social or business relationships. The risk of homicide was greatest in the victim's residence (44.2%) or in a public place (19.8%). Since 1978, when GUN CONTROL legislation came into effect, the proportion of homicide committed with firearms declined from 37.8% to 31.5%, while stabbings increased from 22.1% to 32.2%. Studies show that sparsely populated territories have Canada's highest rate of increase, while in the US the increase is highest in the major metropolitan areas, but this discrepancy may reflect the location of the 2 countries' socially alienated populations, America's blacks in urban slums, Canada's native peoples in the North (*see* NATIVE PEOPLE, LAW). Less than 2% of the Canadian population, the INUIT, INDIANS and MÉTIS, comprised 16% of the homicide victims between 1961 and 1974. In 1986, 4 police officers were murdered, a number consistent with the average 1976-85.

The causes of homicide and of varying homicide rates in different nations remain unclear, although various and usually contradictory theories ascribe both to biological, psychological or sociological factors. LAW REFORM, such as it is, appears to have little or no effect on reducing homicide. Whether the reform involves the abolition or restoration of CAPITAL PUNISHMENT, the restriction or distribution of firearms, or lowering the level of brutality in prison life (*see* PRISON), the proponents of either side typically conduct their arguments from emotional or moral positions without reference to objective analysis, an unsatisfactory state of affairs that will undoubtedly continue. ELLIOTT LEYTON

Reading: Canadian Centre for Justice Statistics, *Homicide in Canada 1976-1985: An Historical Perspective* (1987).

Homosexuality [from the Greek, "homo," meaning same], also called inversion, can be characterized generally as sexual preference for one's own gender. Homosexuals may be male (now widely called "gay") or female (now widely called "lesbian"). Exclusive homosexuality, like exclusive heterosexuality, is uniquely human. Homosexual preference takes many and varied forms. Some persons in whom it is limited to fantasy may try to lead asexual lives, or they may attempt to suppress their inclinations by marrying. Many, however, eventually lead double lives, anxiously hiding from their friends, spouses and children a secret world of homosexual liaisons. Some persons (widely known as bisexual) are able to combine homosexual and heterosexual activity. Where homosexual preference is allowed social expression, it tends to increase in frequency (like other stigmatized action, eg, divorce). In recent years growing numbers of homosexuals have accepted their preference as natural and inherent to their personalities. Some take pride in it and form organizations to promote gay liberation. Like heterosexual behaviour, homosexual behaviour ranges from anonymous sex, promiscuity and prostitution to romantic affairs and lifelong faithful relationships.

Homosexual practices are among the most ancient manifestations of human sexuality and different societies have reacted to them in various ways, from toleration and permissiveness to condemnation. In a 1951 study it was found that 49 of 76 societies condoned some forms of homosexuality, regarding them as normal and even encouraging them for certain groups of individuals. Some societies believed homosexuals possessed magical powers, and conferred SHAMAN status upon them. The ancient Greeks considered homosexuality normal as well. In certain societies homosexuality has generally been more tolerated for certain groups, eg, artists, actors, sailors, or among the noble "favourites" in certain royal courts.

At various times in Western history homosexuality has been savagely punished. This intolerance is rooted in the ancient Judeo-Christian disgust for sexual acts associated with paganism and decadence. Leviticus 20:13 condemns homosexuals to death. Though there is no Gospel record of Jesus' opinion on the topic, the early Christian church under the leadership of Paul condemned homosexuality, and ecclesiastical and secular law attempted to prevent, control and eradicate it. In certain periods of Western Christendom, allegations of homosexuality were enough to condemn the accused to torture and death by fire; the last recorded Christian burning of homosexuals occurred in Amsterdam in 1730.

In the 19th century the medical definition of homosexuality as an illness began to displace the religious definition of it as sin. To denote the practice without using the traditional epithets (sodomite, bugger, queer, etc), the Austro-Hungarian doctor and sexologist K.M. Benkert in 1869 coined the word homosexual. In their search for causes of homosexuality, scientists and clinicians have proposed heredity, hormones, genital malfunction, childhood crisis, inadequate parenting, adolescent peer relationships and mental disorder, among other causes, but there is no conclusive evidence to support any of these as a single cause, and some have been effectively disproved. Recent investigations have challenged Freud's influential theory that homosexuality is an expression of a biological bisexuality common to all human beings by suggesting that human beings are psychosexually neutral at birth and that homosexuality is an adaptive response to a combination of certain experiences. Drugs, electric shock, behavioural therapy and psychotherapy are among the treatments used to cure homosexuals, but none can claim significant success.

The search for causes is frustrated because the same person, at different times and with different partners, may achieve sexual gratification homosexually and heterosexually. Some persons change from a predominantly homosexual lifestyle to one that is heterosexual, or in the opposite direction. Homosexuality and heterosexuality are probably both caused by learning experiences and social conditions. Change in social conditions, eg, confinement in prison, may result in a change of sexual preference, and release from prison may or may not result in another change. That homosexuality is simply a sexual variation (as is chastity or polygamy) won considerable international support in the 1920s as a result of the work of Dr Magnus Hirschfeld's Institute of Sexual Science in Berlin. In 1897 Dr Hirschfeld formed the Scientific Humanitarian Committee to lobby for the abolition of the criminal laws against homosexuals. But in 1933, at the instigation of the Nazi press, students raided the premises and burned the institute's books and documents. Later, from 100 000 to 400 000 homosexuals in Nazi-occupied Europe were killed in concentration camps; others were forced to wear an identifying badge, a pink triangle, which has since become the emblem of gay liberation movements.

In 1948 American biologist Alfred Kinsey published a survey of American male sexual activity, shocking many by revealing statistical estimates that 37% of males had enjoyed homosexual orgasm at least once and that exclusive homosexuals were at least as large a minority as American blacks. The black struggle for equal civil rights inspired a similar movement among homosexuals. Nevertheless, most homosexuals must hide their preference in order to obtain employment and accommodation and many still dare not tell parents or close friends. Because social tolerance is greatest in large cities, many young homosexuals gravitate there and indeed only in modern industrialized societies do homosexuals develop specific subcultures. In some districts of large Canadian, American and European cities, gay men and lesbians form a large enough minority to develop their own social world, comparable to an ethnic community. The "gay world" of a city such as Montréal, Toronto or Vancouver includes bars, discos, sports teams, political and religious groups, gay businesses, medical and legal services, newspapers and publishing houses and even charitable foundations. Smaller centres have some of these facilities, but they are more covert. In the 1960s, gay urban communities became the base for political action. Gay liberation groups encouraged many secret homosexuals in prestigious positions to "come out of the closet."

In 1974, following studies revealing that no particular physical or personality type was associated with homosexual preference and public revelation that many homosexuals were respected and effective members of society, the American Psychiatric Association removed homosexuality from its catalogue of illnesses (it is now classified as "sexual orientation disturbance"). Since then, a wide range of churches, corporations and academic organizations have adopted more tolerant positions, but other groups have strongly opposed toleration of homosexuality.

From Confederation to 1969, under Canada's criminal law, homosexuality was punishable by up to 14 years in prison. In 1969 the law was amended by exempting from prosecution 2 consenting adults of at least 21 years of age who engaged in these "indecent acts" in private. However, homosexual acts before age 21 or with a third person present are still illegal. According to the most recent federal survey, conducted in 1981, only 33% of Canadians would support laws allowing homosexuals the same civil rights as heterosexuals, but some large cities, eg, Ottawa and Toronto, and one province, Québec, have enacted laws against discrimination on the basis of sexual preference. In several Canadian cities, however, including Toronto, police continue to enjoy public support for massive arrests of homosexuals. It is clear that homosexuality will continue to be a controversial issue in Canada for years to come. In the late 1980s one of the main issues involving homosexuals has been the spread of auto-immune deficiency (AIDS). JOHN ALAN LEE

Honderich, Beland Hugh, newspaper executive (b at Kitchener, Ont 25 Nov 1918). As head of the TORONTO STAR, Honderich has transformed a sensationalist but profitable working-class paper into a better modulated and equally profitable middle-class one that is less rigid in its liberalism. He began his career on the Kitchener-Waterloo *Record* in 1935 and went to the *Star* in 1943 as a reporter. Later its financial editor, he became editor in chief (1955), president and publisher (1966) and chairman and publisher (1969), and is now chairman of TORSTAR, the parent company. The *Star* is Canada's largest circulation newspaper but Honderich remains little known outside the business.

Honeysuckle, common name for plants, usually woodland shrubs, of genus *Lonicera*, family Caprifoliaceae. Honeysuckle leaves were a favourite goat food, hence the name *caprifolium* [Lat, "goat's leaf"]. More than 150 species of *L onicera* are widespread in the Northern Hemisphere; 9 are native to Canada. They are distributed transcontinentally, from the subarctic to southern Canada. Flowers are in pairs or 6-flowered whorls, and are showy in some species commonly under cultivation, eg, Japanese honeysuckle (*L. japonica*), woodbine (*L. periclymenum),* trumpet honeysuckle (*L. sempervirens*) and Tatarian honeysuckle (*L. tatarica*). The most common Canadian species are: *L. canadensis, L. dioica* and *L. oblongifolia,* which are red berried; and *L. involucrata* and *L. villosa,* which are black berried. All of these have yellowish flowers. Seven species, including *L. caprifolium* (Italian woodbine), *L. periclymenum* (woodbine honeysuckle) and *L. tatarica,* have been naturalized in Canada from garden escapes. Woodbine and the related climbing honeysuckles are limited to the mildest regions of Canada. Tatarian honeysuckle is very cold hardy and a valuable prairie ORNAMENTAL. Berries are generally nauseously bitter and purgative. N American Indians used berries and root bark for digestive problems and gonorrhea, and as a tonic. ROGER VICK

Hong Kong In 1940 the British regarded their crown colony of Hong Kong and its 20 000-man garrison as expendable in the event of war with Japan and decided against reinforcing it. But in Sept 1941 the Canadian government agreed to send the Royal Rifles of Canada (a Québec unit) and the Winnipeg Grenadiers, although they were not considered fit for action. They arrived on 16 Nov 1941 and 22 days later the Japanese attacked the colony's New Territories on the mainland. On Dec 18 the Japanese crossed to the island of Hong Kong and on Christmas Day the governor surrendered. Of 1975 Canadians, 557 were killed or died in prison camps. Political pressure at home forced the Canadian government to appoint a royal commission to investigate the circumstances of Canada's involvement. The sole commissioner, Chief Justice Sir Lyman DUFF, misinterpreted or ignored evidence and exonerated the Cabinet, the Department of National Defence and senior members of the General Staff. In 1948 a confidential analysis by Gen Charles FOULKES, chief of the general staff, found many errors in Duff's assessment, but concluded that proper training and equipment would have made little difference. *See also* WORLD WAR II.

BRERETON GREENHOUS

Reading: Carl Vincent, *No Reason Why* (1981).

Honours The achievement of excellence in any field of endeavour has always won popular respect and acclaim. From earliest times, heroism, military and athletic prowess, outstanding leadership and civic merit have been rewarded in tangible and symbolic ways. The conferment of honours was formerly a prerogative of emperors and kings, but is nowadays the practice of even the most egalitarian regimes. The many forms of honour include the victor's triumph in ancient Rome and the astronauts' ticker-tape parade, the accolade received from the sovereign's hand and the award of the NOBEL PRIZE, the badge of knighthood and the silk rosette worn in the buttonhole.

Marks of royal favour have been known in what is now Canada from the earliest times of European habitation. Settlers in New France at the beginning of the 17th century took for granted that their governor and his principal officials would be of noble rank. Contrary to the Old World tradition, in the colony the acquisition of land did not affect the owner's status: the SEIGNEURS did not gain entry into "la noblesse" merely because they were landholders. Some were ennobled by Louis XIV, however, for their part in developing and defending the colony (*see* CROIX DE SAINT LOUIS).

When the colony came under the British Crown after 1760, titles were not uncommon among the officials sent out to conduct civil and military affairs. Titular distinctions from the French period gradually fell into disuse. No indigenous form of honours was introduced to recognize the contributions of those who were instrumental in the growth of responsible government and the maturing of the colony's institutions, but an attempt was made to include such a provision in the arrangements leading up to Confederation. In 1866 Lord MONCK, then governor general of British North America, sent a dispatch to the Colonial Office in London recommending the creation of an order of knighthood for Canada as an incentive to public service. Awards would be made by the new Dominion's governor general on behalf of the sovereign. In order to underline

Letters of nobility granted to the Canadian François Hertel, Paris, Apr 1716 (*courtesy Archives municipales, Rochefort, France*).

the award's Canadian character, he suggested calling it the "Order of St Lawrence." The proposal was quietly shelved by the home government. To relinquish control of honours, in the opinion of the colonial secretary, must inevitably lead to a weakening of the imperial tie. It was concluded that there should be no separate order for Canada but that the governor general would be asked to name a few persons each year for appointment to existing British orders. This policy, to which successive British ministers adhered, was a source of recurring friction between Ottawa and London until honours for Canadians were discontinued entirely after WWI.

Sir John A. MACDONALD, Canada's first prime minister, did not contest the British policy, but he pressed constantly for a more generous annual allotment of places. Alexander MACKENZIE, prime minister 1873-78, would accept no title himself but became incensed upon learning that London planned to honour a prominent Canadian entirely without reference to Ottawa. In response to Mackenzie's protest to the governor general, the colonial secretary replied that if the choice of recipients were controlled by the colonial government, party affiliation would be bound to override all other factors, and he stated flatly that the responsibility to advise the sovereign in these matters was his alone.

Preparing the honours lists each year troubled PM Sir Wilfrid LAURIER in his turn, and resulted occasionally in strained relations with the governor general. Honours was a touchy subject with members of Cabinet, and its frustration led to a renewed attempt to gain some control of the nominations process. In 1902 an order-in-council was passed which would require the governor general to seek the advice of the ministry about the annual honours lists, but the response from the Colonial Office was little different from the position taken 25 years earlier.

By 1911, when Sir Robert BORDEN became prime minister, titles in Canada were being viewed with growing public disfavour. A knighthood conferred on Max AITKEN, an expatriate Canadian who had been elected to the British Parliament, provoked widespread criticism. There were further shock waves a few years later when Sir Max Aitken, with the help of influential political friends, received in quick succession a baronetcy and then a peerage, and entered the House of Lords as Lord Beaverbrook. Abuses were becoming more frequent, and Canadian public opinion hardened with the announcement of some of Borden's candidates for titles during WWI. When the Union Government took office after the 1917 election, the matter came to a head. A parliamentary committee recommended and the House of Commons in 1919 adopted the "Nickle Resolution," which brought to an end the granting of both titular and nontitular honours to Canadians.

There was a brief revival of the defunct honours policy during the Conservative administration of Prime Minister R.B. BENNETT, and several knighthoods and lesser distinctions were awarded 1934-35, but shortly after the Liberals were returned to office in 1935 the prohibition was reinstated. Consequently, at the outset of WWII Canadians in the armed services were not entitled to receive awards in the orders of chivalry for which other Commonwealth personnel were eligible. A parliamentary committee appointed in 1943 recommended that the ban on nontitular honours be lifted, thus clearing the way for many members of the military and civilians to receive recognition for wartime services. A further recommendation, favouring the creation of a Canadian order, led to the establishment of the "Canada Medal," a single all-purpose national honour. An initial list of suggested recipients was drawn up but was rejected by the prime minister. Mackenzie KING had a deep distaste for the concept of honours, and on reflection he decided that instituting the Canada Medal had been a mistake. No award was ever made.

After the war the subject was kept alive, chiefly in military circles. In 1951 Vincent MASSEY, chairman of the Royal Commission on NATIONAL DEVELOPMENT IN THE ARTS, LETTERS, AND SCIENCES, was asked by PM Louis ST. LAURENT to include a report on the subject of honours. In response a draft scheme was submitted favouring the creation of an elaborate 5-tier Canadian order. The proposal came to nothing.

Fifteen years later the approaching centenary of Confederation brought the notion of national honours back into focus. PM Lester PEARSON seized the opportunity of the CENTENNIAL celebration to reinforce the theme of Confederation: the fruitful union of diverse elements in a vigorous and independent state. In 1965, in the face of loud and sometimes bitter opposition, he piloted a bill through Parliament giving Canada a national flag (*see* FLAG DEBATE). In the spring of 1967, not a dissenting voice was heard when he announced the creation of the ORDER OF CANADA. On 1 July 1967, the proposal made by Lord Monck a century before at last became a reality. Five years later the honours system was fleshed out with the addition of the ORDER OF MILITARY MERIT and a group of DECORATIONS FOR BRAVERY. The administration of honours is the responsibility of the Chancellory of Honours, Government House, Ottawa. *See also* MEDAL; GEORGE CROSS; VICTORIA CROSS.

CARL LOCHNAN

The Hudson's Bay Co ships *Prince of Wales* and *Eddystone* bartering with the Inuit, Hudson Strait, 1819, by Robert Hood (*courtesy National Archives of Canada/C-40364*).

Hood, Hugh John, writer, academic (b at Toronto 30 Apr 1928). Hood's extensive writings present a view of Canadian experience in this century realistic in detail and emblematic in intent. A Roman Catholic, he has dealt with characters and situations embodying religious, philosophical and allegorical themes. Numerous short stories have appeared in such volumes as *Flying a Red Kite* (1962), *Around the Mountain* (1967), *The Fruit Man, the Meat Man and the Manager* (1971), *Dark Glasses* (1976) *None Genuine Without This Signature* (1980) and *August Nights* (1985). *Selected Stories* appeared in 1978. Among his novels, *White Figure, White Ground* (1964) is noteworthy and 5 works in his New Age series (12 vols) have appeared: *The Swing in the Garden* (1975), *A New Athens* (1977), *Reservoir Ravine* (1979), *Black and White Keys* (1982) and *The Scenic Art* (1984). He has also published 2 essay collections and a sports biography. Educated at U of T, he has taught in the English department of U de M since 1961. A novella, *Five New Facts About Giorgione*, was published in 1987.

DENNIS DUFFY

Hood, Robert, arctic explorer, artist (b at Portarlington, Ire 1797; d near Starvation Lk, NWT 20 Oct 1821). Hood joined the Royal Navy at age 14. In 1819 his artistic abilities gained him an appointment with the arctic land expedition led by Sir John FRANKLIN. As primary surveyor and draftsman, Hood plotted accurately from a birchbark canoe thousands of kilometres of rivers and lakes and nearly 1000 km of the northern coast of N America. He was the first to demonstrate that the AURORA BOREALIS is an electrical phenomenon, and made important observations on climatology, anthropology and natural history. Returning across the Barren Lands, already weakened by starvation and only 50 km from the previous winter's buildings, Hood was shot by Michel, a voyageur turned cannibal.

C. STUART HOUSTON

Reading: C. Stuart Houston, ed, *To the Arctic by Canoe, the Journal and Paintings of Robert Hood* (1974).

Hoodless, Adelaide, née Hunter, educational reformer, founder of the Women's Institutes (b at St George, Canada W 26 Feb 1857; d at Toronto 26 Feb 1910). Hoodless was jolted out of a comfortable middle-class life when an infant son died in 1889 after drinking impure milk. Thereafter she devoted herself to women's causes, specifically to the better education of women for motherhood and household management. She campaigned for domestic science (home economics) in the schools and advised the provincial department of education on this subject. In 1897 she founded the first Women's Institute (Stoney Creek, Ont); within a few years this movement spread across Canada and around the world. Working with Lady ABERDEEN, she helped found the NATIONAL COUNCIL OF WOMEN, VICTORIAN ORDER OF NURSES and the national YWCA. Basically conservative, Hoodless believed women's natural destiny lay in the home, and she never supported the suffragette cause. She was the author of *Public School Domestic Science* (1898).

ROBERT M. STAMP

Hoodoo Rock, a strange, often fantastically shaped, naturally carved rock or earth pedestal, pillar or column. Hoodoos may range from a few centimetres to several metres in height. They result from the combined erosional action of wind, rain and running water, which together with a variety of physical and chemical weathering processes sculpt the material into different shapes. Use of the term appears to be largely restricted to western N America. Hoodoos tend to be best developed in horizontally bedded rocks or strata in which relatively soft units are interspaced with more resistant ones, eg, alternating layers of shale and sandstone. Differential weathering and erosion is enhanced, the soft material being removed more rapidly than the hard. Hoodoos are often capped by a resistant layer (cap rock) which protects the lower units. Removal of the cap rock results in rapid destruction of the unprotected base. Hoodoos are well developed in the BADLANDS of Alberta near Drumheller, in DINOSAUR PROVINCIAL PARK and near the MILK R. Excellent examples also occur in glacial-outwash deposits on the COLUMBIA RIVER N of Cranbrook, BC, and in glacial-lake sediments in the OKANAGAN VALLEY near Penticton, BC.

I.A. CAMPBELL

Hoodoo rocks, Yoho National Park, BC. Hoodoos are formed by the combined erosional action of wind, rain and running water (*courtesy Environment Canada, Parks*).

Hope, BC, Town, pop 3046 (1986c), 3205 (1981c), inc 1929, is located on the Trans-Canada Hwy, 150 km E of Vancouver; it sits on the E bank of the FRASER R, surrounded on 3 sides by mountains. The junction of the Trans-Canada and the transprovincial Hwy No 3 makes it the gateway to the interior. Hope was established 1848-49 as a HBC post at the W end of their Brigade Trail from Fort Kamloops, and may have been so named in the hope that this trail would provide an all-British route between Fort Kamloops and Fort Langley. A townsite was laid out by the Royal Engineers in 1858 during the rush for gold on the nearby sandbars of the Fraser. In 1860 Edgar Dewdney opened the first pack trail, the Dewdney Trail, to the E. Hope became a station on the CPR mainline in 1886 but further growth awaited the advent of automobile traffic. Today logging, tourism and mining in the district are the town's economic base. Local attractions are the Hope Slide (1965), the Coquihalla Canyon and the wilderness of Manning Provincial Park. Hope is at the W entrance to the newly completed COQUIHALLA HWY, although it is bypassed by the highway itself.

JOHN R. STEWART

The dramatic Hope Slide (1965) is a local attraction near the town of Hope, BC (*photo by Valerie L. May*).

Hopedale, Nfld, Comm, pop 477 (1986c), inc 1969, is located on a small peninsula jutting into the N Atlantic N of Deep Inlet on the Labrador coast. The community was established in the

1780s as a mission station of the MORAVIAN Church, but the area had been long used by native peoples because of its proximity to a variety of land and marine resources. The Moravians built and maintained commercial premises, churches and schools for native people and a slowly growing number of European settlers. In the 1920s the Hudson's Bay Co became the principal commercial operator until succeeded by Newfoundland government agencies in the 1940s. During the early 1950s a DEW-Line radar station was constructed at Hopedale. Today it has a government-run fish holding plant, a nursing station and an airstrip. ROBERT D. PITT

Hopkins, John Castell, journalist, encyclopedist (b at Dyersville, Iowa 1 Apr 1864; d at Toronto 5 Nov 1923). He became assistant editor of the Toronto *Mail and Empire* in 1890 and wrote a number of pamphlets, biographies and histories, including the deferential *Life and Work of the Right Hon. Sir John Thompson* (1895) and *Progress of Canada* (1901, rev as *The Story of Canada*, 1922). He edited *Canada: An Encyclopaedia of the Country* (6 vols, 1898-1900) – Canada's first ENCYCLOPEDIA – and succeeded George Morang as editor of the *Annual Review of Canadian Affairs.* DAVID EVANS

Horetzky, Charles George, photographer, explorer, civil servant (b at Edinburgh, Scot 20 June 1838; d at Toronto 30 Apr 1900). An employee of the HBC, he was at Ft Garry in 1869 during the RED RIVER REBELLION. In 1871 he was hired by the CPR survey primarily for his abilities as an amateur photographer. He is best known for his 1871-79 survey photographs of northern BC and northern Ontario. Though intelligent, fearless and innovative, he was impatient and quick to take offence, traits that cost him his job in 1880. He worked for the Ontario government supervising public works 1883-1900 and wrote *Canada on the Pacific* (1874) and 2 other pamphlets. ANDREW BIRRELL

Horn, Kahn-Tineta, meaning "she makes the grass wave" in Mohawk, political activist, fashion model, civil servant (b at New York C, NY 16 Apr 1940), member of the Mohawk Wolf Clan of Caughnawaga, Qué. She attracted national attention to Indian causes in the 1960s and early 1970s by her lively and controversial criticisms of Indian conditions. She had already been a model and public speaker for some years when in 1964 she was fired from her posts in the National Indian Council in a controversy over policy and organization of centennial celebrations. Throughout the 1960s she took part in numerous Indian protests, including one in which she dumped rats in a government meeting to illustrate illegal dumping on her reserve. She advocated "Indian apartheid" or separate development, including preservation of the reserve system, teaching by Indians only, and the banning of Indian-white intermarriage. She founded and directed the Indian Legal Defence Committee, 1967-71. Since 1972 she has held various positions in the social, community and educational development policy sections of the federal Dept of Indian Affairs. BENNETT MCCARDLE

Hornby Island lies in the Str of GEORGIA between VANCOUVER I and mainland BC, SE of the island community of COURTENAY. It is a wooded island with a shoreline of sandbanks and rock shelves. Whaling was carried out in the 19th century from a shore station on the E coast; today it is a busy recreation area. Sandstone ledges along the shore show good examples of Indian petroglyphs. The name refers to Rear-Adm G.T. Phipps Hornby, commander of the Pacific Station 1847-51. DANIEL FRANCIS

Horne-Payne, Robert Montgomery, financier (b in Eng; d at Brentwood, Eng 30 Jan 1929). Long an invalid, he rarely visited Canada, but his financial skills left an imprint on the landscape and a northern Ontario town (Hornepayne) bears his name. He has been credited with directing $500 million of British capital to Canada 1894-1928, through the British Empire Trust Co, which he founded. So influential was Horne-Payne that when he warned British investors in June 1913 of reckless Canadian municipal borrowing, several western mayors protested. As chief fund raiser for William MACKENZIE and Donald MANN, he was London director of the Canadian Northern Ry from 1901 until the Canadian government took it over in 1918. From its inception in 1897 until its sale to Canadian interests in 1928, he was an active chairman of the board of the BC Electric Ry. He was also a director of other Canadian firms and was associated with Canadian capitalists in Latin American utility companies, notably Brazilian Traction, Light and Power Co, Ltd. PATRICIA E. ROY

Hornell, David Ernest, aviator (b at Lucknow, Ont 26 Jan 1910; d at sea 25 June 1944). He was awarded the VICTORIA CROSS for destroying a German U-boat while under extreme fire, and for fortifying his comrades in the ordeal after their flying boat crashed. Blinded and exhausted, Hornell died shortly after being rescued at sea. JAMES MARSH

Horner, John Henry, "Jack," rancher, politician (b at Blaine Lk, Sask 20 July 1927). He has carved a controversial public career since his election to the House of Commons in 1958. Supported by his central Alberta constituency, Horner soon earned a reputation as a spokesman for western farmers and as an arch-Conservative; later he was known as one of the "DIEFENBAKER cowboys." After his failure to gain the Tory leadership in 1976, Horner crossed the floor of the House on 20 Apr 1977 to become a Liberal and the next day was appointed minister without portfolio. In Sept he became minister of industry, trade and commerce, but he was rejected by his constituents in the 1979 election. He was soon appointed to the board of the Canadian National Railways and in June 1982 was named chairman of the board. Since 1984 he has been administrator of the Prairie Grain Agency. PATRICIA WILLIAMS

Reading: J.H. Horner, *My Own Brand* (1980).

Horner, Ralph Cecil, evangelist, church leader (b in Pontiac County, Canada E 22 Dec 1854; d at Ivanhoe, Ont 12 Sept 1921). After a short, stormy career as Methodist minister, he founded and led a series of HOLINESS CHURCHES. Converted and sanctified in Methodist camp meetings (1872), Horner studied theology at Victoria College, Cobourg, Ont, 1883-85 and oratory in Philadelphia 1885-86. A powerful preacher, already active in evangelistic missions, he was ordained by the Montreal Conference of the Methodist Church in 1887. Mounting criticism of his teaching and methods, and failure to submit to conference discipline brought his deposition 1894-95. Taking some Methodist clergy and laity with him, he joined the Wesleyan Methodists of NY and in 1897 formed an independent Holiness Movement Church, becoming its bishop. By 1900 his movement had a Bible college and a publishing house in Ottawa, and claimed some 6000 adherents, mainly in eastern Ontario and on the Prairies. In 1916 criticism of his leadership resulted in schism, and Horner founded the Standard Church of America. R. GERALD HOBBS AND HELEN HOBBS

Hornet, common name for larger WASPS of family Vespidae, order Hymenoptera. The striking, black and white, bald-faced hornet (*Vespula maculata*) is common across Canada. The European hornet (*Vespa crabro*), a large yellow and black, introduced species, is found in southern Ontario. In addition, queens of various species of yellow jacket wasp, being considerably larger than workers, are sometimes called hornets. All are social wasps. They build nests of wood fibres, masticated into coarse paper, usually greyish in colour. Nests are attached to trees or shrubs, or suspended from eaves. Occasionally they may build in cavities in walls, hollow trees or under the ground. In fall workers and males die, but young, mated queens hibernate. In spring each queen may initiate a new colony. M.V. SMITH

Horse (*Equus caballus*), herbivorous MAMMAL possessing single toes or hoofs (ie, ungulate), contributing to its speed. Customary gaits are walk, trot, canter and gallop. Horses are friendly, moderately intelligent animals, capable of being excellent helpers and companions for humans. Indeed, the horse can share with the dog the distinction of being man's best friend. Giving more than friendship, horses have for hundreds of years been mankind's most faithful slaves, furnishing muscle and stamina for heavy work in AGRICULTURE and endurance to cope with heavy loads on long trails in pioneer transportation. When forced from traditional occupations by mechanical power, horses were immediately returned to service in new and important roles in sport and recreation. In some parts of the world, horse meat is a common item of diet but Canadians have never shown much interest in eating their best animal friends. Selection for different purposes led to wide variations and many breeds. In size, for example, the range in height would be from 10-12 hands in the case of some Shetland ponies to 17 hands in certain big breeds. A hand, the horseman's unit in measuring height at the withers, is about 10 cm. More than 25 recognized breeds have been introduced and bred in Canada.

The horse is a pioneer in these parts and should be treated with appropriate respect. With the exception of the turkey, it is the only member of Canada's barnyard community whose family was native to the Americas, and much of the 40-million-year family history is written, convincingly, in the rocks. FOSSIL evidence of the primitive horse's existence has been found elsewhere, but nowhere is there such a long, unbroken paleontological record as on this continent. Written here is the step-by-step story of change from the small and primitive *Eohippus* (the size of a wirehaired terrier) to horses which, in size and appearance, resemble those of modern times. The "dawn horse" had 4 toes on each foreleg, 3 on each hindleg. The little fellow, without much means of protection, lived in swamps. There may be doubt about its diet, but from the shape of its feet, the relatively small size of stomach even today and the survival of canine teeth in males, there is reason to suspect that *Eohippus* was not a strict vegetable feeder.

Members of the race must have been extremely numerous on this continent, at least until struck by disaster and extinction in the Americas. Horses were still here when the first humans arrived (*see* PREHISTORY). Early N American humans feasted on horse meat and left the proof at campfire sites, where horse bones, arrowheads and ashes have been found together. Some horses of that period passed from N America to Asia by way of the land bridge that admitted the first humans to this continent. Thus, they escaped extinction and spread across Asia. It is believed that the first domestication was in China, and eventually domesticated stock reached the Mediterranean and N Africa where improvement took place. Some of the improved horses, taken by invaders to Europe, were left behind and imprinted their quality upon the horse stock of Spain and France. Columbus, on his second voyage westward in 1493, may have taken Spanish horses to the West Indies. In any case, Hernando Cortez, a Spanish conquistador, landed 16 or 17 horses on the N American mainland in 1519. After a long absence, American horses were back on their native soil.

Horses for Settlers North American Indians were quick to adopt the use of horses, and horses moved from one tribe to another, generally by theft. By Arthur Silver Morton's estimates, horses in the possession of the Indians were seen in the valley of the Bow R in 1730. Before long, Indians of all the western tribes had horses and, when the Selkirk settlers arrived at the RED RIVER in 1812, urgently needing livestock, they rejoiced at the prospect of obtaining horses from tribesmen.

The first horses in eastern Canada were brought from France for the use of settlers beside the St Lawrence. In 1665, Louis XIV directed the shipment of 21 mares and 2 stallions from the royal stables. From these and later importations came the Québec strain of hardy black horses, ultimately recognized as the French Canadian or Canadian breed, still prized by many Québec farmers.

For settlers coming into Upper Canada and then westward to Manitoba and the Territories, power was one of the most crucial needs. Some used oxen for a while because they were more readily available and could "live off the land," but ultimately every farmer wanted horses and then better horses. Improvement depended on the importation of sires of approved breeds. The first purebred stallion in the West was Fireaway, a Norfolk trotter brought from England by the Hudson's Bay Company for the benefit of Red R settlers. He was an overwhelming success. Thereafter, demand was for stallions of heavy breeds. British settlers wanted breeds from their homeland (eg, Clydesdale, Shire, Suffolk). Settlers from Europe and the US favoured Percherons and Belgians. Canadian farms became scenes of the mighty "Battle of the Breeds." Reflecting an early predominance of British settlers, the Scottish Clydesdale, with stylish white markings and showy action, led in popularity, but in time the bigger Percherons of French origin and the still bigger Belgians took the lead.

By 1921, when almost every Canadian farmer was a horseman, the horse population stood at 3.5 million. Saskatchewan had one million, mainly of Clydesdale, Percheron and Belgian breeding. The interbreed rivalry continued and reached the point where Clydesdale supporters were known to sit on one side of a country church, while Percheron and Belgian devotees sat on the other. But while the breed debates continued, the supremacy of heavy horses was being challenged by mechanical power, first by the heavy steam tractors introduced on big farms in the West. These huge steamers were excellent for belt work but slow and awkward for field work, and by 1908, when the world's first agricultural motor competition was held at the Winnipeg Industrial Exhibition, heavy, gasoline-driven tractors outnumbered them. During WWI, when farmers were urged to increase production but were denied the needed workers, gasoline and kerosene-driven tractors of smaller kind became attractive. Horse fortunes were about to change.

Horses in Decline It was a landmark event in 1918 when the federal government contracted to buy 1000 2-plow Ford tractors and sell them to farmers at cost (about $800 delivered). These light, 4-cylinder, high-speed tractors signalled a new day for farm power and horse breeding slumped. More and more horses were unemployed and seen

Ploughing on the prairies, *c*1900-1910 (*courtesy National Archives of Canada/PA-37793*).

as surplus. By 1944 farmers and ranchers were becoming impatient with the thousands of unsalable horses eating valuable grass. In March, at a meeting held at Val Marie, Sask, the Western Horse Marketing Co-operative was organized, with a double purpose: horsemen hoped to realize a return from the surplus and to make more grass available for cattle and sheep. By Oct 1945, horsemen were in the meat business, with their gaze fixed upon postwar food needs in Europe. Slaughtering and processing plants were established at Swift Current, Sask, and Edmonton and by 1952 officers could report almost 250 000 horses marketed for a return of about $19 million. Most of the return came from canned meat shipped to Europe. In 1986 horse-meat exports totalled over 17 000 t, valued at $41.1 million. Principal buyers were France and Japan. Usually, old or crippled animals are slaughtered; horses are not bred for the purpose.

The Ascendancy of the Light Horse Heavy horses almost disappeared from Canadian farms; horse-drawn machinery was abandoned; harnesses went to pieces. Familiar old terms such as hame strap, martingale and whippletree were forgotten. But all was not lost. With the decline of the heavy or draft horse and the coming of an age when people had more leisure, Canadians discovered new interests in light horses. The ascendancy of light horse breeds was no less dramatic than the decline of heavy ones. Every type and breed of light horse was useful to some degree. A few, such as the western stock or cowboy horse, were so useful and so irreplaceable that their popularity has never changed. But the search for horses suitable for new sport and recreational uses brought a score of little-known breeds to public attention. The 2 ancient breeds, Arabian and Thoroughbred, have been influential in building and improving other breeds, which include the Hackney, French Coach and German Coach, classified as heavy harness types; American Standardbred and Morgan, seen as roadsters or trotters; American Saddle Horses, Tennessee Walking Horses and Quarter Horses, all of US origin; and the recently popular colour breeds, Palomino, Appaloosa, Pinto and Buckskin. Various pony breeds (eg, Shetland, Welsh, Dartmoor, Exmoor, Fell, Highland, Iceland, New Forest) have been registered.

Breaking a wild horse, Alberta, 1912 (*by permission of the British Library*).

Horse racing is known as "The Sport of Kings" (*see* THOROUGHBRED RACING). A succession of English kings gave it their enthusiastic support and Charles II went so far as to order importation of 40 Barb, Turk and Arab mares which became the foundation of the Thoroughbred breed. Every urban centre has its racetracks and seasonal racing programs. Thoroughbreds and Standardbreds are the principal racing breeds, the former in flat racing under saddles, the latter in HARNESS RACING, with drivers seated in sulkies. The Standardbred, developed in the eastern states, was the original American roadster, a trotter that might be trained to pace. The trotting gait is a diagonal movement, with diagonally opposite legs advancing together. The pace, which some horses do naturally and others by training, is a lateral gait, with both legs on the same side moving together. Good horses with either gait can cover a mile in under 2 minutes.

Light-horse shows became numerous and popular and the Canadian Horse Shows Association furnished uniform rules for contests. Over the years, Canadian horses made many notable records, for example that of the jumper, Confidence, in the East and Barra Lad in the West. The former, owned by Sir Clifford SIFTON, cleared the bars at 245.11 cm at an Ottawa show to establish a world's record, and the latter, foaled at Essondale, BC, and exhibited by Peter Welsh of Calgary, made the incredible jump of 247.65 cm for 6000 spectators at New Westminster in 1925. It was a new world's record but ended tragically; the great horse died later the same evening.

Canadian horse shows reached their highest state of competition and glitter at the Royal Agricultural Winter Fair in Toronto, started in 1922. In the West, the excellent facilities of Spruce Meadows, near Calgary, have become internationally important. Among the many other light-horse events are RODEO, which reaches its pinnacle at the CALGARY STAMPEDE, and trail riding in mountain regions, started in an organized way by John Murray Gibbon after his arrival in Canada in 1913. Dressage attempts to present the art of training with show-ring finish. For the friends of the Quarter Horse and lovers of stock saddle events, there are the cutting-horse contests. *See also* SABLE ISLAND HORSES.

GRANT MACEWAN

Horses, Wild Canada's few remaining wild (feral) horses – aside from those on SABLE I – are restricted to BC, Alberta and Saskatchewan. Saskatchewan residents boast of a few grazing unmolested in the Cypress Hills area; also, some 60 head are purportedly preserved on a section of land owned by a sympathetic Outreach rancher. Alberta has the largest number of wild horses: 2000 in the 1980s. The Alberta government preserved them 1973-80s; but now the animals are being exterminated by the government, which considers abandoned horses (owned by someone) and wild horses (unowned, who have fended for themselves for generations) one and the same. British Columbia has only a few hundred wild horses, mostly in the remote Chilcotin, and they are systematically reduced by permit holders. However, sanctuary has been given to a few by a Kootenays landowner and a Nicola native band. Some ranches still function entirely by using captured wild horses as saddlers and packers, and tillers of land.

NORMA BEARCROFT

Horsetail, perennial plant of genus *Equisetum*, the only living representative of the very ancient and primitive class Sphenopsida, tree-sized members of which were prominent in the land vegetation of the Carboniferous era (360-286 million years ago). The stems are usually hollow, have cylindrical sheaths of reduced leaves at the nodes, and arise from creeping rhizomes (underground stems). When present, branches are often in whorls at the nodes. Stem internodes are commonly ridged longitudinally, the ridges bearing silica-containing tubercles or bands. They are herbaceous or shrubby and rarely exceed 1 m in height. Horsetails show a form of alternation of generations (a sexual phase alternating with an asexual one), in which each generation is an independent plant. Spores are produced in spore cases borne on stalks which form a fruiting, terminal cone on the fertile stem. The spores germinate, forming plants (prothallia) on which are borne antheridia and archegonia (structures producing sperm and eggs, respectively). The prothallium is the sexual generation. The fertilization of the egg and its subsequent development produces the familiar horsetail plant, the asexual generation.

Fifteen species of *Equisetum* (mostly of worldwide distribution) and many sterile hybrids (some widespread) now exist. Ten species occur in Canada: smooth scouring rush (*E. laevigatum*) mainly in the central regions; giant horsetail (*E. telmateia*) on the West Coast and in the Okanagan Valley; common horsetail (*E. arvense*) and variegated horsetail (*E. variegatum*) transcontinentally and far N of treeline. Six other species are transcontinental, but do not occur in the High Arctic. Most species occupy moist environments. Common horsetail and scouring rush (*E. hyemale*) are sometimes considered weeds. Settlers used silica-encrusted stems of both these species for cleaning and sanding. The former is still used to hone woodwind reeds. Common horsetail has been reported poisonous to livestock in Canada.

W.J. CODY

Horton Plain, 71 000 km^2, is the most northeasterly part of the Interior Plains, extending to Amundsen Gulf on the Beaufort Sea, NWT. It consists of a series of dissected plateaus, generally below 800 m elevation, underlain by flat-lying Paleozoic sedimentary rocks in the W and by Precambrian sedimentary bedrock in the E. Drainage is provided by 2 scenic rivers, the HORTON and the Hornaday. Among its numerous small lakes, the Bluenose (400 km^2) and Horton (166 km^2) are noteworthy. The vegetation is low arctic tundra in the N, dominated by dwarf shrubs and grasses, and woodland in the S, consisting of scattered, stunted spruce with a lichen carpet. The summer range and calving grounds of the large Bluenose caribou herd lie within this region. Paulatuk on Darnley Bay is the only permanent settlement in the area.

S.C. ZOLTAI

Horton River, 618 km long, rises N of GREAT BEAR LK in the NWT and empties into Amundsen Gulf. Shallowly entrenched in the upper part of its course, it cuts a deep (up to 200 m) valley into the soft Cretaceous bedrock in its lower course. It originally reached the BEAUFORT SEA at Harrowby Bay, but one of its meanders cut a channel to Amundsen Gulf around 1800, shortening its course by some 100 km. Near the present delta are the Smoking Hills, where lignite and jarosite beds are burning, giving off sulphurous smoke. These beds were already burning in 1826 when John RICHARDSON mapped the shoreline. The river is shallow, but navigable by small craft. Its valley is wooded to within 100 km of its mouth, where the treeless, shrubby tundra begins. A trading post operated at the delta 1918-31, but there are no settlements along the river.

S.C. ZOLTAI

Horwood, Harold Andrew, columnist, politician, editor, novelist (b at St John's 2 Nov 1923). Horwood supported J.R. SMALLWOOD in the campaign which brought Newfoundland into Confederation, and he represented Labrador in the Assembly 1949-51. Horwood relinquished his editorial responsibilities with the St John's *Evening Telegram* in 1958 and became a free-lance writer and novelist. His best-known works are 2 novels – *Tomorrow Will Be Sunday* (1966) and *White Eskimo* (1972) – and *The Foxes of Beachy Cove* (1967), a thoughtful little book on the back-to-nature theme. Recent works include *Remembering Summer* (1987) and *Dancing on the Shore* (1987). He is founding editor of a literary magazine, *The New Quarterly*.

D.R. BARTLETT

Hose, Walter, naval officer (b at sea 2 Oct 1875; d at Windsor, Ont 22 June 1965). After 21 years in the Royal Navy, Hose transferred to the Canadian navy in 1912. Until 1917 he commanded the RAINBOW on the Pacific coast, then the trade defence forces on the Atlantic coast in 1917-18. In 1921 he became director of the Naval Service (chief of the naval staff after 1928), an appointment he held until his retirement in 1934. Cuts in defence spending in 1922 and 1933 threatened the navy's survival, but Hose saved the service through determined leadership and by developing the naval reserves founded under his direction in 1923.

ROGER SARTY

Hospital Canada has numerous types of hospital, including general public (879) and special public (245), both of which are under provincial jurisdiction. As well, there are 64 private hospitals and the federal government has jurisdiction over 50 more.

Historical Development The first HÔTEL DIEU in New France was established in 1639 by 3 sisters of Augustines de la Miséricorde de Jésus in Québec City. This hospital is still in operation. By 1694, 3 other religious hospitals had been constructed, including the Hôtel-Dieu in Montréal, and in 1819 and 1829, respectively, general hospitals were opened in Montréal and York [Toronto]. The York hospital had been built several years earlier but had been used as a temporary home for the government after Upper Canada's parliament buildings burned down in Dec 1824.

The first general hospitals were charitable institutions, relying on donations from benevolent organizations and prosperous citizens. The patients paid very little, if anything, and government support was erratic and undependable. In 1867 the Toronto General closed for a year because of lack of funds, and it was partly because of this that the Ontario government passed an Act in the early 1870s providing for annual grants to the hospital and to other charitable institutions. Today nearly all hospital operating revenues come from federal and provincial governments.

Until the early part of the 20th century, hospitals were generally devoted to the treatment of the poor, who suffered in particular from infectious and nutritional diseases, eg, influenza, pneumonia, tuberculosis, gastroenteritis and scurvy. Because the relationship between public sanitation and personal hygiene and disease was largely unknown, and because of the lack of therapeutic drugs, infectious diseases spread uncontrollably. Dirty and overcrowded hospitals were often traps for infection, and most prosperous citizens, who were treated at home, avoided them.

This situation persisted throughout the early 1900s when tuberculosis hospitals were established to sequester the "incurables" from the general public. "Feebleminded" individuals were dealt with in a similar way and mental hospitals began to expand in both number and size. Between WWI and WWII, however, and before the advent of antibiotics or vaccination programs became widespread, infectious-disease mortality rates began to decrease as a result of enforced PUBLIC HEALTH measures.

By the 1880s, the introduction of safe anesthesia, asepsis (ie, prevention of infection) and of improved surgical techniques led to decreased mortality from conditions such as postoperative hemorrhage and gastrointestinal abnormalities (*see* MEDICINE, HISTORY OF). Because these techniques required sophisticated equipment, specially trained personnel and longer periods of observation, the use of hospital facilities increased, and hospitals became centres for curative therapy, for teaching and for MEDICAL EDUCATION and research.

In 1945 the federal government submitted recommendations for changes to the health-care system in Canada to the Dominion-Provincial Conference on Reconstruction. The recommendations proposed a series of grants and low-interest loans to the provinces to improve existing health services and to construct new hospitals. Because the conference representatives failed to reach agreement, the proposals were left in abeyance, but in 1948 the plans were resurrected in the National Health Grant Program. Funds granted to the provinces were to be used to construct new general and mental hospitals, to strengthen public health services, and to develop programs for specific diseases, eg, tuberculosis and SEXUALLY TRANSMITTED DISEASES, and for specific patients, eg, crippled children.

In 1958, following the lead of Saskatchewan, the federal government passed the Hospital Insurance and Diagnostic Services Act, which empowered it to negotiate agreements with each province to share the cost of provincially administered insurance programs providing for the payment of the basic cost of acute treatment, and for convalescent and chronic care in approved hospital facilities. These hospitals were guaranteed reimbursement for services rendered. By 1961, all provinces were providing federally assisted hospital insurance (*see* HEALTH POLICY).

In 1961 the federal government established the Royal Commission on Health Services to investigate the health-services system and to recommend measures to "ensure that the best possible health care is available to all Canadians." The commission's final report (1964) became the cornerstone of Canada's health-care system.

Both the Health Grant Program and the Hospital Insurance Act encouraged a reliance on hospital care and diagnostic service – the most expensive elements of any health-care delivery system. In response to these rising health-care costs and the royal commission recommendations, the federal government passed the Medical Care Act in 1967 empowering it to share the cost of medical insurance plans in each province. Within 3 years, all provinces had such plans; the combination of national hospital and medical insurance is called medicare.

In 1966 the federal government established the Health Resources Fund under which $500 million was granted to the provinces to plan, build and renovate facilities to be used to train health professionals or conduct research. The money was distributed over a 14-year period ending in 1980; $400 million of this fund was used to build new facilities or renovate old ones. The remaining funds were used to replace outdated equipment. The bulk of the $500 million was spent on teaching hospitals, all of which are general hospitals. Some of the money was spent on medical schools, but because of the intimate relationship between such schools and teaching hospitals, it is difficult to determine precise amounts.

In the 1970s the federal and provincial governments re-evaluated their health-care funding arrangements. It was felt that the federal matching of provincial spending on hospital and medical care encouraged an overreliance on these expensive components of health care. The federal government wished to place some controls on health-care expenditures and to give provincial governments an incentive to be efficient and the latitude to meet their needs. These considerations led to the 1977 Federal-Provincial Established Programs Financing Act (EPF). Through a complex combination of cash grants and tax transfers that differ for each province, the federal government pays for part of the cost of provincially administered hospital and medical insurance plans, but does not automatically match provincial expenditures. In response, provinces have introduced innovations, eg, home care, day surgery, and outpatient care. All indications are that the federal government's strategy has halted the rise in hospital expenditures, though total health expenditures continue to grow.

A new Canada Health Act, which combines the 2 previous Acts (hospital insurance and medical insurance), went into effect in Apr 1984.

Resources Provisional figures for 1985 indicate that health and hospital costs accounted for 8.62% of Canada's Gross National Product. In the same year, all hospitals accounted for 40% of health expenditures or $16 billion (3.5% of GNP). An average of 68% of hospitals' operating expenses are allocated for gross wages and salaries; they employed 432 281 people in 1984-85. In addition to the employees, volunteers devote millions of hours and millions of dollars' worth of free labour to hospitals annually. In 1987 some 119 421 people volunteered their time; of these, 11 783 were teenagers and 3192 were males.

Most hospitals are given an annual inflation-adjusted global budget by the provincial government. With these resources hospitals provide surgical suites, nursing care and a wide range of diagnostic, therapeutic and rehabilitative services. Hospitals feed and house the inpatients, offer numerous community, outpatient and emergency services, and provide training programs for health-care professionals. They also undertake research projects. Hospitals not only train new physicians, nurses and other health-care personnel, but they are committed to educating patients in the maintenance of health and in coping with disabilities.

In the 1985-86 fiscal year, general and allied hospitals provided a total of 50.6 million patient days (ie, the number of days spent in hospital by all patients for a given period) to patients who had 3.7 million hospital stays. This measure does not take into account the outpatient, research and community services that hospitals provide, but it is a commonly used indicator of hospital services. The average cost per patient day in 1984-85 was $295.05. However, the cost of operating special intensive-care units can be twice as high although, because of medicare, Canadians do not have to pay these costs out of their own pockets.

Personnel in hospitals includes technologists, therapists and administrative staff. Although physicians powerfully influence the operation of hospitals, very few are hospital employees. Except in the rare cases of laboratory and emergency-room specialists, and some senior professional staff in teaching hospitals, physicians do not receive payment from hospitals, although only physicians can admit patients to a hospital (patients cannot admit themselves). Physicians have complete authority to order surgery, drugs, diagnostic and therapeutic service, and nursing services for their patients. They are also the only health-care professionals qualified to discharge a patient from hospital (patients can discharge themselves but usually do not do so). Nurses, on the other hand, are hospital employees and are responsible for delivering most of the patient care in hospitals. In 1984-85 there were about 250 000 hospital-employed nursing personnel in Canada, 197 877 of whom were full- and part-time registered nurses.

Atrium in the Walter Mackenzie Health Sciences Centre, Edmonton (*courtesy UHSC Architects Groups, Zeidler Roberts Partnership/Architects Groves Hodgson Palenstein/ Architects, Woods and Gardener Architects/photo by Balthazar Korab*).

Patients in hospital are usually described by their age and sex, or by their illness. By age and sex, the largest users of hospital services are the elderly (people over 65 make up about 10% of the population and are responsible for about 50% of Canada's patient days) and women in their child-bearing years. By illness, the major cause of hospital use is HEART DISEASE (accounting for 22% of all patient days and 11.3% of all discharges).

Future A number of factors are changing the way in which health-care services are being delivered, eg, population AGING, increase in chronic illness, advance in medical technology. Hospitals of the future will need to provide increasingly specialized technological care and yet meet an opposing demand for more personal, generalist care for patients with chronic conditions. It is expected that there will be a greater emphasis on community services and on outpatient and home care.

JEAN-CLAUDE MARTIN

Hospitallers of St Joseph, female religious congregation founded in La Flèche, France, in 1636, by Jérôme le Royer de la Dauversière and Marie de la Ferre. The principal goal was to establish a religious congregation of hospitallers in New France. On her visit to France in 1657 Jeanne MANCE recruited some of the sisters from La Flèche to staff the HÔTEL-DIEU at VILLE-MARIE [Montréal], and in 1659, by letters patent of Louis XIV, the Hospitallers of St Joseph took over the Hôtel-Dieu de Montréal. They later established other Hôtel-Dieu hospitals. Each convent was autonomous, responsible solely to the bishop (without any superior general). Various movements arose in the 20th century to unite the nuns who could trace their origins to La Flèche: in 1953 the American and Canadian convents became one congregation, which the French congregations then joined in 1965. The generalate is in Montréal; in 1986 there were 700 sisters in 63 convents.

MICHEL THÉRIAULT

Hotel Accommodation for travellers in Canada derives from 2 traditions: the inn or roadhouse, and the urban hotel. In early settlements many households took in overnight guests; those with inn licences could charge for the service, a practice which formalized the roadside inn. Willard's Hotel (1795) and Cook's Tavern (1822), both from Williamsburg Township, Ont, and now at UPPER CANADA VILLAGE, were stopping places for commercial travellers and immigrants in coaches along the King's Hwy and on bateaux on the St Lawrence R. Symmes Inn (1831) at Aylmer, Qué, strategically located at a boat landing on the Ottawa R and immortalized by William Henry BARTLETT, boasted a table supplied "with the best the country affords."

Not all roadhouses offered such amenities. An 1860s visitor at Hat Creek House, a ranch on the CARIBOO ROAD leading to BC's goldfields, complained that "the bunks were hard as a board... and the dark looking blankets had unwrapped too many sweaty, dusty travellers since last washed." Inns were often built to resemble large

Neptune Inn at the Foot of Mountain Street Looking up Toward Parliament House, Quebec, Lower Canada (1830), watercolour by J.P. Cockburn (*courtesy National Archives of Canada/C-40368*).

The imposing Château Frontenac at Québec City (1892-93) helped begin a tradition of château-style hotels that became a characteristically Canadian architectural form (*photo by Yves Tessier/Reflexion*).

houses, but often with the addition of 2 tiers of verandahs.

In the early 19th century, some hotels in large Canadian cities were planned on a lavish scale. Rasco's Hotel in Montréal, opened in 1836 and still standing today, is a 5-storey stone building that once accommodated 150 guests. Larger hotels designed in the most fashionable styles of the day achieved high levels of luxury. The Windsor Hotel in Montréal (G.H. Worthington, 1876-78), in the Second Empire style, was the most gracious in the city.

The railway age heralded a new era in hotels, one that blurred the distinction between the 2 traditions. The CPR built a series of "dining stations," with sleeping rooms, in the BC mountains to feed travellers and accommodate guests. Glacier House (architect T.C. Sorby, 1886), perched at the summit of the Selkirks, recalled a Swiss chalet. The original wood-framed Banff Springs Hotel (Bruce Price, 1886-88) was an elaborate resort hotel in the scenic Alberta Rockies. Together with the Château Frontenac in Québec City (Price, 1892-93), the Banff Springs Hotel began a tradition of château-style railway hotels that became a peculiarly Canadian architectural form. The CPR's Empress Hotel, Victoria (F.M. RATTENBURY, 1904-08), and the Grand Trunk Ry's Château Laurier, Ottawa (Ross and MacFarlane, 1908-12), are notable examples of the genre. The contemporary descendants of roadside inns and urban hotels cater to both commercial travellers and tourists, and are often managed by international chains. The motel (or motor hotel), located along a highway or on the edge of the city, caters to the automobile traveller. Popularized in the US in the 1930s, the motel is typically one or 2 storeys high, with each room accessible from the parking lot. Many city hotels have become tall slab towers; they serve as convention centres, with large meeting rooms and internal shopping arcades. The Toronto Hilton (William Tabler and Campeau, 1975) has 967 guest rooms in 2 towers, one of which is topped by a revolving restaurant. The 500-room Pan Pacific Hotel in Vancouver is part of Canada Place (Downs/Archambault, Muson Cattell and Partners, and the Zeidler Roberts Partnership, 1983-86), built for Expo 86 and now used as a trade facility and cruise ship terminal. Highway and city come together in Montréal's Hotel Bonaventure (AFFLECK, Desbarats, DIMAKOPOULOS, LEBENSOLD and Sise, 1967-68), in which a motellike series of rooms arranged around open landscaped courts is perched atop a monolithic trade and retail structure. *See also* ARCHITECTURE; ARCHITECTURE DEVELOPMENT; TOURISM.

HAROLD D. KALMAN

Hôtel-Dieu, name given to HOSPITALS established by nursing orders of nuns. The first in NEW FRANCE and one of the first hospitals in America was the Hôtel-Dieu de Québec, funded by the duchesse d'Aiguillon, who in 1637 obtained a site for the hospital at Québec (as well as a fief on the outskirts). Construction began in 1638 but was not completed by Aug 1639 when the first 3 Augustines de la Miséricorde de Jésus and a servant (all from Dieppe, France) arrived in Québec to take up their work. They established a hospital at the nearby reserve at Sillery to treat Indians with smallpox, though the building there was still under construction when they moved into it in 1640. Harried increasingly by Iroquois raids (*see* IROQUOIS WARS), in 1644 they moved to the Hôtel-Dieu's present site on Québec's rue du Palais. The foundation of this building still exist; the oldest section of the present building dates from 1696.

The Hôtel-Dieu de Montréal was founded by Jeanne MANCE and funded by Mme de Bullion, the widow of one of Louis XIII's superintendents of finance. Mance began treating patients on her arrival in VILLE-MARIE [Montréal] in 1642; in 1644 the hospital was granted land outside the fort and in 1645 the building was completed. Mance ran the Hôtel-Dieu until her death in 1673, assisted in her latter years by the HOSPITALLERS OF ST JOSEPH (this order took over the hospital in June 1659 by letters patent of Louis XIV); 3 times the building was destroyed by fire and rebuilt, and in 1861 the Hôtel-Dieu moved to its present site on Mont Ste-Famille, Montréal. It is affiliated with U de M as a teaching hospital.

Photograph of the Hôtel-Dieu, Québec City, taken *c*1870-80. Founded 1639, it has provided medical care by its nursing sisters for almost 350 years (*courtesy National Archives of Canada/C-35634*).

Both groups of hospitallers later built other hospitals, including those at Tracadie, Chatham and Campbellton, NB; Kingston and Windsor, Ont; Chicoutimi, Arltabaska, Lévis and Gaspé, Qué (1884); Winooski, Vt; and in some mission countries.

MARCEL CADOTTE AND MICHEL THÉRIAULT

Reading: Michel Allard, *L'Hôtel-Dieu de Montréal (1642-1973)* (1973); H.R. Casgrain, *Histoire de l'Hôtel-Dieu de Québec* (1878).

Houde, Camillien, politician (b at Montréal 13 Aug 1889; d there 11 Sept 1958). He tried careers in banking, biscuits and bon-bons, sat in the Québec legislature and House of Commons, but from his first election as mayor on 2 Apr 1928 until his retirement on 18 Sept 1954, Houde so incarnated his city that he was called "Mr Montréal." He first won fame as a Conservative MLA, elected in Ste-Marie in 1923. He was beaten in 1927, but his opponent's shady victory was overturned by the courts and Houde was returned in a 1928 by-election. He won the Québec Conservative Party leadership the same year but lost his seat as his party was defeated in the 1931 general election. Houde resigned as leader in 1932, leaving the way clear for that dominant conservative nationalist, Maurice DUPLESSIS. As Duplessis cast a giant shadow over Québec, Houde did the same in Montréal, serving as mayor 1928-32 and 1934-36; he was then re-elected in 1938. Astonishingly, his mayoralty was suspended on 5 Aug 1940 when after calling for defiance of registration for military service, Houde was arrested at city hall by the RCMP and interned in Ontario for 4 years. Like many nationalist French Canadians of the period, he supported the ideology of Mussolini's Italy and Vichy France. Yet he still remained loyal to the British Crown, which had made him a CBE in 1935. At least 50 000 Montréalers welcomed Houde triumphantly after his release 18 Aug 1944, and he was quickly re-elected mayor, a position he held comfortably through elections in 1947 and 1950. Houde's mastery of Montréal and longevity in office were exceeded only by his successor, Jean DRAPEAU. Houde was elected to the House of Commons in 1949 from Montréal Papineau, but he gave the position scant attention. An enormous man with a Cyranoesque nose, a wonderful sense of humour and a penchant for black Tueros cigars, Houde generously dispensed patronage and largesse from his city hall office through the worst years of the Great Depression and beyond. He winked at the city's brothels and blind pigs, its gangs and gangsters. This was Duplessis's Québec and Houde saw corruption of much of city council, the police and the press as a fact of life. His obsession was immortality, not money. The flamboyant style of his political passion is reflected in his crypt at Montréal's Côte de Neiges cemetery – an Italian marble replica of Napoleon's.

BRIAN MCKENNA

Reading: Hertel La Rogue, *Camillien Houde* (1961).

House usually refers to a building that serves as living quarters for one or several families. House forms and building styles have changed through

Birchbark tipi and Ojibwa Indians at Lake Winnipeg, Man, 1884 (*courtesy Geological Survey of Canada/595*).

out history in response to socioeconomic forces as well as to climatic conditions inherent to particular geographic locations. In effect, houses are like mirrors that reflect both the living conditions and the cultural heritage of their builders.

The earliest dwellings in Canada were built and inhabited by Indians and Inuit. Viewed superficially, these buildings appear primitive, but although simple, they were sophisticated adaptations to a particular lifestyle and habitat, and in greater harmony with nature than most houses are today. The simplest dwellings were built by food gatherers and hunters, nomadic people who roamed Canada's extensive grasslands, forests and the arctic barrens of the North. Their nomadic existence precluded the establishment of permanent settlements, so these migrating peoples built temporary shelters. Some were constructed of available building materials near the campsite, and others were made of materials easily transported from camp to camp.

Perhaps the most fascinating dwelling is the IGLOO, a snowhouse built by the INUIT living in the treeless tundra. These circular, dome-shaped structures had a raised sleeping platform facing the low entranceway. Working from the inside, the builder placed one snow block next to another in upward-spiraling rows, each block tipped slightly inward to narrow the circle until a dome structure resulted. The spiraling rows made scaffolding during construction unnecessary. Although snow may seem to be an unlikely building material for shelter, it has excellent insulating qualities. Insulation of the interior was often improved by lining walls and ceilings as well as the sleeping platform with caribou hides and seal skins. When the igloo began to melt in summer, it was abandoned and replaced by a seal-skin tent called *tupiq*, a portable dwelling like the TIPI, consisting of a framework of poles covered with seal skins.

The tipi was an ingenious dwelling used by several tribes, but mostly associated with the Plains Indians, who followed the immense bison (buffalo) herds that roamed the plains. The skeletal structure of the tipi was composed of 3 or 4 poles tied together at the top and then erected; up to 20 additional poles were placed against the tripod or tetrapod thus formed. A tailored buffalo-hide cover was placed on this skeleton and was staked or weighted down with stones all around the bottom edge. A smoke hole was left on top at the intersection of the poles and could be closed or adjusted with the help of 2 flaps of the hide cover, each attached to a separate freestanding pole. The fire was built near the centre, below the smoke hole, and the bedsteads of the family members were placed on the ground around the walls of the tipi, except at the doorway, which always faced the rising sun. Dome- or beehive-shaped and tipilike structures were the basic forms of indigenous temporary shelters in Canada, and were used by many Indian tribes.

The LONGHOUSE of the agricultural Indians of Canada's northeastern woodlands was a communal dwelling. The interior was subdivided into a number of bays, each allocated to a single family. Each bay had a low sleeping bench against the outside wall, and between the facing bays ran a wide corridor down the length of the building. These longhouses were not substantial, since after a few years of tilling without fertilization, the exhausted soil nearby produced scanty crops and the Indians abandoned their houses and moved on. A series of poles, arched to form a barrel-vault skeleton, supported the bark roof shingles and matting of the walls. Although each bay or cubicle was only about 2 m wide, the length of the longhouse would often exceed 20 m, from which we may conclude that it was not unusual for 20 families to live in one building.

More substantial dwellings were built by the coastal Indians of British Columbia. Living in a temperate climate, with a plentiful supply of good building materials, the coastal Indian tribes built large communal houses, each inhabited by a number of families. Their rich environment allowed a settled existence, which is reflected in the permanence of their homes. These impressive structures were low-pitched and gable-ended rectangular structures built of massive cedar posts and beams. Their interior arrangement, 2 facing rows of bays with sleeping platforms separated by a central corridor, was similar to the buildings of the eastern woodlands. Hearths were tended in the centre of the corridor, with the smoke escaping through apertures made when the roof planks were thrust aside by means of a pole. Most communal buildings had only a single entrance at one of the gable ends. The more leisured existence of the coastal Indians led to a significant art form of ornamentation of their dwellings and TOTEM POLES.

With the European settlement of the St Lawrence Valley in the 17th century, a new house form was introduced to Canada. The early French Canadian settlers created a building tradition reminiscent of French architectural styles, but using Canadian building materials. Initially the farmhouses of the habitants were low, broad buildings constructed of wooden planks with a shingled high-pitched roof and gable verges. They were rectangular and usually divided into 2 rooms of unequal size, with a large masonry chimney rising from the cross wall. Timber was later replaced by fieldstone gathered from the clearing of the fields. Concurrently, other changes were introduced in response to the harsh climate: floor levels were raised well above grade and eaves became wider; the pitch of the gable verges became steeper until the hip was superseded by a gable; with the introduction of a second fireplace, chimneys were placed at the gable ends; a further extension of the eaves led to the typical curving bellcast roof covered with sheet metal. The verandah house with a gallery passage above snow level and wide eaves supported by a row of columns was a further evolution of the Québecois rural house.

The typical urban house in Québec had raised masonry gables with double chimneys and wall head corbels, and the roof structure was covered with sheet metal or tin tiles. These precautions were made necessary by the hazard of fire when houses were multistoreyed and had stone masonry walls with wooden floors and roofs. However, the use of wood planks for walls was also widespread in urban houses and, in later years, wood was often used in conjunction with an external cladding of brick. Many of the early urban houses were attractive structures with well-proportioned windows and doors, having few ornaments but characterized by a simple elegance.

After the Conquest (1760), European traditions in rural house construction continued, not only with the application of the heritage brought from the British Isles but also with an American colonial architectural influence transplanted into Canada with the influx of the Loyalists. Stone masonry walls were gradually replaced by red-brick masonry, but wood continued to be the dominant building material for rural houses. On the prairies, where wood was scarce, early settlers often built SOD HOUSES.

During the 19th century the most prevalent urban dwelling form in central and eastern Canada was the townhouse, in either attached or detached dwelling units. Reminiscent of the Georgian and Victorian townhouses of Great Britain, the Canadian townhouse, like its American

The double house, built *c*1870 in London, Ont, displays classical elements (*photo © Hartill Art Associates, London, Ont*).

The Barnum House (*c*1817) in fall, near Grafton, Ont (*courtesy SSC Photocentre/photo by Paul Von Baich*).

counterpart, was less formal. Since few households had servants, Canadian townhouse dwellers placed their kitchen and scullery on the first floor, rather than in the basement, along with the principal reception rooms. In the Canadian townhouse, the living room, the entrance vestibule and stair hall occupied the front end of the house, and the dining room, kitchen and scullery the rear; the living and dining rooms were often separated from each other by an archway, with or without recessed sliding doors, a double-parlour type of arrangement. The bedrooms were located on the upper floors, with the master bedroom facing the street. The width, size and appointment of the townhouse reflected the wealth of its occupants, but usually townhouses were 2 storeys high, with the ground-floor level raised half a floor above sidewalk level. Tenements and apartment buildings also made their appearance in cities during the 19th century. Tenements were built as minimum-standard living accommodation for low-wage earners, and apartment buildings were more commodious, designed as rental flats for the middle-income group. Neither type constituted a large proportion of the Canadian urban-housing stock and consequently the dire housing conditions experienced in Great Britain and in many large American cities never existed in Canada.

At the beginning of the 20th century, first the wealthy and later others moved to the outskirts of the cities to live in houses on large lots along treed avenues to escape increased air pollution, crime, overcrowding and noise; this desire for a healthier living environment eventually resulted in the proliferation of dormitory suburbs. Single-family suburban homes are usually 2-storey dwellings with a spatial organization not unlike that of townhouses. The principal rooms invariably occupy the front, or street side, of the house overlooking the front lawn, and the secondary rooms are placed towards the rear yard.

The mixture of the garden-city home and new forms such as the bungalow – one of the most popular 20th-century dwelling types – can be seen in the urban landscape of Vancouver in the years 1886-1930. Vancouver's rate of home ownership ran as high as 80% in those years. Unpleasant memories of the industrial cities of Britain were still fresh, and the detached house became the ideal, appearing in surprising "imported" styles, such as Italianate and Queen Anne, as well as in simple frame houses and cottages. Within the suburbs, the most prevalent form was the California bungalow, a style which spread across N America. The bungalow bespoke a new life-style associated with the easier climate and informality of California. It featured indoor-outdoor rooms, deep verandahs and patios. Meanwhile, Vancouver's elite areas favoured fancier mansions and villas displaying a more pastoral imagery based on the lines of old English farmhouses or the use of half-timbered decoration in Tudor revival mansions. These houses attempted to create an instant sense of history, of homes where generations had dwelt. This half-timbered motif was found elsewhere in Canada but was especially prevalent in Vancouver. Equal enthusiasm was shown for the simple English farmhouse, characterized by rough stucco surfaces and exaggerated rooflines. The appeal of the English Tudor cottage in Vancouver and Victoria was symbolic of the strong ties with the "Old Country," as was the California bungalow of BC's presence in the new. Only later, in recognition of an earlier heritage, did British Columbians recognize in the woodwork of the Northwest Coast Indians and in the coastal rain forests an alternate regional style, characterized by cedar siding and the shed roof.

In comparison with the traditional multi-storeyed house, the single-level bungalow acquired increasing popularity across Canada and was used extensively in suburbs where land prices were more reasonable. Today, the suburban bungalow is usually built of wood with an external cladding of wood or masonry and gyproc on the inside. It is prevalent among every income group, as the modest home and as the luxurious rambling ranch house.

The suburban sprawl has, however, resulted in increased distances between the city and new suburbs. To economize on land, and in response to the effects of the energy crisis on transportation, alternatives to the bungalow have been introduced, such as the split-level house, followed more recently by a return to 2 traditional house forms: the 2-storey, single-family home and the attached townhouse.

Along with the proliferation of single-family dwellings in the suburbs, multifamily residential accommodations in cities also underwent changes during this century. The apartment house attracted people who could not afford larger accommodation or who preferred to live in the city for proximity to work and entertainment. To spread more equitably the higher cost of urban land as well as to share the maintenance costs of amenities such as swimming pools, apartment houses evolved into large building complexes, including fitness and entertainment centres and sometimes retail space. Masonry load-bearing construction was replaced by steel or concrete structural frames, paralleling the development of office towers. With higher buildings, upper-storey apartments offered more dramatic views, and the ultimate in luxurious urban living became the penthouse apartment (*see* CONDOMINIUMS).

The principal shared features in 20th-century Canadian housing design are informality, functionalism and hygiene. Informality has been encouraged by the increasing unavailability of servants and with it the abandonment of inconvenient and redundant features of housing design, such as sculleries, butler's pantries and service corridors. The *en suite* arrangement of drawing and dining rooms has been replaced by a less formal, open plan, where the principal living spaces flow into each other. New socioeconomic realities place an emphasis on functionalism; functional houses are designed not so much to impress occasional visitors as to make living in them comfortable.

Perhaps the design, size and location of the kitchen in modern houses best illustrate the new movement; the ill-equipped, dark kitchen relegated to an obscure corner of the old house has been replaced by a well-equipped, sunny and efficient space adjacent to the dining area, or often combined with it. Much greater attention is given to the layout of bedrooms and bathrooms so that reasonable privacy can be enjoyed by each member of the family. Healthful living conditions imply ample access to light and air, as well as good sanitary services. Large picture windows and glass walls in domestic architecture place a new focus on views and thereby a greater awareness of the outdoor environment. Areas such as terraces, patios and gardens are perceived as extensions, or outdoor rooms, of the house. Their connection with the interior, as well as their landscape treatment, have become important design features.

Until the 1970s the choice of housing accommodation in Canada was polarized between low-density, single-family suburban houses and high-density, multifamily urban apartment houses. With the emergence of demographic changes and a greater awareness of diminishing energy supplies, new dwelling forms are being developed that avoid both extremes. Medium-density and medium-rise urban dwellings that are well lit and ventilated, often having more than one exposure, have already made an appearance in large cities of Canada. Another emerging trend involves mixed zoning, whereby housing can be built in combination with commercial and office buildings. Occupying the upper floors of a building, this housing resembles penthouse accommodation with ample access to sun, air and view, away from street noises, but still close to the urban and cultural facilities of a lively city.

Demographic shifts and socioeconomic forces in this century have brought into existence a variety of specialized housing for the elderly and the handicapped, and for single persons, students, communards and others. The same common design criteria of informality, functionalism and hygiene also govern the layout of specialized housing.

The energy crisis which began in the early 1970s stirred the consciousness of many designers to conserve energy. The simplest approach was the use of passive solar energy, by means of an optimum orientation of the dwelling towards the sun. Another approach entailed the active collection of solar energy through solar panels and storage in some form of thermal mass until required. The obvious advantages inherent in subterranean structures led to the earth-shelter movement, which promised warmth, quiet and energy efficiency, but underground homes have

Contemporary condominium and mixed housing in the St Lawrence neighbourhood of Toronto (*photo © Hartill Art Associates, London, Ont*).

Second home built by Ivan Mihaychuk at Arbakka, Man, 1903 (*courtesy National Archives of Canada/PA-8788*).

yet to gain popularity. *See also* HOUSING AND HOUSING POLICY. NORBERT SCHOENAUER

Reading: T.B. Dennis, *Albertans Built* (1986); A. Gowans, *Building Canada* (1966); M. Lessard and H. Marquis, *Encyclopédie de la maison québecoise* (1972); Norbert Schoenauer, *6,000 Years of Housing*, (3 vols, 1981).

House, Christopher Maxwell, dancer, choreographer (b at St John's 30 May 1955). Resident choreographer of the TORONTO DANCE THEATRE since 1981, he has won international acclaim for the intelligence and craftsmanship of his work. House turned to dance after beginning a degree in political science at U of Ottawa. He graduated from York University with a BFA in dance and joined the Toronto Dance Theatre in 1979. While continuing to perform, he has created a repertoire of dances in a personal, modern-dance style. His mostly non-narrative choreographies are distinguished by a firm sense of structure and by the imaginative use of a diverse range of music. His work has helped the Toronto Dance Theatre increase its audience appeal significantly. His choreographic honours include the Chalmers Award (1983), Clifford E. Lee Award (1986) and Dora Mavor Moore Award (1986).
MICHAEL CRABB

House Leader, nonofficial title of MP nominated by each party to serve as head strategist and tactician in the House of Commons. The government House leader, a Cabinet member with the honorific title of president of the Privy Council, negotiates among parties about the Commons timetable. In each party the House leader is responsible for the PARTY WHIP and manages matters ranging from office space to salary negotiations. House leaders meet weekly to discuss the government's timetable and to choose speakers. They have sufficient power to hold their parties to the negotiated agreements. ROBERT J. JACKSON

House of Anansi, a small literary press established in Toronto by Dave GODFREY (whose African experiences provided the inspiration for its name) and Dennis LEE in 1967 at the height of the Centennial revival and with a commitment to the work of new writers emerging in the late 1960s. The press quickly became a rallying point for contemporary writing, both in Toronto and nationally, with its interest in experimental fiction, current poetry, criticism and the translation of young Québec writers. It became identified with strong nationalist sentiment, opening the critical debate of the 1970s with the publication of Northrop FRYE's *The Bush Garden: Essays on the Canadian Imagination* (1971) and scoring a major success with Margaret Atwood's SURVIVAL (1972) and Dennis Lee's *Savage Fields: An Essay in Literature and Cosmology* (1977). Managed by Ann Wall, and with a modest program averaging 6 titles a year, the press continues to be a force in Canadian writing. MICHAEL GNAROWSKI

House of Commons, elected lower house of PARLIAMENT. It consists of a Speaker (traditionally chosen from the party in power but now elected at large from the House as a whole by secret ballot); the prime minister and his Cabinet (though Cabinet ministers may also be appointed from the Senate); members of the governing party; members of the opposition parties and the Opposition's shadow, or alternate, government, and including backbenchers or private members (members who do not belong to the Cabinet and are not designated, on the Opposition side, as party critics). There are sometimes a few Independents. The 282 members of the House (called Members of Parliament, or MPs; number to be increased to 295 in the next general election) are elected in single-member constituency ELECTIONS or by-elections. Under the CONSTITUTION ACT, 1867, the Queen and the GOVERNOR GENERAL and the Queen's ministers and other public servants, not the House of Commons, govern Canada. The House, often incorrectly referred to as Parliament, is important constitutionally because no new statutes of any kind may be made except in response to bills that have been passed by it, and politically because, unlike the SENATE, it is an independent, elected body. Ministers are responsible to the House, not to the Senate.

Interior view of the House of Commons in the Parliament Buildings in Ottawa. The Speaker's chair is at the far end, with the public gallery above (*courtesy SSC Photocentre*).

Nonfinancial bills may be introduced in the Senate as well as in the House, but under the Constitution Act, 1867, both taxation bills and appropriation bills must have passed the House before going to the Senate. Although private members may introduce taxation bills, under the Act (s54), only the CROWN may initiate spending (supply) business; if the House could decide on its own to vote money for new purposes or to increase the amounts requested by the Crown, it would be well on the way to becoming the Government.

The House has important functions deriving from the Government's dependence on its co-operative support. Its constitutional function is to maintain a government for a reasonable time; to defeat one ministry after another in rapid succession would be anarchistic, a point which becomes highly relevant when no party wins a majority, as happened in 6 of the 11 elections between 1957 and 1987. The political function of the House is to foster government acceptable to the people, and it has the power to insist ministers account for their conduct and their bills and policies in their present portfolios. (In 1979 the CONSERVATIVE government proposed that Cabinet ministers, but not former ministers still in the House as backbenchers, be required to answer questions about activities that occurred during earlier portfolios). Some questions may be written down and placed on the Order Paper to receive a printed reply but during oral question period (45 minutes daily) ministers may be questioned directly (*see* PARLIAMENTARY PROCEDURES). Usually, leading Opposition speakers and selected backbenchers on the Opposition side of the House ask the questions. Dissatisfied questioners may indicate they will raise a matter on adjournment later in the day.

"Responsible" means both accountable and reasonable, conscientious or justifiable. Responsibility in the first sense helps ensure that ministers act responsibly in the second sense. The House could bring down a bad government by refusing to vote it money, but if the system is working well this should rarely, if ever, happen. Elections were brought on by defeats in the House of minority governments in 1963, 1974 and 1979. In recent years the controversy over ministerial responsibility and growth of executive power (sometimes referred to as "Cabinet dictatorship") has generated considerable debate over the role and function of the House. The governments of Western democracies have changed fundamentally since the 19th century and, in Canada, Parliament serves increasingly as an auditor of executive government, examining their bills, policies and conduct. House COMMITTEES are particularly useful for these purposes. The basic difficulty is how to improve the House's effectiveness as auditor and critic without abandoning the principle that the government is responsible for policy.

In a sense the House is part of a permanent election, so the role of the media in transmitting parliamentary debate and generating public opinion is very important. The decision of the House to publish its debates in the form of HANSARD and to use television were prompted in part by dissatisfaction with the news media.

The House is divided into the ministers and their supporters and those opposed to the government. Since 1921 there always has been at least one third party on the field, and occasionally 2 or more third parties. Since 1974 the election ballots have shown the candidates' party allegiances, if any. Independents usually are not successful. Members do leave their parties in the House in protest to sit as Independents, but rarely.

The Opposition is allotted up to 25 days in 3 supply periods to determine the subject of debate. Supply periods occur when the government is seeking passage of appropriation bills (*see* BUDGETARY PROCESS). The Opposition may also move adjournment of the House to discuss an urgent, unexpected matter. The SPEAKER may hold over such motions until the evening. The debate on the SPEECH FROM THE THRONE and the debate on the budget are general debates.

At the beginning of each Parliament the privileges of the House of Commons are confirmed by the governor general. At Westminster it was found that if the House was to participate effectively in parliaments it had to have certain privileges, certain exemptions from the ordinary law that were and are the special rights, not of individual members, but of the House. For a long time one of the foremost privileges at Westminster was that its members could not be imprisoned for debt. The foremost privilege of the Canadian House is the right of its members to speak freely – without being liable to prosecution in the courts – in proceedings of the House and its committees. This does not mean members can say anything they please; the privilege appertains to the House, which has a responsibility to control its members, to protect ordinary citizens from vilification. The House can forbid the publication of its debates and controls the taking of pictures and the making of notes in the galleries. The content of parliamentary papers, eg, Hansard, is privileged, but the decision of whether or not to broadcast proceedings has created difficulties: eg, does the freedom from legal penalties extend to broadcasters using the official tape? If so, might not the protection of ordinary citizens against libel be abridged?

MPs may be accused of contempt (which embraces breach of privilege and disrespect for the honour and dignity of the House) and of misleading the House not only in statements about their own conduct but possibly in ministerial answers to questions: eg, in 1982 the SPEAKER took under consideration a breach-of-privilege complaint against the minister of justice. A member of the public may be accused of contempt for publishing an attack on the Speaker, a charge against a member outside legal process, or a false or ridiculing account of proceedings in the House or in a committee. When a matter of privilege or contempt is raised in the House, the Speaker decides if there is a *prima facie* case; if so, the case is normally sent by the House to the Standing Committee on Privileges and Elections for investigation. The committee has the great power to send for persons and papers and may take sworn evidence. The House may admonish or censure offenders and is empowered to imprison them for the balance of the session. Genuine questions of privilege and contempt are serious but very rare; however, many of the members use points of privilege, which take precedence over most other business, to get the floor merely to voice complaints or to make corrections.

All speeches in the House are addressed formally to the Speaker, although direct exchanges often break out in the heat of debate. Private members are referred to by the name of their constituencies – "the Honourable Member for Peace River" – and ministers by office – "the Honourable the Minister of Finance." The terms, "the Prime Minister" and "the Leader of the Opposition" are in order. The House does not permit members to use unparliamentary language because it fosters bitterness and reflects on the honour of the House. Some expressions ruled unparliamentary in recent years include "sick animal," "pompous ass," "has not got the guts," "lies," "nazi" and "stinker."

The Speaker is the chief officer of the House. His or her election is the prime order of business when the House reassembles after an election. The Speaker, although usually a government MP, is responsible not to the government but to the House. The Speaker presides – deciding who is to have the floor, applying the rules of procedure, making rulings, putting the questions and managing the administration of the House and its permanent employees. There have been attempts to make the position permanent. The Deputy Speaker (House-elected) is usually proficient in the official language that is not the Speaker's first language and occupies the Speaker's chair if he or she is absent and chairs the committee of the whole. The Clerk, or Secretary of the House, who holds a deputy minister's rank, is not an MP but is appointed by the governor-in-council. He and one or more of the table officers are expert parliamentarians (procedure experts) and supply the Speaker with advice and information. The Clerk is also the Speaker's chief executive officer in staffing and servicing the House and is responsible to the Speaker for all the papers and the debates (Hansard), but is assisted in this work by expert branch officials.

When the first parliaments were held at Westminster, the king sent a royal sergeant-at-arms, bearing a royal mace, to attend upon the House of Commons, showing that the House was under the king's protection and was not to be threatened or molested. The sergeant-at-arms, who is appointed by the Crown, occupies a special chair in the centre aisle just inside the Bar; he leads the procession when the Speaker enters the chamber or proceeds to the Senate chamber for speeches from the throne, royal assents and prorogations. When the Speaker appears, representing the House, the mace (symbol of the authority of the House vested in the Speaker), borne by the sergeant-at-arms, is at his side.

The House of Commons normally meets in the Commons chamber at the west end of the Centre Block of the Parliament buildings. At Ottawa, unlike Westminster, every member has an assigned place in the chamber and must be in his place to speak and vote in the House (but not in committees of the whole House). There are 5 rows of desks down each of the long sides of the room; these 2 banks of desks face each other across a wide centre aisle. The Chair is at the north end of the centre aisle. This arrangement, far different from that in Paris or Washington, supposedly originated in the days when the English House met in St Stephen's Chapel, and it well suits the adversarial nature of our responsible government system. The main doors are at the south end of the centre aisle; on these the Gentleman Usher of the Black Rod raps when he comes to summon the Commons to the Senate chamber. There is a telescoping brass rail known as the Bar at the foot of the centre aisle, just inside the main doors, which can be extended across the aisle. One of its original functions at Westminster was to keep strangers from mingling and perhaps voting with the members. Occasionally, strangers have been summoned to appear at the Bar of the House to be questioned or censured.

The ministers and parliamentary secretaries are the only members of the government in the House; they receive salaries from the Crown in addition to their indemnities as members from the House. The government and its backbench supporters sit on the Speaker's right, facing east. The leader of one of the opposition parties – normally the largest – has the official role of leader of the Opposition, and in addition to his indemnity as a member receives a salary and various other benefits – including a residence, STORNOWAY. He generally assigns particular topics – finance, external affairs, transport, etc – to members of his team (the shadow Cabinet), but it cannot be presumed that the assignments would be the same if he became prime minister.

The prime minister occupies the 13th place in the front row on the west side; the leader of the Opposition sits directly opposite. The other ministers are grouped in a block of seats around the prime minister; the leader of the Opposition has his key followers around him. Former ministers – styled "the Honourable" as members of the Privy Council – are given seats in the front rows, at either the north or south end. The leader of each party, through the PARTY WHIP, fixes the party seating plan – invariably by class (year of first election) and alphabetically within classes. After each election, survivors from the previous House move closer to the centre aisle. There are 296 places in chamber for the 282 members (1987). Third parties are placed down beyond the official Opposition.

At the end of most sittings the Speaker adjourns the House – at 6:00 PM Monday to Friday – under the terms of a standing order of the House. Normally a sitting takes no more than one day but may extend beyond midnight and usually does when there is an emergency debate. The sitting of 4 May 1982 continued until about 7:00 PM the following day. In 1913, before there was a fixed time for adjournment, 2 sittings each extended throughout an entire week. A new record was set in 1982, during the "long-bell sitting," which began Mar 2 and did not end until Mar 17. The Parliamentary Calendar specifies the time of the year that the House sits. Sessions of Parliament begin with a summons by the governor general and end with prorogation by him. Minority parliaments recently have lasted only one or 2 sessions. Between 1867 and 1938 the annual sessions lasted only a few months; now they normally run a full year, with 3 long adjournments. The main purpose of prorogation is to wipe clean the Order Paper. All business unfinished at the end of a session – unanswered questions and all orders relating to bills and motions – die on the Order Paper. The House controls its own adjournments, but the Crown controls both the length of a session and the life of a Parliament.

JOHN B. STEWART

Reading: C.E.S. Franks, *The Parliament of Canada* (1987); John B. Stewart, *The Canadian House of Commons: Procedure and Reform* (1977).

House Sparrow (*Passer domesticus*), small, granivorous and insectivorous songbird with conical bill and chunky body. Males have a grey crown, black bib, streaked-brown upperparts and greyish white underparts; females are grey-buff overall. They are English SPARROWS (not related to N American sparrows but rather to African weavers) and were introduced 1850-52, from Europe, to Brooklyn, NY, to control INSECT PESTS. Through subsequent introductions and dispersals, the species spread across N America, reaching Québec City (1854), Ontario (1870) and across Canada (mid-1880s). In eastern Canada, it is now common to 48° N. Farther N it occurs in isolated colonies. In the West, it is found N to Ft Simpson, NWT, and W to Vancouver I. House sparrows are permanent residents of cities and farms. They build bulky, domed nests, intricately woven of grasses, on buildings, in natural cavities or in trees and shrubs. Two to 3 clutches of 3-7 eggs are laid from Apr to Aug. House sparrows nest singly or in small groups. Small flocks form in summer, reaching several hundred individuals in winter. The song is repetitive, metallic and unmusical. House sparrows are agricultural pests and fierce competitors of native birds. They are important for studies of rapid adaptation to new environments.

J.C. BARLOW

Housework can be defined as all work performed within a household related to housekeeping functions, childcare and personal services to an adult. Until very recently, housework was not defined as work by most social scientists unless it was performed by a servant who was paid for it. It is only since feminist scholars have pointed out the extraordinary significance of housework for the functioning of the economy and for society that it has received any attention.

During this century, although housework has been industrialized (the products of housework can now be purchased, and services, eg, childcare, nursing the sick, cooking, cleaning, etc, can be bought), no less time than before is actually spent on unpaid housework. The nature of the work performed, however, and the conditions under which it is being performed have changed. Some neo-Marxists argue that, counter to previous assumptions, housework must be understood as productive work, but because it produces use value rather than exchange value, it has long been miscategorized as unproductive. One of its important functions includes the reproduction of society's labour power. Other analysts argue that Marxist analysis cannot suitably be applied to unpaid housework. Even today, economists tend to view housework as a noneconomic activity if no money changes hands. Neither have sociologists and historians given much thought to the subject, although recent work has revealed that unpaid housework does constitute an extremely important part of the overall amount of work performed within Canadian society; if calculated as part of the gross domestic product, it would increase it by about 33%. Housework has historically been, and continues to be, a predominantly female activity; although the majority of married women belong to the LABOUR FORCE (from 1941-1987 the number of married women in the labour force increased from about 4.5% to 56.3%), time-budget studies reveal that women continue to do most of the housework even when they have a paying job. In 1924, for example, American housewives spent about 52 hours a week doing housework; by the 1960s it had increased to 55 hours. Until very recently, housework was commonly regarded as a natural part of the female role, and even though the majority of people now believe it should be shared between the spouses when both of them have paying jobs, this attitude has not been reflected in actual behaviour. Significantly, various provincial family law reform Acts, starting with the Ontario Act of 1978, have recognized unpaid housework as a contribution to the family's well-being, therefore entitling the performer of this work to part of family assets upon divorce. M. EICHLER

Reading: M. Proulx, *Five Million Women, A Study of the Canadian Housewife,* Advisory Council on the Status of Women (1978).

Habitat, Montréal, designed by Moshe Safdie for Expo 67 to illustrate futuristic housing concepts (*courtesy Canapress Photo Service*).

Housing and Housing Policy Housing policies and programs are actions taken by governments to affect the quantity, quality and price of housing. The objectives of Canadian housing policies have been to ensure that dwellings of a decent standard are available to all Canadians at prices they can afford. Government assistance may be provided through grants and loans to developers or consumers. In 1986 there were 9 million dwelling units in Canada, of which 58% were single-family detached, 1% movable, 9% high-rise and 32% lower density multiple housing. Some 65% of this housing had been built since WWII. Construction had averaged only 39 000 units a year during the Great Depression and the war years, but it increased rapidly after the war to meet the needs of returning veterans, immigrants, and people moving from rural to urban centres. Annual additions to Canadian housing averaged 77 000 units in the 1950s, 155 000 in the 1960s, and 229 100 in the 1970s. The early 1980s saw a reduced demand for housing as a result of the economic recession and the fact that most of the postwar BABY BOOM had already entered the housing market (eg, only 184 600 units were built in 1986).

In Canada, all levels of government are involved in housing programs, though the constitutional authority for housing is vested in provincial governments. They, in turn, may delegate housing responsibility to regional and CITY governments. Local governments are usually responsible for enforcing adequate housing standards and for land-use planning that affects the location and type of housing (*see* URBAN AND REGIONAL PLANNING; ZONING). At the national level, a variety of economic and social concerns, all of which have an impact on the housing sector, caused the Government of Canada to become involved in housing policy. Canadian housing policies have addressed 2 tasks: to assist the housing market to produce enough housing to meet the needs of most Canadians (*see* DEVELOPMENT INDUSTRY) and to provide extra assistance to people whose housing needs cannot be adequately met through the normal housing market. Prior to 1970, government programs assisted just over one-third of all housing starts. Most of this assistance was directed to market housing, and less than 5% of all starts were specifically designed to house lower-income Canadians. During the 1970s, government programs assisted 40% of all housing completions; changing funding priorities resulted in a reduction in housing assistance in the mid-1980s. By 1986, government programs assisted only 14% of completions, 8% of completions were targeted to lower income Canadians.

Before 1970 Canadian housing programs were almost exclusively the preserve of the federal government. The first national housing legislation, the Dominion Housing Act of 1935, provided $20 million in loans and helped finance 4900 units over 3 years. The Federal Home Improvement Plan (1937) provided subsidized interest rates on rehabilitation loans to 66 900 homes. In 1938 the first National Housing Act was passed. These acts served the dual purposes of providing housing and creating employment opportunities.

The federal government continued to be active in the housing market during WWII. A crown corporation, Wartime Housing Corp, built 45 930 units at a cost of $253 million over 8 years, and assisted in the repair and modernization of existing houses. New programs stimulated the private housing market by providing mortgage money and favourable interest rates to encourage home-ownership and the construction of limited dividend rental housing. In 1946 the assets of Wartime Housing Corp were transferred to Central Mortgage and Housing Corporation (*see* CANADA MORTGAGE AND HOUSING CORPORATION).

A significant milestone in Canadian housing legislation occurred in 1954 when the federal government agreed to insure mortgage loans made by private investors against borrower default. The Bank Act was also amended to allow Canada's chartered banks to lend money for mortgages. These initiatives enabled the federal government to reduce its direct involvement in lending and to become an insurer of mortgages and a lender of last resort.

During the 1970s the federal government continued to assist the private housing market by insuring mortgages and by providing direct loans in smaller communities that were otherwise not well served by private lenders. Incentives were introduced to stimulate home ownership such as tax-exempt Registered Homeownership Savings Plans, Assisted Homeownership Program, and changes to the Tax Act (1971) that excluded principal residences from capital gains tax. In the early 1980s the Canadian Home Stimulation Program provided grants to home buyers; the Canada Mortgage Renewal Plan assisted those who were experiencing difficulty renewing their mortgages at higher interest rates; and the Graduated Payment Mortgage Plan helped homeowners offset the rising costs of home ownership by lowering initial monthly mortgage payments. Some 37% of Canadians are renters, most of whom live in urban areas. During the 1970s the federal government also assisted the construction of private rental housing through a combination of grants, preferential loans and taxation concessions, eg, Multiple Unit Residential Building deductions, the Assisted Rental Program and the Canada Rental Supply Plan. Most market rental assistance programs had ended by the mid-1980s.

The housing industry is supported by a continuing commitment from all levels of government to improve housing quality and community standards. The National Building Code and the National Fire Code encourage uniform building and safety standards across Canada. Municipalities inspect to ensure that standards are maintained and, through zoning bylaws, regulate what can be built and where. Municipalities are also responsible for planning and for providing water, sewer, roads, parks, schools and other public services. In unincorporated or rural areas, regional districts or provincial governments regulate land use and provide services.

Government programs have assisted cities in improving the quality of housing and services. During the 1950s the federal government funded land assembly programs. In the 1960s cities received funds for urban renewal and municipal infrastructure. During the 1970s the federal government shifted funds into residential rehabilitation assistance, neighbourhood improvement and home-insulation programs. Most cities used the neighbourhood improvement program to upgrade and preserve older neighbourhoods. Homeowners and landlords used the rehabilitation and home-improvement funding to upgrade over 315 000 homes between 1974 and 1986.

The provision of housing for lower-income Canadians has been another continuing concern of governments. Social, public, community or nonmarket housing are terms used interchangeably to describe housing for people whose needs for adequate and affordable shelter cannot be met through market housing. Nonmarket units are built by governments and nonprofit or co-operative societies and are operated and assisted by government subsidies to ensure a continuing stock of affordable housing. The first Canadian social housing legislation was introduced in 1938 when the National Housing Act made provision for construction of low-rent housing. In 1949 the NHA was broadened to include federal-provincial programs (sometimes with city participation) to build publicly owned and provincially managed housing for low-income families, seniors and the disabled. From 1947 to 1986, 253 500 public housing units were built across Canada. Ontario has the largest share (43%), followed by Québec (22%), BC (8%), Manitoba (7%) and Alberta (5%). The location of public housing reflects the ability of provincial governments to participate in cost-shared programs and, to a lesser extent, in areas with traditionally low vacancy rates.

Between 1969 and 1974 the public housing program underwent extensive evaluation. A $200-million program in 1970 stimulated innovative solutions for housing low-income Canadians; the Ministry of State for Urban Affairs, 1971-78, initiated research and implemented policy, and included CMHC in its mandate. In 1974 the NHA was amended: existing public housing was to continue to provide accommodation for low-income households; rural and native programs were added; and new social housing was to be built by municipalities, nonprofit organizations and co-operatives. The legislation encouraged consumers to be more involved in the design and management of housing, and encouraged a mix of modest and lower-income households. Funding for social housing was provided mainly by the federal government, with some assistance from the provinces and cities. More than 220 000 units were provided between 1974 and 1986 to house families (50%), seniors (40%) and others (10%) (*see also* NATIVE PEOPLE, GOVERNMENT PROGRAMS).

During the 1970s provincial and city governments assumed a more active role in housing. Prior to 1970 Ontario had the most active provincial housing agency. By the mid-1970s all 10 provinces had created new or stronger housing departments and assumed more responsibility for policy development and for setting priorities for spending housing funds. Most provinces offer home-ownership grants and contribute to the cost of nonmarket housing. Some provinces assist renters by providing tax credits, shelter allowances, and through rent control. Amendments to the NHA in 1978 and negotiations surrounding the CONSTITUTION ACT, 1982, supported provincial housing activities and, in turn, senior governments encouraged cities to create municipal nonprofit corporations to build and manage social housing.

Social housing programs underwent an extensive review from 1979 to 1984. Governments examined the ongoing cost of housing subsidies and changing housing demand, as a result, housing funds were reduced and directly targeted to low income people and the number of programs reduced with more emphasis placed upon renovation of existing housing. ANN MCAFEE

Reading: M. Dennis and S. Fish, *Programs in Search of a Policy: Low Income Housing in Canada* (1972); *Report of the Task Force on Housing and Urban Development* (1969); M.A. Goldberg, *The Housing Problem* (1983).

Housing Co-operatives Continuing housing co-operatives emerged during the 1960s when many Canadians, especially families with children, could no longer afford home ownership and faced difficulty finding good-quality rental housing. In the mid-1960s the first continuing co-op, the 200-unit Willow Park Housing Co-operative in Winnipeg, served as a demonstration that this new housing tenure was not only practical but also socially desirable because of the sense of community created by the co-operative form of ownership and management. To promote co-op housing, the Canadian Labour Congress, the Co-operative Union of Canada and the Canadian Union of Students established the Co-operative Housing Foundation of Canada in 1968. Housing officials eventually agreed that socially mixed housing co-operatives were an improved alternative to providing assisted housing, and in 1973 the National Housing Act (NHA) was amended to create a co-op housing program. Since then, 1300 housing co-ops have been built, providing self-managed affordable housing for over 46 000 households. Groups who wish to build a co-op are assisted by a national network of nonprofit co-op housing development societies, known as resource groups. Co-ops combine features of owning and renting while having a different form of tenure from both. Residents co-own the buildings and pay a monthly housing charge for the use of their unit. As with home ownership, co-op members have security of tenure and make all decisions regarding their housing. As with renting, members make no down payment and do not sell their unit if they move out. The co-op is jointly owned on a nonprofit basis, with each member having one vote.

The first kinds of housing co-operatives in Canada were building co-ops and student co-ops. The former are temporary rather than continuing co-ops, through which members secure individual home ownership by helping build one another's houses. Over 20 000 houses have been co-operatively built since a group of miners in Tompkinsville, Cape Breton, built the first 11 houses in 1938. Student co-ops emerged in the 1930s and began to appear in larger numbers on or near university campuses after 1964 when NHA funding was made available. In the mid-1980s there were 1750 student co-op housing units in Canada. J. DAVID HULCHANSKI

Reading: A.F. Laidlaw, *Housing You Can Afford* (1977).

Houston, BC, District Municipality, pop 3905 (1986c), situated in the geographical centre of BC, midway between Prince George and Prince Rupert on the Yellowhead Hwy 16 and at the confluence of the Bulkley and Morice rivers; lumber, mining and cattle ranching form the economic base. Originally called Pleasant Valley, it was renamed in 1910 after John Houston, a railway surveyor and the first newspaperman in Prince Rupert. The town has grown rapidly from about 100 people in the 1960s to nearly 4000 by 1986. A large sawmill, owned by Weldwood and Eurocan, and a lumber and pulp mill, Northwood Pulp and Timber Ltd, are the major employers. An important open-pit silver mine, Equity Silver Mine, opened nearby in 1980. JOHN STEWART

Houston, James Archibald, artist, author, filmmaker (b at Toronto 12 June 1921). Houston studied art in Toronto before serving in WWII. After studies in France (1947-48), he spent 14 years in the Canadian Arctic, serving as civil administrator at W Baffin, teaching the Inuit the techniques of printmaking, and popularizing their art in the US and southern Canada. He formed the West Baffin Co-operative to control production. From 1962 to 1972, he was with Steuben Glass of NY. Houston's first children's story, *Tikta'liktak: An Eskimo Legend* (1965) was named Canadian Children's Book of the Year. *The White Archer* (1967) and *River Runners* (1979) won the same award. Houston has been active on many national and international boards, promoting native art. A fellow of the Royal Soc of Art and an Officer of the Order of Canada, he holds several honorary doctorates.

Houston's children's books are of 3 types. Some, such as *Tikta'liktak, Long Claws* (1981) and *The Falcon Bow* (1986) are expanded versions of legends he has been told by the Inuit. Others portray the growth to maturity of West Coast native youths. Four novels, *Frozen Fire* (1977), *River Runners* (1979), *Black Diamonds* (1982) and *Ice Swords* (1985), have modern settings. Houston has illustrated all these books himself. His adult novels – *The White Dawn* (1971), *Spirit Wrestler* (1980) and *Eagle Song* (1983) – depict the powerful emotions involved in confrontation between traditional native cultures and Europeans. He spent the summer of 1987 at Cape Dorset preparing for the production of a major feature film. *See also* INUIT PRINTMAKING. JON C. STOTT

Howard, John George, né John Corby, architect, surveyor, artist (b at Bengeo, Eng 27 July 1803; d at Toronto 3 Feb 1890). Emigrating from England in 1832, Howard enjoyed a successful career, primarily in Toronto, as an architect, surveyor and artist. He produced fine watercolours (many of which survive), was instrumental in organizing the Toronto Soc of Artists in 1834, and was drawing master at Upper Canada Coll from 1833 to 1856. He received many contracts for street improvements following the incorporation of the city of Toronto in 1834 and was city surveyor 1843-55. One of the busiest architects in the city, he was responsible for many private and public buildings. His most important commission was the Provincial Lunatic Asylum (1845-49, demolished 1976), but he is best remembered for bequeathing his estate, High Park, and his home, Colborne Lodge, to the city. VICTOR L. RUSSELL

Howard, Robert Palmer, physician, educator, medical administrator (b at Montréal 12 Jan 1823; d there 28 Mar 1889). Best remembered as a superb teacher, Howard combined enthusiasm with sincerity and dignity, inspiring his pupils with his own zeal and love for medicine. One of those pupils was William OSLER, who often expressed his admiration for his former teacher. By 1860 Howard was professor of the theory and practice of medicine at McGill, and he was dean of the McGill medical faculty from 1882 until his death. His role as a teacher takes precedence, but he rendered distinguished service in other areas, and through his leadership, writings and addresses raised the standards of MEDICAL EDUCATION throughout Canada. EDWARD H. BENSLEY

Howe, Arthur Thomas, entrepreneur, orchardist, sportsman (b at Pavenham, Eng 27 Mar 1855; d at Vernon, BC 7 Oct 1947). Howe arrived in Canada at the age of 20; after working in the leather trade in Toronto, he formed his own successful tanning and leather goods business which became a principal supplier to The T. EATON COMPANY. In 1913 he moved to Vernon, where he built up holdings of fruit orchards, dairy herds and processing plants, and became one of the largest independent farmers in Canada and the largest grower of McIntosh apples in the British Empire. He was responsible for a number of important measures designed to bring order to the troubled BC fruit industry and to establish it as a strong element of the provincial economy. A.S. HENRY

Howe, Clarence Decatur, engineer, politician (b at Waltham, Mass 15 Jan 1886; d at Montréal 31 Dec 1960). Howe was the most successful businessman-politician of his day, and provided a link between the Liberal Party and Canadian industry. Although he claimed relationship to the Nova Scotian Liberal statesman Joseph HOWE, C.D. Howe's Canadian connections were remote until he came N to Halifax with an engineering degree from the Massachusetts Institute of Technology to teach engineering at Dalhousie. Howe's years there (1908-13) were successful, if unexciting, and he readily abandoned academia in 1913 to work with the Canadian Board of Grain Commissioners designing wheat elevators across the Prairies. Howe found the job congenial and in 1916 formed his own engineering firm, specializing in grain elevators. Between 1916 and 1935 the C.D. Howe Co built elevators in Vancouver, Saskatoon, Churchill, Pt Arthur, Toronto and Prescott, as well as Buenos Aires, Argentina. Howe became the foremost grain-elevator builder of his day. His straightforward, blunt personality, and his ability to build elevators at a fixed price, commended him to his customers, especially in western Canada. But the 1930s Depression ended his business, and in 1935 he entered politics and Parliament as a Liberal, representing Pt Arthur (Thunder Bay, Ont). He was promptly made a member of Mackenzie KING'S Cabinet, becoming minister of transport in 1936. In that capacity Howe helped create Trans-Canada Airlines (later Air Canada).

C.D. Howe, who made his fortune building grain elevators, went on to become a powerful Cabinet minister through the 1940s to 1956 (*courtesy National Archives of Canada/C-472*).

Gordie Howe in action against Toronto goalie Johnny Bower (*courtesy Canada's Sports Hall of Fame*).

In 1940 Howe became minister of munitions and supply, with the task of running Canada's war-production program. He succeeded brilliantly, working beside a group of largely Conservative businessmen who came to appreciate his efficient and daring conduct of economic affairs. This stood him in good stead when in 1944 he was asked to preside over the new Dept of RECONSTRUCTION. He reconverted the Canadian economy to a free-enterprise system, with minimal government controls. During the 1950s Howe was concerned with developing certain sectors of the Canadian economy, such as steel, and with expanding Canada's trade, as minister of trade and commerce. In that capacity, in 1956, he sponsored a trans-Canada pipeline, with government aid to a private firm. The move stirred up a parliamentary storm, and Howe's increasingly short-tempered response to criticism helped undermine the government's position. In 1957 the Liberals were defeated, as was Howe. ROBERT BOTHWELL

Reading: Robert Bothwell and W. Kilbourn, *C.D. Howe* (1979).

Howe, Gordon, hockey player (b at Floral, Sask 31 Mar 1928). Gordie Howe's record of 32 outstanding seasons in hockey may be the most remarkable example of longevity in professional sport. He played junior in Saskatoon and Galt, Ont, before turning professional with Omaha and joining Detroit Red Wings in 1946. His career started slowly with 7, 16 and 12 goals in his first 3 years and in his third year he suffered a severe head injury after colliding with Ted KENNEDY and crashing headlong into the boards. He won the ART ROSS TROPHY (leading scorer) 4 straight years 1950-54 and again in 1957 and 1963, the HART TROPHY (most valuable player) in 1952, 1953, 1957, 1958, 1960 and 1963 and was NHL all-star 21 times. Howe retired from Detroit in 1971, but returned to hockey in 1973 to join his 2 sons, Mark and Marty, with the WHA Houston Aeros. He finished his career, at age 52, with Hartford Whalers of the NHL in 1980.

Gordie Howe was doubtless the finest athlete ever to play hockey. He possessed great physical strength, stamina and speed, and his wrist shot was clocked at 183 km/h. His professional totals, including playoffs, are 2421 games, 1071 goals, 1518 assists and 2589 points. Though the NHL does not recognize his 6 WHA seasons, he holds the NHL records for most seasons (26), most games, including playoffs (1924), most goals (869), most assists (1141) and most points (2010). Howe dominated his sport as much by his intimidating strength as by his mastery of skills; he also accumulated 2419 minutes in penalties. JAMES MARSH

Howe, Joseph, journalist, politician, premier and lt-gov of NS (b at Halifax 13 Dec 1804; d there 1 June 1873). Taking over the *Novascotian* in 1828, Howe quickly made it the leading provincial newspaper. Originally defending the political status quo, he gradually became convinced through personal experience that serious ills abounded throughout the government. Charged with criminal libel in 1835 for criticizing local government officials, he was acquitted in the province's most celebrated trial. He entered politics in 1836 and was primarily responsible for the election of a majority of Reformers (Liberals). A conservative Reformer, he entered a coalition with the Tories in 1840, hoping to achieve his aims step-by-step. Having failed, he prepared the way for the Reformers' success in the election of 1847. As a result, Nova Scotia secured RESPONSIBLE GOVERNMENT in Feb 1848, the first colony to do so, and Howe could boast that it had been done without "a blow struck or a pane of glass broken."

Seeking to rise above "the muddy pool of politics," he tried unsuccessfully to arrange the building of the Halifax to Québec Ry. As chief commissioner, he began the Nova Scotia Ry in 1854, however, and saw completion of the lines from Halifax to Windsor and Truro. Devoted to Britain, he recruited forces in the US in 1855 for the CRIMEAN WAR, one outcome of which was a rupture with the Catholics and the defeat of the Reformers in 1857. Following the Liberal victory of 1859, he was premier 1860-63 and imperial fishery commissioner 1863-66 under the RECIPROCITY Treaty of 1854. Between 1866 and 1868 he led the movement against CONFEDERATION on the grounds that it was being effected without popular consent and that it conflicted with his plans for the organization of the British Empire. Although overwhelmingly successful in the provincial elections of 1867, as a delegate to Britain in 1866-67 he could not prevent passage of the BNA Act or, a year later, secure its repeal. Having no further means of opposition he entered the federal Cabinet in Jan 1869. In a celebrated

Nova Scotian patriot Joseph Howe (*courtesy National Archives of Canada/C-22002*).

midwinter by-election in Hants his health was so impaired that he never fully recovered. As a federal minister, he played a prominent role in bringing Manitoba into the union. Becoming lieutenant-governor of Nova Scotia in 1873, he served only 3 weeks before his death.

Despite his failings, many consider Howe to have been the greatest of all Nova Scotians. The Nova Scotian patriot par excellence, he could use his oratorical powers to influence his compatriots as no other man has ever done. He sought, in his own words, to elevate them to "something more en[n]obling, exacting and inspiring, calculated to enlarge the borders of their intelligence, and increase the extent and area of their prosperity." J. MURRAY BECK

Howe Research Institute, (now C.D. Howe Institute), a nonprofit organization established in 1973 to conduct nonpartisan research and analysis of Canadian economic-policy issues. Branch offices are located in Montréal and Calgary; and the head office, in Toronto, publishes an annual *Policy Review and Outlook* surveying Canada's economic performance and policy options. The institute has published several books since 1983, concerning important aspects of the Canadian economy such as the deficit and free trade. GREGORY WIRICK

Howse, Joseph, fur trader, explorer, linguist (b at Cirencester, Eng *c*1774; d there 4 Sept 1852). In 1795 Howse signed on with the Hudson's Bay Co as a "writer." After 4 years at York Factory, he was put in charge of the company's Saskatchewan District, staying for varying periods at Carlton House, Chesterfield House and Fort Edmonton. From Edmonton, Howse explored the Rocky Mountain House – Columbia River continental divide (1809-11). Howse's fight with the Nor'Westers in 1814 and 1815 may have forced his retirement to England. Active in the Church Missionary Soc, and the Royal Geographical Soc, he also authored the important *Grammar of the Cree Language*... (1844) and published several articles in the *Proceedings of the Philological Society*. Howse Pass is named for him. FRITS PANNEKOEK

Hoyles, Sir Hugh William, politician, judge, prime minister of Newfoundland (b at St John's 17 Oct 1814; d at Halifax 1 Feb 1888). The son of Newman Hoyles, a wealthy merchant and politician, he was educated in St John's and Nova Scotia, and was called to the Newfoundland Bar in 1837. He participated in various political, social and religious organizations, and in 1848 was elected Conservative member of the House of Assembly for Fortune Bay; he sat in the House until 1859 and again 1860-65. Hoyles quickly became a major force within his party, and succeeded to its leadership in 1855. In the late 1850s and early 1860s long-standing tensions between the Island's Irish Roman Catholic and English Protestant inhabitants flared up in severe civil disorders. In Feb 1861 Gov Alexander Bannerman dismissed the Liberal administration of Catholic John KENT and called on Church of England member Hoyles to form a government. Hoyles was subsequently confirmed in office in a bitter, violence-marred election. His main concern as prime minister was to ease ethnic and religious tension. Although his efforts met with mixed results, his conciliatory actions helped prepare the ground for later accommodations. Hoyles resigned as prime minister in 1865 and subsequently served as chief justice of Newfoundland 1865-80. GEOFF BUDDEN

Hubert, Jean-François, Roman Catholic bishop (b at Québec City 23 Feb 1739; d there 17 Oct 1797). Educated at the SÉMINAIRE DE QUÉBEC and ordained a priest in 1766, he became in Dec 1774 the first Canadian superior of the Séminaire, but he resigned in 1778 and joined the church's Illinois mission. Coadjutor bishop in 1786, in 1788 he became bishop of Québec, and in 1789 he successfully opposed establishment of a nonconfessional university at Québec. He supported the British government against revolutionary France in the 1790s and was allowed to bring refugee French priests to his diocese, which was suffering an acute shortage of clergy. Worn out by a momentous and active episcopacy, during which he favoured moderation and traditionalism, Hubert resigned in Sept 1797 and died the next month. JAMES H. LAMBERT

Hudon, Normand, caricaturist, painter, fantasist (b at Montréal 5 June 1929). After his studies at École des beaux-arts de Montréal, he lived in Paris, then made a flamboyant entry as a caricaturist and fantasist when television came to Montréal in the early 1950s; the series "Ma Ligne maligne," with Robert LAPALME, stamped the age with its vivacity. At the same time, Hudon was showing his paintings and drawings in galleries and was becoming one of the most biting caricaturists. On 9 July 1965 he signed a cover for *Time* magazine and that year also prepared a huge composition for a pavilion at Expo 67. After a more difficult period, he began working seriously again (1972) and in a few years had completed a body of work which treated, with tender irony, certain aspects of the Québec heritage: nuns on bicycles or priests on skates, mischievous children or picturesque villages, tiptilted houses or shops, and court scenes that could rival those of Daumier. GUY ROBERT

Hudson, Henry, explorer (*fl* 1607-11). Little is known of him before the famous voyages of his last 4 years. He searched twice (1607, 1608) for a polar route to Asia via Norway and Russia, and in the service of the Dutch East India Co ascended the Hudson R in 1609. English patrons financed his search for a NORTHWEST PASSAGE in 1610. He sailed in the DISCOVERY to Iceland and entered HUDSON STR in early June, navigating his tiny vessel through fog and ice, passing through the narrow gap between Cape Wolstenholme and Cape Digges (named for his patrons). He descended the E shore into desolate JAMES BAY, tacking to and fro in a futile search for an opening to the Spice Islands. He beached the *Discovery* and spent a bleak winter, likely by the Rupert R. Resentment among his crew broke into mutiny in the spring when Hudson announced his intention to continue the search. The leaders, Henry Greene, Robert Juet and William Wilson, forced Hudson, his son and 7 others into a shallop and cut it adrift in the open sea. Robert BYLOT piloted the *Discovery* home. Greene and Wilson were killed by natives at Cape Digges; Juet died of starvation. Four of the 9 survivors were tried for murder but acquitted – saved as much by mercantile interest in their knowledge of the Northwest as by the blame laid on the dead. Nothing is known of Hudson's fate. He did not discover Hudson Str – both M. FROBISHER and J. DAVIS had noted its entrance – but in navigating its treacherous course he far outdistanced his predecessors and discovered a route to the continent's interior of inestimable value to England. However, his favouritism and weak leadership vitiated his accomplishment. The quaint, contentious account by Abacuk Pricket, a survivor, is the sole record of the voyage and mutiny. JAMES MARSH

Hudson Bay, 637 000 km^2, is an immense inland sea that penetrates deeply into northeastern Canada. It is virtually landlocked but is joined to the Arctic Ocean to the N by Foxe Channel and Fury and Hecla Str, and to the Atlantic Ocean on the E by HUDSON STR. Baffin I lies athwart the entrance to the bay, and Southampton, Coats and Mansel islands are lodged across the northern gap. The W coast is devoid of islands, but lying off the E is a string known as the Sleepers, Ottawa, Nastapoka and BELCHER groups. The maximum length of the bay is 1500 km and its greatest width 830 km. The bay, including Hudson Str, is fed by numerous rivers, large and small, including, from W to E, the KAZAN, THELON and DUBAWNT, flowing into the bay via Chesterfield Inlet; HAYES, NELSON and CHURCHILL on the W; WINISK and SEVERN in the SW; Grande, EASTMAIN, Nottaway, Moose and Abitibi, ALBANY, ATTAWAPISKAT and Nastapoca flowing into James Bay; and KOKSOAK flowing into Ungava Bay. The total area of the Hudson Bay drainage is about 4 million km^2 and the mean discharge of all the rivers flowing into it is 30 900 m^3/s – greater than those dis-

York Fort, Hudson's Bay (1921), watercolour by Peter Rindisbacher. Hudson Bay played a crucial role in the early development of Canada and York Fort was long the main depot of the HBC (*courtesy National Archives of Canada/C-1918 2-I-18*).

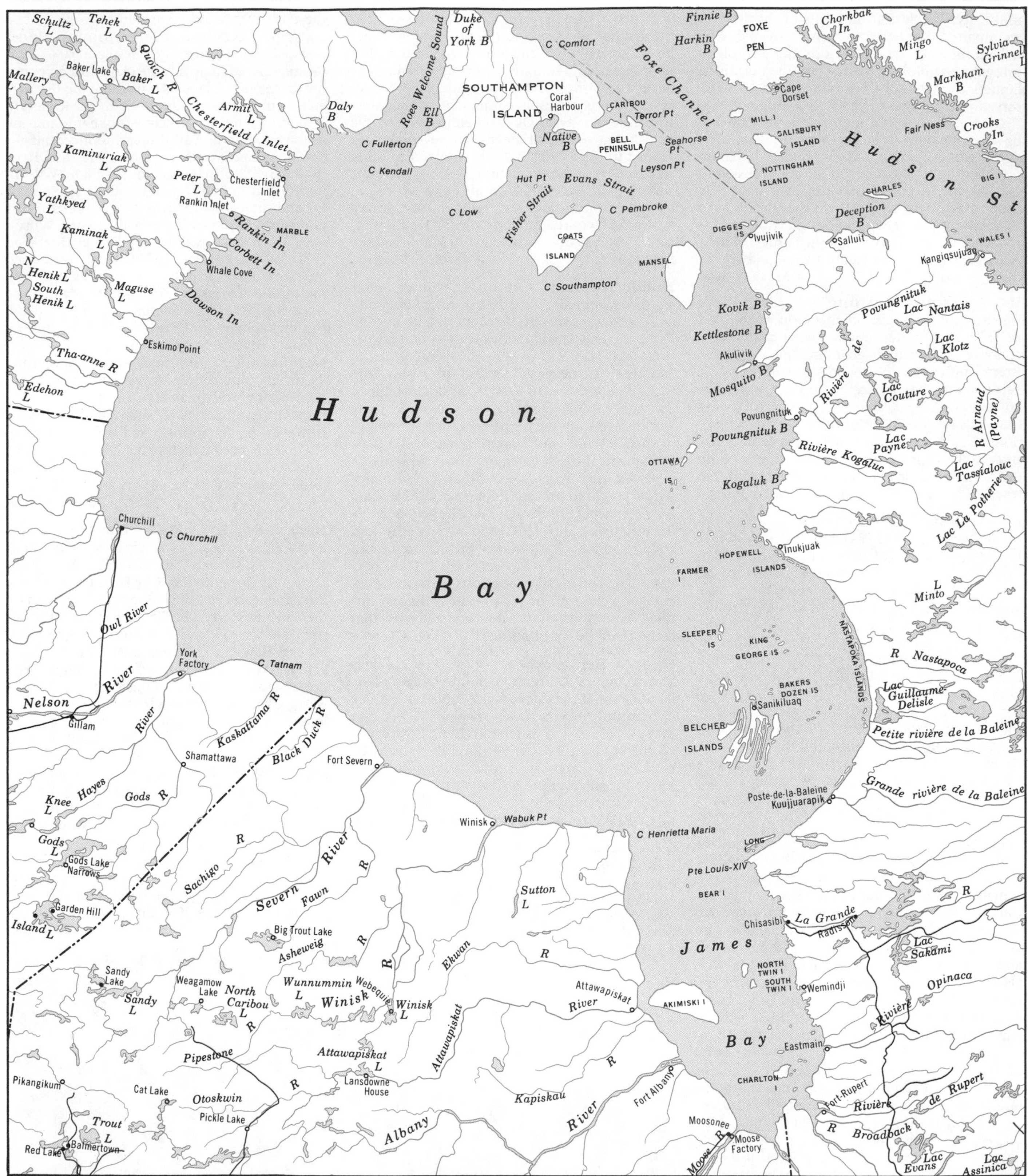

charging into the Atlantic and Pacific oceans combined.

The bay lies in a huge saucer-shaped basin, fringed by uplands of the Canadian SHIELD. The basin was inundated by seawater after the retreat of GLACIATION some 7500 years ago. The bay is generally shallow, and the land is rising steadily at around 60 cm per 100 years because of isostatic uplift, exposing more and more of the coast. The surrounding Hudson Bay Lowland (*see* PHYSIOGRAPHIC REGIONS) is a low plain, locked in PERMAFROST and characterized by marshes, peat and innumerable ponds. Much of the hydroelectric potential of the area develops at the point where powerful rivers surge out of the Shield on to the lowlands. An almost unnatural feature of the E coast is the great, semicircular bight, centering on the Belcher Is, which it has been suggested was caused by a stupendous meteor strike. The W coast is generally without indentation, low and bleak up to Eskimo Pt, and increasingly broken and indented farther N, particularly at the great gashes of Chesterfield Inlet and Rankin Inlet. The shores are mostly covered with brushes, aspen, willow and dwarf birch growing among moss, lichen and grass. Cliffs of ancient sedimentary rocks are found at points on the E coast.

The climate of the region depends largely on the water surface. In Jan and Feb the bay is covered with pack ice, preventing any warming effect on the air, and temperatures are consequently very low. The ice begins to melt in May and rapidly disappears in June, when cloudiness and fog increase. The water temperature rises up to 10°C in July and Aug as a result of the influx of fresh water. During Oct and Nov the waters of the bay yield heat and moisture, bringing showers of rain and snow. Fog is most frequent in June, July and Aug, as warm air cools over the colder water. Winds are strong in all but the summer months and rise to 110 km/h and even 150 km/h in autumn. Hudson Bay contains great quantities of nutrient salts and small CRUSTACEANS occupy the open waters, providing food for molluscs, starfish, sea urchins, worms and other invertebrates. Cod, halibut, salmon and polar plaice are the most common fish. Walrus, dolphins and killer whales live in the northern regions and polar bears migrate S to hunt seals among the ice. Some 200 species of birds, including ducks, snow geese, gulls, swans, sandpipers, owls and crows gather on the coasts and islands.

Archaeological evidence has shown that the shores of the bay have been occupied for thousands of years. Many of the excavated campsites are far from the present, receding coastline. At the time of the appearance of Europeans, Algonquian groups inhabited the area around James Bay and Chipewyan groups the Churchill area, and Inuit groups were found on the N and E coasts. NORSE seafarers possibly found, and even colonized, the bay, but if so their discovery was forgotten. Martin FROBISHER mistakenly sailed into Hudson Str in 1578 but Henry HUDSON was the first European we know to have braved the dangers of the strait and sailed into the bay (1610). He was followed by BUTTON (1612), BYLOT and FOX [Foxe] (1631) and JAMES (1631) in a futile search for a passage to the Orient. The voyages were perilous, often disastrous; in 1619 only 3 members of Jens MUNK's expedition survived. The mutiny of Hudson's crew passed into exploration mythology. The journals of Luke Fox found their way into Coleridge's harrowing tale, "The Rime of the Ancient Mariner." The W coast was not mapped until the 1820s and the first detailed investigation was carried out from 1929 to 1931.

The bay played a crucial role in the early development of Canada after it was realized that it provided a direct route to the fur resources of the North-West. In 1668 DES GROSEILLIERS, in the service of the English, sailed into the bay and built a small post at the mouth of the Rupert R. In 1670 RADISSON founded what later became YORK FACTORY at the mouth of the Nelson R, and the trading rights to the entire watershed of the bay were granted to the HUDSON'S BAY CO. Posts were later built at the mouths of the Moose and Albany rivers and drew Indian traders from a vast area of the Shield, with the CREE playing an important middleman role. From 1682 to 1713, the French made a determined effort to rout the English from the bay. Temporary successes were achieved by de TROYES overland (1686) and IBERVILLE in several expeditions by sea. However, after the Treaty of UTRECHT in 1713, the bay was firmly in the hands of the English, and after the HBC merger with the NORTH WEST CO in 1821, it became the primary route to the interior. On the transfer of RUPERT'S LAND to Canada in 1870, sovereignty over the bay and its watershed passed to Canada. Since that time it has ceased to play an important role as a transportation route and it has been sparsely populated. The primary occupants continue to be Indian and Inuit bands, living by fishing and hunting. The largest settlement is CHURCHILL, Man (pop 1217, 1986c), at the mouth of the Churchill R, Churchill and MOOSONEE, Ont, are connected by railway to the interior, but their potential as saltwater ports is more often talked about than exploited. The bay remains much as it has been designated for conservation purposes – a *mare clausum* ("closed sea"). JAMES MARSH

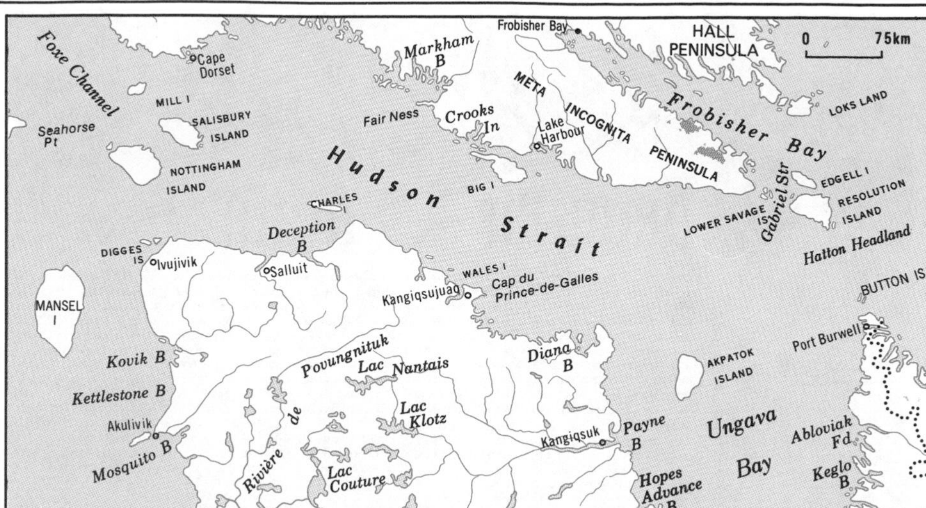

Hudson Bay, Sask, Town, pop 2133 (1986c), 2361 (1981c), inc 1946, 209 km N of Yorkton. Established (1906) as a siding for logging interests by the Canadian Northern Ry on a line laid earlier (1901) through the Porcupine and Pasquia forest reserves,it was called Etoimami, an Indian word describing a nearby point where 3 rivers join. When the CNR built from the village to The Pas (1908) as the first phase of the HUDSON BAY RAILWAY, Etoimami became Hudson Bay Junction. To forestry and the railway was added agriculture when federal authorities opened parts of surrounding forest reserves to settlement by returned soldiers and later by civilians (1920s). Additional settlement occurred when people moved north to escape the drought (1930s). By the end of WWII the community had grown sufficiently to obtain town status, a fact emphasized by dropping "Junction" from its name (1947). Since then, while growth has continued, the economy has been modified. The railway has reduced its work force, but the agricultural sector and especially forestry, Hudson Bay's mainstay, have become more sophisticated. Since 1960, 3 mills manufacturing various wood products and an alfalfa dehydration plant have arisen.

C.O. WHITE

Hudson Bay Railway Two of western Canada's earliest railway charters, granted in 1880, authorized construction, with government help, of railways paralleling old water transportation routes to Hudson Bay. The projects were amalgamated in 1883 and the first 64 km built northward into the Manitoba interlake region. Financial problems and a political scandal led to the abandonment of the original mileage in 1888, and the subsequent absorption of the charter by the CANADIAN NORTHERN RAILWAY. The Canadian Northern, with government aid designated for the Hudson Bay Ry, built a new northwesterly line from Winnipeg to Hudson Bay Junction (1908) as part of its east-west system. The Canadian Northern refused to build north of Hudson Bay Junction without further massive government assistance.

In 1909 the federal government undertook rail construction north of Hudson Bay Junction and improvement of harbour facilities at the proposed terminus of Nelson. During WWI work was suspended, and in 1923 the project became a part of CANADIAN NATIONAL RAILWAYS. Construction advanced only slowly and at great expense, particularly when Nelson was abandoned and the line deflected to the more northerly port of CHURCHILL. The railway opened officially on 10 Sept 1929 as the Hudson Bay Ry. Total cost exceeded $45 million. Intended as a grain road, the railway was a disappointment until mineral discoveries around The Pas and Thompson, Man, generated larger traffic volumes. T.D. REGEHR

Hudson Strait, arm of the sea connecting the Atlantic Ocean with HUDSON BAY and Foxe Channel and separating BAFFIN I from the Ungava Peninsula of Québec. The eastern gap is between Cape Chidley, at the northern tip of Labrador, and Resolution I. There are 250 km of open sea across UNGAVA BAY and the strait trends NW from Cape Hopes Advance to Cap de Nouvelle-France and then westerly to Cape Wolstenholme. Across the western gap is a group of 3 islands: Mill, Salisbury and Nottingham. The strait is never completely frozen over, and open water adds heat and moisture to the air, creating precipitation, cloud and fog. Resolution I is one of the foggiest places on Earth, with fog reported an average of one day in 2. The "insurance date of entry" into the strait is July 23, but ICEBREAKERS extend the sailing season.

Hudson Str provides access by sea to the heart of Canada and has been used commercially for 3 centuries, chiefly in connection with the FUR TRADE. Hudson's Bay Co vessels have used it since 1670. Navigation of the strait is not intricate; the route is wide and free from shoals. However, fog, current and the tidal stream made it tricky for early sailing vessels. The NORSE almost certainly knew the route. Martin FROBISHER mistakenly entered the strait in 1578, but Henry HUDSON – for whom it is named – was the first European known to have explored it and followed it into the bay. JAMES MARSH

Hudson 70 Expedition In 1970 the CSS *Hudson* completed the first circumnavigation of the Americas on the Hudson 70 expedition. The ship left Halifax in Nov 1969 and steamed south in the Atlantic to spend 2 months working in the Chilean fjords and south of Cape Horn. A south-to-north transect of the Pacific followed with the ship arriving in Vancouver in June 1970. After periods of work off the Canadian west coast and in the Beaufort Sea, the *Hudson* passed through the Northwest Passage to arrive back in Halifax in Nov 1970.

The expedition was undertaken to give scientists from Canada and other countries the opportunity to further their studies of the oceanography and biology of the S Atlantic, the Pacific and the Arctic. Over 120 scientific staff took part in the expedition and obtained a wealth of information. Highlights of the expedition were a comprehensive description of the oceanography and biology of the Chilean fjords, which was completed for comparison with the fjords of British Columbia and Norway; measurement

Detail of the charter granted to the Hudson's Bay Company by King Charles II, Westminster, 2 May 1670. Prince Rupert, shown in the upper left, had persuaded the king, merchants and noblemen to back the venture (*courtesy Hudson's Bay Company*).

of the strength of the antarctic circumpolar current as it passes between S America and Antarctica; studies of the geophysical structure of the sea floor off western Canada, which were to be considerably expanded in the years to come; and the first complete description of the marine geology of the Beaufort Sea. C.R. MANN

Hudson's Bay Company, chartered 2 May 1670, the oldest incorporated joint-stock merchandising company in the English-speaking world. Formerly headquartered in London, Eng; since 1970 its head offices have been situated in Winnipeg. The HBC is the largest retailer in Canada, operating about 400 stores in 4 retail groups: The Bay; SIMPSONS, LIMITED; Zeller's; and Field's. It is actively involved in REAL ESTATE development through Markborough Properties.

Médard Chouart DES GROSEILLIERS and Pierre-Esprit RADISSON were the first to propose a trading company to reach the interior of the continent via HUDSON BAY. After failing to obtain French support on their terms, in 1665 they went to England and interested Prince Rupert, cousin of Charles II. Rupert persuaded the king and some merchants and noblemen to back the venture. The first ships, the *Eaglet* and the NONSUCH, were dispatched in 1668 and the royal charter was proclaimed on 2 May 1670. The "Governor and Company of Adventurers" were granted wide powers, including exclusive trading rights in the territory traversed by rivers flowing into Hudson Bay. This vast region was named RUPERT'S LAND.

Unlike most contemporary trading concerns, the HBC evolved as a joint-stock company with a centralized bureaucracy. At the annual General Court, shareholders elected a governor and committee to organize fur auctions, order trade goods, hire men and arrange for shipping. They appointed a governor to act on their behalf in the bay area. Each post was commanded by a chief factor (trader) and his council of officers. The London governor and committee set all the basic policies implemented in Rupert's Land, basing their decisions on annual reports, post journals and account books supplied by the officials on the bay.

Until 1763 the HBC struggled with the French for control of the fur trade of southern Rupert's Land. In the early years a series of naval and land battles took place on Hudson and James bays. In 1713, by the Treaty of UTRECHT, France acknowledged England's claim to Hudson Bay. For the next 60 years the HBC erected posts only at the mouths of major rivers flowing into the bay, with the single exception of Henley House, a small outpost erected in 1743 on the Albany R, 200 km from the coast. After the Treaty of PARIS (1763) the company's French rivals were replaced by a much more formidable opposition, the Montréal-based overland trade network taken over by the British.

By 1774 HBC trade had been undercut enough that the governor and the committee embarked on an aggressive policy of inland expansion beginning with the building of CUMBERLAND HOUSE on the lower Saskatchewan R. Intensive competition with the NORTH WEST COMPANY spilled beyond Rupert's Land into the Mackenzie drainage basin and the Pacific slope, combining economic conflict with occasional physical violence (*see* SEVEN OAKS INCIDENT). In 1821 a merger of the 2 parties was arranged, and the British Parliament confirmed and extended the company's monopoly privileges to include the North-West Territories.

The bringing together of different business traditions required changes in the administrative structure of the new company. BRITISH NORTH AMERICA was divided into trading departments which were then subdivided into districts. District managers met annually in departmental council meetings presided over by the governor in N America, a post held 1826-60 by Sir George SIMPSON. These councils passed regulations governing local trade, determined the deployment of men and posts and established the logistical requirements of the various districts. The officers had a vested interest in these concerns since they shared in the profits of the trade according to the terms set out in deed polls in 1821, 1834 and 1871. Council members theoretically had an equal voice and vote, but Simpson had considerable power, and the London governor and committee could overrule council decisions.

After 1821 a group of independent free traders among the Métis population at the RED RIVER COLONY opposed the company's monopoly rights, which had been renewed by Parliament for another 20 years in 1838. The issue culminated in the famous SAYER TRIAL of 1849, in which Pierre-Guillaume Sayer was tried and convicted of trading with the Indians in violation of the company's legal privileges. Fearing a Métis riot, however, the court did not pass sentence. The decision effectively opened the trade of southern Rupert's Land to many small-scale competitors.

Although the company's primary concern remained the fur trade, it became increasingly involved in providing government for settlers in the Red River Valley and on Vancouver I. Between 1812 and 1834 the governors of ASSINIBOIA were agents of the SELKIRK estate, although they were overshadowed by the HBC. In 1834 the company resumed jurisdiction and, until transfer to Canada, provided the Selkirk colony's government. In 1849 Britain granted to the HBC the colony of Vancouver I, which was to be developed as an agricultural settlement. In 1851 Chief Factor James DOUGLAS was appointed governor. In 1858, following the discovery of gold, the mainland colony of British Columbia, including most of present BC, was created out of NEW CALEDONIA. Douglas was required by the British government to resign his HBC commission before becoming governor of BC. In this way the company began to relinquish its colonial responsibilities.

In 1863 the International Financial Society bought controlling interest in the HBC, signalling a shift in the company's outlook: most of the new shareholders were less interested in the fur trade than in real estate speculation and economic development in the West. Negotiations conducted with the COLONIAL OFFICE and, after 1867, with the Canadian government eventually resulted in the sale of Rupert's Land to Canada in 1870. As part of the agreement the company received £300 000 and one-twentieth of the fertile areas to be opened for settlement. In addition, it retained title to the lands on which it had built trading establishments. The terms of the agreement strongly influenced company development after 1870. By retaining large landholdings on the prairies and the parcels adjacent to its posts, many of which were located in developing urban centres in the West and North, the HBC was able to become one of the most important developers in western Canada. Since the 1874 establishment of the Land Commissioner's Office, the company has continued to be a major real-estate developer, acquiring control of Markborough Properties in 1973.

Involvement in natural-resource development stemmed naturally out of the HBC's fur-trade and real-estate activities. In 1926 it cofounded Hudson's Bay Oil and Gas, and in 1973 acquired 35% of Siebens Oil and Gas. In 1979, the same year it was acquired by Kenneth THOMSON, it disposed of the latter and in 1980 bought controlling interest in Roxy Petroleum. In 1982 the HBOG investment was sold to Dome Petroleum.

As economic development in the PRAIRIE WEST accelerated after 1870, the company did an increasing amount of business with settlers. Initially most of this activity was carried on at its trading posts. Since it differed in many respects from the Indian trade, separate sales shop accounts were kept. From this modest beginning the HBC's retail and wholesale divisions eventually emerged, with outlets entirely separate from the fur trade. Expansion was augmented by the 1978 acquisition of controlling interest in the Simpsons and Zeller's retail chains. With 41 000 employees, the HBC in 1986 had sales of \$5.7 billion (ranking 9th in Canada) and assets of \$4.3 billion (ranking 21st). Foreign ownership stood at 3%, and the Woodbridge Co Ltd owned 74% of the shares. In the mid-1980s some streamlining became necessary. The London and Canadian fur sales operations were sold in 1986, and the following year the Northern Stores Division and Hudson's Bay Wholesale were both sold. Since 1972 most of the Bay's senior officers have been located in Toronto, although the official headquarters of the company remain in Winnipeg. ARTHUR J. RAY

Reading: E.E. Rich, *The History of the Hudson's Bay Company 1670-1870* (3 vols, 1960) and *The Fur Trade and the Northwest to 1857* (1967); Douglas Mackay, *The Honourable Company* (1966); Peter C. Newman, *The Company of Adventurers* (1985) and *Caesars of the Wilderness* (1987).

Hudson's Bay Record Society, est 1938 by the HUDSON'S BAY CO to publish selections from its extensive company records accumulated since 1670. Under an agreement with The CHAMPLAIN SOCIETY, 12 volumes appeared, 1938-49. Thereafter the publications became the sole responsibility of the London-based HBC. Since 1960 the volumes have been published biennially; they are available only to the approximately 1150 members. The society's headquarters was transferred to Winnipeg in 1974, and the following year Hartwell Bowsfield of York U became the first Canadian general editor. By 1983, 33 volumes of minutes, correspondence and journals of trade and exploration dating from 1671 to 1889 had been published. In 1983 the society was disbanded, but the publications have continued under the auspices of the Rupert's Land Research Soc (est 1984). This society promotes Canadian history through biannual colloquia, newsletters and publications such as the *Native Canadian Anthropology and History: A Selected Bibliography*.
SHIRLEE ANNE SMITH

Hughes, Edward John, painter (b at N Vancouver 17 Feb 1913). A realist landscape painter, he has produced work that is as unique an expression of BC's geography as is that of Emily CARR. He studied under F.H. VARLEY and Jock MACDONALD at Vancouver's School of Decorative and Applied Arts 1929-34. With colleagues from the art school, he established a commercial art firm which executed pencil portraits and designs for calendars and posters, and did several mural commissions. Hughes enlisted in the army in 1939 and was appointed a WAR ARTIST in 1940, in that post producing about 1600 works. During these years, his style became more decorative and expressive, influenced by his study of Mexican artists and the French primitive painter Henri Rousseau. Hughes returned to Victoria after the war and tried unsuccessfully to make a living as a landscape painter. In 1951 he moved N to Shawnigan Lk and signed a contract with Max Stern of Dominion Gallery, Montréal.

Hughes's love of privacy has kept him in seclusion on Vancouver I. Though concentrating on scenes of Vancouver I, Hughes has produced paintings of the BC interior, Alberta and major Canadian cities. He usually includes people or evidence of a human presence in the landscape – ships, boats or buildings. *Dawson's Landing, River's Inlet* (1963) is typical of his mature style with its balanced composition and clear, strong colours. His drawings range from light landscape sketches to highly finished graphite studies and elegant pencil portraits. JANE YOUNG

Hughes, James Laughlin, educator, author (b near Bowmanville, Ont 20 Feb 1846; d at Toronto 3 Jan 1935), elder brother of Sir Sam HUGHES. Educated at Toronto Normal School, he became principal of its associated Model School at age 24. In 1874 he was appointed inspector of public schools for Toronto, and later chief inspector, a position he held until his retirement in 1913. During these years Hughes adapted Toronto's public schools to the demands of an emerging urban-industrial order, increasing pupil attendance, improving the quality of instruction, and introducing kindergartens and manual-training classes. In the 1890 provincial election he was defeated as the EQUAL RIGHTS candidate in Peel constituency. Throughout his life he was active in the Orange Lodge, the Methodist church and Toronto athletic organizations. He wrote a number of educational books, including *Froebel's Educational Laws* (1898) and *Dickens as an Educator* (1900), plus several volumes of poetry, including *Songs of Gladness and Growth* (1915) and *In Nature's Temple Shrines* (1921). ROBERT M. STAMP

Hughes, Monica, née Irse, author (b at Liverpool, Eng 3 Nov 1925). Before immigrating to Canada in 1952, Hughes lived and studied in Cairo, London, Edinburgh and Zimbabwe. Since beginnning writing professionally in 1971 she has published 18 novels and has won nearly every major Canadian award for young-adult fiction. Her central characters are psychologically credible adolescents struggling towards maturity. Twelve of the works are nominally classed as SCIENCE FICTION though Hughes's plots centre on contemporary dilemmas: *Crisis on Conself 10* (1975) and *Earthdark* (1977) on feeding an overpopulated world and *Devil on My Back* (1984) on the consequences of over-dependence on technology. *Beyond the Dark River* (1979) and *Ring-Rise, Ring Set* (1982) forms on Canadian Indian, Inuit and Hutterite sub-cultures. Her best work, *Hunter in the Dark* (1982), studies a 16-year old athlete struggling to come to terms with his mortality on a solitary hunting expedition during a period of remission from a possibly fatal disease. *Blaine's Way* (1986) deals with an Ontario farm boy's coming of age in WWII. GERALD J. RUBIO

Hughes, Sir Samuel, teacher, journalist, soldier, politician (b at Darlington, Canada W 8 Jan 1853; d at Lindsay, Ont 24 Aug 1921). A Conservative and an enthusiastic supporter of Sir John A. Macdonald's NATIONAL POLICY, Sam Hughes was elected to Parliament for Victoria North in 1892. Vain, colourful, charming and splenetic, Hughes made a 30-year public career of politics and militia service. A longtime proponent of the volunteer militia and the imperial connection, he helped force PM LAURIER to send Canadian troops to the SOUTH AFRICAN WAR in 1899. Hughes was dismissed from that war for military indiscipline and public exposure of incompetent British generalship. These experiences produced a Canadian nationalist slant to Hughes's imperialist leanings. By 1911, with years of solid caucus and parliamentary service – including 10 years as Opposition militia critic – and personal loyalty to R.L. BORDEN behind him, Hughes won the militia portfolio in Borden's new government. Hughes promoted citizen-soldiers over professionals (to the latter's detriment), and preached the social value of military training and national preparedness.

Early in WWI, Hughes was hailed as the genius of the war effort. Unfortunately, favouritism, confused civil-military functions, disrespect of Cabinet, administrative incompetence and scandals such as the ROSS RIFLE fiasco (*see* ARMAMENTS) forced Borden to fire Hughes in Nov 1916. He died in 1921, a reluctant and sometimes bitter Conservative-Unionist MP for Victoria-Haliburton. Although Hughes was a sincere Canadian and a successful constituency politician, his erratic talents never matched the demands of high office during total war. RONALD G. HAYCOCK

Reading: R.G. Haycock, *Sam Hughes: The Public Career of a Controversial Canadian 1885-1916* (1987).

Hughes, Stanley John, mycologist (b at Llanelly, Wales 17 Sept 1918). A naturalized Canadian, Hughes worked as an assistant mycologist, Commonwealth Mycological Institute, Kew, Eng (1945-52), and in 1952 joined Agriculture Canada in Ottawa as a research scientist. Hughes initiated a new era in the systematics of conidial fungi by focusing attention on the mechanisms of spore ontogeny. He has also contributed an elegant taxonomic analysis of the "sooty-mold" complex. He has received several honours including the Jakob Eriksson Gold Medal, Swedish Academy of Science (1969) and the George Lawson Medal, Canadian Botanical Assn (1981). In 1975 he was president of the Mycological Soc of America, and from 1971 to 1983 VP of the Intl Mycological Assn. Since then he has been honorary research associate, Biosystemics Research Centre, Central Experimental Farm, and in 1986 he was elected a foreign member of the Linnean Society of London. K.A. PIROZYNSKI

Huguenin, Anne-Marie, author, journalist (b at Rimouski 5 Oct 1875; d at Montréal 21 Oct 1943). A pioneer of women's journalism in Canada, in 1897 Huguenin began writing for *Le Monde illustré* under the assumed name Myrto. A founding member of *La Bonne Parole*, in Nov 1919 she established *Le Revue moderne*, which she edited for 8 years. In 1928 she founded another review, *La Vie canadienne*, which she merged with *La Revue moderne* in Oct 1929. Author of several books, including *Premier Péché* (1902), *Le Long du chemin* (1912), *Le Meilleur de soi* (1924) and *Portrait de femme* (1938), her writing is marked by its patriotic fervour and her sympathy for the poor. Her journalistic and charitable work during WWI won her La Reconnaissance française in 1920 and La Reconnaissance belge Roi Albert in 1921.
CARMAN MILLER

Huguenots, a popular term used since 1560 to designate French Protestants, some of whom became involved in the Newfoundland fishery and Canadian fur trade, and in abortive colonization attempts in Canada (1541-42), Brazil (1555) and the Carolinas (1562-64). The Edict of Nantes (1598), granting limited toleration, enabled Pierre Chauvin and the Sieur de MONTS to found bases at TADOUSSAC (1600) and PORT-ROYAL (1605), and Reformed pastors to serve fishermen and sailors. Missionary work was restricted to Roman CATHOLICS, however, and after 1627 in Canada and 1659 in ACADIA neither Protestant worship nor Protestant teaching was permitted. A trickle of Protestants came to Canada as merchants, soldiers, indentured servants and even FILLES DU ROI. Under British rule the term "French Protestant" came into use, and Huguenot immigration to Nova Scotia and recruitment of Channel Island pastors for Québec were encouraged.

In 1834 the independent Lausanne Missionary Society established a centre at Grande-Ligne, Lower Canada. In 1839 the French Canadian Missionary Society was organized in Montréal, and in 1846 a Bible college was established at Pointe-aux-Trembles, and the publication *Le Semeur canadien* was launched in 1853. The Montréal Presbyterian College, est 1867, assured the training of French Reformed clergy after 1880. In 1875 a synod was called to organize a national Reformed church, but the scheme was abandoned in 1877 in favour of independent local congregations. Although the Grande-Ligne missions joined the BAPTISTS, many French Protestants affiliated with the PRESBYTERIANS, eventually to become francophone congregations of the UNITED CHURCH OF CANADA. CORNELIUS J. JAENEN

Reading: Marc-André Bédard, *Les Protestants en Nouvelle-France* (1978); Cornelius J. Jaenen, *The Role of the Church in New France* (1976).

Hull, Qué, City, pop 58 722 (1986c), 56 225 (1981c), inc 1875, is located on the N shore of the OTTAWA R, W of the Rivière Gatineau, across from OTTAWA. Part of the National Capital Region (NCR) and of the Communauté régionale de l'Outaouais (CRO), it is the hub of the AYLMER-

Federal government building complex at Hull, Qué. Ottawa, Ont, is located across the river (top of photo) (*photo by Jim Merrithew*).

Hull-GATINEAU urban area and the regional capital of western Québec, which is commonly called the *Outaouais*.

History Prior to the arrival of Philemon WRIGHT from Woburn, Mass, in 1800, Hull shared a common history with all the areas along the Ottawa R, which was the primary water route to the West. Explorers, missionaries, fur traders and the military of the French and English regimes used the portage paths that crossed Hull. One of these, the Second Chaudière Portage, situated in Brébeuf Park, still shows the crudely hewn stone steps built there by the VOYAGEURS. Hull was the first permanent town established on the Ottawa R. Wright and his associates were given ownership of large tracts of land in Hull and Templeton townships. The small agricultural community, called Wrightstown, quickly turned to the production of squared timber for the British market. The first lumber raft from the area, the "Colombo," reached Québec City in 1806, heralding the beginnings of the lumber industry in the Ottawa Valley.

Ezra Butler EDDY, a citizen of Vermont, settled in Hull in 1851 and built up his equity by manufacturing handmade matches, washboards and clothespins. In the 1870s he became one of the leading sawmill operators at the Chaudière Falls. His match and indurated fibreware production, as well as his pioneering efforts in pulp (1889) and paper manufacture (1890), made Hull one of the main centres of the pulp and paper industry. Axe factories, meat-packing establishments, textile firms and other related industries followed. This industrial development attracted numerous French Canadian workers to Hull and radically changed its ethnic and religious composition. From 1861 to 1871, Hull Township's French-speaking population increased tenfold (from 420 to 4461) while its English-speaking population grew by less than 20% (from 3291 to 3857). Today, 89% of Hull's citizens have French as their mother tongue, 6% English and 5% Portuguese and other languages. Some 97% are Roman Catholic. On its incorporation in 1875, the town was renamed Hull after a city in Yorkshire, Eng.

Economy The Hull economy, essentially based on manufacturing in the 1940s, has changed radically. The majority of its labour force are now white-collar workers, with civil servants forming the largest bloc. The change began after WWII, with the closing of steel foundries and textile factories. The Trudeau government's decision to relocate a large number of federal civil servants in Hull accelerated the rate of change.

The political decision to transform Hull into the capital city's left bank has been interpreted by some as a growing dependancy of Hull on Ottawa and by others (especially representatives of the leftist, nationalist and social pressure groups of the Island of Hull) as outright "dépossession." But for a vast majority of Hull residents this bulldozing away of inferior housing and worker tenement buildings has been heralded as progress and as the end of a way of life that was too closely identified to poverty and blue-collar values. In fact, Hull's economy has been closely linked to that of Ottawa ever since the building of the Rideau Canal (1826-32). The changes that Hull has witnessed since the early 1960s have probably had an opposite impact. The creation of Hull's Roman Catholic Diocese (1963), the large-scale expropriation of land and the transfer of federal government employees (1970-80), the building of infrastructures (water, sewer, roads, bridges) vital to any modern development, the birth of institutions such as the Université du Québec and the CEGEP, and the arrival of large shopping centres have repatriated a good deal of cultural and commercial activity. Hull has slowly become similar to Ottawa. In some ways it is now capable of being a rival of Ottawa, although there is still a very long way to go before Hull can boast to being an equal of Ottawa. In order to do so, the 3 sister cities of the Québec side of the national capital (Hull, Gatineau and Aylmer) will have to put aside the often intense rivalry that plagues the left bank's development.

Cityscape The city of Hull covers some 3 km^2; its core is an island linked to Ottawa by 4 bridges. It has been shaped by its original division into half lots by the Wrights, for rental purposes, and by the Great Fire of 1900, which destroyed two-thirds of the town. In the early 1960s it was a typical medium-size industrial Québec town, with 2-storey brick worker dwellings surrounding a few public parks and buildings, linked together by its business section. As fire, demolition and renovation took their toll, the main public landmarks fell, the city core was changed radically and large developments – Place du Portage and Terrasses de la Chaudière – were built. The city extended into suburbia, with typical bungalows and shopping centres, and the old business section started to decline. Hull's population fell from 63 580 in 1971 to 58 772 in 1986, while that of its suburban sister cities (Gatineau and Aylmer) swelled from a combined 72 163 in 1971, to 110 220 in 1986.

Hull's cultural and social life is closely linked to that of Ottawa, Gatineau and Aylmer. It offers services that do not exist in the surrounding Québec municipalities, such as U du Québec à Hull, the Conservatoire de musique de l'Outaouais, the Centre régional des Archives nationales du Québec, the Palais des Congrès convention centre and the Théâtre de l'Île. In 1988 the Canadian Museum of Civilization will move from Ottawa to a new building located in Hull. It is well served by radio, TV and newspaper, though some of these are based in Aylmer, Gatineau and Ottawa. Many Hull residents attend U of O, and Carleton and Saint Paul universities. Two festivals highlight Hull's yearly calendar of events: the Festival international de la bicyclette de Hull (Aug) and Bal de neiges (Feb). The city is the gateway to Gatineau Park (administered by the NATIONAL CAPITAL COMMISSION), giving access to lakes, parks and 40 km of cycling paths. *See also* statistical table in the OTTAWA entry. PIERRE-LOUIS LAPOINTE

Hull, Robert Marvin, hockey player (b at Pointe Anne, Ont 3 Jan 1939). He played junior hockey in Hespeler [Cambridge], Woodstock and St Catharines and joined Chicago Black Hawks in 1957. Though he scored only 31 goals in his first 2 seasons, Hull developed a fearsome slapshot (clocked at 187 km/h) and went on to become the highest-scoring left-winger in hockey history. His nickname "Golden Jet" aptly described him in motion, and his speed, power and drive epitomized the sport of hockey. He led Chicago to its first STANLEY CUP victory in 23 years (1960-61), dramatically equalled the record of 50 goals in a season (1961-62) and raised it to 54 (1965-66) and 58 (1968-69). He won the ART ROSS TROPHY 3 times, the HART TROPHY twice and the LADY BYNG TROPHY once, scoring 610 goals and 1170 points in 15 NHL seasons. In 1972 he accepted $1 million to jump from the NHL to the WINNIPEG JETS, giving immediate credibility to the fledgling WORLD HOCKEY ASSN. He continued his prolific scoring, with 77 goals in 78 games in 1974-75, adding 303 goals and 638 points to his totals. He attempted a comeback in 1980-81 with NY Rangers but was released in training camp. JAMES MARSH

Human Rights, claimed by individuals and groups, are considered so fundamental to human dignity that they receive special protection under the law and usually under the constitution of a country. They differ from CIVIL LIBERTIES, which refer to traditional Western values, eg, freedom of religion and expression, in that they require government intervention rather than restriction of government action. The distinction was even more crucial in Canada before the entrenchment of the CANADIAN CHARTER OF RIGHTS AND FREEDOMS; rights were defended by law, but liberties were merely tolerated and could be removed by government. After WWI, and more particularly after WWII, it became apparent that other needs basic to human dignity were not being met through civil liberties restrictions. To protect those who suffered discriminatory treatment from private persons, groups or governments or who suffered economic deprivation because of loss of health or job, legislatures began to enact laws to forbid discrimination, to provide administrative assistance to victims of discrimination and to provide compensation for injury or loss of employment to the economically deprived.

A series of treaties after WWI imposed upon

several European countries the obligation for the protection of racial, religious and national minorities and authorized the LEAGUE OF NATIONS to supervise the execution of these obligations. In 1948 the UNITED NATIONS General Assembly proclaimed the Universal Declaration of Human Rights as the "common standard of achievement for all peoples and all nations to the end that every individual and every organ of society, keeping this declaration constantly in mind, shall strive by teaching and education to promote respect for these rights and freedoms, and by progressive measures national and international, to secure their universal and effective recognition and observance." Included were the fundamental freedoms and legal rights (known internationally as civil and political liberties or rights), as well as those of equality, and economic, social and cultural rights. The declaration was accepted by unanimous vote, with the 6 members of the Soviet bloc, Saudi Arabia and the Union of S Africa abstaining. In 1966, the 1948 declaration was supplemented by 2 binding covenants – the International Covenant on Civil and Political Rights and the International Covenant on Economic, Social and Cultural Rights. Canada ratified both covenants in 1976 (with the unanimous consent of the provinces) and they are now binding upon Canada in INTERNATIONAL LAW. Canada also ratified the Optional Protocol to the Civil and Political Rights Covenant so that every individual in Canada can now complain to the Human Rights Committee if a Canadian government is not meeting covenant requirements. Canada also accepted another optional obligation, accepting complaints of other states – parties to the covenant – which have also accepted this state party-to-state party complaint procedure.

The human rights of equality have only recently been proclaimed in Canada. Before the British Emancipation Act of 1833 (effective a year later), SLAVERY was practised in the colonies, and after Confederation discriminatory laws were enacted to discourage the immigration of nonwhites (*see* IMMIGRATION POLICY). Those who had already entered or continued to do so despite the restrictions, as well as native peoples, were subject to laws placing them in segregated schools, denying them the franchise, restricting their entry into professions and certain types of employment, restricting their areas of residence, prohibiting their consumption of alcohol and even denying them equal access to public facilities. In the 19th century, women and children were treated as chattels; property rights were restricted (*see* MURDOCH CASE), and the male head of the family could disinherit his wife and children in his will. Women did not gain the federal vote until WWI and did not gain the provincial vote in all provinces until 1940. Women were not considered "persons" eligible for appointment to the Senate until 1929. By WWII most laws restricting rights of women and children were changed, but some racist laws continued for a few years thereafter, while those denying the franchise to native people were not altered until after the enactment of the CANADIAN BILL OF RIGHTS in 1960.

The history of the Bill of Rights reveals how recently, in Canada, the concept of human rights has been expanded to include equality rights. The result of 2 petitions submitted to Parliament by the JEHOVAH'S WITNESSES, many of whom were arrested in Québec during the 1940s, the Bill was championed by John DIEFENBAKER, who had been a strong defender of the Witnesses during WWII. The Bill of Rights was not entrenched, however, and could be amended in Parliament by the normal legislative process. Moreover, it applied only to the federal jurisdiction.

Although Saskatchewan had had a Bill of Rights since 1947, fair-accommodation and fair-employment-practices Acts were enacted throughout Canada only after 1951, followed by equal-pay Acts for women. In the 1960s the provinces started to consolidate fair-practices statutes into comprehensive human-rights codes, administered and enforced by permanent human-rights commissions. By 1975 every province had done so. The federal Canadian Human Rights Act and Commission were created in 1977. Alberta, Saskatchewan and Québec also provide protection for the fundamental freedoms, and Saskatchewan and Alberta added limited legal-rights protections in their Human Rights Code and Bill of Rights. The Québec Charter of Rights and Freedoms (1975) provides for extensive legal-rights protections, and even proclaims certain economic and social rights.

Human rights are better promoted through administrative agencies than through the courts. In addition to creating human-rights commissions, most Canadian jurisdictions have established the institution of the OMBUDSMAN, to which people can complain against unfair exercise of valid discretionary power, or failure to exercise it. To protect cultural rights, government funds have to be expended. This is particularly true with economic and social-welfare rights, which require positive government action rather than judicial restraint.

The Constitution Act, 1982, not only provides for future amendment of all Constitution Acts to be made in Canada, but includes the Canadian Charter of Rights and Freedoms guaranteeing fundamental freedoms, democratic rights (of participation in elections), mobility rights (to and from and within Canada), legal rights, equality rights (including equal rights of men and women, and protection of the multicultural heritage of all Canadians), language rights (and minority-language education rights), as well as the right to enforce these. But although the Constitution is "the supreme law of the land" and "any law that is inconsistent with the provisions of the Constitution is, to the extent of the inconsistency, of no force or effect," the adoption of the Charter does not of itself guarantee human rights. Although its primary purpose is to restrain government action through judicial enforcement, the scope of civil liberties such as freedom of expression will not be known for some time. To what extent is censorship inconsistent with the Charter? When is it reasonable to limit freedom of assembly for reasons of public security or order? Are actions taken under the WAR MEASURES ACT a reasonable restriction on civil liberties? These questions can only be answered by the courts. However, because s33 of the Charter permits any government to enact laws "notwithstanding the Charter," a majority government wanting to do so must be restrained through the combined action of individuals, public-interest groups, political parties, the media and members of the legislature.

WALTER S. TARNOPOLSKY

Humane Societies are societies for the prevention of cruelty to animals (SPCA). Following a long struggle by Richard Martin, British landowner and parliamentarian, and others to secure legislation against cruelty to children and livestock, the first SPCA was begun in England in 1824. Although Martin was a founding member, the organization was formed by the Rev Arthur Broome, an Anglican clergyman, and Lewis Gompertz, a Jewish author. At Queen Victoria's command, the society became known as the Royal Society for the Prevention of Cruelty to Animals in 1840. The RSPCA was the forerunner of the Children's Aid Society.

The humane or animal-welfare movement was introduced to N America by Henry Bergh. Following a visit to the RSPCA, he organized the American SPCA in New York in 1866. In the same year the first law for the protection of animals was passed. The first humane society in Canada was the Canadian SPCA in Montréal (est 1869). Societies were soon established in Québec (1870), Ottawa (1871) and Toronto (1873). Humane societies now exist in major Canadian cities and in some 85 municipalities throughout the provinces. All are nonprofit, charitable organizations; most operate shelters, which take in lost and abandoned animals (mostly CATS and DOGS). They are often also responsible for municipal animal-control activities. Many operate under provincial SPCA or Animal Protection Acts, with authority to investigate complaints of cruelty to animals and to lay charges where necessary. Society inspectors may use the Cruelty to Animals Section of the Criminal Code of Canada. They may not carry firearms but may, with court permission, remove suffering animals from the possession of their owners.

As the number of SPCAs involved in animal-welfare work at the provincial and municipal levels increased, so did the need to respond collectively to problems of national scope, eg, transportation and slaughter of food animals. Thus, in the mid- to late 1950s Dr A.E. Cameron, a retired veterinary general of Canada, Lt-Col Richard Taylor, president of the Ottawa Humane Society, Senator F.A. McGrand and K. Switzer, managing director of the Ottawa Humane Society, organized meetings to discuss formation of a national SPCA. The Canadian Federation of Humane Societies received its federal charter in 1957 and has its headquarters in Ottawa. It is an umbrella group for 42 autonomous member societies across Canada; most are SPCAs but other organizations concerned with specific animal-welfare issues are included. CFHS does not engage in the daily activities of shelter operations, but addresses issues that have broader implications. CFHS interacts with 10 federal government departments having jurisdiction, in some way, over national, international and interprovincial aspects of man's use of animals.

NEAL R. JOTHAM

Reading: C.G. Niven, *History of the Humane Movement* (1967); J. Turner, *Reckoning with the Beast* (1980).

Humber River, 153 km long, drainage basin 7680 km^2, is the principal river of western Newfoundland. Named for the English river, it rises in the LONG RANGE MOUNTAINS W of White Bay and flows SE and then SW to Deer Lk, where it is joined by a tributary draining the 100-km-long Grand Lk. The Humber flows SW from Deer Lk into Humber Arm at CORNER BROOK and on into the Bay of Islands, having fallen nearly 660 m from its sources. The river is rich in ATLANTIC SALMON and was, from the 1800s, a waterway for European trappers. Though its mouth had been charted by James COOK in the 1760s, there was little permanent settlement in the region until the mid-1800s. Flowing through great stands of timber, the Humber has been used by loggers since the late 1800s.

ROBERT D. PITT

Humboldt, Sask, Town, pop 5089 (1986c), 4705 (1981c), inc 1907, is located at a CNR-CPR junction, 112 km E of Saskatoon. Founded on the arrival of the Canadian Northern Ry (1904), it assumed the name of a nearby Dominion Telegraph Line office named for the German scientist, author and explorer Alexander von Humboldt, who travelled extensively throughout N and S America. Situated on the Carlton Trail, the town originally served as a stage depot on the main cart and stagecoach trail from Ft Qu'Appelle to Ft Carlton. Its designation as a railway divisional point fostered growth, as did the establishment of St Peters

Colony (50 townships) by the Roman Catholic Order of St Benedict (1903). Situated on the black soil of the aspen parkland in a relatively risk-free crop area, Humboldt became the colony's largest centre and is now the province's largest town. While certain early commercial enterprises such as wholesale grocers and a tannery have disappeared, others (eg, a flour mill) still operate, and the town continues to grow as an agricultural service centre. It is also a judicial and administrative centre and in 1975 became the Prairie provinces' central testing station for agricultural equipment with the opening of the Prairie Agricultural Machinery Institute. C.O. WHITE

The rufous hummingbird (*Selasphorus rufus*) is one of 4 species in Canada (*photo by Tim Fitzharris*).

Hummingbird, common name for New World family Trochilidae, which numbers 341 species. It is one of the largest bird families and contains the smallest known bird (bee hummingbird, 2 g). Males, in particular, come in an astonishing variety of sizes, shapes, colours and plumage. In flight, the wings of some beat so rapidly that they produce a humming sound (hence the name). They are the only birds able to hover in midair and fly backwards. Their energy comes from flower nectar; small insects supply protein for growth. The hummingbird has a very fast metabolism. Feeding on almost 1000 flowers daily, it consumes almost half its body weight in sugar. At night and in periods of bad weather, certain species fall into a semiconscious state to conserve energy. Four species nest in Canada, breeding as far W as Alberta. The ruby-throated hummingbird (*Archilochus colubris*) is the only species in eastern Canada. The black-chinned, small calliope and rufous hummingbirds (*A. alexandri, Stellula calliope, Selasphorus rufus*, respectively) nest only in western Canada, only the last in widespread areas. Canadian species nest in trees, laying 2 white eggs. Hummingbirds can be attracted into gardens if flowers with long corollas are grown or small flasks of sugar water are set out, and can be induced to perch on a person's finger while feeding. JEAN-LUC DESGRANGES

Humorous Writing in English It is perhaps paradoxical that the first major work of Canadian humour – Thomas MCCULLOCH'S "Letters of Mephibosheth Stepsure" (1821-23) – should have been written by a man whose other credits included *Popery Condemned* and *Calvinism*. There has always been a perception of something dour, grim and northern about our national literature; critics seeking our defining images have talked of "survival" in a "harsh and lovely land." Our stories are often of failures and victims, our heroes freeze in snowdrifts, and our marriages (like most of our shipping) end up on the rocks.

One major factor inhibiting the early growth of a humorous tradition in Canadian literature was that most writing in the 19th century was dominated by a colonial mentality which looked to the "high seriousness" of English romanticism for its model. A poet who takes himself solemnly (which is not quite the same thing as taking himself seriously) finds it difficult to devote a whole poem to anything as trivial as a joke. One mark of an immature writer, or indeed of a whole literature which has not yet attained self-confidence, is the straining after big, "serious" topics. Robertson DAVIES comments that as late as 1920 to 1935, "we were not sufficiently sure of ourselves in this country to realize that a humorist may be a serious literary artist." The Canadian inferiority complex (which even today leads to much unprofitable anguish over the need to supply a recipe for "the Canadian identity") did not allow a writer the luxury of making a fool of himself in public.

The Canadian tradition of humorous writing has generally been stronger in prose than in poetry. McCulloch's satirical letters, which began appearing in the Halifax weekly *Acadian Recorder* in 1821, have been described by Northrop FRYE as exhibiting a tone "quiet, observant, deeply conservative in a human sense, [which] has been the prevailing tone of Canadian humour ever since." McCulloch's use of a satirical persona – the "conventional, old-fashioned, homespun" farmer – places him in a classical tradition which reaches back to Addison and Swift, and forward to Davies's Samuel Marchbanks and John METCALF'S James Wells in *General Ludd* (1980). Whereas McCulloch's style was dry, subtle and understated, his immediate successor, Thomas Chandler HALIBURTON, proclaimed similarly conservative social values through the brash, colloquial, overstated persona of Sam Slick, the Yankee Clockmaker. From his first appearance in *The* CLOCKMAKER (1836), Sam Slick proved immensely popular and ironically has influenced American humour as much as Canadian.

After these promising beginnings, however, Canada had to wait until 1910 for the appearance of its next major comic writer. That year *Literary Lapses* launched the national and international reputation of Stephen LEACOCK. Leacock's masterpiece, SUNSHINE SKETCHES OF A LITTLE TOWN (1912), was followed 2 years later by the finely satirical *Arcadian Adventures with the Idle Rich*. In Leacock's more than 30 books of humour there was much inferior work; Robertson Davies ascribes his failure to develop into a major comic novelist as due, at least in part, to his unwillingness to carry through the darker implications of his comedy. Critical debate on *Sunshine Sketches* continues to centre on the balance between its irony and its indulgence, and between Leacock's criticism of the townspeople and his nostalgic affection for them.

One of Leacock's more permanent legacies was the establishment of the Stephen Leacock Medal for Humour, of which a most worthy early recipient was Paul HIEBERT'S *Sarah Binks* (1947). Hiebert offers a broad but telling pastiche of the academic biography, but the true genius of the book lies in the creation of what John Moss has called "some of the world's best bad poetry." The verses of the "sweet songstress of Saskatchewan" are fine parodies of Canadian poetry. SARAH BINKS is a comic creation which derives from Canadian literature while simultaneously making a contribution to it. In this it has few rivals, though one may be George BOWERING'S *A Short Sad Book* (1977).

As we move into the period of the full maturity of the Canadian novel, we find an increasing use of humour, in many forms. There is the good-natured humour of W.O. MITCHELL, a born teller of tall tales, as reflected in the conservative, traditional comic world of WHO HAS SEEN THE WIND (1947). A much sharper edge of satire is to be found in the work of Mordecai RICHLER, but even in a novel such as *The* APPRENTICESHIP OF DUDDY KRAVITZ (1959), the most memorable scenes are those – like the Bar Mitzvah movie or the epileptics' newsletter – in which the exuberance of comic exaggeration outstrips the strict necessities of satirical mordancy. A blacker, wilder, more fantastic strain of humour illuminates the novels of Leonard COHEN, especially BEAUTIFUL LOSERS (1966). And in novels such as Sheila WATSON'S *The* DOUBLE HOOK (1959) humour deepens into a more profound sense of comedy as a redemptive vision of life.

Recent Canadian comic novels have moved towards an exuberant, overstated comedy of exaggeration and fantasy. This is evident in Ray SMITH'S *Lord Nelson's Tavern* (1974) and in Leo Simpson's *The Peacock Papers* (1973), in which an angel announcing the end of the world regrets particularly the demise of the Hamilton Tiger-Cats. (Like Simpson, Robertson Davies, in *The Rebel Angels*, 1981, pays homage to the comic novels of Thomas Love Peacock.) The sharp satirical observation of Margaret ATWOOD'S novels may not strike some readers as exaggerated at all. Robert KROETSCH, however, has elevated the Prairies' beer-parlour tall tale to mythic proportions in *The* STUDHORSE MAN (1969). In Kroetsch's *What the Crow Said* (1978) the exuberance of invention attests the influence of S American novelists such as Gabriel García Márquez. The same influence may be traced in the equally extravagant comedy of Vancouver I's Jack Hodgins, especially in *The Invention of the World* (1977). The full range of a comic voice following the possibilities of inventive licence to their limit may be heard in the short stories of Leon ROOKE and in his novel, *Shakespeare's Dog* (1982).

Although much 19th-century Canadian poetry may strike the contemporary reader as unintentionally comic, as W.A. DEACON proved in his satirical *The Four Jameses* (1927), this period contains few and scattered examples of truly humorous verse. The first major Canadian poet for whom humour formed an essential and serious part of his vision was F.R. SCOTT. "The Canadian Authors Meet" (1927) remains a wickedly accurate deflation of literary pretension and colonial mediocrity. Unlike the prose satirists, Scott operated from left of the political centre; his poetry was only one aspect of a most distinguished career in Canadian cultural and political life. During the Depression, Scott's satire, like that of Dorothy LIVESAY, was aimed against the "efficiency" of an economic system which left so many unemployed and impoverished. In his *Trouvailles* (1967), Scott also used the "found" poem to great satiric effect.

Scott coedited with A.J.M. SMITH the first major anthology of Canadian "satire, invective and disrespectful verse," *The Blasted Pine* (1957). Although many of the poems in this collection are not necessarily funny, it was a milestone in the development of Canadian humour. Adopting a more eclectic editorial stance and insisting on the importance of "poetry" rather than "verse," Douglas BARBOUR and Stephen SCOBIE coedited the anthology *The Maple Laugh Forever* (1981).

Scott's tradition of acerbic classical wit has been notably carried on by George JOHNSTON and Francis SPARSHOTT, but the majority of Canadian comic poems are more boisterous or fantastic in tone. Earle BIRNEY has twisted language into many ingenious and whimsical games, though his laughter often seems a thin disguise for his deeper pessimism. Irving LAYTON has used a loud and sometimes crude humour as part of his general assault on stuffy proprieties. Most impressively, Al PURDY has created a kind of comic persona for himself, shambling, expansive and all-embracing, which provides the ideal medium for his widespread range of poetic concerns.

Among younger poets, there is a similar use of the comic persona in Tom WAYMAN'S creation of himself in the distanced third person of *Waiting for Wayman* (1973). The seemingly naive idealism of bill BISSETT is accompanied by shrewd irony and a poker-faced relation of the modern world's sometimes lethal absurdities (as in "Th Emergency Ward"), and Frank DAVEY has also exploited an apparently neutral style of description, which allows the material to reveal its own satiric potential, in his "War Poems" and in *Capitalistic Affection!* (1982). Dennis LEE has written whimsical children's poems which shade, as the age of the intended audience grows, into pointed political satire. The influence of Atwood's bitter satirical treatment of sexual relations in *Power Politics* (1971) is extended by younger women such as Sharon THESEN, in *Artemis Hates Romance* (1980), and Mary Howes, in *Lying in Bed* (1981).

For most Canadian poets, humour has now become one element in a wider and more complex view of the world. In his animal poems, Michael ONDAATJE juxtaposes the "strange case" of his beagle's sexual proclivities with the stranger horrors of the animal man; in his "Letters & Other Worlds," the absurd eccentricities of his parents' characters are inseparable from the tragedy of their lives. *The Martyrology* (1972 and continuing), by bp NICHOL, begins with a play on words: all words beginning in *st* are concealed saints' names (eg, *stand* is written as *St And*). On this is built a whole cosmology, a life-work-poem which stands at the centre of contemporary Canadian literature.

Humour in Canadian drama is less advanced than it is in either fiction or poetry, though comic elements were present in the complex poetic plays of James REANEY and in the multimedia extravaganzas of Wilfred WATSON. Recent works such as *Billy Bishop Goes to War* (publ 1981), by John GRAY and Eric Peterson, and Linda Griffiths's *Maggie and Pierre* (publ 1980) indicate a new willingness to get out on satirical limbs. Canada has a strong comic tradition in shorter dramatic forms, such as the review sketches of many years' *Spring Thaw*, and this tradition has found fertile ground in radio (*Royal Canadian Air Farce*) and television (*SCTV*). Indeed, next to Leacock, the Canadian comedians who were best known internationally in the early 1980s were *SCTV*'s McKenzie brothers, whose precisely timed mockery of Canadian gullibility and boorishness ("Take off, eh?") harks back to the deepest roots of Canadian humour. Sam Slick was fully familiar with "hosers."

STEPHEN SCOBIE

Humorous Writing in French Humorous writing, like humour itself, can be subjective, subtle and difficult to define. Emerging from the marriage of specific social, historical and cultural forces, it also reflects the vagaries of fashion and popular taste. Although there is no French Canadian counterpart to the Leacock Medal for Humour, there is a strong tradition of humorous writing in French Canada, dating to the early 19th century and most evident after the Quiet Revolution of the 1960s. The 2 original strains influencing more traditional genres are folklore and political journalism.

Folk humour and more formal satire are responses to the Roman Catholic Church's domination of culture and politics in 19th-century French Canada, a domination that lasted until the end of the DUPLESSIS régime. ULTRAMONTANISM, a nationalistic type of religious and political conservatism, led to censorship even after the ban on theatre (1694-1763), and political satire is one of the first recorded types of humour, associated with the proliferation of newspapers and magazines edited by European expatriates from 1830 to 1880. Napoléon Aubin is a prototype here: his unfinished novella, *Mon Voyage à la lune*, his journals, *Le Fantasque* (1837-45) and *Le Castor* (1843), and his theatre troupe, Les Amateurs typographiques (est 1839), all satirizing public life in French Canada, led to his brief imprisonment in 1839 for his outspoken views. This cosmopolitan tradition culminates in the journalism of Arthur BUIES, the editor of *La Lanterne Canadienne* (1868-69), one of the most irreverent, satirical journals published in 19th-century French Canada.

The few plays published or produced before 1960, mostly light comedies influenced by French boulevard theatre and the works of Molière, all tend to ridicule local manners and morals. Joseph QUESNEL'S *L'Anglomanie, ou le dîner à l'angloise* (1803), for example, criticizes the imitation of English customs, as does Pierre PETITCLAIR's *Une Partie de campagne* (1865). More serious but no less witty closet dramas attack specific figures: the anonymous *Les Comédies du status quo* (1834) ridicules local politics, while *Le Défricheteur de langue* (1859) by Isodore Mesplats, the pseudonym of Joseph LaRue and Joseph-Charles Taché, mocks the Parisian manners and the lurid historical romances of Henri-Émile Chevalier, editor of Montréal's *La Ruche littéraire* (1853-59). Félix-Gabriel Marchand's light comedy, *Les Faux brillants* (1885), was revived in 1971 by Jean-Claude GERMAIN, a contemporary dramatist whose unpublished plays include the parodies *Don Quickshot* and *Rodéo et Juliette*.

Theatrical satire ended in 1903 with Louvigny de Montigny's *Les Boules de neige*, criticizing hypocrisy among Montréal's bourgeoisie, and eventually re-emerged in 1968 with the production of Michel TREMBLAY's controversial joual play *Les Belles Soeurs*, which blends realistic comedy and allegorical satire to explode the official vision of French Canadian society as a peaceable rural kingdom. Among the many dramatists influenced by Tremblay, Jean BARBEAU stands out for his extensive use of puns and popular culture (especially sports and film) to depict Québec culture; his best known play is the unpublished *La Coupe stainless* (1974). According to Laurent Mailhot, "Barbeau believes that all the great Québécois tragedies will be humorous ones because our greatest misfortune occurred in 1763 and nothing worse awaits us." His comment provides one more serious context for the lighthearted revues such as *Broue* (1979), a collective creation which successfully toured English Canada as *Brew* (1982).

Much humorous fiction in French Canada revisits and transforms the oral tradition of shanty tales, folk songs and "esquisses de moeurs" which formed the richest vein of humour in the nineteenth century. While most of these folk tales remain uncollected and unpublished, the figures of the storyteller José in Philippe AUBERT DE GASPÉ'S *Les* ANCIENS CANADIENS (1863) and of "le père Michel" in Joseph-Charles Taché's FORESTIERS ET VOYAGEURS (1863) provide an example of popular folk humour. Jacques FERRON in Québec (*Contes du pays incertain*, 1962) and Antonine MAILLET in Acadian New Brunswick (*La Sagouine*, 1974, and PÉLAGIE-LA-CHARRETTE, 1979) are 2 contemporary authors of international repute whose ironic fiction and theatre rely extensively on folk humour and the popular tradition.

If Ferron's fiction approaches satire, Maillet's work is closer to comedy. These 2 dimensions of humour are both present in contemporary Québec writing. The satirical novel is the modern form for the vision which found its expression in theatre and journalism during the 19th century. Rodolphe Girard's MARIE CALUMET (1904) employs Rabelaisian humour in its portrait of clerical and rural life, and it led to the author's dismissal from *La Presse*. Jean-Charles HARVEY's *Les Demi-civilisés* (1934), a savage attack on the domination of Québec society and culture by English and Catholic elements, also resulted in severe criticism of the author. Gérard BESSETTE's *Le Libraire* (1960) is another literary landmark, satirizing censorship during the Duplessis régime. More recently, Jacques GODBOUT, in SALUT GALARNEAU! (1967) and especially in *Les Têtes à Papineau* (1981), employs allegorical symbolism to satirize contemporary society with the irony of a gentle humorist. Louky Bersianik's *L'Euguélionne* (1976) turns to the genre of utopian science fiction to communicate its humorous but nonetheless scathing analysis of patriarchy.

The comic novel, once less prevalent, is experiencing a new surge of popularity. The classic example of picaresque comedy in the writing of French Canada is Roger LEMELIN'S LES PLOUFFE (1948), a novel which formed the basis for a long-lived television series before the emergence of the film version in both official languages (1980). Yves BEAUCHEMIN'S novel LE MATOU (1981) is the most recent and most significant addition to this comic tradition; its conventionally realistic story and style unexpectedly and repeatedly devolve into linguistic play, enhancing the humour without detracting from the internal logic of the narrative. Finally, no mention of humour in the novel would be complete without reference to the work of Roch CARRIER; in particular, *Le Jardin des délices* (1975) reveals his characteristic blend of surrealism and black humour.

Poetry has provided a few examples of parody and the mock epic, notably in Réjean DUCHARME'S novel *La Fille de Christophe Colomb* (1969). However, radio, TV and film are the media that have best served French Canadian humorous writing. During the Depression, the popular poetry of Jean Narrache (the pseudonym of Émile Coderre) offered a bittersweet, gently critical portrait of the French Canadian everyman, while in the 1940s the *Fridolinades* of Gratien GÉLINAS, adapting live theatre for the radio, created an audience for the personality Fridolin. The popular stage and television performer Yvon DESCHAMPS (*Monologues*, 1973) emerges from this tradition, employing the monologue as a distinctly French Canadian humorous genre.

A new breed of Québec singer-songwriters have turned to the recording industry rather than to live theatre to earn a living while satirizing contemporary manners and morals. As early as the 1930s, "La Bolduc" (Mary Travers) turned to radio to popularize her satirical songs. Robert CHARLEBOIS and Michel Rivard, from the 1960s to the present, have remained notorious for their witty musical parodies of local and American trends, while Plume Latraverse continues to extend parody into the domain of scatological verse. Finally, the cinema provides some of the most sophisticated and successful artistic outlets for humour: "writing" in this genre includes the award-winning films *Deux Femmes en or* (1970) and *Le Déclin de l'empire américain* (1986), among others.

The importance of live performance in the domain of humour cannot be overemphasized; even film and television underscore the extent to which "humour" is an oral tradition in French Canada. Perhaps because until recently they have feared the effects of censorship, authors of "humorous writing" in French Canada have tended to question the "status quo" in ephemeral but no less

Jack Humphrey, *Charlotte* (1939), oil on canvas (*courtesy Art Gallery of Ontario/gift from the Albert H. Robson Memorial Subscription Fund, 1940*).

scathing terms through popular culture, reserving literature for subtler ironic statements.

MICHÈLE LACOMBE

Humphrey, Jack Weldon, painter (b at Saint John 12 Jan 1901; d there 23 Mar 1967). Humphrey was the most significant eastern Canadian painter of his generation. He studied under Charles Hawthorne at NY's National Academy of Design from 1924 to 1929 and with Hans Hofman in Munich in 1930. He later visited Europe, Mexico and New York, but his deepest sentimental attraction was to his birthplace, in spite of its isolation from artistic developments. Humphrey's paintings of the harbour, streets and workers of Saint John established his reputation as a regional artist and his work extended to numerous portraits of friends and the city's children. Making no concessions to fashion, Humphrey's tough, honest approach made him a respected member of Montréal's CONTEMPORARY ARTS SOCIETY and the Canadian Group of Painters. Returning from France in 1954, he developed abstract and nonobjective tendencies in gouache and oil landscapes, while his beautiful watercolours focused on the intimate details of nature. J. RUSSELL HARPER

Humphrey, John Peters, lawyer, diplomat, scholar (b at Hampton, NB 30 Apr 1905). Humphrey was called to the Québec Bar in 1929 and entered the private practice of law before joining the Faculty of Law of McGill U in 1936, briefly becoming the dean a decade later. In 1946 he was appointed director of human rights for the UN Secretariat, where with the assistance of others he authored the original draft of the Universal Declaration of Human Rights. Passed as a resolution of the General Assembly, the declaration has been referred to as "Magna Carta of mankind." It heralded a revolutionary change in the theory and practice of INTERNATIONAL LAW because of its recognition that human rights are a matter for international concern. Although the principles of the declaration are routinely violated, it is one of the UN's most important achievements for it has become part of the customary law of nations. Humphrey retired from the UN in 1966 and rejoined McGill U, remaining active in international affairs and the protection of human rights.

WILLIAM KAPLAN

Reading: John P. Humphrey, *Human Rights and the United Nations: A Great Adventure* (1984).

Hungarians Until the late 19th century, very few Hungarians came to Canada and even fewer stayed for more than a brief period. In the 1880s Hungarian immigrants to the US began migrating to Canada and, through the efforts of immigration agent Paul Oscar Esterhazy (*see* ESTERHAZY, Sask), they established colonies in the "old" North-West Territory. In time these pioneers were followed by about 100 000 other Hungarian immigrants. Today, there are about 145 000 Canadians of Hungarian descent. They constitute a culturally and socially diverse group whose members live throughout most of the country and can be found in all walks of life.

Origins Before 1914 Hungarians came to Canada from Austria-Hungary, along with numerous SLOVAKS, CROATS, GERMANS and other nationalities. Since WWI Hungarians emigrated from Hungary, or from Czechoslovakia, Romania or Yugoslavia, countries with substantial Hungarian minorities. Throughout most of the past 11 centuries, Hungary occupied the entire Middle Danube Basin and was the home of Hungarians as well as a few other nationalities. Prior to WWI, uneven economic development, lack of agrarian reform, a nationality problem and other factors caused hundreds of thousands of Hungarians to emigrate. After the defeat of the Austro-Hungarian Empire, Hungary was dismembered. The resulting economic and social malaise drove still more Hungarians to emigrate, while Hungarians who had been transferred to neighbouring states often chose immigration to Canada over life in a hostile political environment. WWII and the imposition of a communist dictatorship forced more Hungarians into exile.

Migration and Settlement Hungarians came to Canada in 4 major waves. In the period before 1914 about 8000 immigrated; from 1925 to 1930 about 26 000; between 1948 and 1952 some 12 000 postwar displaced persons arrived, and between 1956 and 1957 about 37 000 Hungarian REFUGEES came to Canada after the collapse of the 1956 uprising against Soviet authority. Since then several hundred Hungarians have immigrated to Canada annually. Most of the pre-1914 settlers were peasants; in general they were disappointed transmigrants from the industrial slums of the US. The interwar arrivals were a somewhat more mixed lot socially, while many of the post-WWII immigrants were from Hungary's dispossessed middle and upper classes. Young adult males predominated in all but the last wave of immigrants.

The first groups of Hungarian immigrants settled mainly on prairie homesteads (Saskatchewan was sometimes called "Little Hungary" before 1914), but later immigrants established themselves in towns and cities. Whether in rural or urban areas they usually congregated in their own residential groups. From the 1920s onwards, more Hungarians settled in cities, especially in central Canada. The Great Depression interrupted these trends, but the shift to the cities, and especially to southern Ontario, resumed after WWII. Today, one out of every 2 people of Hungarian origin lives in Ontario, and 4 out of 5 live in a city, although residential concentrations have all but disappeared.

Economic Life Most of the early Hungarian immigrants worked as homesteaders, miners, navvies and loggers. The post-1945 immigrants tended to be more skilled and better educated. In times of prosperity most Hungarians did well, in times of recession they were particularly hard hit. During the Depression most of them lost their jobs, farms or businesses. Today, many are economically comfortable and a few have become rich.

Social and Cultural Life The majority of Hungarians are Roman Catholic. Others belong to various Protestant faiths; still others are Jewish or Eastern Rite Catholics. Many of their churches double as social and cultural centres and provide instruction in the Hungarian language for children.

To smooth the effects of social isolation and to reduce economic instability, Hungarians have maintained various types of organizations since the establishment of their first settlements.

Today, many of these clubs and churches are members of the Hungarian Canadian Federation, the national umbrella organization of Hungarians in Canada. Among the local, regional or professional organizations mention might be made of the Széchenyi Society of Calgary which had been instrumental in the establishment of a permanently endowed Hungarian studies program at the U of T, the first of the so-called "ethnic studies chairs" in Canada. In Toronto, the Hungarian Helikon Society has been active in cultural and social affairs since the 1950s. Also in Toronto, the Hungarian School Board co-ordinates several programs providing schooling in the Hungarian language at both the elementary and secondary level. The Hungarian Cultural Centre in the same city is one of the largest such centres outside Hungary.

Hungarians began publishing Hungarian-language newspapers before 1914. Today, Toronto is the centre of Hungarian publishing activity in Canada; publications include *Kanadai Magyarság* (*Canadian Hungarians*), *Magyar Élet* (*Hungarian Life*) and many more specialized papers. *Menorah Egyenlöség* is the largest Hungarian language Jewish newspaper in N America.

Group Maintenance Adjustment to Canadian life tended to come first in the workplace and last in the family home. Hungarian women acquired greater influence as they gained more economic power. Hungarian customs and rites have gradually been abandoned, and the process of adjustment has often been followed by that of assimilation. Social and economic stratification among the immigrants has often hindered intra-ethnic unity and interaction and thereby has hastened the loss of the immigrant cultural heritage.

Although maintenance of the native culture was encouraged at home and within the immigrant community's institutions, the adjustment to Canadian conditions has been promoted through the schooling of children in regular English- or French-language schools. Some of the most remarkable contributions of Hungarians to Canadian culture have been in fields in which the immigrant heritage is compatible with the Canadian environment, eg, in arts, sciences and music.

N.F. DREISZIGER

Reading: G. Bisztray, *Hungarian-Canadian Literature* (1987); J. Kosa, *Land of Choice: Hungarians in Canada* (1957); N.F. Dreisziger et al, *Struggle and Hope: The Hungarian-Canadian Experience* (1982).

Hungerford, Samuel James, railway executive (b near Bedford, Qué 16 July 1872; d at Farnham, Qué 7 Oct 1955). After beginning as an apprentice machinist for the Southeastern Ry in 1886 and holding various positions in the operating departments of the CPR, Hungerford joined the Canadian Northern Ry as superintendent of rolling stock in 1910. During the 1920s, as a VP of operation, maintenance and construction, he played an important role in the integration and expansion of the CNR. Appointed president of the CNR in 1934, Hungerford reduced operating expenditures and defended the company's autonomy amid demands for amalgamation with the CPR. He retired from the presidency in 1941. First president of TRANS-CANADA AIRLINES and president of National Ry Munitions Ltd, a crown corporation that produced guns and gun carriages in WWII, he was created CMG for his wartime services. J. LINDSEY

Reading: G.R. Stevens, *History of the Canadian National Railways* (1973).

Hunt, George, ethnographer, museum acquisitions collector (b at Fort Rupert, BC 1854; d there Sept 1933). Most of our knowledge of traditional KWAKIUTL culture is based on Hunt's rich ethnographic notes and artifact collection. Son of an English HBC trader and a Tlingit mother, Hunt lived at Fort Rupert, a trading post and Kwakiutl settlement. He spoke Kwakiutl as his first language, married a high-ranking Kwakiutl woman and achieved a prestigious position in the native culture. Most of anthropologist Franz BOAS's Kwakiutl publications are based on Hunt's ethnographic notes; their collaboration extended for over 40 years until Hunt's death. Hunt greatly assisted most other leading Northwest Coast fieldworkers and artifact collectors of the day, even arranging and directing an ethnographic film for Edward S. Curtis. KATHLEEN MOONEY

Hunt, Henry, Kwakiutl artist (b at Fort Rupert, BC 16 Oct 1923; d at Victoria 13 Mar 1985), grandson of George HUNT, father of Tony HUNT. A principal carver at the BC Provincial Museum for nearly 20 years, Henry Hunt began his career apprenticed to his father-in-law, Mungo MARTIN, and Arthur Shaunnesy, another well-known Kwakiutl carver. From 1962 to 1974 he was chief carver at the BC Provincial Museum, the successor to Martin. There he trained his sons Tony, Stanley and Richard. He and his sons created the magnificent Mungo Martin memorial pole at Alert Bay (1971) and an impressive pole for the Totem Marina at Shuswap Lk. Hunt's works are found in international museum collections. CAROL SHEEHAN

Hunt, Nadine, trade union executive (b at Kingston, Ont). A graduate of the Labour College of Canada in 1971, Hunt served as vice-president of the Saskatchewan Federation of Labour 1970-71 and as treasurer 1974-78, before becoming the first woman in Canadian history to lead a labour federation when she was elected president of the organization in 1978, a post she has held ever since. As well as being a worker's representative at the International Labour Organization, where she served on a committee to establish international standards for the treatment of workers with family responsibilities, she has assisted in the establishment of the Labour Studies Program at U Sask and is active on several educational and political advisory boards. STANLEY GORDON

Hunt, Thomas Sterry, chemist, geologist (b at Norwich, Conn 5 Sept 1826; d at New York C 12 Feb 1892). After studying at Yale under Benjamin Silliman Jr, Hunt joined the GEOLOGICAL SURVEY OF CANADA in 1846 as a chemist and mineralogist. While in this position, he taught at Laval 1856-62 and McGill 1862-68. In 1872 he left Canada to accept the geology chair at Massachusetts Institute of Technology. He officially retired in 1878, but continued to conduct research, remaining an important member of the scientific community. As a chemist and geologist with original and controversial ideas, Hunt was known for his contributions to defining the Laurentian and Huron geological systems. In 1859 he was elected fellow of the Royal Soc of London and was appointed president of both the American Institute of Mining Engineers (1877) and the American Chemical Soc (1880). Throughout his career, he maintained close ties with Canada. He helped found the RSC in 1882 and became its president in 1884. RAYMOND DUCHESNE

Hunt, Tony, Kwakiutl artist (b at Alert Bay, BC 24 Aug 1942). He is a leader in the social and ceremonial life of Alert Bay, a master of traditional performance as well as of the visual arts, and has established an international reputation as a carver of Kwakiutl-style NORTHWEST COAST INDIAN ART, after studying with his illustrious grandfather, Mungo MARTIN, and his father, Henry HUNT. He was assistant carver (1962-72) at the BC Provincial Museum's Thunderbird Park. In 1970 he established the Arts of the Raven Gallery, overseeing an apprenticeship program for aspiring young native carvers. Among his major works are TOTEM POLES in Victoria's BC Provincial Museum and Bastion Square. In 1982 he was commissioned to do a 4 tonne stone sculpture for the Canadian Museum of Civilization, called "Raven Transforming into Man." CAROL SHEEHAN

Hunter, Thomas James, Tommy, singer (b at London, Ont 10 Mar 1937). Hunter and his weekly CBC-TV show have long been important in Canadian country music. He got his start on "Main Street Jamboree," on CHML Radio in Hamilton in 1953 and by 1956 was a rhythm guitarist on CBC-TV's "Country Hoedown," which in 1965 was replaced by the "Tommy Hunter Show." The show has become one of the longest running network variety shows and has provided national exposure for Canadian country singers. Hunter won the Juno Award from 1967 to 1969 as Canada's best male country singer. Tommy Hunter is now a regular on the American Nashville Network. In 1986 he released an album of gospel readings. RICHARD GREEN

Hunter v Southam Case Acting under the authority of s10 of the Combines Investigation Act, the director of the Investigation of the Combines Branch authorized several civil servants to enter the offices of Southam Inc in Edmonton. The company claimed that subsections 1 and 3 of s10 of that Act were incompatible with s8 of the CANADIAN CHARTER OF RIGHTS AND FREEDOMS, which states "Everyone has the right to be secure against unreasonable search or seizure." On 17 Sept 1984 the Supreme Court of Canada declared that in the first place warrantless searches are on the face of it unreasonable under s8 of the Charter. The individual who wishes to justify a warrantless search must rebut the presumption of the unreasonable nature of that search. On the merits of the case, the Supreme Court came to the conclusion that subsections 10(1) and 10(3) of the Combines Investigation Act are "inconsistent with the Charter and of no force and effect, as much for their failure to specify an appropriate standard for the issuance of warrants as for their designation of an improper arbiter to issue them" (Chief Justice Dickson). The Supreme Court added that the person who authorizes the search must be in a position to appreciate, in an entirely neutral and impartial fashion, the opposing rights of the state and the individual. GÉRALD-A. BEAUDOIN

Hunters' Lodges, largest of the SECRET SOCIETIES pledged to liberate the Canadian provinces from "British thraldom," founded in early 1838 in the northern US by Canadian rebels who had fled there after the REBELLIONS OF 1837. The movement quickly became American, with support from widely varied groups in the border states and membership estimated at 40 000-60 000. Abandoning plans to invade Upper Canada on 4 July 1838, the "patriot hunters" attempted numerous unsuccessful incursions in the following months. Rebels were soundly defeated at Napierville, Lacolle and Odelltown, LC, and at Prescott (in the Battle of the WINDMILL) and Windsor, UC. They then undertook a series of border provocations calculated to drive Britain and the US to war, including burning the steamship *Sir Robert Peel* in the Thousand Is and blowing up the Brock monument at Queenstown, UC. On 25 Sept 1841, US Pres Tyler warned them to disband, and within a short time the lodges were a thing of the past. CURTIS FAHEY

Hunting is the purposeful pursuit to the death of wild animals. People hunt for different purposes: subsistence, trade, WILDLIFE CONSERVATION AND MANAGEMENT, training, recreation and prestige. Subsistence hunters are dependent on wild animals for food and shelter or for cultural survival. Evidence suggests that the earliest humans, and their ancestors, hunted animals; some claim that the earliest tools were weapons. Subsistence hunters or their traces have been found on all continents except Antarctica, and from tropical to polar climatic zones. The varieties of technique and organization seem almost endless. Weapons have included the trap, gorge, noose, net, pitfall, deadfall, bolo, throwing-stick or boomerang, club, knife, spear, javelin, blowpipe, bow and arrow, and harpoon. Dogs and horses have often been employed in tracking and pursuit. There can be little doubt that Pleistocene (Ice Age) hunters exterminated some, perhaps many, species.

In Canada, hunting at will for food is possible for natives belonging to groups that obtained that right when they ceded lands under treaty, and for natives belonging to other groups by virtue of acknowledged aboriginal title. Some spokesmen for native associations have claimed rights over the disposition of all game in Canada (*see* INDIAN ACT; LAND CLAIMS).

Presumably, commercial hunting began as trade developed: first, for surplus commodities, between communities of subsistence hunters; later for commodities to be traded on a wider scale. Besides ivory, from walrus and elephant, commercial products of the hunt include feathers, skins, furs and meat. Such products have been traded for millennia. Excessive harvesting has been a recurrent problem and has become chronic in the last 200 years, with widespread affluence creating demands which are filled by efficient means of hunting, transport and trade. Species bearing the most valuable products (eg, SEA OTTER) have suffered severe depletion. Several species are now endangered by commercial hunting, particularly certain whales, sea turtles, rhinoceroses and elephants. Commercial hunting for feathers and plumes declined early in the 20th century with the imposition of strict import controls in Europe and N America. Fur animals have generally proved well able to sustain harvesting. The FUR TRADE, although subject to the swings of fashion, remains viable; its future depends perhaps on philosophical rather than resource issues. In many countries, the meat of hunted animals enters the market, where it competes with domestic meats and returns money to landowners, collectives or hunting associations to set against management costs. The culling of herds and the reduction of vertebrate pest populations are examples of hunting directed to husbandry or the protection of economically important resources.

Trophy hunting is a kind of recreational hunting and demands time, money and effort. It is essentially competitive in nature, the object of the trophy hunter being to get a large specimen. The measurements used for N American trophies are formally detailed by the Boone & Crockett Club, which appoints qualified judges, adjudicates conflicts, provides standards and, in particular, rules on questions of whether or not specimens were taken in "fair chase." A similar system exists for ranking trophies taken by archery.

Today, most hunting in Canada is recreational and motivated by the tangible as well as intangible rewards of success. Under the common law, game is public property until killed or crippled or "brought to bag," although in the case of game on private land the owners control access. Under administrative laws and regulations, competent jurisdictions set out rules governing hunters. These rules may include strictures on age and qualifications of applicants for hunting licences, as well as defining hunting zones, seasons and bag limits. The rules, largely designed to divide hunting opportunities among participants and reduce the risk of accidents, are enforced by provincial game officers and federal migratory bird convention enforcement officers, including members of the RCMP. They are under continuing review by local clubs making up provincial fish and game associations, which are loosely affiliated to the CANADIAN WILDLIFE FEDERATION.

Recreational hunting opportunities are found in all parts of Canada, except in preserves such as national parks and provincial WILDLIFE PRESERVES. All game resources are under provincial administration except migratory birds, which are managed by the CANADIAN WILDLIFE SERVICE with the co-operation of the provinces. Populations of WATERFOWL, which breed in agricultural parts of Canada, have declined in recent years, and the conservation of wetlands, although greatly assisted by governments and by the private agency DUCKS UNLIMITED (Canada), needs continuous effort. Arctic-nesting geese, particularly Canada geese and snow geese, although subject to the vagaries of weather on their breeding grounds, have prospered in contrast to southern-nesting species. As human populations and demand on limited hunting opportunities increase, there must be international co-operation to ensure equitable sharing of these migratory resources.

Judging by the some 400 000 waterfowl licences sold each year in Canada, it can be estimated that perhaps 1 million Canadians hunt. Canada also attracts hunters from all over the world to enjoy its unique hunting opportunities. A stay at a goose camp in the coastal marshes of James Bay is unforgettable. The expected encounter with an excited, antlered bull makes a late Sept moose-calling hunt the experience of a lifetime. Superb landscapes await the hunter on a packhorse trip through mountain valleys, searching the heights for bighorn or Dall rams. For the hardy and daring, a spring hunt for grizzly or polar bear is sure to prove memorable. However, not all Canadians approve of recreational hunting. Some are opposed to it on ethical grounds, and some native Canadians are opposed to non-native Canadians hunting because of violations to native treaty rights.

Canada possesses many upland game birds, from the rock and willow ptarmigan of the arctic tundra to the sage and sharp-tailed grouse of the short-grass prairies. They and the introduced gray partridge and ring-necked pheasant vary in numbers from year to year. There is a tendency for some species, particularly the ruffed grouse of the mixed forest and scrublands, to exhibit a cycle in numbers. These cycles may be related to similar rhythms shown by snowshoe-hare populations, and by their predators.

The most widely distributed big-game species of settled Canada is the white-tailed deer, formerly confined to the eastern provinces but now found as far west as the Okanagan Valley. The western mule deer is common in river valleys and rough terrain; in coastal BC, it is replaced by its relation, the black-tailed deer. The moose, adapted to deep snow with its long legs and typical of boreal and subalpine forests, is well distributed from coast to coast, and now prospers in Newfoundland, to which it was successfully introduced in 1904.

Woodland caribou also frequent the boreal forest. Barren-ground caribou migrate seasonally between the barrens, where they calve early in June, and the northern coniferous forest, where they pass the snowiest parts of winter. They are hunted only by natives and residents of the northern territories. The George River herd of Ungava caribou is hunted both by residents and nonresidents. Of more localized interest are the pronghorn of the southern prairies, the mountain goat, bighorn, stone and Dall sheep of the western cordillera, and the muskox of the High Arctic. Other game species include black, grizzly and polar bears, grey wolf and cougar.

In 1987 roughly 2.5 million ducks and 625 000 geese were harvested in Canada, and about 363 000 beaver, which are used for food as well as pelts. Of the hoofed mammals taken, 248 688 were white-tailed deer, 63 141 moose, 53 266 woodland caribou, 25 559 mule deer, 7535 elk and about 1000 each of mountain sheep and mountain goat. Some 21 359 bears were taken, of which 20 343 were black bear and the rest polar and grizzly. More than any other animal, the grouse and snowshoe hare populations vary greatly from year to year and the hunter harvest is not reported in all provinces. A.H. MACPHERSON

Reading: M. Brander, *Hunting and Shooting, from the Earliest Times to the Present Day* (1971).

Huntsman, Archibald Gowanlock, marine biologist, administrator, editor, teacher (b at Tintern, Ont 23 Nov 1883; d at St Andrews, NB 8 Aug 1973). Huntsman was a provocative thinker and innovator who decisively influenced fisheries science in Canada. His professional career, characterized by keen intellect, verve and indefatigable effort, combined fisheries research with postgraduate teaching and was intimately linked 1904-53 with what later became the Fisheries Research Board of Canada. In serving 1934-53 as the board's scientist, curator, director, editor and consulting director, Huntsman helped shape the research philosophies, the staff of the biological and technological stations and their programs. As professor of marine biology at University of Toronto 1927-54, he taught most fisheries research scientists trained during the 1920s and 1930s. In his lifetime he was honoured frequently by scientific societies in Canada, the US and the UK and in 1952 was awarded the RSC Flavelle Medal.
L.M. DICKIE

Huntsville, Ont, Town, pop 12 131 (1986c), 11 467 (1981c), inc 1900, is located 215 km N of Toronto on a short section of the Muskoka R connecting Vernon and Fairy lakes. Settlers took up land in the area after surveys of the township in 1862 and extension of the Muskoka road to the site in 1870. Capt George Hunt, for whom the town is named, first visited in 1868 and settled here in 1869. He was superintendent of the road, first postmaster and opened the first store. The railway arrived in 1885 and, with a population of 400, the village was incorporated the following year. The export of local white pine supported 6 sawmills in the town at one time. Huntsville still has a small lumber industry, but is sustained primarily by the year-round tourist trade, being within easy access to the Lake of Bays resort area to the SW and to ALGONQUIN PROVINCIAL PARK some 30 km NE. Madill Church, 6 km S, is one of the few remaining pioneer square-timber churches; it was built 1872-73 by Wesleyan Methodists. JAMES MARSH

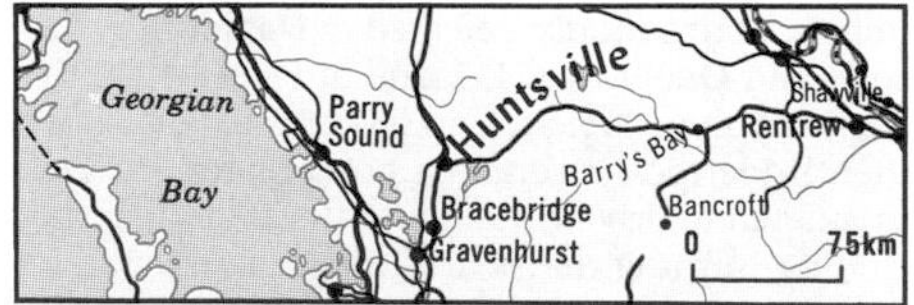

Huot, Charles, painter (b at Québec C 1855; d there 28 Jan 1930). The director of the École normale Laval in Québec organized a subscription fund to help him enrol in 1874 at Paris's École des beaux-arts; he spent much time there in the studio of painter Alexander Cabanel and won a silver medal. The French government bought his painting, *Le Bon Samaritain*, during the Universal Exposition of 1878. In 1898 he finally returned to Québec and produced works for numerous churches throughout the province. He won a contract to decorate Québec's parliament building, and produced 2 large historical murals, *Séance du premier parlement du Bas-Canada, le débat sur la langue* and *Le Conseil souverain de 1663*; he also painted *Je me souviens* for the ceiling of the Assemblée nationale, and *Je puise mais n'épuise* for the massive library stained-glass window. He illustrated many books as well.
MICHEL CHAMPAGNE

Huron, a confederacy of 5 Iroquoian-speaking tribes who occupied northern Simcoe County, Ont, during the first half of the 17th century. The nickname "Huron" was given to them by the French and means "ruffian" or "boar's head," from the hairstyle of Huron men. Their own confederacy name was *Ouendat* (Wendat), commonly thought to mean "people of the island." The tribes of the confederacy were the Attignawantan ("bear people"), Attigneenongnahac ("cord makers"), Arendaronon ("rock people"), Tahontaenrat ("deer people") and Ataronchronon ("swamp people"). By the early 17th century the latter 3 tribes had migrated into Huron country from southern and eastern Ontario to join the other 2 tribes in a loose defensive alliance against their common enemy, the 5 IROQUOIS tribes of upper New York state.

Prior to 1600, the Huron numbered from 20 000 to 25 000, but between 1634 and 1640 they were reduced to about 9000 by a series of epidemic diseases, particularly the smallpox epidemic of 1639. The Huron lived in 18 to 25 villages, some with up to 3500 people. Their subsistence economy was based on corn, beans, SQUASH and fish. Hunting was of minor importance. At the time of French contact (1615-49), these efficient farmers occupied a territory of about 880 km^2, achieving an average population density of 23 people per km^2. Most villages were well fortified with palisades. Villages usually stood on a slight rise, adjacent to a permanent water supply and close to good farming soils. Every 10-15 years, when soils and firewood were exhausted, villages were moved.

The Huron formed monogamous nuclear families; however the fundamental socioeconomic group was the matrilineal extended family, made up of a number of families whose female members traced common descent to a mother or grandmother, who was in charge of daily affairs. The extended family lived in LONGHOUSES, which were about 7 m wide and varied in length with the size of the family. Houses up to 90 m in length have been reported from archaeological work. Huron individuals belonged to one of 8 matrilineal clans. Clan members considered themselves cousins and were not permitted to marry each other. Village affairs were run by 2 councils, one in charge of civil affairs, the other of war. All men over 30 were members. In theory, matters were decided by consensus, but in reality the old men and elected chiefs of large families decided things because of their community standing and powers of oratory.

The Huron were experienced traders, with close relations to the PETUN, NEUTRAL, OTTAWA, Nipissing and ALGONQUIN bands of the Ottawa Valley. In 1609 they contacted the French under Samuel de CHAMPLAIN and concluded a military and trading alliance which drew the French into the Huron-Iroquois conflict (*see* IROQUOIS WARS). Récollet missionaries were sent to the Huron in

1615, followed by the Jesuits in 1625. By the 1620s the Huron had become the most important suppliers of furs to the French, with a trade network that encompassed most of Ontario and western Québec. The Iroquois defeated and dispersed the Huron in 1649. Many Huron joined the Iroquois; others fled westward with remnants of the Petun and now live on the Wyandot Reservation in Oklahoma. The largest surviving group settled near Québec City at Loretteville. *See also* NATIVE PEOPLE: EASTERN WOODLANDS and general articles under NATIVE PEOPLE. C.E. HEIDENREICH

Reading: B.G. Trigger, *The Children of Aataentsic: A History of the Huron People to 1660* (1976) and, ed, *Handbook of North American Indians,* vol 15: *Northeast* (1978).

Huron, Lake, 59 600 km^2, elev 176 m, 332 km long, 295 km wide, max depth 229 m; total shoreline length, including islands, 6159 km. Lk Huron is the second largest of the GREAT LAKES and fifth-largest lake in the world. Samuel de CHAMPLAIN visited GEORGIAN BAY and Lk Huron with the French scout Étienne BRÛLÉ and a fleet of Indian canoes in 1615. Four interconnected bodies of water – the main lake, Saginaw Bay, the North Channel and Georgian Bay – form the lake. Major inflows are the Straits of Mackinac and the St Marys, Mississagi, Saginaw, FRENCH and Spanish rivers. Lk Huron discharges into Lk ERIE through the ST CLAIR R, Lk ST CLAIR and the DETROIT R. The longest suspension bridge in the world (Mackinac, 2625 m) spans the Straits of Mackinac between Lks Huron and Michigan.

Air masses from the Arctic, Pacific and Atlantic oceans and the Gulf of Mexico converge on the lake, which therefore experiences 4 distinct seasonal patterns and extremes of weather conditions. Its basin is composed of Precambrian SHIELD and Phanerozoic rocks and it was formed during the most recent ice age, with its present form developing only 2000-3000 years ago. The Canadian side of the basin is primarily covered with mixed forest consisting of pine, hemlock, birch, maple, oak, beech, walnut and hickory.

The northern basin is an isolated, underdeveloped hinterland, with a few settlements engaged in the exploitation of forest and mineral resources. Southern settlement is founded on lumbering and agriculture. Important industries include mining, pulp and paper, food processing, chemical production, transport equipment and metal fabricating. SUDBURY, the centre of the mining and smelting industry, is the only major urban centre in the area. One of the world's largest nuclear power plants is located at Douglas Pt on the BRUCE PENINSULA. The lake supports commercial fishing (whitefish, perch, walleye, chub, carp) and sportfishing (bass, perch, walleye, pike, rainbow trout). The Canadian side of Lk Huron is renowned for the beauty of its scenery. The North Channel and Georgian Bay shorelines provided subject matter for several of the GROUP OF SEVEN painters. Excellent beaches extend from the Bruce Peninsula to SARNIA. The basin offers wide, unpolluted waters for swimming, boating, cottaging and camping. M. MUNAWAR

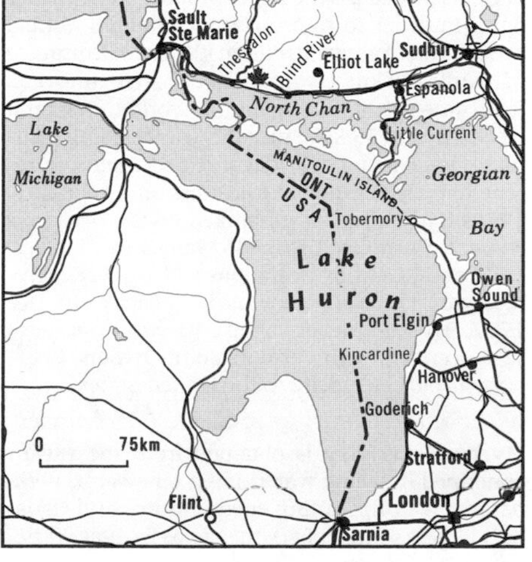

Huronia To all early travellers the territory occupied by the Huron was called *le pays des Hurons* ("the country of the Huron"). A resident in the HURON country described himself as being *aux Hurons* ("among the Huron"), or in *le pays des Hurons.* On 17th-century maps the Huron country is usually given as *Contree des Hurons, Pays* (or *pais*) *des Hurons,* or simply *Hurones* or *Hurons.* The name "Huronia" does not occur in any of the early 17th-century sources. The earliest reference in that form seems to be in a Jesuit vocabulary written in 1745, which refers to *la défunte huronie* ("the deceased or defunct Huronia"). The term came into common usage during the late 19th century. Today, it refers to the area occupied by the Huron during the period of direct French contact (1615-50) as well as a tourist area comprising the townships of Simcoe County, Ont, N of Barrie.
C.E. HEIDENREICH

Hurricane Hazel, tropical storm which struck southern Ontario in 1954. It was one of the mightiest storms ever to hit N America. It germinated off Grenada 5 Oct 1954 and swept over Haiti Oct 12, destroying 3 towns and killing 1000 people. Gaining power, with winds up to 200 k/hr, it rampaged over the coast of N Carolina and poured torrential rains onto Washington, DC, and New York City. When the storm reached Toronto Oct 15, its winds had waned to 120 k/hr, but its warm, tropical air collided with a cold front moving eastward; the ensuing rains swelled creeks and rivers and inundated the watershed of the Humber and Credit rivers. Over 18 cm of rain fell in less than 24 hrs. Low-lying HOLLAND MARSH was submerged, roads were obliterated, houses swept away and 4000 families were left homeless. The storm played itself out over James Bay, leaving 81 people dead and property damage at tens of millions of dollars. As a result of Hurricane Hazel, several flood-control dams and channels were built in the Toronto area and residences were moved from the flood plains, which now provide some of the area's most beautiful recreational settings. JAMES MARSH

Reading: Betty Kennedy, *Hurricane Hazel* (1979).

Hurtubise, Jacques, painter (b at Montréal 28 Feb 1939). He studied at the École des beaux-arts de Montréal. A grant in 1960 enabled him to spend time in New York and become acquainted with the art of the abstract expressionists and he was there for much of the 1960s. Hurtubise's energy-filled canvases reflect a combination of his personal experience and the forces of nature. In the early 1960s he began using the hard-edge technique, producing a unified surface with well-defined edges. Geometric patterns and repeated motifs combine with controlled "splashes" of paint to produce an effect of a foreground that recedes into an emerging background. In 1967 his research into the effects of light led him to produce fluorescent canvases and, later, neon works. As of 1970, the principal structure of his works became the square. In 1977 he began to use shapes and chromatic contrasts on a neutral background to produce linear motifs, evoking abstract landscapes (*Takarakas,* 1979). His "spontaneous" works combine impulse and rigour. LOUISE BEAUDRY

Hutchison, Alexander Cowper, architect (b at Montréal 2 Apr 1838; d there 1 Jan 1922). One of Victorian Montréal's most prolific and prestigious architects, he epitomized the generation of native-born, self-taught men who shaped the city during the second half of the 19th century. Trained as a stonemason, he supervised the cut-stone work on Montréal's Christ Church Cathedral and the East Block of the Parliament Buildings, Ottawa, before establishing a private practice in Montréal shortly after 1865. The firm was known until 1890 as Hutchison and Steele, thereafter as Hutchison and Wood. Hutchison deserves credit for the careful detailing that characterizes all of the firm's output, including the Redpath Museum, testimony no doubt to his apprentice years as a craftsman-builder. Hutchison and Steele gained international reputation as ice-palace designers. JULIA GERSOVITZ

Hutchison, William Bruce, journalist, author (b at Prescott, Ont 5 June 1901). Hutchison grew up in the Kootenay region and in Victoria, BC, becoming a reporter for the Victoria *Times* in 1918. He travelled throughout Canada, the US and UK gathering material for his columns on national and international affairs. He was associate editor 1944-50 of the *Winnipeg Free Press,* editor 1950-63 of the Victoria *Times,* and in 1963 was appointed editorial director of the *Vancouver Sun.* His many books include descriptions of Canada past and present, political histories of its prime ministers (eg, *The Incredible Canadian,* 1952, on W.L.M. KING) and studies of Canadian-American relations. Written with feeling and humour, all seek to define the national identity of what he called in 1942 *The Unknown Country,* in 1957 *Tomorrow's Giant* and in 1985 *The Unfinished Country*. JEAN O'GRADY

Reading: Bruce Hutchison, *The Far Side of the Street* (1976).

Hutt, William Ian deWitt, actor, director (b at Toronto 2 May 1920). From his novice days at Hart House Theatre, he has been a distinguished leading player in Canada, the US and England. After making his professional debut in 1948 in summer stock, he worked at Ottawa's Canadian Repertory Theatre. He joined the STRATFORD FESTIVAL in its inaugural 1953 season and appeared in more than 60 Stratford productions, playing nearly every great role in the Shakespearean canon, including Lear, Hamlet, Macbeth, Prospero, Falstaff and Titus Andronicus. He toured N America for several years with the Canadian Players and in Noël Coward's *Sail Away* (1961). In 1964 he created the lawyer in Edward Albee's *Tiny Alice* on Broadway. He was made a Companion of the Order of Canada in 1969 and in 1975 won ACTRA and Canadian Film Awards for his portrayal of Sir John A. Macdonald in CBC's telecast of Pierre BERTON's *The National Dream.* In 1969-70 he was appointed an associate director of the Festival Stage Stratford and in 1976 became artistic director of Theatre London (Ont), overseeing the rebuilding of the Grand Theatre. In 1983-84 he was featured in Robin Phillips's London season and in his Canadian movie, *The Wars*. For the Vancouver Playhouse he was starred in *The Dresser* (1982) and *Masterclass* (1987); also *A Man for All Seasons* (1984), a role he repeated in 1986 at Stratford (and the NAC in Ottawa) when he returned after a 4-year absence to play Cardinal Wolsey in Henry VIII. DAVID GARDNER

Hutterites are one of 3 major sectarian groups (the others are the MENNONITES and the Amish) surviving today and the only group to insist rigorously on the communal form of existence. Hutterite history dates to 1528 when to escape religious persecution a group of about 200 Anabaptists established a communal society in Moravia (now a region in Czechoslovakia). Under the initial leadership of Jacob Hutter, they established the basic tenets of Hutterian beliefs which they have followed with little deviation to this day. These be-

Hutterite colony near Cayley, Alta (*photo by Jim Merrithew*).

liefs, based on early Christian teachings and a belief in a strict separation of church and state, include a form of communal living, communal ownership of property, nonviolence and opposition to war, and adult baptism. Also, they have retained the dress, the customs, the language and the simple austere life-style of their ancestors.

Migration and Settlement Because of their beliefs, Hutterites were subjected to periodic persecution which invariably resulted in migration. They moved from Czechoslovakia to Hungary, Romania, Tsarist Russia, the US, and finally to Canada. They immigrated en masse to Canada in 1918 because of harrassment and persecution in the US that resulted from their refusal to participate in any type of military service. Initially, they settled in Manitoba and Alberta; later settlements were established in Saskatchewan and some were re-established in the US. In 1987 the total Hutterite population was about 30 000 – more than 66% of whom live in Manitoba, Saskatchewan and Alberta, while the remainder are in the US.

Social and Cultural Life Hutterites believe that their society can be best preserved in a rural setting, and hence agriculture has become a basic way of life. Their belief in communal living has led them to establish village-type settlements on each of their farms (or colonies, as they are known). In Manitoba the average size of a colony is about 1600 ha, but in Saskatchewan and Alberta, because of drier conditions, the colonies are each about 3200 ha. Despite these relatively large landholdings, each Hutterite family has about 50% of the land of a typical single-family farm on the prairies. The average colony has about 13 families with a total population of about 85. When the population reaches 125 to 150, the settlements subdivide and form new colonies, on the average every 16 years. In 1987 there were 78 colonies in Manitoba, 46 in Saskatchewan and 119 in Alberta.

The Hutterite respect for the nuclear family is reflected in their provision of private apartments for each family in the row houses they traditionally build. Kindergarten facilities are provided for children from the age of 2½ years. The regular curriculum is studied in colony schools by all students until the eighth grade, after which about 50% of students proceed to grade 10 by means of correspondence courses. Following this a few Hutterites may proceed to take special diploma courses off the colonies such as animal nutrition or veterinary science, and some take teacher training. There are now several fully qualified Hutterite teachers.

The structure of Hutterite colonies remains unchanged, although the nature of the particular economic activity in which they are involved may vary. Each colony elects an executive council from the managers of various enterprises, and together with the colony minister, the executive deals with important matters that will be brought before the assembly (all baptized male members – in effect, men 20 years of age and older). Although women have an official subordinate status, their informal influence on colony life is significant. They hold managerial positions in the kitchen, kindergarten, the purchase of dry goods, and vegetable production.

Although there is co-operation among the colonies, each colony operates as an independent economic unit. The Hutterites practise a highly mechanized and efficient mixed-farming economy. Because of their well-managed, large-scale operations, when compared to the amount of land they own, the Hutterites produce more than their proportionate share of agricultural produce within the prairie economy. Until fairly recently, the basic nature of the Hutterite settlements had been misunderstood, especially in regard to the relatively small amount of land that they own, and their productivity and contribution to the economy had been unappreciated. This had resulted in the past in various restrictions and forms of discrimination against the Hutterites.

Group Maintenance The survival of the Hutterites and their unique way of life is largely the result of their ability to retain their basic and fundamental beliefs, while simultaneously adopting all the features of contemporary society essential for their economic and social well-being. This strategy of survival includes uncompromising adherence to their religious beliefs and customs, retention of their ancestral German dialect, insistence on their own colony schools and a sound agricultural economy. Although some young people leave the colonies, most return, hence assimilation is not a serious problem for the Hutterites. *See also* COMMUNAL PROPERTIES ACT CASE. JOHN RYAN

Reading: J.A. Hostetler, *Hutterite Society* (1974); John Ryan, *The Agricultural Economy of Manitoba Hutterite Colonies* (1977) and "Hutterites," *Horizon Canada*, vol 2, 21 (1988).

Hutton, Sir Edward Thomas Henry, soldier (b at Torquay, Eng 6 Dec 1848; d at Chertsey, Eng 4 Aug 1923). Hutton was general officer commanding the Dominion militia, 1898-1900, historically the most significant of the 8 British officers who held that appointment between 1880 and 1904. He conspired with the governor general, Lord MINTO, and the British colonial secretary, Joseph Chamberlain, to involve Canada in the SOUTH AFRICAN WAR, quarrelled with government over the issue of political patronage in the militia, and was finally recalled to London at the Dominion government's request. Hutton subsequently commanded Canadian troops serving in South Africa, 1900-01. BRERETON GREENHOUS

Hydro-Québec, a provincially owned corporation based in Montréal, is Canada's largest ELECTRIC UTILITY and, judged by assets ($30.6 billion in 1986), Canada's second largest corporation. More than 95% of its production is from renewable HYDROELECTRICITY. First created as a legal entity in 1944, Hydro-Québec did not become a major force until the early 1960s. René LÉVESQUE, then resources minister in the Liberal government of Jean LESAGE, oversaw the nationalization of the province's larger private electrical utilities. In the late 1970s and early 1980s, Parti Québécois governments led by Lévesque further reorganized Hydro-Québec. The utility enjoys formidable economic advantages: once dams are in place, operating costs are very low; furthermore, it has a contract to buy power from the CHURCHILL FALLS project in Labrador at 1969 prices until the year 2041. Hydro-Québec can thus underbid ONTARIO HYDRO in the US export market, provide cheap power within Québec and still pay a dividend to the provincial government.

Québec's first hydroelectric-generating stations were built by private entrepreneurs at the end of the last century. In 1903 N America's first long high-voltage transmission line was placed in service. The 50 kV line ran 135 km from the Shawinigan powerhouse to Montréal. Although the new industry attracted many entrepreneurs, regional monopolies soon dominated the market. Responding to public criticism of poor service and high rates, the Québec government expropriated Montreal Light, Heat and Power Consolidated and its subsidiary, Beauharnois Light, Heat and Power Co, and empowered the Québec Hydro-Electric Commission to administer these 2 companies. Thus, Hydro-Québec was born on 14 Apr 1944.

On 1 May 1963 Hydro-Québec extended its activities to cover the whole province. It purchased the shares of nearly all remaining privately owned electrical utilities then operating in Québec and took over their debts. The total amount involved was $600 million. Hydro-Québec subsequently undertook construction of the Manic-Outardes hydroelectric complex. The project's Daniel Johnson dam is the world's largest arch-and-buttress dam; its Manic 2 is the largest hollow-joint gravity dam. In order to transmit the complex's annual production of about 30 billion kWh over a distance of nearly 700 km, Hydro-Québec had to innovate. It became the first utility in the world to transmit electricity at 735 kV. Since then, its research institute, created in 1967, has pursued intensive research in electric-power transmission. In the early 1970s Hydro-Québec embarked on the JAMES BAY PROJECT. Completed in 1986, James Bay's LG-2, LG-3 and LG-4 power stations added 10 282 MW to Hydro-Québec's generating capacity. In Dec 1987, Hydro-Québec signed its first long-term sales contract, with Vermont Joint Owners, to export surplus electricity to the United States.

ANDRÉ BOLDUC

Hydroelectricity is obtained from the ENERGY contained in falling water; it is a renewable, comparatively nonpolluting energy source and Canada's largest source of ELECTRIC-POWER GENERATION.

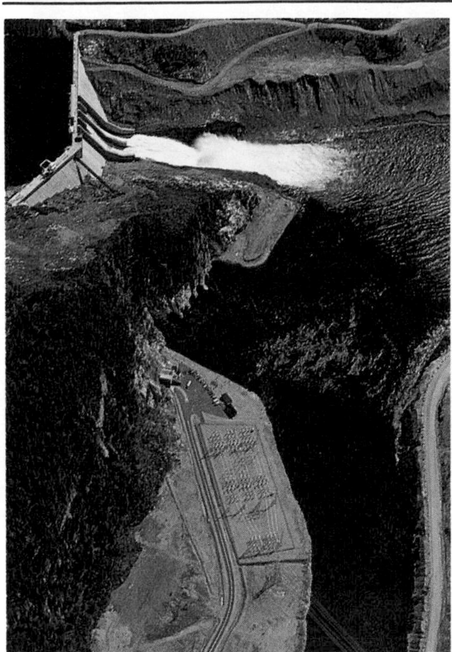

Manic 3 dam on the Manicouagan R in northern Québec (*photo by J.A. Kraulis*).

In N America in the 1850s the energy content of moving water was exploited through the use of small-capacity waterwheels and turbines for the direct drive of machinery, for example, in gristmills and sawmills. By the 1860s many hundreds of turbines, ranging up to 1000 HP capacity, were manufactured annually in the US and by the early 1870s the production of at least one Canadian factory was averaging about 20 machines per year. Hydroelectricity was introduced in the 1880s, soon after Thomas Edison began manufacturing direct-current (DC) electric generators, which were initially belt driven by steam engines. It was not long before enterprising mill owners began to install generators of up to 10-12 kW capacity, with belt drives from existing mill turbines, to provide electric lighting in the mills and adjacent premises. The manifest advantages of electric lighting spawned a ready and increasing market for such service. Where waterpower was close at hand, turbines were installed for the express purpose of driving electric generators for lighting service, initially provided during evening hours only. By the late 1880s generation of electricity by waterpower had become well established. Early use of hydroelectric generation was limited by the capacity of the generating station, which was governed by the waterpower resource (streamflow and net height of fall), or by the electric-lighting load near the station. Beyond a few kilometres, the resistance loss inherent in the transmission of direct-current electricity became excessive. Copper conductors large enough to ensure satisfactory service over longer distances were prohibitively expensive. High-voltage alternating current (AC) transmission, made possible by the development of commercially viable transformers in the 1890s, permitted transmission of ELECTRIC POWER over significant distances without excessive loss, and made possible the development of more remote hydroelectric sites. For example, in 1896 hydroelectric power was transmitted approximately 32 km from NIAGARA FALLS to Buffalo, NY, at 11 000 volts (then considered a phenomenally high level). The possibility of long-distance transmission encouraged great increases in the capacity of hydroelectric-generating equipment: by the early 1900s, 5000-HP directly coupled turbine-generator sets were being produced. For comparison, hydroelectric turbine-generator units of over 600 000-HP capacity are now in service. Beginning in the early 1900s, there was rapid growth in the development of hydroelectric-power sites and progressive increases in transmission-voltage levels. More remote sites were exploited and transmission lines were extended to supply the gradual but strong growth in demand for electric power. In 1903 electric power was transmitted to Montréal from a hydro station at Shawinigan, Qué, via a 135 km long, 50 000 volt transmission line; by 1910 ONTARIO HYDRO was transmitting hydroelectric power from Niagara Falls at 110 000 volts.

By 1900 a total of 133 000 kW of hydroelectric-generating capacity had been installed in Canada. Most of this capacity was in Québec and Ontario, where attractive hydroelectric-power sites were found reasonably near urban centres; there were some smaller developments in the Maritimes, Alberta and BC. In the next 10 years, major hydro-generating stations were established in all provinces except for PEI and Saskatchewan and, in 1910, a hydro development was constructed by a gold-mining company in the Yukon. By the early 1950s, hydro facilities were serving both northern territories. Hydroelectric generation was not developed in Saskatchewan until the early 1960s, when the S Saskatchewan R Development provided control and regulation of the province's major river system.

Growth of hydroelectric generation in Canada continued at a modest rate until the mid-1920s, followed by 10 years of more intensive development, then at a much slower rate through WWII. After 1945, there was a sharp increase in hydro- and thermal-power installations to meet the progressive growth in demand. This growth, which in some provinces exceeded 10% annually, did not slacken until the mid-1970s, when the impact of the international energy crisis of 1973 on economic activity led to a decline in the annual growth rate of electric-power consumption.

In the years 1920 to 1950, hydroelectric stations accounted for over 90% of Canada's total generating capacity. Hydro's share of this capacity declined after 1950, dipping to under 60% in 1976. The decline occurred because fossil-fuel-fired thermal-generating stations then offered a cost-competitive alternative, and because few good hydro sites remained near major population centres and the cost of transmission substantially increased the cost of more remote facilities. However, the cost of competing sources of electricity, principally NUCLEAR POWER and thermal stations burning coal, oil and natural gas, has risen substantially since 1973, and hydro is expected to maintain its 55-60% share of Canadian electrical-generating capacity at least through the 1990s.

Because most hydroelectric installations have been sized to extract the maximum amount of energy available at the power site, based on historical data of average annual streamflow, many stations are able to operate at full output for 70-100% of the time; most other utility systems have annual load factors (rates of average to peak demand) of 50-60%. Consequently, in 1981 approximately 76% of the consumption and 69% of the production of electrical energy in Canada was generated by hydroelectric stations that contained only about 59% of Canada's total electrical-generating capacity.

Waterpower resources basically depend on topography and climate, and development of such energy sources is related to the magnitude and proximity of load centres and to the availability and price of competing energy sources such as coal. The development of hydroelectric power and its share of the total electrical production in Canada varies considerably from province to province. Practically all hydroelectric-power sites in Canada that are reasonably close to load centres have been developed, as have several of the more remote large-scale sites. However, a significant amount of hydroelectric potential remains untapped, chiefly in northern Québec, Manitoba and BC, and in Labrador and the YT. Although this potential is far from existing or foreseeable load centres, much of it may well be developed over the next 2 or 3 decades. The main drawbacks of conventional, large-scale hydroelectric power are the initial high capital cost, the long construction period and the environmental effects of flooding. These factors are offset by the long life and low operating costs of hydro facilities. Interest in smaller-scale or "micro-hydro" projects has revived recently.

Factors that influence the viability of technically feasible hydro sites are almost exclusively economic. Hence, development of such sites would require significant decline in construction and financing costs, greatly enhanced costs of competing energy supply from other sources, development of markets for large amounts of power within reasonable proximity of such remote sites, or prices that would support the cost of transmission to southern markets. Development of the 35 000-40 000 MW of theoretical capacity which is considered not technically feasible is restricted primarily by environmental constraints. Of the 100 000 MW of technically feasible potential, 10-15% is made up of comparatively small-scale sites of less than 50 MW capacity. Most large-scale sites would exceed 500 MW capacity; several would exceed 1000 MW, and at least 2 sites in each of Québec and BC are approximately 3000 MW capacity. The foregoing estimates are mostly preliminary assessments on the basis of map studies with minimal actual site inspection; more comprehensive studies and economic analysis will be required to confirm or reject many of these potential sites on technical or economic grounds.

These estimates of hydroelectric potential do not include the long-recognized but still undeveloped TIDAL POWER potential of the Bay of Fundy in NS, a major source of low-head hydro power adjacent to populated areas of NS and NB. Like river-based hydro, tidal power is a natural hydraulic source that can be converted directly to mechanical and electrical energy by means of a turbine. However, tidal power is very expensive to develop, and the cyclical nature of the energy makes it less useful than river-based hydro.

E.W. HUMPHRYS

Hydrogen (H), the simplest, lightest and most abundant chemical element, is the main fuel for the NUCLEAR FUSION reactions which power the sun. Intensive research is underway to harness fusion energy but hydrogen also shows considerable promise as a potential replacement for conventional fuels.

At normal temperatures and pressures, molecular hydrogen is a tasteless, odourless, colourless gas in which 2 atoms are combined as a diatomic molecule, H_2. It has substantial energy content, reacting readily with oxygen to give pure water and heat as the only products. Using hydrogen as a fuel eliminates the POLLUTION caused by burning conventional hydrocarbons. Hydrogen can be manufactured from a wide variety of renewable and nonrenewable energy sources; however, compared to other fuels, it is still very expensive and difficult to produce, store and transport. In Canada, most molecular hydrogen is produced by the reaction, at high temperature and pressure, of steam with methane (natural gas). Hydrogen also can be produced by applying energy (electricity, heat, solar energy, or some combination) to split water into hydrogen and oxygen. Hydrogen is now used in a wide variety of chemical processes and some scientists and energy planners expect it will become an important fuel for transportation and other applications.

The International Energy Agency maintains an active program of research and development on the production of hydrogen from water, to which Canada is a contributor. In its 1981 report "Energy Alternatives," the House of Commons' Special Committee on Alternative Energy and Oil Substitution recommended that Canada make major investments to establish a leading position in hydrogen technology and systems. In its Oct 1981 report, the Ontario government's Hydrogen Energy Task Force reached similar conclusions. In 1985, the federal government commissioned a report from the federal Advisory Group on Hydrogen Opportunities. The report, entitled *Hydrogen – National Mission for Canada* (June 1987), predicted that the world will move over the next several decades to the major use of hydrogen, first in upgrading fossil fuels such as oil sands and coal, and later as an environmentally clean energy commodity in its own right. A unique opportunity was identified for Canada in leading development of the required technology. An important initiative in this respect has been formation of the Montréal-based Hydrogen Industry Council (1982), which reflects the interests of approximately 50 industrial members.

Applications Alberta and Saskatchewan have rich deposits of BITUMEN in oil sands and heavy oils, which could satisfy Canadian energy needs for generations. The key to producing pipeline-quality fuel from these resources is to increase their hydrogen-to-carbon ratio. In processing plants now in operation, this increase is achieved by coking to reduce the carbon content, but the trend in future could be towards hydrogen addition, to extend the hydrocarbon resource. Similarly, hydrogen could be used to produce methanol from BIOMASS: for example, with hydrogen addition, the dry wood required to produce 1000 t of methanol can be reduced from 2300 t to 900 t.

The substitution of hydrogen for gasoline and other hydrocarbon fuels is a long-term prospect, especially because of the requirements for on-board hydrogen storage. Liquid hydrogen is attractive as an aircraft fuel because its energy content per unit weight is 3 times that of conventional fuels. It is the fuel of the US Space Shuttle and is being considered for use in commercial aircraft. In small vehicles, however, the cost and weight of the cryogenic container for this very low-temperature liquid fuel is likely to be prohibitive.

Production After a decade of intensive work, direct electrolysis of liquid water remains the most viable technology for large-scale hydrogen production from nonfossil energy sources. Groups working in Belgium, Canada, the Federal Republic of Germany, France, Japan and the US have made advances which have sharply reduced capital costs and increased energy conversion efficiency to 85% and more. Canada is in the forefront of these developments. The experimental plant which was opened at Varennes, Qué, in June 1982, is the first commercial-scale demonstration of advanced hydrogen-production technology. The technology has now been applied commercially in plants in Bécancour, Qué (HydrogenAl Inc, fall 1987), and Curitiba, Brazil (Peroxidos do Brasil Ltda, winter 1987-88).

RODNEY L. LEROY

Hydrography is the science of surveying, charting and describing physical features of OCEANS, seas, RIVERS and LAKES. Originally, hydrography encompassed much of OCEANOGRAPHY, plus the general observation, measurement and description of scientific phenomena at sea, but since the voyages of HMS CHALLENGER (1872-76) there has been increasing specialization in the marine sciences. Oceanography has developed as a separate field and hydrography now concentrates on seafloor surveys, studies of tidal phenomena and provision of navigational charts and associated publications. These publications include TIDE and current tables, current atlases and sailing directions ("pilots"). European oceanographers sometimes refer to the measurement of the physical properties of water as hydrography.

The transportable "sweep" system provides total bathymetric survey coverage for the charting of harbours *(courtesy Dept of Fisheries and Oceans/Bedford Institute of Oceanography/photo by Roger Bélanger)*.

Data collected in the field are considerably refined and condensed. Only a representative set including all critical information, such as the least depth over shoals, appears on the published chart. Typically, there is a scale reduction of 2-4 times from the field document to the chart. The chart also includes data from other sources, foreign surveys and charts, engineering drawings of wharves and structures, dredging plans, details of navigational aids (eg, LIGHTHOUSES, BUOYS), etc. Tidal data are analysed for astronomical influences and are used to predict future tides. An international depository of worldwide tidal information is held at the Marine Environmental Data Service (MEDS) in Ottawa. The charts are complemented by "Sailing Directions," providing a written description of information which cannot be shown clearly on the chart itself. These volumes are referenced to the chart and include information on courses, environmental conditions, dangerous hydrographic features (eg, shoals, strong currents) and port facilities. One volume includes the history of early arctic exploration.

Nautical surveying can be traced to medieval times, and a form of sailing directions is reputed to have been available much earlier. Major advances in marine CARTOGRAPHY took place in the 16th century in conjunction with the expansion in EXPLORATION. Early hydrographic surveys and charts resulted from private initiatives. The establishment of national hydrographic departments in France (1720) and Great Britain (1795) was important to Canada, as early surveys of the Canadian coast were conducted by these agencies, with contributions by the Spanish on the Pacific coast. On the Atlantic coast the surveys of Joseph Frederick Wallet DESBARRES and Captain James COOK were particularly notable. Cook's surveys of the St Lawrence R contributed to the success of the British navy in bringing Wolfe's troops to Québec in 1759. In the Arctic, early hydrographic knowledge was gained from the explorations for the British navy of William Edward PARRY and John FRANKLIN, and from those who came in search of Franklin in the latter part of the 19th century. In 1883, following the loss of the steamship *Asia* in Georgian Bay, the first Canadian survey, the Georgian Bay Survey, was formed under Staff Commander J.G. Boulton, RN. In 1904 the Canadian government formed the Hydrographic Service, taking over completely from the British the charting of Canadian COASTAL WATERS. However, the task of completing the work is so great that today many charts still include data collected by British and French naval hydrographers.

Over the years the Canadian Hydrographic Service has evolved, and today operates from headquarters in Ottawa and regional offices in Sidney, BC; Burlington, Ont; Mont-Joli, Qué; and Dartmouth, NS. The Canadian Hydrographic Service, headed by the Dominion hydrographer, is now part of the Department of Fisheries and Oceans. The service is responsible for conducting surveys of all navigable Canadian waters, including inland waterways. It maintains over 1000 navigational charts. During recent years there has been a determined effort to develop expertise in hydrography in industry, and an increasing proportion of the work, particularly that required for offshore oil and natural-gas exploration, is now done outside government. Hydrography is now taught as a specialization of survey engineering at U of New Brunswick. Hydrographic surveyors are usually graduates of technical survey courses or university mathematics or engineering programs who receive special training, often from the CHS. Humber College (Toronto) offers a diploma program in hydrographic surveying.

Canada is a member of the International Hydrographic Organization (est 1921), which has its headquarters in Monaco. This organization works towards ensuring chart uniformity and chart exchange on a worldwide basis and, in collaboration with the Intergovernmental Oceanographic Commission, is responsible for the General Bathymetric Chart of the Oceans. Canada has been particularly active in contributing to this mission.

A.J. KERR

Hydrology studies the behaviour of water: its origin, distribution and circulation; its physical and chemical properties; and its interaction with the physical and living environment. Applied hydrology is primarily concerned with precipitation, with the occurrence and movement of frozen, impounded or flowing water (on or below the Earth's surface) and with evaporation. More specifically, hydrology generally refers to the study of water on or over land rather than in the ocean. Hydrology is concerned with gathering information to determine quantities and rates of movement of water. Quantitative measurements of rainfall, snowfall, the rate at which water penetrates into and moves through soil, streamflow, the rise and fall of lake and groundwater levels, and the evapotranspiration of water into the atmosphere are vital. The science encompasses study of the physical laws governing the movement of water through the hydrologic cycle and the interaction of water with the rest of nature, depending upon various mathematical techniques to define and describe empirical relationships between the movement of water and the conditions and forces influencing it.

History Practical application of hydrological principles preceded a thorough understanding. As early as 4000 BC the Sumerians developed a complicated, extensive irrigation system which lasted some 5000 years. Large-scale FLOOD-irrigation agriculture in the Nile Valley developed at least as early as 3400 BC. In China waterworks date from before 2000 BC. The earliest known hydrological measurements date to 3500-3000 BC, when nilometers were first used to measure the levels of the Nile. Primitive rain gauges existed in India as early as the 4th century BC.

A few early thinkers seem to have had an exceptional understanding of hydrology, but it was not until 1580 AD when Bernard Palissy, a French natural scientist, wrote that rivers and streams were sustained by rain and snow, that the scientific world possessed a realistic description of the hydrologic cycle. A century later, Pierre Perrault and Edmé Mariotté, French physicists, measured rainfall and runoff in the Seine River Basin and proved that rainfall was sufficient to account for river discharge. Soon afterward the English astronomer, Edmond Halley, measured evaporation and demonstrated that evaporation from the Mediterranean Sea could supply the rivers discharging into it. In the late 1600s and 1700s the Italians Giovanni Cassini, Bernardino Ramazzini and Antonio Vallisnieri pioneered the theory of artesian water pressure, and important advances took place in hydraulic theory and instrumentation. Advances in GEOLOGY near the end of the 18th century set the stage for progress in groundwater hydrology. In the latter half of the 19th century, pressure to develop water supplies in Europe forced an intensive study of the field.

In the New World, early emphasis was placed on the measurement of streamflow. In the US and Canada, government programs to measure streamflow and compile records began before the 1900s. A network of climatological observation stations was also started. A statistical and empirical approach to analytical hydrology developed from continuous data collection. For example, using probability theory and the assumption that a record of rainfall or river flow is representative of the rainfall or flow in the future, hydrologists have derived methods for describing the likelihood of occurrence of hydrological events. Approximate relationships between temperature and snowmelt, rainfall rate, ground cover and runoff, DRAINAGE BASIN area and flood magnitude, permeability and groundwater yield, radiation and evapotranspiration, etc, have been defined and used in the solution of practical problems.

Education In 1948 the first Canadian university course titled "Hydrology" was established by R. H. Clark for engineering students at U Man. Thirty years later courses in various aspects of hydrology were being offered in over 40 universities across the country, generally by ENGINEERING and GEOGRAPHY departments. All CIVIL ENGINEERING students now receive some training in hydrology. While there are no faculties dedicated exclusively to hydrology, several universities have hydrological postgraduate programs. Enrolment in these courses varies from year to year; approximately 40 MSc and PhD students graduated annually from Canadian universities during the late 1970s. Postgraduate courses tend to concentrate on the same topics (surface water, erosion, etc) touched on more briefly at the undergraduate level. The computer has made hydrological modelling an important field of graduate study.

Relationship to Other Fields Because of the interrelatedness of water and nearly every other aspect of the natural environment, the lines dividing hydrology from other fields of study are blurred. Meteorology is concerned with precipitation and evapotranspiration, geomorphology with runoff patterns, geology with groundwater flow, soil science and soil mechanics with subsurface flow and plant physiology with transpiration. Supporting sciences, such as physics and mathematics, are necessary for detailed work.

Applications Hydrologists advise water managers in the use and manipulation of water, for example, allocating limited water supplies among various users; sizing structures (eg, spillways, bridges) designed to pass flood flows safely; planning water management or HYDROELECTRIC systems intended to make optimum use of available supplies; forecasting floods and low flows; designing and operating RESERVOIRS, dikes and floodways; designing EROSION-control structures; discovering, inventorying and allocating water from deep underground sources; applying hydrologic principles to soil-plant-water relationships to aid in the production of food and fibre.

Societies and Journals Canadian hydrologists enjoy professional contacts and journalistic outlets through a variety of associations. The Associate Committee on Hydrology of the NATIONAL RESEARCH COUNCIL sponsors hydrological symposia at regular intervals. The journal of the Canadian Meteorological and Oceanographic Society is *Atmosphere-Ocean.* The Canadian Water Resources Association publishes the *Canadian Water Resources Journal*. The Canadian Society for Civil Engineering publishes through the *Canadian Journal of Civil Engineering.* The *Canadian Journal of Earth Sciences* serves the groundwater hydrologist. The American Geophysical Union's *Water Resources Research* and various publications of the American Society of Civil Engineers and the National Water Well Association serve both American and Canadian needs. The International Association of Hydrological Sciences, and the International Assn of Hydrogeologists which produces the *Hydrological Sciences Journal,* provide worldwide scientific communities for the hydrologist. The *Journal of Hydrology* and *Agriculture and Forest Meteorology* are also important journals. UNESCO's International Hydrological Decade, which promoted worldwide research in scientific hydrology 1965-74, was followed by its International Hydrological Programme. In both cases, Canadian scientific and management participation has been significant. R.K. DEEPROSE

Hymns The simple verse-songs of the early Christian church and the chorales and metrical psalms of the Reformation have been sung by Canadians since the 17th century. Prior to the 20th century, hymn singing was not only a method of propagating religious doctrine but also a popular social activity and a means of cultivating knowledge of music. A missionary working among natives near Québec recorded in 1676 that the natives had "much aptitude and inclination for singing the hymns of the church" that were rendered into their language. Annals of 17th-century New France abound in similar comments. The "Huron Carol" ("Jesous Ahatonhia"), attributed to Jean de BRÉBEUF, adapted a French folk melody to Huron words; it remains in popular use at Christmas.

The singing-school movement of 18th-century England and New England became transplanted 1760-1800 to NS, NB and the Canadas by immigrants and Loyalists. After 1800, tune books in Canada catered to the psalm and hymn styles of this movement. Significant publications were Stephen Humbert's *Union Harmony* (1801), notable for its emphasis on fuguing; Mark Burnham's *Colonial Harmonist* (1832); Zebulon Estey's *New Brunswick Church Harmony* (1835); *The Harmonicon* (1836); Alexander Davidson's widely used *Sacred Harmony* (1838); Lemuel C. Everett's *The Canadian Warbler* (1863), adapted from a US collection, and one of the first tune books addressed specifically to children; George Linton's *The Vocalist* (1865 or 1867). During the same era several publications for Anglican worshippers appeared, notably George Jenkins's *A Selection from the Psalms of David* (1821); William Warren's *A Selection of Psalms and Hymns* (1835); James Paton Clarke's *The Canadian Church Psalmody* (1845). For francophone Catholics there was Theodore Molt's *La Lyre sainte* (1844 or 1845) and for Protestants, *Chants évangéliques* (1862).

In the later 19th century, publication became more diversified; several books of hymn texts in native languages appeared, and the "gospel" style attracted popularity. Church authorities began making their own compilations, pioneer instances being *The Presbyterian Psalmody* (1851) and *Methodist Tune Book* (1881). The interdenominational *Canadian Hymnal* (1889) had wide popularity. A Canadian hymnologist, Stanley L. Osborne, remarks that the number of recognized Canadian composers writing hymns appears larger than the number of Canadian poets. Exceptionally productive, however, was David WILLSON (1778-1866), founder of the Children of Peace sect, whose published and unpublished hymn verses total over 1400.

The sect's barrel organ, renovated and in working order at the temple-museum, Sharon, Ont, provides valuable evidence of how the early settings sounded. Despite denominational distinctions, a large common repertoire unites the publications noted. At the same time, all contain originally composed tunes.

In 20th-century Canadian hymnbooks, a notable selection of locally composed tunes continues. *The Canadian Baptist Church Hymnal* (London 1902), the *University Hymn Book* (Toronto 1912) and especially the *Methodist Hymn and Tune Book* (Toronto 1917) contain tunes by prominent musicians such as A.S. VOGT, Alfred Whitehead, W.H. Hewlett, H.C. Perrin and the youthful Ernest MACMILLAN. *The Presbyterian Book of Praise* (London 1897) and *The Hymnary of the United Church of Canada* (Toronto 1930) place less emphasis on locally written music, but set new levels of editorial accuracy. Alexander MacMillan (1864-1961), a major figure in Canadian hymnology, worked on both publications. A Toronto magistrate, James Edmund Jones (1866-1939), was partially responsible for the Anglican Church's *Book of Common Praise* (Oxford 1908), although the influence of the composer Healey WILLAN is strong in the 1938 edition. Of the handsome joint effort *The Hymn Book of the Anglican Church of Canada and the United Church of Canada* (Toronto 1971), Osborne, secretary of the joint committee, states that 10% of the tunes are by Canadians. Responding to revised congregational usages following the Second Vatican Council of the early 1960s were the *Livret des fidèles* (1966) and the *Catholic Book of Worship* (1972).

Whatever changes in taste and performance habits have affected hymn singing, Canadians still respond familiarly to a repertoire embracing "Our God's a fortress firm and sure" (Luther's "Ein'feste Burg," in the 1971 translation by Canadian poet Jay Macpherson) as well as "What a friend we have in Jesus" (with its text by a Canadian, Joseph Scriven, 1819-86) – although extensive Canadian-composed additions to that repertoire await revival. Questions of taste and standards often concern hymnologists and editorial committees as much as the cultivation of a broad repertoire. In 1851 Presbyterians were exhorted to sing their hymns "without any grace notes or ornamental flourishes"; in 1908 Anglicans were allowed such beloved hymns as "Tell me the old, old story," with the reminder that these "would be out of place in many churches"; and in the *Encyclopedia of Music in Canada* (1981) Osborne judged that hymn singing in the 1970s showed immense improvement over that of the 1920s and 1930s. Recordings and radio broadcasts in the mid-20th century were a prevalent means of fostering hymn singing. An outstanding tradition is found in Winnipeg with the work of W.H. Anderson's Choristers and the CBC "Hymn Sing" directed by Eric Wild. *See also* RELIGIOUS MUSIC. JOHN BECKWITH

Reading: J. Beckwith, ed, *Hymn Tunes* (vol 5 of *The Canadian Musical Heritage*, 1986), and ed, *Sing Out the Glad News: Hymn Tunes of Canada* (1987); S. Osborne, *If Such Holy Song* (1976).

Ian and Sylvia, folk music duo composed of singer-songwriter Ian Dawson Tyson (b at Victoria 25 Sept 1933) and Sylvia Fricker Tyson, (b at Chatham, Ont 19 Sept 1940). An accident when he was 19 ended Ian's ambition to be a rodeo cowboy, but the guitar he obtained while recuperating opened up new opportunities. In 1959 he moved to Toronto, started to sing in coffeehouses, and met Sylvia Fricker. Sylvia had grown up in southern Ontario and been exposed to a wide repertoire of music. By 15 she knew she wanted to be a folksinger and, after finishing high school, moved to Toronto.

They soon became full-time professionals and, with their first recording (1961), among the leaders of the folk-music boom in N America. Their repertoire expanded to include their own songs – "Four Strong Winds," written by Ian, was an international hit in 1962, and Sylvia's "You Were on My Mind" was a hit for We Five in 1965 – songs by contemporaries such as Bob Dylan, Gordon LIGHTFOOT, and Joni MITCHELL, and songs taken from their knowledge of country and blues. They were among the first of the "folk" musicians to use electric guitars, strings and other instrumentation. By 1970 their music was a synthesis of country, rock and folk, and they had created a band, The Great Speckled Bird, to help achieve that sound.

In 1970 they started a CTV Network show, "Nashville North," subsequently known as "The Ian Tyson Show" with Sylvia as an occasional guest. As the 1970s began, Ian and Sylvia's professional and marital lives began to split. (They had been married in 1964.) Since 1975 they have appeared together 3 times (in 1979, 1982 and 1986; the last, a concert, was later televised and received a 1987 Gemini for best variety program).

In 1974 Sylvia began to host a CBC Radio show, "Touch the Earth." During its 5-year run, the show provided important exposure for Canadian folk artists and established Sylvia as an independent personality. In 1975 she recorded the first of 2 solo albums for Capitol Records and in 1978 established her own company, Salt Records, to handle her albums and recordings by other folk artists. She has done a CBC TV series and numerous TV specials. In 1986 she produced *Big Spotlight,* her first album in 7 years.

After he took his TV show off the air in 1975, Ian tried unsuccessfully to establish himself in Nashville, Tenn. Following a tour of Canada in 1978, he devoted most of his time to his cattle ranch in Alberta, limiting his musical life to periodic club dates. In 1983 he returned to the recording scene with the critically acclaimed album *Old Corrals and Sagebrush,* and in 1984 followed it with the equally successful *Ian Tyson.* In 1986 he produced and distributed *Cowboyography.* In 1987 he won the Juno Award for Best Country Male Vocalist. RICHARD GREEN

Iberville et d'Ardillières, Pierre Le Moyne d', soldier, adventurer (bap at Ville Marie [Montréal] 20 July 1661; d probably at Havana, Cuba 9 July 1706), third and most famous of Charles Le Moyne's 12 sons. Iberville displayed his bravado on the expedition led by de TROYES against the English on James Bay, and was rewarded with the governorship of the conquered posts. He returned to the bay in 1688, 1690 and 1694, raiding English posts and seizing furs. On 5 Sept 1697, his lone ship *Pélican* defeated 3 English warships near YORK FACTORY, sinking 2.

Iberville's fierce courage and ruthlessness were forged in desperate colonial competition and savage border wars. In 1689, he took part in a brutal guerrilla attack on Corlaer, New England, in which some 60 settlers were massacred. In 1696-97, he led militia, Indians and French soldiers on a rampage across Newfoundland, burning, looting and killing some 200 men. In 1698-99, 1699-1700 and 1701-02, Iberville commanded expeditions to Louisiana, establishing Forts Maurepas, Mississippi, Louis (Old Mobile), collecting furs and negotiating with the Indians. His last campaign (1706), the plundering of the English colony of Nevis in the West Indies, was clouded by controversy. Iberville died that year, likely of yellow fever, but was convicted of various charges, and most of his estate was seized in reparation. His career was an uneasy mixture of commercial ambition and military zeal but, though his conquests were ephemeral and his actions often cruel, his daring roused the admiration of even his enemies. He was the first native Canadian to receive the CROIX DE SAINT LOUIS (1699), for valour. JAMES MARSH

Ice, including snow, is the solid phase of water. It is useful to think of it this way rather than as "frozen water" because water can achieve the solid phase through the freezing of liquid water or by direct deposition (sublimation) of water vapour, its gaseous phase. These different processes can produce distinct ice forms in the atmosphere or on or below the Earth's surface. The form taken by the solid phase of water is often important in determining its environmental and other roles. Snow is one distinctive form of ice; others include GLACIER ice, river ice, lake ice, SEA ICE, ground ice of various types, HAIL, CLOUD crystals, hoar and rime. Ice crystals are typically hexagonal, a direct result of an internal symmetry produced by the orderly packing of the 3-atom water molecules (H_2O) of which each crystal is composed. This crystal form is found in cloud crystals considerably under 1 mm in diameter to crystals of over 10 cm diameter found in some glaciers.

Ex-voto painting commemorating Iberville's victories. The saint is depicted in the upper portion, Iberville below, and above him a ship depicting one of his naval encounters (*courtesy Basilique Ste-Anne-de-Beaupré*).

Snow is one type of solid precipitation originating in the atmosphere and falling to the surface of the Earth. At below -40°C, ice crystals may be initiated from water droplets in the atmosphere by a spontaneous change from the liquid to the solid phase of water. At much lower temperatures spontaneous change from gas to solid can occur. Tiny hexagonal crystals produced in these ways form cirrus clouds and the flickers of "diamond dust" often seen on cold, sunny days. Once in existence within clouds of supercooled water droplets, such ice crystals may grow into snow crystals through the deposition of water vapour because air has a lower capacity for holding water vapour in the presence of ice. The particular hexagonal form achieved by the growing crystal is determined by prevailing humidity and, especially, temperature conditions. When a crystal begins to fall through its cloud, further growth occurs by the accretion of supercooled cloud droplets, or riming. This is growth by freezing as distinct from vapour deposition. Graupel, heavily rimed snow, is an extreme product of this process. Rime, ice produced by the freezing of tiny, supercooled droplets, is not only important in the atmosphere, where it can cause aircraft to become iced up, but also on the Earth's surface. While falling, many snow crystals may combine to produce a snowflake.

In the warmer portions of the cloud, or outside the cloud en route to the surface, snow crystals may melt or evaporate (sublimate). Much of the rain which falls in Canada results from snow melting on its way to the surface. Hail, a type of solid precipitation characterized by layers of ice which are a record of alternate freezing and thawing in turbulent thunderclouds, is a good example of the involvement of the various changes of phase of water in the production of a distinctive ice form. Much of the cloud seeding in RAINMAKING or hail-suppression experiments is aimed at producing ice in water clouds.

On reaching the Earth, snow often forms a snowpack. The general tendency is for the pack to compact and densify before either melting and running off or turning into glacier ice. Melting and freezing may quickly produce layers of "real ice" in the pack, but in cold areas it may take many years for the pack to compact into ice.

The freezing of water droplets or the nucleation of water vapour, in the atmosphere and elsewhere, produce various distinctive ice crystals which may combine to form bulk ice composed of many crystals. On and below the Earth's surface such bulk ice, produced by the freezing of substantial amounts of water or by the densification of the snowpack, forms most of the ice present (*see* PERMAFROST; PERIGLACIAL LANDFORM).

Ice forms on freshwater bodies when surface temperatures fall slightly below freezing point. As the maximum density of water is achieved at close to 4°C, lake surface water cooled to that temperature becomes heavier than warm water below it and sinks. The warmer water, displaced from below, is cooled in its turn and also sinks. Thus, before ice can form on a lake, the entire water column has to cool to 4°C through overturning so that freezing temperatures can be achieved at the surface. When ice does form, much of the lake will still be at 4°C. In rivers, the turbulence of flow prevents freezing until the entire water column

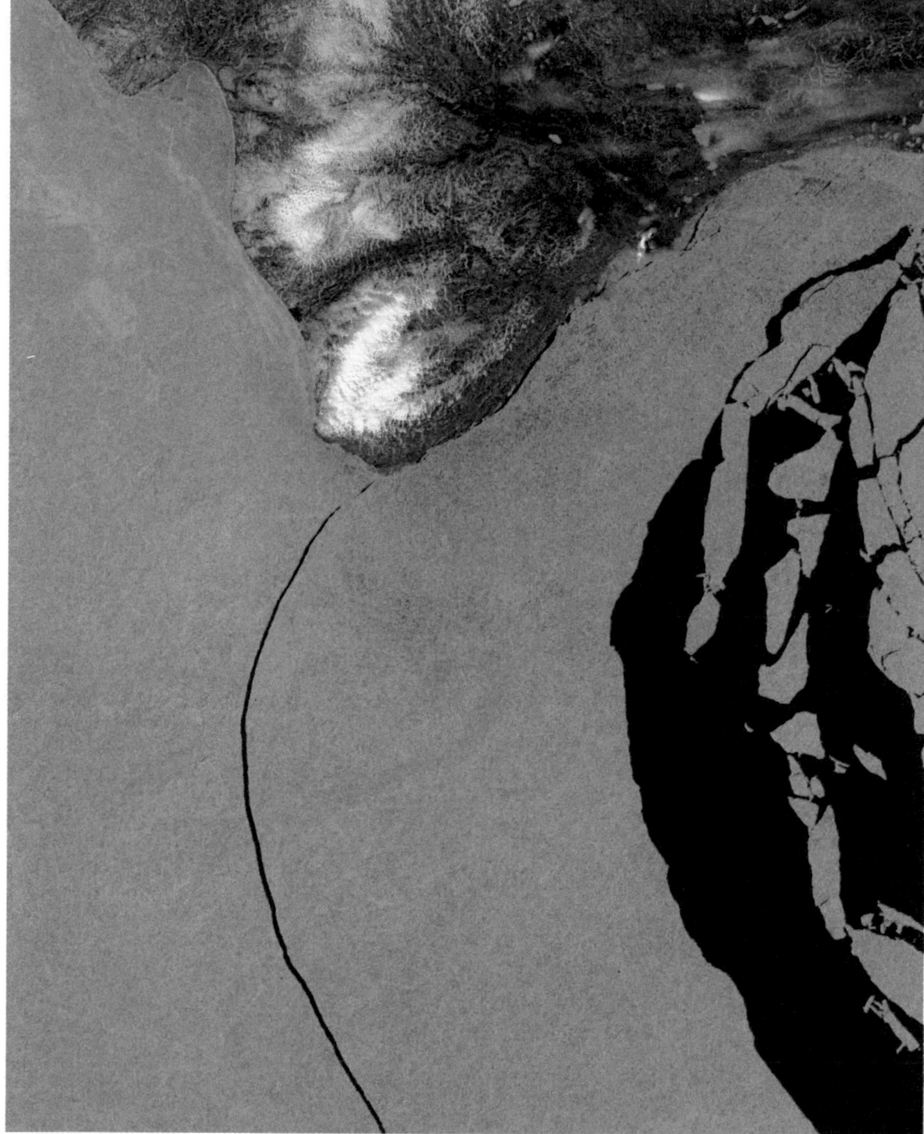

Ice types in Amundsen Gulf, tip of Banks I (centre top). The dark area shows first year ice; the lighter shows multi-layer ice. On the right is a rarely seen large fissure (*courtesy Canada Centre for Remote Sensing, Energy, Mines & Resources Canada*).

has been reduced to 0°C. On lakes, the initial random orientation of ice crystals on the water surface tends to be replaced, as the ice thickens, by vertically oriented 6-sided columns. This process forms a clear sheet of "black ice." The columns often become loose during spring breakup to form distinctive "candle" crystals. Flooding of snowpack lying on a lake produces slush which, on refreezing, forms a distinctive white ice composed of randomly oriented crystals.

These 2 types of ice provide a good illustration of relationships between the process of ice production, the form of ice and the environmental implications of that ice. For example, black ice with its orderly arrangements of crystals is effectively transparent to light; white ice reflects or absorbs most light falling upon it.

Most major forms of ice have been found buried beneath the Earth's surface. It is not unusual for large pieces of glacier ice to be buried and preserved or for snowbanks to be buried in rock avalanches. Ice also actually forms and survives beneath the Earth's surface. Ice beneath the Earth's surface can affect drainage, the condition of surface topography and the development of vegetation. Year-round ground ice proper is a feature of PERMAFROST regions, where its presence is made readily apparent by such features as PINGOS (*see* PERIGLACIAL LANDFORM). In such regions it presents a considerable problem for construction.

Ice, particularly snow, is a major control of the flow regimes of Canadian rivers. Most rivers achieve peak annual flow in spring, as the accumulated precipitation of many months runs off in a period of days or weeks. In colder areas most annual precipitation runs off at this time. Rivers flowing from the mountains, as in the case of some prairie rivers, may, of course, be snow- or glacier-fed all summer. The nature of winter precipitation also controls the low-flow phase of many of our rivers. Except in warmer southern areas, where high evaporation and evapotranspiration offset rainfall to produce late summer droughts, Canadian rivers tend to achieve minimum flows in late winter. At this time, they have been deprived of runoff for months, as precipitation has been held up in the snowpack. In the North and in permafrost regions generally, flows can reach zero where rivers freeze to their beds. Naleds or "icings" are an ice form which may result in such situations. Even Niagara Falls is mainly ice at this time of year.

As a northern temperate region, the populated part of Canada has ice and snow in abundance, ensuring that most areas of the country have sufficient fresh water for society's needs. Snow provides other benefits, ie, to winter recreation as an insulator of the ground, etc. But there are also attendant climate hazards. Snow-removal costs exceed $1 billion per year in Canada; indirect costs (ie, increased fuel consumption, travel delays, etc) are even greater. The centres in Canada which receive most snow are Goose Bay, Nfld, with 409 cm annually; St John's, Nfld, 364 cm; Québec City, Qué, 336 cm; Kapuskasing, Ont, 322 cm; and Charlottetown, PEI, 305 cm. *See also* GLACIATION; AVALANCHE. PETER ADAMS

Reading: D.M. Gray and D.H. Male, eds, *Handbook of Snow* (1981).

Ice Age, the Pleistocene epoch of geologic time, during which periodic, extensive glacial activity occurred in many parts of the world. The Pleistocene is generally considered to encompass the time beginning 2-3 million years ago and ending 10 000 years before the present. *See also* GLACIATION; GEOLOGICAL HISTORY. N.W. RUTTER

Ice Cap, large mass of ICE that originates on land by compaction and recrystallization of snow. Ice caps flow outwards in several directions and submerge most or all features of underlying land. An ice mass constrained by bedrock to flow in one direction, usually along a valley, is called a GLACIER. This distinction is not sharp; for example, an ice cap surrounded by mountains may be drained by a series of valley glaciers. Ice caps and glaciers form where annual snowfall exceeds the amount lost by melting in summer. As a layer of snow is buried by subsequent falls, it is gradually transformed to ice. The ice flows outwards under gravity, carrying the overlying snow with it. At lower elevations, all of the previous winter's snow and some of the ice are removed by melting and runoff, and in some cases by calving of ICEBERGS into an ocean or lake. The surface profile of the ice mass does not change much from year to year, however, because the ice that flows out of the accumulation area approximately balances that lost from the lower reaches.

If snowfall increases or summers become colder, so that melting is reduced, the ice starts to thicken and, after some years, the ice front starts to advance. Conversely, a reduction in snowfall or an increase in summer warmth eventually produces a retreat. Interpretation of the record of advances and retreats is complicated because each ice mass has its own characteristic response time which depends on its size and speed.

Mountain ranges in western Canada contain many ice caps. The best known is the COLUMBIA ICEFIELD, a major tourist attraction on the Banff-Jasper hwy. It has an area of over 300 km^2 and is drained by several valley glaciers, including Athabasca Glacier. Its surface elevation varies from about 2600 to 3500 m, the large range being a reflection of the peaks and valleys in the bedrock underneath. The icefield's average thickness is probably no more than 100-150 m, although the thickness of parts of the outlet glaciers is more than double this. Velocities range from a few metres per year in the centre to about 100 m per year in Athabasca Glacier. About 4 m of ice is melted from the lower part of the glacier each summer. Present flow from the icefield does not quite compensate for this; thus, the glacier is retreating from the position it reached about 100 years ago, after a long period when the CLIMATE was colder than it is today.

The largest ice caps in Canada are on ELLESMERE I, where 3 have areas exceeding 20 000 km^2, and on AXEL HEIBERG, DEVON and BAFFIN islands. The ice in some of these caps is up to 1 km thick. Because both snowfall and melting in the Arctic are much less than in western Canada, the arctic ice caps are less active. Although few measurements have

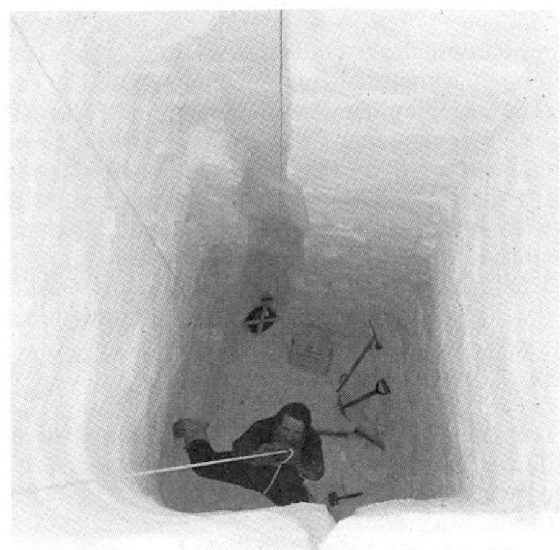

Man descends an ice hole for glaciology studies, Mer de Glace Agassiz Ice Cap, 1977 (*photo by Peter Reshitnyk*).

been made, velocities are probably only a few tens of metres per year.

The world's largest ice caps, covering Antarctica and Greenland, are usually called ice sheets. The Antarctic Ice Sheet has an area of over 12 million km^2 and a maximum thickness of about 4.5 km. If it were to melt, world sea level would rise as much as 75 m. The Greenland Ice Sheet has an area of 1.7 million km^2 and a maximum thickness of about 3.2 km. Glaciers in West Greenland produce icebergs hazardous to shipping and drilling rigs in the N Atlantic.

Taking samples from the central part of a polar ice cap by drilling through it provides a continuous record of past snowfalls. Annual layers can sometimes be distinguished; if not, the ice can be dated by other means. Chemical analyses of core samples from Greenland, Antarctica and arctic Canada have given detailed records of past climates, particularly temperatures, extending in some cases over as much as 100 000 years. Small amounts of other materials such as volcanic ash, wind-blown dust, pollen and, in recent snow, acids and fallout from nuclear tests have been found. W.S.B. PATERSON

Ice Skating probably originated in Scandinavia over 2000 years ago as a means of transportation. It was also practised on the canals of Holland during the Middle Ages. Early references to skating in England date from the 17th century. The first skates were made from the shank or rib bones of elk, reindeer and other animals, and the word "skate" likely derives from the early German word *schake*, meaning shank. As a social and recreational pastime, skating was popular in Britain and France during the 18th century, and the world's first skating club was formed in Edinburgh in 1742.

In Canada, according to legends, the Iroquois had skated, tying animal shinbones to their footwear with leather thongs; and in Acadia, French explorers were skating as early as 1604. Skating as a sport was introduced into Canada by British garrison officers in the 1840s, and quickly gained a strong following. It was thought especially appropriate for girls and women, and thus became an important social pastime. Canada led the world in the development of early skating rinks, and the first prepared outdoor commercial rink in the country was opened in Montréal in 1850. The first covered rink in the world was built in Québec City in 1852. The early rinks were built with natural ice; large sheds provided the skater with shelter from the wind and snow. The most famous of these early rinks was the Victoria Skating Rink in Montréal, built in 1862 and at that time the largest in the world. From this rink the game of ice hockey took its standard rink size. The first artificial rinks in Canada were built in Victoria and Vancouver, BC, during the winter of 1911-12, and artificial rinks are now found in most sizable communities. However, Canadians still skate for pleasure on frozen lakes, ponds and rivers. Ice skating is fundamental to the game of ice HOCKEY and competitively takes the form of FIGURE SKATING, SPEED SKATING and ice dancing.

The evolution of the skate to the modern steel blade or tube variety passed through several stages. Skates made entirely of iron were introduced in the 17th century. Steel skates, fastened with screws and clamps to the wearer's shoes, were first made in the 1850s. In 1861, John Forbes of Dartmouth, NS, developed the first spring-skate; adjusted with a single lever, it eliminated the need for screws and plates. Eventually, this style was replaced by the skate with blade permanently attached to the boot. In 1887 the Amateur Skating Assn of Canada was founded, in Montréal, for both speed and figure skating. In 1939 figure skaters formed the Canadian Figure Skating Assn. BARBARA SCHRODT

Reading: Nigel Brown, *Ice Skating: A History* (1959).

Iceberg [Dan or Nor, *isberg*, "ice mountain"], a piece of ice that has become detached from its parent GLACIER by a process known as calving. The glacier may be flowing into a FJORD, or may be an ice shelf (floating glacier of large dimensions extending beyond the coastline). Icebergs thus created may melt or disintegrate, giving rise to smaller pieces called growlers and bergy bits. Icebergs calve from a parent glacier as a result of the manner in which the glacier enters the water or, subsequently, from tidal and wave action or possibly as a result of EARTHQUAKE shocks. Less commonly, icebergs may suddenly emerge from below water level as a result of forces acting on part of a glacier protruding under the water.

Appearance Most icebergs are white except along freshly calved ice cliffs, which tend to appear blue. Others may appear green, brown or black, or combinations of these colours. These icebergs have usually rolled over, exposing basal ice, or have emerged from below water level. The various colorations are caused by differences in density, air-bubble content and impurities. For example, black ice is of high density and bubble free; dark layers indicate the presence of rock materials derived from the base of the parent glacier. Occasionally, rocks may be found on the original upper surface of the iceberg. As the iceberg melts, these materials precipitate into marine or lake sediments.

Occurrence and Dimensions Some icebergs are trapped in lakes; the vast majority occur in oceans. Flat-topped tabular bergs are sections of almost flat ice shelves. In the Antarctic they are commonly several tens of kilometres square and several hundred metres thick. One of the largest tabular bergs seen measured 160 km x 72 km and one of the longest measured 185 km. A typical height above waterline would be 35-45 m, implying a total ice thickness of 250-320 m, although much greater thicknesses are possible. In the Arctic Ocean, the term ice island is applied to pieces of floating shelf ice that form principally on the N coast of ELLESMERE I. These thin tabular icebergs are 20-60 m thick, often up to 100 km^2 in area, and typically protrude 2-6 m above water. Irregularly shaped icebergs are more typical of coastal Greenland and northern Canada. Many irregular bergs originate in Greenland fjords containing fast-flowing outlet glaciers coming from the inland ice sheet. Because these glaciers usually terminate below the snowline and because they are often extremely broken up in their journey to the sea and then by tidal and wave action, they can give rise to very irregular bergs of almost pure ice, their spires occasionally reaching 100 m above sea level.

Iceberg in the Labrador Sea. Icebergs are usually white, except along freshly calved ice cliffs, which tend to appear blue (*photo by John deVisser*).

Aerial view of an ice island in surrounding frozen arctic waters. The outline of the island shows clearly through in the ice pack, along with gentle ridges on the island (*courtesy Energy, Mines & Resources Canada*).

Dynamics and Stability The composition of antarctic tabular bergs gradually changes from snow on the top surface to ICE by about the waterline. This fact, combined with their tabular shape, makes them much more stable than typical arctic icebergs, which quickly tilt and finally roll on their voyage to destruction. Calving from an already tilted iceberg may shift the centre of gravity sufficiently to cause the iceberg to roll, posing a threat to ships. On the long term, icebergs are driven principally by ocean currents, but other forces produced by wind shear and wave action especially during storm conditions may significantly influence the short term motion of an iceberg. The Coriolis force also influences the drift path of icebergs. Melting below sea level takes place continuously; above sea level, intermittently, according to location. Depending on the shape of the iceberg and rock content, the volume of ice submerged compared to the total ice volume is in the ratio of the density of the ice to that of seawater, or about 0.88 in arctic and 0.85 in antarctic icebergs. The above-water shape of an irregular iceberg does not necessarily provide information about its underwater geometry. This may be discovered through the use of airborne RADAR or side-scan SONAR from a ship. These studies and others (eg, towing tests and iceberg-stability investigations) are carried out at the Centre for Cold Ocean Resources Engineering (C-CORE), St John's, Nfld.

Because the ocean transmits wave energy, icebergs respond to wave action. Thus, in addition to drifting with ocean currents, icebergs are known to oscillate vertically and to roll with a periodic motion. Since icebergs possess natural periods of oscillation dependent on their density and their thickness, they may tune in to certain ocean waves. Waves possessing the right period will tend to cause resonance in the iceberg, with a consequent increase in the size of oscillation. This behaviour changes continually with the changing shape and thickness of the iceberg. An ideal, rectangular block iceberg with a mean thickness

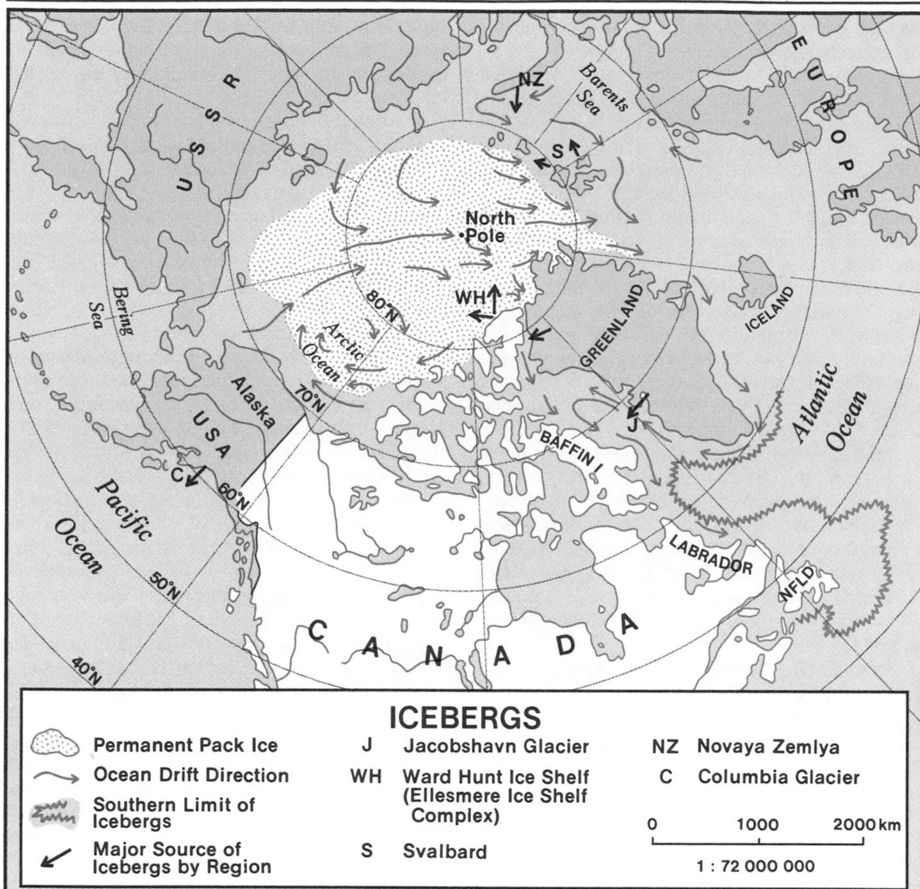

of 200 m would have a natural period of oscillation of about 26 seconds, which is in the range of common wave-swell periods. The thinner arctic ice islands have a much lower natural period of oscillation and, having horizontal dimensions much greater than their thickness, tend to absorb ocean waves as filtered travelling waves, which induce flexing of the ice. As the ice island thins by melting, this process may lead to its fracturing and breaking into smaller pieces. Most Greenland bergs melt before reaching 40° N lat (roughly opposite Philadelphia, Pa), although occasionally some bergs reach almost 30° N. Satellite imagery has been used to track large bergs (*see* REMOTE SENSING).

Applications T3 and other arctic ice islands on which aircraft can land have been used intermittently by the US and USSR as mobile research platforms for about the last 30 years. Since 1985 a Canadian station has been maintained on an ice island that calved from the Ward-Hunt Ice Shelf in 1983. Because many ice islands become trapped in Arctic Ocean current gyres, they survive for many years, melting and crumbling at the edges only slowly. In 1977 and 1980 conferences were held to investigate the possibility of moving antarctic icebergs to places where water shortages are frequently acute, eg, Australia, California and Saudi Arabia. This controversial project, however, has not yet materialized.

Hazards In the Northern Hemisphere icebergs present a threat to human activities. Off the coasts of Labrador and Newfoundland, recent petroleum explorations necessitate the presence of drill platforms, which may be endangered by icebergs. In the vicinity of Valdez, Alaska, the Columbia Glacier is showing signs of disintegration in its terminal region. As a result, bergs will drift into Prince William Sound and pose a danger to oil tankers operating from the port of Valdez. US Geological Survey glaciologists have posted iceberg forecasts. Oil and gas operations in the Beaufort Sea and between the Queen Elizabeth Is are threatened by collisions between even small ice islands and platforms and bottom structures (eg, PIPELINES). The threat to shipping in the N Atlantic is now minimal, as a result of the establishment of the International Ice Patrol after the sinking of the TITANIC (Apr 1912).

G. HOLDSWORTH

Reading: L.H. Howard, *Icebergs* (1986).

Icebreakers Canada has had an icebreaker capability for over 100 years. Indeed, one of the promises of Confederation – a guaranteed year-round ferry service between Prince Edward Island and the mainland – resulted between 1876 and 1899 in the construction of 3 small icebreaking FERRIES. At the turn of the century Canada's first full icebreakers, the *Champlain* and *Montcalm,* were built to break up ice barriers and dams that caused annual flooding at narrow points along the St Lawrence R. Icebreakers were first used in the Canadian Arctic in the 1920s to deliver supplies and services to native and isolated settlements during the short summer season, and to back up claims of Canadian sovereignty over the NORTHWEST PASSAGE and Arctic Archipelago. In the 1930s the port of Churchill was opened for grain shipments and in 1957 the government undertook the annual supply of Distant Early Warning (DEW) line sites across the Arctic. Recent economic development in northern Canada, particularly the extraction of raw materials, has again increased the demand for icebreaker services.

Canada operates 22 of the world's estimated 100 icebreakers: 18 owned by the CANADIAN COAST GUARD (CCG) as part of Transport Canada and 4 by private oil companies. An icebreaker's chief function is to break, separate or divert ice in ice-covered waters, and the CCG icebreaker fleet has been designed and built for specified Canadian needs: to assist shipping in lakes, oceans and river mouths; to keep channels open through the ST LAWRENCE SEAWAY system; and to support government supply and economic development operations in the Arctic. The CCG icebreakers are classified as heavy (8 vessels), medium (7 vessels), and light (3 vessels). Canada's most powerful icebreaker, the *Louis S. St. Laurent* of 13 800 tons displacement (dwt), is smaller than the two 23 500 dwt nuclear-powered icebreakers of the Soviet Union's *Rossiya* class (one in service, one being completed). However, the "Polar 8" icebreaker, designed as a 35 000 dwt ship with 100 000 shaft horsepower (shp), will be the world's largest conventionally powered icebreaker. In 1987 a Vancouver-based joint venture group was awarded the $7.85 million design contract; award of the construction contract is still pending. Construction is to be completed in 1992 at an estimated cost of $347 million. One of the CCG's heavy icebreakers, the *John Cabot,* is also equipped for submarine cable laying and repair. The *Canmar Kigoriak* (7200 dwt) owned by DOME PETROLEUM LTD, though now inactive, was used to convoy other kinds of marine units working in Arctic ice, such as drilling rigs; it was basically experimental, the prototype for the gigantic 200 000 dwt icebreaker-tanker of the future.

Canada, like all nations with icebreakers (Argentina, Finland, Sweden, Japan, W Germany, the US and the USSR), operates many other kinds of ships built to function in ice conditions. These ice-strengthened marine units range from experimental cargo ships, such as the M.V. *Arctic,* to the mobile arctic caissons owned by large private companies involved in offshore oil drilling in the Beaufort Sea.

Heavy icebreakers in the CCG fleet generally operate in southern waters in the winter months and the Arctic during the summer. Though the *Louis S. St. Laurent* has worked in Hudson Bay in December, no serving Canadian icebreaker is able to penetrate Canadian Arctic water during the severe winter season from November to May. The "Polar 8," which has the category of an Arctic 8 type ship, could operate year-round in Arctic waters. This Arctic numbers classification is part of the Canadian Arctic Shipping Pollution Prevention Regulations instituted in 1970. For example, an Arctic 3 icebreaker, which is the category assigned to the 3 "R" or *River* class of CCG heavy icebreakers and tthe *Canmar Kigoriak,* can maintain a speed of 3 knots through ice 0.9 metres (3 feet) thick in what

The *Terry Fox,* a Canadian-built icebreaker, which is classified as Arctic 4, is used in the Beaufort Sea by Gulf Canada Ltd (*photo by Ranson Photographers, Edmonton, for Gulf Canada*).

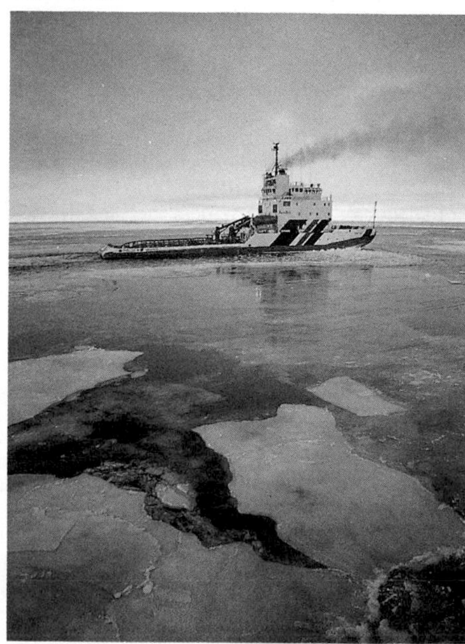

is called "the continuous mode." This expression refers to the steady movement forward of the icebreaker through the water. An Arctic 7 icebreaker can maintain a speed of 3 knots through ice 7 feet thick. The icebreakers owned by GULF CANADA LTD, the *Terry Fox* and *Kalvik*, are classified as Arctic 4. Under severe ice conditions Arctic 3 ships such as the CCG's "R" class and Gulf Canada's 2 Beaufort Sea vessels have operated beyond their category up to Arctic 4 and 5, respectively.

Canada's future need for advanced icebreakers is not likely to be as large as that in the USSR. The composition of Canada's icebreaker fleet depends on the level of demand for their services in ice-covered waters. For example, the transportation of oil and gas from the Arctic by water would result in a considerable increase in the icebreaking capability in Canada. JOHN D. HARBRON

Icelanders, coming by way of Greenland, were the first European visitors to what is now Canada. ERIC THE RED established a settlement in Greenland in about 985 AD, and in 986 BJARNI HERJÓLFSSON made the first known sighting by Europeans of the NE coast of Canada. Archaeological excavations at L'ANSE AUX MEADOWS demonstrate that Norse settled in Newfoundland. KARLSEFNI'S son Snorri was probably the first European born in what is now Canada.

Origins Iceland, an island settled in the 9th century AD by renegade NORWEGIAN chieftains and their followers, is warmed by the Gulf Stream and has a fairly moderate climate. Its uninhabitable interior is a volcanic mountain plateau of glaciers, lava fields and desert, but the treeless coast provides grazing land for sheep and cultivation. The Icelandic *Althing* (est 930 AD) is the oldest parliament in the world. The nation has the highest literacy rate in the world, with more books, periodicals and newspapers published per capita than anywhere else.

Through the centuries Icelanders suffered many natural calamities. By 1800 the national population was reduced to only 47 000 by disease, starvation and volcanic eruptions. In the 19th century, new disasters, including sheep epidemics, a deterioration in the climate and more volcanic eruptions, followed. The Danish government, which controlled Iceland at the time, offered to relocate the entire population to Denmark. The Icelanders declined, although small parties immigrated to Brazil and Wisconsin. The first Icelander to land on Canadian shores since his Norse ancestors was 22-year-old Sigtryggur Jonasson, who arrived in Québec City on 12 Sept 1872.

Migration In 1873 about 150 more Icelanders arrived in Québec, encouraged by Jonasson. They were given free transportation to Ontario by the Canadian government, as well as offers of free land. Rosseau, in the Muskoka district, was selected as a site, but government employment, which had been promised until the land was cleared, was not adequate, and most settlers soon left, leaving behind a small permanent settlement. A second party arrived in 1874, settling in Kinmount, Ont. A Nova Scotian immigration officer induced a large number to relocate at what the Icelanders called Markland, NS, near Halifax, with offers of land, household appliances and financial aid. The land was not arable, however.

Settlement Patterns In 1875, 235 Icelanders travelled N by flatboat on the Red R from Winnipeg, Man, to the W shore of Lk WINNIPEG. There they had been promised an Icelandic reserve in what was then an unorganized part of the North-West Territories. This reserve, established by an order-in-council, became New Iceland, a unique political structure in Canadian history. In 1876, 1200 others joined the first group. Fifty immigrants had remained in Winnipeg the first year, and 200 the second, creating the basis for the first permanent urban Icelandic settlement in Canada.

In New Iceland the settlers created their own laws, maintained their own schools, and generally managed their own affairs. A series of natural disasters, including floods and a smallpox epidemic 1876-77, decimated the population, until in 1878 a general exodus to Winnipeg and North Dakota began. By 1881 the population of the New Iceland area had declined to about 250. In 1881 as well the provincial boundaries were extended N, and New Iceland became part of Manitoba, though remaining, to this day, heavily Icelandic. The main settlement in New Iceland was GIMLI. Other rural areas of Manitoba settled by Icelanders include Lundar (on Lk Manitoba); Glenboro, in the SW region of the province; SELKIRK, N of Winnipeg; and Morden to the S.

Icelanders continued to immigrate to Winnipeg throughout the last 20 years of the 19th century. Later settlements were established in rural Saskatchewan and Alberta, but these were largely settled by families and individuals moving from Manitoba and from Icelandic settlements in the US. Descendants of Icelanders now live across Canada. Between 1978 and 1984, 105 Icelanders immigrated to Canada.

Economic Life Most of the immigrants remained in farming, generally their profession at home. Agricultural settlement in Ontario and Nova Scotia proved unsuccessful and conditions in New Iceland were not much better. The freshwater fishery contributed to the economic viability of New Iceland.

The immigrants sent their children to universities whenever possible, which may have influenced the pattern of assimilation. Icelanders did not encounter much prejudice and there was a fairly high rate of intermarriage between Icelanders and the settled population. Typically, Icelanders entered the professions, particularly medicine, law and education.

Social Life and Community From the time New Iceland was settled, Icelanders have preserved elements of traditional Icelandic society, culture and language. Factionalism, however, has permeated almost all of the Icelanders' endeavours, and this is reflected in their many voluntary associations, most of which, in New Iceland, were organized around religious themes and topics. The most important association historically, the Icelandic National League of N America, was founded in 1919 to assist Icelanders to adapt to Canada and to preserve elements of Icelandic heritage. Chapters of the league were established in almost every traditional Icelandic settlement and in the cities to which children of the immigrants had relocated. Icelandic Canadian clubs now exist in many Canadian cities. In 1942 the Icelandic Canadian Club began publishing the first English-language Icelandic publication in N America, the *Icelandic Canadian* magazine.

The Icelandic associations have traditionally hosted events for social and educational reasons, the most important being the Icelandic Festival (*Islendingadagurinn*), held annually since 1932 in Gimli on August 2. Originally, the purpose was to commemorate the granting of a constitution to Iceland in 1874, but in time it has also become an event to honour the Icelandic pioneers in Canada.

Religion and Cultural Life The Lutheran Church (the state church in Iceland) has been the most prominent, and the Icelandic Evangelical Lutheran Synod of America held its first conference in Winnipeg in 1885. The Unitarian Church was the second-largest church among Icelanders, although it is not clear how this situation developed. The first Unitarian Church opened in 1892. Considerable political and theological rivalry existed between members of the 2 denominations in Winnipeg and this carried over into many of the smaller, rural communities. The United Church is now the second-largest denomination among Icelanders.

The first Icelandic newspaper in N America was *Framfari* (*The Progress*), published in New Iceland between 1877 and 1880. Between 1879 and 1910, 8 other publications originated in Gimli. In 1886 the Icelandic newspaper *Heimskringla* (*The World*) was founded. *Lögberg* (*The Tribune*) was founded in 1887, partly in opposition to *Heimskringla*. They were amalgamated in 1959 into *Lögberg-Heimskringla*.

Literature dating the sagas and the settlement of Iceland is probably the most unifying theme in Icelandic culture. The Icelanders in Canada have produced many poets and novelists writing in both English and Icelandic. Stephán G. STEPHANSSON is considered by many critics to be the foremost Icelandic poet of this century. Stephansson's contemporary, Guttormur J. Guttormsson, was born in New Iceland in 1878 and did not visit Iceland until 1939. He was best known, perhaps, for the poem *Sandy Bar*, a tribute to the Icelandic pioneers in New Iceland. Contemporary Icelandic writers include Laura Goodman SALVERSON, first editor of the *Icelandic Canadian* magazine and author of *The Viking Heart* and *Confessions of an Immigrant's Daughter*, and William Valgardson, author of *Bloodflowers* and other works.

Education In Iceland literacy has long been a requirement for marriage and everyone was expected to have an intimate knowledge of the early sagas. In New Iceland a request was made for provision of a school even before homes had been built. In Winnipeg, Icelandic was first taught at Wesley College (now U of Winnipeg) in 1901. In that same year the Manitoba Department of Education approved the teaching of Icelandic in provincial schools (when requested by parents) and U of Manitoba accepted it as a second language for incoming students. In 1951 the Chair in Icelandic Language and Literature was established at U of Manitoba. The Icelandic collection in U of Manitoba library now has a full-time curator and over 14 000 volumes.

Politics Icelanders are not identifiable with any particular political ideology or Canadian political party, although many have distinguished themselves in political service. In 1898 Sigtryggur Jonasson was elected to the Manitoba legislature to represent St Andrews. Thomas H. Johnson was appointed attorney general and minister of public works for Manitoba in 1915, becoming the first Icelandic Cabinet minister in Canada.

J. MATTHIASSON

Reading: William Kristjanson, *The Icelandic People in Manitoba: A Manitoba Saga* (1965).

Ice-Worm, common name for *Mesenchytraeus solifugus*, a dark-pigmented oligochaete worm (*see* ANNELIDA) up to 4 cm long, found in tangled masses in melting ice of GLACIERS in the Pacific Northwest; similar ice-worms are also reported from Greenland and the USSR. The specific name *solifugus* aptly means "flees the sun": in spring and summer the worms feed on algae at the surface of the ice only at twilight, since they are vulnerable to temperatures above 7° C. Curiously they are not freezing-resistant, although they can tolerate supercooling down to -7° C. In winter the overlayer of snow insulates the worms from the lethal effects of freezing, and they can select optimum temperature zones by vertical migration. The woolly ice-worm of the High Arctic is a caterpillar of lepidopteran *Gynaephora*, which is tolerant of freezing and overwinters in exposed conditions. The term "ice-worm" is also applied to the primitive insect *Grylloblatta campodeiformis*, a slender, wingless animal, creamy white in colour, sometimes found at edges of melting glaciers in the Canadian Rockies. Scott of the Antarctic referred to ice-worms on the underside of spring pack ice, but these were filamentous diatoms (*see* ALGAE). Ice-worms are part of Canadian folklore. An Inuit myth refers to Sikusi, "a woolly and mischievous ice-worm" and a notorious melter of igloos, which freed an Inuit from Tuktoyaktuk who was frozen in ice. Robert SERVICE wrote the "Ballad of the Ice-worm Cocktail," whose subject was a piece of dyed spaghetti with painted eyes.

R.G.B. REID

Igloo, or snowhouse, was a winter dwelling utilized by INUIT across the Arctic. Some Inuit spent most of the winter in semisubterranean houses made of driftwood and whalebone and only used the igloo when travelling. Others relied on igloos for housing through the entire winter. The dome-shaped igloo was built spirally from within. The structure derived its strength from the key block, inserted at the apex of the roof. A series of these domes were constructed, connected by passageways, to house 15-20 people. Furniture consisted of cooking pots, oil lamps and low platforms. Temperatures inside the igloo were just below freezing or warmer.

RENÉ R. GADACZ

Igloolik, NWT, Hamlet, pop 857 (1986c), 746 (1981c), is located on an island off the MELVILLE PENINSULA in the FOXE BASIN Lowlands, 1641 air km NE of Yellowknife. The area provides a unique record of unbroken INUIT habitation, with the oldest site established about 2000 BC. Sir Thomas BUTTON was the first *qallunaaq* ("white man") to visit the area, in 1613. Umik, a local Inuk, set up a mission at the site in the early 1920s where he preached his own brand of Christianity. A Roman Catholic mission was established in the area 10 years later and an HBC post in 1939. The community's residents subsist on hunting, fishing and sealing.

ANNELIES POOL

Igloolik Sites, archaeological sites located on the islands at the northern end of FOXE BASIN, in the vicinity of the village of IGLOOLIK. They appear to have been continuously occupied for the past 4000 years. Prehistoric hunters were attracted to the area by rich sea-mammal resources, principally seals and walrus. Isostatic uplift has resulted in a series of raised beaches, so that the archaeological remains of older beach occupations are at present found at greater elevations above sea level than are those of more recent occupations. This situation has allowed archaeologists to demonstrate an unmatched sequence of occupation and cultural development throughout the Paleoeskimo period between about 2000 BC and 1000 AD. The area was also occupied after 1000 AD by prehistoric THULE CULTURE Inuit, whose descendants continued to use the region through the historic period. *See also* ARCHAEOLOGY; PREHISTORY.

ROBERT MCGHEE

Iglulik Inuit (or Igluligmiut) are known by the name of an important settlement site which translates as "it has houses." Iglulik country extends from Chesterfield Inlet on NW Hudson Bay northward along MELVILLE PENINSULA and across the northern third of Baffin I. Population estimates of about 500 were made in 1822 and in the 1920s. There were about 2650 Igluligmiut in 1985. A dialect of Inuktitut is spoken and main contacts in traditional times were with the BAFFIN ISLAND INUIT in the NW and the NETSILIK in the southern part of the area. Intermarriage with those groups has occurred since the late 19th century. Important Igluligmiut habitation sites have been used since as early as 2000 BC. First European contact dates from the early 19th century. Explorers PARRY, RAE and HALL all travelled in Iglulik country. From 1860 to 1910 a number of US and Scottish whalers wintered in the area and were the first forces of change. After 1920 trade in white-fox furs and the influence of missionaries and police brought more change. The reports of the Danish Fifth Thule Expedition, 1921-24, are the main source of information on Igluligmiut traditional culture. The oral traditions, religion, social and material culture differ only in details from that of neighbouring groups. However, occurrence of superior marine resources, especially walrus and several species of whales, made possible a high level of subsistence.

In recent years settlement has concentrated around Repulse Bay, Mittimatalik [Pond Inlet], Hall Beach, Arctic Bay and Igloolik, which were formerly centres of trade. In 1972 Igloolik became the site of extensive scientific research with the studies of the International Biological Program. Later, a permanent research station was established. In 1974 a silver, lead and zinc mine was opened at NANISIVIK in northern Baffin I, providing employment for a number of Igluligmiut. *See also* NATIVE PEOPLE: ARCTIC.

Ignatieff, George, diplomat (b at St Petersburg, Russia [Leningrad, USSR] 16 Dec 1913). Ignatieff joined the Dept of External Affairs in 1940 and developed an expertise in East-West relations, particularly at the UN, where his service included terms as Canadian ambassador 1966-69 and president of the Security Council 1968-69. He was also ambassador to Yugoslavia 1956-58 and permanent representative to NATO 1963-66. After retirement he spoke eloquently on behalf of disarmament causes, and he was named disarmament ambassador by PM John TURNER. He was provost of Trinity Coll, U of T, 1972-79 and chancellor of U of T 1980-86. In 1986 he was Brockington lecturer, Queen's U. His memoirs, *The Making of a Peacemonger,* were published in 1985.

ANNE HILLMER

Igneous Rock, one of 3 rock classes, the others being SEDIMENTARY and METAMORPHIC rocks. Igneous rocks are the product of the solidification of magma, molten rock generated by partial melting caused by heat and pressure in the deeper parts of the Earth's crust or in the upper mantle. These hot magmas have lower densities than their source rocks and rise buoyantly to the surface. On the way, they cool and may crystallize partially or completely. Early formed, dense crystals may separate from the magma, causing a change in the composition of the residual melt. This process of differentiation, along with compositional variations inherited from the original source material during partial melting, accounts for most of the diversity of igneous rocks. The coarse grain size of granites implies crystallization of a magma under conditions of slow cooling at depth; the finer grain size of basalts indicates more rapid cooling upon extrusion onto the Earth's surface. Glassy rocks imply conditions of rapid chilling with no time for crystal nucleation and growth.

Today, the floors of the oceans are composed largely of basalts; granites are a major component of the continental crust. Igneous activity has been present throughout the Earth's GEOLOGICAL HISTORY, and igneous rocks occur throughout the geological column in Canada (*see* GEOLOGICAL REGIONS). However, because internal temperatures were higher in the early stages of the Earth's history, the rate of magma production has probably declined over time. Granites and basalts are well represented in the old rocks of the Precambrian SHIELD regions of Canada and in the younger, flanking mountainous regions of the Appalachians and the western CORDILLERA. Some of the best examples of the most recent volcanism in Canada can be found in BC: the Mt Garibaldi belt in the S; several centres in Wells Gray Provincial Park in central BC; and Mt Edziza and Level Mt in the N. Dates as young as 1340 years ago have been recorded for the latest activity at Mt Edziza and 220 years ago for a flow at Aiyansh, near Terrace, BC. Some of these volcanic centres are possible sources of GEOTHERMAL ENERGY.

C.M. SCARFE

Île-à-la-Crosse, Sask, Northern Village, pop 1030 (1986c), 1035 (1981c), located on an expansion of the upper CHURCHILL R, called Lac Île-à-la-Crosse. The name may derive from the shape of the lake – supposedly resembling a bishop's staff – or from an island in the lake on which the Indians played lacrosse. The lake provides a connecting route from the Churchill R to Methye Portage and was thus a strategic spot in the FUR TRADE. Montréal-based trader Thomas FROBISHER and others were active in the area in the 1770s and the HBC built a post on the lake in 1799. From here the Athabasca brigades headed NW. In 1846 Fathers LAFLÈCHE and TACHÉ established a mission. Their episcopal "palace" was a crude log shelter smeared with mud. In 1860 Sisters Agnes, Pépin and Boucher founded a convent. A landing strip was cleared in the late 1940s as a base for BUSH FLYING. Today the community is a centre for trapping and fishing.

JAMES MARSH

Illustration, Art The earliest printed image relating to Canada is a bird's-eye-view of HOCHELAGA and environs, published by Giovanni Ramusio in Venice in 1556. This fanciful view owes more to the unknown artist's preconceptions about the nature of the country surrounding the future Montréal than to his immediate source, Jacques CARTIER'S written description of his visit to the Iroquois village in 1535.

Subsequent graphic renderings of the bare facts brought home by explorers and traders were to depend upon the interpretative facilities of engravers who had never visited the sights they depicted. This may likewise be said of the primitive sketches of Samuel de CHAMPLAIN, published in his narratives of his voyages between 1604 and 1632; of Marc LESCARBOT in his *Histoire de la Nouvelle France* (1609); of the botanist J.P. Cornut in his *Canadensium Plantarum* (1635-62); of Fr François Du Creux in his *Historia Canadensis* (1660); and Father Louis HENNEPIN, in whose *Nouveau Voyage d'un pais plus grand que l'Europe* (1698) is to be found the first recorded impression of Niagara Falls and perhaps the first true illustration of a Canadian landscape. In each case, firsthand experience was translated by second and third parties.

New France did not produce its own engraved imagery until after 1760, as it lacked both the market and the presses required for the printing of copper plates. The spread of British settlement in the Maritimes and in Upper Canada, however, included not only printers and publishers – and readers – but artists and engravers. The published views and charts of the topographers Thomas Jefferys, Richard Short and Capt Hervey Smyth in the early 1760s, of J.W. DESBARRES, author of *The Atlantic Neptune*, in the 1770s and 1780s, and of Joseph Bouchette in the 1830s, are testament to the interest that had been sparked in England by the establishment of a British presence in N America. These delineations of Halifax, Québec and other sites and sights may be described as "illustrations" only insofar as they were issued in multiple, reprographic formats, usually as bound or loose portfolios, with minimal letterpress.

After conquest and colonization came exploration and exploitation. Almost from the beginning, probers of Canada's far-western, far-northern, Pacific coast, and high-arctic regions felt duty-bound to back up their reports with their own or with colleagues' sketches and watercolours. This tradition, inculcated in the naval and military colleges as a discipline to sharpen perception and assist in the positioning of ordinance, extended roughly from the 1770s to the 1870s. It embraces the published journals and voyages of the likes of James COOK (whose shipboard artist was John Webber), John MEARES, Samuel HEARNE, George VANCOUVER, Sir John ROSS (whose 1819 *Voyage of Discovery ... in His Majesty's Ships Isabella and Alexander* features an aquatint after a drawing by a Greenland Inuit stowaway, John Sackhouse or Saccheuse), Edward PARRY, G.F. Lyon, Robert Huish, and F.W. BEECHEY.

Undoubtedly the most accomplished of the author-artists associated with boreal latitudes was George BACK, whose on-site watercolours were first reproduced along with those of the equally gifted Robert HOOD in Sir John FRANKLIN'S 1823 and 1828 narratives of northern expeditions. Back's own sketches, engraved by Edward Finden, grace his *Narrative of the Arctic Land Expedition to the North of the Great Fish River...* (1836), but the stresses of his last, near-disastrous voyage, related in his *Narrative of an Expedition in HMS Terror ... in the Years 1836-37*), forced him to turn over the draftsman's role to his first lieutenant, William Smyth.

The disappearance of Sir John Franklin's 1845 expedition led to a renewal of public fascination with the polar and subpolar regions, as documented by numerous illustrated narratives. By the turn of the century, however, and the attainment of the North Pole and the traversing of the NORTHWEST PASSAGE, the attention of readers and publishers had turned to the Antarctic; the Arctic archipelago and islands would not be reclaimed for Canada until the expeditions undertaken for artistic purposes by members of the GROUP OF SEVEN in the 1920s and 1930s.

By the 1770s, a new genre had entered the picture in the form of the illustrated land-travel narrative and its fictional and poetical counterparts (*see* EXPLORATION AND TRAVEL LITERATURE). A vast literature was an outcome of the arrival in the New World of entrepreneurs, settlers, tourists, naturalists, surveyors and fur traders with a penchant for diarizing and description. This printed material, as often as not, was complemented by engraved and lithographed interpretations of the scenery, buildings and peoples encountered during the course of journeys along waterways and the westward-advancing trails, roads and rails. Perhaps the most pleasing such volume, from an artistic as well as literary point of view, is *Travels Through the Canadas* (1807), by a talented amateur exponent of the prevailing Picturesque style, George HERIOT. The year 1842 saw the appearance in London of 2 especially accomplished and influential publications: Coke Smyth's *Sketches in the Canadas*, and N.P. Willis's *Canadian Scenery from Drawings by W.H. Bartlett*, the former illustrated by lithographs, the latter by engravings. By mid-century, however, British interest had begun to wane, and N American publishers took over the issuing of travel and immigrants' guides, narratives and collections of views for European and – increasingly – domestic readerships.

The introduction of printing into Nova Scotia and Québec in the 1760s and 1770s, and Upper Canada in the 1790s, did not initially accommodate visual artists. What is considered to be Canada's first printed picture – a view of Halifax – appeared in the *Nova Scotia Calendar* in 1776. Possibly the first engraved landscapes to be executed in Canada appeared in 1792 in John Neilson's *Quebec Gazette*: a view of Québec and another of Montmorency Falls, by J. Painter and J.G. Hochstetter, respectively. The first known engraved portrait, also by Hochstetter, was printed in the *Quebec Magazine* in the same year. The capital of Lower Canada remained the hub of the graphic arts and printing industries until the ascendancy of Montréal in 1850s, and of Toronto in the 1870s and 1880s. *The Picture of Quebec*, authored and illustrated by George Bourne, was published by David Smillie & Sons in Québec in 1829; Adolphus Bourne brought out views of Québec by R.A. Sproule in 1830 and, most significantly, Thomas Cary and Sons issued *Quebec and its Environs* by the military topographer James P. COCKBURN, in 1831. Bosworth Newton's *Hochelaga Depicta* (1839), featuring lithographs after paintings by James D. Duncan, was published in Montréal, while *The British American Cultivator* (1842), with wood-engravings by Frederick C. Lowe, was published in Toronto.

The Narrows of the Saint John River, watercolour by George Heriot, a talented exponent of the Picturesque style (*courtesy of the Royal Ontario Museum*).

Up to this time, improvements in the standards of published illustrations were thwarted by the lack of trained engravers and lithographers to translate drawings or paintings into reproducible form. Work usually had to be sent to Europe or the US until skilled practitioners could be lured to Canada from abroad. Lithography, though invented in 1776, was not introduced into Upper Canada until Samuel Tazewell briefly established his lithographic press in Kingston in 1830. It remained for Toronto's Hugh Scobie to make a success of the new technology, however, and the possibilities of this economical if cumbersome mode of reprography did not begin to be explored fully until tintstone lithography and its successor, chromolithography, and their abettor, the steam-driven rotary press, came to the fore in mid-century. As late as 1859, Paul KANE, author of perhaps the single-most important Canadian illustrated book of the 19th century, *Wanderings of an Artist*, had to resort to a London publisher to ensure that his paintings and watercolours were properly translated into chromolithographs and wood-engravings. Agnes Dunbar Chamberlin had to make do with hand-colouring the black-and-white lithographs taken from her own watercolours to illustrate Catherine Parr TRAILL'S *Canadian Wild Flowers* (1868), which did not appear in chromolithographic form until 1885.

The most common use to which lithography was initially put was the illustrated county atlas; later, it was adapted to the creation of advertising posters, billboards, trade-cards and labels. A specialist in all these forms was the Toronto Lithographing Co, able to boast in the 1890s of being one of N America's largest and most advanced such firms. Its art department employed a number of the period's best-known artist-illustrators, among them W.D. Blatchly, William Bengough, J.D. Kelly, C.W. JEFFERYS and J.E.H. MACDONALD. In 1909 the company was absorbed by Stone Ltd, which in turn joined Rolph and Clark to become Rolph, Clark, Stone in 1917. Hamilton, Montréal and Ottawa also supported major lithography houses.

Wood-engraving came to Toronto in 1849 with the arrival of John Allanson, a Newcastle native who had trained under the master of the white-line block, William Bewick. Allanson's *Anglo-American Magazine* and *Canadian Journal*, both launched in 1852, were illustrated with views of Hamilton, Kingston and Toronto. Quality remained variable, however, until the immigration from London to Toronto of Frederick Brigden Sr. Buying out his partners, the Beale brothers, he renamed the company first the Toronto Engraving Co and then Brigden's Ltd. Catalogue, newspaper and trade-periodical work became its forte. Adapting to the new photomechanical processes that came along in the 1880s, the company flourished under the directorship of his artist son, F.H. Brigden. Brigden's opened a Winnipeg branch which, like its Toronto counterpart, attracted many well-known illustrators who also made reputations as painters and printmakers – among them Charles COMFORT, H.E. Bergman, and Fritz BRANDTNER.

The scarcity of expert engravers in Montréal, and the growing numbers of skilled photographers, may have induced engraver William A. LEGGO to formulate the world's first halftone reprographic process, Leggotype, in 1869. That year, the world's first magazine halftone appeared in the first issue of *Canadian Illustrated News*, published by G.E. DESBARATS. The magazine survived until 1883 and was illustrated with Leggotypes up to 1871, when technical problems caused Desbarats to return to line-engravings as his mainstay. Among prominent illustrators in his employ were William CRUIKSHANK and F.M. BELL-SMITH, who covered the Toronto scene, and Henri JULIEN, the weekly's Montréal artist. Though its population base and advertising clientele were not large enough to sustain so ambitious an undertaking, the paper inspired imitators, including Desbarats' own *L'Opinion Publique* (which shared visual content with *CIN* but was editorially independent) and *Dominion Illustrated News*, *Canadian Graphic*, and SATURDAY NIGHT, which celebrated its 100th anniversary of continuous publication in 1987.

Grip was a journal devoted to politics produced by J.W. BENGOUGH. He was author of *A Caricature History of Canadian Politics* (Toronto, 1886) and set up the Grip Printing and Publishing Co, which in collaboration with the Toronto Litho Co issued *Canadian War News* covering the 1885 North-West Rebellion. Grip Ltd, the graphic design company that grew out of the publishing concern, went on to employ Tom THOMSON and most of the future Group of Seven – all trained as photoengravers, lithographers or illustrators. The departure of their art director, A.H. Robson, in 1912, induced them to follow him to the rival firm of Rous and Mann Ltd or to seek careers as full-time painters of the Canadian wilderness. Group members Franklin CARMICHAEL and A.J. CASSON were subsequently lured to the leading Toronto silkscreening establishment, Sampson-Matthews.

The most ambitious Canadian publishing venture involving wood-engraving was *Picturesque Canada*. With text by George Monro GRANT, it appeared in serial form in 1882-84 under the imprint of the Art Publishing Co, and in 2-volume book form in 1884. The publishers, H.R. and R.B. Belden, were American expatriates who had started out in Canada as producers of illustrated county atlases. The art director, L.R. O'BRIEN, began to choose his subjects and commission artists and engravers as early as 1880. He encountered controversy almost immediately, however; his contention that the paucity of skilled Canadians meant that outsiders had to be given the task of depicting his country roused the fury of his chief rival, John A. FRASER, and precipitated Fraser's decamping for the US in 1882. The Canadian contributors were O'Brien himself, Henry Sandham, Fraser, O.R. Jacobi, the marquess of LORNE, William RAPHAEL, F.M. Bell-Smith and Robert HARRIS; the American contingent, headed by Frederick B. Schell and J. Hogan, vastly outnumbered its Canadian counterpart.

The disappointment associated with *Picturesque Canada* and the economic depressions of the 1870s and 1890s drove more and more Canadians southward, led by Fraser and Sandham who both enjoyed a measure of success as book and periodical illustrators in the last decades of the so-called "golden age of black-and-white." Their breakthrough into the American market attracted swelling numbers to follow in search of well-paying magazine, newspaper and book-illustration jobs. The wave, which had been anticipated by cartoonist Palmer Cox (inventor of "The Brownies"), portraitist Wyatt EATON, and animal artist and writer Ernest Thompson SETON included J.A. Fraser's brother, W.L. Fraser, who edited *Century Magazine*; Jay Hambidge, later a prominent art theoretician, Charles Broughton and William Bengough, whose departure from Toronto in 1892 inspired coevals C.W. Jefferys, David F. Thomson and Duncan McKellar to follow. Although the call of home and the displacement of the illustrator's role by that of the photographer made many return to Canada, a select few stayed to garner the rewards still to be won: Arthur Crisp, Arthur William Brown, Harold Foster, Robert Fawcett and Norman M. Price, the latter a book and magazine illustrator who had first made a name for himself in London as a founding member of Carlton Studios. This innovative advertising and publishing graphics house, fd 1902, was the brainchild of 4 former employees of Grip Ltd and members of the Toronto Art Students' League – Price, A.A. Martin, Arthur Goode and T.G. Greene – employed J.E.H. MacDonald in 1904-07. Martin's adoptive father, Thomas Mower MARTIN, painted the watercolour landscapes for the most lavish successor to *Picturesque Canada*, Wilfred Campbell's *Canada* (1907), the front cover of which bears the Carlton Studios logo.

The Toronto Art Students' League (est 1886) fostered the cause of Canadian illustration and Canadian nationalism alike through the annual souvenir calendars it published between 1893 and 1904. Active contributors of decorative borders, lettering and drawings, which after 1895 were on explicitly Canadian themes, were C.W. Jefferys, C.M. Manly, Robert Holmes, F.H. Brigden, A.H. Howard, D.F. Thomson, J.D. Kelly, T.G. Greene, A.A. Martin, Norman Price and J.E.H. MacDonald. Especially brilliant are the *art-nouveau* cover designs of the otherwise obscure R.W. Crouch. Intended to show off not only the skills of its contributors to potential clients and critics but the level of reproductive quality achieved by their printers, the calendars are proof that the supplanting of hand-engraving by photoengraving was not such a disaster as some opponents of the new medium had predicted. While betraying the influence of the leading American and European illustrators and designers of the day, they strike a distinctly native note in both style and content.

Though the league disbanded in 1904, to be replaced by the Maulstick Club, the Graphic Arts Club (later the Canadian Society of Graphic Arts) and the Arts and Letters Club, its legacy survived not only in the work of its most prolific and high-profile member, Jefferys, but in the paintings, illustrations and teaching activities of Manly, Holmes, Brigden and MacDonald, spiritual leader of the Group of Seven. Jefferys went on to become Canada's most versatile all-round illustrator, adept at editorial and book as well as at newspaper and advertising work. *Uncle Jim's Canadian Nursery Rhymes* (1908), with text by David BOYLE and

The Betrothal (*c* 1928-1933), gouache, by Clarence Gagnon (*courtesy The McMichael Canadian Coll/gift of Col R.S. McLaughlin*).

drawings by Jefferys, may well be Canada's first colour-illustrated children's book, but owing to the bankruptcy of its British printer it was never distributed in the country of its origin. Similarly, his crowning illustrative achievements were the pen-and-inks he prepared for a projected but abortive edition of the works of Thomas Chandler HALIBURTON in 1915 (although it was published in 1956, after his death, under the title *Sam Slick in Pictures*). His only serious competitors as historical artists were his contemporary, J.D. Kelly, best known for his series of paintings for Confederation Life, and Kelly's successor, Rex Woods, probably the most technically accomplished practitioner in the field. His Québec equivalents were Henri Julien (as a master of pen-and-ink) and E.J. MASSICOTTE, who after 1918 produced hundreds of drawings, paintings and engravings depicting French Canadian habitant life and customs.

These subjects were the stock-in-trade of F.S. Coburn, remembered as an illustrator for his interpretations in oils and pen-and-ink of the dialect poetry of W.H. DRUMMOND, published in New York by G.P. Putnam's Sons. More ethnically authentic are the images provided by Symbolist painter Ozias LEDUC to Dr E. Choquette's *Claude Paysan* (1869) and to Benjamin Sulte's *Contes canadiens* (1899); J.C. Franchère's decorations for his own *Chansons canadiennes* (1907); and M.A. SUZOR-COTE for the most frequently illustrated piece of Québec fiction, Louis HEMON's *Maria Chapdelaine* (1916). The exquisite tempera paintings executed by Clarence GAGNON for a deluxe Paris edition of this novel probably constitute the finest suite of book illustrations to be produced in this country, though Gagnon's pictures for L.F. Pouquette's *Le Grand Silence Blanc* (1929) come a close second.

Nor were "legitimate" English Canadian artists reluctant to try their hands at illustration and design in the first third of this century, encouraged as they were by the enlightened editorial and art-directional policies of such supportive publishers as McClelland and Stewart, Ryerson Press (headed by Dr Lorne PIERCE), Ottawa's Graphic Press, Macmillan (Canada), J.M. Dent (Canada) Ltd, Musson, and Rous and Mann Press Ltd. Group of Seven members J.E.H. MacDonald, F.H. VARLEY, A.Y. JACKSON, Arthur LISMER, F.H. JOHNSTON, Frank Carmichael and Edwin HOLGATE all made significant contributions to the modernizing of the illustrated book in the 1920s and 1930s, as did their contemporaries Stanley Turner, W.J. PHILLIPS, Bertram BROOKER, J.W.G. MACDONALD, Robert PILOT, Charles Comfort and A.C. Leighton. Thoreau MACDONALD, J.E.H.'s son, through his highly characteristic black-and-white work for *Canadian Forum*, Ryerson Press and his own private Woodchuck Press, deserves the title of Canada's most adept and well-loved book designer and illustrator. His production spans 6 decades, from the 1920s to the 1970s and, though much imitated, has never been equalled.

During both great wars, Canada's graphic artists, like its painters and sculptors, were called upon to support the national effort by contributing to the propaganda campaigns organized both by the federal government and by private industry (WAR ARTISTS). The most noticeable form their endeavours took was the poster, WWI's most gifted exponent of which was Arthur Keillor. WWII's Harry Mayerovitch was a protegé of John GRIERSON of the National Film Board.

After WWII there was a brief flourishing of magazine illustration – both editorial and advertising-related – on the American model, though the popular printed media were more and more heavily dominated by photography. Several artists made considerable illustrative and graphic-design reputations for themselves in this period, including painters who exhibited regularly in the tradition of double callings established in Canada in the 1880s and 1890s: eg, Franklin Arbuckle, William Winter, J.S. Hallam, Jack BUSH, Oscar CAHÉN and Harold TOWN. The magnet of the US again attracted many of the finest talents. Unlike his ex-compatriot Doug Johnston, who reached the top of his profession in New York in the 1970s, James Hill came back to his native Toronto late in the same decade: though less lucrative, the Canadian commercial-art marketplace is also less voraciously competitive than its American cousin.

Periodical illustration has enjoyed a renaissance in the past decades, thanks to a half-dozen or so art directors who have given opportunities to a new generation of illustrators. Several of its members have taken advantage of the doors opened for them by the departure southward of their patrons and mentors and made entrées in the glossy big-circulation magazines. The precariousness of the Canadian publishing scene, as exemplified by the demise of such former venues as *Liberty, Canadian Home Journal, Mayfair* and *Weekend Magazine*, means that secure markets for quality work remain few and rates of pay are comparatively low. The highest degree of experimentation and innovation at present and likely for some time to come is to be found in the specialized field of computer graphics.

Book illustration over the past 30 years has become increasingly restricted to CHILDRENS' LITERATURE and school texts on the one hand, and to the limited-edition *livre d'artiste* on the other. Among the most conspicuous names associated with the former category in the period 1950s-70s are Fred J. Finley, Selwyn Dewdney, John A. Hall, Leo Rampen, John Marden, Lewis Parker, Vernon Mould, Frank Newfeld, Carlos Marchiori, Elizabeth Cleaver and Laszlo Gal. Many of this company also authored the words they illustrated: witness R.D. Symons, Annora Brown, Illingworth KERR, Clare Bice, James HOUSTON, William KURELEK, Shizuke Takashima, Ian Wallace and Ann BLADES. Bice, Kerr and Kurelek are typical of the serious painters and printmakers who have made noteworthy forays into the field of book illustration in the past few decades, including Jean-Paul LEMIEUX, D.C. MacKay, Jack SHADBOLT, Eric Aldwinckle, Philip SURREY, Allan HARRISON, Lorne Bouchard, Saul Field, Laurence Hyde, Joe Rosenthal, Aba BAYEFSKY, Louis de NIVERVILLE, Dennis BURTON, Tony URQUHART, Gordon RAYNER, Greg CURNOE and Vera FRENKEL, Paul Fournier, Charles Pachter and Glenn Priestley.

A related phenomenon is the incidence of books illustrated (and, occasionally, written) by

Rebels of 1837 Drilling in North York, 1898, by C.W. Jefferys, whose historical illustrations have been reproduced in virtually every Canadian history textbook (*courtesy Art Gallery of Ontario*).

native Canadians, a genre that begins with Christie Harris's *Raven's Cry* (1966), illustrated by Bill REID, and George CLUTESI's *Son of Raven, Son of Deer* (1967), and continues with Norval MORRISSEAU's paintings for H.T. Schwartz's *Windigo and Other Tales of the Ojibways* (1969), PITSEOLAK ASHOONA's *Pitseolak: Pictures Out of My Life* (1971), Francis Kagige's images for Prunella Johnston's *Tales of Nokomis* (1975), Peter PITSEOLAK's *People from our Side* (1975) and Ruth Tulurialik's *Qikaaluktut: Images of Inuit Life* (1986).

Out of the tradition established by E.S. Thompson have emerged the school of so-called "wildlife artists" whose highly detailed work better fits the description of illustration than of fine art, and which has found itself between the covers of stacks of full-colour, folio-format books, most of them printed outside of Canada. The best-known of these pictorial naturalists are the ornithological painters J. Fenwick Lansdowne and T.M. SHORTT, followed by George Maclean, Glen Loates, Robert BATEMAN and their numerous imitators.

Today few, if any, Canadian illustrators can make a living from book or editorial work exclusively. Illustration as a craft and as an art survives because of the love and respect for it shown by a handful of publishers, authors, critics, historians, collectors, readers and the artists who keep the flame alive. ROBERT STACEY

Reading: W. Colgate, *Canadian Art: Its Origins and Development* (1943); R. Stacey, *The Canadian Poster Book: 100 Years of the Poster in Canada* (1979).

Ilsley, James Lorimer, jurist, politician (b at Somerset, NS 3 Jan 1894; d at Halifax 14 Jan 1967). Educated at Acadia and Dalhousie, Ilsley practised law until his election to Parliament as a Liberal in 1926. Re-elected in 1930 and 1935, he became minister of national revenue in 1935 and minister of finance in 1940. He successfully managed the nation's finances through WWII. He believed that the Canadian federal system required renovation, but his proposals presented to a 1945-46 dominion-provincial conference on reconstruction were rejected by Ontario and Québec. Deeply disappointed, Ilsley became minister of justice in 1946, but retired to practise law in 1948. Appointed to the NS Supreme Court in 1949, he became chief justice in 1950. Between 1954 and 1960 he chaired the Royal Commission on PATENTS, COPYRIGHT AND INDUSTRIAL DESIGNS. ROBERT BOTHWELL

I'm Alone, a rumrunner based in Lunenburg, NS, one of several hundred vessels that supplied illicit liquor to a PROHIBITION-bound US during the 1920s. In Mar 1929 a US Coast Guard cutter sighted it with engine trouble in the Gulf of Mexico. Coast guard vessels chased it out to sea and sank it with the loss of one crewman. Intense diplomatic negotiations followed. In 1935 the US apologized and paid damages to captain and crew. ERNEST R. FORBES

Imax Systems Corporation, formed in 1967, created and manufactures IMAX (large screen) and OMNIMAX (dome screen) motion picture projection systems. IMAX was first unveiled at EXPO 67 when the NATIONAL FILM BOARD presented *Labyrinth* and *Polar Life,* both critically acclaimed multi-screen films. The films' 3 producers, Graeme FERGUSON, Robert Kerr and Roman Kroitor, became convinced that the giant-screen experience could be used effectively in a new generation of motion picture theatres. They formed Multiscreen Corp (now Imax Systems Corp) to develop a new system using a single, powerful projector, unlike the multiple projectors used at Expo. With the help of high technical standards, high-fidelity images were projected on the largest screens in cinema history. As well, both systems use the largest film frame in motion picture history: a 70 mm, 15-perforation format. Imax Systems Corp is headquartered in Toronto. It designs and builds cameras and projectors, and licenses their use worldwide; designs theatres; produces and distributes films; and is engaged in research and development. There are more than 50 IMAX/OMNIMAX theatres worldwide.

Immigrant Children On 14 Apr 1826, an obscure police magistrate in London, Eng, Robert Chambers, told a committee of the British Parliament dealing with emigration: "I conceive that London has got too full of children." Chambers was alarmed at the number of youngsters, victims of east-end London's chronic poverty, who were begging in the streets and sleeping in the gutters. He had a recommendation which may well have been in the minds of others and which was to become reality several decades later in one of the most Draconian movements in the history of emigration. Chambers recommended that Britain's surplus children be sent to Canada as farm labour.

Four decades later, in 1859, 4 women – regarded as social visionaries of the day – were poised to do just that, setting up refuges in London and Liverpool which were in effect way stations from which the children were shipped across the sea to the supposed bright promises of Canada. The most prominent of these women was Annie Macpherson, who along with her sisters Rachel and Louisa sent almost 14 000 children to Canada over many decades. Another of these women was Maria Rye, a strong-willed woman whose children, all girls, were sent from London to "Our Western Home" in Niagara-on-the-Lake, Ont, from which they were subsequently distributed as household help but usually ended up as labourers in the farms of southern Ontario.

At its peak, in the years immediately before and after 1900, dozens of individuals and small organizations were sending children to Canada, mostly youngsters whose parents lived in hopeless poverty, or else waifs found where they were left – in blankets or baskets in the hope someone else would care for them. The most famed figure of child emigration was Thomas John Barnardo, whose work, begun in 1870, grew to large proportion under his zeal. He trained in medicine and theology and after an aborted plan to go to China as a missionary he set up several refuges for children in London's east end. Over the history of the movement, Barnardo's organization sent roughly 30 000 children to Canada, to homes he established in Peterborough and Toronto and, for a time, to a farm he set up in Russell, Man.

The children (most of whom were from 8 to 16 though there were many who came at 4 and 5 years of age) were almost always taken first to receiving homes in Belleville, Stratford, Niagara-on-the-Lake and Toronto in Ont. Advertisements were usually placed in local papers announcing the arrival of another shipment of children and inviting farmers to visit the home for a prospective "home boy" or "home girl." The child was only rarely adopted but was indentured, the farmer in return providing lodging, a modest allowance (to be placed in a bank account ostensibly in trust until the child reached maturity) and schooling. Very often, few of these obligations were met. There were, as might be expected, a great many cases of abuse of all kinds, physical, emotional, mental. Children were often returned to the home as being unsuitable – too small, too slow, too difficult.

In many cases those who sent the children and those in Canada who oversaw their placement had high motives. They believed that life in the clean air of the new land, along with hard work and healthy discipline, would assure them of a wholesome development. Often, too often, this was simply a naive dream, with no understanding of the needs of a child and no awareness of the conditions in which they were placed. From its very early years, the practice of sending children from Britain to Canada was the subject of investigation and high controversy. Only 4 years after it began, a British commissioner who spent several weeks in Canada visiting the homes in which the children were received and then the farms on which they were placed, severely criticized the random nature of the entire operation, both in the selection of farm families receiving the children and the later supervision of their placement which in the case of Maria Rye's was virtually nonexistent. It is testimony to the influence of market demand for cheap labour that despite this early and severe criticism, the schemes were to continue well into the 20th century.

Some youngsters fared reasonably well. These were, in most cases, very young children who being too young to work were taken into families simply as children, not as workers. But quite apart from the numerous youngsters who suffered great physical or emotional abuse – isolated on farms with virtually no oversight and where farm labourers were often undesirable wanderers – the very practice of child emigration must be viewed with deep scepticism simply because it uprooted children at the most crucial period of their lives, shipped them like commodities, placed them in a foreign environment and set them to work. They were robbed of childhood.

By the 1920s, serious voices in Canada were questioning the principle of child emigration. In the summer of 1924, Charlotte WHITTON, the director of the Canadian Welfare Council, said that the schemes were inhumane. James S. WOODSWORTH, the respected MP and later first leader of the CCF, added his opinion in the House of Commons: "We are bringing children into Canada in the guise of philanthropy, and turning them into cheap labourers."

Also in 1924, the Bondfield Commission came from Britain with the same purpose that a one-man British Commission had in the earliest years of child emigration: to inspect the homes and examine the welfare of the children. That November

Immigrant children from Dr Barnardo's homes at Landing Stage, Saint John, NB (*c*1905-1931) (*courtesy National Archives of Canada/PA-41785*).

it offered the opinion that only children over 14 (school-leaving age) should be permitted to emigrate. For the remaining years of the 1920s, only older teenagers came to Canada. Then as the economy of the country began its downturn, and the labour movement stepped up its longtime opposition to the programs, the number began to dwindle. In the end, while child emigration was questioned by men and women in Canada who saw its numerous flaws and its primitive attitude toward children, it was not enlightened understanding which drew the curtain upon this long career of Canadian history. It was the Great Depression. *See also* CHILD LABOUR.

KENNETH BAGNELL

Reading: Kenneth Bagnell, *The Little Immigrants* (1980).

Immigrant Labour Canada, which is essentially a country of immigrants, has consistently required the importation of skilled and unskilled workers to assist its economic development. Prior to Confederation (1867) a vast number of immigrant workers, most of whom were from the British Isles, had already assumed an important role within the predominantly agricultural and extractive economies of the British N American colonies. Perhaps the most controversial of these immigrant workers were the IRISH, who flooded into N America during the 1840s and 1850s in a desperate search for a new life. Because of their propensity for hard work and their ethnic cohesiveness, they virtually monopolized certain jobs in the lumber camps, on the docks, and within a sprawling network of canal and railway camps which stretched from Lk Superior to the Atlantic Ocean.

Immigrant labour was also extensively used during the construction of the CPR, when thousands of British, American and European navvies resolutely pushed the ribbon of steel westward, while CHINESE navvies, many of them imported specifically for this purpose, performed the even grimmer task of building eastward through the BC mountain ranges.

The tendency to import labour became particularly pronounced after 1870, when Canada began actively participating in the transatlantic labour market. The rapid expansion of ocean and rail transportation made it possible for British and European workers to hunt for jobs in N America on a mass scale; according to one source about 900 000 unskilled and skilled workers (other than agriculturalists) arrived between 1907 and 1930. British artisans, with their industrial experience and specific skills, were in high demand, particularly in the rapidly expanding industries of central Canada and BC. Although Canada officially maintained that only agriculturalists were being imported, in practice thousands of the immigrants who came from central and southern Europe (1880-1930) became either full-time or part-time unskilled industrial workers because industrialists and farmers were able to link their economic interests in demanding an "open door" IMMIGRATION POLICY.

Canada has remained a self-proclaimed homeland for immigrants seeking work, but the type of work available has often depended on ethnic background. "Preferred immigrants" (ie, British immigrants, AMERICAN immigrants of English "stock," and skilled workers from western Europe) encountered less PREJUDICE AND DISCRIMINATION than eastern and southern European immigrants, who as "foreigners" met with a decidedly mixed reception, the attitude of their hosts varying with time and economic circumstances. Asians and BLACKS fared even worse and many of them were only employed for the most grinding labour.

From 1945 onwards, however, and with the advent of postwar prosperity and an improved attitude towards human rights, the status of non-British immigrant workers substantially changed. At the same time, 3 new waves of immigrant workers entered Canada: European displaced persons, many of whom were highly educated and soon left the unskilled labour market for professional and skilled jobs; immigrants from "preferred countries" (Britain, Germany, Netherlands, etc), who generally gravitated into prestigious jobs upon arrival in this country; and immigrant workers from the low-wage countries of southern Europe and, increasingly, the West Indies (*see* WEST INDIANS). It is this latter group of predominantly unskilled immigrants who have largely filled the low-paying, hazardous and itinerant or seasonal jobs that Canadians would not accept. However, most of these jobs are no longer on the frontier, and now it is to urban factories, construction sites or service industries – most notably in Toronto and Montréal – that the vast majority of unskilled immigrant workers tend to gravitate.

DONALD H. AVERY

Reading: Donald H. Avery, *Dangerous Foreigners* (1979).

Slavic immigrants working on the Ontario and Rainy River Railway, 1908. In spite of the vital economic role of workers from eastern Europe, many Canadians demanded restriction of immigrants along ethnic and racial lines (*courtesy National Archives of Canada/C-38828*).

Immigration, the movement of nationals of one country into another for the purpose of resettlement, is central to Canadian history, from the native peoples, whose ancestors migrated across the Bering Strait from Asia, to the most recent arrivals. The story of Canadian immigration is not one of orderly population growth; it has been and remains both a catalyst to Canadian economic development and a mirror of Canadian attitudes and values; it has often been unashamedly and economically self-serving and ethnically or racially biased.

Throughout the 17th and much of the 18th century European colonial administrations, charged with overseeing what would become Canada, did not consider settlement a priority. French or British governments initially seemed unprepared to expend vast quantities of money or energy necessary to encourage settlement. Nor was migration to the New World popular in France or Britain. Adventurers, explorers and particularly traders acting for British or French interests feared the interference of settlers in the lucrative trade with the native people. However, policy eventually changed and colonial authorities carefully and slowly encouraged settlement in Canada, hoping that settlers would guarantee the sovereignty of colonial land claims, would Christianize the native peoples, and would exploit the natural resources, often on behalf of European investors. Settlements grew gradually and not without difficulty. New France's population at the time of the British CONQUEST (1759-60) was about 65 000. In NS a transplanted Scottish community was supplemented by German and Swiss settlers, and in the late 1700s Irish settlers reinforced Newfoundland's population.

Although the British victory brought an end to migration from France, it did not instigate a tide of English-speaking immigrants. Except for a handful of British administrators, military personnel and merchants who filled the vacuum left by their departing French counterparts, few English-speaking settlers seemed interested in Canada. Indeed, it is doubtful whether settlers would have been welcomed by the new British administrators, who feared that an influx of English-speaking, Protestant settlers would complicate administration in a recently conquered Roman Catholic, French-speaking territory. Most British immigrants were far more inclined to seek out the more temperate climate and familiar social institutions of the British colonies to the south.

Many of Québec's new British rulers, content to leave the colony to languish as a quiet backwater of the Empire, were soon forced to accept many thousands of English-speaking, largely Protestant settlers displaced by the American Revolution. Known as United Empire LOYALISTS, they were largely political REFUGEES. Many of them migrated northward not by choice but by default, either because they did not wish to become citizens of the new American republic or because they feared retribution for their public support of the British. For these Loyalists, who eventually formed the core of the colony's ruling oligarchies, Canada was a land of second choice, as it would be for countless future immigrants who came because to remain at home was undesirable and entry elsewhere, often the US, was restricted. The Loyalist migration was neither uncontrolled nor unassisted, however. Imperial authorities and military personnel offered supplies to the new settlers and organized the distribution of land. Despite the hardships the settlers endured, their plight was undeniably made less severe by the intervention of government agents, a practice to be repeated in Canada many times.

Throughout the mid-19th century, the colonies, Canada West in particular, returned to a pattern of painfully slow and erratic economic growth. Officially encouraged immigration from England, Scotland and even the US gradually filled the better agricultural lands in the colony and bolstered new commercial or administrative towns. The new immigrants were generally of ethnic stock and outlook similar to that of the established community. But the great Irish potato famine and to a lesser degree a series of abortive European rebellions in 1848 sent new waves of immigrants to N America. Of these tens of thousands, many were Irish settlers, whose arrival in Canada initiated major social and economic changes. In many respects the IRISH were Canada's first enormous wave of foreign immigrants. Although they generally spoke English, they did not mirror the social, cultural or religious values of the majority. Roman Catholic intruders in a Protestant domain, their loyalty to the Crown appeared suspect in a Canada where ardent loyalty was demanded as insurance against the threat of American republicanism. Furthermore, after escaping a life in which farm tenancy and capricious nature made agriculture synonymous with poverty and dependency, some of the famine-stricken Irish had little or no enthusiasm for farm life. Canadian cities and larger towns quickly developed Irish sections or wards. The Anglo-Protestant majority measured the Irish contribution economically and the Irish deficiencies socially, religiously and racially. On the one hand, many of the Irish created a labour force ready and able to fill the seasonal employment demands of a newly expanded canal system, lumber industry and burgeoning railway network; on the other hand, because of their low income, their Catholicism, the seasonal separation from their families and differences in their way of life, they were a conspicuous minority group. They filled working-class neighbourhoods and inflated majority fears of social evils previously dismissed as peculiar to the US. For some years the Irish supplied the base of a working-class labour force necessary for the slow advance of communication, commerce and industry, but they remained an adjunct to, rather than a central component of, mainstream N American economic and social life – the basis of which was commerce and agricultural activity. Policy tied population increase to land settlement. Gradual commercial and industrial development usually serviced the agricultural sector, and, because many Irish were not farmers, Irish labourers were seen as rootless.

If agricultural roots and commitment were measured, in part, by land tenure, Canada underwent a shock when arable land began to disappear from the market. Without a large industrial base, with a relatively low death rate, a high birthrate and a small but continual inflow of immigration largely from the British Isles, the immediate post-Confederation era had its overpopulation problems. The US, with its seemingly boundless supply of free fertile land, attracted thousands of new immigrants and Anglo-Canadians, while French Canadians were drawn to jobs in the factories of New England. Canadian history has been compared to a journey through the Bible, beginning in Lamentations and ending in Exodus, but in the late 19th century Canada's future Prairie provinces were opened to settlement, although it was not until a market developed for the prairie agricultural output that serious settlement began. The demand for farm goods, especially hard wheat, coincided with the election of Wilfrid Laurier's government, which immediately encouraged the settlement of the West with large-scale immigration. Canada's new and aggressive minister of the interior, Clifford SIFTON, organized a revamped and far-reaching program and was prepared, if reluctantly, to admit agricultural settlers from places other than the British Isles, N Europe and the US, explaining, "A stalwart peasant in a sheepskin coat, born on the soil, whose forefathers have been farmers for ten generations, and a stout wife and a half-dozen children is good quality." The Sifton comment, however, no matter how often repeated, is not an accurate reflection of government policy. From 1896 to the 1930s, Canadians, their politicians and immigration officials were not receptive to peasants in sheepskin coats. Immigration policy did not involve just an aggressive peopling of the Prairies. It was enacted within the framework of the British Empire, in which Sifton, the Canadian government and most English-speaking Canadians believed. For English-speaking Canadians the traditional definition of ideal immigrants may have been modified but was not radically altered. Unabashedly colonial, the government defined immigrants who did not originate from the British Isles as foreign; and, unabashedly N American, excluded white, English- speaking immigrants from the US from this category. The ideal immigrants were still British or American independent farmers who would settle in the West. Sifton and the government may only have reflected their times, but Canadian immigration policy and public opinion were nevertheless racist.

Pressed to increase immigration by business and railway interests with visions of an insatiable world demand for Canadian resources, Sifton and his immigration authorities balanced their ethnic anxieties against a frantic search for settlers. They listed ideal settlers in a descending preference. British and American agriculturalists were followed by French, Belgians, Dutch, Scandinavians, Swiss, Finns, Russians, Austro-Hungarians, Germans, Ukrainians and Poles. Close to the bottom of the list came those who were, in both the public and the government's minds, less assimilable and less desirable, eg, Italians, South Slavs, Greeks and Syrians. At the very bottom came Jews, Asians, gypsies and blacks.

Ottawa, however, did not have the only voice when it came to immigration. The British North America Act also gave the provinces a voice in immigration if they chose to run it. Québec, partly in response to the expansion of English-speaking Canada and partly in an effort to stem if not reverse the flow of rural Québec youth to waiting jobs in New England factories, set up its own immigration department. In co-operation with federal authorities, immigration agents were sent into New England to encourage French Canadians to return home to recently opened marginal agricultural lands. The program met with only limited success, but Québec's active determination of its own immigration priorities continued.

In spite of government precautions, not all immigrants committed themselves to resource exploitation or agriculture. Like the Irish before them, many of the "foreign" immigrants, non-English speaking and largely non-Protestant, rejected a life of rural isolation, choosing to work in cities. Furthermore, many of these foreigners saw themselves as living in Canada or N America only temporarily, earning enough money to buy a piece of land at home, to assemble a dowry for a sister or to pay off a family debt. But the many who adopted N American definitions of success or who were unable to return home because of political upheavals established themselves in Canada, bringing wives and children to join them. If these Jews, Italians, Macedonians, Russians, Finns, Chinese, etc, had been content to play the role reluctantly left for them, if they had accepted rural isolation as the price of their admission into Canada, hostility toward them might have been minimal; but by making their way into Montréal, Winnipeg, Toronto, Hamilton and Vancouver and other centres they awakened the old ethnic and religious anxieties and prejudices previously reserved for the Irish. They had been allowed into Canada to satisfy the need for a cheap labour force or a pool of skilled craftsmen adaptable to factory and construction. They were prepared to accept seasonal labour in mining or lumbering (which forced them to drift back into cities during the off-season), but for many Canadians the sudden influx of strange peoples so recently subject to foreign czars, kaisers and gods seemed to threaten the very fabric of Protestant Canadian society. Some Canadians responded with a dignified tolerance. They recognized that these foreigners were here to stay, that their labour and skills were necessary, their living conditions subject to improvement and, perhaps most important, that their children would become integrated, given education and time. But in spite of the vital economic role these immigrants played in urban centres – laying streetcar tracks, labouring in the expanding textile factories and digging the sewer sytems – many Canadians demanded strict enforcement of immigration regulations and restriction of admission along ethnic or racial lines.

During WWI, anti-German hysteria erupted in Canada, directed largely against immigrants born in the now enemy countries or those who entered Canada as subjects of enemy monarchs, but also against foreigners who had been born in now allied countries or had come to Canada as subjects of allied monarchs. Despite Canadian military manpower needs, British and Canadian authorities alike felt that, where possible, foreigners belonged in foreign armies. Groups such as Italians, Serbians, Poles and some Jews were encouraged to return to the armies of their mother country or were recruited into specific British army units reserved for allied foreigners of various origins. Without national armies of their own to join, many Jews, Macedonians and Ukrainians volunteered for the Canadian Army.

Once in Canada, many thousands of immigrants did find a place for themselves and their families, but Canadian immigration policy and administration, which bowed to economic necessity by allowing these southern and eastern Europeans into Canada, could not bend enough to admit other would-be immigrants. Head taxes, landing taxes, bilateral restriction agreements and travel restrictions virtually prohibited the immigration of Asians. Canadian authorities refused to allow the settlement of female Asian immigrants, fearing this would encourage Asian men temporarily in Canada as railway or mine labourers to settle permanently and, perhaps more importantly, become the parents of yet another generation of the "yellow peril." In 1914 almost 400 East Indians aboard the immigrant ship KOMAGATA MARU languished in Vancouver harbour while Canadian authorities debated what to do with them. Canada's new navy, in action for the first time, escorted the ship from Canadian waters while many Vancouver residents cheered approvingly from shore. In 1910 and 1911 rumours had spread that a group of blacks was preparing to migrate to central Alberta. Descendants of freed slaves, they were being pushed from their land in Oklahoma territory, where they had been granted holdings and hoped to build new lives. Public and political response in Alberta was immediate and predictable. Federal authorities initiated an ingeniously simple scheme. Nothing in the Immigration Act specifically barred black Americans, but any immigrant could effectively be denied access to Canada for health reasons under the Act's medical provisions. The government merely instructed immigration inspectors and their medical aides along the American border to reject all blacks as unfit for admission on medical grounds. There was no appeal. Blacks were warned they should not waste their time and money by considering immigration to Canada.

As a result of the dramatic and devastating economic collapse caused by the GREAT DEPRESSION, the need for the government's selective encouragement of immigration faded. Immigration authorities worked not to stimulate admissions but to prevent them. By 1933 Hitler ruled Germany, and millions of political opponents and Jews might have survived if Canada or other countries had offered innocent victims a home. Although many Canadians responded to the refugees with a mixture of sympathy for their desperate plight and embarrassment at the lack of government aid, others, including the federal Cabinet, many in the diplomatic corps and, of course, immigration policymakers, reacted with alarm to any pressure to accept Jews or political refugees escaping Germany. As a result, few refugees were able to break Canadian immigration restrictions.

In the postwar years, perhaps in response to new winds of antidiscrimination blowing across the Western world, perhaps in response to pressure from an earlier generation of well-integrated immigrants to Canada and their increasingly middle-class children, the government gradually removed many of the racial or ethnic barriers in immigration policy. Furthermore, if immigration was still primarily an economic policy, it now reflected the new urban industrial reality; an economic boom had generated a demand for labour. To satisfy it, tens of thousands of displaced persons and eastern or southern Europeans who would previously have been labelled undesirable were admitted. Canada also responded to the plight of refugees by admitting many Hungarian, Czechoslovakian, Ugandan, Chilean and Southeast Asian refugees (although Canada was generally able to attract the younger, healthier and better-educated candidates).

By the early 1970s, because of improved transportation, growing recognition of Canada as a land of opportunity, increased difficulty in immigrating into the US and a seeming liberalization of both Canada's attitudes and its immigration policy, Canada became a major magnet for immigrants, including many from the Third World. Throughout the 1970s and 1980s, the reunification of families remained a key factor in immigrant arrivals. Emigration from less-developed or Third-World countries also remained proportionately high. But under the Mulroney Conservative government, elected in 1984, there were several shifts in immigration emphasis. The ongoing concern for the economic place of independent immigrants intensified as it became almost essential for would-be immigrants to have a sponsoring Canadian family, a waiting job, or a job for which there proved no equally qualified Canadian. In addition, the government laid new emphasis on the immigration of those with capital ready to invest in areas that would generate jobs in Canada. For example, as the long shadow of an impending communist Chinese takeover of Hong Kong loomed closer, Canada encouraged a sharp increase of capital investment from Hong Kong along with an accompanying upswing in investor immigration.

During the 1980s, Canada was also looked upon by frightened refugees as a safe haven. Canadian immigration authorities continued to process pre-set numbers of refugees located outside Canada for admission, including those fleeing the turmoil of war in Central America and the political chaos of Poland. But as part of Canada's international obligation to refugees, the Canadian government originally allowed that persons arriving in Canada and declaring themselves refugees were entitled to a hearing to determine the legitimacy of that claim. If the claim was validated, the claimant was allowed to remain. Fears grew that nonrefugees were abusing this system and choking up the review process, forcing lengthy delays in hearings. In addition, immigration personnel argued that allowing individuals to claim refugee status on arrival in Canada short-circuited Canada's ability to pick and choose those refugees best-suited to the country. After several controversial boatloads of refugees arrived in Canada, the government clamped down. According to its critics, however, the government's new controls removed the protection of Canadian soil from legitimate refugees, not just false claimants. *See also* IMMIGRATION POLICY.

HAROLD TROPER

Reading: H. Cowen, *British Emigration to British North America* (1961); E.C. Guillet, *The Great Migration* (1963); F. Hawkins, *Canada and Immigration* (1972); R. Hurney and Harold Troper, *Immigrants: A Portrait of the Urban Experience* (1975); Troper, *Only Farmers Need Apply* (1972).

Immigration Policy Canada's IMMIGRATION policy is the most explicit part of what might be described as a POPULATION policy. In a liberal democratic state such as Canada only the prevailing rates of immigration and not those of mortality, fertility and EMIGRATION can be effectively regulated. By regulating the means of selection and by controlling the number of entrants, the government seeks to fulfil a variety of national objectives.

According to the 1870-71 census, Canada's total population was 3.6 million. In addition to native peoples (about 136 000 in 1851) the 2 largest groups were the French (1 million) and the British (2.1 million). Excepting the Germans (203 000), other groups (Dutch, American blacks, Swiss, Italians, Spanish, Portuguese) were much smaller. During the next century, about 9.3 million people immigrated to Canada and, although many went on to the US or eventually returned to their native lands, by 1986 Canada's population had surpassed 25 million. During the 19th century, the movement of individuals and groups to Canada was largely unrestricted, although in 1885, under pressure from BC, an Act was passed restricting Chinese immigration through the imposition of a head tax, the first of a series of such measures directed at the Chinese and continuing until the late 1940s. Otherwise immigration policy was concerned mainly with quarantine stations, the responsibilities of transportation companies, and the exclusion of criminals, paupers, the diseased and the destitute. But after the massive immigration between 1903 and 1913, WWI and subsequent political upheavals and economic problems, a much more restrictive immigration policy was implemented and remained unchanged until 1962, when Canada's present universal and nondiscriminatory policy was introduced in stages.

Three different departments or agencies have been responsible for immigration policy in Canada since WWII – the Department of Citizenship and Immigration (1950-65), the Department of Manpower and Immigration (1966-77) and the Canada Employment and Immigration Commission (est 1977).

Under the provision of s95 of the CONSTITUTION ACT, 1867 (formerly BNA Act), responsibility for immigration matters is a concurrent power divided between the provincial and federal governments. Ottawa, for most of Canada's history, has dominated this policy area, although Ontario since WWII, and Québec since the mid-1960s, have been particularly concerned with immigration. More than half the total number of immigrants in recent years have settled in Ontario. Québec created its own Department for Immigration (now called the Department of Cultural Communities and Immigration) in 1968. Its major concerns have been, first, to recruit as many French-speaking immigrants as possible (or immigrants with a good knowledge of French), and second, to ensure that immigrants who settle in Québec form part of the francophone community. Québec was the first province to have a special immigration agreement with the federal government (there are now agreements with several other provinces). The federal government is also involved in the difficult task of increasing the numbers of French-speaking immigrants to Canada.

During the 1970s, immigration and population policies were officially reviewed, and a Green Paper on Immigration Policy and a report to Parliament (1975) by a Special Joint Committee of the Senate and the House of Commons were prepared. Almost all the committee's recommendations were accepted by the Liberal government and absorbed into a new Immigration Act (1976, proclaimed in 1978) which established for the first time the fundamental objectives of Canada's immigration policy. They include the promotion of Canada's demographic, economic, social and cultural goals; family reunion; nondiscrimination; the fulfilment of Canada's international obligations in relation to REFUGEES; and co-operation between all levels of government, as well as with the voluntary sector, in promoting the adaptation of newcomers to Canadian society.

The current Immigration Act, along with subsequent procedures adopted by the Canadian Employment and Immigration Commission, have significantly broadened the constituency that today has a role in the shaping of policy and the establishing of annual immigration levels. By means of an extensive, ongoing consultation process, provincial governments, potential employees, ethnic groups and humanitarian organizations all have the opportunity of having their views weighed by appropriate immigration officials. Following such consultation, the government since 1980 has annually tabled in Parliament 1- to 3-year projections of the desired immigration levels. For several of the years since this practice has been adopted, the actual number of arrivals per year has fallen considerably below the figures appearing in projections. For example, in 1985, the immigration level was set at between 115 000 and 125 000 while, in fact, the number of newcomers reaching Canada numbered barely 100 000.

In addition to the provisions encouraging an open consultation process, the Immigration Act contains sections modernizing policy relating to security and the determination of refugee status, and streamlining provisions concerned with overall control and enforcement. The basic statute also established the Immigration Board, created in 1967 as a fully independent body whose decisions cannot be overruled by government except in relation to security matters.

Immigration and refugee policies are planned and must be considered together. In keeping with Canada's international responsibilities as a signatory to the UN Convention Relating to the Status of Refugees, refugees normally constitute approximately 10% of the annual flow of newcomers. During major international emergencies, such as the unexpected outpouring of humanity from Southeast Asia 1978-81, the figure reached 25% of all new arrivals in Canada. Since the late 1970s but especially during the mid-1980s more and more persons reaching Canadian ports of entry, without first having been processed by Canadian immigration offices, have sought to gain admission to Canada by claiming to be refugees. In this way, such persons seek to jump the queue of regular immigrant applicants and become established in Canada, although there is little if any evidence to indicate that such persons have been the objects of persecution in their last state of residence. During the last half of 1986 alone, in excess of 10 000 persons sought to shortcircuit normal immigration procedures by resorting to claims of refugee status.

The connection between economic and immigration policies usually arises out of the realization that a relationship exists between the size of the immigration flow and LABOUR MARKET requirements. From decade to decade, or even from year to year, the need for professional, skilled or unskilled persons fluctuates significantly. The pool of available labour in any country also alters over time because of the birthrate and the acceptance, for example, of women in the work force. For most of Canada's history, the government's tools for matching the requirement of the labour market with the flow of immigrants have not been particularly refined or effective. In recent years, this has begun to change. Today, with the help of computers, improved communications networks and the co-operation of employers, it is possible to tune more precisely the flow of incoming persons bound for the work place.

During the 1980s, immigration policymakers instituted a program to encourage businessmen and entrepreneurs to immigrate to Canada bringing their managerial skills and capital so as to create additional employment opportunities. More than 2000 entrepreneurs with substantial capital settled in Canada during 1985 and as many as 4000 were expected during 1987.

Immigration regulations provide for the admission of 3 categories of immigrants: family class (closely related persons), independent immigrants (admitted on the basis of skill, capital and labour-market requirements) and refugees. When processing applicants, immigration officers are instructed to give priority to persons seeking family reunification and to refugees. Independent applicants without family but with required skills or capital are considered next. Many new arrivals in the family or refugee categories have tended to be unskilled or else to possess talents inappropriate to the region or community where they have settled. These priorities, then, can disrupt the labour market; the resulting economic insecurity can create disappointment and hostility among the immigrants or among Canadians who feel threatened by the newcomers.

Canada's immigration policy also encourages the dispersal of immigrants across the country. In the decades following the resurgence of immigration after WWII, Montréal, Vancouver and especially Toronto received up to 66% of all immigrants entering Canada. Current policy has attempted to encourage immigrants to settle in smaller communities in the less-populated provinces.

Administrative arrangements and practices adopted by Employment and Immigration Canada and the Immigration Bureau of the Department of External Affairs significantly affect how policy is implemented and whether it achieves its purposes. Since 1967 the selection of applicants for admission has occurred without discrimination on the grounds of ethnicity or geographic region, but because immigration officers are not situated in many states of the Third World, persons in these countries are in effect excluded from Canada even if they are members of an admissible category, unless they are able and prepared to travel to a distant immigration office in another country. The number of applicants being processed at an overseas immigration post can also be easily regulated merely by the size of the staff assigned to this task. The discretionary powers of immigration officials in Canada and abroad necessarily influence the daily administration of policy. Criticism of these discretionary powers can become especially intense because there are no grounds or mechanisms for appeal against negative decisions by officials in the field. Because these and other features of Canada's immigration practices can affect this country's relations with other governments (particularly if these governments perceive Canadian procedures or policies as inequitable), immigration policy is part of Canadian foreign policy. This fact was acknowledged by the government of Canada in 1981, when much of the responsibility for the administration of immigration programs was transferred from Employment and Immigration Canada to the Immigration Bureau in the Department of External Affairs.

While considerable discussion both within and outside government regarding the development of a population policy for Canada has taken place since the early 1970s, explicit moves to formulate and implement such a policy or to carry out demographic research only commenced in the mid-1980s. In a report to Parliament in 1985 by the minister responsible for immigration, reference was made to the establishment of a small secretariat to review the social and economic implications of Canada's prevailing population patterns. The review is to be completed by 1989 and interim reports with recommendations may be tabled in Parliament. The 1985 report to Parliament as well as subsequent reports on immigration indicate the existence of a consensus among relevant government departments, employers, ethnic groups and labour organizations supporting the gradual increase in the number of immigrants annually admitted to Canada. It is agreed that a moderate and controlled increase in arrivals is required if Canada's present population size is to be maintained or to grow marginally. Moreover, without additional immigration, the decline in fertility in Canada over the past generation will by the early years of the next century result in an inadequate number of working age Canadians being burdened with the cost of health and social programs for the much increased number of elderly citizens. Today, estimates suggest that an annual intake of between 125 000 and 140 000 immigrants would be both acceptable and appropriate for Canada's needs.

Among the lengthy list of organizations within Canadian society that expect a role in the formulation of immigration policy and regulations are church groups, employers, organized labour and community-based and ethnic organizations. Many of these nongovernmental bodies seek to promote family reunification and to attain financial assistance for immigrant-adjustment schemes. The government has had to acknowledge as well the existence of a not altogether latent sentiment among a portion of Canadian society favouring a reduction or even a halt in the selection of immigrants. The entry into Canada of a sizable number of nonwhite immigrants (about 33% of Canada's immigrants are from Europe, 33% from the Americas (including the Caribbean), and 33% from Asia, Africa and elsewhere) has created what has been called a visible minority, one that has occasionally been the target of abuse and violence. While the government and interested voluntary associations have attempted to strengthen among the Canadian public a sense of tolerance and compassion for newcomers, the task is not easy. Immigration is an extremely emotional subject, especially when the fate of family members or personal economic security is involved.

Canada's immigration policy is nondiscriminatory regarding ethnicity; however, individuals suffering diseases likely to endanger public health, or those without any apparent means of financial support, or those known to be criminals or terrorists can be excluded. An undetermined number of persons in these undesired categories gain entry every year to Canada by practices and tactics contravening the spirit and letter of prevailing immigration legislation. Still others who may have been properly admitted to Canada, such as students and visitors on short-term visas, choose to remain beyond the time permitted by Canadian law. The problem of illegal aliens, while not a new one, has in recent years become more awkward for the Canadian government to resolve, especially as the total number of persons entering Canada at border crossings and airports has grown constantly. Once in Canada, illegal aliens may easily escape notice unless they try to acquire some public service which would bring them to the attention of government authorities.

The number of illegal aliens in Canada is obviously impossible to determine accurately. Estimates by police and immigration personnel range between 50 000 and 200 000. Where possible, without infringing upon traditional civil liberties, the government is endeavouring to close any remaining loopholes that have in the past facilitated the admission of persons not authorized under prevailing immigration legislation and regulations. Fraudulent claims for refugee status by aliens trying to avoid normal overseas screening and processing constitute one of the more serious headaches confronting immigration officials.

The practice of admitting to Canada highly skilled persons from less-developed countries continues to provoke some controversy. The governments of the less-developed countries, from which a growing number of immigrants to Canada originate, regard with apprehension the exodus of people they can ill afford to lose. While the view has been expressed within and beyond Canada that Canada should not encourage the outflow of trained individuals from "have-not" regions of the world, Canada, like other liberal democracies, stoutly defends the concept of freedom of movement for all persons.

GERALD E. DIRKS

Immunology, branch of MEDICINE that studies the body's ability to defend itself from foreign substances, especially DISEASE-causing organisms, and seeks means of controlling that ability. Immunology had its origin perhaps 900 years ago, when the Chinese discovered how to vaccinate against smallpox. Although vaccination has an ancient history, it was only in the early 1960s that modern immunology began to unravel the mechanisms by which the body defends itself from the incredible variety of potentially lethal micro-organisms surrounding it. The subject has expanded into many fields of modern medicine and microbiology; eg, immune-system research has provided insights into the ways in which cells differentiate and function.

Students with a background in BIOCHEMISTRY, GENETICS, medicine or microbiology may receive advanced training in immunology at a number of centres across Canada, including the universities of British Columbia, Alberta, Manitoba, McMaster, Toronto, McGill and Laval. Research is carried on at the major teaching centres, and is funded primarily by the MEDICAL RESEARCH COUNCIL of Canada. Some funding also comes from the provinces, eg, the Alberta Heritage Savings Trust Fund for Medical Research provides substantial grants for work pursued in Alberta. In addition, research is ongoing and training is offered at the INSTITUT ARMAND-FRAPPIER. Canadian immunologists may belong to the Canadian Society of Immunology and to many international associations. Canadian research findings are published in various national and international journals.

Impaired Driving, also known as drunken driving, driving while impaired (DWI) and driving under the influence (DUI), has been a serious social problem as far back as the beginning of this century, when social scientists took note of the often deadly combination of alcohol and motor vehicles. Today in Canada, on any given night, 25% of the drivers on the road have been drinking; 6% of them are legally impaired. It is estimated that alcohol is involved in 50% of all fatal traffic accidents and in 30% of traffic injuries. Approximately 2500 Canadians die each year as a result of impaired driving. Impaired driving costs society several billion dollars annually in the form of medical and hospital care, property damage and lost working hours.

Although Scandinavian countries took action against impaired drivers in the early 1900s, introducing the use of chemical tests to measure blood alcohol concentrations, it was not until the late 1960s that the legal use of such tests came into wide use in N America. In 1969 Parliament enacted the Canadian Criminal Law Amendment Act, commonly known as the "Breathalizer Legislation." Modelled on the British Road Safety Act of 1967, this legislation made it illegal per se to operate a motor vehicle with a blood alcohol concentration (BAC) of more than 80 mg of alcohol in 100 millilitres of blood (also expressed as 80 mg% or simply .08). It also gave peace officers the authority to demand pre-arrest roadside breath samples and made it an offence to refuse one.

In Dec 1985 amendments to the Criminal Code provided for stiffer penalties for impaired drivers, allowed for the taking of a blood sample where a breath sample could not be obtained, and introduced 2 new impaired driving charges. Referred to collectively as Bill C-19, the amendments raised the minimum fine from $50 to $300 for driving while impaired, driving with more than 80 mg of alcohol in 100 millilitres of blood, and refusing to provide a blood or breath sample. In addition, the courts were authorized to sentence the offender to up to 6 months in jail, for a summary conviction, or up to 5 years if the charge was indictable. Mandatory jail sentences of 14 days for a second offence and 90 days for subsequent offences were also called for. The 2 new impaired driving charges introduced by Bill C-19 are impaired driving causing bodily harm and impaired driving causing death. Conviction on the former charge provides for a prison sentence of up to 10 years, the latter for up to 14 years. In addition, the judge may order a driver's licence suspension of up to 10 years. The legislation also called for a mandatory driver's licence suspension of at least 3 months for a first offence, 6 months for a second, and one year for a subsequent offence.

The courts have been taking a stronger view of impaired driving offences since enactment of Bill C-19. Fines are higher on average than previously and prison sentences are handed down more frequently. In 1986 the Supreme Court ruled that 24-hour suspensions were not contrary to the provisions or spirit of the CANADIAN CHARTER OF RIGHTS AND FREEDOMS. Police forces across Canada make use of the 24-hour suspension as an alternative to arresting an accused.

A number of other initiatives have been taken to deal with impaired driving, especially since the 1970s. Roadside "Check Stop" programs and intense public awareness campaigns have become commonplace. The media has begun to take an increased interest in impaired driving. Provincial governments across Canada run rehabilitation courses, or violators' schools, for convicted impaired drivers, usually under the auspices of an agency such as the Alberta Alcohol and Drug Abuse Commission (AADAC). In light of its finding that 25% of the attendees were repeat offenders, AADAC started offering a special course for repeat offenders in 1986, unique in Canada. In the fall of 1985, the federal Dept of Justice launched a multifaceted campaign against impaired driving, including an extensive media campaign. It has also provided funds to assist in the implementation of community countermeasures and for further research.

Much of the public attention focused on impaired driving during the 1980s has been the result of efforts by grass-roots organizations such as Mothers Against Drunk Drivers (MADD), People Against Impaired Drivers (PAID), and Students Against Driving Drunk (SADD). The citizen movement began in 1980 in the US but it quickly spread to Canada. Groups like MADD and PAID lobby various levels of government for changes to impaired driving legislation and exhort the judiciary to crack down on impaired drivers.

In Canada one of the agencies at the forefront of research into impaired driving is the Traffic Injury Research Foundation of Canada (TIRF) located in Ottawa. TIRF has prepared a number of reports and has been actively involved in efforts to reduce the incidence of impaired driving in Canada. A major research study prepared by TIRF observed that high blood alcohol concentrations are overrepresented among apprehended drivers or drivers involved in accidents compared to others on the road. Young people, especially those aged 20 to 34, show up most frequently in the statistics; 16 to 19-year olds account for 23% of fatalities, 18% of injuries, 15% of those at-risk and 11% of those arrested for alcohol-related driving offences. Males predominate in all groups of drinking drivers, but TIRF has found that women are increasingly represented in the statistics, particularly among fatalities. Finally, a substantial number of impaired drivers involved in accidents and arrested for alcohol-related driving offences are problem drinkers or alcoholics. The TIRF study concluded pessimistically that the "alcohol-crash problem has not gone away; in fact, it appears resistant to virtually all attempts to reduce its magnitude." Although it varies somewhat from province to province, 25% to 40% of all Criminal Code matters dealt with by the courts are for alcohol-related driving offences. Convictions for those offences account for 20% to 25% of all provincial jail admissions. Repeat offenders are especially troublesome because they don't seem to respond to the sanctions currently in place.

Most agencies involved with the impaired driving issue agree that the long-term solution to the problem lies only in a change in public attitudes and behaviour. There is already some indication that public attitudes are changing. Recent research indicates that during the month of December, arrests for alcohol-related driving offences are down, despite (and possibly because of) increased enforcement; alcohol sales in private premises drop, designated driver programs become popular and taxis become the socially acceptable way to travel to and from holiday get-togethers. KAREN WALKER

Imperial Munitions Board, est Nov 1915 in Canada by the British Ministry of Munitions, with Canadian government approval. Headed by J.W. FLAVELLE, a prominent Toronto businessman, the board was responsible for letting contracts on behalf of the British government for the construction of war materials in Canada. It began to establish "national factories," which it owned outright, to produce munitions that private manufacturers were unable to turn out. Under IMB direction Canada produced a wide variety of war materiel including shells, ships, explosives and training planes. The IMB was dissolved in 1919.
D.J. BERCUSON

Imperial Oil Limited, with head offices in Toronto, is an energy company incorporated in 1880 as the Imperial Oil Co. An American company, Standard Oil, bought a majority interest in 1898, and the present name was adopted in 1959. In 1978 Imperial Oil formed Esso Resources Canada Ltd to handle its resource operations. Active in all phases of the PETROLEUM INDUSTRY, Imperial Oil is the largest marketer and refiner of petroleum products and the largest producer of crude oil in Canada. It also manufactures and sells chemicals, fertilizers and building materials, and has mining exploration and development interests. Through Syncrude Canada Ltd, in which it holds a 25% interest, Imperial Oil is also participating in a plant producing synthetic crude oil from the Athabasca oil sands. In 1986 it had sales or operating revenues of $6.9 billion (ranking 8th in Canada), assets of $8.6 billion (ranking 9th) and 12 516 employees. In 1987 Imperial bought Sulpetro, a Calgary-based natural gas producer. The company is 78% foreign owned, with Exxon Corp of New York holding 70% of the shares.
DEBORAH C. SAWYER

Imperial Order Daughters of the Empire (IODE) was founded in 1900 by Margaret Polson Murray of Montréal who envisioned an organization of women devoted to encouraging imperialism. Beginning with an educational mandate promoting Britain and British institutions through the schools, it became actively involved in both world wars in supporting Canada's efforts on behalf of Britain and the allies. Other areas of interest included immigration, child welfare, community health and social services. In recent years the IODE has concentrated more on community affairs, supporting Canadian educational, cultural and social developments. Although its membership has declined, it remains an active women's organization, with 14 000 members in 567 branches in 1986.
NANCY M. SHEEHAN

Imperialism In the late 19th century various nations entered a phase of territorial expansion often called the second great era of imperialism. Britain, France, Germany, the US and others sought colonies for commercial, military and religious motives. This imperialism coincided with growing concern in Canada about its relationship to the British Empire. Britain was still responsible for EXTERNAL RELATIONS and funded defence for Canada and other Dominions. Such colonial vestiges were increasingly unacceptable, yet there were strong loyalties to Britain and a fear that total independence would lead to absorption by the US.

Thus Canadian imperialism was born. When British imperialists founded the Imperial Federation League in 1884, Canadian supporters established branches. They sought a way for Canada to develop beyond colonial status without separating from the empire. Led by G.M. GRANT, G.R. PARKIN, G.T. DENISON and others, the movement mixed Christian idealism and anti-Americanism with an effort to have people accept the principle that the Dominions should participate in foreign policy at the imperial level.

Imperialist rhetoric late in the 19th century began to emphasize the potential of united strength. The appointment of ardent imperialist Joseph Chamberlain as colonial secretary in 1895 created a new impulse for action on specific problems. During the SOUTH AFRICAN WAR, aid to Britain was enthusiastically supported by Canadian imperialists but resisted by many elements in the population. PM Wilfrid LAURIER allowed a volunteer force, but the war served notice that imperialism had become controversial. Participation in the power of empire now also implied participation in imperial wars. From 1900 to 1914 a lively and often acrimonious debate was carried on between those who saw the imperial burden as Canada's burden and those who preferred autonomy.

WWI brought imperialism to its most advanced stage and also led to its collapse in Canada. The Dominions insisted upon joint planning and policy formation, and meetings in 1917 implied postwar consultation on matters of shared interest among the self-governing parts of the empire. However, the toll of Canadian casualties in Europe was creating a reaction which led to a postwar spirit of N American isolationism. Throughout the 1920s the Mackenzie KING government worked to establish a separate Canadian presence in foreign affairs. The empire thereafter devolved into the much more loosely connected COMMONWEALTH. D.R. OWRAM

Reading: Carl Berger, *The Sense of Power* (1970).

Imperialist, The, novel by Sara Jeannette DUNCAN (Toronto, 1904), is set in Elgin, Ont (modelled on Duncan's native BRANTFORD). *The Imperialist* conducts its exploration of Canadian attitudes toward the mother country through the development of 2 romances. One involves Lorne Murchison, a fervent imperialist, with the pretty but shallow Dora Milburn, who eventually marries an asinine Englishman; the other pairs Lorne's sister Advena with Rev Hugh Finlay, who was already engaged to an older woman before he immigrated to Canada, but submits to New World imperatives and his love for Advena. The novel is at once a delightful comedy of manners and a thoroughgoing analysis of Canadian society as it looks back to England, south to the US and into its own evolving idea of itself. NEIL BESNER

Imports consist of goods or services purchased from residents of foreign countries by Canadian residents. For 1986 these totalled $155 billion, or $10 billion more than all receipts from EXPORTS. The 3 major import divisions were merchandise of $110 billion (71%), services of $21 billion (13.5%) and payments for foreign lending to and investing in Canada of $24 billion (15.5%).

Merchandise The share of Canadian imports coming from the US has remained much the same for the last 6 decades – about 69%. Apart from the US, Canadian imports are from widely diverse places, with nearly 7% from Japan, over 11% from the EEC (including the UK) and over 13% from a wide variety of other nations.

As with exports, commodity imports are dominated by automotive products which account for 30% of all merchandise bought abroad. Of these, 83% come from the US, largely as a consequence of the Canada-US Autopact of 1965 (*see* CANADA-US AUTOMOTIVE PRODUCTS AGREEMENT). Japan has become an increasingly important source of supply and now accounts for over 9% of all automotive imports. Most remaining automotive products come from the EEC, Sweden and S Korea. Another large component of imports, amounting to 28% of the total, is machinery and equipment of many types – industrial machinery, communications and electronic equipment, aircraft, agricultural machinery and miscellaneous equipment. The overwhelming proportion of this category comes from the US, although Japan is becoming a major competitor, particularly in electronic equipment, construction machinery, and small equipment and tools. Other important purchases from abroad include many food products and beverages, a wide range of crude materials (including petroleum) and fabricated materials made out of wood, metals and other minerals.

Imports have been growing at about the same rate as exports over the last 15 years, nearly 13.5% compounded annually. Of this expansion about half is attributable to increases in prices and the other half reflects a growth in the quantity of imports. The most rapidly increasing imports in volume terms during the 1980s have been office machinery, petroleum products, precious metals, automobiles, apparel and apparel accessories.

Services The major purchases of services abroad by Canadians consist of foreign travel expenses (36% of total services); payments for freight and shipping on foreign transportation systems (20%); and outlays for a wide variety of business services such as payments for management fees and technology by foreign subsidiary firms in Canada to their parent firms, royalties, patents and trademarks, film rentals, financial services and equipment rentals (36%). Payments by governments for diplomatic and military people abroad make up most of the remaining service outlays. About 75% of business services and 60% of other service outlays go to the US.

Investment Income Because Canada has been a net international debtor for many decades (more of its industry is foreign-owned than for any other nation), it has to make large annual payments of interest, dividends and miscellaneous charges to the foreign holders of these debts. Canadian provincial governments and corporations, and to a lesser extent the federal government, have been borrowing abroad particularly heavily during the 1980s. Consequently, interest payments have become the largest component of these outlays, amounting to 54% in 1986. Dividends and miscellaneous charges are each about 23% of the total. Dividend payments as recorded by Statistics Canada seriously understate the costs of foreign ownership, because the retained earnings of foreign subsidiaries in Canada, which are used to expand the magnitude of foreign assets in this country, are not counted. If they were, as they should be if we were to follow the approach to BALANCE OF PAYMENTS accounting recommended by the International Monetary Fund, it would expand total payments for direct FOREIGN INVESTMENT in this country by about 200%. In 1984, undistributed earnings of foreign-owned corporations in Canada amounted to $5.3 billion. *See also* INTERNATIONAL TRADE. BRUCE W. WILKINSON

Improvement District, a municipal corporation whose powers are exercised by a trustee or board of trustees appointed by the provincial government. Unlike most municipalities, which are subject to the supervision of both the province and local electors, trustees are under provincial supervision only. Normally, improvement districts are established either in a sparsely settled but vast territory which requires MUNICIPAL GOVERNMENT and services because of new development or the residents' desire for local government; or in new towns, which are more compact geographic entities designated for major development, usually a new resource industry. Once the new community is established, with basic services and a sizable population, it is often replaced by a conventional municipal corporation with a local council. KATHERINE A. GRAHAM

In Search of Myself, by Frederick Philip GROVE (1946; repr 1974), in part a sequel to Grove's *A Search for America* (1927), was ostensibly autobiographical, but the self Grove sought was a complicated one. As a cultivated European immigrant, Grove looked back on his life and attempted to explain and justify his failure to realize his youthful promise and attain his early dreams. The book begins with an account of his affluent childhood and reckless youth among the artistic and literary members of European society. This golden past is sharply contrasted with Grove's adventures as a menial itinerant worker in the US, and finally with his poverty-stricken, isolated life as an immigrant teacher, lecturer, writer and part-time farmer in the uncongenial Canadian wilderness. The book won the Governor General's Award for nonfiction in 1946, but the presence of puzzling inconsistencies and omissions eventually led Canadian scholar D.O. Spettigue to investigate Grove's self-revelations. Spettigue's findings – that Grove had fabricated and indeed aggrandized much of his youthful past – are published in *FPG: The European Years* (1973). Regardless of Grove's curious intermingling of fact and fallacy, his stilted prose style and his slightly bitter tone, the book nonetheless sheds valuable light on his own efforts as a creative writer, and provides an insightful analysis into the singular difficulties which plagued the artist in a pioneering Canadian community. DONNA COATES

Inco Limited, with executive offices in Toronto, is the world's leading producer of NICKEL and a substantial producer of copper, precious metals and cobalt. In addition, Inco is the world's largest supplier of wrought nickel alloys as well as a leading manufacturer of blades, discs, rings and other forged and precision-machined components made from special alloy materials. The company is a major producer of sulphuric acid and liquid sulphur dioxide, and has other interests in metals, venture capital, mining equipment manufacturing and engineering and technology. In 1916, the International Nickel Company of Canada, Ltd was established as a Canadian operating subsidiary of the International Nickel Co in New Jersey. In 1928, the Canadian subsidiary became the parent company through an exchange of shares. In 1929, Inco acquired the Mond Nickel Co, Ltd, a British firm incorporated in 1900 to mine in the SUDBURY Basin. Inco's principal mines and processing operations are located in the Sudbury area of Ontario, in the Thompson area of Manitoba and, through a 98%-owned subsidiary (P.T. International Nickel Indonesia), on the island of Sulawesi, Indonesia. The company also has additional metals refineries in Port Colborne, Ont, Clydach, Wales, and Acton, Eng, and has an interest in nickel-refining in Japan through 2 affiliated companies.

The company, through its 2 principal alloy products and forging businesses, Inco Alloys International and Inco Engineered Products Ltd, produces and markets a wide range of alloy products. Inco Alloys International has rolling mill operations in Huntington, West Virginia, in Burnaugh, Kentucky and in Hereford, Eng. Inco Engineered Products Ltd is headquartered in Birmingham, Eng. In 1986, Inco Ltd had sales of $2.017 billion (converted from $US), assets of $4.1 billion and 20 171 employees. Inco Ltd's shares were widely held and foreign ownership stood at 60%.

Income Distribution refers to the share of total income in society that goes to each fifth of the population, or, more generally, to how income is distributed among Canadian households. Annual income is usually chosen as the indicator of a household's ability to meet its needs, primarily because the necessary statistical data are easily accessible. Economic well-being, however, also depends on other important factors.

Determining Factors of Income Distribution In a capitalist economy such as Canada's, people derive their income from wages if they are employed, from INTEREST if they own financial capital, from profits (or dividends) if they are entrepreneurs and from rent if they own property. The earnings of production factors determine what is known as the distribution of "primary" income; wages and salaries alone account for roughly 85% of this income (*see also* CAPITAL AND WEALTH).

The interaction between supply and demand in each market determines the income of each individual and ultimately the distribution of primary income. For example, a hockey player's salary depends upon the supply and demand in the market for hockey players' services. Because a number of variables influence the supply of and demand for factors of production, the income generated is not the same for everyone, with the result that everyone does not receive the same share of primary income. The following variables influence this distribution: skills, education, professional training and experience, working hours, compensatory salary differences, institutional restrictions, discrimination, differences in property wealth (including inherited wealth), opportunity, and age and health. Primary income distribution is also modified by government intervention. The government influences income distribution in various ways, eg, through TAXATION, TRANSFER PAYMENTS and the provision of social goods and services.

Income Distribution in Canada Statistics Canada annually conducts a survey of approximately 35 000 households, including families and single persons. According to Statistics Canada's classification, an "economic family unit" is a group of persons who share a common dwelling unit and who are related by blood, marriage or adoption. An "unattached individual" is a person living alone or in a household with others to whom he is not related. Total income includes wages and salaries, net income from self-employment, investment income (interest, dividends, rental income), retirement pensions, miscellaneous income such as scholarships and alimony, as well as government transfer payments (welfare, old-age security, family allowance, unemployment insurance, etc). This concept of total income, therefore, corresponds to primary income before taxes and after transfer payments.

Once information about income has been gathered, families are classified by increasing levels of income, from the poorest to the richest. They are divided into 5 groups, known as "quintiles," each representing 20% of all families. The first (or lowest) quintile comprises the poorest families and the last (or highest) quintile includes the richest. The income of the families of each quintile is then calculated in proportion to the income of all families. The percentage of income going to each group in society can thus be measured. In 1985 families of the lowest quintile accounted for 6.3% of the total income, while those of the highest quintile earned 39.4%. Families of the first quintile had an annual income of less than $17 928 and those of the fifth quintile an income greater than $53 398 (*see* ELITES).

Other Statistics Canada figures reveal that families of the lowest quintile depend on government transfer payments for nearly 60% of their income. This group is composed mainly of welfare recipients and the elderly (who receive the old-age security pension and guaranteed income supplements), as well as single-parent families. However, wages and salaries account for nearly 80% of the income of families in the highest quintile, where there are often 2 breadwinners.

Income Distribution of Families by Quintiles (%)
(Source: Statistics Canada)

Quintile	*1951*	*1961*	*1971*	*1981*	*1985*
Lowest	6.1	6.6	5.6	6.4	6.3
Second	12.9	13.5	12.6	12.9	12.3
Middle	17.4	18.3	18.0	18.3	17.9
Fourth	22.4	23.4	23.7	24.1	24.1
Highest	41.1	38.4	40.0	38.4	39.4
Total	100.0	100.0	100.0	100.0	100.0

Income distribution, as measured by Statistics Canada, has been very stable over the past 30 years; ie, the share of income going to each quintile has varied only slightly. Such stability in income distribution is surprising because, during the same period, Canada experienced considerable economic growth and the average family income, corrected for INFLATION, nearly tripled. Moreover the WELFARE STATE, which came into existence during this time, brought a considerable increase in government transfer payments. Two factors are generally used to explain this stability. First, the differences in primary income have become more pronounced because of changes in life-style. Young adults and the elderly tend to live as independent households more often than they did a few decades ago, and the rise in the divorce rate has resulted in more single-parent families. Because these households generally have low incomes, the inequality of primary income has increased. Second, government transfer payments, a portion of which are earmarked for poorer people, narrow the disparities among total income.

Government intervention is not limited to transfer payments. The government also taxes income and provides social goods and services. The net redistributive impact of taxation and government expenditures is difficult to determine, but a number of hypotheses concerning those who carry the burden of taxation and those who benefit from government expenditures have been developed. Some observers claim that, using 1969 data, there is a slight shift in income distribution from the richest families to the poorest. The richest families, representing roughly 25% of family units, provided a net contribution of 6.2% of total income. The effect of government redistribution is certainly less than might be believed at first glance, however, because only some government programs are designed specifically for the poorest people; most consist of transfers within the middle class itself.

Percentage of Low-Income Families and Unattached Individuals, 1985 (%)
(Source: Statistics Canada)

	Families	*Unattached Individuals*
Canadian average	13.1	36.6
By region		
Atlantic provinces	15.7	39.2
Québec	15.7	46.3
Ontario	10.0	31.7
Prairie provinces	13.3	32.0
British Columbia	14.7	35.8
By age of head of household		
24 years or less	32.0	47.9
25-34 years	15.8	22.1
35-44 years	12.8	21.5
45-54 years	9.0	32.3
55-59 years	10.4	39.7
60-64 years	13.8	47.3
65 years and over	9.8	46.1
By sex of head of household		
Male	9.4	30.4
Female	42.0	41.6

A number of adjustments are required to define the "real" distribution of income in Canada. First, Statistics Canada's concept of income underestimates income derived from transfer payments, particularly from welfare. Some income, such as income in kind (eg, accommodation in low-rental housing), capital gains and transfers between persons, is not included. Household production as well as income obtained from the UNDERGROUND ECONOMY are also omitted. In addition, since income varies with age, consideration should be given to income obtained throughout a person's life. Lastly, the size of the family should also be taken into consideration. These adjustments are difficult to make, and, as a result, the "real" distribution of income in Canada remains unknown.

Poverty POVERTY, a complex social phenomenon, is not caused only by inadequate income, although this is certainly a major factor. The poor in Canada are defined as those whose standard of living is below a certain level (usually called the "poverty line") and those who have serious difficulties participating actively in the life of society. Defined in this way, poverty is a relative phenomenon that can be measured by income levels.

Statistics Canada establishes the poverty thresholds (more precisely known as "low income cutoffs") most commonly used in Canada. The thresholds are derived from a family expenditure survey conducted in 1978, which revealed that the average Canadian family spent 38.5% of its income on the basic needs of food, clothing and shelter. Statistics Canada then adds 20% to this share and considers that a family that must spend more than 58.5% of its income on basic needs is low income. It then defines low-income thresholds and indexes them annually to reflect increases in the CONSUMER PRICE INDEX. For example, the low-income thresholds of Canadian families living in large urban areas in 1985 were $10 233 for single persons and $20 812 for families of 4 persons.

In 1985, 13.1% of Canadian families and 36.6% of unattached individuals (representing 15.9% of the population or 3.9 million persons), were numbered as poor. Poverty is more common in the Atlantic provinces and Québec (*see* REGIONAL ECONOMICS), among young people and the elderly and in families (usually single-parent families) in which a woman is the head of the household. In deciding whether Canada's income distribution in 1985 was slightly or very unequal, it is necessary to apply an ethical standard. If the standard adopted is that of "equal sharing" of income, which would result in equal distribution, it is possible to measure and visualize the inequality using a Lorenz curve. The vertical axis reveals the cumulative proportion of the total income, and the horizontal axis reveals the cumulative proportion of the population. If each family earns an identical income, 20% of families will enjoy 20% of the income, 40% of the families 40% of the income and so on. Income distribution will therefore be represented by the straight line of complete equality. The curve located under the straight line represents income distribution in Canada in 1985. The farther the curve is from the straight line, the more unequal the distribution.

Canadian society is ambivalent in its support of the standard of "equal sharing," although numerous government income-security programs do attempt to compensate somewhat for the disparity in results. Moreover, the principle of

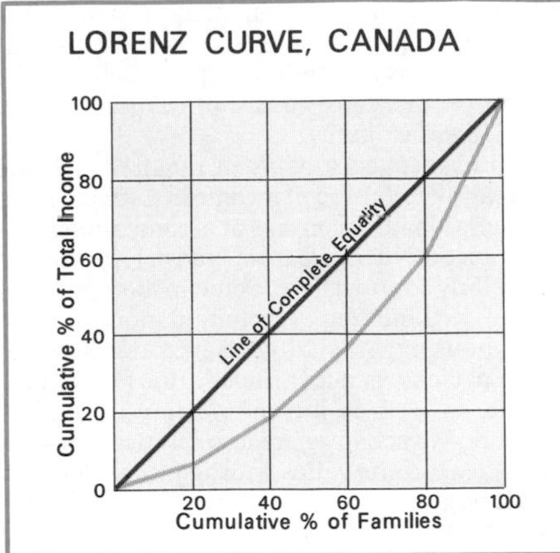

"equal opportunity" probably corresponds, at least partly, to the moral philosophy of Canadian society. A number of government policies focusing on education for young people, for example, are based on this principle. But even if absolutely equal opportunity were achieved for children, certain income disparities would persist in their adult life because of wealth and other advantages, and because of different attitudes towards education, work and savings.

Guaranteed Annual Income Since the early 1960s, a universal solution to poverty and income disparities has been proposed regularly in N America: guaranteed annual (or minimum) income (known as "negative income tax" when incorporated into the tax system). It has 2 components. First, a guaranteed annual income level is determined, below which no family's income is allowed to fall. This income level is based on the needs of each family (by size) and could be the same as the poverty threshold. Such an income is theoretically now provided through welfare payments. Second, while welfare payments are now taxed at $1 for each $1 earned in addition to the welfare payments, a guaranteed annual income would be reduced at a lower tax rate (eg, 50¢ for each $1 of earnings).

Many people share the view that income disparities could be narrowed considerably if the government had the political will to tax the rich more heavily and redistribute wealth to the poor (*see* TAXATION, ROYAL COMMISSION ON). However, any significant redistribution would imply a major rise in taxation for families with an income over $40 000, and it is highly unlikely that these families, considered middle class, would want to accept such a tax hike. PIERRE FRÉCHETTE

Indian, the term used by Europeans to identify aboriginal people of S, Central, and N America, is believed to have originated with Christopher Columbus, who thought he had reached Asia when, in fact, he had arrived in the Caribbean. The term persisted and has been used indiscriminately to refer to all aboriginal peoples on these continents except the INUIT of the Canadian Arctic and the Greenland and Alaska Eskimo. Indians are identified along with Inuit and MÉTIS as the aboriginal peoples of Canada in Sec 35(2) of the Constitution Act, 1982.

In Canada, the legal definition of an Indian is contained in the Indian Act, legislation which first passed in 1876, but which stemmed from similar pre-Confederation laws. People legally defined as Indians are known as status Indians. Nonstatus Indians are of Indian ancestry but, through intermarriage with whites or by abandoning their status rights, have lost their legal status while retaining their Indian identity. Among status Indians there are 2 groups: treaty Indians and registered Indians outside treaty areas. Treaty Indians are people who "took treaty." A treaty is an agreement between the Crown and a specific group of Indians who are held to have surrendered their land rights for specified benefits (*see* INDIAN TREATIES). Registered Indians are people who reside in areas of Canada such as the NWT, BC and YT where treaties were never made or people of Indian status in treaty areas who, for a variety of reasons, have not taken treaty. With the exception of specific promises contained in treaties, treaty Indians and registered Indians outside treaty areas receive identical benefits and privileges from the federal government. Status Indians and nonstatus Indians reside across Canada in every province and territory. Approximately 70% of the status Indian population reside on reserves.

In 1985 the federal government introduced Bill C-31 which enabled Indian women who lost their legal status through marriage to men who did not possess Indian status, to regain their status. Bill C-31 also enabled all first generation children of these marriages and any Indian who had enfranchised, to regain their legal status as Indians. There were about 360 000 status Indians in 1987. HARVEY MCCUE

Reading: P. Cumming and N. Mickenberg, *Native Rights in Canada* (2nd ed, 1972); B. McCardle, *Indian History and Claims: A Research Handbook* (1982).

Indian Act, the principal federal statute dealing with INDIAN status, local government and the management of reserve land and communal monies. The present Act was passed in 1951, but its provisions are rooted in colonial law. The earliest Indian legislation was directed at regulating trade with the Indians and non-Indian settlement in Indian territories. Prior to Confederation, laws to protect Indian lands were enacted in Upper and Lower Canada and in NS, NB, PEI and BC. The concept of Indian status was originally developed to determine entitlement to live in Indian reserve communities, but this changed after 1985 amendments to the Act which now treat Indian status, band membership and residency as separate issues (*see* NATIVE PEOPLE, LAW).

The CONSTITUTION ACT, 1867 assigned to Parliament legislative jurisdiction over "Indians and Lands reserved for the Indians"; 2 separate powers cover status and civil rights on the one hand and Indian lands on the other. The first federal Act was passed in 1868, drawing heavily on earlier legislation of the PROVINCE OF CANADA. Subsequent legislation promoted assimilation into non-Indian society: Indian status was seen as a transitional state, protecting Indians until they became settled on the land and acquired European habits of agriculture. ENFRANCHISEMENT, first legislated in 1869, was the vehicle for assimilation, and was originally a voluntary relinquishment of Indian status. The first Indian Act, so called, was passed in 1876 and was expanded considerably over the years to promote assimilation policy. Traditional Indian practices such as the SUN DANCE and POTLATCH were officially suppressed. Enfranchisement in certain circumstances became involuntary.

During the 1970s, much public attention focused on the statutory rule that an Indian woman lost status on marriage to a non-Indian. A 1973 decision of the Supreme Court of Canada was widely criticized when it held that this rule did not discriminate against women even though Indian men kept their status if they married non-Indians (*see* Jeannette LAVELL). Equality provisions in the CONSTITUTION ACT, 1982 finally led government to amend these provisions. Those who had lost status through marriage were reinstated as Indians and as band members. Their children gained Indian status, but would not gain band membership for 2 years. This interval was intended to give Indian bands time to enact their own membership codes which could exclude the children, but not their mothers. If a code was not enacted prior to June 1987, the children gained band membership as well.

The effect of this amendment was to increase substantially the number of status Indians in Canada, placing pressure on band budgets and land resources. At the same time, few bands have enacted codes because of time limitations and the requirement that a majority of electors approved the code and the necessary votes could not be obtained. The ability to enact a code remains, but persons already on the band list cannot be removed. The 1985 amendments also provide for greater band regulation of liquor and residency on reserves, although the scope of these powers is unclear. Constitutional challenges of such bylaws are certain to be brought in the future. These amendments fall short of the kind of self-government Indian people have argued for. Support was signalled by a special committee of Parliament which reported in 1983, but constitutional conferences in 1985 and 1987 held to entrench an aboriginal right of self-government failed owing to lack of provincial support. For its part, the federal government seemed content to deal with self-government by way of LAND CLAIMS negotiations in some regions and band-specific legislation in others.

Indians remain concerned that the artificial increase of their numbers, coupled with general government austerity and increasing involvement of provinces in Indian issues, signal a general lack of commitment to their special needs and rights. Parliament has been notably reluctant to exercise the full scope of its legislative powers over Indians, and despite acknowledged shortcomings, the Indian Act remains an essentially Victorian statute that continues to resist change. WILLIAM B. HENDERSON

Reading: R. Bartlett, *The Indian Act of Canada* (1980); J. Leslie and R. Maguire, eds, *Historical Development of the Indian Act* (2nd ed, 1978); D. Smith, *Canadian Indians and the Law* (1973); S. Weaver, *Making Canadian Indian Policy* (1981).

Indian Affairs and Northern Development, Department of, est 1966 to replace the Department of Northern Affairs and National Resources. A 1968 reorganization created 3 program areas apart from support services and an engineering and architectural branch: Indian and Inuit Affairs, Northern Affairs and Parks Canada. Parks became the responsibility of the minister of the environment in 1979. An Office of Native Claims was established in 1974 to represent the government in claims negotiations with native groups. The Northern Affairs Program is responsible for a wide range of activities north of the 60th parallel, eg, management of all natural resources (except game), protection of the environment and government-sponsored economic development. The department, commonly called DIAND, is responsible for the administration of the resources and affairs of the NORTHWEST TERRITORIES and the YUKON TERRITORY. Its 1986-87 budget was $2.5 billion.

Indian Art The history of Indian art in Canada begins many thousands of years ago with the migration of the native peoples across BERINGIA (*see* PREHISTORY). The development of native art is in many ways more complex than that of the relatively recent European settlers, and may be divided into 3 distinct periods: prehistoric art, contact or "historic" art, and contemporary native art.

While historians of native art must rely to a large extent upon archaeological finds in the study of the prehistoric period, the work of ethnographers, ethnohistorians and historical archaeologists is of vital importance for knowledge of historic Indian art. Ethnographers have shown that a correct interpretation of the function and meaning of native artworks depends upon an understanding and appreciation of the ways of life, aesthetic values and principles of the peoples themselves. Ethnohistorians have examined early visual sources and written documents such as maps, paintings, captains' logs and accounts by explorers, traders and travellers, and from these documentary fragments have traced the history of native peoples from initial contact to the 20th century. Historical archaeologists have excavated postcontact sites, which give precise, chronological evidence of the interaction between native and European peoples, and also give evidence of the introduction of new materials, techniques and working methods to native artists and crafts people.

Prehistoric Art

Prehistoric art is the period of native art least known in Canada, and its terminal date varies from region to region across the country. While initial contact with the French in the Maritimes and St Lawrence Valley took place in the 16th century, the Indians of the West Coast did not see Europeans until the late 18th century.

Discovery, knowledge and relative dating of prehistoric works of art depend upon meticulous excavation and careful interpretation. Recent important discoveries include the location in NW Ontario of what may be Canada's oldest artwork, a petroglyph site perhaps 5000 years old; a carving of a smiling human head, 5000-3000 BC, from the Coteau-du-Lac site on the St Lawrence R in SW Québec; and the verification that the spectacular art forms of coastal BC – most notably the TOTEM POLES – are not the product of European contact as formerly believed, but have a continuous on-site development dating back at least 2500 years. Since the wet, acidic soils of much of Canada's northland do not permit the survival of artworks in wood, fibre, hide or other perishable materials, much of Canada's prehistoric art has been lost. One major exception has been rock art: paintings in red ochre and carvings incised upon natural rock surfaces (*see* PICTOGRAPHS AND PETROGLYPHS).

Prehistoric art varies not only in genre, style, function, imagery and meaning from region to region but has undergone changes from period to period. These changes accelerated almost everywhere in Canada after about 1000 BC as a consequence of a variety of influential factors: the introduction of pottery, agriculture and settled village life from the Eastern Woodlands of the US and ultimately from Mexico, where New World civilizations developed independently from those of the Old World.

There are several outstanding manifestations of prehistoric art in Canada. The Marpole culture, 500 BC-500 AD, which was centered on the Fraser R Delta and the surrounding Gulf Is of the southern BC coast, produced an abundant variety of stone and bone carvings (ceremonial bowls, effigies and utensils) that in many ways anticipate the style and iconography of postcontact NORTHWEST COAST INDIAN ART. Precontact Iroquoian culture, 900-1600 AD, in southern Ontario (the ancestors of the Huron, Petun, Neutral) produced a pottery of high technical quality and visually pleasing effects decorated with representational and geometric designs. Iroquoian art in the Upper St Lawrence Valley is noted for its clay and stone effigy pipes of fascinating shape and iconographic variety. Both pipe bowls and stems were carved or modelled in high relief or incised with human and zoomorphic images of lizards, turtles and birds, all important power animals in the iconography of Great Lakes religious art. These tiny masterpieces had a sacred function – the ritual smoking of tobacco in the context of Indian spiritual beliefs (*see* CALUMET).

Stone human-effigy pipe bowl, late Iroquoian, post-1500 AD, Simcoe County, Ont (*courtesy the Royal Ontario Museum*).

Postcontact Art

Postcontact or "historic" art is well known, mainly because examples have been collected, sketched and written about by explorers, traders, missionaries, artists and scholars for over 300 years and are now deposited in museums throughout the world. The various regions into which native art is customarily divided are based upon the distribution and cultural character of native groups in the early contact period, but this emphasis on the "ethnographic present" has resulted in a frozen time perspective, an erroneously narrow view of the great time depth, and of the diversity and richness of native art history.

Native art in Canada may be divided into 7 regional subdivisions: Eastern Subarctic (eastern Canadian Shield); Western Subarctic (western Canadian Shield and Mackenzie drainage area); Southern Great Lakes and Upper St Lawrence Valley; Prairies (southern Manitoba, Saskatchewan and Alberta); Plateau (interior southern BC); Northwest Coast (BC coast); and Arctic (arctic coastline and offshore islands eastward to Newfoundland).

Eastern Subarctic The art of the Eastern Subarctic is the most archaic in Canada, the majority of prehistoric and early contact rock-art sites being located in this region. The largely Algonquian-speaking peoples – the Ojibwa, Cree, Algonquin, Ottawa, Montagnais, the Naskapi of Ontario and Québec, and the Micmac and Maliseet of the southern Maritimes – continued a nomadic way of life based on hunting and the gathering of wild foods.

The art of the MICMAC and MALISEET of NS and NB remained distinctive until well into the 20th century. The Micmac are noted for their moosehair embroidery and porcupine quillwork on birchbark and basketry containers, hide and textile clothing. Glass beads introduced by European traders were welcomed early by Micmac and other Indian women artists as substitutes for the more difficult quills and moosehair. The use of beads, their richness of colour and diversity of size and transparency, inevitably changed the aesthetic character of Micmac design. Micmac women's art in quills, moosehair and beads was largely 2-dimensional, secular in function and abstract in style, in contrast to that produced by men who worked in 3 dimensions with harder, more resistant materials such as wood and stone.

A well-known characteristic of Micmac design is the so-called "double-curve" motif, a bilaterally symmetrical arrangement of 2 opposing spirals or curves that is suggestive of plant forms. It appears as the basic, underlying pattern in much 2-dimensional design throughout the Eastern Subarctic and becomes highly elaborate among the central Algonquians and Iroquoians of the Great Lakes area. Although this elaboration may have been influenced by young Indian girls taught needlework by Ursuline nuns, the pattern was rooted in an existing culture, for plants and their medicinal and magical properties played an important role in subarctic Indian belief and shamanistic herbal practice.

The art of the nomadic Naskapi is also remarkable for its 2-dimensional design. Especially noteworthy are caribou-hide coats incised and painted with linear geometric patterns and with the double-curve motif. Throughout the Subarctic and Great Lakes areas, the colour red plays an important symbolic role, expressive of life's renewal and the continuity of the life-force in both animals and men.

The OJIBWA of subarctic Ontario and Manitoba are noted for a number of distinctive sacred art forms. The artwork of Ojibwa women was similar in technique, function and genre to much of that produced throughout the subarctic area: quillwork and beadwork on clothing, bark and basketry in both geometric and floral patterns. Ojibwa men, responsible for works of sacred, ceremonial function, produced an art that was largely symbolic, representational and documentary. Sacred art was intended to embody specific meanings, to portray spirit helpers and record ritual and mythological events and experiences. This division of artistic labour appears to have been the general pattern throughout native America: men producing public art for religious

Smoking bag (*courtesy National Museums of Canada/Canadian Museum of Civilization/K75-950*).

Man's summer jacket (*courtesy National Museums of Canada/Canadian Museum of Civilization/K75-956*).

and ceremonial functions, women producing personal art, largely for the sake of sheer visual pleasure or "beauty," but often using motifs symbolizing spiritual and cosmological concepts such as the Four Quarters or the zigzag lightning of THUNDERBIRD. Ojibwa medicine men (or SHAMANS) were responsible for much of the rock art produced in Ontario and Manitoba, recording their visionary spirit encounters well into the 20th century. One of the most important forms of Ojibwa religious art in the historic period was the sacred birchbark records – rectangular pieces of bark measuring from several centimetres to over 3 m in length, which were incised in an almost imperceptible, fine-line technique with highly esoteric and symbolic images. These records served as documents of sacred lore or as memory aids for ritual, and the most detailed, extensive and valued were those produced by the MIDEWIWIN or Grand Medicine Society.

Least studied to date has been the art of the subarctic CREE. Aesthetic expression among the Cree is highlighted by exquisite quillwork and moosehair embroidery, noted for its perfection of technique and delicate colour harmonies. As nomadic hunters, living a precarious existence in a harsh climate from east of James Bay to northern Saskatchewan and Alberta, the Cree had to carry their goods on their person, so items of clothing, especially their painted and embroidered coats, moccasins and mitts became a focus for personal aesthetic expression. Sacred art, eg, shamans' painted drums and ceremonial animal hides executed with symbolic motifs, are lesser known but equally important as aesthetic objects among both Cree and Ojibwa.

Western Subarctic What has been described for the Cree of the Eastern Subarctic is largely applicable to the Western Subarctic, a region of similar environmental conditions occupied by Athapaskan-speaking peoples. Although linguistically distinctive from the eastern subarctic Algonquians, the DENE NATION, as the Athapaskans prefer to be called, share a similar culture and art with their subarctic neighbours. Decoration of personal gear and clothing was the major form of artistic expression, as caribou and moose hide was embellished with porcupine quills, moosehair embroidery, beads and commercial threads in geometric and floral patterns. Compared to southerly groups such as the Ojibwa and Iroquois, the subarctic peoples revealed in their embroidery their delicate colour sense and exquisite precision in design.

Southern Great Lakes and Upper St Lawrence Valley From the late prehistoric to the early historic period, the Iroquoian-speaking peoples of this region – the HURON, NEUTRAL, PETUN, and later the IROQUOIS proper – underwent more rapid changes than the natives in any other region in Canada. Because they were farmers, living in relatively permanent villages, their political and social institutions found expression in suitable works of art. By the 19th century, however, many of the Indians had migrated westward or eastward, or were settled in reserves throughout the area. Art came to have a new purpose, as a commodity for sale to outsiders – to tourists and collectors of Indian "arts and crafts." In prehistoric times this region was already subject to outside influences. The Iroquois in particular had trade connections to the south with the highly complex and economically advanced "Mississippian" cultures of the Eastern Woodlands, which in turn were stimulated by Mexican cultural innovations (ceramic technology entered Canada from this source). In the early contact period they made alliances with Europeans through the FUR TRADE.

The history of art in this region is too complex to detail, except for a few highlights. While on the whole there is considerable homogeneity in quillwork and beadwork throughout the subarctic and Great Lakes area, Huron work is distinctive in the later historic period. Huron "personal art" favoured moosehair embroidery in floral motifs of exquisite beauty on black-dyed hide. The quality of trade goods, unmatched elsewhere in Canada, had peaked by 1830, long after the Huron had left western Ontario to settle at Lorette, Qué. Hide and yarn shoulder pouches and bags, executed with a wide variety of geometric, naturalistic and mythological motifs, were the predecessors of the more recent loom-woven and heavily beaded "Bandolier" bags of the western Great Lakes area. The most common motifs were Thunderbird and the Underwater Panther, finely rendered in quills, moosehair and beads. Typical as well were finger-woven sashes interwoven with white beads, burden straps of twined Indian hemp, wooden ball-headed clubs incised and carved in high relief, and elaborately decorated knife sheaths. The noted Assomption Sash was a trade item, although, as with silverwork, the Indians adopted European techniques and designs. Even the splint baskets, prized by collectors as a typical Indian craft, employed a technique learned from Swedish settlers in the Delaware Valley.

The Iroquois proper, or Six Nations, did not settle in Canada until after the American Revolution. The most noteworthy art forms of the historic Iroquois are the False Faces, wooden masks with metal eyes and sometimes horsehair, which were carved by the men for use in curing ceremonies (*see* FALSE FACE SOCIETY). Strongly sculptural in character, with a variety of mouth types and painted in red or black or both, they are sacred objects believed to contain the life-force of the living tree. The masks represent mythological beings, the most notable being "Crooked Face," the one who challenged the Creator and had his nose broken. Other masks, plaited from dried cornhusks, were worn in agricultural ceremonies and represent a second group of earth-oriented supernaturals, those who taught mankind how to grow crops.

In addition to personal art (clothing) and sacred art (False Faces), the Iroquois produced another kind of art object of "political" function and meaning. WAMPUM strings and belts of several centimetres width and sometimes metres in length were made of purple and white shells traded in from the Atlantic coast. In the absence of writing, yet with the high degree of political

Painted caribou skin (*courtesy National Museums of Canada/Canadian Museum of Civilization/A77-1849*).

sophistication these Iroquoian-speaking peoples had achieved, these wampum belts with their symbolic motifs served as a visual record of particular treaties and events. As such, the wampum belt became a symbol of friendship and co-operation between political groups, both Indian and European.

Prairies Prairie Indian culture, as it emerged in the 19th century, was a synthesis of native and white cultures, the product of postcontact European influences such as the horse and the gun which provided increased mobility and effectiveness in the BUFFALO HUNT. The art produced by the BLOOD, BLACKFOOT and ASSINIBOINE is similar to that of their eastern subarctic and western Great Lakes neighbours in techniques, materials and motifs, as westward migration, the consequence of new hunting opportunities, the fur trade and advancing colonization, brought eastern influences into prairie culture.

Art produced by prairie people was essentially 2-dimensional, in which painting on hides was the major genre. Large TIPIS that required the hides of up to 40 buffalo were their major architectural form. Among the Blackfoot of southern Alberta, tipis of important men were often lavishly painted with naturalistic and geometric motifs. Dream images depicted on rawhide shields rival contemporary surrealist paintings in visionary and aesthetic impact. As images of the warrior's personal guardian spirits, they were believed to protect him in warfare and help in the hunt. Painted buffalo robes were another major art form, with motifs ranging from the abstract, concentric "sunburst" pattern to representational images. Personal art was the focus of aesthetic attention, as deer-hide moccasins, jackets, dresses, leggings and shirts were embellished with porcupine quillwork and beads. Painted PARFLECHES, rawhide containers of various shapes and sizes, were unique to this area, and no design was exactly the same as another.

Plateau The plateau region of central BC is often ignored in surveys of Indian art but is unique in many ways. The interior SALISH left behind a major body of prehistoric pictographs. The Lillooet, Thompson, Okanagan and Shuswap of the historic period are noted for their finely crafted, watertight baskets made by the coiling technique and decorated with geometric motifs. Little research has been done on the art of the plateau peoples, on their blankets woven of mountain-goat wool, their clothing, or the religious beliefs that provide the context for art interpretation in many Indian cultures.

Northwest Coast and Arctic The historic art of the Northwest Coast and of the Arctic has been the subject of considerable attention in recent years,

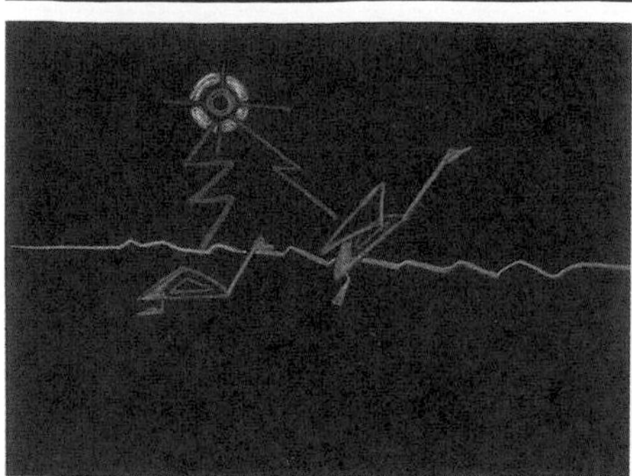

Geese, by Jackson Beardy, an Ojibwa artist from Manitoba (*courtesy Department of Indian and Northern Affairs*).

to a large extent because of the intrinsic importance of INUIT and Northwest Coast Indian art in the context of world art.

Indian art of the prehistoric and postcontact periods is "traditional" art. Even though native art was strongly affected by European materials, techniques and motifs during the historic period, it was still largely shaped by the context of Indian cultures. In contrast, contemporary native art, like contemporary art the world over, fulfils a new purpose: that of self-expression.

Contemporary Indian Art

Contemporary Indian art is so recent in origin that its directions are not clear and, contrary to appearances, its interpretation and aesthetic assessment are not complete. Many significant and fundamental questions – such as criteria for critical judgement – have not been systematically addressed. Three major centres of native art, however, clearly dominate the contemporary scene in Canada: Inuit art, West Coast Indian art, and the Woodlands art of eastern Canada. A scattered group of Indian artists work independently, in the context of mainstream Western art, and may be described as internationalist in scope and intent. The Woodlands school gained recognition in the 1970s with the rise to fame of Norval MORRISSEAU, an Ojibwa from northern Ontario. The majority of Woodland artists have been influenced by Morrisseau and are known as "Legend Painters" for their rendering of tales and mythological characters in their work. Other painters include Carl RAY, from northern Ontario, Daphne ODJIG and Blake DEBASSIGE, from Manitoulin I, and Jackson BEARDY, from Man.

Man Changing Into Thunderbird by Norval Morrisseau (*courtesy National Museums of Canada/Canadian Museum of Civilization/S82-786*).

The internationalist artists tend to work alone, seeing themselves as independent of any "school," and are often highly trained in contemporary Western techniques of painting. They view themselves as "artists" above all who "happen to be Indian." Nevertheless, their paintings evoke in form and content an indisputable link with Indian sensibilities. Outstanding in this group are Alex JANVIER, a Chipewyan from northern Alberta; Arthur SHILLING from Orillia, Ont, who was well known for his portraits of Ojibwa; and Sarain STUMP, a Shoshone-Cree from the Prairies, who was a painter of surrealistic-symbolic compositions. The Iroquois George Longfish from Ohsweken, Ont, though he works essentially in an abstract expressionist manner, is able to communicate Indian spirituality through formal means alone. The portrayals of INDIAN RESERVE life by Allen SAPP are reminiscent of 19th-century realist works and typify the conservative trend among many Indian artists today.

JOAN M. VASTOKAS

Reading: T.J. Brasser, *"Bo'jou, Neejee!": Profiles of Canadian Indian Art* (1976); C.F. Feest, *Native Arts of North America* (1980); Nancy-Lou Patterson, *Canadian Native Art* (1973).

Indian Head, Sask, Town, pop 1886 (1986c), 1889 (1981c), inc 1902, is located in the heart of Saskatchewan's richest farming area, S of the Qu'Appelle Valley, 68 km E of Regina. Its first settlers moved into the district in 1882, a few months ahead of the CPR. Indian Head was named for a low range of hills a few km to the SW of the townsite. The town remains very prominent in the agricultural industry of the province. Not only is it a prime wheat-growing area, it is also the site of an Agriculture Canada experimental farm, established 1887, and a tree nursery, established 1902 and now operated by the Prairie Farm Rehabilitation Administration.

DON HERPERGER

Indian Pipe (*Monotropa uniflora*), a perennial plant, is the only native species of genus *Monotropa,* one of 8 genera of the wintergreen family (Pyrolaceae) found in Canada. The genus is sometimes raised to family level (Monotropaceae), or WINTERGREENS may be included in the heath family (Ericaceae). Indian pipe grows transcontinentally in shaded woodlands but is hard to find, not always appearing in the same place each year. Lacking chlorophyll, it cannot manufacture its own food and lives on partially decayed vegetation in soil, with the aid of a fungus (*see* MYCORRHIZAE). The plant is 10-20 cm tall. The nodding, one-flowered stalks are often clustered. The flower and stalk vaguely resemble a smoker's pipe, hence the common name. It is also called corpse plant because of its shining, translucent white colour. If the plant is touched, the spot turns black. Indian pipe was used by the BLACKFOOT to heal wounds, and by various groups for convulsions and epileptic seizures.

PATRICK SEYMOUR

Indian Reserve The earliest Indian reserves in Canada appear to have been established on seigneurial holdings by Catholic missionary orders and private persons in New France (*see* SILLERY). Later reserves were set aside by treaty and various forms of crown grant in the British Maritime colonies, Lower Canada and Upper Canada. After Confederation, reserves were formed either under the numbered treaties or by special arrangement with individual bands. The actual means by which reserves were created is not yet fully understood.

In Canada there were 2251 reserves in 1985, with a total area of about 2.6 million ha. Reserves are lands set aside for the exclusive use of status Indians. A BAND is the term used to describe a community of Indians residing on one or more reserves, but some Indian bands have no reserves. In 1987 there were about 360 000 status Indians and 542 bands. In June 1985 Parliament passed Bill C-31 which, among other changes to the Indian Act, has allowed some 100 000 people to claim Indian status. So in the 1980s there will be a dramatic increase in the number of status Indians; 17 000 had been added in this way by the beginning of 1987. In the NWT and the Yukon, where few reserves have been established, the bands have been gathered into communities known as settlements, on lands which are generally held by the Crown for their benefit but which do not have reserve status. There are reserves in most parts of southern Canada, but about 65% of the INDIAN population is on reserves in areas designated "rural" or "remote" (*see* NATIVE PEOPLE, DEMOGRAPHY). A majority of bands in Canada have fewer than 1000 members.

The INDIAN ACT stipulates that only status Indians may reside permanently on a reserve. Bylaws enacted by individual band councils enable some persons who are not status Indians to reside on reserves until such time as they may be asked to leave. Many bands have leased or otherwise disposed of portions of their reserve lands to non-Indians for various purposes, including natural-resource exploitation, rights of way for transportation or transmission, farming, ranching and recreational land use. Although many Indians believe that reserves are legally their property, the Indian Act states that the title to reserves is vested in the Crown. This legal relationship with the federal government concerns Indians, who believe that the status of Indian lands is in jeopardy as long as legal title remains outside Indian control. The Indian Act forbids the "surrender" and sale of reserve land by an Indian or a band to anyone other than the Crown. Individual Indians who occupy particular plots of land in a reserve cannot obtain an ordinary deed or title to the land, but they may acquire certificates giving them varying degrees of protection from claims by other parties. This individual title or "location" may be transferred among members of the same band. Land in a reserve which is not assigned to individuals is held as common property for the benefit of the entire band.

Social conditions in most reserves reflect the historical and political neglect that Canada has shown towards people of Indian ancestry (*see* NATIVE PEOPLE, SOCIAL CONDITIONS). The location of most reserves in isolated and remote areas has contributed to the high rate of unemployment among Indians, which remains at about 35% of the working-age population, rising to much higher levels on the remote reserves where traditional economies have been eroded. Of those Indians who are employed, 75% work on a reserve (*see* NATIVE PEOPLE, ECONOMIC CONDITIONS).

In spite of these and other conditions which have contributed to a host of problems among people who reside on reserves, the reserves remain the physical and spiritual home for many Indians, especially in the southern regions. Indian reserves have often been called rural ghettos or retreats where Indians can escape the demands of modern society. People who perceive reserves in this way believe that without reserves Indians would be forced to assimilate into Canadian society and that with assimilation, many of the problems which affect reserve populations today would vanish. This view ignores the political and legal status that reserves have in Canada and overlooks the fact that most Indians do not want to be assimilated. It also ignores the situation in the NWT, the Yukon and northern Québec, where status Indians who do not live on reserves still maintain a separate identity, language and culture.

To many Indians, reserves represent the last visible evidence that they were the original people of this country. The reserve nurtures a community of "Indianness" and reinforces spiritual unity among Indians. Despite the manifest poverty, ill health, poor housing and lack of services, the life-style on reserves, traditional values, kinship affiliations and the land itself all contribute to an Indian's identity and psychological well-being. The relative isolation of most reserves enables Indians to socialize their children to values important to their culture: reticence and noninterference, consensus decision making and nonverbal communication. Reserves, since they are set apart both physically and legally, help Indians to maintain an ethnic identity within Canada. HARVEY MCCUE

Reading: P.A. Cumming and N.H. Mickenberg, *Native Rights in Canada* (2nd ed, 1972); W.B. Henderson, *Land Tenure in Indian Reserves* (1978).

Indian Summer, popular expression for a period of mild, summerlike weather which occurs in the autumn, usually after the first frost. The origins of the name are obscure, but it was in use in Canada early in the 19th century and even earlier in the US. The Toronto Meteorological Observatory (est 1839) recorded the date of certain periodic events, such as Indian summer, until 1871. Almost invariably, its records show that this phenomenon occurred in late Oct or the first half of Nov and lasted from a few days to about a week. Although it cannot be precisely defined, Indian summer continues to arrive most years just as thoughts of the summer past are fading into thoughts of the winter to come. MICHAEL J. NEWARK

Indian Trade Goods are items of European manufacture that were traded with the indigenous peoples of Canada for furs. For the initial stages of culture contact such goods were stray bits of metal (eg, an old iron axe or knife, a handful of nails) and pieces of rope and used clothing. During this period, most of the trade in furs was carried out by fishermen who had gone ashore to dry their catches. Although the volume of trade was small, the profits were relatively large because items of little value to a European could be traded for furs that commanded an excellent price in the home market. During the 16th century, however, the FUR TRADE gradually developed into a separate branch of commerce. Ships solely engaged in trade were sent to the eastern seaboard with cargoes of manufactured goods. At this stage, decisions had to be made about the type of trade goods that would be in greatest demand and produce most furs at the best prices.

From the beginning, one of the most important items of trade was the iron axe. Axes were imported into French Canada in such numbers that they were literally "harvested" in many parts of southern Ontario, forming the first cash crop of the settlers who were breaking the land. The axes were formed by bending a short length of bar iron around a mandrel to form a wedge-shaped eye, then welding the ends of the bar together and hammering it into a long heavy blade. A thin piece of steel was usually set into the blade so that the tool would take and hold a sharper edge. These early French felling axes are found throughout eastern Canada and are scattered across New York and Ohio and down the Mississippi drainage; however, they are concentrated in southern Ontario and western New York, the homeland of the Iroquoian-speaking peoples. Although generations of children were raised with the impression that the old trade axes were weapons, archaeological evidence suggests that they were used, primarily by women, for breaking up the dead limbs and brush that were used for firewood. They would, of course, have been used for many other purposes as well.

While the heavy French felling axe was quite acceptable to the sedentary Iroquoian peoples, it was much too cumbersome for the hunters and gatherers of the northern forests. Hence the French introduced the lighter, more slender Biscay axe. This axe was probably introduced into the trade towards the end of the 17th century, at about the same time that the HUDSON'S BAY COMPANY was establishing trading posts on James Bay. The English also found their axes too cumbersome for the Algonquian-speaking peoples with whom they traded and introduced a lighter, hatchetlike tool. The minor stylistic differences between axe types were probably not significant to the native peoples. But to the archaeologist and historian such minor differences are of primary importance because the distribution of the different types across an area allows reconstruction of the trade routes that stretched out from the various commercial centres. In addition, if the dates at which different styles were introduced into the trade are known, the information can be used in dating archaeological sites. For example, the earliest flintlock musket that the HBC traded into James Bay had a flat cock and lock plate; however, in 1682 the Oakes pattern, with rounded outer surfaces on the cock and lock plate, was introduced. These rounded surfaces remained characteristic of the Northwest gun throughout its history. Any archaeological site which produces the Oakes-pattern musket must postdate 1682.

Styles in trade goods changed through time. Although few such changes can be precisely dated, many are known with reasonable precision. For example, a collection of kaolin pipes can usually be dated to within a 10-year period, as can a collection of glass bottles. Glass beads and brass kettles are much more difficult to date, although some clues are available. For example, larger star beads are associated only with early French sites; small brass kettles with vertical sides seem to appear only on very late sites that were supplied by the HBC.

Native peoples adopted items of European manufacture because of their technological superiority: flintlock muskets, iron axes and knives and brass kettles simply were more efficient than the bows and arrows, stone tools and birchbark baskets they replaced. Similarly, for much of the year, woolen clothing was vastly superior to skin clothing. Trade goods, however, were not limited to utilitarian objects. A pipe of tobacco may not have made a trapper more efficient, but it did make him more serene; and his wife and daughters could have tied back their hair with strips of skin, as had their ancestors for countless generations, but they found a brightly coloured ribbon more attractive.

The volume of goods that was imported during the early fur-trade period was impressive. For example, in 1684 the HBC shipped 300 flintlock muskets, 2000 iron axes, 2160 kaolin tobacco pipes, 3000 jackknives and 5000 butcher knives to its Albany post. During this period, the fur trade was dominated by those historic rivals, the French and English. The French led the way westward, following the ancient canoe routes of the Indians. Even after the conquest of New France, the commercial rivalry continued, with the Montréal traders pushing farther and farther west. At the height of their power, they were following a well-established "Voyageurs' Highway" that stretched from Montréal on the St Lawrence to Fort Chipewyan on Lk Athabasca. The trade goods they carried, the muskets, kettles, beads, pipes, woolen clothing, blankets, etc, were the currency of the fur trade, a trade that opened up half a continent and gave Canada its basic configuration.

WALTER A. KENYON

Indian Treaties in Canada are agreements between the Crown and Indian groups by which native people exchange some of their interests in specific areas of their ancestral lands in return for various kinds of payments and promises from crown officials. On a deeper level, treaty documents are sometimes understood as representative of solemn pacts establishing the future basis of relations between those for whom Canada is an ancient homeland, and those whose deepest family roots lie in other countries.

During the 17th and 18th centuries, competing British and French colonial officials entered into various bargains with native groups of northeastern N America involving trade, military relations and, to a lesser extent, interest in land. Some of these early understandings were documented and can be correctly described as Indian treaties, although most had minimal effect on establishing permanent terms of native-newcomer relations. The Indian people of the Maritime provinces in Canada base part of their claim for recognition of their ABORIGINAL RIGHTS on various commitments made by the British in these old treaties, agreements that are now generally understood to pertain more to peace and friendship than to the exchange of interests in land.

Pre-Confederation Treaties The particular thrust of Indian treaty making whose legitimacy is today most widely recognized in Canada has its origin in the Great Lakes-Ohio Valley region after the Seven Years' War. The ROYAL PROCLAMATION OF 1763 claimed for King George III sovereign dominion over all land formerly occupied by the French, while also reserving to Indian "nations" as their "hunting grounds," those territories lying W of lands drained by rivers flowing into the Atlantic Ocean. The proclamation further stipulated that if any part of this immense Indian reserve was desired for colonial settlement in the future, the native inhabitants would be free to sell their aboriginal interests in the soil at some public meeting arranged for the purpose. Such purchases, it was stipulated, could be made only by properly authorized officials acting directly on behalf of the British monarch. Thus the constitutional basis for Indian treaties in Canada was established in a way that tended towards the Crown becoming the exclusive agency of land transfers between native groups and arriving non-native settlers.

Efforts to enforce systematically the treaty-making stipulations of the Royal Proclamation were first made in Upper Canada, a colony formally created in 1791. The first agreements were negotiated rather haphazardly and were docu-

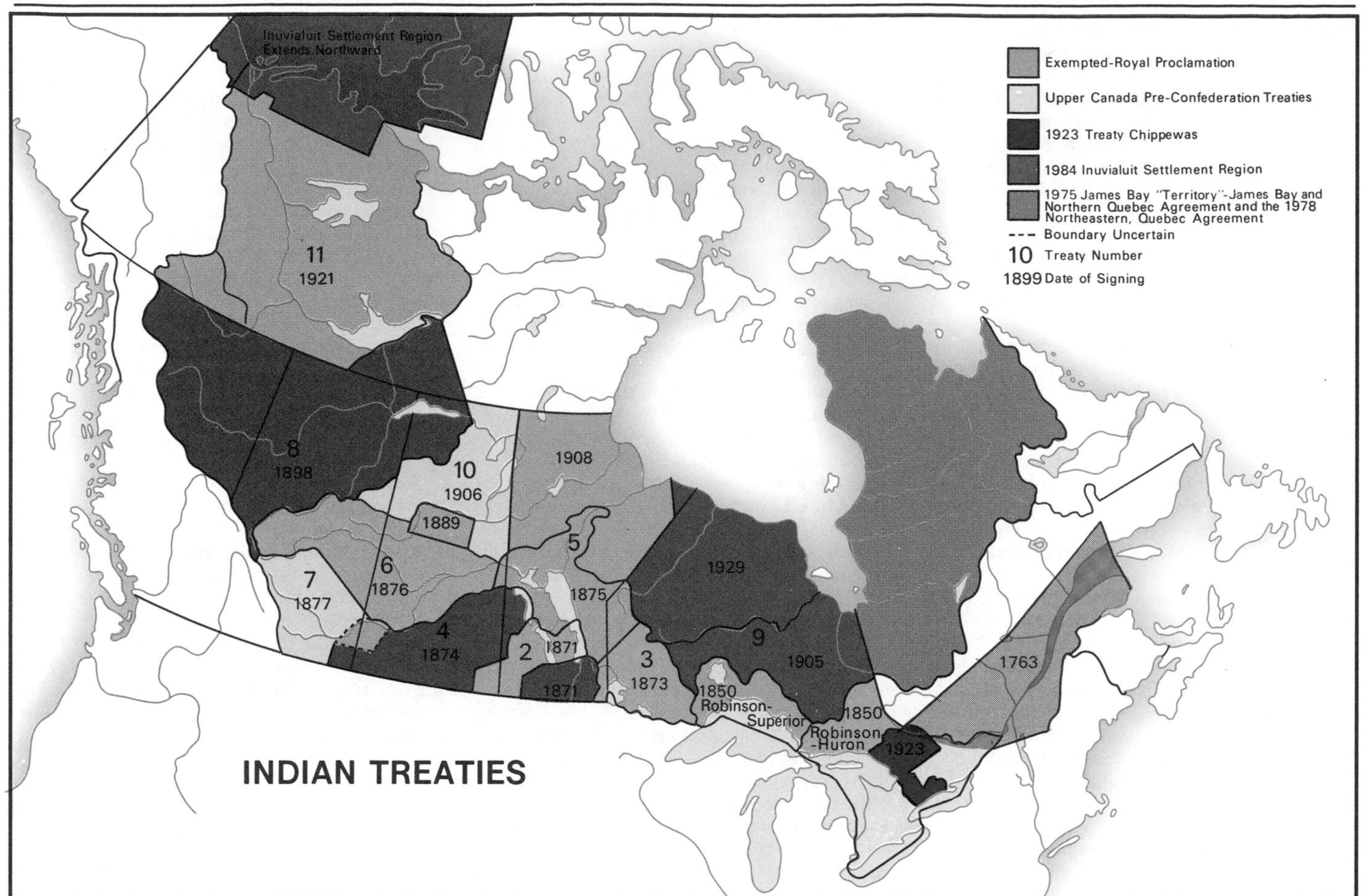

mented only informally, if at all. As a result uncertainties exist about the status of Indian land title in the easternmost townships of the province of Ontario. In 1794, Gov Gen Lord Dorchester attempted to regularize the process of buying aboriginal interests: he detailed that proper records of all treaty transactions should henceforth be made and preserved, that special precautions be made against the use of alcohol during the negotiations, and that "all purchases" were to be made "with great solemnity and ceremony according to the ancient usages and customs of the Indians." With some notable exceptions, Dorchester's instructions were incorporated into subsequent treaty-making procedures in Canada.

Through a series of individual treaties, the Crown obtained by the late 1830s unencumbered title to most Upper Canadian territory south of the Precambrian Shield. By and large Indian groups readily accepted the terms offered them by government representatives: a good deal of trust existed between native people north of the Great Lakes and British military authorities who generally shared an intent to keep in check the land-grabbing expansionism of the US. Thus many of the earlier Upper Canadian treaties were negotiated as part of a well-established ebb and flow of relations between allies holding compatible understandings of their own strategic interests. The treaty agreements usually stipulated a transferring of interest in territory in return for a single presentation of money and merchandise, together with the promise of a regular annual payment in perpetuity. Only gradually did the concept develop of including provision to create well-defined INDIAN RESERVES for the native groups involved.

The principle that treaties could create a secure form of tenure for Indian reserves was advanced in 1850, when crown representative William Benjamin Robinson secured agreement from Indian leaders to "cede, grant and convey unto Her Majesty" about 50 000 square miles (129 500 km^2) N of the Upper Great Lakes. These transactions, known as the Robinson-Huron and Robinson-Superior treaties, included provision for the creation of 21 new Indian reserves, each to be held by the Crown for the "use and benefit" of the respective native groups whose leaders' names and marks were listed on the agreements. Also part of the bargain were initial payments worth a total of £4000, plus "perpetual" annuities valued at £1100 to be distributed among all the Indians covered by the treaties. Officials of what was now the Province of Canada had been pressured to authorize treaty negotiations on the one hand by Gov Gen Lord Elgin, and on the other by Chief Shinguakouce and his followers. In a relatively minor confrontation given the overblown title of the Michipicoten War, the latter had asserted in 1849 their uncompromised aboriginal interest in Precambrian Shield territories where Canadian entrepreneurs had already begun minor mining operations. In the Robinson treaties which resulted, a crown commitment was made that Indians could hunt and fish throughout the ceded territory "as they have heretofore been in the habit of doing." This promise, the first of its kind in an Indian treaty, was made, explained Robinson, so that Indians could not make future claims of support in return for loss of "their usual means of support."

The 2 final major pre-Confederation treaties were signed in 1854 and 1862. They cover, respectively, the Saugeen Peninsula north of Owen Sound, and part of Manitoulin I on Lake Huron. By the terms of rather unusual treaties obtained in 1836 by Upper Canadian Lt-Gov Sir Francis Bond Head, both of these regions had been specifically reserved for Indians, which was one of the factors heightening the atmosphere of acrimony that generally characterized the making of the remaining settlements of the pre-Confederation era. In both instances, Indian sanction of the deals was secured under sordid and somewhat dubious legal circumstances. It seems that Crown regard for native interests had diminished with the declining military significance of the Indians in the international balance of power in the Great Lakes area.

The Saugeen and Manitoulin treaties stipulated that native groups involved would receive regular interest payments on funds obtained from all crown sales of the ceded territories. This promise, the subject of controversy in the future, proved insufficient to attract the participation of an entire community of Roman Catholic Odawa [Ottawa] Indians on the eastern portion of Manitoulin I. In concert with the Jesuit missionaries who lived among them, these Odawas successfully resisted efforts of crown officials to persuade or coerce them into signing the Manitoulin treaty. As a result, to this day Wikwemikong, Ont, remains an unceded Indian reserve.

The Numbered Treaties Confederation in 1867 set the stage for Canada's purchase from the Hudson's Bay Co of Rupert's Land and the North-West Territories. The various legal instruments which formalized the transfer included stipulations that the Canadian government would assume responsibility for the "protection" and "well-being" of the region's aboriginal residents. Moreover, the duty of compensating Indians for any interest they maintained in the annexed territory was to fall to the Dominion. Hence, the system of Indian treaty making that had evolved in Upper Canada was exported westward. Between 1871 and 1877 crown representatives met with Indian delegations to negotiate a series of transactions covering most of the present-day Prairie provinces as well as NW Ontario. These resulted in the first 7 of Canada's 11 so-called "numbered treaties."

The development of the treaty system throughout much of western Canada was based as much on economic pragmatism as it was on any particular legal view of aboriginal rights. During the 1870s the US government was spending over $20 million a year fighting plains Indians. This amount was larger than the entire budget of the whole central government in Canada; with these facts of finance before them, federal officials chose to rely heavily on treaties to bring about a relative degree of peaceful acquiescence among the 35 000 Indian inhabitants of the territories scheduled to be opened up for settlement.

Crown officials conducting the initial numbered treaty negotiations were instructed to offer Indians terms approximately similar to those detailed in the Robinson treaties. The native delegations in these and subsequent bargaining sessions, however, made it clear that more was expected. Typically, the Indian participants in Treaty No 1 to Treaty No 7 sought commitments from the Dominion government, including the building of schools on newly established Indian reserves, the supply of farm implements, seeds, farm animals and instruction in agricultural techniques, and the prohibition of the liquor trade in native communities. Generally such demands were met by the Crown in agreements which also made the more traditional provisions for hunting and fishing rights, annuities, the furnishing of medals, flags and chiefs' uniforms, and initial lump-sum payments. The most comprehensive of all the agreements was Treaty No 6. Its native negotiators exacted a commitment that their people would be supplied with medicine when needed. Similarly, an explicit promise was obtained that if Treaty No 6 Indians were to experience "any pestilence" or "general famine," Crown officials would undertake to do all that was necessary to relieve them of the calamity.

In deciding whether or not to enter these agreements with the Crown, the Ojibwa, Cree and Assiniboine Indians often faced a horizon of fairly limited choices. It was generally made clear to them that non-native newcomers would soon be taking control of most of their lands whether or not treaty deals were reached. Thus they had the option either of fighting to resist the incursion of outsiders, perhaps ineffectively, or they could accept some government assistance in making adjustments to the enormous changes that were surely coming down on the land. For native people on the Prairies, the demise of the great life-sustaining buffalo herds made the prospects for the future seem especially bleak. Thus, to some Indians the treaties seemed to present an avenue of adaptation at a moment when all other paths of survival appeared blocked.

Nevertheless, not all Indian groups believed that their interests were best served by entering into treaty relationships with the Crown. And among those who favoured treaties, there were significant disagreements about the nature of the demands that should be made of the young Dominion government. Generally, crown negotiations dealt first with the leaders of those Indian factions most desirous of securing payments for their land. The strategy was gradually to isolate the most conservative groups, who eventually would accept the terms of treaties once the outcome they held out for the Indians was made to appear as inevitable. These tactics were especially prominent in the negotiations by which Alexander MORRIS obtained for the Crown the territory covered by Treaty No 3. However, in attempting to follow a similar course in 1876, when the N Saskatchewan R became the major site of the Dominion's treaty-making initiatives, Morris met with particularly uncompromising resistance. Those Cree families following BIG BEAR, Little Pine and Lucky Man steadfastly refused to accept the treaty offers extended to them. They could not bring themselves to settle for a future confined to the narrow boundaries of Indian reserves, at least as long as there were still buffalo left to hunt. In later years, however, the pressure of starvation eventually forced most of them into various treaty adhesions. Perhaps the most determined holdout was Big Bear; however, in 1882 even he accepted treaty payments in order that his few remaining followers could survive the winter.

By and large the Indian leaders who most readily accepted the treaties were Christians. Their missionaries were often important go-betweens in encouraging a degree of trust between crown representatives and native groups. Also prominent among those advancing the treaty process were a number of MÉTIS, who were perhaps best placed to act as intermediaries between Indians and newcomers at this crucial time of transition for both societies. The Canadian government attempted to acknowledge the special relationship of the Métis to the treaty proceedings, by paying half-breeds for their aboriginal inheritance in the form of dollar-valued land certificates known as scrip. Unfortunately, however, efforts to implement this program were often undermined by the largely fraudulent activities of "jobbers," who succeeded in amassing to themselves the major portions of the resources originally earmarked for the Métis communities.

The newly formed NORTH-WEST MOUNTED POLICE also became an important factor in the negotiation process. Following their arrival in 1874 in the area of present-day SW Alberta, the NWMP became especially influential among many of the region's Blackfoot, Piegan, Blood, Sarcee and Stoney inhabitants. The police force had earned esteem with the demonstrated capacity to protect Indians from the outrageous exploitative practices of the American whisky traders who had become so domineering in that part of the country. It was in the newly created atmosphere of relative law and order that CROWFOOT, Red Crow and many other Indian leaders felt assured enough of the Crown's benevolence to sign Treaty No 7.

The 1885 NORTH-WEST REBELLION demonstrated for the Dominion government the importance of making some effort to fulfil the Crown's treaty obligations. A large-scale Indian rebellion had been shown to be a real possibility, unless positive moves were made to keep native people at least minimally appeased. After 1877, however, the process of making new treaties was to be put aside until the Klondike Gold Rush in the 1890s.

With the opening of a new resource frontier in the North, there was pressure once again to extinguish aboriginal title. The level of native sanction for the terms of Treaty No 8 was limited at best. Moreover, the 1899 agreement made provision for the allocation of Indian reserves, many of which were never established. These basic features of the treaty were essentially duplicated by the transaction formalized in 1921, following the discovery of oil in the Mackenzie Valley. Some Indian signatures were obtained on Treaty No 11, a document whose provisions were never implemented in any meaningful way. Hence, the DENE residents of the Mackenzie Valley would in later years pursue LAND CLAIM settlements with the federal government based on the premise that for them, Treaty Nos 8 and 11 are of no legal force.

The remaining numbered treaties, 9 and 10, cover territories in N Ontario and N Saskatchewan, respectively. The negotiation of the former in 1905 saw the participation of Ontario government officials along with federal authorities. The implication was that the costs of purchasing aboriginal title were to be shared between the 2 levels of government. This is the only example of provincial participation in any of the numbered treaties. When Treaty No 10 was made the following year, Saskatchewan officials were not included for, unlike Ontario, this newly created provincial jurisdiction then lacked any direct constitutional powers over natural resources.

This major round of treaty making which had begun so boldly in the 1870s came to a whimpering close in 1923. Investigation of various archives had revealed an absence of papers formalizing native land cessions for parcels of territory in central and southern Ontario. As a result, government officials quietly went about gathering Indian signatures on a treaty document intended to patch over a series of historical oversights which together placed in question legal title to some of the most valuable real estate in Canada.

Modern Treaties It was in Ontario and the Prairie provinces, then, where the development of a system of land tenure was most firmly founded on the negotiation of Indian treaties. Elsewhere in the country, ie, in most of BC, the Yukon, the NWT, Québec and the Maritimes, larger scale non-native settlement proceeded without prior purchase by the Crown of aboriginal title. Even so, reserves were allocated for Indians living on provincial unceded territories. These reserves became the home of registered Indians who, while lacking treaties, nevertheless fell under the direct administrative control of the Department of Indian Affairs in Ottawa. This ministry has tended to feel itself more governed by the details of the federal INDIAN ACT than by the provisions of specific Indian treaties. Hence, the fine legal distinctions between treaty Indians and registered Indians not covered by treaties have tended to become blurred under the standardizing regime of the Indian Act. Similarly, throughout most of the 20th century there has been little inclination on the part of the majority population to grapple politically with the legal fact that aboriginal title has never been ceded over large parts of the country.

Indians from BC were largely responsible for breaking through the weight of political inertia that had set in around aboriginal land questions since the early 1920s. Although some treaties had been made in the 1850s on Vancouver I, BC officials since then have consistently resisted the view that native people throughout the unceded portion of the province have inherent aboriginal rights. The NISHGA people of the Nass R valley have long been particularly forceful in opposing this position. Their activism eventually resulted in the Supreme Court of Canada passing down in 1973 a split decision which suggested that aboriginal title may indeed be a legally identifiable layer of interest still at the basis of the land tenure system throughout most of BC.

The Supreme Court's finding on the Nishga case was one of several key developments which helped cast the whole subject of aboriginal rights into the spotlight of public attention in Canada during the 1970s. The pivotal event had been the publication in 1969 of a federal White Paper on Indian policy, which reflected the political ideology of the PM Pierre Trudeau. He advocated the eventual removal of special status for Indians by, among other initiatives, drawing Indian treaties to a close. To Trudeau, whose political career had largely been built in opposing special constitutional status for the province of Québec, it was an "anomaly" to have treaties between groups within Canadian society. Native people strongly opposed the White Paper and became far more organized and vocal as a result. Their bargaining hand was considerably strengthened in 1973 by the Supreme Court's Nishga decision.

The result of these developments was a change in federal policy. An Office of Native Claims was established as a forum to resolve land disputes between aboriginal groups and government authorities. The ONC defines 2 types of claims, specific and comprehensive; it is the latter type that essentially amounts to modern-day treaty negotiations. A comprehensive claim can be made for any part of Canada where aboriginal title has never been ceded.

The 1975 JAMES BAY AGREEMENT could be described as a modern-day treaty. As in earlier times a move to open up a new resource frontier – in this case to develop the hydroelectric potential of the rivers flowing into the eastern half of James Bay – led to the negotiations with native people. Although the enormous hydroelectric project was initiated in the early 1970s without their sanction, the area's Cree and Inuit forced their assertion of unceded aboriginal rights on provincial and federal officials through an aggressive use of both the courts and the media. In the complex negotiated settlement that resulted, a variety of new features were added to those more similar to older Indian treaties. Most significantly, the agreement established a basis for various institutions of Cree and Inuit self-government, such as school boards and health and social service agencies. In 1978 the Northeastern Québec Agreement was concluded with the Naskapi band of Shefferville. It is basically an adjunct of the James Bay Agreement.

The only other comprehensive claim successfully negotiated since the process was initiated is the 1984 agreement between the federal government and the 2500 Inuvialuit people of the NWT's oil- and gas-rich Beaufort Sea area. Although an agreement-in-principle was reached in 1978, the precise details of the final bargain were not worked out until 1983. The settlement reserves to the Inuvialuit 95 000 of the 430 000 km^2 that they traditionally used. Moreover, it is made explicit that the Inuvialuit are to receive royalties on any oil or gas extraction that takes place on their land. In order to hasten this development, a provision was added that any such royalties would remain tax-free until the year 2008. Moreover, the agreement foresaw the participation of the Inuvialuit in a limited form of local self-government through the creation of the Western Arctic Regional Municipality.

As promising as the new comprehensive claims process may have appeared in 1973, this administrative adaptation by and large has not produced the significant breakthroughs that were initially envisaged. By 1985, for instance, over $100 million had been spent on the negotiations by the federal government and aboriginal groups, with only 3 agreements to show for the expenditure. One of the dramatic outpourings of frustration for the inadequacies of the process was the confrontation between Haida and loggers that erupted in 1985 on Lyell I, in BC's Queen Charlotte Archipelago. That same year the federal Task Force to Review Comprehensive Claims Policy submitted a report to the newly elected government of PM Brian Mulroney. In a document entitled *Living Treaties: Lasting Agreements*, this body, chaired by Murray Coolican, recommended a major modification in the federal approach to the whole matter. It argued that a key factor in the virtual breakdown of the comprehensive claims process was the government's insistence that aboriginal groups must agree to the complete extinguishment of their title in ancestral lands as a precondition for successful completion of a negotiation. To expect native people to accept a termination of their inherent aboriginal rights as the basis of their gaining new delegated rights, maintained the Task Force, was simply unrealistic, unjust and inconsistent with the finer spirit of s35 of the Constitution Act, 1982.

Treaty Rights and Constitutional Patriation Aboriginal and treaty rights have been one of the most controversial and difficult issues faced both in the lead up and the aftermath to the patriation of the Canadian Constitution with a CHARTER OF RIGHTS AND FREEDOMS. In 1980, when the federal government was prepared to push unilaterally for patriation without the sanction of the provinces, native groups were briefly courted by a commitment that the new Charter would include a positive affirmation of aboriginal and treaty rights. When a decision of the Supreme Court forced the Trudeau government to seek support for a patriation scheme from a reasonable number of provinces, the federal position soon changed. On 5 Nov 1981, 9 provincial governments (excluding Québec's) entered into the federal government's patriation plan on the condition that the draft constitution's assertion of aboriginal and treaty rights be stripped from the document. However, this modification soon resulted in a compromise. Section 35 of the Constitution Act recognizes and affirms *existing* aboriginal and treaty rights. Premier Lougheed of Alberta was instrumental in inserting the word "existing," in the expectation that it would eventually lead to a more limited judicial interpretation of s35.

An important part of the political manoeuvering leading up to patriation was the development in London, Eng, of a native lobby made up largely of treaty Indians. The objective was to assert the historical fact that aboriginal and treaty rights have long been recognized and, to an extent, guaranteed by the imperial Crown. Therefore Canada, the Indians argued, lacked the authority to sever the old relationship between native people and the imperial Crown without aboriginal consent. Their challenge to the legality of patriation ultimately led to the judgement made by Chief Justice Lord Denning in Jan 1982, in which he confirmed that treaty relationships entered by native people in Canada before 1923 had indeed been with the Crown in respect of the UK. Through constitutional evolution, however, this Crown had gradually split apart so that the treaty rights of aboriginal peoples had come to be vested exclusively with the Crown in the right of Canada. "No parliament," proclaimed Lord Denning, "should do anything to lessen the worth of these guarantees."

In 1983 a FIRST MINISTERS CONFERENCE took place to give greater definition to s35 through a process of constitutional amendment. Representatives of 4 national aboriginal organizations were invited to take part as consultants. The result of the proceedings was an accord to entrench constitutionally the principle that "treaty rights" as described in s35 include rights that then existed or would be acquired through land claims agreements. Furthermore, the principle was adopted that aboriginal and treaty rights are "guaranteed equally" to male and female aboriginal persons.

No other accords have been forthcoming. By 1987, however, the first ministers conferences had been instrumental in drawing the issue of aboriginal self-government into the forum of focused political debate in Canada. In the final FMC (1987), the federal government attempted to advance a constitutional amendment that would have recognized self-government as an aboriginal treaty right. The details of the proposed amendment, however, required that the actual jurisdictional powers of the new aboriginal governments would have to be derived from the sanctioning vote of provincial and federal parliaments. This plan – one that would have made aboriginal self-government a "contingent right" – did not receive the support of a sufficient number of first ministers to become a constitutional amendment. The proposal was also rejected by all 4 aboriginal groups who held to their conviction that aboriginal self-government is an "inherent right," and must be constitutionally recognized as such. In the MEECH LAKE ACCORD of 1987 the first ministers, while expanding provincial jurisdiction and recognizing Québec as a "distinct society," again failed to recognize this right.

Summary Indian treaties, then, constitute a thread of continuity woven throughout the fabric of our history from the earliest beginnings of the Canadian state until today. And if the words often spoken at the time of their negotiation are true, they are to last "as long as the sun shines and the water flows." In their archetypal form treaty documents present powerful images of some of the key traditions which together have combined to form the adventure which is Canada. The ornate handwritten script which covers much of the older treaty documents expresses well the legalistic twists of that imperialistic frame of mind that once carried forth an expanding British Empire to the far corners of the Earth. At the bottom of the documents Indian leaders often marked their approval by drawing a picture of the animal dodem of their clan. In these carefully etched designs are important representations of other attitudes towards law, government, nature and society which have also been incorporated, however imperfectly, within the institutional structures of Canada. It is in the juxtaposition of these 2 very different modes of recording a shared agreement, that we find essential meaning of the treaties.

The initiative to patriate the Canadian constitution has been an important factor in stimulating a vigorous contemporary debate over the precise legal status of Indian treaties. They have been viewed as everything from domestic contracts to international treaties between sovereign powers. An important aspect of this debate has been a sincere effort on the part of some to rediscover the underlying spirit originally at the basis of treaty agreements. What did the various parties who sanctioned Indian treaties understand they were doing in formulating the bargains? How were the terms of the treaties interpreted for Indian people in their own languages? What is the essential informing element of these founding covenants between peoples? And how might the original exchanged promises be honourably renewed in light of the changing experience of Canada?

In spite of the apparent inadequacies in the negotiation, maintenance and renewal of Indian treaties, the process itself demonstrates that Canada has grown and developed according to constitutional principles wherein recognition of aboriginal rights is essential. These founding agreements between peoples constitute fundamental, if often neglected and misunderstood, features in the unfolding drama of Canadian federalism. As Canada becomes home to an increasingly diverse population whose deepest ethnic roots lie in all quarters of the globe, the task of interpreting the significance of Indian treaties for new generations of Canadians becomes evermore challenging. ANTHONY J. HALL

Reading: M. Boldt and J. Anthony Long, eds, *The Quest for Justice: Aboriginal Peoples and Aboriginal Rights* (1985); G. Brown and R. Maguire, *Indian Treaties in Historical Perspective* (1979); Canada, *Indian Treaties and Surrender* (3 vols, 1891-1912, repr 1971); M. Coolican et al, *Living Treaties: Lasting Agreements, Report of the Task Force to Review Comprehensive Claim Policy* (1985); P.A. Cumming and N.H. Mickenberg, eds, *Native Rights in Canada* (2nd ed, 1972); W.E. Daugherty, *Maritime Indian Treaties in Historical Perspective* (1981); R. Fumoleau, *As Long as This Land Shall Last: A History of Treaty 8 and Treaty 11, 1870-1939* (1973); A. Morris, *The Treaties of Canada with the Indians of Manitoba and the North-West Territories* (1880, repr 1971); R. Price, ed, *The Spirit of the Alberta Indian Treaties* (1979).

Indonesians are one of the smallest (about 3500 people in 1986, and one of the more recently arrived ethnic groups in Canada (1443 between 1978 and 1985). They have almost all emigrated since the 1960s when political instability in Indonesia threatened certain ethnic and political groups. About 90% of the Indonesians in Canada are of CHINESE origin, but because of language differences they have tended not to be strongly associated with the Chinese community. Though most Indonesians have come to Canada directly from Indonesia, others born there have come to Canada via the Netherlands, Hong Kong, China and more recently, Vietnam. Most have settled in Ontario (47%), BC (31%) and Alta (14%), in Toronto and Vancouver. Most Indonesian immigrants are highly educated and have sought occupations in the scientific, managerial or clerical fields. Indonesians are best known to a majority of Canadians for their distinct style of cooking and their famous batik fabrics. DAVID S. MOYER

Industrial Design, as defined by the International Council of Societies of Industrial Design (ICSID), "is a creative activity the aim of which is to determine the formal qualities of objects produced by industry. These formal qualities include the external features, but are principally those structural and functional relationships which convert a system to a coherent unit both from the viewpoint of the producer and the user. Industrial design embraces all aspects of human environment that are conditioned by industrial production." Though allied to the disciplines of ARCHITECTURE and ENGINEERING, industrial design has a shorter history and did not come into being until the mid-19th century. Prior to this time, the production of everyday products was mainly the result of individual manual effort within a craft-based economy, but the Industrial Revolution made possible the mass production of these same products. Thereafter, artist/craftsmen were largely excluded from the industrial process. The need for a balance between art and industry was expressed by concerned groups and individuals, and led to industrial design as we know it today.

The major early developments in industrial design took place in continental Europe, especially in Great Britain and Germany. In Britain, William Morris founded a crafts-based school of design and "production" that was anti-industry, and Henry Cole advocated the introduction of art to industry; in 1837 the Normal School of Design (later named Royal College of Art) was founded; in 1849 the *Journal of Design* began publication; and in 1851 the Great Exhibition was held in London. A comparable development occurred in Germany. In 1907 industrialists, businessmen, artists and architects joined to form the Deutscher Werkbund; their manifesto protested the ugliness of the built environment and demanded the revival of artistic, moral and social ethics. This philosophical direction culminated in the establishment, in 1919, of the Bauhaus, the design school which has profoundly influenced the development of contemporary industrial design. In the US, the profession of industrial design began as a method of sales promotion, concerned with product styling and packaging. During the Depression this approach was used by designers such as Norman Bel Geddes, Henry Dreyfuss, Raymond Loewy and Walter Dorwin Teague.

Industrial design became firmly established in Canada only after 1945, as a direct result of the development of secondary industry during the war. C.D. HOWE, minister of reconstruction, was concerned that this industrial potential be preserved. He requested that a display of industrial discoveries by the NATIONAL RESEARCH COUNCIL be arranged. The exhibit, organized by Donald Buchanan to show that design and technical competence are not mutually exclusive, opened in June 1946 at the annual convention of the Canadian Manufacturers' Association, then travelled across Canada. Buchanan pushed for further exposure to industrial design both through the NATIONAL GALLERY and in several small publications. In June 1947 he received a government grant to investigate the role of industrial design in Canada and later that year he proposed a list of recommendations, one of which led to the Industrial Design Act of 1961 and the founding of the National Design Council. During the same postwar period, industrial designers began to organize as a profession. In 1946 the Affiliation of Canadian Industrial Designers was formed, which by 1947 had incorporated itself as the Assn of Canadian Industrial Designers.

Industrial design education was not formalized in Canada until the late 1940s, when the first course was offered at the ONTARIO COLLEGE OF ART. In Québec, l'Institut des arts appliqués, formerly l'École du meuble, began the first design program, followed after 1969 by degree programs at U de Montréal and U du Québec. The School of Industrial Design at Carleton and several Ontario community colleges offer industrial design programs, as do the universities of Alberta and Calgary.

Several Canadians are well known as industrial designers. Jacques Guillon, Julien Hébert and Frank Dudas were pioneers in the profession and worked in transportation (Montréal's Métro in the 1960s, Via Rail's LRC in the 1970s), and in exhibition (Expo 67, Expo 70) and furniture. More recently, Douglas Ball has become known internationally for his office furniture. Ian Bruce played a significant role in designing the Laser sailboat and in arranging for its manufacture in many countries. John Tyson, Morley Smith and André Morin have influenced several everyday products, including telephones, snowmobiles and housewares. Thomas Lamb, Keith Muller, Jan Kuypers, André Jarry and Michel Dallaire are known in Canada and abroad as leading furniture designers. A number of Canadian manufacturers have also contributed to a better utilization of design in industry, notably Bombardier, Sunar-Hauserman, Cooper, Bell Canada, NCR, Danesco, Kinetics and Ambiant. Within Canada, both industry and the general public are slowly developing a growing awareness of the value of industrial design. JACQUES GIARD

Industrial Quality Control uses scientific techniques to determine product and service capabilities, to enable an organization to provide economically a product or service suitable for its intended purpose. The objective of a good quality-control program is to enable all people and machines concerned to do their jobs right the first time and to provide assurance to the customer that this has been done. The detailed techniques vary from product to product and from service to service, but the principles remain the same, ie, knowing the requirements for the product, service or process, verifying that these can be met, maintained and improved, and taking corrective action where necessary.

In Canada, quality control started in the military, aviation and electronic fields. For many years, the only standards available were those issued by the Dept of National Defence. In line with the understanding of the early DND standards, many major companies prepared their own quality-control standards, insisting that their suppliers meet these standards. In the early 1970s the electric power UTILITIES recognized the problem caused to many sections of industry by this mass of similar standards. The utilities, regulatory bodies involved and major suppliers formed a Canadian Standards Association (CSA) Technical Committee to develop a common standard. The result was the initial series of CSA-Z 299 Quality Program Standards. The Standards Council of Canada assigned to CSA the responsibility for developing a series of quality assurance standards. Thus, the latest revisions of the CSA-Z 299 series and other related quality and relability standards are National Standards of Canada, under the cognizance of the CSA Steering Committee on Managing for Quality and Reliability.

Canadians have been equally active in the field of international quality standards, with NATO for military Standards, the International Standards Organization (ISO) and the International Electro-technical Commission (IEC) for non-military standards on quality and reliability, respectively. The chairmanship and secretariat for the ISO Technical Committee on Quality Assurance (ISO/TC 176) were awarded to Canada at the initial meeting.In 1946 the American Society for Quality Control (ASQC) was formed as the first industrial quality control technical society on this continent. This society now has over 40 000 members worldwide. Canadians have been active in the society virtually from its inception. The Canadian region, comprising sections or subsections in Hamilton, London, Kitchener, Montreal and Winnipeg, is represented on the board of directors by the regional director. Other members have held elected positions on the board and the executive of the society.

Educational courses in the discipline are available at a number of community colleges across Canada, plus a limited number of universities eg, U of Manitoba and Concordia U. C.A. MILLS

Industrial Relations are concerned with all aspects, individual and collective, of the relationship between employers and employees. The individual aspects include planning and staffing, the selection and placement of appropriate candidates, their integration into the organization, training and development, their performance appraisal and proper compensation, productivity and discipline. Where the employees have formed a union, the relationship with management comprises labour-organization problems, union-certification procedures, the COLLECTIVE BARGAINING process, strike and dispute resolution, grievance procedure and arbitration. The employment contract, some basic employment standards, health and safety questions, and all matters concerning antidiscrimination laws and charters of rights have both individual and collective implications (*see also* EMPLOYMENT LAW).

Law, because it regulates the employer-employee relationship, and economics, because the basic and fundamental problem of industrial relations is always the distribution of the outputs of production, are central to industrial relations. Sociology, psychology, political science, business administration, organizational behaviour, philosophy and computer science also contribute to a better understanding and functioning of individual and collective relationships. An important controversy exists over whether industrial relations is a discipline in itself – with its own theory and special methodology – or a subject matter to be studied with a variety of tools. The controversy, which will probably never be resolved, partly explains the variety of approaches in the study of industrial relations as well as the different structural arrangements found in institutions that teach it.

In some cases a teaching department, complete with its own staff and students, has been created as a distinct unit; in other places a centre for industrial relations functions as a forum where professors of law, economics, sociology and other disciplines gather to discuss topics of mutual interest concerning employer-employee relationships. Courses in industrial relations can all be gathered under one faculty or department, eg, a faculty of management or business administration, a department of economics or sociology, or they can be divided according to subject, eg, the study of wages in a department of economics, of trade-union movement and labour organizations in sociology, of collective bargaining and collective agreement in business administration. Some of these centres have developed courses and seminars for both management representatives and trade-union leaders and members. The activity can be the exclusive responsibility of the centre or part of the university extension or adult-education services.

Queen's University in Kingston, Ont, was the first Canadian university to offer structured teaching in industrial relations, through its Industrial Relations Section, est 1937. In 1944 U Laval opened its department of industrial relations, and U de Montréal inaugurated its own teaching department a few months later. To put these dates into perspective, the first industrial-relations section of a N American university was created at Princeton, N J, in 1922, and the famous New York State School of Industrial and Labor Relations at Cornell University, from which many Canadian specialists graduated, opened in 1945. At McGill U the Industrial Relations Centre was established (1948) in the department of economics and political science and transferred to the Faculty of Management in the early 1960s. The Institute of Industrial Relations at UBC was established in 1960 but closed in the 1970s. The Centre for Industrial Relations at U of T was founded in 1965.

At the undergraduate level, Laval and Montréal have teaching and degree-granting departments as well as programs leading to master's and doctoral degrees. Queen's had a teaching department until 1961, and now has an Industrial Relations Centre. In the late 1970s, U of T opened a graduate course leading to a master's degree in industrial relations (MIR) and in the early 1980s a course leading to a PhD.

The 2 universities with teaching departments have always offered courses in human-resources management and collective relationships. There are about 50 undergraduate courses, 15 of them obligatory, distributed among 5 or 6 fields of study: theory and methodology, business and personnel administration, trade unionism and collective bargaining, labour legislation, labour and manpower economics. Graduate courses are offered in the same fields. In other universities, industrial-relations courses, eg, industrial relations, labour relations, collective bargaining, labour law and arbitration procedures, usually concentrate on institutional aspects of collective-relationship problems. Subjects likely to be taught in the corresponding departments include labour economics and labour market analysis, industrial sociology, industrial psychology and labour history. Personnel administration and human resources are dealt with primarily in the administration curricula, eg, personnel administration, organizational behaviour, human-resources management, human relations.

In 1987, in 60 Canadian universities almost 1000 courses were taught in industrial relations and human-resources management. The majority of them are undergraduate courses and are offered by faculties and departments of management and administration. They are attended by over 50 000 students. At the college level, courses on the same subjects are given especially to commerce and administration students, who are likely to be given less theory and more application to prepare them as technicians rather than professionals.

Demonstrations following the closure of the 2 wood-processing plants at Lac-des-Îles, Mont-Laurier, Qué, Feb-Mar 1971 (*courtesy National Archives of Canada/ Montreal Star/PA-137179/Daggett*).

Industrial-relations graduates work mainly in personnel and human-resources departments of large and medium-size companies, in trade unions and labour organizations as researchers, organizers and consultants, and in governments and industrial-relations agencies, eg, labour-relations boards and arbitration services. A few operate their own consulting firms. All these graduates compete directly with other professionals working in the same field – lawyers, administrators, industrial psychologists and on-the-job company trainees. In Québec there is a corporation of industrial-relations specialists.

Laval and Queen's are responsible for most academic publications in industrial relations. The Laval journal *Relations industrielles/Industrial Relations*, published since 1945 and bilingual since 1964, has been recognized internationally. Queen's publishes a variety of studies; the best known is its annual *Current Industrial Relations Scene in Canada*. In 1978 Montréal started an important series of monographs on legal aspects of industrial-relations problems. Several universities publish the proceedings of their annual conferences, as does the Canadian Industrial Relations Association, a nonprofit, voluntary organization founded in 1963 that promotes industrial-relations research in Canada. The Laval journal is also the association's official publication. The longest-lived serial publication, *The Labour Gazette*, put out by the federal Department of Labour since 1900, fell victim to government economic constraints in 1980. GÉRARD HÉBERT

Industrial Research and Development Technological innovation is essential for economic growth and for the improvement of the quality of life, and industrial research and development (R & D) is at the heart of the innovative process. While R & D is carried out in sectors other than industry, mainly government and the universities, industrial R & D is the sector most clearly linked to technological innovation and hence to economic growth.

In 1985 industrial R & D expenditures in Canada amounted to $3 billion, about 53% of the total domestic expenditures on R & D. Canada's spending on industrial R & D, at about 0.8% of the domestic product of industry, is similar to that of the middle rank of OECD countries but less than half of that of leaders such as W Germany, US and Japan. From 1965 to 1985 expenditures on industrial R & D in Canada have increased tenfold (about threefold in constant dollars) but Canada's position relative to other OECD countries did not improve during the period. The history of industrial research and development (R & D) and innovation in Canada is unique and certainly has not yet been fully explained or understood. Prior to WWII, Canadian industry depended largely on imported TECHNOLOGY. The few indigenous innovations were the work of individual inventors rather than the result of systematic, planned research and development. During WWII, the MANUFACTURING industry grew spectacularly and the R & D to support it grew almost as rapidly. Canada emerged from the war with the world's fourth-largest manufacturing output, exceeded only by the US, UK and USSR. No one expected Canada to maintain this position when countries such as Japan, Germany, France and Italy recovered from the war, but Canada's steady descent to 13th place in 1981 was not forecast.

In the primary industries, Canadian R & D has been significant but not spectacular. There have been some important innovations in most such industries, including mining, agriculture and pulp and paper. In other areas Canada has been a competent user of technology, making many minor innovations but has not been a world leader in development.

After the war, Canada had a substantial lead over most other countries in many HIGH-TECHNOLOGY fields. The Defence Research Board (DRB) and the Armed Forces, supported in some areas by the NATIONAL RESEARCH COUNCIL and other government agencies, made a valiant but usually unsuccessful effort to maintain this lead. The history of industrial R & D and innovation in Canada from 1945 to the present can be told vividly by tracing the history of some of these defence-initiated activities (*see* DEFENCE RESEARCH). The outstanding technological success of the postwar period has been nuclear power and the evolution of the CANDU reactor. Canada became involved in building a heavy-water reactor for producing plutonium as part of the US-British-Canadian atomic bomb effort. Credit for getting the projects started so quickly and so successfully must go mainly to C.J. MACKENZIE, then acting president of the NRC who had the support of C.D. HOWE, then minister of munitions and supply. Credit for the success of the design of the early reactors NRX and NRU goes to the team led by Sir John Cockcroft from Cambridge, England. British and French involvement made a significant contribution in the early stages but, over the years, the CANDU venture has become almost completely Canadian. Final success was due to the impetus provided by John ROBARTS, then premier of Ontario, who decided that ONTARIO HYDRO would order the first commercial CANDUs. The result was a series of nuclear reactors, designed and built in Canada, that remain among the most successful power-producing reactors in the world.

Private enterprise with, in some cases, effective support from government has made significant advances. At the end of the war, Canada had developed a substantial electronic research capability partly in government and partly in industry. The Defence Research Board set out to maintain and expand this capability by supporting industry financially and through work in its laboratory, the Telecommunications Research Establishment, Shirley Bay, Ont. The NRC Division of Radio and Electrical Engineering was also involved in the venture. This initiative contributed to the establishment of the Bell-Northern Research Laboratory, also at Shirley Bay, and to the worldwide success of Northern Telecom Ltd, Mitel Corp and many other Canadian electronics ventures (*see* ELECTRONICS INDUSTRY). Work at Bell-Northern Research led to advances in digital and electronics switching technology that have made Northern Telecom one of the world's major manufacturers of telephone switching equipment. In 1976 the Telecommunications Research Establishment was taken over by the Dept of Communications, which has continued the policy of supporting industry in areas such as SATELLITE COMMUNICATIONS and TELIDON.

Development in the AEROSPACE INDUSTRY has been much more complex. Col W.W. Goforth, creator of the DRB, talked about the advent of satellites as early as 1945. From the beginning, DRB programs included work on rockets and electronics for guided missiles. The DRB laboratory at Shirley Bay designed and built the first Canadian satellites, the Alouette and Isis series. RCA Victor in Montréal, involved as a subcontractor, was chosen by the government in 1962 as prime contractor for research and planning for the first Canadian COMMUNICATIONS satellite. Telesat Canada was then formed and gave the contract for construction to Hughes Aircraft in California. RCA Victor was anxious to follow its successful R & D by production of both satellites and Earth stations; instead it was given another research contract to work on the next generation of communications satellites. In Jan 1977 RCA sold its R & D facilities outside Montréal to Spar Aerospace Ltd, Toronto, and abandoned satellite research in Canada. The DRB laboratory, by then transferred to the Dept of Communications, continued to work on future satellites with Spar.

In 1954 the Canadian Armed Forces expressed interest in possible future uses of technology using infrared radiation for various purposes. DRB gave DE HAVILLAND CANADA a contract for R & D work under which a specialist team was brought over from England to transfer this technology to Canada. Work began in the special projects and applied research division of de Havilland, which was later purchased by L.G.A. Clarke and became Spar Aerospace Ltd. After many years of successful participation in the US space program, Spar broke into the headlines in 1981 with the CANADARM, the remote-manipulator system built for the US Space Shuttle. Spar has also worked with Hughes Aircraft on the Anik series of communications satellites and was completely responsible for Anik D, launched in 1982. The company built 2 similar satellites for Brazil. In 1984 Spar negotiated a multimillion-dollar contract for the development of infrared detection equipment for the US Navy.

Canadian universities showed an early interest in COMPUTER SCIENCE. In 1951 the NRC and DRB supplied the U of T with one of the world's big computers, the FERUT, made by the Ferranti Co in England. Shortly thereafter, Ferranti established a research lab in Toronto and DRB gave it a major contract. Many of the present leaders of computer technology in Canada were trained in this laboratory. Its first major project was Datar, an information management system for the Canadian navy that pioneered new concepts and technology in information management. It was so far ahead of its time that no other navy adopted it, though it served as a model for later systems.

Under the impetus of defence production, Canada emerged from WWII with a relatively large, successful and innovative aircraft industry. At the end of the war the industry was largely government owned but, because of C.D. Howe's commitment to private enterprise, it was soon sold to British and US companies. In Toronto, the A.V. Roe Co designed, developed and produced the AVRO CF-100 fighter and the Orenda engine, both thoroughly competent and successful ventures by world standards. At the same time, as a private venture, A.V. Roe designed and built the AVRO JETLINER which first flew in 1949, only a few days after the de Havilland Comet flew in England. However, Howe ordered work stopped on the transport. By 1959 the AVRO ARROW, a new supersonic fighter, had made several spectacularly successful test flights and its Iroquois engine was

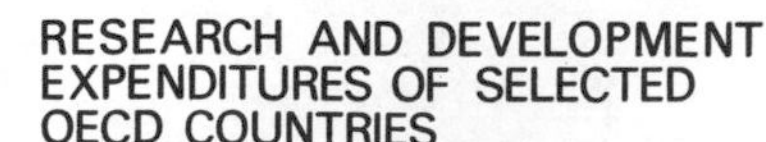

RESEARCH AND DEVELOPMENT
EXPENDITURES OF SELECTED
OECD COUNTRIES

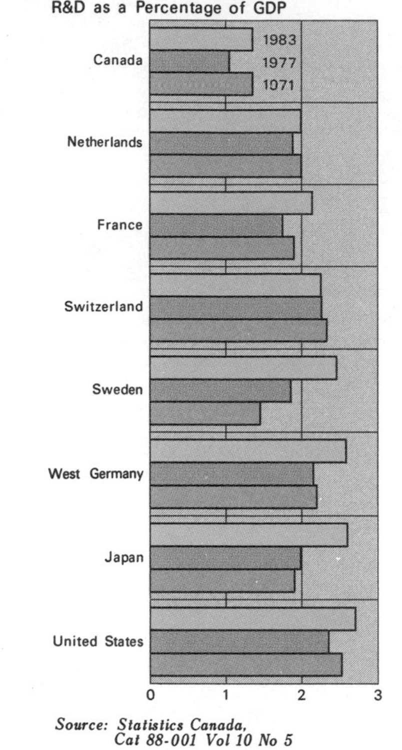

Source: Statistics Canada, Cat 88-001 Vol 10 No 5

doing very well on the test bed. However, costs had greatly outrun estimates and the US Air Force refused to place an order for the aircraft. PM John DIEFENBAKER ordered the project stopped and all prototypes and parts not just scrapped but physically destroyed. Economic and industrial historians will probably identify the cancellation of the Arrow as the turning point in Canada's history as a manufacturing nation. Subcontracts from the Arrow and other aircraft production supported a large and growing number of small companies capable of high-quality innovation and production. Although they were supported by the Arrow contract, their services stimulated progress in many related industries.

These few examples of the history of industrial R & D and innovation in Canada explain in part why Canadian high-technology industry has not prospered. Successive governments have failed to give continuing support to innovation and have, in many cases, not only failed to support success but have discouraged ventures that seem to be on the verge of breaking into new markets. Yet government cannot do it all. Certainly, a stable and encouraging political environment is a necessary but not a sufficient condition for success. With just a few outstanding exceptions, Canadian financial institutions have been timid and conservative and Canadian entrepreneurs and managers have been well behind their counterparts in other countries in the art and practice of technological innovation and entrepreneurship.

The ever-increasing rate of industrial innovation, the sharply increasing international competition and the speed with which all markets are becoming global in action and outlook are all changing the competitive position of companies and countries. These factors are also changing government attitudes towads industrial R & D. National governments have always given support to science and technology, but increasingly they perceive technological leadership in industry as a national issue and responsibility, since it greatly affects the strength and growth of the national economy. As a result many are providing very substantial funding for national R & D programs designed to reinforce or increase the international competitiveness of their industry and their economy. By the end of 1987, the federal and some of the provincial governments, particularly Ontario, were adopting this view and moving in the direction of strong support for industrial R & D.

Despite the uncertainties of governmental and managerial support, the genius of Canadians continues to break through. The aircraft industry has continued to be moderately innovative with the DE HAVILLAND OTTER, which dominates northern flying, the Dash 7 and Dash 8, the CANADAIR CHALLENGER, the Pratt and Whitney (United Aircraft) PT6 gas turbine (which powers the Twin Otter) and other successful aircraft. Through companies such as Northern Telecom, Mitel and others, the Canadian communications and electronics industry is now a front runner in fibre optics, digital data management, microprocessors, computer software, Telidon technology, etc. Canada has repeatedly demonstrated that it has the human, educational and research resources to do first-class industrial R & D. Success, measured in industrial jobs and exports, depends on a climate favourable to R & D at all levels - industry, government and universities - and a bold and aggressive attitude in industry towards technological innovation and entrepreneurship. If these can be created and maintained, Canada will be reindustrialized in the next generation. *See also* INVENTORS AND INNOVATIONS; SCIENTIFIC RESEARCH AND DEVELOPMENT.

OMOND SOLANDT AND W.R. STADELMAN

Industrial Strategy is a term that generally refers to any attempt by government to apply a coherent and consistent set of policies that are designed to improve the performance of the ECONOMY. These policies are frequently directed at the manufacturing sector, but an industrial strategy could also center on the performance of a number of other sectors in the economy, ranging from resource production to services. Industrial strategies are oriented towards correcting imbalances in the economy's performance, and involve the assumption by government of a prominent role in facilitating or effecting economic change. Sometimes the means deployed are very direct (what is now called "interventionist"), but attempts to restructure an economy can be undertaken using a laissez-faire, free-market approach.

While the debate about industrial strategy is fairly recent, the concept of using the powers of government to shape the economy is not new. In the late 19th century, there were major efforts in Canada to build an integrated national economy through tariff protection, the construction of the transcontinental railways and the encouragement of immigration to settle the West. Each of the initiatives complemented the others to yield a national framework for development which became known as the NATIONAL POLICY. The intention was to encourage manufacturing in central Canada through the use of tariffs. Markets for the manufactured goods would be expanded by creating a wheat-based agricultural economy in western Canada through settlement policies (*see* IMMIGRATION POLICY). The western wheat economy would, in turn, provide the agricultural exports needed to support the new western population and to pay for eastern manufactured goods. All this economic activity would be tied together by a transcontinental railway. Like many economic strategies, the National Policy was driven by an external imperative: the rapid growth of the US economy after the Civil War, which was expected to create pressures for the annexation of the Canadian West and for north-south economic integration (*see* CANADIAN-AMERICAN RELATIONS). The politicians of the time feared that if political means were not used to promote the emergence of a national transcontinental economy, Canada's future as an independent country would be seriously compromised.

The current interest in industrial policy has also been prompted by external factors, most notably the rapidly changing environment of INTERNATIONAL TRADE. By the end of WWII, Canada had emerged as a middle-level power both militarily and economically. In the postwar era, Canada's economic strengths lay in resource exports (principally to the US) and in the expansion of manufacturing (primarily through foreign-owned subsidiaries oriented towards domestic, as opposed to export, markets). However, by the early 1960s the manufacturing sector was under pressure. Europe had fully recovered from war and was expanding its industrial base. Moreover, the US dominated the international trading system. Thus, while international demand for traditional resource products such as pulp and paper and minerals was still strong among Canada's industrialized trading partners, international trade in manufactured goods became more competitive and the manufacturing sector began to experience increasing difficulties. This resulted in a national debate about the future prospects of the Canadian ECONOMY, including the issue of whether Canada would revert to its former status as a resource producer or whether it would succeed in expanding its manufacturing base.

Even in the early 1960s, there was a fairly developed national consensus about the nature of the problem. Manufacturing firms in Canada were internationally uncompetitive because they tended to be oriented towards the domestic market, because they were not sufficiently concerned with export activity, and because they were poorly managed, did little in the way of innovation or research and development (R & D), and often operated at a level of production too low to allow economies of scale (ie, lowering of the average costs of production). Debate revolved around the origins of this problem and the possibility of solutions. The majority of economists (but by no means all) argued that the root of the difficulties facing the manufacturing sector lay in tariff protection (a remnant of the National Policy) and advocated a steady reduction in the level of tariff protection enjoyed by Canadian firms and a fuller integration of the Canadian economy into the international economic system, eg, through active government support for international agreements and institutions that promoted the liberalization of world trade, such as the GENERAL AGREEMENT ON TARIFFS AND TRADE (GATT). An increase in competition, generated by an increase in imported products, and wider export opportunities for domestic producers were expected to improve the health of Canadian industry.

Another school of thought stressed the structural problems of the manufacturing sector, such as the relatively small size of most firms, excessive concentration on domestic as opposed to export markets, and a failure to give sufficient emphasis to industrial design and innovation. From this perspective, one of the major causes of the problems in the manufacturing sector was the high level of foreign ownership. Foreign ownership, it was argued, had encouraged firms to increase the purchase of parts and services from their parent firms, to rely on innovations from abroad, and to concentrate on the domestic market so as to minimize export competition with the parent firm or its other foreign subsidiaries. Economists of this school stressed the need to reduce the level of foreign ownership in the economy and to improve the competitive capability and export orientation of Canadian-owned companies through various forms of government assistance, ranging from support for R & D to the promotion of leading sectors of industrial growth. These economists rejected the use of tariff reductions or FREE TRADE as a means of restructuring the Canadian economy, arguing that a weak Canadian economy would be adversely affected by trade liberalization. Instead, they advocated a degree of restructuring before tariff barriers were lowered to ensure that Canadian industry would be strong enough to take advantage of new international markets and would be able to compete with increased imports. Restructuring in this context meant the development of an industrial strategy focused on Canada's key economic sectors.

Over the years, the federal government's approach to the question of industrial policy has embodied major elements of the trade liberalization approach. During the last 30 years tariffs have been gradually reduced, and Canada has been a strong supporter of the GATT system and of other attempts to liberalize international trade. In the mid-1960s a modified form of sectoral free trade in automobiles manufactured in Canada and the US was introduced, allowing the major N American car manufacturers to import and export cars free of duty, provided that certain minimum production levels were maintained in both countries (*see* CANADA-US AUTOMOTIVE PRODUCTS AGREEMENT). Most recently, the Conservative administration of PM Brian MULRONEY has launched an intensive set of negotiations with the US, with the aim of establishing a bilateral free-trade agreement. This initiative, based on a desire to ensure access for Canadian industry to an increasingly protectionist US market, is seen by some of its advocates as providing, through increased trade and competition, a powerful instrument for restructuring the Canadian economy and making it more efficient. However, federal (and provincial) industrial policy has involved more than trade promotion and tariff reductions.

During the 1960s the federal government took a number of steps designed to improve the structural characteristics of Canadian industry. In 1963 the Department of Industry was created and was charged with assisting Canadian manufacturing firms to improve their competitive capability. This department was then fused with the Department of Trade and Commerce to form the Department of Industry, Trade and Commerce (ITC) in 1969. The 2 departments developed a number of industrial assistance programs designed to encourage investment, to improve firms' marketing capacities both at home and abroad, and to increase corporate spending on R & D. The 1960s also witnessed the emergence of a number of specialized federal departments, some of which were designed to improve the government's management of the economy (eg, the Departments of Employment and Immigration, Communications, and Regional Economic Expansion); others were special-purpose agencies designed to assist industry in meeting foreign competition (eg, the Export Development Corporation). While all of these initiatives were intended to facilitate industrial development and sometimes to encourage industry to restructure, there was little, if any, attempt to lend these initiatives coherence through the development of an industrial strategy.

During the 1960s and early 1970s, however, there was strong pressure to develop such a strategy. A number of studies commissioned by the federal government raised the problem of foreign ownership in the Canadian economy (*see* FOREIGN OWNERSHIP AND THE STRUCTURE OF CANADIAN INVESTMENT, TASK FORCE ON). These reports, and others, also suggested that a broader approach to the problems of the structure of the Canadian manufacturing sector was required. In addition, the growing importance in international trade of the newly industrializing countries of the Third World, the emergence of HIGH TECHNOLOGY (an area in which Canadian industry was weak) as a major factor in international trade, and increased uncertainty in the international trading system (caused by a worldwide increase in protectionism and the subsidization of exporting industries) seriously challenged Canadian firms in their efforts to expand export markets and to fight off import competition. These factors encouraged the federal government to deal with the problems of the manufacturing sector in a more comprehensive manner.

In 1974 an explicit attempt was made to control the flow of FOREIGN INVESTMENT into Canada through the activities of the FOREIGN INVESTMENT REVIEW AGENCY. Later a number of other measures were taken in an effort to address specific structural problems in individual industries. Grants for R & D and investment were offered to the AEROSPACE INDUSTRY, and the government took over the country's 2 leading airframe manufacturers to ensure the development of new aircraft projects. Restructuring initiatives or financial assistance programs were also undertaken in other sectors, ranging from clothing and footware to forest products.

Although these diverse initiatives were not part of an overall industrial strategy, several federal agencies, such as the Privy Council Office (PCO) and ITC, made attempts to design one in the 1970s; but no agency was able to design a strategy that met with general acceptance within the federal bureaucratic system. In fact, the ITC initiative, which had started as an ambitious effort to construct a strategy encompassing a large number of public policy objectives, gradually evolved into a more modest industrial consultation process that concentrated on sectoral competitiveness.

Despite these failures, the industrial strategy issue kept re-emerging. When the Liberal government of Pierre TRUDEAU was returned to power in 1980, there was another attempt to formulate an industrial strategy, inspired by the government's NATIONAL ENERGY PROGRAM. This attempt also failed, partly because of growing American objections to Canadian energy and foreign-ownership policies. In the end, the federal government did succeed in developing a strategy, which appeared in an economic development White Paper published with the 1981 federal budget (*Economic Development for Canada in the 1980s*). This paper assumed that resource developments both in eastern and western Canada would be the future engine of growth, and that these resource developments would both provide industrial benefits for central Canada and expand and diversify economic activity in the regions. Unfortunately, this strategy also came to grief with the collapse in energy prices in 1981-82.

In part as a reaction to these failures, by the mid-1980s many observers, including the Royal Commission on the ECONOMIC UNION AND DEVELOPMENT PROSPECTS FOR CANADA (the Macdonald Commission), were advocating a less interventionist approach to industrial strategy – an approach that would place a greater reliance on market forces to shape the competitive structure of the Canadian economy. In its approach to industrial policy, the Conservative federal government seems to be following this advice. While not abandoning the use of industrial assistance programs, the new government has tended to rely more heavily on market-oriented industrial policies, such as deregulation (especially in the transport sector), privatization of crown corporations (eg, CANADAIR and DE HAVILLAND) and the pursuit of a free-trade agreement with the US.

There are various explanations for Canada's continued lack of an industrial strategy, despite the immense effort and large sums of money that the federal government has expended on industrial policy. One viewpoint holds that much of the problem centres on the nature of the bureaucratic system in Ottawa, in which various CENTRAL AGENCIES compete with individual departments for influence over policy. Different federal departments have evolved very different concepts of an industrial strategy, and some departments do not even believe that a strategy is needed. Politicians also find it difficult to commit themselves to a specific course of action in the industrial sphere because, if the industrial goals of an economic development strategy are not attained, they can be held accountable for its failure. The chances of failure are high because industrial strategies are highly dependent upon ECONOMIC FORECASTING, which is a very imperfect art, as the federal government found to its detriment with oil prices.

The highly diversified nature of the Canadian economy is another reason why it has been difficult to implement an industrial strategy for secondary manufacturing in Canada. In Canada, manufacturing accounts for less than 20% of total economic activity, compared to between about 25% and 33% in many European countries and in Japan. In fact, manufacturing has played a far less significant role in Canada than in virtually any other industrialized country. Moreover the growth of manufacturing in Canada has been based as much on foreign-owned branch plants as on domestically owned firms. Even in the relatively homogeneous economies of Europe and Japan, a consensus on industrial issues has never been easily achieved, but the structure of traditional, industry-government relations in these countries and the bias towards manufacturing allows the development of a consensus on specific issues. In Canada, manufacturing interests are overshadowed by the resource sector and are fractured by disputes between large and small business and between domestic and foreign-owned firms.

In addition, and perhaps more importantly, there are marked differences of economic and industrial interest between the various regions within Canada (*see* REGIONAL ECONOMICS). For example, an industrial policy designed to assist the AUTOMOTIVE INDUSTRY will be seen by the western provinces, whose economies are based primarily on resource development and agriculture, as being favoured treatment for central Canada. Indeed the export markets of these provinces may be threatened if a policy for restructuring the automobile industry includes import restrictions on cars from a country, such as Japan, that is a major export market for western grain or coal.

The Canadian economy, with its highly industrialized centre and resource-producing periphery, frequently displays contradictions of this kind. Indeed, it was these very contradictions that in the end caused the breakup of the original National Policy. These contradictions explain, moreover, why provincial governments became much more active during the 1970s in implementing their own provincially based industrial policies. The provinces have fairly homogeneous economies, based on fewer and less diverse economic activities, and it is easier for them to develop coherent strategies that command a reasonable degree of local public support. The challenge at the federal level is to prevent the balkanization of the Canadian economy on regional lines, and at the same time to develop a national industrial strategy that is sensitive to regional aspirations.

MICHAEL JENKIN

Reading: R.D. French, *How Ottawa Decides* (1980); Michael Jenkin, *The Challenge of Diversity*, (1983); R.W. Phidd and B. Doern, *The Politics and Management of Canadian Economic Policy* (1978); *Report of the Royal Commission on the Economic Union and Development Prospects for Canada*, II (1985); Science Council of Canada, *Canadian Industrial Development: Some Policy Directions* (1984).

Industrial Unionism, the dominant form of labour organization. An industrial union is one which, for organizational purposes, includes all workers in a particular industry (eg, steel, automobile) regardless of whether they are skilled or unskilled. The union's bargaining power is based upon the number of its members. In contrast, CRAFT UNIONS (plumbers, electricians) limit their membership to workers with a specific trade or skill. Their power is based upon the scarcity of highly skilled labour. Craft unions, established first, dominated the labour scene until the 1930s but are now largely confined to the construction industry. The first significant attempt to organize on an industrial basis was undertaken in the 1880s by the KNIGHTS OF LABOR, which opposed craft unionism, advocated unity of the producing classes, and (more practically) opposed employer blacklists and discrimination. It was briefly successful in organizing not only unskilled male workers but also women and minorities. After the demise of the Knights in the 1890s, the idea of industrial unionism persisted as craft unions came to be regarded as anachronistic in an increasingly industrialized society. Organizations such as the Catholic union movement in Québec in the 1920s (*see* CONFEDERATION OF NATIONAL TRADE UNIONS) and the All-Canadian Congress of Labour (est 1927) sought to combine the principles of nationalism and industrial unionism. In the 1930s, the Workers Unity League, a communist-sponsored organization, became interested in organizing all workers in the emerging mass-production industries.

The difficult task of organizing the bulk of the industrial labour force was not accomplished until WWII under the Congress of Industrial Organizations (CIO). This movement originated 1935 in the US in opposition to entrenched craft unions, but it also attracted thousands of Canadian workers into what would become established industrial unions such as the United Automobile Workers (*see* OSHAWA STRIKE) and the United Steelworkers. It was successful because the political and economic climate was ripe for a pragmatic form of "business unionism" which combined organization on an industrial basis with a philosophy emphasizing collective bargaining and strike action to improve wages and working conditions. In Canada, the new industrial unions also formed a lasting alliance with the CCF/NDP. In the 1960s and 1970s new white-collar unions have emerged which follow the industrial-union model, but their composition and characteristics are somewhat different from those of their blue-collar predecessors.

LAUREL SEFTON MACDOWELL

Industrial Workers of the World (popularly known as "Wobblies"), a REVOLUTIONARY INDUSTRIAL UNION fd 1905 in Chicago. The IWW's rapid expansion in the Canadian West demonstrated the influence of American labour ideology on the region's labour movement. Wobblies were mostly unskilled, low-status migrant workers ("blanketstiffs") – miners, loggers, navvies and harvesters – who were recruited to the West primarily from southern and eastern Europe and were brutally exploited in the booming economy. The IWW doctrine which attracted them was a peculiar form of syndicalism (an international doctrine based upon the primacy of industrial unionism and the use of the general strike in the settlement of class struggles). Wobbly syndicalism was essentially pragmatic; it advocated the organization of all workers into one body and supported direct action as the only form of protest open to immigrant workers, who were excluded from the electoral process. IWW propaganda was disseminated primarily in street meetings. In 1912, when Vancouver authorities tried to ban street demonstrations, the Wobblies started and won a spectacular free-speech fight. Soon afterwards the IWW led 7000 workers out on strike against the CANADIAN NORTHERN RAILWAY in BC's Fraser Valley. The Wobblies lost, and massive state repression, combined with employer resistance and economic depression, began the process of the union's collapse. The Wobblies' days of glory ended before 1914, but their syndicalist ideology was adopted by the ONE BIG UNION.

A. ROSS MCCORMACK

Reading: A. Ross McCormack, *Reformers, Rebels, and Revolutionaries* (1977).

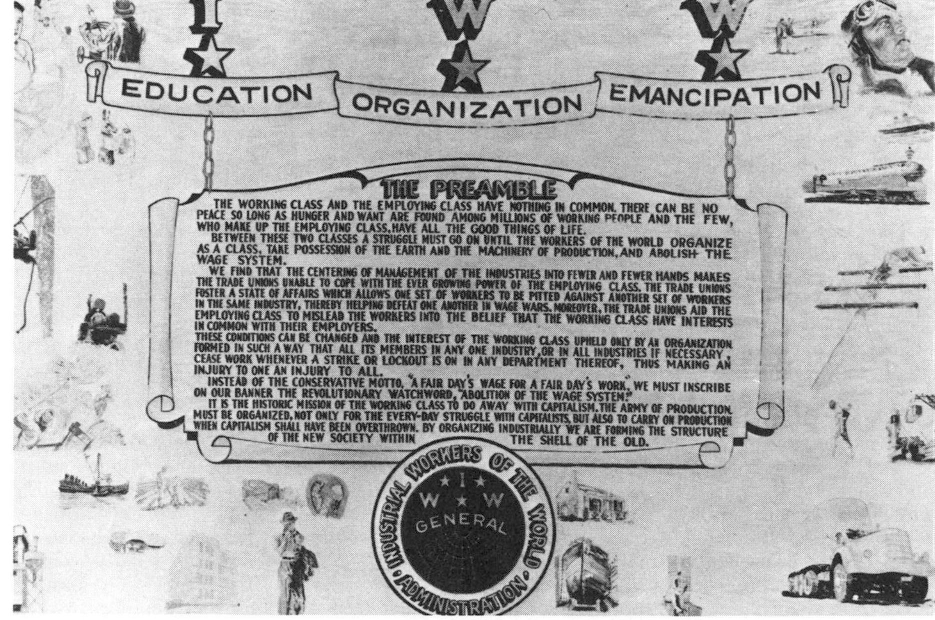

Preamble of the manifesto of the Industrial Workers of the World (*courtesy National Archives of Canada/C-57200*).

Industrialization is a process of economic and social change which shifts the centres of economic activity onto the focus of work, wages and incomes. These changes took 2 forms in the Canadian case. First, economic and social activities were transformed from being based on agriculture and the raw production of natural resources to manufacturing (both primary and secondary) and to services that were complementary to other activities. Second, economic and social activities shifted from rural and cottage industries to an urban core of industrial pursuits where production took place under the factory system, where technology used greater amounts of fixed capital equipment, and where a larger proportion of the population expected to be wage earners for all of their working lives. Therefore, industrialization brought major changes in the way society was organized and in the relations among different groups in society. These 2 changes point to the fact that the personal or human aspects of industrialization were paramount in the shifts that took place in Canada. The human aspects of industrialization were found, for example, in the growth of urbanized areas, in the greater labour force participation of women, in the decline of the family farm, and in the growth of unions in manufacturing and services. In the 20th century, policies were introduced and modified to deal with some of the societal problems which were part of industrialization such as pollution, personal income inequality, regional economic inequality, monopoly practices by firms, and unfair labour practices.

WILLIAM L. MARR

This small iron foundry near Trois-Rivières (now a historical interpretation centre) saw virtually the only industrial activity in Canada before 1800 (*courtesy Gauthier, Guité & Roy*).

Industry, in its broadest sense, includes all economic activity, but for convenience commentators divide it into 3 sectors. The primary sector includes establishments involved in the exploitation and initial processing of natural RESOURCES. For example, COAL MINING includes establishments that break, wash, grade or otherwise prepare coal for use as a fuel. The secondary, or MANUFACTURING, sector is made up of primary manufacturing establishments, ie, those that process raw materials to produce IRON AND STEEL, PULP AND PAPER, PETROLEUM products, etc, and secondary manufacturing establishments, ie, those that produce consumer goods (eg, CLOTHING) and capital goods (eg, ships). The tertiary or SERVICE INDUSTRIES sector includes establishments in both the private and public sectors. These range from bakeries to the BANK OF CANADA. All these elements make up Canada's industrial system, which has become increasingly complex over time.

Industrial development has long been linked to the exploitation of Canada's rich resource endowment. In the earliest years of the FUR TRADE, there was little related industrial development. Emphasis was on commercial activity related to the exportation of resources. But as settlement proceeded, domestic industry began to grow in areas that facilitated the exploitation of resources, such as RAILWAY equipment, SHIPBUILDING and farm machinery. A small IRON foundry was operating near Trois-Rivières, Qué, as early as the 18th century. In the 19th century, industrial development began in earnest. By 1850 there were paper mills and foundries in both Canada East and Canada West. Steam engines and farming implements were also being produced. To spur industrial development, the NATIONAL POLICY was set in place in 1879 by the Conservative government of John A. MACDONALD. The policy had 3 thrusts: stimulation of domestic industrial development through the establishment of tariff barriers; encouragement of immigration to develop the agricultural potential of the West and to create a large domestic market; and completion of the CANADIAN PACIFIC RAILWAY to the West Coast as rapidly as possible. The policy did succeed. With the settlement of the West, AGRICULTURE, MINING, lumbering and fishing expanded. The government supported this type of industrial development by encouraging development of appropriate infrastructures (eg, railways, ships, grain elevators, roads).

Manufacturing industries that supported development of Canada's natural resources were centered along the St Lawrence R and the Great Lakes in Québec and Ontario. These developments were accompanied by the emergence of the service sector (eg, commercial and financial institutions, public administration). Canada became a major trading nation, sending raw and semiprocessed natural resources to the large metropolitan markets of Europe and the US. Industrial development was given a further boost by WWI. War materials poured out of Canadian plants, strengthening manufacturing.

This growing strength encouraged the great expansion of the 1920s. By 1929 pulp and paper, the largest single industry, had captured 64% of world trade. Government continued to encourage the development of infrastructure and undertook large programs, such as mineral exploration conducted by the GEOLOGICAL SURVEY OF CANADA and plant breeding research (eg, for hardy WHEAT strains), which directly assisted the private sector in industrial development.

While primary industries dominated the scene, manufacturing in areas such as the AUTOMOTIVE INDUSTRY grew as well. This great postwar expansion required large-scale capital investment, much of which came from the US in the form of direct investment in branch plants of US firms, which were thus able to serve the Canadian market and circumvent tariff walls set up by the National Policy. In fact, US capital rapidly replaced the British capital of the previous century, which had been mainly in the form of portfolio investment. By 1920 US capital represented over 50% of FOREIGN INVESTMENT in Canada, compared with 15% in 1900.

This rapid industrial expansion came to a sudden halt with the GREAT DEPRESSION of the 1930s. Between 1929 and 1933, Canada's export income dropped by 67%. Firms closed and unemployment soared. Export-oriented industries (wheat, fish, lumber, pulp and paper) were most severely affected. Industries such as manufacturing, established to serve the Canadian market principally and situated mainly in central Canada, suffered least and were in a much better position to respond to the industrial requirements of WWII. The war brought demands for sophisticated products such as aircraft parts, cars and trucks. Many of these products required new techniques of production, which became integrated into Canada's industrial system.

Modern Industry

Because the ravages of war had not touched Canada, the country's industrial structure was intact and it adapted readily to the requirements of a peacetime domestic economy and to the demands of postwar reconstruction in Europe. These activities shaped Canada's current industrial structure.

Structure Canada has an open economy, with about 26% of its 1986 gross domestic product ($488.4 billion) being exported; over 70% of this trade is with the US. This state of affairs is reflected by a current account balance that indicates a large merchandise trade surplus, caused primarily by the export of crude and semiprocessed natural resources. Canada's strength in primary industries is not matched by a strong secondary manufacturing sector. In fact, as a proportion of GDP, the manufacturing sector has shrunk from a peak of 40% in 1973 to about 20% today.

There has always been a trade deficit in fully manufactured goods in the postwar period, but this deficit increased from about $3 billion in 1970 to $20.6 billion in 1986, reflecting a growing erosion. The service sector has continued to expand. Canadians now belong to what has been called "The Information Economy," based on the manipulation of information. Over the past 30 years, the number of Canadians employed in information has grown twice as fast as the work force as a whole. Today, over 40% of Canadian workers are in information fields, up from 20% in 1931. The shift towards a service economy based on information is a characteristic of industrialized countries.

Regional Dimension The industrial strength of Canada lies in Ontario and Québec where two-thirds of all primary and secondary industrial activity takes place, along with 80% of secondary manufacturing. The resource strength lies in the other provinces. Canada is said to have regional economies with distinct characteristics. Thus the West is strong in primary industries – agriculture, FISHERIES, FORESTRY, mining – with some development in the resource-processing sector – wood products, paper and allied products, primary metals and nonmetallic minerals, petroleum and coal. Ontario and Québec are strong in low-technology industries – FOOD AND BEVERAGES, TOBACCO, labour-intensive secondary processing (TEXTILES, FOOTWEAR, FURNITURE, etc), metal fabricating, TRANSPORTATION (excluding aircraft and parts), and electrical products (excluding major appliances, COMMUNICATIONS and industrial equipment). Inroads are being made in the high-technology fields – aircraft and parts, electrical products (major appliances, communications and industrial equipment), chemicals and chemical products and miscellaneous scientific and professional equipment. The Atlantic region is characterized by low-technology, and primary and resource-processing industries. The resource strengths of Atlantic Canada (fishing, mining) differ from those in western Canada (oil and gas, forestry).

The differences in regional economies lead to differing emphases in industrial development and international orientation. The resource-dependent provinces seek free-trade arrangements that encourage resource exports. Ontario and Québec, which are more vulnerable to foreign competitors in manufacturing, do not favour complete free trade and seek the support of the federal government to assist their industries to sell abroad. The near independence of the industrial structures of the regions makes it very difficult to develop a pan-Canadian INDUSTRIAL STRATEGY. Industrial policymaking is becoming increasingly regional in orientation.

Foreign Ownership The National Policy of 1879 did encourage industrialization, but of a peculiar nature. The policy was designed to force foreign (particularly US) industrialists to build factories in Canada if they wished to reach the Canadian market. The tariff brought direct (or equity) investment, which resulted in a branch-plant economy of unique proportions. For example, Canada's dependence on US direct investment in 1970 was some 10 times higher than the average of a group of 13 of the most industrialized countries belonging to the Organization for Economic Cooperation and Development. Some 52% (1984) of manufacturing industries have come to be foreign owned through equity investment; these industries are largely in central Canada. In some sectors (eg, oil and gas), foreign ownership is even higher (71% in 1984). The issues related to foreign-owned firms are now well known. They include truncated operations, ie, establishments which do not possess all the functions that are normally part of a business; production of a broad range of products mimicking those of their parent company, with very limited product and production specialization; a tendency to be import intensive; a tendency not to export because they are geared to serve the Canadian market; and limited linkages with Canadian suppliers, since the parent company tends to provide the components for assembly.

This type of industrialization has resulted in ever-growing BALANCE OF PAYMENTS deficits in manufactured finished goods ($20.6 billion in 1986). Our overall merchandise trade balance is thus dragged down and it becomes increasingly difficult to balance our international accounts because of the growing deficits in service transactions (largely caused by massive interest and dividend payments on foreign borrowings and investment, and payments for foreign-management services). By the end of the 1970s the situation had reached the stage where the federal government felt that it had to establish policies favouring development of Canadian-owned industries. The most striking example was the National Energy Program of 1980, which aimed at increasing Canadian ownership of Canada's PETROLEUM INDUSTRIES to 50% by 1990, up from 28% in 1980. Under this policy, Canadian ownership of assets had increased to 40.6% by 1984.

Since foreign direct investment resulted in an unacceptable industrial structure, the federal government established a mechanism, similar to that in other countries, to control it. The FOREIGN INVESTMENT REVIEW AGENCY (now Investment Canada) was created to evaluate the intentions of foreign investors and to try to extract maximum benefits for Canada. Both federal and provincial governments try to redress unacceptable situations with policies (eg, on procurement) that favour Canadian industrial development.

Research and Development Expenditures on INDUSTRIAL RESEARCH AND DEVELOPMENT as a proportion of Gross Domestic Product, have come to be taken as a barometer of industrial health and sophistication within OECD countries. Canada, with an R & D expenditure level of about 1.3% of GDP, is in the company of the smaller industrialized countries. Since about half of R & D is performed in publicly funded institutions, many technological innovations emerge from these laboratories, eg, the TELIDON interactive videotex system and communications SATELLITES. In fact, federal government laboratories in the Ottawa area are credited with being instrumental in the development of the HIGH-TECHNOLOGY industrial community that has established itself in the area since the 1960s.

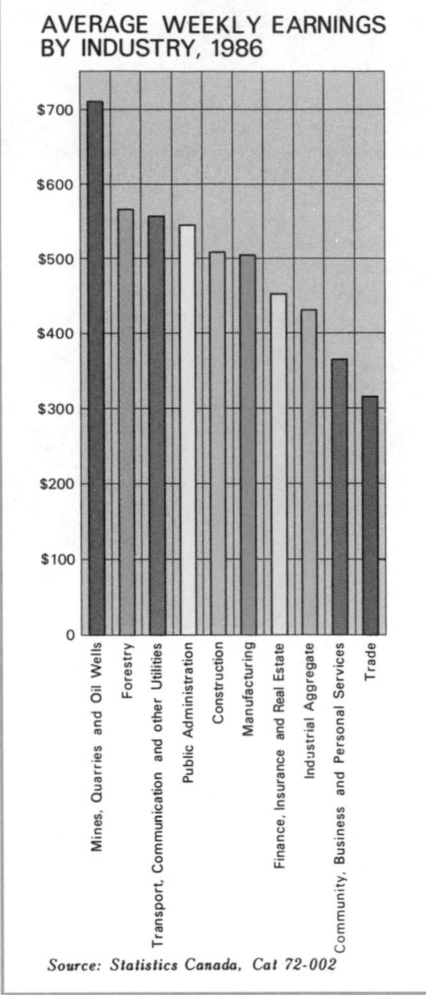

Source: Statistics Canada, Cat 72-002

Both the federal and provincial governments have played key roles in developing scientific and technological capabilities. Governments have not only provided public funds to support the private sector, but have become directly involved when the private sector considered the risks too great (eg, Panarctic Oil Ltd), where the private sector failed (eg, CANADAIR LTD), or where the market system was deemed not to act in the national or provincial interest (eg, PETRO-CANADA; ONTARIO HYDRO; HYDRO-QUÉBEC; ALBERTA OIL SANDS TECHNOLOGY AND RESEARCH AUTHORITY). Eight provinces have their own provincial research organizations. The involvement of governments in economic development has resulted in a large amount of R & D being sponsored by and performed within government agencies. However, the share of industry-funded R & D is increasing and Canadian expenditures on R & D are expected to reach 1.5% of GDP by 1990.

Canadian and US Industrial Structures

Because of close economic ties with the US, Canadians tend to believe that they have a similar economy and industrial structure. If the industrial structures of both countries were approximately the same, there would be little difference proportionally in the output of their various industrial groups. However, Canada's greatest relative strength is in the primary manufacturing industries, which are linked to resource development; its greatest weakness is in higher technology manufacturing areas. In fact the structure of Canadian industry complements that of the US; we export relatively unsophisticated products to the US, while it ships finished goods to us. This long-standing relationship reflects Canada's historical role as a resource hinterland, first to France, then to Britain, now to the US (*see* ECONOMIC NATIONALISM).

Canada is now in search of a new national policy to restructure its industry around areas of strength to compete in a new international marketplace. Other industrialized countries are assisting industries to move into new technological domains, while newly industrializing countries (eg, Taiwan, Mexico, Brazil) are moving into our traditional manufacturing industries. Any new national policy cannot be built around tariffs, as in 1879, since these barriers to trade are being eliminated by international agreement. Moreover the issues of foreign ownership, quasi-independent regional economies, and dependence on the US market must be addressed. *See also* ECONOMIC HISTORY; REGIONALISM; REGIONAL ECONOMICS; TECHNOLOGY. R.D. VOYER

Reading: J.N.H. Britton and J.M. Gilmour, *The Weakest Link* (1978); M. Lamontagne, *Business Cycles in Canada* (1984); A. Rotstein, *Rebuilding From Within* (1984); R.D. Voyer and M. Murphy, *Global 2000: Canada* (1984).

Inflation popularly means rising general prices, most frequently calculated by the CONSUMER PRICE INDEX (CPI) – a measure of the cost of a basket of commodities purchased by a typical family. The rate of inflation refers to the percentage increase in the price level and is usually expressed at an annual rate; if the CPI rose from 100 to 132 over 2 years, then the price level rose by 32%; that is, the rate of inflation was about 16% annually. Most of the sharp inflation of the 19th and 20th centuries has been associated with major wars, and since WWII prices have generally risen.

The average annual rate of inflation in consumer prices from 1970 to 1975 was 6.5% in the US, 7% in Canada, 6% in West Germany, 12% in the UK, 18% in Yugoslavia, 50% in Argentina and 112% in Chile. In 1981 Canadian inflation reached an annual rate of 12.5%; by 1986 this figure stood at 4.1%. In the US, the average annual consumer price index rose only 1.1%, the lowest gain in 25 years. In an inflationary period, distinctions must be made between money income (measured in dollars) and real income (measured in purchasing power). If money income rises by the same percentage as prices of goods, then real income is unchanged. For real income to increase, money income must rise more than prices. Inflation does not necessarily harm everyone; its main consequence is the redistribution of real income. If prices are stable (the rate of inflation is zero) and A borrows $100 from B at a 2% interest rate, in 1 year B expects to receive $102 in real income. However, if prices rise by 5%, then $102 will not buy what $100 would have bought a year ago; B's real income will be reduced and A's real income will be higher. Unexpected inflation therefore redistributes real income from lenders to borrowers. Pensioners who contributed to PENSION funds when inflation rates were low and are repaid with dollars that are worth much less than anticipated are among those harmed by inflation.

The relationship among prices, employment, wages and profits is complex. Inflation can be halted by decreasing aggregate demand (total spending), achieved with FISCAL POLICY by reducing government expenditure or raising taxes, and with monetary policy by restricting the growth in the supply of money in the economy, thereby raising interest rates and reducing credit. However, much of the initial impact of the reduced aggregate demand is reflected in lower output and employment rather than in prices (even in the 19th century, falling prices were generally associated with fairly high levels of unemployment), so governments have chosen alternatives such as wage and price controls, although these alone will not lastingly affect inflation. However, if controls are used in conjunction with appropriate monetary and fiscal policies, they may help reduce inflation, with fewer harmful side effects. Economists generally agree that inflation will not continue unless the money supply is allowed to increase; monetarists tend to emphasize control of the money supply, while Keynesians favour other tools such as wage and price controls. *See also* ECONOMY STAGFLATION. W.C. RIDDELL

Influence d'un livre, L' (1837) by Philippe AUBERT DE GASPÉ, Jr, regarded as the first French Canadian novel, offers a subtle satire of spiritual poverty in Québec through an account of Charles Amand's quest for gold. Amand's alchemical misadventures, influenced by a treatise on magic, alternate with the courtship of his daughter Amélie by a young medical student, and take him from the countryside near St-Jean-Port-Joli to Québec and to Ile d'Anticosti. Written probably in collaboration with Aubert de Gaspé's father, author of *Les* ANCIENS CANADIENS (1863), the novel is remembered for its documentary and folkloric elements, incorporating into its plot the legend of Rose Latulipe and the murder of the peddler Guilmette as well as superstitious beliefs and customs. *Le Chercheur de trésors* (1864), a bowdlerized edition by Abbé H.R. CASGRAIN, was replaced in 1968 by Léopold Leblanc's edition, appending 4 of many excised passages. MICHÈLE LACOMBE

Influenza, an acute infectious epidemic disease caused by a filterable virus. There are 4 main types of the virus – A, B, C and D – and many strains. The virus enters the body through the respiratory tract, but soon spreads to cause symptoms that include fever, chills, headache, sore throat, cough, gastrointestinal disturbances, muscular pain and neuralgia. An attack provides temporary immunity, but only to the particular strain involved. Outbreaks of the disease typically demonstrate high morbidity but low mortality rates, usually killing only the very old and the very young (deaths in these cases are usually related to the complications such as bacterial pneumonia). There is no cure for influenza. The best treatment is a combination of bed rest and increased fluid intake. Neither is there a sure means of prevention. Vaccines are available, but they do not provide complete immunity from all viruses.

It was only with the eradication, through advances in PUBLIC HEALTH and medicine, of more major infectious diseases, that influenza was recognized as a serious threat. In Canada, influenza appeared in EPIDEMIC proportions on at least 7 occasions during the 19th century. The effects of the epidemic of 1832 were masked by cholera and those of the epidemic of 1847-48 by typhus, but the eradication of other diseases was not the only reason influenza grew in importance by the end of the 1800s. The epidemic of 1889-90 was particularly virulent, affecting 40% of the world's population.

The most damaging epidemic of influenza – for Canada and the world – appeared after WWI. The Spanish Flu of 1918-19 killed some 21 million people, including about 50 000 Canadians. It demonstrated a perverse tendency to kill the young and hearty. A long-term consequence for some victims was the development of a Parkinsonian syndrome, including a marked tremor. The Spanish Flu was brought into Canada by returning troops and made its way into even the remotest communities. In Labrador and Québec, which were the hardest hit, some villages were exterminated by the disease. Some areas unsuccessfully tried quarantine. All medical facilities and personnel were soon overtaxed and volunteers organized infirmaries in schools and hotels.

The epidemic brought not only death but social and economic disruption as well. Children were left parentless and many families found themselves without the chief wage earner. Armies on both sides were temporarily debilitated. Businesses lost profits because of lack of demand for their products or because they were unable – as a result of a reduced work force – to meet the demand. Municipal governments, in an attempt to halt the spread of the disease, closed all except necessary services, and provinces enacted laws regarding quarantine and enforced the wearing of masks in public. Although the Canadian population unhappily accepted these restrictions, it defied the federal government's request that WWI victory celebrations be postponed until Dec 1. The influenza strain, although decreasingly virulent, remained active in Canada until the mid-1920s. The establishment of the federal Department of Health in 1919 was a direct result of the epidemic.

Although influenza is a yearly affliction, it is unlikely that another epidemic of such magnitude could occur today. Pneumonia contracted by a sufferer weakened by influenza rather than influenza itself was the major cause of death, and pneumonia lost its impact with the discovery of penicillin, which Canada began to manufacture during WWII. Health facilities are also much improved, the population generally is in a better state of health, and the virus itself is better understood. JANICE DICKIN MCGINNIS

Information Society Information has become very significant in the economies of Canada and other technologically advanced countries. The first half of the 20th century was characterized by a shift in the dominant economic activity from agricultural to industrial production. The second half has been characterized by a shift toward the production, processing, storage, retrieval and consumption of information: not only the familiar press, radio, television, film and library information, but also specialized computer banks of data (ie, information) that are sold to subscribers over TELECOMMUNICATIONS lines. This development is made possible by major technological improvements in microelectronics, computers and telecommunications that have continually reduced the costs of processing and transmitting information.

The Canadian government has adopted a policy of promoting rapid adjustment to the information society, with its potential improvements in economic efficiency. This policy is not without problems. Information technologies often promote centralization, and since much Canadian information is already stored outside Canada, the Canadian economy could become even more dependent on the US and multinational corporations. Personal privacy may become even more difficult to protect. Employment opportunities in Canada may be reduced. Information that used to be generally available, eg, in libraries, may have to be purchased from a databank. With information treated as a primary marketable commodity in the information society, unless social policies are adjusted accordingly, the wealthy may improve their position to the detriment of the poor. *See also* COMMUNICATIONS TECHNOLOGY; COMPUTER COMMUNICATIONS; SATELLITE COMMUNICATIONS.

WILLIAM H. MELODY

Reading: Science Council of Canada, *Planning Now for an Information Society: Tomorrow Is Too Late* (1982); S. Serafini and M. Andrieu, *The Information Revolution and Its Implications for Canada* (1980); K. Valaskakis, *The Information Society: The Issues and the Choices* (1979).

Ingersoll, Ont, Town, pop 8451 (1986c), 8494 (1981c), inc 1865, situated on the Thames R, 36 km E of London. Founded as Oxford Village in 1818 by Charles Ingersoll, it was renamed Ingersoll for his father, Thomas, and incorporated as a village in 1852. Following the opening of the Great Western Ry in the 1850s, its population grew rapidly to about 4000 by 1871, and increased gradually thereafter. Its economy, based initially on the export of wheat and hardwood lumber, shifted to the production of cheese and agricultural implements in the mid-1860s. Ingersoll was the commercial centre for Canada's first cheese export trade and the Canadian Dairyman's Assn was founded there (1867). In 1866 the town sent a 3300 kg "Mammoth Cheese" – celebrated in verse by James McIntyre, the "cheese poet" – to exhibits in NY state and England. Now a manufacturing and residential centre, Ingersoll celebrates its past with an annual heritage day. GEORGE EMERY

Inglis, Charles, Anglican bishop (b at Glencolumbkille, Ire 1734; d at Aylesford, NS 24 Feb 1816). Having gained influence and preferment as a Tory cleric and pamphleteer in New York C during the American Revolution, he was named to NS as the Church of England's first colonial bishop in 1787. The diocese initially included what are now the Atlantic Provinces, Québec and Ontario, and was established at a time when the colonial church was combatting internal weakness and external competition. Given such difficulties, it is clear that Inglis's bishopric was more successful than has been contended. He used patience and discretion to overcome early antipathy from his clerics, and travelled as much as possible within his diocese to foster a stronger commitment from both clergy and laity. The establishment of King's College in 1788-89 was an enduring tribute to his determination to provide a

Charles Inglis, the Church of England's first colonial bishop (*courtesy Public Archives of Nova Scotia/N-875*).

locally trained clergy, although it perpetuated a reactionary Church of England ascendancy in the colony. LOIS KERNAGHAN

Reading: B. Cuthbertson, *The First Bishop: A Biography of Charles Inglis* (1987); J. Fingard, *The Anglican Design in Loyalist Nova Scotia 1783-1816* (1972).

Inglis, John, Church of England bishop (b at New York 9 Dec 1777; d at London, Eng 27 Oct 1850). Son of Charles INGLIS, the Church of England's first bishop of Nova Scotia, he entered the ministry in 1802, after studying at King's College, Windsor, and soon took charge of diocesan church affairs for his ailing father and then for the nonresident second bishop until his own episcopal appointment in 1825. His diocese included NS, PEI, until 1839 Newfoundland and Bermuda, and until 1845 New Brunswick. Inglis's preoccupations were maintenance of the privileges of the established church; opposition to evangelical tendencies within his own denomination which produced serious divisions, especially in Halifax; and fund raising for the church in a period of declining British grants and increasing colonial hostility to his exclusivist aims. An eloquent speaker and a relentless publicist for Anglican rights, he found himself out of step within the liberal climate of the reform era and his minimal achievements left him embittered. JUDITH FINGARD

Ingonish, Victoria County, NS, UP, pop 447 (1986c), 471 (1981c), a picturesque coastal area consisting of Ingonish, Ingonish Centre, Ingonish Beach (pop 573), South I Harbour and Ingonish Ferry, is located on the Cabot Trail, 94 km N of Baddeck. The origin of the name may be Portuguese, named by fishermen who wintered here as early as 1521, or it may be Micmac. The Portuguese settlement was destroyed in conflicts with the Micmac and French, who later, in the 1600s, operated Port d'Orléans, a thriving fortified centre producing the prized salt cod. By 1740, there were 54 fishing boats at Ingonish. During the Seven Years' War, the settlement was destroyed and its inhabitants moved to St Anns. After 1802, the first English-speaking settlers arrived to farm and fish. Today, Ingonish provides facilities for the tourists who flock to the Cape Smokey Ski Area, to the famous hotel, Keltic Lodge, and to Cape Breton Highlands National Park, whose eastern entrance is at Ingonish Beach. JUDITH HOEGG RYAN

Injunction is an equitable judicial remedy issued at the court's discretion. It usually takes the form of an order preventing or restraining a person from performing an act. The order may also take a mandatory form by compelling someone to do something. It may be sought as a final remedy or at a preliminary stage before trial (the interlocutory injunction). The injunction is designed to provide more effective and appropriate relief than an ordinary common-law award of damages. In many circumstances applicants prefer to have an act prevented or performed rather than to receive compensation after the fact. J. BARNES

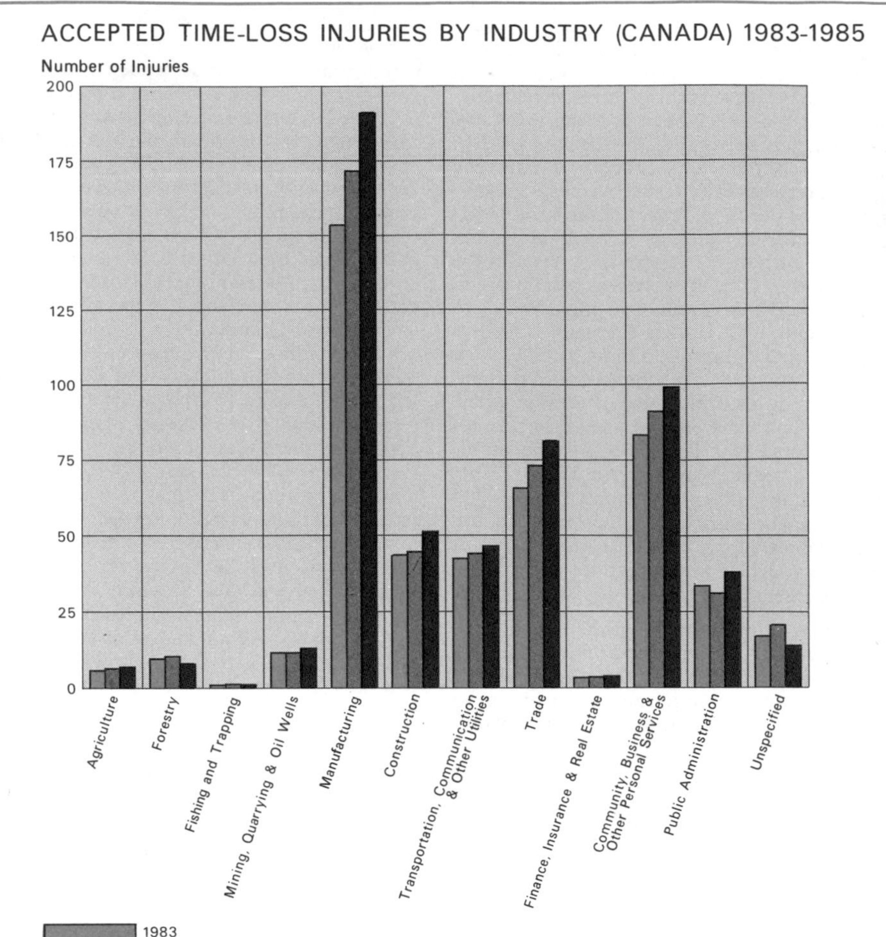

Source: Statistics Canada, Cat 72-208

Injury and Prevention Some 2000 Canadians between the ages of one and 19 are killed each year because of injury, and over 85 000 are hospitalized. With the control of infectious diseases, injury has become the leading cause of death and disability in Canadian children and youth. The most frequent causes of fatal injury are traffic related, drowning, burns, suffocation, falls and poisoning. The vast majority of childhood injuries (95%) are the result of impact by moving objects, such as motor vehicles and hockey sticks; or impact of the victim against stationary surfaces, such as car windshields. Burns account for 3% of all injuries; electric energy, poisoning and radiation, 2%. The head and face are the parts of the body most commonly injured in motor vehicle crashes, in falls, and in other home injuries. Because of the incidence of brain injury and the significant level of neurologic impairment resulting from moderate or severe levels of head injury, and the evidence that mild injury may have significant unfavourable consequences, these injuries are a significant public-health problem. Under a medicare system, the treatment costs to a family are minimal and are measured mainly in days lost from school or work. However, the costs to the community for the care of victims of injury are staggering. In Canada, $16 billion was spent in 1985 on the treatment of injuries.

Injury and Child Development Many injuries are distinctly age related and developmentally determined. Infants, for example, are very susceptible to falls; and about 85% of injuries from birth to one year are due to falls, with baby boys being at greatest risk and head injury being the most frequent result. Scalds from hot bath water or spilled hot beverage account for 10% of injuries to infants, poisoning for 5%. The average infant travels some 8000 km annually in cars. If not protected by car safety seats or air bags, the threat of serious injury or death is significant. Regulations relating to size of soothers and toy objects have decreased choking deaths.

Children who have learned to walk and are able to explore their environment are at especially high risk to injury. In fact this is the most vulnerable stage for injury to girls. Overall, one in 10 toddlers is treated in a hospital emergency room each year for trauma or poisoning; the latter accounts for 12% of injury. Burns and scalds are common, but injury due to falls still predominates. Pedestrian and motor vehicle occupant injuries are the leading cause of death in this age group and the death rate from drowning is higher at this stage than at any other.

From 3 to 6 years of age, the child's environment extends from the home to the neighbourhood. Pedestrian injuries are the most common cause of death and serious injury at this age. The use of tricycles and bicycles also leads to more injuries than the use of any other product. During the ages 7 to 18, the child enters the world of sports, recreation and traffic; 98% of injuries result from mechanical objects, particularly, until the teenage years, from playground hazards and bicycles. The Canadian Institute of Child Health is currently developing safety standards for playgrounds in Canada. A gradually increasing ability on the part of children to recognize hazards and to protect themselves accounts for the low death rates around age 10 from almost all injuries.

Comprehensive data on sports injuries are lacking in Canada. The reduction in eye injuries since the compulsory use of hockey face masks is a notable Canadian accomplishment. Release bindings have reduced the incidence of leg fractures to skiers. In 1986 the Royal Lifesaving Society completed a national study of injury due to diving. The same year, Dr Charles Tater, head of neurosurgery at U of T, completed a study on 115 cord injuries of hockey players of all levels.

During the teenage years, the rate of traffic injury reaches epidemic proportions. Over 50% of all deaths and serious injuries in this age group are traffic related, mainly to youths as drivers or passengers of motor vehicles. Transport injuries are the leading cause of brain injury (48%) and as a result produce more new quadriplegics and paraplegics each year than all other causes combined. Injuries to the brain are also the leading cause of epilepsy and of handicapping conditions in people between one and 19 years of age.

Injury Prevention has received relatively little scientific attention. It is commonly believed that bad luck and chance are the cause of "accidents" and that fate is the main predisposing factor. The first step in influencing public policy would be a general realization that injuries are rarely accidental and most are preventable, and that the medical, social and human toll of injuries warrants a major investment in prevention. Some preventive measures require the co-operation of relatively few individuals but can influence the lives of many (eg, reduction of crib slat spacing resulting in the eradication of crib strangulation deaths of infants). Preventive measures directed at changing human behaviour, on the other hand, require the co-operation of many individuals (eg, car seats that require parents to buckle up their child with each ride).

Preventive strategies (eg, preventing the creation of the hazard in the first place, separating the hazard by time or space or physical barriers, and countering damage already done) are an important conceptual contribution to the field of injury control. If implemented, as interrelated approaches applicable to all types of injury, they could drastically reduce the incidence of injury in Canada.

Occupational Fatalities and Injuries One out of 10 working Canadians, or over 1 million persons each year, are injured on the job. About half of them receive first aid and return to work. The remainder require time off work (554 793 in 1985) or die as a result of their injuries. There were an estimated 844 occupational fatalities in Canada in 1985.

Over 15 million work days were lost in 1985 as a result of injuries and OCCUPATIONAL DISEASES, at a cost of over $3 billion nationally. The ECONOMIC COUNCIL OF CANADA has suggested that indirect costs of employment injuries and illnesses, including failure to meet customer demands, decreased efficiency, lowered employee morale, etc, could range from 2 to 10 times that of direct costs (ie, medical aid, compensation and administration of claims). Therefore, the total cost of employment injuries and illnesses in Canada (1985) can be estimated at between $6 billion and $30 billion.

Injury rates are highest for younger workers, and are higher for workers in hazardous industries such as fishing, forestry, mining and construction. The most frequent types of occupational injury are strains or sprains, bruises, cuts or lacerations, and fractures or dislocations. The body parts most frequently affected are the back, hands, feet and eyes. Occupational injuries result most frequently from overexertion (in lifting, pushing, pulling or carrying objects), being struck by objects, falls and being caught in machinery or between objects.

Occupational safety can be improved through proper design, guarding and maintenance of tools and machinery, and through proper design of work procedures and methods. Workers can protect themselves in many cases through the use of protective equipment such as hard hats, safety shoes, eye protection and breathing apparatus. Worker instruction and training regarding safe work procedures and the proper handling of chemicals and other dangerous substances is also important. Safety information and educational programs are available through provincial and federal government agencies responsible for occupational health and safety, labour and employer organizations, national and provincial safety associations, and the Canadian Centre for Occupational Health and Safety.

JOHN H. READ AND ROBERT ORFORD

Innis, Harold Adams, political economist, and pioneer in communication studies (b at Otterville, Ont 5 Nov 1894; d at Toronto 8 Nov 1952). Innis's earlier writings in economics and economic history gave rise to a distinctively Canadian approach to these subjects, and his later attempts to analyse the crisis in Western civilization led the way to a new emphasis on the importance of different modes of COMMUNICATIONS for understanding the nature and development of a society.

A veteran of WWI, Innis studied at McMaster and U of Chicago. His choice of a Canadian thesis topic, a history of the CANADIAN PACIFIC RAILWAY, was his first step towards a reorientation of many fields of study relating to Canada, especially in the social sciences. In 1920 Innis joined U of T's political economy department where he remained until his death. During the 1920s he became increasingly dissatisfied because he believed that the American- and British-trained scholars who predominated in Canadian universities were applying inappropriate models to their analysis of Canada's economy. Innis's first major work, *The Fur Trade in Canada* (1930), established his reputation and introduced the STAPLE THESIS of economic development. Innis also opposed the continentalist school and argued that Canada's political boundaries were the logical outcome of Canada's economic history – contrary to the tenets of CONTINENTALISM. Appointed head of U of T's political economy department in 1937, Innis continued to work on his second major study, *The Cod Fisheries* (1940). Although he had trouble finding a suitable publisher because of his cumbersome writing style, this work established him in the forefront of the world's economic historians. Whereas *The Fur Trade* had set Canada off from the US, *The Cod Fisheries* underscored Canada's European roots.

During the 1930s and WWII, Innis rose to the challenge of defending the integrity of the universities and of scholarship which he saw as imperiled by the general atmosphere of crisis. He was active in establishing societies, such as Canadian Political Science Assn and the American Economic History Assn, and he used his connections and prestige to secure funding for Canadian research. More controversially, he vigorously opposed the efforts of fellow academics such as F.W. UNDERHILL who were involved in the LEAGUE FOR SOCIAL RECONSTRUCTION. To a considerable extent, the detachment of our contemporary Canadian academic community from political involvement derives from his attitudes and efforts.

Innis's scholarly reputation led to an invitation to visit the Soviet Union in 1945. His posthumously published *Russian Diary* shows his deep concern with the problems of Western civilization. In drawing attention to the impact of the media of communications on the extent and duration of a civilization, Innis's communications researches culminated his lifelong attempt to explain the interpenetration between Canada and Western civilization. He expressed these concerns in his 1947 presidential address to the Royal Soc of Canada, titled "Minerva's Owl," although his arguments were little understood at the time. He contended that western Europe and N America were in a state of profound crisis. This crisis was rendered more severe because the dominant media of communication fostered an obsessive preoccupation with the present, with the consequence that politicians and scholars were neither able to understand their circumstances nor able to devise an appropriate remedy for their problems. Innis continued his researches amidst increasingly heavy administrative responsibilities. In 1947 he became dean of U of T's graduate school, and in 1948 he visited England to deliver the Beit lectures, material which he later included in *Empire and Communications* (1950). This synoptic study of ancient Egypt to the present explores the theme of the interconnection between the vitality and durability of countries and empires and the modes of communication that dominated in them. Innis was still working on these ideas at the time of his death.

Harold Innis, brilliant political economist and pioneer in communications studies (*courtesy National Archives of Canada/C-19694*).

Innis had few followers during his life, though since his death he has secured admirers from several different academic disciplines, ranging from Marshall MCLUHAN in communications to Canadian Marxists interested in his study of the interrelations between economics, politics and society. However, few of Innis's disciples have had the courage and the genius to follow him in the breadth of his reading and theorizing.

WILLIAM CHRISTIAN

Innis, Mary Emma Quayle, author (b at St Mary's, Ohio 1899; d at Toronto 10 Jan 1972), wife of H.A. INNIS. She attended U of Chicago (PhB, 1919) before establishing careers in Canada as an economic historian and literary writer. She received an LLD (Queen's U, 1958) and a DLitt (U of Waterloo, 1965) and was dean of women at University College, U of T (1955-64). Some of her wide-ranging publications include *An Economic History of Canada* (1935), an authoritative but summary work; *Stand on the Rainbow* (1943), a novel recounting a year in the life of a mother of a young family; *Unfold the Years* (1949), the history of the YWCA; *Essays in Canadian Economic History* (1956), an edition of her husband's work; as well as poems, short stories and articles in many Canadian and American magazines. Other works include *The Clear Spirit* (1966) and (ed) *Nursing Education in a Changing Society* (1970).

MARYLYNN SCOTT

Innisfail, Alta, Town, pop 5535 (1986c), inc 1899 is located on the CPR line 121 km N of Calgary. Originally known as Poplar Grove, the settlement emerged as a regular stopping place on the Calgary-Edmonton Trail during the early

1880s. In 1882, the Alberta Lumber Co of Montréal opened a grist mill near the eventual townsite, which was surveyed the following year. Though the North-West Rebellion of 1885 hindered settlement of the area, the rich soil, plentiful timber and abundant wildlife began to attract numerous settlers shortly thereafter. With the arrival of the railway in 1891, the first post office was opened and a school district was established. The settlement was then renamed after the Irish town of Innisfail. It was incorporated as a town in 1903, and has remained the prosperous centre of a mixed farming district. Significant oil discoveries in the area were made after WWII, and today local businesses cater to the servicing of the oil and gas industry that has developed since then.

DAVID LEONARD

Innu, *see* MONTAGNAIS-NASKAPI.

Innuitian Region is a physiographic subdivision of the great arc of younger, mainly stratified sedimentary rocks that surround the stable, ancient SHIELD core of Canada. It comprises a triangle-shaped area of 540 000 km^2 between the Shield and the Arctic Ocean, most commonly referred to as the QUEEN ELIZABETH IS. Its geological history and present form are best understood by visualizing it as the uplifted, drowned edge of the continent. In Cambrian and Upper Devonian times, an ocean-covered area of subsidence and sedimentation, known as the Franklinian geosyncline, bordered the Shield landmass. Deformation occurred in the Middle Devonian, thrusting up a belt of mountains that today stretch in an arc from the rugged peaks of NE ELLESMERE I, 2000 m high, and the highlands of AXEL HEIBERG I, before the ranges progressively broaden and flatten into the plateaus of the western PARRY IS. About 330 million years ago, the Sverdrup Basin developed as a regional depression in which successive formations were built up over 270 million years to thicknesses as great as 12 250 m. During the opening up of the Arctic Basin these rocks were subjected to enormous forces, being pushed towards the unyielding Shield and folded and buckled into a chain of mountains running 2250 km from the Grantland, British Empire and United States ranges of northwestern Ellesmere, through the mountains of central and western Axel Heiberg. Less disturbed Sverdrup sedimentary rocks now form shale and sandstone lowland areas of rolling topography, though intrusion and piercement by evaporite domes has occurred. A narrow strip of thin, unconsolidated sand and gravel deposits is found along the Arctic Ocean coast.

DOUG FINLAYSON

Inquiry Into Certain Activities of the Royal Canadian Mounted Police, Royal Commission of (McDonald Commission), was a federal commission, est 1977, following allegations of crimes by the RCMP Security Service. Matters referred to the commission included a break-in at a data-processing company and the theft of a PARTI QUÉBÉCOIS membership list; 400 break-ins without warrants, mainly in BC (since 1970); electronic surveillance of at least one member of Parliament; unauthorized mail openings; the burning of a barn in Québec; widespread monitoring of election candidates; theft of dynamite; and use of forged documents. Former RCMP Commissioner William Higgitt and former Security Service Director General John Starnes testified that they knew subordinates occasionally broke laws in performance of duties. RCMP officers also claimed that they had informed their ministers of various activities, but PM Pierre Trudeau and other ministers testified that they had received no such information. In its final report, issued in 1981, the commission recommended, among other things, that police comply strictly with the law; that the RCMP be permitted to open mail with judicial authorization; and that a civilian security agency, divorced from the RCMP, be created. The new civilian agency, called the CANADIAN SECURITY INTELLIGENCE SERVICE, came into existence in July 1984 and was given broad powers.

JEFF SALLOT

Insect, small animal (more than 75% of known species are less than 6 mm long) with 3 pairs of legs, 1 or 2 pairs of wings, and a segmented body. Wings did not evolve in some primitive insects (Apterygota) and have been secondarily lost in some advanced groups (eg, fleas and lice). Although a few species occur in fresh water, in the intertidal zone of the seashore, or on the ocean surface, the vast majority are terrestrial. They are especially abundant in the tropics but may be found in all except the most extreme latitudes and altitudes. For example, about 300 species (mostly flies) live N of the 75th parallel, on Canadian arctic islands. A few species even occur in Antarctica, as parasites of birds or seals.

The diversity of insects is staggering: the 750 000 recorded species are estimated to represent only 10-50% of the world total. In Canada, about 55 000 species have been described. Insects owe their success to their adaptability and to their long and varied evolution; they were among the first terrestrial animals. As Arthropoda, insects possessed a light, strong, waterproof cuticular external skeleton (exoskeleton), which was critical in the evolution of the group. Their small size enables insects to hide easily from predators and to feed on scarce materials. Smallness, together with flight, facilitates dispersal by wind into new habitats, leading to geographic isolation of populations and ultimately to the evolution of new species. Reproductive capacity and life history have also been important. The production of large numbers of eggs, combined with short generation time, has enabled insects to adapt rapidly to changing environments. The evolution of a pupal stage, between larva and adult, has permitted specialization of the life history such that the primary function of the larva is accumulation of food reserves; those of the adult are reproduction and dispersal. For many insects, the pupa has developed into a highly weather-resistant stage which, together with the restriction of feeding activity to the larva, has enabled these insects to colonize habitats where conditions are suitable for development only at limited times of year.

Insects inhabiting regions (including most parts of Canada) where adverse conditions (eg, lack of food, and temperatures unsuitable for growth and reproduction) regularly occur survive by becoming dormant. Dormancy may occur at any stage in the life history, the stage varying with species. Thus, many grasshoppers overwinter in the egg stage; some damselflies survive as larvae frozen in ice; many butterflies and moths overwinter as pupae; and some mosquitoes survive as adults. Usually the overwintering stage is laid in or seeks out locations where conditions may not be so extreme, eg, under leaf litter or bark, in soil or in holes in the ground. In addition, some species develop antifreeze molecules that prevent frost damage. An alternative strategy is migration; using wind currents, some insects may migrate several thousand kilometres to more suitable conditions. For example, monarch butterflies, which spend early summer in southern Canada, move S in Aug-Oct to overwintering sites in southern US, returning the following spring.

CEDRIC GILLOTT

Reading: Cedric Gillott, *Entomology* (1980).

Insect, Beneficial Most insects are beneficial; less than 1% are pests. The largest group of insects, the parasitic wasps (about 200 000 species), attack other, often harmful, insects. Insects play a major ecological role and many systems would fail without them: they are the principal food of many animals, and the survival of insect-pollinated plants depends on them. Bees are not the only important pollinators; in northern Canada POLLINATION is largely by flies and butterflies. Plant-feeding insects also function in maintaining plant diversity: if they are removed, a few plant species tend to displace the others. Similarly, if plants or plant-feeding insects are introduced without their natural enemies, they often become pests. The solution, called biological control, involves introducing enemy species. Before 1930, the European spruce sawfly was spreading across eastern Canadian spruce forests. The introduction of parasitic wasps and a VIRUS disease reduced the sawfly from a major threat to an economically unimportant insect. Biological control is also used against weeds, particularly introduced species causing problems in permanent pasture and wild areas. In the interior of BC in 1950, St John's-wort (an introduced European weed) was excluding native forage. A specialized European beetle was introduced which, in most areas, reduced the weed to scattered plants, without damaging other vegetation. This approach is often the cheapest solution and avoids possible side effects from herbicides but may take 20 years. There are currently projects to control leafy spurge and to diffuse knapweed in western Canada using European insects. Insects can also feature in biological control of wastes, as in Australia, where beetles were introduced to control the accumulation of cow dung in pastures and an associated fly problem.

In some parts of the world, insects are used directly as food (eg, grasshoppers). There is a Canadian account, in Samuel HEARNE'S diary for 1771, of eating warble-fly grubs, which were said to taste like gooseberries. The most widely used insect product is honey (*see* BEEKEEPING); others include silk from the cocoon of the silk-worm moth; shellac from the secretions of a scale insect on fig trees in Asia; and red dye from the cochineal insect on cactus. Cochineal is now returning as a red food colouring because the coal-tar dyes that displaced it have been implicated as carcinogens. Insects are important tools for GENETICS and population-dynamics research. Last but not least, butterflies, dragonflies and beetles have been an inspiration for art, literature and music.

PETER HARRIS

Insect Classification A classification system acts as an efficient storage mechanism for information about each taxon or group. A natural classification also attempts to present the genealogical (historical, phylogenetic) relationships known or hypothesized to exist among them. Necessarily, such a classification is closely linked to and dependent on an understanding of the group's evolution. In the case of insects, different entomologists have different viewpoints on evolutionary history, and are likely to propose quite different classification schemes. Insects are classified primarily on the basis of wing structure, mouthpart structure and type of metamorphosis. It is estimated that about 55 000 insect species occur in Canada, categorized in 569 families, belonging to 32 orders. This number includes all Arthropods (segmented, jointed-limbed animals) which have a body divided into head, thorax and abdomen, and 3 pairs of thoracic legs. The class Insecta, as so defined, includes 3 taxa (Protura, Collembola and Diplura) that some workers would exclude from a strict definition of an insect.

All 3 groups have mouthparts withdrawn into pouches in the head, and are sometimes considered to constitute a natural group, the Entognatha [Gk, "internal jaw"]. While all 3 are primitively wingless, they are very different morphologically. Protura (telsontails) lack antennae and have a 12-segmented abdomen with the female genital opening behind segment 11; 8 species are estimated to occur in Canada. Collembola (springtails and snowfleas) have musculated antennal segments and a 6-segmented abdomen; 520 species are estimated to occur in Canada. Diplura (no common name) have 3-4 spiracles (tracheal openings) on the thorax and a specialized method of leg suspension; 5 species are estimated to occur in Canada.

Insects, defined in a restricted sense, have nonmusculated terminal antennal segments; 6 legs, each having 2 points of articulation with the thorax; and an 11-segmented abdomen. Two apterygote (wingless) orders have protruding (ectognathous) mouthparts: the Microcoryphia (bristletails, 13 species estimated in Canada), which have mandibles with a single point of attachment to the head capsule; and the Thysanura (firebrats and silverfish, 12 species estimated in Canada), which have mandibles with a double point of attachment to the head capsule.

Within the subclass Pterygota (winged insects), the infraclass Paleopterygota contains insects unable to fold the wings back and down onto the abdomen. Two very different and rather unrelated orders are represented in the living paleopterygotes, the Ephemeroptera (mayflies, 411 species estimated in Canada) and the Odonata (dragonflies and damselflies, 197 species estimated in Canada). In the infraclass Neoptera, all adults are able to fold the wings over the body and flat down onto the abdomen. The group originally had chewing mouthparts, but members of several descendant groups have departed widely from this condition.

Three subdivisions (cohorts) are recognized within the Neoptera, each representing an independent evolutionary line. The Polyneoptera are generally characterized by chewing mouthparts, a distinct anal lobe to the hind wing, abdomen with cerci (appendages), numerous Malpighian tubules (long vessels functioning primarily in excretion), and an incomplete metamorphosis. In incomplete metamorphosis, juveniles in later instars (periods between molts) closely resemble adults and have the same feeding habits, habitat and type of mouthparts.

Eight orders of Polyneoptera can be recognized in the Canadian fauna: Plecoptera (stoneflies, 310 species estimated in Canada); Dictyoptera (cockroaches and mantids, 16 species estimated in Canada); Isoptera (termites, 3 species native to Canada); Notoptera (grylloblattids, 5 species estimated in Canada); Dermaptera (earwigs, 5 species estimated in Canada); Grylloptera (long-horned grasshoppers and crickets, 96 species estimated in Canada), which are often grouped in the next order; Orthoptera (short-horned grasshoppers, 140 species estimated in Canada); and Cheleutoptera (stick insects, 2 species estimated in Canada). Orthoptera are the most common worldwide. Notoptera is a very interesting group of secondarily wingless, predaceous insects living in the western mountains, often associated with ice and snow fields. Since they have a rather primitive morphology, they are regarded by some entomologists as living fossils.

The second cohort of the Neoptera, the Paraneoptera, usually have piercing and sucking mouthparts, a hindwing with a very small or no anal lobe, abdomen without cerci, 4 or fewer Malpighian tubules and an incomplete metamorphosis. Four orders can be recognized in the Canadian fauna: Psocoptera (bark and book lice, 103 species estimated in Canada), Phthiraptera (bird and mammal lice, 775 species estimated in Canada), Hemiptera (true bugs, 4226 species estimated in Canada) and Thysanoptera (thrips, 246 species estimated in Canada). Hemiptera are the most abundant worldwide.

The third cohort, the Oligoneoptera, characteristically have a complete metamorphosis, with distinct egg, larval, pupal and adult stages. Such a life cycle permits larvae and adults to diverge in form and habits. The generalized mouthparts are of the chewing type; however, the 10 orders represented in the Canadian fauna have very different ways of feeding. The commonest order worldwide, the beetles (Coleoptera, 9116 species estimated in Canada), are distinguished by chewing mouthparts and forewings modified as stiff, hard, protective elytra. Next most common are the true flies (Diptera, 14 464 species estimated in Canada), distinguished by having only one pair of wings, the forewings. The most familiar group is probably the Hymenoptera (bees, wasps and ants, 16 665 species estimated in Canada), with constricted waists allowing stinging movements. The remaining orders of Oligoneoptera are, in order of Canadian representatives: Lepidoptera, butterflies and moths, with 6734 species estimated in Canada; Trichoptera, caddisflies, 546 known; Siphonaptera, fleas, 190 estimated; Neuroptera, lacewings, etc, 87; Mecoptera, scorpionflies, 32; Megaloptera, dobsonflies and alderflies, 20; and Raphidioptera, snakeflies, 6. *See also* individual species entries. G.G.E. SCUDDER

Insect Pests Insects and humans cohabit the Earth and have developed complex relationships. Insect pests (less than 1% of all species) are those insects that feed on, compete for food with, or transmit diseases to humans and livestock. Many insects are forced to adapt to human-dominated ecosystems, and thus may become pests, or may become extinct.

Effects on Humans The human body provides food and shelter for the crab louse and 2 forms of human louse (head and pubic lice). Fleas and bedbugs obtain food from human bodies and inhabit human dwellings between blood meals. Out of doors, humans are attacked by blood-sucking flies (mosquitoes, black, horse and stable flies), which torment victims and may cause toxic or allergic reactions. In Canada, human dwellings, barns and other buildings are essential for the survival of insects from warmer climes (eg, cockroaches, clothes moths, carpet beetles, silverfish and some species of ants).

Many blood-sucking insects are vectors of human diseases, picking up the disease organism while feeding on an infected host (human or animal) and infecting subsequent victims. Human lice are important vectors of trench fever, relapsing fever and epidemic typhus; fleas can transmit plague bacilli from rodents to humans; and different species of mosquitoes transmit malaria and encephalitis. In these diseases, the insect is an essential part of the chain of development of the disease organism, but other diseases are transmitted mechanically. The house fly, which occurs almost worldwide, breeds on organic wastes and can carry disease organisms to food.

Attacks on Livestock Livestock are attacked by the same types of insects as humans. Each type of livestock is attacked by one or more species of lice, which causes lack of vigour and stunted growth. Blood-sucking flies (eg, the introduced stable fly, face fly and horn fly) feed on and pester cattle, reducing growth and milk production. In some areas, mosquitoes or black flies may be so abundant that they reduce cattle feeding and may cause stampedes. Native black flies can cause severe anemia and even death. Cattle raised in black-fly areas are somewhat resistant to attack, but animals brought in for herd improvement lack resistance and suffer severely or die.

In Canada, short growing seasons and cold winters restrict most insects to one generation annually. This reduces the number of pest species and the amount of injury they cause, in comparison with the impact of pest species in warmer parts of the world. Nevertheless, insects cause significant losses, and their control adds to the cost of many agricultural and FORESTRY products.

Cultivated Crops Intensive agriculture encourages the development of insect pests by concentrating food items (CROP plants and stored food) on which insects can feed. Food-plant concentrations, often in monoculture, also may reduce the effectiveness of natural enemies attacking pest species in natural environments. Insects may attack any part of the plant, at any stage of development. Seed grains and potatoes are attacked by wireworms; newly germinated seedlings of almost all crops are attacked by cutworms, while flea beetles are a major pest of newly germinated canola and other cruciferous crops; the growing plant is fed on by climbing cutworms, armyworms, aphids, Colorado potato beetles, etc; corn ears are fed on by corn borers and grain ears by several species of aphids. Several species of beetles and moths may infest stored grain, and other species of these groups feed on flour and processed foods.

Losses, caused by insect attack, and costs of control are difficult to determine and little information on this subject is available. Yield losses of up to 5% per year and maximum losses of 25% are estimated to occur on CEREAL grains in western Canada. The production of canola was estimated to have been reduced, in 1979, by 10% by flea beetles, despite expenditure of about $12 million for insecticides.

Transmission of Plant Diseases Sucking insects that transmit infections from diseased to healthy plants seriously affect several crop plants in Canada. Serious damage can be caused by very few infected insects. Aphids are the only vectors of barley yellow-dwarf virus of cereals, which drastically reduces grain yields. Leafhoppers transmit aster yellows, which affects not only asters but also lettuce, celery, carrots and potatoes. Aphids also transmit virus diseases of potatoes, a continuing threat to production in eastern Canada. In BC, cherries and peaches may be infested by the little cherry virus disease carried by leafhoppers.

Damage to Forest Trees and Wood Products Canadian forests are composed mainly of a few tree species, and these stands were normally subject to attack by insects, especially when they reached maturity. Insects (eg, spruce budworm, hemlock looper and various species of bark beetles) killed old trees to make way for regeneration. They now compete with man for forest resources. In Ontario, Québec and the Atlantic provinces, outbreaks of spruce budworm have occurred periodically for many centuries. Since 1950, PESTICIDES have been used to prevent tree death and to maintain sustained tree-harvesting programs. Unfortunately, spraying has prolonged the outbreaks so that some parts of these forests must be sprayed yearly. Bark beetles occupy a similar position in western forests, normally attacking overaged or weakened trees. They not only compete with man for wood but also are pests in parks, where overaged stands are maintained for aesthetic reasons.

The interior of lumber, poles and wooden portions of buildings may be hollowed out to form nests by black carpenter ants. In addition to serious structural damage, these large ants can be household pests, feeding on moist foodstuffs and

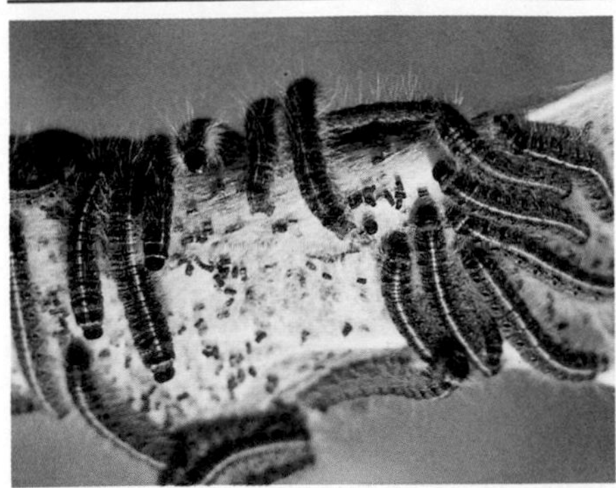

Pesticides have been used since 1950 against such tree pests as tent caterpillars (shown here) (*photo by Norman Lightfoot*).

sometimes damaging fabrics and paper products. Termites can cause serious structural damage to buildings. In Canada they occur only in southern BC and southern Ontario. *See also* individual species entries. W.J. TURNOCK

Reading: D.J. Borror et al, *An Introduction to the Study of Insects* (1981).

Insectivora, order of MAMMALS containing 7 living families: SHREWS (Soricidae), MOLES (Talpidae), hedgehogs (Erinaceidae), tenrecs (Tenrecidae), otter shrews (Potamogalidae), golden moles (Chrysochloridae) and solenodons (Solenodontidae). There are approximately 350 living species, widely distributed in Africa, Eurasia, N America and northern S America. The 22 species found in Canada belong to the Talpidae and Soricidae. Generally, insectivores are small, ranging in size from 2 g (Etruscan shrew, *Suncus etruscus*, the world's smallest mammal) to about 1.5 kg (moon rat, *Echinosorex gymnurus*). Insectivores demonstrate primitive characteristics, although some (eg, moles) show adaptations to highly specialized ways of life. They are plantigrade (ie, walk on sole and heel) and have 5 clawed toes on each foot. The nose tends to be pointed and tubular; eyes and ears are generally small. The tail may be long or greatly reduced. The skull is primitive in form, with a low brain case and a small cranial cavity containing a brain with smooth cerebral hemispheres. The teeth are adapted for crushing or cutting. Although insectivores primarily eat insects, some species are omnivorous. Many, perhaps all, other orders of placental mammals evolved from the early insectivores. The order has been traced back to the Cretaceous (144-66.4 million years ago) in Asia and N America. Ancestors of shrews can be traced back to the Oligocene (36.6-23.7 million years ago) in Europe and N America; those of the males to the late Eocene (about 40 million years ago) in Europe.
C.G. VAN ZYLL DE JONG

Reading: C.G. van Zyll de Jong, *Handbook of Canadian Mammals I, Marsupials and Insectivores* (1983).

Insolences du Frère Untel, Les (1960), by Jean-Paul DESBIENS (published anonymously), is an eloquent plea for educational reform couched in a whimsical, occasionally irreverent but always incisive style. Anticipating the formation of Québec's Ministry of Education in 1964, the essays attack the cultural and linguistic poverty which the author, a teaching friar, attributed in part to the inadequacies of an antiquated and repressive parochial education. Reproducing controversial letters between André LAURENDEAU, Desbiens and others which had been published in the newspaper *Le* DEVOIR, the introductory essay analyses the prevalent, exclusive use of JOUAL by secondary-school students as reflecting an insular, anti-intellectual form of discourse. Desbiens presented his arguments in a nationalist text which became one of the classics of the QUIET REVOLUTION. Often reprinted, it was translated by Miriam Chapin as *The Impertinences of Brother Anonymous* (1962). MICHÈLE LACOMBE

Institut Armand-Frappier In 1938 the Institut de microbiologie et d'hygiène de Montréal was established as an autonomous, nonprofit organization. In 1972 it was integrated into U du Québec and, in 1975, became the Institut Armand-Frappier (IAF), after its founding director Armand FRAPPIER. Four complementary objectives make IAF unique in Québec and Canada: research in microbiology and related sciences, with applications for preventive MEDICINE and industry and other nonmedical aspects; graduate and technical teaching; services to public-health authorities, hospitals, universities, industry and the community (including viral and immunological diagnosis, epidemiological investigations, vaccinations and consultation); and the manufacture of BIOLOGICAL PRODUCTS (vaccines, serums, etc), diagnostic products and biological reagents. This work is done in 6 centres specializing in bacteriology, epidemiology and preventive medicine, IMMUNOLOGY, comparative medicine, applied food sciences and virology. Practical, production-related activities include commercial production and quality control. IAF is located in Laval, employs 450 people, including 42 scientists, 47 professors and 90 technicians, and receives over 90 graduate students and other research trainees. Recent concerns include BIOTECHNOLOGY, particularly GENETIC ENGINEERING and modern fermentation techniques.

Institut canadien, fd 17 Dec 1844 in Montréal by a group of young French Canadian intellectuals who wished to establish a centre of patriotism and culture. The institut quickly became a political and cultural force in francophone society, and similar organizations were established in about 60 other centres. At first politically neutral, it fell under the spell of Louis-Joseph PAPINEAU and developed leftist leanings in harmony with *L'Avenir*, a newspaper fd July 1847, to which a number of members contributed articles. In 1854, 11 members were elected to Parliament. But their radical nature, which earned them the nickname "rouges" (*see* PARTI ROUGE), and their stand favouring annexation to the US caused the Liberal-Conservative Party and the clergy to join forces against them. In 1858 the opposition of the bishop of Montréal, Mgr Ignace BOURGET, led to the resignation of 138 members, to Rome's condemning the institut and placing its 1868 yearbook on the index of forbidden books, and to the GUIBORD AFFAIR. Conservative public opinion turned against the institut, beginning a decline virtually completed by 1885. The Institut canadien had sponsored the most liberal and innovative discussions of the period, and its library was a collection of major scientific, legal and literary works. An ultraconservative political, social and religious climate ruined the hopes raised by its foundation. PHILIPPE SYLVAIN

Institut québecois du cinéma (IQC) was created 19 June 1975 by the adoption of the Loi sur le cinéma to meet long-standing demands from Québec cinematic groups. Its mandate was to promote and support the creation, production, distribution and showing of high-quality films in Québec. The law also defined certain requirements in dubbing, subtitling, children's films and film research that were designed to strengthen the Québecois presence in the industry. The 7 members of the IQC represented all sectors of the industry and its clientele. In 1987 the government introduced a bill to modify the institute's role; thereafter, while it would still be composed of representatives from the world of film, it would have no mandate but to advise the government on cinematographic issues. The annual budget is around $4 million. The IQC has made possible many works which otherwise would not have been produced. PIERRE VÉRONNEAU

Insulin is a peptide protein hormone. It is secreted by the beta cells in the "internal" secretory portion as distinct from the "external" (digestive enzyme) secreting portions of the pancreas. It has a molecular weight of 5800 and is composed of 51 amino acids. The molecule is composed of an A and a B chain connected by 2 disulfide bridges. One milligram equals 24 international units. When synthetic insulin is released into the blood, the liver retains 20-60% of it. The liver is also the major site for insulin degradation. The synthesis and release of insulin is regulated by a moment-to-moment relationship between concentrations in body fluids of substances and receptors on beta cells such as glucose, amino acids and hormones; as well as the activities of the sympathetic nervous system. Among the former substances, glucose is the principal stimulant and among the latter activities alpha-adrenergic action of epinephrine is the principal inhibitor.

Insulin is the most potent hormone of fuel storage, affecting carbohydrate, fat and protein throughout the body. Acting through binding to receptors on cell membranes, the principal targets of insulin are in liver, fat and muscle. Concentrations of glucose, free fatty acids and amino acids decrease in the circulation as a result of augmented insulin action, and fuels are thus stored. The breakdown of these fuels (catabolism) and the release of their breakdown products into the circulation are inhibited and tissue growth is facilitated by augmented insulin action.

During exercise, when there is need for fuel mobilization for the requirements of contracting muscles, there is co-ordinated inhibition of insulin release in association with the release of counter-regulatory hormones such as epinephrine, glucagon, cortisol and growth hormone. Insulin has been made available for treatment of DIABETES MELLITUS by extraction from beef and pork pancreatic islets since the discoveries of F.G. BANTING, C.H. BEST, J.B. COLLIP and J.J.R. MACLEOD in 1921-22. Recently, through GENETIC ENGINEERING, biosynthetic human insulin has become available. G.D. MOLNAR

Insurance can be defined as an agreement under which some or all economic losses are transferred to an insurer who, for a premium, promises to compensate the insured for the losses resulting from specified risks (*see* INJURY AND PREVENTION) during the term of the agreement.

The modern world is full of hazards. While the perils – accident, fire, sickness or death – may result in financial losses, it is the hazards that create the potential for losses. "Risk," a term used to reflect the likelihood of a loss, is faced continually by individuals, organizations and society as a whole. The need for safety and security is deeply entrenched in human nature, and most people fear the threat of loss posed by risk. It is therefore not surprising that attempts to cope with risk have been developed since early in man's history.

The idea of pooling risks originated in ancient civilizations. Chinese merchants divided their cargo among several ships during dangerous trips in China's waterways. Through such pooling, no single merchant would suffer a total loss as a result of a shipping disaster. Various forms of risk sharing were practised in ancient Greece and Rome and by the trading nations of the Middle Ages. The concept of transferring the economic consequences of risk, ie, the purchasing of insurance protection, is an important constituent of risk management.

Although a number of parish and municipal fire-insurance companies operated in the mid-1830s in Lower and Upper Canada, the first Canadian life-insurance company was founded in 1847 in Hamilton, Ont. The formation of major insurance companies (Mutual Life, Sun Life, Confederation Life and London Life) in the 1870s was prompted by the passing of the first Canadian insurance law in 1868. With industrialization and the introduction of new technologies, the insurance industry developed rapidly.

Underlying Principle of Insurance Insurance involves an agreement between the insured, who pays a premium, and the insurer, who promises to reimburse the insured for financial losses incurred from specified risks. For an insurer to enter such an agreement with an individual or an organization, a large enough number of agreements covering similar risk characteristics are required. By combining many risk exposures, it is possible to predict the collective losses quite accurately. The underlying principle is the law of large numbers which – in the context of insurance – states that with an increasing number of risk exposures the actual losses approach their expected value quite closely. The expected collective loss is then shared proportionally by all the insured in the form of premiums. With insurance, individuals or organizations exchange the risk of uncertain but potential losses.

Operation of Insurance An insurance agreement is a contract between the insurer and the insured defining the risk to be covered, specifying the conditions under which the contract applies, and outlining the procedure for settlement. Insurers are either privately owned corporations or government-operated agencies. Most private insurers are stock and mutual companies. Stock companies are profit oriented and owned by shareholders; mutual companies are owned by the insurer, and any excess of income over claim settlements and expenses is returned to the insured in the form of dividends or reduced premiums. An association of individuals can also act as insurers. In such an arrangement the individual insurers characteristically assume the risks personally and are therefore liable for loss settlement with their personal assets. The best known of such associations is Lloyd's of London, which operates worldwide and insures large risks that other insurers may have rejected.

Government-operated agencies also provide protection, typically mandatory, against certain risks. Such programs are termed social insurance (*see* SOCIAL SECURITY) and include WORKERS' COMPENSATION plans, automobile insurance in certain jurisdictions, and some pension plans. Such programs do not necessarily operate on the implicit assumption that sufficient funds are accumulated in advance for the payment of losses; payments are made from general tax revenues.

Supervision and Regulation The insurance industry is regulated for a number of reasons, eg, because premiums are paid in advance and benefits may be paid in the (far distant) future to the insured or to others with little or no power to protect their interests; to protect consumers from unfair practices; and because unreasonably low or high premiums can lead to insolvency or to unwarranted profits. In addition to self-regulation through industry associations, the responsibility for supervision of insurance in Canada is shared by the federal and provincial governments. The federal Department of Insurance is responsible for the registration and licensing of federally registered companies and is concerned with their ability to meet obligations to policyholders. This is accomplished by requiring insurance companies to submit financial statements to establish that they have sufficient financial resources (through solvency tests) and by restricting the investment of the funds of insurance companies. The provincial superintendents of insurance prescribe statutory contract conditions, regulate the licensing of agents, brokers and adjusters, and regulate (in several provinces) the rates for automobile insurance. Nevertheless, insurance companies can and do go bankrupt (although this is quite rare), leaving the insured – particularly after a loss – in a difficult position, because little if any compensation for their losses can be expected.

Insurance "Products" A large variety of different forms of insurance protection are available, eg, life insurance, which provides financial resources to support the survivors of the insured or to pay for the obligations (credit insurance) in case of the death of the breadwinner. While term life insurance protects against the risk of (premature) death during a specified term, whole life insurance pays the face value of the policy whenever the insured dies. Under an endowment life contract the face value of the policy is payable upon death or at maturity of the policy; thus it carries the added function of capital accumulation. Disability insurance, which protects the insured against the loss of income due to disability, is similar to life insurance.

The other major category of insurance protection in this area is health insurance. Sickness or accidents may lead not only to considerable loss of income but also to substantial medical expenses. Life-insurance companies therefore offer health insurance (as do other types of insurance companies). Health insurance offered by government-operated agencies is now mandatory in Canada (*see* HEALTH POLICY).

Another major form of insurance is the protection against liability claims resulting from wrongdoings by individuals or organizations. The legal basis for liability exposures are TORTS and contracts (*see* CONTRACT LAW). While liability claims from contracts arise from violation of contract obligations, tort claims arise from wrongdoings occurred by intentional interference (eg, trespass, defamation) or by negligence. If a wrongful act leads to losses to others, the wrongdoer is liable for the financial consequences. To meet these obligations to others (third parties), liability insurance in our litigious society has become essential. Under a liability coverage, payment of damage or losses only arises if the insured is legally liable. Liability insurance is offered to individuals to cover losses arising from bodily injury or property damage or both; it is offered to businesses (eg, product liability) and more recently to professionals (eg, to protect medical doctors from MALPRACTICE claims).

Automobile insurance is probably the most widely held insurance coverage. Auto insurance policies providing protection against liability claims are typically mandatory and a prerequisite for licensing a vehicle. Both fault and no-fault automobile insurance plans exist. In no-fault plans there is no determination of blame, in the courts, for an automobile accident before payments for bodily harm and perhaps property damages are made by insurance companies. The elimination of fault must be approved by provincial legislation. Saskatchewan introduced the world's first no-fault system of automobile insurance in 1946; Québec introduced a similar plan in 1978. Policies providing protection against physical damage to the automobile from collision and other risks such as theft, storm and fire are voluntary.

Fire insurance indemnifies the insured in the event of damage or destruction of property by fire. Over the years standard forms of fire policies have been developed. Fire insurance is typically part of the homeowner's policy, which includes, in addition, protection against break-ins, theft, water damage and personal liability. In fact the homeowner policy is a so-called "multi-line" contract which provides convenience and cost advantages to the insured.

Many other forms of property insurance exist, including marine and aviation insurance, hail, windstorm and earthquake insurance, insurance against fraudulent computer use, and even insurance against a rained-out vacation. Ransom and kidnapping as well as skyjacking insurance can now be purchased.

Future Issues Insurers attempt to reduce costs of premiums by mass marketing; group insurance is part of this development. A major concern is the increase in fraud, arson and crime and its implications for insurance. Another important trend is the increasing internationalization of economies, which has sparked further need for insurance of export credit risk. Not only has the insurance volume increased worldwide – domestic and foreign insurers compete in the same market – but the need for reinsurance (ie, the assumption of part of the risk insured by one insurance company, by a second insurance company, to reduce the risk) has also grown. International aspects of insurance significantly affect the national BALANCE OF PAYMENTS (ie, the export and import accounting).

The question of HUMAN RIGHTS may also affect future trends in the insurance industry. The principle of insurance (ie, that insurance companies come together to share their risks in a class or group) is in many respects opposed to the principle of human rights (ie, that no individual should be assigned or characterized by the characteristics of a group). Various segments of the Canadian population, eg, women and the handicapped, have expressed their concern over what they believe are discriminatory insurance rates.

From a regulatory point of view, it is necessary to guarantee that the insurance industry is viable and financially solvent, and that insurance is available to so-called substandard risks. Continued supervision, the possibility of establishing a scheme that protects the insured in case of BANKRUPTCY, and the creation of "pools" may contribute to these goals. With the increasing potential for catastrophic losses (eg, supertankers) and the shifting relationships in the socioeconomic system, the insurance business faces considerable challenges in the future.

C. HAEHLING VON LANZENAUER

Reading: D. Bickelhaupt, *General Insurance* (1979); R. Mehr and E. Cammack, *Principles of Insurance* (1976).

Intellectual History is a record of the thought of groups and individuals who may or may not be academics or "intellectuals." The study of intellectual history often includes the treatment of sensibilities, emotions and ideological or cultural preoccupations as well as systematic thought, and touches on the concerns of historians in areas such as SCIENCE, POLITICS, EDUCATION, ECONOMICS, PHILOSOPHY, RELIGION, LITERATURE and JOURNALISM.

French Canada

Intellectual history in Québec, somewhat unfocused before 1760, became more distinctive after the CONQUEST. Its development was marked by the establishment of printing (1764) and was strongly affected by local political events (establishment of a house of assembly) and international ones (American Revolution, 1775-83, and French Revolution, 1789). Intellectual debate focused on civic or political issues; the press – *The Quebec Mercury* (1805), Québec's *Le Canadien* (1806), Montréal's *La Minerve* (1826) – was the most important medium of expression of the new liberalism. After about 1820 schooling led to increasingly polarized ideological stands, with a rising bourgeoisie in the liberal professions pitted against a still somewhat disorganized Roman Catholic Church preoccupied by its educational responsibility. At the time of the Lower Canada REBELLIONS OF 1837, a time of economic crises and parliamentary impasses, anglophone cultural institutions were particularly active.

During the Union period (1841-67) the gazettes were intellectually lively, and cultural institutions were increasingly polarized between an ultramontane Catholic Church consolidating its position and a bourgeoisie weakened by the rebellion. The long search for a "national" literature began in the 1840s, and gained momentum with the publication of HISTOIRE DU CANADA (1845-48) by François-Xavier GARNEAU. New papers kept appearing. There was a proliferation of voluntary associations, such as the liberal INSTITUT CANADIEN, where members could read local and foreign newspapers, borrow library books or take part in rhetoric-laden discussions. The generation of 1845 had access to a much larger network of schools under the new Surintendant de l'instruction publique (1841), to classical colleges and to UNIVERSITÉ LAVAL (fd 1852).

The entire 19th century was marked by the ideology of a church inclined toward Rome, supporting the priority of church over state, justifying thereby its intervention in intellectual, academic and social domains. Post-1870 liberal thinkers failed to implant the values of the bourgeois revolutions: respect for the freedoms of conscience, opinion, speech and association, and the idea of the separation of church and state. Wilfrid LAURIER was the first (in 1877) to attempt a courageous public distinction between political liberalism – that of the Liberal Party – and Catholic liberalism, condemned by a church closely linked with the Conservative Party.

After 1867 political life and especially partisan politics dominated. The public torpor was shaken by the 1885 hanging of Louis RIEL, the defeat of French minorities on the school question in Manitoba, New Brunswick, Keewatin and Ontario, and the sharp awareness that the French language – and "race" – were threatened, even in Québec. Henri BOURASSA clashed with Laurier over IMPERIALISM and NATIONALISM. Bourassa became the rallying point for a new nonpartisan political awareness. With Olivar Asselin, founder of *Le Nationaliste* (1904), and Jules Fournier, Bourassa founded *Le* DEVOIR (1910), the first exception to the rule of a partisan and "servile" press. A new linguistic awareness set the tone for the establishment (1902) of the Société du parler français, the first Congrès de la langue française (1912) and the creation of the Ligue des droits du français (1913). A new religious awareness among young people led to CATHOLIC ACTION, realized in the nationalist Association catholique de la jeunesse canadienne-française (1903-04).

The great intellectual movement 1917-28 was ACTION FRANÇAISE, which, according to its guiding light, Abbé Lionel GROULX, was to synthesize the scattered ideas of nationalist thinkers. This "intellectual action" was also the uneasy response to transformations in Québec society caused by urbanization, industrialization, Americanization and conscription. These social phenomena had preoccupied *Action française* and concerned workers' unions and then legislators before the church finally put together a Catholic SOCIAL DOCTRINE. The church's hesitant involvement in social issues is the key to intellectual history after the Great Depression. It brought the church closer to working-class circles and provided training for young lay people to learn the elements of political action. But until the mid-1930s, all these "actions" – Catholic, intellectual, social or national – were ideologically continuous with the 19th century, when the church had dominated the educational and social fields.

Evidence of a growing state role in cultural life was the new dynamism of the provincial secretariat, where Athanase David directed, 1919-36, an "intellectual action." In this context discussions took place about the existence of a unique French Canadian literature. Modern social patterns received little examination but nevertheless were felt in a life-style whose pace was set by movies, automobiles and new household technologies. Modernism was already present in painting in 1928, the year painter Paul-Émile BORDUAS left to study in France.

The Depression deeply disturbed the generation then coming of age, whose search for a program of social, economic and spiritual recovery was taken up by the new ACTION LIBÉRALE NATIONALE (1934) and in movements and journals (JEUNE-CANADA, L'ACTION NATIONALE, *La* RELÈVE). This generation was the last to believe in "the primacy of the spiritual." The social situation finally undermined the ULTRAMONTANISM of a church increasingly mocked by the Depression. All who participated from the early 1940s in the lay action movements – Catholic, student, worker or rural – lived through the near paralysis of spiritual values as those values were overwhelmed by temporal and material life. The "social" church cracked during the ASBESTOS STRIKE (1949) and finally broke at the end of the 1950s. The shock of the Depression also served to root the university in reality as its faculties of applied sciences multiplied and the social sciences started to develop.

The Depression also created an uneasiness about the future, which led intellectuals toward a new subjectivity expressed by the poets, eg, Hector de Saint-Denys GARNEAU and Alain GRANDBOIS, at the time of the war. In painting, the move from figurative to abstract around the end of the 1930s, eg, by Borduas and Alfred PELLAN, was as radical an intellectual break as the social challenge of the REFUS GLOBAL manifesto published in Aug 1948.

The intellectual and cultural landscape of Québec at the start of the 1950s was radically altered by postwar prosperity and consumption, movies, radio, the automobile, and the arrival of television in Sept 1952 – the later QUIET REVOLUTION would reveal a monument already virtually in place. The first writings seriously examining the intellectual history of Québec had appeared at the end of WWII. In 1945, amid works by Benjamin Sulte, Claude de Bonnault, Robert de Roquebrune, Séraphin Marion and Auguste Viatte, Marcel Trudel published *L'Influence de Voltaire au Canada*. The writers of intellectual history began to focus on precise topics: the cultural significance of the Conquest (Claude Galarneau); the reverberations of the French Revolution in Québec and the state of subsequent cultural relations with France (Mason Wade, Michel Brunet, Gustave Lanctot and, after 1960, Jean-Pierre Wallot, John Hare and Philippe Sylvain); the start of a printing industry and the beginning of NEWSPAPERS (Wade, Brunet and Lanctot); and, in the 1970s and 1980s, liberalism and ultramontanism (Sylvain, Pierre Savard, Jean-Paul Bernard, Nadia Eid, Yvan Lamonde and Marcel Lajeunesse). A passion to defend the liberals of 1837 and thereafter coincided with the beginnings of the Quiet Revolution, that great "collective undertaking" that was to inspire new research into ideologies; this trend, publicized in *Recherches sociographiques*, first peaked in 1969 with a special issue, "Idéologies au Canada français 1850-1900." Other publications about the ideologies of the 19th and 20th centuries followed. This research, based on accounts of major figures, groups and movements, soon revealed its limitation: a privileged position for the written word. Intellectual history thus found itself challenged to include those who had no voice. In the 1980s Québec's intellectual history was at this point in the debate: Is there a satisfactory intellectual or cultural history which is not first of all a SOCIAL HISTORY?

YVAN LAMONDE

English Canada

Much of Anglo-Canadian thought in the first century after the Conquest in 1760 attempted to preserve British and Christian values in a colonial environment, or to establish some acceptable middle ground between a European heritage and an American geographical circumstance. Some of the first such exercises were in the form of humorous social satires (*see* HUMOROUS WRITING), such as Thomas MCCULLOCH'S "Letters of Mephibosheth Stepsure" (1821-23) and Thomas Chandler HALIBURTON'S *The* CLOCKMAKER (1836). McCulloch helped initiate a tradition of moralistic social criticism present in English-Canadian intellectual history since 1820.

McCulloch was a Presbyterian minister and, as founder of Pictou Academy and first principal of DALHOUSIE UNIVERSITY, a major Canadian educator. Elsewhere in English Canada, serious intellectual effort also arose at the pulpit and the lectern. Between 1850 and 1900 many intellectuals were preoccupied with the apparent conflict between science and religion, especially with regard to the implications of evolutionary theory (*see* EVOLUTION; SOCIAL DARWINISM) and HIGHER CRITICISM. Clerics and professors sought to defend social and religious orthodoxy against an increasingly materialistic science by upholding the premises and conclusions of the Scottish "common sense" school of philosophy, the antispeculative Baconian method in science and an evangelical pietism in religion.

From 1870 to WWI there appeared accommodation to the philosophy of evolution, most noticeably through a Hegelian idealism professed by philosophers such as George Paxton YOUNG and John WATSON. This idealism dominated academic thought and writing in English Canada into the 20th century, for it appeared to reconcile religious and scientific claims by subsuming the latter within the former. The ROYAL SOCIETY OF CANADA facilitated the development of a national academic community. New publishing ventures, most notably the *Canadian Monthly and National Review* (1872), *The Week* (1888), QUEEN'S QUARTERLY (1893) and *University Magazine* (1907), provided creative outlets for social critics, including William Dawson LESUEUR, Goldwin SMITH, Agnes Maule Machar and Andrew MACPHAIL. While differing in emphasis and audience, these magazines reflected a consensus of values marked by a broadly conservative social philosophy set within an acceptance (sometimes an uneasy one) of the workings of a capitalist market economy.

These years also saw the emergence of a preoccupation by English Canadians with the nature and implications of nationalism. By the turn of the century this took the form of an intense debate between those such as George PARKIN and G.M. GRANT who placed Canadian nationalism within the context of the British Empire, and those such as Goldwin Smith and John S. EWART who insisted that nationalism was hollow unless it pointed towards constitutional autonomy and away from colonial status. For the half century following WWI, English Canadian thought was thus beset with competing forms of nationalism, one based on sentiment and the other on rationalism. In this respect, historians Harold INNIS and Donald

CREIGHTON may be seen as intellectual heirs of Parkin and Grant, just as F.H. UNDERHILL and Ramsay COOK follow Smith and Ewart.

The emergence of the professional writing of history was testimony to the increasing importance of the university in shaping the direction of English Canadian thought (*see* HISTORIOGRAPHY). By the 1920s, U of T had begun to dominate academic affairs, particularly in the humanities and social sciences; McGill U maintained its high status in medical and scientific research; and Queen's U established a tradition – largely inspired by the example of Adam SHORTT and O.D. SKELTON, but derived from the idealist heritage – of commitment by intellectuals to public service in government agencies. This latter trend was paralleled in religious affairs by the Protestant SOCIAL GOSPEL movement, which held an organic view of society, a belief in the immanence of God and a desire to achieve the Kingdom of God on Earth. One result was a further erosion of traditional denominational commitment and the creation in 1925 of the UNITED CHURCH OF CANADA, which committed itself to Christian engagement in the activities of secular social agencies. Implicit in the Social Gospel was a criticism of Canadian society, a criticism that took the form of a Christian socialism typified in the careers of J.S. WOODSWORTH and Salem BLAND.

Between the wars, research in the emerging social sciences, particularly political economy and history, became more empirical – if not materialistic – in causal inference. Writing in the humanities tended to bear witness to the continued importance of idealism. But some intellectuals became actively engaged in public social issues, particularly during the Great Depression of the 1930s. By the mid 1930s the LEAGUE FOR SOCIAL RECONSTRUCTION, consisting largely of progressive university academics such as Eugene FORSEY and F.R. SCOTT, had in the collectively written *Social Planning for Canada* formulated a major critique of Canadian society and public affairs. Such social concern, together with the considerable intellectual effort that undergirded the federal Royal Commission on DOMINION-PROVINCIAL RELATIONS (reported 1940), pointed toward a major redirection of social assumption and constitutional arrangement after 1945.

Directions in English Canadian intellectual life after WWII were largely derived from a recognition of the American domination of world affairs. The Royal Commission on NATIONAL DEVELOPMENT IN THE ARTS, LETTERS AND SCIENCES (the "Massey Commission," reported 1951) warned of the threat to Canadian cultural life by American-dominated mass media. Throughout the 1950s, as a result, a vigorous cultural nationalism was given forceful expression by a number of social commentators, especially Hilda NEATBY, historian and member of the Massey Commission, who in *So Little for the Mind* (1953) criticized the Canadian educational system for accepting the American values implicit in the "progressive education" movement. The creation of the CANADA COUNCIL in 1957 reflected this enlarged concern for the future of Canadian cultural traditions. But by 1957 nationalist thought was beginning to shift from cultural to economic matters. Walter GORDON'S Royal Commission on CANADA'S ECONOMIC PROSPECTS (reported 1957) was a strong statement of the need for ECONOMIC NATIONALISM. Throughout the 1960s a lively and productive debate took place on the merits of national industrial policy and on the problems – political, sociological and philosophical – inherent in a technology of mass communications dominated by the US. Was it possible to maintain real autonomy in the era of the "universal and homogeneous State"? This question was posed in different forms by philosopher and critic George P. GRANT, most forcefully in LAMENT FOR A NATION (1965). Economic, political and historical writing during these years by Mel Watkins, Abraham Rotstein, Donald CREIGHTON, W.L. MORTON, Ramsay Cook and others provided abundant fuel for animated debate both in the academic community and before the public.

The intellectual efflorescence of the 1960s, coupled with a vast expansion of the country's university system, bore much fruit in the 1970s. The work of Marshall MCLUHAN, himself inspired by Harold Innis, helped assure that Canadians would pay attention to the theory and technology of communication; that of Northrop FRYE nourished a self-confident generation of novelists, poets and critics whose work fused intellect and imagination. The greater division of labour afforded by larger university faculties vastly increased the quality and quantity of scholarly "production." With this specialization, however, also came a more tentative approach to large-scale generalization in all academic fields. In history, for example, the older theme of "nation-building" as fundamental to the thematic ordering of scholarship broke down in the face of intensive research based on newly discovered regional, thematic and ideological "realities."

Canadian scholarship has entered an age of analysis rather than synthesis. Still concerned with questions of nationalism, English Canadians also seek to establish degrees of limitation in social identity and to articulate the cultural differences imposed on the nation by region and ethnicity. This more cautious approach to reflections on national life holds true in the realms of the intellect, the imagination and public affairs.

A.B. McKILLOP

Reading: L. Armour and E. Trott, *The Faces of Reason* (1981); C. Berger, *The Sense of Power* (1970) and *The Writing of Canadian History* (2nd ed, 1986); R. Cook, *The Maple Leaf Forever* (1977) and *The Regenerators* (1985); A.B. McKillop, *A Disciplined Intelligence* (1979) and *Contours of Canadian Thought* (1987); S.E.D. Shortt, *The Search for an Ideal* (1976); S.M. Trofimenkoff, *The Dream of Nation* (1983).

Intelligence and Espionage are controversial areas of government activity, generally shrouded in secrecy, and often the subject of considerable public fascination and sometimes misapprehension. Canada is often thought of as a country innocent of such activities, or of devoting little in the way of government resources to them. Yet Canada has evolved an intelligence community, with a relatively dramatic, if recent, history which belies this picture of inactivity.

Intelligence is information gathered to enhance the security of the state. It divides naturally into 2 kinds of material and activities: foreign intelligence, designed to enable the state to conduct effective diplomatic, military and economic activities in the international arena; and domestic intelligence, utilized by the state to monitor perceived threats to order within its territory and to counter the activities of foreign intelligence services. Espionage is a special kind of intelligence activity, which denotes the work of secret organizations whose task is to gather information by covert means. Espionage, thus, usually represents only a small part of the overall system of intelligence and this has been especially true in the Canadian case. Canada has never developed a secret intelligence service on the model of the British MI6, the American CIA or the Soviet KGB. The country's geopolitical position, alliance membership, and relative power have never required such an espionage organization. While Canada has no secret service, it does possess an intelligence community whose origins can be traced to the mid-19th century.

The first organized intelligence work to take place in Canada was a characteristic blend of both foreign and domestic espionage. In the early 1860s, the Canadian government became alarmed about the FENIAN threat and created a frontier intelligence service to monitor the activities of this exiled Irish group who sought to mount an invasion from bases in the US. On the occasions of the Fenian raids of 1866 and 1870 (both unsuccessful), Canadian secret agents were able to provide the government with considerable advance warning of the Fenians' plans. Herein the government enjoyed its first taste of the uses of organized intelligence for national security purposes.

A second notable, if embryonic, development of the mid-19th century was the decision to establish Guide units in the newly formed Canadian militia, to provide scouting and intelligence skills. Such units saw some action in the Riel Rebellion in western Canada and, in a volunteer contingent, in the SOUTH AFRICAN WAR at the end of the century. But their intelligence-gathering skills were rarely tested and they were generally employed as mounted infantry.

Despite these innovations, Canada enjoyed no genuine intelligence system when WWI broke out in 1914. The war proceeded to give an impetus to the development of areas of intelligence expertise, particularly tactical military intelligence skills developed by Canadian forces fighting on the Western front, and domestic counter-intelligence. The latter was stimulated above all by the fear of an intensive German campaign of sabotage mounted against the country, and particularly against its chief economic achievement, the national railways. The German military attaché in Washington, Capt Franz von Papen (later to serve as Cabinet minister and ambassador during the Hitler regime) did devote his energies to planning sabotage in Canada, but all to no avail. The plotting fizzled out in 1916, after a bungled bomb attack on a Canadian railway bridge near the Maine border.

The Canadian government responded by pressing the DOMINION POLICE, the Royal North-West Mounted Police, military intelligence and even private detective agencies such as Pinkerton's, into action against potential saboteurs. After 1917, and the successful Bolshevik revolution in Russia, attention turned to the threat posed by radical political movements in Canada.

Towards war's end, in Sept 1918, a fledgling Canadian intelligence system survived inevitable pressures for demobilization and a return to peacetime practices. Within the army, a skeletal military intelligence directorate kept in touch with world events through its access to a regular flow of information from London. The newly created ROYAL CANADIAN MOUNTED POLICE (RCMP) turned some of its attention to monitoring domestic political radicalism. The achievement of continuity, linking the activities of WWI with the post-1918 era, provided the framework for future growth in the Canadian intelligence system. But it would take the massive demands placed upon the military and society in WWII before a more fully fledged intelligence community would emerge.

In essence, Canadian intelligence resources in 1939, upon the outbreak of WWII, were little changed from those available to the country in 1914. It was the totally unexpected defeat of France in 1940 that, more than anything else, set change in motion. Canada found itself, in the summer of 1940, thrust into a prominent position as Britain's principal surviving ally. Military and industrial mobilization created a potentially massive internal security problem, owing to the need to create a secure home front and fears of foreign "fifth column" activity. Concern about the prospect of a British collapse prompted a move to create an independent Canadian foreign intelligence capability. Fears of Vichy French or German espionage activities in Canada, and of the extension of the "secret war" across the Atlantic prompted greater attention to domestic intelligence work.

These responses were sustained by the exploitation of new forms of intelligence, once the Grand Alliance of Great Britain, the Soviet Union and the US took shape in 1941 and Canada settled into a role as a junior wartime ally. It was in the forefront of intelligence work, in signals intelligence, that Canada found opportunities to develop an independent capability that was at the same time a useful contribution to the wider intelligence alliance that had been created among the Allies. During the crucial Battle of the ATLANTIC, a submarine tracking room in Ottawa provided naval signals intelligence to convoys in the western Atlantic, warning of threatening U-BOAT activity. A small and highly secret code-breaking establishment, known as the "Examination Unit," was set up in 1941 and enjoyed considerable success in intercepting and decrypting German agent traffic and Vichy French and Japanese diplomatic radio messages.

Canada was also drawn into the secret resistance war, providing personnel and resources to the British organizations created by Winston Churchill to "set Europe ablaze" – the Special Operations Executive (SOE). Canadian volunteers served with distinction in SOE, particularly on missions to aid the resistance in occupied France. A special camp, known as CAMP X, was established near Oshawa, Ont, to provide basic training to SOE recruits. Camp X also housed a top-secret communications centre, known as "Hydra," for the transmission of sensitive material across the Atlantic.

Individual Canadians made their own contributions to intelligence, outside the sphere of the Canadian intelligence community. The most famous of these persons is undoubtedly Sir William STEPHENSON ("Intrepid") who was chosen by Churchill to head the British secret service at New York during the war.

On the home front, the RCMP and military intelligence combined their resources to provide internal security during the war, concentrating their attention on Axis espionage and subversion. The RCMP had good success in infiltrating the few pro-Nazi groups that grew up in Canada, and also managed to capture at least 3 German agents sent to Canada (2 arrived by submarine in the Maritimes).

At the war's end the authorities in Ottawa were convinced of the utility of a Canadian intelligence effort and were determined to carry on the work in peacetime. Canada looked to sustain its membership in a special intelligence relationship with the United States and Great Britain after the war. This desire was substantiated by Canadian adherence to the provisions (still undisclosed) of the 1947 UKUSA Pact, which allocated signals intelligence tasks and exchanges between Britain, the Commonwealth countries and the United States. The Examination Unit's work was continued after 1945 to provide Canadian material for this common intelligence pool. The unit itself was renamed after the war; it is now called the Communication Security Establishment, based near Ottawa, and is operated under the aegis of the Department of National Defence.

Canadian military intelligence authorities also made plans to sustain their work into the postwar years and to create a peacetime foreign intelligence system. Their plans, however, were upset by the impact of the GOUZENKO Affair, perhaps the most startling instance of espionage to occur on Canadian soil. On 5 Sept 1945, a cipher clerk in the Soviet embassy in Ottawa defected (not without some difficulty) to the Canadian authorities. He revealed to the RCMP that a number of Soviet espionage rings were operating in the country and had penetrated into some highly sensitive positions, including the Department of External Affairs' cipher room, the British High Commissioner's Office and the atomic research facilities at Chalk River. These revelations caught the RCMP unawares, as they had devoted little attention to Soviet activities in Canada during the war. The government hurriedly attempted to patch the holes in its internal security by augmenting the role of the RCMP in counterintelligence, and by creating a powerful Security Panel to serve as a watchdog over standards of security and loyalty in government service.

The Gouzenko Affair and the entry of Canada into the UKUSA signals intelligence alliance were the 2 key events of the immediate period after the Second World War. They established the pattern for much that was to follow. Since 1945, Canadian activity in the foreign intelligence sphere has centered on the country's membership in the NATO and NORAD alliance systems. Canadian signals of intelligence, including material derived from the Arctic radar chain, continue to play a large role in the context of these defence alliances, from which Canada gains access to a wider pool of strategic intelligence.

The Gouzenko Affair alerted the government and public to the realities of international espionage and prompted the growth of a counterintelligence service within the RCMP. Since 1945, Canada has continued to be targeted for espionage by a variety of foreign powers, largely because of Canadian proximity to the US and Canada's role as a Western alliance partner. The final report of the McDonald Commission (*see* INQUIRY INTO CERTAIN ACTIVITIES OF THE RCMP), issued in 1981, indicated that there have been 20 cases of persons charged with espionage offences under the Official Secrets Act and 42 diplomats had been expelled from the country for espionage-related activities since 1945.

The RCMP remained the principal authority in domestic intelligence work until July 1984, when the CANADIAN SECURITY INTELLIGENCE SERVICE (CSIS) came into existence to carry out the same mandate as did the RCMP Security Service, but as a separate, civilian service. The Security Service was disbanded largely in response to mounting criticism of its performance. When CSIS was similarly reprimanded in late 1987, a series of reforms were introduced to force it to shed its RCMP past, which had persisted because the bulk of its officers and procedures had been inherited from the Security Service.

One exotic concern that CSIS will undoubtedly inherit from the RCMP Security Service is the nightmare of the "mole," double agent or penetration agent, who gains access from within to the secrets of intelligence work. The Canadian record shows no Kim Philby, but at least one RCMP Security Service officer, James Morrison, code-named "Long Knife," has been convicted of espionage on behalf of the Soviet Union. Leslie James Bennett, a long time counterespionage officer, was forced to retire under a cloud of suspicion, never proven, that he was a Soviet agent. More recently, controversy has been revived over the case of a senior Canadian diplomat, E. Herbert NORMAN, who committed suicide in Apr 1957 while under investigation by the RCMP. Yet new problem areas are encroaching on domestic intelligence work: TERRORISM, the international drug trade, illegal immigration and technological and economic espionage, which may ultimately thrust such traditional counterespionage concerns as the fear of the mole deep into limbo.

The Canadian intelligence community, though small, has evolved over time into an established part of government. In the era of computer-age technology and fierce international competition and violence, it would appear likely that the community will continue to evolve and to play a role in the maintenance of national security.

WESLEY K. WARK

Intendant of NEW FRANCE, office created in 1663 when Louis XIV established a system of colonial government, including a GOUVERNEUR and SOVEREIGN COUNCIL. Second in rank to the governor, the intendant controlled the colony's entire civil administration. He gave particular attention to settlement and economic development, and to the administration of justice. Because he also managed financial matters, he had the most sweeping powers in the colony's government. Appointed by a royal commission and subject to recall at will, the intendant reported to the minister of marine (*see* MINISTÈRE DE LA MARINE). He ensured that the king's decisions were implemented, appealed to the minister over difficulties with new policies and presented a detailed annual report on the colony. He acted either by direct order or by decree of the Sovereign Council, which he chaired. Intendants were usually chosen from influential circles outside the nobility and were noted for the competence and care with which they performed their duties. New France's best-known intendants were Jean TALON, Gilles HOCQUART and François BIGOT.

JACQUES MATHIEU

Intercolonial Railway Construction of a railway linking the Maritime colonies and the Province of Canada was proposed as early as the 1840s. Surveys were carried out and deputations were sent to England to solicit financial support. A line was opened between Halifax and Truro, NS, in 1858 and from Saint John to Shediac, NB, in 1860. In 1865 Sandford FLEMING presented a report recommending a route along Chaleur Bay, through the Matapedia Valley and along the St Lawrence because it was far from the American border and passed through rich timber country. Completion of the railway was made a condition of CONFEDERATION, in 1867, and construction began shortly after. Fleming was appointed engineer in chief and was involved in many heated controversies with officials.

The first section between Truro and Amherst, NS, was opened on 9 Nov 1872, and that between Rivière-du-Loup and Ste-Flavie [Mont-Joli], Qué, in Aug 1874. The link between Campbellton and Moncton, NB, was completed 1875 and the gap between Campbellton and Ste-Flavie was closed in 1876. Fleming declared the railway (some 1100 km long) ready for traffic on July 1 of that year. Construction of the railway did not require spectacular engineering feats, but presented numerous difficult challenges and was built to high standards. At Fleming's insistence, all but 3 of the BRIDGES were built of iron.

The Intercolonial acquired the GRAND TRUNK RAILWAY line from Rivière-du-Loup to Point Lévis, Qué, in 1879 and 10 years later gained running rights into Montréal from the GTR. It added the Cape Breton Railway in 1891, providing ferry service across the Strait of Canso. Built to fulfil the terms of Confederation, the Intercolonial was never a commercial success. Nevertheless, it provided employment, developed towns and villages along its route, and was a customer for Maritime coal. Up to 1918 it was administered by the Dominion government under the minister of railways and canals. Freight rates were kept low in order to promote trade, and deficits were met by the government. In 1919 the Intercolonial became part of the CANADIAN NATIONAL RAILWAYS.

JAMES MARSH

Interest is the price paid by a borrower for the temporary use of someone else's money or, conversely, the price charged by a lender for the temporary use, by someone else, of his money. In ancient and medieval times, the difference between a moderate interest payment and a high rate of interest based on the desperation of the borrower was not clearly understood. All interest was called "usury," a term reserved now for exorbitantly high interest rates.

Interest is stated as a rate, ie, a percentage of the amount borrowed (principal) to be paid for an agreed period of time (usually a year) that the money is on loan. It has often been estimated that the basic rate of interest, the simple payment to the lender for waiting, is about 3% annually, but other factors add to this rate. First, there is a risk that the borrower cannot or will not repay the money. The risk of lending to the federal government is not large (although even countries, or "sovereign" borrowers as they are sometimes called, have defaulted on loans), but it rises somewhat on loans to provinces and even more on those to large companies.

On loans to individuals, risk is often reduced by a mortgage on property or collateral, ie, something valuable, such as a bond deposited with the lender as security. The lender can then seize something valuable belonging to the borrower if the loan is not repaid. Unsecured consumer loans carry a high risk (*see* CONSUMER LAW), and therefore have high interest rates. Second, risk increases the longer the money is loaned. The borrower's ability to repay money may not change much in a month or a year, but over 10 or 20 years it may change radically, as may the need of the lender for the use of his own money.

Third, INFLATION affects the buying power of the money when it is repaid to the lender. On a $100 loan at 5% interest, the lender will lose money if inflation runs at 10%, because the $105 paid in principal and interest at the end of a year will buy only what about $95 would have bought when the loan was made. The inflation that must be taken into account, however, is not the inflation rate at the time the loan is made or over the year; it is the future rate, which can only be guessed by lender and borrower. If inflation is generally expected to drop, short-term loans may cost more in interest than long-term loans, because the greater risk of default on the longer-term loan is more than balanced by the hope of lower inflation.

In the 1970s and 1980s, economists found that uncertainty also affected interest rates. "Real" interest rates, that is, the stated rate minus the expected inflation rate (usually 3%), had risen to 7%, because in a time of economic instability, lenders had attempted to protect themselves from uncertainty.

There is always a range of interest rates, depending on the borrower and the risk of the loan. For example, in 1987, when the federal government was paying 9.5% to buyers of its bonds, large corporations were paying 9.75% as the "prime-rate" for bank loans (the prime rate is the interest charged by banks to their best-secured corporate customers); companies were paying around 10% on money borrowed by issuing bonds for longer periods than the shorter-term prime-rate loans; mortgage loans were costing as much as 13%. Interest rates on credit-card loans ranged from 15.9% to as high as 28.8%. This whole range of rates moves up and down, more or less together, as changes occur in the general level of interest rates (which in Canada is determined by the MONETARY POLICY of the BANK OF CANADA, by the demand for loans, by interest rates in the US and by inflation rates).

The Bank of Canada fixes the BANK RATE, ie, the amount it charges for the relatively infrequent loans it makes to the commercial banks. More importantly, the bank rate signals the direction in which the Bank of Canada wants interest rates to move. In the 1970s the bank rate was fixed for months at a certain percentage rate and then changed by a Bank of Canada announcement, but in March 1980 the Bank of Canada shifted to a system under which the bank rate was changed each week in step with changes in the rate paid by the federal government to borrow money for 90 days by selling treasury bills.

Under this system the Bank of Canada could affect the bank rate directly by bidding at the auction held each Thursday when treasury bills are sold, mostly to the commercial banks. With the bank rate set at 0.25 of a percentage point above the average interest rate on 90-day treasury bills, the Bank of Canada could raise the rate by bidding up the treasury bill rate. Small changes in the bank rate may be ignored by other lenders, but when the bank rate rises significantly in a short period, the commercial banks raise their prime rates and other interest charges follow.

In 1975 the Bank of Canada began trying to cut inflation by raising interest rates. This move was based on the theory that with high interest rates, consumers are unwilling to borrow for goods such as houses and cars, and businesses are unwilling to invest; thus a rise in interest rates cuts down the demand for goods and services, which reduces the upward pressure on prices. This policy (use of interest rates to cut inflation) culminated in 1981 when the bank rate rose above 21% and the prime lending rate was 22.75%.

Canadian rates might not have reached such levels had it not been for the rise in rates in the US where a similar monetarist policy was in effect (*see* MONETARISM). When American rates rise and Canadian rates do not follow, money tends to flow to the US as lenders seek the higher return on their loans. This outflow pushes the value of the Canadian dollar down in terms of American funds. Imported goods then cost more in Canadian dollars, and this tends to raise the inflation rate in Canada. One way to break the close connection between Canadian and American interest rates is to control the flow of money in and out of Canada, as was done during the Second World War by a system of exchange controls.

The general level of interest rates is also affected by the demand for borrowed money, which tends to rise and fall with the economy. In times of RECESSION, businesses and consumers are less interested in borrowing, and this tends to reduce the general level of rates. But with economic recovery, businesses want to expand and consumers want to buy on credit, and this increases the demand for loans and pushes interest rates up. If the interest rates rise so high that consumers and business executives are discouraged, another recession will ensue. This swing of interest rates, from low in recession to high in recovery, is one reason for the pattern of ups and downs in the economy, a pattern no economic theory or policy has so far succeeded in fully explaining or controlling. *See also* BANKING; ECONOMICS; ECONOMY. D. McGILLIVRAY

Intergovernmental Finance In a federal state, to ensure that regional and cultural differences are respected while national interests and policies are pursued, responsibilities and corresponding powers are divided between 2 levels of government, each of which is autonomous within its own designated sphere of responsibility (*see* DISTRIBUTION OF POWERS). The CONSTITUTION ACT, 1867, assigns to the federal government responsibilities for the regulation of trade and commerce, the postal service, money and banking, the criminal law and the PEACE, ORDER AND GOOD GOVERNMENT of Canada in relation to all matters not assigned exclusively to the provinces.

The national government was authorized to legislate for the raising of money by any system of taxation, or "the borrowing of money on the public credit," but each province was assigned exclusive authority to legislate concerning management and sale of public lands and timber; prisons, hospitals and charitable institutions; municipal institutions; and local works and undertakings other than those involving transportation facilities extending beyond the limit of the province or those declared by Parliament to be "for the General Advantage of Canada or for the Advantage of Two or more of the Provinces."

Provincial legislatures were also assigned responsibility for property and civil rights in the province, and for all local or private matters. They were assigned the power to raise revenues through direct taxation both within the province and through the administration of the public lands. Agriculture and immigration fall concurrently under both federal and provincial jurisdictions, but provincial legislatures were assigned exclusive jurisdiction over education subject to provisions regarding rights of minority groups, in which area the federal government has the authority to pass remedial legislation. Local or municipal governments are generally responsible for fire and police protection, health and safety inspection, local works and land use, sanitation, etc. While many of these services are financed directly from property taxes or by transfers from the provincial or (to a much lesser extent) federal government, municipalities, as creatures of provincial governments, derive their responsibilities and taxing powers from provincial legislation.

It has been said that until 1937, in its judicial interpretation of the Constitution Act, 1867, the JUDICIAL COMMITTEE OF THE PRIVY COUNCIL narrowly interpreted the residuary powers of the federal government associated with peace, order and good government and broadly interpreted the property and civil-rights clause, but recent and explicit constitutional amendments may have extended the reach of federal powers. As circumstances change, however, the revenue sources or taxing powers assigned to different levels of government may become inadequate, in which case 4 solutions are possible. First, taxing powers (tax room) can be transferred by legislation. Second, transfer payments to other governments can be authorized as direct expenditures. Third, a particular responsibility may effectively be assumed by another level of government. Finally, through regulation, expenditure obligations (or compliance costs) can be transferred to agents outside government.

Revenue Sources In a federal system, the powers to raise revenues must somehow be matched to the expenditure responsibilities of each level of government and must also somehow be coordinated, because the same taxpayers support both. The Constitution Act, 1867, assigned customs duties, excise taxes and all indirect levies exclusively to the national government. The relatively unimportant (at that time) direct taxes on local inhabitants were assigned to provincial governments, whose responsibilities were not expected to grow, and small statutory subsidies were established for anticipated shortfalls in provincial revenues. The century of economic expansion and national development after Confederation, however, dramatically altered this calculated balance. The provinces, searching for new revenues, claimed increased subsidies and introduced a widening array of licences and taxes, succession duties and, for the first time, income taxes. Federal income tax, purportedly temporary, was introduced to finance WWI. Industrialization and urbanization led to rapid increases in provincial expenditure responsibilities during the subsequent 15 years, until the GREAT DEPRESSION brought several provincial and municipal governments to the brink of bankruptcy and the nation to an unco-ordinated mesh of conflicting and overlapping direct TAXATION measures characterized as a "tax jungle."

By 1939 direct income taxes were a critical source of government revenue and until 1962, under tax rental agreements made at the time, the federal government collected personal and corporate income taxes on its own behalf and on behalf of all the provinces, returning an agreed portion of these revenues to provincial governments, although Québec had opted out in 1947 to establish its own corporate and personal income-tax collection system and Ontario its own corporate income-tax collection (both provinces continued to adhere voluntarily to the federal government's definitions of taxable income). In 1962, the tax-rental agreements were replaced by a tax-collection agreement, according to which the federal government collected income taxes levied by provincial governments under their own provincial legislation, and returned to the province the taxes collected in that province. After 10 years of bitter debate over the appropriate sharing of the available tax room and then over federal proposals for tax reform, in 1972 the agreements were changed again; provincial tax rates were defined as a percentage of basic federal tax and it was emphasized that provincial tax revenues resulted from provincial tax legislation and were not simply an agreed share of some total revenue pie. The principle of access or joint cultivation of tax fields implied in these arrangements reinforces the ability of provincial governments to raise additional revenues independently to finance their expenditure commitments. It is a transition from tax sharing to an attempt at co-ordinating simultaneous federal and provincial government exploitation of the common income tax base. Unfortunately, this co-ordination through tax-collection agreements is threatened by the opting-out of Québec, Ontario and now Alberta (since 1981) from the corporate tax-collection agreements, and threats by Ontario, Alberta and BC to join Québec in adopting their own personal income-tax collection systems if the federal government proves unwilling to administer a sufficiently rich variety of special provincial tax provisions. Both this issue and the acute intergovernmental struggle for shares of revenues derived from the exploitation of natural resources are extremely sensitive areas of intergovernmental finance.

Federal-Provincial Grants and Programs Instead of transferring taxing powers or tax room, governments also transfer to each other direct annual payments (or cash transfers). Several different types of transfer exist, the most important distinction being between unconditional, or general purpose grants, and conditional, or specific purpose, grants. Unconditional grants require no particular commitment by the recipient government, but conditional grants must be spent for a specific purpose, for programs complying with conditions decided by the donor government. Examples include incentive grants (to stimulate expenditure by the recipient government on particular activities), matching or shared-cost programs, and closed- or open-ended grant schemes (the former being those in which payments will be made to designated limits, the latter involving a payment share of a specific fraction of approved expenditures for a designated purpose, without reference to the size of the expenditures). The most important category is the shared-cost program, an open-ended matching grant in which the donor is committed to meet an agreed fraction of approved program costs, in contrast to both block-funding arrangements in which, despite general conditions, the amounts transferred are determined by a formula independent of actual expenditures and to deficiency payments designed to make up an estimated shortfall of revenues below expenditure commitments. Unconditional payments reflect the federal government's responsibility enshrined in the Constitution Act, 1982, "to ensure that provincial governments have sufficient revenues to provide reasonably comparable levels of public services at reasonably comparable levels of taxation" (*see* EQUALIZATION PAYMENTS). This responsibility was implicit in the Constitution Act, 1867, in the provision requiring the Dominion government to make unconditional per capita payments to each of the federating provinces to enable them to meet their expenditure obligations with the revenue sources assigned to them. These statutory subsidies are now trivial as compared to the equalization program itself, however. Estimated at $5.9 billion for the 1987-88 fiscal year, these payments represent over one-quarter of a total $21.5 billion federal-provincial cash transfers for that year, and from as much as 25% of total revenues for some provincial governments.

A variety of other federal-provincial transfers designed to encourage provincial expenditures in particular areas, eg, health, education and social services, which are generally thought to fall within exclusive provincial jurisdiction, are controversial. The transfers include first, cash contributions (about $9.2 billion for 1987-88) under the Federal-Provincial Fiscal Arrangements and Federal Post-Secondary Education and Health Contributions Act of 1977, determined on the basis of block funding, to support provincial programs in hospital and medical insurance, extended health care and post-secondary education. The post-secondary education component is unconditional; the health-care component is broadly conditional upon compliance with conditions legislated in the Canada Health Act of 1984, but not directly related to provincial expenditures. The second type of transfer is cost-shared programs or matching grants, eg, Canada Assistance Plan (CAP), in which the size of the federal transfer for provincially administered social services and social assistance (about $4.7 billion for 1987-88) is directly determined by provincial expenditures on eligible services. Third are special purpose grants, or grants-in-aid, eg, those for economic development or bilingualism in education. Fourth are direct federal payments, eg, those under the Canada Manpower Training Plan, for services rendered by provincially funded agencies.

Under the Established Programs Financing arrangements, (1977, amended 1982) hospital insurance, medical insurance, and post-secondary education were no longer funded under 3 separate cost-sharing arrangements, reflecting the view that these arrangements infringed too severely upon provincial discretion in setting priorities and provided inadequate incentive for control of costs. However, in 1982 the programs were again separated, reflecting both a concern that program objectives, including a national interest in universal access to an adequate level of services, were adversely affected by provincial efforts at expenditure restraint and the federal government's desire to reduce its own expenditure growth and to correct what it viewed as a critical imbalance in fiscal powers between it and the provincial governments. At one extreme in the controversy over conditional grants is the argument for complete federal control over the uses of federal revenues disbursed in the national interest even when the expenditures impinge on provincial jurisdictions; at the other extreme is the argument for complete discretion on the provincial governments' part in deciding the allocation of funds for programs for which they are responsible.

Shared-cost programs may distort provincial priorities, reduce the degree of control over costs and create forecasting problems for the federal government. Block-funding arrangements reduce the federal government's accountability for and influence on the allocation of resources to programs, while increasing the federal control over the level of payments. Of the choices, reassigning revenue sources until all provinces have sufficient revenues to meet their expenditure obligations, accepting continuing transfers of federal revenues to provincial governments to finance provincially administered programs, or transferring to the federal government responsibilities earlier assumed by provincial governments, neither the first nor the third are generally acceptable and an uneasy balance exists between the desires of the federal government to extend its control and of the provincial governments to increase their discretionary powers. Conditional grants are an attempt to reconcile powers assigned to the provinces in 1867 with the reality that the exercise of these powers is no longer of only local or particular interest.

Intergovernmental Economic Issues Tax transfers and cash transfers form only one part of an apparatus of government which also includes regulatory powers, direct services and a maze of production activities. The issue of power over the economy affects fiscal FEDERALISM first because the distribution of taxing and spending powers influences the ability of the federal government in particular to maintain appropriate levels of aggregate economic activity. Although recent studies conclude that the requirements of federal FISCAL POLICY need not preclude further transfer of tax points by the federal government, in recent years the budgets of provincial governments have sometimes run counter to federal STABILIZATION efforts, reducing the leverage of the federal government to influence the budget of the government sector as a whole. Economic federalism also affects interprovincial flows of goods, services and productive resources. When competition among provinces for productive activities intensifies, tax concessions – incentives to locate economic activity in one province rather than another – are commonly introduced. Such outright regulation can reduce the effectiveness or even threaten the existence of a Canadian common market. Federal-provincial tax-collection agreements to ensure tax harmonization thus become essential to the preservation of a strong economic union. The structure of intergovernmental financial flows also influences organization, eg, the extent of decentralized decision making. Measured by relative shares of total government revenue, or by relative expenditure after intergovernmental transfers, decentralization in Canada would appear to have diminished sharply from the late 1920s to the late 1940s and to have increased strongly from the late 1940s to the late 1970s, although after the mid-1970s the Liberal government declared as its objective the reversal of this trend and the establishment of greater national control of fiscal and economic matters. Balance between regions, or the degree of regional influence in national matters, is also affected by the devolution of authority to regional agencies of the federal government and by regional representation in national institutions.

In neither respect, however, can it be argued that decentralization has been significant in recent years. Finally, intergovernmental finance will undoubtedly be affected by constitutional developments concerning the ownership, management and taxation of offshore resources; provision for the taxation of state enterprises, mobility rights and the flow of people or materials across provincial boundaries; and regional representation in national economic and financial institutions.

A.R. DOBELL

Interior Design is a process for solving the physical and aesthetic needs of people using interior spaces for living, working, personal care, worship or recreation. The interior designer deals with a variety of design problems in private residences, commercial businesses and corporations, and public and private institutions. The designer must identify and analyse the client's problems, creatively develop the best solution and supervise the installation of the project. The design solution will include such elements as furnishings, lighting, colour, interior architectural components, decorative accessories and art. These elements will be organized for the client according to function, architecture, climate and individual needs and preferences. Interior designers must be competent in design theory and aesthetics, history, analysis, space planning and programming, specifications and inspections, as well as related aspects of environmental design. Technical knowledge should include interior construction; building systems and related codes; equipment; business, graphic and written-communication skills.

Interior decoration as a career began in the US late in the 19th century, receiving its initial impetus from Candace Wheeler, who published an article in 1890 entitled "Interior Decoration as a Profession for Women." Until 1950 the decorator was principally concerned with the selection and arrangement of interior furnishings for the affluent. After WWII the rapid expansion of industry, the extensive development in commercial and domestic building, and the increasing desire for better living and working conditions greatly stimulated the demand for qualified interior designers. Canadians who have distinguished themselves in the field since 1950 include Jacques Guillon in Montréal, Alison Hymas, Robert Meiklejohn and Murray Oliver in Toronto, Grant Marshall and Margaret Rose Stinson in Winnipeg, Arthur P. Fishman in Calgary and Robert Ledingham in Vancouver. Others work under company or team identification, or as in-house designers for corporations or government agencies.

In Canada there are a number of interior-design programs. Community colleges offer 2-year certificates and 3-year diploma courses in almost every province W of the Maritimes. There are only 2 degree-granting 4-year programs in Canada, at the U of Manitoba and at Ryerson Polytechnical Institute in Toronto. Interior Designers of Canada (IDC) in Ottawa, and provincial organizations of interior designers provide assistance in educational planning. The Foundation for Interior Designers Education Research (FIDER), the accrediting body for interior-design programs in N America, publishes a directory of undergraduate and graduate interior-design programs, available through its New York office. The Interior Design Educators Council (IDEC) is a joint American and Canadian association. The future of interior design will be affected by technological advances as well as by an increasing emphasis on professionalism. Designers must be prepared to accept greater responsibility and accountability for the environments they shape.

GEORGE R. FULLER

International Boundary Commission, comprising a Canadian and an American commissioner, is responsible for the maintenance and supervision of the boundary line between the US and Canada under the terms of the 1925 Boundary Demarcation Treaty. The Canadian section is empowered by the International Boundary Commission Act; it is administered by the Department of Energy, Mines and Resources but reports to the secretary of state for external affairs. The commissioners meet at least once a year, alternating between Ottawa and Washington. *See also* TERRITORIAL EVOLUTION.

International Council for Canadian Studies (ICCS) is a nonprofit organization with registered charity status. Its members are national or multinational associations devoted to the advancement of Canadian Studies around the world, each of which is composed of scholars and other persons involved in teaching, research and publishing about Canada. Established to promote co-operation and communication between Canadian Studies organizations, the council publishes a biannual *Newsletter* and holds a biennial conference in Canada. One representative from each member association plus an elected president constitutes the executive committee which meets once a year.

The ICCS was formed during the LEARNED SOCIETIES annual meeting at Dalhousie U in June 1981. Founding members included the Canadian studies associations in Canada, Australia, New Zealand, Ireland, Italy, France, Japan, US, Britain and some German-speaking countries. Since 1981, the Nordic Association for Canadian Studies, as well as similar associations in China, the Netherlands, Israel and India have become members of ICCS. The council is responsible for the administration and the adjudication of the Northern Telecom International Canadian Studies Award and the Northern Telecom Five Continents Award in Canadian Studies. The ICCS has a permanent secretariat located in Ottawa.

ALAN F.J. ARTIBISE

Reading: *International Directory to Canadian Studies* (1986).

International Development Research Centre, established as a public corporation by Parliament in 1970 to support research designed to adapt science and technology to the specific needs of developing countries. The first chairman was Lester B. PEARSON. Headquartered in Ottawa, it has regional offices around the world. Seven program divisions fund projects – agriculture, food and nutrition sciences; information sciences; health sciences; communications; social sciences; fellowships and awards; co-operative programs (the only division supporting co-operative research projects between Canadian and Third World institutions). Funded by the federal government, IDRC reports annually to Parliament through the minister for external affairs.

GREGORY WIRICK

International Economics is the branch of ECONOMICS concerned with international trade and investment. It includes the role of international economic institutions, the world monetary system, capital flows, commodity agreements and the international co-ordination of economic policy. Canada could undoubtedly survive in complete isolation from the rest of the world, producing sufficient food and other necessities to provide at least a subsistence level of income, but certain metals (eg, tin) would not be available and certain fruits and vegetables (eg, oranges and bananas) could only be produced at great cost. The main cost of such isolation, however, would be the loss of access to foreign markets for goods that can be produced more efficiently abroad and the loss of markets for Canadian products.

Just as it is to the advantage of individuals to specialize in specific tasks, so it is to the advantage of nations to specialize in producing specific commodities. Different countries may enjoy comparative advantages because they possess plentiful resources, highly developed technological skills or the economies of large-scale production. Canada benefits from importing commodities from countries that are most efficient at producing them and from paying for these imports with exports in which Canada has a production advantage. Canada, for example, has enough arable land to produce more food than Canadians could consume, while in many Asian countries, because of high population-to-land ratios and low wages, labour-intensive products (eg, clothing) can be produced at relatively low cost.

International markets, through which these products are exchanged, do not operate on a barter system but through a complex international financial structure (*see* INTERNATIONAL TRADE). Before WWI, most international transactions used the GOLD STANDARD, but this system was abandoned when it proved unfeasible, partly because it imposed severe restraints on domestic policymakers. In recent history the American dollar has served as the principal international medium of exchange and other currencies are usually quoted in $US. For Canada the $US is of particular importance because a large proportion of Canadian trade is with the US. Trade is facilitated through well-developed foreign-exchange markets where domestic currencies can be traded for one another.

The value of the Canadian dollar against the US dollar has traditionally been determined by market forces, that is, by the demand for and supply of Canadian dollars, which is in turn determined partly by relative rates of INFLATION, by the demand and supply of Canadian (and foreign) trade goods and by expectations of future economic circumstances and events. The $Cdn has, over the last few decades, ranged from over $1.05 US in the 1960s to about 75¢ US in 1987, reflecting, it is generally believed by economists, government policy rather than any deficiency in foreign-exchange markets.

Canada in the World Economy A variety of international organizations have developed to facilitate the complex interactions among nations. Among the most important are the World Bank and the GENERAL AGREEMENT ON TARIFFS AND TRADE (GATT). Canada belongs to both organizations. The World Bank was established to act as an international central bank to assist financial transactions among countries and to help developing countries obtain loans and credit. GATT was created to stabilize trading relations and provide uniform trading regulations for signatories; for example, the articles of GATT prohibit preferential treatment of individual countries so that a specific tariff rate available to one country must be made available to all. Exemptions for the formation of customs unions and free-trade areas have been granted and justified on the argument that they have advanced the cause of FREE TRADE.

Measures such as NATIONAL INCOME per capita vary widely among world nations. The World Bank publishes an annual *World Development Report* providing statistics on all countries of the world. Countries are categorized as low-income, middle-income, industrial-market and nonmarket-industrial; capital-surplus oil-exporting countries have recently been added as a fifth group. In 1986 the low-income countries (eg, Bangladesh, India and China) had an average per capita income of $260 (all figures are in $US 1986), with a range of $110 to $380. Middle-income countries, eg, Egypt, Cuba, Mexico, Israel and Indonesia have average per capita incomes of $1250, with a range of $450 to $7260. The 19 industrial market economies have an average per capita income of $11 430 and a range of $4440 (Spain) to $16 330 (Switzerland). Canada, with an average per capita income of $13 280, is fourth from the top of this group, just below Norway, the US and Switzerland and just above Sweden, Australia and Denmark. These comparative statistics, however, are very sensitive to currency values.

This subdivision of nations is somewhat arbitrary, but the relatively small group of industrial-market economies do share a number of characteristics apparently associated with high levels of development: high LITERACY rates, long life expectancies, well-developed capital markets, relatively stable governments and high industrial productivity. In all of them only a small percentage of the LABOUR FORCE is involved in agriculture (7% on average for industrial economies, 70% and 44% respectively for low- and middle-income countries) and a large percentage is involved in service sectors (58% of the labour force in the industrial countries compared to 15% and 34% for low- and middle-income countries). Among these countries the percentage of exports comprising primary commodities (including fuels and minerals) ranges from 78% (New Zealand) to 3% for Japan, with an average of 26%. The percentage in Canada, 45%, is well above that for industrial countries but well below the averages for low- and middle-income countries.

Canada participates in the world economy through trade and FOREIGN INVESTMENT. Both have been important in establishing Canada as a high-income industrialized nation, although the presence of foreign companies in Canada, despite the resulting benefits, has also inspired controversy. Canada also participates in the world economy through its banks, which invest in foreign countries (*see* BANKING). JAMES MELVIN

Reading: W.T. Easterbrook and M.H. Watkins, eds, *Approaches to Canadian Economic History* (1967); W. Ethier, *Modern International Economics* (1983).

International Hockey Hall of Fame and Museum, located in Kingston, Ont, was founded in 1943. The present building was constructed in 1961-62 and opened in 1965. Originally sanctioned by the NATIONAL HOCKEY LEAGUE and the Canadian Amateur Hockey Assn, the hall is now independently and community operated. It has inducted, with one exception (Fred J. "Bun" Cook) the same players, builders and referees as the HOCKEY HALL OF FAME in Toronto. It stresses the international and historical aspects of amateur and professional HOCKEY, and features an outstanding collection of early skates, sticks and memorabilia that trace ice hockey's evolution and rules. One room is dedicated to Capt James Thomas Sutherland (1870-1955), who devoted the last 13 years of his career to the establishment of the world's first recognized hockey hall of fame. J.W. FITSELL

International Joint Commission, the oldest of Canadian-American intergovernmental organizations, was established by the BOUNDARY WATERS TREATY of 1909 to deal mainly with the apportionment, conservation and development of water resources (including hydropower) along the international boundary. Since beginning its work in 1912 it has reported on over 50 issues affecting the US and Canada, has produced decisions on even more applications for diversion of waters, and has supervised dozens of decisions for Canadian-American joint boards and committees. The IJC has a wide range of investigative, quasi-judicial, administrative and arbitral functions. It can also act as a final court of arbitration on any issue between Canada and the US, but has never been used thus. The IJC comprises 3 Canadian and 3 American commissioners and maintains offices in Ottawa and Washington. It has limited staff and budget, yet enjoys a great deal of independence. It has been highly successful, and suggestions have often been made that the IJC model, especially its fact-finding techniques, be applied to other problem areas. *See also* JOINT COMMISSION. N.F. DREISZIGER

International Law is the body of rules that governs the conduct of STATES and other international associations, such as the UN, although in the human rights area international law, in some instances, may be directly applicable to individuals as well as to states. Modern international law has its origins in 16th- and 17th-century Europe. Created to regulate relations among a few states with common religious backgrounds and common commercial interests, international law has developed from a system that sought merely to secure peaceful co-existence within the international community to a system that seeks to protect the common interests and achieve the common aims of states. Today, Canada is one of at least 160 countries that consider themselves bound by the principles, customs and standards of international law.

The peace settlement following WWI led to the creation of the LEAGUE OF NATIONS, the first attempt by the international society to promote international co-operation and to achieve international peace and security. An important feature of the league was its use of unanimity of decision. The league was unable to prevent WWII but it provided a valuable precedent for an international organization after that war. The post-WWII period saw major developments in international law, including the establishment of the UNITED NATIONS, the successor to the league. Canada was a founding member of the UN. A number of former colonies that obtained independence after WWII joined the community of nations as full-fledged members. By 1939, when Canada declared war independently of Britain, it had already established a separate identity.

Today the scope of international law is very extensive, covering laws pertaining to war, recognition of governments and states, LAW OF THE SEA, AIR LAW AND SPACE LAW, international obligations, treaties (*see* TREATY-MAKING POWER), INTERNATIONAL ECONOMICS, international political and economic institutions, HUMAN RIGHTS and dispute resolution. Since the inclusion in the international community of nations at varying stages of economic development, issues related to economic justice have begun to play a significant role in international law.

The UN serves not only as a forum for discussion and deliberation of international issues among the nations of the world, but through its organs it is instrumental in multilateral PEACEKEEPING, in the progressive development of international law, in dispute resolution and in the promotion and fostering of common economic, political and social goals. Canada has been active in the support and development of international law and has played a leading role in the areas of peacekeeping, human rights, the law of the sea, and international economic law at the UN and other international forums.

Sources of International Law Canada's obligations, rights and responsibilities in international law may be found principally in treaties, in the conduct and practice of states, and to a lesser extent in general principles of law, in judicial decisions, in writings of highly respected scholars and in certain UN General Assembly resolutions. Treaties, which may be either bilateral or multilateral, are international agreements between states that are binding in international law. Treaties that reflect customary international law are binding even on nonsignatories of the treaty. For instance, Canada regarded itself bound by many of the provisions of the Vienna Convention on the Law of Treaties, even before it became a signatory to the convention. Treaties concluded by Canada are published in the Canada Treaty Series and are registered with the UN. There are about 200 treaties between Canada and the US alone.

Canada, as all other states, is also bound by customary rules of international law. Custom is evidenced by the general practice of states acting upon a recognition that the practice is legally binding. Canadian courts have accepted the view that customary international law forms part of the law of Canada. However, most custom that formed a source of international law is now incorporated in multilateral conventions. The 1961 Vienna Convention on Diplomatic Relations, for example, codified some rules of customary international law that were centuries old. Largely because of the heterogeneous nature of the community of nations, general principles of law recognized by nations, judicial decisions and writings of highly qualified publicists are treated as subsidiary sources of international law.

Some Current Issues in International Law Since the end of WWI the international community has been preoccupied with maintaining the peace. The UN Security Council, which consists of 5 permanent members and 10 rotating members, has the primary responsibility for maintaining international peace and security.

Under the UN Charter, all members of the UN agree to accept and carry out the council's decisions. When a dispute leads to fighting, the Security Council attempts to bring an end to the hostilities and has on some occasions sent UN peacekeeping forces to the site of the troubled area. Canadian troops have sometimes been part of ad hoc UN peacekeeping forces.

Since its creation, the UN has given priority to the international protection of human rights. In 1948 the Universal Declaration of Human Rights, which set forth basic rights and fundamental freedoms to which all people are entitled, was adopted by the UN membership without a dissenting vote. It has been suggested that the resulting influence of the declaration as well as repeated invocation of the declaration has made it a part of customary international law. A Canadian, Professor John HUMPHREY, served as the first director of the UN Human Rights Division. In 1976 Canada acceded to an important multilateral human rights treaty, the International Covenant on Civil and Political Rights and its accompanying Optional Protocol. By signing these documents, Canada has bound itself to an international standard of human rights protection and has opened the possibility for individual Canadians to submit to the UN Human Rights Committee complaints of human rights violations by the Canadian legal system.

One of the major post-WWII achievements of multilateral negotiations is the 1982 UN Convention of the Law of the Sea (UNCLOS). Canada's extensive coastline has given it a long-established interest in maritime issues and Canada played a leading role in UNCLOS negotiations. The convention, which was signed by Canada in 1982, sets out a comprehensive framework of laws to regulate the peaceful uses of the sea. Canada's main objectives during the UNCLOS negotiations were to a large extent satisfied by the provisions of the convention. Canada sought and obtained jurisdiction over fisheries within a 200-nautical-mile (370 km) limit of its coast and over all the resources of the Continental Shelf within and beyond the 200-mile limit. It obtained only limited powers to control POLLUTION along its coastline, but it ensured its ability to take antipollution measures in the Arctic. Canada also supported the innovative UNCLOS idea that the international seabed be reserved for peaceful purposes and that the area be designated the "common heritage of mankind."

The growing gap between rich and poor nations has led many of the latter to challenge the norms of international law and to charge that international institutions protect and maintain the economic interests of Western capitalist countries. In 1974 the majority of UN members voted in favour of the Declaration on the New International Economic Order, which called for a new set of rules to govern international economic relations. Canada abstained from voting on the declaration and its complement, the Charter of Economic Rights and Duties of States. In practice, however, Canada has pursued a policy of supporting the efforts of economically less developed countries to increase their share of world trade and foreign investment. One illustration of Canada's commitment to changing established patterns of trade is the General Preferential Tariffs legislation which grants preferential treatment to poorer countries.

Dispute Resolution The UN Charter clearly prohibits the use of force by states except in self-defence. Canada may settle a dispute with another state in any one of a number of ways: diplomatic negotiation, mediation, international arbitration or, as a final recourse, it may present its case to the 15-member International Court of Justice (ICJ), a UN organ. The ICJ may preside over disputes between states that agree to submit to its jurisdiction; a decision by the court is binding only upon those states that are party to the dispute in question. Canada and the US submitted their dispute over the maritime boundary in the Gulf of Maine area to a chamber of the ICJ. This was the first time a chamber was utilized instead of the full court. The decision came out in Oct 1984.

The responsibility for Canada's conduct in external relations is handled primarily by the Department of EXTERNAL AFFAIRS and its ministers. *See also* EXTERNAL RELATIONS. EMILY F. CARASCO

International Monetary Fund (IMF), is the principal independent international financial agency concerned with the management of the international monetary system. It was formed in 1944 by 45 nations participating in a Monetary and Financial Conference called to seek international co-operation in avoiding the protectionist trade practices and competitive EXCHANGE RATE devaluations of the GREAT DEPRESSION. The UK was represented by renowned economist John Maynard Keynes. Until the early 1970s, the IMF was remarkably successful in providing a framework for managing stability and adjustments in the world monetary system, and more recently it has devised mechanisms to support countries with serious short-term BALANCE OF PAYMENTS difficulties. Headquartered in Washington, with a voluntary membership of 151 countries, the IMF is governed by an executive board of 22 members, each representing a group of countries. Each member nation contributes to the fund's reserves in amounts commensurate with its role in the world's economy, excluding the Soviet bloc; eg, the US contributes 19.91%, Canada 3.27%. The IMF employs a professional secretariat, surveys economic policy in each member country, holds annual conferences of ministers in conjunction with World Bank meetings and maintains a research and publications program. T.K. SHOYAMA

International Polar Year, 1882-83, was the first worldwide co-ordinated scientific enterprise and the most significant single event in the founding of the science of geophysics. Between 1 Aug 1882 and 1 Sept 1883, 15 expeditions, sponsored by 11 nations, including Canada, went to the Arctic and Antarctic to carry out carefully planned and simultaneous observations in the earth sciences. Measurements of magnetism, aurora, meteorology, earth currents, ground temperatures, geodetic location, tidal behaviour, and atmospheric electricity were collected for subsequent analysis and added to the variety of other geological, oceanographic and natural science observations made during the year. By extending scientific fieldwork into the polar regions, the data from some 35 established observatories in Europe, Asia, and N and S America, were greatly enhanced and permitted the first attempts at comprehensive synoptic marine meteorology for the N and S Atlantic oceans. The planning and co-ordination of the observational fieldwork marked an entirely new approach to science as an international and co-operative activity. Both rigorous observations and the sharing of results strongly influenced the future concept of science in all disciplines. The Department of Indian Affairs and Northern Development created the Centenary Medal to mark the 100th anniversary of the International Polar Year, and to give recognition of Canada's part in this first international scientific endeavour. The medal together with a prize of $5000 is awarded annually to an individual who has made distinguished contributions to northern Canada through scientific activity.

International Trade is the purchase and sale of goods or services between residents of different countries. The traders may be individuals, private businesses or government agencies. Canadian exports of merchandise and services amount to about 30% of the nation's total production, the merchandise accounting for 25% while services and investment receipts are about 5%. Since 1960 (except 1975) Canada has exported more commodities than it has imported and has had a merchandise trade surplus. Services and our payments for borrowed capital have always greatly exceeded the export of services and receipts from investments, so that there has generally been a sizable deficit in combined trade in commodities and services.

Merchandise Trade The US, which purchases 78% of Canadian merchandise exports (and which supplies about 69% of all merchandise imports) is Canada's most important trading partner. Reliance upon the US as a market for Canadian products has been growing for 100 years. Until WWII the US and the UK frequently exchanged positions as the first and second most important destinations for Canadian exports. However, the UK now imports only 2% of all Canadian shipments, and only 3% of Canadian imports now come from the UK (over one-third of these imports consist of crude petroleum).

Japan has supplanted the UK as Canada's second most important trading partner, although it is not nearly as important as the US. Almost all imports from Japan are highly manufactured commodities, such as automobiles and electronic equipment, whereas exports to Japan are almost entirely raw materials, such as lumber, metals, coal and farm products.

The relative significance of Canada's trade with the European Economic Community countries (except the UK) has fallen since the mid-1960s, and now accounts for only 4.5% of exports. Imports from the EEC have risen and now are about 8% of total purchases abroad. Trade with other nations has been expanding slowly. The largest single import is crude oil from Venezuela and Mexico, but other goods such as automobiles, tropical products, labour-intensive goods (in which the developing countries have a comparative advantage) and highly manufactured goods come from developing countries, newly industrialized countries such as S Korea, and a few eastern European nations. Exports to other nations comprise about 11% of total Canadian sales abroad, including wheat, grains, agricultural products, lumber, newsprint, chemicals, metals, minerals, and various types of industrial, telecommunications and transportation machinery and equipment.

Composition of Canada's Merchandise Trade, 1986
(Source: Statistics Canada, *Summary of Canadian International Trade: December 1986)*

	Billions$			*Percentage*	
	Exports (1)	*Imports* (2)	*Balance* (1)-(2)=(3)	*Exports* (4)	*Imports* (5)
Agricultural products	8.78	6.89	1.90	7.5	6.1
Fishing and marine	2.39	.61	1.78	2.1	0.5
Forest products	17.55	1.97	15.58	15.1	1.7
Crude minerals (except energy products)	5.45	2.45	3.00	4.7	2.2
Energy products	11.29	5.14	6.10	9.7	4.5
Semiprocessed minerals	9.20	3.59	5.61	7.9	3.2
Automobiles and parts	34.23	33.92	.31	29.4	30.0
Other highly manufactured goods	27.27	56.60	-29.33	23.4	50.1
Special transactions (trade)	.32	1.77	-1.45	0.3	1.6
Total	116.48	112.98	3.50	100.0	100.0

Over 50% of Canadian exports are automobiles and other highly manufactured goods. Crude and semiprocessed materials from the farm, forest, mining and energy sectors make up the remainder. In contrast, about 80% of Canadian imports are automobiles and other highly manufactured products; 20% are crude and semifabricated goods. Consequently, Canada has a consistent surplus on commodity trade in raw and semiprocessed goods and a deficit on highly manufactured goods, a pattern throughout Canadian history. In its early development, Canada depended upon its natural resources for its export base, relying first on fish, furs and lumber, then on farm products, especially grains; pulp and paper; and various metals and minerals. Since WWII petroleum and natural gas, uranium, iron ore, sulphur, potash, coal, electricity and canola have augmented the nation's raw material exports.

Today, relatively few products dominate the export trade in each broad category. Wheat accounts for over one-third of all agricultural exports. Softwood lumber, wood pulp and newsprint comprise about 85% of forest-product foreign sales. Iron, copper, nickel and precious metal ores and concentrates, asbestos and sulphur total nearly 75% of crude mineral exports. Automobiles account for over 29% of total exports or over 55% of all highly manufactured commodities.

Highly manufactured goods are, in volume and value, among the most rapidly growing segment of Canada's exports. They are also among the fastest-growing imports in volume, but because the value of such imports greatly exceeds the value of exports, the absolute dollar gap between these sophisticated imports and exports is still

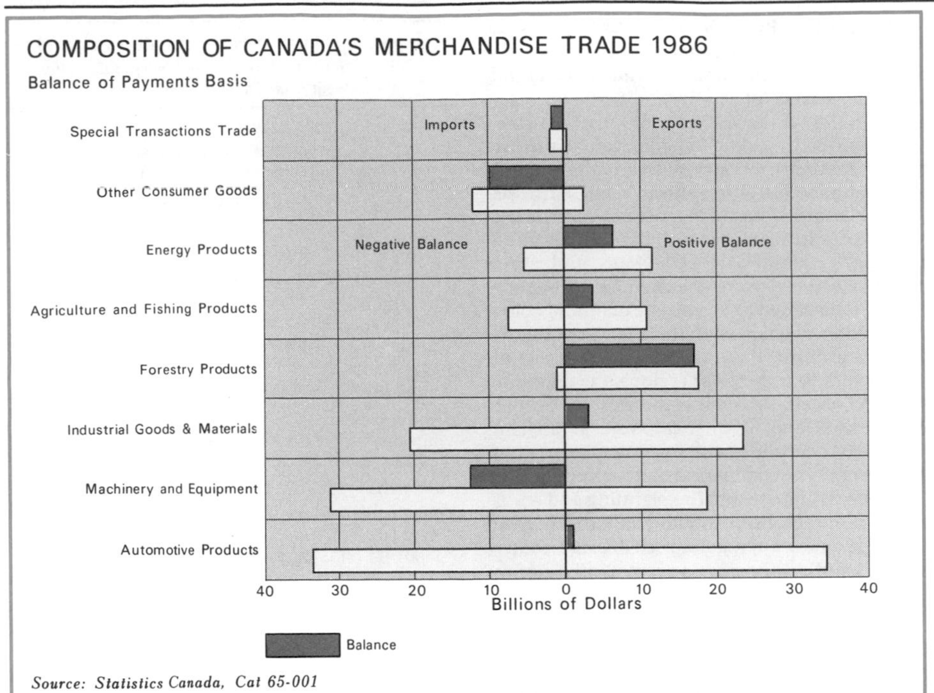

widening. Other rapidly growing imports of value are petroleum products, precious metals, apparel and apparel accessories.

Canada's particular mix of merchandise trade is attributed mainly to its generous endowments of both renewable and nonrenewable natural resources. They provide the foundation for comparative advantage in, and the massive shipments abroad of, crude and semiprocessed minerals as well as energy and agricultural and forestry products. Even highly processed exports from the chemical sector rely on natural gas and petroleum deposits. Some recent advances in exports of sophisticated manufactures may be related to increased production by firms under licence from foreign parents or holders of technology. In other instances, economies of scale have been achieved through domestic rationalization of industry, making domestic industries more competitive with those abroad. In still other cases new technological advances in Canada have been influential. However, Canadian research and development in the manufacturing sector has been meagre, and the adoption of foreign technology slow, leaving firms in Canada at a comparative disadvantage in technology-intensive products. Much reliance has been placed upon imports of these commodities; hence the large proportion of highly processed manufactures imported. This proportion is also related to the high percentage of FOREIGN INVESTMENT and control of Canadian industry, because foreign firms import a larger share of their purchases than domestic firms do. The importation of new US-manufactured products to satisfy Canadian demand patterns influenced by those in the US has also grown.

Organization of production and productivity of labour, which affect the long-run competitiveness of industry and Canada's comparative advantage, are also influenced by taxes, education, skill and aggressiveness of management, education and training of labour, and labour-management relations.

Canada's terms of trade, that is, the price of exports relative to the price of imports, have fallen about 8% during the 1980s because of the substantial declines in many raw material prices. The largest single decline – 3.7% – occurred in 1986 primarily as a result of the drop in world prices of grains and energy products. The 1986 terms of trade loss was responsible for an almost $4 billion reduction in Canada's trade balance.

Commercial Policy Trade is also affected by Canada's commercial policy, especially import tariffs (which are decreasingly important) and import quotas. The former are taxes or duties levied, usually as a percentage of declared value, on imported merchandise; the latter are specific quantitative restrictions on imports of particular commodities.

In the early years of Confederation, tariff revenues comprised about 75% of total federal government revenues. Today they make up less than 5%. The NATIONAL POLICY of 1879 increased tariffs, providing a sheltered market in which domestic and foreign firms could establish manufacturing plants. They have also been used to bargain down other nations' tariffs. When the GREAT DEPRESSION began, rates were again raised dramatically. The hope has always been to increase domestic processing; therefore the tariff structure has tended to be graduated – lower rates on raw material imports and higher rates for processed products. A British Preferential System was initiated (1897) in an attempt to encourage trade with Britain and other members of the Empire but it had little noticeable effect and is now phased out as it applies to the UK, Ireland and South Africa.

In 1986 Canada concluded the Caribbean agreement with the Commonwealth countries and territories of the Caribbean, thereby permitting tariff-free entry for all products from those lands with the exception of several product lines such as clothing, textiles, footwear and leather goods. Canada also is a party to the Generalized System of Preferences which gives either the British Preferential rate, one-third off the Most-Favoured Nation rate, or tariff-free access to products from virtually all developing nations in the world. For those developing countries considered as newly industrialized countries, Canada has, however, withdrawn the Generalized Preferential Tariff on a wide range of steel products.

Canadian tariffs are now at their lowest level,

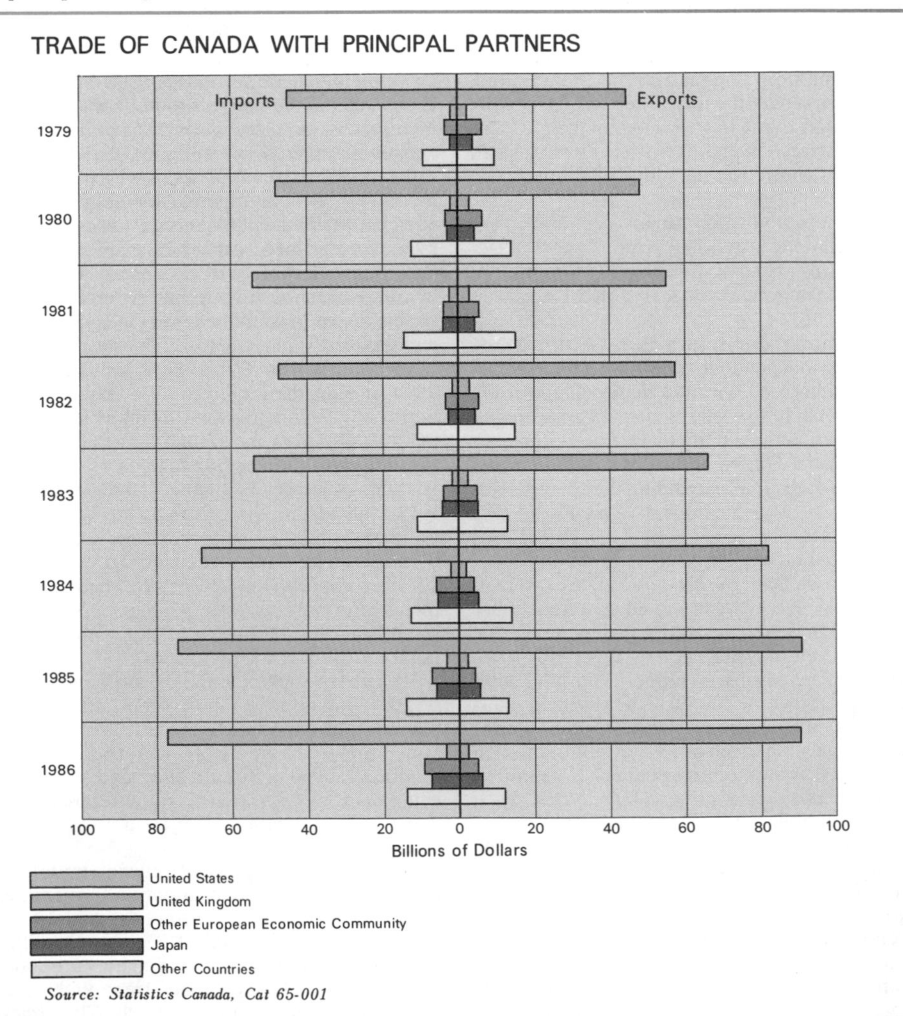

Canada's Trade in Services and Investment Income, 1986[1]

Services	Exports (Receipts) Billions$	%	Imports (Payments) Billions$	%	Balance Billions$
Travel and tourism	6.4	26.1	7.4	16.5	-1.0
Freight and shipping	4.6	18.8	4.3	9.6	.3
Business Services	5.5	22.0	7.7	17.2	-2.2
Government transactions	0.6	2.4	1.2	2.7	-0.6
Other Services	0.4	1.6	0.4	0.9	0.0
Subtotal	17.4	71.0	20.9	46.7	-3.5
Investment Income					
Interest	0.5	2.0	12.9	28.8	-12.4
Dividends	2.7	11.0	5.5	12.3	-1.6
Miscellaneous	3.9	15.9	5.5	12.3	-1.6
Subtotal	7.1	29.0	23.9	53.3	-16.8
Total Services and Investment Income	24.5	100.0	44.8	100.0	-20.3

Notes:
1.Excluding all transfer items such as inheritances and immigrant funds, personal and institutional remittances, Canadian as well as foreign withholding taxes, and official contributions by government.

amounting to about 4% on average for all imports and less than 12% on dutiable imports. Nondutiable imports account for over 65% of all purchases from abroad. Various bilateral and trilateral agreements before WWII and postwar multilateral negotiations under the General Agreement on Tariffs and Trade (GATT) have reduced the Great Depression tariff rates. The Tokyo Round of multilateral negotiations, completed in 1979, involved average reductions in tariffs of about 38% by Canada. These were completed over the years up to 1 Jan 1987. Post-Tokyo Round duties on dutiable imports are expected to be at an all-time low of 9%.

Under tariff protection, more domestic and foreign-owned manufacturing plants have been established in Canada than have been needed to supply the market efficiently. Consequently, economists argue that plants have either been too small to achieve the lowest production costs or, more often, have produced too many product lines so that lengths of run have been shorter and therefore cost more than in foreign plants. As tariffs are lowered and firms attempt to increase their productivity, Canadian plants may become more competitive with those in foreign countries. And increasingly, because of technological changes, economies of scale are becoming a less-important determinant of comparative advantage.

Quotas There are also quantitative restrictions on imported merchandise. Under the GATT Multi-Fibre Arrangement, renewed 30 July 1986, Canada has been negotiating bilateral agreements with about 25 countries, limiting imports of textiles and clothing. Some ladies' and girls' footwear imports are also restricted under GATT rules. Voluntary export restraints on automobiles have been negotiated with Japan too. Agricultural products, including eggs, chickens, turkeys, milk and other dairy products also face quantitative import restraints. These are used to support domestic supply management programs. Beef, veal and grains too are also on the regulated list of imports, even though there are no comprehensive domestic agricultural marketing programs or marketing boards for these products. Where international commodity agreements exist, Canada discriminates against nonmember countries in its imports of products such as sugar and coffee.

Quantitative restrictions on imports provide clearer limits than tariffs and are therefore often preferred by those wishing to protect certain industries. Where labour costs and hence prices on foreign products are particularly low, as with clothing, textiles or footwear from developing countries, quotas preclude the need for high tariffs and have the same limiting effects on commodity inflows. In addition to quotas, a host of other domestic policies are being interpreted by Canada's trading partners, especially the US, as nontariff forms of protection of imports or subsidization of exports. These are called nontariff measures or NTMs. They include federal and provincial "buy-domestic" policies, government loans or grants to industries, low royalties or stumpage fees on resources, and any other government policies that appear to give preferences to domestic producers over foreign ones.

Tariffs, quotas, subsidies on domestic production and other methods to encourage domestic industry at the expense of industry abroad may mean higher prices for domestic consumers or inefficient use of domestic labour, capital and other resources. These economic costs must be weighed against the benefits of such industry-preservation programs.

Services Trade Canadians purchase a range of services abroad. The most important items are travel and tourism; freight and shipping; and business services such as the charges that foreign parent firms make to their subsidiaries in Canada for management advice and technology, plus arm's-length payments for royalties, patents, film rentals and some financial services. Governments also make foreign payments for diplomatic, military and trade purposes. At the same time, Canada receives revenues from foreign residents for similar types of services provided to them. Consistently, total payments to nonresidents exceed receipts from them.

Investment Income When Canada borrows funds, either by issuing bonds or other types of debt, or by welcoming foreign firms establishing subsidiaries in Canada, payment must be made for the use of the capital involved. This may take the form of interest, dividends or corporate undistributed earnings, which are reinvested to increase the foreign ownership of Canadian industry. Similarly, Canada receives payments from foreigners for the use of the capital its residents invest abroad. Canada has borrowed much more than it has lent abroad, however, especially since WWII, and now has a sizable annual deficit in service charges on capital – nearly $24 billion in 1986. This deficit would be several billions greater if the undistributed earnings of the net foreign direct investment in Canada was shown in the Balance of International Payments as a cost of foreign investment – as the International Monetary Fund recommends should be done. Such reinvested earnings account for 82% of the increase in the book value of foreign direct investment in Canada from 1975 to 1984. BRUCE W. WILKINSON

Reading: Statistics Canada, *Canada's International Investment Position 1981 to 1984* (1986) and *Quarterly Estimates of the Canadian Balance of International Payments* (Fourth Quarter, 1986).

International Woodworkers of America, formed in 1937 as part of a drive towards industrial unionization mounted by the Committee for Industrial Organization (later Congress of Industrial Organizations). The IWA quickly moved into BC where it absorbed earlier unions such as the Lumber Workers' Industrial Union, which had grown out of major strikes in logging and sawmilling earlier in the 1930s. A successful strike and organizing drive in 1946 established the IWA as western Canada's largest union, a position that it has generally held since then. In 1948 the IWA's then-communist leadership was replaced with a CCF-NDP tradition that has continued to the present.

Until 1986, the IWA's Canadian membership was divided into the Western and Eastern Regions at the Manitoba-Ontario border. The best-known activity of the Eastern Region was the NEWFOUNDLAND LOGGERS' STRIKE of 1957, following which Prem SMALLWOOD enacted universally condemned legislation barring the IWA from that province. The 2 regions amalgamated in 1986 under the presidency of Jack MUNRO, who had led the Western Region since 1973. The present 50 000 members of the Canadian Region belong mainly to the logging and sawmilling sectors of the BC forest industry.

Internment, detention or confinement of a person in time of war. In Canada such persons were denied certain legal rights, notably habeas corpus, though in certain cases they had the right to appeal their custody. Though not strictly PRISONERS OF WAR, civilian internees were generally treated according to international POW standards.

During WORLD WAR I enemy aliens (nationals of Germany and of the Austro-Hungarian and Turk-

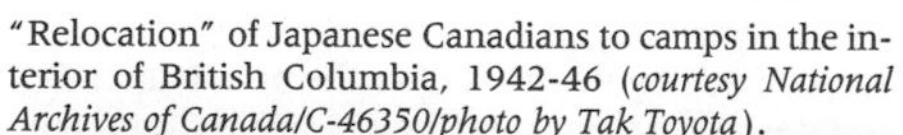

"Relocation" of Japanese Canadians to camps in the interior of British Columbia, 1942-46 (*courtesy National Archives of Canada/C-46350/photo by Tak Toyota*).

ish empires) were subject to internment, but only if there were "reasonable grounds" to believe they were engaged in espionage or otherwise acting illegally. Some municipalities "unloaded" indigents, many of them recent immigrants, on internment camps. In 1916-17, many Austrians were paroled to fill labour shortages. Of 8579 men at 24 camps across Canada, 5954 were Austro-Hungarians, 2009 Germans, 205 Turks and 99 Bulgarians; 81 women and 156 children, dependants of male internees, were voluntarily interned. Although responsibility shifted in 1915 from the Dept of Militia and Defence to the Dept of Justice, Maj-Gen Sir William OTTER remained officer commanding (later director of) internment operations.

In WORLD WAR II the minister of justice could detain anyone acting "in any manner prejudicial to the public safety or the safety of the state." Thus both enemy nationals and Canadian citizens were subject to internment. Precise statistics are not available but the number of internees was less than during the earlier war. Most of the Germans were members of German-sponsored organizations or leaders of the Nazi Party in Canada. After Italy entered the war, a number of prominent Italians and Canadian fascists, notably Adrien ARCAND of Montréal, were interned. Immediately after Pearl Harbor the RCMP interned 38 Japanese nationals; later, an additional 720 Japanese, mainly Canadian citizens and members of the Nisei Mass Evacuation Group who resisted separation from their families, were interned. Contrary to common usage, the approximately 20 000 Japanese Canadians who were removed from the Pacific Coast in 1942 were not interned. Although many were housed in isolated areas and had their activities severely restricted, they were not formally imprisoned. Because citizens could be interned for belonging to such outlawed organizations as the Communist Party, some claimed that internment was used as a weapon against labour leaders, eg, J.A. "Pat" Sullivan, president of the Canadian Seamen's Union, interned 1940. Along with about 90 other communists, he was released in 1941 after the USSR joined the Allies. Most prominent, however, was Mayor Camillien HOUDE of Montréal, interned 4 years for denouncing national registration in 1940 as a prelude to CONSCRIPTION.

Administration was divided between the army and the secretary of state. A total of 26 camps operated in Ontario, Québec, Alberta and New Brunswick, but only 2 held primarily Canadians. In WWI, Canada had accommodated 817 internees from Newfoundland and British Caribbean colonies; in WWII Canadian camps housed POWs and merchant seamen captured by the British, as well as some British civilians. At the peak in Oct 1944, Canada held 34 193 persons for the UK. Provision for internment continues. An emergency planning order approved May 1981 by Cabinet authorizes the solicitor general to establish civilian internment camps in wartime.

PATRICIA E. ROY

Reading: D.J. Carter, *Behind Canadian Barbed Wire* (1980).

Inuit of Little Whale River, with harpoon and white porpoises, *c*1865 (*courtesy National Archives of Canada/C-8160/photo by G.S. McTavish*).

Inuit simply means "people." Inuit were earlier known by Europeans as "Eskimos" – a pejorative, roughly meaning "eaters of raw meat," applied to them by INDIAN groups. They are one of the original groups to inhabit the northern regions of Canada, populating small, scattered communities and villages throughout the Arctic from Alaska to E Greenland. In 1981 Statistics Canada estimated that the Inuit population in Canada was 25 000. There are 8 main tribal-groups: the LABRADOR, UNGAVA, BAFFIN ISLAND, IGLULIK, CARIBOU, NETSILIK, COPPER and Western Arctic Inuit (who replaced the MACKENZIE INUIT). They speak a common language known as Inuktitut, or Inuttituut, divided into 6 different dialects (*see* NATIVE PEOPLE, LANGUAGES). Traditionally, the Inuit were hunters and gatherers who moved seasonally from one camp to another. Large regional groupings were loosely separated into smaller seasonal groups: winter camps (called "bands") of around 100 people and summer hunting groups of fewer than a dozen. Each band was roughly identified with a locale and named accordingly, eg, the Arvirtuurmiut of Boothia Pen, "baleen whale-eating people."

During roughly 4000 years of human history in the Arctic, the appearance of new people has brought continual cultural change. The ancestors of the present-day Inuit, who are culturally related to Inuppiat (N Alaska), Katladlit (Greenland) and Yuit (Siberia and W Alaska), arrived about 1050 AD. As early as the 11th century the NORSE exerted an undetermined influence on the Inuit. The subsequent arrival of explorers, whalers, traders, missionaries, scientists and others began irreversible cultural changes. The Inuit themselves participated actively in these developments as guides, traders and models of survival. Despite adjustments made by the Inuit over the past 3 centuries and the loss of some traditional features, Inuit culture persists – often with a greater reflective awareness. Inuit maintain a cultural identity through language, family and cultural laws, attitudes and behaviour, and through their acclaimed INUIT ART.

The Inuit have never been subject to the INDIAN ACT and were largely ignored by government until 1939, when a court decision ruled that they were a federal responsibility.The Inuit have proposed Nunavut ("Our Land") to the federal government to define Inuit and DENE lands in the NWT. Some Inuit still follow a nomadic way of life, but others are involved in the administration and development of northern Canada – in business, local and territorial politics, teaching, transportation, medicine, broadcasting and the civil service. *See also* NATIVE PEOPLE: ARCTIC.

MINNIE AODLA FREEMAN

Inuit Art The Eskimo word "Inuit" is a fairly recent Anglo-French Canadian term and will be used in this article only with reference to the historical and modern Canadian ESKIMO. Greenlanders, who speak a dialect similar to the Canadian Inuktitut and whose art and artifacts are often almost identical to those found in the Canadian Arctic for the past 4000 years, call themselves Katladlit. Siberians (or Asiatic) Eskimos and Eskimos of W and SW Alaska call themselves Yuit. They speak a dialect called Yupik, and their art forms, except during THULE CULTURE, bear few stylistic resemblances to those of the Canadian Arctic. Yet there exist strong iconographic (image) and thematic (content) relationships between the art forms, indicating a common ancestry or various cultural diffusions and interchanges, or both. Obviously, the words Inuit and Eskimo do not have identical meanings and therefore careful differentiations must be made.

Culture Phases The history of Eskimo cultures and the art of the various regions and times can only be understood if the myth of a homogeneous Eskimo culture is discarded altogether. Though it

Men Hunting Animals by Alasi Audla (*courtesy La Fédération des co-opératives du Nouveau-Québec*).

has not been possible to determine the exact origin(s) of the Eskimo, nor of the various Eskimo cultures, 5 distinct cultures have been established in the Canadian area: PRE-DORSET, DORSET, Thule, Historic and Contemporary.

Pre-Dorset Culture developed out of the migrations of people coming from Siberia via the Bering Strait 4000-4500 years ago (*see* PREHISTORY). While few art objects of this period seem to have survived, the exquisitely shaped artifacts discovered – particularly the projectile points of harpoon heads and lances fashioned from carefully selected lithic material (stones) – are not merely functional but also of considerable aesthetic value. These objects can in fact be called art even though they lacked imagistic intentions. Through their simple splendour and sensitive craftsmanship they exude intentions of magic that perpetuated themselves in the succeeding Dorset culture. Pre-Dorset culture lasted for over 1000 years, and it extended into the beginning of the first millennium BC.

Dorset Culture started to evolve between 700 and 500 BC, and can be called the first native Canadian Arctic culture. It spread from Coronation Gulf to the bottom tip of Newfoundland and to the entire west coast of Greenland. Several problems have arisen in dating Dorset art, particularly its origins. In the chronology established by Danish archaeologist Jørgen Meldgaard for the Igloolik area, with the highlights occurring between 500 and 1000 AD, art emerges only in the Middle Dorset period, 400-500. Yet the well-known Tyara maskette, made with the same perfectionist artistry that characterizes the best of Dorset art, has been dated to before 600 BC. The explanation may lie in faulty carbon dating, or in the possibility that the maskette is a work from the Pre-Dorset culture that somehow survived. Two Pre-Dorset maskettes from the Igloolik area exist which are similar in appearance. In Pre-Dorset culture imagistic supernatural objects may have been destroyed or discarded after use, as in other prehistoric and preliterate cultures, and the Tyara maskette could have been an incidental survivor, used or preserved in the later culture. Or perhaps the fine craftsmanship and aesthetic beauty of both the maskette and Pre-Dorset artifacts point to a magical purpose in their creation: that form does not merely follow function but increases efficacy.

High Dorset art appears to be largely magico-religious in its purpose; this appears to be so particularly for the "excaved" (hollowed out and perforated) Dorset bears and falcons relating in shape to harpoon heads. The points of the harpoon heads become the bear heads; the line-hole openings become the front legs attached to the body (or bent backwards in a swimming motion), and the basal spurs become the hind legs (more or less abstracted). The excaved falcons resemble the excaved forms of the harpoon heads and simultaneously the skeletons of birds. The image of disembowelled creatures refers to a ritualistic technique used in shamanic initiations in many parts of the polar world from Siberia to Greenland: the SHAMAN had to think of himself as a durable skeleton, devoid of flesh and blood, so that the helping spirits might consider it worthwhile to come to him. The skeleton designs incised (not etched) into many of the animal carvings have a similar origin and hint at several supernatural meanings: the body as spirit or dematerialized essence, as a kind of ritual form, or as an instrument for magico-religious purposes.

Linear or incised signs on many of the carvings – joint marks and crosses – can also be found in other prehistoric and preliterate cultures. They too seem to have supernatural associations and reinforce the largely magico-religious content of Dorset art. Several other image types exist in Dorset culture, such as the antler or wooden "face clusters," wooden masks, maskettes, human figures, multiple animal images, various birds, and land and sea mammals (some with and some without skeleton markings). While their purposes are largely unknown, they do have common characteristics: most are carved in ivory or, to a lesser extent, in bone, antler or wood; they are very small – anywhere from 1 to 10 centimetres; all are 3-dimensional, carved with strong or expressionistic features and with decisive strokes of the knife or graver. Except for the wood and antler carvings, they have a remarkably smooth finish despite their small size and expressionist form.

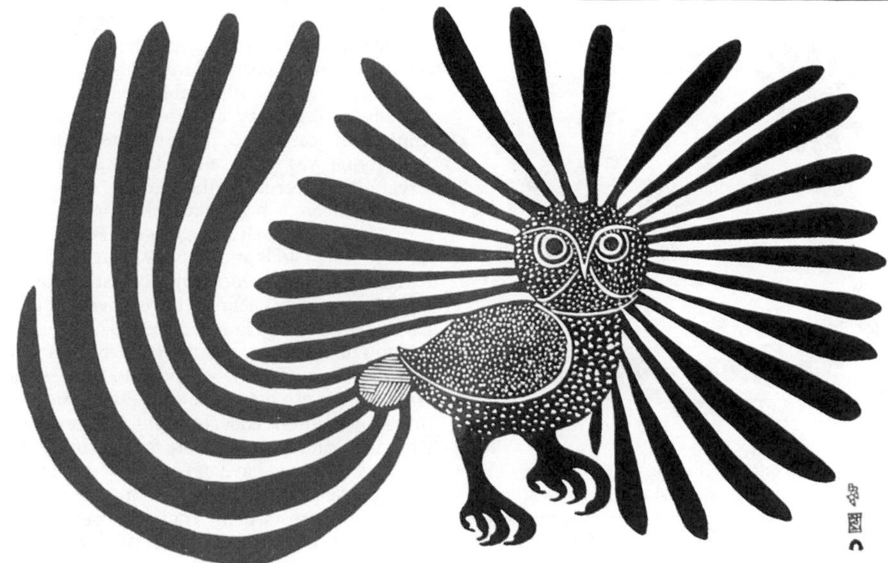

The Enchanted Owl by Kenojuak Ashevak (*courtesy West Baffin Eskimo Co-operative, Cape Dorset, NWT*).

Petroglyphs have been cut in soapstone outcroppings near the sea at Wakeham Bay in Ungava (Nouveau Québec), faces or maskettes not unlike the previously mentioned face clusters (*see* PICTOGRAPHS AND PETROGLYPHS). The shapes themselves, however, are reminiscent of the Tyara maskette, which comes from nearby Sugluk (Salluit). While this similarity asserts a Dorset origin for the Tyara maskette, it brings the date of its origin further into question.

Thule Culture is much easier to define and to date, but again some anomalies exist. Thule culture migration from northern Alaska into the Canadian Arctic began after 1000 AD and reached eastern Greenland by 1200. Thule is the most uniform of the Eskimoan cultures, covering as it did the entire Arctic of the western hemisphere, including the eastern tip of Asiatic Siberia. That manifest uniformity was responsible for giving Eskimos the appearance of homogeneity, which is misleading except for Thule culture artifacts. Thule art across the Arctic was not as uniform as many social scientists once believed, and therefore the less conspicuous art forms of the Thule people in comparison to powerful Dorset and Old Bering Sea art (of Alaska) have led to the revision of many misjudgements by a new generation of archaeologists.

The Thule people, whose pre-Thule ancestry can be traced to SW Alaska but who had evolved into their new culture type in N Alaska, were themselves the true ancestors of the contemporary Inuit. In Canada, however, the art forms of these 2 cultures reflect little of this relationship. This is in contrast to the Thule art tradition in Alaska, which continued well into the late 19th and early 20th centuries.

The most frequent types of Thule art in Canada are combs, needle cases and "swimming figurines" (birds, spirits and humans), as well as various kinds of female effigies and utensils. In contrast to Dorset art, which had hardly any stylistic similarities to contemporaneous Alaskan art forms, Canadian Thule art is almost totally dependent on Alaskan prototypes of the same culture and period.

While Dorset art, in its stark and expressionist form and technique, has a definite masculine quality, which in form and content relates to weapons and tools used by males, Thule art relates in almost every detail to female images, forms and uses. Utensils such as combs, thimble holders, needle cases, bodkins and pendants are obviously women's practical and decorative equipment; the "swimming figurines" too are either female representations or relate to them in their shape. They are identical in their basic structure, with only the upper parts of their bodies shown; the parts underneath the waterline, not being visible, are therefore not shown. These figurines obviously had a common origin, probably as amulets or for similar magico-religious purposes. It is therefore difficult to believe that these carvings were gambling pieces (*tingmiujang*), though they were the prototypes for the gambling pieces used after the breakup of traditional Thule whaling culture in the 17th and 18th centuries.

Besides being small, elegantly shaped and often beautifully decorated, almost all female figurines and statuettes of Thule art are faceless, in contrast to the Dorset figures, with their strongly expressed mostly male faces. The 2 notable Thule exceptions with beautifully carved (almost Dorset-like) faces are a comb from the Pelly Bay region and a marrow fork (or perhaps a bodkin for tents or UMIAKS) from Strathcona Sound. There are a few other carvings with vaguely incised faces and also a few stick figures on combs, as well as a unique bow drill from Arctic Bay.

The Historical Period begins with the demise of Thule culture, as the climate became colder and the whales disappeared, and the coinciding arrival of the white man in the Arctic in the 16th century. The unified art style also broke down, though some Thule effigies persisted into the 20th century, such as the swimming figurines that turned into gaming pieces and the female statuettes that turned into dolls. Certain women's utensils also continued, but carved in much cruder and less stylish forms.

Worshipping the Rising Sun by Agnes Nanogak (*courtesy Holman Eskimo Co-operative, Holman Island, NWT*).

At the start of the 19th century, the dolls, toys and animal carvings that were exchanged with whalers, sailors and explorers (who had then begun to visit on a more or less regular basis) gradually turned into trade and souvenir art, often quite exquisite. In fact, the trade carvings display a much greater skill than carvings made by the Inuit for themselves. By 1920 trade art (which was largely made out of ivory or bone) had lost all of its indigenous magico-religious meanings, and many carvings became replicas of tools and weapons of both Inuit and white men. In several areas liturgical art (replicas of Roman Catholic figurines) were produced regularly, as were inlaid or incised cigarette boxes, match holders, cribbage boards and sailing vessels. Even though the Inuit had lived a largely traditional life-style before WWII, their art forms – but not the techniques or processes for making their objects (*pinguaq* or "toy-like representations") – became increasingly oriented to the white man's tastes and uses.

The Contemporary Phase was a logical outcome of the transitional and acculturated art forms of the historic period, and coincided with the gradual "opening up" of the North after WWII, with the launching of the DEW Line (Distant Early Warning system) and, most of all, with the emerging interest of Western nations in the art and culture of preliterate societies. Largely owing to the insights and promotional energy of James A. HOUSTON, a young artist from Toronto, "Eskimo art," or "Inuit art" as we know it today, came into existence in 1948-49. He encouraged the Inuit to use their "natural talents" in creating art objects to help solve their economic problems. In this regard they were assisted by the INUIT CO-OPERATIVES.

Soapstone and ivory carvings from Povungnituk and Inukjuak (Port Harrison) in Nouveau Québec were the first art forms to appear for sale in the south. Salluit (Sugluk), Cape Dorset and Repulse Bay followed, and soon the entire central Arctic was covered, from Coppermine to Arctic Bay, with other areas to join later in the 1960s and 1970s. The whole enterprise resulted largely from the support Houston and the Inuit received from the federal government, the former Canadian Handicrafts Guild and the Hudson's Bay Company. In 1957-58 Houston also introduced printmaking into Cape Dorset; in the next 20 years, this craft spread to Povungnituk, Holman, Baker Lake, Pangnirtung and, to a lesser extent, into several other arctic communities, including Clyde. The role of economics in contemporary art production is of great importance.

In the new carving activities the emphasis is largely on soapstone and serpentine, which have become increasingly scarce, and stone is often imported from the south. Stone differs greatly from the organic materials used in prehistoric and historic times. Ivory is still used in several areas, especially at Pelly Bay and Repulse Bay, where miniature carvings predominate. Beached whalebone was first used at Arctic Bay but had largely disappeared by the mid-1970s. Instead, large whalebone fragments taken from prehistoric Thule culture sites became extremely popular in the late 1960s and early 1970s, especially at Pangnirtung and Spence Bay. The use of this material had steadily declined, largely because of the US embargo on endangered species.

Though carving is still the largest art activity, INUIT PRINTMAKING has become the most steady and the one providing the greatest financial returns for southern collectors and "art investors." Drawings and paintings are also produced in quantity, but they have never enjoyed the popularity of the prints. Every printmaker draws, but only a few artists paint (notably PUDLO PUDLAT from Cape Dorset and Davie Atchealak from Pangnirtung). Wall hangings (embroidered, appliquéd or woven) are probably the most impressive of the new 2-dimensional art forms but, though highly valued by connoisseurs, they have not achieved the wide acceptance of the prints either.

The new art forms do not have the uniform style and content characteristics found in Dorset and Thule art, but rather exhibit local and individual characteristics. Inuit art is easily recognizable as such, but only because of a predictable subject matter or a definite personal or local style. Most Inuit art shares a predominantly narrative or illustrative content that depicts the traditional life-style and techniques of survival, the animals of the North, the spirits of those animals, or the shamans and mythologies which were the links to that spirit world. But here the similarity ends. In Baker Lake, for instance, MAKPAAQ and Ekoota have initiated a style of massive stone carving, whereas Ikseetaryuk developed out of the antler characteristic images and compositions of his own which have no stylistic relationship to the stone carvings. Baker Lake printmakers and producers of wall hangings such as OONARK, Tulluq, ANGUHADLUQ, William Noah and Simon Tookoome also have their own individual styles, as have at least 10 others.

Sliding in the Sun by Peter Aliknak (*courtesy Holman Eskimo Co-operative, Holman Island, NWT*).

A similar situation exists at Cape Dorset, where all the well-known artists are highly individualistic, including carvers AQJANGAJUK SHAA, QAQAQ ASHOONA, KIAWAK ASHOONA, Kumwartok, Latcholassie, Osuitok. IPEELEE and PAUTA SAILA, and printmakers PARR, PITSEOLAK and Pudlo. Collectively, however, they are typical of Cape Dorset art, and it is possible to speak of a Cape Dorset style with its definite and crisp shapes and often quite original ideas.

In Povungnituk, too, the principal artists all have their own style and subject matter. The stylistic individuality of artists such as DAVIDIALUK, Joe TALIRUNILI and Josie Paperk is noticeable in both carvings and prints. These 3 artists were seldom imitated, but ideas of Charlie SIVUARAPIK, Isapik, and Eli Sallualuk were followed by many of the lesser artists. These multiple Povungnituk styles have one common feature – high finish and craftsmanship. This characteristic applies to both the highly representational and the fantastic art of Povungnituk, but not to the works of Davidialuk, Talirunili and Paperk which, though also narrative, have retained a definite feeling of simple rawness and forceful, personal expression.

Keeviak's Sea Journey by Nancy Pukingrnak (*courtesy Sanavik Co-operative, Baker Lake, NWT*).

Comparisons could be drawn between Pelly Bay, Repulse Bay and Eskimo Point, all of which have styles that could easily be related to FOLK ART, but here too there are many subtle and individual exceptions. In general, Eskimo Point carvings of stone and antler are carved more crudely than the stones and ivories of the other 2 communities, yet PANGNARK's abstract work from Eskimo Point is extraordinarily elegant and sophisticated. Artists using whalebone, especially the vertebrae, which have naturally fantastic shapes, have a certain advantage, leading often to unusual sculptures. This applies particularly to Spence Bay artists such as KAROO ASHEVAK and Anaija, but interesting work has also been coming out of the eastern and northern regions of Baffin I.

The contemporary phase is rapidly evolving and changing. Collectors and museums are starting to pay extremely high prices for older pieces or prints, and the production of new art has increased frighteningly, accompanied by a general decline in quality. Although a great deal of good art is still produced, the collective standard of quality can only be maintained if the creation of art is limited to those of real talent. The Inuit and their co-operatives are fully aware of this danger, but only they can remedy it. GEORGE SWINTON

Reading: "The Eskimo World," *artscanada* 27 (Dec 1971-Jan 1972); S. Cole, ed, *We Don't Live in Snowhouses Now* (1976); B. Driscoll, *The Inuit Amautik* (1980) and *Uumajuk: Animal Imagery in Inuit Art* (1985); H. Goetz, *The Inuit Print/L'Estampe inuit* (1977); George Swinton, *Sculpture of the Eskimo* (1972).

Inuit Co-operatives were initiated in the NORTH by the federal government as a way of introducing the Inuit of the eastern Arctic to a money economy. The first co-operative was established in 1959 at George River in Nouveau-Québec as a logging and fishing operation. Others followed rapidly, the best-known being the West Baffin Co-operative at Cape Dorset, which began as an INUIT PRINTMAKING organization and then became involved in Inuit carvings.

The first co-operatives were involved in the production of northern goods for local consumption or export; from this beginning it was a natural expansion to consumer co-operatives, importing goods from the south for retailing in the north. Many co-operatives have also undertaken various municipal services, and have operated fishing lodges and hotels. The first co-operative conference was held in Iqaluit [Frobisher Bay] in 1963 with 16 co-operatives represented, 11 from the NWT and 5 from northern Québec.

In 1966 representatives of 24 co-operatives met in Povungnituk and decided to form a federation to provide central services, information and advice. The Fédération des co-opératives du Nouveau-Québec was organized in 1967 by the co-operatives in northern Québec, but it was not until 1972 that the Canadian Arctic Co-operatives Federation was established in the NWT. In the meantime, Canadian Arctic Producers had been set up with government encouragement as a central marketing agency for INUIT ART and crafts. In 1983 Canadian Arctic Producers merged with the Canadian Arctic Co-operatives Federation to form Arctic Co-operatives Ltd.

The CO-OPERATIVE MOVEMENT in the North, as might have been expected, has suffered from inexperienced management, both among the Inuit and the staff hired from southern Canada, and from being undercapitalized; it has known failures as well as successes. Government assistance has frequently been necessary, but co-operatives are, after governments themselves, the largest employers of native people in the North. They have been their most important influence in education and commerce, as well as in increasing self-confidence. There were 46 co-operatives, 11 in the Fédération des co-opératives du Nouveau-Québec and 35 in the NWT in 1986 with a volume of almost $40 million. GEORGE SWINTON

Inuit Myth and Legend A myth is usually defined as a poetic attempt to explain some phenomenon of nature or ancient tradition that cannot be understood rationally. A legend is a story handed down by tradition but loosely based on history. Both these forms are widely used by preliterate societies. The INUIT were just such a society until the mid-20th century.

Inuit who make their homes across the vastness of Canada's Arctic belong to a much larger Eskimoid family that extends from the Bering Sea through Alaska and northern Canada to Greenland (*see* ESKIMO). These imaginative, hardy and resourceful people are linked not only linguistically but by a distinctly similar culture and way of life. Songs, dances, myths, legends and art forms all link these widely flung, seminomadic people (*see* INUIT ART). Their earliest myths and legends, along with their hunting techniques, must have travelled with them out of Asia (*see* PREHISTORY). Their songs and story forms of myths and legends, linguistically as well as stylistically, relate most closely to Siberian, Finno-Ugric and early Hungarian (Magyar) traditions. Language and legend may give clues to ancient routes of migration.

Inuit myths and legends perform a useful function by answering, at least in part, many puzzling questions. The Inuit designated the powers of good and evil to deities living in a spirit world (*see* NATIVE PEOPLE, RELIGION). For the Inuit that spirit world was closely entwined with the starkly beautiful northern world in which they lived.

The ancient Inuit oral traditions were employed as the most important method of conveying and preserving ideas, augmented sometimes by small carvings that may have served as illustrations for events. Songs and dances also enhanced the meanings of myths and legends which upheld the existing system, bolstered the traditional customs of Inuit society and verbalized a sense of right and wrong. These early tales may have preceded the priesthood that grew around them, developing into Siberian and Eskimo shamanism (*see* SHAMAN).

Inuit myths and legends are usually short dramatic forms dealing with the wonders of the world: the creation, the heavens, birth, love, hunting and sharing of food, respect for the aged, polygamy, murder, infanticide, incest, death and the mystery of an afterlife. Even in recent times Inuit storytellers will remodel old myths and create new legends, subtly disguising the true identities of the persons involved.

Inuit myths are rarely simple, usually abounding with curious behavioural codes that may only be fully understood by those living within that society. Inuit believe that they have a close relationship with all of nature and that animals have the magical power to hear and understand the human word. For this reason, hunters in their camps, when singing or speaking of walrus or seal, may carefully refer to them as maggots or lice, or call caribou lemmings, thus confusing the animals that are necessary for their survival.

Until modern times Inuit agreed that there were other worlds beneath the sea, inside the Earth, and in the sky where some gifted *angakoks* (shamans) had the power to journey in trances and in dreams, visiting places that ordinary mortals would only experience in some afterlife.

Dreams have always played an important part in the lives of Inuit, perhaps serving as the basis for some myth forms. Dreams are interpreted with care. Dreams of white bears are said to have sexual overtones. Dreams of weasels suggest troubles. Bird dreams forewarn of blizzards.

Some Inuit myths are thought provoking in any language. An extremely short example is as follows: Onto a boy's arm came a mosquito. "Don't hit! Don't hit!" it hummed, "Grandchildren have I to sing to." "Imagine," the boy said, "So small and yet a grandfather."

Among the most famous of the vast array of myths is the legend of the sea goddess who has various names (Sedna, Nuliayuk, Taluliyuk), the legend of Lumiuk (Lumak, Lumaag), the legend of Kiviok and the legend of Tiktaliktak.

Once, on south Baffin Island, I saw a myth come alive. Some young children were playing near a tidal ice barrier with many dangerous hidden cracks. Their grandmother crept with great care down among the ice hummocks and from a hidden position called out, "Oohhwee, Oohhweee!" The children ran back onto the land and said the sea goddess Taluliyuk had frightened them. Later, the grandmother said, "I told them about the woman who lives under the sea. Now she will keep them away from the dangerous places." The grandmother was referring to the powerful sea goddess in this central arctic song:

That woman down there beneath the sea,
She wants to hide the seals from us.
These hunters in the dance house,
They cannot mend matters.
They cannot mend matters.
Into the spirit world
Will go I,
Where no humans dwell.
Set matters right will I.
Set matters right will I.

The legend of the sea goddess, though known in various regions by different names, is one of the most widespread. One version is that some time ago, during a violent blizzard, a handsome young stranger entered a family IGLOO. He was wearing a necklace with 2 large canine teeth. He was welcomed into the bed and slept with the entire family. When they awoke next morning, the young man was gone. The father, seeing only animal tracks outside, said, "We were deceived. That must have been my lead dog disguised as a man." When his daughter became pregnant, the father was ashamed of what she might produce. He made his daughter lie on the back of his kayak while he paddled her out to a small island where he abandoned her. His lead dog secretly swam to the girl, leaving her tender pieces of meat. Thus she remained alive and gave birth to 6 young. Three of them were Inuit children, but the other 3 had bigger ears and snoutlike noses. The young mother did not know how to build a kayak. Instead, she sewed some sealskins into one large slipper, and placing the 3 strange children inside, she pushed them off toward the south, calling out, "*Sarutiktapsinik sanavagumarkpusi*" (You shall be good at making weapons). Some Inuit say that all white men and Indians are descended from those 3 dog children and only through them are they related to Inuit.

The second part of the story, usually told on the following night, tells of the father going in an UMIAK, a large skin boat, and taking his daughter off the island. On their way home a storm rose and it was feared that the overloaded boat would capsize. The boatmen decided that to lighten the load they must throw the daughter overboard. When she tried to climb back into the boat, her father cut off her fingers. These became the seals in the sea. She tried again and he cut off her hands and they became the walruses. She made one last attempt and he cut off her forearms which became the whales of the oceans. After that she sank into the depths and became Sedna, or Taluliyuk, the woman who controls all the sea beasts, and became half woman and half fish. Many songs are sung to this powerful goddess. In new seasons, pieces of liver of the first-killed sea mammal are returned to the waters, imploring Sedna to release her bounty to the hunters so that they might feed their families.

A number of anthropologists agree that although many ethnic societies wished to preserve their history, they preferred to record it in myths and legends. Perhaps this was because these were close societies where every man knew his neighbour well. Until recently, Inuit had no need for last names. This also suggests that to repeat the tale of a wife-stealing or a feud leading to a massacre within a tribal group would be not only socially unacceptable but dangerous. But by transforming enemies into mythical beasts and family members into heroes, the story might travel safely down within the tribe through many centuries.

Ancient tools and art objects may lie preserved in the permafrost unharmed for countless centuries waiting to be discovered. But oral myths and legends, and songs and dances that are parts of Inuit culture, represent a valuable intellectual possession. Once lost, they have no way of returning. For this reason, every effort should be made to record the important Inuit myths and legends that are a part of the priceless heritage of Canada before they slip away. In the past, explorers and anthropologists performed this task, but in recent years Inuit have become concerned with preserving their traditions. JAMES HOUSTON

Reading: Z. Nungak and E. Arima, *Eskimo Stories: Unikkaatuat* (1969).

Inuit Printmaking While their language does not have a specific word for art, the INUIT have decorated garments and carved small items since prehistoric times. Contemporary carving activities were promoted by James A. HOUSTON, artist and administrator, who in 1948 travelled to the Arctic with the objective of exploring artistic ventures that could supplement Inuit incomes. In 1957 printmaking was introduced at Cape Dorset, also with Houston as the catalyst.

Inuit printmaking is unique in that it does not have historical precedents. It might be postulated that printmaking has affinities with the Inuit's incised carvings on bone or antler, women's facial tattoo marks, or inlay skin work on clothing, mitts and footwear. Stone, bone, antler, wood and ivory were available for carvings, but paper and drawing and writing tools were introduced to the Inuit by early explorers and missionaries. While print activities have a short history in the Arctic, and differ markedly from those carried out to the south, the Inuit have shown a high aptitude, ability and enthusiasm for this new art medium and have used it to provide a visual record of traditional life.

The Inuit were encouraged to establish co-operatives to assist in the production and marketing of the art. The methods of production were patterned on traditional workshop practices; Houston studied with the Japanese print artist, Un'ichi Hiratsuka, for 5 months in 1958 and returned to Cape Dorset with Japanese papers and practices. Many of the western and oriental methods and work patterns refined at Cape Dorset were adopted by other print workshops.

Inuit artists usually make the initial drawings in their homes. The finished drawings are brought to the co-operative to be exchanged for money. If a drawing is selected for print editions, the artist who drew the image does not commonly transfer it to the print medium; this is done by another skilled individual, and, in several co-operatives, a third person prints the image onto paper. Most frequently, a print will be signed or stamped with the names of the drawer and the printer. Traditionally, the print will have 2 other symbols or stamps, one pictographic symbol denotes the co-operative from which the print originated (eg, Cape Dorset, a stylized igloo; Holman I, an ulu inscribed with the word Holman) and the other is the stylized syllabics stamp or blind-embossed symbol of the Canadian Eskimo Arts Council indicating that the work is authentic and meets approved standards. Inuit prints are not released individually but as an annual portfolio. The selection of the prints comprising the annual collection is carried out in the south by a government-appointed jury, the Canadian Eskimo Arts Council.

The Woman that Lives in the Sun by Kenojuak Ashevak (*courtesy West Baffin Eskimo Co-operative, Cape Dorset, NWT*).

Marketing, including quality, quantity and price control, is co-ordinated by Canadian Arctic Producers (prints created in the NWT) and by the Fédération des Coopératives du Nouveau-Québec (prints from arctic Québec), and sold through designated commercial galleries. The number of prints per edition is controlled. The first prints were issued in series of 30, now the size of the edition is usually 50.

Inuit prints also differ in their subject matter and their formal concerns. Traditionally, the content of Inuit prints is based on the animals, birds and marine life of the Arctic; on traditional ways of life; on legends and mythologies; and on shamanistic events, creatures and spirits. The artists rarely incorporate contemporary life styles, pure landscape, or abstract or non-objective imagery. Artists, such as PUDLO PUDLAT, Etidloie Etidloie and Jessie OONARK have incorporated such objects as airplanes, helicopters, snowmobiles and rifles, but they are exceptions. Inuit printmakers also differ from their southern colleagues in their use of space. Inuit artists may indicate space by overlapping or may have a ground line, but in general, they are not concerned with showing figures and objects existing as 3-dimensional bodies in a believable space. Most images are flat and are more concerned with depicting pattern and decoration than volume.

The preferred print technique is that of the stone cut which evolved through experimenting with such material as bone, wood and linoleum. The stone cut is similar to the wood cut and is part of the relief technique. The stencil technique was initiated from the traditional inlay designs that women employed to adorn skin garments. Later, the techniques of serigraphy and lithography were added; techniques that are particularly adaptable to colour. In order to stimulate more immediate artist involvement, intaglio techniques were also introduced, enabling artists to draw directly on the plate.

Because Inuit artists have not until recently left their settlements to engage in formal art training, learning from each other and those living in their community, artists' ideas tended to be contained within each regional centre. Printmaking began in the community of Cape Dorset in 1957, with the first exhibition of prints occurring in 1959. Other centres also produced prints: Povungnituk 1962, Holman I 1965, Baker Lake 1970, Nouveau Québec at large 1972, Pangnirtung 1973 and Clyde River 1981. Frequently, each community developed a common style as the artists worked closely together.

Cape Dorset Cape Dorset, with the longest history and the most continuous and professional management, has consistently produced prints of high aesthetic and technical quality. KENOJUAK ASHEVAK and LUCY QINNUAYUAK are both well known for the birds which they depict. Kenojuak's centrally located birds, often emblematic owls like the one on the 6-cent postage stamp issued in 1970, are elegant and decorative images that rely partly on shapes, partly on colour for im-

Inuk artist Kenojuak Ashevak preparing a drawing that will be made into a print, Cape Dorset, NWT (*courtesy SSC Photocentre*).

pact. Lucy's birds tend to be depicted in an asymmetrical manner and shown with a good deal of humour and whimsy. Pitseolak, a prolific artist, created many images that provide visual narrations of the nomadic Inuit life, showing how families were very much dependent on the Arctic creatures for survival. Jamasie Teevee who also uses lithography and stone cut, has drawn and printed his own copperplate engravings. He often fills the paper's rectangular space with many, tightly arranged, figures. PARR, one of the oldest Cape Dorset artists, depicts animals and hunters in a direct and simplified, almost primeval, manner. Pudlo Pudlat is among the very few who has also pursued landscape as a subject matter.

Povungnituk The whole stone block plays a significant role for Povungnituk artists. Many prints show the irregular outlines of the block, which boldly frames the interior scene and powerfully participates in the visual statement. Contrary to practices in other centres, many Povungnituk artists partake in the drawing, cutting and sometimes the printing facets of an image. At times, they even skip the step of tracing the drawing, but carve the image directly onto the stone. Joe TALIRUNILI was a carver and an early printmaker. He often used events of his own life, stories of other hunters, or the migration theme as the basis for his narrative prints where activities are arranged akin to the modular formula used in comic strips. He frequently inscribed a syllabic explanation as part of the print. A renowned storyteller, DAVIDIALUK preferred isolated and specific scenes or figures and often inscribed the name of the story or its protagonist in the stone itself. Josie Paperk uses bird imagery in many works, rendered in a lyrical and decorative manner.

Holman Island The stone cuts of Holman I have utilized local limestone blocks. Storyteller, shaman and printmaker, Helen KALVAK communicated ordinary, legendary and spiritual events through her prints. Mark Emerak depicted hunting scenes and Agnes Nanogak has drawn many powerful images relating historical and legendary practices that have been printed in bold black shapes on the white paper. Their prints have traditionally tended to de-emphasize colour or use it sparingly.

Baker Lake The original inhabitants of Baker Lake in the Keewatin district depended on caribou and fish. While now settled in an urban community, they still rely on those creatures as a main source for their artistic imagery as may be evidenced by Luke Anquhadluq's prints. Jessie Oonark and her daughter, Victoria Mamnguqsualuk, often depict scenes from legends, and may have several events depicted within the same composition. Oonark, also a fine textile artist, frequently used bold, decorative and colourful patterns in prints with a single figure. William Noah and Simon Tookoome are among the few artists who print their own images. Tookoome is known for his unique treatment of faces; for instance, he may insert animal figures into the cheeks of human faces, or he may arrange human faces within and along all limbs of a figure.

Pangnirtung The initial Pangnirtung collection was issued in 1973. The prints focus on daily activities and on whaling as the area has served as a whaling centre since the 18th century. Whaling scenes are included in prints by Jeetaloo Akulukjuk and Atoomowyak Eesseemailee. Mosesee Keyjuakjuk, with Solomon Karpik, has created some simple but effective hunting scenes using the stone cut technique.

Clyde River The most recent of the print centres, the Igutaq Group of Clyde River was organized in 1974 and launched its first collection in 1981. It has employed the stencil technique extensively and the artists are interested in soft gradations of colour, as competently demonstrated in the prints by Lydia Jaypody, Jeanie Tiqulliaraq and Elishah Sanguya. BENTE ROED COCHRAN

Reading: Sandra Barz, ed, *Inuit Artists Print Workbook* (1981); Helga Goetz, *The Inuit Print* (1977); James A. Houston, *Eskimo Prints* (1967); W.T. Larmour, *Inunnit: the Art of the Canadian Eskimo* (1967).

Inuit Tapirisat of Canada (ITC, formerly the Inuit Brotherhood) was founded in 1971, when an organizing committee of Inuit decided it was time to speak with a united voice on various issues concerning development of the Canadian NORTH and preservation of INUIT culture. Headquarters were first established in Edmonton, but in 1972 the offices were moved to Ottawa. In 1983 ITC was a national organization representing over 25 000 Inuit in the NWT, northern Québec and Labrador, as well as 6 regional associations: the Committee for Original People's Entitlement (COPE) in the western Arctic, the Baffin Region Inuit Assn, the Kitikmeot Inuit Assn, the Keewatin Inuit Assn, the Makivik Corp in Québec and the Labrador Inuit Assn. As of 1987-88, COPE is in the process of changing its title of association to Inuvialuit. The presidents of the regional associations constitute ITC's board of directors, along with 4 other members who are elected for 2-year terms at annual general meetings. All Inuit over 18 years of age are now eligible to vote.

The goals of ITC are to preserve Inuit language and culture; to promote a sense of dignity and pride in the Inuit heritage; to provide a focal point for determining the needs and wishes of all Inuit; to represent Inuit on matters affecting their well-being; to improve communications to and between Inuit communities; and to help Inuit achieve full participation in Canadian society. ITC is a nonprofit organization; its funding sources are mainly government agencies and private foundations in Canada.

MINNIE AODLA FREEMAN

Inukpuk, Johnny, sculptor (b at Inoucdjouac, Qué 1911). Anecdotal Inuit sculpture reflects an austere, sometimes violent, way of life. By contrast, Inukpuk's balloon-breasted mothers nurse plump contented babies, assuring them and the viewer a life of love and abundance. An anachronic flaw, a harelip, is invariably shared by both figures. His explanation, probably tongue-in-cheek, is that "white people think Eskimos look like that." He was still prolific in 1987.

MARY M. CRAIG

Inuvik, NWT, Town, pop 3389 (1986c), 3147 (1981c), inc 1970, is located on the MACKENZIE R delta, 97 km S of the BEAUFORT SEA and 1086 air km NW of Yellowknife. The name is from the Inuit and means "place of man." The community was constructed in the late 1950s and early 1960s to replace the existing settlement of AKLAVIK, which was threatened by floods and erosion. Inuvik is the administration, communications and fur-trading centre of the lower Mackenzie R area and is the largest community N of the ARCTIC CIRCLE. Much of its economy is centered on nearby oil and gas exploration. In 1986 energy exploration companies left the town and the nearby army base was closed, becoming Arctic College's Aurora Campus. ANNELIES POOL

Inuvik, NWT, is the administrative centre of the lower Mackenzie area and the largest community N of the Arctic Circle (*photo by John deVisser*).

Inventors and Innovations Innovation is the successful application in a real economic or social context of something new which may or may not be an invention. Economic Council and Science Council investigations 1968-78 defined innovation as of fundamental importance in SCIENCE POLICY and special government programs were created to promote it.

In 1967 J.J. Brown's *Ideas in Exile,* a history of Canadian inventions, concluded that something wrong with the Canadian character had denied many good inventions the economic success they deserved. His assessment was not unique. It corresponds to the idea that Canadian artists, eg, actors and writers, are not recognized at home until after they have earned reputations in Europe or the US. Some sociologists such as S.D. CLARK attribute economic differences between the US and Canada to different social traditions.

History suggests Canada has produced many inventors and innovators. Simple examples include Anna Sutherland Bissell, inventor of the carpet sweeper, and Albert C. Fuller, founder of the Fuller Brush Co. He was an innovator (not being the inventor of the brush) and she both an inventor and an innovator, and manager of the Bissell Carpet Sweeper Co for several decades after her husband's death. Both developed their ideas and earned their fortunes in the US since its much larger market promised greater returns.

There is a long record of both successes and failures in Canada. Successes include the A.V. Roe Co's aircraft, the use of computers to design the St Lawrence Seaway, the CANDU nuclear reactor and Bell-Northern Research Ltd. BNR exemplifies some of the paradoxes of innovation. The Canadian telephone company began large-scale research chiefly because an American legal decision cut off the flow of free technology from US laboratories to Canadian factories in 1958. In the last 25 years BNR has become the largest research organization in Canada and earned a worldwide reputation as an innovator. Five types of innovation were defined by the economist Joseph Schumpeter in 1911: a new thing; a new process for making a familiar thing; a new market to which to sell; a new source of supply or raw material; and industrial reorganization, eg, establishing a monopoly. Only the first 2 of these 5 types are likely also to be inventions. (The assembly line, usually attributed to Henry Ford, is not so much an invention as case 5, reorganization of the flow of materials through a factory.)

The Schumpeter scheme suggests how difficult it is for governments to support or promote innovation, even when they believe it an important agent of economic growth and prosperity. No rules have yet been devised to predict whether a firm (or a nation) would get more benefit by investing resources in a new invention or in something else, eg, marketing. Economic historians have recently suggested that, although there have been so many invention-based innovations in the last 100 years, they are relatively rare: most profits from innovation can be traced to the cumulation of many small improvements. The all-metal aircraft and the jet engine are notable inventions; but their economic success appears to depend on hundreds of small-scale improvements, not necessarily by the original inventors of the airframe and engine.

An illustration is the IBM Personal Computer, of which the unique components were the Intel 8088 computer chip and the MS-DOS operating system. Both these inventions came from other firms and neither was particularly advanced in 1981. In combination with IBM's reputation and its sales organization they constituted a revolutionary innovation. The results were both a huge new market for microcomputers and a new technological standard. Even so, IBM could not monopolize the benefits of its success, and may in fact have profited less than other firms adopting its standard.

Before 1960, most historical thinking about technology amounted to little more than anecdotes about inventions. When the systematic economic analysis of innovation began, science policy theoreticians hoped it would reveal shortcuts to economic prosperity and security. These hopes were disappointed. Current scholarship suggests that innovation is more an aspect of total systems than a separate function. It is possibly a skill like cooking – recipes and the chemistry of cooking – can be scientifically analysed, but they do not make a good cook.

Innovation studies failed to discover what their pioneers wanted, but this makes Canada no worse off than any other country. The practical point is to use what has been discovered, along 2 main lines. One is that the general economic environment now seems to be more important than was previously assumed, and inventive genius is less important. Other important elements are luck, attitude and scale. We can never know how many potential inventors get disillusioned and give up. And the financial risks of innovation which a large firm could absorb might threaten the survival of a small firm. Industrial innovation is risky and expensive. Firms cannot afford to abandon their methods and machinery just because something new has been invented; at the same time they must recognize the risks of falling behind their competitors.

The other approach to managing or promoting innovation is awareness of its secondary characteristics: that economic and social benefits seem to depend on the total context more than individual inventions, and that innovation does not have to mean risking everything on brand-new technology. Detailed studies of new industries and the history of staple products such as wheat and steel suggest that greater economic successes have come more from the cumulation of dozens of incremental improvements than from each major technological revolution. This seems equally true of non-industrial domains such as health and medicine, which have also been transformed in the last 100 years. The benefits cannot be attributed exclusively to specific discoveries, such as antibiotics, independently from general principles, eg, infection, sanitation and scientific nutrition.

These general conclusions suggest that, even if innovations cannot be predicted, there is still scope for governments and business managers to cultivate the economic and cultural seedbed where innovations can happen. Important factors include the size of the domestic market, the structure of Canadian industry (eg, foreign control of certain industries), economic dependence

The rotary snowplow was a turn-of-the-century Canadian invention (*by permission of the British Library*).

on primary industries, psychological attitudes to risk (Canadians' preference to save money in life insurance or bank accounts, rather than investing in the stock market on the same scale as Americans) and the level of technical education, as well as political priorities.

For discussions of inventors and inventions, *see* the following articles: Thomas AHEARN; Alexander Graham BELL; J. Armand BOMBARDIER; Gerald Vincent BULL; Karl Adolf CLARK; William Harrison COOK; Georges-Édouard DESBARATS; Charles FENERTY; Ivan Graeme FERGUSON; Reginald Aubrey FESSENDEN; Robert FOULIS; Abraham GESNER; William Wallace GIBSON; Frederick Newton GISBORNE; Uno Vilho HELAVA; INDUSTRIAL RESEARCH AND DEVELOPMENT; George KLEIN; George Craig LAURENCE; Eric William LEAVER; PATENTS, COPYRIGHT AND INDUSTRIAL DESIGNS, Royal Commission on; Lloyd Montgomery PIDGEON; Frank Morse ROBB; Edward Samuel ROGERS; SCIENTIFIC RESEARCH AND DEVELOPMENT; Sir William Samuel STEPHENSON; TECHNOLOGY; W.R. TURNBULL; T.L. WILLSON.

DONALD J.C. PHILLIPSON

Reading: J.J. Brown, *Ideas in Exile* (1967); Science Council Special Study No 23, *Innovation and the Structure of Canadian Industry* (1972); Economic Council Publication No 22-113, *The Bottom Line: Technology, Trade and Income Growth* (1983).

Invermere, BC, Village, pop 1998 (1986c), 1969 (1981c), inc 1951, is located on the NW shore of Windermere Lk in the ROCKY MOUNTAIN TRENCH, 130 km N of Cranbrook and 120 km SE of Golden. Prehistoric KOOTENAY located here to net and spear salmon. David THOMPSON built the first trading post in the Columbia Dist near here 1807. In 1862 the first placer-gold miners arrived, and mining continued with the Paradise and Mineral King mines. Invermere became a centre for mountaineers in the Purcell Mts 1900-30, after Conrad KAIN, a prominent guide, made the area his home. Agriculture was established, along with beef production. Forestry is now the leading resource industry, but tourism also plays an important role, particularly at nearby Radium and Fairmont hot springs, and at Panorama Ski Resort. WILLIAM A. SLOAN

Inverness, NS, UP, pop 1910 (1986c), 2013 (1981c), is located 150 km W of Sydney, Cape Breton I. Inverness was settled in 1803 by Scottish immigrants who landed at Pictou, NS, and later drifted east to Cape Breton I in search of unoccupied farmland. During the 1800s it grew as an agricultural settlement. After the discovery of coal in 1863, Inverness came to depend more and more on mining. American industrialist William Penn Hussey formed the Broad Cove Coal Co in 1894 and put his expertise into developing the Inverness mines. The mines were sold to Inverness Ry and Coal Co in 1899, and the town prospered. It was named Inverness in 1904 (pop 3000) for the Scottish home of many of its settlers. The mines reached peak production just after 1910, with an average annual output of almost 300 000 t, but decreasing demand, rising costs and hazardous underground problems drove the company into receivership by 1915. The NS government attempted to revive the dying industry, which finally ceased operations in the 1950s; mining was completely abandoned by 1965. Today, Inverness serves as a minor regional centre for rural western Cape Breton I. DEBRA MCNABB

Invertebrate, animal without a vertebral column (backbone). As a group, invertebrates are extremely diverse, differing as much among themselves as they do from the VERTEBRATES, which they greatly outnumber. Some 95% of all animal species are invertebrates, 85% being arthropods. They populate all major environments: marine, freshwater and terrestrial; some are parasites in other animals. Invertebrates may be carnivores, herbivores or omnivores. Some even culture bacteria or plant cells in their tissues (in symbiosis), making use of the by-products. There are invertebrates that swim, float, fly, walk, crawl or burrow, and others that are fixed in one spot. Some of these sessile forms have no power of movement (eg, the glass SPONGES). Endless variations exist in the mechanisms whereby physiological functions (respiration, excretion, movement, co-ordination, etc) are carried out. Some groups (eg, INSECTS, NEMATODES) have developed extraordinarily successful designs. Other designs, though simple, have endured virtually unchanged for hundreds of millions of years (eg, BRACHIOPODS).

While invertebrates are certainly conspicuous on land, they are far more so in the sea. The most elaborate of all marine communities, the coral reef, is dominated by invertebrates. Marine PLANKTON includes representatives of all major invertebrate phyla. The copepod CRUSTACEANS, in both numbers of species (7500) and numbers of individuals, exceed all the rest of metazoan multicelled plankton combined. Some invertebrates, eg, crabs, shrimp, mussels, oysters and squid, are of economic importance. While shellfish cannot compete with fish in sheer volume caught, they are important in cash value.

The origins of most invertebrate groups are buried in early geological history. Surprisingly advanced forms, including ANNELID worms and MOLLUSCS, have been found in rocks from the Canadian Arctic dating from the Precambrian period (more than 570 million years ago). Many once-important groups have dwindled; others have become extinct as new forms emerged. Because of the patchiness of the FOSSIL record, it is often hard to decide on evolutionary relationships in different invertebrate groups, but comparison of structure and development of existing forms may give clues to their ancestry. Thus, the annelids and molluscs, though seemingly very different as adults, show remarkable similarities in their development; both are considered offshoots from the line of evolution leading to the arthropods. Specialists are fairly well agreed upon the broad outlines; however, classifications change continually as new facts come to light.

Invertebrates in Canada Canada's climatic and ecological diversity is matched by an equivalent diversity of invertebrate types. Scorpions and sun spiders live in the hot, dry country around Medicine Hat, ICE-WORMS in the Columbia Icefields; midges and mosquitoes plague the inhabitants of many regions; leeches and flatworm larvae bother bathers in some prairie lakes ("swimmers itch"); starfish and sea anemones delight the eyes of wanderers along the seashore; and the invertebrate fossils of the BURGESS SHALE are famous throughout the world. In Canada research on invertebrates is largely concentrated on insects important to agriculture and forestry, eg,

Phylum	*Habitat*	*Examples*
Cnidaria (9 000 species)	mainly marine	sea anemone, hydra coral, jellyfish
Ctenophora (50 species)	marine plankton	comb jelly, sea gooseberry
Platyhelminthes (12 700 species)	mainly parasitic	flatworm, fluke, tapeworm
Nemertea (600 species)	mainly marine	ribbon worm
Acanthocephala (500 species)	parasitic	spiny-headed worm
Rotifera (1 800 species)	marine and fresh water	wheel animal
Nematoda (10 000 species)	all habitats many parasitic	round worm
Brachiopoda (280 species)	marine benthos, and intertidal	lampshell
Bryozoa (4 000 species)	aquatic	moss animal
Pogonophora (80 species)	deep-sea benthos	beard worm
Mollusca (100 000 species)	all habitats	clam, snail, octopus, squid
Annelida (8 700 species)	aquatic or in damp soil	earthworm, leech, tube worm
Arthropoda (923 000 species)	all habitats	insect, spider, crustacean
Chaetognatha (50 species)	marine plankton	arrow worm
Echinodermata (6 000 species)	marine benthos and intertidal	sea urchin, starfish
Protochordates	marine	sea squirt

spruce budworm, parasites of fish and domestic animals; and on edible marine molluscs and crustaceans (shellfish), copepods and other marine planktonic invertebrates. However, specialists in most of the invertebrate groups are scattered across the country in government laboratories, research institutes and universities. Published works on invertebrate species in Canada are generally regional in nature and of interest primarily to specialists. The Biological Survey of Canada (attached to the National Museums) develops and co-ordinates work on invertebrates, and publishes a newsletter. Invertebrates are far less well known than are higher animals. Of the 2000-4000 new animal species discovered annually, most are invertebrates from remote places (eg, the Alpha Ridge of Canada's ARCTIC ARCHIPELAGO). G.O. MACKIE

Reading: Robert D. Barnes, *Invertebrate Zoology* (1980).

Ipeelee, Osuitok, earlier known as Oshaweetok B, sculptor, printmaker (b 1923). Unlike many Sikusalingmiut living on the SW coast of Baffin I, Osuitok Ipeelee's forefathers were native to that region. His family had not been part of the migration from Arctic Québec to the Fox Pen near the turn of the century. Osuitok came from a family of carvers. Among the Inuit in the early 1950s, Osuitok had the highest reputation of any ivory or stone carver. He also tried his hand at printmaking with great success (*Four Muskoxen* and others) but soon returned to his spirited style of stone carving. Over the years, Osuitok has built an outstanding reputation as a sculptor and has probably gained greater financial success than any other artist. His carvings possess an exceptional sense of life and movement. His work is represented in art museums and important private collections throughout the world. JAMES HOUSTON

Iqaluit [formerly Frobisher Bay], NWT, Town, pop 2947 (1986c), 2333 (1981c), inc 1980, is located near the NE head of FROBISHER BAY on southern BAFFIN I, 1944 air km N of MONTRÉAL. The town is near a traditional South Baffin Inuit fishing camp, where a temporary summer camp was established each year to fish for arctic char. The first European contact was made by Sir Martin FROBISHER on his search for the NORTHWEST PASSAGE in 1576. In 1942 the US Air Force used nearby flats as a landing strip in their efforts to resupply the USSR's war effort. By the 1950s, the landing strip had become part of the DEW Line's network of supply bases and a strategic focal point for US Air Force activities. Today, there is a mixed population of whites and Inuit, and many in the community still subsist on fishing, sealing, trapping and carving. It is the government administrative, communications and transportation centre of the eastern Arctic. On 1 Jan 1987, in keeping with the NWT government's decision to restore aboriginal names, the town became the first arctic community to revert to its original name: Iqaluit, "the place where the fish are." ANNELIES POOL

Iranians Iran, formerly known as Persia, is a predominantly Muslim country in southwestern Asia with a population of more than 50 million. About 90% of the population is Shi'ite Muslim; 8%, Sunni Muslim; and 2% is made up of diverse religious groups, including Zoroastrians (the most ancient of all Iranian minorities), Jews, Assyrians (eastern Christians), Armenians and Baha'is.

There is no record of Iranian immigration to Canada prior to WWII. Between 1946 and 1965, less than 300 Iranians immigrated to Canada; many of them were students who remained in Canada after their studies. From 1966 to 1984, 12 395 Iranian immigrants arrived, including 10 665 from 1976 to 1984. Assuming continuation of recent immigration trends, an addition 4000 to 5000 would have arrived 1985-87. Some of these immigrants came from the US, and others from Britain, W Germany, France, Italy and Spain. Many factors have contributed to Iranian immigration, but the most significant are economic and educational opportunities in Canada and estrangement from the Islamic regime.

Like many emigrants from other parts of the world, Iranian immigrants to Canada are a youthful group, with a slight male majority. They have come as individuals or as individual family units. Most possess exceptionally high educational or occupational qualifications.

It is estimated that by 1987 the Iranian community in Canada numbered 18 000-20 000, the majority in urban centres in Ontario (50%), Québec (20%) and BC (20%). The majority of Iranian immigrants are Muslim, but the eastern Christians and Baha'is are overrepresented proportional to their distribution in Iran. The Iranian Canadian community is one of the newest additions to Canada's ethnic mosaic, but it is in the process of development and will doubtless soon establish its own institutions and distinctive mode of adaptation to the new environment. BAHA ABU-LABAN

Irish While it has been argued (with little supporting evidence) that Irish explorers such as Brendan the Bold preceded the Norse to Canada, such wishful thinking is not necessary to establish the significance of the Irish contribution to Canada. Since the 17th century, because of political and military links between France and southern Ireland, the Irish have lived in what is now Canada. The Irish may have constituted as much as 5% of the population of New France. Indeed, some "French Canadian" and "Acadian" surnames derive from a corruption of Irish names, eg, Riel (from Reilly) and Caissie (from Casey). There have also been Irish in NEWFOUNDLAND since the early 18th century, if not before. "Bristol" fishing vessels habitually stopped at Wexford and Waterford to take on provisions and an Irish crew and labourers for the Newfoundland fishery. There is some indication from New France and Newfoundland that among the Irish at this time there existed a measure of group consciousness, especially in Newfoundland where the Irish population continued to increase until the middle of the 19th century. During the 18th century, smaller groups of Irish began to arrive in the new British colonies. During the 1760s a group of Ulster Presbyterians settled at TRURO, NS, and an undetermined number of Irish were part of the LOYALIST migration.

All of the above were precursors of the main waves of Irish immigrants that arrived during the first half of the 19th century. By the 1850s, over 500 000 Irish had immigrated to British N America, although many of them had moved on to the US (in NY and Boston there were 4 million Irish out of a total population of 24 million) or elsewhere. Today the descendants of these Irish immigrants comprise more than 10% of the Canadian population and have helped define the meaning of "Canadian." Because they spoke English, the Irish could participate more directly in Canadian society than many non-English-speaking immigrants, and they brought to bear on Canadian life many values that were Irish in origin. In particular, education, law and politics have felt the impact of the Irish mind. Well-known Irish in Canada have included Edward BLAKE, Edmund BURKE, Sir Guy CARLETON, Benjamin CRONYN, John Joseph LYNCH, D'Alton MCCARTHY, John O'Conner, Eugene O'KEEFE, Michael Sullivan, Timothy Sullivan, Thomas D'arcy MCGEE and Brian MULRONEY.

Migration and Settlement The migrations of the 17th and 18th centuries had little permanent impact on Canada, except in Newfoundland where many Irish worked as fishermen and lived in the kind of dire poverty they had hoped to escape by migration to the New World. Newfoundland had acquired a name in the Irish language – *Talamh an Eisc* – a singular distinction in the New World. In the 19th century, the growing population and deteriorating economy of Ireland forced a growing stream of Irish to emigrate, particularly after 1815. Simultaneously the economy of the mainland colonies of British N America expanded, offering better opportunities for immigrants. However, because they were relatively poor immigrants with little money for moving across Canada, the Irish tended to settle in the Maritimes.

By the 1830s Nova Scotia, New Brunswick, PEI and Upper and Lower Canada had significant Irish populations. Some immigrants spread throughout the countryside, partly because land from recent timber operations was cheap, but generally because the Irish tended, unlike the SCOTS or ENGLISH, to remain in the ports, such as Halifax, and Saint John, where they provided cheap IMMIGRANT LABOUR. Even in rural districts, many Irish preferred to seek employment instead of, or in addition to, setting up farms. By the 1830s Cumberland County in Nova Scotia; Kings, Queens, Carleton and Northumberland counties in New Brunswick; Queens in PEI; and virtually the whole of Upper Canada E of Toronto and N of the older Loyalist settlements were notably Irish in character.

The Great Famine of the late 1840s drove 1.5 to 2 million destitute Irish out of Ireland, and hundreds of thousands came to British N America. This wave was so dramatic that most Canadians erroneously think of 1847 as the time "when the Irish came." The famine immigrants tended to remain in the towns and cities, and by 1871 the Irish were the largest ethnic group in every large town and city of Canada, with the exceptions of Montréal and Québec City.

The "Famine Irish," who supplied a mass of cheap labour that helped fuel the economic expansion of the 1850s and 1860s, were not well received. They were poor and the dominant society resented them for the urban and rural squalor in which they were forced to live. But the Famine Irish had another characteristic: the propensity to immigrate to the US. Thousands had left for the US by the 1860s, establishing a tradition that remained unbroken well into the 20th century. As a result, in Canada today "Irish" districts and communities are generally those that were established before the famine. For example, in the Maritimes, only Saint John has a significant Famine Irish element. Today, Ontario has the largest population of Irish outside the Atlantic provinces. By the 20th century, there was a significant Irish community in Winnipeg and in a few rural districts of Manitoba, but the impact of the Irish in the West has not been as important as in the East.

Social and Cultural Life The most important single feature of the Irish, both in Ireland and in Canada, is that they have been divided into 2 different and mutually hostile groups. This division is so fundamental that the Irish might be considered 2 ethnic groups. Although it is common practice to refer to Irish people as either Catholic or Protestant, religion itself has never been much more than the easiest determinant of a group affiliation that consists of many factors. The Catholics perceive themselves to be the representatives of the original inhabitants of Ireland, while the Protestants represent the Scots and English colonists who arrived in Ireland when it was under British rule. Because the Catholics were socially and politically disadvantaged in Ireland, they arrived in Canada with few advantages other than a familiarity with the English language and British institutions. They lacked the means to establish themselves securely within the economy and had little impact on the business community. The Catholic Church, an important institution for the Catholic Irish in Ireland, was shared by the Irish in Canada with the Highland Scots and the French, and helped the Irish in the difficult process of integration into Canadian society.

The Protestant Irish, in contrast, generally had more money and found it significantly easier to re-establish themselves as farmers. They became one of the most agrarian of groups in 19th-century Canada. Because their religion made them more acceptable to the dominant society, they were able to move much more freely in Canadian society.

Both groups were rich in cultural traditions, but with significant differences. The Catholic Irish tended to keep alive traditions of being Irish whereas the Protestants tended to glory in their contributions to British civilization. Neither group has preserved much lore about the actual migrations, even the trauma of the famine, but both groups tend to be aware of the more recent experiences in Canada.

Group Maintenance The Protestant Irish tended to stress the importance of the British connection in order to distance themselves from their Catholic compatriots. The ORANGE ORDER, the original purpose of which in Ireland was to preserve British rule (at least in Ulster), was essential in Canada as a vehicle by which the Protestant Irish could gain acceptance from their Scots and English neighbours. Individual Orange Order lodges existed in New Brunswick and in Upper Canada from the early part of the 19th century, and the order was consolidated in 1830 as the Grand Lodge of British N America. Whenever British institutions in Canada seemed to be in peril, Orangemen were fond of bringing up the Protestant victory over the Catholics at the River Boyne in 1690, and the anniversary of that battle (July 12) remains the great Orange celebration. During the latter half of the 19th century, the lodge became increasingly nativist, and today it is difficult to detect a specific Protestant Irish tradition that is distinct from a broad British tradition.

Irish emigrants arrive at Cork – a scene of the quay, from *The Illustrated London News*. Massive emigration from Ireland led to fears that the island would be depopulated (*courtesy National Archives of Canada/C-3904*).

Over the past 150 years, the term Irish has acquired a Catholic connotation. The Catholic Church, the institutional bedrock of the Catholic Irish community in Canada, laboured to gain acceptance for its people, which meant that Irish priests and bishops were often opposed to any manifestations of sympathy for nationalism in Ireland. For the Irish in the US, there was no such problem, because there it was possible to be a good Irishman, a good Catholic and a good American. But in Canada, where citizenship remained British for so long, it was extremely difficult to be Irish politically and a good citizen as well. It was also difficult at times to be Irish and a good Catholic. For example, the Fenian Brotherhood, whose aim was to free Ireland by force of arms, was very popular among the Irish in the US, but in Canada the Fenians (though few in number) were considered seditious by the government, were considered dangerous by the Protestants, and were viewed as an embarrassment by the Catholic Church and by respectable Catholic Irish. FENIAN RAIDS from the US against British N America inspired hostility towards the Catholic Irish and provoked attestments of loyalty from the church and from respectable Catholic Irish. The later and more benign Ancient Order of Hibernians was also dedicated, if less violently, to the cause of Irish nationalism, but it too fell afoul of the Catholic Church.

As English-speaking Catholics, the Catholic Irish in Canada found themselves at odds with French-speaking Catholics as well as with the Protestant majority. Because of the sense of isolation among the Catholic Irish, a sense of identity was stronger among them than among the Protestant Irish.

The Protestant Irish have sustained a powerful belief in institutional strength, and have clung to structures tenaciously. Stability is seen to be their greatest virtue. By contrast, the Catholic Irish define power in personal terms to a degree which may seem anarchistic, but which represents a survival of the patron-client relationship, the basis of politics in rural Ireland. The talent of the Catholic Irish in Canada and elsewhere has been that they could translate this personal approach to politics and to power brokerage in the modern setting. PETER TONER

Reading: C.J. Houston and W.J. Smyth, *The Sash Canada Wore* (1980); W.S. Neidhardt, *Fenianism in North America* (1975).

Irish Moss is the common name for a red ALGAE (*Chondrus crispus*), but may also refer to 1 or 2 other red SEAWEEDS (*Gigartina stellata* and *Furcellaria lumbricalis*). *C. crispus*, the only species of the genus in the Atlantic Ocean, occurs from New Jersey to Labrador, and is most abundant in NS and the lower Gulf of St Lawrence. The plants are perennial, grow on rock in lower tidal and subtidal zones, and arise from disclike "holdfasts." Commonly, the fronds are up to 15 cm high, branched (usually in one plane only) and fan-shaped. The colour varies (dark red, purple, yellow-green), depending on physiological conditions. Dried plants are nearly black. A life cycle consisting of 2 independent and structurally similar phases (sexual and asexual) has been demonstrated in the laboratory. Irish moss is Canada's most valuable commercial seaweed. Originally used in blancmanges and milk jellies, it is still available in "natural food" stores. The dried plants are used to clarify beers, wines, coffee and honey. Since WWII, major exploitation has been for extraction of hydrocolloids (substances yielding gel when water is added, eg, carrageenians) used in convenience foods. Carrageenin is not processed in Canada, and thousands of tonnes of Irish moss are exported annually. AQUACULTURE trials, in tanks and pools, have been carried out in NS. J. McLACHLAN

Iron and Steel Industry includes establishments involved in smelting IRON ORE, in steelmaking (ie, alloying iron and carbon) and in using these materials to fabricate a range of products essential to an industrialized society. Iron is the fourth most plentiful element in Earth's crust, after oxygen, silicon and aluminum. It occurs as iron-ore minerals, the most important, in order of iron content, being magnetite, hematite, goethite, pyrrhotite, siderite and pyrite. Steel is primarily an alloy of iron and carbon in which the carbon content varies from about 0.02% (eg, sheet metal, wire) to 1.5% (tool steels). Alloy steels contain additional elements (eg, manganese, nickel, chromium, vanadium, molybdenum) which give them greater strength and specific properties (eg, chromium makes steel stainless).

Canada is the world's sixth-largest producer and fourth-largest exporter of iron ore. In 1986 iron ore was produced by 5 companies (6 iron mines), directly employing about 7000 people and supporting 9 communities. In 1986 Canada shipped 36.1 million t of iron ore valued at $1.25 billion, of which some 31.0 million t valued at $1.1 billion were exported. Canada imports 5.4 million t annually, mainly from the US, and consumes nearly 10 million t annually to produce iron and steel. The Québec-Labrador region accounts for most of Canada's total production; Ontario and BC produce the remainder.

During the period 1939 to 1970, annual Canadian steel production increased from just over one million to 11 million t. The Canadian steel industry is made up of 5 major, fully integrated iron and steel producers, 26 steel foundries and 28 other primary steel manufacturers. In 1986 these companies produced over 11.7 million t of raw steel, making Canada the world's ninth-largest steel producer. Most of Canada's steel output is concentrated in Ontario in the "Big 3" steel companies: Stelco, Dofasco and Algoma. These companies are recognized as among the most efficient and innovative steelmakers in the world. As well, in 1986 there were 34 firms producing steel ingots, steel castings and pig iron, and 21 firms producing rolled steel products.

In Canada the FORGES SAINT-MAURICE, near Trois-Rivières, Qué, produced iron from local bog iron ore and charcoal to supply settlers and the military (*see* BLACKSMITHING). The first ironworks in Upper Canada, the Marmora Ironworks, near Peterborough, Ont, began production in 1822. It consisted of 2 charcoal-fired blast furnaces, a forge with 2 sets of waterpowered hammers and special hearths for the production of iron bar. At the time it was the largest ironworks in Canada and probably the most advanced in N America. In the late 19th century both the Marmora and the St-Maurice ironworks were closed. They could no longer compete with more modern ironworks in Ontario and NS, which employed coke-fired blast furnaces.

Steel products were first manufactured in Canada in the 1880s. By the early 1900s steelmaking centres had been established in HAMILTON and SAULT STE MARIE, Ont, and in SYDNEY, NS. These centres had easy access to iron-ore deposits recently discovered near Lk Superior and on Bell I, Nfld, and to coking coals from the Appalachians and Cape Breton. Iron and steel production grew slowly until WWII and the postwar economic boom created a tremendous demand for steel.

Processing Iron and steel production first involves bringing together the required raw materials: iron ore, coal, limestone, and iron and steel scrap. The iron ore is then smelted to produce an impure metal called hot metal, if liquid, or pig iron, if solid. The hot metal is refined to remove impurities and to develop the required composition. The liquid steel is then cast in sand or ingot molds, or continuously cast into blooms, slabs or billets. Finally the ingots, blooms, slabs and billets are processed into the desired shapes in rolling mills or by forging.

Large integrated steel plants are located wherever it is convenient to bring together the large quantities of raw materials required. The big steel plants in Canada have been built at Sault Ste Marie (ALGOMA STEEL CORPORATION LTD) and Hamilton (STELCO, DOFASCO), Ont; Contrecoeur (SIDBEC-DOSCO LIMITÉE), Qué; and Sydney (SYDNEY STEEL CORPORATION), NS, ie, along the Great Lakes-ST LAWRENCE SEAWAY system and the Atlantic seaboard. These are areas to which iron ores from northern Ontario, Québec, Labrador, Minnesota, Wisconsin and Michigan, and COAL from Pennsylvania, West Virginia and Kentucky can be transported most economically. Scrap iron and steel, which are collected for recycling, require adjustment of composition and casting before the finishing operations. Thus, many small steel plants, each making a few thousand tonnes of steel annually, have been built throughout the country where scrap is available and a ready market for the finished steel exists. Examples of such facilities include Western Canada Steel Ltd, Vancouver; Stelco, Edmonton; Western Canada Steel Ltd, Calgary; Interprovincial Steel and Pipe Corp Ltd, Regina; Manitoba Rolling Mills (Canada) Ltd, Selkirk, Man; Burlington Steel Division of Slater Steel Industries Ltd, Hamilton, Atlas Steels, a division of Rio Algom Ltd, Welland, Lake Ontario Steel Co Ltd, Whitby, and Ivaco Ltd, L'Orignal, Ont; and Atlas Steels, Tracy, Qué.

Iron ore mining at Carol Lake, Labrador (*courtesy Iron Ore Company of Canada*).

Iron Making Iron ores consist primarily of hematite or magnetite, associated with variable amounts of other unwanted minerals (eg, quartz), which are collectively known as gangue. An ore may be high- or low-grade, depending on the relative proportions of iron minerals and gangue. High-grade ores (in excess of 50% iron) may often be smelted in blast furnaces without preliminary preparation, other than crushing and sizing. Low-grade ores must be upgraded to remove excess gangue before smelting. This operation requires fine grinding of the ore to liberate the iron minerals from the gangue, followed by a concentrating process that separates out the iron minerals. Magnetite ores are particularly suitable for concentration because of their magnetic properties. Ground concentrates must be agglomerated into larger particles before smelting, either by rolling them into small pellets ("pelletizing") or by heating the fine particles until they stick together ("sintering"). Ores containing siderite (the iron carbonate mineral) are less often used because they must be heated by sintering before smelting in order to convert the iron carbonate to an iron oxide. Since 1939 Algoma Steel Corp Ltd has operated one siderite mine at Wawa, northern Ontario. Pyrite and pyrrhotite, although plentiful, are rarely used as iron ores because of the objectionable amounts of sulphur they contain (*see* ACID RAIN).

Following WWII, MINING and processing of iron ores expanded greatly in Canada. The IRON ORE CO OF CANADA operates mines in Québec and at Carol Lk, Labrador, with concentrating and pelletizing plants at Labrador City. In Labrador, Wabush Mines carries out mining and concentrating operations at Wabush Lk and pelletizing at Pointe Noire. Dofasco produces pellets at Adams Mine, Kirkland Lake, Ont, and Sherman Mine, Temagami, Ont. The Québec-Cartier Mining Co mines and concentrates at Lac Jeannin, Qué.

Blast furnaces are heated by burning high-quality coke, a substance high in carbon and low in ash and sulphur, which is distilled from coal. The future of the blast-furnace process is largely dependent on adequate resources of suitable coking coals. A blast furnace is a tall, cylindrical shaft furnace in which ore, coke and limestone are charged to the top and liquid iron and slag are tapped at regular intervals from the hearth at the bottom. The iron melts and dissolves carbon from the coke. The carbon content of the hot metal is about 4.5%. Limestone is added to the charge to provide basic lime, which reacts with the acidic gangue to form slag. Proper proportioning of the acidic and basic constituents forms a low-melting, free-running liquid slag that absorbs most of the sulphur in the charge. Liquid slag does not mix with liquid iron and is separated during furnace tapping.

In recent years, several solid-state reduction processes have been developed in which iron ore is converted to metallic iron without melting. There is no separation of iron from gangue and the use of high-grade ores or concentrates is essential. Many of these processes use natural gas, avoiding the use of expensive coke. Sidbec-Dosco operates such a process at Contrecoeur, Qué, and Stelco has a solid-state reduction plant at the Griffith Mine. Solid-state reduced ore and pellets are melted in electric furnaces and converted to steel in the same way as scrap metal. Separation of the gangue takes place at this stage. Reduced pellets are superior to scrap in purity and uniformity of composition but are not economically competitive with scrap.

Steelmaking Hot metal and pig iron contain silicon, phosphorus, sulphur and often other elements in addition to carbon. These must be removed during steelmaking and the carbon level adjusted by oxidation. The Bessemer process, invented in England in 1856 and used extensively in Europe until the 1960s, was the first large-scale steelmaking process. This method was followed by the invention, a few years later, of the open-hearth process, which from about 1900 to the early 1960s accounted for most of the steel production in the Western world. The open-hearth process is now rapidly disappearing in favour of the basic oxygen process that originated in Austria, where the first plants were built in 1952-53, and was introduced to N America in 1954 by Dofasco in Hamilton, Ont. In this process oxygen gas is blown into a bath of hot metal. Lime is added to produce a slag with the oxidized silicon and phosphorus and to absorb the sulphur. Carbon burns to carbon monoxide. Scrap metal is added to control the temperature. When the carbon content reaches the desired level, alloying elements are added as required, and the liquid steel is cast into molds and solidified.

In the early 1960s, Guy Savard and Robert Lee of Canadian Liquid Air designed an injector that made it possible to introduce pure oxygen through the bottom of vessels normally used for the Bessemer process. This method was developed to industrial scale in W Germany. The first industrial plant was converted in 1968. The conversion of all remaining Bessemer plants in Europe was completed in the next 4 years. It thus became possible to make all grades of high-quality steel and to increase the scrap charge from 5% to 25%.

In 1985 a total of 566 million metric t of crude steel in the form of ingots were produced in non-

To reach the iron ore beneath a lake at Steep Rock, Ont, the entire lake was drained. Here the successive levels of mining show on the face of the rock (*photo by John deVisser*).

communist countries: two-thirds by oxygen processes; about one-quarter by the electric-furnace process; and the remainder by the open-hearth process.

Products The greatest tonnage of liquid steel is formed into large ingots or is continuously cast. Ingots are large, rectangular blocks of steel, most of which are shaped into finished products by rolling mills. The first finishing step is the hot rolling of ingots into blooms, slabs or billets. Continuous casting eliminates this stage: liquid steel is poured into the top of the mold and the bloom, slab or billet is discharged continuously from the bottom. The first successful continuous casting machine for steel in N America was developed by Atlas Steels, Welland, Ont, in 1954. For the most part, blooms, slabs and billets are reduced in rolling mills to finished products such as sheet, plate, strip, rail, structural steel, bar, pipe and wire products. Most shapes are hot-rolled at temperatures above 800°C. Some steels (eg, sheet, strip) are finished by cold-rolling at room temperature to obtain close dimensional tolerances, high-quality surface finish and an exact degree of hardness. *See also* MINERAL RESOURCES.

H.U. ROSS AND J.G. PEACEY

Reading: A.R. Dunn, *The Early History of Iron in Canada* (1980); C.S. Russell and W.J. Vaughan, *Steel Production* (1976).

Iron Ore, is a MINERAL substance that yields metallic iron (Fe) when heated in the presence of a reducing agent such as COAL. Iron ore usually consists of iron oxides. Its most important mineral forms are magnetite (Fe_3O_4, 72.4% Fe), hematite (Fe_2O_3, 69.9% Fe) and goethite or limonite ($Fe_2O_3.3H_2O$, 62.9% Fe). When mined in its natural state, iron ore is called crude ore; when slightly processed by crushing and screening, it is called direct-shipping ore. Concentrates result from processing an ore to raise its iron content. Concentrates and finely divided ores must be agglomerated into pellets, sinter or briquettes before being reduced to iron in blast furnaces. Almost all iron ore mined in Canada must be concentrated to produce a commercial product, because Canadian crude ores are low-to-medium grade. The major steps in processing include crushing, screening and the use of gravitational, magnetic and flotation concentration methods. Concentration increases the iron content from an average of 36% to 63%. Iron was among the first ores mined in Canada (*see* FORGES SAINT-MAURICE). In 1986 Canada shipped 36.1 million t of iron ore valued at $1.25 billion.

M. BOUCHER

Iron Ore Company of Canada, incorporated 1949 by Labrador Mining and Exploration and Hanna Mining interests to exploit the some 400 million t of open-pit IRON ORE reserves proved in central Québec and Labrador in the late 1940s. In order to bring the ore to the port of SEPT ÎLES on the St Lawrence R, the company undertook construction of the QUEBEC NORTH SHORE & LABRADOR RY (573 km long, completed 1954), 2 hydroelectric power stations, a huge shipping terminal at Sept-Îles, roads, mine spurs and crushing plants at the mine sites, and the townsites of Sept-Îles and SCHEFFERVILLE. Construction required a huge airlift, 13 landing strips and some 6900 workers. The first shipment of ore left Schefferville 15 July 1954. The company opened mining facilities, a crushing plant, a pellet plant and offices in LABRADOR CITY in the early 1960s. In 1954-55 IOC built facilities at Contrecoeur, on the S shore of the St Lawrence between Québec and Montréal, to transfer ore to lake carriers. The transfer was no longer necessary after the opening of the ST LAWRENCE SEAWAY, but the docks are still used. In 1983 the company shut down its Schefferville operations.

Iroquois is a term which designates a confederacy of 5 tribes originally inhabiting the northern part of New York state, consisting of the SENECA, CAYUGA, ONEIDA, ONONDAGA and MOHAWK, also known as the League of the Five Nations or the League of the Iroquois. When the Tuscarora joined the confederacy early in the 18th century, it became known as the Six Nations. The 5 tribes of the Iroquois League occupied an area from the Genesee R on the W, through the Finger Lks regions, to the Hudson R on the E. They used the metaphor of the LONGHOUSE to describe their political alliance; hence the Seneca, as the most westerly, were known as "keepers of the western door," and the Mohawk have been called the "keepers of the eastern door." A very rough estimate of the Iroquois population at the time of European contact would be approximately 10 000-15 000 people.

The Iroquois were linguistically related to neighbouring tribes, such as the HURON, PETUN and NEUTRAL, and to more distant tribes including the Cherokee and Tuscarora. There are also suggestions of ancient relationships to the Siouan and Caddoan language families of the Great Plains.

The ancestors of the Iroquois can be traced backwards in New York state by archaeological evidence to at least 500 BC, and possibly as far back as 4000 BC. The distinctive Iroquois culture of the historic period seems to have developed by about 1000 AD. Archaeology suggests that during the 15th century individual villages joined together to form the 5 historic tribes, and that by the 16th century the continuation of this process had resulted in the formation of the League of the Iroquois. With the coming of the FUR TRADE in this historic period, the Five Nations embarked on successful campaigns to subjugate or disperse neighbouring groups. The Huron were forced to abandon their homeland after 2 villages were destroyed in 1649; the Petun, Neutral and Erie all succumbed to Iroquois arms in the next decade. Their military reputation was well respected in territory as distant as the Maritime provinces and the western Great Lakes.

The French maintained trading and military alliances with many of the enemies of the Iroquois, hence Iroquoia and NEW FRANCE were often at war (*see* IROQUOIS WARS). During periods of peace some Iroquois were converted to Catholicism and persuaded to settle on the St Lawrence. The Iroquois remained firmly tied to the Albany, NY, trade and rivalry between the French colony and the Dutch and English at Albany precluded a lasting peace between New France and the Iroquois. The Iroquois frequently raided French settlements on the St Lawrence and, in 1660 at the Long Sault and in 1689 at Lachine, Qué, sent large armies to attack the colony. France successfully attacked Iroquois towns in 1666, 1687, 1693 and 1696.

Treaties with both the French and English in 1701 marked a shift in Iroquois policy toward neutrality with European powers in N America. At this time population losses for the league, owing to both disease and war, had been considerable, even though the Iroquois had absorbed large numbers of war captives and refugees and had incorporated them into their society. Despite official neutrality, the Mohawk under the influence of Sir William JOHNSON did on occasion take the field as English allies, and the Seneca at times fought beside French armies, as at the defeat of General Braddock in 1755.

Except for the Oneida, who fought for the American cause, the Iroquois supported the LOYALISTS and British in the American Revolution, joining that conflict in 1777. The Mohawk lost their homes to neighbouring rebel settlers, and most Seneca, Onondaga and Cayuga towns were burned in 1779. In turn the Iroquois and their allies, under the leadership of Joseph BRANT and others, repeatedly attacked and burned rebel forts and settlements, driving the frontier E to Schenectady, NY. After the war, many Iroquois followed Brant to settle on a land grant secured for them by Gov Frederick HALDIMAND on the Grand R and others settled on the Bay of Quinte.

Before the disruption of their culture by the events of the historic period, the Iroquois were horticulturalists, living year-round in stockaded villages of several hundred people. Social structure was based on matrilineal principles. The basic unit was the matrilineage, consisting of the descendants, through females, of a single woman. Female members lived together with their husbands (who belonged to other matrilineages) in a

The False Face Society was the best known of the Iroquois curing societies. The masks played an important role in curing ceremonies (*courtesy National Museums of Canada/Canadian Museum of Civilization/S75-641*).

single longhouse; a village would contain anything from a few small longhouses to as many as 50. Several matrilineages formed the matrilineal clan which, besides being of symbolic and ceremonial importance, served to regulate marriage patterns. Marriage was forbidden between members of a clan. The Mohawk and Oneida had 3 such clans; the other Iroquois nations had from 8 to 10 clans. For the most part these clans bore animal names (eg, Bear, Wolf, Turtle, Hawk). The league was governed by a council of 50 sachems, with each of the 5 founding members of the confederacy represented by a delegation of 8-14 members. Each of these positions was hereditary within a matrilineage. The individual tribes and villages were governed by councils of their own sachems and chiefs.

Today, some 30 000 Iroquois are dispersed among several reserves in Canada. Among the largest concentrations of Iroquois in Canada are the Six Nations Reserve near Brantford, Ont, the Mohawks of Akwesasne near Cornwall, Ont, and Kahnawake outside Montréal. *See also* general articles under NATIVE PEOPLE. PETER G. RAMSDEN

Reading: L.H. Morgan, *League of the Ho-dé-no-sau-nee* or *Iroquois* (1861, repr *League of the Iroquois*, 1962); A.A. Shimony, *Conservatism among the Iroquois at the Six Nations Reserve* (1961); B.G. Trigger, ed, *Handbook of North American Indians*, vol 15: *Northeast* (1978).

Iroquois Falls, Ont, Town, pop 6191 (1986c), 6339 (1981c), inc 1915, is located NW of NORTH BAY. The town received not only its name but its *raison d'être* from its location at the falls on the Abitibi R, which supplies hydroelectric power for the community's economic lifeline, the pulp and paper industry. Area timber rights were first granted to the Abitibi Power & Paper Co (today ABITIBI-PRICE INC) in 1912. Abitibi constructed a carefully planned, model COMPANY TOWN 1915-20, the first of its kind in northern Ontario. In the 1920s company president Frank Anson initiated a beautification program that transformed Iroquois Falls into the "Garden Town of the North." The closed company-town phase ended in the 1950s. Historically paralleling the growth of Iroquois Falls was the development of the neighbouring noncompany communities of Ansonville and Montrock, and in 1971 these were amalgamated with Iroquois Falls. MATT BRAY

Iroquois Wars, a series of 17th-century conflicts involving the Five Nations IROQUOIS confederacy (MOHAWK, ONEIDA, ONONDAGA, CAYUGA and SENECA), numerous other Iroquoian groups and the French. As the Iroquois grew dependent on European trade goods, pressure was exerted on the rich beaver-producing areas S of the Canadian Shield. After Dutch traders on the Hudson R [NY] provided them with firearms, the Iroquois grew more militant. In 1628 they pushed the Mohicans E, and in the 1630s the Mohawk began to raid the ALGONQUIN in the Ottawa Valley. By the early 1640s the Mohawk and Oneida were attacking NEW FRANCE and raiding the colony's Algonquian and MONTAGNAIS allies throughout the St Lawrence Valley.

By 1642 the French had begun to halt these raids by building a chain of fortified settlements as far upriver as Montréal. The French tried to counter the Mohawk acquisition of muskets by giving muskets to their HURON and Algonquian allies, but the Jesuits persuaded officials to restrict their sale to reliable Christian converts. As a result, the Iroquois had a numerical and psychological advantage.

One of the profound effects of the Iroquois Wars was the dispersal of numerous native groups. The policy of the Seneca was to disperse the Huron, which left them free to raid the hunting peoples to the N. Their raids, beginning in 1642 with the more isolated Huron villages, culminated in 1649 with over 1000 Seneca and Mohawk attacking 2 main villages. Some Huron tried to hold out on a nearby island but were forced to disband; some fled to Québec and others joined the NEUTRAL. In the winter of 1649-50 the Iroquois attacked the Nipissing and the PETUN. The Neutral were decisively defeated in 1651. With the Huron nation destroyed and the Neutral crushed, the Iroquois increased their raids on the Mohican, Sokoki and ABENAKI, while in Québec they raided as far E as Tadoussac and N beyond Lac Mistassini. Faced with stiff resistance from the Susquehannock and the Erie, the Iroquois Confederacy entered into peace with the French in 1653. After concentrated Iroquois attacks, the Erie were absorbed in 1657. Renewed hostilities in 1659-60 on a wide front greatly strained the confederacy, and the Iroquois again sought peace with the French. But a treaty embracing all groups was not arranged until 1667, after the CARIGNAN-SALIÈRES REGIMENT had burned Mohawk villages and food supplies. By 1675 the Susquehannock to the S had been absorbed and the Iroquois moved westward into the Ohio Valley, where they fought the Illinois and Miami nations.

The Iroquois succeeded in breaking every one of the groups that surrounded the confederacy. However, the victories did not bring them the prosperity they sought. The treaty of 1667 had allowed the French to extend their trade in the N and, with Louis JOLLIET, they advanced through the Great Lakes to the Mississippi R. In Sept 1680 a large Iroquois force attacked a small French party under Henri de TONTY which was trading in an Illinois village; the Iroquois were persuaded to desist on condition that the French leave the Illinois country. As part of a broader conflict between French and English, the Iroquois attacked Lachine in force in 1689 (*see* LACHINE RAID). However, with the aid of some 1500 TROUPES DE LA MARINE, the defenders eventually forced the hard-pressed Iroquois to make peace. In a treaty ratified July 1701 at Montréal, they agreed to remain neutral in wars between the English and French.

Massacre of Hurons by the Iroquois, painting *c*1828 (long after the event) by Joseph Légaré. The French-Huron trade network excluded the Iroquois and exacerbated the ancient enmity between the 2 Iroquoian peoples, ending with the annihilation of the Huron in 1649 (*courtesy Musée du Québec/photo by Patrick Altman*).

Irrigation is warranted where the CLIMATE is essentially arid or semiarid and is characterized by low and unpredictable precipitation (*see* RAIN). In certain areas, such as the southern PRAIRIES, southern BC and SW Ontario, irrigation can be used to supplement limited rainfall to achieve desirable crop yields. In Canada irrigation is a relatively recent phenomenon. Before the 1890s, all irrigation was developed by private individuals. From 1898 to 1915, the major incentive was provided by private investment companies and corporations, including the CANADIAN PACIFIC RY. Since 1915 provincial governments have helped local communities organize irrigation developments, resulting in rapid increases in irrigated areas. In 1935 the federal government, through the PRAIRIE FARM REHABILITATION ADMINISTRATION, initiated a program to provide technical and financial assistance for the development of individual farm, community or large-scale WATER storage projects throughout the plains area. During the 1950 to 1960 period, the PFRA designed and constructed 2 major irrigation projects in co-operation with the governments of Alberta and Saskatchewan. The St Mary and Waterton dams and several internal storage reservoirs led to the development of the St Mary River Irrigation District in southern Alberta, Canada's largest, which comprised 132 600 ha in 1986. In south-central Saskatchewan, the GARDINER DAM, a multipurpose development, also established Saskatchewan's largest irrigation block of some 21 000 ha. Smaller project developments by PFRA and all the western provinces have continued through the 1970s and 1980s, including rehabilitation of older projects and major irrigation works.

About 747 625 ha of Canadian farmland was irrigated in 1986. Statistics Canada reports the total by region as follows: Atlantic provinces, 2038 ha; Qué, 15 284 ha; Ont, 52 535 ha; Prairie provinces, 559 954 ha (of which 466 291 ha were in Alta); BC, 117 811 ha. The most intensive irrigation development has taken place in southern Alberta. In 1970, the Alberta government, together with 13 irrigation districts, launched a major cost-shared irrigation rehabilitation program. During the period 1970-86, the province invested some $525 million for capital works rehabilitation and the districts expended $97 million, including their share for operation and maintenance. Rehabilitation of capital works has continued since 1970 to date on the 86:14 formula basis, which economic studies have determined as the ratio of "societal" accrued benefits and direct benefits to irrigation farmers.

Other provinces have established different policies and cost-sharing agreements with the

Furrow irrigation with syphon tubes from a field border ditch in southern Alberta (*courtesy Alberta Agriculture/Irrigation and Conservation Div*).

federal government for new developments, notably Saskatchewan, which announced a $100-million irrigation development agreement in 1986. Lack of sufficient rainfall is most limiting to crop production and agricultural diversification throughout the southern prairies. Within this region the soils and growing season are conducive to irrigation development on upwards of 2 to 3 million ha. However, future irrigation expansion is significantly curtailed by limited availability and location of major water sources, the high cost of capital works development, ie, storage dams, diversions and distribution networks, and by global market competition in agricultural commodities.

In Alberta, for example, while only 4% of arable land is irrigated, the production from this acreage accounts for approximately 18% of the province's gross annual agricultural production (approximately $850 million annually). Some 5800 irrigation farms are sustained in a region which otherwise could support perhaps fewer than 1000 dryland wheat and range cattle operations. Irrigation development and related services and processing industries account for the employment of some 35 000 people in Alberta, and sustain one of the most productive and diversified agricultural regions of Canada. EGON RAPP

Irvine, Acheson Gosford, soldier, police officer, prison warden (b at Québec C 7 Dec 1837; d there 9 Jan 1916). The third commissioner of the NWMP, Irvine's reputation was ruined by the NORTH-WEST REBELLION. A businessman active in the militia, he served with the Quebec Rifles on the RED RIVER EXPEDITION). He remained in Manitoba in command of the Provisional Battalion of Rifles until he joined the police in 1875. As assistant commissioner (1876-80) and commissioner (1880-86), he was responsible for policing the Indian tribes while they were settled on reserves. His warnings that the harsh Indian settlement policy could lead to rebellion were ignored. When rebellion broke out in 1885, he led a column of police to Prince Albert where he remained until the end of the fighting. His inaction was widely criticized and he resigned. Subsequently, he was warden of Stony Mountain Penitentiary (1892-1913) and Kingston Penitentiary (1913-14). A.B. MCCULLOUGH

Irvine, William, Unitarian minister, MP, journalist, political organizer (b at Gletness, Shetland, Scot 19 Apr 1885; d at Edmonton 27 Oct 1962). Irvine played a significant role in Canadian politics for 50 years, 17 as an MP. He organized Alberta farmers and labour to enter the political arena, and in 1921 was first elected to public office as the federal labour representative from Calgary E. Along with his close friend J.S. WOODSWORTH, at that time the only other labour MP, Irvine conducted a vigorous campaign against the economic power of large corporations and financial institutions. Irvine, Woodsworth and others in the radical GINGER GROUP advocated a form of democratic socialism. Their efforts culminated in the founding of the CO-OPERATIVE COMMONWEALTH FEDERATION (1932). In his later years, Irvine worked tirelessly for world peace and urged the necessity of coexistence among world powers despite differences in ideology. ANTHONY MARDIROS

Reading: Anthony Mardiros, *William Irvine* (1979).

Irving, John Allan, philosopher (b in Blenheim Township, Ont 6 May 1903; d at Toronto 3 Jan 1965). As an instructor in philosophy he was first at Princeton, and then at UBC. Later he became head of the dept of philosophy at Victoria Coll, Toronto, where he helped found the Canadian Philosophical Assn. His book *The Social Credit Movement in Alberta* (1959) is a definitive work. Irving's pioneering work on the history of philosophy in Canada, *Philosophy in Canada: A Symposium* (1952), stressed a belief of George BRETT that ideas are best grasped in historical contexts. Irving continued the Canadian tradition of taking philosophy to the public and was well known through his CBC radio programs.

ELIZABETH A. TROTT

Irving, Kenneth Colin, industrialist (b at Buctouche, NB 14 Mar 1899). Founder of an empire that ranges from pulp and paper and oil refining to publishing and broadcasting, he has been called New Brunswick's first modern entrepreneurial industrialist. He was born into a prosperous Scots Presbyterian family in Kent County, where his father ran a lumber business, and he attended Dalhousie and Acadia universities for short periods before going to England for service in the Royal Flying Corps. After WWI Irving took charge of a Ford motor agency and gas station, and in 1924, after a dispute with Imperial Oil, he borrowed enough money to establish the Irving Oil Co. He expanded rapidly into service stations and garages for storing and repairing cars, and in the 1930s took over bus and trucking companies that were heavily in debt to Irving Oil. By 1936, from his office in the Golden Ball Building in Saint John, he was directing the manufacture of buses and trucks and the purchase of ships and tanks for the transportation of his oil.

On the death of his father in 1933, Irving acquired J.D. Irving Ltd, the family lumber business, and in 1938 he bought Canada Veneers, which thrived on wartime sales to become the world's largest supplier of aircraft veneers. The growth of this company led to the acquisition of the New Brunswick Railway Co for its huge tracts of timberland. With the establishment in 1951 of Irving Pulp and Paper Ltd, Irving dominated the NB timber industry. By then, he also owned a number of Maritime newspapers.

Controversy surrounds the Irving empire. His decision to invest in NB industry has altered the course of that province's development, but his critics claim that his interests have often been served at the expense of the taxpayers and the environment. Irving's domination of the NB media symbolizes for many the negative aspects of the power he wields. Although he settled in Bermuda in Dec 1971, many in the province would still agree with the statement that "K.C. Irving *is* New Brunswick." In June 1987 he had a theatre in the new John Flemming Forestry Centre in Fredericton named for him. *See also* IRVING GROUP.

MARY HALLORAN

Irving Group, controlled by the K.C. IRVING family, dominates 90% of English-language NEWSPAPER circulation in NB. The New Brunswick Publishing Co Ltd, led by K.C. Irving and sons Arthur and James, is the owner and publisher of the *Telegraph Journal* and the *Evening Times-Globe* in Saint John. Another son, John, controls the Moncton Publishing Co Ltd, publisher of the Moncton *Times-Transcript*, and University Press New Brunswick Ltd, publisher of the Fredericton *Gleaner*. The New Brunswick Publishing Co Ltd also owns and controls New Brunswick Broadcasting Co Ltd, which owns and operates CHSJ-TV in Saint John and, through rebroadcasters, provides CBC English-language television to almost all of NB. This concentration of ownership has been the focus of court action and a CRTC investigation. In 1972, K.C. Irving, Ltd. and associated companies were convicted under the merger and monopoly provisions of the Combines Investigation Act after members of the Irving family had acquired controlling interest in all 5 of NB's English-language newspapers. An appeal in 1975 overturned the conviction and in 1978 the Supreme Court of Canada upheld the appeal decision. In Jan 1987 the CRTC reversed a 1981 ruling preventing the conglomerate from buying more broadcasting companies, granting it licences for new TV stations in Saint John, Fredericton, Moncton and Halifax. PETER S. ANDERSON

Irwin, William Arthur, editor, diplomat (b at Ayr, Ont 27 May 1898). He is best known as the man who made *Maclean's* truly "Canada's National Magazine." A confirmed nationalist, he saw his task as "interpreting Canada to Canadians." A tough editor, and a brilliant spotter of talent who believed in careful research, Irwin attracted and helped train an entire generation of young writers who served either as staff members or freelance contributors. These included Blair Fraser, Ralph Allen, Pierre Berton, Fred Bodsworth, Sidney Katz, June Callwood, Trent Frayne and many others. He lured cover artists of the calibre of A.J. Casson, and fiction writers of the quality of W.O. Mitchell and Morley Callaghan. He served overseas in WWI before working as reporter and Ottawa correspondent for 2 Toronto newspapers. He joined *Maclean's* in 1925. Although the titular editor was a voluble Englishman, H. Napier Moore, the taciturn Irwin quickly became the magazine's motivating force, long before he assumed the editor's chair in 1945. George Drew's unmasking of the BREN GUN SCANDAL in the early war years was largely owing to Irwin's behind-the-scenes manipulation. In 1950 he left *Maclean's* to become commissioner of the National Film Board where he met and married the poet, Patricia K. PAGE. From 1953 to 1964 he held several high diplomatic posts overseas, returning to Canada as publisher of the *Victoria Times* until 1971. PIERRE BERTON

Isaac Todd, a 350-ton ship built in 1811 at Québec for John McTavish, a partner in the NORTH WEST COMPANY. This vessel's mission was to secure Astoria at the Columbia R mouth from the American PACIFIC FUR COMPANY, to annihilate American fur-trade competition on the NORTHWEST COAST, and to initiate NWC trade with China. The *Isaac Todd* sailed 25 Mar 1813 from Portsmouth, Eng, escorted by Royal Navy ships assigned to protect her from US warships, since the WAR OF 1812 was in progress. But she was a slow sailer and fell behind her escort. Thus, HMS RACOON reasserted British control over Astoria on 30 Nov 1813, about 6 weeks after Nor'Westers approaching overland had purchased the fort from Pacific Fur Co traders. The *Isaac Todd* arrived 23 Apr 1814. She sailed for China Sept 26, initiating the first Anglo-Canadian transpacific trade with China, and she took tea back to England for the EAST INDIA COMPANY. BARRY M. GOUGH

Isbister, Alexander Kennedy, schoolmaster, explorer, lawyer (b at Cumberland House, Rupert's Land [Sask] June 1822; d at London, Eng 28 May 1883). A Métis whose maternal grandmother was Indian, Isbister explored the Mackenzie R basin (1838-42) while employed by the HBC. He published a much-quoted treatise on the geology of portions of the Arctic and northwestern N America. This included the first chromolithograph map produced in England (1855). In 1842 Isbister left for Britain to become a schoolmaster and barrister championing the rights of Métis and the country-born against the HBC monopoly. He willed a personal fortune and 5000 books to U of Man. W.O. KUPSCH

Iseler, Elmer Walter, choir conductor (b at Port Colborne, Ont 14 Oct 1927). Iseler is considered the foremost Canadian choir conductor of his time. His international reputation was earned as founding conductor (1954-78) of the FESTIVAL SINGERS OF CANADA, a highly versatile group noted for virtuoso technique and beautifully blended voices, which in 1968 became Canada's first professional choir. Also conductor of the TORONTO MENDELSSOHN CHOIR from 1964, Iseler has appeared widely in Canada and Europe with both ensembles, performing music of all periods and showing special dedication to the promotion of contemporary Canadian music. In 1978 he founded a new professional choir, the Elmer Iseler Singers. BARCLAY MCMILLAN

Iskowitz, Gershon, painter (b at Kielce, Poland 1921; d at Toronto 26 Jan 1988). A survivor of concentration camps at Auschwitz and Buchenwald, Iskowitz studied painting briefly with Oscar Kokoschka in Munich. In 1949 he immigrated to Canada. His first paintings after his arrival in Toronto were dark memories of his past, but gradually he began to paint landscapes, first around Toronto, then in the Parry Sound area. Though his works were at first representational, the landscapes that later developed were abstracted from nature. After a Canada Council grant in 1967 enabled him to take a helicopter ride over Churchill, Man, his abstract paintings became reminiscent of aerial views of the landscape. Building layer on layer of oil paint, Iskowitz delighted in the experience of making the paintings and in the joy of the landscapes and the colours. In 1985, recognizing the value of the Canada Council's assistance over the years, Iskowitz established a prize of $25 000 to be awarded by the council each year to a mature, practising artist. MARILYN BURNETT

Islam, one of the major religions of the world. Its adherents are estimated at over 900 million people concentrated in S and W Asia and N and E Africa. It is the fastest-growing religion, with believers found worldwide. The word "Islam" is derived from the Arabic *silm,* meaning submission, obedience, surrender and peace. Followers of Islam, called Muslims (Moslems), believe that Islam is the religion of God (Allah), which he ordained for the guidance and benefit of humanity. To accept Islam is to choose to live life according to the revealed will of God, to surrender the self to his mercy and strive to maintain righteousness in the world. Individual and communal obedience to the tenets of the faith, coupled with Islam's message that all men are equal, leads to the elimination of discord. The teachings of Islam are grounded in the Qur'an (Koran), the scripture Muslims believe to have been revealed by God through the angel Gabriel, in Arabic, to the Prophet Muhammad between 610 (when he was 40 years old) and 632 AD (the year of his death). These teachings distinguish between the practice and the beliefs of Islam. For although Islam has no clergy and no sacraments, it does require certain ritual practices in obedience to God's commandments. Often referred to as the "Pillars of Islam," there are 5 acts of worship incumbent on all believers at appropriate times. To avoid formalism, each is to be approached with a conscious purification of intent that recognizes God's lordship over the world.

All acts of worship are Islam. The *Shahadah* (affirmation of faith) is repeated daily: "I bear witness that there is no god but God and that Muhammad is the Messenger of God." It attests commitment to a radical monotheism, specifying that the revelation to Muhammad is the final truth. It is whispered in the ear of the newborn to remind him of a primordial covenant made by each individual with God and in the ear of the deceased in preparation for the questioning of the grave. *Salat* (ritual prayer) is prescribed for all believers 5 times a day (at dawn, noon, afternoon, at dusk and evening). Its performance stamps daily life with a steadfast devotion to God. It is to be preceded by ablutions requiring the washing of hands, mouth, nostrils, face, arms (up to the elbow), head, ears, neck and feet (up to the ankle). The believer must remove his shoes and be properly clad: women must cover the whole body except for face and hands, and men must cover at least from the navel to the knees. The prayer involves standing, bowing and kneeling.

Zakat (the tithe) is perceived as an act of purification. The Qur'an teaches that prayer and tithing are irrevocably bound together. One's commitment to God is incomplete without the fulfilment of responsibility toward the community. The tithe is assessed at 2.5% of one's total assets and is to be given to the poor, orphans and widows. During *Sawm* (fasting the lunar month of Ramadan, 29-30 days) believers refrain from food, drink and sex from before dawn (when one cannot distinguish a white thread from a black thread) to dusk. Fasting is a time of repentance and discipline; it binds the community together in a shared experience of deprivation as well as gratitude and celebration at the end of the day. *Hajj* (pilgrimage to Mecca) is incumbent on believers who can afford it at least once in their lifetime. It commemorates Abraham's obedience to God and his willingness to sacrifice his son. The ceremony begins with repentance and the donning of 2 pieces of white cloth; it includes abstention from worldly pleasures, meditation at Mt Arafat, pelting the devil, offering a blood sacrifice, cutting the hair and nails, and circumambulation of the Kaaba, the central building of the mosque at Mecca.

The essential credal statement of Islam as it appears in the Qur'an specifies belief in God, his messengers, his books, the angels and the Last Day. God is the Lord of the world who reveals himself in nature and history. He has provided humanity with guidance through prophets and messengers, beginning with Adam and ending with Muhammad. Each messenger was entrusted with a book (eg, Moses with the Torah, Jesus with the Gospel), all of which were falsified by their followers. The Qur'an, God's revelation to Muhammad, is preserved in perfect form; it stands in judgement of all previous scriptures.

The Qur'an teaches that God created the angels, his servants, out of light. Gabriel brings revelation, Izrail causes death, Munkar and Nakir question the dead, Michael blows the trumpet announcing Resurrection. Muslims believe that on the Day of Judgement all humans will give account for every intent, thought and act. The righteous will be rewarded in the Garden while the wrongdoers will be consigned to fire.

Islam in Canada The 1981 census (the most recent census figures available) shows over 98 000 Muslims in Canada, from over 60 countries, speaking a variety of languages and adhering to their respective ethnic cultures. This Islamic mosaic is the consequence of various factors, including changes in Canadian IMMIGRATION policies as well as the economic and political upheavals affecting Muslims in their home countries. Over 60% of Muslims in Canada are foreign-born, having immigrated during the last 20 years. The 1871 census recorded only 13 Muslims. Their number had increased to 645 by 1931, mostly from Lebanon, Albania, Syria, Yugoslavia and Turkey. The influx of immigrants after WWII raised the number to 33 370 by 1971. The majority of this wave were highly educated, westernized professionals who came to settle in Canada to share in its economic prosperity. They were mostly from Lebanon, Syria, Indonesia, Morocco, Palestine, Egypt, Iraq and the Indo-Pakistani region. From 1966 to 1970 those of Indo-Pakistani background became the majority as thousands of unskilled labourers came to Canada to escape discrimination in East Africa and Britain. More recently arrived Muslims include unskilled workers from S Lebanon, fleeing their war-torn country, and political REFUGEES from Iran and Afghanistan. Early settlements were concentrated in Ontario and Alberta, with a shift towards Québec in the 1930s. Those arriving in Canada since the 1960s have settled in urban areas. Two-thirds of all Muslims now live in Ontario, with others dispersed throughout the nation.

The first Canadian mosque was built in Edmonton in 1938. Other mosques and centres were not organized in major urban areas until the 1950s and 1970s. The majority of Muslims in Canada are Sunnis with a substantial number of Shia and adherents of other sects. The differences among the groups reflect early political divisions in Islamic history. Sunnis are those who live according to the guidance of the Qur'an and the teachings of Muhammad. The Shia believe that Ali (Muhammad's son-in-law) was designated as his successor, and that leadership of the community is restricted to his descendants. Both groups believe that the revelation through prophets has ceased, the Shia, however, accepting Imams as divinely ordained leaders providing a continuing source of Muslim doctrine. The majority of the Shia in Canada are Ismailis (estimated at 22 000), whose present leader is the Aga Khan. The Twelver Shias believe that with the disappearance of the Twelfth Imam in 878 AD the leadership of the community is in the hands of the religious leaders, the Mujtahids. Their opinion is currently sought from the centres in Iraq and Iran. Other Islamic groups in Canada include Sufis (followers of the mystic traditions) and sects that are deemed non-Islamic by the majority, such as the Druze, the Alawis and the Qadyanis.

For Sunni Muslims, Canada offered a special challenge since they lacked designated leadership. Efforts at organization are principally at the local level. The Federation of Islamic Associations of the US and Canada was formed in the 1950s by second-generation Muslims of Arab background. With headquarters in Detroit, Mich, it has sought ways to help American-born Muslims maintain their Islam. In 1962, the Muslim Student Assn was formed to instil Islamic consciousness in Muslim students in N America. A number of its alumni have opted to remain in Canada, forming the independent Council of Muslim Communities of Canada in 1972. The council's early leaders were Pakistani professionals, who attempted to integrate Muslims of other ethnic and linguistic groups. Its objectives have changed, from forming links between Canadian Muslims and other national and international groups to organizing youth camps, providing scholarships for Muslims, and publishing school textbooks and books on Islam for use by parents. The Council of Muslim Communities of Canada (CMCC) joined the Council of Masajid (with headquarters in Saudi Arabia) in 1982.

Islamic temple in London, Ont. Muslims have come to Canada from over 60 countries (*courtesy Canapress Photo Service*).

Attempts by second- and third-generation Muslims to integrate into Canadian society are not welcomed by recent immigrants. Islamic law has provided over the years a description of what constitutes Islamic behaviour to the minutest detail. This the immigrant finds hard to implement because of the pressures of what some consider to be a "Christian" and others a "materialistic" environment in Canada. There are no public reminders for prayer 5 times a day, nor are allowances made by employers for fasting. Some Muslims question the need to pay the tithe since the Canadian government takes care of the poor and the widows through tax money. Islamic prohibition of usury raises the fear that paying interest on purchases is disobeying God. Islamic dietary restrictions against consumption of improperly slaughtered meat, of pork and pork by-products and of liquor cause concern since they impede social integration, perceived by Canadians as necessary for professional promotion.

The area of greatest stress appears to be in male-female relations, since Islam teaches that there should be a segregation of the sexes and that Muslim women cannot marry non-Muslims. Islamic laws respecting personal status (marriage, divorce, inheritance) are not in complete harmony with Canadian laws, a circumstance which leads to numerous problems.

The Islamic organizations are attempting to deal with these problems. The CMCC has sought support from other Canadian organizations for the implementation of certain Islamic laws in the Canadian settings. Efforts are also made to establish good relations with other religious organizations through Christian-Muslim and Christian-Muslim-Jewish dialogue. Islam West Associates aims at promoting mutual understanding between Muslims in Canada and all other Canadians. Efforts also focus on sensitizing Canadian society to the prejudicial content of educational material in textbooks and SUNDAY SCHOOL texts.

There have been efforts recently to acquaint Canadian society with the Islamic contribution to culture, science and art. Travelling exhibits as well as videotape presentations have been prepared and a speakers' bureau has been organized. While welcoming the opportunities that Canadian human rights provide for Muslims, as well as the support of multiculturalism, Muslim leaders continue to voice concern over Canadian foreign policy in the Middle East and against prevailing social discrimination and underemployment of Muslims. YVONNE Y. HADDAD

Reading: S.A. Nigosian, *Modes of Worship* (1981); E.H. Waugh, B. Abu-Laban and R.B. Qureshi, eds, *The Muslim Community in North America* (1983).

Island, a piece of land surrounded by water. By custom it is agreed that this definition does not apply to the 5 largest pieces of land that form the continents (*see* PLATE TECTONICS). The largest island in the world is Greenland (2 175 596 km^2); the largest in Canada is Baffin I (507 451 km^2). Seventeen other Canadian islands exceed 10 000 km^2 in area. The islands lying N of the mainland in the District of Franklin, NWT, are generally referred to as the Canadian ARCTIC ARCHIPELAGO. They include the QUEEN ELIZABETH ISLANDS, those lying N of the strait (known successively from W to E as M'Clure Str, Viscount Melville Sound, Barrow Str and Lancaster Sound), which extends E-W approximately along 74° N lat. MANITOULIN ISLAND (2766 km^2), the largest island in the world located in a freshwater lake (as distinct from a flowing river), itself contains 17 lakes containing islands.

The total number of islands in Canada has never been established, but it is very large. It is estimated that there are some 30 000 islands along the eastern shore of GEORGIAN BAY alone (the Thirty Thousand Is). The *Canadian Gazetteer Atlas* (1980) records the names of 1016 individual islands and 129 groups or archipelagoes. Of these islands, 259 were recorded as inhabited in the 1976 census of Canada. At that time, Île de Montréal had the greatest population (1 869 641); the 1986 census lists the population as 1 752 582.

Origin of Islands Islands are formed through a variety of geomorphic processes. Canadian islands fall into 2 categories: those resulting from the action of running water on an upland that has recently undergone GLACIATION, and those formed by the rise in sea level that normally follows an ICE AGE. GLACIERS and ice sheets are able to scoop hollows out of hard rock. If an ice age is followed by a humid period, the hollows will be filled with lakes; if the surface is sufficiently irregular, islands will occur within the lakes. The islands of the Great Lakes belong to this class. When large rivers flow over an irregular, glaciated surface, their channels may divide to form islands (eg, those on which the cities of Montréal and Laval are found, and also the Île d'ORLÉANS). Ice not only scoops out hollows by EROSION, it also deposits as till the material it has gathered up. The till can form natural dams impeding the flow of the rivers that drain a land surface where ice has melted. Irregularities left in glacial till may then form islands in the lakes ponded behind such dams (eg, those in Rice Lk, 95 km NE of Toronto). The second major group of islands, those formed by the rise in sea level following an ice age, include the uncounted islands of Canada's Pacific, Arctic and Atlantic coasts. In most cases, the erosional action of ice causes the irregularities in the land surface that result in islands as the margins of a continent are flooded. Some islands, however, result from the deposition of till (eg, those near LUNENBURG in Mahone Bay, NS).

Islands are also formed by the deposition of alluvium where the flow of water in a river is checked at or before the delta (eg, Lulu and Sea islands at the mouth of the Fraser R), and by the drifting of sand and gravel along seashores or lakeshores (eg, Toronto Is). In some parts of the world, islands have been formed by the eruption of volcanoes and by the growth of coral. No examples of either type occur in Canada. Finally, islands can result from human action. One, René-Levasseur (2020 km^2), was formed when the waters of Lk Manicouagan, rising behind the Daniel Johnson Dam, surrounded Mt Babel (elev 952 m). Approximately three-quarters the size of Manitoulin, it is the largest island in Canada formed by human activity, and may be the largest such island in the world. *See also* COASTAL LANDFORM; PHYSIOGRAPHIC REGIONS; RIVER LANDFORM. O.F.G. SITWELL

Largest Canadian Islands

Name	*Area (km^2)*	*General location*
Baffin	50 7451	S Arctic Archipelago
Victoria	21 7290	S Arctic Archipelago
Ellesmere	19 6236	Queen Elizabeth Is
Newfoundland	10 8860	Atlantic Coast
Banks	7 0028	S Arctic Archipelago
Devon	5 5247	Queen Elizabeth Is
Axel Heiberg	4 3178	Queen Elizabeth Is
Melville	4 2149	Queen Elizabeth Is
Southampton	4 1214	Hudson Bay
Prince of Wales	3 3338	S Arctic Archipelago
Vancouver	3 1284	Pacific Coast
Somerset	2 4786	S Arctic Archipelago
Bathurst	1 6042	Queen Elizabeth Is
Prince Patrick	1 5848	Queen Elizabeth Is
King William	1 3111	S Arctic Archipelago
Ellef Ringnes	1 1295	Queen Elizabeth Is
Bylot	1 1067	S Arctic Archipelago
Cape Breton	1 0311	NS

Israel, Werner, physicist (b at Berlin, Germany 4 Oct 1931). He was educated at Capetown U (BSc, 1951, MSc, 1954) and Dublin Institute for Advanced Studies (PhD, 1960). He came to U of A as an assistant professor in the Mathematics Department in 1958. Since 1972 he has been a professor of physics at U of A. His research encompasses several areas, including relativity theory, BLACK HOLES, cosmology, relativistic thermodynamics and quantum gravity. He is well known for his pioneering work on gravitational collapse, the concept of event horizon and the uniqueness of static black holes. He has also made important contributions to relativistic kinetic theory and the thermodynamics of black holes. He has been recognized internationally for his contribution to the fields of relativity, gravitation, relativistic thermodynamics and cosmology by the award of the following prizes and fellowships: Fellow of the Royal Society of Canada (1972); Sherman-Fairchild Distinguished Scholar, CALTECH (1974-75); Canadian Association of Physicists Medal of Achievement in Physics (1981); University of Alberta Research Prize in Natural Sciences and Engineering (1983); Izaak Walton Killam Memorial Prize (1984); Fellow of the Royal Society, London (1986); and Senior Research Fellow, at the Canadian Institute for Advanced Research (1986-91). A.N. KAMAL

Issajenko, Angella, sprinter (b in Jamaica 28 Sept 1958). Known as "Angella Taylor" for most of her athletic career since 1978, Issajenko has been one of Canada's outstanding international sprinters. She has won medals at Commonwealth, Olympic, Pan-American and World University Games, in addition to other prestigious championships. A Canadian senior record holder since 1980, she has received several athletic awards, including the CFTA Phil Edwards Memorial Award for Top Track Athlete (1982); Sport Excellence Award (1983), and the Velma Springstead Trophy for Female Athlete of the Year (1980 and 1982). In 1985 she became a Member of the Order of Canada. In June 1987 she won the women's 100 m at the Olympic International meet in Athens, Greece, and in Aug 1987 she won her 7th Canadian championship in 8 years in the 100 m event. GERALD REDMOND

Italian Writing From its beginning in the 1920s, Italian Canadian writing has existed in English, French and Italian. Liborio Lattoni wrote in Italian while Francesco M. Gualtieri published in English. *La Ville sans femmes* (1945) by Mario Duliani appeared in both French and Italian. Gianni Grohovaz, Elena Albani and Guglielmo Vangelisti (*Gli Italiani in Canada*, 1956), who published in the 1950s in Italian, were followed by authors who participated in both the growth of Canadian literature and the flowering of MULTICULTURALISM, thus making an impact on mainstream English and French Canadian writing. The bilingual tradition continued with Alexandre Amprimoz's *Selected Poems* (1979), *Sur le damier des tombes* (1983) and *Bouquet de Signes* (1986); Filippo Salvatore's *Suns of Darkness* (1980) and *La Fresque de Mussolini* (1985); Romano Perticarini's *Quelli della fionda* (1981); and Maria Ardizzi's *Made in Italy* (1982). Poets, who outnumber novelists, have received awards and recognition through inclusion in major anthologies. Narrative verse in Pier Giorgio DI CICCO's *The Tough Romance* (1979), Mary DI MICHELE's *Mimosa and Other Poems* (1981), George Amabile's *The Presence of Fire* (1982), Len Gasparini's *Breaking and Entering* (1980) and the work of Antonino Mazza and Antonio Corea show strong autobiographical elements. Diverse themes have begun to appear in the books of younger poets: Pasquale Verdicchio (*Moving Landscape*, 1985), Dorina Michelutti (*Loyalty to the Hunt*, 1986), and Salvatore di Falco and François d'Apollonia.

In fiction the need to chronicle the immigrant experience is demonstrated; thus Frank PACI's *Black Madonna* (1982) and *The Father* (1984) are novels in the realist tradition. Caterina Edwards's *The Lion's Mouth* (1982) and *Terra Straniera* (1986) explores women's views on ethnic identity, whereas anecdotal stories by C.D. Minni (*Other Selves*, 1985), Darlene Madott (*Bottled Roses*, 1985), Gianni Bartocci and Dino Fruchi highlight the ironies and joys of life. The women mentioned, along with Matilde Torres, Genni Donati Gunn, Carole Fioramore David, Roberta Sciff-Zamaro and Lisa Carducci, have produced a significant feminist voice in Italian Canadian writing.

Québec poets Fulvio Caccia, Tonino Caticchio, Mary Melfi and Antonio D'Alfonso (*The Other Shore*, 1986) focus on ethnic identity. Dominique De Pasquale's plays in French and Marco Micone's *Gens du silence* (1982), *Addolorato* (1984) and *Bilico* (1986) explore linguistic and political relationships. The anthologies *Roman Candles* (1978, ed Di Cicco), *Quêtes* (1983, eds Caccia and D'Alfonso) and *Italian Canadian Voices* (1984, ed C.M. Di Giovanni) include many other writers. The Association of Italian-Canadian Writers has been formed to promote their work. *See also* ETHNIC LITERATURE; ITALIANS.

JOSEPH PIVATO

Reading: Joseph Pivato, ed, *Contrast: Comparative Essays on Italian-Canadian Writing* (1985), *Canadian Literature* 106 (1985).

Italians The earliest Italian contact with Canada dates from 1497, when Giovanni Caboto (John CABOT), an Italian navigator from Venice, explored and claimed for England the coasts of Newfoundland or Cape Breton I. In 1524 another Italian, Giovanni da VERRAZZANO, explored part of Atlantic Canada for France. Under the French regime, the Italian Henri de TONTY acted as LA SALLE's lieutenant in the first expedition to reach the mouth of the Mississippi R in 1682. Italians served in the military of New France (eg, in the CARIGNAN-SALIÈRES REGIMENT), in which several distinguished themselves as officers. Some Italians also served with the DE MEURON and de Watteville Swiss mercenary regiments in the British army during the War of 1812. Following the example of Italian ex-soldiers in New France who settled on the land in the late 17th century, some 200 or more of the mercenaries took up lots granted by Britain.

By the late 18th century, a small number of Italians, many in the hotel trade, resided in Montréal. In the mid-19th century, Italian craftsmen, artists, musicians and teachers, primarily from northern Italy, immigrated to Canada. By the 1860s, Italian street musicians (hurdy-gurdy men, street singers) were seen in Canada, and by 1881 almost 2000 people of Italian origin lived in Canada, particularly in Montréal and Toronto.

In 1897 Mackenzie KING, then working as a journalist, described the first street entertainer who lived in Toronto in the 1880s. This early Italian immigrant, King wrote, had worn out 5 street pianos and earned an average of $15 daily in his first years in Toronto. Some of the wandering street musicians eventually settled down to teach music or to organize bands and orchestras.

In the late 19th century, millions of peasants migrated to South America, the US and Canada. Professional recruiters and the example of successful migrants who returned to Italy encouraged Italians to set out for North America where work was available on the railways, in mining and in industry.

Although many Italians expected to achieve economic and social well-being by migrating to Canada, they were not always successful. In 1901 a series of articles appeared in a Milanese newspaper describing an unscrupulous system of recruitment from Chiasso on the Swiss-Italian border to Liverpool through Montréal to the Canadian North. Labourers were often misled through this system into permanent migration to labour camps in northern Ontario, or found themselves unemployed and destitute in Canada's major cities. In 1902 the General Commissariat for Emigration in Rome sent Egisto Rossi, a commissioner, to tour Canada and report on the situation of working Italians. Rossi documented even more common routes of recruitment through the US, especially New York, and confirmed that several powerful *padroni* (labour agents) in Montréal were in league with railway and steamship agents in Europe to recruit cheap labour for a quick cash return. Rossi concluded that the abuses suffered by Italians were grave enough that their migration should be suspended until the problem of exploitation was addressed.

Origins Over 75% of Italian immigrants to Canada have come from southern Italy, especially from the regions of Abruzzi-Molise and Calabria, and about three-quarters of these immigrants were small-scale farmers or peasants. Unlike northern Italy, which dominated the newly formed (1861-70) Italian state, and continued to industrialize, southern Italy remained rural and traditional. Overpopulation, the fragmentation of peasant farms, poverty, poor health and poor educational conditions, heavy taxation and political dissatisfaction resulted in heavy emigration. After WWI the number of immigrants from the war-devastated northeastern part of Italy increased.

Early Migration and Settlement Italian immigration to Canada occurred in 2 main waves, from 1900 to WWI and from 1950 to 1970. During the first phase, 119 770 Italians entered Canada (primarily from the US), the greatest number in 1913. About 80% of these people were young males. The 1911 census of Italian-born in Toronto listed 2200 males and 800 females, most of them resident in "Little Italy." Many labourers eventually decided to settle permanently in Canada, and by WWI Italians were to be found not only in major urban centres but also in Sydney (NS), Welland, Sault Ste Marie and Copper Cliff (Ont) and Trail (BC).

Thousands of Italian labourers, however, settled in the growing cities of central Canada, working as construction and factory workers and building tradesmen, as food and fruit merchants or as artisans. Out of modest beginnings, a few, eg, Onorato Catelli of Montréal in the food-processing industry and Vincent Franceschini of Toronto in road construction, were highly successful. While the great majority of immigrants settled in urban centres, agricultural colonies were established at Lorette, Man, and Hylo, Alta. In the Niagara Peninsula and Okanagan Valley Italian proprietors of orchards, vineyards and vegetable farms prospered. Many Italian truck farmers on the cities' outskirts grew small crops for local consumption.

Despite tighter immigration restrictions following WWI, over 29 000 Italians had entered Canada by 1930. Many of them were farm labourers or wives and children sponsored by breadwinners in Canada. This movement, however, virtually ended with the Great Depression.

Throughout the 1930s strong family networks and thrift helped Italian Canadians absorb some of the economic shock of unemployment and deprivation. Their problems were compounded after 1935 when Canadian hostility towards FASCISM was directed against Italian Canadians, many of whom were sympathetic towards Mussolini. As a consequence of Italy's alliance with Germany in WWII, Italian Canadians were designated "enemy aliens" and were the victims of widespread PREJUDICE AND DISCRIMINATION. Men lost their jobs, shops were vandalized, civil liberties were suspended under the War Measures Act, and hundreds were interned at Camp Petawawa in northern Ontario. While some of these men had been active fascists, many were not; and they, as well as their families, who were denied relief, bore the brunt of hostilities. As a result, many Italians later anglicized their names and denied their Italian background.

After WWII the widespread shortage of labour caused by a booming economy, as well as Canada's new obligations within NATO, once again made the country receptive to Italian immigration. Postwar immigrants comprise almost 70% of the Italian Canadian group. Many Italians initially immigrated under the auspices of the Canadian government and private firms. The Welch Construction Co, for example, which was founded at the turn of the century by 2 former navvies, Vincenzo and Giovanni Veltri, specialized in railway maintenance. Men often arrived under one-year contracts to do hard physical labour similar to that of their earlier compatriots, though now the great majority came as permanent settlers, later sponsoring wives, children and other relatives. Family "chain migration" from Italy was so extensive that in 1958 Italy surpassed Britain as a source for immigrants. Starting in 1967, new regulations based admissibility on universal criteria such as education; this "points system" restricted the sponsorship of relatives, so that Italian immigration dropped significantly.

Settlement and Economic Life In 1981, 65% of Italian Canadians lived in Ontario, 22% in Québec and 7% in BC. About 95% of Italian Canadians live in towns and cities. The most significant concentrations are in Toronto, where in 1981 Italian Canadians numbered 297 205 (10% of the population), and in Montréal, where they numbered 156 535 or almost 6% of the population. Other cities in which Italian Canadians numbered 10 000 or more were (in descending order) Hamilton, Vancouver, St Catharines, Windsor, Ottawa, Sault Ste Marie, Calgary and Edmonton. Preliminary figures from the 1986 census estimated 709 500 Italians in Canada.

In cities where Italians have settled in sufficient numbers they have tended to create ethnic neighbourhoods. These "Little Italys," with their distinctive shops, restaurants, clubs and churches are easily recognizable, but they have rarely been ghettos segregated from the rest of society. Over the years, these immigrant areas have decreased significantly in size, though they have generally survived as viable socioeconomic centres. While the movement out of immigrant neighbourhoods to more prosperous residential areas has been significant, even in the suburbs it is still common to find small concentrations of Italian Canadians who have chosen to live near one another because of kinship or village ties. Seventy-five percent post-WWII immigrants were employed in low-income occupations, but this changed dramatically with the second and subsequent generations. The children of immigrants have achieved a higher level of education, reflected in their increasingly important positions in professional and semiprofessional occupations.

Community Life Mutual-aid societies, many of which grew out of village organizations, were among the earliest institutions established by Italian immigrants. The Order of Italy (the first Canadian branch was established in Sault Ste Marie in 1913) was open to all people of Italian heritage. In 1926 some Québec lodges, opposed to the order's profascist leanings, broke away to form a parallel structure which in 1926 became the Order of Italo-Canadians. Wartime hostilities inhibited the work of the societies, but their decline was really made inevitable by the growing influence of the WELFARE STATE and insurance companies.

After WWII, numerous new clubs and societies were established around regional, religious, social or sporting functions. In the early 1960s the Centre for Organizing Technical Courses for Italians (COSTI) was founded in Toronto to provide technical education and upgrading, as well as English courses and counselling. In the mid-1970s, COSTI also established a special program to meet the needs of immigrant women.

In 1971 the Italian Canadian Benevolent Corporation (ICBC) was founded in Toronto. Undertaking what was the largest project of its kind in N America, the ICBC built a multifaceted complex with senior citizens' housing and a community centre offering recreational, cultural and social services.

The founding in Ottawa in 1974 of the National Congress of Italian Canadians was an attempt to bring national cohesion to the group and increase its political influence. The congress co-ordinated the raising of millions of dollars from across Canada to provide relief for the victims of earthquakes that devastated Friuli in 1976 and Campania a few years later. Notwithstanding recent success in forging community-wide cohesion, however, Italian Canadians are divided by rival regional, political and even religious organizations, and along class lines. The Canadian Italian Business and Professional Men's Association and the Italian Chamber of Commerce represent the interests of employers and professionals, while working-class Italian Canadians have sought to protect their interests through the various organized labour movements. Comprising a conspicuously large proportion of the labour force in both the construction and textile industries, they have been especially prominent in the International Labourers Union and the Amalgamated Clothing Workers of America.

Cultural Life Like the major community organizations, the Italian Canadian press and media have promoted cohesion and have mediated between their constituency and the wider society. The first Italian newspaper in Canada was published in Montréal in the late 19th century; by 1914 several others had been founded from Toronto to Vancouver. After 1950, dozens of Italian newspapers and magazines, many aimed at particular regional, religious or political markets, proliferated across Canada. By the mid-1960s, Italian-language publications had a readership of 120 000. Currently the most influential of these are *Il Corriere Italiano* of Montréal and *Il Corriere Canadese* of Toronto. Since WWII, Italian has become, after English and French, the most widespread language in Canadian broadcasting. The owner of *Il Corriere Canadese* has launched a multilingual television station in Ontario which transmits in Italian (as well as other languages) daily.

Italian Canadians have altered society's tastes in architecture, fashion and recreation, thus helping to bring a new cosmopolitanism to Canadian life. They have also made important contributions to the arts. Mario BERNARDI of Kirkland Lake, Ont, for example, was appointed the first conductor of Ottawa's National Arts Centre Orchestra in 1968 and helped guide it to international stature. The avant-garde paintings of Guido MOLINARI of Montréal now hang in leading galleries. At the more popular level, Bruno GERUSSI, a former Shakespearean actor, has become a well-known radio and TV personality. J.R. COLOMBO is a best-selling author of reference works and literature (*see also* ITALIAN WRITING; ETHNIC LITERATURE).

Education and Religious Life Dante Alighieri societies throughout Canada offer films, lectures, Italian-language courses and other programs to foster knowledge of Italy. In 1976 the Canadian Centre for Italian Culture and Education (*CENTRO*) was founded in Toronto to design and institute Italian-language programs in schools. Also important are the cultural institutes run by the Italian government, the Italian-language holdings of public libraries, and the many Italian clubs in high schools and universities.

Over 90% of Italian Canadians are Roman Catholic, and the church has involved itself in immigrant aid, education and recreation. Since there have been many Italian-speaking priests, especially in the national parishes run by orders such as the Servite or Fransciscan fathers, the church has also contributed toward the preservation of Italian Canadians' language and culture.

Politics In 1938 Hubert Badanai of Fort William (later called Thunder Bay) became the first mayor of Italian background and in the early postwar years was elected the first Italian federal member of Parliament. In 1952 Philip Gaglardi of Mission City, BC, appointed to the provincial Cabinet, was the first Italian Canadian to become a minister. In 1973 Laura Sabia, a former St Catharines alderwoman, became chairperson of the Ontario Council on the Status of Women and a leading activist in the women's movement. In 1981 Charles Caccia was appointed minister of labour, the first federal Italian Canadian minister. Italian Canadians have been most successful federally as candidates for the Liberal Party, and in Ontario as candidates for the New Democratic Party. In the 1984 federal election the Progressive Conservative Party made gains among the group, especially in Québec where 2 Montréal candidates of Italian background were elected.

Group Maintenance The most significant social institution among Italian Canadians has been the extended family. Commonly, in the traditional family in Italy the roles were clearly defined. The husband was considered family head and provider; the wife was expected to be a good homemaker and mother. Children were to show obedience and respect towards their parents. Each member was to act for the betterment of the whole family rather than for his or her individual interest. Many Italian immigrants have attempted to maintain such family patterns. Because traditional ways differed markedly from what was expected in the wider Canadian society, the resulting conflict has often been at the root of many social problems. At times the children of immigrants have found that their aspirations for upward mobility and individual expression conflicted with the family's insistence on solidarity and the fulfilment of traditional roles. The second-generation Italian Canadian family, however, has changed considerably. While usually maintaining an emphasis on family cohesion, respect and loyalty, it has increasingly moved toward a greater equalization of roles between husband and wife. Nevertheless, the family still provides its members with important support, and the extended family is frequently reunited at weddings, baptisms and similar events. Often friends are drawn from the extended family and economic favours are exchanged among family members. Related to this, local loyalties among Italian Canadians from the same village often link extended families into a much larger group connected by personal bonds.

This is not to suggest, however, that Italians have wished to live as an ethnic enclave. Prewar Italian Canadians, by 1941, had a higher rate of intermarriage (45%) than most other major ethnic groups. In the postwar group, by 1961, almost 24% of males and 18% of females were married outside the group. In Québec, Italian Canadians integrate more easily into the francophone society than do many other ethnic groups. Over 80% of Italian Canadians are able to speak French, giving them one of the highest levels of French-language facility of any ethnic group in the province.

FRANC STURINO

Reading: R.F. Harney, *Italians in Canada* (1978); H. and J. V. Scarpaci, eds, *Little Italies in North America* (1981); A.V. Spada, *The Italians in Canada* (1969).

Ittinuar, Peter Freuchen (b at Chesterfield Inlet, NWT 19 Jan 1950). The first Inuk MP, Ittinuar is the grandson of Danish explorer Peter Freuchen. He has had a varied and colourful career as teacher of Inuktitut linguistics and Inuit culture at U of O, executive director of the INUIT TAPIRISAT OF CANADA, CBC announcer, northern medical counsellor, pilot and hunter. After his election to the Commons in 1979 as the member for Nunatsiaq and his reelection the following year, he became the northern development critic for the NDP. In 1982 he crossed the floor to join the Liberal Party, where he directed his attention to the establishment of Nunavut, one of the 2 territories to be created by the proposed division of the NWT. He was defeated in the Sept 1984 federal election. JOHN BENNETT

Jack, Annie L., née Hayr, writer, horticulturist (b at Northamptonshire, Eng 1 Jan 1839; d at Châteauguay, Qué 15 Feb 1912). Our first professional woman garden writer, she moved to Canada from Troy, NY. She managed an extensive garden of flowers, fruits and vegetables for profit and experimentation. The garden was written up in American publications and brought her to the attention of N American horticulturists. Jack wrote and published inspirational short stories and poems, articles of social interest, and practical, wide-ranging horticultural articles, but she was most widely known for the gardening articles she wrote for Montréal newspapers and major horticultural and agricultural magazines of the day. Her popular book, *The Canadian Garden: A Pocket Help for the Amateur* (1903), remained the only Canadian gardening manual available until the end of WWI. EDWINNA VON BAEYER

Jack, William Brydone, mathematician, astronomer, educator (b at Trailflatt, Scot 23 Nov 1817; d at Fredericton 23 Nov 1886). An outstanding natural scientist and educator, Jack built an astronomical observatory in Canada on the campus at King's College [U of New Brunswick], Fredericton, in 1851. Now named the Brydone Jack Observatory, it was marked by an official plaque in 1955 which identified the building as the "First Astronomical Observatory in Canada." In 1854 (professor 1840-85, president 1861-85), Jack introduced an engineering course there to train students in practical surveying. Two decades later he established the first "standards laboratory" in Canada for surveying instruments. He gave numerous public lectures on ASTRONOMY and related topics. Under his distinguished presidency, UNB became a centre of excellence and produced many outstanding Canadian scholars. J.E. KENNEDY

Jackman, Arthur, mariner, nicknamed "Viking Arthur" (b at Renews, Nfld 1843; d at St John's 31 Jan 1907). He commanded his first sealing steamer, *Hawk*, to the ice fields in 1872. His other vessels, in later years, included *Aurora*, *Falcon*, *Terra Nova* and *Eagle*. Over 36 years, Jackman took 552 510 seals, losing none of the 8000 men in his charge. For several summers, he participated in the whale hunt around Greenland, and in 1886 he took explorer Robert Peary on his first trip to the Arctic. At the time of his death, he was marine superintendent for Bowring Brothers in St John's. JOHN PARSONS

Jackman, Henry Newton Rowell, "Hal," financier (b at Toronto 10 June 1932). Educated at Upper Canada College, U of T and the London School of Economics, Jackman in 1987 was head of the family group of companies, assembled by his father, that includes E-L Financial Corp, Empire Life Insurance Co, National Victoria and Grey Trust, Dominion and Anglo Investment Corp, the Casualty Co of Canada and Dominion of Canada General Insurance. From 1978 to 1983 he was a VP, director and member of the executive committee of ARGUS CORP, the Toronto conglomerate which he and Conrad and Montegu BLACK took over. In 1987 he sat on the board of directors of 25 corporations and 5 charities. His financial empire controls assets worth over $10 billion. JORGE NIOSI

Jackman, William, sealing captain, sailing master (b at Renews, Nfld 20 May 1837; d at St John's 25 Feb 1877). William, like his famous brother, Capt Arthur JACKMAN, was at an early age involved in the Labrador cod fishery and in the seal hunt. From 1867 to 1876 he was in charge of 2 Bowring Brothers sealing steamers. He is remembered for the dramatic sea rescue at Spotted Is, Labrador, on 9 Oct 1867, which is one of the

greatest stories of heroism ever recorded. In harbour to ride out a storm, Jackman went ashore, where he saw a wooden fishing vessel, the *Sea Clipper*, being dashed to pieces on a reef some distance from shore. Jackman threw himself into the icy water and, though battered by the surf, was able to rescue 11 of the 27 aboard unassisted. Then, with a rope and the help of others, he swam out 16 more times to bring the remaining men and women ashore. JOHN PARSONS

Jackson, Alexander Young, painter, writer (b at Montréal 3 Oct 1882; d at Kleinburg, Ont 5 Apr 1974). As a leading member of the GROUP OF SEVEN, Jackson helped to remake the visual image of Canada; as a sparkling storyteller, he ensured the Group's notoriety. His early art training was partly on the job (he worked at various lithography firms in Montréal 1895-1906 and Chicago 1906-07) and partly at night schools, including the Conseil des arts et manufactures in Montréal 1896-99 under Edmond DYONNET. Anxious to become a painter rather than a commercial artist, Jackson saved assiduously and in Sept 1907 enrolled in the Académie Julian, in Paris, under Jean-Paul Laurens. He stayed in Europe until Dec 1909, studying, travelling and sketching.

Soon after his return to Montréal, Jackson painted *Edge of the Maple Wood*, a canvas that brought him in contact with his future friends in the Toronto-based Group of Seven. Fed up with advertising work and with Montréal's indifference to his painting, Jackson moved to Toronto in the fall of 1913. Soon he was sharing his studio with a shy, uncertain painter, Tom THOMSON. The 2 quickly became firm friends, to their mutual advantage: Jackson taught Thomson aspects of technique, especially colour, while Thomson taught Jackson about the Canadian wilderness. Anxious to experience Thomson's north country, Jackson went up to Canoe Lk in Algonquin Park in Feb 1914. Here he found not only excellent painting country but also an image of Canada. After a trip to the Rockies, he was back in the park that fall with Thomson, Arthur LISMER and Fred VARLEY, and painted *The Red Maple*, a sketch in which art-nouveau composition is balanced by bold coloration.

In 1915 Jackson enlisted in the army and was sent to Europe. Two years later he was appointed an artist with the Canadian War Records and was immediately required to paint a portrait, despite his lack of experience with such themes. His subsequent works were more in keeping with his preference for landscape. Back in Canada in 1918, Jackson continued his perambulations, a tradition he maintained all his life. He spent the summer of 1919 painting in Georgian Bay, and in Sept joined Lawren HARRIS, J.E.H. MACDONALD and Franz JOHNSTON in a boxcar trip into Algoma. These and subsequent expeditions provided the material for the first Group of Seven exhibition held in Toronto in May 1920. Jackson's active participation in 7 other Group exhibitions and in many contemporary shows, including the controversial British Empire Exhibition in Wembley, Eng, 1924, ensured that his images of a rolling, unpopulated land became indelibly imprinted on the Canadian consciousness.

All his life Jackson remained a leading proponent of the Group's land-based nationalism. Once his painting style was established it shifted only to accommodate newly explored territory.

A.Y. Jackson, *Barns* (1926), oil on canvas (*courtesy Art Gallery of Ontario/gift from the Reuben and Kate Leonard Canadian Fund, 1926*).

Never abandoning his interest in landscape, he painted Canada's most distinct and identifiable climates, especially favouring winter, and sought remote regions, including the Arctic, which he visited in 1927 and 1930. But he frequently returned to the gentler regions of his youth, including Québec and Georgian Bay. In Québec in 1926, he painted *Barns*, a canvas that exemplifies his use of simple, curvacious forms and temperate colour to present a powerful, enduring image. Jackson was also one of the Group's most effective propagandists. In numerous articles and in his engaging autobiography, *A Painter's Country* (new ed 1976), all written in appealingly colloquial language, Jackson gently presses home his nationalistic vision. ANN DAVIS

Jackson, Clarence Shirley, trade union leader (b at Ft William [Thunder Bay], Ont 1906). Jackson worked first in the northern Ontario bush and later in Montréal and Toronto. His interest in left-wing politics brought him into organizing work for the fledgling Congress of Industrial Organizations. In 1937 he became a full-time organizer and later Canadian VP of the United Electrical Workers (UE), one of the most internally democratic of the new industrial unions in Canada. Despite his internment for his radical politics in 1941, he led left-wing opposition to the CANADIAN CONGRESS OF LABOUR (CCL) leadership in the 1940s, running several times for president. The CCL expelled his union in 1949, but Jackson and his fellow unionists held their membership together and by 1972 had re-entered the mainstream by affiliating with the CANADIAN LABOUR CONGRESS. For the 4 decades before his retirement in 1980, Jackson had been one of the most articulate, well-informed, though controversial, labour leaders in Canada. CRAIG HERON

Jackson, Donald, figure skater (b at Oshawa, Ont 2 Apr 1940). Winner of the Canadian senior men's FIGURE SKATING title 1959-62, Jackson won the bronze medal in the Olympic Games and placed 2nd in the world championships in 1960. His greatest achievement was in the 1962 world championships, when he moved from a distant 2nd place after compulsory figures to win the title with a spectacular performance in free skating. His winning routine included the 1st triple-lutz jump in competition. Jackson joined a professional ice show in 1962, and in 1970 won the world professional figure-skating championship. He became a coach in 1969. Some authorities consider him the finest skater Canada has ever produced. BARBARA SCHRODT

Some consider Donald Jackson to have been Canada's finest figure skater. He is shown here performing a triple salchow (*courtesy Canada's Sports Hall of Fame*).

Jackson, Henry, "Busher," hockey player (b at Toronto 19 Jan 1911; d there 6 June 1966). He joined TORONTO MAPLE LEAFS in 1929 and played left wing on the famous "Kid Line," with Joe Primeau and Charlie CONACHER. He led the NHL in scoring 1932-33 and compiled a record of 241 goals and 475 points, adding 18 goals in playoffs. He was long denied recognition of his fine career, even nomination to the HOCKEY HALL OF FAME, because of his alleged drinking problem. He gained entry in 1971, 5 years after his death. JAMES MARSH

Russ Jackson is rated by many the finest quarterback ever to have played in Canada (*courtesy Canada's Sports Hall of Fame*).

Jackson, Russell Stanley, Russ, football player (b at Hamilton, Ont 28 July 1936). Jackson was prominent in baseball, hockey, basketball and FOOTBALL as a youth. After graduation from McMaster, he refused to allow his name to stand as one of that university's Rhodes scholarship candidates and went on to play football with the OTTAWA ROUGH RIDERS as a defensive back and quarterback (1958), becoming starting quarterback after the 1962 season. A poised passer, strong runner and capable leader, Jackson finished his 12-year career with 1341 completed passes (53%) for 23 341 yards and 184 touchdowns; he also rushed for 5045 yards while scoring 55 touchdowns and 330 points. In his last season, 1969, he led Ottawa to a Grey Cup championship. He won numerous awards, including the Schenley as outstanding player (3 times), and was twice chosen Canada's male athlete of the year. A 1979 US survey of all professional football rated Jackson as the finest of all time. He always combined teaching with football, except for his term as head coach of the TORONTO ARGONAUTS (1975-76), and he went on to become a high-school principal. FRANK COSENTINO

Jackson, William Henry, also known as Honoré Joseph Jaxon, Louis RIEL's secretary immediately before the NORTH-WEST REBELLION, labour leader (b in Toronto 13 May 1861; d in New York C, NY 10 Jan 1952). After his family moved from Ontario to Prince Albert, Sask, Will Jackson joined them, abandoning his classics course at U of T. Having completed 3 years there, he was one of the best-educated men in the area. He became secretary of the local farmers' union, and in this capacity he met Riel in the summer of 1884. Sympathetic to the Métis cause, he went to live at BATOCHE, Sask, to serve as Riel's secretary, converted to Roman Catholicism and later accepted Riel's new religion. After the failure of the rebellion, Jackson was tried and committed to the lunatic asylum at Ft Garry, Man. Escaping 2 months later, he walked to the American border and eventually settled in Chicago, Ill. As Honoré Joseph Jaxon he worked as a union organizer for over 2 decades. "Riel's Secretary" moved to New York after WWI, where he died. DONALD B. SMITH

Jacobs, Jack, "Indian Jack," football player (b at Holdenville, Okla 1920; d at N Greensboro, NC 12 Jan 1974). A Creek Indian, Jacobs joined the National Football League from U of Oklahoma; playing mostly on defence, he was a sure-handed and solid tackler. He joined the CFL's WINNIPEG BLUE BOMBERS in 1950. Jacobs's fierce desire, competitiveness and brilliant quarterbacking helped popularize professional football in Winnipeg and Canada. Over his CFL career he passed for 11 094 yards and 104 touchdowns and punted for a 41-yard average. He coached London Lords (ORFU), and was an assistant coach with Hamilton, Montreal and Edmonton (CFL). FRANK COSENTINO

Jacobs, Peter, or Pahtahsega, meaning "one who makes the world brighter," Methodist missionary (b near present-day Belleville, Ont *c*1807; d at Rama Reserve, Lk Simcoe, Ont 4 Sept 1890). An early Mississauga (Ojibwa) convert to Methodism, Jacobs served first as a prayer leader and interpreter, and later as an ordained minister in Rupert's Land at Lk of the Woods, and at Ft Alexander and Norway House. Twice he visited England on missionary tours (1842-43, 1850). His published journal of his return trip in 1852 from central Canada to York Factory on Hudson Bay provides a graphic account of the perils of such an overland journey. Expelled by the Methodists (1858) for soliciting funds in the US without the church's approval, he settled at Rama, where he worked as a schoolteacher, merchant and guide. DONALD B. SMITH

Illustration from Peter Jacobs's journal showing mid-19th-century Indian fancy winter dress. An Ojibwa, Jacobs was an early convert to Methodism (*from Peter Jacobs's* Journal, *2nd ed 1858*).

Jaeger, any of 3 species of rapacious, gull-like SEABIRDS of genus *Stercorarius*. With their close relatives the skuas (*Catharacta*), they are placed by some taxonomists in the GULL family (Laridae), or in a family of their own, Stercorariidae. Jaegers are hook-billed, long-winged, swift and predatory. They mercilessly harass other birds, forcing them to disgorge food which the jaeger then snaps up with a graceful swoop. They are polymorphic (ie, have light and dark colour phases) and adults have elongated central tail feathers. Breeding range is northern circumpolar. All 3 species, pomarine (*S. pomarinus*), parasitic (*S. parasiticus*) and long-tailed (*S. longicaudus*), nest widely on the arctic tundra where they feed on small mam-

Parasitic jaeger (*Stercorarius parasiticus*) (*artwork by Claire Tremblay*).

mals, birds, fishes and invertebrates. Because they winter on the open oceans, they are scarce in the southern interior of their breeding grounds at any time. W. EARL GODFREY

Jalna, novel by Mazo DE LA ROCHE (Toronto, Boston and London, 1927). The first of 16 books about the Whiteoak family, *Jalna* is the book which determined the course of de la Roche's career. *Jalna* shows de la Roche's genius for keeping her readers engaged in the improbably fascinating developments in her characters' lives. The novel has been described (and dismissed) as escape literature, as romance, as soap opera and as an "Upper Canadian dream," and there is some truth in all these epithets. The Whiteoaks are, indeed, an impossibly romantic and imperialist concoction; Jalna is too preposterously the British dream of a country estate, set down intact in Ontario; the intertwining affairs (and names) of Renny and Alayne, Eden and Pheasant do anticipate the TV melodrama of *As the World Turns;* and yet *Jalna* has proven magically readable for generations, not only in English, but in French, German, Swedish, Danish, Norwegian, Czech, Polish, Finnish and Portuguese. NEIL BESNER

James, Thomas, explorer (b 1593; d 1635). He sailed from Bristol to Hudson Bay in 1631, 2 days before Luke FOX left on a rival voyage from London. The 2 met by chance at Cape Henrietta Maria (the name of James's ship). The only independent exploration made by James was of the W coast of the bay to which he gave his name. He beached his ship off Charlton I and spent a miserable winter – the first European to winter deliberately in the North. James's voyage was less productive than that of Fox, who was the superior navigator, but the harrowing tale so richly described in his masterly narrative discouraged further attempts to seek the passage for nearly 100 years. The circumstances of his death are unknown.
JAMES MARSH

James Bay, southern appendix of HUDSON BAY. It is about 160 km wide between Pointe Louis-XIV on the E coast and Cape Henrietta Marie on the W. The Québec-Ontario border is at the bottom of the bay, and its numerous islands are administered by the NWT. Akimiski is the largest island with an area of 3002 km². The bay was discovered in 1610 by Henry HUDSON and named for Thomas JAMES who entered the bay in 1631 and spent a difficult winter on Charlton I. The bay was long a centre for trade as CREE brought furs down the many rivers draining the surrounding area. The major rivers, from E to W, are LA GRANDE RIVIÈRE (formerly Ft-George R), EASTMAIN, RUPERT, Nottaway, Harricana, MOOSE, ALBANY and ATTAWAPISKAT. Ft Rupert, Moose Factory and Ft Albany – at the mouths of the rivers of the same names – were active HBC posts. MOOSONEE, Ont, the largest settlement in the area, is the northern terminus of the Ontario Northland Ry. There are native settlements at Chisasibi (formerly Ft-George), Eastmain and Attawapiskat. Polar Bear Provincial Park borders on the NW coast. *See also* JAMES BAY PROJECT. JAMES MARSH

James Bay and Northern Québec Agreement of 1975 is the first major agreement between the Crown and the native people in Canada since the numbered treaties of the 19th and early 20th centuries. This agreement was negotiated after 4 years of politics, court cases and bargaining following the 1971 announcement of plans to build a system of hydroelectric dams in northern Québec (*see* JAMES BAY PROJECT). The natives of the James Bay area insisted on and received a permanent right to control the hunting, fishing and trapping of all economically important species of game in northern Québec; a strong degree of self-government in their own communities; the relocation of the site of the first dam; the clearance of timber from reservoir basins before flooding, with the Cree given first refusal rights on clearing contracts; and $225 million to be paid over a 25-year period to the Cree and Inuit.

The lands were divided into 3 categories: 13 700 km² in and around native communities to be controlled solely by residents; Cree to have 70 000 km² and the Inuit 81 600 km² of exclusive hunting, fishing and trapping territories; and in the remaining lands natives to have exclusive rights to 22 important species of game and freedom to cut timber for their own needs. In addition, provision was made for a minimum family-income plan for those in wildlife harvesting; native languages to be included as official languages of administration; and a James Bay Native Development Corporation to handle investments. The dynamic and complex nature of the agreement is evidenced by 7 amending agreements, 4 additional spinoff agreements and 22 pieces of related legislation. The agreement has been recognized by the constitution. In 1984 the promise of self-government was recognized when Parliament enacted the Cree-Naskapi (of Québec) Act, the first of its kind in Canada.

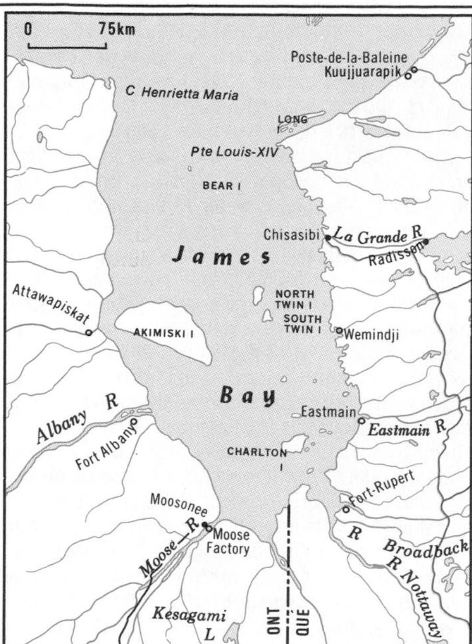

Implementation of certain parts of the agreement continues to be a source of controversy, between native people and the federal government in particular, and the Cree communities have claimed that the federal government has breached the agreement related to the financing of self-government. JOHN A. PRICE

Reading: John A. Price, *Native Studies: American and Canadian Indians* (1978); R.F. Salisbury, *A Homeland for the Cree: Regional Development in James Bay, 1971-1981* (1986).

James Bay Project, a monumental hydroelectric-power development on the E coast of JAMES BAY. The $15-billion project entailed massive diversions of water from the EASTMAIN, Opinaca and Caniapiscau (KOKSOAK) rivers to dammed reservoirs on LA GRANDE RIVIÈRE; the average flow of La Grande Rivière will be increased from 1700 to 3300 m³/s. A tiered spillway, 3 times the height of Niagara Falls, has been blasted from the bedrock, and La Grande-2 (LG-2), which was completed in 1982 and has the world's largest underground powerhouse, generated 5328 MW of electric power. The completion of LG-3 (Feb 1984) and

The massive underground powerhouse of LG-2, blasted from solid bedrock, is the largest underground powerhouse in the world (*courtesy SSC Photocentre*).

LG-4 (May 1984), which ended Phase I of the project, increased Hydro-Québec's production capacity to more than 10 000 MW. Five reservoirs will total 11 900 km^2 – half the size of Lk Ontario – and 8 dams and 198 dikes will have been built.

The project has raised controversy for its effect on the native people and environment. Announced by Québec Premier Robert BOURASSA in 1971, it was contested by the Cree, who had not even been notified. In 1975 the Cree surrendered their LAND CLAIMS for $225 million (*see* JAMES BAY AND NORTHERN QUÉBEC AGREEMENT), retaining special hunting and fishing rights. The village of Ft-George (pop 2373) at the mouth of La Grande R was uprooted and relocated upstream. It is now called Chisasibi. Eastmain (pop 356) now lies in a saltwater estuary, as the Eastmain R has been reduced to a trickle. Vast areas of wilderness have been inundated and forests incinerated in an attempt to clear debris. Phase II of the project, which will start in 1989 with the development of LG-1 at the mouth of La Grande R where it empties into James Bay, calls for 5 more powerhouses with a total generating capacity of 2500 MW. An additional generating capacity of 11 600 MW will be added in the James Bay area at the turn of the century with the construction of the Grande Baleine complex (2900 MW) and the Nottaway-Broadback-Rupert (NBR) complex (8700 MW).

JAMES MARSH

James Norris Memorial Trophy is awarded annually to the player selected by hockey writers as the best defenceman in the National Hockey League. It was first presented in 1953 by the children of James Norris, former owner of Detroit Red Wings. Bobby ORR won the trophy 8 times and Doug HARVEY 7 times. JAMES MARSH

James Richardson & Sons, Limited Started as a one-man enterprise by James Richardson in Kingston, Canada W, in 1857, this family-owned company has emerged as a major international organization, employing more than 4000 people. Through wholly owned subsidiaries, it engages in grain merchandising, storage and shipping; feed and fertilizers; pipeline construction; real-estate development; and a major securities division – Richardson Greenshields of Canada Limited, one of Canada's largest and most diversified investment firms, operating in 50 offices in Canada as well as others in the US, UK, Europe and the Far East and providing a full range of investment services with a staff of 2400 people. A notable pioneer in several fields, the company was the first to establish radio stations on the prairies, to broadcast grain and stock market prices, to make use of teletype for the transmission of business and, through its Canadian Airways Limited, the first to establish a coast-to-coast airline. All these accomplishments predated WWII. As part of its centennial celebration in 1957, the company made a gift of the then recently issued 10-volume *Encyclopedia Canadiana* to more than 400 universities and libraries. Few business organizations have played a more distinguished role in the growth of the nation's economy. ARTHUR E. GREGG

Jameson, Anna Brownell, née Murphy, writer, feminist, art historian (b at Dublin, Ire 17 May 1794; d at London, Eng 17 Mar 1860). Anna spent her early adulthood as a governess in England, in 1825 publishing *A Lady's Diary* (later *Diary of an Ennuyée*), a fictionalized account of a European tour. She married lawyer Robert Sympson Jameson in 1825, but the couple were separated in 1829 when Jameson became a judge in Dominica, and later in Upper Canada. By 1836, when she joined her husband temporarily in Toronto, Anna Jameson was a well-known author. She chronicled her 8-month stay in Canada in the frank, informative *Winter Studies and Summer Rambles in Canada* (1838), its "Winter Studies" a lively but uncomplimentary portrait of Toronto, and its "Summer Rambles" an enthusiastic recounting of her journey through southwestern Ontario, up the lakes to Sault Ste Marie and back. On her return to England, legally separated from Jameson, she began a 6-vol compendium of Christian art, popularly known as *Sacred and Legendary Art*. In later years she was the mentor of the young feminists who founded the *Englishwoman's Journal* and Girton College. CLARA THOMAS

Jamieson, Donald Campbell, broadcaster, politician, diplomat (b at St John's 30 Apr 1921; d at Swift Current, Nfld 19 Nov 1986). He first achieved prominence as a broadcaster in the 1940s, in time becoming Newfoundland's most recognized radio and TV personality and cofounder of a communications empire. In the Confederation debate of the late 1940s, he advocated a Newfoundland-US economic union over union with Canada. Elected to the House of Commons as a Liberal in 1966, he served in the federal Cabinet 1968-79, most notably as minister of external affairs 1976-79. He became leader of the Newfoundland Liberal Party in May 1979, a month before the Liberals were defeated in a general election, and resigned in 1980. Jamieson was appointed to his last public post, Canadian high commissioner to Great Britain, in 1982. Upon leaving public life in 1985, he was much in demand as a public speaker and had intended to write his political memoirs. GEOFF BUDDEN

Jamieson, Elmer, educator (b on the Six Nations Indian Reserve, Ont 30 Aug 1891; d at Toronto 18 Apr 1972). He received his BA from McMaster in 1913. He enlisted in the army, and censorship of his letters led him to write home in Mohawk. When censors could not "crack his code," he was called in to reveal its secrets. With his fellow Mohawks he set up the first Amerindian communications network, an idea adopted by the US Army in WWII. After the war he took an MA at McMaster in 1922, and then a doctorate in pedagogy at U of T in 1928. He was head of the chemistry and biology dept at North Toronto Collegiate 1922-57. ROY WRIGHT

Jamieson, John Kenneth, oil man (b at Medicine Hat, Alta 28 Aug 1910). Educated at U of A and Massachusetts Institute of Technology (1931), he worked for 3 years as a labourer on railway and highway construction and prospecting for gold in the Cariboo area of BC, before obtaining an engineering job with a Northwest Stellarene refinery. After the company was acquired by British American Oil Co (BA), Jamieson became manager of BA's refinery at Moose Jaw, Sask, then transferred to head office in Toronto. After WWII, in which he had worked for the federal government's Oil Controller's Department, he joined Imperial Oil (1948), a subsidiary of Standard Oil Co of New Jersey (now Exxon Corp), and later became a VP (1953). He was named president of one of Standard's principal Latin American subsidiaries (1959), and then VP of the American operating subsidiary. Appointed president of Standard in 1965, Jamieson became chairman and chief executive officer in 1969. When he became president, Standard was the world's largest company, with revenues twice that of the Canadian federal government. The biggest challenge of the job was maintaining corporate relations with governments throughout the world, often involving conflicting producer and consumer interests. Jamieson retired as Exxon chairman in 1975 and as a director in 1981. He remains active as a management consultant and director of several corporations from his home in Houston, Tex. EARLE GRAY

Jansenism, a theological doctrine which urged greater personal holiness, espoused predestination and was linked to some extent with GALLICANISM. Supported by the writings of St Augustine, it was synthesized by Cornelius Jansen (1585-1638), Roman Catholic bishop of Ypres, in his posthumous *Augustinus* (1640, condemned by Pope Urban VIII, 1642). At odds with Rome and particularly critical of the Jesuits, Jansenism was, after 1650, the object of a series of condemnations which shook the church of France. It soon took on a moralistic tone and rigorously opposed all laxity; it also became the vehicle for opinion hostile to Roman centralism. New France, firmly under Jesuit control, was little touched by doctrinal Jansenism, although there were a few enthusiasts. Nevertheless the moral rigour of Mgr de SAINT-VALLIER and his successors drew on Jansenist morality, for it was inspired by the same Augustinian source, though it had different theological bases; yet it was sometimes nourished by the reading of certain Jansenist texts. The ULTRAMONTANIST religious movement of the mid-19th century swept away the last traces of this indirect influence in Canada, without in the process eliminating the rigour itself. NIVE VOISINE

Janvier, Alex Simeon, painter (b at Le Goff, near Bonnyville, Alta 28 Feb 1935). A Chipewyan, he graduated from the Southern Alberta College of Art in 1964 and had his start painting a mural for the Indians of Canada Pavilion at EXPO 67. He returned to Alberta in 1968 to teach adult classes at the Saddle Lk Indian School, St Paul, and Alberta Newstart Inc, Fort Chipewyan. Late in 1971 he decided to paint full time. In 1973 he was a founding member of the Professional Native Artists Inc (Winnipeg), a group of 7 Indian artists seeking to market their own work. Janvier's abstract linear work is characterized by whiplashing pools of colour on negative space. In 1975 he painted a mural for the Muttart Conservatory (Edmonton) and for the County of Strathcona Building (Sherwood Park, Alta). Janvier was invited to Sweden in 1977 to paint and exhibit. He did *The Seasons* for the National Museum of Man 1978-81 and a mural for the 1983 World University Games (Edmonton). In 1987 his work was included in 2 major shows in California.

GERALD R. MCMASTER

Japanese The first known Japanese immigrant, Manzo Nagano, settled in Victoria, BC, in 1877. By 1914, 10 000 Japanese had settled permanently in Canada. The 1986 census estimated that there were 40 240 Canadians of Japanese ancestry. The history of Japanese Canadians is characterized by discrimination and turmoil in the past and success today.

Migration and Settlement The first wave of Japanese immigrants, called *Issei* (Ee-say), arrived between 1877 and 1928. Until 1907 almost all immigrants were young men. In 1907, at Canada's insistence, Japan limited immigration of males to Canada to 400 per year. As a result, most immigrants thereafter were women coming to join their husbands. In 1928 Canada restricted Japanese immigration to 150 persons annually, a quota seldom met. In 1940 Japanese immigration was stopped altogether, and it did not begin again until 1967.

The Issei were usually young and literate, the product of poor and overcrowded fishing and farming villages on the islands of Kyushu and Honshu. Most settled in or near Vancouver and Victoria, on farms in the Fraser Valley and in fishing villages and pulp towns along the Pacific coast. A small number also settled in Alberta, near Lethbridge and Edmonton.

The culture of the second wave of Japanese immigrants, who began arriving in 1967, is very different from the pre-WWI peasant culture brought by the Issei. Highly educated products of Japan's industrialized urban middle class, the culture of the recent immigrants also includes many traditional Japanese skills such as paper folding and flower arrangement, skills no longer practised by descendants of the Issei. Scattered in numerous urban centres across Canada, the new immigrants have made it possible for young Japanese Canadians to learn their ancestral arts, crafts and language.

Discrimination From the beginning Japanese Canadians, both Issei immigrants and their Canadian-born children, the *Nisei* (Nee-say), faced massive discrimination. Until the late 1940s, BC politicians pandered to white supremacists and passed a series of laws intended to force Japanese Canadians to leave Canada. The politicians denied the right to vote to all Japanese Canadians, including the Nisei and veterans of the Canadian Army from WWI. They excluded Japanese Canadians from most professions, the civil service and teaching. They passed labour and minimum-wage laws which ensured that Caucasian employers would hire Asian Canadians only for the most menial jobs and at lower rates of pay than Caucasians. In the 1920s the federal government tried to exclude Japanese Canadians from their traditional livelihood of fishing by limiting the number of their fishing licences. During the Great Depression of the 1930s Japanese Canadians received only a fraction of the social assistance paid to whites. Before 1945, BC's politicians would not let the Nisei enlist in the Canadian armed forces, since enlistment would give them the vote. Of the political parties, only the CO-OPERATIVE COMMONWEALTH FEDERATION sought equality for Japanese Canadians and other Asians.

Community Development Excluded from Canadian society by discrimination, Japanese Canadians congregated in their own enclaves and developed their own social, religious and economic institutions. On Powell St in Vancouver, in Steveston, Mission City and other Fraser Valley villages, and in coastal centres such as Tofino and Prince Rupert, Japanese Canadians built Christian churches and Buddhist and Shinto temples, Japanese language schools and community halls, and hospitals staffed by doctors and nurses trained in the US and Japan. They formed co-operative associations to market their fruits, vegetables and fish, and community and cultural associations for self-help and social events. By 1941 there were more than 100 clubs and organizations within the tightly knit community, 55 for the Nisei alone.

Before the 1950s discrimination also forced the Nisei to seek employment in the Japanese community. Growing up fluent in English, with a reputation as good students and hard workers, and equally familiar with their parents' culture and that of Canadian society in general, the Nisei in the 1930s were ready and eager to make their mark in Canadian society. Discrimination meant that even university-educated Nisei, as capable as Thomas SHOYAMA, were forced to seek employment within the Japanese enclaves; outside them they could work only as labourers.

World War II WWII destroyed the Japanese Canadian community. Twelve weeks after Japan attacked Pearl Harbor and Hong Kong, the federal government, at the instigation of racist BC politicians, used the WAR MEASURES ACT to order the removal of all Japanese Canadians residing within 100 miles of the Pacific coast. Officially they were removed for national security reasons, although the order was opposed by Canada's senior military and police officers who stated that Japanese Canadians posed no threat to Canada's security. No Japanese Canadian was ever charged with

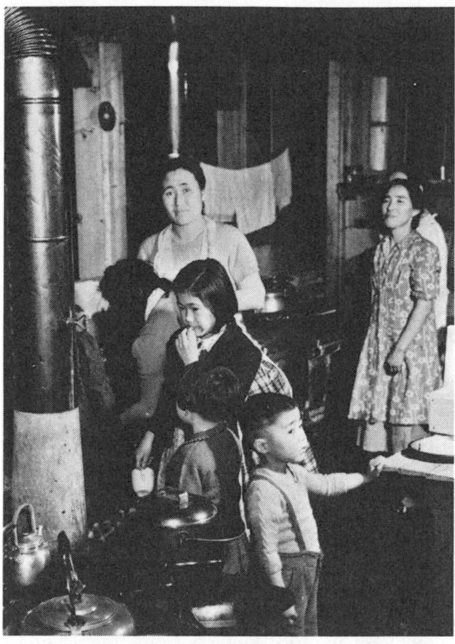

Community kitchen at the hastily built detention camp at Greenwood, BC, 1943, one of 7 camps which received thousands of displaced Japanese Canadians during WWII (*courtesy National Archives of Canada/C-24452/NFB*).

disloyalty to Canada. Later in the war, the government claimed it was only protecting Japanese Canadians from mobs in BC, a doubtful claim since it is normal to punish the mob not its potential victims. Government records also show that the federal government received only 150 anti-Japanese letters and resolutions before ordering the uprooting of Japanese Canadians.

In 1942, 20 881 Japanese Canadians, 75% of whom were Canadian nationals, were removed from their homes, processed through a temporary camp in Vancouver, and shipped to detention camps in the interior of BC or to sugar beet farms in Alberta and Manitoba. Between 1943 and 1946 the federal government sold off all Japanese Canadian property – homes, farms, fishing boats, businesses and personal property – and deducted from the proceeds any welfare received by the owner while confined unemployed in a detention camp. In 1945, Japanese Canadians were forced to choose between deportation to war-ravaged Japan or dispersal east of the Rocky Mts. Most chose the latter, moving to Ontario, Québec and the Prairie provinces. In 1946 the government attempted to deport 10 000 Japanese Canadians but was stopped by a massive public protest from all parts of Canada. Only in 1949 did Japanese Canadians regain their freedom and become enfranchised.

Postwar Community In the 1950s Japanese Canadians, through hard work and educational achievement, rebuilt their lives. The postwar economic boom and the rejection by Canadian society of racism as a political tactic opened new opportunities for Japanese Canadians who moved rapidly into the urban and suburban middle class. The third generation, the *Sansei* (San-say), born in the 1950s and 1960s, grew up entirely in Canadian society. The remnants of the prewar Japanese Canadian community persist only in a few churches, temples and community clubs in the larger cities. Scattered without contact with other Japanese Canadians, the Sansei speak English and French but little or no Japanese and know little of their cultural heritage. As a group they are more highly educated than their Caucasian counterparts and are found in disproportionately large numbers in academia, the professions and the arts. The changes since the Second World War are perhaps best illustrated by the fact that more than 75% of the Sansei have married non-Japanese.

Redress of the wrongs suffered at the hands of racist politicians during WWII is the primary issue unifying Japanese Canadians today. The National Association of Japanese Canadians (NAJC) is trying to persuade the federal government to acknowledge those wrongs, to pay compensation to those who were wronged, and most importantly to make changes to Canada's laws to prevent other Canadians suffering similar wrongs.

Well-known Japanese Canadians include Joy KOGAWA, David SUZUKI, Thomas Shoyama, Raymond MORIYAMA, Yuki Yoshida, Mitch Kawasaki, Takeo Nakano and Zenichi Shimbashi. *See also* INTERNMENT; PREJUDICE AND DISCRIMINATION.

ANN SUNAHARA

Reading: K. Adachi, *The Enemy That Never Was: A History of the Japanese Canadians* (1978); B. Broadfoot, *Years of Sorrow, Years of Shame: The Story of Japanese Canadians in World War II* (1977); J. Kogawa, *Obasan* (1981); Ann Sunahara, *The Politics of Racism: The Uprooting of Japanese Canadians During the Second World War* (1981); P. Ward, *White Canada Forever* (1980).

Jarvis, Alan Hepburn, art connoisseur, sculptor, editor, author (b at Brantford, Ont 6 July 1915; d at Toronto 2 Dec 1972). Educated at Parkdale Coll (Toronto), U of T (BA, 1938) and Oxford (Rhodes scholar, 1938-39), Jarvis accepted – after learning sculpting with Toronto art collector Douglas Duncan – a scholarship to the Inst of Fine Arts at New York U. Returning to England in 1941, be became a consultant in the Ministry of Aircraft Production. After WWII, he held a number of appointments there, including director of public relations, UK Council of Industrial Design (1945-47); director, Pilgrim Pictures (1947-50); head, Oxford House (1950-55); chairman, London's Group Theatre; and director, British Handcraft Export Corporation. In 1955, Jarvis accepted the position of director at the National Gallery, Ottawa. He visited many Canadian galleries, stressing the collection of 20th-century painting and sculpture and encouraging regional art. After a purchasing disagreement concerning European masters, he was asked to resign in 1959. In 1961, Jarvis helped organize the first Canadian Conference of the Arts in Toronto. He edited, and wrote articles for several magazines, and his books include *The Things We See* (1946), *David Brown Milne, 1882-1953* (1955), *Frances Loring, Florence Wyle* (1969) and *Douglas Duncan, A Memorial Portrait* (1974). ELSPETH CHISHOLM

Jasmin, Claude, novelist, playwright, essayist, arts chronicler and scenographer (b at Montréal 10 Nov 1930). He received his diploma in applied arts at the École du meuble in Montréal and became a scenographer with Société Radio-Canada in 1956. He did his first radio scripts for R-C, 10 years before the publication of his first novel, *Et puis tout est silence*, in *Les Écrits du Canada français* in 1960. That same year, he won the award of the Cercle du livre de France for *La Corde au cou*. Part of the QUIET REVOLUTION generation, he was preoccupied with political questions, aligning himself with the PARTI PRIS writers, though he never officially joined them. He won the Prix Arthur B. Wood for his play *Le Veau dort* (1963), the Prix France-Québec for his novel *Ethel et le terroriste* (1964) and the Prix France-Canada for *La Sablière* (1980), a novel from which Jean Beaudin created the screenplay for the successful film, *Mario*. He abandoned political and national questions sooner than other writers of his generation, turning to the fictionalized autobiography that won him the greatest success of his career. First published as a novel in 1972, *La Petite Patrie* became from 1974 to 1976 a popular TV series in Québec. His most recent works take their inspiration from many different sources, such as *Le Loup de Brunswick city* (1976) and *L'Armoir de Pantagruel* (1982). During his career, he has been the arts chronicler for various publications and his polemical style quickly won him the title of enfant terrible of Québec letters. In fall 1986 he made his TV debut as a host for the Quatre Saisons network in Montréal. GUY CHAMPAGNE

Jasper, Alta, UP, pop 3742 (1986c), 3269 (1981c), is located at the junction of the Miette and Athabasca rivers, 362 km W of Edmonton. First called Fitzhugh, it was named after Jasper House, a nearby NWC post, and acted as a supply depot for the mountain trade across ATHABASCA PASS. Possibly established as early as 1801, it remained open with occasional interruption until 1884. Its modern development can be said to have started in Sept 1907, when the Jasper Park Reserve was established. Tourism in Jasper began as early as 1915 and the first major hotels, the Athabasca and Jasper Park Lodge, opened in 1921 and 1922 respectively. The coming of the Grand Trunk Pacific and Great Northern railways (1911-12) and construction of the all-weather road to Edmonton by late 1936 spurred Jasper's growth, not only as a tourist town, but also (from 1912 to 1916 and again after consolidation of the 2 rail companies in the 1920s) as a railway divisional point. FRITS PANNEKOEK

Jasper National Park in winter. The park attracts over 2 million visitors each year (*courtesy SSC Photocentre/photo by Doug Curran*).

Jasper National Park (est 1907, 10 880 km^2) rests amid the unforgettable splendour of the Rocky Mountains. It is the most northerly of the 4 adjoining mountain parks (*see* BANFF, KOOTENAY, YOHO). The combined forces of wind, water and glacial ice have carved Jasper's U-shaped valleys, which sweep upwards to mountain peaks as high as 3747 m. The resulting landscape supports a rich blend of alpine meadows, subalpine forests and montane vegetation. Wildlife is a main attraction in the park. Many species can be seen along park roads, including moose, elk, mule deer, black bear, coyote and bighorn sheep. Grizzly bears roam the back country. The highest ledges are inhabited by mountain goats, golden eagles, ptarmigan and ravens. The park's history is rich with the adventure of the fur trade and of exploration for a route to the West Coast, including David THOMPSON'S 1811 discovery of the ATHABASCA PASS and Jasper Hawes's establishment of a trading post near the present town of JASPER. The COLUMBIA ICEFIELDS Parkway provides direct access to outstanding scenery. Snow-capped peaks, mineral springs and glacier-fed lakes and rivers attract more than 2 million visitors each year. LILLIAN STEWART

Jay, medium-sized bird of the CROW family (Corvidae). Most jays have crests and are brightly coloured. Thirty-seven species are recognized, with 3 occurring in Canada: blue jay (*Cyanocitta cristata*), gray jay (*Perisoreus canadensis*) and Steller's jay (*C. stelleri*). All are mainly permanent residents. Gray jays breed from the northern YT to Nfld, but are generally absent from SE Alta, southern Sask and SW Man. Blue jays breed in central Alta, Sask and Man and southward across Ont to Nfld. Steller's jay is restricted to western and southeastern BC and SW Alberta. Essentially, jays are woodland birds of coniferous and mixed forests. Blue jays are also very common in shade trees in urban areas. Jays tend to nest in conifers and lay clutches of 2-6 eggs. They are omnivorous, feeding on various fruits, insects and grains, and are noted for storing food in crevices in trees. Scientists speculate that this behaviour may be a means of ensuring a constant food reserve. LORRAINE G. D'AGINCOURT

The blue jay (*Cyanocitta cristata*) is one of 3 species of jay found in Canada (*artwork by John Crosby*).

Jay's Treaty, signed 19 Nov 1794 in London by the US and Britain and named for John Jay, US chief justice and a signatory. This primarily commercial agreement was intended to settle disputes which threatened war, such as British retention of frontier posts in American territory after the Treaty of PARIS (1783), American-Indian disputes over the Ohio Valley, and American anger over British seizure of shipping. The treaty stipulated that Britain would evacuate western posts by 1 June 1796, and that merchants of both countries would have free access to lands on either side of the border; that the Mississippi R would be open to both countries; that a commission to settle debts to Britain since the start of the American Revolution would be established; and that American shipping would not be hindered in trade with British possessions. The treaty marks the revival of arbitration in international relations, since commissioners were appointed to settle outstanding boundary problems caused by the peace of 1783. *See also* JOINT COMMISSION. STUART R.J. SUTHERLAND

Jazz, improvised music of Afro-American origin, is a synthesis of elements from African folk music and European art music. The term "jazz," covering a succession of styles historically, has been given various derivations, most of a scatological nature, but like the music itself, its exact genesis is vague. The music called jazz coalesced in the cultural hotbed that was New Orleans at the turn of the 20th century, drawing on ragtime, blues, spirituals and band music and establishing the melting-pot principle that would see it take in many other cultural influences (eg, Latin, Indian) and musical styles (eg, classical, rock) in the following decades.

Jazz was disseminated throughout the US by its proponents' subsequent northern migration – to Chicago, New York and other cities – and, after 1917, by recordings. Its evolution has been the result of both personal initiatives (Louis Armstrong, Charlie Parker, John Coltrane, etc) and popular movements, the latter eventually bringing jazz to Canada. American jazz musicians were present here as early as the 1920s (among them the self-professed inventor of jazz, New Orleans pianist Jelly Roll Morton, in Vancouver *c*1920), but it was not until the late 1940s that jazz was woven even loosely into the Canadian musical fabric, the result of popularizing efforts of men such as cornetist Jimmy (Trump) Davidson (1908-78), clarinetist Bert NIOSI, saxophonist Lance Harrison and trumpeter Johnny Holmes.

Its styles, from traditional and the related dixieland, through swing, mainstream and bebop to free and fusion, have had their adherents in Canada. The full historical spectrum is practised here in the 1980s: trad-dixie, particularly by the European musicians who immigrated during the 1960s (eg, Scotsmen Jim McHarg, Charlie Gall and Jim Galloway), as well as Canadians Lance Harrison and Ken Dean; mainstream by Galloway, Fraser MacPherson and Oliver Jones; bebop by Moe KOFFMAN, P.J. Perry, Dave Turner and Wray Downes; free jazz by Claude Ranger, Paul Plimley, Bill Smith and the musicians of the CCMC [not an acronym but the full name] and of the Ensemble de musique improvisée de Montréal; and the jazz/rock "fusion" style most notably by the bands Skywalk, Uzeb and Manteca.

Many of the country's best known jazzmen have been equally well known for their work in the pop music and studio worlds: Koffman, Perry, MacPherson, big-band leader (Boss Brass) and trombonist Rob MCCONNELL, flugelhornist Guido Basso, vibraphonist Peter Appleyard and pianists Chris Gage (1927-64), Vic Vogel and Tommy Banks. Some have established their reputations on their work in jazz alone: pianist Oscar PETERSON, indisputably the most popular Canadian in jazz; guitarists Ed BICKERT and Sonny GREENWICH; bassist and pianist Don Thompson; composer and big-band leader Phil NIMMONS; and flugelhornist and composer Fred Stone (1935-86).

Most of Canada's jazz musicians have been white. Notable exceptions include pianists Peterson, Jones and Downes, and guitarists Greenwich and Nelson Symonds. Several Ontario-born blacks taken to the US at an early age enjoyed international careers, among them pianist Kenny Kersey, trumpeter Arthur Briggs and bassist Albert Lucas; several white, Canadian-born musicians, including arranger Gil Evans, saxophonist Georgie Auld and trombonist Murray McEachern achieved even greater international renown after similarly youthful departures. Others, including the trumpeter and big-band leader Maynard FERGUSON, the pianist Paul BLEY and the trumpeter and composer Kenny WHEELER left Canada in the early 1950s as mature musicians to enjoy major and influential careers in jazz.

Characteristically an urban music, jazz has had centres of support in most major Canadian cities. It has been heard in concert and, beginning in the 1950s, in nightclubs, eg, The Cellar in Vancouver; the Yardbird Suite, through several incarnations, in Edmonton; the Colonial and Town taverns, George's Spaghetti House and Bourbon Street in Toronto; Rockhead's Paradise, the Café St-Michel, La Jazztek and Le Jazz Hot in Montréal; Pepe's in Halifax. Summer jazz festivals have flourished in the 1980s. The oldest, at Toronto's Harbourfront, began in 1979, and the 2 most significant, in Edmonton (Jazz City) and Montréal, in 1980. The 10-day Festival International de Jazz de Montréal drew more than 400 000 people in 1986 and has become one of the country's major cultural events and

Outside stage of Festival International de Jazz de Montréal, Canada's foremost jazz festival (*courtesy Festival Internationale de Jazz de Montréal*).

equally one of the world's great jazz festivals. Other festivals of varying importance have been mounted in Toronto, Vancouver, Victoria, Ottawa, Calgary and Victoriaville, Qué.

Notwithstanding its high festival profile, jazz has remained as a minority-interest music in Canada, as it is elsewhere, recorded by only a few Canadian companies (eg, Sackville, Toronto; Parkwood, Windsor, Ont; Justine Time and the CBC's Jazzimage, Montréal) and documented sporadically by the media. The Toronto magazine *Coda*, which was established in 1958, has maintained a small, though international circulation. Jazz has had limited TV exposure, but many long-running radio programs, both on the CBC and on private stations, attest to its continuing, if limited, popularity. MARK MILLER

Reading: J. Litchfield, *The Canadian Jazz Discography 1916-1980* (1982); Mark Miller, *Jazz in Canada: Fourteen Lives* (1982) and *Boogie, Pete and the Senator: Canadian Jazz in the Eighties* (1987).

Jefferys, Charles William, painter, illustrator, muralist, writer, teacher (b at Rochester, Eng 25 Aug 1869; d at Toronto 8 Oct 1951). Determined to explore both "the true nature of our landscape" and the historical (and prehistorical) background that shaped Canadian society, Jefferys was a strong advocate of artistic nationalism. Beginning work as a newspaper artist in 1889, Jefferys served as an illustrator on the *New York Herald* 1893-1901, and as art editor of the satirical periodical *The Moon* (1902-03). He was appointed chief illustrator of the *Toronto Star* (1905) and art director of Toronto *Star Weekly* (1910), before launching a free-lance career. He also taught at the School of Architecture, U of T, 1911-39. Jefferys is one of the most frequently reproduced of Canadian illustrators and is best known for his "visual reconstructions" of Canadian history. ROBERT STACEY

Reading: C.W. Jefferys, *Dramatic Episodes in Canada's Story* (1930), *Canada's Past in Pictures* (1934) and *Picture Gallery of Canadian History* (3 vols, 1942-50); Robert Stacey, *Charles William Jefferys: 1869-1951* (1976).

Jehin-Prume, Frantz, violinist, composer, teacher (b Jehin at Spa, Belgium 18 Apr 1839; d at Montréal 29 May 1899). As the first foreign musician of international fame to settle in Canada, with his wife Rosita del Vecchio, he played an important role in the development of musical life in Montréal. He enjoyed a brilliant career in Europe, Russia and Mexico. He came on a fishing and hunting trip to Canada in 1865 at the invitation of violinist Jules Hone and in 1867 settled in Montréal. For performances of Gounod's *Jeanne d'Arc* (1877), he was choirmaster and solo violinist under the direction of Calixa LAVALLÉE, his friend and collaborator. He was president of the Académie de musique de Québec (1877-78) and one of the founders of the Association artistique de Montréal (1891). After a final tour of France and Belgium (1885), he returned to Montréal where he devoted himself to teaching. Jehin-Prume composed numerous works, most of which have not survived. HÉLÈNE PLOUFFE

Jehovah's Witnesses, religious denomination known internationally for tireless door-to-door EVANGELISM, large conventions, and members' refusal to bear arms, salute flags or accept blood transfusions. Witnesses are thoroughgoing MILLENARIANS who believe that Christ came invisibly in 1914, and that through witnessing they are carrying out a "harvest work" by which mankind is separated into the saved and the damned. Accordingly the world will be destroyed at Armageddon, which will occur before the generation old enough to witness events in 1914 has all died. Witnesses deny the Trinity and hold to an Arian theology, which asserts that the Son of God is not co-eternal with the Father and is "a god" of a lesser degree. They teach that 144 000 will eventually dwell in heaven, but the rest of the saved will live eternally on a restored paradisical earth. In 1985 only 9051 proclaimed a heavenly hope out of more than 3 million active members worldwide. The Witnesses are mortalists and believe that most humans will be resurrected physically during the millennium. They hold that other religions and the secular state are demonic.

Jehovah's Witnesses grew out of the Bible Student movement developed by Charles T. Russell in the 1870s at Pittsburgh, Pa. In 1876 he adopted the "biblical" chronology of Nelson H. Barbour, which has been basic to the date-setting apocalypticism of the Bible Students and Witnesses ever since. Russell founded the Watch Tower Society in 1881 to spread this view. In 1931, Russell's successor, Joseph F. Rutherford, gave the name Jehovah's Witnesses to those Bible Students loyal to the Watch Tower Society. He abandoned many of Russell's teachings, rearranged Barbour's chronology and established a firm leadership for followers of the movement. Nathan H. Knorr (1905-77) was largely responsible for their growth into a worldwide movement.

Bible students appeared in Ontario about 1882 and soon spread throughout Canada. During both world wars they suffered much persecution because of their evangelical fervour, abhorrence of patriotic exercises and conscientious objection to military service. In 1918 their literature was banned, and they were outlawed 1941-43 under the WAR MEASURES ACT. Their most serious problems occurred in Québec after WWII (*see* RONCARELLI V DUPLESSIS; SAUMUR V CITY OF QUÉBEC). Consequently, to obtain religious freedom they popularized the idea of a Canadian Bill of Rights and established numerous libertarian precedents before Canada's highest courts (*see* HUMAN RIGHTS). Recently they have come under severe public criticism for the practice of disfellowshipment (excommunication) and the shunning of dissenters expelled from their ranks. They also continue to come under public scrutiny because of their opposition to the administration of blood transfusions to their children. Some 143 000 Canadians claimed to be Jehovah's Witnesses in the federal census of 1981. In 1986 there were 83 130 active Canadian Witness "publishers," or evangelists. *See also* EVANGELISM.

M. JAMES PENTON

Reading: J.A. Beverley, *Crisis of Allegiance* (1986); R.V. Franz, *Crisis of Conscience* (1983); M. James Penton, *Jehovah's Witnesses in Canada* (1976) and *Apocalypse Delayed: The Story of Jehovah's Witnesses* (1985).

Jellyfish, common name for free-swimming medusae of INVERTEBRATES of phylum CNIDARIA. Jellyfish are characterized by an umbrella-shaped body containing a jellylike substance (mesoglea), between upper and lower surfaces, which acts as a buoyancy aid. Three types are recognized: true jellyfish (Scyphozoa), hydromedusae (Hydrozoa) and colonial Siphonophora and Chondrophora. About 110 species are found in Canadian waters. They can occur in incredible densities; eg, moon jellies (*Aurelia aurita*) may clog boat cooling systems. Their effectiveness in capturing other planktonic animals makes jellyfish an integral part of oceanic food chains. Stinging cells (cnidoblasts) used to capture food have made some species notorious: sea wasp (*Chironex fleckeri*), off Australia's Queensland coast, can kill unwary bathers; the sting of the Portuguese man-of-war (*Physalia physalis*), however, is probably never fatal. Most Canadian species are harmless. Jellyfish buoy themselves by mesoglea or by gas-filled bladders. Siphonophores and chondrophores are supported by bladders and may be buoyant enough to float at the surface (eg, *Physalia* and *Velella*). Sail-by-the-wind-sailor (*Velella*) has a sail which usually keeps it away from shore by enabling it to tack across the wind. After periods of prevailing onshore winds, these jellyfish may become stranded on the outer BC coast in such numbers that beaches turn violet. Jellyfish move by jet propulsion, using powerful muscles to squeeze water out of the cavity formed by the umbrella. A.N. SPENCER

Moon jellyfish (*Aurelia aurita*) can occur in incredible densities (*artwork by Claire Tremblay*).

Jenkins, Ferguson Arthur, baseball player (b at Chatham, Ont 13 Dec 1943). The finest Canadian-born baseball player, Jenkins began his major-league career in Philadelphia before joining the Chicago Cubs in 1966. In 1967 he began a 6-year string of 20 or more pitching victories per season. A control pitcher, he rebounded from a disappointing 1973 season to win 25 games for the Texas Rangers, the team to which he had been dealt in 1974. He was traded to the Boston Red Sox (1976) and, after another period with the Texas Rangers (1977-81), signed with the Chicago Cubs again in 1982. Released by the Cubs prior to the 1984 season, his pitching record includes 284 wins, 3192 strikeouts, a remarkable strikeout-to-walk ratio of 3.20 and the modern major league lifetime record of 363 putouts by a pitcher. He won the Cy Young Award for pitching excellence (1971), the LOU MARSH TROPHY as Canada's outstanding athlete (1974) and was Canadian male athlete of the year 4 times. He made an unsuccessful bid as a Liberal candidate in the 1985 Ontario provincial election and, since 1984, has farmed near Chatham, Ont. In 1987 he was elected to the Canadian Baseball Hall of Fame, and he is the pitching coach of Canada's national baseball team. WILLIAM HUMBER

Jenness, Diamond, anthropologist, arctic scholar (b at Wellington, New Zealand 10 Feb 1886; d near Ottawa 29 Nov 1969). Canada's most distinguished pioneer anthropologist, he was educated at U of NZ and Oxford. After fieldwork in New Guinea in 1911-12, he joined the Canadian Arctic Expedition under V. STEFANSSON 1913-18 at the request of the National Museum of Canada. His participation in the traditional life of the COPPER INUIT around Coronation Gulf, NWT, laid the base for his later work. After service with the Canadian field artillery in WWI, he joined the museum staff and began his remarkable series of publications in Canadian ethnology, linguistics, physical and applied anthropology, and archaeology. *The People of the Twilight* (1928) is probably the best single book on the Canadian Inuit. His classic *The Indians of Canada* (1932), based on field projects among native peoples across the country, has been republished repeatedly. In 1925 he authored a brilliant paper on the prehistoric culture of Arctic Canada. His excavations at Cape Prince of Wales, Alaska, in 1926 resulted in his definition of the Old Bering Sea culture, still a fundamental discovery in Alaskan prehistory.

Jenness became chief anthropologist of the National Museum in 1926. He subsequently represented Canada at many international conferences and served as president of the Soc for American Archaeology in 1937 and the American Anthropological Assn in 1939. Before 1939 he developed the antiquities legislation vital to the protection of archaeological resources in the NWT. Deputy director of intelligence for the RCAF in 1940 and then chief of the Inter-Service Topographical Section of the Dept of National Defence, he later organized the Geographical Bureau from this section and served as its director until 1947. In 1962 he published an economic history of Cyprus. Between that date and 1968 the Arctic Institute of N America issued his 5 volumes on Eskimo administration in Alaska, Canada and Greenland, adding to his bibliography of some 100 titles.

A kind, quiet, modest man, Jenness was the recipient of honorary degrees from 5 universities and was associated with many learned institutions in Canada and abroad, among them the Royal Canadian Geographical Soc, whose Massey Medal he was awarded in 1962. Diamond Jenness Peninsula on Victoria I was named for him, and in the fall of 1969 he was appointed a Companion of the Order of Canada, his country's highest honour. WILLIAM E. TAYLOR, JR

Diamond Jenness (left) and W.L. McKinley aboard the *Karluk*, 1913 (*courtesy National Archives of Canada/C-86412*).

Jerome, Harry Winston, track and field athlete, consultant, teacher (b at Prince Albert, Sask 30 Sept 1940; d at Vancouver 7 Dec 1982). He was the first man to share world 100-yard and 100 m records. While attending U of Oregon on an athletic scholarship in 1960, Jerome ran the 100 m in 10.0 sec, tying German Armin Hary's world record; in 1962 he ran the 100 yards in 9.2 sec, equalling the mark of Frank Budd and Bob Hayes. An Olympic representative for Canada in 1960, 1964 and 1968, he won the 100 m bronze in the 1964 Tokyo Olympics; he took the 100 m gold in the 1967 Pan-American Games. After retirement, Jerome taught, consulted for Sport Canada and travelled Canada inspiring youngsters to try TRACK AND FIELD sports. TED BARRIS

Jessup, Edward, soldier, Loyalist, founder of Prescott (b at Stamford, Conn Dec 1735; d at Prescott, UC 29 June 1809). He supported the British cause throughout the American Revolution, raising the King's Loyal Americans and serving during the BURGOYNE campaign of 1777. His corps and others were reorganized to form the Loyal Rangers or Jessup's Corps in Nov 1781. After limited service on frontier raids, the rangers were disbanded in Dec 1783. In common with other Loyalist units, they were assigned lands in present-day Ontario. Jessup settled in Augusta Township, serving as justice of the peace and lt-col of militia. He went to England seeking Loyalist compensation but eventually returned to the area of the upper St Lawrence and founded the town of PRESCOTT. ROBERT S. ALLEN

Jesuit Relations (*Relations des jésuites*), the voluminous annual documents sent from the Canadian mission of the Society of Jesus to its Paris office, 1632-72, compiled by missionaries in the field, edited by their Québec superior, and printed in France by Sébastien Cramoisy. As a result of Cardinal Richelieu's decision to enlist the Jesuits in colonizing French N America, the early history of settlement was systematically and colourfully documented by priests attempting to convert the Indians and also to attract support at home for their project. The journals and letters of Paul LE JEUNE, Jérôme LALEMANT, Jean de BRÉBEUF and Paul Ragueneau, among others, dramatize tribal warfare in Huronia and the day-to-day life of colonists in ACADIA; these are supplemented by "relations" of Jesuit participation in colonial matters throughout the New World. Invaluable as ethnographic and documentary sources, the *Jesuit Relations* were avidly and widely read in the 18th century, along with the works of Cartier and Champlain, as exciting travel literature. Reuben Gold Thwaites edited 73 volumes as *The Jesuit Relations and Allied Documents, Travels and Explorations of the Jesuit Missionaries in New France 1610-1791* (1896-1901), presenting annotated parallel versions of his translations and the French, Latin and Italian original texts. MICHÈLE LACOMBE

Jesuits The Society [or Company] of Jesus was founded in Paris in 1534 by Ignatius Loyola (later St Ignatius Loyola), a Spanish soldier who underwent a profound religious experience while recovering from serious wounds. The Jesuits, as the religious order came to be known, were authorized by Pope Paul III in 1540 and participated actively in world affairs thereafter. Spurred by the inspirational writings of their founder (*Spiritual Exercises*) and unswerving in their obedience to the papacy, the Jesuits quickly became known as the schoolmasters of Europe – teaching not only the tenets of the Catholic faith but also subjects as varied as the Latin classics and dancing.

As part of their missionary endeavour, the Jesuits came to New France in 1625. Their activities are well documented in the JESUIT RELATIONS,

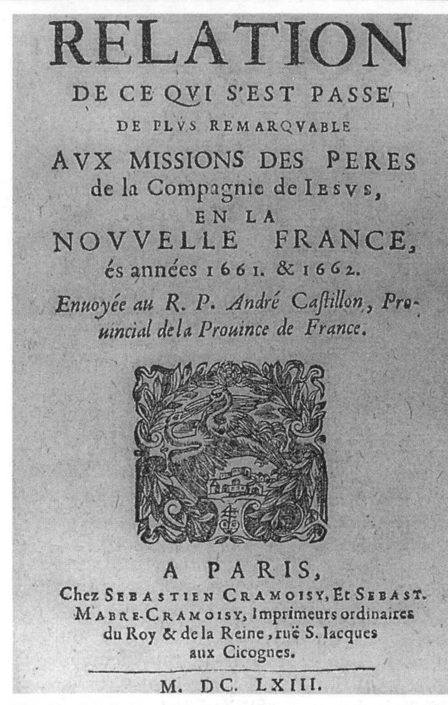

RELATION
DE CE QVI S'EST PASSE'
DE PLVS REMARQVABLE
AVX MISSIONS DES PERES
de la Compagnie de IESVS,
EN LA
NOVVELLE FRANCE,
és années 1661. & 1662.
Enuoyée au R. P. André Castillon, Prouincial de la Prouince de France.
A PARIS,
Chez SEBASTIEN CRAMOISY, Et SEBAST. MABRE-CRAMOISY, Imprimeurs ordinaires du Roy & de la Reine, ruë S. Iacques aux Cicognes.
M. DC. LXIII.

The *Jesuit Relations* were annual documents compiled by Jesuit missionaries in New France and were avidly read in Europe for their colourful depiction of the early days of colonization (*courtesy National Library of Canada*).

which include details of both the successes and failures of the Jesuits in their attempts to convert native peoples (*see* STE MARIE AMONG THE HURONS). In 1763, after the British CONQUEST, Jesuits in Canada were effectively suppressed by a ban on recruitment – the last, Father Casot, died in 1800. Ten years later, Pope Clement XIV dissolved the order in response to increasing pressure from secular governments; however, the papal brief had to be proclaimed publicly, and Bishop Briand of Québec's refusal to do so rendered it technically invalid in Canada. Pope Pius VII reconstituted the order in 1814, and by 1842 Jesuits had reappeared in Québec. Since the 1840s, Jesuits have been instrumental in founding parishes, schools and post-secondary institutions throughout Canada. There were 687 Jesuits in Canada in 1986. MICHEL THÉRIAULT

Jesuits' Estates Act During the French regime JESUITS were granted considerable property and seigneuries, which they used for educational purposes and for their Indian missions. After the CONQUEST, ownership of these estates passed to Britain, which held them 1763-1800, when the last Canadian Jesuit died. In 1831 London awarded the estates to Lower Canada. In 1838 Catholic bishops began to petition unsuccessfully for the appropriation of the Jesuits' estates in accordance with the wishes of the donors.

A view of the Jesuit College and Church (Québec) *c*1761, engraving by R. Short (*courtesy National Archives of Canada/C-354*).

The Jesuits, re-established in Canada in 1842, were authorized by Rome in 1871 to begin negotiating a settlement of their estates with the Québec government, the estates' owner since Confederation. Archbishop Elzéar-Alexandre TASCHEREAU of Québec then intervened, arguing that revenue from these estates should be divided among Catholic schools rather than being given to the Jesuits, who wished to establish a university in Montréal to rival Québec's UNIVERSITÉ LAVAL. As Québec's Roman Catholic hierarchy quarrelled, Québec Prem Honoré MERCIER called upon Pope Leo XIII to arbitrate the dispute. In July 1888 the Legislative Assembly unanimously passed the Jesuits' Estates Act, which provided a monetary settlement: the Jesuits would receive $160 000 and surrender all claims; $140 000 would go to U Laval and $100 000 to selected dioceses. A further $60 000 was allocated to Protestant institutes of higher education. Since Pope Leo XIII had been arbiter, the ORANGE ORDER in Ontario vehemently opposed the settlement as a papist intrusion into Canadian affairs. A heated debate occupied the House of Commons in Mar 1889; the motion to disallow the Québec law was defeated by 188 votes to 13. The Jesuits' Estates Act put additional strain on English Protestant-French Catholic relations. PHILIPPE SYLVAIN

Jeune-Canada, a FRENCH CANADIAN NATIONALIST movement, fd 1932 in Montréal during the Great Depression. Its membership of some 20 university students included André LAURENDEAU, Pierre DANSEREAU and Gérard FILION. They supported a conservative form of nationalism based on the protection of francophone rights in Canada and the defence of Québec as a Catholic, French, rural and agricultural society whose destiny was one of economic and political independence. For 5 years its members led an awakening of Québec nationalism, speaking at meetings, publishing pamphlets and attacking economic monopolies and governments. By 1938, as the Depression neared its end, the movement faded. RÉAL BÉLANGER

Jeunesses musicales du Canada/Youth and Music Canada Founded in 1949 in St-Hyacinthe, Qué, by Gilles LEFEBVRE, J.H. Lemieux, Anaïs Allard-Rousseau and Alice Desruisseaux-Boisvert, this nonprofit organization encourages the pursuit of music among young Canadians and helps the talented composers and performers in developing their careers in Canada and abroad. In 1950 JMC joined the International Federation of the JM; next year it established a summer music camp which, in 1967, became the JMC Orford Arts Centre, run since 1972 by an independent JMC corporation. Following the initiative of Lefebvre and the JMC, the World Orchestra of JM was created in 1969. By 1987 some 50 JMC centres and sections across Canada presented more than 250 concerts each year. Other JMC activities include artists' competitions and tours, instructional workshops, Sunday concerts and recordings. Jean-Claude Picard was director general of this Montréal-based organization 1976-87, succeeding Lefebvre (1953-72) and Gaston Germain (1972-76). In 1983 the name Youth and Music Canada, in place of Jeunesses musicales of Canada, was adopted for anglophone members. HÉLÈNE PLOUFFE

Jewellery and Silverware Industry includes establishments that manufacture jewellery (including costume jewellery, emblems, watch bracelets and precious metal cigar and cigarette cases) and silverware (including sterling or plated flatware and hollowware, and trophies), and those which rerefine or roll precious metals and produce precious metal alloys.

The jewellery industry in Canada dates back to the 17th century and includes clockmakers and watchmakers as well as silversmiths who emigrated from the British Isles. Canada has a tradition of SILVER crafting, as seen in the Henry BIRKS Collection of antique Canadian silver at the Royal Ontario Museum. François Ranvoyzé (1739-1819), acclaimed as Canada's outstanding silversmith, developed a beaten technique that made his work both beautiful and distinctive. During most of the 19th century, the silversmith's craft in Canada revolved around 2 Montréal workers, Robert Hendery and John Leslie. First as master and apprentice, later as partners, they fashioned silver for dealers in nearly all large population centres. They so dominated the trade that perhaps more than half the silver made in Canada in the last half of the century bears their mark.

Toward the end of the 19th century, a craftsman commonly described himself as a "watchmaker, jeweller and silversmith" and, as his position in the community consolidated, he became a merchant who employed watchmakers and silversmiths. Hence, by the beginning of the century the jeweller was firmly established as a link between the public and the craftsman. In this period, there were about 2000 jewellery firms in Canada. Many jewellers acted as opticians or worked closely with them in the early years when spectacle frames were made of silver.

Formal government intervention in the industry began in 1906, when the Precious Metals Marking Act was introduced to control the quality of precious metals used in jewellery. In 1918 the government placed a discriminatory 5% excise tax on jewellery; by 1986 the tax was 10%, in addition to the 12% federal sales tax. In Jan 1982 the industry became one of the first in Canada to implement metric conversion.

The Dept of Industry, Trade and Commerce (Regional Economic Expansion) encourages export of Canadian jewellery by sponsoring foreign trade missions for jewellery manufacturers. Markets are sought in the US, Japan and Britain. In 1986 Canada exported over $10 million in jewellery, including fashion (costume) jewellery. In recent years, Canadian jewellery has received worldwide attention through international competitions in which Canadian designers have received awards. This recognition has led foreign buyers to take a greater interest in Canadian jewellery products. The Canadian gold maple leaf, a consumer jewellery item produced by the federal government, is also popular in international markets.

Various native craftsmen are also producing a range of jewellery (necklaces, brooches, bracelets) in a variety of materials (eg, gold, silver, copper, bone). Foremost among these is Northwest Coast artist Bill REID, who in 1951 began to produce jewellery in Vancouver. His work, like that of other native craftsmen, is characterized by the adaptation of traditional native style and iconography to new materials and forms.

In 1983 the industry included 2908 retail outlets with total annual sales of nearly $1 billion. In 1984 there were 379 manufacturing firms, employing 4931 persons; 57% are small companies, each employing up to 4 people. Often, several generations of a family have carried on in a business. Most jewellery and silverware manufacturers are located in Ontario and Québec, with some in BC, Alberta and Manitoba. A single organization, the Canadian Jewellers Assn (CJA), represents manufacturers, wholesalers and retailers. It was formed in 1918 to promote sales and to represent the industry to government. The CJA publishes *Jewellery World* and *Jewellery World Plus* which, along with regional associations, keep members informed of national activities such as developments in insurance, excise tax, appraisals, ethics, precious-metals marking regulations and metrication. The educational branch of the CJA, the Canadian Jewellers Institute (incorporated 1945), offers courses at various levels of expertise, beginning with the 2-term Retail Jewellers Training Course. Completion of this course leads to a diploma and the designation "Graduate Jeweller" (GJ). Other educational and training courses are offered by the Québec Jewellers Corporation, the Canadian Gemmological Association and community colleges. These courses and practical training have increased the professionalism of Canadian jewellers. Three trade publications serve the jewellery industry in Canada: *Bijou*, *Canadian Jeweller* and *Canadian Gemnologist*.

DOROTHY A. LENARCIC

Jewett, Pauline, educator, politician (b at St Catharines, Ont 11 Dec 1922). Educated at Queen's, Radcliffe, Harvard and London School of Economics, she was a professor of political science (1955-74) and head of the Institute of Canadian Studies (1971-74) at Carleton before being appointed president of SFU (1974-78), the first woman to head a major coeducational university in Canada. Jewett was a Liberal MP for Northumberland from 1963 to 1965 and in 1966 she was vice-president of the national Liberal Party. In 1979, 1980 and 1984 she was elected MP for New Westminster-Coquitlam for the New Democratic Party. In Parliament she has acted as NDP critic on education and external affairs and in 1987 was critic on the constitution, federal-provincial relations, arms control and disarmament.

HARRIET GORHAM

Jewish Writing in Canada is characterized by linguistic and thematic influences derived from successive waves of immigration, and it appears mainly in Yiddish, Hebrew, English and French. Some Jewish writers work in other languages, such as German and Hungarian, reflecting the countries of their origin. Jewish concerns have also been treated by non-Jewish authors; eg, Gwethalyn Graham's *Earth and High Heaven* (1944) deals with intermarriage and anti-Semitism, Philip Child's *Day of Wrath* (1945) is concerned with Jewish persecution in Nazi Germany, and Yves THÉRIAULT's *Aaron* (1954) concentrates on the rejection of orthodoxy and the question of assimilation.

Yiddish and Hebrew writing began to appear in Canada before WWI when large numbers of Jews arrived after fleeing pogroms in tsarist Russia. In 1851 there were barely 450 JEWS in Canada; in 1901 there were almost 17 000, and suddenly there was a Yiddish reading public. By 1931 there were about 156 000 – mainly in Montréal, Toronto and Winnipeg – of whom 95% claimed Yiddish as their mother tongue. Yiddish was at its crest 1930-45, being used by Jewish communal institutions, 3 daily newspapers and numerous journals. For another decade Yiddish was bolstered by the influx of Holocaust survivors, including famous writers such as Melech Ravitch (1893-1976) and Rochl Korn (1898-1982), who continued the "internationalism" of Yiddish literature in Canada begun 1912 by the great Yiddish-Hebrew author Reuben Brainin (1862-1939) when he was editor of the Montréal Yiddish daily *Kanader Adler*.

Unlike most immigrant groups, Jews brought writers who tended to write with a "foreign" perspective for a worldwide public. Early in the 1920s, J.I. Segal (1896-1954) led a group of poets who were raised or began writing in Canada. Most notable of these were A.S. Shkolnikov (1896-1962), A. Almi (1892-1963), Ida Maze (pseudonym for Ida Massey, 1893-1963) and Sholem Shtern (b 1907). Together, they established Montréal as a centre of Yiddish creativity. The most distinctly Canadian is Shtern, whose 2-volume epic *In Kanada* (1960; 1963) narratively describes the Jewish immigrant experience in Canada. With Shabtai Perl (1906-76) and 3 noteworthy Toronto "native" poets – Abraham Nisnevitch (1886-1955), Shimon Nepom (1882-1939) and Judica (Yehudit Zik, 1898-1979) – Shtern belongs to a group loosely called "proletarian" because of Marxist influences.

The writers who arrived after WWII intensified the "international" tendency; and their influence, and that of the Holocaust, became dominant. Korn's dark but strangely undespairing poetry has been translated by Seymour Mayne and others in *Generations* (1982), and the "Auschwitz" poems of Joseph Rogel (b 1911) have appeared in English and French as well as Yiddish. Novelists Yehuda Elberg (b 1912) and Chava Rosenfarb (b 1923) are known worldwide for their description of Jewish life in Poland before and during WWII. In Toronto fabulist Peretz Miransky (b 1908), lyricist Simcha Simchovitch (b 1921), and poet and critic Itzchak Goldkorn (b 1911) are also recognized for Holocaust writing. Two younger survivors, Jack Kuper (b 1932) in *Child of the Holocaust* (1973) and Abraham Boyarsky (b 1942) in *Shreiber* (1982), have written in English about wartime experience. Most mainstream Jewish writers publishing in English, such as Eli MANDEL, Irving LAYTON and Phyllis GOTLIEB, have also attempted to deal artistically with the tragedy.

The use of Yiddish declined in Canada as succeeding generations turned to English; recent arrivals from Arab countries, Israel and Russia know no Yiddish. Iraqi-born Naim KATTAN writes in French about acculturation in his novels *Adieu Babylone* (1975, trans Farewell Babylon, 1976) and *Les Fruits arrachés* (1977, trans *Paris Interlude*, 1979), and in the collection *The Neighbour and Other Stories* (1982); he is perhaps the most important Jewish writer in French Canada. Michel Solomon (b 1919 in Romania) is also widely known in Québec for his memoirs *Magadan* (1971) and *Mon Calvaire roumain* (1976), and his novel *Eden retrouvée* (1980).

Most of those writing in Hebrew were usually also Yiddish writers, the exception being authors of religious works. Until WWI Yiddish was widely regarded as too vulgar for serious literature. Later it had to compete with the Zionist revival of Hebrew. Thus, most of the rabbinic sages who settled here – such as world-renowned Rabbi Judah Rosenberg, grandfather of Mordecai RICHLER – wrote mainly in Hebrew, although Rabbi Rosenberg also published several books on legends in Yiddish. The only poet composing exclusively in Hebrew is Miriam Schneid (b 1924), but poet and educator Isaiah Rabinovitch (1904-72) and novelist Joshua Altman (1898-1980) also wrote in Hebrew.

Jewish writers publishing in English in Canada share certain concerns with their immigrant predecessors: immigrant acculturation, the Holocaust, Zionism and the birth of the state of Israel, and fear of assimilation. Thus, nostalgia for the vanished traditions of European Jewish life, dominant in the work of Segal and the early Yiddish writers, reappears in A.M. KLEIN's attempt to synthesize Jewish culture and English language. His shock at the collapse of European Jewry during the Nazi ascendancy produced the first Canadian Holocaust poetry in *Hath Not A Jew* (1940) and in the bitter hyperbole of his satire *The Hitleriad* (1944), and scenes of Jewish wartime suffering in *The Second Scroll* (1951), his powerful, symbolic Zionist novel.

Klein is thus a pivotal figure; others followed his example. Although Mandel, Layton, Miriam WADDINGTON, Joseph ROSENBLATT and Leonard COHEN represent some of the most important influences of mainstream Canadian poetry, they also reflect in various ways their Jewish heritage, eg, in Cohen's darkly satiric *Flowers for Hitler* (1964) and his *Death of a Lady's Man* (1978), in which he attempts to blend romantic and Holocaust visions. Layton's poetry, especially after the Arab-Israeli war of 1967, has become increasingly concerned with Jewish, rather than artistic, alienation and with anxiety over Israel's survival. Among novelists these concerns surface in *The Sacrifice* (1956) by Adele WISEMAN, in *The Rich Man* (1948) and *The Betrayal* (1964) by Henry KREISEL, and in Mordecai Richler's fiction, particularly *The* APPRENTICESHIP OF DUDDY KRAVITZ (1959) and *St Urbain's Horseman* (1971). The shorter fiction of Jack Ludwig and Norman LEVINE also reflects facets of the Jewish experience in Canada, as do the plays of Leonard Angel, Sharon POLLOCK, Ted Allan and Beverley SIMONS.

Canada's Jewish population is predominantly urban, but its concentration in a few major cities has not led to a marked regionalism in Jewish writing. The eastern Ontario novels of Matt COHEN are an exception, and Richler's St Urbain Street can be seen as an urban "region" akin to Hugh GARNER's Cabbagetown or Ethel Wilson's Vancouver. Even the radicalism of playwrights Rick SALUTIN and Janis Rapoport, while it has its own form of regionalism, is actually in the tradition of Yiddish socialist writing. In their concern over identity, Canadian Jewish writers are related to their American counterparts and reflect the international orientation of their immigrant predecessors. Through the unique linguistic and cultural experience of its authors, Jewish writing continues to enrich the Canadian identity. *See also* ETHNIC LITERATURE. ADAM G. FUERSTENBERG

Jewison, Norman Frederick, film director and producer (b at Toronto 21 July 1926). Jewison has an international reputation as a filmmaker of talent and integrity. Though the bulk of his career has been spent outside Canada, Jewison believes his Canadian perspective has brought an important objectivity to his work. He was a graduate of U of T and worked as an actor and writer for both the British and Canadian broadcasting corporations before moving on to direct live TV in Canada and the US. In 1963 he directed his first film, *Forty Pounds of Trouble*, for Universal Pictures. Since that time, Jewison has maintained complete artistic control of all the films he has directed, and has, in most instances, functioned as both producer and director. These films include *The Cincinnati Kid* (1965), *In The Heat Of The Night* (1967; Academy Award for best picture), *Fiddler on the Roof* (1971) *Jesus Christ Superstar* (1973), *And Justice For All* (1979), *A Soldier's Story* (1984) and *Agnes of God* (1985). Jewison has also produced a number of films which he did not direct, such as *The Landlord* (1969), *Dogs of War* (1980) and *The Iceman* (1983). In all his work, Jewison has attempted, with frequent success, to balance popular appeal and serious social comment.

Jewison moved back to Canada in the late 1970s, with the desire to make a significant contribution to Canadian filmmaking. In June 1986 he was honoured with a retrospective of his career at the Vancouver Film Festival, and in Nov 1986 he initiated the establishment of the Canadian Centre for Advanced Film Studies near North York, Ont. KAREN LAURENCE

Jewitt, John Rodgers, armourer (b at Boston, Eng 21 May 1783; d at Hartford, Conn 7 Jan 1821). Jewitt was an armourer aboard the American fur-trading ship *Boston*. He and one companion were spared by NOOTKA chief MAQUINNA, whose followers destroyed the ship in Nootka Sound 22 March 1803. Jewitt agreed to remain as Maquinna's gunsmith and blacksmith. Immersed in Nootka culture, Jewitt was initiated into the Winter Ceremonial and took a Nootka wife. His journal was published in 1807, 2 years after his rescue, inspiring Richard Alsop to interview Jewitt at length. The result was *A Narrative of the Adventures and Sufferings of John R. Jewitt* (1815) – a classic of captivity literature – and a broadside ballad "The Poor Armourer Boy," which Jewitt hawked around New England. Jewitt was a shrewd observer, and his accounts are valuable records of Northwest Indian culture. DEREK G. SMITH

Jews The first Jews to make their permanent home in Canada arrived with General Jeffery AMHERST, who entered Montréal in 1760, eg, Aaron Philip Hart, who settled in Trois-Rivières. Most of the original Jewish settlers emigrated from the US and the majority settled in Montréal. The 1831 census recorded 107 Jewish residents in Upper and Lower Canada; by 1851 this number had increased to 451. These pioneering Jewish settlers were not, in one sense, a typical immigrant group. Most belonged to the middle class, were well educated and were engaged in trade, commerce and industry. Many played an important role in the economic growth of the country.

Between 1850 and 1900 the nature of Jewish immigration changed. The 1850s marked the beginning of a period of intensive emigration from Europe (which was torn by wars, revolutions, national rivalries and religious conflicts) to the New World, which needed labour power for development. It has been estimated that between 1850 and 1900, some 15 000 Jewish immigrants arrived in Canada. The 120 000 Jews who immigrated between 1900 and 1920 were primarily from eastern Europe, but those who arrived between 1920 and 1940 (60 000) and from WWII to the present (135 000) included Jews from the US, North Africa and the Middle East. The Jews migrated for the same reasons that other peoples did, except that economic and social discrimination, social and political inequality, and racial and religious persecution in their native lands made the position of Jews more precarious, and thus made the drive for migration very strong. Emigration was often synonymous with survival.

Between 1850 and 1914, immigrants wishing to emigrate to Canada encountered relatively unrestricted admission provisions, but restrictions tightened after WWI, at the same time that upheavals in Europe forced many Jews, particularly those of Russia, Poland, Austria-Hungary, Romania and the Baltic states, to emigrate. As a result of virulent anti-Semitism, thousands of European Jews were massacred or were driven from their homes, or fell victim to disease and starvation. The rise of Nazism in the mid-1930s threatened Jews throughout Europe, yet it became difficult for Jews to find refuge because the traditional countries of immigration, including Canada, had imposed restrictions on immigration. As a result, millions of Jews and non-Jews perished. Canada's record was particularly dismal. In the middle of the 19th century, Jews were largely a European people, but today only 25% of all Jews live in Europe, most of them in the Soviet Union. The largest number (6 million) live in N America, some 300 000 of whom are in Canada.

During the first century of settlement Jews lived primarily in Upper and Lower Canada, but by the 1850s they had settled in all the provinces. Although they generally settled in "urban centres" (a census term, in 1851, for all nonrural areas), there were also Jewish farm colonies in various parts of Canada. The 1986 census estimated that there were 245 860 Jews in Canada, distributed roughly as follows: Ontario (131 320), Québec (90 355), Manitoba (14 950), BC (13 170), Alberta (9460), Nova Scotia (2090), Saskatchewan (1515), New Brunswick (720), Newfoundland (285), PEI (80) and Yukon and Northwest Territories combined (80).

Economic Life Economic and occupational distribution among Jews has been diversified (ie, they have entered a variety of occupations), although there has been a relative concentration in specific fields. Jews in Canada have been victims of overt discrimination (eg, restricted admission to universities and professional schools) and subtle discrimination, which has tended to diminish during the last 30 years (*see* ANTI-SEMITISM; PREJUDICE AND DISCRIMINATION).

Religion, Social and Cultural Life The synagogue has served as a house of worship and of study and as a place of bringing together the members of the community for social and philanthropic work. Several forms of religious expression exist within Canadian Jewry, such as orthodox, conservative, liberal and reconstructionist (*see* JUDAISM). Certain other groups practise specific religious philosophies.

Orthodox Jews follow the 16th-century laws of the authoritative code of religious observance known as the "Shulchan Aruch," which is based on the Halakha, or legal part of Talmudic law. Conservative Judaism, an essentially American movement whose influence is spreading, maintains that Judaism can retain its distinctiveness and still be responsive to the changing social, economic, religious and moral needs of Jews. Reform Judaism, which originated in the past century, has advocated the abolition or modification of some traditional religious practices and beliefs that are considered anachronistic. According to reconstructionism, which originated in the US in 1935, Judaism is not only a religion but a dynamic religious civilization. It supports the re-establishment of the "Land of Israel" as the historic home of Jewish civilization, organic Jewish communities outside of Israel, free inquiry and acceptance of diversity in Jewish thought, and respect for traditional cultural values. Adherents of various Hasidic religious movements are strictly orthodox.

As the Jewish community grew, organizations were established to serve specific functions, eg, to support local and national philanthropy; to provide health and social services; and to aid immigrants and refugees. There are also fraternal organizations, mutual and self-aid societies, Jewish groups of various ideological leanings, Jewish labour groups, organizations related to Zionism and Israel, and organizations to promote Jewish culture. National organizations include the National Budgeting Conference of Canadian Jewry, the Canadian Jewish Congress (which is sometimes known as "the parliament of Canadian Jewry" and is the most representative of national organizations as far as general community participation is concerned), the Jewish Immigrant Aid Services of Canada, the Canada-Israel Committee, the B'nai B'rith, the Canadian Zionist Federation, and the National Council of Jewish Women. As an integral part of the world Jewish community, the organizational structure of Canadian Jewry aims to maintain local communal agencies while providing a bond between scattered communities in Canada and in other countries.

The Jewish community is served by one Yiddish and 4 Anglo-Jewish weeklies, one monthly magazine, a number of house organs of general interest and periodic publications.

The Canadian Jewish community has contributed significantly to various forms of cultural expression. Jewish poets and writers, artists, musicians and performers include Lloyd Bochner, Pauline DONALDA, Lorne GREENE, John HIRSCH, Johnny WAYNE and Frank SHUSTER, Mordecai RICHLER, A.M. KLEIN, Irving LAYTON, Leonard COHEN, Peter C. NEWMAN, Alexander BROTT and Louis APPLEBAUM.

Education Most Jewish children in Canada attend public schools, but almost every Jewish community provides facilities for religious and Jewish education through supplementary schools. In the larger communities, there is also a network of Jewish day schools that combine a program of secular and Jewish education at the elementary and high-school levels. Some Canadian universities have developed programs of Judaic studies. There are several orthodox rabbinical schools. Jewish education is considered vital for group identity, and every community attempts to provide schools, synagogues, publications, etc, usually with the assistance of national organizations devoted to this purpose.

Politics Ezekiel Hart, son of Aaron Hart, was elected to the legislature of Lower Canada in 1807, but was unable to take his seat because the law prescribed that an oath be taken "on the true faith of a Christian." This condition was removed by legislation 5 June 1832 and Jews were granted the same civil and political rights as other Canadians – some 25 years before similar legislation in England. Canadian Jews are represented in all Canadian political parties and voting patterns on a national level appear to follow general trends. Jews are represented in the provincial legislatures, the House of Commons, the Senate, the Judiciary (eg, the late Supreme Court Chief Justice Bora LASKIN) and have served or are serving as members of the provincial and federal Cabinets.

David LEWIS, former leader of the national New Democratic Party, was of Jewish origin. Herb GRAY was the first Jewish Cabinet minister and David CROLL was the first Jewish senator. Jews have also figured prominently in the Canadian labour movement; the Jewish Labour Committee, formed shortly after WWII, promoted human rights legislation in Canada. About 17 000 Canadian Jews served in the Canadian armed forces during WWII.

Group Maintenance Ever since the biblical origin of the Jews and throughout their history – including their history of migration and resettlement in various countries – religion has been the major force of group cohesion, not only as a faith but as the fountainhead of education and social and communal organizations.

Three major historical events have affected the Jews during the 20th century: intensive migration, which resulted in the formation of new or enlarged communities in N and S America, Australia, Africa, the UK, France and Israel; the decimation of the Jews during the Nazi persecutions and WWII; and the establishment of the state of Israel in 1948, which posed a number of political, social and economic challenges to Jewish communities throughout the world. Finally, Jews have had to face the difficulty of maintaining Jewish identity in a relatively open society during the transitional stage between generations. More and more Canadian-born Jews are identifying themselves by religion rather than ethnic origin, and English and French are replacing Yiddish as the mother tongue.

Although the decline in formal religious identification with the synagogue has been replaced by other manifestations of Jewish identity, eg, identification with Israel, the task of Canadian Jewry is to evolve specific programs designed to aid the retention of Jewish values and cultural life.

JOSEPH KAGE

Reading: A. Horowitz, *Striking Roots: Reflections on Five Decades of Jewish Life* (1979); E. Kallen, *Spanning the Generations: A Study in Jewish Identity* (1977); H. Troper and I. Abella, *None is Too Many* (1982).

Jiles, Paulette, poet, novelist, playwright, journalist (b at Salem, Mo 1943). A graduate, in Spanish literature, of U of Illinois, Jiles came to Canada in 1969. After a group of her poems appeared in *Mindscapes* (1971), she published *Waterloo Express* (1973) before moving to the North for 10 years. A juvenile novel, *The Golden Hawk* (1978), was her only book until *Celestial Navigation* (1984), which won 3 awards, including a Gov Gen's Award in 1985. Her poetry is philosophical, ironic and witty, yet capable of profound emotional insights. Two recent novels, *The Late Great Human Road Show* (1986) and *Sitting in the Club Car Drinking Rum and Karma Cola* (1986), give her wild, comic talent free reign, and signal that hers is a career moving into high gear.

DOUGLAS BARBOUR

Jiu-jitsu is a martial art developed by the warrior class of Japan. The modern martial ways of JUDO, Aikido, Hapkido, Nippon Shorinji Kempo and some systems of KARATE-doh all have their roots in Jiu-jitsu. Jiu-jitsu is a generic or collective term which when translated means "the art of flexibility or adaptability." In Canada, in addition to a combat self-defence art, Jiu-jitsu is practised as a healthy and exciting sport at the provincial, national and international levels. The Canadian Jiu-jitsu Association, founded in 1963 by Ronald W. Forrester, sent its black-belt team to Honolulu, Hawaii, in 1977 to win top honours in the first recorded international Jiu-jitsu team tournament. At the 1978 Canadian National Exhibition, the Canadian Jiu-jitsu black-belt team defeated teams from the US and West Indies; in addition, Canadian Jiu-jitsu athletes won the first 5 places in individual competition, male and female divisions. In 1981 the Canadian Jiu-jitsu team defeated the Florida State black-belt team by winning 7 matches out of 8. The first world Jiu-jitsu championships, in which countries from 4 continents participated, were held in 1984 in Niagara Falls, Ont. The Canadian Jiu-jitsu team won first place in the team, heavyweight and lightweight divisions. The second world Jiu-jitsu championships were held in 1986 in London, Eng, where Canada swept the championships with first-place victories in the team, heavyweight, middleweight, and newly created senior divisions (over age 45). The third world Jiu-jitsu championships are scheduled to be held in Brisbane, Australia, in 1988. Jiu-jitsu now ranks as one of the most popular of the martial arts, and one of the most effective systems of self-defence. Its ultimate aim is to produce well-adjusted individuals through recreation.

RONALD W. FORRESTER

Joachim, Otto, composer, viola professor (b at Düsseldorf, Germany 13 Oct 1910; Canadian citizen 1957). After violin and viola studies in Germany, he spent 15 years in the Far East, establishing his performing and teaching career. In 1949 Joachim settled in Montréal and became first a member of and then viola soloist with the symphony orchestra and the McGill Chamber Orchestra. With his brother Walter (cellist and teacher) and other colleagues, he founded the Montréal String Quartet, and was its viola player 1955-63. He also founded the Montréal Consort of Ancient Instruments (1958), for which he built replicas of ancient instruments. Joachim taught at McGill U 1956-64, Montréal Conservatory 1956-77 and Conservatoire du Québec 1961-67. His talents as a composer have developed in Canada, and almost all his works are built on a 12-tone base. He composed *Katimavik* for the Canadian Pavilion at Expo 67 in Montréal, which was the result of several years' experimentation in electronic music in his private studio, and he is also the author of some daring works. Some of his pieces have been recorded by his brother Davis, a guitarist, publisher and composer. HÉLÈNE PLOUFFE

Jobin, Louis, sculptor (b at St-Raymond, Qué 26 Oct 1845; d at Ste-Anne-de-Beaupré, Qué 11 Mar 1928). In 1870, after 4 years of apprenticeship in Québec City and New York, Jobin opened his own studio in Montréal. He filled many naval and commercial orders: ships' figureheads, signs and furniture. Moving to Québec in 1875, he increasingly specialized in large religious statues in metal-covered wood for the exterior of buildings. He did many Calvary scenes, monuments to the Sacred Heart, and numerous angels and saints. The huge Notre-Dame-du-Saguenay statue (7.5 m) is his most famous creation of this period (1881). After an 1896 fire in his workshop, Jobin moved to Ste-Anne-de-Beaupré where, until his retirement in 1925, he continued to serve his religious clientele. Here he made his celebrated monument of St George on horseback for St-Georges-de-Beauce (1912). After his prolific 60-year career, Jobin was "rediscovered" by the anglophone and francophone intelligentsia, and his works are now much sought after. MARIO BÉLAND

Saint-Georges et la dragon, sculpture by Louis Jobin who specialized in large religious statues (*courtesy Musée du Québec/photo by Patrick Altman*).

Jobin, Raoul, teacher, administrator, civil servant (b Joseph Roméo Jobin at Québec C 8 Apr 1906; d there 13 Jan 1974). He was the greatest francophone tenor of his age. His studies, begun at U Laval, were continued in Paris. Throughout a long and fruitful career, he was frequently asked to interpret strong characters such as Samson, Don José and Lohengrin. He was first tenor at the Opéra-Comique de Paris during the 1930s before joining the Metropolitan Opera in New York (1940-50). He taught at the music conservatories in Montréal and Québec (where he was also director 1961-70). Cultural consultant with Québec's general delegation in Paris 1970-73, he was made a knight of the Légion d'honneur in France (1951) and a Companion of the Order of Canada (1967). HÉLÈNE PLOUFFE

Jodoin, Claude, labour leader (b at Westmount, Qué 25 May 1913; d at Ottawa 1 Mar 1975). During the Depression he worked in the garment industry, becoming in 1937 an organizer for the International Ladies' Garment Workers Union. Selected president of the Montréal Trades and Labour Council in 1947, he was elected VP of the TRADES AND LABOR CONGRESS in 1949. During 1953-54 he played an important role in arranging a "no raiding pact" between the TLC and the CANADIAN CONGRESS OF LABOUR, setting the stage for the complete amalgamation of the 2 by 1956. President of the TLC 1954-55 and 1955-56, he was selected first president of the new CANADIAN LABOUR CONGRESS (CLC) in 1956, retaining the position for 10 years. Labour unity, in his view, was essential if organized labour was to influence the social, economic and political life of Canada and raise the standard of living of working people. Despite his early opposition to organized labour's involvement in politics, he supported the CLC's decision to back the New Democratic Party in 1961. M.D. BEHIELS

Jogues, Isaac, Jesuit missionary, martyr (b at Orléans, France 10 Jan 1607; d at Auriesville, NY 18 Oct 1646). Jogues entered the Society of Jesus in 1624. Sent to the Canadian missions in 1636, he was captured and tortured by the Iroquois in 1642. A year later, Dutch traders arranged his escape to France. Nevertheless, Jogues returned to Canada in 1644 and in 1646 volunteered for a peace embassy to the Iroquois. He was murdered that year on his second trip into Iroquois country. In 1930 Jogues and 7 other martyrs of the Huron missions were canonized. JOHN S. MOIR

Johannsen, Herman Smith, "Chief Jackrabbit" (from his Cree name), ski pioneer (b at Horten, Norway 15 June 1875; d at Tønsberg, Norway 5 Jan 1987). One of the best all-round skiers in Norway during the early 1890s, he became a salesman of heavy machinery and made Montréal his headquarters in 1919. In 1932 he settled in Piedmont, Qué, and began spreading ski trails throughout the Laurentians. A pioneer in all forms of skiing, Johannsen acted as organizer, instructor, coach and official well into his nineties. He was patron of the CANADIAN SKI MARATHON, and in 1979 became involved in the Jackrabbit Ski League, a nationwide children's ski program started in his honour. Although awarded the Order of Canada (1972) and inducted into the Canadian Sports Hall of Fame, it is the 8500 (1987) young skiers who provide the most fitting tribute to this extraordinary man. MURRAY SHAW

"Jackrabbit" Johannsen skiing at age 90 years. He was a pioneer in all forms of skiing (*courtesy Canadian Ski Museum*).

John Labatt Corporation, with head offices in London, Ont, is a management holding company which was begun as a small family brewery in 1847 by John Kinder LABATT. The company was incorporated in 1911 (in 1930 it was reconstituted to increase the number of shares available for distribution – 2500 (1911) to 90 000) and became public in 1945. Today, it has interests in 3 areas: brewing, packaged food and agricultural products. The principal company in the brewing group is Labatt Brewing Company of Canada; Ault Foods, Ogilvie Flour Mills and Catelli are parts of the packaged foods group. John Labatt Corporation has also been involved, with Casco, in the Zymaize experiment, producing high-fructose syrup from corn. The corporation has made significant investments in the US. As of Dec 1986, it had $3.2 billion in annual sales or operating revenue (ranking 29th in Canada), assets of $1.79 billion (ranking 61st) and 14 200 employees. BRASCAN, LTD holds 40% of the shares. DEBORAH C. SAWYER

Johnny Canuck, a personification of Canada and a member of the same family of figures as John Bull (Great Britain), Uncle Sam (US), and Marianne (France). Since the 1860s, editorial cartoonists have depicted Johnny Canuck as a wholesome, if simpleminded, young man wearing the garb of a habitant, farmer, logger, rancher or soldier. He is often drawn resisting the blandishments or bullying of John Bull or Uncle Sam. Johnny Canuck is also the name of a Canadian comic-book hero introduced in 1941, a caped strong-man who protected Canadians from the Nazi menace. The use of such stock figures declined after WWII; however, another comic-book character, Captain Canuck, a superhero instead of just a hero, was introduced in 1975. He wore red tights and "electro-thermic underwear" for warmth and on his forehead sported a red maple leaf. JOHN ROBERT COLOMBO

Johns, Harold Elford, physicist, educator (b at Chengdu [Chengtu], W China 4 July 1915). Educated at McMaster and U of T, Harold Johns devoted his career to the application of physics to medicine and biology and to training students with similar interests. He is best known for his development at U of Sask of cobalt therapy units which revolutionized the radiation treatment of cancer worldwide, and for his pioneering efforts in a variety of areas of medical physics and photochemistry. His work was at all times characterized by the application of imagination and experimental skill backed by theoretical rigour to the solution of major problems, largely related to cancer diagnosis and treatment. An inspiring and enthusiastic teacher and lecturer, he was the initiator of Canada's first department of medical biophysics at U of T and gained international recognition for his research and educational efforts. He is the author of numerous scientific papers and *The Physics of Radiology* (4th ed, 1983), and he served as chairman of the Healing Arts Radiation Committee, 1981-82. Among his awards and honours are Officer of the Order of Canada (1977); Gold Medal, American College of Radiology (1980); the R.M. Taylor Award, Canadian Cancer Society (1982); and the W.B. Lewis Award, Canadian Nuclear Society (1985). GORDON WHITMORE

Johnson, Albert, the "Mad Trapper" (b ?; d on the Rat River, Yukon 17 Feb 1932). Johnson (who sometimes called himself Arthur Nelson) was shot and killed by RCMP officers on the Rat River, northern Yukon Territory 17 Feb 1932. On 31 Dec 1931, an RCMP constable investigating a complaint about traplines was shot and seriously wounded by a trapper living west of Ft McPherson, NWT. The ensuing chase lasted 48 days and covered 240 km in temperatures averaging -40°C, and at its end another policeman was badly wounded and a third, Constable Edgar Millen, had been killed. The killer, tentatively but never positively identified as Albert Johnson, was so skilled at survival that the police had to employ bush pilot "Wop" MAY to track him. No motive for his crimes has ever been established. A request for the exhumation of Johnson's body – to allow a fingerprint comparison – was refused by the NWT's government in June 1987. WILLIAM R. MORRISON

Reading: Dick North, *The Mad Trapper of Rat River* (1972).

Johnson, Ben, track and field athlete (b at Falmouth, Jamaica 30 Dec 1961). In 1976 Johnson immigrated to Canada and was attracted to competitive sprinting, initially in the 100 and 200 m. In 1978 he entered national competition with the Scarborough Optimists track club in Toronto under coach Charlie Francis (later national sprint coach). Johnson's first sprint record was on the Canadian senior 4 x 100 m relay team against the US in 1982. But right from the beginning, Johnson and Francis set their sights on mastering the 100 m sprint. In 1978 he broke 11 sec, in 1980 10.62 sec, sixth behind US gold-medalist Carl Lewis. Johnson was the dominant 100 m sprinter in 1985, winning the 60 m in Japan and France, and defeating Lewis and teammate Calvin Smith in Switzerland. Also in 1985, he ran the 100 m in 10.02 sec, the fastest time ever run by a Canadian on native soil, and set the World Cup record at 10.00 sec. In 1986 he again beat Lewis and Smith at the Moscow Goodwill Games, running the 100 m in 9.95 sec, the fastest time ever run at sea level and the second-fastest time in track and field history. In 1987 he set world indoor records in the 60 m (6.41 sec) and the 50 m (5.55 sec). On 30 Aug 1987, at the world championships at Rome, Johnson won the 100 m sprint in the record-breaking time of 9.83 sec (again defeating Lewis), becoming "the fastest man on earth." In December 1987, Johnson was awarded the Lou Marsh Trophy as Canada's outstanding athlete and he was named male athlete of the year as well as top international sports personality of the year.

TED BARRIS

Ben Johnson at the Commonwealth Games, 27 Aug 1986 (*courtesy Canapress Photo Service*).

Daniel Johnson became premier of Québec in 1966 and continued the reforms of the Quiet Revolution (*courtesy National Archives of Canada/PA-117516*).

Johnson, Byron Ingemar, "Boss," businessman, politician, premier of BC (b at Victoria 10 Dec 1890; d there 12 Jan 1964). After service in WWI, Johnson and his brothers formed a building supply company in Victoria. Elected as a Liberal in Victoria in 1933, he was defeated in 1937. During WWII he was in charge of building RCAF airports in BC. In 1945 he was elected Coalition (Liberal) MLA for New Westminster and in 1947 succeeded John HART as premier. The coalition disintegrated in 1952 and Johnson was personally defeated in the election. His government introduced compulsory hospital insurance and the retail sales tax, negotiated the Alcan agreement, promoted highway expansion and began extension of the Pacific Great Eastern Ry.

PATRICIA E. ROY

Johnson, Daniel, lawyer, premier of Québec (b at Ste-Anne-de-Danville, Qué 9 Apr 1915; d at the Manic Dam near Baie-Comeau, Qué 26 Sept 1968). Elected Union Nationale MNA for Bagot in the 1946 by-elections, he did not enter the Cabinet until 1956, when Maurice DUPLESSIS made him minister for hydraulic resources. Chosen party leader in 1961, he worked to reorganize the UNION NATIONALE by giving it a solid program and democratic structures. In 1965 Johnson published *Égalité ou indépendance* and had his party adopt the principle – political equality between the 2 founding peoples of Canada – that was his government's touchstone on the subject of constitutional reform. Having won power in 1966, the new premier continued and even accelerated the major reforms of the QUIET REVOLUTION; for example, he created the U du Québec and Radio-Québec and laid the foundations for the future health-insurance system. PM Pierre TRUDEAU strongly disagreed with Johnson's defence of Québec's interests in FEDERAL-PROVINCIAL RELATIONS and his search for a new constitutional arrangement. Johnson was the father of Pierre-Marc JOHNSON, who was leader of the Parti Québécois 1985-87 and premier of Québec until his party was defeated by the Liberals under Robert Bourassa in Dec 1985. He was also the father of Daniel Johnson, a member of the Québec Liberal Party and a minister in Bourassa's government since Dec 1985. DANIEL LATOUCHE

Johnson, Edward, tenor, opera administrator (b at Guelph, Ont 22 Aug 1878; d there 20 Apr 1959). After amateur experience in Guelph and success in a Broadway operetta, Johnson studied singing in Italy, made his opera debut in Padua in 1912 and for 8 years, calling himself Edoardo Di Giovanni, won a devoted Italian following. In 1919 he joined the Chicago Opera Co and in 1922 went to New York's Metropolitan Opera where for 13 seasons he remained one of its most highly acclaimed singers. During this period he made a few recordings. As the Metropolitan Opera's general manager 1935-50, Johnson expanded the company's repertoire and introduced to the public many of opera's most spectacular personalities. Retiring to Canada in 1950, he helped establish the Edward Johnson Foundation to support public music education. BARCLAY MCMILLAN

Reading: R. Mercer, *The Tenor of His Time* (1976).

Johnson, Emily Pauline (she adopted the native name Tekahionwake, meaning "double wampum"), Métis poet, entertainer (b at Six Nations IR, Canada W 10 Mar 1861; d at Vancouver 7 Mar 1913). The daughter of a Mohawk chief and an Englishwoman, Pauline Johnson is best known for her poetry celebrating her Indian heritage, such as "The Song My Paddle Sings." Her work was well received by critics and was popular with the public during her lifetime, but faded into obscurity after her death. Much of her writing might be seen as an early expression of nationalism since it deals with Canadian themes. Between 1892 and 1910 she undertook a series of speaking tours in Canada, the US and England. She crisscrossed Canada, giving poetry readings in many remote settlements that saw few other forms of entertainment. Characteristically dressed as an Indian princess, she acted as a Canadian cultural ambassador throughout her travels. Her first collection of poems, *White Wampum*, was published in 1895, followed by *Canadian Born* (1903); *Flint and Feather* (1912); a volume of tales, *Legends of Vancouver* (1911); and a novel, *The Shagganappi* (1913). HARRIET GORHAM

Emily Pauline Johnson, best known for her poetry celebrating her Indian heritage. She is shown characteristically dressed as an Indian princess (*courtesy National Archives of Canada/PA-111473/Cochrane*).

Johnson, Harry Gordon, economist, teacher, author (b at Toronto 26 May 1923; d at Geneva, Switz 9 May 1977). He obtained his formal education at Cambridge (BA), U of T (MA) and Harvard (PhD). He held permanent teaching positions in Canada and Europe and visiting positions at universities worldwide. His most influential associations were with U of Chicago (1959-77) and simultaneously London School of Economics (1966-74). Johnson was one of the most prolific economists of his generation, publishing many works that advanced the frontier of economic science, most notably in international and monetary economics theory. Some of his contributions to the theory of tariffs and the monetary approach to the balance of payments have been standard readings for graduate students in economics worldwide. He also wrote many more rhetorical works aimed at the general public and policymakers. In his policy-oriented writings, he was a staunch defender of personal freedom and markets. He retained a lifelong interest in Canadian economic policies and often criticized the country's nationalist and interventionist policies, as is evidenced by his collection of papers in *The Canadian Quandary*. As an editor of economics journals – especially the prestigious *Journal of Political Economy* – he influenced strongly the nature and quality of economics research. HERBERT G. GRUBEL

Johnson, Sir John, soldier, Loyalist, public servant (b at Mohawk Valley, NY 5 Nov 1742; d at Mount Johnson, near Montréal 4 Jan 1830). He was the son of Sir William JOHNSON and heir to the Johnson family's massive Mohawk Valley estates. With the outbreak of the American Revolution, he moved to Montréal and organized and commanded the 2 battalions of King's Royal Regiment of NY, a Loyalist Provincial corps. In Mar 1782 Johnson was appointed to command the British Indian Dept, a position he held until 1828. He assisted in resettling the Loyalists, especially along the upper St Lawrence. Appointments to the legislative councils of Québec in 1787 and Lower Canada in 1796 followed. During the WAR OF 1812, he commanded the Six Township Battalions of Québec Militia. ROBERT S. ALLEN

Johnson, Pierre-Marc, politician, premier of Québec 1985 (b at Montréal 5 July 1946), younger son of Québec Prem Daniel JOHNSON. Very political, even as a youth, Johnson studied at Collège Jean-de-Brébeuf, U de M and U de Sherbrooke. He was admitted to the Québec Bar, and in July 1975 received his diploma from the Faculty of Medicine at U de Sherbrooke. He played an active role in student associations and practised medicine in Montréal before becoming a Parti Québécois candidate in Nov 1976. During the 2 PQ terms in office, he served in various Cabinet positions, including attorney general (1984-85). He was responsible for Bill 45 (labour relations), better known as the "Anti-Scabs Act." In May 1985, Johnson announced the Québec government's terms for supporting a constitutional agreement (including recognition of the special situation of Québec and the right to a veto, or provisions for opting-out with financial compensation, should there be federal-provincial agreements made without Québec). He succeeded René LÉVESQUE as PQ leader in Sept 1985, following a leadership vote open to all party members, the first leadership convention of its kind in Canada. Although his government was defeated by the Liberals under Robert BOURASSA 2 Dec 1985, he was re-elected in County Anjou for the third time. In June 1987 he consolidated his leadership at a party convention with his plan to defer independence while working for "national affirmation." In Nov 1987, however, a week after the death of Lévesque, Johnson announced his resignation as party leader. CLINTON ARCHIBALD

Johnson, Thorvaldur, plant pathologist (b at Arnes, Man 23 Oct 1897; d at Winnipeg 15 Sept 1979). Johnson became Margaret NEWTON's assistant at the Winnipeg Rust Research Laboratory in 1925 and was its head from 1953 until his retirement in 1962. His chief work was the plant-disease survey, especially for wheat. Following the discoveries of J.H. CRAIGIE, a constant watch was kept for new varieties of crop-plant diseases, and genetic material was collected for C.H. GOULDEN to breed into new disease-resistant wheats. Johnson later wrote the standard history, *Rust Research in Canada* (1961), and an informal memoir of the rust laboratory and its staff 1925-67. DONALD J.C. PHILLIPSON

Johnson, Sir William, superintendent of northern Indians (b at Smithstown, County Meath, Ire *c*1715; d at Johnson Hall, near Johnstown, NY 11 July 1774). As a landowner and militia officer Johnson amassed a fortune in the Mohawk Valley, NY, and cultivated close relations with the Six Nations Indians. Superintendent of Indian affairs, he solved a number of problems of Indian-white relations and led Indians and irregulars in several actions in the SEVEN YEARS' WAR, including at Lk George (1755), Ft Niagara (1759) and Montréal (1760). Johnson's devoted companion was Mary BRANT, sister of Joseph BRANT. CARL A. CHRISTIE

Johnston, Francis Hans (later Franz), painter (b at Toronto 19 June 1888; d there 9 July 1949). Among those who founded the GROUP OF SEVEN in 1920, Johnston was unusually well trained in academic practice, first at Toronto's Central Technical School with Gustav Hahn and at the then Central Ontario School of Art with William CRUIKSHANK and G.A. REID. After a stint at Grip Ltd in 1908, he studied at Philadelphia and did commercial work in New York before returning to Toronto in 1915. In 1917-18 he was commissioned by the Canadian War Memorials to record the activities of Canadian flying personnel training for overseas duty. Johnston's landscapes reflect his knowledge of turn-of-the-century ideals, being more atmospheric than those of the Group. The difference in ideology and technique may partially explain why he participated only in the Group's first show (1920). Johnston may have felt also that the adverse publicity generated by the show might affect his sales. He was principal of the Winnipeg School of Art (1922-24) and taught at the Ontario College of Art (1927-29). JOAN MURRAY

Batchawana Falls (1918), tempera on illustration board, by Franz H. Johnston, who participated in the Group of Seven's first show in 1920 (*Collection of The Winnipeg Art Gallery, Ernest P. Mayer/Franz Johnston/Paul Rodrik Foundation*).

Johnston, George Benson, poet, translator (b at Hamilton, Ont 7 Oct 1913). Johnston is best known for lyric poetry that delineates with good-humoured wisdom the pleasures and pains of suburban family life. After serving as an RCAF pilot in WWII and studying at U of T, Johnston joined the department of English at Carleton, where he taught until retirement in 1979. He is the author of *The Cruising Auk* (1959), *Home Free* (1966), *Happy Enough: Poems 1935-72* (1972), *Taking a Grip: Poems, 1971-78* (1978), *Auk Redivivus: Selected Poems* (1981), *Ask Again* (poems, 1984), *Carl: Portrait of a Painter* (biography of Carl Schaefer, 1985) and *Collected Poems of George Whalley* (ed, 1986). His translations of poetry from Old Norse include *The Saga of Gisli the Outlaw* (1963), *The Faroe Islanders' Saga* (1975), *The Greenlanders' Saga* (1976) and *Wind over Romsdale: Poems by Knut Odegard* (1982). Johnston has also translated *Pastor Bodvar's Letter*, by O.J. Sigurdsson (1985). JAMES STEELE

Johnston, James William, lawyer, politician, judge (b in Jamaica 29 Aug 1792; d at Cheltenham, Eng 21 Nov 1873). The son of a prominent Loyalist, Johnston migrated to Nova Scotia, where he became a lawyer and married into Halifax's social establishment. Proud and quick-tempered, Johnston became notorious as a duelist and debater. A quarrel with the Anglican hierarchy resulted in his emerging as a leader of NS's baptist community. Dissenter credentials, along with links to Halifax's business elite, enabled Johnston to move into politics. For more than a decade he led the moderates who sought compromise between Tory oligarchy and Liberal democracy.

Ousted from power in 1848 by Joseph HOWE, Johnston continued as leader of the Conservative Party. Restored to the premiership in 1857, Johnston soon moved to the bench, allowing Charles TUPPER to become his successor. A persistent critic of colonial democracy, Johnston advocated Confederation as a remedy for the alleged failings of RESPONSIBLE GOVERNMENT. His reward came in 1873 when Ottawa named him Nova Scotia's lieutenant-governor, but ill health and then death frustrated the appointment. D.A. SUTHERLAND

Johnston, Lynn, cartoonist (b at Collingwood, Ont 28 May 1947). Canada's most widely syndicated cartoonist produces her daily comic strip "For Better or For Worse" in a lakefront log cabin at Corbeil in northern Ontario. A former commercial artist and medical illustrator, Johnston introduced N American newspaper readers to "Elly" and "John" and their children, "Michael" and "Lizzie" (patterned after her own family), on 9 Sept 1979. By 1981, she had an estimated 50 million daily readers around the world. She had already produced 3 books: *David, I Think We're Pregnant* (1974), *Do They Ever Grow Up?* (1976) and *Hi Mom! Hi Dad!* (1977). Her daily and Sunday strip is syndicated to more than 450 newspapers in 19 countries by Universal Press Syndicate of Kansas City, Mo. In 1986, she became the first woman cartoonist to win the US National Cartoonists Society's Reuben Award. PETER DESBARATS

Johnston, William, outlaw (b at Trois-Rivières, Qué 1 Feb 1782; d at French Creek (Clayton), NY 17 Feb 1870). The "Pirate of the St Lawrence," Bill Johnston was a bandit and smuggler who operated in the Thousand Islands district. During the War of 1812 he deserted to the Americans, serving them as a spy and raider. In 1838, following the REBELLIONS OF 1837, Johnston enlisted in the rebel cause as "Commodore of the Navy." He terrorized river traffic, raided farms on the Canadian shore, and plotted an attack on Ft Henry. On 29 May 1838, he seized and burned the steamer *Sir Robert Peel*, carrying off $175 000 in cash and plunder. He participated in the attack on Prescott, Nov 12, but fled when the fight turned against the rebels. The Americans imprisoned him on charges of piracy, but he was granted a full pardon by Pres William Henry Harrison. EDWARD BUTTS

Joint Commission, a mechanism used extensively by Britain and the US to settle bilateral disputes mainly of a technical nature. Bodies composed of one or more representatives from each country, occasionally with a neutral chairman, are appointed to collect the facts of a dispute and offer recommendations for its solution. The ancient principle of arbitration was revived in N America by JAY'S TREATY, 1794, which set up 3 commissions to resolve intractable British and American differences. One, identifying the "true" ST CROIX R mentioned in the Treaty of PARIS (1783), was outstandingly successful and began the use of mixed commissions to clarify the route of the Canadian-American border. The method was also applied to the determination of merchant-shipping losses in naval warfare and to disputes over the N Atlantic fisheries. When joint commissions failed, matters were referred to diplomatic negotiation (eg, ASHBURTON-WEBSTER TREATY, of 1842) or to arbitration by a friendly power (eg, San Juan Is decision by the German emperor, 1872).

Following the US Civil War the practice began of referring a range of questions to a joint or mixed commission for simultaneous decision. The most famous of these bodies was the 10-member commission (among whose members was PM Sir John A. MACDONALD) that resulted in the 1871 Treaty of WASHINGTON. Another commission, meeting in Québec City and Washington 1898-99 and including PM Sir Wilfrid LAURIER and 2 Cabinet ministers among its members, failed to settle the ALASKA BOUNDARY DISPUTE. The most successful mixed commission has undoubtedly been the permanent INTERNATIONAL JOINT COMMISSION (1909). Joint commissions between Canada and the US have dealt with a number of diverse topics: fisheries, defence, the marking of the boundary and the reconciliation of trade statistics. Parity of membership has enhanced Canada's standing in an asymmetrical relationship, and both countries have benefited from the disposition to solve problems constructively. D.M.L. FARR

Joliat, Aurèle, hockey player (b at Ottawa 29 Aug 1901; d at Ottawa 1 June 1986). Left-winger for the MONTREAL CANADIENS 1922-38. In 644 games, and despite his 170 cm height and meagre 61 kg weight, he amassed 270 goals and 190 assists. A member of the all-star team of 1931, he was with the Canadiens for 3 of their Stanley Cup victories (1924, 1930 and 1931) and was winner of the Hart Trophy (most valuable player) in 1934. YVON DORE

Joliette, Qué, City, pop 16 845 (1986c) 16 987 (1981c), inc 1863 and as a city in 1918, is located 60 km NE of Montréal on the banks of the Rivière L'Assomption, close to the Laurentians and surrounded by a prosperous agricultural region. It was founded about 1824 by Barthélemy Joliette, seigneur de Lavaltrie, who wanted to become involved in the forestry industry. The lumber mill was one of the first buildings constructed. The town's economy diversified rapidly with the establishment of stone quarries and a foundry. Joliette himself sought to establish new businesses, including a distillery (1839) and a railway (1848-50). After his death in 1850, diversification continued and the town has always had a varied manufacturing base, ranging from food products to ceramics, textiles, tires, building materials and specialized metal products. As of 1847, a classical college drew students to Joliette from surrounding areas. In 1858 the town became a seat of the district court, and toward the end of the century built a hospital. Establishment of the Joliette diocese in 1904 confirmed the town as a regional service centre. Today, Joliette still plays a dual role as a small industrial and service centre, with 2 hospitals, several educational institutions, a CEGEP, a museum of art and government offices. JEAN-CLAUDE ROBERT

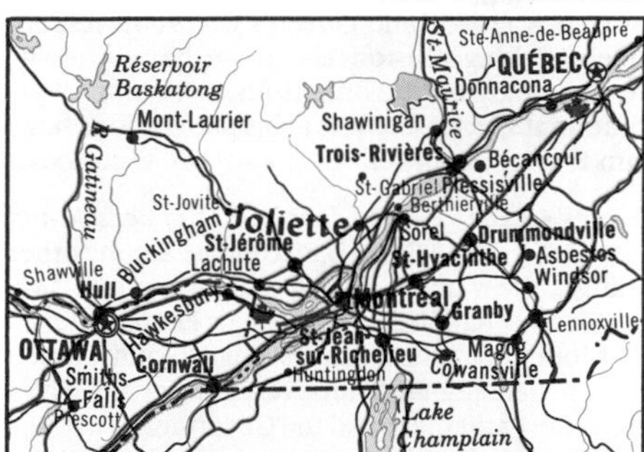

Jolliet, Louis, explorer, cartographer, king's hydrographer, fur trader, seigneur, organist (bap at Québec 21 Sept 1645; d near Île d'Anticosti late summer 1700), best known as the co-discoverer of the Mississippi. In 1656 Jolliet entered the Jesuit college at Québec where he studied for the priesthood and became an accomplished organist. He took his minor orders in 1662 but left in 1667 to become a fur trader. In 1672 he was chosen by Intendant Jean TALON to lead an expedition to determine whether the Mississippi, known from native accounts, flowed into the Gulf of Mexico or the Pacific Ocean. By 17 June 1673, Jolliet, with Father MARQUETTE and 5 others, was on the Mississippi and in mid-July he reached 33°40′ N lat near the mouth of the Arkansas R, sufficiently far S to prove that the river flowed into the Gulf of Mexico. Upon his return to Québec, Jolliet was denied a fur concession he sought for the Illinois area and joined his father-in-law about 1676 in a company trading at Sept-Îles. In Mar 1679 Jolliet was granted a trade concession at MINGAN in the Gulf of St Lawrence to which Île d'Anticosti was added in 1680. After an overland voyage to Hudson Bay in 1679, Jolliet concentrated on trade and fisheries at his concession until 2 raids by the English in 1690 and 1692 dealt him a financial blow from which he never recovered. Jolliet was commissioned in 1694 to chart the Labrador coast, a task he accomplished to 56°8′ N lat near the present Zoar. In 1697 he succeeded Jean-Baptiste-Louis FRANQUELIN as king's hydrographer and teacher of navigation. C.E. HEIDENREICH

Joly de Lotbinière, Sir Henri-Gustave, lawyer, politician, premier of Québec 8 Mar 1878 to 31 Oct 1879 (b at Épernay, France 5 Dec 1829; d at Québec C 15 Nov 1908). He represented Lotbinière in the Assembly of the Province of Canada 1861-67, in the Québec Assembly 1867-85 and in the House of Commons 1867-74. Leader of the Liberal Party of Québec from 1867, he was asked to replace BOUCHER de Boucherville as premier. Joly was unable to govern effectively, lacking majority Liberal support, and his government was defeated in the Assembly in the fall of 1879. He returned to federal politics in 1896 and joined PM LAURIER's Cabinet as controller (later minister) of inland revenue 1896-1900. He was lieutenant-governor of BC 1900-06.

Jonas, George, author (b at Budapest, Hungary 15 June 1935). Coming to Canada in 1956, Jonas became a producer of radio and TV programs for the CBC. His writing career started with poetry. In recent years, he has concentrated on prose, principally nonfiction, though he has written a novel, *Final Decree* (1982), a narrative that examines the wayward slowness of the legal system. This interest in the law began with his painstaking account, co-authored with Barbara Amiel, of a Canadian crime in *By Persons Unknown: The Strange Death of Christine Demeter* (1977). He has also written an examination of the plans by Israeli investigators to track down the terrorists responsible for the shootings at the 1972 Munich Olympic Games – *Vengeance: The True Story of an Israeli Counter-Terrorist Team* (1984), used as the basis for the feature movie *Sword of Gideon.* Jonas has also written libretti for 2 operas by Tibor Polgar: *The European Lover* (1966) and *The Glove* (1973), and his play *Pushkin* was produced by THEATRE PLUS in Toronto (1978). His most recent publication, *Crocodiles in the Bathtub and Other Perils* (1987), is a collection of his newspaper articles. PETER STEVENS

Jones, Alice, writer (b at Halifax 26 Aug 1853; d at Menton, France 27 Feb 1933). Developing international themes and the "New Woman" figure in her novels, Jones counterpointed the superficiality of European life against the vitality of Canadian society and character. Besides short stories and travel pieces for periodicals, she wrote *The Night-Hawk* (1901, pseud Alix John), *Bubbles We Buy* (1903, repr in England as *Isobel Broderick,* 1904), *Gabriel Praed's Castle* (1904), *Marcus Holbeach's Daughter* (1912) and *Flame of Frost* (1914). In 1903 a reviewer in the *Canadian Magazine* called her "the leading woman novelist in Canada," a consideration encouraged by her practice of including Canadian characters and settings in her fiction even after she had moved to France in 1905. GWENDOLYN DAVIES

Jones, Douglas Gordon, poet, literary critic, editor, translator (b at Bancroft, Ont 1 Jan 1929). Jones ranks among the major lyric poets in English in Canada. He has written 5 books of poetry: *Frost on the Sun* (1957); *The Sun Is Axeman* (1961); *Phrases From Orpheus* (1967); *Under the Thunder the Flowers Light up the Earth* (1977), which won the Gov Gen's Award; and *A Throw of Particles: New and Selected Poetry* (1983). Furthermore, his work as an editor of *ellipse* has been vital in making poets of English and French Canada mutually intelligible. Although chiefly inspired by rural Ontario and Québec, his work is not "nature" poetry, but rather a Taoist meditation on language, love and art whose roots are in Archibald LAMPMAN as well as Ezra Pound and William Carlos Williams. One of the crucial aspects of this poetry is its development from a central Canadian "garrison mentality" to neo-romanticism, expressed in the leitmotif of his book on Canadian literature, *Butterfly on Rock* (1970): "Let the wilderness in." In recent years, he has translated (with Marc Plourde) *Embers and Earth: Selected Poems of Gaston Miron* (1984) and *The Fifth Season,* by Paul-Marie Lapointe (1986). E.D. BLODGETT

Jones, George Clarence, naval officer (b at Halifax 24 Oct 1895; d at Ottawa 8 Feb 1946). Jones joined the RCN in 1911 and spent WWI at sea in British warships. From 1940 to 1942 he was commanding officer Atlantic coast, at that time the senior Canadian naval appointment on either coast. He became chief of the naval staff 15 Jan 1944, overseeing Canada's acquisition of major warships, including 2 cruisers and a light fleet aircraft carrier, and supervising the demobilization of the navy for peacetime. He died in office. ROGER SARTY

Jones, Henry, community founder (b at Plympton St Maurice, Eng 21 or 22 May 1776; d at Maxwell, Ont 21 Oct 1852). A Royal Navy purser, Jones was probably the first socialist in British N America. Retiring in 1815, he was attracted to the teachings of Welsh socialist Robert Owen who conceived self-sufficient communities – "villages of unity and cooperation" – to solve unemployment among workers displaced by machinery. Jones helped found a community near Glasgow, Scot, which failed in 1827. That year he sailed to New York and then moved to land on Lake Huron. He recruited settlers in Scotland, and in 1829 the first 20 arrived at the site, which Jones called Maxwell. A community building with family apartments and a common kitchen was built, with school and store run on Owenite principles. About 80 people joined the community, which disintegrated after the main house burned in 1834. Jones left for England in 1835, and efforts to revive the community from a distance failed. He returned to Canada a theoretical rather than an active socialist and his utopian ideas have had no lasting influence on Canada. GEORGE WOODCOCK

Jones, Hugh Griffith, architect, artist (b at Randolph, Wis 3 Dec 1872; d at Montréal 16 Feb 1947). Trained in Minneapolis, he practised in Chicago and New York, and came to Montréal in 1908 to work as a designer and assistant chief architect for the CPR. In 1913-14 he was one of the designers of Toronto's UNION STATION, but his outstanding achievement was a redevelopment plan for the downtown core of Montréal on property owned by the CNR; the plan occupied his interest 1923-32 but was thwarted by the world financial slump. Besides enjoying a successful private practice, Jones received wide recognition for his watercolours and oils, examples of which are in the Musée des beaux-arts de Montréal.
ROBERT LEMIRE

Jones, John Walter, farmer, politician, premier of PEI (b at Pownal, PEI 14 Apr 1878; d at Ottawa 31 Mar 1954). An unsuccessful Progressive candidate in the federal election of 1921, Jones was first elected to the provincial legislature as a Liberal in 1935. In 1943, following Premier Thane CAMPBELL's appointment as chief justice, he became premier. A student of agricultural science and a successful farmer, "Farmer Jones" championed rural interests. As premier he took on the powerful PEI Temperance Federation when in 1945 he favoured strict government regulation of intoxicants rather than PROHIBITION. When the lt-gov, a prohibitionist, refused assent to the necessary legislation, Jones, characteristically, proceeded by order-in-council. During a 1947 Canada Packers strike, his government, claiming to "protect the farm interest," seized the plant, employed scab labour and outlawed unions affiliated with national or international labour organizations. Colourful, outspoken and popular, Jones was appointed to the Senate in 1953.
DAVID A. MILNE

Jones, Peter, or Kahkewaquonaby (Sacred Feathers), Methodist minister, chief, translator (b at Burlington Heights [Hamilton], UC 1 Jan 1802; d at Brantford, Canada W 29 June 1856). Son of a white surveyor and a Mississauga (Ojibwa) woman, he became the first native Methodist missionary to the OJIBWA after his conversion to Christianity in 1823. With his brother John, he prepared the earliest translations of the Bible from English into Ojibwa. Elected chief of 2 Ojibwa bands, he argued articulately for Indian land rights. His *Life and Journals* (1860) and *History of the Ojebway Indians* (1861) were published posthumously. DONALD B. SMITH

Jones, Richard Norman, scientist (b at Manchester, Eng 20 Mar 1913). A British-educated specialist in infrared SPECTROSCOPY, which is used to elucidate molecular structure, he retired from 3 decades of service with the NATIONAL RESEARCH COUNCIL in Ottawa in 1978. Among his contributions was the harnessing of computers to refine instrumented spectrometric information. He was one of Canada's most "international" scientists, giving lectures and working on committees across the academic world. He developed strong links with Japanese colleagues and was a guest professor at the Tokyo Institute of Technology 1979-82 and again in 1985-86. He has also been Distinguished Visitor and Adjunct Professor at U of A (1983) and Queen's U (1984), respectively. Having a historical bent, he has written illuminatingly on the origins and evolution of vibrational spectroscopy, and his publications have run to over 200 titles. N.T. GRIDGEMAN

Jones Case (1975) In *Jones* v *A.G. of Canada and NB* the Supreme Court had to judge, among other things, the validity of the federal OFFICIAL LANGUAGES ACT (challenged by Mayor Leonard Jones of Moncton), which makes English and French the official languages for everything that derives from the Parliament and the Government of Canada, by granting their use equal status, rights and privileges in all institutions of Parliament and of the government in Canada. The judges unanimously found that by virtue of its residual power Parliament could enact such a measure.
GÉRALD-A. BEAUDOIN

Jones Konihowski, Diane, pentathlete, track and field coach (b at Vancouver 7 Mar 1951). Educated at Saskatoon, Jones first competed internationally for Canada in 1967, and has been a member of 3 Olympic teams since 1972, finishing out of the medals each time; she won gold medals in the 1975 and 1979 Pan-American Games pentathlon, and in the XI Commonwealth Games at Edmonton (1978) with a Canadian record 4768 points. Throughout her amateur career, she has spoken for Canada, for athletes in general and for women in sport. In 1987 she was an administrator with the Alberta Sport Council. TED BARRIS

Jonquière, Qué, City, pop 58 467 (1986c), pop 60 354 (1981c), inc 1975, is located at the confluence of the SAGUENAY R and Rivière aux Sables, 5 km W of CHICOUTIMI and 200 km N of Québec City. Regional metropolis of the Saguenay-Lac Saint-Jean area, the present city includes the amalgamated municipalities of Jonquière, Arvida, Kénogami and the parish of Jonquière. It was named after J.P. de Tafanel, marquis de La Jonquière, governor of New France 1749-52.

As the industrial axis of the region, its history is closely tied to the history of big business, specifically to that of the Price and Alcan companies. An agricultural parish founded in 1847, Jonquière began developing in 1900 when a group of citizens built a pulp mill on the Rivière aux Sables. The mill was soon bought by William PRICE, who turned it into a paper mill. In 1911 the company built a larger paper mill near the town, which, like the town built to house its employees, was called Kénogami. By 1912 Jonquière was the major producer of newsprint in Canada. In 1925 the Aluminum Co of America (Alcoa, later ALCAN) built the aluminum plant that gave rise to Arvida on the plain between Jonquière and Chicoutimi. Arvida (from the name of *Ar*thur *Vi*ning *Da*vis, then president of Alcoa) was a fine example of a legal company town. Its 1926 charter contained many deviations from the Québec law for cities and towns. The company ran every aspect of the townspeople's lives, from the urban plant to education (the school board), sports and health.

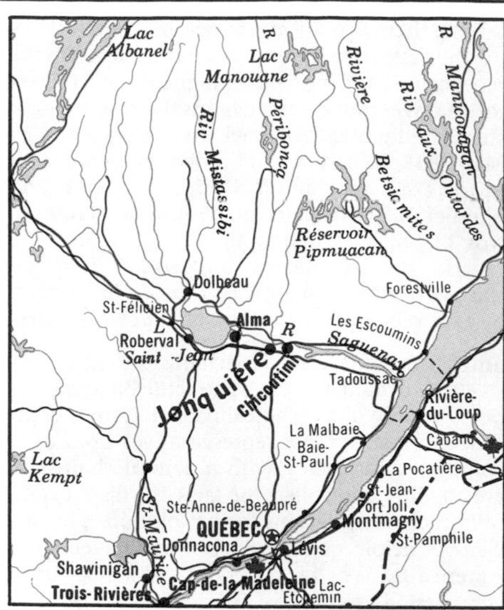

Besides factories, Alcan built a hydro station on the Saguenay near Jonquière, which was finished in 1931. During WWII Alcan boosted its production capacity at Arvida and built the Shipshaw hydro station, at the time the largest aluminum production centre in the Western world, a title it still holds. Basically an industrial centre, Jonquière began to change in the 1960s as services began to develop. Along with its commerce and professional services the city has since 1975 become home to the regional offices of a number of Québec government ministries. As well, the Collège de Jonquière (1967), part of the CEGEP network, has an admirable reputation at the provincial level. MARC ST-HILAIRE

Joual is a type of Canadian French language. The term, often used pejoratively, derives from a colloquial pronunciation of the word *cheval* ("horse"), which came to symbolize this form of speech. Just as Canadian English is different from English spoken elsewhere, French in Canada is different from that of France. But the standard has traditionally been set in France alone. The more an individual's speech diverges from standard French (this usually depends on education), the more it is considered joual, but there is no clear dividing line between joual and simply Canadian French. Features such as *moé (moi), m'as partir (je vais partir), achaler (ennuyer)*, and the extensive use of words borrowed from English are often construed to be joual; but such features are found in informal Canadian French.

The significance of joual is as much political and cultural as linguistic. The word was first given prominence in the early 1960s, at the beginning of the QUIET REVOLUTION, by André LAURENDEAU, editor of *Le* DEVOIR, and Jean-Paul DESBIENS, author of *Les* INSOLENCES DU FRÈRE UNTEL, who attacked the "incorrectness" of Québec French as one of the evils of their society. At the same time, many Québec writers, especially those of the review PARTI PRIS, began using joual in their novels, plays, poetry, radio and TV scripts, and popular songs. For the first time, a substantial proportion of such material was being written in the real language of the people, rather than in an asepticized, artificial French. Most of these works were set among the working class, and while joual enhanced the social realism, it also symbolized the degradation suffered by the people as a result of English Canadian economic and political domination. The joual movement was controversial: many believed that such language should not be made public. For that reason Michel TREMBLAY's play *Les Belles-soeurs* was refused a government subsidy for a European tour. Today, "joual" is no longer a watchword. The role of a spoken variety of Canadian French in popular culture is firmly established. SINCLAIR ROBINSON

Reading: M.M. Orkin, *Speaking Canadian French* (1971); Sinclair Robinson and D. Smith, *Practical Handbook of Quebec and Acadian French* (1984).

Joudry, Patricia, writer (b at Spirit River, Alta 18 Oct 1921). Joudry grew up in Montréal but moved to Toronto in 1940 to write and act for radio. Over the next decade, she became one of the most successful radio comedy writers in N America. During the 1950s, she turned to more serious dramatic writing for radio, television and stage. Her best known play, *Teach Me How to Cry* (1955), had productions in New York and London, won the DOMINION DRAMA FESTIVAL's best play award and was made into a feature film. Joudry was one of the few Canadian dramatists of her era with an international reputation, based on plays such as *The Sand Castle* (1955), *Walk Alone Together* (1960) and *Semi-Detached* (1960). Author of 2 novels and 2 volumes of autobiography, Joudry continues to write plays from her home near Saskatoon. JERRY WASSERMAN

Journalism is the occupation of a diverse group of people who earn their living by writing or editing material of current interest for dissemination via print or electronic media. The libertarian norms of "freedom of the press," the unofficial status of a "fourth estate," and the notion that modern society is greatly influenced by the content of the mass media all suggest an impressive and privileged role for the journalist in Canadian society. In an age of mass media administered by corporate executives, and rapid advances in electronic communications, the character of journalism is by no means simple to define.

Journalism has always been conditioned by a series of institutional constraints: the state, the party system, the business imperatives of MEDIA OWNERSHIP, and the impact of technological innovation. These factors have interacted throughout the development of Canadian journalism to condition the standards, style, social status and freedom of journalists. The professionalization of journalism is best understood as a historical process in which journalists responded to these various constraints with a variety of strategies to defend their group integrity. This process, however, has not amounted to a simple progression towards "freedom of the press." Instead, escape from one institutional constraint has led to a new one, usually more subtle, and posing even greater obstacles to the ideal of professionalization.

As a colony of the centralized Bourbon monarchy of France, NEW FRANCE was not allowed a printing press before 1760. Journalism came to NS in 1751 in the wake of the British expedition to found Halifax, and to Québec in 1764 after the British Conquest. The character of publishing and the nature of society, however, provided little scope for journalists. Most of the population was still illiterate and circulations were small. The typical journalist was usually a publisher, editor and printer all in one. The weekly newspaper "gazettes" that developed were dependent on government printing for revenue. Journalists were subject to arbitrary arrest and they often had to post bond to ensure good behaviour. A publisher could be convicted of criminal or seditious libel merely for criticizing public officials.

In an age of revolution abroad and political reaction at home, the outspoken journalist was associated with rebellion, sedition and treason, an impression reinforced by the defection of Joseph WILLCOCKS to the Americans in 1813. Colonial elites looked upon the press as a convenience of the state, otherwise intolerable. The suppression of *Le Canadien* and the imprisonment of Pierre BÉDARD and François BLANCHET in 1810 is just one example of this intolerance. Most journalists, however, accepted the state patronage, toed the official line, and served a faction of the ruling oligarchy.

The libel case of Joseph HOWE in 1835 established the press as a vehicle of legitimate dissent in Canada. Impatient with the slow pace of reform, Howe used his paper the *Novascotian* (acquired 1827) to criticize public policy and the magistrates who administered it. He was sent to jail and indicted for criminal libel. At his trial, he gave an impassioned defence of a free press and submitted evidence substantiating his allegations. Although he was clearly guilty, for the only issue of law before the court was whether or not he had published the defamatory remarks, the jury nonetheless acquitted Howe. The real and psychological threat of criminal libel that colonial regimes had held over the heads of publishers was now practically removed.

Further augmenting journalistic independence was the growth of commerce, literacy and the mechanization of printing. Colonial society began to experience serious tensions that gave rise to competitive political parties, first in Lower Canada, after 1800, then in Upper Canada in the 1820s, and later in the Maritime colonies. Political conflict gave scope for the newspaper as a vehicle for dissent, a ready readership for such "opinionated" journalism, and the backers necessary to supply operating capital when necessary. In this changed environment, journalism began to take on a different character. The chief offering of the mid-Victorian press was opinion, usually partisan. Partisan or not, the Victorian journalist entered his "profession" because he had something to say. It might be William Lyon MACKENZIE attacking the FAMILY COMPACT, or Egerton RYERSON defending the dissenting majority of Upper Canada in his *Christian Guardian.* "Personal" journalism flourished.

Individuality in journalism was often achieved at the expense of profit for the paper. Even large dailies were short-lived before Confederation. In the face of commercial uncertainties and the heat of political battle over RESPONSIBLE GOVERNMENT, journalists readily allied themselves with political parties. George BROWN, for example, was encouraged by the Reform Party in 1844 to start the Toronto *Globe.* He employed the *Globe* as a party organ to expand readership, and thereby to attract advertising revenue. The influence Brown gained as publisher helped consolidate his position as leader of the reconstituted Grit Reform Party after 1854, which in turn gave him tremendous editorial freedom as a journalist. Other successful newspaper entrepreneurs such as Edward WHELAN of the Charlottetown *Examiner* or Étienne PARENT of *Le Canadien* exercised influence and enjoyed editorial latitude through their combined role of publisher-politician.

The payoffs of the party connection were real enough: partisan publishers gained access to patronage, power, even office. The progressive revision of libel laws to limit the liability of journalists, the formative conventions of the PARLIAMENTARY PRESS GALLERY, and favourable postal rates for periodicals were all effected at the high tide of party journalism. Partisan journalism, however, meant biased reporting. The maverick publisher faced financial reprisals, boycotts, loss of patronage and the threat of a new party-sponsored rival.

Party papers only gradually asserted their editorial independence after Confederation, 1867, leaving the norms of partisan conformity at least outwardly intact until 1914. Yet, even in the pioneer communities of the West, dependent party publishers such as Nicholas Flood DAVIN of the Regina *Leader* or Frank OLIVER of the Edmonton *Bulletin* could offer quality in their news and editorial columns. Ultimately, party journalism did not prevent the achievement of better standards.

By the 1880s a revolution in the pattern of daily competition had begun. A new type of paper, the "people's journal," was developing in industrial cities to win a mass readership. Their style varied greatly, but they abandoned close affiliation with political parties and emphasized not opinion but news, especially sensational news. They were challenged by revamped quality papers, such as the Montréal *Gazette* or the Toronto *Mail,* which strove to win an elite readership by offering extensive coverage of political and business affairs. The dailies separated the functions of reporters, desk men, city and news editors, and columnists.

The personnel of journalism was changing in other ways as well. By the turn of the century, the increased complexity of the newspaper enterprise had encouraged the appearance of professional editors, such as John W. DAFOE of the *Manitoba Free Press.* The poorly paid reporter became the workhorse of the 20th-century newspaper office, and job pressures weeded out all but careerists. At the TORONTO STAR, Joseph E. Atkinson experimented in recruiting a few university men. Women were also able to gain entry into journalism, as Kit Coleman at the *Mail and Empire* and Edouardina Lesage ("Collette") at *La* PRESSE, for example, started their careers in the new "women's sections" (*see* CANADIAN WOMEN'S PRESS CLUB). E. Cora HIND, agricultural specialist of the *Manitoba Free Press,* and Simma Holt, crime reporter for the Vancouver SUN, found other ways to establish reputations.

The initiative in creating the original people's dailies was taken by individual entrepreneurs. Publishers were still people with something to say – and many failed precisely because they considered what they had to say more important than profits. Those who found a balance became the characters of their age: Hugh GRAHAM of the Montréal *Star,* E.E. Sheppard of *Saturday Night,* Wilson Southam and Harry SOUTHAM of the Ottawa *Citizen,* and Joe Atkinson of the Toronto *Star.* Among the weeklies of the western frontier, Robert (Bob) EDWARDS of the Calgary *Eye Opener* (1902-22) and Margaret "Ma" MURRAY of the *Bridge River-Lillooet News* gained national notoriety.

The growing business imperatives of newspapers altered the conventions of the old party journalism. In Montréal, the sensationalist *La Presse* (1884) of Trefflé Berthiaume almost wiped out the old-style dailies. Party organs imitated the people's journals to survive. Beneath the gloss and diversity of the new popular style, however, a second more subtle revolution was occurring which proved more fundamental in shaping journalism as a profession: the industrialization of newspapers into big business. In the face of rising costs and factionalized advertising revenues, the chief imperative of all newspapers was to find the formula to maximize readership and attract the most ADVERTISING. Papers that fell behind were doomed to extinction. Between 1914 and 1931, the trend was established for the single newspaper city and the newspaper chain. Successful publishers became associates of the corporate elite. The model of journalism based on the "independent" editor-publisher was obsolete.

Ironically, journalism as a profession had only escaped its partisan master to face a new order of big business. By the 1920s big-city dailies settled down in their rationalized markets to a superficial formula of day-to-day headline journalism. The rough edges of personal idiosyncracy were smoothed away and newspapers came to be more and more alike. The scoop, the stunt or the human-interest story substituted for editorial character. In this atmosphere a new ideal of objectivity or balanced coverage defined the professional ethos of career journalists, though the ideal was honoured no more consistently than the "principled" standards of the personal journalism it had superseded.

The triumph of a business ethos at big-city dailies prompted a variety of strategies to achieve a new degree of professionalism. The Canadian Press Assn and its successor, the Canadian Daily Newspapers Assn (CDNA), were effective publisher lobbies which helped to rationalize the business side of newspapers. The CDNA contributed to the defence of publishers' prerogatives in such classic challenges to freedom of the press as the arbitrary Alberta Press Act of 1937 (*see* ALBERTA PRESS ACT REFERENCE). John M. Imrie of the EDMONTON JOURNAL received a Pulitzer Award for leadership in the fight.

News services developed at the initiative of publishers, eg, CANADIAN PRESS emerging out of a rebellion of western newspapers against the Canadian Pacific Telegraph Co. By 1923 CP had become a nationwide co-operative of member papers, controlling the rights to the Associated Press world report. CP and its rivals were influential in developing the contemporary ideal of objective reporting, as they sought to serve an editorially diverse constituency. Also conducive to professional standards after 1900 was the Press Gallery which, by the 1920s, had become a voluntary, self-governing body. Admission gave entry to a competitive "jungle" in which political reporters sharpened their investigative skill.

By the mid-20th century the tempo of change accelerated. Journalism was transformed by the internal need of working journalists to develop new strategies to define role and status, and by the external pressure from the communications businesses to find a successful formula in the competition for advertising. With the advent of television in the 1950s, old newspaper formats no longer assured a market share. In the resulting uncertainty, journalists found greater latitude for initiative. The PIPELINE DEBATE of 1956 seems to have been a turning point, at which the Press Gallery began to act like a public watchdog, criticizing the government. Canadian political journalism (Jack Scott, Bruce Phillips, Douglas FISHER, Charles LYNCH) suddenly became "opinionated" again – but this time in an adversary role with the politicians. Public-affairs programs on television, whether a newsmagazine such as THIS HOUR HAS SEVEN DAYS or a special documentary such as "Air of Death" (1967), were particularly prone to editorializing about perceived public wrongs.

Technology gave greater latitude to the photo, film and broadcast journalists. René LÉVESQUE, for example, capitalized on the novelty of television to launch himself as a media star and leading personality in Québec politics. Gordon SINCLAIR settled for media stardom and personal wealth by simultaneously pursuing careers in 3 media.

The expanded opportunities for journalists did not translate into an improvement of working conditions, and journalists turned to union organizations to deal with problems of poor pay and job security, irregular hours and arbitrary management. The most successful union was the American Newspaper Guild (ANG), which signed its first collective agreement with the Toronto *Star* in 1949. By 1960 union rates, if not unionization, set the standards for the industry.

French Canadian journalists, following the bitter strike of French-speaking CBC personnel in 1958-59, became the militant vanguard. The radical idea of using collective bargaining to achieve editorial independence for staff members, however, was defeated in the bitter strike at *La Presse*

CBC radio reporter (later premier of Québec) René Lévesque interviewing a soldier during the Korean War, 14 Apr 1951. Many of Canada's leading political figures began their careers in journalism (*courtesy National Archives of Canada/C-79009/DND Post-WWI Collection/ MacLean*).

in 1964. Though the 1969 contracts at *La Presse* and *Le* SOLEIL contained "professional clauses," the legal language deprived them of much substance. Declarations of editorial policy at management initiative, eg, at the Toronto *Star*, provided the most ambitious professions of standards in the industry, but could not resolve the tension between working journalists and the management of mass media organizations. A survey of Canadian journalists at major dailies in 1973 showed that 50% of those surveyed had their copy altered significantly without prior consultation. Unionized journalists took compensation in better working conditions, hours and pay, and thereby attracted a new generation of university graduates, including women, into their ranks.

After WWII some universities in Canada introduced courses in journalism. Carleton U and Ryerson Polytechnical Institute established the first full undergraduate programs, while U of Western Ontario became an innovator in specialty seminars and graduate programs oriented to working journalists. In 1968 Laval U introduced the first journalism program at a Québec university. By the 1970s dozens of universities, community colleges and CEGEPs offered an array of diplomas, certificates and degrees in communications studies or journalism. By 1985, 9 universities offered graduate programs. The changes in educational standards were evident by 1973: over 40% of working journalists at city dailies had a university degree of some kind.

By the 1960s journalists had become more self-critical about their craft. Organizations of working journalists, eg, la Fédération professionnelle des journalistes du Québec or the Institute for Investigative Journalism, provided a forum for journalists to develop a common sense of professionalism, as did radical "alternative" magazines such as *Content*. A few newspapers and the CBC (after 1967) provided training programs, though these initiatives were weakened rather than strengthened by community college programs. Some newspapers initiated summer training schools for select university undergraduates. Since 1962 the Southam chain has offered fellowships for a year of study at U of T, and by the 1980s journalists were often granted a leave of absence to further their university studies.

The trends in unionization, university education and professional development contributed to a rising debate about the role of the press and its freedom. Critics came up with a variety of catch phrases to rationalize a new degree of professional independence and to indict the status quo. Under the influence of communications theory, newly affluent journalists became self-conscious about bias created by "snarlwords," social class, or "pack journalism"; about their ideological role as gatekeepers, and the behavioural effects of the mass media. Proposed reforms included advocacy journalism, investigative reporting and the more radical notions of an alternative press, "staff democracy," or reporter control. The New Journalism, however, was far less radical than the rhetoric would imply. Compromise on standards was made possible by the technological nature of the new media environment. Efficient use of news-gathering technologies required some delegation of authority and editorial independence, at least to the more experienced reporters. Moreover, changes in technology made it imperative to find journalistic formats that attracted the attention of a more affluent and sophisticated audience. *See also* MAGAZINES; NEWSPAPERS.

BRIAN BEAVEN

Reading: W.H. Kesterton, *A History of Journalism in Canada* (1967); P. Rutherford, *Making of the Canadian Media* (1978).

Journals of Susanna Moodie, The, by Margaret ATWOOD (1970). In these poems, Atwood recreates the life of a 19th-century English settler in Canada, exploring the irrational and mythic dimensions of human experience. Journal 1 (1832-40) follows Susanna Moodie as she lands at Québec and, alien and dispossessed, struggles to accommodate the confusion and terror of life in the bush; Journal 2 (1840-71) finds Mrs Moodie in Belleville, haunted by dreams of the wilderness, but beginning to accept an alternate reality and a dual vision; and Journal 3 (1871-1969) takes Mrs Moodie into death and beyond, when she appears in the present, fully a part of the land she once despised. This collection, with its laconic style and intricate structure, is considered one of Atwood's major poetic achievements.

CAROL W. FULLERTON

Juan de Fuca Strait is an inlet of the Pacific Ocean between VANCOUVER I and Washington state, connecting the Str of GEORGIA and Puget Sound to the outer ocean. The international boundary with the US follows its 160 km length. Tides are complicated and dangerous for ships using it to approach mainland harbours. It was named for mariner Juan de FUCA, whose voyages to the area were likely apocryphal. In 1787 the trading captain Charles Barkley entered the strait and named it. For many years it was considered a possible entrance to a NE passage to the Atlantic.

DANIEL FRANCIS

Juba, Stephen, businessman, Manitoba MLA 1953-59, mayor of Winnipeg 1957-77 (b at Winnipeg 1 July 1914). The son of Ukrainian immigrants, Juba was imaginative, colourful and politically independent, refusing PM John Diefenbaker's offer of a Senate seat in the early 1960s. He helped liberalize liquor laws and sweepstakes, and the 1967 Pan-American Games and the 1972 "anti-metro" unification of Winnipeg and its suburbs came to Manitoba mainly as a result of his efforts. He built a new city hall, promoted tourism and tried to get a monorail for public transportation. His dramatic intervention stopped the cutting of a giant elm tree on Winnipeg's Wolseley Avenue in 1957, resulting in international publicity. Similarly, in 1973, he protested the construction of a controversial public washroom by dumping a portable toilet on the Manitoba Legislature grounds. He received the Order of Canada in 1970.

MICHAEL CZUBOKA

Judaism is the religion of Jews. Canadian JEWS, with few exceptions, find their religious heritage in Rabbinic Judaism, which emerged after the destruction of the Temple in Jerusalem in 70 AD, an event precipitated by a Jewish revolt against the Roman Empire. By the 7th century Rabbinism was the religion of virtually all Jews in the Middle East, N Africa, Asia Minor and Europe. It remained the dominant form of Judaism there through the late 19th and early 20th centuries, the period of massive immigration of Jews to N America.

The Rabbinic Judaism of the immigrants had provided them in their homelands with a comprehensive cultural system. According to the ancient rabbis (teachers; religious leaders), the God of Israel, YHWH, having made a covenant with the ancestors of the people of Israel, vouchsafed to Moses on Sinai a dual revelation (Torah). One, in written form, they hold, is the Pentateuch (the first 5 books of the Hebrew Bible); the other Moses communicated orally to the first of successive generations of Israel's (religious) leaders. The rabbis claim religious "mastery" because of their knowledge of the whole Torah. Although their writings – the Mishnah (oral law recorded about 200 AD), the Palestinian and Babylonian Talmuds and subsequent codes and commentaries – are expressions of Torah, ultimately Torah resides in the persons and pronouncements of rabbis and their disciples. The content of this whole Torah of Moses, "our Rabbi," is open-ended; under the authority of the rabbi's Torah come not only such matters as prayer, synagogue ("house of assembly") and religious fasts and festivals, but also family, business, civil and criminal law, and the court system by which these are legislated and enforced. Thus the Rabbinism of the immigrants provided them with all requisites of religion, society and culture.

The N American context provided Jews and Judaism with a cogent challenge. Free and open participation by a Jewish minority in N America's secular society (overwhelmingly indebted to Protestantism for its culture) meant relegating their life as Jews to something other than an all-encompassing cultural system. This was now defined by the Canadian and N American milieus, in which a reasonable level of participation was not only desirable but a requisite of economic survival. Canada was and remains a society in which cultural differences are permitted, even encouraged. But societies depend for their cohesiveness upon shared values and life-styles. The costs of not conforming are social prejudice and limited economic opportunity. Insofar as Jews overwhelmingly opted to remain, in some significant sense, Jews, and to contribute fully to, and benefit from, Canadian life, they have adopted distinctive definitions of "Juda-ism" and "Jewishness" – all by means of an unofficial consensus, without regard to the authority of tradition, which is vested in the rabbi.

Canadian Jews generally practise Rabbinic Judaism highly selectively. Rabbinic legal injunctions (the *halakhah*, the "way") concerning such matters as refraining from all labour on the Sabbath and on festivals (New Year, Day of Atonement, Booths, Passover and Pentecost) seem little honoured. So too are dietary laws, injunctions regarding daily prayer, distinctive dress, menstrual taboos, regular study of Torah and the like. Most laws governing business and the courts have been laid aside in deference to Canadian law and jurisprudence. Synagogues as the locus for communal prayer suffer infrequent and sporadic attendance, although formal affiliation through membership dues remains relatively high.

That Jews have abandoned much of their traditional religion is not surprising; most Canadians have done so. Nevertheless, Canada's Jews appear remarkably persistent in those parts of their traditional religion they do practise. For example, prayer services on the New Year (Rosh Hashanah) and Day of Atonement (Yom Kippur) see heavy attendance, along with fasting on the latter. Whereas laws pertaining to the Passover (Pesach) may not be observed, the family service and feast (*seder*) marking the first 2 eves of the Passover find widespread participation. Many families still gather at a Friday evening meal ushering in the Shabbat (Sabbath), although Sabbath observances are honoured by relatively few Jews. The festival of Hanukkah, commemorating the successful Jewish revolt against the Seleucid Empire in the 2nd century BC, also retains a considerable following. Further, there is general consensus among Canadian Jews that they should marry within the faith, even though intermarriage is increasingly common.

The consistency in what has been selected for continued observance is explained in part by Canadian Jewry's commitment to participation in N American life. Traditional practices which impinge upon an "appropriate" level of participation in Canadian life have been abandoned. But Canada's Jews remain Jews and wish to invest that identity with some transcendent, or religious, legitimacy and meaning. Hence, most contemporary Jewish practice stresses the importance of family and people. In all the retained ritual activity, Jewish peoplehood and its constituent unit, the Jewish family, are endowed with ultimacy. God and Torah seem either conspicuously absent or carefully hidden.

This selective practice has its counterpart in other activities recently incorporated into the "religion of Jewish peoplehood." The destruction of European Jewry in WWII's Holocaust and the establishment of the state of Israel have come to constitute powerful symbols to Canadian Jewry of the "eternity" of the people, guaranteed by a deity of whom few Jews will speak. Thus a mythic Israel (not entirely identified with the political state) appears a phoenix rising out of the ashes of Auschwitz (one of the most notorious death camps, where millions of Jews were killed), the ultimate symbol of those forces bent upon destroying the people. These events function as sacred stories, endowing Jewish peoplehood with transcendent meaning, but the actual events that brought about both the mass murder of Europe's Jews and the politics of Israel have relatively little significance. Thus, Holocaust Memorial Day (and the functions related to the Holocaust) and Israel's Independence Day have come to constitute major "religious" commemorative festivals for Canadian Jews.

In sum, the dynamics of the religion of Canada's Jews lie in 2 principal commitments: first, to full participation in Canadian life and society; second, to retention, in some significant way, of the Jewish identity.

Institutions Canadian Jewish institutions are both instruments for the realization of ideas selected from European and N African rabbinical traditions, and a social reality in themselves. Belonging to virtually any Jewish group, which may range from a weekly bridge club to a Zionist association or a Jewish hospital, has become a definition and measure of being Jewish. Statistics are not available, but participation is high.

Jewish religious organization in Canada is not limited to the spiritual, to Torah learning, or to the ritual. It reflects communal, social and educational, as much as theological, concerns. This is true of synagogue membership and even of its leadership. From 1770 to 1860 each local community established one synagogue. Montréal alone had 3 by 1882. In the 1880s, with the strong informal organizational traditions of the great migration, orthodox congregations in Montréal, Toronto and Victoria multiplied beyond record. By the mid-1920s there were many congregations.

After WWII congregations reorganized and consolidated, thus reducing the total number, despite increased Jewish population and a larger proportion of it willing to identify with a synagogue. In 1963 Max Bookman counted 210 Canadian congregations, but in 1982 there were 113 synagogues, 57 of them in Montréal, Toronto and Winnipeg, the rest in 40 other centres. Fifty-two are Orthodox, 45 Conservative, 15 Reform, and one (in Montréal) Reconstructionist. The distinctions are not rigid; there is a wide gradation, but no clear demarcation. There are no true denominations in the Christian sense, and all divisions are in communion. Each synagogue creates its own place in the order, as in fact does each Jew.

The synagogue is probably a greater focus for family life than it was in the past, and it is a major vehicle for Jewish culture and tradition. The cantor (one who sings liturgical music and leads a congregation in song and prayer) has won a key role which he has not had for 1000 years. Musicologists may find in the Canadian synagogue a very high quality of performance. In larger cities, synagogues (and to some extent their clergy) compete for congregations in a common pool of potential members – in a manner somewhat akin to the merchandising philosophy of consumerism; frequently the product is bland and noncontroversial. The ancient decisive role of custom and consensus has dominated, but probably for the first time it has been a popular, not a learned, consensus. The rabbi has taken to pastoral and organizational work and to sermonizing frequently. He speaks in the language of contemporary sociology, not that of Talmud studies. In the Canadian synagogue there is not a deterioration but a new Jewish religious civilization slowly taking shape.

The centrality of Jewish organization dates mainly from the 17th-century Hassidic revolution and the emergence of secularism. In the new world of industrialization, cosmopolitanism and other concomitants of the American and French revolutions, the survival of Judaism could not depend solely on the expectation of divine intervention or on patient suffering of cataclysmic violence. From western Europe Judaism imported the fundamental philosophical value of organizing information, and of organizing a disunited society as an instrument of action. To counteract geographic dispersion, poverty, anti-Semitism and even the lack of a common language, the communal ideal of voluntary organization arose. This inspiration led to the Zionist organization to restore statehood, the syndicalist Bund to bring nearer the other messianic objective of justice and equality, and other organizations. Since Jewish communities in the New World either were formed by migration of secularists or were quickly secularized, it was here that this philosophy flowered.

In Canada, local structures for voluntary self-taxation, such as the United and Combined Jewish appeals and welfare funds, enrol citizens for voluntary effort and financial contribution. This structure reaches nearly every Jewish citizen above the level of social aid recipients. The oldest such agency, the Hebrew Benevolent Society of Montréal (later Allied Jewish Community Services), was founded in the 1860s when a wave of eastern European migrants arrived. This group's prevailing civic religion altered, as it became ever more integrated into Canadian middle-class society, and its ethic moved from the religious to the philanthropic. Simultaneously, power and honour within the community moved from learning and piety to participation in organized services.

The Toronto, Winnipeg, Victoria and Saint John experiences were similar. At present their UJAs comprise nearly all the agencies dealing with the Jewish community's needs, from welfare to libraries and legal aid. The community's representatives apportion large budgets, study performance and, in effect, constitute the agencies' executive. In Canada, where the state is deeply involved in social work, contact with the political machinery is inevitable. The people selected for these processes must be devoted, skilled and trusted. They clearly constitute an elite, constantly required to justify their appeals to the total voluntary community.

The need for efficiency in communal concerns justifies the enrolment of available talent, regardless of individuals' commitment to the society's fundamental principles. But mobilization of "useful" manpower helps to cement more and more persons into organizational structures, thus strengthening the Jewish community and the (secular) Jewish identity of individual participants. This condition has opened participation and leadership in the community to women, who form a large talent pool. The National Council of Jewish Women, an old parallel to the Canadian Council of Women, has been influential from coast to coast, and has for decades searched out the vanguard of social thought and has worked to introduce hitherto neglected areas of welfare.

Canadian Jews also consider themselves well served nationally by the Canadian Jewish Congress (fd 1919). This body deals with nationwide responsibilities, eg, co-ordinating immigrant reception, advancing civil rights, sponsoring historical interests and acting for Canadian Jewry on perennial international questions, especially those related to Israel. The congress works closely with the World Jewish Congress and other such institutions. The democratically structured CJC comprises representatives of Jewish groups across Canada. At its triennial plenary sessions virtually every Jewish man and woman has full opportunity of expression and is represented on its committees.

Another national organization is the B'nai B'rith, with both men's and women's chapters. It advances general Jewish causes and co-operates in adult education, welfare, camp programs and combating anti-Semitism. Because of its large membership it exerts some influence in the community, but it shuns controversy and does not pretend to innovation. Jewish Immigrant Aid Services is atypical in being an independent service organization, formulating and executing its own programs nationwide, though it co-operates closely with related agencies. Another structure independent of the central network is that of the Young Men's and Young Women's Hebrew associations (parallel to the YMCA and YWCA), with large memberships, broad programs and long traditions.

The Zionist movement is central in importance. It began with the thesis that scattered persons, by uniting, propagandizing and structuring their adherents, can accomplish politically what 2000 years could not achieve through communion, prayer and traditional communication. Zionism has had a simple purpose: to establish a publicly assured Jewish state in Palestine. Its history in Canada has involved gathering disparate Canadian Jews and forming local groups; raising funds; pleading with the outside world; and winning more and more of the Jewish community until the state took shape. Organization in Canada came early – even before Theodore Herzl crystallized the world movement in 1896. Remarkably, Canadian Zionists had broad support. The movement's structure was largely "political," divided

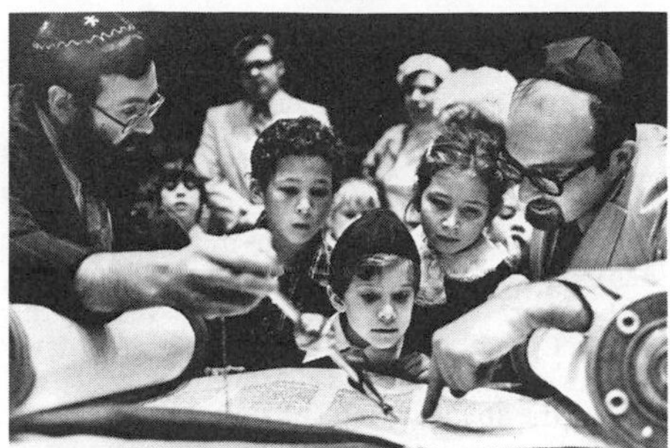

Schoolchildren viewing Old Testament scrolls at the Machzikel Hades Synagogue in Ottawa. The synagogue is a focus of Jewish tradition (*courtesy Canapress Photo Service*).

along lines parallel to the division in world Zionism: labour Zionists (Po'alei Zion), religious Zionists (Mizrachi) and free enterprise (General) Zionists, each group engaged in such ideological programs but all supporting the advancement of the Jewish state.

The sectarian programs are still vigorous, notably the women's institutions such as Hadassah-WIZO and Pioneer Women (labour-oriented). But since WWII Zionism has become central, and Israel is conceived generally as essential to Jewish survival. Dissidents are hard to find. Although there are extensive organizations devoted entirely to Zionism, the major Canadian contribution to the Jewish state is provided not by strictly Zionist institutions, but by the total organizational structure of the community.

It is in education that the voluntary and democratic options of organization have their widest range. Every parent must decide whether his or her child is to receive training for living as a Jew, the nature of this education, and the relation between it and the Canadian provincial curricula. These questions, complicated by unavoidable ideological problems, have faced Canadian Jews (as they have, in some ways, faced Canadian Roman Catholics) for 2 centuries, and have evoked imaginative resolutions. Historically, solutions have included private tutors (*melammedim*), exclusive private schools and sections in established schools, universities and other institutions. Until recently, special schools (Talmud Torahs) have operated after public school hours. The children learn Hebrew, the Bible, religious practices and traditions, Jewish history and current affairs. Although many such schools are now in systems, a number continue to operate independently, and here Yiddish has remained a factor; Canada has been among the world pioneers in Yiddish education and literature.

Over 50 years ago Jewish day ("parochial") schools ventured to provide an integrated double curriculum, combining Jewish and public system curricula within the traditional public school timetable. This daring program succeeded and was widely adopted. The Jewish system of day and afternoon schools is essentially private, but the community has virtually assumed the additional cost of public education, even as Jewish parents continued to pay school taxes. Some provincial governments have begun contributing to the public education programs of Jewish day schools. *See also* JEWISH WRITING.

JACK N. LIGHTSTONE AND DAVID ROME

Reading: B.G. Sack, *History of the Jews in Canada* (1965).

Judicial Committee of the Privy Council, a board of the British Privy Council which, until 1949, served as a court of final appeal for Canada. Drawn from persons who had held high judicial office in Britain, together with a sprinkling of Commonwealth judges, it was formally constituted and given jurisdiction over all colonial courts by acts of the British Parliament in 1833 and 1844. In 1875 when the SUPREME COURT OF CANADA was established, Justice Minister Edward BLAKE made an unsuccessful attempt to abolish appeals to the Privy Council. The clause intended to carry out this purpose was found to be inoperative and appeals continued from Canada to the Judicial Committee. It was agreed, however, that Canada possessed the authority to regulate the category of appeal which could be taken to London. Thus Canada abolished appeals in criminal cases in 1888. In 1926 the Privy Council ruled that this limitation was invalid since the Canadian law on which it was based conflicted with the 1844 British statute expressly extending the Judicial Committee's jurisdiction to Canada. The STATUTE OF WESTMINSTER (1931), by giving Canada legislative equality with Britain, allowed the Canadian Parliament to re-enact the prohibition of criminal appeals. Appeals in civil cases would also have been discontinued but for WWII, which postponed hearings on the question. In 1947 the Judicial Committee held that the Parliament of Canada was competent to abolish appeals in civil cases. This was done in 1949, when an amendment to the Supreme Court Act transferred ultimate appellant jurisdiction to Canada.

The Judicial Committee provided 173 major judgements interpreting the BRITISH NORTH AMERICA ACT. Many of these decisions were believed by Canadian lawyers to contradict the intentions of the Fathers of Confederation, as well as the text of the act, by showing a bias towards provincial powers. The judgements drastically curtailed federal jurisdiction in fields such as trade and commerce and made the general powers of the Dominion, found in s91, subordinate to the specific powers enumerated in s91 and s92. The decentralizing current of the Judicial Committee's decisions, often couched in abstract language, was criticized as showing an unfamiliarity with the problems of Canadian federalism. In the 20th century many Canadian lawyers also felt that it was demeaning for Canada to have to go outside the country for final decisions respecting the constitution. *See also* CONSTITUTIONAL HISTORY.

D.M.L. FARR

Reading: G.P. Browne, *The Judicial Committee and the British North America Act* (1967); D.M.L. Farr, *The Colonial Office and Canada, 1867-1887* (1955).

Judiciary, judges of the courts, collectively; also the branch of government in which judicial power is vested. Judges are public officers appointed to preside and administer the law in a court of justice. The CONSTITUTION ACT, 1867, provides for the establishment and operation of Canada's professional judiciary. It gave the federal government exclusive lawmaking power over CRIMINAL LAW and CRIMINAL PROCEDURE (but not over criminal courts), and it gave the provinces exclusive lawmaking power over the administration of justice in each province. The federal government appoints the judges of the SUPREME COURT and the FEDERAL COURT, and under s96 of the Constitution Act it also appoints judges to some provincial courts. Sometimes referred to as "section 96 judges," they sit in the provincial Supreme Court or Court of Appeal or in equivalent courts such as the Court of Queen's Bench, the Divisional Court or the Superior Court. Provincial or municipal governments appoint judges of provincial lower courts, magistrates, justices of the peace, coroners, sheriffs and other officers of provincial courts. Provincially appointed judges deal with both provincial and federal legislation.

Whether it presides over criminal prosecutions or civil lawsuits (*see* CIVIL PROCEDURE), the role of the judiciary is to serve as an impartial arbiter. The court's impartiality flows from the essential feature of our judicial system – independence of the judiciary. Although the judiciary is sometimes regarded as equal to the executive and legislative branches of government, and although appointment, removal and remuneration of judges are dependent upon the other branches, the quality of justice to which Canadians are accustomed can only be maintained if an independent judiciary is jealously guarded. The notion of judicial independence has been shaken by some provincial court judges who have refused to rule on various cases, claiming they are not independent of the provincial government, which sets their salaries and working conditions.

The Constitution Act and the federal Judges Act provide the basis for the appointment, removal, retirement and remuneration (including matters such as pension) of federally appointed judges. Similar provisions contained in various provincial enactments, which vary to some extent from province to province, exist for provincially appointed judges. Most federal appointments are made by the minister of justice after Cabinet consultation and approval, but some, eg, to the Supreme Court and to the various chief and associate chief justiceships and judgeships, are made by the prime minister, again after Cabinet consultation and approval. Prospective federal appointments are usually considered through the office of a special assistant to the minister of justice and are reviewed and rated by the Judicial Appointments Committee of the Canadian Bar Association. Provincial appointments are made by the attorney general of the province, after provincial Cabinet consultation and approval. Although there is no formal review by a Canadian Bar Association committee, in some provinces the attorney general appoints a judge only after consideration of the application by a special committee constituted for that purpose.

Federally appointed judges must be lawyers who have been members of a provincial bar for at least 10 years. Although "horizontal" appointments from bar to bench have been traditional, judges are now frequently elevated from a lower to a higher court. The composition of the judiciary is changing with the recent appointment of women (in June 1987 Alice Desjardins, a member of the Québec Superior Court since 1981, was the first woman named to the Federal Court of Appeal), younger persons, academics and others. Provincially there is no minimum requirement of 10 years at the bar, and other eligibility rules vary among provinces. In some provinces prospective judges must have been members of the bar for 5 years, while in others they need not even be lawyers. Many police magistrates are retired members of national or local police forces. However, even in provinces where judges need not be lawyers, only lawyers are now appointed.

Federally appointed judges hold office during "good behaviour" and can be removed only by Joint Address of the House of Commons and the Senate. Under the federal Judges Act, however, matters not constituting good behaviour are given broad definition to include conditions such as senility. The Judges Act also created the Canadian Judicial Council, comprising the various federally appointed chief justices and associate chief justices, whose president is the chief justice of Canada. The Judicial Council provides continuing education for federally appointed judges, makes recommendations to the minister of justice following investigation and review of complaints against them, and recommends, when appropriate, their removal. While no federally appointed judge has been removed this way, some have resigned in the course of or under the threat of the invocation of this impeachment process. Similar but varying guidelines for judicial behaviour exist for provincially appointed judges. Some provincially appointed judges have been removed by an impeachment process which in certain provinces follows investigation and review by a provincial judicial council similar to its federal counterpart. Judges have been disciplined or removed for the commission of crime and for moral turpitude and gross addiction.

Federally appointed judges hold office until their mandatory retirement at age 75 if they are serving on a superior court, or at age 70 if they are serving on a county or district court. After they have served 15 years on the bench and have reached the age of 65 or more, or, in the case of superior-court judges, after they have served 10 years on the bench and have reached the age of 70, they can partially retire or go "supernumerary," sitting on cases from time to time. The retirement age of provincially appointed judges (usually age 70) is set out in statutes creating the provincial courts.

The process of judicial appointment has always been surrounded with secrecy, which has perpetuated the belief that political considerations influence the appointment of judges. It is widely held that to become a judge it is beneficial to be politically affiliated with the party in power – a fact generally regarded by the public in a somewhat negative way. However, a person should not be disentitled from a judicial appointment because of past political affiliation. This matter became the subject of public debate during the 1984 federal election following a spate of PATRONAGE appointments by the outgoing Trudeau Liberals. Since the early 1970s, all federal judicial appointments are externally reviewed by the Judicial Appointments Committee of the Canadian Bar Association. This review served as a buffer against the usage of judicial appointments as political patronage. This procedure was not followed in a 1984 appointment and the CBA publicly expressed its concern and created a national committee to study judicial appointments.

Most newly appointed judges are persons trained and experienced in the law. A great deal is expected of them by society, yet they possess no superhuman qualities. In return for special legal and ethical constraints imposed upon them, society provides them with status, prestige and trust. Because they are also entrusted with the ultimate responsibility of adjudicating personal, sensitive, delicate and emotional disputes as well as resolving the major social, economic and occasionally political issues that arise in some legal contexts, the judiciary helps mold the social fabric governing our lives. GERALD GALL

Judique, NS, UP, pop 181 (1986c), 925 (1981c), is located 189 km SW of Sydney, Cape Breton I. The name is likely of French origin, perhaps a corruption of the name for Judith. Judique is an administrative district extending along Cape Breton's western shore from Port Hood to Port Hastings and including several small settlements. Known for its green meadows and many fine inlets and coves, Judique was settled by Highland Scots who immigrated to Pictou, NS, in the late 18th century in search of unoccupied farmland and finally settled on Cape Breton I. Judique became a prominent Catholic centre in western Cape Breton during the 19th century owing to the uninterrupted residency of Catholic priests. The area depended on mixed farming and fishing for its livelihood, but poor docking facilities discouraged development of the latter; out-migration of Judique's youth led to agricultural failure. Today, there is a little fishing and forestry, but there are no major industries. DEBRA MCNABB

Judo literally means "the gentle way." It is a sport developed from JIU-JITSU, a group of self-defence methods, but with certain harmful techniques eliminated or modified for safety's sake. Judo incorporates ethics, art and science into a sport which uses the opponents' strength against themselves. Judo was begun in June 1882 in Tokyo, Japan, by Dr Jigoro Kano in a small hall which became the Kodokan, the mecca of judo. Kano defined the purpose of judo as the training of one's mind and body to use energy efficiently, in competition and everyday life, toward the goals of physical development, contest proficiency and mental and moral development.

Around 1924 judo was introduced on the Canadian West Coast by pioneers such as S. Sasaki, first director of the Vancouver Judo Club. WWII moved many Judokas east of the Rockies, establishing new centres to practise the sport. Judo Canada, the governing body for the sport, was established in 1956. Each province has affiliated associations to help govern and promote judo. Participants are graded from 6th *Kyu* (white belt) to *Ikkyu* (brown belt) provincially, and from 1st *dan* (degree), or black belt, to 9th *dan*. The highest rank in Canada at present is the 8th *dan*.

Judo received Olympic recognition at the 1964 Tokyo Olympics, at which Doug Rogers won a silver medal for Canada in the heavyweight class. Since then, Canada has been represented at all Olympics, world championships and Pan-American Games. Other highlights for Canada were the 1981 world championships in Maastricht, Holland, where Phil Takahashi and Kevin Doherty both won bronze medals in the 60 kg and 78 kg classes respectively. Later Takahashi, Brad Farrow (65 kg) and Louis Jani (86 kg) won bronze medals at the 7th world university championships in Jyväskylä, Finland, August 1982. Mark Berger won a bronze medal in the 95 kg class at the 1984 Olympics and Tina Takahashi won a gold medal in the 48 kg class at the 1984 world university championships. In the 1987 Pan-Am Games, Sandra Greaves of Thunder Bay, Ont, won a gold medal in the 66 kg class; other members of the Canadian team won 2 silver and 3 bronze medals. YOSH SENDA

Jukes, Joseph Beete, geologist (b near Birmingham, Eng 10 Oct 1811; d at Dublin, Ire 29 July 1869). Jukes had attended geology lectures at St John's College, Cambridge, graduating with a BA in 1836. In 1839 he became Newfoundland's geological surveyor and began a scientific search for mineral resources, prospecting many coastal areas. After a fruitless search he returned to England in Oct 1840. *Excursions in and about Newfoundland* (1842), a rich record of colonial Newfoundland society 1839-40, emphasized negative results and discouraged "rash speculation" in mining. In 1842 Jukes was naturalist on a surveying expedition into Australasian waters. His career culminated in 1850 with the directorship of the Geological Survey of Great Britain's Irish Branch. RICHARD DAVID HUGHES

Julien, Octave-Henri, painter, illustrator (b at Québec C 14 May 1852; d at Montréal 17 Sept 1908). He began his career as engraver and lithographer with Desbarats's printing firm (about 1868), where he also learned drawing and painting. He accompanied the expeditionary force of NWMP sent to suppress the liquor traffic on the Prairies (1874) and prepared illustrations of western life for the *Canadian Illustrated News*. He became art director of the Montréal *Star* in 1888, where he developed his skill for capturing portraits with a few strokes of a pencil. He soon became Canada's foremost newspaper illustrator, executing brilliant cartoons of Sir Wilfrid LAURIER and his Cabinet. His keen interest and sharp sense of humour produced some of the best political comment of the time. He also worked in watercolours and oils, exhibiting regularly with the ROYAL CANADIAN ACADEMY OF ARTS. JAMES MARSH

Julien, Pauline, singer, actress, songwriter (b at Trois-Rivières, Qué 23 May 1928). She studied drama in Paris and made her debut there as a singer about 1957. She first appeared in Montréal at a cabaret called Au Saint-Germain-des-Prés, and she introduced the songs of Kurt Weill and Bertolt Brecht to Québec, soon adding songs by Raymond Lévesque and Gilles VIGNEAULT to her repertoire. Julien made her first album in 1962 and 2 years later took second prize at the International Festival of Song in Sopot (Poland), singing "Jack Monoloy" by Vigneault. In 1968 she began to write some of the words for her songs. Feminism is only one of the topics she treats with fiery passion. As an actress she has appeared in several films, including *La Mort d'un bûcheron*. Her albums *Suite québécoise* and *Où peut-on vous toucher* won the Grand Prix du disque from the Académie Charles-Cros in Paris in 1970 and 1985 respectively. Julien received the 1974 Prix de musique Calixa-Lavallée, and in 1986 she announced her retirement from solo performing. HÉLÈNE PLOUFFE

Juliette, stage name of Juliette Augustina Sysak, singer, entertainer (b at St Vital, Man 26 Aug 1927). She started her singing career as a child, making her CBC radio debut at 15. After regular CBC appearances, "Our Pet, Juliette" ran her own program 1954-66. Her folksy pop style created one of CBC's most popular shows. This success was followed by several TV specials and regular CBC-TV performances: "After Noon" (1969-71) and "Juliette and Friends" (1973-75). After 1975 Juliette began to reduce her public performances, the last being a Christmas telethon in Vancouver 1984. ANN SCHAU

Jumbo Pass, elev 2270 m, is situated in the central Purcell Mts of BC, between the headwaters of Jumbo Cr, flowing E into Toby Cr, which empties into Windermere Lk, and Glacier Cr which flows W to Duncan Lk. Lumber roads pass within 2 km of the pass in both drainages. There is no significant history attached to the pass, but it may have been used by Indians in days past, as there was at one time a rough trail over the pass. With the recent increase in popularity of mountaineering, hiking and skiing, improved trails now lead up to the pass from both sides, where a 4-man hut is located at the pass's N end. GLEN BOLES

Juneau, Pierre, administrator, broadcasting executive (b at Verdun, Qué 17 Oct 1922). After a distinguished administrative career at the NFB, 1949-66, Juneau was appointed vice-chairman of the Board of Broadcast Governors, 1966-68, and was chairman of the CANADIAN RADIO-TELEVISION AND TELECOMMUNICATIONS COMMISSION 1968-75. His assertive application of commission regulations governing Canadian content in broadcasting won him a reputation as a cultural nationalist (the Canadian recording industry's Juno Awards were named partly in his honour) that was only marginally dimmed by the commission's failure to devise effective controls for cable transmissions. In 1975 he was named minister of communications, but he resigned after failing to win election to Parliament. From 1975 to 1982 he held several senior administrative posts at Ottawa, and in 1982 he became president of the CBC, agreeing to serve until 1989. Faced with sharply reduced government funding, nationalists feared an increase in foreign programming, but with Juneau's mandate to make the CBC 95% Canadian and the 1987 licence for an all-news channel, they foresee a victory for Canadian sovereignty. STANLEY GORDON

Common juniper (*Juniperus communis*), with flowers (left) and fruit (*artwork by Claire Tremblay*).

Juniper, evergreen CONIFER, genus *Juniperus* of cypress family (Cupressaceae). About 60 species occur worldwide, primarily in the Northern Hemisphere; 4 are native to Canada. Of these, eastern red cedar (*J. virginiana*) of the Great Lakes region, and Rocky Mountain juniper (*J. scopulorum*) of arid regions of BC, reach tree size. Common juniper (*J. communis*) and creeping juniper (*J. horizontalis*), both shrub species, occur in the boreal forest and on the prairies. Scalelike or awl-shaped leaves usually have a distinct resin gland on the surface. The round, berrylike seed cones are composed of fleshy, fused bracts (modified leaves) and scales. Male pollen cones and female seed cones usually grow on separate trees. POLLINATION occurs in spring; cones mature in the second or third year, turning blue. They have been used as flavouring (eg, gin). The seeds are small, with 2 lateral wings, and the wood is hard, heavy, aromatic, purplish red and decay resistant. Juniper trees are usually too small to be commercially valuable in Canada but are widely used as ORNAMENTALS. JOHN N. OWENS

Juno Awards, annual awards given by the Canadian Academy of Recording Arts and Sciences (CARAS) in honour of the best of the Canadian music industry. The award system was established by RPM magazine as a readers' poll with winners listed in the magazine. The awards ceremony was staged as the Annual Gold Leaf Awards in 1970, and the following year the name was changed to the Juno Awards in part after a Roman goddess and in part after Pierre JUNEAU. As head of the Canadian Radio-television and Telecommunications Commission, Juneau instituted regulations aimed at ensuring a minimum of Canadian content on AM radio. The Juno Awards were first broadcast nationally in 1975. There are 26 award categories, 12 of which, including Album of the Year, Single of the Year, Male Vocalist of the Year and Female Vocalist of the Year, have nominees selected by sales figures. Winners are then selected by a ballot vote of members of CARAS. Four other categories, Composer of the Year, and the Most Promising Female Vocalist, Male Vocalist and Group, have nominees chosen by a panel of experts and winners chosen by a vote of CARAS members. The Best Children's Album is chosen by schoolchildren from across Canada, while the remaining categories, including Producer of the Year, Best Jazz Album, Best Classical Album (contains 2 categories) and Best Video, have both nominees and winners chosen by panels of experts. The Hall of Fame award and the Walt Grealis Special Achievement Award honour those making special contributions to the Canadian recording industry. JOHN GEIGER

Jurisprudence, literally "knowledge of law," is used in several different senses. Occasionally, it simply means law in general or of a particular kind, eg, "medical jurisprudence"; rarely, it denotes the study of law, eg, an Oxford degree in jurisprudence. Today, when using it, civil lawyers (*see* CIVIL LAW) usually mean a body of case law or court decisions, and common lawyers (*see* COMMON LAW) usually mean a philosophical inquiry into problems about rather than of law, such as "What is law?" or "What is the relationship between law and justice?" In this sense jurisprudence in English-speaking countries has traditionally been divided into legal theory, analysis of specific legal concepts, and sources of law. Legal theory, generally considered the most important, focuses on the definition of law and the analysis of the notion of a legal system. It has generated most of the jurisprudential literature and spawned many theories: including the theory of natural law, expounded originally by Aquinas, which views law as comprising rules that accord with right reason, and therefore claims that an intrinsic connection exists between law and morality; the theory of legal positivism, according to which law is distinct and separate from morality, the validity of a law deriving from its pedigree rather than its content; the theory of legal realism, according to which, as expressed by some American scholars, law is only the practice of the courts and various officials (and as expressed by certain Scandinavian philosophers, the concept is a fiction); pure theory, according to which law is a system of norms deriving from a basic norm; and Hart's theory of law, according to which laws are special kinds of social rules, legal systems depending on an interplay between them. Recently, legal theory has gained attention not only from academic lawyers but from philosophers who have created an American Society of Philosophers of Law. A Canadian section was set up in 1982 originally under the director of the Westminster Institute for Ethics and Human Values in London, Ont.

Today, with accelerating change and law reform, it is becoming evident that fundamental questions of law are really questions of politics, and these in turn are ultimately questions of morality. Students of ethics, philosophers and students of jurisprudence are needed to assist in their exploration. This is clear in the work being done at the Westminster Institute, at the Center for Bioethics in Montréal and at the Law Reform Commission of Canada, as well as in the more general investigations in Canada into the nature and justification of criminal law itself. It will become even clearer in future analysis of human-rights problems arising from the new CANADIAN CHARTER OF RIGHTS AND FREEDOMS.

PATRICK FITZGERALD

Jury A group of citizens summoned by law to render verdict on a question submitted in a court of justice. Originally, jurors testified too and decided issues on the basis of their own community knowledge, but since the admission of sworn testimony, jury verdicts have been based on evidence submitted at the trial.

Statute governs the right to jury trial. In criminal cases, summary and minor indictable offences are tried without jury (*see* MAGISTRATE). Serious offences, eg, murder, treason, sedition and hijacking, require trial by jury in a superior court, although such charges may be tried without jury with the consent of the accused and the attorney general. With many less serious indictable offences the accused may elect jury trial. In civil proceedings (proceedings governed by provincial statutes), parties may elect to dispense with the jury except in cases involving libel, slander, seduction, malicious arrest or prosecution and false imprisonment. Even in those cases the jury may be dispensed with if both sides agree (in fact juries in civil trials are becoming the exception), and in highly complicated and technical cases, and in some instances where the assessment of damages is involved, the courts frequently refuse a jury trial.

Because provinces are responsible for the constitution and selection of juries, qualifications vary from province to province. Normally, all Canadian citizens between ages 18 and 65 or 69 who do not suffer mental or physical handicaps that might impede the performance of their duty and who have not been convicted of an indictable offence are qualified to serve as jurors. Certain classes of persons (and occasionally their spouses) are exempt, including members of the Privy Council, provincial Cabinets, the Senate, the House of Commons and provincial legislatures, lawyers, law students, judges, police, law-enforcement officers, clergy, doctors, dentists, veterinarians in active practice and employees of some essential services.

Jury lists (arrays) are prepared annually from a random selection of names from the county assessment roles or voters' lists. In Manitoba, Québec and NB the use of either official language in the courts is an entrenched right, and in many other areas the accused has the right to trial by a jury speaking his or her official language.

The county SHERIFF is responsible for the summoning and attendance of the jury. Persons normally qualified to serve may be excused on the grounds of illness or if undue hardship would result.

The jury in criminal cases comprises 12 jurors, except in the Yukon and the NWT, where there are 6. The jury's verdict must be unanimous and based on evidence presented in court. If, after a reasonable time, there appears to be no hope of a jury reaching agreement (a "hung" jury), the judge may call for a new jury or set the case for retrial. Fewer jurors (usually 6) are required in civil cases, and unanimity is not necessary; it is sufficient that 5 agree.

The grand jury was the forerunner of the petit jury. The grand jury decided whether reasonable grounds existed for sending a case to trial. If so, it brought in a "true bill." Qualifications for grand jurors were the same as those for petit jurors. The grand jury has been abolished in Canada.

The jury in criminal cases has historically been regarded as the "foundation of our free institutions," although others have said it "puts a ban upon intelligence and honesty, and a premium upon ignorance and stupidity and perjury." Most surveys on the value of the criminal jury have supported its retention with minor changes, but juries in civil trials are becoming the exception, mostly as a consequence of the extra costs and time involved and the more complex and technical nature of the cases. K.G. McShane

Reading: Canada, *The Jury* (1982); P. Devlin, *Trial by Jury* (1956).

Justice, Department of, est 1868 by Act of Parliament. The responsibilities of the department include being the legal adviser of the governor general, superintending many matters concerned with the administration of justice in Canada (excluding the jurisdiction of provincial governments) and seeing that the administration of public affairs is in accordance with law. The minister is also attorney general of Canada responsible for the conduct of all litigation for or against the Crown or any public department. The department carries out, on behalf of the federal government, the legal functions and services customarily performed by a law firm for its clients. The Tax Review Board, LAW REFORM COMMISSION OF CANADA, CANADIAN HUMAN RIGHTS COMMISSION and SUPREME COURT OF CANADA report to the minister. The department's 1986-87 budget was $165 million.

Justice of the Peace, also called magistrate, stipendiary and JP. An ancient public office that originated in medieval England (a 1361 statute authorized the office and defined its duties), and is still in use in common law countries. The Tudor monarchs found them invaluable for administering local affairs, and the duties of local government were only replaced in the 19th century in response to the new ideologies and urbanization associated with the industrial age. Little noticed by historians, JPs were present bearing the burdens of local administration in all American and BNA colonies from the earliest days: in NS from 1721, in Québec (where captains of militia were used like JPs) from 1760, and in the Ontario region from the 1780s. Justices of the peace in quarter sessions were the local government in central and eastern Canada until supplanted by elective county councils, NS being the last (with the Counties Incorporation Act) in 1879. The Canadian West opened under HBC administration, limiting JPs to their judicial functions. Red R (Winnipeg) had JPs from 1821 and Victoria from 1849. Stipendiary magistrates with the "powers of two JPs" were the principal judges of the early prairie West, while NWMP commissioners and superintendents held JP commissions.

Justices of the peace are appointed in numbers, never in single isolation, to specific districts. Essentially they are private citizens – most have not been lawyers – of good standing in their community, appointed by the provincial government to hear "informations" and "complaints (of crimes)" and to initiate appropriate legal process. In their day, they have provided workable and reasonably effective local government. The office of JP continues to evolve.
Paul G. Cornell

Jutra, Claude, filmmaker (b at Montréal 11 Mar 1930; d there c5 Nov 1986). Jutra was best known as the director of *Mon oncle Antoine* (1971), one of the best-loved and most popular films made in Canada. He joined the NFB in 1956 and made a number of shorts before leaving for Africa, where he co-directed *Le Niger, jeune république* (1961) with Jean Rouch. Back in Québec he joined NFB's famed French unit, and directed several short films before attempting his first feature *A tout prendre* (1963), the film that launched the new Québec cinema. With *Mon oncle Antoine,* Jutra established his reputation as an accomplished film director. Set in a small Québec town on Christmas Eve, the film sensitively shows a young boy approaching manhood, and won many awards. *Kamouraska* (1973), an adaptation of Anne HÉBERT's novel, did not match expectations. After *Pour le meilleur et pour le pire* (1976), Jutra worked in English for the CBC. "Ada" (1977), "Dreamspeaker" (1977) and "The Wordsmith" (1979) are among the most distinguished TV films produced in Canada. Jutra returned to the theatrical feature with *Surfacing* (1981), based on the Margaret ATWOOD novel, and *By Design* (1982). His warmth and ironic humour were evident in all his work. He returned to Québec to make *La Dame en couleurs* (1984). Apparently suffering from Alzheimer's disease, he disappeared in Nov 1986. Five months later, on 19 Apr 1987, his body was found in the St Lawrence R at Cap-Santé, Qué. Piers Handling

Claude Jutra, during the filming of *La Dame en couleurs,* 1984 (*courtesy Cinémathèque Québécoise/Alain Gauthier*).

Juvenile Delinquency, in social science, refers primarily to social acts of juveniles that are defined and evaluated as deviant or antisocial by legal or social norms and that are usually, though not always, socially learned. When children are designated "juvenile delinquents," it is a precise definition of their legal status and makes them wards of the court subject to its discretion (*see* JUVENILE JUSTICE SYSTEMS). In Canada provisions for special institutions and treatment for young people were available in 1857, but the first federal legislation dealing with juvenile delinquents was the Juvenile Delinquents Act passed in 1908 and revised in 1929. Under the Act, the definition of delinquency encompasses more than the adult crimes in the Criminal Code and includes "sexual immorality or any similar form of vice" as well as cases of neglected, abused or uncontrollable children. The Act established the state as a sympathetic guardian which treats the juvenile as a misguided child requiring care and supervision. Courtroom procedures are informal, allowing the judge wide discretion in deciding juvenile proceedings. Dispositions vary from a reprimand, fine or probation to committal to an institution.

In recent years the Act has been attacked for its paternalism, informality and failure to protect the basic rights of the child. The new Young Offenders Act (passed July 1982, effective Apr 1984) eliminates all status offences such as truancy and sexual morality; thus, delinquency is confined to federal offences, and applies only to young people between 12 and 18 years of age. Additionally, indefinite terms have been replaced by maximum 3-year sentences, and juveniles have the right to legal representation and strict rules of evidence and proof throughout the court proceedings.

The official statistics on delinquency gathered from the records of public agencies, eg, the police, juvenile courts and correctional institutions, and published by the Centre for Justice Statistics, Statistics Canada, are valuable but reflect the actions of officials rather than children and limit understanding of the nature of delinquency and the process by which an individual becomes delinquent. The behaviour of children varies widely, and since all youngsters likely act in ways that can result in legal action, it is not correct to presume that children are either delinquents or nondelinquents. Moreover, clinically normal children are responsible for most of the delinquency in society, and although some maladjusted children do violate the law, there is no necessary correlation between delinquency and defective personalities. Also, police statistics do not reveal all the delinquency that occurs in society. Self-reported questionnaires on delinquent acts, administered to high-school students, reveal that juveniles from all social classes are responsible for a wide variety of delinquent acts, although according to a Montréal survey the toughest kinds of delinquency usually occur in urban slums. Other recent studies underscore the significance of poverty in explaining the distribution of delinquency.

Maximum delinquent activity occurs during middle adolescence. In 1983 the highest proportion (26.3%) of youths designated delinquent were 15 years old (juveniles aged 15 and 16 accounted for about 49% of all offences). Ratios were higher for boys, as expected, but the ratios for offences relating to immorality (where girls were higher) and education were more balanced. Of the total number of officially reported delinquencies in 1983, 25% were for breaking and entering. Theft under $200 accounted for 14% of delinquencies; 5% were categorized as mischief. However, the violation of provincial statutes, which include less serious offences such as truancy, drinking under age and traffic violations, accounted for 21%. Of the 556 sexual offences (541 boys, 15 girls), juveniles aged 13 accounted for 16%, while youths aged 14 and 15 accounted for 51%. At 16 years of age this decreased to 16%. In 1983, 4 provinces accounted for 80% of all juveniles designated delinquent: Québec 29.1%, Manitoba 18%, BC 17% and Ontario 16%. In Alberta there was a decrease to 10%. The NWT, PEI and the Yukon accounted for 1% of all officially designated delinquents.

Recent Research Research in CRIMINOLOGY and delinquency in Canada has increased considerably during the past 25 years, and the schools of criminology at the universities of Montréal, Toronto and Ottawa have developed into important centres of study. A new school of criminology has been founded at Simon Fraser U. Canadian research has been strongly influenced by American theory, eg, psychiatric theories, which argue that delinquency is a solution to psychological problems resulting from early, damaged family relationships; "sociogenic" theories, which emphasize the importance of learned behaviour; "subcultural" theories (gang and subcultural delinquency in Canada is not yet well documented), according to which working-class youths generate a new subculture of norms and expectations in which virtue consists of defying middle-class morality; labelling theories, according to which a delinquent career is a response to institutional processing by official agencies; and finally control theories, proponents of which emphasize the importance of socialization in helping individuals develop appropriate emotions, beliefs and concerns that bond them to society.

In Canada techniques and mechanisms to control delinquency have not been effective. Treatment (a term that unfortunately implies that delinquents have defective personalities that should be cured) programs are well established and include individualized treatment and counselling, group therapy and self-help groups, but their impact on delinquency has been no more impressive than behaviour-modification programs. Nonintervention programs are an attempt to minimize contact between the offender and the criminal justice system. This approach usually includes the idea of restitution and is likely to be successful with those who have committed harmless violations; however, modifications in the criminal justice system are not likely to have much effect on delinquent behaviour. Our understanding of delinquency will not develop without a considerable increase in the extent and quality of our knowledge of Canadian society (and its seemingly endemic disparities in wealth, power and opportunities) and the common motivations for crime and delinquency. Without a willingness to accept widespread reforms and solutions that require major readjustments to our way of life, a vast reduction in delinquency will never be achieved. EDMUND W. VAZ

Juvenile Justice Systems On 7 July 1982, Parliament enacted the Young Offenders Act (effective Apr 1984, some sections not until 1985), which the government claimed would bring about a long-overdue reform of Canada's juvenile justice system. This Act replaced the 74-year-old Juvenile Deliquents Act under which juveniles who contravened any federal, provincial or municipal laws were tried, convicted and sentenced. The system that evolved under that Act had permitted many injustices, eg, different age limits for juveniles from province to province, informal court proceedings, the criminalizing of young persons for acts and behaviour that were not illegal for adults, the subjecting of young offenders to indeterminate sentences that were not always related to the seriousness of the offence, and an arbitrary review process whereby the young offenders could be brought back to court at any time until they reached 21 to have new sentences imposed.

The main theme of the Young Offenders Act is that, although young people should be held responsible for their behaviour, they nevertheless have special needs which demand a lesser standard of accountability than that imposed on adults. At the same time, they should have the same right as adults to fair and equal treatment before the law.

Under the Canadian Constitution, CRIMINAL LAW is a federal jurisdiction, so this Act applies to persons between the ages of 12 and 17 inclusive who commit crimes and other offences that are defined in federal statutes. Persons under the age of 12 cannot be convicted of such offences, and those 18 and over who commit such offences must answer for them in adult court.

Generally a young person charged with committing an offence under this Act has the same rights and privileges as an adult who is charged with a crime, including the right to bail, to a hearing conducted according to the rules of evidence, to a lawyer, to a determinate sentence and to appeal. In addition, there are special safeguards for young persons charged under this Act; eg, offences are tried by a special Youth Court; notice of a young person being charged, arrested and detained is to be given to his or her parent(s); a young person, if detained in custody, is to be kept apart from adult prisoners; information which may identify young persons who are involved in Youth Court proceedings (as an accused, a witness or a victim) may not be published; the court may exclude persons from the courtroom; and access to a young offender's record is restricted.

Dispositions or sentences too are related to the needs and circumstances of young offenders. Where young persons are found guilty of an offence, the court may impose a variety of dispositions or sentences. These include an absolute discharge; a fine (not exceeding $1000) and an order to pay compensation to the victim (in kind or by way of personal service); an order to perform community services; the placement of a young offender on probation for up to 2 years (or, in the case of certain serious offences, up to 3 years); and the placement of a young offender in custody for a period of up to 2 years or, for certain serious offences, up to 3 years.

Custody of a young offender may be open, ie, in a residential centre, group home, child-care institution or wilderness camp; or it may be secure, ie, the young offender is contained, either intermittently or continuously. An offender may only be sentenced to secure custody under certain circumstances related to the seriousness of the offence and to the offender's age and previous criminal record, and in cases where secure custody is considered necessary by the court for the protection of society and having regard to the offender's needs and circumstances. During the course of a disposition or sentence, it may be reviewed by the court (or by a review board, appointed by the province) and varied, if it is deemed necessary, because of changed circumstances of the offender or of the services available to him.

Where a young person 14 years of age or over is charged with certain serious offences, he or she may be ordered to stand trial in adult court, depending on the interests of society and the young person's needs having regard to the offence, the person's age, maturity, character and background, and the availability of treatment or correctional services.

The provinces, through provincially appointed officials, are responsible for providing care and supervision of persons dealt with under this Act. Youth workers prepare the predisposition reports for the court, supervise young offenders on probation, and assist young offenders in complying with their sentences. Provincial directors have certain authority to release young offenders from custody temporarily for medical, compassionate or humane reasons, for rehabilitative purposes, or to allow them to attend school or obtain employment. The provincial director may, under certain circumstances, transfer offenders from secure custody to open custody. The Act permits a province to set up "alternative measures" whereby, instead of answering in court for an offence, young offenders accept responsibility for it and agree to make compensation to the victim or to participate in a program of community service, education or rehabilitation.

Because the Young Offenders Act only applies to offences against federal statutes, the completion of the reform required that each province enact similar legislation governing the treatment of young offenders against provincial laws. By 1986 most provinces, though critical of the Act, had taken some action, either passing new Acts or modifying old ones. Most of the special safeguards contained in the federal Act were incorporated, but differences remain in the manner with which young offenders are dealt with in each province. There is a varying degree of commitment to the "alternative measures" program: most provinces have them, but they vary sharply in quality and effectiveness. Provincial courts have tended to be conservative and legalistic in their interpretation of the law, and contrary to expectation the number of young offenders in detention has increased. Amendments have been made and some of the criticisms muted, but the Act remains controversial. MARGARET DONNELLY

Kabalarian Philosophy, *see* NEW RELIGIOUS MOVEMENTS.

Kabloona (or non-Eskimo), the name given by Inuit to white Canadians who are long- or short-term residents in northern communities. The Kabloona include missionaries, teachers, police, government personnel and their spouses or companions. Kabloonamuit, or "people of the white man," are those Inuit who are consciously imitative of Kabloona ways. They follow Kabloona-like customs, they have a dependence on manufactured food and clothing, and they seek wage employment whenever possible. RENÉ R. GADACZ

Reading: F.G. Vallee, *Kabloona and Eskimo* (1962).

Kahane, Anne, sculptor (b at Vienna, Austria 1 Mar 1924). Kahane is nationally recognized for dense, monumental and 3-dimensional figures carved in wood, portraying political satire, humour and human foibles. She immigrated with her parents in 1925, settling in Montréal at age 5. Kahane studied at Cooper Union School, New York C, 1945-47. Her entry took a prize at the first International Sculpture Competition sponsored by the Institute of Contemporary Arts, London, 1953. *Delegation* (Venice Biennale, 1953) is a strong statement on frustration and red tape. In the 1960s she carved large decorative panels for the Winnipeg airport and Winnipeg General Hospital, and figures for Montréal's Place des Arts. By 1978 Kahane had abandoned wood for thin, strong sheets of aluminum, which gave flexibility to figures flattened into abstraction. This new technique was first shown at McMaster U, where she taught 1980-82. ANNE MCDOUGALL

Kain, Conrad, mountain guide (b at Nasswald, Austria 1883; d at Cranbrook, BC 2 Feb 1934). Kain received his first guiding job on a local cliff in 1903 and after 5 seasons of extensive climbs in the Alps was invited to become the first official guide of the ALPINE CLUB OF CANADA (1909), based in Banff, Alta. Kain was an independent spirit, admired for his prolific climbing achievements and loved for his warmth and humour. In addition to guiding wealthy climbers in Canada and abroad, he was an assistant to early surveying teams at the Rogers and Yellowhead passes. He built the first ski jump in Banff (1911), ushering in the sport of recreational skiing, and led the first ascents of Mt Robson (1913) and Mt Farnham (1914), highest mountains in the Canadian Rockies and Purcells, respectively. Kain's 1916 ascents of Mt Louis, Mt Howser and the Bugaboo Spires involved climbing techniques that were ahead of their time and not repeated for many years. He settled in Wilmer, BC, on the edge of the Purcells in 1920, trapping in winter and guiding in summer. His solo snowshoe ascent of Mt Jumbo (1919) was the first winter ascent above 3350 m in Canada, and his last climb, in the Purcells, was of a 3352 m peak (1933) which later came to be called Mt Conrad. Kain died of encephalitis lethargica in hospital at Cranbrook. PAT MORROW

Kain, Karen, dancer (b at Hamilton, Ont 28 Mar 1951). One of Canada's finest dancers, Kain graduated from the NATIONAL BALLET SCHOOL in 1969 and became a principal of the NATIONAL BALLET OF CANADA in her second season when she danced the Swan Queen in *Swan Lake.* In 1973 she won the women's silver medal and, with Frank AUGUSTYN, the prize for the best *pas de deux* at the Moscow International Ballet competition. Kain's strong technique, breadth of movement, sensitive musicality and daring attack are widely admired in both classical and contemporary works. She created major roles for Roland Petit (*Les Intermittences du coeur, Nana, Tales of Hoffmann*) and Constantin PATSALAS (*Inventions, Rite of Spring, Oiseaux*

exotiques) and has been a guest artist with the Bolshoi Ballet, Petit's Ballets de Marseille, and, with Rudolf Nureyev, around the world. Kain starred in Norman CAMPBELL's films of *Giselle* and *La Fille mal gardée*. In 1986 she danced *The Merry Widow* and *Giselle* with the National Ballet, and during the Christmas season she toured with *Cinderella* (1984-86). In 1987 she performed in the world premiere of Glen Tetley's *La Ronde. See also* BALLET. PENELOPE DOOB

Reading: D. Street, *Karen Kain, Lady of Dance* (1978).

Kaiser, Edgar Fosburgh, Jr, entrepreneur, merchant banker (b at Portland, Ore 5 July 1942). The scion of one of the world's major industrial dynasties, he was educated at Stanford U (BA) and Harvard (MBA). After serving in Vietnam with the US Agency for International Development, he became White House Fellow under Pres Lyndon Johnson. He spent a dozen years in various capacities, ultimately as chief executive officer with Kaiser Resources Ltd, which acquired some of BC's most important coal and energy reserves, later selling Ashland Oil to Dome Petroleum and coal operations to BC Resources Investment Corp – both at large profits. He became a Canadian citizen on 17 Feb 1980, and has since made significant contributions, through his family foundations, to the research and prevention of drug abuse. Between 1984 and 1986, he was chairman of the Bank of BC, which was absorbed by the Hongkong Bank when the failure of 2 Alberta banks decimated the fiscal viability of regional banking. Through his many international connections and personal commitment to social and economic reform, rare among his kind, Kaiser has turned himself into an influential figure in the evolution of Canada's Pacific Rim future. PETER C. NEWMAN

Kale (*Brassica oleracea,* Acephala Group), cole crop (like CABBAGE, cauliflower, etc), belonging to the Cruciferae family. Native to the Mediterranean, kales are now more common in northern temperate parts of the Eastern Hemisphere. Types with attractive curly foliage and coloured centres are used as ornamentals. Kales are cold hardy but not heat tolerant; thus, they do best as spring or fall crops. Curly kales are 35-45 cm high, 65-75 cm wide. Upright, straight-leaved cultivars (commercial varieties) attain 75-90 cm in height. They mature in 55-65 days. They are vulnerable to aphids, cabbage worms, loopers, root maggots, damping-off and blackleg. Kales produce neither heads nor edible flowers, but are used mainly as a potherb, and are rich in vitamins A, B_1 and C. They are widely grown in Canadian gardens, but commercial production is limited. V.W. NUTTALL

Kallmann, Helmut, music historian, librarian (b at Berlin, Germany 7 Aug 1922). He is the foremost scholar of Canadian MUSIC HISTORY. The publication of his *A History of Music in Canada 1534-1914* (1960), the subject's first comprehensive treatment, delineated the field and encouraged other researchers. Kallmann headed the Music Division of the National Library of Canada 1970-87, building there an unsurpassed collection of musical Canadiana – printed material, manuscripts and recordings. With K. Winters and G. Potvin, he was editor of the ENCYCLOPEDIA OF MUSIC IN CANADA (1981) and responsible for its overall content. He became a Member of the Order of Canada in 1987. BARCLAY MCMILLAN

Reading: J. Beckwith and F.A. Hall, *Musical Canada: Essays and Music in Honour of Helmut Kallmann* (1987).

Kalm, Pehr, botanist (b in Sweden 6 Mar 1716; d in Finland 16 Nov 1779). Kalm was educated in Finland and Sweden. He met the leading European naturalist, Linnaeus, in 1741, and under his influence became an expert on botanical applications to agriculture. Linnaeus proposed a trip to N America to discover plants that might be viable in Scandinavia and chose Kalm, who reached Philadelphia in Sept 1748, to meet the foremost American naturalists. Arriving in New France in July 1749, he botanized near Lk Champlain before moving on to Montréal and Québec. His work there was financed by the French as a favour to Sweden. He met the leading scientific lights, including Jean-François GAULTIER and Gov LA GALISSONIÈRE. He returned to New York that autumn but made a botanical foray to Niagara during the summer of 1750. Returning to Sweden in 1751, he took up a professorship at Åbo. Kalm's record of his visit to New France, published 1753-61, offers one of the best studies of intellectual and social life during the final years of the French regime. Besides providing new botanical information, it brought Canada to European attention. In his diary he stated that the scientific interest exhibited by the French was superior to that of the British Americans. RICHARD A. JARRELL

Reading: P. Kalm, *The America of 1750: Peter Kalm's Travels in North America,* ed A.B. Benson (1927, repr 1966).

Kalvak, Helen, graphic artist (b on Victoria I, NWT 1901; d at Holman, NWT 7 May 1984). Although Kalvak only began to draw in her early sixties, she created over 3000 drawings vividly portraying the traditional life of the COPPER INUIT. Kalvak showed a deep interest in spiritual traditions, and her drawings are rich with references to legends, shamanism and ceremonial life. In the print *Kidnapper* (1973), Kalvak portrays Arnakafaluk, the legendary woman who appears out of the sea to kidnap children who wander away from their parents' camp. A recurring

Helen Kalvak, whose remarkable career as an artist did not begin until her early 60s (*photo by Tessa Macintosh*).

theme in her work is the interrelationship between the human and animal worlds. In the print *Don't Be So Noisy* (1969), the festive spirit of a drum dance attracts the curiosity of a polar bear. Kalvak's drawings, interpreted in stone relief or stencil prints by the printmakers of Holman, have drawn international attention. She was elected a member of the Royal Canadian Academy of Arts in 1975. *See also* INUIT ART. BERNADETTE DRISCOLL

Kamloops, BC, City, pop 61 773 (1986c), 64 048 (1981c); inc 1893, amalgamated with N Kamloops (1967) and surrounding residential areas (1973) to form the new city of Kamloops, is located in southern BC 420 km (325 km via the COQUIHALLA HWY) NE of Vancouver. It is situated at the confluence of the N and S THOMPSON rivers near their entrance into Kamloops Lk, and covers an area of 31 141 ha. Kamloops has a rapidly expanding role in mining, is the centre of BC's cattle industry, and is bidding to overtake PRINCE GEORGE as the largest city in the BC interior. It is governed by a mayor and 8 aldermen.

The region's first inhabitants were members of the Shuswap tribe of the SALISH nation, who named the area *cume-loups,* likely meaning "meeting of the waters." David Stuart of the Pacific Fur Co spent the winter of 1811 in the area and was impressed with the fur-trading possibilities. He built the first trading post, Ft Kamloops, in Sept 1812 – the first white settlement in southern BC. In Nov the NWC arrived and constructed a post, Ft Thompson, on the other side of the river. The HBC took over Ft Kamloops after the union with the NWC in 1821. In the 1850s gold seekers arrived; Kamloops became a depot for the region and farming began. The completion of the CPR 1885 encouraged further development, and by 1893 Kamloops had a population of 6000. Since the late 1950s, it has grown rapidly as a regional metropolis.

Served by the CPR and CNR and by Pacific Western Airlines, and situated at the junction of 2 large rivers and 3 major highways, Kamloops is the natural trade and distribution centre in the southern BC interior, and is the financial, travel, cultural and administrative centre for Thompson-Nicola, Lillooet and Southern Cariboo regions. Initially, ranching and fruit and vegetable growing dominated the economy, but by the 1960s, the forest industry and mining had become more important. A large pulp mill and the province's only copper smelter are located here. Tourism is growing as well; the region's more than 200 lakes offer excellent fishing and boating, and several ski resorts are found nearby. Kamloops is served by the Royal Inland Hospital, by numerous provincial and federal agencies and by Cariboo Community College. It now has one newspaper (*Kamloops News*), a second (*Kamloops Sentinel*) closed down in late 1987, a museum, art gallery, symphony orchestra and theatre company.
ALAN F.J. ARTIBISE

Reading: M. Balf, *Kamloops: A History of the District up to 1914* (1969); R. Balf, *Kamloops, 1914-1945* (1975).

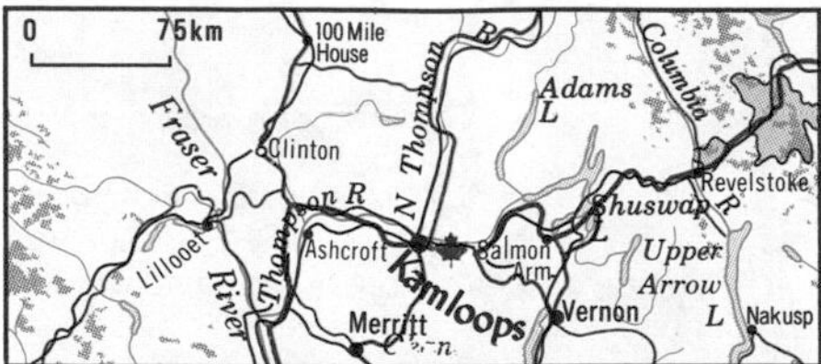

Kamouraska, Qué, Village, pop 398 (1986c), 442 (1981c), inc 1858, is located on the S shore of the ST LAWRENCE R, 125 km NE of Québec City. In Algonquian its name means "rushes at the water's edge." In 1674 a seigneury was granted to Olivier Morel de la Durantaye. In 1714 the parish of St-Louis was founded. In the 18th century, Kamouraska was one of the largest settlements on the S shore. At the start of the 19th century, the seigneury belonged to the Taché family, one of whose members, Sir Étienne-Paschal TACHÉ, served as prime minister of the Province of Canada 1855-57. Agriculture prospered in the area and the region was called "the granary of Lower Canada." In 1849 the first superior court outside Québec City was established here. Kamouraska was an important tourist area in the 19th and early 20th centuries. People came to admire the countryside, breathe the salt air and bathe in the sea. As parishes grew in size, a number of them such as St-Pascal, St-Denis and Ste-Hélène separated from St-Louis, thus accounting for its small population today. Anne HÉBERT's novel KAMOURASKA recounts tragic events that occurred here in 1839. ANTONIO LECHASSEUR

Kamouraska, novel by Anne HÉBERT (1970), is a psychological gothic romance based on an actual murder committed in 1839 in the village of KAMOURASKA, Qué, by a female ancestor of the author. The action takes place in Elizabeth's mind on the night of her second husband's impending death, transmuting the facts surrounding an earlier crime of passion into a haunting study of internalized guilt and the search for freedom. Attending Jérome Rolland's sickbed, she revisits in dream and memory her stifling childhood; her escape into an unhappy marriage to the squire of Kamouraska; an affair with Dr Nelson, with whom she plotted to kill her husband; her trial and acquittal; and her subsequent quest for respectability, leading to her second, equally stifling marriage. A fragmented juxtaposition of first- and third-person narration communicates Elizabeth's inner turmoil in an interior monologue with feminist overtones. Claude JUTRA's film *Kamouraska* (1973) captures the poetic quality of Hébert's writing. MICHÈLE LACOMBE

Kamsack, Sask, Town, pop 2565 (1986c), 2688 (1981c), inc 1911, is located in E-central Saskatchewan, about 86 km NE of YORKTON and 27 km from the Manitoba border. The general area was fur-trading territory for many years, and the town was named after a well-known Indian. A DOUKHOBOR settlement was located nearby at the turn of the century. Kamsack primarily serves as an agricultural service centre for the surrounding district, which contains both grain and mixed farms. As a service centre, it provides a modern shopping area, medical, dental and hospital services, elementary and secondary schools, and a range of recreational facilities. DON HERPERGER

Kananaskis Country comprises 5200 km^2 of the front range of the Rocky Mts W of Calgary and adjoining the Trans-Canada and Kananaskis highways. It includes 4 zones. On the E are rolling sandstone foothills, with dry grassy areas and patches of lodgepole pine and aspen. Mammals include deer, hare, coyotes, moose and black bears. Higher up is a montane zone with a cooler, wetter climate that supports spruce, fir and birds (eg, warblers, thrushes, wrens). The alpine meadow zone displays carpets of wildflowers amid islands of larch and whitebark pine. Between 1830 m and 2440 m is an alpine barren zone of rock, lichen and saxifrage, with glaciers prevailing along the Continental Divide. STONEY and SARCEE long occupied the area and, in the 19th century, numerous explorers, including John PALLISER (1858), penetrated the area searching for routes through the mountains. It is likely that the area was named for a legendary Indian. As settlement increased to the E, the area was exploited for RANCHING, logging, COAL MINING and HYDROELECTRICITY. Today, it is managed primarily for nature conservation and recreation. The area contains 2 splendid golf courses and 3 provincial parks. Bragg Creek Park on the E (121 ha) offers swimming, fishing and camping. Bow Valley Park in the N has an extensive campground with many services. Peter Lougheed Provincial Park (name changed from Kananaskis Provincial Park Nov 1985), a 508 km^2 section of mountain wilderness including an amphitheatre of glacier-clad peaks around the Kananaskis Lks, is 60 km S. It provides opportunities for outdoor recreation and will be a site of the 1988 Winter Olympics.
JOHN S. MARSH

Kananginak Pootoogook, sculptor, designer, draughtsman, printmaker (b at Ikerrasak camp, S Baffin I, NWT 1935). Son of the great camp leader Pootoogook, he came to Cape Dorset in 1957. In 1958, when James HOUSTON brought PRINTMAKING to the North, he became one of the 4 original printers. Kananginak works in all media, but he excels as an engraver and lithographer, particularly of wildlife art, which he has mastered completely while retaining a personal style with definite abstract qualities. His sister Napatchie and brother Paulassie are also good artists. *See also* INUIT PRINTMAKING. GEORGE SWINTON

Dance of Love by Kananginak Pootoogook (*courtesy West Baffin Eskimo Co-operative, Cape Dorset, NWT*).

Kanata, Ont, City, pop 27 519 (1986c), inc 1978. Located in the Regional Municipality of Ottawa-Carleton, urban Kanata is an award-winning "new town," begun W of the capital's greenbelt by developer William Teron in 1964. Teron's original concept was as much an attempt at social engineering as at urban development. Kanata was to consist of clusters of houses within distinctive village communities, revolving around a city centre and separated by naturally landscaped open spaces. Business mergers favoured increased residential density, but important components of the original concept were retained after the then March Twp established a planning committee with extensive powers to amend development proposals. In the original plan, 120 ha were allotted to a research and development area, and during the 1970s microchip revolution Kanata became a centre of high technology. Former employees of Bell-Northern Research, one of the first firms to relocate, established businesses such as Mitel Corp, which began in a basement and rapidly became a multinational (*see* ELECTRONICS INDUSTRY). The rural ward contains a historic site, Horaceville – the mansion of Hamnett Pinhey (1784-1857) and location of an annual heritage festival. BRUCE S. ELLIOTT

Kane, Elisha Kent, explorer, physician, naval officer (b at Philadelphia, Pa 3 Feb 1820; d at Havana, Cuba 16 Feb 1857). A graduate of U of Pennsylvania medical school, he travelled widely in the Far East. In 1845 Kane joined the US Navy as assistant surgeon, and saw action in the Mexican-American War of 1848. He served in the Grinnell expedition of 1850-51 sent north to search for the lost Franklin expedition (*see* FRANKLIN SEARCH), and became an advocate of the

idea of an "open polar sea." From 1853 to 1855 he commanded an American-sponsored polar expedition. Based at Kane Basin, the expedition, though plagued by disease and insubordination, achieved a "farthest north" of 81° 22′. Trapped by ice, the men travelled 2100 km by small boat and on foot to Upernavik, Greenland; 3 did not survive. Kane has been widely hailed as America's greatest explorer, and it was he who pioneered the idea that northern explorers should adopt the Inuit way of life, particularly in clothing and diet.
K.S. COATES

Kane, Paul, painter (b at Mallow, Ire 3 Sept 1810; d at Toronto 20 Feb 1871). The most famous of all Canadian artist-explorers, Kane immigrated with his family to York [Toronto] before 1822. He worked as a decorator of furniture and in 1841-42 visited Italy to copy old masters. An exhibition of George Catlin's American Indian paintings in London so excited him that he returned to Canada determined to paint a similar series in the Canadian North-West. Kane left Toronto in 1845 to sketch Indians in their homelands and collect Indian legends. He travelled around the Great Lakes but, warned of the dangers of a solitary trip to the Pacific, he contacted Sir George SIMPSON, superintendent of the HBC, who arranged for him to accompany the fur-trade canoe fleets to the West. He joined the traders at FT WILLIAM [Thunder Bay, Ont] in May 1846 and travelled W with them to Ft Garry. He witnessed the last great BUFFALO HUNT in that region, continued to Norway House, and followed the Saskatchewan R to Ft Edmonton. After crossing the mountains on horseback, he descended the Columbia R to Ft Vancouver and sketched Mt St Helens and the coastal tribes around Victoria. He returned to Toronto in 1848, having made 700 sketches of western scenery and of Indians from some 80 tribes.

Kane lived quietly in Toronto after his return. He painted canvases from his sketches, rendered in a contemporary European genre style. One hundred canvases bought by George Allan are now in the Royal Ontario Museum, while 12 bought by the Canadian government are in the National Gallery. Kane's account of his travels was published in 1859 and translated into Danish, French and German. A Canadian classic, full of anecdotes, it complements his sketches in its vivid description of the life of Indians, Métis, HBC traders and missionaries in the 1840s. *See also* NATIVE PEOPLE; PAINTING.
J. RUSSELL HARPER

Reading: J. Russell Harper, *Paul Kane's Frontier* (1971).

Paul Kane, the most famous of Canada's artist-explorers, shown here in his *Self-Portrait*, oil on paper (*courtesy Stark Museum, Orange, Tex*).

Kane Basin is a broad expanse of water, about 3900 km², that leads northward between the eastern shore of ELLESMERE I and the W coast of Greenland. It is relatively shallow; for the most part depths reach 180 m. Ice conditions are a severe impediment to navigation. The persistence and heaviness of sea ice prevent the southward drift of icebergs from the Arctic Ocean and those calved from glaciers coming off Greenland, which collect in groups at the glaciers' mouths. Favourable sea-ice conditions paradoxically increase the iceberg hazard, since these result in a marked increase in the outflow of formerly trapped icebergs.
DOUG FINLAYSON

Kangaroo Rat, solitary, strictly nocturnal rodent of the N American family Heteromyidae. The family comprises 75 species (*see* POCKET MOUSE). Of the 14 species of kangaroo rat only one occurs in Canada. Ord's kangaroo rat (*Dipodomys ordii*) of the Great Sand Hills of SW Saskatchewan and Alberta is one of Canada's rare desert-dwelling mammals. Its front legs are weak; hindlegs, long and powerful. The tail, longer than the body, is used for support and balance. These features enable the rat to move by jumping. The kangaroo rat grows up to 30 cm long. Its body is tawny with white underparts. White patches occur on the upper lip, above the eyes and behind the ears; white stripes across the hips. Cheek pouches are used to carry grain to the burrow, where kangaroo rats shelter in winter. Insects are also eaten. Kangaroo rats drink little water, having adapted to minimal water loss. Although very agile, they are preyed on by carnivorous mammals, birds and snakes. The reproductive cycle is not fully understood: mating occurs in spring; gestation lasts 29-30 days. Females can produce 2 or more litters annually, each averaging 3-4 young.
JEAN FERRON

Kangirtugaapik (formerly Clyde River), NWT, Hamlet, pop 471 (1986c), is located on the W shore of Patricia Bay on the E coast of BAFFIN ISLAND, 2153 air km NE of Yellowknife. Situated on a shallow gravel ridge and surrounded by high hills, the community was not established until 1922 when the HUDSON'S BAY CO set up a post named Clyde River until 1987. The Inuit place-name means small inlet or bay. At that time, the company relocated many Inuit from the Baffin region to Clyde River to exploit the plentiful fur resources in the area. A US Coast Guard weather station was established here during WWII and provided the Inuit with an alternate form of employment. Although the Inuit here have become renowned for their soapstone and whale-bone sculptures as well as their silkscreening designs, many still live a quiet, traditional life closely tied to the land.
EDWARD STRUZIK

Kaplan, Robert Phillip, politician, lawyer (b at Toronto 27 Dec 1936). Kaplan received a BA in sociology (1958) and an LLB (1961) from U of T, and was called to the Ontario Bar in 1963. He specialized in corporate and tax law during stints with 2 Toronto legal firms, and between 1972 and 1974 he lectured on Canadian affairs for the Hudson Institute in Croton-on-Hudson, NY. Elected Liberal MP for Don Valley (Toronto) in 1968, he lost the seat in the 1972 general election. Kaplan switched ridings and was elected in York Centre (Toronto) in the 1974, 1979, 1980 and 1984 elections. He became solicitor general in 1980, ushered in the Young Offenders Act (1982), and removed national security responsibilities from the RCMP by creating the CANADIAN SECURITY INTELLIGENCE SERVICE. Kaplan has been Liberal justice critic since 1984.
DEAN BEEBY

Kapuskasing, Ont, Town, pop 11 378 (1986c), 12 014 (1981c), inc 1921, located on the Kapuskasing R, 493 km NW of North Bay. The name derives from a Cree term meaning "branch" (the Kapuskasing R being a branch of the Mattagami) or "place where the river bends." Although the area had been explored since the 18th century by HBC and NWC fur traders, the site itself only came into existence in 1910 as a station along the National Transcontinental Ry, a line linking Québec City and Winnipeg, incorporated into the CNR system 1922. During WWI an internment camp was established near the town, its prisoner-of-war and "enemy alien" occupants developing what is now a federal experimental farm. After the war the community's agricultural base was further expanded by a government soldier-resettlement program. Kapuskasing's future lies in its rich surrounding forests; and since the 1920s the pulp and paper industry, represented by the Spruce Falls Power and Paper Co, and tourism have become its chief economic mainstays. Half of Spruce Falls's daily newsprint output goes to the *New York Times*.
MATT BRAY

Kap'Yong On 23 Apr 1951, during the KOREAN WAR, the 27th British Commonwealth Infantry Brigade was ordered to protect the withdrawal through the Kap'Yong R valley, about 20 km S of the 38th parallel in central Korea, of the ROK (S Korean) Division, which had been dislodged by a major Chinese offensive. The 2nd Battalion, Princess Patricia's Canadian Light Infantry, and the 3rd Battalion, Royal Australian Regiment, were assigned forward hilltop positions, the Canadians on the west side of the valley and the Australians to the east. The Australians bore the brunt of the initial attack and were forced to retreat, with 155 casualties, late Apr 24. The Chinese then turned their attention to the PPCLI, which managed in heavy all-night fighting on Apr 24-25 to stop their advance. Canadian casualties were 10 killed, 23 wounded. The battle contributed significantly to the defeat of the general Chinese offensive. Both the Canadians and the Australians received Distinguished Unit Citations from the American government.
DENIS STAIRS

Karate, which translates as "empty hands," is a form of unarmed combat employing a variety of punches, open-hand strikes, kicks and blocks. Developed on the small Japanese island of Okinawa, karate's exact origins remain unclear, though it probably derived from a combination of native and Chinese fighting arts. It reached a level of lethal efficiency after the Japanese Satsuma clan conquered the kingdom of Okinawa in 1609 and banned weapons. Karate masters had to develop extraordinary skills in order to fight armed samurai with only bare hands, feet and modified farm implements. Its spread to the rest of Japan started after Okinawan master Gichin Funakoshi moved to Tokyo in 1922.

Canadian karate began with Masami Tsuruoka. Born in Canada, he studied Chito-Ryustyle karate in Japan for almost a decade before returning in 1956 to open a dojo (school) in Toronto. Tsuruoka helped oversee the spread of karate across Canada and founded the National Karate Association in 1964. Though an undetermined number of schools operate outside its jurisdiction, the NKA is the official governing body of karate in Canada, holding an annual tournament and representing more than 10 000 members from all the major karate styles.

Although karate originated primarily as a means of self-defence, it later assumed a spiritual and ethical basis in which self-mastery is paramount. In karate tournaments, contestants' blows are pulled and judged according to the damage they would have caused if unrestrained. Karate is not yet an Olympic sport, though there are international meets. John Carnio of Toronto won second place in the open-weight sparring of the first world tournament in Tokyo in 1970, and in 1986 Manuel Monzon of Montréal won bronze in the 65 to 70 kg division of the eighth World Championships in Sydney, Australia. *See also* JIU-JITSU; JUDO. PETER GIFFEN

Karlsefni, common name for Thorfinnr Thordarson (*fl*1000-20). Sometime between 1003 and 1015 AD Karlsefni set out to colonize Vinland. Evidence for his adventure, based on the *Eric the Red's Saga* and the *Greenlanders' Saga* is vague and the location of the colony impossible to identify, but excavations at L'ANSE AUX MEADOWS ended doubts that the Vikings had reached America. *See also* NORSE VOYAGES. JAMES MARSH

Karluk, whaling ship, 251 t, 39 m long, sunk in the Arctic Ocean 11 Jan 1914. Eleven of the 25 survivors died before rescue from Wrangel I on 7 Sept 1914. The loss of these men and the ship caused a half-century of dispute about the leadership and technical skills of Vilhjalmur STEFANSSON, leader of the CANADIAN ARCTIC EXPEDITION of 1913, and Robert Bartlett, captain of the *Karluk*. The *Karluk* was trapped by ice in the Beaufort Sea 300 km short of the planned base, HERSCHEL I. While Stefansson was away hunting seals, the weather changed and the ship was carried westward towards Siberia for 4 months until crushed by ice. The shipboard group occupied themselves with hunting for meat and making winter clothing, which had not been previously issued, and, according to one report, the 12 scientists and officers had only 9 bowls, 7 mugs and 10 seats between them. After sending out 4 scouts, who disappeared, the *Karluk* survivors took 6 weeks to walk 128 km to Wrangel I. Six days later, Captain Bartlett left with one Inuk to get help and eventually reached the Russian port of Cape North, travelling 1120 km on foot. During the 6 months the others waited for rescue, more men died. There were quarrels about food, tobacco and ammunition, and one death by gunshot – it was never determined whether it was suicide or murder.

DONALD J.C. PHILLIPSON

Reading: W.R. Hunt, *Stef: A Biography of Vilhjalmur Stefansson* (1986); W.L. McKinley, *Karluk: The Great Untold Story of Arctic Exploration* (1976).

Karoo Ashevak, artist (b near Spence Bay, NWT 1940; d there 19 Oct 1974). Gaining recognition only late in his short artistic career, Karoo is now acknowledged as an important figure in contemporary Canadian INUIT ART. He grew up living the traditional life on the land and began carving in the late 1960s after moving into Spence Bay. About 5 years later, he and his wife perished in a fire at their home. Karoo brought to his work a lively imagination, a knowledge of traditional culture, a love of gadgets and tremendous skill as a carver. Working primarily in whalebone with stone, baleen and ivory highlights, he gave to his subjects – people, shamans, animals and birds – a sense of life, humour and spirituality. The approximately 250 sculptures he produced during his lifetime are now eagerly sought after.

JEAN BLODGETT

Karpis, Alvin, gangster (b Albin Karpowicz at Montréal 1908; d at Torremolinos, Spain 26 Aug 1979). Nicknamed Old Creepy, he was among the most notorious of the Depression-era bandits in the US. As a henchman of the infamous Barker Gang, he robbed numerous banks and participated in 2 sensational kidnappings. After the FBI broke up the Barker Gang and killed such legendary hoodlums as John Dillinger and George "Baby Face" Nelson, Karpis became Public Enemy No 1. He was captured in New Orleans in 1936, allegedly by J. Edgar Hoover, chief of the FBI. After serving a long prison term, including a record 26 years in Alcatraz, Karpis was paroled and deported to his native Canada in 1969. His autobiography, *Public Enemy Number One* (1971), is a graphic and chilling account of his criminal career. EDWARD BUTTS

Karsh, Yousuf, photographer (b at Mardin, Armenia-in-Turkey 23 Dec 1908). As a boy Karsh survived the Armenian massacres and then immigrated to Canada in 1924 to live with a photographer-uncle, George Nakash. Later he apprenticed under photographer John H. Garo of Boston, Mass, where he decided to concentrate on photographing people of influence. He opened a studio in Ottawa in 1932, where he learned the dramatic use of lighting that characterizes his work at the Ottawa Little Theatre. In 1941 he photographed the visiting British PM Winston Churchill. That portrait, the first to carry the copyright "Karsh of Ottawa," ran on the cover of *Life* magazine and brought him international fame; it remains one of the most widely reproduced portraits in the history of photography. Karsh photographed famous personalities on every continent and his portraits of political, literary, artistic, theatrical and scientific figures made being "Karshed" (Field Marshal Bernard Law Montgomery's term) a mark of achievement. His work hangs in major art galleries in Europe and N America, including the Museum of Modern Art, the Metropolitan Museum of Art in New York, the National Portrait Gallery in London, Eng, and the National Gallery of Canada, where he was the first photographer to have a one-man exhibition (1959). His *Portraits of Greatness* (1958) set new standards for Canadian publishing, and numerous other books (*Karsh Portraits,* 1976, and *Karsh: A 50-Year Retrospective,* 1983) have followed. In 1965 Karsh was awarded the Canada Council Medal and in 1968 the Medal of Service of the Order of Canada. In Apr 1987, the National Archives of Canada paid $3.5 million for Karsh's lifetime collection, including 250 000 negatives, 12 000 colour transparencies and 50 000 original prints. IAN MONTAGNES

Reading: Y. Karsh, *Karsh: A Fifty-Year Retrospective* (1983) and *In Search of Greatness: An Autobiography* (1962).

Yousuf Karsh, a photo montage of the internationally known portrait photographer, Sept 1960 (*courtesy National Archives of Canada/PA-123864/Duncan Cameron*).

Karst Landform, feature created on the Earth's surface by the drainage of water into the ground or by its discharge at springs. The term derives from an area on the coast of Yugoslavia where these features (eg, sinkholes, caves, natural bridges, sinking streams, etc) are common. Karst landforms are an important variant of landforms created by flowing water. In the former, water is routed underground via solutional cave systems, instead of flowing at the surface in normal river channels (*see* RIVER LANDFORM). The development of karst landforms is limited to areas where comparatively soluble rocks, principally limestones and dolomites (carbonate rocks) and gypsum and anhydrite (sulphate rocks), occur. Approximately 8% of the Earth's land surface is karst terrain. There are 1.2 million km^2 of karst rock outcroppings in Canada. They are common in all geological regions except the Canadian Shield.

There are 2 solution processes important to karst terrain formation. Gypsum, anhydrite and very soluble substances such as natural salt dissolve in the presence of water. For example, gypsum dissociates until there are 2500 mg dissolved per litre of water (at 25°C). The solution is then saturated and may precipitate gypsum crusts, eg, at mineral springs. Calcite (the limestone mineral) and dolomite are dissolved by carbonic acid produced by the solution of atmospheric carbon dioxide (CO_2) in water. Rates of limestone solution are determined, therefore, by the amounts of water and CO_2 available in an environment. CO_2 may build up to high concentrations in soils, where it is dissolved by rainwater. Rates of limestone solution range from less than 5 m^3 per km^2 per year in deserts and very cold regions to more than 100 m^3 in rain forests.

The most widespread surface karst landforms are small solution pits, grooves and runnels, termed karren. Individual features are rarely longer or deeper than 10 m, but frequently they are densely clustered to dissect larger areas, termed limestone pavement. Solution pavement is particularly well developed in Île d'Anticosti, Qué; and Bruce Peninsula and Manitoulin I, Ont. Small patches may be seen within the city limits of Hamilton, Montréal, Ottawa, etc. In Winnipeg, approximately 3500 km^2 of solution pavement is preserved beneath later glacial-lake clays and forms an important industrial water store.

The diagnostic karst landform is the sinkhole (doline). This is a bowl-, funnel- or cylinder-shaped depression feeding water underground. There may be a periodic or permanent pond in the base. The length or diameter of sinkholes ranges from 10 to 1000 m. Most are formed by solution focused in the funnel or by collapse of the roof of an underlying cave. In southern Saskatchewan, collapse-solution cavities in salt have extended through as much as 1000 m of overlying insoluble rocks to produce shallow sinkholes at the surface. Sinkholes often occur in lines or clusters. In some karsts (eg, central Kentucky) their frequency exceeds 500 per km^2, giving the terrain a shell-pitted appearance. Thousands are known in southern Canada, from gypsum terrains in western Newfoundland to limestones on Vancouver I. There are many large, spectacular examples in WOOD BUFFALO NATIONAL PARK, in the Franklin Mts, and W of Great Bear Lk where limestones and dolomites have collapsed into cavities in gypsum. Some new collapses occur each year, the hole appearing in a matter of seconds. These are a hazard to settlement on gypsum terrains in parts of Newfoundland and NS.

Larger karst landforms include dry valleys and gorges, carved by past rivers which now flow underground, and poljes, which are major sinkholes with alluviated, flat floors. Medicine Lk in Jasper National Park is a polje measuring 6 km by 1-2 km. The Maligne R drains into it and floods it to a depth of 25 m during the summer melt season. In winter, the lake reduces to small pond sinkholes in the polje floor. The sinking water is discharged 16 km NW at some 60 springs in the floor of Maligne Canyon. With an aggregate discharge that may exceed 65 m^3 of water each second, these are the largest karst springs known in Canada.

Karst landform development is rather limited in Canada when compared to countries that have not undergone repeated GLACIATION. Glacier action has eroded or infilled much karst. Our finest karstland, Nahanni Karst, is found in a region of the Mackenzie Mts, NWT, which has escaped glaciation for the past several hundred thousand years. Major karst forms have developed without interruption or destruction and include hundreds of sinkholes up to 150 m deep, giant solution grooves intersecting to form a natural labyrinth, several poljes and dry canyons. Parts of the karst have reached a very advanced stage, displaying residual rock towers and natural bridges, features rarely seen in northern latitudes.

Alpine karst, comprising fields of karren and shaft sinkholes above the treeline that drain into deep caves, is well developed in parts of the Rocky Mts and Vancouver I. The largest icefield in the Rockies, Columbia Icefield, is mostly drained by sinkholes surviving in the limestone beneath it. The waters flow in great caves through a mountain, to emerge as spectacular springs in the valley of Castleguard R. D.C. FORD

Kasemets, Udo, composer, educator, writer (b at Tallinn, Estonia 16 Nov 1919). Following musical studies in Estonia and Germany, Kasemets immigrated to Canada in 1951 where he established himself as a teacher, conductor and music critic in the Hamilton-Toronto area. In the 1960s, he was involved in several performance groups specializing in experimental music and multimedia presentations. He derived his experimental aesthetic in large part from the controversial work of American composer-philosopher John Cage. The result has been, since 1960, the creation of a series of musical and mixed-media works exploiting chance operations and game situations with the intention of blurring the lines of demarcation between composer, performer and listener, thereby enhancing the sensory awareness of audiences by involving them more directly in the creative process itself. ALAN M. GILLMOR

Kaska live in the mountainous region drained by the LIARD R of the southern Yukon and northern BC, primarily in the communities of Lower Post, Upper Liard (near Watson Lake), and Ross River in the Pelly drainage. With their TAHLTAN and TAGISH neighbours, they speak dialects of a single variety of Athapaskan and number about 500. The territory was one of the last regions explored by the HUDSON'S BAY COMPANY after 1834. At that time parts of the region were only seasonally exploited, in winter by the Tahltan and in the spring by Kaska from the upper Pelly R. The Tahltan considered much of this district their territory and defended their middleman trade position between the coast and interior groups against the HBC.

Early contact period Kaska material culture and subsistence was basically similar to that of other Athapaskan peoples of the subarctic plateau, especially those who similarly lacked salmon and migratory herds of barren-ground caribou. Woodland caribou, moose, Dall sheep, berries and whitefish are among the principal traditional resources of the rugged upper Liard R region.

During the middle to latter half of the 19th century there were 4 regional Kaska bands – Frances Lake, Upper Liard, Dease R and the Nelson Indians – though these divisions were not cohesive social units. The primary unit of Kaska society was the local band, consisting of an extended family with a male leader. Although most Kaska belonged to one of 2 exogamous matri-moieties, Wolf and Crow, with reciprocal obligations, moiety bonds appear to have been weak.

Many Kaska only formed village communities following the 1873 Cassiar gold rush, when other Indians, Métis, Europeans and Chinese entered the region. By 1888 the number of miners had dwindled, but many natives, referred to as Cascar, remained. The backgrounds of the families aligned with the Lower Post and McDame trading posts were diverse, though Athapaskan speakers made up the majority, but intermarriage between the offspring of the immigrants represented the first step towards integration of the communities. As wage-labour opportunities declined, hunting and fur trapping provided the most stable resources. Their exploitation played a primary role in the emerging social pattern, especially through the formation of trapping alliances. Upon marriage, each couple had to consider the situation at hand and there were no simple rules regarding exogamy, postmarital residence or household composition.

After the 1920s, when Lower Post was linked into the air route between Edmonton and Whitehorse, Euro-Canadian influences increased again. The WWII period provided good returns from trapping and wage labour: Watson Lake was a supply station during construction of the ALASKA HIGHWAY, and Lower Post became a depot. After the war governmental services increased dramatically, though interaction with Euro-Canadians, which was now channelled into administrative and educational functions and mining operations, became more formal. *See also* NATIVE PEOPLE: SUBARCTIC. A. MCFADYEN CLARK

Reading: J. Helm, ed, *Handbook of North American Indians,* vol 6: *Subarctic* (1981).

Kaslo, BC, Village, pop 858 (1986c), 854 (1981c), inc 1893, located 70 km N of Nelson, overlooking Kootenay Lk. It was established 1892 to service the silver-mining boom sweeping the Kootenays; destroyed 1894 by the great flood on the Kootenay-Columbia system, it was immediately rebuilt. Mining declined at the end of WWI, but fruit farming and logging grew in the 1920s. In 1942, 964 JAPANESE were relocated there. Lumbering was spurred by the need for housing and other services. Kaslo protested the removal of this energetic community to New Denver in 1946. The present population is supported mainly by logging, sawmilling, mining and catering to the increasing flow of tourists exploring the region's excellent fishing and sightseeing. Kaslo is the anglicized spelling of a Kootenai expression for "place where the blackberries grow." WILLIAM A. SLOAN

Katimavik, a youth program founded by the social activist and author Jacques HÉBERT in 1976 and funded, until 1986, by the federal government. It replaced, to some extent, the defunct COMPANY OF YOUNG CANADIANS, but unlike its predecessor it kept out of trouble and, by and large, out of the public eye. In its heyday, Katimavik sent about 1700 young Canadians across the country to work in youth programs of a useful kind; its volunteers got room and board and a dollar a day, or $1000 if they completed their full term of service of 9 months. In the winter of 1986, the Mulroney government moved to cancel Katimavik, which precipitated a 22-day fast by Hébert – who was by then a senator – in the Senate lobby. The program continued on a much reduced scale in 1988, with the financial support of labour, business, student and church organizations. ROBERT BOTHWELL

Kattan, Naim, writer, literary critic (b at Baghdad, Iraq 26 Aug 1928). Kattan studied law at U of Baghdad before studying literature at the Sorbonne. His fictionalized memories of these years appeared as *Adieu, Babylone* (1975) and *Les Fruits arrachés* (1977). He immigrated to Canada in 1954 and in 1984 became head of the writing and publishing division of the Canada Council. Kattan has contributed to magazines and newspapers in the Near East, Europe and N America, and has written several books, distinguishing himself in the genres of essay, novel, short story and theatre. In *Le Réel et le théâtral* (1970), a collection of essays that won the Prix France-Canada (1971), Kattan pondered the elements that over the ages have differentiated and distinguished cultures and civilizations, the relationship of oriental and occidental man with nature, other men and the beyond. He continued this reflection in *La Mémoire et la promesse* (1978), *Le Désir et le pouvoir* (1983) and *Le Repos et l'oubli* (1987). In addition, Kattan has long been interested in Canadian, American and Latin American writers. His 3-vol *Ecrivains des Amériques* (1972, 1976 and 1980) has helped to make these writers better known in Canada. *See also* JEWISH WRITING. JACQUES COTNAM

Kavik, John, sculptor and potter (b in Gjoa Haven, NWT 1897). Having moved inland to hunt in the Barren Lands, he almost died during "the great starvation" of the 1950s. He eventually moved via Baker Lk to Rankin Inlet, where he took up carving in the early 1960s, as well as working in clay in 1964. Like the work of his great friend John TIKTAK, Kavik's work is primary and stark, but is also filled with narrative content. This is particularly evident in his totally original pots, which are covered with 3-dimensional protruding figures full of humour and folklore. *See also* INUIT ART. GEORGE SWINTON

Kawartha Lakes are 14 interconnected lakes stretching across Peterborough and Victoria counties in S-central Ontario. Ranging in size from 5 to 45 km^2, they are Katchiwano, Clear, Stony, Lovesick, Lower Buckhorn, Buckhorn, Chemong, Pigeon, Sturgeon, Cameron, Scugog, Balsam, Mitchell and the man-made Canal Lk. Lake Katchiwano in the SE drains through the Otonabee and Trent rivers to Lk Ontario. On the W the chain drains into Lk SIMCOE. The resources of these beautiful, wooded lakes were first exploited by native people, chiefly the Mississauga, who were occupying the region when European settlers arrived early in the 19th century. There is an Indian reserve on Chemong Lk.

Once the centre of a thriving logging industry, the island-studded lakes became a popular vacation area after 1890, especially for sportfishermen. Steamboats carried visitors to several palatial resort hotels. Today, cottages line the shores and pleasure craft crowd the waters. The lakes form part of the Trent-Severn navigation system linking Lk Ontario and Georgian Bay. Locks at 9 locations allow pleasure boats to connect with all the lakes. Major towns include LINDSAY, Fenelon Falls and Bobcaygeon. The name is a corruption of a Huron word meaning "bright waters and happy land." DANIEL FRANCIS

Kayak All Inuit groups used some form of kayak, except for the most northerly polar Eskimo. Essentially a one-man closed-deck hunting craft, it was employed sometimes for transport of goods. Fast and seaworthy and ranging from 4 m to 7 m in length, it was built to hold from one to 3 persons. Covered with dehaired seal or caribou skins, the frame was often made of driftwood, with ribs of willow branches. Both single and double-bladed wooden paddles were used. To make the entire craft watertight, even when tipped, the hunter wore a parka which was tied around the hatch-hole rim. RENÉ R. GADACZ

Kazan River, 732 km long (from Ennadai Lk), rises in the SE NWT near the Saskatchewan border. Flowing N it follows an irregular course through several lakes, draining a large part of the Barren Lands. It joins the THELON R on the S shore of Baker Lk, not far from the Inuit hamlet of the same name. It is a popular wilderness canoe route. The name comes from a Chipewyan word for white partridge. DANIEL FRANCIS

Kean, Abraham (Abram), "Killer Kean," master mariner, legislative councillor (b at Flowers Island, Nfld 8 July 1855; d at St John's 18 May 1945). The archetypal sealing captain, Kean is accused, in legend and popular mythology, of responsibility for the loss of 77 lives in the *Newfoundland* sealing disaster of 1914. William COAKER accused Kean of irresponsibly leaving 132 men from his son's ship on the ice where many froze to death during a violent storm. Exonerated by a court of inquiry, Kean kept his formidable reputation as "the greatest seal killer of all time." In 1934, when he surpassed his personal goal of more than 1 million seals killed (with 1 008 100), he was fêted by the Board of Trade, awarded the Blue Ensign and created OBE. He wrote his autobiography, *Old and Young Ahead* (1935). LINDA WHALEN

Reading: C. Brown, *Death on the Ice* (1972); G.A. England, *The Greatest Hunt in the World* (1969).

Kedgwick, NB, Village, pop 1129 (1986c), inc 1966, is a francophone community (99%), located 80 km SW of Campbellton. The area is at the height of land between the Kedgwick, Restigouche, Nepisiguit and Saint John rivers. It was the site of many 19th-century lumber camps and was known then as Grand Forchee, but it was not settled until after 1909 when the railway between Campbellton and Saint-Léonard was built through the area. It was called Richard's Station from 1909 to 1915, at which time the current name, derived from the Micmac *madawamkedjwik,* possibly meaning large branch or flowing underground, was adopted. The sawmills, which the advent of the railway facilitated, were taken over by major companies in the 1920s and continue to operate, with the smaller logs being shipped to pulp mills in Edmundston and Atholville. About 60% of the work force is engaged in primary forest activities. BURTON GLENDENNING

Keefer, Samuel, engineer (b at Thorold, UC 20 Jan 1811; d at Brockville, Ont 7 Jan 1890). The first chief engineer of the Board of Public Works of the Province of Canada in 1841, he built the first suspension bridge in Canada in 1843 spanning the Ottawa R at Chaudière Falls. He resigned his government post in 1853 to become an engineer for the GRAND TRUNK RY. As supervising engineer for the Brockville and Ottawa Ry, he built the first railway tunnel in Canada at Brockville. In 1857 he re-entered government service as inspector of railways and deputy commissioner of public works; having selected the plans for the Parliament buildings in Ottawa in 1859, he directed their construction. He retired again from public service in 1864 and 5 years later built the Clifton Bridge over the Niagara R. For the design and construction of this bridge, he received the 1878 Gold Medal at the Paris Exposition. PHYLLIS ROSE

Keefer, Thomas Coltrin, civil engineer (b at Thorold, UC 4 Nov 1821; d at Ottawa 7 Jan 1915). He was involved in a number of important engineering works, and his pamphlet *Philosophy of Railroads* (1849) was widely used. He himself began the survey for a railway connecting Kingston, Ont, and Toronto (1851), was in charge of the survey for a line between Montréal and Kingston, and determined the site for the Victoria Bridge over the St Lawrence R at Montréal. His essay *The Canals of Canada* (1850) brought him work in hydraulic ENGINEERING. He served as chief engineer of the Montréal Water Board and designed the water-supply system for Hamilton, Ont (1859), as well as the waterworks in Ottawa (1874). His Hamilton Pumping Station, with its working Gartshore beam engines, has been declared a national historic site. Keefer was a founding member and first president of the Canadian Soc of Civil Engineers (1887). As the "dean of Canadian engineers," he received many honours, including the presidency of the American Soc of Civil Engineers. PHYLLIS ROSE

Keen, George, salesman, co-operative leader (b at Stoke-on-Trent, Eng 8 May 1869; d at Brantford, Ont 4 Dec 1953). Keen immigrated to Canada in 1904. In 1906 he helped organize the Brantford Co-operative Soc, a consumer co-operative. In 1909 he called the meeting that organized the Co-operative Union of Canada, the national organization for co-operatives in English Canada, and was its general secretary 1909-45. Keen believed that all economic activities should be organized co-operatively and was particularly devoted to encouraging consumer co-operatives. Between 1922 and 1939 he visited western Canada annually and Atlantic Canada frequently, thereby playing a significant role in developing the CO-OPERATIVE MOVEMENT in those regions. He also became an authority on legislation for the co-operative movement, and he frequently defended it before provincial and federal governments. IAN MACPHERSON

Reading: G. Keen, *The Birth of a Movement* (1952).

Keene, Minna, née Bergman, photographer (b at Arolsen, Germany 5 Apr 1861; d at Oakville, Ont Nov 1943). A self-taught photographer, she was a member of the Linked Ring and the London Salon, societies devoted to the promotion of pictorial photography. In 1908 she became the first woman to be admitted as a fellow to the Royal Photographic Society. Immigrating to Canada about 1913, she was commissioned by the CPR to photograph the Rockies (1914-15), opened a studio in Toronto in 1920 and relocated to Oakville in 1922. Keene travelled, exhibited and lectured widely. She received medals for photographic excellence in Japan, S Africa and Australia. Her photographs are in the collections of the National Archives of Canada and the Smithsonian Institution, Washington, DC. LAURA JONES

Keenleyside, Hugh Llewellyn, public servant (b at Toronto 7 July 1898). Joining the Dept of External Affairs in 1928, Keenleyside served in Tokyo 1929-36. During WWII he was secretary of the Canadian section of the PERMANENT JOINT BOARD ON DEFENCE, and an opponent of the internment of Japanese Canadians. He was ambassador to Mexico 1944-47 but then left the department, disillusioned with diplomatic life. He was deputy minister of mines and resources and commissioner of the NWT, 1947-50, and director-general, UN Technical Assistance Administration, 1950-58. Chairman of the BC Power Commission 1959-62 and the BC Hydro and Power Authority 1962-69, he was deeply involved in the COLUMBIA RIVER TREATY negotiations. Keenleyside wrote *Canada and the United States* (1929, rev ed 1952) and 2 impressive volumes of *Memoirs* (1981-82). He received the Pearson Peace Medal of the UN Assn of Canada (1982). NORMAN HILLMER

Kejimkujik National Park (est 1968, 375 km^2). Tranquillity is the keynote of this glacier-scarred park situated 170 km SW of Halifax in central NS. Its brooding forests and dark waters are disturbed only by the loon's cry or the swirl of a paddle. In the past, most of the park was logged over and burned, but the primeval character of the forest is once again intact, and scattered stands of ancient hemlocks can still be found. The wildlife is diverse. The park's marshes, bogs and shallow lakes support more species of reptiles and amphibians than occur anywhere else in Atlantic Canada, including such rarities as the ribbon snake and Blanding's turtle. The woods are home to mammals common to eastern Canada, eg, black bear, mink, flying squirrel, red fox. The area's first inhabitants, the MICMAC, left hundreds of petroglyphs (*see* PICTOGRAPHS AND PETROGLYPHS) depicting legends and events. The waterways linking the Atlantic Ocean and the Bay of Fundy provided the Micmac and French with a major canoe route, and the park is still a canoeist's paradise. Scottish and Irish immigrants settled as early as the 1760s, and wealthy Boston families used the area as a summer retreat in the late 1800s. The name derives from a Micmac word referring to the exertion required in paddling across the lake. LILLIAN STEWART

Kelesi, Helen Mersi, tennis player (b at Victoria 15 Nov 1969). By the time she was 12, she was the top junior player (under 18) in western Canada. At age 13, she won the Canadian Junior Nationals and the Taipei International Junior Open. Her best world junior ranking was third in 1985, after she had reached the semifinals in the Junior French Open and at Junior Wimbledon. With such a record, she turned professional and was initially ranked eightieth in the world. By the time she was 16, in 1986, she had achieved victories over Helena Sukova (ranked seventh) and Hana Mandlikova (ranked third), her world ranking had jumped to twenty-fifth, and she had won her first professional tournament, the Japan Open. In 1987 she won the Canadian Women's Tennis Championship. JOHN J. JACKSON

Kellett, Sir Henry, naval officer, arctic explorer (b at Clonabody, Ire 2 Nov 1806; d there 1 Mar 1875). Kellett joined the British navy in 1822 and served in the West Indies and on survey vessels in Africa, the Far East and Central America. From 1846 to 1850 he commanded *Resolute* and *Intrepid* as part of the expedition led by Sir Edward BELCHER to search for Sir John Franklin (*see* FRANKLIN SEARCH) in the eastern Arctic. In the winter of 1853 his ships were trapped by ice in Barrow Strait, and in Apr 1854, under protest, he obeyed an order to abandon them; a later court-martial quickly absolved him of responsibility for this action. Denied credit and a share of the reward for his role in the discovery of the NORTHWEST

PASSAGE, he subsequently served in the W Indies and China. W.R. MORRISON

Kelly, Leonard, "Red," hockey player (b at Simcoe, Ont 9 July 1927). He was a star with the powerhouse St Michael's College junior teams of the 1940s and was one of the best defencemen in the NHL with Detroit, winning the JAMES NORRIS TROPHY in its first year. In 1960 he was traded to TORONTO MAPLE LEAFS, where as a centreman he was a key figure in 4 STANLEY CUP victories. He coached Los Angeles, Pittsburgh and Toronto. A smooth skater and effective playmaker, he scored 281 goals, 542 assists in regular season play, and 33 goals, 59 assists in playoffs. He won the LADY BYNG TROPHY 4 times. He served 2 terms as an MP for the Liberal Party. JAMES MARSH

Kelly, Peter Reginald, Methodist-United Church of Canada cleric, Indian activist and leader (b at Skidegate, BC 21 Apr 1885; d at Nanaimo, BC 2 Mar 1966). A member of the Haida nobility, Kelly was educated at Coqualeetza Institute and Columbia College, both Methodist institutions. Before becoming a lay preacher, he taught school for 5 years at Skidegate. By 1911 he had begun to distinguish himself in the BC LAND CLAIMS issue and in 1927, as president of the Allied Tribes of BC, he testified on Indian grievances before a special parliamentary committee. Prominent in the Native Brotherhood of BC in the 1930s, he was a key figure in the consultations of the late 1940s that led to a revision of the Indian Act. A clergyman as well, he also served in several pastorates and as captain of the *Thomas Crosby III* and *Thomas Crosby IV* mission ships. E.P. PATTERSON

Kelowna, BC, City, pop 61 213 (1986c), 59 916 (1981c), inc 1905, located in S-central BC on the E shore of Okanagan Lk. The area was first visited by David Stuart, a Scottish fur trader, 1811. Oblate missionaries built a mission on the present site 1859, and planted the first fruit trees 3 years later. The townsite was laid out in 1892, and the name chosen – from an Indian word meaning "grizzly bear." At incorporation, population was 600, and shortly after there were 11 sawmills, 3 fruit-packing plants and 2 canneries. Main-line rail service did not arrive until 1925, and population increased to 5100 in 1941, reaching 13 000 by 1961.

Kelowna is the main marketing and distribution centre of the central OKANAGAN VALLEY. The city's large area contains many orchards and vineyards, numerous canning plants and BC's largest winery (started 1932). A bridge, with a long section floating on pontoons, was built across the lake in 1958. The city is served by road to Calgary and Vancouver, and has the third-busiest airport in BC. It has the Sunshine Theatre Co, a symphony orchestra, a museum and an art gallery. Okanagan College, begun 1963, offers adult education and a 2-year transfer program. With the largest beach on Okanagan Lk, a sunny climate and a pretty harbour for thousands of boat owners, the city is a popular tourist centre. The main summer attraction is the Kelowna Regatta, begun 1906. JAMES MARSH

Kelsey, Henry, explorer (b at East Greenwich? Eng 1667?; d there and buried 2 Nov 1724). He was apprenticed to the HBC in Mar 1684 and served the company nearly 40 years – all but 3 of them at Hudson Bay. He is chiefly remembered for his journey to the Canadian plains 1690-92. His exact route is unknown, but he left York Factory in June 1690 and with his Indian guides travelled the Hayes and Saskatchewan rivers and wintered near The Pas, Man, before striking out on foot across the prairie, possibly as far as the Red Deer R. Kelsey's journal of the trip, which opens with some curious, rhyming doggerel, describes buffalo, grizzly bears and an Indian group – possibly the Sioux or Gros Ventres. The company's hold on the bay was tenuous, and Kelsey twice negotiated surrender of York to Pierre Le Moyne d'IBERVILLE (1694 and 1697). His reward for loyal service was his appointment as chief trader at Albany (1705) and governor of all the bay posts (1717). *The Kelsey Papers,* a single, paperbound volume dated 1693, were not known to historians before 1926, and mysteries still surround them. JAMES MARSH

Kelso, John Joseph, social reformer (b at Dundalk, Ire 31 Mar 1864; d at Toronto 30 Sept 1935). While a reporter for the *World* and the *Globe*, Kelso founded the Toronto Humane Society in 1887 for the prevention of cruelty to children and animals, the Fresh Air Fund and the Santa Claus Fund in 1888 to provide excursions and cheer for poor women and children, and the Children's Aid Society in 1891. In 1893 he was appointed the first superintendent of neglected and dependent children in Ontario and, until his retirment in 1934, directed the establishment of children's aid societies throughout Ontario and played a key role in their acceptance in other provinces. He also advocated special juvenile courts, mothers' allowances and the legalizing of adoption, and was active in closing reformatories and organizing playgrounds. In these reforms he was not an original thinker but a popularizer and promoter of policies and programs developed elsewhere. After 1895 he was recognized as Canada's leading expert in child welfare and gloried in the title the "children's friend." ROSEMARY SHIPTON

Reading: A. Jones and L. Rutman, *In the Children's Aid: J.J. Kelso and Child Welfare in Ontario* (1981).

Kemp, Sir Albert Edward, businessman, politician (b at Clarenceville, Qué 11 Aug 1858; d at Pigeon Lake, Ont 12 Aug 1929). After establishing himself in business as owner and president of a sheet-metal manufacturing company, Kemp was a Conservative MP for East Toronto, 1900-08 and 1911-21. As minister of militia and defence 1916-17 and minister of the overseas military forces 1917-20, Kemp helped restore order to the chaos created by former defence minister Sam HUGHES, but he was careful not to surrender ministerial authority to the soldiers. He served in the Senate from 1921 until his death. STEPHEN HARRIS

Kempt, Sir James, soldier, colonial administrator (b at Edinburgh, Scot 1764; d at London, Eng 20 Dec 1854). He attained the ranks of lieutenant (1784), captain (1794) and major (1803) in the British army. He saw active service during the Napoleonic Wars in the Mediterranean, the Peninsular War and the Battle of Waterloo. He was promoted lieutenant-colonel and served as quartermaster general of British N America 1807-11, as lieutenant-governor of Nova Scotia 1820-28 and as administrator of the Government of Canada 1828-30. Although seen as little more than a caretaker administration, Kempt's short term in Canada temporarily eased the tensions that had arisen between Gov DALHOUSIE and the Parti patriote led by Louis-Joseph PAPINEAU. DAVID EVANS

Kemptville, Ont, Town, pop 2597 (1986c), 2362 (1981c), inc 1963, located on Kemptville Cr, a branch of the Rideau R, 60 km S of Ottawa. Named after Sir James KEMPT, it was first called Clothier's Mills after Lyman Clothier, who developed it on an 81 ha site. Its growth speeded with the arrival of the Bytown and Prescott Ry, then of the CPR. Once an active manufacturing centre of stoves and leather, it is now an agricultural servicing centre, site of the Kemptville School of Agricultural Technology and of a provincial forestry station. It was the birthplace and home base of G. Howard FERGUSON, premier of Ontario 1923-30. K.L. MORRISON

Kenderdine, Augustus Frederick, painter (b at Manchester, Eng 31 Mar 1870; d at Saskatoon 3 Aug 1947). With James Henderson, he was the most significant painter in Saskatchewan before 1950. He arrived at Lashburn to farm in 1907 and began recording prairie life in his paintings. He trained at the Manchester School of Art and the Académie Julian in Paris, exhibited at the Royal Academy in London, and had an established commercial reputation in England. In keeping with his training, Kenderdine's interpretation of the prairie landscape was romantic. He relied on rich tonal effects and subtle colour to convey with European dignity a sensuous ruggedness in the mood of the Prairies. Kenderdine joined the art department at U Sask in 1920, and in 1935 started the Summer School of Art at Emma Lk, Sask. KATHLEEN LAVERTY

Kennedy, Garry Neill, artist, teacher (b at St Catharines, Ont 6 Nov 1935). Since 1967 he has been president of the Nova Scotia College of Art and Design (Halifax), Canada's only degree-granting art college. Kennedy's other life is that of a nihilist artist, rooted in conceptual art, suspicious of art systems and traditions, and doubtful that valid art is possible unless founded in irony and disenchantment. A series of 1976-77 paintings began from the premise that the traditional reasons for painting were exhausted and that only the craft and the material conditions of painting – paint, brush, canvas – were realities. Scornful of references to taste, he produced a series of unexpectedly strange and beautiful works. With a shrewd sense of humour his subsequent work has probed the systems that operate in museums, commercial galleries and the art world in general. In July 1987, his show "Superstar Shadow" appeared in the Stride Gallery, Calgary. ROALD NASGAARD

Kennedy, Sir John, civil engineer, harbour authority (b at Spencerville, UC 26 Sept 1838; d at Montréal 25 Oct 1921). Educated at McGill, he first worked under Thomas KEEFER on the St Lawrence Ship Channel below Montréal. Attracted by early railway building, he moved to Ontario and became a divisional chief engineer of a branch of the GREAT WESTERN RY. In 1875 he returned to Montréal as chief engineer, Montreal Harbour Commission. For 44 years he was in charge of developing the port to its international status. In 1907 he became blind but continued as consulting engineer to direct all ENGINEERING work for the harbour. A man of wide interests, he presided over the founding meeting of the Canadian Engineering Standards Assn. R.F. LEGGET

Kennedy, John Leo, poet, critic (b at Liverpool, Eng 22 Aug 1907). After immigrating to Montréal in 1912, Kennedy helped change the direction of Canadian poetry in the 1920s and, through critical manifestos and literary journals, shared in avant-garde literary movements (1925-38). After

only 6 years of education, Kennedy took to the sea and then had a variety of jobs. Friend of A.J.M. SMITH, F.R. SCOTT, A.M. KLEIN and Leon EDEL, he contributed to the *McGill Literary Supplement, McGill Fortnightly Review* and *Canadian Mercury* and was part of a politically active circle of intellectuals in Montréal and Toronto in the 1930s and an editor of *New Frontier* 1936-38. In 1933 he published *The Shrouding* (poems) which, marked by a fascination with death and symbolic resurrection, reflects his wit and forceful personality. Most of his life he worked as a copywriter in the US; recently he has lived in Montréal, writing poems for children, satiric verse and broadsides.
PATRICIA MORLEY

Kennedy, Theodore Samuel, Ted or "Teeder," hockey player (b at Humberstone, Ont 12 Dec 1925). He played senior hockey at Pt Colborne and joined TORONTO MAPLE LEAFS 1942-43. Hardworking and tenacious, he typified the powerful, tough checking Maple Leaf teams built by Conn SMYTHE. He lacked skill as a skater but was a resourceful playmaker and scored 231 goals and 560 points in 696 games. He won the HART TROPHY (most valuable player) in his last full season, 1955. He later operated a thoroughbred training centre in St Mary's, Ont. In 1966 he was inducted into the Hockey Hall of Fame. JAMES MARSH

Kennedy, Thomas Laird, farmer, politician, premier of Ontario (b at Dixie [Mississauga], Ont 15 Aug 1878; d there 13 Feb 1959). An army officer in WWI and later a militia brigadier, he was a Conservative member of the Ontario Legislature 1919-34 and 1937-58, serving as minister of agriculture 1930-34 and 1943-53. An amiable, homespun man, he was widely popular and respected among farmers. He was appointed premier temporarily (1948-49) in recognition of long public service. ROGER GRAHAM

Kennedy, William, explorer (b probably at Cumberland House, Rupert's Land 26 Apr 1814; d at St Andrews, Red River Settlement 25 Jan 1890). He was the son of a fur-trading father and an Indian mother, was educated in the Orkney Is and worked for the HUDSON'S BAY CO, 1833-45, serving mostly at posts in Québec. In 1851-52 he led the 13th expedition in search of Sir John FRANKLIN. In what was unknown territory, he and Joseph-René Bellot sledged along the E coast of Somerset I, crossed Bellot Str to Ommanney Bay on Prince of Wales I, then trekked N to Cape Walker and back to base at Batty Bay. Kennedy settled at St Andrews, Man. He was a strong advocate of the annexation of Rupert's Land to Canada and worked diligently for an all-Canadian route from Toronto to the RED RIVER COLONY, and for the development of the seaport at Churchill.
SHIRLEE ANNE SMITH

Kennedy, William Paul McClure, historian, jurist, educator (b at Shankill, Ire 8 Jan 1879; d at Toronto 12 Aug 1963). He was educated at Paris, Vienna and Berlin, and at Trinity College, Dublin, where he majored in modern history, jurisprudence and constitutional law. He came to Canada in 1913 and taught English at St Francis Xavier. In 1915 he was hired by U of T as lecturer in English and history. He was a special lecturer on federal institutions in the dept of political economy 1922, and became professor of law and political institutions 1926. Largely through his efforts a separate department of law was created in 1930, and he became its first head. Kennedy was founder-editor of the U of T *Law Journal* and a prolific author. Through such books as *The Constitution of Canada* (1922) he influenced a generation of students with his "Actonian" view of nationalism. He advised many government commissions, including the federal Royal Commission on DOMINION-PROVINCIAL RELATIONS (1937). He was respected rather than liked; his colleagues found him "mercurial" and "somewhat erratic."
M. BROOK TAYLOR

Reading: C. Berger, *The Writing of Canadian History* (1976).

Keno City, YT, located 122 km NW of the Klondike Hwy, 466 km by road N from Whitehorse. In 1919 Louis Beauvette staked the Roulette silver-lead claim on top of Keno Hill in the Mayo district. The Keno Hill Ltd, a subsidiary of the Yukon Gold Co, purchased Beauvette's claim and 5 others and began mining in 1920. The company established a supply depot and reloading point at the base of the hill. Under the name Keno City, it evolved from a scattering of tents to a settlement with cabins, stables, hotel, assay office, school and liquor store. In the 1930s, falling silver prices and the exhaustion of the principal deposits on Keno Hill reduced mining activity and residents left for work elsewhere. The school was closed in 1931 and the liquor store in 1933. Soon afterward, the site was virtually abandoned and remains as a historic site. Keno gave its name to a popular game of chance played in western mining communities. H. GUEST

Kenojuak Ashevak, artist (b at Ikerrasak camp, S Baffin I, NWT 3 Oct 1927). She is perhaps the best-known Inuk artist because of her famous print *The Enchanted Owl.* The first woman to become involved with the newly established PRINTMAKING shop at Cape Dorset, Kenojuak began drawing in the late 1950s; her works have inspired about 200 prints produced since then. Her drawings, primarily of birds, are characterized by a strong sense of composition, colour, design and draughtsmanship. Although best known as a graphic artist she also carves, making sculptures and (with her late husband Johnniebo) a mural for the 1970 World's Fair in Osaka, Japan. The recipient of numerous awards, including the Order of Canada (Companion in 1982) and participant in many exhibitions, Kenojuak has travelled to southern Canada and Europe. She was featured in a NFB film in 1962 and in a limited-edition book published in 1981. Kenojuak became a member of the Royal Canadian Academy of Arts in 1974 and was given a 30-year retrospective of her work at the McMichael Canadian Collection Gallery (Kleinburg, Ont) in 1986. *See also* INUIT ART; INUIT PRINTMAKING. JEAN BLODGETT

Reading: Jean Blodgett, *Kenojuak* (1985).

Kenora, Ont, Town, pop 9621 (1986c), 9817 (1981c), located on LAKE OF THE WOODS, 50 km E of Manitoba border, seat of Kenora Dist (about 441 000 km^2). The LA VÉRENDRYES built Ft St-Charles on the NW arm of the lake in 1732. Incorporated as Rat Portage by Manitoba 1882 during a boundary dispute with Ontario, and subsequently by Ontario 1892, the current site was renamed Kenora 1905. The name derives from *Ke*ewatin, *No*rman and *Ra*t Portage, interdependent communities clustered where the lake spills into the Winnipeg R. Kenora's scenic location on a major international waterway determined its growth patterns. A prehistoric dependence on caribou, fish and wild rice continued through the FUR-TRADE era. By 1836 the HBC established a post within the present town limits. Construction on the Canadian Pacific railway beginning 1879 brought lumbering, steamships, gold mining, fisheries, hydroelectric development and flour milling. Seaplanes and the TRANS-CANADA HWY (1953) swelled summer traffic. Kenora's economy is based on a pulp-and-paper mill, tourism, CP Rail and government offices. Neighbouring reserves affirm a significant OJIBWA presence.

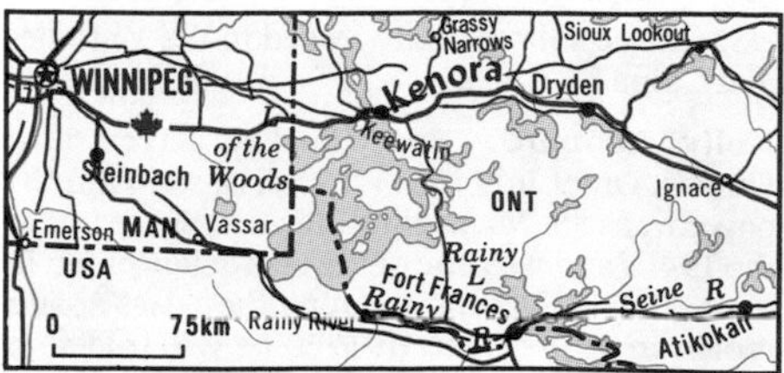

Nearby Manitoba and the US exert a strong social, economic and political influence. ELINOR BARR

Reading: F. Mead, ed, *Through the Kenora Gateway* (1981); F.E. Jackson, *North Wind Blowing Backwards* (1977).

Kensington, PEI, Town, pop 1105 (1986c), 1143 (1981c), is situated 13 km NE of Summerside and 48 km NW of Charlottetown. The largest inland community in the province, Kensington developed at the focus of 5 roads. In 1820, Thomas Barrett and family emigrated from Ireland and settled at "Five Lanes' End." When Barrett established an inn and a tavern, a village began developing, and it was eventually renamed Barrett's Cross. After the change to Kensington was suggested at a town meeting in 1862, the community was again renamed. Owing to its crossroads location, the town received a station when the PEI Railway was constructed in 1873. Today, Kensington is still a commercial centre, although it competes with the larger port town of SUMMERSIDE. W.S. KEIZER

Kent, BC, District Municipality, pop 3741 (1986c), 3394 (1981c), named after the county of Kent in England, and located in the upper Fraser Valley in the lower mainland region of southwestern BC about 127 km E of Vancouver, is bound by the Fraser R on the S and the Harrison R on the W. Farming began in the fertile lowlands of the district in the early 1800s and the Harrison R and Harrison Lk were important during the gold rush of the late 1850s as a route to the interior of BC. Major settlement did not begin until construction in the 1880s, and development was encouraged by highway construction in the 1930s, 1950s and 1960s. The municipality contains the settled areas of Harrison Mills and Agassiz, which is the main population and commercial centre. At the S end of Harrison Lk, but with a separate municipality, is the famous resort and convention centre of Harrison Hot Springs. The federal government's experimental farm at Agassiz was established in 1886 and today Kent is largely agricultural and devoted to dairy and mixed farming. JOHN STEWART

Kent, John, merchant, politician, premier of Newfoundland (b at Waterford, Ire 1805; d at St John's 1 Sept 1872). First elected to the Assembly in 1832, Kent championed Catholic rights and aroused sectarian disorders that led to a modified constitution, 1842-48. Thereafter the Reform movement stalled, especially when Kent accepted an executive appointment as collector of customs 1849-52. However, when Philip LITTLE, a more Reform-minded and less intemperate leader, led the province to self-government in 1855, Kent became colonial secretary and in 1858 succeeded Little as premier. Easily re-elected in 1859 Kent was forced to the polls in 1861 when his government was dismissed by the governor. Kent's campaign, fought along sectarian lines, led to murderous riots and a narrow victory for Protestant Conservatives. He soon retreated from the Liberal leadership and joined a coalition government favouring denominational amalgamation and confederation. His tenure as receiver general, 1865-69, concluded his illustrious political career. JOHN GREEN

Kent, Thomas Worrall, journalist, public servant (b at Stafford, Eng 3 Apr 1922). An Oxford graduate, Kent worked for the *Manchester Guardian* and *The Economist* before coming to Canada, where he became editor of the *Winnipeg Free Press* (1954-59). From 1963 to 1966 he was PM PEARSON's principal policy adviser. He then served as deputy minister in the Departments of Manpower and Immigration and Regional Economic Expansion. He headed Devco (1971-77) and Sydney Steel (1977-79) in NS, headed a royal commission on the press (1980-81), and became dean at Dalhousie (1980-83). He was also fellow-in-residence at the Institute for Research on Public Policy (1985). ROBERT BOTHWELL

Kentville, NS, Town, pop 5208 (1986c), 4974 (1981c), inc 1886, is located on the Cornwallis R, 103 km NW of Halifax. Kentville was settled in the 1760s by New Englanders with lots at the western end of Horton, one of 13 townships established by the NS government after the expulsion of the Acadians. Known to the Micmac as *Penook* ("fording place") and to the New Englanders as Horton Corner, it was, because of its location at a bend in the Cornwallis R, a natural crossing point between Horton and Cornwallis townships. It became shire town of Kings County at the end of the 18th century and, being at the junction of 7 roads, grew into a commercial centre, serving agricultural villages and hamlets in the Annapolis Valley. Named Kentville in honour of Prince Edward, Duke of Kent, in 1826, the community thrived when the Windsor-Annapolis Ry (later Dominion Atlantic) established its headquarters there in 1868 and began shipping Annapolis Valley apples to British markets. Government facilities followed, including a militia installation at Camp Aldershot (1904) and the 183 ha Kentville Regional (agricultural) Research Station (1910), which has been renovated and is now one of the most modern and sophisticated research centres in Canada. Although the British fruit market collapsed with WWI and trucking of freight replaced rail transport, Kentville has survived, remaining the area's financial centre. DEBRA MCNABB

Kenyon, Walter Andrew, archaeologist, museum curator (b near Brantford, Ont 21 Feb 1917; d at Toronto 10 Sept 1986). He joined the ROYAL ONTARIO MUSEUM in 1956 as assistant curator of ethnology, later earning Canada's first PhD degree in ARCHAEOLOGY (U of T, 1967). In 1977 he was appointed curator of the Department of New World Archaeology, a position he held until his retirement in 1982. A specialist in Ontario archaeology, his work led to a greater understanding of European settlement and the developmental history of the HURON and NEUTRAL. His many publications include *The Miller Site* (1968), *The Grimsby Site* (1982), *Mounds of Sacred Earth: Burial Mounds of Ontario* (1986) and *The History of James Bay* (1986). *See also* INDIAN TRADE GOODS. RENÉ R. GADACZ

Keremeos, BC, Village, pop 839 (1986c), 830 (1981c), inc 1956, is located in the fertile bench beside the Similkameen R, 42 km S of Penticton. Its name likely derives from a Salish phrase meaning "wind channel in the mountain." Site of a prehistoric Indian village, the area was visited by fur trader Alexander ROSS in 1813. An HBC post located at Cawston was moved to Keremeos in 1864 and was shut down in 1872. Barrington Price, an Englishman, pre-empted land in 1873, founded a cattle ranch and built a gristmill in 1877. Keremeos Land Co, mainly interested in orchards, was formed in 1906. The Great Northern Ry arrived in 1907. Hedley Camp, an important gold producer, operated nearby 1904-58. Agriculture is the most important economic sector today, with grape growing recently showing an increase. Many roadside stands service the travelling public. Mining is still an important activity. WILLIAM A. SLOAN

Kerr, Illingworth Holey, "Buck," painter, illustrator, writer (b at Lumsden, Sask 20 Aug 1905). Kerr attended Central Technical School, Toronto, and Ontario College of Art. He also studied at Westminster School of Art, London, in 1936 and, returning to Canada, taught at Vancouver School of Art (1945-47). In 1947 he became director of the art department of the Provincial Institute of Technology in Calgary. His early landscape style reflects the influence of Lawren HARRIS in his long, curving brush strokes and emphasis on design. He applied paint heavily, giving relief to an otherwise flat, spatial quality in his work. In later works Kerr has used a broken brushstroke style that creates visual tension to counteract this 2-dimensionality. Named to the Order of Canada in 1983, he was given a retrospective exhibition ("Harvest of the Spirit") at 9 major galleries in 1985. KATHLEEN LAVERTY

Kerr, Robert, track and field athlete, coach (b at Enniskillen, Ire 1882; d at Hamilton, Ont 12 May 1963). Despite the "marathon craze" of the time, Kerr took advantage of the speed required for his occupation as a Hamilton fireman and won the 100-, 440- and 880-yard races at the 1902 Coronation Games. He could not afford to attend the unofficial 1906 Athens Olympics, but at the 1908 London Olympics he won the 220-yard gold and 100-yard bronze. Though he set the 50-yard record and was selected to the 1912 Stockholm Olympics team, Kerr chose retirement. He was captain of the 1928 Olympics team and manager of the 1932 team, the last to win an Olympic gold medal in TRACK AND FIELD for Canada. TED BARRIS

Kerwin, John Larkin, physicist, research director (b at Québec C 22 June 1924). Kerwin joined Laval's physics department in 1946 after study at St Francis Xavier, U of T and Massachusetts Inst of Technology and, after earning his DSc at Laval, rose to become its rector in 1972. He was one of the first French Canadians to specialize in atomic physics, the first layman to become rector of Laval, and the first French Canadian appointed president of the NATIONAL RESEARCH COUNCIL (since 1980). At the NRC he prepared a 5-year expansion plan focused on industrial research and laid the foundations of a closer relationship between the NRC and the Cabinet. In Dec 1987 he received the Outstanding Achievement Award, the highest award for federal public servants. DONALD J.C. PHILLIPSON

Kestrel, *see* FALCON.

Ketchum, Jesse, businessman, politician (b at Spencertown, NY 31 Mar 1782; d at Buffalo, NY 7 Sept 1867). Ketchum moved to Upper Canada as a youth and became a leading merchant and landowner in York [Toronto]. A noted philanthropist, he is most often remembered for his dedicated work to establish common schools, though he himself had little formal education. However, he generously donated time and money to set up benevolent and relief societies, to construct churches, Sunday schools and Bible societies, and the York Mechanics' Institute. In politics Ketchum opposed the FAMILY COMPACT, and helped organize numerous Reform committees and associations. He held office once – from 1828 to 1834 he was in the House of Assembly. He did not participate in the REBELLIONS OF 1837 but following its collapse moved his business to Buffalo. There, Ketchum was soon similarly successful, becoming a leading merchant and a generous philanthropist. VICTOR RUSSELL

Kettle Valley is a dry, forested area in the Okanagan Highland of southern BC. The name relates either to rock formations in the falls at the confluence of the Kettle and COLUMBIA rivers in Washington state or to the shape of baskets woven by Salish there. Bypassed during the gold rush into nearby boundary country in the 1880s, the Kettle Valley developed a stable silver-mining industry after becoming the final link of the railway system between the Kootenays and the Pacific coast. Begun in 1910, the CPR's Kettle Valley Division included a passenger service between Midway and Penticton (terminated 1964) popular with railway buffs. The Highland Bell mine complex has produced silver-bearing ore continuously since 1922. The valley's forests supply sawmills at Midway and Grand Forks and local cattle ranches with forage. PETER GRANT

Keynesian Economics is a method of analysing the behaviour of key aggregate economic variables such as output, employment, inflation and interest rates. British economist John Maynard Keynes initially developed this analytic structure (and as a result virtually established the modern field of macroeconomics) during the 1930s, as a method of understanding the GREAT DEPRESSION. Prior to this time, economists generally believed that cyclical swings in employment and output would be relatively small and self-correcting. This classical approach argued that if overall demand in the economy weakened, causing a temporary drop in production and jobs, the resulting slack labour and product market conditions would force a rapid drop in both wages and prices, which in turn would operate to restore full employment.

The trauma of the Depression severely challenged such an optimistic view of macroeconomic behaviour. In his *General Theory of Employment, Interest and Money* (1936) Keynes argued that rigidities existed that would prevent the necessary equilibrating fall in wages and prices. As a result, a drop in demand could cause a fall in output and employment that was not quickly self-correcting and, indeed, might endure for some time. Keynes also identified a number of characteristics of market economies that would cause any demand decrease to be magnified into an even larger decline in overall demand. For example, worsening business conditions can cause firms to reduce investment in new plants and equipment with a consequent drop in overall expenditures. Keynes argued that the answer to such destabilizing private-sector behaviour was an activist public-sector STABILIZATION policy. He specifically argued for increased government expenditures and lower taxes to raise demand and pull world output and employment out of their Depression slump. Subsequently, some other economists used Keynesian ideas to assert that stabilization policy could be used not only to prevent prolonged economic declines, but also to dampen inflationary booms and to promote high economic growth.

Canadian economics scholar Mabel TIMLIN's book, *Keynesian Economics* (1942) influenced thinkers in Canada and abroad and affected economics teaching in Canadian universities. Canadian government policy also was affected by the new Keynesian concepts, chiefly through the persuasion of several able young civil servants, especially Robert BRYCE, who eventually became deputy minister of finance. Indeed Canada was one of the first countries of the world to commit itself to active use of fiscal (and later monetary) policy to stimulate domestic output and employ-

ment. The buoyant economic period of the 1960s and 1970s seemed to support the appropriateness of such a Keynesian approach. However, the higher rates of both unemployment and inflation from the mid-1970s through the early 1980s caused critics, in academic and government circles, to argue on both theoretical economic and political grounds that Keynesian-style interventions are more likely to increase, rather than dampen, economic fluctuations. Furthermore, they claim that such actions have an inherent inflationary bias which has created severe long-term economic problems both in Canada and in other countries. Keynesian economists counter that many of the difficulties of the last decade can be attributed to events (such as the rapid rise in world oil prices) that are largely outside the control of national economic policies. Furthermore, while they acknowledge that some policy errors have been made, they assert that the application of Keynesian principles has kept the world from experiencing another Depression. In the mid- and late 1980s, the use of active Keynesian FISCAL POLICY in Canada became limited by the large deficits experienced by the federal government. The magnitude of these deficits left very little scope for either stimulative tax cuts or new expenditures. *See also* ECONOMICS.
RONALD G. WIRICK

Keys, David Arnold, physicist (b at Toronto 4 Nov 1890; d at Ottawa 28 Oct 1977). He was a much-loved professor at McGill 1922-47 and thereafter the "mayor of Chalk River" – administrative manager of the Canadian atomic project. After research on antisubmarine warfare with J.C. MCLENNAN in WWI, Keys earned PhDs at both Harvard and Cambridge before joining the McGill physics department in 1922, where he became Macdonald research professor in 1941. His own special field was geophysics, for which he wrote one of the earliest textbooks in 1929. During WWII he was research director of the bureau of technical personnel and organized special classes at McGill that trained 2000 radar technicians for the RCAF. The NATIONAL RESEARCH COUNCIL appointed Keys VP in charge of the Chalk River Nuclear Laboratories in 1947 and he retired in 1961 after serving as London liaison officer for ATOMIC ENERGY OF CANADA LTD. DONALD J.C. PHILLIPSON

Khaki University (initially Khaki College), an educational institution set up and managed by the Canadian Army in Britain, 1917-19 and 1945-46. The program was rooted in the study groups of the Canadian YMCA and the chaplain services of the Canadian Army. The planning and organization of the institution was the work of Dr Henry Marshall TORY, originating in a special report on discharged men from the army, which he wrote at the request of the National Council of the YMCA. In it he recommended that an educational institution be established in one central camp in England, to be called the Khaki College of Canada, with an extension department providing services for every other camp in Great Britain. Tory, on leave as president of U of A, became president of the Khaki College in 1917. By that year, 19 centres of education had been organized in the camps and hospitals in England, with about 50 000 men taking courses – in such subjects as agriculture, business education, mechanics, teacher training, legal studies and medical instruction – through a scheme of popular lectures and the promotion of small study and reading groups. Supporting libraries were established and a uniform set of textbooks was approved by all Canadian provinces. In 1918, the educational work of Khaki College became the educational services of Canadian forces overseas under the general staff of the Canadian Army. Khaki College claims an important place among Canadian educational institutions, and its concept became the forerunner of similar educational programs in the military forces of other countries. Apart from providing morale for demobilized personnel, the university provided many Canadians with an opportunity to continue their education. *See also* ADULT EDUCATION. JAMES A. DRAPER

Reading: E.A. Corbett, "The Khaki University," in *Henry Marshall Tory* (1954).

Khorana, Har Gobind, scientist (b at Raipur, India 9 Jan 1922). His mother was illiterate and his family impoverished. His first class was in the open on the edge of the Rajastan Desert. Khorana's brilliance was obvious early and, with scholarships, he earned degrees in organic chemistry at Punjab U. He obtained a PhD at Liverpool (1948) and then spent 3 years studying proteins and nucleic acids at Cambridge. In spite of his ability, his race precluded him from appointment as a professor in Britain. In search of an outstanding young scientist, Gordon SHRUM, a physicist from UBC, hired Khorana to do organic chemistry at the BC Research Council in Vancouver in 1952. Gifted with a photographic memory, relentless drive, high standards and exquisite experimental dexterity, Khorana soon made an international reputation. Attracting a group of brilliant scholars, he succeeded in synthesizing pure ATP, the cellular source of energy. He made co-enzyme A, a complex molecule, important in metabolism. He showed how enzymes break down DNA, studied cyclic precursors of DNA, and discovered how to join building blocks into chains of DNA. Each discovery opened up new vistas for research.

In 1960 Khorana went to the US where he proved the triplet DNA code and synthesized a gene in a test tube. When he earned a Nobel Prize for medicine in 1968, he pointed out the importance of the Vancouver work and acknowledged 3 scientists, all at UBC. DAVID T. SUZUKI

Kicking Horse Pass, elev 1627 m, straddles the Continental Divide on the BC-Alberta border, 10 km W of LAKE LOUISE. Sir James HECTOR and a party of the PALLISER EXPEDITION explored the pass in 1858. The peculiar name derives from an incident in which Hector was kicked in the chest by a packhorse. The pass was selected as the route for the transcontinental CANADIAN PACIFIC RY, despite its severe inclines; construction was completed in 1884. The steep rail grades of 4.5% on the BC side of the pass were lessened to 2.2% by construction of Spiral Tunnels (1909), now a popular tourist attraction. The pass, which connects Yoho and Banff national parks, is also crossed by the Trans-Canada Hwy. GLEN BOLES

Below Kicking Horse Pass. Despite its severe inclines the pass was chosen as the route for the CPR and later the Trans-Canada Hwy (*photo by J.A. Kraulis*).

Kidd, James Robbins, "Roby," adult educator, internationalist (b at Wapella, Sask 4 May 1915; d at Toronto 21 Mar 1982). Founder and first secretary-general of the International Council for ADULT EDUCATION (ICAE), Kidd was a leader in the movement to recognize adult education as an important field of endeavour in Canada and abroad. Kidd's own formal education was completed while he worked for the YMCA (1935-47) in Montréal, Ottawa and New York, and he was the first Canadian to hold a doctorate in adult education, awarded by Columbia U in 1947. He joined the Canadian Assn for Adult Education in Toronto, in 1947, and worked there 13 years, the last 10 as director. During this period, Kidd was also first executive secretary of the Canadian Film Awards and the Canadian Radio Awards (1947-58). In 1959 he founded the Overseas Book Centre (now Canadian Organization for Development through Education), and in 1961 the Overseas Institute (now Canadian Council for International Cooperation). The ICAE was incorporated in 1973, with 26 countries as members; more than 70 national and regional associations were members in 1984. Kidd was the first chairman of the department of adult education (OISE) from 1965 to 1972 and continued as professor from 1972 until his death; he participated fully in international activities, notably as chairman of the Second Unesco World Conference on Adult Education at Montréal in 1960, and as chairman of the International Committee for the Advancement of Adult Education, 1961-66. He defined the central goal of education as "learning to be, learning to become, learning to belong." His best known book, *How Adults Learn* (1952, rev 1973), has been translated into 14 languages.
SUSANNE MOWAT

Kidder, Margot, movie actress (b at Yellowknife, NWT 17 Oct 1948). With no theatrical training, she performed in numerous Canadian TV shows as a teenager, before being cast in the American movie *Gaily, Gaily* (1969) by director Norman JEWISON. With *The Amityville Horror* (1979) and *Superman* and *Superman II* (1978, 1981), where she played reporter Lois Lane, Kidder achieved widespread recognition. Her starring role in Don SHEBIB's *Heartaches* (1981) won her praise. In the mid-1980s Kidder resumed making TV movies, with *Honky Tonk* (1984), *Picking up the Pieces* (1985) and *Hoax* (1986). During this period she also starred in feature films, including *Trenchcoat* (1983) and *Keeping Track* (1985). ALLAN M. GOULD

Kidnapping, historically, indicated the seizing and carrying away of children to make them slaves or servants or for some other nefarious purpose, eg, the marriage of an infant heiress to acquire a claim to her property. The term now applies to any taking or carrying away of persons against their will, either by transporting them out of the country or by confining them within the country to secure a ransom or some other concession in return for their freedom. Kidnapping is expressly condemned in the Canadian Criminal Code. Anyone who confines or imprisons another against his will, or causes another to be sent without lawful justification out of Canada, or, and this is the most usual and popular conception of the offence, holds another against his will for ransom or services is liable to life imprisonment. It is also an offence to imprison a person unlawfully, not necessarily holding him in a jail, but, for example, without lawful cause detaining him for any purpose, even without seeking a ransom or other concession for his freedom (*see* CIVIL LIBERTIES). Such unlawful imprisonment is punishable by a 5-year sentence. The code treats the kidnapping of a female or a child under 14 as the distinct offence of ABDUCTION, regarding such an act as usually being for sexual purposes. In 1985, there were 1327 reported cases of kidnapping, and 284 charges were laid against 168 males, 80 females and 9 juveniles.

Perhaps the most famous recent case of kidnapping (1970) in Canada was that of James Cross (a

British trade commissioner) and Pierre LAPORTE by the Front de libération du Québec (see OCTOBER CRISIS). The 1973 Treaty on the Prevention and Punishment of Crimes against Diplomats made the kidnapping of diplomats criminal by international law. Canada is a party to this treaty, and under the Criminal Code (s381.1) the kidnapping of a diplomat is recognized as a separate crime.

In connection with activities against terrorism, a number of countries have amended their criminal codes to enable them to try terrorists for acts affecting their nationals, regardless of the nationality of the terrorist or the place where the act of terrorism occurred. Occasionally, this has meant that the offender has been unlawfully captured by authorities of the country in question and his arguments condemning his kidnapping have been rejected, since by international law only a state can complain if its territory or its ships on the high seas are interfered with in any way. L.C. GREEN

Kielley, Edward (or Kielly), surgeon, naval officer (b at St John's *c*1790; d there 8 Mar 1855). A Catholic at peace among Protestants and a conservative who had no wish to engage in the bitterly partisan politics of his day, Kielley was nevertheless catapulted into a controversy that resulted in one of Newfoundland's most celebrated cases in constitutional law. After heated words with a Reform member of the legislature Kielley was arrested, charged with contempt and imprisoned on a warrant issued by the speaker of the assembly. He issued a counterclaim, alleging false imprisonment, and the resulting case, *Kielley* v *Carson*, was carried to the Privy Council. The decision, delivered 11 Jan 1843, supported Kielley, and thereby defined a limit to the powers claimed by colonial assemblies in the British empire, denying them the authority to commit anyone for contempt, a privilege exclusive to the Parliament in London. STANLEY GORDON

Kierans, Eric William, economist, politician, businessman (b at Montréal 2 Feb 1914). Educated at Loyola Coll and McGill, Kierans was director of the School of Commerce at McGill 1953-60, president of the Montreal Stock Exchange 1960-63, and then minister of communications and postmaster general of Canada 1968-71. He achieved political prominence despite brief service in only 2 governments, partly because those governments – Jean LESAGE'S QUIET REVOLUTION (in which he served as minister of revenue 1963-65 and as minister of health 1965-66) and Pierre TRUDEAU'S first Cabinet – made beginnings of significance to Canadian politics and partly because Kierans stirred up controversy outside government. Examples include his attack on Walter GORDON'S 1963 budget; his 1967 challenge to René LÉVESQUE to abandon separatism or quit the Québec Liberal Party; his candidacy for the national Liberal leadership in 1968; and his sustained criticism of Trudeau's economic policies. Although he is often labelled an "economic nationalist," his views are rooted more in his belief in the primacy of politics over economics, his distrust of economic, political and intellectual "monopoly," his insistence that Canada's natural resources belong to the public, and his conviction that things do not improve unless somebody speaks out. Kierans has been visiting lecturer and fellow at UBC (1984), Memorial U (1985) and the Institute for Research on Public Policy (1985). JOHN MCDOUGALL

Reading: J. Swift, *Odd Man Out* (1987).

Killaly, Hamilton Hartley, engineer, civil servant (b at Dublin, Ire 1800; d at Picton, Ont 28 Mar 1874). Killaly attended Trinity Coll, Dublin, and worked as an engineer on canal projects before immigrating to Upper Canada in 1835. He worked on the WELLAND CANAL and in 1841 was appointed chairman of the Board of Public Works of the Province of Canada. Canada was then building CANALS between Lk Erie and Montréal, a program Killaly pursued vigorously and competently. Unfortunately, he was notoriously casual about financial controls and resistant to political restraint, and by 1846 the government had removed him. In 1851, however, he was appointed assistant commissioner of public works. He was soon challenging the chief commissioner, and in 1859 legislative action forced him out. Thereafter, Killaly, responsible for so many public works, worked in various temporary government positions, including a royal commission on fortifications in 1862. DOUG OWRAM

Killam, Izaak Walton, financier (b at Yarmouth, NS 23 July 1885; d at Grand-Cascapedia, Qué 5 Aug 1955). Born into a family of merchants and shipowners, Killam had little formal education but great entrepreneurial drive. He joined the Union Bank of Halifax as a clerk in 1901 and was transferred to head office 2 years later. He befriended Max AITKEN and like him gravitated to Montréal. From 1909 to 1913 Killam managed the London office of Aitken's Royal Securities Corp. In 1915 he became president and 4 years later bought out Aitken, remaining president until 1954. Killam built an investment empire in Canada and Latin America with holdings in publishing, utilities (International Power, Calgary Power, Ottawa Valley Power Co), pulp and paper (BC Pulp and Paper, Mersey Paper), construction and films. The epitome of the financial power of Montréal's St James Street, secretive and austere, Killam was said to be the richest Canadian of his day. In 1922 Killam married Dorothy Brooks Johnston (b at St Louis, Mo 1900?; d at Villefranche-sur-Mer, France 27 July 1965). After his death she more than doubled her $40-million inheritance and carried out her husband's wishes to assist the arts, education and sciences. Initial funding for the CANADA COUNCIL (1957) was largely provided from some $50 million in inheritance taxes on the Killam estate, with a similar amount from the estate of Sir James P. DUNN. Mrs Killam left $30 million to Dalhousie U, $30 million to be divided among 3 other universities, $8 million to the Izaak Killam Hospital for Children in Halifax, $4 million to the Montreal Neurological Inst and a further $15 million to the Canada Council. The Killam Memorial Prize honours Canadian scholars, and Killam research fellowships are presented to Canadian scientists and scholars. DUNCAN MCDOWALL

Reading: D. How, *Canada's Mystery Man of High Finance* (1986).

Killam, Thomas, merchant, shipowner, politician (b at Yarmouth, NS 8 Feb 1802; d at Digby, NS 15 Dec 1868). He became the central figure in a group of related families who dominated the commercial and social activities of Yarmouth from the 1840s into the 1860s. He was the senior partner of Thomas Killam and Co 1849-62, a marine-insurance company director 1837-57, and on the board of the Bank of Yarmouth 1865-66. He emerged from municipal politics to become an influential member of the Legislative Assembly 1847-67 and the first MP for Yarmouth County in 1867. GERRY PANTING

Killarney, Man, Town, pop 2318 (1986c), 2356 (1981c), inc 1903 (village), 1907 (town), is an agricultural and recreational centre on Killarney (formerly Oak) Lk, 230 km SW of Winnipeg and 20 km N of the Canada-US border. The area and nearby Turtle Mt were traversed by native hunters, fur traders and explorers. Métis settled near Rock and Pelican lakes in the mid-1800s. Eastern Canadian and British squatters followed in the late 1870s, and then French, Belgian, Dutch, Mennonite and central European homesteaders. A struggling crofter settlement of Scottish labourers and fishermen was established in 1888-89. Although Killarney was founded in 1880-81, it did not boom until the arrival of the Manitoba Southwestern Colonization Railway (1885). The boom lasted until about 1911. In later years, Killarney became a key service and shipping centre for area farmers. By 1896 cottages had appeared at Killarney Lk, beginning one of several recreational resources in the area. D.M. LYON

Killiniq Island, 269 km^2, is located off the northern tip of the Labrador Pen on the S side of the entrance to HUDSON STR. The provincial boundary passes across the island, so that its eastern portion belongs to Newfoundland and the rest is part of the NWT. It is only 29 km long and about 13 km wide, with a high, rocky coastline, and is separated from the mainland by the narrow, steep-sided Maclelan Str. Port Burwell [Kiliniq] on the SW side of the island has been an important arctic harbour since the 1880s. Sheltered behind precipitous cliffs, it has been the site of an Inuit camp, a trading post and a MORAVIAN mission. . DANIEL FRANCIS

Kimberley, BC, City, pop 6732 (1986c), 7375 (1981c), inc 1944, is located on the slope (elev 1120 m) of Sullivan and North Star mountains, 29 km NW of Cranbrook. Since the Sullivan and North Star mines were discovered 1892, Kimberley has been mainly a mining centre. Consolidated Mining and Smelting gained control of the Sullivan Mine 1920 and used advanced technology to separate the ore components. By 1937 the Sullivan was the largest zinc-lead-silver mine in the world, producing 10% of the world's output. Tin and iron were processed at Kimberley until 1972. By-products led to the building of a fertilizer plant. Cominco has begun mechanization of its methods to increase productivity and improve working conditions. Renowned for its sports, Kimberley won the Allan Cup and the World Hockey Championship 1937-38 and the Allan again 1978. Its downtown renewal on a "Bavarian" theme and potential expansion of ski facilities promise a future as a tourist centre. WILLIAM A. SLOAN

Kincardine, Ont, Town, pop 5833 (1986c), 5778 (1981c), inc 1875, is located along the shore of Lk Huron, about 225 km NW of Toronto and 80 km SW of Owen Sound. In the earliest settled part of Bruce County, the community was first named Penetangore (1848). It was subsequently named (1851) for the earl of ELGIN and Kincardine, governor general of N America 1847-54. By 1867 it had 5 hotels and numerous services and small

Lighthouse and Huron Terrace Bridge at Kincardine Harbour, Ont (*photo by Sean Murphy*).

industries, including cabinet shops, 4 carriage and wagon shops, waterpowered gristmills and sawmills, 2 foundries, pearl-ash factories, woolen factories, blacksmiths, tinsmiths, tanneries, harness and saddlery shops, a bakery and confectionery, and a brewery. Until the mid-1960s the town still had some notable furniture factories, but today it depends on summer tourists and particularly on the Bruce Nuclear Power Development about 16 km N. More than 1000 ONTARIO HYDRO employees live within the municipality, despite the closure of the Douglas Point plant – one part of the Bruce development – in May 1984. JAMES J. TALMAN

Kindergarten, conceived by Friedrich Froebel in 19th-century Germany, refers to a program of education of 4- and 5-year-old children. Although Canada's first public-school kindergartens were established in Berlin [Kitchener], Ont (1882), Toronto (1883) and Hamilton (1885), kindergarten programs in public schools are not yet available to all Canadian children. Whether public or private, kindergartens continue to reflect Froebel's belief that education must be attuned to the child's level of development and his belief in play as an avenue for learning. Recently, however, the extent to which kindergarten should emphasize the preparation of children for the school's academic program has become an issue. Some educators see such emphasis as desirable; others believe it would detract from kindergarten's historic concern with the development of the "whole child."
ELLEN M. REGAN

Kindersley, Sask, Town, pop 4912 (1986c), 3969 (1981c), inc 1911, is located in W-central Saskatchewan, 200 km SW of Saskatoon and 65 km E of the Alberta border. The town quickly developed into a service centre for the surrounding agricultural area after the CNR laid steel through the townsite in 1909. By 1911 it had a population more than 1000. Sir Robert Kindersley, a heavy stockholder in CNR at that time, was honoured by having the town named after him. Agriculture remains the most important element in Kindersley's economy; however, oil and natural-gas wells north of the town have provided some diversification. DON HERPERGER

Kindle, Edward Martin, paleontologist, sedimentologist (b at Franklin, Ind 10 Mar 1869; d at Ottawa 29 Aug 1940). Educated at U of Indiana, Cornell and Yale, Kindle moved from the staff of the US Geological Survey to that of the GEOLOGICAL SURVEY OF CANADA as an invertebrate paleontologist in 1912. He was chief of the PALEONTOLOGY division 1919-38. His early work was mainly on the Palaeozoic fossils of north-central US, Greenland, Alaska and northern Canada. Later, he made pioneer observations and experiments on the origin and significance of sedimentary deposits. He wrote on the resources and development of the N American Subarctic, and he inaugurated a catalogue of Devonian type fossils. Under him the paleontological research and museum displays of the Geological Survey were greatly expanded. L.S. RUSSELL

King, Allan Winton, filmmaker (b at Vancouver 6 Feb 1930). King was involved in the Vancouver Film Society before joining CBC Vancouver in 1954. He formed his own company in England in 1961 to produce documentaries, and at the time shot his first dramatized documentary, *Running Away Backwards* (1964). He returned to Canada in 1967 and soon commanded international attention with 2 documentaries, *Warrendale* (1967) and *A Married Couple* (1969). His growing interest in fiction resulted in the "staged" documentary *Come on Children* (1973). Devoting his attention to drama, he directed a number of distinguished films for the CBC: *A Bird in the House* (1974), *Six War Years* (1975), *Red Emma* (1976) and *One Night Stand* (1977). He made a successful transition to the fiction feature with his adaptation of W.O. MITCHELL'S WHO HAS SEEN THE WIND (1977); his second dramatic feature, *Silence of the North* (1981), was not a commercial or critical success. He returned to the documentary form with the controversial film on unemployment, *Who's in Charge?* (1983). King was given a retrospective of his work at Canada House, London, Eng, in 1985. PIERS HANDLING

King, George Edwin, lawyer, politician, judge, premier of NB 1872-78 (b at Saint John 8 Oct 1839; d at Ottawa 7 May 1901). First elected MLA for Saint John in 1867, he was minister without portfolio in the Confederation Cabinet of A.R. WETMORE. In 1870 he won the election as government leader but resigned to a stronger leader, G.L. HATHEWAY. As attorney general, King was chief architect of the NB Common Schools Act of 1871, which aroused religious and cultural animosity (*see* NEW BRUNSWICK SCHOOL QUESTION). In 1872 he was chosen Liberal-Conservative premier, retiring in 1878. He was appointed judge of the NB Supreme Court in 1880 and was raised to the Supreme Court of Canada in 1893.
DELLA M.M. STANLEY

King, William Frederick, astronomer (b at Stowmarket, Eng 19 Feb 1854; d at Ottawa 23 Apr 1916). King worked as a Dominion land surveyor and topographical surveyor in western Canada. With E.G. DEVILLE and O.J. KLOTZ he formed the astronomical branch of the Dept of the Interior and was appointed chief astronomer in 1890. A small observatory, built in 1890, was succeeded in 1905 by the larger Dominion Observatory, of which he was named first director. He directed plans for the 72-inch (1.8 m) telescope at the Dominion Astrophysical Observatory in Victoria, BC, but died before its completion. He was appointed superintendent of the Geodetic Survey of Canada, was named international boundary commissioner several times and was awarded the CMG for his work. He was a president of the Royal Soc of Canada and founding president of the Ottawa centre of the Royal Astronomical Soc of Canada. MALCOLM THOMSON

King, William Lyon Mackenzie, politician, prime minister of Canada 1921-26, 1926-30 and 1935-48 (b at Berlin [Kitchener], Ont 17 Dec 1874; d at Ottawa 22 July 1950), grandson of William Lyon MACKENZIE. Leader of the LIBERAL PARTY 1919-48, and prime minister for almost 22 of those years, King was the dominant political figure in an era of major changes. King graduated from U of T in 1895 and studied economics at Chicago and Harvard. In 1900 he became Canada's first deputy minister of labour; in 1908 he was elected in North York as a Liberal and in 1909 entered Sir Wilfrid LAURIER's Cabinet as minister of labour.

His interest in labour coincided with an expansion in manufacturing and a concern with industrial relations. King acted as conciliator in a number of strikes, his major legislative achievement being the Industrial Disputes Investigation Act of 1907, which delayed strikes or lockouts in public utilities or mines until a conciliation board achieved a settlement or published a report. He was defeated in the 1911 federal election and the 1917 CONSCRIPTION election. He maintained his connections with the Liberal Party, but during the war acted as a labour consultant and was employed by the Rockefeller Foundation. His book *Industry and Humanity* (1918) outlined his view that there were 4 parties to industry – capital, management, labour and society – and that the government, acting on behalf of society, had an interest in the peaceful resolution of industrial disputes.

William Lyon Mackenzie King
Tenth Prime Minister of Canada

Name: William Lyon Mackenzie King
Birth: 17 Dec 1874, Berlin [Kitchener], Ont
Father/Mother: John/Isabel Mackenzie
Father's Occupation: Lawyer
Education: Harvard U, U of T, U of Chicago; Cambridge, Mass
Religious Affiliation: Presbyterian
First Occupation: Civil servant
Last Private Occupation: Civil servant
Political Party: Liberal
Period(s) as PM: 29 Dec 1921 - 28 June 1926; 25 Sept 1926 - 7 Aug 1930; 23 Oct 1935 - 15 Nov 1948
Ridings: Waterloo North, Ont, 1908-11; Prince, PEI 1919-21; York North, Ont, 1921-25; Prince Albert, Sask, 1926-45
Other Ministries: Labour 1909-11
External Affairs 1921-26
Died: 22 July 1950 at Ottawa
Cause of Death at Age: Pneumonia at 75
Burial Place: Toronto
Other Information: Longest total duration as PM

(photo 8 May 1945, courtesy National Archives of Canada/C-26989.)

At the 1919 Liberal convention King was appointed Laurier's successor. Two years later the Liberals won a bare majority in the federal election and King became prime minister. He set out to regain the confidence of the farmers in Ontario and western Canada who had supported the new PROGRESSIVE PARTY, but his reductions in tariffs and freight rates were not enough, and after the 1925 election the Liberals could stay in office only with Progressive support. During the first session of the new Parliament, when it was clear this support would be withdrawn because of a scandal in the Dept of Customs, King asked Gov Gen Viscount BYNG for a dissolution. Byng refused and called on Arthur MEIGHEN to form a Conservative government, which was defeated in the House a few days later. In the 1926 election King stressed the alleged unconstitutionality of Meighen's government, but the Liberal victory stemmed from the support of Progressives who preferred the Liberals to the high-tariff Conservatives (*see* KING-BYNG AFFAIR).

In the prosperous years after 1926 the Liberal government provided a cautious administration which reduced the federal debt. Its only initiative was an OLD-AGE PENSION scheme. King insisted on Canadian autonomy in relations with the UK and contributed to the definition of Dominion status at the 1926 Imperial Conference. In 1930 he was reluctant to acknowledge that there was an economic crisis and the Liberals were defeated by the Conservatives under R.B. BENNETT.

King was an effective Opposition leader, keeping his party united as he attacked Bennett for unfulfilled promises and rising unemployment and deficits. His only alternative policy, however, was to reduce trade barriers. In 1935 the Liberal Party campaigned on the slogan "King or Chaos," and was returned to office with a comfortable majority. King negotiated trade agreements with the US in 1935 and with the US and Great Britain in 1938. The economic downturn in 1937 left the government with high relief costs but no coherent economic response. King was forced to pay more attention to international affairs, from the Ethiopian crisis to the Munich crisis, and he hoped war could be averted through appeasement. He insisted that the Canadian Parliament would decide on Canada's participation if war came, and to make such a decision more palatable, particularly to French Canadians, he promised there would be no conscription for overseas service. Britain declared war on Germany in Sept 1939; the Canadian Parliament was recalled in an emergency session, and, with only token opposition, declared that Canada was at war.

King called a snap election early in 1940 and his government was returned with an increased majority. Co-operation between the government and business and labour leaders shifted Canadian industrial production to a wartime footing. The remarkable industrial expansion involved special financial arrangements with the US and economic planning on a continental scale. Early German victories led some Canadians to advocate conscription but, fearing a political crisis, King tried to compromise. He introduced conscription for the defence of Canada in 1940. In a 1942 plebiscite a majority of Canadians favoured relieving the government of its promise not to introduce conscription for overseas service, but Québec voters were opposed. High casualties in 1944 and a declining rate of voluntary enlistment led to prolonged debates within the government and the resignation of the minister of defence, James Layton RALSTON. In Nov, King abruptly agreed to send some of the home-defence forces to Europe, a decision grudgingly accepted, even by French Canadians.

To placate Canadians who feared the return of the Depression after the war and who looked to the government for greater social security, King introduced UNEMPLOYMENT INSURANCE in 1940, and his reconstruction program, based on KEYNESIAN ECONOMICS, included family allowances and proposals for health insurance. The Liberals narrowly won the 1945 election. King did not play a decisive role in the postwar era, preferring a minimal role for the government at home and abroad. He was persuaded to resign as prime minister in 1948 and was succeeded by Louis ST. LAURENT. He died 2 years later.

Mackenzie King has continued to intrigue Canadians. Critics argue that his political longevity was achieved by evasions and indecision, that he failed to provide creative leadership; his defenders argue that King gradually altered Canada, a difficult country to govern, while keeping the nation united. Recent revelations show that this apparently proper and colourless man was a spiritualist, in frequent contact with his mother and other dead relatives and friends.

H. BLAIR NEATBY

Reading: R.M. Dawson wrote the first vol of the official biography *W.L. Mackenzie King 1874-1923* (1958), followed by 2 vols by H. Blair Neatby for the years 1923-32 and 1932-39 (1963, 1976). J.W. Pickersgill and D.F. Forster edited King's diary as *The Mackenzie King Record* (4 vols, 1960-70); C.P. Stacey, *A Very Double Life* (1976), and J.E. Esberey, *Knight of the Holy Spirit* (1980), discuss King's personality.

Of 87 species of kingfisher worldwide, only one occurs in Canada: the belted kingfisher (*Megaceryle alcyon*), which dives headfirst into water to capture prey, often submerging completely (*photo by Tim Fitzharris*).

King-Byng Affair The 29 Oct 1925 federal election returned 101 Liberals (government), 116 Conservatives and 28 Progressives, Labour and Independents. The new Parliament supported the minority Liberal government until 25 June 1926, when it defeated a motion to remove censure from a motion of censure. PM Mackenzie KING asked Gov Gen VISCOUNT BYNG to dissolve Parliament, the motion of censure being still under debate. Byng refused. A request for dissolution while a motion of censure was under debate was unprecedented. The previous election, only 8 months before, had been held at King's request; an alternative government in the existing Parliament seemed possible. King resigned, and Conservative leader Arthur MEIGHEN was asked to form a government and did. The new government won 4 critical votes, including one of censure of the King government, but was defeated on a fifth. The House had now censured both governments; no alternative in the existing House was now possible. Byng granted Meighen a dissolution, and King won the ensuing election.

EUGENE A. FORSEY

King George's Sound Company (Richard Cadman Etches and Co), fd 1785 in London to trade for furs on the Northwest Coast. Nathaniel Portlock and George Dixon, veterans of James COOK's third voyage, commanded the company's first 2 vessels, which were licensed by the SOUTH SEA COMPANY and the EAST INDIA COMPANY. The company effectively merged on 23 Jan 1789 with that of John Meares, and its commercial activities virtually ended with the NOOTKA SOUND CONTROVERSY that year.

BARRY M. GOUGH

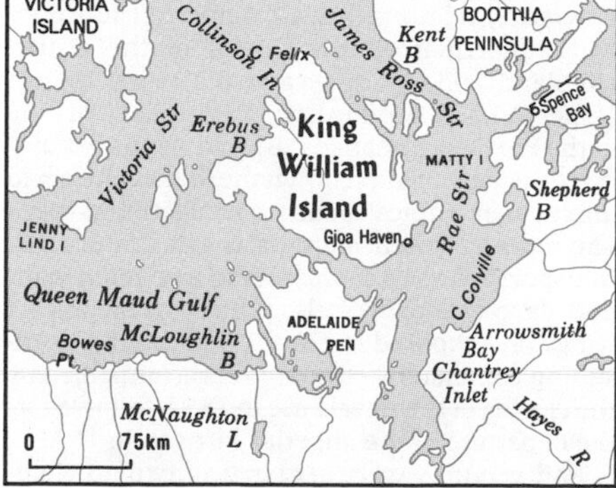

King William Island, 13 111 km², in the ARCTIC ARCHIPELAGO, is a lake-studded, gently rolling plain, with a maximum elevation of 137 m. Its vegetation, a polar semidesert, serves as summer range for mainland caribou. It was discovered 1830 by Sir John ROSS and named after the British monarch King William IV. Remains of the ill-fated Franklin expedition have been found here. *See also* FRANKLIN SEARCH.

S.C. ZOLTAI

Kingbird, *see* FLYCATCHER, TYRANT.

Kingfisher (Alcedinidae), family of robust birds, with large heads, strong, pointed bills, short tails and small feet. The middle and outer toes are joined together for over half their length. The family comprises 87 species worldwide. The only representative in Canada, the belted kingfisher (*Megaceryle alcyon*), is 30-33 cm long, white underneath and blue grey on the back, with a large, ragged, double crest on its head. Belted kingfishers defend feeding territories along edges of water bodies.

Kingfishers perch on dead branches, watching for minnows, frogs and large aquatic insects. They dive headfirst into the water to capture prey, often submerging completely. Prey are returned to the perch, struck against it several times, tossed into the air and swallowed headfirst. Nests are burrows, 1-3 m long, dug into dirt banks. Once the female starts incubating the 5-8 white eggs, the male feeds her on the nest. Newly hatched kingfishers intertwine into a compact mass for warmth. Burrows are often reused in subsequent years, regurgitated fish scales and bones from the previous season supplying nesting material.

PHILIP H.R. STEPNEY

Kinglet, tiny, highly active, insectivorous songbird, olive grey with brightly coloured crown, sharp, slender bill and short, stubby tail. Kinglets belong to the large (about 1400 species) Old World family Muscicapidae, subfamily Sylviinae (Old World warblers). This subfamily was sometimes elevated to family status. In Canada, it is represented by golden-crowned kinglet (*Regulus satrapa*), ruby-crowned kinglet (*R. calendula*) and blue-gray GNATCATCHER. Kinglets summer in forested parts of Canada, from Aklavik, NWT, southeast to northern Québec and then into the US, parts of Mexico and the Guatemalan highlands. They are migratory, although both species winter in southern Canada, where they frequent coniferous and mixed-deciduous woodland. Breeding occurs from mid-May to mid-July. Nests are pensile (suspended) or semipensile, made of moss and lichens, and take up to a month to build. Clutch includes 5-11 eggs. Kinglets are parasitized, rarely, by brown-headed cowbirds (*Molothrus ater*). Ruby-crowns have a loud, bubbling, musical song; that of golden-crowns is similar but higher-pitched. The scrub-dwelling arctic warbler (*Phylloscopus borealis*) occurs only accidentally in Canada. J.C. BARLOW

Kings Landing Historical Settlement, an outdoor museum covering about 160 ha, established in the early 1960s in the tranquil beauty of the Saint John R valley about 40 km W of Fredericton, NB. It is a crown corporation under the New Brunswick Historical Resources Administration, a provincial government department. Officially opened in 1974, the settlement contains more than 70 restored buildings, including homes, a school, store, church, forge, carpenter's shop and inn. This living-history site depicts the period from the LOYALIST era to late Victorian times. A unique attraction is a reproduction of a pre-Confederation Saint John R woodboat. ROBERT S. ALLEN

Kings Landing, NB (*photo by Malak, Ottawa*).

King's Posts, a name applied during the French regime to FUR TRADE and fishing posts in the King's Domain (Domaine du Roy), the vast territory N of the St Lawrence R to the Hudson Bay watershed, between the E end of the seigneury of Les Éboulements (E of Québec City) and Cape Cormorant. The land was owned by the king but leased to a private company; posts included TADOUSSAC, CHICOUTIMI, SEPT-ÎLES and LA MALBAIE. The term "King's Posts" was also applied to forts farther N toward Hudson Bay, such as Mistassini, and farther W, such as Lachine, FT FRONTENAC, Ft Rouillé and FT DUQUESNE. After the CONQUEST the King's Domain was leased to private individuals and companies, including the HBC (1842-59). In 1859 the government took over the administration of the land, continuing to lease fishery and timber rights, while the HBC continued to operate several fur-trade posts. *See also* CARTOGRAPHY.

Kingsmere, Qué, a property left to the nation by former PM William Lyon Mackenzie KING (although it is not named for him, but an early pioneer family), is administered by the NATIONAL CAPITAL COMMISSION. Located in Gatineau Park 12 km from Hull, Qué, it began as a small lakefront property purchased by King in 1903. It grew over the years into an estate of some 240 ha where King would walk his guests – among whom were the Duke of Windsor and Winston Churchill – over miles of nature trails and where from May to October he conducted much of the nation's business. It included 5 country homes, barns, garages, gardens and the Moorside ruins, a peculiar collection of materials from old Ottawa buildings. "The Farm" is the residence of the Speaker of the House of Commons. CLAUDINE PIERRE-DESCHÊNES

Kingsmill, Sir Charles Edmund, naval officer, public servant (b at Guelph, Canada W 7 July 1855; d at Portland, Ont 15 July 1935). He joined the Royal Navy as a midshipman in 1869, served in the Sudan in 1884 and as British vice-consul and agent at Zeyla, Aden. He rose to captain by 1898 and subsequently commanded ships on the Australia, China and Home stations. In 1908 he retired from the RN as a rear-admiral and took charge of the Canadian Marine Service. He played a prominent role in the founding of the Royal Canadian Navy in 1910, and, as vice-admiral, became the first director of the Naval Service. He commanded the RCN throughout WWI and was promoted admiral in 1917. MARC MILNER

Kingston, Ont, City, pop 55 050 (1986c), 52 616 (1981c), located at the eastern end of Lk ONTARIO, 170 km SW of Ottawa. Former capital of the PROVINCE OF CANADA, its position at the junction of the Great Lks and ST LAWRENCE R has been crucial to its economic and political history.

Settlement and Development The French entered the region 1673 and constructed a fort and trading post on the site, Ft Cataraqui, which developed into the elaborate FT FRONTENAC, and became an important base for mounting military forays against the Iroquois and the British to the S and explorations along the lakes to the W. In 1758 the fort was captured by the British.

In 1784 the British government negotiated with the Mississauga who were occupying this area for lands on which to settle LOYALISTS from the American colonies. King's Town, as it was then named (in honour of King George III), was made capital of the new district (Mecklenberg) encompassing townships along the Upper St Lawrence and eastern end of Lk Ontario. The town was not negatively affected by the WAR OF 1812. Instead the significant military and naval presence there stimulated the local economy. Being at the junction of lake and river transport, Kingston was also the site of much transshipment activity for the chief staples of the export trade, lumber and grain, and for inward-moving merchandise and passengers. The construction of the RIDEAU CANAL, linking Upper and Lower Canada by the Ottawa R rather than the vulnerable St Lawrence, reinforced this commercial function. Kingston remained the capital of the district (Midland) and rapidly became the largest town in Upper Canada, serving briefly as capital 1841-43 of the Province of Canada. By mid-century, however, the flow of grain down the St Lawrence had diminished; improvements in navigation of the St Lawrence allowed more through traffic; rail transport became a competitor to water transport, and larger lake vessels posed problems for Kingston's exposed and shallow harbour. The resulting commercial erosion was accompanied by the closing of the naval base in 1852, followed by the departure of the imperial garrison in 1871.

The Customs House is one of the imposing 19th-century buildings preserved in Kingston (*courtesy Environment Canada, Parks/Heritage Recording Services*).

Rail ventures were explored to extend Kingston's hinterland, leading to its inclusion in 1856 in the E-W GRAND TRUNK RY system. By the 1880s the Kingston-Pembroke railway had trains running over 160 km N to Renfrew. Despite offers of bonuses and tax relief, Kingston could not attract significant capital. Not until WWII, with its stimulus of shipbuilding and other productivity, did large new industries (Alcan Aluminium, DuPont Nylon) enter the city's economy.

Kingston's society and economy have a distinctive institutional base instead. FORT HENRY, the ROYAL MILITARY COLLEGE, the National Defence College and the extensive military establishment at Barriefield are part of a continuing military presence in the city. Similarly the Provincial Penitentiary, opened in 1835, led governments to locate a number of other federal and provincial correctional institutions in Kingston and its environs. "Queen's College at Kingston," a college of the Presbyterian Church in Canada, was founded in 1841, developed into QUEEN'S UNIVERSITY, and by the early 20th century had a national reputation in arts and science, medicine and theology. Finally, hospitals and other medical establishments, along with branch offices of government agencies, are part of the institutional presence in Kingston. Lacking dominant industries and significant population increase, Kingston retains much of the physical fabric and employment structure of its 19th-century form.

Cityscape As in the original town plot of 1783, Kingston's downtown continues to be focused on the few blocks around Princess (Store) and Brock streets between Barrie and Ontario, near the waterfront. Apart from commercial activities, it is characterized by edifices of institutional and architectural note. The imposing KINGSTON CITY HALL and magnificent St George's Cathedral are the focal points of several buildings from the last century. The Customs House, Grand Trunk and Kingston and Pembroke stations, MARTELLO TOWERS and Ft Frontenac all reflect a former way of

The Kingston City Hall was begun in 1842, after Kingston had been named capital of Canada. It was completed in 1844 though the capital had been moved the previous year (*courtesy Environment Canada, Parks/Heritage Recording Services*).

life. A few blocks away are Kingston's residential areas, featuring the city's traditional limestone construction. There are grand contemporary residences as well, making Kingston a pleasing mixture of architectural styles reflecting the community's different periods of construction and social structure.

Since 1945, suburbanization – particularly to the W in Kingston Township and Ernestown Township (in such communities as La Salle Park, Collins Bay and Amherstview) – has been a feature of Kingston's urban growth. After a shift of much retailing to suburban shopping malls in the 1960s and 1970s, the city's waterfront has witnessed a major revitalization through the introduction of condominiums, hotels, restaurants, apartment houses and boutiques.

Population Kingston's failure to grow economically in the 19th century on a scale with other large Ontario communities such as Toronto, Hamilton and Ottawa has meant a slow population growth, even some periods of decrease. From a permanent population of about 2000 just after the War of 1812, the city grew to almost 12 000 by mid-century and 14 000 by 1881. With 30 000 in 1941, population expanded beyond the city limits after WWII into the Kingston Urban Area. By 1986 approximately 54 000 of the KUA population resided outside the city, in Kingston, Ernestown and Pittsburgh townships.

Kingston was bypassed by the immigrants of the late 19th and early 20th centuries. From 59% in 1851, its foreign-born population decreased to 14% in 1951. Over 75% of this group were British, Irish or American born. Only in the 1960s and 1970s did a more ethnically diverse population develop, with substantial groups of PORTUGUESE, ITALIANS, DUTCH and Asians. Even so, the city remains predominantly Anglo-Celtic in its heritage and social structures.

Economy As commercial activities eroded in the late 1800s, institutional employers, such as the university, penitentiaries, the military and hospitals, became more important in the city's economy. In the period up to 1940 some industries such as Canadian Locomotive Co and Kingston Cotton Mills were attracted, but these were the exceptions. Others were added by the early 1950s – Alcan, DuPont and Celanese Canada. By 1987 these 3, with Northern Telecom, employed 3698, whereas institutional employers, with more than 18 000, still dominate the employment picture.

Government and Politics Though governed by English law as part of Upper Canada under the CONSTITUTION ACT, 1791, Kingston was a "police town" until well into the 19th century, administered by the Court of Quarter Sessions. In 1838 Kingston was incorporated as a town with a mayor and elected aldermen and councillors serving 4 wards. John A. MACDONALD promoted Kingston's incorporation as a city (1846), and a new 20-man council of councillors and aldermen who elected the mayor from among themselves was created. In 1850 Kingston extended its limits to annex some outer suburbs, but not until 1952 were the city's limits again extended – W to Cataraqui Cr and N to the present Hwy 401. With the city's shortage of land for industrial and residential development – readily available in the adjoining townships – some are promoting a regional government system for the KUA.

Cultural Life Kingston has a diverse cultural life, with a symphony orchestra of some distinction, several local theatre groups, the Agnes Etherington Art Centre and a full calendar of visiting artists, scholars and entertainers. Queen's and the military have long contributed to the musical, theatrical and general cultural scene, and St George's Cathedral choir has achieved recognition beyond the community. The *Whig Standard* is

one of Canada's oldest newspapers. Among Kingston's tourist attractions are Ft Henry, BELLEVUE HOUSE (the home of Canada's first prime minister), the Thousand Islands, the Rideau Canal and the architecture of "Old Kingston."

Kingston's chief claim to sporting fame rests on Queen's football "Gaels," the Kingston Canadians hockey team, and the superlative sailing throughout the waters of the Bay of Quinte area. Portsmouth Village site, developed for the 1976 sailing Olympics, hosts the annual Canadian Olympic Regatta Kingston. BRIAN S. OSBORNE

Reading: Brian S. Osborne and Donald W. Swainson, *Kingston: Building on the Past* (1988); J. Roy, *Kingston: The King's Town* (1952).

Kingston, George Templeman, meteorologist, (b at Oporto, Portugal 5 Oct 1816; d at Toronto 21 Jan 1886). For successfully promoting and organizing one of Canada's first scientific services, Kingston has been called the father of Canadian METEOROLOGY. He was a Cambridge graduate and came to Canada in 1852; 3 years later he became professor of meteorology at U of T and director of the Toronto Observatory, a position he held until 1880. He was founding director of the national meteorological service 1871-80. With new federal resources in 1871-72, he initiated a daily exchange of weather data with the US and a few years later began the dissemination of daily storm warnings and weather forecasts to eastern ports and cities. MORLEY THOMAS

Kingston City Hall and market was begun in 1842, a year after Kingston had been named capital of the Province of Canada. Designed by George BROWNE Sr, one of Canada's leading architects of the 19th century, it was an ambitious plan for the period. All civic offices – the town hall, municipal offices, post office, custom house, police station, market hall and mechanics' institute – were to be housed in one massive complex. Its heroic scale would have dwarfed all surrounding buildings and reflected the pride of the city fathers in the new status and future growth of their city. Though the capital was moved in 1843, the building was completed the following year. The city hall and market was Browne's most important commission and the design, with its dome and monumental portico which dominated the main façade, represented a superb example of civic architecture in a neoclassical style. *See also* ARCHITECTURE, DEVELOPMENT OF. JANET WRIGHT

Reading: M. Angus, *The Old Stones of Kingston* (1966).

Kinsella, William Patrick, writer (b at Edmonton 25 May 1935). Educated at U of Vic and U of Iowa, Kinsella taught at U of C 1978-83. In 7 books of stories and 2 novels to date, he has created 2 quite disparate fictional universes. The first, set largely on the Hobbema Reserve in central Alberta, focuses sympathetically on the lives of Indians in their perennial skirmishes with blundering white institutions and bureaucracies. The second – which has won Kinsella an American audience – deals with the world of baseball, a world often leavened with a touch of the surreal, the magical or the fantastic. *Dance Me Outside* (1977) was the first of Kinsella's several story collections; the novel *Shoeless Joe* (1982), which won both the Houghton Mifflin Literary Fellowship in 1982 and the *Books in Canada* Award for First Novel in 1983, is the best known of his baseball fictions. His recent works are a novel, *The Iowa Baseball Confederacy* (1985), and 3 collections of short stories, *The Alligator Report* (1985), *The Fencepost Chronicles* (1986, won the 1987 Stephen Leacock Medal) and *Red Wolf, Red Wolf* (1987). NEIL BESNER

Kinsmen Clubs, The Association of, a uniquely Canadian organization of young business and professional men between the ages of 21 and 45 gathered together for personal development, community service and social activities. Kinsmen is Canada's largest national service organization, with more than 18 000 members, including its associates the Kinettes, who are spouses of Kinsmen. There are more than 600 Kinsmen clubs and nearly 500 Kinette clubs. Kinsmen was founded in Hamilton 20 Feb 1920 by Harold (Hal) Rogers, a WWI veteran. During WWII, under Rogers's leadership, Kinsmen raised more than $3 million to send 57 million litres of milk to children in Britain. Kinsmen raise more than $26 million annually for community service work, medical research and international development and donate more than $1 million to research into the children's disease cystic fibrosis (CF), making Kinsmen the largest single contributor to CF research in the world. Recent activities have included the establishment of a medical relief camp in Ethiopia during the 1984-85 famine crisis and sponsorship of Rick HANSEN's Man in Motion World Tour. The Kinsmen national headquarters is located in Cambridge, Ont.

Kirby, Michael J.L., politician, administrator (b at Montréal 5 Aug 1941). Educated at Dalhousie U and Northwestern U, Kirby was teaching at Dalhousie when he became assistant to Premier Gerald Regan of Nova Scotia in 1970, a post he held for 3 years. He returned to teaching in 1973 but entered the federal service the next year as assistant principal secretary to PM Trudeau. In 1976 Kirby became a member of the Nova Scotia Commissioners of Public Utilities, and then president of the Institute for Research on Public Policy in 1977. In 1980 he was named secretary to the Cabinet for federal-provincial relations and in 1981 deputy clerk of the Privy Council. He was a major architect of Ottawa's constitutional patriation strategy, earning a place in the demonology of provincial politicians second only to Trudeau's. In 1982 he became a vice-president of Canadian National Railways, simultaneously chairing Ottawa's task force on the Atlantic fisheries; in 1984, Trudeau made him a senator. With the Liberals in opposition, Kirby was national campaign co-chairman, with Raymond Garneau, of the federal Liberal Party. J.L. GRANATSTEIN

Kirby, William, novelist, journalist (b at Kingston-upon-Hull, Eng 23 Oct 1817; d at Niagara-on-the-Lake, Ont 23 June 1906). Author of a classic English Canadian historical novel, *The* GOLDEN DOG (1877), Kirby also edited the *Niagara Mail.* Immigrating with his parents to the US in 1832, Kirby arrived in Niagara in 1839, where his house still stands. A grandmother had been a United Empire Loyalist. He married into a family of prominent LOYALISTS and established himself as a major figure in that tradition, delivering the principal address at the 1884 UEL centennial celebration. Still in print in an abridged edition, *The*

Golden Dog is a swashbuckling historical romance. Based upon historic figures, the product of meticulous research, the novel depicts moral progress leading from the corruption of the last days of New France to French Canada's incorporation into the loyal, upright Canadian state. A Loyalist version of history also informs his epic poem, *The U.E.: A Tale of Upper Canada* (1859).

DENNIS DUFFY

Kirk, Lawrence Eldred, agriculturist (b at Bracebridge, Ont 27 May 1886; d at Saskatoon 27 Nov 1969). Kirk's most significant contribution was the breeding and introduction in 1932 of Fairway, the first variety of crested wheat grass, to the great plains of Canada. The use of this grass was a contributing factor in bringing the "dust bowl" of the 1930s under control. Fairway crested wheat grass is still the main grass used to reseed rangeland. Kirk taught at U Sask and Moose Jaw Collegiate Inst before joining the Experimental Farms Service as Dominion Agrostologist in Ottawa. He then became dean of agriculture at U Sask before moving to Rome as head of the plant-industry branch in the UN Food and Agriculture Organization, a position he held until retirement in 1954.

T.H. ANSTEY

Kirkconnell, Watson, translator, poet, university administrator, Baptist lay leader (b at Port Hope, Ont 16 May 1895; d at Wolfville, NS 26 Feb 1977). Master of more than 50 languages and dialects, Kirkconnell introduced English-speaking Canadians to the literature of "New Canadians" through his own English translations. More prolific than original, he dealt eloquently and clearly with broad themes in more than 170 books and brochures of poetry, literary criticism and social commentary. During WWII he was the architect of the government's "Nationalities Branch" (1940), later the Citizenship Bureau; the Humanities Research Council (1943); and the Baptist Federation of Canada (1944). After decades as a professor in Manitoba and Ontario, he became a formidable president of Acadia U (1948-64). Although he was intolerant of biblical fundamentalists and mistrustful of communists, his infectious generosity towards all others influenced many Baptists and Anglo-Canadians.

TOM SINCLAIR-FAULKNER

Kirke, Sir David, adventurer, governor of Newfoundland (b at Dieppe, France *c*1597; d near London, Eng 1654). Accompanied by his brothers **Sir Lewis** (b at Dieppe *c*1599; d 1683), **Thomas** (b at Dieppe *c*1603; d after 1641), **John** and **James**, he captured TADOUSSAC in 1628. His demand that CHAMPLAIN surrender QUÉBEC was refused and he retired, capturing a French supply fleet off Gaspé. He returned in 1629 and the destitute French surrendered Québec July 19. Thomas was left in charge of the post as governor. The brothers were ordered to restore Québec to the French in 1632, but David was made coproprietor and became first governor of Newfoundland in 1637. He took possession of FERRYLAND, but came into conflict with the fishing merchants and was recalled in 1651 to answer charges of withholding taxes. He was imprisoned on a suit resulting from his seizure of Ferryland and died in jail. A hero to some English writers and a pirate in the eyes of the French, Kirke remains controversial.

JAMES MARSH

Kirkland Lake, Ont, Town, pop 11 604 (1986c), 12 219 (1981c), inc 1972, located 241 km NW of North Bay. Named after a secretary in the Ontario Dept of Mines, Winnifred Kirkland, the lake around which the town grew has been filled with the tailings of the GOLD mines that brought the town to prominence. Sir Harry OAKES was not the first prospector into the district in the summer of 1911, but he and others such as Bill Wright and the Tough brothers were responsible for discovering and developing the gold mines (Lake Shore, Wright Hargreaves, Kirkland Minerals) that were the basis for the town's growth and prosperity during the 1920s and 1930s. The population reached a peak of nearly 25 000 at the outbreak of WWII. Since then, downward fluctuations in gold mining have deflated the town's fortunes, although the decline was ameliorated in the 1960s and 1970s by the growth of iron ore mining and tourism. A resurgence of gold mining occurred in the 1980s with the discovery of new goldfields in Harker (Holloway Townships and the sinking of Lac Minerals (Macassa Div) No 3 single-lift shaft to a depth of more than 2200 m.

MATT BRAY

Reading: S.A. Pain, *Three Miles of Gold: The Story of Kirkland Lake* (1960).

Kitamaat The contemporary Kitamaat Band is an amalgamation of the 2 Haisla-speaking tribes, the Kitamaat of upper Douglas Channel and Devastation Channel and the Kitlope of upper Princess Royal Channel and Gardner Canal in BC. The Kitamaat call themselves *Haisla* ("dwellers downriver"); and the Kitlope *Henaaksiala* ("dying off slowly"), a reference to their traditional longevity. The official designations *Kitamaat* ("people of the snow") and *Kitlope* ("people of the rocks") were adopted from the names used by their TSIMSHIAN neighbours. The Haisla language is the northernmost of the North Wakashan division of the Wakashan language family.

No formal estimates of precontact population exist, although native tradition asserts that each tribe numbered about 1000. Epidemics and endemic diseases brought by Europeans reduced that population, and after the 1918 influenza pandemic, fewer than 300 survived. The decline was arrested around 1930, and by 1986 the population of the combined tribes had reached 1100. There are also additional persons of Haisla ancestry who have lost their status (*see* INDIAN ACT).

Unlike those of other Wakashan-speaking tribes, the Kitamaat and Kitlope social system was based on the matrilineal CLAN. This principle was also followed by the Tsimshian tribes, with whom the Haisla enjoyed close economic and social relations. Aboriginally, there were 8 clans (Eagle, Beaver, Raven, Crow, Killer Whale, Salmon, Wolf and Frog), each composed of a number of family units or lineages, occupying one or more communal dwellings housing up to 30 individuals (*see* HOUSE). The highest-ranking members of each house or lineage formed a council of nobles for the clan chief, who himself acted as counsellor to the tribal chief. Each clan controlled its own resource sites within the general tribal territory, and each occupied an independent winter village. With the population decline, the Wolf and Frog clans disappeared entirely. The survivors of other clans formed linkages, in which they united to occupy a common winter village, and co-operated economically and socially, as in the planning and amassing of wealth for the POTLATCH. Eventually the whole tribe began to occupy the same village, although clan distinctions and linkages remain.

The remoteness of their villages, situated far up northern inlets, enforced isolation on the Kitamaat and Kitlope until the 1890s, when a mission and residential school were established at Kitamat. Missionaries and government agents believed that the flamboyant, theatrical aspects of traditional culture were impediments to "civilization" and should be eradicated. They exerted pressure to abandon feasts, dancing and potlatches; the traditional communal houses were pulled down, and the children were forbidden to speak the native language. During the same period, the decline in population shattered the clans and lineages and disrupted orderly lines of succession to titles and property in the traditional social order. After several decades of strain and dislocation, a culture has emerged that combines elements of both their traditional heritage and Euro-Canadian culture. *See also* NATIVE PEOPLE: NORTHWEST COAST and general articles under NATIVE PEOPLE.

JOHN PRITCHARD

Reading: R. Olson, "The Social Organization of the Haisla of BC," *Anthropological Records* 2, no 5 (1940).

Kitchener-Waterloo are twin cities in central SW Ontario, 110 km SW of Toronto. Each retains its own political culture and its own historical development, though both have shared a general socioeconomic development. Kitchener, larger of the 2 (pop 150 604, 1986c; 139 734, 1981c), was the county seat and judicial and financial centre of Waterloo County, and it continues to have a predominant influence in the Regional Municipality of Waterloo (pop 329 404, 1986c; 305 496, 1981c) formed in 1973 by combining several communities and cities, including WATERLOO (pop 58 718, 1986c; 49 428, 1981c) and the newly formed city of CAMBRIDGE.

Settlement The cities and entire regional area were originally part of a tract of over 243 000 ha set aside by the British Crown in 1784 as a reserve for the Six Nation Indians. In 1798 this land was subdivided and sold, Block 2 becoming the future Waterloo Township. Purchased first by speculators, then in 1805 by Pennsylvania MENNONITES, it was the nucleus of a large German-speaking settlement, swelled by the 19th-century exodus from Germany of skilled craftsmen, artisans and tradesmen as well as farmers and agricultural labourers. Both communities were included as villages in the 1850s, Kitchener being known then as Berlin. (It was renamed for Lord Horatio H. Kitchener during WWI.)

Development of the communities was determined primarily by the entrepreneurial skills and cohesive nature of the German community. Even in 1911, 70% of the inhabitants of Berlin and Waterloo were of Germanic origin. Economic growth was aided by Berlin's location on the GRAND TRUNK RY. An effective system of municipal

Population: Kitchener 150 604 (1986c), 139 734 (1981c); Waterloo 58 718 (1986c), 49 428 (1981c); 311 195 (1986, CMA), 287 801 (1981, CMA); 329 404 (1986, Regional Municipality), 305 496 (1981, Regional Municipality)

Rate of Increase (1981-86): Kitchener 7.8%; Waterloo 15.8%; CMA 8.1%

Rank in Canada: Twelfth (by CMA)

Date of Incorporation: Kitchener 1912 (Town of Berlin 1876); Waterloo 1943

Land Area: Kitchener 135.13 km^2; Waterloo 64.45 km^2 CMA 823.64 km^2

Elevation: 343 m

Climate: Average daily temp, July 20.6°C, Jan -6.9°C; Yearly precip rain 745 mm, snow 152.3 cm; Hours of sunshine 1936.4 per year

support and "bonusing" for industrial growth led by prominent German Canadian families aided Berlin's industrial pre-eminence in the area. After 1900 external investment and branch-plant industries, particularly in rubber and automotive parts, brought Kitchener and Waterloo more fully into Canada's economy. The transmission of inexpensive Niagara hydroelectric power to Berlin in 1911 – the first inland Ontario community to be able to have access to this new source of power – reinforced the industrial growth of the communities.

Cityscape The swampy terrain along the Great Road from Dundas determined the location of the first urban settlement of Berlin and Waterloo. Population slowly encroached on existing farmlands, but without large annexations from nearby townships until the rapid population growth of the 1950s. Early housing, generally of white or yellow brick, featured a unique Germanic vernacular. After WWI, styles began to conform to national stereotypes: bungalows, "ranch style," and row housing. Strenuous efforts began in the 1980s to halt the erosion of the cities' central cores, but little of the 19th-century ambience remains.

Population Though the prevalent German language and culture of Kitchener and Waterloo at the turn of the century made them unique in Canada, immigration from the fatherland ceased with the outbreak of war in 1914. The rise of Hitler, the Great Depression and WWII stifled subsequent German immigration, and by 1941 less than half the population saw itself as German. However, new German refugees who had fled or been expelled from eastern Europe (Romania, Yugoslavia, Poland and the USSR) reached Kitchener and Waterloo after the war. By the 1970s the cities were once more extolling their German identity through an annual Oktoberfest, which became a national tourist attraction. Other ethnic groups – POLES, GREEKS, PORTUGUESE, ITALIANS, CHINESE and WEST INDIANS – created a new population mixture throughout the 1960s and 1970s. With more than 45% of the population being British by ethnic origin as well, the community, like the nation, had become multicultural.

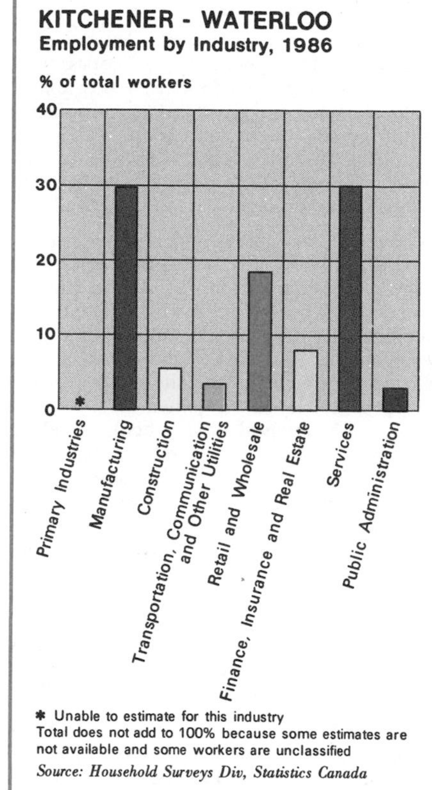

* Unable to estimate for this industry
Total does not add to 100% because some estimates are not available and some workers are unclassified
Source: Household Surveys Div, Statistics Canada

Economy and Labour Force The business and artisan skills of the German immigrants created a diversified industrial base. J.M. Schneider, a meat packer, began making sausage. Joseph E. SEAGRAM'S distillery was an auxiliary enterprise to a gristmill. Kuntz brewery (now Labatt's) began producing German lager beer, and Electrohome was aided in its early growth by the presence of skilled craftsmen. Some 20 furniture companies flourished in the early 20th century. Fire-insurance companies, particularly the Economical in Kitchener, and life-insurance companies in Waterloo, such as Mutual, Dominion and Equitable Life, drew on the local community's stability. The rubber industry came with the automobile era, as B.F. Goodrich, Uniroyal and Kaufman established factories and head offices in Kitchener. An excellent road and rail transportation system gave access to the Canadian and American markets, and a stable and efficient labour force (about 37% unionized) provided additional incentives. Technically oriented Conestoga College and the UNIVERSITY OF WATERLOO (which has Canada's largest engineering school and co-operative work-study programs with industry) have continued the community's original orientation.

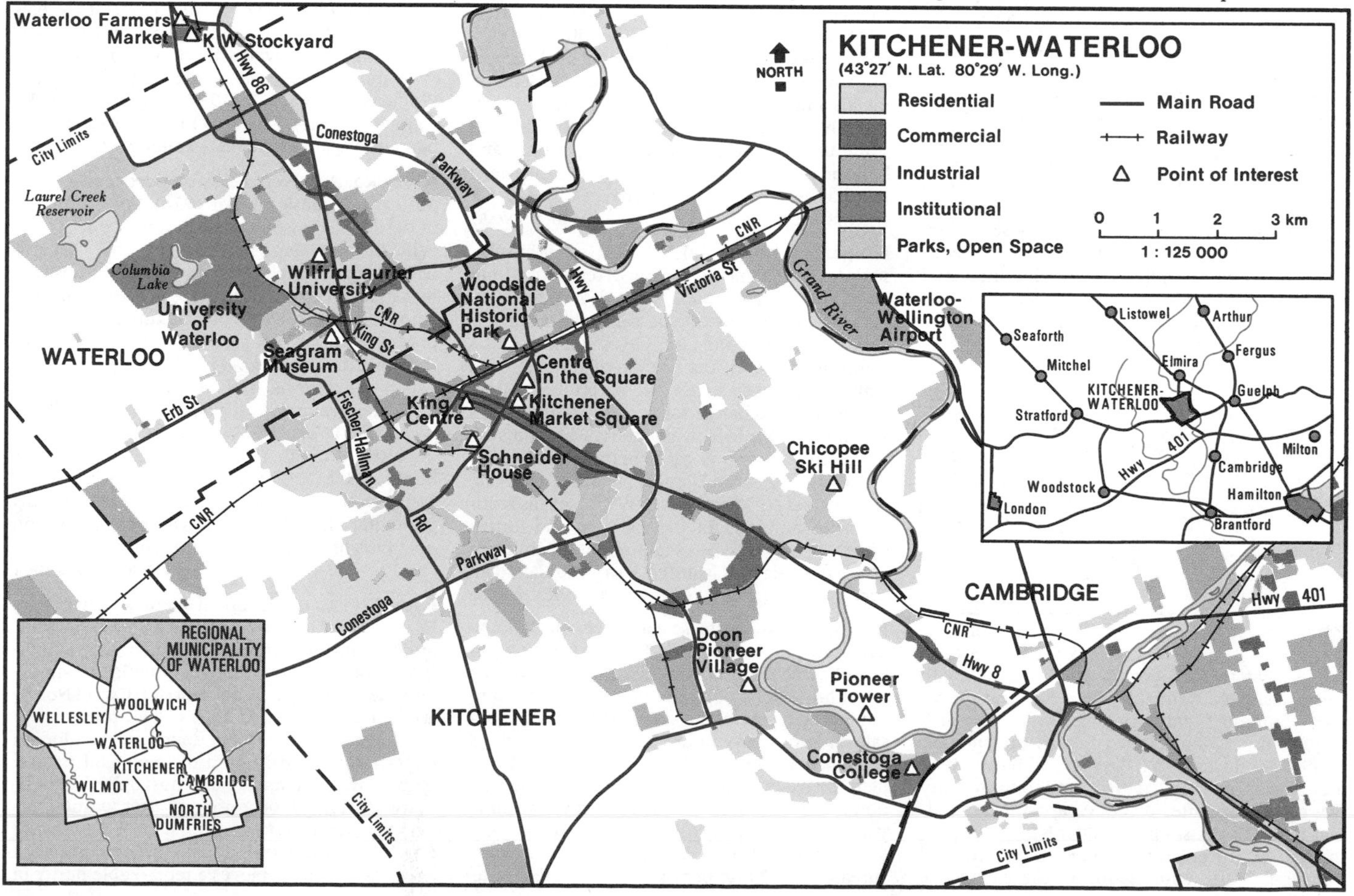

Government and Politics From the beginning, Kitchener and Waterloo maintained independent municipal governments with few shared services or mutual concerns. With the establishment of a 2-tiered REGIONAL GOVERNMENT in 1973, city councils remained, but the regional government assumed control over services such as police, health and social development and some planning and engineering services. Rather than drawing Kitchener and Waterloo more closely together, their rivalries were now provided with a forum for discontent. Administrative bureaucracies expanded dramatically and professionals and elected officials asserted control. Kitchener and Waterloo created or encouraged "neighbourhood" or residents' associations to make their councils more amenable to the wishes of constituents. Though local politics have lacked the fractiousness of some municipal governments, Kitchener has had its share of maverick mayors.

Cultural Life German cultural events predominated in the 19th century: *saengerfests, turnvereins* and celebrations of the birthdays of Kaiser Wilhelm and Chancellor von Bismarck were highlights. The love of music has survived and flourished in the 20th century, particularly the symphonic and choral traditions as well as a penchant for band music. Live theatre, by contrast, has not fared well. Organized sports, particularly hockey, have a prominent role in the community. WILFRID LAURIER UNIVERSITY and U of Waterloo, Kitchener's multipurpose Centre-in-the-Square theatre, the Kitchener-Waterloo Symphony Orchestra and Art Gallery provide local access to international performances. Kitchener's Saturday Farmers' Market is a popular southern Ontario attraction. K.M. McLaughlin

Kitimat, BC, District Municipality, pop 11 196 (1986c), 12 814 (1981c), inc 1953, is located at the head of Douglas Channel, 110 km E of Prince Rupert. Named for the nearby KITAMAAT ("people of the snow") by the HBC around 1837, its modern founding occurred in the early 1950s. Although Kitimat was developed by ALCAN for a single industrial purpose, it is perhaps unique in that consideration was given to ultimate diversification. Planning provided a basis for this potential future growth and from the beginning the residents managed their own affairs. The Alcan aluminum smelter was located at the head of the Douglas Channel because it provided a deep-water port with access to world markets; the alluvial plain of the Kitimat R provided flat land for the smelter and town. The massive hydroelectric power required for the smelting of ALUMINUM was provided by a dam on the Nechako R, which diverted its flow westward through a tunnel to a gigantic generating station at Kemano. Although one of the great metallurgical plants in the world, Alcan is no longer the only employer. The Eurocan pulp-and-paper complex plays a secondary role and logging also extracts timber for conversion at southern mills. The Ocelot methanol plant has pioneered a potential for petrochemical activities, and natural-gas export may also prove important. The construction of a new ammonia plant was under way in 1986.

William A. Sloan

Kitsilano, a 549 ha waterfront section of Vancouver, BC, inc with Vancouver 1886, S from English Bay to 16th Avenue and E from Alma to Burrard streets. Named by the CPR, after the famous Squamish chief *Khahtsahlanogh*, the area filled with single-detached homes in 2 phases, 1905-12 and after 1932. German, Sikh and Greek immigrants have settled there, and some industry was established after WWII. As apartment buildings replaced houses in the older NE corner from the mid-1950s on, Kitsilano became a centre of transient youth, culminating in the emergence between 1967 and 1969 of Fourth Avenue as Vancouver's "Hippie Haven." Shops selling psychedelic posters, incense and love beads attracted thousands of young people. The passing of Vancouver's "summer of love" gave way to purposeful shopping and chic boutiques. Kitsilano's beachfronts and parks include the Vancouver Centennial Museum, the Maritime Museum, the Gordon Southam Observatory and the H.R. MacMillan Planetarium. Peter Grant

Kittigazuit Site, archaeological site located at the mouth of the MACKENZIE R, was the largest INUIT village in arctic Canada during the 19th century. It was occupied by the Kittegaryumiut band of the MACKENZIE INUIT, who used it primarily as a summer beluga-hunting camp. As many as 1000 people lived in the village during the WHALING season and up to 200 kayakers joined in communal hunts, which involved driving herds of beluga onto shoals in the river. Several hundred of the small whales could be killed in a single day by this technique. During the winter a much smaller population remained at the village, living in large multifamily houses built of driftwood and covered with turf. Archaeological research indicates that the site had been used in this way for about 500 years. Most of the Kittegaryumiut died in a measles epidemic in 1902, and the village was abandoned except for occasional use as a trading post. *See also* ARCHAEOLOGY. Robert McGhee

Kitwanga Fort, a Northwest Coast Indian village on the Kitwankul R in BC, was part of a complex trading network. In 1979 field research conducted at Kitwanga, combined with records of oral traditions, indicated that intertribal trade and warfare were prevalent along the coast. Periods of war involving Kitwanga Ft began before 1700, continuing to the 1830s. Twenty-two trails were plotted along the Skeena, Nass, Stikine R system where this trade and warfare activity took place. Archaeological discoveries showed that after 1741 trade was undertaken primarily with Russian traders. Warfare was motivated by the desire to gain control over new resources, particularly metals and weapons. The exploits of Nekt, a warrior who became a legendary archetype, demonstrate the struggle for economic superiority and honour along the Northwest Coast. Kitwanga Fort has been declared a national historic site. *See also* ARCHAEOLOGY. Lillian Stewart

Kiugak Ashoona (also known as Kiawak), sculptor (b 16 Sept 1933). Son of renowned Inuit artist PITSEOLAK Ashoona, Kiugak recounts that his own prodigious artistic career began in his childhood, while the family was still living at a camp on the land. His first carving, made from walrus tusk, was taken by his brother QAQAQ Ashoona to exchange for supplies at the Baffin Trading Co. While focusing on typical Inuit subject matter – people engaged in traditional activities, mythological and fantasy creatures – Kiugak, who resides at CAPE DORSET, NWT, earns his reputation as an artist for the elegance and formal beauty of his work. His sculpture of the Inuit sea goddess Sedna was featured on a 1980 Canadian stamp. *See also* INUIT ART. Marie Routledge

Kives, Philip, business executive and innovative marketer (b at Oungre, Sask 12 Feb 1929). A farm boy of Turkish extraction, Kives showed a youthful passion for salesmanship. After completing high school, he gravitated into itinerant salesmanship in Winnipeg and at fairs, hawking gadgets as far away as Atlantic City, NJ. In 1962, he returned to Winnipeg to create K-tel International Inc, and used it to sell novelty consumer wares such as the "Veg-O-Matic" food slicer and the "Miracle Brush" lint gatherer. In 1965, a "greatest hits" line of records was added. K-tel eventually expanded to serve 34 national markets, and in the early 1980s diversified into oil and gas and other ventures, such as films. Kives's success lay in his ability to cut out the middleman, selling directly to the customer by mail and in his "hard-sell" television advertising. Kives excelled in identifying innovative products (eg, "jazzed up" classical melodies played by the Royal Philharmonic Orchestra). Financial overextension led to receivership in both Canada and the US in 1984. Undeterred, Kives reactivated K-tel in the US and Europe and launched a new company, K-5 Leisure Products, in Canada. By 1987 reorganization of K-tel International had been completed and the company was again profitable. Duncan McDowall

Kiugak Ashoona's *Woman Holding Fish*, typical of the elegance and formal beauty of the artist's work (*courtesy West Baffin Eskimo Co-operative, Cape Dorset, NWT*).

Kiyooka, Roy Kenzie, artist, poet, teacher (b at Moose Jaw, Sask 18 Jan 1926). After studying under J.W.G. MACDONALD, I.H. Kerr, James Pinto, Will Barnet, Barnett Newman and Clement Greenberg, he explored the problems of abstraction in relation to prairie space in a series of large canvases. In the late 1960s, he turned to poetry, photography and collage. The first 2 are united in the brilliant *StoneDGloves* (1970), the last 2 in *The Fontainbleau Dream Machine* (1977). Photographs also interweave with Kiyooka's rewriting of the *utanikki* in *Wheels* (1987), a poetic diary concerning a trip through Japan. In these, and in other books such as *Kyoto Airs* (1964), *Nevertheless these eyes* (1967) and *transcanadaletters* (1975), as in his photographic collections, it is Kiyooka's amazing openness to experience that stands out.

Douglas Barbour

Klee Wyck, collection of literary sketches by Emily CARR (Toronto 1941). *Klee Wyck* – the Indian name given Carr, meaning "Laughing One" – is an evocative work that describes in arrestingly vivid detail the central influence on Carr of Northwest Coast Indian life. Carr's clear, poetic prose summons up TOTEMS, abandoned villages, Indian character, broken-English dialogue and natural scenery without lapsing into nostalgic sentimentality, sociology or romance. Her writing inevitably invites comparison with her PAINTING: Carr's gifts with words are of a different but not a lesser order; she achieves a remarkable purity of effect through her careful translation of images, perceived by a keenly sympathetic eye, into translucent language. *Klee Wyck* won a Gov Gen's Award for nonfiction (1941) and has been translated into French (Montréal, 1973). NEIL BESNER

Klein, Abraham Moses, poet, writer (b at Ratno, Ukraine 14 Feb 1909; d at Montréal 20 Aug 1972). One of Canada's greatest poets and a leading figure in Jewish-Canadian culture, Klein was raised in the working-class Jewish immigrant district of Montréal. He studied classics and political science at McGill (1926-30) and as a student began to publish poetry and prose in Canadian and American periodicals. An excellent speaker and debater, he became active as a writer, editor and educator in the Zionist youth organization Young Judaea. His close friends at McGill included David LEWIS, F.R. SCOTT, A.J.M. SMITH, Leo KENNEDY and Leon EDEL. After graduating from Université de Montréal law school (1933), he practised law until his retirement in 1956. Editor and principal columnist (1938-55) of the weekly *Canadian Jewish Chronicle,* he worked as a ghostwriter and public-relations consultant for Samuel BRONFMAN during the same period. He was a visiting lecturer in poetry at McGill (1945-48) and was affiliated with the *Preview* group of Montréal poets. In 1949 he ran unsuccessfully as a CO-OPERATIVE COMMONWEALTH FEDERATION candidate. In the early 1950s he suffered a mental breakdown, withdrew from public activity and gradually lapsed into silence for the remainder of his life.

Much of Klein's verse (*Hath Not a Jew,* 1940; *Poems,* 1944) was infused with Jewish images and ideas. In *The Hitleriad* (1944) he vented his spleen against the Nazis. His last and finest collection, *The Rocking Chair* (1948), is a satirical portrayal of Québec. His short allegorical novel *The Second Scroll* (1951) was based on his 1949 journey to Europe, Israel and Morocco. Klein also published many newspaper articles, stories, book reviews and translations from Hebrew and Yiddish. His work is remarkable for its linguistic exuberance, wit, learning and moral fervour.

Abraham Moses Klein, whose work is remarkable for its linguistic exuberance, wit and moral fervour (*courtesy National Archives of Canada/C-64042*).

Prospectors' camp at Teslin, BC, June 1898, en route to the Klondike (*courtesy National Archives of Canada/PA-16141*).

Klein has rightly been called the "first contributor of authentic Jewish poetry to the English language." His writings articulate the feelings of a generation that witnessed the destruction of European Jewry and the fulfilment of the Zionist dream. USHER CAPLAN

Reading: Usher Caplan, *Like One That Dreamed: A Portrait of A.M. Klein* (1982); Caplan and M.W. Steinberg, eds, *A.M. Klein: Literary Essays and Reviews* (1987).

Klein, George John, design engineer (b at Hamilton, Ont 15 Aug 1904). Possibly the most productive inventor in Canada in the 20th century, he spanned in his career the "stick and string" era of aviation to the Space Shuttle. Klein worked 1929-69 at the NATIONAL RESEARCH COUNCIL and as a consultant after retirement. He designed the NRC's first wind tunnels and undertook research on fitting skis to aircraft, which led in turn to designing the Weasel army snowmobile (mass-produced in the US as the M-29) and ultimately to studying the mechanics of snow, on which he became an authority. Gearing systems were a lifelong specialty. During WWII he designed aiming systems for artillery and naval antisubmarine mortars and in his seventies he was chief consultant on gear design for the CANADARM. In 1951 he invented the STEM (*S*torable *T*ubular *E*xtendible *M*ember), a radio antenna that can be retracted into a flat reel and rolled out again on command. First used in space by the Alouette 1 satellite of 1962, the STEM increased the maximum size of satellite antennas from 6 metres to 45 metres, and was subsequently adopted as standard space technology. In 1944-45 Klein headed the team that designed the Zero Energy Experimental Pile, the first atomic reactor outside the US. His other inventions have ranged from a wheelchair for quadriplegics to a microsurgical staple gun used to suture blood vessels. DONALD J.C. PHILLIPSON

Reading: W.E.K. Middleton, *Mechanical Engineering at the National Research Council of Canada, 1929-1951* (1984).

Kleinburg, Ont, straddles a hogback between 2 branches of the Humber R, 40 km NW of Toronto. It has no legal entity, being part of the sprawling rural Town of Vaughan (formerly Vaughan Township), and therefore no official boundaries; but its population is generally reckoned at 1250. Founded around 1847 by an Alsatian immigrant, John Kline (*sic*), who built the first gristmill, it is known today as the site of one of Canada's largest art galleries, the McMichael Canadian Collection; for the Toronto International Film Studios, a major centre for TV and motion-picture production; and for the annual Binder Twine Festival, which attracts 30 000 people to the main street each Sept. Once an important farming centre, it has become a bedroom community for Toronto, its residents lured by the unspoiled beauties of the Humber Valley and the rural atmosphere of the village they struggle fiercely to preserve.

PIERRE BERTON

Klinck, Carl Frederick, literary historian, educator (b at Elmira, Ont 24 Mar 1908). Klinck helped make CANADIAN STUDIES a central part of the curriculum: his *Canadian Anthology* (edited with R.E. Watters, 1955, 1974) established a canon of poetry, short fiction and critical essays. A graduate of Waterloo College (U of Western Ontario) and Columbia, Klinck taught Canadian works in a continental context. Introductions to Frances BROOKE'S *The History of Emily Montague* (1961), Susanna MOODIE'S ROUGHING IT IN THE BUSH (1962) and John RICHARDSON'S WACOUSTA (1967) stirred interest in early Canadian novels. Perceptive and historically searching articles, and book-length studies of W.W. CAMPBELL (1943), E.J. PRATT (1947), "Tiger" DUNLOP (1958) and Robert SERVICE (1976) were capped by his integrative work as general editor of *The Literary History of Canada* (1965, 1976). He is a fellow of the RSC and an Officer of the Order of Canada.

ELIZABETH WATERSTON

Klondike Gold Rush, touched off by the 17 Aug 1896 discovery of placer gold on Rabbit (later Bonanza) Creek, a tributary of the Klondike R, by George Washington Carmack and his Indian brothers-in-law, "Skookum Jim" and "Tagish Charley." This accidental find was the result of a tip by a Canadian prospector, Robert Henderson, now credited as codiscoverer. The gold rush that followed was confined that first year to the Yukon interior. Miners already on the scene staked every creek in the Klondike and Indian river watersheds, including the fabulously rich Eldorado.

The world did not learn of the strike until some of these newly rich pioneers reached the West Coast by steamship in mid-July 1897. The Seattle *Post-Intelligencer*'s description of "a ton of gold" actually touched off the stampede. The effect on the depressed economy was instantaneous as hoarded funds were freed to finance some 100 000 amateur goldseekers who started N that fall and winter. The rich went all the way by water; the poor struggled over the WHITE PASS and CHILKOOT PASS, then down the Yukon R in handmade craft; the foolhardy took the "all-Canadian" routes through BC or out of Edmonton and found themselves spending 2 years on the trail. Soon much of Alaska and the Canadian Northwest was speckled with men and pack animals. Every Canadian community from Winnipeg to

Victoria was permanently affected by the boom. The Canadian North was seen as something more than frozen wasteland: Klondike fever was the catalyst for a chain of later mineral discoveries. Sixty steamboats plied the Yukon. The new town of DAWSON at the Klondike's mouth, with a floating population of some 30 000, became the largest community N of Seattle and W of Winnipeg, boasting telephones, electricity and motion picture theatres. Prostitution was tolerated; saloons, dancehalls and gaming parlours ran wide open except on Sundays. The North-West Mounted Police kept Dawson a law-abiding town while the YUKON FIELD FORCE, a military unit, maintained Canadian sovereignty in the face of a predominantly American population. The Spanish-American War and the news of a strike at Nome, Alaska, ended the stampede in the summer of 1898. By then, it is estimated, the gold-seekers had spent some $50 million reaching the Klondike, a sum about equal to the amount taken from the diggings in the 5 years following Carmack's discovery. *See also* GOLD RUSHES.

PIERRE BERTON

Reading: Pierre Berton, *Klondike* (1958).

Klotz, Otto Julius, astronomer (b at Preston, Canada W 31 Mar 1852; d at Ottawa 28 Dec 1923). With W.F. KING and E.G. DEVILLE, Klotz was responsible for the formation of the astronomical branch of the Dept of the Interior, and for the building of the Cliff Street Observatory in 1890. With King he planned the Dominion Observatory and succeeded him as director in 1917 after the post had been vacant for 18 months. As an astronomer he established positions along the CPR right-of-way through BC in 1885, participated on the team that determined the longitude of Montréal W of Greenwich, and in 1903-04 extended the longitude from Vancouver across the Pacific along the new cable route, closing the link previously established from England eastward to Australia.

MALCOLM THOMSON

Kluane National Park (est 1972, 22 000 km^2) is an area of unclimbed peaks, vast ice fields, clear lakes, GLACIERS and spectacular wildlife. Tucked in the SW corner of the YT, 150 km W of Whitehorse, the park contains Canada's highest peak, Mt LOGAN. Surrounding its jagged 6050 m summit and dominating the park is the world's largest concentration of ice fields and glaciers. The landscape includes alpine meadows, tundra and lush, forested valleys. The park is well known for its abundant wildlife, including ground squirrels, mountain caribou, moose, grizzly and black bears, Dall sheep and mountain goats. Over 170 bird species, from golden eagles to golden-crowned sparrows, inhabit the park. Archaeologists believe humans may have lived in the area at least 30 000 years ago. More recently the TUTCHONE hunted there. Explorers, prospectors, climbers and hunters settled around Kluane beginning in the 1890s. Today, those seeking adventure can camp at Kathleen Lakes, hike and climb, or fish (June-Aug). There are winter facilities for cross-country skiing, ice fishing and camping. Nearby towns of HAINES JUNCTION and Destruction Bay on the ALASKA HWY provide essential services. The park is a UNITED NATIONS WORLD HERITAGE SITE. The supt of Kluane is also the supt for North Yukon National Park (est 1984).

LILLIAN STEWART

Kluane Ranges, the easternmost of the St Elias Mts in the Yukon, extend 350 km NW from the Tatshenshini R to just beyond the Yukon-Alaska boundary. The ranges rise in a wall-like front at the SW edge of Shakwak Valley to elevations of 2000-2800 m and are bordered on the W by a succession of valleys and plateaus collectively known as the Duke Depression. Several large valleys drained by wide, braided rivers cut across the ranges. Although not as high as the Icefield Ranges farther W, the Kluanes show a unique ruggedness typified by serrated narrow ridges, steep slopes and long talus screes. They are sculpted mainly from Paleozoic and Mesozoic volcanic and sedimentary rocks that are laced with faults, some of which may still be active. Spruce forest is common below about 1200 m elevation, but the upper slopes of the ranges are treeless. The area supports an abundance of wildlife, including grizzly and black bear, timber wolf, Dall sheep, mountain goat, caribou and moose. The ranges are partly within KLUANE NATIONAL PARK and are a popular destination among hikers and climbers.

JOHN J. CLAGUE

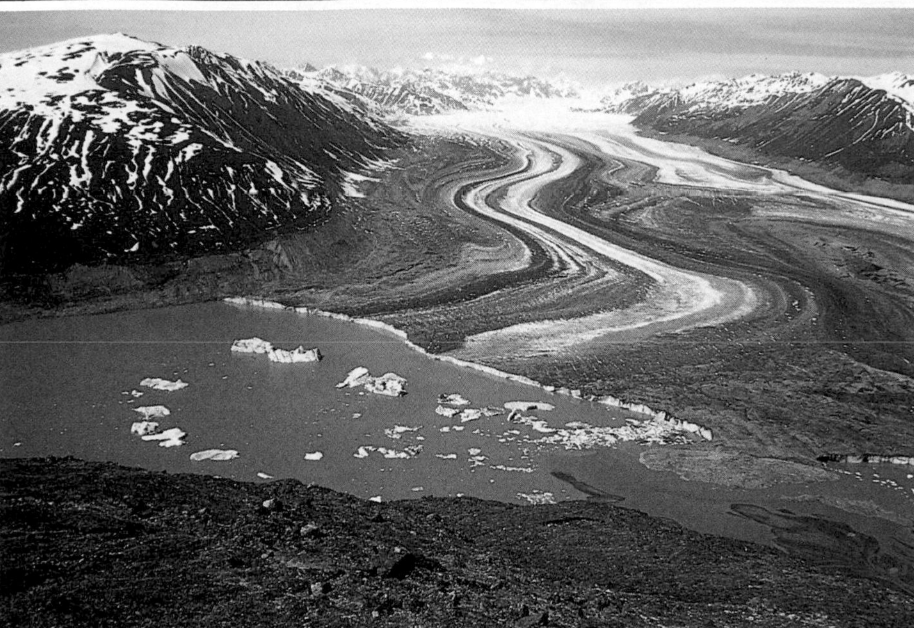

Lowell Glacier, in Kluane National Park, YT. The park was established in 1972 (*courtesy Environment Canada, Parks/Prairie and Northern Region*).

Knight, Harry Upperton, photographer (b at Tillington, Eng 6 July 1873; d at Victoria 28 Dec 1973). After operating a PHOTOGRAPHY studio in Cranleigh, Eng, Knight immigrated to Canada in 1910. He sold real estate in Vancouver, and in 1917 he established a studio in Victoria. Knight spent the next 47 years taking portraits and creating a vision of the city that mixed Old World sentiment with soft-focus pictorial moodiness. Although his career spanned nearly half a century, and although he witnessed profound social and cultural changes, his style remained rooted in turn-of-the-century concepts of photography as an inferior cousin of painting.

DAVID MATTISON

Knights of Labor, the major labour reform organization of the late 19th century, organized Dec 1869 by Philadelphia garment cutters. Growing slowly in the 1870s, the secret organization emphasized co-operation and education. The Knights believed in organizing all workers, without regard to skill, sex or race. Their major organizational breakthrough was the mixed assembly of various types of workers, which allowed the order to expand into small towns and villages. Entering Ontario, perhaps in 1875, and certainly in 1881 in Hamilton, the order organized some 450 local assemblies across Canada. Strongest in Ontario, Québec and BC, the Knights also enjoyed success in Nova Scotia and Manitoba and established locals in New Brunswick and present-day Alberta.

In Ontario and Québec, leading Knights played key roles in organizing the TRADES AND LABOR CONGRESS OF CANADA, and were prominent in independent labour political campaigns in the 1880s and 1890s and in considerable parliamentary lobbying. The Knights peaked in Ontario and the West in 1886, but were most successful in Ottawa and Québec in the 1890s. Their expulsion for dual unionism from the TLC in 1902 at Berlin [Kitchener] abetted the development of distinctive Québec unions. Key Knights' strongholds were Toronto, Hamilton, Montréal, Québec, Ottawa, St Catharines, St Thomas, London, Kingston, Winnipeg and Victoria. Canadian Knights such as A.W. WRIGHT, Thomas Phillips THOMPSON and D.J. O'DONOGHUE made important contributions in the US as well. The Knights' major contributions to the Canadian working class lay in the notion of the organization of all workers and in their efforts to formulate social alternatives to the growth of monopolistic capitalist society.

G.S. KEALEY

Knister, Raymond, writer (b at Ruscom, Ont 27 May 1899; d at Stoney Pt, Ont 29 Aug 1932). He attended Victoria College, U of T, briefly and took courses at Iowa State U, Iowa City (1923-24). To his own writing and criticism, Knister brought a mind attuned to new literary developments. Farm work provided him with realistic details for his stories and his first novel, *White Narcissus* (1929). He wrote in various literary forms as well as many journalistic pieces. After a brief stay in Montréal (1931-32) he was offered an editorship with RYERSON PRESS, which had accepted his novel, *My Star Predominant*. Just before taking up that position, he was drowned in Lk St Clair. A representative collection of his prose is *The First Day of Spring and Other Stories*, ed by Peter Stevens (1976).

PETER STEVENS

Knowles, Dorothy Elsie, artist (b at Unity, Sask 7 Apr 1927). Knowles studied at U Sask, with Eli BORNSTEIN, and was stimulated by the Emma Lake Artists' Workshops (Sask), where in 1962 Clement Greenberg encouraged her interest in landscape. Her work is distinguished by a delicate, broken touch influenced by Cézanne and by thin paint surfaces that owe to a suggestion from Kenneth Noland. Knowles's long-standing interest in watercolours aligns her with the traditions of English landscape painting so

The River Valley (1985), acrylic on canvas, by Dorothy Knowles (*courtesy Woltjen/Udell Gallery*).

important in Saskatchewan since the arrival in 1907 of Augustus KENDERDINE. An important exhibition of her work, organized by the Edmonton Art Gallery, opened at the Norman Mackenzie Art Gallery in Regina in Apr 1983 and in Edmonton Feb 1984, followed by exhibitions at Canada House in London and Paris, the Chicago and Los Angeles art fairs, and most recently in Vancouver in Dec 1987. KEN CARPENTER

Knowles, Stanley Howard, politician (b at Los Angeles, Calif 18 June 1908). The best-known and respected of Canada's Opposition MPs, Knowles represented Winnipeg N Centre for the CCF/NDP 1942-58 and 1962-84, using a legendary knowledge of parliamentary procedure to promote social justice. Born in the US of Nova Scotian/New Brunswick parentage, Knowles had a profoundly religious upbringing in the SOCIAL GOSPEL tradition of the Methodist Church. He never forgot his mother's death from tuberculosis in 1919 or his father's firing from a machinist's job in 1932; both incidents marked his choice for theological studies at United College, Winnipeg, and then for political action via the CO-OPERATIVE COMMONWEALTH FEDERATION in 1935. He had to change laws rather than souls. From 1942 (when he won the by-election following the death of J.S. WOODSWORTH), he did so by an increasing mastery of the rules of procedure: for almost 40 years he badgered successive governments into enlarging Canada's nascent WELFARE STATE. The PIPELINE DEBATE of 1956 was the most publicized illustration of his parliamentary skills; the founding of the NDP in 1961 confirmed his promotional abilities. Knowles's political life took a heavy personal toll but his sense of duty, his will power and the public esteem he commanded sustained him through multiple sclerosis (since 1946), marital estrangement (since the 1950s) and a massive stroke (1981). In 1984 Parliament, in an extraordinary retirement gift, named him an honorary officer of the House with a place, for life, at the Clerk's Table. He was appointed an Officer of the Order of Canada in 1985. SUSAN MANN TROFIMENKOFF

Reading: G. Harrop, *Advocate of Compassion: Stanley Knowles in the Political Process* (1984); S. Knowles, *The New Party* (1961); Susan Mann Trofimenkoff, *Stanley Knowles* (1982).

Knox, Walter, track and field athlete (b at Listowel, Ont 1878; d at St Petersburg, Fla 3 Mar 1951). Knox was one of the most versatile and successful performers in Canadian sport. From 1896 to 1933, he obtained 359 firsts, 90 seconds and 52 thirds in competition. He won 5 Canadian titles in one afternoon in 1907 – 100 yards, broad jump, pole vault, hammer throw and shot put – and he defeated various champions during his international career as a gambling "gypsy athlete." In 1914 Knox defeated British champion F.R. Cramb for "world all-round championship" at Manchester, Eng, winning 6 of 8 events. Coach of the Canadian track and field team at the 1920 Antwerp Olympics, he also coached Ethel CATHERWOOD, gold-medal high-jump winner at the 1928 Amsterdam Olympics. GERALD REDMOND

Knudson, George, golfer (b at Winnipeg 28 June 1937). Knudson was introduced to golf as a teenager at St Charles Country Club, Winnipeg, and later moved to Toronto. Fascinated with the golf swing, he was determined to make his reliable and efficient. He became known as a superior ball-striker and, turning professional in 1958, won 8 events on the US tour. In 1968 he won consecutive events in Phoenix and Tucson, Ariz, and in 1969 finished 2nd by a stroke in the prestigious Masters. In the late 1970s he turned to teaching. Knudson was scheduled to publish an instructional book in 1988. LORNE RUBENSTEIN

Koerner, Leon Joseph, lumberman, philanthropist (b at Nový Hrozenkov, Austria-Hungary [Czechoslovakia] 24 May 1892; d at Vancouver 26 Sept 1972). Born into a prominent Austro-Hungarian lumbering family, Koerner was a founder of the European Timber Exporters Convention and once served as Czechoslovakia's timber controller. After the dismemberment of Czechoslovakia in 1938, Koerner, who was of mixed Slav and Jewish ancestry, came to Vancouver where 3 brothers joined him. In 1939 he bought a defunct lumber mill in New Westminster. Applying curing techniques developed in Europe and using his British trade connections, his Alaska Pine Co sold hemlock, hitherto a waste wood in BC, as Alaska Pine. In 1955 he and his wife established the Leon and Thea Koerner Foundation which continues to provide financial aid for higher education, cultural and creative arts, and public welfare (*see* FOUNDATIONS). BC was a special beneficiary of Koerner's philanthropy. PATRICIA E. ROY

Koffman, Morris, "Moe," flautist, saxophonist (b at Toronto 28 Dec 1928). One of Canada's most popular instrumentalists, Koffman began as a saxophonist with dance bands in Toronto and, from 1950 to 1955, the US (Sonny Dunham, Jimmy Dorsey, etc). He moved to the forefront of Toronto's jazz and studio worlds, especially with a flute recording in 1957 of his "Swinging Shepherd Blues," a tune subsequently recorded by more than 300 artists. Koffman's pop-jazz bands have been a fixture at George's Spaghetti House restaurant in Toronto for over 25 years; he has been a soloist with other Toronto jazz bands, including Rob MCCONNELL's Boss Brass. His recordings (21 albums 1957-86) combine versatility with a sure commercial instinct, mixing jazz lightly with other styles of music, from classical (*Moe Koffman Plays Bach, Master Sessions*) to disco (*Jungle Man, If You Don't Know Me by Now*). MARK MILLER

Kogawa, Joy Nozomi, poet, novelist (b at Vancouver 6 June 1935). During WWII she and her parents were among the thousands of JAPANESE Canadians forcibly removed from the coastal areas and interned in the interior of BC: an experience Kogawa dealt with in her 1981 novel *Obasan*. Prior to its publication she was known mainly as a poet, as evidenced in *The Splintered Moon* (1967), *A Choice of Dreams* (1974) and *Jericho Road* (1977), collections of tightly controlled verse in which her Japanese ancestry becomes a growing preoccupation. Her cool appraisal of such themes and her natural dignity and understated literary power have won her numerous awards. Kogawa's latest publications include another collection of poetry, *Woman in the Woods* (1985), and a children's book, *Naomi's Road* (1986).

Kohlrabi (*Brassica oleracea*, Gongylodes Group), sometimes called stem turnip or cabbage turnip, an important Canadian garden vegetable of the Cruciferae family. Seedlings and leaves resemble those of most cole crops (eg, BROCCOLI; CAULIFLOWER). Plant height ranges 25-40 cm. The edible part of the kohlrabi is an enlargement of a small portion of the above-ground stem. In shape the swollen stem varies from nearly round to a flattened globe; in outer colour, from greenish white to reddish purple. Kohlrabi is cold tolerant, like CABBAGE. It matures in 45-60 days and can be direct seeded, but a greenhouse or hotbed start results in earlier maturity. Insect pests and diseases include aphids, cabbage worms, damping-off and blackleg. Kohlrabi is a good source of potassium. It is a common Canadian garden crop, but the commercial production is limited to large-city market gardens. V.W. NUTTALL

Koje-Do, island 40 km SW of Pusan, S Korea, location of a series of disorders in American-operated POW camps during the KOREAN WAR. Quartered in huge compounds containing as many as 6000 men, the 160 000 N Korean and Chinese prisoners were inadequately controlled, and in May-June 1952 had to be dispersed with the help of tanks after they captured the camp commander and extorted a "confession" of inhuman treatment. Hoping to distribute POW administration more widely among UN powers, the Americans, without consulting the governments concerned, requested the help of British Commonwealth units. A company of the Royal Canadian Regiment was thus sent to Koje-Do on May 25 and without bloodshed helped to reorganize part of the camp and guard some of the prisoners. Fearing political repercussions at home, however, Ottawa in the meantime had delivered a public diplomatic protest to the US government, officially on the grounds that it was government policy to keep Canadian troops unified under Canadian command. American authorities were accommodating, although privately infuriated, and the RCRs were relieved of their POW duty 8 July 1952. DENIS STAIRS

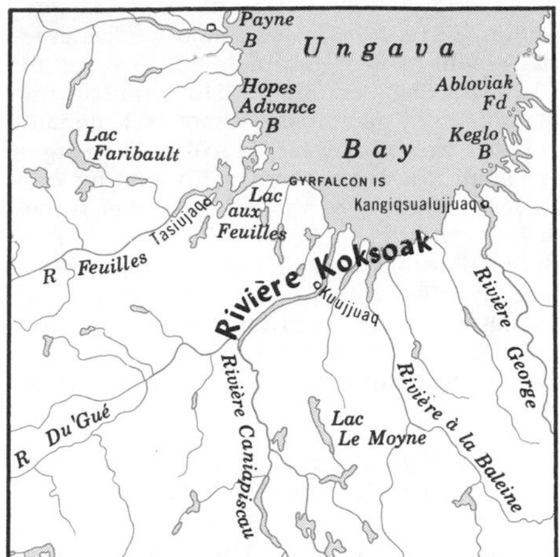

Koksoak, Rivière, 874 km long (to head of Caniapiscau R), final leg of a river system that drains a vast area (133 000 km^2) of northern Québec. The main branch is formed by the Caniapiscau R, which rises in Lac Caniapiscau, and its main tributary, the Rivière Swampy Bay, and flows generally NNW. The more westerly branch is formed by Rivière aux Mélèzes and its tributaries R du Gué and R Delay. The Caniapiscau and Mélèzes join to form the Koksoak, which flows N 145 km past Kuujuak to UNGAVA BAY. The name is likely a translation of an Inuit word meaning "big river," and the Koksoak is over 1600 m wide near its mouth. A dam on the Caniapiscau R has tripled the size of Lac Caniapiscau, and water is being diverted to the JAMES BAY hydroelectric development via LA GRANDE RIVIÈRE. JAMES MARSH

Komagata Maru, a Japanese-owned freighter chartered out of Hong Kong in Apr 1914 by 376 Punjabis, mostly SIKHS, bound for Canada. At the time, East Indians were kept out of Canada by an order-in-council requiring them to come to Canada by continuous passage from India, when no steamship line provided the service. Before the Canadian government, under tremendous pressure, closed the door in 1908, about 2000 Sikhs had settled in BC. In 1913, 38 Sikhs contested the continuous-passage order and were admitted. This encouraged others to charter the *Komagata Maru.* When it arrived at Vancouver in May 1914, most of the passengers were detained on board. They waited for 2 months while immigration officials maneuvered to keep them out of court and, after they had lost their case, while their leaders negotiated departure terms. The arrival of the RCN cruiser RAINBOW on July 20 added to the Canadian pressure, and on July 23 *Komagata Maru* sailed for Calcutta, where it was met by police suspicious of the organizers' politics. On disembarkation, 20 passengers were killed in a shooting exchange. The affair strengthened Indian nationalist feeling, but did not significantly soften Canadian immigration law.

HUGH JOHNSTON

East Indian immigrants waited for 2 months aboard the *SS Komagata Maru* while immigration officials maneuvered to keep them out of Canada (*courtesy Vancouver Public Library/6232*).

Kootenay are divided into "Upper" and "Lower" divisions, respectively occupying eastern and western portions of their plateau habitat. The Kootenay R in southeastern BC served as the unifying centre of their aboriginal territory and culture, provided many of their subsistence needs, and was also the location for their villages and a means of transportation. The term "Kootenay" is an anglicized form of either a Peigan or an old Kutenay word. Kutenay is a language isolate.

The various bands of the Upper and Lower Kootenay were well adapted to their somewhat different natural environments. The Upper Kootenay exploited a greater abundance of big-game animals (deer, caribou, elk, mountain sheep and goat) while the Lower Kootenay relied more on fish and other aquatic resources. The Upper Kootenay undertook annual bison hunts over the Divide, probably after acquiring the horse. This intensified their contact with Plains cultures, resulting in their adoption of a veneer of Plains culture traits apparent after 1800 (*see* NATIVE PEOPLE: PLAINS).

The lands along the Kootenay R were segmented into BAND or group territories. Shifting residence patterns allowed utilization of various economic resources according to the season. Men fished, hunted and, when necessary, cared for horses. In addition to child rearing, women were responsible for root gathering, preparation of food and hides, and making clothing. The Kootenay kinship system was bilateral but lacked lineages or clans (*see* CLAN). Reciprocal exchange among relatives was the principal means of redistributing economic goods, acquiring protection and achieving social status. When the Kootenay bands were in their winter villages, each was under the relatively informal leadership of a man respected for his success in accumulating wealth and for his generosity. With adoption of the horse, certain bands came to rely more on the bison, and more powerful leaders emerged. A principal sodality, the "Crazy Dogs," was composed of warriors who functioned as a police unit within the band and during bison hunting and was probably borrowed from the Plains. Other sodalities included the "Crazy-Owl" society for women and shamanistic groups such as the Conjuring or Blanket societies (*see* SHAMAN).

As seen in their mythology, Kootenay regarded the Earth as an island surrounded by water, covered by the dome of the sky. The supernatural side of man was his soul, but humans also possessed numerous personal spirits who were often associated with the rivers and their cascades. The spirits offered their powers to the Kootenay, who sought them through "vision quests." The principal ceremonies today are the Conjuring or Blanket ceremony and the SWEAT LODGE ceremony. Other rites include the SUN DANCE, the Bluejay Dance and the Grizzly Bear, Game Calling and First Fruits ceremonies.

Although semisubterranean pit houses have been reported, the Lower Kootenay usually occupied long, mat-covered lodges similar to those of the neighbouring Interior SALISH. During summer, temporary conical lodges covered by boughs of spruce or fir bark were used. After adopting the horse, the Upper Kootenay replaced brush shelters by the skin-covered TIPI.

Most of the contemporary Kootenay of Canada are located on 5 INDIAN RESERVES: Columbia Lake, Lower Kootenay, St Mary's, Shuswap and Tobacco Plains. Although severely decimated by EPIDEMICS in the 18th and 19th centuries, the Kootenay population appeared to stabilize in the late 19th century. There were 515 Kootenay in 1986. They earn their living from wage labour and a few tribal enterprises. Their tribal councils are working to improve health and education, and are participants in the movement to secure LAND CLAIMS settlements for their extensive aboriginal territory. *See also* NATIVE PEOPLE: PLATEAU and general articles under NATIVE PEOPLE.

DEWARD E. WALKER, JR

Reading: H. Turney-High, *Ethnography of the Kutenai* (1941).

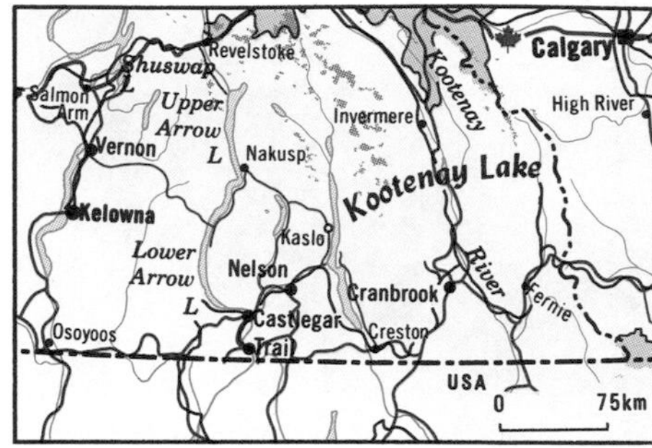

Kootenay, Lake, 407 km^2, elev 532 m, is situated in the mountainous SE interior of BC. A long, narrow lake squeezed between the SELKIRK and PURCELL mountain ranges, it is a widening of the Kootenay R, which rises in the Rocky Mts and flows S into the US before looping sharply N back into Canada. The lake drains W to the COLUMBIA R. The town of NELSON is on the W arm. David THOMPSON visited in 1808 during one of his fur-trading ventures across the Rockies and found the area occupied by the Kootenay. Late in the century the logging and mining industries moved into this corner of the province. The name derives from a Kootenay word meaning "water people."

DANIEL FRANCIS

Kootenay National Park (est 1920) is located on the W slope of the Continental Divide. The park, stretching N and S for 104 km, is bounded on the E by BANFF and on the N by YOHO. Vegetation ranges from alpine tundra to forests of Douglas fir. Large mammals found in the park include mountain goat, bighorn sheep, elk, mule deer, black bear and the occasional grizzly, as well as numerous smaller mammals and over 150 species of birds. Kootenay has always been a travel route. Ancient pictographs (*see* PICTOGRAPHS AND PETROGLYPHS) suggest that plains and mountain Indians met regularly at what is now Radium Hot Springs. Later the Kootenay settled there but still made regular trips across the Rockies to hunt bison on the plains. David THOMPSON, who was

Radium Hot Springs in Kootenay National Park. Ancient pictographs suggest that plains and mountain Indians met regularly at these hot springs (*courtesy Environment Canada, Parks/Ted Grant*).

exploring a route to the Pacific, was the first European to travel through the area. Today the Banff-Windermere Parkway passes through the park and provides dramatic views of snow-capped peaks and narrow canyons. The park offers year-round camping and swimming at the hot springs, as well as outdoor recreational facilities. LILLIAN STEWART

Korean War (1950-53) In Dec 1947 PM Mackenzie KING chastised his external affairs department for agreeing to membership on the UN Temporary Commission for Korea. Nevertheless, on 27 July 1950, after King's funeral, his former colleagues decided in principle to contribute a Canadian Army unit to assist UN forces in Korea. In the government's view, Canada would fight not for Korea but for the UN and the principle of collective security.

The war had begun 25 June 1950. The next day Gen Douglas MacArthur informed US Pres Harry Truman that S Korean defences were collapsing and defeat was imminent. The Americans decided to help the south defend itself against the communist north, but through the UN. The UN General Assembly was dominated by Western countries and, since the Soviets were boycotting the Security Council because of the UN's refusal to seat the new communist Chinese regime in Council, they could not exercise a veto. The Security Council thus condemned the N Koreans and called on UN members "to render every assistance" to the beleaguered south. The Americans quickly offered air and naval assistance. On 28 June 1950 Lester PEARSON, Canada's secretary of state for external affairs, commended them, believing that Canada must respond as well through the UN and under US military leadership.

In 1950, perhaps the worst period for COLD WAR fears, Canadians accepted and even encouraged American leadership in resistance to communist expansion. There was, however, some fear that the Americans were too impetuous in defending the "free world." Pearson therefore emphasized that Canada's participation was part of a UN, not an American, operation. Initially, Canada contributed 3 destroyers and an air-transport squadron. The Americans, thinking this inadequate, used UN Secretary General Trygve Lie to pressure Canada and other nations to expand their efforts. The Canadian government needed little external pressure; domestic interests exerted the necessary influence. Even the socialist CCF urged the government to commit ground forces. Canada's major difficulty was the weak state of the armed forces, but on Aug 7 Prime Minister ST. LAURENT announced rearmament measures and plans for a Canadian Army Special Force (CASF) to carry out Canada's UN obligations.

At first it appeared that Canadian soldiers would never fire a shot. Under MacArthur UN forces drove the N Koreans back to the border at the 38th parallel. Canadians and most others expected MacArthur, having vanquished the aggressor, to halt. To Pearson's shock and disappointment, he did not. Canada nevertheless publicly supported the US decision to carry the war into the north. Now the Canadians sought to restrain the American-dominated military action lest the Chinese communists be drawn into battle. By the end of Oct Chinese "volunteers" crossed the Yalu R, driving back the UN forces. Pearson's concern was expressed publicly in mid-Nov when he emphasized that Canada had always sought a "confined and localized" war that did not imperil the security of "Korea's neighbours." MacArthur did not exaggerate when on 28 Nov 1950 he called it "an entirely new war." Canadians would not escape the battles.

In Dec 1950 the 2nd Battalion of the Princess Patricia's Canadian Light Infantry landed in Korea, and in May the CASF followed. The Canadians fought on rough terrain and in an unfamiliar environment. The UN forces established a stable front near the 38th parallel, and until the war ended 27 July 1953, the fighting took place along this line. Canadians distinguished themselves in a major engagement at KAP'YONG Apr 1951. There were 21 940 Canadians who served in the army and approximately 3600 naval personnel. Eleven army officers, 298 other ranks and 3 sailors fell in action. Fifty-nine officers and 1143 other ranks were wounded or injured. By all accounts, the Canadians performed admirably.

Pearson and his colleagues had thought American leadership essential, but its character became increasingly troubling. First, there were careless remarks by Pres Truman about Gen MacArthur's right to decide alone on the use of atomic weapons. Then, MacArthur clearly indicated that he wanted to expand the war into China, an action that might have caused World War III. Even Truman's firing of MacArthur on 10 Apr 1951 failed to remove many concerns. During the war, Canadian diplomats sought to "constrain" the American decision makers from the risky actions they sometimes considered. Certainly the Canadians worked with exceptional zeal and skill in UN corridors and in Washington offices to advance arguments for a negotiated peace. Their influence, however, remains open to question. Although some Canadians believe Canada's actions did restrain American aggressiveness, it must be admitted that American evidence offers little support. The Korean War has thus become part of a larger historical controversy concerning the nature of CANADIAN-AMERICAN RELATIONS. *See also* KOJE-DO. JOHN ENGLISH

Reading: L.B. Pearson, *Mike,* II (1973); J.W. Pickersgill and D.F. Forster, *The Mackenzie King Record,* IV (1970); D. Stairs, *The Diplomacy of Constraint* (1974); H.F. Wood, *Strange Battleground* (1966).

Koreans Korea is a mountainous peninsula E of China and W of Japan. After WWII, the country was divided into northern (communist) and southern (American-influence) zones. It was this division that led to the KOREAN WAR in the early 1950s. Almost all Korean immigration to Canada has been from the S. The earliest known contacts with Canadians occurred in 1890 through Canadian missionaries working in Korea. Subsequently, Koreans immigrated to Canada through these same church connections, seeking opportunities for economic independence and a future for their families. Immigrants came not only from S Korea, but also via Europe, Vietnam, S America and the US. Most Korean Canadians are highly skilled workers or professionals, eg, doctors, professors, engineers, or are engaged in business, eg, food stores, gas bars, restaurants, printing shops, real-estate and insurance agencies. Others have entered the labour force as skilled and semiskilled workers.

Most Koreans have settled in urban centres, particularly in Toronto, Vancouver, Edmonton and Calgary. The number of Koreans in Canada today is 27 685 (1986e).

Social and Cultural Life In traditional Korean social structure, the clan system, with its emphasis on hierarchical relationships, is important. Customs derived from Confucianism, the philosophical system of traditional Korea, have been retained by Korean Canadians, although CHRISTIANITY, with its modern education system, has had a profound effect on the shaping of modern Korea. The first Korean United Church was established in Vancouver; 9 United Church congregations now serve Koreans in Vancouver, Winnipeg, Edmonton, Toronto, Hamilton, Windsor and Montréal. The Korean Presbyterian and Korean Catholic churches are also well established. Koreans are rich in folk traditions. Contributions to Canadian culture range from dance, music and Tae Kwon Do (the art of self-defence) to specialized Korean cuisine such as *bul-go-gi* and *kimchee*.

Club Coreana was founded in 1970 for social gatherings of Korean students at U of T. Other organizations include the Cultural Centre for Korean Canadians and the Association of Korean Scholars. A Korean Canadian association in Toronto has started a Korean-language school. The Ad Hoc Committee for the Orientation of Korean Immigrants (1972) in Vancouver was founded to assist new immigrants, as was the Korean Human Rights Council in Ontario, which also serves the community.

Canada News and *New Korea Times* are weekly publications, as is the Korean journal *Sangjo,* published by the Korean Vancouver Society.

Although there is a tendency for them to be integrated into the Canadian way of life, Koreans are also conscious of maintaining their independent identity. National celebrations include National Independence Day on March 1, which is related to the 1919 movement for independence. DAVID BAI

Kotcheff, William, "Ted," filmmaker (b at Toronto 7 Apr 1931). He studied literature at U of T, joined the CBC in 1952 and soon began directing. He left for England in 1957, directing many TV productions, stage plays and his first films. After making *Outback* (1971) in Australia, he returned to Canada to adapt Mordecai RICHLER's novel about a young Jewish hustler living in Montréal. At the time, *The* APPRENTICESHIP OF DUDDY KRAVITZ (1974) was the most expensive privately financed film produced in Canada, but it did not sacrifice artistic integrity for commerce. Although most of Kotcheff's subsequent work was produced in the US, he returned to adapt another Richler novel, *Joshua Then and Now* (1985). PIERS HANDLING

Kouchibouguac National Park (est 1969, 238 km^2), on the eastern NB shore of Northumberland Str, is a delicate blend of beaches, sand dunes and salt marshes framed by a mixed maritime forest. A 25 km long barrier-island system shelters placid lagoons from the often violent sea. LILLIAN STEWART

Kraft, Norbert, classical guitarist (b at Linz, Austria 21 Aug 1950). He was brought to Canada in 1954 and took up classical guitar relatively late, at age 17, but has gone on to establish himself as one of the world's finest guitarists. He was the first N American to win the prestigious top prize in the Andrés Segovia International Guitar Competition, held in Palma de Majorca, Spain. Kraft's other accomplishments include winning the Grand Prix at the CBC Talent Festival in 1979, recording with the Winnipeg Symphony and the Boston Pops, and numerous engagements with symphony orchestras nationwide. He is professor of guitar at the Faculty of Music, U of T, and has edited and compiled many musical publications, including the official graded repertoire series for the Royal Conservatory. Kraft is chairman of competitions for the International Guitar Festival in Toronto. D'ARCY GREAVES

Krajina, Vladimir Joseph, scientist, educator (b at Slavonice, Austria-Hungary [Czechoslovakia] 13 Apr 1905). He earned his doctorate *summa cum laude* in 1927 at Charles U, Prague, where he remained on staff until 1948. His botanical studies were interrupted during WWII when, as a leader of the Czech underground resistance, he was active in gathering and transmitting information to the British War Office. This work earned him high military and civilian honours.

Elected to the Czech parliament in 1945, and forced to seek safety abroad in 1948, he immigrated with his family to Canada where he joined the botany department of UBC. Here his major work was to develop and introduce an ecology-based system of vegetational classification, now widely used (*see* VEGETATION REGIONS). His leadership in securing establishment in Canada of more than 100 ecological reserves is also widely acknowledged. Recognition of the value of his work includes scientific awards, honorary degrees (DSc, LLD) and membership in the Order of Canada (1981). CLAYTON O. PERSON

Kreiner, Kathy, alpine skier (b at Timmins, Ont 4 May 1957). She began skiing at age 3, racing at 7 and World Cup competition at 14, winning her first World Cup race at Pfronten, W Germany, in 1974. She won Canada's only 1976 Olympic gold medal in the giant slalom, for which she was named Canada's Outstanding Female Athlete of 1976. She is at present a colour commentator for CBC sports. MURRAY SHAW

Kreisel, Henry, novelist, professor, administrator (b at Vienna, Austria 5 June 1922). He was one of the first people to bring the experience of the immigrant to modern Canadian literature. Drawing on personal knowledge of fascist pre-WWII Austria, Kreisel has powerfully dramatized the anguish experienced by Jews there. He left Austria for England in 1938 and was interned for 18 months during WWII. After studying at U of T, he began teaching in 1947 at U of A, where he has remained. He served as vice-president, 1970-75 and in 1975 was named University Professor. In both Kreisel's novels, Canadian security is contrasted with European turbulence. In *The Rich Man* (1948), an immigrant who has achieved modest success in Toronto returns to Vienna to discover that his claims to wealth deceive and harm his despairing Austrian relatives. *The Betrayal* (1964) explores questions of guilt and revenge that arise when a man who has escaped from the Nazis finds his would-be betrayer in Edmonton. *The Almost Meeting* (1981) is a collection of short stories with a variety of Canadian and European settings. Kreisel's internment diary and other autobiographical materials have been combined with essays on his work by 8 critics in *Another Country: Writings By and About Henry Kreisel* (1985). He became an Officer of the Order of Canada in 1988. THOMAS E. TAUSKY

Krieghoff, Cornelius David, painter (b at Amsterdam, Holland 19 June 1815; d at Chicago, Ill 8 Mar 1872). Krieghoff's colourful paintings of Québec habitants, sporting life and Indians have fascinated succeeding generations. Of German parentage, Krieghoff spent his youth in Düsseldorf and Schweinfurt, Germany, and studied at the Düsseldorf Academy, famous for its genre painters. He and his brother Ernst immigrated to America 1835 or 1836 and fought with the Americans in the Seminole War in Florida. He met Louise Gauthier (or Gautier) from Boucherville, Qué, in New York and by 1840 they were living in Montréal, where he worked as a musician and painter. He was in Rochester, NY, in 1842-43, but went to Paris for study in 1844.

Krieghoff lived in Longueuil, a village across the St Lawrence from Montréal, from 1845 to 1849. He also maintained a studio in Montréal, where he was establishing himself as a major artist. His paintings of local habitant life embodied satirical humour, ironical anecdote and brilliant colours. Typical is one which portrays with suppressed mirth a priest tyrannically guarding his parishioners' morals by catching them eating meat during Lent. In others, men cheat at cards, lovers flirt on winter evenings, and neighbours gossip. Indians greet each other along the frozen river while Montréal gentlemen sweep by in handsome sleighs. All Krieghoff's canvases read like gripping narratives. The family moved to Montréal in 1849, where he continued painting, but sales of his works were poor.

Cornelius Krieghoff, *The Habitant Farm* (1856), oil on canvas (*courtesy National Gallery of Canada/gift of the estate of the Hon W.C. Edwards, 1928*).

Krieghoff moved to Québec, likely in 1853, at the urging of John Budden, whose auction firm sold his canvases. For 11 years he fraternized with the affluent Québec sporting fraternity of wealthy lumber merchants, army officers and businessmen, and painted many well-known canvases. *Merrymaking* is a rowdy winter party at a country inn. Others picture incidents on winter hunting and sleighing trips and fishing expeditions in autumn woods. There are picturesque waterfalls and Indian groups in the forest. Habitant life is the theme in paintings such as *Spill My Milk!*, in which a girl is being scolded for carelessness. In *Bilking the Toll*, youths evade the old keeper unable to collect the fee from a speeding sleigh. Krieghoff was commissioned to paint canvases for the chamber of the new Québec Legislative Assembly.

The artist left Québec in late 1863 or early 1864 and lived in Paris and Munich, where he painted additional versions of Canadian subjects. He visited Québec in 1867 and moved back in 1870. His former patrons, the garrison officers, had returned to England, and he could not pick up his old carefree life. Krieghoff moved to Chicago late in 1871, where his daughter was living, only to die there suddenly. His 2000 canvases of popular, anecdotal, genre subjects had brought new dimensions to the Canadian scene and a colourful romanticism unsurpassed by contemporary artists. J. RUSSELL HARPER

Reading: J. Russell Harper, *Krieghoff* (1979).

Kroetsch, Robert, writer, editor, teacher (b at Heisler, Alta 26 June 1927). He grew up on his father's farm and studied at U of A, and U of Iowa. He taught at State University of NY, Binghamton, until the late 1970s, meanwhile writing a series of novels set mostly in Alberta that won him a growing critical reputation.

Kroetsch's first novel, *But We Are Exiles* (1966), was a serious affair lacking the ribald comic energy of his later works. His major theme of Dionysian chaos versus Apollonian order was present, though he had not found the proper style to explore it. In *The Words of My Roaring* (1966), he began to use the tall-tale rhetoric of prairie taverns. Both *The* STUDHORSE MAN (1969), which won the Governor General's Award, and *Gone Indian* (1973) call the conventions of realistic fiction hilariously into question. *Badlands* (1975), a comic triumph, could be called an example of feminist fiction-making because of the questions it raises about masculine conventions of behaviour and storytelling. In 1975 Kroetsch also published his first 2 books of poetry, *Stone Hammer Poems* and *The Ledger*. The latter, along with *Seed Catalogue* (1977), *The Sad Phoenician* (1979) and *Sketches of a Lemon* (1981), are parts of *Field Notes* (1981), a "continuing poem" which interrogates problems of genre, structure and the very possibility of writing literature in the New World. *Advice to My Friends* (1985), the second volume of *Field Notes*, was followed by *Excerpts From the Real World* (1986) and "Spending the Morning on the Beach," which appeared in a special new edition of *Seed Catalogue* (1986). *What the Crow Said* (1977), an experiment in magic-realism, and *Alibi* (1983), the first volume of a trilogy, testify to his continuing commitment to fiction.

Kroetsch is a synthesizer of new literary theory. Through interviews and essays, he has encouraged critical thinking about contemporary writing. Perhaps the most significant example is *Labyrinths of Voice: Conversations with Robert Kroetsch* (1982) by Shirley Neuman and Robert Wilson. *Open Letter* published his collected criticism (1983), and a special issue devoted to his work (1984). Through his teaching, at U of C and U of Man during the 1970s and 1980s and Saskatchewan Summer School of the Arts, as well as through his writing, Kroetsch has powerfully influenced recent writing on the Canadian Prairies and elsewhere. DOUGLAS BARBOUR

Krol, Joseph, "Joe King," football player (b at Hamilton, Ont 20 Feb 1919). He played collegiate football in Windsor, and at Western he helped the Mustangs win the 1939 intercollegiate title. After playing with the Hamilton Wildcats, Grey Cup winners 1943 and finalists 1944, he joined the TORONTO ARGONAUTS, leading them to 3 consecutive Grey Cups (1945-47). Krol and receiver Royal Copeland – "the gold dust twins" – were a potent passing combination, and Krol was an effective runner and kicker. His passing and kicking accounted for all the Argos' points in their 1947 cup win over Winnipeg. He retired after 1952 but returned in 1955 to punt for the Argos. FRANK COSENTINO

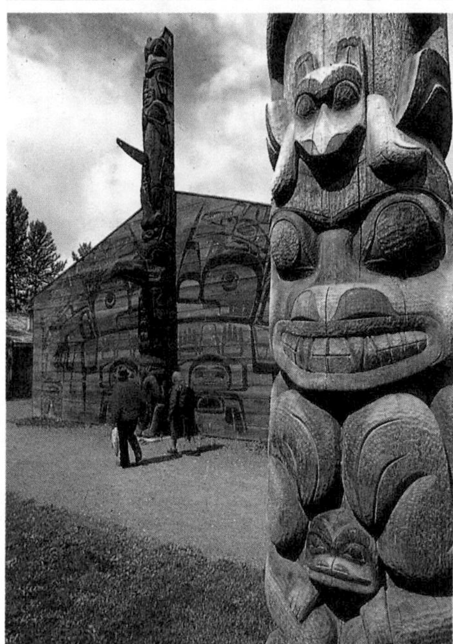

Ksan, a reconstruction of an early 1800s Gitksan village in Hazelton, BC, where Indian villages have stood for thousands of years (*photo by John deVisser/Masterfile*).

Ksan is a reconstructed Gitksan (TSIMSHIAN) Indian village located at the junction of the Skeena and Bulkley rivers in Hazelton, BC, where Indian villages have stood for thousands of years. Ksan, the Gitksan name for the SKEENA R ("River of Mists"), is the result of a joint project by Indians and non-Indians to help solve the area's social and economic problems by promoting a better understanding of local Indian culture and reviving its artistic traditions. In 1958 the Hazelton Library Assn raised $10 000 and constructed the Skeena Treasure House for exhibition of ceremonial regalia on loan from many Gitksan chiefs in the area. Following the decision of the volunteer planning committee to build a replica of an Indian village of the early 1800s, construction began in 1968, with the combined financial help of the Ksan Assn and the provincial and federal governments. Ksan was officially opened 12 Aug 1970. Buildings, modelled on communal houses with painted fronts, include a carving school and workshop, a shop for sales of carvings and Gitksan and CARRIER native crafts, and a museum where the regalia of chiefs are housed and displayed until needed at ceremonial feasts (*see* POTLATCH). A 19th-century Wolf Crest HOUSE prepared for a feast and a prehistoric Frog Crest house with displays depict traditional activities.

Some Ksan buildings are open year-round, and tours and dance performances are scheduled during the summer. In Gitksan villages near Ksan, visitors can see some of the oldest TOTEM POLES still in a native setting and learn more about the local history. *See also* NORTHWEST COAST INDIAN ART.

V. JENSEN AND J.V. POWELL

Ku Klux Klan [Gk *kuklos*, "circle"], an ultraconservative, secret fraternal organization dedicated to the supremacy of an Anglo-Saxon, Protestant society. Formed in Pulaski, Tenn, in Nov 1865 by 6 ex-Confederate soldiers, it was outlawed in 1871 because of violent and outrageous acts against blacks and northerners. Revived Nov 1915 in Atlanta, Ga, it drew its support from middle- and lower-class Americans who feared the loss of conservative and rural values. In 1921 the Klan was reported active in Montréal; by 1925 "klans," or locals, had been established all across Canada. Like their American counterparts, Canadian Klansmen had a fanatical hatred for all things Roman Catholic and feared that the purity of the Anglo-Saxon race was being jeopardized by new immigration. Moreover, they were not averse to stepping outside the law to achieve their goals.

The Klan appealed to few Canadians and remained relatively obscure, except in Saskatchewan. After American organizers absconded with approximately $100 000 of Klan funds in 1927, the Saskatchewan organization regrouped and, at its height, just after the 1929 provincial election (in which it was instrumental in ending 24 years of Liberal rule), it boasted of having 40 000 members. Thereafter the Saskatchewan Klan declined rapidly, as did the organization in the rest of Canada. In the late 1970s the Klan attempted once more to organize in Canada, notably in Ontario, Alberta and BC. The organization's avowed white-supremacist stance and further outrages committed by the American Klan during this period have done little either to increase membership or to establish the Klan's credibility in the eyes of the Canadian public. *See also* PREJUDICE AND DISCRIMINATION.

PAUL BANFIELD

Reading: J. Sher, *White Hoods* (1983).

Kudelka, James, choreographer, dancer (b at Newmarket, Ont 10 Oct 1955). Acknowledged as the leading Canadian ballet choreographer of his generation, he has evolved a unique style that fuses classical ballet and modern-dance idioms of movement to produce emotionally powerful works. Kudelka first choreographed while a student at the NATIONAL BALLET SCHOOL. He continued to choreograph while a leading dancer of the NATIONAL BALLET OF CANADA, 1972-81, becoming a company resident choreographer, 1980-82, and winning serious critical attention for such overtly dramatic ballets as *A Party* (1976) and *Washington Square* (1979). After joining Les GRANDS BALLETS CANADIENS in 1981, Kudelka's choreography shifted to a more abstracted style in such acclaimed works as *In Paradisum* (1983) and *Alliances* (1984). He was named resident choreographer of Les Grands Ballets in 1984 and contributes regularly to the repertoire, eg, *Le Sacre du printemps* (1987). Kudelka now also choreographs increasingly for a range of other companies in Canada and abroad. Among his recent works are *Dracula* (Montréal, 1985), *The Heart of the Matter* (U of Iowa, 1986) and *Collisions* (Expo 86).

MICHAEL CRABB

Reading: U. Kareda, *The Turning Point* (1985).

Kuerti, Anton Emil, pianist, teacher, composer (b at Vienna, Austria 21 July 1938). Kuerti began performing at age 9 as soloist with the Boston Pops Orchestra. He continued studies at the Peabody, Cleveland and Curtis institutes, and before moving to Canada in 1965 had performed with every major N American orchestra and given solo recitals in most large N American and European cities. An interpreter and performer particularly of Beethoven, Schumann, Mozart, Brahms, Schubert, Scriabin and Bach, Kuerti is one of Canada's leading pianists. Very much an individualist, Kuerti eschews high concert fees and performs in many smaller centres, always with his own piano. His recording of the 32 Beethoven sonatas won a Juno Award in 1976. As a teacher at the Faculty of Music, U of T, Kuerti has encouraged several notable young pianists, and as an international performer has premiered some of his own works and those of Oskar MORAWETZ and S.C. ECKHARDT-GRAMATTÉ. He has also initiated individual concerts and festivals, including the Festival of the Sound, established at Parry Sound, Ont, in 1980. In 1986 Kuerti held a Beethoven concert at Toronto's Massey Hall with the Kitchener-Waterloo Symphony Orchestra and also released a recording of 5 Beethoven concertos which he made with the Toronto Symphony Orchestra.

MABEL H. LAINE

Kulesha, Gary, composer, arranger, conductor, radio producer (b at Toronto 22 Aug 1954). A composer of concert and theatre music, Kulesha has written vocal, instrumental and electronic works, including incidental music for productions at the STRATFORD FESTIVAL where he was principal conductor between 1983 and 1985. After studying with John McCabe in London, England, and with John Corigliano in New York, Kulesha returned to Toronto in 1982. Since then, he has composed prolifically and in a wide range of styles. He acknowledges the influence of such 20th-century composers as Bartok, Ligeti and Schoenberg (which can be heard in his *First, Second* and *Third Chamber Concertos*), as well as jazz and African music (heard in his *Nocturne and Toccata* and *Suite For Percussion Quartet*). Kulesha has also worked as a producer for CBC Radio in its Winnipeg station.

COLIN EATOCK

Kurelek, William (Wasyl), painter and writer, evangelist (b near Whitford, Alta 3 Mar 1927; d at Toronto 3 Nov 1977). Influenced by Bosch and Brueghel and by prairie roots, his UKRAINIAN heritage and Roman Catholicism, Kurelek's realistic and symbolic paintings record his historic culture and religious vision. The oldest of 7 children, he was expected to help run the farm. His lack of mechanical aptitude attracted harsh criticism from his father, as did his wish to be an artist. He studied at Winnipeg, Toronto and San Miguel, Mexico. In England (1952-59), he sought psychiatric help and was hospitalized for severe emotional problems, depression and eye pain. He converted to Roman Catholicism (1957), credited God with his healing, and began to paint the Passion of Christ according to St Matthew. This series of 160 paintings is housed in the Niagara Falls Art Gallery and Museum.

Returning to Toronto, he was established by the early 1960s as an important painter, alternating realistic works depicting his prairie roots with didactic series. In the 1970s he began to publish his paintings with simple texts. His books for children (*A Prairie Boy's Winter*, 1973; *Lumberjack*, 1974; *A Prairie Boy's Summer*, 1975; and *A Northern Nativity*, 1976) have become modern classics.

William Kurelek showing himself at work in *The Painter* (1974), mixed media (*courtesy the Isaacs Gallery, Toronto*).

His autobiography, *Someone With Me* (1973, rev ed 1980), ends with his marriage to Jean Andrews (1962). Kurelek was an outstanding artist with a unique idealistic and pragmatic vision. A modern Jeremiah, he painted a coming apocalypse – divine justice on a materialistic, secular society. PATRICIA MORLEY

Reading: Patricia Morley, *Kurelek: A Biography* (1986).

Kushner, Donn, author, scientist (b at Lake Charles, La 29 Mar 1927). He studied at Harvard (BSc, 1948) and McGill (MSc, 1950; PhD, 1952). He has lived in Canada since 1948 and is a Canadian citizen. Kushner has taught biology at U of O since 1965 and is the author of numerous scientific articles and editor of *Microbial Life in Extreme Environments* (1978). From 1977 to 1983 he co-edited the *Canadian Journal of Microbiology* and in 1986 was recipient of the Ottawa Biological and Biochemical Society Award. Although he has published one collection of short fiction for adults, *The Witness and Other Stories* (1981), he has secured his literary reputation as a children's writer. In 1981, *The Violin Maker's Gift* won the Canadian Library Assn Book of the Year Award. This highly imaginative saga has been translated into Dutch, German, French and Polish. In 1984, he published *Uncle Jacob's Ghost Story*. Kushner's cerebral blend of fantasy and fiction has resulted in a distinctive voice, winning him critical acclaim as a modern fabulist with echoes of Antoine de Saint-Exupéry. SHARON DRACHE

Kutchin, the northernmost of all N American Indians, occupied a broad sweep of territory located primarily N of the Arctic Circle and extending across the Mackenzie drainage and northern tributaries of the Yukon R into NW Alaska. Their northern boundary abuts Inuit land. They speak an Athapaskan language, unintelligible to all other Athapaskans except possibly the HAN.

Depending on an upland or lowland habitat, the 9 or 10 regional bands concentrated on moose hunting or salmon fishing, though caribou, captured in impressive corrals, were available to all bands. Even though big game supplied the greater part of their food and hides for clothing and shelter, the Kutchin also caught whitefish, hare and other small game. Kutchin knowledge of their environment was extensive; one anthropologist recorded 400 Kutchin names for plants and animals. Kutchin technology was similar to that of other subarctic Athapaskans, with distinctive western elements, including large metal knives with double recurved handles, sleds, chair-style birchbark baby carriers, partially decked-over kayak-canoes, and portable domed caribou-skin tents. Adults and children alike wore V-tailed summer shirts decorated with red ochre, dentalium (beads made with seeds) and dyed porcupine quills. Women tattooed their chins and, on ceremonial occasions, men coiffed their hair with red ochre mixed with grease and sprinkled with down.

A pair of same-sex siblings with their nuclear families customarily formed a household. Several households related to one senior person or "chief" made up a local band, which worked together to build caribou surrounds and large fish traps, but sometimes larger groups met to hunt. Several local bands formed a regional band, maintained through intermarriage and other interactions between constituent families within a single geographic area. Regional bands assembled for annual festivities and ceremonies. Kutchin identity was achieved through language. Crosscutting the band structure were 3 matrilineal clans which regulated marriage.

The Kutchin world view included beliefs in animal spirits, spirit beings, bushmen (wild Indians with supernatural attributes), and the culture hero-trickster Raven (crow), recorded in culture hero myth cycles and raven myths.

In 1789 the Kutchin were contacted by Alexander MACKENZIE, S of the Mackenzie Delta. Within 2 decades they were trading extraterritorially at posts on the Mackenzie R and, in 1840, FT MCPHERSON was built on the Peel R. The HUDSON'S BAY COMPANY established Ft Yukon, Alaska, in 1847. The Kutchin became middlemen in trade between the coastal Eskimo and interior tribes and between the Mackenzie and Yukon and resented establishment of European trading posts in their territory. In the 1980s Kutchin population was approximately 2500 persons, with slightly more than half living at OLD CROW, Ft McPherson and Arctic Red River or in the mixed Inuit/Indian/white communities of Aklavik and Inuvik. The remainder live in Alaska. *See also* NATIVE PEOPLE: SUBARCTIC and general articles under NATIVE PEOPLE. A. MCFADYEN CLARK

Reading: J. Helm, ed, *Handbook of North American Indians*, vol 6; *Subarctic* (1981).

Kwakiutl The "kwakwaka'wakw" (often referred to as Kwakiutl, which is the name of the Ft Rupert band, and Kwagulth) occupy coastal areas of BC extending from Smith Inlet in the N to Cape Mudge in the S, W to Quatsino and E to Knight Inlet. Originally, there were 28 tribes, all speaking dialects of Kwakwala, from which comes the people's name for themselves, *Kwakwaka'wakw*. The first census in 1835 recorded the total population as 8575. A member of the Wakashan language family, Kwakwala is related to other languages such as Westcoast (NOOTKA), Heiltsuk (BELLA BELLA), Oowekyala (Rivers Inlet people) and Haisla (KITAMAAT). The culture of the Kwakiutl is similar to that of their northern neighbours, the Bella Bella and Rivers Inlet peoples. Trails across Vancouver I made trade possible with Nootka villages on the West Coast. Archaeological evidence shows habitation in the Kwakwala-speaking area for at least 8000 years. In precontact times Kwakiutl fished, hunted and gathered, according to the seasons, securing an abundance of preservable food. Consequently, this allowed them to return to their winter villages for several months of intensive ceremonial and artistic activity.

In 1792 Spanish explorers Dionisio Alcalá-Galiano and Cayetano Valdés and Capt George VANCOUVER encountered most of the south Kwakiutl groups, and Vancouver wrote detailed descriptions of them. Farther N, in 1849 the HUDSON'S BAY CO established Ft Rupert, which operated until 1877, when it was sold to Robert Hunt, the last factor. George HUNT, Robert's son, became anthropologist Franz BOAS's assistant, and together they wrote a large body of material on the language and culture of the Kwakiutl.

Kwakiutl wolf mask. In 1921 a number of Kwakiutl were arrested for conducting a potlatch and their masks and other items were confiscated. In 1967 the National Museums agreed to return the masks (*courtesy National Museums of Canada/Canadian Museum of Civilization/K81-361*).

Kwakiutl wedding party returns to the groom's village, photograph by Edward S. Curtis (*courtesy British Columbia Provincial Museum*).

A federal law of 1884 prohibiting the POTLATCH threatened to destroy the heart of the culture. In 1921 a large potlatch at Village I resulted in the arrest of 45 people, of whom 22 were imprisoned, their ceremonial goods confiscated. Knowing that these masks and other ritual objects had been wrongfully taken, the *Kwakwaka'wakw*, in 1967, initiated efforts to secure their return. The National Museums of Canada agreed to return that part of the collection held by the Canadian Museum of Civilization, on the condition that 2 museums be built, the Kwakiutl Museum in Cape Mudge and the U'mista Cultural Centre in Alert Bay (*see* NORTHWEST COAST INDIAN ART).

Today, most Kwakiutl children speak English as their first language, and many schools in the area sponsor programs in Kwakwala and traditional dance and art. Traditionally fishermen, the *Kwakwaka'wakw* continue to fish commercially in a highly competitive industry. Hereditary chiefs still pass on rights and privileges at potlatches, but band government is conducted by elected councillors.

A number of original villages have been abandoned as inhabitants moved to communities such as Alert Bay, Campbell River and Port Hardy, to be close to schools and hospitals. Only 9 villages are now inhabited, with a total population of about 4100 for the area. *See also* NATIVE PEOPLE: NORTHWEST COAST and general articles under NATIVE PEOPLE. GLORIA CRANMER WEBSTER

Reading: F. Boas, "The Social Organization and the Secret Societies of the Kwakiutl Indians," *Smithsonian Institute Annual Report for 1895* (1897), and *Kwakiutl Ethnography* (ed H. Codere, 1966); R. and E. Rohner, *The Kwakiutl* (1970).

Kwong, Normie, "The China Clipper," football player (b Lim Kwong Yew at Calgary 24 Oct 1929). As a running back over 14 seasons in Calgary and Edmonton, he was a Canadian Football League all-star 5 times, twice won the Schenley Award as outstanding Canadian player (1955-56) and was Canada's athlete of the year (1956). Together with teammate Johnny BRIGHT, Kwong gave EDMONTON ESKIMOS a potent running attack. From 1950 to 1961 he gained 9022 yards, averaging 5.2 yards per carry, and scored 74 touchdowns. In 1987 Kwong was inducted into the Alberta Sports Hall of Fame. He is also one of the owners of the Calgary Flames hockey team.

GERALD REDMOND

La Baie, Qué, City, pop 20 753 (1986c), 20 935 (1981c), inc 1976, is located at the end of Baie des Ha! Ha! on the SAGUENAY R, 10 km E of CHICOUTIMI and 200 km N of Québec City. Seaport and cradle of the Saguenay-Lac Saint-Jean region, La Baie is the amalgamation of 4 former municipalities: Bagotville, Port-Alfred, the parish of Grande-Baie and the parish of Bagotville. La Baie was founded in 1838 by employees of the Société des vingt-et-un, a Charlevoix forestry company bought by William PRICE in 1842. Price's sawmills were soon joined by port facilities, making La Baie, a natural harbour, a major port on the Atlantic coast. A paper mill was built there in 1917 (Consolidated Bathurst) and an aluminum plant in 1979 (Alcan). The Musée du fjord shows the maritime character of La Baie. The Monument des vingt-et-un and the Fêtes du Saguenay, held each June, are reminders that this city is the oldest municipality of the Saguenay-Lac Saint-Jean region. MARC ST-HILAIRE

La Barre, Joseph-Antoine Le Febvre de, governor of New France 1682-85 (b in France 1622; d at Paris, France 1688). La Barre's administration in New France was disastrous, particularly from a military point of view. Like many governors, he enriched himself in the FUR TRADE. Joining forces with several Canadian merchants, he attempted to secure the trade with the Illinois by confiscating the posts of Cavelier de LA SALLE, protégé of the previous governor, FRONTENAC. Some said it was to secure this business that La Barre launched his ill-planned expedition against the Iroquois in 1684. His troops were so weakened by disease that he was forced to sign a humiliating peace. This failure, and La Salle's complaints, led to his dismissal. *See also* IROQUOIS WARS. ALLAN GREER

La Brosse, Jean-Baptiste de (1712-82), Jesuit missionary in the Saguenay-St Lawrence Gulf region remembered for having predicted his own death on 11 April 1782. Upon his death, darkness is said to have covered the SAGUENAY R, and in all the parishes where he had preached the bells began ringing without anyone going near them. NANCY SCHMITZ

La Galissonière, Roland-Michel Barrin de La Galissonière, Marquis de, naval officer, commandant general of New France (b at Rochefort, France 10 Nov 1693; d at Montereau, France 26 Oct 1756). He was born into a powerful family and rose to lieutenant-general of the French naval forces. He was in NEW FRANCE from 19 Sept 1747 to 21 Oct 1749, during which time he strongly advocated building a line of garrisoned posts down the Ohio Valley to hold the English colonies along the coast. He enthusiastically promoted the colony's interests, seeing it as a viable economic asset in classic mercantilist terms, as well as a military distraction to the English. La Galissonière had broad humanistic and scientific interests and had his officers collect botanical specimens from across the colony. His report on France's colonies, found in *Mémoires des commissaires du roi* (1755-57), contained a lucid account of colonial policies and of the potential riches of Canada. Despite his brief stay in Canada, La Galissonière's engaging personality, intelligence and fervent activity on the colony's behalf made him popular and left a lasting impression. In the year of his death, he commanded the French fleet at Minorca that defeated Admiral Byng. JAMES MARSH

La Grande Rivière, 893 km long, rises in the rugged forest highlands of central Québec and drains W into JAMES BAY. Its 97 600 km^2 drainage basin is the third-largest in Québec. The river has

long been populated by CREE, whose hunting territories stretch along to its banks and tributaries. In 1803 the establishment of a fur-trade post at the river mouth marked the origins of the modern native settlement of Fort George. For many years the river too was called the Fort George. During the 1970s it was transformed by the JAMES BAY PROJECT, a scheme to divert major rivers flowing into eastern James Bay for hydroelectric development. Phase one of the project involved erecting huge dams on the La Grande and flooding low-lying areas to create reservoirs. After a prolonged legal dispute, an agreement was signed with the native people who feared the destruction of their wildlife resources, and construction on the river was completed. DANIEL FRANCIS

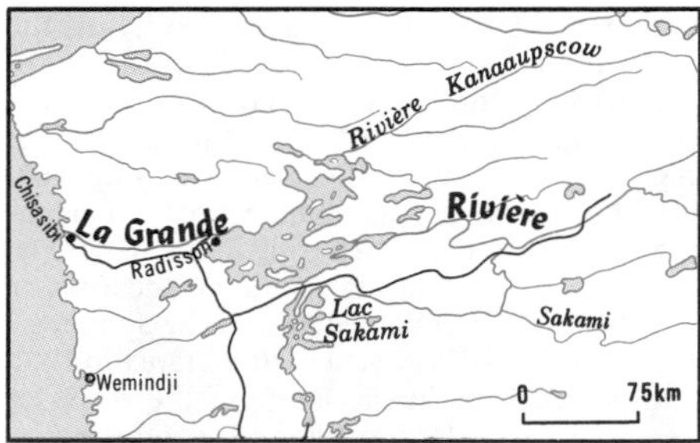

La Jonquière, Jacques-Pierre de Taffanel de La Jonquière, Marquis de, naval officer, governor general of New France, appointed 1746, served 1749-52 (b near Albi, France 18 Apr 1685; d at Québec 17 Mar 1752). In 1746 La Jonquière was a veteran of 49 years in the French navy. War raged with England at the time; he served in the expedition of the duc d'Anville in 1746 and was taken prisoner of war in 1747. He finally reached Québec in 1749. France and England were theoretically at peace during his administration, but La Jonquière's main concern was to prepare for the next armed struggle, reinforcing his troops and fortifying posts on the Great Lakes and along the frontier of Acadia. He was implicated in some of the speculations of intendant François BIGOT. ALLAN GREER

La Malbaie, Qué, Town, pop 3948 (1986c), 4030 (1981c), inc 1958, is situated on the lower N shore of the ST LAWRENCE R at the mouth of Rivière La Malbaie, 150 km E of Québec City. Named *malle baye* by CHAMPLAIN in 1608 for its difficult anchorage, La Malbaie is the seat and centre of Municipalité regionale de comte Charlevoix-Est. Some of New France's first rural settlements were located in the area. Two Scottish soliders, John Nairne and Malcolm Fraser, the first resident seigneurs, called it Murray Bay. They occupied grants on either side of Malbaie R until about 1815 and introduced many visitors to the area. The county's renowned resorts are among the oldest on the continent and include Manoir Richelieu in Pointe-au-Pic and hotels situated in Cap-à-l'Aigle. Tourist accommodation, outdoor recreation and market gardening are the main activities of the La Malbaie economy. A poultry abattoir and an aluminum-products plant are its largest industries. PAULA KESTELMAN

Reading: G.M. Wrong, *A Canadian Manor and Its Seigneurs* (1926).

La Mauricie National Park (est 1970, 544 km^2) is situated about 220 km NE of Montréal. The gently rolling Laurentian Hills form a backdrop for the park's billion-year-old Precambrian granite and gneiss landscape, sculpted by the action of GLACIERS during the last Ice Age. The same glaciers scraped out the numerous lakes dotting the park. La Mauricie has a mixed forest vegetation. Coniferous species typical of the boreal forest share the hillsides with deciduous species found more abundantly in the ST LAWRENCE LOWLANDS. Wildlife includes moose, black bear, lynx, red fox and wolf. Some 116 bird species nest in the park. The lakes and bogs support 17 species of amphibians and reptiles. The remains of red-ochre rock paintings testify that nomadic tribes hunted and fished here over 2000 years ago. Explorers and missionaries inhabited the area from the mid-1600s, but the lumber industry did not become established until 1825. The abandoned camps are a reminder of the colourful history of the lumberjacks and log drivers. The ST-MAURICE R still carries millions of logs to mills in nearby towns. LILLIAN STEWART

La Palme, Béatrice, soprano, violinist, teacher (b at Beloeil, near Montréal 27 July 1878; d at Montréal 8 Jan 1921). She was the second Québec vocalist, after Emma ALBANI, to appear on the great lyrical stages. She studied violin with Frantz JEHIN-PRUME and Fernandez Arbos, and sang with Gustave Garcia and Nelly Rowe. At the suggestion of Albani, she decided to devote herself exclusively to song. She appeared before Massenet, and sang various times 1905-09 at the Opéra-Comique de Paris. She then toured with the Montreal Opera Company. After 1914 she taught in the studio run by her husband, French tenor Salvator Issaurel. HÉLÈNE PLOUFFE

La Peltrie, Marie-Madeleine de Gruel de, née Chauvigny, patron of Ursuline nuns in New France (b at Alençon, France 1603; d at Québec C 18 Nov 1671). Born into the aristocracy, widowed at 22, Mme de La Peltrie was influenced by *Relations des Jésuites* to devote her life and fortune to Amerindian missions. Introduced to MARIE DE L'INCARNATION, she sailed with her and 2 Ursulines to Québec to found a convent in 1639. Except for an 18-month absence to help found the utopian colony of VILLE-MARIE [Montréal] in 1642, she lived cloistered with the nuns she supported. When she died her body was buried in the Ursuline chapel and her heart was sent to the Jesuits. CORNELIUS J. JAENEN

La Prairie, Qué, Town, pop 11 072 (1986c), 10 627 (1981c), inc 1909, a suburb of Montréal, is located on the S shore of the St Lawrence R. It took its name from the land called "La-Prairie-de-la-Madeleine," occupied by the Jesuits as of 1647 and granted by the Abbé de La Ferté de La Madeleine, a member of the COMPAGNIE DES CENT-ASSOCIÉS. After the CONQUEST, British merchants immigrated to La Prairie and soon controlled its economy, which was linked to river transportation. In 1836 the first Canadian railway, linking La Prairie with St-Jean, was inaugurated. After construction of the Victoria Bridge, goods trains coming from the east were diverted from the town. Around 1890 the establishment of brickyards gave the town new vigour; one of these yards is still among the largest in Canada. In the 20th century, La Prairie's economy has undergone little growth. Other industries (electrical equipment, electronics, printing and food processing) have been established, but in the service sector, La Prairie is largely dependent upon Montréal. SYLVIE TASCHEREAU

La Presse Strike The strike at the newspaper *La* PRESSE began as a classic work conflict but became a major sociopolitical confrontation. The paper, the most important French-language daily in Québec, had been owned since 1967 by Paul DESMARAIS, president of Power Corp. At the end of July 1971, after 6 months of negotiations, management decided to lock out the typesetters belonging to 4 unions affiliated with the Québec Federation of Labour (Fédération des travailleurs du Québec). The unions refused to modify their collective agreements and to allow the loss of unionized jobs. The paper appeared until Oct 27, when the strikers forced it to close down. Two days later, the 3 main UNION CENTRALS defied a municipal ban to organize a huge march in solidarity with the newspaper workers. More than 12 000 people clashed with 100 Montréal policemen. The outcome was some 50 arrests, several dozen injuries and one death from natural causes. These events had a powerful impact, especially among the QFL leaders, whose critique of society became radicalized as a result. The strike came during a period of intense frustration for the union movement, tested the preceding year by the OCTOBER CRISIS. However, negotiations resumed soon after the demonstration and 3 months later, 7 Feb 1972, management and workers reached a satisfactory compromise. JACQUES ROUILLARD

La Rocque, Marguerite de, co-seigneuress of Pontpoint (place and date of b and d unknown). She was a close relative of the Sieur de ROBERVAL and accompanied him on his 1542 voyage to Canada. Shocked by Marguerite's conduct in taking a lover, Roberval set her ashore of Île des Démons, in the St Lawrence R, with her lover and a servant girl. (A more romantic version of the story has the young man put ashore and Marguerite joining him.) The young man, the servant and a child Marguerite bore all died. Marguerite managed to survive and was rescued some years later by fishermen. JAMES MARSH

La Ronge, Sask, Town, pop 2696 (1986c), 2579 (1981c), inc 1976, is located on the W shore of LAC LA RONGE in northern Saskatchewan. Origin of the name is uncertain but it is likely associated with the beaver and the French verb *ronger* ("to gnaw"). Fur traders such as the FROBISHERS and Peter POND frequented this site in the 1770s, and HBC posts operated intermittently in the area into this century. Occupation of the present townsite started when Archdeacon John Alexander Mackay established an Indian residential school and sawmill (1898). Not accessible by road until 1947, the basically native community grew very slowly for many years. But it has more than doubled in size since 1971, expanding as a tourist and administrative centre and departure point for prospectors. C.O. WHITE

La Salle, René-Robert Cavelier de, would-be Jesuit, fur trader, explorer, intriguer, discoverer of the Mississippi delta (b at Rouen, France 21 Nov 1643; assassinated 19 Mar 1687 in Texas). In 1658 La Salle began his noviciate in the Society of Jesus. Mental instability caused his release from his vows in 1667. He crossed to NEW FRANCE and 2 years later, falsely claiming to speak fluent Iroquois, he joined a Sulpician exploration expedition. Upon their encountering some Seneca he had to admit his total ignorance of their language and went off on his own. In 1673 he joined the coterie of Gov Gen FRONTENAC, with whose support he obtained letters of nobility. At the French Court, meanwhile, 2 clerics, Abbés Eusèbe Renaudot and Claude Bernou, to advance their own careers on La Salle's coattails, obtained a commission for him to explore the mid-west. In 1678 he began establishing a chain of trading posts, and then in 1682, with a small party of French and Indian guides, he descended the Mississippi to its mouth. On Apr 9 he claimed the entire region for Louis XIV.

Returning to France he fell in with a scheme of Bernou's to establish a base at the mouth of the Rio Grande for the conquest of Mexico. To make it seem more feasible to the king he falsified geography, situating the Mississippi over 600 miles W of its true course. Given command of the expedition, he displayed incompetence and paranoia. That, and his earlier duplicity, caused him to land in Feb 1685 at Matagorda B [Texas] which he claimed to be an outlet of the Mississippi. Most of the expedition's supplies having been lost and the Indians alienated, starvation loomed. In Apr 1686 La Salle set off with 20 men to seek help at Ft St-Louis-des-Illinois. Dissension in his party and at the base resulted in desertion and murder, and finally in the assassination of La Salle. The wonder is that his men had not killed him long before.

A romantic hero to 19th-century historians, La Salle was in fact a victim of his own incapacities. His one claim to fame is his descent of the Mississippi, upon which French claims to Louisiana were to be based. W.J. ECCLES

La Sarre, Québec, Town, pop 8622 (1986c), 8861 (1981c), inc 1949, is located in the western part of the Abitibi region, near Lac ABITIBI and the Ontario border. Founded in 1917, it was one of the first agricultural centres to be settled when the transcontinental railway opened up the Abitibi region around 1910. The place was originally called *Wabakin,* an Algonquin expression meaning "white fish river," referring to the Rivière La Sarre which flows through the town and into Lac Abitibi. It was later named after the La Sarre regiment, which had been sent to New France in 1755 and gained fame at the Battle of the PLAINS OF ABRAHAM. La Sarre's agricultural and forest industries have made it one of the principal urban centres in Abitibi-Témiscaming. The town is located in the heart of rich, agricultural lands around Lac Abitibi. Its economy is largely dependent upon its sawmills and wood-processing plants. The Normik-Perron plant, one of the largest timber companies in eastern Canada, is also located here. BENOÎT-BEAUDRY GOURD

La Tour, Charles de Saint-Étienne de, colonizer, trader, governor of Acadia (b at Champagne, France 1593; d at Cap de Sable, Acadia 1663). La Tour possibly reached Acadia as early as 1606, living there permanently from 1610. When Charles de BIENCOURT died in 1623, La Tour assumed leadership of the colony and 8 years later received a royal commission as lieutenant-general. Shortly afterwards he became embroiled in a dispute with the governor, Charles de MENOU D'AULNAY. With support at the French court, d'Aulnay had La Tour discredited and in 1645, in La Tour's absence, attacked and captured his base at Ft La Tour, treacherously killing its defenders. Mme Françoise LA TOUR, who had commanded the fort, died 3 weeks later. La Tour returned to Acadia following d'Aulnay's death in 1650, but was captured by an English invading force in 1654. Eventually, he came to terms with his captors and returned to an Acadia under English occupation. During the short-lived Scottish occupation of NS 1629-32, he had been given the title of knight-baronet of Scotland, and in the 1650s he allowed this title to be used to give legitimacy to the English conquest. This arrangement has frequently been termed treachery and opportunism by La Tour's critics, but La Tour had tenaciously defended his settlements when necessary and his commitment to Acadia can be measured by his lifelong residence there. JOHN G. REID

La Tour, Françoise-Marie de Saint-Étienne de, née Jacquelin, Acadian heroine (b in France 1602; d at Ft La Tour [NB] 1645). Civil war raged in Acadia in 1640 when she married Charles de Saint-Étienne de LA TOUR, one of 2 claimants to the colony's governorship. She proved to be his most courageous and resourceful supporter, travelling to France, England and Boston to secure supplies and men to fight his rival, Charles de MENOU D'AULNAY. During her husband's absence in 1645, she took command of Ft La Tour at the mouth of the St John R when d'Aulnay attacked. Despite her stout defence over 3 days, her outnumbered forces were defeated. Mme La Tour surrendered on d'Aulnay's assurance of giving "quarter to all." However, he went back on his word and forced Mme La Tour to watch, a rope around her neck, as the garrison was hanged. She died 3 weeks later. ALLAN GREER

La Tuque, Qué, Town, pop 10 723 (1986c), 11 556 (1981c), inc 1911, is located on the Rivière ST-MAURICE, 165 km N of Trois-Rivières. Isolated in a huge forest zone in the heart of the Maurice region, the town was built at the start of the 20th century on the site of a former trading post. It owes its name to a mountain shaped like a triangular woolen hat, popularly known as a "tuque." In 1904 the Brown Corp, an American paper company, bought the falls and neighbouring lands and in 1907 built a pulp mill powered by electricity from a dam. The town born of this industry grew and became the gathering point for forest workers. The hydroelectric station, whose power was increased in 1943, is used by HYDRO-QUÉBEC. In 1954 the Canadian International Paper Co (CIP) bought the pulp mill, which it operates today. La Tuque lives primarily from FORESTRY and its derivatives: mills and construction wood. CIP makes industrial wrapping paper, cartons and bleached kraft paper. CLAUDINE PIERRE-DESCHÊNES

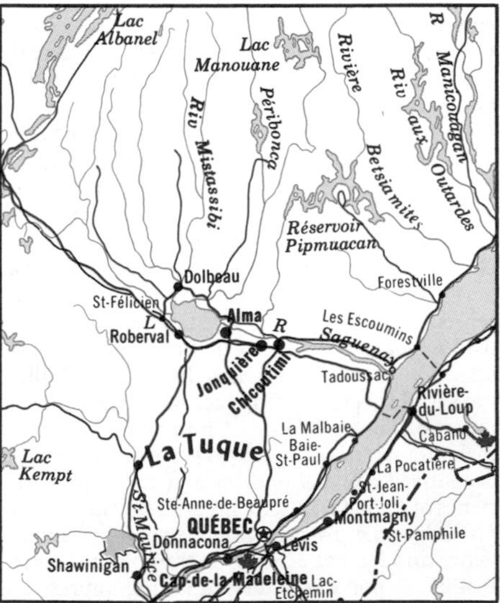

La Vérendrye, Jean-Baptiste Gaultier de, fur trader, explorer (b on Île Dupas 3 Sept 1713; d at Lac des Bois [Lake-of-the-Woods] 6 June 1736). He was the eldest son of Pierre Gaultier de Varennes et de LA VÉRENDRYE. In 1731 he was a member of the first group to head west under his father's command. In autumn 1731 he completed the building of Ft Saint-Pierre at Rainy Lake. In spring 1733 he travelled as far as the Winnipeg R and built a small fort there. In Jan 1734 he was left by his father among the Cree, who adopted him as one of theirs. He built the first Fort Maurepas (about 10 km N of present-day Selkirk, Man) on Red River in 1734 and remained there until 1735. He spent the winter of 1735-36 at Ft Saint-Charles and on June 5 left with Father Aulneau and 19 others to fetch provisions at Michilimakinac. The party was surprised by Sioux warriors and all killed on a small island in Lake-of-the-Woods. The bodies were found on June 20 and brought for burial at Ft Saint-Charles.

JAMES MARSH

La Vérendrye, Louis-Joseph Gaultier de, "Chevalier," explorer, fur trader, military officer (b at Île aux Vaches, New France 9 Nov 1717; d at sea 15 Nov 1761). Youngest son of Pierre Gaultier de Varennes et de LA VÉRENDRYE, Louis-Joseph is best known for having led the first European exploration across the Missouri R into the Great Plains. He joined his father's westward explorations in 1735 and helped him re-establish Ft Maurepas (1736) and build Ft La Reine (1738). In 1738 he accompanied his father to the Mandan country (near Bismarck, N Dakota) and in 1739 was sent N to explore Lk Winnipeg. It is likely that he reached THE PAS on the lower Saskatchewan R. In 1742 Louis-Joseph, his brother François Gaultier Du Tremblay and 2 other Frenchmen undertook their epic 15-month journey SW of the Mandan in search of the fabled "western sea." Having reached what were probably the Big Horn Mtns (Wyoming) they returned along the Cheyenne and Bad rivers, and buried a lead plaque at Pierre (S Dakota), unearthed in 1913. After 1743 Louis-Joseph served as post commander at Chequamegon, Kaministiquia and Michipicoton.

In the east, he participated in the Mohawk campaign (1748) and on Lk Champlain (1759) during the SEVEN YEARS' WAR. The most active and gifted of the 4 La Vérendrye sons, Louis-Joseph died in a shipwreck off Cape Breton.

C.E. HEIDENREICH

La Vérendrye, Pierre Gaultier de Varennes et de, military officer, farmer, fur trader, explorer (b at Trois-Rivières 17 Nov 1685; d at Montréal 5 Dec 1749). The expeditions organized by La Vérendrye and spearheaded by his sons were the first to open the country from Lk Superior to the lower Saskatchewan R and the Missouri R to the French fur trade.

Early in life La Vérendrye had chosen a military career. He saw action during the American phase of the WAR OF THE SPANISH SUCCESSION and, in 1708, was wounded and taken prisoner in France. Released in 1710 he returned to Canada in 1712, married and became a farmer on his wife's land on Île aux Vaches and Île Dupas in Lac St-Pierre. Tiring of this life, he decided to join his brother Jacques-René when he became commandant of the posts along the N shore of Lk Superior in 1726. After succeeding his brother as commandant in 1728, La Vérendrye began to revive the old dream of discovering a route to the hypothetical "western sea," believed by some geographers to be a large gulf in the western interior that opened to the Pacific. With permission from the minister of the marine, Maurepas, but no financial backing, La Vérendrye sought and received a 3-year monopoly on the fur trade of the area in 1731. He formed a partnership with a number of merchants and between 1731 and 1737 he was active building posts from Lk Superior to Lk Winnipeg promoting the fur trade, and gathering native information. These accounts mentioned 2 rivers leading west. La Vérendrye named them *Rivière Blanche* (Saskatchewan) and *Rivière de l'Ouest* (Missouri). Dissatisfied with La Vérendrye's progress in exploration (6 years to get to Lk Winnipeg), Maurepas demanded action. Accordingly, La Vérendrye struck SW in 1738 to the Mandan country on the Missouri R. It was the only journey of exploration in which he had not been preceded by one of his sons or his nephew Christophe Dufrost de La Jemerais. Unsure of what he had found, exhausted physically and financially, La Vérendrye returned to Ft La Reine [PORTAGE LA PRAIRIE] and left further exploration to his sons. In 1742-43 his sons Louis-Joseph and François Gaultier Du Tremblay journeyed SW beyond the Mandan proving that the sea did not lie in that direction. In the meantime La Vérendrye continued the development of the fur trade in the Manitoba Lks area. Expectations for a major discovery were so high that Maurepas lost patience, blaming La Vérendrye for diverting energies from exploration to trading, and suggested to Governor BEAUHARNOIS that he be replaced. In 1743 La Vérendrye resigned but was reappointed in 1746. He planned the exploration of the Saskatchewan R but died before he could undertake it.

C.E. HEIDENREICH

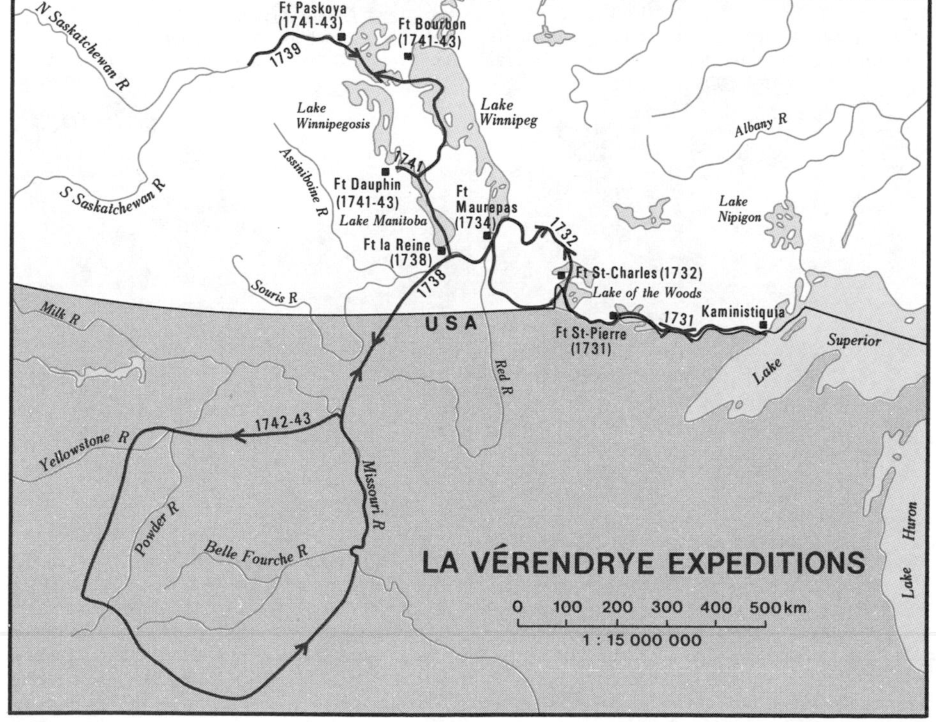

Labatt, John, brewer, entrepreneur (b in Westminster Twp, Middlesex County, Upper Canada 11 Dec 1838; d at London, Ont 27 Apr 1915). Third son of John Kinder LABATT, he was educated at Caradoc Academy and secondary school in London. He studied under an English brewer in Wheeling, West Virginia, 1859-64. Two years later, on his father's death, he entered into partnership with his mother to manage and then own the London Brewery, changing its name to John Labatt. Specializing in an English-type India pale ale, he marketed beyond the local region by the use of railways and bottling agencies, advertising by using prizes won at international expositions. Though he invested in other ventures, even founding an implement company to compete with Massey-Harris, none succeeded. Finally he confined himself to brewing, resisting merger first with Carling and then with O'Keefe. In 1911 he finally incorporated the firm as JOHN LABATT CORP, with a capital of $250 000 and a capacity of some 30 000 barrels annually.

ALBERT TUCKER

Labatt, John Kinder, farmer, brewer (b at Mountmellick, Ire 1803; d at London, Canada W 26 Oct 1866). Descended from French Huguenot exiles who had become Anglican, he emigrated from Ireland to England and thence to Upper Canada in 1833 with his wife. They settled on land of the Canada Co in Westminster Twp, Middlesex County. After 13 years Labatt sold his farm and invested as a partner in a small London brewery near the forks of the Thames R. In 1855 he became sole owner, and went on to build the business into a successful enterprise which combined the making of malt with the brewing of English types of ale.

ALBERT TUCKER

Labatt, John Sackville, brewer (b at London, Ont 10 Mar 1880; d at Port Stanley, Ont 8 July 1952). The eldest son of John LABATT, he was educated at Trinity College School and McGill. Succeeding his father, he was president of John Labatt Ltd 1915-50. Not a dynamic man, he combined ingenuous charm with the sense to maintain family control through the years of prohibition in Ontario (1916-27) and in the US (1920-33). During these years the company made large profits from the sale of beer and whisky across Lk Erie and the Detroit R. These profits made him the target for kidnapping in Aug 1934, when he became the first important Canadian business figure to be kidnapped for a high ransom. The ransom was never paid, and he was released unharmed. In the subsequent trial he mistakenly identified the wrong man, who was imprisoned. The experience made Labatt apprehensive and defensive. Though maintaining his visibility as president and his cordial relations with employees, he depended on others for direction through the period of expansion in the 1930s and 1940s.

ALBERT TUCKER

Labelle, François-Xavier-Antoine, Roman Catholic priest (b at Ste-Rose, Qué 24 Nov 1833; d at Québec C 4 Jan 1891). One of the best-known and most popular figures in Québec at the time, Curé Labelle was instrumental in promoting colonization of the Ottawa Valley. Appointed parish priest of St-Jérôme de Terrebonne in 1868, he dreamed of a francophone and Catholic reconquest of northern Canada, from Montréal to Winnipeg, through the establishment of a chain of colonies. A remarkable orator and assiduous lobbyist in Québec C and Ottawa, the huge priest devoted most of his energy to the first stage of this project: the settlement and agricultural, commercial, mining and manufacturing development of the area northwest of Montréal. An ardent supporter of building the CPR in 1872, he was sent as an envoy to Europe by the Canadian government in 1885 and the Québec government in 1890. In 1888 Prem Honoré MERCIER appointed him deputy minister of agriculture and colonization. Although Labelle encountered innumerable obstacles over the years and saw his most grandiose dreams crumble, he contributed to the establishment of some 20 parishes. GABRIEL DUSSAULT

Labelle, Huguette, née Rochon, nursing teacher and administrator (b at Rockland, Ont 15 Apr 1939). She began her career as a general staff nurse at the Ottawa General Hospital. After changing to teaching, she became founding director of the Vanier School of Nursing in Ottawa. In 1973 she was appointed principal nursing officer with Health and Welfare Canada, nursing's highest administrative post. A past president of the Canadian Nurses' Assn, she was undersecretary of state 1980-85 and since 1985 deputy clerk of the Privy Council and associate secretary to the Cabinet. As well, she is a senior adviser to the Government of Canada. DANIEL FRANCIS

Laberge, Albert, journalist, author (b at Beauharnois, Qué 18 Feb 1871; d at Montréal 4 Apr 1960). Laberge began school at the Académie Saint-Clément in Beauharnois and later attended Collège Sainte-Marie in Montréal, which he left in 1892. In 1894 he studied law at the École de Leblond de Brumath. His first poetic tales appeared in *Le Samedi* (1895). From 1896 to 1932 he worked at *La* PRESSE. He helped found the École littéraire de Montréal but did not participate in it until 1909. *La Scouine* (1918), a novel of rural customs, established Laberge as a naturalist writer. Besides *La Scouine,* Laberge published 10 collections of stories, 3 essays and some literary criticism – all at his own expense. His autobiographical novel, *Lamento*, was unfinished. Laberge tried to describe life as he saw it and placed particular emphasis on the dark side of life. Some of his stories have become classics: "La Femme au chapeau rouge" (1947), "Les Noces d'or" (1950), "La Rouille" (1950), "Le Dernier Souper" (1952) and "Madame Pouliche" (1963). PAUL WYCZYNSKI

Laberge, Louis, aircraft mechanic, labour leader (b at Ste-Martine, Qué 18 Feb 1924). At age 22, after working 2 years for Canadair, Laberge became shop steward of his union. Three years later (1948), he became the union's business officer and was president 1956-63 of the Conseil des métiers et du travail de Montréal. His election as president of the Fédération des travailleurs du Québec in 1964 came when it was losing ground to the Confédération des syndicats nationaux. Under his leadership, the FTQ, while defending the advantages of international ties and allegiance to Canada, also incorporated Québec neonationalist objectives. During the 1960s and 1970s, the FTQ sought greater independence from the CANADIAN LABOUR CONGRESS, supporting the PARTI QUÉBÉCOIS and moving ideologically to the left. Laberge has been re-elected easily at every congress since 1964. Although since 1985 the FTQ has not followed Laberge's recommendation that it endorse the PQ, he is still the longest-serving president of any federation of labour. JACQUES ROUILLARD

LaBine, Gilbert, prospector, mining promoter (b at Westmeath, Ont 10 Feb 1890; d at Toronto 8 June 1977). He and his brother Charlie formed ELDORADO Gold Mines (1926) in Manitoba. When the mine petered out, he used the company's remaining funds to finance prospecting trips around Great Bear Lk, where in 1930 he discovered a valuable deposit of silver mixed with pitchblende (radium). After establishing a refinery at Port Hope, Ont, LaBine entered the world radium market in 1933. His mine was forced to close in 1940, but American demand for uranium reopened it in 1942. That year the government secretly bought control of Eldorado, and in 1944 the company was nationalized. LaBine remained president until 1947. A brilliant prospector and creative promoter, LaBine was less at home with routine administration. His other interests included Gunnar Mines and Nesbitt-LaBine Mines. ROBERT BOTHWELL

Under Louis Laberge, the Fédération des travailleurs du Québec incorporated nationalist and independentist objectives (*courtesy Canapress Photo Service*).

Labour Canada, est 1900 as the Department of Labour under the Conciliation Act (now Department of Labour Act) to "aid in the prevention and settlement of trade disputes." The department's objectives are to promote and protect the rights of parties involved in work and to ensure equitable access to employment opportunities in enterprises subject to federal labour jurisdiction. Its functions are implemented through the Federal Mediation and Conciliation Program, which appoints conciliation officers in labour disputes; Program Developments and Central Operations Program, which produces labour-related data; the Policy Co-ordination and Liaison Program, which co-ordinates Canada's participation in the International Labour Organization; and the Administrative Policy and Services Program, responsible for the department's personnel relations. The Canada Labour Relations Board reports to the minister. The department's 1986-87 expenditures totalled $192 million.

Labour Day, honouring organized labour, is a legal holiday observed throughout Canada on the first Monday in Sept. The contribution of organized labour to Canadian society has been recognized since 1872, when parades and rallies were held in Ottawa and Toronto. The earliest American labour parades were not held until 1882 and in Europe Labour Day has been celebrated since 1889 on May 1, thereby merging traditional May Day festivities with labour celebrations. This spring date was briefly observed in Canada, but the N American need for a long weekend at the end of summer was recognized by Parliament in 1894. JOHN ROBERT COLOMBO

Labour Force, total of the adult population available to the LABOUR MARKET at a specific time; defined by Statistics Canada as "that portion of the civilian noninstitutional population 15 years of age and over who, during the reference week [in which the employment survey was taken], were employed or unemployed." Employed persons include all those who worked, part or full time, and those who would have been at work were it not for illness, disability, family responsibilities, bad weather, labour disputes or vacations. The unemployed include those without work but seeking work, those laid off for less than 6 months but available for work or those who have not sought work in the previous 4 weeks but have a job to go to within 4 weeks. This definition is a technical one for gathering statistical data and has been refined and modified over the years both for operational reasons and to reflect social and economic changes. For instance, earlier in this century the labour force was considered those 10

Since 1872, Labour Day has continued to be celebrated with parades, such as this one in what is now Thunder Bay (*courtesy Thunder Bay Historical Museum Society*).

The Canadian Labour Force: 1911-1987
(Source: Census of Canada 1971,1981; *The Labour Force*, June 1987)

Year	Labour Force (000s) Total	Male	Female
1911	2 698	2 341	357
1921	3 144	2 658	485
1931	3 908	3 245	663
1941	4 184	3 352	831
1951	5 277	4 114	1 162
1961	6 458	4 694	1 764
1971	8 688	5 698	2 990
1981	12 054	7 155	4 899
1987	13 186	7 362	5 824

Note: Excludes the Yukon, the NWT and, prior to 1951, Newfoundland. Excludes the unemployed who have never been employed and those on active service in 1941. Prior to 1951 the concept used was the "gainfully occupied" rather than the "labour force"

years of age and over. This changed to 14 years in 1941 and 15 years in 1961, reflecting the decline of an agriculturally based economy.

The size of the labour force is determined by the size of the adult population (potential labour force) and the proportion of that population willing and able to work (actual labour force); it is calculated from a monthly survey of 55 000 households across Canada, from which unemployment rates, employment rates, reasons for leaving the labour force, etc, are also calculated. The proportion of the adult population in the labour force is referred to as the participation rate, which varies by region and by demographic factors such as age or sex. PAUL PHILLIPS

Labour History, *see* WORKING-CLASS HISTORY.

Labour Law governs COLLECTIVE BARGAINING and other collective relations among employers, their unionized employees and trade unions. In Canada a distinction is commonly made between labour law narrowly defined in this way and EMPLOYMENT LAW, the law of individual employment relationships. In England, labour law describes both, and of course a close relationship exists between them. In most provinces these matters are covered in separate statutes, but the Canada Labour Code, Parliament's major labour-law enactment for industries within federal jurisdiction, also regulates labour standards and occupational health and safety.

As soon as there were unions in Canada there were labour laws (*see* WORKING-CLASS HISTORY), but it was not until 1944 that a full system of collective labour-relations law was established by regulation PC 1003, under federal government emergency powers. After the war it was replaced by federal and provincial legislation (*see* LABOUR RELATIONS), eg, Industrial Disputes Investigation Act 1948. These statutes, variously called labour codes, labour or industrial-relations Acts or trade-union Acts, are all based on the idea, expressed in the preamble to Part V of the Canada Labour Code, that "the common well-being" is promoted "through the encouragement of free collective bargaining and the constructive settlement of disputes." At the heart of labour law lies the volatile ideological issue of how completely the state should regulate the use of economic power by both labour and management in bargaining over wages and other terms or conditions of employment.

The Canada Labour Code and each equivalent provincial statute protects the right of employees to join the union of their choice by making it an unfair labour practice for an employer to discriminate against employees for joining a trade union or participating in any of its lawful activities. Moreover, the employer is required by law to bargain in good faith with the union chosen as bargaining agent by a majority of his employees. To protect these rights each statute provides for the appointment of a labour relations board, to which complaints of unfair labour practices may be taken and which, upon application for certification, decides whether a majority of the employees in question wish to be represented by that union. In deciding whether to certify a union the board must determine the "appropriate bargaining unit," ie, the group of employees by whom and for whom the selection of the bargaining agent is to be made. Once the appropriate bargaining unit is determined the labour relations board must ascertain the wishes of the majority by examining dues receipts and other evidence of membership in the union or by administering a secret-ballot vote, or both. In addition to the legislation there are regulations, practices, countless decisions by labour boards and many court judgements that make up the labour law governing unfair labour practices, union certification and the duty to bargain in good faith.

Once a union has been certified it is entitled to require the employer to meet with its representatives and bargain over the terms and conditions of employment that will form the collective agreement for the employees in the bargaining unit. Either the union or the employer may apply to the minister of labour for the province (or for Canada if the industry is under federal jurisdiction) for conciliation. If no collective agreement is reached by that process, and in some provinces after a STRIKE vote, the employees can lawfully strike. Legally, a strike is a concerted withdrawal of labour; at that same point in the process the employer can legally lock the employees out. Usually in a strike or lockout everybody loses something: the employer his profits and continuing costs, the employees their wages and the union its strike funds. It is generally believed that the fear of this mutual loss is the driving force behind collective bargaining. In most cases the union and the employer sign a collective agreement without a strike. The agreements are usually for one or 2 years and during that time any strike is illegal. When the agreement expires the process of collective bargaining, conciliation and strike or lockout starts again.

The ordinary CRIMINAL LAW and the law of TORTS and DELICTS determine the legal limits on picketing and other union activity in support of a strike, although in some provinces special laws limiting such activities are administered by labour-relations boards. Strikes are usually lawful and peaceful and are concluded by the signing of a collective agreement, but not necessarily. If the employer wins the strike or lockout so completely that no collective agreement is reached, the employees' jobs are protected only by the unfair-labour-practice laws and individual employment law. Aside from the legal aspects of strikes, their economic, political, social and personal implications may be very important.

In public sector collective-bargaining relationships, federal or provincial law may substitute interest ARBITRATION (which is otherwise noncompulsory) for the right to strike, particularly when essential services are involved. The interest arbitrator's function is to establish the terms of the collective agreement upon which the parties have been unable to agree, usually the amount of the wage increase, but certain nonmonetary conditions of employment can be equally or even more contentious.

When a collective agreement is in force, it becomes, in effect, the private law of the employer, the employees and the union. Disputes over the application, interpretation or breach of the collective agreement are settled through a grievance procedure which leads finally to grievance arbitration, but arbitration is not always the final step because application may be made to the courts if arbitrators do not perform their functions properly. The enormous number of arbitration awards and court judgements relating to arbitration comprise the most practically important, if not the most newsworthy, component of labour law. For every strike there are tens of thousands of grievances that are settled by the people involved and hundreds of grievance arbitrations.

Labour law is also concerned with the relationships between unions and their members. Since collective agreements can legally make union membership mandatory, employees may need protection against their own unions. Generally employees are hired and then required by "union shop" provisions to join the certified union. In some industries, eg, longshoring and construction, because of closed-shop provisions union membership is a prerequisite to being hired. The common, or judge-made, law, the Canada Labour Code and the labour statutes of some provinces protect employees against unfair union disciplinary procedures and, in the case of the statutes, limit the reasons for which an employee can be expelled from a union or fired as a consequence.

The central issues of labour law are the central issues of our society. How much state regulation should exist? Can economic justice be defined and administered, or must the free market be given more play? Is there a breakdown in order as competing interests vie for public sympathy and support? Paradoxically, the trend in the 1980s appears to be toward greater state regulation of all aspects of the employment relationship, including the wage bargain. Labour relations is increasingly a matter of labour law. INNIS CHRISTIE

Labour Market is a generalized concept denoting the interaction between the supply (number of persons available for work) and the demand (number of jobs available) and the wage rate. Labour-market analysis is complicated by the need to consider not only the short-term supply and demand for labour, but their allocation among regions, occupations and industries. In addition many institutions influence and regulate the distribution of workers.

The many labour markets in Canada are indistinctly divided and sometimes overlap. The most obvious types are geographical and occupational. The market for unskilled labour would normally be the local area, while that for highly trained professionals would be international. However, there are exceptions. Canada has been importing agricultural workers from Caribbean countries rather than paying wages and providing working conditions adequate to induce Canadian workers to accept jobs in this seasonal industry. By contrast, because of the surplus of trained teachers in most major urban centres, school boards rarely need recruit beyond the local area. In this sense the size of the labour market is determined by worker mobility – the ability and willingness of workers to move from one labour market to another, occupationally as well as geographically. To complicate matters further, a significant number of firms, particularly large ones, do not hire on the open market except to fill low-level positions or "entry ports." Otherwise their jobs are filled from internal labour markets through promotion. Legislation may also affect how people choose or are chosen for jobs; eg, lawyers and doctors are restricted from practising within a province unless they are certified by that province. Under current immigration laws, employers may not seek workers outside Canada unless they can demonstrate that there are no qualified personnel available in Canada. Some union agreements stipulate that employers may not hire from outside the local union. Various professions and technical jobs require certificates attesting to an individual's training, eg, a university degree or a journeyman's certificate attained by apprenticeship.

The total supply of labour is determined by the size of the adult population, defined statistically as all those 15 years of age and over. Only a portion of the potential LABOUR FORCE actually participates in the labour market, the main determinants of participation being age and sex, economic conditions, social institutions and attitudes. Many young people, until their mid-twenties, attend school or training institutions, and participation declines rapidly as people approach and pass the age of 60. The participation rate of women, particularly those between the ages of 25 and 64, has traditionally been much lower than that of men, although this is changing as more married women enter the labour force. Increasing participation of WOMEN IN THE LABOUR FORCE has been attributed to changing social attitudes, declining birthrates and family size (which may be a consequence rather than a cause), higher education levels, growing availability of jobs, the need to maintain a family and economic pressures.

The total labour supply is not evenly distributed among regions or even subregions, nor between rural and urban labour markets. Its size in any local labour market is affected not only by the size and participation rates of the local population and the rate of natural increase, but also by migration into or out of markets. The rate of migration into or out of a labour market varies directly with economic opportunities. The relative growth of the labour force in different regions has reflected Canada's economic development. In the early 20th century, the advent of the wheat economy brought explosive growth to the Prairies. Later, expansion was concentrated in central Canada but, more recently, shifted again to the West until the downturn in the western economy in the 1980s.

For practical and administrative purposes and because of geographical limits, Canada has been divided into 99 labour-market areas in the labour-force survey; but the 460 Canada Employment Service areas, within each of which is a Canada Employment Centre, are a better measure of the number of local labour markets, except that major urban areas have a number of centres, which may result in an overestimation of the number of markets. Occupationally, it is possible to make a rough estimate of the flow of new workers with certain occupational skills into the labour market by monitoring the output of education and training institutions, formal on-the-job industrial and apprenticeship programs, and the occupational skills of immigrants. Such an estimation would be imprecise, however, because it does not include informally acquired skills and workplace training, which are not normally recorded, and does not record the number of workers employed at jobs that do not utilize their actual skills. According to a one-time study for Employment and Immigration Canada, in 1976, 37.7% of university graduates and 25.3% of community-college graduates 2 years after graduation were employed in jobs that did not utilize their qualifications. There is also no accurate record of the skills lost to the country by EMIGRATION. The actual occupational distribution of the labour force is therefore more accurately determined by measuring the demand for skills, rather than the supply of them. The prolonged reliance upon immigrants for certain skills and repeated complaints of employers in periods of low unemployment of a shortage of available tradesmen are evidence that the domestic supply of certain skills has fallen behind the demand.

Market Demand for Labour The demand for labour is indirectly determined by the demand for the goods and services that labour produces. Demand for labour has geographical and occupational dimensions, but is also affected considerably by the industrial distribution of demand and the organization of industries. Geographically, the demand for labour will not normally equal the geographical distribution of supply. Consequently, differences in both unemployment rates and in average wage levels for essentially similar jobs will often exist.

Regional Differences in Average Wage Rates and Unemployment: 1986-1987
(Source: *The Labour Force*)

Region (%)	*Average Weekly Earnings (Industrial Aggregate)*	*Unemployment Rate (Annual Average)*
Atlantic provinces	$404.36	15.2
Québec	$432.32	11.0
Ontario	$454.13	7.0
Prairies	$433.09	8.9
British Columbia	$455.06	12.6
Canada	$442.56	9.6

According to the industrial distribution of the employed labour force, the difference between male and female distribution is again quite pronounced, primarily because of differences in the occupational composition of the demand for labour in the various industries. The figures reveal more rapid growth of employment in the service-producing industries, similar to the occupational distribution trend towards increasing numbers of white-collar workers.

Wages and Unemployment In an economist's ideal model of the labour market, wages would adjust to eliminate all unemployment and, over time, labour would move between regions, occupations and industries until real wage rates were equalized when adjusted for differences in skill, education and training, and nonmonetary costs and benefits of individual working environments. In fact, such ideal conditions do not exist and disparities in the supply and demand for labour persist, particularly between regions and between jobs with similar skills, in training requirements and working conditions and in wide differences in unemployment rates between occupations and regions. Analysis of these disparities is extremely complex, but regional disparities reflect how far the Canadian situation falls short of the equilibrium of supply and demand posited by the economic theory of labour markets.

Occupational Distribution Experienced Labour Force: 1981-1987
(Source: Census of Canada 1981; *The Labour Force*, June 1987)

Occupation	*% of Labour Force 1981*			*1987*		
	Total	*M*	*F*	*Total*	*M*	*F*
Managerial	8.9	11.3	5.5	11.2	12.6	9.3
Professional	15.5	12.5	19.8	16.0	12.6	20.5
Clerical	18.9	7.0	36.3	16.2	5.9	29.7
Sales	9.0	8.7	9.4	9.2	9.0	9.6
Service	12.0	9.6	15.7	13.6	10.1	18.1
Agriculture	4.1	5.3	2.2	4.4	5.8	2.5
Fishing, Hunting and Trapping	0.4	0.6	0.1	0.4	0.6	0.1
Forest and Logging	0.7	1.1	0.1	0.6	1.0	0.1
Mining and Quarrying	0.7	1.1	a	0.5	0.9	a
Processing	4.1	5.3	2.3	3.0	4.1	1.6
Machining	2.7	4.1	0.5	2.3	3.7	0.3
Product Fabrication	8.1	10.2	4.9	8.0	10.9	4.1
Construction Trades	6.6	10.9	0.3	6.1	10.6	0.3
Transportation Equipment Operators	4.0	6.2	0.6	3.9	6.3	0.7
Materials Handling	2.1	2.7	1.2	2.6	3.7	1.2
Other Crafts	1.2	1.6	0.7	1.2	1.6	0.6
Not Classified or not stated	1.3	1.9	0.5	0.9	0.6	1.2
All occupations	100.0	100.0	100.0	100.0	100.0	100.0

a = less than .05%

The concept of a labour market must be considered a complex and imperfect tool for analysing the system by which the total supply of Canadian labour, including employers, managers and the self-employed, is allocated among the total of employment opportunities in the economy.

Participation Rates, the proportions of people within any given age/sex group that participate in the labour market, have been undergoing quite marked changes in recent years as a larger percentage of women enter the market. In 1961 less than 30% of Canadian women were in the labour market; by 1986 this had risen to 55.1%, mainly as a result of fewer women leaving the labour force for marriage or for raising families. Male participation, on the other hand, has remained relatively constant despite a steady decline in participation by males 65 years of age or older as a result of improved retirement provisions. The participation rate of males 15 years or age or older has remained considerably higher than the female rate despite this trend, standing at 77.4% in May 1987 compared to the female rate of 56.4%.

PAUL PHILLIPS

Labour Mediation is the process of trying to effect a collective agreement between a union and management (*see* LABOUR LAW and COLLECTIVE BARGAINING). Since 1907 Canadian labour legislation has required unions to try "conciliation" before they can legally strike (*see* STRIKES AND LOCKOUTS). The responsibility for labour conciliation is generally that of conciliation officers who are civil servants expert in the field, but in some provinces 3-person conciliation boards are used in difficult or major labour disputes. The term "labour mediation" is often used interchangeably with "labour conciliation," but strictly speaking, under most Canadian labour legislation, mediation is a special attempt to achieve agreement, usually after the regular conciliation process has failed, by an independent expert.

INNIS CHRISTIE

Labour Organization The first labour organizations in Canada appeared in the early 19th century, but their major growth came only in the 1940s as a result of the industrial development spurred by the war industries and the postwar boom, and from new legislation (1944) permitting union certification and forcing employers to accept collective bargaining with employee representatives. Thus, during the 1940s, membership in labour organizations more than doubled, from less than 400 000 to 1 million, and the level of unionization rose from 20% to 30%. The degree of unionization reached 34% in 1954, but returned to 30% in the late 1950s and beginning of the 1960s. Even in absolute numbers, union membership declined between 1959 and 1963. In the 1960s efforts were made to tap new sources of members, eg, office workers and some professional employees. In the late 1960s all Canadian jurisdictions (except Saskatchewan, which had done so in 1944) granted public-sector employees the right to organize and bargain collectively. The level of unionization consequently rose to 40% of Canadian nonagricultural paid workers in 1983. Since then it has declined slightly (37.6% in 1987).

The distribution of union members by province is uneven, the most highly unionized being BC and Newfoundland (around 50%), and the least, Prince Edward Island (25%). The distribution has also changed over time. Between 1962 and 1984 (2 years for which relatively comparable data are available) the degree of unionization has increased in most provinces; it has remained relatively stable, around 35%, in Ontario, Nova

Scotia and Manitoba. An important advance (from 25% to 41%) has occurred in Québec, mainly because of an almost complete unionization of public-sector employees. Besides the exceptional case of Newfoundland, in recent years, BC has always been the most unionized of all Canadian provinces, while Ontario and Nova Scotia, former strongholds of Canadian unions, are losing ground.

Union membership and unionization rate also vary greatly from industry to industry. They also change through time, reflecting basic changes in the ECONOMY, such as the extraordinary development of service industries, and changing social attitudes. During the first half of the 1980s, the number of union members in service industries has increased by 66%, and the degree of unionization has jumped from 25% to 40%, while both measures have decreased in manufacturing and in construction. In public administration, the number and degree of unionization have advanced only slightly, because the main changes in that sector had occurred in the 1970s and the late 1960s.

The advance of unionism in the public sector is particularly obvious when one considers the 10 largest unions in Canada. In the mid-1980s, the 3 groups with the highest number of members are public-sector unions; the CANADIAN UNION OF PUBLIC EMPLOYEES (CUPE), the National Union of Provincial Government Employees (NUPGE) and the Public Service Alliance of Canada (PSAC). Altogether they represent 750 000 members. Only after these 3 come the most powerful unions of the private sector, the Steelworkers, the Food and Commercial Workers, and the Autoworkers. Twenty years ago, the Steelworkers and the Autoworkers were the biggest of all Canadian unions.

At the turn of the century, international unions represented 90% of all union members of Canada. From 1930 to 1960, the proportion remained constant, at around 70%. In 1975 it was down to 50% and in 1987 down again to 35%, so strong has been the movement towards Canadianization of unions, through both the development of Canadian-born unions, and the peaceful secession of Canadian locals from several American-based international unions.

Despite the frequent stance of solidarity, the labour movement has always been divided internally. With the reunification of the TLC and Canadian Congress of Labour in 1956, the CANADIAN LABOUR CONGRESS became the mouthpiece of close to 80% of all union members. New divisions developed in the 1970s. Unaffiliated or independent unions grew in number and importance; in the early 1980s they accounted for 20% of all union members in Canada. A major split among CLC-affiliated unions occurred in 1982 when the building trades seceded to form the Canadian Federation of Labour (CFL), resurrecting the name of an old federation that had existed from 1902 to 1927. The split came because for many years the CLC sided with the industrial unions against the building trades on different questions, eg, regarding whether certain types of works should belong to the shop employees or to the construction workers. Because of fragmentation, the CLC represented, in the mid-1980s, only 58% of all union members in Canada.

In the 1980s labour organizations in Canada face a number of challenges from both inside and outside their ranks. Ideological divisions still exist. Unions preoccupied with social reform have a tendancy to become radical, more in the public than the private sector. Many members from private-sector unions have viewed public-sector salary increases as coming directly from the taxes they themselves have to pay. Although no split

Membership in Labour Organizations (000s)
(Source: *Labour Organizations in Canada*)

	TLC	*CLC*	*CCL*	*Labour Total*	*% of paid nonagri workers*
1901	8				
1911	57			133	
1921	174			313	16.0
1931	141			311	15.3
1941	145		125	462	18.0
1951	497		360	1 029	28.4
1961		1 071		1 447	31.6
1971		1 654		2 231	33.6
1981		2 369		3 487	37.4
1987		2 213		3 781	37.6

TLC: Trades and Labor Congress, established in 1883
CCL: Canadian Congress of Labour, established in 1940
CLC: Canadian Labour Congress, established in 1956, integrating the TLC and the CCL.

has actually occurred, serious tensions have been felt between the 2 groups, especially within the ranks of smaller central labour bodies, such as the CNTU. Another source of controversy has been the divergent views of various labour organizations regarding co-operation with management and governments. So-called "tripartism" has been a source of contention among unions. Some consider such mechanisms the only feasible and practical avenue of the future; others regard them as a downright betrayal of their members and of worker in general.

As serious as these internal divisions may be, other problems may be more menacing, eg, unsupportive government interventions, decreasing support of public opinion, tougher management and the problems raised by new technology.

In the 1970s most governments introduced extended and more sophisticated employment standards, together with more constraining health and safety measures. Some have called these new standards the "collective agreement of the unorganized." These measures may either curtail or enhance the unionization of the 60% of workers still not covered by any collective agreement.

A more drastic type of government intervention has to do with the substance of collective bargaining, eg, wage controls (*see* WAGE AND PRICE CONTROLS) of the mid-1970s and the curtailing of bargaining rights of public-sector employees in the early 1980s. These interventions have considerably reduced the influence of labour organizations on the Canadian economy. Their bargaining power has also been curtailed by the many instances of back-to-work legislation adopted at various times – federally and in all large Canadian provinces. These laws, according to some observers and practitioners, amount to a denial of the right to strike.

The support of such government intervention by many Canadians reflects the diminishing support of labour organizations among the public. Public-opinion polls in the late 1970s revealed that the Canadian people trusted management and business representatives more than labour-union spokesmen. On the other hand, employees realize that as a group perhaps the only opportunity available to them to secure better working conditions still lies in unionization and collective bargaining.

Another factor influencing the future of labour organizations in Canada is the uncompromising position management has taken at the bargaining table since the recession: in the early 1980s it became commonplace for employers to try and rescind advantages already conceded. Also, the nonunion sector of private industries has been growing steadily. World competition has made employers aggressive. Labour organizations have grown at different rates around the world, and industry and consumers have taken advantage of the poorer working conditions in other countries. HIGH TECHNOLOGY will also cause drastic changes in the labour movement and its organizing tactics, as well as affecting various methods of production; and diversified economic structures may further the balkanization of the labour movement rather than increase its bonds of solidarity.

GÉRARD HÉBERT

Reading: Labour Canada, *Labour Organizations* (publ annually).

Labour Party That workers should have political representatives of their own class has been a recurrent theme in Canadian labour history. No one organization has provided a permanent home for this idea. Labour candidates and workers' parties emerged during the 1870s and 1880s, often backed by local unions. In 1874 Daniel J. O'DONOGHUE, an Ottawa printer, was elected to the Ontario legislature, and in 1888 A.T. Lépine, a Montréal leader of the KNIGHTS OF LABOR, was elected to Parliament. Many union leaders have preferred to advance their cause through established political parties. Also, acceptance of trade unionists and hybrid candidates by the major parties inhibited the formation of independent labour parties.

Nevertheless, the TRADES AND LABOR CONGRESS showed a growing interest in political action, and in 1900 A.W. PUTTEE, a Winnipeg Labour Party founder, and Ralph SMITH, TLC president, were both elected to Parliament. While rejecting the more radical SOCIALIST PARTY OF CANADA, the TLC in 1906 endorsed the creation of provincial labour parties based on the TLC's platform. Although there were labour candidates from all 9 provinces in the 1921 federal election, only J.S. WOODSWORTH, Winnipeg, and William IRVINE, Calgary, were elected. Labour candidates had greater success at the provincial level, winning seats in NS, Manitoba and BC in 1920, and participating in the Farmer-Labour government in Ontario (1919-23). In 1920 also, more than 100 mayors and municipal councillors were elected as labour candidates. Nevertheless, attempts to create a cohesive Canadian Labour Party failed. Since then working-class representation has found a place in the COMMUNIST PARTY, the CO-OPERATIVE COMMONWEALTH FEDERATION and the NEW DEMOCRATIC PARTY, though labour parties have continued to appear occasionally, especially at the local level.

DAVID FRANK

Labour Policy includes policies concerned with relations between employers and employees and those concerned with manpower or the LABOUR MARKET. INDUSTRIAL RELATIONS in Canada were governed through the common law of conspiracy in restraint of trade until 1872 when, as a result of the jailing of striking Toronto printers in a dispute with George BROWN, PM John A. MACDONALD introduced the Trade Unions Act legalizing unions. While professing neutrality in labour matters, government has often intervened without legal basis on behalf of employers. The first direct legislative intervention in labour-management relations came with the Industrial Disputes Investigation Act (1907) prohibiting STRIKES AND LOCKOUTS in public utilities and mines until a dispute had been investigated. The Act had been prepared by Mackenzie KING who, in 1909, became the first full-time labour minister.

Jurisdiction over labour relations was transferred to the provinces in the interwar period until wartime emergency and rising labour discontent led to the passage of wartime order-in-council PC 1003 (1944), which provided for the right to organization and to engage in COLLECTIVE BARGAINING. After the war, jurisdiction over most labour relations returned to the provinces, though governments at both levels have generally adopted the principles of the wartime measures. Since that time conflicts and disagreements over industrial relations are normally referred to provincial or federal tribunals or boards for adjudication.

Labour policy has been aimed at maintaining, allocating and ensuring a plentiful supply of labour; implementing strategies to increase the mobility of labour, including relocation and retraining; job creation and enhancement; managing the unemployed; and implementing appropriate social policies. It has always reflected economic policy which has traditionally involved hinterland resource exploitation, eg, the squared-timber industry in the Maritimes and northern Québec and Ontario. A comprehensive manpower policy was introduced (excluding wartime) only in the 1960s. Most provinces have their own policies, not all of which are in harmony with those of the federal government.

The earliest Canadian labour-market policy was the attempt during the time of Jean TALON, in the late 17th century, to consolidate French control of the St Lawrence region through settlement. Although opposed by the fur-trading monopolies, efforts were made to increase population through encouragement of immigration, the shipment of young women from France, the settlement of demobilized soldiers and the promotion of natural increase through state subsidies for early marriage and large families. In the FUR TRADE, the native people provided much of the labour as suppliers and transporters, and French Canadian traders, COUREURS DE BOIS and VOYAGEURS located new resources and brought the furs to port. The HUDSON'S BAY CO developed another de facto policy. The native peoples acted as suppliers and brought the furs to the Bay until Orkney labourers began to handle transport to the interior. Métis communities developed as suppliers of PEMMICAN, guides and labourers; the English were merchants, traders and managers. The encouragement of immigration and settlement continued after the Conquest (1760), reaching its peak in the late 19th century and the first decade of the 20th. Massive numbers of immigrant workers were imported to build the transcontinental railway. A royal commission (reported, 1908) revealed that 2 CPR subcontractors alone had imported some 6000 oriental labourers. The federal government and the CPR also co-operated in an ambitious recruiting campaign to populate the Prairies, first in England, Scandinavia and W Europe and then, by necessity, in eastern and southern Europe. Many of these immigrants supplied a labour reserve for mines, highways and factories as well as breaking land on the Prairies. The policy of importing workers was opposed by labour, which was able to persuade government to intervene, eg, in passing the Alien Labour Law (1897).

Government support of manpower development was not restricted to encouraging immigration. Soon after the Conquest, agricultural societies and exhibitions were promoted as a means of providing agricultural education. Beginning in Ontario, public education spread across much of Canada in the second half of the 19th century, one of its explicit aims being the preparation of young men for the labour market. Prior to WWII there were a number of sporadic and ad hoc incursions into labour-market policy by all levels of government, usually in response to high unemployment. Several municipal governments in the larger centres established employment exchanges or became involved in public relief work, as did provincial governments.

By 1914 "relief work" was a common response to the growing numbers of unemployed men who were given bed and meals in exchange for performing menial or odd jobs, eg, cutting firewood and sewer work. During the GREAT DEPRESSION the federal government resorted to deportation and work camps. In 1930, at the urging of provincial and municipal governments, 4000 people were deported, some 45% of whom had been receiving public assistance, several hundred of whom were ill. Relief work was reinstituted and in 1932 work camps administered by the Department of National Defence were established. Around 17 000 men were detained in 10 camps in remote areas of Alberta alone. The Conservative government under Prime Minister R.B. BENNETT did attempt unsuccessfully to introduce an unemployment insurance program in 1935, but it was not until a constitutional amendment to the BNA Act in 1940 that the federal government became directly involved in employment exchanges.

The establishment of the Unemployment Insurance Commission (UIC) and its affiliated National Employment Service (NES), which derived from the wartime registration program (1940), marks the first systematic labour-market policy. The NES was to match unemployed workers with unfilled job vacancies, using the employment centres as clearing houses. Almost immediately it began allocating labour to priority wartime work and administering the selective-service system, but in the generally buoyant economic conditions after the war it returned to its placement work.

In the late 1950s, unemployment and concern with structural unemployment (unemployment created by regular cyclical crises and that created by technological change, corporate conglomeration and shifting world markets) began to rise, resulting in the Technical and Vocational Training Assistance Act (1960), a shared-cost program with the provinces for the provision of occupational training and training facilities. The central importance of the labour-exchange function of labour-market policy was consequently downgraded. In 1966 the government established the Department of Manpower and Immigration (DMI), responsible for all manpower policy except UNEMPLOYMENT INSURANCE. The Adult Occupational Training Act (1967) under the Canada Manpower Training Plan (CMTP) emphasized training; it was federally funded but no longer included capital grants for facilities and was restricted to adults only.

In the 1970s the persistence of unemployment and poverty particularly among disadvantaged youth, women, natives, the handicapped and residents of areas suffering high unemployment prompted a new interest in the management of unemployment and in the containment of potential crises. Training, counselling and relocation strategies proved inadequate and governments again resorted to job creation. In the 1950s they had funded winter-works programs to combat seasonal unemployment.

In the 1970s Opportunities for Youth (OFY), a summer scheme for students, Local Initiatives Program (LIP) for winter unemployment, and Local Employment Assistance Program (LEAP) to aid the hard-core unemployed were introduced under the Job Creation Branch of the DMI. In 1975 a joint scheme with the provinces was added, the Community Employment Strategy. In addition, the federal and provincial governments attempted to stimulate activity in the private sector through a variety of incentives, eg, tax considerations, loan guarantees, direct grants and subsidies and infusions of equity. The government also reunited its labour-market and immigration branch with the UIC in 1976. The new department, Employment and Immigration, supervises the Canadian Employment and Immigration Commission, which is responsible for implementing programs and the insurance scheme. Under revisions to the Unemployment Insurance Act, funds also became available for job creation and work sharing.

The election of the Mulroney Conservative government in 1984 resulted in a reorganization of labour programs, under the title of the Canadian Jobs Strategy, introduced in 1985. The major programs under this strategy are job development, work experience and training for the long-term unemployed through job subsidies; job entry, a combination of training with on-the-job experience to facilitate the entry of youths and women into the labour market; skill shortages, subsidization of employers who provide on-the-job training and classroom instruction to develop skills currently in short supply or where shortages are anticipated; skill investment, wage subsidies and tuition fees to undergo retraining for workers whose jobs are threatened by technological or market change; community futures, funding for job development in communities with chronic unemployment problems or facing the loss of a major employer; and innovations, financial support for pilot or demonstration projects facilitating labour-market adjustment.

In 1986-87, 3 million people were referred to regular employment by the 460 Canada Employment Centres (CECs) across the country and 287 other university centres and itinerant employment services in remote communities. Employers registered 1 104 000 vacancies, which included casual, temporary and seasonal labour. Referrals resulted in 829 600 placements, 16% of them for casual labour. There were also special placements under the Agriculture Employment Service (formerly the Farm Labour Pool) and the Outreach program for disadvantaged workers. In 1986-87, almost $1.5 billion was spent on the Job Strategy programs, the biggest proportion, 56%, for job development. Job entry received 23% of the funds while the 2 skill development programs received only 16%. Under this revised manpower policy, emphasis has shifted from institutional training to subsidized, private-sector, on-the-job training. Of those who participated in the various programs, 42.5% were women and 15.1% were natives, visible minorities or disabled.

Mobility programs have played a considerably smaller role in manpower policy because high rates of unemployment are now country-wide; 1986-87 expenditures on worker relocation, grants for job seekers and for seasonal and agricultural work totalled $8.0 million. Immigration, which for most of Canada's history was a significant labour-market policy tool, is now less important, although immigrants fill a disproportionate number of job openings in certain skilled trades, particularly in manufacturing. PAUL PHILLIPS

Labour Relations refers to the relations between employers and employees. They are affected by a number of factors, including labour organizations, COLLECTIVE BARGAINING, LABOUR MARKET, government policy, the structure of the economy, LABOUR LAW and technological change. Because labour relations are commonly associated with unions, it is significant that in Canada, until the 1970s, a majority of unions and union members belonged to American-based craft and industrial unions. American employers are also influential – more than 4000 branch plants and subsidiaries of American corporations exist in Canada. In Dec 1987, Statistics Canada estimated that US-based unions acquired $56.5 million more from their members in Canada than they spent in Canada in 1985. During this century, labour relations in Canada and the US have been remarkably similar; a 1959 survey of 15 countries over more than 15 years described them as "a single system."

The outstanding feature of N American industrial relations, according to some observers, has been the unusually high incidence of STRIKES. Studies have also disclosed that the incidence of violence and illegality arising out of labour disputes has been much higher in the US and Canada than in other comparably industrialized countries – characteristics attributed to a few political and institutional factors that Canada, until the 1960s, shared with the US. They included the relatively recent development of large-scale "mass unionization," a considerable residue of tension and mutual hostility arising from the widespread, protracted and frequently violent opposition of employers to unions; intense organizational and leadership rivalries among unions; the highly decentralized structure of labour organization and collective bargaining in most industries; and the absence of a strong or dominant labour party capable of gaining power at the national level. Despite these broad similarities, however, labour relations in Canada have differed from those in the US in some important respects, which appear to have widened in recent years. For example, until the late 1950s the incidence of strikes in Canada was well below that of the US. Canada was less industrialized, with a smaller proportion of unionized workers. It underwent rapid industrialization and union growth during and after WWII and by the mid-1950s had reached virtual parity with the US in percentage of nonagricultural workers unionized. There was another dramatic upsurge in the later 1960s and the 1970s with the growth of public-sector unions. By 1987, 37.6% of nonagricultural workers in Canada were unionized, as compared to less than 20% in the US.

The relative strength of organized labour in Canada was also affected by cultural and ethnic divisions among workers, particularly the formidable gap between Francophones and Anglophones, which was exemplified by the formation of the separate francophone CONFEDERATION OF NATIONAL TRADE UNIONS in Québec. Pronounced geographic and political divisions also precluded effective unionization and often set the interests of the workers in one region against those in another. For example, the interests of packinghouse workers in the food-processing industry in eastern Canada have often conflicted with those of their western counterparts, particularly regarding transportation, international trade and government subsidies. Politically, the labour movement had been divided since the turn of the century, when the TRADES AND LABOR CONGRESS, backed by the American Federation of Labor, evicted the militant KNIGHTS OF LABOR. Conflicts over opposing ideologies, programs and organizational objectives became less intense with the formation of the CANADIAN LABOUR CONGRESS in 1956. Since then numerous unions have broken away from traditional American-controlled organizations in a drive for national autonomy. Some are in the CLC and some in the recently formed Confederation of Canadian Unions. Government intervention is another factor increasingly influencing labour relations. Since W.L. Mackenzie KING, as federal deputy minister, introduced the Industrial Disputes Investigation Act of 1907 to curb western Canada's militant coal-mine workers, governments in Canada have acted to maintain "law and order" and to protect employers' property and latitude of action rather than to protect the rights of employees to organize and bargain collectively. This tendency is evident in a history of expeditious resort to compulsory intervention, such as back-to-work legislation and binding arbitration, to settle disputes.

As far as employers are concerned, the Canadian situation differs from the American in that employers in most major industries in Canada have been relatively larger and more concentrated in their respective labour and product markets, and in earlier decades enjoyed relatively stronger bargaining power vis-à-vis organized labour. Where they have operated as subsidiaries or "branch plants," their strength has increased because their freedom to invest selectively and to relocate physically have provided them with an advantage in dealing with unions.

Labour relations changed dramatically during and after WWII, and Canadian and American positions were, in some respects, reversed. Union organization and membership grew more rapidly in Canada, and for the past several years union members have comprised a considerably larger percentage of the labour force. Since the 1950s the incidence of industrial conflict has also risen far more rapidly in Canada, and has remained at a considerably higher level for more than 20 years. Rapidly growing but highly erratic and irregular waves of industrial disputes developed in Canada from the mid-1960s to the mid-1980s, reaching record peaks in the numbers of strikes, workers involved and person-days lost in 1965, 1966, 1968, 1972, 1974, 1975 and 1976 (the all-time high) and 1980 and 1981. During this period Canada shared with Italy the rather dubious distinction of having the world's highest annual average time loss per 1000 workers, with the US a distant third. Illegality and violence arising from labour disputes also increased in Canada during this period, particularly in Ontario and Québec, in a pattern reminiscent of the 1930s and earlier. As a result, and in response as well to the emergence of powerful public-sector unions, governments in Canada severely restricted organized labour. Strikes were banned in essential services, and in 1975 the federal government imposed a mandatory incomes policy administered by an ANTI-INFLATION BOARD. "Six and five" legislation followed in the early 1980s, and various provincial governments imposed wage-guideline policies.

Labour relations have also been affected by the structure of the Canadian economy. During the 1960s and 1970s Canada's LABOUR FORCE grew more rapidly than that of any other industrial country and was accompanied by and dependent upon an unusually high rate of capital investment, particularly by American corporations. Postwar economic expansion, however, produced an economy heavily reliant upon primary-resource extraction and export, susceptible to "boom-and-bust" cycles. Canadian governments, owing partly to the inability of a highly decentralized federal system of government to do so and partly to tradition, have not generally introduced measures to promote long-term stability or planning in the economy. Instability, inflation and unemployment have all generated corresponding instability in labour relations. The concentration of strikes in cyclically sensitive industries seems to indicate a close relationship between economic instability and industrial conflict. Over the past 2 decades, only 6 industries, employing less than 15% of the labour force, accounted for more than 50% of all person-days lost and for more than 66% of the unusually large and protracted strikes. In order of percentage of time loss from strikes, they were construction, mining and smelting (particularly nickel), and (in manufacturing) transportation equipment (mainly automobiles), primary metals (mainly iron and steel) and wood products (mainly lumber and pulp and paper).

A by-product of Canada's rapid but unstable pattern of economic growth and one particularly provocative of industrial conflict has been the problem of wage disparities. During periods of rapid expansion, greater disparities have tended to develop within the general wage structure of Canada than within that of other industrial countries, primarily because of widely unequal rates of growth and profitability among different industries and regions and because of wide differences in bargaining power among unions. In Canada's very decentralized labour movement, collective bargaining is highly localized and competitive. Three-quarters or more of all collective agreements are negotiated with individual employers, and multi-employer bargaining is usually local or district wide. The resulting differences in wages and fringe benefits have made it difficult for unions to achieve their general goal of parity among workers and have tended to provoke widespread conflict.

The problem of unequal growth during the 1960s and early 1970s particularly affected the public sector, partly because of growing intervention of government at all levels in disputes and strike settlement procedures in other industries under the aegis of postwar labour legislation. The (implied) responsibility of governments for the gains in wages and benefits in the private sector and the wage lag in various public and publicly controlled sectors has resulted in the formation of militant unions, the enactment of new legislation providing for union certification and collective bargaining, and numerous large and protracted strikes among public-service workers.

The onset of a severe recession and serious unemployment in the 1980s greatly weakened the bargaining power of unions. On the other hand, new demands and policies by various public and private employers have been viewed as serious threats to job and union security and, in the mid-to-late 1980s, have provoked numerous incidents of picket line violence, injuries and arrests in labour disputes. STUART M. JAMIESON

Reading: Stuart M. Jamieson, *Times of Trouble* (1968) and *Industrial Relations in Canada* (1973).

Labrador, mainland section of the province of NEWFOUNDLAND, lies almost entirely N of the Island, 20 km across the Strait of Belle Isle, and some 800 km S of Greenland. The long (1125 km) Labrador coast is indented by innumerable fjords, bays and inlets, notably HAMILTON INLET (Lk MELVILLE), which penetrates the rocky interior for over 250 km. Geologically, Labrador is part of the Canadian SHIELD, a massive granite plateau rising some 300 m from sea level to the interior watershed. Most of coastal and northern Labrador is bare rock and barren tundra, but river valleys S from Lk Melville and the deep interior contain valuable forest reserves. The TORNGAT MTS of the far N rise in splendid isolation – the highest peaks E of the Rockies. Though in the same latitude as the British Isles, Labrador's forbidding terrain and extreme climate support only sparse settlement. The Labrador Current, sweeping S from arctic waters, chills the coast and clogs harbours with ice from Dec to May. The primary settlements in 1986 were CARTWRIGHT, Rigolet, Makkovik, Postville, Hopedale and NAIN S to N along the coast; North West River and HAPPY VALLEY-GOOSE BAY on Lk Melville; and Churchill Falls, Wabush and LABRADOR CITY in the interior.

The Labrador coast has been occupied for a very long time. Evidence of Maritime Archaic Indian occupation, dating back at least 7000 years, has been found at L'ANSE AMOUR BURIAL SITE in the S. Labrador was likely the "Markland" of the Viking sagas, which described the anomalous silvery beaches near Groswater Bay. BASQUE fishermen established a great whale fishery, centered at RED BAY on the NE coast of the Str of Belle Isle, even before Jacques CARTIER explored the coast in

Cape Mugford, Labrador. Labrador contains some of the most rugged and splendidly isolated scenery in N America (*photo by John deVisser*).

the early 16th century. Maritime Archaic culture was displaced about 4000 years ago by southward expansion of Paleoeskimos from the Arctic, who were in turn displaced by the ancestors of the MONTAGNAIS-NASKAPI and Inuit. Portuguese explorers were active along the coast and the name "Labrador," which was first applied to the coast of Greenland, likely derives from the Portuguese explorer João FERNANDES, a *lavrador* or "landholder" in the Azores. Early European occupation was entirely focused on the coastal fishery and was fiercely opposed by the Inuit to the N and the Naskapi in the S. Control of the coast was contested by the British and French, but control by either was tenuous. In the early 19th century, thousands of New England fishermen and whalers descended on the coast annually.

Settlement was haphazard, begun by a few fishermen who stayed on each winter (called LIVEYERS), while thousands of "stationers" (those who fished from land bases in summer) and "floaters" (those who used schooners as their bases) came and went with the fishing season. George CARTWRIGHT established a business at Cape Charles in 1770 and persevered for 16 years. The Moravians set up a mission at Nain in 1771 that has been in continuous operation since. The HBC established its first post at Rigolet in 1834, another at North West River in 1836 and a third at Cartwright. HBC employee John MCLEAN explored the interior in 1839, but the fur trade remained marginal in Labrador. In the 1890s geologist A.P. LOW reported the massive iron-ore deposits of the interior and in 1937 and 1939 Finnish geographer V.A. Tanner compiled the most detailed designation of Labrador to date. The small coastal settlements of Labrador were among the most isolated, deprived and neglected in the world. With the exception of the Moravian mission at Nain, Labrador was without medical care, schools or adequate housing until the heroic efforts of Wilfred GRENFELL in the 1890s. Grenfell and his associates established hospitals, schools, orphanages and co-ops – financed by fund-raising tours around the world.

The break with the traditional dependence on the fishery alone came during WWII when the airport at Goose Bay was built as a staging point for FERRY COMMAND. It later continued as a USAF base and by the early 1950s was the second-busiest airport in the world. Happy Valley grew up nearby. Meanwhile the completion of the monumental QUÉBEC NORTH SHORE AND LABRADOR RY (1954) opened the vast iron reserves of the interior, and BRINCO tapped the huge power of the Churchill R at CHURCHILL FALLS – the second-largest hydroelectric development in Canada.

The LABRADOR BOUNDARY DISPUTE was one of the most celebrated legal cases in British colonial history. Though Newfoundland's claim to the watershed of all rivers flowing into the Atlantic Ocean is recognized in the Constitution Act, many Quebecers still consider Labrador part of "Nouveau-Québec." JAMES MARSH

Labrador Boundary Dispute The territorial limit between Québec and Newfoundland in the LABRADOR peninsula, at over 3500 km long, is the longest interprovincial boundary. It has not yet been surveyed and marked on the ground. A dispute concerning the ownership of Labrador arose in 1902 when the Québec government protested NEWFOUNDLAND's issuing a timber licence on the CHURCHILL R. Two years later Québec asked Ottawa to submit the controversy to the JUDICIAL COMMITTEE OF THE PRIVY COUNCIL in London. This reference to an outside impartial body was appropriate, since Canada and Newfoundland were separate members of the British Empire and neither could have settled the issue through its own courts. Only Canada and Newfoundland were admitted as parties to the case, and Québec had no direct representation.

The dispute dragged on, and in 1922 Canada and Newfoundland agreed to ask the Privy Council to decide only "the location and definition of the boundary as between Canada and Newfoundland in the Labrador Peninsula under the statutes, orders-in-council and proclamations." The panel of 5 judges was confined to this question; it could not create a new boundary or suggest a territorial compromise. The main point in the case was the meaning of "coast," for that was how Labrador was legally described. Newfoundland traced its claim of ownership to the commission issued to Gov Thomas Graves in 1763, which extended his jurisdiction to the "Coasts of Labrador." Canada argued that a royal proclamation later that year merely placed the territory under the governor's "care and inspection" for fishing purposes. In 1774, it was pointed out, Labrador was transferred by statute to Québec, but in 1809 it was reannexed to Newfoundland; in 1825 the coast of Labrador W of a line extending due N from the bay of Blanc-Sablon to the 52nd parallel of latitude was once again restored to Lower Canada [Québec].

The judicial committee refused to accept Canada's contention that "coast" meant a strip of land one mile (1.6 km) wide along the seashore. It found that the evidence supported Newfoundland's inland claim as far as the watershed line or height of land. The court's decision in Mar 1927 settled the boundary in its present location. When Newfoundland joined Confederation in 1949, its boundary in Labrador was confirmed in the Terms of Union (now the NEWFOUNDLAND ACT), enshrined in the CONSTITUTION ACT, 1982. A 1971 Québec royal commission decided that Québec's case against the 1927 boundary was not worth pursuing; by 1987, although the province did not consider the issue to be settled, the dispute appeared to be dormant.

ALEC C. MCEWEN

Reading: Alec C. McEwen, "The Labrador Boundary," *Canadian Surveyor*, vol 36, no 2 (June 1982); F.W. Rowe, *A History of Newfoundland and Labrador* (1980).

Labrador City, Nfld, Town, pop 8664 (1986c), 11 583 (1981c), inc 1961, is located in western Labrador near the Québec border and the base of the Wapussakatoo Mts, adjacent to one of the richest iron-ore formations in Canada. The ore was discovered in 1892, and the mineral rights were acquired in 1936 by the Iron Ore Co of Canada (IOC). In 1958 formal mining operations began at Carol and Smallwood Mines, and by 1959 construction of a planned townsite had begun by the shore of Carol Lk. In 1960 a railway linked Carol Lk to Québec. When incorporated in 1961, Carol Lk was renamed Labrador City. By 1968 the town, with a population of nearly 8500, was the largest in Labrador. Constructed by IOC, by 1960 it had an airstrip, a hospital and numerous churches and schools. Because Labrador City's economic fortunes are tied to those of world markets for iron ore, employment has fluctuated accordingly.

JANET E.M. PITT AND ROBERT D. PITT

Labrador Current, famous for icebergs and cod fish, is a southeasterly flow of water over the continental shelf and slope E of Newfoundland and Labrador, between Hudson Strait and the southern tip of the Grand Banks. About 80% of the flow is concentrated in a 50 km-wide, high-speed stream over the upper continental slope, where surface speeds up to 0.8 m/s have been recorded, in contrast to 0.1 – 0.2 m/s elsewhere in the current. The water, coming from Baffin and Hudson bays, Foxe Basin and the West Greenland Current, is colder (0.0°C) and contains less salt (.0334) than water of the deep ocean (4.0°C, .0347). JOHN R.N. LAZIER

Labrador Highlands extend 400 km S from Cape Chidley, at the northern tip of LABRADOR, almost to NAIN. The uninhabited highlands contain 3 mountain groups: the TORNGAT, Kaumajet (Inuktitut, "shining top") and Kiglapait ("sawtooth"). The highest summits are Mt Caubvick (1652 m) in the Torngat, Brave Mt (1220 m) in the Kaumajet and Man O'War Peak (1050 m), which rises just S of the main range of the Kiglapait. Formed of ancient Precambrian rocks and heavily glaciated in recent times, the mountains support more than 70 small glaciers, the southernmost in eastern N America. Bold cliffs fall sheer to the LABRADOR SEA or the narrow water of FJORDS, while the valleys support only arctic vegetation and wildlife. R.J. ROGERSON

Labrador Inuit, who sometimes refer to themselves as Labradormiut, have occupied most of

Inuit woman, 18th-century, oil on canvas, by Angelica Kauffmann (*National Archives of Canada/C-95201*).

the Atlantic coast of LABRADOR during the historic period. In early historic times they ranged even farther to the south, crossing occasionally to northern Newfoundland and travelling far into the Gulf of St Lawrence. However, the nature and extent of former Inuit presence in southern Labrador is uncertain. The Inuit appear to have made contact with European explorers, fishermen and whalers in the south of Labrador by the late 16th century. In spite of frequent misunderstanding and bloodshed during the first few centuries of contact, an intermittent trade was already well established when Britain acquired Labrador in 1763. The Inuit had obtained a wide variety of European goods, including wooden sailing boats, in exchange for their baleen (horny plates in the jaws of certain whales), sealskins and blubber. Until they obtained firearms in the 1780s, the Labrador Inuit tried to avoid contact with their sometimes hostile Indian neighbours, the MONTAGNAIS-NASKAPI, who had been armed earlier by French fur traders.

The traditional Labrador Inuit, who numbered about 1500 during the late 18th century, derived most of their livelihood from the sea. While coastal waters remained unfrozen (mid-June to mid-December), the men hunted walrus, beluga and seal from their KAYAKS. In late autumn they hunted the giant Greenland whale from their open skin-covered UMIAKS. During winter they hunted seals. Large winter houses, made of sod, stone, timber and whalebones, were usually shared by several families.

Most Labrador Inuit now live in NAIN, Hopedale and Makkovik, settlements which were founded by Moravian missionaries in 1771, 1784 and 1896. Since WWII some have moved to the inland communities of Happy Valley and North West River. Those who had migrated even farther to the south in earlier times were decimated by various contagious diseases, and their survivors have been largely absorbed through intermarriage with European settlers. As a result of government relocation projects in the 1950s there are no longer any permanent Inuit settlements on the coast N of Nain. Nevertheless, many people still travel north from Nain each summer to fish for arctic char, one of the main sources of earned income for the modern Labrador Inuit. *See also* NATIVE PEOPLE: ARCTIC.

J. GARTH TAYLOR

Reading: C. Brice-Bennett, ed, *Our Footprints Are Everywhere: Inuit Land Use and Occupancy in Labrador* (1977).

Labrador Sea is the body of water between Greenland and the coast of Labrador. It is 3400 m deep and 1000 km wide where it joins the N Atlantic and shallows to less than 700 m where DAVIS STR separates it from BAFFIN BAY. The NW Atlantic Mid-Ocean Channel, a 100-200 m deep channel some 1.5-2.5 km wide in the seafloor, follows the axis of the Labrador Sea, some 3800 km from the mouth of HUDSON STR, southward into the N Atlantic. The sea's circulation is anticlockwise. At the surface the West Greenland Current transports warmer, more saline water northward, while the LABRADOR CURRENT transports cold, less saline water southward. At a depth of 2500-3000 m the dense outflow from the Greenland Sea flows around the basin and then southward as a bottom boundary current. A water mass, the Labrador Sea water, is formed in the western Labrador Sea by wintertime cooling and spreads into the NW Atlantic at depths of 1500-2000 m.

The northern and western Labrador Sea is ice-covered from Dec through June. This pack ice is the whelping and breeding area for harp and hooded SEALS in early spring. The Labrador and Greenland banks are commercially fished for cod. As well, a shrimp fishery has developed in recent years. The Labrador Sea is a feeding ground for ATLANTIC SALMON and several species of marine mammals. Icebergs, carried southward in the Labrador Current, are an impediment to the exploitation of natural-gas fields off Labrador.

ALLYN CLARKE AND KEN DRINKWATER

Labrador Tea (*Ledum groenlandicum* and *Ledum palustre*), also called Hudson's Bay or Indian tea, shrubs of the heath family (Ericaceae). They grow up to 2 m high in wet, acidic soil throughout much of northern Canada and in peat bogs to the south. Some 4 species of genus *Ledum* exist worldwide, 3 in Canada. The third, *L. glandulosum* (trapper's tea), should not be used for tea. Labrador tea leaves are elliptical, up to 6 cm long, with revolute (backward-rolled) margins and dense, whitish to rust-coloured fuzz on the lower surfaces. The flowers are white and clustered. The aromatic young twigs, leaves and flowers have been used, fresh or dried, as "tea" by native peoples and settlers. Tea should be weak; a small handful of leaves steeped in boiling water for 5 min yields a pleasant beverage. *See also* PLANTS, NATIVE USES.

NANCY J. TURNER

Labrosse, Paul-Raymond Jourdain, *dit,* joiner-sculptor, organ builder (b at Montréal 20 Sept 1697; d there 8 June 1769). He was hired in 1721 to repair an old organ and build a new 7-stop instrument for the Cathedral of Notre-Dame in Québec (now Basilica of Notre Dame de Québec). The leading Montréal joiner-sculptor from 1730 to 1760, he trained at least 3 apprentices. He sometimes worked as a joiner, but was usually employed as a wood sculptor by a dozen Montréal-area parishes, creating for them retables, tabernacles and statues as well as various liturgical accessories. Few of his works remain. One is the richly ornamented tabernacle (1741) originally in the old Longueuil, Qué, church, now in the National Gallery of Canada. There is also the vigorous *Christ* (1741) in Notre-Dame de Montréal, and some small baroque-style statues.

JOHN R. PORTER

Lac La Biche, Alta, Town, pop 2553 (1986c), inc 1951, headquarters for Improvement District 18 (south), is located 225 km NE of Edmonton on the S shore of the lake of the same name. Posts established as early as 1798-99 indicated the lake's early position on FUR TRADE ROUTES. "Portage La Biche," between the waters of the Lac La Biche R and Beaver Lake, connected the Athabasca/Mackenzie R system with the Saskatchewan R system from Hudson Bay. In 1853 both an Oblate mission and the HBC's Lac La Biche post were located where the townsite would be established after the Alberta and Great Waterways Ry from Edmonton reached that point in 1914. French Canadian settlers joined Métis and other original occupants. Tourism began when railwayman J.D. McArthur opened the McArthur Inn in 1916 and continued after WWII. The province created Sir Winston Churchill Island Park in 1965.

CARL BETKE

Lac La Ronge, 1414 km^2, elev 364 m, is located in the rugged, sparsely populated Canadian Shield country of central Saskatchewan, 235 km N of Prince Albert. About 58 km long and studded with many islands, it drains NE via the Rapid R into the CHURCHILL R. When the first Europeans arrived, the area was inhabited by Cree. Peter POND built a fur-trade post in 1781; the village of LA RONGE on the W shore is one of the oldest settlements in Saskatchewan. Today the area is a tourist centre catering to campers, fishermen and hunters. The name probably comes from the French verb *ronger*, "to gnaw," referring to the local beaver population.

DANIEL FRANCIS

Lac-Mégantic, Qué, Town, pop 5732 (1986c), 6119 (1981c), inc 1912, is located on the NE shore of Lac MÉGANTIC, 85 km E of SHERBROOKE. On nearby Mont Mégantic (1100 m) are located the oratory of St-Joseph de la Montagne, a pilgrimage site built in 1855, and an astronomical OBSERVATORY. The observatory, with its 1.6 m diameter telescope, is shared by Université de Montréal and Laval. The Rivière CHAUDIÈRE starts in Lac-Mégantic, the name of which in Abenaki means "the place of fish." The river was a traditional Indian route. The first settlers (SCOTS), arrived in Lac-Mégantic in the mid-19th century. After 1895 a branch of the Quebec-Central rail line linked Lac-Mégantic to LÉVIS. Today the city, a commercial and industrial crossroads and tourist site, is a service centre for the surrounding region and features the large Baie des Sables recreational complex. The Manesokanjik museum traces local history.

CLAUDINE PIERRE-DESCHÊNES

Lac Ste Anne, Alta, UP, pop 20 (1986c), 34 (1981c), is located 75 km NW of Edmonton on the lake of the same name. The Rev Jean-Baptiste Thibault, an Oblate priest, named the lake for his patron, Ste Anne de Beaupré, and the shrine became a PILGRIMAGE destination in 1889, when rain fell following prayers. Thousands still visit the shrine on the feast day of Ste Anne (July 26), and bathe in the lake, which is believed to have curative powers.

ERIC J. HOLMGREN

Lacewing, common name for small, fragile insects of the 2 most common families (Chrysopidae, green lacewings; Hemerobiidae, brown lacewings) of order Neuroptera. Most green lacewings have golden or copper eyes and are found on foliage. They are poor, erratic flyers and strongly attracted to light. Some 25 species occur in Canada, the most common (*Chrysopa carnea* and *C. oculata*) in all provinces and territories. Eggs are laid on foliage or other objects, singly or in groups of 20 or more. Larvae are voracious predators, seizing small insects or arachnids with pincerlike jaws. Thus the possibility of rearing and releasing large numbers for biological control of INSECT PESTS has been studied. When fully grown, larvae spin cocoons, usually in secluded places. Brown lacewings resemble greens but are generally smaller and less common. They frequent wooded areas. About 23 species are found in Canada; the most common, *Hemerobius humulinus*, occurs throughout the country. Beaded lacewing (family Berothidae) and giant lacewing (Polystoechotidae) have one species each in Canada: *Lomomyia occidentalis* (southern BC), and *Polystaechotes punctatus* (BC, Alberta, Ontario and Québec).

J.E.H. MARTIN

Lachance, Louis, priest, philosopher (b at St-Joachim de Montmorency, Qué 18 Feb 1899; d at Montréal 28 Oct 1963). His *Nationalisme et religion* (1936) provided the base for a nationalism based on reason – distinct from that advocated by Lionel GROULX which was based primarily on feeling. His pioneering *Philosophie du langage* (1943) helped give Thomism a contemporary relevance and direction. Among philosophers, he is best known for *Le Droit et les droits de l'homme* (1959) which develops the theory that human rights are meaningless if seen merely in the context of the individual and his desires. They depend upon the community and must be related to the common good and to basic social responsibilities.

Lachance studied at the Petit Séminaire de Québec and then joined the Dominican order at St-Hyacinthe, the traditional stronghold of Québec Thomism. He studied and taught in Ottawa until 1936, apart from the years 1929-31 when he studied in Rome. In 1936 he returned to Rome to teach at Angelicum U. His career there was cut short by WWII and he returned to Canada as a priest, and in 1943 moved to U de M as professor of philosophy. LESLIE ARMOUR

Lachine, Qué, City, pop 34 906 (1986c), 37 521 (1981c), inc 1907, is located on the S bank of Montréal I and forms part of the MONTRÉAL urban community. In 1669 Cavelier de LA SALLE travelled inland in search of China, whence the derisive nickname Lachine applied to his land grant. In 1689 it was the site of a battle between the French and IROQUOIS (*see* LACHINE RAID). Lachine remained the nerve centre in the Canadian FUR TRADE for several decades, and the HBC maintained a trading post there for many years. The development of the Lachine Canal in the 19th century, the establishment of the MONTREAL AND LACHINE RAILROAD in 1847, and the expansion of the trucking businesses in the 20th century gave Lachine a major role in the trade network extending to SW Canada and the US. The town's industrialization, one of the most rapid in Canada, attracted a large working-class population. Its economy is dominated by steel plants and by the electrical-appliance and electronics industries. SYLVIE TASCHEREAU

Lachine Raid French westward expansion in the 1670s and 1680s cut off the IROQUOIS Confederacy from new sources of beaver and threatened New York's fur trade. As long as France and England were at peace, little could be done to impede French traders, but New York authorities could encourage the Iroquois on the warpath. On the morning of 5 Aug 1689 some 1500 warriors fell on the little settlement of Lachine just W of Montréal, killing 24 settlers and capturing more than 60 others. The ferocity of this attack terrorized the inhabitants of the Montréal region, who were to suffer many more such raids in the following decade. *See also* IROQUOIS WARS. JOHN A. DICKINSON

Lachute, Qué, City, pop 11 586 (1986c), 11 729 (1981c), inc 1885, is located on the Rivière du Nord where the first Laurentian foothills meet the plain of Montréal. Having developed through its close connection with the paper and textile industries, its economy is now increasingly diversified. The first settlers, who arrived in 1789, came from Jericho, Vermont. Early in the 19th century, population grew so rapidly that the settlers needed a flour mill to grind their grain, and built one at the foot of a rapids that stretched across the Rivière du Nord at a spot subsequently called "Lachute." GILLES BOILEAU

Lacombe, Alta, Town, pop 6080 (1986c), inc 1902, county seat for County of Lacombe, is situated in rolling parkland some 118 km S of Edmonton. Settlement appeared as early as 1883 but increased after construction of the Calgary-Edmonton Ry 1890-91. The new railway townsite was named for Father Albert LACOMBE. Growth between 1900 and WWI stabilized when it became clear that Lacombe would not become a major divisional point or the terminus of a line to the Brazeau Collieries. The town has served an agricultural region featuring cereal crop production and mixed farming, an emphasis notable in the work of the Dominion experimental farm at the Lacombe Research Station, originally established in 1908. More recently, the town has also become a residential dormitory for some of Red Deer's work force. From modest origins in 1909, the Seventh-Day Adventist Canadian Union College has developed as a vocational and academic junior college. CARL BETKE

Lacombe, Albert, Oblate priest, missionary (b at St-Sulpice, LC 28 Feb 1827; d at Midnapore, near Calgary 16 Dec 1916). A successful missionary to the CREE and BLACKFOOT, Lacombe used his trace of Indian blood to gain an entry to the hearts and minds of the Fort Edmonton Métis and Indians in 1852 when he came to serve them. In due course, he either founded or ministered at the Alberta missions of Lac Ste Anne, St Albert (1861) and St Paul des Cris (Brosseau) 1865. After 7 years as a travelling missionary among the Indians, he moved to Manitoba in 1872 and took over St Mary's parish, Winnipeg. On his return to Alberta in 1882, he became priest of Calgary's St Mary's parish and also served in southern Alberta at Fort Macleod and from his "Hermitage" at Pincher Creek. In 1883, when the CPR came into conflict with the Blackfoot, who threatened to block the route across the reserve, Father Lacombe successfully negotiated on behalf of the railway with Chief CROWFOOT. In 1894 Lacombe was principal of an industrial school at Midnapore; he initiated the colony of St Paul des Métis in 1895, and in 1909 he started the Midnapore Old Folks' Home. As the church's spokesman for the prairies, he played a significant part in influencing government policy, as well as helping settle the prairies. His love for the native people never faded. Called by the Indians "The Man of the Good Heart," he wrote both a Cree grammar and a dictionary. J.G. MACGREGOR

Reading: J.W. Grant, *Moon of Wintertime* (1984).

Lacroix, Richard, printmaker, painter, sculptor (b at Montréal 14 July 1939). He learned etching, lithography, silk-screen and block printing in Montréal with Albert DUMOUCHEL. Under an Arts Council of Canada grant (1961) he went to Paris, where he studied with Stanley Hayter at Atelier 17 and learned that studio's method of multicolour printing from one plate, a technique unknown in Canada. Shortly after his return to Montréal in 1964, Lacroix set up his own workshop and quickly drew other artists eager to learn the new techniques. Committed to reaching the widest audience possible, he established La Guilde graphique (1966) to generate public interest by distributing prints. In 1964 he and several other artists had formed Fusion des arts in an attempt to reflect the concerns of Québec society through a Québec popular art. Fusion's activities were later politically scrutinized, resulting in police raids on its offices and the loss of a group commission for Expo 67. Lacroix himself provided a kinetic sculpture and produced a show for this event.

Lacroix's prints are often highly organized geometrics or carefully orchestrated abstractions of great technical expertise. By pioneering colour printing in intaglio, working to establish the print as an "original" work of art and attempting to make the public more aware of the print medium, he has greatly increased respect for Canadian prints. In 1985, 2 surveys of his work were held in Montréal, at the Musée du Québec and at the Galerie Estampe Plus. CAROL ANN POPE

Lacrosse originated among the Algonquian tribes of the St Lawrence Valley in eastern Canada. For this reason, it is often described as the oldest organized sport in N America. The game has 2 forms. Field lacrosse is played outdoors on a ground that is 110 by 64 m, by teams of 10 players each. A hard rubber ball is passed and thrown between players by means of large, curved sticks with a pocket of netting or webbing. The object is to score points by tossing the ball into the opposing team's goal. The field game is played in England, Australia and New Zealand and by colleges along the eastern seaboard of the US. Although this form is Canadian in origin, box lacrosse or "boxla" is more commonly played in Canada. In the latter form, 7-man teams play on an indoor surface the size of a standard hockey arena.

Historians have recorded that the French missionary Jean de BRÉBEUF first saw the game in 1638 and called it *la crosse* because the sticks reminded him of a bishop's crozier or *crosse*. The Indian term for the original game was *baggattaway*, derived from the Ojibwa word *pagaadowewin* or "ball." Thus, white men named the game from the stick used, while the Indians named it after the ball. Lacrosse had an important role in Indian society, as it held religious significance and functioned in the training of young warriors. Since wagers were frequently taken on the outcome of matches between tribes, it also could play an economic role, raising or lowering a tribe's fortunes. Indian baggattaway was a rough melee. Matches could last 2 or 3 days and goals, marked by bushes or trees, could be 450 m or more apart. The arrival of French and later English fur traders and the consequent opening of trade routes throughout N America may have helped spread the game to other Indian nations. Perhaps the most famous incident in the game's history occurred in 1763. Ojibwa used the game as a cover to gain entry to Ft Michilimackinac and massacred the English soldiers camped inside. In 1834 a team of Caughnawaga first demonstrated the game before a white audience on the St Pierre racecourse in Montréal. The first all-white lacrosse team was formed in 1842 as part of the Montreal Olympic Athletic Club. Next year, the first game between whites and Indians took place. Until 1867 lacrosse's growth was slow and uneven and largely confined to Montréal and the towns of the Ottawa Valley.

One of the game's primary exponents at this time was George BEERS, who in 1860 at age 17 had been goalkeeper in a match played before the Prince of Wales. That same year, he set down lacrosse's first code of rules. A strong Canadian nationalist, Beers saw lacrosse as a way to encourage fitness and bravery among the young men of the new nation. In Sept 1867 he organized a convention in Kingston, Ont, at which the National Lacrosse Assn was formed. Beers was an ardent promoter of the sport and it was he who gave rise to the enduring misconception that lacrosse is the officially recognized national game of Canada. If lacrosse is not by law Canada's national game, it can be said that by 1889 its popularity was such that it was in fact the national game. Through the 1880s, it enjoyed sustained growth, spreading from coast to coast, and by 1900 its position seemed secure. It was also beginning to be played outside of Canada. In 1868 the first international match had been held in Buffalo, NY. Tours of Canadian teams to England were organized in 1876 and 1883 to introduce the game there. In 1901 Gov Gen Lord MINTO presented the Minto Cup for the senior amateur Canadian championship. Within 3 years it had become emblematic of the professional championship and, in 1910, the gold Mann Cup was donated for the Canadian amateur title. Although Canadian teams won Olympic gold medals in 1904 and 1908, the sport during this period was embroiled in unending disputes over professionalism. Finally, in 1912, the Amateur Athletic Union of Canada stepped in to form the Canadian Amateur Lacrosse Assn. By then, lacrosse was being played by only a small portion of the population. It had no minor system to develop young players and was not played in the country's schools, as was FOOTBALL. Following WWI, BASEBALL replaced lacrosse as a summer sport. The automobile's growing popularity affected the game as well, as it took potential players and spectators out of the cities on weekends and holidays. After struggling with these problems, the Canadian Amateur Lacrosse Assn decided to adopt box lacrosse as its official game. It was hoped this move would increase the game's popularity, as well as make use of unoccupied arenas during the summer months. An attempt was made to start up a professional lacrosse league in Montréal and Toronto, but by 1937 the professional game was gone and the Minto Cup was placed in junior competition.

The game is now largely played on Canada's West Coast and in medium-sized towns in Ontario. In fact, both national championships are held alternately in BC and Ontario. The switch to box lacrosse also effectively isolated the Canadian game from international competition. Eventually, supremacy by Canadians in the game they invented was severely challenged. In 1967, a world field lacrosse championship was held in Canada as part of the centennial celebrations. The US won. The best Canada could do at the 1974 world lacrosse series in Australia was a 2nd-place tie. In 1978, however, at the first true world championship, in Stockport, Eng, the Canadian team won after a dramatic last-minute goal in the final game. In 1982 the US took the title, while Canada finished third. In 1986 Canada lost to the US in the final.

J. THOMAS WEST

Reading: W.G. Beers, *Lacrosse: The National Game of Canada* (1869); C. McNaught, *Birth and Development of Canada's National Game* (1873); S.F. Wise and D. Fisher, *Canada's Sporting Heroes* (1974).

Lady Byng Trophy is awarded annually to the NATIONAL HOCKEY LEAGUE player chosen by hockey writers as best combining sportsmanship and skill. It was first presented in 1925 by Lady Byng, wife of the governor general. After Frank BOUCHER won the trophy 7 times, he was given it to keep, and another was donated to the league.

JAMES MARSH

Lady's Slipper, common name for some members of the ORCHID family in which modified petals (labella) fold inward to make the toe of the "slipper." Insects must pass through the structure to obtain nectar, pollinating the plant in the process. Only the genus *Cypripedium* is hardy enough to withstand the Canadian climate. Its 50 species are scattered throughout northern temperate regions of America and Eurasia. Of the 13 N American species, 8 are native to Canada. The pink or stemless lady's slipper (*C. acaule*), also known as moccasin flower, has 2 leaves at the base of the plant and produces a single flower. The 5 cm long slipper is split along its length. This spring-flowering plant grows in moist places, preferably in acidic soil, from Newfoundland to Manitoba. The lady's slipper was selected (1947) as the PROVINCIAL FLORAL EMBLEM of PEI. The showy lady's slipper (*C. reginae*) was chosen first but, because it is rare, was replaced in 1965 by the pink lady's slipper. As it is difficult to grow, the lady's slipper should not be disturbed in its native stands. The sedative qualities of a root infusion of yellow lady's slipper (*C. calceolus*) or of moccasin flower were known to Canadian native people. *See also* PLANTS, NATIVE USES.

CÉLINE ARSENEAULT

Montreal Lacrosse Club team, 1867. Until Confederation lacrosse was largely confined to Montréal. Within 20 years it was virtually the national sport (*courtesy Notman Photographic Archives*).

Ladysmith, BC, Town, pop 4393 (1986c), 4558 (1981c), inc 1904, is located on the E coast of VANCOUVER I, 95 km N of Victoria. It is situated on Oyster Harbour on the northern edge of a lucrative farming area. Indians were attracted here by the abundance of oysters. The area's COAL mines and Ladysmith's fine harbour spurred development in the late 1890s. Initially designed by Premier James DUNSMUIR as a recreation area and dormitory for miners, it was named after the relief of Ladysmith in the SOUTH AFRICAN WAR. In the 1930s lumbering became the economy's mainstay. Commercial fishing is also important, and tourism is developing.

ALAN F.J. ARTIBISE

A species of orchid, the pink lady's slipper (*Cypripedium acaule*), is the floral emblem of PEI (*photo by Mary W. Ferguson*).

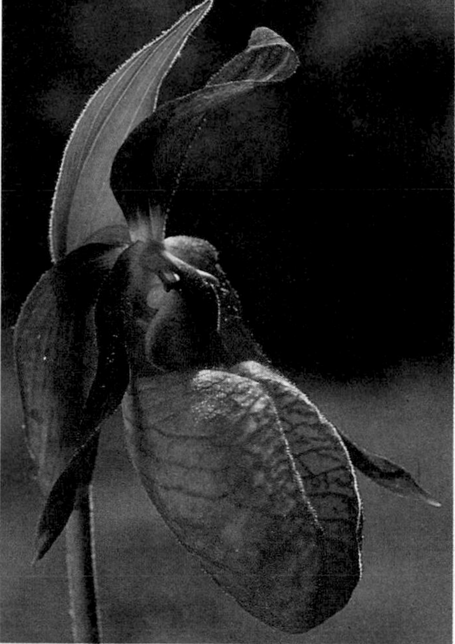

Lafitau, Joseph-François, priest, Jesuit missionary, legal philosopher (b at Bordeaux, France 1681; d there 3 July 1746). He was the discoverer of GINSENG in N America, and his landmark study of the laws and customs of the IROQUOIS, *Moeurs des sauvages amériquains, comparées aux moeurs des premiers temps*, was published in 4 vols in Paris in 1724, subsequently translated into Dutch and German, and even circulated in China. Stationed at Sault-St-Louis [Caughnawauga] in NEW FRANCE by his Jesuit superiors in 1713, Lafitau spent 5 years observing the customs of the Iroquois with a view ultimately to illuminating those of the ancient civilizations he had studied at several European universities through comparison and contrast with Iroquois practices. *Moeurs*, the result of this empirical ethnography, bears a striking resemblance to philosopher Montesquieu's famous *De l'esprit des lois*, published in 1748, although Montesquieu did not cite Lafitau. Largely ignored by other Enlightenment thinkers, this early philosopher has only received prolonged attention in the 20th century, principally as a result of the favourable review of his work by such contemporary historians of ideas as Arnold Van Gennep, Gilbert Chinard, Alfred Métraux and Peter Stein.

G. BLAINE BAKER

Laflamme, Joseph-Clovis-Kemner, priest, educator, scientist (b at St-Anselme, Canada E 18 Sept 1849; d at Québec C 6 July 1910). After studying at the SÉMINAIRE DE QUÉBEC and later spending periods at Harvard and in Europe, Laflamme became professor of geology and mineralogy at Laval in 1870. He also taught physics 1875-93. From 1880 on, he was given several assignments to conduct explorations in Québec on behalf of the GEOLOGICAL SURVEY OF CANADA. Despite his contributions in this field, he is better known for his activities in education and in the dissemination of scientific knowledge. A founding member of the RSC, he became its president in 1891. In 1893 he was appointed rector of Laval. Through his lectures, science manuals and numerous newspaper articles, Laflamme made French Canada aware of the major scientific discoveries of his era, particularly the new uses of electricity, the telephone and X rays. At the end of his life he was unanimously recognized as the leading scholar of French Canada.

RAYMOND DUCHESNE

Laflèche, Louis-François Richer, Roman Catholic bishop (b at Ste-Anne-de-la-Pérade [La Pérade, Qué], LC 4 Sept 1818; d at Trois-Rivières, Qué 14 July 1898). After a diversified career as missionary to RUPERT'S LAND (1844-56), professor and administrator of the Collège de Nicolet (1856-61) and diocesan bursar (1861-66), he became bishop of Trois-Rivières (coadjutor, 1867-70; titular, 1870-98). A faithful disciple of Mgr Ignace BOURGET, he was a member of the intransigent Ultramontane group that battled liberalism and opposed Archbishop E.A. TASCHEREAU and his allies over the Programme catholique, the university question, the issue of undue clerical influence in electoral campaigns and the reform of the CIVIL CODE; after 1876 he was the recognized and unyielding leader of the group. Despite his weakened standing within the office of the archbishop and in Rome he again took up the cudgels over the MANITOBA SCHOOLS QUESTION and was supported by most Québec bishops. When the pope refused to condemn the compromise policy of Wilfrid LAURIER, Laflèche acquiesced and until his death devoted himself to his religious duties. His ideas, summarized in his *Quelques considérations sur les rapports de la société civile avec la religion et la* *famille* (1866), had a long-lasting influence on nationalist and Catholic circles in Québec. *See also* ULTRAMONTANISM. NIVE VOISINE

Reading: Nive Voisine, *Louis-François Laflèche, deuxième évêque de Trois-Rivières* (1 vol to date, 1980).

Lafleur, Guy Damien, hockey player (b at Thurso, Qué 20 Sept 1951). His outstanding 1971 junior exploits (130 goals and the Memorial Cup for his team, the Québec Remparts) made him a much heralded rookie with the MONTREAL CANADIENS. In his first 3 professional seasons Lafleur struggled to meet the high standards expected of him, but in 1975 he turned his career around dramatically. His fluid skating style, instinctive playmaking and accurate shot carried him to 6 consecutive 50-goal seasons and selections (1975-80) as NHL all-star right winger. He won the HART TROPHY 1977-78, the ART ROSS TROPHY 1976-78, and while contributing to Montréal's STANLEY CUP wins of 1973 and 1976-79 was awarded the 1977 CONN SMYTHE TROPHY. On 20 Dec 1983 he became only the tenth player in NHL history to reach the 500-goal plateau. He retired early in the 1984-85 season. In Jan 1987 Lafleur began working as a commentator for Montréal radio station CKAC on Montreal Canadiens home games. DEREK DRAGER

LaFontaine, Sir Louis-Hippolyte, also La Fontaine, politician (b at Boucherville, LC 4 Oct 1807; d at Montréal 26 Feb 1864). Educated at the Collège de Montréal, LaFontaine was called to the bar of Lower Canada in 1828. He began his political career with election to the Lower Canadian Assembly in 1830. Although a radical follower of PAPINEAU, he opposed the 1837 call to arms, and travelled to London to plead with the imperial government for constitutional reform. He was arrested in 1838, but released without trial. He then became leader of the French Canadian moderate reformers.

After the 1841 union of Upper and Lower Canada, he worked with Robert BALDWIN and Francis HINCKS to found a united party of Upper and Lower Canadian reformers. He insisted on speaking French in the Assembly, and because of his action the imperial government later repealed the ACT OF UNION clause prohibiting official use of French. In 1842 he formed an administration with Baldwin, but resigned in Nov 1843 to protest Governor General Sir Charles METCALFE's political actions. In 1848, he was again called to form a ministry, this time by Lord ELGIN, who fully recognized RESPONSIBLE GOVERNMENT. LaFontaine thus became the first prime minister of Canada in the modern sense of the term. During this second administration, he demonstrated the achievement of responsible government by the passage of the REBELLION LOSSES BILL, despite fierce opposition and violent demonstrations. His ministry also passed an AMNESTY ACT to forgive the 1837-38 rebels, secularized King's College into U of T, incorporated many French Canadian colleges, established Université Laval, adopted important railway legislation and reformed municipal and judicial institutions.

LaFontaine retired to private life in 1851 but was appointed chief justice of Canada E in 1853. In 1854 he was created a baronet by Queen Victoria and a papal knight by Pius IX. A tall, portly man, resembling Napoleon I, LaFontaine was a master politician who commanded respect and inspired many others with his high ideals and patriotism. JACQUES MONET, S.J.

Reading: J.M.S. Careless, *The Union of the Canadas* (1967); Jacques Monet, s.j., *The Last Cannon Shot* (1969).

LaFontaine, a portly man who resembled Napoleon I, was instrumental in the achievement of responsible government and was in effect the first PM of Canada (*courtesy National Archives of Canada/C-5961*).

Lagemodière, Jean-Baptiste, also spelled as Lagimodière, Lagimonière and Lajimodière, fur trader (b at Trois-Rivières, Qué 26 Dec 1778; d at St-Boniface, Man 7 Sept 1855). Going west as a hunter and trapper about 1800, he returned to Québec in 1806, where he married Marie-Anne Gaboury. Taking her west, he was a free trapper near the RED RIVER COLONY and later near Ft Edmonton. In 1815, during the troubles at the Red River settlement, he was given despatches to take to Montréal for the Hudson's Bay Co, informing Lord SELKIRK of the dangerous situation in the West. He made the arduous 3000 km journey in 5 months, but on his return was captured near Ft William and held prisoner by the North West Co for 56 days. Upon his release and return to Red River, he was given a land grant across the river from Ft Garry. HUGH A. DEMPSEY

Lagemodière, Marie-Anne, née Gaboury, western pioneer (b at Maskinongé, Qué 2 Aug 1780; d at St-Boniface, Man 14 Dec 1875). Married to Jean-Baptiste LAGEMODIÈRE, a fur trader, in 1806, Marie-Anne went to the Red River and Ft Edmonton areas with him, becoming one of the first white women on the western prairies. Her daughter, Reine (b 1807), was the first legitimate white child in the West. Of Marie-Anne's 8 children, the second youngest, Julie, was the mother of Louis RIEL. HUGH A. DEMPSEY

Lagomorpha, order of mammals containing 2 families: the RABBITS and HARES (Leporidae), with long ears and hindlimbs, small tufted tail and hopping gait; and the small, lesser-known PIKAS (Ochotonidae), with smaller, rounded ears, hindlegs and forelegs of approximately the same length, no apparent tail and running gait. Approximately 61 species are found in a wide variety of habitats, on every continent except Antarctica. Seven species are native to Canada (5 leporids, 2 ochotonids); 2 leporid species have been introduced. They range from the US border to the arctic islands and are a familiar sight to almost every Canadian. All lagomorphs are terrestrial, herbivorous and active year-round. Pikas are most active during the day, rabbits and hares mainly in the evening and at night. Both groups exhibit coprophagy (the reingestion of feces), which allows them to extract maximum nutritional value from fibrous plant food and is somewhat reminiscent of chewing the cud in ruminant mammals. Two types of fecal pellets are produced: soft, moist pellets which are eaten, and hard, fibrous ones which are discarded. The lagomorphs were classified as rodents until formally separated, in the early 1900s, on the basis of numerous differences in dentition, skeleton and musculature. Rodents are no longer considered to be even close relatives. The origin of the lagomorphs is uncertain. M.L. WESTON

LaHave, NS, UP, pop 207 (1986c), 195 (1981c), is located at the mouth of the LaHave R, 11 km SW of LUNENBURG. The Micmac called it *Pijelooeekak* ("having long points"). In 1604 de MONTS gave the name La Hève to the nearby cape. In 1632 de RAZILLY brought with him from France several families to settle the area. A fort was built to protect the settlement; a school, said to have been the first Acadian school, was established. The settlement was later transferred to PORT-ROYAL, though a few families remained behind. By the 1760s an English fishing base had been established at the former Acadian settlement. The 19th century saw industries connected with the fisheries, such as shipbuilding and sawmills, become an important part of the LaHave R economy, while farming remained a support industry. At this time the centre of development shifted upriver to Bridgewater. Today, residents are mostly of German descent. JEAN PETERSON

LaHave River Estuary is a narrow, shallow inlet of the Atlantic Ocean extending 24 km from Bridgewater, NS, to the coast. This lovely sheltered waterway is favoured for recreational sailing and fishing, especially for salmon and striped bass. The principal industry is fishing, with smaller amounts of farming and shipbuilding. East LaHave was the first land reached by de MONTS in 1604 and later became the site of one of the earliest European settlements in the province. (It was named after Cap de la Hève, near Le Havre, France.) In the early 1800s LaHave was used as a depot by pirates preying on New England shipping. Cape LaHave I is the largest of a group of islands extending 7 km offshore from the mouth of the estuary. P.C. SMITH

Lahontan, Louis-Armand de Lom d'Arce, Baron, officer, author (b at Lahontan, France 9 June 1666; d in Europe before 1716). During Lahontan's 10 years in New France (1683-93), he fought the Iroquois, explored the Mississippi and helped defend Québec in 1690 and Newfoundland in 1693 against English attacks. Lahontan's fame rests on the 1703 publication of his colourful travels and memoirs (*Nouveaux Voyages dans l'Amérique septentrionale; mémoires de l'Amérique septentrionale*) and on a supplementary volume of imaginary dialogues with an Indian chief that contributed to the vogue of the "noble savage." The 3 volumes, retouched in 1705 by an unfrocked Benedictine monk, Nicholas Gueudeville, were frequently republished and translated for European readers during the 18th century. DAVID M. HAYNE

Laidlaw, Alexander Fraser, co-operative leader, educator, writer (b at Port Hood, NS 12 Jun 1908; d at Ottawa 30 Nov 1980). He worked with Moses COADY as part of the ANTIGONISH MOVEMENT (1944-56) and after 2 years with co-ops in India, became general secretary of the Co-operative Union of Canada (1958-68). He supported housing co-ops while on the board (1959-68) and on staff (1971-74) of Central (Canada) Mortgage and Housing Corp. Retired in 1974, Laidlaw became a conscience and inspiration for Canada's CO-OPERATIVE MOVEMENT through his writings and speeches, while he continued to consult for co-ops overseas. A lucid and prolific writer, he published regularly in the *Maritime (Atlantic) Co-operator* and wrote several books, including *The Campus and the Community* (1961), *The Man from Margaree* (1971), *Housing You Can Afford* (1977) and *Co-operatives in the Year 2000* (1980).

VICKI L. DAVIS

Laidler, Keith James, chemist, professor (b at Liverpool, Eng 3 Jan 1916). After studying at Oxford and Princeton, and holding appointments at the National Research Council and Catholic U, Washington, DC, he joined University of Ottawa in 1955. He is coauthor of *The Theory of Rate Processes* and has published a large number of research papers, research monographs on chemical kinetics and chemistry textbooks. His research has covered the fields of chemical-reaction kinetics, fundamental theoretical aspects of kinetics and experimental study of many types of systems. Elected a fellow of the RSC in 1960, he received the Chemical Inst of Canada Medal in 1971, the Queen's Jubilee Medal in 1977 and the Henry Marshall Tory Medal in 1987.

B. CONWAY

Laird, David, editor, politician, lt-governor, Indian commissioner (b New Glasgow, PEI 12 Mar 1833; d at Ottawa 12 Jan 1914). He was Liberal leader in the PEI legislature, was elected to Parliament 1873, was minister of interior (1873-76); then, to 1881, he was appointed first (separate) lt-gov of the North-West Territories. Treaty No 7 was signed 23 Sept 1877 by Chief CROWFOOT and other chiefs and by Commissioner Laird and Lt-Col MACLEOD, CO of the NWMP. Owing to virtual extinction of buffalo soon thereafter the Plains Indians neared starvation. An uprising was feared, but disaster was averted, largely because of the Indians' respect for the NWMP and the mutual trust between the chiefs and Laird based on many personal contacts and his honoured promises. Appointed Indian commissioner for the West at Winnipeg 1898, he negotiated Treaty No 8 in 1899 with Indians of the vast Athabasca area N of Edmonton. From 1909 to 1914 he was adviser to the Indian Affairs Dept at Ottawa.

Lake The hydrologic cycle supplies the world's landmasses with water as precipitation. In areas where precipitation is neither totally retained as ICE nor totally evaporated, excess water must find its way back to the sea via surface runoff, RIVERS and GROUNDWATER percolation. Where these flows are intercepted by a naturally occurring impervious basin or depression, a lake may result. A lake represents a short-term dynamic balance and a long-term evolution. A constant water level is maintained only if inflows from precipitation, runoff and groundwater percolation balance losses from outflow, evaporation or groundwater movement. Over geological time, lakes are transient; inflows carry dissolved and suspended material washed from the surrounding high ground, and biological productivity adds organic material to the accumulating sediments. These sediments gradually fill the basin. Human activities in a lake's DRAINAGE BASIN can accelerate the aging and infilling processes through increased EROSION accompanying agricultural and urban developments and through addition of biologically active materials or nutrients.

The 6 most important geological processes involved in lake formation are described in order of importance.

Glacial Movements of ice sheets and valley GLACIERS in past ice ages have scoured basins in underlying terrain. Glacial deposits (eg, MORAINES, ESKERS, DRUMLINS) may create favourable sites for lakes and ponds. Most Canadian lakes are of glacial origin.

Tectonic Movements of the Earth's crust, ie, folding and faulting, can create basins later filled by lakes. Lake Superior has been formed by glacial and tectonic processes.

Canada's Fifteen Largest Lakes
(Source: *Canadian Survey on the Water Balance of Lakes*, UNESCO, 1973)

Lake	*Province*	*Area (km^2)[a]*
Superior[b]	Ont	82 100
Huron[b]	Ont	59 600
Great Bear	NWT	31 300
Great Slave	NWT	28 600
Erie[b]	Ont	25 700
Winnipeg	Man	24 400
Ontario[b]	Ont	19 000
Athabasca	Alta/Sask	7 940
Reindeer	Sask	6 650
Nettiling	NWT	5 540
Winnipegosis	Man	5 370
Nipigon	Ont	4 850
Manitoba	Man	4 630
Lake of the Woods[b]	Ont	4 350
Dubawnt	NWT	3 830

[a] Total lake area, including islands
[b] Includes portion located in the US

Coastal Waves contribute to erosion and generate coastal currents which move sediments along the shore to zones of relative calm. The sandbars thus formed may block the entrance to a bay, forming a lagoon. If fresh water drains into the lagoon, a coastal lake, separated from the sea by a narrow barrier, may result. Many small lakes so formed occur along the Atlantic coast of NS, and several good examples occur within Lk Ontario, eg, Hamilton Harbour.

River Processes In floodplains, river meanders can be separated from the main flow and become oxbow lakes or sloughs. Deposition of sediments across the mouths of tributaries can flood the upstream tributary valley. At river mouths, where a DELTA is formed, a combination of river and coastal processes can form shallow deltaic lakes.

Volcanic Centres of volcanic cones may collapse into craters, forming crater lakes, often very deep in relation to their surface area. Lava flows may dam rivers to form lakes.

Solution Relatively soluble rock may be slowly eaten away by percolating groundwater, creating caverns which may collapse into water-filled depressions or solution lakes. This process occurs most frequently in limestone or gypsum regions.

Lakes in the shield country near Killarney, Ont. It is estimated that there may be as many as 2 million lakes in Canada (*photo by Karl Sommerer*).

A somewhat analogous process occurs in the Arctic when collected surface water melts underlying PERMAFROST, forming a thaw lake.

Distribution of Lakes in Canada

Recent surveys suggest that there may be as many as 2 million lakes in Canada. About 7.6% of Canada's nearly 10 million km^2 is covered by fresh water; enough water is contained by these lakes and rivers to flood the entire country to a depth of over 2 m. Canada possesses nearly 14% of the world's lakes having surface areas over 500 km^2. Although Canada stores a disproportionate share of the world's surface fresh water, the amount available for use depends more on the volume supplied annually than on that stored over many years. Therefore, despite an apparent abundance, the freshwater resource must be managed carefully.

Surface geology and climate govern the nature and distribution of lakes. It is convenient to describe lakes in relation to the PHYSIOGRAPHIC REGIONS of Canada. Many lakes are distributed through a 1000 km swath of land surrounding Hudson Bay, the Canadian SHIELD. Nearly all are of glacial origin. Thin soils and high resistance of the rocks to weathering tend to make the lakes clear, biologically unproductive and relatively long-lived because of slow sedimentation. The Shield is dome-shaped in cross section, dipping to contact the softer SEDIMENTARY ROCKS of the Hudson Bay Lowlands and the Western Interior Lowlands. The lowlands along the SW shore of Hudson Bay have only recently emerged from the sea as the land rebounds from the last GLACIATION. This region of poor, disorganized drainage is carpeted with MUSKEG and peat bogs. Within the peatlands are many small, shallow lakes and ponds having a teardrop shape aligned to the prevailing winds, the result of wave action on the fragile shorelines. Close to the coast, ancient beach ridges define long, narrow, shore-parallel lakes and ponds. Old river channels, abandoned as the land rises, are frequently occupied by lakes in this region.

The line of contact between the Shield and the Western Interior Lowlands is marked by a band containing Canada's largest lakes, ranging from Great Bear Lk, NWT, to the Great Lakes, Ont. Glaciers pouring off the Shield and carrying with them hard granitic debris, gouged deeply into the thin edge of the softer sedimentary rocks before spreading over the lowlands. Glacial deposition of till, rather than extensive scouring, marks the effect of glaciers on the plains. Unlike Shield lakes, prairie lakes are formed in a thick overburden of clay, till and soil. Lakes in the Western Interior Lowlands tend to be more shallow, more rapidly filled by sediments and more biologically productive than Shield lakes.

Annual rainfall decreases and evaporation increases from NE to SW; the corresponding trend in lake distribution is for fewer, sometimes seasonally transient lakes, carrying higher concentrations of dissolved materials. In the dry SW, numerous alkali lakes and ponds occur in which concentrations of dissolved materials reach saturation and evaporite crystals, usually sodium sulphate, precipitate out. Glacial deposition in the SW has left the ground pocked with small depressions which fill to become ponds or sloughs in spring, often drying up by late summer. Although the total water volume of these ponds is small in comparison with well-established lakes in other places, they are important to agriculture and as WATERFOWL habitat. In the Far North, parkland and forest yield to the boreal forest proper, with extensive areas of muskeg and bog lakes.

Lakes in the rugged terrain W of the Great Plains are relatively sparse compared with those of eastern Canada (covering less than 2% of surface area), but they are extremely varied. Lakes in western Canada are mainly of glacial origin: large lakes in BC and the YT are generally confined to deep, glaciated valleys; smaller scour lakes are found on upland plateaus. Tectonic processes associated with mountain building provide other natural basins. The Cariboo region (Southern Interior Plateau) of BC, in the rain shadow of the Coast Range, is relatively arid and contains alkali ponds and lakes. Some lakes occupy the heads of ancient FJORDS near the coast. Powell Lk, near Vancouver, was formed when isostatic rebound (the tendency for land to rise once the heavy ice cover melts) isolated a fjord from the sea. Although this took place thousands of years ago, the lake's bottom water is still salty, a fossil seawater.

The Atlantic provinces lie in a region of ancient mountains, a northern extension of the Appalachians. This land was also heavily glaciated. The many lakes in areas underlain by hard IGNEOUS or metamorphosed rocks closely resemble the lakes of the Shield. More permeable sedimentary rocks underlie eastern NB, northwestern NS and PEI, and hence fewer lakes occur in these areas. Many small coastal lakes occur in NS.

The St Lawrence Lowlands and lower Great Lakes region contain some of Canada's richest farmland, but compared to the scoured region of the Shield, small- and medium-sized lakes are rare. However, this region is adjacent to the Great Lakes, which together constitute the largest body of fresh water on Earth. Lakes SUPERIOR and HURON lie across the contact between Shield rocks and the more recent sedimentary rocks. Lakes Michigan, ERIE and ONTARIO are underlain by sedimentary rocks with thick overburdens of glacial deposits. The geology of the drainage basins has affected the primordial character of each lake and has determined the settlement patterns, which in turn have had a considerable impact on Lakes Erie and Ontario.

Biological Properties

Lakes are ecosystems: biological energy flows through a food chain and spent organic matter is recycled into materials that are again available to living organisms. The first and most important stage, primary productivity, is photosynthesis, where nutrients are combined into organic matter through the energy of sunlight and the action of chlorophyll contained in plant cells. Most lake plants are single-celled microscopic ALGAE (phytoplankton), which are suspended in the water and move with it. In abundant quantities, they may colour the water, rendering it turbid. A host of tiny ZOOPLANKTON graze on the phytoplankton and, in turn, are eaten by fish. Bacteria decompose dead material into constituents available for new cycles of life. Carbon, hydrogen and oxygen are usually freely available in sunlit surface waters. Usable forms of nitrogen and phosphorus may be scarce, limiting primary productivity. Nutrients may be supplied by inflows and by local runoff; their distribution within a lake is controlled by physical processes.

Physical Properties

Water movements in lakes are governed by 3 sources of energy: the flow of water from inlet to outflow and the stirring action of wind (both mechanical sources), and heat energy, gained in spring and summer, lost in fall and winter. The longest time scales of motion, having perhaps a yearly cycle, are those associated with the flow of water through a lake from inlet to outlet (hydraulic component of flow). Outflow removes dissolved and suspended materials along with the water. Since lakes vary widely in size and rate of outflow, it is useful to define a flushing time as the volume of the lake divided by the average rate of outflow (ie, the time required to drain the lake at the mean outflow rate). Permanent lakes with flushing times much less than a year are quite rare, and their behaviour is strongly marked by vigorous flow, biological productivity usually being depressed. At the other extreme, lakes with flushing times greater than 10 years are considered sensitive to external changes; recovery from a polluted state requires at least one flushing time.

Superimposed on this motion are movements driven by wind and by convection caused by surface cooling or heating. Wind-driven motions, mechanically the most important, include surface waves, turbulent mixing and systems of currents circulating around the lake. These motions distribute dissolved and suspended materials through the lake.

Lakes gain heat from solar radiation; they lose heat as water evaporates from the surface; they may gain or lose heat directly from the atmosphere. Except for solar radiation, these fluxes are absorbed or emitted in the top few centimetres of the water column. Solar radiation, which powers photosynthesis in addition to heating the water, may penetrate effectively to a depth of 30 m in a very clear lake, or may be absorbed in the top metre of a lake made turbid by suspended sediments or an abundance of plankton. A kilogram of water must absorb or lose 4200 joules of heat to raise or lower its temperature by 1°C. This is one of the largest "specific heats" of all substances. Compared with the land, lakes can store and release huge amounts of heat; therefore, large lakes may moderate the climate near their shores. Stone fruits can be grown on the Niagara Pen because it is protected from severe winter weather by the open waters of Lk Ontario.

As the surface water warms or cools in response to the surface heat flux, its density changes. Fresh water is most dense not at freezing point (0°C) but at 4°C. As water is warmed above or cooled below 4°C, its density decreases (it expands). If the heat flux acts to increase the surface density (fall cooling or early spring warming), surface water tends to sink and mixing by convection takes place. If the heat flux decreases the surface density (winter cooling just before freezeup, spring and summer warming), the lighter surface water tends to float on the heavier underlying water. Wind mixing may not be strong enough to overcome this extra stability, particularly in summer, and a layered distribution of warm and cool water can persist through the summer in deep lakes. These lakes are said to be thermally stratified, and it is usually possible to define 3 layers: a warm, actively wind-stirred upper layer called the epilimnion; a cool, relatively homogeneous bottom layer called the hypolimnion; and a transitional layer called the thermocline between the warm and cool layers.

Stratification strongly affects all other physical, biological and biochemical processes. It influences the horizontal distribution of nutrients, and the speed with which nutrients trapped in the hypolimnion and in bottom sediments are made available to algae in the surface waters. Furthermore, inflows and outflows often occur at shallow depths within the epilimnion. If the inflowing water is of equal or lesser density than the surface water of the receiving lake, the hydraulic flow and attendant flushing is confined to the epilimnion. This restriction may retard the effective flushing of a contaminant from a lake since much of it will be stored in the sheltered hypolimnion.

Seasonal thermal stratification has other important consequences. Diversity of habitat encourages diversity of living organisms; therefore, stratified lakes may permit the coexistence of warm-water fish (eg, bass) and cool-water fish (eg, trout). Diversity may be limited by the interaction of stratification with primary productivity and bacterial decomposition, which may be influenced by human activities.

Overfertilization by sewage or agricultural runoff may lead to an increase in algal growth, with a corresponding rise in dead organic material in the cool waters of the hypolimnion. This results in depletion of oxygen, caused by increased bacterial decomposition, and may lead to the loss of cool-water fish species. If the system has been pushed far enough, recovery may become impossible, even with greatly reduced external loading of nutrients. Also poor FORESTRY practices (eg, extensive clear-cutting in inappropriate areas) can have similar effects because increased runoff carries soil nutrients into nearby lakes. Logging and settlement in the basins of Lakes Ontario and Erie are thought to have modified these lakes considerably.

Other Human Impacts

Overenrichment (cultural eutrophication) is not the only problem in lake management. Many compounds used in agriculture or industry are dangerous toxins; the more insidious have chemical affinities to natural organic material and enter the food chain, becoming increasingly concentrated (*see* HAZARDOUS WASTES, WATER POLLUTION). Another serious problem arising from human activities is ACID RAIN, which results from the burning of fossil fuels. The effects of the fallout on lakes are strongly governed by the region's surface geology. Shield lakes are vulnerable to these effects, which may include a complete loss of fish. Lakes in limestone-rich areas are less vulnerable because acidity is neutralized by dissolution of limestone.

In Canada many lakes have been created by damming rivers for RESERVOIRS for hydroelectric developments, sources of water for irrigation and domestic use, and for flood control. Reservoir design and management draw on all aspects of lake science. For example, the large fluctuations in water level accompanying reservoir operation can cause accelerated shore erosion and are potentially harmful to fish spawning in shallow water.

F.M. BOYCE

Lake Carriers, or "lakers," are ships whose design is unique to the GREAT LAKES of N America. The lake carrier's long and flat shape reveals its basic purpose – to move bulk cargoes through the ST LAWRENCE SEAWAY and Great Lakes, a total distance of almost 4000 km. The *John B. Aird,* a typical modern Canadian lake carrier, was launched in 1983 by Collingwood Shipyards on Georgian Bay, is 219 m long and has a deadweight tonnage of 30 700 tonnes. Similar to an increasing number of lake carriers of its size which are fitted with cranes or conveyor belts, the *John B. Aird* is a self-unloading lake carrier.

Ships of this size can carry one million bushels of wheat on a single voyage (27 000 tonnes). Wheat and other feed grains account for about 40% of all cargoes carried by Canadian lake carriers, followed by coal, iron ore and limestone. The annual 9-month shipping season of the lake carriers does not include the winter months of late December to early March when the seaway is closed and ice covers much of the Great Lakes.

Most of the 199 lake carriers in service in 1986, down from 247 in 1984, belonged to member companies of the Dominion Marine Assn (DMA) of Ottawa, founded in 1903, and the Lake Carriers' Assn of US, formed in Cleveland, Ohio, in 1880. Of these vessels, 131 are Canadian ships on the DMA register, down from 143 in 1984, and the remaining 68 are US-owned vessels. The Canadian lake-carrier fleets carried cargoes weighing 72.1 million tonnes in 1986.

The modern Canadian lake carrier is the result of more than 100 years of continually changing Great Lakes ship design and modification (*see* SHIPBUILDING AND SHIP REPAIR). Earlier types of cargo carriers on the Great Lakes, all of them built for the bulk transit of goods, included the exotically named hermaphrodite barquentines of the age of sail and the whalebacks and canalers of the age of mechanical propulsion. As becomes the name "hermaphrodite," which means having 2 opposite qualities, this class of sailing ship had 2 masts, with square-rigged sails on the foremast for maneuvering in and out of dock and in narrow passages, and fore-and-aft rigged sails on the mainmast for speed. Except for their tall funnels and awkward deck structures, the whalebacks of the age of coal-fired steam engines, squat and broad-beamed, looked like the modern nuclear submarine. The whalebacks were also called "pig boats" because their bows ended in a steel snout built above the waterline. The later canalers were designed to fit snugly into the narrow locks of the old Welland Canal, linking Lakes Erie and Ontario and passing near St Catharines, Ont, and the canal system between Lk Ontario and Montréal which terminated at the Lachine Canal. The canaler was one-third the length of the *John B. Aird.* In 1959 canalers were replaced in the wider and longer locks of the St Lawrence Seaway system by upper lakers, which had previously been restricted to the upper lakes above Niagara because of their size. These locks can take ships up to 222.5 m in length and 23.2 m in breadth.

Some of these larger carriers, though designed primarily for the inland lakes, have been built for both the coastal trade and deep-sea service and are called ocean lakers. This is not entirely a new trend since some earlier lakers were requisitioned to serve on the N Atlantic during WWII, and a few of them were sunk by German U-BOATS.

The Great Lakes have been a graveyard for hundreds of ships, most of them lost during the age of sail between 1750 and 1870, in storms, fires and collisions. Despite their size, even modern lake carriers can be victims of severe ice conditions and storms. The tragic sinking on 10 Nov 1975 of the *Edmund Fitzgerald,* a 222 m long US iron-ore carrier, was commemorated in song by Gordon LIGHTFOOT. After battling 7.5 m waves and record 125 km/h winds on Lk Superior, the ship suddenly plunged to the bottom with the loss of the entire crew of 29, including her experienced captain. JOHN D. HARBRON

The *John B. Aird,* a bulk carrier with a self-unloading system. The lake carrier's characteristic shape, long and flat, reveals its purpose of moving bulk cargoes (*courtesy Lucas Photographics, Thunder Bay*).

Reading: H.C. Campbell, *Early Days on the Great Lakes: The Art of William Armstrong* (1971); J. Lesstrang, *Lake Carriers: The Saga of the Great Lakes Fleet* (1979).

Lake Louise, 2.4 km long, elev 1731 m, is located in BANFF NATIONAL PK in SW Alberta; its outlet is a stream flowing into the BOW R. Indian guides took CPR workman Tom Wilson to the site in 1882; he named it Emerald Lk, but the name was changed (1884) to honour Princess Louise Caroline Alberta, fourth daughter of Queen Victoria and wife of Gov Gen the marquess of LORNE. The community of Lake Louise, UP, pop 688 (1986c), 355 (1981c), is near the lake, on the site of the former CPR station, Laggan, which was base camp for 12 000 workers in 1884, when CPR construction proceeded through KICKING HORSE PASS. The jewellike lake, framed by blue mountains and gleaming snowfields, is one of the most famous mountain vistas on the continent. Chateau Lake Louise stands atop the huge glacial moraine that dams the lake. JAMES MARSH

Known only to local Indians a century ago, Lake Louise is perhaps the world's most famous mountain lake. Its creamy turquoise colour is caused by suspended rock flour, fine particles which are carried down in the melt-water from glaciers (*photo by J.A. Kraulis*).

Lake of the Woods, 4350 km^2 (of which 3149 km^2 are in Canada), elev 323 m, fed by Rainy R from the S and drained to the NW by the WINNIPEG R; it is a remnant of former glacial Lake AGASSIZ. The S shore is regular, low and sandy, contrasting with the granite edge, myriad channels, peninsulas and 14 632 islands of the N shore. Thrust into the lake from the E is Aulneau Peninsula, named for the Jesuit priest Jean-Pierre Aulneau (1705-36) who, along with Jean-Baptiste LA VÉRENDRYE and 19 others, was killed on an island in the lake by Sioux warriors. The French explorer Jacques de Noyon reached the lake in 1688, and La Vérendrye built Fort Saint-Charles on the N shore (1732). The lake was part of the main FUR-TRADE ROUTE, and voyageurs frequently lost their way among its islands. Cree, Ojibwa and Sioux lived in the area first, and rock paintings have been found at several sites. About 2000 native people still live around the lake in numerous reserves. The Canada-US border runs NNW from the mouth of Rainy R across the lake, leaving a small peninsula of US territory above the 49th parallel.

The scenic lake attracts a thriving tourist trade. In early August, sailboats from Canada, Britain and the US take part in the Lake of the Woods Regatta, a 7-day race from KENORA around the lake. The lake's islands are wooded, but the name is likely a mistranslation of an Indian word meaning "inland lake of the hills."

JAMES MARSH

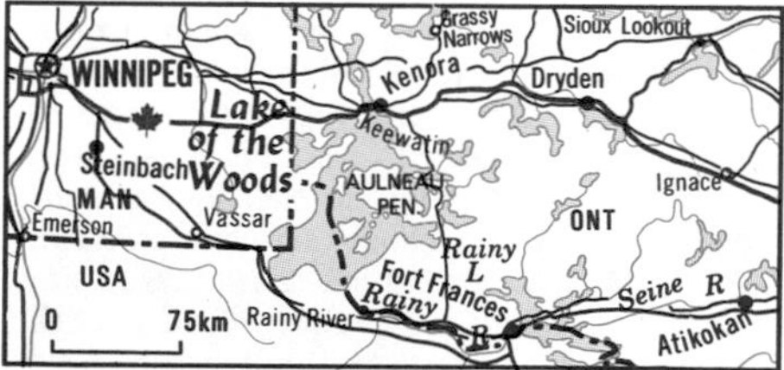

Lake Superior Provincial Park (est 1944, 1540 km^2), located N of SAULT STE MARIE, Ont, includes part of the wild shoreline of eastern Lk SUPERIOR and a hinterland of rugged, forested Canadian SHIELD country. Pink granitic hills and boulders dominate the landscape but lavas are found near Cape Gargantua and sandstones on the offshore islands. The mixed forest of maple, birch, poplar and spruce produces a magnificent display of colour in autumn. The commonest mammal is the moose, but visitors may also see white-tailed deer, red squirrel, chipmunk, beaver, bear, wolf and some 250 species of birds, including Canada goose, heron and sandhill crane. Except for garter snakes, there are few reptiles. Animals such as caribou, lynx and pickerel feature prominently in the PICTOGRAPHS visible especially along the coast. These rock paintings reflect some 10 000 years of Indian occupation. There has been sporadic mining for copper and gold, commercial fishing and lumbering. Early in this century the region attracted the attention of the GROUP OF SEVEN painters. Lake and river fishing and, in autumn, moose hunting are possible.

JOHN S. MARSH

Lakehead University, THUNDER BAY, Ont, was founded in 1965. Its roots date back to 1946 when Lakehead Technical Institute was established. Its name was changed to Lakehead College of Arts, Science and Technology in 1956, and in 1957 the city of Port Arthur donated the land for a new college campus. In 1965 Lakehead became a university with all degree-granting powers. In addition to its full-time programs, Lakehead provides students in the region with spring, summer and extension programs. Through Innovation North, the university makes available its researchers and consultants. The Resource Centre for Occupational Health and Safety is a joint venture with the province. B. BEATON

Enrolment: Lakehead University, 1985-86
(Source: Statistics Canada)

Full-time Undergrad	*Full-time Graduate*	*Part-time Undergrad*	*Part-time Graduate*
3 478	147	1 575	106

Lalemant, Charles, Jesuit missionary, first superior of the Jesuits at Québec (b at Paris, France 17 Nov 1587; d there 18 Nov 1674), brother of Jérôme LALEMANT. He organized the first Jesuit mission to Canada in 1625, returning to France in 1627 to counter the objections of merchants and Protestants to mission work. He came back to Canada in 1634, having been taken prisoner of war and shipwrecked twice in the meantime. He ministered to the French immigrants at Québec until 1638 when he returned to Paris to serve as first procurator of the missions of New France until 1650, a period when missions and fur trade were complementary. He brought together *dévots* of the Compagnie du Saint-Sacrement who organized the Société de Notre-Dame de Montréal, founders of the utopian colony of VILLE-MARIE on Montréal I in 1642. In addition to many letters, he wrote a devotional treatise on the Eucharist. CORNELIUS J. JAENEN

Lalemant, Jérôme, Jesuit missionary (b at Paris, France 27 Apr 1593; d at Québec City 26 Jan 1673), brother of Charles LALEMANT. He arrived in Canada in 1638 and was named superior of the Huron mission. He completed the first census of a native nation, introduced *donnés* (lay workers) and in 1639 centralized operations at STE MARIE AMONG THE HURONS, a fortified headquarters and model community. Author of *Relations des Jésuites*, 1639, 1644, and much of the *Journal des Jésuites*, he was superior at Québec 1645-50. In 1649 the Huron mission was destroyed, and in 1656 he returned to France and taught at La Flèche college. Recalled as superior at Québec 1659-65, he helped resettle Huron refugees. CORNELIUS J. JAENEN

Laliberté, Alfred, sculptor, painter, memorialist (b at Ste-Élisabeth de Warwick, Qué 19 May 1878; d at Montréal 13 Jan 1953). In 1896 he began studying modelling and design at the Conseil des arts et manufactures (CAM), Montréal. In 1902 he left for Paris, where he studied at the École des beaux-arts, met SUZOR-COTÉ and had several showings at the Salon du printemps. He was named a professor at the CAM, Montréal, in 1907, and had his first showing at the Art Assn. His work totalled some 925 bronze, marble, plaster and wooden statues, plus about 500 canvases of lesser interest. He sculpted busts, historical statues (BALDWIN, BRÉBEUF), public and commemorative monuments (LAURIER, Louis HÉBERT), allegorical and religious statues, and over 200 small bronzes illustrating legends, customs and rural trades. While influenced by various sources, his work reflects the nationalist and conservative ideology of his Québec contemporaries who gloried in their national history and were strongly attached to the land. Three of Laliberté's manuscripts appeared in 1978 under the title, *Mes souvenirs*. JOHN R. PORTER

Lalonde, Édouard, "Newsy," hockey and lacrosse player (b at Cornwall, Ont 31 Oct 1887; d at Montréal 21 Nov 1970). He excelled at both sports and gained notoriety and fame for his intense competitiveness. He picked up his nickname during a stint as reporter and printer for the Cornwall *Freeholder*. He played hockey with Cornwall and turned professional with Sault Ste Marie. He was a member of MONTREAL CANADIENS at their inception (1910) and rejoined them in 1913, winning the scoring title 4 times and scoring 124 goals in 98 games over the next 5 years. He had an explosive temper, and feuds with opposing players, notably Joe Hall, often erupted into brawls. Lalonde was the best LACROSSE player of his generation and was in great demand across Canada; a Vancouver team paid him $6500 for one season. He was voted Canada's outstanding lacrosse player of the first half century. JAMES MARSH

Lalonde, Marc, politician (b at Île-Perrot, Qué 26 July 1929). Educated at U de M, Oxford and U of Ottawa, Lalonde at first sought a legal and academic career but interrupted it to become special adviser in 1959-60 to E. Davie FULTON, minister of justice under PM DIEFENBAKER. After practising law in Montréal, Lalonde returned to Ottawa as special adviser to PM PEARSON in 1967, and stayed on in the PMO as Pierre TRUDEAU's principal secretary 1968-72. In 1972 he ran successfully for Parliament and under Trudeau held various portfolios, including minister of national health and welfare, minister of state for federal-provincial relations, minister of energy, mines and resources (1980-82) – in which capacity he implemented the National ENERGY POLICY – and minister of finance under both Trudeau and PM TURNER (1982-84). Lalonde was closely identified with Trudeau and his various causes and was a vigorous federalist advocate in Québec and Ottawa. He retired from politics in 1984, following the resignation of Trudeau, and returned to private business. ROBERT BOTHWELL

Lamarche, Gustave, priest, dramatist (b at Montréal 17 July 1895). He is best known for the vast dramatic frescoes on religious themes, often reminiscent of medieval passion plays, that he began to compose and direct in Québec in the 1930s, especially his *Jonathas* and *Tobie* (both 1935), *La Défaite de l'enfer* (1938), *Notre-Dame-des-Neiges* (1942) and *Notre-Dame-de-la-Couronne* (1947), the latter 2 performed outdoors before thousands of spectators. His collected 6-vol *Oeuvres théâtrales* (1971-75) include 34 plays. In restoring the respectability of stage arts, long considered suspect in French Canada, Lamarche has made an important contribution to contemporary Québec culture. L.E. DOUCETTE

Reading: René Pageau, *Gustave Lamarche, poète dramatique* (1976).

LaMarsh, Julia Verlyn, "Judy," lawyer, politician, broadcaster, novelist (b at Chatham, Ont 20 Dec 1924; d at Toronto 27 Oct 1980). Liberal MP for Niagara Falls 1960-68, Judy LaMarsh was a controversial member of PM PEARSON's Cabinet and was responsible for some of that government's more innovative legislation. Under her aegis as minister of national health and welfare 1963-65, the CANADA PENSION PLAN was implemented and Canada's "medicare" system designed. As secretary of state 1965-68, she brought in the Broadcasting Act, presided over the CENTENNIAL YEAR celebrations, and established the Royal Commission on the STATUS OF WOMEN IN CANADA. Her books include *Memoirs of a Bird in a Gilded Cage* (1968). HARRIET GORHAM

Lamb, William Kaye, librarian, archivist (b at New Westminster, BC 11 May 1904). Educated at UBC (BA, 1927; MA, 1930), the Sorbonne and London School of Economics (PhD, 1933), Lamb served as provincial librarian and archivist in BC 1934-1940 and librarian at UBC 1940-1948 before being appointed Dominion Archivist in 1948. In that post, and as national librarian from 1953, he played a decisive role in the development, over the next 20 years, of 2 important cultural institutions. His aggressive program of documentary acquisition and his introduction of improved records management systems vastly enhanced the value of the National Archives as a research institution; and his role in the planning and development of the National Library, from its creation in 1953, was similarly concerned with making that institution useful and accessible. In addition to his professional duties, Lamb established an imposing presence in scholarly publishing, achieving particular excellence is his editions of historical documents, of which *George Vancouver, A Voyage of Discovery 1791-1795*, 4 vols (1985), is an impressive culmination. STANLEY GORDON

Lambert, Betty, née Elizabeth Minnie Lee, playwright (b at Calgary 23 Aug 1933; d at Burnaby, BC 4 Nov 1983). Author of some 70 adults' and children's plays for radio, TV and stage, Lambert also taught at Simon Fraser from 1965 until her death. Often called a feminist, she was concerned with injustice to and victimization of men as well as women, concerns which appear as ironic wit in her comedies and as compassion and a profound sense of evil in her tragedies. She is author of the children's play *The Riddle Machine* (performed 1967, published 1974); *Sqrieux-de-Dieu* (1975, 1976); the novel *Crossings* (1979); and *Jennie's Story* (1981, 1982). ANN MESSENGER

Lambeth, Michel, filmmaker, writer, photojournalist, teacher, publisher (b at Toronto 21 Apr 1923; d there 9 Apr 1977). He served in the Canadian Army 1942-45, and then studied art in London and Paris. Returning to Toronto in 1948, he supported himself with clerical work and freelance writing. By 1959 he had become a committed photojournalist, and during the 1960s he worked for the *Star Weekly, Saturday Night, Maclean's, Time* and *Life*. He had numerous shows and the National Film Board of Canada toured his exhibition *Encounter* nationally. He was honoured with the Canadian Centennial Medal in 1967. During the 1970s he taught and became a spokesman for Canadian Artists Representation. His photography reflects a love for working people, and the reality of street life and the social conditions of the disadvantaged. MAIA-MARI SUTNIK

Lament for a Nation: The Defeat of Canadian Nationalism, by George GRANT (1965; repr 1970 with an introduction by the author), is a short book which eloquently argues that Canada has ceased to be a nation. Grant argues that this demise was inevitable, for although Canadians had hoped to build a more ordered and stable society than the liberal experiment in the US, that county's emergence as a leader in modern science, technology and corporate capitalism precluded the preservation of Canada's indigenous culture. Grant places blame on the LIBERAL PARTY's willing surrender to CONTINENTALISM, which inexorably reduced Canada's role to a mere branch plant of American corporate capitalism. He further suggests that while John DIEFENBAKER's government struggled to reverse the trend, in a last gasp of nationalism, it did not succeed. Although some critics praised Grant's theories as brilliant and profound, others rejected them as overstated and simplistic; nevertheless, Grant's analysis did provoke a lively debate on the issue of Canada's capability to maintain some independence from the American empire. DONNA COATES

Lamèque, Île, 150 km^2, is located off the NE corner of New Brunswick at the entrance to CHALEUR BAY. Originally called Shippegan I, its present name was confirmed in the 1970s and derives from a MICMAC word describing tidal flows in the area. Nineteen km long and 11 wide, the island is sandy and flat, covered in grasses and a few stunted trees. Originally inhabited by Micmac, its modern residents are mainly French speaking. As well as a small fishing industry, the island features vast bogs of peat moss, sold primarily to the US. The island is connected by bridge across the Shippegan Sound to the mainland community of Shippegan and by ferry to MISCOU I, its sister island to the N. DANIEL FRANCIS

Lamontagne, Joseph-Georges-Gilles-Claude, air-force officer, politician, lt-gov of Québec (b at Montréal 17 Apr 1919). Lamontagne stud-

ied at the Collège Jean-de-Brébeuf and the École des hautes études commerciales in Montréal. A bomber pilot in the RCAF, he was shot down over Holland and was a prisoner until 1945. He bought an importing firm in Québec C in 1946, was elected mayor of Québec C in 1965, and was Liberal member to the House of Commons for Langelier in 1977. In 1978 he became postmaster general and in 1980 minister of national defence. Since 28 Mar 1984 he has been lt-gov of Québec.
JEAN PARISEAU

Lamontagne, Maurice, economist, politician (b at Mont-Joli, Qué 7 Sept 1917; d at Ottawa 13 June 1983). A graduate of Laval and Harvard, Lamontagne taught at Laval 1943-54. In 1954 he became a federal civil servant and in 1957 professor of economics at U of Ottawa. He also served as an adviser to Lester PEARSON, 1958-63, and ran for the House of Commons in 1958 and 1962, finally getting elected in 1963. Lamontagne, a strong federalist, promoted bilingualism and biculturalism and worked to strengthen the Liberal Party's base in Québec. After serving as president of the Privy Council and secretary of state in Pearson's Cabinet, 1963-65, he was appointed to the Senate in 1967. ROBERT BOTHWELL

Lamothe, Arthur, film director, producer, editor (b at St-Mont, France 7 Dec 1928). Lamothe immigrated to Canada in 1953 and joined the NFB in the late 1950s as a researcher and writer. His first film was *Bûcherons de la Manouane,* a documentary made in 1962 about lumber camps. He soon left the NFB to start his own production company where he directed a full-length fictional film, *Poussière sur la ville* (1965), which was not a commercial success. Lamothe returned to documentaries, particularly those with a social perspective. In 1970 he produced for the CONFEDERATION OF NATIONAL TRADE UNIONS a full-length film on the working conditions of construction workers. *Le Mépris n'aura qu'un temps* firmly determined the direction of Lamothe's future work: social and economic criticism designed to promote change. In 1973 he began work on *Carcajou et le péril blanc* (1973-76), a series of 8 films on the Montagnais culture and the first such film study to adopt the Indian viewpoint. He continued this theme in a more political series of 4 films, *Innu Asi/La Terre de l'homme* (1979-80), and a more anthropological one of 3 films, *Mémoire battante* (1983). He returned to fiction with *Equinoxe* (1986). PIERRE VÉRONNEAU

Lampman, Archibald, poet, civil servant (b at Morpeth, Canada W 17 Nov 1861; d at Ottawa 10 Feb 1899), one of the "Confederation" group of poets. He was the son of a clergyman of modest means, although the family was not without distinction. He was educated at Trinity College School, Port Hope, and Trinity College, Toronto, from which he obtained a BA in 1882. After a false start as a teacher, Lampman secured a position in the Post Office Dept in Ottawa in 1883 where he remained until his death.

Lampman began as a writer in the pages of his college magazine, *Rouge et Noir,* graduating to the more prestigious pages of *The Week*, and winning an audience in the major American magazines of the day such as *Atlantic Monthly, Harper's* and *Scribner's*. In spite of this success, Lampman was unable to find a publisher for his first collection, *Among the Millet* (1888), which he published himself. In 1896, after some difficulty and delay, a Boston publisher released his second book, *Lyrics of Earth* (1895; restored text 1978). His third collection, *Alcyone and Other Poems* (1899), which was in preparation at the time of the poet's death, was issued privately in a few copies. Its contents were incorporated in *The Poems of Archibald Lampman* (1900), devotedly assembled and edited by his friend, memorialist and fellow poet, D.C. SCOTT. Later important collections of his poetry include *Lyrics of Earth: Sonnets and Ballads* (1925); *At the Long Sault* (1943), a joint project of D.C. Scott and E.K. BROWN based on Lampman's manuscripts; and the *Selected Poems* (1947). Lampman's *Selected Prose* was published in 1975.

Archibald Lampman, generally considered the finest of Canada's late 19th-century poets in English, was at the height of his powers when observing and contemplating nature (*courtesy National Archives of Canada/C-68854*).

Reportedly reclusive and shy, Lampman enjoyed a circle of friends drawn mainly from the community of writers and intellectuals in Ottawa. With Scott and W.W. CAMPBELL he wrote a thoughtful and lively column, "At the Mermaid Inn" (1892-93) for the Toronto *Globe*. He was also associated with various literary and scientific groups in Ottawa before which he would read his poems or deliver the occasional paper. As a poet Lampman is noted for his carefully fused poems of nature closely observed in moods of delight and solemn contemplation. Although he showed great skill and some range with the sonnet, Lampman could also be a discursive poet given to narrative and, on occasion, to strong criticism of contemporary industrial civilization.

Afflicted by poor health and frequently of a moody disposition, Lampman appears to have been unhappy with his situation in the civil service but did little to change his life. His poetry, with its tableaux of nature, its oft-encountered dream states, its idealized communities and relationships, was the preferred world of his imagination and poetic experience. In the last years of his short life there is evidence of a spiritual malaise which was compounded by the death of an infant son and his own deteriorating health. Lampman was elected a Fellow of the Royal Society of Canada in 1895. MICHAEL GNAROWSKI

Reading: D.C. Scott, ed, *The Poems of Archibald Lampman* (1900; repr together with *At the Long Sault* and with an intro by Margaret Whitridge, 1974); M. Gnarowski, ed, *Archibald Lampman* (1970); Carl Y. Connor, *Archibald Lampman: Canadian Poet of Nature* (1929; repr 1977); L.R. Early, *Archibald Lampman and his Works* (1983).

Lamprey, group of primitive VERTEBRATES which, together with HAGFISH and various extinct forms comprise the fish class Agnatha. Lampreys have a cartilaginous skeleton and an eellike body form. They lack scales and paired fins, but have 1 or 2 dorsal fins. Seven external gill openings appear on each side of the body, near the head. Development begins with a larval stage, the wormlike ammocoete, which has a life span longer than that of the adult. The ammocoete has a broad, hoodlike structure overhanging the mouth. Its principal food is microscopic algae. Eyes are rudimentary and hidden under the skin. For respiration and feeding, water enters the mouth and is extruded through the gill openings. At the onset of metamorphosis the ammocoete shrinks in length. In adults, water for respiration enters and exits only through the gill openings. Metamorphosed individuals acquire a sucking disc with horny teeth. They may be nonparasitic, lacking a functional intestine and not feeding after completion of metamorphosis; or parasitic, retaining a functional intestine and feeding primarily on the blood and body fluids of fish. Of the 37 Northern Hemisphere species, about 15 are parasitic. Nonparasitic species are confined to freshwater habitats. Although adults of certain species can live in salt water, all species spawn only in fresh water in specially prepared nests, and die shortly after. Before spawning, mature males and females shrink in length. Eggs are small (1 mm diameter); 1000-260 000 may be laid, depending on the length of the female.

Lampreys occur in both Northern and Southern hemispheres. About 41 extant species are known, as well as FOSSIL forms dating from the Mississippian and Pennsylvanian (360-286 million years ago) in the US. Twenty-three species are found in N America, of which 21 are indigenous. Twelve species occur in Canada. Three N American species are very destructive to FISHERIES: Atlantic sea lamprey (*Petromyzon marinus*), 900 mm maximum length, spends some time in the Atlantic and becomes landlocked in the Great Lakes; Pacific lamprey (*Entosphenus tridentatus*), 690 mm maximum length, found in the West; and arctic lamprey (*Lententeron japonicum*), 625 mm maximum length, of arctic regions of N America and Eurasia. These species attack other fish, attaching themselves by their oral discs and sucking the blood and flesh of the host. In the Great Lakes, the Atlantic sea lamprey contributed to the decline of the lake trout and other fishes. The species always lived in Lk Ontario, but was first found in Lk Erie in 1921, apparently having passed through the Welland Canal, and was established in the Great Lakes by 1940. The Canadian and American governments have instituted a program to reduce the population. Although *Lampetra fluviatilis* is considered a delicacy in Europe, lampreys are little eaten in N America, except by the natives of the West Coast. *See also* PARASITOLOGY. VADIM D. VLADYKOV

Lancaster, Ronald, football player, coach (b at Fairchance, Pa 14 Oct 1938). He quarterbacked the OTTAWA ROUGH RIDERS from 1960 with Russ JACKSON and was later traded to Saskatchewan (1963-78). In his 19-year playing career Lancaster completed 3384 passes for 50 535 yards and 333 touchdowns. He set 30 Canadian Football League records, was twice selected the outstanding player in the country, and 17 times led his team into the playoffs (and to 2 Grey Cup wins). His quick, analytic play and determination earned him the nicknames "little general" and "little assassin" – he is 178 cm tall. He was head coach of the SASKATCHEWAN ROUGHRIDERS (1979-80), and through 1987 was a commentator on CFL telecasts. FRANK COSENTINO

Lancaster Sound, arm of BAFFIN BAY and major passage through the ARCTIC ARCHIPELAGO, 400 km long and some 100 km wide. It lies at the N end of BAFFIN I and is connected to Barrow Str on the W. As a result of the interaction of currents, the

sound is rich in nutrients and supports a biologically varied community of birds, mammals and fish. It provides breeding grounds for some 3 million seabirds alone. The area has provided sustenance for INUIT cultures for thousands of years: ringed seals, walrus and polar bears, and narwhals, belugas, killer and bowhead whales. Arctic fox is trapped in almost every inlet, and arctic char is taken at the mouths of rivers. European interest began in the 17th century, with the search for the NORTHWEST PASSAGE, and William BAFFIN was likely the first to discover the sound (1616). It was named for English navigator Sir James Lancaster (d 1618). WHALING became important at the end of the 19th century, and trading posts were established at Port Leopold, Button Pt, Albert Harbour, Arctic Bay, Pond Inlet and Dundas Harbour. Today, interest centres on geological evidence of petroleum, and on mining sites at Mary River (iron), Arvik (lead-zinc) and Nanisivik, where some 150 000 tonnes of lead-zinc are being taken. With ICEBREAKERS, the passage could be used year-round for local shipping and for tankers from the BEAUFORT SEA. Increased human activity threatens the area's wildlife, which is concentrated at a few sites and therefore highly vulnerable. JAMES MARSH

Lanctot, Gustave, archivist, historian (b at St-Constant, Qué 5 July 1883; d at Montréal 2 Feb 1975). After studying at U de M, Oxford and the Sorbonne, he went to work in 1912 for the Public Archives of Canada (now NATIONAL ARCHIVES OF CANADA). He became Dominion Archivist in 1937 and retired in 1948. His abundant historical work was spread over some 40 years. His main works are *François-Xavier Garneau* (1926), *Histoire du Canada* (1960-64) and *Montréal sous Maisonneuve* (1966). A specialist in the French régime, he wanted to write a scrupulously accurate history, free from the "racism," which he felt marred the school of Lionel GROULX, and the tendency to present New France in unduly heroic terms. His ideas weakened his prestige with traditionalists and with nationalist intellectuals, all the more so in that he lacked the elegant style which might have disarmed his critics.

PIERRE TRÉPANIER

Land, in law, is an area of the Earth's solid surface which is the property of an individual, group or state. Hence, the Canadian polity controls a total of 9 167 165 km^2 of land, and 755 165 km^2 of fresh water, for a total territory of 9 922 330 km^2. In popular usage, "land" refers simply to the rock and soil that make up the solid part of the Earth's surface.

Land has a finite capability to withstand the natural processes of EROSION. One of the most remarkable illustrations of this limitation comes from the volcanic slopes of Mt St Helens in Washington, where over 100 000 cubic metres of volcanic material have been removed from each square kilometre of the northern slope by the natural processes of surface wash and debris flow. At the other extreme, bedrock areas on gentle slopes in the Canadian SHIELD lose about one cubic metre of material or less per square kilometre per year through WEATHERING, slow soil creep and surface wash. Commonly, when various uses are imposed on land, the rates of landscape change alter. When natural events interact with society, however indirectly, they are called natural hazards: a FLOOD or LANDSLIDE in an uninhabited part of the Canadian Arctic is a geophysical event; a flood or landslide in the Lower Fraser Valley is a natural hazard.

Recognition that the capability for use of the land resource varies from region to region is a relatively recent development in Canadian environmental awareness (*see* ENVIRONMENTAL PLANNING). The CANADA LAND INVENTORY program (1965-75), which assessed and mapped the natural capability of approximately 25% of Canada's land area, contributed to a new sensitivity to land-quality problems. The underlying concepts in this program were that land has a finite capability to sustain a given type of land use, that it has a finite capability to assimilate pollutants and that it is possible to define optimal uses for a given land unit. The 1973 Cabinet decision to establish an Environmental Assessment and Review Process (EARP) was also important in establishing public awareness of land use issues.

Specific geomorphological processes and natural hazards tend to be associated with specific terrain units: ROCKSLIDES are relatively common in areas of dipping stratified rocks; slumps, earthflows and debris flows tend to occur on finely textured materials (eg, lacustrine silts, clays, tills); finely textured materials also encourage surface erosion and gullying; all active fluvial areas adjacent to river channels are flood-hazard zones; piping, causing collapse and settling, is associated with lacustrine silts; sinkhole development is associated with limestone and gypsum lithologies. EARTHQUAKE hazard is not restricted to a specific terrain unit, but the severity of the effect is greatest in thick deposits of those materials. All these hazards become intensified as land-use activities increase in sensitive locations. Only laboratory and field testing can ultimately confirm these inferences from photographs, but it is impossible to test all field sites over a large region. Terrain mapping, selective sampling and testing provide a practical approach at the local scale.

As ability to extrapolate the effects of human activities on land quality improves, so the input of information into environmental impact-assessment reports becomes more precise and the relationships between society and environment become better understood. OLAV SLAYMAKER

Reading: Wendy Simpson-Lewis et al, *Canada's Special Resource Lands* (1979); Lands Directorate Environment Canada, *Stress on Land in Canada* (1984).

Land Claims are dealt with by a process established by the federal government to enable INDIANS, INUIT and MÉTIS to obtain full recognition of their rights under treaties or as the original inhabitants of what is now Canada (*see* INDIAN TREATIES; ABORIGINAL RIGHTS). At the core of the process is negotiation between native groups and the federal government, and in some cases the provincial and territorial governments and other third parties. The process is formally based on legal concepts such as land title and treaties, and is intended to make economic and social adjustments between 2 different societies.

Historical Basis, 1763-1969 The ROYAL PROCLAMATION OF 1763 reserved an unspecified area of what is now Canada for the use of Indians, and forbade any unauthorized purchase or possession of those lands by non-Indian settlers. The British government, followed after 1867 by successive Canadian governments, concluded treaties with various groups of Indian people to legitimate European settlement in their lands.

The gradual occupation of Canada by immigrants, with or without treaties, has continued for almost 400 years and has made the native people a small minority within an industrial nation. In some cases Indian bands that had concluded treaties have lost control of reserve lands, and in others the reserve lands promised according to treaty were not requested or allocated (*see* INDIAN RESERVES). Native people, many of whom had been nomadic, often found themselves isolated on reserves with little or no access to wildlife and no money, skill or natural resources to make a living from their reserves. For those Indians, Inuit and Métis who did not sign treaties or take reserve land, the impact of being surrounded or overrun by agriculture, industry, cities and "foreign" institutions has been similar to that on the treaty Indians. They have suffered the shock of great change in virtually every aspect of their lives and in their homelands.

Development of the Claims Process Although native people have from the beginning struggled to maintain their identity, the "movement" for aboriginal rights and native claims which began for a few bands in the 19th century did not become prominent until the 1960s. Many factors contributed to the expression of native aspirations. Minority rights of all kinds and concern for the environment became worldwide causes. The search for new sources of oil, gas and hydroelectricity brought the native people of the NORTH into the mainstream of Canadian life. At the same time, although an imposed education system threatened native languages and cultures, it also prepared young native people to enter and challenge the "white man's" political and legal system (*see* NATIVE PEOPLE, POLITICAL ORGANIZATION).

Canada has been influenced by the treatment of claims and aboriginal rights in other countries. In 1946 the US government created an Indian Claims Commission and in 1971 legislated the Alaska Native Claims Settlement. Australia passed an Aboriginal Land Rights Act in 1976, and in 1980 Denmark granted home rule to Greenland. Proposals to establish a body similar to the US Indian Claims Commission in Canada resulted in the drafting of 2 bills, 1963 and 1965, which proved unsatisfactory to the Indian people and were never enacted. In 1969 the federal government appointed Lloyd Barber as commissioner of Indian claims to determine and recommend appropriate means of resolving native claims. Early in the 1970s the government set up a system of research funding for native political and cultural associations to enable them to document and organize their land claims.

In 1972 the Indians of Old Crow in the Yukon Territory presented a petition to Parliament concerning oil and gas exploration on their hunting grounds. In the CALDER CASE in 1973 the Supreme Court of Canada split 3 to 3 in recognizing the aboriginal land title of the Nishga Indians of British Columbia, and in the same year the Yukon Indian Brotherhood presented a formal claim to the federal government.

In 1973 Justice Morrow of the NWT recognized the aboriginal title of the Dene of the Mackenzie R Valley (*see* DENE NATION) and in 1973 Justice Malouf of Québec recognized the title of the CREE and Inuit of Québec. These decisions were later appealed and overturned, but they gave important weight to the native cause.

The Process On 8 Aug 1973 the federal government, wishing to clear the way for industrial development of the North and to improve the position of native peoples in Canada, announced a new policy for the settlement of native claims. The policy confirmed the responsibility of government to meet its lawful obligations through fulfilment of the terms of the treaties and to negotiate settlements with native groups in those areas of Canada where native rights based on traditional use and occupancy of the land had not been dealt with by treaty or superseded by law. The policy emphasized that the co-operation of provincial and territorial governments would be required. The Indian interpretation of "lawful obligations" was broader than that of the government, and the debate over the meaning of "lawful" as opposed to "legal" or purely technical obligations remains an obstacle to the claims settlement process.

In order to carry out the new policy, an Office of Native Claims (ONC) was created in 1974 within the Dept of INDIAN AFFAIRS AND NORTHERN DEVELOPMENT. Under the leadership of an assistant deputy minister, negotiators, lawyers and researchers dealt with 2 main types of claim: specific and comprehensive. *Specific claims* are based on problems arising from the administration of Indian treaties, the INDIAN ACT, Indian funds and disposition of Indian land. Although negotiation is the preferred course of action to settle these claims, settlement may also be reached by administrative remedy or court action. Specific claims are usually made by Indian groups living in the provinces, as opposed to the territories, and most settlements consist of compensation and land (sometimes land only). *Comprehensive claims* are based on the traditional use and occupancy of land by Indians, Métis or Inuit who did not sign treaties and were not displaced from their lands by war or other means. These claims, which are settled by negotiation involve the 2 territories and the northern parts of some provinces. The areas of land and the numbers of native people involved are usually greater than in the case of specific claims. Settlement of these claims comprises a variety of terms including money, land, forms of local government, rights to wildlife and rights protecting native language and culture.

The federal government provides funding in the form of contributions to native associations for the research and presentation of their claims. Once claims are submitted, lawyers of the Dept of Justice and officials of the ONC are supposed to determine whether or not the claims are acceptable according to government policy and law. If they are, additional funding is granted in the form of loans to the associations for further research and for negotiation. These loans must be reimbursed from the proceeds of the eventual claims settlements.

In 1980 the government appointed the first chief government negotiator from outside the public service to bring a fresh and more neutral perspective to the negotiation of comprehensive claims. These claims are now negotiated by such appointees, who work on contract, assisted by negotiating teams in the ONC.

The Progress of Specific Claims By Aug 1987, a total of 470 specific claims had been submitted to the federal government from all the provinces except Newfoundland. Of these, 34 had been settled, 109 rejected or withdrawn, 111 under negotiation, and 216 under review or referred for solution by administrative programs. Provincial participation is essential in the resolution of most specific claims, and in Ontario, for example, a provincial Indian Claims Commission has facilitated the process of negotiation.

The Progress of Comprehensive Claims Comprehensive claims cover about half of the total area of Canada. Problems include the differing powers and objectives of federal and provincial governments; the different legal status and goals of Indians, Métis and Inuit; the overlapping of native territorial claims; the divergence of native desire for independence and government's wish to exercise control; conflict caused by industrial development and political evolution in the North and constitutional changes in Canada.

By Aug 1987, 32 comprehensive claims had been submitted to the federal government. Of these, 3 had been settled and the results legislated (James Bay and Northern Québec Agreement, Nov 1975; Northeastern Québec Agreement, Jan 1978; Inuvialuit Final Agreement, June 1984). Two claims from Newfoundland and Nova Scotia, respectively, had been rejected, 15 claims (mostly from BC) had been accepted for negotiation, and negotiations were under way on 5 regional claims (Nass Valley, BC; Yukon Territory; Mackenzie Valley, NWT; central and eastern NWT; central and eastern Qué). Seven claims from BC were under review.

Recent Developments During more than a decade of formal treatment of comprehensive claims, the circumstances that gave rise to the claims have changed. Improved transportation and communication and the educational nature of the claims process itself modified the differences between native and non-native people. In the northern territories, native people gained effective political influence, and national economic conditions reduced both the scale of industrial development and the native opposition to such development.

In administrative changes, in 1985 and 1986, the Office of Native Claims was abolished within the Dept of Indian Affairs and Northern Development. The responsibilities for specific claims, comprehensive claims and the implementation of settled claims were divided among various sectors of the department.

In Dec 1986 the federal government revised its policy with respect to comprehensive claims, in light of its policy on aboriginal self-government, of the experience gained during 12 years of negotiation and of recommendations made by a task force commissioned to examine the whole business of comprehensive claims. The new policy, explained in a booklet entitled *Comprehensive Land Claims Policy* (1987), addresses such topics as the mandates of negotiators, constitutional guarantees, the parameters of negotiation and the planning and implementation of settlement agreements.

For almost 50 years the Lubicon Lake Band of Indians have pressed their claim to lands in NW Alta. The claim has been dealt with by the federal and provincial governments outside the normal processes used for specific and comprehensive claims. As of Aug 1987 the matter was unresolved, and the band was continuing its representations to the United Nations. KEITH CROWE

Reading: P. Cumming and N. Mickenberg, *Native Rights in Canada* (2nd ed, 1972); G. Dacks, *A Choice of Futures* (1981); R.C. Daniel, *A History of Native Claims Processes in Canada* (1980).

Land God Gave to Cain, The, was Jacques CARTIER's description of the N shore of the Gulf of St Lawrence, which he first sighted in 1534. Cartier was presumably alluding to Genesis 4, in which Cain, having killed his brother, is condemned to till land that is barren.

Land Question, PEI In 1767 the British government decided to allocate, prior to settlement, virtually all of PEI to proprietors who would become semi-feudal resident landlords paying annual quitrents to the Crown to finance the cost of governing and colonizing the Island. Most proprietors remained absentees, their quitrents perpetually in arrears and their colonizing obligations unfulfilled. Soon after 1770, PEI residents sought to force the proprietors either to live up to their obligations or to surrender their land to those in actual possession. An attempt by Walter PATTERSON's Island government to force the sale of land by distraint proceedings (seizure of property) in 1780-81 failed. The question had already taken on a circular quality it was never to lose. The Island's elite insisted that the terms of the grants, which were unrealistic, be fulfilled or the land be forfeited, whereas the proprietors insisted that they could not fulfil the terms because the actions of the Island's elite and government made any investment insecure.

Escheat, the process by which unimproved lands would revert to the Crown and become subject to reallocation, became the rallying cry throughout the 19th century, although it shifted considerably in meaning. Under Edmund Fanning, lieutenant-governor 1787-1804, and his immediate successors, escheat implied little more than the transfer of proprietorship from absentee to resident landlord. But the 1830 enfranchisement of Roman Catholics, most of them tenants, led to the emergence of a popularly based Escheat Party, which called for distribution of the land to those in actual occupation. The British government, ever protective of property rights, opposed escheat without compensation. Gradually the absentees were eliminated. By the 1880s most of PEI was owned by the small yeoman farmers in actual occupation. But resentment over the Land Question remained, particularly against Britain for its refusal to respect the popular will, and in some quarters against Island governments which had acquiesced in the principle of compensation.
J.M. BUMSTED

Landform Regions, *see* PHYSIOGRAPHIC REGIONS.

Landlord and Tenant Law, governed by provincial statutes and judge-made law, varies considerably from province to province. Essentially, a landlord and tenant relationship is contractual (*see* CONTRACT LAW). The tenant acquires an interest in land and the right to exclusive possession of defined premises. However, not every person permitted to occupy the premises of another is a tenant in the eyes of the law; for example, boarders or lodgers, who are not granted exclusive possession, would not qualify. Most leases are either for a fixed period, eg, one year, or for a periodic term, eg, from month to month. If the latter, the lease may be terminated by either party by giving appropriate notice (usually set out by statute). Leases do not have to be written, although in some provinces long-term leases must be in written form and signed by the parties. Many of the obligations owed by the landlords and tenants to each other defy precise definition; in the absence of express, agreed terms upon which they generally depend, the law will imply certain obligations. The tenant's primary responsibility is to pay rent; the landlord's corresponding obligation is to provide the premises to the tenant, together with the assurance that the tenant has the right to enjoy possession of the premises. Consequently, a landlord who interferes with this possession, even indirectly, eg, by permitting noxious fumes to seep into the rented premises, may be in breach of the terms of the lease agreement.

Within the last 20 years statutory reforms have greatly redefined the obligations of both landlords and tenants, but they have been primarily concerned with residential leases and have not greatly altered the existing law respecting commercial leases. They have tended to enhance the legal position of the tenant, and many new tenant rights cannot be altered by a contrary provision in the lease. In commercial tenancies, landlords are under no statutory obligation to keep the premises in a good or even reasonable state of repair, but under the reforms the landlord of residential property must undertake all major repairs. The tenant's only obligation is to maintain the property in a reasonably clean condition and to use it suitably. Tenants have a right to assign or sublet the rented premises to others, unless the lease provides otherwise. Sometimes the tenancy agreement will require the landlord's consent to any assignment or sublease, in which case the landlord may not unreasonably or arbitrarily withhold consent. If a tenant violates the tenancy agreement by failing to pay rent or by abandoning the premises prior to the termination of the lease or in other ways, a landlord may sue the tenant to recover arrears of rent or damages. A landlord may sue to repossess the premises, in which case a court order may be necessary if the tenant does not consent. M.M. LITMAN AND BRUCE ZIFF

Landry, Sir Pierre-Amand, lawyer, politician, judge (b at Memramcook, NB 1 May 1846; d at Dorchester, NB 28 July 1916). He was the first NB Acadian Cabinet minister and Supreme Court judge, and the only knighted Acadian (1916). He articled with Albert J. SMITH and practised in Dorchester. In 1870 he was elected MLA for Westmorland County. Defeated in 1874, he was re-elected in 1878 and in 1883, serving as commissioner of public works and provincial secretary. Elected MP for Kent County in 1883 and 1887, he carried Acadian support to John A. MACDONALD and lobbied for Acadians and for NB. In 1890 he was appointed a county court judge and was raised to the NB Supreme Court bench in 1893. DELLA M.M. STANLEY

Landsat Island A small island 20 km off the NE Labrador coast, named in recognition of the fact that it was first detected on imagery from the satellite Landsat-1. This satellite, designed for Earth-monitoring, was the first of a continuing series launched by the US having transmissions received in Canada. The island has significance, not because of its size, which is only 25 m wide and 45 m long, but rather because it marks the eastern extremity of the Canadian landmass on this part of the coast. After detection in 1976 by the Surveys and Mapping Branch, Dept of Energy, Mines and Resources (EMR), it was surveyed and charted by the Hydrographic Service, Dept of the Environment (DOE), in the same year, and later used to define the coastal boundary of Canada. Because of its location, an additional 68 km^2 were added to the area of Canada.

E.A. FLEMING

Landscape Architecture refers to the conscious modification and shaping of outdoor environments for human use. In the past, those who conceived and implemented landscape designs were trained in such diverse skills as horticulture, gardening, ARCHITECTURE, agriculture, SILVICULTURE and hydraulics. Although the field was generally regarded as horticultural, adoption by mid-19th century of the term landscape architecture was meant to convey the growing significance of both environmental concerns and professionalism in landscape design. Today's landscape architects are often involved in projects relating more to planning or URBAN DESIGN. While they continue to work extensively with plant materials and landforms, they do so with regard to ecological considerations, resource conservation and the creation of outdoor spaces rather than simply for the aesthetic qualities of plants.

European and American influences have affected landscape architecture in Canada. Publications and immigrants from both regions were sources of ideas about gardening styles, park design, new-town planning, garden suburbs and city beautification. Americans were also influenced by British ideas, but they expanded the scope of landscape architecture beyond garden design to include large-scale planning. European and American landscape architects were brought to Canada to work on important projects such as the National Capital Region Plan, Mount Royal Park, the Niagara parks and numerous city planning schemes in the early 20th century. Since a university degree in landscape architecture was not offered in Canada until 1964, many Canadians went to the US to study and to work before returning to practise in Canada.

The work of early Canadian practitioners clearly indicates their varied origins and training. George Laing and Charles Woolverton came from an agricultural and horticultural tradition, as their gardenesque designs for large estates indicate. H. Dunnington-Grubb and his English wife Laurie were trained in the aristocratic traditions of the beaux-arts style, of which the Oakes Garden at Niagara Falls is a surviving example. Others such as Gordon Culham, Frederick Todd, Humphrey CARVER and Carl Borgstrom were more concerned with social issues and the integration of nature into urban environments. The National Capital Region is probably the best example in Canada of the continuing influence of landscape architects in the design process, though the work done by Calvert Vaux at the Houses of Parliament no longer exists and that of Frederick Todd was never implemented as he had envisioned (*see* NATIONAL CAPITAL COMMISSION).

Since WWII opportunities for landscape architects in Canada have greatly increased. Rapid urban expansion, economic growth and various government programs have meant more involvement in urban design, regional planning, and the design of recreational areas, housing environments and industrial sites (*see* URBAN AND REGIONAL PLANNING; ZONING). The Canadian Society of Landscape Architects was established in Toronto in 1934 and professional programs at Canadian universities have been developed; both the society and the programs have encouraged landscape architecture that is better adapted to Canadian needs and conditions. Major projects such as EXPO 67, Don Mills, campus planning, urban open-space systems and Olympic development have helped to bring public recognition to the profession and establish its role in the environmental design process (*see* DEVELOPMENT INDUSTRY).

Landscape architecture involves economical and efficient use of land, together with a concern for its visual appearance and social purpose. Projects may range in scale and emphasis from detailed site design to comprehensive development plans. Though landscape architects work primarily on recreational, commercial and institutional projects, they are now becoming more involved in large-scale planning, landscape rehabilitation and reclamation, visual resources management and historic landscape conservation and restoration. These new specializations require additional training in environmental psychology, HERITAGE CONSERVATION, soils chemistry, and public-participation processes, although the basis of the profession continues to lie in an ethic of conservation and stewardship of the land.

The universities of Guelph and Manitoba and the NATIONAL ARCHIVES OF CANADA house important archival material relating to landscape architecture in Canada. Of particular interest are the J. Austin Floyd Papers at NAC and the collected drawings of H. Dunnington-Grubb at Guelph. Evidence suggests that landscape architects have worked in Canada since the early settlement period, but little is known about them or their works. Protection and restoration of some important examples of landscape architecture have been undertaken by Parks Canada (eg, MOTHERWELL HOMESTEAD, Sask), and other groups are also becoming increasingly active in preservation.

The first professional landscape architecture program in the world was established at Harvard in 1900. The first Canadian professional degree program was instituted at Guelph in 1964 and is available at both a bachelor's and master's level. The U of Man offers a master's degree, and U of T, U de M and UBC offer Bachelor of Landscape Architecture degrees. Diploma courses in landscape technology and architecture are available from several colleges and technical schools.

The Canadian Society of Landscape Architects deals with matters pertaining to maintenance of high standards of professional practice in Canada, including ethics, publicity, education and archives. In matters of licensing and registration, associations from each province (the Maritimes has a joint association) are the controlling bodies.

SUE DONALDSON

Reading: S. Buggey and J. Stewart, "Canada's Living Past: Historic Landscapes and Gardens," *OALA Review* 2 (Aug 1976).

Landslide, downward and outward movement of a SOIL mass that formed part of a slope. Although the term landslide often has a broad meaning, this entry is restricted to landslides in soils and excludes creep movements, falls and ROCKSLIDES. A landslide may occur with or without any apparent disturbance and involves a soil mass ranging from a few to several million cubic metres. Slope failure may occur within a few minutes or take several months or even years. Landslides occur in every province in Canada and in both natural and man-made slopes. Slope failures have been responsible for loss of life, destruction of property, reduction in property values, loss of productivity of agricultural and forested land and disruption of transportation systems.

The common landslide types (circular-arc failure and noncircular-arc or translational failure) can be analysed and the risk of failure calculated. The major causes of slope failure are the removal of material at or near the base of a slope by natural EROSION or human excavation; additional weight placed on the upper part of a slope by natural or human agencies; an increase of water pressure within the slope by rainfall or snowmelt, local irrigation or leaking sewer or water mains. Land-use studies in the design stages of a project can avoid or minimize subsequent landslide activity.

Clayey soils were deposited in the CHAMPLAIN SEA which invaded the St Lawrence and Ottawa River lowlands between some 10 000 and 12 000 years ago. These sediments are termed sensitive CLAYS and transform from a brittle soil to a viscous fluid when sufficiently disturbed. This transformation occurs quickly and with little warning. The remolded mass can flow for long distances. Thousands of landslides have been identified on air photographs. In 50 large, documented landslides in sensitive clays in eastern Ontario and Québec over 100 people have been killed and 40 000 ha of land destroyed. The South Nation River landslide (16-17 May 1971) occurred at a site 48 km E of Ottawa and involved nearly 28 ha. Debris from the failure was carried upstream and downstream, filling nearly 2.5 km of the riverbed to a depth of 11 m. At St-Jean-Vianney, Qué, another major landslide in the sensitive clay destroyed 27 ha and 36 homes, and killed 31 persons in 5 minutes (4 May 1971).

Landslides contribute to the retreat of the stiff clay bluffs along the N shore of Lk Erie and the Scarborough Bluffs E of Toronto on Lk Ontario. In Winnipeg, slope instability along the Red and Assiniboine rivers has long been a problem.

Over large areas of the western Canadian PRAIRIE, a thin veneer of late Pleistocene deposits rests on the soft rocks of Upper Cretaceous age. During deglaciation, some 10 000 years ago, RIVERS were diverted from their preglacial courses and rapidly eroded deep, steep-walled, postglacial valleys (*see* GLACIATION). Geologic evidence indicates that the rivers have been eroding laterally for about the last 6000 years (*see* RIVER LANDFORM). This lateral erosion, which removes support at the base of the slopes, results in reactivation of ancient landslides and creates many recent landslides. Because the soil strata are flat lying, the failed mass undergoes a dominantly translational movement. At a site on the South Saskatchewan River, S of Saskatoon, erosion at the toe of the slope is causing slope failure. Many similar cases have been documented in Saskatchewan and Alberta. A landslide, largely the result of toe erosion, is endangering the bridge across the Little Smoky River N of Valleyview, Alta. The bridge was completed in 1957; movement was noticed the following year. The distribution of landslides along major rivers in southern Alberta shows that clayey bedrock deposited in ancient marine seas is most prone to failure. Slope failures in Saskatoon appear to be caused mainly by erosion from groundwater seepage, augmented by lawn watering. In the Edmonton area, many landslides have been induced by human activity.

In the Vancouver area, the most common and destructive landslides are debris AVALANCHES and debris flows. These failures are triggered by heavy rains that saturate the surface layer of soil. As this saturated mass moves down the steep slopes, it gains volume and velocity. The major result is damaged and destroyed property near the base of the slope. Dikes were installed at Port Alice on Vancouver I to protect the town from debris flows such as those which occurred in 1973 and 1975.

In the PERMAFROST areas of the western Canadian Arctic, many landslides are caused by melting ground ice which is exposed by sea or river erosion or by the destruction of vegetation on slopes by forest fires. The ice melts during summer and the overlying soil collapses and is carried away by the meltwater. S. THOMSON

Landymore, William Moss, naval officer (b at Brantford, Ont 31 July 1916). He joined the Royal Canadian Navy in 1936 and was promoted lieutenant in 1940. Landymore saw action in the Arctic, Atlantic and Pacific oceans during WWII and commanded the destroyer *Iroquois* off Korea, 1951-53. He was promoted captain in 1953 and held a series of posts until 1963 when, as rear-admiral, he became flag officer, Pacific coast. In 1965 he was appointed officer commanding, Maritime Command, but a bitter public disagreement over unification led to his early retirement in 1966. MARC MILNER

Lane, George, rancher (b near Des Moines, Iowa 6 Mar 1856; d at Bar U Ranch, near Pekisko, Alta 24 Sept 1925). Lane came to the Canadian West from Montana in 1883 and was hired as a ranch foreman by the North West Cattle Co. In 1891 he went into the stock business for himself and, with the 1905 purchase of the Bar U Ranch, became the owner of one of the largest ranches in Alberta. Lane also developed one of the continent's outstanding Percheron breeding herds and was one of the "Big Four" who organized the first CALGARY STAMPEDE. DAVID H. BREEN

Lane, Patrick, poet (b at Nelson, BC 26 Mar 1939). Lane began publishing himself and others in the 1960s when still leading a nomadic knockabout life in northern BC logging camps, small towns and mines, and his poetry has remained true to the ideals of brutal honesty and self-reliance. Important early collections were *Letters from the Savage Mind* (1966) and *Separations* (1969). There were also many chapbooks and broadsides published from wherever the poet happened to be at the moment and distributed to other poets. Such people constituted his primary readership until the publication by Oxford University Press of *Poems New and Selected* (1978, Gov Gen's Award). Lane's poetry at its most characteristic deals straightforwardly, yet with lush descriptive imagery, with man's rough treatment of his environment and of his fellow human beings. Several of his books are illustrated with his own graphic works. Lane is the brother of the near-legendary poet Red Lane (1936-64) and he edited the *Collected Poems of Red Lane* (1968). In 1987 *Poems Selected and New* was published.
DOUGLAS FETHERLING

Lang, Alexander Matheson, expatriate actor-manager, dramatist (b at Montréal 15 May 1879; d at Barbados 11 Apr 1948). A tall, good-looking, classical actor he was renowned for his tours of Commonwealth countries. He began professionally at Wolverhampton, UK, in 1897 with Louis Calvert, followed by extended engagements with Frank Benson's Company and, after 1915, with his own. He had successes as Romeo, Benedick (opposite Ellen Terry), Orsino, Othello, Hamlet, Petruchio and Shylock, at the Old Vic. In 1913 he created the Chinese character Mr Wu, with which he was always associated. He first toured to America 1902-03 with Lillie Langtry and subsequently toured to the W Indies, Australia, S Africa, India, the Far East and Canada (in 1926-27). His autobiography, *Mr. Wu Looks Back*, was published in 1941. DAVID GARDNER

Lang, Charles Benjamin, industrialist (b at Thornton, Ill 17 Sept 1887; d at Montréal 23 Feb 1958). For 44 years Lang was an executive of the Dominion Steel and Coal Corporation (DOSCO), Maritime Canada's largest integrated steel producer. After working with the Brownell Improvement Co and several Chicago-area steel companies, Lang went to Montréal in 1914 as manager of Peck Rolling Mills. By 1920 he was managing director. In 1930 he joined DOSCO as a vice-president. He had a sound knowledge of the steel industry and utter devotion to his company. In 1948 he became president of DOSCO and its subsidiary companies and was chairman from 1950 until he retired in 1957. The unexpected death of his successor as president obliged Lang to return to DOSCO at age 70. He died in office.
DUNCAN MCDOWALL

Langevin, André, writer (b at Montréal 11 July 1927). His first 3 books made him one of the most celebrated novelists in Québec before 1960, first year of the QUIET REVOLUTION. These books introduced a new outlook on life into Québec letters, inspired by existentialism and Albert Camus's humanism; *Poussière sur la ville* (1953) is still the best known. With its sympathetic presentation of secular (rather than the traditional, church-dominated) culture and its tragic but nonpuritanical view of love, the novel foreshadowed value changes that have since become part of Québec. Two later novels had a more contemporary treatment, especially *L'Elan d'Amérique* (1972), which borrowed aspects of the French nouveau roman. *Une Chaîne dans le parc* (1974) in some ways echoed *Évadé de la nuit* (1951), with its autobiographical themes. Langevin's novels are moving, packed with meaning and carefully written. All deal with man's vain efforts to escape fate, which sometimes wears the Christian face of an evil Providence. Langevin is also a playwright and columnist (notably in *Le Magazine Maclean*, 1961-69), dealing with culture, education and politics.
ANDRÉ BROCHU

Reading: André Brochu, *L'Evasion tragique: essai sur les romans d'André Langevin* (1985).

Langevin, Sir Hector-Louis, lawyer, journalist, politician (b at Québec C 25 Aug 1826; d there 11 June 1906). He was admitted to the bar on 9 Oct 1850 and turned to journalism in 1847, becoming editor of *Mélanges religieux* and a contributor to *Journal d'Agriculture;* editor of *Le Courrier du Canada* in 1857; political editor of *Le Canadien* 1872-75; and owner of *Le Monde* in 1884. He began his political career as mayor of Québec C (1857-61) and was elected in 1857 to represent Dorchester County in the Assembly, serving as solicitor general for Canada East 1864-66 and postmaster general 1866-67. He was also head of the ST-JEAN-BAPTISTE SOCIETY in Québec C 1861-63 and of the INSTITUT CANADIEN 1863-64.

Langevin was a FATHER OF CONFEDERATION, defending Québec's interests at the CHARLOTTETOWN and QUÉBEC CONFERENCES in 1864 and at the LONDON CONFERENCE in 1866. After 1867 he represented Dorchester County in both Québec and Ottawa until dual representation was abolished in 1874. In Ottawa he was secretary of state and superintendent of Indian affairs in John A. MACDONALD's Cabinet 1867-69 and minister of public works 1869-73. He succeeded George-Étienne CARTIER as leader of the Québec wing of the Conservative Party 1873-91. He was implicated in the PACIFIC SCANDAL and did not stand in the next federal election. His return to active political life in 1876 was delayed by a contested election in Charlevoix, but in 1878, after a defeat in Rimouski County, he was elected for Trois-Rivières. Langevin had considerable influence in the Macdonald government following the 1878 election. He headed the post office 1878-79 and then public works 1879-91. Compromised by another scandal and linked to Thomas McGreevy's patronage, Langevin was forced out of the Cabinet after Macdonald died. He retired from politics in 1896. ANDRÉE DÉSILETS

Reading: Andrée Désilets, *Hector-Louis Langevin* (1969).

Langford, Sam, "The Boston Tar Baby," boxer (b at Weymouth Falls, NS 4 Mar 1886; d at Cambridge, Mass 12 Jan 1956). Langford fought professionally in the lightweight, welterweight, middleweight and light-heavyweight ranks, finishing as a heavyweight. His best weight was just over 77 kg, though he retired weighing over 90.7 kg despite his 167 cm height. He has been considered one of the best heavyweight boxers ever to fight, though he never fought for the world championship. He was denied a title bout with champion Jack Johnson, because Johnson's management claimed that 2 blacks would not draw. Langford held the Welsh middleweight crown and the heavyweight championships of England, Spain and Mexico; he won the last despite being declared legally blind at the time of the 1923 fight. Canadian Press named him "Boxer of the Half-Century." A.J. "SANDY" YOUNG

Langham, Michael, director (b at Bridgwater, Somerset, Eng 22 Aug 1919). Educated at Radley College and the U of London, he studied law until enlisting in 1939. His interest in theatre developed while incarcerated as a prisoner-of-war, and he launched his professional career running repertory theatres in Coventry (1946-48), Birmingham (1948-50) and Glasgow (1953-54). He first directed at Stratford-on-Avon in 1950, and made his West End and Old Vic débuts in London 1951. He succeeded Tyrone GUTHRIE as artistic director of the STRATFORD FESTIVAL (Ont) 1955-67, doing memorable productions of *Henry V* (mixing a French and English cast), *King Lear, Love's Labour's Lost* and *Cyrano de Bergerac,* among others. Although he continued to mount plays in Britain, he became more permanently based in N America. In 1968 he staged *The Prime of Miss Jean Brodie* on Broadway and in 1971 assumed the leadership of the Guthrie Theatre in Minneapolis.

Further appointments include directorships of New York's Juilliard School of Theatre 1980 and, in 1983, the Dallas Theater. He returned to the Juilliard in 1987. DAVID GARDNER

Langley, BC, District Municipality, pop 53 434 (1986c), 44 617 (1981c), inc as a city 1955, is located about 45 km E of Vancouver. The colony of British Columbia was incorporated 19 Nov 1858 at FORT LANGLEY, an HBC post built 1827 and now restored. It was named after HBC director Thomas Langley. Gov Douglas bowed to pressures and on 14 Feb 1859 proclaimed the site of the capital to be New Westminster. Before the advent of the Trans-Canada Hwy in the early 1960s, the area had an economy based largely on agriculture; Langley City was its trade and service centre and continues to exist as a separate corporation. Improved access and land suited for subdivision led to a residential construction boom. Large industrial estates have drawn numerous manufacturing and warehousing operations and made Langley a regional commercial and industrial centre. Enterprises include a distillery, a cedar-products firm, machine shops and meat packers. Poultry production, dairying, beef farming and berry growing are part of a thriving agricultural economy on the 85% of the municipality protected for the purpose. Attractions include historic Fort Langley. ALAN F.J. ARTIBISE

Langstaff, Annie, née MacDonald, feminist, legal scholar, aviatrix (b at Alexandria, Ont 1887; d at Montréal 29 June 1975). First woman graduate of McGill's professional schools and first woman graduate in law in Québec (first-class honours, 1914), she achieved notoriety as a result of litigation against the Québec Bar, in which she sought permission to take its qualifying examinations. Defeated, Langstaff returned as a para-legal in 1916 to the Montréal law firm of her sponsor and advocate, Samuel W. Jacobs. She wrote several articles on FAMILY LAW published in popular women's journals, as well as the unique *French-English, English-French Law Dictionary* (1937), and she continued to agitate for the admission of women to law practice in Québec until it was achieved in 1942. Langstaff herself was never admitted to the bar. G. BLAINE BAKER

Reading: M. Gillett, *We Walked Very Warily* (1981).

Langton, Hugh Hornby, librarian, editor, historian, translator (b at Québec C 29 Aug 1862; d at Toronto 30 Sept 1953), son of John LANGTON. Educated at U of T, he was the first full-time registrar of the university 1887-92 and its librarian 1892-1923. He established the library on a firm footing after the fire of 1890, and he developed the collection, staff, services, procedures and traditions from which the present system has grown. He also brought high standards to his role as the first general editor of the university's scholarly publishing program, 1897-1923, and as joint editor with George M. WRONG of the *Chronicles of Canada* (32 vols 1914-16) and of the *Review of Historical Publications Relating to Canada* (1897-1919), which at his initiative became the CANADIAN HISTORICAL REVIEW. After retiring in 1923 he continued to translate for the CHAMPLAIN SOCIETY, to edit and to write biographies. His last publication was an edition of journals and letters of his aunt Anne Langton, *A Gentlewoman in Upper Canada* (1950). ROBERT H. BLACKBURN

Langton, John, first auditor general of Canada (b at Blythe Hall near Ormskirk, Eng 6 Apr 1808; d at Toronto 19 Mar 1894). Educated at Cambridge, he immigrated to Canada in 1833 where he established a farm near Fenelon Falls, Upper Canada. He represented Peterborough in the Assembly of the Province of Canada 1851-55. His grasp of administration led in 1855 to his appointment as first auditor for the Province of Canada. As auditor he established systematic and responsible accounting, and after Confederation he became the first auditor general of the Dominion. When the Treasury Board was founded in 1869 he was its secretary. From 1870 until his retirement in 1878 he was in the unique and somewhat anomalous position of being both auditor general and deputy minister of finance. As vice-chancellor of U of T, elected in 1856, he pushed ahead with plans to convert a large part of the endowment into the University College building, a project he managed to get planned and completed within 3 years. ROBERT H. BLACKBURN

Language is a term that covers a vast array of concepts best understood through a series of basic distinctions. Language is a form of communication – specifically, a communication system based on human sounds. There are several types of communication systems, which can be based on touch, scent, movement, colour, gesture and even the electrical impulses that pass through computers. A bee is able to communicate the location of nectar by performing a dance for other bees in the hive, just as the peacock can communicate by displaying brightly coloured feathers and strutting about. However, such forms of communication do not match the marvelous complexity of human language.

Linguists agree that there are some universal features of human language that distinguish it from other forms of communication. Perhaps most important is "productivity," a feature implying that there are no limitations to what speakers can express through language. We can talk about anything; we are able, with no effort, to utter and understand sentences that we have never heard before. Language is an arbitrary (or conventional) system: it does not matter what sequence of sounds is used to symbolize a thing or idea, as long as it is mutually agreed upon by the speakers in the community.

A user of language employs syntax (including word order), morphology (word roots, affixes), phonology (functional sounds) and prosody (intonation, stress, tone) in order to categorize things, events and ideas. What is expressed in one language by differences among words may be expressed in another language by differences in grammar or intonation. For example, the difference between the French words "personne" and "n'importe qui" can be rendered in English by a difference in the intonation of such utterances as "I don't lend my books to anyone" ("je ne prête pas mes livres à – personne/n'importe qui").

A further distinction within the concept of language should be made between natural and artificial languages. Some artificial languages were invented in response to a desire for a universal medium of communication. Esperanto, Novial, Interlingua and several hundred other artificial languages have been proposed over the past few centuries, but none of them has met with universal acceptance. Computer technology has brought about another kind of artificial language: FORTRAN, BASIC and COBOL are some of the codes with which humans can communicate with machines, but none of them is nearly as elaborate as a natural language. Natural languages have evolved within communities, some of them over many millennia; they are all based on human speech sounds, with the exception of sign languages (used by the deaf). An infant surrounded by individuals speaking a particular language will learn that language just as he learns the behaviours expected of him by family and community.

Only those who succeed in speaking a language to the satisfaction of a given linguistic group are eventually integrated into the group. It is as if the speech community were to say, "this person, who speaks like one of us, must be one of us." Language, even more than religion, social behaviour, dress, food or custom, is the most integrative and exclusive component of culture. As a living monument fashioned by countless generations of users it has encoded all that its speakers have considered important. It has also left uncoded that which was considered unimportant. For example, nomadic Canadian Inuit on the fringes of the Arctic seas had little interest in distinguishing different types of trees; what they needed were words to talk about snow. In some Inuit dialects, more than 50 words referring to ice and snow are in use. All cultures have words that reflect their needs.

Language, Dialect and Register It has been said that no 2 people, not even twins, speak the same language in exactly the same way. Every individual has an *idiolect*, yet the degree of individual difference cannot be such as to make mutual comprehension impossible. Groups of people who communicate frequently develop a common speech and a threshold of tolerance for individual speech differences. Consequently, people living in the same region are likely to speak in a similar way; ie, they speak the same *dialect*. Dialects have traditionally been described along 2 parameters, geographic and social. Just as people tend to speak in a manner similar to that of those living nearby, their speech usually resembles that of their socioeconomic peers. An example of a dialect based on social position is the British *RP* ("received pronunciation"), the "public school" accents of English as spoken by the people educated in the private schools of Great Britain. Language varies in degree of formality depending on the occasion and on the relative familiarity of the speakers. Thus many people use a number of different *registers*. What is appropriate in speaking to a family member may not be acceptable to a group of strangers at a public meeting, and we adjust our speech accordingly.

Languages of the World Since the difference between adjacent speech communities is one of degree, there has not always been total agreement on what dialect belongs to which language, and in some cases there is debate as to whether a given dialect is, in fact, a separate language. This has influenced estimates of the number of languages there are in the world: counts have ranged from 3000 to about 8000. The latest (1984) inventory (Barbara Grimes, ed) lists the names of 5445 languages, exclusive of dialects. Recognition of a dialect as a language is a matter of circumstance. In the past, the dialect of the royal court, the capital city or the seat of national government was usually selected as a state's language (*see* ENGLISH LANGUAGE; FRENCH LANGUAGE). Today linguists seek more objective criteria (eg, mutual intelligibility) for recognizing a language. If 2 speech communities can understand each other they are commonly thought to speak dialects of the same language, whereas 2 communities using mutually unintelligible speech might claim to be speaking 2 different languages. This is generally the way in which distinctions are made today, although political boundaries still have an influence on linguistic classification.

Languages are grouped into families, a language family being a number of languages that have all developed historically from the same *protolanguage* (source language). There are a number of families in the world, including Sino-Tibetan, Afro-Asiatic, Uralic-Altaic, Austronesian and Uto-Aztecan. The languages of Canada's native people have been grouped into Algonquian, Athapaskan, Salishan, Wakashan and other families (*see* NATIVE PEOPLE, LANGUAGES). One of the world's largest and most widespread language families is Indo-European, whose members include English, French, Irish, Spanish, Romanian, Russian, Greek, Farsi (Persian), Armenian and Hindi. The English language belongs to the so-called Germanic branch of this family, as do German, Dutch, Yiddish, Danish, Icelandic and many others. French belongs to the Italic branch, which includes Italian, Latin, Portuguese, Spanish, Italian, Romanian and others.

Language Change Language differentiation is a function of time and space. When a group of people emigrates from its home community, the farther away it goes and the longer it remains isolated, the more different its language might become from that spoken in the area of origin. Although related languages may be mutually incomprehensible, it is possible, using techniques of comparative reconstruction, to establish sound-to-sound and word-to-word relationships – even if the speakers have lived apart for a thousand years or more. The same techniques that permit the identification of related languages also show how one language evolves into another. By comparing forms of the same word in documents of different dates, linguists have demonstrated, for example, the conditions under which the Latin of the Roman legions and their subjects developed into Spanish in Spain, French in France and Romanian in Romania. The process continues today, as the Haitian language clearly shows: on the early plantations of Haiti, the African slaves speaking mutually incomprehensible languages developed their own simplified version of the speech of their French-speaking supervisors; in a few generations, this creole developed into the vernacular of all Haitians.

Official Languages A nation in which many languages are spoken may choose to do all its legal, administrative and other official business in one or more official languages. Canada, which has a great many languages as a result of both indigenous development and immigration, has adopted 2 OFFICIAL LANGUAGES, English and French. A language may be official according to 2 principles, the principle of territoriality and the principle of personality. According to the first, it is the individual who must accommodate to the language of the state. According to the second, it is the state that must accommodate to the language of the individual. The principle of territoriality was adopted for the first time in 1974 as the basis for Québec's Official Languages Act. By contrast, in 1969 both Canada and New Brunswick had formalized through their Official Languages Acts the application of the principle of personality in all dealings, in English or French, between the government and its citizens. *See also* BILINGUALISM; DICTIONARY; ETHNIC LANGUAGES; LANGUAGES IN USE; LINGUISTICS; TRANSLATION. WILLIAM F. MACKEY

Language Policy, official efforts to affect the relative status and use of one or more languages. Language policies of one sort or another have featured in human history from the earliest times. Latin was carried along with the military conquests of the Romans; French, once one of several dialects within France's borders, was deliberately developed as a unifying national tongue at Cardinal Richelieu's instigation.

In a strictly monolingual society, language policy is usually concerned exclusively with promoting an approved, standard grammar of the common language, but in Canada the term is more often associated with a situation in which several languages are in contact or even in conflict. Language policy in Canada is designed to influence the relative use of the various languages in whatever ways are currently judged to serve the general interest. As those perceptions change over time, so does the consensus about what constitutes linguistic justice. Language policy is not a fixed law, but an evolving accommodation to changing linguistic circumstances and the social and political climate.

The History of Language Policy in Canada Canadian language policy is the fruit of the historical relationships among various language communities. The national language debate has often focused on the use of English and French (*see* FRANCOPHONE-ANGLOPHONE RELATIONS), but both Canada's official languages were preceded by the languages of the Inuit and Indian races and succeeded by many other European and non-European languages (*see* NATIVE PEOPLE, LANGUAGES).

Of the 3.5 million inhabitants of the 4 original Canadian provinces in 1871, over 2 million were British in origin and over 1 million were French. By 1986, the proportion of those of British origin in the population had decreased substantially. Of 25 309 000 Canadians, 6.3 million claimed French as mother tongue; 15.7 million claimed English, and 2.9 million claimed a language other than English or French. As well, 900 000 claimed English and one or more languages. The English-speaking community is distributed fairly evenly across Canada, but French-speaking Canadians are concentrated in Québec, New Brunswick, Ontario and parts of Manitoba.

It may be assumed that the earliest language policy in the colonies resulted from the usual highly pragmatic and commercial decisions that characterize new contacts between language groups, eg, decisions about which of the available native or European languages best suited the task at hand. But as the confrontation between the 2 colonizing powers spread to N America, the stage was set for generations of conflict over language and the development of distinctively Canadian language policies. Since the concerns of Indian and Inuit languages were seldom given serious attention, the heart of the Canadian language question became the relative standing and sanctioned uses of English and French.

The terms of the treaty by which the French territory was ceded to the British in 1763 were, on the surface, quite tolerant for the times. The right of the francophone population to practise the Roman Catholic religion was recognized, so far as the laws of Great Britain permitted. The FRENCH LANGUAGE continued to assert itself in practice, since the QUEBEC ACT of 1774 had restored, in civil law, earlier legislation and customs of the country which were of French origin. Moreover, the CONSTITUTIONAL ACT of 1791 had divided the Province of Québec into 2 separate colonies, Upper Canada and Lower Canada, and provided each with an elective assembly. In Lower Canada, the majority of elected parliamentarians were Francophones who saw to it that their language was used alongside English and that it enjoyed equality of status in the parliamentary process. Assembly member Alain Chartier, the marquis of Lotbinière, declared during a parliamentary debate in 1793: "As the largest number of our voters finds itself in a peculiar situation, we are obliged to set aside the ordinary rules and to demand the use of a language which is not that of the Empire; but being as fair to others as we hope they will be to us, we would not wish our language to banish the language of the other subjects of His Majesty. We ask that both be permitted."

The view that it was politically unwise to foster the coexistence of 2 linguistic communities within a single state was expressed by Lord DURHAM in his report. The ACT OF UNION (1841) reunited Upper and Lower Canada into one province. Section 41 of that Act sanctioned unilingualism in the legislature of the Province of Canada, although it did not prevent translations of documents being made for other purposes. However, they were not deemed to have the force of an original record. This section provoked such sharp protests from francophone members that it had to be repealed in 1848 by the British Parliament.

The French language in Canada, through a combination of "habitant" resilience and official tolerance, remained vigorous in many domains of public and private life. By consecrating some of the more institutional uses of French – in laws, in the federal Parliament and in the Québec Legislature, and before federal and Québec courts – the CONSTITUTION ACT, 1867, was in effect formalizing policies that had already taken root in the developing country. Parents' rights to educate their children in English or French were not enshrined in that Act, but the right to maintain denominational schools was and often has been interpreted as a guarantee of the language of education.

If the French language held its own until Confederation, the next 50 years of Canadian expansion and modernization took a heavy toll on both the use of French and the policies believed to support it. During the late 19th and early 20th centuries, several public Acts, such as the abrogation of official bilingualism in Manitoba in 1890 (*see* MANITOBA SCHOOLS QUESTION), the abolition of French schools in Ontario in 1912 (*see* ONTARIO SCHOOLS QUESTION) and the strict limitations imposed on French-language instruction in other provinces, were deliberately aimed at repressing the use of French. Moreover, because the ENGLISH LANGUAGE was the language of N American commerce, the attractiveness of French tended to decline as the continental economy expanded.

By 1963, when the Royal Commission on BILINGUALISM AND BICULTURALISM was created by PM Lester Pearson, the relative status of the French language had declined to an unacceptable extent. The commission, asked to review and assess Canadian language policy, was primarily concerned with promoting a concerted federal-provincial response to what it called the "crisis" in English-French relations. It also had to take account of the fact that increasing numbers of Canadians no longer had any inborn allegiance to either English or French. Language relations had entered a new era, but language policy had not kept pace. The B & B Commission found that French had fallen behind English, eg, in the public service, to a politically and socially unacceptable extent. It urged that a "new charter for the official languages of Canada, a charter founded on the concept of equal partnership" be implemented by both the federal and provincial governments. In 1969, in response to the Commission's recommendations, Parliament passed the OFFICIAL LANGUAGES ACT, which was supported by all parties in the House. As part of the ambitious program that followed, the federal government sought to improve its own capacity to deal with Canadians in the official language of their choice and to allow public servants to use either language at work in certain areas.

Reaction to federal government reforms was sometimes extremely negative. Besides overseeing federal efforts to comply with the Act, the Commissioner of OFFICIAL LANGUAGES (appointed 1969) and others have had to devote much energy to persuading Canadians that these reforms are necessary and just. Some provinces, eg, Ontario and New Brunswick, provide government services in both languages and have tried to implement their own language policies, particularly in regard to minority language and second-language education.

The principles of the Official Languages Act and other important components of language policy were enshrined in the 1982 Constitution through the CANADIAN CHARTER OF RIGHTS AND FREEDOMS. The impact of the Act, particularly on the field of minority education, has been somewhat slow to make itself felt; nor does the Charter make federal and provincial language policies complementary in every respect. Some language-policy initiatives by the Québec government appear to be based on a conviction that it is vital that the interests of the province's French-speaking majority be fully protected before significant concessions can be made to any other language group, including the anglophone community. In 1977 Québec adopted the Charter of the French language, BILL 101, making French the only official language of the province and strengthening its position as the most important language of work, commerce and community life. The right to choose English as the language of schooling has been restricted to those parents who meet a rather narrow definition of "English-speaking," and certain public uses of languages other than French have been limited. However, as the use of French has become more firmly established, provincial governments have more recently shown some willingness to relax these restrictions. New Brunswick has its own provincial Official Languages Act, parallel English and French school systems and legislation requiring equal government treatment of both language groups. In 1986 Ontario, home to the largest French-speaking population outside Québec, implemented the French Language Services Act (Bill 8) guaranteeing provincial services in French in those parts of the province where the vast majority of Franco-Ontarians live. The province has also passed legislation making French an official language of the courts. Manitoba, under the terms of its entry into Confederation (1870), formally recognized the use of English and French in its laws, its legislature and its courts. It failed, however, to abide by these provisions. Following a 1979 Supreme Court decision requiring reinstatement of institutional bilingualism, the province has been engaged in debating whether to comply retroactively with the Manitoba Act of 1870 or to devise a compromise that would attempt to give contemporary expression to the bilingual spirit of that fundamental law. The matter was submitted to the Supreme Court of Canada, which unanimously declared that all enactments (and ensuing rules and regulations) of the Manitoba legislature printed and published in English only are, and always have been, invalid. However, in the interests of public order and the rule of law, the Court declared at the same time that existing enactments would be deemed to have full force and effect until the deadline set for their translation expires.

Language policy strongly influences EDUCATION POLICY across Canada. Many provinces, supported financially by the federal government, have extended and improved their minority and second language education programs (*see* SECOND-LANGUAGE INSTRUCTION). During the 1970s and 1980s several provincial governments that had not previously done so took steps to provide elementary and secondary schooling in French. In spite of recent developments, the English educational network in Québec remains the most complete minority language educational system in Canada. In English-speaking provinces the number of students enrolled in French immersion has increased dramatically, and English as a second language is still a compulsory subject for French-speaking children in Québec through a large part of their elementary and secondary schooling.

In 1984 the Court of Appeal of Ontario, in a reference on minority language educational rights, was of the opinion that 4 sections of the provincial Education Act were inconsistent with s23 of the Canadian Charter of Rights and Freedoms, that the quality of education to be provided to the minority must be on a basis of equality with the majority and that the representation of the linguistic minority on local boards or other public authorities which administer minority language instruction or facilities should be guaranteed. On 1 Oct 1986, the government of Ontario followed the recommendation of the Court of Appeal and passed Bill 75 to amend the Education Act and make it consistent with the Charter. In another connection, Ontario enacted legislation in 1986 on full funding of Catholic separate schools, many of which provide education in French.

The MEECH LAKE ACCORD (Constitution Amendment, 1987), reached by Canada's 11 first ministers in June 1987, will, if adopted by all provincial legislatures, entrench the concept of Canada's linguistic duality in the Constitution. The entire Constitution should then be interpreted in a manner consistent with the recognition that the existence of French-speaking Canadians, centered in Québec but present elsewhere in Canada, and English-speaking Canadians, concentrated outside Québec but present in Québec, constitutes a fundamental characteristic of Canada; and the recognition that Québec constitutes within Canada a distinct society. Parliament and the provincial legislatures would commit themselves to preserving the fundamental characteristic of language duality, while the legislature and government of Québec would have the role of preserving and promoting its own distinct identity.

There are over 100 languages spoken in Canada, and in some places people of non-English and non-French origin are more numerous than those of English or French extraction, a fact often ignored in the continuing struggle between English and French communities over power sharing. Some social services are available in languages other than English or French, but although Canadian governments officially endorse MULTICULTURALISM, they are vague about the rights and privileges to be accorded these other languages. Whereas the various Inuit and Indian languages are receiving some belated institutional recognition, the so-called "heritage" languages, brought to Canada from all over the world, only rarely enjoy a degree of official support, usually in the form of educational privileges. Some languages, eg, Ukrainian and German, are relatively well established in certain parts of Canada, but many others are maintained voluntarily, almost completely within the family or the community. No clear policy toward all Canadian language groups has been devised. OFFICE OF THE COMMISSIONER OF OFFICIAL LANGUAGES

Reading: *Annual Reports of the Commissioner of Official Languages*; R. Wardhaugh, *Language and Nationhood: The Canadian Experience* (1983).

Languages in Use Canada has 2 official languages (*see* ENGLISH LANGUAGE and FRENCH LANGUAGE), but the country's linguistic wealth is much greater. Beginning with the oldest languages, there are no fewer than 53 Indian and Inuit tongues, some of which seem to be disappearing. According to the 1971 census, 25% of those claiming one of these languages as their mother tongue no longer used that language in the home, at least not as their main language. This is not a new phenomenon; in 1971 those whose mother tongue was an Indian or Inuit language comprised only 58% of those who stated that they were of the corresponding ethnic origin. Since "mother tongue" is defined as the first language learned in childhood and still understood, this figure means that the parents or ancestors of 42% of those with Inuit or Indian backgrounds had already abandoned their ancestral languages (*see* NATIVE PEOPLE, LANGUAGES).

The dominant languages in Canada – English and French – are those of the colonizers. In 1763, when New France was ceded to England, there were about 70 000 French and 9000 English in the territory that is now Canada. Forty years later, the English were becoming dominant, and by the mid-19th century a state of equilibrium had been established. Although the relative size of the language groups fluctuated in subsequent years, the balance remained fairly constant. Only since 1931 have Canadian censuses provided information on mother tongues for the country as a whole; for earlier periods it must be calculated from information concerning population distribution by ethnic origin. In 1871, however, there was probably not much difference between mother tongue and corresponding ethnic origin.

English representation has risen almost to its 1871 level. French representation fluctuated between 27% and 31% until 1961, and has since decreased. The other language groups grew in relative size until 1931 but since then have declined. The explanation for these movements is very complex, but 2 factors appear primarily responsible – first, the arrival of immigrants who spoke languages other than English or French, which initially increased the size of the "other" group; and second (and more decisive in the long term), the adoption of English by their descendants.

According to the 1981 census, English gained 1 742 000 but at the expense of the 2 other groups; French lost 204 000 and other languages, 1 198 000. The relative loss of the "other" languages was thus 69%. However, closer examination reveals that abandonment of that "other" language, especially in favour of English, is even greater. Among adults with "other" mother tongues, 80% of those born in Canada (40% if born abroad) generally speak a language other than their mother tongue at home. Of adults whose mother tongue is English and who were born in Canada, only 1% (3% if born abroad) do not generally speak English at home, while 8% of those whose mother tongue is French (20% if born abroad) do not generally use their French at home. The long-term ability of the other languages to survive thus appears to be weak. Some, however, are still quite strong. According to the 1986 census, each of 35 languages, other than English and French, is the mother tongue of at least 10 000 people; of these, 19 are spoken by between 10 000 and 25 000 people each; 4 by between 25 000 and 50 000 people; 4 by between 50 000 and 100 000 people; and 8 by between 100 000 and 530 000 people. Comparison of the numbers for mother tongue and home language in 1971 reveals the losses suffered by these languages (except English), and particularly by German, Ukrainian, Dutch and Polish.

A distinction does exist between Québec and the rest of Canada. In Québec, 98% of Francophones keep their mother tongue all their lives; this is also the case for 90% of Anglophones (about 10% have adopted French as their home language), and for about 70% of persons with other mother tongues. Yet in Québec, which is nearly 85% French speaking, about 66% of immigrants who have chosen to learn one of the 2 official languages have chosen English (although this may alter as a result of the effects of BILL 101). In the rest of Canada, the situation is more clear cut; almost all Anglophones keep their language; almost all non-English-speaking people who abandon their language choose English; and about 40% of adults with French as their mother tongue speak mostly English at home. In 1981, 95.1% of Anglophones (home language) lived outside Québec; on the other hand, 88.8% of all Francophones lived in Québec. The percentage of Anglophones in Québec (12.7% in 1981) will probably be between 9% and 12% by the year 2000; that of

Number of persons whose mother tongue (1986 and 1981) and home language (1981) were one of the 10 most widely spoken languages in Canada
(Source: Canadian censuses, 1986 and 1981)

	*Mother Tongue**		*Home Language**
*Language***	1986	1981	1981
English	15 334	14 684	16 426
French	6 160	6 127	5 923
Italian	456	500	365
German	439	485	164
Chinese	267	213	187
Ukrainian	208	259	95
Portuguese	154	159	131
Dutch	124	137	24
Polish	123	116	56
Greek	110	117	95

* In thousands
** Based on "single response"

Francophones in the rest of Canada (only 11.2% in 1981) between 2.5% and 3.5%.

English-French bilingualism is not very widespread. It is especially prevalent though among mother-tongue Francophones and Anglophones living in Québec. For Canada as a whole, 7% of those with English as their mother tongue and 46.2% of those with French as their mother tongue are bilingual. In Québec the figures are 44.9% and 37.8%, and for the rest of Canada, 4.4% and 88.8%.

Here we find another aspect of English language dominance in Canada: while the majority of Anglophones in Québec can ignore the French language, the same is not true for Francophones in other provinces with respect to English. It is conceivable, however, that fewer and fewer Anglophones will be able to live exclusively in English if they wish to remain in Québec.

JACQUES HENRIPIN

Languirand, Jacques, dramatist, essayist (b at Montréal 1 May 1931). In the 1950s and 1960s he was Canada's most important exponent of the theatre of the absurd, having been much influenced by playwrights in vogue during his stay in Paris, 1949-53. Several of his dramatic texts were performed on radio in Montréal before his first stage play, *Les Insolites,* which was performed in 1956 (pub 1962) and awarded the prize for best Canadian play at the Dominion Drama Festival. Other successes were *Les Grands Départs* (1958) and the musical comedy *Klondyke* (1970). Although his plays focus on the isolation of the individual in a modern society bereft of traditional values, they failed to attract Québec audiences after the onset of the QUIET REVOLUTION. Languirand has since abandoned theatre in favour of more esoteric pursuits in works such as his mystical *La Voie initiatique* (1978) and *Mater Materia* (1980).

L.E. DOUCETTE

Reading: M. Genuist, *Languirand et l'absurde* (1982).

Lansdowne, Henry Charles Keith Petty-Fitzmaurice, 5th Marquess of, politician, governor general of Canada 1883-88, viceroy of India 1888-93 (b at Lansdowne House, London, Eng 14 Jan 1845; d at Clonmel, Ire 4 June 1927). Henry was educated at Eton and Balliol Coll, Oxford. He entered the Lords as a Liberal and served as a lord of the Treasury 1869-72, as undersecretary for war 1872-74 and, after Gladstone's Liberals returned to power in 1880, as undersecretary of state for India. A model governor general, he presided over the turbulent political period of the NORTH-WEST REBELLION without incident. Soon after he arrived in Canada he organized the despatch of the NILE EXPEDITION. Lansdowne seemed to regard his Canadian years as a respite from the more arduous duties of British public life.

CARMAN MILLER

Portrait of the marquess of Lansdowne, by E.M. Merrick, oil on canvas (*courtesy House of Commons, Speaker's Office/National Archives of Canada/C-116827*).

L'Anse Amour Burial Site, located on the Str of Belle Isle coast of southern LABRADOR, was occupied between at least 5500 and 2000 BC by Maritime ARCHAIC Indians who used the area for fishing and hunting harp seals and walrus. The earliest known portion of the site consists of a burial mound which has been radiocarbon dated to between 5500 and 5000 BC. The mound, 8 m across and covered with large boulders, protected an empty burial cist of upright slabs extending one metre below the surface; ½ metre farther below was found the skeleton of an adolescent child covered with red ochre and accompanied by several stone and bone spearpoints and knives, a walrus tusk, a harpoon head, an ivory carving and a bone whistle. It is estimated that the burial ceremony must have involved at least one week's labour for the local hunting band. L'Anse Amour site is the earliest mound burial of this type known at present anywhere in the world. *See also* ARCHAEOLOGY; PREHISTORY.

ROBERT MCGHEE

L'Anse aux Meadows, the first authentic Norse site found in N America, is located on the northern tip of Newfoundland's Great Northern Peninsula. Newfoundlander William A. Munn suggested in 1914 that Norse landings had occurred on this spot, but remains were not discovered until 1960 when the Norwegian explorer and writer Helge Ingstad and his wife, archaeologist Anne Stine, searched the area. The site was excavated by Anne Stine Ingstad, 1961-68, and by Parks Canada, 1973-76. The Norse remains consist of 3 building complexes, each comprising a large dwelling and associated workshops. Finds show evidence of ironworking and carpentry, the first known iron smelting in the New World. Distinctive artifacts include a bronze pin, a spindle whorl, sewing tools and broken wood objects. Building types, artifacts and radiocarbon dates indicate an occupancy of short duration between 990 and 1050 AD. The site also contains evidence of Groswater, Maritime ARCHAIC and DORSET occupations predating the Norse, and several Indian occupations ranging in date between 900 and 1600 AD. Since 1977 L'Anse aux Meadows has been a national historic park administered by Parks Canada. The site was declared a UNITED NATIONS WORLD HERITAGE SITE in 1978. The modern settlement was established as a French fishing station; in 1835 William Decker, an English seaman, founded the present community which derives most of its income from inshore fishing. *See also* NORSE VOYAGES; ARCHAEOLOGY; PREHISTORY.

BIRGITTA LINDEROTH WALLACE

Reading: H. Ingstad, *Westward to Vinland* (1969).

L'Anse aux Meadows, Nfld, showing the excavations of the 8 structures built there and subsequently covered again with turf. The excavations provided proof of Norse occupation (*courtesy Ron Redfern, Random House Inc*).

Lapalme, Georges-Émile, politician (b at Montréal 14 Jan 1907; d there 5 Feb 1985). Leader of the Québec Liberal Party 1950-58, he left his mark as a reformer of the party and thus helped prepare it for its role as catalyst of the QUIET REVOLUTION. The Liberal member for Joliette-L'Assomption in the federal House of Commons, 1945-50, he was afterwards the Liberal member of the Québec Assembly for Outremont 1953-66. He served as deputy premier 1960-64 and attorney general 1960-63, but his greatest contribution was as the first minister of cultural affairs 1961-64. As such, he supervised the creation of the department and was responsible for the actions of the Québec state in cultural matters. After retiring from active political life, he was first chairman of the CANADIAN FILM DEVELOPMENT CORP in 1968 and headed the Commission des biens culturels (1972-78). He published his memoirs 1969-73.

DANIEL LATOUCHE

LaPierre, Laurier, television personality, author, editor, academic (b at Lac-Mégantic, Qué 21 Nov 1929). Brought up in rural poverty in the Eastern Townships, LaPierre received a PhD in history from U of T in 1962, and taught French Canada studies at U of Western Ontario, Loyola College in Montréal, and, from 1962 to 1978, at McGill. He established a national reputation as co-host of the CBC's popular television program THIS HOUR HAS SEVEN DAYS (1964-66) where his charm and his articulate and occasionally emotional interviewing style captured the attention of his audience. However, it was considered unprofessional by CBC management, particularly the incident, on 20 Mar 1966, when he was so moved by an interview with the mother of young Steven Truscott (*see* R V TRUSCOTT) that he shed a tear on camera. More recently, he became widely known as host of a daily show on CKVU-TV in Vancouver where he now lives. ERIC KOCH

Reading: Eric Koch, *Inside Seven Days: The Show That Shook the Nation* (1986).

Lapointe, Ernest, politician (b at St-Éloi, Qué 6 Oct 1876; d at Montréal 26 Nov 1941). Educated at Rimouski Coll and Laval, he was called to the bar in 1898 and practised law in Rivière-du-Loup and Québec City. He was elected Liberal MP for Kamouraska in 1904. In 1919 he shifted to Québec E, the former riding of Sir Wilfrid LAURIER, which he represented until his death. Lapointe was a little-noticed backbencher in his early years, but the burly, slow-moving member learned English and gradually won respect for his sound judgement and unswerving loyalty to the party. In Laurier's last years he was the most prominent among the younger French Canadian members, and led the debate on the controversial ONTARIO SCHOOLS QUESTION. Under PM Mackenzie KING, Lapointe was minister of marine and fisheries (1921-24), minister of justice (1924-30, 1935-41) and, more importantly, was recognized as King's Québec lieutenant and his most influential adviser. He shared King's commitment to Canadian autonomy, accompanied him to the Imperial Conference of 1926 and chaired the Canadian delegation in the discussions that led to the STATUTE OF WESTMINSTER in 1931. In domestic affairs he was identified with the low-tariff wing of the Liberal Party and with provincial autonomy. As minister of justice he disallowed some of ABERHART's Social Credit legislation in Alberta because of its encroachment on the federal sphere. He did not disallow DUPLESSIS's PADLOCK ACT, despite its threat to civil liberties, because he believed DISALLOWANCE would strengthen Duplessis's political position in Québec. In 1939 Lapointe's prestige, coupled with his guarantee that there would be no CONSCRIPTION for overseas service, was instrumental in winning French Canadian support for Canadian participation in WWII. His intervention in the Québec provincial elections of Nov 1939 contributed to Duplessis's defeat and the election of a more co-operative Liberal government under GODBOUT. Under Lapointe's leadership, Québec was a federal Liberal stronghold, a pattern that survived long after his death in 1941. H. BLAIR NEATBY

Lapointe, Gatien, poet, professor, publisher (b at Sainte-Justine-de-Dorchester, Qué 18 Dec 1931; d at Trois-Rivières, Qué 15 Sept 1983). He studied at the Petit Séminaire de Québec, the École des arts graphiques in Montréal, U de Montréal (MA), the Collège de France and the Sorbonne. He published *Jour malaisé* in 1953 and *Otages de la joie* 2 years later. In 1962 he won the award of the Club des poètes for *Le Temps premier*. He received the Prix Du Maurier, the Prix du Québec and the Gov Gen's Award for *Ode au Saint-Laurent*, which appeared in 1963. He again won the Prix du Québec in 1967 for *Le Premier Mot*. He taught at the military college in Saint-Jean-sur-Richelieu and became a professor at U du Québec à Trois-Rivières in 1969. While teaching, he also started and ran Écrits des Forges, a publishing house almost exclusively devoted to poetry. In 1980, after 13 years of silence, he again began publishing his work, bringing out, in order, *Arbre-radar, Barbare inouï, Corps et graphies, Corps de l'instant* and *Le Premier Paysage*. In these later collections, he moved away from lyricism and themes of the land to an entirely modern focus on the body and the moment. But his writings always had the same intensity and sensitivity which provided the unity and value of his work, one of the richest of all Québec poetry. FRANÇOIS DUMONT

Lapointe, Louise-Marguerite-Renaude, politician, journalist (b at Disraeli, Qué 3 Jan 1912). She obtained her diploma in music from the Dominion College of Music (1927) and certificates in foreign language from Laval (1937-42). She started as a journalist with *Le Soleil* (1939-59). At first responsible for music criticism and women's issues, she then wrote editorials. She also became a correspondent for *Time, Life* and the international service of Radio-Canada. After 20 years at *Le Soleil* she went over to *La Presse* and then to *Le Nouveau Journal*. She published *L'Histoire boulerversante de Mgr Charbonneau*, which sold 50 000 copies. The death of *Le Nouveau Journal* (1963) sent her back to *La Presse* where she became the first woman editorial writer (1965) and was named "journalist of the year." She left the paper (1970) and became an information officer for the federal ministry of Indian and Northern Affairs. Appointed to the Senate 10 Nov 1971, she was Speaker of the Senate 1974-79; she is the first French Canadian woman to hold this prestigious position. She resigned from the Senate 3 Jan 1987. MARTHE LEGAULT

Lapointe, Paul-Marie, writer, journalist (b at St-Félicien, Qué 22 Sept 1929). His unique synthesis of a surrealist heritage and a profoundly N American outlook, along with the richly imaginative nature of his writing, make him one of Québec's greatest poets and among those with the widest influence and audience.

After studies in Chicoutimi and at the École des beaux-arts in Montréal, he published *Le Vierge incendié* (1948), a piercing and violently surrealistic collection, just when Paul-Émile BORDUAS and his friends put out their REFUS GLOBAL manifesto. He then was silent for 12 years while pursuing a career in journalism. He was with *L'Événement Journal* 1950-54, *La Presse* 1954-60, was information officer with the short-lived *Nouveau Journal* 1963, and then was editor in chief of *Le Magazine Maclean* 1963-68, before joining Radio-Canada where he became programming director for radio. Lapointe published *Choix de poèmes: Arbres* (1960) and *Pour les âmes* (1964), which were republished in 1971 along with *Le Vierge incendié* in his retrospective *Le Réel absolu* (Gov Gen's Award). His poetry was relatively unaffected by the 1960s nationalism, but is imbued with rebellion and sensuality, is close to nature, and is shot through with a keen awareness of Western history. His works have been translated for various anthologies and foreign magazines and in 1976 he won the prize of the International Poetry Forum in the US. Other collections, including *Tableaux de l'amoureuse* (1974) and *Écritures* (1980), have joined this exclusively poetic body of work. PIERRE NEPVEU

Laporte, Pierre, politician (b at Montréal 25 Feb 1921; d there 17 Oct 1970). Kidnapped by the FRONT DE LIBÉRATION DU QUÉBEC on 10 Oct 1970, he was killed on Oct 17 and his body was found in St-Hubert, Qué. Originally a journalist and parliamentary correspondent for *Le Devoir*, 1945-61, he was one of Prem Maurice DUPLESSIS's fiercest opponents. He was elected Liberal member for Chambly in a 1961 by-election and served as minister of municipal affairs 1962-66 and cultural affairs 1964-66 during the Jean LESAGE administration. Defeated as a candidate for the Québec Liberal Party leadership in 1970, he held the posts of minister of immigration and of manpower and labour in Robert BOURASSA's government until his death. His murder intensified the OCTOBER CRISIS, occurring a day after the federal government applied the WAR MEASURES ACT.

Eastern larch, or "tamarack" (*Larix laricina*), with young fruit (pinkish) and older cones (*artwork by Claire Tremblay*).

Larch is the Lat name for CONIFERS of genus *Larix* of the PINE family (Pinaceae). All 10-12 species of *Larix* grow in the Northern Hemisphere; 3 are in Canada. Tamarack (*L. laricina*) is a small tree of cold, wet areas from eastern BC to the Atlantic provinces. Alpine larch (*L. lyallii*) occurs at high elevations in southern BC and Alberta. Western larch (*L. occidentalis*) is a large tree of southern BC and southwestern Alberta. Larches are slender, with straight, gradually tapering trunks and narrow, irregular crowns. Larches are the only Canadian deciduous conifers, turning golden and shedding their leaves in fall. The leaves are needlelike, soft and borne in clusters on dwarf twigs. The cones are 1-4 cm long and composed of smooth scales and pointed bracts (modified leaves). Western larch is the most important timber-producing larch. Tamarack is used for pulp. Tannin, for tanning leather, can be extracted from the bark of the larch. JOHN N. OWENS

Lark, common name for small songbirds of the primarily Old World family Alaudidae. Larks inhabit open country and are ground dwelling. Characteristically, they run or walk, rather than hop. The hind claw is long and sharp; wings are long and pointed. Both sexes are similarly coloured, mainly in subdued browns, which blend with their usual surroundings; young are spotted. Many larks have elaborate, impressive flight songs. Of the world's 75 species, 2 occur in Canada. The horned lark (*Eremophila alpestris*) is a native, holarctic species found throughout Canada. Fond of open expanses, it breeds across prairies, arctic and alpine tundra and seacoasts, even in airports, cultivated fields and pastures. In settled areas, horned larks eat quantities of weed seeds and insects. Although migratory, larks begin nesting before the snow disappears (late Mar). The female constructs the nest, a grass-lined cup dug into the ground, and incubates 3-6 eggs. Horned larks winter from southern Canada southward, congregating in loose flocks. The Eurasian skylark (*Alauda arvensis*), introduced in 1902-03, is now resident on southern Vancouver I. The population remains low and has spread little. The skylark's song is immortalized in English poetry and prose. The MEADOWLARK is not a lark. PHILIP S. TAYLOR

Larsen, Henry Asbjorn, mounted policeman, seaman, explorer (b at Fredrikstad, Norway 30 Sept 1899; d at Vancouver 29 Oct 1964). He went to sea in a square-rigger at 15; inspired by the career of his countryman Roald AMUNDSEN, he

Captain Henry Larsen, who was called Hanorie Umiarjuag ("Henry with the Big Ship") by the Inuit, is shown aboard RCMP patrol schooner *St. Roch* in the Arctic (*courtesy National Archives of Canada/C-70771*).

dreamed of exploring the Arctic. After a voyage to the Beaufort Sea he became a Canadian citizen in 1927, and in 1928 joined the RCMP. He was assigned as first mate to RCMP schooner ST. ROCH on her maiden voyage to the western Arctic in 1928; later that year he was made skipper, a position he retained until 1948. Under Larsen, called by the Inuit "Hanorie Umiarjuag" or "Henry with the Big Ship," the *St. Roch* patrolled the Canadian Arctic coast, often wintering in the North. The first ship to traverse the NORTHWEST PASSAGE from W to E (1940-42), it was the first to make the passage in both directions (1944); later it was the first ship to circumnavigate N America (1950). Larsen retired with the rank of superintendent in 1961.
W.R. MORRISON

Reading: Henry Larsen, *The Big Ship* (1967).

Lartigue, Jean-Jacques, Roman Catholic bishop of Montréal (b at Montréal 20 June 1777; d there 19 Apr 1840). A member of the Séminaire de Saint-Sulpice in Montréal from 1806 to 1820, he was given oversight of the district of Montréal in Jan 1821, when he was consecrated a titular bishop and auxiliary bishop to the bishop of Québec. For some 15 years, he was the target of the hostility of the Saint-Sulpice priests, jealously defending the influence they had exercised in Montréal since 1657, and of the British authorities who found him too nationalistic for their liking. An ULTRAMONTANE, he tried to bring about a Christian society which would revolve around the church. In pursuit of this objective, he had to face the revolt of a lay minority which opposed Church control, especially over education. Named the first bishop of Montréal on 13 May 1836, he drew upon himself the wrath of the radical PATRIOTES whom he condemned energetically in his pastoral letter of 24 Oct 1837.
GILLES CHAUSSÉ

Laser (*l*ight *a*mplification by *s*timulated *e*mission of *r*adiation), device used to generate high-intensity light. Unlike light from conventional sources, which is emitted incoherently (ie, light waves are unsynchronized or scattered) and over a range of frequencies, laser light is coherent (waves move in unison) and monochromatic (of a single colour/frequency). The frequency of the light emitted is determined by the nature of the atoms and molecules making up the laser medium. The maser is a similar device that emits coherent radiation at microwave frequencies. The 3 major components of a laser are the laser medium, an optical cavity for producing feedback (eg, pairs of mirrors), and a means of exciting the laser medium, thereby increasing the energy level (excitation) of the constituent atoms and molecules (eg, a flash lamp).

Types Maser emission was first demonstrated in 1954 by J.P. Gordon, H.J. Zeiger and C.H. Townes at Columbia U. Arthur L. Schawlow, a graduate of U of T, and Townes proposed a technique for obtaining laser emission in a paper published in 1958. Operation of the first laser was reported by American physicist Theodore Maiman in 1960. This device had a ruby crystal medium.

The first gaseous laser, demonstrated in 1960, used a mixture of helium and neon as the laser medium and had an output power of 15 milliwatts. In 1960 John C. POLANYI, working at U of T, suggested a new type of laser based on the exchange of molecular vibrational energy in a gas. In 1964 this suggestion led to the development by C.K.N. Patel of the carbon dioxide laser, which operates in the infrared. Carbon dioxide lasers are the most powerful CW lasers available, with outputs of up to 100 000 W. An important advance in carbon dioxide laser technology, made in 1970 by A. Jacques Beaulieu, a scientist at the Defence Research Board laboratory in Valcartier, Qué, allowed these lasers to operate efficiently under pulsed conditions and has resulted in many new industrial applications for these devices. A recent advance permits pulsed operation using a mixture of halogen and inert gases (eg, fluorine and krypton). These excimer lasers operate in the ultraviolet with a combination of high-pulse energy and rapid repetition rate.

Applications Lasers are widely used in many areas of technology. In industry the high power and narrow beams available have led to applications in materials forming, joining, machining, heat treating and marking. Lasers are extensively used in the manufacture of semiconductor elements and devices (*see* MICROCHIPS). The monochromaticity of laser radiation has opened up new areas in chemistry, through the use of laser radiation to modify chemical reactions and separate isotopes. In COMMUNICATIONS, lasers are used as optical transmission links, often through optical fibres. The science of holography, the generation of 3-dimensional pictures, has expanded with laser development. In medicine, lasers are routinely used in eye surgery and, in the case of the carbon-dioxide laser, as a scalpel in various surgical techniques. Optical lasers, used to read the digital information on compact discs, have revolutionized the home audio industry. The ability of a laser to project a beam of light over vast distances has resulted in the use of lasers for REMOTE SENSING of atmospheric pollutants. Several studies are proceeding in which very high-power lasers are being used in an effort to achieve NUCLEAR FUSION. *See also* PHYSICS.
W.W. DULEY

Laser beam reflecting at an angle of 90 degrees at the National Research Council in Ottawa (*courtesy SSC Photocentre/photo by Bob Anderson*).

Lash, Zebulon Aiton, lawyer, civil servant, businessman (b in Nfld Sept 1846; d at Toronto 24 Jan 1920). Called to the Bar of Upper Canada in 1868, he joined the federal Dept of Justice in 1872 and was deputy minister 1876-82. In this period the department assisted in defining the central government's powers by reviewing provincial legislation and frequently recommending DISALLOWANCE. The department also played a key role in the colonization of the PRAIRIE WEST. Lash administered the MANITOBA ACT to encourage maximum dispersal of the MÉTIS, thus freeing over 1.2 million ha for Ontarians who wanted to settle in Manitoba. He then entered private practice in Toronto with Edward BLAKE and developed many links with business, especially firms with interests in the West. Lash was also a leading imperial federationist. His publications include *The Banking System of Canada* (1907) and *Defence and Foreign Affairs* (1917).
D.N. SPRAGUE

Bora Laskin, chief justice of Canada (1973-84), was well known as a civil libertarian and brilliant legal scholar (*courtesy SSC Photocentre*).

Laskin, Bora, lawyer, judge (b at Fort William [Thunder Bay], Ont 5 Oct 1912; d at Ottawa 26 Mar 1984). After graduating from U of T (BA 1933, MA 1935), Laskin received an LLB from Osgoode Hall in 1936 and an LLM from Harvard in 1937. Called to the Ontario Bar in 1937, he taught law at U of T from 1940 to 1945, Osgoode Hall from 1945 to 1949, and returned to U of T from 1949 to 1965. He was appointed QC in 1956, to the Ontario Court of Appeal in 1965, and a puisne judge in the Supreme Court of Canada in 1970. Named chief justice of Canada in 1973, he died in office. Known throughout his career as a civil libertarian and as a brilliant legal scholar, especially in constitutional and labour law, he was author of *Canadian Constitutional Law* (1963) and *The British Tradition in Canadian Law* (1969).
FREDERICK VAUGHAN

Lasnier, Rina, poet (b at St-Grégoire d'Iberville, Qué 6 Aug 1915). She studied at the Collège Marguerite Bourgeoys, Montréal, and at U de M. Her first publication was *Féerie indienne* (1939), a religious play followed by several others: *Le Jeu de la voyagère* (1941), *Les Fiançailles d'Anne de Noüe* (1943), *Notre-Dame du Pain* (1947). Her predominant interest lies in poetry and in the renewal of its forms and themes. After *Images et proses* (1941) and *Madones canadiennes* (1944), in which prose poems accompany pictorial equivalents, Lasnier published *Le Chant de la montée* (1947), a biblical

Portrait of Rina Lasnier by artist Ruby Boardman (*courtesy Rina Lasnier*).

meditation upon the human antecedents of the Incarnation. *Escales* (1950) demonstrates the richness and complexity of her mature poetic style. After travelling in Europe (1953-54), she published in 1956 *Présence de l'absence*, which symbolically expresses inner conflict and sorrow. *Miroirs* (1960) consists of autobiographical prose texts while *Mémoire sans jours* (1960) envisions poetic creation as an arduous submarine quest. Much recognition has come her way, including the Prix Duvernay (1957), the MOLSON PRIZE (1971), the Prix France-Canada (1973) and the Prix David (1943 and 1974). Her symbolic vision continues to unfold through her work of the 1960s and 1970s: *Les Gisants* (1963), a meditation on death and eternity; *L'arbre blanc* (1966), dramatizing the poetic vocation in today's Québec; *La Salle des rêves* (1971) with its measured response to the intuitions of psychology. Her poetry was collected in *Poèmes I et II* (1972), but she has published many works since that time: *L'Invisible* (1969), *Le Rêve du quart jour*, (1973), *Amour* (1975), as well as the prose poems *L'Echelle des anges* (1975), *Les Signes* (1976), *Matin d'oiseaux* (1978), *Paliers de paroles* (1978), *Entendre l'ombre* (1981) and *Voir la nuit* (1981), in which she continues to probe for the unity that may lie beyond sensory experience. EVA KUSHNER

Last Post Fund On a winter day in 1909, an old South African war veteran was carried into Montreal General Hospital suffering exposure and starvation. He died a few hours later and his body was consigned, in the custom of the time, to a pauper's unmarked grave. But a hospital orderly, a veteran himself, Arthur Hair, intervened and raised money for a proper burial. He then canvassed prominent Montrealers and, with their help, organized the Last Post Imperial Naval and Military Contingency Fund, officially inaugurated 19 Apr 1909, in the vestry of Trinity Church, Viger Square, Montréal.

Until 1921, the fund, supported entirely by voluntary contributions and limited to Québec province, provided an honourable funeral and burial and a granite grave marker for 276 indigent veterans. The fund acquired its present name, Last Post Fund, when it received a Dominion charter and annual government grant of $10 000 in 1921, enabling it to extend services across Canada. The fund pays all or part of the cost of a dignified funeral and burial for any indigent former member of Canada's armed forces or merchant marine, in Canada or abroad. Members of Allied forces who die in similar circumstances in Canada are also eligible. The Fund maintains its own military cemetery at Pointe Claire, Qué. Its national headquarters are in Montréal and it has 11 branches across Canada, one in Britain, and 3 in the US. DAVE MCINTOSH

Latin Americans are among the most recent cultural groups to arrive in Canada. According to unofficial figures released by several community agencies there are about 200 000 people of Latin American extraction now living in Canada.

Origins Most historians and sociologists studying Latin America have generally done so from a colonial Spanish and Portuguese perspective; as a result, Latin Americans see themselves as a product of the Spanish conquest in the 16th century, and as a consequence the history of the region is wrongly considered to have begun with the Spanish arrival in the New World. The Inca, Aztec and Maya civilizations are merely looked upon as "prehistory." The region's culture, however, is a mixture of European elements (primarily Spanish and Portuguese, but also Italian, German and Dutch) and native elements. There are 19 countries in Latin America.

Migration The first wave of Latin American immigrants arrived in Canada between 1970 and 1973. (Official figures show that Canada's total Latin American population was less than 3000 before 1970.) The influx of Latin Americans (some 68 000) in the early 1970s can be partly attributed to Canada's "open door" IMMIGRATION POLICY. From 1969 to 1972 it was possible to arrive in Canada as a tourist without a visa and later apply for landed immigrant status from within the country. At the same time, due to a growing demand for labourers willing to perform jobs with low social status (*see* IMMIGRANT LABOUR), Canada relaxed its immigration requirements. Argentinian immigrants, who before 1970 had arrived at a rate of 200 yearly, numbered 948 in 1973, 1088 in 1974 and 674 in 1975. The vast majority of Chilean political REFUGEES immigrated to Canada by way of Argentina after the overthrow of the Allende regime. From 1963 to 1973, only 2135 persons were recorded as emigrants from Chile; by 1976, 4600 had immigrated to Canada as part of the Special Chilean Movement initiated by the Canadian government. During the early 1970s about 20 000 Ecuadorians in search of a better life immigrated to Canada, primarily to Montréal and Toronto. By the late 1980s several hundred Central Americans had arrived as refugees.

Settlement Pattern Most Latin Americans settled originally in the downtown areas of Toronto and Montréal. But since industry, and above all light manufacturing requiring semiskilled workers, is located in the suburbs of Toronto and Montréal, the need to live near their work forced many Latin Americans to move to some of the more isolated neighbourhoods. Hundreds of Latin American families have migrated west, mostly to Alberta, in search of work. There are now Latin Americans settled in all provinces and territories.

Economic Life The service industry, light industry manufacturing and the garment industry are the areas of employment to which Latin Americans gravitate. There is a perceptible shift, over time, from lower skilled jobs obtained upon arrival to positions requiring greater skills. With the growth and stabilization of the Latin American community in the mid-to-late 1980s, a number of its members have entered occupations such as insurance, real estate, restaurants and travel agencies. Also, a growing number of professionals and academics, mostly from Chile and Argentina, have now revalidated their qualifications in Canada and are entering their professional fields of expertise.

Social Life and Community The social life of Latin Americans is centered around community activities and family gatherings. Clubs regularly hold dances and sporting events. These mutual-aid clubs serve to maintain group ties and keep cultural heritage alive. Latin American associations include the Centre for Spanish-Speaking Peoples in Toronto and the Latin Association de Sud Americanos in Montréal.

The community is not divided by class or income (although a small number of professionals and executives see themselves as a separate group) but rather by nationality. Chileans have formed organizations such as the Winnipeg Chilean Association, which has committees for education and culture, finance, women and social welfare. In Toronto and Montréal, the Ecuadorian-Canadian Soccer League holds weekly matches.

The biggest challenge so far for the Latin American community seems to be the newly gained independence of women. Feminist self-assertion, which comes from living in a more liberal N American environment, is a constant source of contention between Latin American couples.

Religion and Cultural Life Although most Latin Americans are baptized as Catholics, many do not consider themselves practising members of the church. In Canada this separation has been reinforced because of the absence of social pressures and the opportunity to engage in various alternative activities.

Spanish-language newspapers, 2 of which are published in Toronto, one in Vancouver, and others in Calgary and Edmonton, serve the Latin American community in Canada. Theatre presentations, poetry recitals and art exhibits are becoming more frequent in the community. Dozens of folkloric groups, both dance and music, are very active. Several Latin American writers, poets, painters and journalists are becoming known in Canada.

Education In 1970, in the combined school systems of Toronto and Montréal, there were 342 students from Latin America. By the 1980s their number had climbed to 9738. The number of students in Canadian universities and technical colleges who claim Spanish as their mother tongue had increased from 67 to 583 by the 1980s. Largely because of emotional and behavioural problems, many Latin American children and parents experience difficulty in their adjustment to Canadian schools. The parents' own difficulties in adjustment and the problem of communication with the school are the major barriers to happy, successful schooling.

Group Maintenance Latin Americans, even those who, as political refugees, may have hoped to return to their countries of origin, have become increasingly involved in Canadian life. Many, as they succeed in Canada, may suffer the loss of their language and some isolation from their communities. WILSON RUIZ

Reading: Wilson Ruiz, *The Latin American Community Survey* (1982).

Latter Rain Movement, *see* NEW RELIGIOUS MOVEMENTS.

Latulippe, Rose, one of many girls in French Canadian tradition who were supposed to have danced with the devil, some to survive, others to be carried off, never to be seen again. Rose

Latulippe neglected her fiancé Gabriel in favour of a handsome stranger whose horse breathed fire and who had claws inside his velvet gloves. Just as the devil tried to put his own necklace around her neck to bind her to him, the local parish priest (curé) rushed in, placed his stole around her shoulders and put the devil to flight, restoring Rose to her fiancé. Such stories were prevalent as sanctions against dancing, particularly during Lent or on Sundays. NANCY SCHMITZ

Latvians Latvia is a small country situated on the eastern shore of the Baltic Sea. Established as an independent state after WWI, Latvia was occupied by the Soviet Union in 1940, by the Nazis 1941-44 and then again by the Soviet Union. In 1945, 110 000 Latvians who had fled to western Europe were classified as displaced persons. Of these, 14 911 eventually immigrated to Canada.

The first Latvians (mainly farmers) to arrive in Canada were refugees from Tsarist Russia in the 1890s. They settled primarily in Manitoba and Alberta, although during the Great Depression many sought work in eastern Canada. The Canadian census of 1941 lists only 975 Canadians of Latvian origin, but by 1986 an estimated 12 615 Canadian residents claimed Latvian ancestry. Of these a majority reside in Ontario, particularly in Toronto, which has become the centre for almost all Latvian cultural, social and political life in Canada.

A very high percentage of post-WWII Latvian immigrants are professionals, eg, doctors, engineers and lawyers. They have been able to integrate into Canadian society with considerable success. The majority of Latvians belong to the Lutheran Church, although there are Baptists and Roman Catholics among them.

All sizable Latvian centres have their own congregations and professional and social organizations. The activities of these local groups are co-ordinated by the Latvian National Federation in Canada, headquartered in Toronto. The Latvian community also supports 10 Latvian-language Saturday schools.

The most spectacular demonstration of the Latvian culture is the song festival, dating from the 19th century. The tradition has been transplanted to N America. The one-week festivals (massed choirs, symphony concerts, recitals, folk dancing, theatre performances and exhibits of fine arts and handicrafts) are held at 2- or 3-year intervals in Toronto and the US alternately. J. MEŽAKS

Laure, Carole, stage name of Carole Champagne, later Carole Lord, actress, singer (b near Montréal 5 Aug 1949?). She studied for a career as a concert pianist and made her theatre debut in an experimental piece by Pierre Moretti called *Equation pour un homme actuel* and acted in the musical comedy *Demain Montréal m'attend* by Michel TREMBLAY. In 1973 she starred in Gilles CARLE's *La Mort d'un bûcheron* (1973). Her career has since paralleled that of Carle with whom she has made 6 films, including *La Tête de Normande St-Onge* (1975), *L'Ange et la femme* (1977), *Fantastica* (1980) and *Maria Chapdelaine* (1983). Her performance in *La Menace* opposite Yves Montand led to her role in *Préparez vos mouchoirs* (*Get Out Your Handkerchiefs*), directed by Bertrand Blier, and Joyce Bunuel's *La Jument vapeur* (*Dirty Dishes*). Laure has recorded 2 record albums in France and once took the extraordinary step of taking over the Bobino Theatre in Paris to sing songs created especially for her by Lewis Furey. Her most recent performance was in *Night Magic* (1986).

Film actress Carole Laure in *Maria Chapdelaine*, directed by Gilles Carle (*courtesy Canapress Photo Service*).

Laurence, George Craig, nuclear physicist (b at Charlottetown 21 Jan 1905; d at Deep River, Ont 6 Nov 1987). Educated at Dalhousie and Cambridge (under Ernest RUTHERFORD), Laurence became the NATIONAL RESEARCH COUNCIL's radium and X-ray physicist in 1930, when J.A. GRAY's pupils at Queen's constituted the only Canadian laboratory for atomic physics. Most of the early NRC work was developing medical and industrial radiology, but in 1939-40 Laurence attempted, virtually alone, to build a graphite-uranium atomic reactor in Ottawa. In 1942 he joined the Anglo-French atomic research team in Montréal that built the ZEEP reactor, the first outside the US, at Chalk River in 1945, and served in the Canadian delegation to the UN Atomic Energy Commission (1946-47). Laurence then became a senior scientist at the Chalk River Nuclear Laboratories and president of the Atomic Energy Control Board (1961-70). DONALD J.C. PHILLIPSON

Laurence, Margaret, née Jean Margaret Wemyss, novelist (b at Neepawa, Man 18 July 1926; d at Lakefield, Ont 5 Jan 1987). She was educated in Neepawa and at United College, Winnipeg, and married Jack Laurence, a hydraulic engineer, in 1947. In 1949 they moved to England and later to Somaliland and Ghana where he worked as a dam builder with the British Overseas Development Service. Their 2 children were born in 1952 and 1954. In 1957 the family moved from Ghana to Vancouver, and in 1962 Margaret Laurence and the children moved to England, settling in the village of Penn in Buckinghamshire. Margaret and Jack Laurence were divorced in 1969, and in 1974 Margaret Laurence returned to live permanently in Lakefield, Ont.

From age 7 she wrote stories; though she wrote throughout high school and college and worked after graduation for the *Winnipeg Citizen*, a labour daily, her first work for publication did not occur until the Somaliland years. In 1954 the British Protectorate of Somaliland published *A Tree for Poverty*, her translations of Somali folktales and poetry. Africa transformed Laurence from an idealistic young western liberal to a mature woman who saw at first hand the problems of emergent nations, empathized with their peoples and read deeply in their history and literature. Her first published fiction was a story, "Uncertain Flowering," published in a Whit Burnett anthology for 1954; it was followed by the stories set in Ghana published in various journals and gathered into *The Tomorrow-Tamer* in 1963. *This Side Jordan*, her first novel, was set and drafted in Ghana and published in 1960. All her African fiction reflects a determined apprenticeship to writing and a burgeoning talent based on a passionate belief in the dignity and potential of every human being.

Back in Vancouver she revised her memoirs of the Somaliland years, published as *The Prophet's Camel Bell* (1963), and then turned her attention to Hagar Shipley, who had developed in her imagination out of her prairie background. *The* STONE ANGEL (1964), the story of Hagar's last journey towards recognition of love and freedom, was a landmark event for Canadian literature and the keystone of Laurence's career. It set the town, Manawaka, firmly in Canada's imaginative landscape and pointed the way for the works to follow. *A Jest of God* (1966) is the story of Rachel Cameron, who, through the ordeal of one summer in Manawaka in the 1960s, finds a fragile but sustaining selfhood. Seven of the 8 stories of *A Bird in the House* were published from 1962 onward; with the addition of an 8th they were gathered together and published in 1970. The maturing of Vanessa MacLeod, their heroine, is based on Margaret Laurence's own experiences. The deaths of her own parents, the changes caused first by loss and grief and then by the practical circumstances of her life are present in Vanessa's story, not in correspondence of detail, but in truth of spirit. Stacey MacAindra of *The Fire-Dwellers* (1969) is Rachel Cameron's sister. Married to a struggling salesman, living in Vancouver and mother of 4, Stacey is the beleaguered housewife of our time. She thinks of herself as commonplace and ordinary, but Laurence's great achievement is to reveal to us her extraordinary qualities of love, fortitude and vitality. *The Diviners* (1974), the story of writer Morag Gunn, is true in its spirit to Laurence's own maturing and is the climactic work of the Manawaka cycle. A complex and profound novel, it brings the Scottish pioneers and the Métis outcasts of Manawaka together and culminates in the joining of past and present and the affirming of the future in the person of Pique, the daughter of Morag and Jules Tonnere.

From time to time Laurence found refreshment in writing children's books. *Jason's Quest* (1970) is a joyfully inventive tale about a mole

Margaret Laurence's novel *The Stone Angel* (1964) was a landmark event for Canadian literature, setting the town of Manawaka firmly in Canada's imaginative landscape (*photo by Doug Boult*).

and his friends, its essence a confrontation between the forces of darkness and light. *Six Darn Cows* (1979) is a carefully crafted story for very young readers, and *The Olden Days Coat* (1979, rev 1982) is a magic Christmas story. *A Christmas Birthday Story* (1980) is the retelling of a work first written when her own children were very young. In 1968 Laurence's continuing interest in African literature was expressed in *Long Drums and Cannons*, her tribute to the upsurge of Nigerian writing in English between 1958 and 1964. In 1976 she collected and introduced a group of her occasional essays, *Heart of a Stranger*.

From her home in Lakefield, she was constantly active in organizations promoting the cause of world peace, particularly in Project Ploughshares. She was awarded the Order of Canada and honorary degrees by 14 Canadian universities. *The Stone Angel* was the first Canadian novel to be required reading for France's prestigious "aggregation" examination. Her works were translated into many languages, and before her last illness she was preparing to journey to Britain, where the Manawaka novels are now being reissued by Virago Press and to Norway, where the translation of *The Stone Angel* has been a best-seller. For 3 years she was chancellor of Trent U in Peterborough, Ont.

She was much beloved and will be remembered for her works and for the personal warmth, strength and humour which she shared so generously. Her final literary legacy, the memoir, *Dance on the Earth*, which she finished before she died, was being edited for publication in 1988.

CLARA THOMAS

Reading: Patricia Morley, *Margaret Laurence* (1981); Clara Thomas, *Margaret Laurence* (1969) and *The Manawaka World of Margaret Laurence* (1975); George Woodcock, ed, *A Place to Stand On* (1983).

Laurendeau, Joseph-Edmond-André, journalist, politician, playwright, co-chairman of the Royal Commission on BILINGUALISM AND BICULTURALISM (b at Montréal 21 Mar 1912; d at Ottawa 1 June 1968). A lifetime French Canadian nationalist, he helped prepare the way for Québec's QUIET REVOLUTION by redefining nationalist aspirations for an urban and industrial society. After completing his classical education at Collège Sainte-Marie in Montréal, he pursued graduate work in literature and history at U de M where he came under the influence of Abbé Lionel GROULX. After a brief sojourn in the separatist youth movement, Jeune-Canada, André Laurendeau spent 2 years in France, 1935-36, taking courses at the Sorbonne, the Collège de France and the Institut catholique. While in Europe he came to embrace the social CATHOLICISM and the personalism of Emmanuel Mounier, Jacques Maritain and Étienne Gilson. He returned home critical of the concept of political independence for the French Canadian nation but determined to reorient FRENCH CANADIAN NATIONALISM toward socioeconomic issues. As editor of L'ACTION NATIONALE, 1937-42, he attempted to pursue this goal.

In 1942 he joined forces with other nationalists to create the Ligue pour la défence du Canada to fight for a "no" vote in the Apr 1942 plebiscite called by PM Mackenzie KING over CONSCRIPTION for overseas service. Following the success of the league — over 80% of French Canadians voted no — a nationalist third party was created in the fall of 1942. The BLOC POPULAIRE fought against the threat of conscription and demanded greater equality for Francophones in the federal system. Laurendeau was selected provincial leader of the Bloc in Feb 1944 and was one of the 4 Bloc members to win election to the Québec Assembly in 1944. He denounced the centralist economic and social policies of the federal government and called upon the Union Nationale regime of Maurice DUPLESSIS to make provincial autonomy meaningful by implementing long overdue socioeconomic reforms.

In Sept 1947 Laurendeau resigned as leader of the Bloc Populaire and, at the invitation of his friend and publisher Gérard FILION, joined the editorial staff of *Le Devoir*. He became editor in chief in 1958 and retained that post until his premature death in 1968. Between 1948 and 1954, he also resumed the functions of director of *L'Action nationale*, which he infused with a new sense of direction, and attracted a new generation of contributors and readers. Along with his nationalist colleagues, Filion, Jean-Marc LÉGER and Pierre LAPORTE, he fought the politically and socially regressive regime of Duplessis, and turned *Le Devoir* into an effective forum for criticism. Laurendeau called for a redefinition of traditional French Canadian nationalism to reflect more clearly the problems and aspirations of an overwhelmingly urban and industrial society. This neo-nationalism was adopted by the Québec Liberal Party of Jean LESAGE prior to the 1960 provincial election in which the Union Nationale was defeated.

Fearing the political and social implications of the rise of SEPARATISM in Québec after 1960, Laurendeau called upon the DIEFENBAKER and the PEARSON governments to investigate the crisis in Québec-Ottawa relations. PM Pearson responded by creating in 1963 the B&B Commission with Laurendeau and Davidson DUNTON as co-chairmen. Until 1968 Laurendeau pursued diligently, but with a growing sense of despair, the challenge of finding a long-term solution that would provide a constitutionally entrenched equality for the French Canadian majority of Québec and the francophone minorities outside Québec. His fellow commissioners, reflecting the divisions within Canadian society at large, could not come to terms with the constitutional implications of linguistic duality and cultural pluralism, and thus the final volume of the report never materialized. The country did respond to the crisis by making room for French Canadians at the federal level through the implementation of the 1969 OFFICIAL LANGUAGES ACT (*see* BICULTURALISM).

In addition to his other work, Laurendeau was a radio and TV personality, and wrote articles, TV dramas, a play, *Deux femmes terribles* (1961), and a novel *Une Vie d'enfer* (1965). He was a member of the Royal Soc of Canada and the Académie canadienne-française.

M.D. BEHIELS

Reading: Michael D. Behiels, *Prelude to Quebec's Quiet Revolution* (1985) and, with Ramsay Cook, *The Essential Laurendeau* (1976).

Laurentia, the name given by geologists to a landmass that, between 600 and 500 million years ago, embraced eastern N America, most of Europe and much of Asia. Writers have also used the word "Laurentia" as their name for a utopian Québec. Jules-Paul TARDIVEL set his futuristic novel *Pour la patrie* (1895; trans *For My Country*, 1975) in the "Laurentian Empire," a state separate from Canada. Lionel GROULX in 1937 defined his "Laurentia" as a separate French, Catholic state. The Latin name is that of Saint Lawrence, the Christian martyr burned to death by the Romans in AD 258. It was on St Lawrence's feast day, Aug 10, that Jacques CARTIER in 1535 named after the saint a bay he discovered; the name was later applied to the river.

JOHN ROBERT COLOMBO

Laurentian Highlands are part of the plateau and dissected southern rim of the Canadian SHIELD in Québec. Viewed from the valleys of the Ottawa and St Lawrence rivers, the S-facing escarpments of the Shield give the appearance of mountains 500-800 m high; looking across the plateau, the relief is more moderate and subdued. These scarps mark the dramatic southern edge of the highlands. Although the other limits are less well defined, the highlands may be considered to extend 75-150 km northward from the scarps and to stretch from the Gatineau R in the W (mean elev 400 m) some 550 km to the SAGUENAY R in the NE. Here they attain their maximum elevation N of Québec City in the Parc des Laurentides (1200 m). Individual summits rise above the plateau surface: Mont Sir Wilfrid (783 m) and Mont Tremblant (968 m) in the W, Mont Ste-Anne (815 m) at Québec, Mont Raoul-Blanchard (1166 m), Mont Bleu (1052 m) and Mont des Conscrits (1006 m) in Parc des Laurentides. Cap Tourmente (579 m) and Mont des Éboulements (770 m) are dramatic examples of the scarp face as it drops precipitously to the St Lawrence R.

The 1000-1700-million-year-old rocks of the Shield are mostly metamorphosed granites and gneiss in this area. They have been faulted, uplifted and eroded. The ice of the Pleistocene glaciation (1 million years ago) scraped the plateau surface bare in many sections, but elsewhere deposited rock, sand and gravel as moraines, resulting in a disrupted drainage system with many lakes and youthful rivers. The ice also overdeepened the valleys that lead southward from the Shield, the most dramatic of which is the fjord of the Saguenay R (500 m cliffs and 600 m depths). When the ice sheets finally melted (about 10 000-20 000 years ago) many of these valleys were partly filled by sands, gravels and other outwash material carried by the meltwaters. Postglacial uplift and continued downcutting by past and present rivers have resulted in the formation of terraces and plains along the river valleys. The resulting local relief of 300-600 m along these valleys adds to the ruggedness and scenic beauty of the highlands. The Rivière ST-MAURICE, flowing from the large GOUIN RESERVOIR on the Shield some 560 km to the St Lawrence at TROIS-RIVIÈRES, is one of the largest rivers, but the Nord at ST-JÉRÔME and the Montmorency and Jacques Cartier, flowing from Parc des Laurentides to the St Lawrence E of Québec, must also be noted.

The southern limits of the vast boreal forest of subarctic Canada cover most of the highlands. Black and white spruce, balsam fir, tamarack, poplar and white birch are the dominant tree species. Along the southern edge of the plateau and in the valleys these mix with white pine and deciduous species common to the ST LAWRENCE LOWLAND – sugar maple, beech, hemlock. These forests attracted the early explorers and settlers from the lowlands for hunting, trapping and eventually for forestry. Lumbering became a major industry and many species of trees were cut and floated down the numerous rivers to sawmills. These were located near rapids or falls where the rivers left the Shield or joined the Ottawa or St Lawrence rivers. Hull and LACHUTE at the mouths of the Gatineau and Nord rivers and Grand-Mère and Trois-Rivières on the St-Maurice are typical. As technology advanced and rivers were harnessed for electricity (SHAWINIGAN, 1899) the lumber mills were joined by other industries such as textiles at Lachute and St-Jérôme and pulp-and-paper mills and chemicals at Shawinigan and Grand-Mère.

The valleys leading from the Shield tempted some hardy, early settlers who, pressed by the scarcity of unoccupied farmland on the lowlands, tried to develop an agricultural base. An early wave in the mid-1800s of Irish and other European immigrants was partly successful in the lower valleys. A second wave of French settlers, inspired by Father LABELLE in the late 1800s, initiated several colonization schemes. St-Jérôme, founded in 1834, became the springboard for the push up the Nord and Rouge valleys. The railway (Petit Train du Nord) reached STE-AGATHE in 1892

The Laurentian Highlands, part of the plateau and dissected southern rim of the Canadian Shield in Québec, have been a centre of outdoor recreation since the 1890s (*photo by John deVisser*).

and a first period of success occurred. The podzolic soils and the humid, cool continental climate proved unsuitable for agriculture, however, and within 2 generations most of this marginal land was abandoned. The farmers found work in the forest industries, which stretched even farther N in search of marketable trees, and in the industries and mills along the rivers.

The physical environment that was hostile to agriculture was ideal for recreation, a fact recognized by some of the colonists. As early as 1894 Ste-Agathe and the surrounding hills, lakes and streams attracted summer and, by the 1920s, winter tourists. Vacationers from the cities, not only nearby Ottawa, Montréal and Québec, but also from the US, began a seasonal migration. Tourists of all ages and incomes flock to the resort areas and family cottages throughout the highlands. The federal and provincial governments established nature and recreational parks to protect the natural environment and provide extensive areas for outdoor recreation. Gatineau Park N of OTTAWA-Hull, Mont Tremblant Park near St-Jovite, La Mauricie NW of Grand-Mère and Laurentides between Québec and Lac SAINT-JEAN offer a wide variety of hunting (moose, deer, grouse) and fishing (trout, perch, pike), camping, swimming and sailing. Winter sports include downhill and cross-country skiing, skating, snowshoeing and snowmobiling. Extensive modern road networks, particularly the Laurentian Autoroute N from Montréal (built in the late 1960s), provide rapid access to such centres as St-Sauveur, Ste-Agathe and Mont Tremblant and, near Québec City, MONT STE-ANNE. R.N. DRUMMOND

Laurentian Thesis, an influential theory of economic and national development set forth by several major English Canadian historians from the 1930s through the 1950s. The theory received its most sustained and sophisticated expression in the writings of Donald CREIGHTON, especially *The* COMMERCIAL EMPIRE OF THE ST. LAWRENCE (1937). Creighton argued that Canadian economic and national development derived fundamentally from the gradual exploitation of key staple products – fur, timber and wheat – by colonial merchants in the major metropolitan centres of the ST LAWRENCE R system. That system provided the means by which both a transatlantic and a transcontinental market economy could be created. In stressing the connection with the metropolitan capitals of Europe, Creighton undermined the CONTINENTALISM implicit in American historian Frederick Jackson Turner's FRONTIER THESIS while emphasizing environmental factors. In Creighton's view, the 1885 completion of the CANADIAN PACIFIC RAILWAY marked an extension of the potential for national development inherent in the St Lawrence system. Creighton's theory was derived in part from the STAPLE THEORY advanced by H.A. INNIS, particularly in *The Fur Trade in Canada* (1930), in which Innis emphasized the importance of European linkages and determining environmental factors.

The Laurentian thesis, given complete expression by Innis and Creighton by 1940, was a major influence on historians writing after WWII. It was not, however, without critics. In a 1946 address called "Clio in Canada: the Interpretation of Canadian History" (published in *University of Toronto Quarterly*), W.L. MORTON warned of the potential for cultural and regional exploitation inherent in the expansion of central Canadian commerce and institutions, nevertheless accepting as historical fact, here and in *The Kingdom of Canada* (1963), the development made possible by the Laurentian waterway. J.M.S. CARELESS'S publication, *Canada: A Story of Challenge* (1953), also built upon the theory, although Careless paid closer attention to regional differentiation and metropolitan influence (*see* METROPOLITAN-HINTERLAND THESIS).

Since 1960 the Laurentian thesis has received much scholarly debate, particularly (as Morton warned) because it rests upon imperial exploitation and control over regional hinterlands. With the regionalization of the historical profession, and with the rise of a SOCIAL HISTORY sensitive to regional and class exploitation, most recent discussion has been critical; nevertheless, even under attack it continues to be the mechanism of historical synthesis against which all others must compete as a means of explaining Canadian history. A. BRIAN MCKILLOP

Reading: Carl Berger, *The Writing of Canadian History* (1976).

Laurentian University, Sudbury, Ont, was founded in 1960; instruction is in both French and English. Laurentian U dates from 1913 when the Roman Catholic Collège du Sacré-Coeur was established in Sudbury. In 1957 it became University of Sudbury. In 1960 and 1963, respectively, representatives from the new Huntington U (United Church) and Thorneloe U (Anglican) joined in a nondenominational federation with the university. Each church-affiliated university provides a college for Laurentian. Nipissing College in North Bay, Collège de Hearst in Hearst, and Algoma College in Sault Ste Marie are also members of the Laurentian federation. The Centre in Mining and Mineral Exploration Research (CIMMER), est 1984, focuses research on the region's most important economic activity. An internationally acclaimed swim club, led until 1987 by Alex BAUMANN, is based at the university. Full-time undergraduate enrolment in 1985-86 was 3312. B. BEATON

Laurier, Sir Wilfrid, lawyer, journalist, politician, prime minister of Canada (b at St-Lin, Canada E 20 Nov 1841; d at Ottawa 17 Feb 1919). As leader of the LIBERAL PARTY 1887-1919 and PM 1896-1911, Laurier was the dominant political figure of his era. A skilful and pragmatic politician with a charismatic personality, he unceasingly sought compromise. Above all, he was a fervent promoter of national unity at a time of radical change and worsening cultural conflict.

After obtaining his law degree from McGill in 1864 and practising in Montréal, Laurier went in 1866 to live in L'Avenir and then Arthabaska, Qué, where he ran the newspaper *Le Défricheur*. Upholding the position of the radical PARTI ROUGE, Laurier, a former vice-president of the INSTITUT CANADIEN in Montréal, vigorously opposed CONFEDERATION. In 1871, when the Catholic Church in Québec led by Bishop BOURGET was ferociously attacking the Rouges and liberalism, he became the Liberal member for Drummond-Arthabaska in the Québec legislature. His lack of interest in regional questions led him to resign in 1874 and, reconciled to Confederation, he was immediately elected a Liberal member to the House of Commons of Canada. Thus began an uninterrupted stay of some 45 years in Ottawa. In Oct 1877, some months after giving a vigorous speech in Québec City in defence of political liberalism, he was appointed minister of inland revenue in Alexander MACKENZIE's Cabinet. The most prominent Liberal of his province, Laurier became the recognized leader of the Québec wing of the party. But his party's defeats in the elections of 1878 and 1882 meant a curb to his ambitions, though he himself was re-elected in Québec-Est, and he took less interest in political debate. In 1885 his ardour was aroused by the hanging of Louis RIEL and he vigorously defended the cause of the Métis leader and the need to unite the French and English in Canada. In 1887 Edward BLAKE, disappointed by the recent electoral defeat, chose Laurier to succeed him as leader of the Liberal Party, despite the opposition of a number of eminent Liberals.

From 1887 on, Laurier devoted himself to building a truly national party and to regaining power gradually. His efforts were divided into 2 distinct phases. The first and less successful, 1887-91, emphasized the policy of unrestricted RECIPROCITY with the US; announced in 1888, the program was rejected in the 1891 general election. Perceived as a continentalist and as anti-British, Laurier was trampled by the Canadian electorate even though, for the first time since 1874, Québec gave a majority of its seats to the Liberals. The second more fruitful phase took place between 1891 and 1896; this was the period when Laurier, more sure of himself, managed to take his party in hand while the Conservatives, after the death of Sir John A. MACDONALD, were mired in difficulties. In 1893 Laurier organized an impressive political convention in Ottawa which approved a new program and the basis for a truly national structure. In the 1896 election, when the education rights of the Catholic minority in Manitoba, curtailed since 1890, became an important issue (*see* MANITOBA SCHOOLS QUESTION), Laurier, more a skilful politician than a sincere defender of the Catholic minority, avoided taking a definite stand. On 23 June 1896, Canadians chose him over Charles TUPPER to lead their country as prime minister.

During the period of prosperity that then ensued, Laurier and his government concentrated on the country's development and on implementing policies designed to heal the wounds to national unity. In 1896, with the signing of the Laurier-Greenway agreement, the prime minister decided the fate of educational rights for Manitoba's Catholic minority: never again would this group have the separate schools it enjoyed prior to 1890, but it would henceforth be possible to obtain, under well-defined conditions, religious instruction during the last half-hour of the school day and instruction in a language other than English. In the name of national harmony and the politics of the "lesser evil," Laurier thus launched his policies of compromise which kept him in power for many years but never completely redressed the wrongs committed against the Catholic minority. After beginning, with Clifford SIFTON, to reorganize the immigration system, and finalizing with William FIELDING the details of a tariff policy based on imperial preference, Laurier participated in 1897 in London, Eng, at his first colonial conference. Guided by his belief in the future independence of Canada, he resisted every effort the British Empire made toward unification. Nonetheless, in 1899 he agreed to help defray the costs of transportation and material of

Canadians wishing to fight for England in the SOUTH AFRICAN WAR; this conciliatory stance would bring reproach from those French Canadians fiercely opposed to any participation. But Laurier and his Liberals easily won the 1900 general election, well supported by Québec which gave them 57 of its 65 seats.

After 1900, Laurier led his country forcefully. Within Cabinet, it was he who directed policy, and he did not hesitate to push aside dissenters such as the powerful Israël TARTE, who was forced to resign in 1902. In this year Laurier also commanded attention outside the country when, at the colonial conference in London, he again opposed all proposals to unify the Empire. In 1903, however, shortly after the failure of the ALASKA BOUNDARY discussions with the US, Laurier revealed the most important policy of his second term: the construction of a second transcontinental railway. The GRAND TRUNK PACIFIC would build the section from Winnipeg westward, while the government would undertake the construction of a line (called the NATIONAL TRANSCONTINENTAL) from Moncton and Québec C to Winnipeg. Indeed, Laurier was so optimistic about the nation's progress that he allowed the CANADIAN NORTHERN RY to build a third transcontinental. By agreeing to this multiplication of railways, much of it at public expense, Laurier mortgaged the future with a heavy financial burden. At the peak of this prestige, Laurier would allow nothing to check his ambitions as prime minister. Moreover, the people agreed and re-elected him with a comfortable majority on 3 Nov 1904.

The progressive decline of the Laurier government began in 1905 despite Laurier's pursuit of ambitious projects such as the creation that year of 2 new provinces, Alberta and Saskatchewan. Although a reflection of the country's development, this undertaking necessitated defining the educational rights of the Catholic minority. Once again, yielding to pressures from Anglophones and Protestants, Laurier took refuge behind the status quo, thus depriving the minorities of separate schools. As a result, the last chance to establish genuine cultural dualism throughout Canada was lost. Offended by this retreat, French Canadian nationalists bitterly criticized Laurier, whose prestige in Québec began to fade. In the years that followed, the prime minister sought chiefly to counter accusations of corruption and patronage within his administration and to rebuild his Cabinet. In the 1908 general election, Canadians once again entrusted him with their destiny. His party's majority, however, though still solid in Québec, was somewhat reduced. After 1908, despite his desire to correct certain abuses arising from the far-reaching changes in society, Laurier focused his attention primarily on 2 bills which, in the final analysis, resulted in his defeat. The first, the NAVAL SERVICE Bill, presented in 1910, was to establish a Canadian navy composed of 5 cruisers and 6 destroyers; the navy was to be ready to fight with Great Britain anywhere in the world. Insufficient in the eyes of English Canadian imperialists, excessive according to French Canadian nationalists led by Henri BOURASSA, this moderate measure would cost Laurier precious support, especially in Québec. The second bill concerned reciprocity with the US, the old Liberal dream of 1891. Brought to the Commons early in 1911, it provided for the free trade of several natural products and reduced duty for an imposing number of Canadian manufactured products entering the US. Despite the attractions of the plan, it raised the ire of Canadian industrialists and provided a target for the Conservative Party under R.L. BORDEN, who accused the Liberals of disloyalty toward England and of leading the country towards political annexation. To settle the issue the prime minister called a general election and, on 21 Sept 1911, suffered a bitter defeat.

Sir Wilfrid Laurier
Seventh Prime Minister of Canada

Birth: 20 Nov 1841, St-Lin, Canada East
Father/Mother: Carolus/Marcelle Martineau
Father's Occupation: Surveyor
Education: McGill U, Montréal
Religious Affiliation: Roman Catholic
First Occupation: Lawyer
Last Private Occupation: Lawyer
Political Party: Liberal
Period as PM: 11 July 1896 - 6 Oct 1911
Ridings: Drummond & Arthabaska, Qué 1874-77; Québec East 1877-1919; Saskatchewan District 1896-1900; Ottawa 1908-11
Other Ministries: Inland Revenue 1877-78
Marriage: 13 May 1868 to Zoê Lafontaine: (1841-1921)
Children: None
Died: 17 Feb 1919 in Ottawa
Cause of Death at Age: Stroke at 77
Burial Place: Ottawa
Other Information: First PM of French ancestry; longest unbroken tenure; KCMG, 1897.

(photo, 1911, courtesy National Archives of Canada/C-16748).

Laurier was an energetic and vigilant leader of the Opposition. If he failed to renew his liberalism as progressive Liberals would have wished, he kept his troops united until at least 1916, and relentlessly attacked the government's failure to address problems such as the rising cost of living. Prior to 1914, he fought mainly against the emergency contribution of $35 million offered to Great Britain to help strengthen its navy and against the financial assistance given to the CANADIAN NORTHERN RY. Out of personal conviction, Laurier vigorously supported Canadian participation in WWI. He ardently promoted voluntary enrolment and proposed a political truce. In 1915-16, at age 75, he held several recruiting meetings. In 1917, when the country was plunged into national crisis following imposition of military CONSCRIPTION, Laurier again turned to compromise. To save Canada's threatened unity, he refused to support this measure which was so repulsive to Québec and proposed instead a referendum and continued voluntary enlistment. This time, because his proposal was not supported by the majority of English Canadians, the formula collapsed in general bitterness. Idolized by his French Canadian compatriots who remembered his vigorous defence of the rights of Franco-Ontarians in 1916, he became a symbol of division within the country. Now even his party disintegrated when several eminent English Canadian Liberals crossed the floor to join the UNION GOVERNMENT in which Laurier refused to participate. In the general election of Dec 1917, Laurier was overwhelmingly defeated by Borden's Unionist Party. The vote was divided along distinctly cultural lines. Laurier died on 17 Feb 1919, just after beginning his courageous effort to restructure his party and to rebuild Canadian unity.

Under Laurier's leadership the country continued its industrialization and urbanization and was strengthened by the addition of 2 provinces and 2 million inhabitants. A clever and eloquent politician, a true legend in his own time, Laurier has been judged in a variety of ways. For some, he was the spiritual successor to Macdonald, who pursued and consolidated Confederation. For others, Laurier, in the name of national unity and necessary compromise, too often sacrificed the interest of French Canadian Catholics to those of a majority little inclined to support the ideals of Confederation. Finally, some think he too often governed his country with only Québec's interest in mind. Support for each of these opinions can be found in Laurier's actions in Ottawa but the last view is most open to argument.

RÉAL BÉLANGER

Reading: R.T. Clippingdale, *Laurier* (1979); J.W. Dafoe, *Laurier* (1922, new ed 1965); H.B. Neatby, *Laurier and a Liberal Quebec* (1973); J. Schull, *Laurier* (1965); O.D. Skelton, *Life and Letters of Sir Wilfrid Laurier* (1921, 2nd ed 1965).

Lauson, Jean de, governor of New France 1651-56 (b *c*1584; d at Paris, France 16 Feb 1666). Long before coming to the colony as governor, Lauson had enjoyed a close and lucrative connection with Canada. As intendant of the COMPAGNIE DES CENT-ASSOCIÉS since 1627, he had accumulated vast estates in the St Lawrence. As governor, Lauson used his authority to enrich himself and his family. In 1654, a time of declining prosperity, he gave himself a virtual monopoly in the fur trade, and 2 years later he seized pelts worth 300 000 livres from DES GROSEILLIERS.

ALLAN GREER

Laval, François de, first bishop of Québec (b François-Xavier de Montmorency-Laval de Montigny at Montigny-sur-Avre, France 30 Apr 1623; d at Québec 6 May 1708). Destined for the church at age 8, a would-be missionary, Laval was initially a political pawn. For 10 years he studied with the Jesuits, who nominated him for bishop of Québec in opposition to a Sulpician candidate, de Queylus, who would have kept the Canadian church within the crown-controlled state church of France, and who wanted to control the Jesuit missionaries serving the European colonists. To preserve their independence, the Jesuits, supported by the queen-regent and other notables, promoted Laval.

In defiance of French bishops and the *parlements* of Rouen and Paris, a papal nuncio in 1658 consecrated Laval bishop of Petraea, a diocese in Muslim lands — there being no diocese of Québec yet. Although he swore allegiance to the French king, Laval was the pope's vicar-general. After his arrival at Québec in June 1659, Laval asserted his primacy over de Queylus and rejected the governor's claim to precedence in religious ceremonies. Before leaving Canada, Governor Voyer d'ARGENSON wrote of Laval's "adherence to his own opinions and . . . zeal that bore him

Lithograph of François de Laval by Guiseppe Fassio after Claude Duflos (*courtesy National Archives of Canada/C-89380*).

beyond his mandate . . . that he listens to no one." On his authority and on morality, Laval was inflexibly single-minded. Although willing to compromise on some issues, such as the scale of tithes, he fought an unrelenting battle against the liquor trade with Indians. With the king's backing and by quiet determination, Laval outlasted vociferous opponents, including governors.

His goal was a diocese of Québec in which all religious were subject to the bishop. To reduce lay control of the clergy, Laval instituted a church court to judge cases involving clerics. In 1663 he founded the SÉMINAIRE DE QUÉBEC as a theological college and a mother house of all secular priests. Curates could be recalled at will and their parishioners' tithes went to the seminary. His reluctance to appoint permanent, resident curates — as was done in France — was criticized. He replied that, until he was bishop of Québec, he could not lawfully create new parishes for curates.

Louis XIV's aggressiveness towards the papacy made Rome delay creation of the Québec diocese. Laval left Canada in 1671 determined not to return except as Québec's bishop; his wish was granted in 1674. Although his faith was austere and self-denying, it was charitable and practical. It resulted in new churches, schools and good works. He resisted any multiplication of religious orders as a burden on the colonists and a threat to the centralized church structure. The king financed Laval's work while containing the bishop's ambitions. The bishop and the Jesuits were counterbalanced by royal protection for the Sulpicians and the reintroduction of the Franciscans, loyal crown agents.

In 1685 infirmity and advancing age prompted Laval to offer his resignation as bishop, although he agreed to remain until the consecration of his successor, Jean-Baptiste de La Croix de SAINT-VALLIER, which took place in 1688. Laval's church seemed firmly established. His headstrong, tactless and improvident successor was a disappointment. With pained and silent resignation, Laval watched the young bishop undo much of his work. In 1700 Saint-Vallier was detained in France, and thereafter Laval acted as bishop of Québec until his own death.

Laval's episcopacy had 2 great consequences. His seminary for colonial priests facilitated the "Canadianization" of the clergy so that, after the British Conquest, the Roman Catholic Church was the national church of French Canada. By keeping his diocese independent of any French see, but still linked to Rome, Laval prepared the way for the Ultramontane politics of 19th-century Québec. PETER N. MOOGK

Lavalin Inc is a privately owned engineering firm based in Montréal. With operations in more than 100 countries, more than 7000 employees and annual revenues of about $1 billion, it is a major presence among the world's biggest engineering and construction contractors and one of Canada's most powerful corporate entities. It enjoys particularly close ties with Québec's political elite, some of whom have been employed, or anticipate employment, in its executive offices.

Much of Lavalin's growth has occurred since 1962, when Bernard Lamarre (b at Chicoutimi, Qué 6 Aug 1931) became a partner in the company founded by his father-in-law in 1936. He brought formidable political and engineering skills to the firm, and under his leadership (he became CEO in 1972) it won its share of the ambitious construction contracts generated by the Quiet Revolution, including a part in the biggest of them, the JAMES BAY PROJECT. Lavalin's involvement in the James Bay development was its major breakthrough; it gained there the money and expertise it needed to compete successfully for rich contracts in Third World countries, as well as in China and the Soviet Union, where, during the past 15 years, its most significant work has been accomplished. In addition, the firm won the contract to construct a roof over the Olympic Stadium in Montréal.

In the past decade Lavalin has acquired numerous subsidiaries as a cushion against the cyclical nature of the construction industry, including the Lafarge Coppée cement manufacturing company of France and a 50% interest in the US firetruck manufacturer, Maxim Inc, in 1987 as part of a corporate strategy to move into the manufacture of mass-transit vehicles. STANLEY GORDON

Lavallée, Calixa, composer, pianist (b at Verchères, Canada E 28 Dec 1842; d at Boston, Mass 21 Jan 1891). Author of the music for O CANADA which became the Canadian national anthem, Lavallée was a pioneer in music both in Canada and the US. Taught first by his father, he studied in Montréal, then left for the US in 1857 and toured S America, the West Indies and Mexico. After returning to Verchères in 1863, he gave concerts and taught. On 24 Jan 1864 he gave a concert in Montréal playing piano, violin and cornet. From 1865 to 1872 he again lived in the US and from 1873 to 1875 studied piano, harmony and composition in Paris; one of his piano studies composed at this time, *Le Papillon,* was particularly successful. He later opened a studio in Montréal with Frantz JEHIN-PRUME and Rosita del Vecchio, was twice president of the Académie de musique de Québec, and tried unsuccessfully to open a conservatory of music. In 1881 Lavallée's comic opera *The Widow* was presented in New Orleans. HÉLÈNE PLOUFFE

Lavell, Jeannette Vivian, née Corbière, community worker (b at Wikwemikong, Ont 21 June 1942). From 1970, Jeannette Corbière-Lavell was at the centre of a controversy over inequities in federal Indian status law. In 1970 she married a non-Indian, thus losing her legal status as an Indian under the INDIAN ACT. Since Indian men do not lose status when they "marry out" (but gain status for their wives and children), Lavell appealed to the Federal Court of Canada, which in 1971 rejected her case. The Supreme Court of Canada in 1973 confirmed this ruling in a complex and much-questioned decision, stating that the 1960 CANADIAN BILL OF RIGHTS did not prohibit this particular kind of racial-sexual discrimination and did not invalidate the Indian Act. Controversy over the LAVELL CASE and similar cases led to censure of Canada by international human-rights groups, as well as to a split in the Indian community arising from differing views on intermarriage. BENNETT MCCARDLE

Lavell Case (1973) In *A.G. (Can)* v *Lavell* the Supreme Court of Canada considered whether s12 of the Indian Act, in providing that an Indian woman who marries a non-Indian lose her Indian status (while an Indian male does not lose his status by marrying a non-Indian), is contrary to the principle of equality before the law entrenched in the CANADIAN BILL OF RIGHTS of 1960. The Court ruled in a divided judgement of 5 and 4 that the measure was valid. In its controversial decision the court held that the concept of equality means equality in the administration or application of the law. Parliament could not exercise its jurisdiction over the Indians without passing legislation listing the characteristics required for a person to have the right to Indian status; according to the court, the Act could be enforced reasonably without infringing upon the rights of Indian women to equality before the law.

In *Lovelace* v *Canada* case the UN Human Rights Committee ruled that the status provision was contrary to the International Covenant on Civil and Political Rights. Section 35 of the Constitution Act, 1982, was amended in 1983 in order that the existing aboriginal and treaty rights of the aboriginal peoples of Canada be guaranteed equally to male and female persons. Section 12 of the Indian Act was repealed in 1985. GÉRALD-A. BEAUDOIN

Law governs the relationship of society's individual members to each other and to society as a whole. Every human society has a legal system, because every society must attempt to resolve the basic conflict between the needs of the individual and those of the community. Law is not synonymous with justice, although it has been described as "part of Western man's dream of a life governed by reason."

Canada has inherited 2 of the world's basic law systems: common law (in the 9 provinces and the territories) and civil law (in Québec). Common law, which originated in England, is unenacted law, as opposed to statutes and ordinances. In theory it is traditional law – that which has always been and still is law, if it has not been overridden by legislation. Civil law, however, is based on ancient Roman law, which, together with laws derived from French custom and legislation, was codified by Napoleon. Most of continental Europe, Scotland, Central and S America, some of the W Indies and much of Africa now use the civil law system. The phrase "common law" has different meanings in different contexts. Sometimes it refers to a whole legal system (in contrast with "civil law" systems). Sometimes it refers to judge-made law, as opposed to statute. Sometimes it is contrasted with equity, discussed below, and sometimes with criminal law.

New France was the first region of Canada to adopt a system based on European law. In 1664 Louis XIV of France ordained that French law existing in the area surrounding Paris was to apply in the colony. This body of law was supplemented by portions of French law as it developed in France during the 18th century and by the laws and regulations developed by the colonial authorities.

In 1763 the SOVEREIGNTY of the territory now identified as Canada was transferred from the French to the English Crown, and in 1774 the QUEBEC ACT guaranteed the place of French civil law (*le droit civil*) in Canada alongside English public or constitutional law and English parliamentary institutions. In 1857 the Province of Canada legislated the drafting of a CIVIL CODE and a Code of CIVIL PROCEDURE, major compilations of Québec private law on property and civil rights and the form and style of proceedings before Québec courts. These works were brought into force just prior to Confederation. Today theorists describe the Québec legal system as mixed. The relationships between and transactions among persons subject to Québec law are regulated by both the Civil Code and the Code of Civil Procedure. At the same time, and as a result of legislation passed in Québec since 1763 and later incorporated into the codes, portions of English law have also found their way into Québec private law.

The Civil Code governs the status of individual persons, the law of marriage and relations between married persons, the relations of parents and children, the law of property and the law of contracts and responsibility for civil (noncriminal) wrongs. Today the decisions of French courts and the writings of French legal commentators may be accorded respect when the provisions of French law remain similar to those in force in Québec, but they have no binding authority in Québec law. Law reform in Québec draws its inspiration as much from legal developments in N America and elsewhere as it does from continental Europe.

The other 9 provinces and the territories have adopted English common law. Each jurisdiction has a statute providing that from a certain date the law of England shall be the law of the jurisdiction unless changed by statute, an important qualification. Until 1949 the highest Canadian court was the JUDICIAL COMMITTEE OF THE PRIVY COUNCIL, which sat in London and was composed largely of English judges; English common-law developments were incorporated more or less automatically into Canadian common law. Since 1949 English court decisions, though not binding on Canadian courts, have been treated with great respect, though the SUPREME COURT OF CANADA has sometimes rejected English authority. Canadian decisions are quite often cited in English cases and have influenced English law. The American states (except Louisiana) also adopted English common law in the 18th century and, although the links with modern English law are naturally weaker there than in Canada, American common law still retains the style of reasoning and argument found in all countries affected by English law. As Canada adopts more legislation based on American models the influence of American law will increase and is likely to be particularly strong in the interpretation of the CANADIAN CHARTER OF RIGHTS AND FREEDOMS incorporated into the Canadian CONSTITUTION, for its origins can be directly traced to the American Bill of Rights.

Sources of Law

The Constitution and Legislation are the most authoritative sources of law. The Constitution outlines the DISTRIBUTION OF POWERS and the legislative jurisdictions of Parliament and the provincial legislatures. Each is granted the right to enact statutes (and in Québec, codes), which are a major source of law, often referred to as primary legislation. Subordinate legislation is legislation (bylaws, ordinances, orders-in-council, regulations) enacted by an individual or group with the delegated power to do so. The courts, bound to give effect to validly enacted legislation, nevertheless retain important powers. First, in the case of a dispute it is up to the courts and ultimately the Supreme Court to determine whether the legislation is validly enacted. Disputes frequently arise over whether a provision is within the powers of the legislature that has enacted it. The rules dealing with the respective powers of the legislatures are a very important part of constitutional law. Secondly, the meaning of words is elusive, and disputes over interpretation of legislation must be resolved by the courts. In interpreting legislation the court must always ask itself, expressly or implicitly, what purpose the legislature had in mind and determine what meaning to give to the words used. By saying, for example, that it presumes the legislature does not intend to take away property from citizens without providing compensation and does not intend to take away other rights unless such a purpose is expressly stated, the court interprets legislation to provide some protection to interests it considers important.

The Canadian Charter of Rights and Freedoms, under which individual interests are more directly protected than in the Constitution, was influenced by British and American traditions. According to the former, protection of individual interests is best secured by Parliament itself, and parliamentary Acts bind the courts even if they are contrary to the court's conception of fundamental justice, though much can be done by the courts through interpretation. In the American tradition, by contrast, the courts, on the basis of the Bill of Rights, can strike down legislation contravening fundamental rights. As the language of any such charter of rights is very general, this gives the highest court the last word on many matters of social and political controversy. A compromise between these views, the Canadian Charter of Rights and Freedoms, was based on the American Bill of Rights, but the principle of legislative supremacy was preserved by including a power in any legislature to declare expressly in an Act that the Act or any provision of it shall operate notwithstanding certain provisions of the Charter. It remains to be seen how frequently this power will be used and how it will be interpreted by the courts.

Judicial Decisions The second most important source of law is judicial decisions, known also as case law. In deciding cases judges often record the relevant facts of a case, the issues of law involved and the reasons for the decision. In the common law, prior decisions of higher courts are binding on lower courts but trial judges are not bound by decisions of judges of the same rank, and it is now established that the Supreme Court of Canada is not bound by its own decisions. Some provincial courts of appeal consider themselves bound by their own prior decisions. Despite this, the doctrine of binding precedent is much less restrictive than it appears. Only the reason for the decision of the prior court is actually binding, and the subsequent court retains the power to define for itself the true reason. The circumstances of cases are never precisely similar, so it is usually possible for the later judge to find between the prior case and the case before him a distinction enabling him to come to a different conclusion. The words used in an earlier case are not construed like statutes but read in the context in which they were spoken. It is essential for the law to retain such flexibility, for a judge can never foresee the infinite varieties of human conduct that will give rise to subsequent disputes, and it would be unduly rigid to apply the words of an earlier judge to circumstances he could not have foreseen. The development of both common and civil law depends on the creation and refinement of distinctions in cases, and the final decision over whether to apply a rule in an earlier case always rests (subject to appeal) with the court called upon to decide the point in the later case.

Legal reasoning in common law is primarily reasoning by analogy. To avoid arbitrary decisions, like cases must be decided alike (*see* STARE DECISIS), but there is always room for argument about which facts of a previous case are relevant and which are not. In this system legal reasoning is an attempt to make persuasive arguments for, or to give a rational explanation for, distinctions between cases. This is a never-ending process, as other cases will always arise; as new decisions are made, the principles and exceptions enunciated as part of that case law form the basis of common law.

In Québec civil law – that is, the portions of Québec private law under the Civil Code – judicial decisions are viewed differently, at least in formal theory. In this system the courts will look to the Code to determine a given principle and then apply the principle to the facts of the case. The primary authority for Québec judges is the Code itself; therefore, they are entitled to apply it without being bound by a prior decision, even that of a higher court. In practice, however, great reliance has traditionally been placed on previous judicial decisions (JURISPRUDENCE), as in the common-law tradition and for the same reasons – that it is unwise as a matter of public policy to revive uncertainty about a law once its sense and meaning have been established. Moreover the techniques adopted by Québec judges for making distinctions between cases are similar to those of their counterparts in other provinces. The real status and weight of earlier decisions therefore depend on whether a jurisprudence has been established, and this itself depends upon a judge's interpretation. There is no rule about the number of such cases necessary to establish them as a truly authoritative source of law.

Although it is not as important as statutes or case law, royal prerogative (*see* PREROGATIVE POWERS) does constitute a source of law. In Canada these powers are vested constitutionally in the Crown, represented by the governor general and the provincial lieutenant-governors. The Crown also has the prerogative to pardon those convicted of crime. Formerly the Crown could not be sued in tort, and some of these restrictions on its liability still survive.

Scholarly Writings have sometimes been considered a source of law. In the common law, writings were until quite recently considered of inferior weight, and it was said that writers could not be considered authorities until they were dead. Nevertheless, lawyers could always adopt the argument of a writer as their own. The courts now readily hear and cite arguments of contemporary legal scholars, although these are not true sources of law until the judges adopt them. In Québec, doctrinal writings (*la doctrine*) of scholars, living or dead, and whether in the form of books, articles or commentaries on individual judicial decisions, have always been freely consulted and cited by legal practitioners and judges, although they are no more a source of law or of binding authority than they are in the tradition of the common law.

Equity, meaning fairness or justice, also describes a special body of rules sometimes considered a source of law. These rules developed in England alongside common law to permit enforcement of legal rights for which common law did not provide appropriate remedies. During the Middle Ages the king retained the power to override decisions of the courts on grounds of equity and began to refer petitions for the exercise of this discretion to the chancellor, who for this purpose established the Court of Chancery. By the 16th century, this court was conducting a large volume of business and, as reasons were given for decisions, an originally unfettered discretion became a body of principles and rules. As a result the English legal system contained the principles of both common law and equity, with 2 sets of courts; if the rules conflicted, equity prevailed because the chancellor's orders were enforced by threat of immediate imprisonment. Ironically, the rules of equity became even more rigid than the common law, so that by the 19th century the Court of Chancery was ridiculed by Charles Dickens. Although in England the 2 courts were united and a similar union has been effected in all Canadian common-law jurisdictions, the principles are not yet fully merged.

In Québec no separate body of rules or courts of equity developed. The legislature, in formulating a provision of law, will attribute a measure of discretion to judges, enabling them to bring into play considerations of fairness and equity, and to respond to changing notions of social justice. This equitable discretion may be more widely framed in areas such as family law than in others, eg, property law.

Fundamental Legal Concepts

Justice is an elusive word. To lawyers it incorporates the notions of rationality and due process. In any disputed case there are always arguments on both sides, and some lawyers would say that often there is no right answer. However, if disputes are determined by fair procedures before an impartial tribunal honestly trying to give rational and consistent reasons for its results, it can be said that justice has been done.

Rule of Law is another elusive phrase with several different meanings. It describes an ordered society, like the phrase "law and order," but it also describes judicial independence of the executive branch of government. According to this principle, the police must obey the law and actions of government officers must be authorized by statute. The phrase is also used to support the reasons given by courts for their decisions; in rational explanation lies the assurance to the losing party that the decision is not just a whimsical exercise of arbitrary power. Another aspect of the rule of law, often called the principle of legality, is the avoidance of retroactive lawmaking. The courts will lean in favour of construing penal statutes to apply only to conduct arising after a statute comes into force, a principle included in the Canadian Charter of Rights and Freedoms.

Divisions of the Law

Public Law The law may be conveniently divided into public and private law. The most important branch of the former is CONSTITUTIONAL LAW, which deals with the powers of governments and the division of powers among different levels of government. The second branch is CRIMINAL LAW, which governs the punishment and deterrence of offences regarded as wrongs against society. Criminal conduct often constitutes a civil wrong as well; eg, an assault is a crime for which the assailant can be punished by the state and a civil wrong for which the person assaulted can recover compensation in a civil court. The distinction is important; because of the consequences of a criminal conviction, greater protection is required for the accused in a criminal case than for the defendant in a civil case, the most important safeguard being the requirement of proof of guilt beyond a reasonable doubt. In contrast, a civil action for damages can succeed on the balance of probabilities. Plaintiffs in civil cases have a right to win if their case is more persuasive, but the complainant in a criminal case has no right to a conviction. The only right to a conviction belongs to the community, and although it is in the interests of the community to suppress crime, it is almost as important not to create a society whose members live in constant fear of wrongful conviction. ADMINISTRATIVE LAW, of increasing importance in a highly regulated society, is the third branch of public law. It governs, among other things, the exercise of government powers, which greatly affect most citizens.

Private Law regulates the relations of citizens among themselves. The main divisions of the civil and common law governing the obligations of individuals to each other are contracts (the law of agreements and promises) and the law of civil wrongs (TORTS in the common law and DELICTS in the civil law). To these must be added the law of PROPERTY (governing the acquisition and transfer of rights in goods, land and intangible property) and the law providing for recovery to avoid unjust enrichment (restitution or quasi contract). There is no consensus on the proper arrangement of further divisions and subdivisions, although much of Québec law is structured in the Civil Code. FAMILY LAW is perhaps the most important branch of private law as far as its impact on ordinary persons is concerned. Another important branch, known as conflicts, or private international law, governs the effect of foreign (or extraprovincial) elements in a dispute. Other specialized branches of law include corporation law, sales, negotiable instruments, security for debt on property, agency or mandate, taxation, evidence, debtor and creditor, insurance, wills and trusts, patents, copyright, trademark law and transfer of land; some of these may be regarded as subbranches of contracts and property. *See also* SUBSTANTIVE LAW; PROCEDURAL LAW. S. WADDAMS AND J. BRIERLEY

Law, Andrew Bonar, statesman, prime minister of Great Britain (b at Kingston, NB 16 Sept 1858; d at London, Eng 30 Oct 1923). The only colonial to become PM of Great Britain, Law grew up in simple surroundings, until at 12 he was sent to live with affluent relatives in Scotland. At 16 he joined the family banking firm and became a prominent iron merchant. He entered Parliament as a Conservative in 1900. Champion of the IMPERIAL PREFERENCE and an opponent of Irish Home Rule and socialism, Law was wartime chancellor of the exchequer. In Oct 1922 he became PM but served only 209 days before retiring because of poor health. He was a close friend of Max AITKEN.

DUNCAN MCDOWALL

Law and Society One of the most historic ideas about the LAW is that it is based on human nature or reason, and therefore simply reflects what is natural or reasonable, enabling society to function in a just and effective manner. According to this conception, the law is also an expression of both the common good and the fundamental values of society. It is the same for everyone and protects everyone's interests. Lawmakers take into account the collective will and formulate the best laws possible. The common good, however, must be defined by certain criteria and interests and does not always correspond to the interests of everyone; it is first and foremost the "good" as seen and defined by certain groups. The law is not above or outside of society; it is the reflection of society at a given moment in its evolution, the result of the balance of power between social groups and one of a number of instruments or means used to impose ideas and defend interests. The law can sometimes be an instrument of discrimination or repression and sometimes an instrument of protection. Everything depends on the power or alliances a group has when legislation is prepared, passed by Parliament and implemented. In addition, there is a difference between what is stated or claimed about law and legislation, and what actually happens.

The profound changes society has undergone since the early 20th century have occurred at an increasingly faster pace since WWII. The law has been and still is the major means by which we attempt to cope with these changes, and as a result legislation and government regulations have proliferated. Canadians can now be liable for some 350 Criminal Code offences, about 20 000 federal and 20 000 provincial offences and all those created by municipal regulations. In Québec, for example, almost as many new offences or penalties were created between 1965 and 1975 as were created during the entire preceding century. After WWI, the federal government took its first major initiatives in health and welfare by creating the Department of Health (1919). Attempts to define precisely the limits of what is healthy and unhealthy, acceptable or not acceptable, normal or pathological have led to increased legislative intervention. The developments in science and technology have also created new problems, eg, those associated with genetic research and pollution, which the law must attempt to resolve. In 1917 individual and corporate income taxes were introduced to fund the expanding public sector, guaranteeing the bureaucracy the means it needed to grow. According to the LAW REFORM COMMISSION OF CANADA (LRCC), federally the activities of the WELFARE STATE grew considerably after WWII. The FAMILY ALLOWANCE Plan (1944), OLD AGE PENSIONS (1952) and the CANADA PENSION PLAN (1965) were added to veterans' assistance programs and UNEMPLOYMENT benefits. The expansion of related legislation has been enormous.

Law as an Instrument of Discrimination The law has the effect of making official, repeating and giving concrete expression to social and economic inequalities. For example, for many years the law expressly deprived women of civil, political and economic rights. It was only toward the end of the 19th century that a woman could consider her salary her own property and not that of her husband, and not until the 1950s did most provincial legislatures recognize that women had the right to the same salary as men. For a long time women were barred from certain professions; eg, in Québec women were not allowed to practise law until 1942. Women could not vote in federal elections until 1918 (and in Québec provincial elections, until 1940). Only after WWII did most provinces allow women to serve on juries, Québec being the last province to give them this right, doing so in 1971.

Indians, Inuit and other groups have also been victims of legal discrimination (*see* NATIVE PEOPLE, LAW). When the CHINESE came to BC to construct the railway in the 19th century, the province withdrew their right to vote, enforced restrictive hiring practices and limited their business opportunities and right to own land. The law also discriminates against those who have been arrested and sentenced or imprisoned for a criminal offence. Many provincial or federal laws deprive them of the right to vote or to run for and hold public office; they also authorize the refusal or revocation of permits or licences and of the right to exercise certain professions.

It is probably in the application of law that inequalities of power and the manner in which law can be a de facto instrument of discrimination are more evident. Until recently, the poor, unable to afford lawyers, had little access to the law. It was only in 1967 that the Ontario government established the first provincially financed LEGAL AID service. In Québec there was no such service until 1973. Only since 1972 has the federal Department of Justice contributed to legal-aid expenditures in criminal matters, though all provinces and territories now provide legal assistance to anyone who might be sentenced to prison or might lose his livelihood, and all jurisdictions, excepting NB, also provide some assistance in civil issues. As late as 1974, however, observers were claiming that divorce was the prerogative of the rich, while the poor, unable to afford such a luxury, simply abandoned their families and lived common law, with all the legal problems such a situation entailed. In testimony before a special Senate committee on POVERTY (1971), the chairman of the Clinical Law Program at the Faculty of Law at Osgoode Hall stated that a study of the Family Allowances Act and other post-WWII legislation preceding it would reveal that these Acts have not been the subject of litigation until recently, that the poor, whose material life is regulated by financiers and whose life is conditioned by many difficulties, have never had the chance to have their rights interpreted or to make these same rights the subject of litigation.

Given the behaviour for which they are condemned, the criminal-law system most often and most severely affects the deprived, blacks, native peoples and disadvantaged groups. In a study conducted some time ago the LRCC found that the prison population contained a disproportionately large number of poor or disadvantaged persons and native delinquents. In 1976, men with 10 years of schooling or less comprised 45% of Canada's male population 15 years of age and over, but 77% of those admitted to penitentiaries. Many economically disadvantaged people go to prison simply because they have not paid fines. In 1974, the LRCC found that the practice of imprisoning for default of payment had for a number of years been the reason for about 50% of admissions to provincial and local detention centres in certain parts of Canada. In some provinces, native people are particularly affected by this sentencing.

Law as an Instrument of Protection The law can also be an instrument of protection and advancement. In Canada, these advances have been fairly recent, and possible largely because of the socioeconomic situation and changes at political and economic levels. Only in the last 30 years have antidiscrimination provisions appeared in legislation, and not until 1947 did a province (Saskatchewan) pass the first Act dealing with human rights. In 1960, Parliament adopted the Canadian Bill of Rights. All provinces have now adopted antidiscrimination legislation and established human rights commissions. The Constitution (1982) now contains an entrenched CANADIAN CHARTER OF RIGHTS AND FREEDOMS which applies to federal and provincial jurisdictions. Other Acts have been passed as well to protect the interests of some traditionally disadvantaged groups. In the 1970s legislation regarding health and safety at work (*see* SAFETY STANDARDS) was revised in most provinces to give workers more protection, and consumers successfully lobbied for laws to protect their interests. Elsewhere in Canada, legislation governing relations between LANDLORDS AND TENANTS was adopted, as was the Small Loans Act, which protects small borrowers, particularly the poor, from excessive interest rates, deceptive methods regarding credit costs and loan sharking.

However, the rights and interests of the disadvantaged are not automatically protected simply because new legislation has been passed. The first antidiscrimination laws were not very effective, because their enforcement depended largely on the initiative of the victims themselves. There was no way to publicize the laws or educate the public; therefore most people did not know the legislation existed. The creation of human-rights commissions to administer this legislation was a major step forward. Unfortunately, although in principle legislation can protect the rights and interests of the powerless, a very large percentage of this group cannot afford to take advantage of it. The Canadian Charter of Rights and Freedoms guarantees that any person arrested or detained is immediately entitled to the services of a lawyer, but no practical procedures have been established for this purpose. Although social legislation passed to reduce inequalities or their effects has undoubtedly helped the most disadvantaged Canadians, it is generally very difficult for them to have it changed, passed, challenged or even adequately enforced. Legislation in fields such as social assistance, the MINIMUM WAGE, social and health services and family allowances often leaves users at the mercy of impersonal decisions made within government BUREAUCRACIES. OMBUDSMEN, whose job it is to ensure that citizens' rights are not violated through injustice, error or negligence arising from administrative action, and whose positions have been created by legislation in several provinces, have helped to improve this situation. Another useful mechanism is the SMALL CLAIMS COURT, established in a number of provinces in the 1970s. According to the Québec minister of justice, the purpose of these courts is to make justice accessible to citizens, strip it of its formal nature, procure a means of reconciliation that will provide social order, guarantee the coercive force of the law and ensure that justice is inexpensively and promptly meted out.

Conclusion Legislation and its enforcement, even if designed to protect the interests of the most disadvantaged groups, are always subject to shifts in the power relationships of a society at a given time. Thus legislation may be stripped of its content or rendered inoperative by subsequent legislative changes. Sometimes political decisions, or lack of them, will virtually paralyse enforcement mechanisms. This will happen, for example, if a chairman or members of a commission are not appointed, or if their budget is not adequate to enable them to operate effectively.

D. LABERGE AND P. LANDREVILLE

Law and the Press Operating in a libertarian climate, the Canadian media are mainly unhampered by licensing and little affected by prior CENSORSHIP. Instead, they are governed by laws dealing with contempt of court, civil defamation, criminal libel, OBSCENITY, COPYRIGHT, privacy and government secrecy. Journalists are more likely to commit constructive contempt than contempt "in the face of the court," except when court rules restricting photographing of trials are violated or when reporters appearing as witnesses refuse to disclose sources. Media reports may scandalize the courts or prejudice a fair trial. For a reporter to publish false "facts" about a case, to report evidence ruled inadmissible in a *voir dire* hearing, or to comment on *sub judice* matters invites legal penalties.

Section 470 of the Criminal Code forbids published mention of confessions considered at preliminary inquiries; s467, at the request of the defendant, empowers the court to forbid the publication of any evidence given at a preliminary inquiry. On 20 June 1985 s467(1) was repealed and the following substituted: "Prior to the commencement of the taking of the evidence at a preliminary inquiry, the justice holding the inquiry (a) may, if the application therefor is made by the prosecutor, and (b) shall, if application therefor is made by any of the accused, make an order directing that the evidence taken at the inquiry shall not be published in any newspaper or broadcast before such time as, in respect of each of the accused, (c) he is discharged, or (d) if he is ordered to stand trial, the trial is ended. (This suggests that whereas defence requests are automatically acceded to, the prosecution must show cause, if its request for a publication ban is to be acceded to.) Other sources of legal danger to journalists include reporting the amount of damages asked by plaintiffs during examination for discovery; publishing amounts of bail as determined in bail-bond hearings; publishing court documents not entered in evidence in open court; imputing improper motives to judges. In many cases the likelihood of legal punishment is determined by when the offence is committed in relation to the trial proper. Canadian journalists may be compelled to divulge sources of their news stories by courts, parliamentary bodies or properly constituted committees of inquiry. By contrast, no law forbids publication of the names of adults charged with crimes, as the law does in several European countries.

In Canada civil DEFAMATION law is more often resorted to than criminal libel. Civil defamation is based on provincial statutes and common law. In most jurisdictions broadcast defamation, though oral, is libel rather than slander. To maintain a libel action 3 conditions must be proved: defamation (the words complained of are capable of a defamatory meaning), publication and identification (of the claimed libelee). Defendants may plead truth, fair comment or privilege, or consent to defend themselves against defamation claims. Proved truth is an absolute defence in Canada's 9 common-law provinces but not in Québec, where public benefit must also be proved. Journalists are able to enjoy only qualified privilege (privilege which malice destroys) except in fair, accurate and contemporaneous reporting of trials. Defendant journalists may avoid paying general (but not special) damages by making apologies and retractions, provided the libelous statement does not impute a criminal conviction or criminal offence, is not actuated by malice or caused by undue carelessness on the journalists' parts. Apologies and retractions must fulfil statutory requirements of prominence and timing.

Defamatory, seditious, blasphemous and obscene libel are all forms of criminal libel covered by the Criminal Code. Truth, fair comment and privilege provide defences against criminal libel charges as they do with civil libel claims, but, as with Québec civil law, public benefit must be proved if the truth plea is to succeed. Incitement to the use of force to bring about a change in government may be punished as seditious libel. However, qualifying stipulations in the Criminal Code are designed to permit political debate, discussion and argument without the incurring of criminal sanctions. In certain sensitive areas the OFFICIAL SECRETS ACT inhibits the media in their investigative role.

The Criminal Code defines blasphemous libel only as intention to commit blasphemy, which it does not define. The code provides that the blasphemy law shall not be construed so as to prevent religious discussion conducted in good faith and in temperate language. Section 159(8) of the Criminal Code says that "Any publication a dominant characteristic of which is the undue exploitation of sex, or of sex, and one or more of the following subjects, namely crime, horror, cruelty and violence, shall be deemed to be obscene."

Journalists cannot copyright the news but they can copyright the language of news reports. For signatories of the Berne Convention, except in the case of serial stories and tales, articles from one newspaper may be copied by another unless such borrowing has been specifically forbidden, but the borrower must indicate the source of those articles.

Privacy does not enjoy complete statutory protection in Canada. Section 178 of the Criminal Code deals almost exclusively with electronic surveillance. Passed in June 1977, in conjunction with the Canadian Human Rights Act but now joined with the ACCESS TO INFORMATION ACT, the federal Privacy Act relates primarily to private information in government files and does not deal with the invasion of personal privacy by private persons. BC, Manitoba, Saskatchewan and Newfoundland have privacy Acts, but they produced no press-related case law. Canada's long-gestating ACCESS TO INFORMATION ACT was passed in June 1982. It was criticized as being a toothless document, by comparison with the American Freedom of Information Act. Critics considered that there were too many exemptions from the government's requirement to disclose information it held. However, the ambit and effectiveness of the new Canadian law will not become clear until the Act is put to fuller use and until a larger body of case law is built up. *See also* HUMAN RIGHTS; JOURNALISM; NEWSPAPERS; POLITICS AND THE MEDIA.

WILFRED H. KESTERTON

Reading: C.F. Beckton, *The Law and the Media in Canada* (1982); Kent Commission Research Studies, *Newspapers and the Law* (1981); Wilfred H. Kesterton, *The Law and the Press in Canada* (1976); S.M. Robertson, *Courts and the Media* (1981).

Law Enforcement refers to the application or threat of legally permitted sanctions to induce compliance with legal rules. Although the enforcement of the LAW may be undertaken by a wide variety of individuals and organizations, law enforcement is often popularly associated with the activities of specialized state agencies, especially the public POLICE forces. Indeed the public police are frequently described as a law-enforcement agency, as if they were the only group engaged in law enforcement and as if the enforcement of laws (especially CRIMINAL LAW) were their primary activity. In fact, the public police are only one of many agencies engaged in law enforcement (*see* POLICING). In addition, research suggests that only about 20% of police work is directly concerned with law enforcement as such.

C.D. SHEARING AND P.C. STENNING

Law of Evidence, the body of regulations governing the proof of the existence of a fact before a court. It falls under federal and provincial legislation. In matters governed by the former, provisions of the Canada Evidence Act must be applied. Common law must also be applied. In criminal law, the rules of evidence are partly unwritten and derive from judgements in English and Canadian JURISPRUDENCE. One of the basic principles of Canadian criminal law, a principle which is now entrenched in the CANADIAN CHARTER OF RIGHTS AND FREEDOMS, is that an accused is presumed innocent until proven guilty beyond reasonable doubt; because no accused person may be forced to testify against himself, the prosecution must supply evidence of the crime. It may be supplied by witnesses, by documentary evidence, by the exhibition of objects or by circumstantial evidence – as long as the rule of relevancy, which determines the admissibility of evidence in criminal cases, is respected and there is no violation of the exclusionary rule. According to this rule, anything that might establish the guilt or innocence of the accused may be admitted as evidence, the most important exception being hearsay. Generally, oral or written statements made outside the court, unless they are made by the accused, are not admissible. As long as it was free and voluntary, any statement by the accused acknowledging commission of the crime may be introduced to establish guilt. Privileged communications between lawyers and clients are also excluded; no lawyers may be obliged to testify concerning matters confided to them in the exercise of their profession. Evidence obtained in a manner that infringed or denied any rights or freedoms guaranteed by the Charter is to be excluded if it is established that its admission would bring the administration of justice into disrepute.

In provincial civil cases the rules of evidence derive from each provincial legislature. The rules governing how evidence is presented are largely the same in all provinces since Québec has adopted the English model, which is based on adversarial procedure, meaning that each party is responsible for proving the facts which it invokes; and in all provinces, witnesses must in principle be heard before an open court where they are first questioned by the lawyer of the party who has called them and then cross-examined by the lawyer of the opposing party. The distinction between the law of evidence in Québec and in the common-law provinces lies in the provisions governing the admissibility of evidence. In the latter, the basic principle is still the rule of relevancy, from which flows the principle of the freedom of means of obtaining evidence. In Québec law, however, evidence concerning contracts must be presented in writing, not orally, although oral testimony may be permitted in a limited number of cases, eg, commercial transactions. Another unique feature of Québec law is called "authentic writing," writing drawn up by a public officer, eg, a notary public. An advantage of an authentic writing is that nobody may prove it false without having first obtained permission from the court to do so and without thereby calling into question the public officer who received it.

In recent years, considerable concern has been expressed regarding the variation of the laws of evidence among provinces and between federal and provincial courts. In 1975 the Law Reform Commission of Canada presented a report to Parliament recommending an evidence code which would replace existing common law. The Ontario Law Reform Commission has also proposed changes in rules of evidence, though its recommendations differ significantly from those of the LRCC. The Uniform Law Conference of Canada, a body composed of commissioners appointed by each provincial government to attend conferences organized for the purpose of promoting uniformity of legislation throughout Canada, responded by recommending a task force to prepare a Uniform Evidence Act which, presented in 1981, was adopted by the conference and proposed as a legislative model for Parliament and the provincial assemblies. Federal and provincial work is being done, but no evidence bills have as yet been passed.

LÉO DUCHARME

Law of the Sea, for about 300 years, was to a large extent determined by principles of customary law. Coastal states claimed sovereignty over a narrow belt of territorial sea; on the rest of the seas (the "high seas"), the basic principle of freedom of the seas reigned. This freedom was interpreted as freedom to navigate, fish, trade, travel, make war, conduct research, etc. In 1967, in response to a perceived need for change in the law of the seas, the UNITED NATIONS began complex and painstaking multilateral negotiations. This ambitious venture consisted of a conference (with several sessions) which spanned 15 years and produced a comprehensive set of laws dealing with the seas known as the United Nations Convention of the Law of the Sea (UNCLOS). Canada signed the Convention in Dec 1982. With the second-longest coastline in the world, Canada has a wide range of interests in the sea and a substantial stake in the proposed new law of the sea. It therefore played a leading role in shaping the convention. In recent years, Canada has focused its attention on issues concerning territorial sea, fisheries, mineral resources, marine environment, passage through international straits and control over the arctic waters. Between 1956 and 1977, Canada moved from claiming the traditional 3-mile territorial seas to claim a 12-mile territorial sea and exclusive jurisdiction over fisheries within 200 miles of its coast and over mineral resources of its continental shelf. Canada accepted the concept of a 200-mile exclusive economic zone (EEZ) that emerged from UNCLOS negotiations. The convention provides that coastal states will have sovereign rights over the exploitation of the resources of the 200-mile EEZ and certain rights in respect of the preservation of the marine environment and the conduct of marine scientific research. Canada was unsuccessful in its attempt to obtain preferential rights to harvest fish stocks beyond 200 miles but was successful in obtaining recognition of its primary interest in the conservation and management of anadromous species, eg, SALMON, throughout the limits of their migratory range.

Canada lent its support to the innovative UNCLOS idea that the international seabed be reserved for peaceful purposes and that the area be designated the "common heritage of mankind." The convention provides for international machinery both to control and to undertake exploitation of the international seabed. Throughout the UNCLOS negotiations, Canada had been particularly concerned about the possible adverse effects of deep-sea mining on Canadian land-based NICKEL production. Canadian mining interests are somewhat protected by a formula in the convention that sets limits to seabed production in relation to land production.

Canada has asserted that the waters of the ARCTIC ARCHIPELAGO, including the NORTHWEST PASSAGE, constitute internal waters. As a manifestation of this claim, in 1970 Canada passed the Arctic Waters' Pollution Prevention Act. The Act gave the Canadian government rights over a 100-mile POLLUTION control zone around the arctic islands. Despite protests by the US, Canada has persevered in its claim over the arctic waters; during UNCLOS negotiations Canada was actively involved in a campaign to obtain coastal-state rights to prescribe and enforce pollution control standards. Although the convention recognizes only limited coastal-state environmental powers, it does include the so-called "arctic exception," which permits Canada to take antipollution measures in ice-covered areas. Canada attempted to project further its claim in the Arctic by ensuring that the Northwest Passage does not become subject to the rules that pertain to passages through international straits. Canada has consistently asserted that the Passage is not a strait and therefore that the right of "transit passage," ie, a right to navigate through the Passage freely, cannot be claimed. In 1985, responding directly to the voyage of the US icebreaker *Polar Sea,* which traversed the Northwest Passage, Canada announced its decision to exercise full sovereignty in and over the waters of the Arctic Archipelago.

Canada's offshore claims have overlapped with those of 3 different countries at 6 points: with Denmark over the area between Greenland and the Canadian Arctic; with France over the area between Newfoundland and the islands of Saint-Pierre and Miquelon; with the US over the Strait of Juan de Fuca, the Dixon Entrance, the Beaufort Sea and the Gulf of Maine. The Gulf of Maine boundary dispute which centered on competing claims to the resources-rich area known as Georges Bank was submitted to a special Chamber of the International Court of Justice. In 1984 the Chamber arrived at an "equitable solution" and determined a single maritime boundary between Canada and the US in a large portion of the Gulf of Maine area.

When the Convention of the Law of the Sea is signed and ratified by the required number of states and comes into effect, it will be binding only upon those states that have signed it. However, many of its provisions, through the practice of states over a period of time, may become customary INTERNATIONAL LAW.

EMILY F. CARASCO

Law Reform is the process of improving, modernizing or clarifying the law on a particular subject, not mere technical change, but a fundamental recasting. Law is "reformed" when it is organized more rationally, expressed more clearly and works more effectively. The 2 principal sources of law are legislation and case law, but it is through the former that most law reform has been achieved. In the 19th century, Jeremy Bentham (1748-1832) argued that legislation as a rational form of law was preferable to a bulky mass of unprincipled case decisions, and when the civil law of France was reformed in 1804, statutory codes were enacted to introduce consistent and uniform rules. However, judicial decisions are important, particularly concerning constitutional documents. The power of ultimate interpretation of the Canadian CONSTITUTION, including the CHARTER OF RIGHTS AND FREEDOMS, rests with the courts; judicial interpretations may materially alter the content and enforcement of criminal law and the general rights and freedoms of individuals. Law reform by legislation is a public and political process. A proposal must be included in a government's legislative program and must therefore be politically acceptable. It may originally be suggested by a private group, eg, a consumers' association or the chiefs of police. Or it may be based on a study by a government department or on a report by a legislative committee or a royal commission. In addition, professional associations such as provincial law societies, the CANADIAN BAR ASSOCIATION and academic lawyers also present law-reform proposals.

Law-reform commissions, usually independent bodies established by statute that report to the minister of justice or to the legislature, are relatively new organizations with a general responsibility to suggest reforms. A commission comprises a small number of distinguished judges, lawyers or academics, assisted by a research staff. The Law Reform Commission of Ontario was established in 1964. Most of the provinces have since created similar bodies. In Alberta it is the Institute of Law Research and Reform, which is associated with U of A. Besides preparing reports recommending reforms, the institute also conducts general legal research. The work of the provincial commissions is restricted to matters which fall within provincial jurisdiction. These include court administration, property law, the law of injury compensation and some aspects of family, commercial and administrative law.

The Law Reform Commission of Canada (LRCC) was established by statute in 1971. It reports to Parliament through the federal minister of justice and is responsible for working towards the modernization and improvement of federal law and the development of new concepts and approaches. It is particularly concerned that the methods of both the common-law and the civil-law traditions be reflected in national laws. It recognizes that the law-reform process requires more than statutory revisions and is of concern to all citizens. It has inquired philosophically into the values law should uphold and has relied on social-science research techniques and public consultation. Much of the LRCC's work has been educational. It recognizes that much genuine reform can be achieved through changes in administrative practices and attitudes, but it is also strongly committed to the need for statutory changes, has produced many studies and reports in the areas of family law, evidence law, criminal law, criminal procedure, administrative law and the protection of life and has recommended new legislation. The LRCC emphasizes the need to simplify the language of the law and in 1985 it established a pilot project on Plain Language. This study focuses on government forms, and it is designed to make these more intelligible to the ordinary citizen through the elimination of "gobbledegook." Provincial law-reform commissions have concentrated on preparing recommendations for statutory changes and have had considerable success in having proposals adopted and enacted by their legislatures. By 1986, 12 of 28 final reports of the LRCC had been partly enacted by Parliament and various other publications by the federal commission had produced legislative initiatives. The slower pace of federal implementation reflects the political and controversial character of much of the LRCC's work. It is, for example, difficult to satisfy all concerns and interests in fields such as criminal law or police powers. The slower pace also reflects differences in the federal commission's approach: it has chosen first to consider and clarify basic principles before proceeding to detailed recommendations. However, following this initial, much-needed period of reflection, the LRCC is now completing a comprehensive new Code of Criminal Law and Criminal Procedure.

J. BARNES

Law Reform Commission of Canada began operation in 1971 as a permanent body to study and make a systematic review of Canadian LAW. The LRCC recommends improvement, modernization and reform of some federal laws and deletion of others, as well as providing a philosophical inquiry into legal issues. As of 1986, 12 of its final reports had been enacted by Parliament and its other publications have produced legislative initiatives as well (*see* LAW REFORM). The LRCC's work also influences the legal community and provincial commissions, exercising an indirect effect on administrative and legislative reform. The courts refer to positions adopted by the LRCC frequently when making judgements.

Lawn Bowling, or "bowls," is a game played on a flat lawn or green at least 36.6 m^2. In a match, the object is to roll bowls, or "woods," so that as many as possible are nearer to the "jack" (a smaller white bowl) than the nearest opposing wood. Bowling can be traced back to ancient Egypt. The game spread to Greece and Rome and thence through medieval Europe to Britain, where it has been played since the 13th century. Scotland, where a code of rules was formulated in 1848, is considered the home of the modern sport.

Lawn bowling was brought to Canada by British garrison officers; the first bowling green in Canada was constructed on the garrison grounds at Annapolis Royal, NS. By 1888, a tournament was staged in Toronto, involving 7 clubs. The game's popularity grew during the latter part of the 19th century. The Dominion Lawn Bowling Tournament was inaugurated in 1892. The game flourished from the turn of the century into the 1930s. In 1901, the "points playing" system was introduced and electric lights were first used for late-evening play. The first Canadian touring team travelled to Britain in 1904, and 2 years later a British team toured Canada. The 1913 Canadian team to Britain was the most successful of such groups; it won 17 matches, lost 13 and tied one.

National organizations have been formed to promote the game. The Dominion Lawn Bowling Assn (later the Canadian Lawn Bowling Council) was founded in 1924; its first national championships were held in 1954. Until 1971, women lawn bowlers were associated with clubs affiliated with the CLBC, but in that year the Canadian Ladies' Lawn Bowling Council was organized, and since 1972 men's and women's national championships have been held jointly. Canadian men bowlers have participated in the British Empire and Commonwealth Games since 1930, winning silver medals in 1930, 1934 and 1954. Men's teams have also entered the world bowls championships since their inception in 1966. In 1980, after a long period of low rankings, the Canadian pairs team won the silver medal at the world championships. Women's teams have entered the women's world bowls championship since 1969, their best showing being a silver medal in the singles event, won by June Bell in 1977. Canada hosted the 1981 women's world bowls in Willowdale, Ont, and in 1982, the women's team entered the first women's Commonwealth Games event. In the 1986 Commonwealth Games, the Canadian men's team earned a silver medal in pairs and fours, fourth place in singles and first overall in team standings.

BARBARA SCHRODT

Lawrence, Charles, military officer, governor of NS (b in England *c*1709; d at Halifax 19 Oct 1760). Though he lacked the backing of any influential patron, Lawrence enjoyed a successful career. He entered the army in 1727, serving in the West Indies and in Flanders [Belgium], and joined the 45th regiment at LOUISBOURG (Cape Breton I) as a major 1747. In 1753 he was put in charge of establishing the settlement of German Protestants at LUNENBURG, NS. He was named lt-gov of "Acadia or Nova Scotia" in 1754, and is chiefly remembered as the architect of the deportation of the Acadians from the colony in 1755. Though this event would likely never have taken place without Lawrence's influence, administrative talent and actions, final responsibility for this tragedy must be shared much more widely. Lawrence was promoted governor in 1756 and in 1758 he commanded a brigade in the successful expedition against Louisbourg. His last years as governor were concentrated on settling migrants, principally from New England, in the colony. On his death, this controversial but respected governor was honoured by his associates with the erection of a monument in St Paul's Church, Halifax.

N.E.S. GRIFFITHS

Lawson, George, botanist (b at Logan, Scot 12 Oct 1827; d at Halifax 10 Nov 1895). Lawson studied natural and physical sciences at U of Edinburgh. Assistant secretary and curator for the Botanical Soc of Edinburgh, he also worked in Britain's first biological laboratory. Lawson became professor of chemistry and natural history at Queen's in 1858. He founded the Botanical Soc of Canada in 1860 and published its *Annals* until 1863. That year he became professor of chemistry and mineralogy at Dalhousie. He was secretary of the NS Board of Agriculture 1864-85, secretary of agriculture for NS from 1885 to 1896 and a charter member of the RSC (1882). In 1891 he founded the Botanical Club of Canada under RSC auspices. As Canada's first professional botanist, Lawson greatly influenced the fields of study of amateur Canadian BOTANY, as well as agricultural and science education policy in NS.

SUZANNE ZELLER

Layton, Irving Peter, né Israel Lazarovitch, poet, short-story writer, essayist, professor (b at Tirgu Neamt, Romania 12 Mar 1912). Since the early 1940s, Layton has been recognized in Canada and abroad as a prolific, versatile, revolutionary and controversial poet of the "modern" school. Layton was brought from Romania to Montréal before age one. He took his BSc in agriculture at Macdonald Coll in 1939. He served briefly in the Canadian Army 1942-43 and then did graduate work in political science at McGill. After graduation Layton tutored immigrants, taught at a high school and lectured part time at Sir George Williams U, Montréal, where he later held a full-time position.

Poet Irving Layton, whose work is proof of his theory that poetry must be intense, subtle and dramatic (*courtesy National Archives of Canada/PA-127567/Gail Turnbull*).

Layton was one of a nucleus of young Montréal poets who believed they were effecting a revolution against insipid romanticism and published their poems in *First Statement* (1942-45), a journal edited by John SUTHERLAND. Layton remained on the editorial board of *Northern Review*, the journal that resulted when *First Statement* merged with *Preview* in 1945. In 1952 Layton assisted Louis DUDEK and Raymond SOUSTER in founding Contact Press, a co-operative publishing outlet for Canadian poets.

Of the poets that emerged in Montréal during this period, Layton was the most outspoken and flamboyant. His satire was generally directed against bourgeois dullness, and his famous love poems were erotically explicit. Layton's first collection was *Here and Now* (1945). He went on to publish numerous volumes of poems of unusual range and versatility and a few of prose. These include *Now Is the Place* (1948), *The Black Huntsman* (1951), *Cerberus* (with Louis Dudek and Raymond Souster, 1952), *Love the Conqueror Worm* (1953), *In the Midst of My Fever* (1954), *A Laughter in the Mind* (1958), A RED CARPET FOR THE SUN (1959), which won the Gov Gen's Award, *Balls for a One-Armed Juggler* (1963), *The Laughing Rooster* (1964), *Periods of the Moon* (1967), *The Shattered Plinths* (1968), *Engagements: The Prose of Irving Layton* (1972), *Lovers and Lesser Men* (1973), *The Pole-Vaulter* (1974), *Seventy-Five Greek Poems* (1974), *For My Brother Jesus* (1976), *The Covenant* (1977), *Taking Sides: The Collected Social and Political Writings* (1977), *Droppings from Heaven* (1979), *The Gucci Bag* (1983), *Una Nuova Glaciazione* (1985), *Dance With Desire* (1986) and a collection, *Final Reckoning: Poems 1982-86* (1987). *Fortunate Exile* (1987), his 47th book, contains previously published poems about Jews. Layton has theorized that poetry should be "vital, intense, subtle and dramatic," and his work is ample proof of his description. He has also edited volumes of poems by other Canadians. The first volume of his memoirs, *Waiting for the Messiah*, was published in 1985.

In 1967 Layton received a Canada Council award on which he travelled to Israel, Greece, India and Nepal. He has been poet-in-residence at a number of Canadian universities and was professor of English at York 1969-78. Layton was nominated by Italy and Korea for the Nobel Prize in 1981. Throughout his career, he has excelled as a dramatic reader of his verses, and some performances have been recorded. ELSPETH CAMERON

Le Ber, Pierre, painter (bap at Montréal 11 Aug 1669; d at Pointe-St-Charles, near Montréal 1 Oct 1707). It is not known where Le Ber studied painting, but his family's position and fortune enabled him to found the Hôpital Général of Montréal with François Charon in 1692 and set up his studio in this building. His best-known work is the portrait of Ste Marguerite BOURGEOYS (1700). From 1697 until his death, he worked on decorating the chapel of Ste-Anne at Pointe-St-Charles. Of his many paintings for churches, only the 3 of St Theresa, St Alphonsus Rodriguez and St Charles Borromée are known. The inventory made of Le Ber's studio after his death suggests substantial artistic output since it lists a quantity of art supplies as well as 12 canvases.

NICOLE CLOUTIER

Le Caine, Hugh, physicist, designer of electronic-music instruments, composer (b at Port Arthur [Thunder Bay], Ont 27 May 1914; d at Ottawa 3 July 1977). He was trained as a physicist at Queen's and later at Birmingham U (Eng). From his youth he also maintained an active interest in music and electronic instruments. In 1939 he joined the NATIONAL RESEARCH COUNCIL (NRC) in Ottawa, working in RADAR development and nuclear physics. By 1945 he had begun work in his home studio on the sackbut, an electronic keyboard instrument now recognized to have been the first "synthesizer." The NRC opened a project in 1954, directed by Le Caine, to design new equipment for electronic music. By his retirement in 1974, he had designed 15 new instruments. He carefully considered their musical expressivity, designing them to accommodate the needs of performers, composers and listeners rather than the demands of the technology. He composed a series of studies at the NRC lab, one of which, *Dripsody* (1955), now a classic of electronic music, uses only the sound of the fall of a single drop of water, transformed by tape-speed changes. The first electronic music studio in Canada, the second in N America, was opened at U of T in 1959. Its unique equipment, designed by Le Caine, used innovative methods of sound production, extending the possibilities available to composers, and attracting many from across Canada and abroad. Le Caine published many articles on his work, primarily in technical journals. Recognized internationally for his contribution to the development of electronic music, he was awarded 3 honorary doctorates in Canada. *See also* ELECTROACOUSTIC MUSIC. GAYLE YOUNG

Le Jeune, Paul, Jesuit missionary and superior at Québec, author (b at Vitry-le-François, France July 1591; d at Paris, France 7 Aug 1664). Converted to Catholicism at 16, Le Jeune was named superior of the Jesuits at Québec in 1632. He advocated language study for missionaries and the settling of nomadic tribes on agricultural reserves. In 1634-35 he accompanied Algonquins on a winter hunt. From 1639 to 1649 he served as missionary priest at Sillery, Tadoussac, Trois-Rivières and VILLE-MARIE [Montréal], lobbying for military support against the Iroquois and supporting the Ville-Marie settlement project. His annual report of 1632, published by the Jesuit provincial in Paris, inaugurated the series of JESUIT RELATIONS published until 1673 to attract recruits and encourage financial support for missionary work. Procurator of Canadian missions 1649-62, Le Jeune was author of 15 of the *Relations* and 2 devotional books. CORNELIUS J. JAENEN

Le Loutre, Jean-Louis, priest, missionary (b at Morlaix, France 26 Sept 1709; d at Nantes, France 30 Sept 1772). Some historians regard Le Loutre as a political agent for France, others as the consummate missionary, using every means to keep the French Catholic ACADIANS from British Protestant domination. After studies in Paris at the Séminaire du St-Esprit and ordination at the Séminaire des missions étrangères, Le Loutre travelled to LOUISBOURG in 1737. Appointed to the parish of Annapolis Royal – in British territory – he worked among the MICMACS at the Shubenacadie mission near Truro, NS.

In 1744, after war was declared between England and France, he helped François DuPont Duvivier in his siege of Annapolis Royal. When the British took Louisbourg in 1745, Le Loutre went to Québec City to consult the governor of NEW FRANCE, who delegated him to meet the duc d'Anville's fleet, which was to arrive to recapture Acadia. Le Loutre thus became the link between the French authorities and the colonists. After the failure of d'Anville's fleet, Le Loutre arrived in France on *La Sirène*. In 1749, after 2 attempts that ended in English prisons, Le Loutre returned to Acadia. From his new mission at FORT BEAUSÉJOUR (near Sackville, NB), Le Loutre encouraged the Micmacs to harass the British and urged the Acadians to abandon their lands and take refuge in areas claimed by France. He returned to France in 1752 but came back the following year still determined to oppose the British. After the fall of Beauséjour in 1755, Le Loutre, who knew a price had been put on his head some years earlier, escaped to Québec City. Captured by the British on his way to France, he was imprisoned until 1763. After his release, he worked for the deported Acadians who wished to live in France. GÉRARD FINN

Le Moyne, Jean, writer (b at Montréal 17 Feb 1913). Le Moyne was a founding member in 1934 of *La Relève*, a magazine produced by a group of young French Canadian Catholic intellectuals. He pursued a career in journalism 1941-59 and then went to the NATIONAL FILM BOARD. In 1961 he published a collection of essays, *Convergences*, which appeared in English in 1966 as *Convergence*. For these he won the Gov Gen's Award in 1961 and first prize in the Québec Literary Competition in 1962. In 1968 he received the Molson Prize. In 1969 he moved to the Prime Minister's Office, where he was an assistant and adviser until retiring in 1978. In 1982 he was made an Officer of the Order of Canada and appointed to the Senate.

Le Moyne de Longueuil et de Châteauguay, Charles, soldier, seigneur (b at Dieppe, France 2 Aug 1626; d at Montréal Feb 1685). He came to New France at age 15 and worked for the Jesuits in Huron country. He settled at VILLE-MARIE [Montréal] in 1646, where he took part in numerous defences against the Iroquois. He distinguished himself as a fighter and was invaluable as an interpreter. In 1668 he received letters patent of nobility and in 1672 he was confirmed in his title to the seigneury of Longueuil; the following year he was granted a seigneury at Châteauguay. He was made governor of Montréal in 1683. He was the patriarch of a remarkable family: almost all of his 12 sons had spectacular careers, displaying the bravery, guile and savagery of the coureurs de bois.

Charles Le Moyne de Longueuil (b at Montréal 10 Dec 1656; d there 7 June 1729) is the only native-born Canadian to be made a baron in New France. As the eldest son of Charles Le Moyne, Sr, he inherited his father's honours, and his baronetcy was confirmed in 1700. He was governor of Trois-Rivières, Montréal and interim administrator of New France in 1725.

Jacques Le Moyne de Saint-Hélène (b at Montréal 16 Apr 1659; d at Québec Dec 1690) accompanied de TROYES on his expedition to drive the English from Hudson Bay, proving himself fierce in battle. In 1687 he led the vanguard in DENONVILLE'S expedition against the Seneca. He was a commander of the punitive raid against

Corlaer (Schenectady), New England, in 1689, in which some 60 settlers were massacred. In Oct 1690 Saint-Hélène was injured in the defence of Québec against the attack of English forces under Sir William PHIPS. He died of his wound in Dec.

The most renowned of Charles Le Moyne's sons was Pierre Le Moyne d'IBERVILLE.

Paul Le Moyne de Maricourt (b at Montréal 15 Dec 1663; d there 21 Mar 1704) also accompanied de TROYES and later sailed to James Bay with Iberville, commanding the captured forts in his brother's absence. To him fell much of the family burden, his father's estate and his brother Saint-Hélène's children. He was a regular emissary to the Iroquois and played a major role in the peace settlement of 1701-02.

Joseph Le Moyne de Serigny et de Louie (bap 22 July 1688 at Montréal; d at Rochefort, France 12 Sept 1734) was the 6th son of Charles Le Moyne. In 1694 he commanded the ship *Salamandre* in Iberville's service and he was left in command of the Bay posts in 1697. He sailed to Louisiana to trade in 1701 and lived in France 1702-06. He took part in Iberville's plunder of Nevis in 1706 and a cloud came over his career for his illicit gains. He returned to Louisiana in 1718 and captured the Spanish base of Pensacola. For this action he was promoted to naval captain and received the coveted Croix de Saint-Louis. He took up residence in Rochefort and was made governor of that French port in 1723.

JAMES MARSH

Le Roy, Donald James, physical chemist, science adviser (b at Detroit, Mich 5 Mar 1913; d at Ottawa 1 Nov 1985). After gaining his PhD at U of T (1939), he joined E.W.R. STEACIE at the NATIONAL RESEARCH COUNCIL, where he carried out important research on molecular fragments called free radicals, which determine the course of many chemical reactions. In 1944 he joined U of T's chemistry department, becoming chairman in 1960. Through his efforts, the department developed a worldwide reputation in fundamental chemical research. Sharing Steacie's conviction that Canada must increase its scientific stature to survive, LeRoy returned to the NRC in 1969 as VP (scientific). In that office (1969-74) and as science adviser at the Science Council (1974-84), he strongly influenced the building of Canada's research capabilities. HARRY EMMET GUNNING

Lea, Walter Maxfield, politician, premier of PEI 1930-31 and 1935-36 (b at Tryon, PEI 10 Feb 1874; d at Charlottetown 10 Jan 1936). A successful farmer and livestock breeder, Lea was the first agriculturalist to lead PEI. Elected to the Assembly in 1915 as a Liberal, he became commissioner (minister) of agriculture in 1919. On 30 May 1930 Lea became premier, attending the Dominion-Provincial Conference (1930), but resigned 29 Aug 1931. Illness during the 1935 general election forced him to direct a campaign from his bed, which resulted in the first sweep of seats in a parliamentary democracy. His second term as premier lasted until his death. PETER E. RIDER

Leacock, Stephen, humorist, essayist, teacher, political economist, historian (b at Swanmore, Eng 30 Dec 1869; d at Toronto 28 Mar 1944). The recipient of numerous honorary degrees, awards and distinctions (the Lorne Pierce Medal, the Gov Gen's Award, a postage stamp issued in his honour, the Leacock Medal for Humour established in his honour), Leacock was the English-speaking world's best-known humorist 1915-25.

He grew up on a farm near Lk Simcoe, Ont, and was educated at Upper Canada College (where he taught for 9 years), U of T and U of Chicago, where he studied economics and political science (PhD 1903). He joined McGill's dept of economics and political science in 1903, rose quickly to become department head, and remained there until his retirement in 1936. A prolific magazine supplier of humorous fiction, literary essays and articles on social issues, politics, economics, science and history, Leacock claimed near the end of his life: "I can write up anything now at a hundred yards." Most of his books are collections of these magazine pieces.

Stephen Leacock was the English-speaking world's best-known humorist, as well as an accomplished economist (*courtesy National Archives of Canada/© Karsh, Ottawa/ Miller Comstock*).

His first book, *Elements of Political Science* (1906), a workmanlike treatment of its subject, was his best-selling book in his lifetime. Although he was not an original or particularly incisive political economist, Leacock's professional opinions on matters such as the need for a gold standard have proved prophetic in their commonsense approach to what he considered a jungle of statistics. His writings on the theoretical and technical aspects of humour are similarly refreshing for their accessibility, as are his views on education.

He was politically active in the Conservative Party in both his home riding of Orillia and nationally. In the 1911 general election, his propagandist writings and public addresses on the issue of RECIPROCITY helped defeat Sir Wilfrid LAURIER'S Liberal government. Although Leacock is a man of many seeming contradictions, generally his stance is traditionally conservative. A Tory in the precapitalist sense, he valued the community over the individual, organic growth over radical change, the middle way over extreme deviation. Such values form the basis of Leacock's satiric norm, the authorial position from which he attacked rampant individualism, materialism and worship of technology. Although frequently unfaithful to his credo that humour be kindly – he was at times racist, anti-feminist and downright ornery – the unique alchemy of compassion and caustic wit remain the elements which accord his humour a timelessness few Canadian writers have achieved.

His 2 masterpieces are SUNSHINE SKETCHES OF A LITTLE TOWN (1912) and *Arcadian Adventures with the Idle Rich* (1914). The first humorously anatomizes business, social life, religion, romance and politics in the typical small Canadian town of Mariposa, whose name has attained mythic significance in the Canadian psyche. Perhaps the greatest creation of *Sunshine Sketches* is the narrator himself, who, in his affection for and bemusement at the community of Mariposa that he so admirably represents, reveals the essential Leacock. *Arcadian Adventures* dissects life in an American city with sharper satire, less qualified by the author's affection and pathos. Taken together, these 2 books reveal the imaginative range of Leacock's vision – the nostalgic concern for what is being lost with the passing of human communities and his fear for what may issue. However, Leacock believed that the best humour resides at the highest reaches of literature. Any list of his own best works, both fiction and nonfiction, would have to include the following selection from some 60-odd books: *Nonsense Novels* (1911), *Moonbeams from the Larger Lunacy* (1915), *Further Foolishness* (1916), *Essays and Literary Studies* (1916), *Frenzied Fiction* (1918), *The Unsolved Riddle of Social Justice* (1920), *My Discovery of England* (1922), *The Garden of Folly* (1924), *Winnowed Wisdom* (1926), *Short Circuits* (1928), *Lincoln Frees the Slaves* (1934), *Humor: Its Theory and Technique* (1935), *Humour and Humanity* (1937), *My Discovery of the West* (1937), *Too Much College* (1939), *My Remarkable Uncle* (1942), *Our Heritage of Liberty* (1942), *Happy Stories* (1943), *How to Write* (1943), *Last Leaves* (1945) and his unfinished autobiography, *The Boy I Left Behind Me* (1946).

GERALD LYNCH

Reading: Donald Cameron, *Faces of Leacock* (1967); Robertson Davies, *Stephen Leacock* (1970); D. Staines, *Stephen Leacock: A Reappraisal* (1987).

Lead (Pb), silver-grey metal commonly found with zinc and copper sulphides as the MINERAL galena. Properties such as a low melting point (327.4°C), high density and malleability, corrosion resistance and a good ability to attenuate gamma radiation and sound vibration have led to a wide variety of uses. Lead oxide was used for pottery glazing as early as 7000 to 5000 BC, and lead was one of the earliest smelted metals. It was used for coinage in China and Greece, and about 100 BC the Romans began using it for plumbing and solder. Roofing and ammunition applications developed during the Middle Ages. Lead-acid batteries, which account for the largest use of lead today, were introduced in 1911. Lead is also used as an additive in gasoline and for solders, chemicals and alloys, plumbing and cable sheathing, and as protective sheathing against X rays and nuclear radiation. Lead is easily recycled; scrap accounts for nearly one-third of Canada's supply, and Canada mines about 300 000 t of lead annually, ranking 3rd in the world (after the US and Australia). Leading producers are BC, NWT, NB and YT. Lead ore is mined, crushed and ground, and the lead-containing mineral is separated by flotation to produce a concentrate. At the smelter, concentrate is roasted to drive off the sulphur and then smelted, usually in a blast furnace, to produce impure lead bullion. Refining by electrolytic or pyrometallurgical means purifies the lead and allows recovery of by-products, including silver, antimony and bismuth (*see* METALLURGY). Smelters at TRAIL, BC, and near BATHURST, NB, convert concentrates to refined metal. In 1986 45.6% of this metal as well as the remaining lead and lead alloy scrap, dross, etc, was exported to the US, Europe, Japan and elsewhere. In 1986 the mined lead was worth $204 427 000. Lead is toxic at high levels of exposure and lead poisoning was formerly an occupational hazard. Its present use, eg, in paints, is regulated and the lead content of gasoline has gradually been reduced. The "lead" of lead pencils is not lead but a mixture of graphite and clay. *See also* POLLUTION.

J. BIGAUSKAS

Leader of the Opposition, usually the leader of the political party with the second-largest number of seats in the HOUSE OF COMMONS. (If the party leader, usually elected at a national LEADERSHIP CONVENTION, does not have a seat, the party HOUSE LEADER temporarily substitutes for the leader.) The leader of the Opposition was first recognized by statute in 1905 and given the same salary and allowances as CABINET ministers. The leader of the Opposition is a parliamentarian hoping to become PRIME MINISTER and is the leading critic of government programs and policies. He directs the party in PARLIAMENT and appoints leading members of the caucus as "shadow ministers" to monitor the work of the ministries. He is usually consulted by the prime minister on the appointment of the SPEAKER and sometimes on the appointment of the GOVERNOR GENERAL. If the government is defeated in the Commons, the leader of the Opposition may be asked to form a government if the prime minister chooses to resign rather than to request a dissolution. Provincial legislatures have leaders of the Opposition with similar responsibilities. STORNOWAY is the official residence of the federal leader of the Opposition. JOHN SAYWELL

Leadership Convention, meeting of party members to select a parliamentary leader. Of the countries deriving their parliamentary system from the Westminster model, Canada alone has adopted and modified the American national party convention as the means for choosing its party leaders. For more than 50 years after CONFEDERATION the parliamentary parties (caucuses) chose their leaders from among their own members – senators and MPs – but in 1919 that system came to an end when Sir Wilfrid LAURIER called a national party convention to discuss policy and organization. Between the time the call went out to the 1135 delegates and the time they assembled some months later in Ottawa, Laurier died. The party executive seized the opportunity to convert the meeting into a forum for selecting the new leader.

The convention came at an ideal time for the Liberals. The 1917 "Conscription Election" had split the party, and its forces in Parliament were small and drawn overwhelmingly from Québec. A truly "national" convention presented the party with the opportunity to widen considerably the number of participants in its leadership-selection process. It was decided that an equal number of delegates was to be sent by each federal constituency association. At the same time the party executive accepted as a second principle the notion that a clear majority of delegates should come from the constituencies – the minority being made up of party officials, MPs, senators and provincial legislators.

Both principles have been applied by the LIBERAL PARTY and the Progressive CONSERVATIVE PARTY (though not the CO-OPERATIVE COMMONWEALTH FEDERATION, now the NEW DEMOCRATIC PARTY, which has based its constituency representation on the size of party membership lists at the local level) in every national leadership convention since 1919. They have lent support to the common claim of Canadian politicians that leadership conventions are more democratic and representative than any alternative method of choosing party leaders. That the delegates (usually between 2000 and 3500 in number) vote secretly and individually, that no additional names may be placed in nomination once the voting has begun, and that the candidate with the fewest votes is dropped after each ballot until one candidate has won a clear majority of the votes – all of these rules stand in marked contrast to those of an American convention and contribute to the rhetoric about the uniqueness of Canadian leadership conventions.

While leadership conventions have compensated to some degree for the regional imbalances of the parliamentary parties, they have at the same time effectively ended the caucus's monopoly over the selection of a party leader, with a curious result. "Outsiders" (those with little or no prior parliamentary experience) stand a greater chance of being chosen party leader than those who have devoted many years to a parliamentary career and who, in many cases, have served for a long period of time on the Government or Opposition frontbenches. The first 5 leaders of the Liberal Party chosen by national leadership conventions, W.L. Mackenzie KING (1919), Louis ST. LAURENT (1948), Lester B. PEARSON (1958), Pierre Elliott TRUDEAU (1968) and John TURNER (1984), fall into this category. For its part, the Conservative Party has selected 3 provincial premiers as national leaders. Not one had stood for election to Parliament before his selection: John BRACKEN (1942), George DREW (1948) and Robert L. STANFIELD (1967). After only 3 and one-half years in Parliament, Joe CLARK defeated 10 other candidates (some of whom had had lengthy political careers) to become, at the age of 36, Canada's youngest national party leader. Clark was succeeded as Conservative leader in 1983 by Brian MULRONEY, a man who had never previously been nominated for or elected to public office at any level of government. Of the Conservative leaders chosen by convention, only R.B. BENNETT (1927) and John G. DIEFENBAKER (1956) had had extensive prior parliamentary experience.

While the leadership convention itself is open and democratic, the real key to a successful candidacy is organization at the local or constituency level. Recently, candidates have focused upon the election of supporters at meetings to select a riding's delegates rather than appealing for a national consensus of impartial delegates. These constituency elections, while normally being an efficient gauge of local party support, have been marred by accusations of "dirty tricks" and last-minute registration of "one-day" party members and have tended to create antagonistic actions within the political party, both at the federal and provincial level. This image of "brokerage" politics at the local level has caused parties to consider new methods of leadership selection. The Parti Québécois, in fact, has adopted one of these methods. At its leadership convention in 1985, following the resignation of René Lévesque, all party members were allowed to vote for the new leader in a one-day convention that featured a central convention site and 6 regional sites hooked via computer and closed circuit to the central convention. It is expected that other parties will soon opt for some form of universal suffrage in selecting their leaders.

Canadian leadership conventions are not held at regular, stated intervals. Thirty years passed between the first and second Liberal leadership conventions – an unrivalled hiatus that would no longer be tolerated by the press, public and politicians. Leadership conventions are now typically called every 8 to 10 years when, for example, the leader no longer feels equal to the task (St. Laurent and Drew); when he is convinced there is little likelihood of the party gaining office under his leadership (Bracken and Stanfield); or when, as prime minister, he is satisfied that the time has arrived for handing over the reins of power (King, Pearson and Trudeau).

Another reason for calling a leadership convention has so far been peculiar to the Conservative Party. It stems from the party's internecine battles from the mid-1960s to the early 1980s over its leadership. By his party's approval of a motion to hold a leadership convention within a year, John Diefenbaker, who was unwilling to step down, was forced to choose between retiring from the position or seeking re-election in a convention open to other contenders. He chose the latter and was defeated. At the Conservatives' biennial meeting early in 1983, when Joe Clark was party leader, 66% of the delegates voted against holding a leadership convention (as they were entitled to do under the leadership review provisions of the party's constitution). Despite the support, Clark interpreted the vote as insufficient endorsement of his leadership and he resigned his office, announcing he would be a candidate at the next convention. At that convention (held June 1983) there were 8 leadership candidates. Although Clark led on the first 3 ballots, he was overtaken on the fourth by Brian Mulroney, who won by a vote of 1585 to 1323. The candidate with the least parliamentary experience defeated the former leader, who, among all the candidates, enjoyed the greatest support of his parliamentary colleagues.

It seems that convention delegates look for qualities other than parliamentary and Cabinet experience when choosing their party's leader. Success in previous provincial elections, reputations earned in administrative, industrial and extra-political spheres, and potential electoral attractiveness count for more than lengthy service in Parliament. It is debatable whether the openness and freedom inherent in the leadership-convention system, with its challenge to established career patterns and recruitment practices, is necessarily beneficial to the larger political system.

JOHN C. COURTNEY

Reading: John C. Courtney, *The Selection of National Party Leaders in Canada* (1973).

Leaf Rapids, Man, Town, pop 1950 (1986c), 2265 (1981c), inc 1974, a mining community located 3 km S of the Churchill R on the Canadian Shield and 976 km NW of Winnipeg. Leaf Rapids was established in 1970 when Sherritt Gordon Mines Ltd decided to open a copper mine at its Ruttan Lake property 25 km E of the townsite. Development of the town differed from past practice in that it was designed and built by a provincial CROWN CORPORATION instead of the mining company. The townsite is also distinctive because its central complex contains stores, schools, offices, arena, curling rink, hospital and other services all under one roof. The Leaf Rapids Winter Carnival held every March features "northern" events that include sled dog and snowmobile races, bannock baking and tea boiling.

JOHN SELWOOD

League for Social Reconstruction, organization of left-wing intellectuals, fd 1931-32 in Montréal and Toronto, largely in response to the GREAT DEPRESSION. Although it soon had almost 20 branches elsewhere in Ontario and the West, the founding branches proved the longest lived and most active in political education. Led by historian Frank UNDERHILL and law professor F.R. SCOTT, the LSR was critical of monopoly capitalism and demanded economic change by parliamentary means. Never formally linked with a political party, it made its sympathies clear with the annual re-election of J.S. WOODSWORTH as its honorary president. The Regina Manifesto (1933) of the CO-OPERATIVE COMMONWEALTH FEDERATION was largely written by LSR members. The league's ideas found fullest expression in the books *Social Planning for Canada* (1935) and *Democracy Needs Socialism* (1938), and in the CANADIAN FORUM, acquired in 1936. Disillusionment with SOCIALISM in the late 1930s weakened the LSR. WWII and the increased organizational demands of the CCF led to the LSR's quiet demise in 1942. Its influence on the CCF was great; its influence on Canada is still a matter for speculation. MICHIEL HORN

Reading: Michiel Horn, *The League for Social Reconstruction* (1980).

League of Canadian Poets, The, was founded in 1966 as a result of a meeting of Toronto and Montréal poets that included Raymond SOUSTER, Earle BIRNEY, John Robert COLOMBO, Louis DUDEK, Ralph GUSTAFSON, Al PURDY, F.R. SCOTT, and others. These senior poets wanted to establish an organization to, in the words of the LCP's constitution, increase "the advancement of poetry in Canada, and the promotion of the interests of poets." The LCP's first annual general meeting (AGM) was held in Toronto in 1968, and chaired by Scott; in succeeding years, these meetings have been held at various locations across Canada. The LCP has 2 categories of membership (figures are to 1986): full (210) and associate (70). Its offices are located in Toronto and it employs a staff of 3. The executive committee consists of the president, 2 vice-presidents, a treasurer, a past president and 8 regional representatives, all of whom are elected annually. Policy is defined by this committee and the AGM, and several standing committees – eg, rights and freedoms, membership, feminist caucus, copyright – tend to ongoing concerns. The LCP gives 3 literary awards annually: The Pat Lowther Memorial Award, The Gerald Lampert Memorial Award, and the F.R. Scott Prize for Translation.

The LCP also runs 2 major touring programs for poets, one nationwide, the other focusing on Poets in the Schools in Ontario. It represents the interests of poets to publishers, all levels of government and the public. As a national, nonprofit organization, it is eligible to receive charitable donations to help with its programs.

ROBERT BILLINGS

League of Nations, international organization established at the Paris Peace Conference (1919) at the end of WWI. It was founded on the principles of collective security and preservation of peace through arbitration of international disputes. American Pres Woodrow Wilson had taken an important part in founding the league, but the US never joined. Sixty-three states were eventually members. With headquarters in Geneva, Switz, it lasted until the founding of its successor, the UNITED NATIONS, in 1945. Canada was a member throughout the league's existence, and served 1927-30 on the council.

The Covenant (the treaty provisions creating the league) established a council, assembly and secretariat. The council met quarterly and comprised the major powers as permanent members, plus non-permanent members elected by the assembly. The assembly consisted of representatives of all member states, and met annually. Under a secretary-general, the secretariat provided the permanent staff. A Canadian, Sir Herbert AMES, was financial director 1919-26, a high administrative position in the secretariat. The league provided opportunities for international discussion of political and legal questions, disarmament, economic relations, the protection of minorities, communications and transit, and health and social questions. Members were required by Article 10 of the Covenant to respect and preserve each other's territory and independence. Aggression against any member would be considered aggression against all, and would lead to collective economic, and possibly military, measures. The purpose of collective security was to avert war, and in the 1920s the league participated in the attempted reconciliation of Germany with France and Great Britain. However, it proved incapable of effective action in the face of territorial aggression in the 1930s by Italy, Germany and Japan. The league ceased to function as a collective-security organization, although its social and economic activities continued until WWII.

From 1920 to 1923 the Canadian government actively but unsuccessfully sought removal of the collective-security guarantees, fearing involvement in European wars. More positively, in 1929, Raoul Dandurand, Canadian representative on the council, successfully proposed strengthening league procedures in overseeing the treatment of linguistic and religious minorities in E Europe. In 1935, when Canada supported the league's sanctions against Italy, Canadian delegate Walter A. RIDDELL proposed stopping all exports of oil, coal and steel to Italy. This action, unauthorized by the new Mackenzie King government, was publicly repudiated. Subsequently, Canada kept a low profile at league meetings.

The League of Nations, even though ultimately unsuccessful in achieving collective security, established a new pattern of international organizational activity. League membership brought Canada its first official contact with foreign governments, helped establish its position as a sovereign state and confronted it with both the opportunities and the dilemmas associated with problems of international co-operation and attempts to prevent war. RICHARD VEATCH

League of Nations Society in Canada, fd 1921 to promote international peace by developing public knowledge of and support for the LEAGUE OF NATIONS. With headquarters in Ottawa, it operated until 1942. Its presidents included such public figures as Sir Robert BORDEN, Sir George FOSTER and Ernest LAPOINTE; John W. DAFOE, Newton W. ROWELL and J.S. WOODSWORTH served on its national council. The society's activities were primarily promotional and educational. It distributed league publications and its own monthly, *Interdependence*, and sponsored speaking tours and radio broadcasts by supporters. It was the first Canadian organization to encourage public interest in and understanding of international affairs.

RICHARD VEATCH

Leamington, Ont, Town, pop 12 828 (1986c), 12 528 (1981c), inc 1890, located on the N shore of Lk Erie, 54 km SE of WINDSOR. Named after a town in Warwickshire, Eng, it developed in the 19th century as a lake port and market-gardening centre. Tobacco growing was a major industry in the surrounding area, along with canning and food processing. Today it is the site of a large H.J. Heinz Co food-processing plant. It is also the gateway to POINT PELÉE NATIONAL PARK. DANIEL FRANCIS

Learned Societies, a term applied in Canada to the large group of scholarly organizations that hold conferences annually from late May to mid-June at a different university location each year. Society members come not only to hear and discuss scholarly papers on the latest work in their fields, but also to renew contacts and share common concerns.

The gathering of these associations in one place over one period is distinctively Canadian and owes more to practical evolution than to planning power. Selecting one site with suitable university accommodation was an answer to Canadian distance that allowed scholars more economical joint arrangements, let them attend meetings of societies besides their own, and encouraged them to visit varied geographical areas. The older ROYAL SOCIETY opened the way by moving from its Ottawa base to annual conferences at Montréal, Kingston or Toronto. Younger, more specialized associations – such as those in history, political science and economics – joined in, holding their own meetings along with, or just following, the senior scholarly society. By the 1930s the practice of holding an annual learned-conference period at a different site each year was well established, though such sites were usually in central Canada, where most larger universities were located. But in 1949 "the Learneds" went to Halifax, and soon afterwards to Winnipeg, Edmonton and Vancouver. Since then the growth of large universities across the country and the multiplication of learned societies – from the Assn of Canadian Archivists to the Canadian Linguistic Assn, the Canadian Institute of International Affairs to the Assn for Canadian Theatre History – have provided still more locations and a greater range of meetings for the organizations of Canadian scholarship. J.M.S. CARELESS

Leatherworking in New France began in the 17th century when the first groups of colonists began farming around Québec City and VILLE-MARIE [Montréal]. In the young colony, trades were not governed by the statutes and regulations of French guilds, despite repeated attempts by Intendant Jean TALON to establish such regulation (*see* APPRENTICESHIP IN EARLY CANADA). New France was unlike the mother country, where trades were highly compartmentalized (eg, skinners, tawers, tawers using Hungarian techniques, strap makers, glovers, belt makers, harness makers, cobblers, trunk makers, last makers, heel makers). For example, tanners used methods which, in France, were reserved for other artisans; cobblers and harness makers ventured beyond the tasks originally assigned to them by guild statutes.

Tanning At first, Québec leatherworkers were supplied with skins processed in the royal factories of France and by local private tanners; the first tannery in the colony was established at Pointe-Lévy in 1668. Headed by a master tanner from France, the company quickly achieved success and sparked enthusiasm among other master tanners and merchants, including Johan, Thibierge, Larchevêque, Perthuis, Fornel and Bégon. The Québec government's 68 tanners and merchants obtained their raw materials on contract mainly from butchers, the principal suppliers of sheepskin and cattle hides. Hunting and fishing supplied other types of skins, eg, walrus, seal, moose, deer, bear. Tanning operations were modelled on methods used in France, with local modifications. Tanning mills were driven by wind, water or animal power. Tanners prepared the skins in the traditional manner by washing the leather, soaking or softening it, placing it in a lime pit, and then graining, scraping and trimming it. The tanners of New France prepared their tannin using the bark of hemlock or spruce, rather than oak or chestnut as in France. Most production was of tough leather for the local manufacture of shoes, work boots and harnesses. The tanneries grew and prospered in New France. Despite the owners' high operating costs, the pressing local need for leather goods and the availability of various skins helped the tanneries survive. Originally established and run by master craftsmen from France, tanneries quickly became the preserve of merchants and dealers who could assume the extremely high investment costs.

Between the arrival of British craftsmen after the Conquest, 1759-60, and the end of the 18th century, the art and techniques of the leather trade underwent little change. The 19th century saw developments in tanneries, including innovations in the forms of energy used, technology and work organization, as well as a concentration of capital. During the 1880s, American tanneries broke new ground by abandoning vegetable tannin in favour of the chrome-tanning process. This process reduced the tanning period from 9 months to 5 or 6 weeks, thereby saving time, lowering production costs and even improving product quality. The tanneries of Ontario quickly adopted the new method, but those of Québec did not begin to do so until 1910. This situation may have been a factor in the decline of Québec's tanneries which, until then, had been the leading Canadian producers of leather goods.

In Ontario, the Davis tanneries in the Kingston and Toronto areas exemplify the evolution of this industry. In the mid-19th century, Andrew Davis operated a tannery where craftsmen produced leather goods for local farmers and independent cobblers. Around 1860 he and his son became interested in mechanization. In the next decade, the family installed steam power and began introducing machines. Then, as the shoe industry began to expand in Ontario, the market grew to the point where mass production and the wholesale trade became viable propositions. New machinery helped accelerate production, reduce costs and provide variety in the colour and types of leather of the finished products. At the end of the 19th century, the Davis family experimented successfully with chrome tanning; in the first decade of the 20th century, running water and electricity were installed. Finally, direct access to the CANADIAN NATIONAL RAILWAY resulted in lower transportation costs. The Davis tanneries continued to prosper, entering American and world markets in the 1930s.

The tanning industry originated in Québec but did not develop to its fullest extent in that province. In 1949, Canada had 70 tanneries, 33 in Québec and 28 in Ontario. Québec's tanneries employed 606 workers and supplied 11% of Canada's leather production; Ontario's 3852 workers supplied 86%. Today, Ontario tanneries have production capacities 4 times greater than those of Québec. In 1985 Canada had 40 tanneries, 32 of which were divided equally between Ont and Qué. Of the total number of workers, 2153, Ont had 1512. The stagnation of Québec's tanneries had been seen as one of the factors in the decline of the FOOTWEAR INDUSTRY.

Cobbling and Footwear Production Between 1660 and 1760, 132 craftsmen were employed as cobblers or harness makers in Québec. Of that number, 55 independent craftsmen with their own shops were known as "masters." The rest were employed on a fixed-salary or contract basis in shops or tanneries, some of which had their own cobbler's workshop. The cobblers of New France made French shoes, MOCCASIN-style shoes and boots, mules and slippers; harness makers produced harnesses, backstraps, saddles, hame straps and collars for dogs and horses. Because of the severe climate, cobblers had to adopt styles that would offer their customers warm as well as hardy footwear. They thus adopted native moccasins and high, soft boots. The effectiveness of Indian footwear lay in the cut and assembly of the pieces: the upper and the sole formed a single piece joined on the upper part to a tightly sewn, rounded tongue, thereby preventing water from leaking in through seams underfoot. The moccasin boot was a variation of the shoe, with the addition of a knee-high, sewn upper. A lace held the boot snugly against the leg. Cobblers also made more delicate shoes by imitating the styles of French footwear brought to the colony by boat. After the Conquest, new models of army-style boots and shoes were introduced.

Cobblers remained shop craftsmen or eventually became employees of combined shoemaking and tanning factories because no large cobbling enterprises could compete with the firmly established, government-funded tanneries. Cobblers were subject to the requirements and decisions of tanneries, which were made on the basis of the availability and quality of leathers and contracts with the army. As they changed from being employees to owners of small shops, tanners and merchants were establishing control over leatherworking. This situation developed despite the cobblers' complaints and their appearance before the Conseil souverain to try to eliminate the discriminatory power of tanneries over the free enterprise of independent cobblers.

In the first half of the 19th century, Canada's cobblers preserved the trade practices of their ancestors. However, such craftsmen were progressively replaced by cobbler-merchants, journeymen hired by factories and specialized workers in the large 20th-century footwear factories. From about 1810 to 1860, 2 types of shoe production coexisted in Québec: the traditional system, in which independent craftsmen produced the entire shoe to a client's order; and the system in which cobbler-merchants employed journeymen who each produced different parts of the shoe, thereby increasing production. Cobbler-merchants stocked both imported and locally produced shoes. During this period, workshops began to grow in size; fabrication was divided into a series of distinct tasks; journeymen worked as paid employees in workshops or at home; and a concentration of capital was organized to meet rising production costs. Hence, the introduction of a new approach to LABOUR RELATIONS (eg, the close master-journeyman-apprentice relationship was replaced by a hierarchical labour-management relationship), of piecework and of a shorter apprenticeship period. Journeymen faced competition from untrained, poorly paid workers and were financially unable to open their own workshops.

In the first half of the 19th century, the technological revolution, fed by discovery of new forms of energy and by mechanization, transformed the cobbler's trade. Perfected in 1845, sewing machines were used to sew vamps and "Howe" uppers and thus replaced work previously performed by women working at home. By 1860 the capacity of these machines increased with the introduction of steam power. A few years later, a worker could sew 90 pairs of soles with the McKay "Soles Sewing Machine" in the time it took to sew one by hand. A favourable economy allied with technological progress led to a boom in the footwear industry. Proof of this rapid growth is the fact that Québec City had 9 shoe factories in 1861, 73 by 1871.

With the exception of refinements of mechanization and greater division of labour, the physical organization of factories at the turn of the 20th century remained essentially unchanged. The ground floor of a 3- or 4-storey building would house several departments: the assembly room, where pins or nails would be used to attach the upper to a false sole on a form; the fitting area, where the sole was joined to the upper; the heel-cutting division; and the finishing and shipping department. The second floor housed the administration, management and sales departments; the third floor was reserved for cutting the leather into uppers, for machine assembly of the handcut parts of the upper, and for storage of rolls of fine leather and cutting patterns.

The industrialization of shoe production produced major changes in organization and labour relations and required a concentration of capital and cost-effective production methods. Owners had to instill a team spirit among managers, production heads and foremen in order to have workers produce at full capacity. This hierarchical structure was motivated by profit. Employees worked in difficult conditions: unsanitary workshops, long days and fatigue induced by the need to earn a decent income from piecework. They also had to face the danger of accidents, the lack of job security at a time of chronic unemployment and the loss of qualifications formerly required of members of a traditional trade. This last phenomenon, the result of increasingly specialized duties (150 manufacturing operations existed in 1910), required workers to accept low wages since they could no longer use their qualifications to compete with unskilled workers (particularly women and children).

Traditionally, Québec's leatherworkers were not members of trade guilds established to defend their rights. Trade unions, the offshoots of American unions, gained ground in the 1860s but were not legally recognized until the 1870s. Under the influence of Mgr Louis-Nazaire Begin, the first national Catholic unions appeared in 1901. The arbitration cases and strikes of that era reveal that workers were fighting mainly for the right to union membership, higher salaries and a slowdown in the introduction of machines.

MARÎSE THIVIERGE AND NICOLE THIVIERGE

Leaver, Eric William, inventor, electronics engineer (b at Langham, Eng 11 Aug 1915). Leaver came to Saskatchewan as a child and after graduation from high school established himself in the 1930s as an inventor of automatic landing systems for aircraft. At the end of WWII he formed Electronic Associates Ltd with colleagues from Research Enterprises Ltd, the government's radar factory, and set out to develop robotic machine tools. Leaver's AMCRO system (Automatic Machine Control by Recorded Operation) was patented in 1947 and, for lack of risk capital in Canada, was developed by American licensees. The AMCRO system was resisted by manufacturers of conventional machine tools and never fully developed.

Electronic Associates diversified to produce electronic instruments, such as portable Geiger counters for uranium prospectors, radar altimeters for accurate aerial surveys, and automatic process controls for industry, notably mines and paper mills. The firm was selling more than $15-million worth of HIGH TECHNOLOGY products a year when Leaver lost personal control in 1974 and became an independent consultant. Renamed Sentrol Systems, the firm was acquired in 1981 by the CANADA DEVELOPMENT CORPORATION. Sentrol and a US subsidiary, now sold off, continue to be successful.

DONALD J.C. PHILLIPSON

Lebensold, Fred David, architect, theatre design consultant (b at Warsaw, Poland 1917; d at Kingston 30 July 1985). Educated in Poland, he went to London, Eng, to study at the Regent Street Polytechnic (1939). He served as a staff captain in the Royal Engineers 1943-47 and then taught design in London. Immigrating to Canada 1949, he was associate professor of architecture at McGill 1949-55. In private practice, he was a founding member of Arcop Associates and emerged as a gifted theatre designer, responsible for the design development of many theatres, including the Queen Elizabeth, Vancouver; Place des Arts, Montréal; National Arts Centre, Ottawa; and City Center Theatre, New York City. Lebensold's practice also included domestic architecture, public building developments and historic building rehabilitation. He was an initiator of restoration work in Vieux Montréal.

NORBERT SCHOENAUER

LeBlanc, Arthur, violinist, composer (b at Village-du-Bois de Saint-Anselme [Dieppe], near Moncton, NB 18 Aug 1906; d at Québec C 19 Mar 1985). A true prodigy, LeBlanc was acclaimed by the age of 5. He attended the École normale de musique in Paris and studied composition with Paul Dukas. Called the "Acadian poet of the violin," he received enthusiastic reviews in N America and Europe. On 6 Dec 1941, he was playing for the president of the US at the White House when word came that Pearl Harbor had been attacked.

In 1948 he created *Concerto No 2,* which Darius Milhaud composed for him. Ill health caused him to retire in 1965. The U de Moncton gave him an honorary doctorate in music in 1982.

HÉLÈNE PLOUFFE

Leblond, Charles Philippe, anatomist, cell biologist (b at Lille, France 5 Feb 1910). Considered a pioneer in cell biology, Leblond was among the first to use synthetic radioactive isotopes in the localization of labelled molecules within tissues. To achieve this he developed, in collaboration with L. Bélanger in 1946, the now universally used technique called radioautography. This consists of placing thin sections of tissues containing radioactive substances in contact with a photographic emulsion. The presence of developed black silver grains over cells or tissues, when examined with the microscope, reveals the source of radioactivity.

Leblond exploited this method to investigate dynamic processes taking place in the body, such as the renewal of tissue components or the elaboration of various substances by the cells. Author of more than 350 scientific articles and professor of anatomy at McGill since 1948, he has received many honours including membership in the Royal Society, London (1965), and in the American Academy of Arts and Sciences (1970), and honorary degrees at Acadia U (1972), McGill U (1982), U de Montréal (1985) and York U (1986).

YVES CLERMONT

Lecavalier, René, sports announcer (b at Montréal 5 July 1918). After classical studies at Mont-Saint-Louis, he joined Radio-Canada, serving as a war correspondent with United Nations radio in N Africa 1942-44. Upon his return to Radio-Canada he worked for a number of different programs, including *P'tit Train du matin* with Miville Couture. But he was drawn to sport, and in 1952 called the first hockey game broadcast by Radio-Canada television; he remained the commentator for *La Soirée du hockey* until his retirement in 1985.

YVON DORE

Leckie, John Edwards, "Jack," soldier, mining engineer, explorer (b at Acton-Vale, Qué 19 Feb 1872; d at Port Hope, Ont 7 Aug 1950). He was best known for engineering and research work around Hudson Bay. Leckie was educated at Bishop's, RMC, and King's College. He saw service in S Africa and France, and was "Malamute Force" commander in the Russian civil war. He developed mines in northern BC and in the Zeballos fields of Vancouver I, explored in Mexico and Venezuela and led a major, though unsuccessful, search for Spanish gold on Cocos I. He was a press censor in WWII. Made a Fellow of the Royal Geographical Society in 1928, he received the DSO and the French Croix de Guerre among other decorations.

ALLAN LEVINE

Leckie, Robert, air marshal (b at Glasgow, Scot 16 Apr 1890; d at Ottawa 31 Mar 1975). A much-decorated flying-boat pilot in WWI, Leckie was the only airman to be credited with downing 2 Zeppelins. He then joined the newly formed RAF and was seconded to Canada as director of civil flying operations, 1919-22. He played a leading role in the first trans-Canada flight in 1920. Returning to Canada after a series of RAF appointments, Leckie was air member for training, 1940-44, the officer in charge of the BRITISH COMMONWEALTH AIR TRAINING PLAN. He transferred to the RCAF in 1942 and was chief of the air staff, 1944-47. Intelligent, sensitive and forceful, Leckie was the most impressive of Canada's senior air officers in WWII.

NORMAN HILLMER

Leclerc, Félix, singer-songwriter, composer, poet, novelist, playwright, actor (b at La Tuque, Qué 2 Aug 1914). He was a radio announcer in Québec C, and was encouraged by Mgr Albert Tessier to publish several radio scripts he had written. In 1939 he made his debut as a singer for Radio-Canada and then, with 2 colleagues, in 1948 founded the VLM troupe, which presented his own plays throughout Québec. Thereafter, he continued to make himself known throughout Europe, particularly in France, as well as in Canada. Some of his most popular songs are "Notre sentier," "Moi, mes souliers," "Bozo" and "Le Train du nord." Recurring themes are love of nature, his homeland and mankind. His poetic work takes its strength from its simplicity. Among other awards he has received the Grand Prix du disque (1951, 1958, 1973) and the Diplôme d'honneur of the Canadian Conference of the Arts (1976). He was made Member of the Order of Canada (1985) and Chevalier of the Légion d'honneur (1986), France's highest honour.

HÉLÈNE PLOUFFE

Leduc, Alta, City, pop 13 126 (1986c), 12 471 (1981c), inc 1906 (town) and 1983 (city), is located 30 km S of EDMONTON. Originally a telegraph terminus and stop on the Calgary and Edmonton Ry, the town grew as an agricultural centre. On 13 Feb 1947, the Leduc No 1 well, several kms NW, successfully tapped the huge Leduc oil field. By the end of 1947, some 30 wells in the field were producing 3500 barrels of oil a day. Today, most of the field is depleted, though Leduc is still a storage and pumping station. It is a farm distribution centre with some light industry connected with oil production, although not as much as formerly. Leduc is a dormitory community for many people who commute to Edmonton or who work at the nearby Edmonton International Airport. It has a hospital, schools, churches, a public library, parks and other recreation facilities. The newspaper is the *Leduc Representative*. Leduc is named for Rev Hippolyte Leduc, OMI, a pioneer priest in the area.

ERIC J. HOLMGREN

Leduc, Fernand, painter (b at Montréal 4 July 1916). Leduc studied at the École des beaux-arts in Montréal 1938-42. In 1941 he met Paul-Émile BORDUAS and became a leading member of the AUTOMATISTES, exhibiting with them and signing Borduas's REFUS GLOBAL in 1948. He spent the years 1947-53 in Paris and then returned to Montréal, becoming the founding president of the Association des artistes non-figuratifs de Montréal in 1956. He returned to France in 1959 and has lived there since, except for the years 1970-74 when he taught at UQAM and Laval. Leduc's work moved from the abstract surrealism of the automatiste movement to the rigorous, hard-edge colour abstraction found in the PLASTICIENS and others.

With Guido MOLINARI and Claude TOUSIGNANT, he gave force to the direction Montréal painting took through the 1960s. In 1970 he began his *Microchromie* paintings, subtle layerings of colour concerned with the character of coloured light. A major retrospective, 111 works from 1943-85, was shown at the Musée de beaux-arts de Chartres, France, in 1985.

DAVID BURNETT

Reading: Jean-Pierre Duquette, *Fernand Leduc* (1980).

Leduc, Jacques, film director, cameraman (b at Montréal 25 Nov 1941). A writer for the magazine *Objectif* 1961-67, Leduc joined the NFB during that period. He worked as a cameraman until 1967 when he began directing. His first major film, *On est loin du soleil* (1970), was based on the spirit of Brother ANDRÉ and established Leduc's style. In the 5 years after *Tendresse ordinaire* (1973), he directed *Chronique de la vie quotidienne,* a series of 8 films that draw upon daily life, recombining its elements into a work of fiction. This was a change from the traditional direct cinema approach used in Canadian feature filmmaking. His *Albédo* (1982) develops and transforms this duality: the aesthetic qualities of an episodic film are highlighted in a work in which documentary and fictional elements intertwine. *Le dernière glacier* (1984), which dealt with the closing of the town of Schefferville, shared the same aesthetic. *Trois journées dans l'histoire recente du Québec* (1986) is a film in 3 parts which reflects on social obligations today.

PIERRE VÉRONNEAU

Leduc, Ozias, painter (b at St-Hilaire, Qué 8 Oct 1864; d at St-Hyacinthe, Qué 16 June 1955). Leduc's interest in drawing was encouraged by a local teacher. Around 1883 he joined a Montréal statue-making firm, then became assistant to Adolphe Rho and Luigi Cappello, who introduced him to mural painting as a profession. He began exhibiting his works at the Art Assn of Montreal's annual spring exhibition in 1891, and in 1892 won a prize for his painting, *Nature morte, livres.* Until the early 1920s his works were periodically displayed at the AAM and at annual expositions of the Royal Canadian Academy.

After working on the decorative interior of the church of St-Paul-l'Ermite (1892), he landed his first important contract, with Joliette Cathedral, where he completed a group of 23 religious paintings. During his career he decorated 31 churches and chapels in Québec, NS and the eastern US. His most important work includes the churches of St-Hilaire (1894-99); St-Ninian's Cathedral, Antigonish (1902-03); St-Romuald, Farnham (1905); St-Enfant-Jésus du Mile-End, Montréal (1916-19); the chapel of the Sherbrooke bishopric (1922-32); the baptistry in Notre-Dame, Montréal (1927-28); Sts-Anges-Gardiens, Lachine (1930-31); and Notre-Dame-de-la-Présentation, south Shawinigan (1943-55). His religious works are closely linked to his still-life paintings and landscapes inspired by the St-

Neige dorée by Ozias Leduc, oil on canvas (*courtesy National Gallery of Canada*).

Hilaire region. His paintings of daily life and nature have both a symbolic and spiritual dimension achieved through flowing but concise, meticulous lines, warm and subdued colours and soft light. In this vein his 1913-21 landscapes *Cumulus bleu, Fin de journée, Effet gris (neige), Pommes vertes, Neige dorée* and *L'Heure mauve*, along with drawings from the series *Imaginations* (1936-42), are among the most outstanding of his career.

As a painter of portraits and allegorical and historical figures, Leduc instilled his small works with great suggestive power. His interest in symbolism probably dated back to his brief stay in London and Paris in 1897. His writer friends, Arsène Bessette, Guy Delahaye, Olivier Maurault, Marcel Dugas, Paul MORIN and Robert de Roquebrune, as well as musician Léo-Pol MORIN, encouraged him in this direction. He collaborated with some of them to establish an art appreciation and criticism magazine, *Le* NIGOG, published in 1918. He also illustrated several books, including *Claude Paysan* (1899) by Ernest Choquette, *Mignonne allons voir si la rose...est sans épines* (1912) by Guy Delahaye and *La Campagne canadienne* (1927) by Adélard Dugré.

Leduc was not influenced by contemporary Canadian artistic currents and trends. He held only one important exposition at the St-Sulpice Library in 1916. By helping to promote the career of Paul-Émile BORDUAS, he became quite popular late in his career. He also left many texts, poems and short reflections on art. His feelings about modern painting are expressed in the mystical thought that man lives searching for the paradise he hopes to regain through a knowledge of nature and the beauty of art. LAURIER LACROIX

Reading: J.R. Ostiguy, *Ozias Leduc* (1974).

Lee, Dennis Beynon, teacher, editor, critic, poet (b at Toronto 31 Aug 1939). A graduate in English from U of T (BA 1962, MA 1965), Lee has taught or served as writer-in-residence for various universities. A founder and highly praised editor (1967-72) of HOUSE OF ANANSI, he later worked as consulting editor for Macmillan (1974-79) and McClelland and Stewart (1981-84), and also wrote songs, with Phillip Balsam, for the TV program "Fraggle Rock" (1982-86). Lee's prose books include *The University Game* (ed with H. Adelman, 1968), in which he calls for freedom from inhibiting educational institutions, and *Savage Fields: An Essay in Literature and Cosmology* (1977). The latter explores the interrelationship between "earth" and "world" – ie, nature and civilization, or instinct and consciousness – all with particular application to a critical analysis of works by Michael ONDAATJE and Leonard COHEN.

Lee disavows much of *Kingdom of Absence* (1967), a sequence of 43 sonnet variations, but some of its concerns — modern ills, alienation, emptiness, colonialism, and their effects on the imagination and even on language – are developed in later books. *Civil Elegies* (1968, rev 1972; Gov Gen's Award) is a free-verse lament for Canada's colonized condition and a meditation on the need to become a full citizen: to occupy, imaginatively and in integrity, one's own life and land. Reclaiming language and liberating imagination, key parts of this process, are best begun in childhood; accordingly, Lee tries to free Canadian children from a colonial mentality by creating poems rooted in the words and activities of their everyday lives, poems which encourage free imaginative play. His 2 best children's books appeared in 1974; *Alligator Pie*, for pre-schoolers, and *Nicholas Knock and Other People* for older children. On the adult level, roots and play (including lovemaking) are further explored in Part 1 of *The Gods* (1979). Part 2, *The Death of Harold Ladoo* (1976),

Poet Dennis Lee has become as well known for his writing for children as for his fine serious poetry (*courtesy Canapress Photo Service*).

is an elegy for Lee's friend, a writer murdered in 1973 during a visit to his native Trinidad. The poem also meditates on the roles of mystical epiphanies and of artistic creation in its attempt to come to terms with the problems of the contemporary world. His most recent work is *The Difficulty Of Living On Other Planets* (1987). JOHN R. SORFLEET

Lee, James Matthew, businessman, politician, premier of PEI (b at Charlottetown 26 Mar 1937). After setting up his own real-estate and development company in 1970, Lee ran unsuccessfully as a PC candidate in 1974. In a by-election on 17 Feb 1975, he was elected to the assembly. He held various portfolios and, after winning the 1981 leadership convention, was sworn in as premier in 1982. In 1983 Lee succeeded in securing Maritime and federal agreement for the establishment of a school of veterinary medicine at UPEI. He lost his own seat in the election 21 Apr 1986 and was subsequently appointed commissioner to the Canadian Pension Commission for a 10-year term. DAVID A. MILNE

Leech (class Hirudinea), segmented ANNELID worm with 34 segments, many external rings and no setae (bristles). Suckers at each end are used in looping movements. Many aquatic leeches can also swim. Some leeches eat detritus; others, soft-bodied animals with red blood (eg, snails, worms). Most are external parasites on VERTEBRATES. Some may invade the bladder or body parts near the exterior, eg, nostrils. About 300 species are known worldwide, most from freshwater habitats; some are marine or terrestrial, especially in tropical areas. There are some 45 Canadian species, if those known from bordering US are included. The traditional medicinal use of leeches to draw blood continues, eg, in draining blood from reattached, severed fingers before natural circulation is fully restored. The leech's gut has a large storage area to hold massive blood meals needed for balanced diet; the intestine is simple, as blood is easily digested and absorbed. R.O. BRINKHURST

Leeson, Thomas Sydney, anatomist, electron microscopist (b at Halifax, Eng 26 Jan 1926). Having received his arts and medical degrees from Cambridge (1946-50), he later obtained an MD (1959) and a PhD (1971) there. He arrived in Canada in 1957 as assistant professor of anatomy at U of T. In 1963 he became professor in the anatomy dept at U of A, also serving as chairman until 1983. His research on the ultrastructure of tissues has gained him international recognition; he is especially well known for his textbook *Histology* (1966, 5th ed 1985), which he coauthored with his twin brother Charles Roland Leeson. K.D. MCFADDEN

Lefebvre, Jean-Pierre, filmmaker (b at Montréal 17 Aug 1941). Lefebvre's remarkable films, most made on low budgets, present a singularly personal body of work. His first 3 features, including the magnificent *Il ne faut pas mourir pour ça* (1967), were made independently, and his work began to attract international attention. In 1967 he joined the NFB, where he made 2 features and produced the films of a number of young Québec filmmakers. He soon left and formed his own company, Cinak. Working consistently with his wife, Marguerite Duparc, who edited and produced almost all his work, Lefebvre advanced his humanitarian view of the world in films such as *Les Maudits sauvages* (1971), *Les Dernières Fiançailles* (1973), *Le Vieux Pays où Rimbaud est mort* (1977), *Les Fleurs sauvages* (1982), *Le Jour "S...* (1984) and *Alfred Laliberté, sculpteur* (1987). PIERS HANDLING

Legal Aid The availability of publicly funded legal services for poor clients in Canada has developed only in the latter half of the 20th century. Previously, lawyers were sometimes willing to provide free assistance to poor clients in meritorious cases, and judges would sometimes appoint lawyers to act for poor clients, but such legal services were essentially charitable. Modest arrangements to provide legal services for clients who could not afford them were begun in some provinces in the 1950s and early 1960s by means of municipal and provincial grants and with contributions from lawyers, but it was not until 1966 that Ontario enacted legislation establishing the first comprehensive provincial legal-aid scheme. This legislation represented a major change in the philosophy of legal-aid services – that legal aid was no longer a charity but a right.

The Impact of Cost-Sharing on Services Legal-aid programs had been adopted by all other provinces and territories by the mid-1970s. Although legal-aid services fall within the provinces' constitutional responsibility for "the administration of justice," the federal Department of Justice became involved in these programs with federal-provincial cost-sharing agreements for legal-aid services in criminal law, a matter within federal constitutional responsibility. These cost-sharing agreements significantly affected the uniform development of provincial legal-aid plans because they specified both minimum standards of services to be provided and financial eligibility requirements for clients. For instance, an indigent client anywhere in Canada must be granted legal aid if that client is charged with an indictable offence, and the client is entitled to choose a lawyer in all serious cases where life imprisonment may result.

By contrast, federal funding has been far less available for legal-aid services in noncriminal cases, and provincial programs usually provide only restricted services or none at all. Notwithstanding the idea of legal aid as a right, provincial legislation creating legal-aid programs generally provides for discretion in granting legal aid to clients who are charged with less serious offences, or who must appear in lower courts in family law disputes, or where the client's case is heard in a small-claims court or before a tribunal. In addition, the provision of legal advice, the preparation of documents, and negotiation on behalf of a client are all usually discretionary matters under legal-aid legislation. Thus, legal aid as a right in Canada exists primarily for those poor clients charged with serious criminal offences.

Financial Eligibility The cost-sharing agreements require provinces to administer a flexible means test to determine whether a client can retain a lawyer without contracting major debts or having to sell modest assets that are necessary for livelihood. Provincial programs generally require an examination of income, of disposable assets, indebtedness, maintenance obligations, etc, to determine eligibility. Clients receiving social assistance will usually qualify for legal aid anywhere in Canada, but there is some variation from province to province in the application of financial eligibility guidelines for other clients. In addition, clients may sometimes be asked to make a contribution to or to repay legal-aid expenses.

Salaried or Fee-for-Service Lawyers? The development of publicly funded legal-aid services in Canada coincided with the expansion of legal aid elsewhere and with the adoption of international commitments to legal aid as expressed, for example, in the International Covenant on Civil and Political Rights that was adopted by the UN General Assembly in 1966. Yet even with broad agreement on the basic objectives of legal-aid services, considerable diversity occurred in their implementation. The US pattern of salaried public defenders in storefront offices contrasted with the delivery model adopted initially in England, where solicitors in private practice provided legal aid to clients and received reimbursement from government. From the inception of modern legal-aid programs in Canada, the issue of the appropriate delivery model – salaried lawyers or private practice lawyers paid on a fee-for-service basis – has been controversial. Several provinces, including Saskatchewan, Manitoba, Québec and Nova Scotia, initially opted for salaried lawyers in storefront locations, while Alberta and New Brunswick adopted the fee-for-service model. BC developed a more "mixed delivery" model, using a combination of salaried lawyers and paralegal workers in storefront clinics, as well as fee-for-service lawyers. The mixed delivery model also developed in Ontario, where the early fee-for-service model was expanded in 1976 and now includes approximately 45 independent community clinics staffed both by lawyers and paralegal workers. Clinics in Ontario provide complementary legal-aid services, particularly for those legal problems excluded from "entitlement" under the fee-for-service program (tenant problems, welfare, workers' compensation, immigration).

By 1980 most provincial legal-aid programs were based, in varying degrees, on this "mixed delivery" model. In addition, many provinces had adopted duty counsel arrangements in courts, and, in the North a duty counsel regularly travelled on circuit. Many programs had experimented, often quite successfully, with legal-education projects and with arrangements designed to create better access to the law for poor clients. Such projects often used the expertise of paralegal or community legal workers and sometimes resulted in successful legal actions on behalf of groups of poor people.

Costs, Control and the Charter By 1980 the strength of the Canadian legal-aid system lay in the combination of its diversity and the maintenance of minimum standards that were effected by the federal cost-sharing agreements. The main issue for legal aid is its cost; total expenditures in 1984-85 reached $182.1 million ($7.22 per capita). Even in provinces where responsibility has been vested in independent legal-aid corporations (BC, Manitoba, Saskatchewan, Québec, Nova Scotia and Newfoundland), fiscal restraint has dramatically affected legal-aid resources. Thus, the issue of access to justice through independent legal-aid services in Canada remains unsolved. Ironically, the fiscal restraint responsible for dismantling legal-aid programs coincided with the CHARTER OF RIGHTS AND FREEDOMS which enshrined the "right to retain counsel" as well as "equality before and under the law," "equal protection" and "equal benefit" of the law. The challenge to create an effective right to legal aid and equal access to justice still lies ahead.

MARY JANE MOSSMAN

Legal Education Because all provinces but Québec inherited the English COMMON LAW, legal education in Canada – training for the practice of law – was in the beginning modelled on that in England. In England, however, the profession was and is divided into 2 mutually exclusive branches – BARRISTERS and SOLICITORS. Solicitors deal with clients, but if there is to be a trial in the High Court a barrister must be retained to act as counsel. Barristers, who have the exclusive right to represent a party at a trial or on appeal, are the "senior" branch of the profession, but until very recently the educational qualifications were very low. Although most barristers have a university degree (not necessarily in law) it is not obligatory, and students can still become barristers without having ever been in court. Solicitors, however, must be articled clerks to practising solicitors and must pass examinations. The basic period was recently changed from 5 years to 4, which can be reduced to as little as 2 if the candidate passes certain qualifying examinations and has a university degree.

In Canada (except Québec) the division of the profession into 2 mutually exclusive branches has not occurred; today a legal practitioner in the common law provinces is invariably both a solicitor and a barrister, though in practice many act in the capacity of one or the other.

Before the establishment of the modern law school, the typical provincial Act governing the legal profession provided that applicants had to spend 5 years under articles and to write periodic examinations, though if they held a university degree the period was reduced to 3 years. When modern law schools were established, the articling period was usually reduced to one year after graduation. In Ontario and Manitoba it was once possible to combine part-time law school with part-time articles, but now these provinces have the same system as the others.

In Canada, as in the US, and unlike England, students do not come directly from high school to law school. The usual minimum is 2 years of university education and most successful applicants have a degree.

The story of the common-law schools can be divided into 2 periods – from the founding of the Dalhousie Law School in 1883 to 1945, and from 1945 to the present. Dalhousie established a full-time 3-year course soon after the school was founded. It had always had links to Harvard Law School and at the end of WWI its curriculum resembled that of Harvard. Following the recommendations of the CANADIAN BAR ASSOCIATION in 1920, this curriculum was widely accepted by other common-law schools.

In Ontario the Law Society created its own law school, OSGOODE HALL, in 1862, though it closed and reopened twice before being put on a permanent foundation in 1889. Later the universities of New Brunswick, Manitoba, Saskatchewan, Alberta and BC established law schools.

Shortly after WWII the Law Society made Osgoode a full-time school. The U of T had long given a degree in law. In 1949 the faculty was reorganized under Dean C.A. Wright and Bora LASKIN so as to make the LLB a professional course that would lead to admission to the bar. However, the Law Society did not give complete recognition to other schools in Ontario until 1957. In 1968 the society gave up its school and Osgoode Hall became a part of York U. By that time there were 6 faculties in Ontario – at the universities of Ottawa, Toronto, Western Ontario, Windsor, Queen's and York – and in other provinces law schools were also established at the universities of Victoria, Calgary and Moncton (where instruction is in French), and a common-law course was begun at McGill. By 1987 the number of full-time teachers had risen from about 20 to about 450 and student enrolment is now in the thousands. Most law schools impose a quota on admissions. One notable postwar trend has been the marked increase in women students and in women law teachers.

The standard curriculum of 1920 remained virtually unchanged until 1945. In 1957 the Law Society of Upper Canada prescribed the courses it would require of "approved" schools, making amendments in 1969. As all the common-law schools are approved, it is clear that the Ontario prescription has influenced the curriculum in all common-law schools. There are 25 subject areas, with 6 compulsory "core subjects." The object is to provide a general education that permits a degree of specialization. In some law schools there is special emphasis on specific topics, eg, taxation or oil and gas law.

The teaching method in common-law schools was originally based on the "case method" created in the 1870s by Dean Langdell at Harvard Law School, who believed that law was a science composed of principles that could be learned from reading decisions of appellate courts. Formal lectures were replaced by discussions in class of assigned cases and by questioning of the Socratic type. By the 1920s, all common-law schools in Canada employed one or other variation of the case method.

Since WWII, the use of the case method, at least after the first year of law school, has been criticized on the grounds that it is unproductive and gives a misleading view of law in action. Legislation tends to be ignored in the reading of cases, although its pre-eminent place is now being recognized. There has been emphasis as well on problem solving and legal writing, and on public law as compared to private. Courses in CONSTITUTIONAL LAW were always fundamental, but now courses on ADMINISTRATIVE LAW, taxation and LABOUR LAW are also important. Another trend is the linking of law with other disciplines, eg, economics, history, psychology and sociology; and, to answer the criticism that law school study ignores pressing social needs, there are courses in poverty law, WOMEN AND THE LAW, and CIVIL LIBERTIES. There has been an effort to strengthen courses on legal theory, the philosophy of law and sociology of law, usually under the rubric of JURISPRUDENCE. Efforts have been made as well to teach ethics and professional responsibility.

The development of these new subjects is not always strong and has to face competition with other subjects. As a result of criticism that law schools fail to teach skills necessary in legal practice – drafting documents, writing opinions, preparing for trial and cross-examination, interviewing and negotiating – there has been increasing emphasis on clinical training. Considerable effort has been made to meet this demand, usually with the help of practitioners and judges. Like every innovation, however, its place in the law school has been debated. The production of legal journals has conspicuously increased. These journals usefully provide scholarly articles and a forum for criticism and for proposals for reform.

In addition, the use of computers is constantly increasing and may soon be indispensable in both law teaching and practice.

The 1983 report of the Arthurs Committee on Legal Education, *Law and Learning,* states that law schools are "eclectic" and still overemphasize training for the professional rather than the academic. The report advocates research at a high level to help the development of a "scholarly" discipline that will not be shunted aside from professional training. The report specifically recommends an expansion and intensification of graduate study (a number of schools give a master's degree and a few offer a doctorate) with a view to the education of future law teachers and researchers, and recommends that these programs should concentrate on those subjects in which the school is strong. Support for graduate research is hampered, however, by the shortage of funds for scholarships.

The advent of the law school did not mean an end to the system of articles. The purpose of articling is to provide "practical" training, ie, an introduction to practice which the law school has not provided. The success of articles depends on the "principal" and the student. The principal is under a duty to see that the student receives instruction in the basics of practice, but there is little or no supervision to this end. For many years after WWII, the business expansion created a demand for students and good articles were comparatively easy to obtain. In recent years, the number of graduates has been more than the market can easily absorb and the adequacy of the articling system has come into question. To supplement articles, most law societies have established a Bar Admission Course. The most notable is that of Ontario, begun in 1957. When students have finished the year of articles they are required to attend a 6-month course in matters such as rules of procedure, forming companies, handling estates, and real-estate transactions. This course is described in a handbook published by the Law Society of Upper Canada. The other provinces, except for PEI, have each provided in legislation for a bar admission course. However, these courses are less ambitious than Ontario's and vary a great deal. Some are given throughout the period of articles while others are offered near the end of the articling period, the length of the course varying from one week to 6.

In the mid-1980s BC replaced its Bar Admission Program by a Professional Legal Training Course. It is 10 weeks in length and offered 3 times a year to articling students. They take part in true-to-life transactions likely to be encountered in practice and receive training in the major skills. This scheme shows promise of being an improvement on the typical bar admission course and other provinces are examining it.

In the US, the requirement of articles is virtually nonexistent. In theory, admission to practice is a matter for the state supreme court. The court in fact delegates its function to bar examiners who set comprehensive exams for those seeking to practise, and who conduct character checks. Another difference between the 2 countries is that the American Bar Association publishes a list of approved law schools, though some unapproved schools still exist; the Canadian Bar Association has no such role and there is no category of unauthorized law schools. Finally, the Canadian type of provincial law society, with statutory control over admission and discipline, is quite different from the type of law society in the US.

Once an individual has been admitted to practice it is important to keep up to date. Legal journals and special lectures and meetings of bar associations are helpful but provide uneven coverage and do not always reach those most in need. In recent years there has been a call for a greater and more systematic program of continuing legal education. In 1978 the Federation of Law Societies of Canada held a Conference on Quality of Legal Services and in 1980 held a workshop on the same subject. It concluded that continuing legal education should be fostered but it was not prepared to recommend mandatory continuing legal education. Organized efforts at programs of continuing legal education are in fact increasing in most provinces.

The legal profession (outside Québec) has never recognized specialties, as does the medical profession, though in some provinces practitioners may now announce a preferred area of practice. The significant fact is that the "practice of law" is not homogenous, and the variations go far beyond the differences between barrister and solicitor. In addition, lawyers work not only in private practice but also in government and business.

In Québec the legal profession is divided. Advocates form the Barreau du Québec while notaries, governed by their own statute, are somewhat like solicitors. An individual cannot belong to both branches. The course leading to a degree in law in Québec takes 3 years, and the prelegal requirement is a diploma equivalent to an arts degree. If law students wish to become notaries, they must declare so by Dec 1 of their third year. Up to that point, the courses are the same for both branches, with emphasis on the CIVIL CODE, which comprises the basic statement of legal relations as between private citizens – contracts, property, inheritance, etc. In many other ways the Québec schools have gone through the same experiences and problems as the common-law schools. The first faculty of law in Canada was established in 1853 at McGill, which now gives a common law as well as a civil law degree (as does U of O). Laval's law faculty was founded in 1854 and that of U de M is over 100 years old. Other law schools exist at Sherbrooke and U de Québec at Montréal.

Practical training occurs after graduation. For advocates there is an 8-month "formation professionelle" (similar to a bar admission course), followed by a "stagiaire" (now similar to BC's new program in skills training) of 6 months, and finally a bar examination. Graduates who wish to be notaries must attend an additional year in notarial practice at a civil law school; finally, they take a notarial examination. W.F. BOWKER

Reading: R.J. Mates and D.J. McCawley, eds, *Legal Education in Canada* (1987).

Légaré, Joseph, painter, art collector, politician (b at Québec C 10 Mar 1795; d there 21 June 1855). Originally a painter and glazier, Légaré became a fine-arts painter around 1819. Self-taught, he never went to Europe for training and learned by copying the work of others. His first efforts to diversify his work were crowned with success when Québec's Société pour l'encouragement des sciences et des arts en Canada gave him a medal of honour (1828) for his painting *Le Massacre des Hurons par les Iroquois.* In all he painted more than 250 oils on canvas or paper, including about one hundred religious copies, occasional portraits, some rural scenes and contemporary events (Québec's 1832 cholera epidemic and 1845 fires), some remarkable historical tableaux (*La Bataille de Sainte-Foy* 1854) and native Indian subjects. Légaré, who taught Antoine PLAMONDON, was the first Canadian-born painter to devote himself to landscapes. He also opened Canada's first art gallery (in 1833), featuring his personal collection of canvases and European engravings; it closed in 1835. From 1838 to 1840 and 1852 to 1855 he again offered Québec C art amateurs access to his ever-growing collection. Since 1874 the former Légaré collection has been held in the Musée du Séminaire de Québec, which also holds the most important body of the artist's own output. Légaré worked ceaselessly to promote fine arts in Lower Canada, and after 1845 was one of the greatest supporters of the creation of a national gallery. A Lower Canadian nationalist, he tirelessly promoted humanitarian, social and political goals. His activities included a stint as member of the first Québec C municipal council (1833-36). A faithful follower of Louis-Joseph PAPINEAU, he was arrested for his part in the REBELLIONS OF 1837, 4 years after becoming one of the founding members of the ST-JEAN-BAPTISTE SOCIETY of Québec. Defeated as a candidate in the by-elections of 1848 and 1850, he was appointed to the Legislative Council in Feb 1855, a few months before his death. JOHN R. PORTER

Joseph Légaré opened Canada's first art gallery in 1833. He painted over 250 oils, among which were a number of fine portraits, such as *Portrait of Josephte Ourné*, c1840 (*courtesy National Gallery of Canada*).

Legault, Émile, director, dramatist, critic (b at Ville St-Laurent, Qué 29 Mar 1906; d at Montréal 28 Aug 1983). Ordained a Catholic priest in 1930, he became a teacher and founded, in 1937, a troupe of young actors at Montréal's Collège de Saint-Laurent. This troupe, the Compagnons de Saint-Laurent, would last 15 years and prove to be the most influential theatrical company in the history of Québec. With Legault's guidance and dedication it moved from an early emphasis on religious theatre to classical and contemporary plays, a tendency heightened after his year of drama studies in Paris. Former members of the Compagnons went on to provide leadership in all aspects of the performing arts in Québec for the next 3 decades. After the troupe disbanded in 1952, Legault turned to composing dramatic texts on religious themes, such as *Premiers gestes* (1954), *Le Grand Attentif* (1956) and *Kermesse des anges et des hommes* (1960). A perceptive critic, he is the author of many articles on stage arts in Canada and of a volume of memoirs, *Confidences* (1955). L.E. DOUCETTE

Léger, Jean-Marc, journalist, social theorist, public servant (b at Montréal North, 1927). After graduate studies at U de M in law, history and social sciences (1949), he attended the Institut d'études politiques, Paris, and returned to Montréal to become a journalist for *La Presse* until 1956

and for Le DEVOIR until the late 1960s. At U de M, with several other colleagues, he had set up the Équipe de recherches sociales to explore the socioeconomic problems of postwar Québec. They concluded that traditional FRENCH CANADIAN NATIONALISM, thanks to spokesmen such as Maurice DUPLESSIS, was synonymous with the exploitation of the working class and the prevention of Québec's modernization. Throughout the 1950s, Léger, through his writings in *L'Action nationale* and *Le Devoir* helped redefine this nationalism in terms of economic, social and political liberation for Québec's francophone majority. He was, thus, one of the ideological founders of the QUIET REVOLUTION. He worked for the "revolution" on the international scene as secretary general of the Assn des universités de langue française, 1961-78, and of the Agence de coopération culturelle et technique, 1969-74. He was Québec's delégué général in Brussels 1978-81, and then an associate deputy minister with the Québec Ministry of Education. In 1986 he was named commissioner general of the FRANCOPHONIE. M.D. BEHIELS

Léger, Jules, governor general of Canada, 1974-79 (b at St-Anicet, Qué 4 Apr 1913; d at Ottawa 22 Nov 1980), brother of Paul-Émile LÉGER. After studies at U de M and the Sorbonne, and working as a journalist, he joined the Dept of External Affairs in 1940 and began a brilliant diplomatic career that would lead him to ambassadorships in Mexico, Rome, Paris and Brussels. In France between 1964 and 1968, he won admiration for his sensitive handling of General de Gaulle's policy towards Québec. As undersecretary of state 1968-72, he provided the administrative underpinning for Prime Minister L.B. PEARSON's foreign policy and the TRUDEAU government's policy on bilingualism and multiculturalism.

Jules Léger was installed as governor general on 14 Jan 1974 and served until Jan 1979. In June 1974 he suffered a stroke which impaired his speech and paralysed his left arm. Although he regained a degree of health, he was thereafter greatly aided by his wife, Gabrielle Carmel, who in 1976 and 1978 shared with him the long reading of the speech from the throne. In 1978 he became the first governor general to exercise all the powers delegated to the office by King George VI in 1947. During Léger's term the country was divided by many acrimonious disputes over Québec SEPARATISM and the alienation of other regions. Throughout he maintained an unshakable and serene confidence in the unity of Canada and inspired a renewed respect for his office by his dignity, kindness, prudence and courage.

JACQUES MONET, S.J.

Jules Léger, governor general of Canada 1974-79; portrait by J. de Lavoye (*courtesy National Archives of Canada/ C-98013*).

Léger, Paul-Émile, cardinal of the Roman Catholic Church (b at Valleyfield, Qué 25 Apr 1904), brother of Jules LÉGER. He was ordained a priest in Montréal in 1929, beginning an ecclesiastical career that took him first to France (1930-33) and then Japan (1933-39). He returned to Valleyfield during WWII (1940-47), was rector of the Pontifical Canadian College in Rome (1947-50) and was then named archbishop of Montréal (1950-67), succeeding Mgr Joseph Charbonneau. Mgr Léger regularly made headlines, thanks to his eloquent speeches, his presence in all the religious and social activities of a city still unable to handle the demands of rapid change, and his clear support for the disadvantaged. He won the affection of the city and a reputation that quickly went beyond the borders of Québec. He was a man of action, with an extraordinary ability to stir people's consciences and energies to participate in projects such as the Foyer de Charité, the Hôpital Saint-Charles-Borromée for the chronically ill. He will also be remembered for his independence from politicians during Maurice DUPLESSIS's premiership of Québec and for his willingness to increase the role of the laity by renouncing certain privileges until then reserved to the church. His nomination as a cardinal in 1953 increased his renown. A member of the preparatory commission leading to Vatican Council II (1962-65), Cardinal Léger played an important role as both a liberal and a progressive. Upon returning to his diocese, he worked to implement the decisions of the council and then, in 1967, decided to step down from the episcopal seat in Montréal to become a missionary among lepers and handicapped children in Cameroon, Africa. Though retired, he sees to the continuity of the missionary activities he helped to launch and continues his humanitarian work from Montréal.

Since 1950, Cardinal Léger has received a great many nominations, decorations and awards. More than 10 Canadian universities have granted him honorary doctorates in theology, letters and law. In 1958, France awarded him the Grande Croix of the Légion d'honneur and he received the Order of Canada in 1968. Copresident of the Canadian Refugee Foundation, in 1969 he received the Pearson Peace Medal and in 1980 the Lester B. Pearson Foundation award for peace. In 1983 he was the first recipient of the Prix Maisonneuve awarded by the Société Saint-Jean-Baptiste of Montréal and he was made a grand officer of the Ordre national du Québec in 1985.

DENISE ROBILLARD

Legge, Francis, soldier, colonial governor (b *c*1719; d near London, Eng 15 May 1783). After an undistinguished military career spent largely in N America, Legge was appointed governor of NS (1773) by his kinsman the earl of Dartmouth. During his first year in office, he studied NS and sought to improve its economic situation and administration, but he soon conflicted with the Halifax merchant oligarchy. An attempt to audit the provincial books and to recover missing funds in the courts completed the process of alienation. By 1775 both Assembly and Council had turned against him, and as open rebellion broke out to the south, NS's military position was weak. Legge was recalled to England and criticized by the Board of Trade in 1776 for want of "Gracious and Conciliating Deportment." Although not formally replaced until 1782, he was not permitted to resume residence in NS throughout the war.

J.M. BUMSTED

Legget, Robert Ferguson, civil engineer (b at Liverpool, Eng 29 Sept 1904). After working in the Canadian construction industry, Legget taught at Queen's and U of T until 1947, when he joined the NATIONAL RESEARCH COUNCIL to establish, and serve as director of, its new Division of Building Research, a position he held until retirement in 1969. He is known internationally for contributions to engineering, geology and building research and standardization. He helped establish co-operation among geotechnical engineers, geologists and pedologists in Canada, and his achievements have been recognized by 13 honorary degrees and many fellowships. Legget has written or edited more than 12 well-known books, including *Canals of Canada* (1975), *Glacial Till* (1976), *Handbook of Geology in Civil Engineering* with P.F. Karrow (1983) and many papers on soil mechanics.

Legume Leguminosae or Fabaceae is the third-largest family of flowering plants, containing up to 650 genera and 18 000 species. Over 4000 species are native to N America, most being members of the bean subfamily, occurring as scattered, secondary components of native vegetation. Over 2000 species of milk vetch (genus *Astragalus*) alone occur worldwide, more than 40 in Canada. Other common native legumes are LUPINES (*Lupinus*), VETCHES (*Vicia*), LOCOWEED (*Oxytropis*) and vetchling (*Lathyrus*). Most legumes, in association with strains of the bacterium *Rhizobium*, "fix" part of their nitrogen requirement and improve soils as green manure. Legumes are widely consumed by animals and humans.

Most agriculturally important legumes in Canada have been introduced. ALFALFA, sweet clover and red and alsike CLOVERS are introduced forage legumes used widely for hay and green manure. They are used sparingly for pasture and are usually mixed with grasses, since they can cause potentially fatal gas buildup (bloat) in grazing animals. Several forage legumes (eg, sainfoin and birdsfoot trefoil) do not cause bloat and are used for pasture in limited areas.

The PULSE crops comprise a second very important group of large-seeded, introduced legumes. Most pulses grown in Canada are cleaned and exported for human consumption. The dry BEAN is the most important Canadian pulse crop. The dry pea or field pea is the second most important crop, followed by LENTILS and FABA BEANS. SOYBEAN (properly an OILSEED, not a pulse) is also produced, although primarily in southern Ontario.

A.E. SLINKARD

Leif Ericsson, Norse mariner (d *c*1020). The son of ERIC THE RED, Leif was likely the first European to set foot on the mainland of N America. In or around the year 1000, according to the *Saga of the Greenlanders,* Leif bought BJARNI'S HERJOLFSSON'S ship and retraced his westward course, sighting 3 areas which he called Helluland (likely Baffin I), Markland (likely Labrador) and Vinland (possibly Newfoundland). Archaeological evidence at L'ANSE AUX MEADOWS confirmed a Viking presence in Newfoundland, but the ruins are not necessarily from Leif's Vinland. Leif earned his nickname "the Lucky" by rescuing shipwrecked sailors. *See also* NORSE VOYAGES. JAMES MARSH

Leliefontein During the SOUTH AFRICAN WAR 90 officers and men of the Royal Canadian Dragoons were assigned to cover the retreat of a British infantry column under attack by several hundred Boer horsemen near Leliefontein farm, E Transvaal. In the action on 7 Nov 1900, in which the Dragoons were supported by 2 guns of the Royal Canadian Field Artillery, 3 dragoons won VICTORIA CROSSES, 3 were killed and 11 were wounded. BRERETON GREENHOUS

Lemelin, Roger, novelist, scriptwriter (b at Québec C 7 Apr 1919). He was born in the working-class St-Sauveur district of Québec C and is mostly self-taught. He has also been a journalist and a businessman with interests in advertising, food processing and lumbering, as well as publisher of the Montréal daily, *La* PRESSE, until 1981. Lemelin has published 4 novels, a short-story collection and some nonfiction. Most successful have been his novels, *Au pied de la pente douce* (1944; tr *The Town Below*, 1948) and *Les* PLOUFFE (1948; tr *The Plouffe Family*, 1950). Critical comment was less favourable to *Pierre le magnifique* (1952; tr *In Quest ofSplendour*, 1955) and especially to *Le Crime d'Ovide Plouffe* (1982; tr *The Crime of Ovide Plouffe*, 1984). Lemelin also wrote the long-lasting TV series based on *Les Plouffe*, a great success on CBC's English and French networks in the 1950s, and the scenarios for the popular screen and TV adaptations of the same novel, directed by Gilles CARLE. Director Denys ARCAND's film, *Le Crime d'Ovide Plouffe* (1984), based on Lemelin's screenplay, reduced some of the original melodrama — the author's major flaw. A pioneer of social realism in French Canada, Lemelin's best writing is characterized by keen observation of his compatriots, with the main targets of his satire being clericalism, nationalism, the conventional Québec family, sexual taboos and ignorance. He is a Companion of the Order of Canada and in 1987 was made an honorary member of the Union des écrivains québecois.

B.-Z. SHEK

Lemieux, Jean-Paul, painter (b at Québec C 18 Nov 1904). Lemieux's artistic universe is often classified as one of northern landscapes, flat, barren and infinite, but this preoccupation is only one characteristic of his work. He studied at the École des beaux-arts in Montréal (1926-34), interrupted by a trip to Paris. After teaching at the École du meuble, he moved to the École des beaux-arts in Québec in 1937, remaining there until 1965. His work draws inspiration from Québec C and from Île aux COUDRES, Charlevoix County, which he holds in particular affection. His first paintings reflected daily life, portraits of relatives and familiar landscapes. In the 1940s, his canvases (*Lazare*, 1941; *La Fête-Dieu à Québec*, 1944) in fresco style summarize the attitudes of a people. His organization of subject and space was then influenced by the Italian primitivist school and early Québec folk art, which he collects avidly. Gradually his subjects became simplified and his style more geometric. It is not, however, a stiff geometry, for the lines still vibrate, and colours are either transparent or pastel. Space opens up (*Le Train de midi*, 1956), and against a line of horizon appear hieratic figures (*L'Été*, 1959). Part of and yet distinct from the background, his figures evoke a world of dream and memory. Often meditative and serious, Lemieux's art can sometimes be humorous and lyrical, as in his illustrations of Gabrielle ROY's books. His work is regularly exhibited in Canada and internationally, and he has been commissioned to paint portraits of a number of public figures. In 1985 Lemieux published a limited edition bilingual collection of prints – one for each province and territory – entitled *Canada-Canada*.

LAURIER LACROIX

J.P. Lemieux, photographed in a physical setting not unlike those of his paintings (*photo by John deVisser*).

Chemist Raymond U. Lemieux holds over 30 patents, mostly on antibiotics and semisynthetic blood-group antigens (*courtesy Ole Hindsgaul*).

Lemieux, Raymond Urgel, professor of chemistry (b at Lac La Biche, Alta 16 June 1920). Internationally recognized for his fundamental and innovative contributions to organic chemistry, especially in the area of carbohydrates, Lemieux obtained his doctorate from McGill (1946). He briefly held research positions at Ohio State U and U of Sask before moving, in 1949, to NRC Prairie Regional Laboratory in Saskatoon as senior research officer. Here he completed the first chemical synthesis of sucrose. He moved to U of O in 1954, where he pioneered the application of nuclear magnetic resonance SPECTROSCOPY to the structure elucidation of natural products. In 1961 he went to U of A, where his research focused on the special bonding properties termed "anomeric effects" and how these controlled the chemical reactions and shapes of carbohydrate molecules. This work led to the first chemical syntheses of the complex carbohydrates found on human cell surfaces and to an understanding of how the shapes of these molecules control their function. In addition to producing more than 200 scientific publications Lemieux holds over 30 patents, mostly on antibiotics and semisynthetic blood-group antigens, and is the founder of 3 research and chemical companies. He is fellow of the Royal Society of London (1955), and among his many awards are the Izaak Walton Killam Award (1981), Canadian Medical Association Medal of Honour (1985) and Gairdner International Award (1985). He is an Officer of the Order of Canada and in 1988 was professor emeritus at U of A.

O. HINDSGAUL

Lemming, stocky northern RODENT related to VOLES and MUSKRATS. About l6 species occur worldwide; best known of the 7 Canadian species are brown and collared lemmings (*Lemmus sibiricus* and the *Dicrostonyx groenlandicus* complex, respectively) from the arctic islands and mainland tundra W of Hudson Bay, and Labrador collared lemmings (*D. hudsonius*) from Ungava and Labrador. The northern and southern bog lemmings (*Synaptomys borealis* and *S. cooperi*) are uncommon. Lemmings rarely exceed 90 g and 15 cm in length. Their extremities are hidden by, or barely extend beyond, their long brown or grey fur. Collared lemmings are the only rodents that molt to a camouflaging white for winter. Lemmings eat willows and herbs. They are intermittently active day and night, and during winter forage beneath insulating snow. They breed rapidly and every 3-5 years reach peak densities of 60-125 per hectare. Subsequent population declines involve cessation of breeding and massive die-offs, but are not caused by predators, disease, starvation or stress from overcrowding. Lemming populations are self-regulating: genetically determined behaviours (aggressiveness and tendency to disperse) change with population density and influence the cycle. Although some Canadian lemmings emigrate from crowded areas and some accidentally drown, they do not make spectacular suicide marches to the sea, as related in folklore. Lemmings are the main food for arctic carnivores, including valuable, fur-bearing arctic foxes and ermines.

DONALD A. SMITH

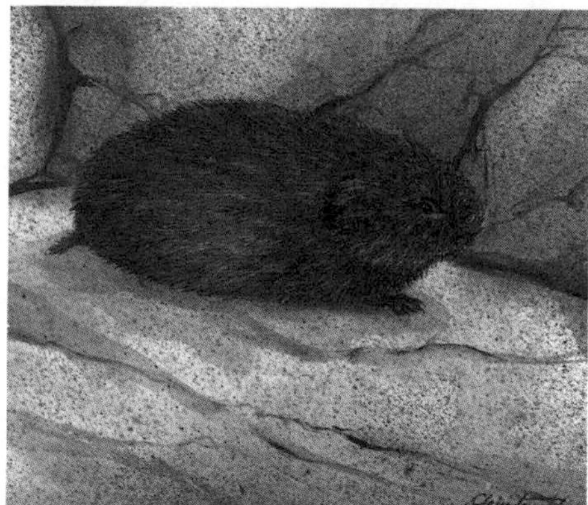

Brown lemming (*Lemmus sibiricus*) (*artwork by Claire Tremblay*).

LeMoine, Sir James MacPherson, folklorist, historian, ornithologist (b at Québec City 24 Jan 1825; d there 5 Feb 1912). Half Scots and half French Canadian, LeMoine was proficient in both English and French and wrote extensively on contemporary and historical Québec. He grew up on the Île aux Grues seigneurie of his grandfather Daniel MacPherson, was educated at the Seminaire de Québec, and was called to the bar in 1850. He was a charter member of the Royal Society of Canada (and president 1894-95). The sketches of "Chateau Bigot" and "The Golden Dog" from his series Maple Leaves (7 vols 1863-1906) formed the basis for William KIRBY's novel *The* GOLDEN DOG (1877). He was knighted in 1897.

CAROL W. FULLERTON

Lend-Lease, an Act of the US Congress passed Mar 1941, providing for the transfer of American war materials to Britain and its allies in return for theoretical deferred payment. Canada's involvement in WORLD WAR II had caused serious deterioration in the BALANCE OF PAYMENTS vis-à-vis the US, and the Lend-Lease Act threatened to divert all British war orders from Canada to the US. To avert a crisis, on Apr 20 PM Mackenzie King and Pres F.D. Roosevelt issued the Hyde Park Declaration, named for the latter's Hyde Park estate, where they met, providing for American war purchases in Canada. American-produced components of war materiel manufactured in Canada for Britain were to be included in the Lend-Lease scheme, an arrangement which alleviated Canada's trade deficit and made it easier for Canada to fill British orders and guarantee financing for them. Lend-Lease, terminated Aug 1945, greatly helped the war efforts of Britain, the USSR and some other Allied powers; it benefited Canada only indirectly. N.F. DREISZIGER

Lenihan, Patrick, trade unionist (b at Kanturk, Ire 11 Apr 1903; d at Calgary 4 Mar 1981). He was a member of the Sinn Féin movement engaged in rebellious activities against British rule in Ireland. In the 1930s he organized workers, farmers and unemployed throughout Alberta. He was elected as a Calgary alderman in 1938, running on the communist slate. Interned for 2 years in 1940 for opposition to the war, after WWII he became a labourer in Calgary and eventually president of the Civic Employees Union. He was instrumental in the formation of the National Union of Public Employees, one of the predecessor unions of today's CANADIAN UNION OF PUBLIC EMPLOYEES. On his retirement in 1968 he was western Canadian director of CUPE. GILBERT LEVINE

Lennoxville, Qué, Town, pop 3898 (1986c), 3922 (1981c), inc 1871, is located in the Appalachians on the Rivière SAINT-FRANÇOIS, at the junction of the Massawippi, 5 km SE of SHERBROOKE. It was named in honour of the then governor general, the duke of RICHMOND (1818-19). The Abenaki and French missionaries often used the site because it was a focal point for canoes and small boats using the tributaries of the St-François. A sawmill and forest-products plant (lumber and potash) preceded the founding of the first village by LOYALISTS around 1794. From 1860 to 1950, there was some copper mining in the region. Development of road and rail networks 1810-84 brought copper manufacturing (1903), asbestos (1935) and, more recently, maple syrup industries. Located here are BISHOP'S UNIVERSITY (est 1843) and Bishop's Coll School (est 1836), which attract students from across Canada and the US. There are as well federal agricultural research facilities. The town is the centre of activities for the anglophone community in the EASTERN TOWNSHIPS.

JEAN-MARIE DUBOIS AND PIERRE MAILHOT

Lentil (*Lens esculenta*), herbaceous, cool-season annual belonging to the legume family. Lentils were one of the first plants domesticated (about 4000 BC). They originated in Asia and spread quickly throughout the Middle East and Europe and, later, the New World. The plants have several ascending branches, varying in height from 15 to 45 cm. The leaves are alternate, with 6 pairs of leaflets per leaf. Each leaf axil bears 2-4 white or pale blue flowers. The slightly inflated pods are 1.5-2.0 cm long and contain 2 doubly convex-lens-shaped seeds. Lentils require 80-130 days to mature and need 15-75 cm of precipitation during the growing season. They are cultivated in Asia, N Africa, Europe and N America. Lentils are a high-protein foodstuff used in soups or dhal. Canadian production, located primarily in Saskatchewan, has increased greatly over the last few years, from 55 000 t in 1983 to 182 400 t in 1986. P. MCVETTY

Leonard, Stan, golfer (b at Vancouver, 2 Feb 1915). Leonard turned professional in 1938. He won the Canadian Professional Golfers' Assn championship 8 times 1940-61, was low Canadian in the Canadian Open 9 times 1945-61, won the BC Open 5 times, the Alberta Open 9 times, and the Saskatchewan Open twice. Until 1955 Leonard's competitive golf was restricted to Canada. Then over 40, he began to compete on the US tour. In 1957 he won the Greater Greensboro (NC) Open, in 1958 the Tournament of Champions and in 1960 the Western Open.

LORNE RUBENSTEIN

Leonowens, Anna Harriette, née Crawford, author, teacher, feminist, lecturer (b at Caernarvon, Wales 5 Nov 1834; d at Montréal 19 Jan 1915). After her officer husband died in Singapore in 1858, she established a school there for officers' children and then became a teacher at the Siamese court (1862-67). Her experiences there were the inspiration for 2 of her books, *The English Governess at the Siamese Court* (1870) and *The Romance of the Harem* (1872), which dealt with the exploitation of women in this exotic environment. These later became the basis for *Anna and the King of Siam* by Margaret Landon (1943) and the play *The King and I* (1951). Moving to Halifax in 1876, Leonowens organized a book club and a Shakespearean society, was active in a suffrage association, and was founding secretary of the Halifax Council of Women. She helped found the Victoria School of Art and Design in Halifax (later the NOVA SCOTIA COLL OF ART AND DESIGN) in 1887, before leaving there in 1897. She then lived in Germany for some years before settling in Montréal.

ERNEST R. FORBES

Lepage, Ernest, priest and botanist (b near Rimouski, Qué 1 June 1905; d there 4 Jan 1981). Lepage was an assistant parish priest until 1933 and then taught at the École moyenne d'agriculture in Rimouski 1936-61. In 1943 he began his professional association with a fellow Oblate, Arthème Dutilly, and his long concentration on arctic and subarctic flora. Their annual trips, 1945-64, which focused for the most part on the James Bay region, were documented in extensive publications, while their personal herbariums grew constantly. Despite health problems, Lepage continued his regional botanizing and his writing until he suffered partial paralysis from a thrombosis in 1976. He left his herbarium and botanical library to Laval. Although Lepage left no individual disciples the herbaria, writings and archives of Dutilly and Lepage contributed enormously to botanical knowledge in Canada. BERNARD BOIVIN

LePan, Douglas Valentine, public servant, educator (b at Toronto 25 May 1914). LePan taught English literature at U of T and Harvard 1937-41, was a personal education adviser to Gen A.G.L. MCNAUGHTON 1942-43, and fought in the Italian campaign with the Canadian Army. He was a member of the Dept of External Affairs 1945-59, developing an expertise in economics and serving in Washington as minister-counsellor, as secretary and director of research for the Royal Commission on CANADA'S ECONOMIC PROSPECTS, and briefly as assistant undersecretary of state. A volume of memoirs, *Bright Glass of Memory* (1979), recalls LePan's early experiences. After teaching at Queen's 1959-64, he returned to U of T as principal of University College 1964-70 and university professor 1970-79. He won the Governor General's Award for his second volume of poetry, *The Net and the Sword* (1953) and for his novel *The Deserter* (1964), both of which are concerned with the experience of war. *Weathering IV: Complete Poems 1948-87* was published in 1987.

NORMAN HILLMER

Leprohon, Rosanna Eleanor, née Mullins, novelist, poet (b at Montréal 12 Jan 1829; d there 20 Sept 1879). Of Irish-Catholic descent and a convent-school education, Leprohon published her first poetry, at age 17, in the *Literary Garland,* followed by serialized novels of manners set in England, published annually from 1848 to 1851. In June 1851 she married a French Canadian, Dr J.L. Leprohon; they had 13 children. Subsequently Leprohon's focus shifted to Québec society. "The Manor House of de Villerai" (serialized in *The Family Herald* 1859-60) is set in New France during the Seven Years' War; *Antoinette de Mirecourt* (1864) in Montréal just after that war; and *Armand Durand* (1868) in early 19th-century Lower Canada. Soon translated, these novels became part of both Canadian literatures; indeed *Le Manoir de Villerai* (tr 1861) precedes P.J. AUBERT DE GASPÉ'S Les ANCIENS CANADIENS (1863) as the immediate literary descendant of Garneau's HISTOIRE DU CANADA, Leprohon's posthumous *Poetical Works* (1881) treat historical and religious subjects, nature and family life. JOHN R. SORFLEET

Lesage, Jean, lawyer, premier of Québec (b at Montréal 10 June 1912; d at Québec C 12 Dec 1980). Known as the father of the QUIET REVOLUTION, he led the Québec government during that period of profound change in the organization of the collective life of Québecois. Elected federal MP for Montmagny-L'Islet in 1945, he was reelected in 1949, 1953, 1957 and 1958. He became, in 1953, minister of resources and development and then of northern affairs and national resources. Upon the defeat of the Louis ST. LAURENT government in 1957, he left federal politics to become leader of the Québec Liberal Party 31 May 1958. He completely reformed the party by attracting dynamic people and by preparing a program of social and political reform.

His party came to power in 1960 and introduced many reforms, including the elimination of patronage and corruption, the creation of ministries of education and of cultural affairs, and the establishment of the Société générale de financement. In 1962 he held an election on the issue of nationalizing the electricity companies and won easily under the slogan of "Maître chez nous," which became the byword of his government. Though his government was defeated in 1966, he remained leader of the Liberal Party until his retirement from political life in 1970.

DANIEL LATOUCHE

Lescarbot, Marc, lawyer, author (b at Vervins, France *c*1570; d in France 1642). A Paris lawyer, Lescarbot sailed for ACADIA in May 1606 at the invitation of one of his clients, colonizer Jean de BIENCOURT DE POUTRINCOURT. He remained there until the summer of 1607, when the colony was abandoned after the revocation of its trading monopoly. Based at PORT-ROYAL, Lescarbot travelled widely in Acadia and took a keen interest in the problems and opportunities of N American colonization as well as the way of life of the region's native peoples. His insights were set down in several published works, most notably his *Histoire de la Nouvelle-France* (1609).

Besides being a vivid account of early colonizing attempts in Acadia, the *Histoire* is a remarkable plea for realism in harvesting the colony's natural resources, as against a futile search for quick profits. Also a poet and playwright, Lescarbot presented his *Théâtre de Neptune* at Port-Royal in 1606, reputedly the first theatrical production in N America. After returning to France in 1607, Lescarbot resumed his law practice, but his interest in the progress of Acadian colonization was lifelong. JOHN G. REID

Reading: Marc Lescarbot, *The History of New France,* ed W.L. Grant (1907-14); John G. Reid, *Acadia, Maine, and New Scotland* (1981).

Lessard, François-Louis, army officer (b at Québec C 9 Dec 1860; d at Meadowvale, Ont 7 Aug 1927). He served in local militia units before joining the Quebec Garrison Artillery (1880). As a lieutenant in the Cavalry School Corps he served during the NORTH-WEST REBELLION. Promoted lieutenant-colonel to command the Corps (1899), he volunteered for service in the SOUTH AFRICAN WAR, and eventually commanded the 1st Battalion, Canadian Mounted Rifles (Royal Ca-

nadian Dragoons). Though promoted major-general in 1912, he was prevented by Sam Hughes, minister of militia and defence, from getting command overseas at the outbreak of WWI. Appointed inspector general for eastern Canada, Dec 1914, he commanded the Halifax Fortress. In Mar 1918 he was called upon to restore order in Québec C following anticonscription riots. After retiring (1919) near Toronto, he often served as judge at horse shows in Canada and the US.
Jean Pariseau

Lesser Slave Lake, 1168 km^2, elev 577 m, located in central Alberta, about 200 km NW of Edmonton. It is fed by numerous small rivers, including the Swan, Driftpile and E and W Prairie, and discharges E via the Lesser Slave R to the Athabasca R. It was named for the Slavey Indians, and "Lesser" was added to distinguish it from its namesake in the NWT. The oldest settlement in the area is Grouard, once a bustling stopover on the Klondike trail. The site of Slave Lake (pop 5429, 1986c) was a gathering place for Indian hunting and war parties. By 1900 the town was a steamboat centre, until the arrival of the railway in 1915. Sandy beaches on the S and NE shore have raised talk of tourism, but it is oil that has given the area new importance. There are several Indian reservations along the S shore and Lesser Slave Lake Provincial Park is on the NE.
James Marsh

Lester B. Pearson College of the Pacific, Victoria, BC, was established in 1974 and named in honour of Lester B. Pearson, who had been much impressed by the United World College project, which aims at the establishment of a chain of international schools and colleges throughout the world. There are 5 other colleges: in Wales, Italy, the US, Singapore and Swaziland. Students live on campus and follow the International Baccalaureate program. Emphasis is given to community service in the belief that international understanding cannot be created in the classroom alone. Over 60 countries are represented by the 200 students who are competitively selected by committees in their native country, and who attend each year on full scholarships funded by donations from corporations, foundations, individuals and governments.
Kate Mansell

LeSueur, William Dawson, critic, historian, civil servant (b at Québec C 19 Feb 1840; d at Ottawa 23 Sept 1917). Of French Huguenot and English parentage, LeSueur became the most important Canadian-born man of letters of his generation, introducing a spirit of critical inquiry into journalism and historical writing. An Ottawa civil servant from 1856, LeSueur rose to prominence in 1871 with the publication of an essay on the French critic, Sainte-Beuve, in the *Westminster Review*. This was followed by articles on science, social philosophy and religion in Canadian, American and British periodicals in the 1870s and 1880s. A convinced Comtean positivist, LeSueur became notorious for the heterodoxy of his religious views. From the 1890s on, however, his attention turning to historical writing and political criticism, he came ironically to be seen as a man harbouring a "Tory" bias. His 1908 biography of William Lyon Mackenzie for the Makers of Canada series was critical of the "patron saint" of Canada's liberal tradition, and protracted litigation prevented it from being published; it finally appeared in 1979.
A.B. McKillop

Letendre, Rita, painter, printmaker (b at Drummondville, Qué 1 Nov 1928). After study at the École des beaux-arts de Montréal, Letendre was influenced by Paul-Émile Borduas and the automatistes. In 1962 she travelled in western Europe and Israel. Her new interest in more structured composition and simpler shapes is seen in her outdoor mural commission in Long Beach, Calif, where she lived (1965-70) with her sculptor husband Kosso Eloul before moving to Toronto. There her painting became more austere, with large geometric forms and vibrant colour. Letendre is well known for her monumental interior and exterior murals.
Sandra Paikowsky

Lethbridge, Alta, City, pop 58 841 (1986c), 54 588 (1981cA), inc 1906, is located 215 km by road SE of Calgary on the steep, coulee-scarred banks of the Oldman R. It is a pleasant, tree-lined service centre for the surrounding agricultural communities. An elected mayor and 8 councillors govern the city with the assistance of an appointed city manager.

History Some 500 generations of Blackfoot inhabited the Lethbridge area before recorded history. In 1869 Montana traders built Fort Whoop-up, one of the notorious whisky forts dotting the region. The North-West Mounted Police stopped the liquor trade in 1874. Soon coal mining became the primary economic activity. Although coal had been mined from the banks of the nearby Belly R (a tributary of the Oldman R) as early as 1872, large-scale mining did not begin until 1885, when the North Western Coal and Navigation Co, directed by Sir Alexander and Elliott Galt, completed a railway from its mines to Dunmore on the CP main line. The colliery created an instant town, soon called Lethbridge (after North Western Coal's president, William Lethbridge), whose population reached 1478 in 1890 when the company completed a rail link with Montana. Railways continued to play an important part in Lethbridge's history. In 1897 the CPR assumed control over the Lethbridge-Dunmore line and extended it through the Crowsnest Pass. In 1905 the transcontinental made Lethbridge a divisional point on its line, expanded the railyards and constructed a station and maintenance facilities. The move firmly established Lethbridge as the region's marketing and distribution centre.

Irrigation has also played a major role in the evolution of Lethbridge. In 1900 the Canadian North-West Irrigation Co, managed by Elliott Galt, completed the first large-scale irrigation system in Alberta. Between the 2 world wars, the Taber and Lethbridge Northern schemes were implemented, and in the postwar period the St Mary R development was realized. Today, pivot irrigation has increased the potential of the area's semiarid lands even more, particularly for market gardening.

Economy The city contains nearly 100 manufacturing and processing firms making everything from cellular mobile telephones to gas transmission line compressors; from table-ready products to farm equipment to recreation products. Manufacturing facilities are located on an industrial park within a short drive from the downtown core. The retail and service sectors employ 58% of the total city work force. The trade area for the Lethbridge retail and service sector is extensive and includes a population of about 150 000 people. In 1985 the CPR was relocated outside the city and redevelopment has taken place on the site.

Cityscape In direct challenge to its dry prairie environment, Lethbridge has built wide, tree-shaded streets, and several wooded parks, which include Henderson Lake, Nikka Yuko Japanese Garden and Urban-River Valley Park. A spacious sportsplex, several arenas and small parks offer a wide variety of sports facilities. Cultural events are regularly staged at the Yates Memorial Centre, the Bowman Arts Centre and the Performing Arts Centre at University of Lethbridge (built 1967 as a Centennial project). Lethbridge also supports a community college.
A.A. den Otter

Lett, Sherwood, soldier, lawyer, chief justice of BC (b at Iroquois, Ont 1 Aug 1895; d at Vancouver 2 July 1964). After distinguished service in both world wars Lett was named first Canadian representative (1954-55) on the International Control Commission established under the auspices of the 1954 Geneva Conference to oversee the ceasefire and disengagement of French forces in N Vietnam and the political stabilization of that country. From 1955 until his death he was chief justice of BC. In 1963 he delivered a judgement of considerable constitutional significance when he declared the expropriation of a private company, BC Electric, by the provincial government in its precipitate efforts to set up the giant government-owned BC Hydro and Power Authority, to be ultra vires and therefore illegal. The government was forced to resume negotiations and ultimately purchased BC Electric at a substantially increased price.
Stanley Gordon

Lett, Stephen, psychiatrist (b at Callan, Ire 4 Apr 1847; d at Kingston, Ont Oct 1905). Having served as assistant medical superintendent of the insane asylums in Malden and London, Ont, 1870-77, he lost out to R.M. Bucke for the post of London's medical superintendent. A lasting antipathy developed between the 2 imperious men and resulted in Lett's transfer to a post at the Toronto asylum. In 1883 he briefly administered the Hamilton asylum until named first superintendent of the Homewood Retreat in Guelph, Ont. He was a specialist in the early treatment of addiction and his gradual withdrawal therapy for "opium neurosis" proved popular with his upper-crust clientele; however, his late-blooming success was cut short by a neurological disorder contracted in youth.
Cheryl L. Krasnick

Lettuce (*Lactuca sativa*), annual vegetable belonging to the Compositae family. Several species of wild lettuce occur in Canada, including prickly lettuce, a common weed that is a probable parent species of garden lettuce. Native to Asia Minor, lettuce was introduced to Haiti by Christopher Columbus. Of the 4 major varieties, head lettuce, which is firm and keeps well, is the most widely grown. The other varieties – small, tender-headed Bibb lettuce, long-headed Romaine lettuce and high-quality leaf lettuce – all lack the firmness required for most marketing purposes. Lettuce thrives in cool climates and is well suited to Canada's organic soils. Being frost resistant, it is usually sown in early spring. Less firm varieties are often grown in greenhouses in autumn. Slugs, aphids and leaf rot are its principal pests. Lettuce provides average food value (head lettuce being the least nutritious) and because of its freshness is a basic salad ingredient. In 1986, 40 900 t were produced, the lowest since 1982.
Roger Doucet

Levasseur Family, master joiners and architectural sculptors active in Québec throughout the

18th century. The dynasty was founded by 2 brothers who had apprenticed in France as master joiners: **Jean** (b at Paris Feb 1622; buried at Québec 31 Aug 1686) and **Pierre** (b 1629; d *c* 1681). From the middle of the 17th century, dozens of Levasseur descendants worked on government and especially RELIGIOUS BUILDINGS in Québec.

Outstanding among them were **Noël** (b at Québec City 28 Nov 1680; d there 12 Aug 1740), a sculptor who introduced the balustraded tabernacle at the chapel of the Hôpital-Général in Québec (1722-23) and elsewhere, and his cousin **Pierre-Noël** (b at Québec City 28 Nov 1690; d there 12 Aug 1770), one of the best architectural sculptors in New France. Pierre-Noël's work is characterized by the early use of the baldachin in church decoration and imbued with the richness and dramatic movement of the Baroque period, exemplified by the statues of St Peter and St Paul (1742-43) in the church of St Charles Borromée at Charlesbourg. Both sculptors participated in the ornamentation of the Ursuline chapel at Québec (1726-36) with its boldly trumpeting angel of the Last Judgement above the pulpit and its classically inspired retable, alive with shimmering saints and robust angels. This magnificent interior in the spirit of Louis XIV is one of the finest examples of wood carving in New France.

Reflecting the shift in taste towards the fussier, more animated Louis XV forms is the work of the next generation, in particular 2 sons of Noël, namely **François-Noël** (bap at Québec C 26 Dec 1703; d there 29 Oct 1794) and Jean-Baptiste-Antoine (bap at Québec C 20 June 1717; d there 8 Jan 1775). Spanning more than a century, the work of the Levasseur family in Québec amply illustrates the cultural transfer of French classical forms to the New World. CHRISTINA CAMERON

Reading: J. Trudel, *Un chef-d'oeuvre de l'art ancien du Québec: la chapelle des Ursulines* (1972); A.J.H. Richardson et al, *Québec City: Architects, Artisans and Builders* (1984); R. Gauthier, *Les Tabernacles anciens du Québec* (1974).

Léveillée, Claude, singer-songwriter, actor (b at Montréal 16 Oct 1932). His works, interpreted notably by Édith Piaf and André GAGNON, are marked by the depth and sincerity of the feelings they express. Léveillée was co-founder of the group Les Bozos (1959) and was the first Québec *chansonnier* to present a one-man show at Montréal's Place des Arts (1964). He has toured Canada, France, the USSR, Poland, Belgium, Switzerland, central Asia and Japan. His musical drama, *Concerto pour Héléne,* was played by the Québec Symphony in 1978. HÉLÈNE PLOUFFE

Lévesque, Georges-Henri, priest, sociologist, administrator (b at Roberval, Qué 16 Feb 1903). After studying at the Dominican College in Ottawa and U de Lille, France, he taught at the College as well as at U de M and Laval. In 1938 he organized the School of Social Sciences at Laval, which became a full-fledged faculty in 1943, and was its dean until 1955. A fervent liberal Catholic deeply committed to democratic norms and values, he used his position, as well as the Faculty of Social Sciences, to create new socioeconomic institutions such as the Conseil supérieur de la coopération and the Société d'éducation des adultes, and to initiate the modernization of Québec's church-controlled social welfare organizations. The faculty was also responsible for producing the first generation of university-educated labour organizers. During the 1950s and 1960s this group contributed immensely to the modernization and democratization of organized labour as well as of Québec society in general. His liberal ideas and endeavours brought him into conflict with Québec's intensely conservative clerical and political elites, especially Premier Maurice DUPLESSIS. With the support of his Dominican order and his numerous friends inside and outside the university, he was able to weather several attempts to undermine his career and destroy the faculty.

In the early 1950s he was a member of the Royal Commission on NATIONAL DEVELOPMENT IN THE ARTS, LETTERS AND SCIENCES, chaired by Vincent MASSEY, which recommended federal grants to universities and the creation of the CANADA COUNCIL. He served as VP of the Canada Council (1957-62), the Association canadienne-française pour l'avancement des sciences and the Royal Society of Canada (1962-63). Between 1954 and 1963 he acted as the director of Maison Montmorency near Québec C, a centre of social, cultural and religious debate and activism. He helped create a faculty of social sciences at Salamanaca, Spain, and was the founder and first rector of the National University of Rwanda in Central Africa (1963-72). He has been a lifelong member of numerous international organizations and has been awarded honorary degrees from over a dozen universities. He received the prestigious Canada Council MOLSON PRIZE (1966) as well as the Royal Bank Award (1982), the Pearson medal for peace (1983), and, most recently, the Fondation Édouard-Montpetit Medal (1985). He was made a Companion of the Order of Canada in 1979 and an Officer of the Ordre nationale du Quebec in 1985. Lévesque's contribution to a more humane, more democratic Canadian society has been immeasurable. M.D. BEHIELS

Lévesque, Jean-Louis, financier (b at Nouvelle, Qué 13 Apr 1911). After graduating from St Dunstan's U, in PEI, and Laval, Lévesque worked for the Banque provinciale du Canada in Moncton, NB. In 1937 he became a salesman for a securities firm and in 1941 founded Crédit Interprovincial Ltée. Lévesque then began buying, reorganizing and selling companies, including Fashion-Craft Manufacturers 1945, Slater Shoe 1951 and Dupuis Frères 1952. Later he merged his securities firm with L.G. Beaubien et Cie to form Lévesque, Beaubien Inc, the largest francophone brokerage house in Canada, specializing in government bonds. A former director of the Banque provinciale du Canada and General Trust of Canada, he still sits on the boards of several companies, including L'Équitable, Compagnie d'Assurances générales, and Hilton Canada. In 1978-79 he sold the companies he controlled and retired. In the 1950s Lévesque became involved in THOROUGHBRED RACING and breeding; his most successful racehorse, L'Enjoleur, won the QUEEN'S PLATE in 1975. In 1952 he received an honorary doctorate from UNB; he has received many other honours including the Order of Canada.

JORGE NIOSI

Lévesque, René, journalist, premier of Québec 1976-85 (b at Campbellton, NB 24 Aug 1922; d at Montréal 1 Nov 1987). A minister on Jean LESAGE's Liberal team, he resigned in 1968 and founded the PARTI QUÉBÉCOIS, whose main objective became Québec sovereignty and the creation of a new form of association with Canada.

A liaison officer and European war correspondent for the American armed forces in WWII, Lévesque joined Radio-Canada International in 1946 and became head of the radio-television news service in 1952. From 1956 he hosted the TV series "Point de Mire" and became one of Québec's most influential TV commentators. After taking part in the 1959 CBC producers' strike, he joined the Québec Liberal Party and was elected MNA for Montréal-Laurier in 1960. He was minister of water resources and of public works 1960-61, minister of natural resources 1961-66 and then minister of family and social welfare. One of the most popular and energetic members of the Lesage government, he was responsible for that government's decision to nationalize private electric utilities and for its efforts at cleaning up political mores.

René Lévesque was one of Québec's most influential television journalists before joining the Cabinet of Jean Lesage. He left the Liberals to found what in 1968 became the Parti Québécois and led the party to power in Nov 1976 (*photo by Jim Merrithew*).

Increasingly critical of his party's stand on constitutional issues and of its relations with the federal government, Lévesque sat as an independent MNA in 1967 and quit the party for good in Nov 1967 to found the Mouvement souveraineté-association, which in Oct 1968 became the Parti Québécois. Having managed to unite the various groups promoting independence and a new political status for Québec, Lévesque's party won 23.2% of the vote in the 1970 elections. In 1973 the PQ became the official Opposition. Lévesque was twice defeated (1970 and 1973) in Laurier and Dorion, but on 15 Nov 1976 he won in Taillon. Campaigning successfully in this election against the unpopular Liberal government of Robert BOURASSA, the PQ promised a REFERENDUM on SOVEREIGNTY-ASSOCIATION. The PQ won a majority of 71 seats, a result that dismayed the rest of Canada.

During its first term the new government passed several progressive measures concerning automobile insurance, rezoning of agricultural lands and the abolition of secret electoral funding. One of the most important pieces of legislation was BILL 101, which formalized the status of French as the official language of Québec. On 20 May 1980 the long-awaited referendum took place after an emotional campaign led on the *Non* side by Liberal Opposition leader Claude RYAN and federal Cabinet minister Jean CHRÉTIEN (with key support from PM TRUDEAU) and on the *Oui*, by Lévesque and his ministers. Lévesque suffered a major personal defeat when the sovereignty-association proposal won only 40 percent of the vote. Against all expectations the PQ was re-elected in 1981 but it suffered another defeat during the 1981-82 constitutional negotiations (see CONSTITUTION, PATRIATION OF), when the other 9 provinces accepted terms rejected by all parties in the Québec National Assembly. In 1982 and 1983 Lévesque's government met with considerable opposition and public disapproval when it attempted to reduce public spending to solve its grave financial problems.

In Nov 1984 a serious crisis affected the PQ government when Lévesque announced his intention of not fighting the next election on the issue of independence while maintaining sovereignty-association as the party's official *raison d'être*. Several ministers resigned in protest but the party reaffirmed Lévesque's leadership at a special convention in Jan 1985. In June 1985, however, he resigned and resumed a broadcasting and journalism career. His *Memoirs* have sold more than 250 000 copies. DANIEL LATOUCHE

Reading: P. Desbarats, *René: A Canadian in Search of a Country* (1976); G. Fraser, *P.Q.: René Lévesque and the Parti Québécois in Power* (1984); R. Lévesque, *Memoirs* (1986).

Levine, Norman, author (b at Ottawa 22 Oct 1923). Raised in Ottawa and educated at McGill (MA, 1949), he lived in England 1949-80. He is author of 2 books of poetry, *Myssium* (1948) and *The Tightrope Walker* (1950); 2 novels, *The Angled Road* (1952) and *From a Seaside Town* (1970); and several collections of short fiction, including *One Way Ticket* (1961), *Canada's Winter Tales* (1968), *I don't want to know anyone too well* (1971), *Selected Stories* (1975), *Thin Ice* (1979), *Why do you live so far away?* (1984) and *Champagne Barn* (1984). His stories have been translated and published throughout Europe. Levine's controversial collection of autobiographical, bittersweet reflections, *Canada Made Me*, published in England in 1958, did not appear in a Canadian edition until 1979. Best described as the ironic nostalgia of a natural alien, its dedication to emotional distancing has become a hallmark of Levine's art. In 1980 Levine returned to Canada and he currently lives and writes in Toronto. SHARON DRACHE

Lévis, Qué, City, pop 18 310 (1986c), 17 895 (1981c), inc 1861, is located on the rocky cliffs opposite Québec City, to which it is linked by ferry. Lévis is characterized by steep streets lined with picturesque old homes. Formerly called Aubigny, it was renamed in 1861 to honour Henri de Lévis, duke de Ventadour and protector of Samuel de CHAMPLAIN, and François-Gaston, duc de LÉVIS, victor in the 1760 Battle of STE-FOY. In the 19th century it was a major station on the GRAND TRUNK RY line and served Québec C, which had no line until 1879. Today, Lévis's economic activity is largely integrated with that of Lauzon, a major industrial centre. Davie Shipbuilding of Lauzon, founded in 1828, is the oldest and largest SHIPBUILDING company in Canada. In Lévis the Caisse populaire is a major employer, as is Baribeau et Fils, a manufacturer of wood items. Its deepwater port can handle 100 000 t tankers.

CLAUDINE PIERRE-DESCHÊNES

Lévis, François-Gaston de, Duc de Lévis, French army officer (b at Château d'Ajac near Limoux, France 20 Aug 1719; d at Arras, France 26 Nov 1787). Lévis, probably the most capable officer sent to Canada during the SEVEN YEARS' WAR, was appointed brigadier and made second-in-command of the French regular army in Canada in 1756. Remarkably fair-minded, he avoided the bitter disputes between his commander, MONTCALM, and Gov VAUDREUIL. During the campaigns of 1756, 1757 and 1758, Lévis directed the defence of the Lk Champlain invasion route, joined Montcalm in the successful attack on Ft William Henry (Lk George, NY), and in July 1758 helped Montcalm repel the British assault on Ft Carillon (Ticonderoga, NY). He played a leading role in the defence of Québec until Aug when he was sent to protect Montréal from a British advance.

On learning that Montcalm was dead and Québec had fallen, Lévis assumed command. In his bid to retake Québec in Apr-May 1760, Lévis dealt James MURRAY a severe blow in the Battle of STE-FOY, but lacked the cannon for an effective siege and had to retreat when British ships relieved the defenders. Besieged in Montréal, Lévis hoped to make a last stand but was overruled by Vaudreuil, and the town capitulated Sept 8. After the fall of New France, he rose to *maréchal*, the highest rank obtainable in France, in 1783 and was created a duke in 1784. IAN CASSELMAN

Lewis, David, né Losh, socialist politician, labour lawyer, university professor (b in Svisloch, Russia 23 June 1909; d at Ottawa 23 May 1981). As a child he lived through the German invasion of Russia in WWI and the Russian Revolution. In 1921 his family moved to Montréal, where Lewis soon mastered English. Active in municipal socialist politics, he attended McGill (1927-31) and won a Rhodes scholarship to attend Oxford (1932-35), where he established extensive contacts with socialists in the British Labour Party. Upon returning to Canada, Lewis practised law in Ottawa, but in 1936 he commenced work as national secretary for the CO-OPERATIVE COMMONWEALTH FEDERATION. During these years he became a key CCF theorist and member of the LEAGUE FOR SOCIAL RECONSTRUCTION. In 1943 he coauthored, with F.R. SCOTT, *Make This Your Canada*. Efforts to gain election to Parliament in 1940, 1943 (by-election), 1945 and 1949 were unsuccessful. From 1943 to 1945 Lewis was the primary target of a vicious antisocialist campaign.

In 1950, with CCF prospects dwindling, Lewis practised labour law, though his involvement with the CCF continued. He held a variety of executive positions and helped draft the Winnipeg Declaration of 1956. Lewis consistently worked to rid the labour movement of communist infiltration and to forge a link between the Canadian socialist and labour movements. He was the key architect in the formation of the NEW DEMOCRATIC PARTY in 1961. Through his efforts the primarily western farm-based CCF was transformed into the more urban, labour-oriented and successful NDP.

Lewis ran for Parliament in York S in 1962, 1963, 1965, 1968, 1972 and 1974, losing only in 1963 and 1974. He quickly became one of Parliament's most devastating debaters. Lewis continued to serve in a variety of NDP executive posts culminating in his election as leader at a long and polarized 1971 NDP convention in which he defeated Jim Laxer, representing the WAFFLE, a left-wing NDP faction. Lewis, campaigning on the theme of "corporate welfare bums," achieved his greatest political prominence in 1972 when he held the balance of power in the Liberal MINORITY GOVERNMENT of 1972 to 1974. This Parliament enacted a new Elections Expenses Act, pension indexing, PETRO-CANADA and the FOREIGN INVESTMENT REVIEW AGENCY.

David Lewis had a long involvement with the CCF and NDP parties. His party held the balance of power in the Liberal minority government 1972-74 (*courtesy Sophie Lewis*).

After his defeat in the federal election of 1974, Lewis stepped down as NDP leader in 1975 and ended his career as a professor at Carleton U. The first volume of his memoirs, *The Good Fight*, was published posthumously (1981). Lewis was sometimes a controversial figure, but few doubted his intellect, energy and sacrifices on behalf of Canadian socialism. ALAN WHITEHORN

Lewis, Stephen Henry, politician, journalist, labour arbitrator (b at Ottawa 11 Nov 1937), son of David LEWIS. After teaching English in Africa, Lewis worked as director of organization for the federal NEW DEMOCRATIC PARTY 1961-62. He was a member of the Ontario legislature for Scarborough W 1963-78 and became leader of the Ontario NDP in 1970. He was active in demanding the 1972 disbandment of the WAFFLE, a left-wing NDP faction. He achieved greatest success in 1975 when the NDP became the official Opposition. A year after the NDP's electoral setback in 1977, Lewis resigned as leader and became a newspaper columnist, radio and TV broadcaster, lecturer and labour arbitrator. In 1984 External Affairs Minister Joe CLARK appointed the articulate Lewis Canada's ambassador to the UNITED NATIONS. In 1986 Lewis was also named a special adviser to the UN's general secretary regarding African affairs.

ALAN WHITEHORN

Lewis, Wilfrid Bennett, physicist, chief scientist for 26 years of Chalk R Nuclear Laboratories (b at London, Eng 24 June 1908; d at Deep River, Ont 19 Jan 1987). Lewis trained under Lord RUTHERFORD and worked in atomic physics throughout the 1930s. Like most of his Cambridge colleagues, he worked on radar during WWII, becoming in 1945 superintendent of the main British airborne radar laboratory. His prewar colleague J.D. Cockcroft, earlier superintendent of army radar, was in 1944-45 scientific director of the Canadian-Anglo-French atomic project. Unexpectedly the British government ordered Cockcroft's return, to refound atomic research in Britain. The existence of the Canadian project hung in the balance, since the Canadian government was unwilling to continue it unless a qualified research director could be found. Lewis's name was eventually suggested. He came to Canada in 1946 as director of the Atomic Energy Division of the NATIONAL RESEARCH COUNCIL and served as the government's chief nuclear scientist until retirement in 1973 as senior VP (science) of ATOMIC ENERGY OF CANADA LTD..

Lewis's career had 2 main facets, scientific and political. When he came to Canada, the ZEEP reactor was already in operation and the NRX reactor under construction (completed 1947). Lewis had to find staff and orchestrate their work into an efficient research program, deal with unforeseen problems (notably the NRX accident of 1952), and at the same time plan ahead for new reactors appropriate to new investigations. By 1949 he decided in principle on a large heavy-water reactor, the specialty of the original wartime Canadian project, that could use Canadian-produced uranium fuel, supply especially high quantities of neutrons for research, and produce plutonium that could be sold to defray costs. This was the NRU reactor, completed in 1957. Its success led to the CANDU reactor program of the 1970s, to generate electricity at competitive rates. Other ventures under Lewis's direction ranged from the Theratron machine for medical radiation to the 1966 proposal to build an Intense Neutron Generator, vetoed by the government as being far too expensive.

Until the late 1950s, Canada was the only "atomic power" in the world dedicated to exclusively nonmilitary uses of nuclear technology.

Thus, when the first "Atoms for Peace" conference was held at Geneva (1955), Canada was in a unique political position, especially attractive to the "unaligned" countries that wanted to develop scientifically without joining the American or Russian camps, such as India and Pakistan, both of which later built Canadian-designed research reactors. Lewis led the Canadian delegation at this and subsequent UN conferences until 1971 and exercised considerable influence. He received numerous honours and awards for his scientific and diplomatic work, including the Atoms for Peace Award in 1967, worth $50 000, which he donated to McGill to buy scientific apparatus.

DONALD J.C. PHILLIPSON

Lewisporte, Nfld, Town, pop 3978 (1986c), 3963 (1981c), inc 1946, is a deep-water port and shipping centre in NOTRE DAME BAY, N-central Newfoundland. Settled around 1876, it was formerly called (Big) Burnt Bay and later Marshallville. It was renamed Lewisport (later Lewisporte) in 1900 after lumber pioneer Lewis Miller, who used the excellent harbour, connected by rail with the interior, as a port for lumber mills at Glenwood and Millertown. A large shipping yard was built at Lewisporte by Newfoundland Timber Estates, which assumed ownership of Miller's holding by 1903. Thus the former fishing, farming and boat-building settlement became a shipping port and sawmilling centre. Today, Lewisporte serves as a major distribution, shipping and supply point for the NE coast of Newfoundland and coastal LABRADOR. It also has large fuel-storage facilities for Gander International Airport.

JANET E.M. PITT AND ROBERT D. PITT

Leyrac, Monique, née Tremblay, singer, actress (b at Montréal 26 Feb 1928). Thanks to her happy combination of gifts for music and theatre, she has been able to give her shows a rare intensity of emotion. She studied with Jeanne Maubourg before starting her acting career on radio in 1943. She began singing a few years later. Slowly she developed an interest in Québec songs, having started her career performing French music (including that of Édith Piaf) and South American songs. In 1965 she won the grand prizes at the International Festival of Song in Sopot, Poland (performing "Mon Pays" by Gilles VIGNEAULT), and at the Festival de la chanson at Ostende, Belgium. She received the 1978 Prix de musique Calixa-Lavallée. Leyrac has acted in several films, including Paul ALMOND'S *Act of the Heart.* In the 1980s she has all but given up her singing career, preferring to act in one-woman shows such as *Monique Leyrac chant et dit Nelligan* and *Divine Sarah.* She is an Officer of the Order of Canada.

HÉLÈNE PLOUFFE

L'Heureux, Jean-Baptiste (b at L'Acadie, LC 25 June 1831; d at Midnapore, Alta 19 Mar 1919). L'Heureux studied for the priesthood but was never ordained; a tradition maintains that he was expelled from the Séminaire de St-Hyacinthe for a criminal offence. He came west in the late 1850s and by the early 1860s was in the Montana goldfields, where he passed himself off to the Jesuits as a priest. A short time later, L'Heureux was apparently caught in the act of sodomy and was sent away. Exposed as a fraud, he joined the Blackfoot and in 1862 went to the Oblate fathers at St Albert mission near Ft Edmonton; a year later, Bishop A.A. TACHÉ commented that the man "wanted to pass for a priest, but he is known by all to be a robber and a liar." The same year, L'Heureux was accused of sending a false sample of gold dust to prospectors in Ft Benton, Mont, claiming he had found a lode and would show them where it was located. A party of men spent weeks searching fruitlessly for him. L'Heureux's name also has been associated with the legend of the LOST LEMON MINE.

L'Heureux spent most of his time with the Blackfoot, performing marriages, baptisms, etc. In their language he called himself *na-okska-tapi,* Three Persons, after the Trinity. He prepared a census of the Blackfoot tribes, wrote a manuscript on stone effigies, described the land features in Blackfoot territory, prepared a Blackfoot-English dictionary and sketched Rocky Mountain House. In an 1871 manuscript, now in the NATIONAL ARCHIVES OF CANADA, he made what is probably the first reference to dinosaur remains in Alberta. He may also have named the St Mary R in southern Alberta and St Mary Lks in Montana. An official witness to Treaty No 7 in 1877, L'Heureux was engaged as interpreter for the Indian department on the Blackfoot reserve about 1880. He remained there until 1891, when he was dismissed for giving religious instruction to preschool children. He became a recluse near Pincher Creek and in 1912 moved to Lacombe Home at Midnapore.

HUGH A. DEMPSEY

Liard Highway is an all-weather road linking northern British Columbia and the Northwest Territories. Beginning 27 km north of Fort Nelson on the Alaska Highway, it runs 400 km north to join the Mackenzie Highway a short distance south of Fort Simpson, NWT. Work on the highway started in 1969, when the federal government began construction south from Fort Simpson; in 1972 the BC government commenced work on the southern section. Jurisdictional disputes delayed the work, and the highway was not finished until 1984. At present, the only facilities for travellers are at Fort Liard, the approximate mid-point of the road.

K.S. COATES

Liard River, 1115 km long, rises in the Pelly Mts in the SE Yukon and flows SE into BC, through the Rocky Mts, then NE through heavily forested land to the Mackenzie R at FT SIMPSON, NWT. Its major tributaries are the SOUTH NAHANNI, Petitot and Fort Nelson rivers. The river is navigable to Ft Liard, about 270 km from its mouth, though much of it is wild and perilous. Named for the liards (a species of poplar) found along its banks, it was called "Courant-Fort" in early days, and appears as Rivière aux Liards on early maps. For many years a fur-trade route, it was first surveyed by R.G. MCCONNELL of the Geological Survey (1887). Gold-hungry prospectors travelled it on the way to the Klondike in 1897-98.

JAMES MARSH

Liberal Party, which has dominated federal politics through the 20th century as the "government party," first developed its formula for political success under the leadership of Sir Wilfrid LAURIER who was prime minister from 1896 to 1911. In clear contrast to its enjoyment of power through the politics of pragmatism in this century, the party's 19th-century history is a record of long decades of opposition to the powerful through the pursuit of reform principles.

Opposition politics took organizational shape in the colonies of British N America with the establishment of representative institutions in Nova Scotia (1758), New Brunswick (1784) and Upper and Lower Canada (1791). Since power in these colonies was concentrated in a governing oligarchy of appointed governors and councils that was not held responsible to the elected assemblies, reformers appealed to the Whig principle of parliamentary supremacy in pressing for the adoption of RESPONSIBLE GOVERNMENT. In the Maritimes Joseph HOWE led a 10-year struggle for responsible government that was finally successful in 1848. In the same year, a Reform coalition led by Robert BALDWIN in Canada West and Louis-Hippolyte LAFONTAINE in Canada East achieved the same breakthrough.

In Canada West, the radical farmers of southwest Ontario, known as the Clear Grits, who had been inspired by the anti-British radicalism of William Lyon MACKENZIE, strongly attacked the CLERGY RESERVES as an institutionalization of the FAMILY COMPACT'S domination and a denial of liberty to the Protestant denominations. With the vocal support of the Reform publisher, George BROWN, whose newspaper, *The Globe,* was the most influential organ in the colony, the Reformers succeeded in eliminating the reserves by the 1850s. Co-operation between the anti-Family-Compact Reformers in Upper Canada and the anti-English-oligarchy *rouges* in Lower Canada broke down in the 1850s over the question of state support for denominational schools (*see* SEPARATE SCHOOL). The liberalism of Protestant Reformers led them to believe that each church should be supported by the aid of its adherents, voluntarily offered. By extension, denominational schools should not receive public funds.

Another characteristic of pre-Confederation Reform politicians was also a product of their belief in the principles of English liberalism. Opposition to government intervention in the economy in the form of tariff protection (*see* PROTECTIONISM), which conservative administrations tended to favour, led mid-century Reformers to advocate free trade with their admired neighbour to the south. The crowning achievement of the Reform administration of Francis HINCKS and A.N. MORIN was the negotiation of a RECIPROCITY treaty with the US in 1854. This proclivity for CONTINENTALISM was to remain a theme of Liberal politics for the next century.

In the early years of Confederation, the Liberals, as the Reform remnants now called themselves, could do little against the political wiles of the Conservative PM Sir John A. MACDONALD and the breadth of his coalition in federal politics. The post-Confederation Liberals developed successful provincial organizations. As premier of Ontario from 1872 to 1896, Sir Oliver MOWAT led the provinces' assault on the power of the Dominion government in the name of provincial rights, a tenet of Liberal thought for several decades. Following the downfall of Macdonald's government over the PACIFIC SCANDAL, the dour stonemason Alexander MACKENZIE formed the federation's first Liberal administration in 1873, but a severe economic depression and Mackenzie's lack of political vision led to Macdonald's re-election in 1878 on a platform of protection. The resulting NATIONAL POLICY of tariff protection was vigorously opposed by Edward BLAKE, a Toronto lawyer and ex-premier of Ontario, who led the Liberal Party from 1880 to 1887. (Blake is the only federal Liberal leader never to have become prime minister.) Blake and Mowat pressed for further reforms of the ELECTORAL SYSTEM and managed to wean their Ontario supporters from the fanatical anti-Catholicism they had retained from the Clear Grits and George Brown.

Meanwhile, in Québec, Wilfrid Laurier was turning the *Rouges* – the radical successors of Papineau's PATRIOTES from the 1837 uprising – from anticlericalism by preaching the principles of William Gladstone's English liberalism and the virtues of racial conciliation. Chosen party leader by the reluctant federal caucus upon Blake's advice in 1887, Laurier gradually broadened the Liberals' base in Québec and, on a platform of provincial rights, won the election of 1896 despite the hostility of the Catholic Church hierarchy and the embarrassment of Manitoba's discrimination against French-speaking Catholics (*see* MANITOBA SCHOOLS QUESTION).

Laurier went on to win the next 3 elections by copying Macdonald's formula for success – a nationwide coalition of forces, an expansionary role for government, and an accommodation between the French and the English – tempering the principles of Liberal reform with pragmatism and PATRONAGE. He built his electoral coalition in English Canada on the organizational backs of Liberal provincial premiers whom he brought into his Cabinet as power brokers for their regions. He endorsed the aggressive IMMIGRATION POLICY to settle the West of his Manitoba minister, Clifford SIFTON, and he entered the same kind of transcontinental railway-building collaboration with the Grand Trunk and Canadian Northern that his caucus had denounced in the 1880s when championed by Macdonald.

Nevertheless, differences of principle still distinguished the Laurier Liberals from their Conservative opponents. In foreign policy, the Liberals showed their affinity to Gladstone's anti-imperialism by their preference for an independent Canadian navy over Canadian contributions to the British navy. In commercial policy Laurier achieved the long-held Liberal goal of a reciprocity agreement with the US. It was a victory that proved his undoing: reciprocity alienated the protection-minded business community whose support he had cultivated, and the Liberals went down to defeat in the 1911 election in the face of the Conservative Party's anti-Americanism. Laurier soldiered on as leader, watching in despair as the WWI military CONSCRIPTION issue nearly destroyed his party by temporarily shaking the solidarity of its English-French alliance.

The political longevity of the Liberals' next, and probably greatest, leader, William Lyon Mackenzie KING, who began his career as a public servant and ended it as the most enduring prime minister in Canadian history (1921-48 except for 2 periods in Opposition, in 1926 and 1930-35) has been ascribed to his uncanny capacity for blurring political issues to maintain support among such ideologically opposed groups as western free-trade farmers and protectionist manufacturers of central Canada; his shrewd recognition of the importance of sustaining Québec support, especially during WWII; his talent for attracting to his Cabinet strong ministers with regional power bases and making the best use of their abilities and connections; and his success in presenting a progressive face to the electorate by gradually initiating social-welfare programs while propitiating the business community. King straddled the middle of the political road while leaning slightly left; his genius for obfuscation was epitomized by his vacuous 1935 campaign slogan "King or Chaos" and his delphic position, "conscription if necessary but not necessarily conscription," with which he walked the tightrope between English-Canadian militants and Québec pacifists during WWII.

King's hand-picked successor, Louis ST. LAURENT, was more admired among the bureaucratic and business elites than was King, but because of his disregard of party organization and his dependence on the Ottawa bureaucracy, his regime saw the collapse of King's great Liberal alliance and the beginning of the party's persistent alienation from western Canada. Since St. Laurent's narrow defeat by John DIEFENBAKER (1957), the Liberal Party has been struggling to regain its status as a truly national party.

It took Lester Bowles PEARSON, a Nobel-peace-prize-winning former diplomat and secretary of state for external affairs who was elected party leader in early 1958, 3 elections before he won back power in 1963. It was largely thanks to the organizational skills and reformist convictions of his close adviser, Walter GORDON, that this most unpolitical of Liberal leaders managed to establish his control over the rebuilt party organization. One price of Gordon's reforms was the alienation of the western provincial organizations from what had become a Toronto-dominated party. Gordon received the credit for winning a minority victory in 1963 and then was blamed for recommending another election in 1965, which returned the Liberals as a MINORITY GOVERNMENT once more. Even when the extraordinary Pierre Elliott TRUDEAU succeeded Pearson in a hotly contested leadership campaign in 1968, the party continued to scramble unsuccessfully to remake its alliance with the West, managing to remain in office until 1979 and then again from 1980 to 1984 despite marked vacillations in its popularity on the basis of its strength in central Canada.

Sir Wilfrid Laurier at Mission City, BC, 15 Aug 1910. Laurier became leader in 1887 and broadened the Liberal base in Québec. He became PM in 1896 and went on to win the next 3 elections (*by permission of the British Library*).

Party Size Liberal party officials in the early 1980s claimed 250 000 adherents. Although structured under its elaborate constitution as a mass democratic party whose leadership, in theory, is controlled by the grass-roots membership, it is in fact run along oligarchic lines. Real power is held by the party leader and his coterie. This top-down structure is modified slightly in periods of Opposition when its leadership is forced to appeal for greater rank-and-file participation in policy-making as an inducement to mobilize the grass roots in a collective struggle to regain power. The number of people belonging to the 282 federal constituency associations in the 1980s cannot easily be compared with its membership in the past, because historically the party was a federation of provincial parties whose membership varied greatly, depending on who was in power in individual provinces. In the early 1980s the Liberals were without a single member in the 4 provincial legislatures west of Ontario, a situation that reflected their federal weakness in the West where they had fallen to third-party stature.

A 1930 election poster characterizing the Liberal Party as the forger of a national consensus (*courtesy National Archives of Canada/C-85940*).

Splinter Groups As in any such broadly based party, there are always small but significant groups that oppose the dominant view of the Liberal leadership. In BC in the 1950s many provincial Liberals formed an electoral coalition with the right-wing Social Credit movement, to the dismay of the federal party. In the 1960s, Ross THATCHER, the Liberal premier of Saskatchewan, strongly opposed the welfare liberalism of PM Lester Pearson. Both conflicts helped destroy the federal party's credibility in the West. Throughout the party's history there has been tension between the forces of continentalism and NATIONALISM within Liberal ranks; it became most obvious during the 1960s when Walter Gordon led the effort to limit the growth of foreign control in the economy (*see* FOREIGN INVESTMENT). Gordon lost his preliminary battles but did not abandon the war, unlike other dissidents, such as James RICHARDSON and Eric KIERANS, Trudeau Cabinet ministers who quit politics when their policy positions were rejected. In the late 1970s and early 1980s, there were again left-right tensions in the party, chiefly between Pierre Trudeau and John TURNER and their respective followers. Though Turner, Trudeau's former minister of finance, quit the Cabinet in 1975, he continued to play the role of Liberal dauphin-in-exile. Two weeks after Trudeau announced he would retire, Turner declared his candidacy for the succession, a goal he achieved on 16 June 1984 at the party's leadership convention. Sworn in as prime minister on June 30, he quickly called a general election hoping to profit from the Liberals' brief surge of popularity in the public opinion polls. Without an adequate organization, platform or personal campaign style, he led the party to the worst electoral defeat in its history. The results were Progressive Conservatives 211, Liberals 40, New Democrats 30 and Independent 1.

Electoral Appeal and Popular Support Since the 1930s the Liberals' electoral appeal has been based on projecting an image of competence and compromise. Ideologically the party has clung to the political centre, modulating its stance in each region and appealing to the upwardly mobile middle class of urban central Canada. In the Atlantic provinces, where the social democrats have traditionally had great difficulty in becoming a third political force, Liberals vie directly with Conservatives in a 2-party seesaw fight for votes. In Québec a strong plurality of the vote has generally translated into an overwhelming majority of seats, with the dramatic exceptions of the 1958 and 1984 elections. In Ontario, electoral support averaging 40% has been transformed into 60% of the seats since the 1930s. But the third-party status of the federal Liberal Party in the West has turned electoral returns of about 30% of the votes into a tiny number of actual Liberal seats.

Financial Support The Liberals traditionally raised election campaign money from big businessmen and to a lesser extent, small entrepreneurs (*see* PARTY FINANCING). Since the introduction of the ELECTION EXPENSES ACT (1974), reliance on business funding has dramatically declined in favour of tax-deductible member donations and direct subsidies from the public purse (*see* PARTY SYSTEM).

Current Issues and Significant Changes in the Party The most significant changes in recent decades in the Liberal Party were heralded by the accession to the party's leadership of Pierre Trudeau in 1968 and his resignation 16 years later. Under his aegis French Canadians achieved greater equity within the Liberal Party and the Government of Canada than ever before. Trudeau's dedication to FEDERALISM and to combatting the separatist forces of Québec nationalism lay at the heart both of his early electrifying appeal to the public and of the strong animosities he later generated among English Canadian voters. His controversial personal style and the vacillations of his policies (eg, withdrawing, then reinforcing, Canadian troops in NATO; opposing economic nationalism, then endorsing the adoption of a dramatic National Energy Program) kept his personality the chief issue of the political scene, notwithstanding his significant achievement in generating a wide consensus for the "patriation" of the CONSTITUTION in 1982. As Trudeau's period in office ended and his successor was plagued by dramatic problems of ideological direction and party organization, some speculated, as they had in 1957 and again in 1979 when the party fell temporarily from power, that the Liberals were on the edge of disappearing from the country's political map. To others it seemed more likely that, with John Turner's commitment to rebuild the party, it would ultimately be able to resuscitate itself, especially in view of the fact that the mid-1980s saw an important revival of its fortunes provincially with Liberal governments elected in Ontario (1985 and a landslide victory in 1987), Québec (1985), PEI (1986) and NB (a complete sweep 1987). *See also* PARTI ROUGE; PARTI PATRIOTE.

CHRISTINA MCCALL AND STEPHEN CLARKSON

Reading: Christina McCall-Newman, *Grits* (1982); J. Wearing, *The L-Shaped Party* (1980); R. Whitaker, *The Government Party* (1977).

Liberalism Long before the political label was coined in 19th-century Spain, liberalism existed as a body of thought dedicated to the proposition that the individual is the unit of supreme value in society.

The English philosopher John Locke (1632-1704) holds pride of place among liberalism's thinkers. Locke was the first to argue that individuals have innate rights of life, liberty and property. These rights exist prior to government. Governments come about only through the agreement of autonomous individuals that their rights are best protected by joint association. If this contract is broken the people have the right to rebel. Locke's ideas justified England's Glorious Revolution of 1688 and animated the American revolutionaries of 1776.

By the early 19th century liberalism was on the march. In 1812 the Liberales, a middle class movement opposed by the nobles and clergy, succeeded in giving the Spanish nation a brief respite from absolutism by winning acceptance of a Constitution. The name caught on when the British Tories used it as a term of abuse to taunt the more progressive Whigs. Nearly 2 centuries after its invention the label still denotes opprobrium in some quarters: Vice-President Spiro Agnew of the US, for example, briefly made a reputation by attacking his opponents as "radic-libs."

Liberals believe that every individual has a special dimension, a uniqueness that cries out to be realized. The purpose of life is to realize that potential, to become whatever it is one is capable of becoming. As a free agent man is able to define and pursue his own definition of happiness, his own version of the good, his own set of values. The role of the state is to produce the conditions under which individuals have the broadest possible choice in deciding upon their definition of the good. Society, meanwhile, should relish this diversity while dispensing equal treatment regardless of one's origins, colour, sex or status in life. In exchange for this respect, the individual must acknowledge responsibility for his own fortunes and for the fortunes of the community.

It is this individualistic essence which distinguishes liberalism from conservatism or socialism. Whatever their disagreements about the ends of society, both conservatives and socialists believe that society is more than a collection of autonomous individuals. Conservatives favour an organic hierarchical society, socialists stress the primacy of class but the central concept for both is a collectivity. Liberalism, therefore, is a particular way of thinking about human needs and the political good. It is not the property of a single political party. In Canada it forms almost as an important a strand in the ideology of the Progressive Conservative and New Democratic parties as it does in the Liberal Party for, whatever the party label, if the primary focus of one's concern is individual self-realization, liberalism has won a convert.

Liberalism came to Canada with the United Empire Loyalists. Devoted to British institutions (especially to the monarchy), the Loyalists bitterly opposed American republicanism; but as N Americans used to economic mobility and representative government, they were equally passionate about individual liberty. The Constitutional Act of 1791 which created the elected assemblies of Upper and Lower Canada was liberalism's first success in Canada. Responsible government, representation by population, minority rights, and the welfare state have followed. The Loyalist settlement set a pattern persisting from that era to our own: influenced in equal parts by British and American developments, with an occasional leavening from the Continent such as the impact of the 1848 Revolution on Les Rouges, liberalism has formed the core of the Canadian public philosophy.

Liberalism is not without its detractors. Noted scholars such as George GRANT criticize the very foundations of the philosophy: they oppose a "possessive individualism" which stresses the acquisition of property by competitive individuals and they favour a more co-operative form of society which has a purpose above and beyond the individual rights and desires of its members.

There is an inner tension too within liberalism that often pits one school of thought against another. Liberals agree that they want to expand choice but how best to do so? The "classical" school of liberalism concentrates on freedom from external interference: government is feared, the market economy is favoured, private autonomy is valued. Positive liberalism, however, points out that having the absolute right to do something is meaningless unless one has the actual capability of doing it. Liberty is more than the absence of restraint, it must include equality of opportunity. Liberal egalitarians demand positive programs to redistribute wealth and to create more fairness in the competition of life.

Despite this basic dispute over whether the state is an obstacle to be removed or an instrument to be used, Canadian liberalism has made one very real contribution to the practice of democratic governance. How best to reconcile ethnic pluralism and minority rights within a national community is a problem that plagues much of the world. India is but one example of a society beset by social and religious discord. Liberals in Canada have always placed a premium on protecting minority rights. In 1982 the CANADIAN CHARTER OF RIGHTS AND FREEDOMS advanced this cause in a quantum way through entrenching into the Canadian Constitution both basic liberties and new linguistic rights for minorities. The overriding purpose of the Charter for its proponents was to entrench rights, especially language rights, where no government could ever take them away. With the Charter as a shield a single citizen can achieve Locke's vision of a society in which rights take precedence over authority.

The proudest achievement of Canadian liberalism has been in the words of Sir Wilfrid Laurier, Canada's most eloquent liberal, the creation of this "regime of tolerance."

THOMAS S. AXWORTHY

Liberation of Holland, begun by American troops, who entered Maastricht on 13 Sept 1944; British troops also played a major part in liberating S Holland, along their axis of advance toward Berlin. The failure of an airborne assault on Arnhem (Sept 17) prevented the liberation of the rest of Holland in 1944. FIRST CANADIAN ARMY, under Gen H.D.G. CRERAR, on the N end of the Allied line, was to clear the Dutch approaches to the key Belgian port of Antwerp, along both banks of the Schelde estuary, a task completed in Nov. There were still more Allied than Canadian troops under Crerar, but in mid-Mar 1945 I Canadian Corps arrived from Italy to replace I British Corps. I Corps pushed N to the IJsselmeer (Apr 18), isolating German forces in W Netherlands, while II Corps drove NE to Groningen (Apr 13) and Leeuwarden (Apr 15), and then E into Germany.

When hostilities ceased 5 May 1945, it fell to the Canadians to liberate W Holland, including the major cities of Amsterdam and Rotterdam and the Dutch capital, The Hague. The Dutch there had suffered through an extremely harsh winter, short of food and fuel, but relief supplies were quickly funnelled into the area. The Canadians were welcomed enthusiastically and the joyous "Canadian summer" that ensued forged deep and long-lasting bonds of friendship between the Dutch and Canadian peoples. *See also* WORLD WAR II. BRERETON GREENHOUS

Reading: D. Kaufman and M. Horn, *A Liberation Album* (1980).

Liberté, bimonthly journal fd 1959 in Montréal by poet Jean-Guy Pilon and other writers including Jacques GODBOUT, Fernand OUELLETTE, Paul-Marie LAPOINTE and Gilles Hénault. Managed in turn by Pilon, Godbout, Hubert AQUIN, again by Pilon and, since 1980, by François Ricard, it occupies a special place because of the quality and biting tone of its writing, its role as a critical forum for all contemporary cultural ideas, its avid interest in other literatures, the number and importance of its special issues and the international writers' conferences it has organized. *Liberté* has published such celebrated works as Lapointe's *Arbres*, Gaston MIRON's *La Vie agonique* (tr *The Agonized Life*, 1980), Aquin's "La Fatigue culturelle du Canada français" (tr "The Cultural Fatigue of French Canada," 1979), Ouellette's "La Lutte des langues et la dualité du langage" and the first collection by the future writers of PARTI PRIS.

Although most major Québec writers have written for *Liberté*, the journal has always welcomed contributions from foreign authors. Major authors and critics such as René Char, Pierre-Jean Jouve, Aimé Césaire, Milan Kundera, Julio Cortazar, Jean Starobinski and René Girard have all contributed. Since 1980, *Liberté* has become more polemical, but continues to diversify its involvement in the cultural field with such undertakings as TV specials, studies of the literary institution and studies of feminism. ANDRÉ BELLEAU

Libraries The earliest libraries in Canada were private collections belonging to immigrants from Europe. The first known library belonged to Marc LESCARBOT, a scholar and advocate who came to PORT-ROYAL in 1606. Early religious orders accumulated libraries: volumes from the Canadian Jesuit Mission of 1632 and the Jesuit College in Québec C (est 1635) still exist. Libraries were maintained in the 18th and 19th centuries in settlements, fur-trade or military posts – at Selkirk's RED RIVER COLONY, at the Hudson's Bay Co post at YORK FACTORY, by John McKay on Vancouver I after 1786, by Roderick McKenzie at Fort Chipewyan [Alta] after 1788, and at the Halifax garrison by Lord DALHOUSIE.

Public Libraries

In the 19th century, mechanics' institutes and subscription, social, school-district, university and professional libraries assumed increasing importance. Most public libraries that existed in the early decades of the 19th century were supported by subscription fees, eg, Governor HALDIMAND established a library at Québec C in 1779, the Montreal Library was founded in 1796, and a library began operation at Niagara in 1800. By mid-century, libraries were firmly established in British N America. The first free tax-supported public libraries date from 1883 at Saint John, Guelph and Toronto. However, the development of the public library as it is known today was a slow evolution through a variety of forms, in response to the geographic, economic, cultural and demographic conditions of each province. Predecessors of the modern, tax-supported public library were school-district libraries, mechanics' institutes and association or social libraries.

School-District Libraries were initiated by Joseph HOWE in NS and Egerton RYERSON in Canada W (Ontario) in 1850. Both men felt that children and adults could be served by local school authorities, with some financial and organizational assistance from colonial legislatures. NB (1858) and PEI (1877) followed this example, but after Confederation school-district libraries were less successful owing to local disaffection with the centralizing tendencies of departments of education.

Mechanics' Institutes originated in Great Britain in conjunction with working men's societies. In 1828 the first Mechanics society was formed at Montréal. They quickly became popular in communities such as Halifax, Montréal, Toronto and Victoria because they offered the working class inexpensive access to books and newspapers. Interest began to wane after Confederation, and many institutes eventually became part of a public library. In Ontario, for example, this process was facilitated when the 1882 Act allowed the establishment of free public libraries in cities, towns and villages and permitted the assets of institutes to be transferred to free libraries. Legislative grants were similarly transferred, with the result that the institutes ceased or were replaced by public libraries.

Association or Social Libraries dedicated to a variety of interests flourished in eastern Canada after 1800. The collection of the LITERARY AND HISTORICAL SOCIETY OF QUEBEC (est 1824) was particularly noteworthy. Most associations provided a meeting place for lectures, discussions, or other programs and a circulating library for members. Like the mechanics' institutes, association libraries were public by virtue of serving a membership beyond class, ethnic or religious limitations because they catered to broader cultural, musical, literary, or sporting tastes; many eventually became free public libraries, though the type still exists in some areas, eg, BC.

Reading area of the Metropolitan Toronto Library, designed by architect Raymond Moriyama (*photo © Hartill Art Associates, London, Ont*).

Free Libraries In 1882 an Act of the Ontario legislature provided for the establishment of free libraries, supported financially by a levy of one-half mill to be assessed on the value of all real and personal property. A local board composed of 9 members appointed by the municipal council and school boards was to provide leadership. The Toronto Public Library was the largest among the first libraries to choose free status. This Ontario pattern of legislating tax support for library services was followed in other provinces: BC (1891), Manitoba (1899), Saskatchewan (1906), Alberta (1907), NB (1929), Newfoundland (1935), PEI (1935, repealed 1936), NS (1937), Québec (1959) and the NWT (1966).

Modern Public Libraries The modern library selects, acquires and organizes books, periodicals, newspapers, government publications, reports, microforms, maps, audiovisual materials, computer tapes and other materials, and makes them available to users. Materials selected to meet user needs are acquired and processed for the shelves using a cataloguing and classification system to provide the user with access to the library collection. Reference service offers assistance to the user in determining what is needed and how to find it. Provision of additional services, eg, children's programs, audiovisual services, and selective dissemination of information, depends on the clientele of the library. Public libraries in Canada are governed by provincial statutes and are primarily financed by local tax revenues, with provincial grants supplementing local funding. Public libraries are normally the responsibility of a local library board with authority to appoint or dismiss employees, control library property, establish policies, and budget for library operations. Service has varied depending on the commitment of local communities and their library boards.

The period in public library development immediately after 1900 was marked by construction of library buildings and expansion of collections and services. With an emphasis on broadening the membership base, open access was permitted, children's departments were introduced, standard cataloguing and classification systems were adopted, library extension in rural areas also commenced. Travelling libraries were introduced to BC, Ontario and Québec shortly before 1900. Similar libraries were operated by the universities of Manitoba, Dalhousie, McGill and Alberta, and by provincial authorities in Saskatchewan, Ontario and Newfoundland. Although public library development was checked during the Depression and WWII, the expansion of service resumed after 1945.

Following the 1960s' emphasis on education, more than 125 new or remodelled public library buildings were constructed in Canada, in part with Centennial grants, and public library service expanded. Library development has been adversely affected by the inflationary period of the 1970s and early 1980s, and libraries are caught between increasing demands from the public for enhanced services and pressures from municipal or regional jurisdictions to reduce or stabilize expenditures. Expansion of services has slackened, though the statistics are still impressive. In 1986 Statistics Canada reported that 1014 public libraries held 51.8 million books, circulated 154.8 million items, spent $57.7 million on materials, and employed over 11 457 people at 3136 service points across Canada.

Regional Libraries Because of Canada's demographic composition, provincial legislatures and professional associations have encouraged the formation of larger units of service such as county, regional and provincial library systems. The first regional systems were demonstrated on a trial basis in the early 1930s in the Fraser Valley and in PEI. After WWII other provinces adopted the regional forms. Some, such as Saskatchewan, have found that a regional system is the best solution to serving small communities separated by great distances – the province's large municipal libraries serve as backup to the regionals. Administrative frameworks and financial support for regional systems differ in each province: some local units are branches in a provincial system whereas others remain autonomous; some provinces provide centralized processing and backup collections for the regional library systems, others do not.

University, College and School Libraries

University and college libraries are integral parts of the academic community in which they are located, and are supported with a percentage of normal operating funds (6-8%), with additional special grants from funding agencies or endowments. A university chief librarian usually reports to an academic official, such as the office of vice-president, academic, and is represented on senior academic decision-making bodies of the university. College libraries receive a smaller percentage of operating funds and the administrative structure varies greatly in and between provinces.

University Libraries The first academic library as they are now known opened in 1789 with the establishment of King's College in Windsor, NS. Though libraries were included in many colleges and universities founded in the early 19th century in eastern Canada, academic collections remained relatively small until 1950, when Canadian academic libraries escalated rapidly in response to a new emphasis on education and research. According to Statistics Canada, in 1984-85, 1.5% ($291 million) of total Canadian university expenditures went to library acquisitions.

Typical of this rapid growth was the establishment of 5 new universities in Ontario, which opened their doors with completely catalogued basic collections thanks to the Ontario New Universities Library Project of the early 1960s, one of the first large-scale uses of library automation in Canada. Other provinces, most notably BC, also funded university library development, and the CANADA COUNCIL, and subsequently the SOCIAL SCIENCES AND HUMANITIES RESEARCH COUNCIL provided special grants for the enrichment of collections of national distinction.

In the late 1960s co-operative programs were introduced to allow the reorganization and sharing of collections. The Ontario Council of University Libraries developed a co-operative library network that included a transit system, a structured interlibrary loan system, automated union list systems for serials and government publications, and interuniversity and reciprocal borrowing agreements. In BC the Tri-University

Libraries initiated a government-funded union catalogue project that included college libraries. Similar activities occurred in Québec under the library council for the universities. The most ambitious project, UNICAT/TELCAT (1974-79), was a union catalogue and support system shared by 18 Ontario and Québec university and government libraries; it was disbanded when newer technologies made local integrated systems linked to each other via TELECOMMUNICATION networks more cost-effective.

College Libraries have developed rapidly in Canada since 1960 – in Québec in Collèges d'enseignement général et professionel, in Ontario in colleges of applied arts and technology, and in the other provinces in technical institutes or community colleges. These libraries are learning resource centres, emphasizing nonprint materials as much as traditional print collections. It was in 1982-83 that Statistics Canada last calculated specific library information. At that time, 86 community college libraries in 9 provinces outside Québec held 3.8 million books, circulated 3.4 million items, spent $7.3 million on materials annually and employed about 1000 people.

School Libraries in Canada are learning-resource centres for students and teachers, and many have become an essential part of the teaching process. The role of the school library depends on the willingness of the individual school board and principal to provide space, personnel, funding and materials. In an effort to maintain quality, supervisors or consultants are employed by many provincial school-library agencies to help organize and oversee libraries. Provincial school-library associations as well as the Canadian School Library Assn have proposed standards for the size of collections, for staff and physical facilities, and for the role of the librarian in curriculum development. In 1981-82 Statistics Canada reported that there were 7528 centralized school libraries holding 47.7 million books, spending $27.9 million on materials annually, and employing 9041 personnel in 9 Canadian provinces. No data were available for Québec and none have become available since.

Special Libraries

Special libraries serve the needs of a sponsoring organization, which may be federal, provincial or municipal governments; companies, associations or industries; or public institutions such as hospitals or museums. Special libraries can also be distinguished by a subject such as law, finance, insurance or health science. The origin of special libraries in Canada dates from the 17th century when 2 libraries at the Hopital general and Hôtel-Dieu in Québec C were opened to provide patients with religious materials. Most special libraries in Canada have been established since WWII. They are represented nationally by the Canadian Assn of Special Libraries and Information Services, and by subject-oriented associations such as the Canadian Health Libraries Assn and the Canadian Assn of Law Libraries.

Government Libraries The federal government funds the Library of Parliament, the NATIONAL LIBRARY OF CANADA, the Canada Institute for Scientific and Technical Information (CISTI), libraries of government departments and crown corporations, the public library service of the NWT and the Yukon Regional Library System, and it contributes to the provision of library service for Indian bands. Federal libraries are responsible to their departments, but co-operate on matters of common interest through the Council of Federal Libraries, whose secretariat is provided by the National Library. The parliamentary librarian reports directly to Parliament; the national librarian, with the status of a deputy head, reports to Parliament through the minister of communications. The growth of provincial departmental libraries has been determined by factors influencing the development of their respective provinces, eg, since 1965 they have developed rapidly in Ontario, Québec and Alberta.

The Parliamentary Library was the only structure left standing after the fire of 1916, and it was preserved in the new Parliament Buildings (*photo by Richard Vroom*).

Legislative Libraries had their beginnings after 1758 when a colonial legislature was created for Nova Scotia; by 1800 legislative libraries were being established in PEI, NB, and Upper and Lower Canada. In 1867 the Library of Parliament was officially established in Ottawa, based on collections from the legislative libraries of Lower and Upper Canada (1791-1841) and the Province of Canada (1841-67). Until the creation of the National Library in 1953, the Library of Parliament received deposit copies of all books published in Canada. It serves as a reference library for MPs and senators. Provincial legislative libraries are financed by provincial governments and serve MLAs and sometimes civil servants. Their holdings are an important resource for the history and development of their areas. In Québec the position of the Bibliothèque nationale is unique; it acts as a depository for all Québec publications, co-ordinates Québec bibliographic projects, and through its mandate to promote literary activity, has entered into cultural agreements between Québec and France.

Professional, Business and Industrial Libraries Among the earliest professional libraries were law libraries. The Law Society of Upper Canada was established in 1797, and by this time law collections were being used at Halifax and Québec C. As industry and business expanded rapidly, larger firms founded libraries: the Grand Trunk Railway's library for its employees, opened at Montréal in 1857, was typical in this regard. Modern industrial libraries, eg, Esso Resources Canada Ltd library in Calgary, tend to be in major cities where there are strong concentrations of business and industry, as in Montréal and Toronto. By the 1980s scientific and technical libraries formed the largest single group of special libraries.

Libraries in Nonprofit Organizations Important literary collections pertaining to fine art, science and technology exist in many libraries attached to nonprofit organizations such as museums and art galleries, in particular the Musée des beaux-arts de Montréal, the NATIONAL GALLERY in Ottawa, the ART GALLERY OF ONTARIO, the NATIONAL MUSEUMS OF CANADA and the ROYAL ONTARIO MUSEUM. Libraries associated with the CANADIAN BROADCASTING CORPORATION and the CANADIAN MUSIC CENTRE in Toronto serve as information centres for broadcasters and composers.

Library Associations

There are over 150 library associations in Canada, including national, provincial, regional, local, and ethnic associations, and groupings by library type such as public, academic, government, school and special libraries. The first was the Ontario Library Assn, established in 1900; other provincial associations followed: in BC (1911), Québec (1932), the Maritimes (1935), Manitoba (1936), Saskatchewan (1942), Alberta (1944) and the NWT (1981). The Yukon is still without a library association.

The Canadian Library Assn (CLA) was formed in 1946 as a bilingual national association but became unilingual in 1973. The CLA is subdivided into 5 type-of-interest associations, eg, the Canadian Assn of College and University Libraries, and it also sponsors a number of co-ordinating groups and committees. Some of the major activities of the CLA have included microfilming of Canadian newspapers of historical importance; compiling and publishing the *Canadian Periodical Index* 1948-86; encouraging publication of reference works; developing standards; maintaining liaison with national and international library associations and with the federal government; and providing opportunities for continuing education for library staff through conference programs.

Association pour l'avancement des sciences et des techniques de la documentation (ASTED) is the national association of francophone libraries. Like CLA, ASTED has a substructure of sections for academic and public libraries.

Contemporary Developments

In the postwar decades all types of libraries in Canada responded to the increasing information requirements of users. Collections changed to encompass such new formats as microforms, audio and video cassettes, compact disks, films, talking books, braille and kits. Programs for cultural or minority groups became an important part of public library service, and information retrieval, frequently from external computer-based bibliographic data bases, became a major component of reference service in public, academic and special libraries. Service to adult learners has become very important in college libraries and is gaining importance in university libraries as well.

These expanding services have been facilitated by local, regional, provincial and national co-operative agreements or resource-sharing networks and encouraged by support from the National Library and CISTI, both of which readily make their own collections available on loan or through photocopy to libraries across the country.

Although some public and university libraries had separate facilities before 1900, the Andrew Carnegie grants for public library buildings led to the construction of 125 Canadian libraries between 1901 and 1923. Influenced by the beaux-arts design common in public buildings of that period, classical columns and other elaborate ornamentation were features of even the smallest buildings. Unfortunately, these early libraries, although functional for the services of that period, proved difficult to modify or expand to meet an increased user population, changing services and new technologies.

A second surge in public library construction in the 1960s and 1970s, with emphasis on internal rather than external monumentalism, led to aesthetically pleasing but not necessarily functional libraries. The Metropolitan Toronto Central Library, which opened in 1977, has attracted international attention for the dramatic access it provides to its collections. Academic library buildings experienced a renaissance during this same period, with new central or divisional libraries constructed on every major university campus in Canada.

Since 1960 the most dramatic influence on libraries of all types has been the introduction of new technologies with implications for services, staff, collections and buildings. At the end of the 1970s advances in mini- and micro-computer technology permitted the development of local systems at costs that most libraries could afford; and information networks, encouraged by the National Library and CISTI, provided mechanisms for resource sharing and data exchange.

Library services were changed and expanded with the introduction of computer-based systems which made available the very latest materials. CISTI made major data bases available through CAN/SDI (selective dissemination of information) and CAN/OLE (on-line enquiry), and encouraged electronic messaging for the transfer of interlibrary loan requests and for the delivery of documents (CAN/DOC). The National Library has made its extensive bibliographic data base (DOBIS) available to other Canadian libraries for on-line searching. U of T Library Automation System (UTLAS), founded in 1971, provides computerized library-related services, products and systems to about 200 libraries. Geac, a Canadian based computer company, sells more online circulation and cataloguing systems worldwide, eg, Vatican Library, Bibliotheque National, Smithsonian Institute, than any other vendor.

Canadian library schools have responded to changed requirements for librarians by adding computer and telecommunication technologies to their curricula and by providing continuing-education programs in the new technologies. Library technician programs have been offered at many community colleges. Requirements for accommodating new and future information systems and resources have become major considerations in the design or renovation of library buildings.

The enhanced potential for gaining access to and sharing library collections, which has been made possible by the new technologies, has presented new challenges. The creation of library systems which combine the resources of all types of library in flexible administrative structures will need to be carefully considered. Support for the library and information networks of the 21st century will have to be co-ordinated at the national level if Canadian libraries are to succeed in meeting the greatly increasing demands of an INFORMATION SOCIETY.

MARGARET BECKMAN, MOSHIE DAHMS, LORNE BRUCE

Reading: "Canada, Libraries in," E.L. Morton, *Encyclopedia of Library and Information Science* 4 (1970), 71-157; "Canada, Libraries in, 1970-1979," B.L. Anderson, ELIS 36 (1983), 94-155; A. Drolet, *Les Bibliothèques canadiennes 1604-1960* (1960); L.S. Garry and C. Garry, eds, *Canadian Libraries in Their Changing Environment* (1977); P. McNally, *Readings in Canadian Library History* (1986); National Library of Canada, *The Future of the National Library* (1979).

Library Science, which encompasses all aspects of library operation, is an organized graduate course of studies taught at university level and producing practitioners with a recognized professional qualification. Until 60 years ago, most Canadian librarians acquired their knowledge from experience; those with formal training usually were graduates of library schools in the US. Beginning in 1904, when McGill U conducted a 3-week library summer school, instructional programs became available in Canada. These were mainly intermittent, short courses, until 1927 when McGill offered a full-year professional course of studies at the undergraduate level. The U of T established a School of Library Science in 1928. In 1931 and 1936, respectively, the McGill and Toronto library schools established postgraduate programs and were accredited by the American Library Assn (ALA). In the 1930s other library schools were established at the U of Ottawa, the École de bibliothécaires in Montréal and Mt St Vincent in Halifax. These 3 schools were never accredited and eventually went out of existence.

McGill and Toronto continued to dominate Canadian library education, but in the period of expansion during the 1960s the need for librarians was greater than they could meet, and new graduate library schools were established at UBC (1961), U de M (1961) and U of A (1968). In general these institutions offered the Bachelor of Library Science (BLS), but since the BLS could be taken only by those already holding an undergraduate degree, it was equated with the Master of Library Science (MLS) awarded in the US. All the above Canadian schools were, and continue to be, accredited by the ALA.

In the early 1970s, Canadian library schools made a notable departure from the US pattern. Because of expanding professional knowledge, the growing need for specialization and the continuing need for generalist preparation, Canadian library schools doubled the length of their programs and awarded an MLS instead of the BLS. McGill had already instituted the 2-year MLS in 1964; by 1972, Toronto, Montréal and UBC followed suit, and U of A did so in 1976. From their inception the library schools at U of Western Ontario (1967) and Dalhousie (1979) offered only the MLS degree. Canadian library-education programs hence are significantly longer than those in the US and other countries. A number of American library schools have taken or are contemplating a similar measure. Other noteworthy developments of the 1970s were the inception of doctoral programs (U of T and UWO), the erection of impressive physical facilities (Toronto) and a rapid increase in enrolment. The U of Western Ontario and U of T are now among the largest on the continent. In 1986-87 the 7 graduate schools awarded 457 MLS degrees, of which Montréal, the only French-language school, accounted for 71. Two Phd degrees were awarded.

Recently there have been considerable revisions in the graduate library-school programs and in the conceptions held about the nature and scope of library science. Traditionally, library science has been equated with the work done in and by libraries. The core elements have been materials selection and acquisition; cataloguing, classification and subject analysis of these materials; services to readers, and such necessary background aspects as the role of the library in society. Though these subjects remain important, the identification of library science with libraries (as institutions) is not nearly as close as it was. Library science is concerned with all aspects of library operation, and more broadly with the entire information-transfer process, whether the medium for such transfer be graphic records or electronically transmitted data. Library science thus conceived overlaps with such disciplines as documentation and information science. All the Canadian library schools include the term "information science" in their names, and all of them give considerable attention to information technology, electronic storage and retrieval, and information and communications theory. The graduates of Canadian library schools are therefore increasingly likely to see themselves as "information professionals" rather than as librarians. Though the majority will still work in public, academic or special libraries, other graduates may take jobs in such non-traditional settings as editing, publishing or research enterprises, law offices and records management, or even set up their own companies. In effect, any position that calls for high-level skills in the selection, organization or retrieval of information materials, for knowledge of telecommunications and videotex technology and for the ability to create data bases is suitable for library- and information-science graduates.

In addition to the graduate library-school programs, undergraduate courses in librarianship are offered by the faculties of education of many Canadian universities. These courses are intended for the training of school librarians or teacher-librarians. The latter term reflects the view that the librarian in the school should be primarily an educator, a partner with the classroom instructor in the effective use of learning materials. With the general implementation of the Canadian School Library Assn's *Recommended Curriculum for Education for School Librarianship* (1981), school librarianship in Canada has become a postgraduate discipline in all provinces except PEI and Saskatchewan.

On the nonprofessional level, library-technician-training programs are well developed in Canada. Beginning in Winnipeg (1962), such programs are now offered in 23 institutions. In the 4 western provinces, the parent institutions are community colleges or technical institutes; in Ontario, colleges of applied arts and technology (CAATs) and Lakehead U, which has a 3-year library-technology program; in Québec, the Collèges d'enseignement général et professionel (CEGEPs). There are no library-technician-training programs in the Atlantic provinces except in NB which offers a library assistant program. In general, the library-technician-training programs are 2-year programs, and half of that period is given to courses in library work. Apart from Québec, most programs follow the well-designed *Guidelines for the Training of Library Technicians* (1982) issued by the Canadian Library Association. The CLA has also sponsored frequent surveys of the programs, which encourages the maintenance of high standards. Here too, Canada has taken a vanguard position in library education and library science. SAMUEL ROTHSTEIN

Lichen, a dual organism composed of FUNGI living in close association with green ALGAE or BLUE-GREEN ALGAE. As composite organisms, they cannot be formally classified within a single kingdom. Names applied to lichens are actually those of the fungal component of the association because, with few exceptions, each recognizable lichen is the product of a different species of "lichen fungus." However, the algal species involved in the lichen consortium might be found in a number of different lichens. The more conspicuous lichens are foliose, lobed or leafy with distinct upper and lower surfaces; or fruticose, hanging like black or yellow hair from trees, or shrubby and erect on the ground. Crustose lichens form a thin crust over rocks or bark and are conspicuous only if brightly coloured. A typical foliose lichen has a complex organization. The algal cells form a layer within the fungal body, just below a protec-

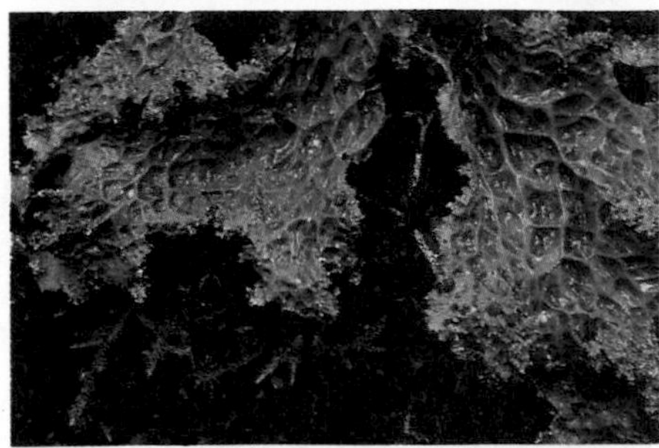

Foliose-type lichen (*photo by Tom W. Parkin/Pathfinder*).

tive cortex of thick-walled fungal cells and above a loosely organized layer of thin-walled cells (medulla). Below the medulla is another protective cortex from which rootlike attachments (rhizines) often arise. Crustose and fruticose lichens have slightly different tissue relationships as well.

Lichens grow extremely slowly (about 0.1 mm per year in some arctic species, 5-8 mm per year in temperate species). Estimating the growth rate of a lichen and measuring its diameter shows that some patches of rock-dwelling crustose lichens in the far North may be several thousand years old. Lichens are found from the tropics to the tundra and grow on many kinds of materials or substrates. There are approximately 18 000 species worldwide, with perhaps 2500 found in Canada. They are most conspicuous in cooler regions: on exposed mountaintops, in northern coniferous forests and on arctic tundra. In the subalpine forests of the western mountains and in some boreal forests, lichens often completely cover dead branches of spruce and fir. The caribou lichens blanket the ground over thousands of square hectares in Canada's subarctic woodland. Across the prairies and in the dry interior of BC, brilliantly coloured species invade exposed soil and cover erratic boulders. In eastern Canada, lichens are especially conspicuous on tree trunks, particularly those of roadside elms and maples. On thin or sandy soil, large mixed colonies of fruticose lichens often develop. Some lichens, restricted to coastal rocks, decorate the sea-splashed outcrops with orange, white and black belts reflecting the specificity of certain species to different tidal and splash zones.

Lichens are of great importance in Canada because of their relative abundance in the North. They make up the greater part of the winter diet of barren-ground caribou and are essential for the survival of the herds which form the most important element in the life of many Indian and Inuit groups. Lichens have little nutritive value and are generally used only as an emergency food, although some Indian peoples of interior BC include in their diet species such as the black, hairlike tree lichen. Bark- and twig-inhabiting lichens are extremely sensitive to AIR POLLUTION.

Beard lichen (*photo by Tim Fitzharris*).

Studies have been made in Canada and elsewhere of the relationship between specific levels of pollutants (especially sulphur dioxide) and the distribution and growth of lichens. Hence, lichens are frequently used in biological estimations of pollution levels and as early indicators of pollution problems. IRWIN M. BRODO

Reading: D.H.S. Richardson, *The Vanishing Lichens* (1974).

Lieutenant-Governor combines the monarchical and the federal principle in provincial governments. Although the lieutenant-governor is appointed by the GOVERNOR GENERAL on the prime minister's advice, in the words of an 1892 decision by the JUDICIAL COMMITTEE OF THE PRIVY COUNCIL, a lieutenant-governor "is as much the representative of Her Majesty, for all purposes of provincial government, as the Governor-General himself for all purposes of Dominion Government." The lieutenant-governor, therefore, possesses all the formal, prerogative and discretionary powers exercised by the monarch or the governor general. These include the duty to open, prorogue and dissolve the provincial Assembly; to assent to (or withhold assent from) provincial legislation and ORDERS-IN-COUNCIL; and to give prior approval to money bills. The lieutenant-governor also has the responsibility to select the provincial premier and, presumably as a last resort, to dismiss a government.

Although the discretionary powers may be obsolescent, they are not obsolete. Five governments have been dismissed, and dismissal has been seriously considered on several other occasions – the latest in Alberta in 1938 and Ontario in 1940. The task of selecting a premier has not always been easy, given the early looseness in party structures. But in the 20th century, lieutenant-governors have, with only 2 exceptions (the latest being in Ontario in 1985), asked the leader of the largest party to form a government or, if one leader died, waited until the party could make its choice known through either Cabinet or caucus.

Dissolution has usually been the result of an uncertain or unstable balance of power within the legislature. Since 1867 there have only been 3 clear cases in which a lieutenant-governor has refused to dissolve the Assembly, although on other occasions the knowledge that a request would be refused forestalled the request. However, the subject has been warmly debated. In 1952 in BC and 1971-72 in Newfoundland the existing government had been defeated, but the new government did not have a clear majority and defeat in the Assembly seemed certain. The question was whether the new government could request and receive a dissolution before the House met (the answer in both instances was negative) or whether a newly defeated government could secure a dissolution rather than resign. In BC the lieutenant-governor granted a dissolution to the defeated government, and in Newfoundland he agreed to a dissolution on the first day of the session, before the government had been defeated.

Lieutenant-governors are also officers of the federal government: they are appointed and paid by, and are subject to instructions from, Ottawa, and can be dismissed for cause. The usual term of 5 years is often extended. By the CONSTITUTION ACT, 1867 (formerly BRITISH NORTH AMERICA ACT), the lieutenant-governor has the power to reserve provincial Bills and is the instrument through which provincial Acts disallowed by Ottawa are proclaimed. One draft of the BNA Act used the word "superintendent," and at the QUÉBEC CONFERENCE of 1864 it was proposed that the subordination of provincial governments be effected, in part, by keeping the power to nominate and dismiss the lieutenant-governor in the central government's hands. Sir John A. Macdonald regarded the lieutenant-governor as one who should serve the Dominion's interests to the greatest possible extent without infringing on the province's right to self-government.

But the principles of provincial autonomy and federal intervention proved to be incompatible. Lieutenant-governors in the early years supported federal interests – eg, during the REPEAL MOVEMENT in Nova Scotia in the late 1860s and the intense federal-provincial disputes in Manitoba – and reserved many provincial Bills on instructions from Ottawa, or because they encroached on federal power or seemed contrary to national policy. As late as 1937, the lieutenant-governor of Alberta reserved 3 Bills, 2 with the concurrence of the federal government. In 1938 the Supreme Court ruled that the power of reservation still existed, but during the constitutional debate of the 1970s there seemed to be unanimous federal-provincial agreement that the provision should be removed from the Constitution. Seventy Bills have been reserved since 1867, but only 4 in the last half century. The last Bill to be reserved was in Saskatchewan in 1961, when the lieutenant-governor believed it was of doubtful validity. The Dept of Justice concluded that the Bill was within provincial jurisdiction and assent was given.

The Constitution Act, 1867, protects the office of lieutenant-governor from any amendment by the provincial government. However, many provinces have scaled down the expenses of the office and some have closed official residences. Mitchell HEPBURN (Ontario) closed Chorley Park in 1937; William ABERHART (Alberta) closed Government House in 1938 during his conflict with Ottawa (although another residence was purchased in 1967), and the CCF government in Saskatchewan did likewise in 1944. Although the cost is modest, there have been frequent suggestions that the office be abolished and that the chief justice perform the routine ceremonial functions. But abolitionists have never received much support, even in the depths of the Depression.

The office has been seen as a form of political patronage. Retired Cabinet ministers, federal and provincial politicians whose day has passed, and party fund-raisers have eagerly sought and been given the position. Among the 10 lieutenant-governors in 1987 were 3 who had been federal Cabinet ministers, 3 retired provincial Cabinet ministers, and one former chief justice. In 1929 the Judicial Committee of the Privy Council ruled that women could be senators, and in 1934 the Dept of Justice decided that women could be lieutenant-governors. However, it was not until the appointment of Pauline MCGIBBON in Ontario in 1974 that the first woman read the Speech from the Throne in a provincial legislature. Pearl McGonigal of Manitoba (1981-86) and Lt-Gov Helen Hunley of Alberta are Canada's other 2 female lieutenant-governors. Lincoln ALEXANDER (Ont, 1985-) was the first black and Ralph STEINHAUER (1974-79) the first native Indian to be appointed lieutenant-governor. JOHN T. SAYWELL

Reading: John T. Saywell, *The Office of Lieutenant-Governor* (1986).

Life Expectancy, *see* POPULATION.

Lightfoot, Gordon Meredith, singer, songwriter (b at Orillia, Ont 17 Nov 1939). Canada's most popular male vocalist during the 1970s, Lightfoot first drew attention in 1965 as the composer of "Early Morning Rain" and "For Lovin' Me," recorded by folk artists IAN AND SYLVIA and Peter, Paul and Mary, among others. At heart a romantic, in voice a baritone balladeer, he moved easily from folk to pop and by 1970 had become a major concert and recording artist throughout the English-speaking world. Other Lightfoot songs

Singer Gordon Lightfoot performing in a 1980 benefit for Canada's Olympic athletes (*courtesy Canapress Photo Service*).

from more than 15 record albums include pop items "If You Could Read My Mind," "Sundown" and "Did She Mention My Name?," as well as the more traditional "Canadian Railroad Trilogy" and "The Wreck of the *Edmund Fitzgerald*." Lightfoot has received many Juno awards (as folksinger, male vocalist and songwriter and, in 1986, the Juno Hall of Fame Award) and in 1971 was named an Officer of the Order of Canada.

MARK MILLER

Lighthouses Functions of lighthouses vary greatly. The great landfall lights at Cape Race, Seal I, Sambro and Race rocks provide the first sight of land for Atlantic or Pacific travellers after days or weeks at sea. Coastal navigation is by a system of major and minor lights, and smaller lights are used on intricate waterways where numerous islands and channels need to be marked. Harbour lights and range lights mark the final approaches to safe havens.

Duties of lighthouse keepers include the traditional "keeping of the light," radio communications and beacons, fog alarms, rescue services and sanctuary. Certain stations provide regular weather observations as part of the national system, and the station at Langara in the Queen Charlotte Is provides part of the tidal-wave warning system in the Pacific Ocean.

The first documented lighthouse, built at LOUISBOURG in Cape Breton in 1734, was almost immediately destroyed by fire and rebuilt. It was levelled by British guns during the siege of 1758 and rebuilt several times. The oldest existing lighthouse was built on Sambro I at the mouth of Halifax harbour in 1758. The second-oldest surviving lighthouse was built in 1809 on Green I (Isle Verte) in the St Lawrence R, opposite the mouth of the Saguenay. In the early 19th century, sea trade between Canada and Europe increased rapidly and so did wrecks and disasters at sea. By 1840 major lights had been placed on Seal I at the entrance to the Bay of Fundy, NS, at several places along the coast of Newfoundland and at the entry to the St Lawrence R. Lights were used on the Great Lakes at Mississauga (1804) and at Gibraltar Pt on Toronto I (1808). The upper Great Lakes remained in darkness until increasing trade forced the lighting of shore lamps throughout the region in the latter half of the 19th century.

On the Pacific coast it was not until 1860 that the first 2 lighthouses, at Race Rocks and Fisgard, near what is now Victoria, came into service. In the latter half of the 19th century lights were used along the outer coast of Vancouver I and the entryways to Victoria, Vancouver and Prince Rupert. Inland waters, such as the Saint John R, Red R and Lake Winnipeg, were marked with lights and buoys by the early part of the 20th century. In arctic waters beacons were installed in the 1930s, with the opening of the port of Churchill.

The first lighthouses were bonfires on the ends of points at harbour entrances, later replaced by towers with similar beacons on top. Candles were used in the 18th and early 19th centuries, but it took many to make even a dim light. Oil lamps with wicks were used extensively by 1800. Eventually, whale oil and a variety of vegetable, fish and seal oils were used in different places, according to the availability of supplies and equipment.

The invention of kerosene by Abraham GESNER in NS in 1846 led to the production of good-quality kerosene lamps, used extensively in Canada from the 1860s because they were cheap, reliable and efficient. The invention of the mantle lamp and experimentation with various oils produced lighthouses of considerable brilliance by the beginning of the 20th century. Electric lights came to lighthouses in Canada about the end of the 19th century and gradually replaced other forms of illumination.

Parabolic reflectors of polished steel or silvered copper greatly increased the effectiveness of lighthouses in the early 19th century, and some of these reflectors are still in use in lights at Red I in the St Lawrence and East Pt, PEI. Reflecting systems are known as catoptric systems. Simple lens systems (dioptric) and combinations of refracting prisms and concentrating lenses (catadioptric) came into use in the mid and latter part of the 19th century. Many of these systems survive, and Canada's greatest lighthouse, at Cape Race, has such a system weighing many tons and casting its beam 48 km into the Atlantic. By 1800 along the coasts of Europe there were such numbers of lighthouses that it became necessary to invent a system of identifying them. An apparatus was attached to the light to produce a different pattern of flashes for each lighthouse. This sequence is noted in the *List of Lights* for each area. By 1890 the revolving light mechanisms were floated in mercury and driven by clockwork with great weights, which were wound up by the keeper at 2- to 4-hour intervals.

In the 1970s electrification was virtually complete. Modern mercury-vapour and xenon bulbs are so powerful that simple optics of pressed glass or plastic have replaced the great revolving masses of glass and prisms. These new lamps revolve in the same way as airport beacons and lights on tall buildings. Automation has replaced the traditional lighthouse keeper in most stations (75 of 266 have been automated since 1980; another 100 or so will be automated by 1990). The man living with his family at a light station in a remote place has been replaced by the helicopter and the travelling technician who changes or charges the bulbs and batteries. Bulbs are changed automatically and remote lighthouse stations are fitted with automatic standby equipment in case something goes wrong.

Along Canadian coasts, where lighthouses must be seen against snow or rocks and where complicated coastlines result in many lighthouses within short distances along the shore, distinctive patterns are painted on the towers in order to distinguish them from one another. These daymarks have great variety, ranging from a red cross at Head Harbour, NB, to black and white horizontal stripes at Race Rocks in BC.

Construction materials vary with the time of building and local conditions. Wooden lighthouse towers are characteristic of the Canadian lighthouse service. Superb examples are to be found at East Pt, PEI, Pachena on the outside of Vancouver I, and at Gannet Rock on the entrance to the Bay of Fundy. The last, despite its exposed position, has stood for 150 years. Stone towers at Race Rocks, Cove I (near Collingwood, Ont) and on Île d'Anticosti were built with what was available nearby and were as much as 30.5 m high. Lighthouses were sometimes built of brick, and for a period in the late 19th century cast-iron plates were hauled ashore from ships and bolted together to produce the lighthouses at Ferryland, Nfld, and Cape North, NS. The latter is now on the grounds of the National Museum of Science and Technology in Ottawa. Reinforced concrete towers have been built in many places in Canada this century, the most distinctive being built around 1910, with central towers up to 30.5 m high and with flying buttresses; examples are the beautiful towers at Father Pt, Qué, Caribou I in Lk Superior and Estevan Pt on the outside of Vancouver I. Steel caissons are set into the riverbed at Prince Shoal and White I Reef in the St Lawrence R, and an open-steelwork tower is on Pigeon I in Lk Ontario. Even fibreglass towers have been tried on the Magdalen Is and in inland waterways. Canadian lighthouses are set in a great variety of environments – in the rain forests of the Pacific coast; in the middle of a downtown park, such as Brockton Pt in Vancouver; and on the tops of high-rounded points of islands so thoroughly windswept that the lighthouses are held down by steel guy wires, as at Gull I. Although often starkly functional in setting and design, the lighthouse has become a romantic symbol both of the country's maritime greatness and of safe haven.

DAVID M. BAIRD

The Bonavista Bay lighthouse, built in 1843, guided Newfoundland mariners until 1966 when it was replaced by a steel tower with an automated beacon (*photo by David M. Baird*).

Lighting From earliest times it has been recognized that artificial light prolongs daytime activities. Relaxation and social interaction necessarily occurred after the day's work was done; therefore, indoor lighting has always had a special association with this aspect of living. The campfire moved indoors to become the fireplace, and from this main source of light a branch could be pulled out and placed in a wrought-iron holder to illuminate other areas, or carried outside to serve as a torch. Small pieces of wood held in a clamp or splint holder would burn for a short period of time. The open flame continued to be the only source of domestic lighting until the incandescent light bulb was introduced in the 1880s. Although the most primitive forms are still in everyday use in some areas, it is possible to view the evolution of lighting as having 3 distinct periods.

Early Period (to 1780) During the first period, which ended in about 1780, fats and oils from animal and vegetable sources were used with various types of wicking. In some cases, dried whole animals or fish fastened to a stick served as torches; for example, in BC, oily SMELTS, popularly known as candlefish, were used in this manner. The earliest lamps were simple covered or uncovered saucers with a wick lying along the bottom and extending to the rim; examples include Roman pottery lamps, European iron cruses, Inuit stone lamps and perhaps shells. Slight improvements, such as a channel or tube to elevate the wick, were incorporated in European spout lamps and in Betty, Kettle and cup-shaped lamps.

A peeled rush, dipped in melted fat, provided a primitive form of candle. Rushlights were rarely used in Canada, but candles were a part of Canadian life from the earliest times of European settlement. The self-supporting column containing a cotton wick was commonly made of tallow during pioneer times. Tallow was superseded by paraffin in the 1860s. Candle production has been maintained because of the visual and psychological association of warmth and romance with the flickering flame. Animal fats were readily available in most households and were used for lamp fuel and in soapmaking as well as for candles.

Middle Period (1780-1880) The second period, beginning about 1780, was one of invention and discovery. Lamps and burners were created for new fuels, such as artificial gas, burning fluid, rosin oil and kerosene, as well as for old fuels such as WHALE oil and lard. GLASS was the most common material, although brass and other metals were popular. The Swiss scientist Aimé Argand is credited with the first significant invention of this period, the Argand lamp. His centre-draft burner, holding a tubular wick and using a glass chimney, is recognized as the beginning of modern lighting. Such chimneys, being fragile and requiring daily washing, were a staple product of the Canadian glasshouses.

Artificial gas, introduced about 1800, required special burners and, more importantly, a distribution and installation system. This innovation took many years to accomplish, and in N America artificial gas was available only in major cities and towns. In Montréal, Québec C and Toronto, distribution of artificial gas began in the late 1830s and the 1840s, primarily to supply public buildings and the homes of the affluent, as well as some street lighting (*see* COAL GASIFICATION).

During the entire second period, the shape of lamps reflected inventions tailored to the characteristics of the fuels used and to the manufacturing technology available, particularly in the glass industry, as well as to the influences of contemporary fashion. From 1830 to 1860, the most common illuminants used in N America were animal fats, burning fluid made from camphene (pine oil) and redistilled alcohol. Burning fluid (known as camphine in England), although inexpensive, was highly volatile and resulted in numerous fatal explosions.

Simple whale-oil burners usually had one or 2 vertical wick tubes extending into the fuel container (font). Burning-fluid burners, although similar, did not extend into the font and had single or multiple, divergent wick tubes, with removable wick caps used to extinguish the flame and to prevent evaporation. Whale oil was also used in more complicated lamps such as the Astral or Simumbra lamps, which had ring-shaped reservoirs that permitted unobstructed light to be cast downward. Lamps with offset fonts and separate reservoirs (the most popular being the kerosene student lamps) were used during the entire second period. Lard lamps featured various arrangements designed to force the fuel to the wick and to conduct heat from the flame to the fuel to keep it melted. In the 1850s the solar lamp, designed for use with lard or whale oil, was the most sophisticated lard lamp in both operation and appearance.

Fuel-burning lamps were invented around 1780 and remained in use well into the electric era. This bull's eye lamp of blue opal glass is from the Diamond Glass Co, Montréal, *c*1902 (*courtesy Royal Ontario Museum*).

Mechanical lamps employed a clockwork mechanism to force highly viscous fuels to the top of the lamp. These were popular in Europe where they were used with Colza (rapeseed) oil (*see* CANOLA). Another type of mechanical lamp popular during the kerosene period used a fan to maintain a continuous flow of air between the wick tube and the draft deflector of the burner. Chimneys were not required with these lamps. Wanzer mechanical lamps were made in Hamilton, Ont, for several decades beginning in the 1880s, by the Wanzer Sewing Machine Co.

In 1846 Abraham GESNER, a physician and geologist from NS, gave the first public demonstration of a revolutionary lighting fuel in Charlottetown, PEI. Kerosene was the name Gesner gave this product in his 1854 US PATENT. It was obtained initially from COAL and later from PETROLEUM. A similar product called Paraffine oil was patented in England in 1850 and in the US in 1852 by James Young from Scotland. These developments, as well as Samuel Kier's contemporary experiments in Pennsylvania, had little effect upon domestic lighting until the late 1850s. Kerosene provided, for the first time, an inexpensive and abundant supply of a safe fuel that could make good lighting available to the general public. It was this dream that sparked the rush to discover and market petroleum, and it was James Miller WILLIAMS of Hamilton who, in 1857, first shipped crude oil from hand-dug wells at Oil Springs, near Petrolia, Ont. American and Canadian patents for kerosene burners and lamps continued long after electric lighting was introduced. In the 1880s a mantle that dramatically increased the intensity of light and could be used with gas or kerosene burners was invented by Karl Auer von Welsbach, an Austrian chemist.

Late Period (1880 on) The Paris World Fair of 1878 had introduced the new mode of electric lighting to the world. Montréaler J.A.I. Craig, impressed by the demonstration, upon his return helped the Jesuits install the first electric light in the city (based on the arc lamp invention of Russian engineer Pavel Jablochkov) in front of the Jesuit college on Bleury St. American inventor Thomas Alva Edison produced the first successful incandescent electric light bulb in late 1879, and his activities in organizing ELECTRIC-POWER GENERATION and ELECTRIC-POWER TRANSMISSION systems ushered in the third period of lighting.

In Canada, although all cities, towns and villages are served by electric power, domestic lighting in remote areas is still provided by lamps using naphtha gas, propane or kerosene. As electric lights become available, all other illuminants will likely be discontinued. However, for those who still derive great pleasure and satisfaction from the psychological attraction, the magic of the open flame will endure.

Nondomestic Lighting Oil (vegetable or animal), gas and kerosene lamps were used extensively for street lighting in North America before electric lamps were introduced. The brilliant carbon-arc lamps invented by Sir Humphry Davy in 1808 were used primarily for large indoor areas and outdoors for streetlights, searchlights and lighthouses. Oil-fueled streetlights were used in Montréal, Québec C and Toronto until replaced by gaslights (1837-47), which were in turn replaced by electric lights.

Horse-drawn vehicles, trains, bicycles, motorcycles, cars and boats had special lighting requirements. To guide the traveller, candles, kerosene, whale oil and carbide lamps were used before battery-powered electric lights. In Ontario, Thomas Leopold WILLSON demonstrated Hamilton's first carbon-arc lamp in the 1880s. Soon after, he went to the US where he discovered a method of producing calcium carbide. This substance was used in vehicle lamps, particularly for bicycles and motorcycles, as well as in lighthouses and in miners' lamps. A controlled trickle of water, combined with the calcium chloride, produced a continuous supply of acetylene gas that was conducted to a special burner. These lamps had worldwide use but, in Canada as elsewhere, have been superseded for transportation purposes by electric lighting, powered by batteries or generators. *See also* TECHNOLOGY. CATHERINE M.V. THURO

Reading: L.S. Russell, *A Heritage of Light: Lamps and Lighting in the Early Canadian Home* (1968); Catherine M.V. Thuro, *Oil Lamps: The Kerosene Era in North America* (1976) and *Oil Lamps II: Glass Kerosene Lamps* (1983).

Lightning, sudden electric discharge that occurs as a giant spark between one portion of an overhead THUNDERSTORM and another portion of the overhead CLOUD or some point on the ground below. Thunder is the noise such a discharge makes as the air is violently heated along the lightning stroke path. In the absence of clouds, the Earth has a downward-directed, fair-weather electric field, with positive electric charges carried in the air on various ions, and a neutralizing negative charge on the planet's surface. As a thunderstorm grows, or a mature storm approaches, this electric field is reversed. In general, the lower part of a cloud is negatively charged; the upper portions, positively charged. A further positive charge is induced on the Earth's surface below a thunderstorm. As the storm develops, the electric field within and below the cloud may reach several thousand volts per centimetre, at which stage an electrical breakdown occurs in the form of lightning. A lightning stroke to the ground starts out as a luminous, erratic path of ionized air that proceeds rapidly from the cloud base. As it nears the

Lightning, Awenda Provincial Park, Ont (*photo by Bill Ivy*).

ground, it is met by an upward-moving column of electric charge originating from some high point on the ground below. On meeting, a violent surge of electric current occurs which constitutes the main stroke. Such lightning is commonly referred to as streak or forked lightning. The sequence of stages is essentially the same when the electrical breakdown occurs between upper and lower portions of the same cloud. In this case the stroke is usually so obscured that only a diffuse flash of light, commonly known as sheet lightning, is seen. The basic mechanism responsible for thunderstorm charging is the interaction of HAIL pellets and supercooled water droplets in colder regions of the growing cloud. Collision of these, followed by partial freezing of the latter, results in the ejection of small, positively charged ice splinters; a net negative charge accumulates on the growing hail pellet. Cloud updrafts then complete the process by carrying the small ice crystals towards the cloud top, leaving the negatively charged pellets at lower levels. Within a vigorous and growing thunderstorm, charge separation by these updrafts rapidly rebuilds the electric field following each lightning stroke, so that another can occur from the same cloud region a few minutes later. J. MAYBANK

Lillie, Beatrice Gladys (Lady Robert Peel), comedienne (b at Toronto 29 May 1894). Her saucy songs and unruly rope of pearls made her a beloved revue entertainer. She began in Ontario as a concert singer with her mother and sister ("The Lillie Trio") and went to England in 1914 where she was hired for a series of wartime revues. She made her New York debut in 1924, and throughout the 1930s alternately headlined at the Palace Theatre in New York and London's Palladium or Café de Paris. In 1936 she had a triumphant return to Toronto in a revue entitled *At Home Abroad.* Following WWII, in which she tirelessly entertained the troops, her important shows were *Inside USA* (1948-50), *An Evening with Beatrice Lillie* (1952-56), *Auntie Mame* (1958) and *High Spirits* (1964), the musical version of Coward's *Blithe Spirit.* In 1972 she published an amusing autobiography *Every Other Inch a Lady.* DAVID GARDNER

Lillooet, BC, Village, pop 1758 (1986c), 1725 (1981c), inc 1946, is located in the southern interior of BC, 325 km NE of Vancouver. It sits at the foot of the Cascade Mts above the W bank of the FRASER R. A larger part of the area's population is native Indian, of the Lillooet tribe of the Interior SALISH.

Miners came by the thousands from the coast to the interior in the 1850s gold rush, travelling up the Harrison, Lillooet, Anderson and Seton Lakes to the present site of Lillooet. The new settlement (1858) quickly became an important town on the route to the Cariboo and Fraser R goldfields. It received its name (meaning "wild onion") in 1860. Shortly thereafter it became mile "0" on the new CARIBOO ROAD, and is said to have grown quickly to 4000-5000 people. The Lillooet route was abandoned when the Cariboo later went through the Fraser Canyon, and the town declined. After the gold rush waned, the area was known for big-game hunting, and many settlers were employed as outfitters and guides. Logging and lumbering have been important; today a sawmill is the major employer. The local newspaper, the *Bridge River-Lillooet News,* achieved notoriety under owner and editor Margaret Ma MURRAY, known for her colourful, commonsense editorials and commentary on public events. JOHN R. STEWART

The madonna lily (*Lilium candidum*) was chosen Québec's floral emblem for its resemblance to the fleur-de-lis (*photo by Mary W. Ferguson*).

Lily, common name for members of genus *Lilium* of the lily family (Liliaceae). The family, comprising over 200 genera and perhaps 3000 species, includes plants as diverse as onion, daffodil and lily of the valley. Some authors divide it into subfamilies; others confer separate family status. Family members are mainly herbaceous; rootstocks form bulbs, tubers, rhizomes, etc. Genus *Lilium* comprises about 80 species native to northern temperate regions. Canada lily (*L. canadense*) and western red or prairie lily (*L. philadelphicum*) are native to Canada. Lilies are among the most popular ORNAMENTALS, and many decorative hybrids have been produced. Since 1941, the western red lily has been the PROVINCIAL FLORAL EMBLEM of Saskatchewan. It grows in abundance in meadows and clearings; however, picking the flowers weakens the plant and causes its progressive disappearance. The tall (1.2-1.5 m) madonna lily (*L. candidum*), an introduced Asian species, has fragrant, trumpet-shaped, white flowers with yellow stamens. Although not indigenous to Québec and somewhat difficult to cultivate, it was chosen as Québec's floral emblem in 1963. It resembles the fleur-de-lis on armorial emblems and on Québec's flag; however, the fleur-de-lis is generally thought to be a stylized version of the flower found along the Lys R in France, probably *Iris pseudacorus.* Blue flag (*I. versicolor*) has been proposed as a new floral emblem for Québec. This pretty, bluish violet flower, 8 cm in diameter, is native to Canada (Manitoba to S Labrador, Newfoundland and NS) and appears in late May or early June. CÉLINE ARSENEAULT

Limestone, a SEDIMENTARY ROCK largely or wholly composed of calcium carbonate ($CaCO_3$). Carbonate rocks are important to the CONSTRUCTION INDUSTRY as building stone and aggregate, and as the primary component of portland CEMENT and lime. Limestones are also used in glass manufacture, as fillers, abrasives and soil conditioners, and in the manufacture of various chemicals. Quicklime is formed by the process of calcination, in which limestones are heated to the dissociation temperature of the carbonates (402-898°C), and held there long enough to release carbon dioxide. Although the word "lime" is used generally to refer to pulverized limestone as well as forms of burned lime, more correctly it refers to quicklime and its products, slaked and hydrated limes. Slaked lime is quicklime mixed with water; hy-

The western red, or prairie, lily shown above (*Lilium philadelphicum*) is the floral emblem of Saskatchewan (*photo by Mary W. Ferguson*).

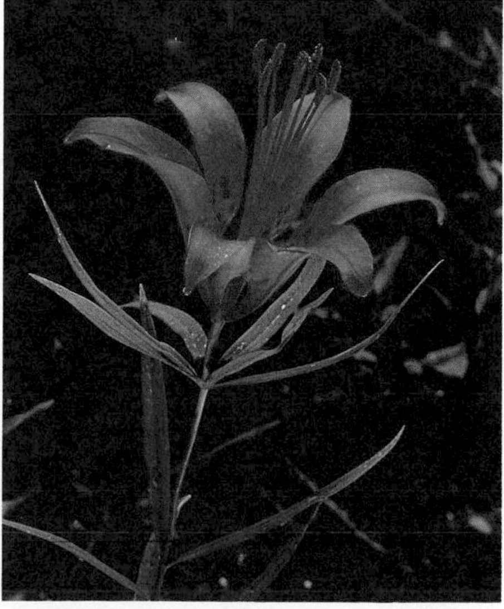

drated lime, slaked lime dried and possibly reground. Lime is used principally in the steel, pulp and paper and mining industries, where its chemical qualities are required as a flux (promoting ease of melting), in digesting liquors and as a neutralizing agent, respectively. Water and sewage treatment and removal of sulphur dioxide from smelter-stack gases and thermal power-plant emissions will require large amounts of lime in the near future. The use of lime in construction (eg, in mortar and sand-lime bricks) has been greatly reduced in recent years.

Lime plants have been established near industrial centres in Canada where reserves of suitable limestone are available and where major consumers are situated. Ontario and Québec produce over 80% of Canada's total lime. A high-bulk, low-cost commodity, lime is rarely shipped long distances because the raw material for its manufacture is so widely available. Calcining is done in kilns of various types, including traditional vertical or rotary types, or more recently developed rotary hearth, travelling grate, fluo-solid and inclined vibratory types. The high cost of energy has required inclusion of preheating facilities in new plants, and environmental regulations have necessitated incorporation of dust-collection equipment. Limestone production was valued at $596.6 million in 1986. D.H. Stonehouse

Lincoln, Ont, Town, pop 14 391 (1986c), 14 196 (1981c), inc 1970, situated in the Niagara Peninsula, immediately W of St Catharines. The town was formed from the townships of Clinton and Louth (part) and town of Beamsville and comprises several distinct communities (Beamsville, Vineland, Jordan, Jordan Station and Campden) interspersed with rural areas. The area was settled in the 1780s, and the various communities grew up in response mainly to agricultural needs. Since 1900 it has been important for tender fruit and grape growing, and Jordan is the home of one of Niagara's oldest wineries. Though people of British origin predominate, Mennonite and, more recently, Dutch people are also important elements in the population. The town, named for Lincoln in Lincolnshire, Eng, has attracted many light industries, particularly close to the QUEEN ELIZABETH WAY, and various tourist facilities, and the federal and provincial governments have agricultural research facilities in Vineland.
H.J. Gayler

Lindbergh, Alta, UP, pop 47 (1986c), 47 (1981c), is located 200 km E of Edmonton. Formerly called Mooswa, it was renamed (1928) in honour of American aviator Charles Lindbergh, after his famous solo flight across the Atlantic. The hamlet declined when the CNR branch line (built 1928) was abandoned in 1946. In the 1940s a SALT bed 300 m thick and several kms long was discovered, and up to 350 t of salt are refined and packed daily at the Canadian Salt Co plant. The salt bed contains enough salt to supply Canada's needs for 200 years. Eric J. Holmgren

Linder, Herman, rancher, rodeo competitor, promoter (b at Darlington, Wisconsin 5 Aug 1907). Born the son of a circus performer who emigrated from Switzerland to N America, young Linder rode yearling steers and unbroken range horses for amusement. From their home in Cardston, Alta, Herman and his brother, Warner, took to rodeoing in the 1920s. His first time at the Calgary Stampede, Linder won both the Canadian Bronc and Bareback Bronc Riding championships. From 1929 to 1939 he was known as "King of the Cowboys" at the Stampede, winning the Canadian all-round championship 7 times, and the N American championship 5 times in a row. In 1936 Linder was one of 61 cowboys who staged the first rodeo cowboy strike at the Boston Gardens; the action precipitated the birth of the Rodeo Cowboys' Association, and later the Canadian Pro Rodeo Association. He later produced rodeo, including one presented at Expo 67 in Montréal. Linder is a member of the (American) National Cowboy Hall of Fame, and an honorary chief of the Blood Indians. Ted Barris

Reading: Cliff Faulknor, *Turn Him Loose, Herman Linder, Canada's Mr Rodeo* (1977).

Lindner, Ernest, artist (b at Vienna, Austria 1 May 1897). Lindner came to Canada in 1926 and worked first as a farm labourer in Saskatchewan. By 1931 he had won local recognition as an artist and by 1933 was beginning to exhibit in eastern Canada. Lindner is best known for his works in watercolour and pencil, although he has produced linocut and wood-block prints and has studied etching and lithography. The subject that has concerned him most is the cycle of life. His preferred metaphor is the plant life of northern Saskatchewan forests. Lindner's images are often composites of human and plant forms, overlapping and blending into each other. He is regarded as a superb craftsman, and is noted for the tenacity of his ideas. He was elected a member of the Royal Canadian Academy of Arts in 1977 and is an Officer of the Order of Canada. Judy Gouin

Reading: T. Heath, *Uprooted: The Life and Art of Ernest Lindner* (1983).

Lindsay, Ont, Town, pop 14 455 (1986c), 13 596 (1981c), inc 1857, located on the Scugog R, which connects it to Sturgeon Lk and the Trent-Severn Waterway, about 95 km NE of Toronto. Originally it was named Purdy's Mills, after William Purdy, an American settler who built gristmills and sawmills on the site in 1828. The dam Purdy built backed up the Scugog R until it formed Lk Scugog out of what had formerly been bog and swamp, but it also flooded surrounding farmland and the farmers marched to town and destroyed the dam. The name Lindsay commemorates a surveyor's assistant who died after being accidently shot on the site. In 1844 the government built a lock which opened the Scugog R to navigation. A new one constructed in 1870 is now one of 43 on the Trent-Severn system. Lindsay developed as a farming and lumbering centre. During the summer it is a jumping-off spot for vacationers visiting the central KAWARTHA LAKES. Now the seat of Victoria County, its riverfront is dominated by a stone gristmill dating from the 1860s. A campus of Sir Sandford Fleming College of Applied Arts and Technology is located here.
Daniel Francis

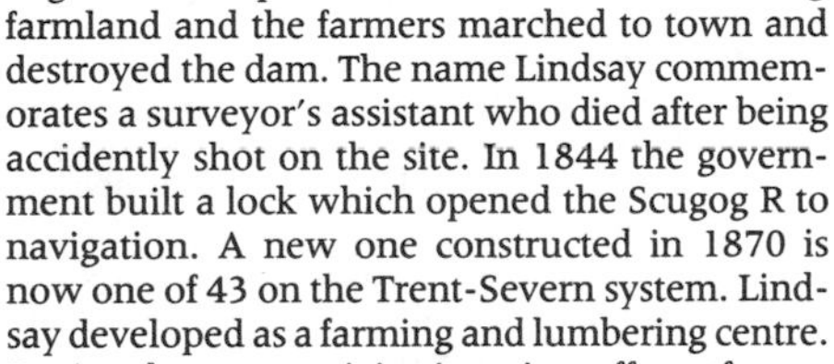

Lindsay, Robert Blake Theodore, "Ted," hockey player (b at Renfrew, Ont 29 July 1925). He joined Detroit Red Wings in 1944 and played left wing on the famous "Production Line," with Sid Abel at centre and Gordie HOWE on right wing. He won the NHL scoring title in 1949-50, but he was best known for his toughness and fearless checking. He was traded to Chicago when Detroit manager Jack Adams discovered his role in forming the NHL players' union. His 379 goals and 472 assists were records for a left winger when he retired. He returned to Detroit for an unsuccessful stint as general manager. James Marsh

Lindsley, Thayer, mining engineer, promoter (b at Yokohama, Japan 17 Aug 1882; d at New York C 29 May 1976). Born of American parents in Japan, Lindsley returned to the US at 15, graduated from Harvard in engineering and worked for the New York City subway. After serving in WWI, he worked up a mine in Oregon, selling it for $30 000 in 1923. With this stake he set up Ventures Ltd in 1928. Ventures prospected, developed and financed mines, and by the mid-1950s owned mines or shares of mines on every continent except Asia. Lindsley's best-known venture was Falconbridge Nickel Mines near Sudbury, Ont, which he and a partner, Joseph Errington, incorporated in 1928. He and his brother, Halstead, also helped establish Sherritt Gordon mines in 1927. Robert Bothwell

Linear Mounds, a cluster of archaeological sites located mainly along the SOURIS R of southwestern Manitoba. Although scattered throughout the northeastern Plains, the linear mounds along the Souris contain the greatest concentration of long prehistoric burial mounds in Canada. These earthen mausoleums, massive undertakings with a technology of stone and bone, consisted of long straight ridges up to 230 m long and 7 m wide, with circular mounds on the ends. They appear to date to 900-1400 AD, and the grave goods, though rare, show that the local Plains tribes were part of vast continental trade networks involving dentalium from the West Coast, obsidian from Yellowstone, brown chalcedony from western N Dakota, copper from Lk Superior, catlinite (red pipestone) from southern Minnesota and items of conch shell traded up the Mississippi R from the Gulf of Mexico. *See also* ARCHAEOLOGY; PREHISTORY.
E. Leigh Syms

Linguistics, the study of LANGUAGE. Language accompanies almost all human activities, and is the medium for many of them. The subject of speculation and inquiry throughout history, in the 20th century its study has come to be called "linguistics," and this term characterizes a modern emphasis, with special methods and techniques.

The foundations of the modern discipline were laid at the beginning of the 20th century. Ferdinand de Saussure, a professor at U of Geneva, is credited with bringing together the results of many types of language study into a coherent discipline. Numerous scholars elaborated and refined de Saussure's framework in the next 3 decades. Among the influential early contributors were Nikolas S. Trubetzkoy and Roman Jakobson (USSR), Edward SAPIR and Leonard Bloomfield (US), J.R. Firth (Britain), Louis Hjelmslev (Denmark) and André Martinet (France). Since 1950 linguistics has become firmly established throughout the world. Much of its rapid growth is due to the stimulating and often controversial work of American linguist Noam Chomsky, beginning with his first book, *Syntactic Structures* (1957). Chomsky's ideas presented challenges not only to the tradition begun by de Saussure, but also to philosophers, mathematicians and psychologists.

Linguistics in Canada Canada is rich in languages, with dozens of native languages (*see* NATIVE PEOPLE, LANGUAGES), 2 official languages (*see* ENGLISH LANGUAGE; FRENCH LANGUAGE) and several flourishing immigrant languages, such as Italian, Ukrainian, Greek and Japanese (*see* ETHNIC LANGUAGES). Much of Canada's political, cultural and social distinctiveness and many of its national issues are rooted in multilingualism. Language and language-related studies have inevitably played an important part in Canadian society, and the recent growth of linguistics as a systematic discipline has found fertile soil in Canada.

Linguists seek to discover the principles that underlie the human capacity for language. They begin with some fairly obvious observations: that all speakers of a language can utter and understand an unlimited number of sentences; that their capability develops rapidly when they are children, without much conscious learning or teaching; that they automatically know whether a sentence is grammatical, sensible or ambiguous; and that they cannot discover the principles of their language abilities simply by thinking about what is going on in their minds while they are speaking.

The mental representation that allows speakers to use language is called the *grammar* (not to be confused with the rules intended to help students write better). Those simple observations about language prove that the grammar is not a simple device: it must be a finite device with an infinite output, because each human being can produce and comprehend a potentially unlimited set of utterances; it is organized on several different levels because speakers can judge sentences in several ways; it is subconscious, or tacit; and it is innate, rather than learned. The study of the grammar makes up the core area of linguistics; several subfields apply the results of grammatical study to numerous types of human interaction. The core and the subfields depend upon one another, and in practice it is not easy to separate them; all linguists work in both areas, often simultaneously.

For many years linguists worked individually in branches of the government, in museums or in ANTHROPOLOGY and language departments at universities. The first department of linguistics (still one of the largest in Canada) was formed at U de M in the late 1940s, when Jean-Paul Vinay gathered together several colleagues from various departments. A decisive step in promoting the discipline occurred at U of Man in 1954, when scholars from all parts of the country gathered to form the Canadian Linguistic Assn. Henry Alexander of Queen's U became the first president (1954-56) and, during the early years, other founding members succeeded him: Gaston Dulong, J.B. Rudnyckyj, E.R. Seary, Vinay, M.H. Scargill, Jean Darbelnet and Walter S. Avis. The founding members also began publishing *The Canadian Journal of Linguistics* which, from its modest beginning in 1954, has come to provide an international forum for linguistic research.

During the 1960s many universities expanded to include departments of linguistics, beginning with Laval in Québec C (1961). Universities in English-speaking Canada caught up a few years later when Memorial, Toronto, Alberta and Simon Fraser expanded their programs into full departments. By 1975, departments had also been established at Sherbrooke, McGill, Québec à Montréal, Ottawa, Carleton, Calgary, British Columbia and Victoria. Now, although no new departments have been formed, most Canadian universities offer instruction in the subject.

J.K. CHAMBERS

Lisgar, Sir John Young, Baron, politician, colonial administrator, governor general of Canada and governor of PEI 1869-72 (b at Bombay, India 31 Aug 1807; d at Bailieborough, Ire 6 Oct 1876). John Young was educated at Eton and Corpus Christi, Oxford. A Tory MP for County Cavan, he served as a lord of the Treasury 1844-46 and chief secretary for Ireland 1852-55. Young's colonial appointments before coming to Canada, the Ionian Is and New South Wales, both ended in controversy. During his term in Canada, Lisgar took an active part in diffusing Canadian-American tensions created by the RED RIVER REBELLION and the Fenian raids. A keen supporter of CONFEDERATION, he tried to mediate the conflict created over the transfer of RUPERT'S LAND and the entry of Manitoba into Confederation and encouraged BC to join. He also organized the Governor General's Foot Guard. Although Lisgar was outspoken and independent, John A. MACDONALD considered him the ablest governor general he had known.

CARMAN MILLER

Arthur Lismer, *A September Gale, Georgian Bay* (1921), oil on canvas. An original member of the Group of Seven, Lismer developed a powerful expressionist style of his own, characterized by raw colour and simplified form (*courtesy National Gallery of Canada*).

L'Islet-sur-Mer, Qué, Village, pop 746 (1986c), 1070 (1981c), on the S shore of the ST LAWRENCE R, 100 km E of Québec City, within the former seigneuries of L'Islet-St-Jean and Bonsecours (granted 1677). Before the arrival of the first resident parish priest in 1745, L'Islet was served by missionary priests, and the parish of Notre-Dame-de-Bon-Secours-de-L'Islet was founded in 1721. Until the end of the 19th century, agriculture was the principal economic activity. The arrival of the railway in 1860 brought some industrial development: several brickworks exploited but soon exhausted the local clay deposits; a foundry that was in operation for several years has more recently become a trailer factory; a large cabinetmaking enterprise also established several shops in the village. These industries have had an influence on urbanization: in 1911 the village separated from the parish municipality (est 1845), and in 1950 L'Islet-Station broke away, eventually becoming a town (L'Islet). The church, built in 1768, is a designated historic building and contains several religious masterpieces. A major maritime museum opened in 1970.

ANTONIO LECHASSEUR

Lismer, Arthur, painter, educator (b at Sheffield, Eng 27 June 1885; d at Montréal 23 Mar 1969). Lismer studied at Sheffield School of Art 1899-1906 and the Académie royale des beaux-arts, Antwerp, 1906-07. He moved to Canada in 1911, seeking work as a commercial illustrator. At the Grip Engraving Co in Toronto, he met J.E.H. MACDONALD, Tom THOMSON and F.H. JOHNSTON, and, shortly thereafter, Frank CARMICHAEL. In 1912 he returned to England to marry and spoke so highly of Canada that F.H. VARLEY followed him to Toronto.

Lismer began his distinguished career as an art educator as principal of the Victoria School of Art and Design (later NS Coll of Art and Design) in Halifax 1916-19. A prodigious worker, he painted views of Halifax harbour and returning troopships for Canadian War Records in 1918-19. He returned to Toronto to become VP of the Ontario College of Art in 1919 and in 1920 became a founding member of the GROUP OF SEVEN.

Lismer's first Canadian paintings were heavily influenced by John Constable, but during the 1920s he developed a powerful expressionist style of his own, characterized by raw colour, heavy impasto, deliberately coarse brushwork and simplified form. But Lismer devoted most of his time to art education. From 1927 to 1938 he was the educational supervisor at the Art Gallery of Toronto (now Art Gallery of Ontario). In 1932 he undertook a nationwide lecture tour; invitations to conferences in Europe and S Africa followed, and he returned to teach in S Africa in 1936-37. In 1938 he was visiting professor at Teachers' Coll, Columbia. He ran the Montreal Children's Art Centre, affiliated with the Montreal Museum of Fine Arts from 1941 to 1967. This activity left Lismer with little time to paint, but he produced many of his most original works after 1930, painting first in the Maritimes and Georgian Bay, and from 1951 at Long Beach, on Vancouver I, each summer. The lurid, intestinal and claustrophobic qualities of many of these paintings were not to contemporary taste, but have gained acceptance in recent years, for they seem to have developed from a form of deep, personal expressionism.

CHRISTOPHER VARLEY

Reading: John McLeish, *September Gale: A Study of Arthur Lismer of the Group of Seven* (1955).

Literacy has been defined both as the ability to read and write one's own name and as the ability to read and understand newspapers, magazines and encyclopedia articles written at a level of sophistication often well above that of the average graduate of grade 10. Such widely varied definitions make it difficult to form a reliable estimate of the number of illiterates in a particular society. Claims by different writers, eg, that illiteracy in the USSR has been eradicated and that 28% of Canadians are illiterate, are not comparable.

Although no precise figures are available for Canada, in Western societies generally the incidence of complete illiteracy is relatively low. Data from a provincial assessment of reading achievement in BC suggest that no more than 2% of Canadians cannot read or write at all (in this context the fact that a number of recent or older immigrants may be relatively illiterate in English or French but literate in their mother tongue must be considered). Estimates of how many Canadians are functionally literate, ie, able to understand the limited basic written communications thought to be essential in order to function in modern society, provide a more meaningful indication of illiteracy. Tests of functional literacy often include excerpts from such documents as bus schedules, drivers' manuals, classified advertisements, cookbooks, etc. Not surprisingly, scholars studying literacy often disagree on exactly what and how much an individual must be able to read in order to "function" in Canadian society. For instance, is someone who cannot read the Revenue Canada tax forms functionally illiterate?

Organizations such as UNESCO consider that anyone in an industrialized society who has less than a grade 5 education is wholly illiterate and that those with less than grade 9 are functionally illiterate. By these standards, nearly one in every 6 Canadians was functionally illiterate in 1987. Though females generally learn to read faster and score higher on reading tests while in school, the proportion of functional illiterates calculated by the grade-completed criterion is nearly identical for males (18%) and females (17.5%). Literacy has often been equated with occupational status. For example, it was calculated that of the population 15 years of age and over in 1987 who can be considered functionally illiterate, in UNESCO terms, only 33.8% are employed.

"Grade completed" however, is a very indirect and inadequate measure of literacy. First, it is not at all clear whether even with 10 or 11 years of schooling individuals can be considered functionally literate in advanced technological societies; moreover, individuals vary greatly in achievement after a specific period of schooling – many grade 8 students perform well above the level of the average grade 10 student; conversely, many grade 10 students perform below the level of the average grade 8 student.

More importantly, such calculations fail to take into account other and possibly more important factors affecting employment and social mobility, ie, class, ethnicity and sex. In the 19th century the majority of Irish Catholic immigrants to Canada were literate, but they occupied the lower economic and social ranks. Women and blacks, regardless of education, fared even worse.

In Canada, since the 19th century, literacy has been perceived as a personal and social "good," although the precise meaning of literacy and the understanding of what individuals are expected to achieve from their instruction in and possession of literacy is unclear. Nevertheless, many individuals exert great effort to become literate, even late in life, and societies with sharply contrasting political systems promote literacy through widespread popular education.

In Canada, literacy has been promoted primarily by school boards, libraries and, to a lesser degree, by private organizations. Public EDUCATION in Canada has fostered and encouraged literacy. Among private agencies, Frontier College, est 1899, was the first Canadian organization to receive a UNESCO medal for exemplary work in promoting literacy (1977). Canada's colleges in general are largely responsible for the provision of basic ADULT EDUCATION programs, including those specifically designed to enhance literacy.

Claims of an absolute increase in illiteracy among Canadians are generally unsubstantiated, but drops in reading performance for specific groups for specific periods of time and for specific skills are recorded occasionally. For example, authorities agree that although basic reading skills at lower grade levels have improved during the last 15 years, a loss among older pupils of higher order skills, such as inferential reading, has been documented. Nevertheless, Canadians in general are gradually becoming more literate and more educated. For example, the proportion of Canadians completing secondary school rose from 62% in 1971 to 82.2% by 1987; during the same period the percentage of Canadians with university degrees increased from 4.8% to 11%.

Although Canadians are now more literate in an absolute sense, it is not known if they keep pace with the demand in new literacy skills, because little work has been done in tracking the changing levels of literacy needed for full participation in society. The ability to read involves 3 major components: reasoning ability, mastery of language, and familiarity with the alphabetic code. The second component, mastery of language, is particularly important. Much of language is coded knowledge. As knowledge expands, so does the language that is needed to describe it. This in effect means that individuals can be or become relatively illiterate because they are or have become ignorant of new knowledge. In order to read anything at all with understanding, individuals must possess sufficient prior knowledge. If, therefore, knowledge expands at a rate faster than the ability to absorb it, the potential of a decline in situational or relative literacy is real.

Over the past few years the terms "visual literacy" and "computer literacy" have become popular. In both instances "literacy" refers to familiarity with and an ability to manipulate the object in question: visual symbiotic material or computers. J.J. TUINMAN

Reading: Harvey J. Graff, *The Literacy Myth* (1979).

Literary and Historical Society of Quebec, fd 6 Jan 1824, is Canada's oldest HISTORICAL SOCIETY. The earl of DALHOUSIE, governor in chief of Canada 1820-28, was a driving force in establishing the bilingual society, which received its royal charter in 1831. It had as its objective the preservation, care and dissemination of the colony's historical records, and was one of the first bodies to collect archival material for these purposes. It achieved considerable success and shared its findings through an active publications program. By its centennial in 1924 the society had published its *Transactions* series for all but its first 5 years, along with numerous monographs. It remains an active organization today. CARMAN V. CARROLL

Literary Bibliography in English The essential foundations of literary scholarship are adequate research tools and definitive texts of the literature itself: both are the products of literary bibliography – the former of enumerative, the latter of textual and analytical, bibliography. Enumerative bibliography aims at recording the literary achievement – past and present, primary and secondary – of a nation. At its best, it enables scholars to determine the structure and perceive the historical shape of their discipline; and on a more practical level it helps them to be selective in their research and to establish, without time-consuming work, the publishing history and transmission of primary texts. The bibliographies themselves may range from mere chronological listings of short titles to elaborate catalogues of quasi-facsimile title pages, and may include any combination of primary, secondary, retrospective and current material. The chief criteria of usefulness are comprehensiveness, accessibility and currency.

The literary scholar's first concern is to know the primary texts. The standard retrospective bibliography in this area of Canadian LITERATURE IN ENGLISH is R.E. Watters's *Checklist of Canadian Literature and Background Materials 1628-1960* (2nd ed 1972) which, though inconveniently organized and now outdated, has contributed greatly to an awareness of the scope of Canadian writing. This work, augmented by such references as Marie Tremaine's *Bibliography of Canadian Imprints, 1751-1800* (1952), library catalogues and current listings in the National Library's *Canadiana* (monthly and annually), goes far towards giving a complete view of Canada's primary texts, but falls far short of the ideal of enabling scholars to ascertain any author's literary *corpus*.

More helpful in doing so are a number of retrospective primary and secondary bibliographies which attempt to define each author's *corpus* and also offer complete listings of critical and historical commentary. R.G. Moyles's *English-Canadian Literature to 1900* (1976), Peter Stevens's *Modern English-Canadian Poetry* (1978) and Helen Hoy's *Modern English-Canadian Prose* (1983) together provide a focused view of Canadian literature up to the 1970s. Intended for students and beginning researchers, these offer primary and secondary bibliographies for over 150 authors, and also introduce the user to other reference guides, major anthologies, literary histories and general criticism, and important literary periodicals.

More intensive and detailed is *The Annotated Bibliography of Canada's Major Authors* (1979-) edited by Jack David and Robert Lecker – each volume containing 5 major writers. When completed the series will have covered 50 authors, detailing not merely the usual primary/secondary work, but such important items as manuscripts, works published in periodicals (very important for poets) and reviews.

The scholar's research will, of course, often lead far beyond creative writing, and into many ancillary disciplines such as history or native studies. Bibliographies in these areas can easily be found through Douglas Lochhead's *Bibliography of Canadian Bibliographies* (1972) and a number of specialized regional guides. Also indispensable are such reference tools as the *Canadian Periodical Index* (annual), the *Canadian Book Review Annual, Canadiana* and the *MLA International Bibliography* (annual); this last, though American, contains a great deal of current Canadian criticism.

Enumerative bibliography in Canada is nevertheless both disparate and idiosyncratic. There is still too little attention paid to textual transmission, variant editions and minor authors. Bibliographical investigation is still too dependent on individual initiative and preference, and a greater effort must be made to produce, by scholarly consensus, a single complete and comprehensive primary/secondary bibliography of Canada's creative literature. But enumerative bibliography has at least made a strong beginning; textual bibliography has not.

It used to be felt that analytical and textual bibliography were necessary only in defining the provenance of very old texts, eg, those of Shakespeare or Milton, where many authoritative variant versions existed. Analytical bibliography examined the text's printing history and textual bibliography applied those findings to the production of a definitive edition. It is now accepted, however, that following the textual path is necessary in producing a critical edition in the following steps: 1) establishing and collecting the authoritative texts; 2) choosing a base text for comparison; 3) thoroughly collating all texts or versions; 4) determining a copy text; 5) preparing a critical apparatus; 6) determining through these steps the extent of emendation and correction needed. In the past this was not done: new editions of Canadian classics were, if not truncated or bastardized, merely reprints of any preceding edition.

In recent years, however, editors of Canadian classics have become aware of and more concerned about textual fidelity. They are indeed following the "textual path" outlined above. New critical editions of such texts as Frances BROOK'S *The History of Emily Montague* (1769) and John RICHARDSON'S WACOUSTA (1832), produced by the Centre for Editing Early Canadian Texts at Carleton U, and the major editorial projects for E.J. Pratt and A.M. Klein, have set new standards for future editors. If they are adhered to, we can be assured that Canadian literature will be as reliably transmitted as that of any other nation.

R.G. MOYLES

Literary Bibliography in French Bibliographies of Canadian LITERATURE IN FRENCH can be roughly divided into 2 groups: retrospective, which list printed items of an earlier period, and current, which record the publication of books and articles as they appear. Québec books printed after the introduction of printing to central Canada (1764) and before 1820 are called *incunabula* (early printed works) and, because of their rarity, are usually described in detail by bibliographers. Québec incunabula are listed in 3 compilations: Marie Tremaine, *Bibliography of Canadian Imprints, 1751-1800* (1952), John Hare and Jean-Pierre Wallot, *Les Imprimés dans le Bas-Canada, 1801-1840* (only vol 1, 1801-1810, has been published, 1967), and *Laurentiana parus avant 1821* (1976). Books of the later 19th and early 20th centuries are listed in the multivolume *Bibliographie du Québec, 1821-1967* (1980-) and in *Canadiana, 1867-1900* (on microfiche; 1981-), both to appear over several years.

Among retrospective bibliographies limited to literary works, the most complete are those contained in the *Dictionnaire des oeuvres littéraires du Québec*, 4 vols to date (1978-). Separate listings by John Hare for the novel, poetry, drama and essays are included in volumes 3-6 of *Archives des lettres canadiennes* (1961-). Specialized bibliographies exist for 19th-century short stories (Aurélien Boivin, *Le Conte littéraire québécois au XIXe...*, 1975), novels (David M. Hayne and Marcel Tirol, *Bibliographie critique du roman canadien-français, 1837-1900*, 1968), travel narratives (John Hare, *Les Canadiens français aux quatre coins du monde*, 1964) and journalism (André Beaulieu and Jean Hamelin, *La Presse québécoise des origines à nos jours*, 6 vols to date (1973-). Plays of both the 19th and 20th centuries are listed in Édouard-Gabriel Rinfret, *Le Théâtre canadien d'expression française...* (4 vols, 1975-78).

Short bibliographies for most Québec writers are provided in Réginald Hamel, John Hare and Paul Wyczynski, *Dictionnaire pratique des auteurs québécois* (1976, expanded edition forthcoming). More detailed references for authors are found in university theses devoted to them or in library science theses submitted to Québec universities. The former are indexed in Antoine Naaman, *Répertoire de thèses littéraires canadiennes de 1921 à 1976* (1978) and in *Canadian Theses/Thèses canadiennes* (1952-). The latter are listed in Jeanne Proulx, *Bio-bibliographies canadiennes-françaises* (1970) and in *Bibliographie de bibliographies québécoises* (1978; supplement 1980). A few authors have been the subject of book-length bibliographies, eg, Paul Wyczynski's *Bibliographie descriptive et critique d'Émile Nelligan* (1973), and Pierre Cantin's *Jacques Ferron, polygraphe* (1984).

For the current bibliography of Québec's greatly increased literary production since 1960, the basic reference is the official monthly *Bibliographie du Québec* (1968-82), which lists all material published in, or about, Québec. An excellent annual review appears under the title *Livres et auteurs québécois* (1969- ; formerly *Livres et auteurs canadiens*, 1961-1968). A comprehensive listing of magazine articles on Québec literature is found in Pierre Cantin, Normand Harrington and Jean-Paul Hudon, *Bibliographie de la critique de la littérature québécoise dans les revues de XIXe et XXe siècles* (5 vols, 1979), with supplements in each issue of the *Revue d'histoire littéraire du Québec et du Canada français* (1979-87).

DAVID M. HAYNE

Literary Magazines in English After a tentative beginning with the publication of the *Nova Scotia Magazine* (1789-92) in Halifax and the *Quebec Magazine/Le magasin de Québec* (1792-94) in Québec City, brief experiments in literary journalism in the British North American colonies appeared more frequently in the 1820s and 1830s with the increase in an educated middle-class population. The earliest magazines largely contained material reprinted from books, newspapers and British and American magazines. The response of contributors grew, however, and patriotic editors encouraged an indigenous literature, so that increasing amounts of original material were introduced. Contributions were generally unsigned or acknowledged by initials or pseudonyms, such as "Canadensis"; the traditional anonymity of contributors was not abandoned until the latter part of the century. Some early titles – the *Christian Recorder* (Kingston and York, 1819-20, the first in Upper Canada), the *Literary Miscellany* (Montréal, 1822-23), the *Canadian Magazine & Literary Repository* (Montréal, 1823-25), the *Acadian Recorder, or Literary Mirror* (Halifax, 1823-25) – indicate the journals' eclectic nature: in them appeared history, current events, travel description, tales and verse. The term "magazine" was used in its most basic sense, meaning "storehouse." Other titles, such as the *Canadian Garland* (Hamilton, 1832-33), the *Colonial Pearl* (Halifax, 1837-40), the *Amaranth* (Saint John, 1841-43) and the *Mayflower* (Halifax, 1851-52) evoke the flowery gentility of their literature. Most successful was the *Literary Garland* published in Montréal by John Lovell and edited by John Gibson, 1838-51. Its most frequent contributor was Susanna MOODIE; others included John RICHARDSON, Charles SANGSTER, Catharine Parr TRAILL and Anna JAMESON. Mr and Mrs Moodie's venture in Belleville, the *Victoria Magazine* (1847-48), followed the more usual pattern of a short life, expiring within a year.

At mid-century, improvements in printing presses and an increase in literacy opened new markets for special interest publications, most notably those devoted to religion. In 1852 the Royal Canadian Institute founded the *Canadian Journal: A Repertory of Industry, Science and Art*. Edited initially by geologist and explorer Henry Y. HIND, it became an important medium for the academics of the newly formed universities of Canada East and West. It was superseded by the *Proceedings* of the institute in 1878. Vying with the popularity of weekly newspapers, and with readers' easy access to American and British magazines, and struggling to overcome problems of distribution to a scattered population, publishers attempted to reach a national audience with the *Anglo-American Magazine* (Toronto, 1852-55), edited by R.J. McGeorge; the *British American Magazine* (Toronto, 1863-64), published by G. Mercer Adam and edited by Hind; John Dougall's *New Dominion Monthly* (Montréal, 1867-69); and *Stewart's Literary Quarterly* (Saint John, 1868-72), edited by George Stewart, Jr.

The *Canadian Monthly and National Review* was launched in 1872, abetted by the new nationalistic fervour abroad after Confederation. Published by Adam and with the early support, both financial and editorial, of Goldwin SMITH, it amalgamated in 1878 with *Belford's Monthly* (1876-78) to become *Rose-Belford's Canadian Monthly and National Review*. During its 10 years of publication most of the leading figures of the day contributed articles, essays, fiction and verse. Intellectual in tone, highly moral in purpose, it became a nonpartisan forum for Canadian writers on controversial issues and lent impetus to the development of a Canadian literature. Smith continued some of its tradition in his review of current events in *The Bystander* (1880-83, 1889-90), and *The Week* (1883-96), whose first editor was the young Charles G.D. ROBERTS. By the century's end, mass circulation weeklies and magazines, such as SATURDAY NIGHT (1887-), *Dominion Illustrated* (1888-95), *Canadian Magazine* (1893-1939) and MACLEAN'S (1896-), began to thrive as advertisers' interest in their potential increased. Several university quarterlies were established (*see* LITERARY PERIODICALS). *The* UNIVERSITY MAGAZINE (1907-20) succeeded *McGill University Magazine* (1901-06). Another group of regional magazines appeared at this time: *New Brunswick Magazine* (Saint John, 1898-1905), *Great West Magazine* (Winnipeg, 1891-1908), *Prince Edward Island Magazine* (Charlottetown, 1899-1905), *Acadiensis* (Saint John, 1901-08) and *Westminster Hall* (Vancouver, 1911-27). These magazines are invaluable in providing a picture of the social and political life of the times and a reflection of the current ideas of writing and literary taste.

MARILYN G. FLITTON

Modern and Contemporary Periods

Until WWI, writers looked to Britain and the US for their literary models, but after 1918 magazines in Canada began to define Canadian literary activity. *Saturday Night* had always noted literary development in Canada and now CANADIAN FORUM (1920-) could point with pride to the achievements of Canadian THEATRE and the GROUP OF SEVEN. The *Dalhousie Review* (1921-) published important essays on emerging Canadian nationalism. The CANADIAN AUTHORS ASSOCIATION (fd 1921) began with its official organ, *Canadian Bookman;* this was succeeded by the *Authors' Bulletin* (1923-33) and *Canadian Author;* in 1940 this became incorporated into *Canadian Author & Bookman*. *Canadian Poetry Magazine* (1936-), also under the aegis of the CAA, was incorporated into *CAB* in 1968. The major forerunner to the exciting literary magazines of later years was the supplement to the *McGill Daily*, founded by Frank SCOTT and A.J.M. SMITH. It evolved into the *McGill Fortnightly Review* (1925-27), from which Scott moved to the *Canadian Mercury* (1928-29), which attacked the traditionalist views of the CAA. Modelled on British examples, the Montréal-based magazine launched a revolution in Canadian poetry inspired by T.S. Eliot and Ezra Pound. Apart from the UNIVERSITY OF TORONTO QUARTERLY (1931-) which brought mature critical standards to Canadian criticism, the Depression years were a barren decade for creative publishing. Short stories were published in *Maclean's* and *Saturday Night* and traditional poems were published in newspapers. BC's first literary magazines were the 2 issues of the *B.C. Argonaut* and the Vancouver Poetry Society's *Full Tide* (1936-66). But during WWII new ground was prepared for serious creative development. It started in Montréal with Patrick Anderson's left-wing *Preview* (1942-45), which published the writing of P.K. PAGE, Scott and A.M. KLEIN. Despite differences in outlook between this magazine and John SUTHERLAND'S *First Statement* (1942-45), the 2 merged as NORTHERN REVIEW (1945-56). The magazine was criticized for its right-wing, traditional and formal poetry, but it published early work by Irving LAYTON, Miriam WADDINGTON, Louis DUDEK and Raymond SOUSTER. From N Vancouver and later Victoria, Alan Crawley published CONTEMPORARY VERSE (1941-52), which later inspired the Winnipeg-based *CV II* (1975-). From Halifax, Raymond Souster published his mimeo magazine *Direction* (1943-46) followed by the Toronto magazines *Enterprise* (1948), CONTACT (1952-54) which evolved into Contact Press, and *Combustion* (1957-60). An expensive but short-lived Toronto publication was the 4 issues of *Here and Now* (1947-49). Other promising magazines lasted an issue or 2.

The 1950s was a decade of literary growth, partly because of the ease of reproduction by mimeograph. *Quarry* (fd 1952 at Queen's U), *CIV/N* (1954-56) and TAMARACK REVIEW (1956-82) under Robert Weaver published sophisticated writing. Marshall MCLUHAN and Edward Carpenter published Canada's first post-modern literary magazine, *Explorations* (1953-59). In Montréal Louis Dudek began *Delta* (1957-66), which was taken over by *Yes* (1956-70) in 1966. In 1945 A.G. BAILEY had founded *The* FIDDLEHEAD as a poetry magazine at University of New Brunswick; under Fred COGSWELL'S editorship (1952-66) it broadened to include prose and scholarship, and became a magazine of national significance. In Vancouver, George WOODCOCK began CANADIAN LITERATURE (1953-), which often publishes poetry alongside literary criticism. A student magazine at UBC, *Raven* (1955-62) was an important publication that introduced many significant poets, especially those associated with *Tish*, and was a forerunner to the finer production values of magazines in coming years.

The 1960s saw the beginnings of literary magazines in every area of the country. Some rare mimeo magazines include Al PURDY and Milton ACORN'S *Moment* (1961) and Toronto's Bohemian Embassy's *The Sheet* (1961) published in less than 100 copies. Photo-offset reproduction methods improved production quality at reasonable cost, and literary manifestations of a surging nationalism were encouraged by the CANADA COUNCIL, by provincial arts funding and municipal grants. James REANEY'S *Alphabet* (1960-71) was inspired by the mythopoeic theories of Northrop FRYE. Frank DAVEY founded *Tish* (1961-65) at UBC, stressing the poem as a developing experience, rather than as a finished product. This mimeo magazine's 45 issues frequently published George BOWERING, Fred WAH, Daphne MARLATT and David MCFADDEN. *Tish* inspired a cluster of magazines and small presses, both in support of its views and in reaction against them. Bowering's *Beaver Cosmos Folio* (1968-71) often published chapbooks devoted to a single poet, and *Imago* (1964-73) was devoted to the long poem. Davey's *Open Letter* (1965-) publishes critical commentary on experimental work. The variety of the 1960s is indicated by such titles as Seymour Mayne's *Cataract* (1961-62); Patrick LANE'S *Up th Tube with One i (Open)* (1961-63); David McFadden's *Mountain* (1962); Bill BISSETT'S radical *blewointment* (1963-72); Henry Beissel's *Edge* (1963-69); *Evidence* (1960-67); *Parallel* (1966-67); and Alan Safarik's *Blackfish* (1971-73). Another important ongoing magazine is bp NICHOL'S *grOnk* (1965-); published irregularly in small runs, it challenges all the conventions of literary publishing. *Culture* (1931-71), one of the few bilingual scholarly magazines, began regular publication in 1965. Another bicultural magazine was *Le Chien d'or/The Golden Dog* (1971-75). *Ellipse* (1971-) publishes translations of Québec and English-Canadian poets, 2 per issue. Magazines such as Fraser Sutherland's *Northern Journey*, Dave GODFREY'S *Porcépic*, and *White Pelican* (closely associated with Sheila WATSON who was on its board of directors) all contributed to the nation's awareness of its literary artists. In Québec, a number of important LITERARY PERIODICALS IN FRENCH performed a similar service for francophone writers and readers.

One significant development in the 1960s was the university-based quarterly; creative writing courses were established, and by mid-decade many universities had literary magazines, including *University of Windsor Review* (fd 1965), *West Coast Review* (Simon Fraser, 1966), *Wascana Review* (U of Saskatchewan, 1966), *Malahat Review* (U of Victoria, 1967), MOSAIC (U of Manitoba, 1967), *Antigonish Review* (St Francis Xavier U, 1970), CAPILANO REVIEW (North Vancouver, 1970) and *Exile* (York U, 1972). These in turn have generated short-lived student- and professor-edited publications on campuses across Canada. Another important feature of the 1960s was the alternative newspaper. Some, such as Vancouver's *Georgia Strait* (which evolved into New Star Books), or Guelph's Marxist *Alive*, grew into SMALL PRESSES. Many magazines of the 1960s evolved into the small press publishers of the 1970s, including *Talon, blewointment, 3¢ Pulp, Alive, Porcépic, Fiddlehead, Square Deal, Blackfish, Quarry, NeWest Review, Delta* and *Potersfield Portfolio*.

Running against the impulse of nationalism were the internationalist magazines such as *Prism International* (1956-), *Contemporary Literature in Translation* (1967-78) and *Exile*. *Descant* (1970-), *Jewish Dialog* (1970-) and *Waves* (1972-) reflected a cosmopolitan awareness. *Malahat Review* became more Canadian, on the other hand, with a change of editors in 1982. The new Canadian writing also found expression in special issues of American, Australian and New Zealand literary magazines. By the 1970s, literary magazines numbered in the dozens. CANADIAN FICTION MAGAZINE (1971-), edited by Geoffrey Hancock, was Canada's first short-story magazine, publishing innovative short fiction, with a special interest in magic realism, metafiction, neo-surrealist stories, and theories of the narrative. The *Journal of Canadian Fiction* (1972-) published traditional stories, bibliographies and critical commentary. *Essays on Canadian Writing* (1974-), BOOKS IN CANADA (1972-), *Canadian Poetry* (1977-) and *Brick* (1977-) took part in the continuing critical examination of Canadian letters. *Poetry Canada Review* (1978-) was the country's first poetry tabloid. Women's magazines reflected the many concerns arising from the women's movement at the populist and academic levels with *Fireweed* (1977-), *Branching Out* (1971-81), *Room of One's Own* (1975-), *Canadian Woman Studies* (1978-), *Atlantis* (1975-), and others such as *Makara, The Other Woman, Kinesis* and *Broadside* that answered particular needs.

A magazine by women of colour, *Tiger Lily*, began in 1986. One innovative feminist collective known as "Tessera" with a special interest in feminist literary theory, "borrowed" existing magazines annually to publish their work. Regional magazines as varied as BC's *Raincoat Chronicles* (1972-), *Arts Manitoba* (1978-), which became *Border Crossings*, and *Cape Breton's Magazine* also addressed specific local literary concerns.

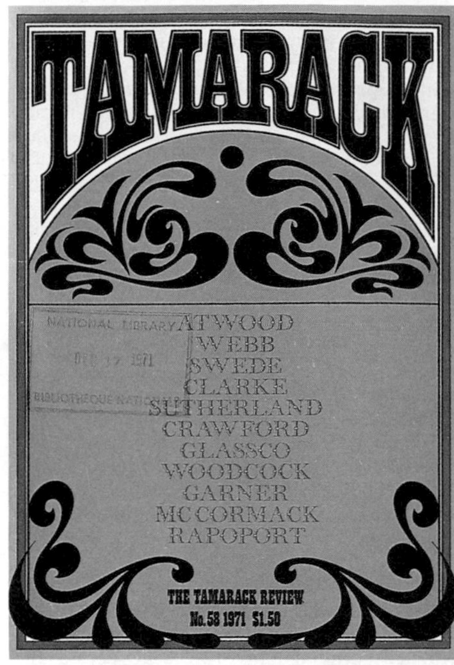

The *Tamarack Review*, which covered all literary genres, set a high standard for later Canadian literary magazines (*cover design by Fred Huffman/used with permission*).

In the 1980s, some ambitious new magazines, like *Ethos* (1983-), strove for international circulation. The short-lived *Canadian Literary Review* (1982) and *Gamut* (1979-) tried to balance the Canadian tradition with international writing. Among the successful university magazines was McGill's *Rubicon* (1983-). Newer magazines opted for a variety of styles, from the conservative paper, *The Idler* (1984-) to the complimentary tabloid, *What* (1985-). As computer technology became readily available, so did the possibility of a database literary magazine; *Swift Current* (1984-) was founded by Frank Davey and is available via modem to subscribers. In addition, seminars organized by the Canadian Periodical Publishers Assn and various provincial writers groups improved production, distribution and promotion of Canadian literary magazines. Committed to new writing, literary magazines continue to keep the literature vital.

GEOFFREY HANCOCK

Reading: Robert Bringhurst, *Ocean/Paper/Stone* (1984); Aileen Collins, ed, *Civ/N: a literary magazine of the 50s* (1983). Frank Davey, ed, *Tish: 1-19* (1977); Louis Dudek and Michael Gnarowski, *The Making of Modern Poetry in Canada* (1966); C.H. Gervais, ed, *Tish: The Writing Life* (1978); Geoff Hancock, *Published in Canada* (1987); Ken Norris, *The Little Magazine in Canada, 1925-1980* (1984).

Literary Periodicals in English In the 19th century, Canada relied mainly on foreign imports for its literary scholarship, and early attempts to provide native periodicals aiming at more than a merely popular standard were generally short-lived. The most successful and long-lasting journals of this kind were the *Canadian Journal* (1852-78), the *Canadian Monthly and National Review* (1872-78, later amalgamated into *Rose-Belford's Canadian Monthly and National Review*, 1878-82) and *The Week* (1883-96). The last 2 were fostered by Goldwin SMITH, and Charles G.D. ROBERTS was the first editor of *The Week*. The 20th century has seen a fragmentation of the audiences, with university-based journals providing academic, learned articles and glossier magazines catering – often superficially – to a more popular audience. In the middle stands the CANADIAN FORUM, which has appeared regularly since 1920. Describing itself as "an independent journal of opinion and the arts," it is not officially connected with any university but draws upon the academic community, mainly in Toronto, for many of its contributors. Although its origins were primarily political, reflecting (in the words of its opening editorial) "a desire to secure a freer and more informed discussion of public questions" and generally presenting a radical or left-wing viewpoint, it has consistently endeavoured to "trace and value those developments of art and letters which are characteristically Canadian."

The first of Canada's 3 main university journals founded to further humanistic scholarship was QUEEN'S QUARTERLY, which first appeared in 1893. It began with the twofold aim of serving the intellectual needs of Queen's University graduates and "promoting the interests of culture in Canada." Its early emphasis was on religious matters, but it soon became a wide-ranging, respected academic publication. It was joined in 1921 by the DALHOUSIE REVIEW, which claimed in its first issue to be a project "of university extension" discussing "problems of general import" in "a style that can be generally understood." Ten years later, the UNIVERSITY OF TORONTO QUARTERLY began with similar goals. Offering itself as "a Canadian Journal of the Humanities," it has generally succeeded in providing a forum for academic discourse where Canadian and internationally recognized scholars can appear side by side. All 3 journals have continued to publish and maintain a high standard.

The most remarkable feature of Canadian periodical publishing in recent years has been the rich crop of scholarly journals devoted to discussion of the nation's own literature. The earliest, and still best known, is CANADIAN LITERATURE, a quarterly founded in 1959 at UBC with George WOODCOCK as its first editor. Since then it has published scholarly articles and reviews on works of Canadian origin, often devoting individual issues to topics of special interest and concern. Initially considered by some to be a premature venture, it not only succeeded in creating its own readership, but has, by its very existence as an outlet for Canadian literary studies, helped to nurture the subject to which it is devoted. Without rivals for many years, it was later joined by several journals with similar aims, notably *Essays on Canadian Writing* (fd 1974, originally with York U) and *Studies in Canadian Literature* (fd 1976, UNB).

The interdisciplinary *Journal of Canadian Studies*, a wider-ranging quarterly embracing history and social studies as well as literature, was founded at Trent University in 1966. The flowering of Canadian fiction and poetry in recent years is reflected in the appearance of 2 journals specifically devoted to each genre: CANADIAN FICTION MAGAZINE (1971-), the *Journal of Canadian Fiction* (1972-), *Canadian Poetry* (1977-) and the *Journal of Canadian Poetry* (1978-). In addition, *Canadian Drama* has been published at University of Waterloo since 1975 and *Theatre History in Canada* appeared in 1980.

A number of Canadian LEARNED SOCIETIES publish their own specialized periodicals, eg, the Association of Canadian University Teachers of English, whose *English Studies in Canada* first appeared in 1975. Of more general interest is the Humanities Association of Canada's *Bulletin* (1951-73), which was replaced with the more ambitious *Humanities Association Review*. Not considered here are the numerous journals from *The* FIDDLEHEAD (1945-) in the Maritimes to the *Malahat Review* (1967-) in BC that concentrate on the publication of creative writing. It will be noticed that the majority of literary periodicals in English that are of scholarly importance were established quite recently, reflecting the expansion of Canadian universities since the late 1950s and the concurrent growth of Canadian LITERATURE IN ENGLISH. *See also* LITERARY MAGAZINES. W.J. KEITH

Literary Periodicals in French Periodicals have always played a leading role in the dissemination and development of Québec literature. In the 19th century, when books were rare, the contributors to periodicals affirmed the need to lay the foundations of a literary identity. Originally patriotic in outlook, the periodicals that coincided with the "Literary Movement of 1860" (*Les* SOIRÉES CANADIENNES, 1861-65, *Le Foyer canadien*, 1863-66 and *Nouvelles Soirées canadiennes*, 1882-88) encouraged the publication of legends and short stories drawn from popular culture, as well as historical facts that had to be rescued from oblivion. *L'Opinion publique* (1870-83), *Le Monde illustré* or *L'Album universel* (1884-1907) and *Revue canadienne* (1864-1922), despite their more diversified content, expanded this concept of an essentially traditionalist and folkloric literature.

Early 20th-century writers preferred to approach the problem of national literature as a choice between regionalism and universalism. Despite their brief existence, *Le Terroir* (fd 1909), whose contributors were members of the École littéraire de Montréal, and *Le* NIGOG (fd 1918) were the 2 poles of a debate waged later by essayists and pamphleteers on the theme of the language of writing. Periodicals such as *Idées* (1935-39), *La* RELÈVE (1934-41) and its successor, *La Nouvelle Relève* (1941-48), and *Gants du ciel* (1943-46) sought to stimulate the mind and arouse a spiritual and humanistic renewal. Far from being folkloric, the literary works of *La Relève's* contributors focused on an expression of the self, the psyche and the spiritual problems that affect modern life. AMÉRIQUE FRANÇAISE (1941-63) extended these reflections by posing the problem facing those who have both French and American backgrounds.

More political than literary, CITÉ LIBRE (1950-66) also had an effect on the ideological climate in which the literature of the 1950s evolved. Opposed to the pervasive conservative trend, contributors encouraged internationalism. This group soon became a target of those writing for PARTI PRIS (1963-68), a political and cultural periodical with 3 objectives: independence, socialism and secularism for Québec. *Parti pris* gave nationalism a leftist stance and articulated the relationship between the literary and the political. LIBERTÉ (fd 1959) debates current issues ranging from cultural fatigue to the language battle, from cultural policies to literary institutions. Although it has published articles by foreign authors, *Liberté* gives prominence to young Québec writers, who have often had their first works published there. After a few years, *Liberté* changed its editorial board and found a new dynamic spirit fueled by concern, humour and vigilant criticism.

While *Parti pris* countered *Cité libre* and supported the leftist *Liberté*, *La* BARRE DU JOUR (1965-76) and *La Nouvelle Barre du jour* (fd 1977) broke with the strictly social concept of literature: the writer is no longer the measure of society's pain. In tune with his own instincts, he translates a writing in gestation in which one sees the encoded writing of modern times – halfway between literary theory and fiction, where even theory becomes fiction and is considered fictitious. Hence an inevitable formalism. *Herbes rouges* (fd 1968) chose to publish only one author in each issue. Here, too, there was talk of the materiality of the text as the setting for questioning and strategy. The texts of *Herbes rouges* are generally more provocative than those of *La Barre du jour*. Everything is material for prose and poetry, from publicity to comics, from social discourse to political conscience. In another vein, *Estuaire* (fd 1976) publishes young writers' poetry. The journal at first highlighted the poetry of oral expression, of proclamation, of sharing. This initial orientation was gradually replaced by more diversified poetry which still sought a level of readability. Between 1960 and 1980 other periodicals had a fairly ephemeral existence. They included *Maintenant* (1962-75), which published a number of manifestos on Québec language and condition, *Mainmise* (1970-78), a voice of the counterculture originating in the US, *Presqu'Amérique* (1970-73), torn between different intellectual attachments, and the Marxist *Chroniques* (1975-78) and *Stratégie* (1972-77). *Les Têtes de pioche* (1976-79) was in the vanguard of radical feminism in Québec.

There are a number of useful surveys of current Québec literary journalism: *Livres et auteurs québécois* (1961-82), an annual collection of reviews of Québec's literary production; *Lettres québécoises* (fd 1976), a systematic review of current publications; and *Spirale* (fd 1979), a periodical of literary criticism that tries to fight clichés and received ideas. In theatre, the excellent *Jeu* (fd 1976) links theory and practice, carefully examines productions, interviews troupes and reports on theatrical activity in Québec.

The many university reviews generally devote each issue to the study of a theme or a writer. This is true of *Études littéraires* at Laval and *Études françaises* at the Université de Montréal. *Voix et images du pays*, published by the Presses de l'université du Québec, is the only journal devoted solely to Québec. In Sherbrooke, *Ellipse* publishes works in translation, while *Présence francophone* reports on activities in various French-speaking countries. In Ottawa, *Incidences* and the *University of Ottawa Quarterly* discuss literary issues.

The most recent journals include *Dérives* (fd 1975), *Possibles* (fd 1976), *Intervention* (fd 1978), *Le Temps fou* (1978-83) and *La Vie en rose* (fd 1980). All favour opening up every field of cultural activity and anti-dogmatism. These periodicals integrate creation within a global view of society and question new cultural practices based on co-operative, self-managed and feminist movements. Three of the newer library journals include *Arcade* (fd 1982), *Dixit. 01* (fd 1984) and *XYZ* (fd 1985). Two are devoted to science fiction: *Solaris* (fd 1974 as *Requiem*) and *Imagine* (fd 1979).

Analysis of cultural periodicals thus reveals a number of co-existing currents struggling for symbolic recognition, whereas Québec's literary history has accustomed us to seeing only one group dominate in any single period. Breaks with established trends are less violent than in the days of the REFUS GLOBAL and *Parti pris*. Writers no longer oppose, simply transpose and transgress.

LISE GAUVIN

Literary Prizes in English Until the 1920s there were no annual literary awards in Canada for writers in English. Ironically, the first such prize was the Québec Literary Competition prize, awarded 1923-70 by the Province of Québec. The oldest literary prize still being awarded is the Lorne Pierce Medal, sponsored by the ROYAL SOCIETY OF CANADA and first awarded in 1926. In 1928 the Royal Society began offering the Tyrrell Medal for contributions to Canadian history. These 2 medals were presented annually until 1966, when a $1000 prize was added to each award and they became biennial.

No other literary awards established in the 1920s are still being offered. The IMPERIAL ORDER DAUGHTERS OF THE EMPIRE National Short Story Competition lasted 1923-33, and the IODE National One-Act Play Competition lasted 1923 to 1936. The Montreal Poetry Contest sponsored by the Montréal branch of the CANADIAN AUTHORS

ASSOCIATION (CAA) was offered 1925-46, and the Maclean's Magazine Short Story Awards were presented 7 times between 1927 and 1955.

Of the awards established in the 1930s, the GOVERNOR GENERAL'S LITERARY AWARDS have become pre-eminent in Canada. Launched in 1937 by the CAA, with the first awards being given for 1936, they were originally made in 3 categories: fiction, nonfiction and poetry or drama. In 1959 the CANADA COUNCIL took over partial responsibility for the awards, created matching categories for works in French, and added a $1000 prize to each award. Finally, in 1971 the Canada Council took over full responsibility for the awards, the value of which increased to $2500 in 1966 and $5000 in 1975. In 1981 a separate category for drama was created.

Two other awards from the 1930s have survived: the Alberta Poetry Contest, established in 1930 by the Edmonton branch of the CAA, and the Canadian One-Act Playwriting Contest, established in 1937 by the Ottawa Little Theatre. The various awards offered 1934-69 by the Dominion Drama Festival were once prominent, but the festival (now Theatre Canada) became noncompetitive in 1970.

The most familiar award created in the 1940s is perhaps the Stephen Leacock Memorial Medal (est 1947), awarded for humour. In 1973 the Manufacturer's Life Insurance Co added a cash prize, for which the Hudson's Bay Co assumed responsibility in 1981. Other prizes established in the 1940s include the Book of the Year Medal for children's books, begun in 1947 by the Canadian Association of Children's Librarians; the IODE Provincial Chapter of Ontario Short Story Competition, established in 1948; the Eaton Short Story Competition, set up in 1948 by the Winnipeg Women's Canadian Club and the Winnipeg branch of the CAA (the present name was adopted in 1960 when The T. Eaton Co began contributing a cash prize); and the Nova Scotia Poetry Contest, created in 1949 by the Nova Scotia Centre of the Poetry Society of England. Also established in the 1940s were the Ryerson Fiction Award, presented by Ryerson Press 14 times between 1942 and 1960; the O'Leary Newfoundland Poetry Awards (1944-55); and the IODE Annual Book Contest (1946-57), sponsored by the Alberta branch.

The 1950s saw the establishment of the University of Alberta National Awards in Letters, Music, and Painting and the Related Arts (1951-); the University of British Columbia Medal for Popular Biography (1952-); the University of Western Ontario President's Medals (1952-), which are awarded in recognition of periodical publications and are meant to complement the Governor General's Literary Awards; the Chauveau Medal (1952-) of the Royal Society (annual until 1966, when a $1000 prize was added and it became biennial); the Government of Newfoundland and Labrador Arts and Letters Competition (1952-); and the Little-Brown Canadian Children's Book Award (1957-). Several others, such as the Maclean's Magazine Novel Award (1953-57), and the Beta Sigma Phi Award (1956-67), awarded for a first novel, lasted only a few years.

The most prestigious awards to come out of the 1960s were the MOLSON PRIZES, made possible by a grant from Molson's to the Canada Council. Two prizes of $50 000 each are awarded annually for distinguished achievement in any area of culture. Among other prizes established in the 1960s and still being awarded are the Vicky Metcalf Award (1963-) for children's literature; the Beaver Trophy (1965-) awarded by the HBC in Edmonton; the CAA, Vancouver Branch, Award (1966-); the Alberta Playwriting Competition (1967-); and the Dr William Henry Drummond National Poetry Contest (1969-). The Doubleday Canadian Prize Novel Award (1961-67), worth $10 000, was another first-novel award that did not survive.

The growth in the number, value and prestige of literary awards is undoubtedly a correlative of both our increasing awareness of our national literature in English and of the increasing quality and quantity of that literature. Although most of these new awards are single, several associations have established series of awards that are intended to compete with the Governor General's Literary Awards. In 1973 the CAA began to award a series of silver medals to replace the Governor General's Awards which they had administered before 1971. In 1975 Harlequin Books added a $1000 prize to the medals, and the prize money now stands at $5000. In 1975 the Canada Council established the Children's Literature Prizes ($5000 annually) for 2 writers in English and in French; in 1980 the award was extended to include illustrators of children's literature. The Canada Council also awards prizes for TRANSLATIONS. In 1980 CBC Radio made its first series of annual CBC Radio Literary Awards. In 1982 the Writers Development Trust and the National Book Festival sponsored the first Writers' Awards, an annual series which includes the Gerald Lampert Memorial Award, the Pat Lowther Memorial Award and the John Glassco Translation Prize. In Alberta in the late 1970s the Edmonton *Journal* set up the Edmonton Journal Awards, and in the early 1980s the Writers Guild of Alberta Awards were established.

Several other single, general awards came into being after 1970: the City of Toronto Book Award (1973-); the Rothmans Merit Award for Literature (1974-); the IODE Book Award (1974-); the Canada-Australia Literary Prize (1976-), given to a Canadian every second year; the Gibson Merit Award for Literature (1977-); the Evelyn Richardson Memorial Award (1978-) for residents of Nova Scotia; the Periodical Distributors of Canada Book of the Year (1977-) and Author of the Year (1981-); and in 1984 the Philips Prize, $5000 plus a new word processor, was awarded for the first time.

First-novel prizes continue to be popular, and several new ones have been set up: the Search for a New Alberta Novelist Competition (1972-); the Books in Canada First Novel Award (1977-); the Gibson First Novel Award (1977-); and the much publicized $50 000 Seal Books First Novel Award (1978-). There are several other new awards for fiction, including the Canadian Booksellers' Association Literary Award (1972-); the Chatelaine Magazine Annual Fiction Competition (1979-); and the Young Canadian Writers Award (1982-). Perhaps the most interesting new fiction award is the Pulp Press International 3-Day Novel Writing Contest (1978-), which has grown quickly and has gained considerable interest in the US.

Most new awards for poetry have been incorporated into the general awards series, with the exception of the Poetry Award of the Federation of Women Teachers Associations of Ontario and the Canadian Author & Bookman Poetry Award. On the other hand, several distinct awards have been established for drama, juvenile literature and nonfiction writing. Among the drama awards are the Alberta Televison Playwriting Competition (1970-); the University of Saskatchewan Playwriting Competition (1971-); the Chalmers Award (1972-); and the Clifford E. Lee Award (1973-). The juvenile literature awards include the Amelia Frances Howard-Gibbon Medal (1971-); the Collier-Macmillan Award (1974-); the Ruth Schwartz Memorial Award (1976-); the Vicky Metcalf Short Story Award (1978-); and the Claude Aubry Award (1981-). New nonfiction prizes include the Sainte-Marie Prize in History (1971-); the Alberta Non-Fiction Award (1973-); the Alberta Regional History Award (1973-); and the Saskatchewan Native Writers' Contest (1976-).

A sign of the vitality of literary awards in Canada is the recent creation of a new category of award: in 1982 the first Malahat Review Awards for Book Design were presented.

ALAN R. KNIGHT

Literary Prizes in French The first literary award in Québec dates from 1809, the year when the Société historique de Québec held its first literary competition. The stated topic was the 50th anniversary of the accession of King George III. Other competitions followed, sponsored by societies or periodicals. These competitions, which gained publicity for their funding bodies, usually dealt with historical or political themes. At the beginning of the 20th century, 2 annual awards were inaugurated which quickly won wide renown: the Action intellectuelle award of the Association de la jeunesse canadienne-française, open to candidates of age 35 or under, and the poetry competition of the Société des poètes canadiens-français.

In 1922, at the insistence of Athanase David, provincial secretary, the Québec government created a number of literary and scientific competitions. Their awards became the most highly valued of all in Québec, as much for their prestige as for their monetary value. The Prix Duvernay and that awarded by the Cercle du Livre de France are the 2 other important prizes created before the 1960s, when an explosion of Québec awards took place, some of which still exist.

The list of literary prizes awarded in Québec now covers a wide number of fields apart from the novel, notably journalism, science, history, literature for young people, the novel and poetry. There are also some regional awards.

The Prix Athanase-David (Prix David), which has existed in its present form since 1968, honours an author for the totality of his work. This prize, the most highly valued in Québec, is for $15 000 and applies to all literary genres. The winners, 1968-86, are Mgr Félix-Antoine Savard, Alain Grandbois, Gabrielle Roy, Paul-Marie Lapointe, Hubert Aquin, Marcel Dubé, Rina Lasnier, Fernand Dumont, Pierre Vadeboncoeur, Jacques Ferron, Anne Hébert, Yves Thériault, Gérard Bessette, Gilles Archambault, Marie-Claire Blais, Gaston Miron, Jean-Guy Pilon and Jacques Godbout.

In 1959, the Canada Council assumed responsibility for the GOVERNOR GENERAL'S LITERARY AWARD ($5000) and created a French division. Instituted in 1937 by the CANADIAN AUTHORS ASSOCIATION, these awards have honoured many authors in all literary fields.

One of the oldest Québec awards (1949), the Prix Esso du Cercle du Livre de France ($5000) for an unpublished work of fiction, has been offered since 1977 by the oil company whose name it bears.

The Prix Molson of the ACADÉMIE CANADIENNE-FRANÇAISE and the UNION DES ÉCRIVAINS QUÉBÉCOIS, awards a $5000 scholarship to a Québec or francophone Canadian novelist.

The Translation Prize of the Canada Council ($5000) goes to the 2 best translations, one French and one English. The same organization also gives a prize for youth literature ($5000), instituted in 1975 and awarded to one French-language and one English-language work.

The Grand Prix de poésie Gatien-Lapointe (1984), to a maximum of $5000, is awarded to a francophone Canadian poet.

In 1979 the Fondation Émile-Nelligan honoured the centenary of Emile NELLIGAN's birth by creating a prize of the same name ($3000) for poets age 35 or under. Winners to date are François Charron, Claude Beausoleil, Jean-Yves Collette, Philippe Haeck and Jocelyne Félix, Lucien Francoeur and Anne-Marie Alonzo.

Created in 1958 as the Prix France-Canada, the Prix Québec-Paris (1982) is jointly administered by the Association France-Canada and the government of Québec. It is awarded to a French Canadian writer whose work has appeared in Canada or in France. The winner receives a $2000 scholarship from the government of Québec plus 4000 NF from the City of Paris.

The Prix France-Québec Jean-Hamelin (formerly the Prix France-Québec) was founded in 1965 by the Association des écrivains de langue française (ADELF) with the help of the DÉLÉGATION GÉNÉRALE DU QUÉBEC. Worth 2000 NF, it is awarded to a French-language writer born in N America.

The Prix Canada-Suisse ($2500), founded in 1980 by the Canada Council and the Swiss Pro Helvetia Foundation, is alternately awarded to a Canadian and a Swiss writer for a work published in French. The same principle applies to the Prix Canada-Communauté française de Belgique ($2500), which is given for the entire body of the winner's work rather than one particular piece, and the Prix de littérature de jeunesse Québec/Wallonie-Bruxelles ($2500).

Created in 1978 by the Salon International du livre de Québec, the Prix Robert-Cliché for unpublished writers offers 3 prizes ($2000, $500 and $300), which are awarded by the newspaper *Le Soleil*. The prize-winning works are published in Québec by Les Éditions Quinze and by Québec-Loisirs, and co-published in France.

The 3 Grands Prix du Journal de Montréal (for poetry, novels and plays) follow from the Prix Littéraires du Journal de Montréal, instituted in 1980. Each of the winners receives a $1500 scholarship.

Finally, the Prix Molson, created in 1963 and managed by the Canada Council, may be awarded to a writer. This highly prestigious prize, worth $50 000, honours Canadians who have distinguished themselves in the arts, the humanities or the social sciences. VÉRONIQUE ROBERT

Literature and Politics This subject is usually examined in 3 categories: the political content in works of literature; the political activities of writers and their organizations to secure respect, recognition and economic independence; and relations between writers and the state respecting the rights of the author and of literature (*see* AUTHORS AND THEIR MILIEU).

From the beginning, Canadian history has presented highly political subjects for our literature. European nations struggled for territorial possession and for favourable boundary decisions. Christian missionaries and settlers struggled with the aborigines for souls and space for settlement. Settlement groups disputed among themselves and with outsiders the nature of the society that was forming. Later, history and literature were shaped by tension between the individual and the community, between "authority" and "personal freedom," between imperial powers and the national will for self-determination. Finally the continuing global tension between socialist and liberal-capitalist ideologies is mirrored in Canadian literature.

Since early times, relations between literature and politics have been manifested in the organization of many literary interest groups, formed to make members' work better known, to encourage production, to pressure governments and other patrons for support, and to secure an atmosphere in which writers can produce well and profitably. Such organizations have been born and have died according to the energy of their members and the liveliness of the political and social issues with which they have been engaged. The first in what is now Canada may have been the ORDRE DE BON TEMPS (Order of Good Cheer), founded by Samuel de CHAMPLAIN in ACADIA in 1606 to entertain the colonists through the long winter with literary creations and scientific studies. Usually claimed as the oldest, however, is the LITERARY AND HISTORICAL SOCIETY OF QUEBEC, fd 1824, a largely English organization despite its location. The later francophone INSTITUT CANADIEN, fd 1844, had over 700 members, a large library and connections with France. It was liberal, and for a short time some members favoured annexation of Canada East (Québec) to the US. The Institut was attacked by Mgr Ignace BOURGET for its willingness to spread secular ideas. It diminished in the 1860s and 1870s largely because of church opposition to its progressive policies, and it faded away at the turn of the century. The École littéraire de Montréal (1895) concerned itself principally with aesthetic matters and is renowned for having among its members Émile NELLIGAN, Albert Lozeau and Albert Ferland.

In English Canada the claims of literature were often expressed in MECHANICS' INSTITUTES, which appeared as early as the 1820s in many cities "to afford instruction in the principles of the arts and in the wonders of science and useful knowledge." Literary and historical societies also developed in Montréal, Toronto, Halifax, Saint John and Winnipeg as the century progressed. One of the most publicly volatile organizations in the 19th century was the CANADA FIRST movement. Formed in Ottawa in 1868, with a platform that united political nationalism and the encouragement of literature and culture, it eventually became a political party. Unsuccessful in politics, it nevertheless had a significant effect on the production of literature and the establishment of a Canadian tradition in the arts.

In 1921 the CANADIAN AUTHORS ASSOCIATION was founded "to foster and develop a climate favourable to the creative arts, to promote recognition of Canadian writers and their work." Support for the CAA was strong, and in its first 3 years it lobbied hard for COPYRIGHT legislation to safeguard the interests of Canadian authors. A francophone section was created in 1922, and it became, in 1936, the Société des écrivains canadiens.

The CAA involved itself with the production of periodicals and poetry anthologies. It helped to create the GOVERNOR GENERAL'S LITERARY AWARDS (1937) and was the precursor of more recently created literary organizations devoted to the rights and well-being of writers, such as the LEAGUE OF CANADIAN POETS (1966), the Newfoundland Writers Guild (1968), Playwrights Canada (1972), the WRITERS' UNION OF CANADA (1973) and the UNION DES ÉCRIVAINS QUÉBÉCOIS (1977).

The claims of writers, and indeed all artists, to organized support by government was considered sympathetically in the 1951 report of the Massey Royal Commission on NATIONAL DEVELOPMENT IN THE ARTS, LETTERS AND SCIENCES. This report led in 1957 to the creation of the CANADA COUNCIL, which has transformed the relation of writers and other artists to government. Today, provincial councils parallel and supplement the Canada Council's work, providing financial and other support for people in the arts. The grants, literary awards and support structures that have developed since 1957 have been criticized; however, some claim that public money is spent badly upon people who have little talent, and for the production of inferior works; others feel that public support of artists introduces political bias in the production of literary work and invites writers to censor themselves in order to please the governments of the day. Nevertheless, Canadian governments follow the pattern of governments elsewhere, actively supporting the production of literature through various agencies.

Naturally, writers espousing political ideas or policies that are distinctly opposed to the governments of the day have found themselves in tense situations, despite the widespread belief that Canadians have full freedom of expression. For example, in 1933 a mock trial drama, *Eight Men Speak*, played to an audience of 1500 in Toronto. The play alleged that Canadian Communist Party leader Tim BUCK, recently arrested with others under an eccentric and unpopular s98 of the Criminal Code, had an attempt made upon his life by a prison guard who acted with approval of people in the government. Police moved in on the play, effectively suspending its life until it was published in book form in 1976. The effect upon the general sense of literary freedom caused by such individual acts of government intervention cannot be measured. But at various times actions initiated or sanctioned by governments and their agencies have made it clear that the state has disapproved of some kinds of literature.

Novels and other literary forms dealing with political events or beliefs are numerous. A few representative works that show Canadian authors' wide range of political interest are Irene Baird's novel *Waste Heritage* (1939), concerned with unemployment in the GREAT DEPRESSION; George RYGA's play *The Ecstasy of Rita Joe* (1967), dealing with the plight of native people; Richard ROHMER's novel *Ultimatum* (1973), about conflict between Canada and the US; Hubert AQUIN's novel PROCHAIN ÉPISODE (1965), dealing with the psychology of Québec separatism; and Ivan Shaffer's novel *The Medicine Man* (1975), exploring conflict arising between large corporate interests and reformist members of the Canadian House of Commons. In a less confrontational way writers have treated the political nature of life in Canada from the earliest times. John RICHARDSON'S WACOUSTA (1832), William KIRBY's *The* GOLDEN DOG (1877) and Philippe AUBERT DE GASPÉ Sr's, *Les* ANCIENS CANADIENS (1863) all deal, each in its own way, with the character of the Canadian community and the nature of the political order. That theme has continued unflaggingly as a subject of literature to our day.

Because modern Canada continues to debate REGIONALISM and centralism, ANARCHISM and communitarianism, national independence and association with US power, socialism and capitalism, and independence or federal association for Québec, the country's literature exhibits a continuing political dimension. Literary associations occupy themselves with many of these questions, and theories of literary creation in Canada tend to be closely associated with the political views of those who construct the theories. Indeed, the character of Canada's internal and external relations ensures that the literature of the country, which began in the midst of strong political tensions, will continue in a similar milieu. Our nation provides an especially clear argument that a country's literature and its politics are inseparable and affect each other on many visible and invisible levels.

ROBIN MATHEWS

Literature in English, written in what is now territorially Canada or written by Canadians abroad, is currently termed "Canadian literature in English." "English-Canadian Literature," although still in use, has been rejected by many who consider it to refer only to the literature of

Canadians of English descent. The terms "Colonial Literature," "Commonwealth Literature," "Littérature améericaine" and "New Literature Written in English" have sometimes referred to Canadian literature in English. The term "Canadian writer" has been applied to long-term visitors such as Malcolm LOWRY, to short-term residents who still hold citizenship such as Brian MOORE, and to travellers and settlers who came before Canada existed as a nation.

Writers have described Canada in many ways: for example, as a French or English colony, a "fifty-first state," a Pacific Rim country, an arctic giant, a friendly territory or an uninhabitable wilderness. Canadian literature has often had to deal with such differences in attitude, not just because many Canadian authors were born elsewhere and brought outsiders' expectations with them, but also because popular attitudes often perpetuated stereotypes of Canada. Three pervasive stereotypes portray Canada as a physical desert, a cultural wasteland and the raw land of investment opportunity. These distortions have created an audience for stereotypes, which Canadian writers sometimes chose to serve by writing romantic adventures of the frozen North, in which everything local was savage and hostile and culture was imported; but in time they sought to record local experience and to use literature to shape their own culture rather than to imitate or defer to that of another society.

Language and Literary Form Canadian writers needed to be able to refer appropriately to local flora, fauna, place-names and events, and to use local vocabulary unapologetically (*see* ENGLISH LANGUAGE). Words such as "moose" and "Medicine Hat," which had been automatically comic because they transgressed English conventions of verbal propriety, became legitimate to use in literature. Native words ("igloo," "muskeg"), borrowings from French ("tuque," "gopher"), adaptations of English ("separate schools," "sky pilot"), regionalisms ("slough," "lakehead," "Bluenose") and vernacular cadences all became accepted during the 19th century. Still, the dominant vocabulary was "international English," neither so highly localized as to impede communication nor different enough to require readers outside the culture to recognize the need to adjust to it.

By the 20th century, irony had become a dominant literary mode, and the documentary and the sequence of short sketches became recurrent literary structures. "Documentary" took several generic forms, from historical report and narrative sketch to drama and long poem. Frequently the effect is more subjective than the word "documentary" implies: the glimpses of history that such works offer are also records of cultural and personal bias. In them, "history" is a fictional structure, a process of perceiving hierarchies of value and of constructing legends to encapsulate these values. Many early long poems took narrative forms, making "history" a "story"; more recent long poems – like the story sequences and some novels and plays – are characteristically discontinuous in form. Often "metatextual," or self-referential, they concern themselves with the language of literature and the processes of understanding as well as with empirical experience. Writer and reader consequently both become active agents in these literary works, interconnecting with the characters and the text. The discontinuity, however, emphasizes the fragmentariness and the bias of understanding, often pointing to the existence of a "subtext" or alternative to the values of received tradition. Several techniques have been used to imply the validity of various "marginal" stories, or regional, ethnic and sexual alternatives to conventional norms. Besides the discontinuous series, these include allegory, folktale, the fractured frame story, parodic humour, and the ironic "embedded story" or *mise-en-scène*. There is more humour in Canadian literature than is commonly recognized – more often in asides and understatement than in broad farce – and HUMOROUS WRITING often addresses serious subjects.

Many writers became highly conscious that what distinguished them and their community was not the tale they told but the manner of telling it. By documenting local experience and using the local voice, they fostered regional and national culture. Newfoundland writers such as E.J. PRATT drew on a tall-tale tradition, Prairie writers such as Robert KROETSCH on an anecdotal tradition, and Ontario writers such as Margaret ATWOOD and Robertson DAVIES on a laconic interplay between irony and moral orderliness. Much of the force of their style derived from their control over regional cadence, which is as important as literal meaning because it reveals the inner motivations of the characters and also the social context. Narrative method is often indirect in Canadian writing (modes of parable and allegory are common); narrators usually hide their true feelings or have limited understanding of events around them, and the oblique or implied meanings are richer and more instructive than the obvious ones.

Motifs and Patterns Some commentators have interpreted literary indirectness politically and psychologically, finding in it a sign of national insecurity and a group feeling of inferiority. Others argue that indirectness is a healthy demonstration of the culture's ability to adapt an inherited tongue to its own purposes. Although the national character is not always the subject of literature, the culture's social attitudes and values can be seen in the language and forms it uses. Several specific narrative patterns recur in Canadian writing: 1) a community walls itself off from the wilderness (the "garrison mentality"); 2) a person leaves the homeland, adjusts to the new world, then finds the "homeland" to be "alien"; or a person born in Canada always feels a stranger in his or her own home; 3) a woman struggles to come to terms with her own creativity and the inhibitions of her cultural upbringing (often told as conflict between colony and empire); 4) an apparently passive observer, surrounded by articulate tricksters and raconteurs, turns out to be able to tell both their story and his own, often ironically; 5) an adventurer turns failure into a form of grace; 6) a child grows up to inherit a world of promise, or a world of loss, or usually both at once; 7) a subjective historian meditates on place and memory; 8) a character celebrates space and wilderness, usually after a struggle to learn to accept that the wilderness provides spiritual therapy only on its own terms. To epitomize the character of their society, many writers have portrayed historical figures, such as Samuel HEARNE, Louis RIEL, Susanna MOODIE, Sir John A. MACDONALD, Emily CARR and William Lyon MACKENZIE, each possessing a vision, but still an ordinary, less than heroic, frail human being.

Settings often possess a symbolic dimension. Catholic Québec recurrently figures as a land of mystery, attractive but enthralling and morally dangerous; Ontario as an enigmatic blend of moral uprightness and moral evasiveness; Atlantic Canada as a repository of old values; the North as a land of vision; the Prairies as a land of isolation and acquisition; and the West Coast as a dream of the future in which people often mistakenly believe. Europe often appears as the home of refinement and discrimination, the US as a land of crass achievement and tangible success, and Africa as the embodiment of all that seems "other" to Protestant rationalism. Although most Canadians live in cities, until recently writers used rural and small-town settings more frequently than urban ones, and they often ignored problems of class, race and poverty. From early on, however, writers such as Frances BROOKE, Susanna Moodie, Sara Jeannette DUNCAN and Nellie MCCLUNG have been important analysts of Canadian political life. Often they sharply pointed out social divisions within Canada that male adventure writers ignored or underplayed. "Regional" writing also conveyed political stances, for by rejecting a single definition of "Canada," it asserted the viability of a nation with a plural character (*see* REGIONALISM IN LITERATURE). Increasingly, moreover, native writers and writers who draw on ethnic backgrounds other than western European ones, examined the social limitations and political opportunities of Canadian pluralism. Among such writers are Beatrice Culleton, Thompson Highway, Rohinton Mistry, Neil Bissoondath, Katherine Vlassie and Paul Yee (*see* ETHNIC LITERATURE).

History

The growth of Canadian literature in English has been affected by numerous factors, from population size to the diverse literary influences of foreign writers.

1620-1867 In the first 2 centuries of Canadian writing in English, writers' techniques reflected changing literary fashions in England. There was Jacobean poetry in 17th-century Newfoundland; epistolary fiction in the English garrison community in late 18th-century Québec; political satire in the LOYALIST communities of the Maritimes and Upper Canada; folksong and folktale, and romantic poetry and fiction in the early 19th century. Fiction writers such as John RICHARDSON and Rosanna LEPROHON demonstrate the European connection both stylistically and thematically; despite their enthusiasm for the wilderness, they continued with European social and literary conventions. The tales translated from Indian and Québec sources were intended for a readership that romanticized Indians. Early poets such as Oliver GOLDSMITH and Charles SANGSTER defined the Canadian landscape as "sublime," using a British literary convention. Early folk traditions in Atlantic Canada derived from Scottish and Irish sources, but they were influenced by a thriving Gaelic literature in the New World and were adapted to local experience and language. Writers continued to use forms from FOLK MUSIC and ORAL LITERATURE well into the 20th century, as in Johnny Burke's "The Killigrews' Soiree" (1904), the tales of Pauline JOHNSON and the popular verses of Robert SERVICE.

Political and AUTOBIOGRAPHICAL WRITING has proved to be some of the most enduring early literary work. The social and moral critiques of Joseph HOWE, Thomas MCCULLOCH and Thomas Chandler HALIBURTON reveal contemporary rhetorical conventions and political stances, and Haliburton's humorous narratives of Sam Slick in *The* CLOCKMAKER (1836) in addition coined many now-familiar phrases. Also important are the journals of explorers, travellers and settlers, primarily those of Samuel Hearne, Alexander MACKENZIE, David THOMPSON, Alexander HENRY, William "Tiger" DUNLOP, Catharine Parr TRAILL, Susanna Moodie and Anna JAMESON (*see* EXPLORATION AND TRAVEL LITERATURE). The travel and settlement narratives vary from romantic tales of captivity and adventure to exact accounts of things seen. Moodie, in *Roughing It in the Bush* (1852), told of her own ill-preparedness to cope with Canada and advised the English middle class not to emigrate, though subsequent editions of her work revealed that she gradually grew to accept her new country. Settlement narratives set in western Canada, eg, those of Susan Allison and Georgina Binnie-Clark, date from the later 19th and early 20th centuries.

As local publishing ventures took root in the Maritimes, Montréal and Upper Canada – often associated with NEWSPAPERS and LITERARY MAGA-

ZINES, such as Howe's *Acadian Recorder* and John Lovell's *Literary Garland* – they encouraged writers to apply their imaginative talents to the local scene. The result was that, by 1867, fanciful tales set in Europe and the Orient flourished in periodicals side by side with realistic sketches of Canada and political and moral commentary.

1867-1914 With Confederation came a quickened interest in the growth of a national culture. This was expressed both in celebrations of the romance of Canadian history and in explorations of the new nation's political destiny, by writers such as William KIRBY, James DE MILLE and Gilbert PARKER. Political life was recorded in new journals, such as *Rose-Belford's Canadian Monthly*, the *Canadian Magazine* and QUEEN'S QUARTERLY. Fredericton and Montréal became major creative centres; the ROYAL SOCIETY OF CANADA was founded in 1882; and in Toronto the *Globe* expanded its political and cultural influence. Yet Canadian writers published also with foreign presses and in British and American journals, and Canadian writing was affected by continental expansion, curtailed by economic pressure and restricted by changes in international COPYRIGHT LAW. Despite their patriotic sentiments, many writers were drawn elsewhere to live for financial or personal reasons; Charles G.D. ROBERTS and Bliss CARMAN went to the US, S.J. Duncan to India. Duncan, who was politically attracted to the cause of imperial federation (*see* IMPERIALISM), noted the impact of American taste and ideas on Canadian culture. Poet Charles MAIR became active in the CANADA FIRST movement, and political causes attracted Goldwin SMITH, William Dawson LESUEUR and John WATSON (*see* PHILOSOPHY).

By 1905 there was literary activity across the Prairies and a thriving cultural centre in Victoria, as the work of Martin Allerdale Grainger attests. Children's writers Margaret Marshall SAUNDERS and L.M. MONTGOMERY, both from the Maritimes, wrote the international best-sellers *Beautiful Joe* (1894) and ANNE OF GREEN GABLES (1908). Early in the century Stephen LEACOCK established an international reputation as a comic writer and lecturer in the Dickensian tradition. He satirized social pretensions and political and literary fads, among them the mannered comedies, melodramas, historical romances and muscular adventures made popular by writers such as Parker, Ralph Connor (C.W. GORDON) and Robert Barr, and early dramatists Charles HEAVYSEGE and John Hunter-Duvar.

The dominant literary figures of the late 19th century were the poets and SHORT-FICTION writers Duncan Campbell SCOTT and Charles G.D. Roberts, and 2 poets with whom they were associated, Archibald LAMPMAN and Bliss Carman. Known as the "Confederation Group," these writers (along with W.W. CAMPBELL and I.V. CRAWFORD) together reshaped Canadian POETRY. Influenced by the later English Romantic poets and the American Transcendentalists, they shunned Sangster's verbal ornamentation, rejected the notion of "sublimity," sought plainer ways to record the beauty and reality of the Canadian landscape, and used natural imagery as a language of spiritual inquiry. Scott's work sympathetically sketched patterns of life in Québec and among the Indians, and it introduced psychological realism into narrative form. Roberts's anthropomorphic animal stories, as well as those of Ernest Thompson SETON, observed nature closely, imaginatively adapting Darwinian scientific method. Though Roberts and Scott continued to write long after WWI, their main work belongs to the 2 decades before the war began.

1914-41 WWI had a profound cultural and political impact. Many creative people were lost in the war, eg, John MCCRAE, author of the rondeau "In Flanders Fields." Attitudes towards empire and nationhood altered as Canada moved to-

SAM SLICK;

THE

CLOCKMAKER.

"I AM SAM SLICK, SAYS I."

Philadelphia:

T. B. PETERSON, No. 306 CHESTNUT STREET.

Cover from Thomas Chandler Haliburton's satiric *Sam Slick: The Clockmaker*, published in Philadelphia *c*1858. (*courtesy National Library of Canada/Rare Book Division*).

wards equality within the COMMONWEALTH; tensions involving Québec's cultural presence in the country increased; emigration patterns changed following the war; and there was a shift in political influence among the country's regions. Pacific cultural contacts with Australia, China, Japan and India diminished, though emigration from Asia increased. The literature of RACISM increased as well. Germanic and E European immigration to the Prairies had a marked literary result in the family sagas of Martha OSTENSO, Laura Goodman SALVERSON and, most notably, Frederick Philip GROVE. Grove was singled out as a writer of substance for his large-scale portraits of immigrant life and his analysis of the Canadian economic class structure. In Ontario, Mazo DE LA ROCHE's family chronicle, the JALNA series (1927-60), continued to celebrate the imperial connection.

In 1921 D.C. Scott reflected that the violence of the new age required poets to express the values of their time in a more discomforting, rebellious, critical fashion. This judgement also applied to fiction. Early war fiction included the harshly realistic work of Charles Yale Harrison (*Generals Die in Bed*, 1930). WWI preoccupied writers for 50 years, from Philip CHILD, Robert STEAD, Edward Meade and Colin McDougall to Douglas Le Pan, Alden NOWLAN, Timothy FINDLEY, David Gurr, George Payerle and John Gray. Class conflict in Vancouver during the GREAT DEPRESSION was the subject of Irene Baird's *Waste Heritage* (1939), while J.G. Sime, Madge Macbeth and (later) Joyce Marshall demonstrated that the lives of women, particularly in urban surroundings, were repeatedly constrained by social and institutional conventions. The fiction of Morley CALLAGHAN portrayed crime and deprivation in Toronto and Montréal, but appealed also to the sustaining force of the Roman Catholic faith. Callaghan's plain style set a new standard for Canadian prose. Callaghan's and John GLASSCO's artful autobiographical accounts of life in Paris in the 1920s date from this time, though they were published (in revised form) much later. Painter Emily CARR wrote of West Coast Indian culture and character, of changes in artistic taste and practice and of her own engagement with the wilderness.

As with prose, the dominant tone of poetry and DRAMA in the postwar decades was critical. In drama, Merrill DENISON's satiric sketches challenged empty nationalism and the pageantry of earlier English-language theatre. Herman VOADEN adapted the techniques of German expressionism to the stage; and Oscar Ryan used drama as a form of direct left-wing social protest (*see* LITERATURE IN POLITICS). In poetry, the "McGill Group" (F.R. SCOTT, A.J.M. SMITH, Abraham KLEIN) emerged in Montréal in the 1920s to praise the GROUP OF SEVEN's revolution in painting, to respond to the international literary influence of T.S. Eliot, W.H. Auden and James Joyce, and to challenge the Confederation Poets' Victorian formalism. Newfoundland poet E.J. Pratt, fascinated by modern science, penned lyric and narrative verse celebrating heroic action and the power of personal and public decision. Raymond Knister and W.W.E. Ross were other significant figures. Still other writers to emerge at this time and to go on to greater formal experimentation were Dorothy LIVESAY and Earle BIRNEY; their work, by turns dramatic, narrative, lyrical, documentary, meditative, ironic and autobiographical, juxtaposes personal experience with social causes. Between 1950 and the 1980s they addressed McCarthyism, African independence, and feminism, poverty and cultural impoverishment within Canada.

1941-59 Hugh MACLENNAN's 1941 novel *Barometer Rising* ushered in a period of liberal reassessment of Canadian culture, a period which declared Canada's freedom from constraint, a Canadian role in world affairs, and the viability of Canadian subjects in literature. It was a time that believed in progress. These themes, given impetus by the humanist and anticlerical stances of francophone writers Ringuet (Philippe PANNETON), Gabrielle ROY, Roger LEMELIN and Germaine GUÈVREMONT (*see* LITERATURE IN FRENCH), were also recorded by Pierre BERTON, Roderick HAIG-BROWN and Farley MOWAT. But MacLennan's 1959 novel *The Watch that Ends the Night* caps the period, placing faith in the land but by then acknowledging a sense of disillusionment in political causes. Prose stylists of the 1940s and 1950s nonetheless demonstrated that the period had a darker side, one that focused on the moral psychology of individualism. Malcolm Lowry in *Under the Volcano* (1947) and Ethel WILSON in SWAMP ANGEL (1954) explored the psychological pressures of alcoholism and women's limited options in society, respectively. Using prairie settings, Sinclair ROSS (AS FOR ME AND MY HOUSE, 1941) and W.O. MITCHELL (WHO HAS SEEN THE WIND, 1947) probed the psychological barriers that often prevent individuals from connecting productively with their community. Thomas RADDALL and Ernest BUCKLER examined similar problems in Maritime contexts, as did Henry KREISEL against a background of European war and cultural displacement. In 1959 the raw satire of Mordecai RICHLER's *The* APPRENTICESHIP OF DUDDY KRAVITZ and the elliptical modernism of Sheila WATSON's *The* DOUBLE HOOK augured a different, more sardonic era of literary attitude and technique. In Québec the QUIET REVOLUTION of the 1960s was to bring about a secular and politically rebellious, separatist literature.

New poetic movements also developed in the shadow of WWII. In Montréal the "cosmopolitan" *Preview* poets (Patrick Anderson, P.K. PAGE) joined briefly with the "proletarian" *First Statement* poets (Louis DUDEK, Irving LAYTON) in John SUTHERLAND's magazine NORTHERN REVIEW. The continuation of old journals (primarily CANADIAN FORUM) and the development of new ones FIDDLEHEAD in Fredericton; *CIV/n* and *Delta* in Montréal; TAMARACK REVIEW and *Here and Now* in Toronto;

Alan Crawley's CONTEMPORARY VERSE in Vancouver; and, after 1960, James REANEY'S *Alphabet* in London) gave poets new opportunities for publication; among those to emerge were Anne WILKINSON, Wilfred WATSON, Robert Finch, A.G. BAILEY, Elizabeth BREWSTER, Fred COGSWELL, Miriam WADDINGTON and Roy DANIELLS. Initially linked as poets of social protest, Dudek, Layton and Raymond SOUSTER went on to explore separate avenues of poetic form and political engagement.

At this time drama was affected by the development of radio and by the growth of play societies and the LITTLE THEATRE MOVEMENT. Outstanding radio playwrights included Mavor MOORE and Fletcher Markle; Gwen Pharis RINGWOOD, James Reaney and Robertson Davies furthered the art of the stage play. Radio dramatizations (W.O. Mitchell's *Jake and the Kid* series, John DRAINIE'S readings, Robert Weaver's *CBC Wednesday Night*) helped foster the short-story form; and radio writers such as Mary Grannan gave a Canadian voice to CHILDREN'S LITERATURE (*see* RADIO DRAMA).

The period closed on the threshold of a new wave of nationalism and creative energy. Several anthologies and critical surveys became available; society was enjoying postwar prosperity; and the report of the Massey Royal Commission on NATIONAL DEVELOPMENT IN THE ARTS, LETTERS AND SCIENCES, which led to the creation of the CANADA COUNCIL in 1957, encouraged concentrated support for Canadian culture in ways that would allow it tangibly to develop.

1959-80s Periods of economic prosperity and adversity sharply affected literary activity during the next decades. The number of publications grew markedly during the 1960s, fostered in part by the Canada Council and the establishment of government support programs for the arts. In the wake of legislation curtailing foreign control over the production and distribution of Canadian writing, SMALL PRESSES developed (including HOUSE OF ANANSI and Oberon) and for several years asserted a pronounced cultural nationalism. New LITERARY PERIODICALS began, among them CANADIAN LITERATURE, *Prism*, *ECW*, *Journal of Canadian Studies*, CANADIAN FICTION MAGAZINE and *Canadian Children's Literature*. An increase in the number of available texts and paperback books (represented by McClelland and Stewart's New Canadian Library), the formation of professional societies (Association for Canadian and Québec Literatures, League of Canadian Poets, WRITERS' UNION OF CANADA), the establishment of several popular festivals and the increase in academic attention to Canadian writing also helped expand the audience for Canadian letters. Influential Québec and Acadian writers were translated, as were several writers who wrote in "unofficial" languages, such as Josef ŠKVORECKÝ.

Technological innovation affected both the manner and matter of publication – charting a change from mimeographed journals such as *Tish* in 1961 (edited by George BOWERING and Frank DAVEY) to the sophisticated design and computer printing systems of a press such as Coach House in the 1980s. Poets mixed media, wrote concrete poetry (bp NICHOL), sound poetry (bill BISSETT), found poetry (J.R. COLOMBO) and popular songs (Leonard COHEN), and tried out other experimental forms in linguistic and visual design (Joe ROSENBLATT). An important development involved the writing of long meditative poetry (Michael ONDAATJE, Kroetsch, John NEWLOVE, Christopher Dewdney). Technology thus became an artistic paradox: as a literary theme it often implied the enervating routine of mechanization, but as an aid to literary production it opened new freedom of technique.

South American writers Jorge Luis Borges and Gabriel García Márquez were particularly influential on Ondaatje and Kroetsch. Northrop FRYE'S theories of myth influenced other writers (Jay MACPHERSON, James Reaney, D.G. JONES); still others were affected by CHRISTIANITY and Black Mountain poetics (Margaret AVISON, M.T. LANE), by traditional format of various kinds, including bardic models, and by an awareness of social inequities (Patrick LANE, Milton ACORN, Tom Wayman, Daryl Hine, David MCFADDEN, George Bowering, Ralph GUSTAFSON, Francis SPARSHOTT, George JOHNSTON, Richard Outram, Kristjana Gunnars), by phenomenology (Daphne MARLATT, Fred WAH, Eli MANDEL), by Asian and native Indian cultural models (Robert Bringhurst, David Day, Gary Geddes), by feminist and linguistic theory (Claire Harris, Lola Lemire Tostevin, Betsy Warland), by vernacular cadences (Al PURDY, Paulette JILES, Alden Nowlan, Marilyn Bowering) and by the conservative Loyalist philosophy of George GRANT (Margaret Atwood, Dennis LEE). Rather more general influences included the views of historians and communications theorists H.A. INNIS, Donald CREIGHTON, W.L. MORTON and Marshall MCLUHAN, and of international social analysts O. Mannoni, Frantz Fanon, Ruth Benedict, Robert Ornstein and Jean Piaget.

Dennis Lee and Robert Heidbreder (in poetry), Dennis Foon and John and Joa Lazarus (in drama), and Mordecai Richler, Gordon Korman, Brian Doyle, Jean Little, Monica HUGHES, Kevin Major and Christie Harris (in fiction) became leading writers of children's literature. Margaret Atwood (in poetry, fiction and criticism) dominated the period, in both poetic craft and nationalist and feminist commentary. Other important prose writers also addressed feminist issues, including Margaret LAURENCE, Audrey THOMAS, Jane RULE, Marian ENGEL and Alice MUNRO. Each of these honed a highly individual style. Political justice was a major concern, as were the nature and source of violence, both in the work of these writers and in that of Timothy Findley, Dave GODFREY, Adele WISEMAN, Hugh HOOD, Richard Wright, Juan Butler, George WOODCOCK, Joy KOGAWA and David Adams Richards. Native writers such as George CLUTESI and Markoosie used English to tell of traditional experience and the possibility of moral continuity. Other writers, notably Jack HODGINS and Rudy WIEBE, took literature as their subject, exposing the imaginative artifice of storytelling and asserting the morality of art.

Major fictional achievements of the period include Wiebe's epic enquiries into the language of different cultures (Mennonite and Cree in particular), Findley's dramatizations of the loss of innocence in the 20th century, Laurence's social mythology of Western woman and Robertson Davies's Jungian rendering of ambition and aspiration in Loyalist Ontario (in his Deptford Trilogy). English-language emigration from the US (Leon ROOKE, Thomas, Rule) and from the Commonwealth (Ondaatje, John METCALF, Moore, Robin SKELTON, Daphne MARLATT, Austin CLARKE, Bharati MUKHERJEE, Sean Virgo) added other dimensions of ethnic sensitivity, stylistic versatility and comic insight to modern Canadian writing. The period, partly under the influence of Québec's politically active theatre, also saw the emergence of strong dramatic talents, including Sharon POLLOCK, George Walker, Rick SALUTIN, David FENNARIO, Cam Hubert (Anne Cameron), George RYGA and Michael COOK.

Critics have recorded the history of Canadian literature in English, observed its connections with other literature, probed its derivation, analysed techniques and charted patterns, and assessed its value as a cultural record. As international attention to Canadian literature increased during the 1970s, Canadian studies organizations were established in Europe, the US, Japan, the S Pacific and elsewhere. By the late 1980s many critics in Canada were turning from thematic to technical subjects; others were writing literary BIOGRAPHY, theorizing about the procedures of criticism, and attempting to establish accurate, scholarly texts of the works of major writers. By the latter part of the 20th century, there were clear but diverse traditions in Canadian literature.

W.H. NEW

Reading: Carl F. Klinck, ed, *Literary History of Canada*, 3 vols (2nd ed, 1976); W.H. New, *A History of Canadian Literature* (1988); William Toye, ed, *The Oxford Companion to Canadian Literature* (1983).

Literature in English: Teaching In colonies, the literary tradition of the mother country normally prevails. This was true in Canada, where it has taken English-speaking Canadians a long time to accept their own literature as a legitimate subject for study. Throughout the late 19th century, English language and literature, with some admixture of CLASSICS, held undisputed sway in the literary curricula of Canadian schools and universities. Outside the institutions, however, the groundwork of an indigenous literature was being laid. The first Canadian anthology was E.H. Dewart's *Selections from Canadian Poets* (1864). Although there is no evidence that this book was used in the schools, it was the first of many anthologies that would support the teaching of Canadian literature as the subject gained recognition. W.D. Lighthall's *Songs of the Great Dominion* (1889) was another landmark volume. BIOGRAPHY and literary history had their beginnings in H.J. Morgan's *Bibliotheca canadensis: A Manual of Canadian Literature* (1867). By the end of the century, to such names as Haliburton, Moodie and Richardson had been added Lampman, Carman, Roberts and Scott. The making of a teaching canon of early Canadian writers was in sight.

Records of pioneering attempts to bring Canadian literature into university curricula are often unreliable. In 1924 the *Canadian Bookman* published the results of a survey undertaken by the Canadian Authors Association on the status of "Canadian Literature in Education." Most universities reported, rather defensively, that they keenly supported the subject. The public schools said they liked to use Canadian authors "to diffuse a sane view of patriotism." These were, however, apparently only token interventions. Desmond PACEY claims that the first undergraduate course was offered by J.B. Reynolds at Macdonald Inst (*see* UNIVERSITY OF GUELPH) in 1906-07. The McGill calendar for 1912-13 listed a course in "American and Canadian Literature." Its instructor, Susan E. Cameron, seems to have taught in this field as early as 1907-08. The "Am-Can" combination (satirized by Robertson DAVIES in *Leaven of Malice*, 1954) soon became a common expedient for allowing Canadian literature a place in the sun. In practice the balance usually favoured the American component. Although U of Toronto was late in giving its formal blessing to the study of Canadian literature (an Honours American-Canadian course was first offered in 1933-34), it had endorsed a series of "popular" lectures emphasizing Canadian subjects at the turn of the century. A full-fledged course in Canadian poetry, given by Alexander W. Crawford, was in place at U of Manitoba, 1919-20.

A more serious claim to the pioneering role comes from Acadia U, where in 1915 John Daniel LOGAN began lecturing on Canadian literature. Logan joined the army in 1916, but in 1919 he returned as "Special Lecturer in Canadian Literature without salary." The *Acadia Bulletin* had called the 1915 series "the first course of lectures on distinctively Canadian Literature which has ever been given in a Canadian University." The appointment of 1919 was hailed by the Toronto *Globe* as "an innovation of national importance." The same year V.B. Rhodenizer taught "The History of Canadian Literature," a half course. Logan later attacked Archibald MacMechan and Dalhousie U in *Dalhousie University and Canadian Literature...* (1922), a broadside discounting their claim to lead the way in teaching Canadian literature by offering a half course in 1921-22.

Expediency and compromise governed the entry of Canadian literature into academe: noncredit courses; courses not acceptable for credit in majors or honours programs; half-credit courses; courses treating Canadian literature as a wayward extension of English literature or as a footnote to American literature were offered. Carlyle King's full-fledged, upper-level and fully accredited course at U Sask in 1946-47 may have been the first of its kind.

In fact, a new, strengthening current reached critical force just before and after WWII. Although the 1920s and 1930s had produced few curricular developments, there had been an increasingly widespread awareness of writers and writing in Canada. The Canadian Authors' Association (fd 1921) had preached literary nationalism and had created the necessary tension to spark the coming of modern poetry to Canada by the decade's end. Moreover, 68 anthologies and collections were published 1920-40. A handful of texts, such as *Our Canadian Literature* (1922) by Watson and Pierce and *A Book of Canadian Prose and Verse* (1923) by Broadus and Broadus were designed specifically for school and university use. J.D. Logan and D.G. French published *Highways of Canadian Literature* (1924), one of 6 literary histories which appeared in the 1920s. It was also important, in the context of teaching, that the criticism of Canadian literature had begun to fall to a new breed of established scholars. W.E. Collin's *The White Savannahs* (1936) brought an urbane manner and sophisticated techniques to bear on the work of selected Canadian poets. E.K. BROWN and a roster of experienced scholars contributed, from 1936 on, incisive annual reviews of contemporary Canadian writing to the "Letters in Canada" supplement of UNIVERSITY OF TORONTO QUARTERLY. Symbolic of a general quickening of literary energies was the publication in 1943 of Brown's *On Canadian Poetry*, the first extensive and scholarly treatment of the tradition of poetry in Canada, and A.J.M. SMITH's *Book of Canadian Poetry*, the first such anthology compiled on scholarly principles. Publication of new poetry was on the upsurge. The return of the war veterans set the stage for the dramatic expansion of university enrolment over the next 20 years.

Until at least 1960 the introduction of Canadian courses continued to face opposition from defenders of the traditional curricula of English departments. American literature, moreover, which had been an expedient for getting Canadian literature into course work, became, especially 1960-70, a threat when a high incidence of American appointments to Canadian departments was reflected in a sometimes smothering expansion of American courses. The establishment of postgraduate studies in Canadian literature at U of T (1947-48) was an important development. C.T. Bissell and R.L. McDougall were early instructors. On the one hand this development marked a first step towards the legitimation of Canadian literature as a subject for advanced study, and on the other it charted the way for the first generation of scholars trained in this specialty. The next 20 years saw strong postgraduate centres established at Carleton, U of New Brunswick, McGill, Queen's, Western, U of Alberta and U of British Columbia. Among those who set the pace were C. KLINCK, Malcolm ROSS, D. Pacey, R.L. McDougall, L. DUDEK, R. Watters, F. COGSWELL, A. Lucas, G. Roper and J. Matthews. The expansion of course work was nourished by (and in turn nourished) the publication of texts and supporting critical material. Landmark publications were Klinck and Watters's *Canadian Anthology* (1956); the New Canadian Library series of reprints (est 1957); the *Literary History of Canada* (1965; rev 1976); and the periodical *Canadian Literature* (est 1959). Finally, demographic, economic and cultural factors produced a dynamic development of Canadian courses and enrolments in the 1960s. The development was fed by the arrival at university age of the youth of the postwar BABY BOOM; it was accelerated by a prosperous economy and the wishes of a generation of students seeking "relevance" in education. It was at the same time fueled by a national movement towards "Canadianization," the term used by Robin Mathews and J. Steele in their highly public efforts to increase Canadian content in the educational system.

By 1970 there seemed little reason to question the status of Canadian literature as an academic subject. In 1948, 10 universities had offered half courses in Canadian literature; 2 offered full courses. In 1972, 38 universities offered 90 full undergraduate courses, for a total enrolment of over 6000 students. At the graduate level, offerings had risen from virtually nothing in 1948 to 30 graduate offerings in 22 universities 1972-73, for a total enrolment of over 200 students. Nevertheless, T.H.B. SYMONS stated in *To Know Ourselves* (1975), the report of the Commission on Canadian Studies, that undergraduate courses in Canadian literature represented only 8% of the total offerings of departments of English. Perhaps more serious was the commission's finding that the atmosphere of denigration which had surrounded the teaching of Canadian literature for the better part of 50 years was far from dead. The 1970s closed with severe financial stringencies imposing new priorities on the universities. There are indications in the 1980s that a period of deregulation, in which Canadian literature will take its natural place in our curriculum for English studies, is in hand. R.L. McDOUGALL

Literature in English: Theory and Criticism
Samuel Taylor Coleridge, a principal source of modern literary theory in English, made little direct impression in 19th-century Canada, largely because literary life in Canada shared the anti-theoretical biases of Victorian England. Thomas Carlyle, John Ruskin and Matthew Arnold, the most powerful arbiters of Victorian taste, were convinced moral determinists. For them, good art was "at root" a matter of good morality, directing the sensuous imagination of artist and audience alike; if the artistic vision was true, then technical details of expression would take care of themselves. In taking "vision" in this sense, these authorities effectively denied access to the mystery of art other than by uncritical, unsystematic procedures. Great or successful literature was the occasion for ostensive definition (comparison with similar points of excellence drawn from Homer, Dante, Shakespeare or Milton) or for the invocation of a moral standard; it was not the occasion for reflection on particular literary arts, or for isolation and analysis of a text's distinctive features.

In Canada, LITERARY MAGAZINES provided the first forum for discussion of literary theory. Long before John George BOURINOT's *The Intellectual Development of the Canadian People* (1881) there appeared essays and reviews in the literary press that identified and attempted to assess the vital issues in contemporary Britain and the US. This was not easy, given limited resources and circulation, and the fact that the migration of ideas is constant and complex. Most striking about the early efforts is the shrewdness and clarity with which they established the topics that have remained at the centre of Canadian theoretical debate: the possibility and desirability of a distinctive Canadian literature, and the nature of literature's contribution to the national life. Although interest in these questions was largely a legacy of the European romantics, Canadians claimed them as their own – not in the first instance through the usual channels of theoretical innovation (new analytical tools and terminology, a new conceptual grounds), but rather through recognition that to address these questions was to deal with the condition of all Canadians, grounded as they were in the historical and geographical reality of Canada itself. There was no lack of derivative and pedestrian commentary on literary genres, literature as the interplay of fact and precept, and similar topics. And it was easy for Goldwin SMITH to assure the readers of *The Week* in 1894 that "no such thing as a literature Canadian in the local sense exists or is ever likely to exist." There was little prospect of original theorizing while Canada's cultural autonomy remained in question. Meanwhile, Canadians could draw on the values and expectations nourished by the Scottish intellectual tradition in immigrants such as Daniel Chisholme, David Wilson and Graeme Mercer Adam, and take heart from the sensitivity shown by native-born Canadians of the calibre of journalist and novelist Sara Jeannette DUNCAN and social commentator John A. Cooper.

The early 20th century witnessed a steady growth in Canadian literary scholarship, but little innovative theory. Despite the stocktaking of J.D. LOGAN'S *Aesthetic Criticism in Canada* (1917) and A.J.M. SMITH'S sardonic demand of 1928, "Wanted – Canadian Criticism," academic conservatism held firm. Canadian PHILOSOPHY and LANGUAGE study continued to be more historical than analytical, while orthodoxy was fortified by scholars such as Pelham Edgar, E.K. BROWN and A.S.P. WOODHOUSE. Even George Whalley's *Poetic Process* (1953) was more of a tribute to Coleridge than an advance beyond him. However, with the work of Marshall MCLUHAN and Northrop FRYE this situation changed dramatically.

Literary essays written by McLuhan between 1943 and 1962 (collected in *The Interior Landscape*, 1969) revealed an erudite but profoundly restive mind moving away from "mere literature" and traditional scholarship towards a new vision of cultural history, human cognition and the challenges facing academe. In *The* GUTENBERG GALAXY (1962) McLuhan anticipates the concerns of European theorists with the impact of technology on man's responses to the world around him, and reflects on the changes wrought on speech and writing by advances in COMMUNICATIONS TECHNOLOGY. He draws on the spiritual and intellectual resources of scholasticism to elucidate the implications of *The Gutenberg Galaxy*, enriching in the process the vocabulary of literary theory, recognizing the advantage of interdisciplinary studies, and dramatizing the idea that criticism enlivened by radical theory and unafraid of analogy can claim to be not parasitism or prostitution, but creative predation.

Frye, like McLuhan, has written one major work of theory and many subsequent validations of it. Since the appearance of ANATOMY OF CRITICISM (1957), Frye has become a highly influential theorist. Lucid, learned and witty, polemical and yet plausible, *Anatomy* is a series of interlocking theoretical essays built upon definitions of symbol ("any unit of any literary structure that can be isolated for critical attention"), criticism (which "begin[s] with, and largely consist[s] of, the systematizing of literary symbolism") and related terms – the whole synoptic scheme being held together by the proposition that "in myth we see the structural principle of literature isolated." In collections such as *The Bush Garden* (1971) Frye refers not to Canadian isolation itself, but to the autonomy-through-isolation enjoyed by "great" literature and literary study. His works have inspired some of the finest contemporary Canadian writers, but have too often occasioned mere condemnation or rapture within the university community, or led his more careful readers into a no-man's-land between autonomous and socially determined performance, as in Francis Sparshott's *The Concept of Criticism* (1967). More recently, however, literary theorists have freed themselves from Frye's bias against structuralism and ideologically motivated criticism. Debate is carried on in the LEARNED SOCIETIES and in publications such as the *Journal of Literary Theory* (1980-), *Taxte* (1982-), Tillottama Rajan's *Dark Interpreter* (1980), and *Identity of the Literary Text*, eds Valdés and Miller (1985).

A strong interest in avant-garde and theoretical approaches to literature was nurtured in *Open Letter* (est 1965), a literary magazine edited by Frank DAVEY. The influence of recent European trends (poststructuralism, deconstruction, narratology, reception theory, etc) can be seen in Linda Hutcheon's *Narcissistic Narrative* (1980, 1984), E.D. Blodgett's *Configuration* (1982) and in *Labyrinths of Voice* (1981), a series of interviews with Robert KROETSCH by Shirley Neuman and Robert Wilson. Perhaps the most important evidence of the new interest in theory is in the works of feminist critics, including Mary Hyquist, Lorraine Weir and the editorial collective "Tessera" (Barbara Godard, Kathy Mezei, Daphne Marlatt and Gail Scott), whose work also links criticism in English Canada with that of critics and writers in Québec, such as Nicole Brossard, Louky Bersianik and Louise Cotnoir. LEONARD M. FINDLAY

Criticism

The work of critics is generally to define, classify, interpret and judge literature, but which of these activities achieves prominence varies from period to period and from place to place. In countries such as France and England, where the classics are widely agreed upon, little need exists to define the national literature (it is simply understood to be these classics) or to promote it (since all agree that the classics should be widely read and taught). When such a consensus exists, critics can devote their time to editing famous texts or to interpreting famous authors. Many English Canadian critics, including Barker FAIRLEY, Douglas Bush, Leon EDEL, Hugh Kenner, Kathleen Coburn, Marshall McLuhan, George WOODCOCK and Northrop Frye, have achieved international recognition for this kind of work on world writers or for their literary theory. If such critics turn their attention to Canadian literature, a new literature with few classics, they often change their approach. In Canada much critical energy has been consumed in attempts to define Canadian literature. Furthermore, critics who feel that Canadian literature deserves an audience must promote its publication, study and popular reception.

The history of English Canadian literary criticism has also involved a struggle to promote Canadian literature by providing it with a literary institution: publishers, readers, reviewers, booksellers, literary associations, journals, reference works, textbooks and university courses (*see* AUTHORS AND THEIR MILIEU; BOOK PUBLISHING). Even before Confederation, Edward Hartley Dewart concerned himself with the economic difficulties of Canadian authors and publishers. Three important later institution builders were Pelham Edgar, head of English at Victoria College, University of Toronto, 1903-18; Lorne PIERCE, literary editor of the RYERSON PRESS, 1922-60; and William Arthur Deacon, book reviewer for the GLOBE AND MAIL and other important Toronto publications, 1922-60. Although these men wrote much about Canadian literature, they also strove to set in place permanent institutional structures to support the growth of that literature. Their projects were precursors to such later ones as the establishment of the NATIONAL LIBRARY (1953) and the CANADA COUNCIL (1957), and the publication of *Literary History of Canada* (1965; rev 1976).

In their attempts to define Canadian literature, critics have been dominated by romantic nationalism. This still-common view sees the nation-state as an ideal association because it is based primarily on linguistic, cultural, social and geophysical unity, rather than on political expediency or the accidents of imperialism. Non-European countries rarely possess the unity required by this theory, and Canada is no exception. For example, Canada has officially recognized BILINGUALISM and MULTICULTURALISM. Critics, therefore, have had the difficult task of identifying national characteristics not shared by Canada and the US or Britain yet common to English and French Canada. Thus Canada's cold climate, northern wilderness and colonial mentality have been seen as crucial in the formation of the nation's literature; more recently, native peoples and myths, French-English relations, and early history have become popular "Canadian" topics. Several general books based on the ideas of romantic nationalism were published; the most representative is perhaps Archibald MacMechan's *Headwaters of Canadian Literature* (1924). E.K. Brown's writings, especially *On Canadian Poetry* (1943), best exemplify the continuing tradition. Lionel Stevenson's *Appraisals of Canadian Literature* (1926) made some interesting revisions to the main tenets of romantic nationalism in order to approach the older generation of Canadian poets more flexibly.

With the 1920s and the introduction of modernist poetics to Canada (documented in Louis Dudek and Michael Gnarowski, *The Making of Modern Poetry in Canada*, 1967) came resistance to romantic taste and to romantic nationalist literary theories. CANADIAN FORUM (1920-) provided the most public medium for the new poetry and its supportive criticism, which was influenced by T.S. Eliot, the Imagists and the French Symbolists. W.E. Collin's *The White Savannahs* (1936) exemplifies this critical approach. A.J.M. Smith, a central figure in the attack on Canadian romantic poetry and criticism, argued that the focus on writing "distinctively Canadian" poetry led to low standards and a parochial ignorance of foreign innovations. In his introduction to *The Book of Canadian Poetry* (1943), he made an influential distinction between "native" writers, who concentrated on "what is unique and individual in Canadian life," and "cosmopolitan" writers, who make a "heroic effort to transcend colonialism by entering into the universal, civilizing culture of ideas." Although Smith himself recanted in later editions of his book, the "native-cosmopolitan" split has been revived in the debate between Frank Davey, a postmodernist who supports McLuhan's concept of the "global village," and Robin Mathews, a left-wing nationalist.

The greatest contemporary influence on Canadian criticism has been the work of Northrop Frye. Although he approved of Smith's modernist taste, Frye has rehabilitated many of the important themes of romantic nationalist criticism. For example, his view that nature is a major determinant of the "Canadian" quality in our literature is similar to that of Dewart, who wrote in 1864 that Canadian "nature unveils her most majestic forms to exalt and inspire the truly poetic soul." For Frye, Canadian nature inspires the "deep terror" that leads to a "garrison mentality." Because of the threat of a "huge, unthinking, menacing, and formidable physical setting," this mentality promotes the human and moral values of the group.

Frye's ideas influenced D.G. JONES's *Butterfly on Rock* (1970), which argues a change from garrison mentality to communication between man and his formerly frightening surroundings, and Margaret ATWOOD'S SURVIVAL (1972). Atwood sees the Canadian literary fixation on survival as arising less from the threat of the real wilderness than from the threat of American cultural domination. Detractors from these and other "thematic" discussions of Canadian literature argue that the emphasis on man's relation to the wilderness is not unique to Canadian literature, and that this approach risks equating Canadian content with quality, oversimplifies Canadian-American relations and overemphasizes the Canadian landscape at the expense of the more time-bound and problematic intellectual, social, economic and political influences.

Frye's ideas have been turned inside out by several writers and critics who, instead of claiming that the land determines the literature, argue that writers invent the land. Eli MANDEL suggests that an environment is "a mental construct, a region of the mind, a myth." Because no one can grasp the variety of the real Canada, we evolve, in art, popular culture, journalism, literary criticism and especially literature, an imaginative version of Canada to stand for the real Canada.

The surge of Canadian self-awareness that accompanied the Centennial of Confederation in 1967 encouraged the expansion of Canadian literature courses (*see* LITERATURE IN ENGLISH: TEACHING) and of Canadian criticism. New journals sprang up to join CANADIAN LITERATURE, which had stood alone since its establishment in 1959: *Journal of Canadian Fiction* (est 1972), *Essays on Canadian Writing* (est 1974), *Studies in Canadian Literature* (est 1976) and many others. By the early 1980s the gains of the previous decade were being consolidated in a number of large-scale projects, including *The Oxford Companion To Canadian Literature* (1983, ed W. Toye), Carleton U's Center for Editing Early Canadian Texts (gen ed Mary Jane Edwards), and ECW Press's proposed 20-volume series, Canadian Writers and Their Works (gen eds Robert Lecker, Jack David and Ellen Quigley). That the bare survival of Canadian literature perhaps need no longer be the central concern of Canadian criticism is indicated also by the recent publication of several major works about individual writers: biographies, volumes of letters and critical monographs.

Recently the traditional borders between literature, literary criticism and literary theory have become blurred in Canadian criticism based upon European theory. Thus avant-garde writers such as Douglas BARBOUR, George BOWERING, Frank Davey, Robert Kroetsch, Stephen SCOBIE and Phylis Webb, comparative literature specialists such as E.D. BLODGETT, Linda Hutcheon and Lorraine Weir, and feminist critics such as Barbara Godard, Daphne MARLATT, Kathy Mezei and Gail Scott (the TESSERA collective), write criticism of Canadian literature based on a variety of internationally current theoretical perspectives. Although definition and promotion will not vanish completely from the Canadian critical repertoire, Canadian literature appears to have achieved the institutional security necessary to support the theoretical and analytical critical writing typical of an established literary culture. MARGERY FEE

Reading: Margaret Atwood, *Second Words* (1982); Carl Ballstadt, ed, *The Search for English-Canadian Literature* (1975); Frank Davey, *Surviving the Paraphrase* (1983); Northrop Frye, *The Bush Garden* (1971) and *Divisions on a Ground* (1982); W.J. Keith, *Canadian Literature in English* (1985); Eli Mandel, *Another Time* (1977), *The Family*

Romance (1986) and, ed, *Contexts of Canadian Criticism* (1971); Shirley Neuman and Smaro Kamboureli, eds, *A Mazing Space: Writing Canadian Women Writing* (1986); A.J.M. Smith, *Towards a View of Canadian Letters* (1973); David Staines, ed, *The Canadian Imagination* (1977).

Literature in French During the 1960s, "Québec literature" became the established term used in Québec to refer to all francophone literature in Canada. Outside Québec the older expression – French Canadian literature – has not disappeared, and Québecois historians themselves continue to use it for other Canadian French-language literatures: Acadian, Franco-Ontarian and western Canadian. The history of this francophone literature of Canada may be divided into 7 periods.

French Origins (1534-1760) This period began with the travel accounts of Jacques CARTIER and ended with the French regime itself. The metropolis had never allowed printing presses to be installed in the colony: works were published in France and sometimes elsewhere in Europe. Though most of the writers were born in France, a good many may be called Canadians, for they came to Canada while very young and lived here for their most active years. The works of this period consisted primarily of the reports of discoverers (Cartier) and explorers; missionaries' letters (*Les Relations des Jésuites;* selections tr *The* JESUIT RELATIONS *and Allied Documents,* 1963); EXPLORATION AND TRAVEL LITERATURE (Gabriel Sagard, Baron de LAHONTAN); histories (François-Xavier CHARLEVOIX); studies of customs and mores (Joseph-François LAFITAU); spiritual writings (MARIE DE L'INCARNATION); annals (Marie Morin); and personal correspondence (Élisabeth Bégon; *see* AUTOBIOGRAPHICAL WRITING IN FRENCH). Few were purely literary works, excepting the writings of Marc LESCARBOT.

Narratives were primarily eyewitness accounts and descriptions. The author was more concerned with educating than amusing his reader, but since he also wanted to be interesting and was often well educated, he frequently wrote in colourful style. His pleasure in writing is contagious: today's reader gains a fresh vision of the country by rediscovering it through eyes that literally looked upon a "New World." It is this aspect that has been most beneficial to many modern writers (Félix-Antoine Savard, Pierre PERRAULT, Jacques FERRON, Gilles VIGNEAULT). These humanistic works also influenced the literature of France and inspired great writers (Rabelais, Montaigne, the Encyclopedists, Rousseau, Chateau-briand), and contributed to the development of a literature spurning socialized man and lauding the "noble savage."

Canadian Origins (1760-1836) After the CONQUEST of 1760, France yielded Canada to Britain in the Treaty of Paris (1763). French Canada was in ruins: it was economically and politically shattered; its administration and commerce had passed into the hands of the conquerors; its educational system had lost its teachers and its resources. The remaining 65 000 Canadiens clustered about their natural leaders: some 125 impoverished seigneurs, 100 or so priests, a couple of dozen men of the law and an equal number of doctors. Isolated from France, loyal to England, involuntarily thrown upon their own resources, they forged their will to live through fidelity to their French origins.

In 1764 the first Québec NEWSPAPER was born, the bilingual *Quebec Gazette/La Gazette de Québec.* Its French translations were appallingly bad and the original Canadien articles either affected in tone or obsequious. A French newspaper, *La Gazette du commerce et littéraire, pour la ville et district de Montréal,* appeared in 1778. It was of good quality but lasted only a year. The first truly Canadien paper, *Le Canadien,* started in 1806. It was devoted to the defence of the rights and liberties of the conquered. With this paper the French Canadian people found their voice and their literature took on a nationalist tone that has been nurtured ever since.

The best writer of the time was journalist Étienne PARENT, editor of *Le Canadien.* He clearly analysed the political battles of the 1830s, and his compatriots, although they did not always listen, respected his independence and lucidity. When he retired from journalism and abandoned politics, he was sought after as an adviser and lecturer; today, he is regarded as the first Québec sociologist. Two orators marked the same era: Joseph-Octave PLESSIS, bishop of Québec, whose traditionalist sermons supported the authorities of the day, and Louis-Joseph PAPINEAU, political leader and charismatic populist member of the legislative assembly. There were no indigenous novels and no theatre. In 1830 an inferior imitator of Boileau, Michel Bibaud, published the first collection of Canadien POETRY. That was the sum of Canadien literary production for this period.

The Literary Homeland (1837-65) The political struggles which stimulated the birth of Canadien literature led first to the REBELLIONS OF 1837 and then to the union of Upper and Lower Canada. French Canadians once again lost their homeland but were intellectually better equipped than in 1760. In 1824 and again in 1829, they had created a respectable network of primary schools. This system was reorganized after the union of the Canadas in 1841. At the secondary level, 7 *collèges* were founded after the turn of the century. The students, molded by their studies of Greco-Latin humanities and the French classics, willingly believed that the glory of a people came from its literature.

Two NOVELS appeared in 1837: *Les Révélations du crime,* by François-Réal Angers, an account of a real incident, and *L'Influence d'un livre,* by Philippe AUBERT DE GASPÉ, Jr, who drew his inspiration from anecdotes and FOLKLORE. The adventure novel made its appearance with *Les Fiancés de 1812* (1844) by Joseph DOUTRE and *Une de perdue, deux de trouvées* (1849) by Georges Boucher de Boucherville. The rural novel was born in 1846 with *La Terre paternelle* by Patrice Lacombe and *Charles Guérin* by P.J.O. CHAUVEAU, a great admirer of Balzac. Antoine GÉRIN-LAJOIE gave substance to Chauveau's dream and that of the majority of his compatriots by creating a whole new parish, a kind of homeland in miniature, for the hero of *Jean Rivard* (1862-64). The glory of the nation had its history, which Philippe AUBERT DE GASPÉ, Sr, evoked in *Les* ANCIENS CANADIENS (1863). Napoléon BOURASSA retold the tragic story of the ACADIAN deportation of 1755 in his touching history of an engaged couple, *Jacques et Marie,* 1865-66. The historical novel, like the rural novel, was to be fashionable for a full century. It owed part of its inspiration and success to the best writer of the age, François-Xavier GARNEAU, author of HISTOIRE DU CANADA, which came out in 3 editions between 1845 and 1859. Garneau had the tone of his romantic French masters but added an entirely Canadien fervour (which did not, however, cloud his objectivity). The most highly acclaimed poet of the age, Octave CRÉMAZIE, enchanted his contemporaries with poems that borrowed heavily from history. Today's reader prefers his death-haunted poems and his letters, which attain the status of literary criticism.

Messianic Survival (1866-95) The preceding era had been ideologically turbulent. The INSTITUT CANADIEN, a kind of popular university founded in 1844, had drawn the ire of Mgr Ignace BOURGET, bishop of Montréal, because of the "liberal" contents of its library. The debate between ULTRAMONTANISTS and liberals such as L.A. Dessaulles stimulated thought and produced some interesting texts. Conservatism triumphed after the 1860s; the nation gained homogeneity but lost originality of thought.

In 1866, Fr Henri-Raymond CASGRAIN established literary doctrine for the coming years. Literature was to be the faithful mirror of a Catholic, religious and moral people. He himself showed the way by theologizing history. His footsteps were duly followed: Joseph Marmette and Laure Conan (Félicité ANGERS) wrote "good" historical novels, while poets imitated the French romantics (particularly Hugo and Lamartine) and sang the praises either of NEW FRANCE (Louis-Honoré FRÉCHETTE) or of the small homeland Québec had become once again after CONFEDERATION (Leon-Pamphile Le May, Nérée Beauchemin). Catholic journalism (Jules-Paul TARDIVEL) was dominant; literary criticism (Adolphe-Basile Routhier) was preoccupied with morality. Tedium threatened on all fronts, though it was escaped by Fréchette, a liberal, and Arthur BUIES, the only real Canadien romantic and the only great writer of the age. Also a liberal, Buies had style and showmanship; a chronicler, he observed well; a philosopher, he had independent ideas.

Exile and the Establishment of Roots (1896-1938) The Liberals who took power in Ottawa in 1896, and then in Québec in 1897 for almost 40 years, were primarily politicians; the ideologues were either dead or silent. The first decades of the 20th century continued the established ideology of the 3 preceding ones: the dominant voice was that of nationalist historian and essayist Fr Lionel GROULX. However, literature grew in importance, thanks to an educational system whose primary and secondary levels, well developed in the 19th century, now prepared students for 2 francophone universities, LAVAL and U DE MONTRÉAL.

There was an abundance of poets. The École littéraire de Montréal sought to modernize both form and themes, though with little success except in the case of one poet of genius, Émile NELLIGAN. Between the ages of 17 and 20 (1896-99), Nelligan produced some 170 poems whose quality lifted him well above his colleagues and elders. Like them, he imitated the poets of France, but with more originality and modernity. A few others, the "exotists" (Paul Morin, René Chopin) and Robert CHOQUETTE, thematically exiled themselves from the homeland. But most poets still devoted themselves to "poetry of the soil," with more success than in the 19th century. This trend reached its ultimate expression in *À l'ombre de l'Orford* (1929) by Alfred DESROCHERS.

Rural novels appeared in large numbers. A Frenchman, Louis HÉMON, gave the style an international audience with his MARIA CHAPDELAINE (1916); *Un Homme et son péché* (1933) by Claude-Henri GRIGNON brought it back to Québec; and the genre produced its best example in *Trente Arpents* (1938) by Ringuet (Philippe PANNETON). Historical fiction peaked in 1938 as well, with *Les Engagés du Grand Portage* by Léo-Paul DESROSIERS, and then fell off. Nationalism found poetic expression in MENAUD, MAÎTRE-DRAVEUR (1937) by Félix-Antoine SAVARD, and was then silent. Criticism, like the novel and poetry, knew a certain strength in this period (Louis Dantin, Marcel Dugas), but it was led by an academic, Mgr Camille ROY, whose literature textbook sustained H.R. Casgrain's influence in the collèges.

Age of Introspection (1939-57) The economic crisis of the 1930s caused French Canadians to rethink their traditional values; WWII forced them to open themselves to the world and new ideas. Urbanization was underway; prosperity returned, and education was available to more people.

People freed their minds from collective thought; the drama of society as a whole no longer overshadowed individual destiny. Writers became more introspective, in the manner of European writers (such as Mauriac, Bernanos, Julian Green, Graham Greene, Ibsen). Canadian publishing also began to develop. Traditional nationalism was transformed. It was now at the humanistic level that one sought to be a better French Canadian.

The great poets of the era (Saint-Denys GARNEAU, Anne HÉBERT, Alain GRANDBOIS, Rina LASNIER) rejected versifying and the cult of the soil for new forms and new rhythms; they travelled through interior landscapes instead. It was a revelation: unsuspected shadows were found swarming there, but light eventually broke through to show a universe of colour and open space where a new awareness was taking shape. What was once felt to be the collective duty, to survive in the face of the English, was now replaced by an appetite for life as individual men and women among other men and women.

Novelists were developing in the same way. Old stereotypes yielded to more earthy characters, as authors of the psychological novel (Robert CHARBONNEAU, André Giroux, Robert Élie, Jean Simard, André LANGEVIN) created individuals searching for themselves, not for collective salvation. French Canadian society was being transformed: it was being observed with care and a certain wariness, especially in the cities, by the first novelists of sociological analysis (Roger LEMELIN, Gabrielle ROY, Yves THÉRIAULT).

THEATRE (*see also* DRAMA IN FRENCH) abandoned melodrama and comedic variety shows for social satire (Gratien GÉLINAS) and intimate dramas of bourgeois family life (Marcel DUBÉ). The historians, except for Guy FRÉGAULT, were no longer purely writers; they sought cold scientific objectivity. Literary criticism marked time, but did so gracefully (Roger Duhamel, René Garneau, Guy Sylvestre).

Québec Literature since 1958 The political and social climate in Québec began to change at the end of the 1950s, the beginning of the QUIET REVOLUTION. Teaching institutions became more democratic; ideologies continued to diversify, and a new nationalism emerged that called for greater sovereignty, even for the independence of Québec. With a few surrealistic flourishes (Gilles Hénault, Roland Giguère, P.M. LAPOINTE) and much lyricism (Gaston MIRON, Jacques BRAULT, Fernand OUELLETTE, Gatien Lapointe, Paul CHAMBERLAND), the poets named their country: no longer Canada, but Québec. The magazine PARTI PRIS (1963-68) added a socialist, populist dimension to the nationalist option. A formalist trend also appeared, however (*La* BARRE DU JOUR, *Les Herbes rouges*), whose stylistic exercises and linguistic experimentation led to intellectualization of literature, despite some Marxist, feminist and rock-inspired contributions (*see* LITERARY PERIODICALS IN FRENCH).

Novelists took the lead in the 1960s. They were preoccupied with the form and structure of their works (Jean Basile, Hubert AQUIN, Réjean DUCHARME, Gérard BESSETTE), and managed to borrow some techniques of the French nouveau roman (new novel) without losing their own originality. Female authors led the way in the creation of the poem-novel (Anne Hébert, Marie-Claire BLAIS, Louise MAHEUX-FORCIER). The traditional novel (Roch CARRIER, André MAJOR) still existed, side by side with a novel that wove its form around its words (Victor-Lévy BEAULIEU). Feminist ideology appeared at the end of the 1970s (Nicole BROSSARD).

Theatre expanded considerably, but moved away from literature in that it became preoccupied with showmanship (Michel TREMBLAY). Even so, it was a platform for new ideologies, such as linguistic populism and feminism. There were a great number of ESSAY writers, and a few of them were literary (Fernand Dumont, Pierre VADEBONCOEUR).

A new criticism was born when Québec literature entered the universities. This criticism attempts to be scientific but as yet lacks originality, since it follows in the wake of its French and American masters. However, it has enormous influence on Québec writers, who are, often simultaneously, both its creators and its followers. Although good writers do produce work for a general audience (Michel Tremblay), the ordinary reader is as likely to turn to American best-sellers. Québec's preoccupation with itself has compelled Francophones in the rest of Canada to look to their own literature. Similarly, the all-powerful nature of the Montréal literary establishment has provoked (with the help of the Québec government) regional movements of self-awareness in other parts of Québec. Montréal has largely replaced Paris as the literary metropolis of the Canadian francophone world. *See also* SHORT FICTION IN FRENCH; LITERARY BIBLIOGRAPHY; LITERARY PRIZES; ORAL LITERATURE; POPULAR LITERATURE IN FRENCH. RENÉ DIONNE

Reading: Pierre de Grandpré, *Histoire de la littérature française du Québec*, 4 vols (1967-69); Réginald Hamel et al, *Dictionnaire pratique des auteurs québécois* (1976); Maurice Lemire, ed, *Dictionnaire des oeuvres littéraires du Québec*, 5 vols to date (1978-88).

Literature in French: Theory and Criticism

No French-language literary critic in Canada seems to have stature among writers equal to that of Bayle, Sainte-Beuve or Barthes in France. Nevertheless, several writers have won a degree of prominence as much (if not more) for their works of criticism as for their other writings. Their ranks include members of the interwar generation: Marcel Dugas, whose critical prose has poetic overtones; Berthelot Brunet, whose breezy histories of French and French Canadian literature have much more life than his vapid novels; Victor Barbeau, sole editor and jack-of-all-trades of *Les Cahiers de Turc*, which appeared Oct 1921-Mar 1922 and Oct 1926-July 1927; Valdombre (pseudonym of Claude-Henri GRIGNON), whose virulent pamphlets (*see* ESSAY IN FRENCH) are as much polemic as criticism. This period also saw the critical publications of Albert Pelletier, novelist and journalist Harry Bernard and poet Alfred DESROCHERS. The list is short, not because criticism has been insignificant, but because it has always been considered a marginal literary activity. And that is the paradox. Criticism, because it has usually favoured the established order, bears responsibility for the fact that Quebecers have generally viewed their literature as a reflection of society.

The earliest French Canadian critics were journalists and a few amateurs, who set themselves the task of judging the few publications that appeared according to the norms of the French language and the rules of classical verse. The first literary critic was Valentin Jautard, a Frenchman, editor of the *Gazette littéraire de Montréal*, fd 1778 by his compatriot, Fleury Mesplet. The versatile Michel Bibaud practised the genre in the many publications which he himself founded in rapid succession, such as *L'Aurore* (1816-19), *Le Courrier du Bas-Canada* (1819-20) and *La Bibliothèque canadienne* (1825-30).

Fr Henri-Raymond CASGRAIN was the first to judge works systematically, according to an explicit theory of literature. His goal was to dictate the guiding principles for all literary production: literature had to be "essentially religious and devout" and was to reflect the "genius" of the nation. He made literature his apostolic mission, thus founding a tradition of clerical and moralizing criticism that was to last almost a century. Nobody had as much prestige and influence in this field as Camille ROY. A professor and later rector at UNIVERSITÉ LAVAL, he transposed to Québec the principles of 19th-century French criticism, with emphasis on the methodology and assumptions of Gustave Lanson and, to an even greater degree, the thought of Ferdinand Brunetière. Roy, however, also believed that allowances had to be made for the infant state of the literature to which these principles were being applied. He therefore lavished praise on many mediocre works and saved his wrath for the defence of Catholic morality and the French classical ideal of clarity. Despite occasional opposition, like that of journalist Jules Fournier, who took him to task for applying to nonentities critical methodologies developed for the study of masterpieces, Roy dominated and guided the perception of French Canadian literature for almost half a century. He had many disciples, including Maurice Hébert and priest-critics Albert Dandurand, Émile Chartier, Henri d'Arles, Marc-Antonin Lamarche and Samuel Baillargeon, who produced pedagogic works imbued with the ideals of French classicism and strict moral tone. In contrast, Louis Dantin, who wrote a remarkable introduction to the poetry of Émile NELLIGAN, was a sensitive aesthete and a man of subtlety, eclectic tastes and freedom from doctrinal limitations.

The pro-establishment narrowness of this literature and literary criticism explains the violence of the clash, which lasted 1918-48 under a variety of forms and pretexts, between the literary schools of the "men of the soil" and the "exotists" – the former seeking a "national" literature expressed in a "Canadien" language, the latter, partisans of French linguistic norms, preaching emancipation from any form of regionalism. The basic argument resurfaced in the 1960s and 70s, this time in the form of a debate about the choice of language and centering on the publications and critiques of PARTI PRIS and the early plays of Michel TREMBLAY.

After WWII, several critics of considerable stature emerged, among them Guy Sylvestre, Pierre de Grandpré, Roger Duhamel and Gilles MARCOTTE; the last three were, at different times, in charge of the literary page of *Le* DEVOIR. From the start of the 1960s, the tradition of journalistic criticism was maintained in the departments or weekly supplements of newspapers such as *La* PRESSE, *Le Devoir* and *Le Droit* and in magazines such as *Lettres québécoises* devoted to current literature. National radio had a few programs of literary criticism, but television (whether Radio-Québec or Radio-Canada) virtually ignored the whole field. The greatest growth of criticism in the last 20 years has been in university literature departments. Though it keeps close watch on French literature, this criticism is primarily concerned with Québec writings. Inspired by the transformations of criticism in France, it has multiplied and diversified its methodologies to thematic analysis, psychocriticism, sociocriticism and, more recently, structuralism and semiotics.

The 3 principal university magazines in Québec are *Études françaises* (U de Montréal), *Études littéraires* (U Laval) and *Voix et images* (U du Québec). The universities have also produced a wide range of monographs and surveys, most of them published in university-press collections: "Lignes québécoises" (Presses de l'Université de Montréal), "Vie des lettres québécoises" (Presses de l'Université Laval), "Cahiers du CRCCF" (Éditions de l'Université d'Ottawa), and "Constantes" and "Littérature" in the "Cahiers du Québec" series (Éditions HMH).

Despite the explosive growth of criticism since 1960 and a tradition that is more than a century old, no history of criticism has yet been written which pays as much attention to its specifically literary evolution as to its ideological evolution. Moreover, critics are now questioning the degree of their dependence on outside – especially French – methodologies and arguing the need to develop their own, along with appropriate literary theories. This may be the trend of the future. *See also* LITERATURE IN FRENCH; BOOK PUBLISHING, FRENCH-LANGUAGE. JEAN-LOUIS MAJOR

Reading: F. Dumont and J.C. Falardeau, eds, *Littérature et société canadienne-française* (1964); G. Laflèche, ed, *Dix ans de recherche québécoise sur la littérature française (1970-1979)* (1980); G. Marcotte, ed, *Présence de la critique* (1966); G. Tougas, *History of French-Canadian Literature* (1966).

Literature in French: Scholarship and Teaching The first substantial publication devoted to French Canadian literature was James Huston's *Répertoire national* (1848-50; repr 1982), a 4-volume annotated anthology of writings culled from early Québec newspapers. During the period of increased literary activity known as the Mouvement littéraire de 1860, Laurent-Olivier David, Henri-Raymond CASGRAIN and Hector Fabre all published inspirational essays on the national literature, and Henry James Morgan's *Bibliotheca canadensis* (1867) included about 100 French-speaking authors. Early anthologies of poems and songs were compiled by Joseph Lenoir (1858), Antonin Nantel (1869) and Louis-Hippolyte Taché (1881). During the 1870s, Casgrain, David, Adolphe-Basile Routhier and Louis-Michel Darveau composed bibliographical or satirical portraits of prominent contemporaries, many of whom were authors, and Edmond Lareau issued the first history, or catalogue, of Canadian literature in both English and French (1874). The death of Octave CRÉMAZIE in France in Jan 1879 prompted several articles on his work, and during the following decade Benjamin Sulte and Pierre-Joseph-Olivier CHAUVEAU published short historical accounts of the beginnings of French Canadian poetry. In general, however, 19th-century writing on Québec literature consisted of either anecdotal chronicles or moralizing comment, the latter typified by Casgrain's eulogistic essay on the novel ANGÉLINE DE MONTBRUN (1884) by Laure Conan (Félicité ANGERS).

In the early 20th century the study of Québec literature became more scholarly. Bibliophiles Philéas Gagnon and Narcisse-Europe Dionne compiled extensive bibliographies of Québec publications. Charles ab der Halden, a French academic, wrote articles and gave lectures in Paris on French Canadian authors; these he published as *Études de littérature canadienne-française* (1904) and *Nouvelles Études...* (1907). Mgr Camille ROY, Québec's first literary historian to have studied the new discipline in Paris, began in 1902 to publish remarkably well-informed articles on contemporary Québec writers and on the early history of the literature. These were later incorporated into his numerous collections of essays, his classic study *Nos origines littéraires* (1909) and the successive printings of his influential *Manuel d'histoire de la littérature canadienne-française* (1907-62). Another literary historian, Mgr Émile Chartier, attempted to synthesize the INTELLECTUAL HISTORY of his province in articles collected in *La Vie de l'esprit au Canada français, 1760-1825* (1941). Genuine aesthetic criticism was rare except in the writings of Louis Dantin and Marcel Dugas. Up-to-date anthologies were compiled by Jules Fournier and Olivar Asselin (1920), Camille Roy (1934) and Guy SYLVESTRE (1942), and secondary-school manuals for the study of French Canadian literature were published by the Sisters of St Anne (1928) and the Brothers of the Christian Schools (1928).

Between the world wars, several theses on French Canadian literature were submitted to French universities: those of Antoine Roy ("Les Lettres, les sciences et les arts au Canada sous le régime français," Paris, 1930) and Laurence A. Bisson ("Le Romantisme littéraire au Canada français," Bordeaux, 1932) are still consulted, as is Louis Le Jeune's *Dictionnaire général...* (1931). Most studies of Québec literature published in the 1930s were impressionistic, but the group gathered around the magazine *La* RELÈVE took an intellectual and universalist position. Serious histories of POETRY (1933) and the NOVEL (1937) were written by Albert Dandurand; an American, Ian Forbes Fraser, compiled the first systematic bibliography of French Canadian poetry (1935), and Jane Mason Turnbull published the best study in English, *Essential Traits of French-Canadian Poetry* (1938). Annual surveys of Québec writing began to appear: the *Bulletin bibliographique* of the Société des écrivains canadiens (1937-59) and the "Letters in Canada" issue of UNIVERSITY OF TORONTO QUARTERLY, which began to include French Canadian letters in 1937.

During WWII publication declined, but Séraphin Marion's *Les Lettres canadiennes d'autrefois* (9 vols, 1939-58) continued to appear. The Archives de folklore de l'Université Laval (1944), the Institut d'histoire de l'Amérique française (1945) and the Bibliographical Society of Canada (1946) were founded. As the war ended Marcel Trudel's thesis *L'Influence de Voltaire au Canada* (1945) and Jeanne Paul-Crouzet's *Poésie au Canada* opened a new period of more rigorous study. The 1950s saw the publication of numerous bibliographical guides by Gustave Lanctot (1951), Marie Tremaine (1952), Gérard Martin (1954), Antonio Drolet (1955), Philippe Garigue (1956) and Gérard Tougas (1958). The outstanding publications of the decade were Luc Lacourcière's critical edition of the poems of Émile NELLIGAN and Auguste Viatte's *Histoire littéraire...* (1954), a pioneering comparative study.

The tremendous upsurge in Québec literary production since 1960 has been accompanied by an unprecedented growth of bibliographical, literary-historical and critical activity. The founding of the Centre de recherche en civilisation canadienne-française at U of Ottawa in 1958 was followed by the creation of similar research centres in Québec universities. Major undertakings such as the DICTIONARY OF CANADIAN BIOGRAPHY (est 1959), Adrien Thério's annual panorama *Livres et auteurs québécois* (1961-82) and the scholarly series "Archives des lettres canadiennes" (1961-), directed by Paul Wyczynski, mark the beginnings of contemporary Québec literary scholarship. The Bibliothèque nationale du Québec (est 1968) implemented a wide-ranging program of bibliographical research and publication. Scholarly journals such as *Incidences* (1962-69; *Co-Incidences* since 1969), PARTI PRIS, (1963-68), *Études françaises* (1965-), *Études littéraires* (1968-), *Voix et images* (1975-), *Jeu* and *Lettres québécoises* (1976-) have published articles, interviews and documents.

Since 1960 all forms of literary study have been actively pursued in Québec. Dozens of anthologies have appeared for individual authors (Arthur BUIES, Albert LABERGE), for particular genres (Laurent Mailhot and Pierre Nepveu, *La Poésie québécoise des origines à nos jours,* 1980), or for the whole literature (Gilles MARCOTTE, *Anthologie de la littérature québécoise,* 4 vols, 1978-80). Numerous bibliographies have been compiled by John Hare (in several volumes of "Archives des lettres canadiennes"), by André Beaulieu and Jean Hamelin (*La Presse québécoise...,* 6 vols to date), by Pierre Pagé and Renée Legris for radio and television scripts, and by the staff of the Bibliothèque nationale du Québec in various fields. Each volume of the *Dictionnaire des oeuvres littéraires du Québec* (1978-) contains extensive bibliographies of authors and literary periods. Modern histories of Québec literature have been published by Gérard Tougas (1960), Pierre de Grandpré et al (1967-69) and Laurent Mailhot (1974), and biographical or critical studies of more than 50 Québec writers are now available. Réjean Robidoux and André Renaud (1966), Maurice Lemire (1970), Gérard BESSETTE (1973), Gilles Marcotte (1976) and Jacques Michon (1979) have written important studies of the Québec novel; Paul Wyczynski (1965), Marcotte (1969) and Pierre Nepveu (1979) have published major works on Québec poetry; and Jean-Cléo Godin and Mailhot (1970, 1980) have produced 2 collections of studies of contemporary Québec theatre. Sociologist Jean-Charles Falardeau has investigated (1967-74) relations between Québec society and its literature. Franco-Ontarian literature has been studied (1978-81) by René Dionne and Acadian literature by Marguerite Maillet et al (1979). Critical editions have been few in number (Nelligan, 1952; Saint-Denys GARNEAU, 1971; Crémazie, 1972-76; Nérée Beauchemin, 1973), but a major collective research project directed by Roméo Arbour, Jean-Louis Major and Laurent Mailhot has 4 editions in print and several in preparation. Other large collaborative projects under way are a critical edition of the works of François-Xavier GARNEAU (Paul Wyczynski and Pierre Savard), a final volume of the *Dictionnaire des oeuvres littéraires du Québec* (Maurice Lemire et al) and an augmented edition of the *Dictionnaire pratique des auteurs québécois* (Réginald Hamel, John Hare and Paul Wyczynski).

Despite the early efforts of Mgr Roy, French Canadian literature had been a marginal element of French literary studies in Québec university courses until the 1950s. During the following decade programs of specialization in French Canadian studies were established at Laval, Montréal, McGill and Sherbrooke universities, and at the new UNIVERSITÉ DU QUÉBEC from its founding in 1968. Québec literature is now the subject of as many university theses in Québec as is French literature. Elsewhere in Canada undergraduate courses in French Canadian literature began in the 1930s or 1940s and graduate study in the 1950s, but on a more limited scale than in Québec. In recent years Canadian COMPARATIVE LITERATURE (English and French) has become a popular field of study, particularly at the universities of Sherbrooke and Alberta. DAVID M. HAYNE

Litherland, Albert Edward, "Ted," nuclear physicist (b at Wallasey, Eng 12 Mar 1928). Litherland received a BSc in 1949 and a PhD in 1955 from the U of Liverpool. He was a National Research Council Fellow (1953-55) and a career scientist (1955-66) with Atomic Energy of Canada Ltd. In 1966 he was appointed a professor of physics at U of T and a university professor in 1979. He was visiting professor at Oxford in 1960-61 and in 1972-73. Litherland published over 100 scientific papers in such areas as: electron-induced fission, nuclear spectroscopy, collective motions in light nuclei and accelerator design. He has recently established the world-class Isotrace Laboratory at Toronto using nuclear techniques in a supersensitive mass spectrometer for archaeological dating, trace element detection, etc. He holds fellowships in the Royal Societies of London and of Canada and in the American Physical Society. Awards include the Gold

Medal of the Canadian Assn of Physicists (1971), the Rutherford Medal of the British Institute of Physics (1974), a Killam scholarship (1980) and a Guggenheim (1986). L. TRAINOR

Lithuanians Lithuania is a small country on the southeastern coast of the Baltic Sea. The first recorded Lithuanian immigrants to Canada were soldiers serving in the British army in the early 19th century. At the end of the 19th century and in the early 20th century, many Lithuanians (for the most part unskilled workers), fleeing Tsarist police or in an attempt to improve their livelihoods, immigrated to Canada and settled in Nova Scotia, Ontario and western Canada. The 1921 census recorded 1970 people of Lithuanian origin in Canada; another 5000 emigrated in the 1920s and 1930s. Most of these early Lithuanian immigrants found work on farms and the railways and in coal mines and factories in Toronto and Montréal. The largest number arrived after WWII, when thousands of Lithuanians, fleeing Soviet occupation, fled westward and found themselves in displaced persons' camps. Calling themselves *Dievo Paukštai* ("God's birds"), almost 20 000 of these refugee Lithuanians, many of whom were well-educated professionals, craftsmen and artists, made their way to Canada. In the 1986 census it was estimated that there were 14 625 persons in Canada of Lithuanian ancestry, of which half also claimed to be able to speak Lithuanian. Most Lithuanian Canadians reside in Ontario, but substantial numbers are settled in Québec, Alberta and BC.

Social and Cultural Life Lithuanians have integrated easily into Canadian society but have maintained a strong sense of their former identity through a variety of clubs and singing and dancing groups. Mutual aid societies were founded in the 1900s. All Lithuanian Canadians are considered members of the Lithuanian Canadian Community (1952), which has 20 chapters; its National Council in Toronto maintains links with the Lithuanian World Federation. The community holds Saturday classes across Canada in Lithuanian language, history, religion and folklore. Lithuanians are predominantly Roman Catholic.

Reading: Adam and Filomena Kantautus, *A Lithuanian Bibliography* (1975; *Supplement,* 1980).

Littérature qui se fait, Une (1962), Gilles MARCOTTE's innovative study of the evolution of LITERATURE IN FRENCH, is an anthology of his early essays about major writers. Analysing the problems confronting authors who have outgrown the old values of church, family and the land without fully articulating new values, Marcotte identifies the experience of vertigo as a constant in urban fiction. The 19th-century poet was isolated from European cultural centres; the modern poet is a double or inner exile, searching for a language with which to inhabit the landscape. Marcotte suggests that Québec writers, successfully voicing the poetics of solitude, express alienation, despair and silence (HÉBERT, BLAIS, Jasmin), or escape into the worlds of death, dream and the past (NELLIGAN, Saint-Denys GARNEAU, Lozeau). With the appearance from 1949 onward of Roland GIGUÈRE's writings, the Québec poets' apocalyptic vision began to confront the physical realities of life. Larry Shouldice's anthology *Contemporary Quebec Criticism* (1979) offers a translation of the chapter "The Poetry of Exile." MICHÈLE LACOMBE

Little, Jean, writer, lecturer (b at Taiwan [Taichung], Formosa [Taiwan] 2 Jan 1932 to Canadian medical doctors). A successful contemporary writer of children's fiction, Little has won the Canada Council Children's Literature Award as well as foreign acclaim. She was educated at U of T and was a special-education teacher before her royalties made her self-supporting. Almost blind since birth, she has nevertheless travelled to 27 foreign countries, and her books are widely translated abroad. Her 11 novels for young readers, and one book of poetry, treat with insight such universal themes as loneliness, alienation, intolerance, family stress, and the difficulties in interpersonal and intercultural relationships. Her best-known book is *From Anna* (1972), which has sold more than 130 000 copies. *Mama's Going to Buy You a Mockingbird* (1985) won the Canadian Library Assn's book-of-the-year-award for children's literature and the Canadian Booksellers' Assn Ruth Schwartz Award. Other recent publications include *Lost and Found* (1985), *Different Dragons* (1986) and *Hey, World, Here I Am!* (1987). MARY RUBIO

Little, Philip Francis, lawyer, judge, politician, premier of Nfld (b in PEI *c*1822; d at Monkstown, Ire 22 Oct 1897). Arriving in Newfoundland in 1843, Little found himself in the midst of the Reform struggle for the right of local Roman Catholics to practise law. The constitution of the Law Society at the time excluded that denomination, which particularly grieved a Reform Party supported almost exclusively by Irish Catholic voters. Little's PEI Bar membership enabled him to become Newfoundland's first practising RC lawyer, and Reformers greeted his arrival as a victory and championed his election to the Assembly in 1850. He soon unified various anti-government forces in demanding self-government. By 1855 he had become premier and attorney general in Newfoundland's first responsible administration. In a short-lived tenure as premier, Little helped stabilize political affairs and led a successful resistance against France's efforts to extend her traditional fishing privileges. Ill health forced his retirement to the bench in 1858, from which he soon retired to Ireland. JOHN GREENE

Little, Richard Caruthers, "Rich," impressionist, actor (b at Ottawa 26 Nov 1938). He is world famous for his uncanny impressions of celebrities and politicians. Little began to develop his talents by an avid listening to radio, attending movies and working in amateur theatre in Ottawa. He received his BA from Lisgar Collegiate in 1957 and among his activities there he was a cheerleader, writing several school cheers. The singer, Mel Tormé, saw Little on a Canadian television variety program and convinced Judy Garland to allow him to make his US debut on her show in 1964. Little has appeared as a regular on numerous television programs since that time, including the "John Davidson Show" (1969), "ABC Comedy Hour" (1972), the "Julie Andrews Hour" (1972-73), and hosting the "Rich Little Show" in 1976 and "You Asked For It" (1981-83). He was named Entertainer of the Year in 1974 and has received many awards for his virtuoso performances in his version of "A Christmas Carol." JAMES V. DEFELICE

Little Theatre Movement Canada's community theatres can be traced back to the beginning of settlement. All THEATRE during the French colonial period was amateur, whether produced by high society, the Jesuit and Ursuline schools, or the military garrisons. These 3 traditions extended into the 18th and 19th centuries, and paralleled the coming of the professional touring companies. Essentially, they were Canada's indigenous theatre until Confederation and beyond. Garrison productions in particular attained high standards while bolstering morale and raising funds for charity. Other highlights were the theatricals inaugurated in 1873 at Rideau Hall by Lord and Lady DUFFERIN, and maintained by various governors general thereafter. With Confederation, 1867, the British troops were gradually replaced by North-West Mounted Police. While the "Mounties" played the cultural role for some years, it was the gentry who assumed the theatrical mantle and the "Little Theatre Movement" as we know it took form. Perhaps the oldest surviving civic, amateur group was the Garrick Club in Hamilton, which began in 1875 and metamorphosed into Hamilton's Players' Guild in 1929. The French-speaking equivalents were literary and theatrical circles; one of the earliest, the Cercle Saint-Henri, dates from 1878. Paul Cazeneuve, a Montréal professional, organized the first French amateur festival in 1908, the Concours de l'île. This was in response to Gov Gen Earl Grey's Musical and Dramatic Competition initiated in 1907, and held in Ottawa, Montréal, Toronto and Winnipeg until 1911. This contest would be the precedent for the famed DOMINION DRAMA FESTIVAL (DDF), created in 1932 and launched in 1933 by yet another governor general and one to be, Lord Bessborough and Vincent MASSEY.

The Little Theatre's golden era occurred between the 2 world wars. Inspired by European troupes, such as André Antoine's Théâtre Libre in Paris and W.B Yeats's and Lady Gregory's Abbey Theatre in Dublin, the movement began as an idealistic reaction to the crass professional fare on tour around the turn of the century. With the rise of films and radio after WWI, the commercial theatre declined and literally hundreds of community theatres blossomed across Canada to fill the vacuum. Hart House Theatre in Toronto (1919-) became the model; some of the finest were the Vancouver Little Theatre (1921-) and Carroll Aikins's short-lived Home Theatre at Naramata, BC (1920-24); Toronto's University Alumnae (1918-); the Cercle Molière in St-Boniface (1925-); the Ottawa Little Theatre (1913-); the Montréal Repertory Theatre (1930-61) and Father Legault's Compagnons de Saint-Laurent (1937-52); and the Halifax Theatre Arts Guild (1931-). Perhaps only with director-playwright Herman VOADEN's "symphonic expressionism" during the 1930s and the left-wing Theatre of Action (1935-40), both in Toronto, did the Little Theatre achieve some new directions. "Agit-prop" theatre was vital across the country throughout the Depression, but the idealism had evaporated and the early experimentation gave way to comic and sentimental plays reflecting the waning colonial ties of Empire, whether French, British or American.

In 1932 the DDF was created, and for a time it was Canada's national theatre, a network of community companies that assembled each spring in a different city for a final week-long competition that distributed coveted awards for acting, directing, design and best production. These finalists had been chosen by a system of regional runoffs. Both the preliminary and final festivals were adjudicated by bilingual professionals usually imported from Britain or France. Until 1951 it was a one-act play festival and did much to foster the writing of original short plays in Canada, as well as developing Canadian actors and directors for the profession. During WWII the DDF was shelved, and many felt it was this break in continuity that triggered the eventual downfall of the organization. The postwar DDF evolved into a full-length play festival, but the rise of professionalism reduced its importance. Increasingly, Canadian adjudicators were hired and colonial ties were broken. In 1967 the DDF distinguished itself by convening an all-Canadian contest at a time when Canadian plays were not seen regularly. The organization was renamed Theatre Canada in 1970 and lovingly documented in Betty Lee's history *Love and Whisky* in 1973. But these were vain attempts to capture former glory. Money and interest dried up, and the Ottawa office of DDF-Theatre Canada closed in 1978.

Amateur theatres today continue to flourish in great numbers, usually in small communities or suburban areas and often still evincing a noticeable London or Parisian accent. They also function as focal points for multicultural expression (*see* THEATRE, MULTICULTURAL). Little theatres still serve an important training role and fill an avocational need. Without the Little Theatres and the DDF, the indigenous theatre would not have bridged the 2 wars. Being avocational, they were able to exist unsubsidized through a decade of economic depression. The roots of a national theatre in Canada were amateur, even though only a small number of groups, such as the Winnipeg Little Theatre, Workshop 14 in Calgary and the London Little Theatre, made the actual transition to professional status. *See also* DRAMA; STAGE AND COSTUME DESIGN. DAVID GARDNER

Liver Disease, *see* CANADIAN LIVER FOUNDATION.

Liverpool, NS, Town, pop 3295 (1986c), 3304 (1981c), inc 1897, is situated near the mouth of the Mersey R, at the head of Liverpool Bay, 115 km SW of Halifax. It occupies the site of a MICMAC village called *Ogomkegea* ("place of departure") and was called Port Rossignol by de Monts. Named after the English city, Liverpool was a fishing centre for New England from at least 1670 but was not settled until 1759, by New Englanders of Pilgrim stock. During the American Revolution, when privateers ran rampant along the coast damaging shipping, the townspeople fitted out the famed Liverpool privateers. As it became a major seaport in the 18th century, its SHIPBUILDING industry flourished and with it the TIMBER TRADE that sent products to Great Britain, the US and the Caribbean. The fall of the Bank of Liverpool, est 1871, ruined the county's fortunes and precipitated a long decline in the shipbuilding and timber industries. This prosperity was partially recovered with the establishment of the Mersey pulp and paper mill in 1929, and (reminiscent of the days of the privateers) with rum-running during the Depression. Fish and timber remain the town's main resources. JEAN PETERSON

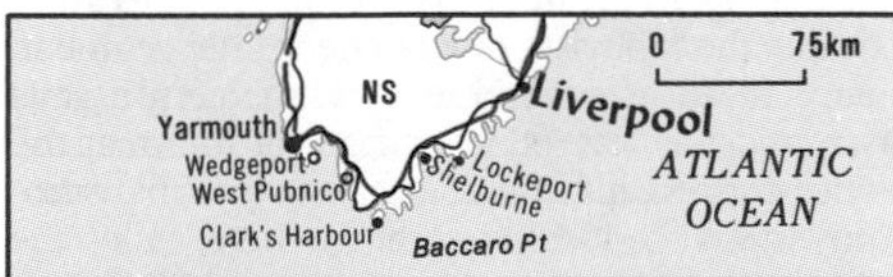

Liverwort, small terrestrial plant belonging, with MOSSES and hornworts, to division Bryophyta. Bryophytes show alternation of generations, ie, have 2 stages in the life cycle: a free-living, perennial gametophyte (sexual generation) and a short-lived sporophyte (asexual generation) that remains attached to and dependent on the gametophyte. The liverwort gametophyte is either a leafy stem or a thallus, ie, a flat, leafless expanse of cells (resembling the lobes of the liver, hence the name). The horizontally growing gametophytes have rhizoids (structures analogous to roots), which serve to attach them to the surface on which they grow. Most leafy liverworts have stems with 2 lateral rows of leaves; many species have a third row of reduced leaves on the underside of the stem. Liverwort sporophytes have a foot, embedded into the gametophyte tissues, and a spore capsule, normally raised above the gametophyte by a fragile stalk and persisting for only a day or so. Spores are released when the capsule wall ruptures, generally into 4 sections. Inside the capsules are hygroscopic cells (elaters), which help to disperse the spores. Many liverworts reproduce asexually by

Liverworts are rarely abundant in Canada, except in the rain forests of coastal BC (*photo by Mary W. Ferguson*).

gemmae, small groups of cells produced on the thallus or leafy stem. Since they lack any conducting tissues (xylem, phloem), liverworts mainly absorb water directly through leaves, stems or thallus. The 2 theories of liverwort evolution state that they developed from a primitive group of vascular plants (ie, those having true conducting tissues) or from some green algal ancestor. They belong to a group that lost much evolutionary potential by having the gametophyte generation dominant and by lacking conducting tissues, so that their size is greatly limited (most range from a few millimetres to 20 cm). Liverworts grow mostly in moist, shady places on rocks, trees, rotten wood, humus or soil. In Canada, they are rarely abundant in ground vegetation except in the temperate rain forests of coastal BC, where they can dominate ground cover and densely clothe branches and tree trunks. Over 7000 species occur worldwide, about 85% having leafy gametophytes. GUY R. BRASSARD

Lives of Girls and Women, a novel by Alice MUNRO (1971), as the title suggests, is a narrative of female experience as gathered in the adolescence of Del Jordan. With startling honesty, it recounts her early encounters with death, the problems posed by religion, and her growing awareness of romance and sexuality. The most remarkable characteristic of the novel is its ability to recapture the past (it is set for the most part in the 1940s) with remarkable skill, to examine some of the more vulgar experiences of sexuality and transform them into humour and art. While ostensibly set in a small town in western Ontario, the novel achieves a certain level of universality by modelling itself on the genre of the artist's novel, acquiring thereby an originality in Canadian letters by portraying the artist as a young woman. E.D. BLODGETT

Livesay, Dorothy, poet (b at Winnipeg 12 Oct 1909). A writer of journalism, short fiction, autobiography and literary criticism, Livesay is best known as a strong, sensitive poet dealing as capably with public and political issues as with personal and intimate emotion and reflection. She was senior woman writer in Canada during active and productive years in the 1970s and 1980s. Her mother, Florence Randal Livesay, journalist, poet and translator, and her father, J.F.B. Livesay, general manager of Canadian Press, encouraged her literary efforts from her first publication, *Green Pitcher* (1928). Educated at U of T and the Sorbonne, she worked in left politics during the 1930s, and subsequently won Gov Gen's Awards for *Day and Night* (1944) and *Poems for People* (1947). She trained as a teacher, taught in Northern Rhodesia [Zambia] 1959-63 and has served as university writer-in-residence. Her prolific publication continues undiminished, and her lifelong concern for women's rights and the identity of the woman artist has ripened with time. A major collection of her poetry, *Collected Poems: The Two Seasons*, was published in 1972. Recent work includes *A Public and Private Voice: Essays on the Life and Work of Dorothy Livesay* (1986). She became an Officer of the Order of Canada in 1987. R.D. MATHEWS

Liveyer (also liveyere, livyer, livier, liver), a Newfoundland term applied historically to a permanent resident of Newfoundland or Labrador, one who was not a migratory resident of the coast during the summer fishing season as was the BYE-BOAT keeper or Labrador stationer. Compared with the island's summer population, the liveyers were small in number throughout the 1600s, fewer than 1 in 6 summer residents remaining year-round. This component expanded during the 18th century so that by 1800 about 90% of the summer population of Newfoundland remained through the winter. ROBERT D. PITT

Lizard, common name for members of the most diverse of the 5 groups of living REPTILES. Most lizards occur in warm, sunny, dry climates. Some 3307 species have been recorded. Six types, ranging from 8-21 cm long, occur in Canada: northern alligator lizard (*Gerrhontus coeruleus principis*) in southern BC, including southern Vancouver I; western skink (*Eumeces skiltonianus*) in south-central BC; pigmy horned lizard (*Phrynosoma douglassii douglassi*) in the extreme S of the Okanagan Valley; eastern short-horned lizard (*P. d. brevirostre*) in SE Alberta and SW Saskatchewan; northern prairie skink (*E. septentrionalis septentrionalis*) in SW Manitoba; and 5-lined skink (*E. fasciatus*) in SE Ontario. Lizards are included with SNAKES in order Squamata of subclass Lepidosauria. Both have dry skin covered with epidermal scales. Most lizards have legs, a long tail, movable eyelids and well-developed ears. Some have adopted snakelike habits and may be very long and slender, with tiny or not externally visible legs. Some burrowing lizards have lost the eyes and ears. Snakes are thought to have evolved from lizard ancestors which underwent reduction of limbs, eyes and ears while adapting to a burrowing life-style.

Most lizards produce eggs which must be fertilized inside the female. Mating is preceded by complex courtship behaviour and by display and combat among males to defend territories and among females against each other. Most lizards form a leathery shell around eggs, which are laid in a protected site and abandoned by the female. In some species (eg, northern alligator lizard, horned lizards), females retain eggs inside their bodies until fully developed young are born. Some whiptail lizards and lacertas occur only as females which lay fertile eggs without mating, one of the few cases of parthenogenesis (a form of asexual reproduction) found among VERTEBRATES. The adaptation may have developed to allow small numbers of lizards to use small, isolated patches of suitable habitat.

Most lizards are predatory, feeding on small invertebrates. The S American tegus and Old World monitor lizards will eat other reptiles and even mammals. The Komodo dragon (a 3.5 m monitor), the world's largest lizard, can kill deer and wild pigs. Tropical New World iguanas and some Old World agamas are the only herbivorous lizards.

Despite their small size, most lizards are capable of fast movement and usually will easily outdistance a predator or human pursuer to cover. The limbs are held in a sprawling position directed outward from the sides, but when lizards run, the body is raised clear of the ground. A few, eg, Australian frilled lizard and basilisks of Central America, have large hind legs and can run with forebody and forelegs off the ground and the tail elevated as a counterweight. Two species, the gila monster of southwestern US and the Mexican beaded lizard, are poisonous. Their alertness, complex behaviour and often bizarre shapes, colours and colour patterns make lizards a rewarding and fascinating subject for study.

K.W. STEWART

Ljungh, Esse Willem, radio-drama producer, actor, director, teacher (b at Malmö, Sweden 1904). Educated in Sweden in arts and law, he immigrated to Canada in 1927, worked as a farmhand for 2 years and acquired his own farm near Radville, Sask. After losing his farm during the Depression he moved to Winnipeg to edit a small Swedish-language farm paper. He acted in the Winnipeg Little Theatre and during the late 1930s became interested in radio, first as an actor, then as audio technician, producer and director. He became famous for his imaginative use of sound, artistic integration of music and inspiring direction of actors. He joined the CBC in Winnipeg in 1942 and was transferred to Toronto in 1946. With Andrew ALLAN and J. Frank Willis he became one of Canadian radio's leading producers. His work ranged from the prestigious "Wednesday Night" series to the popular "Jake and The Kid" programs written by W.O. MITCHELL, the long-running soap opera "Brave Voyage" and the musical "G.E. Hour." He tried TV in the late 1950s but returned to radio and was national supervisor of radio drama when he retired in 1969. He was awarded the Diplôme d'honneur by the Canadian Conference of the Arts and the John Drainie Award for distinguished contribution to Canadian broadcasting. He is a Member of the Order of Canada. JOHN L. KENNEDY

Lloyd, Gweneth, ballet director, choreographer, teacher (b at Eccles, Eng 15 Sept 1901). As founding director and choreographer of what became the ROYAL WINNIPEG BALLET, Lloyd exemplifies the spirit of initiative and imagination that helped build Canada's cultural institutions. Trained first as a physical education instructor in England, she later studied Greek dance and BALLET. In 1927 she opened her own dance school in Leeds. In 1938, with former student Betty FARRALLY, Lloyd immigrated to Canada, settling in Winnipeg. There she quickly opened a school and Winnipeg Ballet Club – from which a full-fledged professional company developed. Apart from a National Film Board production of Lloyd's *Shadow on the Prairie* (1952), little record remains of the more than 30 ballets she choreographed for her company, 1939-52. The records of her ballets were destroyed in a 1954 fire at the Royal Winnipeg's studios. Lloyd left Winnipeg in 1950 to found a school in Toronto. In 1946 she helped establish, and began a long association with, the BANFF CENTRE'S summer dance program, becoming director of the program in 1950. With Farrally, Lloyd resettled in Kelowna, BC, in 1957, opening a new school. Lloyd's many honours include the Order of Canada (1977) and the Dance in Canada Award (1984). She is now retired.

MICHAEL CRABB

Lloyd, Woodrow Stanley, educator, politician, premier of Saskatchewan 1961-64 (b near Webb, Sask 16 July 1913; d at Seoul, South Korea 7 Apr 1972). Lloyd was best known for his fight for free universal medical care in Saskatchewan and for his contributions in the field of education. From 1939 to 1944, as vice-president and then president of the Saskatchewan Teachers' Federation and on the executive of the Canadian Teachers' Federation, Lloyd worked for better teaching conditions and higher standards. As minister of education in the CCF government 1944-60, he introduced larger school units to improve financing and facilities and articulated the "lighted school house" concept of continuing education for all. He became premier 7 Nov 1961, inheriting a bitter dispute over medical care which culminated in the withdrawal of doctors' services on 1 July 1962. He refused to abandon the principle of a universal government health plan, and his calmness, restraint and dignity in an explosive situation led to a settlement on July 23 (*see* SASKATCHEWAN DOCTORS' STRIKE). Lloyd resigned as leader of the Saskatchewan NDP on 6 July 1970 and left politics in 1971. He became representative of the UN Development Program in S Korea.

JEAN LARMOUR

Lloydminster, Alta-Sask, City, pop 17 356 (1986c), 15 031 (1981c), is located on the Saskatchewan-Alberta border, 300 km W of Prince Albert and 235 km E of Edmonton. It came into being with the arrival of the BARR COLONISTS in 1903. "Britannia Settlement" was the name in common usage before it was changed to Lloydminster in 1903 to honour Rev George Exton Lloyd, an Anglican minister who guided the destiny of the colonists after the departure of Rev Isaac Barr. When Saskatchewan and Alberta were created in 1905, the townsite found itself divided between the 2 provinces. The problem was solved in 1930 when the Saskatchewan town of Lloydminster and the Alberta village of the same name were amalgamated as the town of Lloydminster by order-in-council in both provinces. The town became the tenth city of both provinces in 1958 when it was raised to city status. Natural resources in the area include oil, natural gas, salt, gravel and coal. DON HERPERGER

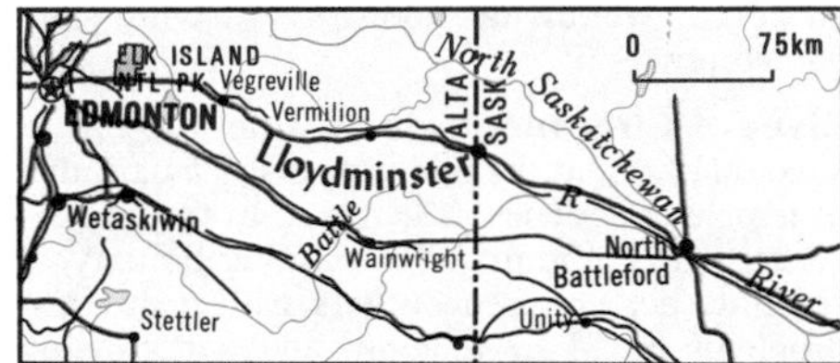

Lobbying The process through which individuals and groups articulate their interests and press them upon governmental decision makers in order to influence the determination of PUBLIC POLICY. Any citizen who attempts to influence a public policy decision is engaged in lobbying and may be considered a lobbyist, but in recent years lobbyists have come to be thought of as individuals who "for compensation" assist others to represent their concerns to government. The term "lobbying" is almost exclusively associated with politics and public policymaking, perhaps because it originated with the tendency of individuals anxious to influence legislation to gather in the lobbies leading to the legislative chamber in order to appeal personally to parliamentarians and congressmen – both Westminster and Washington claim to have originated the term – as they entered the chamber to debate and vote.

Lobbying is as ancient as the art of politics, but it first attracted widespread public interest and concern at the end of the 19th century when crusading journalists and reformers exposed its extensive abuse and corrupt application in American politics. By 1890 Massachusetts proclaimed an anti-lobbying Act which served as a model for the legislation of Maryland (1900), Wisconsin (1905) and a few of the other states. Based upon the publicity principle it required counsel and other legislative agents to register with the sergeant-at-arms giving the names and addresses of their employers and the date, term and character of their employment. Lobby regulations were passed in 9 other states in the single year of 1907. Improper lobbying was a felony in California, Georgia, Utah, Tennessee, Oregon, Montana and Arizona, though it was to be 1946 before similar measures were taken at the federal level.

Lobbying has been a part of Canadian politics from the earliest colonial period. The grants, monopolies and concessions that made possible the early voyages of Cartier, Gilbert, Frobisher, Hudson and others were obtained through lobbying at court; the decisions that favoured the FAMILY COMPACT and the CHÂTEAU CLIQUE were the result of lobbying the British Cabinet and Parliament. Once responsible government was attained, and then Confederation, lobbyists turned their attention to the federal and provincial governments. At first they focused on the political party, the legislature and the government of the day, but as government became more complex and its influence extended into virtually every aspect of social and economic life, lobbyists came to pay more attention to the bureaucracy and the Cabinet than to the legislature and to political parties. This is generally the case today, though in recent years the restoration to Parliament of a more significant voice in policy debate has encouraged some lobbyists to attempt to influence Members of Parliament as well as ministers and officials.

Popular stereotype depicts the lobbyist as a well-dressed, cigar-smoking individual who corrupts public officials in order to obtain their support for the schemes of moneyed interests. This figure is not entirely apocryphal. It derives from historical accounts and press reports of the many scandals – from the PACIFIC SCANDAL to the Oerlikon affair – that Canada, in common with other political systems, has experienced. But very few lobbyists work to achieve their ends through venal lobbying. The great majority earn their salaries by applying their knowledge of how policy is made and how to obtain access to the policy processes. Although we do not know how many lobbyists actually work in Ottawa and the provincial capitals, it is likely that the majority are salaried employees of interest groups, corporations and unions.

When we describe what lobbyists do we must first remember that knowledge is their chief tool; knowledge about the substance of policy and also about the policy process. Expert knowledge is the key that opens the door to government offices and permits the lobbyists to exercise influence, for in many instances government lacks expertise of its own and has few other sources of information. Policy-process information is also valuable since knowing who does what, and where, helps the lobbyist make the best use of the information he or she possesses. For example, the experienced lobbyist will know what minor technical problems can be handled by which junior officials, and where and when to take major policy issues to senior public servants and ministers. He or she will know which problems can be resolved with a single telephone call, and which will require the formation of coalitions of interests and the building of supportive public opinion that can be harnessed in mass public "lobbying."

The lobbyist's knowledge is brought to bear in one or other of 3 ways: by representing interests to government, by providing a "dating" service, or by "mapping" decision processes for clients. Representation involves articulating to officials, politicians and sometimes the general public the needs and views of particular interests. The permanent employees of trade associations and other pressure groups spend a great deal of time in this sort of activity. The "dating" service puts clients in touch with appropriate officials and advises them on how best to present their case. "Mapping" services are more elaborate and expensive since the lobbyist has to help the client develop a strategy for taking the proposal through the entire decision process. Many of the activities are quite routine and would not necessitate the establishment of lobbying concerns were it not that the public service has become extremely complex and regulation quite baffling for those who do not work regularly with government.

Most lobbyists seldom tackle broad policy issues. Rather they work on a "project basis"; they are concerned with helping their clients obtain such things as government supply contracts, industrial incentive grants; fisheries licences, access to natural resources or minor regulatory changes. Nor does this have to involve influence peddling. Instead, in the words of one lobbyist, it is the "dull, repetitive, time-consuming and expensive" task of advising clients as to how to apply for grants and submit proposals.

Even though it is generally above-board and frequently makes a positive contribution to government, in recent years lobbying has aroused a degree of public suspicion that has at times been expressed in calls for its regulation. This concern is rooted in a growing awareness of the role interest groups and lobbying firms have come to play in the policy process. There is an appreciation on the one hand that political parties have lost much of their traditional capacity to satisfy individual and local needs, and on the other that access to decision makers is increasingly hard to obtain. Those with the time or money to form interest groups have a competitive edge in the struggle to obtain access to the process. Not surprisingly, fears have grown that inequities are becoming entrenched in the policy process, giving the wealthy a degree of access denied to the average citizen. In addition to the problem of equity a succession of scandals – the Skyshops affair, the Hamilton harbour dredging scandal, the Oerlikon affair – have suggested that the integrity of the policy process may be too easily abused, prompting reformers to argue that lobby regulation is necessary to ensure openness in government.

In Sept 1985 Prime Minister Mulroney acknowledged these concerns by incorporating in a general policy statement on public-sector ethics a promise that the government would introduce legislation providing for the registration of lobbyists. Although this legislation did not materialize immediately, the PM's statement did initiate a debate on the registration issue. A government discussion paper was prepared and referred to the House of Commons Standing Committee on Elections, Privileges and Procedure which held hearings on the matter and reported in Jan 1987. The committee noted that some aspects of lobbying are already regulated, through, for example, the Criminal Code, which prohibits bribery and influence peddling, and various guidelines which have been provided for Parliamentarians, cabinet ministers and officials. The latter, however, have limited authority and the Cabinet deals with major abuses. Their capacity to foster openness and equity in government is limited. Consequently, the committee recommended instituting a limited system of registration. It defined lobbyists as individuals who, for compensation, represent third party interests directly or indirectly to government employees, or officers of nongovernment organizations who receive compensation to perform duties that include lobbying; individuals conducting mass mailings or advertising campaigns intended to influence government through public opinion, and lawyers and other professionals hired to carry out lobbying activities. The committee concluded that those seeking to influence government decisions should make their interests known both to the officials with whom they are dealing and to the public at large. It recommended that they be required to register with the deputy registrar general their own names and that of their firm, along with the names and places of business of their clients and the issue that is the object of their lobbying activity. The committee also urged lobbyists themselves to establish a method of self-regulation.

Lobster boats, Skinners Pond, PEI. Several Atlantic coast communities are dependent on the lobster fishery (*photo by Richard Vroom*).

The government will introduce legislation in accordance with the committee's recommendations. The recurrent abuse of the policy process by a small group of lobbyists virtually guarantees that the public will insist on a closer regulation of the ways in which the lobbying industry as a whole participates in public decision making.

A. PAUL PROSS

Reading: J. Sawatsky, *The Insiders: Government, Business and the Lobbyists* (1987).

Lobster, term applied to 4 groups of decapod ("10-footed") CRUSTACEANS: the coral, slipper, spiny and clawed lobsters. They comprise 163 species. The American lobster (*Homarus americanus*), found along the Atlantic coastline and Continental Shelf from Labrador to N Carolina, is the only species occurring in Canadian waters. It attains the greatest weight of any living arthropod: the largest male *H. americanus* on record weighed over 19 kg. Lobsters are not native to the Pacific coast of Canada, but from 1896 to 1966 there were at least 11 separate introductions of American lobsters into BC waters, and even more along the US West Coast. In Canada, introductions probably totalled no more than 5000 adults. Although American lobsters seem able to survive in the Pacific, there is no evidence that any of the introductions has resulted in a reproducing population. The clawed *Homarus* genus is the *homard* of French cuisine. The clawless spiny lobster [Fr *langouste*] is also known as CRAYFISH. *See also* CRUSTACEAN RESOURCES.

D.E. AIKEN

Lobstick (or lopstick) is a tall, conspicuously situated spruce or pine tree with all but its topmost branches stripped or lopped off. This was done by northern Indians, and later by voyageurs, to turn trees into talismans, landmarks or memorials.

JOHN ROBERT COLOMBO

Local Elections are the procedures by which citizens in a community choose the MUNICIPAL GOVERNMENT. Federal and provincial election systems are generally designed by a nonpartisan independent agency, and since the 1960s responsibility for redesigning constituency boundaries for local elections has sometimes been delegated to independent boundary commissions (*see* REDISTRIBUTION), reducing the possibilities for gerrymandering or for the drawing of election rules to the advantage of incumbents.

Constituency boundaries, known as "wards" in municipal elections, may conform to one of 3 types. In smaller urban centres, election at-large is common; the municipality as a whole is the constituency. Vancouver is the largest city using this system, which works to the advantage of corporate, professional and blue-ribbon civic groups. To reduce the costs of city-wide campaigning, other large cities such as Edmonton, or Winnipeg prior to 1971, have adopted division into a few multi-member "strip" wards that do not respect natural geographic or community boundaries. Wards may also be drawn in a "block" design to encompass neighbourhoods, a system favoured by left-of-centre politicians and spokesmen for community associations and some minority groups. Montréal, Toronto and now Winnipeg elect on this basis.

Canadian local elections are nominally nonpartisan. City elections, unlike provincial and federal elections, are held at a fixed time (designated by the Municipal Government Act). Parties are not identified on the ballot (names are listed alphabetically), and most candidates are elected as independents or are loosely attached to a local party. Voter turnout is low (30% is considered good), and incumbents enjoy a considerable advantage because voters recognize their names. At-large elections magnify these problems because the voter must make so many ballot choices. To become a candidate usually requires only a nominal cash deposit and the filing of a petition on the candidate's behalf by a small number of electors.

Historically the right to vote was tied to property holdings, and the property had to be of a certain value (although this restriction became unimportant in the 20th century because the required values were not adjusted for inflation). The tenant of a house is a property holder; a lodger is not. An apartment dweller may or may not be considered a property holder, depending on the relevant legislation. The practice of plural voting, ie, being entitled to vote in each municipality or ward (sometimes in each polling division) where property is owned, was widespread until the last 2 decades. Nonresident property owners still possess a local vote in several provinces (eg, Ontario). Since the mid-1960s, the provinces have widely extended the FRANCHISE so that it is virtually universal and a right of citizenship. There is frequently a municipal enumeration before an election. Votes are normally tabulated on a plurality basis, and the person (or persons, where there is a multi-member ward or at-large election) receiving the most votes is declared elected; in the past, various provinces, eg, Manitoba, have permitted their municipalities to employ a form of proportional representation using a transferable ballot. Finally, unlike federal and provincial politicians, municipal councillors are elected for an established term of 2 or 3 years, which may have policy implications, eg, unpopular or controversial decisions would not normally be expected of a council in the months immediately prior to the fixed voting date. *See also* CITY POLITICS. JAMES LIGHTBODY

Reading: D.J.H. Higgins, *Urban Canada: Its Government and Politics* (1977).

Local Government, the level of government below the provinces. The most important local governments are the MUNICIPAL GOVERNMENTS. Under the constitution, the provinces have exclusive jurisdiction over municipal affairs (*see* MUNICIPAL-PROVINCIAL RELATIONS). Each province has established a slightly different system of municipal institutions, but there is a strong family resemblance among these systems, because they are all derived from British or American models. Canada's first uniform municipal system was established in 1849 in what was then Canada West [Ontario]. The other provinces followed the Ontario example, and most of the populated area of Canada is now organized into municipalities, although there are great tracts of sparsely populated land that remain unincorporated for municipal purposes. In the latter areas, local administration falls to the PROVINCIAL GOVERNMENT or the territorial government, although in some places quasi-municipal institutions, such as improvement districts, have been formed.

A local government is distinguished from a local administrative office of the province in that it is chosen by and held accountable to the local community, conventionally by means of LOCAL ELECTION. Other local administrative bodies may also be elected. This is generally true not only for SCHOOL BOARDS, but may also be true for public utilities commissions, parks boards and other special-purpose agencies. The municipal council is therefore not the only elective local government in most Canadian communities. There is a further complication in that many other more or less autonomous local agencies – harbour commissions, library boards and police commissions – have been established by the provincial or federal governments or by the municipalities themselves. However they are constituted, these agencies often operate like independent local governments. In no Canadian community is the situation quite similar to that in metropolitan Chicago, where more than 1000 special-purpose and general-purpose local governments are at work, but the system of local government is everywhere complex and is unique to the community concerned. The bigger the community, the more complex the system: in metropolitan TORONTO, for example, researchers have identified more than 100 authorities that could be classified as "local governments."

Despite these complexities, the municipalities remain the most important elements in systems of local government. In most places, the municipalities are the only general-purpose governments at the local level and the municipal council is therefore usually the focus of attention in local politics. The council is expected to concern itself with matters of general interest to the community and to represent the community in its relations with the outside world. The powers granted to the municipalities under the Municipal Acts of the various provinces reflect this, for municipal councils are the repositories for local government functions not assigned to other agencies. The multiplication of special-purpose bodies at the local level itself is testimony to the role of the municipalities, since these bodies have been formed to relieve the general-purpose governments of the ostensibly specialized functions that they are ill equipped, as general governments, to perform.

In each province, there are different classes of municipalities. The most important distinction is between urban and rural authorities. The latter – called TOWNSHIPS, parishes, districts, rural municipalities, etc – have the most limited functions. Generally, their most important duty is to maintain roads. People in rural areas have rarely been willing to pay for very active local government. On the other hand, in urban areas where there is a need and demand for more government activity, the situation is different. Urban municipalities are classifed by size as villages, towns and cities; to be reclassified upwards means an increase in prestige and in the powers of the municipal council. City councils are the most active municipal governments and have played a major role historically in developing new public services and the regulations necessary to modern life.

The relative increase in the activities of the provincial governments since 1945 is partly the result of an effort to make city-quality services available elsewhere. In the course of this effort, functions once performed at the municipal level (if they were performed at all) have been taken over by the provincial governments. This applies particularly to social services. What remains at the core of municipal activity is a set of economic functions. Municipal councils have always been expected to serve as agencies for local economic development. Most of them regard it as their first responsibility to provide the infrastructure for the local economy, eg, physical facilities such as roads and sewers, and basic services such as POLICE and fire protection. Since 1945, the urban municipalities in particular have attempted to play a more positive role by using physical planning controls to set the pace and determine the form of economic development. Planning issues have thus become central to municipal politics.

Municipal councils and other elective local authorities in Canada are generally quite small. Most comprise from 5 to 15 members; only the largest municipalities are liable to have bigger councils. It is usually feasible for the council (or school board) to act as its own Cabinet, with the mayor (or chairman) taking the leading role. Because most councillors are theoretically nonpartisan, collegial decision making is possible. Most councils divide themselves into committees for the different municipal functions, and this eases the burden on the central body. The traditional tendency to delegate duties to semi-autonomous agencies (whose boards are largely appointed by the municipal councils) further reduces the scope of responsibility at the centre. Since the beginning of this century, critics have been pointing to the problems arising from this dispersal of municipal responsibilities and from the connected emphasis on lay participation in administration. As a result, there have been constant efforts to make local government more professional and to centralize managerial control. In some municipalities, full administrative responsibility is given to a single manager or administrative board, acting under the political direction of the council. Elsewhere – especially in large communities – the function of executive control has been taken over by a committee of the council. In either case, ordinary councillors have become more removed from day-to-day business and stronger managerial control has been established.

Municipal governments must generally depend on real property taxes for most of their own revenues. This limits their financial capacity, and forces them to rely on provincial grants, which limit municipal discretion. Indeed, the municipalities and other local governments have been used increasingly as mere administrative agencies of the province and have been subjected as such to tight controls. Even when local governments are acting independently, using their own revenues for their own purposes, they are subject to the laws and regulations of the province. These may severely restrict local freedom of action, and force the governments concerned to seek provincial approval for capital spending, land-use regulations and other items of local concern. The provincial department of municipal affairs is normally the most prominent agency of control, but other departments and administrative tribunals (eg, the Ontario Municipal Board) are also involved. Local governments simply do not have the autonomy in relation to the provinces that the latter enjoy in relation to Ottawa.

Many critics have claimed that local government could be strengthened by consolidating existing authorities into larger units with wider responsibilities. This would mean eliminating most, if not all, of the special-purpose local governments and redrawing municipal boundaries to bring suburbs and satellite towns under the control of city councils. In rural areas, whole regions or counties might be unified. However, the provinces have little incentive to create local governments that would rival them in power and prestige. Thus, the trend throughout Canada has been to make comparatively minor adjustments in boundaries and functions, and to preserve local government arrangements in the face of socioeconomic change.

The most obvious recent development has been the double-tiering of municipal government. The COUNTY councils of central Canada have traditionally provided a second-level of municipal government outside the cities. These councils are composed of representatives of neighbouring rural and small urban municipalities and exist to provide common facilities and services. This model for joint action was not adopted in major urban areas until 1953, when the municipality of Metropolitan Toronto was established. The new authority was in effect a metropolitan county council for Toronto and its suburbs. To deal with problems of metropolitan development and planning, it was given greater powers than any ordinary county, and it was successful enough to inspire many imitators in Canada and elsewhere. Most of the major cities in Canada now have metropolitan or regional governments of this sort. The model has also been applied outside the metropolitan areas to strengthen or replace existing county government (as in Ontario) or to create a new level of regional municipal government (as in BC).

The creation of new units of regional municipal government reflects a more general tendency in the past few decades to enlarge the scale of local administration. Health, education and welfare administration – traditionally entrusted to special-purpose local authorities – has generally been regionalized, if not provincialized. Thus the independent local authorities that remain in these fields tend to be on a larger scale. The municipalities have been less affected by consolidation than have the school boards; generally they have maintained their existence even when overarching REGIONAL GOVERNMENTS have been established. Some consolidation has occurred, especially of very small municipalities, but there are still some 5000 municipal governments in Canada, and new ones continue to be formed. It is difficult for provincial governments to persuade local communities to take responsibility for their own affairs without organizing municipal councils. Once created, these councils become symbols of local autonomy and are not easily eliminated.

To those concerned about comprehensive planning and administrative co-ordination, the fragmentation of authority at the local level among thousands of municipalities and even more numerous special-purpose bodies is the source of much anxiety. However, it is not clear that consolidation would increase the efficiency or effectiveness of local government, because bureaucratic centralization creates its own problems. Whatever advantage there is in the present system arises from the opportunities it affords for local initiative and citizen participation. To simplify present arrangements and consolidate authority in the hands of strong regional councils would be to close off many of these opportunities. This may occur regardless, but so long as the demand remains for effective local control over local public activities, the system of government at this level will remain as complex as it is now. WARREN MAGNUSSON

Reading: D.J.H. Higgins, *Local and Urban Politics in Canada* (1986); Warren Magnusson and Andrew Sancton, eds, *City Politics in Canada* (1983); C.R. and S.N. Tindal, *Local Government in Canada* (2nd ed, 1984).

Lochhead, Kenneth Campbell, painter (b at Ottawa 22 May 1926). He attended the Pennsylvania Academy of Fine Arts, 1945-49, and in 1950 was appointed director of the School of Art, Regina. He was one of the REGINA FIVE and was instrumental in the establishment of the Emma Lake Workshop for Artists. His non-referential works of the 1960s reflected the New York aesthetic imparted via workshop leaders, such as American artists Barnett Newman and Kenneth Noland, and he was included in Clement Greenberg's 1964 "Post-Painterly Abstraction" exhibition. Lochhead taught at U of Man 1964-73, York U 1973-74 and U of Ottawa from 1975. In the 1970s he reintroduced recognizable subject matter into paintings which nevertheless remain largely intuitive, colourist exercises. Lochhead's contribution as an artist and educator has been affirmed by several notable commissions and awards, including the Order of Canada in 1971. A major survey exhibition of his paintings was organized by the Art Gallery of Windsor in 1977. NORMAN ZEPP

Lock, Édouard, choreographer (b at Casablanca, Morocco 3 Mar 1954). He first attracted attention with *Rémus* in 1978, choreographed for Nouvelle aire. He founded Édouard Lock and Dancers 1981 (later Lock/Danseurs; currently LA LA LA). His major works include *Lily Marlène in the Jungle* (1981), *Oranges* (1982) and *Businessman in the Process of Becoming an Angel* (1983), a musical. Lock aspires not to aesthetics in style but to maximum risk, emphasizing high energy, contradictory physical impulses and gestural detail. A predilection for on-stage litter indicates that he may be veering towards performance art. He received the Jean A. Chalmers Choreographic Award in 1982. During 1985-86 the troupe toured Canada, the US and Europe with its production of *Human Sex.* KATI VITA

Locke, John Lambourne, astronomer (b at Brantford, Ont 1 May 1921). After service in the Royal Canadian Navy in WWII, Locke graduated from U of T in 1946. He received his doctorate in 1949 and was appointed astrophysicist at the Dominion Observatory, Ottawa, that year and chief of its stellar physics division in 1959. From 1959 until 1962 he was officer in charge of the new Dominion Radio Astrophysical Observatory near Penticton, BC. In 1966 he was appointed radio astronomer in the radio and electrical engineering division of the NATIONAL RESEARCH COUNCIL. He became associate director of the division in 1970 and was first director of the council's Herzberg Inst of Astrophysics from 1975 to 1985. Locke was a member of the Canadian team that in 1967 successfully combined simultaneous observations from radio telescopes thousands of kilometres apart, and the team received a Rumford Premium from the American Academy of Arts and Sciences. A.H. BATTEN

Lockhart, Grace Annie, pioneer of women's university education (b at Saint John 22 Feb 1855; d at Charlottetown 18 May 1916). On 25 May 1875, Lockhart received a bachelor of science and English literature from Mt Allison Coll, Sackville, NB, and thus became the first woman in the British Empire to receive a bachelor's degree. Although her later life was spent in a more conventional role, as the wife of the Methodist minister J.L. Dawson, Lockhart's academic achievement as a student provided clear evidence of the justice of women's claim to full rights in the field of higher education. JOHN G. REID

Locomotives and Rolling Stock A locomotive is a self-propelled vehicle which hauls nonpowered vehicles on railway track. The first locomotive used in Canada was the *Dorchester*, built by Robert Stephenson and Co in England (1835). It ran between La Prairie and St-Jean, Qué, on Canada's first railway, the CHAMPLAIN AND SAINT LAWRENCE (1836). It had a 0-4-0 wheel arrangement (no front truck, no rear truck, 4 main wheels) with 1.2 m diameter driving wheels. In working order it weighed $5\frac{1}{2}$ t and ran at an average speed of 23 km/h. The first locomotive to be constructed in Canada was built by the James Good family (1853) of Toronto. Named *Toronto*, the locomotive had a set of 4 driving wheels and 4 small front wheels for better travel through curves. This wheel configuration, 4-4-0, was referred to as the American type and was the predominant style of locomotive during the 1850-90 period. By 1887 the CANADIAN PACIFIC RAILWAY owned nearly 400 of these locomotives.

The *Toronto* was the first locomotive manufactured in Canada. On 16 Apr 1853, it was moved out of the James Good plant, Toronto, for use by the Ontario, Simcoe & Huron Union Rail Road, the first steam-operated railway in Ontario (*courtesy Canadian National*).

The Pacific locomotive was introduced in Canada in 1905 to provide faster service for passenger trains. This locomotive had larger cylinders than the American, greater boiler capacity and tremendous hauling power. During the first part of the 20th century. locomotives continued to grow in size and power output. In 1927 CANADIAN NATIONAL RAILWAYS introduced the Northern locomotive. It had wheels in 4-8-4 configuration and was used for freight and passenger service east of the Rockies. At about the same time, CPR brought into service 2 types of locomotives, the Royal Hudson (4-6-4 configuration) and the Selkirk. The Royal Hudson locomotive was used for high-speed passenger service. The Selkirks (2-10-4 configuration) were the largest locomotives to operate in Canada and were used in the Rockies between Calgary and Kamloops.

The diesel engine, invented by Rudolf Diesel in the late 1890s, was first used in a diesel-electric locomotive in the US (1924). CN Railways operated the first diesel-electric locomotive in Canada. Built in 1929, it was actually 2 locomotives coupled, developing 950 kW of power each. Until the end of WWII diesel locomotives in use in Canada were low-horsepower switching engines. After the war, railways began to use diesel-electric locomotives for main-line freight and passenger service. By 1960 both CN and CP railways had stopped using steam locomotives in regularly scheduled trains.

The diesel-electric locomotive uses a diesel engine to power an electric generator. The generator provides electrical energy to drive the motors on each locomotive axle. Diesel-electric locomotives are more economical to operate than steam locomotives. They have higher fuel efficiency, lower maintenance requirements and fewer breakdowns. Several units can be coupled for long trains, requiring only one engineer to operate all of them. Today most freight trains are hauled by units of approximately 220 kW (3000 hp) with 4 or 6 axles. Locomotives for passenger trains have higher gearing which gives them a higher normal operating speed.

The first electric locomotives in Canada went into service in 1906, when the St Clair tunnel at Sarnia was electrified to overcome problems with steam locomotive smoke. The Mount Royal tunnel in Montréal was electrified in 1915. Electric locomotives are clean and have low maintenance. They are not dependent on a single energy source; they can use electricity generated by coal, oil, nuclear or hydropower. Electric locomotives have the ability to withstand overload power levels for short periods, making them well suited to mountainous regions where steep grades and heavy trains predominate. Their fast acceleration makes them preferable for passenger service. They have 2 major disadvantages: they can run only where overhead wire (catenary) for electric power has been installed; and they and their power supply equipment are expensive and thus economical only in regions of heavy traffic.

Rolling stock consists of nonpowered railway cars for the transport of freight and passengers. On the earliest railways, passenger cars were merely modified stagecoaches. Freight cars were of 2 basic types: open-deck flatcars and enclosed boxcars. Until 1910 most rolling stock was constructed of wood on iron or steel frames. Today, freight and passenger cars are constructed of steel and aluminum. Modern freight cars are capable of carrying up to 100 t of freight. Freight cars are of a wide variety: boxcars for general merchandise; tank cars for liquids; refrigerator cars for perishable goods; hoppers and covered hoppers for bulk commodities; flatcars for large machinery, containers and highway trailers; tri-level automobile carriers; plus various special-purpose freight cars. The caboose, the last car in the freight train, provides office space for the train crew as well as a position from which to observe the train.

The passenger coach is the standard piece of railway passenger rolling stock, seating usually 60 to 90 people. Commuter cars used in short runs have higher-density seating. Club cars are the premium of passenger rolling stock, providing more room per passenger as well as an attendant for service. For long-distance rail travel, sleeping cars provide berths and small rooms for overnight accommodation. On-board meals are provided in a dining car, and at the seat in club cars.

Locomotives are constructed in Canada by General Motors Diesel of London, Ont, which builds locomotives from the designs of the Electro-Motive Division of General Motors in the US. Freight cars are constructed in Canada by the following companies: Hawker Siddeley (Trenton, NS); CanCar Rail (Thunder Bay, Ont); National Steel Car Corporation of Hamilton, Ont; Procor, Ltd, of Oakville, Ont (builders of tank cars); and Marine Industries of Sorel, Qué. Passenger cars are constructed by Bombardier and CanCar Rail.

Future designs of locomotives will be influenced by fuel economics. Diesel-electric locomotives will probably be made more fuel-efficient.

Electric locomotives may be placed in service as the price of diesel fuel increases. Research is being carried out on the use of coal as a fuel in diesel locomotives. For passenger service, higher-speed trains will be placed in service, perhaps in advanced electric or magnetically levitated and propelled trains. Freight cars will become more lightweight in construction. Containerization of cargo will increase the ability to transfer freight between the various transportation modes. Highway tractor-trailers with railway wheels for train service will reduce the need for flatcars and hence reduce train weight. *See also* RAILWAYS, TRACKS AND YARDS. JEFFERY YOUNG

Locoweed, common name for plants of genera *Astragalus* and *Oxytropis* of the pea family (Leguminosae), notorious for causing livestock poisoning. *Astragalus* is also known as milk vetch. Both genera have pealike flowers and featherlike leaves. *Oxytropis* flowers have lower "keel" petals prolonged to points; plants are usually stemless. *Astragalus* species have blunt keels; stems are evident. Both grow in clumps of spikes; height and colours vary. Over 1000 *Astragalus* and about 300 *Oxytropis* species are found worldwide, 40 and 15, respectively, in Canada. Arctic or alpine species are unimportant to domestic animals. The most important Canadian plains species are *Oxytropis lambertii,* southern Manitoba and Saskatchewan; *O. campestris,* BC to Manitoba; and *O. sericea,* Alberta. Poisonous *Astragalus* species include *A.bisulcatus, A. racemosus* and *A. pectinatus,* all found in Canada. *Astragalus* species accumulate selenium from soil, but the toxic principle is not clearly established. "Loco," Spanish for "crazy," refers to peculiar movements of poisoned horses. In Canada most poisonings occur among cattle. *See also* POISONOUS PLANTS. J.M. GILLETT

Lodge, Rupert Clendon, philosopher (b at Manchester, Eng 1886; d at St Petersburg, Fla 1 Mar 1961). He went to the US in 1914, then to U of A and finally to U of Man, where he spent most of his career. Lodge was the most widely read of all philosophers in Canada and his books were popular in the US. *An Introduction to Logic* (1920) portrays his commitment to idealism, though his later philosophy of pluralism was his public trademark. Throughout a series of books, he developed his tripartite theory: there will always be 3 kinds of responses to every philosophical question – that of a realist, a pragmatist and an idealist. His publications include several works on Plato. Lodge's theory of philosophical pluralism is applied rigorously in his books *The Questioning Mind* and *The Philosophy of Education* (1937), *The Philosophy of Business* (1945) and *Applying Philosophy* (1951). *The Great Thinkers* (1949, 1964) continues to be consulted. ELIZABETH A. TROTT

Log Houses are associated with pioneer settlement, past and present, and Canada's forests provided ready building material. West Coast Indians used log frames for their large plank houses long before the arrival of European settlers. Most of the first farmhouses in New France were constructed of posts driven vertically into the ground, a technique used in NW France and by some local Indians. Later, the posts were placed on a sill or foundation above ground level. This method was displaced by the *pièce-sur-pièce* technique: roughly squared, relatively short logs were laid horizontally, to meet at rabbeted corners. Tapered ends of the logs fitted into slotted vertical posts at house corners and along the walls. Fur traders carried this technique into the Red River valley and the HBC adopted it as its standard building form (called "Red River frame" or "Hudson's Bay Co frame") for its posts across the continent.

A wide variety of size and complexity in log houses characterized southern Ontario settlements. LOYALIST settlers introduced "Pennsylvanian" or "American" log houses, with horizontal logs interlocked at the house corners by a variety of techniques, a style originating with 17th-century Swedish-Finnish colonists on the Delaware R, refined by later German settlers and adopted by far-ranging Scots-Irish pioneers. Although most log houses were later replaced by houses constructed of other materials, many are still occupied as residences. Later immigrants to the PRAIRIE WEST often patterned their first log houses after customary forms of their homelands (eg, Ukraine). In the subarctic forests, log houses still provide comfortable shelter for trappers and woodsmen. Their attractive appearance and thermal efficiency make them popular not only with summer cottagers across Canada, but among many people with a renewed interest in traditional housing. WILLIAM C. WONDERS

Reading: T. Ritchie et al, *Canada Builds 1867-1967* (1967); William C. Wonders, "Log Dwellings in Canadian Folk Architecture," *Annals of the Association of American Geographers,* 69:2 (1979).

Mt Logan, named for Sir William Logan, is the highest mountain in Canada (*photo by Richard Harrington*).

Sir William Edmond Logan, a brilliant geologist who, as the first director of the Geological Survey of Canada, forged Canada's first public scientific endeavour (*courtesy National Archives of Canada/C-119978*).

Logan, John Daniel, writer, teacher (b at Antigonish, NS 2 May 1869; d at Milwaukee, Wis 24 Jan 1929). Though engaging in many occupations during his life and publishing poetry, literary and music criticism, literary history and composition texts, Logan is probably most renowned for his claim to have taught the first university course on Canadian literature (at Acadia in 1915) and for a ferocious battle he conducted with Archibald MacMechan of Dalhousie about the teaching of Canadian literature there. A brilliant student, completing BA, MA and PhD degrees, he worked in advertising, archives and journalism as well as teaching for many years in American colleges and universities. R.D. MATHEWS

Reading: J.D. Logan and D. French, *Highways of Canadian Literature* (1924).

Logan, Mount, elev 5950 m, is Canada's highest mountain, named after Sir William E. LOGAN by Prof I.C. Russell who first saw it during an attempted ascent of Mt St Elias in 1890. Situated in the Yukon T's St Elias Mts, it is one of the world's most massive mountain blocks, rising abruptly 4150 m above the flat Seward Glacier on the south side. The mountain is largely composed of granodiorite, a granitic rock of intrusive origin. Multiple summits rise above a NW-SE elongated snow and ice plateau varying in elevation between 4500 m and 5400 m and extending over a distance of 19 km. Three of the summits exceed 5890 m in elevation. In 1925, a joint Canadian-US expedition, led by A.H. MACCARTHY, made the first ascents of the Weak Peak (5915 m) and the High Peak (5950 m, then believed to be 6050 m high). The mountain has now been climbed by 13 different routes. For more than a decade, ending in 1980, a high-altitude physiology research program was conducted by a joint US-Canadian medical team from a camp at 5303 m, supported by the Arctic Institute of North America and the Canadian Armed Forces. Meteorological and glaciological research has been carried out on the NW col (5340 m). GERALD HOLDSWORTH

Logan, Sir William Edmond, geologist, first director of the GEOLOGICAL SURVEY OF CANADA (b at Montréal 20 Apr 1798; d at Castle Malgwyn, Cilgerran, S Wales 22 June 1875). Logan identified and mapped the major geological structures of the Province of Canada, in particular the Laurentian and Huronian series of the Precambrian SHIELD. He attended Alexander Skakel's school in Montréal and the Edinburgh High School, Scotland. In 1816 he took a year of medical studies at the U of Edinburgh before entering an uncle's business. From 1831 Logan managed the Forest Copper Works near Swansea, in South Wales. A systematic thinker by nature, and anxious to find a reliable source of coal, he mapped the nearby coal seams topographically and cross-sectionally. These highly accurate maps were adopted by the Geological Survey of Great Britain. In 1840 Logan read to the Geological Soc of London his theory of the *in situ* formation of coal, which enabled geologists to determine the location of workable deposits of carboniferous strata. Logan's reputation as a geologist, his Canadian birth, and his social and family connections in Montréal secured him the position of geologist of the Province of Canada in Apr 1842.

By 1844 Logan and one assistant, Alexander MURRAY, had divided the geological formations of the province into 3 main divisions; he concluded reluctantly that none could be expected to yield coal. But Logan justified continued public funding of the Survey in other ways. He founded a geological museum; mapped the often uncharted lands he surveyed; analysed the copper-bearing N shore of Lk Superior. As a result of his outstanding collection of Canadian minerals and his geological map of Canada, exhibited at London's Crystal Palace in 1851, Logan became the first native Canadian inducted into the Royal Society of London for achievements in Canada. Similarly, at the Paris Exposition in 1855, he was awarded the Cross of the Legion of Honour. A knighthood followed in 1856. While the Survey continued investigations in both laboratory and field, Logan in 1863 published *Geology of Canada*, followed in 1865 by an atlas and in 1869 by a larger geological map. This masterly analysis of Canada's geological structures and economic minerals earned Logan the Royal Soc's Gold Medal in 1867.

The enormous expansion of the Geological Survey after Confederation had been anticipated by Logan as a natural development. He retired to South Wales in 1869 and was succeeded by A.R.C. SELWYN. Undaunted by the "Herculean task," Logan had forged Canada's first public scientific endeavour from its initial precarious decades into a permanent institution.

SUZANNE E. ZELLER

Reading: B.J. Harrington, *Life of Sir William E. Logan* (1883); Morris Zaslow, *Reading the Rocks* (1975).

Logo, a symbol, mark or word used by a corporation or other organization to distinguish its products, services or identity from those of anyone else. First used in 1937, the term was originally an abbreviation for "logogram" or "logotype" (both derived in part from Gk *logos*, "word"). It came into general use in Canada among marketers and designers in the 1960s, and by the mid-1970s it had become, to the layman, a synonym for "trademark."

One of the first details a new company must consider is its corporate image, reflected in the design of a symbol to be used in advertising and on packaging, vehicles and stationery. A long-established company may redesign an old trademark or adopt a new one, as CANADIAN NATIONAL RAILWAYS did in 1960. For many years CNR had used a realistic maple leaf as a frame for a dark square within which appeared "Canadian National Railways" in white, each word under the next. The designing of a new mark was entrusted to James Valkus of New York, who asked Toronto designer Allan R. Fleming to take on the assignment. After months of work, Fleming joined the letters C and N into one continuous flowing line, to symbolize the movement of people, materials and messages across the country. The design, accepted by CN, created a national controversy. There were complaints that it looked like a "tapeworm rampant" or the numeral 3 on its back; but around the world the idea of having a simple, bold logo had come into vogue.

Many Canadian firms adopted new corporate symbols such as the M for the BANK OF MONTREAL, designed by Hans Kleefeld of Stewart & Morrison Ltd, who also designed the AIR CANADA symbol of a maple leaf within an open circle. Burton Kramer of Burton Kramer Associates created the animated C symbol for the CANADIAN BROADCASTING CORPORATION-Société-Radio-Canada. The Canadian Confederation Centennial symbol, a maple leaf composed of 11 equilateral triangles to represent the 10 provinces and the territories, was the work of Stuart Ash of Gottschalk & Ash Ltd, and Georges Beaupré designed the NATIONAL FILM BOARD symbol representing the eyes of mankind seeing the world. *See also* GRAPHIC ART AND DESIGN.

FRANCES E.M. JOHNSTON

Reading: Yasaburo Kuwayama, *Trademarks & Symbols*, 2 vols (1973); C.J. Werkman, *Trademarks* (1974).

VIA Rail logo (*courtesy Canapress Photo Service*).

Lombardo, Guy (Gaetano Alberto), bandleader, violinist (b at London, Ont 19 June 1902; d at Houston, Tex 5 Nov 1977). His dance band, the Royal Canadians, was the most popular in N America, selling some 300 million records in over 50 years, despite critical disdain for its bland style. In 1923 Lombardo went to Cleveland, Ohio, together with other London musicians, including his brothers: Carmen (1903-71), a saxophonist, singer and later successful songwriter ("Coquette," "Boo Hoo," etc), and Lebert (b 1904), a trumpeter. In 1924 they took the name Royal Canadians. Their New Year's Eve broadcasts (later telecasts) from New York's Roosevelt Grill – the band's base 1929-62 – were a traditional part of N American celebrations, known especially for their "Auld Lang Syne" theme. MARK MILLER

London, Ont, the seat of Middlesex County, is centrally located in the SW peninsula of the province, on the Québec-Windsor corridor midway between Toronto and Windsor. Due S lies Lk Erie, with Lk Huron to the NW. London's market and service area to the N and NE includes much highly productive farmland. To the SW and SE lie intensive cash-crop areas, especially Canada's main tobacco-growing area. Noted as a financial, educational and medical centre, London is also a regional base for business and government.

Settlement Originally within the territory of the Attiwandaronk nation (NEUTRALS), London began as a 405 ha site reserved by John Graves SIMCOE 1793 as the future provincial capital. There were then few European settlers W of Lk Ontario, but after Thomas TALBOT's colonization scheme expanded N from Lk Erie, it became expedient to relocate the seat of the London Dist at the reserved townsite. Construction of the masonry courthouse – a fortresslike structure with crenellated towers – followed the beginning of formal settlement in 1826.

Population: 269 140 (1986c), 254 280 (1981c); 326 817 (1986 CMA), 283 668 (1981A CMA)
Rate of Increase: (*1981-86*): (City) 5.8% (CMA) 4.7%
Rank in Canada: Eleventh (by CMA)
Date of Incorporation: Town 1847; City 1855
Land Area: (City) 177 km (CMA) 2105.07 km
Elevation: 278
Climate: Average daily temp, July 20.3 C, Jan -6.6 C; Yearly precip 909.4 mm; Hours of sunshine 1894.6 per year

Development SW Ontario saw a large influx of settlers during the 1830s and the new town grew apace. The REBELLIONS OF 1837 led to the stationing in London of the largest body of troops W of Toronto; from this time dates London's reputation as a "garrison town." During the 1840s improved road links stimulated commercial growth, and the many hotels, merchants, banks and newspapers reflected the town's regional primacy. The opening of the GREAT WESTERN RAILWAY (Niagara-Hamilton-Windsor) in 1854 ensured London's growth as a regional centre. In 1855 it was incorporated as a city (pop 10 060). It thereafter became the seat of a Roman Catholic and an Anglican diocese (Huron). With further railway construction and settlement, and an oil boom to its W, the city's economy grew and London began to develop a financial role with the formation of companies, now nationwide, such as London Life Insurance, Canada Trust Co and Avco Finance. Manufacturing, especially brewing, developed as well. Both John LABATT and John CARLING were associated with London; the headquarters of JOHN LABATT LTD is still here.

In 1863 the Anglican Huron College, precursor of UNIVERSITY OF WESTERN ONTARIO (1878), was founded. In the following decades, schools and colleges of other denominations were added. A Provincial Asylum (1870) was the first regional hospital. University Hospital, famous for neurosurgery, is one of 3 current general and teaching hospitals.

Cityscape London's older central portion is a grid of wide streets laid out on level ground between N and S branches of the Thames R. The city's suburban expansion post-1945 has moved N, W and S, on somewhat higher land. Distinct neighbourhoods centered on shopping plazas now extend in a nearly complete circle around the older core, which is still a lively office and shopping precinct. London's 19th-century houses are commonly built of a pale yellow ("white") brick, frequently with a distinctive keyhole- or horseshoe-shaped side window.

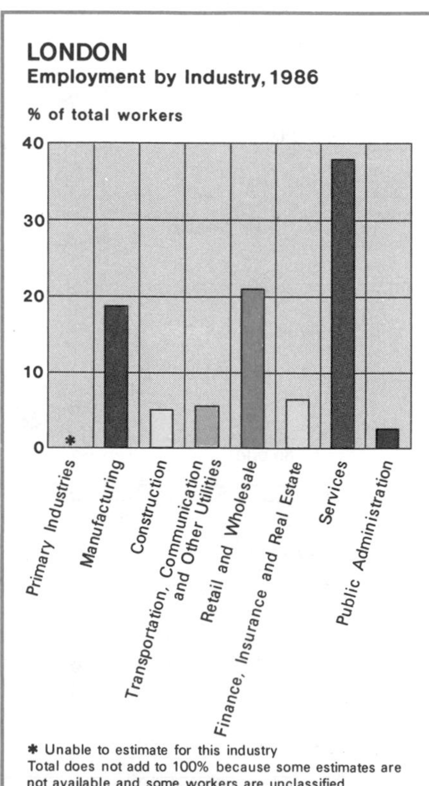

Known as the "Forest City," its many 19th-century street-side plantings are chiefly of large silver maples. The total city area includes one-sixth in open space; Springbank, the largest park (78 ha), contains Storybook Gardens, a childrens' zoo and Play World. Planning activity occurred sporadically until 1946, when a planning board was formed, leading to the first official plan and zoning bylaw in 1949. A massive annexation doubled the city's area in 1961, and in 1987 the city was looking into a further expansion of its boundaries.

Population For most of its history, London's population has grown more by in-migration than by natural increase. The city's population in 1986 was predominantly of British stock.

Economy and Labour Force London's hinterland contains some of the best agricultural land in Canada, and the city's regional centrality is constantly being strengthened by improved communications. Of a total 1986 labour force of 160 000, 38% were in service industries, 19% in manufacturing, 20.6% in trade, 6.2% in financial work, 3.4% in public administration, 5.1% in construction and 5.6% in transportation and communications. Manufacturing in the mid-1980s had a value-added of over $1.3 billion – about 18% of the SW Ontario region.

Transportation From the mid-1850s, London has been a major railway junction and division point. The London and Port Stanley Railway provided connections with Lk Erie until 1976. As many as 11 trains a day run between London and Toronto. A regional highway node in the 1930s and 1940s, London is connected by freeways to Windsor, Sarnia and Hamilton-Toronto (Hwys 401 and 402). These connections have encouraged a considerable tourist industry. The local airport supports feeder services to Toronto, Ottawa, Montréal, Sarnia and Cleveland, Ohio, with a daily flight to and from western Canada. Internally, a horsecar system gave way to streetcars in 1895 and since 1940 the city has used buses only.

Government and Politics During its history London has for the most part been governed by a mayor and aldermen representing 4 wards. After the 1961 annexation, the city added 3 wards and adopted a board of control (mayor plus 4 directly elected controllers) in addition to the 14 council aldermen. City politics are not strongly polarized, and issues tend to concentrate on control over peripheral expansion, attraction of business, viability of the city core, etc. The public and separate (Catholic) school boards and the Public Utilities Commission are also elected bodies; the latter also administers parks and recreation.

Cultural Life An active community of artists, both creative and interpretive, gives the region's cultural life great vitality. London has been home

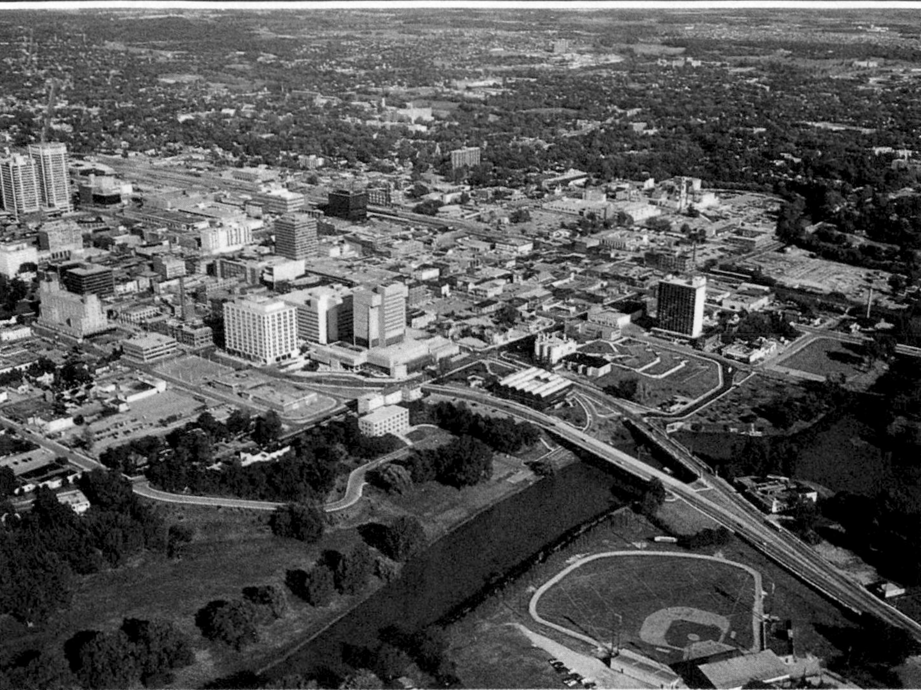

London, Ont, a regional base for business and government, with the Thames R in the lower right (*photo by Ron Nelson Photography Ltd*).

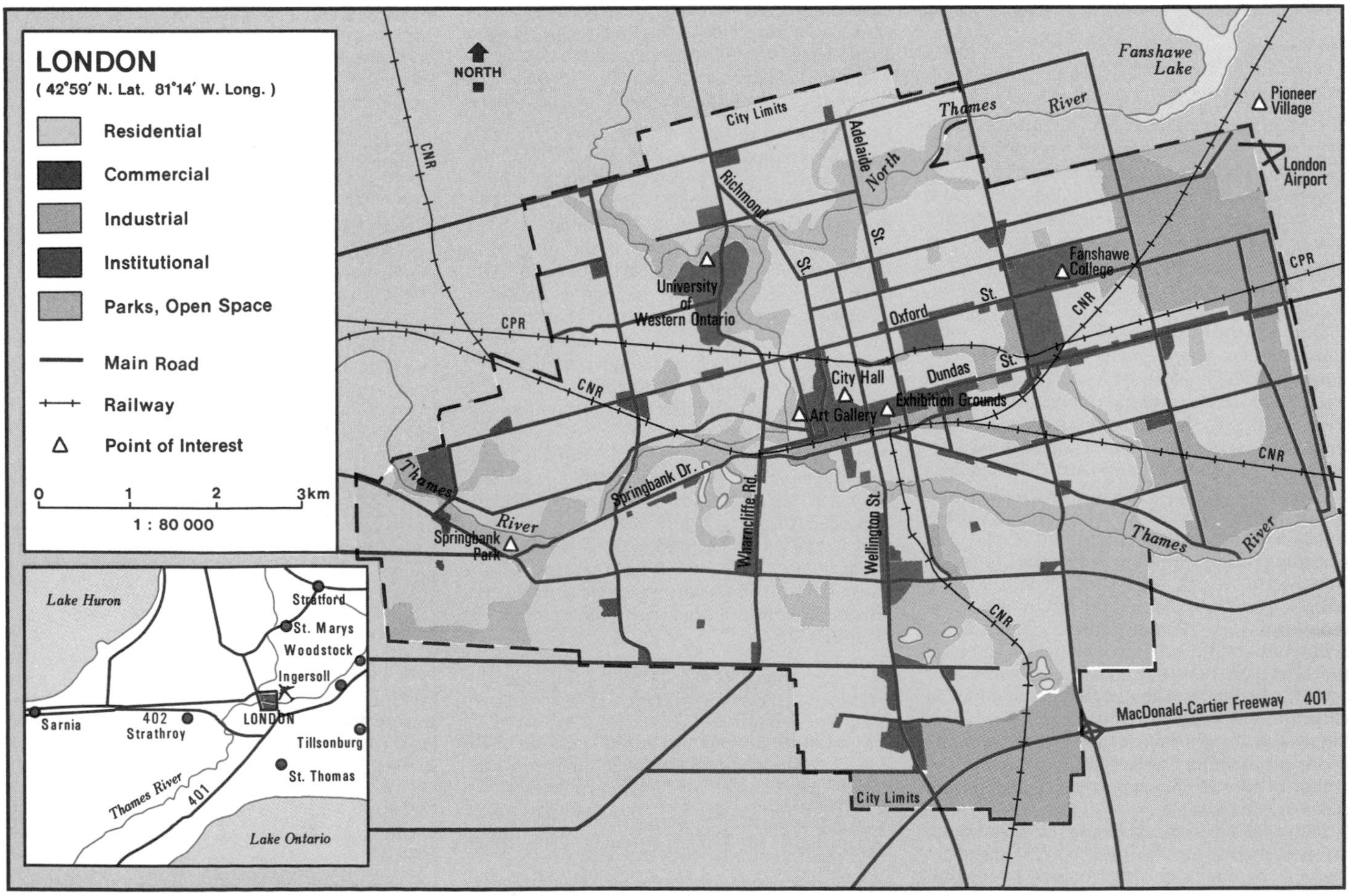

to several nationally and internationally known artists – notably Paul PEEL, Greg CURNOE and Philip Aziz. The Regional Art Gallery (1980) supports the visual arts. Western's Faculty of Music has contributed greatly to vigorous musical activity; there are orchestras, including Orchestra London, choirs and outstanding organists. There is also a professional theatre company, The Grand Theatre, which has 2 stages and shows 6 plays per season. Museums include a pioneer village and Indian site.

One TV and 5 radio stations operate from London; there is one daily newspaper, the *Free Press*. London competes in Major Junior A hockey (the Knights) and various amateur sports; the many university teams also attract city spectators.

C.F.J. WHEBELL

Reading: F.H. Armstrong, *The Forest City: An Illustrated History of London, Canada,* ed, J. Mosher (1986).

London and Bristol Company, est 1610, the first formal attempt to colonize NEWFOUNDLAND. A group of merchant "adventurers" from London and Bristol, Eng, obtained a royal charter giving them title to Newfoundland's E coast. The first governor of the colony at CUPIDS, in Conception Bay, was John GUY, a respected Bristol resident. After brief success, disillusionment brought about by climatic severity, hostility from English West Country merchants who sent out ships seasonally to fish in Newfoundland waters, PIRACY and the realization that nonfishery activities were unprofitable, led to the company's demise in the 1620s.

F.W. ROWE

London Conference, beginning 4 Dec 1866, in which Canadian, Nova Scotian and New Brunswick delegates met with the British government in London, Eng, was the important transitional stage between the 1864 QUÉBEC CONFERENCE and the 1867 BRITISH NORTH AMERICA ACT. The major issue was the educational clauses of the Québec Resolutions. There was strong lobbying in London by bishops from the Maritimes, notably Archbishop Connolly of Halifax, to get guarantees for Roman Catholic separate schools – schools that existed by custom, though not by law – in all 3 provinces. Maritime delegates resisted, and what emerged was Section 93 of the BNA Act, which protected whatever separate schools existed by law at the time of CONFEDERATION. This guaranteed the separate school systems in Québec and Ontario, but not in Nova Scotia or New Brunswick. Early in 1867 the London Resolutions were redrafted into the BNA Act.

P.B. WAITE

Lonergan, Bernard Joseph Francis, Jesuit priest, philosopher-theologian (b at Buckingham, Qué 17 Dec 1904; d at Pickering, Ont 26 Nov 1984). Lonergan was a brilliant, original thinker of the highest rank. For many years his ideas have been studied by scholars in various fields. In addition to the original Lonergan Research Centre, founded in 1971 at Regis Coll, Toronto, where Lonergan had his academic and spiritual home, there were, by the time he died, 9 similar centres around the world. The originality of his work lies principally in the area of method where through a penetrating study of the mind in action he demonstrated the methodical interrelation of the natural and social sciences, philosophy and theology. Lonergan was a professor at the Gregorian U, Rome (1953-65), at Harvard (1971-72) and at Boston Coll (1975-83). His honours include Companion of the Order of Canada and Fellow of the British Academy. Lonergan's work is too rigorously intellectual and specialized to be widely known, though popular journals have taken note of congresses held to study his ideas. His works include *Insight: A Study of Human Understanding* (1957) and *Method in Theology* (1972).

WILLIAM O. FENNELL

Long-Distance Running refers to the running, both on and off the track, of distances longer than 3000 m. During the 1970s the upsurge of interest in long-distance running in Canada and elsewhere gained much of its impetus from the growing popularity of running as a form of exercise to improve FITNESS. Increased numbers of entries in clubs and organized races forced improvements in race categorization. The simple 4-division arrangement of men's and women's novice and men's and women's open was enlarged to include men's and women's masters, with 10-year age stages and under-18 age divisions. However, the 26-mile, 385-yard (42 195 m) marathon, for most, remained the golden challenge. The marathon commemorates an event in ancient Greece; Pheidippides's run from the battlefield at Marathon to Athens (*c*35 km) to announce victory. The first marathon race was in the 1896 Olympics; in the 1908 Olympics, the 26-mile distance from Windsor to London, Eng, came up a little short of the place at Windsor Castle from which the Royal Family was due to observe the start. This was corrected by adding 385 yards. By an administrative quirk the extra yards were adopted in the official distance in 1924.

The burgeoning interest in running has revived some defunct Canadian races. The Old Home Summer 10-Miler resurrected the Halifax Herald Modified Marathon, which was first run in 1907. It drew crowds until 1942, when WWII halted its continuation. In 1926, responding to his father's bribe of a trip to compete in the Boston Marathon, a 21-year-old miner from Sydney, NS, John C. Miles, ran the Modified and finished first. In Boston, Miles battled reigning Olympic champion Albin Stenroos and the race favourite, Bostonian Clarence DeMar, to win the 1926 Marathon in a time of 2:25:40, 4 minutes faster than the previous course record. In 1987 N America's oldest race, the Hamilton "Around-the-Bay" race, had been run 77 times since its inception in 1894. The route, now standardized at 30 km, a little short of its original distance, launched the career of another great runner, Tom LONGBOAT. In 1906 Longboat defied gamblers' odds of 60-1 in winning the Hamilton race. He won the Boston Marathon in 1907 and, despite a US protest about his amateur status, competed for Canada in the marathon of the 1908 London Olympics, but did not finish. Other Canadians who have won the Boston Marathon are Jack Caffery (1900, 1901), Fred Cameron (1910), James Duffy (1914), Édouard Fabre (1915), Dave Komonen (1934), Walter Young (1937), Gérard Coté (1940, 1943, 1944, 1948), Jerome Drayton (1977) and Jacqueline Gareau (women's open, 1980). Another noteworthy victory was William Sherring's first-place finish at the mid-Olympiad festival in Athens, Greece, in 1906.

Newer races offer unique challenges to racers. The Nanisivik Midnight Sun Marathon is run on a 32 km trail of rubble, virtually the only road in the area, some 725 km above the Arctic Circle. It takes place in June, when the sun never sets in the Arctic. Where Nanisivik, like many other races, is a test of individual endurance, the Banff-Jasper Relay is a test of team endurance. In 1982 the Toronto Olympic Club set a new course record of 16:47:45.

Marathons are staged in most major Canadian cities. These and shorter races are run by notable men's open racers such as Jerome Drayton, Canadian marathon record, 2:10:09, Fukuoka, Japan, 1975; Paul Bannon, 1978 Commonwealth Games marathon medallist; Peter Maher, 1987 Ottawa Marathon, 2:12:58; Art Boileau, 1987 Los Angeles Marathon winner, 2:13:08; Dave Edge, PB-2:11:51 and Peter Butler, Canadian 10 km record holder with a time of 28:19:07. Women's open notables include Cynthia Hamilton, 1982 New York Marathon, 2:38:12; Linda Staudt, 1981 Montréal Marathon, 2:33:33; Odette Lapierre, 4th place women's open, 1987 Boston Marathon, 2:31:36; S. Ruegger, PB-2:31:53; and Jacqueline Gareau. Another promising woman runner is Lynn Williams who holds the Canadian women's records for the indoor mile (4:34:7$\frac{1}{2}$) and the indoor 3000 m (8:50:80) and won the 1987 Sun 10 km in 32:14. As well, there is a wide field of master's competitors in every race. Men's master Bob Moore was 7th in the Vancouver International Marathon with a time of 2:24:10 and 10th in the Bermuda Marathon at 2:30:50. Women's master Diane Palmason became master Canadian and N American female champion when she was 3rd overall woman finisher in the 1981 Oakland marathon. World record holder Art Taylor had times in the 1982 N American and Canadian championships, 50+ age division, of 35:08 for 10 000 m and 17:04:08 for 5000 m. Some athletes are enticed to run even greater distances. Al Howie holds the Canadian records for several ultra marathon distances – 50 km in 3:12:46, 50 miles in 5:35:12, 100 km in 7:30:31, 100 miles in 14:06:18 as well as the Canadian 24-hour race record with a distance of 150 miles, 352 yards. Before attempting unsuccessfully to break his own 24-hour race record in the 1983 Sri Chinmoy 24 Hour Race, Howie ran from Winnipeg to Ottawa, a distance of 1500 miles. However, this distance is overshadowed by Kanchan Stott's achievement. On 29 Nov 1983, 37-year-old Stott reached Halifax, NS, 207 days after leaving Victoria, BC, completing the first cross-Canada run by a woman and the longest recorded run (6688 km) by a woman.

CAROLYN HLUS

Long Lance, Buffalo Child, writer, actor, impostor (b Sylvester Long at Winston-Salem, NC 1 Dec 1890; d at Arcadia, Calif 20 Mar 1932). Of mixed Indian and white (and possibly black) ancestry, he was able to escape the segregated southern US because he looked "Indian." Presenting himself as a Cherokee he gained entry to the famous Carlisle Indian School in Pennsylvania. As "Sylvester Long Lance" he fought in the Canadian Army in WWI and then settled in Calgary. In the early 1920s he worked for several western Canadian newspapers. Adopted by the Blood as Buffalo Child in 1922, he began a free-lance writing career as Chief Buffalo Child Long Lance. In 1928 he published his fictitious "auto-biography," *Long Lance,* which won acclaim as a Blackfoot reminiscence of growing up in the last days of freedom on the plains. In 1930 he starred in *The Silent Enemy,* a feature film about northern Canadian Indians before the Europeans. Long Lance's fortunes turned as rumours of his true origins began circulating and early in 1932 he took his own life.

DONALD B. SMITH

Reading: Donald B. Smith, *Long Lance: The True Story of an Impostor* (1982).

Long Range Mountains are the highest and most extensive mountain range of insular Newfoundland, extending more than 500 km along the island's W coast, up the Great Northern Pen from Cape Ray in the south. A part of the Canadian Appalachians, the Long Range Mts are an average 610 m high; the Lewis Hills, elev 814 m, the S-central portion of the range, are the highest on the island. The range, generally steep on the coastal side and scarred by deep glaciation and faulting, reaches highland plateaus and flat-topped peaks before sloping away more gently to the E. In places deep fjords and bays cut into its

Tom Longboat, celebrated long-distance runner who won the Boston Marathon in 1907 (*courtesy Canada's Sports Hall of Fame*).

base, and rivers, such as the HUMBER R, flow through its valleys. GROS MORNE NATIONAL PARK, N of CORNER BROOK, contains some of the mountain range's most spectacular vistas. ROBERT D. PITT

Longboat, Thomas Charles, distance runner (b at Ohsweken [Six Nations IR], Ont 4 July 1887; d there 9 Jan 1949). Largely because of his ability to dominate any race and his spectacular finishing sprints, Longboat was one of the most celebrated pre-WWI athletes. He won the Hamilton "Around-the-Bay" (1906), the Boston Marathon (1907), the Toronto Ward's Marathon (1906-08), the "World's Professional Marathon Championship" (1909), and broke numerous records. He was one of the most sought-after performers in the brief (1908-12) revival of professional racing that followed the controversial 1908 London Olympics marathon, in which Longboat and Dorando Pietri collapsed, likely from drug overdoses. Longboat's desire to train himself led to several well-publicized conflicts with managers. Despite constant and sometimes racist criticism, he stuck to his own methods. He bought up his contract in 1911 and ran better than ever. In 1912, he set a professional record of 1:18:10 for 15 miles, 7 mins faster than his amateur record. Longboat raced successfully during WWI while serving as a dispatch runner in France. After the war he lived and worked in Toronto until 1944, when he retired to the Six Nations Reserve.
BRUCE KIDD

Longden, Johnny, jockey (b at Pontefract, Eng 14 Feb 1907). He enjoyed a distinguished career that many regard as one of the finest in THOROUGHBRED RACING history. Longden's family settled near Taber, Alta, when he was 2 years old. While still a teenager, he went to work in the coal mines and spent his weekends racing quarter horses. In 1927 he visited Salt Lake City and managed to ride a horse named Hugo K. Asher in a race, which he won, beginning a career that lasted until his retirement in 1966. During those years, he rode 6032 horses to victory, a record for that time. He was the first N American jockey to ride 4000 winners.

One of Longden's greatest achievements was training and riding Count Fleet, winner of the N American Triple Crown in 1943. In 1950 he rode the Irish-bred Noor to 4 victories over Citation, one of N America's finest thoroughbreds. Longden retired to train horses and has been successful there as well. In 1969 he trained Majestic Prince, the Kentucky Derby winner. J. THOMAS WEST

Longhouse, the basic house type of northern Iroquoian peoples such as the HURON and IROQUOIS, sheltered a number of families related through the female line. It was established throughout the Iroquoian area by the 12th century. They were 8 m wide but of variable length (one 94 m long was uncovered at the Moyer site in southern Ontario). Longhouses described by the early French explorers and by the Jesuit missionaries in the 17th century were somewhat shorter. In the 18th century, longhouses were replaced by single-family dwellings for residences, but continued as political and ceremonial structures. Followers of the HANDSOME LAKE RELIGION continue to refer to the buildings that house their ceremonies as longhouses.

The 17th-century dwelling was constructed by driving flexible poles into the ground at fixed intervals. These were then bent over and lashed together. Horizontal poles strengthened the frame, and cedar-bark (Huron) or elm-bark (Iroquois) sheathing covered the structure. Sleeping platforms ran the length of the house. Each of the 3 to 5 hearths, 6 m apart down the middle of the longhouse, was shared by 2 nuclear families of 5 or 6 persons. Firewood was stacked in vestibules near the entrances at either end of the structure. The Iroquois characterized their confederacy as a longhouse of 5 fires. RENÉ R. GADACZ

Longpré, Ephrem, historian, philosopher (b at Woonsocket, RI 24 Aug 1890; d at Paris, France 19 Oct 1965). His defence of the philosophy of Joannes Duns Scotus played a role in the background of Vatican II and in the opening of Catholic thought to traditions other than that of St Thomas. Longpré's French Canadian parents returned to farm at Upton, Qué, when he was 4. He was educated at Montréal, where he joined the Franciscan order. He was cured of a serious illness at age 18 after an intervention by Brother ANDRÉ. Longpré studied in Rome and then worked in Florence and Paris. His study of Scotus, whose philosophy combines a subtle metaphysics of community with a strong sense of the importance of individuality, strengthened his convictions about human freedom, and he was hunted by the Gestapo throughout much of the war. His resistance work was acknowledged by the French and British governments. His most important work is *La Philosophie du B. Duns Scot* (1924). LESLIE ARMOUR

Longhouse at Ste Marie Among the Hurons, Midland, Ont. The reconstruction is a lively tourist attraction (*photo by Richard Vroom*).

Loon (family Gaviidae), common name for a distinctive group of 4 large, swimming birds, all confined to the Northern Hemisphere and all occurring in Canada. Loons nest on inland lakes and rivers, migrating to the sea for winter. Summer plumages are black or grey, streaked and spotted in bold patterns with white. Underparts are all white. For winter, dense plumage molts to an unspotted grey. During molting, loons are flightless: common, yellow-billed and arctic loons (*Gavia immer, G. adamsii, G. arctica,* respectively) molt in late winter and red-throated loons (*G. stellata*) in autumn. Sexes are similar. Bills are strong, straight and pointed; necks, long and stout; tails, very short. The legs, set far back on the body and with flattened sides and fully webbed toes, are well adapted to swimming. Walking is accomplished only with difficulty. As the wings are comparatively small, loons must run along the water surface to become airborne. They come to shore only to nest, usually laying 2 olive brown eggs with darker spots, on a heap of vegetation near the water's edge. Both parents incubate for about 4 weeks and assist in rearing young. The uniformly greyish young leave the nest soon after

Red-throated loon (*G. Stellata*) (*artwork by John Crosby*).

hatching and often ride on their parents' backs. Loons eat mainly fish, diving to depths of 75 m, usually for less than one minute.

Loons are known for their various cries, particularly a weird, mirthless laugh and an eerie, wolf-like howl. These unique sounds are symbolic of Canada's North. R.D. JAMES

Loranger, Françoise, dramatist, novelist (b at St-Hilaire, Qué 18 June 1913). Her novel, *Mathieu* (1949), a gloomy portrayal of Québec society in the DUPLESSIS era, received critical acclaim, but it is chiefly on her dramatic texts, many televised nationally, that her reputation rests. Hers is a constantly evolving theatre, reflecting changing social realities in her province. She began writing radio scripts in 1939, but her first published stage plays date from the 1960s. *Une Maison...un jour* (1965) is a psychological study of the intense pressures destroying a middle-class family; *Encore cinq minutes* (1967) is one of the earliest texts to treat feminist concerns in French Canada. Contemporary political events are the focus of plays such as *Le Chemin du roy* (1969) written in collaboration with Claude Levac, a savage satire depicting, in the guise of a penalty-filled hockey game, the confrontations between Québec City and Ottawa provoked by French President de Gaulle's visit in 1967, and *Médium saignant* (1970), dealing with conflict over language rights in the atmosphere of Québec's controversial BILL 63. Most of Loranger's plays have been successfully transposed to television, and works such as *Une Maison...un jour* have been well received abroad. L.E. DOUCETTE

Loranger, Jean-Aubert, poet, storyteller, journalist (b at Montreal 26 Oct 1896; d there 28 Oct 1942). Loranger belonged to a family known for its lawyers (the Lorangers), writers (AUBERT DE GASPÉ) and military officers (Charles de SALABERRY). He excelled at journalism, working for *La Patrie* 1923-27 and 1939-42, *La* PRESSE 1927-30, *Le Jour* 1938-39 and *Montréal-Matin* for 6 weeks in 1942. During WWI he associated with young intellectuals and artists who had lived in Paris (including his cousin, Robert de Roquebrune) and met regularly in the Westmount drawing room of architect Fernand Préfontaine. In 1918 this group started the first arts magazine in Québec, *Le* NIGOG, to which Loranger contributed. Admitted to the École littéraire de Montréal on 17 Nov 1920, he broke definitively with this group, unwilling to participate in activities that fell far short of his own creative ambitions. His 2 collections, *Les Atmosphères* (1920) and *Poëmes* (1922), introduced blank verse to Québec and showed his obsession with modernity and escapism. But peasant life fascinated him and inspired his realistic, yet ironic and amusing, short stories. In 1979 he was posthumously awarded the Prix France-Québec for his 2 volumes of short stories. BERNADETTE GUILMETTE

Loranger, Thomas-Jean-Jacques, politician, judge,political theorist (b at Yamachiche, Qué 2 Feb 1823; d at Ste-Pétronille, Qué 18 Aug 1885). Upon completion of his classical education at the Seminary of Nicolet he studied law and was admitted to the bar in Lower Canada in 1844. After several years of practice in Trois-Rivières and Montréal, he set up, in 1858, a law firm with his 2 brothers, Louis-Onésime and Jean-Marie.

He began his short and stormy political career in Aug 1854 as a deputy in the Legislative Assembly of the United Canadas. Re-elected in 1857, he became provincial secretary for Canada E. When he broke ranks with the executive by voting against its motion to transfer the capital to Ottawa, he was not reappointed when the Liberal-Conservatives returned to office in Aug 1858. Loranger's nationalist sentiments brought him to criticize Cartier for accepting legislative measures that would anglicize French Canadians. In 1862 he broke ranks once again and voted against the militia bill, thereby contributing to the defeat of the administration. He remained a deputy until 9 Mar 1863 when he was named Superior Court judge, a position which he held until 1879.

Loranger had a very perceptive juridical mind. During the 1850s he contributed his talents to the resolution of the numerous legal problems created by the abolition of the SEIGNEURIAL SYSTEM. His interpretation was very favourable to the habitants. While on the bench he wrote a 2-vol *Commentaire sur la code civil du Bas-Canada* in which he affirmed the Church's claim that it had sole jurisdiction over all matters pertaining to marriage. While professor of administrative law at Laval U, he helped found a legal journal, *Thémis*, and proceeded with the arduous work of codifying the statutes of the province of Québec. As one of the first French Canadians to specialize in constitutional law, Loranger applied his nationalist vision to the federal system. In his *Lettres sur l'interprétation de la constitution fédérale...* (1883-84), he advanced the compact theory of confederation, a theory which was quickly adopted by the provinces in their struggle for greater autonomy. M.D. BEHIELS

Lord, John Keast, naturalist, veterinarian (b in Cornwall, Eng 1818; d at Brighton, Eng 9 Dec 1872). After receiving his veterinarian diploma in 1844, he practised briefly, then disappeared and wandered through several only partially recorded endeavours, including a whaling voyage, trapping in Minnesota and parts of Canada, and artillery service in the Crimea. When British Columbia was established as a colony, he worked as naturalist to the boundary commission surveying the FORTY-NINTH PARALLEL from 1858 to 1862, wintering on Vancouver I. During this period he sent numerous faunal collections to the British Museum, named 2 new mammals and reported his observations in 2 vols, *The Naturalist in Vancouver Island and British Columbia* (1866). MARTIN K. MCNICHOLL

Lord's Day Alliance of Canada (renamed People for Sunday Assn of Canada in 1982), a lay organization fd 1888 under the aegis of the PRESBYTERIAN Church and supported by the other Protestant churches to combat increasing Sabbath secularization. In the early phases of Canada's industrialization and urbanization, Sunday was usually the only day of rest: the issue was whether that day should be a holy day or a holiday. The churches faced growing competition for the loyalty of potential churchgoers: industrial concerns, such as railways, demanded Sunday labour from their employees; more important, new leisure pursuits beckoned. Technological advances, particularly electric urban transit systems, increased people's mobility, allowing them to escape the cities. Commercial recreation activities such as sporting events, ice cream parlours and theatres were equally tempting. Many Canadians seemed inclined to make Sunday a day both of religion and recreation.

The Alliance became one of the most effective lobbies of the early 20th century. It gained the crucial support of the French Canadian Catholic hierarchy and, with its promise of a legislated weekly rest day, of organized labour. In 1906, this combination of forces and the Alliance's sophisticated lobbying techniques persuaded PM Sir Wilfrid LAURIER to introduce a Lord's Day Act. Although strong opposition existed among the transportation and manufacturing concerns and among French Canadians, the Act became law in Mar 1907. It aimed to restrict Sunday trade, labour and recreation. The struggle to secure enforcement has occupied the Alliance since then. Because the Act required provincial authorization for each prosecution, the Alliance battled in many arenas, with varying success. The Sunday shopping issue still provokes intense debate, uniting labour, retail merchants, churches and the People for Sunday Assn in opposition. Canadians' pursuit of Sunday pleasure has doubtless defeated the association's main aim – Sunday is primarily a holiday and only partly a holy day. *See also* SUNDAY SHOPPING. SHARON P. MEEN

Reading: R. Allen, *The Social Passion* (1973); C. Armstrong and H.V. Nelles, *The Revenge of the Methodist Bicycle Company* (1977).

L'Orignal, Ont, Village, pop 1914 (1986c), 1819 (1981c), inc 1876, seat of Prescott and Russell counties, located on the Ottawa R, 88 km E of Ottawa. Named after nearby Pointe à l'Orignal [Fr, *orignal,* "moose"], it was granted as part of the Seigneurie de Longueuil by the Co of New France to Françoise Prevost in 1674. With La Salle's Cataracoui [Kingston] it was the only seigneury granted in the French regime in what is now Ontario. It was acquired in 1796 by Nathaniel Tredwell, a wealthy American from Plattsburg, NY. In 1812 when Tredwell refused to swear allegiance to the British Crown, his property was confiscated and he fled to the US. He returned in 1840, but meanwhile his son Charles had recovered it and sold it to some 100 settlers. The village was made capital of the new Ottawa district. Preserved from its past are St Andrew's church (1832), a pioneering Presbyterian congregation and a fine example of Regency architecture. The District Court House and Jail (built 1821 and still in use) is the oldest remaining courthouse in Ontario. The village is roughly 80% French speaking. K.L. MORRISON

Loring, Frances Norma, sculptor (b at Wardner, Idaho 14 Oct 1887; d at Newmarket, Ont 5 Feb 1968). From the time she settled in Canada in

Frances Loring, *Luna* (1950-51), poplar wood (*courtesy MacDonald Stewart Art Centre/University of Guelph Coll*).

1913 she worked tirelessly, both in the development of her own work and in fostering a climate that made sculpture possible for others. She had first studied sculpture in Geneva, Munich and Paris 1901-06. A fascinating, compelling personality of keen intelligence and warm understanding, she assailed public and official indifference to SCULPTURE as a founding member of the Sculptors' Soc of Canada and a chief organizer of the Federation of Canadian Artists and the National Arts Council. For over 50 years she shared studio quarters with fellow sculptor Florence WYLE in a converted Toronto church that was widely considered the salon of Canada's art world. Her own work was architectural in nature, and among her best-known public monuments were the lion formerly situated at the Toronto entrance to Queen Elizabeth Hwy, and war memorials at St Stephen, NB, and Galt, Ont. REBECCA SISLER

Reading: Rebecca Sisler, *The Girls* (1972).

Lorne, John Douglas Sutherland Campbell, Marquess of, later 9th duke of Argyll, governor general of Canada 1878-83 (b at London, Eng 6 Aug 1845; d on the Isle of Wight 2 May 1914). Private secretary to his father, the secretary of state for India 1868-71, Lorne represented Argyllshire as a Liberal in the House of Commons 1868-78. His appointment to Canada in 1878, at age 33, had much to do with his marriage 7 years previously to Princess Louise, Queen Victoria's fourth daughter, and the British government's attempt to enhance the prestige of the queen's representative in Ottawa. In Canada Lorne helped to reconcile BC to CONFEDERATION and supported the Canadian government's efforts to establish a Canadian high commissioner to the UK, though it reduced his own viceregal authority. A devoted patron of the arts and letters, Lorne founded the ROYAL SOCIETY OF CANADA in 1882 and the Royal Canadian Academy of Arts in 1880, a precursor to the National Gallery of Canada. An author of prose and poetry, his writings include *Memories of Canada and Scotland* (1884), *Imperial Federation* (1885), *Canadian Pictures* (1885), *Passages from the Past* (2 vols, 1907) and *Yesterday and To-day in Canada* (1910). CARMAN MILLER

Lortie, Louis, pianist (b at Montréal 27 Apr 1959). His major piano instructors were Yvonne Hubert and Marc Durand in Québec, Dieter Weber in Austria and Menahem Pressler and Leon Fleisher in the US. He distinguished himself in competitions: 5-time winner of the Canadian Music Competitions (1968-72), the Orchestre symphonique de Montréal competition (1972), the Concertino Praga (1973, 1975), the CBC Talent Festival (1975), the International Stepping Stones of the Canadian Music Competitions (1975), first-prize at the Busoni international competition (Italy, 1984) and fourth-prize winner at the Leeds international competition (GB, 1984). Lortie is a violinist whose interpretations reveal great maturity, strong personality and impeccable technique. His repertory includes Beethoven, Chopin, Liszt and Ravel. He was invited to join the Toronto Symphony for its tour of Japan and China 1978 and returned to China in 1983. The Canada Council gave him its Virginia P Moore Award in 1984. In 1987 the British company Chandos released recordings by Lortie of the Chopin *Études* and Liszt's *Piano Sonata in B minor.* HÉLÈNE PLOUFFE

Lost Lemon Mine, a legendary gold deposit reputedly somewhere between the CROWSNEST PASS and the Highwood R in SW Alberta, discovered about 1870 by prospectors Frank Lemon and "Blackjack." Lemon allegedly murdered Blackjack at the mine and went mad. Two Stoney witnesses were sworn to secrecy by Chief Bearspaw. Later, Lemon was unable to direct other prospectors to the mine. Thousands have since searched for the fabulous lode; many have died mysteriously. King Bearspaw, descendant of the chief, claimed to know the secret location and led many expeditions into the mountains – all in vain. FRANK W. ANDERSON

Reading: D. Riley, et al, *The Lost Lemon Mine* (1968).

Loto-Canada Inc, established May 1976 to be responsible for continued operation of the Olympic lottery. It was to turn over 82.5% of net revenues to help with the expected deficits of the OLYMPIC GAMES and to help with the COMMONWEALTH GAMES; other portions of the revenues would go to the provinces and to the federal government's national sports, fitness and recreation programs. The federal government agreed to close down Loto-Canada in return for a payment of $6 million from the provinces, paid annually. A last draw was held in late 1979. *See also* LOTTERY.

Lottery, a centuries-old concept, is an arrangement for distributing prizes by lot, chance or mixed chance and skill. Under the Criminal Code (s189) it is an indictable offence to conduct any of a number of activities related to "any proposal, scheme or plan for advancing, lending, giving, selling or in any way disposing of any property, by lots, cards, tickets, or any mode of chance whatever." A 1969 amendment (rewritten 1985) provides for exceptions. Section 190(1) of the code now permits provincial governments to conduct and manage lottery schemes; and permits provinces to license charitable or religious organizations, agricultural fairs and exhibitions, and persons at public places of amusement to conduct and manage lottery schemes.

Federal Government Under s10 of the Olympic (1976) Act, passed in 1973, the Organizing Committee of the 1976 Olympic Games, a Québec corporation, was authorized to run a lottery scheme to raise money for the 1976 Olympic Games in Montréal and was allowed to sell tickets in any province where the government of that province agreed, provided that the proceeds were used to provide financial assistance for the Olympics and for the development of amateur sport in the participating provinces. In the 9 draws between 1973 and 1976, $230 million was raised for the Olympics, $25 million for the provinces and $190 million was awarded in prizes.

LOTO-CANADA INC, a federal crown corporation, was established in 1976 to raise money through lotteries to help Québec pay for its Olympic deficit. This lottery was strongly opposed by the provinces which regarded lotteries as their exclusive field of operation. Under a 1979 agreement, Loto-Canada Inc was wound up by the federal government in return for the payment by the 10 provincial governments quarterly to the federal government of $6 million, adjusted according to the Consumer Price Index; 82.5% of the profit of Loto-Canada had gone to the Olympic debt, 12.5% to the provinces, and 5% to the federal government in support of programs in fitness and amateur sport, recreation, the arts and culture.

In 1983 the federal government passed the Athletic Contests and Events Pool Act and established the Canadian Sports Pool Corp, which has the power to conduct and manage virtually every type of lottery scheme in addition to sports pools. Charging that this constitutes a breach of the 1979 agreement with the provinces, in Mar 1984 the provinces started legal proceedings in the federal court.

A game called "Sports Select Baseball" was launched in May 1984, but was discontinued in Sept 1984 after substantial losses had been incurred. An agreement among the federal government and the provinces was reached in June 1985 whereby the federal government agreed to withdraw from the field of lotteries, to amend the Criminal Code and to remove all existing legislation authorizing it to conduct lotteries; the provinces agreed to continue their payments under the 1979 agreement and to pay an additional $100 million over a period of 3 years. In pursuance of the agreement, s190 of the Criminal Code was amended in Dec 1985 to remove the provision authorizing the federal government to conduct lotteries.

Provincial Governments All the provinces and the 2 territories are involved in conducting and managing lotteries. BC, Alberta, Saskatchewan and Manitoba incorporated the Western Canada Lottery Foundation under the Canada Business Corporations Act in 1974. The name has since been changed to the Western Canada Lottery Corp, and BC is no longer involved. The Yukon and the NWT participate as associate members. Each province and territory operates its separate ticket-distribution system and makes separate provision for its share of the profits. Programs in recreation, amateur sport, culture, community service and health research are the principal beneficiaries. In the fiscal year 1985-86, the corporation distributed to its member provinces and territories over $122 million, some of which covered local expenses. In BC, since 1985, lotteries have been managed and conducted by the British Columbia Lottery Corp. In 1985-86, $104 million went to the BC government.

The Ontario Lottery Corp was established in 1975. The profits (about $320 million in 1985-86) accrue to the provincial treasurer of Ontario but are earmarked for a number of grant programs, which would not normally qualify for government assistance, for sports, fitness, recreation, culture, research in health and environment, hospital capital projects and social-service programs run by volunteers in the private sector.

In Québec the lottery authority is the Société des loteries et courses du Québec, better known as Loto-Québec. Constituted in 1969, it began operations in 1970. It made a profit in 1985-86 of $302.7 million for the government of Québec, none of which has been designated for any specific programs.

New Brunswick, Newfoundland, Nova Scotia and PEI jointly incorporated the Atlantic Lottery Corp in 1976. In 1985-86 the net profit was $45.8 million which was distributed to the 4 provincial governments as general revenue, none of which was earmarked for specific programs.

The Interprovincial Lottery Corporation, constituted in 1976, currently has as its shareholders the governments of the 10 provinces of Canada. It conducts 3 national lottery schemes: Loto 6/49, Super-Loto and the Provincial. These national lotteries are managed by the 5 provincial organizations within their respective territories.

In the 1985-86 fiscal year, despite the recession, lottery sales in Canada climbed nearly $2.7 billion. All lottery games are based on the same principle; it is details such as the price and prize structures, the frequency of the draw and the technology for choosing winners that change. Games are usually "passive," ie, players match a preprinted number on a ticket against a winning number; "active," ie, players choose their own numbers; or "instant," ie, prizes are awarded based on the matching of hidden numbers or symbols. J.F.C. WRIGHT AND JOSEPH W. KANUKA

Lou Marsh Trophy, named after a former sports editor of the *Toronto Star,* is awarded annually to Canada's best athlete, as decided by a committee of Toronto sports writers. Louis Edwin Marsh died on 5 Mar 1936 after 43 years as a journalist, and was regarded as the dean of Canadian sports journalism. In his youth he was an excellent all-round athlete. He played on the Toronto Senior Argonaut football team and was a good sprinter and strong swimmer, being credited with some 15 rescues in the water. He raced iceboats and small speedboats, for which he coined the term "sea fleas," and was a highly regarded referee in boxing and ice hockey. His daily sports column in the *Toronto Star* 1925-36 was entitled "With Pick and Shovel," describing his tenacious ability to obtain an in-depth analysis of the sporting scene. Made of black marble, the trophy stands about 75 cm high. The words "With Pick and Shovel" appear above the engraved names of the winners. Among the latter are Dr Philip Edwards (first winner, 1937), Marilyn BELL, Petra BURKA, Wayne GRETZKY and Russ JACKSON. The trophy is kept on exhibition at Canada's Sports Hall of Fame in Toronto. J. THOMAS WEST

Loudon, James, educator, physicist (b at Toronto 24 May 1841; d there 29 Dec 1916). President of U of T from 1892 to 1906, Loudon devoted his life to the university. Gold medalist in MATHEMATICS in 1862, he became tutor in mathematics at University College in 1863 and the first Canadian professor of the university in 1875, succeeding his teacher John Bradford Cherriman. In 1873 he was elected to the university senate. In 1878, at Loudon's recommendations, the School of Technology (renamed the School of Practical Science) was affiliated with the university. Loudon also encouraged the federation of the principal colleges of the university, and his construction program included the Chemistry Building (1895), Convocation Hall (1907) and the Physics Building (1907). Loudon continuously promoted research and established a PhD program in 1897 although, not surprisingly, he had little time for research himself. Loudon also organized the Alumni Assn and used it to persuade the government to finance its university adequately. YVES GINGRAS

Reading: H.H. Langton, *James Loudon* (1927).

Lougheed, Edgar Peter, lawyer, premier of Alberta (b at Calgary 26 July 1928), grandson of Sir James LOUGHEED. He was educated in Alberta, received a BA (1951) and LLB (1952) from University of Alberta and briefly played football for the Edmonton Eskimos (1949 and 1950). He earned an MBA from Harvard (1954) and practised law in Calgary before joining the Mannix Corporation as secretary, rising to VP (1959) and director (1960). In 1965 he was elected leader of the small Alberta Progressive Conservative Party and began building a grass-roots organization. Although SOCIAL CREDIT had maintained an iron grip in Alberta since 1935, and the Conservatives had not been a provincial political force for 40 years, Lougheed was elected to the legislature in 1967 by the largest majority of any candidate. He and the 5 other elected PCs became the official Opposition. When Prem Ernest C. MANNING retired in 1968 and was replaced by Harry STROM, Lougheed effectively characterized the Social Credit government as burned out.

In Aug 1971 he was swept into office with 49 of the 75 seats. His first major action was to increase royalties paid to the province by oil companies. Lougheed proved to be a tenacious negotiator and an adept manager of relations with the media. His government's major initiatives were increasing Albertans' return on their natural resources, promoting industrial development and urban decentralization, and improving health care and recreation (new hospitals and medical research, urban parks and the large "Kananaskis Country" park).

Peter Lougheed, former premier of Alberta, whose overwhelming support in Alberta gave him a strong voice in national politics (*courtesy Public Affairs Bureau/Government of Alberta*).

Lougheed's industrial-development policies encouraged an expanding petrochemical industry backed by the province's huge stocks of natural gas. By 1983, many large plants were producing ethylene, methanol, benzene and other chemicals. Recognizing that Alberta's conventional oil reserves were finite, Lougheed encouraged development of the huge reserves of heavy oil and oil sands through tax policy and direct investment. In 1978 the Syncrude Canada oil-sands project – the world's largest single synthetic-fuels complex – was completed with provincial participation. The government created the ALBERTA OIL SANDS TECHNOLOGY AND RESEARCH AUTHORITY (AOSTRA) to develop improved technology for nonconventional oil production. Lougheed was also interested in agricultural diversification – an expanded food-processing industry, increased irrigation and a wider diversity of crops – and the Alberta Heritage Foundation for Medical Research. He conceded that his ultimate goal – to diversify the province's economy and ensure its prosperity beyond the oil and gas era – was constrained by Alberta's small population, its distance from foreign markets, and federal control of tariffs and other factors; he said it would not be accomplished in his lifetime.

The centrepiece of the premier's determination to maximize provincial revenues and to ensure a healthy long-range future for the provincial economy was the creation in 1976 of the ALBERTA HERITAGE SAVINGS TRUST FUND, which put aside a portion of oil and gas revenues and deposited them in long-term investments.

In the 1970s Lougheed pushed for a stronger role for Alberta in national decision making – a role commensurate with the province's then-growing economic strength. He sharply resisted what he saw as federal incursions into provincial rights. In the negotiations that led to the CONSTITUTION ACT, 1982, he was a driving force behind the amending formula that gave no province a veto but allowed dissenting provinces to opt out of amendments that would reduce their powers. He personally championed the clause that ensures the supremacy of the legislatures over the courts. His major confrontation with Ottawa over oil revenues ultimately led to the 1981 Energy Pricing Agreement and subsequent accords, which had the effect of ensuring federal negotiation of oil and gas prices and revenues, rather than unilateral federal action.

Albertans thought highly of Lougheed's managerial competence, integrity and commitment to the province's welfare, as shown in his overwhelming electoral victories in 1975, 1979 and 1982. By the mid-1970s, Canadians at large had come to take him seriously as a major western spokesman.

He dominated the province's politics as Manning had a generation earlier and gave voice to Albertans' frustrated pride and determination to be taken seriously on the national stage. He stepped down in fall 1985, returning to private business. In 1987 he and Donald S. MACDONALD headed the Canadian Alliance for Trade and Job Opportunities to promote FREE TRADE with the US, and in that year he was made a Companion of the Order of Canada. JOHN J. BARR

Lougheed, Sir James Alexander, lawyer, senator (b at Brampton, Canada W Sept 1854; d at Ottawa 2 Nov 1925). He practised law in Toronto and Calgary where he was in partnership with R.B. BENNETT. In 1889 he was appointed to the Senate and was its Conservative leader 1906-21. Created privy councillor in 1911, for 7 years he was minister without portfolio in the administration of Sir Robert BORDEN. He then held several portfolios until Mackenzie KING took office in 1921. In 1928 a mountain W of Calgary was named after him. ERIC J. HOLMGREN

Louie, Alexina Diane, composer, pianist, teacher (b at Vancouver 30 July 1949). Stylistically influenced by her Chinese cultural heritage, Louie is one of the leading composers of Canada's post-WWII generation. After studying at UBC and at U of California at San Diego she moved to Toronto in 1980. Louie has composed works for chamber ensembles (including *Lotus, Lotus II* and *Pearls*), for electronic media (*Molly*), and has been particularly active in the field of orchestral music. Her *O Magnum Mysterium*, dedicated to the memory of pianist Glenn Gould, has been performed by major Canadian orchestras. Other orchestral works by her include *The Ringing Earth, The Eternal Earth* and *Songs of Paradise*. In 1986 Louie was named Composer of the Year by the Canadian Music Council. COLIN EATOCK

Louis-Marie, Trappist priest, botanist, teacher (b Louis-Paul Lalonde at Montréal 17 Oct 1896; d there 3 Nov 1978). Trained at U de M by Frère MARIE-VICTORIN (LSc, 1924) and at Harvard (PhD, 1928), Father Louis-Marie taught botany and genetics at the Institut agricole in OKA, near Montréal, 1923-62. Under his direction the institute's herbarium grew until it contained nearly 100 000 specimens. Known as the Herbier Louis-Marie, it is now at Laval. Author of many scientific articles, Father Louis-Marie is known especially for his *Flore manuel* (1931), reissued various times, through which several generations of amateur botanists have been introduced to the study of Canadian flora. RAYMOND DUCHESNE

Louisbourg, 18th-century fortified town, capital and major settlement of the French colony of Île Royale (Cape Breton I), 1713-58. In the 17th and 18th centuries, France and Britain competed both for territorial control of Atlantic Canada and for domination of the valuable cod FISHERIES off its coasts. In the Treaty of UTRECHT (1713), France ceded Newfoundland and ACADIA to Britain. That year the French colonized Île Royale and founded Louisbourg, which quickly became a substantial town and seaport. Unlike the other communities of New France, Louisbourg and its outports carried on little agriculture; instead the export of cod paid for almost all the colony's supplies. From its base in the fishing industry, Louisbourg devel-

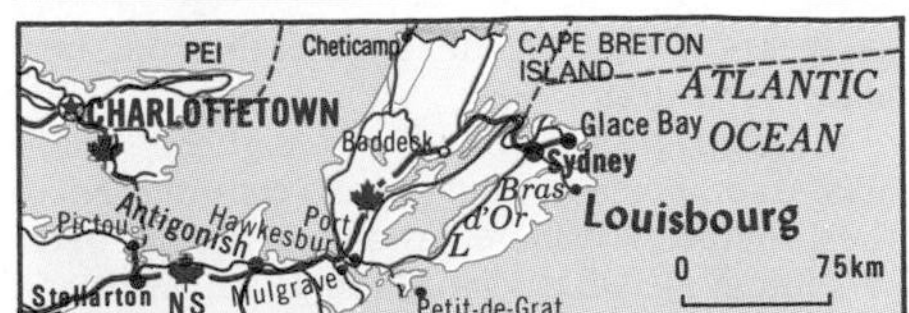

oped diversified shipping links. The port annually welcomed trading vessels from France, the Caribbean, the British American colonies, Acadia and Québec. BASQUE, Breton and Norman fishermen joined the fishing industry each summer, and the town's settled population, drawn partly from France, partly from other parts of New France, grew to roughly 2000 by 1740 and double that in the 1750s.

Though its governor was subservient to the governor general of New France at Québec, Île Royale functioned as a separate colony. The centre of French power in the region, Louisbourg was an important military base with a permanent garrison. A major fortification program began in 1719 and by the 1740s cannon-bearing, stone-and-mortar ramparts encircled the town. Military engineers under Jean-François VERVILLE shaped the town in accordance with the FORTIFICATION theories of Le Prestre de Vauban (1633-1707) and the urban design theories of early 18th-century France.

Louisbourg was besieged in 1745, during the WAR OF THE AUSTRIAN SUCCESSION by troops from New England supported by the Royal Navy, and in 1758 by the British army and navy. Each time, the town was obliged to capitulate after suffering serious damage from artillery fire and naval blockade, and the population was exiled to France. After the first siege, France recovered the colony by treaty, but soon after the second the fortifications were demolished and the town permanently abandoned. The fall of Louisbourg, with the capture of Québec in 1759 and Montréal in 1760, ended France's military and colonial power in N America, although SAINT-PIERRE AND MIQUELON, acquired by France in 1763 after the SEVEN YEARS' WAR, partly replaced Île Royale as a base for the fishing industry.

The modern town of Louisbourg, a small fishing port, grew up at the other end of Louisbourg harbour. The fortress of Louisbourg became a national historic site in 1928, and in 1961 Parks Canada began reconstruction based on comprehensive archaeological investigation and the colony's well-preserved historical records. Part of the fortifications, the citadel buildings, the town quay and several streets with their homes, shops and taverns are now rebuilt in intricate detail.

Open to the public from spring to fall and interpreted for visitors by guides, costumed animators and museum displays, the reconstruction of 1744-era Louisbourg is today a major visitor attraction, an important contributor to Cape Breton's tourist economy and a world-class model of historic-site reconstruction. CHRISTOPHER MOORE

Reading: C. Moore, *Louisbourg Portraits* (1982).

View from the Clocktower, Louisbourg, 1744, acrylic on canvas, by Lewis Parker (*courtesy Fortress of Louisbourg National Historic Park and Lewis Parker*).

Louisiana was born in 1682, when the explorer LA SALLE reached the Mississippi Delta and claimed for France the whole area drained by the river and its tributaries. Politically, however, Louisiana was French for only 84 years. It was ceded to Spain in 1763 by the Treaty of PARIS. France got it back in 1800 by the secret Treaty of San Ildefonso, and 3 years later Napoleon sold it to the US for $15 million.

Despite its strategic location and immense territory, Louisiana was never a profitable colony for France and was thus badly neglected. In 1766, when Spain occupied the colony, its population may have been as few as 7500 people. The restitution of Louisiana to France in 1800 and Napoleon's intention of occupying it might have changed French attitudes toward the colony, but his plan fell short. Napoleon's fear that Louisiana might fall into British hands prompted him to sell it to the Americans.

In 1803, when Louisiana became American, its population had grown to 50 000, mostly through immigration. For the Spaniards, as for the French, Louisiana was a remote frontier territory. Its only merit was as a buffer zone between Anglo-America and New Spain's northern frontier. Because of Louisiana's marginal location inside the Spanish Empire in N America, few settlers from Spain or Mexico were attracted to the area. Ironically, a large part of the immigration during Louisiana's Spanish period was French. Many of the displaced ACADIANS found their way to Louisiana after the revolution in Saint-Domingue (1791), present-day Haiti.

Today, there may be as many as one million Francophones in Louisiana, and they can be divided into a few subgroups reflecting the diversity of their origins: 1) the white Creoles: the descendants of the colonial French and colonial gallicized Germans; 2) the black Creoles: blacks with a French culture; 3) French-speaking Indians; and 4) "Cajuns," ie, Acadians and other immigrants (Germans, Italians, Scots-Irish, Spanish, etc) who have been acculturated to Acadian ways. The Louisiana French are mainly concentrated in the southern part of the state, which since 1971 has been officially designated by the Louisiana legislature as "Acadiana." They are the fragile remains of the 17th- and 18th-century French Empire in America. YVES BROUSSEAU AND CÉCYLE TRÉPANIER

Reading: C.L. Dufour, *Ten Flags in the Winds: The Story of Louisiana* (1967); M. Savelle, *Empires to Nations: Expansion in America, 1713-1824* (1974); J. Smith-Thibodeaux, *Les Francophones de Louisiane* (1977); J. Gray Taylor, *Louisiana: A History* (1976).

Lount, Samuel, blacksmith, politician, rebel (b at Cattawissa, Pa 24 Sept 1791; d at Toronto 12 Apr 1838). Variously employed after settling south of Lk Simcoe, Upper Canada, in 1815, Lount was best known as a blacksmith. A generous, concerned man he became a Reformer in the 1830s, serving in the Assembly from 1834 until defeated by corrupt practices in 1836. He led a large party to join the REBELLION OF 1837. Captured, he was tried and executed. RONALD STAGG

Loup-Garou, the werewolf, known but less widespread in French Canadian tradition than in Europe, is not always a wolf or dog, but may also take the form of a calf or small ox, a pig, a cat or even an owl. A person could fall under suspicion of being a werewolf if one had not made one's Easter duty for 7 years in a row. NANCY SCHMITZ

Louse, common term broadly used for certain INSECT PESTS of mammals, birds, plants (aphids), books (book lice), etc, and for CRUSTACEANS (sea lice), living commensally with aquatic mammals and fish. More commonly, the term refers to biting and bloodsucking insects adapted as wingless, dorsoventrally flattened external parasites of birds and mammals. Lice have short legs with large claws. Eyes are reduced or absent. Under the most favourable conditions, lice cannot survive off the host for more than a few days. Sucking lice, of which over 200 species have been described, are blood-feeding parasites of mammals, including humans. They have piercing and sucking mouthparts and subsist entirely on nutrients derived from the host's blood. Biting lice, estimated to comprise even more species, are parasites mainly of birds but also of mammals. They have chewing mouthparts, and feed on epidermal debris and exudates. Each species is confined to one host or a few closely related ones, and at least one species is known for almost every terrestrial, warm-blooded animal. Lice harbour and transmit disease organisms to and among animals (eg, those causing relapsing fever and typhus in humans). Lice spread rapidly to cause epidemics in crowded, unsanitary conditions. W.O. HAUFE

Lousewort (genus *Pedicularis*), herbaceous plant of figwort family (Scrophulariaceae). Five hundred species occur in the Northern Hemisphere; 22 throughout Canada. Most Canadian species are perennial; heights vary (10-100 cm). Louseworts occur in alpine situations and in damp, marshy ground in association with grasses. They are semiparasitic: green leaves produce some food and suckers connect to, and absorb food from, grass roots. Parrot-beaked, often

Large-flowered lousewort (*Pedicularis capitata*), growing on a dry, alpine slope (*photo by Julie O. Hrapko*).

brightly coloured flowers usually occur in showy, terminal spikes. *P. arctica,* with pink flowers on stout stems (up to 15 cm), are often abundant in alpine situations. *P. groenlandica,* common in boggy areas, grows to 50 cm and has reddish purple flowers. Common lousewort or wood betony (*P. canadensis*), now considered poisonous, was eaten and used as animal feed by settlers. N American Indians used it for food, to cure rattlesnake bite, to reduce swellings, and as an aphrodisiac.
PATRICK SEYMOUR

Loverboy, a Vancouver-based rock group, is a top international concert draw. The band – Paul Dean (guitar), Mike Reno (vocals), Matt Frenette (drums), Doug Johnson (keyboards) and Scott Smith (bass) – won 8 consecutive Juno Awards 1977-84. The worldwide success of the 1980 debut album *Loverboy* was followed by *Get Lucky,* which sold over 3 million copies in the US. *Lovin' Every Minute of It* (1985) had 3 hit singles.
JOHN GEIGER

Lovitt, William Dodge, vessel owner, entrepreneur (b 21 July 1834; d 1 Jan 1894). He purchased new sailing vessels at YARMOUTH, NS, Port of Registry during the 19th century. As an entrepreneur, he was at the centre of a family connection, including the Burrills and the Canns, that succeeded the KILLAMS as the dominant family group in Yarmouth. Beginning as a vessel owner in the late 1850s, Lovitt was a director of the Exchange Bank 1874-86 and of insurance companies by the 1870s. As the Canadian sailing-ship industry settled into an irreversible decline, he invested in railway and textile companies during the 1880s. He was president of the Yarmouth Duck and Yarn Co, a local textile mill that was profitable into the 20th century. GERRY PANTING

Low, Albert Peter, geologist, explorer (b at Montréal 24 May 1861; d at Ottawa 9 Oct 1942). Low joined the GEOLOGICAL SURVEY OF CANADA on graduation from McGill. The Québec-Labrador border was eventually defined on the basis of his 1893-95 explorations. He resigned in 1901 to prospect for iron on Hudson Bay, but returned to government service and spent the winter of 1903-04 on board the *Neptune* at Cape Fullerton on the W side of Hudson Bay. Low became director of the Geological Survey in 1906 and deputy minister of mines in 1907; illness led to his retirement in 1913. DONALD J.C. PHILLIPSON

Lowden, John Alexander, "Sandy," pediatrician (b at Toronto 21 Feb 1933). After graduating in medicine from U of T in 1957, Lowden studied for his doctorate at the Montreal Neurological Inst. Appointed to the medical staff of the Hospital for Sick Children, Toronto, in 1964, he is currently professor of pediatrics and clinical biochemistry, associate director of the HSC Research Inst and president of the Research Development Corp. The author of over 80 scientific and medical publications, Lowden is a recognized authority on genetic-metabolic diseases, particularly those involving lysosomes and hydrolases.
JOHN W. CALLAHAN

Lower, Arthur Reginald Marsden, historian (b at Barrie, Ont 12 Aug 1889; d at Kingston, Ont 7 Jan 1988). Professor at Wesley College, Winnipeg (1929-47), and Douglas Professor of Canadian History at Queen's U, Kingston (1947-59), Lower, the son of English immigrants, was the first of his family to attend university (U of T, Harvard). His first books, *The Trade in Square Timber* (1932), *Settlement and the Forest Frontier in Eastern Canada* (1936) and *The North American Assault on the Canadian Forest* (1938), detailed the role of the forest in Canadian development, following the STAPLE THESIS elaborated by Harold INNIS. In *Colony to Nation* (1946), written during WWII, Lower sought a basis for a sense of national community which might unite French and English Canadians. Recipient of the Gov Gen's Award (1946, 1954), the Tyrrell Medal of the Royal Soc of Canada (1947), and a Companion of the Order of Canada (1968), Lower was also an honorary chief of the Ojibwa; his native name, *Kikugaygawbigoneden*, meant "The Recorder of His People's Tradition." MARGARET E. MCCALLUM

Reading: A.R.M. Lower, *My First Seventy-Five Years* (1967).

Lower Canada, the southern portion of present-day Québec, existing as a separate British province from 1791 to 1840. In 1791 Britain took the decision to divide the PROVINCE OF QUEBEC into UPPER CANADA and Lower Canada. The decision could have been foreseen, since Britain had followed a policy of territorial division in the 17th and 18th centuries when the American colonies were being founded; in 1769 when Prince Edward Island was detached from Nova Scotia; and in 1784 after the wave of LOYALIST immigration (which occurred in Québec as well) when the provinces of Cape Breton and New Brunswick were created. After the Conquest of NEW FRANCE, Great Britain wanted to redraw the boundaries of its new colony so as to make room in the fisheries and the fur trade for the rival merchants of Québec and Montréal. The QUEBEC ACT of 1774 was a formal recognition of the failure of the project, as the borders were adjusted in closer conformity to the needs of a transcontinental economy.

In 1791 the fur trade still played a determining role for the merchants and seasonal workers drawn from the rural population. These and their dependants still felt that their territory included both the St Lawrence Valley and the huge western expanse from the Great Lakes to the Pacific. In the early 19th century, however, the economic bases for this perception grew blurry and, for most francophone Lower Canadians, took on the dimensions of the St Lawrence Lowlands from Montréal to the Gulf of St Lawrence. When in 1822 Louis-Joseph PAPINEAU attacked the proposed union of the 2 Canadas, he described Lower Canada as a distinct geographic, economic and cultural space, forever destined to serve the HABITANT as a Catholic and French nation.

This Québecois vision found little support among the anglophone merchants, who continued to challenge the 1791 decision and who, from Montréal, largely controlled the economic development of Upper Canada. These businessmen, who owned the banks and means of transportation and who fervently advocated the building of canals on the St Lawrence R, were involved primarily in the grain trade to England and in transporting Upper Canadian forest products to the port of Québec; they occupied an economic space that overflowed the borders of the St Lawrence Valley. After the unsuccessful attempt to unite the 2 Canadas in 1822, they began clamouring for the annexation of Montréal to Upper Canada and continued until after the failure of the REBELLIONS OF 1837, when a single province was formed.

An Economy in Crisis Around 1760 the colonial economy was still dominated by the FUR TRADE and a commercial AGRICULTURE based on wheat. The FISHERIES, the timber trade, shipbuilding and the FORGES SAINT-MAURICE were all secondary. The fur trade was still expanding northwards and towards the Pacific: towards the end of the century, 600 000 beaver skins and other furs worth over £400 000 were being exported annually to England. All this activity, transcontinental and international by its very nature, was largely concentrated in the hands of the bourgeoisie of the NORTH WEST COMPANY – the Montréal-based company that had triumphed over its American rivals and the HUDSON'S BAY COMPANY. However, after 1804, growing pressure from these rivals reduced profits to such an extent that in 1821 the NWC had to merge with the HBC.

The wheat trade underwent equally important transformations. After about 1730 wheat farming, the basis for a subsistence agriculture, started to become a commercial activity, thanks to the development of an external market. This market was mainly the West Indies until 1760, and then it expanded until, by the beginning of the 19th century, it included southern Europe and Britain. Thereafter, production fell off so sharply that around 1832 Lower Canada had to import over 500 000 minots (about 19.5 million L) of wheat annually from Upper Canada. The deficit became chronic. Oats, potatoes and animal husbandry occasionally brought profits to some farmers, but most grew these crops for subsistence. The increasing difficulties in agriculture and in the fur trade adversely affected the population's standard of living.

This was the context for the rapid growth of the TIMBER TRADE after 1806. Increased production and export of forest products occurred during Napoleon's Continental Blockade when England, to guarantee wood supplies for her warships, introduced preferential tariffs that were maintained at about the same level until 1840, despite successive price drops. Again there was abundant seasonal help in Lower Canada. The forest industry, with Québec City as its nerve centre, was especially active in the Ottawa Valley, the EASTERN TOWNSHIPS and the Québec and Trois-Rivières areas. Squared pine and oak, construction wood, staves, potash and shipbuilding were the industry's mainstays.

Lower Canada's economy, transformed in the climate of crisis of declining fur and local wheat shipments, was increasingly Québec-centered and yet more dependent for its exports on surplus production in Upper Canada. This produced an urgent need for credit institutions and for massive investments in road and canal construction.

Overpopulation From the early 18th century, French Canadian population had grown without significant help from immigration. With a birthrate of about 50 births per thousand population and mortality of about 25 per thousand, the population doubled every 25-28 years. Post-Conquest British immigration hardly affected this demographic trend except for a limited time during the Loyalist wave, whereas land was so abundant and people so scarce that French Canada's vigorous increase continued until the end of the century. It was in the seigneur's interests to grant lands upon request in order to have the largest possible number of rent payers, but early in the 19th century this policy, combined with the high birthrate, led to decreasing accessibility of good lands; as well the seigneurs, prompted by the rising value of their forest products, began to limit the peasants' access to real estate. As the scarcity of land, real or artificial, became more widespread, a rural proletariat began to develop, which by 1830 made up about one-third of the rural population. French Canadian immigrants to the US (*see* FRANCO-AMERICANS) came largely from this group and from the impoverished peasantry.

After 1815, population pressure was intensified in the rural communities along the St Lawrence and Richelieu rivers by a massive wave of British immigrants looking for land and jobs. Peasants and the proletariat in rural Québec felt threatened by the strangers, who sought land in the Townships, where French Canadians had long thought their own excess population could settle. The rapidly rising urban anglophone population was even more alarming to them: in Québec City in 1831, Anglophones formed 45% of the population and topped 50% among the day labourers; in Montréal in 1842 the percentages were 61% and 63%, respectively. These factors helped sharpen the Francophones' feeling that their culture was in danger and helped strengthen the nationalist movement, tormented by class struggle (*see* FRENCH CANADIAN NATIONALISM).

Class Struggles and Political Conflicts The society that had developed in New France was one in which the military, nobility and clergy were dominant and the bourgeoisie was dependent on them. After 1760 British military personnel, aristocrats and merchants replaced their francophone equivalents. But the development of class consciousness within the 2 bourgeoisies, the English and the French, helped set off a conflict between the middle class and the aristocrats over the introduction of parliamentary institutions. The outcome in 1791 showed both the progress of the middle class and the economic and social decline of the nobility. Towards the end of the century, the power of the nobility was entirely dependent on the privileges and protection guaranteed by the heads of the colonial state.

Economic and demographic changes after 1800 produced a deterioration of social relationships, the emergence of new ideologies and a reorientation of the old ones. This was the context for a struggle among 3 classes for the leadership of society: the anglophone bourgeoisie, the French Canadian middle class and the clergy. The anglophone merchant bourgeoisie, the main beneficiary of the 1791 reform and of recent economic expansion, felt that its status and power were threatened by the widespread changes. The efforts of these merchants to have the St Lawrence R canalized and their desire to stimulate the construction of access roads into the Townships were parts of a larger program seeking to increase immigration, create banks, revise the state's fiscal policies and abolish or reform the SEIGNEURIAL SYSTEM and customary law.

But these measures required political support from the francophone nationalists, who were on the rise and held a majority in the legislative assembly. Income from continued TIMBER DUTIES was uncertain since it depended, after the 1815 peace, on both the goodwill of this nationalist element and the failure of England to introduce free trade. Anglophone merchants dominated business circles in the cities (in 1831 they constituted 57% and 63% of the merchant class in Québec City and Montréal, respectively) and played a disproportionately large role in the countryside. Nevertheless, they felt vulnerable in a colony numerically dominated by Francophones. Not surprisingly, Anglophones tended to seek the political support of governors, colonial bureaucrats and even the government in London. Their attitude is explained by their inability to form a party capable of dominating the majority, slight though it was, in the Legislative Assembly. Their successive political defeats over 30 years forced them to defend the imperial connection and the constitutional status quo and to support conservative political ideas.

After the turn of the century, this bourgeoisie began to clash with the French Canadian middle class, in particular with the professionals who were then developing a national consciousness. These professionals, whose numbers were rapidly growing and who aspired to form a national elite, became sharply aware that major economic activities were increasingly controlled by Anglophones. Regarding this as the result of a serious injustice done their fellow Francophones, they tended to view the anglophone merchants and bureaucrats as the most dangerous enemies of the French Canadian nation. Their ideology, warmly welcomed among small-scale merchants in French Canada, became steadily more hostile to the activities on which anglophone power was based. The francophone petite bourgeoisie glorified agriculture, defended the COUTUME DE PARIS and the seigneurial system (which it wanted to see extended throughout the province) and opposed the BRITISH AMERICAN LAND CO, loudly insisting that Lower Canadian territory was the exclusive property of the French Canadian nation.

Place d'Armes, Montréal (1830), line engraving and etching by R.A. Sproule (*courtesy Royal Ontario Museum*).

To promote its interests, the French Canadian bourgeoisie fashioned the PARTI CANADIEN (which in 1826 became the Parti PATRIOTE). Party leaders explained economic disparities by the British control of the political machine and the distribution of patronage. They therefore developed a theory that, though it provided for political evolution along traditional British lines, also justified rule by the majority party in the legislative assembly. Party leader Pierre BÉDARD was the main architect of this strategy, which was inspired by a desire to apply the principle of ministerial responsibility. (Its obvious consequence was to transfer the bases of power to the francophone majority and to reduce the governor's powers.) In 1810, in the context of revolutionary and imperial wars, perpetual tension with the US and current ideas about colonial autonomy, these reformist plans seemed so radical that the suspicious Gov CRAIG arrested the editors of *Le Canadien*, suppressed this nationalist party organ and dissolved the legislative assembly.

After the WAR OF 1812, Papineau, the new leader of the decapitated party, realized that it was necessary to seek more limited results. He focused on the struggle over control of revenues and on complaints, with the immediate objective of sharing power with his party's opponents. Papineau hoped in this way to control the clergy and win over the Irish Catholics, thus warding off accusations of nationalist extremism; it is from this perspective that the leadership roles in the party of John Neilson and, later, E.B. O'Callaghan can be explained. Only after 1827 did the pressure of events and from the militants cause Papineau to become more radical, and the idea of an independent Lower Canada then began to take root. The desire initially to win power by ordinary political means was at the heart of this adjustment of political ideology. But the British model was replaced by the American model, which justified the elective principle for all posts that exercised power, from justices of the peace and militia officers to legislative councillors and even the governor.

As the political struggle intensified, the Parti patriote gained strength in French Canadian circles, stirred up by nationalism, but lost popularity among Anglophones, who tended to align themselves with the anglophone merchants. Though they agreed on the main objective – national independence – Patriote militants disagreed about the kind of society that should follow their victory: the majority, which backed Papineau, wanted to continue the social *ancien régime*, whereas a minority hoped to build a new society inspired by authentic liberalism. These opposing views were to play a major role in the failure of the rebellions.

The clergy, a class solidly enthroned on a complex institutional network that generated great revenues, naturally became engaged in the struggle for power. Having seen the effects of the French Revolution and the intervention of the Protestant colonial state in Québec education at the turn of the century, Québecois clerics were already aware of the threat to their social influence. They became even more aware when conflict flared between the Parti canadien and the merchants' party, which was supported by the governor. The ecclesiastical leaders became convinced that a local group was using parliamentary institutions to achieve its revolutionary intentions. Consequently, during the crisis of 1810, Mgr PLESSIS asked his priests to support (with little success) the government's candidates. When the War of 1812 began, it is not surprising that the episcopacy strongly denounced the Americans and demanded, on pain of religious sanction, that the population actively defend its territory.

After 1815, reassured by peace and the more conciliatory attitude of the Parti canadien leaders, who opposed the Sulpician fathers (still French in origin) and supported the clergy's efforts to create a diocese in Montréal, clerical leaders began fighting for the restoration and extension of the privileges of their class. They sought control of primary education, perceiving that school was one of the main instruments of socialization. With Papineau's support the clergy won a dramatic but brief victory over the Protestant and state threat when the Parish Schools Act was passed in 1824.

The clergy gained new strength when Mgr J.J. LARTIGUE became bishop of Montréal and devoted himself to reorienting clerical ideology and strategy to fight the lay and Protestant threat. He was well suited to the role: he was one of the first priests to break with GALLICAN ideology and to be won over by ULTRAMONTANE and theocratic doctrine. He followed the new form of nationalism, now detached from its liberal roots and justifying the dominant role of the clergy in a Catholic society. He hoped to restore to the church full control over educational institutions and to bring the clergy closer to the people so as to deepen church influence. But after 1829 the Parti patriote decided to establish assembly schools (nurseries for future patriotes), sought to democratize the management of the parishes and adopted a liberal and republican rhetoric. A break between the clergy and the French Canadian middle class became inevitable.

Rebellions of 1837-38 The 3-way power struggle became more violent in Mar 1837, when the British government, to break the political and financial deadlock, adopted the Russell Resolutions, which effectively rejected the Patriotes' demands. The Patriotes were not well enough organized to jump immediately into a revolutionary venture, so they developed a strategy that provided for the possibility that the state would refuse to yield to the pressure of a mass movement while it gave them time to prepare an armed insurrection to begin after winter set in.

The great parish and county assemblies began in May 1837 and spread agitation from parish to parish. For the present, action was supposed to stay within legal limits, but these assemblies, pushed by radicals, soon went beyond. Government leaders saw the uproar as a huge blackmail operation, but the better-informed clergy immediately understood the Patriotes' real objectives. By July 1837 Bishop Lartigue had given precise instructions for his priests in case of armed uprising. Agitation increased until the end of Oct, when the Patriotes held the "Assembly of the Six Counties" in ST-CHARLES-SUR-RICHELIEU. It was marked by a declaration of rights and by the adoption of resolutions suggesting a desire to overthrow the government.

Meanwhile, militant Patriotes had been extremely active in Montréal, where they set up the FILS DE LA LIBERTÉ, an association that publicly advocated revolution, held military drills and paraded through the streets amid great commotion. A Nov 6 battle between the Fils de la liberté and anglophone members of the DORIC CLUB led to government intervention, something long and anxiously sought by country dwellers who were being harrassed by the Patriotes. A few days later the government issued warrants for the arrest of the Patriote leaders, who hastily left Montréal and took refuge in the countryside.

A General View of Quebec From Pointe Levy by Richard Short (*courtesy Musée du Québec/photo by Patrick Altman*).

Armed confrontation came well ahead of the Patriotes' intended timetable. Following an incident in Longueuil on Nov 16, the governor sent troops into the Richelieu Valley. On 23 Nov 1837 the Patriotes, led by Wolfred Nelson, took ST-DENIS, but 2 days later were defeated at ST-CHARLES. Having scattered the last insurgent ranks S of Montréal, Gen COLBORNE attacked ST-EUSTACHE on Dec 14 and ended Patriote resistance.

Papineau, supreme commander, had hidden in St-Hyacinthe before taking refuge in the US under an assumed name. Many refugees gathered in the US and, until Lord DURHAM tried to calm tempers, attempted to plan an invasion of Lower Canada. Their efforts were complicated by a rift within Patriote ranks between the radicals, such as Coté and Nelson, and the more conservative elements led by Papineau. When Durham left Canada in early Nov 1838, a second rebellion broke out, led by the radicals. Even though the revolutionary organization, through the efforts of the Société des frères chasseurs (HUNTERS' LODGES), spread throughout the territory, the Patriotes had no more luck than the year before. By about mid-Nov 1838 order had been re-established in the Richelieu Valley.

In 1837 Durham had exiled a few of the most seriously compromised political prisoners, but was rebuked by London. In 1838, 850 suspects were arrested; 108 were brought before a court-martial and 99 were sentenced to death; only a dozen were hanged and 58 were deported to Australia. The main winners in the revolution were the clergy, with its special vision of a French, Catholic nation, and the anglophone bourgeoisie, with its plans for development through economic measures. In 1840 the ACT OF UNION was passed in Britain, providing for the 1841 unification of Upper and Lower Canada into the single PROVINCE OF CANADA. FERNAND OUELLET

Reading: Fernand Ouellet, *Lower Canada 1791-1840* (1980).

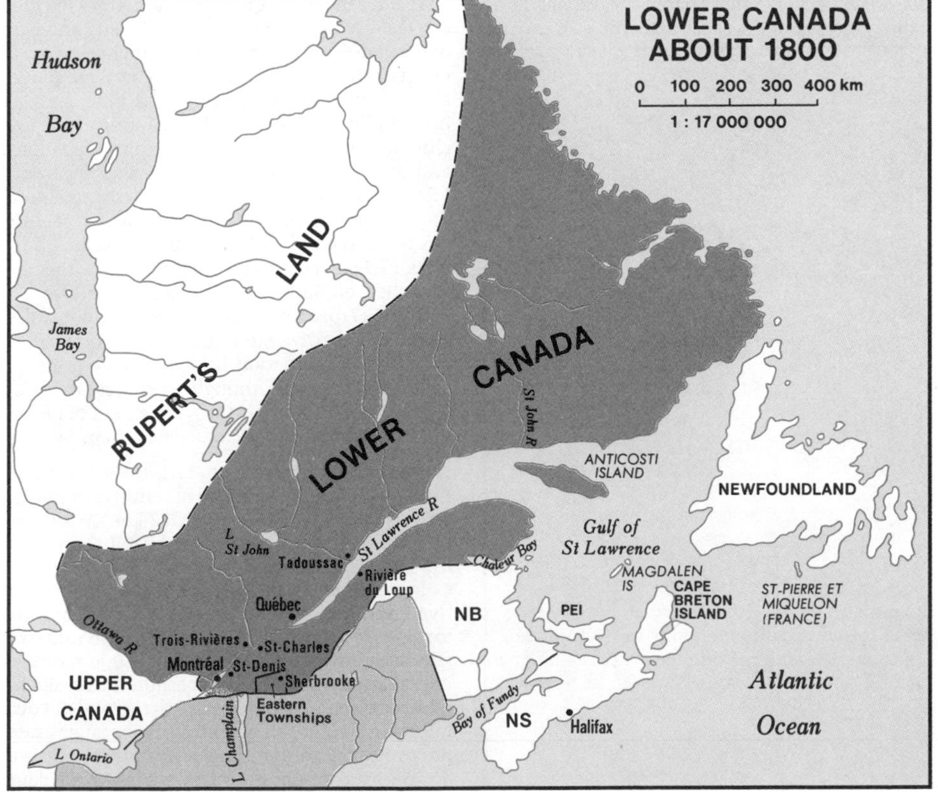

Lowry, Clarence Malcolm, novelist (b at New Brighton, Eng 28 July 1909; d at Ripe, Eng 27 June 1957). Although he was not born in Canada, the years he spent in Dollarton, BC, (1940-54) were the happiest and most productive years of his chaotic life. Much of his later fiction is set in BC. All of Lowry's work is to a degree autobiographical. *Under the Volcano,* one of the great books of modern literature, was inspired by his months of alcoholic depression in Mexico (1936-38). From 1941 to 1944 he worked with his wife Margerie in their Dollarton shack tirelessly revising the manuscript, and in 1946 it was accepted for publication. In the character of the consul, a drunken diplomat without official duties, and in the infernal Mexican setting, Lowry found his perfect symbols. His supple and allusive style lends tragic dignity to the consul's sufferings, and gives the novel its unique combination of humour and horror. Much of Lowry's fiction (*Ultramarine,* 1933; *Lunar Caustic,* 1968; HEAR US O LORD FROM HEAVEN THY DWELLING PLACE, 1961) is memorable, but it is *Under the Volcano* that has established Lowry as one of this century's great writers. *October Ferry to Gabriola* (1970) was published posthumously. TRACY WARE

Reading: Douglas Day, *Malcolm Lowry* (1973); S. Salloum, ed, *Malcolm Lowry: Vancouver Days* (1987).

Lowther, Patricia Louise, poet (b at Vancouver 29 July 1935; d there 24 Sept 1975). Lowther devoted herself to the promotion of poetry, lecturing in creative writing at UBC, and to the advancement of the NEW DEMOCRATIC PARTY, for which she was constituency secretary. She was elected cochairman of the League of Canadian Poets in 1974 and subsequently to the BC Arts Council. Widely anthologized, Lowther published 4 collections of poetry (*This Difficult Flowering,* 1968; *The Age of the Bird,* 1972; *Milk Stone,* 1974; and *A Stone Diary,* 1977) in which the 2 pivotal aspects of her work, socialist politics and the politics of sex, are mirrored. She is survived by 4 children and her husband Roy, who was sentenced to life imprisonment in 1977 for his wife's murder. The Pat Lowther Award is given annually by the LEAGUE OF CANADIAN POETS.

CATHERINE AHEARN

Loyal Electors, political group active in Prince Edward Island 1806-12. Either during or shortly after the elections for the PEI House of Assembly in 1806 a loose alliance of 5 members of the House came together as the Club of Loyal Electors, opposed to the supporters of former governor Edmund Fanning who dominated colonial politics at the turn of the 19th century. A leading member of the Loyal Electors was James Bardin PALMER, a Charlottetown lawyer, but the membership included a number of other leading residents of the Island, most of whom were recent immigrants. The group had some success in by-elections and following a general election in 1812 emerged with 7 members in the 18-seat assembly. As some of the members of the House refused to attend the sessions, the Loyal Electors won effective control of the Assembly. The group, however, had no real platform of reform and, while opposed to the "family compact" which dominated Island politics, did not offer a substantial alternative. Their success was further limited owing to charges of disloyalty brought against several members and following the arrival of a new governor late in 1812 the power of the group was severely diminished. Some historians have seen in the Loyal Electors the beginning of a reform party tradition in PEI, but it is more accurate to identify the Electors as a short-lived political grouping who reacted to particular circumstances in the colony. H.T. HOLMAN

Loyalists, American colonists of varied ethnic backgrounds who supported the British cause during the AMERICAN REVOLUTION (1775-83). In 1789 Lord Dorchester (*see* CARLETON), governor-in-chief of BRITISH NORTH AMERICA, proclaimed that the Loyalists and their children should be allowed to append "UE" to their names, "alluding to their great principle, the Unity of Empire"; hence the phrase "United Empire Loyalist," or UEL. (The term applied initially in the Canadian colonies alone; it was officially recognized in the Maritimes only in the 20th century.) In determining who was eligible for compensation for war losses, Britain used a fairly precise definition: Loyalists were those born or living in the American colonies at the outbreak of the Revolution who rendered substantial service to the royal cause during the war, and who left the US by the end of the war or soon after. Those who left substantially later, mainly to gain land and to escape growing intolerance of minorities, are often called "late" Loyalists.

The Loyalists supported Britain for highly diverse reasons. Many evinced a personal loyalty to the Crown or a fear that revolution could bring chaos to America. Many agreed with the rebels that America had suffered wrongs at the hands of Britain, but believed the solution could be worked out within the empire. Others, seeing themselves as weak or threatened within American society and in need of an outside defender, included linguistic and religious minorities, recent immigrants not fully integrated into American society, blacks and Indians. Sympathy for the Crown was a dangerous sentiment: those who defied the revolutionary forces could find themselves without civil rights, subject to mob violence or flung into prison. All the states finally taxed or confiscated Loyalist property.

During the Revolution over 19 000 Loyalists served Britain in specially created provincial corps, accompanied by several thousand Indians. Others spent the war in such strongholds as New York City or in refugee camps such as those at Sorel and Machiche, Qué. Between 80 000 and 100 000 eventually fled, about half of them to Canada. The vast majority were neither well-to-do nor particularly high in social rank; most were farmers. Ethnically, they were quite mixed, and many were recent immigrants. White Loyalists brought sizable contingents of slaves with them. Free blacks and escaped slaves who had fought in the Loyalist corps and as many as 2000 Indian allies, mainly Six Nations Iroquois from NY, settled in Canada.

The main waves of Loyalists came to what is now Canada in 1783 and 1784. The MARITIME PROVINCES became home for upwards of 30 000; most of coastal NS received Loyalist settlers, as did Cape Breton and St John's I [PEI]. The 2 chief settlements were in the Saint John R valley and temporarily at SHELBURNE, NS. The Loyalists swamped the previous population of 20 000 Americans and French, and in 1784 New Brunswick and Cape Breton were created to deal with the influx.

Of about 2000 who moved to present-day Québec, some settled in the Gaspé on Chaleur Bay and others in the seigneury of Sorel at the mouth of the Richelieu R. About 7500 moved into what would become Ontario, most settling along the St Lawrence R to the Bay of Quinte. There were also substantial settlements in the Niagara Peninsula and on the Detroit R, with subsidiary and later settlements along the Thames R and at Long Point. The Grand R was the main focus of Loyalist Iroquois settlement. The Loyalist influx gave the region its first substantial population and led to the creation of a separate province, UPPER CANADA, in 1791. Loyalists were instrumental in establishing educational, religious, social and governmental institutions. Though greatly outnumbered by later immigrants, Loyalists and their descendants, such as Egerton RYERSON, exerted a strong and lasting influence. Modern Canada has inherited much from the Loyalists, including a certain conservatism, a preference for "evolution" rather than "revolution" in matters of government, and tendencies towards a pluralistic and heterogeneous society. *See also* UNITED EMPIRE LOYALISTS.

BRUCE G. WILSON

Reading: W. Brown, *The Good Americans* (1969); M.B. Fryer, *King's Men* (1980); B. Graymont, *The Iroquois in the American Revolution* (1972); Bruce G. Wilson, *As She Began* (1981); E.C. Wright, *The Loyalists of New Brunswick* (1955).

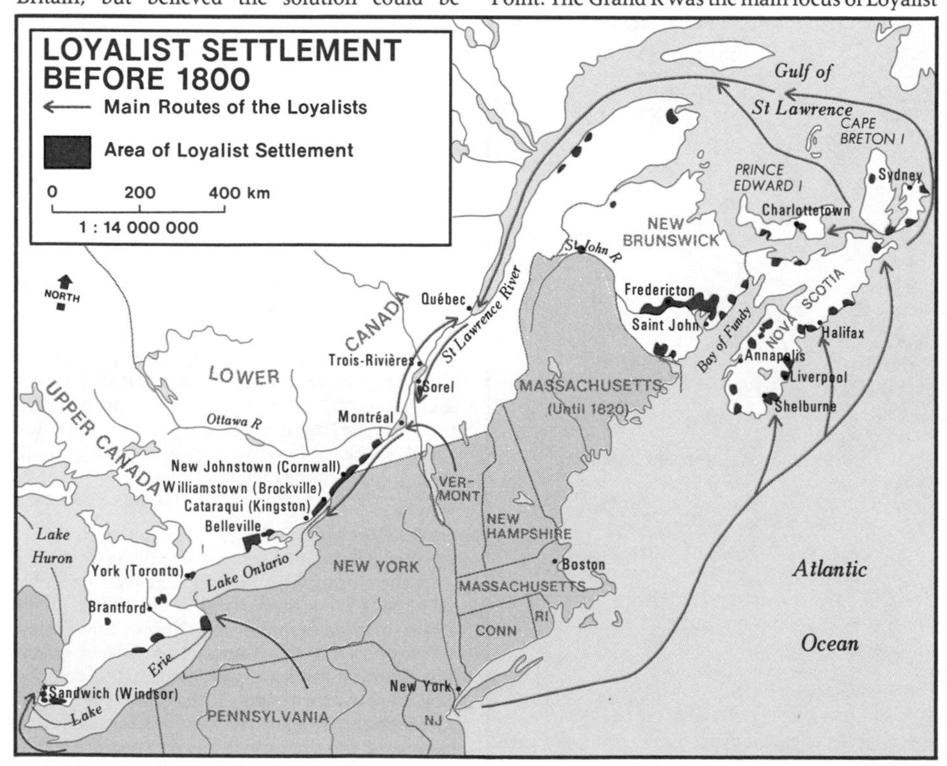

Loyola College, *see* CONCORDIA UNIVERSITY.

Luard, Richard George Amherst, army officer (b in Eng 29 July 1827; d at Eastbourne, Eng 24 July 1891). A British military officer, he was general officer commanding the Canadian Militia 1880-84, following active service in India, the Crimea and China. Scornful of the Militia's fancy dress and lack of expertise, he advocated expansion of Canada's tiny permanent force at the expense of the part-time soldiers in rural regiments. With displays of his fearsome temper at military gatherings, this policy led him into conflict with politically influential officers. Adolphe CARON, minister of militia and defence, perceived his attempts at departmental reform as interference with political patronage. Although new permanent-force units were raised in 1883, Luard resigned under pressure soon after. O.A. COOKE

Luc, Frère, Récollet, painter, architect (b Claude François at Amiens, France, May 1614; d at Paris 1685). He studied in Paris and Rome, received the title "king's painter" for his work in decorating the Louvre (1640-42), joined the Récollets (1644) as Frère Luc, and worked in New France from Aug 1670 to Oct 1671. He designed the chapel for the rebuilt Récollet monastery in Québec C, now the oldest chapel in Canada and part of Hôpital-Général, and a wing of the SÉMINAIRE DE QUÉBEC (1677-78). Since works of art were generally imported from France at this time, he was most influential through his paintings for local churches, both during his sojourn in the colony and after his return to France. The *Assomption de la Vièrge*, which he painted in 1671 for the retable of the Récollet chapel, is his best-known work. He has been credited with a few portraits, including ones of Jean TALON and Bishop LAVAL, and the churches of Ste-Anne-de-Beaupré and of St-Philippe (Trois-Rivières) possess his colourful if sentimental VOTIVE PAINTINGS. Most accomplished paintings of the period have variously been attributed to him and, though recent research discredits many of these claims, the extent of his influence cannot be denied. ROSEMARY SHIPTON

Lucan, Ont, Village, pop 1728 (1986c), 1616 (1981c), inc 1872, is located in southwestern Ontario, 90 km NE of SARNIA and 22 km NW of LONDON. It was first settled 1829-30 by refugee BLACKS from the US and was known as the Wilberforce Colony. In 1832 settlers from southern Ireland arrived and the community was renamed Marystown. When the main line of the GRAND TRUNK RY was built through the village in 1860, it received its present name after a suggestion by a resident who had been coachman on the estate of Lord Lucan in Ireland. In recent years, because of its proximity to London, Lucan has prospered as a dormitory community for that city. The village has received unwelcome notoriety because of its connection with the savage massacre of the DONNELLYS in 1880 on a nearby farm. ORLO MILLER

Lucania, Mount, elev 5226 m, the third-highest mountain in Canada, is located 29 km E of the Alaska border and 50 km N of Mt LOGAN in the Yukon's St Elias Range. It was named by the duke of Abruzzi, who viewed it from Mt St Elias in 1897. Mt Lucania is joined to its neighbour to the NE, Mt STEELE, by a high saddle. Bradford Washburn and Bob Bates were flown to Walsh Glacier and made the first ascent 9 July 1937, then proceeded over Mt Steele – that mountain's second ascent. GLEN BOLES

Lucy Qinnuayuak, artist (b near Sugluk, Qué 1915?; d at Cape Dorset, NWT 10 Sept 1982). One of the most popular Inuit graphic artists, noted primarily for fanciful arctic birds, Lucy began to draw in the late 1950s at the time James HOUSTON started INUIT PRINTMAKING experiments at Cape Dorset. "We would draw our art in camp and then when a dog-team went to Cape Dorset to get supplies we would take our drawings and give them to Saumik" (ie, to Houston). Well over 100 of her drawings have appeared as prints; the stone for her early *Large Bear* (1961) was donated to the Tate Gallery, London, by admirer Sir Charles Gimpel and is displayed at the Scott Polar Research Institute, Cambridge. Widely collected, her work has appeared on an Olympic banner and in many exhibitions. *See also* INUIT ART.
DOROTHY HARLEY EBER

Luge, *see* BOBSLEDDING.

Lumber and Wood Industries Canada's lumber and wood industries include manufacturers that convert logs (by mechanical processes of sawing, peeling, slicing or chipping) into lumber, veneer, plywood, particle board and wafer board, and that produce, as residual by-products, wood chips, sawdust and shavings. Lumber and plywood are the most significant products in volumes manufactured. Over 60 000 people are employed directly in manufacturing lumber, plywood, veneer and wood-based panels. The market value of primary wood products in 1985 was $8.2 billion, of which 84% was attributed to lumber sales. Over 80% of softwood lumber production is exported, therefore this industry makes a significant contribution to Canada's BALANCE OF PAYMENTS.

The primary wood-products industry consumes about half the roundwood cut in Canada; the PULP AND PAPER INDUSTRY uses the remainder. Over 95% of logs used to manufacture lumber, plywood and other wood-based panels are softwoods (primarily CONIFERS); the rest are hardwoods (deciduous TREES). In Canada the principal softwood lumber species are DOUGLAS FIR, SPRUCE, PINE, HEMLOCK and western red CEDAR; BIRCH and MAPLE are the predominant hardwood species. Between 1970 and 1986, Canadian softwood lumber production rose dramatically by 64%. In 1986, 99% of the 33.1 million m^3 of lumber manufactured in Canada was softwood (of which BC produced 65%). In that year, 2 million m^3 of plywood was manufactured from softwoods, with BC responsible for 84%. Hardwood lumber and plywood are produced mainly in Ontario and Québec.

About 20% of Canadian lumber production is consumed in the domestic market; 80-85% of exported lumber is purchased by the US. During the 1980s, Canadian lumber producers were subjected to a number of impositions by the US on their penetration of that market, resulting in a tax imposed on softwood lumber exported to the US (*see* SOFTWOOD LUMBER DISPUTE). The European Economic Community and Japan are also important markets, with lesser volumes going to Australia and Latin America. More than 85% of the softwood plywood produced is used domestically; over 70% of exported plywood goes to Britain and other EEC countries. The US imports about 19% of Canadian export plywood, having itself a strong domestic industry. Around 80% of Canadian particle board and wafer board are consumed in Canada; the majority of exports goes to the US.

During the period 1970 to 1985, the number of sawmills decreased from an estimated 1800 to 1327 because of the trend towards larger, more technically efficient manufacturing complexes. A significant innovation in this period was the development of high-volume, small-log processing systems.

Lumber and Plywood Manufacturing Merchantable timber is felled and cut into logs for transport to sawmills. Mechanical or hydraulic debarking is the first step in converting a sawlog into lumber. In conventional sawmills, large logs are placed on a moving log carriage and passed repeatedly through a band or circular saw, each pass producing boards that normally require further processing on edgers, resaws and trimsaws. In sawmills processing small logs, the primary unit may be a chipper-canter with integrated sawing units, or a system of multiple-band or circular saws, designed to operate at speeds up to 100 m per minute. About three-quarters of the lumber produced in Canada is further processed in planer mills that smooth the rough surfaces and dimension the pieces. Over half the lumber is dried to remove excess moisture, either in dry kilns for several days at temperatures sometimes exceeding 80°C, or by air for several months.

Plywood is wood reduced to thin sheets of veneer, glued together with the grain direction of adjacent sheets at right angles. This cross-lamination makes the panel stable and redistributes the inherent directional-strength properties. Plywood is an engineered product. Veneers are produced by holding a log firmly at each end in a lathe and rotating it against a knife that moves towards the axis of rotation. The veneer exits from the lathe knife in a continuous ribbon of wood that is clipped to desired widths or to eliminate defects. After drying the veneers are sorted into sets, each of which will form a plywood panel of the desired thickness and size. Alternate sheets are coated with glue, which forms a waterproof bond when subjected to high temperature and pressure in a hot press. The rough plywood panels are then trimmed and may be sanded.

To ensure uniform quality, lumber and plywood are graded into categories by standardized procedures. Most of the lumber produced in Canada is used in CONSTRUCTION, mainly for house building; it is classed as dimension lumber and is graded into width and use categories. Other classes of lumber include clears, factory lumber and shop lumber, used to manufacture high-quality moldings, panelling and flooring, or to obtain clear cuttings for components in such items as doors and windows. Softwood plywood is produced in 3 grades: sanded (for high-quality finishing), unsanded (for construction use), and unsanded and overlaid (for special uses). For general construction and other structural purposes, the most common type of panel is sheathing, the unsanded grade. About half the plywood used in Canada is for house building and agricultural construction; industrial uses take up another third; the balance is consumed in a multitude of miscellaneous uses.

Particle Board and Wafer Board Wood particle board is a panel product manufactured by bonding particles of wood together with an adhesive in a press. Since the product is manufactured from small pieces of wood, properties of the finished board, such as density, hardness and elasticity, can be engineered into the panel. The furnish for particle board is sawdust or planer shavings or solid wood flaked or chipped specifically for that purpose. The various wood elements are screened and separated by size and shape so that their integration in the finished product can be controlled. The particles are then dried by heat and circulation and mixed with thermosetting bonding agents. The mixture is then meshed together in a layup for final pressing under heat.

The most common type of particle board manufactured in Canada is the 3-layered, graduated mat-formed variety. By preparing the core and surface material separately, segregating the coarser materials into the centre and the finest particles on the surface, the manufacturer can create a board that can be sanded to an even, smooth surface, and that has the desired mechanical properties in each layer. The fibre lengths of the particles are distributed in a random pattern, so that internal stresses average to zero, resulting in an extremely stable finished product. Major uses of particle board are furniture and cabinet panels and cores, and floor underlay; minor uses include interior wall sheathing and mobile-home decking.

Wafer board is an engineered, structural panelboard made from large, thin wafers cut from roundwood. These wafers are mixed with waterproof phenolic resin and interleaved together in thick mats, which are then bonded together under heat and pressure. The result is a solid, uniform building panel with high strength and water resistance, properties that make wafer board suitable for most construction applications. Some examples of uses are wall and roof sheathing, subflooring and underlay, cladding and soffits. The panels are also widely used for farm structures, industrial packaging, crating and warehouse pallets. DAVID MILTON

Lumonics Inc, *see* ELECTRONICS INDUSTRY.

Lumsdon, Cliff, long-distance swimmer (b at Toronto 1 Apr 1931). At age 6 Lumsdon joined the Lakeshore Swim Club in Toronto, coached by the famous Gus Ryder. In 1949 he claimed the first of 5 men's world marathon swimming championships by beating a field of 70 in the CNE 15-mile (24 km) swim with a time of 7 hrs 55 mins. He received the LOU MARSH TROPHY as Canada's athlete of the year in 1949. He continued to do well after 1954, when the shorter waterfront marathon was replaced by a 30-mile (48 km) swim across the lake. In 1956 he won the Atlantic City 26-mile (42 km) event and became the first to conquer the Juan de Fuca Strait. Later, he coached his daughter Kim and assisted Cindy NICHOLAS and other marathon swimmers.
GERALD REDMOND

Lund, Alan, choreographer (b at Toronto 23 May 1925). A specialist in musical theatre, he trained in Toronto and first established a performance reputation as a dance team with his wife Blanche, appearing during WWII in the revue *Meet the Navy*. Turning to choreography in the 1950s, Lund contributed to various productions, including *Spring Thaw*, the CANADIAN NATIONAL EXHIBITION Grandstand Show and at the STRATFORD FESTIVAL. From 1966 to 1986 he was artistic director of the CHARLOTTETOWN SUMMER FESTIVAL, where he directed Canada's most successful musical, *Anne of Green Gables*, and several others. His own *The Legend of the Dumbells* premiered there in 1977. Lund was given an honorary degree by UPEI and is a Member of the Order of Canada. He continues to direct and choreograph productions, such as *Kiss Me Kate* (Toronto, fall 1986).
JILLIAN M. OFFICER

Lundrigan, James, Conception Bay fisherman (*fl* 1818-30). In 1819 Lundrigan and fellow fisherman Philip Butler were involved in a court case which gave great impetus to the agitation for representative government. The men were tried at a surrogate court by the captain of one of His Majesty's Ships, in Harbour Grace. Lundrigan, who did not appear on a summons, was held in contempt of court and sentenced to receive 36 lashes on his bare back, which he was given until he fainted under the severity of the punishment. In Nov 1820 a committee of 13 with Patrick Morris as chairman passed a resolution condemning the cruel punishment inflicted for such trifling causes; the committee began to pursue such legal and constitutional means necessary to have the law which sanctioned such arbitrary proceedings repealed. Prowse, the historian, contends that the case of Lundrigan and Butler were taken up solely for the purpose of being used as a lever to obtain a Legislature for the colony. In 1824 "An Act for the Better Administration of Newfoundland" was passed which established the Supreme Court of Newfoundland. This put an end to the centuries-old tradition of naval officers holding courts of civil jurisdiction. TONY HOLLIHAN

Lundy's Lane, site of a battle fought between American troops and British regulars assisted by Canadian fencibles and militia on the sultry evening of 25 July 1814, almost within sight of NIAGARA FALLS. The action swayed to and fro, as the troops attacked each other with reckless abandon in pitch darkness. The British regulars, mainly the Royal Scots and the 8th, 41st and 89th regiments of foot, were steadfast in defence and bold adversaries in attack. Sir Gordon DRUMMOND, the Canadian-born British field commander, was wounded; his second-in-command was captured. Nonetheless, by midnight the British and Canadians held the field as the Americans retired toward Ft Erie. Casualties were high on both sides, the Americans suffering more killed. The battle was the toughest and most bitterly contested of the WAR OF 1812. ROBERT S. ALLEN

Lunenburg, NS, Town, pop 2972 (1986c), 3014 (1981c), inc 1888, shire town of Lunenburg County, is located on Lunenburg Bay, 90 km SW of Halifax. The centre of NS's fishing industry, it was known first as Merliguesche, and was home to some 50 ACADIANS as late as 1749. In 1753 the British government settled 1453 "Foreign Protestants" here; recruited from southwestern Germany and the Montbéliard district of France and Switzerland, these mostly German-speaking people were intended to help counter the French and Catholic presence in NS. (The settlement was named for the royal house of Brunswick-Lüneburg, whence came King George I of England.) Each settler was granted a free town-and-garden lot and farm acreage in the county. The town's gridlike plan mirrored that of Halifax.

Despite initial hardships, by the late 18th century Lunenburg supplied Halifax with many agricultural products. Lunenburgers had also entered the offshore fishery, today the foundation of the local economy. They first fished off the Labrador coast, but with the introduction of new trawling techniques in the late 1860s, the town's schooner fleet turned to the GRAND BANKS of Newfoundland and the Western Bank, SW of Sable I. The "Lunenburg cure" of dried cod found steady markets in the West Indies, particularly Puerto Rico.

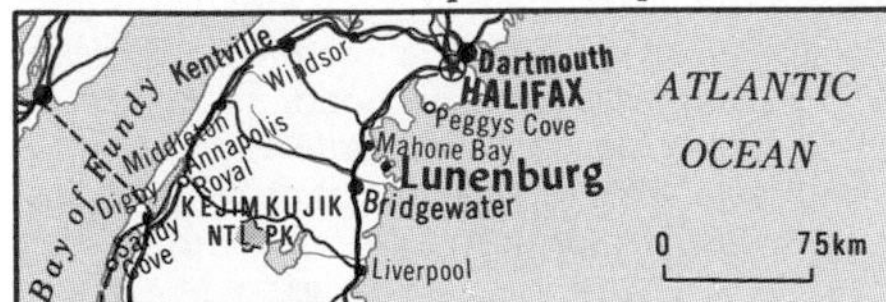

Lunenburg, NS, settled in the mid-18th century, is the base for Atlantic Canada's largest fish-processing plant and deep-sea trawler fleet (*photo by Jim Merrithew*).

"A boom of splendid proportions" (Lunenburg *Progress*, 1888) did not persist, however. The fish export trade became centralized in Halifax, where fast steamships left directly for the West Indies and US markets. Moreover, a preference appeared for fresh instead of dried fish. Local entrepreneurs, especially the Smith and Zwicker families, made adjustments to recapture lost trade. Beginning in the late 1920s, cold-storage equipment, processing plants and diesel-powered trawlers replaced cod-drying flakes and traditional schooners. Today, Lunenburg is the base for Atlantic Canada's largest fish-processing plant and fleet of deep-sea trawlers, owned by National Sea Products of Halifax, the successor to several Lunenburg-owned firms.

The fishery is celebrated annually in the NS Fisheries Exhibition and Fisherman's Reunion; and the Fisheries Museum of the Atlantic is found here. The famous racing schooner BLUENOSE was launched from a local shipyard. Several churches, including Canada's oldest Presbyterian (St Andrew's 1754) and Lutheran (Zion's 1772), and second-oldest Anglican (St John's 1753), as well as rich architectural tradition, testify to Lunenburg's historical significance. L.D. MCCANN

Reading: M.B. DesBrisay, *A History of Lunenburg County* (1895); Lunenburg Heritage Society, *A Walk Through Old Lunenburg* (1979).

Lupine [Lat *lupus*, "wolf," from belief that it robs the soil], annual or perennial herbaceous plant, genus *Lupinus* of family Leguminosae or Fabaceae. Worldwide, there are about 200 species with 2 principal areas of distribution: western mountains of N and S America, and the Mediterranean basin. In Canada, 28 species are recognized, most from southern Saskatchewan to BC; *L. arcticus* and *L. nootkatensis* reach the western Arctic; *L. perennis* occurs in southern Ontario; the western species, *L. polyphyllus*, is naturalized in eastern Canada. Some cultivated lupines escape along roadsides. Palmately compound leaves (ie, leaflets radiate from central point) and showy flower spikes make lupines admirable ORNAMENTALS (eg, Russell hybrids). Some species are grown for fodder, green manure and food (eg, the Balkan species, *L. albus*, cultivated in Europe and S. Africa). In Canada, lupines are used as a cover crop in reforestation projects. Lupines grow on and enrich nitrogen-poor soils. Quinolizidine alkaloids make lupine seeds poisonous to livestock, although vegetative plants are not. When treated, seeds provide a protein source for livestock. *See also* POISONOUS PLANTS. J.M. GILLETT

Luscombe, George, director, producer, playwright (b at Toronto 17 Nov 1926). As artistic director of Toronto Workshop Productions (1959-86), Luscombe is considered the founder of the "alternative" theatre movement in English Canada in the late 1960s. Working as an actor with Joan Littlewood in England 1952-56, he was influenced by her experimentation with new performance styles and belief in a socially committed theatre. His productions are characterized by ensemble acting rather than a written script orientation – what he calls "group" theatre. At TWP he pioneered original Canadian scripts, adaptations of classics and collective creations. His most noteworthy productions, combining a lively theatricality with significant social commentary, include *Hey, Rube!* (1961, 1973), *Mister Bones* (1969), *Chicago 70* (1970), *Ain't Lookin'* (1980, 1984) and, particularly, *Ten Lost Years* (1974, 1975, 1981). ANTON WAGNER

Lutherans, adherents to the Christian church founded by 16th-century Protestant reformer Martin Luther, whose central doctrine, justification by grace through faith alone, concentrates on God's favour to man and not on man's actions. Because the understanding of that favour depends upon proclamation and interpretation of the Word, preaching is the Lutheran church's hallmark. Lutheranism also reduced the number of sacraments from 7 to 2: baptism and the Lord's Supper (*see* CATHOLICISM). An emphasis upon pure doctrine derived from Lutheran orthodoxy and the influence of pietism are post-Reformation shifts imported to Canada principally from the US. The doctrinal stance of the Lutheran Church is determined by the acceptance of the Scriptures as sovereign over church tradition and as normative for faith and life, and by subscription to the Lutheran Confessions, composed 1530-80. Century-long doctrinal disputes which have divided American Lutherans have also impeded inter-Lutheran merger in Canada.

With the exception of Baltic congregations in exile, Lutheran state church congregations abroad and a few Wisconsin Synod congregations, there are now 2 Lutheran jurisdictions in Canada: Evangelical Lutheran Church in Canada (ELCIC) and Lutheran Church – Canada (LCC). The ELCIC, a merger of the Lutheran Church of America (LCA) and the Evangelical Lutheran Church of Canada, effective 1 Jan 1986, is headquartered in Winnipeg. Matters of inter-Lutheran concern are handled through the Lutheran Council in Canada (fd 1967). Originally rural and small town in orientation, concentrated in NS, Ontario and the Prairies, the Lutheran churches were greatly affected by urbanization after WWII. Major strength now is around Kitchener-Waterloo,

Winnipeg and Edmonton, with new missions in many cities. The slowness of Lutheran ethnic minorities to adjust to the dominant culture has to some degree inhibited Lutheran involvement in Canadian society.

Lutheran history in Canada has been determined by US affiliations. Congregations were established 1752 in Halifax, NS, and 1784 in Dundas County, Ont. From the beginning the mission suffered from lack of personnel and fiscal support from the parent US body; conflict with Anglicans; rivalry among the Lutheran denominations; and imposters posing as evangelical ministers. Confined principally to German settlements, churches associated with the New York Ministerium and the Pittsburgh Synod later found themselves competing with the Lutheran Church, Missouri Synod (LCMS). In the mid-19th century the Pittsburgh Synod created a Canada Conference, and in 1876 the Nova Scotia Conference. These and an English Conference became units of the General Council (GC), then of the successor United Lutheran Church in America (ULCA) in 1918. In 1962 they combined into a single synod upon formation of LCA. Meanwhile, in 1879 LCMS had formed its Canada District (renamed Ontario District in 1922), and the English District in 1911. The Canadian congregations of LCMS have been federated since 1958 as LCC, which became autonomous in Canada in Jan 1988.

In western Canada work began among Icelanders near Gimli, Man, in the 1870s, Germans in Winnipeg in 1888, Swedes in New Stockholm, Assiniboia (now Sask), in 1889, Norwegians in Vancouver in 1890 and Danes at Dickson, Alta, in 1903. By 1910 there were 3 German, 1 Swedish, 1 Danish, 1 Icelandic and 4 Norwegian Lutheran church bodies in the West, using at least as many languages. Except among Norwegians, the mergers of US parents did not follow ethnic lines. As a result, the German Manitoba Synod of the GC became a synod of ULCA in 1918; the Icelandic Synod joined this body in 1943 as a nongeographic synod; and these and the Canada Conference of the Swedish Augustana Synod became 2 synods (Man-Sask and Alta-BC) in LCA in 1962.

The Norwegian Lutheran Church and the Haugean Synod, the constituent units of the United Norwegian Lutheran Church, became in 1917 a district of the successor Evangelical Lutheran Church. This district, plus the Canadian District of the German Ohio Synod (later American Lutheran Church, 1930) and the Danish United Evangelical Lutheran church district, became a single district in the 1960 merger forming the American Lutheran Church. In 1967 this district became autonomous as ELCIC.

Lutheran Church polity is nonepiscopal, LCA's recent introduction of "bishops" notwithstanding (the title reflects American influence). The pastorate is the fundamental office of the church and the prerequisite for official functions. Ministerial recruitment is the responsibility of the church body; LCA and ELCIC ordain women, but women's rights remain restricted in LCC.

Youth work is carried out through the Luther League (Walther League in LCC) and university-campus ministry through inter-Lutheran Student Centres. The best-known men's organization is the Lutheran Laymen's League of LCMS, which in N America sponsors such programs as radio's Lutheran Hour. Women's auxiliaries have been major supporters of foreign mission and service projects. Education has received high priority among Lutherans, not only through the SUNDAY SCHOOL system and the earlier Saturday and Monday schools, but also through parochial schools, particularly in LCC; Bible schools such as those at Outlook, Sask, and Camrose, Alta, in ELCIC; and high schools and junior colleges such as Luther College, Regina, and Concordia College, Edmonton. WILFRID LAURIER UNIVERSITY in Waterloo was formerly Waterloo Lutheran U. Theological education has been pursued for some 75 years at seminaries in Waterloo and Saskatoon. An LCC seminary opened in 1976 in St Catharines, Ont, and another at Edmonton in 1984. Lutheran Life, a fraternal insurance society, provides scholarship support to Lutheran students and institutions. In the mid-20th century, health care mushroomed with the establishment of auxiliary hospitals and senior-citizens' homes. WALTER FREITAG

Reading: C.R. Cronmiller, *A History of the Lutheran Church in Canada*, (vol 1, 1961); G.O. Evenson, *Adventuring for Christ* (1974); V.J. Eylands, *Lutherans in Canada* (1945); Walter H.P. Freitag, *Prospect and Promise of Lutheran Unity in Canada* (1974); J.E. Herzer, *Homesteading for God* (1946); N. Threinen, *A Sower Went Out* (1982).

Lutin, elf or imp in French Canadian tradition who rides horses throughout the night, leaving them with plaits or knots in their hair, which are very difficult to remove. In some cases, it is believed that only a woman wearing a wedding ring can loosen the knots. NANCY SCHMITZ

Lyall, William, philosopher (b at Paisley, Scot 11 June 1811; d at Halifax 17 Jan 1890). He arrived in Halifax in 1850 as a minister trained in the classics. Most of his teaching (about 32 hours a week) was done at Dalhousie in Halifax. His major work, *Intellect, The Emotions and The Moral Nature* (1855), attempted to bring together the emotions and intellect in man. Lyall relied on commonsense realism and Augustinian Neoplatonism to achieve his goal. He argued that the emotions, of which love was most important, were a source of knowledge. This position influenced his ethical theory, which in turn was reflected in the moral tone of Maritime literary works of his day. ELIZABETH A. TROTT

Lyle, John MacIntosh, architect, urban planner, teacher, designer (b at Connor, Ire 13 Nov 1872; d at Toronto 19 Dec 1945). He attended the Hamilton School of Art and trained as an architect at the Yale School of the Arts before enrolling (1894) in the École des beaux-arts, Paris. Lyle's training was reinforced by 12 years' work in New York for several large firms. Upon return to Canada in 1906 he was instrumental in disseminating the beaux-arts ideals to the architectural profession through Atelier Lyle's lectures at University of Toronto. His early works reflect the beaux-arts style – Royal Alexandra Theatre (1906) and UNION STATION (1913-27) in Toronto – as do his later works – Memorial Arch, RMC, in Kingston (1923) and Bank of Nova Scotia in Ottawa (1923-24). Later in the 1920s, through an examination of Canada's architectural heritage, Lyle went on to develop a distinctively Canadian style. His integration of Canadian floral and faunal motifs into the design of his buildings parallels the artistic developments of the GROUP OF SEVEN. For example, in 1929 he designed 3 bank branches that codified his nationalistic feelings: Dominion Bank (Yonge and Gerrard, Toronto), Bank of Nova Scotia (8th Avenue SW, Calgary) and Bank of Nova Scotia (head office, Halifax). In these buildings he integrated elaborate sculptural motifs in stone, metal, plaster, fresco, glass and mosaic to express the Canadian heartland. In 1930 he built the Runnymede Library, Toronto, which combined colonial Georgian and early Québec styles.

Lyle's work in URBAN AND REGIONAL PLANNING made him a leader in the City Beautiful movement, and he developed visionary designs for Toronto's Civic Improvement League. His designs submitted to the Dominion Coin Competition (1936) influenced the adoption of animal and leaf motifs used in contemporary Canadian coinage. GEOFFREY HUNT

Reading: Geoffrey Hunt, *John M. Lyle: Toward a Canadian Architecture* (1982).

Lyman, John Goodwin, painter, author, teacher (b at Biddeford, Maine 29 Sept 1886; d in Barbados, West Indies 26 May 1967). Apart from trips to Canada in 1913 and 1927, he spent the years 1907-31 in Europe. He attended several art schools there but, while these provided him with basic technical competence, the Académie Matisse (1910) exercised a deep influence on his art and thinking. Upon his return to Canada, his "gentlemanly" life-style gave way to a commitment to improve artistic conditions. As a critic (the *Montrealer*, 1936-42) he showed an aware-

John Goodwin Lyman, *The Card Game*, oil on canvas. As a critic, Lyman considered the Group of Seven reactionary. His own work reflects more advanced formal concerns (*courtesy National Gallery of Canada*).

ness of art's elusive quality and rather than dictate to people tried to help them respond to art. He saw the GROUP OF SEVEN as a reactionary institution standing in the way of progress, and was a key figure emphasizing internationalism in Québec. Though he often seemed to express formalist views about art, he never insisted on values of the medium alone, admitting the interplay of raw material and subjective states. Like Matisse, he emphasized the role of instinct and the expression of feelings. As an organizer (Eastern Group of Painters, Contemporary Arts Soc) Lyman sought to improve exhibiting conditions for artists. Here, however, as in his teaching (Atelier, McGill), he was careful not to become dogmatic. Lyman the artist is a controversial figure. Though many dismiss his role as a painter, his works reflect advanced formal concerns and a personal vision. Neither anecdotal nor picturesque, and simplified in form, they state the everlasting quality of things. LOUISE DOMPIERRE

Lynch, Charles Birchell, journalist, author (b Cambridge, Mass 3 Dec 1919). Lynch came to Canada age 2 weeks and was educated at Saint John, NB. At 17 he began his newspaper career as a reporter with the Saint John *Citizen*. At the end of 1943 he joined Reuters as a correspondent and went to London in 1944. He reported the troops storming ashore on D-Day (1944), and until war's end he covered the First Canadian and 2nd British armies. Later, he was a Reuters correspondent covering the war crimes trials in Nuremburg. He was chief of Southam News Services and for 2 decades wrote a 5-times-weekly column for the Southam chain. At age 61 he assumed a new role as freelance columnist. His publications include *You Can't Print That!* (1983) and *A Funny Way to Run A Country* (1986). JEAN MARGARET CROWE

Lynn Lake, Man, LGD, pop 1665 (1986c), a mining community located some 1060 km by road NW of Winnipeg on the Canadian Shield. The townsite was developed by Sherritt Gordon Mines Ltd and the Manitoba government. It was named after Lynn Smith, then chief engineer of the mining company. Nickel was discovered at Lynn Lake in the late 1930s but awaited development until 1952 when Sherritt Gordon began moving its operations up from Sherridon, 250 km to the south. The move, which included 150 houses, school, churches as well as mining and milling equipment, was by tractor train and took 8 winters to complete. In 1985 the town faced collapse with the closure of the nearby Fox Lake copper and zinc mine but received new vitality with the development of the MacLellan gold and silver mine by SherrGold Ltd, a subsidiary of Sherritt Gordon. Tourism is of growing importance to the community with fly-in fishing and hunting being major attractions. Each June the town hosts the Northern Pike Festival. JOHN SELWOOD

Lynx, medium-sized, carnivorous mammal of family Felidae. Canada lynx (*Lynx canadensis*) is distinguished from N American BOBCAT by its tufted ears, large feet, long legs and lack of a white patch below the tail tip. The buff grey, indistinctly spotted fur is long behind the jaws, on the sides of the body and back of the hind legs. Males are larger than females and size ranges widely (5-13 kg). Lynx inhabit northern mainland N America and Newfoundland, and occur accidentally on Baffin I. Once found throughout Canada, they have now been eliminated from settled areas in the south. Their chief food is snowshoe hares, although other small mammals and birds are taken. Individuals become mature at one year. Females bear 1-4 (rarely 5) kittens about 63 days after breeding in Mar-Apr. Kittens are born in a den under a windfall or some natural shelter, and are brownish with blotched upper parts. They become independent in autumn of their second year, when fully grown. Lynx fur is prized by furriers, and overtrapping coupled with elimination from settled areas has seriously reduced the population. Eurasian lynx (*L. lynx*) occupies forested parts of northern and central Europe and northern Asia. C.S. CHURCHER

Lyon, George Seymour, golfer (b at Richmond, Canada W 27 July 1858; d at Toronto May 1938). Lyon was undoubtedly one of Canada's most amazing athletes. At 18 he set a Canadian record in the pole vault. He played baseball, rugby and soccer successfully, was an excellent curler and lawn bowler, and he represented Canada at cricket (scoring 238 not out for his club, a Canadian record). At age 38 he took up golf and between 1898 and 1914 won the Canadian Amateur title 8 times. At age 46 he won one of only 2 Olympic gold medals awarded in golf, defeating US champion H. Chandler Egan 3-and-2 at St Louis, Mo (1904). One of his drives in the semifinal match was estimated at 299 m. In 15 tournaments for the Canadian senior championship, he won 10 times and came second on 4 occasions. GERALD REDMOND

Lyon, Sterling Rufus, lawyer, politician, premier of Manitoba (b at Windsor, Ont 30 Jan 1927). Lyon, elected to the Manitoba Legislature in 1958, spent the next 11 years as a minister in the Roblin-Weir PC administrations. Defeated by Walter WEIR in a bid to succeed Duff ROBLIN in 1967, he left politics 1969, but returned in an unsuccessful attempt at a federal seat in 1974. He became leader of the Manitoba Tories in 1975 and premier in 1977. His administration, despite its policy of restraint in government spending, passed some progressive social legislation. As chairman of the provincial premiers' conference in 1980-81, Lyon played a leading part in opposition to the federal government's proposed constitutional changes. His government was defeated in 1981. In Opposition, Lyon strenuously opposed the PAWLEY government's proposal to entrench Franco-Manitoban rights in the constitution. He resigned from the leadership in 1983, and was not a candidate for re-election to the legislature in 1986. That year he was appointed to the Manitoba Court of Appeal. GEOFFREY LAMBERT

Lytton, BC, Village, pop 368 (1986c), inc 1945, is located on the Trans-Canada Hwy, 260 km NE of Vancouver, at the junction of the THOMPSON and FRASER rivers, in one of the driest and warmest spots in Canada. The village is on the former site of a Thompson R Indian village called Camchin, or Thilkumcheen, meaning "great forks," and of the later HBC post Fort Dallas. In 1858 the settlement was named after Sir Edward Bulwer-Lytton, British colonial secretary. The area was important during the GOLD RUSH on the Fraser in the late 1850s and was a stopping point on the CARIBOO ROAD from the 1860s. A bridge over the Thompson built there in 1866 was nearly swept away in the great flood of 1894. Lytton today is supported by sawmilling, tourism and the CN and CP railways. Tourism has greatly increased the number of popular raft trips down the rapids of the Thompson R. JOHN R. STEWART

Maass, Otto, educator, scientist (b at New York C, NY 8 July 1890; d at Montréal 3 July 1961). Maass was educated at McGill and Harvard (PhD 1919). In 1920 he joined McGill's staff and in 1923 became Macdonald Professor of Chemistry there, a position he retained until 1955. He was also chairman of the McGill department of chemistry (1937-55). Other positions he held were as director general of the Pulp and Paper Research Inst of Canada (1940-55); assistant to the president, NATIONAL RESEARCH COUNCIL (1940-46); director of the Directorate of Chemical Warfare and Smoke (1940-46); and chairman of various governmental committees during WWII.

Maass was instrumental in the establishment of the Defence Research Board and contributed to the eminence of the NRC. He established the first graduate school in science at McGill and there directed the work of 137 graduate students. He published more than 200 papers in such areas as calorimetry, critical-state phenomena, preparation and properties of pure hydrogen peroxide (first prepared by him and used today as a rocket fuel), basic study of cellulose and cellulose systems, and chemical pulping of wood. Awarded many honorary degrees and other awards, Maass was a member of the RSC (1940). A brilliant teacher, experimentalist and organizer, Maass was one of the great scientists in Canadian history.

LEO YAFFE

McAdam, NB, Village, inc 1966, pop 1658 (1986c), 1857 (1981c)located in York Co, in the Canadian Appalachian region of southwestern NB, 10 km from the Canada/US border. The first name applied to the area about 1850 was City Camp for the number of logging camps nearby. The name was changed about 1876 to McAdam Junction in honour of the MLA from the area, John McAdam, and to denote the crossing point of 2 railways. By 1941 it was simply called McAdam. It had become a major rail centre by 1890 with 16 regular trains per day, and the CPR, which operated the E-W line, opened a repair and refit shop in 1924. With the moving of the repair facilities to larger centres and the reduction in the number of trains, as well as the closing of most of the lumber mills in the area, the village has been forced to seek new industries and to develop its tourist potential. The large granite CPR station has been designated a national historic site.

BURTON GLENDENNING

Macallum, Archibald Byron, biochemist, physiologist, educator (b at Belmont, Canada W 7 Apr 1858; d at London, Ont 5 Apr 1934). Macallum was a pioneer of medical and biological research and teaching in Canada, best remembered for his contributions to the Faculty of Medicine of U of T and to the early years of the NATIONAL RESEARCH COUNCIL. Born on a farm, he taught school before going to U of T to graduate in natural sciences in 1880. With Professor Robert Ramsay WRIGHT, he carried out research while teaching high school, returning to U of T in 1883 to lecture in biology and work toward both a doctorate (Johns Hopkins, 1888) and a medical degree (U of T, 1889). As professor of physiology (1890-1908) and of the new science of biochemistry (1908-16), he included among his students Maud L. Menten and James Bertram COLLIP. In 1917 he became the first chairman of the wartime Advisory Council on Scientific and Industrial Research (later the NRC), and in 1920 went to McGill as professor of biochemistry, retiring in 1928 after a distinguished scientific career. Macallum's early research was on the microchemical distribution of inorganic ions (especially iron and potassium) within cells. Later, as an active member of the Biological Board of Canada (FISHERIES RESEARCH BOARD), he carried out fieldwork at its marine stations, and developed his

theory that the body fluids of animals represent living "fossil" evidence of the ancient ocean environments in which they had evolved.

SANDRA F. MCRAE

McAskill, Angus, the Cape Breton giant (b at Harris, Scot 1825; d at Englishtown, NS 8 Aug 1863). The tallest nonpathological giant on record, at maturity he was 236 cm (7'9") tall, weighed 193 kg (425 lbs) and had a shoulder width of 112 cm and palms measuring 20 cm by 30 cm. He was born a normal baby in the Scottish Hebrides and moved with his family to St Anns, NS. Though many stories about him are apocryphal, he is known to have possessed prodigious strength and reputedly could lift 635 litre barrels and beams as long as 18 m. Having joined a travelling show he toured Lower Canada, the US, the West Indies and Cuba 1849-53. He then returned to Cape Breton and engaged in business until his death, which was attributed to "brain fever."

EDWARD BUTTS

Macaulay, John, merchant, journalist, office-holder, politician (b at Kingston, UC 17 Oct 1792; d there 10 Aug 1857). A prosperous merchant and an immensely capable, perceptive man, Macaulay came to attention as coeditor and owner of the *Kingston Chronicle* 1818-22. The paper gave, as his friend John Beverley ROBINSON put it, the "highest satisfaction to every well-wisher of *Church & State*." Supported by John STRACHAN, Macaulay soon became an influential adviser of Lt-Gov MAITLAND's administration. He served on a host of committees and commissions, the most important of which concerned internal navigation. His reports together with Robert NICHOL's report on internal resources provided the framework for a provincial strategy for economic development. In his columns, he popularized the idea of development, especially canals. In 1836 he moved to Toronto upon his appointments as legislative councillor and surveyor general, serving until he became civil and private secretary to Lt-Gov Sir George ARTHUR in 1838. That year he took up the inspector generalship and held it until 8 June 1842. He remained a councillor until his death. Intensely private, fervently pious and somewhat diffident, he suffered almost unremitting affliction in his family life.

ROBERT L. FRASER

Angus McAskill, the Cape Breton giant, standing with a man of ordinary size. At maturity he was 236 cm (7'9") tall (*courtesy Public Archives of Nova Scotia/N-232*).

MacBraire, James, soldier, merchant, shipowner, justice of the peace (b at Enniscorthy, Wexford, Ire 1760; d at Berwick on Tweed, Eng 24 Mar 1832). He is first recorded in Harbour Grace, Nfld, in the 1780s working as a clerk for a Bristol firm engaged in the cod fishery. A judicious marriage to the daughter of a Bristol merchant who had ships and property in Harbour Grace helped him launch an independent mercantile career. Following the outbreak of the Napoleonic Wars MacBraire rejoined the army and was appointed a commissioned officer of the Royal Newfoundland Regiment, based in St John's. MacBraire acquired extensive premises on the St John's waterfront in 1799 and, as captain of his regiment, he procured houses and land which he leased to soldier families. As prices for cod rose rapidly in the European markets, his trade expanded rapidly along the shore south of St John's, westwards to Burin and north to Trinity and Bonavista Bay. Apart from the wealth he accumulated, MacBraire is best remembered for his role in the creation at St John's of the Benevolent Irish Society in 1806 and the Society of Merchants in 1807. He was treasurer and president (1807-17) of the Irish Society, a charitable organization which helped immigrants in distress. He made major efforts to secure better terms of trade for the local mercantile community and the redress of economic grievances. An Anglican and staunch loyalist, his popularity among the Catholic Irish community was unique and his humanitarian exertions earned him a permanent place in Newfoundland mythology.

JOHN MANNION

McBride, Richard, lawyer, politician, premier of BC (b at New Westminster, BC 15 Dec 1870; d at London, Eng 6 Aug 1917). He was educated in New Westminster and at Dalhousie U (LLB, 1890) and was first elected MLA in 1898. The personable McBride briefly (1900-01) served in the Cabinet of James DUNSMUIR and, after the government of E.G. PRIOR resigned, he formed the first BC administration based on party lines 1 June 1903. In the subsequent election, McBride and the Conservatives won a narrow majority. To restore financial stability his government cut expenditures and introduced new taxes; to secure socialist support, it made many minor reforms, especially of labour laws. By 1909 a booming provincial economy allowed McBride and his government to plan for a provincial university and to promise continued prosperity through such means as the construction of railways. In the 1909 and 1912 elections, the Conservatives almost completely eliminated the Opposition from the legislature.

McBride also won popular approval for his persistent agitation for "better terms" from the federal government. He campaigned for the Conservative Party in the federal elections of 1908 and 1911 and successfully delivered the BC vote. An ardent imperialist (KCMG, 1912) and friend of

Winston Churchill, McBride enthusiastically supported the idea of a Canadian contribution to the imperial navy. When WWI began, BC was virtually undefended. On his own initiative, McBride had the province purchase 2 submarines, later sold to the federal government. By 1914, however, the province was economically depressed and in danger of having to meet heavy railway debts. Moreover, McBride paid scant attention to such popular reform movements as WOMEN'S SUFFRAGE and PROHIBITION. On 15 Dec 1915, McBride resigned as premier and accepted the position of BC's agent-general in his beloved London, where he also hoped to get treatment for Bright's disease, which ultimately took his life.
PATRICIA E. ROY

MacBrien, James Howden, soldier, policeman (b at Port Perry, Ont 30 June 1878; d at Toronto 5 Mar 1938). MacBrien served in the militia, the NWMP and then the S African Constabulary 1901-06. A staff officer at the outbreak of WWI, he took command of the 12th Infantry Brigade in 1916. Chief of the general staff, Overseas Forces, 1919-20, he presided over the formation of the Dept of NATIONAL DEFENCE, retiring in 1927. He was a founder of the Canadian Aviation League and commissioner of the RCMP from 1931 until his death. W.J. MCANDREW

McCain, H. Harrison, executive (b at Florenceville, NB 3 Nov 1927). The son of an exporter of seed potatoes, McCain graduated from Acadia U and worked as a sales executive for Irving Oil Co. In 1957 he and his brother Wallace used their $100 000 inheritance from the family seed potato business at Florenceville, NB, to build the first frozen french-fry plant in eastern Canada. Facing stiff competition in the US market, they opened a food-processing plant in Britain and acquisitions and other overseas expansion followed at a rapid pace. Harrison is chairman of the board of McCain Foods Ltd, now one of the largest firms of its kind in the world and the parent company of the McCain Group, whose holdings include a shipping wharf at Bayside, NB, 3 trucking companies, an orange juice company, 3 cheese plants in rural Ontario and Thomas Equipment Ltd (which manufactures harvesting and industrial equipment). McCain Foods Ltd employs over 7000 people in 7 countries and in 1985 topped $1 billion in sales. In 1987 the company had operations in the US, Australia, Belgium, France, the UK, W Germany, Japan and the Caribbean and was preparing to crack markets in Brazil, Argentina, Chile and China. MARY HALLORAN

McCalla, Arthur Gilbert, cereal chemist (b at St Catharines, Ont 22 Mar 1906; d at Edmonton 30 Apr 1985). At U of A, McCalla was one of the elite students of Robert NEWTON; like the others, after taking a 2-year MSc degree under Newton, he was awarded a PhD (U of Calif, Berkeley, 1933) extraordinarily quickly, in only 2 years. He returned to Edmonton to join the university staff, where he remained throughout his career. He took his family to Sweden for advanced study 1939-40 and was trapped there by the German invasion of Norway. They had to return via the USSR, on the Trans-Siberia Ry. McCalla was U of A's dean of agriculture 1951-59 and dean of graduate studies 1957-71. He sat on the National Research Council 1950-56 and was a member of its influential Prairie Regional Committee. The U of A now awards 10-15 Arthur G. McCalla research professorships to promote research at that university. DONALD J.C. PHILLIPSON

MacCallum, Elizabeth Pauline, diplomat, scholar (b at Murash in the Ottoman Empire [Turkey] 20 June 1895; d at Ottawa 12 June 1985). The daughter of missionaries, MacCallum graduated from Queen's and Columbia and taught in the Yukon. After working for the Foreign Policy Assn in New York City and the League of Nations Soc in Ottawa, she joined the Department of External Affairs in 1942, serving as adviser to the delegation to the 1945 San Francisco Conference, which established the UN, and as Middle Eastern specialist at many general assemblies. Chargé d'affaires in Beirut in 1954, she was the first woman head of mission. After retiring, she spent 4 years in Turkey before returning to Ottawa. She wrote extensively on Middle East and Balkan subjects. JOHN W. HOLMES

MacCallum, William George, pathologist (b at Dunnville, Ont 18 April 1874; d at Baltimore, Md 3 Feb 1944). After graduating in 1894 from U of T, he entered Johns Hopkins Medical School and graduated with an MD in 1897. He took up the study of pathology after a year as intern. This study took him first to Columbia U and finally in 1917 to professor of pathology at Johns Hopkins. Besides writing a textbook of pathology which went through several editions, he made discoveries on the life cycle of the malarial parasite and the physiology of the parathyroid gland, and studied valvular lesions of the heart and the pathology of influenza. In 1919 he discovered the stain, known as MacCallum's stain, which is used to render influenza bacilli visible under a microscope. A.L. PURDON

MacCarthy, Albert H., mountaineer (b at Ames, Iowa 1876; d at Annapolis, Maryland 11 Oct 1956). Though by vocation a US naval officer and entrepreneur, MacCarthy was by avocation a mountaineer with a passion for pioneering new climbs in western Canada. After joining the ALPINE CLUB OF CANADA in 1911, he participated in many difficult ascents, including Mt ROBSON (3954 m, in 1913), the highest summit of the Canadian Rockies. He is best remembered, however, as the leader of the team that conquered Mt LOGAN, at 5950 m the highest peak in Canada. The expedition, 65 gruelling days of wilderness travel through Alaska and the Yukon, met success on 23 June 1925. BART ROBINSON

McCarthy, D'Alton, lawyer, politician (b near Dublin, Ire 10 Oct 1836; d at Toronto 11 May 1898). He came to Canada with his parents in 1847, and was educated in Barrie, Canada W. He was called to the Bar of Upper Canada in 1858, and was elected to Parliament as a Conservative 1876. He was re-elected in 1878 to the constituency of N Simcoe, which he represented continuously until his death. McCarthy was at the centre of the most heated political issues of his day. He was president of Canada's Imperial Federation League for 7 years, although he was forced to resign because of his support for unilingualism. He relentlessly opposed the use of the French language outside Québec, and voted against his leader over the JESUITS' ESTATES ACT. After the 1891 election he began to advocate reform of the protective tariff, a divergence from Tory policy that led in 1893 to a break with the party. During the 1890s he continued his vehement opposition to French-language schools and his support of Manitoba's eradication of denominational schools as a way of suppressing French instruction. Consequently, he and his McCarthyite League worked to defeat the federal Conservatives in the election of 1896. He was rumoured to be about to enter LAURIER's Cabinet at the time of his death. J.R. MILLER

Reading: J.R. Miller, "'As a Politician He Is a Great Enigma,'" *Canadian Historical Review* LVII, 4 (1977).

McClelland, John Gordon, Jack, publisher (b at Toronto 30 July 1922). Educated at U of T, he joined the navy in 1941 and volunteered for duty on a motor torpedo boat; promoted captain of MTB 747 in 1944, he saw action in the English Channel. He joined MCCLELLAND AND STEWART (founded by his father John McClelland, Sr, in 1906), became executive VP in 1952 and president in 1961. He transformed the company into English Canada's best-known publishing house by encouraging, supporting and publishing Canadian writers such as Farley MOWAT, Irving LAYTON, Margaret LAURENCE, Leonard COHEN, Peter NEWMAN, Mordecai RICHLER, Pierre BERTON, Margaret ATWOOD, Brian MOORE and others. He published many Canadian BEST-SELLERS, such as Berton's *The National Dream* (1970) and Newman's *The Canadian Establishment* (1975). McClelland stepped down as president in 1982, sold the firm to Avie Bennett in 1985 and announced that he was severing all ties with the company in Feb 1987. He became an Officer of the Order of Canada in 1976.

McClelland and Stewart Limited, publishing company founded in 1906 by John McClelland and Frederick Goodchild as McClelland and Goodchild Limited. When George Stewart joined the firm in 1914, his name was added to the title, but the present form was adopted after Goodchild's departure in 1918. The company began as a library supply house, representing British and American firms, and went on to publish Canadian authors such as C.W. GORDON (Ralph Connor), Bliss CARMAN, D.C. SCOTT, Stephen LEACOCK, L.M. MONTGOMERY and F.P. GROVE. Jack MCCLELLAND, the founder's son, became executive vice-president in 1952 and president in 1961, and continued to develop a vigorous Canadian BOOK PUBLISHING program that made a most notable contribution to the publishing and marketing of Canadian literature. Through the New Canadian Library Series (est 1958) and Carleton Library Series (est 1963) the company made accessible classic works in Canadian literature, history and social sciences, and greatly aided the growth of Canadian studies. The company published the first 2 volumes in its Canadian Centenary Series – an 18-volume history of Canada – in 1963. Widespread publicity and concern was aroused by the announcement in 1971 that M&S was for sale. The Ontario government decided to provide a $1-million loan to prevent its sale to American interests. In 1984 the government again stepped in, freeing M&S from its debt obligation (some $4 million). This action depended on McClelland being able to raise over $1 million from the private sector; his success at this endeavour was an acknowledgement of M&S's contribution to Canadian culture. However, M&S was sold in 1985 to real-estate developer Avie Bennett and McClelland resigned his position as "publisher" with the firm in 1987.

McClintock, Sir Francis Leopold, explorer (b at Dundalk, Ire 8 July 1819; d at London, Eng 17 Nov 1907). One of the British navy's most experienced arctic explorers, he participated in several expeditions to search for Sir John FRANKLIN. On the first of these (1848-49), he learned the techniques of northern sled travel which he later used to great effect. After 3 unsuccessful attempts, McClintock discovered the fate of Franklin and his men on his last voyage to the Arctic 1857-59. McClintock rose to senior rank in the navy and retired from active service in 1882. DANIEL FRANCIS

McClung, Nellie Letitia, née Mooney, suffragist, reformer, legislator, author (b at Chatsworth, Ont 20 Oct 1873; d at Victoria 1 Sept 1951). From 1880 she was raised on a homestead in the Souris Valley, Man, and did not attend school until she was 10. She received a teaching certificate at 16 and then taught school until she

Nellie McClung, writer, reformer and women's advocate (*courtesy National Archives of Canada/PA-30212*).

married Robert Wesley McClung in 1896. In Manitou, where her husband was a druggist, she became prominent in the WOMAN'S CHRISTIAN TEMPERANCE UNION, of which her mother-in-law was provincial president. In 1908 McClung published her first novel, *Sowing Seeds in Danny*, a witty portrayal of a small western town. It was a national best-seller and was followed by numerous short stories and articles in Canadian and American magazines. In 1911 the McClungs and their 4 children moved to Winnipeg, where their fifth child was born. The Winnipeg women's rights and reform movement welcomed Nellie as an effective speaker who won audiences with humorous arguments. She played a leading role in the 1914 Liberal campaign against Sir Rodmond ROBLIN's Conservative government, which had refused women suffrage, but moved to Edmonton before the Liberals won in Manitoba in 1915. In Alberta she continued the fight for female suffrage and for PROHIBITION, dower rights for women, factory safety legislation and many other reforms. She gained wide prominence from addresses in Britain at the Methodist Ecumenical Conference and elsewhere (1921) and from speaking tours throughout Canada and the US, and was a Liberal MLA for Edmonton, 1921-26.

In 1933 the McClungs moved to Vancouver I, where Nellie completed the first volume of her autobiography, *Clearing in the West: My Own Story* (1935, repr 1976), and wrote short stories and a syndicated column. In all, she published 16 books, including *In Times Like These* (1915, repr 1975). Her active life continued: in the Canadian Authors Assn, on the CBC's first board of governors, as a delegate to the League of Nations in 1938 and as a public lecturer. Forgotten for a decade, she was rediscovered by feminists in the 1960s. Although some criticized her maternalistic support of the traditional family structure, most credited her with advancing the feminist cause in her day and recognizing the need for further progress such as the economic independence of women. *See also* WOMEN'S MOVEMENT.

M.E. HALLETT

Reading: Candace Savage, *Our Nell* (1979).

McClure, Robert Baird, medical missionary (b at Portland, Ore 23 Nov 1900). The son of Canadian medical missionaries in China, Dr McClure went to Henan [Honan], China, in 1923, serving as surgeon and medical educator and helping to establish the Hwaiking rural medical system. When war broke out between Japan and China in 1937, he became field director for the International Red Cross in central China. From 1941 to 1946, he led the Friends Ambulance Unit in China, providing supplies, medical treatment, public-health services and mobile surgery to the war-ravaged country. With the end of foreign missions in China, McClure provided medical service to the Palestinian refugees in Gaza 1950-54, and superintended the Ratlam hospital in India 1954-67. As always, he combined his surgery with public health and training for local medical personnel. He returned to Toronto in 1968 and served as the first nonordained moderator of the UNITED CHURCH OF CANADA 1968-71. He has spent his retirement practicing medicine in Borneo, rural Peru, the Caribbean, Zaire and a native community on the BC coast. In his eighties, he has continued his fight for the welfare of the Third World. His strong will, independence and quick temper have exasperated generations of friends as well as critics; yet his heroic self-sacrifice on behalf of the distressed around the world makes him one of the true humanitarians of the 20th century. In 1985 McClure received the Man of the Year Peace Award of the Lester B. Pearson Peace Park.

NEIL SEMPLE

Reading: M. Scott, *McClure: The China Years of Bob McClure* (1977) and *McClure: Years of Challenge* (1979).

McClure, Sir Robert John Le Mesurier, explorer, adventurer (b at Wexford, Ire 28 Jan 1807; d at London, Eng 17 Oct 1873). McClure obtained a lieutenancy for his 1836-37 service on *Terror* under George BACK in the ice of Hudson Bay. He served on Sir James Clark ROSS's abortive Franklin rescue mission in 1848-49, and in 1850 was appointed commander of *Investigator* in the expedition led by Capt Richard Collinson, who was taking 2 ships to the Arctic via Bering Str. This commission brought McClure fame and success. He proved brave, lucky and inordinately ambitious. Arriving ahead of Collinson at Bering Str, he decided to continue on alone. From Aug to Oct 1850 he coasted E hundreds of kilometres to Cape Parry, wheeled N to Banks I and reached and wintered in Prince of Wales Str, the last link in the fabled NORTHWEST PASSAGE, which he undoubtedly discovered. Sir John FRANKLIN's earlier claim, for which all witnesses were dead, was only discovered by Sir Francis MCCLINTOCK in 1859.

McClure encountered great danger in Prince of Wales Str and in rounding Banks I in 1851. He was forced to winter in Mercy Bay and was frozen in. His crew was saved from starvation in 1853 by Capt Henry KELLETT of the *Resolute* and finally returned to England in 1854. McClure ungenerously informed a parliamentary committee that he could have kept his men alive without Kellett's aid, thereby denying his rescuers a share in the £10 000 voted to the discoverers of the passage. McClure served on the China Station 1856-61 and died a vice-admiral.

L.H. NEATBY

McConachie, George William Grant, airline executive (b at Hamilton, Ont 24 Apr 1909; d at Long Beach, Calif 29 June 1965). McConachie's family moved to Edmonton in 1910 and he was educated there. In 1931 he acquired an aircraft and flew fish from northern lakes and barnstormed prairie communities. He cofounded, then became president of, Independent Airways, and founded United Air Transport (later called Yukon Southern Air Transport) in 1933. He pioneered airmail and passenger service between Edmonton and Whitehorse (1939) and performed aerial exploration for the Alaska Hwy and Canol projects. Canadian Pacific Railway bought out his firm and 11 others in 1941 and appointed him general manager of the western lines (1942) and president of CP Air (1947). He inaugurated CP Air passenger services to Australia, Japan and Hong Kong and by 1957 had added a further 25 000 km of flight paths. He was awarded the MCKEE TROPHY in 1945 for his pioneering efforts in forging air service to the North.

ROBERT BOTHWELL

McConnell, John Wilson, publisher, businessman (b in Muskoka, Ont 1 July 1877; d at Montréal 6 Nov 1963). McConnell was the owner of the *Montreal Star*, the largest English-language newspaper in Québec, and as such was a force in the land. He went into business in Toronto as a young man. In 1900 he moved to Montréal as manager of Standard Wood Chemical Ltd, but in 1906 he went into finance as an investment broker. By 1912 he had control of the St Lawrence Sugar Refineries. He bought the *Montreal Star* in 1925 from Hugh GRAHAM, Baron Atholstan, and took control in 1938 on the latter's death. In 1939 he threw his paper's support to the Liberals and against Premier Maurice DUPLESSIS in the Québec general election; he thereafter remained close to Mackenzie KING. King offered him a Cabinet post during WWII, but McConnell refused. He was also a philanthropist of note, helping such artists as Maureen FORRESTER.

J.L. GRANATSTEIN

McConnell, Richard George, geologist, explorer (b at Chatham, Canada E 26 Mar 1857; d at Ottawa 1 Apr 1942). In 1879 he graduated from McGill and began working for the GEOLOGICAL SURVEY OF CANADA in Québec. For some 30 years he studied geological phenomena in Canada, particularly in the W and NW. In 1882 he assisted G.M. DAWSON in exploring the southern Alberta Rockies as well as the Waterton Lks region, St Mary R and Cypress Hills. Five years later, he explored a large portion of northern BC, the Mackenzie Valley and the Yukon Territory. In 1889-90 he conducted an extensive study of the Athabasca tar sands of northeastern Alberta and explored the Peace-Athabasca region. In 1914 he became federal deputy minister of mines, retiring in 1921. He was elected a fellow of the Royal Society of Canada in 1913.

ERIC J. HOLMGREN

McConnell, Robert Murray Gordon, jazz musician (b at London, Ont 14 Feb 1935). McConnell studied with Gordon Delamont in Toronto and then played valve trombone in the bands of Maynard FERGUSON (New York, 1964) and Phil NIMMONS (Toronto, 1965-69). As a prominent Toronto studio musician, McConnell formed the Boss Brass in 1968 to record pop song arrangements for radio programs serviced by the Canadian Talent Library. By 1987 they had more than 15 albums. By 1976 the band of 22 musicians had evolved into an uncompromising jazz ensemble, and McConnell was praised widely for his arranging ability. The Boss Brass, now considered one of the major big bands in jazz, although it performs only sporadically, has received Grammy nominations for several of its dozen recordings, and won a Grammy for *All In Good Time* in 1983. Recent recordings include *Old Friends, New Music* (1984) and *Boss Brass and Woods* (1985) and in 1987 the Boss Brass played in concert with the Calgary Philharmonic.

MARK MILLER

McCowan, Daniel, naturalist, lecturer, writer (b at Crieff, Scot 20 Jan 1882; d at Cloverdale, BC 19 Feb 1956). After an early education in Scotland, he moved to Banff, Alta, where he soon acquired expertise on the local flora and fauna. His thousands of photographs of scenery, flowers, birds and mammals enabled him to travel widely, lecturing on nature in the Rockies, and he wrote extensively for several newspapers and popular magazines. His lectures on CBC Radio were

among the first by naturalists. In addition to these early important contributions to the popularization of nature and thus conservation concepts in Canada, he published 6 nature and photography books, all illustrated with his own photographs: *Animals of the Canadian Rockies* (1936), *A Naturalist in Canada* (1941), *Outdoors with a Camera in Canada* (1945), *Hill-top Tales* (1948), *Tidewater to Timberline* (1951) and *Upland Trails* (1955).
MARTIN K. MCNICHOLL

McCrae, John, physician, poet (b at Guelph, Ont 30 Nov 1872; d at Boulogne, France 28 Jan 1918). Educated at U of T, he was appointed fellow in pathology at McGill in 1900. He served in the SOUTH AFRICAN WAR as an artillery subaltern 1899-1900. The author of a number of medical texts, he also contributed poetry to various magazines. In 1914 McCrae enlisted in the CANADIAN EXPEDITIONARY FORCE as a medical officer. He died of pneumonia at the hospital of which he was in charge in 1918. "In Flanders Fields," his most enduring poem, was first published in *Punch* in 1915. A book of the same title was published posthumously in 1919. His birthplace in Guelph is now a historic site. DAVID EVANS

John McCrae, poet and physician known for his poem "In Flanders Fields," shown with his dog Bonneau, *c*1914 (*courtesy National Archives of Canada/C-46284*).

McCreight, John Foster, lawyer, first premier of BC (b at Caledon, Ire 1827; d at Hastings, Eng 18 Nov 1913). Educated in England and Ireland, McCreight immigrated to practise law in Melbourne, Australia, but moved to Vancouver I in 1860, being admitted to the BC Bar in 1862. In Aug 1871 he entered the first provincial legislative assembly as a member for Victoria. Designated premier in Nov, he was defeated on a speech from the throne in Dec 1872. He continued as a private member, retiring in 1875. In 1873 he was made a QC and in 1880 a Supreme Court justice. After serving in the Cariboo, he moved to New Westminster, BC, in 1883, living there until his retirement in 1897. Soon after, he returned to England. SYDNEY W. JACKMAN

Reading: Sydney W. Jackman, *Portraits of the Premiers* (1969).

McCulloch, Thomas, educator, theologian, author (b at Ferenze, Scot 1776; d at Halifax 9 Sept 1843). One of the most prominent educators and theologians in the Maritimes, McCulloch was a prolific letter writer, as well as the author of books on theology and *Letters of Mephibosheth Stepsure.* Educated at Glasgow U and at Divinity Hall, Whitburn, McCulloch was a member of the secession branch of the Presbyterian Church. He set out for PEI in 1803 as an ordained minister but landed, because of bad weather, at PICTOU, NS. Here he accepted a call to the church and soon became involved in many other public activities. He founded Pictou Academy (incorporated 1816) but was unable to obtain government financial assistance or the privilege to confer degrees. The question of public support for all educational endeavours, not just the Anglican schools and colleges, became a lively political issue. McCulloch and his supporters founded a reform newspaper in Pictou, the *Colonial Patriot* (1827), in which they set forth their views. He expanded his educational interests by founding a theological college at West River, Pictou County. Some of McCulloch's theological students were granted degrees by Glasgow, an institution with which he maintained close connections throughout his life. McCulloch was an inspired and versatile teacher and was named first president of Dalhousie in 1838, a position he held until his death. During his busy life he devoted much time to his scientific interests and collected a large number of bird specimens, which came to the attention of John James Audubon who visited him in Pictou in 1833.

McCulloch's best-known fictional work, "Letters of Mephibosheth Stepsure" first appeared in serial form (22 Dec 1821-Mar 1823) in the *Acadian Recorder.* The letters were reprinted in 1862 and then in 1960 as *The Stepsure Letters.* In an effort to arouse his fellow Pictonians to improve their farming practices and style of life in general, he chided them in a humorous, satirical fashion. His writings influenced Thomas HALIBURTON's Sam Slick. He also wrote 2 highly moral tales, called *William and Melville* (1826), about the fortunes and misfortunes of immigrants to the New World.

On the subjects of education and religion, McCulloch's works included *Popery Condemned by Scripture and the Fathers* (1808), *Popery Condemned Again* (1810), *The Nature and Uses of a Liberal Education* (1819) and *Calvinism: The Doctrine of the Scriptures* (1849). The titles of these substantial works provide some indication of McCulloch's dedication to his role as an educator and theologian in 19th-century NS. DOUGLAS LOCHHEAD

McCurdy, James Frederick, "father of biblical studies in Canada" (b at Chatham, NB 18 Feb 1847; d at Toronto 30 Mar 1935). A graduate of UNB he taught grammar school, then entered Princeton Seminary in 1868 to study biblical languages. He taught there 1871-82, but resigned when his "modernist" views on the Bible were attacked. After studying in Germany he was hired by U of T in 1885, and taught there until retirement in 1914. As head of the oriental languages department he made biblical studies an important and popular discipline in a secular university, and trained a generation of outstanding scholars who later taught in Canadian and other universities. His 3-volume *History, Prophecy and the Monuments* (1894-1901) won him international critical acclaim. JOHN S. MOIR

McCurdy, John Alexander Douglas, aviation pioneer (b at Baddeck, NS 2 Aug 1886; d at Montréal 25 June 1961). With F.W. BALDWIN and A.G. BELL he formed the Aerial Experiment Assn to test the feasibility of powered flight. He made more than 200 short flights in experimental aircraft in the US before flying the SILVER DART at Baddeck 23 Feb 1909 – the first controlled flight by a British subject in the British Empire. McCurdy is also credited with making the first ocean flight, from Florida to Cuba, and with sending and receiving the first messages while aloft. He was assistant director of aircraft production for the Canadian government in WWII and was lieutenant-governor of NS 1947-52. He was awarded the MCKEE TROPHY (1959) on the 50th anniversary of the flight of the *Silver Dart*. JAMES MARSH

McCutcheon, Malcolm Wallace, lawyer, businessman, politician (b at London, Ont 18 May 1906; d there 23 Jan 1969). Director of over

J.A.D. McCurdy flew the Silver Dart at Baddeck, NS, 23 Feb 1909, the first flight of an aircraft in Canada (*courtesy City of Toronto Archives/SC 244-79*).

20 companies and financial institutions, McCutcheon resigned them in 1962 when he became minister without portfolio in the DIEFENBAKER government. Called to the Ontario Bar in 1930, he soon found his talents lay in the executive suite and the boardroom. A member of the WARTIME PRICES AND TRADE BOARD, he went to Argus Corp where he was VP and managing director when called to the Senate in 1962. A lifelong Tory, he was an important fund raiser and Bay Street (Toronto) contact for the Diefenbaker government. He ran unsuccessfully for the Tory leadership in 1967. PATRICIA WILLIAMS

McDermott, Dennis, trade unionist (b at Portsmouth, Eng 3 Nov 1922). McDermott came to Canada after WWII and in 1948 worked in Toronto as an assembler and a welder. In 1954 he became an organizer for the United Automobile Workers (UAW). Known as a social activist, he supported the United Farm Workers' campaigns in Canada on behalf of the California grape workers, and has participated in the Canadian Civil Liberties Assn. In 1968 he was elected UAW director for Canada and in 1970 international VP. He also became a general VP of the CANADIAN LABOUR CONGRESS, and in 1978 succeeded Joe MORRIS as president. In that job, he opposed wage controls and any infringement on collective bargaining for public or private sector employees, and chided the government about the high level of unemployment and the state of the economy. He also served on the executives of the NDP in Ontario and federally. In 1986 he was appointed Canada's ambassador to Ireland by the Mulroney government. LAUREL SEFTON MACDOWELL

MacDonald, Angus Bernard, educator, cooperative leader (b at Glassburn, NS 21 Nov 1893; d at Ottawa 13 Sept 1952). Following study at St Francis Xavier U and at NS Agricultural Coll, MacDonald worked in government agriculture positions in NS and Ontario and studied at Ontario Agricultural Coll and U of T. He returned to NS in 1925 as inspector of schools for Antigonish and Guysborough counties. In 1930 MacDonald joined St FX's extension department as associate director. A good administrator and powerful personality, he became a vitally important leader in the ANTIGONISH MOVEMENT, as the department's program came to be called. MacDonald also organized several credit unions and became managing director of the NS Credit Union League when it was formed in 1934. During 1943 he became involved with a reorganization of the Co-operative Union of Canada and in 1944 was appointed its national organizer. In 1945 he joined the CUC as general secretary (subsequently national secretary), a post he held until his death. MacDonald's accomplishments with the CUC included the sponsoring in Canada of CARE, the international aid program. IAN MACPHERSON

Macdonald, Angus Lewis, lawyer, professor, politician and premier of NS 1945-54 (b at Dunvegan, NS 10 Aug 1890; d at Halifax 13 Apr 1954). An officer in the Canadian Expeditionary Force (WWI), educated at Saint Francis Xavier, Dalhousie and Harvard, Macdonald was assistant deputy attorney general of NS 1921-24 and professor of Dalhousie Law School 1924-30 before being elected leader of the NS Liberal Party in 1930. Victorious in the election of 1933 during the Great Depression, Macdonald implemented old-age pensions and relief for the unemployed, and launched an inquiry (Jones Commission) into the effects of the tariff on the NS economy. In 1940 PM King recruited him to become minister of defence for naval services. Macdonald presided over the creation of a wartime Canadian Navy and convoy service for the Allies. A conscientious administrator, he was a poor politician, putting defence priorities before party considerations in the CONSCRIPTION crisis. King triumphed over the conscriptionists and Macdonald resigned from the Cabinet in Apr 1945. He returned to NS and resumed the premiership, resisting the centralizing policies of the King governments but, sapped by overwork and illness, he was unable to restore the spark that had characterized his prewar government. When he died in 1954, Macdonald left a party that had languished too long in his shadow. His personal reputation in the NS Liberal Party was second only to that of Joseph HOWE. MARGARET CONRAD

Reading: J. Hawkins, *The Life and Times of Angus L.* (1969).

Macdonald, Bernard Donald, Roman Catholic bishop of Charlottetown (b at Allisary, PEI 25 Dec 1797; d at St Dunstan's College, near Charlottetown, 30 Dec 1859). In 1812 Macdonald was one of the first 2 Island boys sent to study for the priesthood at the Grand Seminary of Québec. He was ordained there on 1 June 1822. After 15 years of missionary work back in his native colony, he was named bishop of Charlottetown on 21 Feb 1837. Created in 1829, his diocese initially included PEI, Magdalen Is and New Brunswick. The bulk of Macdonald's episcopate was concerned with ensuring a succession of clergy and establishing Catholic institutions for his charge. To that end, his most significant accomplishment was the opening of St Dunstan's College in Jan 1855 as a preparatory school for seminarians. Religious controversy and ill health (likely tuberculosis) marred the last years of Macdonald's episcopate. Nevertheless, he successfully guided the diocese through a difficult adolescence. G. EDWARD MACDONALD

Macdonald, Brian, choreographer (b at Montréal 14 May 1928). Macdonald was a radio whiz kid, child actor, swimmer and skater before entering McGill at 16. Inspired by the visit of Ballet Theatre (later American Ballet Theatre) in 1944, he began dance training. Leaving university, he became music critic for the *Montreal Herald* while continuing his training, and in 1951 he became a founding member of the NATIONAL BALLET OF CANADA. Two years later a severe injury ended his performing career and he returned to teach and choreograph in Montréal during a period of intense artistic activity in the city. His first major success was the 1957 McGill student revue *My Fur Lady,* which ran for 18 months. The ROYAL WINNIPEG BALLET has been commissioning works from him since 1958, and on a number of these, including *Rose Latullipe* (1966) and *The Shining People of Leonard Cohen* (1970), he has collaborated with composer Harry FREEDMAN. Macdonald has created many works for companies in Canada, Europe and the US. He was artistic director of the Royal Swedish Ballet 1964-67, the Harkness Ballet 1967-68, Batsheva Dance Theatre 1971-72 and Les GRANDS BALLETS CANADIENS 1974-77, where in 1987 he was resident choreographer. Macdonald has been associated with the BANFF CENTRE since 1960 and has taught at the National Theatre School. He directs or choreographs for TV, musicals, operas and operettas. Macdonald is also associate director of the Stratford Festival where his productions of Gilbert and Sullivan operettas have been highly successful; his production of *The Mikado* became the longest-running Canadian musical on Broadway. Of a driving and sometimes volatile personality, he has created ballets for almost every professional ballet company in Canada. He became an Officer of the Order of Canada in 1967 and won the MOLSON PRIZE 1983. In 1987 his new ballet, *Breaks*, premiered as part of the Banff Festival of the Arts. He is married to Annette AV PAUL. JILLIAN M. OFFICER

MacDonald, Donald, trade unionist (b at Halifax 12 Sept 1909; d at Ottawa 25 Sept 1986). At age 17 MacDonald became a coal heaver on the Sydney docks. He joined the United Mine Workers and at age 21 became president of Local 4560. When the local struck in 1940 for a guaranteed weekly minimum wage, MacDonald was fired and blacklisted. He had a long and active interest in the CO-OPERATIVE MOVEMENT, which gave him a job. He helped to organize successful co-operative ventures in NS in housing, credit union and consumer fields. In 1941 he was elected CCF MLA from Cape Breton S. He was CCF party leader in the legislature until 1945. In 1942 he joined the organizing staff of the CANADIAN CONGRESS OF LABOUR, becoming regional director of the Maritimes in 1945 and secretary-treasurer and chief executive officer of the CCL in 1951. He played a major role in the merger negotiations which created the Canadian Labour Congress in 1956 from a merger of the CCL and the Canadian Congress of Labour, being elected secretary treasurer at the founding convention. He was appointed acting president of the CLC in Sept 1967 and was elected president in 1968. He was re-elected in 1970 and 1972 and resigned in 1974. In 1972 he was the first non-European to be elected president of the International Confederation of Free Trade Unions, retiring in 1974. Among his many honours were the Order of Canada, the Canadian Centennial Medal and the Federal Republic of Germany Award of Merit. LAUREL SEFTON MACDOWELL

Macdonald, Donald Stovel, politician, lawyer (b at Ottawa 1 Mar 1932). Elected to the House of Commons as member for Toronto Rosedale in 1962, Macdonald entered the Liberal Cabinet in 1968 and, as minister of energy, mines and resources between 1972 and 1975, resisted economic and provincial pressures to move to world oil prices. In Sept 1975 he became minister of finance and introduced WAGE AND PRICE CONTROLS. He resigned from Cabinet in 1977 to enter private law practice in Toronto. In 1982 Pierre TRUDEAU appointed Macdonald chairman of a royal commission on the ECONOMIC UNION AND DEVELOPMENT PROSPECTS FOR CANADA. The report, which was released in Sept 1985, has been influential in debates on economic policy, particularly that on FREE TRADE. In Mar 1987 he and Peter LOUGHEED agreed to head the Canadian Alliance for Trade and Job Opportunities to promote FREE TRADE. JOHN ENGLISH

MacDonald, Flora Isabel, politician (b at N Sydney, NS 3 June 1926). Between 1956 and 1965 she worked at the Progressive CONSERVATIVE PARTY headquarters, where she was executive secretary for 5 years. She was then national secretary of the PC Assn 1966-69 while working at Queen's U. In 1972 she was elected MP for Kingston and the Islands and immediately became Conservative critic on Indian affairs and northern development in Robert STANFIELD's "shadow cabinet." She made an unsuccessful bid for the Conservative leadership in 1976, her promised support failing to materialize at the leadership convention polling stations. As an MP MacDonald has been outspoken on constitutional issues, on national defence, external affairs and reform of the penitentiary system. In the brief CLARK government (1979-80) she was secretary of state for external affairs, the first woman to hold such an important federal Cabinet post. After the Sept 1984 election, she served as minister of employment and immigration. She became minister of communications in the MULRONEY Cabinet in 1986. HARRIET GORHAM

Macdonald, Sir Hugh John, lawyer, politician, magistrate, premier of Man (b at Kingston, Canada W 13 Mar 1850; d at Winnipeg 29 Mar 1929), the only surviving son of Sir John A. MACDONALD. Educated at U of T, he was called to the Ontario Bar in 1872. In 1882 he moved to Winnipeg where he entered partnership with J. Stewart Tupper, eldest son of Sir Charles TUPPER. He saw active military service on 3 occasions: the 1866 Fenian invasion, the 1870 Wolseley Expedition and the 1885 North-West Rebellion. Elected for Winnipeg in the 1891 general election, he resigned in 1893. In 1896 he joined the short-lived Tupper government as minister of the interior. After the courts overturned his election, he became leader of the Manitoba Conservatives and led them to victory in 1899. Touted as successor to Tupper, he resigned as premier to run in Brandon against Clifford SIFTON in the 1900 federal election. He retired to private life after his defeat. Macdonald's shyness and nervousness in public made the path he chose even more difficult and it was his lot to be measured against his eminent father, and inevitably he was found wanting. HAL GUEST

MacDonald, James Edward Hervey, painter (b at Durham, Eng 12 May 1873; d at Toronto 26 Nov 1932). Among the GROUP OF SEVEN, of which he was a founder, J.E.H. MacDonald was one of the best trained, first at the Hamilton Art School from about 1887 and, after 1889, in Toronto lithography houses and at the Central Ontario School of Art and Design, where he studied with William CRUIKSHANK. In 1895 he joined Grip Ltd, an important commercial art firm, where he encouraged the staff (which included Tom THOMSON from about 1907) to develop as painters. MacDonald was a key member of the later Group. Lawren HARRIS recalled that a show of MacDonald's in 1912 at the Ontario Soc of Artists gave him his first recognition of the Group's "ethos."

MacDonald was Harris's greatest early friend among the Toronto painting community. Together in 1913 they went to the Albright Art Gallery in Buffalo, NY, to see the survey of Scandinavian landscape painting which was to influence their work. Around this time MacDonald introduced more colour into his dark panels. Algoma, N of Lk Superior, which he visited several times with Harris's help from 1919, became the country of his heart. His best paintings were done there, often of great vistas in a turbulent, patterned style. The sketch *Mist Fantasy, Sand River, Algoma* (1920, National Gallery of Canada) shows how he used the sketches he made in Algoma: the finished canvas (1922, now in the Art Gallery of Ontario), with its long ribbons of mist, was noted by a later

J.E.H. MacDonald's *Mist Fantasy* (1922), oil on canvas, has been called the height of the artist's way of stylizing form (*courtesy Art Gallery of Ontario/gift of Mrs. S.T. Williams in memory of J. Elinor Williams, 1927*).

critic as the height of MacDonald's way of stylizing form. In 1924 he made the first of 7 trips to the Rockies, another favourite painting place.

MacDonald's palette was dark, tough and rich, like A.Y. JACKSON's, but his colouring was more fiery and his style more elegant. His sense of composition was oriented towards his meditation on design, a subject in which he was a master (he was the greatest calligrapher of the period and a designer of consequence). Like other members of the Group, he loved Chinese and Japanese art.

Among other tasks he performed was the decoration of St Anne's Church, Toronto (1923), and teaching at the ONTARIO COLLEGE OF ART. He also wrote poetry after a nervous breakdown in 1917. He was an eccentric gardener and enjoyed playing on a set of chimes made of old plough points. One of his favourite authors was Henry David Thoreau, for whom he named his son, illustrator Thoreau MACDONALD. JOAN MURRAY

Reading: Paul Duval, *The Tangled Garden* (1978).

Macdonald, James Williamson Galloway, "Jock," artist, educator (b at Thurso, Scot 31 May 1897; d at Toronto 3 Dec 1960). Educated in Scotland, he enlisted in 1915, and was wounded in France in 1918. He entered the Edinburgh Coll of Art, graduating with a diploma in design and an art specialist's teaching certificate in 1922. He was employed as a designer and educator in England, and was appointed head of design at the Vancouver School of Decorative and Applied Arts in 1926. He began to paint in oils under the tutelage of Fred VARLEY in a style strongly influenced by the GROUP OF SEVEN.

Although he painted landscapes throughout his life and drew inspiration from nature, Macdonald's best paintings show his struggle to find an abstract form of expression. Among the first abstract artists in Canada, he immersed himself in painting the experience of his environment at NOOTKA SOUND on NW Vancouver I in 1935-36. One of the most important teachers in modern Canadian art history, he and Varley founded the innovative BC College of Arts (1933-35). He taught at the Provincial Institute of Technology at Calgary (1946-47) and, from 1947 until his death, at the Ontario College of Art, Toronto. Numerous Canadian artists acknowledge the impact he had on their development. Instrumental in founding the Calgary Group in 1947, he was a key figure in the influential Ontario abstract group PAINTERS ELEVEN, and was active in most Canadian art societies. He is best remembered for his free-flowing abstract watercolours and the often majestic paintings of his last years – without question his masterpieces. JOYCE ZEMANS

Macdonald, John, merchant, churchman, philanthropist, politician (b at Perth, Scot 27 Dec 1824; d at Toronto 4 Feb 1890). Macdonald accompanied his officer father to NS in 1838. Educated at Dalhousie and Bay Street Academy (Toronto), he worked in Gananoque, Toronto and Jamaica and in 1849 opened a dry-goods business in Toronto. Within a decade his firm, John Macdonald and Co, became the largest wholesaler in Canada. He was elected to Parliament as an independent Liberal in 1863 and 1875; PM John A. Macdonald appointed him to the Senate in 1887 for his periodic support of Tory legislation and for his strong opposition to commercial union with the US. A devout Methodist and a strict employer, Macdonald was the author of *Business Success*, a manual that exemplified his commitment to Christian morality in business life. JOSEPH LINDSEY

Macdonald, Sir John Alexander, lawyer, businessman, politician, first prime minister of Canada (b at Glasgow, Scot 10 or 11 Jan 1815; d at Ottawa 6 June 1891). He was the dominant creative mind which produced the BRITISH NORTH AMERICA ACT and the union of provinces which became Canada. As the first prime minister of Canada, he oversaw the expansion of the Dominion from sea to sea. His government dominated politics for a half century and set policy goals for future generations of political leaders.

Macdonald was brought to Kingston, UC, by his parents when he was 5 years old and he grew up and attended school there and in rural Lennox and Addington and Prince Edward counties. At age 15 he began to article with a prominent Kingston lawyer. Both at school and as an articling student he showed promise. At 17 he managed a branch legal office in Napanee by himself, and at 19 opened his own office in Kingston, 2 years before being called to the Bar of UC. Macdonald's early professional career coincided with the rebellion in UC and subsequent border raids from the US. He was in Toronto in Dec 1837 where, as a militia private, he took part in the attack on the rebels at Montgomery's Tavern. In 1838 he attracted public notice by defending accused rebels, including Nils von Schoultz, leader of an attack on Prescott.

He remained in the practice of law for the rest of his life with a series of partners, in Kingston until 1874 and then in Toronto. His firm engaged primarily in commercial law; his most valued clients were established businessmen or corporations. He was also personally involved in a variety of business concerns. He began to deal in real estate in the 1840s, acquired land in many parts of the province, including commercial rental property in downtown Toronto, and was appointed director of many companies, mainly in Kingston. For 25 years (mostly while he was prime minister) he was president of a Québec City firm, the St Lawrence Warehouse, Dock and Wharfage Co, and in 1887 became the first president of the Manufacturers Life Insurance Co of Toronto. Macdonald's personal life was marked by a number of misfortunes. His first wife, his cousin Isabella Clark, was an invalid during most of their married life. His first son died at the age of 13 months. His second marriage, to Susan Agnes Bernard, was saddened by the chronic illness of his only daughter Mary.

Macdonald entered politics at the municipal level, serving as alderman in Kingston 1843-46. He took an increasingly active part in Conservative politics and in 1844 (at age 29) was elected for Kingston to the Legislative Assembly of the PROVINCE OF CANADA. Parties and government were in a state of transition, a modern departmental structure had begun to evolve but RESPONSIBLE GOVERNMENT had not yet been conceded, and the role of the governor was still prominent. In this context Macdonald's political views proved cautious; he defended the imperial prerogative and state support of denominational education, and opposed the abolition of primogeniture. Above all, he emerged as a shrewd political tactician who believed in the pursuit of practical goals by practical means. His obvious intelligence and ability brought him his first Cabinet post as receiver general in 1847 in the administration of W.H. DRAPER which was defeated in the general election that year.

Macdonald remained in Opposition until the election of 1854, after which he was involved in the creation of a new political alliance – the Liberal-Conservative Party – in which the Conservatives were attached to the existing alliance of Upper Canadian Reformers and the French Canadian majority political bloc. Once returned to office, he assumed the prestigious post of attorney general of UC. On the retirement, which he helped to engineer in 1856, of Conservative leader Sir Allan MACNAB, Macdonald succeeded him as joint-premier of the Province of Canada, along with Étienne-Paschal TACHÉ (and then with George-Étienne CARTIER, 1857-62, with the exception of the 2-day Brown-Dorion administration in 1858).

During the years 1854-64 Macdonald faced growing opposition in his own section of the province to the political union of Upper and Lower Canada. The Reform view, voiced by George BROWN of the Toronto *Globe*, complained that the legitimate needs and aspirations of UC were frustrated by the "domination" of French Canadian influence in the government of Macdonald and George-Étienne Cartier. By 1864 the political and sectional forces in the province were deadlocked and Macdonald reluctantly accepted Brown's proposal for a new coalition, to include the Upper Canadian Reformers, designed to solve the constitutional difficulties through the adoption of a federal system, applied if possible to all the colonies of British North America. While conceding the necessity of a federal arrangement to accommodate strong racial, religious and regional differences, Macdonald's preference was for a strong, highly centralized, unitary form of government. Macdonald took the leading part in the drafting of a federal system in which the central government held unmistakable dominance over the provincial governments. His great constitutional expertise, ability and knowledge received immediate recognition from the imperial government. Created Sir John A. Macdonald, KCB, he was chosen to take office as first prime minister of Canada on 1 July 1867.

During his first administration, 1867-73, he became a "nation builder." To the original 4 provinces were added Manitoba, the North-West Territories (present-day Sask and Alta), BC and PEI. The INTERCOLONIAL RY between Québec City and Halifax was begun and plans were made for a transcontinental railway to the Pacific coast. These undertakings involved unprecedented expenditures of public funds and did not proceed without incident. Manitoba entered the union following an insurrection led by Louis RIEL against the takeover of the area by the Dominion government, thereby forcing Macdonald's government to grant provincial status much sooner than had been intended and to accept a system of separate schools and the equality of the French and English languages. Macdonald's involvement in the negotiations for a contract to build the CANADIAN PACIFIC RAILWAY to BC involved him eventually in the PACIFIC SCANDAL; during the 1872 election large campaign contributions had been made to him and his colleagues by Sir Hugh ALLAN, who was to have headed the railway syndicate. Macdonald claimed that his "hands were clean" because he had not profited personally from his association with Allan, but his government was forced to resign in late 1873 and in the election of 1874 was defeated. Some of these political problems stemmed from the fact that he, like many of his contemporaries, was at times a heavy drinker. At the time of the election of 1872 and of the negotiations with Allan it is clear that there were periods of time of which he later had no recollection. His drinking subsequently became more moderate.

Fortunately for Macdonald his defeat coincided with the onset of a business depression in Canada which gave the Liberal administration of Alexander MACKENZIE a reputation for being ineffectual. In 1876, at the instigation of a group of Montréal manufacturers, Macdonald began to advocate a policy of "readjustment" of the tariff – a policy which helped him return triumphantly to power in 1878. He remained prime minister for the rest of his life. The promised changes in tariff policy, introduced in 1879 and afterwards frequently revised, in close collaboration with leading manufacturers, became Macdonald's NATIONAL POLICY, a system of protection of Canadian manufacturing through the imposition of high tariffs on foreign imports, especially from the US. Appealing to Canadian nationalist and anti-American sentiment, it became a permanent feature of Canadian economic and political life. However, the economy as a whole continued to suffer slow growth, and the effects of the policy were uneven.

The great national project of Macdonald's second administration was the completion of the transcontinental CPR, which proved an extremely difficult and expensive undertaking requiring extensive government subsidization. Macdonald played a central role in making the railway a reality. He was involved in awarding the contract to a new syndicate headed by George STEPHEN, which called for a government subsidy of $25 million and 25 million acres (10 million ha) of land, and on 2 occasions, in 1884 and 1885, he agreed to introduce legislation for the further financial support of the railway. Its completion in Nov 1885 made feasible the future settlement of the West.

The physical linking of the Canadian community was accompanied by the first steps towards eventual autonomy in world affairs. Macdonald did not foresee Canadian independence from Britain but rather a partnership with the mother country. He himself represented Canada on the British commission which negotiated the Treaty of Washington of 1871; in 1880 the post of Canadian high commissioner to Britain was created; and Finance Minister Charles TUPPER represented Canada at the Joint High Commission in Washington in 1887.

Sir John Alexander Macdonald
First Prime Minister of Canada

Birth: 11 Jan 1815, Glasgow, Scot
Father/Mother: Hugh/Helen Shaw
Father's Occupation: Businessman
Education: Royal Grammar, Kingston, LC; Oxford U
Religious Affiliation: Anglican
First Occupation: Lawyer
Last Private Occupation: Lawyer
Political Party: Conservative (formerly Liberal-Conservative)
Period(s) as PM: 1 July 1867 - 5 Nov 1873; 17 Oct 1878 -6 June 1891
Ridings: Kingston, Ont, 1844-78; 1887-91; Marquette, Man, 1878-82; Victoria, BC, 1878-82; Carleton and Lennox, Ont, 1882-91
Other Ministries: Pre-Confederation Legislative Assembly: Receiver-General 1847-48; Attorney-General 1854-56; 1862; and others
Marriage: 1 Sept 1843 to Isabella Clark (1811-56); 16 Feb 1867 to Susan Bernard (1836-1920)
Children: 1) 2 boys; 2) 1 girl
Died: 6 June 1891 in Ottawa
Cause of Death at Age: Heart failure at 76
Burial Place: Kingston, Ontario
Other Information: First PM in Confederation; KCB 1867.

(photo courtesy National Archives of Canada/C-10144).

The last stage of Macdonald's public career was plagued by difficulties. The NORTH-WEST REBELLION, which occurred at a time when he himself was superintendent general of Indian affairs, and the subsequent execution of Louis Riel in 1885 greatly increased animosity between French-speaking and English-speaking Canadians and cost Macdonald political support in Québec, where Riel was regarded as a martyr to the forces of Anglo-Saxon imperialism. A series of successful legal challenges to the powers of the central government, mainly emanating from Ontario Premier Oliver MOWAT, resulted in a federal system much less centralized than Macdonald had intended. The federal power of DISALLOWANCE, freely used at first, was virtually abandoned in the face of provincial opposition.

Macdonald's contribution to the development of the Canadian nation far exceeded that of any of his contemporaries, yet he was not by nature an innovator. Confederation, the CPR, the protective tariff were not his ideas, but he was brilliant and tenacious in achieving his goals once convinced of their necessity. As a politician he early developed shrewdness and ingenuity. He kept a remarkable degree of personal control over the functioning of the party and was adept in using patronage for political advantage. He was a highly partisan politician, partly because he genuinely believed it essential to maintain certain political courses – especially the British connection and legal-parliamentary tradition in Canada against the threat of American political and economic influences. Macdonald was an Anglophile but he also became a Canadian nationalist who had great faith in the future of Canada. His nationalism was primarily central Canadian and English Canadian; his concern with Québec was largely political. He accepted the existence of a unique French Canadian community and especially a French Canadian claim to a due share of government patronage, but after Cartier's death in 1873 he did not share equal political power with a strong "Québec lieutenant" nor did he give senior Cabinet positions to French Canadian politicians. His overriding national preoccupations were unity and prosperity. An 1860 speech summed up his lifelong political creed and political goals: "one people, great in territory, great in resources, great in enterprize, great in credit, great in capital."

J.K. JOHNSON

Reading: D.G. Creighton, *John A. Macdonald,* 2 vols (1952-55); J.K. Johnson, ed, *Affectionately Yours, the Letters of Sir John A. Macdonald and his Family* (1969); P.B. Waite, *Macdonald* (1975).

Macdonald, John Sandfield, lawyer, politician, premier of Ontario 1867-72 (b at St Raphael, UC 12 Dec 1812; d at Cornwall, Ont 1 June 1872). "Sandfield" served as a subsurname for Macdonald's Highland Scottish family. After brief schooling, he articled in the offices of A. McLean and W.A. DRAPER, prominent Conservatives. He was called to the bar in 1840 and opened a practice in Cornwall. The following year he was drafted by local Conservatives and successfully contested the Glengarry seat for the first Assembly of the United PROVINCE OF CANADA. He was unique in that he served in all 8 parliaments of the United Province. Annoyed by the intransigent position of old-line Tories, he identified increasingly with Governors SYDENHAM and BAGOT. He supported Bagot's Council of Reformers in 1842 and followed his new associates into opposition when they clashed with Governor METCALFE in 1843. Thenceforth, he would remain a Reformer. From 1849 to 1851 he served as Robert BALDWIN's solicitor general for Canada W. When Francis HINCKS became Reform premier, he passed over Sandfield, who, though bitter, accepted election in

John Sandfield Macdonald was a strong opponent of Confederation. He later became the first premier of Ontario (*courtesy National Archives of Canada/C-10896/Notman & Fraser, Toronto*).

1852 as Speaker of the Assembly – a post he filled with great distinction. During political maneuvres of 1854, which led to the formation of a Liberal-Conservative ministry under Sir A.N. MACNAB, he severely criticized Lord ELGIN for alleged improprieties and thus became a leading figure in the disrupted Reform opposition, a role he shared with George BROWN. The 2 Reformers became bitter antagonists, however, with Brown championing REP BY POP and a centralized federation and Sandfield advocating the "double majority," a requirement that the Cabinet hold the confidence of majorities from both Upper and Lower Canada, which would have ensured that the duality of the province would be more fully represented.

When the government of G.É. CARTIER fell in 1862, Lord MONCK called on Sandfield to form a Reform administration. Associating himself with the moderate L.V. SICOTTE, Sandfield, who served also as attorney general west, attempted to govern the increasingly divided province on the basis of his constitutional formula, but was thwarted by the Upper Canadian separate-school crisis. Reorganized with A.A. DORION as his associate and with more Rouge and Grit involvement, his ministry struggled on until it fell in Mar 1864. It was Sandfield who then introduced the idea of a coalition. Yet the GREAT COALITION of June 1864, which brought together John A. MACDONALD, Cartier and Brown, isolated Sandfield, who opposed both the concept of FEDERALISM and the notion of union with the Maritimes. He particularly feared Toronto domination of his St Lawrence Valley region. He denounced the federal plan as being too conservative and its process of implementation as arbitrary and even unconstitutional. Nevertheless, being basically a Reform-minded pragmatist, by early 1867 he gently bowed to the inevitable.

John A. Macdonald became prime minister and helped engineer the selection of Sandfield as the first premier of Ontario. "Hunting in pairs," the 2 Macdonalds won the concurrent federal and provincial elections. Sandfield's ministry was of considerable distinction, frugal yet creative, and despite opposition assertions to the contrary he was no puppet of the prime minister. By 1871, however, he was gravely ill and, after an inconclusive election that was followed by the desertion of a few coalition Reformers, he resigned that Dec. In his place, Edward BLAKE inaugurated 34 years of Liberal rule.

BRUCE W. HODGINS

Reading: Bruce W. Hodgins, *John Sandfield Macdonald* (1971).

Macdonald, Ronald St. John, international jurist, teacher, (b at Montréal 20 Aug 1928). He was educated at St Francis Xavier U (BA, 1949), Dalhousie (LLB 1952), London and Harvard (LLM 1954-55). He went straight to law teaching, first at Osgoode Hall, then Western Ontario and then U of T, where he was dean of law, 1967-72. He then returned to Dalhousie as professor of international law and dean, holding the latter post until 1979. He served as arbitrator in the Republic of Cyprus, 1974-78, and was frequently adviser and consultant to the Prime Minister's Office and to External Affairs. In 1980 he was appointed judge of the European Court of Human Rights at Strasbourg, on which court he still sits (1987). Vigorous, charming, witty, gregarious, Macdonald is as unlike the usual stereotype of a judge of international law as possible. He was awarded the Order of Canada in 1984. P.B. WAITE

MacDonald, Thoreau, illustrator, designer, painter (b at Toronto 21 Apr 1901). Thoreau MacDonald was self-taught but worked with his father, J.E.H. MACDONALD. Colour blindness forced him to work mainly in black and white. His illustrations, particularly for the RYERSON PRESS and the magazine CANADIAN FORUM, typify a whole period of Canadian ILLUSTRATION in the 1920s and 1930s. Certain technical mannerisms characterize his work: skies are always a series of parallel horizontal lines; clouds are simplified amoeboid shapes; trees look like the skeletons of conch shells; and his animals recall the art of the ancient Near East, appearing full face or, more usually, in profile. In general his subjects recall his father's, but he favoured Ontario farmland. He was one of the first artists in Canada to study factories and construction, but his work is most memorable for his delight in nature. JOAN MURRAY

Macdonald, Sir William Christopher, manufacturer, philanthropist (b at Glenaladale, PEI 1831; d at Montréal 9 June 1917), son of Donald Macdonald, president of the Legislative Council of PEI. Educated at Central Academy, Charlottetown, Macdonald began his career as a Montréal commission merchant. Within a few years he became a tobacco manufacturer, founding the Macdonald Tobacco Co and amassing a large fortune. A man with neither family nor frivolous tastes, Macdonald became the greatest educational philanthropist of his generation. He was a generous benefactor of McGill and Ontario Agricultural Coll (now part of U of Guelph) and founded and endowed Macdonald College at Ste-Anne-de-Bellevue, Qué, and Macdonald Hall at Guelph, Ont. With James ROBERTSON, he financed a number of elementary-school innovations: the Macdonald Manual Training Movement, the Macdonald Rural Schools Fund and the Macdonald Consolidated School Project. Knighted in 1898, he was for many years chancellor of McGill.

ROBERT M. STAMP

MacDonald, Wilson Pugsley, poet, poetaster, performer (b at Cheapside, Ont 5 May 1880; d at Toronto 8 Apr 1967). MacDonald was a barnstorming versifier with unbending faith in his own greatness. He graduated in 1902 from McMaster, and his first collection of poems, *Song of the Prairie Land*, appeared in 1916. Many others, which he himself hawked at his "recitals," followed at intervals. Best known are *The Miracle Songs of Jesus* (1921) and *A Flagon of Beauty* (1931). It is surprising the extent to which MacDonald was often taken seriously as an artist and equally surprising that genuine poems or hints of them can sometimes be discovered in his collections by those willing to wade through his vapid romanticism and pre-modernist conventions. Some satirical light verse may also stand re-examination. *Wilson MacDonald's Western Tour*, edited by Stan Dragland (1976), includes some of the poet's correspondence with his long-suffering publishers. There were once Wilson MacDonald poetry societies in several cities, sustained no doubt by the bombast of MacDonald himself, and at least one such group still survives.

DOUG FETHERLING

Macdonell, Alexander, Roman Catholic bishop (b at Fort Augustus, Glengarry, Scot 17 July 1762; d at Dumfries, Scot 14 Jan 1840). Ordained in 1787, Macdonell spent the next few years in the Scottish Highlands. In 1793 he persuaded the British government to establish a Catholic corps, the Glengarry regiment, of which he was chaplain. In 1802 the regiment was disbanded. Two years later, with a government promise of 200 acres to every soldier who emigrated, Macdonell and a large group of settlers left for Glengarry County, Upper Canada.

Central in the religious and political life of the colony, Macdonell was appointed vicar general in 1807 and vicar apostolic in 1820, and was consecrated bishop of Kingston or Regiopolis in 1826. During his tenure thousands of IRISH immigrants arrived, and by 1840 there were 34 priests and 48 parishes in Upper Canada for which Macdonell had secured financial assistance from the local and British governments. A firm conservative, Macdonell was a legislative councillor from 1831 and soon came under fire from the Reform movement. Macdonell died while in Britain to solicit funds for Regiopolis College and recruit more Catholic emigrants. Buried in St Margaret's Convent, Edinburgh, his remains were brought to St Mary's, Kingston, in 1861. CURTIS FAHEY

Reading: J.E. Rea, *Bishop Alexander Macdonell and the Politics of Upper Canada* (1974).

Macdonell, Sir Archibald Cameron, KCB, CMG, DSO, police officer, soldier (b at Windsor, Canada W 6 Oct 1864; d at Kingston, Ont 23 Dec 1941). After graduating from the Royal Military College of Canada in 1886, Macdonell joined the army but subsequently transferred to the NORTH-WEST MOUNTED POLICE, as an inspector, in 1889, and was posted to the North-West. In 1897 he played a prominent part in tracking down ALMIGHTY VOICE. Two years later he joined the 2nd Canadian Mounted Rifles for service in the SOUTH AFRICAN WAR, where he was decorated for his bravery under fire. He returned to the NWMP, was promoted to superintendent and then, in 1907, joined what became Lord Strathcona's Horse. Named commanding officer in 1912, he took his unit to France in May 1915 and, because of his success, was promoted to command the 7th Brigade in Dec 1915, and the 1st Division in June 1917. After the war he was commandant of RMC until his retirement, as lt-gen, in 1925.

STEPHEN HARRIS

MacDonell, Miles, soldier, governor of Assiniboia (b in Scot *c*1767; d at Pte-Fortune, LC 28 June 1828). Immigrating with his family to New York in 1773, Miles eventually followed them to Upper Canada, where he began farming. He was appointed a captain in the Royal Canadian Volunteers in 1796, but after the corps' disbandment in 1802, he came to Lord SELKIRK's attention in 1804. Selkirk supported his unsuccessful efforts in 1806-07 to raise a force of Glengarry Fencibles and backed his ultimate appointment as sheriff of the Home District in 1807. Called to England by

Selkirk in 1810, he was appointed first governor of ASSINIBOIA in 1811, and led the initial party of settlers to the RED RIVER COLONY in 1812. His belligerent attitude exacerbated conflict between the colony and the NORTH WEST CO, and he suffered severe emotional instability. Arrested and sent to Montréal in 1815 by the Nor'Westers, he was back in Assiniboia as governor in 1817, but soon returned to Montréal. His last years were spent in semiretirement on his farm near Osnaburgh, UC.
J.M. BUMSTED

Macdonnell, Daniel James, Presbyterian minister (b at Bathurst, NB 15 Jan 1843; d at Fergus, Ont 19 Feb 1896). After graduating from Queen's U in 1858, Macdonnell taught school before studying theology in Scotland and Germany. Called to a church in Peterborough in 1866 and to St Andrew's, Toronto, in 1870, he became renowned as one of the most influential preachers in late Victorian Canada. An original theological thinker and friend of philosopher G.P. YOUNG, Macdonnell publicly voiced his doubts about certain Calvinistic doctrines. He was tried for heresy in 1876 and acquitted 2 years later. JOHN S. MOIR

McDougald, John Angus, "Bud," financier (b at Toronto 14 Mar 1908; d at Palm Beach, Fla 15 Mar 1978). An intensely private man fascinated by power, Bud McDougald developed ARGUS CORPORATION into one of Canada's dominant corporate entities. The son of a wealthy Toronto financier, McDougald began his career as a clerk for Dominion Securities at age 18. He quickly worked his way up through the corporate structure while at the same time developing outside financial activities. He left DS in 1945 to form a partnership with E.P. TAYLOR in a promotional company, Taylor, McDougald and Company Ltd. Ten years later he was made a director of Argus Corp, a holding company set up by Taylor to control his industrial interests. In 1969 McDougald became chairman of Argus which by then controlled 6 of Canada's leading industrial concerns, a position which saw him safely ensconced as a dominant member of Canada's BUSINESS ELITE.
CHRISTOPHER G. CURTIS

McDougall, Barbara Jean, née Leamen, politician, financial analyst (b at Toronto 12 Nov 1937). She received a BA in political science and economics from U of T in 1960, and from 1964 to 1974 was an investment analyst. She became investment manager for the North West Trust Co of Edmonton in 1974, and in 1976 VP of A.E. Ames and Co Ltd of Toronto. Throughout this period, McDougall was also a business journalist and commentator for magazines, newspapers and television. She worked in several Tory campaigns in Toronto, and in 1984 was elected MP for St Paul's (Toronto). As minister of state for finance, she fielded most of the criticism over the government's response to the decline and collapse of 2 Alberta banks in 1985. In June 1986, she became minister of state for privatization and was given responsibility for women's issues. A month later, responsibility for regulatory affairs was added to her portfolio. DEAN BEEBY

McDougall, Elizabeth, née Boyd, frontier woman (b in Grey County, Canada W 1853; d at Calgary 31 Mar 1941). McDougall is less known for her own activities than for aiding her Methodist missionary husband John MCDOUGALL. She was the first white woman in the Alberta foothills, arriving at Morley in 1873 after a particularly hazardous journey during which she often drove the wagon across the plains. The couple lived among and worked to convert the STONEY on their reserve for 25 years. When her husband travelled as a church superintendent, McDougall went with him by canoe and dogsled, despite having 6 children. In 1898 she moved to Calgary where she became president of the Southern Alberta Pioneer Women and Old Timer's Assn. Speaking to the group, she voiced her conviction that frontier women had made possible their husbands' activities, citing the large number of bachelors who had found it necessary to leave the prairies when unsupported by the labour and sympathy of women. ELIANE LESLAU SILVERMAN

McDougall, George Millward, missionary, pioneer, negotiator (b at Kingston, UC 9 Sept 1821; d in a blizzard N of Calgary 25 Jan 1876). Born of Scottish parents, McDougall attended Victoria College in Cobourg, UC and was ordained deacon 1852 and minister 1854. He went on to work at or establish a series of Wesleyan missions: Garden River (1851-57), Rama (1857-60), Norway House (1860-63), Victoria (1863-71), Edmonton (1871-74) and Morley (1873-76). Each of these postings meant extreme hardship for McDougall and his family, ranging from land-clearing chores and isolation to smallpox epidemics. Aside from teaching religion and establishing schools, he was an area superintendent, overseeing native affairs and settlement activities within his regions of the vast North-West. In his later years, McDougall gave lectures in eastern Canada, England and Scotland on the potential of the country and the plight of the natives. MARK RASMUSSEN

McDougall, John Chantler, Methodist minister, missionary (b at Owen Sound, Canada W 27 Dec 1842; d at Calgary 15 Jan 1917), son of George MCDOUGALL and husband of Elizabeth MCDOUGALL. Educated at Victoria College, Cobourg, 1857-60, and ordained in 1874, McDougall served for many years as missionary to the Indians of western Canada, continuing the work he began under his father's tutelage before his ordination. He served the federal government in both the 1869-70 and 1885 rebellions and drew government attention to the plight of the Indians after the disappearance of the buffalo. He retired in 1906 and lived in Calgary for the remainder of his life. He wrote several books including *George Millward McDougall* (1888) and *Forest, Lake and Prairie* (1895). ERIC J. HOLMGREN

McDougall, Pamela Ann, diplomat, public servant (b at Ottawa 9 May 1925). After studying chemistry at Mt Allison and U de Paris, McDougall joined the Department of EXTERNAL AFFAIRS in 1949. She served at the embassy in Bonn, W Germany, as political adviser to the Canadian commissioners in Vietnam; in the high commission in New Delhi, India, as deputy head of the Far Eastern Division in Ottawa; and as ambassador to Poland (1968-71). From 1971 to 1974 she was in the Privy Council Office as assistant secretary to the Cabinet, and in 1976 she became chairman of the Tariff Board. Her report as royal commissioner on conditions of foreign service was presented in 1981. JOHN W. HOLMES

MacDougall, Sir Patrick Leonard, military officer, author (b at Boulogne-sur-Mer, France 10 Aug 1819; d at Kingston Hill, Eng 28 Nov 1894). Adjutant general of the Canadian militia 1865-68, MacDougall served in Canada from 1844 to 1854 and had written *Emigration* (1848), proposing a railway from Halifax to Québec. In *Forts versus Ships* (1862), he underlined the importance of British control of the Great Lakes. During the difficulties with the FENIANS, he organized isolated volunteer companies into battalions and formed mobile brigades. From 1878 to 1883 MacDougall commanded the British troops remaining in N America. O.A. COOKE

McDougall, William, lawyer, politician, first lieutenant-governor of the North-West Territories (b near York [Toronto] 25 Jan 1822; d at Ottawa 29 May 1905). A member of the Assembly of the Province of Canada (1858-67), he was commissioner of crown lands, 1862-64, and provincial secretary, 1864. He attended all 3 CONFEDERATION conferences and as minister of public works in John A. MACDONALD'S government (1867) introduced the resolution that led to the purchase of RUPERT'S LAND. He was appointed lieutenant-governor of the area in 1869, and was repulsed by Louis RIEL'S men, who prevented him entering the territory he had come to govern. This failure, and the fact that he had been a Clear Grit in his early political life but had switched to the Conservatives in 1867 (which had earned him the tag "Wandering Willie"), destroyed his political credibility. Although continuing in politics (Ontario MPP, 1875-78; MP, 1878-82), he was given few political plums. FRITS PANNEKOEK

McDowall, Robert, pioneer Presbyterian minister (b at Balston Spa, near Albany, NY 25 July 1768; d at Fredericksburgh, Canada W 3 Aug 1841). In 1790 the Dutch Reformed Church sent McDowall as a missionary to what is now southern Ontario. Invited to be a permanent minister in the Bay of Quinte area, he settled near Bath, UC, in 1798 after completing his theological education at Schenectady, NY. McDowall formed several congregations between Belleville and Brockville, performed some 2500 baptisms and 1300 marriages in the next 40 years, and also made missionary trips. He was elected first moderator of the Presbytery of the Canadas in 1819.
JOHN S. MOIR

McDowell, Charles Alexander, physical chemist (b at Belfast, Ire 29 Aug 1918). McDowell came to Canada in 1955 as head of the chemistry department of UBC. In his 26-year tenure, he built up this department to a point at which it could sometimes be counted the largest in N America, with great breadth in its activities. His sensitivities to physicochemical sophistication and fashionable trends in science led to a concentration in his department of big-machine methods for studying molecular structure. This field includes his own substantial research in mass spectrometry, magnetic resonance and photoelectron SPECTROSCOPY. Unlike many scientists, he seems able to pursue science itself and the politics of science as an essential unity. He was president of the Chemical Inst of Canada, 1978-79. He was university professor at UBC 1981-84, then university professor emeritus. In 1986 he became a full member of the European Academy of Arts, Sciences and Humanities, and an honorary member of the Canadian Society for Chemistry.
LIONEL G. HARRISON

MacEachen, Allan Joseph, professor, politician (b at Inverness, NS 6 July 1921). After serving as head of the dept of economics and social sciences at St Francis Xavier U he entered federal politics; from 1953 to 1984, except for 1958-62, he represented Inverness-Richmond (later Cape Breton Highlands-Canso) in the Commons, gaining wide recognition for looking after his constituency and for his ability as a political tactician. After 1963 his prestige grew steadily; for 2 decades he has been recognized as the federal Liberal leader in Nova Scotia. He headed a succession of departments including finance and external affairs. During 2 stints as government leader in the Commons (1967-68 and 1970-74) he proved an able tactician, though his Nov 1981 budget was highly controversial and evoked considerable criticism. For most of the time from 1977 to 1984 he was deputy PM and always a leading party strategist. A close confidant of Pierre TRUDEAU, he helped devise the strategy that brought down the

CLARK government in 1979 and he helped plan the 1980 Liberal victory. He did not run in the 1984 federal election and was appointed to the Senate that year, acting as government leader from June to September, and opposition leader there since that time. He was widely seen as the driving force behind the Liberal-dominated Senate's opposition to the Conservative government's controversial prescription drug legislation in 1987. J. MURRAY BECK

MacEachern, Angus Bernard, Roman Catholic bishop of Charlottetown (b at Kinlochmoidart, Scot 8 Feb 1759; d at Canavoy, PEI 22 Apr 1835). In a missionary career spanning 5 decades, MacEachern firmly rooted Catholicism in pioneer Prince Edward Island and New Brunswick. He came to the Island a young missionary in 1790 to join his emigrant family, but his duties compelled him to crisscross the priest-poor Maritime region endlessly. Fluency in English, French and Gaelic enabled him to minister effectively to his scattered Scots, Irish and Acadian flock. Charm and tact won the respect of civil authorities. As titular bishop of Rosen, MacEachern became vicar general for much of the Maritimes in 1819, but by the mid-1820s he was convinced that the only cure for the region's spiritual ills was independence from the sprawling, neglectful archdiocese of Québec. In 1829 the diocese of Charlottetown, comprising PEI, NB and the Magdalen Is, was created, with MacEachern its first bishop. The next year he saw Catholic Emancipation, a cherished dream, promulgated. In 1831 he founded St Andrew's College at his home in St Andrew's, PEI, to provide preliminary training for prospective seminarians. Much beloved by his people, MacEachern acquired near-mythic stature in his lifetime. G. EDWARD MACDONALD

Reading: F.W.P. Bolger, "The First Bishop," in *The Catholic Church in Prince Edward Island* (1979).

McEachran, Duncan, teacher, administrator (b at Campbelltown, Scot 27 Oct 1841; d at Ormstown, Qué 24 Oct 1924). He graduated from Edinburgh Veterinary Coll in 1861 and came to Canada in 1862 to practise in Woodstock, Canada W. He lectured at the Montreal Veterinary Coll at McGill in 1866, the name being changed to Faculty of Comparative Medicine and Veterinary Science in 1889. He served as professor and dean until it closed in 1903. McEachran established contagious-disease-control programs for Canada in 1875 and was chief veterinary inspector 1884-1902. He was succeeded by J.G. RUTHERFORD, who took over disease control and founded the Health of Animals Branch of the federal Dept of Agriculture. McEachran established the first animal-disease quarantine station at Lévis, Qué.

R.G. THOMSON

Macedonians Contemporary Macedonians are the South Slavic and slavicized population that inhabit the territory comprising roughly the Macedonia of antiquity: that population which in its own language calls itself *Makedonci*. This territory falls today within 3 Balkan countries: Bulgaria, Greece and Yugoslavia. Throughout history this region has been the locus of contradictory political, cultural and economic interests.

Migration and Settlement While it is difficult to establish exactly when the first Macedonians arrived in Canada, it is believed that they were probably the participants in the Ilinden uprising against the Ottoman Empire which at that time ruled over Macedonia. They were forced to flee Macedonia and the first group arrived in Toronto from the village of Zhelevo [Andartikon, Greece] in 1903, followed by a group from Oshchima [Trigonon, Greece] in 1904.

It is equally difficult to establish the exact number of Macedonians in Canada. According to J.S. Woodsworth, there were between 1000 and 2000 Macedonians in Toronto in 1909, and according to the *Canadian Family Tree* of 1967 there were 6000 Macedonians in Canada prior to WWI. Until 1981 the Canadian census did not list Macedonians or the Macedonian language. According to that census 10 045 people (preliminary estimate in 1986 was 11 355) in Canada declared themselves to be Macedonians (9905 in Ontario) and 10 165 people spoke the Macedonian language. These figures, too, are inaccurate because many Macedonians declare their country of origin as their ethnic origin and their language as Greek or as Yugoslav, or they declare themselves Canadians. Most Macedonians in Canada are concentrated in the region that includes Metro Toronto, Mississauga and Hamilton. Based on their membership in various churches and other associations, it is reasonable to assume that there are many more Macedonians in Canada than the census data indicates.

Many early Macedonian immigrants found work in Toronto, either as workers in meat-packing plants or in grocery stores and restaurants. From these jobs, they quickly, progressed to the ownership of a great number of restaurants, grocery stores and butcher shops. The majority of Canadian-born Macedonians are employed in the professional, clerical and service sector of the economy.

Social Life and Community The social life of early Macedonian immigrants centred around village-based associations such as the benefit society, St Nicholas, formed in 1907 by immigrants from the village of Oshchima. Similar associations were formed by immigrants from other localities in Macedonia. The first Macedonian church, Sts Cyril and Methody, was based on representatives from different villages and was formed in 1910 in Toronto. The second church, St George, was established in 1941, and the third, and most popular among recent arrivals, St Clement of Ohrid, was established in 1962 in Toronto. In addition, there are other small Macedonian or Macedono-Bulgarian churches in Toronto. Most of the social life is centred around the churches and affiliated associations.

Religion, Cultural Life and Education Macedonians belong to the Eastern Orthodox branch of Christianity and now have their own autocephalous Macedonian Orthodox Church centred in Ohrid, Yugoslavia. The cultural life of Macedonians revolves around their churches, their numerous radio and television programs and their newspapers, notably the *Newspaper of United Macedonians* and *Makedonija*. The children of Macedonian immigrants are integrated in the mainstream of Canadian cultural life, gaining prominence in film, television, music, newspapers, etc. The Macedonian language belongs to the South Slavic group of languages. Various dialects of the language are spoken and maintained in the home and the literary language is taught to children in special classes.

HARRY V. HERMAN

Reading: R. Harney and H. Troper, *Immigrants* (1975); Harry V. Herman, *Men in White Aprons* (1978).

MacEwan, John Walter Grant, author, historian, lieutenant-governor of Alberta (b at Brandon, Man 12 Aug 1902). Educated at schools in Brandon and Melfort, Sask, MacEwan graduated from Ontario Agricultural College in 1926 and from Iowa State College in 1928. He was professor of animal husbandry at U Sask and department head from 1928 to 1946, and dean of agriculture, U Man, from 1946 to 1951. He was the Liberal candidate in the federal by-election in Brandon in 1951 but was defeated. He moved to Calgary and was elected alderman in 1953, 1955, 1957 and 1959; he was mayor from 1963 to 1966. Elected MLA in 1955, he became Alberta Liberal leader in 1958, but was defeated in the election of 1959 and resigned the leadership in 1960. Between 1936 and 1987 he published 4 agricultural texts (2 collaborations) and 39 books on historical subjects, averaging latterly a book a year. His most recent publications are *Frederick Haultain: Frontier Statesman of the Canadian Northwest* (1985), *Heavy Horses: Highlights of Their History in Canada* (1986) and *Paddy Nolan: He Left Them Laughing When He Said Goodbye* (1987). He was lt-gov of Alberta from 1965 to 1974 and was made a Member of the Order of Canada 1975. R.H. MACDONALD

McEwen, Clifford MacKay, "Black Mike," fighter pilot, air vice-marshal (b at Griswold, Man 2 July 1896; d at Toronto 6 Aug 1967). He was credited with 22 victims while flying with 28 Squadron RAF in Italy in 1918. He joined the Canadian Air Force and reached the rank of air commodore in 1941, commanding training formations and 1 (Maritime) Group, RCAF in St John's, Nfld. In 1944 he took command of 6 (Bomber) Group in Yorkshire, Eng, and flew missions over Germany. His forceful leadership made his formation one of the most successful in Bomber Command. He retired 27 Apr 1946, becoming a consultant to aircraft manufacturers and a director of TRANS-CANADA AIRLINES.

BRERETON GREENHOUS

MacEwen, Gwendolyn, writer (b at Toronto 1 Sept 1941; d at Toronto 29 Nov 1987). A sophisticated, wide-ranging and thoughtful writer, she began her career with the poetry collection *The Drunken Clock* (1961). Through many other, larger poetry collections – especially *The Rising Fire* (1963), *A Breakfast for Barbarians* (1966), *The Shadow-Maker* (1969, Gov Gen's Award) and *Afterworlds* (1987 shortlisted for Gov Gen's Award) – she displayed a commanding interest in magic and history as well as an elaborate and penetrating dexterity in her versecraft. Her fiction included 2 novels, *Julian the Magician* (1963) and *King of Egypt, King of Dreams* (1971), and a collection of stories, *Norman* (1972). In addition, she published plays, a translation, a children's book and a travel narrative, *Mermaids and Ikons: A Greek Summer* (1978), which reminds us of the international outlook and gift for languages obvious in her novels and sometimes in her poems.

McEwen, Jean, painter (b at Montréal 14 Dec 1923). Essentially self-taught, he worked in Paris in the early 1950s. Returning to Montréal, he was committed to nonfiguration, influenced by French impressionism and American abstract expressionism. Though McEwen has always employed a hieratic symmetrical composition, his works are experiments in sensual colour, light and gesture. Recipient of several Canadian awards and international honours, he was president of the Non-Figurative Artists Assn of Montréal in the early 1960s and has received several Canadian awards and international honours. A "lyrical abstractionist," he celebrates the potential of colour through a knowledgeable and skilful use of paint. In 1987 a major retrospective of his 20 years' work was held at the Musée des beaux-arts de Montréal. SANDRA PAIKOWSKY

McFadden, David William, poet, novelist (b at Hamilton, Ont 11 Oct 1940). McFadden joined the *Hamilton Spectator* as a proofreader, later becoming a reporter. Following publication of 6 poetry collections, he left the *Spectator* in 1976 to begin free-lance editing and writing. He became writer-in-residence at Simon Fraser U in 1979 and instructor in the writing program of David Thompson U Centre in Nelson, BC, 1979-82. Through irony, self-parody and mock ingenuousness, McFadden's writing illuminates conflicts between the ordinary citizen and an increasingly surreal and commercial society. His most noteworthy books are the mock picaresque novel *A Trip Around Lake Erie* (1980) and selected poems, *My Body was Eaten by Dogs* (1981), and his most recent is *Gypsy Guitar* (1987).

FRANK DAVEY

McGarrigle, Kate and Anna, singing duo and songwriters. Sisters, Kate (b at Montréal 6 Feb 1946) and Anna (b at Montréal 4 Dec 1944), began playing in coffeehouses and colleges in the Montréal area during the early 1960s. Kate moved to New York in 1970; however, they continued to perform together occasionally and both began to write their own songs. Several of these were recorded by other artists, including Linda Ronstadt. In 1975 the singers were reunited as a duo, releasing their self-titled debut album the following year. The critically-acclaimed album was followed by *Dancer With Bruised Knees* (1977) and *Pronto Monto* (1978). Prior to the release of *Lover Over And Over* in 1982, the McGarrigles released *Entre Lajeunesse et la sagesse*, an album in French. A third sister, Jane, has served as manager for the duo as well as contributing backing vocals and piano to some songs.

JOHN GEIGER

McGee, Thomas D'Arcy, politician, journalist, poet, historian (b at Carlingford, Ire 13 Apr 1825; d at Ottawa 7 Apr 1868). Probably the most eloquent FATHER OF CONFEDERATION, D'Arcy McGee was one of the few Canadian politicians to be assassinated.

Most of McGee's short life was spent outside Canada. He emigrated from Ireland to the US at age 17 and took over the editorship of the *Boston Pilot* 2 years later. He returned to Ireland in 1845 and helped edit the nationalist newspaper *Nation*. After he participated in the rebellion of 1848, he fled to the US. McGee spent the next 10 years editing newspapers in the US. Preoccupied with the welfare of hundreds of thousands of IRISH immigrants, he became discouraged by lack of support for his many projects. McGee moved to Montréal in the spring of 1857 at the request of the Irish community and began another newspaper, *New Era*, advocating a "new nationality." He called for the federation of British N America, a transcontinental railway, the settlement of the West, a protective tariff and the development of a distinctive Canadian literature.

McGee was elected to the Legislative Assembly of the Province of Canada from Montréal in 1858. He worked at first with George BROWN and the Reform Party but broke with them after becoming discouraged with the lack of enthusiasm shown by the Reformers for his national projects. He then fell in with John A. MACDONALD and George-Étienne CARTIER. He was in the "Great Coalition" leading up to Confederation and attended the Charlottetown and Québec conferences. By 1866, however, he had alienated many Irish voters and was dropped from the Cabinet. In addition to editing newspapers and pursuing his active political career, McGee was an excellent public speaker, published over 300 poems and wrote many works on Irish history. He was bitterly opposed to the FENIANS and their plans to obtain Irish independence by revolution and the conquest of Canada. When he was assassinated a week before his 43rd birthday, it was generally believed that a Fenian conspiracy was involved.

ROBIN BURNS

Reading: E.J. Phelan, *Ardent Exile* (1951); T.P. Slattery, *The Assassination of D'Arcy McGee* (1968) and *"They Got to Find Me Guilty Yet"* (1972).

The Irish radical D'Arcy McGee was an eloquent spokesman for Canadian Confederation. He was assassinated, likely by a Fenian extremist. Photo *c*1868 (*courtesy National Archives of Canada/C-21543*).

McGeer, Gerald Grattan, "Gerry," lawyer, politician, mayor of Vancouver 1935-36, 1947 (b at Winnipeg 6 Jan 1888; d at Vancouver 11 Aug 1947). He first distinguished himself as counsel for BC on freight-rate hearings in the 1920s which brought enduring financial benefits to BC. Elected mayor of Vancouver in 1934 by a landslide, his 2-year term was marked by tragedy and triumph: the riots of the unemployed, the ON-TO-OTTAWA trek, the serious waterfront strike, the desperate plight of Vancouver citizens; conversely the highly successful Golden Jubilee Celebrations of 1936 and, culminating his mayoralty, construction of the superb city hall. He gave Vancouver a sense of destiny. Twice elected to Parliament, and appointed senator in 1945, he chafed at federal politics and, after being re-elected mayor in 1946, died in office. An early proponent of monetary reform, mixing Keynesian economics with SOCIAL CREDIT theories of Major Douglas, he, with his powerful oratory, became a national figure.

DAVID RICARDO WILLIAMS

Reading: David Ricardo Williams, *Mayor Gerry - The Remarkable Gerald Grattan McGeer* (1986).

McGibbon, Pauline Emily, née Mills (b at Sarnia, Ont 20 Oct 1910). After years of volunteer positions, including national president of the IMPERIAL ORDER DAUGHTERS OF THE EMPIRE (1963-65), president of the Alumni Assn (1953-54) and chancellor of U of T (1971-74), McGibbon held her first salaried position as Ontario's lieutenant-governor (1974-80). She was the first woman lieutenant-governor in Canada. Although she attributed her success to a sense of humour and love of people, she acknowledged that her appointment would have been impossible but for the WOMEN'S MOVEMENT. She was chairperson of the National Arts Centre (1980-84), member-at-large of the board of trustees, Toronto School of Theology (1984-87) and since 1980 has been a director of Massey Hall/Roy Thomson Hall.

MARGARET E. MCCALLUM

MacGill, Elizabeth Muriel Gregory, "Elsie," aeronautical engineer, feminist (b at Vancouver 27 Mar 1905; d at Cambridge, Mass 4 Nov 1980). First woman graduate in electrical engineering at U of T (1927) and with a masters degree in aeronautical engineering from U of Mich (1929), MacGill worked in Montréal in the 1930s for Fairchild Aircraft Ltd and as chief aeronautical engineer of the Canadian Car and Foundry Co, designing the Maple Leaf Trainer aircraft. During WWII she headed Canadian production and designed a winterized version of the Hawker Hurricane fighter plane in Fort William, Ont. After 1943 she practised privately in Toronto as a consulting aeronautical engineer. An active feminist, MacGill was president of the Canadian Federation of Business and Professional Women's Clubs (1962-64) and was a member of the Royal Commission on the STATUS OF WOMEN. In addition to several technical papers, her writings include *My Mother the Judge* (1981), a biography of her mother, BC journalist, suffragist and judge Helen Gregory MACGILL.

DAVID FRASER

MacGill, Helen Gregory, née Helen Emma Gregory, feminist, reformer, judge (b at Hamilton, Canada W 7 Jan 1864; d at Chicago, Ill 27 Feb 1947). She was the first woman graduate of Trinity Coll, Toronto (BA, MA), and, although never a career woman, she wrote and published all her life. As a reporter, she travelled alone across the Canadian West to Japan, marrying her first husband en route. Widowed young, she married James MacGill in 1903 and spent the remainder of her life in Vancouver. MacGill served for 23 years as judge of the Juvenile Court there; she was the first woman appointed judge in the region (1917) and the third in Canada. The Court itself had been created because of the pressures for reform exerted by women's groups in which MacGill was active. Elsie Gregory MACGILL's biography *My Mother the Judge* (1981) – also in part an autobiography – is a valuable document of the WOMEN'S MOVEMENT.

NAOMI BLACK

McGill, James, merchant, philanthropist (b at Glasgow, Scot 6 Oct 1744; d at Montréal 12 Dec 1813). One of the Montréal merchants primarily concerned with the FUR TRADE S of the Great Lakes in the 1770s and 1780s, he began diversifying his commercial activities in the 1790s to include land speculation and by 1810 had withdrawn from the fur trade altogether. Showing an unusually strong affection for his adopted city, he was also active in its public life, holding several important appointments in municipal and provincial affairs. When he died, reputedly the community's richest citizen, he willed, among other philanthropies, an endowment of land and money with which to establish the university which bears his name.

STANLEY GORDON

McGill University, Montréal, was founded in 1821. To meet demands for public education, the Royal Institution for the Advancement of Learning was established in 1801. In 1813 merchant James MCGILL died, leaving his estate outside Montréal and an endowment of £10 000 for a college, naming the Royal Institution as trustee. It acquired a charter for "the University of McGill College" in 1821. McGill's heirs contested his will; the trustees, on gaining the estate, adopted in 1829 the Montreal Medical Institution, a teaching arm of the Montreal General Hospital, as the new university's Faculty of Medicine. The litigation regarding the endowment was finally settled in the trustees' favour, and the nondenominational McGill College was built on the founder's farm. A faculty of arts was established in 1843.

In 1852 the Royal Institution merged with McGill University. The governors appointed as principal John William DAWSON, a young Nova

Enrolment: McGill University, 1985-86
(Source: Statistics Canada)

Full-time Undergrad	*Full-time Graduate*	*Part-time Undergrad*	*Part-time Graduate*
13 587	4 427*	2 446	1 216

* Includes medical interns and residents

Scotia geologist, and his driving genius began to build McGill into an internationally renowned institution. His interest in public education led to the establishment of McGill Normal School. He also formulated a scheme for affiliated schools and colleges across Canada, which taught the McGill curriculum. Further, he established the tradition of enlisting the sympathies of wealthy benefactors, notably the MOLSON family, Lord Strathcona (*see* D.A. SMITH) and Sir William MACDONALD. McGill received minimal public funding until the early 1960s.

Dawson's successor, William Peterson, supported McGill's inclination towards the medical, biological and physical sciences. In 1898 he brought Ernest RUTHERFORD from Cambridge U to a full professorship of physics. Peterson encouraged H.M. TORY to found McGill College in Vancouver (now UNIVERSITY OF BRITISH COLUMBIA). He persuaded Macdonald to found Macdonald College in Ste-Anne-de-Bellevue as a constituent of McGill, to further agriculture, food science and teacher training.

During the principalship of Sir Arthur CURRIE, Canada's brilliant WWI corps commander, the McGill graduate school began to share with Toronto the development of postgraduate studies in Canada. Medicine remained pre-eminent, with such names in the interwar years as J.B. COLLIP and Wilder PENFIELD; chemistry was tremendously encouraged by Otto MAASS and physics by J.S. FOSTER. The McGill Social Science Project, begun 1930 by Leonard MARSH, strongly influenced Canada in the development of the welfare state.

Cyril James, principal 1940-62, led the fight for federal funding of universities. During his tenure an immense flood of returning veterans swelled enrolment, which increased from about 3400 in 1939 to over 8000 in 1948. After the war humanistic studies increased, and now every aspect of human culture is actively studied on campus. In the 1960s and 1970s McGill survived the "student revolt" and came to terms with reviving FRENCH CANADIAN NATIONALISM. McGill is a constituent of the provincial university network but has considerable freedom in maintaining its tradition of excellent education and research. The university comprises 14 faculties: medicine, arts, law, education, engineering, dentistry, agriculture, music, management, science, religious studies, nursing, physical and occupational therapy, and graduate studies and research.

STANLEY B. FROST

Reading: Stanley B. Frost, *For the Advancement of Learning*, 2 vols (1980-84).

McGillivray, Duncan, fur trader (b in Inverness-shire, Scot *c*1770; d at Montréal 9 Apr 1808), brother of William and Simon MCGILLIVRAY. One of a family of boys attracted into the Canadian FUR TRADE by their uncle Simon MCTAVISH, McGillivray joined the NORTH WEST CO sometime before 1793. He traded out of posts on the N Saskatchewan R for most of his career and may have made an early crossing of the Rocky Mts. In 1802 he returned to Montréal where he became an agent for the NWC, travelling to the summer rendezvous at FORT WILLIAM each year until his death.

DANIEL FRANCIS

McGillivray, Simon, merchant (b at Stratherrick, Scot 1783; d at London, Eng 9 June 1840), brother of William and Duncan MCGILLIVRAY. Owing to physical disability, he did not enter the Canadian FUR TRADE actively like his brothers. Instead he turned to the financial end of the business, working in London, Eng, and Montréal for subsidiaries of the NORTH WEST CO. In 1821 he was instrumental in bringing about the union between the NWC and the HBC. His association with the fur trade and Canada ended in 1830.

DANIEL FRANCIS

McGillivray, William, fur-trade merchant (b Scot *c*1764; d at London, Eng 16 Oct 1825). Attracted to the fur trade by his uncle, Simon MCTAVISH, McGillivray was a wintering partner in the NORTH WEST CO for several seasons. From 1794 he represented the Montréal end of the business at the annual rendezvous at GRAND PORTAGE [Minn]. Eventually he became superintendent of the northwestern trade, and when his uncle died in 1804, McGillivray was made chief director of the NWC. During the War of 1812 he commanded a company of voyageurs, assisting Gen BROCK at the capture of Detroit. As leader of the NWC, he presided over a period of intense competition with the HBC that ended when the companies united in 1821. Afterward, he was a director of the newly organized company. FORT WILLIAM, the NWC depot at the head of Lk Superior, was named after him.

DANIEL FRANCIS

Reading: M.W. Campbell, *Northwest to the Sea: A Biography of William McGillivray* (1975).

William McGillivray, chief director of the North West Co. He led a company of voyageurs during the War of 1812 and assisted Gen Brock in the capture of Detroit (*courtesy National Archives of Canada/C-167*).

McGregor, Gordon Roy, engineer, aviator, airline executive (b at Montréal 26 Sept 1901; d there 8 Mar 1971). After attending McGill U, he joined Bell Telephone Co of Canada as an engineer in 1923, where he remained until joining the RCAF in 1938. He went overseas in 1939, seeing action in the Battle of BRITAIN and becoming one of the first 3 RCAF officers to receive decorations in WWII. As a group captain, he obtained a posting to London where, in a brilliantly conceived and executed movement for which he later received the OBE, he led an echelon of the Second Tactical Air Force HQ onto the continent in June 1944 – the first allied air unit to base itself on the continent after D-DAY. In addition to the DFC and OBE, he was awarded the Order of Orange Nassau by the Netherlands, the French Croix de guerre and the Czechoslovakian War Cross. McGregor joined TRANS-CANADA AIRLINES in Dec 1945 and became president in Feb 1948. During his tenure, the airline's routes and traffic volume grew enormously. In 1968, the year of his retirement, McGregor was invested as a Companion of the Order of Canada.

McGregor, James, Presbyterian minister (b in Comrie Parish, Scot 1759; d at Pictou, NS 1830). Ordained in 1780 by the General Associate Synod (Antiburgher) of Scotland, McGregor was sent as an unpaid missionary to PICTOU, where he remained as minister until his death. Under extremely difficult physical conditions, he made several missionary tours of NS, PEI and NB between 1791 and 1805. Founder of the first Canadian Auxiliary Bible Society, he revised Gaelic publications for the British and Foreign Bible Society and was the author of 2 pamphlets and a volume of Gaelic poetry.

JOHN S. MOIR

MacGregor, James Gordon, physicist (b at Halifax 31 Mar 1852; d at Edinburgh, Scot 21 May 1913). Educated at Dalhousie U, MacGregor was awarded a Gilchrist scholarship in 1871 and studied under Peter Guthrie Tait at Edinburgh and Gustav Wiedeman at Leipzig. When he received a doctorate from London in 1876, he had already had 4 papers published in the *Proceedings* of the Royal Society of Edinburgh. In 1879 Dalhousie offered him its newly established chair of physics. During his 22 years there he published about 60 papers on several aspects of the electrical and thermal properties of solutions and was elected to both the Royal Soc of London and the Royal Soc of Edinburgh. He helped found the ROYAL SOCIETY OF CANADA and was a charter member. In 1888 he published *An Elementary Treatise on Kinematics and Dynamics*. He succeeded P.G. Tait at Edinburgh in 1901.

YVES GINGRAS

McGuigan, James Charles, cardinal, archbishop of Toronto (b at Hunter River, PEI 26 Nov 1894; d at Toronto 8 Apr 1974). The shy, anglophilic grandson of Irish Catholics who fled Ulster immediately before the Great Famine, McGuigan graduated from St Dunstan's Coll and Laval. In 1930, when only 35, he was appointed archbishop of Regina and engaged in vigorous efforts to help the poor, but 5 years later was delegated as archbishop of Toronto. McGuigan retrenched Toronto's archdiocesan finances and despite his professed ecumenism extended its separate school system against hysterical opposition lead by the Orange Order and Thomas Todhunter SHIELDS. On 23 Dec 1945, McGuigan was nominated Canada's first non-French cardinal. Two years later, Pius XII appointed him legate to Ottawa's Marian Congress; as well the cardinal, a liberal, attended Vatican Council II. However, failing health, beginning with a traffic accident in 1957, lead to his semi-retirement in 1961.

PETER MCGUIGAN

MacGuigan, Mark Rudolph, academic, politician (b at Charlottetown 17 Feb 1931). A graduate of St Dunstan's Coll and U of T, he taught law at U of T, Osgoode Hall and U of Windsor, where he was also dean. In 1968 he was elected to Parliament for Windsor, succeeding Paul MARTIN, and in 1980 PM TRUDEAU appointed him minister of external affairs. From 1982 to 1984 he was minister of justice. In 1976 he ran unsuccessfully for the leadership of the Ontario provincial Liberals and in 1984 was an unsuccessful candidate for the leadership of the national Liberal Party. He then retired from politics and since then has been a judge of the federal Court of Appeal.

ROBERT BOTHWELL

McHenry, Earle Willard, "Mac," professor, scientist, author (b at Streetsville, Ont 25 Jan 1899; d at Toronto 20 Dec 1961). McHenry's initial discipline was chemistry; however, an interest in nutrition emerged when he was appointed lecturer in the dept of physiological hygiene at U of T. Ultimately a separate dept of public-health nutrition was established in 1946 with McHenry as professor and head (1946-61). His interest in nutrition encompassed both basic research and the nutritional health of the general public. He was the first president of the Nutrition Soc of Canada (est 1957), and was an outspoken, articulate contributor to several governmental committees on nutrition education and policy in N America. McHenry wrote 2 books, *Basic Nutrition* and *Foods without Fads,* which expressed his commonsense philosophy towards nutrition and his impatience with unscientific thinking. At his death he was coediting the 3-volume *Nutrition: A Comprehensive Treatise.* M.J. BAIGENT

Machinery and Equipment Industry includes establishments that produce pumps and compressors, rolling-mill and metalworking equipment, forestry equipment, mining equipment, farm machinery, construction equipment and service industries equipment. The largest resource industry users of machinery in Canada are mining, forestry, petroleum and electric-power generation. Among Canadian manufacturing industries, the largest purchasers of machinery and equipment are the metalworking industries, including steelmaking, the automotive industry and the machinery industry itself. Other large user industries are food processing, packaging and air and water purification. Machinery and equipment are made in foundries, machine and welding shops and assembly plants.

It was not until the 1850s, when a reciprocity treaty opened the booming US market to Canadian manufacturing industries, that machinery and equipment production moved from small forges and metalworking shops to the early versions of today's large plants. It is estimated that, at the time of Confederation (1867), about 30 to 40 firms were manufacturing machinery and equipment for other industries; by 1967 there were 15 Canadian machinery firms 100 years or older. Some, such as Dorr-Oliver Canada Ltd in Orillia, Black Clawson-Kennedy Ltd in Owen Sound and Babcock-Wilcox Canada Ltd in Cambridge, are now among the country's largest. The earliest companies manufactured primarily steam engines, hydraulic turbines, pumps, woodworking machinery, machine tools and flour-mill, cement-making and sawmill machinery. The plants were initially powered by waterwheels, water turbines or steam engines. At the end of the 19th century, the advent of large thermal and hydroelectric power plants, with their far-flung distribution systems, started a new phase in machinery manufacturing. Factories were located near markets and transportation networks. The availability of large, efficient electric motors permitted the design of more powerful machinery.

As its customer industries proliferated and expanded, machinery manufacturing grew. WWI accelerated the demand for more and newer types of machinery, giving the industry maturity and a permanent place in Canada's economy. It expanded until the Great Depression of the 1930s, when all sectors encountered nearly a decade of minimal growth. With WWII, enormous demands were again imposed on the industry. The boom was followed in 1945 by a period of conversion and expansion for production of peacetime materials and goods for the domestic market and for the immense rebuilding requirements in Europe. These events called for new machinery on an unprecedented scale. Annual plant shipments of Canadian machinery and equipment grew from $60 million in 1938 to $460 million in 1950. The industry enjoyed a continuous and above-average growth rate until 1981, after which it followed the rest of the Canadian economy into a severe recession. Industry sales dropped from $6.1 billion in 1981 to $4.86 billion in 1982. Production has since then risen steadily and reached $6.4 billion in 1985.

The Modern Industry

The modern Canadian machinery and equipment industry is heavily dependent on export markets: between 1975 and 1985, exports accounted for 62% of the industry's real growth. Increasing exports were necessary to sustain growth because the indigenous Canadian market is too small, even for manufacturers who concentrate on producing machinery for larger Canadian industries. In 1985 the industry exported 51% of its production, with $2.8 billion or 75% of exports going to the US. Conversely, a country with Canada's small population cannot manufacture the entire range of machinery and equipment needed by all its industries. In fact, in recent years Canadian machinery and equipment manufacturers have never managed to capture more than about one-third of the domestic market. A 1977 study of the 17 largest Western industrial nations by the OECD showed that Canada had the lowest machinery self-sufficiency in the group (32%). By comparison, figures for some of the other countries were Italy 60%, W Germany 70%, France 74%, the US 91% and Japan 95%. A 1985 study showed Canada's machinery self-sufficiency still to be only 31%.

Location of Plants About 64% of the machinery and equipment industry (by dollar value of plant shipments) is found in Ontario; Québec has 20%; the Prairie provinces 9%; BC 6%; and the Maritimes 1%.

Ownership It is estimated that in the 1980s about 225 firms in the Canadian machinery sector, accounting for about 62% of its total output, were subsidiaries of American parent companies. Only about 25% came from Canadian-controlled companies. FOREIGN INVESTMENT has provided ready access to the technical, financial and marketing resources of parent corporations. It has also created an outflow of profit capital and, in some cases, has restricted company activity.

Work Force Machinery and equipment manufacturing is a labour- and technology-intensive industry, employing large numbers of engineers and skilled tradesmen. The industry work force has grown, but in less than direct proportion to the value of its shipments because of productivity improvements. Employment increased from 13 500 in 1949 to 112 000 by 1967, to 132 000 by 1981. By 1983 the work force was down to 102 000. While the industry's output increased by 33% from 1983 to 1985, its work force increased by only 8%. The low employment increase primarily resulted from large productivity gains provided by the implementation of new computer-assisted design and manufacturing technologies during this period. The 3 major unions are the International Assn of Machinists and Aerospace Workers, the United Steelworkers of America and the Canadian Auto Workers.

Associations The Machinery and Equipment Manufacturers Assn of Canada was established in 1955 in Ottawa to provide a forum for technical, economic, educational and other deliberations, and for representation to the government, the public and the media. J.R. ROMANOW

Machray, Robert, Church of England priest, bishop (b at Aberdeen, Scot 17 May 1831; d at Winnipeg 9 Mar 1904). Educated at King's College, Aberdeen, and Sidney Sussex College, Cambridge, he received prizes in mathematics, philosophy and divinity. He was ordained in 1855, served in English parishes and was dean of Sidney Sussex College 1859-62. He succeeded David ANDERSON as bishop of RUPERT'S LAND and was consecrated in June 1865. During his years there he helped extend and consolidate the church's work and built up St John's College, Winnipeg. He became first metropolitan of the new ecclesiastical province of Rupert's Land in 1875, with the title of archbishop, and first primate of Canada in 1893. He died in office. F.A. PEAKE

McIlwraith, Thomas, businessman, ornithologist (b at Newton, Scot 25 Dec 1824; d at Hamilton, Ont 30/31 Jan 1903). He is best known for his 1886 treatise on Ontario birds, the first major annotated provincial bird book in Canada. McIlwraith came to Canada in 1853 and became a successful Hamilton businessman and alderman. He published several papers on birds in Canada West, and was credited with instructing wildlife artist Allan BROOKS in the proper preparation of bird skins. He was one of 25 founders of the prestigious American Ornithologists' Union and served on its council. The name of the McIlwraith Field Naturalists of London, Ont, honours his memory. MARTIN K. MCNICHOLL

McIlwraith, Thomas Forsyth, anthropologist (b at Hamilton, Ont 9 Apr 1899; d at Toronto 29 Mar 1964). McIlwraith graduated from McGill and Cambridge and, as field assistant at the National Museum of Canada, conducted research on the Northwest Coast, 1922-24. In 1925 he joined U of T and was a professor and head of the dept of anthropology from 1936 to 1952. At U of T, McIlwraith built a department in which archaeological, linguistic, physical and ethnological anthropology all found a place. His own research interests lay in ethnology and later in the effects of change on Canadian native peoples. In 1939 he edited (with C.T. Loram) *The North American Indian Today* and in 1948 published the *Bella Coola Indians.* Chairman of the Social Science Research Council, president of the Royal Canadian Institute and the RSC, fellow of the Royal Institute of Great Britain and Ireland, he remained a research associate of the National Museum and the Royal Ontario Museum. TOM MCFEAT

McInnes, William Wallace Burns, lawyer, politician, commissioner of Yukon T, judge (b at Dresden, Ont 8 Apr 1871; d at Vancouver 4 Aug 1954). McInnes entered U of T at 14 years of age and graduated at 18 in 1889, the youngest graduate to that date. After studying at Osgoode Hall, he was called to the BC Bar in 1893 and practised in Nanaimo and Vancouver. A Liberal, he won the federal constituency of Nanaimo in 1896. He represented Alberni in the BC legislature 1900-05, serving as provincial secretary and minister of education in the short-lived Prior administration. In 1905 he was appointed commissioner of Yukon T and his term was characterized by reform and political harmony. He unsuccessfully sought election in 1907, 1908 and 1917, and was appointed to the County Court of Vancouver (1909-17). He served as police magistrate in Vancouver for 10 years, beginning in 1944, and was known for the severity of his sentences. HAL GUEST

MacInnis, Grace Winona, née Woodsworth, politician (b at Winnipeg 25 July 1905). Following in the footsteps of her father, J.S. WOODSWORTH, and husband Angus, Grace MacInnis became a key member of the CO-OPERATIVE COMMONWEALTH FEDERATION and later the NEW DEMOCRATIC PARTY, as well as a respected MLA in BC (1941-45) and an MP (1965-74). A backroom politician *par excellence,* she was influential within provincial and national party circles, leading one reporter to call her in 1949 the true leader of the CCF executive. In BC and Ottawa she worked hardest for low-income housing, consumer rights and women's equality. She also took great interest in international affairs, serving as Canada's representative during a number of international conferences. For her contributions MacInnis received several awards, including the Governor General's "Persons Award" (1979), marking the 50th anniversary of the PERSONS CASE. In 1953 MacInnis published *J.S. Woodsworth: A Man to Remember.* SUSAN WALSH

MacInnis, Joseph Beverly, physician, diver, poet (b at Barrie, Ont 2 Mar 1937). After completing his MD at U of T (1962) and interning at Toronto General Hospital (1963), he lectured at U of Penn (1964), but he has spent most of his career on underwater projects. He was the life-support physician for a man-in-sea project (1964), directed 75 dives at the Linde Research Lab (1965) and was a consultant to Sealab III (1967) to the TITANIC project (1985) and to the American Medical Assn *Journal* (1966).

In 1969 MacInnis developed an underwater contained environment in Georgian Bay and then designed a transparent non-corrodible undersea refuge. In 1972, at Resolute Bay, this became, as one of 10 arctic underwater expeditions (1970-74), the first-named station under ice, including the first under the North Pole. MacInnis has participated in many diving expeditions, including a 700-foot dive (213 m) from the first lock-out submarine (1968), and an arctic dive in which BREADALBANE, a ship sunk in 1853, was discovered off Beechey I (1980). His interest in merging arts with science has found expression in *Underwater Images* (1971), in which his own photographs of underwater life are accompanied by his poems, and in several films and TV programs. A film, *Deep Androsia,* received a Gold Medal of Excellence at the International Film Festival, Santa Monica (1965). Many of his dives are documented in his book *Underwater Man* (1974). In Aug 1987 MacInnis joined the French team diving to investigate the wreckage of the *Titanic.* MARTIN K. MCNICHOLL

McIntosh, John, farmer, apple breeder (b in the Mohawk R valley, NY 1777; d at Dundela, Canada W 1845). After a family disagreement, McIntosh immigrated to Iroquois, Upper Canada, in 1796. In 1811 he moved to the site of Dundela, where in clearing the forest he discovered about 20 apple trees in a previously cleared area. He transplanted several, one of which produced a superior fruit that he cultivated with mixed success. In 1835 his son Allan learned the art of grafting and the family began to produce the apples on a major scale. The vigorous, hardy and productive trees produced the popular dessert fruit of wide climatic and cultural tolerance, first known as "Granny" and later "McIntosh Red." The original tree lived until about 1910, bearing fruit for over 90 years until 1908. MARTIN K. MCNICHOLL

McIntosh, William, fur trader (b at Grand Rapids, US 1784; d 16 Feb 1842). By 1816 a wintering partner in the NORTH WEST CO, he had previously been positioned at Lesser Slave Lk (1803) in the Peace R country (1805) and at Ft Vermilion (1815). He was arrested at Grand Rapids in 1819 along with several other senior NOR'WESTERS by the governor in chief of the HUDSON'S BAY CO. McIntosh pretended illness, feigned suicide and escaped to FT WILLIAM. In the 2 preceding years he had completely disrupted HBC attempts to capture the Athabasca country, driving one of their officers to near starvation.

After the 1821 union of the NWC and HBC he served as chief trader and after 1823 as chief factor, variously at Nelson House (1825-29), CUMBERLAND HOUSE (1829-32) and Dunvegan (1832-34). He retired in 1837 after 2 furloughs. Although McIntosh served the HBC for 16 years, his prominence in the wars between the 2 fur-trade giants may have engendered the hatred of Sir George SIMPSON, the governor of the HBC. In his private "Character Book," Simpson described McIntosh as "A revengeful cold blooded black hearted Man whom I consider capable of anything that is bad: possessing no abilities beyond such as qualify him to cheat an unfortunate Indian and to be guilty of a mean dirty trick: Suspicious, Cruel & Tyrannical without honour or integrity." FRITS PANNEKOEK

McIvor, George Harold, businessman, public servant (b at Portage la Prairie, Man 1894). Starting in the grain business at 15, McIvor rose from work at a country elevator to the Winnipeg Grain Exchange. In 1935 he joined John I. McFarland as assistant chief commissioner of the CANADIAN WHEAT BOARD. He became chief commissioner of the board in 1937, and held the post until 1958 when he became chairman of Robin Hood Flour. He was closely linked to C.D. HOWE and was blamed by many for Howe's unpopular policies during the wheat glut of the mid-1950s. ROBERT BOTHWELL

Mackay, Angus, prairie agriculturist (b near Pickering, UC 10 Jan 1841; d at Indian Head, Sask 10 June 1931). Mackay is reputedly the man who introduced "summer fallow," which some historians consider more important than any other discovery in allowing successful agriculture on the Canadian prairies. A farmer's son and a farmer, Mackay moved west at age 40 and took up virgin land at Indian Head. The prairie farmer's main problem is drought. Mackay appears to have discovered independently about 1885 that cultivating land and leaving it fallow for a year allows it to store moisture and yield a good crop the next year. In 1888 Mackay was appointed to create the first Dominion Experimental Farm in the Canadian West. He became the chief propagandist for summer fallow and a powerful influence in western agriculture. DONALD J.C. PHILLIPSON

McKay, Arthur Fortescue, painter (b at Nipawin, Sask 11 Sept 1926). He studied at the Provincial Institute of Technology and Art, Calgary, 1946-48; Académie de la grande chaumière, Paris, 1949-50; Columbia U, and Barnes Foundation, Merion, Pa, 1956-57. He first began to teach at U Sask, Regina, in 1950. Appointed associate professor in art 1956-74, he served as director of its School of Art 1964-67. Since 1978 McKay has been associate professor at U of Regina. One of the REGINA FIVE, he was influenced in the 1960s by Barnett Newman at the Emma Lake workshops and was included in Clement Greenberg's 1964 "Post-Painterly Abstraction" exhibition. McKay is most noted for his scraped enamel "mandalas" which utilize circular and rectangular formats to create highly contemplative images reflecting his interest in Zen Buddhism. In the 1970s, he continued to paint abstractions but also reintroduced the landscape in his work. NORMAN ZEPP

McKay, Donald, designer and builder of clipper ships (b at Jordan Falls, NS 4 Sept 1810; d at Hamilton, Mass 20 Sept 1880). As a boy he learned the shipbuilder's trade in his father's and uncle's shipyards on the Jordan R. He immigrated to New York in 1827 and at age 16 bound himself an apprentice to Isaac Webb. After his indenture was up he became a free-lance shipwright, worked in the Brooklyn Navy Yard, then in Wiscasset, Maine, and in 1841 formed a partnership in Newburyport, Mass, where he made a reputation building fast packet ships. In 1845 McKay opened his own shipyard in E Boston, where he began building the great clipper ships – *Flying Cloud, Great Republic, Sovereign of the Seas* – that set long-standing records for fast passages and carried his name throughout the world. MARION ROBERTSTON

MacKay, Elmer MacIntosh, politician (b at Hopewell, NS 5 Aug 1936). Educated at Acadia and Dalhousie, MacKay was called to the NS Bar in 1961 and practised law in Pictou County. Elected a Conservative MP for Central Nova in a 1971 by-election, he was a tenacious and vocal Commons critic of Liberal governments, taking particular aim at security questions. He was minister of regional economic expansion and the political minister for NS in the 1979-80 Joe CLARK government. An early and prominent supporter of Brian MULRONEY'S successful campaign to become PC chief in 1983, he resigned his seat so that the new leader could run for Parliament. MacKay was re-elected in Central Nova in 1984 and served as solicitor general 1984-85 and then as minister of national revenue in the Mulroney government. NORMAN HILLMER

Mackay, George Leslie, Presbyterian missionary (b at Zorra, Oxford County, Canada W 22 Mar 1844; d in Formosa [Taiwan] 2 June 1901). A graduate student in Edinburgh, Mackay decided to become a missionary after hearing Alexander Duff, the "apostle to India," call for foreign evangelism. He was sent to mainland China in 1871 by the Canadian Presbyterian Church but settled in Tamsui, Formosa. Although natives destroyed several of his churches, his knowledge of elementary medicine won him respect. Nicknamed "the blackbearded barbarian," Mackay built a hospital, a girls' school and Oxford College, and established 60 mission stations in 20 years. JOHN S. MOIR

McKay, James, trader, guide, entrepreneur, politician (b at Edmonton House, NWT 1828; d at St James, Man 2 Dec 1879). Son of a Scottish boat-brigade guide and Métis mother, McKay spoke English, French, Ojibwa, Cree and Sioux. A massive, powerful man, he was Hudson's Bay Co postmaster and clerk 1853-60 before starting his own business, freighting, trading, carrying mails, running a stagecoach from Winnipeg to Edmonton, and outfitting and guiding hunters and travellers. On the Council of Assiniboia 1868-69, McKay played a moderating part at the time of the first RIEL rising. He served Manitoba as president of the Executive Council, Speaker of the Legislative Council and minister of agriculture, and was on the Council of the North-West Territories 1873-75. As adviser for Treaties No 1, 2 and 3 and commissioner for Treaties No 5 and 6, he played a crucial role. McKay converted from Presbyterianism to Catholicism and his marriage to a daughter of John Rowand brought him wealth and social status. His home, Deer Lodge, became a meeting place for the Indian and Métis and elite newcomers from Ontario. His career linked the old fur-trading, buffalo-hunting West to the new order of business, settlement and organized government. IRENE SPRY

MacKay, Robert Alexander, political scientist, diplomat (b in Victoria County, Ont 2 Jan 1894; d at Ottawa 25 Nov 1979). MacKay served overseas in WWI and studied at U of T and Princeton. Professor of government and political science at Dalhousie 1927-47, he also served on the Rowell-Sirois Commission on Federal-Provincial Relations. Wartime assistant in the Dept of External Affairs, he rejoined the dept in 1947. In addition to his work as a negotiator of union with Newfoundland, he was deputy undersecretary, permanent representative to the UN (1955-58) and ambassador to Norway (1958-61). He taught political science at Carleton 1961-72. His publications include *The Unreformed Senate of Canada* (1926); with E.B. Rogers, *Canada Looks Abroad* (1939); and *Documents on Canadian Foreign Policy 1945-1954* (1971). JOHN W. HOLMES

Mackay Case (1980) In *Mackay v the Queen*, private R.C. Mackay, accused of trafficking in drugs and of being found in possession of drugs, invoked in his defence the principle of equality before the law found in the CANADIAN BILL OF RIGHTS of 1960, because the prescribed penalty was higher for a service person than for a civilian. The Supreme Court of Canada enunciated the principle that, based on the Constitution Act, 1867 (s91.7), Parliament could, for a valid federal purpose, provide a more severe penalty for a serviceman than for a civilian and for the same reasons could provide that these cases should be conducted by a military attorney before a court martial. GÉRALD-A. BEAUDOIN

McKee Trophy, award given annually for contribution to the advancement of Canadian aviation. It was donated by J. Dalzell McKee, an American sportsman pilot, who completed the first flight of a seaplane across Canada in 1926. The selection was made by a committee established by the Dept of National Defence. It was first awarded 1927, retired in 1968, and transferred to the custody of the Canadian Aeronautics and Space Institute in 1971 for re-presentation. Among recipients are C.H. DICKINS (1928), W.R. MAY (1929), G.W.G. MCCONACHIE (1945), J.A.D. MCCURDY (1959) and C.C. AGAR (1950). T.M. Reid (1942, 1943) and P.C. GARRATT (1951, 1966) are the only 2-time winners. JAMES MARSH

McKellar, Andrew, astrophysicist, molecular spectroscopist (b at Vancouver 2 Feb 1910; d at Victoria 6 May 1960). McKellar received the MBE in 1947 for his work in WWII as a research officer in the RCN. He was astronomer at the Dominion Astrophysical Observatory in Victoria 1935-39 and 1945-60 and was internationally regarded as one of Canada's greatest astronomers. His 73 scientific publications include evidence that the source of energy of cool carbon stars is a nuclear reaction involving carbon and nitrogen, and the deduction that the temperature of interstellar gas is 2.3 Kelvin. It was more than 20 years before his result was confirmed and used to support the theory of the explosive creation of the universe. His final paper, a biography and a list of his publications appear in the *Journal of the Royal Astronomical Society of Canada* 54 (1960). E.H. RICHARDSON

McKenna, Frank Joseph, lawyer, politician, premier of NB (b at Apohaqui, NB 19 Jan 1948), educated at St Francis Xavier U, Queen's U and UNB, McKenna was admitted to the bar in 1974 and practised law in Chatham, NB. He was elected to the legislature for Chatham in 1982 and was chosen leader of the provincial Liberal Party in May 1985. In Oct 1987 he led the Liberals to a stunning election victory, ending Richard HATFIELD's 17-year reign as premier by winning all 58 seats. It was only the second sweep in a provincial election in Canadian history. During the campaign, McKenna voiced concerns about the MEECH LAKE ACCORD – supported by his predecessor – but by Jan 1988 he expressed his support of the Accord and of the Mulroney FREE TRADE pact. JAMES MARSH

Mackenzie, BC, District Municipality, pop 5542 (1986c), 5890 (1981c), area 20 285 ha, inc 1966, is situated in northern BC on the shores of the man-made Williston Lk Reservoir in the ROCKY MT TRENCH. It was created by the flooding of the Peace, Finlay, Omenica and Parsnip rivers caused by damming the Peace R at the W.A.C. Bennett Dam. Governed by a mayor and 6 aldermen, Mackenzie (after the explorer Alexander MACKENZIE) was a preplanned, instant town designed to exploit the region's rich natural resources. The local economy features the reserves of the Mackenzie Forest Dist, which support 2 pulpmills and 5 sawmills, and the minerals of the Rocky Mt Trench. Mackenzie quickly gained all the services of typical Canadian towns and today has schools, churches, an arena, swimming pools, a ski hill, a library, an arts and craft centre, a hospital and numerous clubs and organizations. ALAN F.J. ARTIBISE

Mackenzie, Ada, golfer (b at Toronto 30 Oct 1891; d at Richmond Hill, Ont 25 Jan 1973). Mackenzie paved the way for women to take GOLF seriously by founding the first club restricted to women, the Ladies' Golf and Tennis Club, in Thornhill, Ont, in May 1925. Mackenzie's own play set high standards. She won the Ont Ladies' Amateur title 9 times and the Canadian Ladies' Open Amateur 5 times. In 1933 she was chosen Canadian athlete of the year. LORNE RUBENSTEIN

Mackenzie, Alexander, builder, newspaper editor, 2nd prime minister of Canada, 1873-78 (b near Dunkeld, Scot 28 Jan 1822; d at Toronto 17 Apr 1892). Immigrating to Canada in 1842, Mackenzie eventually settled in the Sarnia area, working in the building trade with his brother. In the early 1850s he became editor of a Reform newspaper, the *Lambton Shield*, and a supporter of George BROWN. He was first elected to the Legislative Assembly of the PROVINCE OF CANADA in 1861. He backed CONFEDERATION but refused the presidency of the Council when Brown left the coalition in 1865. Mackenzie was elected to the House of Commons, and subsequently to the Ontario legislature in 1867. He sat in the Ontario legislature until dual representation was abolished and sat in the Commons until his death.

In 1873 Mackenzie formed the first Liberal administration in Canada after Sir John A. MACDONALD's government was brought down by the PACIFIC SCANDAL. A hardworking man of exceptional integrity but little imagination, Mackenzie served as his own minister of public works, and his attempt to build a transcontinental railway on a self-financing basis met with some success but little public approbation. Many felt his diligence in his portfolio detracted from his leadership in the Commons. Nevertheless, in his short tenure the Supreme Court and the Auditor General's office were created, and the groundwork for the modern electoral system was laid. Macdonald's party defeated Mackenzie's in the 1878 elections, which were fought on the issue of the NATIONAL POLICY proposed by the Tories.

Mackenzie remained leader of his party for only 2 more years when failing health or a threatened party revolt led him to step down in favour of Edward BLAKE. He refused several offers of a knighthood, and wrote several books in his retirement, including *The Life and Speeches of George Brown* (1882). J.M. BUMSTED

Reading: D.C. Thomson, *Alexander Mackenzie, Clear Grit* (1960).

Alexander Mackenzie
Second Prime Minister of Canada

Birth: 28 Jan 1822, Dunkeld, Sask
Father/Mother: Alexander/Mary Fleming
Father's Occupation: Contractor
Education: Parish school, Scot
Religious Affiliation: Baptist
First Occupation: Contractor
Last Private Occupation: Editor
Political Party: Liberal/Reform
Period(s) as PM: 7 Nov 1873 - 8 Oct 1878
Ridings: Lambton, Ont, 1861-82; York East, Ont, 1882-92
Other Ministries: Public Works 1873-78
Marriage: 28 Mar 1845 to Helen Neil (1826-52); 17 June 1853 to Jane Sym (1825-93)
Children: 1) 1 girl; 2) none
Died: 17 Apr 1892 in Toronto
Cause of Death at Age: Stroke at 70
Burial Place: Lakeview Cemetery, Sarnia, Ont
Other Information: First liberal PM; Declined knighthood.

(*photo courtesy National Archives of Canada/C-20052*).

Mackenzie, Sir Alexander, fur trader, explorer (b at Stornoway, Scot 1764; d near Dunkeld, Scot 12 Mar 1820). Mackenzie's father took him to New York in 1774, and in 1778, because of the Revolutionary War, he was sent to school in Montréal. There in 1779 he entered the employ of the fur-trading firm of Finlay and Gregory, later Gregory, MacLeod and Co. In 1784 he became a partner and spent the years 1785-87 in charge of the post at ÎLE-À-LA-CROSSE. In 1787 the company coalesced with the NORTH WEST CO and Mackenzie became a partner in the larger concern.

He was assigned to the post on the Athabasca R as second-in-command to Peter POND, who had explored the region extensively and would be leaving it in the spring. Pond was convinced that Cook's R (Cook Inlet, Alaska) on Capt COOK's chart was the mouth of the large river that flowed westward out of Great Slave Lk, and that it would provide a travel route to the Pacific. This association with Pond was decisive; Mackenzie later declared that "the practicability of penetrating across the continent" was the "favourite project of my own ambition," and this resulted in the 2 remarkable expeditions upon which his fame rests. He and Pond had founded FT CHIPEWYAN on Lk Athabasca, and he set out from it in 1789 to test Pond's theory, but found that the river (the MACKENZIE R) led to the Arctic, not the Pacific. Undaunted, he planned a second expedition. Having wintered at Ft Fork, on the upper waters of the Peace, he headed westward in May 1793. Crossing the divide from the watershed of the Peace to that of the Fraser, he was advised by Indians to complete his journey to the Pacific overland, instead of following the Fraser to its mouth. The

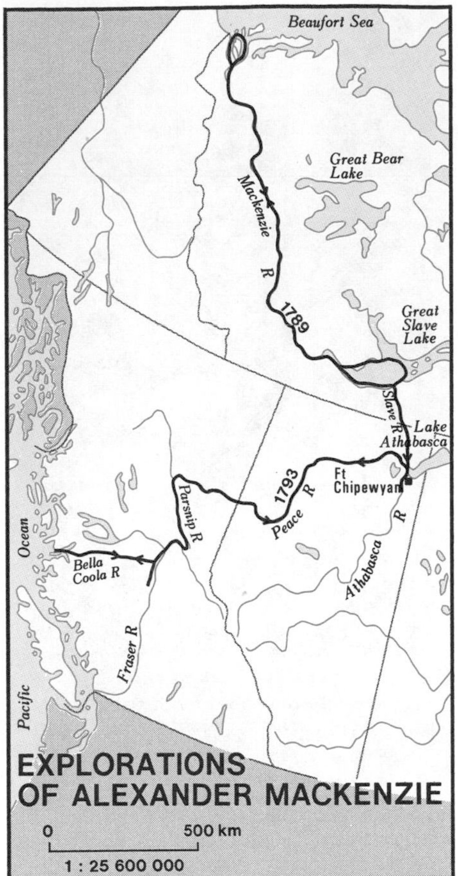

EXPLORATIONS OF ALEXANDER MACKENZIE

last stage of this first crossing of the full width of N America was down the Bella Coola R. The speed and efficiency with which Mackenzie travelled were astonishing; he brought both his crews home safely and in spite of numerous contacts with Indians never fired a shot in anger.

Mackenzie left the West in 1795, and after serving as a partner in McTavish, Frobisher and Co, which managed the NWC, he went to England in 1799. His *Voyages* were published in 1801 and he was knighted in 1802. His ambition was to form a trading concern that would span the continent and involve a union of the NWC and the HBC, but his efforts to bring it about failed. He married in 1812 and retired to an estate in Scotland.

W. KAYE LAMB

Reading: W. Kaye Lamb, ed, *The Journals and Letters of Sir Alexander Mackenzie* (1970).

Mackenzie, Sir Alexander, lawyer, businessman (b at Kincardine, Canada W 30 June 1860; d there 12 July 1943). Son of a Scottish farmer, Mackenzie left school at 17 and articled with a Toronto legal firm, being called to the bar in 1883. In 1899 Z.A. LASH, Canada's pre-eminent corporate lawyer, sent Mackenzie to oversee the legal arrangements of the São Paulo Tramway, Light and Power Co in Brazil. Fluent in Portuguese and conversant with the Brazilian legal and political systems, in 1904 he joined the Rio de Janeiro Tramway, Light and Power Co and served both companies as resident VP until their merger into Brazilian Traction in 1912 (BRASCAN). When F.S. Pearson, Brazilian Traction's founder, drowned on the *Lusitania* in 1915, Mackenzie assumed the presidency, and under his leadership Brazilian Traction became Canada's largest single overseas investment. He retired in 1928, remaining a company director. In 1919 he was knighted for his services in bringing Brazil into WWI.

DUNCAN MCDOWALL

Mackenzie, Chalmers Jack, engineer, research manager (b at St Stephen, NB 10 July 1888; d at Ottawa 26 Feb 1984). He was the single most important figure in the postwar growth of Canadian science. He was trained in civil engineering at Dalhousie and Harvard and served in the Canadian Army in WWI (MC, 1918) before moving to Saskatchewan (where he had worked 1910-15). Part-time lecturing at the U of Sask led to his becoming dean of engineering 1921-39. During this period he organized important research in protecting concrete buildings from attack by "alkali salts" in the soil, supervised the design and construction by his students of a highway bridge in Saskatoon, and served as chairman of the Town Planning Council.

Mackenzie was appointed to the NATIONAL RESEARCH COUNCIL in 1935, and his abilities were recognized by NRC Pres A.G.L. MCNAUGHTON who personally chose him as acting president in 1939. Mackenzie was thus the government's chief scientist in WWII and became the right-hand man of C.D. HOWE in planning postwar SCIENCE POLICY. His war work included the tenfold expansion of the NRC Laboratories, top-secret war gas, aviation, radar and atomic bomb research, membership on the US-British-Canadian Combined Policy Committee, allocating uranium supplies, and even the chore of telling Winston Churchill that "Habakkuk," the British PM's pet project of an iceberg-aircraft carrier, was impossible.

Mackenzie was NRC president in his own right 1944-52, president of ATOMIC ENERGY OF CANADA LTD 1953-54 and president of the Atomic Energy Control Board 1948-61. In the postwar years he and E.W.R. STEACIE laid the foundations of the Canadian scientific system as it is today. He had a hand in the GOUZENKO investigations, the NRC's entry into basic research through Gerhard HERZBERG and others, governmental responses to the Russian atomic bomb (1949) and Sputnik (1957), the foundation of the DEFENCE RESEARCH Board and MEDICAL RESEARCH COUNCIL, the expansion of NRC university grants to equal its internal budget, the Industrial Research Assistance Programme of 1962, the enlargement of CANADA COUNCIL grants 1963-69, and he served as chancellor of Carleton U 1954-68. Though nominally retired in 1961, Mackenzie remained a member of the Advisory Panel on Science Policy to 1963, acting as chairman during Steacie's terminal illness; in 1964 he provided a "second opinion" for the government about the science policy reforms proposed by the Glassco Royal Commission Report of 1963, which were implemented 1964-70, and he maintained an office at the NRC until his 90th year. He received many honours and awards including the CMG (1943), US Medal of Merit (1947), Companion of the Order of Canada (1967), Royal Bank Award and fellowship in the Royal Soc of Canada and that of London.

DONALD J.C. PHILLIPSON

Mackenzie, Sir Colin John, soldier (b 26 Nov 1861; d at London, Eng 7 July 1956). A conscientious Scot who came to Canada as Chief of the General Staff, 1910-13, Mackenzie resigned after a series of disagreements with the free-wheeling Minister of Militia and Defence, Sir Sam HUGHES. He protested against Hughes' neglect of his advisors, his contempt for permanent force officers, and his wish to be his own commander-in-chief. Hughes, no lover of the British, accused Mackenzie of acting "ignorantly, illegally, unconstitutionally, tyrannically and contemptuously." PM Sir Robert Borden wrote friendly letters to the British War Office, but Mackenzie's Canadian appointment was his last.

NORMAN HILLMER

Mackenzie, Ian Alistair, politician (b at Assynt, Scot 27 July 1890; d at Banff, Alta 2 Sept 1949). After sitting in the BC Assembly 1920-30, the gregarious Mackenzie entered Parliament in Ottawa. He was minister of national defence, 1935-39, overseeing the rearmament of Canada's armed forces. Although a superb constituency politician, he was not (as the BREN GUN SCANDAL illustrated) an effective minister, and he was swept aside upon the outbreak of war. As minister of pensions and national health, 1939-44, Mackenzie pushed for the expansion of social benefits. He was not sufficiently influential, however, to seize leadership of the social reform movement. As BC's representative in the Cabinet, he was the key figure in the decision to intern JAPANESE Canadians. Minister of veterans affairs, 1944-Jan 1948, Mackenzie entered the Senate in 1948.

NORMAN HILLMER

McKenzie, Kenneth George, neurosurgeon (b at Toronto 13 June 1892; d there 11 Feb 1964). After graduating with an MB from U of T in 1914, he saw medical service overseas during WWI. Following a period of general practice, he studied for a year with Dr Harvey Cushing in Boston before joining the staff at the Toronto General Hospital. The first neurosurgical unit in Canada, which he founded there in 1923 and directed until 1952, became widely recognized for its excellent care and training. President of the Harvey Cushing Soc 1936-37 and the Soc of Neurological Surgeons 1948-49, he made many contributions to his field, including a scheme for training general surgeons to treat head injuries; new methods of treating torticollis, chronic subdural hematoma and acoustic neuroma; the use of skull tongs for traction of patients with spinal fractures; a technique for dividing the vestibular nerve in Ménière's disease; and a long-term analysis of the results of frontal lobotomy. His greatest influence was as a master surgeon and an exemplary teacher.

WILLIAM FEINDEL

MacKenzie, Norman Archibald MacRae "Larry," international lawyer, university president (b at Pugwash, NS 5 Jan 1894; d at Vancouver 26 Jan 1986). His education at Pictou Academy was all his family could afford; he went west in 1909 to work for his 2 brothers homesteading near Qu'Appelle, Sask. He attended Dalhousie in 1913, but in 1915 he joined the Canadian Army and spent the next 4 years in the trenches, escaping death by miracles and earning the Military Cross and Bar. Returning to Dalhousie, he graduated in law and went on to Harvard and Cambridge, specializing in international law. He went to the International Labour Office in Geneva in 1925 and in 1926 became professor of international law at U of T, where he remained until 1940. He then became president of U of New Brunswick, where he was a great success. In 1944 he went to UBC as its president; it was his *spiritus movens* that helped to make UBC into a great university. He resigned in 1962. He remained a vigorous elder statesman, working on countless boards and commissions. His most famous was the Massey Commission, 1949-51; he was instrumental in persuading Massey to accept the necessity for federal grants to universities.

P.B. WAITE

Reading: P.B. Waite, *Lord of Point Grey: UBC's Larry MacKenzie* (1987).

McKenzie, Robert Tait, educator, sculptor, orthopedic surgeon, author (b at Almonte, Canada W 26 May 1867; d at Philadelphia, Pa 28 Apr 1938). He was a student at McGill 1885-92, and became well known for rehabilitative methods he developed as a medical officer during WWI. He later joined McGill as a lecturer in anatomy and a gymnastics instructor. He became equally famous for his sculpture. His early models – *Violent Effort, Breathlessness, Fatigue* and *Exhaustion* – were praised by artistic and scientific authorities; his statuette *The Sprinter* graced US President Theodore Roosevelt's desk at the White House. Among McKenzie's later works were *The Joy of Effort, Brothers of the Wind,* numerous medallions and many statues and war memorials throughout Great Britain, Canada and the US. He restored the Mill of Kintail outside Almonte, and the mill's museum contains more than 70 of his works. He was director of physical education at the U of Pennsylvania 1904-30. GERALD REDMOND

MacKenzie, Roderick Andrew Francis, priest, scholar (b at Liverpool, Eng 15 Nov 1911). He came to Peterborough, Ont, with his family in 1924, then entered the Society of Jesus at Guelph, Ont, in 1928. After several years' study and teaching, he was ordained in Montréal in 1941. He completed doctoral work in sacred scripture at the Pontifical Biblical Institute, Rome, 1946-49. From 1950 to 1963 he lectured on the Old Testament at Regis College, Toronto. He was rector of the Pontifical Biblical Institute 1963-69, and continued as professor there until 1975. During that time he was *peritus* (consultant) at Vatican Council II and was a member of the council on the liturgy and of the commission for a new version of the Latin Bible. He returned to Regis College in 1975 as professor emeritus, and retired 10 years later. Among his many activities he has been president of the International Organization for Old Testament Studies (1965-68), editor in chief of *Biblica* (1969-75), associate editor of the *Catholic Biblical Quarterly* (1952-63) and consultant for the *New Catholic Encyclopaedia* (1961-63). In addition to numerous articles, reviews and commentaries, he has written *Introduction to the New Testament* (1961), *Faith and History in the Old Testament* (1963), *The Psalms: A Selection* (1966) and *Sirach* (1983). D.M. STANLEY, S.J.

Mackenzie, Sir William, railway entrepreneur (b in Eldon Twp, Peterborough County, Canada W 17 or 30 Oct 1849; d at Toronto 5 Dec 1923). Though he was both a teacher and local politician, his chief interest was business. He was a gristmill and sawmill owner in his native Kirkfield, Ont, and then a railway contractor 1874-91 in Ontario, BC, Maine and the North-West Territories. In 1891 he became part owner of the Toronto Street Ry, the first of many such investments on 3 continents. In 1899 he helped found a company later called Brazilian Traction (BRASCAN), and was its first chairman. With Donald MANN, in 1895 Mackenzie had begun to assemble prairie railway lines and charters that would form the nucleus of the CANADIAN NORTHERN RY. Completed in 1915 from Halifax to Victoria, it was one of 3 Canadian transcontinental railways. In 1911 both Mackenzie and Mann were knighted. National and personal economic difficulties resulted in the nationalization of the Canadian Northern in 1918. Eventually, with the Grand Trunk and Intercolonial railways, it became part of the CANADIAN NATIONAL RAILWAYS system. Mackenzie's career personifies the optimism and energy of the economic boom, 1896 to 1913. R.B. FLEMING

Reading: T.D. Regehr, *The Canadian Northern Railway* (1976); G. Stevens, *History of the Canadian National Railways* (1973).

Mackenzie, William Lyon, journalist, politician (b at Dundee, Scot 12 Mar 1795; d at Toronto 28 Aug 1861). Mackenzie, as journalist, MLA, first mayor of Toronto and a leader of the REBELLIONS OF 1837, was a central figure in pre-Confederation political life. He arrived in UPPER CANADA in 1820 and, after a few years in business at Dundas, moved to Queenston. In May 1824 he published the first issue of the *Colonial Advocate,* which immediately became a leading voice of the new Reform movement.

To be closer to the provincial Parliament, Mackenzie moved his operation to York [Toronto] in the fall of 1824. His forthright and forceful manner together with his ardent denunciation of the FAMILY COMPACT contributed much to his popularity, and in 1828 he was easily elected to the House of Assembly for York County. In 1832 he visited England to present his political supporters' grievances before the imperial government. The sympathetic hearing he received outraged Upper Canadian conservatives. Moreover, Mackenzie's venomous attacks on the local oligarchy brought reprisals in the form of libel suits, threats and physical assaults, as well as an attack on his printing office, which left his press wrecked and the type thrown into the lake.

William Lyon Mackenzie, fiery journalist who in Dec 1837 led an abortive armed revolt against the Upper Canadian establishment (*courtesy National Archives of Canada/C-1993*).

The diminutive Scot's scathing attacks on his opponents also led to his repeated expulsion from the Assembly, although he was continually re-elected by his rural constituents. In 1834, when the Reformers won a majority on the newly created Toronto City Council, he was elected its first mayor. At the end of 1834, he was elected to the provincial Parliament again. However, he was defeated at the polls in 1836, and in Dec 1837 an embittered Mackenzie turned his mind to armed revolt. On Dec 6, convinced that he would gain spontaneous support, he led an erratic expedition down Yonge St towards Toronto, seemingly more intent on damaging the property of Tory supporters than taking control of the government. As the force neared Toronto it was dispersed by a few shots from loyalist guards. On Dec 7 loyalists marched N to Montgomery's Tavern and easily defeated the rebels. Mackenzie fled to the US and tried to muster a new scheme from Navy I in the Niagara R. Canadian militia bombarded the island and sank the rebel supply ship *Caroline.* Mackenzie moved to New York where he founded *Mackenzie's Gazette.* However, he was convicted of violation of the US neutrality laws and imprisoned for a year, falling ill and deeper in debt. He spent the next 10 years in the US, eventually finding employment as a correspondent for the *New York Daily Tribune.*

During exile he wrote several books, including *The Sons of the Emerald Isle* (1844), *The Lives and Opinions of Benjamin Franklin Butler and Jesse Hoyt* (1845) and *The Life and Times of Martin Van Buren* (1846). Mackenzie returned to Canada in 1849 following a government pardon. Undaunted, he quickly resumed both his journalistic and his political careers, serving with characteristic energy as MLA for Haldimand until retirement in 1857 and occasionally publishing a political squib usually entitled *Mackenzie's Weekly Message.* The fiery and principled Scot died at his home on Bond St, now one of Toronto's historic sites and museums. VICTOR L. RUSSELL

Reading: D. Flint, *William Lyon Mackenzie* (1971); W. Kilbourn, *The Firebrand* (1956); Victor L. Russell, *The Mayors of Toronto, 1834-1899* (1982).

Mackenzie-Grease Trail extends approximately 345 km in the QUESNEL- Bella Coola region of central BC. In 1982, under an agreement between the BC and federal governments, it became a designated and protected historic-trail corridor. The trail is nationally significant because it formed a final link in the crossing of N America. Alexander MACKENZIE followed it in 1793 in his search for the Pacific. For several hundred years previously, the trail was a main trade route of several Indian tribes including the Bella Coola, the Chilcotin and the CARRIER. The name "grease" originated from the processed oil of the oolichan, a smeltlike fish, which was a principal trading item of the Bella Coola tribe. Much of the trail is in its original condition; it comprises back-country roads, horse trails and hiking routes. The trail will be upgraded so that its unique history can be shared by hikers of today. BART DEEG

Mackenzie Highway, begun in 1945, runs from Peace River, Alta, through Hay River, NWT, around the SW end of Great Slave Lake to Wrigley on the Mackenzie R, a distance of about 1200 km. 80 km NW of Enterprise, a ferry connects with the highway to Yellowknife, and connecting roads serve Fort Resolution and Fort Smith. An all-weather road, it is the principal highway route into the NWT. W.R. MORRISON

Mackenzie Inuit aboriginally occupied the western Canadian arctic coast from Barter I in the W to Cape Bathurst in the E, as well as the northern portion of the Mackenzie R Delta. Numbering about 2000 during the 19th century, they formed the densest Inuit population in arctic Canada. They were divided into 5 regional groups of 200-1000, each with a way of life adapted to the resources of its own area. The group W of the Mackenzie R spent the summer fishing and hunting caribou, and the winter sealing; those at Cape Bathurst in the E hunted the large bowhead whale during the summer and seals during the winter. The largest group lived in the Mackenzie Delta, centered at the village of Kittigazuit at the mouth of the main river channel. Here, people gathered during the summer to hunt beluga feeding in the shallow estuary. The area was a natural trap for beluga, which were driven upstream onto shoals by groups of up to 200 hunters in kayaks; a single hunt might kill several hundred small whales, providing food and fuel for winter use. The remainder of the year was spent in fishing, hunting caribou and sealing. During winter the people moved to smaller settlements of a few houses each. Winter houses were built of driftwood logs, heavily banked with turf insulation, heated and lighted by stone or pottery lamps burning whale oil, and each accommodated about 6 families. Social organization was family-based; most marriages were monogamous, although polygamy was practised by wealthy individuals. Families or individuals owned such items as houses, tents, KAYAKS and UMIAKS. There is some evidence that the regional groups had hereditary chiefs, with the office passed through the male line. Little is known about the aboriginal religion, but it was based on shamanism, and important religious festivities occurred when the population gathered during the period of total darkness in December.

Archaeology indicates that the ancestors of the Mackenzie Inuit have lived in the area for approximately 1000 years, having derived from a Thule population that moved eastward from Alaska about 1000 AD. Through the following centuries they maintained trading and cultural ties with the Alaskan Inuit to the W, and were the most easterly group to share in the relatively rich Alaskan Inuit way of life. The Mackenzie Inuit became involved in the European FUR TRADE during the 19th century, at first by indirect trade with the Russian posts in Alaska and later with posts established in the Mackenzie Delta. During the late 19th century they became heavily involved with the American whalers who began to hunt and winter in the area. Because of a series of epidemic diseases, their population had been reduced to less than 10% of aboriginal levels by 1900, and their territory had been taken over by Alaskan Inuit and Europeans who moved into the area as trappers. The descendants of the Mackenzie Inuit now live in the communities of Inuvik, Tuktoyaktuk and Paulatuk, where they form a minority of the local Inuit populations. *See also* NATIVE PEOPLE: ARCTIC.

ROBERT MCGHEE

Reading: Robert McGhee, *Beluga Hunters* (1974); Nuligak, *I, Nuligak*, tr M. Metayer (1966).

Mackenzie King Island, 5048 km^2, is one of the central islands in the QUEEN ELIZABETH IS of the Arctic Archipelago. Low-lying, with only occasional points over 300 m, it consists of lowlands and plateaus developed on horizontal or gently folded sedimentary rocks. The general absence of resistant strata is responsible for the lack of salient features. Only on harder sandstone do more prominent landforms, such as the Leffingwell Crags, develop. Material at the surface, being derived from the fine-grained underlying bedrock, is particularly susceptible to solifluction; and Mackenzie King I has some of the best examples of this process in the Arctic. In 1915, mistaking a strait for a bay, V. STEFANSSON mapped Borden and Mackenzie King islands as one – an error uncorrected until a 1947 RCAF aerial survey.

DOUG FINLAYSON

Mackenzie Mountains Named after PM Alexander MACKENZIE, they are a northern continuation, 800 km long, of the eastern system of the ROCKY MTS, composed almost entirely of folded sedimentary strata. They consist of several ranges trending in a NW-SE orientation, straddling the greater part of the NWT-Yukon boundary. The main core, the Backbone Ranges, is a mass of peaks and ridges reaching a maximum height, in Mt Sir James MacBrien, of 2759 m, the highest peak in the NWT. The Mackenzie Mts lie in the precipitation shadow of the SELWYN MTS farther W and are relatively dry. The timberline is low, leaving their slopes bare and rock covered.

DOUG FINLAYSON

Mackenzie-Papineau Battalion, collective designation for some 1300 Canadian volunteers who served in international brigades recruited to assist the communist-supported republican government against Franco's fascists during the Spanish Civil War (July 1936-Mar 1939). There was also an actual battalion, named after the leaders of the REBELLIONS OF 1837, mustered into the XVth "English-Speaking" International Brigade on 1 July 1937, in Albacete, Spain. Other Canadians joined the Abraham Lincoln Battalion, the British Battalion and other units, including medical and transportation detachments. Dr Norman BETHUNE, undoubtedly the most famous Canadian there, created and led a blood transfusion service. The "Mac-Paps" fought in 5 major campaigns, including the assault on Fuentes de Ebro on 13 Oct 1937, the defence of Teruel in Dec-Jan, the "Retreats" in Mar-Apr 1938, and a counterattack across the Ebro R in the last summer of the war. The battalion was led by Edward Cecil-Smith, the military commander and a Toronto labour journalist, and Saul Wellman, a New York union organizer and the unit's political commissar. When the Mac-Paps withdrew from the conflict in Sept 1938, it is said, only 35 men were left on their feet. Although celebrated by well-wishers on their arrival home in early 1939, the survivors, half the original number, received no official welcome. In Apr 1937 the Canadian government had passed the Foreign Enlistment Act, outlawing participation by Canadians in foreign wars, and the Customs Act, which provided for government control over arms exports. The Mac-Paps were an official embarrassment, and so languished in obscurity until the 1970s when a number of books, films and plays documented their history.

VICTOR HOWARD

Reading: V. Hoar, *The Mackenzie-Papineau Battalion* (1969).

The Mackenzie Mountains straddle the Yukon-NWT border (*photo by Hans Blohm/Masterfile*).

Mackenzie River, 4241 km long (to head of the Finlay R), next to the Mississippi R the longest river in N America. Its total DRAINAGE BASIN of 1.8 million km^2 is the largest of any river in Canada and its mean discharge of 9910 m^3/s is second only to that of the St Lawrence. The river's peak discharge occurs in June, but its flow is generally uniform because of the flat barren lands E of the river and the many large lakes in the system. The lakes and rivers of the Mackenzie and its tributaries are open from mid-June to Nov 1 in the northerly areas.

The river's sparsely populated basin is one of the few great unspoiled areas of the world. The main headwaters are the Peace R and the ATHABASCA R, while the main stream issues from the shallow swamps and mudbanks of the West Arm of GREAT SLAVE LK. It flows W to Ft Providence and Head-of-the-Line, where scows, canoes and YORK BOATS were hauled upstream. At FT SIMPSON the turbulent LIARD R pours its muddy waters into the S bank. Near the N Nahanni R the Mackenzie trends WNW through a rolling plain and deflects N past an escarpment of the MACKENZIE MOUNTAINS which lie parallel to the river. The Redstone and Keele rivers and other streams cut through the mountains and pour into the lowlands through deep canyons. At FT NORMAN the clear, cobalt waters of Great Bear R enter over a shallow gravel bar. Past NORMAN WELLS the Mackenzie continues through weedy channels and beneath ribbed cliffs, widening to 5 km, its path braided among countless islands. At Sans Sault Rapids a rocky promontory juts into midstream, and rough water endangers navigation. A few kilometres above Ft Good Hope the river widens and constricts again, between limestone cliffs called The Ramparts, then resumes its meandering NW, its channels clogged with islands and shifting sandbars. The Arctic Red R enters 270 km from the sea, and at Point Separation the delta begins.

Delta The Mackenzie Delta is a vast fan of low-lying alluvial islands, covered with black spruce, thinning northward. These trees are large enough to be used for construction of log buildings and are widely used as fuel. The delta is a maze of channels, cutoff lakes and circular ponds, which are home to a large muskrat population. The delta is 80 km across, bordered by the Richardson Mts in the W and the Caribou Hills in the E. Below Point Separation the river splits into 3 main, navigable channels: East Channel, which flows past Inuvik on the easterly edge of the delta; Peel Channel in the W which flows past AKLAVIK; and Middle Channel, which carries the main outflow into the BEAUFORT SEA. TUKTOYAKTUK, NE of the delta, is the transfer point for river and ocean cargo, its harbour open from July to late Sept.

The Mackenzie Delta is a vast fan of low-lying alluvial islands and a maze of channels, cutoff lakes and circular ponds (*photo by John deVisser*).

Lowland The Mackenzie R Lowland is a great northward extension of the central plains. On the W side rise the Mackenzie Mts, and on the eastern edge lie the rocky outcrops of the Canadian SHIELD. The valley is underlain by sedimentary rock, but its surface is mostly glacial gravel, sand and clay. The plains of MUSKEG are broken by stunted spruce and fir, bog, swamp and lakes. Much of the terrain is underlain by PERMAFROST, which presents a challenge to construction of buildings and transportation.

History In 1778 Peter POND traversed Methye Portage [PORTAGE LA LOCHE], connecting the FUR-TRADE ROUTES of Hudson Bay with the Mackenzie Basin. Alexander MACKENZIE came in 1789, following the full length of the river aptly named for him. Other traders followed, establishing posts along the way. From the 1820s supplies were carried by York boats. The first steamer plied the Athabasca R in 1884, and in 1886 operated N of Ft Smith. From 1920 to 1940 flat-bottomed sternwheelers plied the river, but after 1945 they were replaced by tugs and barges. The tugs are now equipped with radar and depth sounders.

The lowland is still sparsely populated. The fur-trade economy dominated until the mining rushes of YELLOWKNIFE and GREAT BEAR LK and the Canol Project of WWII. Fur remains important to the local residents; mining has been dominant although its fortunes have fluctuated in the 1980s. Most mining has been concentrated in the E, in the Shield. The key centres are Yellowknife (gold), Echo Bay – formerly Port Radium (uranium), Uranium City, Flat R (tungsten), Norman Wells (oil and gas) and Faro. Great potential for future development lies at the S end in the Athabasca tar sands and at the N in the Beaufort Sea. The fine clay soil would support agriculture, but climate prevents it. The only waterpower sites are on the Snare and Talston rivers, supplying local power, but controversial development is under way on the Slave R. The river and the delicate

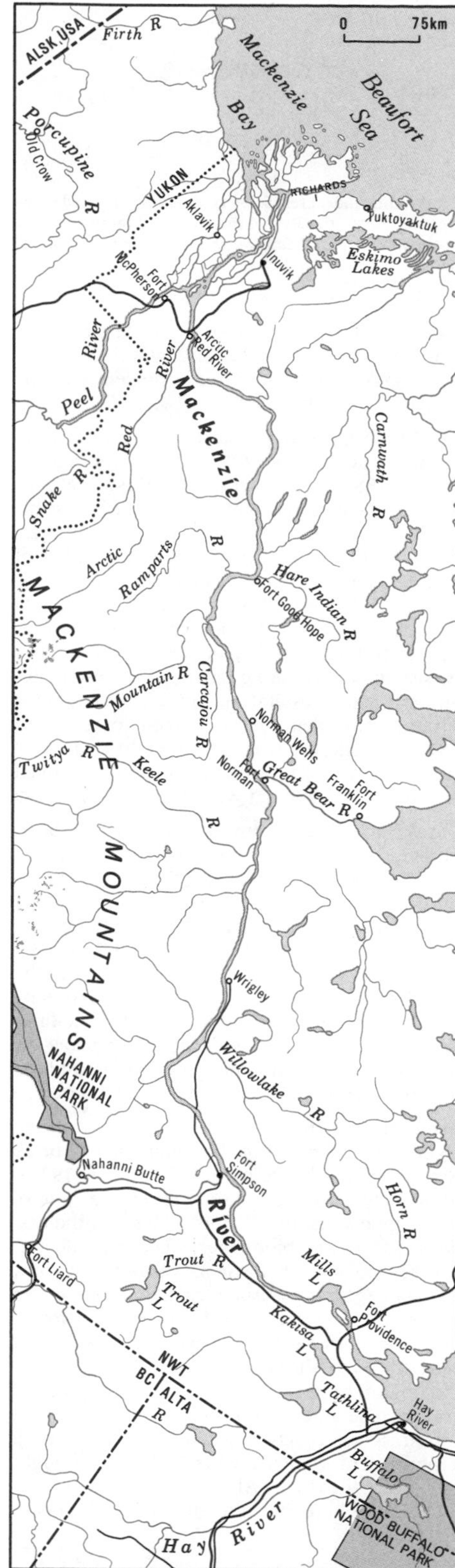

environment of the NORTH were brought to the national consciousness during the debate over the MACKENZIE VALLEY PIPELINE. JAMES MARSH

Mackenzie Valley Pipeline, proposed PIPELINE for the transport of natural gas and later oil from the Arctic Ocean to Alberta. The proposal of a pipeline corridor from the NORTH was put forward by the federal government in the 1970 Pipeline Guidelines and provoked a spate of engineering and environmental studies, public-policy reviews and economic analyses unequalled in Canadian history.

Detailed proposals were promulgated by 2 consortiums. Canadian Arctic Gas Pipeline Ltd, composed of 27 Canadian and American producers (including Exxon, Gulf, Shell and TRANSCANADA PIPELINES), proposed a route from the Prudhoe fields in Alaska, across the northern Yukon to the Mackenzie Delta and then S to Alberta. Foothills Pipe Lines Ltd, formed by Alberta Gas Trunk Line [NOVA] and Westcoast Transmission, proposed a shorter route from the Mackenzie Delta to Alberta. The Arctic Gas pipeline would have been the longest in the world (3860 km) and the greatest construction enterprise ever undertaken. In either case, the engineering problems of building a pipeline over PERMAFROST were monumental (both proposals entailed refrigerating the gas) and the impact on the North would have been significant.

A federal royal commission, led by Judge Thomas BERGER, was appointed in Mar 1974 to consider the proposals and their social and economic impact on the North. The commissioners held community hearings across the North, beginning in 1975 and ending Nov 1976, dealing with the concerns of native people and environmentalists. The commission's report, issued April 1977, concluded that a pipeline from the Mackenzie Delta down the Mackenzie Valley to Alberta was feasible, but should proceed only after further study and after settlement of native LAND CLAIMS; it recommended, successfully, a 10-year moratorium. However, the commission was adamantly opposed to the building of a line across the delicate environment of the northern Yukon. Amid controversy and uncertain economic conditions, both plans were shelved. The commission itself became a *cause célèbre* because of its broad interpretation of its mandate and its illumination of the complex problems facing northern development. JAMES MARSH

Reading: Minister of Supply and Services, *Northern Frontier, Northern Homeland,* Report of the Mackenzie Valley Pipeline Inquiry 1 (1977); P.H. Pearse, *The Mackenzie Pipeline* (1974).

Mackerel (Scombridae), family of pelagic (open-sea) fishes of class Osteichthyes. The family also includes TUNAS, albacores, skipjacks, bonitos and ceras. The name mackerel, more commonly used for members of genus *Scomber,* is also applied to fishes of genus *Auxis* (bullet and frigate mackerels), genus *Scomberomorus* (Spanish mackerels) and family Gempylidae (snake mackerels). Three species of true mackerels, genus *Scomber,* occur in the temperate waters of the Atlantic and Pacific oceans. Two of these occur in Canada's coastal waters: in the Atlantic, the chub and Atlantic mackerels; in the Pacific, the chub mackerel. The Atlantic mackerel (*Scomber scombrus*) is an elongate, streamlined fish, resembling a miniature tuna. Few exceed 52 cm in length. Located behind the widely spaced dorsal fins and the anal fin are 5 small finlets on the dorsal and ventral surfaces. The chub mackerel (*S. japonicus*) resembles the Atlantic mackerel but is smaller. Swiftly swimming mackerel form huge schools in surface waters off coasts facing the open sea. They are highly migratory: those in Canadian Atlantic waters move inshore and northward along the coast as far as Labrador in summer; southward and offshore in late fall. This population is thought to overwinter in deep waters between Sable I and Cape Cod. In Canadian waters, spawning occurs from late May to July. An average-sized female may produce up to 500 thousand buoyant eggs. Mackerel feed primarily on PLANKTON, eating a wide variety of small organisms. The chub mackerel supports a fishery in California waters but not in Canadian. Atlantic mackerel is an important food fish on both sides of the Atlantic and is used fresh, frozen, smoked and salted. In Canadian waters, it is fished com-

The Atlantic mackerel (*Scomber scombrus*) is fished commercially from the Bay of Fundy to Labrador (*courtesy National Museums of Canada/National Museum of Natural Sciences*).

mercially from the Bay of Fundy to Labrador, primarily by purse seines, but also by weirs and trap nets. Mackerel are also prized by anglers, particularly in US waters. W.B. SCOTT

Mackieson, John, physician, officeholder (b at Campsie, Scot 16 Oct 1795; d at Charlottetown 27 Aug 1885). A pioneer of the PEI medical profession, Mackieson was most distinguished by his work with the insane. A physician when he arrived in PEI in 1821, he served in a number of public-health posts before being appointed medical superintendent of the PEI lunatic asylum in 1848. His treatment of patients exhibited humanity and an understanding of new techniques, but persistent underfunding caused conditions to deteriorate at the hospital and ultimately his administration was denounced. Forced to resign in 1874, Mackieson was nevertheless cleared of charges of neglect. Subsequently the improved facilities he had sought were built. P.E. RIDER

Mackinaw Boat, a strong flat-bottomed boat, pointed at each end and with a hold in the middle, was used by fur traders during the French regime for running downstream. It was later adapted for open water by the addition of 2 sails and a steering oar. By the 1870s a distinctive type, 6.7 m to 8.7 m long and schooner rigged, had evolved in the Strait of Mackinaw, and gave its name to the vessel. A further development called the Collingwood skiff was widely used throughout GEORGIAN BAY for gill-netting and pleasure sailing until the advent of the outboard motor. JAMES MARSH

McKinney, Louise, née Crummy, women's rights activist, legislator (b at Frankville, Ont 22 Sept 1868; d at Claresholm, Alta 10 July 1931). McKinney achieved national renown as one of the 5 appellants, the "Famous Five," in the PERSONS CASE. Her ambition was to become a doctor. She became a teacher instead, leaving that work to organize for the WOMAN'S CHRISTIAN TEMPERANCE UNION. In 1903 she helped organize its North-West Territories branch, remaining president of its successor, the Alberta and Saskatchewan Union, for 20 years. A Methodist Sunday school teacher, she urged that TEMPERANCE education be introduced into schools, and she was a strong proponent of women's rights. McKinney brought her convictions to the Alberta legislature, as MLA 1917-21, where she also urged social-welfare measures for immigrants and widows. She, along with Lt Roberta MacAdams of Calgary, was one of the first women to be elected to a Canadian legislature. ELIANE LESLAU SILVERMAN

Distinctive mackinaw boats tied up at Killarney, Ont, on Georgian Bay. The boat was developed for use in the Strait of Mackinaw (*courtesy National Archives of Canada/ PA-85551/ W.J. Topley*).

Mackintosh, William Archibald, (b in Madoc, Ont 21 May 1895; d at Kingston, Ont 29 Dec 1970). He attended Queen's (BA) and Harvard (MA and PhD). At Queen's he came under the influence of O.D. SKELTON, particularly his historical approach to economics and his interest in public affairs. After teaching briefly at Brandon College, Mackintosh returned to Queen's as a faculty member in 1920. He remained on staff there until WWII, writing influential works, including the 1923 article, "Economic Factors in Canadian History," and *The Economic Background of Dominion Provincial Relations* for the Rowell-Sirois Report. During this period he also served as an adviser to government in many capacities, including acting as a member of the National Employment Commission in the 1930s. When WWII broke out he was brought in to the Dept of Finance by W.C. Clark. Mackintosh served in a senior capacity with Finance and then Reconstruction until 1946. While in the civil service he was especially interested in reconstruction problems and drafted the key federal policy document, the White Paper on EMPLOYMENT AND INCOME. In 1947 he returned to Queen's where he became vice-principal and then, 1951-61, principal. DOUG OWRAM

McLachlan, James Bryson, labour leader (b at Ecclefechan, Scot 9 Feb 1869; d at Glace Bay, NS 3 Nov 1937). Born into a family of cotton weavers and farm labourers, McLachlan graduated from the Lanarkshire coalfields to become the fiery leader of the Nova Scotia coal miners and a popular spokesman for labour radicalism in Canada. Influenced by social critics such as Thomas Carlyle and labour leaders such as Keir Hardie, McLachlan believed it was the mission of the working class to "redeem the world from the chaos of capitalism." Immigrating to Cape Breton in 1902, McLachlan challenged the conservative policies of the Provincial Workmen's Assn, and was elected secretary-treasurer of District 26, United Mine Workers of America, on its formation in 1909. The UMWA was disbanded in 1915 and re-established 1919; McLachlan served as an officer of the 2 interim organizations 1916-18. Blacklisted from the mines, McLachlan was instrumental in the achievement of collective bargaining in the NS coal industry during WWI. In the strikes of the 1920s he was known for his imaginative tactics, including the "strike on the job" and the "100 per cent strike." Never defeated in a union election, McLachlan remained an officer of the miners' union until July 1923, when he was removed by UMW president John L. Lewis for promoting a sympathetic strike in support of Sydney steelworkers. Convicted of seditious libel in Oct 1923, he was sentenced to 2 years in Dorchester penitentiary but was released in Mar 1924. He returned home to become editor of the *Maritime Labor Herald*, which he had helped establish in 1921, and later edited the *Nova Scotia Miner* (1929-35). He belonged in turn to the Socialist Party of Canada, the Independent Labour Party of Nova Scotia and the Communist Party of Canada, running 6 times for the provincial and federal parliaments and polling almost 9000 votes at the peak of his influence in 1921. Nationally he was prominent as president of the Workers Unity League, 1930-36. McLachlan was known for his fierce dedication to the workers' cause, and his "economic gospel," borrowed from the Old Testament (Proverbs), is inscribed at his grave: "Open thy mouth, judge righteously, and plead the cause of the poor and needy." DAVID FRANK

MacLaren, Donald Roderick, fighter pilot, businessman (b at Ottawa 28 May 1893). MacLaren joined the RFC in 1917, served in 46 Squadron in France, and was credited with 54 "kills" (48 aircraft and 6 balloons) in less than 8 months, an unparalleled record. He was briefly director of air services for the CAF, but left in 1919 to enter commercial aviation. From 1945 until his retirement in 1958, he was executive assistant to the president of Trans-Canada Airlines. BRERETON GREENHOUS

McLaren, Norman, director of animated films (b at Stirling, Scot 11 Apr 1914; d at Montréal 26 Jan 1987). He followed John GRIERSON to the NATIONAL FILM BOARD in 1941 and remained there, except for 2 UNESCO missions (to China in 1949 and to India in 1952). He participated in the series *Chants populaires* (1944-46) and produced *Begone Dull Care*, set to the music of Oscar PETERSON (1949). Constantly innovative, McLaren tried techniques such as drawings scratched directly on film, cutout animation, painting directly on film, etc. During the COLD WAR in 1952, using a technique of stop-motion cinematography called pixilation, he made *Neighbours*, a political fable on the futility of using violence to resolve conflict. After this – his ultimate ideological statement – his films concentrated more on aesthetics and technique than on content. His work earned him increasing international recognition, and for over 30 years he produced roughly one film per year. Some of the more interesting examples are *Blinkity Blank* (1954), the didactic *Rythmetic* (1956), the absurd humour of *Il était une chaise* (1957) and the fantasy of *Le Merle* (1958). Many of his films were co-directed by Evelyn Lambart. In *Lines Vertical* (1960), *Lines Horizontal* (1962) and *Mosaic* (1965), he opted for an austere, abstract style and exercises in which technology took precedence. He began a series of films about ballet and the beauty and harmony of movement with *Pas de deux* (1967); it was followed by *Ballet adagio* (1972) and *Narcissus* (1983). He also produced more didactic films on the art of animation, such as *L'Écran d'épingles* (1973) and *Animated Motion* (1977). McLaren's creative genius made him Canada's leading director of animated film. His life work of 72 films was donated in 1985 to the Museum of Modern Art, NY, and Academy of Motion Picture Arts and Sciences, Los Angeles. PIERRE VÉRONNEAU

McLarnin, Jimmy, boxer (b at Belfast, Ire 19 Dec 1907). McLarnin moved at age 3 to Vancouver and started boxing at 12. As a 16-year-old pro in 1923-24 he went undefeated in 19 bouts. He started boxing regularly in Los Angeles, then moved to New York where he was called the "Irish Hero." He won the world welterweight championship in 1933 by knocking out "Young" Corbett III at 2:37 of the first round. His most

Innovative filmmaker Norman McLaren was Canada's leading director of animated film (*courtesy National Film Board of Canada*).

famous fights were with world-renowned Barney Ross. He lost his title to Ross in 1934, won it back the same year, then lost again in 1935. He retired in 1936. In 77 fights he won 63 (knocking out 20), lost 11 and drew 3.

A.J. "SANDY" YOUNG

McLauchlan, Murray Edward, singer, songwriter, guitarist (b at Paisley, Scot 30 June 1948). McLauchlan came to Canada at age 5. At 17 he was making the rounds of Toronto's Yorkville coffeehouses and in 1966 first appeared at the Mariposa Folk Festival. American singer Tom Rush recorded 2 of his songs in 1968, "Child's Song" and "Old Man's Song." He recorded for True North Records 1971-86 and in 1972 his "Farmer's Song" established him across Canada as a popular singer with both folk and country audiences. With the formation of his band, The Silver Tractors (1975), he attempted to shift his music more towards rock, but the move did not pay off as international success continued to elude him and his popularity in Canada waned. In 1983 he returned to his folk and country roots, and to commercial success, with the album *Timberline*, and also produced a critically acclaimed series for CBC Radio. McLauchlan has won 7 Juno awards. He signed with Century City Artists and in 1987 recorded his 16th album.

RICHARD GREEN

McLaughlin, Isabel, painter (b at Oshawa, Ont 10 Oct 1903). An important early modernist in Canada, she is preoccupied with design, bright colour and the study of tangible space, and her paintings are highly subjective. Her friends and mentors have included Arthur LISMER; painter Yvonne McKague Housser, with whom she studied at the Ontario College of Art; Lawren HARRIS; and A.Y. JACKSON. She studied in Paris in 1929 and Vienna in 1930, and twice with Hans Hofmann in the period 1947-52. Her development has been characterized by constant self-renewal and by an awareness of her own roots. Her *Tree* (1935) received notoriety in the press and the respect of peers. In 1939 McLaughlin was elected president of the Canadian Group of Painters, the first woman to head an important Canadian art society.

JOAN MURRAY

McLaughlin, Robert Samuel, industrialist (b at Enniskillen, Ont 8 Sept 1871; d at Oshawa, Ont 6 Jan 1972). After a 3-year apprenticeship in the carriage business owned by his father, Robert McLaughlin, and work in similar establishments in New York, McLaughlin entered into partnership with his father and his brother George in the McLaughlin Carriage Works, Oshawa (1892). When fire destroyed the company's Oshawa factory (1899), 15 municipalities offered financial assistance for relocation near them, but the company stayed in Oshawa, in return for a $50 000 loan repayable "as convenient." In 1908 McLaughlin began producing Buick car bodies for William Durant, owner of the Buick Motor Co in Flint, Michigan. When Durant moved on to Chevrolets, McLaughlin began producing them too (1915). The business was purchased by General Motors in 1918, and incorporated as GENERAL MOTORS OF CANADA, with McLaughlin as president. He also served as VP of the American parent. By the mid-1920s, the Oshawa plant had 3000 employees and produced more cars for the Canadian and Commonwealth market than the rest of the country combined. McLaughlin retired from active management in 1942, becoming chairman of the board, a position he held until 1967. In recognition of his support for Canadian educational and medical facilities, including the McLaughlin Planetarium in Toronto, and his work in the Boy Scout movement, McLaughlin received honorary degrees from several Ontario universities. He was named a Companion of the Order of Canada in 1967.

MARGARET E. MCCALLUM

McLaughlin, Samuel, photographer, publisher, watchmaker (b in Ire 28 Jan 1826; d at Los Angeles, Calif 26 Aug 1914). McLaughlin issued Canada's first publication of photographs – *The Photographic Portfolio* (1858-60), a series of his views in and around Québec C. He also published Québec C directories 1854-57 and had been a watch and chronometer maker in that city. In 1861 he became the first official photographer for the Province of Canada. He provided impressive documentation of many Canadian public-works projects, including the initial construction and development of the Parliament Buildings, Ottawa.

RICHARD J. HUYDA

McLean, James Stanley, meat packer, philanthropist (b in Clarke Twp, Durham County, Ont 1 May 1876; d at Toronto 1 Sept 1954). A graduate of U of Toronto (1896), McLean became a clerk at the Harris Abattoir Co, Toronto, in 1901. The president, Joseph FLAVELLE, taught him the importance of careful accounting and, as president himself in the 1920s, McLean, through cost cutting and weekly budgeting, made profits for his company when other Canadian meat packers lost money. In 1927 he merged Harris and 3 other firms into CANADA PACKERS LTD, and was president until 1954. Under his autocratic leadership, Canada Packers dominated the industry and developed numerous by-products. A member of the United Church and a patron of Canadian art, McLean endowed the J.S. McLean Junior Farmer Scholarship and made generous donations to hospitals.

JOSEPH LINDSEY

McLean, John, fur trader, explorer (b at Dervaig, Scot 24 July 1798; d at Victoria 8 Mar 1890). In charge of HBC trade at Ft Chimo [Qué] 1837-43, he searched relentlessly for an overland route to Ft Smith [North West River], on Hamilton Inlet. In 1839, he ascended the George R, travelled overland to Petitsikapau Lk, moved SE to the CHURCHILL R, and was the first European to see CHURCHILL FALLS. In 1841, he found a route into the interior, circumventing the falls. McLean did not receive the promotion he thought he deserved, and resigned after a stint at FT SIMPSON (1846). He managed a bank in Guelph, Canada W, for 9 years, but his career ended when he took responsibility for the loss of £1300 from his branch. By 1857 he was in Elora, where he was clerk of division court for 25 years. McLean published *Notes of a Twenty-Five Years' Service in the Hudson's Bay Territory* (1849), a valuable account of the FUR TRADE.

JAMES MARSH

MacLean, John, or *Am Bàrd MacGilleathain,* meaning "The Bard MacLean," Scottish Gaelic poet (b at Caolas, Tiree, Scot 8 Jan 1787; d at Addington Forks, NS 26 Jan 1848). At an early age, he displayed a talent for composing poetry, a skill which earned him the patronage and friendship of Alexander, 14th MacLean of Coll. Apprenticed to a shoemaker at age 16, he later went to Glasgow to work at his trade but returned to Tiree about a year later. Shortly after the publication of his first book of poems he decided to emigrate to Canada and he and his family left Tobermory, Mull, in 1819 on the ship *Economy*. They eventually settled near Barney's River, Antigonish County. The hardships which he endured as a pioneer are graphically depicted in the most famous of his poems "A'Choille Ghruamach" ("The Gloomy Forest"). His songs constitute an important source of information on the way of life in a 19th-century Scottish Gaelic community.

MAUREEN WILLIAMS

MacLean, John Angus, farmer, politician, premier of PEI 1979-81 (b at Lewes, PEI 15 May 1914). After serving in WWII, MacLean returned to PEI and contested unsuccessfully the federal elections of 1945 and 1948. First elected in 1951, he served for more than 2 decades as MP for Queens County, then left federal politics to lead the provincial Conservatives to victory in 1979. Stressing the virtues of rural community life, his government banned new shopping malls and cancelled participation in New Brunswick's Point Lepreau nuclear reactor project. MacLean resigned as premier on 17 Nov 1981 and vacated his seat immediately prior to the 1982 election.

DAVID A. MILNE

MacLean, John Bayne, publisher (b at Crieff, Canada W 26 Sept 1862; d at Toronto 25 Sept 1950). Maclean (who also spelled his name McLean and MacLean) was a teacher, reporter and the financial editor of the Toronto newspaper *The Mail* before founding a highly successful trade magazine, *Canadian Grocer* (1887). It was followed by an arrary of similar magazines which made him Canada's leading producer of trade publications. Under his and his successor's direction, the company became the diversified media conglomerate Maclean Hunter. Horace Talmadge Hunter was made a printer (1919), named president (1933), and his name was added to the corporate title (1945).

Maclean's solid base of trade magazines allowed him to found wider interest publications such as the *Financial Post* (1907), *Farmer's Magazine* (1910), *Mayfair* (1927) and *Chatelaine* (1928). As well, he purchased *Canadian Homes and Gardens* (1925) and *Busy Man's Magazine* (1905) which became his namesake *Maclean's* in 1911. By the 1930s, his company had become Canada's leading magazine publisher and had established branches in the US (1927) and Great Britain (1930).

Maclean's publishing success made him wealthy and he had a long militia career ultimately achieving the rank of Lieutenant Colonel. Though a staunch Conservative in politics, Maclean steadfastly maintained his publications' non-partisan status. Still, he frequently contributed editorials which criticized both parties and championed efficient government and increased industrial productivity.

R. NEIL MATHESON

Reading: F.S. Chalmers, *A Gentleman of the Press* (1969).

MacLean, John Duncan, politician, premier of BC 1927-28 (b at Culloden, PEI 8 Dec 1873; d at Ottawa 28 Mar 1948). He taught in prairie schools and in BC, and became a principal in Rossland, BC, before going to McGill. He graduated with a medical degree in 1905 and was practising in Greenwood, BC, when elected a Liberal MLA in 1916. Appointed provincial secretary and minister of education, he became minister of finance in 1924. When John OLIVER's failing health became known to his party in 1927, MacLean was made leader designate and, on Oliver's death, became premier, serving for one year. Though a competent Cabinet minister, he was an unimaginative, colourless premier who took office when his party's fortunes were on the wane. The Liberals were defeated by the Conservatives in the 1928 election. After an unsuccessful bid for a federal seat, MacLean was appointed chairman of the Canadian Farm Loan Board in Ottawa and held the post until his death.

ROBIN FISHER

McLean Gang, BC outlaws (*fl* 1879). Consisting of Allan, Charlie and Archie McLean and Alex Hare (all 4 of mixed blood), the gang lived by banditry and violence. On 8 Dec 1879 they killed John Tannatt Ussher, a Kamloops policeman who was arresting them for horse theft, and James Kelly, a shepherd. A posse trapped them in a cabin near Douglas Lk and after a short siege the gang surrendered. At the time Allan was 24, Charlie and Alex 17, and Archie 15. Tried in New Westminster, they were executed in a group hanging on 31 Jan 1881. EDWARD BUTTS

Maclean Hunter Limited is a diversified communications company, with assets in 1986 totalling $990 million and revenues of $1.15 billion. As the largest publisher of national MAGAZINES and periodicals in Canada, its list includes *Flare*, *L'*ACTUALITÉ and English and French editions of CHATELAINE. The FINANCIAL POST was purchased from Maclean Hunter by Toronto Sun Publishing Corp in late 1987. The company publishes over 130 Canadian special-interest, consumer and business magazines, directories and manuals, as well as 70 business periodicals in the US and Europe. It has a majority interest in Toronto Sun Publishing Corporation, publishers of the *Toronto Sun*, *Edmonton Sun and Calgary Sun*.

Maclean Hunter's broadcasting holdings include the CTV affiliate CFCN-TV in Calgary and Lethbridge and 22 radio stations located in Calgary, Edmonton, Toronto, Kitchener-Waterloo, Chatham-Wallaceburg (Ont), Ottawa, Sarnia, Leamington and throughout the Maritimes. As Canada's third-largest CABLE-TELEVISION operator, with 16 cable systems in 20 Ontario municipalities, Maclean Hunter provided service to 715 000 subscribers in Ontario and the US. Other interests include book distribution, commercial printing, business forms, trade shows and specialized information services. PETER S. ANDERSON

Maclean's was acquired by John Bayne MACLEAN in 1905 and was the first consumer magazine to be published by him. Between 1896 and 1910 the magazine had a number of titles, including *Business, The Business Magazine, The Busy Man's Magazine* and *Busy Man's*. It was officially named *Maclean's* in 1911. Initially, the new magazine was a general-interest digest for businessmen, ordinarily devoting most of its space to reprints of articles from the world's periodicals. By 1914, however, Maclean and his editor, T.B. COSTAIN, saw that Canadian NATIONALISM might be a profitable line, and by the boom years of the 1920s *Maclean's* had its formula. There were always articles on Canadian men and women, Canadian politics and problems, Canadian fiction, and regular features at the "back of the book." Occasionally, as when George DREW denounced the arms manufacturers, there was a crusading air, but ordinarily the magazine was firmly middlebrow.

The high point was the early 1950s. Blair FRASER was the Ottawa correspondent, and his regular column presented the best grade of political gossip while his longer pieces were the decade's best political reporting. In Toronto, editor Ralph ALLEN tried for a liberal mix of thoughtful and light pieces, good illustration and occasional fiction. The magazine was successful in circulation and revenue.

In the 1960s *Maclean's* experienced difficulties. ADVERTISING revenues fell as television cut into the periodical market, and even able writers such as Peter GZOWSKI, Peter C. NEWMAN and Christina McCall could not arrest the decline. What saved *Maclean's* was the conversion to a weekly newsmagazine format. Under Newman as editor, the magazine took advantage of the opening that resulted from *Time* leaving Canada to create Canada's first newsmagazine. The result has been a success in advertising sales and in reader response. Newman resigned in 1982, succeeded by Kevin Doyle as editor. Although the new *Maclean's* still relies on stringers for most of its foreign news, its Canadian coverage is good and provides a welcome supplement to the pallid fare in most newspapers. As of June 1987 average total paid circulation was 648 545. There are 6 bureaus, located in Ottawa, Montréal, Calgary, Vancouver, London, Eng, and Washington, US. *See also* MAGAZINES. J.L. GRANATSTEIN

McLearn, Frank Harris, paleontologist (b at Halifax 27 Feb 1885; d at Ottawa 7 Oct 1964). Educated at Dalhousie and Yale, he served on the GEOLOGICAL SURVEY OF CANADA from 1913 to 1952. His thesis on the Silurian fossils of Nova Scotia is accepted as definitive, but he is best known for his studies on the Mesozoic faunas of western Canada. Fieldwork in the Crowsnest Pass and along the Athabasca and Peace rivers enabled him to establish the stratigraphy and correlation of the Cretaceous and Triassic formations of those areas. He also contributed greatly to the paleontological knowledge of the Queen Charlotte Is, the plains of southern Saskatchewan and the Manitoba Escarpment. His correlations were fundamental to the development of petroleum geology in western Canada. L.S. RUSSELL

McLennan, Sir John Cunningham, physicist (b at Ingersoll, Ont 14 Apr 1867; d at Paris, France 9 Oct 1935). After graduating in physics from U of T in 1892, McLennan worked as a demonstrator and in 1898 went to the Cavendish Laboratory in Cambridge, Eng. In 1900 he received the first doctorate in physics from U of T. He spent his career at that university, bringing his physics laboratory to the forefront of research in radioactivity, spectroscopy and low-temperature physics. During WWI McLennan was scientific adviser to the British Admiralty. In 1915 he was elected to the Royal Soc of London (receiving its gold medal in 1928) and in 1917 received the OBE. After the war he returned to U of T but spent each summer in Britain, becoming president of the scientific section of the British Association for the Advancement of Science in 1923. President of the Royal Canadian Institute in 1916, he helped found the NATIONAL RESEARCH COUNCIL and was a member of the ONTARIO RESEARCH FOUNDATION (est 1928). He resigned from U of T in 1932 and moved to England where he continued his pioneering research in the use of radium to treat cancer. He was knighted in 1935. YVES GINGRAS

MacLennan, John Hugh, novelist, essayist, professor (b at Glace Bay, NS 20 Mar 1907). MacLennan is best known as the first major English-speaking writer to attempt a portrayal of Canada's national character. His education consisted of an ever-widening circle of experience that began in Nova Scotia, took him as a Rhodes scholar from Dalhousie to Oxford, from where he travelled on the continent, and culminated in a PhD in classics at Princeton, NJ. Returning to Canada in the mid-1930s to take a teaching job at Lower Canada College near Montréal, MacLennan continued work on a novel, begun at Princeton, in which he hoped to convey his personal interpretation of all he had witnessed during his travels abroad. The failure to publish this novel – and an earlier one on a similar theme – induced him to take another tack. The events that preceded WWII sparked him to recall what he had witnessed of the Halifax naval base during WWI. By way of experiment, he wrote *Barometer Rising* (1941), focusing on the HALIFAX EXPLOSION he had survived as a 10-year-old. The success of this shift from international to national subject matter (brought to the fore by the favourable criticism of Edmund Wilson) induced him to theorize that writers in Canada must now both set the stage and recite the country's dramas to the world at large. *Barometer Rising* and his essay collection *Cross-Country* (1949) ushered in a new phase in Canadian literature.

Hugh MacLennan, novelist and essayist who was the first major English-speaking writer to portray a Canadian national character (*photo by Nakash/Cameron*).

Though he would now focus directly on aspects of contemporary Canadian life, MacLennan eschewed regionalism. "I have always seen Canada as a part of the history of the world," he maintains. Although TWO SOLITUDES (1945) deals with English-French tensions in Québec, *The Precipice* (1948) with puritanism in small-town Ontario and *Each Man's Son* (1951) with the Cape Breton mining community, each novel expands from its specific situation to consider, respectively, the rapid transition instigated by WWI, the contrast between American and Canadian societies, and the effect of Calvinism, wherever it is found. With his last 3 novels – *The Watch that Ends the Night* (1959), *Return of the Sphinx* (1967) and *Voices in Time* (1980) – he has increasingly moved outwards from the specific base of Montréal (where he taught in McGill's English dept 1951-81) to encompass those universal themes that arise from local political, social and human interests. Because his works transcend their particular settings, he is the most widely and most successfully translated Canadian novelist to date.

MacLennan now holds a position of exceptional respect in Canada. He has won the GOVERNOR GENERAL'S LITERARY AWARD 3 times for fiction (*Two Solitudes*, *The Precipice*, *The Watch that Ends the Night*) and twice for nonfiction (*Cross-Country* and *Thirty and Three*). In 1984 he won the $100 000 Royal Bank Award, and in 1987 he became the first Canadian to receive Princeton U's James Madison Medal, awarded annually to a graduate who has distinguished himself in his profession. He has garnered many other awards and honorary degrees. Despite this success, critics have long debated the merit of his work. Many have endorsed Wilson's early praise; others have argued that the didactic aspect of MacLennan's fiction forces the stereotyping of characters, the predominance of the authorial voice, and reliance on outdated Victorian techniques of narrative and structure. Still others see MacLennan as overly ambitious in subject matter; especially in his treatment of French Canada is his lack of firsthand experience an artistic drawback. However, almost all critics have singled out MacLennan's skill in descriptive writing, whether of episode, action or natural landscape. Although MacLennan is primarily a novelist, his essays (the best of which are collected in *The Other Side of Hugh*

MacLennan, 1978) have elicited more consistent critical admiration. In these, MacLennan ranges over a variety of subjects with a civilized mind, impish humour, warm humanity and sharp intuition. He and Robertson DAVIES are Canada's finest essayists.

Ironically, MacLennan's own international aspirations are generally overlooked. As time passes, he has taken on mythic proportions as the Canadian nationalist who pioneered the use of Canadian scenarios in fiction. To him, writers such as Robertson Davies, Margaret LAURENCE, Robert KROETSCH, Leonard COHEN and Marian ENGEL owe the sense that Canada is a place worth writing about. ELSPETH CAMERON

Reading: Elspeth Cameron, *Hugh MacLennan* (1981).

McLeod, Alan Arnett, aviator (b at Stonewall, Man 20 Apr 1899; d at Winnipeg 6 Nov 1918). He received the VICTORIA CROSS for heroic action, in which he received 5 wounds, against 8 enemy aircraft. He was injured again rescuing his observer, A.W. Hammond, after their aircraft crashed. The youngest of 3 Canadian fliers to win the VC in WWI, he died of influenza while recuperating in Winnipeg. JAMES MARSH

Macleod, James Farquharson, police officer, judge (b on Isle of Skye, Scot 25 Sept 1836; d at Calgary 5 Sept 1894). Commissioner of the NWMP, member of the NWT Council and judge, Macleod was a respected and popular figure in the southwestern prairies. Educated in Ontario, he practised law near Bowmanville, Ont, in the 1860s. He served as brigade major with the WOLSELEY expedition in 1870. Joining the police as a superintendent, he was assistant commissioner 1874-75. He resigned to become a stipendiary magistrate, but returned as commissioner in 1876. He founded Ft Macleod, suppressed the whisky traffic and, having won the confidence of the Blackfoot chiefs, negotiated Treaty No 7. Nevertheless, he lost the confidence of the government and resigned in 1880. He continued to act as a magistrate and in 1887 was appointed a judge of the Supreme Court of the NWT. A.B. MCCULLOUGH

Macleod, John James Rickard, physiologist, codiscoverer of INSULIN (b at Cluny, Scot 6 Sept 1876; d at Aberdeen, Scot 16 Mar 1935). Trained at the universities of Aberdeen and Leipzig and the London Hospital Medical Coll, J.J.R. Macleod immigrated to America in 1903 to teach at Western Reserve U, Cleveland. He gradually developed an international reputation as an expert in carbohydrate metabolism and general physiology, and in 1918 was appointed professor of physiology at U of T. In the spring of 1921 Macleod gave F.G. BANTING laboratory space, equipment, advice and one of his student assistants (C.H. BEST) to investigate the hypothetical internal secretion of the pancreas. Contrary to Banting's and Best's later distorted accounts, Macleod was an active, essential supervisor of a research effort that, by the spring of 1922, had resulted in the discovery of insulin. His elaboration of the early crude results, his handling of the clinical trials, and his highly professional presentations of the research particularly impressed the Swedish investigators who rightly recommended that he share the 1923 Nobel Prize for medicine or physiology with Banting.

Macleod's contribution to physiology and Canadian science was not properly recognized in Toronto or Canada for many decades. He left Canada in 1928 to become regius professor of physiology at U of Aberdeen, where he died in 1935, honoured in his native country but not in his adopted one. MICHAEL BLISS

Reading: Michael Bliss, *The Discovery of Insulin* (1982).

Macleod, Mary Isabella, née Drever (b at Red R 11 Oct 1852; d at Calgary 15 Apr 1933). At age 17, during the RED RIVER REBELLION (1869-70), Drever showed the steady nerve for which she became famous in western Canada when she evaded detection by Métis guards and safely delivered an important dispatch addressed to Col WOLSELEY. Accompanying Wolseley's troops was James MACLEOD, soon commissioner of the newly formed NWMP; they were married in 1876 and settled in Ft Macleod. She was one of several women to sign Treaty No 7 at Blackfoot Crossing Sept 1877. She frequently accompanied her husband on his inspections and tours of duty, and she was universally admired by NWMP officers and their wives. SUSAN JACKEL

McLeod, Neil, lawyer, politician, premier of PEI, judge (b at Uigg, PEI 15 Dec 1842; d at Summerside, PEI 19 Oct 1915). Called to the PEI Bar in 1872, McLeod was elected to the Legislative Assembly in 1879. Re-elected in 1882 and 1886, McLeod, a Conservative, was premier 1889-91. In 1892 he was appointed county court judge for Prince County. NICOLAS J. DE JONG

McLeod, Norman, Presbyterian minister (b at Point of Stoer, Scot 29 Sept 1780; d at Waipu, NZ 14 Mar 1866). McLeod, a teacher and lay preacher, moved to Pictou, NS, in 1817. His forceful preaching attracted a large congregation that joined him on "The Ark" in 1820 to sail to Ohio but landed instead at St Ann's Harbour, Cape Breton. McLeod made himself a moral dictator over his followers, imposing severe punishments for trivial "sins." Despite his fanaticism they obeyed his command to migrate to Australia in 1851, but McLeod was unhappy and moved them to Waipu, NZ. In the 1850s, almost 900 persons left NS to join him in his search for "righteous" surroundings. JOHN S. MOIR

MacLeod, Pegi Nicol née Margaret Kathleen Nicol, painter (b at Listowel, Ont 4 Jan 1904; d at NY 12 Feb 1949). MacLeod's images of the contemporary world helped form the first wave of Canadian modernism. Her gift lay in her ability to present life's spontaneity and energy. After studies with Franklin BROWNELL at the Ottawa Art Assn, she attended Montréal's École des beaux-arts with fellow students Goodridge ROBERTS and Marian SCOTT. The breakthrough in her style is revealed in her 1933 watercolours of schoolchildren in a garden. In 1936, with Douglas DUNCAN, she helped found the Picture Loan Soc. In 1937 she moved to New York but frequently visited Fredericton where she helped found (and taught at) the Observatory Art Centre. She painted numerous works of the women's division of the armed forces (1944-45) and her *oeuvre* is composed of almost 1000 works in many media, including designs of hooked rugs. JOAN MURRAY

Reading: Joan Murray, *Daffodils in Winter: The Life and Letters of Pegi Nicol MacLeod* (1984).

McLeod Young Weir Limited The company was established in 1921 by Donald I. McLeod, Ewart Young and J. Gordon Weir with an initial capital of $40 000, which has since expanded to $300 million. From its inception the firm was first in the industry to adopt 2 basic principles: productive staff were given the opportunity to participate as shareholders and no father and son alliances were permitted. The firm pioneered a number of new products now commonplace in the industry. Best known perhaps is its "McLeod Young Weir Bond Averages," a yardstick of bond yields, maintained and perfected over many years as a service to investors and the industry. With 1600 staff in 43 offices throughout Canada as well as others in Britain, Europe, US and the Far East, the company is a recognized leader in all facets of the industry. The Bank of Nova Scotia acquired 100% control of the company in Dec 1987. ARTHUR E. GREGG

Pegi Nicol MacLeod, *Saint John, New Brunswick* (1947), oil on canvas (*courtesy Art Gallery of Hamilton/Mrs Jane MacLeod Pappidas*).

McLoughlin, John, fur trader, physician, merchant (b near Rivière-du-Loup, Qué 19 Oct 1784; d at Oregon City, Ore 3 Sept 1857). He studied medicine but in 1803 joined the NORTH WEST CO, becoming a partner in 1814. Greatly worried by the rivalry between the NWC and the HUDSON'S BAY CO, he attempted to bring about a settlement. When a coalition between the 2 took place, under other auspices, in 1821 he became a chief factor in the HBC. Governor George SIMPSON, concerned about the Columbia District, put McLoughlin in charge when he visited it in 1824-25, and McLoughlin was its superintendent for 2 decades. In later years differences arose between McLoughlin and Simpson over how to defeat American trading ships on the coast and how to deal with American immigrants to Oregon. McLoughlin favoured a chain of forts along the coast; Simpson favoured the use of ships. Simpson wanted the immigrants treated ruthlessly; McLoughlin, the man on the spot and a humanitarian, dealt with them kindly, realizing that an eventual American takeover of the area was inevitable. The 2 finally parted company over the murder of McLoughlin's son at Ft Stikine in 1842. After a prolonged dispute, McLoughlin retired in 1846 and lived the rest of his life at Oregon C. His holdings included flour and sawmills and he engaged in an export trade in lumber and other commodities. He has long been known as "the Father of Oregon." W. KAYE LAMB

McLuhan, Herbert Marshall, communication theorist (b at Edmonton 21 July 1911; d at Toronto 31 Dec 1980). Professor of English at U of T, McLuhan became internationally famous during the 1960s for his studies of the effects of mass media on thought and behaviour. Trained in literature (PhD, Cambridge, 1943), he laid the basis of his later work in his erudite dissertation, "The Place of Thomas Nash in the Learning of his Time." McLuhan thought of himself as a grammarian studying the linguistic and perceptual biases of mass media. A deeply literate man of astonishingly wide reading, he gravitated intellectually to the cutting edge of modern culture where the "irritation," he said, was greatest. His contribution to COMMUNICATIONS has been compared to the work of Darwin and Freud for its universal significance. Still, he was misunderstood by many because of his revolutionary ideas and their expression in an aphoristic prose style. He emphasized the connectedness of things and built what he called "mosaic patterns" of meaning, rather than offering mere argument using one-dimensional specialist logic.

McLuhan studied changes in perception created by electric media competing with print and machine process, the old strategy of fragmenting reality into informational categories. With the integrating, interdisciplinary force of electric process, information shifts its focus from specialist emphasis on detail towards a need to interpret the contexts created by media forms. The environment, overloaded with detailed information, can be ordered meaningfully, McLuhan said, through enhanced pattern-recognition skills, the ability to deal with open systems undergoing continual change at electric speed. He stressed how electric processes decentralized information, bringing simultaneous awareness to every point in a network. The perception of reality then becomes dependent upon the structure of information.

His famous distinction between "hot" and "cool" media referred to the different sensory effects associated with media of higher or lower definition. High-definition ("hot") media, such as print or radio, are full of information and allow for less sensory completion or involvement on the part of the reader or listener than low-definition ("cool") media, such as telephone or television, which are relatively lacking in information and require a higher sensory involvement of the user. The form of each medium is associated with a different arrangement, or ratio, in the order among the senses and thus creates new forms of awareness. These transformations of perceptions are the bases of the way in which the message *means*. In this sense, "the medium is the message."

Controversy always raged around McLuhan's work, for he was initiating a new paradigm which required that we recognize the form our information takes as basic to the way that knowledge is perceived and interpreted. *The Mechanical Bride* (1951) documents the power of advertising to manage public consciousness. *The* GUTENBERG GALAXY (1962) presents a pattern of insights into the cultural transformation created by print technology, and with the publication of *Understanding Media* (1964) McLuhan's reputation became worldwide. Of the several books that followed, *The Medium is the Message* (1967), *Through the Vanishing Point* (1968, coauthored with Harley Parker), *The Interior Landscape: The Literary Criticism of Marshall McLuhan* (1969), *From Cliché to Archetype* (1970, with Wilfred WATSON) and *Take Today: The Executive as Dropout* (1972, with Barrington Nevitt) are the most important.

McLuhan received numerous N American and European honours and awards, including the Schweitzer Chair (1967), which he spent at New York's Fordham U. The Centre for Culture and Technology that he founded is still functioning under the guidance of his disciples at U of T. The McLuhan Teleglobe Canada Award was created in 1983, as a memorial to McLuhan; it carries a cash award of $50 000. A volume of his letters was published in 1987. FRANK D. ZINGRONE

Reading: A. Kroker, *Technology and the Canadian Mind: Innis/McLuhan/Grant* (1984); D.F. Theall, *The Medium is the Rear View Mirror: Understanding McLuhan* (1971).

Marshall McLuhan, world-famous communications innovator (© *Karsh, Ottawa/Miller Comstock*).

Maclure, Samuel, architect, artist (b at Sapperton [New Westminster], BC 11 Apr 1860; d at Victoria 8 Aug 1929). The foremost BC domestic architect from 1900 to 1929, Maclure established a building style and form that gave Victoria and parts of Vancouver a distinctive Canadian West Coast flavour. Noted mainly for his large Tudor-revival house designs with 2-storey central halls and lavishly finished interiors, he also pioneered the shingle style, worked in traditional board-and-batten, and later turned to a severe Edwardian classicism. Much of his work survives, as do the watercolour landscape sketches for which he was noted during his lifetime. MARTIN SEGGER

Reading: Martin Segger and D. Franklin, *Victoria* (1979).

McMahon, Francis Murray Patrick, industrialist (b at Moyie, BC 2 Oct 1902; d at Hamilton, Bermuda 20 May 1986). He began as a driller working for mining companies in BC, and in 1927 established a small business as a diamond-drilling contractor. In 1930-31 he participated in drilling in the Fraser R Delta in search of natural gas for nearby Vancouver, and when that failed he proposed a 1000 km pipeline to transport gas from the Peace R district of northeastern BC. In 1936 he acquired for $100 an option on 32 ha of oil and gas rights near an oil discovery at Turner Valley, Alta. A successful oil well on this property led to the establishment of Pacific Petroleums Ltd, which became one of the most successful oil- and gas-producing companies in western Canada. In 1957, 25 years after he had first promoted the plan, McMahon completed construction of the Westcoast Transmission pipeline from the Peace R, Canada's first large natural-gas pipeline. In 1979 Petro-Canada acquired ownership of Pacific Petroleums for $1.5 billion. EARLE GRAY

Reading: Earle Gray, *Wildcatters* (1982).

McMaster, Ross Huntington, industrialist (b at Montréal 11 Oct 1880; d there 3 Jan 1962). For over 50 years, McMaster was a senior executive of the Steel Company of Canada (STELCO). He began his career with the Sherwin-Williams Paint Co. In 1903 he became general manager of Montreal Rolling Mills, where his father had worked. When the company was merged into Stelco in 1910, McMaster became Montréal manager of the new steel company, Canada's largest. He became Stelco president in 1926 and chairman in 1945, a post he held until 1960. Refusing to burden the company with undue debts, especially in the stagnant 1920s, McMaster insisted throughout his presidency on a strong profit margin. He introduced a "gaited" (cost plus profit) sales policy, replacing the old "Pittsburgh plus" pricing schedule. He introduced modern accounting practices to Stelco. A lifelong Montréal resident, he also took a business interest in the Montréal *Gazette*. DUNCAN MCDOWALL

Reading: W. Kilbourn, *The Elements Combined: A History of the Steel Company of Canada* (1960).

McMaster, William, businessman, banker, philanthropist (b in County Tyrone, Ire 24 Dec 1811; d at Toronto 22 Sept 1887). After immigrating to America he came to York [Toronto] in 1833 and entered a dry-goods firm. He shrewdly concentrated on wholesaling and turned his enterprise into one of Toronto's most profitable. Eager to curtail Montréal's control of the western economy, he joined George BROWN'S Reformers. Their opposition to the Church of England and its Conservative friends also appealed to McMaster who, as a Baptist, wished to advance the cause of his coreligionists.

At mid-century he ventured into banking, and in 1867 played a major role in establishing the Canadian Bank of Commerce, in large part as competition for the Bank of Montreal. During his presidency the bank surpassed all others in Ontario and was second only to its Montréal rival. After his death, his will revealed his desire to further Baptist education. Having supported the Canadian Literary Institute (Woodstock College) and Toronto Baptist College, he gave his estate of nearly $1 million to establish a Baptist institution of higher learning in Toronto. MCMASTER UNIVERSITY opened its doors in 1890 as an independent institution, after refusing federation with U of T. C.M. JOHNSTON

McMaster University, fd in 1887 as a BAPTIST institution, opened in Toronto in 1890 and moved to Hamilton in 1930. Chartered by the provincial legislature, the university was named for William MCMASTER, who bequeathed to it the bulk of his estate. It incorporated 2 older Baptist educational enterprises: Woodstock College (fd 1857) and Toronto Baptist College (1881). While in Toronto, McMaster had to overcome the opposition of theological conservatives to the instruction it presented. In 1930, under Chancellor Howard P. Whidden, a fresh start was made in nearby Hamilton, which offered an ample setting for McMaster's 500 students and considerable private support from its citizens. This arrangement honoured the traditional Baptist refusal to accept financial assistance from any public body.

Although WWII threatened enrolment, the demand for trained scientific personnel in industry and the armed forces prompted feverish activity in the university's laboratories. The war also led to the recruitment of the chemistry department's H.G. THODE for crucial wartime nuclear studies. Stimulated by scientific and technological demands, McMaster underwent a structural reorganization so that it might receive vital public aid, a process directed by George P. Gilmour, Whidden's successor. As a result, Hamilton College was established in 1948 as a nondenominational affiliate which would be eligible for governmental funding. By this time doctoral programs in the sciences had either been implemented or were being planned. Under Thode's leadership, engineering and nuclear studies expanded. A nuclear reactor was constructed on campus, the first such university facility in Canada.

In 1957, when it became evident that Baptist resources alone were insufficient, McMaster became a fully nondenominational private institution. The Baptist connection continued, however, through the incorporation and affiliation of McMaster Divinity College. Rapid growth during the 1960s was highlighted by the establishment of doctoral programs in humanities and social sciences, the organization of a business school and the planning of a college of health sciences. In

Enrolment: McMaster University, 1985-86 (Source: Statistics Canada)			
Full-time Undergrad	*Full-time Graduate*	*Part-time Undergrad*	*Part-time Graduate*
9 712	1 471	2 870	896

* Includes medical interns and residents

1967 McMaster, with the exception of its Divinity College, was reorganized into divisions. These have since become 6 faculties: Humanities, Social Sciences, Science, Engineering, Business and Health Sciences. C.M. JOHNSTON

McMicken, Gilbert, politician, magistrate (b at Wigstonshire, Scot 1813; d at Winnipeg 6 Mar 1891). He arrived in Canada in 1832, going into business at Chippawa, UC. From 1857 to 1861 he represented Welland in the legislative assembly. Appointed stipendiary magistrate for Canada W in 1864, he led a detective force which prevented Confederate agents from using Canada as a military base. The spy network he established served him again in the mid-1860s when as chief commissioner of Dominion Police, he kept the radical FENIAN movement under close observation, greatly diminishing its threat to Canada. In 1871 McMicken was appointed Dominion Lands agent for Manitoba, assistant receiver general and auditor and manager of the Dominion Savings Bank. From 1874 to 1877 he was an inspector of the Manitoba penitentiary. In 1879 he was elected to represent Cartier in the Manitoba legislative assembly and became speaker the following year. He retired in 1883. EDWARD BUTTS

MacMillan, Alexander Stirling, businessman, politician, premier of NS 1940-45 (b at Upper South River, NS 31 Oct 1871?; d at Halifax 7 Aug 1955). After a successful career in lumbering and construction, he was appointed chairman of the Nova Scotia Highways Board in 1920 and served briefly as minister of highways in 1925. A Liberal member of the Legislative Council 1925-28, he held a seat in the NS Assembly 1928-45. In 1933 he again assumed the powerful highways portfolio and in 1940 also took on the posts of premier, provincial secretary and minister of public works. A tough debater and a shrewd politician, the aging MacMillan found wartime leadership burdensome. He willingly relinquished the premiership to Angus L. MACDONALD and retired from public life in 1945. MARGARET CONRAD

MacMillan, Sir Ernest Alexander Campbell (b at Mimico [Etobicoke] 18 Aug 1893; d at Toronto 6 May 1973). Internationally known as a conductor of symphonic and choral music, he was also an organist and pianist, an educator, a spokesman for music, and a leading figure in Canadian musical organizations. He left about 20 compositions and many arrangements; his extensive writings and talks cover many subjects, from folk song to musical pedagogy. By his cultivation, skill, energy and travels, he became the most influential Canadian musician of his time.

A prodigy, he had composed several songs and played the organ publicly by age 10. During his teens, he audited music classes at Edinburgh U and attained both an organ diploma and an Oxford baccalaureate in music. He held a professional position as an organist in Toronto at age 15. Interned in Germany as an enemy alien, 1914-18, he developed his talents through prison-camp shows and concerts. In the early 1920s in Toronto he performed as church organist and choir director, wrote for journals and taught music. Most of his original works belong to this phase of his career. In 1923 he directed the first of 30 annual presentations of Bach's *St Matthew Passion.* He was active in the annual CPR folk festivals (1927-

Sir Ernest MacMillan, known as the statesman of Canadian music, was the first person to be knighted outside the UK for contributions to music; photo taken in 1964 (© *Karsh, Ottawa/Miller Comstock*).

31), and edited *A Book of Songs* (1929; reissued as *A Canadian Song Book*, 1937), widely used as a school text, and an anthology of essays, *Music in Canada* (1955). He was principal of the Toronto (later Royal) Conservatory of Music 1926-42; dean of the Faculty of Music, U of T, 1927-52; and toured all regions of the country as festival adjudicator and as Conservatory examiner. MacMillan's fame as a conductor grew rapidly after 1931, when he became conductor of the Toronto Symphony Orchestra. He led the TSO until 1956, and for the last 14 of those years was also conductor of the TORONTO MENDELSSOHN CHOIR. He was guest conductor with major orchestras in the US, Australia and Brazil, and conducted the first commercial recordings of his home organizations. Bach was his specialty, but he exposed audiences to a gamut of music and championed numerous works by Canadian composers.

MacMillan was knighted in 1935 and received the Canada Council Medal (1964), the Order of Canada (Companion, 1970), the Canadian Music Council medal (1973, awarded posthumously), the Richard Strauss Medal (GEMA, W Germany), honorary diplomas from the 2 royal music schools (London, England), and honorary doctorates from 8 universities. Named after him were the MacMillan Theatre and the annual MacMillan/CAPAC Lectures (Toronto); and the Sir Ernest MacMillan Fine Arts Clubs (Vancouver). MacMillan's papers have been acquired by the National Library of Canada. The Sir Ernest MacMillan Memorial Foundation, established by his family in 1985, aims to assist gifted young professional musicians. JOHN BECKWITH

MacMillan, Harvey Reginald, entrepreneur (b at Newmarket, Ont 9 Sept 1885; d at Vancouver 9 Feb 1976). After studying at the Ontario Agricultural Coll and the Yale Forestry School, MacMillan worked on the BC coast as a timber cruiser in 1907. Although he was hired as assistant inspector of forest reserves for western Canada in 1908, tuberculosis forced him to spend the next 2 and a half years in a sanatorium. In 1912 he became chief forester for BC, a post he kept until WWI, when he became timber-trade commissioner for the federal government, assistant manager of the Chemainus plant of Victoria Lumber and Manufacturing Co and, by the end of the war, an employee of the IMPERIAL MUNITIONS BOARD. In 1919 MacMillan, backed by British timber merchant Montague Meyer, launched the H.R. MacMillan Export Co. His manager and later partner was W.J. Van Dusen, and the 2 men developed the company into a major exporter of lumber. Competition was met with aggressive marketing, the purchase of sawmills and timber limits, and the building of a plywood plant in 1935. During WWII MacMillan was chairman of Wartime Shipping Ltd, a crown corporation. After the war he continued to expand his company, building the Harmac Pulp Mill in 1947. In 1951 the company merged with Bloedel, Stewart and Welch. In 1956 MacMillan resigned as chairman and in 1970 he and Van Dusen resigned as directors, but MacMillan maintained his interest in MACMILLAN BLOEDEL until his death.

CHRISTOPHER G. CURTIS

Reading: Donald McKay, *Empire of Wood* (1982).

MacMillan, William Joseph Parnell, physician, premier of PEI 1933-35, lieutenant-governor (b at Clermont, PEI 24 Mar 1881; d at Charlottetown 7 Dec 1957). After a brilliant career as a scholar and physician, MacMillan entered politics in 1923. Ten years later he became premier during the Island's worst economic depression. The dynamic premier implemented many relief programs and greatly increased government expenditures to relieve the needy Islanders. Nevertheless, MacMillan and the Conservative Party were swept from office when the Liberal Party captured all 30 seats in the 1935 election. In 1957 MacMillan was appointed lieutenant-governor only days before his death. LEONARD CUSACK

MacMillan Bloedel Limited, with head offices in Vancouver, is Canada's largest forest-products company. It began in 1909 as the Powell River Paper Company Ltd, and it was reorganized as the Powell River Co in 1911. Upon merging in 1960 with MacMillan and Bloedel Ltd (est 1951), its name was changed to MacMillan, Bloedel and Powell River Ltd. The present name was adopted in 1966. Between 1964 and 1980 the company made various acquisitions, mainly of corrugated case, lumber and paper companies. With integrated operations in Canada, the US and overseas, "MacBlo" produces newsprint, paper, lumber, panelboard and containers. It also owns timberland in BC. In 1986 it had revenue of $2.5 billion (ranking 36th in Canada), assets of $2.2 billion (ranking 46th) and 15 102 employees. Noranda Forest holds 49% of the shares and the company is 7% foreign owned.

DEBORAH C. SAWYER

Reading: Donald MacKay, *Empire of Wood* (1982).

MacNab, Sir Allan Napier, soldier, lawyer, businessman, politician (b at Newark, UC 19 Feb 1798; d at Hamilton, Canada W 8 Aug 1862). A forceful though enigmatic personality, MacNab had a deep influence on many aspects of pre-Confederation Canada. As a youth he served with conspicuous gallantry in the WAR OF 1812. Moving in 1826 from York [Toronto] to Hamilton, he set up a thriving law practice, but he owed his fortune to speculation in real estate. He was an entrepreneur as well; with Glasgow merchant Peter Buchanan, he was chiefly responsible for the construction of the GREAT WESTERN RY.

In the first phase of his political career (1830-35), MacNab vigorously promoted economic development and moderate Tory policies. In the second (1836-49) he became an extreme Tory. Knighted for his zeal in suppressing the REBELLION OF 1837-38, he vainly stressed loyalty as an issue in public policy. In the third (1850-56) he declared that "all my politics are Railroad," but as leader of the Conservatives he was also concerned to move his party back from extremism. In 1854 he played an important role in the formation of the Liberal-

Conservative alliance and became premier of the Canadas (1854-56). Dundurn, his stately 37-room mansion, still stands today in Hamilton.
D.R. BEER

Reading: D.R. Beer, *Sir Allan MacNab* (1984).

McNab, Archibald, 17th chief of Clan Macnab (b in Perthshire, Scot *c*1781; d at Lannion, France 12 Aug 1860). McNab came to Upper Canada in 1822 to flee his creditors in Scotland. His settlement scheme was approved Nov 1823 and he was given land on the Madawaska R. The township was surveyed and called McNab in 1824 and he brought about 15 families from Scotland in 1825 who, with others recruited in Canada, settled the township on terms laid down by McNab. For the next 15 years he plundered these people and pursued them in the courts. He was supported at first by his politically well-placed friends in Toronto and at Perth, but his position, unassailable in the 1830s, was wholly undermined in the 1840s by his excessive greed. Ultimately he was driven from the township by the determination of the settlers to work together and to petition the councils of Upper Canada and Canada W. He lived in Hamilton until at least 1851 before leaving Canada and dying in exile in France. With 4 children and a wife abandoned in Scotland, he fathered at least one illegitimate child in McNab Township, and another upon his return to England in the 1850s.
JULIAN GWYN

McNair, John Babbitt, lawyer, politician, judge, premier of NB 1940-52 (b at Andover, NB 20 Nov 1889; d at Fredericton 14 June 1968). First elected MLA for York in 1935, he was attorney general in the DYSART government and president of the provincial Liberal Party. Defeated in 1939, he was re-elected in 1940 for Victoria and in 1944 for York. In 1940 he succeeded Dysart as party leader and premier, and in 1943 passed the Civil Service Act providing security of tenure for public servants. Following the defeat of his government in 1952, McNair left politics and returned to legal practice. In 1955 he was named chief justice of NB and in 1957 he headed the royal commission examining the fiscal status of Newfoundland. He was appointed lieutenant-governor of NB in 1965.
DELLA M.M. STANLEY

McNaughton, Andrew George Latta, army officer, scientist, diplomat (b at Moosomin, NWT [Sask] 25 Feb 1887; d at Montebello, Qué 11 July 1966). He was trained as an engineer at McGill, enlisted in the nonpermanent militia in 1909 and took the 4th Battery of the CANADIAN EXPEDITIONARY FORCE overseas in 1914. His scientific approach to gunnery brought him rapid advancement; he was twice wounded and ended the war commanding the Canadian Corps artillery. He joined the permanent force in 1920 and became deputy chief of the general staff in 1922. As chief of the general staff, 1929-35, he began the mechanization of the permanent force and the modernization of the nonpermanent militia. From 1935 to 1939 he was president of the NATIONAL RESEARCH COUNCIL OF CANADA.

McNaughton returned to soldiering in WWII as commander of the 1st Canadian Infantry Division in 1939. Senior Canadian officer in the UK while the force there grew to a corps (1940) and then an army (1942), he endeavoured to hold the Canadians together in one formation and deeply involved himself in the scientific aspects of soldiering. He initiated an improved method of airburst ranging and the development of "sabot" antitank ammunition. But his tactical judgement was weak – he endorsed the ill-fated DIEPPE plan – and he never properly mastered the relationship between politics and high command in war. By late 1943 the crusty Canadian's uncompromising opposition to fragmentation of the Canadian Army Overseas was causing resentment in Ottawa; he was out of favour with his own minister of national defence, J.L. RALSTON, and British criticism of his generalship was mounting. Under pressure and in declining health, he resigned in Dec 1943.

General A.G.L. McNaughton with Mackenzie King (*Central Press Photo/Miller Comstock*).

McNaughton remained a favourite of PM Mackenzie KING (he had earlier been a confidant of PM R.B. BENNETT) and was slated to become the first Canadian-born governor general. Instead he was lured briefly and unsuccessfully into politics; he served as minister of national defence 1944-45 but was unable to stave off CONSCRIPTION for overseas service or to win a seat in Parliament. A compelling public figure for almost 2 decades after 1945, McNaughton was Canadian representative on the UN Atomic Energy Commission, and president of the Atomic Energy Control Board of Canada, 1946-48; permanent delegate to the UN, 1948-49; chairman of the Canadian Section of the INTERNATIONAL JOINT COMMISSION, 1950-62, and of the PERMANENT JOINT BOARD ON DEFENCE, 1950-59. He was a determined, independent-minded proponent of his view of the national interest, and in his last great campaign he bitterly opposed the COLUMBIA RIVER TREATY.
NORMAN HILLMER AND BRERETON GREENHOUS

McNaughton, Duncan Anderson, track and field athlete (b at Cornwall, Ont 7 Dec 1910). Raised at Kelowna and Vancouver he attended U of Southern Calif, joining its track team as a high jumper. His "diving" western-roll technique disqualified him at the 1930 British Empire Games and nearly excluded him from the 1932 Los Angeles Olympics. Ultimately, he was allowed to compete and, in a dramatic jump-off to break a tie, he cleared the bar at 6 ft 6 in (2 m), beating Americans Bob Van Osdel and Cornelius Johnson and the Philippines' Simeon Toribio for the gold. A year later McNaughton retired; he distinguished himself in the RCAF and later as a petroleum geologist.
TED BARRIS

McNaughton, Violet Clara, née Jackson, journalist, feminist leader (b at Borden, Eng 11 Nov 1879; d at Saskatoon 3 Feb 1968). In 1912 the McNaughtons joined the Saskatchewan Grain Growers' Assn and jointly became secretary-treasurer of the Hillview local. Violet's insistence on being recognized as a delegate to the 1913 SGGA convention led to a special "Women's Congress," and an organizing committee for a women's section, with Violet as secretary, was created. When the section was organized in 1914, McNaughton was elected president (1914-17). She sparked in 1915 the formation of the Saskatchewan Equal Franchise League, which was primarily responsible for gaining the franchise for women a year later. In 1919 she became president of the Interprovincial Council of Farm Women and, in that post, became a prominent national feminist leader. She was elected to the board of the SGGA in the early 1920s and was important in the Saskatchewan and national Progressive movements, helping to formulate the platform for the PROGRESSIVE PARTY in 1921. From 1925 to 1950 she edited the "Mainly for Women" page in *The Western Producer*.
IAN MACPHERSON

McNeil Case G. McNeil, a journalist who wanted to see a film (*Last Tango in Paris*) banned in his province (NS) by a provincial regulatory body, challenged the constitutionality of the provincial Theatres and Amusement Act. The Supreme Court of Canada, in a divided decision, ruled that the provincial measure was valid. In its opinion, this local control over the film was justified by the Constitution Act, 1867 (s92.13 and s92.16). The court distinguished between criminality and provincial interest in morality. A provincial Act that establishes standards of decency is not necessarily an infringement on criminal law. According to Mr Justice Ritchie, tastes and mores may vary from region to region and the decision about what is morally acceptable to the public may be considered a matter of local and private nature.
GÉRALD-A. BEAUDOIN

Macoun, John, explorer, naturalist (b at Maralin, Ire 17 Apr 1831; d at Sidney, BC 18 July 1920). Champion of the agricultural capabilities of the western interior, Macoun was also Canada's foremost field naturalist and amassed a collection of Canadian flora and fauna which became the foundation for the National Museum of Natural Sciences. Macoun developed his expertise as a plant geographer himself; he was a

John Macoun, Canada's foremost field naturalist, whose large collection of flora and fauna became the foundation for the National Museum of Natural Sciences (*courtesy National Museums of Canada/Canadian Museum of Civilization/31874*).

graduate of Syracuse U (MA). In 1872 he took part in the first of 5 government surveys of western Canada led by Sandford FLEMING. Over the next decade, he declared in various reports and public lectures that western lands were ideally suited for agriculture. Though the route for the CPR main line was located through the grasslands essentially for strategic reasons, Macoun provided the agricultural justification for that route.

In 1882 Macoun was appointed to the GEOLOGICAL SURVEY OF CANADA as Dominion botanist and began a study of the range and distribution of Canada's flora, adding fauna when he became survey naturalist and assistant director in 1887. Macoun established a Dominion Herbarium of over 100 000 specimen sheets and discovered approximately 1000 new species, many of which were named after him. By the time he retired to Vancouver I in 1912, the Geological Survey boasted the finest collection of Canadian flora and fauna in the country. He was a charter member of the Royal Society of Canada in 1882. His son **William Tyrrell Macoun** (1869-1933) was the first Dominion horticulturalist and received numerous awards for his research into apple breeding. W.A. WAISER

Macphail, Agnes Campbell, politician, reformer (b at Proton Twp, Grey County, Ont 24 Mar 1890; d at Toronto 13 Feb 1954). Macphail was the only woman elected to Canada's Parliament in 1921, the first federal election in which women had the vote. She served until defeated in 1940. In 1943 she was elected to the Ontario legislature, one of the first 2 women there. She lost her seat in 1945 but was again in the legislature 1948-51. She was also the first woman appointed member of a Canadian delegation to the LEAGUE OF NATIONS, where she insisted on serving on the Disarmament Committee. Macphail began as a country schoolteacher and was active in the Ontario agricultural CO-OPERATIVE MOVEMENT and the UNITED FARMERS OF ONTARIO. She entered politics to represent the farmers of her region; in office she came also to see herself as representing other women. As MP she first sat as a member of the PROGRESSIVE PARTY, with which the UFO was then affiliated. She later sat as an independent and finally as a representative of the CO-OPERATIVE COMMONWEALTH FEDERATION; as MPP she represented the CCF. Although involved in founding the CCF, she distrusted partisanship and did not acknowledge party discipline.

Though modern accounts have tended to deny it, in her own time Macphail was recognized as a feminist. Rural issues such as a protective tariff were always primary for her, but she gave major attention to so-called "women's issues" such as prison reform. She was the founder of the Elizabeth Fry Society of Canada and was largely responsible for the establishment in 1935 of the Archambault Commission to investigate Canada's prisons. Her feminist antimilitarism included active participation in the WOMEN'S INTERNATIONAL LEAGUE FOR PEACE AND FREEDOM (but she reluctantly voted for Canada's entry into WWII). She supported women's acquisition of civil rights, although she was not an active suffragist. She was a friend of Nellie MCCLUNG and admired Thérèse CASGRAIN's suffragist efforts in Québec, and she welcomed the decision in the PERSONS CASE. She was responsible for Ontario's first equal pay legislation (1951). After her electoral defeat, she supported herself by journalism, public speaking and organizing for the Ontario CCF, but she suffered from lack of money and poor health. She died just before a Senate appointment was to be announced. NAOMI BLACK

Reading: D. French, "Agnes Macphail," in *The Clear Spirit*, ed Mary Quayle Innis (1966); M. Stewart and D. French, *Ask No Quarter* (1959).

In her time Agnes Macphail was recognized as a feminist, though she was primarily concerned with issues such as the tariff (© *Karsh, Ottawa/Miller Comstock*).

McPhail, Alexander James, farmer, farm leader, businessman (b near Paisley, Ont 23 Dec 1883; d at Regina 21 Oct 1931). In 1913 McPhail joined the Saskatchewan Dept of Agriculture, but resigned in 1918 out of loyalty to his superior, P.F. Brendt, who had been dismissed because of his German nationality. Returning to Elfros, Sask, McPhail became a livestock drover, selling mostly on the Winnipeg market. He became an active organizer for the PROGRESSIVE PARTY and joined the moderate wing of the Saskatchewan Grain Growers' Assn, becoming secretary later that year. McPhail was a leading proponent of the wheat pool movement and was elected first president of the SASKATCHEWAN WHEAT POOL board in 1924. As president, he faced several difficult issues. He reluctantly carried out the pool's purchase of the elevator system owned by the Saskatchewan Cooperative Elevator Co. He was the principal organizer of the Central Selling Agency, established by the 3 Prairie wheat pools to market grain internationally. A firm believer in voluntary marketing, McPhail campaigned against compulsory marketing, a controversial issue in Saskatchewan during the late 1920s. After the market crash in 1929, the Saskatchewan pool, like the others, avoided bankruptcy only because of government support. IAN MACPHERSON

Reading: H.A. Innis, ed, *The Diary of A.J. McPhail* (1940).

Macphail, Sir Andrew, physician, man of letters, professor of medicine, soldier (b at Orwell, PEI 24 Nov 1864; d at Montréal 23 Sept 1938). Macphail studied at Prince of Wales College, Charlottetown, before proceeding to McGill, where he received degrees in arts and medicine. After practising medicine and teaching at Bishop's U medical faculty in Montréal 1893 to 1905, Macphail in 1907 was appointed McGill's first professor of the history of medicine, a chair he occupied for 30 years. In 1911 he became founding editor of the monthly *Canadian Medical Association Journal,* a position he held until enlisting as a medical officer in WWI. Beginning in 1905 he published more than 10 books and scores of shorter pieces, most on nonmedical themes. Many of his essays appeared in *The* UNIVERSITY MAGAZINE, an outstanding Canadian quarterly he edited 1907-20, with the exception of his 4 years overseas. Most of his writings in this period were political commentary or social criticism. His particular concerns were to define the imperial connection between Canada and the UK, and to expose fallacies in, eg, feminism or modern education. He was knighted for his literary and military work on 2 Jan 1918. The book to which he devoted most care, and which he considered his best, appeared posthumously: *The Master's Wife* (1939, repr 1977), a semiautobiographical reminiscence of PEI. IAN ROSS ROBERTSON

McPherson, Aimee Semple, née Kennedy (b at Ingersoll, Ont 9 Oct 1890; d at Oakland, Calif 27 Sept 1944). At age 17 Aimee married Robert Semple, a Pentecostal missionary who died in China in 1912. She returned with her newly born daughter to the US, married H.S. McPherson and conducted tent revivals in the Atlantic seaboard states. Her evangelistic success took her to Los Angeles in 1918 where, 5 years later, she opened her debt-free, 5000-seat, $1.25-million Angelus Temple of the Foursquare Gospel.

"Sister Aimee's" theatrical pulpit techniques made her the most publicized revivalist in the world — she toured the US, Canada, Britain and Australia. In 1926, shortly after divorcing McPherson, by whom she had a son, Aimee disappeared and was presumed drowned; she reappeared weeks later claiming to have been kidnapped, apparently to cover her affair with her radio station manager. During the next decade she was connected with moral and financial scandals, including divorce from her third husband. Her public image never fully recovered and her health deteriorated. She died of an apparently accidental drug overdose. JOHN S. MOIR

Macpherson, Cluny, doctor, inventor, businessman, justice of the peace (b at St John's Mar 1879; d there 16 Nov 1966). Educated at McGill and later in Edinburgh and Paris, he was commissioned a surgeon and magistrate in Battle Harbour, Lab, where he helped Wilfred GRENFELL contain a smallpox epidemic. He returned to private practice in St John's in 1904 and was appointed registrar of the Nfld Medical Board, a position he held with few interruptions until his death. He was decorated in May 1915 for his invention of the gas helmet to provide protection against poison gas. Active as the director of the Grenfell Assn of Newfoundland and a director of the International Grenfell Assn, president of the Medical Council of Canada, 1954-55, and president of a commission of the Newfoundland Supreme Court, Macpherson was also prominent in business. STEPHEN O. JACKSON

Macpherson, Crawford Brough, political theorist, professor (b at Toronto 18 Nov 1911; d there 22 July 1987). Educated at U of T and U of London, he returned to U of T in 1935 to begin 4 decades of teaching in the department of political economy, interrupted only by work for the WARTIME INFORMATION BOARD (1943-44) and by visiting professorships in Britain, the US and Australia. His various writings on the development of liberal-democratic theory brought him international acclaim. Turning first to the work of 17th-century English theorists such as Thomas Hobbes and John Locke, Macpherson identified what he called "possessive individualism" as the ideology of a rising bourgeois class. His uniquely humanist analysis drew on a Marxist critique of emergent capitalism, but also on the ethical promise of liberalism: the individual freedom to realize one's full human potential, which he believed was overshadowed by capitalist market relations. In an early work he turned his analytical skills on a particular strand in Canadian liberal-democratic thought, the ideology of the early 20th-century Alberta farmers' movement. His major publications include *Democracy in Alberta* (1953), *The Political Theory of Possessive Individualism* (1962), *The Real World of Democracy* (1965), *Democratic Theory: Essays in Retrieval* (1973), *The Life and Times of Liberal Democracy* (1977) and *Burke* (1980). He was made Officer of the Order of Canada in 1976.

CRAIG HERON

Macpherson, Sir David Lewis, politician, businessman (b at Castle Leathers, near Inverness, Scot 12 Sept 1818; d at sea 16 Aug 1896). After a successful start in his elder brother's transportation firm, he combined his administrative skills with the engineering expertise of Casimir GZOWSKI in the early 1850s on a number of key construction projects, including the GRAND TRUNK RAILWAY west of Toronto and the International Bridge across the Niagara R. Macpherson was elected to the legislative council in 1864 and appointed to the newly created Senate in 1867; he was a valuable Conservative organizer and fundraiser in the province of Ontario. However, in the early 1870s, he withdrew his support of Macdonald over the granting of the CANADIAN PACIFIC RAILWAY contract to the Montréal-based syndicate. He later resolved his differences with Macdonald and was appointed Speaker of the Senate in 1880 and minister of the Interior in 1883. His single-minded obsession with reducing costs and increasing revenues made him an excessively rigid administrator of the politically sensitive land policies in the North-West. The outbreak of the NORTH-WEST REBELLION in 1885 demonstrated his weaknesses and worsened his failing health, and lead to his resignation from public life.

KEN CRUIKSHANK

McPherson, Donald, figure skater (b at Windsor, Ont 20 Feb 1945). World figure-skating champion in 1963, McPherson was the first Canadian to win the Canadian, N American and world championships in the same year. He competed in the 1960 Squaw Valley, Calif, Olympics at age 15, and at 18 was the youngest man to win the world title. Not strong in compulsory figures, McPherson performed free-skating routines that were brilliant and near-perfect. After the 1963 competitions, he retired from amateur competition. He skated for 11 years with a professional ice show and won the 1975 world professional title.

BARBARA SCHRODT

Macpherson, Duncan Ian, political cartoonist (b at Toronto 20 Sept 1924). Macpherson is one of the most influential editorial cartoonists in N America, though the influence is a result of his much-copied visual style rather than of his political views. His association with the *Toronto Star* began in 1958, and his renderings of John DIEFENBAKER soon reached the same state of vitriolic perfection as BENGOUGH'S of John A. MACDONALD some 80 years earlier. He has produced collections of his cartoons and has illustrated various other works. In 1971 the Canada Council awarded him the Molson Prize, and in 1973 he became a member elect of the Royal Canadian Academy of Arts. He has won 6 national newspaper awards for his work. In 1980 the *Star* donated 1220 cartoons to the National Archives of Canada and in 1985 the NAC acquired, by purchase and donation from Macpherson, 2485 items, a collection now constituting Canada's largest by one artist. It is valued at more than $500 000.

Macpherson, Jean Jay, poet, teacher (b at London, Eng 13 June 1931). She was brought to Newfoundland in 1940 and, educated at Carleton, McGill and U of T, she has been teaching English at Victoria Coll, U of T since 1957. She began publishing poetry in CONTEMPORARY VERSE in 1949, had her first book published in 1952 and won the Governor General's Award for poetry for *The Boatman* (1957), a cycle of pellucid lyrics unified by symbols of fall and redemption. From 1954 to 1963 she published the works of Canadian poets in 8 Emblem Book pamphlets. Her subsequent work includes other poetry, a classical mythology for secondary schools and an authoritative study of patterns in the late romances of 2 continents.

JEAN O'GRADY

Reading: Jay Macpherson, *Poems Twice Told: The Boatman and Welcoming Disaster* (1981) and *The Spirit of Solitude* (1982).

McTaggart-Cowan, Ian, zoologist, educator (b at Edinburgh, Scot 25 June 1910). A distinguished contributor to zoology, in particular to the biology of mammals, birds and molluscs, McTaggart-Cowan has been a pioneer in the application of science to the management and conservation of wildlife. An acclaimed teacher and orator who served at UBC as a professor, department head, dean and member of the Senate (1940-75), he pioneered science on television with shows widely featured beyond Canada's borders. His public service includes consulting on national parks in Canada and abroad, acting as vice-president of IUCN, president of The Wildlife Society and Biological Council of Canada, chairman of Canadian Environmental Advisory Council, and as member or executive of numerous local, provincial and national councils and boards. Cowan's achievements have been widely honoured, including fellowship in the Royal Society of Science, the Leopold Medal (1970), Einarsen Award in Conservation (1970) and Officer of the Order of Canada (1972). Following retirement he served as chancellor of U Vic (1979-85), chairman of the Canadian Committee on Whales and Whaling, Academic Council (BC), Habitat Conservation Board (BC), and other public service bodies.

VALERIUS GEIST

McTaggart-Cowan, Patrick Duncan, meteorologist (b at Edinburgh, Scot 31 May 1912), younger brother of Ian MCTAGGART-COWAN. McTaggart-Cowan's family immigrated to Canada in 1913; he graduated from UBC and was a Rhodes scholar at Oxford. As officer-in-charge of the meteorological service in Newfoundland from 1937 to 1942, he pioneered weather services for the first passenger transatlantic flights. During WWII he was chief meteorologist for the RAF FERRY COMMAND. In 1946 he became assistant director of the Canadian weather service, and when Andrew THOMSON retired in 1959, he became director. Named the founding president of SIMON FRASER U in 1963, he guided the university until his appointment as executive director of the SCIENCE COUNCIL OF CANADA in 1968. In 1970 he directed Operation Oil to clean up the *Arrow* oil spill in Chedabucto Bay, NS. The recipient of several medals and honours, in 1986 he became an honorary life member of the Canadian Meteorological and Oceanographic Society. He was created member, OBE, in 1944 and Officer of the Order of Canada in 1979.

DAVID PHILLIPS

McTavish, Simon, fur-trade merchant (b in Stratherrick, Scot *c*1750; d at Montréal 6 July 1804). He immigrated to N America at age 13, probably as an apprentice to a merchant. After engaging in the fur trade out of Albany, NY, he moved to Montréal in the mid-1770s. He is not known to have travelled west of Lk Superior but he financed trading expeditions to the Saskatchewan R and the Northwest generally. In 1779 he was a key figure in the creation of the first NORTH WEST CO and he may have been behind the reorganization of 1783. After joining Joseph FROBISHER in 1787 to form McTavish, Frobisher and Co, chief outfitter and sales agent for the NWC, his control of the latter firm tightened. His pre-eminent position in Montréal business circles and his personal style were reflected in his nickname, "The Marquis."

DANIEL FRANCIS

Made Beaver Soon after its founding in 1670, the HUDSON'S BAY COMPANY found it necessary to devise a unit of value that would accommodate Indian bartering to European bookkeeping methods. A Standard of Trade was established, based on the made beaver (one prime beaver skin in good condition). Prices of all goods were set in MB. Later the HBC issued brass tokens in denominations of one MB and fractions thereof. *See also* FUR TRADE.

JENNIFER S.H. BROWN

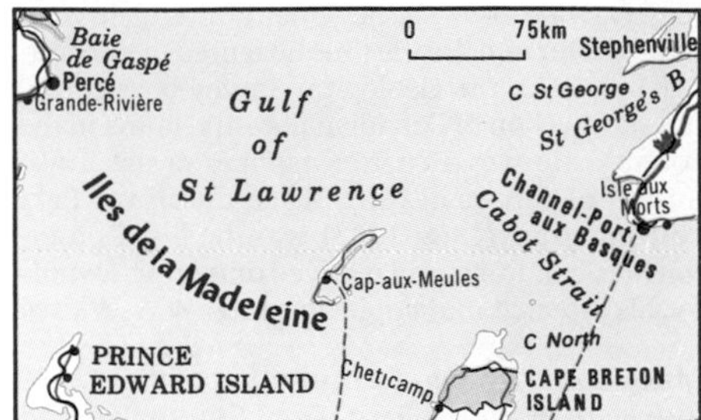

Madeleine, Îles de la (Magdalen Islands), Qué, pop 14 532 (1986c), 14 130 (1981c), 202 km^2, is an archipelago located in the middle of the Gulf of ST LAWRENCE, 288 km SE from the GASPÉ Pen, 112 km N from PEI and 88 km NW from CAPE BRETON I. The 100 km, hook-shaped archipelago consists of 16 islands, islets and outcroppings.

Preceded by BASQUE fishermen, Jacques CARTIER arrived at Île Brion in 1534; he named it in honour of the great French admiral. He christened the islands "Les araynes" because of the endless beaches of very fine white sand. Later CHAMPLAIN referred to them as the "Ramées." The definitive name was given in honour of Madeleine Fontaine, wife of the islands' first seigneur. Real colonization began in 1755, when the ACADIANS were deported, and several families landed on the islands. The Treaty of PARIS (1763) gave all N American French possessions to England, except Saint-Pierre and Miquelon; in 1775 George III gave the islands to Capt Isaac Coffin, who subjected the inhabitants to seigneurial tenure. These hardships forced the islanders into exile and they founded several villages on Québec's North Shore. In 1895 Québec legislation enabled the islanders to buy back their land and the islands then began to develop and prosper.

The largest islands are inhabited: Havre Aubert, CAP AU MEULES, Havre aux Maisons, Île de GRANDE ENTRÉE, Grosse Île and Île de L'Est, which are linked by long sandspits; Île Brion lies out to sea. The red and grey sandstone cliffs are spectacularly sculpted and the 300 km of beaches are dotted with harbours and picturesque bays. Fishing represents 45% of the island's economic base. Herring, cod, plaice, halibut, mackerel and scallops are shipped all over the world from plants where the fish are canned, frozen or smoked. Lobster is kept in ponds and shipped live. Since 1972 the tourist industry has developed to such an extent that the population of the islands triples during the summer season, despite the long waits for the ferry. The tapping of salt deposits at Grosse Île became one of the mainstays of the islands' economy, and aquaculture of MUSSELS began in 1986. The capital is Cap-aux-Meules.

JEAN-MARIE DUBOIS AND PIERRE MAILHOT

Magazines are paper-covered publications issued at regular intervals, at least 4 times a year. Paid magazines are sold on the newsstands or delivered through the mail to subscribers; unpaid or

The red and grey cliffs of the Îles de la Madeleine have been sculpted from the islands' sandstone (*photo by J.A. Kraulis*).

controlled-circulation magazines are deposited free of charge at the homes or offices of specific groups of people defined as a target audience. These 2 groups incorporate consumer, literary, academic, trade and professional journals and are designed to entertain, inform, educate and provoke commentary. With rare exception, all of them carry ADVERTISING, usually in the proportion of 60% advertisements to 40% editorial. In the last decade, magazine supplements in newspapers have all but disappeared while regional (particularly city) and specialty magazines (eg, those dealing exclusively with fashion, travel or women's issues) have flourished.

The history of magazines in Canada is not a story of ideas or particular writers. Canadian innovations in form and content have been slight, contributions to belles lettres competent but not dazzling, and association with trends affirmative rather than provocative. The story of magazines in Canada is a political saga of small independent interests struggling to survive in an environment dominated by foreign interests. The struggle has always been between preserving cultural autonomy and permitting the free flow of ideas. The Canadian market is small, divided into 2 linguistic camps, and stretched through a narrow corridor that makes distribution awkward and expensive. More important is the impact of the US: in 1984, of the paid-circulation consumer magazines, 65% were imported foreign magazines and 35% were magazines produced in Canada. However, almost half of the circulation of Canadian-produced consumer magazines was accounted for by *Time, Reader's Digest* and *T.V. Guide*, all of which make extensive use of American editorial material.

The Audit Bureau of Circulations (ABC) show that the top American magazines coming into Canada in 1987 were *National Geographic* (798 825), *National Enquirer* (389 699) and *Star* (306 367). The top Canadian-produced paid-circulation magazines were *Reader's Digest* (1 710 110, French and English editions), CHATELAINE (1 359 090, French and English editions), *T.V. Guide* (803 859), *Canadian Living* (655 986, French and English editions), MACLEAN'S (648 545) and *Legion Magazine* (504 278). The largest circulation unpaid magazines were *Recipes Only* (2 million, French and English editions) and *Homemaker's* (1 410 000, French and English editions). Despite 3 royal commissions struck at least in part to recommend measures to protect the ailing magazine industry, Canadians quite simply prefer to read American magazines.

Canadian periodicals were first established in NS by transplanted New Englanders. The first Canadian magazine, edited by the Rev William Cochran and printed by John Howe, father of reformer Joseph HOWE, was *The Nova Scotia Magazine and Comprehensive Review of Literature, Politics, and News*. It commenced publication in 1789, lasted 3 years, and was concerned more with British than colonial affairs. The bilingual *Le Magasin de Québec* was established by Samuel Neilson in Lower Canada's capital and published from 1792 to 1794. It marked the first attempt at drawing the 2 cultures together through a printed medium.

Until the late 19th century, high production costs, poor distribution and low circulation meant that most attempts at magazine publication in British North America were short-lived and derivative. Various efforts were made to launch literary magazines for select audiences, but they were largely overwhelmed by the newspaper boom of the 1820s. Some notable productions were J.S. Cunnabell's *Acadian Magazine* and *Halifax Monthly Magazine*, John Gibson's *Literary Garland* from Montréal, and Michel Bibaud's various efforts: *La Bibliothèque canadienne, l'Observateur, Le Magasin du Bas-Canada* and the important *l'Encyclopédie canadienne*. Many eminent Canadians were published in these outlets, including Susanna MOODIE and John RICHARDSON in the *Literary Garland*.

By mid-century, Toronto had become an important centre for English-language production with magazines such as *The Canadian Journal, Anglo-American* and *British Colonial*. All were consciously literary and all soon failed. The introduction of regular train service, the electric telegraph, and the coming of Confederation gave great impetus to the Canadian magazine industry. American magazines such as *Harper's* were freely circulating in the country and many people felt Canadian counterparts were necessary to help give substance to the newly minted nationality. Montréal was also an influential centre, with magazines such as John Dougall's *New Dominion Monthly*, which pursued an aggressive national bias and achieved in only a few years a circulation of 8000.

The technique of photoengraving was pioneered in Canada and used first in the immensely successful *Canadian Illustrated News*, which began operations in 1869 and gained a large following principally because of its vivid portrayal of scenery and its stirring images of the NORTH-WEST REBELLION. Its French counterpart was the technically more accomplished, but generally less commercially successful, *L'Opinion publique illustré*. Other significant magazines of the period were religious in orientation. Particularly important were the *Northern Messenger* and *Methodist Magazine and Review*, a magazine of opinion on Canadian affairs. Goldwin SMITH's *Canadian Monthly, National Review, Nation* and *The Bystander* contributed to serious discussion, as did *La Revue canadienne* and 2 university-based journals, QUEEN'S QUARTERLY (1893) and *University Magazine* (edited by Sir Andrew MACPHAIL at McGill). Toronto's satirical *Grip* flourished from 1873 to 1894 and a number of national cultural magazines appeared, such as *Canadian Monthly* and *The Week*. Interest in a definitive national cultural expression dimmed after the turn of the century, however, and was only revived in magazine format after WWI with the launching in 1920 of the CANADIAN FORUM.

National news and politics found an outlet in *Toronto Saturday Night* (1887), which dropped the city name in 1889 (*see* SATURDAY NIGHT). This consumer magazine, a feisty combination of social news and political crusades against issues such as divorce or the exploitation of labour, soon developed a highbrow following, and circulation reached 10 000. *The Canadian Magazine*, launched in Toronto in 1893, was another attempt at a national organ, although this time the object was to challenge quality American competition such as *Scribner's* and *The Atlantic*. *The Canadian* was a mouthpiece for "Wasp" Ontario; it did not often stretch its definition to include French Québec, the Maritimes or even the West, except as an Ontario fief.

The mid-1890s saw yet another attempt to stem the flood of American consumer magazines with the publication of what would become *Maclean's* magazine. Called the *Busy Man's Magazine*, 1896-1911, it was at first no more than a digest of previously published pieces. The magazine was successful in attracting advertisers, both from overseas markets and the US, especially after the adoption of American trim size. *Maclean's* expressed the Canadian national voice of the time – decidedly British and imperial – but it also frequently published such local writers as Lucy Maud MONTGOMERY and Robert SERVICE.

As the Canadian population stretched westward, magazines of regional and specialized interest began to appear. *The Manitoban* was launched in 1891 and the *British Columbian* followed 2 decades later. *Busy East* (eventually *Atlantic Advocate*) appeared in 1910, as did the *Canadian Home Journal*. The latter catered to the growing awareness of women as an important segment in society, although its content focused on recipes and housework. The market for trade and business magazines led J.B. MACLEAN to launch a series that included *Canadian Grocer* and *Dry Goods Review*. From the end of the 19th century also, farm weeklies increased in popularity, eg, Montréal's *Family Herald and Weekly Star*.

Circulation of Canada's top half dozen magazines never amounted to more than 300 000 during WWI, though American magazines flooded the country. In 1927 some foreign materials, mainly fiction, were denied free entry, but this had no appreciable effect on the home industry, and talent continued to drain south. However, *Mayfair* and *Chatelaine*, both modelled on American formats, were launched in the late 1920s, with *Chatelaine* gaining almost 60 000 readers in its first year (1928). Government was finally beginning to listen to the woes of industry, which had greatly increased with the advent of commercially sponsored radio programs in 1928. "The world is listening, not reading" was the slogan that wooed many advertisers, at least temporarily, away from print and into broadcast. In 1931 R.B. BENNETT's Conservative government imposed a content tax on US magazines devoting more than 20% of their space to advertising, with the result that some 50 American magazines began printing in Canada. Mackenzie KING removed the tax when his Liberals regained power in 1935, arguing that it was a tax on thought and literary art. The American magazines immediately returned home and Canadians returned to importing them.

The coming of WWII caused magazine circulations, particularly of opinion and information magazines, to increase considerably. *Maclean's*, for example, reached a circulation of 275 000 in 1940. Canadian editions of American magazines were introduced as well – *Time Canada* appeared in 1943 – and the American *Liberty* magazine increasingly used Canadian content.

The influence and sheer presence of American magazines was felt even more after the war. B.K. SANDWELL, editor of *Saturday Night*, complained that Canada was the only country in the world in which the largest percentage of reading matter was foreign controlled; 86 489 copies of US-owned magazines were bought by Canadians in 1948. A year before Mackenzie King had banned the importation of pulp magazines and comic books, but had exempted supplements distributed with newspapers. The STAR WEEKLY in Toronto became the exclusive carrier of the most popular comics from the US, thus playing havoc with the circulation of the *Montreal Star*'s rotogravure supplement, the MONTREAL STANDARD. In retaliation, the *Montreal Star* launched WEEKEND MAGAZINE as a supplement in 1951, with an initial circulation of 900 000. In 1952 the combined circulation of *Weekend* and *Star Weekly* was almost 2 million – 300 000 more than the total circulation of the 4 leading Canadian magazines of the time.

Television advertising began in 1952 and within one year it accounted for $1 335 000 in sales. The combined threat of weekend supplements, television and American magazines seemed unbreachable, until in 1956 the Liberal government imposed an advertising tax on Canadian editions of US magazines. The following year, however, the Conservatives repealed it.

In 1960 Grattan O'LEARY, editor of the OTTAWA JOURNAL, was appointed chairman of a 3-member Royal Commission on Publications to study the "position and prospects of Canadian magazines and other periodicals with special attention to foreign competition." The commission found that 75% of the general-interest magazines bought in Canada were American publications, that *Time* and *Reader's Digest* took 40 cents out of every dollar of magazine advertising, and that there were only 5 Canadian general-interest consumer magazines, of which *Maclean's* and *Liberty* were in poor financial shape (*Liberty* ceased publication in 1964). When the commission tabled its report in June 1961, its major recommendations were that expenditures made for advertisements in imported publications aimed at the Canadian market be disallowed as income tax deductions and that foreign periodicals containing Canadian domestic advertising be banned from entering Canada.

The DIEFENBAKER government accepted the recommendations but made special reservations for foreign periodicals already established in the country, specifically *Time* and *Reader's Digest*. Before these changes could be implemented, the Liberals under Lester PEARSON came into office

The process of photoengraving was first used in the highly successful *Canadian Illustrated News* (courtesy National Archives of Canada/C-75551).

and the magazine question was shelved until the Special Senate Committee on the Mass Media was struck (1969) under the chairmanship of Liberal Senator Keith DAVEY. The Davey Committee recommended in its report, "The Uncertain Mirror," in 1970 that the O'Leary Commission findings be implemented. Between the time of the O'Leary Commission and the Davey Report, *Reader's Digest* circulation had climbed from 1 million to nearly 1.5 million, *Time*'s circulation had increased from 215 000 to 444 000 and its advertising revenue had nearly tripled from $3.9 million to $9.5 million. At the same time, television attracted an increasing proportion of brand-name advertising and destroyed the economic base of mass consumer magazines.

Matters continued to drift until yet another official investigation was launched. The Ontario Royal Commission on Book Publishing delivered its final report with some 70 recommendations on 22 Feb 1973. On 7 Oct 1974 *Saturday Night*, the country's oldest surviving magazine, suspended publication. That same year a group of Canadian magazine publishers, headed by Michael de Pencier, publisher of *Toronto Life* (founded in 1966 and premier publication of Key Publishers), banded together to form the Canadian Periodical Publishers' Assn to foster a Canadian-owned and -controlled magazine publishing industry. Incorporated in 1974, the group offers promotion and distribution services, professional development and lobbying. In 1987 the group had 260 members.

On 18 Apr 1975 the Liberal government introduced Bill C-58 to eliminate, among other things, the tax concessions enjoyed by Canadian editions of foreign-owned publications such as *Time* and *Reader's Digest*. Four days later *Saturday Night* resumed publication. After the bill passed in Feb 1976, *Time* announced the end of its Canadian edition and the last issue appeared on 1 Mar 1976.

One of the greatest beneficiaries of Bill C-58 was MACLEAN HUNTER (with 109 magazines, the largest magazine publisher in Canada), which had long wanted to revamp *Maclean's* into a newsmagazine. The launch of such a publication, which Secretary of State Hugh Faulkner had informed the Commons was a major purpose behind the bill, occurred on 18 Sept 1978 under the editorship of Peter C. NEWMAN.

The most obvious contemporary trend in magazine publishing (other than the continuing and overwhelming presence of foreign publications) is the emergence of life-style and specialty magazines, some of which, such as *Toronto Life* or *Western Living*, are regional in nature. Sophisticated market research techniques have meant that target audiences – career women, homemakers, travellers, lawyers, or even smaller groupings such as lawyers who travel – can be identified readily and an editorial product designed to deliver appropriate advertising material to the designated consumer. The Kent Commission (1981), discovered that slightly over three-quarters of the population were magazine readers, and that readership was higher among the young and better educated.

The term "general-interest magazine" has little relevance in the contemporary market. Nowhere is that more apparent than in the increasing prominence of controlled-circulation magazines. The largest publisher of such magazines is COMAC, which was founded in 1966 and has 8 magazines including *Homemaker's/Madame à foyer*, *Quest* (which folded in late 1984) and *Western Living*. In late 1983 a rival company launched the largest circulation Canadian magazine, *Recipes Only*, which has a controlled circulation of 2 million readers and is a prime example of the current trend toward publishing for a narrow and specific market. All these magazines endorse doctrines of affluence and have a clear middle- and upper-middle-class consumer bias. They reflect a glistening internationalism rather than a parochial nationalism and, in that sense, are a mirror of contemporary Canadian middle-class aspirations. *See also* LITERARY MAGAZINES IN ENGLISH; LITERARY PERIODICALS IN ENGLISH.

SANDRA MARTIN

Magazines in French

Early magazines aimed not simply to inform their readers but to instruct them and entertain them. This vision guided Samuel Neilson when he launched *The Quebec Magazine/Le magasin de Québec* (1792-94), a 64-page bilingual monthly, containing excerpts from European and American publications, and illustrated by what may have been the first engravings ever published in a magazine. Two similar publications – *Le Courrier de Québec* (1807-08) and *L'Abeille canadienne* (1818-19) – met with less success. The *Bibliothèque canadienne* (1825-30) of Michel Bibaud contained selected excerpts from journals, poetry, anecdotes and local events, as well as a unit of Bibaud's *Histoire du Canada*. Though the magazine had readers from Québec to Detroit, it was a semi-success at best, for it reached only the élite. *La Bibliothèque* thus gave way to *L'Observateur* (1830-31) which being a weekly could report local news and thus interest the larger public. But in his *Magasin du Bas-Canada* (1832) and *L'Encyclopédie canadienne* (1842-43), Bibaud returned to the *Bibliothèque* format, concentrating once again on culture.

At this time magazines began a battle which was to prove decisive for their future, against the Roman Catholic Church, all-powerful in Québec in the 19th century. One of the first major conflicts occurred in 1851 when Narcisse Cyr revealed abuses committed by church officials in *Semeur canadien*, a magazine declared to be heretical and dangerous, whose readers were threatened with excommunication by the archbishop of Montréal. The battle escalated in 1864 when Pope Pius IX published his *Syllabus*, banning certain books. Mgr Ignace BOURGET then threw himself into a crusade aimed at preventing the appearance of any new publications in Québec. The Index included about 20 000 titles and more than 8000 authors, causing the eventual disappearance of a number of publications, including *Le Canada* (1889-1909), which had denounced the Catholic school system and abuses of authority committed by the church. It quickly found its place in The Index and sales plummeted from more than $350 a month to a bare $25 in Dec 1893.

Purely literary publications, such as *Les Soirées canadiennes* (1861-65), felt less pressure from the church. In fact, this extremely popular monthly – with prestigious contributors such as François-Xavier GARNEAU, Antoine GÉRIN-LAJOIE and Abbé Henri-Raymond CASGRAIN – caused its own demise when an administrative quarrel split the editorial group. *Le Foyer canadien* (1863-66), a monthly publishing poetry and critiques, is considered by many as the best literary Canadian magazine of the 19th century, with a press run of 2075 copies and readers from Chicoutimi to Detroit. At the end of the 19th century, the lack of money made life even riskier for francophone magazines. It was under these circumstances that Georges Desbarats had to cease publication after 3 years of *Le Foyer canadien*, and of *L'Opinion publique illustrée* (1870-83), a francophone counterpart to the *Canadian Illustrated News*. *Les Nouvelles Soirées canadiennes* (1882-88) said farewell in very similar circumstances.

In 1888, Frédéric Poirier launched *Le Samedi* (1888-1963), a little magazine which, along with Trefflé Berthiaume's *Le Monde illustré* (1884-1907), quickly became one of the most important periodicals of the first decade of the 20th century. At first a humour magazine, *Le Samedi* became a general-interest one after WWII and turned to sensationalism in 1963, known from then on as *Le Nouveau samedi*. *Le Monde illustré*, for its part, carried on from *L'Opinion publique*. It held, along with *Le Revue canadienne* (1863-1922), a major place in the life of francophone intellectuals early in the century.

Growing urban concentration and more widespread education meant that traditional magazines no longer met the needs of their readers, who were increasingly drawn from the masses. These readers wanted popularization, variety and light entertainment, as found in American and French magazines. And so *La Revue populaire* was born (1907-63), whose circulation rose in less than 50 years from 5000 to more than 125 000. Aimed at the whole family, it published short stories, a family column, various pieces of information and, during WWI, news from the Front. But the postwar period was fatal both for it and the austere *Canada français* (1918-46): faced with ever more competitors, magazines fought for survival by attracting readers with a tempting layout, winning advertisers and, above all, by specializing. *La Revue populaire* tried to attract a female readership, but they remained faithful to *La Revue moderne* (1818-1960), one of the first magazines to be run by a woman (Madeleine Huguenin). Very visual, and financed as much by advertising as by sales, this magazine caught the attention of Maclean Hunter Ltd. In Oct 1960, *La Revue moderne* merged with a French version of CHÂTELAINE. Five months later, *Châtelaine* printed 125 000 copies; the age of modern magazines had definitely come to French Canada.

The specialization which began after WWII increased in the second half of the 20th century. Professional publications appeared on the market and consumer magazines became increasingly important. According to a study by Statistics Canada, in 1984 there were more than 270 francophone magazines, aimed at numerous special interests among the public, from arts, agriculture and astrology to computers and data processing, youth, literature, leisure and sports, fashion and health. While literary magazines are much less prominent, rising educational levels have led to the success of general-interest magazines such as *Sélection du Reader's Digest* and have caused the explosion of newsmagazines such as L'ACTUALITÉ (270 000 copies in 1986). Other social trends are evident in magazines such as *Age d'or/Vie nouvelle* (35 000 copies in 1986); *La Vie en rose* (25 000 copies in 1986); the immutable *Châtelaine* (300 000 copies in 1986); and *Super Ecran* (180 000 copies in 1986) for pay-TV subscribers.

Another phenomenon seems both characteristic of the present and a guarantor of the future: concentration of ownership. Survival in the world of magazine competition increasingly depends on access to huge financial resources, more often to be found in corporations' pockets than in private ones. That is why such different groups as Nordais, Maclean Hunter Ltée, QUÉBECOR Inc, Télémédia Publishing and Québecmag (1984) have all specialized in magazine publishing, or have at least developed a magazine section. All this suggests that even in our computerized age, this particular media genre is still in demand. It allows the reader to learn more about a whole variety of subjects and delivers a target demographic group to the advertiser. In short, far from being outdated, the francophone magazine in Canada has entered its golden age. *See also* LITERARY PERIODICALS IN FRENCH.

SONIA SARFATI

Reading: H.F. Angus, ed, *Canada and her Great Neighbour* (1938); P. Audley, *Canada's Cultural Industries* (1983); Canada, Royal Commission on Publications, *Report* (1961); F.S. Chalmers, *A Gentlemen of the Press* (1969); I. Litvak and C. Maule, *Cultural Sovereignty: The Time and Reader's Digest Case in Canada* (1974).

Magic is a performance or demonstration of events which appear to occur in defiance of natural law. It has been employed for centuries in the practice of witchcraft and religious rituals by so-called prophets, witch doctors and medicine men, in support of their claims to possess supernatural powers. Its practice and fascination for mankind can be traced in Egyptian records as far back as 2700 BC. Native peoples of N America were performing magic long before the arrival of Europeans. Archaeologists have uncovered Migis (Cowrie shells) which were widely used by magic practitioners in the region. It is believed they were used not only for ritual use but also for the practice of sleight-of-hand. Ojibwa played a "moccasin game" which bore a close resemblance to the notorious "shell game" still popular in modern magical entertainment.

The first known white magician to appear in Canada has been reported as one Maginnis, performing in Halifax in 1875. As Canadian magicians toured the country in the late 1800s along with others from abroad, the popularity of magic increased, not only as a performing art but also as a hobby. The art of magic involves an unusually diverse range of mental and physical talents, artistic, creative and histrionic. In Canada, its devotees include about 1700 professional and part-time performers, amateurs and hobbyists. The hitherto jealously guarded secrets of magic are available to the public in bookstores and most public libraries. Manufacturers of magic apparatus and stage illusions publish magazines and catalogues for their customers. Magic societies have their own journals for private circulation among their members. The largest among these is the International Brotherhood of Magicians (IBM) which is an affiliate of Magic Clubs in more than 60 countries. The movement was founded in Winnipeg in 1922 by Melvin G. McMullen (stage name Len Vintus); head office of IBM is now located in the US.

Many Canadian magicians are recognized internationally. Notable among them are Sid Lorraine, Ross Bertram, Howard Lyons, Bruce Posgate and Norman Houghton, all of Toronto; Stewart James of Courtright, Ont; Romaine and Tom Auburn of Montréal; Mel Stover and Brian Glow of Winnipeg; and Mickey Hades of Calgary. Among famous Canadians resident in the US are John Booth, Dai Vernon and Randi; foremost among them is Douglas James Henning (b at Winnipeg 3 May 1947) who gave his first public show at age 14. He graduated in psychology at McMaster U, but medical ambitions were deferred when a Canada Council grant enabled him to advance his magical studies. These led to his production of "Spellbound," a full evening magic show at the Royal Alexandra theatre in Toronto. This in turn led to his "The Magic Show" on Broadway, where it ran for over 4 years. In 1974 his first "TV Spectacular" magic show, seen by 60 million people, created a great surge of interest in magic. Subsequent TV specials have been followed by successful world tours.

BRUCE POSGATE

Magistrate, historically, retired police officers, now lawyers appointed by the lieutenant-governor-in-council. Magistrates are now known as provincial court judges; they are judicial officers with summary jurisdiction in both criminal and civil actions, hearing minor indictable offences and those where the accused may elect mode of trial. They may preside over family court or small-claims court, and are ex officio COMMISSIONERS FOR OATHS.

K.G. MCSHANE

Magnussen, Karen Diane, figure skater (b at North Vancouver 4 Apr 1952). An accomplished free-skating performer, Magnussen won the women's title at the Canadian championships in 1968. In 1969 she withdrew from world competition because of stress fractures in both legs, but recovered in 1970 to recapture the Canadian title, which she held until 1973. She won silver medals in the 1972 Sapporo Olympics and world championships. In 1973, when free skating – Magnussen's strength – was given a larger percentage of the total marks, she won the world championship in Bratislava, Czechoslovakia, with a brilliant performance. She received the Velma Springstead Trophy as Canada's outstanding woman athlete 1971-73 and was awarded the Order of Canada in 1973. She was an adviser for the 1988 Calgary Winter Olympics.

BARBARA SCHRODT

Magog, Qué, City, pop 13 530 (1986c), 13 604 (1981c), inc 1950, is situated on the Magog R at the outlet of Lac Memphrémagog (Abenaki, "expanse of water") in the EASTERN TOWNSHIPS. Economic links have been strong with both SHERBROOKE, 25 km E, and MONTRÉAL, 122 km NW. Formerly an Indian campsite and subsequently known as The Outlet, its first settlers were LOYALISTS and other Americans. Today's population is predominantly French Canadian. Built in 1884, A.H. Moore's Magog Cotton and Print Co, the first calico-printing plant in Canada, was amalgamated with Dominion Cotton Mills in the 1890s. Moore's Magog and Waterloo Railroad was sold to the CPR. Currently at the centre of the city's economy, the Dominion Textile Co employs one-fifth of Magog's population. Other important employers include the food-processing, clothing, printing and iron-products industries. Lac Memphrémagog and nearby Mont Orford have made Magog a traditionally popular resort area, which also hosts a summer theatre, swim meet and music festival.

PAULA KESTELMAN

Magpie, common name for birds of several genera in the CROW family. Of the 17 species known worldwide, only the black-billed magpie (*Pica

pica) is found in Canada. This permanent resident breeds from southern YT to western Manitoba, wandering farther E in winter. Magpies have extended their range eastward in historical times. They possess heavy bills and short, rounded wings. Their tails often make up over half their total length of some 50 cm. Magpies are black with white scapulars (feathers at the base of the wing) and underparts. They are weak fliers, adapted to ground foraging in open habitats. Their elaborate nests, requiring about 6 weeks for construction, are composed of a domed mass of sticks with one or more entrances leading to a cup of mud. Magpies are believed to mate for life.

LORRAINE G. D'AGINCOURT

Maguire, Thomas, Roman Catholic priest (b at Philadelphia, Pa 9 May 1776; d at Québec C 17 July 1854). Educated at the Séminaire de Québec, he was ordained in 1799 and was parish priest at Berthier (Berthier-sur-Mer) 1805-06 and Saint-Michel, 1806-27. Dedicated to education as a means of raising clerical prestige, he was director of the Collège de Saint-Hyacinthe 1827-31. As chaplain at the Ursuline convent, Québec 1832-54, he updated the curriculum and teaching practices in its boarding school for girls. A remarkable administrator, he saved both the college and convent from impending financial ruin. He was emissary from the Canadian bishops to Rome (1828-29, 1833-35) during their struggle against the Sulpicians to establish the episcopal authority of Jean-Jacques LARTIGUE. Maguire was an impassioned polemicist against attacks on the church by British Protestants and Canadian liberal professional men. From 1835 until his death he was vicar general of the bishop of Québec.

JAMES H. LAMBERT

Maheux-Forcier, Louise, writer (b at Montréal 9 June 1929). After extensive musical studies, she decided to devote herself exclusively to writing. Her first novel, *Amadou* (Prix du Cercle du livre de France, 1963), one of Québec's first poetic novels, developed the then taboo theme of lesbianism. While revealing her as a subtle, lucid and courageous writer, the novel aroused passionate controversy among critics. The author pursued her quest for primal beauty in her other novels (*L'Île joyeuse*, 1965, trans as *Isle of Joy*, 1987; *Une Forêt pour Zoé*, 1969, Gov Gen's Award; *Paroles et musique*, 1973; *Appassionata*, 1978), as well as in her short stories (*En toutes lettres*, 1980) and films for television. The ever-present androgynous character exerts a strong attraction on the living sources of this dream world, finding expression in a visual and rhythmical perfection of writing.

GABRIELLE POULIN

Mahone Bay, NS, Town, pop 1093 (1986c), 1228 (1981c), is located on the "Lighthouse Route" of Nova Scotia's S shore, 10 km NW of LUNENBURG. A quiet residential community and retirement haven, it is known for its beautiful bay, dotted with hundreds of islands. Its name is derived from the French *Mahonne*, "Venetian boat," referring to the long, low boats used by pirates who frequented the area. In 1754 Capt Ephraim Cook brought English, French and Swiss settlers to the area. Farming and fishing were mainstays of life until the mid-1800s, when shipbuilding became an important industry. Today the construction of pleasure craft has replaced that of seagoing vessels. Mahone Bay has been able to adapt to the 20th century by concentrating on the manufacturing, service and tourism industries. Although many young people have left the town, it has shown a consistent growth rate over the last 50 years.

HEATHER MACDONALD

Mahovlich, Francis William, Frank, hockey player (b at Timmins, Ont 10 Jan 1938). He played junior hockey at St Michael's College, Toronto, and joined TORONTO MAPLE LEAFS 1957-58, winning the CALDER TROPHY (best rookie). A powerful skater with an explosive slap shot, he led Toronto in scoring 1960-66, and played a large part in Toronto's 4 STANLEY CUP victories of the 1960s. His obvious capabilities led to great expectations and pressures from fans and management, and he left the team twice, distressed with his treatment. In 1962 Chicago owner James Norris offered $1 million for him in a much-publicized incident. He was traded to Detroit 1968 and then Montréal 1971, where he set a new playoff scoring record that year (14 goals and 13 assists). He finished his career with Toronto Toros, later Birmingham Bulls, of the WHA, retiring in 1978. In 17 NHL seasons he scored 533 goals and 570 assists, adding 51 goals and 67 assists in playoffs.

JAMES MARSH

Maillard, Pierre, priest of the Séminaire des missions étrangères, missionary (b in the diocese of Chartres, France *c*1710; d at Halifax 12 Aug 1762). Missionary to the MICMAC, Maillard was a brilliant linguist who perfected a system of written symbols for the Micmac language. He was sent to Île Royale [Cape Breton I] in 1735, and during the winter of 1737-38 worked out his system of hieroglyphics. In subsequent years he compiled a Micmac grammar and dictionary. Although (unknown to Maillard) there had been 2 earlier attempts to put Micmac in written form, Maillard's system alone had lasting impact. During the WAR OF THE AUSTRIAN SUCCESSION, he urged the Micmac to support the French cause. He was captured in 1745 and sent to France, but returned in 1746. In 1759 Maillard made peace with the British and, from 1760 until his death, lived in Halifax.

JOHN H. YOUNG

Reading: H.J. Koren, *Knaves or Knights?* (1962).

Maillet, Antonine, novelist (b at Buctouche, NB 10 May 1929). After the success of *La Sagouine* (1971; tr 1979) and PÉLAGIE-LA-CHARRETTE (1979), Maillet dominated contemporary Acadian literature. The latter won the Prix Goncourt, bringing her overnight fame in France, where it sold over 1 million copies. Her imaginary universe is rooted in the geography, history and people of ACADIA. Her novels, often reworked for the theatre, fuse adventure, desire, frustration, agony and joy to offer a new image of the original Acadia, restructured to fit an epic vision. She presents a simple event (conflict between 2 characters, a collective struggle to conquer the land, the long trip back to the homeland), rich in every kind of development. As the characters work through these developments, they become symbols. The language of these pieces, a fusion of "ancient and sonorous words" and literary language, is an original creation. The narrator is often presented not as an individual but as a collective being–the memory of the Acadian people. Maillet is a storyteller; only *La Sagouine* is not a narration. Here the character is autonomous and has an authenticity and complexity that lifts her above the other characters in the piece.

Maillet's renown coincides with an Acadian cultural revival. *La Sagouine*, as well as being a genuine literary success, appeared at the right moment to give voice to the Acadians. We find in that voice wisdom and lucidity, verve and reserve, humour and anger. As the author herself says, to recognize her works is to recognize the people to whom she belongs. Among her other works are *Pointe-aux-Coques* (1985), *Don l'Orignal* (1972), *L'Acadie pour quasiment rien* (1973), *Evangeline Deusse* (1975), *Les cordes-de-bois* (1977), *La gribouille* (1982) and *Le huitième jour* (1986, tr 1987). She has taught literature and folklore at Laval and is a Companion of the Order of Canada.

YVES BOLDUC

Antonine Maillet, whose novel *La Sagouine*, as well as being a great literary success, gave voice to her Acadian people (*courtesy Canapress Photo Service*).

Maillou, *dit* **Desmoulins, Jean-Baptiste,** builder, architect (b at Québec City 21 Sept 1668; d there Sept 1753). The brothers Joseph and Jean Maillou were successors of Claude BAILLIF and, because of their knowledge of classical and French Renaissance design, were employed by merchants, clerics and government officials. Joseph's death in 1702 left Jean-Baptiste in control of a flourishing business constructing houses, churches, religious houses, public buildings and fortifications. The French Crown's military expenditures sustained the colony, and Maillou profited from the defences built at Québec and Crown Point (NY). He received the title "Architect to the King" in 1719. Having been a land surveyor and expert estimator, he was appointed deputy overseer of highways in 1728. Royal patronage was vital to social advancement in NEW FRANCE and, under the Crown's aegis, this former stonemason became a propertied and influential bourgeois of Québec. Maillou House, built by Maillou beginning 1736, displays the traditional textures of 18th-century domestic architecture in Québec.

PETER N. MOOGK

Reading: Peter N. Moogk, *Building a House in New France* (1977).

Mainguy, Edmond Rollo, naval officer (b at Chemainus, BC 11 May 1901; d at Nanaimo, BC 29 Apr 1979). After graduating from the Royal Naval College of Canada, he served in various posts until 1939, when he took command of the destroyer *Assiniboine*. Following a year as captain (destroyers), Newfoundland, Mainguy became chief of naval personnel in 1942 and ended the war in command of the cruiser HMCS *Uganda*. A capable and well-liked officer, he chaired a commission in 1949 investigating several mutinies in the fleet. The resulting "Mainguy Report" recommended improvements in the handling of lower-deck grievances. He was promoted rear admiral and appointed chief of the naval staff in 1951. Mainguy retired from the navy in 1956 and was president of Great Lakes Shipping until 1965.

MARC MILNER

Maintiens le Droit [Fr, "Uphold the Right"], the official motto of the ROYAL CANADIAN MOUNTED POLICE. The use of the motto by the NORTH-WEST MOUNTED POLICE was first advocated in 1873 and adopted 2 years later. The expression "They always get their man," associated with the force since 1877, has no official standing.

JOHN ROBERT COLOMBO

Mainwaring, Sir Henry, pirate (b near Ightfield, Eng 1587?; buried at Camberwell [London], Eng 15 May 1653). A skilled navigator who was commissioned by the Crown in 1610 to capture the pirate Peter EASTON, he failed and turned to piracy, basing himself in N Africa. In 1614 he sailed for Newfoundland to reprovision his ships and recruit men. He took over Easton's old base at HARBOUR GRACE and terrorized Spanish and Portuguese shipping in the region. His audacious attacks almost destroyed the peace between England, Spain and Portugal. Pardoned in 1616 by James I, he returned to England where he was knighted, elected to Parliament and made a vice-admiral. A Royalist, he was ruined during the English Civil War and died in poverty.
EDWARD BUTTS

Reading: G.E. Manwaring, ed, *The Life and Works of Sir Henry Mainwaring* (1920-22).

Mair, Charles, writer, civil servant (b at Lanark, UC 21 Sept 1838; d at Victoria 7 July 1927). Mair's memory rests on 3 bases: his inflammatory activities surrounding the RED RIVER REBELLION of 1869-70; his role in the formation of CANADA FIRST, an early nationalist movement; and his composition of the drama *Tecumseh* (1886). Mair represented to an extreme the contemptuous Upper Canadian dismissal of the Métis claims. Imprisoned by Louis RIEL at the outbreak of the rebellion, Mair escaped and on his return to Ontario agitated tirelessly for the suppression of the uprising. Canada First, of little immediate, practical influence, remains significant as the first of a series of Canadian nationalist groups. While not outstanding from a literary viewpoint, *Tecumseh* was important in the development of Canadian drama. It presents a vision of Canada as a co-operative enterprise in contrast with the self-seeking individualism of the US. DENNIS DUFFY

Reading: Norman Shrive, *Charles Mair: Literary Nationalist* (1965).

Maisonneuve, Paul de Chomedey de, officer, founder of MONTRÉAL (bap at Neuville-sur-Vanne, France 15 Feb 1612; d at Paris, France 1676). He was chosen by the Société Notre-Dame de Montréal to found a missionary colony on Montréal I. The expedition, which included Jeanne MANCE, left La Rochelle 9 May 1641 and arrived at Québec late in 1641. Maisonneuve began construction of VILLE-MARIE [Montréal] in 1642 and within a year had established a fort for defence, a hospital, chapel and lodging for about 70 persons who lived there. Maisonneuve was a skilful organizer and tireless defender of the colony, particularly against the constant attacks of the Iroquois. However, he did not always enjoy the favour of the governors general and he was recalled to France in Sept 1665. He lived out his life in seclusion in Paris. The history of the early years is told in DOLLIER DE CASSON'S *Histoire du Montréal, 1640-1672* (1868; tr *A History of Montreal*, 1928).
MARY MCDOUGALL MAUDE

Maitland, Ont, UP, pop 635 (1986c), 667 (1981c), located on the St Lawrence R, 8 km E of Brockville. During the SEVEN YEARS' WAR (1756-63) it was the site of a fort and shipyard, Pointe au Baril, where the last French warships to sail on Lk Ontario were built. The founders of Maitland were Ziba Phillips, a Loyalist who with his brother Jehiel acquired property there in 1821, and George Langley who in 1822 purchased land where the village now stands. A townsite was laid out in 1822 and named after Sir Peregrine MAITLAND, lt-gov of Upper Canada at the time. St James's Church, built in 1826, survives as a fine example of early Gothic revival architecture. Barbara Heck, founder of N American Methodism, settled here after the American Revolution. Never developing beyond a small settlement, Maitland has profited from the commercial traffic along the St Lawrence corridor and retains much of its early charm in its restored buildings. DANIEL FRANCIS

Maitland, Sir Peregrine, soldier, civil administrator (b in Hampshire, Eng 6 July 1777; d at London, Eng 30 May 1854). At age 15 he joined the Grenadier Guards. He served with distinction at the Battle of Waterloo and was knighted in 1815. In 1818 he was appointed lt-gov of Upper Canada, where he became identified ideologically with the conservative element later known as the FAMILY COMPACT. Continually at the centre of political controversy, he believed that democratic and American tendencies in Upper Canadian society had to be resisted to maintain the imperial connection. By the end of his tenure, Reform elements were demanding that the lt-gov choose his advisers from elected members of the Legislative Assembly, one of the issues that led to the REBELLIONS OF 1837. As lt-gov of NS 1828-34 he left little mark on the province's political history. Appointed commander in chief of the Madras army in 1836, he resigned 2 years later. In 1844 he became governor of Cape of Good Hope, but was replaced during the Kaffir War, being considered ineffective. HARTWELL BOWSFIELD

Major, André, writer, literary critic, journalist (b at Montréal 22 Apr 1942). Since 1973 Major has been a producer of cultural programs for the Radio-Canada network. He first became known in 1961, with the appearance of 2 collections of poetry: *Le Froid se meurt* and *Holocauste à deux voix*. By 1963 he was also publishing short stories. That same year he helped found PARTI PRIS, to which he contributed until 1965. In this same period Major was especially interested in the often tragic problems of young people struggling to contain personal rebellion. Since 1968, without ceasing to express himself politically, Major has published poems and several novels. One novel, *Les Rescapés* (1976), won the Gov Gen's Award. His newest stories are *La Folle d'Elvis* (1981) and *L'hiver au coeur* (1987). Major is also interested in theatre and has written 2 radio plays and a stage play.
JACQUES COTNAM

Makers of Canada, The, a series of books designed to present a history of Canada through a study of its major figures. The original series contained 20 volumes which appeared between 1903 and 1908; an index volume was added in 1911 and a 21st volume in 1916. The publisher was George M. Morang of Toronto, and the editors were poet Duncan Campbell SCOTT and Professor O. Pelham Edgar of Victoria College; a third advisory editor, William Dawson LESUEUR, was added later. The series sold extremely well and Morang brought out 2 less expensive 11-volume editions in 1910. Scott's *John Graves Simcoe*, with its excellent prose, and Adam SHORTT'S *Lord Sydenham* and Jean Newton McIlwraith's *Sir Frederick Haldimand*, with their thorough research, received high praise. Overall, though, the series was deemed deficient because of its overtly whiggish orientation, particularly in the selection of its subjects. This partisan charge is best exemplified in the case of LeSueur's biography of William Lyon Mackenzie; Mackenzie's relatives, in particular his grandson, W.L. Mackenzie KING, complained that the biographer was too critical. Between 1908 and 1913, 5 controversial court cases ensued over LeSueur's manuscript; Morang refused to publish it and LeSueur was prohibited from publishing it elsewhere. It did not appear until 1979, as part of the Carleton Library Series.

In 1926, the Oxford University Press brought out a 12-volume edition of The Makers of Canada, with historian W.L. Grant as editor; several volumes were discarded, some recommissioned, and the remainder thoughtfully revised and brought up to date. A notable addition, originally published in 1903 by Morang, and subsequently hailed as a distinguished example of political biography, was Sir John Willison's *Sir Wilfrid Laurier and the Liberal Party: A Political History*. The U of T Press, which now owns the rights to the series, has reissued several volumes. DONNA COATES

Malaria Early settlers in Ontario experienced a disease called "fever and ague," which occurred as far north as the present site of Ottawa, and interfered seriously with the construction of the RIDEAU CANAL in the 1830s. Most instances of "fever and ague" were what we now know as malaria. The variety that existed in Ontario, benign tertian malaria, rarely was fatal but caused regularly recurring bouts of severe fever, shaking chills and anemia, and thus severely sapped the energy of its victims. Fortunately, the symptoms could be controlled by taking Peruvian bark, or cinchona, which later was found to contain quinine. Malaria was so common in the period from the 1780s to the 1840s that it was considered remarkable if any newcomer failed to acquire the disease within a year or two. Rich or poor, old or young, almost all suffered with "fever and ague."

Malaria is a disease conveyed by the bite of infected MOSQUITOES of the genus *Anopheles* several species of which still live in Ontario. However, progressive drainage of the large tracts of marshy land that once existed in the southern part of the province have removed most of the breeding grounds. Malaria now occurs in Canada only when imported from malarious parts of the world, particularly central Africa and parts of Southeast Asia, where the disease continues to be endemic. CHARLES G. ROLAND

Malartic, Qué, Town, pop 4474 (1986c), 4833 (1981c), inc 1939, is located 70 km E of ROUYN-NORANDA in northwestern Québec. It was established by Québec's Ministry of Mines, which hoped to end the proliferation of squatter camps that had sprouted up around the gold mines in this part of the Abitibi region during the gold rush of the mid-1930s. The town was named after the first gold mine, which was possibly named after the comte de Malartic, Montcalm's aide-de-camp. It developed near 3 of the largest gold mines in Québec – the Canadian Malartic, E Malartic and Malartic goldfields – and the population reached its peak (5983) in the early 1950s. Malartic's economic and urban structure was deeply affected in the 1960s by the decline in the region's mining industry and the closure of the major mines. Despite these problems, the town lives on, its economy still based on its gold mines.
BENOÎT-BEAUDRY GOURD

Malaspina, Alejandro, explorer (b at Mulazzo, Italy 5 Nov 1754; d at Pontremoli, Italy 9 Apr 1810). Born to an illustrious but impoverished family, Malaspina entered the Spanish naval service. In 1784 he sailed around the world in the frigate *Astrea*. Impressed by the important scientific voyages of James COOK and the comte de la Pérouse, Malaspina in 1788 approached the Spanish government with a plan for scientific explorations. He received full command in July 1789 and sailed from Cadiz with 2 corvettes, *Descubierta* and *Atrevida* July 30 and rounded Cape Horn. Malaspina planned to investigate the Sandwich Is [Hawaiian Is], but new orders from Spain redirected his ships to the NORTHWEST COAST. The 1789 NOOTKA SOUND CONTROVERSY with the British and persisting beliefs in the existence of a NORTHWEST PASSAGE led to the side trip.

In search of the fabled STRAIT OF ANIAN, Malaspina sailed to 59° N lat. On 27 June 1791 the corvettes entered Mulgrave Sound (Yacutat Bay, Alaska). Reconnaissance dashed hopes that a Northwest Passage was accessible by this route, but the scientists collected samples and studied Tlingit culture. Malaspina coasted farther W along the Alaskan shore before heading S to Nootka Sound, arriving 12 Aug 1791.

Returning to Mexico, Malaspina made recommendations which led to the 1792 voyage of the SUTIL AND MEXICANA. He visited the Marianas, the Philippines, New Zealand and Australia before returning via S America to Spain 1791-94. Although the expedition was highly successful, court intrigue soon destroyed his career and prevented publication of his reports; the account did not reach print until 1885. *See also* SPANISH EXPLORATION. CHRISTON I. ARCHER

Reading: Iris H.W. Engstrand, *Spanish Scientists in the New World* (1981).

Malaysians Malaysia was constituted in 1963 out of the Federation of Malaya and the former British colonies of Singapore (until 1965), Sarawak and North Borneo (Sabah). The population of Malaysia includes the Malays (about 46%), Chinese (about 35%) and Indians (about 9%). The term "Canadian Malaysian" therefore does not indicate membership of a discrete ethnic, linguistic or religious community, but simply a shared experience of national origin.

Migration and Settlement Between 1973 and 1984, 6872 Malaysians immigrated to Canada. In 1984, of the 356 arrivals, 172 planned to reside in Ontario; 99 in BC; 44 in Alberta; 12 in Manitoba; 10 in Québec; 6 each in Saskatchewan and NB; 4 in NS; and 3 in Newfoundland. The largest single occupational group was clerical, followed by fabricating, assembling and repairing; science, engineering and math; medicine and health; managerial or administrative; service; entrepreneurial; sales; and construction.

Group Maintenance Although Malaysians do not belong to a single ethnic community, there is a sense of cultural identity (shared to a considerable extent with Singaporeans), which results from the fusion in the Malay world, over many centuries, of influences from China and India. It is this sense of common background that distinguishes Canadian Malaysians from other Asian communities in Canada. Community organizations in Toronto and Vancouver and Malaysian student associations on several university campuses encourage an awareness of aspects of Malaysian cultural traditions. Since English is one of the languages widely used in Malaysia, assimilation of immigrants appears most likely to occur in anglophone Canada. H.E. WILSON

Maliseet (Malecite) have long been associated with the SAINT JOHN R in NB and Maine, and early extended as far as the St Lawrence. These Algonkian (Algonquian) speakers referred to themselves as *Welustuk* ("of the beautiful river"). Their lands and resources are bounded on the E by MICMAC, on the W by Passamaquoddy and Penobscot. Local histories depict many encounters with IROQUOIS and MONTAGNAIS. Contact with European fisher-traders in the early 17th century and with specialized fur traders developed into a stable relationship which lasted for nearly 100 years. Despite devastating population losses to European diseases, these Atlantic hunters held on to coastal or river locations for hunting, fishing and gathering, and concentrated along river valleys for trapping.

With the general unrest as European hostilities concentrated between Québec and PORT-ROYAL, and as increasing sporadic fighting and raiding took place on the lower Saint John (English against the French), the eastern fur trade faltered. Maliseet women took over a larger share of the economic burden and began to farm, raising native crops which previously had been grown only S of Maliseet territory. Men continued to hunt, though with limited success, but they proved useful to the French as support against the English, and for a short period during the late 17th and early 18th centuries Maliseet men became virtually a military organization. With the gradual cessation of hostilities in the first quarter of the 18th century, and with the beaver supply severely diminished, there was little possibility of a return to traditional lifeways. Native agriculture on the river was curtailed by the coming of white settlers; all the farmland along the Saint John R, previously occupied by Maliseet, was taken, leaving the native peoples virtually displaced persons. With evidence of widespread hunger and wandering, pressure came to bear on government officials who established the first INDIAN RESERVES during the 19th century, at Oromocto, Fredericton, Kingsclear, Woodstock and Tobique.

As late as the 19th century, the Maliseet practised some traditional crafts, especially building WIGWAMS and birchbark CANOES, but major shifts had taken place during the previous 2 centuries as Maliseet acquired European cutting tools and containers, muskets and alcohol, foods and clothing. In making wood, bark or basketry items, or in guiding, trapping and hunting, the Maliseet speak of themselves as engaged in "Indian work." The growth of potato farming in Maine and NB created a market for Maliseet baskets and containers. Other Maliseet work in pulp mills, construction, nursing, teaching and business.

The Maliseet of NB experience problems of unemployment and poverty common to native people elsewhere in Canada, but they have evolved a sophisticated and intricate system of decision making and resource allocation, especially at Tobique where they support community enterprises in economic development, scouting and sports. Some are successful in middle and higher education and have important trade and professional standings; individuals and families are prominent in native and women's rights; and others serve in provincial and federal native organizations, in government and in community development. *See also* NATIVE PEOPLE: EASTERN WOODLANDS and general articles under NATIVE PEOPLE. TOM MCFEAT

Reading: A.G. Bailey, *The Conflict of European and Eastern Algonkian Cultures, 1504-1700* (2nd ed, 1969); H.F. McGee, ed, *The Native Peoples of Atlantic Canada* (1984); W. Mechling, *Malecite Tales* (1914); W.D. and R.S. Wallace, *The Malecite Indians of New Brunswick* (1957).

Malloch, Archibald Edward, surgeon (b at Brockville, Canada W 14 June 1844; d at Hamilton, Ont 6 Aug 1919). Educated at Queen's and at U of Glasgow, where he graduated in 1867, he served as house surgeon for Joseph Lister when the latter was beginning to publish accounts of antiseptic surgery. He became a firm believer in the method and, after his return to Canada in 1869, was likely the first in the country to use it in its fully developed form. A skilful surgeon, he was not prominent outside medicine, nor was he active in medical circles outside his practice in Hamilton. His only formal relationship with a medical school – as professor of anatomy at Victoria College, Toronto – lasted less than 2 years. He was not as vociferous an advocate of antiseptic surgery as he might have been. By the 1890s, however, most Canadian surgeons were using antisepsis or its successor asepsis.
CHARLES G. ROLAND

Malone, Maurice Joseph, hockey player (b at Sillery, Qué 28 Feb 1890; d at Montréal 15 May 1969). He turned professional with Québec Bulldogs in 1909, playing 7 years with them, 4 with MONTREAL CANADIENS and 2 with Hamilton Tigers. Some of his scoring feats have never been matched. He once scored 9 goals in a game, but it was his 7 goals on 31 Jan 1920 that was still the NHL record in 1988. He scored 142 goals in 125 NHL games; a total of 338 goals in 271 professional games. JAMES MARSH

Malpeque, PEI, UP, pop 157 (1986c), 160 (1981c), is a compact, attractive village located on the northeastern shore of MALPEQUE BAY, 60 km NW of Charlottetown. First called *makpaak* ("the big water") by the Micmac, the current name is an Acadian modification. When Samuel HOLLAND surveyed the Island after the British Conquest of New France, he believed that through the bay's excellent anchorage a major colonial seaport would develop in the area. Thus, he founded there the capital of Prince County. However, the development of the Malpeque Bay area was cut short by sandbars at the bay's entrance that discouraged shipping. Because of the navigability of Bedeque Bay on the county's southern shore, Malpeque was eventually displaced as the capital by SUMMERSIDE. Today, most of the residents of Malpeque are farmers and fishermen, and oysters are the area's most important product.
W.S. KEIZER

Malpeque Bay is a picturesque bay so deeply indented into the NE coast of PEI that its southern edge lies within 7 km of the S coast of the Island. Aptly named from the Micmac word *makpaak,* (ie, "the big water"), it contains several islands and many small rivers and creeks flow into it. Its waters support a thriving shellfish industry, most notably its world-famous cultivated oysters. These are grown on "farms," where the young seed oysters are sown and later harvested from the mud on the bottom of the bay with long-handled, rake-ended tongs that are worked like scissors. P.C. SMITH

Malpractice is intentional or negligent failure by any professional, eg, doctor, lawyer, accountant, to meet the standards of reasonable competence in his field. These standards are set taking into account the circumstances in which the professional is acting. Specialists must meet the higher standards of a reasonably competent specialist; beginners must meet ordinary standards, inexperience being no excuse. Professionals are expected to keep up to date and to act only within the sphere of their own competence, and those acting otherwise will be judged according to the standards of practitioners by whom the task should have been undertaken. Québec's Civil Code contains a standard similar to that existing in the common law of TORT which, with the law of contract, governs malpractice in the other provinces. The damages awarded in malpractice suits vary enormously, depending on the loss to the plaintiff. Generally, they are much higher in the US than in Canada. MARGARET SOMERVILLE

Maltese There are over 50 000 people of Maltese origin in Canada, most of whom emigrated after WWII from the islands of Malta (pop 315 000) and Gozo, which are situated in the Mediterranean, S of Sicily. Maltese trace their ethnic and linguistic origins to the Phoenicians. In 58 AD, when the Apostle Paul was shipwrecked on Malta, they were converted to Christianity. The Maltese, who speak a Semitic tongue, celebrate their national day on March 31. In Canada the Maltese settled first in Ontario; although significant immigration occurred in 1840, around 1907, and between 1918 and 1920, there were few Maltese in Canada until after WWII. Between 1946 and 1981 over 18 000 came to Canada and between

1982-84, 279. Preliminary figures from the 1986 census estimated 15 345 Maltese Canadians. Toronto has the largest Maltese community (some 25 000) with a heavy concentration around Dundas St W, where the Maltese Franciscan fathers have built a church. Maltese clubs and societies are located in this area. Other Maltese communities are found in Ontario and in Montréal, Winnipeg and Vancouver. GEORGE BONAVIA

Mammal The word mammal is derived from the milk-producing mammary glands that are unique to the class Mammalia. Mammals, including man, are generally regarded as the most evolved or advanced of the vertebrates (animals with a backbone and spinal cord). Some of the typical diagnostic features of mammals may be shared with other vertebrates or be absent in some groups, as defined in the following list of characteristics: 1) mammary glands which produce milk for nourishing the young; 2) all give birth to living young, except the order Monotremata (eg, duck-billed platypus) which is egg laying; 3) endothermic (warm blooded, shared with birds) – the ability to maintain a constant body temperature; 4) a body covering of hair (unique to mammals, but reduced in some forms) or a subcutaneous layer of blubber (in whales where hair is extremely reduced or absent in adults); 5) sweat glands in the skin aid in heat loss; 6) lower jaws of only one bone on each side which articulates directly with the cranium; 7) 3 middle earbones; 8) a large complex brain allowing for learning and quick reactions and flexible behaviour; 9) 4-chambered heart which provides for a closed circulation of non-nucleated blood cells; 10) teeth that are typically differentiated into incisors, canines, premolars and molars; 11) the vertebral column has vertebrae differentiated into cervical (usually 7), thoracic, lumbar, sacral and caudal (tail).

Most mammals are typically quadrupeds with the feet modified in many ways for terrestrial (running, hopping or leaping), fossorial (digging), arboreal (tree climbing) and aquatic living, but some have developed modified appendages such as the whales, manatees and dugongs who have lost the rear appendages, modified the tail as horizontally flattened flukes for propulsion and modified the front appendages as flippers. Bats have modified the front limbs as wings, and are the only mammals capable of true flight. In size, mammals range from some tiny shrews and bats that weight little more than a 10-cent piece to the giant blue whales which measure over 35 m and weigh more than 100 tonnes – the largest animals that have ever lived.

Origin and Evolution Modern or living mammals represent only a surviving fraction of the great number that evolved since the transition from mammal-like reptiles at about the end of the Triassic period some 208 million years ago. Mammals are thought to have evolved from a group of mammal-like REPTILES (subclass Synapsida) which dominated the vertebrate fauna during the Permian period beginning 286 million years ago, long before the first DINOSAURS appeared. Among the order Therapsida were a number of different mammal-like reptiles that developed one or more characteristics typical of mammals.

The earliest known true mammals date from the middle or late Jurassic (187-144 million years ago) and all were quite small. Even though dinosaurs and other reptiles dominated the Earth for over 100 million years, mammals persisted as small, inconspicuous and perhaps nocturnal creatures before they finally became dominant when the dinosaurs became extinct (97.5-66.4 million years ago). By the late Cretaceous the stage was set for the evolution of a wide diversity of mammals, some to become extinct and some to survive until today. Beginning in the Cenozoic (66.4 million years ago), the "Age of Mammals" emerged and there was a trend for mammals to adapt to exploit all available "niches" that were open to them. With changing environmental conditions, many species had either to adapt or become extinct.

Ecology The overall success of mammals as a group can be correlated with their ability to adapt to virtually every environment of the Earth. Although most species are terrestrial, some have taken to both the sea and air as well as underground. Only bats developed wings and the ability to fly in competition with birds and succeeded by becoming nocturnal, whereas most birds are diurnal. Whales and sirenians (manatees and dugongs) moved to the seas, whereas others exploited the sea but maintained a terrestrial or ice-flow retreat (primarily for breeding, eg, seals, sea lions, walruses and sea otters). Aquatic environments have been exploited by a number of mammal groups, including platypuses, insectivores, carnivores, rodents and hippopotamuses. Some species became arboreal, spending much of their time in the tree tops, as typified by some marsupials, dermopterids (flying lemurs), sloths, various primates, carnivores, rodents and others. From this arboreal home, some species developed the ability to glide considerable distances by means of an extension of skin between the hind and front limbs. Included here are marsupials (sugar gliders), dermopterids (flying lemurs) and rodents (flying squirrels).

Other species retreated underground to become fossorial, including insectivores (moles) and rodents (pocket gophers and many others), and to use underground burrows as homes as has been done by a wide variety of species. Other terrestrial environments such as deserts, tundras, prairies, marshes and forests have been utilized by a wide array of mammal species. Mammals have become adapted to a wide variety of food resources, basically divided into plant and animal. Plant feeders include both grazers (grasses and herbs) and browsers (trees and shrubs) as well as certain types of aquatic plants and nectar and pollen of flowers. Animal feeders utilize insects and other invertebrates (insectivores), fish, birds and their eggs as well as amphibians, reptiles and other mammals.

Intertwined in this matrix of ecological adaptations are competition with other species for space, food and a place to reproduce and the predator-prey relationship, as well as parasites and diseases. Human occupiers of many environments have imposed many special conditions which have affected the survival of many mammal species. Some have been extirpated, become rare, ENDANGERED or extinct while a few have managed to adapt to co-habitation with man.

Relation to Man The interrelations of man and other mammals had their beginning with common prehuman ancestors in the early evolution of mammals. While man tends to set himself apart from other mammals, there are many ways in which mammals have played a vital role in the history and development of human civilization unrelated to the evolution of *homo sapiens*. From prehistoric times, mammal flesh has been an important source of man's food. Hides and fur have provided clothing, and bones have been used to fashion tools. Blubber and fat were used for food and fuel (and still are by Inuit). Mammals were domesticated long before the dawn of written history, perhaps over 9000 years ago. There is evidence that dogs were kept by the inhabitants of what is now Denmark about 6000 years ago, and of Jericho about 6800 years ago; the Chinese are thought to have started swine husbandry more than 5000 years ago, and the Egyptians kept cats prior to 2100 BC. Mammals have been used as guardians and as aids in hunting and killing other forms of life, as beasts of burden, as draft animals and in warfare. Some species even assumed a holy role and were worshipped or were assumed to be sacred. With the advance of civilization, mammal products became prime articles of commerce and played a major role in man's exploration and settlement of new lands. Early land transportation was almost wholly dependent on horses, cattle and camels. The early development of agriculture was built around mammals for draft animals and animal husbandry in many forms. They now include milk, cheese, butter, fat, oils, blood products, felt, leather products, wool, bristles, ivory, wax, whalebone and fertilizers.

Some mammals play an increasingly important role in the search for knowledge by which man may better understand himself. Mammals have been used in various experiments to help shed light on the psychology of human behaviour. Surgery and most forms of medical research have been advanced immeasurably by the use of laboratory mammals. Mammals and mammal products are used in the development and production of serums, vaccines, hormones and other biological products such as insulin, that are now used in modern medicine. As specimens for dissection, mammals are indispensable in training science students – particularly in medicine and other branches of biology. Mammals are also fundamentally involved in research in many divisions of the biological sciences.

However, not all of man's relations with other mammals have been beneficial. The fear of actually being killed and eaten by them was very real to early man. There have always been species which plagued man by consuming or damaging his stores of food, his crops, his livestock or his equipment. Some species became carriers of infectious diseases or parasites which were transmitted either to him or to his livestock; some competed with domesticated livestock for grass.

Native mammals are an integral part of the renewable natural resources – soil, water, forest and wildlife – and sound conservation of any one of these resources calls for some understanding and appreciation of the interrelations of the multitude of facets of the total environment. A major disturbance of the equilibrium within an environment has many far-reaching and complex results. For example, when man introduced domestic cattle, sheep or goats to an area and attempted to eliminate native grass-eating ungulates such as bison, pronghorn, deer or wapiti (to reduce the competition for food), he found that native carnivores began to prey on his livestock instead. When he attempted to eliminate these predators he found his land plagued with rabbits and rodents which provided just as much competition for the vegetation needed as food for the livestock as did the original native ungulates. Viewed in relation to man's own interest, no species of mammal is entirely beneficial or entirely detrimental.

Each species attains a state of harmony with its environment through gradual adaptations, modifications and evolution, and must adapt to continual changes. Now that man has become capable of making profound and rapid alterations in the environment, the future survival of most species is becoming more and more dependent upon his actions.

Major Groups of Mammals in Canada (excluding humans)
Numbers refer to native species

Order	Family	Examples
Marsupialia	Didelphidae(1)	opossum
Insectivora	Soricidae(16)	shrews
	Talpidae(6)	moles
Chiroptera	Molossidae(1)	free-tailed bat
	Vespertilionidae(*c* 18)	common bats
Carnivora	Canidae(6)	dog, wolf, fox
	Felidae(3)	cats
	Mustelidae (*c* 14)	weasel, skunk, otter, wolverine
	Odobenidae(1)	walrus
	Otariidae(3)	eared seals
	Phocidae(*c* 7)	hair seals
	Procyonidae(1)	raccoon
	Ursidae(3)	bears
Cetacea:		
Odontoceti	Delphinidae(*c* 11)	dolphins
	Monodontidae(2)	white whale, narwhal
	Phocoenidae(2)	porpoises
	Physeteridae(2)	sperm whales
	Ziphiidae(*c* 8)	beaked whales
Mysticeti	Balaenidae(2)	right or baleen whales
	Balaenopteridae(5)	fin whales
	Eschrichtiidae(1)	grey whale
Perissodactyla	Equidae*	horse
Artiodactyla	Antilocapridae(1)	pronghorn
	Bovidae(5)	bison, sheep, muskox, goat
	Cervidae(5)	moose, deer, caribou
	Suidae*	hog
Rodentia	Aplodontidae(1)	mountain beaver
	Arvicolidae(*c* 23)	muskrat, vole, lemming
	Capromyidae*	nutria or coypu
	Castoridae(1)	beaver
	Cricetidae(*c* 7)	native mice
	Dipodidae(4)	jumping mice
	Erethizontidae(1)	porcupine
	Geomyidae(2)	pocket gophers
	Heteromyidae(3)	pocket mice, kangaroo rats
	Muridae*	Old World mice and rats
	Sciuridae(*c* 22)	squirrel, marmot
Lagomorpha	Leporidae(2)	hare, rabbit
	Ochotonidae(5)	pika

*Introduced or domesticated

While the vital role that mammals have played in man's past and their many contributions to his present well-being leave no doubt of their basic importance and economic worth, mammals should also be considered in a cultural or aesthetic context. They have played a part in the history of religion, art, mythology and literature. A person who observes mammals in their native habitat even casually cannot help but be attracted to them in one way or another. He may be fascinated by their activities, enthralled by their beauty of form and the speed, power, agility and grace of movement, envious of their apparent sense of purpose and self-sufficiency, curious about their adaptations for survival or their vocal sounds and other means of communication.

Mammalian Fauna of Canada Although Canada has a rich and diverse mammalian fauna, very few species are uniquely Canadian, as our known fauna is shared with Greenland, Alaska and the northern US. A few exceptions are the Vancouver Island marmot, Gaspé shrew and Ungava lemming. Of the N American terrestrial mammal fauna, many reach their northern limits of distribution somewhere in Canada. Our marine and arctic mammals tend to consist of northern circumpolar species. There has been an interchange of species with the Old World across the Bering Strait which includes caribou (reindeer), wapiti, moose, bears, weasels, walruses, various rodents and others. Other species have made their way to Canada from the neotropics. These include the opossum, raccoon and porcupine. One of the truly endemic species of N America is the pronghorn antelope, found in the plains of Canada and the US. The fur-bearing mammals figured prominently in the early years of exploration and settlement of Canada and have been an economically important resource throughout the years (*see*, for example, FUR TRADE).

Compared with most nations of the world, Canada is particularly fortunate in still having substantial wilderness areas which provide suitable habitat for many mammals and therefore has fewer rare or endangered species than most. As lands are being more and more exploited by ever increasing human populations, the safeguarding of our native mammalian fauna through wise conservation becomes increasingly important and critical. *See also* entries on individual species.

R.L. PETERSON

Reading: A.W.F. Banfield, *The Mammals of Canada* (1977).

Mance, Jeanne, founder of the HÔTEL-DIEU hospital at Montréal (bap at Langres, France 12 Nov 1606; d at Montréal 18 June 1673). When young and unusually interested in foreign missions, Jeanne Mance was introduced to Mme de Bullion (who dedicated a small fortune to establishing a hospital at Montréal) and to the Société Notre-Dame de Montréal and its associates. Mance joined the association, which planned a utopian settlement on Montréal I, and sailed in 1641 with MAISONNEUVE and the first settlers for VILLE-MARIE, spending her first winter at the Sillery reserve. The hospital was not completed until 1645 but there were patients from 1642. She returned to France in 1645 to make new financial arrangements and again in 1657 after losing the use of an arm as a result of a fall. She claimed that the application of a relic of the Sulpician founder healed her so she was able to return to Montréal, bringing the Hospitallers from La Flèche to staff her hospital.

CORNELIUS J. JAENEN

Mandel, Eli, author (b at Estevan, Sask 3 Dec 1922). The son of Russian Jewish immigrants, he was raised on the Prairies during the Depression, an experience that left its mark on his poetry. Mandel has taught English and creative writing at the universities of Alberta, Victoria, Toronto and York. He is the author of 8 books of poetry including *Fuseli Poems* (1960), *Black and Secret Man* (1964), *Out of Place* (1977) and *Dreaming Backwards* (1981). His third book of poetry, *An Idiot Joy* (1967) shared a 1968 Gov Gen's Award. The title, which comes from Saul Bellow's *Herzog*, sums up Mandel's attitude to the craft of writing: his role as obsessive namer, capturing his own life experience in language. Mandel has edited 5 anthologies of poetry and in 1987 published a volume of literary criticism, *The Family Romance*.

SHARON DRACHE

Mandel, Miriam, née Minovitch, poet (b at Rockglen, Sask 1930; d at Edmonton 13 Feb 1982). An English graduate from the U of Saskatchewan, Mandel began writing poetry in her late 30s, shortly after her 20-year marriage with author Eli MANDEL dissolved. She long suffered from manic depression, which plagued her until her death by suicide. Mandel's poetry explores her personal suffering with courage and honesty. Her first collection, *Lions at her Face* (1973), won the Gov Gen's Award. It was followed by 2 other collections. Sheila Watson paid posthumous tribute to Mandel by editing her work in *Collected Poems of Miriam Mandel* (1984).

MARLENE ALT

Manery, Jeanne Fisher, biochemist (b at Chesley, Ont 6 July 1908; d at Toronto 9 Sept 1986). She was educated at U of T, did postdoctoral studies at the universities of Rochester and Harvard, and taught part time at U of T from 1932 to 1948, becoming full time in 1953 and full professor in 1965; she retired in 1976 but remained active in teaching, research, publishing and administration. An expert in the physiology of transport into and out of cells of water and the ions essential for many cellular functions, especially the generation of energy, Manery succeeded in isolating and characterizing the enzyme of the cellular membrane which catalyses cation transport, work described in numerous scientific papers in journals and monographs. Manery's honours in recognition of her scientific accomplishments included an honorary doctorate (1983) from Memorial U. Her scientific work and her feminist endeavours brought women a new status in her field.

ROSE SHEININ

Manicouagan Réservoir, 1942 km², elev 360 m, located in southeastern Québec about 140 km from the Labrador border, is the second-largest lake in Québec and was created by a meteorite millions of years ago. The circular-shaped reservoir contains a centrally situated island, capped by 952 m Mont de Babel. Fed by the Rivières Hart Jaune and Mouchalagane, it drains S, via the Rivière MANICOUAGAN, and empties into the St Lawrence R near BAIE-COMEAU. Hydroelectric developments have resulted in the damming of the water flow at the 214 m high Daniel Johnson (Manic 5) Dam, one of the world's largest, situated 40 km S of the reservoir (1968). The availability of power has attracted several industries over the years, yet the area still retains its attraction for canoeists, fishermen and wildlife enthusiasts. Its name is possibly of Cree origin and might mean "where there is bark" (for canoe making). It could also be a French form of *Manicouaganistiku*, meaning "drinking place." The lake appears on Jonathan Carver's map of Québec (1776) as Lk Asturagamicook, and is shown to be drained by the Manicouagan or Black R.

DAVID EVANS

Manicouagan River, 455 km long, rises in E-central Québec near the Labrador border and flows S to the ST LAWRENCE R near BAIE-COMEAU. It drains a rugged, heavily forested watershed of 45 900 km², and has been an important artery for moving logs S to supply pulp and paper mills at its mouth. Several hydroelectric power plants (Manic 1 completed 1967, 184.4 MW; Manic 2

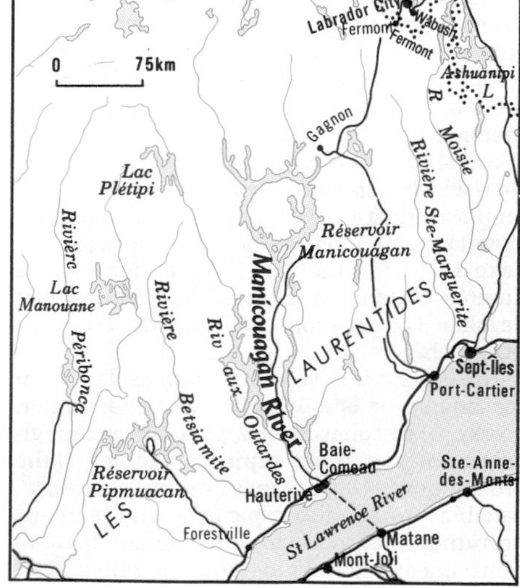

completed 1967, 1015.2 MW; Manic 3 completed 1976, 1183.2 MW; and Manic 5 completed 1971, 1292 MW) have harnessed the river's power, some of which is carried under the St Lawrence by a submarine cable to the Gaspé area. Iron ore is mined in the river's upper reaches. The name may come from an Indian word meaning "where there is bark" (ie, for making canoes).

DANIEL FRANCIS

Manion, Robert James, politician, physician (b at Pembroke, Ont 19 Nov 1881; d at Ottawa 2 July 1943). After receiving a medical degree at Trinity College (Toronto) in 1904, Manion continued training in Edinburgh until 1906, then returned to Fort William, Ont, where he was elected alderman 1913-14. He became military surgeon with French forces during the WWI, later joined the 21st Canadian Battalion and was decorated for heroism at VIMY RIDGE. He was elected MP for Fort William in 1917 as a Liberal-Unionist, and re-elected as a Conservative in every general election until 1935 when he lost the seat. His longest Cabinet posting was as minister of railways and Canals, 1930-35, under PM R.B. Bennett. In July 1938 he was elected leader of the Conservative Party in the hope his Roman Catholicism and French Canadian marriage would win Québec votes. Manion won a by-election in London later that year and opposed CONSCRIPTION after WWII broke out. The defeat of Prem Duplessis in Oct 1939 deprived Manion of an effective entrée in Québec. This, combined with hostility from hard-line Toronto Tories over his nonconscription policy, contributed to the party's poor showing in the Mar 1940 election. He lost his own seat and resigned his party leadership in May of that year.

DEAN BEEBY

Manitoba is the "keystone" province located in the heart of Canada. Created by the Manitoba Act of 1870, the province was at first a tiny rectangle comprising little more than the RED RIVER COLONY radiating from the juncture of the Red and Assiniboine rivers. After lengthy and often difficult provincial-federal negotiations the boundaries were extended in 1881 and 1884. In 1912 they were finally set at 49° to 60° N and 101°30′-102° W to 95° W, angling NE at about 53° N on the E boundary. For 200 years the FUR TRADE dominated the area known as Rupert's Land. Settlement, particularly from eastern Canada and eastern Europe, eventually created a sound agricultural tradition. Postwar political and economic efforts have enabled the economy to diversify industry and develop primary resources, while maintaining agricultural strength.

Land and Resources

The regions of Manitoba are derived chiefly from its landforms. Since the final retreat of the continental ice sheet some 8000 years ago, many physical forces have shaped its surface into 4 major physiographic regions: Hudson Bay Lowland, Precambrian Upland, Lake Agassiz Lowland and Western Upland. Manitoba provides a corridor for the Red, Assiniboine, Saskatchewan, Nelson and Churchill rivers. Three large lakes, Winnipeg, Winnipegosis and Manitoba, cover much of the Lake Agassiz Lowland. They are the remnants of Lake AGASSIZ, which occupied S-central Manitoba during the last ice age. The prolonged duration of this immense lake accounts for the remarkable flatness of one-fifth of the province, as 18-30 m of sediments were laid on the flat, preglacial surface. Antecedent streams, such as the Assiniboine, Valley and Swan rivers, carved the SW part of the province (Western Upland) into low plateaus of variable relief, which with the Agassiz Lowland provide most of Manitoba's arable land. The Precambrian Upland is composed of hard granite and other crystalline rocks that were subject to severe glacial scouring during the Ice Age; its thin soil, rock outcrop and myriad lakes in rock basins are inhospitable to agriculture but are amenable to hydroelectric-power sites, freshwater fishing, metal mines and some forestry. Flat sedimentary rocks underlie the Hudson Bay Lowland, and the climate is extremely cold. Little development or settlement exists other than at CHURCHILL, Manitoba's only saltwater port. A line drawn from SE Manitoba to Flin Flon on the W boundary separates the arable and well-populated section to the S and W from the sparsely inhabited wilderness to the N and E. The latter comprises about two-thirds of the area of the province.

Geology The bedrock underlying the province varies from ancient Precambrian (Archean) to young sedimentary rocks of Tertiary age. The former has been identified as 2.7 billion years old, among the oldest on Earth, and forms part of the Canadian Shield, a U-shaped band of Precambrian rocks tributary to Hudson Bay. It consists principally of granites and granite gneisses in contact with volcanic rocks and ancient, metamorphosed sedimentary rocks. Contact zones often contain valuable minerals, including nickel, lead, zinc, copper, gold and silver – all of which are mined in Manitoba. Along the flanks of and overlying the ancient Precambrian rocks are sedimentary rocks ranging from Paleozoic to Tertiary age. Lake Agassiz Lowland comprises a surface cover of lacustrine sediments superimposed on early Paleozoic rocks of Ordovician, Silurian and Devonian age, from which are mined construction limestone, gypsum, clay, bentonite, sand and gravel. In favourable structures petroleum has also been recovered from rocks of Mississippian age.

West of Agassiz Lowland rises an escarpment of Cretaceous rocks, which comprise the surface formations of the Western Upland. For long periods the escarpment was the W bank of glacial Lk Agassiz. East-flowing rivers such as the Assiniboine, the Valley and the Swan once carried the meltwaters of retreating glaciers, eroding deep valleys (spillways) that opened into this lake. The former lake bottom and the former valleys of tributary streams were veneered with silts and clays, which today constitute the most fertile land in western Canada. Both the Western Upland and the bed of Lk Agassiz comprise the finest farmlands of Manitoba. In the SW the geologic structures of the Williston Basin in N Dakota extend into Manitoba and yield small amounts of petroleum. A vast lowland resting on undisturbed Paleozoic sediments lies between the Precambrian rocks of northern Manitoba and Hudson Bay. Adverse climate, isolation and poorly drained peat bogs make this region unsuitable for agriculture.

Terrain Minor terrain features of Manitoba were formed during the retreat of the Wisconsin Glacier at the close of the last ice age. The rocks of the Shield were severely eroded, leaving a marshy, hummocky surface threaded with a myriad of lakes, streams and bogs. Relief is rolling to hilly. Much of Agassiz Lowland, the largest lacustrine plain in N America (286 000 km^2), is suitable for irrigation. Much is so flat that it requires an extensive drainage system. Its margins are identified by beach ridges. The Western Upland is now covered by glacial drift. Rolling ground moraine broken in places by hilly end moraines has a relief generally favourable to highly productive cultivated land.

Drainage Since southern Manitoba is lower than the regions to the W, E and S, the major rivers of western Canada flow into it. Including their drainage basins, these are the SASKATCHEWAN RIVER (336 000 km^2); the RED and ASSINIBOINE (285 000 km^2) and WINNIPEG rivers (138 000 km^2). Lakes Winnipeg, Manitoba and Winnipegosis receive the combined flow of these basins. In turn the water drains into Hudson Bay via the NELSON R. These together with the CHURCHILL, HAYES and other rivers provide a hydroelectric potential of 9748 MW.

Climate, Vegetation and Soil Situated in the upper middle latitudes (49° N to 60° N) and at the heart of a continental landmass, Manitoba experiences large annual temperature ranges: very cold winters and moderately warm summers. The southward sweep of cold, dry arctic and maritime polar air masses in winter is succeeded by mild, humid maritime tropical air in summer. Nearly two-thirds of the precipitation occurs during the 6 summer months, the remainder appearing mostly as snow. The frost-free period varies greatly according to local conditions, but as a general rule

Manitoba

Capital: Winnipeg
Motto: None
Flower: Prairie crocus
Largest Cities: Winnipeg, Brandon, Thompson, Portage la Prairie, Selkirk
Population: 1 063 016 (1986c); rank fifth, 4.2% of Canada; 72.1% urban; 29.2% rural; 1.9 per km^2 density; 3.6% increase from 1981-86; 5.3% increase from 1976-86
Languages: 71.3% English; 4.3% French; 18.6% Other; 5.8% English plus one or more languages
Entered Confederation: 15 July 1870
Government: Provincial — Lieutenant-Governor, Executive Council, Legislative Assembly of 57 members; federal — 6 senators, 14 members of the House of Commons
Area: 650 087 km^2; including 101 592 km^2 of inland water; 6.5% of Canada
Elevation: Highest point — Baldy Mountain (832 m); lowest point — Hudson Bay shore
Gross Domestic Product: $15.9 billion (1985); $19.9 billion (1986e)
Farm Cash Receipts: $2 billion (1986)
Electric Power Generated: 15 544 GWh (1987)
Sales Tax: 6% (1987)

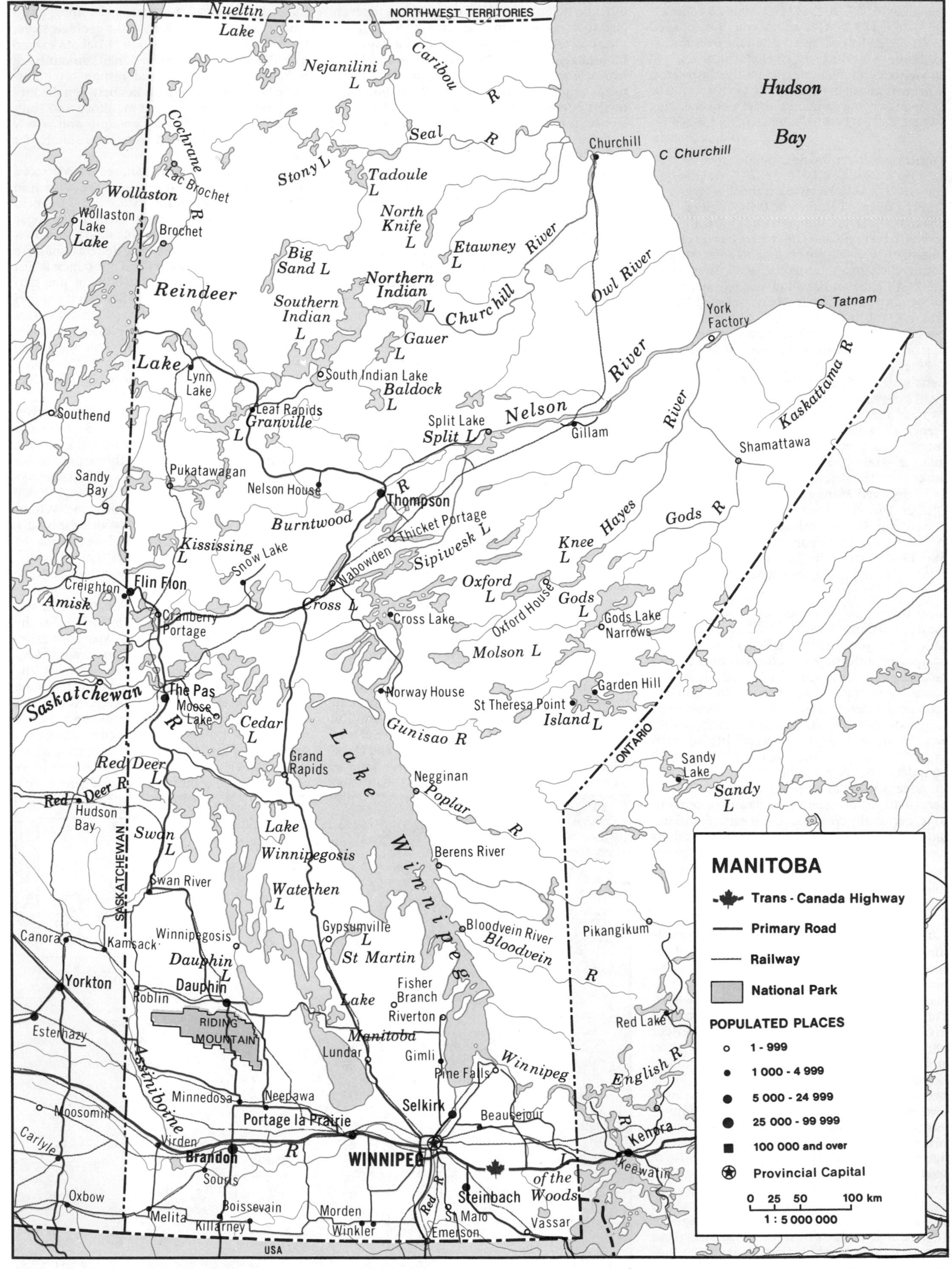
MANITOBA
Trans - Canada Highway
Primary Road
Railway
National Park
POPULATED PLACES
1 - 999
1 000 - 4 999
5 000 - 24 999
25 000 - 99 999
100 000 and over
Provincial Capital
0 25 50 100 km
1 : 5 000 000
NORTHWEST TERRITORIES
Hudson Bay
Churchill
C Churchill
C Tatnam
York Factory
Nueltin Lake
Nejanilini L
Caribou R
Seal R
Cochrane R
Lac Brochet
Brochet
Wollaston Lake
Reindeer Lake
Stony L
Tadoule L
North Knife L
Etawney L
Big Sand L
Northern Indian L
Southern Indian L
Churchill River
Owl River
Gauer L
South Indian Lake
Baldock L
Nelson River
Lynn Lake
Leaf Rapids
Granville L
Southend
Split Lake
Split L
Gillam
Kaskattama R
Hayes River
Shamattawa
Sandy Bay
Pukatawagan
Nelson House
Thompson
Burntwood R
Thicket Portage
Sipiwesk L
Knee L
Gods R
Kississing L
Snow Lake
Wabowden
Oxford L
Oxford House
Gods L
Gods Lake Narrows
Creighton
Flin Flon
Amisk L
Cranberry Portage
Cross L
Cross Lake
Molson L
Saskatchewan R
The Pas
Moose Lake
Norway House
Garden Hill
St Theresa Point
Island L
Cedar L
Gunisao R
ONTARIO
Grand Rapids
Lake Winnipeg
Sandy Lake
Sandy L
Red Deer L
Red Deer R
Hudson Bay
Negginan
Poplar R
Swan L
Lake Winnipegosis
Berens River
SASKATCHEWAN
Swan River
Waterhen L
Canora
Kamsack
Winnipegosis
Gypsumville
Bloodvein River
Bloodvein R
Pikangikum
Dauphin L
St Martin L
Yorkton
Dauphin
Roblin
Fisher Branch
Riverton
RIDING MOUNTAIN
Esterhazy
Lake Manitoba
Red Lake
Lundar
Gimli
Pine Falls
Winnipeg R
English R
Assiniboine R
Minnedosa
Neepawa
Moosomin
Selkirk
Portage la Prairie
Beausejour
Carlyle
Virden
Brandon
WINNIPEG
Kenora
Keewatin
Souris
Red R
Steinbach
Lake of the Woods
Oxbow
Boissevain
Morden
St Malo
Vassar
Melita
Killarney
Winkler
Emerson
USA

Manitoba landscape west of Winnipeg (*photo by J.A. Kraulis*).

the average 100-day frost-free line extends from Flin Flon SE to the corner of the province. Spring comes first to the Red R valley, which has a frost-free period of about 120 days, and spreads to the N and W. As a result, the mean number of growing degree days (above 6°C) varies from 3000 to 2000 within the limits defined. Snowfall tends to be heaviest in the E and diminishes westward. Around Winnipeg the average snowfall is 126 cm per year. Fortunately, 60% of the annual precipitation accompanies the peak growing period for grains: May, June and July. Late Aug and early Sept are dry, favouring the harvest of cereal grains.

Subarctic conditions prevail over N Manitoba. Churchill occupies a position on Hudson Bay where abnormally cold summers are induced by sea temperatures. Manitoba's climate is best understood with reference to air masses. During the winter, low temperatures and humidities are associated with the dominance of cA and cP air. During spring abrupt seasonal changes introduce mT air from the S, which is unstable and warm. The usual sequence of mid-latitude "lows" and "highs" brings frequent daily temperature changes. Some Pacific air moves E, moderating at intervals the extreme cold of winter.

Manitoba's natural vegetation ranges from open grassland and aspen in the S, to mixed forest in the centre, typical boreal forest in the N and bush-tundra by Hudson Bay. In the S high evaporation rates discourage the growth of trees, which are replaced by prairie. Both tall-grass and mixed-grass species were extensive before settlement. Elm, ash and Manitoba maple grow along stream courses, and oak grows on dry sites. With increase in latitude and reduced evaporation, mixed broadleaf forest replaces parkland. The northern half of the province is characteristically boreal forest, consisting of white and black spruce, jack pine, tamarack, aspen and birch. This pattern continues with decreasing density nearly to the shores of Hudson Bay, where the cold summers and short growing period discourage all but stunted growth of mainly spruce and willow and tundra types of moss, lichens and sedges. Spruce, fir and pine are processed for lumber and large pulp mills are found at Pine Falls and The Pas.

In general the province's soil types correlate closely with the distribution of natural vegetation. The following soil descriptions are in order of decreasing agricultural value. The most productive are the black soils (chernozems), corresponding to the once dominant prairie grassland of the Red R valley and SW Manitoba. They differ in texture from fine in the former to medium in the latter. Coarse black soils are found in the old Assiniboine delta and the Souris Valley, the former extending from Portage la Prairie to Brandon. Sand dunes are evident in places. In areas of transition to mixed forest, degraded black soils and grey-wooded soils are common, notably in the area from Minnedosa to Russell S of Riding Mountain. Large areas of the former Lk Agassiz, where drainage is poor, are termed "degraded renzina" because of high lime accumulation. Soils derived from the hard granites and other rocks of the Shield, typically covered with coniferous forest, are described as grey wooded, podsol and peat; they are rated inferior for agriculture.

Resources and Conservation Manitoba's principal resource is fresh water. Of the 10 provinces it ranks third, with 101 592 km² in lakes and rivers, one-sixth its total area. The largest lakes are WINNIPEG (24 400 km²), WINNIPEGOSIS (5370 km²) and MANITOBA (4630 km²). Other freshwater lakes of more than 400 km² are SOUTHERN INDIAN, MOOSE, Cedar, ISLAND, Gods, Cross, Playgreen, Dauphin, Granville, Sipiwesk and Oxford. Principal rivers are the Nelson, which drains Lk Winnipeg, and the Red, Assiniboine, Winnipeg, Churchill and Hayes. Lk Winnipeg is the only body of water used today for commercial transportation, but the Hayes, Nelson, Winnipeg, Red and Assiniboine rivers were important during the fur-trade and early settlement eras. The network of streams and lakes today is a source of developed and potential hydroelectric power; its installed generating capacity is 3644 MW. Possessing 70% of the hydroelectric potential of the Prairie region, Manitoba promises to become the principal contributor to an electric grid that will serve Saskatchewan and Alberta as well as neighbouring states of the US. Flooding along the Red R and its principal tributaries, the Souris and Assiniboine, has affected towns as well as large expanses of agricultural land. Major flood-control programs have been undertaken, beginning with the Red R Floodway and control structures completed in 1968. A 48 km diversion ditch protects Winnipeg from periodic flooding. Upstream from Portage la Prairie a similar diversion was built between the Assiniboine R and Lk Manitoba. Associated control structures include the Shellmouth Dam and Fairford Dam. Towns along the Red R are protected by dikes.

Agricultural land is the province's second major resource, with over 4 million ha in field crops in addition to land used for grazing and wild-hay production. Based on "census value added," agriculture leads by far all other resource industries; mining follows in third place after hydroelectric-power generation. Nickel, copper, zinc and gold account for about two-thirds by value of all minerals produced. The fuels, mainly crude petroleum, are next, followed by cement, sand, gravel and construction stone. Of the nonmetallics, peat and quartz are important.

Most of Manitoba's productive forestland belongs to the Crown. The volume of wood cut averages 1 600 000 m³ annually, from which lumber, plywood, pulp and paper are produced. Manitoba's freshwater lakes yield large quantities of fish; the leading species by value are pickerel, whitefish, perch and sauger. Hunting and trapping support many native people.

Conservation of resources has been directed mainly to wildlife. Fur-bearing animals are protected by quotas, by licensing trappers and allotting traplines. Hunting is restricted by a series of wildlife Acts, which began in 1870. Of 270 kinds of bird common to the province only 12 lack legal protection. In 1961 a system of wildlife management areas was established and now consists of 59 tracts of crown land encompassing 29 540 km² to provide protection and management of game birds and animals. Since Manitoba is on the staging route of the North American Flyway, many migratory birds use the protected areas. Hunting of all species of game is totally restricted or closely managed in management areas, including the shoreline of Hudson Bay, a natural breeding ground for POLAR BEARS. Hunting and fishing are also closely controlled in provincial parks and forest reserves. Forest conservation is limited to fire protection, insect control, controlled cutting and reforestation programs. Surveillance of 332 553 km² of forestland by aircraft and from numerous widely dispersed fire towers reduces significantly the incidence and spread of forest fires. Insects and disease are controlled by aerial spraying, tree removal and regulated burning. Among the more virulent pests are jack pine budworm, spruce budworm, aspen tortrix, forest tent caterpillar and birch beetle. Winnipeg is fighting desperately to contain dutch elm disease. In 1985, more than 10 million seedlings, mainly jack pine, red pine and white spruce, were planted for REFORESTATION on 14 569 ha. To ensure future supplies of commercial timber, operators must make annual cuttings by management units on a sustained yield basis.

Since southern Manitoba is lower than regions to the W, E and S, the major rivers of western Canada flow into it towards Hudson Bay. Shown here are the Kettle Rapids on the turbulent Nelson R, one of the province's many sources of hydroelectric power (*photo by Richard Vroom*).

People

Between 1682, when YORK FACTORY at the mouth of the Hayes R was established, and 1812, when the first Selkirk settlers came to Red R, settlement consisted of fur-trading posts established by the HUDSON'S BAY CO, the NORTH WEST CO and numerous independent traders. As agriculture spread along the banks of the Red and Assiniboine rivers, radiating from their junction, the Red R Colony was formed. In 1870 the British government paid the HBC $1.5 million for control of the vast territory of RUPERT'S LAND and opened the way for the newly formed Dominion of Canada to create the first of 3 Prairie provinces. Manitoba in 1870 was little larger than the Red R valley, but by 1912 its current boundaries were set. Settlement of the new province followed the Dominion Lands Survey and the projected route of the national railway. The lands of the original province of Manitoba were granted to settlers in quarter-section parcels for homesteading purposes under the Dominion Lands Act of 1872. The remainder of what is now Manitoba was still the North-West Territories at the time. After 1878 settlers could obtain grants of quarter-section parcels of land in those areas provided they managed to improve the land. By 1910 most of S Manitoba and the Interlake and Westlake areas were settled. Railway branch lines brought most settlers within 48 km (30 mi) of a loading point from which grain could be shipped to world markets. Rural population peaked in 1941, followed by a steady decline resulting from consolidation of small holdings into larger farm units, retreat from the submarginal lands of the frontier because of long, cold winters and poor soils, and the attraction of the larger cities, especially Winnipeg. Overpopulation of submarginal lands in the Interlake and the Westlake districts and along the contact zone with the Shield in the SE caused a substantial shift from the farm to the city. Hamlets and small towns have shrunk or disappeared; large supply centres are more easily reached with modern motor vehicles, and children are bused to schools in larger towns and cities. Elimination of uneconomic railway branch lines also has left many communities without services.

Manitoba's population is disproportionately distributed between the "North" and the "South." A line drawn from lat 54° N (N of The Pas) to the SE corner of the province sharply divides the continuous settled area, containing 95% of the people, from the sparsely populated N. Settlement of the N is confined to isolated fishing stations and mining towns, scattered Indian reserves and Churchill, a far N transshipment centre on the shores of Hudson Bay.

Urban Centres Until 1941 the rural population component exceeded the urban. The rural population subsequently declined in absolute and relative terms until today it is 29.2% of the total. "Rural" includes farm and nonfarm residents and people living in towns and hamlets that have populations under 1000. Centres designated as "urban" (more than 1000) now comprise 72.1% of the total. More than half of the urban total live in Winnipeg, which together with its satellite, Selkirk, accounts for about 60% of the provincial total. WINNIPEG began in the shadow of Upper Fort Garry. In the 1860s free traders, in defiance of the HBC monopoly, located there and competed for furs. After 1870 the tiny village rapidly became a commercial centre for the Red R Colony. Located at "the forks" of the Red and Assiniboine rivers, it commanded water and land travel from the W, S and N and became the northern terminus of the railway from St Paul, Minn, in 1878. Following the decision to have the CANADIAN PACIFIC RAILWAY cross the Red R at Winnipeg (1881), the centre became the apex of a triangular network of rail lines that drew commerce from Alberta eastward, and it eventually became a crossroads for E-W air traffic. Since WWII Winnipeg has experienced modest growth and commercial consolidation in a reduced hinterland. It is the provincial centre of the arts, education, commerce, finance, transportation and government.

Although Winnipeg's pre-eminence is unchallenged, certain urban centres dominate local trading areas. BRANDON, Manitoba's second city, is a distribution and manufacturing centre for the SW, as is the smaller PORTAGE LA PRAIRIE, set in the Portage Plains, one of the richest agricultural tracts in the province. In the N, Thompson and Flin Flon service the mining industry. The major towns of Selkirk, Dauphin and The Pas were founded as fur-trading forts and today serve as distribution centres for their surrounding communities. Lynn Lake, Leaf Rapids and Bissett are small northern mining centres. A network of smaller towns in SW Manitoba fits the "central place theory" modified by the linear pattern of rail lines emanating from Winnipeg. Grain elevators approximately every 48 km (30 mi) became the nuclei of hamlets and towns. Eventually, with the advent of motor transport, branch lines were eliminated and with them many place-names that once stood for thriving communities. The present pattern is a hierarchy of central places, from hamlets to regional centres, competing to supply a dwindling farm population.

Demographic Trends and Labour Force Since 1961 Manitoba's population growth has been slow but steady, rising from 921 686 in 1961 to 1 063 016 in 1986, despite a fairly constant amount of natural increase, about 8000 per year. The significant factor in population growth during this period has been migration. During periods of economic health Manitobans have been less likely to move away and in fact often return home from other provinces. When the economy is in decline, Manitobans tend to migrate, primarily to Ontario and the other western provinces. These cyclical periods, normally 3 to 5 years, either negated or enhanced the natural population growth so the population has experienced short periods of growth followed by short periods of decline, resulting in very slow overall population growth.

The labour participation rate is higher for men than women although the figure for women increased steadily in the years 1977 to 1987, as a reflection of an increase in the total participation rate. The unemployment rate is slightly higher for men than women. When Winnipeg is considered separately, its unemployment rate is slightly higher than that in rural areas. Compared with other provinces, Manitoba in July 1987 had the second-lowest unemployment rate (6.4%) – following only Ontario.

Manitoba's largest employers of labour by industry are service 165 000, trade 87 000, manufacturing 57 000, transportation, communication and utilities 45 000, and agriculture 44 000.

Language The dominant "mother tongues" in 1986 are English (71.3%), German (6.2%), Ukrainian (3.9%) and French (4.3%). The concentration of those reporting their "mother tongue" as English is higher in urban centres than in rural areas. The reverse is true for French, Ukrainian and German, the latter mainly because of the large MENNONITE farming population. In 1870 the Manitoba Act gave French and English equal status before the courts and in the legislature. In 1890 a provincial Act made English the only official language of Manitoba. This Act was declared *ultra vires* in 1979, and since 1984 the provincial government has recognized both English and French as equal in status. The Department of Cultural Affairs provides a program in MULTICULTURALISM, which produces foreign-language pamphlets for specific ethnic groups. In schools the *Français* program provides instruction entirely in French for Franco-Manitobans and the French-immersion program gives all instruction in French to students whose mother tongue is not French. Some schools offer instruction in the majority of subjects in a minority tongue, eg, Polish, Ukrainian, German. The mother tongues of native Indians are Saulteaux, Cree, Chipewyan and Sioux. The native people of the N speak mainly Cree; Saulteaux is the mother tongue of most bands in the S although English is most often spoken.

Ethnic Composition Of all Canadian provinces Manitoba contains the largest diversity of ethnic origins. The relative proportions are British (41.9%), GERMAN (12.4%), UKRAINIAN (11.5%), FRENCH (8.7%), native Indians (4.3%) and POLES (4.0%). British descendants have decreased proportionately since 1921 (57.5%); numerically they are strongest in urban areas, whereas the minorities are relatively more numerous in rural areas. The distribution of the larger ethnic groups, especially in rural areas, is related to the history of settlement. The Mennonites are concentrated in the southern Red R valley around Steinbach and Winkler; the Ukrainians and Poles live in the Interlake district and along the frontier. Many French live south of Winnipeg close to the Red R. Those of ICELANDIC origin are found around the SW shore of Lk Winnipeg. Native Indians live mainly on scattered reserves, primarily in central and N Manitoba, although some have moved to a very different life-style in Winnipeg.

Religion To some extent religious denominations reflect the pattern of ethnicity. Three groups comprise more than half the population: UNITED CHURCH (23.7%), Roman CATHOLIC (26.5%), ANGLICAN (10.6%). Most Ukrainians are members of the Ukrainian Catholic (4.8%) and Greek Orthodox (2.6%) churches. Those of German and Scandinavian backgrounds support mainly the Lutheran faith (5.8%) and 6.6% are Mennonite.

Manitoba GDP
1985 at factor cost ($000 000's)

Agriculture	1307
Forestry	22
Fishing	14
Mining	516
Manufacturing	1801
Construction	531
Utilities	545
Goods Producing Industries	4735
Transportation & Communication	1827
Trade	1814
Finance	2871
Services	3773
Public Administration	974
Service Producing Industries	11 260
Total	15 995

Economy

Hunting and trapping constitute Manitoba's oldest and today's smallest industry. For 200 years the HBC dominated trade in furs across western Canada as far as the Rocky Mts. Alongside the fur trade, buffalo hunting developed into the first commercial return of the plains; Indians, Métis and voyageurs traded meat, hides and PEMMICAN, which became the staple food of the region. Until 1875 the fur trade was the main business of Winnipeg, which was by then an incorporated city of 5000 and the centre of western commerce. In the city the retail/wholesale and real-estate business grew in response to a new pattern of settlement and the development of agriculture. Red Fife wheat became the export staple that replaced the beaver pelt. After the westward extension of the main CPR line in the 1880s, farmers and grain traders could expand into world markets and an E-W flow of trade began, with Winnipeg the "gateway" city. Over the next 20 years this basically agricultural economy consolidated. Lumbering, necessary to early settlement, declined and flour mills multiplied. During the boom years, 1897 to 1910, there was great commercial and industrial expansion, particularly in Winnipeg, and agriculture began to diversify. The following decades of depression, drought, labour unrest and 2 world wars sharpened the realization that the economy must diversify further to survive, and since WWII there has been modest growth and commercial consolidation. Today, manufacturing leads all industrial groups, followed by agriculture, the production of hydroelectric power and mining. The primary industries (including electric-power generation) represent about half of the total revenue derived from all goods-producing industries. Manufacturing and construction account for the rest.

Agriculture The prominent role of agriculture in the provincial economy is evident from both numbers employed (44 000) and value by goods-producing industries (28%). There are diverse sources of income from agriculture. In 1986 farm cash receipts for crops amounted to $1.3 billion compared with livestock at $782 million. Wheat cash receipts are 3 times those from barley and oats combined. Barley ranks second, followed by CANOLA, flaxseed and rye. Hay crops are important because of a secondary emphasis on livestock production. Cash receipts from livestock are highest by far from cattle ($316 million in 1986), followed by hogs, dairy products, poultry and eggs. Wheat is grown throughout southern Manitoba, primarily where there are medium- to fine-textured black soils, especially in the SW. Barley used as prime cattle feed is tolerant of a range of climatic conditions, but is intensively grown S and N of Riding Mtn and in the Swan R valley. Prime malting barley prefers the parkland soils and cooler summer temperatures. Cultivation of oats is general, concentrated in areas of livestock farming; it is frequently tolerant of less productive soil. Flax is grown mostly in the SW on black soil, and canola is significant on the cooler lands near the outer margin of cultivation. Specialized crops, including sugar beets, sunflowers, corn (for both grain and silage) and canning vegetables are concentrated in the southern Red R valley, where heating degree days are at a maximum and soil texture is medium. Beef cattle are raised on most farms in western Manitoba but are less important in the Red R valley. Dairy cattle are raised mainly in the cooler marginal lands, which extend in a broad arc from the SE to the Swan R valley. Poultry is heavily concentrated in the Red R valley, but hogs have a much wider distribution, influenced by a surplus of barley and fresh milk. Market gardening occupies good alluvial soil around Winnipeg and the Red R, from which water is obtained for irrigation during dry periods.

Neighbouring farmers set up co-operatives, which vary in scope and purpose from the common purchase of land and machinery to processing and marketing members' products. Two large co-operatives, Manitoba Pool Elevators and United Grain Growers, were founded to handle and market grain, and now deal in livestock and oilseeds and provide members with reasonably priced farm supplies. Manitoba's 8 marketing boards are producer bodies that control stages in the marketing of specific commodities. Wheat, oats and barley for export must be sold to the national CANADIAN WHEAT BOARD.

Agriculture is never likely to expand beyond the limits imposed by shortness of growing season (less than 90 days frost free) and the poor podsolic soils associated with the Shield. Plans for irrigating the southwestern Red R valley, known as the Pembina Triangle, are under study. Periodic flooding of the upper Red R (S of Winnipeg) has damaged capital structures and reduced income. Approximately 880 000 ha of farmland are under drainage, mostly in the Red R Valley and the Interlake and Westlake districts. The Prairie Farm Rehabilitation Act (PFRA) encourages conservation of water through check dams and dugouts.

Mining Mining contributed 11% of the value of goods-producing industries in 1985. Of Manitoba's income from all minerals, 71.4% is derived from metals, chiefly nickel, copper, zinc, tantalum and gold, with minor amounts of precious metals. All metals are found in the vast expanse of Precambrian Shield. Diminishing amounts of petroleum are recovered from sedimentary rocks of Mississippian age in the SW corner of the province near Virden and Tilston, accounting for 12.5%. Industrial minerals, principally quarried stone, gravel and sand, account for 16.0%. The famous Tyndall stone is a mottled dolomitic limestone quarried near Winnipeg and distributed across Canada. Gypsum is mined in the Interlake district near Gypsumville and in the Westlake area near Amaranth. Silica sand comes from Black I in L Winnipeg. Nonmetals account for 2.5%.

Manitoba's most productive metal mines are at Thompson. Reputed to be the largest integrated (mining, smelting and refining) operation in N America, Thompson accounts for most of Manitoba's nickel production. The province's oldest mine still in production, dating from 1927, is at Flin Flon; along with its satellite property at Snow Lake, it is a major producer of copper and zinc and small amounts of gold and silver. A third major centre is Lynn Lk which, with its sister mine at Leaf Rapids, produces nickel and copper. Ore from these mines is smelted at either Fort Saskatchewan, Alta, or Flin Flon. Local supplies of clay are obtained at Fort Whyte for making cement in Winnipeg.

Energy Other than a small amount of petroleum, the province's resources in energy are derived from hydroelectric power. Thermal plants depend mostly on low-grade coal imported from Estevan, Sask, and on diesel fuel. Manitoba Hydro, a crown corporation, is the principal authority for the generation, development and distribution of electric power, except for Winnipeg's inner core, which is served by Winnipeg Hydro, a civic corporation. Hydraulic power plants were first built along the Winnipeg R and 6 of these plants still operate. The availability of cheap power within 100 km of Winnipeg has made the city attractive to industry for many years. Since 1955 hydroelectric development has been in the N. In 1960 a plant was commissioned at Kelsey on the Nelson R, and in 1968 the Grand Rapids plant was built near the mouth of the Saskatchewan R. Increased demand led to the construction of 3 additional plants on the Nelson: Jenpeg, Kettle Rapids and Long Spruce. Downstream another plant at Limestone will be the largest in Manitoba when completed by 1992 with a 1280 MW capacity. In addition, 2 thermal plants powered by coal from Estevan are located at Brandon and Selkirk; they supplement hydro sources at peak load times. Installed generating capacity is 3644 MW with a further potential of 6104 MW. Manitoba sells surplus power, mostly during the summer period, to Ontario, Saskatchewan, Minnesota and N Dakota. Its transmission and distribution system exceeds 76 000 km. Manitoba Hydro serves over 400 000 customers, who consumed 23.4 billion kWh in 1986. Natural gas from Alberta, which is used mainly for industrial and commercial heating, supplies one-third of Manitoba's energy requirements.

Forestry FORESTRY in its primary stage (logging) accounts for 0.5% of the value of goods-producing industries. The most productive forestlands extend N from the agricultural zone to lat 57° N; N and E of this line timber stands are sparse and the trees are stunted, gradually merging with tundra vegetation along the shores of Hudson Bay. The southern limit is determined by the northward advance of commercial agriculture. On the basis of productivity for forestry, 25% of the total provincial land area is classified as "productive," 22% as nonproductive and 53% as nonforested land. Of the total productive forestland of 140 000 km², 95% is owned by the provincial government. From 1870 to 1930 lands and forests were controlled by the federal government; after the transfer of natural resources in 1930, the province assumed full responsibility. In 1930 there were 5 forest reserves, and 4 additional reserves totalling 14 000 km² have since been added. RIDING MOUNTAIN NATIONAL PARK, on the Manitoba escarpment, is the province's only national park. Manitoba has over 150 provincial parks of various types. The 12 natural parks are the most commonly used and include Whiteshell in the W and Duck Mountain in the East. There are also 44 recreation parks, 107 wayside parks, 5 heritage parks, 4 special-use parks and the province's first wilderness park, Atikaki, which was opened in 1985 and is Manitoba's largest park. Timber cutting practices are restricted around roads, lakes and rivers. In order of decreasing volume, the most common commercial tree species are black spruce, jack pine, trembling aspen (poplar), white spruce, balsam poplar and white birch. Other species common to Manitoba include balsam fir, larch (tamarack), cedar, bur oak, white elm, green ash, Manitoba maple and red and white pine. The government proposes annual cuts for each management unit on a sustained yield basis. In addition to its reforestation program, the government provides planting stock to private landowners for shelterbelts and Christmas trees.

Fisheries Inland fisheries contribute 0.2% of the value of Manitoba's primary industries. Water covers 16% of Manitoba, of which an estimated 57 000 km² is commercially fished. Two-thirds of the total catch comes from the 3 major lakes – Winnipeg, Manitoba and Winnipegosis – and the balance is taken from the numerous smaller northern lakes. The total value of the 1984-85 catch was $19 million and some 2000 fishermen were employed. Between 200 and 300 fish-receiving stations are located on the larger lakes as far N as Lac Brochet, and processing plants with quick-freezing facilities are also widely distributed. All the commercial catch is processed by the Freshwater Fish Marketing Corp, a crown agency based in Winnipeg, and 90% is exported to large northern cities in the US. Fourteen commercial species, dressed and filleted, include whitefish, pike, walleye and sauger. Pickerel, pike, walleye, trout and bass are principal sport fish. The Manitoba Department of Natural Resources maintains hatcheries for walleye, whitefish and trout.

Industry Today, Manitoba has a firm base in its processing and manufacturing industries, as shown by the value of production: 1290 manufacturers employing 51 303 people produced goods exceeding $5 billion (1984) and accounted for about 40% of the value of goods-producing industries. About two-thirds of the value of industrial production comes from the following industries: food processing, distilling, machinery (especially agricultural); irrigation and pumps; primary metals, including smelting of nickel and copper ores, metal fabricating and foundries; airplane parts, motor buses, wheels and rolling-stock maintenance; electrical equipment; computers and fibre optics. There are also the traditional industries: meat packing, flour milling, petroleum refining, vegetable processing, lumber, pulp and paper, printing and clothing. Winnipeg accounts for 75% of the manufacturing shipments. Half of all manufactured goods are exported, one-third to foreign countries.

Transportation Winnipeg's strongest asset has always been its location. In the heart of Canada and at the apex of the western population-transportation triangle, this city historically has been a vital link in all forms of E-W transportation. The YORK BOATS of the fur trade and the RED RIVER CARTS of early settlers gave way first to steamboats on the Red R, then to the great railways of the 19th and early 20th centuries. Subsequently, Winnipeg provided facilities for servicing all land and air carriers connecting E and W. Today, rail and road join the principal mining centres of N Manitoba. During the long, cold winter the myriad of interconnected lakes creates a network of winter roads. Major northern centres are linked to the S via trunk highways. Since 1926 BUSH FLYING has made remote communities accessible; several small carriers serve the majority of northern communities. Transcontinental routes of Air Canada and Canadian Airlines International pass through Winnipeg, and Air Canada operates daily flights S to Chicago, connecting with the American network. Canadian Airlines International also has links with northern Manitoba. Perimeter Airlines also serves northern points and Nordair has eastern connections as far as Montréal. Canadian Airlines International, Air Canada and Wardair provide international flights direct from Winnipeg to Europe and Hawaii. Northwest Airlines connects with Minneapolis, and Frontier Airlines with Denver and Los Angeles. Southern Manitoba has 6630 km of trunk highways and 12 377 km of provincial roads (mainly gravel).

Because Winnipeg is Canada's principal mid-continent rail centre, both CNR and CPR have extensive maintenance facilities and marshalling yards in and around the city. Wheat has the largest freight volume, but diverse products from petroleum and chemicals to motor cars and lumber are transported by rail. The CN owns Symington Yards, one of the largest and most modern marshalling yards in the world. At Transcona it maintains repair and servicing shops for rolling stock and locomotives and at GIMLI a national employee-training centre. In addition to repair shops and marshalling yards, the CPR has a large piggyback terminal; Weston shops, one of 3 in its trans-Canada system, employs about 1600 people. Via Rail operates Canada's passenger train service, which uses the lines of the 2 major railways and provides direct service between Vancouver and Halifax and Saint John. In 1929 the HUDSON BAY RY, now part of the CNR system, was completed to the port of Churchill, where today major transshipment facilities handle annually some 500 000 t of grain between July 20 and Oct 31. Formerly an army base, Churchill is also a research centre and a supply base for eastern arctic communities.

Tyndall stone (quarried near Winnipeg) and life-size bronze bisons in the ground stairhall of the Manitoba Legislative Building (*photo by Henry Kalen*).

Government and Politics

On 15 March 1871 the first legislature of Manitoba met for the first time; it consisted of an elected legislative assembly with members from 12 English and 12 French electoral districts, an appointed legislative council and an appointed executive council who advised the government head, Lt-Gov Adams G. ARCHIBALD. When the assembly prorogued, systems of courts, education and statutory law had been established, based on British, Ontarian and Nova Scotian models. The Legislative Council was abolished 5 years later. Since 1871 the province has moved from communal representation to representation by population and from nonpartisan to party political government. Today the LIEUTENANT-GOVERNOR is still formal head of the provincial legislature and represents the Crown in Manitoba. The government is led by the PREMIER, who chooses a CABINET, whose members are sworn in as ministers of the Crown. Her Majesty's Loyal Opposition is customarily headed by the leader of the party winning the second-largest number of seats in a given election. Laws are passed by the unicameral Legislative Assembly, consisting of 57 elected members. The judiciary consists of the superior courts, where judges are federally appointed, and many lesser courts that are presided over by provincial judges. The RCMP is contracted to provide provincial police services and municipal services in some centres; provincial law requires cities and towns to employ enough police to maintain law and order. Manitoba is federally represented by 14 MPs and 6 senators.

Local Government Local government is provided by a system of municipalities. Manitoba has 5 incorporated cities (Winnipeg, Brandon, Selkirk, Portage la Prairie and Thompson), 35 incorporated towns and 40 incorporated villages. (An incorporated municipality has a greater degree of autonomy, especially in taxing and borrowing power.) There are 105 rural municipalities ranging in size from 4 to 22 TOWNSHIPS, many of which contain unincorporated towns and villages. Locally elected councils are responsible for maintaining services and administering bylaws. In remote areas where population is sparse, the government has established 17 local government districts (LGDs) with an appointed administrator and an elected advisory council. The Department of Northern Affairs has jurisdiction over remote areas in northern Manitoba and uses the community council as an advisory body. Community councils are elected bodies, mostly in Métis settlements, through which the government makes grants. Each has a local government "co-ordinator" to represent the government.

Public Finance For the fiscal year ending 31 March 1986 the province had revenues of $3.12 billion and expenditures of $3.645 billion, with a net deficit of $251 million. Income taxes garnered $777 million (1985-86) and other taxes, including 5% sales tax and gasoline and resources taxes, totalled $428 million. Liquor revenues were $139 million. Unconditional transfer payments and shared-cost receipts from federal sources covering education, health and economic development are estimated at $1.1 billion. More than 50% of government expenditures go toward education, health and social services.

Health and Welfare Manitoba Health Services Commission, with generous support from Ottawa, provides nonpremium medical care for all its citizens. A pharmacare program pays 80% of the cost of all prescription drugs above $75 ($50 for senior citizens). The province and Winnipeg each has a free dental-care program for all elementary-school children.

The departments of Health and of Community Services and Corrections provide services in public and mental health, social services, probations and corrections. The government is responsible for provincial correction and detention facilities and through the Alcoholism Foundation administers drug and alcohol rehabilitation facilities. Manitoba has 82 provincially supported hospitals, including 10 in Winnipeg, and 113 personal care homes in addition to elderly persons' housing. Winnipeg is an important centre for medical research; its Health Sciences Centre includes Manitoba's chief referral hospitals and a number of specialist institutions, among them the Children's Centre and the Manitoba Cancer Treatment and Research Foundation.

Politics While Manitoba's system of RESPONSIBLE GOVERNMENT was maturing during the 1870s, communal loyalties rather than party politics dominated public representation. As the 1880s advanced, however, a strong Liberal opposition to John NORQUAY's nonpartisan government developed under Thomas GREENWAY. After the election of 1888, Greenway's Liberals formed Manitoba's first declared partisan government until defeated in 1899 (on issues of extravagance and a weak railway policy) by an invigorated Conservative Party under Hugh John MACDONALD. When Macdonald resigned in 1900, hoping to return to federal politics, R.P. ROBLIN became premier, a position he held until 1915, when a scandal over the contracting of the new legislative buildings brought down the government in its fifth term. In 1920, against the incumbent Liberal government of T.C. NORRIS, the United Farmers of Manitoba

Premiers of Manitoba 1870-1988

	Party	*Term*
Alfred Boyd*	Nonpartisan	1870-71
Marc A. Girard*	Nonpartisan	1871-72
Henry J. Clarke*	Nonpartisan	1872-74
Marc-A. Girard	Nonpartisan	1874
Robert A. Davis	Nonpartisan	1874-78
John Norquay	Nonpartisan	1878-87
David H. Harrison	Nonpartisan	1887-88
Thomas Greenway	Liberal	1888-1900
Hugh John Macdonald	Conservative	1900
Rodmond P. Roblin	Conservative	1900-15
Tobias C. Norris	Liberal	1915-22
John Bracken	United Farmers of Manitoba	1922-28
John Bracken	Coalition	1928-43
Stuart S. Garson	Coalition	1943-48
Douglas L. Campbell	Coalition	1948-58
Dufferin Roblin	Conservative	1958-67
Walter C. Weir	Conservative	1967-69
Edward R. Schreyer	NDP	1969-77
Sterling Lyon	Conservative	1977-81
Howard Pawley	NDP	1981-

* chief minister, not premier

Lieutenant-Governors of Manitoba 1870-1988

	Term
Adams G. Archibald	1870-72
Alexander Morris	1872-77
Joseph E. Cauchon	1877-82
James C. Aikins	1882-88
John C. Schultz	1888-95
James C. Patterson	1895-1900
Daniel H. McMillan	1900-11
Douglas C. Cameron	1911-16
James A.M. Aikins	1916-26
Theodore A. Burrows	1926-29
James D. McGregor	1929-34
William J. Tupper	1934-40
Roland F. McWilliams	1940-53
John S. McDiarmid	1953-60
Errick F. Willis	1960-65
Richard S. Bowles	1965-70
John W. McKeag	1970-76
Francis L. Jobin	1976-81
Pearl B. McGonigal	1981-86
George Johnson	1986-

first entered provincial politics and returned 12 members to the Legislative Assembly, heralding a new era of nonpartisan politics. The promise was fulfilled in the election of 1922, when the UFM won a modest majority and formed the new government. Manitoba was returning to its roots, reaffirming rural virtues of thrift, sobriety and labour to counter rapid change, depression and the aftereffects of war. The farmers chose John BRACKEN as their leader, and he remained premier until 1943 despite the UFM withdrawal from politics in 1928. Bracken then formed a coalition party, the Liberal-Progressives, which won a majority in the Assembly in 1932 but only gained a plurality in the 1936 election, surviving with Social Credit support. He continued as premier in 1940 over a wartime government of Conservative, Liberal-Progressive, CCF and Social Credit members. Bracken became leader of the federal Conservatives in 1943 and was replaced by Stuart S. Garson. In 1945 the CCF left the coalition, the Conservatives left it in 1950 and the Social Credit Party simply faded. From 1948 the coalition was led by Premier Douglas CAMPBELL, although after 1950 it was predominantly a Liberal government. From 1958 the Conservatives under Duff ROBLIN governed the province until Edward SCHREYER's NDP took over in 1969 with a bare majority. His government survived 2 terms; during its years in office many social reforms were introduced and government activity in the private sector was expanded. In 1977 Sterling LYON led the Conservative Party to victory on a platform of reducing the provincial debt and returning to free enterprise, but his government lasted only one term. In 1981 the NDP returned to power under Howard PAWLEY. They were re-elected in 1985. The Lyon government, in fact, was the only one-term government in Manitoba's history. The political tradition of the province has been notable for its long-term stability, particularly during the era of the UFM and later coalition governments.

Education

The denominational school system was guaranteed by the Manitoba Act of 1870 and established by the provincial School Act of 1871: local schools, Protestant or Roman Catholic, might be set up on local initiative and administered by local trustees under the superintendence of the Protestant or Roman Catholic section of a provincial board of education. The board was independent of the government but received grants from it, which the sections divided among their schools. Until 1875 the grants were equal; disparity in the population and the ensuing Protestant attack on dualism in 1876 made it necessary to divide the grants on the basis of enrolment in each section. After 1876 the British (predominantly Protestant) and French (Roman Catholic) coexisted peaceably and separately, until agitation against the perceived growing political power of the Catholic clergy spread W from Québec in 1889. A popular movement to abolish the dual system and the official use of French culminated in 1890 in the passage of 2 provincial bills. English became the only official language and the Public Schools Act was altered. Roman Catholics could have private schools supported by gifts and fees, but a new department of education, over local boards of trustees, was to administer nondenominational schools. French Catholic objections to violations of their constitutional rights were ignored by the Protestant Ontarian majority, who saw a national school system as the crucible wherein an essentially British Manitoba would be formed. Intervention by the courts and the federal government eventually produced the compromise of 1897: where there were 40 (urban) or 10 (rural) Catholic pupils, Catholic teachers were

School Treat, St Paul's, Man, 1883, albumen by W. Hanson Boorne *(courtesy Notman Photographic Archives/McCord Museum)*.

to be hired; where at least 10 pupils spoke a language other than English, instruction was to be given in that language; school attendance was not compulsory, since Catholics were still outside the provincial system. After 20 years of decreasing standards and linguistic chaos, the Public Schools Act was amended in 1916; the bilingual clause was removed and the new School Attendance Act made schooling compulsory for Catholics and Protestants alike, whether publicly or privately educated.

Since 1970, Franco-Manitobains can receive instruction entirely in French through the *Français* program; as well, non-French students in French immersion are taught all subjects in French. Instruction in a minority tongue in the majority of subjects is possible in some schools. Both English- and French-medium schools are organized in 48 school divisions, each administered by an elected school board, under the Department of Education. There are 14 school districts of which 6 are financed mainly from sources other than provincial grants and taxes; these include private schools sponsored by church organizations and by the federal government. School boards are responsible for maintaining and equipping schools, hiring teachers and support staff and negotiating salaries. The Manitoba Teachers Federation negotiates with the boards.

Institutions In 1986 enrolment in the public schools of the province totalled 198 948, and 12 700 teachers were employed. Elementary schools consist of kindergarten through grades 1 to 9, and larger urban centres offer a junior-high-school program for grades 7-9. Senior high school, grades 10-12, has a varied curriculum with core subjects and several options. Special, practically oriented programs are available at 35 vocational-industrial schools, and vocational-business training is given in 106 schools. There are also schools for the disabled, the blind, the deaf and those with learning disabilities.

COMMUNITY COLLEGES provide a wide variety of career-oriented adult educational and vocational programs, and day, evening and extension programs – full-time and part-time – are offered in more than 120 communities. Assiniboine Community College operates in and outside Brandon; it is responsible for all community college agricultural training in the province. Keewatin College offers 25 certificate courses of one year or less, mostly in northern Manitoba, as well as a mineral sciences course. Red River College, located in Winnipeg, provides 25 two-year post-secondary courses leading to recognized diplomas, as well as over 50 certificate courses of one year or less, including courses in applied arts, business administration, health services, industrial arts and technology. During 1986 there were over 6000 full-time and 25 000 part-time students enrolled in community colleges in Manitoba.

In 1877 St-Boniface (French, Roman Catholic), St John's (Anglican) and Manitoba (Presbyterian) united as UNIVERSITY OF MANITOBA. Later, they were joined by other colleges, but in 1967 a realignment of the constituents resulted in 3 distinct universities. The U of Manitoba is one of the largest universities in Canada, with numerous faculties and with 4 affiliated colleges that provide instruction in French: St John's and St Paul's (Roman Catholic), St Andrew's (Ukrainian Orthodox) and St-Boniface. In 1985-86, 12 860 full-time and 6379 part-time students were enrolled. BRANDON UNIVERSITY offers undergraduate programs in arts, science, education and music, with an enrolment of 1358 full-time and 1471 part-time students. The UNIVERSITY OF WINNIPEG, located in central Winnipeg, provides primarily undergraduate instruction, teacher training and theological studies for 3008 full-time and 4280 part-time students. Teachers are trained at all 3 universities and at Red River College.

Cultural Life

To a large degree, Manitoba's cultural activities and historical institutions reflect the varied ethnic groups that comprise its fabric. The provincial government, through its Department of Cultural Affairs and Historical Resources, subsidizes a wide range of cultural activities. Many annual FESTIVALS celebrate ethnic customs and history: Icelandic Festival at Gimli; Winnipeg Folk Festival; National Ukrainian Festival at Dauphin; Opasquia Indian Days at The Pas; Pioneer Days at Steinbach; Fête Franco-Manitobaine at La Broquerie; the midwinter Festival du voyageur in St-Boniface, the N Manitoba Trappers' Festival at The Pas and Folklorama sponsored by the Community Folk Art Council in Winnipeg. Manitoba's historic past is preserved by the Museum of Man and Nature (Winnipeg), considered one of the finest interpretive museums in Canada; by the Living Prairie Museum, a 20 ha natural reserve; St-Boniface Museum, rich in artifacts from the Red R Colony; and the Provincial Archives and Hudson's Bay Co Archives. The Planetarium is among the finest in N America. The Winnipeg Zoo in Assiniboine Pk has a major collection of more than 1000 animals.

The Arts The Manitoba Arts Council promotes the study, enjoyment, production and performance of works in the arts. It assists organizations

Lionel LeMoine FitzGerald spent almost his whole life in Winnipeg, drawing and painting contemplative scenes. The painting *The Jar* (1938), oil on canvas, displays his use of glistening daubs of paint *(courtesy Mr and Mrs Earl Green/Collection of The Winnipeg Art Gallery, Ernest P. Mayer; donated by the Women's Committee)*.

involved in cultural development; offers grants, scholarships and loans to Manitobans for study and research; and makes awards to individuals. The Winnipeg Symphony Orchestra, ROYAL WINNIPEG BALLET, Manitoba Theatre Centre, Le Cercle Molière, Manitoba Opera Association, Manitoba Contemporary Dancers and Rainbow Stage all contribute to Winnipeg's position as a national centre of the performing arts. Among well-known and respected Manitoban writers are the novelists Margaret LAURENCE and Gabrielle ROY, essayist, historian and poet George WOODCOCK and popular historian Barry Broadfoot. The Winnipeg Art Gallery, in addition to traditional and contemporary works, houses the largest collection of Inuit art in the world.

Historic Sites Among the fine historic sites associated with the settlement of the West is the HBC's Lower Fort Garry (*see* FORT GARRY, LOWER). Situated on the Red R 32 km NE of Winnipeg, this oldest intact stone fort in western Canada was built in 1832 and preserves much of the atmosphere of the Red River Colony. Among a number of historic houses is Riel House, home of the Riel family; York Factory, located at the mouth of the Nelson R and dating from 1682, was a transshipment point for furs. The partially restored PRINCE OF WALES'S FORT (1731-82) at the mouth of the Churchill R was built by the HBC and destroyed by the French. Other points of historical significance are St-Boniface Basilica, oldest cathedral in western Canada and the site of Louis RIEL's grave; Macdonald House, home of Sir H. J. MACDONALD; Fort Douglas; Ross House; Seven Oaks House; and the Living Prairie Museum.

Communications Manitoba has 8 daily newspapers: *Winnipeg Free Press, Winnipeg Sun, Brandon Sun, Dauphin Daily Bulletin, Portage la Prairie Daily Graphic, Swan River Report, Flin Flon Daily Reminder* and *Roblin News.* Sixty-two weekly and biweekly papers service suburban Winnipeg and rural areas, with emphasis on farming, and several trade and business journals are published. The French-language weekly, *La Liberté*, is published in St-Boniface, and Winnipeg produces more foreign-language newspapers than any other centre in Canada.

The province has 16 AM radio stations, including the French-language station CKSB, and 8 FM radio stations; as well, the CBC has 24 English-language and 6 French-language rebroadcasters. Four television stations operate from Winnipeg and one from Brandon, and CABLE TELEVISION is available in 16 centres. The Manitoba Telephone System, a crown corporation, provides telecommunications facilities for all Manitoba. (In 1908, because of high rates and inefficiency, the provincial government began appropriating Bell Telephone and established Manitoba Government Telephones in 1908, the first publicly owned system in N America). Three microwave radio networks join N and S Manitoba, bringing CBC television and radio to most communities of 500 or more. CNCP Telecommunications maintains its Prairie region offices in Winnipeg. Manitoba Data Services, providing data processing to government and private sectors, is one of the largest computer utility operations in Canada.

History

Exploration The history of exploration in Manitoba did not begin in the S but in the coldest and most remote area – the shores of Hudson Bay. A succession of navigators, Henry HUDSON (1610), Thomas BUTTON (1612), Jens MUNK (1619), and Luke FOX and Thomas JAMES (1631), searched the shoreline for the NORTHWEST PASSAGE. Two French Canadian explorers interested in the fur trade, DES GROSEILLIERS and RADISSON, persuaded Charles II of England to establish the Hudson's Bay Co in 1670, granting it a huge territory (part of which is modern Manitoba), to be called RUPERT'S LAND. Trading posts were soon established along the shores: Fort Nelson (1682), Fort York (1612), Fort Churchill (1688), Prince of Wales's Fort (1731). Henry KELSEY, an HBC employee, penetrated SW across the prairies 1690-92. The LA VÉRENDRYE family travelled W via the Great Lakes, building Fort Maurepas on the Red R (1734), then 4 other posts within the present area of Manitoba. The subsequent invasion by independent traders of lands granted to the HBC stimulated an intense rivalry for pelts, which ended only with amalgamation of the HBC and the North West Co in 1821. About 20 forts existed at various times S of lat 54° N, but the early explorers left little permanent impression on the landscape.

Settlement Agricultural settlement began in 1812 with the arrival of Lord SELKIRK's settlers at Point Douglas, now within the boundaries of Winnipeg. Over the next 45 years the Red R Colony at Assiniboia survived hail, frost, floods, grasshoppers, skirmishes with the Nor'Westers and an HBC monopoly. Expansionist sentiment from both Minnesota and Upper Canada challenged the HBC's control over the NW and the Red R Colony. In 1857 the British government sponsored a joint expedition with the Canadians to assess the potential of Rupert's Land for agricultural settlement; the PALLISER EXPEDITION reported a fertile crescent of land suitable for agriculture extending NW from the Red R valley. The conflict between agricultural expansion and the rights of the Métis broke out in 2 periods of unrest (*see* RED RIVER REBELLION; NORTH-WEST REBELLION). Eventually the HBC charter was terminated and the lands of the North-West were transferred to the new Dominion of Canada by the Manitoba Act of 1870, and quarter sections of land were then opened to settlement. It was soon evident that the diminutive province needed to expand; settlers were rapidly moving to the North-West and spilling over the established boundaries. In 1881, after years of political wrangling with the federal government, the boundaries were extended to their present western position, as well as being extended farther E, and to lat 53° N. Between 1876 and 1881, 40 000 immigrants, mainly Ontario British, were drawn W by the prospect of profitable wheat farming enhanced by new machinery and milling processes. Mennonites and Icelandic immigrants arrived in the 1870s, the former settling around Steinbach and Winkler, the latter near Gimli and Hecla. Immigration then slowed until the late 1890s and it was limited mostly to small groups of Europeans. Between 1897 and 1910, years of great prosperity and development, settlers from eastern Canada, the UK, the US and eastern Europe – especially Ukraine – inundated the province and the neighbouring lands. Subsequent immigration was never on this scale.

Development From 1897 to 1910 Manitoba enjoyed unprecedented prosperity. Transportation rates fell and wheat prices rose. Grain farming still predominated, but mixed farms prospered and breeders of quality livestock and plants became famous. Winnipeg swiftly rose to metropolitan stature, accounting for 50% of the increase in population. In the premier city of the West a vigorous business centre developed, radiating from the corner of Portage Ave and Main Street: department stores, real-estate and insurance companies, legal firms and banks thrived. Abattoirs and flour mills directly serviced the agricultural economy; service industries, railway shops, foundries and food industries expanded. Both the CPR and the Canadian Northern Railway (later CNR) built marshalling yards in the city, which became the hub of a vast network of rail lines spreading E, W, N and S. In 1906 hydroelectricity was first generated at Pinawa on the Winnipeg R, and the establishment of Winnipeg Hydro 28 June 1906 guaranteed the availability of cheap power for domestic and industrial use.

The general prosperity ended with the depression of 1913; freight rates rose, land and wheat prices plummeted and the supply of foreign capital dried up. The opening of the Panama Canal in 1914 ended Winnipeg's transportation supremacy, since goods could move more cheaply between E and W by sea than overland. During WWI, recruitment, war industry demands, and cessation of immigration sent wages and prices soaring; by 1918 inflation seemed unchecked and unemployment was prevalent. Real wages dropped, working conditions deteriorated and new radical movements grew among farmers and urban workers, culminating in the WINNIPEG GENERAL STRIKE of May 1919. Ensuing depression followed by an industrial boom in the late 1920s tilted the economic seesaw again. By 1928 the value of industrial production exceeded that of agricultural production; the long agricultural depression continued into the 1930s, aggravated by drought, pests and low world wheat prices, and the movement from farm to city and town accelerated. Cities were little better off: industry flagged and un-

A view of the Post dog trains leaving Fort Garry for St Paul, 1851; watercolour by W. Armstrong, 1901 (*courtesy National Archives of Canada/C-10503*).

employment was high. To eliminate the traditional boom/bust pattern attempts have been made to diversify the economy. The continuing expansion of mining since 1911 has underlined the desirability of broadening the basis of the economy. The demands of WWII reinforced Manitoba's dependency on agriculture and primary production, but the postwar boom gave the province the opportunity to capitalize on its established industries and to broaden the economic base.

Since WWII, the Manitoba economy has been marked by rapid growth in the province's north. The development of rich nickel deposits in northern Manitoba by Inco Ltd led to the founding of the city of Thompson, whose fluctuating fortunes have mirrored swings in world commodity prices. The region has been the site of several "megaprojects," including the Manitoba Forest Resources operation at The Pas, and the huge limestone hydro-electric generating plant on the Nelson R. The economic future of Manitoba is thus a mixed one – a continuing agricultural slump, offset by growth in light industry, publishing, the garment industry, and the export of power to the US.

The past 20 years has seen a dramatic realignment of provincial politics, with the virtual disappearance of the provincial Liberal Party and the rise to power of the New Democratic Party, under Edward Schreyer and Howard Pawley. Typical of the social democratic initiatives of the NDP are the introduction of a government-run automobile insurance plan and the 1987 plan to purchase Inter-City Gas Co. The government's attempt to increase bilingual services within the province aroused old passions, however, and was abandoned.

T.R. WEIR

Reading: J. Brown, *Strangers in Blood* (1980); K. Coates and F. McGuinness, *Manitoba, The Province & The People* (1987); W.L. Morton, *Manitoba: A History* (2nd ed, 1967); G. Friesen, *Prairie West* (1984); X. McWillams, *Manitoba Milestones* (1928); Alan Artibise, *Winnipeg: An Illustrated History* (1977).

Manitoba Act, which received royal assent 12 May 1870 and went into effect 15 July, provided for the admission of Manitoba as Canada's fifth province. It marked, as well, the legislative resolution of the struggle between inhabitants of the RED RIVER COLONY and the federal government (*see* RED RIVER REBELLION). Local anxiety, especially over MÉTIS land rights, had provoked the inhabitants' determination to have a voice in the terms under which the community would be incorporated into Canada. A popularly elected convention, reflecting the settlement's cultural diversity, supported a provisional government dominated by Louis RIEL. Four successive lists of rights were drafted by the provisional government; the final version became the basis of federal legislation. Despite PM Macdonald's reluctance, Manitoba entered Canada as a province, not a territory. English- and French-language rights were safeguarded, as were Protestant and Roman Catholic educational rights; the right to education in either English or French was not protected. The Dominion retained control of natural resources, in particular unallocated land, which was to be sold to support the building of a Pacific railway and to be the magnet for a vast IMMIGRATION (*see* DOMINION LANDS POLICY). The new province of Manitoba, severely circumscribed in size, thus entered as a province unlike the original 4, and its creation revealed Ottawa's resolve to control western development.

J.E. REA

Manitoba, Lake, 4630 km^2, elev 248 m, is one of 3 large lakes occupying the southern half of Manitoba. A narrow, irregular lake, about 200 km long with marshy shores, it is fed mainly from Lk WINNIPEGOSIS, which lies to the NW, and drains NE via the Dauphin R to Lk WINNIPEG. The marshes at its southern end, which lie just 24 km N of PORTAGE LA PRAIRIE, are an important waterfowl research area. When Pierre LA VÉRENDRYE arrived in the mid-1730s, he found the area populated by Assiniboine. For many years it formed part of an important trade route along which furs were transported via Lk Winnipeg and the northern rivers to Hudson Bay. Subsequently a commercial fishery was established. Early French traders called it Lac des Prairies; the modern name probably refers to the Indian spirit MANITOU.

DANIEL FRANCIS

Manitoba Research Council (MRC) was established by an Act of the Manitoba legislature in 1963. In 1971, after a period of inactivity, MRC began to provide technical assistance to industry and small research grants to university and business scientists. Federal-provincial funding provided permanent facilities: in 1978 a laboratory for research on food, beverages and feeds; in 1979-80 a centre to encourage manufacturers to use existing knowledge effectively, especially in the areas of ELECTRONICS, materials research and building systems. MRC falls under the Manitoba Dept of Industry, Trade and Technology, which provides most of the funding. Facilities include the Canadian Food Products Development Centre, Portage la Prairie, and the Industrial Technology Centre, Winnipeg. MRC provides free to low-charge technical advice to small businesses, administers grants for research, and advises government ministers on the allocation of funds for scientific and technical research.

MARTIN K. MCNICHOLL

Manitoba Schools Question, the most complex and far-reaching of Canada's several crises involving minority school rights. The 1870 MANITOBA ACT established a dual system of Protestant and Roman Catholic schools. Through Anglo-Protestant settlement largely from Ontario during the 1870s and 1880s, the proportion of Roman Catholics and French to the total Manitoba population fell dramatically. In Mar 1890 Manitoba's Liberal government under Thomas GREENWAY abolished public funding of Catholic schools. Two Privy Council decisions, 1892 and early 1895, upheld the validity of the Manitoba law but affirmed the federal government's power to restore the lost school privileges.

After much delay and several federal Cabinet crises, the faltering Conservative government introduced remedial legislation in March 1896. Liberal leader Wilfrid LAURIER, energetically supported by explicitly anti-French and anti-Catholic voices such as D'Alton MCCARTHY's, forced the bill's withdrawal. The June 1896 federal election was fought primarily on this explosive issue. Laurier defeated the government largely by winning 49 of 65 seats in Québec. Laurier circumvented danger from pro-remedial Québec Catholic bishops by promising a less abrasive but presumably more effective "sunny ways" approach to the province. The Laurier-Greenway compromise of late 1896, prompting an amendment to the Schools Act in 1897, did not restore separate schools, but it did allow Catholic teachers to be employed in certain circumstances and it did give some religious-instruction privileges within the public schools. Not until the late 1970s were more favourable arrangements made by Manitoba. In modern Québec, the Manitoba Schools Question is viewed as Canada's most significant loss of French and Catholic rights outside Québec.

PAUL E. CRUNICAN

School in Rapid City, Man, *c*1890. Opponents of Catholic schools and French-language rights argued that schools should be used to assimilate newcomers to the dominant Anglo-Protestant culture, symbolized by the Union Jack (*courtesy Provincial Archives of Manitoba*).

Manitoba Theatre Centre was created in 1958 as the first of Canada's professional regional theatres when cofounders Tom HENDRY and John HIRSCH merged the pre-existing amateur Winnipeg Little Theatre and the semi-professional Theatre 77. Named in 1962 by the CANADA COUNCIL as a model for others to follow, the centre's programming energy under its cofounders – particularly in the areas of education, touring and training – made it widely influential throughout N America. Under succeeding artistic directors Edward Gilbert, Kurt Reis, Len Cariou (who began as an actor with MTC), Arif Hasnain, Richard Ouzounian and James Roy the centre has narrowed the breadth of its responsibilities while consolidating its position as one of Canada's most securely based theatres. Its main stage attracts one of Canada's largest subscription audiences, and in The Warehouse, a second stage where new Canadian work is gradually regaining the importance it had during MTC's founding years, a new, younger audience is growing. Guided by artistic director Rick McNair (1987), MTC is administered by a volunteer board of directors.

TOM HENDRY

Manitou, an Algonquian word meaning "mysterious being," or simply "mystery," that represents the unknown power of life and the universe. The notion is connected to the veneration of the sun and is related to the concept of *mana*, a personal supernatural force, common among native peoples of N America.

RENÉ R. GADACZ

Manitoulin Island, 2766 km^2, the largest island in the world located in a lake, is part of an archipelago at the top of Lk HURON that straddles the Ontario-Michigan border. Its northern shore encloses the North Channel, which leads to the St Marys R at Sault Ste Marie. It has an irregular, rocky shoreline and many interior lakes. In the 17th century it was part of the territory occupied by the OTTAWA. Jesuit missionaries arrived in 1648, but their mission was short-lived. The island was sporadically inhabited until the 1830s when it became the centre of Indian administration for northern Ontario. Indians from across the region were settled here and others visited to receive their annual presents from the British government. In 1862 the provincial government puchased most of the island from the Indians. By this time settlers

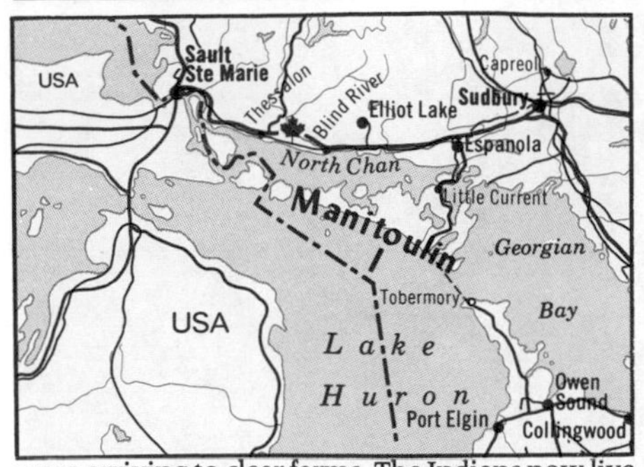

were arriving to clear farms. The Indians now live on small reserves.

Though the island is fertile only in spots, farming has always been a major economic activity. Turkey production thrived after 1920 and by 1930 the island was one of the most important sheep-rearing areas in Ontario. Logging dates from the 1860s and commercial fishing for whitefish and trout was also an economic mainstay; however, both these industries have declined. Since the 1920s the island has become a popular outdoor recreation area, and tourism and agriculture are now the principal activities. Little Current is the main populated centre and is linked to the mainland by road and railway. The name refers to the *Manitou* (Algonquian for "spirit"), believed to dwell on the island. DANIEL FRANCIS

Manitouwadge, Ont, Twp, Thunder Bay District, pop 3522 (1986c), 3185 (1981c), is located in northwestern Ontario 397 km NE of Thunder Bay. Manitouwadge is an Ojibwa word meaning "cave of the Great Spirit." The area's rich mineral resources – copper, lead, silver and zinc – were first identified in 1931, but the absence of gold deposits and the inaccessibility of the area delayed active development until 1953 when 2 Geraldton men, William Dowd and Roy Barker, staked their claims. This touched off a prospecting stampede, out of which emerged General Engineering Co Ltd (GECO) and Willroy Mines Ltd, both going into production in 1956. The demographic growth of Manitouwadge dates from the construction of the CPR and CNR branch lines and the highway southward to the Trans-Canada Highway in 1954. As a mining camp Manitouwadge was unique because, although the companies owned most of the residential properties, the Ontario government itself designed the physical layout of the town so as to create a model urban community. MATT BRAY

Manitowaning, Ont, UP, pop 473 (1986c), 518 (1981c), is located on the NE shore of MANITOULIN I. In 1835 T.G. Anderson, superintendent of Indian affairs for Upper Canada, selected it as administrative headquarters of the newly created Indian reserve on Manitoulin I. Though OJIBWA and OTTAWA began to move onto the island in 1836, permanent settlement dates only from 1838. Anderson's dream of making this Indian community a model of Anglican prosperity failed in the 1840s and 1850s, partly because of the lack of sustained government support and partly because of the more effective Roman Catholic missionary activities at nearby Wikwemikong. The opening of the island to non-Indian settlement in 1862 brought Manitowaning a brief economic boom; by 1880 it was the island's largest village. During the next 20 years, Gore Bay and Little Current surpassed Manitowaning, and since 1900 it has been mainly a trade and tourist centre. MATT BRAY

Mankiewicz, Francis, filmmaker (b at Shanghai, China 15 Mar 1944). His parents fled Nazi Germany, landing in France, then China and Montréal. He studied film in England at the London School of Film Technique and made industrial films after returning to Canada in 1968. With *Le Temps d'une chasse* (1972), the story of a hunting weekend as seen by a young boy, he made a stunning directorial debut in feature films. He then directed 2 dramas for the CBC in English and a feature film for TV in French. His next film, *Les Bons Débarras* (1980), in which a young girl manipulates the adult world around her, was a popular and critical success. His latest film, *Les Portes Tourantes* (1987) is based on a novel by Jacques Savoie. He is a second cousin of US director Joseph Mankiewicz. PIERS HANDLING

Mann, Cedric Robert, physical oceanographer (b at Auckland, NZ 14 Feb 1926). He came to Canada in 1949 to study physics at UBC and was involved in marine acoustics research 1953-61 at the Naval Research Establishment, Dartmouth, NS. He initiated, developed and led the deep-sea OCEANOGRAPHY program of the Atlantic Oceanographic Laboratory at the BEDFORD INSTITUTE OF OCEANOGRAPHY 1961-75 and was director of the laboratory 1975-78. Director general of the Bedford Inst 1978-79, he was appointed director general of the Institute of Ocean Sciences, Pat Bay, BC, in 1979. He is best known for his work on the Gulf Stream system, oceanic silicate distributions, the overflow of deep water in Denmark Str, and his leadership of the HUDSON '70 expedition around the Americas. In 1974-75 he undertook a study of physical and chemical oceanography in Canada and since the mid-1970s has been active in the organization of climate research and as chairman of the Sea Use Council. G.T. NEEDLER

Mann, Sir Donald, railway builder (b at Acton, Canada W 23 Mar 1853; d at Toronto 10 Nov 1934). Mann studied for the Methodist ministry but took up work in the lumber camps of Ontario and Michigan. In 1879 he was in charge of the barge that brought the first railway locomotive to Winnipeg. He completed a number of earth-moving and grading contracts on the CPR's prairie and mountain main line in the 1880s. With James ROSS, William MACKENZIE and Herbert HOLT, he built a number of branch lines in western Canada, Maine, and in S America and China. In 1895 he joined Mackenzie to purchase and complete the Lk Manitoba Ry and Canal Co, which later became the CANADIAN NORTHERN RY. Rapid expansion and numerous amalgamations transformed the Canadian Northern Ry into a transcontinental system by 1915. Financial difficulties, however, led to nationalization in 1918 and the subsequent merger of the Canadian Northern with other government railways to form CANADIAN NATIONAL RAILWAYS. After 1918 Mann devoted himself to mining and other smaller business ventures. He was created a KB in 1911. T.D. REGEHR

Reading: T.D. Regehr, *The Canadian Northern Railway* (1976).

Mann, Kenneth Henry, freshwater and marine biologist (b at Dovercourt, Eng 15 Aug 1923; naturalized Canadian). Mann is an aquatic biologist whose wide experience ranges from the taxonomy and biology of freshwater leeches to the production of inshore marine ecosystems. He is best known for his work in the analysis of the production of aquatic systems, and was influential in the International Biological Programme, in which production of many ecosystems was compared. Mann's production studies have included fish in the R Thames in England and the lobster/sea urchin/kelp complex off eastern Canada. He has written several books and more than 100 research papers in his field and has lectured and worked widely overseas. Mann was chairman of the biology dept at Dalhousie 1972-78 and professor 1972-80. He was director of the Marine Ecology Laboratory, BEDFORD INSTITUTE OF OCEANOGRAPHY, Dartmouth, NS, 1980-87, and then became senior research scientist there.

Mann v the Queen A. Mann had been charged in 1966 with careless driving pursuant to a provincial highway traffic Act. He challenged the constitutional validity of the provincial offence, arguing that Parliament, by establishing an offence of dangerous driving, had made the matter a question of CRIMINAL LAW, which according to the Constitution Act, 1867, falls under the exclusive legislative jurisdiction of Parliament.

A majority of the Supreme Court of Canada upheld the constitutional validity of the careless driving provision, stating that the province could legitimately create driving offences that required proof of mere negligence. In their view, the charge of dangerous driving under the CRIMINAL CODE required proof of both negligent driving and MENS REA. In other words, they held that the offence of dangerous driving required proof of advertent negligence, while that of careless driving under the provincial legislation was concerned with inadvertent negligence. However, the court did not define what it meant by "advertent negligence." It is not clear whether the accused must have actual foresight that his or her driving could create a dangerous situation or whether it is sufficient that a reasonable person would have realized the situation was dangerous. A. PRINGLE

Manning, Edward, Baptist minister (b in Ireland 16 Oct 1766; d at Upper Canard, NS 12 Jan 1851). Manning came to Nova Scotia with his Irish Catholic family about 1769. Greatly influenced by the New Light movement begun by Henry ALLINE, he was converted on 27 Apr 1789 and shortly thereafter became a New Light Congregational minister, as an itinerant and then as pastor of the Cornwallis, NS, church. In 1797 he was baptized by immersion and by 1807 was pastor of the Cornwallis Baptist Church, which he founded. Over the next 40 years he was responsible for establishing BAPTIST churches in all 3 Maritime colonies. In 1800 he was a key organizer of the NS Baptist Assn, the forerunner of the present United Baptist Convention of the Atlantic Provinces. Although possessing little formal education himself, Manning's pressure for a denominational school resulted in the founding of Horton Academy (1828) and Acadia College (1838), both in Wolfville, NS. He was also a driving force behind support for foreign missions, the TEMPERANCE movement and home missions. Poorly supported by his congregation, Manning farmed and doctored his neighbours to augment his uncertain income. BARRY M. MOODY

Manning, Ernest Charles, politician, Christian layman, premier of Alberta 1943-68 (b at Carnduff, Sask 20 Sept 1908). From modest beginnings as a student at William ABERHART's Prophetic Bible Institute in Calgary, Manning eventually became premier of Alberta and one of Canada's most effective provincial leaders. He was re-elected 7 consecutive times and retired in 1968 at the peak of his power. Manning grew up in a conventional Saskatchewan farm family and as a teenager was drawn to Aberhart's religious radio broadcasts. He studied with Aberhart and later became the institute's executive secretary. He joined Aberhart's Cabinet as provincial secretary, but his role in policymaking was initially limited by a bout of tuberculosis. Nevertheless, he enjoyed Aberhart's confidence, and when Aberhart died from liver disease in 1943 Manning was chosen leader of the SOCIAL CREDIT Party and premier. His first challenge was the wartime popularity of the CO-OPERATIVE COMMONWEALTH FEDERATION; in the 1944 election he opposed the CCF's demand for nationalization of private utilities and won handily.

Manning's stewardship of Alberta affairs for the

next 25 years was marked by cautious financial conservatism and cautious social reformism. After the discovery of the giant LEDUC oil field in 1947, the government saw the promise of rich revenues to finance "good government"; successful oil policies attracted capital and maximized oil exploration and development. The industry grew rapidly, provincial revenues soared, and funds were poured into planned expansion of the educational, health and transportation facilities that brought Alberta into the modern era. Manning's administration was clear of corruption and, despite huge budgetary surpluses, government growth was controlled.

The combination of low taxes – Alberta has been free of a sales tax except for a few months in 1936 – and efficient services, plus Manning's unchallengeable rectitude, proved politically invincible. His unease at the "leftward" drift of federal politics, especially after the election of Lester PEARSON's Liberals in 1963, led him to oppose several federal policies, including compulsory national medicare. He fielded his own non-compulsory, subsidized medical-care scheme, but in the end Alberta was forced to join the federal plan.

Frustrated by the major parties' unwillingness to offer the voters clear-cut philosophical choices, Manning published an appeal for a reordering of Canadian politics. In *Political Realignment: A Challenge to Thoughtful Canadians* (1967), he called for a regrouping of forces into a social-democratic party and a "social conservative" party, offering a free economy plus a humanitarian concern for the truly needy. None of the parties showed much interest in this proposal.

In 1968 Manning resigned as premier. He left no designated successor, and 3 years later the Social Credit government, under Premier Harry STROM, was defeated. Manning was a senator 1970-83. He was given honorary degrees by several universities and was made a Companion of the Order of Canada. In 1981 he was the first recipient of the Alberta Order of Excellence, and he received the National Humanitarian Award from B'nai B'rith in 1982. He continued his weekly religious broadcasts on radio stations across Canada and the US.

JOHN J. BARR

Ernest Manning posing at a wartime housing project, June 1943 (*courtesy Provincial Archives of Alberta/A. Blyth Coll*).

Mannix, Frederick Charles, businessman (b at Edmonton 21 Oct 1913). As a young man he worked in the construction camps of his father's company, Fred Mannix Co. The elder Mannix sold control of the company to a US-based firm in the 1940s, but Frederick Charles regained control after his father's death in 1951 and built it into an international giant with diverse interests in oil, coal, pipelines, earth moving and industrial plants. By 1983 Mannix owned or controlled a network of 132 companies, including Loram International, Techman Engineering, Pembina Resources and Manalta Coal (the largest coal producer in Canada), and commanded corporate assets estimated at $1 billion. He was also director of the Royal Bank and Stelco. An intensely private man, Mannix was involved in a widely publicized court battle with the Alberta government over the expropriation of his ranch, S of Calgary, for a park. In 1985 in the face of the slump in megaproject and pipeline construction contracts, Loram International Ltd was put on hold and its $12 million worth of heavy equipment sold. Mannix is a laureate of the first Canadian Business Hall of Fame and an Officer of the Order of Canada.

EARLE GRAY

Reading: Earle Gray, *Wildcatters* (1982).

Mannumi, Davidee, earlier known as Munamee-kotak, sculptor, character actor (b Cape Dorset region, SW Baffin I 1919). Mannumi immigrated to Iqaluit [Frobisher Bay] in the DEW-line construction period mid-1950s but has now returned to Cape Dorset. One of the Arctic's outstanding early carvers, his sculptural work *Mother and Child* was presented to Her Majesty Queen Elizabeth II by the people of Canada on the occasion of the royal tour 1954. Mannumi also proved to be an outstanding actor in his portrayal of Sowniapik in Paramount Pictures' *The White Dawn*, filmed on south Baffin I 1973. Along with his other talents, Mannumi is well known among Inuit as a graceful dancer, thus confirming a long-held Inuit belief that a talented human is the true art object. Such a person should be capable of performing many skills – carving, storytelling, singing and dancing – outward evidence of *inulariak*, a worthy human being.

JAMES HOUSTON

Mansel Island, 112 km long by 48 km wide, is the smallest of 3 islands lying across the entrance to HUDSON BAY. Its topography features a gently undulating limestone lowland with elevations not exceeding 100 m. The entire island was submerged under higher sea levels at the end of the last glaciation. A legacy of this marine transgression is the particularly striking relic beach deposits and elevated former shoreline features. The island itself is an outcrop of ancient resistant marine sediments and is part of an elongated escarpment extending 725 km along the N and E margin of Hudson Bay.

DOUG FINLAYSON

Manske, Richard Helmuth Frederick, scientist (b at Berlin, Ger Sept 1901; d at Guelph, Ont 7 Sept 1977). In 1906 Manske immigrated with his family to Macklin, Sask. After studying at Queen's and U of Manchester and spending 5 years in the US, he returned to Canada in 1931 to the National Research Council, Ottawa. Appointed director of Dominion Rubber Co (now UniRoyal) Research Laboratories at Guelph, Ont, in 1943, he retired in 1966 and joined U of Waterloo as adjunct professor of chemistry. His studies of the plant alkaloids span some 50 years and resulted in over 150 research publications and 17 volumes of a standard reference monograph. His other interests ranged from music, astronomy, bird-watching and Greek philosophy to the culinary arts. Elected to the RSC (1935), he was president (1964) and honorary fellow (1967) of the Chemical Inst of Canada and received its medal (1959) and the Morley Medal of the American Chemical Society (1972).

RUSSELL RODRIGO

Manuel, George, Shuswap Indian, political organizer, author (b at Neskonlith IR, BC 17 Feb 1921). A widely respected, self-educated man and clever political strategist, Manuel was second president (1970-76) of the National Indian Brotherhood during intense local-level Indian protest and numerous important court decisions affecting Indians. He helped establish the NIB and its member organizations as a force to be reckoned with in Indian affairs. A worldwide traveller in support of indigenous peoples, he emulated the principles of frugality, community development and leadership-by-example as espoused by Tanzanian president Julius Nyerere. Manuel thrust Canadian Indian affairs onto the world stage at the UN and elsewhere and in 1975 became founding president of the World Council of Indigenous Peoples, from which post he promoted the concept of indigenous peoples as the "Fourth World." He became Officer of the Order of Canada in 1986.

J. RICK PONTING

Manufacturing in Canada had its beginnings early in the 18th century, but it was not until the late 19th century, with the development of electricity and a national political objective, that it achieved significant growth. Throughout the 20th century, manufacturing has contributed significantly to the economic well-being and prosperity of Canadians. Manufacturing provides equipment for exploring, developing, extracting, processing and distributing resources from land, oceans and forests; for example, hydroelectric generators, fishing vessels, railway locomotives, farm machinery, mining equipment and supplies, machines for making paper, and machinery for transforming oil and natural gas and coal into chemicals, textiles, paints, etc. Durable goods are manufactured for housing, transportation, communications, education, recreation, entertainment, personal and health care – ranging from refrigerators, automobiles, telephones, pianos, aircraft, windows and doors to tea kettles. Personal goods are manufactured for clothing, footwear, recreation, entertainment, health care; for example, dresses, shoes, suits, boots, bandages, books, video displays, toys and games, etc. Manufactured edible goods include beverages, butter, bread, cheese, milk, processed fruits, fish, meats and vegetables. Manufacturing also includes machinery and equipment to package, handle, distribute, store and record all other manufactured goods.

The export of manufactured goods enables Canadians to earn foreign currencies for travel and vacations and to purchase imported goods. In 1987, about one-third of the total production of Canadian factories was exported. Manufacturing is a major purchaser of raw materials and services; Statistics Canada data show that, for every 3 new jobs created in manufacturing, about 3 more jobs are created, ie, one each in the service sector, the resource sector and in a related manufacturing industry. To illustrate this point, steel is manufactured from iron ore, coal and other materials, which are mined and transported by railways, ships, trucks and conveyors (all manufactured goods). Executives, salespeople, engineers and others in the steel companies use all modes of transportation and types of accommodation and purchase many services (eg, data processing, communications, legal, accounting).

Manufacturing in Canada began with flour mills. The first gristmills were built in New France in the 17th century and, by 1840, there were 400 in UPPER CANADA and LOWER CANADA producing flour for domestic and foreign sale (*see* FLOUR MILLING INDUSTRY). Iron smelting began in the 1730s at the FORGES ST-MAURICE near Trois-Rivières, Qué. By the mid-1740s, this foundry supplied some of New France's armament requirements as well as stoves and household utensils. The first steamboat made in Canada, the ACCOM-

MODATION, was built in 1809 by the Eagle Foundry of Montréal, which made all of the more than 100 parts for its engines. The engines of the ROYAL WILLIAM, which was, in 1833, the first ship to cross the Atlantic almost continuously under steam power, were manufactured by St Mary's Foundry in Montréal.

Several events in the last half of the 19th century stimulated substantial growth in Canada's manufacturing industries. The first was CONFEDERATION in 1867. With political unification and self-government came geographic expansion, construction of the CANADIAN PACIFIC RAILWAY, and new settlement bringing population increases, skills and capital. In 1871 a group of businessmen founded the CANADIAN MANUFACTURERS' ASSN (CMA) dedicated to promoting the growth of manufacturing. Eight years later, John A. Macdonald's NATIONAL POLICY established protective tariffs to encourage domestic processing of Canadian materials. Newly established factories, processing products for domestic consumption (eg, lumber, grains, animal products), survived and prospered even during the economic depression of the late 1870s and early 1880s. During this period, the discovery of electricity and the subsequent harnessing of some of Canada's vast hydro resource provided industry with an efficient, low-cost source of electrical energy (*see* HYDROELECTRICITY). At the same time the extent of the mineral wealth beneath the Canadian Shield began to be realized, stimulating great interest in Canada's growth potential. WWI stimulated industrial development and diversification, especially in such industries as steel, shipbuilding, nonferrous metals and pulp and paper. By 1920 manufacturing directly employed 600 000 workers, about 17% of the total labour force at that time. The worldwide depression of the 1930s reduced economic activity and stifled industrial progress in Canada as in other countries, but Canadian industry expanded and diversified dramatically during WWII. There was swift growth in heavy industries (vehicles, aircraft, armaments, shipbuilding and steel) and spectacular development in aluminum, electrical apparatus, communications equipment, toolmaking and chemicals. By the end of the war, manufacturing directly employed over 1 million workers, more than 25% of the labour force.

Postwar Developments

Between 1945 and the 1980s, manufacturing has accounted for 22-24% of Canada's total real output of goods and services. Employment has roughly doubled, from 1 to 2 million, but this represents a decline in the proportion of total employment because output per worker in manufacturing has risen about two-thirds again as fast as national productivity. Manufacturing productivity gains have, in fact, contributed about one-third of the gains in real per capita income since WWII. In this period Canada's manufacturing industry has been strongly affected by developments in ELECTRONICS, energy-price escalation (especially in the mid-1970s) and trade liberalization resulting from renegotiation of parts of the General Agreement on Tariffs and Trade (GATT) and from the drastic changes in the state of international competition.

Electronics The first industrial computer was introduced in Canada in 1957, and since then computer TECHNOLOGY has found widespread use in manufacturing – for production and sales planning, inventory control, accounting and payroll, personnel records, market analysis, business planning, evaluating strategies, etc. The use of computer-aided design (CAD), computer-aided manufacturing (CAM) and ROBOTICS technologies has increased rapidly. Electronics spurred the explosive growth of Canada's TELECOMMUNICATIONS industry, which reached worldwide stature by the 1980s. Canadian manufacturers participated in the AEROSPACE INDUSTRY by designing and producing communication satellites and components for spacecraft and aircraft (*see* SPACE TECHNOLOGY).

Energy The rapid rise in world oil prices in the 1970s had a stimulating effect on the development of Canada's rich energy resources, ie, oil, bitumen, gas, coal, hydro and uranium. Demand increased for machinery and equipment for exploring and developing energy resources, for producing energy in a usable form and distributing it. The increase permitted Canadian manufacturers to achieve internationally competitive scales of operation, and Canadian-manufactured machinery and equipment have been used in energy development and production throughout the world.

Trade Four developments in trade policies and practices in this period affected Canadian manufacturers substantially: the Canada-US Autopact; the GENERAL AGREEMENT ON TARIFFS AND TRADE (GATT); the world competitive environment, particularly the emergence of lesser developed countries; and the bilateral FREE TRADE agreement with the US reached (though not yet ratified) in late 1987. The 1965 CANADA-US AUTOMOTIVE PRODUCTS AGREEMENT (known as the Autopact) between Canada and the US created a conditional, duty-free environment which has allowed the Canadian and US industries to rationalize according to appropriate economies of scale, resulting in efficient industries that serve an integrated Canada-US market. The Autopact benefited both countries at different times. Canada did gain substantially more production, an increase in trade and productivity, a greater share of N American automotive employment and lower consumer prices.

Canada was one of 23 major trading nations that signed the original GATT treaty in 1947. GATT is a multilateral agreement signed by 85 nations and 30 provisional signees; its rules call for elimination of discriminatory treatment in international commerce in order to maximize the use of world resources and thereby raise living standards. GATT membership is a national commitment to the principle of "freer trade." There have been 8 rounds of GATT negotiations (1947, 1949, 1951, 1956, 1961, 1967, 1979 and 1986-underway). Between 1966 and 1986 the share of Canadian production exported increased from 18.8% to 39%; increases occurred in almost all product categories. The value of export shipments of manufactured goods in 1986 was $98 billion. With "freer trade," the volume of manufactured goods imported into Canada has increased. Canada's degree of trade exposure is high by international standards, though it varies from sector to sector. For example, groups of industries that operate on a localized basis (eg, parts of food and beverages, metal-fabricating and nonmetallic mineral products) naturally have low trade exposure, and activity in the domestic economy is more important. Resource-oriented sectors (eg, primary metals, paper and wood products) have a high export orientation and a lower import penetration of the domestic market. Sectors that tend to be more rationalized on a N American basis (eg, the MACHINERY AND EQUIPMENT INDUSTRIES) have offset high import penetration with success in export markets. Sectors such as textiles, leather products and ELECTRICAL APPLIANCES have been facing high import penetration with little offsetting exports (although exports are increasing in many categories).

The state of international competition has changed drastically since the late 1950s and early 1960s. At that time, Europe and Japan were largely preoccupied with postwar rebuilding and with the development of internal markets; Canada's share of the world's exports of manufactured goods rose from 4.5% to 6%. The emergence of Japan and Europe as industrial powers has meant tougher competition across the board for Canadian manufacturers. But, as these economies have become more advanced and as costs have risen, competition has been based increasingly on product quality and technology rather than on price (*see* INDUSTRIAL QUALITY CONTROL). This emphasis has meant intensified competition in the domestic and international markets in such sectors as transportation equipment (including automobiles), machinery and electronic equipment. At the same time, industrialization among lesser developed countries (LDCs) has focused on sectors producing labour-intensive, low-technology, highly transportable goods. Therefore, increasing import penetration from LDCs has created significant problems in Canada in such sectors as clothing, certain textiles, the lower range of the footwear market, and consumer electrical products.

Canada's Manufacturing Structure

The value of goods shipped by Canada's 47 000 manufacturing establishments was almost $250 billion in 1986; fuel and electricity costs were $7.3 billion; materials and supplies $136 billion; wages and salaries $43 billion. Despite remarkable expansion in manufacturing in the western provinces, Ontario and Québec still dominate most industries, accounting for over half and just under a quarter of Canada's manufacturing output, respectively. Many consumer goods industries are concentrated in these 2 provinces, which have well over half the country's population. Among these industries are food and beverages, TOBACCO, shoes and leather products, clothing, FURNITURE AND FIXTURES, transportation equipment, electrical products, and scientific and leisure goods (*see* SPORTING-GOODS INDUSTRY). Resource-based manufacturing industries are spread more evenly across the country, eg, wood industries, newsprint, pulp and paper, steel and primary metals, nonmetallic minerals, petroleum refineries and chemicals. As resource development continues in the 1980s, resource-based manufacturing will grow in the western and Atlantic provinces. The western provinces now account for a significant and growing proportion of the metal-fabricating and machinery output. The CMA strongly supported the free trade agreement proposed by the Mulroney government, arguing that it will create significant investment and employment opportunities for Canadian manufacturers. LAURENT J. THIBAULT

Maple (*Acer*), genus of trees and shrubs of the maple family (Aceraceae). Of the 125 species found worldwide, over two-thirds grow in China; 10 are native to Canada. Maples are a major constituent of eastern deciduous forests. Sugar, black, silver, red and striped maples are found in the East; mountain maple occurs eastwards from Manitoba; Manitoba maple in Saskatchewan and Manitoba; bigleaf, Douglas and vine maples in BC. The tree may be large, medium-sized or small, depending on species. The leaves are opposite, usually simple, lobed and have 3-9 veins. The paired, winged fruits are a food source for birds and small mammals; deer and moose eat young twigs and leaves. Maples grow in various soils and at varying altitudes but prefer deep, moist, fertile soils. The great commercial value of the hard, durable maple wood is overshadowed by the worldwide fame of MAPLE SUGAR and syrup. The maple leaf has long been considered an appropriate emblem for Canada. Maple leaves were used in coats of arms granted (1868) to Ontario and Québec and the new Canadian coat of arms granted in 1921. The leaf was used on regimental badges in WWI and WWII and was confirmed as an official national symbol in 1965 with the proclamation of the national flag.

ESTELLE LACOURSIÈRE

Maple Ridge, BC, District Municipality, pop 36 023 (1986c), 32 232 (1981c), area 26 709 ha, inc 1984, is located 40 km E of Vancouver, bounded by the FRASER R on the S and on the N by the Golden Ears Mountains. The largest of the 6 communities within the municipality was formerly named Haney, after a pioneer. Its northern area is rugged and mountainous; the western section flat and open. Rapid growth in recent years stems from the development of large tracts of residential land. Forestry and agriculture are the leading resource sectors, along with lumber mills on the Fraser, logging in the northern area, dairying in Pitt Meadows and mixed farming in Maple Ridge. Golden Ears Provincial Park at Alouette Lk has the highest day use in the province. Whonnock Lake Municipal Park is heavily used as a swimming and picnic area. ALAN F.J. ARTIBISE

Maple Sugar Industry Maple syrup is a unique agricultural product. The sweet sap of the sugar MAPLE (*Acer saccharum*) was known and valued by the native peoples of eastern N America long before the arrival of European settlers. An Iroquois legend tells of the piercing of the bark of a maple and the use of the "sweet water" to cook venison, a happy accident which established the culinary tradition of maple-cured meats. French settlers probably learned from the Indians how to tap trees to obtain sap and how to boil it to reduce it to sweet syrup or sugar slabs to be stored for later use. The Ojibwa called the "sugaring off" period the "maple moon" or "sugar month." The tradition of sugaring off became established in communities in the deciduous forests of N America and has survived to the present time.

World production of maple sugar is limited to the Maple Belt, the hardwood FOREST stretching from the midwestern US through Ontario, Québec and New England and into the Canadian Maritimes. In the fall, the sugar maple lays down concentrated sugars in the rays of the tree; these sugars mature during winter and are harvested while the frost is still in the ground. The sap flow is stimulated in spring as the days become warmer and temperatures rise above 0°C during daylight, followed by below-freezing nights. Within the tree, positive pressures (as high as 165 kPa or 1.6 atmospheres) produce a natural flow of sap that is tapped by boring holes into the tree. The clear sap rushes out of these holes and into the collection system. As the pressure drops during the day, the sap flow slows down and stops. Negative pressure is then found within the tree, and it begins to absorb water through the root system. The next day, as the tree warms up, positive pressure is restored and the pumping action yields another flow. The process continues for about 6 weeks in early spring. At the end of that time the sap takes on a cloudy appearance and the sugar content drops off dramatically. During the height of the sugaring season, sap contains about 2.5% sugar; towards the end of the season less than 1%. During the maple harvest, the tree will give up about 7% of its sap; tests confirm that this does no long-term damage to the tree. Many of the tapped trees are well over 100 years old.

There are various sap-gathering methods. Traditional bucket collection, although still used throughout the Maple Belt, is being replaced by a vacuum-tubing system that reduces labour and creates a more sanitary environment for collection. Once the maple sap is collected, it is evaporated into syrup. The dilute raw material is reduced to remove excess water; nothing is added. It takes approximately 151.4 L of maple sap to produce 3.8 L of pure maple syrup. Water can be removed from sap by using various systems, from wood-fired evaporators to reverse osmosis systems that separate water from the sugar molecules at high pressure. However, the sugarhouse remains the focal point of maple-syrup production; each sugar maker has one of his own.

Mature sugar maple tree (*Acer saccharum*), with details of leaf (*artwork by Claire Tremblay*).

There are about 20 000 maple-syrup producers in N America. In Canada, Québec is the major producer. In 1986 the province produced 9010 kL of maple syrup; Ontario, 628 kL; NB, 44 kL; and NS, 51 kL. Total production in 1986 amounted to 9733 kL. Maple syrup is a pure, natural sweetener, the only other liquid natural sweetener being honey. Maple syrup has an abundance of trace minerals that are essential to good nutrition: potassium, magnesium, phosphorus, manganese, iron, zinc, copper and tin, as well as calcium in concentrations 15 times higher than honey. It contains only one-tenth as much sodium as honey, an important consideration for those on a salt-restricted diet. Maple syrup is graded according to colour, flavour and density; standards are prescribed by law. It must be in the range of 65-67% Brix (a hydrometric scale for sugar solutions) or 32-34% on the Baumé scale (for liquids heavier than water). Anything less or more cannot be graded and sold as pure maple syrup. In 1986, 9022 t of maple syrup were exported. The US is the major consumer (82%). Small amounts are exported to Europe and Japan. In the early part of the 1970s, the traditional buyers were the large food companies. When the US Food and Drug Administration reduced the minimum volume of maple syrup that must be listed as an ingredient in products sold as "maple syrup" and "maple sugar" from 15% to 2%, sales plunged dramatically and the industry experienced a major crisis. Efforts were made to develop a new market aimed directly at the consumer and the growth of this market has rejuvenated the industry. Production of pure maple syrup has been encouraged by provincial and federal governments, resulting in an expansion of the crop over the last several years. Research conducted in both Canada and the US provides necessary production innovations to make the industry more efficient. But for the foreseeable future, the traditional sugarhouse and the family operation, so evocative of Canada's pioneer past, will remain.

LEO H. WERNER

Mapping, Computer-Assisted One of the fundamental changes to CARTOGRAPHY during the 20th century has been the introduction and use of computers and computer-driven machinery (especially drawing and graphic devices) to mapping. There are many ways to encode graphic images in the form of numbers, such as with Cartesian co-ordinate geometry, and computers are marvelous tools for encoding, storing, sorting and calculating with numbers.

Straight lines may be accurately defined by the X,Y co-ordinates of their end points, ie, pairs of numbers recording distance of a point to the right of and above (orthogonal directions) a defined origin. Wiggly lines may be similarly recorded by streams of X,Y co-ordinates. Images registered by a television-cameralike apparatus may be recorded as a table of numbers representing the colour intensity for every cell of the picture. These cells ("pixels") are usually organized in a fine rectangular grid ("raster") in a television camera or video tube.

Numerical data representing map images or geographic phenomena may be collected from aerial photographs, or by tracing from existing map documents. There are numerous ways that such data may be collected. Resembling a drafting table with a pointer attached by an electronic wire, a cartographic digitizer measures the position co-ordinates of that pointer and records them in a computer. The position of points can be recorded at frequencies high enough to sense every nuance of hand movement. The first patent holder for a cartographic digitizer is Prof A.R. Boyle of U Sask. Also available are devices which automatically scan documents into data representing a fine-resolution raster grid. They require complex computer programs to convert them into forms usable for mapmaking. Lines and shapes traced by a digitizer or recorded by a scanner may then be redrawn by a computer-driven graphic device.

The stored map, in the form of computer-stored numbers, may be processed by the computer through algebraic computations between recording and plotting. This opens countless possibilities, such as bringing together data representing overlapping or abutting maps, or data from different types of maps. Arithmetic operations required for changing scale or transforming the map through the various map projections are also easily done, and maps in the form of numerical data can be transmitted over telecommunication lines. Maps at different scales and of high graphic quality, with elaborate and accurately drawn symbolism, may be produced from the data in amazingly short time periods. One important contribution of digitized mapmaking is the potential to produce differently symbolized maps from the same data quickly enough that operators may experiment with the symbolism.

Photogrammetry, the science of measuring from photographs, has direct application to the mapmaking process. Much research has been done by photogrammeters in applying computers to measuring map information from aerial and space photographs.

A major problem with map data in the form of numbers in a computer is finding and correcting errors. But as a result of recent improvements in computer science and technology, map information may now be displayed on a screen and immediately manipulated by the terminal operator. Features identified by pointing to the graphic image may be moved, stretched, squashed, modified or erased. While the operator manipulates the image on the screen, the numerical data from which the image is generated are simultaneously altered. Systems designed for such functions are often referred to as "interactive mapping systems."

Other types of data manipulation are possible, eg, the mapping of the 3-dimensional characteristics of topographic maps. A surface can be numerically recorded and different types of symbolism, such as relief shading, contours or perspective views, can be generated from the data record. Another important application is in overlapping information from maps of different subject matter of the same area, and in calculating the areas of the new set of regions thus created. A map of soil capability may thus be compared with a map of current land use, and the areas of each class of match and mismatch may be listed in a convenient table. Systems designed for such calculation are generally termed GEOGRAPHICAL INFORMATION SYSTEMS. Computer mapping has also made possible the mapping of statistical, socioeconomic and demographic data (eg, census information). Such maps were formerly rare because the tedious handwork required to produce a single map was not often seen to be worth the effort.

In the late 1960s the Surveys and Mapping Branch of the Dept of Energy, Mines and Resources started a computer-aided mapping program, and it has recently shifted much of the development into an operational environment. Now reorganized, the Topographic Mapping Div has established a National Digital Topographic Computer Mapping Data-base. This provides a framework for efficient map maintenance and for special applications by clients. Satellite imagery is used extensively to locate areas of change and to assist in the planning of aerial photographic survey missions required to revise the large-scale map series. The "electronic atlas" project, established by the Geographical Services Div in the 1980s, offers geographical analysis capabilities from computerized atlas maps for government decision making and for education. Hydrographic charting by computer has progressed steadily from its beginnings in the early 1970s, and Statistics Canada has led in the development and implementation of statistical mapping systems. Many provincial mapping agencies started programs in the middle and late 1970s. Recognized pioneers in the development of computerized geographic information systems have been Environment Canada and its predecessors. Owing to the research activities of government agencies and numerous universities, Canada is acknowledged to be one of the leaders in the field. THOMAS K. POIKER AND DAVID H. DOUGLAS

Maquinna, or **Mukwina,** meaning "possessor of pebbles," Nootka chief (*fl* 1778-95?). Maquinna was the ranking leader of the Moachat group of Nootka Sound Indians on the W coast of Vancouver I during the early years of European contact. Following James COOK's 1778 visit, NOOTKA SOUND became an important fur-trading centre. Maquinna controlled the FUR TRADE and emerged as the dominant Indian leader in the Sound, operating as a middleman. Maquinna was also involved in dealings with British and Spanish representatives who visited Nootka Sound as the 2 nations asserted rival claims to the area. While Maquinna had achieved his position among the NOOTKA by traditional means, he was a leader whose role was changing because of the Europeans' impact. His power and prestige were enhanced by new wealth from the fur trade but, at the same time, he had to lead his people through new and sometimes difficult situations. His successor assumed the name of Maquinna.

ROBIN FISHER

Reading: Robin Fisher, *Contact and Conflict* (1977).

Marani, Ferdinand Herbert, architect (b at Vancouver 8 Aug 1893; d at Toronto 18 July 1971). Marani graduated from U of T in 1920 and shortly thereafter established a practice in Toronto. His partnerships include Marani and Morris (1947-59) and Marani, Rounthwaite and Dick (1964-71). His designs, which are noted for his contemporary translation of the Georgian tradition, include the original BANK OF CANADA building in Ottawa, the Medical Arts Building in Toronto and the Canadian Forces HQ in Washington, DC. Marani served in WWI and WWII and was a chairman of the Ontario Assn of Architects and of the Ontario College of Art. ANDREA KRISTOF

Marathon Swimming takes place on open water for distances in excess of 1500 m. Most marathon swims are across established bodies of water such as channels, lakes or straits. The best known and most prestigious is the crossing of the English Channel, a distance of approximately 34 km. Marathon swimmers aim to win races or set records such as first crossing, fastest time, youngest or oldest swimmer, first double or triple crossing, or most crossings by the same person. Most are professionals and swim for the prize money available to winners or record breakers. Matthew Webb, the first person to swim the English Channel without the aid of a life jacket, tried to cross the rapids and whirlpool below Niagara Falls in 1883 but drowned in the attempt.

Canadian long-distance swimmers have been among the world's best. The first to draw public attention was Toronto's George Young. In Jan 1927 he won the first Catalina Swim (32 km). His feat stimulated an interest in long-distance swimming, and was responsible for the introduction of the Marathon Swim, a highlight of the CANADIAN NATIONAL EXHIBITION in Toronto. In Aug 1927, the first "Professional Swim Championship of the World," for 21 miles (34 km), was staged at the CNE. Young did not win this event until 1931. In 1950, he was named the Canadian swimmer of the half century. The CNE world championship swims, at various distances, continued until 1937, then were cancelled owing to waning public interest. They were resumed in 1948, and by 1949 Cliff LUMSDON, of New Toronto, had emerged as an outstanding swimmer. He won the CNE men's world championship in 1949 and repeated this feat in 1950, 1952 and 1953. In 1955, he won the Marathon Swim of 32 mi (51.5 km), and was perhaps the finest swimmer of his day in the world. Marilyn BELL, of Toronto, became a household name in 1954. In July she was the first woman to complete the 26-mile (42 km) Atlantic City, NJ, marathon race, and in Sept became the first person to complete the arduous 64 km crossing of windswept Lake Ontario. In 1955 she was the youngest to swim the English Channel, and in 1956 crossed the dangerous Juan de Fuca Strait in record time. Bell was awarded the LOU MARSH TROPHY in 1954 as Canada's outstanding athlete. Both Lumsdon and Bell were coached by Gus Ryder, founder and coach of the Lakeshore Swim Club of New Toronto.

In the 1970s, 2 Canadian swimmers dominated long-distance swimming. Cindy NICHOLAS, of Scarborough, Ont, at age 16 made a record crossing of Lake Ontario in 1974, and one year later made her first of 10 English Channel crossings, setting a record for the crossing from France to England. In 1976 she was the women's world marathon-swimming champion, and in 1977 set the Channel round-trip speed record. By 1978, she had earned the title "Queen of the Channel" for the most crossings by a woman (6), and in 1979 she lowered her time for the 2-way crossing of the Channel. Loreen Passfield, of Etobicoke, Ont, was ranked the world's top woman marathon swimmer in both 1977 and 1978. In Aug 1987 Vicki Keith swam across Lake Ontario and back in 56 hours. BARBARA SCHRODT

Marchand, Félix-Gabriel, lawyer, journalist, playwright, premier of Québec 1897-1900 (b at St-Jean, LC 9 Jan 1832; d at Québec City 25 Sept 1900). Marchand, one of the last "vrai rouges" and an important transitional figure in Québec political life, assumed leadership of the shattered provincial Liberals in 1892 and led them to victory in 1897, promising, in a direct challenge to the Roman Catholic Church, to restore political control over education. The church blocked Marchand, however, and controlled education until the 1960s. Under Marchand the Liberal Party became an agent of industrial expansion, welcoming foreign capital and technology, developing Québec's vast hydroelectric-power potential and exploiting its forest resources. Although bitterly criticized, these policies were the foundation of Liberal political success for more than a generation. BERNARD L. VIGOD

Marchand, Jean, union leader, politician (b at Champlain, Qué 20 Dec 1918). After completing a social-science degree in labour relations at Laval (1942), he became an organizer for the Fédération de la pulpe et du papier and for the Confédération des travailleurs catholiques du Canada (1944). Secretary general of the CTCC from 1947, he was elected president 1961. During the 1950s, with other unionists, intellectuals and reform members of the Québec Liberal Party, he helped bring about the defeat of the Union Nationale government (1960). His union central, renamed the CONFEDERATION OF NATIONAL TRADE UNIONS in 1960, worked closely with the Liberal government of Jean LESAGE and won some legislative reforms, such as the right of government employees to form unions and to strike. Critical of the rise of SEPARATISM in Québec in the early 1960s, he was persuaded by PM Lester PEARSON to be a member of the Royal Commission on Bilingualism and Biculturalism and to join the federal Liberal Party in 1965. His presence was designed to enhance the francophone presence in Cabinet and to defend the cause of federalism in Québec. He agreed on condition that 2 longtime friends, Pierre TRUDEAU and Gérard PELLETIER, be allowed to join him. He held several important Cabinet posts, resigning in 1976 to run in the Québec provincial election to try to prevent the PARTI QUÉBÉCOIS from coming to power. He failed in both objectives. He was appointed to the Senate in Dec 1976; selected Speaker in Mar 1980, he played a central role in the 1981 debate over reform of the Constitution. After his resignation from the Senate he was president of the Canadian Transport Commission 1983-85, when he became a director of Ports Canada and vice-chairman of the Québec Port Corp. In 1986 he became an Officer of the Order of Canada. M.D. BEHIELS

Marchand, Leonard Stephen, politician, agronomist (b at Vernon, BC 16 Nov 1933). Len Marchand was the first Indian federal Cabinet minister and the second native member of the federal Parliament after Louis RIEL. Through early involvement with the N American Indian Brotherhood, he left a career as agricultural research scientist in 1965 to work as special assistant to 2 successive Cabinet ministers. He was elected Liberal MP for Kamloops-Cariboo in 1968, and was minister of state for small business 1976-77 and minister of state for the environment 1977-79. Defeated in 1979, he returned to BC as administrator for the 5-band Nicola Valley Indian Administration. He has been a senator since 1984. A low-profile politician considered successful in his ministerial roles, Marchand represented a liberal-individualist approach to business, environmental and Indian issues. This, and his qualified support for his party's native policies, set him apart from the mainstream, both of Indian and of environmentalist activism. BENNETT MCCARDLE

Marchildon, Philip Edward, baseball player (b at Penetanguishene, Ont 25 Oct 1913). He was pitching in a semipro Ontario league when discovered at a Barrie tryout camp. He joined the Philadelphia Athletics in 1940 and, despite a 3-year interruption for war service, won 68 major league games before retiring in 1950. In 1947, 14 of his 19 wins for the 5th-place Athletics were against first-division teams. WILLIAM HUMBER

Marco Polo, sailing ship of 1625 tons launched in April 1851 from the building yard of James Smith, Courtney Bay, Saint John, NB. She was the most famous ship built in NB, cutting a week off the previous record run from England to Australia, completing the round trip in less than 6 months and earning the title "Fastest Ship in the World." She remained in the Australian trade for 15 years before being bought by Norwegian owners for the Québec timber trade. She ran ashore at Cape Cavendish, PEI, in 1883. JAMES MARSH

Marcotte, Gilles, journalist, critic, professor, novelist, essayist (b at Sherbrooke, Qué 1925). Marcotte has been one of the best-known and most-respected Québec intellectuals. First a journalist at *La Tribune*, then at *Le Devoir* and *La Presse*, Marcotte worked for Radio-Canada and the NFB before becoming literature professor at U de M in 1965. He has been active in publishing, notably *Écrits du Canada français*, since 1954 and has written a series of columns in *L'*ACTUALITÉ. Often consulted and interviewed, the winner of many major prizes, Marcotte has been at the centre of every kind of literary activity. He has written 2 novels, *Le Poids de Dieu* (1962) and *Retour à Coolbrooke* (1965) and a spare and sombre narrative, *Un Voyage* (1973). As a novelist, Marcotte, a master of narrative technique, sometimes lacks daring and spontaneity; he has some difficulty in *seeing* and being seen. The critic has no such problems. Marcotte's collection of essays, *Une* LITTÉRATURE QUI SE FAIT (1962), is a benchmark in the evolution of Québec critical thinking, opening new horizons on Saint-Denys GARNEAU and on such themes as solitude, exile and vertigo. *Le Roman à l'imparfait* (1976) is an original analysis of the experiences of 5 novelists struggling with characters who are themselves writers, storytellers, readers: Bessette, Ducharme, Blais, Godbout and Ferron. He published an important study on the prose of Rimbaud in 1983. In *La Littérature et le reste* (1980), an exchange of letters with André Brochu, Marcotte develops and systematizes his theoretical ideas with grace and wit. LAURENT MAILHOT

Marcuse, Judith Rose, née Margolick, dancer, choreographer, teacher, director (b at Montréal 13 Mar 1947). Her broad international background in ballet and modern dance has made Marcuse a versatile choreographer. Trained initially in Montréal, Marcuse attended Britain's Royal Ballet School 1962-65 and studied subsequently in Canada and the US. She danced with a number of leading companies, notably Les GRANDS BALLETS CANADIENS, 1965-68, the Bat-Dor Dance Co of Israel 1970-72, and England's Ballet Rambert 1974-76. Although Marcuse still performs, she has become increasingly occupied as a choreographer, creating works for Canadian and foreign troupes. She has been artistic director of the Judith Marcuse Dance Project Soc since its founding in 1980 and of the Repertory Dance Co of Canada since 1984. Marcuse has won both the Jean A. Chalmers Award for Choreography (1976) and the Clifford E. Lee Award for Choreography (1979). MICHAEL CRABB

Margarine (oleomargarine), butter substitute consisting mainly of refined, hydrogenated vegetable oils (canola and soybean), milk powder and water, with added salt, preservatives, emulsifiers, vitamins A and D, artificial flavour and vegetable colour. The soluble and insoluble ingredients are processed and heated in separate vats, then churned to form an emulsion, which is passed through heat exchangers to be cooled and hardened.

Invented by a Frenchman, Hyppolite Mège-Mouries, in 1869, margarine was soon patented and manufactured in many countries. Originally, beef fat and lard were used but later, with modern processing techniques, vegetable oils were introduced. More recently, concern about the role of saturated fats and oils in health has brought a greater use of polyunsaturated oils.

Dairy farmers vigorously opposed the sale of margarine, and as a result it was regulated or prohibited in many countries. In Canada, the manufacture and sale of margarine was forbidden by an Act of Parliament in 1886. The ban was enforced until 1917, when wartime shortages of butter brought legalization; it was banned again in 1923. A lengthy conflict persisted between farmers and consumers, so that margarine did not become permanently legal until 1948, when Parliament referred the issue to the Supreme Court. Despite federal law, some provinces forbade the colouring of margarine; today the provinces permit it but control the colour.

Production in Canada began quickly, rising from about 53 000 t in 1954 to 129 000 t in 1986. The output would be much greater if margarine were available in restaurants, but provincial laws require that eating places which serve margarine must display in large letters "Oleomargarine is served here." Thus the Canadian dairy farmer still has a measure of protection. ERWIN KREUTZWEISER

Maria Chapdelaine (serialized in Paris 1914, publ in Montréal 1916), a novel embodying the spirit of French Canada at its most lyrical, was based by author Louis HÉMON, an expatriate Frenchman, on his experiences in the Lac Saint-Jean district of Québec. Church and farm provide a physical and symbolic setting for the romance, as the seasons and feast days provide a mythic temporal framework for its action. Following the death of her mother and that of her lover François Paradis, Maria must choose between 2 suitors: Lorenzo Surprenant, who tempts her with the riches of America, and Eutrope Gagnon, the boy next door. She unselfishly accepts Gagnon, thereby ensuring the survival of family and community and affirming the traditional values of rural French Canada. Frequently reprinted both in Canada and in France, *Maria Chapdelaine* has been filmed 3 times, most recently by Gilles CARLE (1983). W.H. Blake's translation (1921), beautifully illustrated with woodcuts by Thoreau MACDONALD, remains the standard English edition. MICHÈLE LACOMBE

Marie de l'Incarnation, née Marie Guyart, founder of Ursuline order in Canada, mystic, author (b at Tours, France 28 Oct 1599; d at Québec C 30 Apr 1672). As a child, Marie Guyart, daughter of a master baker, showed unusual spirituality. Her husband, Claude Martin, died in 1619 after 2 years of marriage, leaving her with a 6-month-old son and a bankrupt business. Urged to remarry, she withdrew into secluded meditation and prayer and on 24 Mar 1620 experienced a mystical and emotional "conversion." She decided to withdraw from the world, but her sister and brother-in-law called on her to help their failing carrier business. Under Marie the business prospered but visions continued to haunt her. In 1632, though heartbroken at leaving her son Claude, she entered the Ursuline cloister at Tours. She took her vows in 1633 and taught Christian doctrine for 6 years. From her reading of the *Relations des Jésuites* and her visions she concluded that her vocation was in Canada. With 2 Ursulines and Mme de LA PELTRIE she landed at Québec 1 Aug 1639 and established a convent in the lower town. In 1642 it moved to a permanent stone building in the upper town. She worked zealously at educating French and Indian girls, wrote numerous theological and spiritual treatises, an Iroquois catechism and Algonquian and Iroquois dictionaries, and kept abreast of public affairs. CORNELIUS J. JAENEN

Reading: J. Marshall, ed, *Word from New France: The Selected Letters of Marie de l'Incarnation* (1967).

Marie-Rose, Mother, name in religion of Eulalie Durocher, educator (b at St-Antoine-sur-Richelieu, LC 6 Oct 1811; d at Longueuil, Canada E 6 Oct 1849). As housekeeper to a brother at the Beloeil presbytery 1831-43, she became alarmed at the lack of rural schools. When Bishop Ignace BOURGET of Montréal was unable to form a local community of the Sisters of the Holy Names of Jesus and Mary, a teaching order in Marseilles, France, Durocher agreed in 1844 to become founder and first superior of a Canadian religious community of the same name. Recognized as a woman of exceptional virtue, she brought to her work unflagging enthusiasm and unequalled ability. In the 1870s Bourget expressed the hope that she would be beatified, and on 23 May 1982 this wish was fulfilled by Pope John Paul II. SISTER MARGUERITE JEAN, S.C.I.M.

Marie-Victorin, Frère, brother in the Écoles chrétiennes community, botanist, teacher (b Conrad Kirouac at Kingsey-Falls, Qué 3 Apr 1885; d at St-Hyacinthe, Qué 15 July 1944). Son of a prosperous merchant, Kirouac grew up in Québec C. At 16 he joined the Frères des Écoles chrétiennes in Montréal. His postulant and early teaching years were often disrupted by illness, but long periods of convalescence allowed him to study BOTANY. As teacher at the Collège de Longueuil from 1905, Marie-Victorin stimulated student life, founded a study circle and published several literary works. However, botany took more and more of his time. Around 1908 he published his first scientific articles. He was named professor of botany at U of M in 1920. There followed 25 years of intense scientific and social activity. At the Botanical Inst, which he founded in 1922, Marie-Victorin gathered a small research team which included Jules Brunel, Ernest Rouleau, and Jacques ROUSSEAU. As his monumental *Flore laurentienne* (1935) shows, Marie-Victorin was above all a taxonomist. However, the importance he gave to phytogeography and the evolution of American flora paved the way for ecologists such as Pierre DANSEREAU.

As ardent propagandist of "scientific cultivation" and of a nationalism like that of Lionel GROULX, Marie-Victorin was a major Québec intellectual and political figure in the 1930s. He took part in founding the Association canadienne-française pour l'avancement des sciences and the Société canadienne d'histoire naturelle, in organizing the Cercles des jeunes naturalistes and, most notably, in creating the Montréal Botanical Garden. He became a member of the RSC in 1924. Marie-Victorin was at the height of his power as a scholar and leader when he died in an automobile accident. RAYMOND DUCHESNE

Marion, Léo Edmond, organic chemist, administrator, educator (b at Ottawa 22 Mar 1899; d there 16 July 1979). After studying at Queen's and McGill and spending a year at University of

Vienna, Marion became R.H.F. MANSKE's assistant at the National Research Council Laboratories. When Manske left NRC in 1942, Marion became chief organic chemist. His dedication to basic research, and the support of E.W.R. STEACIE and C.J. MACKENZIE, enabled him to build an internationally recognized school of alkaloid chemistry. At the NRC he directed the pure chemistry division 1952-65 and acted as VP (scientific) 1963-65. He was president of the RSC, and editor in chief of the *Canadian Journal of Research*, and contributed to the early growth of the chemistry departments of U de M and Carleton, ending his career as dean of pure and applied science at Ottawa. He received an OBE, many honorary doctorates and awards. O.E. EDWARDS

Mariposa Folk Festival, *see* FOLK FESTIVALS.

Maritime Provinces PRINCE EDWARD ISLAND, NOVA SCOTIA and NEW BRUNSWICK cover 134 584 km^2 – just a little more than 1% of Canada's land surface. The populations of Nova Scotia at 873 199, New Brunswick at 710 422 and PEI at 126 646 constituted about 7% of the Canadian total of 25 354 064 (1986c). As part of a nation that has placed great stress on unlimited size and almost limitless space, and also on western development, Maritimers have often found themselves, as the 20th century has unfolded, pushed to the periphery of Canadian development.

The Maritimes constitute a cluster of peninsulas and islands which form the NE extension of the Appalachian highlands and are also significantly affected by the Atlantic Ocean. The tension between the pull of the continent and that of the Atlantic has, over the centuries, shaped the region's cultural, social, political and economic development. For much of its human period – both before and after European settlement – the Maritime region was a homeland for a distinctive group of people. Before the arrival of the first Europeans, the MICMAC, who constituted a single linguistic and cultural entity, inhabited all of present-day peninsular Nova Scotia, Cape Breton I, PEI and southern and eastern New Brunswick. Only in the upper Saint John R valley were the MALISEET, who spoke a somewhat different Algonquian dialect but had much in common with their Micmac neighbours. With the coming of the French, especially in the early 17th century, the Micmac-Maliseet hegemony over the region was challenged. From its beginnings in 1604 French ACADIA gradually came into existence, a territory roughly encompassing that now covered by the Maritime provinces. Though made up largely of isolated settlements, Acadia was united by a common language, culture and economy. By 1763 France was compelled to surrender its last remaining outpost in Acadia-Nova Scotia (*see* LOUISBOURG) to the British. Thus, in 150 years, the region had passed from Micmac-Maliseet control to the French; then, after 1713, to the dual sovereignty of France and Britain; and finally after 1763 to undisputed British control.

Once Britain controlled the entire region, ethnic heterogeneity characterized its settlement. Acadians, New Englanders, foreign Protestants from present-day W and E Germany and Switzerland, English, Irish, Scots and a mixture of LOYALISTS provided Nova Scotia, New Brunswick (created in 1784 for the Loyalists) and PEI with their unique ethnic composition. This basic Anglo-Saxon and Acadian ethnic mix was virtually unaffected by the hundreds of thousands of European immigrants who, bypassing the Maritimes, flooded into Canada, especially after 1900.

At CONFEDERATION in 1867, the Maritime provinces had little in common with Canada. The region's development had been radically different, and furthermore a Maritime distinctiveness had been significantly influenced by the interplay of 3 major forces: those of the Atlantic, New England and Britain. The Atlantic was for many inhabitants of the area a frontier of space and abundance, and for them its metaphors coloured many of the cultural expressions of their region. Its powerful appeal helped to provide, for some, not only an escape from the grim and often mundane realities of everyday existence, but also a sense of acute fatalism affected by the conviction that the environment could never effectively be mastered.

The second formative force, not only at Confederation but also throughout the post-Indian period, was that of neighbouring New England. Until the AMERICAN REVOLUTION shattered the Anglo-American empire, the Maritime region was "New England's Outpost," and even in the 1980s economic, cultural, religious and social ties between the regions have been surprisingly strong.

The British connection was the third formative force. After France's direct exercise of power in N America was eliminated, Britain's influence over the Maritimes was unrivalled. The arrival of thousands of Loyalists during and after the American Revolution, and the tens of thousands of British immigrants who settled in the region during the 19th century, reinforced Britain's influence. The interaction of these forces before 1867 gave the inhabitants of NS, NB and PEI a strong sense of provincial identity. They did not view themselves as Maritimers, and certainly not as Canadians, but rather as British Islanders, British Nova Scotians or British New Brunswickers.

It may be argued that the Maritime provinces have never fully recovered psychologically from the traumatic experience of Confederation and the sudden end in the late 19th century of the golden age of "Wooden Ships and Iron Men" (*see* SHIPPING HISTORY). Before Confederation, many Maritimers believed that their region had unlimited economic potential and that theirs was the most sophisticated and best administered of all the British colonies possessing RESPONSIBLE GOVERNMENT. It was felt that the Maritimes had a special role to play in the evolution of a new British Empire. The development of this sense of destiny came to a sudden halt after Confederation when the Maritimes found themselves left out of the westward transcontinental thrust of the new Canada, bypassed by immigrants to the interior, and lacking natural and human resources for industrialization. Most Maritimers believed the identity of the villain was obvious: the federal government in Ottawa. The proof was there – before Confederation there had been widespread prosperity and the entire region had shared a feeling of optimism and pride. After Confederation there were prolonged economic recessions and a growing sense of inferiority and bitterness.

The anti-Confederation feeling, especially strong in Nova Scotia, provided the emotional substance to much of Maritime regional protest, particularly 1867-1930. Maritimers tended to remain quiet until those periods of extreme economic crisis when their discontent and their suspicion of "Upper Canada" and "Upper Canadians" could be channelled into regional political protest (*see* REPEAL MOVEMENT). The MARITIME RIGHTS Movement of the 1920s was the last significant manifestation of regional protest and anti-Confederation feeling. Because the movement had never sought political involvement outside the traditional 2-party system, it could not transform the regional grievances into a permanent political framework. Even the Conservatives, who had been champions of the movement, soon became Conservatives first and Maritime Righters second. Maritime Rights made good political rhetoric. It could help win elections, could be carefully stored until the next election, and did not demand political action or political sacrifice. It made more sense for pragmatic Maritimers to avoid the possible confrontation towards which the thrust of their regional complaints was driving them. To deviate from the 2-party system was considered political suicide. Evidently, central Canadian progress and development could not be reversed by "paranoid" regional protest separated from "power politics."

The mood of the Maritime region had obviously changed by the end of the 1920s. One reason was economic resurgence after 1927, when a construction and tourism boom encouraged the first signs of hope in nearly a decade. The staples industries also revived, as did the traditional markets in Britain and the US. Capital development gave new importance to the pulp and paper industry. But revival was largely restricted to areas such as the Annapolis Valley, Cape Breton, Halifax County and Saint John. Elsewhere the decline continued, and consequently there was a steady exodus of young Maritimers – at least 300 000 from 1900 to 1930, of whom fully three-quarters went to the US. The social costs of such emigration are incalculable, but it seems reasonable to assume that those with ambition and initiative more often left the region than stayed. The remaining population resigned itself to a collective fate only as promising as their individual prospects of success. For most, the Maritime Rights Movement had led to "cynicism and apathy"; a feeling of dependence had replaced regional pride and the cutting edge of alienation had been worn smooth by a prevailing indifference to change.

By the late 1970s the Maritimes had undergone a remarkable transformation of collective identity. No longer were Maritimers the most vociferous critics of Confederation and Canada; they had become, in an ironic twist of historical development, ardently Canadian. They had been able to move beyond the point of merely stressing their Maritime distinctiveness to a position where they could, at the same time, freely discuss and contemplate their powerful emotional attachment to Canada. When a person is able to admit to being an ardent Islander, New Brunswicker or Nova Scotian and an ardent Canadian at the same time, it reveals an ability to integrate 2 quite different, but not incompatible, levels of identity. According to Northrop FRYE, this dynamic tension between the imaginative sense of locality and the attachment to Canada is the essence of whatever the word "Canadian" means. Nova Scotians are Nova Scotians, Islanders are Islanders, and New Brunswickers are New Brunswickers, because as one Maritime premier put it in 1967, "we're Canadians before we're anything else." *See also* ATLANTIC PROVINCES.

GEORGE A. RAWLYK

Reading: Ernest R. Forbes, *The Maritime Rights Movement, 1919-1927* (1979); W.S. MacNutt, *The Atlantic Provinces* (1965); George A. Rawlyk, ed, *Historical Essays on the Atlantic Provinces* (1967).

Population of the Maritime Provinces (000s)

	NS	*NB*	*PEI*
1871	388	286	94
1891	450	321	109
1911	492	352	94
1931	513	408	88
1951	643	516	98
1971	789	635	112
1981	847	696	123
1986	873	710	127

Maritime Rights, regional protest that climaxed in the 1920s. Essentially a reform movement, it was triggered by the region's declining influence in CONFEDERATION and its inability to protect important interests in transportation, tariffs, port development and federal subsidies. Promoted by newspapers, boards of trade, Maritime clubs, Acadian "national" conventions, farm organizations and some trade unions, the agitation included frequent delegations to Ottawa, economic conferences, propaganda pamphlets and cross-country speaking tours. An amorphous movement, its leadership was legion, and included Nova Scotians H.S. Congdon, W.H. Dennis and F.B. McCurdy; New Brunswickers A.M. Belding and A.P. Patterson; and Prince Edward Islander A.E. MacLean.

Regional issues encouraged major shifts in the popular vote against unsympathetic federal governments. In 1921 Liberals swept 25 of 31 seats; in 1925, amid worsening economic depression, Conservatives won 23 of 29. In 1926 the Mackenzie King government appointed British lawyer Sir Andrew Duncan to investigate Maritime discontent. His recommendations of freight-rate reductions and subsidy increases were implemented, but suggestions for subsidies based on fiscal need and transportation use to encourage regional development were ignored. Hopes once raised turned to cynicism in the Great Depression and regional resentment along with vestiges of co-operation remained the movement's legacies.

ERNEST R. FORBES

Reading: Ernest R. Forbes, *The Maritime Rights Movement, 1919-1927* (1979).

Marlatt, Daphne, née Buckle, writer, editor (b at Melbourne, Australia 11 July 1942). When she was 9, Marlatt moved from Malaysia to Vancouver, which has been the ground of her imagination since. She attended UBC in the early 1960s and has lived and worked in Vancouver since 1970. In its insistence upon the particulars of perception, Marlatt's writing has sought to represent the flux of existence; as a result her densely accumulative style has sometimes proved difficult to the uninitiated. An editor with *The Capilano Review, periodics* and *Island*, she also did 2 documentaries for the BC Provincial Archives: *Steveston Recollected* (1975) and *Opening Doors* (1979). Her many books include *Steveston* (1974/1984), with photographer Robert Minden, *Zocalo* (1977), *Selected Writing: Net Work* (1980), *How Hug a Stone* (1983) and *Touch to My Tongue* (1984), all of which express her intense apprehension of the continually changing world. In 1988 she published *And Historic* and *Double Negative,* the latter a long poem written with Betsy Worland.

DOUGLAS BARBOUR

Marmot, large, diurnal, burrowing rodent of the SQUIRREL family, native to Eurasia and N America. Marmots are rotund and stocky, weigh 2-9 kg, and have thick fur, short bushy tails and small ears. Of 13 species, 4 occur in Canada, inhabiting grassy areas and rocky slopes of mountains and lowlands. Yellow-bellied, hoary and Vancouver Island marmots (*Marmota flaviventris, M. caligata, M. vancouverensis,* respectively) are found only in the western provinces; the woodchuck (possible corruption of Cree, "*wuchak*") or groundhog (*M. monax*), in patchy distribution throughout Canada, excluding Newfoundland. The Vancouver Island marmot, found only in Canada, inhabits a few subalpine sites on the island. Marmots eat green plants and can become pests in vegetable gardens. They signal danger by shrill calls. Marmots hibernate in burrows for 4-8 months in winter; on awakening they may be almost half their autumn weight. Females bear 2-9 young after hibernation. The whimsical observance of Groundhog Day (Feb 2) recognizes marmots' impending emergence from a long winter's rest (much later in colder climates). *See also* ENDANGERED ANIMALS.

J. MARY TAYLOR

Marquette, Jacques, Jesuit priest, missionary, explorer (b at Laon, France 10 June 1637; d at the mouth of a river later called the Père Marquette R, Mich 18 May 1675). Contemporaries regarded Marquette as a gifted linguist who founded the St-Ignace Mission and opened the Illinois country to missionaries. In the popular mind he is inextricably bound to Louis JOLLIET and the discovery of the Mississippi.

Father Marquette was ordained on 7 Mar 1666 and sailed for New France, where he served at Sault Ste Marie and at the mission to the Huron and Ottawa at Chequamegon (SW shore, Lk Superior) before he founded the mission of St-Ignace on the Straits of Mackinac. Late in 1672 Marquette received orders from his superior, Father Dablon, to accompany Louis Jolliet. The expedition departed St-Ignace for the Mississippi on 17 May 1673 and reached 33°40′ N lat near the mouth of the Arkansas R by mid-July. On Sept 30 they returned to the mission of St-Francis-Xavier (DePere, Wis) by way of the Illinois R and Lk Michigan. Exhausted and ill from the Mississippi voyage, Marquette journeyed back to the Illinois late in 1674 and opened the mission of La Conception among the Kaskaskia (an Illinois tribe). By spring 1675 he was too ill to continue his work and departed for St-Ignace but died on the NE shore of Lk Michigan.

C.E. HEIDENREICH

Marquis Wheat, a hybrid variety of WHEAT originated by the cerealists of the Dominion Department of Agriculture at the Central Experimental Farm, Ottawa. The crossing that resulted in Marquis was done under the direction of Percy Saunders, but credit is due to his brother Charles E. SAUNDERS for selecting, naming, testing and distributing the variety. By Charles Saunders's own account, it is impossible to put a specific date on the origin of Marquis. The first cross between an early-ripening Indian wheat (Hard Red Calcutta) and Red Fife made by Percy Saunders likely took place at the experimental farm at Agassiz, Man, in 1892. It remained mixed, however, with other varieties until discovered by Charles Saunders in 1903, and it was first grown in a pure state in 1904 in Ottawa. It was first sent to the prairies in 1907, where it was thoroughly tested, and by 1911 it was commercially established. Because of its early maturing quality, Marquis greatly extended the area where wheat may be safely grown. Its head is resistant to heavy winds and it yields flour of high quality. By the early 1920s, Marquis made up at least 90% of the spring wheat in western Canada and over 60% of the spring wheat in the US.

Marriage and Divorce Marriage remains one of the most important social institutions in Canada. Marriages can be dissolved through annulment or divorce, both of which involve a judicial decree, and remarriage to another person can occur only after a previous marriage has been legally terminated through either device. There is, however, another form of marriage (the so-called common-law marriage) that does not involve a legal ceremony. This is a form of cohabitation that gradually confers rights and obligations to its participants which are not identical with but are similar to those acquired through legal marriage. They are acquired through the act of living together and, where applicable, having a child together. Different provinces have different laws recognizing common-law marriages under different circumstances. Québec does not recognize common-law marriages.

Since the 1960s, marriage and divorce in Canada have been undergoing profound changes which have substantially altered the meaning of marriage, the probability of its ending in divorce and the circumstances attached to marriage. The vast majority of people (over 90%) marry at some point in their lives, although a substantial proportion will eventually divorce. In 1985 the average age at first marriage was 24.6 for brides and 26.7 for grooms. This has implications both during the marriage and towards its end. Women live on average longer than men (the life expectancy for a female born in 1986 has been estimated at 76.9 years and for a male born in the same year at 70.2 years) and a woman is therefore much more likely to die as a widow while a man is much more likely to die as a husband.

Until very recently, a rather strict division of labour between husbands and wives was the rule in most marriages. In general, husbands were held responsible for the economic well-being of the family, and were considered the breadwinners, while wives were considered responsible for child care, HOUSEWORK, keeping the FAMILY in good emotional and physical health, and generally for many of the service functions associated with families. In addition, farm wives worked on the farm and many wives in working-class households took in boarders or sold their household services in other ways to nonfamily members, contributing directly to their family's income. Since the early 1980s, however, the majority of Canadian wives have been earning an independent income and participating in the economic functions traditionally associated primarily with husbands. This situation has reduced the economic dependency of wives on husbands and has therefore shifted the balance of power within marriages. It has also meant that the majority of preschool children are cared for by somebody other than a parent during substantial portions of their day. In 1981, 52.2% of all preschool children (up to age 5) were in some form of shared child-care arrangement. In 1986, 70.4% of all married women aged 20-44 were in the labour force. Nevertheless, housework still tends to be seen primarily as a female task. Since 1978, all provinces have substantially changed their FAMILY LAWS (some more than once), generally assigning equal responsibility to husbands and wives for all types of family responsibilities, including housework, child care and provision for the financial well-being of the family. As a consequence, in divorce settlements, housework and child care are now generally recognized as contributions to a family's overall economic well-being, and through which a spouse develops some claim to matrimonial assets. Overall this legislation does not seem to have improved the economic situation of ex-wives and children after divorce. A comprehensive California study demonstrated that after the introduction of no-fault divorce legislation, on average divorced women and their minor children experienced a 73% decline in their standard of living, while the former husbands experienced a 42% rise in their standard of living. While no comparable Canadian study exists, indications are that the situation here is similar.

Divorce law is under federal jurisdiction. In 1968 Canada's first unified divorce law was passed. At the time, divorce was made easier to obtain, although considerable legal and other difficulties remained. Divorce could be obtained on the basis of a matrimonial offence (previously the only basis on which divorce was available) or on the basis of marriage breakdown. However, in the latter case, a couple had to have lived 3 years apart before they could obtain a divorce. In 1986 a revised Divorce Act (1985) was proclaimed in force. The sole reason for divorce now is marriage breakdown, which is defined as either living apart for at least one year or committing adultery or treating the other spouse with physical or mental cruelty. The divorce rate has been steadily rising in the latter part of this century but, following the final change in the divorce law, there was a sharp increase (from 54.8 divorces per 100 000 population in 1968 to 124.2 in 1969). Since that time the increase continued at an accelerated pace until by 1980 there was a 40% chance that a marriage would end in divorce. In 1985 the divorce rate had risen again to 244.4 per 100 000 population as 61 980 divorces were granted that year. The rate is likely to increase again, now that the new Divorce Act is in force.

Divorce rates alone are not a sufficient indicator of marriage breakdown because they do not include judicial separations, divorces granted in other countries, and desertions. Reasons for the tremendous rise in the divorce rate, a phenomenon that has occurred in virtually all industrialized countries, are not entirely clear, but contributing factors probably include longer life expectancies, which increase the possibility of differences in the individual development of wives and husbands; the greater labour force participation of women and improved SOCIAL SECURITY, which has meant wives are less economically dependent on their husbands than in the past; the lessening of religious and social sanctions against divorce; and the movement towards a more individualistically oriented ethic which stresses self-actualization over maintenance of the family unit. All of these factors suggest that an increased divorce rate may be an indication that expectations about marriage have risen and that many people prefer a divorce to an unhappy marriage.

Where there are dependent children involved (this tends to be the case of slightly more than 50% of all divorces in the 1970s and the mid-1980s) divorce usually leads to the formation of one-parent households (*see* POVERTY). These households are primarily female-headed, because more than 75% of all dependent children involved in divorce are assigned to the custody of the mother, and about 15% are assigned to the custody of the father. This pattern has been remarkably stable between 1971 and 1985.

Given that a high proportion of marriages end in divorce, a substantial group of people in their middle years again become available for marriage. The majority of people who divorce remarry, although men are more likely to remarry than women. In 1985, 29.7% of all Canadian marriages contracted involved at least one partner who was previously married, and by far the largest component came from divorced rather than widowed people. Remarriage families involving dependent children who have 2 parents who are still alive but not married to each other have only recently become important as a large-scale social phenomenon. Questions of overlapping and competing responsibilities and rights of stepparents versus biological nonresidential parents are still in the process of being socially defined. Other questions involve the right of access of other relatives (such as grandparents) and the relationship between step-siblings.

The trends that have been noted for Canadian families (eg, rising divorce rate and greater numbers of WOMEN IN THE LABOUR FORCE) are not restricted to Canada but are typical of all highly industrialized nations, although significant national differences remain. Another common trend among industrialized countries is a sharp decline in fertility rates. In Canada, between 1960 and 1985, fertility rates dropped by more than 50% in all age categories. While the average number of children per woman was 3.9 in 1960, by 1985 that figure had dropped to 1.7. At the same time, rate of births to unmarried women increased, from 4.3% of all live births in 1960 to 12.8% in 1980 and 17.8% in 1985.

Incidence of Divorce in Canada by Year: Frequencies and Rates (per 100 000 population)
(Source: Statistics Canada, *Vital Statistics.*)

Years	*Frequencies*	*Rates*
1921	558	6.4
1931	700	6.8
1941	2 462	21.4
1951	5 270	37.6
1961	6 563	36.0
1967	11 165	54.8
1968	11 343	54.8
1969	26 093	124.2
1970	29 775	139.8
1971	29 685	137.6
1972	32 389	148.4
1973	36 704	166.1
1974	45 019	200.6
1975	50 611	222.0
1976	54 207	235.8
1977	55 370	237.7
1978	57 155	243.4
1981	67 671	278.0
1982	70 436	285.9
1983	68 567	275.5
1984	65 172	259.4
1985	61 980	244.4

Marriage is now legally defined as a partnership of equals. Nevertheless, the economic consequences of divorce tend to be negative for women and children and neutral or positive for men. The increase in divorce, with the consequent increase in remarriages, coupled with the increase in the proportion of women who give birth outside of marriage, has led to a discrepancy between marital and parental roles: an increasing proportion of the people who are parents together are not necessarily married to each other. This discrepancy has different consequences for each sex: most women continue to live together with most of their dependent biological children, while many men do not share a household with (all) their biological children. For children this means that they may have parents living in 2 separate households, or that they may live with a step-parent. The availability of divorce has underlined the voluntary rather than compulsory character of marriage. M. EICHLER

Marriage and Divorce, History of Canadians have always followed the marriage pattern dominant in Western societies, eg, relatively late marriage, companionable unions and a significant proportion of individuals who remain unmarried. Before WWII, 9 out of 10 adults in Canada apparently had married at least once in their lives. The average age of grooms at first marriage was between 25 and 29, of brides, between 20 and 25.

Then, as today, 3 basic factors influenced the opportunity to marry and the timing of marriage. First is the ratio of marriageable males to females. In Canada this ratio has varied widely over time. Normally the numbers of bachelors and spinsters have been more or less equal, but unmarried men often outnumbered unmarried women in times of high immigration and in frontier areas, while the converse was generally true in the growing industrial cities of central Canada from 1850 onward. Second, the strong tendency of men to marry women younger than themselves has affected the marriage chances of prospective brides and grooms in quite different ways. The selection of potential spouses for a woman has always been greatest when she was young; for males, on the other hand, the choice of mates expanded steadily as the males aged. Third, economic factors have always affected marriage opportunities, especially for men. Until recently a man could not marry until he could support a wife and the children who, almost inevitably, would soon follow.

Long before the founding of Canada, the Catholic and Protestant churches had established that marriage was a lifelong, exclusive union of one man and one woman who freely consented to join their lives for procreation and mutual comfort. But the various Christian denominations were divided on several issues. The Roman Catholic Church held marriage to be a sacrament; Protestants simply considered it sacred or blessed by God. Catholics believed the marriage bond lasted until death while Protestants admitted the possibility of divorce and remarriage in limited circumstances. Catholicism prohibited a broad range of unions among kinfolk, but offered some leeway in enforcing its rules; Protestantism imposed fewer restrictions on who one could marry, but did so absolutely. Despite these differences, broad agreement on the fundamentals of Christian marriage existed in western Europe after the Reformation.

From the dawn of European settlement in Canada, the marriage system reflected these traditions. As a result, the Christian concept of marriage has predominated throughout the history of Canada, even though notable exceptions have persisted in special circumstances, eg, marriages *à la façon du nord,* the consensual unions of white men and Indian or mixed-blood women in the northwestern fur trade.

Some evidence suggests the existence of arranged marriages among bourgeois families in New France, but for the most part men and women have always chosen their own spouses. Ethnicity, religion and class have played an important role in the process of mate selection, for Canadians have tended to marry within their own social groups. No doubt, material concerns have never been far from view in many matches as well. Yet within these boundaries (and occasionally outside of them) personal attraction has been the most important motive for marriage in Canada. Historically the romantic basis of marriage was regarded with ambivalence. Although unions founded on personal choice and emotional attachment offered the promise of happiness and personal fulfilment through companionship, they also required lengthy, private courtship and contained hidden dangers, eg, the possibility of imprudently choosing a spouse by yielding to the dictates of the heart and not the mind. Another danger was the prospect of sexual intimacy before marriage, which was an offence against respectable opinion and religious teaching, and one which carried the risk of childbirth outside marriage. Censure of nonmarital sexual intercourse served 2 important functions. It affirmed high ideals of personal conduct, particularly for women, and it also constituted protection for the interests of women and children whose greatest economic security, before the age of the WELFARE STATE, lay in marriage and family life.

For these reasons, family and community influences exerted strong control over courtship in Canada until almost the end of the 19th century. Couples exploring the possibility of marriage courted largely in their own homes under the watchful gaze of their families. They also passed time together in the homes of relatives and friends, in church, at community events, and out of doors on strolls, sleigh rides and incidental pastimes. These circumstances gave parents an effective control over courtships, especially those of their daughters. In urban middle-class circles, where "calling" and "at homes" formed part of customary social life, a mother admitted to the home only those young men who she considered fit companions for her daughters. The annual "coming out" ceremonies, so carefully arranged by mothers, formally placed young women in a marriage market regulated by adults. Urban working-class families had less influence over their courting young, for their children often worked and boarded away from home after mid-adolescence. Instead, the families with whom youths lived often oversaw their conduct, though perhaps with something less than due parental care. In rural communities courtship also fitted in and around the common customs of social visiting, church attendance and everyday recreations.

From the 1880s onward the controls on courtship and youthful social life in Canada gradually relaxed. Parents exercised less formal oversight of late adolescence, though they continued to wield indirect influence through youth clubs, schools, residences, church groups and other institutions which increasingly framed the lives of the young. The transportation revolution after the turn of the 20th century also increased youthful independence. Greater mobility brought freedom from parental and community supervision, especially in larger cities. Generally speaking, the urban young achieved earlier and more extensive freedom than their rural counterparts, for they had easier access to the quasi-privacy that anonymity offers to city dwellers. In these circumstances courtship became an increasingly private matter.

Throughout the history of marriage in Canada the decision to marry has always belonged to the couple. But until the 1880s, a young woman's choice of a spouse was commonly subject to her parents' approval. From time to time, fathers and mothers refused to allow a daughter to wed the man of her choice, the usual justification being that the alliance was not in her best interest. In these circumstances a woman might defy her parents and marry against their will, but she did so at the risk of estrangement from her family. The parental veto, however, was a heavily qualified power. Its strength declined as a daughter's age increased, and it could not be used more than once or twice without inviting defiance. During the 1880s women began to free themselves from this restriction, as they did from so many other constraints which until then had affected their lives. Thereafter, they usually married whom they pleased. Men, by contrast, had always been far less limited by parental wishes when choosing a spouse. From the earliest days of colonial settlement they were relatively free agents on the marriage market.

In the past, marriage in Canada was usually a religious rite. Civil marriage has always been possible, at least since the end of the French era, but until recently has been relatively uncommon. The secular custom of a honeymoon after the wedding developed slowly during the 19th century. Initially, only the well-to-do had money and leisure enough for a postmarriage vacation, but after 1850 the practice spread gradually throughout all social levels. The purpose of the honeymoon has changed considerably over time as well. At first, it took the common form of 19th-century social visiting. The recently married couple often travelled with relatives and visited friends and relations in distant communities. But by the end of the century, the honeymoon had become a private holiday for the newly wedded pair.

The history of divorce in Canada contrasts sharply with that of marriage for, while most Canadians married, divorce was extremely uncommon until after WWII. In fact, until that time, Canada had one of the lowest divorce rates in the Western world. Respectable opinion – articulated by social and religious leaders – condemned divorce as a threat to the family, and the strength of this opinion prevented relaxation of Canadian divorce laws. Consequently, access to divorce in Canada was extremely limited until 1968. For most of Canada's first century adultery was virtually the only ground for divorce and, before WWI, only NS, NB and BC had divorce courts, although Alberta, Saskatchewan and Ontario created them during the interwar period. In provinces without access to judicial divorce, the only alternative was an appeal to Parliament for a statutory divorce, an expensive process that limited relief to the wealthy. The most common alternatives were desertion, legal separation and divorce in an American jurisdiction which, though it had no legal force in Canada, seemed to satisfy public opinion. PETER WARD

Marriott, Joyce Anne, poet (b at Victoria 5 Nov 1913). Marriott was a productive poet and poetry-educator in the 1940s, when she was also on the board of the famous pioneer literary magazine CONTEMPORARY VERSE and otherwise active as an editor. She was renowned especially for the narrative poem "The Wind, Our Enemy." Her best-known collection was *Sandstone and Other Poems* (1945), though one of her earlier ones, *Calling Adventurers* (1941), won the Gov Gen's Award. After the war, Marriott stopped writing, only to return eventually with *Countries* (1971), *The Circular Coast: Poems New and Selected* (1981), *A Long Way to Oregon: Selected Short Stories* (1984) and *Letters from Some Island: New Poems* (1985). She thus proved herself a hardy survivor of the gifted generation of poets whose leading lights were and remain figures such as Earle BIRNEY and Irving LAYTON.

Marsh, Leonard Charles, social scientist, professor (b at London, Eng 24 Sept 1906; d at Vancouver 10 May 1982). Marsh came to Canada in 1930 after studies at the London School of Economics. He was director of an interdisciplinary social-science research program at McGill 1930-41 and an early member of the group of social reformers which eventually became the LEAGUE FOR SOCIAL RECONSTRUCTION. He made major editorial contributions to the league's influential book, *Social Planning for Canada* (1935, repr 1975). His *Canadians In and Out of Work* (1940), written almost 2 decades before John PORTER'S *The* VERTICAL MOSIAC, was the first significant analysis of the impact of social class on Canadian society. Marsh was research adviser on the federal Committee on Post-War Reconstruction 1941-44 and published his *Report on Social Security for Canada* in 1943 (repr 1975). Although the government paid little attention at the time, most of the major elements in his program had become law by 1966 and are the basis of the modern Canadian SOCIAL SECURITY system.

Marsh was welfare adviser to the UN Relief and Rehabilitation Administration (1944-46), professor and director of research at the School of Social Work, UBC (1948-64) and professor of educational sociology, UBC (1964-72). He retired in 1973 but continued to write and lecture, his writings reflecting his interests, which ranged from cats to music. His contribution to society, considered unparalleled by some, has not yet been adequately evaluated. ALBERT ROSE

Marshall, Donald, Jr (b at Sydney, NS 13 Sept 1953). The case of Donald Marshall has become one of the most controversial in the history of the Canadian criminal justice system. Accused of the 28 May 1971 stabbing death of a black youth, Sandy Seale, in Sydney, NS, Marshall, a 16-year old Micmac was convicted of murder and sentenced to life imprisonment. After he had served 11 years in a penitentiary, a re-examination of the case found him innocent of the murder, as he had maintained all along. Roy Ebsary was charged and convicted of manslaughter, and Marshall was acquitted in May 1983. Marshall's long incarceration for a crime he did not commit, and his subsequent struggle with provincial and federal governments for compensation, have drawn great interest from the general public, prison reform groups and organizations opposed to the reinstatement of capital punishment. The alleged mishandling of his case has brought the police and judicial systems under severe criticism. In Sept 1987 a royal commission of inquiry began to investigate the Marshall case. EDWARD BUTTS

Reading: M. Harris, *Justice Denied: The Law Versus Donald Marshall* (1986).

Marshall, Lois Catherine, soprano (b at Toronto 29 Jan 1924). Lois Marshall began voice lessons at age 12 with Weldon Kilburn, whom she married 32 years later. Her first major engagement was in 1947 as soprano soloist in Bach's *St Matthew Passion*, with Sir Ernest MACMILLAN conducting the TORONTO MENDELSSOHN CHOIR and the TORONTO SYMPHONY. In 1950 she won the Royal Conservatory of Music's Eaton Graduating Scholarship and 2 years later won the Naumberg Award and made her New York debut. Her career included performances of all the great oratorios with the leading orchestras of the world, and she toured Europe, Britain, the USSR, Australia, New Zealand and N America in solo recitals, orchestral performances and concerts. She appeared with most of the important Canadian orchestras, performed at festivals, and joined other soloists such as Glenn GOULD, Louis QUILICO and Maureen FORRESTER. Though crippled by polio as a child, Marshall managed a limited opera career with companies such as the CBC Opera Co, the CANADIAN OPERA CO and the Boston Opera Co. In the mid-1970s Marshall turned to the mezzo-soprano repertoire, especially German lieder. She has received the Molson Prize, is a Companion of the Order of Canada and was music director of Tribach, the festival commemorating J.S. Bach's 300th birthday held in Edmonton in 1985. That year she also became honorary president of the Toronto Mendelssohn Choir. In 1987 she was awarded the Toronto Art Award for music. MABEL H. LAINE

Marshall, Tom, poet, critic (b at Niagara Falls, Ont 9 Apr 1938). With David HELWIG, Marshall was at the centre of a group of writers active in Kingston, Ont, where he began teaching at Queen's in 1964. As a poet, he is known for 4 linked collections (published between 1969 and 1976) of philosophical, meditative verse. *The Silences of Fire* (1969) is perhaps the best known of these, though all of them are neatly represented in a fifth book, *The Elements* (1980). He is also the author of 2 novels, *Rosemary Gaal* (1978), a satire of academic and literary life, and *Adele at the End of the Day* (1987), as well as other works. Most important critically are *The Psychic Mariner: A Reading of the Poems of D.H. Lawrence* (1970) and *Harsh and Lovely Land* (1979), an incisive, insightful survey of contemporary Canadian poets and poetry.

Marsupialia, order of mammals belonging to the infraclass Metatheria, comprising about 250 living species, of which two-thirds are found in Australia. The Virginia OPOSSUM (*Didelphis virginiana*) is the only marsupial found in Canada. Marsupials differ from placental mammals in many anatomical details, especially in the reproductive system. In the vast majority of marsupials, no placenta is formed and the young are born in a premature state after a brief gestation. The young complete their development attached to a teat and protected by skin folds or a fully formed pouch (marsupium). Marsupials and placental mammals evolved at about the same time in the Cretaceous period (144-66.4 million years ago) from a group of primitive mammals, the pantotheres. The oldest FOSSILS are from the Upper Cretaceous (97.5-66.4 million years ago) of N America. Marsupials are found in N and S America and Australia, which they may have colonized, via Antarctica, before continental drift moved Australia to its present location.

C.G. VAN ZYLL DE JONG

Reading: C.G. van Zyll de Jong, *Handbook of Canadian Mammals I, Marsupials and Insectivores* (1983).

Martello Tower, distinctive masonry FORTIFICATION used in defence of British N America in the first half of the 19th century. The name is likely derived from references to a stone tower on Cape Mortella in Corsica, which had proven particularly resistant to an English attack during the French Revolutionary wars. Round towers had begun to replace square towers about the year 1000 AD, reflecting improved skills of masons. The advantage was that a round tower offered fewer blind spots to shelter an attacker and better deflected projectiles. The 16 squat, flat-roofed towers built in British N America from 1796 to 1846 were distributed as follows: Halifax (5), Saint John (1), Québec C (4) and Kingston (6). The Kingston towers, constructed 1846-48 at the height of border tensions with the US, were the most complex in design. None of the towers was ever subject to attack; 11 have survived. JAMES MARSH

Carleton Martello Tower, Saint John, NB, one of the 16 distinctive towers built in British N America (*photo by Malak, Ottawa*).

Marten (*Martes americana*), slender WEASEL specialized for life in the northern coniferous forests; found from Alaska and BC to Newfoundland and into the US. Males average 60 cm long and weigh 1 kg; females 54 cm and 650 g. The bushy tail is half the body length; feet are large with sharp climbing claws. The colour is shades of brown with a yellow chest spot and blackish legs and tail. The large ears are whitish. Marten are solitary, except for the female and kits, which may travel as a group for several months. Expert climbers, they hunt in trees for squirrels and bird nests and on the ground for mice, voles, hares and birds. Insects, berries and even carrion are also eaten. Mating is in July-Aug and the litters of 1-4 young are born Mar-Apr. Sexual maturity occurs at 2 years. The species is highly valued for its soft, lustrous fur. The annual catch in Canada is 20 000 to 50 000 but was once as high as 180 000. Forest fires and overkill have been the main causes of the decline. *See also* FUR TRAPPING.

IAN MCTAGGART-COWAN

Martial Arts, *see* JIU-JITSU, JUDO, KARATE.

Martin, Claire, pseudonym of Claire Montreuil (b at Québec C 18 Apr 1914). She studied with the Ursulines (in Québec City) and the Dames de la Congrégation (in Beauport). She won the Prix du Cercle du livre de France (1958) for her first book, a collection of short stories called *Avec ou sans amour*. This was followed by 2 novels, *Doux-Amer* (1960) and *Quand j'aurai payé ton visage* (1962). Her 2 autobiographical books, *Dans un gant de fer* (1965) and *La joue droite* (1966) confirmed her reputation and won her the Prix du Québec (1965), the Prix France-Québec (1965) and the Gov Gen's Award (1967). A final novel, *Les Morts* (1970), was presented in 1972 at the THÉÂTRE DU RIDEAU VERT in an adaptation. Her style focuses on love, its risks and "illnesses" and a sharp denunciation of prejudice and social conventions. Her work is characterized by pure, beautifully crafted language, plus a fine irony that sometimes in her autobiography turns acid and pitiless.

GILLES DORION

Martin, Joseph, lawyer, politician, premier of BC (b at Milton, Canada W 24 Sept 1852; d at Vancouver 2 Mar 1923). Elected as a Liberal to 4 legislatures, he was an agitator more suited to opposition than government. He was elected to the Manitoba legislature in 1883, became attorney general in the GREENWAY government in 1888, and in 1890 sponsored legislation ending the official use of French and public support for separate schools (*see* MANITOBA SCHOOLS QUESTION). He represented Winnipeg in the House of Commons 1893-96, and then moved to Vancouver to practise law. Elected to the BC legislature in 1898, he served as attorney general until 1900. In Feb 1900 he was asked to form a government but, unable to muster support, resigned after 3 months. He speculated in real estate and practised law 1903-08 and in 1907 edited and published the *Vancouver Guardian*. His legal business took him to Britain, where he represented East St Pancras at Westminster 1910-18. He nevertheless contested the Vancouver mayoralty in 1914 and founded the *Evening Journal* there in 1916. H. GUEST

Martin, Mungo, or Nakapenkim, meaning a potlatch chief "ten times over," or Datsa, meaning "grandfather," Northwest Coast carver, painter, singer, songwriter (b at Fort Rupert, Vancouver I *c*1879-82; d at Victoria 16 Aug 1962), stepson of Charlie James (a recognized Kwakiutl carver), and tutor to Henry HUNT and Tony HUNT. As an authority on various aspects of his culture, Mungo Martin helped renew pride in Kwakiutl heritage. Martin was carving during the prohibition of the POTLATCH, and his first commissioned totem pole, *Raven of the Sea*, was carved *c*1900 at Alert Bay. In 1948 UBC asked Martin to take over their TOTEM POLE restoration program. Martin was not only considered an exceptional carver but was of invaluable service to the ethnographers, in the early 1950s recording 200 songs at UBC and at the BC Provincial Museum, Victoria. In 1952 he moved to Victoria to begin a replication program of old poles; the work continues in 1984 with Richard Hunt (son of Henry Hunt) being a carver-in-residence. In 1958 Martin finished the World's Tallest Pole, which stands in Beacon Hill Park, Victoria, and in 1961 he carved his last pole, which rests in Mexico. GERALD R. MCMASTER

Marten (*Martes americana*), a slender weasel whose habitat is the northern coniferous forests (*photo by Wayne Lankinen/DRK Photo*).

Martin, Paul Joseph James, politician, statesman (b at Ottawa 23 June 1903). First elected to the House of Commons in 1935, Martin quickly took a prominent place in Liberal ranks because of his impressive educational background in philosophy, international relations and law. PM KING appointed him parliamentary assistant to the minister of labour in 1943; he entered Cabinet in 1945 as secretary of state, and in 1946 became minister of national health and welfare. Faced with a government becoming increasingly conservative on social issues, Martin managed to introduce a system of health grants and, by threatening resignation, made PM ST. LAURENT accept national health insurance. He also undertook diplomatic assignments for the King and St. Laurent governments. In 1955 he negotiated an agreement that allowed the expansion of UN membership. Martin ran unsuccessfully for the Liberal leadership in 1948 and 1958. In 1963 PM PEARSON appointed Martin secretary of state for external affairs, a portfolio he held until 1968, when he tried again for the leadership but lost to Pierre TRUDEAU. He was appointed government leader in the Senate (1968-74) and high commissioner to Britain (1975-79). His memoirs, *A Very Public Life*, have been published in 2 volumes (1983, 1986). JOHN ENGLISH

Martin, Paul Edgar Philippe, business executive (b at Windsor, Ont 28 Aug 1938). After graduation from U of T (BA 1962, LLB 1965), Martin joined POWER CORP OF CANADA in 1966 as executive assistant to Paul DESMARAIS. In 1969 he was made a Power Corp vice-president, in 1971 vice-president of special projects at Consolidated-Bathurst (a Power Corp subsidiary), and in 1973 vice-president of planning and development at Power Corp. In 1974 he became president of CANADA STEAMSHIP LINES (renamed CSL Group in 1980), which in 1981 he and a partner bought from Power Corp. The son of Paul MARTIN, he has occasionally been suggested as a potential leader for the national Liberal Party and in late 1987 announced his intention to run in the Montréal riding of La Salle. STANLEY GORDON

Martin, William Melville, lawyer, premier of Saskatchewan (b at Norwich, Ont 23 Aug 1876; d at Regina 22 June 1970). He was the second premier of Saskatchewan 1916-22, serving with considerable skill during a difficult transition period. Educated at U of T and Osgoode Hall, Martin moved to Regina in 1903 to practise law. Elected to the House of Commons for Regina in 1908 and re-elected in 1911, he resigned from Parliament in 1916 and led the provincial Liberals. He was elected to the legislature in a by-election in 1916 and was re-elected in the general elections of 1917 and 1921. On his voluntary retirement from politics in 1922 he was appointed a judge of the Saskatchewan Court of Appeal. He became chief justice of the Supreme Court of Saskatchewan in 1941 and held that post with distinction until 1961. D.H. BOCKING

Martínez Fernández y Martínez de la Sierra, Esteban José, naval officer (b at Seville, Spain 9 Dec 1742; d at Loreto, Mexico 28 Oct 1798). In 1774 he sailed with Juan Pérez HERNÁNDEZ on an exploratory voyage from San Blas, Mexico, to the northern Queen Charlotte Is and Nootka Sound.

In 1778 he was sent on a reconnaissance of Russian fur-trading posts in the Aleutian Is, learning that the Russians planned to establish a post at Nootka the next year. To assert Spanish presence on the Northwest Coast, Viceroy Flórez sent Martínez in 1789 to establish a temporary post at Nootka before the Russian arrival. Martínez found British and American trading ships there, and the British about to construct a trading post. He seized the British ships and crews, built a military post at Nootka, and abandoned it in the autumn. British accounts portray Martínez as impetuous and hot-headed; nevertheless, he prevented the British from establishing a post in territory claimed by Spain. *See also* NOOTKA SOUND CONTROVERSY. JOHN DEWHIRST

Martini, Paul, figure skater (b at Toronto 2 Nov 1960). Favoured to win the 1984 Olympic gold medal in pair skating at Sarajevo, Yugoslavia, Martini and partner Barbara UNDERHILL gave 2 disappointing performances and finished in 7th place. They made a comeback a month later to defeat the Olympic gold medallists, Elena Valova and Oleg Vassiliev from the Soviet Union, and won the gold medal at the world championships in Ottawa. TERESA MOORE

Martre, Lac la, 1777 km^2, elev 265 m, max length 76 km, is located in the NWT, 50 km W of Rae-Edzo and 150 km NW of Yellowknife, and 346 km S of the Arctic Circle. The settlement of Lac la Martre is located at the SE corner of the lake. The lake is fed by Lac Grandin and several smaller lakes and streams, and drains SE into the North Arm of GREAT SLAVE LK. Originally, it appeared as Martin Lk (in Aaron Arrowsmith's map of MACKENZIE's journey of 1789), but later took on its present name, presumably owing to the abundance of pine marten (*Martes americana*) in the area. DAVID EVANS

Martyrology, The Books 1 and 2 of *The Martyrology* appeared in 1972, and subsequent volumes have been published in 1976, 1982 and 1987. After several attempts to "finish" it, bp NICHOL now sees his poem as an open-ended, ongoing work; its very lack of closure challenges traditional ideas of what constitutes a single, unified poem. Starting from plays on words beginning with the letters st ("stand" interpreted as "St. And"), *The Martyrology* has expanded into a wide-ranging exploration of world mythology and personal experience, of the forms of language and of human community. Increasingly experimental in technique and presentation, it has rightly been described as "the most courageous body of work in Canada today" (Frank Davey). It is also, for all its apparent difficulty, among the most entertaining. STEPHEN SCOBIE

Marxism is a basic world view first developed by Karl Marx and Friedrich Engels in the 19th century. It has been adopted as the official ideology of communist governments in Europe, China, Cuba and elsewhere. It has spawned diverse movements, eg, Marxist-Leninism, Maoism, Christian Marxism, Marxist Humanism and Trotskyism, all of which can be found to some degree in Canada.

As a method of analysis, Marxism emphasizes the development of the forces of production – machinery, technology, labour skills, and the interaction among SOCIAL CLASSES, ie, who does the work and who gives the orders, who has the right to possession, ownership or consumption of the product. It also examines (in a method called "dialectical materialism") the way this "economic base" influences and shapes the superstructure of society, ie, the FAMILY, school system and political system as well as art and culture, religion and all systems of ideas.

Marxism recognizes that massive historical transformations have produced new social systems, eg, slavery, feudalism, capitalism and socialism, which alter every aspect of daily life. But all hitherto existing social systems, according to Marxism, are divided into socioeconomic classes. The ruling class expresses its dominance through its ability to force the subordinate classes to turn over a portion of the products they produce (or the value of these products) to itself. One social system is distinguished from another in the way this economic surplus is extracted and the manner in which it is utilized. Surplus extraction is the basis of exploitation in the Marxist analysis and the basis of class conflict, which in turn is the fundamental dynamic in historical transformations. According to the Marxist analysis, when capitalism can no longer extract sufficient "surplus value," a major element of which is profit, the result is economic crises and widespread UNEMPLOYMENT. Marxist theory holds that these problems are inherent in the capitalist organization of society, through which ownership of the means of production is confined to a handful of people while the vast majority of people must sell their labour power in order to live, and that only the creation of a new economic order can overcome these problems. It advocates a planned economy that replaces the profit system as the motor force of the economy; public ownership of the major means of production; and economic democracy with community control over economic priorities and worker control over the organization of work.

Marxism was brought to Canada by British worker intellectuals in the first years of the 20th century. It was the dominant ideology in the earliest socialist parties of Canada and was fully adopted by the COMMUNIST PARTY OF CANADA when it formed in 1921. During the Stalin years, Marxism became a religious faith rather than a social science and stagnated in Canada as it did elsewhere, but over the past decade it has flourished, gaining a significant presence in Canadian scholarship. Prominent Canadian Marxist scholars include C.B. MACPHERSON (d 1987), Stanley RYERSON, Leo Panitch, Bryan Palmer, Gregory Kealey, Michael Lebowitz, Dorothy Smith, Varda Burstyn, Patricia Connelly, R. James Sacouman, Pauline Vaillancourt, Jorge Niosi, Gilles Bourque, Carl Cuneo and John Saul. C. GONICK

Mary Celeste, brigantine built in 1861 at Spencer's I, NS, and originally named *Amazon*. She was wrecked off Cape Breton in 1867, salvaged, sold and in 1868 registered at New York and renamed *Mary Celeste*. In 1872 she was found adrift off the Azores, with no sign of her crew. The mysterious disappearance caused wild speculation, but the fate of the crew will never be known. JAMES MARSH

Marystown, Nfld, pop 6660 (1986c), 6299 (1981c), inc 1951, is a shipbuilding and fish-processing centre, comprising the settlements of Marystown (formerly Mortier Bay) and Creston, on the E side of the Burin Pen. Marystown, having one of the finest natural harbours in Newfoundland, has been promoted historically as a free port. Probably frequented by French and BASQUE fishermen in the 16th and 17th centuries, the area was settled predominantly by English and Irish fishermen by the early 1800s. In 1966 a shipyard and fish plant were constructed, providing much-needed alternative employment. One of the most efficient and best-equipped shipbuilding and ship-repair facilities of its size in N America, the yard is a crown corporation and produces mainly stern trawlers for the Newfoundland fishing industry, although it has the capacity to design and build vessels of all types up to 85 m long. JANET E.M. PITT

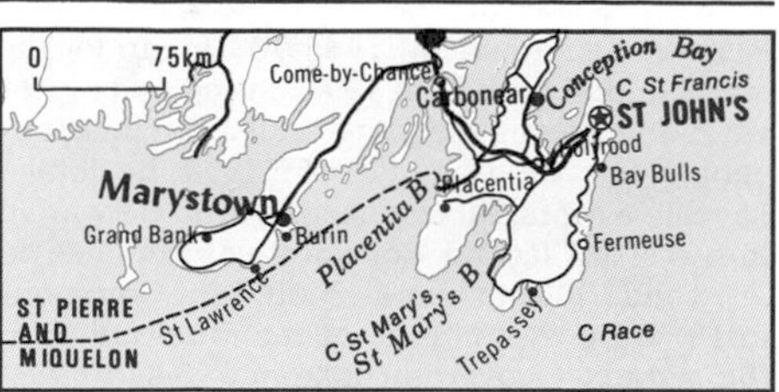

Mascarene, Paul, born Jean-Paul, military officer, colonial administrator (b in Languedoc, France 1684/85; d at Boston, Mass 22 Jan 1760). A Huguenot émigré, Mascarene served throughout New England and Atlantic Canada 1710-40 as a military engineer and fluent negotiator with the Acadians and Indians. He was one of the first (1720) to analyse Great Britain's weakness in Nova Scotia, recommending a stronger military presence and unqualified loyalty from the ACADIANS. Mascarene became interim colonial administrator 1739, governor 1744, and successfully held Annapolis Royal against repeated French attacks 1744-46. He attributed his victory to the military support sent by Gov William Shirley of Massachusetts, and to his own policy of extracting neutrality rather than loyalty from the truculent Acadians, a tactic he vigorously defended as politically expedient. Mascarene returned to New England in 1751 and eventually settled in Boston. LOIS KERNAGHAN

Mason, John, governor of the English colony in Newfoundland (b at King's Lynn, Eng 1586; d at London, Eng 1635). In 1615 he was appointed the second governor of the colony at Cuper's Cove (Cupids, Nfld), succeeding John GUY, and arrived in 1616 accompanied by his wife. He explored much of the island and used his findings in the first English map known to be based on personal survey and in writing *A Briefe Discourse of the New-Found-Land* (1620). He left in 1621 for New England, where he founded the colony of New Hampshire. MICHAEL J. MCCARTHY

Masse, Marcel, politician (b at St-Jean-de-Matha, Qué 27 May 1936). He was a student of history and political science at U de M and abroad in London and Paris, and taught high school in Joliette, 1962-66. A strong Québec nationalist, he was a member of the Québec Assembly, 1966-73, and held several ministerial posts in the UNION

Portrait of Marcel Masse, minister of communications and later minister of energy (*courtesy SSC Photocentre*).

NATIONALE government, 1966-70. He ran for the leadership of the UN in 1971, losing by only 21 votes and leaving the party to sit as an independent a few months later. In 1974 he joined Lavelin, a Montréal engineering firm. He was an unsuccessful federal Conservative candidate in 1974 and 1980 but won election to the Commons in 1984. He was minister of communications in the MULRONEY government from 1984 to 1986, where he proved a resourceful defender of Canadian culture before being moved to the energy portfolio during a troubled period of low oil prices. NORMAN HILLMER

Masset, BC, Village, pop 1529 (1986c), located on the northern tip of Graham I, the largest of the QUEEN CHARLOTTE ISLANDS off the northern coast of BC. The islands are the traditional home of the Haida and the name Masset is derived from the Haida word *maast.* The first area on the island to attract non-native settlers, the townsite was originally called Graham City but was renamed Masset in 1909. When amalgamated with the adjacent community of Delkatla, Masset became the first incorporated village on the Queen Charlotte Is in 1961. Today Masset is the largest settlement on the Queen Charlottes and the economic base comes from commercial fishing, a crab cannery, logging and sawmilling. The old Haida village of Masset [Haida] is renowned for its gold and silver smiths and carvers. JOHN STEWART

Massey, Charles Vincent, politician, diplomat, governor general (b at Toronto 20 Feb 1887; d at London, Eng 30 Dec 1967). Vincent Massey is best remembered as Canada's first native-born GOVERNOR GENERAL. He was the grandson of Hart MASSEY who developed the farm-implement company started by Daniel MASSEY into a powerful international corporation, and the brother of actor Raymond MASSEY. His education was at U of T and Balliol College, Oxford, and he lectured in history at Victoria College, U of T, 1913-15. He then joined the army and served as a staff officer in Canada, ultimately working for the war committee of the Cabinet. He was president of Massey-Harris Co Ltd, from 1921 until 1925 when he joined PM Mackenzie KING's Cabinet. But he failed to win a seat in Parliament, and in 1926 King made him Canada's first minister to the US where he served until 1930. In 1935 King named him high commissioner to Britain, a post he held until 1946. As a diplomat Massey was more successful on the social side than in the hard-slogging details of negotiation, but there was no doubt that in Britain particularly he had access to the highest quarters. His own prime minister, however, mistrusted his judgements on imperial questions, and the relations between the 2 were formal and tense. After the war, PM Louis ST. LAURENT placed Massey in charge of the Royal Commission on NATIONAL DEVELOPMENT IN THE ARTS, LETTERS AND SCIENCES, a post for which Massey's status as a patron of the arts well fitted him, and his report in 1951 recommended the formation of a CANADA COUNCIL (est 1957). In 1952 Massey became governor general, a post he filled with distinction and in a manner that minimized the break with the past that the appointment of a Canadian represented. In 1959 Massey left RIDEAU HALL and went into an active retirement. J.L. GRANATSTEIN

Reading: C. Bissell, 2 vols, *The Young Vincent Massey* (1981) and *The Imperial Canadian* (1986).

Massey, Daniel, manufacturer (b at Windsor, Vt 24 Feb 1798; d at Newcastle, Canada W 15 Nov 1856). A prosperous Methodist farmer near Cobourg, Upper Canada, Massey became interested in farm machinery in the 1830s and invested in a foundry at Bond Head in 1847. In 1849 he moved to Newcastle and established the Newcastle Foundry and Machine Manufactory. Massey's industrious habits and religious temperament were passed on to his son Hart, whose aggressive marketing technique and acquisition of patent rights to the latest American farm-machinery designs contributed to the firm's later success as the Massey Manufacturing Co. In 1891 the firm merged with its chief rival, A. Harris, Son & Co Ltd, to become Massey-Harris Co Ltd (MASSEY-FERGUSON LTD), Canada's largest manufacturer of farm implements. JOSEPH LINDSEY

Vincent Massey was Canada's first native-born governor general (© *Karsh, Ottawa/Miller Comstock*).

Reading: P. Collins, *Hart Massey* (1977); M. Denison, *Harvest Triumphant* (1948); M. Gillen, *The Masseys* (1965); E.P. Neufeld, *A Global Corporation* (1969).

Massey, Hart Almerrin, manufacturer, philanthropist (b in Haldimand Twp, Upper Canada 29 Apr 1823; d at Toronto 20 Feb 1896). Son of Daniel MASSEY, he propelled his father's Newcastle Foundry into a dynamic farm-implement producer by mergers, spirited sales and advertising techniques, and acquisition of patents for labour-saving American mowers, reapers and binders that transformed the productivity of Canadian agriculture (*see* AGRICULTURAL IMPLEMENTS). In 1870 he incorporated the Massey Manufacturing Co, which relocated in Toronto in 1879 and expanded significantly with the purchase of the Toronto Reaper and Mower Co, an American branch plant. Massey directed the firm's successful entry into foreign markets; it was the first N American firm of its kind to go abroad. In 1891 he merged A. Harris, Son & Co Ltd and other Canadian rivals to form Massey-Harris Co Ltd, of which he was president, 1891-96. A stern employer but genial Methodist patriarch who regarded his business as a trust from God, he contributed to many charitable, educational and religious institutions, and erected Toronto's Massey Music Hall (*see* MASSEY HALL) and Fred Victor Mission in memory of his sons Charles Albert (1848-84) and Frederic Victor (1867-90). Massey's son Walter Edward Hart (1864-1901) was president of the firm 1896-1901 and active in advertising and sales activities. He promoted the pasteurization of milk and encouraged cultural endeavours, producing some of Canada's first staff magazines, including the literary journal *Massey's Magazine,* merged (1897) with the *Canadian Magazine.* Hart Massey's last surviving son, Chester Daniel (1850-1926), relinquished in 1901 his managerial responsibilities to Massey-Harris, an increasingly complex public corporation. He devoted himself to public service, administering Hart Massey's estate, reorganized in 1918 as the Massey Foundation, which supported numerous philanthropies and constructed HART HOUSE and MASSEY COLLEGE at U of T. JOSEPH LINDSEY

Massey, Raymond Hart, actor (b at Toronto 30 Aug 1896; d at Los Angeles, Calif 29 July 1983), brother of Vincent MASSEY. His distinctive voice and craggy good looks made him indelibly associated with the role of Abraham Lincoln both on stage and in film. In Siberia, in Feb 1919, Massey mounted an army minstrel show with the Canadian forces before turning professional in July 1922 with the Everyman Theatre in England. He had already been an amateur at Appleby Coll, Oakville, Ont (1913-14), Oxford (1919-20) and Hart House Theatre, U of T (1921-22). In 1924 he played 2 parts with Sybil Thorndike in *Saint Joan* and in 1931 made his debut on Broadway as Hamlet. Notable New York revivals of Bernard Shaw plays in which he starred were *The Doctor's Dilemma* (1941), *Candida* (1942) and *Pygmalion* (1945). His distinguished film career began in 1931 and included over 70 movies ranging from *The Scarlet Pimpernel* to *East of Eden.* In the late 1950s and 1960s he became known to a new generation as Dr Gillespie in the "Dr. Kildare" TV series. DAVID GARDNER

Massey College, Toronto (designed by R.J. THOM, completed in 1963). At the height of international-style architecture in Canada, the design of Massey College seemed to break ranks, to look backwards or sideways, rather than forward. Considered 2 decades later, it appears ahead of its time, a remarkable anticipation of new directions in architecture. It is, as well, simply among the best buildings in Canada. Thom's design was the result of a 2-stage, limited competition held in 1960 by the Massey Foundation. In response to Vincent MASSEY's desire for a building that evoked his Oxford experience, Thom combined informality of layout and richness of detail with all-embracing order, a limited palette of materials dominated by brick. MICHAEL MCMORDIE

Massey-Ferguson Limited (now Varity Corp), with headquarters in Toronto, manufactures farm machinery and other equipment. Established in 1847 by Daniel MASSEY as the Newcastle Foundry and Machine Manufactory, the company became a sole proprietorship under his son, Hart Almerrin MASSEY, in 1855, and in 1870 it became the Massey Manufacturing Co. The firm moved to Toronto in 1879 and merged with its chief competitor, A. Harris, Son & Co Ltd (est 1857), in 1891. The new Massey-Harris Co Ltd was incorporated in 1891, becoming the largest company of its kind in the British Empire. In 1953 the company merged with the Ferguson companies to form Massey-Harris-Ferguson Ltd; Massey-Ferguson Ltd was adopted in 1958; and in 1987 it was renamed Varity Corp, although subsidiaries retained variations of the old names, eg, Massey Combines Corp of Brantford, Ont.

From its earliest days the company acquired the rights to innovative machinery, making agricultural history with the Toronto Light Binder during the late 19th century and in 1927 acquiring the Wallis Tractor. The ideas of Harry Ferguson, developed during the 1920s, also gave the company an edge in tractor technology. In spite of financial difficulties in the 1980s (necessitating federal government assistance from 1981), Varity continues to manufacture and sell farm and industrial equipment such as tractors, balers and multipurpose diesel engines. It operates plants in Canada and overseas. In 1986, in order to become less dependent on the cyclic agricultural sector, it acquired Dayton Walthier, an automotive and building products supplier. In 1986 it had sales or operating revenue of $1.8 billion (ranking 49th in Canada), assets of $1.8 billion (ranking 60th) and 17 251 employees. Its shares are widely held; foreign ownership stands at 82%.

DEBORAH C. SAWYER

Massey Hall, designed by C.R. Badgely, was built on Shuter St in Toronto by Hart A. MASSEY as a gift to the city at a cost of $150 000. Known first as Massey Music Hall, it opened on 14 June 1894. Seating capacity of 4000 was reduced to 2765 when the building was redesigned in 1933. Until the 1920s, when other cities began to erect CONCERT HALLS, it was the only building in Canada designed primarily for musical performances. Massey Hall was the home of major local ensembles such as the TORONTO MENDELSSOHN CHOIR and TORONTO SYMPHONY, and the site of performances by great artists of the world, including Ignacy Jan Paderewski, Enrico Caruso and Vladimir Heifetz. It also has been used for many other types of events: a speech by Winston Churchill (1900), boxing matches, movies and folk, rock and jazz concerts. ROY THOMSON HALL, completed in 1982, is now the main concert facility, but Massey Hall continues to be used for performances.

FREDERICK A. HALL

Massicotte, Edmond-Joseph, artist, illustrator (b at Montréal 1 Dec 1875; d at Sault-au-Récollet, near Montréal 1 Mar 1929). After studying at Montréal, Massicotte in 1892 began contributing illustrations depicting the popular customs and traditions of French Canada to such periodicals as *Le Monde illustré* and *L'Almanach du peuple*. The illustrations frequently record traditional customs no longer practised in Massicotte's lifetime. Drawn primarily from his imagination and accumulated documentation (some of it supplied by his brother, archivist Édouard-Zotique), and less frequently from on-the-spot sketches, his works betray a certain lack of dynamism. They give only an impression of authenticity and often impart moralizing, religious and nostalgic sentiments. By reducing and simplifying the number of pictorial elements, he sacrificed a certain sense of lively interaction, which allowed, however, for easy recognition of the subject. His illustrations, which glorify Québec rural life, traditions and customs, have become iconographical images for Quebecers. *See also* ILLUSTRATION, ART.

ELIZABETH H. KENNELL

Masson, Henri Leopold, painter (b at Spy, Belgium 10 Jan 1907). Largely self-taught, Masson combines his narrative abilities with a fluid GROUP OF SEVEN style. He lived in Ottawa from 1921 and began exhibiting nationally in 1938 and internationally in 1946. His themes reflect his belief in the unity of nature and art. Cityscapes and landscapes reveal a sense of place and time. Still lifes and paintings of monks and choirboys, musicians, children and a great variety of commonplace activities deal with subjects that he considers to convey the essence of life. He uses a loose, vigorous brush style in many media. His best works are full of detail and movement, with a broad range of colour, and convey a sense of immediacy to the viewer.

KATHLEEN LAVERTY

Master of the Mill, The, novel by Frederick Philip GROVE (Toronto, 1946; repr 1961), has been criticized for being, with its frequently shifting time frame and points of view, and its complicated subplots, too technically demanding. In spite of these drawbacks, the novel is a painstakingly researched, prophetic attempt to trace the effects of industrial mechanization on individuals, societies and civilization. Set in northwestern Ontario in 1938, the ambitious book focuses on the conflicts between the 4 generations of the Clark family, owners of a flour mill. The story is primarily told through the recollections of Senator Samuel Clark, the elderly humanitarian hero of the novel who, before he dies, longs to explain and justify his responsibility and guilt in the creation of the colossal empire which has turned both his father and his son into false masters, slaves of the mill. But Grove's nightmarish, bleak vision of a sterile, automated society which ultimately robs humans of dignity, purpose and joy, is tempered at the end, as he affirms his conviction in the collective capacity of the human mind to triumph.

DONNA COATES

Advertisement for a self-propelled combine developed for the Massey-Harris Co in the 1930s (*courtesy Varity Corporation*).

Masterless Men of Newfoundland, legendary outlaw society (*fl* late 18th, early 19th centuries). According to tradition, for which there is little documentary evidence, they were Royal Navy deserters and runaway indentured servants from Newfoundland fishing plantations who fled inland to escape their harsh life. Led by Peter Kerrivan, an Irish-born deserter *c*1750, the Masterless Men are said to have inhabited the wild Butter Pot barrens of the Avalon Pen. Regarded as criminals by the authorities, they lived by hunting, fishing, stealing and illegally trading in isolated villages.

They reputedly blazed Newfoundland's first roads, some for practical purposes, others as blind leads to confound pursuers. Two, possibly 4, of them were captured and hanged, but authorities never succeeded in breaking up the outlaw society, nor did they capture Kerrivan, who became a folk hero in Newfoundland lore. In the early 19th century, as social conditions improved, the Masterless Men allegedly moved to outports where they could work as independent fishermen.

EDWARD BUTTS

Matane, Qué, City, pop 13 243 (1986c), inc 1845, located in the Gaspé region on the S shore of the St-Lawrence R 100 km NE of Rimouski. Its name is a derivative of the local Micmac word for "beaver pond." Jacques CARTIER visited the site in 1542 and noted its abundant stocks of fish and game. Jesuit missionaries established contact with the Micmac in 1643, while the first seigneury was granted in 1672. Permanent European habitation dates to the building of fishing camps in 1688. Agricultural development began in the late 18th century and the population remained very small until the growth of the lumber and forest products industries. In the 1950s, the closing of several paper mills resulted in widespread unemployment. A decade later, however, the recognition of Matane's port as an important regional transportation and distribution point revived interest in the city. The International Paper Co opened a mill in Matane in 1965; in early 1987, plans were announced for the building of another large paper mill. Shrimping is another important activity. Over 92% of the population is of French origin and the city is served by a community college (CEGEP).

SERGE DURFLINGER

Mathematics is the SCIENCE of numbers and spatial relationships. It is customary to distinguish pure mathematics and applied mathematics. Pure mathematics can be divided roughly into 3 major fields: geometry and topology, algebra and arithmetic, and analysis. It is complemented by logic, which deals with sets, the basic mathematical objects, their axioms and rules of inference.

Geometry studies figures, especially with regard to their rigid properties, and as a deductive science it began, like mathematics itself, with the Greeks. Straight lines, triangles, circles, spheres and cubes are among the first figures studied. A typical theorem, or general statement arrived at deductively, is that a right-angled triangle is characterized by the Pythagorean property (ie, the square of the hypotenuse is equal to the sum of the squares of the other 2 sides). In the early period (600 BC-100 AD), the theory of conic sections (ellipses, hyperbolas, parabolas) was developed, as was trigonometry, which was important for ASTRONOMY. In addition, formulas for the area or volume of special figures were discovered and proved. The principal later developments were the introduction of co-ordinate geometry (Descartes) and of curvature (Gauss), the central notion of differential geometry. The discovery of non-Euclidean geometry is, in comparison, minor.

In co-ordinate geometry the points of a plane are labelled by 2 co-ordinates, its distances from the 2 axes, and familiar figures become the loci of points satisfying an algebraic equation. Thus, geometry is incorporated into algebra and the way is opened for the introduction of spaces of arbitrarily large dimension, important in mechanics. Curvature, in its simplest form, is a number attached to a surface at a point. The flatter the surface, the smaller the number (positive for a sphere, negative for a saddle-shaped surface).

Topology studies properties of figures or spaces that are invariant under deformation. It has had its greatest successes in higher dimensions and studies spaces by attaching algebraic and numerical invariants to them. For example, closed oriented surfaces are characterized by their genus. For the surface of a ball, $g = 0$; of a doughnut, $g = 1$; and of a pretzel, $g = 2$. The classification of 3-dimensional spaces, of much current interest, is still incomplete. The Gauss-Bonnet theorem connects topology and geometry in a typical way: the integral of the curvature over a closed surface equals 4π (1-g).

Algebra studies general properties of the solutions of one or several equations; arithmetic or number theory is the study of solutions in specific domains or fields of numbers. Linear algebra, the highly developed theory of equations of degree one, is of importance thoughout mathematics. The notion of eigenvalues and eigenvectors, which appear geometrically as the principal axes of an ellipsoid, is critical. All of algebra is pervaded by the concept of a group, a collection of elements which can be multiplied, such as operations on a Rubik's cube. The theory of finite groups has made great strides in recent years.

Analysis begins with calculus, the calculation of velocities and tangents (derivatives), lengths, areas and distances traversed (integrals), and maxima and minima. The central notion is that of a function, which expresses the way one variable depends upon another. The integrals of very few functions can be calculated explicitly; the attendant problems for algebraic functions have greatly influenced the development of geometry and arithmetic.

A differential equation is one connecting a function and its derivatives. Differential equations arise in all sciences. The equation is ordinary if there is only one independent variable and 2 of the basic problems are stability and the existence of periodic solutions. Much is known but the empirical data, found by computer, outstrip our theoretical understanding. The equation is called partial if there is more than one independent variable. Partial differential equations appear in the study of the propagation of waves and matter. In spite of an enormous theory, there are still basic phenomena that we do not understand, such as turbulence, and to which ideas from probability, a discipline in its own right, are often applied. Derivatives and integrals require the use of limits, as do expansions of functions in infinite series, such as a power series or Fourier series. The use of Fourier series, which express a function as an infinite sum of sines and cosines, is indispensable in the study of partial differential equations.

ROBERT P. LANGLANDS

Applied Mathematics

Applied mathematics is any valid mathematics that arises in the evolution and dispatch of real problems. It may use all of the techniques of "pure" mathematics; the 2 differ in the sources of problems addressed and the uses to which solutions will be put. Therefore, applied mathematics can involve ENGINEERING, PHYSICS and other fields, as well as pure mathematics. The evolution and solution of a real problem may be divided into roughly 6 stages, each requiring somewhat different skills. However, there are no sharp boundaries between the stages.

Recognition In industry, the realization that a problem exists will usually come from an engineer, scientist or manager involved in the practical applications of a technology, and in a position to recognize that something needs improvement or that something is going wrong.

Data Collection After a problem has been recognized, some specific data will be required to define it. Such data may be experimental, statistical or both. Therefore, experimental design and statistical analysis are important tools of the applied mathematician.

Formulation When enough data has been collected to define the problem, it must be formulated in a way that is precise enough to work on, ie, a mathematical model must be made of the situation. The model must be simple enough to permit a complete analysis, but also sufficiently close to reality to be relevant to the real problem being considered. In the process, all irrelevant details, and all details of only minor importance, must be suppressed. This narrowing focus permits concentration on major effects. To decide what is of major and what is of minor importance demands considerable *savoir faire* and makes model building probably the most valuable and difficult task of the applied mathematician.

Solution After recognition, data collection and formulation comes solution. Different formulations of a problem are usually possible and, as one formulation may be easier to handle than another, the solution may vary in complexity. Often, general mathematical methods that are applicable in principle are not actually useful. This situation is especially true when a numerical answer, correct to a specified degree of accuracy, and at a reasonable cost of time and manpower, is required. The neatness and simplicity of most textbook problems cannot be guaranteed in the real world; however, neatness or elegance in a solution frequently comes with real understanding of the problem.

Computation Most problems require not only understanding but also an actual numerical solution. Computation of the relevant numbers frequently may be done more quickly and economically without using a computer; however, should a computer be required, proper programming is important. If a fast computer costs $500/h of machine time, a good mathematician can effect a considerable saving through the way he prepares the problem for computation. For example, such problems arise in the computation of 3-dimensional partial differential equations involved in calculations of elasticity, weather predictions, etc.

Communication Since an applied mathematician must make his findings accessible to the people he works for, he must present his work in a style less compact and easier for a nonspecialist to read than that common in most mathematical journals.

MURRAY KLAMKIN

History in Canada

Every Canadian university has a mathematics department and offers one or more programs in this field. The same is probably true of almost every university throughout the world, a reflection of the importance of mathematics in contemporary society. Mathematics came to prominence as a scientific discipline after the Renaissance, during the period historians call the Scientific Revolution (1450-1700), when brilliant astronomer-mathematicians such as Copernicus and Newton discovered the true nature of the solar system, with the sun at the centre and the planets revolving around it. The role that mathematics played in these major discoveries gave the discipline the stature it has maintained to this day.

The evolution of mathematics in NEW FRANCE followed closely on the heels of this newly acquired stature. Although there were no new discoveries, the quality of teaching was virtually equal to that found in colleges in France. The Jesuits founded Collège de Québec in 1635 and started to teach intermediate mathematics there in 1651. Until 1760 students were taught arithmetic, the rudiments of second-degree or quadratic equations, trigonometry, geometry and a little differential and integral calculus – all in one of the 2 final years of the 8-year course of studies. The first full professor was Martin Boutet de St-Martin. In 1678 Louis XIV appointed him to the new royal chair of mathematics and HYDROGRAPHY in Québec City, his wish being that pilots for the St Lawrence R and surveyors and cartographers be trained in the colony. The chair was not abolished until the end of the French regime. The most celebrated appointee to this chair was Louis JOLLIET, the discoverer of the Mississippi R. Soon after Jolliet's death, the chair officially passed to the Jesuits.

After the Conquest, 1759-60, the Collège de Québec had to close, but the SÉMINAIRE DE QUÉBEC, which took over its operations, retained the same classical course structure. Encouraged by Abbé Jérôme DEMERS, the teaching of science and mathematics flourished, particularly around 1840. Soon, however, for sociological and religious reasons, it fell into disfavour. It was not until 1920 that the importance of science was re-established among Québec Francophones. In that year, U Laval (Québec City) organized its École supérieure de chimie (which became its faculty of science in 1937) and U de M established its Faculty of Science.

Nothing significant in the field of mathematics occurred in English Canada until 1855. Of the few English-language universities in Canada, only U of T offered programs with specializations, one being in mathematics and natural philosophy (the latter term signifying the physical sciences). However, each university had a mathematics and natural philosophy professor. Trained in Great Britain, these few professors brought with them the idea that science and TECHNOLOGY were central to the Industrial Revolution. A Canadian scientific community thus began to take shape and the need for communication among its members was felt almost immediately. In 1856 the *Canadian Journal of Science, Literature and History,* published under the aegis of the Royal Canadian Institute, accepted articles on mathematics and continued to do so until 1912. Professor J.B. Cherriman (U of T) was in charge of the section on mathematics and natural philosophy.

In the 1870s the idea arose of more specialized university studies. In 1877 U of T launched its mathematics and PHYSICS programs, which became models for the rest of Canada during the first half of the 20th century. Other universities, eg, Queen's, McGill and Dalhousie, gradually moved in the same direction. During this time, science departments were being subdivided and by 1890 almost all universities (with the exception of McGill) had at least one mathematics (no longer a "mathematics and natural philosophy") professor. At the same time, bursaries were offered for studies in mathematics, 2 each at University of Toronto and Dalhousie.

Three mathematicians merit special mention for the impetus they gave to the establishment and development of mathematics programs at their respective universities: James LOUDON of U of T, Alexander Johnson of McGill and N.F. Dupuis of Queen's. In 1890 all were members of the ROYAL SOCIETY OF CANADA. Founded in 1882, this society was originally divided into 4 sections, one of which was mathematics and natural philosophy. The society reserved a place for the mathematics publications of its members in its *Proceedings and Transactions,* thereby offering a new means of communication for the mathematics community. In 1878 the *American Journal of Mathematics* was founded at Johns Hopkins University, Baltimore, followed in 1886 by the American Mathematical Society which, from 1891 on, published its *Bulletin* and from 1900 on, its *Transactions.* Canadian mathematicians contributed regularly to these journals.

The number of mathematics departments increased during the first 2 decades of this century, as a result of the growing importance of mathematics in professional fields (eg, engineering). The U of Toronto was the first N American university to move into the field of actuarial science (ie, the calculation of INSURANCE and annuity premiums and dividends). The Canadian Institute of Actuaries, a professional society, was founded in 1907. In 1915 U of T awarded the first Canadian doctorate in mathematics to Samuel Beatty, who later became the head of that institution's mathematics department. McGill conferred the second Canadian mathematics doctorate in 1917. The U of T was increasingly taking the lead in Canada and held it until the end of the 1950s. One of the most notable figures in the department was undoubtedly J.C. FIELDS, renowned for his work in algebraic functions and one of those who managed to revive the International Congress of Mathematics, meetings of which had been suspended after WWI. The first meeting after the war was held in Toronto in 1924. Fields, reacting to the lack of a Nobel Prize for the field of mathematics, began working to establish an equivalent prize. These efforts were successful in 1932, a few months after his sudden death. The Fields Medal, named in his honour, is now universally recognized as the greatest honour that can be conferred on a mathematician. In 1936 the algebraist and geometer Harold S.M. Coxeter joined the department. An example of the high calibre of teaching then being provided in Toronto can be seen in the first years of the American William Lowell Putnam Mathematics Competition. Only undergraduates could participate in this competition and each university entered a team of 3 students. In the first year, 1938, the U of T team won first place over all the N American universities. The competition rules prevented U of T from entering a team the following year, but in 1940, it won again, as it did in 1942 and 1946. In the 1986 competition, teams from 2 Canadian universities (UBC and Waterloo) ranked among the top 10 (the others being Harvard, Washington U St Louis, U of California Berkley, Yale, MIT, California Inst of Technology, Princeton and Rice.

The end of WWII was a turning point for mathematics in Canada. During the war Canadian mathematicians became aware of their isolation, even within Canada. If they wished to meet, they had to participate in meetings of the American Mathematical Society. They therefore organized the first Canadian mathematical congress, held in Montréal in June 1945. This very successful gathering led to the creation of the Canadian Mathematical Society. In 1949 the society began publishing the *Canadian Journal of Mathematics*, an internationally recognized publication, to which was added the *Bulletin* in 1958. In 1950, still under the aegis of the congress, Professor R.L. Jeffery, from Queen's, organized a Summer Research Institute in Kingston, which brought together 10 mathematicians to conduct joint research. This type of meeting proved so fruitful that summer research institutes have been held annually in some universities. In the 1950s mathematics departments developed very quickly. Toronto lost its leadership, not because its quality of teaching had declined, but because departments in other Canadian universities had improved – a case of students surpassing their teachers. Graduate studies burgeoned everywhere. Because of the development of STATISTICS, operations research and COMPUTER SCIENCE, industry showed increasing interest in mathematics graduates. However, forecasts of major increases in the student population in the 1960s indicated that there would be a high demand for university professors. With the launching of the first Sputnik by the USSR in 1957, mathematics once again found itself in the public eye, and the "New Math" movement began. In the same year, the NATIONAL RESEARCH COUNCIL OF CANADA began to give grants to mathematician-researchers and 2 new societies were founded: the Canadian Information Processing Society and the Canadian Operational Research Society. The prodigious development of computer science and diversified interests among mathematicians and computer scientists later led to the subdivision of mathematics departments in almost all universities into a mathematics department and a computer science department, the most striking example being the creation in 1966 of the Faculty of Mathematics at the U of Waterloo, with its 5 constituent departments: pure mathematics, applied mathematics, combinatorics and optimization, applied analysis and computer science, and statistics.

In Québec francophone universities returned to the Canadian mainstream around 1945 after successfully overcoming the difficulties generated by the prolonged lack of a scientific tradition in that province. By 1970 the department of mathematics at U de M had acquired an international reputation under the direction of Maurice L'Abbé, and had established a Centre de recherche en mathématiques appliquées. The early 1970s were truly a golden age for mathematicians in Canada. In 1961 Canadian universities had awarded 11 PhDs in mathematics; this number increased to 94 in 1973. The National Research Council in 1960-61 gave $87 500 for mathematics research; the figure for 1972-73 was $2 461 500. The figure in 1986-87 was $8 419 000. In 1961 there were about 250 university mathematics professors (assistant rank and higher) in Canadian universities; in 1973, about 1300. The Canadian Society for History and Philosophy of Mathematics was founded in 1973 and, a few years later, the Statistical Society of Canada, which now publishes the *Canadian Statistical Review*. In 1974 the International Mathematical Congress again met in Canada, this time in Vancouver.

The Canadian mathematics community, like other scientific communities, is affected by the movement of promising graduates to the US, a fact that further testifies to the level of excellence of instruction in Canadian departments. Mathematicians with international reputations who received their early training in Canada include Cathleen Morawetz (U of T), Courant Institute of Mathematical Sciences, New York; Robert Langlands (UBC), Institute for Advanced Study, Princeton; Israel Herstein (U of Man), U of Chicago; Irving Kaplansky (U of T), U of Chicago; Louis Nirenberg (McGill), New York U; G.F. Duff (U of T), emeritus professor, U of T; Leo Moser (U of Man), U of A (d 1970); W.O. Moser (U of Man), McGill; Raoul Bott (McGill), Harvard. The new generation of Canadian mathematicians includes Robert V. Moody (now working at U de M), John Mallet-Paret (Brown U, Rhode I), Jerry Marsden (Berkeley), Robert Steinberg (UCLA), Frank Clarke (U de M), Jack Edmonds (U of Waterloo), Stephen Cook (U of T), Marvin Shinbrot (U of Victoria) and David Brillinger (Berkeley).

The Canadian mathematics community faces a number of challenges. Connections seem to have been made among university departments, industry and government in such fields as statistics and computer science, where the future appears to hold promise. However, other areas of mathematics appear more sensitive to difficult economic conditions. LOUIS CHARBONNEAU

Reading: K.P. Beltzner et al, *Mathematical Sciences in Canada* (1976).

Mathematics and Society The involvement of a society in MATHEMATICS is determined by cultural and functional factors. Mathematics has its own intrinsic beauty and aesthetic appeal, but its cultural role is determined mainly by its perceived educational qualities. The achievements of mathematics are recognized as being among the greatest intellectual peaks attained by mankind and, therefore, are seen as being worthy of study in their own right, while the heavy reliance of mathematics on logical reasoning is seen to have educational merit in a world where rational thought and behaviour are highly valued. Furthermore the potential for sharpening the wit and problem-solving abilities fostered by study of mathematics is also seen as contributing significantly to the general objectives of acquiring wisdom and intellectual capabilities. These cultural aspect affect all Canadians to some degree through our formal educational processes, reflecting the degree to which Canadian society is committed to "liberal" or "humanist" education. In particular, it is a point of view adopted by many professional mathematicians in their teaching and research activities.

The "functional" aspect of mathematics stems from its importance as the language of SCIENCE, ENGINEERING and TECHNOLOGY, and its role in their development. This involvement is as old as mathematics itself and it can be argued that, without mathematics, there can be neither science nor engineering. In modern times, adoption of mathematical methods in the social, medical and physical sciences has expanded rapidly, confirming mathematics as an indispensable part of all school curricula and creating great demand for university-level mathematical training. Much of the demand stems directly from the need for mathematical and statistical modelling of phenomena. Such modelling is basic to all engineering, plays a vital role in all physical sciences and contributes significantly to the biological sciences, medicine, psychology, economics and commerce.

In addition, the rapid development of computing power has created its own demand for mathematical techniques and has permitted the implementation of large-scale mathematical models that would have been impractical before. Indeed, development of COMPUTER SCIENCE itself owes much to the contributions of mathematicians, and its continuing explosive growth draws on, and contributes to, mathematical science. For example, the analysis of algorithms, the structure of formal languages, ROBOTICS, logical design, and large-scale scientific computation may be seen as important components of computer science which require, and stimulate, mathematical analysis in their development.

The pervasive and ever-increasing use of mathematical methods in science, commerce and government implies that a well-informed public must be mathematically literate to some degree. In practical terms this means that, in the mainstream of primary and secondary education, there must be effective mathematical education, bringing students to a point where they can readily calculate and think in quantitative terms, where information presented graphically or in statistical terms is easily comprehended, and where the logic and precision demanded in communication with computers is appreciated. There is an ever-increasing need for people who are well trained in mathematics and are confident with the mathematization of problems in the world around us.

In any country, the place of mathematics in society depends on the nature of the society and its ambitions. Canadian society has inherited the European traditions of cultural and scientific freedoms and it is reasonable to assume that these will be maintained. Also, from a prosperity based on the extraction of primary resources, Canada aspires to a leading role on the international scene as an industrialized nation and as a producer of consumer goods and HIGH TECHNOLOGY products. These aspirations are strongly influenced by the proximity of the US and, in particular, by Canadian economic dependence on that country. The role of mathematics in Canada, and of all the basic sciences, depends partly on the degree of economic independence chosen by Canadians now and for the future.

This discussion sets the context in which the past and present role of mathematics in Canada must be assessed and suggest a context for the future. It implies, first, that building on existing programs a relatively high level of mathematical literacy must be an objective of the primary and secondary school systems. This is necessary if the layman is to cope with the computer and information revolution and with the ever-increasing use of quantitative methods in governmental decision making. It is also a necessary foundation for the appreciation of modern scientific activities and the history of sciences, as well as for those wishing to participate in more advanced technical, scientific or mathematical subjects. At the post-secondary level, Canada should maintain a strong tradition for mathematics education in all its forms and must continue to maintain an active community of mathematicians engaged in research, if it is to maintain a viable position in the world's scientific and technological enterprise.

The extent to which such a commitment to mathematics is explicity accepted by society and the Canadian public is questionable. For the great majority, exposure to mathematics is limited to something less than a current grade 12 high-school curriculum. Hence, the corresponding view of mathematics is narrow, extending little further than arithmetic, with a smattering of algebra, geometry, trigonometry and, possibly, formal calculus. Such exposure cannot extend in any substantive way beyond the state of mathematical knowledge achieved in the 17th century. With this limited view, it is practically impossible to conceive of the extraordinary volume, diversity and value of modern mathematical developments. Consequently, there are widely held misconceptions about the significance and usefulness of mathematics that leave the subject vulnerable to periodic and shortsighted popular demand for functional education. There is also evidence that a negative attitude, or a feeling of anxiety, towards mathematics is common in Canadian society and is even shared by many teachers of mathematics, especially at the primary level. Such considerations put responsibility on the mathematics community to recommend improvements in methods and curricula, and on governments and local authorities to ensure that high standards and, especially, proper hiring practices are maintained.

It is necessary to recognize difficulties (like those mentioned in the preceding paragraph) with the development of skills in mathematics, and of awareness of the importance of mathematics in Canadian society. Nevertheless, mathematics has a respected place in the Canadian cultural and educational spectrum. The necessary educational and organizational infrastructures exist, and the subject is alive and well in Canada in both its cultural and functional forms.

PETER LANCASTER

Reading: K.P. Beltzner et al, *Mathematical Sciences in Canada* (1976); L.A. Steen, editor, *Mathematics Today* (1978); P.J. Davis and R. Hersch, *The Mathematical Experience* (1981).

Mather, Bruce, composer, pianist, educator, administrator (b at Toronto 9 May 1939). He studied first in Toronto, notably with Godfrey RIDOUT, Oskar MORAWETZ and John WEINZWEIG; then at the Paris Conservatoire with Darius Milhaud, Simone Plé-Caussade and Olivier Messiaen; at Stanford U, Calif; and with Pierre Boulez in Switzerland. A teacher at McGill from 1966, he has also taught at the Brodie School in Toronto and as a visiting teacher at the Paris Conservatoire. He has been a member of the executive of Ten Centuries Concerts and a director-member of the Société de musique contemporaine du Québec. He has performed several pieces of contemporary music, both solo and with his wife, pianist Pierrette LePage. In 1979 he won the Prix Jules-Léger for new chamber music, for his *Musique pour Champigny*. Many of his compositions are for small ensembles. HÉLÈNE PLOUFFE

Matheson, Ont, UP, pop 605 (1986c), 966 (1981c), is located 296 km NW of NORTH BAY. Originally a fur-trading post called McDougall's Chute, its name was changed in 1912 in honour of the Ontario provincial treasurer. Located on the Temiskaming and Northern Ontario Ry (Ontaro Northland), it initially served as a supply centre for the surrounding lumbering and agricultural communities. It is widely known for the devastating fire of 1916 that officially claimed 233 lives, although the loss was probably much greater. In the 1920s and 1930s gold and asbestos mining began in the area, and more recently tourism has become important. MATT BRAY

Matheson, Alexander Wallace, lawyer, politician, premier of PEI 1953-59 (b at Bellevue, PEI 11 June 1903; d at Charlottetown 3 Mar 1976). First elected to the PEI Legislature in 1940, Matheson became minister of health and welfare under Premier J. Walter JONES and premier in 1953 when Jones retired to the Senate. Matheson vigorously promoted rural electrification to protect and strengthen farm life. Although the provision of modern services did improve life, the erosion of rural communities continued. Matheson resigned as party leader in 1961 following the defeat of the Liberals in the 1959 provincial election, but was re-elected by a large majority. He served as leader of the Opposition until his retirement from politics in 1965. In 1967 he was elevated to the bench. DAVID A. MILNE

Mathieson, John Alexander, lawyer, politician, judge, premier of PEI 1911-17 (b at Harrington, PEI 19 May 1863; d at Charlottetown 7 Jan 1947). Educated at Prince of Wales College, Charlottetown, he was a schoolmaster and lawyer before his election to PEI's Assembly as a Conservative in 1900. He became premier in Dec 1911 after the resignation of the Liberal government. Within a month he led his party to a landslide election victory. As premier he obtained a constitutional guarantee that PEI would have at least 4 federal MPs. In 1917 he resigned to become chief justice of the provincial Supreme Court. He retired in 1943 because of infirmity.

IAN ROSS ROBERTSON

Mathieu, André, pianist, composer (b at Montréal 18 Feb 1929; d 2 June 1968). Called the "Canadian Mozart," he started composing at age 4, gave a recital of his own works at age 6 and made his radio debut in 1936 as the soloist in his own *Concertino No 1* for piano and orchestra. He studied first with his father, Rodolphe MATHIEU, then in Paris. After distinguishing himself with a Town Hall concert in New York (1940) he settled there and, aged 13, appeared at Carnegie Hall. He returned to Montréal (1943), then to Paris (1946) where he studied with Arthur Honegger (composition) and Jules Gentil (piano). He then put himself on display in "pianothons." This publicity disillusioned those who believed in his talent which, sadly, never reached its full potential. His youthful compositions echoed Prokofiev; later he became a post-romantic of the Rachmaninov type. Excerpts from his writings were the basis for the song of welcome and the music for the XXIst Olympic Games (1976). HÉLÈNE PLOUFFE

Mathieu, Rodolphe, composer, teacher, writer, pianist (b at Grondines, near Québec C 10 July 1890; d at Montréal 29 June 1962). Considered too avant-garde for his time because of Debussy's influence on his music, he gained recognition too late to inspire the generation that followed. Impressed first by the works of Scriabin, to which he was introduced by Alfred La Liberté, he devoted himself to composing only after studying with Alexis Contant (*c*1910). He then studied in Paris with Vincent d'Indy. In 1923 he received the first grant given to a composer by the Québec government. He taught in several institutions and, in 1929, founded the Canadian Institute of Music.

HÉLÈNE PLOUFFE

Matonabbee, Chipewyan leader (b at Prince of Wales's Ft *c*1737; d Aug 1782). A leading hunter of caribou on the Barren Lands, Matonabbee grew up in and around PRINCE OF WALES'S FT and was an important middleman in the fur trade between the HUDSON'S BAY CO and other DENE tribes farther W. In the 1750s he was an ambassador among the Cree and made at least one trip to the Coppermine R. Samuel HEARNE is justly famous for his overland journey to the Arctic Ocean (1770-72), but it was Matonabbee who made the trip possible, with his leadership and knowledge of the Indian way of travel and living off the land. He was a "leading Indian" of Prince of Wales's Ft – an important position in the fur trade, but not of broader political significance. Bound to the fortunes of the fur trade, he committed suicide when the French destroyed the fort in 1782. DAVID LEE

Matsqui, BC, DM, pop 51 449 (1986c), 42 000 (1981c), area 21 920 ha, inc 1892, is located between the Fraser R and the US border, 70 km E of downtown Vancouver on the Trans-Canada Highway. Its name, of West Coast Salish origin, likely means "a stretch of higher ground." It is situated in the Central Fraser Valley Regional Dist, with LANGLEY to the W, ABBOTSFORD to the E and MISSION to the N. Its economic base is primarily agricultural, including dairy production, eggs, poultry and such labour-intensive activities as berry and horticulture production, as well as cash-crop production. Matsqui produces over 90% of Canada's raspberry crop. Other elements in the economy include resource extraction (primarily sand and gravel), manufacturing, food processing, aircraft modification, transportation, and trade and services. Clearbrook, the main business and residential area, is the valley's regional town centre with a developing office, professional and administrative function. Matsqui has experienced rapid population growth, increasing by more than 20 000 residents in the period from 1976 to 1986. The Abbotsford Airport and its renowned International Airshow are located in Matsqui. Matsqui is served by the Fraser Valley College and is home to several denominational colleges and the Mennonite Central Committee. Rural settlements include Clayburn Village, the original home of Clayburn Industries brick and tile manufacturers, Matsqui Village, Mt Lehman and Bradner. ALAN F.J. ARTIBISE

Matthews, John, army officer, farmer, politician (b probably in Eng *c*1763; d probably in Eng 20 Aug 1832). Retiring as captain after 27 years in the Royal Artillery, he immigrated to Canada in 1819, apparently on the promise of the gov gen, the duke of Richmond, to put him in charge of a new military settlement. Arriving after Richmond's unexpected death, he claimed the patronage of the lt-gov of Upper Canada, Sir Peregrine MAITLAND, but his extravagant demands alienated Maitland. Settling in the London District, he became a spokesman for critics of the local administrative elite. Elected as MPP for Middlesex in 1824, he adopted a radical political posture in the Assembly. Matthews became a political "martyr" in 1826, when he was stripped of his military pension and ordered to report to Royal Artillery HQ in England after allegedly leading a theatre audience at York [Toronto] in pro-American songs. In 1828 the pension was restored, but not before this transparently oppressive action, probably provoked by Matthews's outspokenly anti-government stance on the ALIEN QUESTION, had helped to discredit Maitland's administration. Matthews went to England anyway in 1829. PAUL ROMNEY

Matthews, Peter, farmer, rebel (b in Marysburgh or Sidney Twp, Qué [later UC] 1789 or 1790; d at Toronto 12 Apr 1838). The son of Loyalists, Matthews was a prosperous farmer and leading figure in Pickering Township. Angry with government development policies, he was persuaded to lead his neighbours to join the REBELLION OF 1837. He was captured, tried and executed.

RONALD STAGG

Matton, Roger, composer, teacher, ethnomusicologist (b at Granby, Qué 18 May 1929). He first studied at the Montreal Conservatory of Music, notably with Claude Champagne (composition) and Arthur Letondal (piano), then in Paris with Andrée Vaurabourg-Honegger, Nadia Boulanger and Olivier Messiaen. He began his career as a composer for Radio-Canada radio and television. After studies with Marius BARBEAU at the National Museum of Canada, he worked as a researcher and ethnomusicologist in the folklore archives of Laval (1956-76), transcribing nearly 300 Acadian songs (1957-59). Most of his works carry the mark of this association with folklore (*Concerto* for 2 pianos and percussion, *L'Escaouette, L'Horoscope, Te Deum*). His *Mouvement symphonique II* was played by the orchestre symphonique de Montréal during its USSR tour (1962) – probably one of the first Canadian symphonies to be presented there. In 1965 he won the award for musical creation at the Congrès du spectacle; in 1969 he received the Prix Calixa Lavallée for music.

HÉLÈNE PLOUFFE

Mauger, Joshua, colonial entrepreneur (bap in the parish of St John, Jersey 25 Apr 1725; d at Warborne, Eng 18 Oct 1788). Mauger arrived in Halifax in 1749 and evolved his position as navy victualler into a commercial and property empire, based initially on contraband trade with the French. He became Halifax's largest shipowner, building vessels, plying the coastal and W Indies trade, and supplying rum, lumber, mercantile goods and fish to a network of outpost stores. His distillery produced 50 000 gallons (190 000 litres) annually by 1766, and in a colony totally dependent on rum revenue, Mauger's position was pre-eminent. Although based in England after 1760, he used agents and his own influence to protect his NS interests and undermine the colonial administration, including Jonathan BELCHER, Lord William CAMPBELL and Francis LEGGE, governors hostile to the mercantile ascendancy. Mauger's complex involvement with NS underscores the bonds of subservience and influence that hindered that colony's early development.

LOIS KERNAGHAN

Reading: J.B. Brebner, *The Neutral Yankees of Nova Scotia* (2 ed, 1969) and *New England's Outpost* (1927).

Maugerville, NB, UP, pop 285 (1986c), 249 (1981c), is located on the SAINT JOHN R, 8 km SE of FREDERICTON. It was founded by New England planters from Essex County, Mass, in 1763-64 and named in honour of Joshua MAUGER, who aided settlers in gaining title to their lands. Situated on rich alluvial soil in the Saint John Valley, it was the first successful English-speaking settlement on the river. During the AMERICAN REVOLUTION most inhabitants openly supported the American cause; several took part in an attack on Fort Cumberland in 1776, the only armed uprising against British authority in NS.

When the province of New Brunswick was created at the end of the war, Loyalist leaders held the old Yankee residents suspect for their past sympathies and divided the township, retaining the name Maugerville for the upper half and renaming the lower section Sheffield. The growth of the mast-and-timber trade brought prosperity and the rich farmlands, flooded annually by spring freshets, provided much of the produce consumed in Saint John and Fredericton throughout the 19th and early 20th centuries. Today the farmers struggle to survive. The river, once bustling with sloops, barges and paddle-wheelers, now carries only pleasure craft. Yet the proud independent character of the first settlers is still evident in the farms tilled by their descendants.

JIM SNOWDON

Mavor, James, scholar (b at Stranraer, Scot 8 Dec 1854; d at Glasgow, Scot 31 Oct 1925). Economist, economic historian, second professor of political economy and constitutional history at U of T, Mavor created a modern department of political economy, introduced the teaching of commerce at the honours level and began Canadian contract research in the social sciences. Educated in Glasgow, Mavor originally inclined towards socialism, but moved to the right before coming to Toronto. His representations brought the DOUKHOBORS to Canada. He wrote on many topics, including the economic history of Russia, Canada's wheat economy, Manitoba government telephones, Ontario Hydro and applied economics. He ceased to teach in 1922 and retired in 1923. His descendants have been prominent in drama and the arts; his influence on Toronto's social sciences was felt into the late 1970s.

IAN DRUMMOND

Maxville, Ont, Village, pop 815 (1986c), 836 (1981c), inc *c*1891, located SE of Ottawa. It began around 1869 and expanded rapidly when the Canada Atlantic Ry established a station there in 1881. It got its name from the many "Macs" of its Highland Scottish neighbourhood. Its population was 749 by 1901, but since has been virtually unchanged. With little industry, its main economic function has been to supply merchandise and services to the surrounding farm community. Less tangibly, but not unimportantly, it has emotional significance for SCOTS as a surviving concentration of the old "Scottishness" of its county, Glengarry. The Glengarry HIGHLAND GAMES, held annually in Maxville since 1948, are among the more successful of their kind, attracting some 20 000 every summer. The novelist Ralph Connor (Charles William GORDON) and British financier Sir Edward Peacock were born at St Elmo, 3 km NW of here.

ROYCE MACGILLIVRAY

Reading: Royce MacGillivray and Ewan Ross, *A History of Glengarry* (1979).

Maxwell, Edward, architect (b at Montréal 31 Dec 1867; d there 14 Nov 1923). He apprenticed in Boston with Shepley, Rutan & Coolidge, who won a competition (1891) for the new Montréal Board of Trade. Maxwell returned to Montréal to supervise construction, and the contacts he made with prominent members of the Board of Trade helped to assure his success. In 1892 jeweller Henry BIRKS hired him to design a new store facing Phillips Square – now one of the city's architectural ornaments. Maxwell also designed numerous CPR stations and hotels, including the major western terminal at Vancouver (1897). The country estate planned for Louis-Joseph FORGET at Senneville, Qué (1899), is a fine example of his residential work.

His younger brother **William Sutherland Maxwell** (b at Montréal 14 Nov 1874; d there 25 Mar 1952) became his partner in 1902. William had studied at the École des beaux-arts in Paris, and the beaux-arts style is reflected in the design and planning of the Maxwells' buildings at this time, eg, in the Royal Bank branch at Westmount (1903) and the CPR station at Winnipeg (1904). Their grandest and most memorable works – the SASKATCHEWAN LEGISLATIVE BUILDING at Regina (1908-11) and the Montreal Art Assn Gallery (1911; now the Musée des beaux-arts de Montréal) – display a skill at planning and composition that ranks with the best beaux-arts designs of the period. Their final achievement was the St-Louis wing and tower block of the Château Frontenac Hotel at Québec C, which was completed in 1924, a year after Edward's death.

Although William continued to practise, his work consisted mainly of additions and alterations to buildings designed earlier by the firm. Without the support of his brother, he seemed unable to revive the high level of creativity that had kept their office at the front rank of the architectural profession in Canada.

ROBERT LEMIRE

"Wop" May, WWI fighter pilot and one of Canada's leading bush pilots in the postwar era (*courtesy National Archives of Canada/C-57580/W.R. May Coll*).

May, Wilfrid Reid, "Wop," airman (b at Carberry, Man 20 Mar 1896; d at Provo, Utah 21 June 1952). He was a novice pilot on the Western Front being hotly pursued by Manfred, Freiherr von Richthofen, when the "Red Baron" was killed on 21 Apr 1918. May might have been his 81st victim but instead went on to become one of Canada's leading bush flyers in the postwar era, winning the MCKEE TROPHY in 1929. During WWII he helped set up the BRITISH COMMONWEALTH AIR TRAINING PLAN and was a pioneer in aerial "search and rescue" techniques.

BRERETON GREENHOUS

Mayflower, common name for the trailing arbutus (*Epigaea repens*), a creeping, woody, evergreen plant belonging to the heath family (Ericaceae) and native to eastern N America. The only other member of the genus (*E. asiatica*) is native to Japan. The name mayflower derives from the very fragrant, white or rose-coloured, bell-shaped blossoms that appear during that month, and sometimes in Apr. Ants are attracted to the globular, capsule-shaped fruit. The mayflower grows in acidic sandy or peaty soils from New-

Mayflower, common name for the trailing arbutus (*Epigaea repens*), the provincial floral emblem of Nova Scotia (*photo by Mary W. Ferguson*).

foundland to Manitoba, and has been the PROVINCIAL FLORAL EMBLEM of NS since 1901. It is grown from seed because transplanting produces poor results. CÉLINE ARSENEAULT

Mayfly, or shadfly, common names for small, fragile, soft-bodied insects comprising order Ephemeroptera [Gk, "living a day"]. About 2000 species are known worldwide; 300 in Canada. Eggs are deposited on clean, flowing water. The larval stage is aquatic and lasts a few months to 2 years, depending on the species. Larvae obtain oxygen through abdominal gills. Most feed on algae and particles of detritus; a few are predatory. Transformation to the terrestrial adult usually occurs at water surface. Mayflies are unique among winged insects, usually having 2 adult stages: the subimago, a rather dull creature with translucent wings, molts again within a few minutes to 24 hours, to the sexually mature adult. Adults do not feed; most live only 1-2 days. Their long, shiny bodies end in 2 long appendages (cerci). The wings are membranous: forewings are large; hindwings, small or absent. Mayflies are an important food for fish and provide models for fishermen's lures. G. PRITCHARD

Maynard, Hannah, née Hatherly, photographer (b at Bude, Eng 17 Jan 1834; d at Victoria 15 May 1918); **Maynard, Richard James,** photographer (b at Stratton, Eng 22 Feb 1832; d at Victoria 10 Jan 1907). The Maynards immigrated in 1852 to Bowmanville, UC, where Richard opened a boot and shoe business. Hannah learned photography, possibly in 1859 when Richard was in BC prospecting for gold. In 1862 they moved to Victoria, where Hannah began her "photographic gallery." Richard, who may have learned photography from her, did a panorama of Victoria harbour in 1864, and a decade later began a 20-year career as a landscape photographer, rivalling Hannah's portrait work. Among Richard's commissions were tours to inspect Indian villages (1873, 1874), an expedition to the Queen Charlotte Is (1884) and a trip to the Pribilof Is (1892). Hannah's most interesting photographs include experiments in the early 1890s with multiple images of herself and a young grandson, and photosculptures, where people are made to resemble statues or busts. DAVID MATTISON

Mayne Island, 2327 ha, is one of the GULF IS in BC. The island is named for British surveyor Lt R.C. Mayne. Excavated Indian middens near Active Pass suggest habitation for at least 5000 years. Active Pass, separating Mayne and GALIANO islands, has large salmon runs and, because of tidal upwellings, large feeding waterfowl populations. Mayne I was the hub of the Gulf Is at the turn of the century on the strength of its resort hotels and wharves, which handled passenger ships plying the Str of GEORGIA between Victoria and New Westminster or Vancouver. Today, with the other islands, it is a retirement and summer tourism centre. PETER GRANT

Mayo, YT, Village, pop 317 (1986c), 398 (1981c), is located on the Stewart R at the mouth of the Mayo R, 407 km N of Whitehorse. Originally called Mayo Landing, it was named after Alfred S. Mayo, an early prospector and trader. It became the landing point for riverboats on the Stewart R after gold was found nearby (1902). In 1919 the discovery of silver-lead deposits at Keno Hill transformed the town into a major transshipment point for ore. In 1949 a road was built to the Klondike Hwy and, as the riverboats went out of service, Mayo declined. H. GUEST

Mayor, *see* MUNICIPAL GOVERNMENT.

Mazankowski, Donald Frank, politician (b at Viking, Alta 27 July 1935). After a period as president and general manager of an automobile and farm machinery dealership, Mazankowski was elected to the House of Commons as Conservative MP for Vegreville, Alta, in 1968. Bright and popular, he chaired the PC caucus 1973-76 and served as minister of transport and minister responsible for the CANADIAN WHEAT BOARD in the CLARK government, 1979-80. He won the respect of the media, Opposition politicians and his officials, and registered a series of solid achievements, notably in the area of rail transportation. He was again a popular and successful minister of transport 1984-86 before becoming PM MULRONEY's deputy prime minister and government house leader in the House of Commons in 1986. In Aug 1987 Mazankowski was given additional responsibility as president of the Treasury Board. NORMAN HILLMER

Meadow Lake, Sask, Town, pop 3976 (1986c), inc 1936, is located 160 km N of North Battleford and 100 km E of the Alberta border. It is one of the more recently incorporated communities in the province but its history dates from the FUR TRADE rivalry between the Hudson's Bay Co, which first exploited the area, and the North West Co. The fur trade remained the dominant activity into the 1930s and provided a market for the ranchers who brought horses and cattle into the area in the early 20th century. During the 1930s many farmers deserted land in the "dust bowl" and moved N to start again. Meadow Lake was a popular destination, and the arrival of a CPR line in 1936 provided an opportunity for further development. Residents and vacationers appreciate the blend of agriculture and wilderness, past and present, in the area. DON HERPERGER

Meadowlark, robin-sized bird with bright yellow breast marked by a black crescent. Like BLACKBIRDS and ORIOLES, it belongs to the Icterinae subfamily. Two species occur in Canada. Although their appearance is very similar, their songs are distinct. The western meadowlark (*Sturnella neglecta*) has an elaborate, flutelike song; that of the eastern meadowlark (*S. magna*) is a shorter, clear whistle. The former species occurs from the West Coast to eastern Ontario, the latter from central Ontario through the St Lawrence Valley. The eastern meadowlark ranges S through Mexico and Central America to Brazil. Although some meadowlarks winter in southern Canada, most migrate a few hundred km S. Meadowlarks nest on the ground in open grasslands, laying 3-7 eggs in a well-concealed, domed nest. They feed on insects during the breeding season and on weed seeds in fall and winter. R.J. ROBERTSON

Meagher, Blanche Margaret, diplomat (b at Halifax 27 Jan 1911). Meagher taught in Halifax 1932-42, when she became one of a few pioneering women in the Dept of External Affairs. She served under H.L. KEENLEYSIDE in Mexico and Norman ROBERTSON in London, Eng, impressing them with her sound and independent judgement. From 1958 to 1961 she was ambassador to Israel, the first Canadian woman to hold that rank. She was from 1962 ambassador to Austria, and at the same time governor for Canada on (and later chairman of) the International Atomic Energy Agency. When ambassador to Sweden, 1969-73, she negotiated with representatives of the People's Republic of China towards the establishment of Sino-Canadian diplomatic relations. Since 1984 she has been a trustee for the NS College of Art and Design. NORMAN HILLMER

Meares, John, sea captain, entrepreneur, fur trader (b 1756?; d 1809). He entered the Royal Navy in 1771, and was promoted to lieutenant in 1778. After leaving the navy in 1783, Meares formed a company for trading furs on the NORTHWEST COAST. His first trading voyage, to Prince William's Sound, Alaska, was tragic, as many sailors died from scurvy. In 1788 Meares sailed with 2 ships to Nootka, where he built a temporary trading post and *North West America*, the first ship built on what is now Canada's West Coast. In 1789 Meares formed a company with other British entrepreneurs, and sent 3 ships to build a permanent trading post at Nootka and to trade widely on the Northwest Coast. They found Nootka occupied by a Spanish naval force which seized the British ships and crews. Meares was an effective propagandist in promoting British political and economic interests on the Northwest Coast. JOHN DEWHIRST

Reading: J. Meares *Voyages Made in the Years 1788 and 1789 from China to the Northwest Coast of America* (1790).

Meares Island, 8477 ha, of remnant coastal rain forest and N Pacific coast tidal areas, is 2 km from Tofino, BC, in Clayoquot Sound. The Indian village of Opitsat is on the island. By oral and botanical record, Meares I's resources were long exploited by the Clayoquot and Ahousaht bands. It has ancient western red cedar trees (a backbone of traditional westcoast crafts and technologies) and many other plant species; salmon runs in small rivers; wildlife and waterfowl and abundant intertidal foods, especially in the extensive mud flats of Lemmens Inlet. Two rugged slopes (792 and 730 m) provide water and a scenic backdrop to Tofino District and, between them, sheltered water for intensive shellfish mariculture. It was named (1862) for John MEARES. Timber licences for Meares I were first granted in 1905 and a small sawmill operated there. In 1955 most of the island's timber was incorporated in 2 Tree Farm Licences and massive clear-cutting began in the area. Following study by a public planning team, MacMillan Bloedel Ltd obtained permits to log on Meares I, but in Nov 1984 protesters blocked the first loggers, the 2 bands having declared the island a "tribal park." Court action over the blockade led to a BC Supreme Court trial (1987) of the claim of aboriginal title to Meares I. Logging is prohibited while the claim is tried. PETER GRANT

Meat-Processing Industry The slaughtering and meat-processing sector in Canada is made up of companies engaged in abattoir or packing operations. Products include fresh, chilled or frozen meats; cured meats (smoked, pickled or dry salted); fresh or specialty sausages; canned meat preparations; animal oils and fats; and tankhouse products such as bone, blood, feather and meat meals and dry rendered tankage.

Meat slaughtering and processing is a highly regulated industry. The first regulations in New France were passed in 1707 and made it illegal for a butcher to kill an animal without first informing a king's officer. The Crown's representative was required to carry out an inspection at the time of slaughter. Another early law, enacted in Lower Canada in 1805, was the Act to Regulate the Curing, Packing and Inspection of Beef and Pork, which required that all beef and pork be inspected upon slaughter. Until the early to mid-1800s, most of the meat processed for human consumption was handled by farm and village butchers, but by 1850 the meat packer had emerged. During the early to mid-1800s, many local packers engaged in slaughtering, curing and packing pork in salt during the winter months (the term "packer" came from the last function). Many leading companies in Canada's meat industry began between 1850 and 1870. F.W. Fearman set up operations, in Hamilton, Ont, in 1852, for sugar curing and smoking meats. William E. Davies, a major force in the late 1800s, began business in Toronto in 1854 and, in 1874, built the first continuous hog-slaughtering facility in Canada in Toronto. In 1867 John Duff opened a retail business in Hamilton that eventually became part of Essex Packers Ltd.

The use of refrigerated railway cars in the 1860s and 1870s had a major impact. During the 1870s, mechanical refrigeration was introduced and soon adopted by meat processors. By 1871 the livestock population (about 2.5 million cattle, 3.2 million sheep and 1.4 million hogs) was large enough to support a sound packing industry. During the 1870s there were 193 packing plants employing 841 people. Annual sales were about $3.8 million.

Pat BURNS initially supplied beef to gangs laying rail and later established P. Burns & Co, later Burns Foods Ltd, western Canada's largest meat-packing company for most of a century. From 1880 to 1890 the industry grew rapidly. The number of plants more than doubled and sales grew from nearly $4.1 million to $7.1 million. Most companies were small but during the 1890s many of them were absorbed into larger operations; by 1900 only 57 packing facilities remained. However, capital investment more than doubled over this period, climbing from $2.2 million in 1890 to $5.4 million by 1900. Employment jumped from 1690 to 2416 and sales climbed to a new peak of $22.2 million.

In 1906 J. G. RUTHERFORD, veterinary director and livestock commissioner for Canada, convened a meeting in Ottawa to discuss federal meat inspection with the major meat exporters. On 3 Sept 1907 federal meat inspection became a reality: the Meat and Canned Foods Act and Regulations required antemortem and postmortem veterinary inspections of all food animals the meat of which would cross provincial or international borders. The law set rigid sanitation standards for plants using the federal inspection service. After 1907 the meat industry grew steadily except for periods following the 2 world wars. In both cases the industry had expanded to meet heavy wartime demand and was left with capacity far exceeding peacetime domestic and export demands. Consequently, some consolidation was needed.

The Modern Industry By 1950 the structure of the industry was firmly in place and 3 classes of companies emerged. Traditional, full-line slaughtering packers slaughter all species and process carcasses into fresh, cured, smoked, cooked and canned meats, sausage products, etc. Nonslaughter processors purchase carcass meat and prime cuts from slaughterers and specialize in one or more secondary processing operations. Purveyors prepare portion-ready cuts, mainly for hotels, restaurants and institutions. There were 157 companies in 1950 and 210 by 1960. Employment increased from 20 522 to 25 946 and annual sales climbed from $757 million to $1.06 billion.

Industry growth continued through to the 1980s. The industry is now represented nationally by the Canadian Meat Council in Scarborough, Ont, with regional offices in Montréal and Winnipeg. All member companies operate federally inspected production facilities. In 1970, 453 plants were in operation; in 1986, 536, distributed as follows: Nfld, 4; PEI, 4; NS, 10; NB, 6; Qué, 133; Ont, 195; Man, 38; Sask, 35; Alta, 71; and BC, 40. Since 1970 employment has fluctuated (31 099 in 1970 and 30 836 in 1984). The annual value of shipments has jumped from about $2.1 billion in 1970 to over $8.28 billion in 1984. But the cost of operations has grown equally dramatically; materials and supplies have increased from nearly $1.7 billion in 1970 to $6.76 billion in 1984. Costs of fuel and electricity have risen from $11.4 million to over $80 million.

Like other FOOD AND BEVERAGE sectors, the meat industry has very low profit margins, usually about 1.8% net profit on sales (in a straight meat-packing operation, it can be as low as 0.75%). Traditionally the industry has been a big exporter; exports are now about 15% of total sales. In 1986 meat products were exported to 58 countries; exports of red and fancy meats and edible by-products earned $980 million. Pork exports accounted for over 25% of Canadian pork output. In 1986 the industry processed 3.6 million cattle and 13.5 million hogs at federally inspected plants. Over 95% of all meat and meat products produced in Canada comes from federally inspected plants. The industry must also comply with provincial legislation and often with municipal health requirements. The main federal agency involved with the meat industry is Agriculture Canada, particularly the Food Inspection Directorate, the Livestock and Poultry Division and the Meat Hygiene Division. ROBERT F. BARRATT

Mechanical Engineering, branch of ENGINEERING that deals with the design, construction and operation of machines. Machines are designed for an enormous variety of purposes, but most fall into 3 broad categories: energy conversion machines, including engines, heat exchangers, refrigerators, heat pumps, furnaces, motors, brakes, windmills and turbines; manufacturing machinery, including lathes, drills, rolling mills, assembly-line robots and hand tools; and transportation machinery, including all vehicles, conveyors and pipelines, with their compressors and pumps. Mechanical engineering plays a role in the production of all goods and commodities; moreover, many consumer goods (eg, domestic appliances) are machines.

History Mechanical engineering can be said to have started with the Industrial Revolution, with the advent of the steam engine. It has evolved as advances in materials, control technology and design methods have led to continued improvements in machines of all kinds. The last 3 decades have seen an acceleration of that evolution, as machines continued to become more efficient, faster, more precise, more economical and capable of performing more functions. The growth in industrial uses of computers in the last decade has increased that acceleration even more. Today, it appears that mechanical engineering stands on the threshold of another revolution, the result of the advent of cheap and reliable microelectronic devices, particularly sensors of various kinds and microprocessors.

Canadian mechanical engineers have made many world-class contributions to technology, including self-propelled combines, harvesting equipment for forest industries, pulp and paper production machinery, and hydroelectric turbine generators. More recent achievements include the CANDU NUCLEAR POWER generating system, the aircraft engines of the PT-6 family developed by Pratt & Whitney Canada, Ltd, the SNOWMOBILES and LRC trains designed by Bombardier, Ltée, and the CANADARM manipulator for the NASA Space Shuttle developed by Spar Aerospace Ltd.

Because mechanical engineering is a very broad branch of engineering, it has developed a number of specialties.

Education and Societies Technical training in Canada probably began in the workshops of railways, factories and some schools. Formal courses in mechanical engineering followed establishment of schools and colleges of engineering or practical science in eastern Canada in the late 19th century. In 1985, 24 Canadian universities offered accredited, 4-year degree programs leading to an honours BA. Most offered postgraduate programs leading to the master's and PhD degrees. Degrees and diplomas in mechanical engineering technology, with courses of study ranging from 2 to 4 years, are offered at institutes of technology and at numerous community colleges.

Canadian mechanical engineers have 2 principal professional and technical organizations: the mechanical engineering branch of their provincial engineering association and the Canadian Society for Mechanical Engineering. CSME was founded in 1970 as a constituent society of the Engineering Institute of Canada. Both the provincial associations and CSME hold technical meetings and produce publications containing professional and technical news. CSME also publishes *Transactions* in which research developments are reported. A biennial technical conference, the Canadian Congress of Applied Mechanics, provides a forum for discussion of current research. Canadian mechanical engineers are also active in many foreign and international technical societies. *See also* ENGINEERING, HISTORY OF.

T.A. BRZUSTOWSKI

Mechanics' Institutes Established first in England during the 1820s, Mechanics' Institutes began as voluntary associations of working men seeking self-improvement through education. The community-based institutes offered evening lectures, lending libraries and periodical reading rooms. Members were supposed to learn the underlying scientific principles of their work as well as the general value of "rational information." The concept spread quickly elsewhere, including British N America where the Montreal Mechanics' Institute opened in 1828 and the York Mechanics' Institute in 1830. Other institutes followed, especially in Ontario but also in NS and BC. In 1895 Ontario included 311 institutes with a total of 31 195 members. Internal contradictions, however, as well as the development of the labour movement, public libraries and ADULT EDUCATION prevented the institutes from maintaining a viable identity into the 20th century.

Despite the name, the central figures who developed the Mechanics' Institutes in Canada were rarely manual workers. Rather, the institutes were controlled by shopkeepers, doctors, ministers and small manufacturers who sought activities for themselves, and more importantly, the growing number of urban wage-earners. The institutes emphasized Victorian discipline and morality while refusing to consider social, economic and political questions. Much debate concerned the reading rooms and libraries which most members frequented for newspapers and popular fiction rather than the works of science, art and religion promoted by institute directors. In Ontario, this debate was transferred to communities at large in 1895 when the provincial government used legislation to transform the institutes into public libraries. The Mechanics' Institutes thus reflected important features of 19th-century Canada: the constant anxiety of local leaders about social order and stability; the widespread hope of self-improvement through education; and the increasing popular thirst for reading material. CHAD GAFFIELD

Medal, usually a small metal disc, ornamented in relief, struck or cast, and awarded for merit or issued to commemorate an event or person. Medals have essentially the same significance in Canada as elsewhere in the Western world; little noticed in everyday life, they are nevertheless highly esteemed. A distinction is often made between medals of the military sort, worn on the person, and others that are not intended to be worn, but there is no generally accepted and understood terminology for this differentiation.

Although a few early medals alluding to Canada were created in France and Britain as commemorative pieces, Canadians became more familiar with medals through the British military; when Canadians began to sponsor medals for their own purposes, after about 1850, they looked primarily to British sources. By the end of the century, many medals were being struck in Canada, notably by P.W. Ellis & Co, of Toronto. Early in the new century the lead in Canadian medal manufacturing passed to Caron Frères Inc of Montréal. Canadians also ordered medals from France as readily as from Britain, but few came from the US. The issuing of medals in Canada ebbed in the period of the Depression and WWII. Since WWII Canadian medals have generally been designed and fabricated at home. There is, however, no specifically Canadian school of design, Canadian medals today reflecting broad international trends rather than particular heritages. Québec, though more influenced by France, does not have a markedly distinctive medallic tradition, but recent Prix du Québec medals have been innovative in design.

The medal collection at the National Archives of Canada, Ottawa, contains medals of all types, and the Canadian War Museum, Ottawa, has the leading military collection. Château Ramezay, Montréal, the Glenbow Museum, Calgary, and the museum at the Seminaire de Québec, Québec, have notable medal collections.

Military Medals and Civilian Bravery Awards Canadians know military medals through the striped ribbons often worn by people in uniform. Emanating from the sovereign, official medals were traditionally the same as the British, until the establishment of Canada's own HONOURS system. Since combat awards effectively lapsed after the KOREAN WAR, most ribbons worn by members of the Canadian forces today represent commemorative or long-service medals, or United Nations medals for PEACEKEEPING operations.

There were many Canadian recipients of the British military gallantry awards that were common to the whole Commonwealth. The VICTORIA CROSS could be won by any rank in any service, the Distinguished Service Order by officers of any service, and the Royal Red Cross by nurses. The Distinguished Service Cross, Military Cross, Distinguished Flying Cross and Air Cross went to officers of the respective services, while the Distinguished Conduct Medal, Conspicuous Gallantry Medal (Navy or Flying), Distinguished Service Medal, Military Medal, Distinguished Flying Medal and Air Force Medal went to other ranks on the same basis. The Canada Medal, established 1943, was never awarded. Current DECORATIONS FOR BRAVERY, instituted within the honours system in 1972, are not military awards.

Campaign medals rewarded participation rather than individual conduct. The first, the Military General Service Medal, covered a period including the WAR OF 1812. Canadian recipients included militiamen and Indians. Among the clasps identifying particular battles were those denoting the Battle of CHÂTEAUGUAY, CRYSLER'S FARM and Ft Detroit. The Canada General Service Medal, for the years 1866 and 1870, recognized service against the FENIAN raids and in the RED RIVER REBELLION, and the North-West Canada Medal recognized service in the NORTH-WEST REBELLION. The first war medal for Canadians only was the Canadian Volunteer Service Medal of WWII, and the first British war medal with a distinct Canadian version was for the Korean War. Canadians receive UN medals for military service under the UN command. Medals also went to members of 19th- and 20th-century arctic expeditions. Military commemorative medals for jubilees and coronations went originally to contingents sent to England, but distribution later widened, eventually to include selected civilians. The 1967 Canadian Centennial Medal and the Canadian 1977 Queen Elizabeth II Silver Jubilee Medal resemble military medals and are worn as such, but they were widely distributed throughout the whole community. Long-service and good-conduct medals, originally British, then for colonial forces, gave way in 1930 to a number of Canadian awards. In 1949 all were replaced by the single Canadian Forces Decoration.

"Kebeca Liberata" medal (reverse), silver, designed by Jean Mauger and struck in France, 1690, commemorated the French victory at Québec that year (*courtesy National Archives of Canada*).

The Canadian honours system now recognizes service in high-risk professions providing public security by such awards as the Police Exemplary Service Medal and the Corrections Exemplary Service Medal. The RCMP Long Service Medal was established in 1933. Other police and fire-fighting medals are awarded by provincial governments, local authorities or unofficial bodies. Before the institution of Canada's own decorations for bravery, Canadians received British awards for heroism in civilian circumstances; these included the GEORGE CROSS, the George Medal and the Albert Medal. Early in this century the Dept of Marine issued, in the name of the Canadian government, medals for lifesaving at sea.

Commemorative and Prize Medals The earliest medal directly pertaining to Canada was the French "Kebeca Liberata" medal celebrating the repulse of a British attack on Québec in 1690. Later French and British medals commemorated Canadian events of the 18th century. Unique to Canada were the special medals which were presented to Indian chiefs at treaty signings and on other significant occasions. These imposing, normally silver, medals were often worn around the neck.

Magnificent allegorical medal that commemorates Confederation in 1867 (*courtesy National Archives of Canada*).

Early Canadian medals included Catholic medalets, TEMPERANCE medals and individually engraved presentation pieces. Educational and agricultural prizes became popular after about 1850, and the 1860 visit of the Prince of Wales inspired an upsurge in medals. CONFEDERATION was commemorated by a magnificent allegorical medal. In 1873 the Governor General Medals, personal gifts awarded mainly for academic achievement, were inaugurated. They portray each successive incumbent with spouse on the obverse, and the coat of arms on the reverse. Originally made by Wyon in England, they have been struck since 1947 at the Royal Canadian Mint. Some provinces issue lieutenant-governor medals as academic awards. Only the Québec series (1884-1966) regularly bore the portraits and arms of the respective incumbents. Until 1934 they were usually struck in France, and thereafter in Montréal by C. Lamond et fils ltée.

Noteworthy commemorative medals were the Québec Tercentenary Medal (1908), the George-Étienne Cartier Centenary Medal (1914) and the Confederation Diamond Jubilee Medal (1927). Many prize medals are given at Canadian universities, the earliest having been awarded at McGill. Agricultural fairs spawned many medallic prizes and souvenirs. The Toronto Exhibition (later CANADIAN NATIONAL EXHIBITION) inaugurated its impressive series in 1879. Other educational institutions, municipalities, learned or professional associations and sports or hobby clubs issue prize or commemorative medals. In 1924 the ROYAL SOCIETY OF CANADA established its first of 12 medals now awarded.

Canada's 1967 CENTENNIAL inspired many medals. Commercial mints, especially the Franklin Mint (formerly Wellings), have manufactured series of commemorative medals directly for the collectors' market. A more sustained recent development, especially strong in western Canada, has been the issuing of municipal "trade dollars." These essentially perpetuate the medallic tradition of striking souvenir pieces for local festivals, anniversaries and visits.

Medallic Art Despite its long-respected status in Europe, the art of the medal has not been much appreciated in Canada until recently. Formerly, medals represented a venerable honorific tradition, but their appearance had only to be dignified and conventionally correct. The earliest medals produced in Canada combined customary heraldic, decorative and typographical elements; some emulated the classical style of the British family of medalists, the Wyons, who supplied many medals to Canada. Early Canadian medals were often the work of unidentified designers, just as many of the stylistically more conservative medals among recent Canadian production are unsigned.

The first medals by well-known Canadian artists were created early in the 20th century by Louis-Philippe HÉBERT and Alfred LALIBERTÉ, both sculptors who had been to France. Emanuel Hahn and Robert Tait MCKENZIE, also distinguished sculptors, designed medals between the wars. Since the 1960s Dora DE PÉDERY-HUNT, a medallist of international reputation, has designed many struck medals but has also familiarized Canadians with the cast medal, now favoured by many European artists. A number of Canadian artists have been inspired by her example, sometimes creating medals purely as works of art. Canadian pieces are regularly included in the major biennial exhibitions of contemporary medallic art staged in Europe and N America by

The prestigious Tyrrell medal is one of 12 awarded by the Royal Society of Canada (*courtesy National Archives of Canada*).

FIDEM (Fédération Internationale de la Médaille). The limited "consumer" base still hampers Canadian medallic art. The Royal Canadian Mint and a few private mints strike medals on commission, sometimes in considerable quantity, while the cast medals favoured by some contemporary artists are produced in small runs through art foundry facilities. *See also* COINAGE.

N.M. WILLIS

Media Ownership Western societies are relying increasingly on communication through various media and relatively less on face-to-face contact to organize and co-ordinate activities, to disseminate knowledge and information, to educate and entertain. It is expected that mediated communications will expand in importance as we enter the INFORMATION SOCIETY.

Conditions of access to the media – the implicit and explicit rules governing who may and who may not distribute messages, the nature of the messages distributed, the terms under which messages may be received and by whom – are of vital political, social and cultural importance. Those individuals and groups that possess and exercise relatively unencumbered rights to distribute messages through the media can influence large audiences and thereby help shape societal development; conversely, those who are prevented from so participating are muted and may be politically ineffectual.

Two important and interrelated factors help determine conditions of access to the media: the pattern of ownership, which shapes incentives for media use; and the bundle of rights accompanying ownership, which can modify, or even eliminate, restrictions that could otherwise inhere in ownership. The bundle of rights and duties is primarily an outcome of law, but also may be influenced by traditions and ethical precepts adhered to by the owner. The pattern of media ownership has 4 major constituents:

Owner Characteristics Owners may be distinguished by the sector in which they reside: government, private, co-operative. Within each sector additional distinctions can be made. For example, government comprises 3 levels, each of which can, in principle, have media holdings. Moreover, managers of government-owned media can have varying degrees of independence from their proprietors, depending on the goals set for the media. Likewise, in the private sector, many variations are possible: ownership can reside with family-run businesses; with large, professionally managed, publicly traded corporations; with religious, political or social organizations for reasons extending well beyond profit incentives; and so on. Particularly troublesome, from a public policy perspective, is conglomerate ownership of the media, whereby media holdings constitute but a portion of the firm's economic domain; conglomerate ownership can create incentives for the manipulation or suppression of news that impinges on the diversified activities of the parent company. Other important characteristics of owners include nationality and language. In media studies, media owners are also often classified by social class in order to detect possible bias resulting from social stratification.

Concentration of Control Concentration refers to the number and size of competing outlets within a market or audience grouping, eg, newspapers in a community. Concentration indicates the degree of monopoly power enjoyed by the media owner(s) and hence the owners' power in determining conditions of access within the relevant market. The "marketplace of ideas" is premised on notions of equitable access to the media by all segments of society.

Cross Ownership refers to common control over different media genres (eg, print, film, electronic). It indicates the extent to which intermedia competition thrives or is restricted.

Vertical Integration is the extent to which media owners create, select or otherwise determine messages. It exemplifies the interrelationship between media ownership and the variable bundle of rights and duties accompanying ownership. The telephone industry, for instance, although largely monopolized and dominated by conglomerate enterprises, is proscribed by law from tampering with the messages transmitted. Moreover, access to telephone facilities for message originators must be provided by telephone companies on a "just and reasonable" basis, without "undue preference" or "unjust discrimination"; regulatory bodies (at the federal level of government, the CANADIAN RADIO-TELEVISION AND TELECOMMUNICATIONS COMMISSION) endeavour to ensure that these conditions are met. In declaring telephone companies to be common carriers, government has reapportioned rights from the owners of the medium to the general public in order to diffuse control over the origination and reception of messages in this inherently monopolized medium.

The Canadian newspaper industry is a contrasting example. Current legal conceptions of press freedom, originating in a former era of greater newspaper competition, endow owners with much autonomy in selecting and creating editorial content, subject to general laws pertaining to libel, sedition, obscenity and official secrecy (*see* LAW AND THE PRESS). In the past, when newspaper competition was more vigorous and entry into publishing easier, this policy of apportioning rights to the owners of the press as surrogates for the public, rather than with the public directly, may not have been unduly restrictive inasmuch as individuals who lacked a forum could (in theory) start a new paper (*see* NEWSPAPERS).

Newspaper competition has dwindled in recent decades, however; indeed, some critics conclude that freedom of the press now resides principally with the few companies that own newspapers. The 1981 Royal Commission on Newspapers (Kent Commission) questioned the desirability of maintaining the owners' current high level of power over editorial content.

During the 1980s daily newspaper publishing remained dominated by 2 chains, Southam and Thomson, together accounting for some 60% of English-language daily circulation and 50% overall. In 1985 Southam's 15 dailies plus the weekly *The Financial Times of Canada* generated $648.3 million of the company's total revenues of $1.3 billion. SOUTHAM INC publishes 47 business and consumer periodicals in addition to the foregoing, as well as directories, annuals, newsletters and so forth. It also has links in broadcasting through shares in SELKIRK COMMUNICATIONS. The other major domestic newspaper chain, Thomson Newspapers Ltd, publishes some 50 dailies and weeklies. Its Canadian operations are, however, diminutive alongside its transnational activities, which include wholesaling and retailing, real estate, oil and gas exploration, insurance, travel and tourism, financial and management services, high technology communications, trucking and publishing. In Canada Thomson controls HUDSON'S BAY CO and its subsidiaries. Other daily newspaper chains in Canada include TORSTAR CORP (*Toronto Star* and numerous weeklies); Toronto Sun Publishing (majority owned by Maclean Hunter) which publishes newspapers in Toronto, Calgary and Edmonton and, beginning in 1988, The FINANCIAL POST); Gesca (a subsidiary of Power Corp); QUEBECOR INC; and Hollinger Inc, controlled by Conrad BLACK, which also acquired SATURDAY NIGHT magazine in 1987.

The monopolistic nature of newspaper publishing can be further highlighted by noting that as of 1984 only 6 communities still enjoyed local competition in the same language from newspapers operated by different owners. Moreover, the major common source of news-gathering and distribution for all dailies, CANADIAN PRESS, is owned by the dailies, with Southam and Thomson being the largest participants. Through subsidiaries, such as Broadcast News, Canadian Press also serves the broadcasting industry.

The Royal Commission on Newspapers recommended measures to stimulate competition, erode monopoly and decrease the editorial autonomy of the owners. None of the commission's major recommendations have been implemented by the government. Ownership of the periodical press is also highly concentrated. MACLEAN HUNTER in 1985 published 125 Canadian periodicals, including *The Financial Post* and *Maclean's*, plus an additional 55 in the US and Europe. It also controls the Toronto Sun Publishing Corp. Its revenues from newspaper and periodical publishing in 1985 were $612.9 million. Maclean Hunter is a multimedia company with a strong presence in the radio and television broadcasting and cable television industries as well as publishing. In the periodical trade its major competitor is Southam.

While a vibrant and competitive domestic BOOK PUBLISHING industry exists in Canada, the industry is nonetheless dominated by foreign-controlled firms. Indeed Canadian-owned publishers account for under 20% of domestic book sales.

Broadcasting, which is predominantly Canadian owned, is less highly concentrated than either telephone or newspapers, although levels of concentration are still quite high. The largest television broadcasting companies are BATON BROADCASTING INC with a station in Toronto, outlets covering most of Saskatchewan, and (subject to CRTC approval) one in Ottawa; Télé-Métropole, centered in Montréal and Chicoutimi; Selkirk Communications Ltd (a station in Hamilton and majority interests in British Columbia Television Broadcasting Ltd); WIC Western International Communications Inc (majority interests in British Columbia Television Broadcasting Ltd); and CHUM Ltd (Toronto, Barrie and the Maritimes). The 3 last-mentioned companies are leaders in private radio broadcasting as well. However, the existence of a strong public-sector component, represented by the CANADIAN BROADCASTING CORPORATION and certain provincially sponsored networks, have increased ownership diversity. These government-owned undertakings do not pursue profit maximization as the private sector does, and consequently conditions of access are liberalized for the system as a whole. In addition, for both the private and public sectors, access is to some extent regulated by the CRTC; without Canadian content quotas as administered by this body, Canadian performers and other creative talent would largely be foreclosed from private-sector television owing to the cost disadvantage facing Canadian productions compared to American imports.

The CABLE TELEVISION industry, termed a component of the broadcasting system by the Broadcasting Act, is also highly concentrated nationally. The largest multisystem owner, ROGERS CABLESYSTEM INC (a subsidiary of Rogers Communications Inc) in 1986 accounted for 1 418 000 subscribers in Canada, about 24% of the Canadian total. Cablevision Vidéotron, centered in Québec and Alberta, accounts for an additional 9%, while Maclean Hunter serves some 6% of cablevision subscribers. Although the industry comprised 827 separate systems (in 1985), ownership is nonetheless highly concentrated, and cable systems are local monopolies.

Industrial incentives for concentration of control stem primarily from the pursuit of profit. Profits can be increased by raising revenues, by lowering costs, or both. Monopoly control gives a firm power to increase prices whereas competition erodes this power; consequently, concentration of control can allow higher revenues. Likewise, costs per viewer or reader can be reduced as a firm increases its audience, since the costs of the content tend to be stable as additional audiences are reached. One method of increasing audience size is by eliminating competitors.

Similarly, vertical integration between the means of transmission (the media proper) and the content transmitted is an outcome of the quest for profit. Vertical integration can shore up or create monopoly at stages of production that otherwise would be competitive. In 1923, for example, Famous Players Canadian Corporation attained dominance of film exhibition through its vertical integration with Paramount Pictures (US); these proprietary links enabled Famous Players, under the guidance of N.L. NATHANSON, to seize control of its principal rival by eliminating the latter's major source of feature films. Today the film exhibition industry in Canada is dominated by 2 rival chains – Famous Players and Cineplex Odeon Corp, both affiliated with US production/distribution companies, namely Twentieth Century Fox and Universal Studios (MCA Ltd), respectively. By 1987 Cineplex Odeon had become a major theatre chain in N America, controlling 1500 movie screens in Canada and the US, with plans to expand into Britain (*see* FILM DISTRIBUTION).

Levels of concentration, cross ownership and foreign ownership are outcomes of government policy, both explicit and implicit. Government bears explicit responsibility for ownership patterns and the accompanying bundle of rights and duties in broadcasting insofar as each broadcasting undertaking is licensed by the government. Government is implicitly responsible for ownership patterns, and for the accompanying bundle of rights and obligations, in nonregulated media industries. Canada's weak combines legislation allowed K.C. IRVING to acquire all 5 English-language daily newspapers in New Brunswick; it sanctioned the same-day closing of rival papers owned by Thomson and Southam in Ottawa and Winnipeg, respectively; and approved Thomson's sale to Southam of its interest in the Vancouver *Province* while Southam was proprietor of the Vancouver SUN. It may well be that the power of media owners to shape public opinion is feared by government to such an extent that monopolies can be formed and can persist with little likelihood of redress.

The existing patterns of ownership are being strained by technological developments, principally the integration of cable television with communication satellites and the replacement of analog transmission by digital transmission techniques (*see* SATELLITE COMMUNICATIONS). These developments have 2 main effects. First, they increase national and international communications at the expense of local and regional communications owing to the economies of scale attained through larger audiences and the technological ease with which these larger audiences can be reached; eg, the electronic transmission of the Toronto GLOBE AND MAIL via satellite to Vancouver (and other communities) for local printing, and the proliferation of specialty television services delivered nationally by cable systems interlinked by satellite. Second, previous distinctions between telephone, television, print, film, data communication and so forth are being eroded as all forms of mediated communication are increasingly encoded digitally for electronic transmission; the differences that remain concern the bandwidth used and the nature of the terminal device to which the messages are destined.

These trends have important implications for ownership patterns and on conditions of access. First, to the extent that national and international communications are economically favoured by these technological developments, access by local groups seeking a local audience may become increasingly difficult; national and multinational ownership of communications firms may be favoured rather than local and regional ownership. Second, since distinctions among hitherto separate media are being blurred, an increasing number of mergers can be expected among erstwhile print, electronic and film concerns that wish to decrease direct competition. Third, inasmuch as the means of transmission exhibits strong monopolistic characteristics (one domestic satellite carrier, Telesat Canada; one cable company in each market; one telephone company in each locality), measures to prevent vertical integration between message origination and selection on the one hand and transmission on the other become even more vital. *See also* COMMUNICATIONS LAW. ROBERT E. BABE

Reading: P. Audley, *Canada's Cultural Industries* (1983); Canada, *Report of the Task Force on Broadcasting Policy* (1986); Royal Commission on Newspapers, *Report* (1981).

Medical Drug Abuse Although medicines have been misused for as long as they have been available, a universally accepted definition of the term "drug abuse" does not exist. Broadly, drug abuse can include any failure to comply with the prescribing physician's orders, eg, forgetting to take medication or taking less or more than directed. Commonly, however, the term "drug abuse" denotes the self-administration of psychoactive substances in a deliberate attempt to alter mood, perception, thought and behaviour. In addition to the illicit drugs, several classes of prescription medications affect brain function in this manner. If a psychoactive substance produces effects perceived as beneficial (either as a pleasurable sensation or as relief from a state of depression or anxiety) the user may take the drug repeatedly. The cycle of administration and reward may become so well established in some users that they become psychologically and possibly physically dependent on the drug, and other more constructive methods of coping with problems become less important. Social problems, family breakdowns and unemployment may result (although it is true that such problems may have initially encouraged the use of mood-altering drugs). Medical complications are also common; individuals develop a "tolerance" for the drug, ie, as the body adapts to the presence of the substance and the desired effect decreases in intensity, users compensate by increasing the dosage, thus also increasing the risk of dangerous side effects (eg, barbiturate-induced cessation of breathing). When administration is discontinued suddenly, the body continues to compensate for the drug; with many drugs, this unmasked compensation causes withdrawal symptoms, which are usually opposite to the initial effects of the drug. For example, withdrawal from sedatives is characterized by signs of hyperexcitable nerve cells (anxiety, tremors and, in severe cases, seizures and hallucinations) while withdrawal from stimulants is characterized by lethargy and mood depression.

The psychoactive prescription drugs subject to abuse can be categorized as opioid analgesics, sedative-hypnotics and stimulants. Other drugs used in PSYCHIATRY, such as the antipsychotic tranquillizers, the antidepressants and lithium, produce effects that normal individuals find unpleasant and they are therefore seldom used for nonmedical reasons. However, they are not always taken as directed, and their misuse can cause untoward effects.

Opioid analgesics (sometimes termed narcotic analgesics) are either derived from the opium poppy or manufactured synthetically. They include heroin, morphine, methadone, meperidine and codeine. They are used medically primarily for the relief of pain, although they are also employed to suppress a cough, and occasionally in the treatment of severe diarrhea. Their dependence liability is generally high, and for this reason, their distribution and sale is strictly controlled. Over the past 10 years, nonmedical users of prescription opioids in Canada have increased so greatly in number that they outnumber street heroin users in some treatment populations and it has become difficult to make these drugs readily available to those who need them, while restricting their availability to illicit users. Users obtain drugs illegally by means of forged prescriptions, by thefts from pharmacies or by feigning the symptoms of a painful, difficult-to-diagnose disorder (eg, low back pain). Favoured drugs include the analgesics meperidine (Demerol ®), oxycodone (in the form of Percodan ®) and codeine, and the cough suppressants hydromorphone and hydrocodone (in Dilaudid ® and Novahistex DH ® cough syrups, respectively). Unlike street heroin, prescription opioids are pure, and many are effective when taken by mouth. Oral use also eliminates the risks associated with injection. Those dependent on prescription opioids suffer the same side effects as heroin users and are treated in the same manner, ie, by methadone substitution or in drug-free therapeutic communities. Because of the high dependence liability of opioids, physicians are more reluctant to prescribe them for patients with chronic pain. Other nonpharmacological therapies are being explored. In terminally ill patients, effective and long-lasting pain relief is of primary importance and analgesics are not withheld unless the side effects become life threatening. After much public debate and discussion, the government has now allowed heroin to be legally administered to these patients. In practice, however, physicians almost always prescribe other potent analgesics instead.

The many prescription drugs that slow the activity of the central nervous system are called sedative-hypnotics. They include the barbiturates, general anesthetics, antianxiety tranquillizers (eg, benzodiazepines) and a number of nonbarbiturate sedatives. These substances are prescribed to relieve anxiety, to induce sleep, to prevent or treat epileptic seizures, or to produce surgical anesthesia. All can create dependence in some individuals.

The barbiturates have been used since the early 1900s. Although their dangers were universally recognized (severe respiratory depression, high-dependence liability and life-threatening withdrawal reactions), safer alternatives did not exist until recently. The number of prescriptions has decreased significantly, however, since the introduction of the benzodiazepines into Canada in the 1960s. The short-acting barbiturates such as secobarbital (Seconal ®) are still used illicitly, since they take effect quickly and produce the most euphoria. They are often administered to enhance the effects of other sedative-hypnotics or to terminate the unpleasant effects of a long stimulant binge.

The benzodiazepines (13 different kinds were being sold in Canada by 1986) were originally thought to be unusually safe and to have a very low dependence liability. For this reason they are heavily prescribed both for treatment of anxiety – eg, diazepam (in Canada sold under 8 trade names, including Valium ®, and generically by 4 companies), chlordiazepoxide (Librium ®), oxazepam (Serax ®) – and for induction of sleep, eg, flurazepam (Dalmane ®) and triazolam (Halcion ®). Physicians agree that these drugs are safe for short-term uses (ie, less than 4 weeks), but the value of long-term drug therapy is questionable. When long-term administration of tranquillizers is stopped, the original symptoms of anxiety often reappear. This state may be temporarily enhanced by the emergence of withdrawal symptoms, which are generally less severe than those induced by barbiturates or alcohol, but can still motivate the individual to resume drug use. Some evidence suggests that the long-term use of these drugs can adversely affect memory and other aspects of brain function. Physicians are increasingly reluctant to prescribe benzodiazepines for longer than a month without supervision. In Canada, as elsewhere, they are prescribed to women about twice as frequently as to men, and to the elderly much more often than to the young (*see* WOMEN AND HEALTH). Those suffering from chronic diseases are also likely to receive these medications. These imbalances have generated considerable discussion about prescribing practices, particularly among those who feel that tranquillizers are being prescribed to women for problems that could be best handled by more constructive means. Although Canadian data suggest that the great majority of benzodiazepine users (between 90-95%) take their medication as prescribed, given the large number of prescriptions, the remaining 5% constitute a significant number of individuals, some of whom require medical assistance to stop use. Benzodiazepines (especially diazepam) are sometimes used nonmedically, often to enhance the effects of other psychoactive drugs including alcohol.

The nonbarbiturate sedative hypnotics offer few therapeutic advantages over the benzodiazepines. Of these, methaqualone has been the most heavily abused, although the problem does not appear to be as severe in Canada as elsewhere. This drug is no longer manufactured legally in the US, although small amounts are still made in Canada. The licit supply available for diversion of this drug to the street has decreased, but illicit consumption of other drugs of this class may increase as a consequence.

The term "stimulants" refers to a broad category of agents that includes the amphetamines and related drugs, as well as cocaine, caffeine and nicotine. The amphetamines were formerly prescribed for several disorders such as obesity, mood depression and lethargy. However, their ability to produce profound stimulation and euphoria led to epidemics of use in Japan, Sweden, the US and other countries. Because of their high dependence liability and their ineffectiveness as long-term appetite suppressants, their use as "diet pills" was strictly curtailed in Canada in 1972. The prescribing of amphetamine and methylphenidate (Ritalin ®) was limited to a few disorders that included the treatment of hyperactive children and of narcolepsy. The use of some drugs (eg, phenmetrazine) was discontinued altogether, and other less potent appetite suppressants such as diethylpropion (Tenuate ®) were reclassified as controlled drugs under the Food and Drugs Act. Since the mid-1970s there has been a significant drop in the abuse of both licitly manufactured amphetamines and illegally synthesized methamphetamine. However, the consumption of illicit cocaine and of over-the-counter mild stimulants (such as ephedrine, phenylpropanolamine, caffeine and propylhexedrine), which are sold as decongestants and "wake-up" preparations, has risen. All of these drugs, when taken in sufficient quantities, can produce toxic side effects. KEVIN O'BRIEN FEHR

Reading: R. Cooperstock and J. Hill, *The Effects of Tranquillization: Benzodiazepine Use in Canada* (1982); M.R. Jacobs and K.O. Fehr, *Drugs and Drug Abuse* (2nd ed, 1987); R.G. Smart, *Forbidden Highs* (1983).

Medical Education There are 3 distinct phases of medical education. The first is undergraduate education, in which students with prior university education (the minimum requirement is 2 years) are taught the basic knowledge, skills and attitudes of the physician. Upon completion of undergraduate study students are awarded the degree of medical doctor (MD). Second, to be eligible for a licence to practise, all MDs must complete at least one year of internship during which time they work under supervision in a hospital or clinic, gaining practical experience and being given increasing responsibility for the care of patients. Many graduates choose to undertake a minimum 2-year training program leading to the certificate of the College of Family Physicians of Canada; others enter 4- or 5-year programs leading to certification in one of the 44 medical specialties recognized by the Royal College of Physicians and Surgeons of Canada. The third and most recently developed phase is continuing medical education. This includes all programs of independent or supervised study through which practising physicians seek to keep abreast of the latest developments in medicine of concern to them.

Undergraduate and postgraduate education was provided exclusively by Canada's 17 university medical faculties in 1987. Continuing education is provided by the medical faculties, by various national, regional or local professional societies, by hospitals or pharmaceutical companies, and by other agencies or groups.

History of Medical Education in Canada The first program of medical education in Canada was created in 1824 at the Montreal Medical Institution, which 5 years later became the Faculty of Medicine at McGill U. By the turn of the century, schools had been established at McGill, U of T, Laval (which had schools both in Québec C and Montréal – the latter eventually becoming the Medical Faculty of U de M), Queen's, Dalhousie, U of W Ontario and U of Man. An eighth school at U of Alta in Edmonton was opened in 1913. By 1950 additional schools had been established at U of Sask, U of O and UBC, and the Montréal branch of Laval had become an independent school.

Two events in the early 20th century profoundly affected the quality of medical education in Canada. The first was the publication in 1910 of *Medical Education in the United States and Canada* by the Carnegie Foundation for the Advancement of Teaching. Written by Abraham Flexner and based on his visits to the 155 schools of medicine then existing in the 2 countries, the publication proposed that acceptable schools of medicine must have high standards for the admission of students, must be part of and subject to the rigorous academic standards of a university, must base their educational programs on a scientific approach to medicine and must encourage the scholarly research of their faculties.

So profound was the impact of the Flexner Report that within 15 years of its release most of the schools identified as substandard (nearly half of the total) had closed their doors forever. Although no Canadian schools were closed, standards at the weakest were greatly improved. The second important influence was the formation of the Medical Council of Canada in 1912. The council established a single standard examination for the graduates of all medical schools in Canada which was eventually accepted by all provincial medical licensing authorities as a criterion for awarding licences. As a result, the quality of medical education across the country became more standardized and, just as important, medical graduates became free to move from one part of the country to another with the reasonable expectation that their credentials would be recognized and accepted.

The next major influence on medical education was the publication in 1964 of the report of the Royal Commission on Health Services. The commission, under its chairman Mr Justice Emmett HALL, was established to investigate the provision of health services. It concluded that the supply of physicians provided by the 12 medical schools was insufficient to meet the country's needs without continued reliance on high levels of immigration of physicians trained in other countries. This led to the almost immediate establishment of new schools at McMaster U, U of C and Memorial U, and to the accelerated development of the school at U of Sherbrooke. Along with the opening of these 4 new schools, existing faculties increased their enrolments. As a result, the total enrolment of first-year medical students in Canada rose steadily from 1133 in 1964, peaking at 1835 in 1985 and then declining to 1767 in 1987.

Different Approaches to Medical Education Prior to WWII the curricula in Canadian medical faculties had generally evolved from that first established at McGill, which was in turn based on the Edinburgh model. Strong emphasis on bedside teaching was introduced at McGill by William OSLER in the 1880s. The curriculum consisted of 2 years of lectures and laboratory exercises in the basic sciences of (with greater or lesser emphasis) anatomy, physiology, biochemistry, bacteriology, pathology and pharmacology, followed by 2 years of clinical instruction in hospital wards. The Flexner tradition, with its emphasis on the theoretical basis of the fundamental medical sciences, shaped the basic sciences teaching. In contrast, clinical instruction emphasized the practical aspects of medical care and was based almost entirely on the exposure of students to hospital patients.

Scientific knowledge, much of which was quickly absorbed into medical practice, increased dramatically during and after WWII. Consequently the already crowded curriculum of medical students expanded as well. At about this time a new breed of clinical teachers appeared in the medical schools. Young men and women, attracted by the increasing support available for research and by the opportunities a research career could offer, were no longer satisfied with training only in the clinical disciplines but sought a broader and more profound theoretical grounding in one or more of the basic sciences. They became the forerunners of the new generation of clinical scientist-teachers who now strongly influence all medical faculties.

By the late 1950s and early 1960s Canadian medical faculties were staggering under the stresses of a rapidly expanding body of knowledge that could not be adequately conveyed in the curriculum then in use. Medical students became increasingly frustrated and vocal about the volume of information they had to learn, the relevance of which was not always apparent. In response, most schools started introducing students to patients in the first rather than the third year, in order to provide a framework of relevance for the basic sciences that still had to be taught. To accommodate the change, basic science laboratory exercises were either reduced in number or eliminated.

Many schools adopted integrated or "systems" curricula in which the basic and clinical features of such systems as the cardiovascular, musculoskeletal, respiratory or digestive were taught in integrated blocks. The students learned, in a co-ordinated sequence, the basic sciences of the particular system as they were learning its clinical features, diagnosis and management. It was expected that the systems approach would provide students with a conceptual framework on which they could base their diagnosis and treatment. In the "new" curricula, lecture and laboratory were no longer relied upon as the principal educational tools. Seminars and tutorials were emphasized. To cope with the growing body of knowledge that had to be absorbed, schools also encouraged students to assume more responsibility for their own education, and to develop their problem-solving skills.

The most radical of the new curricula, and one that attracted worldwide attention, was the "problem-based learning" approach adopted at McMaster. In this curriculum, small groups of students, under the guidance of an instructor, worked together in collecting and integrating information, either from books and journals or from faculty consultants, to solve problems devised for them by the faculty. The program emphasized teamwork between students and faculty. The faculty made no pretence at providing students with an encyclopedic fund of medical knowledge, but assumed that after the experience of a problem-based curriculum students would have developed the ability and self-reliance to deal with the clinical problems they might encounter in practice. Critics of the program claim that the performance of its graduates has been consistently below the average for graduates of other Canadian schools and that failure rates have been higher. On the other hand, graduates of McMaster have been accepted into some of the most prestigious postgraduate training programs in N America and elsewhere, where they have received highly favourable ratings. The curricula at McMaster and Calgary are both concentrated into 3 undergraduate years, with only a month of vacation per year. Both faculties admit older students, generally in their mid- or late twenties, who are assumed to be mature and experienced enough to cope successfully with such demanding programs of study.

In contrast, the universities of Montréal and Saskatchewan admit younger than average students. The 5-year programs of these schools are designed to provide students with greater opportunities to "ripen" into their roles as future physicians. The other medical schools have 4-year curricula, as have almost all others in N America.

Accreditation of Medical Schools Since 1934 schools in Canada have been regularly accredited by the US body now called the Liaison Committee on Medical Education. With the advent of universal medicare in Canada in 1970, the patterns of medical care and practice in the US and Canada began to diverge, making it necessary for Canada to adopt a system of accreditation more appropriate to the country's needs. Accordingly, in 1979 the Committee on Accreditation of Canadian Medical Schools was formed as an independent body to examine and attest to the quality of educational programs in Canadian medical schools. Schools in Canada are now jointly accredited by both bodies, with the assurance that Canadian schools meet Canadian standards.

Emerging Issues During the remainder of the 20th century medical educators will need increasingly to adapt their teaching to the changing environment in which physicians must practise. Advancing technologies related to such things as organ TRANSPLANTATION, dialysis, GENETIC ENGINEERING and reproduction now make it possible for more and more people to survive to an advanced age in which health-care costs are likely to be highest. Not only must students learn the new technologies, they will also be required to understand the social and ethical implications of caring for patients whose lives have been ever-more precariously prolonged. Students of the future will have to be prepared to advise other care givers and legislators on the economic and social costs of new technologies and on the integration of medical advances into Canada's unique health care system. As well, medical students of the 1990s and beyond will increasingly be required to use and understand computers, both as part of their education and as an adjunct to diagnosis, prognosis and patient care.

The worldwide epidemic of Acquired Immune Deficiency Syndrome (*see* AIDS) of the 1980s adds emphasis to the need to expand medical teaching in both epidemiology and virology. Educators must prepare themselves to exploit advances in both these fields quickly, not only in relation to AIDS but in spin-off applications to other viral diseases such as influenza and the common cold, whose costs in human productivity are astronomical.

While the medical needs of the future cannot be accurately predicted, we can be sure that all concerned with the health-care system will need to be conditioned more and more to a flexible state of adaptability to unexpected demands. Of particular concern in this regard will be the medical disorders that can result from "lifestyle" changes in human behaviour – substance abuse, obesity, promiscuity, etc. Fads and fashions in behaviour can develop rapidly and unpredictably and many of them can be expected to result in health problems that require prompt medical or political response. DOUGLAS WAUGH

Reading: S.E.D. Shortt, ed, *Medicine in Canadian Society* (1981).

Medical Ethics are concerned with moral questions raised by the practice of medicine and, more generally, by health care. Because of the increasing importance of health care to an aging population within a society wealthy enough to afford it, and because of the increased complexity of health care, and the reduced reliance upon tradition and authority in moral matters, debate over issues in medical ethics has grown more intense. Certain issues present particularly difficult ethical dilemmas.

Physician-Patient Relationship How much information is a patient entitled to receive before accepting or refusing treatment? Is a physician or other health provider ever permitted to deceive or withhold information from a patient? To what extent, if any, may a physician's personal moral or social beliefs influence his or her relationship with and advice to a patient? The Hippocratic Oath, which is still administered in many (but not all) medical schools, omits any reference to a moral obligation on the part of physicians to be honest with their patients. Traditional medical ethics were paternalistic; information was given or withheld as doctors thought best. Since the beginning of the 20th century, however, courts in the US, Britain and Canada have ruled that a "mentally competent" adult patient is entitled to all information necessary to give "informed consent" to treatment. Nevertheless, ascertaining the true wishes of a patient may not always be easy, eg, the patient may be seriously ill, drugged, in pain, depressed, and may be less than fully rational and competent. As a result, physicians are not necessarily released from the obligation of using their own judgement to determine, at least in the short run, what is best for the patient.

Reproductive Technology and Medical Interventions Besides the issue of ABORTION, questions have been raised about artificial methods of inducing pregnancy (eg, by donor artificial insemination and *in vitro* fertilization); about gestation, eg, surrogate motherhood; and about various contraceptive techniques and surgical sterilization procedures.

Death and Dying When breathing and heartbeat are temporarily sustained by machine in a patient without brain function, is that patient alive or dead? Should it be permissible, for example, to harvest organs from such an individual for the purpose of organ TRANSPLANTATION? Is a health practitioner permitted to provide life-sustaining treatment to a patient who has forbidden medical treatment? Does the dying patient have the right to be assisted should he or she wish to commit suicide? In these questions the value of "sanctity of life," that every life must be preserved at all costs, is frequently at odds with the value of the "quality of life," according to which an individual has a right to a humane and dignified death. Whether and when to use technology to prolong the life of infants with severe genetic diseases is one of the most difficult decisions health-care practitioners and society must make, and it involves again the conflict between "sanctity" and "quality." Those who advocate what is sometimes called "medical vitalism" support the former and argue that the potential abuse of quality-of-life judgement is enormous; their opponents argue that concern for relief of suffering and a dignified death will help promote a society more sensitive to human life (*see* DEATH AND DYING).

Special Patient Populations Who should decide treatment on behalf of severely handicapped newborns (or any group who cannot speak for themselves), and on what basis should these decisions be made? In some ethnic groups, an extended family (including grandparents) is involved in the rearing of children. Are there therefore special circumstances in which the extended family should be involved in medical decisions regarding newborns?

Economic and Social Policy Do patients have a right to health care regardless of expense? When patients' needs exceed available health-care resources, how should those resources be distributed? Considerations of social welfare have traditionally been used to justify intervention into the physician-patient relationship, eg, physicians have been required to report on patients with gunshot wounds or communicable diseases. The question arises, to what degree should health professionals act in accordance with the best interests of their society?

Research and Experimentation upon Human Beings When is experimentation upon children justified? Is it ethical to proceed with an experiment that requires the subject of research not to know whether the drug he is taking is a sugar pill or pharmacologically active?

Individuals and Organizations Involved in Medical Ethics Legal and governmental bodies are concerned primarily with the public regulation of health practices. The Law Reform Commission of Canada established the Protection of Life Project in 1976. This group has issued reports and recommendations on topics such as the definition of death, euthanasia and the withholding of treatment, and behaviour control techniques. Provincial law-reform commissions have also issued reports on aspects of ethics and health care, eg, children's consent to medical procedures (Alberta, 1975); artificial insemination (Saskatchewan, 1981); and new forms of human reproduction (Ontario, 1984). Views of legislators on some issues of medical ethics may be expressed in provincial Acts governing the conduct and licensure of the health professions, as well as in special enactments (eg, Manitoba's Act on defining death, and the Human Tissue Gift Acts, governing transplantation, that were adopted by a number of provinces). Cases brought before courts may involve the judges in intricate questions of medical ethics, such as whether physicians are obliged to advise patients against relatively useless surgery (*Zamparo* v *Brisson*, Ontario Court of Appeal, 1981); whether a physician, when informing a patient of the risks and benefits of a medical procedure, should take into account the patient's economic situation (*Reibl* v *Hughes*, Supreme Court of Canada, 1980); and whether the parent of a person with a mental handicap may authorize that person's surgical sterilization (*Re Eve*, Supreme Court of Canada, 1986).

Organizations of health professionals are involved in establishing codes of ethical behaviour on behalf of their membership. Some have committees charged with enforcing ethical behaviour, or with studying ethical problems that arise in the profession. A code of ethics for physicians established by the Canadian Medical Association (CMA) has been revised on a number of occasions. In 18th-century England, a long, highly detailed code was formulated, but current codes usually consist of a brief set of abstract principles that need to be supplemented by guidelines governing implementation. The codes do not, of course, preclude the occurrence of serious conflicts and ambiguities, and in fact may sometimes help inspire them. Also, while a code may represent the ethical view of the profession, physicians are not necessarily familiar with it. As far back as 1880, an editorial in the *Canada Lancet* complained that most doctors were not familiar with the code, and a 1983 survey of 300 Toronto physicians found that 68% had never read the code and 84% could not say whether references were made in it to abortion or to organ transplantation.

Legislation may require professional associations to establish committees to monitor ethical conduct. Independent committees on ethics have been established by the CMA, the Royal College of Physicians and Surgeons of Canada and the Canadian Pediatric Society. Some lay associations and church groups also issue statements representing members' views on specific issues in medical ethics, eg, the United Church of Canada issued a report on ethics and genetics in 1978.

Courses on medical ethics became widely available in the 1970s. Most Canadian universities and some colleges offer at least one and sometimes several undergraduate courses. Graduate instruction is also available in some Canadian universities, largely within departments of philosophy, theology or religious studies. Because of year-to-year variations, it is difficult to say what proportion of medical schools include ethics within the curriculum. For several decades prior to the 1970s, however, formal ethical instruction included within the medical curriculum was the exception; today, it is the rule.

Research into aspects of medical ethics is conducted by individual scholars from many disciplines, including the health professions, the humanities and the social sciences. In addition, research institutes investigating questions of medical ethics have been established in a number of Canadian cities including Montréal (Centre de Bioéthique and the McGill centre for Medicine, Ethics and the Law) and London, Ont (the Westminster Institute). Institutions involved in research have commonly established ethics committees to review the ethics of proposed research programs. These committees are likely to refer to guidelines on the ethics of research established by the Medical Research Council of Canada (1978; revision prepared 1986) and by the Social Sciences and Humanities Research Council of Canada (1979). Increasingly, hospitals and other institutional providers of health care are establishing internal ethics committees to consider their own practices and those of their staff. *See also* BIOETHICS.

BENJAMIN FREEDMAN

Reading: T.L. Beauchamp and J.F. Childress, *Principles of Biomedical Ethics* (1979); *Journal of Medicine, Ethics and Law* (1988-); Law Reform Commission of Canada, *Euthanasia, Aiding Suicide and Cessation of Treatment* (1983), *Criteria for Determination of Death* (1979) and *Medical Treatment and Criminal Law* (1980); W.T. Reich, ed, *The Encyclopedia of Bioethics* (1978); *Synapse* newsletter.

Medical Jurisprudence, broadly defined, covers the relationship between a patient and a health-care provider such as a doctor, nurse, dentist, physiotherapist, or even an institution such as a HOSPITAL. The law has established standards, it regulates practice and provides a mechanism for patients to claim compensation in the case of an injury. The source of the law may be statutes (provincial or federal) or judge-made law. While the legal principles set out by judges in case law are generally consistent throughout Canada, there are some variations in legislation from province to province.

Medical jurisprudence is concerned with many basic and profound issues, such as a patient's right to consent to health care. Every person, including children who understand the nature and consequences of treatment, has the right to be fully informed of the risks of a procedure and to choose whether to proceed with it or not (*see* MEDICAL ETHICS), even if refusing treatment will result in the death of the patient. In 1980 the Supreme Court of Canada stated that the standard for the disclosure of risks must be what the reasonable patient would want to know and not what health-care professionals customarily choose to explain. Another basic legal principle is the requirement that in carrying out health care, a person or institution must exercise reasonable skill, knowledge and judgement. This standard is derived from the custom or common practice of the profession or group, ie, that a doctor must perform as a reasonable doctor would in the circumstances (*see* MALPRACTICE). If this standard is not met and a patient suffers injuries as a consequence, the health-care provider may be found negligent and have to pay monies to the patient as compensation. Very complex issues arise when the proposed medical treatment is experimental or when it involves organ transplantation, artificial insemination or *in vitro* fertilization. Then, not only must the right of the individuals involved be considered but the values and goals of society as well.

A number of problems have emerged from modern medical practice where the "team" approach to health care is used and where the hospital assumes a major role as a health-care provider. Very often a patient may be cared for by many highly trained doctors and nurses, and frequently there is an overlap in their functions; in many cases that have gone to court it is clear that each member of the team has deferred to the others his or her responsibility in decision making or communication, with the result that the patient has received substandard care. Cases have also arisen concerning whether or not a nurse should carry out a doctor's orders when he or she believes that they will be harmful to the patient. The law states that if a nurse carries out such an order he or she may be negligent and, as in the case of a lethal overdose of a drug, might even be charged under the CRIMINAL CODE.

Hospitals have assumed a greater role in providing health care and are increasingly being held accountable to patients. The earliest hospitals were charitable institutions and were shielded from liability by the courts, but modern hospitals are large, complex organizations that as far as the public is concerned constitute the heart of the health-care system. A hospital as an employer is liable when any employee is held to have injured a patient through negligence. However, a hospital also has certain direct responsibilities to a patient, including the duty to select competent and qualified employees and to instruct and supervise them; to provide proper facilities and equipment; and to establish systems necessary to the safe operation of the hospital. Courts have recently noted that the public expects hospitals to provide competent medical treatment. For example, in the emergency department of a hospital a patient may receive medical treatment by a doctor who is provided by the hospital but who is not an employee of the hospital. Whether the hospital should be liable when such treatment is substandard remains to be resolved by the courts.

Law suits by patients against health-care providers are increasing. Resort to the legal process brings difficulties for all parties. In some provinces the patient may have to make a preliminary application to the court for an order allowing him to gain access to his health records. Litigation is slow and costly, and those sued are usually concerned that the allegations made against them may affect their reputations. Even if the patient is successful, money can never compensate for the loss suffered. However, there is at present no alternative to the law suit for resolving a patient's claim for compensation. The alternative of reporting a health-care professional to his or her governing body for discipline, while sometimes effective for that purpose, does not result in compensation to a patient.

ELLEN PICARD

Reading: Ellen Picard, *Legal Liability of Doctors and Hospitals in Canada* (2nd ed, 1984).

Medical Research ranges from fundamental research to applied technology. Fundamental research involves investigation into biological functions; knowledge thus derived may then be applied in clinical research to help understand specific diseases and to develop cures or methods of prevention. Applied technologies result from both fundamental and clinical research in the form of vaccines, drugs, instrumentation, diagnostics, prostheses and other health-care products. Physicians, biologists, biochemists, biomedical engineers, chemists, dentists, veterinarians, health economists, nurses, physicians and pharmacists are among the health professionals involved in medical research.

The discovery of INSULIN in 1922 by Frederick BANTING, J.J.R. MACLEOD, Charles BEST and James COLLIP, the most celebrated event in Canadian medical research, spurred development of biomedical research in Canada and led to the establishment of the CONNAUGHT LABORATORIES and the Banting Institute at U of T. Since that time, research in Canada has been conducted into areas such as molecular biology, immunology, nutrition and metabolism, reproductive biology,

CANCER, behavioural sciences, genetics, developmental biology, DENTISTRY, microbiology, drugs, OCCUPATIONAL DISEASE, health-care organization, environmental health hazards, and the biology of human populations. In addition, Canadian researchers are examining the function and diseases of particular organs such as the skin (dermatology), the blood system (hematology), the kidney (nephrology), the eye (ophthalmology), the ear, nose and throat (otolaryngology), the stomach and intestines (gastroenterology), the endocrine glands (endocrinology), the respiratory system (respirology), and connective tissue disorders. The range of accomplishments is impressive. Research at U of T in cardiovascular surgery alone has contributed significantly to the overall treatment of HEART DISEASE. Canadians have been responsible for major developments in heart pacemakers, heart-lung machines to oxygenate blood and correct heart defects, and the first coronary care units. Hans SELYE broke new ground in the understanding of STRESS. In the neurosciences Canadians have made major contributions to the knowledge of the central nervous system and its related diseases. The Montreal Neurological Institute (MNI est in 1934), is an important centre for neuroscience research. Its founder, Wilder PENFIELD, not only pioneered the technique of brain-mapping, which is conducive to the better understanding of localized functions of the brain, but also built the MNI into an internationally known training centre. Research at the MNI has led to improved surgical and nursing techniques for the management of spinal lesions, to the development of electroencephalography to treat conditions such as epilepsy, and to a deeper understanding of cognitive and other behavioural changes associated with brain lesions. Noninvasive imaging techniques, in conjunction with a new understanding of neurotransmitters, help researchers understand the way the various parts of the brain and nervous system grow, develop, take on specific tasks, and repair and replenish themselves.

The federal government, provincial governments, voluntary agencies and private foundations, industry and foreign sources all contribute to the support of biomedical research in Canada, including equipment, operating costs, research training and technical assistance.

Federal Funding Agencies The MEDICAL RESEARCH COUNCIL OF CANADA was established by Parliament in 1969 to promote, assist, and undertake basic, applied and clinical research in the health sciences and to advise the minister of the Dept of National Health and Welfare on matters of health research. MRC evolved from the Associate Committee of Medical Research, established in 1938 at the National Research Council of Canada. During WWII, the committee divided into a number of subcommittees; after the war, the Division of Medical Research replaced the committee and this subsequently became the MRC.

MRC supports about 50% of direct medical research expenditures in Canada. It provides support, on the basis of scientific excellence as determined by national peer review, for research and for training of health-science researchers in the health-science faculties. These include the departments and laboratories of the 16 medical schools, 10 dental schools and 8 pharmacy schools and their affiliated HOSPITALS and institutes across the country. In 1986-87 the MRC spent $164 million contributing to medical research across Canada.

In an effort to encourage private sector participation in research, the federal government instituted a matching grants policy, effective for 5 years beginning April 1987. The budget of the MRC will remain constant except insofar as the private sector provides new funds, which the federal government will match up to a maximum of 6% of the annual budget. This policy, with no built-in allowance for inflation or growth, could impose severe limitations on the levels of research activity in Canada.

Research relating to health-care delivery has been supported at the federal level primarily by the National Health Research and Development Program in the Dept of National Health and Welfare, a program which grew out of the annual Public Health Grants started in 1948. (The MRC was precluded from support of public health research until 1976 when Parliament removed this restriction.) NHRDP provides grants to encourage research that is required by the department to fulfil its mandate to promote, protect, maintain and restore the health of Canadians. Researchers may belong to any of the 4 general health fields of health-care organization, environmental health hazards, life-styles or the biology of human populations.

To address the issue of AIDS, the federal government has established a national program, which includes a significant research component.

Provincial Funding Agencies Provincial agencies in Alberta, BC, Manitoba, Ontario, Québec and Saskatchewan contribute to medical research and training through such organizations as the Alberta Heritage Foundation for Medical Research and le Fonds de la recherche en santé du Québec.

Voluntary Funding Agencies Voluntary agencies, which are generally "disease specific," play a major role in medical research. For example, the Canadian Cancer Society supplies 80% of the National Cancer Institute of Canada's granting monies for research into cancer.

Research costs, such as salary support, capital expenses to construct laboratories and animal-care facilities, are generally paid by the institutions where the research is conducted. They receive funds for this purpose through provincial governments and private donations.

Structure of Medical Research

Medical research is highly decentralized in universities and teaching hospitals and their affiliated institutions throughout the provinces. Canada is one of a small minority of countries which does not have significant government laboratories devoted to biomedical research. While this decentralization links research with professional training and health-care delivery, it makes it difficult to define or maintain a national focus for concerted programs, especially as health care and education are provincial responsibilities. However, in 1982 federal and provincial representatives identified several health areas of national concern (cancer, accidents, arthritis and joint disorders, cardiovascular and cerebrovascular diseases, maternal and infant health problems, MENTAL HEALTH and respiratory diseases). The MRC and other funding agencies are providing support for research in these areas. In 1983, the federal Cabinet approved in principle a federal framework for medical research that emphasizes the provision of high-quality training, a balance between basic and applied research, and a balance across regions and disciplines (with special attention to areas of national health concern), and the utilization of new knowledge for improved health care. Within this federal strategy, elaborated in the MRC's Five Year Plan, the MRC undertook to continue the development of a strong research base, and to promote research in areas of national concern and in the more efficient transfer of new knowledge to health-care systems. In 1986 the MRC adopted an additional objective, to enhance the interaction between researchers in the health sciences and industry by implementing joint university-industry programs.

Issues in Medical Research Some critics of medical research claim that advances in medical research have led to little improvement in health status. Some blame this on inadequate communication among workers in the health sector and recommend an increase in the number of clinicians conducting research to improve the introduction of new knowledge into health care and increase treatment-oriented research. Others charge that the conservative nature of the peer review system precludes progress of innovative science, and they advocate the participation of a greater variety of health professionals in medical research, eg, nurses and pharmacists, who have received less support in Canada than basic and clinical researchers. The absence of a strong health-care sector industry with a solid commitment to research, or of adequate long-term funding, are other problems that have been identified. There is also ongoing debate about the appropriate balance between curiosity-driven and targeted research, and between research which is oriented towards costly, technologically sophisticated medical treatments and more broadly based epidemiological and environmental medicine.

Ethics is another important issue in medical research. Although the MRC has helped to establish guidelines (favoured by many because of their flexibility) for safe and ethical practices with respect to human experimentation, research with animal subjects and use of hazardous and infectious substances, these are technically only binding on researchers supported by the MRC. In fact, many groups voluntarily comply with these guidelines. Some critics advocate legislation defining safe and ethical medical research practices on the grounds that laws are more enforceable than guidelines. Canada has no law that protects research volunteers or ensures that they are fully informed of the purpose or possible dangers of the drug or procedure being tested. Through its committee on Ethics of Experimentation the MRC is currently revising its ethical guidelines. Major issues addressed in these revisions include accountability of the ethics review process, means to improve the quality and uniformity of ethics review, ways to reduce both the number and the suffering of animals in studies which must precede trials in human subjects, research with vulnerable groups and research with embryos.

International aspects of research are becoming more critical with the increase both in health problems such as AIDS which face many nations and in multinational studies to examine such problems. The International Summit Conference on Bioethics, held in Canada in 1987 and sponsored jointly by the MRC and the Dept of National Health and Welfare provided one important forum for Canada to work with other nations "Towards an International Ethic for Research with Human Subjects."

Future of Medical Research The health-care system in Canada is changing. Developments such as the increased recognition of the contribution of environmental and behavioural factors to mental and physical health, the growing focus on cost containment and the allocation of scarce resources, the significant rise in the number of women in medicine, the increased need for chronic-disease care in an aging population, the trend towards home care and away from hospital care, and the increase in hospital-based research institutes will all influence the nature and extent of medical research.

Many of the discoveries of medical research, such as those which have recently offered new abilities to manipulate genes, to perform *in vitro* fertilization and embryo experimentation, to transplant organs and to screen for genetic problems, will continue to require excellent research by scientists. However, the growing social and ethical issues raised by medical research will necessitate closer co-operation between scientists and the Canadian public. Scientists can help the public understand the implications of new knowledge, and the public needs to exercise its responsibility in guiding the extent, conduct and application of medical research in Canada.

JUDITH MILLER

Reading: Michael Bliss, *Banting: A Biography* (1984); Donald Jack, *Rogues, Rebels and Geniuses* (1981); S.E.D. Shortt, ed, *Medicine in Canadian Society* (1981).

Medical Research Council of Canada (MRC) is a crown corporation established by Act of Parliament in 1969 to promote, assist and undertake basic, applied and clinical research in Canada in the health sciences. It was set up initially as a unit within the NATIONAL RESEARCH COUNCIL (1960) and was reorganized to report to the minister of health and welfare in 1966. The council has a full-time president and 21 other members representing the scientific and lay communities. MRC has also created standing committees to assist it in formulating policies and procedures for ethics in experimentation, research funding, etc. In addition, there are 35 committees to review applications for research projects and awards. The council has no laboratories of its own. Its responsibilities are to support research and research training in health sciences in universities, affiliated hospitals and institutes. The MRC's support of research, which in 1986-87 was $164.2 million, represents about half of the health sciences research in Canada.

Medicine, Contemporary The years since 1939 have seen great changes in Canadian medicine. In the armed forces, which were served during WWII by many of Canada's most talented medical practitioners and specialists, medical services were responsible for advances in the management of wounds and shock, for research on infections, motion sickness and high-altitude aviation, and for perfecting methods of preventing blackout during rapid descent of fighter planes.

The effectiveness of penicillin against many bacterial infections was established when the drug was provided (largely through the efforts of the CONNAUGHT LABORATORIES in Toronto) to the Canadian armed forces at the time of the invasion of Europe after D-Day.

During the early postwar years the Dept of Veterans Affairs organized medical and HOSPITAL services for veterans. Some of the hospitals were closely associated with university medical schools, with the result that medical teaching and research were carried out in the hospitals and the staffs of the hospitals were in most cases members of the medical faculty. This arrangement, which ensured a high level of medical care for veterans and provided universities with teaching facilities, continued until the 1970s when the Dept of Veterans Affairs' hospitals were converted to general hospitals under the provincial hospital programs.

In the 1940s Saskatchewan and BC developed hospital insurance programs; Saskatchewan also provided medical coverage.

In 1957 the federal government began to give assistance to the provinces for programs of hospital services and in 1966 a countrywide medical-care program was developed (*see* HEALTH POLICY). In 1984 the federal government passed new legislation designed to discourage user fees for hospital services and extra billing by physicians.

Gairdner Foundation International Awards

Date of award	*Canadian recipients*	*Area of achievement*
1959	W.G. Bigelow	hypothermia method of open-heart surgery
	A.C. Burton	cardiovascular physiology
1963	M.L. Barr	insight into cell genetics and discovery of the Barr body
	J. Genest	vascular physiology and hypertension
1964	G.D.W. Murray	cardiac physiology and pathology and cardiac surgery
1965	C.P. Leblond	autoradiography for cellular biology and research on the thyroid gland
1967	D.H. Copp	calcium homeostasis, identification of the hormone calcitonin which alters blood calcium levels
	P.J. Moloney	immunology and diabetes
	J.F. Mustard	the role of platelets in thrombosis and atherosclerosis
	B. Chown	human blood groups and hemolytic disease of the newborn
1969	R.B. Salter	musculoskeletal disorders and orthopedic surgery
	E.A. McCulloch & J.E. Till	spleen-colony technique for leukemia treatment
1971	C.H. Best	insulin
1972	O. Hornykiewicz	Parkinson's disease and physiology of the brain
1973	H.E. Johns	cobalt and high-energy radiotherapy
1974	J.H. Quastel	biochemistry
1975	J.D. Keith	congenital heart disease
	W.T. Mustard	cardiovascular surgery
1976	K.J.R. Wightman*	educator, physician and leader
1977	H.G. Friesen	biochemistry and physiology of hormones which stimulate milk production (lactogenic hormones)
1978	S.O. Freedman & P. Gold	carcinoembryonic antigen
1979	C.R. Scriver	genetic disease
	C. Fortier*	scientist, teacher and scientific adviser
1980	I.B. Fritz	regulation of fatty-acid metabolism
1981	J.H.C. Wang (with W.Y. Cheung)	discovery of calmodulin
	L. Siminovitch*	geneticist, adviser on science policy, leader of Canadian academic community
1984	K. Krnjevic	research on the mechanisms of brain cell communication
	R.L. Noble	discovery of important anticancer drug vinblastine
	D.G. Cameron*	educator, physician and initiator of training programs for both clinicians and clinician-scientists.
1985	R.U. Lemieux	organic synthesis and structural analysis of oligosaccharides with human blood-group antigens specificity
1986	A. de Bold, T.J. Flinn & H. Sonnenberg	discovery and characterization of atrial natriuretic factor
	M. Smith	development and use of technique of site-specific mutagenesis
	A. Rothstein	medical scientist, scientific administrator

* Indicates receipt of the Gairdner Foundation Wightman Award, an award for demonstrated outstanding leadership in medicine and medical science.

Diagnostic and Treatment Methods Many advances in diagnosis and DISEASE treatment have occurred since 1945. The development of a large number of antibiotics has provided means of combatting bacterial infections (the successful treatment of tuberculosis is an outstanding example) although the ability of some bacteria to develop resistance to antibiotics is still of increasing concern.

Many viral diseases are now controlled by the use of vaccines. For example, the last epidemic of poliomyelitis in Canada occurred in the mid-1950s; because of effective vaccination programs it is not the threat it once was. The use of ultrasound and radioactive isotopes and the recently developed nuclear magnetic resonance method of examination has enabled cardiologists to assess the state of the heart muscle. Surgical procedures involving correction of congenital heart defects, valvular abnormalities and coronary artery disease are being carried out in many centres across Canada. The widespread use of cardiopulmonary resuscitation in hospitals and by paramedical personnel has resulted in recovery in many cases of cardiac arrest. Pacemakers have enabled patients with life-threatening cardiac rhythm problems to survive many years. The development of coronary care units and intensive care units in hospitals has resulted in the much improved management of patients suffering from severe illness or injury.

Canada has made a significant contribution to the field of CANCER diagnosis and early detection with the "Pap" smear tests for uterine cervical cancer. Programs for the early detection of breast cancer by self-examination and mammography have also been developed. Canadian scientists were responsible for the development of the "cobalt bomb" used in radiation treatment of cancer, and for the discovery of the vinca alkaloids, chemotherapeutic agents used in the treatment of many types of cancer. Cancer diagnostic treatment and research centres have been established in all major cities in Canada.

The availability of radioactive isotopes (used in the diagnosis of many conditions, including cancer and disease of the lungs) has led to the development of the specialty of nuclear medicine. The diagnosis and treatment of certain conditions, eg, thyroid disease, has been greatly improved. The development of dialysis units and kidney transplants for chronic kidney failure have enabled patients to carry on useful lives, in many cases, for years.

Centres for the treatment of the many types of ARTHRITIS have been established in many Canadian communities, greatly assisted by The Arthritis Society. These centres provide an integrated program of treatment including medical, physiotherapy and occupational therapies and social service assistance. New medications and developments in surgery involving replacement of joints with plastic or metal materials have improved the outlook of patients suffering from chronic arthritis.

The management of patients with mental illness has changed quite markedly in recent years. Patients suffering from depression and schizophrenia can now be treated with various types of medication, thus avoiding long periods of hospital care. Outpatient community treatment clinics and departments of PSYCHIATRY based in general hospitals have also been established.

Early ambulation after surgical operations has been very effective in preventing postoperative complications such as venous clotting, lung congestion and general muscle weakness. Anesthetic methods have improved so that extensive surgical procedures can be performed even on elderly patients. Cardiac surgery and neurosurgery have made great advances. TRANSPLANTATION of organs is much more common and raises new ethical questions for the medical profession. Surgery of the blood vessels has progressed with the use of artificial replacement materials. The provision of blood transfusions by the Canadian RED CROSS SOCIETY has made possible many of the advances in surgery. Emergency departments of hospitals have been provided with personnel and equipment to handle serious injuries, because trauma continues to be a major cause of disability requiring surgery. Microsurgery has made possible the repair of small blood vessels and operations on the ear to relieve deafness. In OPHTHALMOLOGY LASERS have been used in the treatment of some retinal diseases.

The understanding and treatment of epilepsy has advanced, and there has been considerable improvement in the outlook of patients with strokes because of extensive study by Canadian neurologists of this common affliction. The treatment of berry aneurysms of the arteries of the brain by neurosurgeons has been an outstanding Canadian development.

The application of ultrasound to many conditions, eg, liver and gall bladder disease, obstetrics, and cardiac function, has improved diagnosis and treatment. The introduction of computerized axial tomography (CAT scanner) revolutionized the diagnosis of intracranial conditions, spinal cord lesions, abdominal masses and other conditions. The application of fiber optics to diagnostic instruments has greatly enhanced the examination of the stomach, duodenum and colon. This modification of equipment has allowed the catheterization of the common bile duct without surgical intervention and in some cases impacted gall stones can now be removed without surgery. Similarly, the lithotripter has been used to smash kidney stones in a safe way that also involves no surgery.

In obstetrics the emphasis has been on careful prenatal investigation, to discover high-risk situations in order to anticipate and prevent complications during delivery. The prenatal programs of preparation of the mother for the birth of the baby have allowed for delivery with a minimum of anesthesia. Other advances in the management of pregnancy include fetal monitoring during delivery, ultrasound examination of the fetus and placenta, and examination of the intrauterine amniotic fluid for genetic abnormalities in the fetus. There has been a complete change in attitudes towards pregnant women, one result of which is increased family involvement. Recently, *in vitro* fertilization of the mother's ovum has been carried out in Canada, resulting in successful pregnancies for women who could not otherwise have borne a child. Departments of PEDIATRICS have changed considerably in recent years. Infectious diseases have declined markedly in incidence, and isolation hospitals have been closed. Emphasis has been directed toward neo-natal intensive care nurseries, congenital diseases, child neoplastic conditions and adolescent problems.

Diagnostic laboratories have also greatly improved with automation and such developments as have been made in electron microscopy. Great advances have been made in the application of immunology and genetics in diagnoses. By the use of monoclonal antibodies there is a much greater detection rate for malignancies and hopes for improved treatment. It is now possible to detect abnormalities in fetuses and to offer prospective parents sound genetic analyses.

Some medical faculties have established divisions of SPORTS MEDICINE to study and treat the special needs of those engaged in athletic activities.

Emphasis has been paid to the rehabilitation of patients after injuries, following the development of disabling illnesses and after surgical procedures such as amputations. A specialty of rehabilitation medicine has been recognized, and rehabilitation centres have been established in many Canadian communities. Patients with paraplegia, strokes and other neurological and musculoskeletal diseases benefit from these programs, which include physiotherapy, occupational therapy, speech therapy and the use of facilities such as therapeutic pools.

Increased medical attention is being paid as well to the particular problems of the AGING population. A large proportion of medical and hospital care is devoted to the needs of individuals above 65 years of age. Many patients in the older age group become disabled to the extent that they require continual hospital care. The need for extended care or chronic care hospital facilities has always been greater than the supply. Recently, geriatrics (the study and care of aging individuals) has been recognized as a specialty.

For patients with terminal malignancies, some hospitals have established special hospice facilities that administer to the patients' physical, emotional and spiritual needs.

The health professions have become increasingly concerned with prevention of disease and injury, not only as a means of improving the health of their patients but also to reduce the cost of health care. To this end they have advocated the use of seat belts and participation in suitable FITNESS activities, and have supported anti-SMOKING campaigns and information programs concerning diet.

The outstanding advances in many branches of medicine in the past 40 years have led to improvement in the treatment and prevention of illness and injuries but have also created problems, eg, the rapidly increasing cost of providing all available health care universally. The health professions and the public must also confront ethical problems that have arisen with technical advances (*see also* MEDICAL EDUCATION; MEDICAL ETHICS; MEDICAL RESEARCH). R.B. KERR

Reading: H.R. Robertson, *Health Care in Canada* (1972); L. Saderstrom, *The Canadian Health System* (1978); S.E.D. Shortt, ed, *Medicine in Canadian Society* (1981).

Medicine, General Practice General practice is the branch of medicine concerned with providing care (known as "primary and continuing care") to patients irrespective of their age, sex or type of problem. In Canada general practice is also known as "family practice" and general practitioners are also known as "family physicians." General practice as a medical discipline is usually referred to as Family Medicine.

A number of features make general practice a distinctive part of the medical profession. General practitioners (GPs) usually enter into a long-term relationship with their patients which enables the physician to treat illness with a full knowledge of a patient's life history, medical history, social and family relationships, and personal values or preferences. GPs see each of their patients on the average 4 times a year. These visits provide excellent opportunities for health education and the early detection of disease. The majority of illness episodes are managed entirely by the GP.

When specialized help is needed, the GP arranges a consultation with or a referral to the appropriate specialist. The growth of specialization and the technological development of medicine have added greatly to the complexity of medical care; GPs are often instrumental in co-ordinating the patient's care and in explaining the implications of diagnostic investigations to patients and their families.

When GPs live in the communities in which they practise, particularly rural communities, they can gain valuable knowledge of the working and living environments of their patients. Some GPs still visit their patients at home and the great majority of general practitioners in Canada admit and care for their own patients in hospital. Prenatal, postnatal and well-baby care are important parts of this kind of medicine.

The Development of General Practice In the 19th and early 20th centuries, virtually all doctors were GPs. Since the 1930s there has been an enormous growth in the number of major medical specialties, and since the 1950s, a great deal of fragmentation into subspecialties. As a result, certain procedures (eg, major surgery) which were formerly the responsibility of GPs have increasingly become the province of full-time specialists. At the same time, many specialists, by limiting their practice to narrower fields, can no longer provide primary care. In some specialties, however (notably pediatrics and obstetrics), there are practitioners who offer primary and continuing care to certain age groups.

The rapid growth of specialization after WWII was followed by a decline in the numbers of GPs, a decline paralleled in other countries and in other professions, where the relationship between generalists and specialists became an issue. Since that time, however, a number of factors have contributed to a renaissance of general practice, including the founding in 1954 of the College of General Practitioners, renamed in 1967 the College of Family Physicians. The college has provided the intellectual and academic leadership that has enabled GPs to redefine their role in a more complex society. Instead of seeing themselves as "jacks of all trades," GPs are now members of a well-defined medical discipline, based on an integrated knowledge of clinical medicine and human behaviour, with special skills in the prevention and early diagnosis of disease and the complex long-term care of patients. The college has encouraged the emergence of general practice as an academic discipline in the universities and the development of postgraduate training programs in family medicine. The first chair of family medicine was established at University of Western Ontario in 1968; today all 16 medical schools in Canada have academic units of general practice and postgraduate training programs. About 450-500 trainees graduate from these programs each year. In 1969 the College of Family Physicians held its first certification examination in family medicine. There were, in 1987, 5629 certificants of the college.

As a result of these developments, Canada's health-care system seems to have attained a balance between generalists and specialists. In 1987 there were estimated to be 15 000 family physicians in Canada. General practice has become a popular career choice for medical graduates, especially women graduates. Some problems still exist, for example, there are insufficient training positions for all graduates entering general practice and a substantial number are therefore entering practice without a specific preparation for their role; and the role of the GP in the large urban hospital – especially the teaching hospital – is in flux and is not yet clearly defined.

In the future, the growing proportion of old people in the population will make the care of the aged an increasingly important aspect of general practice, and the high cost of hospital care and the complexity and fragmentation of medicine will make it essential to have a well-trained and highly skilled body of generalists.

IAN R. MCWHINNEY

Medicine, History of Medicine in Canada arguably began centuries before the French settled the shores of N America, but because the native people passed on their traditions orally, the only written accounts of their practices and beliefs were recorded by the white explorers and settlers. Most aspects of native medicine were integral to a religious system in which disease was ascribed to magical causes and therefore required magical cures, provided generally by a SHAMAN, or medicine man. But native people also treated illness with some highly effective plant remedies (eg, oil of wintergreen, bloodroot, high bush cranberries, *see* PLANTS, NATIVE USES) and physical procedures such as SWEAT LODGES and massages. It was from an Indian that Jacques Cartier learned of a cure (brewed from twigs and bark of white spruce or hemlock) for scurvy. Systems of native medicine began to break down after prolonged contact with European settlers and their imported, often EPIDEMIC diseases (eg, measles, typhoid, typhus, diphtheria and smallpox; *see* NATIVE PEOPLE, HEALTH).

European medicine at the time of settlement was evolving into an identifiably scientific discipline, although theories and knowledge about disease developed very slowly. Most of the first medical practitioners from France were barber surgeons, trained only by a rough and ready apprenticeship, or apothecaries who were theoretically limited to providing remedies ordered by a doctor but usually functioned as semi-trained general practitioners. Many of these men were of questionable character but others, eg, Robert Giffard and Michel SARRAZIN, dedicated their lives to serving the colonists. Giffard, a barber surgeon who arrived in Québec in 1627, was the first physician at the HÔTEL-DIEU, a HOSPITAL (4 rooms, 2 closets) originally founded by a religious order from France (*see* NURSING). The practice of combining the offices of barber and surgeon may have derived from the almost universal custom of bleeding patients as a panacea for virtually every ill. All that was required was a sharp knife and a knowledge of where to locate the major veins. Surgery was limited to operations on the arms, legs and the surface of the body and head. Internal operations usually resulted in the patient's death. The use of drastic measures to induce vomiting and purging were also commonplace.

Sarrazin, who arrived in New France in the second half of the 17th century, was appointed surgeon-major of the French troops in Canada and later official physician of the Hôtel-Dieu. In that capacity he became famous for helping hundreds of colonists recover from typhus. He was also an acclaimed botanist.

Despite the combined hazards of climate, disease, hunger and Indian attack, by 1763, when New France was ceded to the British, Montréal and Québec City were thriving small cities. The medical system imported by the British was similar to that used by the French. Military surgeons continued to dominate the practice and organization of the profession. However, there was a change in that the anglophone doctors took control of the cities, leaving the francophone doctors to serve the poorer areas.

Arriving in what was to become Ontario, LOYALISTS brought army surgeons with them as well as civilian physicians. These men usually had great difficulty making a living because the population was small, the fees low and the prestige of the medical profession very shaky. They often held other jobs, such as operating a farm or a store.

The settlers in Upper Canada were afflicted by acute infectious diseases, injuries of all kinds, periodic malnutrition and serious recurrent illnesses such as "fever and ague" (malaria). When they could obtain the services of a physician they often did, but frequently treated themselves with home remedies and botanic cures based on native peoples' prescriptions. Midwives usually assisted at childbirth. The situation was much the same in the Maritime colonies. Halifax, the largest city in the area, had a substantial medical population, including many military surgeons, and a number of hospitals. The poor could obtain some medical services from dispensaries or the workhouse. Many early Maritime doctors established successful second careers. Abraham GESNER, educated in London, was a doctor, geologist, mineralogist and the discoverer of kerosene. Dr J. Webster was also an historian, Sir Andrew MACPHAIL a writer, Dr Charles TUPPER a politician. Another Maritime doctor, David Parker, who worked in the asylum for the poor in Halifax, was the first physician in Canada to operate with the help of anesthesia.

In the West, most of what was to become the Prairie provinces and BC were controlled by the Hudson's Bay Co, which employed its own doctors. William Fraser TOLMIE, who immigrated to Vancouver as a surgeon and trader for the HBC, and for whom Mt Tolmie in BC is named, was a botanist, geologist and later, a member of the legislature. He may have performed one of the first modern operations on the West Coast when he removed a tumour from the breast of a sailor. Tolmie had brought stethoscopes from Scotland; surgical instruments provided to him on his arrival in BC included "an Amputating, two trephining, two eye instruments, a lithotomy and a cupping case, beside two midwifery forceps, and a multitude of catheters, flexible and silver sound bougies, probangs, tooth forceps." A colleague of Tolmie's, Dr John MCLOUGHLIN, born in Lower Canada, became representative of the HBC in the West.

During the 19th century, immigration to Canada, particularly from Britain and the US, increased dramatically. Among the immigrants were many notable physicians, such as Christopher Widmer (who became known in Upper Canada as the "Father of Surgery") and W.R. Beaumont, a prolific inventor of surgical instruments. Widmer practised at York Hospital (later the Toronto General). The first medical schools in Upper Canada had been established in the 1820s. One of the first, the Talbot Dispensary, was opened by the reformer Dr Charles DUNCOMBE, but closed when its benefactor, Thomas TALBOT, withdrew his support, suspecting correctly that Duncombe was using the dispensary as a stepping stone into politics. Indeed, many of Canada's early doctors became actively involved in politics. A second school, which eventually (1870) became the medical department at Victoria U, was founded by the reformer Dr John ROLPH. In late 1823 the Montreal Medical Institution, established by Dr. W. Caldwell and his associates and later absorbed by the medical faculty of McGill U, began to give classes.

The founding of medical schools in Canada was inspired by various motives, including the desire of doctors (who invariably founded the schools) to teach along lines of which they approved and to ensure a source of income for themselves. They were supported by those who felt that many Canadians who sought education in the US were being inadequately trained and were being exposed to dangerous democratic principles. In the US, many medical schools became commercial operations, willing to lower standards to attract students, but in Canada the schools sought affiliation with universities and in an effort to discourage charlatans and to raise the low esteem in which doctors were held by the public, they maintained high standards of entry. By the 1850s, students in medical schools in Canada typically attended lectures on "Materia Medica and therapeutics, Anatomy and Physiology, Principles and Practices and Surgery, Midwifery and the Diseases of Women and Children, and Medical Jurisprudence." There was some dissection but little laboratory work (it was not until the mid-1870s, when William OSLER took over the chair at McGill, that microscopes would be used in any extensive way). The dissecting rooms were known as "dead-houses." The one associated with the medical school established in London, Ont, was not untypical. In makeshift quarters (a dining room of an old cottage), the room contained "two tables, a few chairs, a pile of sawdust, a shovel in the corner, old coats and aprons and hooks along the walls. A trapdoor in the floor led to the cellar where 2 large vats, filled with ancient wood alcohol and other things, permeated the whole building with their odours." New medical students were initiated into dissecting by being forced down to the cellar to retrieve the cadavers. Dr D.C. MacCallum has left a record of the situation at McGill in the mid-19th century, where he prepared the dissections that were to be part of the anatomy professor's lectures the following day. He was compelled to pass several hours at night in the dissecting room, which was "dismal and foul-smelling." He wrote that his only company was "several partially dissected subjects and numerous rats which kept up a lively racket coursing over and below the floor and within the walls of the room." The procuring of cadavers, used for anatomical studies and medical research, was often risky. Some students in Québec paid their medical fees by taking bodies from the cemetery near Côte des Neiges. Such incidents led finally to amendments in the Act regarding anatomy and thus indirectly aided the development of Canadian medicine.

From the late 1700s, efforts to regulate the medical profession had provoked controversy between universities and boards of examiners over whether a medical degree constituted a licence to practise. The number of charlatans and incompetents practising medicine had proliferated, partly because the public preferred them, having no social or scientific reason to choose regular doctors. In both Upper and Lower Canada licensing bodies had existed since the late 1800s. In Lower Canada a board appointed by the governor had been formed under the authority of a British Act of Parliament to prevent unlicensed persons from practising medicine. Later attempts to define the profession in Lower Canada produced tension between French and English doctors until the College of Physicians and Surgeons of Lower Canada was finally created in 1847. In 1849 the Act creating the corporation was amended to provide automatic membership in the college to those engaged in practice in 1847. In 1839 a group of Toronto physicians, many of them trained in Britain, were incorporated as the College of Physicians and Surgeons of Upper Canada, but its incorporating act was disallowed in 1840. In 1869, under the Ontario Medical Act, a new College of Physicians and Surgeons of Ontario, empowered to examine would-be practitioners and university graduates, was incorporated. In 1867 the CANADIAN MEDICAL ASSOCIATION was formed. Overall, the mid-19th century was a turbulent period in the Canadian medical profession, which was torn by divisions between English and French doctors, and between those trained in Canada and those trained elsewhere.

As the population of British N America increased, so did its susceptibility to EPIDEMICS. In 1832, 1834, 1849 and during the 1850s, CHOLERA epidemics ravaged the country. In 1832 the disease spread from Québec City to most of the towns and cities in Upper Canada in only 3

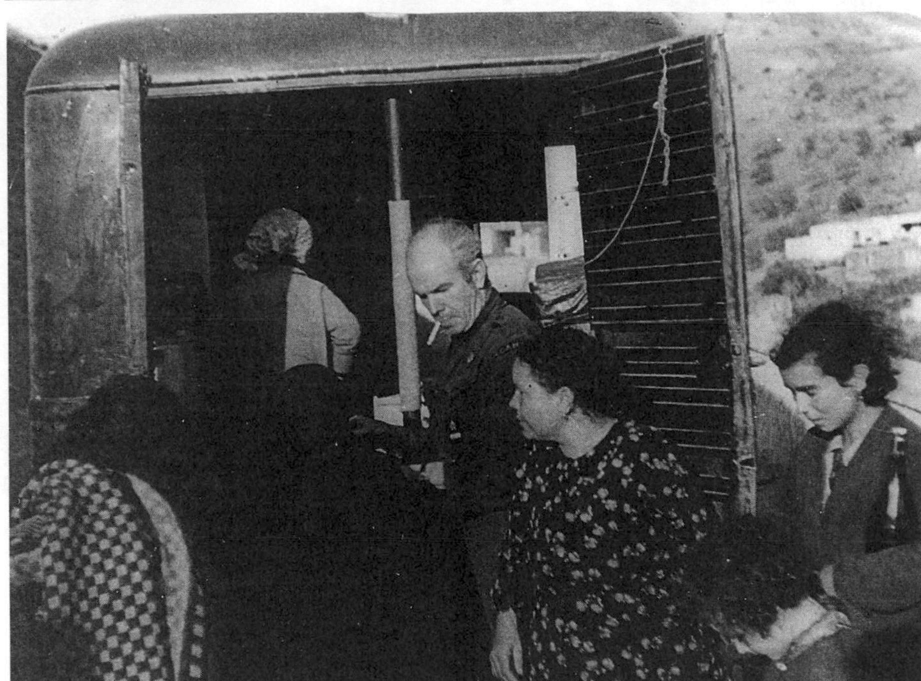

Norman Bethune, shown here during the Spanish Civil War, in which he organized the first mobile blood-transfusion service (*courtesy National Archives of Canada/PA-124407*).

weeks. In 1854 an Italian, Filippo Pacini, had described the cholera vibrio visible through a microscope, but it was not until the germ theory, established by Louis Pasteur, was reluctantly accepted that the cause of cholera was isolated. Robert Koch, a German researcher building on the discoveries of Pasteur, also discovered the germs that caused diphtheria, typhoid and tuberculosis.

During the cholera years in Canada, doctors disagreed over whether the disease was contagious. There was a tendency to see it as a disease of the blood; treatments included bleeding, massive doses of calomel and opium, and cauterizing. As early as 1834, however, William Kelly, a surgeon of the Royal Navy, had suggested there was a relationship between diseases and sanitation, particularly clean water. Local boards of health were established to enforce quarantine and sanitary laws. By the end of the 19th century PUBLIC HEALTH was being promoted through a variety of enactments regarding IMMIGRATION restrictions, protection against the sale of tainted food, and provision of adequate sanitation. Public resistance to these measures was intense, as it was to compulsory vaccination. For example, although a smallpox vaccine was introduced into Canada in the early 1800s by a Nova Scotia doctor, smallpox epidemics ravaged the country until the 1900s, when the value of the vaccination was finally understood.

Two other major discoveries in medicine also occurred in the mid-1800s. The first was the discovery, in the 1840s, of anesthetic, which rendered surgery painless. Two Canadian doctors later made major contributions to developments in anesthesiology. In 1923, W.E. Brown of U of T established the value of ethylene as an anesthetic, and in 1942 Dr Harold Griffith advanced the science of anesthesia by his use of curare (commercially, Intocostrin), a plant extract used by South Americans as an arrow poison. The second discovery, by the Englishman Joseph Lister, derived from Pasteur's work. Lister proved that the recovery rate of patients suffering wounds could be drastically improved if the wounds were disinfected (Lister first used carbolic acid for this purpose). At that time, surgeons at the Toronto General, like surgeons everywhere, operated in frock coats, usually holding their knives, when not in use, in their mouths. Instruments were washed in a cursory fashion or wiped on a towel. Lister's antiseptic treatment was described in Canadian journals within a few months of Lister's experiments and was being used in operating rooms of the Toronto and Montreal General Hospitals by 1869, but most Canadian physicians initially resisted the technique and the attempts by Archibald Malloch, an Ontario surgeon who had worked with Lister in Glasgow, to teach Lister's principles of antisepsis. Thomas RODDICK is credited with being the first doctor to base procedures at the Montreal General on these principles.

By the 1850s Canadian women had begun to demand access to medical schools, but until the 1880s virtually all female physicians practising in Canada (eg, Emily Howard STOWE, Jennie Kidd TROUT) had trained with doctors or in schools outside Canada. In 1883 the Women's Medical College, affiliated with Queen's, and the Woman's Medical College, affiliated with U of T and the University of Trinity College, opened. Both institutions offered only the required course work, not degrees, but after 1895 students of the Ontario Medical College for Women, successor to the Toronto school, could take the exams of the medical school of their choice. Medical training for women was subsequently offered at Dalhousie (1890), U of Western Ontario (1890s) and U Man (1891), but the universities of McGill, Laval and Montréal did not open their doors to women until much later. Early female practitioners, such as Elizabeth Matheson in her work in the NWT and Maude ABBOTT in her work on congenital heart disease, among other accomplishments, made significant contributions to Canadian medicine.

Many Canadian doctors, eg, John SCHULTZ, John Sebastian HELMCKEN, Clarence HINCKS, and John RICHARDSON, helped influence the development of their own country not only as physicians but as politicians, inventors, explorers, writers, soldiers and community leaders. Many others, including Robert MCCLURE (whose work was described in W.H. Auden's and Christopher Isherwood's *Journey to War),* Florence Murray, Davidson BLACK and Norman BETHUNE, became known for their work outside of Canada in countries such as China and India. Of the 19th-century doctors who contributed to the prestige of Canadian medicine abroad, the most eminent was William Osler. Educated at the Toronto School of Medicine and at McGill, over time he was professor of medicine at U of Pennsylvania, was appointed to Johns Hopkins Hospital and Medical School, and became Regius Professor of Medicine at Oxford. Author, in 1892, of *The Principles and Practice of Medicine* (which indirectly helped inspire the foundation of the Rockefeller Institute of Medical Research), he contributed to science through his discovery of blood platelets and his investigations into heart disease, malaria and tuberculosis. His emphasis on the study of anatomy and on bedside teaching transformed medical teaching in N America. His colleague, Dr Francis SHEPHERD, introduced new scientific methods of teaching at McGill and, like Osler, emphasized the importance of a grounding in anatomy in understanding medicine.

Tentative advances in medical research in Canada were accelerated by the discovery (1922) of INSULIN by Frederick BANTING, Charles BEST and J.J.R. MACLEOD. Because of their success and the increased interest in medical research, government became involved in financing and more studies and institutes of medical research were established. For example, in 1934, Wilder PENFIELD, funded by the Rockefeller Foundation, founded the Montreal Neurological Institute, which drew together the disciplines of neurosurgery, neuropathology, neurology and related basic sciences and consequently transformed the study of the brain.

As WWII approached, medical practice was changing slowly, influenced by the discovery that a number of serious diseases could be controlled by immunization. Health in general was improving, largely because of better diet and nutrition and more effective public-health measures. Hospitals had become safer places for the sick, and surgical procedures were more sophisticated and more likely to achieve satisfactory results. The discovery of sulfa drugs in the 1930s was a harbinger of the discovery of antibiotics. In the early 1950s, a vaccine, which the CONNAUGHT LABORATORIES at U of T had helped develop, defeated the feared disease of polio. CHARLES ROLAND

Medicine Bundles were the focus of most Plains Indian rituals. A bundle might be a few feathers wrapped in skin or a multitude of objects such as animal skins, roots, or stone pipes inside a rawhide bag. Every article had significance and called for a special song whenever its owner exposed it to light. Songs and a sacred myth belonged to the bundle itself. Fixed rules of inheritance governed the sale of a particular bundle. Formal transfer was a solemn ceremony and the new owner had to learn the significance of all objects in the bundle, details of visions to which they owed their origins, and songs that established their validity. Feasts were given for bundles by both owners and nonowners. *See also* NATIVE PEOPLE, RELIGION. RENÉ R. GADACZ

Medicine Hat, Alta, City, pop 41 804 (1986c) 40 380 (1981c), inc 1906, is located on the CPR main line and the Trans-Canada Hwy about 300 km E of CALGARY. Nestled in the valley of the south SASKATCHEWAN R, it is a park-studded retreat amidst the surrounding flat and treeless prairies. A council of 8 aldermen and a mayor govern the city.

History According to an Indian legend, a Cree medicine man lost his headdress while fleeing across the S Saskatchewan from a bloody battle against the Blackfoot. His disheartened tribesmen surrendered and were massacred. This is the most likely explanation of Medicine Hat's name. With the arrival of the CPR here in 1883, a tent town sprouted up around the station and slowly a community emerged. The commercial production of natural gas and clay led to the manufacturing of pottery, bricks and tiles. Milling, canning, brewing and some smelting followed. Medicine Hat grew most rapidly during the first decade of the 20th century. By 1911 it had a population of 5600.

Economy Although Medicine Hat is located in an agricultural region of large ranches, wheat farms and some irrigated lands, the abundance of natural gas permitted it to build a small but vigorous industrial sector. In 1921 Medalta Stoneware became the first western Canadian plant to sell a manufactured product E of the Lakehead. Northwest Nitro Chemicals (now Western Co-operative Fertilizers) built a large fertilizer plant in the city in 1955. Five years later Medicine Hat built Brier Industrial Estates, which welcomed as one of its first occupants a Goodyear tire plant. Both the greenhouse and petrochemical industries have profited from local supplies of natural gas.

Cityscape Medicine Hat is an oasis with many parks and sporting facilities. Its college, art gallery, museum, Fire Hall Theatre and Little Symphony Orchestra enhance local cultural life. The Medicine Hat Tigers play in the Western Canadian Junior Hockey League. The Medicine Hat Blue Jays baseball team is a farm team of the Toronto Blue Jays.

A.A. DEN OTTER

Medicine Wheels are circular structures of fieldstones and small boulders arranged to resemble spoked wheels, and are found atop prairie hills. Built by natives in prehistoric and possibly historic times, many of several dozen located in Alberta, Saskatchewan (Moose Mountain wheel) and across the northwestern plains (Big Horn wheel in Montana) are over 6 m in diameter. Perhaps dating to the time of Stonehenge in England and as puzzling as that famous structure, they could have been ancient calendars, memorials to important native chiefs, ceremonial sites associated with buffalo hunting, or simply guide posts for travel. Their exact meaning remains a problem in ARCHAEOLOGY. Sometimes artifacts such as stone scrapers, knives and points are found in association with them. *See also* BRITISH BLACK CAIRN; NATIVE PEOPLE, RELIGION.

RENÉ R. GADACZ

Medley, John, bishop (b at Chelsea, Eng 19 Dec 1804; d at Fredericton 9 Sept 1892). As the first Anglican bishop of Fredericton, Medley spent 47 years building up the church physically and spiritually. Educated at Wadham Coll, Oxford, and friend of Edmund Pusey, he was active in the English ecclesiological movement, which stressed the improvement of church music and architecture. A known Tractarian, his High Church sympathies were viewed with suspicion by his LOYALIST congregation. Consecrated bishop of Fredericton in 1845, he embarked on a series of annual parish visitations and dedicated himself to building a cathedral at Fredericton and developing a cathedral choir school. The cathedral, designed by architect Frank Wills with furnishing designed by William Butterfield, was consecrated in 1853. Medley supported free pews, free-will offerings and the development of diocesan synods. He was

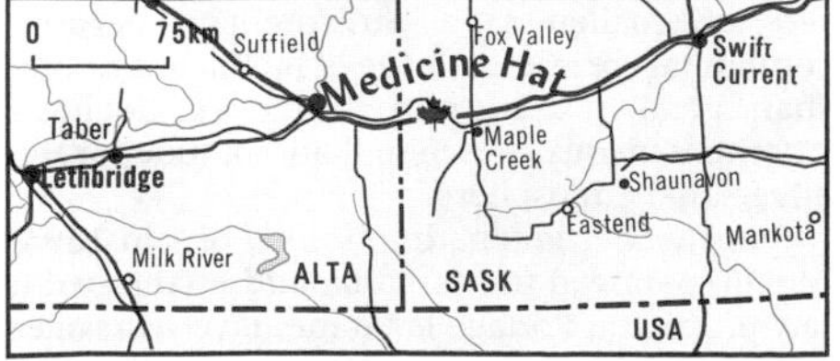

Medicine Hat City Hall was completed in 1983 and is built on the banks of the S Saskatchewan R (*courtesy City of Medicine Hat*).

the author of *Hymns for Public Worship in the Diocese of Fredericton* (1855, 1863, 1870).

TERRY THOMPSON

Meech Lake Accord Québec's refusal to accept the constitutional terms agreed to by the other provinces at the Nov 1981 conference in Ottawa, dealing with the patriation of the Constitution and the entrenchment of the CANADIAN CHARTER OF RIGHTS AND FREEDOMS, led to continuing negotiations. Although legally bound by the CONSTITUTION ACT, 1982, which gave effect to the 1981 Nov conference (the Supreme Court having held that Québec had no veto in law or by convention and that the federal authorities had substantial support from the provinces), Québec was desirous to join the agreement, politically, with certain conditions. Prem René LÉVESQUE in 1985 proposed some conditions and in 1986 Prem Robert BOURASSA established 5 minimal conditions. Bourassa's conditions were finally agreed upon by PM Brian MULRONEY and all premiers at Meech Lake, Qué, on 30 Apr 1987 and put into legal and final form in Ottawa 3 June 1987. The National Assembly in Québec adopted the terms of the Accord 23 June 1987. Saskatchewan ratified the Accord 23 Sept 1987 by a vote of 43 to 3. Nationally, a special joint committee of the Senate and House of Commons began hearing witnesses and representations 4 Aug 1987. The committee accepted the Accord on 21 Sept 1987, as did the House of Commons on 26 Oct 1987, by a vote of 242 to 16. Provincial premiers were not unanimous in their support. Premiers David PETERSON of Ontario and Howard PAWLEY of Manitoba, in particular, expressed doubts. Strong dissent was expressed by a number of women's groups and native groups.

The 5 points of the Accord pertain 1) to the linguistic duality of Canada and the distinct society of Québec; 2) to the federal spending power (right for a province to opt-out with compensation, in share-cost programs in exclusive provincial fields); 3) to increased power of the provinces in immigration; 4) to constitutionalization of the Supreme Court and its civilian composition, and the appointment by the federal authorities of Supreme Court judges and senators from provincial lists; and 5) to the amendment formula (unanimity rule extended to cover central institutions). The 11 first ministers agreed to hold a conference (a second round) before the end of 1988 and to consider the reform of the Senate and the question of fisheries.

GÉRALD-A. BEAUDOIN

Mégantic, Lac, 26 km^2, elev 395 m, 75 m deep, is located in southern Québec, 6 km from the US border. The lake is the source of the Rivière CHAUDIÈRE; the town of Lac Mégantic is nearby. Discovered in 1646 by Father Druillettes, it was only settled about 1700 by the ABENAKI, who gave it the name *Namesokanjik,* meaning "place of the fish." Bordered to the S and E by the Appalachians, the lake is fed by a network of valleys that drain the surrounding forests. Once used to float timber, it is now popular with fishermen and vacationers. In 1776, during the American Revolution, Col Benedict ARNOLD's troops used Lac Mégantic and the Chaudière to attack Québec City from Boston.

JEAN-MARIE DUBOIS AND PIERRE MAILHOT

Mégantic Hills, part of the Appalachian Region of Québec – a region 800 km long by 60-150 km wide lying S of the St Lawrence R between the American-Canadian border and the Gulf of St Lawrence. The region, formed by the alignment of many mountain chains (the chief ones being the Notre Dame mountains in Gaspé), spreads to the SW into New England, as the White and the Green mountains, and to the NE into Newfoundland. The highest peaks are Jacques Cartier (1268 m) and Albert (1151 m) in Gaspé, and Mégantic (1100 m) in the EASTERN TOWNSHIPS. The region's main city is SHERBROOKE (pop 74 438, 1986c) in the Eastern Townships. Colonized primarily by LOYALISTS in the 18th century, it was the principal mining region in Canada in the 19th century, especially for COPPER. It now produces ASBESTOS and lumber as well as fish products in the Gaspé. One of the loveliest tourist regions in all Québec, it has some of the province's finest salmon rivers.

JEAN-MARIE DUBOIS

Megantic Outlaw, *see* MORRISON, DONALD.

Megaprojects The term megaproject was already inappropriate when, in the early 1970s, it was first applied to very large capital projects such as the JAMES BAY PROJECT and the Syncrude oil-sands project in northern Alberta. "Mega" denotes a factor of millions; in fact the proper prefix for Canada's giant ENGINEERING schemes of the 1970s and 1980s would have been "giga" (ie, billions) because their common characteristic was a price tag of billions of dollars. In the energy field alone, construction of major projects costing more than $200 billion was initially planned in Canada during the 1980s. A single offshore oil-production platform, serving up to 36 undersea wells, may carry a price tag of billions of dollars.

The whole concept of "megaprojects" was thrown into question when the long list of megaprojects proposed in the 1970s was wiped out by the recession of the early 1980s. Megaprojects can only thrive in an atmosphere of certainty. Ten-year, 20-year, or even 50-year commitments, involving billions of dollars and thousands of man-years, can only be undertaken with assured finances, good product demand, a supportive political environment and fail-safe technology. Without this certainty, megaprojects can easily become white elephants.

Canada is a huge country blessed with a great wealth of natural RESOURCES – the ideal environment for megaprojects. Its history is often told as a sequence of what were, in the context of their times, megaprojects: Ontario's WELLAND CANAL and RIDEAU CANAL; the CANADIAN PACIFIC RAILWAY and CANADIAN NATIONAL RAILWAYS; the war mobilizations; the HYDROELECTRIC systems; the Trans-Canada and Westcoast natural-gas PIPELINES; the Interprovincial and TransMountain oil pipelines; the TRANS-CANADA HIGHWAY, ALASKA HIGHWAY and Canol pipeline; the ST LAWRENCE SEAWAY; the Canadian deuterium-uranium (CANDU) nuclear reactors; and the Syncrude oil-sands project. All were built for one or more of 3 overriding national purposes: transportation, energy or defence.

In addition to mere size and scope, megaprojects involve a long-term perspective that often verges on crystal-ball gazing. Megaprojects are usually designed for a future that will not begin for 5-10 years and will extend for a further 25-30 years. Moreover, the megaproject usually does not enter the economic system gradually but represents a quantum leap in productive capacity. Hence, there must be a huge, unsatisfied demand to be met when the project begins operation, or the project must meet old demands more cheaply and efficiently. Old suppliers (eg, clipper ships around Cape Horn, imported oil, oil-fired electrical plants) are abruptly displaced by the arrival of a railway, heavy-oil plant or massive hydroelectric development.

The earliest and most persistent critics of major projects are usually accountants. Even proposing a project carries substantial financial risk: the Canadian Arctic Gas consortium spent over $100 million before its MACKENZIE VALLEY PIPELINE was rejected in 1977; the Alsands group spent a similar amount before abandoning the oil-sands venture in 1982. In Canada, where the long-term real return on capital has averaged 7%, investors want a potential profit at least 7% higher than the expected rate of inflation. Hence, investors require assurances from governments about tax rules, prices and regulations that will apply. Governments have a parallel concern that the social benefits of a project exceed its social costs, and that the same benefits (eg, oil supply, transportation, employment) could not be obtained more cheaply by other means. For example, megaprojects are generally built in the hinterland but benefit metropolitan centres – sometimes out of the province or even out of the country (*see* CHURCHILL FALLS). Governments must judge whether the boom-and-bust trauma suffered by remote regions is worth the benefit to the industrial heartland.

The calculations of "opportunity cost" and "benefit/cost" are intimately entwined with the basic economics of the projects themselves. During the 1970s the inflation rate for energy projects was a daunting 1.5 times greater than the general rate. With the recession of the early 1980s came the concern that there might not be a demand for the megaprojects' high-priced production when it eventually came to market. Forecasts of annual energy-demand growth in Canada were reduced from as high as 7% to around 2%, with some predictions of zero or negative growth rates for many years. Consequently, several projects were shelved. The collapse of expected energy price increases dimmed enthusiasm for virtually all megaprojects. Long-term national strategy (for energy security, BALANCE OF PAYMENTS, economic infrastructure, defence, etc) can override discouraging economic factors, but such planning demands extraordinarily clear long-range vision, seldom evident among politicians facing election every few years. Federal and provincial elections, such as Manitoba's 1981 campaign, have centered on megaprojects (*see* ENERGY POLICY). Uncertain political support was frequently cited by businessmen as the reason they abandoned oil-sands megaprojects in the early 1980s.

Even after the cancellation in early 1982 of the $13-billion Alsands tar-sands project and the postponement until the mid-1980s of Esso Resources Canada Ltd's $12-billion COLD LAKE heavy-oil project, nearly 200 major, energy-related projects, with a total cost of $226 billion, were planned to start in western Canada between 1982 and 1995. Proposals included completion of a world-scale PETROCHEMICAL complex in BC and Alberta, development of major coal mines, the tapping and transporting of arctic oil and gas, liquefying BC natural gas for shipment to Japan, upgrading heavy oil, adding new electrical production and transmission capability, and increasing railway capacity.

The largest single megaproject underway in 1982 was the $15-billion James Bay hydroelectric development in northern Québec; in 1987 it was the $12-million Darlington nuclear generating station in Ontario. Other proposed megaprojects in eastern Canada included more CANDU nuclear reactors in NB, Québec and Ontario; developing TIDAL ENERGY projects in the Bay of FUNDY, NS; tapping the oil and gas off NS and Newfoundland; building natural-gas pipelines through Québec and the Maritimes; and producing synthetic fuels from Cape Breton coal.

Fort McMurray area 20 July 1973, before work had progressed on the oil-sands project (*courtesy Canada Centre for Remote Sensing/Energy, Mines & Resources Canada*).

Fort McMurray area 10 Aug 1981, showing the massive changes after work on the oil-sands project (*courtesy Canada Centre for Remote Sensing/Energy, Mines & Resources Canada*).

All of these technologies attempt to take advantage of "economies of scale," ie, the larger a facility, the lower its unit cost of production. This was the conventional wisdom for generations of engineers and economists, but much of its validity rests on an assumption of financial, economic and political stability. Amid the uncertainties of the 1980s the tenet was re-examined critically and found wanting for a number of reasons. First, a very large project is vulnerable to malfunction. Thus, it would be unwise to depend too much on one technology (oil-sands projects or CANDUs) that might be shut down completely by some hidden flaw or hazard. The Syncrude project, for example, was plagued in its first years by fires, freeze-ups, breakdowns and accidents that abruptly halved or even cut off its 125 000-barrel/day output. Nearby, the Suncor oil-sands plant suffered the latest of several debilitating times in 1987. Second, smaller projects can be built in modules, with a continuing labour force and design improvements as mistakes are found in earlier models; cash flow from the first units can help pay for subsequent ones (substantially reducing the financial risks), and the timing of additional units can be altered to match shifts in price, demand and competition. Third, the regulatory process is simpler and quicker for smaller projects. Fourth, some technologies (eg, *in situ* oil-sands extraction, high-pressure oil processing) are not notably cheaper on a huge scale. Other technologies (mining, pipelining, railroading) have obvious economies of scale, but even they were being questioned in the new climate of the 1980s.

Some previously ignored concepts, eg, free-running turbines to tap the hydroelectric power of tides and rivers without dams, could revolutionize project engineering in the coming decades. Companies are hedging their bets on megaprojects, eg, "prebuilding" the profitable southern portion of the Alaska Highway gas pipeline and postponing the riskier $40-billion northern portion.

In retrospect, many technologies seem to go through a dinosaur age, an era of eventually untenable gigantism, followed by a focus on smaller, more manageable ventures. The one certainty is that not all the megaprojects on the drawing boards will be built. ROBERT D. BOTT

Megarry, Archibald Roy, publisher (b at Belfast, N Ire 10 Feb 1937). Megarry has been publisher and chief executive officer of the Toronto *Globe and Mail* since 1978 and was responsible for establishing its national edition. Megarry moved to TORSTAR CORP, the owners of the *Toronto Star*, in 1974 as vice-president of corporate development. Four years later, he switched to the *Globe and Mail*, where he maintained that paper's reputation for quality while expanding foreign and business coverage, and introducing 4 new magazines. J.L. GRANATSTEIN

Meier, Rolf Georg Walter, electronics designer, amateur astronomer (b at Bremen, W Germany 24 July 1953; immigrated to Canada 1958). Meier made unique discoveries of 4 new COMETS, all named after him. Educated at Carleton U (B Eng, 1977), he was employed by Mitel Corp. Meier started building his own telescopes in the late 1960s and joined the Royal Astronomical Society of Canada (RASC) 1970. In 1974 he commenced a systematic search for new comets, using the 400 mm telescope of the RASC, and discovered Comet Meier 1978f on 26 Apr 1978, a first for a Canadian astronomer observing in Canada. He was awarded the Chant Medal of the RASC in 1979. He followed up his initial success by additional discoveries in 1979, 1980 and 1984. His total search time for all 4 comets was under 200 hours, a remarkable observational record which he attributes to using a larger aperture than normal in comet hunting. PETER M. MILLMAN

Meighen, Arthur, lawyer, politician, businessman, prime minister of Canada (b at Anderson, Ont 16 June 1874; d at Toronto 5 Aug 1960). As MP, 1908-26; leader of the Conservative Party 1920-26, 1941-42; PM, 1920-21, 1926; and senator, 1932-41, Meighen was a prominent, controversial public figure for nearly 30 years. He was unequalled as a parliamentary debater, combining great knowledge of public business, a sharply analytical and critical mind, a gift for lucid extemporaneous speech and an aptitude for the adversarial atmosphere.

Shortly after graduating from U of T in 1896, Meighen moved to Manitoba and established a law practice at Portage la Prairie. Five years after entering the House of Commons in 1908 he was appointed solicitor general in Sir Robert Laird BORDEN's ministry and 2 years later added the post of secretary of state. In the 1917 Union government he became minister of the interior and one of the Cabinet's dominant members. He was instrumental in devising and defending a number of disputed measures, among them the Military Service Act, the Wartime Elections Act, and bills nationalizing several private transportation companies and uniting them with others in the CANADIAN NATIONAL RAILWAYS. As acting minister of justice in 1919, he was prominent in ending the WINNIPEG GENERAL STRIKE, thus incurring the bitter enmity of part of the labour movement.

Meighen succeeded Borden as PM in 1920 against the advice of most of his fellow ministers, who believed he was temperamentally unsuited and handicapped by his connection with these contentious policies. His one notable achievement in that office came at an imperial conference, where he argued successfully against the British government's plan to renew the Anglo-Japanese alliance. At home, things went from bad to worse in a situation complicated by the rise of a new political force, the PROGRESSIVE PARTY, which attracted much support in the Prairies and rural Ontario. In the general election of Dec 1921 his government was defeated and he became leader of the Opposition to the Liberal administration of Mackenzie KING. During the ensuing 4 years the Conservatives made a strong recovery and in the election of Oct 1925 won a plurality of seats. King was able to retain office with the support of the remaining Progressives until a serious scandal in the Customs Dept was exposed. Faced with a motion of censure that seemed certain to pass, King sought to have Parliament dissolved. When Gov Gen Viscount BYNG refused, King resigned and Meighen again took office. But his government was soon defeated in the Commons and in the resulting election, whereupon he retired as party leader and joined a Toronto investment company. In 1932 PM BENNETT appointed him to the Senate, which he reluctantly left after 9 years to resume the Conservative leadership. His attempt to re-enter the House of Commons in a 1942 by-election failed and, disillusioned with politics, he retired once again to devote himself to his business interests. ROGER GRAHAM

Reading: Roger Graham, *Arthur Meighen,* 3 vols (1960-65); J.L. Granatstein, *The Politics of Survival* (1967).

Arthur Meighen
Ninth Prime Minister of Canada

Birth: 16 June 1874, Anderson, Ont
Father/Mother: Joseph/Mary Bell
Father's Occupation: Farmer
Education: U of Toronto
Religious Affiliation: Presbyterian/United
First Occupation: Teacher
Last Private Occupation: Lawyer
Political Party: Conservative
Period(s) as PM: 10 July 1920 - 29 Dec 1921; 29 June 1926 - 25 Sept 1926
Ridings: Portage la Prairie, Man, 1908-21; 1925-26; Grenville, Ont, 1922-26
Other Ministries: Solicitor General 1913-17; Secretary of State 1917; Interior 1917-20
Marriage: 1 June 1904 to Isabel J. Cox (1882-1985)
Children: 2 boys, 1 girl
Died: 5 Aug 1960 in Toronto
Cause of Death at Age: Heart failure at 86
Burial Place: St Mary's, Ont

(photo courtesy National Archives of Canada/C-5799).

Meighen, Maxwell Charles Gordon, financier (b at Portage la Prairie, Man 5 June 1908), son of PM Arthur MEIGHEN. After studying at RMC and U of T and serving in WWII, Meighen took over the group of investment companies founded by his father. Chairman and director, Canadian General Investments Ltd, in 1961 he entered the consortium of financiers, headed by J.A. MCDOUGALD, that owned the huge Argus Corp. As an Argus director he was also a member of the boards of some of the largest Canadian companies, including Domtar, Massey-Ferguson, Dominion Stores and Hollinger Mines. He resigned from Argus in 1978, when it was taken over by Montegu and Conrad BLACK and H.N.R. JACKMAN. In 1987 he was chairman and director of Canadian General Investments Ltd. JORGE NIOSI

Meisel, John, educator, public servant (b at Vienna, Austria 23 Oct 1923). He is known to academics as a leading student of Canadian politics and to the public as chairman of the CANADIAN RADIO-TELEVISION AND TELECOMMUNICATIONS COMMISSION (CRTC). Meisel was educated at schools in Czechoslovakia and, after his family came to Canada, at U of T and London School of Economics. In 1949 he joined the politics dept of Queen's and, after switching research interests from international relations to politics, he published ground-breaking work on the 1957 and 1962 general elections as well as other studies on the Canadian political system. He served on a number of royal commissions in research capacities, and in Dec 1979 the Clark government named him head of the CRTC. He served there until Oct 1983 and presided over the introduction of pay-TV into Canada. Since 1983 he has been Sir Edward Peacock professor of political science at Queen's. J.L. GRANATSTEIN

Melfort, Sask, City, pop 6078 (1986c), 6010 (1981c), inc 1907, is located in central Saskatchewan, 85 km SE of Prince Albert. The first settlers came to this area in 1892 and began a settlement called Stoney Creek about 2 km SE of the present townsite. In 1902 the settlement was moved to its present location where it was surveyed by the CNR. Mrs Reginald Beatty, the first woman to settle in the district, was asked by railway officials to name the town and chose the name of her birthplace in Scotland. The rail line, which arrived in 1909, made Melfort a trade and cultural centre for the surrounding area. It was incorporated as a village in 1903, as a town in 1907 and a city in 1980. Melfort is the service centre of one of Saskatchewan's richest agricultural areas, the Carrot R valley, a territory that has never known drought or severe crop failure. DON HERPERGER

Melon (*Cucumis melo*), annual, viny plant of the Cucurbitaceae family. The most important cultivated groups are cantaloupe (*C. melo* var. *cantalupensis*), muskmelon (*C. melo* var. *reticulatus*), winter melon (*C. melo* var. *inodorus*) and sugar melon (*C. melo* var. *saccharinus*). Watermelon (*Citrullus vulgaris*) belongs to a different genus of the same family. Melons originated in Asia and were found by Christopher Columbus on Isabella I in 1494. Cantaloupe is grown mainly in Europe. What are known as cantaloupes in N America are muskmelons; they have a pleasant flavour and aroma and can be served as an entrée or dessert. Winter melons ripen late and lack the scent and rough rind of the muskmelon. Melons need warm temperatures and a frost-free growing season of at least 120-140 days; these factors limit their cultivation in Canada to southern Ontario, the OKANAGAN VALLEY of BC, southern Alberta, southern Manitoba, and drier parts of the ANNAPOLIS Valley, NS. A hardy variety of muskmelon, Far North, was introduced by Ukrainian settlers in the southern prairies. To hasten their development, muskmelons may be grown in greenhouses or under cover in the field. Irrigation is important during dry spells, especially in the period up to formation of the melon. Melons are susceptible to wilt diseases and mildew, and to cucumber beetles and aphids.

HUGUES LEBLANC

Melvill Jones, Geoffrey, physiologist, medical doctor (b at Cambridge, Eng 14 Jan 1923). Jones is a pioneer in aviation medical research in Canada, specializing in research on the body's vestibular system (balancing organs in the inner ear) and its role in problems of disorientation in flight environments. He has also studied the brain's ability to adapt to conflicting information from several bodily sensory systems, particularly the relationship between vestibular and visual sensory information. Melvill Jones began his aviation-related medical research as an RAF scientific officer, studying problems in high-altitude respiration and escape, long-duration flying fatigue, and pilot disorientation. In 1961, after coming to Canada, he inaugurated McGill's Aviation Medical Research Unit as its director. He has examined physiological adaptation to zero-gravity among Skylab astronauts and has collaborated in research on physiological zero-g adaptation among space-shuttle astronauts. He has received numerous awards and honours. LYDIA DOTTO

Melville, Sask, City, pop 5123 (1986c), inc 1960, is located 130 km ENE of Regina. Established by the Grand Trunk Pacific Ry in 1907-08, it was named after the president of the GTPR, Sir Charles Melville HAYES, who died aboard the *Titanic*. The community's growth beyond that of others in the area came as a result of its designation as a divisional point by the railway. The impact of the railway was balanced somewhat by its role as a service and processing centre for the poultry, livestock and grain farmers in the area. Despite its diminished role as a CNR service centre, Melville achieved city status in 1960. It is noted as a good sports community with stars such as Sid Abel in hockey and Terry Puhl in baseball going on to the major leagues. The Melville Millionaires won the Allan Cup in 1914.

DON HERPERGER

Melville, Lake, 3069 km^2, is a tidal extension of HAMILTON INLET on the rugged E coast of Labrador. Linked to the inlet on the E by a narrows, the lake extends 140 km inland to its 2 western arms, Goose B and Grand Lk. At places the water reaches depths of 300 m. Circled by rocky mountains and hills, the lake receives several major rivers that drain a large part of Labrador, including the Naskaupi and the CHURCHILL. An air-force base was built at HAPPY VALLEY-GOOSE BAY during WWII; another settlement is North West River, a former trading post. The name refers to Viscount Melville (1742-1811), a prominent British politician.

DANIEL FRANCIS

Melville Island, 42 149 km², fourth-largest of the QUEEN ELIZABETH IS, NWT. Its western half is hilly, with elevations reaching 775 m, and sustains small ice fields. The eastern half is a rolling plateau with elevations generally below 300 m. Vegetation is scant, but well-vegetated broad valleys and coastal flatlands support a relatively high muskoxen population. Caribou numbers are low, owing to recent adverse climatic events. The island was discovered in 1819 by Lt W.E. PARRY, who named it after Viscount Melville, first lord of the Admiralty. Promising natural-gas and oil deposits were found recently on and around the island.

S.C. ZOLTAI

Melville Peninsula, NWT, approximately 400 km long and 100 km wide, joined to the Canadian mainland by Rae Isthmus, is bounded on its W side by Committee Bay and separated from BAFFIN I in the N by Fury and Hecla Str; it faces FOXE BASIN in the E. Uplifted through faulting associated with the Foxe Basin structural depression, it is an erosional remnant of a once widespread sheet of sedimentary rocks that mantled the core of the Canadian SHIELD. It is made up of 2 distinct physiographic regions, with by far the larger part consisting of a dissected plateau that becomes quite mountainous on the W side, rising as high as 900 m. In the NE corner is a narrow, low-relief coastal plain of more recent limestone. The Precambrian material forming the upland is 1600 million years old, metamorphosed and granitized Shield. Most of the rocks have been moderately folded and more intensive folding raised the low mountains in the W. The faults and intrusions associated with the peninsula's general uplift have become the focus of erosion, and steep-walled canyons, 90-175 m deep, have developed. In conjunction with some of the intrusions, formations of iron-ore deposits have been found, assessed as an important addition to Canada's iron-ore inventory. The high concentration of natural uranium in lake sediments and waters of S Melville Pen has been traced to igneous rocks intruded into the Shield bedrock.

DOUG FINLAYSON

Member of Parliament, member of the HOUSE OF COMMONS elected in single-member constituencies. Predominantly from densely populated areas, as a group they have a high level of education and many are lawyers. They are mostly male and most are middle-aged. Most are elected on a party "label" but some may sit as independents. In recent years few have had prior experience, politically, in public office, although many have had local officeholding experience. Their careers are usually short-lived, because of electoral vicissitudes. Policymaking is the domain of Cabinet and the senior public service; MPs as a group have less effect in policy formation, although some MPs claim a strong voice in CAUCUS and in Commons committees. Part of an MP's representative role is responding to the grievances of constituents. There are 282 MPs (1987) but the number will be increased to 295 at the next general election.

ROBERT J. JACKSON

Members of Provincial Legislatures In 1987, 759 Canadians were elected to seats in 10 provincial and 2 territorial legislatures. They are designated as Members of the Legislative Assembly (MLA), with the exception of Ontario where they are Members of the Provincial Parliament (MPP), Québec where they are Members of the National Assembly (MNA), and Nfld and NS where they are Members of the House of Assembly (MHA). Members of legislatures represent constituencies which have different boundaries to those of federal MPs. The largest provincial constituency, in population, is Scarborough N in Ontario (pop 161 000). The smallest is Victoria in NS (pop 5000). Ontario, with 130 seats, is the largest legislature. PEI, with 32 seats, is the smallest. Most members work in legislative buildings constructed 75 to 100 years ago (*see* GOVERNMENT BUILDING). However, the legislatures of Newfoundland, the Yukon and the NWT meet in more modern buildings.

The job of a provincial member is now considered to be full time in the larger provinces. Québec members, followed by Ontario, are the highest paid. Principal work for all "backbench" members is providing services to constituents; policymaking in conjunction with the party caucus in the House; and being members of various committees reviewing legislation.

During the past decade provincial legislatures have gone through a period of considerable change and modernization. Total operating budgets exceed $200 million and more than 3000 employees staff Canada's legislatures. Members in the largest legislatures have as many as 4 full-time assistants. Computers and computer networks are having a considerable impact on the work of members. Legislatures in Québec, Ontario and Saskatchewan have full-time television coverage. Almost all legislatures now have boards or committees of internal economy made up of elected members who are responsible for financial policy and controls, reflecting the independence of the legislature from government.

ROBERT J. FLEMING

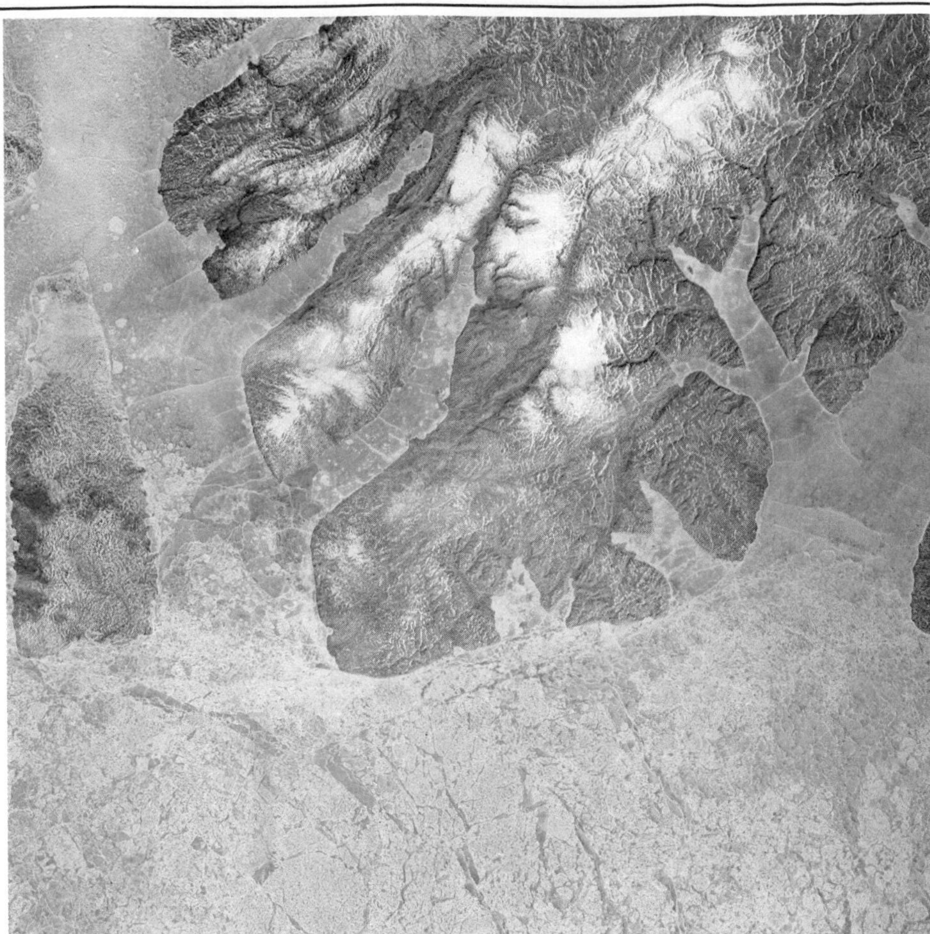

Melville Island, NWT, showing different ice types: dark ice; first year ice; lighter multi-layer ice, various fracture lines and ice flows (*courtesy Canada Centre for Remote Sensing/Energy, Mines, Resources Canada*).

Mémoires de l'Amérique septentrionale, a learned and entertaining natural history of Canada, was the journal kept by Louis-Armand de Lom d'Arce, baron de LAHONTAN, during his travels in New France, 1683-93. Published as vol II of *Nouveaux voyages* (1703), the memoirs duplicate information from vol I, an epistolary travelogue. Lahontan's memoirs describe the geography, native peoples and flora and fauna of the colony, and outline its trade and politics and its importance to Europe. Lahontan's lists and essays, occasionally unreliable, include false accounts of fictitious tribes from the Long R, which he claimed to have discovered; his portrait of the Indian helped to create the image of the "noble savage" popular in 18th-century Europe. The complete *Voyages* went through 13 editions in 14 years, including the author's own English translation (1703; ed R.G. Thwaites, 1905). A facsimile of the 1703 French text was published in Montréal (1974).

MICHÈLE LACOMBE

Memoirs of Montparnasse, autobiography by John GLASSCO (Toronto, New York, 1970). Glassco, born into a prominent Montréal family, and feeling intellectually stifled, cast off a promising future in the establishment. Seeking a less repressive atmosphere, the 17-year-old McGill student arrived in Paris in the 1920s, and quickly became a member of the expatriate literary avant-garde. Candidly declaring himself a hedonist, "sunk in greed, sloth and sensuality," he began confidently to document his experiences, essentially composed of dazzling all-night parties and daring escapades. His memorable impressions of encounters with Morley Callaghan, Gertrude Stein, Ernest Hemingway, James Joyce and Kay

Boyle, meticulously recorded, provide a fascinating glimpse into a long-vanished era. The first chapter was written soon after the events occurred, but the bulk of the *Memoirs* are the vivid recollections of a wiser and older Glassco and are tinged with the artist's melancholic recognition of the end of his youth. DONNA COATES

Memorial Cup, trophy presented for the Canadian championships of major junior hockey teams in national competition. It was presented in Mar 1919 in memory of Canadian hockey players who had died in WWI. The trophy sparked interest in junior hockey across Canada. The Ontario Hockey Assn (OHA) assumed responsibility in the first 2 years. U of T won the first series in 1919. The first victory for a western team was Winnipeg Falcons in 1921. In 1970 junior hockey was divided into 2 classifications, Major Junior and Junior "A." The OHA, Québec Junior Hockey League and Western Canadian Junior Hockey League were placed in the Major Junior category leading to the Memorial Cup.
JAMES MARSH

Memorial University of Newfoundland, St John's, fd in 1925 as Memorial University College, a memorial to Newfoundlanders who died in WWI. Memorial received university status in 1949 after Newfoundland joined Canada. In 1961 it moved from its crowded, centrally located campus to 89 ha on the city's northern outskirts. A second campus, the Sir Wilfred Grenfell College, was opened 1975 in Corner Brook on the island's W coast. Memorial has 6 faculties (arts, science, education, medicine, engineering and business administration) and 9 schools (graduate studies, nursing, physical education and athletics, social work, general studies, continuing studies and extension, music, fine art and pharmacy). Because it is the province's only university, Memorial has to meet a wide variety of needs. It has therefore established a number of special divisions that promote research in areas of particular regional concern. These include the Centre for Cold Ocean Resources Engineering, the Centre for Earth Resources Research, the Archaeology Unit, the Folklore and Language Archive, the Institute for Educational Research and Development, the Labrador Institute of Northern Studies, the Marine Sciences Research Laboratory, the Maritime Studies Research Inst, the P.J. Gardiner Institute of Small Business Studies, the Oxen Pond Botanical Garden. The Institute of Social and Economic Research, the Newfoundland Institute of Cold Ocean Science and the International Reference Centre for Avian Haematozoa. Memorial is the largest university in Atlantic Canada, with high academic standards in teaching and research and a broad, multipurpose program.
SHANNON RYAN

Enrolment: Memorial University, 1985-86
(Source: Statistics Canada)

Full-time Undergraduate	*Full-time Graduate*	*Part-time Undergraduate*	*Part-time Graduate*
9 714	638*	4 092	532

Menaud maître-draveur (1937), novel by Félix-Antoine SAVARD, is the last classic example of the didactic Québec *roman du terroir,* "novel of the land," basing its lyrical descriptions of rural life and its appeal to colonize the interior upon the author's firsthand experiences as a pastor in new settlements near La Malbaie. Savard revisits MARIA CHAPDELAINE (1916), incorporating excerpts into his novel and effectively writing a sequel to Hémon's romance. A farmer who prefers logging, Menaud bemoans the exploitation of Québec's resources by unnamed strangers, encouraging his daughter Marie to marry le Luçon rather than le Délié, who would sell his inheritance to "foreigners." Following his son's death in a log jam, Menaud, rendered insane by his quest to confront the enemy, obsessively tracks the elusive le Délié. Savard revised his poetic novel in 1938, 1944, 1960 and 1964; Alan Sullivan translated the first edition as *Boss of the River* (1947), Richard Howard the 1964 text as *Master of the River* (1976). MICHÈLE LACOMBE

Mennonites, a Protestant religious-cultural group, numbering over 730 000 adult members in 41 countries. Mennonites first arrived in Canada from the US in 1786 and there are now about 100 000 members of Mennonite churches in Canada. They date their separate Christian identity to the ANABAPTIST movement of the early 16th-century Reformation. Baptism (not of infants but of mature voluntary believers) and a communion service, which included foot washing as a symbol of humility and service, were the Anabaptists' only ordinances. The movement soon spread to the northern German states and the Netherlands, where Menno Simons (after whom the Mennonite denomination is named) assumed the leadership in 1536. Through prolific writing, preaching and tireless organizational work he strengthened his people. However, even the peaceful "Mennists" were persecuted and thus scattered in all directions. The Swiss-South German Mennonites went mostly westward, settling in Alsace and the Palatinate and, by the end of the 17th century, in Pennsylvania. The Dutch-N German went mostly eastward, forming settlements in present-day Poland, and by the end of the 18th century in Russia. The Mennonites' relative isolation and self-sufficiency within closed communities, combined with their conviction that religion was a way of life, produced a unique socioreligious culture. Thus the Mennonites who came to Canada, all of whom spoke Germanic dialects, were perceived as a minority group with both religious and ethnic characteristics.

The first migration into Canada brought about 2000 Swiss Mennonites from Pennsylvania to Upper Canada after the American Revolution. They acquired land from private owners in the Niagara Peninsula and in York and Waterloo counties. This group was followed by Amish Mennonites (named after Bishop Jacob Ammon, a conservative leader of the late 17th century). From 1825 to the mid-1870s about 750 settled on crown land in Waterloo County and nearby.

In the 1870s the russification policies of the Russian government caused 18 000 Dutch Mennonites – one-third of the total in Russia – to leave for N America. The promise of land, cultural and educational autonomy, and guaranteed exemption from military services attracted about 7000 of them to southern Manitoba. The opening up of HOMESTEAD lands in the North-West Territories attracted Mennonites from Prussia, Russia and the US between 1890 and WWI. They were joined by many from Manitoba, who established 2 reserves in Saskatchewan, and others from Ontario. Conscription in the US in 1917 brought more Mennonites to the Canadian Prairies. The largest immigration occurred in the 1920s, when 20 000 Mennonites took the opportunity to escape the effects of the Bolshevik Revolution. Most of this group settled on the Prairies. WWII caused over 12 000 Mennonite "displaced persons" to migrate from the USSR and Germany. Most of them settled in urban areas, the most rapidly growing urban community being Winnipeg. In recent decades many Mennonites have emigrated from the US, Mexico and Paraguay.

The basic unit of Mennonite institutional life is the congregation. There are nearly 1000 congregations throughout Canada, tied together in about 30 congregational families of 2 types: those representing older and more conservative traditions whose unity is symbolized by a single membership register and a single bishop (eg, Old Order Mennonite Churches); and those representing newer structures called "conferences" (eg, the Conference of Mennonites in Canada. Most congregational families are members of provincial, national and continental central committees. The headquarters of the Canadian Mennonite Central Committee is in Winnipeg. An annual budget of more than $13 million is applied to foreign and domestic programs which include development, relief and peace projects (*see* PACIFISM; PEACE MOVEMENT). Canadian Mennonite periodicals include the German-language *Mennonite Rundschau, Der Bote* and *Die Mennonitische Post,* and the English-language *Mennonite Brethren Herald* and *Mennonite Reporter.* Two scholarly journals are also published: *Journal of Mennonite Studies* and *Conrad Grebel Review.* Their total circulation is about 45000. Mennonite voluntary associations promote music, the arts, folk and heritage festivals, research and writing, welfare institutions, nursing homes, retirement centres, psychiatric units, insurance and tourism.

Mennonites differ in their attitudes toward innovation in religious and cultural life. Some

Arrival of the first Mennonites in Winnipeg, Man, 1874 (*courtesy Glenbow Archives, Calgary*).

believe that lives of discipleship in communities separated from the world is of the essence. Here attempts are always made to control change. Others insist that penetration of, adaptation to, and involvement in the world is essential to the Christian mandate. Among both the Swiss and the Dutch are conservative groups that have successfully perpetuated traditional rural modes of life, unchanging clothing styles, the German language and liturgical forms. The Old Order Amish and Old Order Mennonites have also succeeded in continuing a traditional farming style. Other Mennonites have adjusted and integrated with society. Mennonites are no longer limited to their Swiss and Dutch traditions and ethnic backgrounds. There are many Canadian Mennonites of French, Chinese, Indian and Anglo-Saxon extraction, and about 40% of Mennonite marriages in 1981 were mixed.

As a church, emphasizing separation from the world and social nonconformity, Mennonites frequently resisted the influence of state-run public schools. In the late 1980s about 10% of 18 000 Mennonite elementary children were in 50 private schools; some 2400 secondary (grades 7-13) students were in 10 private high schools; and over 1000 post-secondary students were in 5 church colleges. A further 5 BIBLE SCHOOLS instruct nearly 300 students annually. Students seeking training for the ministry usually go to one of 4 Mennonite seminaries in the US.

Politics have represented a problem for Mennonites. On the one hand, they discourage any involvement in an evil world in which force and violence are used even as instruments of the state. On the other hand, they encourage application of the ethics of Jesus: love, peace and justice in all areas of life, including potentially the state. Today, most Mennonites vote. A number serve in elected office and many more are active as civil servants, public school teachers, etc.

Except for conservative minorities, Mennonites in Canada are undergoing rapid change; but a strong emphasis on the family and the role of religion, specific programs to keep the young people (youth organizations, camps, choirs, service programs), special schools and a dynamic congregational life minimize the losses to the larger, secular community.

FRANK H. EPP AND RODNEY J. SAWATSKY

Reading: Frank H. Epp, *Mennonites in Canada*, 2 vols (1974, 1982).

Menou d'Aulnay, Charles de, sea captain, governor of ACADIA (b in France *c*1604; d at Port-Royal [Annapolis Royal, NS] 1650). Although best known for his disputes with rival Acadian governor Charles de Saint-Étienne de LA TOUR, d'Aulnay was a determined and resilient colonial promoter who grappled over a 15-year period with the intractable problems associated with the colonization of Acadia. Of noble descent, he saw naval service as lieutenant to his cousin Isaac de RAZILLY, and went to Acadia 1632 when Razilly became governor. On Razilly's death in 1635, d'Aulnay assumed his powers and was later formally commissioned to govern Acadia. La Tour claimed similar powers, and their rivalry was only ended by d'Aulnay's military victory on the Saint John R 1645, in which he ruthlessly executed the defenders. Military supremacy did not solve for d'Aulnay the problem of how to bring real social and economic stability to the colony. After his accidental death by drowning in 1650, Acadia lapsed again into internal strife. His most lasting achievement was the establishment of the Acadian people at PORT-ROYAL.

JOHN G. REID

Mens Rea, "guilty mind" (Lat), refers to the mental state that must generally accompany a prohibited act before it can legally be considered a crime. Different offences require different mental states; some require intention, eg, to commit theft; some knowledge, eg, that property possessed is stolen. In the case of some offences (viz, those of "strict" and "absolute liability"), no mens rea requirement exists.

LEE PAIKIN

Mental Health, in the early years of the mental-health movement, was often defined as the absence of symptoms of mental illness. Since that time, attempts have been made to relate mental health to a concept of psychological well-being and to certain capacities of individuals, eg, the capacity to perceive reality "objectively," to be flexible in meeting new situations and to understand another's point of view. However, no clear line divides the mentally healthy from the mentally unhealthy, and in addition, the definition of mental health is relative and is dependent on cultural context. The characteristics of a mentally healthy person in one milieu may seem very different from those of a mentally healthy person in another. The World Health Organization's definition of health as "a state of complete physical, mental and social well-being, and not merely the absence of disease or infirmity" implies that perfect "health" is an unattainable ideal, and this point of view is also reflected in the concept of mental health, as no person will exhibit all the symptoms of mental health all the time. Freud's definition of health as the capacity "to work and to love" is widely accepted by mental-health specialists as simple and accurate, and does not reflect the legal or moral considerations which often colour attempts to describe mental health.

Hippocrates was one of the first writers to challenge the belief in supernatural causes of mental illness, a belief that had prevailed since ancient times. Hippocrates claimed that mental disease had a physiological and natural basis. An astute observer, he described in clinical detail a number of mental conditions now known as phobias, mania, depression and paranoia. By the Middle Ages, however, attempts to explain mental illness through rational mechanisms were replaced by theories of demonology and witchcraft. Those who opposed the habit of attributing mental disorders to possession by the devil included Johann Weyer (1515-88), considered the father of PSYCHIATRY, and Paracelsus (1493-1541). Philippe Pinel (1745-1826), director of 2 institutions in Paris for the mentally ill, was one of the first reformers to advocate a humane approach to mental patients. In England the Society of Friends (Quakers) supported the work of reformer William Tuke (1732-1819) who established a country retreat for the mentally ill, who, although treated kindly, were expected to undertake manual labour. In the 19th and 20th centuries the work of Sigmund Freud revolutionized the psychological understanding of individuals and the concepts of mental health.

Mental Health in Canada In 1714 the HÔTEL-DIEU in Québec provided a ward for women who were mentally ill and later took in about 12 men, but treatment of the mentally ill both in New France and British N America was primarily a family responsibility, and patients who could not be cared for at home were placed in jails and poorhouses under deplorable conditions, eg, overcrowding, poor sanitary conditions, inadequate food and heating, and no intervention or treatment. The mentally ill, often caged or kept in barred rooms, were thought to be morally unfit and were treated essentially as sinners. Asylums for the insane were opened in 1835 in Saint John, NB, and in 1841 in Toronto. The latter, which was begun in an abandoned jail, was transferred to a wing of the Parliament Buildings and finally to headquarters at 999 Queen Street.

Changes in care in Canada and the US were initiated by Dorothea L. Dix (1802-1887), Richard M. BUCKE, Charles K. CLARKE, Clifford W. Beers (1876-1943) and Clarence M. HINCKS (1885-1964). Dix, a Massachusetts schoolteacher, wrote, lectured and informed the public and legislators about the deplorable conditions in mental institutions. She was successful in influencing a number of state legislatures either to establish or improve their mental institutions, and because of her efforts a mental hospital was built in St John's in 1885. She also lobbied the Nova Scotia legislature and oversaw the building of a hospital for mental patients in that province. Dr Richard Bucke was appointed superintendent of the Asylum for the Insane in Hamilton in 1876 and a year later of the asylum in London, Ont. He believed mental illness was a "failure of the biological process by which mankind adapts to change." In his attempts to reform the crude treatment of mentally ill patients he abandoned the practice of pacifying the inmates with alcohol, ceased to "restrain" the patients, opened an infirmary to treat physical ills, and inaugurated regular cultural and sports events in which the patients were encouraged to participate.

Dr Charles Clarke was an assistant superintendent at Hamilton asylum in the early 1880s, and later superintendent of the asylum at Kingston, Ont. By 1887 he had changed the asylum from a jail to a hospital and was instructing nurses and attendants in the care of the mentally ill. He ceased to restrain inmates. By 1893 he was advocating that the term "asylum" be dropped and that special hospitals be constructed for the mentally ill.

A Connecticut engineer and founder of the mental-health movement in N America, Clifford Beers had suffered an episode of mental disorder at the age of 18 while a sophomore at Yale University. At one point he was hospitalized in the Hartford Retreat, which had been founded by Dr Eli Todd 71 years earlier. He was also housed in other psychiatric institutions, and was aware of the appalling treatment and physical abuse suffered by patients. On his release, he wrote *A Mind That Found Itself,* in which he described his experiences. In 1908, the year his book was published, he founded the National Committee for Mental Hygiene. Dr Clarence Hincks was born in St Mary's, Ont, the only child of a schoolteacher and a Methodist minister. His interest in mental health was partly the result of his own experiences with severe depression. In 1918, with Beers's help, he organized the Canadian National Committee for Mental Hygiene, which later became the Canadian Mental Health Association. Both organizations were influential in promoting mental-health issues in both the US and Canada. After WWI, he toured asylums across Canada, and was shocked by what he found. In 1920, with Beers, he organized the International Committee for Mental Hygiene (which in 1948 became the World Federation for Mental Health, headquartered in London) and helped plan the first International Congress on Mental Hygiene, which was held in Washington in 1930. Hincks was one of the first physicians to recognize the value of prevention and of treating sufferers of mental illness before they were incapacitated. His work led to the development of child-guidance clinics for the early detection and prevention of mental illness. Perhaps because of the psychoanalytic focus on the development of children or because of Hincks's conviction that mental health began in childhood, academic interest in child development began in earnest during this time. Hincks persuaded benefactors to fund the St George's School for Child Study at U of T and the McGill University Nursery School and Child Laboratory in Montréal in 1925. A psychologist, Samuel

The Toronto asylum was first located in an abandoned jail, then a wing of the Parliament Buildings before being moved to this facility on Queen Street (*courtesy National Archives of Canada/PA-112173*).

Laycock (1882-1971), came under the influence of the charismatic Hincks during one of Hincks's visits to the West. He became professor of educational psychology in 1927 at University of Sask and director of education for the Mental Hygiene Committee in 1929.

WWII profoundly affected attitudes towards mental health. The medical examinations of recruits revealed that thousands of apparently healthy adults suffered mental difficulties. This knowledge affected public attitudes towards mental health, and stimulated research into preventive measures and methods of treatment. It has also led to a better understanding of the emotional needs of children and of the role of stress in causing mental disorder. Indeed, it is commonly held today that symptoms of much mental illness are a response to everyday or unusual stresses and are probably transitory.

Treatment of Mental Illness Mental illness is the most pervasive health problem in Canada. Universal medicare in Canada includes coverage for psychiatric illness (as well as any other medical condition), but all mental-health problems are not necessarily psychiatric problems, and there has been a significant increase in demand for care for the full range of behavioural and adjustment problems. Mental illness may be treated by family physicians, psychiatrists, psychologists, social workers and psychiatric nurses, but these professional groups have not met all of the mental-health needs. Specific problems, such as those involving ALCOHOLISM or SMOKING, have led to the development of very large and sophisticated self-help groups, eg, Alcoholics Anonymous, founded in 1935. There are other groups whose aim is the development of healthier life-styles or healthier dietary habits and who offer structured programs and group support to achieve these ends.

In the past 2 decades, research towards evaluating the psychotherapeutic, behavioural and biochemical interventions for mental-health problems has increased. For example, both effectiveness and cost studies of home treatment versus hospital psychiatric treatment have recently been carried out in Montréal. Findings from these studies have allowed a clearer understanding of the usefulness of such interventions and have pointed the way toward innovative approaches.
JOHN T. GOODMAN

Mer de l'Ouest ("Western Sea"), originally the goal of EXPLORATION during the French regime, was the stuff of wishful thinking obligingly corroborated by Indians. Initially thought to be an inland sea somewhere W of the Great Lakes, it gradually blended in imagination with the Pacific. The search for the Mer de l'Ouest had a useful function, since the argument that exploration must be financed by the FUR TRADE served ambitious traders well in their efforts to secure monopoly privileges from the royal authorities. The imaginary Mer de l'Ouest finally came to rest in the region around Lk Winnipeg, where, in the middle of the buffer zone marked off by the Cree and Assiniboine around the English at Hudson Bay, LA VÉRENDRYE, his sons and their successors established a network of trading posts after 1730.
TOM WIEN

Merasty, Angelique, *see* BIRCH-BARK BITING.

Mercantile Bank of Canada has head offices in Montréal. The Mercantile Bank operates a general banking business through 13 branches and one representative office. As of Oct 1983, it had annual sales or operating revenue of $476 million, assets of $4.1 billion (ranking 18th among banks and financial institutions in Canada) and 826 employees. In 1986 the bank became wholly controlled by the National Bank of Canada.
DEBORAH C. SAWYER

Mercantilism, economic theory that there is a fixed amount of wealth in the world and that a nation's prosperity depends on its success in accumulating wealth by exporting more than it imports. European nations of the 17th-19th centuries attempted to put it into effect through commercial policies designed to produce a favourable balance of trade, through acquisition and development of colonies as exclusive markets and sources of raw materials, and, in England, through NAVIGATION ACTS, which made the shipping and marketing of colonial goods the monopoly of British merchants and shippers. Mercantilism was intended to benefit European powers, but it was not wholly disadvantageous to the colonies, providing a protective mantle for early development. However, it has been argued that mercantilist policies left colonial economies dependent on staple production (*see* STAPLE THESIS) and obstructed their industrial development. Though less rigid than the French system, English mercantilism brought no fundamental changes to the colonial economy after the CONQUEST of New France (1760). The system was dismantled with the repeal of the CORN LAWS in 1846 and the Navigation Acts in 1849, and the elimination of duties that had favoured colonial timber. JAMES MARSH

Mercier, Honoré, lawyer, politician, premier of Québec (b at St-Athanase, Qué 15 Oct 1840; d at Montréal 30 Oct 1894). A founder of the PARTI NATIONAL, he was the first Québec political leader to assert that the Québec government was the national government of Quebecers, and is therefore considered a father of Québec nationalism.

A Liberal, he helped found the short-lived Parti national in 1872, in an attempt to win electoral support by dissociating the Liberals from the PARTI ROUGE, and won election to the House of Commons for Rouville. Defeated federally in St-Hyacinthe in 1878, he won the provincial election in that riding the following year. In 1883 he became leader of the provincial Liberal Party, and in 1885 he headed a group of Liberals and dissident conservatives who rejected their parties' respective stands on the Louis RIEL affair. At the head of the revived Parti national, Mercier was the first Québec leader to win large popular support; by keeping alive the feelings aroused by Riel's hanging, he and his party won the election held late in 1886 after the Conservatives failed to cling to power and he took office as premier 29 Jan 1887. In office he settled the issue of the JESUITS' ESTATES as well as the quarrels that surrounded the creation of a distinct university in Montréal. Mercier's government encouraged railway building and colonization of undeveloped lands, creating a department of agriculture and colonization in 1888, with Curé Antoine LABELLE as deputy minister. Mercier also called the first interprovincial conference of premiers since Confederation and led the movement to force the federal government to recognize the principle of provincial autonomy in administrative and fiscal matters. Implicated in the BAIE DES CHALEURS SCANDAL, Mercier was removed by the lieutenant-governor in Dec 1891. A subsequent investigation could not prove that Mercier was personally involved and he was re-elected in 1892 provincial elections, but his party was soundly beaten. A man of considerable style and a noted orator, Mercier collected various foreign honours during his premiership.
DANIEL LATOUCHE

Map by Delisle and Buache, 1752, showing the imaginary Mer de l'Ouest in the lower right (*courtesy National Archives of Canada/NMC-21056*).

Mercure, Pierre, composer, producer, bassoonist, administrator (b at Montréal 21 Feb 1927; d accidentally near Avallon, France 29 Jan 1966). Mercure, always seeking a new, multimedia language, learned French music and became an orchestrator with Claude CHAMPAGNE. He studied in Paris, notably with Nadia Boulanger and Darius Milhaud and in 1951, in Tanglewood, Mass, was introduced to dodecaphony by Luigi Dallapiccola. Mercure was the first producer of TV music programs on Radio-Canada. Influenced by Pierre Schaeffer during a second stay in Europe, he turned to ELECTROACOUSTIC MUSIC and, after organizing the Semaine internationale de musique actuelle (1961), returned to Europe to study electronic music. He left a legacy of ballet music (eg, *Structures métalliques I* and *II* and *Tétrachromie)* and of chamber, electronic, vocal and orchestral music. His *Cantate pour une joie* has been performed several times, eg, during the Olympic Games in Montréal in 1976. HÉLÈNE PLOUFFE

Mercury (Hg), silvery white metal, also known as quicksilver. It is the only common metal existing as a liquid at ordinary temperatures (melting point: -38.87°C) and is a good conductor of heat and electricity. Mercury and its compounds have been used for centuries, eg, in the making of vermillion, a red paint, and in early treatments for syphilis. Mercury was used to extract gold from rock and sand. Production of caustic soda and chlorine in mercury cells is gradually being replaced because of mercury's toxicity. Because it has a high rate of thermal expansion, it is used extensively in thermometers. Its primary use is in electric switches, mercury-vapour lamps, batteries, catalysts and dental and agricultural compounds. Mercury and many of its compounds are toxic and mercury chloride is used as an insecticide and rat poison. Mercury is recovered primarily by roasting ores containing the MINERAL cinnabar, a red mercury sulphide. Historically, the major producers have been Spain, the US, Italy and Yugoslavia. Virtually all mercury produced in Canada was obtained from the Pinchi Lk deposit in north-central BC, which closed in 1976.

Mercury is a cumulative poison and becomes increasingly concentrated in the food cycle of aquatic life and may reach dangerous levels in fish. Highly toxic levels can cause irreversible damage to the nervous system and the brain. The phrase "mad as a hatter" refers to the occupational disease resulting from contact with the mercury used in the early manufacture of felt hats. Mercury poisoning has occurred among native people dependent on fish and much of the freshwater fishery in Canada has been destroyed by mercury pollutants such as industrial wastes and agricultural insecticides *See also* GRASSY NARROWS.

J.J. HOGAN

Meredith, John, painter (b at Fergus, Ont 24 July 1933), brother of William RONALD. John Meredith Smith (known professionally since 1951 as John Meredith), studied at the Ontario College of Art 1950-53, and had his first solo exhibition in 1958. Meredith's work is informed by a belief in the human presence as the ultimate subject of art; it is based on knowledge gained through experience rather than theory, on instinctive understanding. In early works (1958-62), abstract vertical stripes, dark and tonal in colour, take on first vegetal and then human connotations, projecting a pervasive sense of primordial mystery. Paintings from the period 1962-66 generally present large-scale images and brilliant colour, often used to optical and psychological effect. Coloured-ink sketches then became the basis for paintings; his work at the same time became increasingly complex, concentrated and obsessive. These exceptional paintings of the later 1960s achieve a forceful presence, not through scale alone but also through an insistent, overall interaction of colour, related and recurring motifs and linear patterning. Works of the early 1970s frequently evoked the Orient through their titles and subtle asymmetries, but by the 1980s his paintings became simplified, looser and more open. In 1986 the Region of Peel Art Gallery in Brampton, Ont, held a 30-year survey of his work.

Reading: M.L. Fleming, *John Meredith: Fifteen Years* (1974); I.M. Thom, *John Meredith: Drawings* (1980).

Meridian, First or Principal, is the line of longitude forming the main backbone of the Dominion Lands Survey System – a plan devised in 1869 for the subdivision of the territory about to be purchased by the federal government from the HBC into a rectangular system of square townships numbered northerly from the FORTY-NINTH PARALLEL and E and W of a given meridian. The Principal Meridian, sometimes referred to as the Winnipeg Meridian, ran northward from a point on the 49th parallel 10 miles (16 km) W of Pembina, where astronomical observations had been made to determine the exact position of the parallel in that location. The point was selected to avoid the settled cultivated areas taken up along the Red R prior to the survey. It has a longitude of 97°27′28″ W. The other initial meridians are spaced at intervals of about 4° of longitude and are numbered westerly and easterly from the Principal Meridian.

N.L. NICHOLSON

Merrickville, Ont, Village, pop 994 (1986c), 984 (1981c), located on the Rideau R, 55 km SW of Ottawa. It was founded by the LOYALIST William Merrick, a millwright, to utilize the local falls for gristmills and sawmills, and became a major lock point on the RIDEAU CANAL. It remains one of the best preserved 19th-century Ontario villages, with over 100 designated historic buildings, including one of 4 blockhouses (1826-32) built to defend the canal, the Merrick sawmill and tavern, and the house in which Col BY lived. Harry F. McLean, railway contractor and eccentric philanthropist, was a longtime resident. The local economy is based on 2 foundries, a pottery, 2 rehabilitation institutions and tourism. K.L. MORRISON

Merritt, BC, City, pop 6180 (1986c), 6100 (1981c), inc 1911, is located in the Nicola Valley of south-central BC, at the junction of the Coldwater and Nicola rivers, about 12 km S of Nicola Lk and 100 km by road S of Kamloops. The Thompson and Okanagan tribes of the Interior SALISH first inhabited the area. Fur trader Alexander ROSS visited the region in the winter of 1813. The great fur brigades, with hundreds of horses carrying packs of fur between Ft Kamloops to the N and Ft Langley on the lower Fraser R, used routes through the valley 1848-60. Settlement began and cattle ranches were established in the 1860s. Coal, discovered in the 1860s, was being mined here in the early 1900s. The town of Forksdale was renamed Merritt in 1907 after William H. Merritt, promoter of the failed Nicola, Kamloops and Similkameen Ry. Merritt became a mining boom town and prospered until the Great Depression, when it went into receivership. The province ran community operations until 1952. The growth of the lumber industry and the opening of large COPPER mines in the region in the 1950s and 1960s made Merritt the commercial centre of the Nicola Valley. The region around Merritt is famous for its fishing lakes and the rolling hills of the cattle country. Nearby Douglas Lk Ranch is the largest in Canada at 220 000 ha and over 15 000 head of cattle. JOHN R. STEWART

Merritt, William Hamilton, soldier, businessman, politician (b at Bedford, NY 3 July 1793; d at Cornwall, Canada W 5 July 1862). "A Projector," as he styled himself, he epitomized what John Beverley ROBINSON called the defining characteristic of American society, the "anticipating spirit." Merritt considered enterprise and commercial activity as the quintessential aspect of the American and English character. He believed that Providence had "ordained that Nature should do her part & leave it to the engenuity [*sic*] of Man so to improve." Confident that the "mind is never satisfied" and certain that industry rather than idleness conferred "the greatest peace of mind," Merritt proposed and undertook policies and projects to transform Upper Canada into a great commercial emporium. Although he was an assemblyman in pre- and post-union Upper Canada and president of the Executive Council in the second Baldwin-LaFontaine administration, politics were secondary, at best complementary, to his policies on public works, transportation and trade. He is best remembered for his role in the construction of the WELLAND CANAL (chartered 1824). The idea likely arose from his plan to connect the water of the Welland R to Twelve Mile Creek to provide water for his mills. Merritt enlisted government support, raised funds and supervised the canal project. He was also very influential in promoting early railway projects, also with government aid.

ROBERT L. FRASER

Messer, Don, and the Islanders For close to 40 years the sounds of "old-time" music meant Don Messer and the Islanders. Donald Charles Frederick Messer (b at Tweedside, NB 9 May 1909; d at Halifax 26 Mar 1973) started playing the fiddle at age 5, learning basic skills and traditional melodies from family and friends. By age 7, he was performing at local dances and social events. In 1929 he began his radio career with a show on CFBO, Saint John. In Sept 1939, he moved to Charlottetown where he formed "The Islanders" for station CFCY. The personnel of the Islanders changed many times but there were several constants: bass player, Julius "Duke" Nielsen; clarinetist and announcer, Ray Simmons; drummer, Warren MacRae; and pianist, Waldo Munro. The singers were Marg Osburne, who joined in 1947, and Charlie Chamberlain, with Don since 1934.

In 1959 "Don Messer's Jubilee" started a 10-year run on CBC TV. Its cancellation (1969) met with great protest and the show was syndicated from CHCH TV, Hamilton, until Messer's death. Messer's TV and radio shows, his extensive personal appearances across the country, combined with more than 30 LPs, brought traditional fiddle and dance music into homes across Canada. His shows provided exposure for younger artists, including Stompin' Tom CONNORS, Fred McKenna, Vic Mullen, Graham Townsend and Catherine McKinnon. Several collections of his music have been published. His papers and music are now kept in the NS Public Archives, and one of his fiddles is on display in the Country Music Hall of Fame in Nashville. RICHARD GREEN

Metallurgy is the art, science and technology of making metals and alloys into forms suitable for practical use. Some metals are found in their "native" or free elemental form (eg, GOLD, SILVER, COPPER), and a limited number can be produced from seawater, notably magnesium. However, most metals are extracted from naturally occurring MINERAL compounds found at or near the earth's surface (*see* MINING). In Canada most nonferrous metals (eg, copper, ZINC, NICKEL, LEAD) are produced from sulphide ores. The steps in extracting metals from their ores are mineral processing, which processes mined ore into concentrates and tailings (wastes); chemical extraction, which separates concentrates into metals and slag and leach residues; and refining, which produces refined metal and by-products.

Mineral Processing

Mineral processing involves the chemical and physical treatment of the ore to upgrade the valuable mineral component before the metal-extraction stage. This processing eliminates as much of the waste portion as possible. Two principal steps are involved: comminution and separation.

Comminution is liberation of the desired mineral (eg, nickel sulphide, copper sulphide) from the waste (gangue) by crushing and grinding. The ore is crushed, by jaw crushers and cone crushers. The crushed ore is then ground in ball mills and rod mills to particle sizes less than 75 μm. Grinding is usually carried out in water to minimize dust. The degree of grinding depends on the size and distribution of the valuable mineral in the ore. Many of the sulphide deposits in Canada require grinding to a product size less than 30 μm.

Separation of the desired mineral from the gangue produces an enriched portion (concentrate) and a discard portion (tailings). Separation is performed by taking advantage of differences in the physical and chemical properties of the minerals, such as density, radioactivity, magnetism, electrical conductivity and surface reactivity. The most commonly used property, surface reactivity, has proven to be very selective, particularly for sulphide ores. The separation process based on this property is called flotation. In flotation, air is bubbled through the pulp (a mixture of finely ground ore and water) in a tank which is agitated vigorously to break the air into fine bubbles. The valuable mineral is picked up by the bubble and floated to the surface to form a stable froth, which is skimmed off. The flotation column is a Canadian invention and a major advance in 1980s flotation technology, it is typically 13 m high by 1-2 m in diameter.

The concentrates produced through mineral processing are drastically reduced in bulk and weight compared to the original ore. For example, 100 kg of copper ore containing as little as 1% metal in the form of a sulphide can be upgraded to 4 kg of concentrate containing 25% copper, a reduction of 96% in the weight of the initial ore.

Chemical Extraction

Unlike metal oxides, metal sulphides cannot be directly reduced to the metallic state. Extraction processes are often referred to as pyrometallurgical (high-temperature processes, eg, smelting, roasting, distilling, etc, involving furnaces) or hydrometallurgical (aqueous-solvent processes, usually operating near room temperature). Most metal-extraction processes use both high temperatures and aqueous solution treatments. There are a number of paths which can be followed to produce metals from sulphide concentrates.

Copper In the case of copper, the principal mineral in the concentrate is chalcopyrite ($CuFeS_2$).

Pouring liquid aluminum, casting centre at Grande Baie, Qué (*courtesy Alcan Aluminium Limited*).

The traditional process for producing copper from this concentrate involved roasting, smelting, converting and refining. Roasting is the heating of the sulphide concentrates in air to temperatures of about 600-700°C to oxidize partially the iron sulphides to iron oxides and sulphur dioxide gas. The solid products of the roaster together with a flux (silica) are then melted in a furnace (smelting) to separate and remove the oxide components as slag and the enriched copper-iron sulphides as matte. The liquid matte is transferred to a converter where the remaining iron and sulphur are removed by air blown through the matte (converting). The iron is oxidized, then slagged with the addition of silica; the sulphur forms sulphur dioxide gas. The resulting product is "blister" copper of more than 98% purity. The impurities are present in the concentrate and remain in the copper during processing. Some of these impurities (eg, zinc, tin, iron and sulphur) may be removed by a fire-refining step, in which air is blown into the molten copper to oxidize the impurities selectively to form a slag or oxide gas. The slag is then skimmed off and the copper is covered with charcoal to prevent further oxidation. At this stage the copper contains approximately 1% oxygen. Traditionally, most of this oxygen was removed by inserting and agitating a freshly cut tree trunk below the copper surface (poling). Today, natural gas is usually used to reduce the oxygen content to about 0.13%. This grade of copper, referred to as "tough pitch" copper, is sold to manufacturers. Sometimes precious metals are present in the copper in very small amounts. These cannot be removed by fire refining and the copper must undergo an additional refining process, electrolytic refining.

In electrolytic refining, fire-refined copper is cast in the form of a large block, which acts as an anode. The block is placed into a copper sulphate solution (an electrolyte, ie, solution in which electrical current is carried by ions) together with a thin sheet of high-purity copper, which serves as the cathode. Direct current is passed through the anode, electrolyte and cathode, resulting in the transfer of copper from the anode to the electrolyte as copper ions and the migration of these ions to the cathode surface, where pure copper is deposited. The precious metals do not dissolve but drop to the bottom of the refining cell. They are referred to as anode slime. The slimes are collected periodically for the recovery of gold, silver and PLATINUM group metals. The refined cathode copper is melted and cast into shapes for industrial use. There are 3 copper refineries in Canada: at Montréal (NORANDA MINES LTD), one of the largest in the world; Copper Cliff, Ont (International Nickel Company of Canada); and Timmins, Ont (Kidd Creek Mines Ltd).

In the late 1940s, INCO LTD developed a new technology, "flash smelting," to smelt copper concentrates at Copper Cliff. By using pure oxygen, INCO technicians were able to ignite the sulphide concentrates spontaneously, thus combining the roasting and smelting steps. This process requires no fuel for smelting and also permits the efficient collection of sulphur dioxide gas for liquefaction. INCO was the first company to use pure oxygen in metal extraction and to produce liquid sulphur dioxide from sulphide concentrates. In the late 1960s, Noranda developed a continuous copper-making process using a single furnace (the Noranda Reactor). This reactor is a horizontal cylinder in which roasting, smelting and converting operations are combined. The concentrates and flux are fed in at one end and the surface of the bath is kept turbulent by oxygen-enriched air (23.5% O_2) blown through tuyeres (nozzles) located at the side of the reactor. The matte or copper produced is tapped from one side and the slag from the end of the vessel. The slag contains substantial amounts of copper and is treated by a mineral-processing operation in which it is crushed as it cools slowly. The copper-containing components are floated to produce a 40% copper slag concentrate for recycling to the reactor. This process has been in operation at Noranda, Qué, since 1973.

Nickel In Canada, 2 main methods are used to produce nickel: one is a leaching process; the other is based on roasting, smelting and converting processes similar to those used in copper production. In the leaching process, developed by Sherritt Gordon Ltd and used at Fort Saskatchewan, Alta, the sulphide concentrate is mixed with ammonia leaching solution and oxygen (compressed air at 689-758 kPa) and heated to 80°C. The nickel, copper and COBALT present in the concentrate form soluble ammonia complexes. The solution containing the dissolved metals is separated from the residue. The copper is precipitated out from the solution as copper sulphide by increasing the acidity of the solution and by use of hydrogen sulphide. Metallic nickel is then produced in powdered form by reducing the solution with hydrogen gas at 3445 kPa and 200°C. The nickel-free solution is then treated with hydrogen sulphide to recover cobalt as cobalt sulphide. The metal-free solution is evaporated to form ammonium sulphate, which is sold as fertilizer.

Three variations of the roasting, smelting and converting route are practised in Canadian plants. At INCO's operation in Thompson, Man, the nickel sulphide concentrate is roasted, smelted and converted to remove iron and part of the sulphur (as in the copper process). The product, nickel sulphide (Ni_3S_2), is cast into anodes and dissolved electrolytically, using a sulphate chloride electrolyte, to produce pure cathode nickel. The anode residues are treated for the recovery of elemental sulphur and precious metals. This is a unique process patented by INCO.

Since the nickel concentrate produced at INCO's Sudbury plant also contains some copper, the product after roasting, smelting and converting contains both nickel sulphide (Ni_3S_2) and copper sulphide (Cu_2S). By slowly cooling a molten mixture of these 2 sulphides in an insulated mold over a period of 3 days, it is possible to produce large crystals of nickel sulphides, copper sulphides and a small amount of copper-nickel alloy containing most of the platinum metals. The nickel sulphide is separated from this mixture by grinding and flotation. The metallic alloy fraction is removed magnetically and treated for recovery of nickel and precious metals.

The remaining nickel sulphide is then oxidized to form nickel oxide by a roasting operation at approximately 1050°C. The nickel oxide is then reduced either with coke (a dense substance distilled from coal) in a reverberatory-type furnace or with hydrogen in a fluid-bed roasting furnace to produce metallic nickel. The nickel is further refined electrolytically at a plant at Port Colborne, Ont. An alternative high-pressure carbonyl process has been developed by INCO and has been in operation since 1973 at their Sudbury plant. In this process, carbon monoxide gas is passed over nickel at a pressure of 6895 kPa and a temperature of 170°C. A nickel carbonyl gas is formed which is purified by distillation. The purified nickel carbonyl is then decomposed at 200°C to form high-purity nickel pellets or powder and carbon monoxide gas which is recycled.

Falconbridge Nickel Mines at Falconbridge, Ont, process their nickel-copper sulphide concentrates by roasting, smelting and converting. The product from the converting operation, a copper-nickel sulphide matte, is shipped to Norway for metal recovery. The sulphur dioxide gas from the roasters is used to produce sulphuric acid.

A number of nonferrous metals are produced from oxide minerals. Two examples are given.

Magnesium is produced in Canada by Chromasco near Renfrew, Ont. The process, invented and developed in Canada during WWII by L.M. PIDGEON, is referred to as the Pidgeon Process. Calcined dolomite (MgO.CaO) is mixed with ferrosilicon and then placed in a tubular stainless steel retort which is evacuated to approximately 0.003 kPa. One end of the retort is heated to about 1180°C; the other is cooled. The magnesium vapour that forms condenses in the water-cooled end as a dense, coherent deposit. The magnesium crystals are removed, melted and cast into ingots.

Uranium In Canada URANIUM is extracted from various minerals such as pitchblende, uraninite and brannerite. The ore containing these minerals is crushed, ground and treated with sulphuric acid to dissolve the uranium. The solution containing the uranium is separated from the solid residue and purified by ion exchange or solvent extraction techniques. The uranium is then precipitated out from the solution as an ammonium or magnesium diuranate. This material is filtered, dried and shipped to the refinery in Blind River, Ont, where it undergoes further purification to produce nuclear-grade compounds such as uranium oxide (UO_2) and uranium fluoride (UF_6).

Environmental Considerations

Canadian metallurgical plants are generally located in sparsely inhabited areas near the mines. As a result, ecological problems were not given much consideration until recently. In general there were no facilities to capture or fix the sulphur dioxide gases; all gases were vented through stacks to the atmosphere. However, with the greatly increased knowledge of the influence of poisonous gases on the environment and in the face of increasing public apprehension, the control of pollutants from metallurgical plants is of utmost concern to modern industry (*see* AIR POLLUTION). The principal pollutants from nonferrous operations in Canada are particulate materials and the sulphur dioxide gas which is responsible for ACID RAIN. The control of solid particulate matter has been brought about by elaborate gas-cleaning equipment such as venturi scrubbers, cyclones, filter bags and electrostatic precipitators. The control of smelter gases is much more difficult. Approximately 98% of the sulphur which enters the plant in the form of sulphides leaves as sulphur dioxide gas. This emission, through the formation of acids and other compounds in the atmosphere, can cause serious damage to human health, vegetation and property. In order to protect the environment it is necessary to capture the sulphur dioxide and convert it to a marketable product or to an inert solid waste which can be safely stored. The most common conversion treatment is to produce sulphuric acid. However, depending on the economics and concentration of the sulphur dioxide gas, other products include elemental sulphur, liquid sulphur dioxide, ammonium sulphate and gypsum. In Canada sulphuric acid and liquid sulphur dioxide are produced by nonferrous smelters. *See also* IRON AND STEEL INDUSTRY; MINING; MINERAL RESOURCES. J.M. TOGURI

Reading: J. Neely, *Practical Metallurgy and Materials of Industry* (1979); A. Street and W. Alexander, *Metals in the Service of Man* (1979).

Metamorphic Rock is one of the 3 major classes of ROCK comprising the Earth's crust, the others being SEDIMENTARY and IGNEOUS ROCKS. Metamorphic rock has been transformed, while in the solid state, by pressure, temperature and deformation. The original MINERAL content, textures or structures have been changed, from those of the rock's sedimentary or igneous parent material, to others that are characteristic of the pressure, temperature and strain of the metamorphic process. No substantial changes of bulk rock composition take place. Two types of metamorphism occur. In kinetic or dynamic metamorphism, mechanical forces (eg, shearing, crushing) produce cataclastic rocks. In true metamorphism, changes of temperature or temperature and pressure produce recrystallized rocks. The latter form of metamorphism takes place at temperatures of 100-1000°C and at pressures of a few hundred to 100 000 atmospheres. In nature, these conditions are achieved in rocks that have been carried to great depths in the Earth by the forces of PLATE TECTONICS.

The names given metamorphic rocks usually highlight aspects of texture, mineral content and physical conditions. Gneiss [Ger, "spark," for its sparkling appearance] is a coarse-grained rock with distinct layers made up of different proportions of minerals. Many gneissic rocks are also foliated, ie, show alignment of leaves or layers of flat or tabular minerals (eg, mica), or of elongate minerals (eg, hornblende). Schist [Gk, "divided"], a strongly foliated rock, is named for the ease with which it can be split into thinner sheets. Mica and chlorite impart the foliation to schist. Phyllite [Gk, "leaf"] is a very fine-grained, foliated rock in which the alignment of plates of minerals can be recognized, although individual grains are difficult to discern without a microscope. Slate [Fr, "splinter"] is a rock, ordinarily derived from mudstone (shale formed by consolidation of mud), that has a well-defined cleavage cutting across the original sedimentary layers. These textural names may be applied to metamorphic rock of any composition and primary origin. Pelite [Gk, "clay"] is a term applied to rocks originally rich in clay minerals and feldspars. Because any rock may become metamorphosed, various adjectival modifiers can be applied to the names of metamorphic rocks. Migmatite [Gk, "mix"] is a metamorphic rock that has a mixed appearance because part of the material has melted during heating. Migmatitic gneisses are common in rocks of the Canadian Shield, which has experienced many episodes of metamorphism at very high pressures and temperatures.

The minerals present in metamorphic rocks can be used to deduce the pressures and temperatures that prevailed during metamorphism. These minerals, different from minerals of unmetamorphosed rocks, form because the change of conditions makes the original low-temperature and low-pressure minerals unstable together. Chemical reactions occur that produce new minerals. Generally speaking, rocks of higher metamorphic grade are coarser grained and have experienced higher temperatures and pressures than rocks of lower grade. For example, the more common metamorphic minerals of pelitic rocks include andalusite, kyanite, sillimanite, staurolite, garnet, cordierite, chlorite, biotite and muscovite, as well as quartz, which is found in most rocks of all origins. Kyanite is characteristic of high pressure; andalusite, of low pressure. Sillimanite is stable only at high temperature, and the others take part in complex reactions in response to changes in pressure and temperature.

The same parent rock, eg, a common pelite or mudstone, would show different metamorphic characteristics if subjected to low, intermediate or high pressure. Thermal metamorphism at low pressure is normally caused by heat given off at the contact of an igneous intrusion and is referred to as contact metamorphism. Plutonic igneous rocks, positioned in the crust at 1-8 km depth, provide a source of heat that can transform pelites: first, chlorite appears, followed, with increasing temperature, by biotite, garnet, cordierite, andalusite and sillimanite. The rocks so formed are referred to as hornfels [Ger, "horn rock"] because of their very fine-grained, hornlike texture. For example, a biotite-cordierite-andalusite hornfels could have been produced at approximately 700°C and 2000 atmospheres. Rocks of this sort may be found in many places in Canada, eg, near the Amulet-Dufault ore body near Noranda, Qué, and in the contact metamorphic rocks of BC's coastal ranges. If the same material were subject to high pressure, it would be changed progressively into chlorite schist, chlorite-biotite schist, biotite-garnet-staurolite schist, garnet-staurolite-kyanite schist, and finally to a sillimanite-bearing gneiss. Among the best Canadian examples are those found in the Shuswap Metamorphic Complex, between Revelstoke and Quesnel Lk, BC.

A volcanic rock would develop a different mineralogy because of its different bulk composition. Chlorite would dominate, biotite would be less common and, at higher grades (500°C upward), amphibole would be the major mineral. These so-called amphibolites are common in the metamorphosed volcanic rocks of the Canadian Shield. A special trajectory is achieved in subduction zones where extremely deep burial, accompanied by a slow rise of temperature, produces a spectacular blue amphibole called glaucophane. These "blueschists" are found only in rocks formed in the last 120 million years and are thus restricted in Canada to the CORDILLERA. The best examples are found near Pinchi Lk, BC.

Polymetamorphic rocks have been subjected to several episodes of metamorphism. Such rocks reveal their complex histories through their textures. Minerals of later episodes can be found growing on top of older minerals, and foliation that originated in an earlier metamorphic period can be seen included in prophyroblasts produced in a later episode. A prophyroblast is a mineral grain that grew in the solid state during metamorphism, enveloping and enclosing mineral grains that had formed previously. Prophyroblasts contrast with phenocrysts, large crystals in igneous rocks which crystallized from molten magma. *See also* GEOLOGICAL REGIONS. H.J. GREENWOOD

Metcalf, John, author (b at Carlisle, Eng 12 Nov 1938; Canadian citizen 1970). Metcalf received a BA from U of Bristol and lived in Eng until 1961 when he immigrated to Canada. He taught school in Montréal. In 1964 Earle BIRNEY published 8 of his stories in *Prism International* and in 1969 had 5 stories published in *New Canadian Writing*. Metcalf has published 3 collections of short stories, *The Lady Who Sold Furniture* (1970), *The Teeth of My Father* (1975) and *Adult Entertainment* (1986); 2 novellas, within *Girl in Gingham* (1978); 2 novels, *Going Down Slow* (1972) and *General Ludd* (1980). He has also edited numerous anthologies of short stories, edited 9 high school texts and has written one book of literary criticism, *Kicking Against the Pricks* (1982). A witty satirist, Metcalf is a master of the short story and is relentless in his jibes against the Canadian literary establishment. He has had 5 writer-in-residence appointments, including one in Bologna, Italy (1985).

SHARON DRACHE

Metcalf, Thomas Llewelin, lawyer, politician, judge (b at St Thomas, Ont 21 Feb 1870; d at Winnipeg 2 Apr 1922). A successful lawyer and partner in a Winnipeg law firm soon after his call to the bar in 1894, Metcalf developed into a well-read legal scholar. At the early age of 39 he was appointed judge of King's Bench, and was elevated to the Manitoba Court of Appeal in 1921. Metcalf was frequently chosen to serve as a royal commissioner; as such, he drafted a major revision of the Criminal Code in 1902. In 1919 he presided at the WINNIPEG GENERAL STRIKE trials. A mirror of the establishment of his day and an extremely able jurist, Metcalf knew better than most what had to be done to secure the conviction of the strike leaders and he did it well. D.H. BROWN

Metcalfe, Charles Theophilus, first Baron, governor general of British N America 1843-45 (b at Calcutta, India 30 Jan 1785; d at Malshanger, Hampshire, Eng 5 Sept 1846). He was educated at Eton and in 1801 joined the Indian Civil Service, where he earned a reputation as a talented and judicious administrator. He succeeded to his father's baronetcy in 1822, and later was appointed provisional governor general of India. Between 1838 and 1842, he served as governor of Jamaica.

Metcalfe arrived in Canada early in 1843 to replace Sir Charles BAGOT, with instructions to make no concessions towards RESPONSIBLE GOVERNMENT, the principle on which was founded Bagot's existing Reform ministry headed by Louis-Hippolyte LAFONTAINE. In Nov 1843 he provoked his ministers' resignation by making appointments without their advice. For some 9 months he carried on the government with the aid of a single minister, Dominick Daly. In Aug 1844 he formed a Conservative administration headed by William Henry DRAPER, and was sustained at the polls by a small majority in Nov 1844.

Afflicted with cancer of the face, Metcalfe laboured under the most difficult personal circumstances, yet he devoted long office hours to official business. He moved the capital to Montréal, negotiated pardons for the rebels of 1837-38 who had been deported to Australia, consolidated Lord SYDENHAM's work in the civil service and gave generous financial support to many cultural and philanthropic causes. In Nov 1845 the progress of his disease giving him no other choice, he resigned his office and left for England. As a reward for his service, he had been created Baron Metcalfe of Fern Hill early in 1845, but his titles became extinct when he died. JACQUES MONET, S.J.

Meteor, Meteorite, Impact Crater The solar system contains many small objects travelling in individual orbits about the SUN. When such a particle collides with Earth, interaction with the upper atmosphere produces a flash of light called a meteor, which typically endures for less than one second near heights of 90 km. Large particles produce spectacular meteors and, in rare cases, part of the object survives to reach Earth's surface and is then called a meteorite. Huge meteorites are not slowed much by the atmosphere and their violent collisions with Earth blast out "impact" or "meteorite" craters.

The vast majority of meteors are fragments of COMETS. When a comet is heated during passage near the sun, particles separate from the nucleus and the more stony material withstands the effect of solar heating and continues in its own orbit, which resembles the comet's orbit. Over thousands of years, the particles disperse around the entire orbit and into a stream of appreciable width. When Earth crosses such a stream, a meteor shower can be seen, and one observer can typically see 5-50 meteors per hour, all meeting Earth from the same direction and with constant velocity. A shower may last only hours or many days and is likely to occur every year. With time, streams disperse so that the meteors blend into a general background of sporadic meteors. Meteors enter the atmosphere at speeds of 11-72 km/s.

RADAR and spectroscopic meteor observations have been Canadian research specialties. A radar beam reflects from the column of electrified gas produced by a meteor's passage; the method is sensitive for very small particles. A meteor's spectrum can be recorded photographically or by television techniques, and spectrum analysis (ie, SPECTROSCOPY) reveals which atoms are abundant in the particle and hence, indirectly, something of the chemical composition of comets.

Except for lunar samples, meteorites provide our only chance to study material from space by laboratory techniques. Most meteorites are "stones," with a thin, black fusion crust; about 5% are "irons," composed of a nickel-iron alloy; a smaller number are "stony-irons." Analysis of meteorites yields vital clues about the early history of the solar system because some have had relatively simple chemical and thermal histories. It is not clear whether any large chunks of cometary material are strong enough to survive impact with Earth's atmosphere. Most meteorites appear to be derived from asteroids by mutual collisions, but at least 3 small ones are fragments blasted from the moon by meteorite impacts there, and a few are suspected to have come from Mars in the same manner. Their orbits appear to have been modified by Jupiter's gravitational field in tens of millions of years to permit collision with Earth. About 3000 different meteorites are known, of which nearly 50 have been found in Canada. Observations with a network of cameras in western Canada indicate that a meteorite of at least 100 g falls somewhere in Canada daily, but very few are ever recovered.

Impact craters are formed by the expanding shock wave when a giant meteorite, weighing hundreds to millions of tonnes, strikes the ground at high velocity. The MOON and several other planets and satellites retain impact craters for very long periods, but on Earth EROSION usually removes the surface evidence in a few million years. Subsurface rock, however, is permanently damaged by the shock wave and can be used to identify very ancient craters. A major program to study impact craters was begun during the 1950s by C.S. BEALS, the Dominion Astronomer. Two dozen features in Canada, ranging from 3 to 95 km in diameter, have been confirmed as impact craters in this pioneer study, of which the Nouveau-Québec Crater is the most recent.

IAN HALLIDAY

Reading: D.W. Sears, *The Nature and Origin of Meteorites* (1978).

Canadian Meteorite Craters

Name	*Latitude*	*Longitude*	*Diameter (km)*
Nouveau-Québec, Qué	61°17′	73°40′	3
Brent, Ont	46°05′	78°29′	4
Manicouagan, Qué	51°23′	68°42′	100
Clearwater LkWest, Qué	56°13′	74°30′	32
Clearwater Lk East, Qué	56°05′	74°07′	22
Holleford, Ont	44°28′	76°38′	2
Deep Bay, Sask	56°24′	102°59′	12
Carswell, Sask	58°27′	109°30′	37
Lac Couture, Qué	60°08′	75°18′	8
West Hawk Lk, Man	49°46′	95°11′	3
Pilot Lk, NWT	60°17′	111°01	6
Nicholson Lk, NWT	62°40′	102°41′	12
Steen R, Alta	59°31′	117°38′	25
Sudbury, Ont	46°36′	81°11′	140
Charlevoix, Qué	47°32′	70°18′	46
Mistastin Lk, Lab	55°53′	63°18′	28
Lk St Martin, Man	51°47′	98°33′	23
Lk Wanapitei, Ont	46°44′	80°44′	8
Gow Lk, Sask	56°27′	104°29′	5
Lac La Moinerie, Qué	57°26′	66°36′	8
Haughton, NWT	75°22′	89°40′	20
Slate Is, Ont	48°40′	87°00′	30
Montagnais, NS	42°53′	64°13′	30

Meteorology is the science that studies the atmosphere and atmospheric phenomena, using data about temperature, humidity, cloud, wind, etc. Its ultimate aim is to explain the structure and functioning of the atmosphere using the basic laws of PHYSICS. The major theoretical divisions are physical and dynamic meteorology (very closely related and often coupled under the title atmospheric physics) and synoptic meteorology. CLIMATOLOGY is the branch of meteorology most concerned with WEATHER, CLIMATE and CLIMATE CHANGE.

Physical Meteorology

Physical meteorology links meteorology and physics in studies of 3 core topics: electromagnetic radiation, meteorological thermodynamics and cloud physics. Related topics include stratospheric physics, atmospheric electricity, optics and ACOUSTICS.

Radiation Solar radiation is received by Earth mostly as visible and near-infrared light. About 30-35% is lost to space by reflection from clouds and the Earth's surface. Most, however, is absorbed by the Earth's surface and re-emitted as infrared radiation, which is absorbed by water, carbon dioxide (CO_2) and pollutants in the air. In the long term, the solar radiation received by Earth and its atmosphere at any point is balanced by infrared radiation emitted to space. Temporary imbalances, eg, the summer surplus and winter deficit in incoming solar radiation in Canada, result in large seasonal temperature changes, except where moderated by oceans. Radiative exchange processes are of central importance in computer models for long-range WEATHER FORECASTS and climate change. Radiation is used extensively in REMOTE SENSING of weather elements from satellites, aircraft and surface instruments.

Meteorological Thermodynamics assumes that air is a mixture of dry air and water vapour, each characterized by temperature, pressure and density, interrelated in an equation of state. Temperature variations cause pressure changes that drive the winds. Local cooling causes condensation and the release of latent heat. Complex interactions among the state variables, clouds, winds and radiation are studied with the aid of the laws of thermodynamics and computer simulation.

Cloud Physics is the study of cloud and precipitation particles and the physical processes that take place in natural and artificial clouds. Water vapour condenses on tiny hygroscopic particles called condensation nuclei to form cloud and FOG droplets. At temperatures far below freezing, water vapour condenses on soil particles and other freezing nuclei to form ice crystal clouds. In favourable circumstances, droplets and crystals grow into raindrops and snowflakes, or even hailstones, by collision and coalescence and by transfer of water vapour from droplets to crystals in a mixed cloud (*see* ICE). Scientific experiments on modification of clouds, fog and precipitation for purposes of rainfall enhancement, HAIL suppression, visibility improvement and forest-fire suppression have been conducted in Canada with mixed results since about 1950 (*see* RAINMAKING).

The stratosphere (upper atmosphere) imposes thermodynamic constraints on air motions in the weather layer (troposphere) below, and acts as a reservoir for gases and fine particles that influence radiation streams. LIGHTNING, ionization and the air-earth current are elements of atmospheric electricity. Electrical processes are thought to be important in the physics of clouds and precipitation. Atmospheric optics and acoustics embrace studies of transmission, reflection, refraction and diffraction of light or sound. The results are applied to such phenomena as RAINBOWS, mirages, scintillation, wind sounds and echoes, and to the use of light and sound in remote sensing as in laseror acoustic RADAR, cloud photography and the sonic anemometer-thermometer. K.D. HAGE

Dynamic Meteorology

Dynamic meteorology is the science of atmospheric motions. Because the Earth's atmosphere is a complex physical system subjected to a number of external influences, such as heating and cooling by the land and ocean masses, a wealth of phenomena involving air motion are observed. The largest is the belt of westerlies, ie, winds blowing from W to E, circling the Earth in the middle latitudes. These westerlies are normally disturbed and forced to wander northward and southward in a snakelike fashion. The core of this meandering current, the jet stream, normally located 10-12 km above sea level, can have winds of over 300 km/h. The wavy structure of the jet stream is caused by the deflecting effect of large mountains such as the Rockies, by heating or cooling by the underlying surface and by travelling vortices measuring as much as a few thousand kilometres in diameter. These vortices can be viewed as clockwise or counterclockwise circulations superimposed on the main westerlies and causing the latter to be deflected around them. Some of the larger vortices can remain nearly stationary for periods of several days; smaller, weaker vortices are swept downstream by the jet current. There is, therefore, an intricate interplay between the jet stream and the vortices, each affecting the other in ways that depend on their relative strengths and configurations.

Near the Earth's surface the circulation is dominated by the vortices because the jet stream becomes feeble at low altitudes. These are the systems seen on sea-level weather maps on which are drawn isobars – lines connecting points of identical pressure. In the Northern Hemisphere, clockwise vortices have a high central pressure (anticyclones), while counterclockwise vortices have a low central pressure (cyclones); in the Southern Hemisphere the opposite circulations around "highs" and "lows" are observed. Lows are normally associated with areas of cloud and, often, precipitation; highs are usually accompanied by clear skies. Far less frequent but much more violent is the hurricane, or typhoon, one of the most intense and feared storms. Ranging in size from about 100-1000 km, they are normally found only in the tropics and subtropics. On a still smaller scale is the THUNDERSTORM, with a typical dimension of 5-10 km, and the destructive TORNADO, typically having a diameter of a few hundred metres and winds estimated at up to 500 km/h.

Dynamic meteorology uses the laws of hydrodynamics and thermodynamics to investigate various types of atmospheric circulations. The former describe how various forces, eg, gravity acting on a parcel of air, will affect its velocity; the latter provide information on the temperature change that results when a certain amount of heat is added or extracted from the air. The procedure may be most easily visualized if the atmosphere is subdivided into a large number of imaginary volumes (cubes or similar shapes). If all forces acting on the volume and the velocity of the air are known, it is possible to compute the displacement of the air over a period of time. Similarly, if at a given instant the temperature inside a given volume is known and the amount of heat entering or leaving it can be determined, it is possible to compute what the temperature inside the volume will be some short time later. This is fundamentally the method used to produce weather forecasts by electronic computers. Calculations are most accurate when volumes are small; hence, forecasts for large regions, such as a continent or hemisphere, are feasible only on powerful computers.

JACQUES DEROME

Synoptic Meteorology

Synoptic meteorology is the analysis of meteorological data, obtained more or less simultaneously from a large geographical area, in order to present a comprehensive and nearly instantaneous picture of the state of the atmosphere. Frequently, data will be obtained over an extended period so that the development of meteorological systems may also be studied. Synoptic meteorology is very closely related to physical and dynamic meteorology and to general climatology, and may be considered a synthesis of these disciplines. Phenomena of interest to the synoptic meteorologist occur on many spatial and temporal scales. Major hemispheric circulation patterns (including jet streams) in the middle and upper troposphere (lower atmosphere) typically span 10 000 kilometres or more and may persist for weeks or months. These major circulation patterns tend to control and interact with smaller-scale phenomena, eg, cyclones and anticyclones.

Cyclones are vortices having a relatively low central pressure. At the Earth's surface, the air tends to spiral inward toward the centre of the cyclone where it is forced to rise. Since the rising air will be cooled by adiabatic expansion (ie, expansion that occurs without the addition of heat) at a rate of about 1°C per 100 m, some of the water vapour will condense to form cloud droplets. If there is sufficient moisture and if the air ascends high enough, precipitation will occur. Anticyclones have a relatively high central pressure. Near the Earth's surface, the air generally spirals outward from the centre. Near the centre of an anticyclone, the air is generally subsiding; consequently, clouds tend to dissipate and fair weather is frequently observed.

Cyclones and anticyclones occur in middle latitudes and are one of the principal means by which heat and moisture are redistributed throughout the atmosphere. Solar heating in equatorial regions and cooling in polar regions will create strong horizontal thermal gradients. These gradients represent sources of potential energy which, under suitable conditions, may become available for conversion into kinetic energy. It is now generally accepted that cyclones form in order to accomplish this energy conversion. During the period of development (cyclogenesis), a cyclonic wind field will be initiated (increase in cyclonic kinetic energy). This will occur at the expense of the thermal gradient (decrease in potential energy). At the same time, the kinetic energy is also being destroyed by friction and other dissipative processes in the atmosphere.

Synoptic meteorology is used in weather forecasting to follow the development and evolution of cyclones and anticyclones, as well as a myriad of associated structures such as air masses and fronts (boundaries between dissimilar air masses). In this task the meteorologist is assisted by mathematical models of the atmosphere which are run on digital computers. This interaction between the synoptic meteorologist and computers is the essence of modern weather prediction.

M.E. TRUEMAN

Meteorology in Canada

The main agency in Canada responsible for weather services is the Atmospheric Environment Service of the federal Department of the Environment. The Service has the primary responsibilities for observing and forecasting the weather and disseminating this information to the Canadian public. Its mandate also includes the provision of information on sea ice, the sea-state, air quality and the provision of climatological services. It further carries out applied research on a wide variety of environmental and atmospheric topics, such as climate change, long-range forecasts, acid rain, and the prediction of intense maritime winter storms.

Current and past weather conditions and short- and long-range forecasts are distributed by the service through 9 forecast centres and 64 weather offices, located in most of the major population centres across Canada. Most weather information is available to the general public through telephone dial-in services, dedicated cable-TV channels, Weatheradio broadcasts and computer access for special users.

The Canadian Forces, in close collaboration with the Atmospheric Environment Service, is responsible for special weather and oceanographic services for its military operations in Canada and abroad. The Forces' Weather Service provides weather and ocean data and special forecasts for such diverse activities as para-drops, arctic maneuvres, anti-submarine patrols by aircraft and ships, mid-air refuelling of fighter aircraft and other military activities.

Private industry in Canada, offers specific meteorological services in support of a wide range of economic activities. Several companies provide weather, sea- and ice-state observations and forecasts for offshore petroleum and gas exploration. Others specialize in such areas as air quality, remote sensing, computer graphic display systems and the dissemination of appropriate information through the media. Several provincial government departments are involved in some meteorological and climatological services.

Atmospheric science programs at the university level are directed at pure and applied research and offer several traditional degree courses. The meteorological research activities are supported through federal subvention programs from the Atmospheric Environment Service, the National Science and Engineering Research Council, provincial governments and private industry. Projects focus on climatological studies, atmospheric chemistry, cloud physics, boundary layer studies, numerical weather prediction, remote sensing of the atmosphere, and the physics of severe summer and winter storms. Undergraduate and graduate degree programs are offered at the following universities: Dalhousie, McGill, Québec at Montréal, Toronto, York, Alberta and British Columbia. The Université du Québec à Montréal offers its programs in French only.

Employment as a professional meteorologist in Canada, such as a weather forecaster, requires graduation from a recognized university with at least an undergraduate degree in meteorology or a degree in physics or engineering combined with a one-year diploma or certificate program in meteorology. Most research positions, however, require either a master's or doctorate degree. A suitable undergraduate program consists normally of at least 3-and-a-half courses in physics, 4-and-a-half courses in mathematics and computer science, and 5 courses in meteorology.

The Atmospheric Environment Service provides an intensive 6-month operational training program for qualified university graduates in either English (Toronto) or French (Montréal). Upon successful completion, these intern meteorologists are then posted as forecasters to a major civil or military forecast centre.

Meteorological technicians form the largest component of those employed in meteorology in Canada. The Atmospheric Environment Service alone employs almost 1000 technicians at more than 100 locations across the length and breadth of Canada, including the High Arctic. These technicians are typically involved with duties in such areas as surface weather (observe, record and transmit weather data), aerological (measure upper atmospheric data using gas-filled balloons with attached instruments), ice (observe ice conditions on board ship or aircraft), presentation (provide weather information to users – pilots, seamen, farmers, radio, TV, public), climatological (data processors, provide services to clients) and inspection functions.

Meteorological technicians are also employed by the Canadian Forces, private industry and the universities. The basic qualification for a position as a technician is normally graduation from a secondary school, but many have more education at the college or university level.

The Canadian Meteorological and Oceanographic Society is the organization which has as its aim the advancement of meteorology and oceanography in Canada. Founded in 1939 as a branch of the Royal Meteorological Society, it evolved into the Canadian Meteorological Society in 1967, and in 1977 the Society broadened its scope to include oceanographers. The Society publishes 2 refereed journals, *Atmosphere-Ocean* and the *Climatic Bulletin*. It also publishes the quarterly magazine *CHINOOK* and the bi-monthly *Newsletter*. Membership is around 1000 and is open to non-Canadians. HANS VAN LEEUWEN

Reading: L.J. Batten, *Fundamentals of Meteorology* (1979); H.J. Spiegel and A. Gruber, *From Weather Vanes to Satellites* (1983).

Methodism, originally a movement within the Church of England in Britain, led by John Wesley (1703-91), who encouraged personal holiness and a disciplined (hence "methodical") Christian life. It was distinctive in its Arminianism, the belief that individuals are free to accept or reject God's grace, and that it is possible to attain "perfection" (the overcoming of a will to sin) in this life. The movement was first represented in what is now Canada by one of Wesley's followers, Laurence COUGHLAN, who began to preach in Newfoundland in 1766. Yorkshire settlers around Chignecto, NS, in the 1770s were the first sizable group of Methodists in the Maritimes. William BLACK, of the next generation, became the greatest Methodist preacher and organizer in the Atlantic colonies. Following the arrival of LOYALIST Methodists after the American Revolution he worked with the American Methodist Episcopal Church, but before long he began to recruit preachers from England and in 1800 Methodists in the Maritimes joined the English Wesleyan Conference. Subsequent immigration strengthened ties with England, making Maritime Methodism dependent on English policies, deferential to dominant Anglican elites, and conservative. Not until 1855 did Maritime Methodists gain partial autonomy, in the new Conference of Eastern British America.

Methodism exercised its strongest influence in Upper Canada. Methodists were among the Loyalist founders and many more among "late loyalists" who flocked into Upper Canada before the WAR OF 1812. With them came Methodist Episcopal "saddle bag preachers" whose zeal and adaptability made them highly effective in frontier conditions. After the war, UC Methodists laboured increasingly under suspicion of being "pro-American" and in 1828 they sought a remedy by severing their American connections. In 1833 they negotiated a union with the more conservative English Methodists who had first entered the colony in 1817. The resulting Wesleyan Methodist Church fell apart in 1840 but was renewed in 1847. Methodists who rejected the union formed a continuing Methodist Episcopal Church in 1834 and attempted to maintain close ties with their American counterparts. Continued English immigration brought more evangelical

Interior of the gallery of the Methodist Meeting House in Hay Bay, Ont, built in 1792 (*photo © Hartill Art Associates, London, Ont*).

groups to UC: Primitive Methodists (1829), Bible Christian Church (1831) and New Connexion Methodists (1837).

Reflecting its Anglican origins, Methodism retained the sacraments of baptism and Holy Communion but placed more emphasis on evangelical preaching and the necessity for individual conversion. The warmth of Methodist services owed much to hearty congregational singing, especially of the hymns of Charles Wesley. Methodists were nurtured in their faith and discipline by the weekly "class meeting." In the pioneer societies of N America the "camp meeting," often lasting several days, was a highly emotional experience for participants. Later, with success and wealth, the church became less rigid in both doctrine and discipline and its services more formal and sedate.

Under Egerton RYERSON, founding editor of the *Christian Guardian*, Methodists became involved in UC politics as a result of their determination to deny the C of E's claim to be the colony's established church (*see* ANGLICANISM). Support for religious and civil equality did not lead to political radicalism and Ryerson's early sympathy for William Lyon MACKENZIE and the Reform Party soon waned. In both the REBELLIONS OF 1837 and the 1844 election, when loyalty was an issue, Ryerson and most Methodists followed a moderate path. Its concern for community life made the Methodist Church the most "Canadian" of denominations and encouraged Methodists to view their church as a nation-building force. Inspired partly by the forces leading to CONFEDERATION, the Wesleyan Methodist Church, the Conference of Eastern British America, and the New Connexion Church united in 1874, and in 1884 the Methodist Episcopal Church and the smaller Methodist bodies were added to form the Methodist Church. The Free Methodists, who entered from the US in 1876, were few and have remained separate. The new Methodist Church was governed by a national quadrennial conference and annual area conferences, with the participation of laymen (but not women) at all levels. It continued earlier missions among Canadian Indians in several regions and conducted overseas work in Japan (1873) and W China (1892).

Methodist commitment to education was expressed in Upper Canada Academy (1836), Cobourg, UC (Victoria College after 1841); MOUNT ALLISON Academy (1843), Sackville, NB, (a university after 1862); and Wesley College (1888), Winnipeg, which joined with the Presbyterian Manitoba College to form United College (1938). Secondary schools included Belleville Seminary (1857), later Albert College (1866); Stanstead Wesleyan College, Qué (1873); Alma College, St Thomas, Ont (1877); and Mount Royal College, Calgary (1910).

With the settlement of western Canada the Methodist Church endeavoured to hold the allegiance of Canadians migrating westward and of British settlers, and to promote the assimilation to Protestant Canadian culture of the thousands of non-Anglo-Saxons who poured into the West before WWI. This endeavour was closely associated with the SOCIAL GOSPEL. Many Methodists saw increased state intervention in economic and social life as essential in establishing the Kingdom of God on Earth. The Methodist Church and most members were vociferously patriotic during WWI, a struggle they believed would purge the nation and prepare the way for a new social order. At the end of the war several church bodies adopted Christian socialist platforms, but subsequent rejection of such policies testified to the church's dominant conservatism. When the Methodists entered the new UNITED CHURCH OF CANADA in 1925, they carried both radical and conservative traditions with them. At that time the church had 2061 ministers, 418 352 members, and many adherents. MARGARET E. PRANG

Reading: M. Bliss, "The Methodist Church and World War I," *Canadian Historical Review* XLIX, 3 (1968); G.S. French, *Parsons and Politics* (1962); J.W. Grant, "Canada," in N.B. Harmon, ed, *Encyclopedia of World Methodism* (1974).

Methye Portage, *see* PORTAGE LA LOCHE.

Métis, one of several historically variable terms (*michif, bois brûlé, chicot,* halfbreed, country-born, mixed blood) used in Canada and some parts of the northern US to describe people of mixed N American Indian-European descent.

It is important to define specific meanings for the term as used in this discussion, while cautioning that writers, past and present, have not achieved consensus on the matter. Written with a small m, *métis* is an old French word meaning "mixed," and it is used here in a general sense for people of dual Indian-white ancestry. Capitalized, *Métis* is not a generic term for all persons of this biracial descent but refers to a distinctive sociocultural heritage, a means of ethnic self-identification, and sometimes a political and legal category, more or less narrowly defined. (For example, Alberta's Métis Betterment Act of 1938 defined Métis as persons "of mixed white and INDIAN blood having not less than one-quarter Indian blood," not including those people already defined under Canada's INDIAN ACT as treaty or nontreaty Indians.) This complexity arises from the fact that biological race mixture (Fr, *métissage*) by itself does not determine a person's social, ethnic or political identity. Many N American whites have some Indian ancestry, and rates of European genetic admixture among status-Indian groups in eastern and central Canada range in some instances from 20 to over 40%. Biologically, *métissage* has gone on since earliest European contact, but over time and in different areas people of that ancestry have grown up and lived out their lives in a vast variety of circumstances, leading them and their descendants to be categorized and to classify themselves by many different criteria.

On Canada's Atlantic seaboard, Métis families and communities were identifiable in the 1600s, although not classified according to race. Early and often casual unions between European fishermen and native women from Acadia to Labrador produced uncounted progeny who matured as Indians among their maternal relatives. Those among the MALISEET were known as "Malouidit" because so many of their fathers came from St Malo on the Brittany coast of France. In Acadia, many French took Indian wives, and some communities became largely Métis. The *capitaines des sauvages* who served the French governors as interpreters, intermediaries and distributors of annual presents to the Indians were commonly of mixed parentage.

Métis traders, *c*1872-75 (*courtesy National Archives of Canada/PA-4164*).

Some such offspring were born of formal church marriages, as Acadian families such as the Denys and d'Entremonts forged both kinship and trading ties with the MICMAC. During the 17th century French officials supported such marriages in hopes of better converting the Indians and building up the population of New France. "Our young men will marry your daughters and we shall be one people," Samuel de CHAMPLAIN reportedly told his Indian allies, and subsequent administrators continued to encourage those mixed unions which were church sanctified.

Problems arose, however. Both the Indians and the French traders who sojourned among them had a distressing tolerance for unions unblessed by Christian rite, and many Frenchmen took up "savage" ways themselves. As New France began its second century, policy shifted against intermarriage – reflecting, too, the increased availability of white wives within the colony, both FILLES DU ROI and native-born. The ideal of "one people" (French, incorporating Indian and Métis) faded. Countless families, both French and Indian, had become genetically mixed, but Indian communities, as such, were not assimilated. Nor did biological *métissage* in eastern Canada yield a biracial population that persisted as socioculturally or politically distinct. Indeed, despite their numbers, people of mixed descent are difficult to identify in early records of New France; they either remained among their mothers' kin as Indians or were baptized with French names, and in almost all instances went on record solely as French.

The official discouraging of mixed unions in New France was probably one among many factors that fostered the growth of the first distinguishably Métis communities, around and beyond the Great Lakes from the 1690s on. Many men who evidently preferred the freedom and opportunities of life in the Indian country to the regulation of church and state in the home colony found livelihoods at the trading and military posts that were carrying French influence into the interior of the continent. Their native families, whom they might or might not legitimize in the missionaries' terms, had formed nuclei of settlement at several dozen localities by the time of the Conquest (1759-60). Numerous American and Canadian towns and cities (eg, Detroit and Michilimackinac in Michigan; Sault Ste Marie in Ontario; Chicago and Peoria in Illinois; Milwaukee, Green Bay and Prairie du Chien in Wisconsin) had their origins in these informal biracial communities. The sizes of these populations are sporadically reported. As of 1700, the Jesuit missionary Étienne de Carheil was deploring the lewdness and apostasy of the hundred or more VOYAGEURS and COUREURS DE BOIS residing with native women around Michilimackinac.

Carheil and other outsider-critics to the contrary, these communities achieved a moral and social order of their own. French Catholicism remained a part of their heritage, even if attenuated by isolation. Indian constraints also set moral limits. Unions with Indian women involved commitments to and reciprocities with Indian kin and neighbours, and earned their own descriptive term, marriage *à la façon du pays*, "according to the custom of the country." Fathers often lived out their lives with these families, whether formally employed at the forts or subsisting as *gens libres*, freemen who supplied the posts or served intermittently as guides, interpreters or voyageurs. Game, fish, wild rice and maple sugar furnished sustenance, supplemented by the small-scale slash-and-burn or "burnt-stump" agriculture that may have caused Great Lakes Métis to be labelled *bois brûlés* or *chicots*.

While these communities were growing during the 1700s, a biracial population of a rather different character was becoming noticeable to the north of the Great Lakes watershed. RUPERT'S LAND, the region draining into Hudson Bay, was granted by Charles II of England in 1670 for the exclusive trade of the HUDSON'S BAY COMPANY. After the Treaty of UTRECHT in 1713 granted Hudson Bay to the British, HBC posts there became permanent residential enclaves among the predominantly CREE Indians, who, as "Homeguard" traders and provisioners, were basic to the company's survival and success. As around the Great Lakes, white women were absent; and Indians eager to consolidate trade and friendship offered wives to the Europeans in "the custom of the country." HBC employees, however, violated strict company rules if they accepted. The HBC directors in London, strongly aware of the costs and problems of maintaining posts so remote from their home base in so northerly an environment, sought rigid controls on the numbers of post dependants. Needs to maintain security at the forts and to minimize expenses and sources of friction with the Indians reinforced company concerns to maintain servants' celibacy and chastity and, in turn, reinforced the employees' efforts to keep transgressions off the record. By the 1740s, however, when officer James Isham reported that traders' native offspring around the posts had become "pretty Numerious," the HBC London Committee had to acknowledge the limits of its control. By 1810 the company had given some attention to both the responsibilities and the rewards of educating and training these progeny into "a colony of very useful hands."

These early Hudson's Bay offspring did not become classed as a separate ethnic/racial entity in these years. Even if the company could not suppress country marriages, it could and did suppress the growth of dependent post communities and free traders by removing from the bay all British servants who retired or were dismissed and by encouraging Indians to disperse to their hunting grounds each winter. A very few HBC officers' native sons gained permission to travel to Britain; most offspring were assimilated among the Cree Homeguard, and a few became company servants, sometimes classed by 1800 as "Natives of Hudson's Bay" or even as "English."

The HBC data to 1810 show that biological mixing in itself was insufficient to occasion Métis "ethnogenesis" – the rise to recognition and self-consciousness of a new racial-political-cultural group. These HBC offspring lacked the distinct community and economic base upon which to build a separate identity. Through much of the 18th century, company rules gave their trader-fathers good reason to be circumspect about their existence. HBC word usage also muted their distinctiveness. It was in New France, and in British Canada after 1763, that Métis, *bois-brûlé*, and later, halfbreed, came into use; HBC men lacked such terms until they picked them up from the Canadians in the early 1800s. If language is any guide to thought, perhaps HBC writers also lacked (although they later learned) the increasingly judgemental racial/blood consciousness shown by some of their Canadian FUR-TRADE counterparts by the early 19th century.

Events of the late 1700s and early 1800s brought great changes for both British and Canadian fur-trade offspring. Around the Great Lakes, Britain's conquest in 1760 of New France may have heightened a Métis sense of separateness as the new regime intruded. The leadership of the Montréal fur trade became British, in fact mainly Highland Scottish, as the NORTH WEST COMPANY gained strength in the 1780s; Francophones whose experience and skills continued to be basic to the trade were relegated to lower ranks. In 1794 JAY'S TREATY fixed the United States-Canadian boundary around the Great Lakes. In following decades, US white settlers and governments displaced and disorganized numerous Métis communities around the lower lakes, leading many to migrate northwest towards Minnesota and Manitoba.

It was in Manitoba that the Métis became conspicuous in Canadian history. By 1810 they had established roles as buffalo hunters and provisioners to the NWC. As NWC supply lines lengthened to ATHABASCA and beyond, the Red R heartland was central to the Montréal traders. Accordingly, when in 1811 Thomas Douglas, fifth earl of SELKIRK, reached an agreement with the HBC to found the colony of ASSINIBOIA with a band of Scottish settlers, the NOR'WESTERS and their native-born employees and associates saw it as a direct threat to their trade, livelihood and territorial interests.

Events of the next decade are well known: the Pemmican War, the SEVEN OAKS killing of Gov Robert SEMPLE and several colonists in 1816, the often violent conflicts between the HBC and NWC, and the final merger in 1821. Less recognized is the fact that each company's RED RIVER COLONY involvement was intensified in part by the presence of its own native-born constituency.

The growing numbers of "Hudson's Bay natives" were a factor in the HBC decision to support the colony. Servants with "country" wives and families lobbied for the founding of a community where they could retire and have lands, livelihoods, schools and other amenities. The HBC itself hoped to reduce costs by relocating dependent post populations in a place where they could become self-supporting under the company's governance.

The Nor'Westers and their Métis associates had a more complex relationship. The NWC claimed less control over its Métis and freemen, many of whose biracial connections long predated its arrival in the Northwest. In the conflict, this fact served the NWC well, for no matter what support it actually gave to Cuthbert GRANT, Jr, and his Métis cohorts, it could and did argue that these men were defending an identity and interest of their own. Nor'Wester William MCGILLIVRAY admitted in a letter of 14 Mar 1818 that Grant and the others were linked to the NWC by occupation and kinship. "Yet," he emphasized, "they one and all look upon themselves as members of an independent tribe of natives, entitled to a property in the soil, to a flag of their own, and to protection from the British government." Further, it was well proved "that the half-breeds under the denominations of bois-brûlés and metifs [alternate form of Métis] have formed a separate and distinct tribe of Indians for a considerable time back."

From 1821 to 1870 Red River's overwhelmingly mixed-descent population continued to reflect its dual origins: Montréal, the Great Lakes and Prairies, and the NWC; and Britain, the Orkney Is (a major HBC recruiting ground) and Rupert's Land. The extent to which these subgroups were allied is debated. Some argue for their solidarity on the basis of their numerous intermarriages, business ties, and shared involvements in the BUFFALO HUNT, the HBC transport brigades, and Louis RIEL's provisional government of 1869-70. A contrary view emphasizes the split between the Roman Catholic Francophones and the Protestant anglophone "country-born," as they were sometimes known. The debate reflects in part the complexity of the evidence and the fact that many individuals, such as members of the Alexander ROSS family, suffered ambivalence about their Indian heritage and about Métis political activism.

Whatever their internal ties and tensions, the rapidly growing population of "halfbreeds" in the Northwest was, by the 1830s, increasingly seen as a racial aggregate as racial interpretations of human behaviour gained ground. As such, they were often stereotyped and disparaged, as by HBC Gov George SIMPSON in his characterizations of the company's "halfbreed" clerks and postmasters from the mid-1820s to 1832. Simpson showed biases that were common among other Europeans (clergy, colonists) arriving in Red River and the fur-trade country and among numerous scientific and popular writers of the period; attributes of race or "blood" were linked with cultural and behavioural traits to produce deterministic judgements that science later proved untenable. Such views, applied to biracial groups, covered a wide range; such hybrids were everything from "faulty stock" or a "spurious breed" to "the natural link between civilization and barbarism," as Alexis de Tocqueville put it in the 1830s. Daniel WILSON, writing of the Red River halfbreeds in 1876, moved beyond such interpretations. Racial traits, he suggested, did not set limits to adaptiveness or potentials. Besides demonstrating "a remarkable aptitude for self-government" in their organization of the buffalo hunt, the Métis also showed "capacity for all the higher duties of a settled, industrious community."

A Halfcast and His 2 Wives, watercolour by Peter Rindisbacher (*courtesy National Archives of Canada/C-46498*).

Events from the mid-1800s onwards offered few outlets for the qualities that Wilson perceived. The 1840s and 1850s saw Métis challenges to the HBC trade and administrative monopoly in Red River: the trial and freeing of trader Pierre-Guillaume SAYER in 1849, and the anti-HBC lobbying efforts in London by Alexander ISBISTER. Other events soon overshadowed the HBC question: the intensifying eastern interest in developing the West (heightened by Henry Y. HIND's glowing report of its agricultural potential), Confederation and the 1870 transfer of Rupert's Land to the Canadian government. The consequent efforts of government surveyors to map Red River without regard for local residents' holdings touched off Louis Riel's establishment of a provisional government and the RED RIVER REBELLION of 1869-70. The Canadian bargaining with Riel led to passage of the MANITOBA ACT, securing the admittance of a small portion of the present province to Canada with provincial status and, most important for the Métis, stating that 1 400 000 acres (566 580 ha) would be allotted for the children of the halfbreeds.

The promised land base was lost in the next decade, however. The settlers and troops who arrived in the new province from 1870 on were hostile to the Métis, many of whom were "beaten and outraged by a small but noisy section" of the newcomers, according to a report by the new governor, Adams Archibald. Métis landholders were harassed, while new laws and amendments to the Manitoba Act undermined Métis power to fend off speculators and new settlers. Of the approximately 10 000 persons of mixed descent in Manitoba in 1870, two-thirds or more are estimated to have departed in the next several years. While some went N and some S to the US, most headed W to the Catholic mission settlements around Ft Edmonton (Lac Ste Anne, St Albert, Lac La Biche) and to the S Saskatchewan R, where they founded or joined St Laurent, BATOCHE and DUCK LAKE.

As they grew, several of the latter communities sought to secure clear land titles from the Canadian government. Lt-Gov Alexander MORRIS thought in 1880 that the claimants' case was clear: "They will, of course, be recognized as possessors of the soil and confirmed by the Government in their holdings." He urged that Métis still depending on the buffalo hunt have land assigned to them as that resource failed. The government ignored Métis concerns while at the same time negotiating the major Indian treaties and pre-empting land for RAILWAYS. In deep frustration, the Saskatchewan Métis took up arms under Riel and Gabriel DUMONT in the NORTH-WEST REBELLION of 1885.

Métis defeat at Batoche and the execution of Riel set off a second dispersal, particularly to Alberta, and a renewed weakening of their political influence and cohesiveness. Sir John A. MACDONALD in 1885 viewed them as without distinct standing: "If they are Indians, they go with the tribe; if they are half-breeds they are whites." Where Métis individuals did receive land allowances (or money equivalents), they usually were granted them in paper scrip – transferable certificates which unscrupulous speculators often pressured them to sell cheaply on the spot (*see* INDIAN TREATIES). The "scrip hunters" who followed the Treaty No 8 Half-Breed Commission in 1900 as it made its awards to Métis in the Dene settlements bought up many $240 scrip certificates for cash amounts of $70 to $130.

From 1885 into the mid-1900s, poverty, demoralization and the opprobrium commonly attached to being "halfbreed" led many people of Indian descent to deny or suppress that part of their heritage if they could. In 1896 Father Albert LACOMBE, concerned for Métis interests, founded St-Paul-des-Métis NE of Edmonton, on land furnished by the government. For financial and other reasons, the colony failed as a formal entity by 1908, and settlers from Québec began to dominate the area.

Some other developments after 1900 were more positive, however. In 1909 the Union nationale métisse St-Joseph de Manitoba, founded by former associates of Riel and others, began to retrieve from Métis documents and memories their own history of the events of 1869-70 and 1885, resulting in A.H. de Tremaudan's *History of the Métis Nation in Western Canada* (1936). The 1920s and 1930s saw the rise of new leaders – notably James Patrick (Jim) BRADY and Malcolm NORRIS – who, as prairie socialist activists, built a new political and organizational base to defend their people's interests. Many Métis and ex-treaty Indians had been squatters on crown lands in N-central Alberta. Threatened by a federal plan to place these lands under provincial jurisdiction, Joseph Dion and others organized petitions and delegations to the Alberta government to seek land title for the squatters. After Brady and Norris joined the movement in 1932, the first of several provincial organizations was founded – the Métis Assn of Alberta, open to all persons of Indian ancestry. Its efforts led to the appointment of the Ewing Commission to "make enquiry into the condition of the Halfbreed population of Alberta" 1934-36. Despite reverses, the association eventually secured land for MÉTIS SETTLEMENTS and passage of the Métis Betterment Act in 1938. In the same year the Saskatchewan Métis Society (later the Assn of Metis and Non-Status Indians of Saskatchewan) was founded.

Since the mid-1960s Métis political activity has intensified with the founding of numerous other organizations, eg, the Manitoba Métis Federation, the Ontario Métis and Non-Status Indian Assn, and the Louis Riel Métis Assn of BC. Confronting such issues as the federal government's White Paper of 1969 and the Constitution of 1982, Métis have repeatedly faced questions about whether to pursue their concerns jointly with status or nonstatus Indians or through their own channels. From 1970 to 1983 the Native Council of Canada represented Métis interests on the national level. For the 1983 First Ministers Conference, however, the 2 NCC seats were both allocated to non-status Indian delegates; and the Métis National Council was formed to secure distinct Métis representation there and elsewhere. In Manitoba the Métis have initiated legal action to pursue claims to lands promised to them under the Manitoba Act.

JENNIFER S.H. BROWN

Reading: Alberta Federation of Métis Settlement Associations, *Métisism: A Canadian Identity* (1982); Jennifer S.H. Brown, *Strangers in Blood: Fur Trade Company Families in Indian Country* (1980) and "People of Myth, People of History: A Look at Recent Writings on the Metis," in Acadiensis 17(1), fall 1987; M. Campbell, *Halfbreed* (1973); *Canadian Journal of Native Studies* 3, 1 (1983); M. Dobbin, *The One-and-a-half Men: The Story of Jim Brady and Malcolm Norris* (1981); T. Flanagan and J. Foster, eds, "The Metis: Past and Present," special issue,

Canadian Ethnic Studies 17(2), 1985; J.W. Friesen and T. Lusty, *The Métis of Canada: An Annotated Bibliography* (1980); R. Fumoleau, *As Long as This Land Shall Last: A History of Treaty 8 and Treaty 11, 1870-1939* (1974); M. Giraud, *Le Métis canadien* (1945, tr 1985); A.S. Lussier and D.B. Sealey, eds, *The Other Natives: The Métis* (1978); D.F.K. Madill, *Select Annotated Bibliography on Métis History and Claims* (1983); E. Pelletier, *A Social History of the Manitoba Métis* (rev ed, 1977); J. Peterson, "Prelude to Red River: A Social Portrait of the Great Lakes Métis," *Ethnohistory* 25, 1 (1978); J. Peterson and Jennifer S.H. Brown, eds, *New Peoples: Being and Becoming Métis in North America* (1985); D. Redbird, *We Are Métis: A Métis View of the Development of a Native Canadian People* (1980); D.N. Sprague and R.P. Frye, *The Genealogy of the First Métis Nation: The Development and Dispersal of the Red River Settlement 1820-1900* (1983). G.F.G. Stanley, ed, *The Collected Writings of Louis Riel/Les Ecrits complets de Louis Riel* (5 vols, 1985).

Métis Settlements Located across the northern part of Alberta, the Métis settlements of Paddle Prairie, Big Prairie, Gift Lake, East Prairie, Buffalo Lake, Kikino, Elizabeth and Fishing Lake form the only MÉTIS land base in Canada. They comprise 501 810.18 ha, much of it covered by forest, pasture and farmland. The present population is about 5000.

Métis settlers are the descendants of European fur traders and Indian women who emerged as a distinct group on the Prairies towards the early part of the 19th century. Following the NORTH-WEST REBELLION of 1885, many Métis moved to the N and W. After a period of political agitation among landless Métis in Alberta during the Depression, the provincial government passed the Métis Betterment Act in 1938. Lands were set aside for Métis Settlement Associations, although 4 of the settlements (Touchwood, Marlboro, Cold Lake and Wolf Lake) were later rescinded by order of the Alberta government. A distinct Métis culture combining Indian and Euro-Canadian values and modes of expression is practised in the Métis settlements. For example, jigging, a favourite form of dance, mixes the reels of Scotland and France with the chicken dance of the Cree. A distinct Métis language combining Cree, French and English words is still spoken alongside English. Most of the residents in Métis settlements still retain Indian spiritual beliefs and customs. Education in most of the settlements is provided by the Northland School Division of the Alberta government. In recent years the settlements have emphasized the need to make their children's schools more responsive to the cultural values and history of the Métis.

Employment in the settlements is generated by commercial fishing, logging, farming, ranching and energy projects. During the past decade Métis settlers have emphasized the economic development of their land. They have established a plan for the development of a mixed economy that will combine traditional economic activities and new industrial and commercial ventures.

The Métis Betterment Act provides for Settlement Associations for each of the 8 communities and a form of settlement government has developed through them. Councils of 5 members are elected by the membership to deal with matters affecting the settlements. In 1971 the settlements started to work together as a federation, and in 1975 the Alberta Federation of Métis Settlement Associations was officially established to act as the political voice of the settlements and to litigate their subsurface rights in court.

In June 1985 in the Alberta legislature, Resolution 18 was unanimously approved committing the province to transfer title to the settlement lands to the Métis and to provide constitutional protection for the lands by means of an amendment to the Alberta Act. This would be effected after a new Métis Settlements Act was passed to replace the out-of-date Act. Since 1985 settlement people have been working with the province to develop the membership, land allocation and government structure provisions for the new Act. This process appears to be nearing completion and it is hoped that the lands will be constitutionally entrenched and protected in 1988.

ALBERTA FEDERATION OF MÉTIS SETTLEMENT ASSOCIATIONS

Metlakatla Pass Sites Metlakatla Pass, or Venn Passage, located 4 km W of PRINCE RUPERT on the northern BC coast, is a narrow, protected channel, 5 km long, separating Digby I from Tsimpsean Pen. The area is noted for its density of archaeological sites: archaeologists have discovered 40 sites along its shores – 27 are shell middens which represent the remains of ancient Indian villages; 13 are petroglyph or rock art sites, which consist of low-relief carvings on boulders or rock outcrops (*see* PICTOGRAPHS AND PETROGLYPHS). The people who occupied the area at the time of European contact were the Coast TSIMSHIAN. Traditionally, all 9 tribes of Coast Tsimshian had permanent winter villages in the Metlakatla Pass area. Excavations conducted at several of these village sites 1966-mid-1970s suggest that Metlakatla Pass has been occupied for approximately 6000 years. DAVID J.W. ARCHER

Metric Conversion is the process of making metric units, eg, metre (m), litre (L), kilogram (kg), degree Celsius (°C), the common units of measurement in Canada. Although the metric system was legalized in Canada in 1871, the British imperial system of units, based on yards, pounds, gallons, etc, continued to predominate. In the 1960s, with rapidly advancing technology and expanding worldwide trade, the need for an international measurement system became increasingly apparent. Britain decided to convert to the metric system and the US was studying a similar move. A number of Canadian associations representing diverse interests, including consumers, educators and professionals, made representations to the government favouring the metric system. In Jan 1970 the White Paper on Metric Conversion in Canada set out Canadian government policy. It stated that a single, coherent measurement system based on metric units should be used for all measurement purposes, including legislation. In line with this policy, the Weights and Measures Act was amended by Parliament in 1971 to recognize the Système International d'Unités (SI), the latest evolution of the metric system, for use in Canada. Also in 1971, Parliament passed the Consumer Packaging and Labelling Act, requiring that metric units be shown on labels of most consumer products.

To implement metric conversion the government established in 1971 a Preparatory Commission, later called Metric Commission Canada. The commission's role was to ensure a planned and co-ordinated conversion in all sectors of the Canadian economy and to disseminate information on metric conversion. Beginning in 1973 the commission organized over 100 sector committees, with members from national associations and major organizations representing business and industry, consumers, labour, health, education and government. Each sector committee was responsible for preparing a sector conversion plan and monitoring its implementation. The commission as a whole approved sector conversion plans developed through consensus.

The process of replacing imperial units with SI units in all kinds of documents, measuring devices, manufacturing processes, products and packages involved a countless variety of tasks. The technical basis for the change to SI units was established by 2 national standards of Canada, the *International System of Units (SI)* and the *Canadian Metric Practice Guide*, first published in 1973 by the Canadian Standards Assn and approved by the Standards Council of Canada. After choosing appropriate SI units, practical approaches to implementation were debated by sector committees, with each sector determining policies and strategies to suit its interests. Soft conversion (arithmetical conversion of pre-existing measurement values) versus hard conversion (round, rational values in metric units, possibly requiring physical change in product size) was a major issue. The use of both imperial and metric measurements was another area of controversy. Dependence on the US for many parts and products was a constraint for many sectors. The dedicated efforts of Canadian industry allowed conversion to proceed with few major problems, although it took 2-5 years longer than planned.

Education and public-awareness programs were important considerations to ensure public understanding and acceptance of the change to metric units. With the co-operation of all provinces, schools prepared to teach mainly the metric system. A series of metric conversion events exposed the public to simple metric units in everyday life; extensive information campaigns accompanied each change. The first such event was the announcement of temperature in degrees Celsius in weather forecasts beginning 1 Apr 1975. From Sept 1975 rainfall and snowfall were quoted in millimetres and centimetres, respectively. The next significant change (Sept 1977) was the introduction of road signs showing distances in kilometres and speed limits in kilometres per hour. Concurrent with this change, cars with speedometers and odometers graduated in metric units were produced. In Jan 1979 service stations started pricing and dispensing gasoline and diesel fuel in litres. In Dec 1980 (the cutoff date for using imperial length units) fabrics and home furnishings were required to be advertised and sold only by the metre and centimetre. Conversion of weighing scales in retail food stores created political controversies. After 3 pilot areas (Kamloops, Peterborough and Sherbrooke) completed scale conversion in the summer of 1979, national conversion was postponed by the government of the day, but was resumed in Jan 1982. Cutoff dates were established for different areas, extending up to Dec 1983. After that, store-weighed food items could be priced and advertised only by kilogram or 100 gram quantities and sold only in metric units. Conversion involved some 35 000 retail food stores across Canada. Steadily metric units became normal for most products and services. However, metric units did not receive support in real estate or in sports (except track and field and swimming).

Metric conversion proceeded voluntarily in many sectors, but federal and provincial legislative action was required in some. Regulations on the use of metric units for WEIGHTS AND MEASURES in retail trade were established and enforced by the government for the protection of consumers and retailers against unfair practices and confusion in comparing products. Even so, the government did not escape criticism for imposing mandatory use of metric units to the exclusion of old units. Opponents of metric conversion pointed to the costs at a time of inflation and economic weakness, the danger of being out of step with the US and the invasion of a foreign language of measurements upon a Canadian heritage bound to imperial measurements. Some challenged metrication through the courts.

The Conservative government of Brian Mulroney reaffirmed the commitment to metric but revoked the required use of metric alone in some cases, eg, gasoline and diesel fuels and home furnishings. In 1985 some small businesses were exempted from the requirement to install metric scales. Defendants of metric measurements have cited many benefits besides export trade and international standardization. SI is simple because of its decimal nature and the absence of a multiplicity of units with conversion factors. The universality of SI symbols (regardless of language) and the convenience of having a single unit for a physical quantity made communications clearer. Upgrading of many technical standards and rationalization of product sizes and containers were side benefits. All these led to long-term cost savings, despite initial conversion expenses. In the final analysis, pressures of technology and of the marketplace made metric conversion inevitable for Canada. N. GANAPATHY

Metropolitan Government is a form of urban REGIONAL GOVERNMENT used in metropolitan centres with a population over 100 000. The modern concept of metropolitan government originated in the US in the early 20th century as an attempt to devise institutions that could cope with urban growth.

The classic dilemma for municipalities in a metropolitan centre is that area-wide concerns are not met by a policymaking apparatus of similar scope. There are 3 basic problems. Policy co-ordination among local units of government is difficult in land-use and transportation planning and decisions made in one locality will frequently have detrimental consequences for its neighbours. Policy inequities result because each municipality provides services based upon its own tax base (*see* MUNICIPAL FINANCE); only those suburbs with extensive industry can provide high-level services with low residential taxation and normally the core city is hard pressed on both counts. Policy accountability is fragmented because the numerous municipalities grapple with individual problems but no one unit of government is responsible for the well-being of the metropolitan region. The idea of federation was central to proposed reforms. Municipalities would unite to provide specific common services by delegating that authority to a new level of metropolitan government but would otherwise remain autonomous. The first steps to metropolitan governance were usually intermunicipal co-operative agencies (often known as special-purpose districts) created to provide water transit or sewerage facilities.

The creation of Metropolitan Toronto in 1953 was an important breakthrough for N American metropolitan government reform. Acting on the recommendation of the Ontario Municipal Board, the province federated the city of Toronto and its 12 suburbs as a metropolitan corporation. Although the municipalities retained their separate existences and a portion of their councillors also served as metro councillors, the metropolitan corporation assumed a wide range of functions that have increased over the years. In 1967, in a comprehensive reorganization, the number of local municipalities was decreased to 6. Metro Toronto served as the model for the regional governments of Ottawa-Carleton (1969), Hamilton-Wentworth (1974) and the metropolitan corporation of Greater Winnipeg (1961-71). But, in Winnipeg, the metro council was directly elected and its responsibilities fewer. Both the Montréal and Vancouver regions have metropolitan governments although they undertake fewer functions than that in Toronto, and Vancouver is technically based upon a system of special-purpose districts. Winnipeg (since 1971) and Calgary each have one local government coterminous with the metropolitan area.

The basic problem with metropolitan government in Canada has been that it is a political compromise. Few governmental responsibilities were transferred entirely to the new level. For example, metropolitan governments would sell water wholesale to municipalities who were responsible for local deliveries; build freeways, although municipalities controlled local roads and parking; issue area-wide plans, but leave municipalities the power to issue building permits. Tension has resulted because 2 levels of government are in competition with each other. The conflict in Winnipeg became so severe that the provincial government was forced to abandon the metropolitan approach in favour of unitary government. JAMES LIGHTBODY

Reading: D.J.H. Higgins, *Urban Canada and its Government* (1977).

Metropolitan-Hinterland Thesis, a theory of historic relations between a large, powerful urban community (metropolis) and the surrounding territory (hinterland) which the metropolis dominates through mainly economic means. Formulated by economic historian N.S.B. Gras in the 1920s, it has since the 1950s been widely applied and extended in Canadian history to illuminate the growth of urban power, REGIONALISM and generally the interplay of central and territorial forces. Gras conceived 4 stages in the rise of a major city to metropolitan dominance: it first harnessed the commercial life of a wide adjacent territory, then centered its industrial activities, built up its transport network and finally provided financial services to, and so more controls over, the hinterland. Later, it appeared that these were better regarded as key attributes of economic metropolitanism than as stages operating in straight sequence. The concept was also widened to include noneconomic aspects such as the political power wielded by metropolitan centres, especially as seats of governments, or the social, cultural and informational holds they may acquire. In any case, metropolitan-hinterland relations remain reciprocal, producing complementariness as well as confrontation in complex patterns that may involve whole sets of urban centres, as well as overlapping, changing hinterlands. J.M.S. CARELESS

Reading: J.M.S. Careless, "Metropolis and Region," *Urban History Review* 3, 78 (1979).

Meulles, Jacques de, chevalier, INTENDANT of New France 1682-86 (d at Orléans, France May 1703). De Meulles, despite explicit instructions, was embroiled in confrontation with Governor LA BARRE throughout his term. In 1685, when the minister, Seignelay, neglected to send cash to pay the troops who were sent to control the increasingly threatening Iroquois nations, de Meulles used playing cards as money, promising redemption the following year. This expedient of using PLAYING-CARD MONEY was frequently resorted to thereafter and was a forerunner of modern paper money. In 1685 the new governor, DENONVILLE, accused de Meulles of greed and illegal trafficking, thereby causing his recall to France. FRANCE BEAUREGARD

Mézy, Augustin de Saffray de, governor of New France (d at Québec C 6 May 1665). De Mézy was chosen first governor of New France under direct royal rule 1663-65. The colonial administration was reorganized on his arrival and the SOUVERAIN COUNCIL established. The question of new appointments to the council led to public quarrels between the governor and Bishop LAVAL, whose civil powers overlapped with those of de Mézy. Bishop and governor also fell out over procedures for the election of a *syndic* to represent the people of Québec. The colonial minister ordered an investigation into de Mézy's rather violent and arbitrary rule, but the governor died before it could be carried out. ALLAN GREER

Mi-Carême Mid-Lent, in French Canadian tradition, is the time when people dress up in disguise and go from house to house asking for treats, singing and dancing in the MUMMING tradition. An interesting variation is found in parts of ACADIA, where the Mi-Carême becomes a kind of St Nicholas figure: a person disguised as an old woman mummer distributes treats to good children. Mi-Carêmes are also used as frightening figures, and as bringers of children (in place of storks or cabbages). NANCY SCHMITZ

Michaux, André, botanist, explorer (b near Versailles, France 8 Mar 1746; d on Madagascar 11 Oct 1803?). He compiled the first N American flora which includes many plants collected in Lower Canada in 1792. Michaux learned about practical horticulture in France before embarking on a series of botanizing expeditions in Europe, Persia (1782-85) and the US (1785-96). After meeting Peter POND in June 1792 he visited Montréal and Québec before proceeding by canoe up the Saguenay R through unexplored territory to Lac MISTASSINI. Michaux kept a diary and collected numerous new plants (his herbarium is in the Musée nationale d'histoire naturelle, Paris). According to contemporary records, Michaux was a quiet, independent and simple man, more at ease with the natives than with his fellow Frenchmen. He wrote *Historie des chênes de l'Amérique* (1801) and *Flora boreali-americana*, 2 vols (1803), both edited by his son, François-André. JUDITH F.M. HOENIGER

Michener, Daniel Roland, politician, governor general of Canada 1967-74 (b at Lacombe, Alta 19 Apr 1900). Educated at U of A (1920), Michener attended Oxford as a Rhodes scholar, where he became friends with L.B. PEARSON. Michener practised law in Toronto from 1924, was an Ontario MPP, 1945-48, and a Cabinet minister 1946-48. Describing himself as "a small 'l' liberal and a capital 'C' Conservative," he was MP for Toronto St Paul's 1953-62. Speaker of the House 1957-62, he was civilized and witty but clashed frequently with PM John DIEFENBAKER. After Michener suffered defeat in the 1962 election, PM Pearson appointed him high commis-

Portrait of Roland Michener by Arthur E.C. Horne (*courtesy National Archives of Canada/C-116806/House of Commons, Speaker's Office*).

sioner to India 1964-67, and governor general in 1967. Michener and his accomplished wife, Norah, democratized the office (curtailing the curtsey, for example), and were among the busiest and most creative of viceregal couples. Among the Michener innovations were frequent state visits abroad, periodic meetings with provincial lieutenant-governors, and the establishment of an Honours Secretariat (the Order of Canada having been instituted in 1967) at Rideau Hall.

NORMAN HILLMER

Michif is a term used to describe the speech of a number of MÉTIS communities in western Canada and the northern US. It is one outgrowth of long contact between Cree and Ojibwa speakers and Francophones from the Great Lakes to the northern plains. Although formerly dismissed as "bad French" or a disorderly mix of elements, it exhibits a complex structure which establishes it as at least a creole language or a dialect of Cree. Most typically, French nouns and noun phrases are combined with Cree syntax and verb structures: "I like fish" – *Li pwesoon nimiyaymow*. While best documented at Turtle Mountain Reservation, ND, it also survives locally in Manitoba and Saskatchewan. Many Métis do not speak Michif, having grown up in settings where English or French dominated or having learned to use those languages plus Cree according to need, as did older generations at Lac La Biche, Alta. Michif persistence, however, is one indicator of the temporal depth and historical distinctiveness of Métis cultural traditions.

JENNIFER S.H. BROWN

Micmac The origin of the name *Micmac,* which identifies both a people and their language, is unclear, though it may derive from *nikmaq* ("my kin-friends") used by the 17th-century French as a greeting for the tribe. Alternative names for the Micmac, which can be found in historical sources, include Gaspesians, Souriquois, Acadians and Tarrantines. At the time of European contact, Micmac-speaking peoples occupied the coastal areas of the Gaspé and the Maritime provinces E of the SAINT JOHN R drainage. They continue to occupy this area as well as settlements in Newfoundland and New England, especially Boston. The number of registered Micmac is 15 300, with another 4500 (approximately) nonstatus persons of Micmac heritage (*see* INDIAN). Estimates of aboriginal population range from 3000 to 35 000, with 20 000 being a reasonable figure.

Micmac is among the Wabanaki cluster of Eastern Algonquian languages, which include the various ABENAKI dialects and the Penobscot and MALISEET-Passamaquoddy languages. Maritime PREHISTORY extends 11 000 years into the past, but the date of arrival of Algonquian speakers into the area remains uncertain.

Aboriginal Micmac settlements were characterized by individual or joint households scattered about a bay or along a river. Communities were related by alliance and kinship. Leadership, based on prestige rather than power, was largely concerned with effective management of the fishing and hunting economy. Painting, music and oratory were encouraged. The Micmac were among the first peoples to be affected by European activities in the New World and underwent early depopulation and sociocultural disruption. They attempted to profit from the FUR TRADE by serving as intermediaries between Europeans and groups farther W. As their trade advantages disappeared, they tried to exploit a military alliance with the French (*see* IROQUOIS WARS).

After British suzerainty was established, the Micmac were subjected to conscious attempts by government to alter their life-style. Most moves to establish them as agriculturalists failed because of badly conceived programs and encroachments upon reserved lands. Their employment as labourers effected irreversible change: crafts, coopering, the porpoise fishery, and road, rail and lumber work integrated the Micmac into the 19th- and 20th-century economy, but left them socially isolated. A forced relocation scheme in the 1950s posed the greatest threat to them as a distinctive people. The Micmac have been able to salvage some of their traditional culture in political decision making, religion and language. The rate of unemployment for reserve communities is extremely high in a region with high unemployment, but there are a number of successful musicians, artists, writers and business and professional persons among the Micmac. *See also* NATIVE PEOPLE: EASTERN WOODLANDS and general articles under NATIVE PEOPLE. HAROLD FRANKLIN MCGEE, JR

Ornate Micmac coat presented to Capt O'Halloran at a Micmac tribal council held at Burn Church Point, NB, 1841 (*courtesy National Museums of Canada/Canadian Museum of Civilization/S77-1834*).

Reading: A.G. Bailey, *The Conflict of European and Eastern Algonkian Cultures, 1504-1700* (2nd ed, 1969); Harold Franklin McGee, Jr, ed, *The Native Peoples of Atlantic Canada* (1984); B.G. Trigger, ed, *Handbook of North American Indians,* vol 15: *Northeast* (1978).

Microbiology is the science that studies micro-organisms and VIRUSES. Micro-organisms are too small to be distinguished by the naked eye (ie, less than 0.1 mm in diameter); hence, their discovery and study occurred only after the introduction of adequate microscopes. These organisms have in common a relatively simple cell structure, although different species may differ in some aspects of their structure. Based on structural aspects, particularly those of the nucleus, micro-organisms are divided into 2 groups, eukaryotes (having a true, membrane-bound nucleus) and prokaryotes (with a primitive nucleus). Protozoa, fungi and most ALGAE are eukaryotic, as are the cells of higher plants and animals. BACTERIA and the BLUE-GREEN ALGAE (cyanobacteria) are the only prokaryotes. Because viruses require host cells to perform their life processes, they are in a class by themselves, being neither eukaryotic nor prokaryotic.

Micro-organisms are of interest, in part, because some varieties cause disease. However, micro-organisms exist in all habitats and are an important component of all normal ecosystems. Soil and the oceans are the most important habitats. Soil supports a wide range of types and, as it is a very stable habitat, protects them for months or years. Micro-organisms decompose organic matter (plant and animal remains, sewage, etc) to simple molecules that can be used by plants, and oxidize or reduce insoluble elements (eg, sulphur) to soluble compounds also usable as plant food. Even pesticides and petroleum products will be broken down to less dangerous forms. The oceans are low in nutrients and over 80% of ocean water is below 4°C; hence the microbial population and rate of growth and metabolism are very low. However, ocean bacteria can grow, albeit slowly, at these temperatures. These bacteria require sodium as a nutrient and some (called barophiles) require great pressures. Marine micro-organisms function like terrestrial ones in decomposing organic matter and converting it to forms available to aquatic plants. For example, a relatively small number of petroleum-decomposing bacteria occur in the oceans, limited by the low level of nutrients. When an oil spill provides an abundant carbon source, the bacterial population increases immediately, provided that enough nitrogen and phosphorus are also present. In the long run, substances that cannot be handled by micro-organisms (eg, heavy metals, some pesticides, thermal pollution) will become the most serious POLLUTION problems. In addition, phytoplankton (photosynthetic algae and some protozoa) form critical links in ocean food chains.

On the negative side, the many disease-causing micro-organisms are undesirable in themselves. Furthermore, micro-organisms cause disease in plants, and constant effort is required to breed disease-resistant (eg, rust-resistant) varieties, especially as the fungi that cause rusts and many other PLANT DISEASES continually evolve new ways of attacking plants. Micro-organisms contribute to pollution by oxidizing organic matter, thus using up available oxygen and causing the death of fish and other oxygen-requiring organisms. Bacteria can cause problems in water systems by oxidizing iron or manganese to insoluble salts that clog pipes. Some bacteria, in the absence of oxygen, will reduce sulphate to hydrogen sulphide, a weak acid that corrodes metal pipes. Crude oil is often very high in sulphur, and bacteria capable of oxidizing sulphur to sulphuric acid are present in oil wells. The acid formed destroys drilling bits and shafts.

Uses of Microbiology

In industrial societies, micro-organisms are put to a variety of uses to enhance the quality of the human environment.

Sewage Treatment Micro-organisms, particularly bacteria, play a major role in sewage treatment. They oxidize organic matter present in wastewater to its basic constituents and thus reduce potential harmful effects on fish and other oxygen-requiring organisms. The first microbiological step of sewage treatment, carried out in the absence of oxygen, produces methane gas. Many sewage plants get all their energy from this source. To complete decomposition, aeration is required and is accomplished in various ways. Aeration has the added effect of killing undesirable bacteria.

Industrial Microbiology The dairy industry has a long history of work with micro-organisms. Pasteurization of milk was introduced soon after 1886 to kill pathogenic bacteria and generally reduce bacterial numbers, thereby increasing the keeping quality of milk. The industry also uses bacteria for producing yogurt, cottage cheese, buttermilk and acidophilus milk are produced by controlling fermentation of milk by various lactic-acid bacteria (especially the *Lactobacilli*).

Various strains of YEAST have been developed that produce ethyl alcohol and flavour compounds from grapes, and are tolerant of high concentrations of alcohol. These yeasts are the basis of the wine industry and problems arise when wild yeasts take over fermentation. Wine must also be protected from bacterial contamination because bacteria may form lactic acid or oxidize alcohol to vinegar.

Brewing also uses yeast to convert sugar to alcohol. In this case, the source of sugar is cereal grain and the yeast does not have to be tolerant of high levels of alcohol. Bottled or canned beer is pasteurized in the container to prevent bacterial attack; keg beer is not pasteurized but relies on refrigeration and rapid use for its desirable qualities. Distilleries use yeast fermentation of grains, molasses, fruits and vegetables to obtain alcohol which is then distilled from the mash, aged and blended.

One of the major industrial uses of micro-organisms is in the production of antibiotics. Penicillin, the first to be discovered, is still the most widely used. Antibiotics act by interfering with the normal metabolic processes of bacteria or other micro-organisms. Thus, penicillin interferes with the synthesis of the cell wall of prokaryotic cells. This cell wall is totally unlike the wall in any eukaryote; hence, penicillin is selective for bacteria and blue-green algae. Over 100 antibiotics are now in use and more than 5000 different types have been produced. In general, the useful antibiotics are produced by fungi and by a special group of bacteria known as the *Streptomyces*.

To an ever-increasing degree, micro-organisms are being used to produce industrial enzymes (complex proteins that catalyze specific reactions). Bacteria, especially, are capable of secreting enzymes from their cells, thus making it much simpler to concentrate and purify the enzyme. The greatest industrial use of enzymes is in the chill proofing of beer, ie, in making the proteins and carbohydrates soluble so that they do not precipitate when the beer is chilled. Microbial enzymes are also used to remove the bitter constituents of grapefruit peel in juice production and to convert glucose (corn sugar) to the much sweeter sugar fructose. The enzyme rennin, used to coagulate milk for cheese making, is now largely obtained from fungi. Single-cell proteins, used primarily for animal feed, are produced using micro-organisms.

Micro-organisms are also used in such industrial processes as the synthesis of methane from cellulose (eg, from PULP AND PAPER INDUSTRY wastes); the process is still largely experimental (*see* BIOMASS ENERGY). Bacteria may be used to dissolve metals from ores, a procedure widely practised in the Canadian MINING industry.

Agriculture Soils are often deficient in nitrogen and, although nitrogen-fixing strains of bacteria are present in soil, they may not occur in high enough numbers to be effective. To safeguard against this possibility, the seeds of legumes (eg, clover, peas, beans) are often preinoculated with the appropriate nitrogen-fixing bacteria. As the seeds germinate and plants grow, the bacteria (genus *Rhizobium*) invade the roots and concentrate in nodules on them. The plant supplies energy from the sun and the bacteria convert nitrogen to ammonia to feed the plant and enrich the soil. There is also some advantage to inoculating nitrogen-poor soils with free-living nitrogen-fixing bacteria of the genus *Azotobacter*. Micro-organisms have also been used to control insect pests that attack plants (eg, spruce budworm and sawflies).

In BIOTECHNOLOGY, a field now attracting a great deal of attention, characteristics from several strains of organisms are combined into a single cell, usually a bacterium. The basic techniques are those of microbial genetics. The production of compounds (eg, INSULIN, interferon) by bacteria is already underway and the potential for the production of important biological compounds is very great.

Microbiology in Canada

Microbiology is a strong science in Canadian universities. In many instances it is centered in medical schools but there are successful departments in faculties of science or agriculture. The NATIONAL RESEARCH COUNCIL, Agriculture Canada and the Dept of Fisheries and Oceans have a long tradition of research in microbiology. Microbiology is more widely accepted as a profession than are other biological sciences. There are all levels of employment for graduates in hospitals, public-health laboratories and private diagnostic laboratories. Within the food and beverage industries, dairying is the chief employer, although breweries, wineries and meat-packing plants routinely employ microbiologists for quality-control work. The training is also considered appropriate for a brewmaster or wine maker.

In many industries, a microbiology background is considered an excellent preparation for a management position. Universities are one of the largest employers of the most highly trained individuals (in research and teaching) and of those with a BSc degree (eg, laboratory demonstrators, research assistants). The pharmaceutical industry employs graduates either in sales or in their research or quality-control laboratories.

In Canada, microbiologists may belong to the professional associations: Canadian Society of Microbiologists, Canadian Assn of Medical Microbiologists, Canadian Assn of Clinical Microbiology and Infectious Diseases, Canadian Genetics Society, Canadian Society for Cell Biology, Canadian Biochemical Society, Canadian Society of Immunology, Canadian Assn of Public Health, Canadian Society of Clinical Chemists and Canadian College of Microbiologists.

J.J.R. CAMPBELL

Microchips and Transistors Microchips or microelectronic chips (also called semiconductors or integrated circuits) are essential components of all computerized systems. They form the basis of a $20-billion, worldwide industry. The breathtaking pace of technological change in microchips (every year or 2 their capacity doubles while prices are halved) permits them to be used not only in sophisticated electronic systems but in many consumer products (eg, personal computers, calculators, video games, cars, sewing machines, video-cassette recorders and microwave ovens). The revolution in consumer electronics of the 1970s and 1980s largely results from microchip advances. If comparable progress had been made in automobiles, a Rolls Royce would cost $10 and could be driven around the world on 5 L of gas.

Microchips are silicon wafers on which intricate patterns of transistors are laid down. Transistors function as switches which control electric signals passing through the chip. In the past 2 decades, researchers have packed increasing numbers of transistors onto wafers about the size of a thumbnail. Chips containing tens of thousands of transistors are called large-scale integration (LSI) chips, while those with hundreds of thousands to a million transistors are called very large-scale integration (VLSI) chips. By the early 1980s, chips with more than 250 000 transistors were on the market, and a million-transistor chip is available today. A 4 million transistor chip is expected by the early 1990s, with a 16 million transistor chip a few years later. This complexity has been compared to a street network: if the simpler chips of the 1960s have the complexity of the street layout of a small town, VLSI chips have the complexity of a street network of big-city density covering the N American continent.

Technologies based on VLSI chips are faster and more reliable, smaller and more portable, cheaper and more energy efficient than those just a generation older. It has been estimated that a product with 10 standard chips will cost 2-3 times more to produce than one using a VLSI chip. Developments in VLSI chips are blurring the traditional distinction between computer hardware (ie, physical components) and computer software (instructions that tell the system what to do) because often the instructions are put right into the VLSI chips. This integration reinforces the growing importance of custom and semicustom chips designed to perform specialized functions. Standard or "off-the-shelf," general-purpose chips dominated in the 1970s and 1980s.

By the end of the 1980s the worldwide market for custom chips had reached $25 billion, more than half the semiconductor market. Semicustom chips are projected to show greatest growth, 62% annually between 1983 and 1986. They are made by combining a number of "cells" in novel ways to create chips that can do special tasks, or by using partially prefabricated chips for special functions. Semicustom chips are cheaper and less complicated to design and make than are full custom chips. New technologies (eg, computer-aided design, automated assembly lines and ion-beam write-on-wafer devices) are expected to reduce greatly the cost of producing specialized chips.

Chip production is divided into 2 phases: design and fabrication. The first is the most expensive and time-consuming: designing a chip with 60 000 to 70 000 transistors can take dozens of man-years and millions of dollars. Computer-aided design (CAD) systems will automate much of this work, but it seems unlikely that human designers will be totally displaced (*see* ROBOTICS). Fabrication involves laying down the intricate patterns of transistors and their connections, often on several layers of silicon. At present, 40 or more processing steps are needed, but new technologies for "writing" circuit patterns onto the wafers may cut this number in half.

A handful of Canadian companies, notably Northern Telecom Ltd of Mississauga and Mitel Corp of Ottawa, have in-house "foundries" (fabrication facilities) to make specialized chips for use in their own products. Canada's only "non-captive" fabrication facility is in Edmonton. It is run by the Alberta Microelectronic Centre (AMC). The AMC's primary concentration is in the design and fabrication of semicustom gate array circuits. In Ontario, the Ontario Centre for Microelectronics provides integrated circuit design and consulting services.

Another problem was that the US, the major source of chips, began restricting the outward flow of microchip technology because it feared a loss of its technological edge and was preparing for a battle with Japan for world dominance in semiconductors.

In 1982 the SCIENCE COUNCIL OF CANADA reported that, unless Canada develops its own custom-chip manufacturing capability, "the electronics industry will forever be dependent on foreign sources." The AMC was formed in 1985 in view of this recommendation. In 1983 the NATURAL SCIENCES AND ENGINEERING RESEARCH COUNCIL, a federal

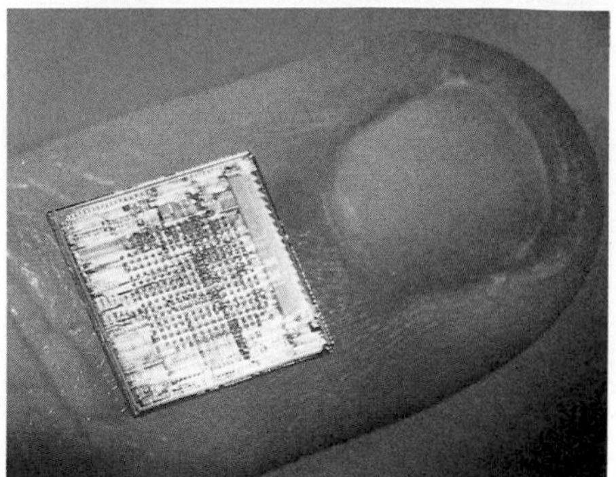

Microchip, the "brain cell" of modern-day computers (*courtesy Canapress Photo Service*).

agency that supports university research, initiated a 5-year, $17.5-million program to establish a nationwide network of CAD stations that will permit universities to do advanced microchip design and testing. LYDIA DOTTO

Middle Power During and after WWII Canadians became increasingly aware that although they should not aspire to the privileges and responsibilities of a great power, they and other countries of comparable consequence could not settle for the role of small powers. In the various conferences at which the UNITED NATIONS was designed, Canada, Australia and medium-sized countries of Europe and Latin America curbed the intentions of the greater powers to dominate all aspects of the UN. In the early postwar years there was a need for middle powers, less directly involved in world economics and politics, to fulfil intermediary UN roles, particularly in conflicts arising from the disengagement of colonial powers in the Middle East, S Asia and Africa. The Scandinavian countries, Canada, Brazil, Yugoslavia and others proved useful in seeking compromises and formulas for agreement, as well as in staffing the PEACEKEEPING operations required when truces were established. The term "middle" thereby developed a mediatory connotation as well. As the 2 superpowers emerged in a special classification, there is a tendency now to refer to Britain, France, W Germany and Japan as middle powers.
JOHN W. HOLMES

Middleton, Christopher, Hudson's Bay Co captain, naval officer, explorer (b at Newton Bewley, Eng late 17th century; d 12 Feb 1770). Middleton served on PRIVATEERING ships during Queen Anne's War 1701-13 and joined the HBC in 1721 as second mate on a voyage from England to York Factory. During subsequent voyages to Hudson Bay he made scientific observations, which were published by the Royal Society in 1726. In 1737 he sailed N of Churchill in a company-sponsored search for the NORTHWEST PASSAGE. In 1741 he joined the navy, and sailed to the northwestern coast of Hudson Bay in command of the first official British expedition to look for the passage. His map of 1743 was the first to show that part of the Canadian North. He retired from the navy in 1748 and died in obscurity. K.S. COATES

Middleton, Sir Frederick Dobson, soldier (b at Belfast, Ire 2 Nov 1825; d at London, Eng 25 Jan 1898). Middleton was educated at Sandhurst and commissioned in the 58th Regiment in 1842. His early service was in Australia, Norfolk I and New Zealand, and he distinguished himself during suppression of the Indian Mutiny. After stationing in England, Gibraltar and Malta, he came to Canada in 1868 with the 29th Regiment and remained as an instructor with the Canadian Militia and then was commandant 1874-84 of Sandhurst. In July 1884 he was appointed commander of the Canadian Militia, and to him fell the task of organizing and leading the expedition during the NORTH-WEST REBELLION of 1885. The organization was accomplished with speed and efficiency, but after an initial brush with the rebels at Fish Creek, Middleton became cautious and his tactics at the decisive battle of BATOCHE were ponderous. Nevertheless the campaign was successfully concluded and a grateful Canadian Parliament voted Middleton a monetary award, while the British government made him a KCMG and promoted him lieutenant-general. He retired in 1890, but his plans to take over the presidency of a Canadian insurance company were spoiled by a minor scandal involving the misappropriation of furs during the North-West Rebellion. In 1896 he was appointed keeper of the crown jewels, Tower of London. R.C. MACLEOD

Reading: Desmond Morton, *The Last War Drum* (1972).

Midewiwin, or Grand Medicine Society, a closed ritual society generally limited to men, is found historically among the Upper Great Lakes Algonquian (OJIBWA and Lk Winnipeg Salteaux), the northern prairies and among some groups in the eastern subarctic. In some Chippewa (Ojibwa) communities members still meet. In the past the society recognized 4 grades of membership (sometimes as many as 8), each with their own initiation rites and initiation fees, periods of instruction and myths, songs, herbal remedies and Midewiwin bags or MEDICINE BUNDLES. An individual's rank in the society was marked by facial painting and by the use of certain animal or bird skins of which the Midewiwin bag was made. Skins denoting specific grades included that of the weasel, mink, the paw of the bear or wildcat, the rattlesnake, the owl and the hawk. The events of initiation ceremonies were recorded in line drawings on bark scrolls, which served as mnemonic devices to those, including the initiates, who were taught to decipher them. The Midewiwin developed in the early 18th century in response to the prosperity brought by the fur trade, and served as a focal point within the multiple CLAN villages that formed during this period. *See also* NATIVE PEOPLE, RELIGION. RENÉ R. GADACZ

Midge, name given to several groups of small, slender-bodied FLIES. In Canada, nonbiting midges (chironomids), biting midges (ceratopogonids) and gall midges (cecidomyiids) are most important. About 500 species of chironomids are known in Canada; many more await discovery. They reach the northern limit of land, forming an increasingly large component of insect fauna in northern latitudes. Larval stages are mostly aquatic and may form much of the diet of fish. Minute ceratopogonids (no-see-ums) can be a scourge in midsummer and seem undeterred by repellents. They are transmitters of bluetongue virus of cattle and sheep, and of protozoan bird diseases. In Canada, 180 species are reported; not all are pestilential. Their predatory larvae inhabit mud or moist soil. Cecidomyiids are known as gall midges, although not all larvae form plant galls. The notorious Hessian fly, whose larvae bore into wheat stems, is a cecidomyiid. Some larvae are fungus feeders, including some serious pests of commercial mushrooms. Others are predatory. Canadian cecidomyiid fauna has been little investigated, with 100 species recorded of a fauna estimated to exceed 1000.
G.C.D. GRIFFITHS

Midland, Ont, Town, pop 12 092 (1986c), 12 132 (1981c), inc as a village 1878 and as a town 1887, is located on Midland Bay, an inlet of GEORGIAN BAY. It is about 145 km by road N of TORONTO. The area was part of HURONIA before the arrival of Europeans and STE MARIE AMONG THE HURONS (some 2 km outside present-day Midland) was the first European settlement to be established inland from the St Lawrence Valley. Constructed by Jesuit missionaries in 1639, Ste Marie was a base for missionary work among the HURON until it was abandoned in 1648-49. The present reconstruction as well as the nearby Jesuit Martyrs' Shrine and Wye Marsh Wildlife Interpretive Centre attract hundreds of thousands of visitors every year. Midland also serves as a "waterway" to the popular Thirty Thousand Islands of Georgian Bay.

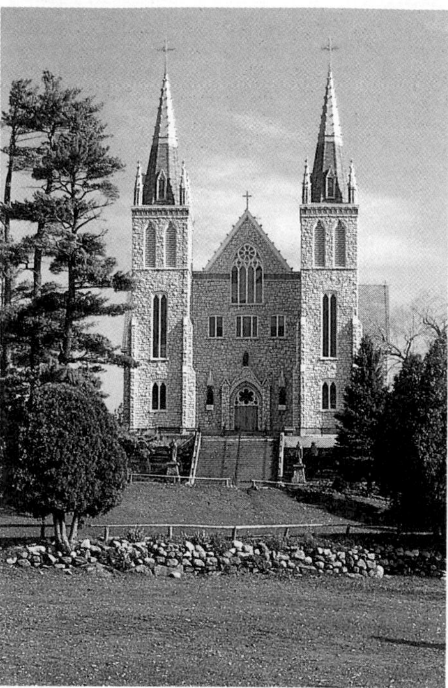

The Martyrs' Shrine, Midland, Ont, commemorates the martyred Jesuit missionaries of the 17th century (*courtesy Canapress Photo Service*).

Modern development of the town began with the arrival of the Midland Railway from Port Hope via Beaverton in 1871. The railway stimulated the logging industry and the town developed extensive harbour facilities and grain elevators. Today, light manufacturing includes world-famous Leica cameras, television picture tubes and automobile parts. PATRICK D. GRUBER

Midnight Sun In the Arctic in the summer, the sun shines all night long. Robert W. SERVICE had this in mind when he used the phrase in his ballad "The Cremation of Sam McGee" (1907). The expression "land of the midnight sun" has often been used to refer to Canada's arctic region and, more loosely, to the Yukon and the Northwest Territories. JOHN ROBERT COLOMBO

Mignault, Pierre-Basile, legal author, judge (b at Worcester, Mass 30 Sept 1854; d at Montreal 15 Oct 1945). Educated in Montreal, where he brilliantly completed law studies at McGill (1878) and later taught civil law (1914-18), Mignault was a prolific writer on various topics in Quebec law. He is now chiefly remembered for his monu mental treatise *Le Droit civil canadien* (9 vols, 1885-1916) which is still cited as an authority in Quebec courts. He sat as a judge of the Supreme Court of Canada (1918-29). Many of his judgements, written in French and English, are considered authoritative statements on CIVIL LAW in Canada. JOHN E.C. BRIERLEY

Migration is defined restrictively as a regular movement between alternate sites, one of which is usually a breeding location. More broadly, it can involve any significant movement of animals (or even plant seeds). Canadians think of migration primarily as the movement of birds: southward in fall, northward in spring. Such movements may be short, as with horned LARKS which nest in the Prairie provinces and winter just S of the border, returning as early as February. Most migrating passerine (perching) birds and SHOREBIRDS go farther, many to Central and S America. The long-distance champion, the arctic TERN, nests at Churchill, Man, and winters in the Antarctic. North-south movements may follow broad fronts or well-defined flyways, as with WATERFOWL. Routes may be identical in both directions or may differ, as with the lesser golden PLOVER which flies S along the Atlantic coast from the Canadian Arctic to Argentina in the fall, but returns N through the Canadian prairies. Similar migrations, southward in fall and northward in spring, are shown by monarch BUTTERFLIES, DRAGONFLIES and some BATS. Some species, however, migrate S in spring, N in fall, eg, Heermann's GULLS which after breeding move from Mexico and southern California to coastal Vancouver I, and various Southern Hemisphere SEABIRDS going to the Atlantic and Pacific coasts. Some birds move altitudinally, usually downslope in winter, up in summer. In contrast, spruce and blue GROUSE move downslope in spring, up in fall.

Barren-ground CARIBOU in northern Canada and Alaska move in a generally circular pattern, wintering near the Peel and Porcupine rivers and calving along the Beaufort Sea. Movements of aquatic animals necessarily follow the configurations of water bodies. SALMON and EEL spawn in fresh water yet spend much of their lives in oceans. Other seasonal movements include those of freshwater FISHES between lakes and rivers and those of SEALS, WHALES and TURTLES in oceanic waters. FROGS, SALAMANDERS and GARTER SNAKES show more localized annual movements. Garter snakes winter and mate in interlake Manitoba and summer in nearby marshy areas.

Many such regular movements involve individuals returning annually to the same breeding area, wintering site or migratory stopover. Species that breed or feed in less stable habitats may alter the precise sites of their activity from year to year but may still migrate regularly. Other migrations are less regular, eg, species such as crossbills and snowy OWLS, which feed on fluctuating food supplies, show "irruptive" or "invasion" types of migration. Some species, such as Clark's nutcracker, undergo much less regular eruptions from their usual range. Other variations are exemplified by partial migrants, such as blue jays and black-capped CHICKADEES, in which only some populations migrate; and by monarch butterflies in which one generation moves south, the next north.

Migratory movements were first documented as a result of observations of diurnally moving flocks, especially along coasts and mountain passes where concentrations occur, or at sites such as POINT PELÉE where night migrants concentrate during the day. Being restricted in time and place, such observations supply limited data. Movements of many species, such as night-migrating birds, underwater animals and wind-blown spiders, are not readily observed. Early observers recognized migratory movements of large birds, but explained the mysterious disappearance of small birds by assuming they hibernated in the mud, rode on the backs of large birds or changed into other species (not entirely foolish, as many species change plumage). Banding or other forms of marking helped in defining migration routes of bats, birds, fishes and dragonflies and, in some cases, in finding the winter range (eg, for chimney swifts, monarch butterflies). Banding has also revealed unexpected patterns of movement, such as the northward movement of Florida-nesting bald EAGLES and the "leap-frog" pattern of some species, eg, the American ROBIN, in which northern-nesting populations winter farther S than do southern-nesting ones. RADAR tracking and transmitters on birds, large mammals and even tiny fishes are helping to define such movements even more precisely. An early observer, seeing birds flying at night silhouetted against the moon, thought they must migrate there. A commentator, thinking that was too far, suggested that PASSENGER PIGEONS moved to an undiscovered satellite between Earth and the moon. Moonwatching has since proved a useful technique in documenting movements.

Factors governing timing, routes taken and reasons for migratory movements are among the great mysteries of science. Experiments performed by William ROWAN in Alberta showed that the effects of photoperiod on physiological processes triggered migration in many birds. Light also governs the daily vertical movements undertaken by some PLANKTON. Weather, although not important in triggering broad timing, is undoubtedly an evolutionary factor and influences precise timing, exact routes and sometimes even reverse movements in birds. Wind is a major influence in movements of some invertebrates and plant seeds that depend on passive dispersal (*see* POLLINATION). The superb navigational skills of many birds, turtles and fishes seem to be determined by a complex array of factors, including landmarks, celestial patterns, the sun's position, magnetic forces and (in fish) chemoreception. The relative importance of each factor remains controversial.

Evolutionary pressures for migration are also controversial. The reasons why migrations occur away from harsh temperatures, dry seasons and scarce food are obvious; return movements from attractive habitats are probably based on longer-term factors, eg, reducing competition for food or other resources, past patterns of glaciation, continental drift and deep-routed traditions. Much remains to be learned about this complex subject. MARTIN K. MCNICHOLL

Reading: R. Baker, ed, *The Mystery of Migration* (1981).

Mikita, Stan, hockey player (b at Sokolce, Czech 20 May 1940). Born Stanislaus Gvoth, he took the name of his uncle after moving to St Catharines as a boy. He played junior hockey for St Catharines and joined Chicago Black Hawks 1959-60. A smooth-skating centre and superb playmaker, he won the ART ROSS TROPHY (leading scorer) in 1964, 1965, 1967 and 1968. He received the HART TROPHY (most valuable player) in 1967 and 1968, and after an early career marred with penalties received the LADY BYNG TROPHY (most gentlemanly player) in 1967 and 1968. He was first all-star centre from 1961-62 to 1963-64 and from 1965-66 to 1967-68. He played his entire career with Chicago, retiring after the 1979-80 season. His 1467 career points in regular season play rank him (in 1987) fifth all-time among NHL scorers; his 926 assists ranked fourth and his 541 goals ranked him ninth. He scored 59 goals and 91 assists and 150 points in playoffs.

JAMES MARSH

Military and Staff Colleges The 3 Canadian military colleges (formerly Canadian services colleges) educate and train officers and officer cadets for ARMED FORCES careers. ROYAL MILITARY COLLEGE opened 1 June 1876 at Kingston, Ont. Royal Naval College of Canada, authorized by the 1910 NAVAL SERVICE ACT, opened at Halifax, NS in 1911; as a result of the 1917 HALIFAX EXPLOSION it moved to RMC, then in 1918 to the former British dockyard at Esquimalt, BC. It closed June 1922, and for 20 years naval cadets attended Royal Naval College, Dartmouth, Eng. As a result of wartime expansion the new Royal Canadian Naval College, Royal Roads, opened near Esquimalt in 1942. It accepted air force officer cadets in 1947 and then, along with RMC, became a tri-service military college in 1948. In 1952 Collège militaire royale (CMR) was established at St-Jean, Qué, primarily for French-speaking officer cadets. Today, both CMR and RMC offer courses in French, and all 3 colleges offer university degrees: RMC since 1959, CMR since 1971 (with UNIVERSITÉ DE SHERBROOKE) and Royal Roads since 1975. Women were admitted to RMC post-graduate degree programs in 1978, and female cadets were enrolled in the Regular Officer Training Plan at all 3 military colleges in Sept 1980.

After commissioning, an officer's professional development and education may include courses at staff schools and colleges. The Canadian Forces Staff School, Toronto (which opened 1960 as RCAF Staff School, a part of Air Force College), prepares junior officers for basic administrative and planning staff duties. The Canadian Land Forces Command and Staff College, Kingston (opened as a Canadian Army Staff College during WWII), offers a tactics-oriented course for operational command and staff duties. The Canadian Forces Command and Staff College, Toronto (opened as the RCAF Staff College in 1943), prepares air, land and naval officers for command and staff positions as lieutenant-colonels. National Defence College, Kingston, est 1947, provides senior officers and civil servants with the opportunity to study broad questions of national policy and international affairs. STEPHEN HARRIS

Military Engineers, soldiers specially trained to apply engineering science and technology to war. Their tasks include building roads, bridges, railways, airfields, field FORTIFICATIONS, and antitank and other obstacles; laying and removing demolition charges and mines; and spearheading amphibious assaults by preparing invasion beaches for subsequent landings. Volunteer companies served in the militia from 1859, and in 1903 the Canadian Engineers Corps was added to the Permanent Force. The "sappers," who were renamed the Corps of Royal Canadian Engineers in 1936, served overseas in both world wars where, in addition to normal duties, they provided mining and tunnelling companies at the front, in Britain, and at Gibraltar. In peacetime, Canada's army engineers have conducted land surveys, built bases and other defence installations, and contributed to northern development through the construction of dams, bridges, roads and airfields. STEPHEN HARRIS

Military History, *see* ARMAMENTS; ARMED FORCES; AVIATION, MILITARY; KOREAN WAR; SOUTH AFRICAN WAR; WAR OF THE AUSTRIAN SUCCESSION; WAR OF THE SPANISH SUCCESSION; WAR OF 1812; WORLD WAR I, WORLD WAR II; and individual battle entries.

Military Recruiting, the practice of persuading people to serve in the ARMED FORCES. Although military service is compulsory in some countries, the Canadian tradition has been to maintain volunteer forces (for exceptions, *see* CONSCRIPTION; IMPRESSMENT). This places considerable pressure on recruiting officers to find sufficient numbers of suitable, willing candidates. When unemployment is widespread, the simple prospect of having a job may persuade young men and women to enlist. In wartime, strong appeals are made to patriotism, honour and the citizen's duty to serve. In peacetime, recruiters may challenge the young adult's love of adventure, but more recently they have emphasized that the trades training and education available in the armed forces are applicable to civilian employment once an individual's military career is over. In 1987 about 512 recruiting officers and civilians in 37 locations visited hundreds of high schools and colleges across the country to attract the personnel required to keep the Canadian Forces up to their established strength of approximately 82 000 officers and men. STEPHEN HARRIS

Military Service Act, 29 Aug 1917, invoked to reinforce the CANADIAN EXPEDITIONARY FORCE in France. The war was going badly, casualties were enormous, and Canada's contribution in manpower compared unfavourably with that of other countries. Voluntary enlistment had been uneven, and the military believed they could not maintain the Canadian Corps at full strength without CONSCRIPTION. Encouraged by English Canadians and the British, PM Sir Robert BORDEN introduced the Military Service Act. Riots broke out in Québec. The Act was unevenly administered, and there were numerous evasions and many exemptions. By the end of the war only 24 132 conscripts had reached the front. The Act's military value has been questioned, but its political consequences are clear. It led to Borden's Union government and drove most of his French Canadian supporters into opposition, as they were seriously alienated by this attempt to enforce their participation in an imperial war.
RICHARD A. PRESTON

Militia, *see* ARMED FORCES: MILITIA AND ARMY.

Militia Acts provided manpower for defence. Until the 1850s, such Acts in Upper and Lower Canada, NS and NB usually imposed compulsory service on males between 16 and 50 or 60, with annual or more frequent enrolment musters. This institution, the Sedentary Militia, was unorganized and untrained. The Acts also authorized service battalions for transport duties, etc, or for operations. This Active Militia was composed of volunteers, supplemented if necessary by the ballot (selection by lot). In 1846 an Active Militia 3000 strong was provided for in the Province of Canada. In 1855 much of Canada's British garrison left for the Crimea, and patriotic excitement enabled approval of legislation for an Active Militia of 5000 to be equipped, trained and paid. In 1856 additional Active Militia companies without pay were authorized.

Fearing invasion during the AMERICAN CIVIL WAR, John A. Macdonald introduced a bill (1862) to provide an Active Militia of 50 000, to be selected by ballot if necessary, and to be equipped and paid for 28 days' training. The bill's defeat brought about the fall of his government. In 1863 PM John Sandfield Macdonald provided that the Sedentary Militia would be retained and service battalions could be called out for 6 days' drill a year; 35 000 volunteers would be equipped but not paid. George-Étienne Cartier's Militia Act of 1868 retained the theory of conscription but recognized voluntary training as the backbone of the Dominion's militia system: 40 000 infantry, organized in companies in military districts, formed an Active Militia. The Militia Act of 1883 added permanent staffs for militia schools, the nucleus of a permanent force.

In 1904, after a series of confrontations between British general officers commanding the Canadian Militia and the minister of militia and defence, a Militia Act set up the Militia Council of civilians and military officials, including a chief of the General Staff. The bill doubled the Permanent Force to 4000 to provide a garrison to replace the British at Halifax. The 1922 National Defence Act brought the Militia, the Naval Service, and the Canadian Air Force together under the Dept of NATIONAL DEFENCE. *See also* ARMED FORCES: MILITIA AND ARMY. RICHARD A. PRESTON

Milk River, located in the extreme SE corner of Alberta, is the only river in Canada to flow into the Gulf of Mexico drainage basin. It has its source in Montana, flows N into Canada and then S to join the Missouri R near Fort Peck, Montana. In Alberta the river cuts a spectacular canyon, 150 m deep and over 1.5 km wide in places, straddling the Canada-US boundary. The river flows through the Canadian Dry Belt where precipitation is as low as 200 mm and temperatures of 38°C are not uncommon. The rare geomorphological process of "piping" along the canyon walls has created a unique landscape of disappearing streams, dry valleys, "sinkholes," blind valleys, waterfalls, natural bridges and caves.
JAMES MARSH

Milkweed is the common name for perennial, herbaceous plants of genus *Asclepias*, family Asclepiadaceae (from Gk physician Aesculapius). One hundred species occur worldwide; 13 are native to Canada. Except for butterfly weed (*A. tuberosa*), all Canadian species have milky juice with toxic properties. Leaves are simple; flowers grow in large clusters. Seed pods are generally large, often containing hundreds of seeds, each with a silky parachute. In nature, several species (eg, butterfly weed) are highly regarded "showy" plants. Six species are listed as Canadian weeds, the most important of these being common milkweed (*A. syriaca*), found from Manitoba to the Maritimes and abundant in southern Ontario and Québec. It spreads by creeping underground rootstocks and by seeds. In Ontario, it was grown for fibre and latex rubber during WWII; other economic uses have been suggested. It is a source of nectar for monarch and other butterflies. Indians valued its medicinal properties and used the fibre for rope and weaving. *See also* PLANTS, NATIVE USES. PAUL B. CAVERS

Millar, Charles Vance, lawyer (b at Aylmer, Ont 1853; d at Toronto 31 Oct 1926). An able lawyer, sportsman and practical joker, he is best known as creator of the Stork Derby. By his will Millar, a bachelor, left the bulk of his estate to the mother who, in the 10 years following his death, gave birth in Toronto to the largest number of children. The ensuing contest inspired worldwide interest and much litigation before the validity of the bequest was upheld by the Supreme Court of Canada and the money distributed among 4 winning mothers. The question of whether Millar intended his will to take effect or merely to amuse his lawyer friends remains in doubt.
MARK M. ORKIN

Millard, Charles Hibbert, labour leader (b at St Thomas, Ont 25 Aug 1896; d at Toronto 24 Nov 1978). Originally a carpenter by trade, Millard helped organize United Auto Workers Local 222, which he led in the historic 1937 OSHAWA STRIKE. From 1938 to 1939 he was Canadian UAW director. Between 1940 and 1943 he was on the executive of the Congress of Industrial Organizations (CIO), the CANADIAN CONGRESS OF LABOUR (CCL), the United Steelworkers of America, and the Packinghouse Workers' organizing committee. Millard helped negotiate the merger of the 2 labour congresses and was elected VP of the CANADIAN LABOUR CONGRESS at its founding convention (1956). In 1956 he also became director of organization for the Confederation of Free Trade Unions in Brussels. A staunch CCF supporter, he was elected to the Ontario legislature twice (1943, 1948). He also ran unsuccessfully for Parliament several times. In 1961, he supported labour's participation in the formation of the NEW DEMOCRATIC PARTY. LAUREL SEFTON MACDOWELL

Millenarianism (from the Lat *mille*, "thousand" and *annus*, "year"). Its religious significance comes from Revelation 20:1-6, where John predicts that Satan will be bound for 1000 years. In Christian theology, millenarianism refers to the expectation of the Kingdom of God on Earth, in which the returning Christ will rule men for 1000 years before the Last Judgement puts an end to history altogether. Although part of the inheritance of all Christian groups, this doctrine has been pushed into the background by most of the larger churches. In contrast, it is vital to many smaller sects active in Canada such as the MORMONS, JEHOVAH'S WITNESSES and SEVENTH-DAY ADVENTISTS. Historically, expectation of millennial deliverance has become particularly intense at times of great social stress, such as the Crusades or Black Death in medieval Europe or the Protestant Reformation. It is in such a context that one should place Louis RIEL, who preached a message of millennial salvation to the Métis of Canada as their society was being overwhelmed by white immigration.

Originally a Judeo-Christian concept, millenarianism is now applied by anthropologists and sociologists to parallel phenomena in non-Christian settings, eg, the Ghost Dance of 1890, when many Plains Indian tribes anticipated the destruction of the white man, accompanied by rejuvenation of the earth and the return of the buffalo in unprecedented numbers. Among thousands of such movements are the "cargo cults" of Melanesia, the Black Muslims of the US, the Rastafarians of Jamaica (now also in Canada), and the followers of the People's Temple who committed mass suicide in Guyana in 1978.

A closely related concept is "messianism." Strictly speaking, messianism refers to a doctrine or movement featuring an individual Messiah, whereas millenarianism is a broader term encompassing expectations of collective salvation; but in practice the 2 terms are often used interchangeably. The concept of messianism is often employed metaphorically in discussions of Québec history to designate the sense of mission deeply embedded in French Canadian culture. In the 19th century, this was the desire to evangelize the N American continent in the Roman Catholic religion; in the 20th century, it is the desire to foster the French language and culture.

Some authors also use the terms millenarianism and messianism to refer to ideologies such as Marxism, Fascism and Social Credit, which posit the fundamental transformation of society through political action. This usage, while also metaphorical, highlights important similarities between religious and political movements.
THOMAS FLANAGAN

Miller, Clarence Horatio, "Dr Big," jazz musician, blues singer, educator (b at Sioux City, Iowa 18 Dec 1922). Miller served his musical apprenticeship in Kansas City and in Wichita, Kans, in the late 1930s. Between 1946 and 1959 he performed and recorded, mainly as a sideman, with Duke Ellington, Jay McShann, Bob Brookmeyer, Count Basie and others. From 1962 onwards Miller began performing in Canada, appearing on the Tommy Banks Show (CBC-TV) in 1963. In 1966 he made Vancouver his home base, then moved to Edmonton in 1969. During the 1970s and 1980s Miller led a succession of small jazz and blues bands, working mainly in western Canada but also touring abroad. Since 1976 Miller has taught master classes at the Banff Centre and has acted as adviser to the Grant MacEwan College

(Edmonton) music department. The subject of an NFB film, he was awarded an honorary doctorate by Athabasca U (1985). He has recorded a number of albums in Canada, including *Jazz Canada – Montreux* (which received a Juno Award), *The Best of Jazz Radio Canada* and *Big Miller Live from Calgary*. DAVID GREGORY

Miller, Frank, politician, premier of Ontario (b at Toronto 14 May 1927). He graduated from McGill U in chemical engineering in 1949. He was a General Motors dealer in Bracebridge, Ont, and operator of several resorts in the Muskoka area. He was councillor in Bracebridge 1967-70 and was elected Conservative MPP for Muskoka in 1971, 1975, 1977 and 1981. As minister of health 1974-77, his move to close some small-town hospitals created public controversy, but he became increasingly adept at defusing confrontation. He was minister of natural resources 1977-78, minister of treasury and economics 1978-83 and minister of industry and trade 1983-85. Considered the most conservative of those who sought to replace William DAVIS, he made a commitment to maintain the social service network built up in Ontario during the previous 41 years of Conservative government. He won the leadership on the third ballot in Jan 1985 and became premier in Feb. His party's popularity fell dramatically at the polls in May 1985 and Miller was unable to form a government. A Liberal-NDP pact made David PETERSON premier, ending a 42-year Tory regime. Miller resigned as leader in Nov of that year. JAMES MARSH

Miller, Frank Robert, engineer, air chief marshal (b at Kamloops, BC 30 Apr 1908). Miller joined the RCAF in 1931 and commanded training schools in WWII before proceeding overseas in 1944 as a station commander. He rose to vice-chief of the air staff 1951-54, but left the air force to serve as deputy minister of national defence 1955-60. He became chairman, Chiefs of Staff, 1960-64, and chief of the defence staff 1964-66. As Canada's first COS, he presided over the integration of the 3 service headquarters and the command organization of the Canadian Armed Forces. Quiet, gracious and known for an ability to cut through to the heart of the matter, Miller is the only man ever to hold both the top permanent civil and military positions in the Dept of National Defence. NORMAN HILLMER

Miller, George Martell, architect (b at Port Hope, Canada W 1855; d at Toronto 17 Apr 1933). Designer of many fine neoclassical structures in Toronto, he came to the city in the early 1880s, taught at the Mechanics' Institute and began to practise architecture in 1885. Among his buildings are the Lillian Massey Building at U of T, the old Havergal College on Jarvis St, and the Toronto General Trust Building. He was also architect for the Canadian General Electric Building, Peterborough, Ont; the Ontario Ladies College and the House of Industry, Whitby, Ont; and the Macdonald Building, Ontario Agricultural Coll, Guelph. ANDREA KRISTOF

Miller, John Henry, actor-manager (b at London, Eng 1 Feb 1859; d at New York 9 Apr 1926). Henry Miller was 14 when his parents brought him to Toronto and in 1876 he made his stage debut at the Grand Opera House, with Mrs Morrison's resident Toronto stock company in *Amy Robsart*, the dramatization of Walter Scott's *Kenilworth*. He achieved recognition with Daniel Frohman's Lyceum Theatre in New York, and toured opposite such Canadian stars as Clara MORRIS and Margaret ANGLIN. Miller evolved into a meticulous director and went into management at New York's Princess Theatre in 1905, building his own Henry Miller Theatre in 1916. DAVID GARDNER

Miller, William Lash, educator, chemist (b at Galt, Ont 10 Sept 1866; d at Toronto 1 Sept 1940). When he died, Miller was described as the greatest chemist Canada had produced; he was certainly the most colourful. A graduate in chemistry from U of T (1887), Miller then earned 2 PhDs in Germany, joining the teaching staff at Toronto in 1891, where he served for 46 years. Possessed of extraordinary clarity of thought and a forceful personality, Miller was an inspiring yet terrifying teacher. His greatest scientific strength lay in his mastery of the chemical thermodynamics of Willard Gibbs, learned from Ostwald at Leipzig. His greatest weakness (also learned from Ostwald) was his refusal to use or teach the atomic and molecular theories that formed the mainstream of 20th-century chemical thinking. Toronto became an important centre of chemical research, and a roster of Miller's pupils includes a remarkable number of important chemists. W.A.E. MCBRYDE

Miller and Cockriell Case (1977) J.H. Miller and V.J.R. Cockriell, charged with the murder of a policeman, argued the incompatibility of the penalty imposed by law with the Canadian Bill of Rights 1960. The Supreme Court ruled that the death penalty for the murder of a policeman or prison guard is not "cruel and unusual punishment" in the sense that the expression is used in the Bill of Rights. Since 14 July 1976, CAPITAL PUNISHMENT has been abolished in Canada, although a narrow provision for it still applies to those in military service. In *McCann et al* v *The Queen et al* (1976), federal court judges found that solitary confinement under particular conditions could be considered cruel and unusual punishment. GÉRALD-A. BEAUDOIN

Millet, general term applied originally to any small-seeded cereal or forage grass used for food or as animal feed. Most are restricted to the tropics or subtropics; they are rare in Canada. The most important exception is proso millet (*Panicum miliaceum*), an annual grown for birdseed in Ontario; it has also been used as livestock feed in most provinces. In the USSR, millet is a major source of grain and flour. In the 1970s, a brown- to black-seeded form of proso millet invaded Ontario and Québec. This weed, resistant to triazine herbicides, has become a serious problem in corn and bean fields. Ripe seeds scatter readily and are distributed primarily by farm machinery. Seeds are strongly dormant and survive for years in the soil. The seed hull remains attached to the root system through the life cycle. If roots can be excavated, this feature allows positive identification. PAUL B. CAVERS

Millidge, Thomas Edward, vessel owner and builder (b probably at Saint John 18 Dec 1814; d there 5 Aug 1894). He was the principal 19th-century registrant of newly built tonnage at Saint John Port of Registry. His mother, Sarah Simonds, and his cousins, the Gilberts, linked him to 2 of the leading families of the town. Although Millidge began acquiring vessels during the 1830s, the bulk of his tonnage was registered in the 1850s. While carrying on a lumbering business, he served as president of the Bank of New Brunswick (to 1858) and also invested in railways and ferries. By the 1860s Millidge was operating the family shipyard on the Kennebecasis R. From that point, his commercial pursuits tapered off. At his death he had no heir to carry on the family business. GERRY PANTING

Millipede (class Diplopoda), terrestrial, usually elongate arthropod, with a small head and short antennae. Typically, the body is very hard and subcylindrical, but often with platelike expansions making the animal appear flattened. The body comprises 11-100 or more similar segments which, except for the first 3-4, consist of fused pairs of true segments. The first and last true segments and the anal plate lack appendages. The second, third and, usually, fourth segments each bear one pair of legs; other segments, 2 pairs. Some appendages, in functional adults, are modified for reproduction. Despite the name millipede ("1000-footed"), the number of legs is less than 400, generally less than 200. Newly hatched millipedes have 3-4 pairs of legs; the number increases following successive molts. About 10 000 species are known worldwide, mostly from tropical regions. More than 60 species are known to occur in Canada. About 10% of these, particularly in the East, have been introduced from Europe. Tropical millipedes sometimes grow to 30 cm; Canada's largest species barely attain 8 cm; many common species are less than 1 cm long and 1 mm in diameter. In western Canada, fossils of marine, millipedelike arthropods, not directly ancestral to any living group, are known from the mid-Cambrian (530 million years ago). Cylindrical millipedes usually burrow in soil; "flat backs" occupy matted, rotting vegetation. A few spend periods on the surface, mainly at night. Millipedes are important in soil formation in some deciduous and tropical forests. Virtually all feed on decayed matter or fresh vegetation. One or 2 species have been considered to be crop pests but, usually, damage done follows other injury to plants. An alarmed millipede typically coils itself into a spiral; some flat-backs are incapable of coiling; very short, exotic species may roll into a ball. Millipedes often protect themselves by noxious body secretions. Those of large, tropical species may cause skin and eye inflammation. Canadian species are harmless. D.K. MCEWAN KEVAN

Millman, Peter MacKenzie, astronomer (b at Toronto 10 Aug 1906). Educated at U of T and Harvard, Millman was an astronomer at U of T 1933-41 and served in the RCAF during WWII. After 9 years at the Dominion Observatory, Ottawa, he transferred to the NATIONAL RESEARCH COUNCIL in 1955 as head of upper-atmosphere research. In 1986 he was awarded the title researcher-emeritus at the NRC. Millman's own specialty was the spectroscopic study of METEORS, for which he was awarded the J. Lawrence Smith Medal of the US National Academy of Sciences. He traced meteors by RADAR and in the 1950s was chairman of the Canadian government's interdepartmental committee on unidentified flying objects. Millman was an officer of the Int Astronomical Union and presided over its committee on planetary-system nomenclature 1973-82. In 1984 Minor Planet No 2904 was named Millman in his honour. DONALD J.C. PHILLIPSON

Milne, David Brown, artist, writer (b near Paisley, Ont 8 Jan 1882; d at Bancroft, Ont 26 Dec 1953). Milne's initial recognition was in the US and he did not enjoy in Canada the attention that his contemporaries in the GROUP OF SEVEN received. Succeeding generations of artists, however, have generally given him (or J.W. MORRICE) the highest acclaim among Canadian painters (*see* PAINTING).

As a child, Milne drew constantly. Before he embarked for New York City in 1903 to become an illustrator, he had taken a correspondence art course and experimented with photography. He studied at the Art Students League (1903-05), attended lectures by Robert Henri and William Chase, and visited galleries, especially Stieglitz' 291. Finally, he decided to be a painter rather than an illustrator. He exhibited vivacious and avant-garde paintings regularly with leading art societies from 1909, at the Montross Gallery, in the famous Armory Show (1913) and in the

Sparkle of Glass (*c*1927), oil on canvas, by David Milne. The artist forged several influences into a unique and powerful expression (*courtesy National Gallery of Canada, Vincent Massey Bequest, 1968*).

Panama-Pacific Exposition (1915) where he won a silver medal.

In 1916 Milne and his wife Patsy (m 1912) moved to Boston Corners in upstate NY, where his work achieved a different power, both productive and innovative. He joined the Canadian Army in 1917 and after WWI painted for the army in England and France. He returned to NY state and painted prolifically, even during summer projects in the Adirondacks. In 1923-24 he spent a winter in Ottawa trying unsuccessfully to establish himself in Canada. He finally returned to Canada in 1929 (separating from his wife in 1933), and from then on painted in Ontario, mainly in Temagami, Toronto and at Baptiste Lk near Bancroft. His work became known after he sought the patronage of Alice and Vincent MASSEY, who organized several exhibitions, the first of which was seen by Douglas DUNCAN, who later became Milne's agent and dealer, and Alan Jarvis, later director of the National Gallery.

Milne's art was formed by both American and French impressionism and by Henri Matisse's fauvism. Claude Monet, especially in the aesthetic unity of his paintings, was the most pervasive influence. Milne forged these influences into his own powerful way of seeing and painting. He endowed the simplest subjects – houses, barns, flowers, trees and still lifes – with majestic stature. Figures appear frequently in his work in New York and Toronto, but the landscape dominated until the last 10 years of his life when a series of fantasies emerged. These may have been inspired by Kathleen Pavey, whom he met in 1938 and who became his second wife, and certainly by the birth of his only child, David, in 1941. Nevertheless the strong biblical references in them suggest a symbolic understanding of life, death, rebirth and resurrection. The *Ascension* series best illustrates his serious intent, but the *Noah and the Ark* series shows also that he could be amused by his biblical reinterpretations.

Approximately half of Milne's paintings are oils and half are watercolours. The National Gallery of Canada and the Winnipeg Art Gallery both have excellent collections of his work. *Billboards* (1912), *Painting Place* (1930), *Boston Corners* (1917), *Raspberry Jam* (1936) and *White Poppy* (1946) are fine examples of his work at different periods. Milne also invented a method of making colour drypoints and returned to this medium sporadically over 20 years (1927-47). Many critics consider these drypoints his finest works. Milne's unpublished letters to his friend James Clarke, to the Masseys and to others, his "Autobiography" (1947) and his journals are a rich store of observations, thoughts and descriptions unparalleled in Canadian art.

DAVID P. SILCOX

Reading: David P. Silcox, *David Milne* (1967); Silcox and David Milne Jr., eds, "David Milne: His Journals and Letters of 1920 and 1921," *artscanada* 30, 3 (Aug 1973); J. O'Brien, *David Milne: The New York Years 1903-1916* (1981).

Milton, Ont, Town, pop 32 037 (1986c), 28 067 (1981c), located 29 km W of Toronto. The area was opened to settlement with the purchase of the Mississauga Tract from Indians, and creation of the York Road (Hwy 5) to London. It was first called Martin's Mills after a pioneer family, and in 1837 was renamed Milton. It was made county seat of Halton in 1853 and a town in 1857. The Robertson "socket head" screw was developed here.

K.L. MORRISON

Minas Basin is the broadest part of the S-eastern head of the Bay of FUNDY and lies entirely within NS. It merges westward into Fundy, through Minas Channel, 5 km wide, and eastward into Cobequid Bay, and is widest (30 km) S of Parrsboro, NS. Its depth, generally less than 40 m, is over 100 m in Minas Channel. The bottom consists of large sand bodies swept by strong tidal currents, changing to mud flats nearer the shore. Its daily tidal range of 15-16 m is among the highest in the world. The N shore is straight, with small coves and islands, and cliffs rising to 100-200 m; the S shore is mainly low, with undulating good agricultural land and hayfields on former salt marshes. Farming includes mixed cattle husbandry, vegetable growing, egg production and apple growing. Coastal marshes in the SW were a focal area of ACADIAN French settlement in the early 17th century. Major towns are WOLFVILLE, WINDSOR and Parrsboro. GRAND PRÉ, dating from Acadian times, is a national historic park.

I.A. BROOKES

The Minas Basin as photographed by satellite, showing its position at the head of the Bay of Fundy. The basin proper is lower centre; Minas Channel is left and Cobequid Bay right (*courtesy Canada Centre for Remote Sensing/Energy, Mines, Resources Canada*).

Miner, William, Bill, outlaw (b at Bowling Green, Ky *c*1847; d at Covington, Ga 2 Sept 1913). Known as the "Gentleman Bandit," Miner achieved notoriety for numerous robberies in the American West. In 1904 after his release from San Quentin Prison, Miner moved to BC where on Sept 13 he successfully robbed a CPR train near Mission. On 8 May 1906, Miner struck the CPR again near Kamloops, but this time the robbery was bungled. Miner and 2 accomplices were captured by the Royal North-West Mounted Police, and the aging robber was sentenced to 25 years in the New Westminster Penitentiary. On 8 Aug 1907, he escaped and fled to the US where he continued to rob banks and trains until his death in a Georgia prison. Miner's bold attacks on the unpopular CPR made him a folk hero to many western Canadians. An award-winning Canadian film, *The Grey Fox*, is based on his career in Canada.

EDWARD BUTTS

Miner, John Thomas, "Jack," conservationist, lecturer (b at Dover Center, Ohio 10 Apr 1865; d at Kingsville, Ont 3 Nov 1944). He moved to Kingsville with his family in 1878 and helped in the family tile business. Miner developed an early passion for nature and spent much of his time in the forest. He became an avid and skilful hunter, known for good humour and boundless energy. A hunting accident fatal to his brother and other family tragedies diverted his energy into religious zeal and passion for conservation. He tried to attract geese to his property (1904), establishing in 1908 one of the first bird sanctuaries in N America, officially declared a provincial crown reserve in 1917.

Miner's many lectures on the sanctuary throughout N America and Europe inspired similar efforts elsewhere and instilled a conservation ethic in many people, eventually earning him the Outdoor Life Gold Medal and the OBE. His attitude towards predators as "evil vermin" has been much criticized, but was typical before the ecological importance of predation was understood. His 1927 warnings against pollution of the GREAT LAKES were prophetic. Miner early recognized the importance of international co-operation in migratory bird conservation and, before banding was regulated, obtained bands from Percy A. TAVERNER and tagged thousands of waterfowl, placing biblical scriptures into the bands. National Wildlife Week, proclaimed in his honour, his sanctuary and 2 autobiographical books continue as his legacy.

MARTIN K. MCNICHOLL

Reading: J.M. Linton and C.W. Moore, *The Story of Wild Goose Jack* (1984); J. Miner, *Jack Miner and the Birds* (1923) and *Wild Goose Jack* (1969).

Mineral, element or chemical compound formed in nature usually by inorganic processes. Minerals may be composed of one element such as carbon (diamond) or gold, or of several elements. Most minerals are characterized by a definite chemical composition, expressed by a chemical formula indicating the types of atoms and their numbers. These atoms are arranged in an orderly 3-dimensional pattern forming a crystalline material. Some solids (including natural glasses) and liquids (eg, water, mercury) lack the orderly atomic arrangement and are referred to as mineraloids. COAL, PETROLEUM and amber, lacking both a definite chemical composition and an orderly atomic structure, are not minerals, although they are referred to as MINERAL RESOURCES. Pearls, CORAL and shells are composed of crystalline calcium carbonate and are referred to as biogenic minerals because they were formed by living organisms. Laboratory grown (ie, synthetic) compounds are also nonminerals, although their chemistry and structure may be identical to naturally occurring minerals.

There are about 3000 known mineral species; about 80 new species are discovered yearly. To establish a new species, all data relating to the mineral, including its chemical, structural, physical and optical properties, must be approved by the Commission on New Minerals and New Mineral Names of the International Mineralogical Assn. The association also judges the acceptability of the proposed name. Minerals are named in various ways, some in honour of a person (eg, weloganite, after Sir William E. LOGAN), a locality (athabascaite), an institution (mcgillite), the chemical composition (cobaltite), or a distinctive property such as colour (azurite) or shape (cylindrite). Many names are derived from Latin or Greek words describing characteristic features, eg, albite [Lat *albus*, "white"] or rhodonite [Gk *rhodon*, "rose"]. All accumulated scientific data concerning the newly named mineral are published in a recognized international journal, such as the *Canadian Mineralogist*, for dissemination worldwide.

Minerals occur as components of ROCKS and, less commonly, as concentrations in rocks. Individual minerals may be readily recognized in coarse-textured rocks (eg, granite) but not in fine-grained rocks (eg, lava, shale). Concentrations of minerals range from small occurrences to large deposits and are formed by various processes, including solidification of mineral-bearing solutions in rock openings (eg, fissures, cavities), precipitation from mineral-rich waters as in springs and saline lakes, and solidification of gases during volcanic eruptions. In each case, minerals grow when appropriate temperature and pressure allow atoms in magma (molten rock), solutions or gases to group together into the basic, mineral-forming building blocks.

Structurally, minerals are grouped into 7 crystal systems, each giving rise to characteristic geometrical shapes. These systems – cubic (isometric), tetragonal, hexagonal, trigonal, orthorhombic, monoclinic and triclinic – are derived from 7 basic boxlike forms, each made up of atoms arranged in a precise and orderly fashion. During crystal growth, these basic building blocks align themselves symmetrically in 3 directions to produce a crystalline solid. If there is sufficient space during growth, a crystal with smooth geometrical faces, reflecting its internal structure, may form; usually, growth conditions are not ideal and minerals form as masses of generally microscopic crystals or in other aggregates (fibrous, powdery, flaky, globular, etc).

Minerals are defined and identified on the basis of their chemical composition and structure. A chemical analysis may range from a test for the presence of one or a few elements to a complete quantitative analysis. The techniques may be simple (eg, a flame test) or may involve sophisticated instruments (eg, electron microprobe, optical spectrograph). Minerals may, however, be identified without use of elaborate laboratory equipment. The most noticeable properties are those influencing appearance.

Form or Habit refers to the characteristic shape in which the mineral is formed. It may be fibrous (asbestos), lamellar or scaly (mica), platy (barite) or globular (hematite). Crystal forms, such as cubes and octahedra (fluorite and magnetite), rhombs (calcite) and 6-sided prisms (quartz and beryl) may also be readily recognized.

Colour, if constant, as in the metallic minerals (gold, copper, chalcopyrite), may be diagnostic. Other minerals (eg, spinel, fluorite, corundum) may occur in various colours. Colour in minerals results from atoms or structural defects (colour centres) that absorb certain portions of the spectrum of light; the unabsorbed portion is reflected or transmitted to the eye as colour. The colour of the powdered mineral (its streak) is more reliable than that of the intact mineral. The streak is produced by rubbing the mineral across an unglazed porcelain plate. Yellow, brown or black sphalerite has a cream-white streak; black or reddish brown hematite has a dark red streak. Some minerals produce a fluorescent colour when exposed to ultraviolet light, eg, the white, tungsten-ore mineral scheelite fluoresces bluish white, a property used in PROSPECTING for it. Minerals that continue to fluoresce after the ultraviolet light source has been removed are referred to as phosphorescent.

Lustre, the reflection of light from mineral surfaces, is classified as metallic or nonmetallic. Various terms are used to describe nonmetallic lustre, including vitreous (glassy), adamantine (brilliant), resinous, waxy or oily, silky, pearly and earthy (dull). Lustre is generally more characteristic of a particular mineral than colour.

Transparency and Opacity depend upon the mineral's ability to transmit or absorb light. Metallic minerals, strong light absorbers, are opaque. Transparent minerals transmit most incident light; these minerals are potential GEMSTONES. Translucent minerals both absorb and transmit light; objects viewed through them appear blurred. Some mineral species vary from transparent to almost opaque, depending upon the degree of impurity and structural defects they contain.

Specific Gravity is the density or weight of a substance, compared to the weight of an equal volume of water (specific gravity, 1). Galena, an ore of lead, has a density of $7\frac{1}{2}$, ie, is $7\frac{1}{2}$ times heavier than water. The atomic weight of elements forming the mineral and the packing arrangement (ie, whether atoms are close or far apart) affect specific gravity. In stream gravels, minerals are separated by their specific gravity, heavier ones settling to the bottom.

Hardness, the relative ability of a mineral to resist scratching or abrasion, is among the most useful diagnostic properties. The Mohs's mineral scale of relative hardness is used to assign an approximate hardness value to a mineral. The scale consists of 10 minerals in order of increasing hardness: talc, 1: gypsum, 2; calcite, 3; fluorite, 4; apatite, 5; orthoclase, 6; quartz, 7; topaz, 8; corundum, 9; diamond, 10. Each mineral will scratch those with lower hardness and be scratched by those higher on the scale. Zircon, which scratches quartz but not topaz, has a hardness of $7\frac{1}{2}$. The hardness of a mineral depends upon the strength of the bonds, or electrical force, holding atoms together; the scratch breaks those bonds.

Breakage Cleavage, a smooth, flat break produced between planes of atoms, results from weakness in the force binding parallel planes of atoms to each other. Minerals may cleave in one or more directions, or not at all. Cleavage is described according to the number and direction of cleavage planes and by the smoothness of the cleavage surface (perfect, good, fair, poor). Mica minerals have a perfect cleavage in one direction and can be split into sheets. Galena has 3 cleavage directions at right angles to each other; each cleavage surface is parallel to a cube face and the cleavage is referred to as cubic. Fracture, a break across planes of atoms resulting in an irregular, nonplanar surface, occurs in minerals having no distinct planes of weakness. All minerals show some type of fracture; minerals that cleave in one or more directions may fracture in others. Fracture is described as conchoidal or shell-like (quartz, glass), hackly or jagged (native copper), splintery (jade) or uneven (feldspar).

Tenacity or Cohesiveness is the breaking strength of minerals. "Tough" minerals (eg, jade) are so difficult to break that boulders are generally sawn. Brittle minerals shatter or crush to a powder when struck; diamond, the hardest mineral known, and talc, the softest, are brittle. Other minerals are deformed more easily than broken: a malleable mineral (gold) can be hammered into sheets; a sectile mineral (silver) can be cut into shavings; a ductile mineral (copper) can be drawn into wire; flexible minerals (graphite) can be bent; and elastic minerals (mica) will spring back after being bent.

Magnetism and Radioactivity, properties shown by only a few common minerals, are easily detected. Magnetism refers to the reaction of a mineral in a magnetic field. Magnetite is strongly attracted to a hand magnet; pyrrhotite and ilmenite are less strongly attracted. Radioactive minerals (uraninite, thorite) contain unstable atoms (uranium, thorium) that emit radiation detectable by a scintillometer or a Geiger counter. In metamict minerals (betafite, allanite) radioactivity causes destruction of the internal atomic structure and the minerals become noncrystalline.

Optical Properties refer to the behaviour of light passing through a mineral. Light travels more slowly in minerals than in air and the amount of slowing varies from mineral to mineral. With the loss of speed, light changes its path, or is refracted. The degree of slowing, referred to as the index of refraction, may be expressed as the ratio of the speed of light in air to the speed in a given mineral. For example, light travels at 299 330 km per second in air (refractive index 1) but slows down to 123 916 km/s in diamond (ie, light travels 2.41 times as fast in air); hence the refractive index of diamond is 2.41.

All minerals, except those in the cubic (isometric) system, split an incoming light ray into 2 rays when it travels along certain crystallographic directions. Each ray is slowed down to a different degree; hence, each ray will have its own index of refraction and the mineral will have 2 indices of refraction along certain directions. Such minerals are referred to as optically anisotropic; minerals with only one refractive index are described as isotropic. To determine the refractive index, mineralogists use the petrographic (polarizing) microscope; gemologists, the refractometer.

X-Ray Powder Diffraction is the most universal laboratory method of mineral identification. The technique uses an X-ray source, a cylindrical camera lined with a strip of photographic film, and a small amount of the mineral powder mounted on a rod inside the camera. A beam of X-rays strikes the mineral, which reflects (diffracts) the X-rays from different sets of parallel planes of atoms; the reflected rays are recorded on the film as a series of concentric lines of varying intensities. The lines represent distances between atomic planes, and the intensities are related to the kind and distribution of atoms in the atomic plane. Since the distances and intensities of the lines (ie, the powder diffraction pattern) are characteristic for each mineral species, the film gives a "fingerprint" of that mineral. An unknown mineral is identified by matching its pattern with a standard pattern.

Classification of Minerals

Modern mineral classification is based on chemical composition. Each chemical class is subdivided into groups or families according to similarities in structure and, to a lesser degree, in chemistry. Minerals in each group have similar properties and were formed in similar geological environments.

Native Elements The 20 or so minerals formed of one element include metals (eg, gold, silver), semimetals (arsenic, bismuth, antimony) and nonmetals (sulphur, carbon as graphite or diamond).

Sulphides, Sulphosalts A sulphide mineral is composed of sulphur with one or more metallic elements (eg, galena, chalcopyrite) or sulphur with a semimetallic element (realgar). A sulphosalt, or double sulphide, is composed of sulphur with both metallic and semimetallic elements (pyrargyrite). Sulphides and sulphosalts are generally opaque, have metallic lustre and a hardness of 1-6, and occur commonly in veins. They include the important ore minerals.

Oxides, Hydroxides Oxide minerals are composed of oxygen with one or more metals or semimetals (eg, hematite). If hydrogen is also present, as in goethite, the mineral is classed as a hydroxide. Oxides generally have simple chemistry and structure.

Halides are minerals composed of the halogen elements (fluorine, chlorine, bromine, iodine) with a metal (eg, halite or table salt, fluorite). Halides are generally soft, brittle and light in colour; some are water soluble. The halides form an important group of industrial minerals, including halite, sylvite (a source of potash), chlorargyrite (ore of silver) and fluorite.

Carbonates, Nitrates, Borates Minerals in these classes have the same basic structural unit (ie, a radical) consisting of 3 oxygen atoms arranged in an equilateral triangle. In each class, a different type of atom is positioned in the centre of the triangle: the centre position in carbonates is occupied by a carbon atom and the radical is CO_3; in nitrates by nitrogen (radical NO_3); in borates by boron (radical BO_3). Each triangular unit is held to similar ones by atoms of metallic elements. Carbonate minerals are most common; calcite and dolomite are the major constituents of limestone and marble. Carbonates are generally soft and soluble in acids; nitrates are water soluble and occur only in arid regions.

Sulphates, Phosphates, Chromates, Arsenates, Vanadates Minerals in these classes have the same type of basic building block (radical), a tetrahedron (pyramid shape) with one oxygen atom at each of its 4 corners and an atom characteristic of the class inside. In sulphates the inner atom is sulphur and the radical is SO_4; the others are phosphorus in phosphates (PO_4), chromium in chromates (CrO_4), arsenic in arsenates (AsO_4) and vanadium in vanadates (VO_4). Atoms of metallic elements unite the tetrahedra to form minerals. Barite and gypsum are important sulphates; apatite is an important phosphate.

Molybdates, Tungstates The radical in minerals in these classes is the tetrahedron of 4 oxygen atoms surrounding an atom of molybdenum in molybdates (MoO_4) or tungsten in tungstates (WO_4). These tetrahedra are distorted by the large atoms inside.

Silicates, minerals containing silicon and oxygen, make up over 90% of Earth's crust and about one-quarter of known mineral species. The basic building block of silicates is the silicon-oxygen tetrahedron (SiO_4). The silicates are classified into 6 groups according to ways in which the tetrahedra are joined to each other: in neosilicates, the basic SiO_4 tetrahedra are held together by atoms of other elements (eg, zirconium in zircon); in sorosilicates, pairs of tetrahedra share one corner atom and the "bow tie" shaped units formed are held together by atoms of other elements (eg, hemimorphite); in cyclosilicates, which have a ring structure, each tetrahedron shares a corner oxygen atom with the 2 adjoining tetrahedra (eg, beryl); in inosilicates, which have a chain structure, each tetrahedron shares an oxygen atom with the 2 adjoining tetrahedra and the chains are aligned and joined by atoms of other elements (eg, pyroxene); in phyllosilicates, which have a sheet structure, each tetrahedron shares 3 oxygen atoms with other tetrahedra (eg, mica minerals); in tektosilicates or framework silicates, all 4 oxygen atoms of each tetrahedron are shared (eg, quartz). ANN P. SABINA

Reading: R.I. Gait, *Exploring Minerals and Crystals* (1972); W.L. Roberts et al, *Encyclopedia of Minerals* (1974).

Agate (quartz) from Lake Superior (left) (*courtesy Geological Survey of Canada*) and arsenopyrite from BC (right) (*courtesy National Museum of Natural Sciences*).

Beryl in feldspar from Lacorne, Qué (left), and beta-uranophane from Faraday Mine, Bancroft, Ont (right) (*courtesy Geological Survey of Canada*).

Weloganite from Francon quarry, Montréal, Qué (left), and grossular garnet from Asbestos, Qué (right) (*courtesy National Museum of Natural Sciences*).

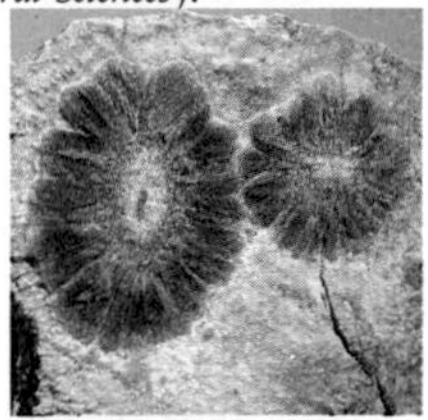

Graphite from Baffin I (left) (*courtesy National Museum of Natural Sciences*) and selenite in gypsum rock from Walton, NS (right) (*courtesy Geological Survey of Canada*).

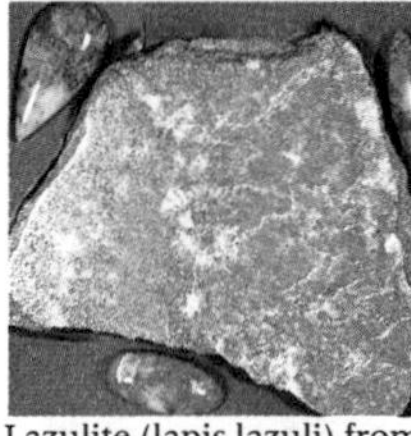

Lazulite (lapis lazuli) from Baffin I (left) (*courtesy National Museum of Natural Sciences*) and phlogopite mica from Otter Lake, Ont (*courtesy Geological Survey of Canada*).

Natrolite from Ice River, BC (left) and pyrite from Mont-St-Hilaire, Qué (right) (*courtesy National Museum of Natural Sciences*).

Uraninite from Payne Mine, Gatineau Park, Qué (left), and stilbite from the Bay of Fundy (right) (*courtesy National Museum of Natural Sciences*).

Mineral and Mining Engineering Mineral engineering is that branch of ENGINEERING concerned with the application of scientific and technical knowledge to the search for and production of valuable MINERALS from naturally occurring surface, underground or below-water deposits. Mining engineering, an essential part of mineral engineering, is also concerned with the construction of civil works such as tunnels, subways, power plants and shelters and, thus, is related to both CIVIL and MECHANICAL ENGINEERING. Minerals are inorganic substances but engineers and economists commonly include materials derived from organic matter (eg, COAL; OIL AND NATURAL GAS) in their classification. A mineral occurrence is called an ore deposit when its valuable minerals can be extracted at a profit.

History in Canada The native people of Canada were known to have used minerals (eg, COPPER) before the arrival of Europeans. Early explorers of N America showed intense interest in the mineral potential of the New World. It was not, however, until the establishment of the GEOLOGICAL SURVEY OF CANADA (1842) that scientific principles were used to determine the extent of Canada's mineral wealth. The mid-1850s (especially the GOLD RUSH) saw the beginning of a series of major finds of economic minerals. To meet the need for qualified individuals to help exploit the newfound wealth, engineering schools were established to teach core courses in civil, mechanical and mining engineering. These included King's College, Fredericton, NB, in 1854; McGill, Montréal, in 1871; School of Practical Science, Toronto, in 1873; École polytechnique, Montréal, in 1873; Royal Military College, Kingston, in 1876; and the School of Mining and Agriculture, Queen's U Kingston, in 1893. The Canadian Institute of Mining and Metallurgy was established in 1898; its membership in 1987 was about 11 000.

Because Canada's economy has remained resource based, mineral and mining engineers and their colleagues who discover and exploit economic minerals (geologists, geophysicists, geochemists, and electrical, mechanical, chemical and metallurgical engineers) continue to play a vital role in Canada's economic well-being. Continual improvements in mining technology have greatly reduced the hazards for mine employees (see MINING SAFETY). Canadian advances in dealing with the logistics of mineral extraction, such as floating a prebuilt processing factory to a remote site, have extended the range of usable resources. Considerable advances have also been made in technologies for extracting the required ore from the rock in which it is embedded.

Applications The normal sequence of mineral engineering activities includes exploration (ie, PROSPECTING), evaluation, financing, development and extraction of the ore and then separation, concentration and refining of the desired minerals, using chemical, physical, electrical and metallurgical systems. The environmentally acceptable disposal of the resultant wastes is an integral part of the process. Exploration activities may still involve the traditional individual prospector looking for surface outcrops or other ready evidence of mineral deposition. Modern mineral exploration, however, makes increasing use of highly organized and specialized REMOTE SENSING methods. The benefits of surface geological mapping can be substantially extended by the use of aerial or satellite photography. Geophysics is concerned with the detection of anomalies related to gravitational, seismic, magnetic, electromagnetic, radioactivity and electrical conductivity measurements in Earth's crust. These changes may indicate the presence of valuable underground mineral occurrences. GEOCHEMISTRY is used to identify unusual concentrations of chemicals in surface soils, water and vegetation, as clues to the proximity of an ore deposit.

The evaluation of mineral occurrences to determine their potential value and to establish proven, probable and possible quantities of ore requires detailed sampling from surface pits and diamond drill holes. Even after extensive drilling has outlined a potential ore body, it may be necessary to carry out bulk sampling from underground shafts, drifts, crosscuts and stopes before the true value of the deposit can be accurately calculated and MINING costs established. Pilot-plant studies may be carried out to confirm or modify mining methods and treatment systems. Because of the highly competitive nature of the mineral industries, the evaluation of relatively low-grade ore deposits is becoming increasingly rigorous. Methods for funding mineral production will depend on the level of risk and the total capital requirement for the recovery procedures involved. Normally, the establishment of a limited liability company and sale of equity shares is necessary. Alternatively, some or all of the funding may be obtained through loans guaranteed by the ore proven in the evaluation stage.

Some mineral resources (eg, PETROLEUM) may be extracted from the earth via drilled holes, using induced pressure and solvents. Dredging is used to mine unconsolidated materials from below the water. Recovery of mineral nodules from the deep-sea bed requires further development of the dredging method (*see* OCEAN MINING). Minerals may also be leached from surface or underground deposits by circulating solvents or microbial fluid, with later precipitation or other suitable disposal of the leached material. Surface and underground deposits may be exploited by open-pit or underground mining methods.

The development phase of mining activity involves mining engineers in complex decisions on rate of ore extraction, methods of mining and treatment of broken ore. A critical path schedule is established and, based on this schedule, equipment is purchased and a work force mobilized. Because many of these decisions interrelate, the mine planner will be involved in selection of equipment for drilling, blasting, waste control, transportation, pumping, power supply, ventilation, ground support and personnel safety. Final mining and process plant design and erection, housing and all of the other complex infrastructure needs will depend on mine location and transport facilities available.

Most mining operations require some form of further processing of broken ore. This processing could be as simple as crushing and washing or may include further steps (eg, grinding, screening, flotation, gravity separation, cyanidation, leaching, precipitation, filtering, roasting), the ultimate purpose being to separate waste from valuable material and to concentrate the latter to meet customer requirements or to prepare for further processing, including smelting and electrical refining (*see* METALLURGY). Environmental considerations require that great attention be given to the disposal of waste products. Atmospheric emissions should be treated to remove unacceptable chemical constituents and solid particulate matter. Processed water should be recycled through the ore-treatment system and, when discharged, should be treated to avoid undesirable constituents reaching rivers or streams. Suspended solids are filtered or settled in restricted basins. When an ore body is completely mined, the site should be returned to an environmentally acceptable condition; eg, plant equipment is removed and access to underground workings sealed, building foundations are normally destroyed and buried, and waste dumps are levelled and contoured to fit in with adjacent topography and seeded or planted.

T.W. KIERANS AND W.G. WEGENAST

Mineral Naming Each MINERAL species is identified by its own appellation, and names have been assigned since antiquity. While there are only some 3000 valid mineral species, nearly 20 000 names occur in the literature. This is partly because researchers working independently have given different names to the same mineral, and partly because distinct names have been applied to minerals that later proved to be varieties or mixtures of already known species. Today a much better control is exercised by the Commission on New Minerals and New Mineral Names established in 1959 by the International Mineralogical Assn.

Two contrasting tendencies can be seen in mineralogical nomenclature. First, there are the names that convey useful information about the mineral itself and are based on the chemical composition, crystal form, colour, lustre or other properties. For example, caysichite, found near Poltimore, Qué, is named after its chemical composition (Ca, Y, Si, C, H). Secondly, there are minerals with names that communicate very little or no information about the composition or properties of the mineral. Such is the case when names of persons are used: some refer to the discoverer or first analyst of the mineral; others recall a famous person or a scientific institution. For example, steacyite was named for H.R. Steacy, a Canadian mineralogist. Moreover, there are names of minerals that convey information about the region where they have been found. Some are quite specific about the location, eg, sudburyite named for Sudbury, Ont; others refer to a much larger area, eg, labradorite. The suffix "ite" is derived from the Gk word *lithos*, meaning rock or stone. While the vast majority of mineral names end in "ite," some have the suffixes "ine" or "ide."

Some 86 new minerals, discovered, analysed or identified by Canadians, have been enshrined in the international nomenclature with Canadian names. Two branches of the Dept of Energy, Mines and Resources (EMR), the GEOLOGICAL SURVEY OF CANADA (GSC) and the Canada Centre for Mineral and Energy Technology (CANMET), rank very high among the leading institutions that identify and publish scientific studies on new minerals; at this time, they have at least half a dozen new species under examination.

A number of Canadian localities, regions and other geographical features are identified by names from the mineral kingdom. A famous example is Cap-Diamant. While investigating the surroundings of the Indian settlement of Stadacona (near Québec City), Jacques CARTIER and his men noticed some sparkling, crystallized minerals attached to the rocks of the nearby cliff, which any modern geologist would describe as a formation of argillaceous limestones and bituminous schists dating back to the Middle Ordovician period (over 458 million years old). This formation forms part of the front of the Appalachians. Understandably, these hexagonal crystals provoked great interest among Cartier's sailors, particularly those specimens showing a range of colours caused by the presence of minute quantities of bitumen. Samples of the newly found "diamonds" were brought back to France, where an informed mineralogist instructed Cartier and his men about the great difference between rock crystal and the most precious stone known to man (*see* DIAMONDS OF CANADA). It is probably this incident that is responsible for an old French saying, still heard in some parts of Normandy and Brittany: "Faux comme un diamant du Canada" [As false as a Canadian diamond]. Samuel de CHAMPLAIN, founder of Québec (1608), made the same discovery some 70 years later, and the promontory was, accordingly, named Cap Diamant.

Many more Canadian geographical names have been derived from minerals. Dozens of lakes, creeks, points, inlets, hills and islands have names such as agate, amethyst, calcite, copper, emerald, garnet, gold, jasper, quartz, ruby, silver, sulphide, topaz and zircon, to name just a few of the minerals and precious and semiprecious stones currently used for this purpose across the country.

JEAN-PAUL DROLET

Minerals Named After Canadian Places

athabascaite	from Martin Lk mine near Uranium City, N of Lk Athabasca, Sask
bytownite	for Bytown, former name of city of Ottawa
carletonite	for Carleton College, now Carleton U, Ottawa, where mineral first recognized
falcondoite	after Falcondo, subsidiary of Falconbridge Nickel Ltd
froodite	for Frood mine, Sudbury dist, Ont
gaspeite	from a site in Gaspé Ouest County, Gaspé Peninsula, Qué
hastingsite	from a site in Hastings County, Ont
hedleyite	from a site near Hedley, SW of Penticton, BC
hilairite	from the site at Mont-St-Hilaire, Rouville County, Qué, one of the Monteregians, where about 125 mineral species have been recognized
labradorite	from Paul I, coast of Lab, official mineral of Nfld
langisite	from Langis mine, Timiskaming dist, Ont
latrappite	from an area near La Trappe, Qué
madocite	from a marble quarry near Madoc, Ont
mattagamite	from a site at Matagami Lake, Qué, spelled Mattagami until 1962
mcgillite	after McGill University, Montréal
montbrayite	from a site in Montbray township, Abitibi, Qué
monteregianite	after the Monteregian Hills, Qué, 8 extinct volcanoes E of Montréal; see above, hilairite
mordenite	from a site near Morden, NS
muskoxite	from the Muskox Intrusion (named by Charles H. Smith) located S of Coppermine, NWT
pellyite	site near the headwaters of Pelly R, YT
romarchite	from Royal Ontario Museum of Archaeology now Royal Ontario Museum, also hydromarchite
spionkopite	site on Spionkop Creek in SW Alta
sudburyite	for Sudbury, Ont
tancoite	site at Tanco mine near Bernic Lake, Man, Tantalum Mining Corp of Canada
temagamite	site near Lake Temagami in northern Ont
tintinaite	site near the Tintina silver mines, YT
tulameenite	site near Tulameen River, BC
wakefieldite	site near Wakefield, Qué
yarrowite	site near Yarrow Creek, SW Alta
yukonite	site near Tagish Lake, YT

Mineral Resources Beyond its importance as one of the main suppliers of food (wheat) to the rest of the world, Canada is probably best known as a storehouse for a host of MINERALS: metals, nonmetals, structural materials and fuels. In fact, few countries can claim a mineral domain that covers nearly 10 million km^2 and embraces 6 main GEOLOGICAL REGIONS, each possessing its characteristic features. Dominating this territory is a massive central upland of Precambrian rocks known as the Canadian SHIELD, which underlies about half the total area of Canada. This vast expanse of ancient IGNEOUS and SEDIMENTARY rocks, bush and bog is one of the world's richest ore-bearing regions, and has been Canada's leading source of a great variety of precious and base metals and has large reserves of ferrous and uranium minerals. Because of its enormous size and favourable geological features, the Shield still has great potential for the discovery of additional mineral deposits. One geological region, the Superior Province of the Shield, has been the greatest source in Canada of copper, lead, zinc, gold, silver, nickel, iron, cobalt, platinum, magnesium, titanium and uranium.

Between the Shield and the Western Cordillera, and stretching from the US border to the Arctic Ocean, lie the Interior Plains (Interior Platform). Under the rich, fertile soil of the southern plains lies a vast storehouse of PETROLEUM, coal, potash and salt, contained in thick sequences of gently dipping sedimentary rocks. The northernmost part of the region holds promise for further discoveries of fossil fuels. Exploration is being extended through most of the plains, including areas in the Arctic Archipelago. The central part contains the famous Athabasca rock formations, where accumulations of heavy-oil sands show reserves and resources equal to any in the world.

West of the Interior Plains is the Canadian Cordillera, composed of high mountains, lower plateaus and valleys, underlain by various sedimentary and volcanic rocks. It covers most of BC, the YT and part of the NWT, and has extensive and varied mineral wealth. Whereas the western and central parts are mainly sources of a great variety of metals, the eastern region of the Cordillera is noted chiefly for coal, gas, petroleum and some industrial minerals. Eastern Canada, SE of the Shield, contains a broad belt of mountains and plains known as the Appalachian Region (Appalachian Orogen). It underlies all of NB, NS and PEI, parts of Newfoundland, and that part of Québec lying S of the St Lawrence R and E of a line between Lk Champlain (US) and Québec City. A great variety of minerals is found there, particularly asbestos (Eastern Townships, Qué) and coal (NS); important deposits of lead and zinc occur in NB and Newfoundland, and industrial minerals (salt, potash and gypsum) in NB and NS.

The Innuitian Region (or Orogen), lying mainly in the Arctic Archipelago, is underlain mainly by folded sedimentary rocks and by gently dipping strata, which contain important petroleum resources (eg, Sverdrup Basin). Older rocks of the Cornwallis Belt contain lead and zinc, including the rich Arvik deposit which supports Canada's most northerly mine, Polaris, on Little Cornwallis I. Other minerals, such as salt and gypsum, have also been identified in the region.

Of increasing importance are the continental shelves extending off the coasts of Canada and underlain mainly by seaward-dipping sedimentary and, in places, volcanic rocks. They include the Pacific, Atlantic and Arctic continental shelves, the last known to extend between the arctic islands, beneath the Beaufort Sea and along the coast of Baffin I. Canada has the second-largest continental margin – that vast submerged area that is the geological prolongation of Canada's landmass into the seas. Increased attention has been paid in recent years to exploration for petroleum and natural gas, particularly off the Atlantic coast where the shelf extends out more than 320 km.

Minerals and Economic Development In the course of its history, and more particularly since Confederation (1867), Canada has taken its place among the richest nations of the world. The people of Canada have discovered and brought into production a rich variety of minerals (metals, industrial minerals and ENERGY resources), making Canada one of the world's leading mineral producers (surpassed only by the USSR and the US for value and diversity of production).

Minerals Named after Canadian People

Mineral	Named after
aplowite	Albert Peter Low
barnesite	William Howard Barnes (b 1903), mineralogist NRC
berryite	Leonard Gascoigne Berry (b 1914), mineralogist, Queen's U, past president of Mineralogical Soc of America (1964), editor of *The Canadian Mineralogist* (1957-75)
boyleite	Robert William Boyle (b 1920), geologist, GSC
cabriite	Louis John Gabri (b 1934), mineralogist, Canmet, EMR
cernyite	Petr Cerny (b 1934), mineralogist U of Manitoba
chapmanite	Edward John Chapman (1821-1904), geologist and mineralogist, U of T
collinsite	William Henry Collins (1878-1937), geologist, former director GSC
dadsonite	Alexander Stewart Dadson (1906-1958), contributed to development of Yellowknife gold deposits
dawsonite	Sir John William Dawson
donnayite	Joseph Dérisé Hubert Donnay (b 1902), mineralogist-crystallographer, McGill and Laval universities; Gabrielle (Hamburger) Donnay, (b 1920) crystallographer-mineralogist, McGill
dresserite	John Alexander Dresser (1866-1954), geologist, author of *The Geology of Québec*, also strontiodresserite
ferrierite	Walter Frederick Ferrier (1865-1950), geologist and mining engineer
frohbergite	Max Hans Frohberg (1901-1970), geologist
gaidonnayite	Gabrielle (Hamburger) Donnay, crystallographer-mineralogist, McGill
gaitite	Robert Irwin Gait (b 1938), curator of mineralogy, ROM
garyansellite	Harold Gary Ansell (b 1943), mineralogist, GSC
gittinsite	John Gittins (b 1932), petrologist, U of Toronto
gormanite	Donald G. Gorman (b 1922), mineralogist, U of Toronto
gunningite	Henry Cecil Gunning (b 1901), geologist, GSC
hawleyite	James Edwin Hawley (1897-1965), mineralogist, Queen's
haycockite	Maurice Hall Haycock (b 1900), former head mineralogy section, EMR
howlite	Henry How (1828-1879), chemist, U of King's College, Windsor, NS, author of *The Mineralogy of Nova Scotia*
jagowerite	John Arthur Gower (1921-1972), mineralogist, UBC
jamborite	John Leslie Jambor (b 1936), mineralogist, CANMET
keithconnite	Herbert Keith Conn (b 1923), Manville Products Corp, provided samples for study
kulanite	Alan Kulan (1921-1977), prospector, Ross River, YT
larosite	Frederick Alfred La Rose, prospector, discovered silver at Cobalt, Ont
lemoynite	Charles Le Moyne, Baron de Longueuil
mandarinoite	Joseph Anthony Mandarino (b 1929), mineralogist, curator, ROM
michenerite	Charles Edward Michener (b 1907), geologist, Canadian Nickel Co, Toronto
moorhouseite	Walter Wilson Moorhouse (1913-1969), geologist, U of Toronto
neyite	Charles Stuart Ney (1918-1975), geologist in charge of early exploration of deposit where mineral discovered
nuffieldite	Edward Wilfred Nuffield (b 1914), mineralogist, U of Toronto
parsonsite	Arthur Leonard Parsons (1873-1957), mineralogist, U of Toronto, ROM
pavonite	Martin Alfred Peacock (1898-1950), [Lat *pavo*, "peacock"], professor, U of Toronto, past president, Mineralogical Soc of America (1948)
penikisite	Gunar Penikis (1936-1979), a discoverer of phosphate occurrence in northeastern YT
petarasite	Peter Tarasoff (b 1934), amateur mineralogist, assistant director, Noranda Research Centre
poitevinite	Theophile Eugene Poitevin (1888-1978), mineralogist, GSC
prosperite	Prosper John Williams (b 1910), South African mineral dealer, Ont and Alta
robinsonite	Stephen Clive Robinson (1911-1981), mineralogist, Queen's and GSC
rucklidgeite	John Christopher Rucklidge (b 1938), mineralogist, U of Toronto
sabinaite	Ann Phyllis Sabina (b 1930), geologist, GSC
satterlyite	Jack Satterly (b 1906), geologist, Ont Dept of Miners and ROM
spencite	Hugh Swaine Spence (1885-1973), Dept of Mines, now called tritomite-(Y)
sperrylite	Francis Lewis Sperry (d 1906), chemist at Sudbury who first found the mineral
spertiniite	Francesco Spertini (b 1937), chief geologist, Jeffrey mine, Asbestos, Qué
steacyite	Harold Robert Steacy (b 1923), mineralogist, GSC
sterryite	Thomas Sterry Hunt
twinnite	Robert Mitchell Thompson (1918-1967), mineralogist, UBC; mineral name derived from Thompson, ie, "son of Thomas," Thomas based on Aramaic for "twin"; the mineral thomsonite existed already
tyrrellite	Joseph Burr Tyrrell
weloganite	William Edmond Logan
wicksite	Frederick John Wicks (b 1937), curator of mineralogy, ROM
yofortierite	Yves Oscar Fortier (b 1914), geologist, former director of GSC

QUARRYING and MINING are among the oldest industries in Canada. The record dates from the time of the early explorers Cartier, Frobisher and Champlain. In the 1850s, gold discoveries in BC, oil finds in Ontario and the expansion of Cape Breton coal production marked a turning point in mineral history from events of primarily local importance to developments destined to have wide-ranging impact. BC's entry into Confederation (1871) came about largely because of the rapid growth of the West Coast colony following the GOLD RUSHES. The discovery of petroleum at Oil Springs [Ont] in 1857, followed by gold finds in Québec in the 1860s, attracted increased attention to the mineral possibilities of eastern Canada. During the 1870s, the country emerged as a major phosphate supplier to the fertilizer industry, with the development of deposits throughout eastern Ontario and southwestern Québec. The mineral potential became more clearly evident with the discovery of asbestos in the Eastern Townships (1877) and the fabulous Sudbury nickel-copper discovery (1883). Cape Breton coal, the development of the Wabana iron mine in Newfoundland (1893), the Intercolonial Railway, industrial expansion of Ontario and Québec assisted by mineral development, and the start of an IRON AND STEEL INDUSTRY, all were important in the subsequent economic development of Canada.

In the years following Confederation through the 1890s, increasing exploration in southern BC led to many gold, silver and base-metal discoveries, including the Rossland copper-gold deposit (1887) and the famous lead-zinc deposit at Kimberley. The Athabasca oil sands of northern Alberta, which were to commence production only in recent years, received attention in a Senate committee report of 1887, following investigations made by the GEOLOGICAL SURVEY OF CANADA a few years earlier. In 1896 placer gold was found in the KLONDIKE, YT, giving rise to one of the world's most spectacular gold rushes. It is reported that between 1898 and 1905 more than $100-million worth of gold was mined from the sands and gravels of creeks near Dawson. Even at this early stage, large deposits of coal, oil and gas were evident in that part of the North-West Territories later to become Alberta. Ontario's mineral potential inspired considerable optimism, especially since good progress was being made in finding the best ways of extracting metals from the Sudbury copper-nickel ore. Asbestos was the leading mineral in Québec at that time, followed by copper. In the Atlantic area, NS coal was the dominant mineral commodity, although Newfoundland's copper had gained world prominence.

Although economic policy, based on railways, immigration and tariffs, did not adversely affect the mineral sector, it was closely linked to the railway-building programs of the 1870s and 1880s. After 1896, a new period of expansion began, particularly in the PRAIRIE WEST. The resulting impetus to the production of capital goods increased demand for more minerals for the manufacturing sector. During WWI, the steel industry almost doubled in capacity. Diversification increased, changing the steel industry from a specialized industry serving the railway-building market to one equipped to supply a range of products to meet the needs of a new industrial economy. In the 1920s the mining and metallurgical base was broadened by the Noranda (Qué) copper-gold enterprise, the Flin Flon copper-zinc operation on the Man-Sask border, and the Britannia copper mine near Vancouver; by metallurgical expansion at Sudbury and the establishment of the Trail smelter in BC; and by many other developments, including the drilling of the first oil well at Fort Norman, NWT, and the discovery of a major deposit of natural gas in the Turner Valley field near Calgary (1914). Mineral development was slower in Saskatchewan. The first copper-zinc ore from the Man-Sask boundary area came from the Mandy mine in 1917. Not until the Flin Flon smelter was built (1930) did the Prairie provinces contribute to Canadian metal production. It was also in 1930 that Gilbert LABINE discovered silver-radium ores at Great Bear Lk, NWT.

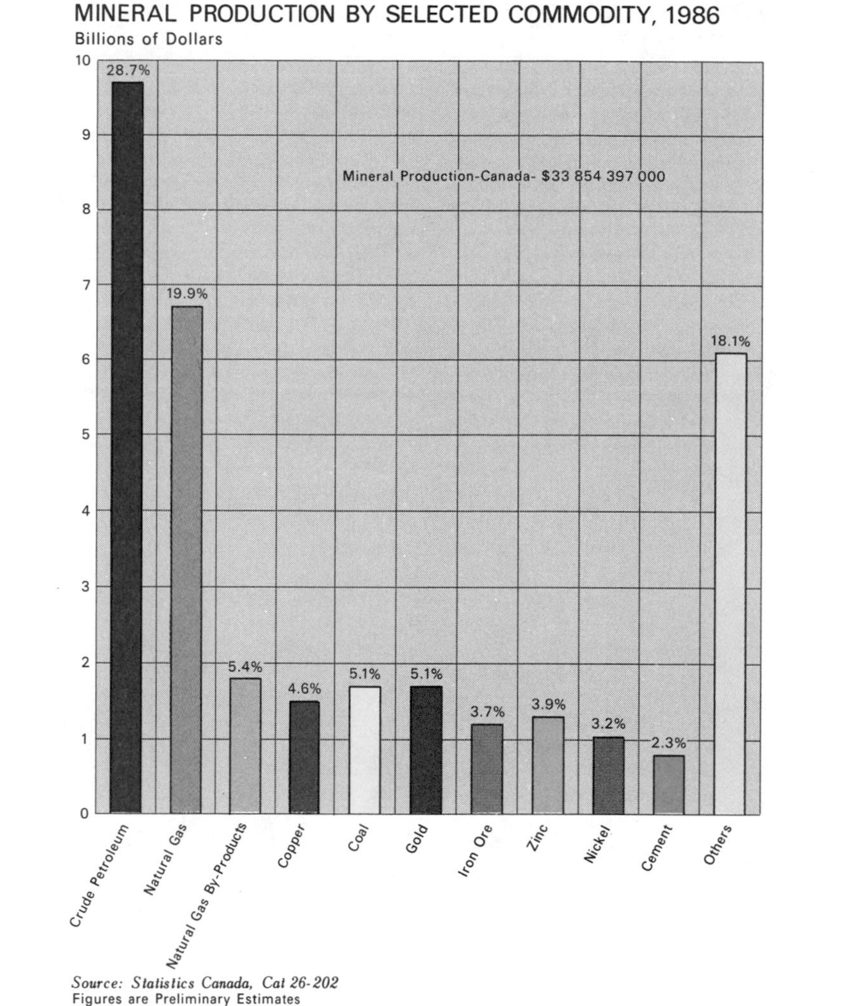

In WWII, Canada became an important source of strategic materials. Expansion of production was particularly great in the steel and nonferrous-metals industries and in the electrical-apparatus, tool and chemical industries. Between 1939 and the peak of the war-materials output, steel production doubled and aluminum output increased fivefold. During the war years, production of nickel, copper, lead and zinc had a value of over $1 billion. The country quickly converted to peacetime activities, and interest in mineral-resource development was renewed after the huge drawdown of resources of the war period. The new discoveries, such as crude oil, iron ore, natural gas, potash, copper, zinc and uranium, not only launched the mineral industry on its greatest period of expansion but also provided an impetus to the capital goods industries.

Total mineral output value in 1986 was nearly $34 billion. There was a sharp drop for the value in 1986 compared to 1985 ($45 billion) because of a severe decline in the price of petroleum. The postwar era has been marked by many major finds: nickel-copper deposits in Manitoba, lead-zinc, molybdenite and copper in BC, base metals and asbestos in Qué, Ont, Man, Nfld, the YT and BC. The discovery of the famous Alberta LEDUC oil field (1947), was followed by great expansion of the fuels industry. In the early 1950s uranium was discovered in Ontario and Saskatchewan, making Canada the owner of the largest known reserves in the world. At this time, iron ore became one of the most important minerals in Canada as the huge deposits in Québec-Labrador were exploited and titanium was discovered on Québec's North Shore. Major base-metal mines were brought into production in NB and made possible an important smelter industry. The

Annual Values of Canadian Mineral Production

Year	*Production (Millions$)*	*Value per capita ($)*
1886	10.2	2.23
1890	16.8	3.50
1895	20.5	4.05
1900	64.4	12.15
1905	69.1	11.51
1910	106.8	15.29
1915	137.1	17.18
1920	227.9	26.63
1925	226.6	24.38
1930	279.9	27.42
1935	312.3	28.84
1940	529.8	46.39
1945	498.8	41.15
1950	1 045.5	76.24
1955	1 795.3	114.37
1960	2 492.5	139.48
1965	3 714.5	189.11
1970	5 722.1	266.58
1975	13 345.4	585.32
1980	31 841.7	1 330.28
1985	44 729.6	1 763.80
1986	32 447.3	1 267.91

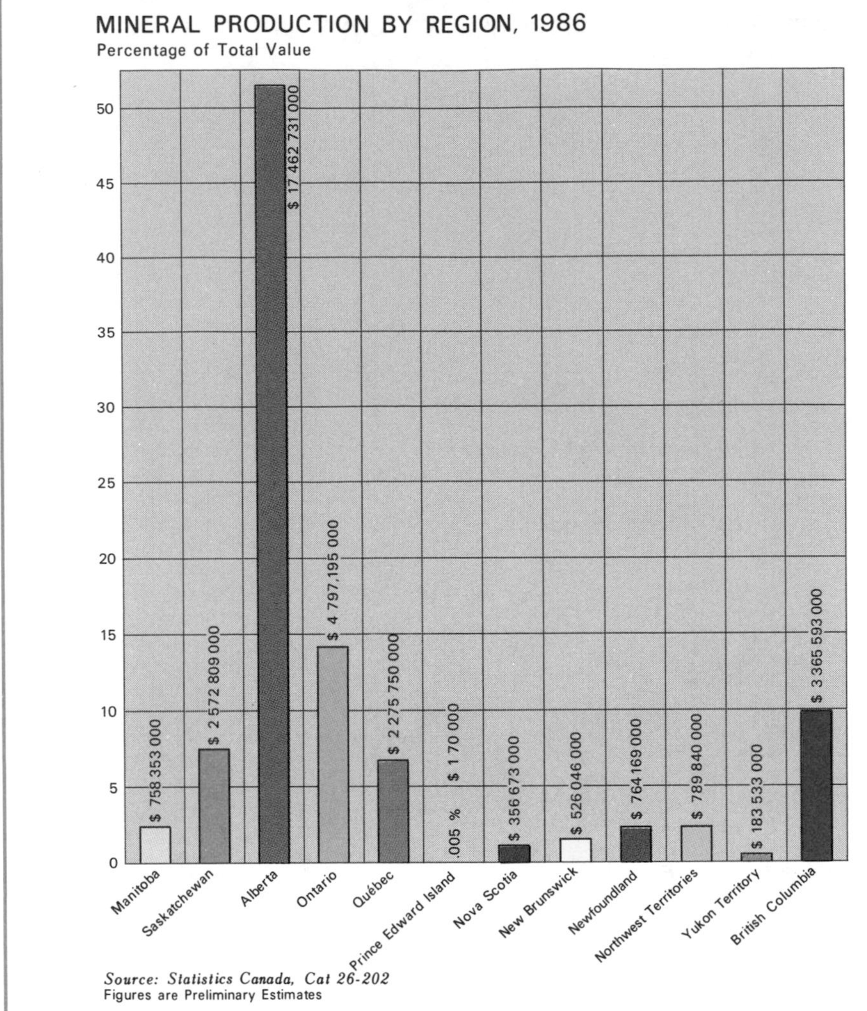

Source: Statistics Canada, Cat 26-202
Figures are Preliminary Estimates

Minerals and Metals Essential to Canada (excluding fuels)

Produced in Canada (surplus exported)

Abrasives (metal)*
Antimony (compounds)*
Arsenic (oxide)
Asbestos*
Bismuth
Cadmium*
Calcium
Cement*
Clays and shales*
Cobalt*
Copper*
Ferrosilicon
Gold*
Gypsum*
Helium
Indium
Iron ore*
Lead*
Limestone and lime*
Magnesium
Mica
Molybdenum (compounds)*
Nepheline syenite* and feldspar
Nickel*
Peat*
Pollucite (cesium)
Potash*
Pyrite*
Pyrochlore (columbium)
Pyrophyllite
Radium*
Salt*
Sand and gravel*
Selenium
Silicon metal
Silver*
Sulphur*
Tellurium
Titanium (dioxide)*
Tungsten (oxide)*
Uranium (oxide)*
Zinc*

Produced in Canada but not in right form (or deficit imported)

Antimony (metal)*
Ball Clay
Barite and celestite
Bentonite
Cesium (metal)
Columbian (metal)*
Fireclays
Gallium
Gemstones*
Granite (black)
Graphite
Platinum group*
Rare earths
Rhenium
Rubidium
Silica sand*
Soapstone (talc)*
Tantalum (metal)*
Thallium
Tin
Titanium (metal)*
Tungsten (metal)*

Not now produced in Canada (imports)

Bauxite
Beryllium
Boron
Bromine
Chromium*
Corundum and emery
Diamonds
Fluorine (fluorspar)
Fuller's earth
Garnet
Gemstones (high quality)
Germanium
Hafnium
Iodine
Kaolin
Kyanite
Lithium
Manganese
Mercury*
Perlite
Phosphorus (phosphate rock)
Pumice
Strontium
Thorium
Vanadium
Vermiculite
Zirconium

**See individual entries*

world's largest deposits of potash were discovered in Saskatchewan and N America's first tantalum mine was opened in Manitoba. The largest known reserves of zinc and silver in the world were discovered near Timmins, Ont.

The development of mining communities has helped to expand the frontiers of the nation and to provide economic activity in RESOURCE TOWNS across the country. Many of these towns are familiar: Labrador City and Wabush in Nfld; Bathurst in NB; Fermont, Sept-Îles, Chibougamau, Rouyn-Noranda, Val d'Or, Matagami, Murdochville, Black Lake in Qué; Wawa, Cobalt, Manitouwadge, Balmerton-Red Lake, Sudbury, Timmins, Temagami, Kirkland Lake, Elliot Lake, Hemlo in Ont; Leaf Rapids, Lynn Lake, Flin Flon and Thompson in Man; Esterhazy in Sask; Blairmore and Grande Cache in Alta; Ashcroft, Logan Lake, Cassiar, Kimberley, Peachland, Sparwood, Stewart and Trail in BC; Yellowknife and Pine Point in the NWT; Whitehorse and Faro in the YT. Canadians are also ushering in a new era to the Far North, mining gold on the fringe of the Arctic Circle and developing the Arvik lead-zinc deposit on Little Cornwallis I, only 100 km from the North Magnetic Pole. Accompanying the development of metal and industrial mineral resources has been an equally significant development of petroleum and COAL. Minerals, vital to a modern industrialized country and to the high standard of living of its people, have had an important impact on the social and economic development of Canada.

The Mineral System The mineral system comprises several components that are circumscribed by geography, economics, politics and the international context in which the system operates. An important element that transcends the whole mineral system is transportation. Mineral development depends on efficient and economical means of transportation (railways, highways, waterways and air), which link the resources to domestic and foreign markets. Crude minerals and products (excluding petroleum) account for over half of all revenue freight moved by Canadian railways; and half of all cargoes loaded at Canadian seaports for international markets are made up of minerals. In turn, materials for mineral development comprise a large portion of the tonnage moved by the transport industry.

Rank Held in the World by Canada as Producer of Minerals (based on 1987 statistics)

Mineral	*Rank*
Uranium concentrate	1st
Zinc	1st
Potash	2nd
Nickel	2nd
Elemental sulphur	2nd
Asbestos	2nd
Gypsum	2nd
Titanium concentrate	3rd
Cadmium	3rd
Aluminum	3rd
Gold	3rd
Platinum group (metals)	3rd
Copper	4th
Molybdenum	4th
Lead	4th
Cobalt	4th
Silver	5th

From mining to marketing, the mineral industry provides much direct and indirect employment, stimulates a broad range of manufacturing and service industries and, through export sales, contributes substantially to Canada's balance of payments. Apart from large amounts of new investment, mineral development also accounts for much of the new railway construction, for several new ports and for many Canadian frontier communities. Mining has helped Canadians attain one of the highest standards of living in the world. But the mineral industries are dependent on the economic well-being of Canada's trading partners in the world economy: production is adversely affected by a severe slowdown of growth rates in the world economy and changing geographic patterns of industrial growth and mineral consumption. Both of these factors have affected the mineral sector in the 1980s. A further problem is the capital expenditure necessary for the opening of new mines to replace depleted deposits. Studies estimate that 200-250 new mines will have to be developed in the 1980s and 1990s, if Canada is to hold its place in world markets.

Present Status of the Mineral Industry The Canadian mining industry not only enjoys good distribution in every major region (from coast to coast and into the North) but is also highly diversified. Over 60 mineral commodities (metals, nonmetals, structural materials and fuels) are produced from nearly 400 mines and quarries, and are processed in hundreds of mills, smelters and refineries. In fact, Canada produces most of its mineral requirements and has substantial proven reserves and undeveloped resources to meet its growing domestic and export needs.

Growth of the mining industry is tied very closely to a number of factors: international demand for minerals, competitive prices in world markets, climate for mineral development in Canada, availability of workers in remote areas and introduction of advanced technology. In 1983 confidence in a potential boom in the mineral industry, after the down cycle of recent years, has been demonstrated by the many new developments in several regions of Canada: coal in BC, potash and uranium in Saskatchewan, gold and silver in Ontario, several new gold mines in Québec, potash in NB and coal in NS. As one of the world's most diversified suppliers and largest exporters of mineral products, the Canadian mining industry will continue to meet future demand on world markets. Canada's known economic mineral reserves and known undeveloped resources, coupled with technical expertise, a favourable energy environment and easy access to world markets (principally the huge US market), offer limitless opportunities. J.P. Drolet

Mingan, Îles de, Québec, are 15 islands and 40 or more islets stretching for 80 km in the Détroit de Jacques-Cartier between Île d'Anticosti and the N Shore of the St Lawrence R, 175 km E of Sept-Îles. They are a striking example of sedimentary rock formations left by retreating glaciers, and are noted for picturesque "flowerpot" rock formations and limestone cliffs. The islands are a sanctuary for migratory birds and seabirds, and a feeding area for blue, fin and other whales. Naturalists have identified 256 species of wildflowers here. Indian burial grounds indicate they were inhabited before Jacques Cartier first reported the islands in 1535. Surveys have also uncovered 16th-century Spanish coins and the remains of Basque habitations. Frontenac gave the islands to Louis Jolliet 1679 for cod fishing and seal hunting, which remained the chief uses. The HBC gained title to the islands 1836 and sold them to Siebens Oil and Gas Co 1973. Dome Petroleum became the owner when Siebens's assets were taken over in 1979. Geological surveys identified industrial uses for the limestone deposits, but they were never exploited. The islands are now a national park (1984). Henry F. Heald

Minimum Wage, lowest hourly wage that an employer is legally permitted to pay to employees. There are 2 sets of minimum-wage laws, reflecting the division of powers between the federal and provincial governments. The federal minimum wage covers employees in designated federal industries while the provincial minimum wage covers most other employees – farm labourers being a notable exception. The 1987 federal minimum wage was $4.00 per hour, a level lower than that of most provinces. Alberta's minimum wage in 1987 was $3.80 per hour, Ontario's was $4.55 and Newfoundland's $4.00. Minimum wages were initially legislated in Canada during the 1920s, but economists have for many years disagreed about their effectiveness, arguing that they may price low-skilled workers out of the market and cause unemployment. D.A. Smith

Mining is the work of extracting rocks and solid minerals of economic value from the Earth. These products include metallic ores (eg, iron, copper, lead, zinc), industrial minerals (eg, limestone, rock salt, potash, gypsum), native metals (principally gold and silver), coal, oil sands, uranium ores and precious stones. Excavation of sand and gravel is a mining activity; quarrying for building and monument stone is a special branch of mining. The creation of underground spaces, such as storage chambers or drainage tunnels,

Rock drilling underground in the Dome Mine, a gold mine at South Porcupine, near Timmins, Ont (*courtesy Placer Dome Inc/photo by Frank Grant*).

uses many mining techniques but is not generally considered to be mining, unless the solids removed also have some value. The production of liquids and gases, as in the petroleum industry, is not usually considered mining. Mining is a major primary industry, as are agriculture, forestry and fisheries, but it differs in being a "one-crop" industry: minerals and rocks, once removed and used, cannot be replaced or regenerated. New mineral deposits must be found continually and new mines opened to replace exhausted ones. Most industrial activities require materials originally obtained by mining. A few mine products can be used in their natural state, but many must be processed by concentration, extraction, purification or fabrication.

History Mining has been practised since prehistoric times, when people began to dig for stones, weapons and pigments. In southern Africa, caves made to get iron-oxide pigments are at least 40 000 years old. In western Europe, pits dug for flints are several thousand years old. Prehistoric people collected loose pieces of native copper, gold, silver and gemstones from streams or the ground. Quarrying was widely practised when Stonehenge and the Pyramids were built. Advances in technology and civilization, indicated by the terms "Stone Age," "Copper Age," "Bronze Age" and "Iron Age," required quantities of materials obtainable only by mining. Thus was necessitated the digging of trenches, caves and pits; operations later extended to the excavation of shafts, tunnels and underground chambers. Ancient operations were restricted by the technology available and by dependence on human labour as the main energy source. The difficulty of removing water prevented deep mining in wet places, and hard ores could be broken only by hammering or wedging, or by heating and dousing with water. By the Middle Ages, advances had been made in mining and metallurgy, although they remained highly dependent on manual labour. Two especially important improvements came later: the application of explosives and steam power. The use of explosives in mining, which began around 1627, eliminated much of the arduous work needed to break rocks. Steam was first applied for industrial power around 1700, in Cornwall, England, for working mine pumps. The invention of steam railway locomotives, mine hoists, etc, followed a few years later.

Cross-section of the Noranda Mine at Hemlo, Ont (*courtesy Noranda Inc*).

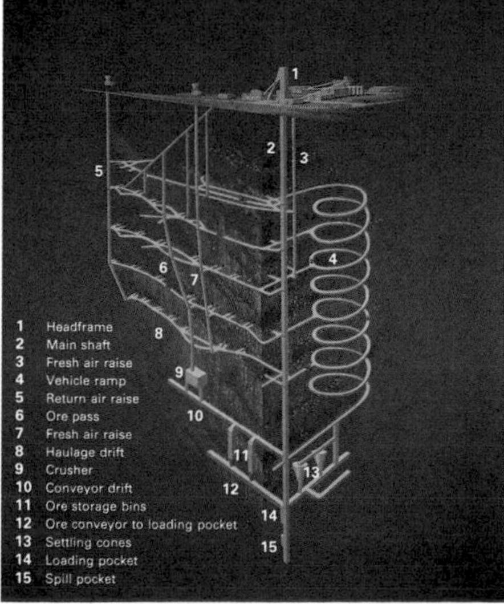

In the Western Hemisphere, no underground hard-rock mining was done before the arrival of the Spanish. Mining had been limited to placer work, chiefly for gold and silver, and to quarrying building stones and digging native copper, flints and obsidian from outcrops. The search for gold was a principal goal of the voyages of many explorers and of the campaigns of the conquistadors. The plundering of the natives' collections was followed by placer mining, then by mining of lode deposits of gold, silver, tin, lead, mercury and copper, often using forced labour.

In N America, British and French explorers were less successful in finding precious metals. In 1577 Martin Frobisher took back to England, from Baffin I, some 200 t of rock; he believed it to contain gold, but it proved worthless. Raleigh, in 1584, had hoped to find gold but, failing in this, turned to colonization. Discoveries of silver and iron, in Acadia, were reported in 1604 by Master Simon, a mining engineer with Samuel de Champlain, and the coal outcrops along the shores of Cape Breton I were known to early sailors and settlers. In 1643 it was reported that a shipment of coal was sent from Grand Lk [NB] to New England, and in 1672 Nicolas Denys prepared a report on the coal resources of the Maritimes for Louis XIV.

Mining and metallurgical operations were started in eastern N America as settlement proceeded. Small ore bodies of lead (for bullets) and of copper were opened; iron deposits were also mined. By the early 1700s, several iron foundries were in operation in the eastern states and at Forges Saint-Maurice at Trois-Rivières, Qué. As the fur traders moved west, they noted that copper ornaments and small tools were widely traded by natives of the Lk Superior district. This copper was obtained from loose pieces and surface outcrops of native metal. Traders sought the sources of the metal but did not establish productive mines. Samuel Hearne journeyed to the Coppermine R (1771) hoping to locate the source of copper carried by northern Indians, but found only small amounts of ore. The first mines of important size in northern N America were opened about 1845 to exploit the Michigan copper ore bodies near Lk Superior; Cornish miners working these brought their knowledge of mining and ore processing to the continent.

The discovery of placer gold near Sacramento (1848) triggered the California Gold Rush (1849). The flow of miners to the goldfields spilled over into other parts of the western US and N into Canada, leading to the discovery of many other mineral deposits. The Fraser R gold rush (1858) brought an influx of miners and traders into interior BC, prompting the formation of a British colonial government. The Klondike gold rush (1896-98) was an exciting but brief episode. Since then, placer mining has received less attention but is still carried out on a small scale in the YT and in northern and central BC.

Cominco lead-zinc smelter at Trail, BC (*photo by Doug Leighton*).

When BC joined Confederation, a transcontinental railway connection was promised. As the CPR was being built, nickel-copper ore was discovered near Sudbury, Ont (1883). Prospectors flocking to the district soon staked many of the deposits there. During the following half century, others ranged farther into northern Ontario and northwestern Québec, finding the silver veins of the Cobalt area, the gold veins of the Timmins and Kirkland Lk areas and the copper and zinc ore bodies of northwestern Québec. PROSPECTING and the establishment of new mines has continued, and about 280 mines are now in operation in Canada.

Coal has been mined in NS and NB since the early days of settlement. In western Canada, coal was first noted at Drumheller [Alta], in 1793, but coal mining began in the 1830s when the Vancouver I coal seams were opened near Nanaimo to serve coastal trade. As railways brought settlers into the Prairies, plains coal seams were mined to provide fuel for local use, and foothill and mountain seams were opened to serve both railways and settlers. Petroleum development (1947-60) caused severe losses of coal markets, forcing many western mines to close. However, recent growth in export markets, particularly in Japan, and in the use of coal for ELECTRIC-POWER GENERATION has revived the industry. It now comprises fewer but larger mines, with over 90% of production from surface operations.

Canadian Mines Mining has been carried out in all provinces and territories, except PEI. Only a brief review can be provided here. In 1987 in the Yukon a large lead-zinc mine reopened, some placer mining was under way and several smaller silver and gold mines were in operation. In the NWT the famous ELDORADO mine, beside Great Bear Lk, was operating by 1933 for the silver and radium in its ores. Operations were suspended in 1940 then resumed in 1942 to meet wartime demands for uranium. It was closed in 1960 and reopened in 1964 as a silver mine, finally closing in 1981. Other mines for gold and for lead and zinc are in production in the NWT, including one on Little Cornwallis I (at lat 75° N) and another on Baffin I.

BC continues to be a major producer of base and precious metals and of coal. Copper and molybdenum ores are obtained from several big open pits, the largest being in the Highland Valley near Kamloops. The underground Sullivan mine at Kimberley has been one of the world's largest producers since the 1920s. Coal from the Crowsnest area in southeast BC and from the Tumbler Ridge area in northeast BC is mined in large open pits; no coal is mined underground now in BC.

Alberta is Canada's major coal-producing province. Half a century ago its coal was being mined from several hundred small underground mines, but except for one small underground operation all coal now comes from a few large strip and open-pit mines. Bituminous sand is mined from 2 large surface mines in northern Alberta.

In Saskatchewan coal for power generation is produced from several surface mines. A few open-pit mines in the northern part of the province mine high-grade uranium ores, accounting for about 60% of Canadian output of uranium. Deep mines in the central part of the province produce about 25% of the world's potash for market.

In Manitoba the towns of Flin Flon, Thompson, Lynn Lake and Leaf Rapids have been established to serve nearby mines for copper, zinc, nickel and precious metals.

Ontario is a major producer of base metals, gold, uranium and precious metals. The Blind River district accounts for about 40% of Canada's uranium output. Its ores, of lower grade than those in the Saskatchewan mines, are obtained by underground methods. The Sudbury district, where the first ore bodies were located 1883-85, is the world's most important nickel mining and smelting area. Large amounts of copper and other valuable metals are also produced. Methods of separating copper from nickel in the smelting and refining processes had to be found before the ores could be profitably exploited. The district boasts several of the largest underground mines in the world. Gold mines, notably in the Timmins and Kirkland Lk districts, have passed peak production but the important recent gold discoveries in the Hemlo district will more than make up the loss. The Kidd Creek Mine near Timmins, which produces principally copper and zinc, is now the largest mine in northern Ontario. The discovery of silver ores around Cobalt in 1903 led to a staking rush which was extended to the discovery of many of the other mines in N Ontario. In the 60 years following the discovery of silver ores in 1903, over 460 million oz (troy) of silver were taken from the mines, but the area is quiet now.

Mines in northwestern Québec have been important contributors to the mineral wealth of the nation since 1926, when the Noranda copper mine came into production. Some of the earliest-worked ore bodies have been depleted but others have been found to sustain production. Numerous gold mines have recently been opened in this region as a result of increases in the prices of gold. Open-pit mines at Thetford-Mines and Asbestos, in the southern part of the province, produce about 18% of the world's asbestos. Concern about health hazards from asbestos has caused reductions in sales and production in recent years.

Coal mining on Cape Breton I has continued for over 200 years and, with the associated IRON AND STEEL works, is the island's most important industry. Mining has followed the seams beyond the shoreline for over 8 km, and mining to greater distances is projected as drilling from ships has established the presence of coal seams far under the ocean floor (*see* OCEAN MINING). In a mining museum at GLACE BAY, visitors can descend into part of an old coal mine.

Large deposits of iron ore are mined from open pits in the Québec-Labrador region, but competition from foreign producers has been curtailing output from the region. T.H. PATCHING

Mining Safety and Health Mining has been considered, with some justification, a dangerous occupation. Disastrous mine fires and explosions receive much publicity, but single injuries and fatalities also occur, as they do in many other industries. Safety statistics for an industry can be expressed in several ways, eg, frequency of fatalities or injuries, number of working days lost through injuries. These differences in standards and methods mean that care must be taken when comparing statistics from different industries or countries, or from different mines. However, surface mining is generally about as safe as work in other heavy surface industries: most injuries result from work with machinery. Workers in underground mines face additional hazards because working space is usually more restricted, illumination and visibility are lower, and ventilation is more difficult. Most underground injuries result from rockfalls and from work around equipment; others from slips, falls and explosions. In COAL mines, accidents and fatalities are often more frequent than in other mines because the rock strata are usually weaker and methane gas may be present. Fires and explosions of methane and coal dust have caused great losses of life, especially because of the carbon monoxide and carbon dioxide produced and the resulting depletion of oxygen.

The frequency of accidents and injuries has been much reduced by the efforts of miners' unions, employers, engineers and research workers. The development of better methane detectors, safety lamps, flameproof electric equipment and safer explosives has greatly reduced the frequency of mine fires and explosions. Shielded and remote-controlled equipment minimizes exposure of miners to dangerous areas; better knowledge of strata control and rock mechanics, and better supports (eg, rock bolts, hydraulic supports and cemented fill) have reduced the frequency of falls of rock. Increased use of personal protective equipment (eg, hard hats, goggles, respirators) has also diminished the number and severity of injuries. The development of proper working methods is also of prime importance in the prevention of accidents.

Safety generally means freedom from injury or fatality; health is a state of well-being, the absence of disease or infirmity. Several occupational diseases may result from prolonged or excessive inhalation of mine dusts: silicosis from dust containing free SILICA; pneumoconiosis (black lung) from coal dust; asbestosis and certain forms of cancer from ASBESTOS dusts. Radon gas, from URANIUM ores, may be related to a higher incidence of lung cancers in uranium miners, notably among smokers. In modern mines, because of increasing attention to dust suppression at source and dust reduction by improved ventilation, the incidence of dust-related diseases has been greatly reduced. Present ventilation standards are expected to prevent the occurrence of such diseases in future.

Hearing loss may develop from working in noisy places for prolonged periods. In mines, the NOISE hazard is often accentuated by the confined spaces. In recent years noise-abatement measures have been developed, eg, the muffling and enclosure of noisy equipment, and where these measures are not feasible, the wearing of hearing-protective devices is generally mandatory.

These improvements in TECHNOLOGY have been accompanied, sometimes forced, by laws, regulations and codes of practice controlling the conduct of mining operations. To ensure that SAFETY STANDARDS are met, mine inspectors are appointed by most governments and given authority to assess penalties for infraction of regulations or to stop work if conditions are unsafe. In coal mines, the qualifications of workers and supervisors must usually be approved by government boards. Regular safety inspections by supervisors are routine in well-managed mines, and frequently miners' representatives are also empowered to make inspections. Increasing emphasis is being placed on training new workers in safe work methods because most accidents are now caused, at least in part, by human error. Aside from human and legal considerations, strict attention to safety standards is warranted for purely economic reasons: as has often been shown, safety and profit are inseparable. Great improvements in safety have been made and some companies now claim that employees are safer at work than at home or on the highways.

In Canada, provincial governments are generally responsible for legislating and enforcing safety and health standards; the federal government is responsible for works in the YT and NWT and for certain mines in the provinces. The federal government tests and certifies equipment and materials, eg, diesel engines, explosives, electric devices and motors. Regulations differ among the various governments and are subject to revision as new information becomes available and as policies evolve. All governments carry out other functions related to worker safety and health, including maintaining records, administering WORKERS' COMPENSATION for injuries and conducting or supporting research programs. *See also* DISASTERS. T.H. PATCHING

Gold miners pose beside ore cars at a typical mining operation in the Yukon, *c*1900 (*courtesy Yukon Archives, Government of Yukon*).

Mining Work Force Mining is estimated to support, directly or indirectly, about 5-6% of all Canadian employment. Metal mines employ 47 000 (1986) people; coal mines, 10 000; quarries, 7300; and nonmetallic mines, 12 000; and about 31 000 are employed in nonferrous smelting and refining plants. Many more are employed in associated industries, eg, iron and steel, manufacturing, transportation, construction, etc. The direct work force diminished by almost 20% in the 1976-86 period owing to mechanization and changes in methods. In Canada mining pays the highest average wages of any major industry; straight wage, bonus, salary and contract schemes are in effect at various mines. Most operations are unionized. The higher costs of living in remote mining communities are often offset by subsidies or other benefits. Some northern mines engage alternating crews of employees to work intensively for periods at the mine site and then take equal periods of leave in their southern homes, thus avoiding the need to establish family accommodation at the northern locations.

Mining has been a predominantly male activity. Laws prohibit employment of juveniles; until recently, the engagement of females as mine workers was generally forbidden. In part, this was a reaction to conditions prevalent 150 years ago, when over half the underground workers in western Europe were women or were children under 12. In recent years, however, legislation has allowed the hiring of women as underground labourers in some provinces. The proportion of women so employed is still small. Some are engaged in surface mining operations, as physical strength is not needed to operate most powered vehicles and machines. In most countries, very few are employed in underground work because, although the operation of some kinds of underground equipment does not require great effort, the environment is not considered attractive, customs are slow to change and some tasks still require considerable strength.

Until recently, mining was a labour-intensive industry. However, wages have increased rapidly in the last 3 decades, and the need to mine larger tonnages of lower-grade ores and to increase productivity has become more urgent. Improvements in equipment, resulting in mechanization of many tasks, have reduced the number of workers required. Consequently the industry has become capital intensive and, in many mines, investment in equipment now exceeds $100 000 per miner. Concurrently the proportion of conventional miners has diminished, while that of mechanics, electricians, technicians, etc, has increased.

Certification of coal mine workers and supervisors is usually required, with minimum standards set by federal or provincial governments. This is to ensure that miners and officials are aware of hazards and will follow approved procedures where explosive gas and coal dust may be present. Government certification in other mining industries is not usually required but employers generally provide training programs. These programs range from simply assigning new employees to work with more experienced workers, to formal courses, sometimes with union and government participation. A recent development in some areas is the awarding of certificates of competence to miners who have achieved certain standards of experience and skill. Many companies also provide apprentice training programs for tradespeople (eg, mechanics, electricians). T.H. PATCHING

Ministère de la Marine, the section of the French government that administered Canada during its last 100 years as a French colony. The Marine, variously described as a ministry, department, or secretariat of state, combined administration of the navy, the colonies and seaborne trade. It was an expression of the MERCANTILIST idea that colonies and the trade they produce are fundamental to the wealth and power of the state, which thus maintains a navy to protect them and to destroy the wealth and power of rivals.

Cardinal Richelieu, Louis XIII's first minister, created the prototype of the Marine in 1624 and in 1626 became "grand master" of navigation and trade. This gave him authority without creating a permanent bureaucracy. It was left to Louis XIV's most trusted servant, Jean-Baptiste Colbert, to create a government department in the modern sense. An edict 7 Mar 1669 established the Marine, to be housed in offices at Versailles, where with a permanent staff Colbert established its policies and procedures. The Marine was divided into *bureaux* headed by *premiers commis* or "first clerks," the powerful civil service mandarins of their day. It was the Bureau du Ponant (from 1710, Bureau des Colonies) that administered Canada.

Under Colbert, France had the largest navy in Europe. But after 1690, even though the colonies were increasing in importance, the French became disenchanted with naval strategy and the fleet was allowed to deteriorate. In the 18th century hard-pressed controllers general kept the Marine chronically short of money. Protection for the colonies declined accordingly, and until the AMERICAN REVOLUTION France did not again attempt to equal Britain upon the seas. *See also* COLONIAL OFFICE. DALE MIQUELON

Ministry of Overseas Military Forces, est Nov 1916 to administer Canadian forces in the UK, especially in the training of reinforcements, and to act as the communications channel between the Militia Dept, the British War Office, and the Canadian Corps in France. When the CANADIAN EXPEDITIONARY FORCE went overseas, no provision had been made for its administration. Sir Sam HUGHES, minister of militia, George PERLEY, acting high commissioner in Britain, and Col Max AITKEN, Canadian military representative at the front, were involved in CEF affairs. To end confusion, PM Borden planned to establish a military council in England. Meanwhile, Hughes established an Acting Sub-Militia Council. Borden then appointed Perley minister of overseas military forces on 31 Oct 1916, and an angry Hughes, requested to resign, did so. Sir Arthur E. KEMP succeeded Perley in Oct 1917, and the office was abolished in July 1920. RICHARD A. PRESTON

Mink The American mink (*Mustela vison*) is a small, amphibious WEASEL, inhabiting wetlands throughout Canada, excluding the tundra, and abundant on the BC seashore. They are dark brown with some white on the chest and abdomen. Although the feet are not webbed, mink swim and dive well. The fur is dense and lustrous and serves as insulation even in water. Males reach 1.8 kg in weight and 60 cm in length; females weigh less than 1 kg. Mink feed on a variety of fish, invertebrates (especially sea crabs), small mammals and amphibians. Except along the Pacific coast, they breed Feb-Mar and give birth in late Apr and May. On the coast they breed May-June and give birth in July. The litter size is usually 5 (range 1-10) and young reach adult weight in 4 to 10 months (females and males, respectively). The mink is the most valuable Canadian furbearer. In 1985-86, 87 972 mink were trapped and 1.4 million were produced on fur farms. *See also* FUR FARMING; FUR TRAPPING.

IAN MCTAGGART-COWAN

The mink (*Mustela vison*) is the most valuable Canadian furbearer (*artwork by Claire Tremblay*).

Minnedosa, Man, Town, pop 2520 (1986c), 2637 (1981c), inc 1883, is located 205 km NW of Winnipeg, on the E side of the Little Saskatchewan R. The area was popular for buffalo hunting. Settlement began in 1870 near a trail to the NW. The site was first called Tanner's Crossing after John Tanner, who established a toll ferry and later a bridge across the river. Competitive communities sprang up nearby, but a gristmill and sawmill operation at Tanner's Crossing attracted trade and settlement. In the 1880s Minnedosa – a name of Sioux origin, meaning "swift water" – became the major supply and grain and livestock trading centre in NW Manitoba. Settlers included Hungarians, Scandinavians and English "gentlemen's sons" sent to Canada to learn farming. When the boom ended, Minnedosa was financially overextended, and NEEPAWA and DAUPHIN soon surpassed it as regional centres. Today, Minnedosa serves the area's grain and livestock farms and has several industries. D.M. LYON

Minnow Many people refer wrongly to any small fish as a minnow. Properly, minnows are small to large freshwater fish of class Osteichthyes, order Cypriniformes, family Cyprinidae. The largest fish family, with over 1500 species (including carp, squawfish, dace, bream, etc), it is found worldwide, excluding S America, Australia and the Far North. Forty-nine species occur in Canada. Some have restricted ranges (eg, redside dace, *Clinostomus elongatus*, of Lk Ontario drainages); others are found coast to coast. Carp (*Cyprinus carpio*) and goldfish (*Carassius auratus*) are familiar Asian minnows that have been introduced and become established in several provinces. Minnows inhabit waters from bogs to large lakes and rivers throughout Canada, except insular Newfoundland, and are often the most numerous fishes, both as species and individuals. Many are quite small, attaining lengths of only 60 mm as adults, eg, the northern redbelly dace (*Phoxinus eos*). The northern squawfish (*Ptychocheilus oregonensis*), unusually large for a minnow, may reach 120 cm in length. Minnows are characterized by toothless jaws (pharyngeal teeth are present); soft fin rays (carp and goldfish have stiffened rays in dorsal and anal fins); and cycloid (smooth) scales, often giving them a silvery sheen. A series of bones, the Weberian apparatus, connects the swimbladder to the ear. This makes their ability to detect sound exceptional and is probably important to their success. Injured minnows release "fright scents" into the water, which cause fear reactions in other members of the species.

Breeding males may be as brightly coloured as tropical aquarium species and may develop obvious tubercles (nodules) on the head, scales and fins. In the breeding season, some species (eg, hornyhead chub, *Nocomis biguttatus*) construct nests a metre in diameter by piling up pebbles with the mouth. Food varies with species. The chiselmouth (*Acrocheilus alutaceus*) of BC has a chisellike cutting edge to its lower jaw, used to scrape algae from rocks. Species with long, coiled intestines feed on algae and bottom ooze; those with short guts feed on insects, crustaceans and molluscs. The northern squawfish preys on other fishes. Minnows are not considered good to eat, and few are large enough to attract anglers. They are important as food for more valuable fish and as bait. Certain species, eg, pugnose minnow (*Notropis emiliae*), are sensitive to urbanization and to agricultural practices that increase the silt load in rivers. Abundance and distribution of such species serve as indicators of environmental conditions. BRIAN W. COAD

Minority Government, one that does not have a majority of MPs attending its caucus. A minority parliament (in which no party can claim a majority of MPs) need not result in a minority government if 2 or more parties are willing to form a coalition government, but since 1867 no peacetime coalition governments and only one wartime coalition (1917) have existed. Since 1921 there have been 8 minority parliaments (1921, 1925, 1957, 1962, 1963, 1965, 1972 and 1979) and 9 minority governments (the 1925 parliaments had both Liberal and Conservative governments), 4 of them Conservative, 5 of them Liberal. Of the former (1926, 1957-58, 1962-63 and 1979-80), none endured for more than a few months and only one (1957-58) did not fall on a vote of confidence. Of the 5 Liberal governments, one (1925-26), under Mackenzie King, left office following the refusal of the governor general to grant a dissolution (*see* KING-BYNG AFFAIR). A second Liberal government (1972-74) was defeated on its budget, but it is generally agreed that it sought defeat in the correct belief that it could win a majority in an election. The remaining Liberal minority governments (1921-25, 1963-65 and 1965-68) were able to gain the support of the third parties.

The balance of power in minority parliaments in Canada has been held by reformist parties of the broad left (Progressives, CCF, NDP) or, occasionally, by a regional French Canadian party (Créditistes) – parties that have feared and distrusted the intentions of the Conservative Party, which was, in any event, unable to compromise its policy positions to accommodate them. The Liberal Party, however, has always been willing to accommodate them, at least minimally. For example, the King government's ability to retain the confidence of the Commons from 1921 to 1925 depended partly on the strong antitariff policy favoured by the PROGRESSIVE PARTY. The Pearson minority governments of 1963-65 and 1965-68 and the Trudeau minority government of 1972-74 wooed the NDP by enacting, or by committing themselves to enact, the Canada Pension Plan, the Canada Assistance Plan, the Guaranteed Income Supplement for old-age pensioners, universal medicare, nonpartisan redistribution of seats in the House of Commons, regulation of election expenses and the establishment of Petro-Canada. Perhaps the Liberal governments would have enacted these measures anyway, but undoubtedly the possibility of being hanged within a fortnight concentrated their minds and imparted an urgency to their legislative programs. In contrast, immediately following the election of the Conservative minority government of 1979-80, PM Joe Clark announced he would govern as if he had a majority. He tried, even to the extent of allying with the Liberal Party and NDP, to deprive the Créditistes of their standing as a recognized political party in the House of Commons, although his government depended for its existence upon the votes of those same Créditistes. As a result, the Créditistes lost their collective right to speak in all matters before the House as well as their right to public funding for their caucus research office. In the non-confidence vote of Dec 1979, the Créditistes withheld their support for the government despite their chances of re-election being slim. D. KWAVNICK

Mint, low-growing perennial herb (genus *Mentha,* family Labiatae) with aromatic leaves and small blue flowers. It spreads rapidly in moist ground. Over 200 species have been described, but this number has been reduced to about 15 valid species: 7 Australian, 7 Eurasian and 1 circumboreal. Field or wild mint (*M. arvensis*) is the only species native to Canada. It was used by N American Indians as a tonic for stomach disorders, heart ailments and chest pains. *M. spicata* (spearmint, garden or green mint), cultivated in Europe for centuries and probably introduced to N America by the Puritans, is now used primarily as a culinary herb. Strongly flavoured peppermint (*M. piperita*) is grown for commercial preparation of menthol. A powerful antiseptic with local anesthetic properties, mint is widely used for toothache, headache, chest complaints and rheumatic pains. An antispasmodic, it is used for seasickness and to relieve stomach cramps. It makes a palatable tea, which is good for colds and insomnia. GILLIAN FORD

Artist's rendition of Canada as seen from far above the Arctic Archipelago. Courtesy Northern Transportation Company Limited.